WISDEN

CRICKETERS' ALMANACK

1981

EDITED BY JOHN WOODCOCK

PUBLISHED FOR THE PROPRIETORS JOHN WISDEN AND CO LTD
BY QUEEN ANNE PRESS, MACDONALD FUTURA LTD, PAULTON
HOUSE, 8 SHEPHERDESS WALK, LONDON N1 7LW

LIMP EDITION £6.95   CASED EDITION £7.95

PREFACE

Delighted as I am to have been appointed *Wisden's* eleventh editor, it is sad that it should have come about through the death of such an old friend as Norman Preston. For 29 years Norman edited the almanack, his father, Hubert, having done so for the eight years before that. Between them they served *Wisden* for no fewer than 85 years, Hubert's work having been first acknowledged by the then editor, Sydney Pardon, in 1895. In this 1981 edition will be found the tribute paid by Denis Compton to Norman at his Memorial Service, held at St Bride's, Fleet Street, on April 10, 1980, as well as a few words from Harry Abel, who collaborated with Norman in the compilation of almost all his *Wisdens*.

Anyone expecting the end of such an era to be marked by sweeping changes will be disappointed. Since, as a small boy, I was admonished for reading *Wisden* in form, I have had a deep affection for it as it is. It seems important, even so, to guard against its becoming any bulkier. If the gradual increase of recent years is maintained, it will fill more than 1,500 pages by the end of the century. The one major revision that I have made concerns Births and Deaths, a section that is as frequently referred to as any in the book. By rewriting the conditions of qualification I have removed, reluctantly, many good friends whose reasons for inclusion were becoming somewhat tenuous.

All Test cricketers are now included, rather than, as in the past, only those who had played in Test matches in England. Robert Brooke, whose life's work is to know when all first-class cricketers were born and when they die, has answered every call on his time with never a murmur of complaint. He tells me that in the final count, 194 names have been removed from the lists and 905 added, of which 505 are Test players. Those who have in their time been Cricketers of the Year are no longer to be found in a separate list. To save space, the letters CY (Cricketer of the Year) appear in their entries in Births and Deaths, together with the year in which they were honoured.

There are some, I know, who consider it incongruous in what is an international publication to devote more than 60 pages to Schools cricket. In time this may have to change, though it may be of interest to readers to know that in the County Championship averages for 1980 there are something like a dozen more former public school boys than there were in 1960. I would very much like to include the *full* scores of *all* first-class matches played throughout the world. Those not already published would just about fit into the space currently allocated to Schools cricket; but how possible it would be to vouch for the accuracy of all those from India and Pakistan is another matter. For the moment the Schools survive – to give pleasure to the 1,500 boys whose names appear each year and interest to future generations who will like to know what, for example, Robin Jackman did at St Edmund's, Canterbury, or Christopher Tavaré at Sevenoaks School.

The days are gone, almost certainly, when the traditional double of 1,000 first-class runs and 100 first-class wickets is within a cricketer's scope. It has not been done since 1967 when F. J. Titmus, in achieving it, bowled 440 more first-class overs than John Emburey, his counterpart, in 1980. In future the almanack will record the achievement, since 1969, of a 'double' of 1,000 runs and 75 wickets, as well as all separate feats of 2,000 runs and 100 wickets. There are other changes and additions to the Cricket Records. I have, for example, restored at least some reference to the series in 1970 between England and the Rest of the World and those who played in it. As the resident statistician, Michael Fordham has performed unfailingly. I would like also to mention Bob Arrowsmith, who takes such good care of the obituaries. These are implemented this time by a special article by Bill O'Reilly on his great spinning partner, Clarrie Grimmett.

The retirement of John Arlott, an integral part of the cricket scene since the end of the Second War, is marked by an article by E. W. Swanton, another of cricket's great narrators. As the only survivor from the England side to play against Australia at Lord's in 1930, G. O. Allen links that match with last summer's Centenary Test. The expanding market in Cricketana is assessed by David Frith, editor of *Wisden Cricket Monthly*, and after a season in which, for the first time, helmets became standard wear in the first-class game, Trevor Bailey discusses their implications. After covering the last England tour of Australia for *The Observer*, Scyld Berry headed off into the Pacific; he tells here of the islanders' enthusiasm for cricket.

Of the Five Cricketers of the Year, Jackman and the South African, Vintcent van der Bijl, chose themselves. A case could have been made for making up the number with three more South Africans. In the event, two of them, Clive Rice, who plays for Transvaal and Nottinghamshire, and Allan Lamb of Western Province and Northamptonshire are joined by the Australian, Kim Hughes, who batted so well in the Centenary Test. Seldom before have there been so many overseas players in the five.

The assistance I have received in putting the almanack together has been wonderfully generous. The readiness with which an invitation to write for *Wisden* is accepted is a healthy indication of the regard in which it is held. Producing it is essentially a team effort, and a very cosmopolitan one at that. Numerous secretaries, especially those of MCC, the TCCB and the first-class and minor counties, as well as Patrick Eagar, Bill Smith and Ken Kelly, the photographers, and the masters-in-charge of schools' cricket have been most helpful. But two people, above all others, must be picked out for special thanks. One is Graeme Wright, my assistant editor, who has been as nearly indispensable as anyone could be, the other his admirable assistant, Christine Forrest. If, as I hope, this 118th *Wisden* is as well received as its predecessors, all of these, together with our printers and the names of those in the list that follows will be the reason why.

JOHN WOODCOCK

LIST OF CONTRIBUTORS

The Editor acknowledges with gratitude the assistance afforded in the preparation of the almanack by the following:

H. E. Abel
G. O. Allen
Jack Arlidge (Sussex)
John Arlott
Robert L. Arrowsmith
Diane Back
T. E. Bailey
Alex Bannister
Geoff Beane (Warwickshire)
Michael Beddow (Worcestershire)
Scyld Berry
J. Watson Blair (Scotland)
Ian Brayshaw
R. T. Brittenden (New Zealand)
Robert Brooke
Kenneth R. Bullock
C. R. Buttery (New Zealand)
John Callaghan (Yorkshire)
Michael Carey (Derbyshire)
Terry Cooper
Tony Cozier (West Indies)
Basil Easterbrook
Paton Fenton (Oxford)
David Field
Michael Fordham
Bill Frindall
David Frith
Nigel Fuller (Essex)
Lawrence Hancock
Ghulam Mustafa Khan (Pakistan)

David Hallett (Cambridge)
Brian Hayward (Hampshire)
Eric Hill (Somerset)
C. G. Howard
Philip Jurd
John Kay (Lancashire)
John Lawson (Nottinghamshire)
Edward Liddle
Barry McCaully
Peter McFarline
Michael Melford
Dudley Moore (Kent)
W. J. O'Reilly
Brian G. Osborne (Australia)
Netta Rheinberg
Dicky Rutnagur
Peter Sichel (South Africa)
Derek Scott (Ireland)
Peter Smith
F. S. Speakman (Northamptonshire)
P. N. Sundaresan (India)
E. W. Swanton
John Thicknesse
J. B. G. Thomas (Glamorgan)
Gerry Vaidyasekera (Sri Lanka)
E. M. Wellings
Geoffrey Wheeler
Crawford White
A. H. Wiggett

★ ★ ★ ★ ★

© QUEEN ANNE PRESS
Limp edition ISBN 0362 02032 9
Cased edition ISBN 0362 02031 0

CONTENTS

No-one argues the decision when this one is given out.

DON'T BE VAGUE. THE DARK BOTTLE'S HAIG.

INDEX

Note: c = catches; d = dismissals; r = runs; w = wickets.

* Signifies not out or an unbroken partnership

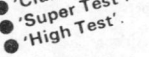

UNBRIDLED DISSENT

[*Southland Times*

New Zealand v West Indies, February 1980. M. A. Holding, the West Indian fast bowler, shows his anger at having an appeal for a catch at the wicket turned down by kicking down the stumps at the batsman's end. The batsman, J. M. Parker, remains unruffled by this disgraceful incident, which occurred in the first Test match at Dunedin which New Zealand won by one wicket.

POLICE PROTECTION AT LORD'S

[*Wisden Cricket Monthly*]

An unhappy reflection of the discontent among MCC members on the Saturday afternoon of the Centenary Test at Lord's was the presence of the police to escort the umpires from the Long Room on to the ground, following a scuffle which had occurred earlier.

THE LONG WALK, THE LONG WAIT

[Patrick Eagar]

The reason why the West Indian over-rate was the slowest ever. M. A. Holding, in the Headingley Test match, approaches the end of his long walk back to his mark. The attitudes of the fielders are indicative of the tedium.

ENGLAND'S CENTENARY TEST TEAM

[Patrick Eagar

The England team which was selected to play Australia in the Centenary Test match at Lord's. *Back row:* M. W. Gatting, C. W. J. Athey, D. I. Gower, J. E. Emburey, P. Willey, D. L. Bairstow, R. D. Jackman. *Front row:* M. Hendrick, G. Boycott, I. T. Botham (*captain*), C. M. Old, G. A. Gooch.

THE AUSTRALIANS IN ENGLAND, 1980

Patrick Eagar

The Australian party which made a short tour of England in August 1980, culminating in the Centenary Test match at Lord's. *Back row:* M. R. Mason (*physiotherapist*), Dr D. Carney (*medical officer*); J. R. Thomson, R. W. Marsh, L. S. Pascoe, A. A. Mallett, G. Dymock, D. K. Lillee, A. R. Border, B. M. Laird, D. K. Sherwood (*scorer*). *Front row:* R. J. Bright, J. Dyson, K. J. Hughes, P. L. Ridings (*manager*), G. S. Chappell (*captain*), G. N. Yallop, G. M. Wood.

SOMERSET'S TEST MATCH CONTRIBUTION

[Ken Kelly]

In the fifth Test match at Headingley between England and West Indies, both captains, both umpires and two others were past or present Somerset players.
L-r: K. E. Palmer, I. V. A. Richards, B. C. Rose, J. Garner, I. T. Botham and W. E. Alley.

ENGLAND CAPTAIN'S FITNESS TEST

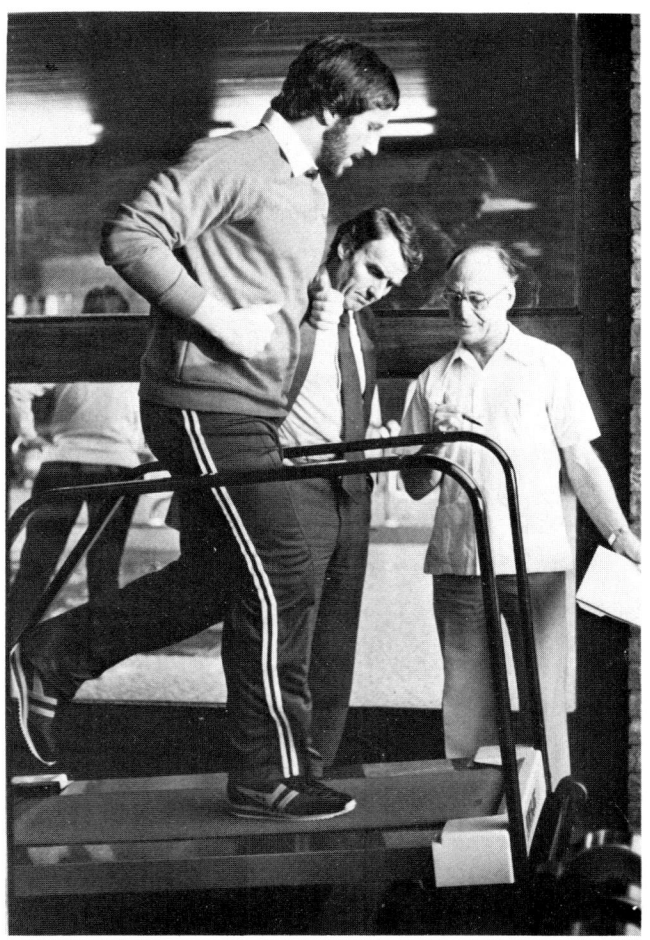

|Ken Kelly

Seven weeks before leading England to the West Indies, Ian Botham satisfies the team manager, Alan Smith, and their physiotherapist, Bernard Thomas, that he will be fit to tour.

FIVE CRICKETERS OF THE YEAR

| Patrick Eagar

R. D. JACKMAN (Surrey)

FIVE CRICKETERS OF THE YEAR

|Patrick Eagar

V. A. P. VAN DER BIJL (Middlesex)

FIVE CRICKETERS OF THE YEAR

|Patrick Eagar

A. J. LAMB (Northamptonshire)

FIVE CRICKETERS OF THE YEAR

[Ken Kelly

C. E. B. RICE (Nottinghamshire)

FIVE CRICKETERS OF THE YEAR

K. J. HUGHES (Australia)

[*Patrick Eagar*

FIVE CRICKETERS OF THE YEAR

K. J. HUGHES

The distinction of scoring the first hundred in Anglo-Australian Tests on English soil belonged, fittingly, to the legendary W. G. Grace. That of scoring the first in the second century of these games went to Graeme Wood with a fine 112, but it was Wood's Western Australian team-mate, KIMBERLEY JOHN HUGHES, to whom the Centenary Test of 1980 at Lord's really belonged. In two innings of the highest quality, Hughes put his manifest talents on display on each of the five days of the game.

His 117 in the first innings was spread over the first three, sadly rain-hit days. He hurried to 47 late on the first day, advanced to 82 in the seventy-five minutes available on the second, and charged to 117 when play finally got under way on the third. This memorable century contained three 6s and fourteen 4s, all put together with an air of casual disregard for the importance of the occasion. As if such a smörgåsbord of strokes was not sufficient for the connoisseur, he tickled the palate with a lot of new ones in the second innings with a breathtaking 84 in 114 minutes, which included two 6s and ten 4s. One of his 6s, hit off paceman Chris Old on the run some three yards down the wicket, landed on the top deck of the members' pavilion, failing by only an extra erg or two to clear the building altogether. Another stroke, from even further down the pitch and also against a pace bowler, was slashed to the point boundary with such speed as to leave standing a fieldsman on the ropes only a yard or two from its scorching path. Such rare batting gave Greg Chappell an opportunity to declare with half a chance of forcing a victory that had seemed beyond all reality after rain had robbed the game of so much play.

The marvellous appeal of Hughes's batting lies in the repertoire of his strokes and his unashamed enthusiasm in playing them. Most are straight from the copybook and executed with the fine touch of the artist's brush; some, however, are of his own design and despatched with a grand flourish. The high backlift, the skipping footwork, the flashing blade and the full-blooded follow-through – all hallmarks of the great stroke-players – are evident at their very best when Hughes is in full flight.

But it hasn't always been such plain sailing for Hughes, born in Western Australia on January 26 (Australia Day), 1954. His talent was obvious from a very early age; he was chosen in an all-Australian side after a national schoolboys carnival at the age of thirteen. Moving into senior club cricket in Perth at the age of fifteen, he was reckoned by good judges close to him to be one of the very few who should have been elevated to first-class ranks when even as young as that. Perhaps it was a somewhat brash nature and an unbridled impetuosity which held him back. But it was at this stage that Hughes's coach and mentor, Frank Parry, himself a former club cricketer, told him, "You could make the Australian side and go on to be a Test captain", and Hughes believed him.

Hughes was so impatient to get to the top that, frustrated at being unable to break into the Western Australian side in the 1974-75 season (he was twelfth man three games in a row), he packed his bags and moved to Adelaide to try his luck there. But having failed to make the South Australian training squad, let alone the State side, he returned home to force his way into the Western Australian eleven the following summer. As if to make the point that he should have been there sooner, he put his name in bright, shining lights in his maiden first-class innings, against New South Wales in Perth on November 2, 1975. Then 21 years old, he set about an attack that included Pascoe, Gilmour, Colley, Walters and O'Keeffe to hammer out 119 runs in 166 minutes of batting glory. In the second innings he almost repeated the dose, picking up 60 in a 108-minute stay.

Australian selector Neil Harvey, watching the game, could not have failed to be impressed. Yet it was to be a long time before Hughes climbed the next step up the ladder into the Australian eleven. Again he had first to do an apprenticeship carrying out the drinks, beginning with the second Test against Pakistan at the Melbourne Cricket Ground in January 1977 and again, soon after, on a short tour of New Zealand, where he filled this rôle in both Tests. He finally won his spurs in the fifth Test against England at The Oval later that year.

The fact that Hughes scored only 1 in his first Test innings is testimony to the contrary nature of cricket – not always does everything come to him who waits. Indeed, it was some time yet before Hughes really made his mark in Test cricket, and it took the advent of World Series Cricket to afford him more frequent opportunities. Even so, his form in the early stages of that era seemed plagued by rushes of blood to the head. To some he was known as "Howie", the "millionaire" batsman, the name taken from Howard Hughes.

Then, thankfully, the coin dropped. In the first Test against England in 1978-79 he scored a century – 129 runs in just under eight hours – and in doing so recognised the need at times to work very hard for runs. That innings cemented his place in the Australian side. When Graham Yallop, who had captained the Test side throughout the summer, injured himself in the days leading up to the second of two Tests against Pakistan in March 1979, there, before his home crowd in Perth, was Hughes, captain of Australia. There was a new enthusiasm about the Australians under Hughes. Against the odds, they beat Pakistan and Hughes was retained as skipper for the tour of India that followed.

Hughes played well in India, scoring a century first-up and following with scores of 86, 50, 40, 92, 64 not out and 80 among his innings in the remaining Tests. That was more like it. Back in Australia for the twin tours by West Indies and England in 1979-80, he showed great character in scoring 130 not out against West Indies in the first Test at Brisbane, celebrating with a 99 against England in Perth and then a 70 in the next Test against West Indies in Melbourne. All it needed was sustained opportunity.

The true entertainers of the sporting arena are few and far between. In cricket, rigid coaching routines sometimes take their toll, stifling the glorious individuality that makes it worth paying twice the entrance fee to watch some players in action. Thank goodness nobody bent to curb the natural brilliance of Kim Hughes. Des Hoare, a tearaway fast bowler for Western Australia who played one Test match, was captain of the side when Hughes made his début in first-grade club cricket in Perth, immediately recognised a rare talent, and has closely watched Hughes's progress ever since. "I have most admired him", said Hoare, "because he has had the courage and ability not to become ordinary". That sums it up. – I.J.B.

R. D. JACKMAN

For ROBIN DAVID JACKMAN, Surrey's lion-hearted opening bowler, there was nothing much wrong with 1980 that a slight adjustment to his birth certificate, fourteen more points in the County Championship, and a different set of Test selectors would not have put right. With 121 wickets in the first-class game, 17 in five Gillette Cup ties and 19 more in other limited-overs matches, he was far and away the country's leading wicket-taker. Yet to the shame of the selectors, sympathy of his peers and indignation of the public, official recognition of his excellence was confined to one Prudential Trophy match and the bitter-sweet experience of watching the Centenary Test against Australia as twelfth man from the balcony of England's dressing-room.

When a fortnight later Jackman was passed over for the tour to the West Indies, deemed by the selectors not to be among England's best five seamers despite having taken more wickets than any two others put together, even a man of his optimistic spirit was inclined to believe that, at 35, his last chance of playing for his country had probably slipped by.

From mid-season there had never been much doubt that, short of a broken bowling arm, he would be among *Wisden's* Five Cricketers. But pleased as he was to be chosen, an even more satisfying honour was in store when he was voted the "Cricketers' Cricketer for 1980", an annual award given by the 250 or so county professionals to the player they considered made the greatest contribution to his team's success – in hard work and dedication as much as, or more than, statistically. As most of them would have had Jackman in their Test team, it is not being too fanciful to read into their verdict a hint that, had the choice been theirs, his coveted first England cap would have been safely in his cricket-bag.

Having set his heart on playing for England, Jackman was honest enough to make no attempt to hide his disappointment when, one after another, the Test teams came along without his name included. He was a strong contender from the third Test onwards, by when his 66 wickets made him by 36 the most prolific English seamer. At the end of the season he was generous enough to admit that "it would have been a bold decision to pick a bowler of my type at 35", but then added pointedly: "All the same, I can't help thinking they'd have picked me if I'd been a 35-year-old batsman and got twice as many *runs* as anybody else!"

The year had begun unpromisingly for him when, minding his own business as he waited to turn out of a T-junction in Salisbury, Rhodesia (Zimbabwe), his car was struck amidships by someone swinging wildly round the corner, throwing him bodily into the road. He escaped with severe bruising, but had to cancel a holiday with his wife in South Africa to return to England, where by continual exercise under supervision he worked himself back to fitness in time to start the season. Fully recovered, he took nine Hampshire wickets in Surrey's opening Championship match and never looked back. Compensating by accuracy, consistency and willingness for the extra yard of pace that would have made him a certain choice for England, he played an indispensable part in Surrey's season, keeping them snapping away at Middlesex's heels till the penultimate Schweppes match and steering them to the final of the last Gillette Cup, in which their batting let them down and, much to their disgust, they were again beaten by their London rivals.

Obviously Jackman didn't do it on his own. Sylvester Clarke, his West Indian opening partner, Alan Butcher and Roger Knight were other key members of the side. But an analysis of his figures shows just how much Surrey owed to him: of his 114 Championship wickets, 67 were in the top five of the order. In cricket parlance, he kept "knocking over" the best players, often before they reached 20. Of his 34 wickets in July (15 of them, for 80 runs, in three Gillette Cup ties) no fewer than 27 were specialist batsmen – and 17 of those were out in single figures. His fortnightly rejections by Alec Bedser's panel made nonsense of the recurrent theme of Test selectors that England teams should invariably be picked to maximise their winning chances.

By giving him incentive, Surrey's challenge for the Championship can only have helped Jackman put his disappointments to one side. But, Jackman being above all a fighter, it would have made no difference to his game had they been lying twelfth instead of second. For whatever limitations he has as a cricketer, lack of heart is certainly not one of them. Of all the thousands of times they have watched him scurry in to bowl during the seventeen seasons since he joined the Surrey staff, his team-mates will not remember many when he spared himself – never when it mattered. He is the sort of bowler any captain would like to have on hand – fit, strong, aggressive and as full of guts and bounce at the end of a day as at the start of it.

Jackman's family background is of a type that has become increasingly familiar among county cricketers since the abolition of the amateur in the early 1960s removed the stigma of public schoolboys playing a game for money. He was born on August 13, 1945 in Simla, where his father, a colonel in the 2nd Gurkhas, was serving the last months of his career in the regular army before being invalided out. He lost a leg in a wartime accident. On his mother's side, Robin has a well-known uncle in the actor, Patrick

Cargill, who long ago did batsmen a bad turn by discouraging his starry-eyed nephew from following him on to the stage.

The Jackmans came back to live in Surrey in 1946 – they are both members of the club and are often to be seen at The Oval – and it was in a net on their lawn that, at five, Robin turned professional. Sixpence from father if he pitched it on a handkerchief, a penny deducted each time he bowled down the leg-side. "He lost", said Robin.

Like his father, Jackman was educated at St Edmund's School, Canterbury, where he blossomed from a skinny off-spinner at twelve into the beginnings of the sturdy (5ft 9½in and 12½st) athlete we know today. In his second year in the Eleven, 1962, he topped both sets of averages, scoring 515 runs, a record, and taking 34 wickets opening the bowling.

He joined Surrey in 1964, but with competition from Arnold, Sydenham, Jefferson, Gibson and Storey, had to wait till 1968 for a regular place and till 1970 for his county cap. Ten years later he has taken more than 1,100 wickets and become one of the most reliable and hard-working bowlers on the circuit. His best two seasons, strangely on the surface, have been the last two (93 wickets and 121). But not to Jackman.

"Put it down to Sylvester Clarke", he said. "It would be over-modest if I didn't say I'd bowled well; but it's made a tremendous difference to a bowler of my type – fast-medium length-and-line – to have a genuine quick one at the other end." – J.D.T.

A. J. LAMB

In 1977, three young South African cricketers arrived in England in search of fame – and the prerequisite of a county contract. All were from the Cape. Allan Lamb and Peter Kirsten (who had played for Sussex against the 1975 Australians) were specialist batsmen; Garth le Roux was a fast bowler. And as their sponsored enterprise had been initiated by Eddie Barlow, then captain of Derbyshire, it was natural that they should base themselves in that county. For Derbyshire's Second Eleven Kirsten returned a spectacular average of 133.50 which led to his remaining with the county. Lamb also did well and le Roux, later to join Sussex, was second in the bowling averages. In the same season, in the "also batted" and "also bowled" for Northamptonshire Second Eleven, lurk the same names of Lamb, Kirsten and le Roux. They fished in several waters. On Saturdays, for example, Lamb was a successful batsman for Holmfirth in the Huddersfield League.

Having advertised the considerable ability which was to take him to the top of the national averages in 1980, ALLAN JOSEPH LAMB returned to the Cape with runs aplenty from his English adventure, but lacking the much-wanted contract. The gods, however, had not forsaken him. Back at Northampton, a serious shortage of class had been created by the departure of Mushtaq Mohammad, Bishen Bedi, John Dye and Roy Virgin. Replacements were a top priority, and over Christmas Roy Barker, a member of the Northamptonshire committee on a business visit to South Africa, appeared like Santa himself with a contract for Lamb.

It was a tough first season. Northamptonshire, ironically, "celebrated" their centenary by finishing last in the Championship. Among several injuries suffered by the team was a broken finger which put Lamb out for a crucial three weeks. The weather was poor, and yet in conditions foreign to him Lamb scored 883 first-class runs with an average of 46.47. In the following year, rich promise ripened into fulfilment with 1,747 runs, an average of 67.19, and general agreement that a new star adorned the county scene. Only Geoff Boycott and Younis Ahmed had better figures. Lamb's aggressive style was reflected in no fewer than 315 boundaries.

Far from being awed by the tall standard he had set himself, Lamb ended the 1980 season with 1,797 runs and first place in the national batting averages with 66.55. He also took the Gold Award for his match-winning 72 in the Benson and Hedges Cup final against Essex, which showed him to be a man for the big occasion. "I thrive before a large crowd", he says. "It excites and challenges me, and Lord's is the perfect setting. I think my best innings for Northamptonshire have been in the major cup competitions."

Born at Langebaanweg, Cape Town, on June 20, 1954, Lamb was imbued with a love for the game by his father, Mickey, a club bowler, and his mother, Joan, an ardent spectator who never willingly missed a match. Both parents came from London. Father helped a lot with the basic principles of batting, and Allan was an apt and eager pupil. His batting flair was evident at Wynberg Boys' High School and Abbots College, and in two Nuffield Schools weeks in Rhodesia and Johannesburg he was outstanding. Towards the end of the 1972-73 season, when only eighteen, he was selected for Western Province in the Currie Cup. Batting at number three, he made 59 and 36 against Eastern Province.

Before leaving for National Service in the South African Air Force, which meant an absence of two years from the first-class game, he had another match against Natal and two one-day outings. After helping to build airfields, he returned to Western Province, this time as an opener. The position did not suit him, and a year later he dropped to number six, where he made an impact with more than 600 runs. Number four, however, was to become his true and permanent position.

Lamb always wanted to play in English county cricket. His coaches in South Africa — Tom Reddick (Nottinghamshire), Don Bates (Sussex), David Steele (Derbyshire) and George Sharp, now a Northamptonshire team-mate, as well as Barlow — nourished his ambition. Yet when the chance came, some technical adjustments were necessary. "After the hard and firm pitches of South Africa I found I had to wait for the ball in England", he explained. And, with some understatement, he added: "by the end of the season I was beginning to get it right."

Like many champions reared on true and trusted surfaces, Lamb is an instinctive stroke-maker and an attacking player. An uncomplicated philosophy is his recipe for success. "I am not a defensive player. My main objective at all times is to score runs, and to look for runs off every ball. I believe that as you are likely to get a good ball sooner or later it is pointless to wait for it with a passive outlook. I look to score off most balls I face, and I dislike leaving the bad ball, such as a wide or a long hop, as some do. Playing in England has not only been a great experience, but has vastly improved my game. I have learned a lot, especially about turning wickets, and I have begun to play spinners better."

Inevitably Lamb's record and healthy methods aroused speculation in 1980 about possible future qualification for England by residence. There are three cogent reasons why he could opt to become available for England – a natural ambition to play at Test level, his English parentage, and his enjoyment at playing and living in Northampton where he has made many friends. But it is a personal decision only he can make. One fact emerges with shining clarity. If he continues his consistent brilliance, it would take an unusually good batsman to keep him out even of a vintage England team. – A.J.B.

C. E. B. RICE

It takes a very special person to absorb the trauma of being sacked by a club and then return to lead them to their most successful season for more than 50 years. But then CLIVE EDWARD BUTLER RICE, born in Johannesburg on July 23, 1949, is someone special.

The 31-year-old South African arrived at Trent Bridge in 1975 – after Nottinghamshire, then under the management of Jack Bond, had switched their attentions from his fellow-countryman, Eddie Barlow – and it was three years later that they decided his aggressive and positive pursuit of success was deserving of the captaincy. His involvement, however, with World Series Cricket, at a time when Nottinghamshire were open critics of Kerry Packer's wheelings and dealings, led to the Trent Bridge hierarchy stripping him both of the leadership and his place on the staff before he had had the opportunity to assert himself. Following threats of protracted legal battles, between club and player, a compromise of a kind was reached with Rice maintaining his position on the books while returning the captaincy to Mike Smedley.

A season and a half later the Nottinghamshire manager, Ken Taylor, reappointed Rice as captain, a move that did not meet with total acceptance by members of the county. But, leading from the front, Rice has in a short time improved Nottinghamshire's fortunes, for so long at a low ebb. In terms of captaincy he had much to learn tactically, his previous experience being limited to leading out his club side, Bedford View, in South Africa, but although listening to and digesting the advice of Taylor and such senior Nottinghamshire players as Mike Harris, Rice has retained his own identity. It is enormously to his credit that the pressures and strains of captaining the side have not detracted too much from his own statistical contribution. "I am sometimes thinking of many other things when I am out in the middle batting", he conceded. Yet if, last season, his output was reduced by some small percentage, this was more than compensated for by the influence he had on those around him. The players, not least Derek Randall, readily acknowledge the spirit, determination and enthusiasm that spread through the dressing-room as a result of Rice's vibrant attitude to the game.

Above all else, Rice, like so many Springboks, is dedicated to winning. To coin a sporting cliché, he leads by example. Whether with the bat, the ball or in the field, he has consistently produced the kind of performances that have uplifted less-talented colleagues. Despite South Africa's continuing absence from Test cricket – a fact which frustrates him to the point of embitterment – Rice has used the county game and South African cricket, as well as his flirtation with WSC, to reveal himself as one of the most complete and competitive of modern all-rounders. As a right-handed bat, he has gained a reputation as a prodigious hitter. There are few more powerful front-foot drivers around, but in no way have his technique and timing been sacrificed for ferocity. At his best he is equally untroubled by pace or spin, and his ability to hit "through" the ball on turning pitches has often saved Nottinghamshire when at their most vulnerable.

It is almost taken for granted at Trent Bridge now that Rice completes 1,000 first-class runs in a season. His best aggregate was in 1978 when he scored 1,871 runs at an average of 66.82. In 1980 he hit five centuries, including two, both unbeaten, in the match against Somerset, and reeled off seven 50s. His run-making has often been best illustrated in the limited-overs competitions, particularly the John Player League. In 1977 he blitzed all previous figures with a total of 814 runs on Sundays alone.

There is something of the showman in his make-up, being often at his best when a ground is full and he can respond to the sort of crowd participation upon which he would thrive if the Test door were open to him. He would almost certainly be guaranteed a place in a South African side for his batting alone, but run-making is just one facet of a multi-talented cricketer who came to prominence in his own country as much for his pace bowling as his stroke-play.

Although troubled by an assortment of injuries, he has given the Nottinghamshire attack the kind of hostility and penetration it has not had for years. At times his partnership with the New Zealander, Richard Hadlee, has all but rekindled memories of the halcyon days of Larwood and Voce. In the last three seasons they have represented, when fit together (which has been too seldom), one of the most formidable opening attacks in county cricket.

Rice is also held in high esteem in South Africa, where he returns annually in search of sun and cricketing success. In 1980 he helped Transvaal win both the Currie Cup and Datsun Shield for the second successive year, his 43-wicket haul taking him to the top of the national averages. However, the Transvaal side being so rich in talent, batting opportunities have been fewer than he would have liked. He had not, in fact, scored a first-class century in South Africa until the winter of 1979-80 when he made two, in successive matches, against Western Province and Natal. But any honours he achieves in South Africa detract in no way from his ambition to take Nottinghamshire to the top of the tree. – J.L.

V.A.P. VAN DER BIJL

Few cricketers have made a bigger impact in a single season of English county cricket than VINTCENT ADRIAAN PIETER VAN DER BIJL made in 1980. He took 85 wickets at 14.72 apiece, finishing virtually top of the first-class bowling averages. He made a massive contribution to Middlesex's victories in the Schweppes County Championship and the Gillette Cup, not only with wickets but also with controlled hitting when runs were needed. When he arrived in April, he had a long tally of broken records behind him in South Africa and, on a variety of pitches in an uneven English summer, he more than justified the reputation which had preceded him of being one of the best fast-medium bowlers in the world. Most of all he brought, as is generally agreed, "a breath of fresh air" with his immense enthusiasm, his love of playing cricket, and his bubbling friendship for other cricketers.

Born in Cape Town on March 19, 1948, he is a member of one of only four South African families to have had three generations of first-class cricketers. His grandfather, V. A. W. van der Bijl, played for Western Province in 1892 and a great-uncle was selected for a tour of England but had to decline.

Vintcent van der Bijl's success in England in 1980 must have given special pleasure to those who knew his father, Pieter, a greatly loved figure as a Rhodes Scholar at Oxford in the early 1930s, as a soldier in the Second World War, and thereafter as a famous schoolmaster in the Cape. Pieter was in the Oxford side of 1932 with two other eminent South African cricketers, Alan Melville and "Tuppy" Owen-Smith. As a resolute opening batsman he made 125 and 97 in the "Timeless" Test in Durban in 1939. Though seriously wounded in the Desert Campaign, he was always closely concerned with cricket afterwards and, after retiring as headmaster of the Diocesan College Preparatory School, Rondebosch – "Bishops" Prep – he was proving a great success as Director of Coaching for the Western Province Cricket Union when he died suddenly in 1973.

He had by then been delighted and surprised by the start of his son's remarkable career in first-class cricket, having thought that Vintcent would be no more than a good club cricketer. I was present in the van der Bijl house at Rondebosch on New Year's Day 1967 when Vintcent, then just leaving Bishops, was setting off for the Nuffield Schools Week, in Rhodesia that year, as captain of the Western Province side. Pieter was asked how good a cricketer Vintcent was. "Oh, I don't know", he said vaguely and with a certain lack of paternal optimism, "but" – this with more certainty – "if they could only get someone the same size to pack down in the second row with him, he'd kick goals for them from all over the field". Vintcent, it seems, was a prodigious place-kicker.

Vintcent van der Bijl had already reached his height of 6ft 7½in but had not long been bowling. It was Tom Reddick, late of Nottinghamshire and for many years a coach of inspiration in Western Province, who had persuaded him to take bowling seriously at the age of fifteen. In 1967 he was still batting high up the order in schools cricket. In the next year or two he probably had two pieces of luck, the first that he went to the University of Natal. This took him away from Cape Town, where the slow, low pitches of Newlands at that time would not have helped a young fast-medium bowler, though he was successful enough there later when in his prime. He stayed on, too, in Natal during one vacation to work and in that time was invited to play for Natal.

He had not been very successful in his first first-class matches for the South African Universities in 1967-68, but under the influence of the Sports Director of Natal University, Trevor Goddard, he was soon bowling well enough for the University in league cricket to go straight into the Natal side, missing out the "B" team. Peter Pollock was another to help him, as van der Bijl began the career with Natal in which in the twelve seasons from 1968-69 to 1979-80, he broke all sorts of records.

He is the highest wicket-taker in Currie Cup history with 420 wickets and the highest for Natal or any other province in first-class matches with 458 wickets. He holds the record of 65 wickets in a season of South African domestic cricket. He has taken more wickets than any South African bowler in history. He holds the Gillette Cup/Datsun Shield record of wickets taken in this limited-overs competition. He has made more appearances for Natal than any other cricketer, including 77 in succession – a compliment in itself to the fitness of one who has an extensive frame to look after and cannot be expected to be as supple as others. Yet he has made himself into a very competent fielder and he is a fine catcher.

In 1976-77 he took over the captaincy of Natal, who duly won the Currie Cup and became the first province to win the 60 overs Datsun Shield in the same season. As Natal's batting declined in subsequent seasons he applied himself more to his own batting and in 1978-79 made his first Currie Cup 50, in fact his first three 50s. The consistency with the bat which was to be so useful to Middlesex was developed. In 1979-80 the Natal Cricket Association paid him the unusual tribute of granting him a benefit. By then, Vintcent van der Bijl would probably have been considered by those who played against him and watched him as the best bowler never to have played in a Test match. He was picked for the tour of Australia in 1971-72 but it did not take place.

Early in 1980, however, an opportunity occurred to break new ground. He had not been a professional cricketer – he was a schoolmaster in Pietermaritzburg who loved playing cricket – and he was not greatly bothered that he was not widely known outside South Africa, where he had taken all his first-class wickets. But because of South Africa's isolation, he had been deprived of the more colourful life and the travelling which other cricketers of his standing take for granted. He had been to England only once, on a private tour with the Wilfred Isaacs' XI in 1969.

Then in 1979 he gave up teaching and went into business. When Middlesex approached him, his employers, Wiggins Teape, generously let him off for six months, as he says, "to fulfil my personal ambition" – and also to gain business experience in Britain. For Middlesex, his arrival in April 1980 and the failure of West Indies to pick Wayne Daniel for their tour promised a Championship-winning partnership. For Vintcent van der Bijl it was a marvellous chance to take his wife, Beverley, and their two daughters, Sarah and Chloe, to England for the first time. As one of the later chapters in his playing career, he would be sampling the different and, to use an overworked word, challenging world of English first-class cricket.

He would have enjoyed it however it had worked out, and would have remembered it all his days. In the event, a lot of others, players and spectators, were to remember it too. – M.M.

STATUS OF MATCHES IN THE UK

(a) Automatic First-Class Matches

The following matches of three or more days duration should automatically be considered first-class:

- (i) County Championship matches.
- (ii) Official representative tourist matches from ICC full member countries, unless specifically excluded.
- (iii) MCC v any first-class county.
- (iv) Oxford v Cambridge and either University against first-class counties.
- (v) Scotland v Ireland.

(b) Excluded from First-Class Status

The following matches of three or more days duration should not normally be accorded first-class status:

- (i) County "friendly" matches.
- (ii) Matches played by Scotland or Ireland, other than their annual match against each other.
- (iii) Unofficial tourist matches, unless circumstances are exceptional.
- (iv) MCC v Oxford/Cambridge.
- (v) Matches involving privately raised teams, unless included officially in a touring team's itinerary.

(c) Consideration of Doubtful Status

Matches played by unofficial touring teams of exceptional ability can be considered in advance and decisions taken accordingly.

Certain other matches comprising 22 recognised first-class cricketers might also be considered in advance.

NOTES BY THE EDITOR

"This leads us to the much greater question of the desirability of further altering the Law of leg before wicket." (*1934*)

"As to the events of the past year, the happiest man in the country must have been the born pessimist. In the course of 16 months our cricketers have lost a rubber in Australia, West Indies and South Africa in turn." (*1936*)

"Of great leg-break bowlers there was none." (*1939*)

"The fast natural pitch, made as level as a billard table by mowing, rolling and watering, would increase greatly the likelihood of a definite result in county matches." (*1944*)

"In short . . . English cricket needs an injection of culture and enterprise." (*1952*)

These extracts are taken from this corresponding article on the last five occasions that a new editor of *Wisden* has taken over, and they all, to some degree, apply today. The Law of leg before is still under discussion; England are still losing successive rubbers to Australia and West Indies; there are now no English leg-break bowlers, let alone any great ones; "fast natural pitches" remain as elusive as ever; and English batsmanship is in need once again of "an injection of culture".

So when I sound a cautionary note, or a sombre one, it will be in the established tradition of these notes. *Deja vu* you may think. There is one aspect, even so, of the year under review which is new and of great concern. This is the manner and frequency with which famous players have flouted the authority of the umpires. In all the years that *Wisden* has been published, there can have been no more shocking photograph than that, to be found in the illustration section, of Michael Holding, the distinguished and richly talented West Indian fast bowler, kicking the stumps out of the ground in a Test match in New Zealand – for no other reason than that he disagreed with an umpire's decision.

Unbridled Dissent

Nor was this an isolated example of such unbridled dissent. In the same Test series Colin Croft, another of the West Indian fast bowlers, having lost his temper, sent an umpire flying as he ran into bowl. In India, at much the same time, the umpires were being denounced by the touring Pakistanis; in Perth, Dennis Lillee, the great Australian, held up play for ten minutes in a Test match between England and Australia while he argued with the umpires and his own captain over the use of an aluminium bat in which he had a proprietorial interest. Technically Lillee had a point, there being nothing in the Laws at that time, though there is now, to say that a bat must be made of wood; morally, as he must have known, he should have done as the umpires asked him.

As disconcerting as these individual cases of defiance was the way in which they were glossed over by those whose responsibility it was to make an example of the players concerned. In New Zealand, the West Indian manager, himself a former Test player, blamed the umpires for what was happening. No wonder that when the West Indians left for home the New Zealand cricketing public, to quote R. T. Brittenden in his summary of the tour, "was glad to see the back of them". In Australia, the Chairman of the Australian Cricket Board said that he could not understand what all the fuss was about over Lillee's insubordination. Ian Chappell, an outstanding batsman and conspicuously successful captain of Australia, was suspended once, and subsequently given a second suspended sentence, for tilting at the precept that the umpire's decision is final; but in Australia, as elsewhere, the standards of cricketing discipline have in recent years been regularly compromised.

Towards the end of 1980, however, it began to seem as though those who administer the game were themselves seeing the red light. In West Indies Gerry Gomez, a member of the West Indian Board of Control, advocated a series of fines aimed at calling the players to order. There was a move among members of the International Cricket Conference to appoint independent "observers" to Test series. From Pakistan came a suggestion that Test umpires should be empowered to send players off the field. Even in Australia the senior players, or most of them, were looking for ways of keeping the hoodlums at bay.

Formidable West Indians

English cricket is certainly not blameless. Many young players, upon entering the county game, are surprised by the language they hear and the distractions they encounter. However, in England last season, among all those who played first-class cricket, there were signs that attitudes were being rethought. The Test matches against West Indies, and later the Centenary Test against Australia at Lord's, were played in a good spirit. Only the weather prevented West Indies from beating England more comfortably than by a single victory. The West Indians, remorseless in certain tactical respects, were a powerful side and less prone than most of their predecessors to self-destruction. They and their manager, Clyde Walcott, were on their guard against such a collapse of morale and discipline as had undermined them in New Zealand earlier in the year.

There can never have been a side more heavily reliant on their fast bowlers than these West Indians, or better served by them. When the fifth Test match ended in August, West Indies had played ten Tests in 1980 and included a spin bowler in only one of them – that when, against all the odds, they lost to New Zealand in Dunedin. It is a pity, none the less, to see them so committed to speed. A balanced attack adds to the joys of watching cricket; to sit through a day's play in which only 74 overs are bowled, as happened in the Oval Test match, does not. In England last year Croft, Garner, Holding, Marshall and Roberts, the West Indian fast bowlers, were formidable in attack and effective in defence. Vivian Richards, one of the two Antiguans in the West Indian side, remains the world's most brilliant batsman. Sir Gary Sobers was the last most powerful single influence on the game; before that, Sir Donald Bradman was.

Rain and More Rain

The summer of 1980 was the wettest since 1958, when the New Zealanders, in England on a full tour, lost the equivalent of a month's cricket. In 1954 the first visit of the Pakistanis took place in a disastrously wet year. While in the 1932 *Wisden*, the editor in his Notes wrote of such deplorable weather being experienced in 1931 "that coming on top of the almost equally wet season of 1930, the loss of money rendered the position of several of the less wealthy counties serious to a degree. . . . In first-class games there were 111 days on which not a ball could be bowled. . . . The wet and cheerless weather not only discouraged people from attending matches owing to the discomfort it created but, in delaying play and destroying interest, exercised a further prejudicial effect upon the receipts." In 1980 a colleague from the provinces went for six consecutive Saturdays without seeing a ball bowled. After a cool but uncommonly dry May it rained for most of the rest of the season.

The Sponsors' Rôle

That the same seventeen counties which made up the County Championship 50 years ago still do so today is due to a large extent to the generosity and abundance of the game's sponsors – from those who invest hundreds of thousands of pounds in it to others who pay perhaps once a season for the players' lunches on a county ground. Each year cricket becomes increasingly dependent upon patronage. In a sense it is on a life-support machine, kept going by good will but threatened, like so much else, by the current recession, and the doubts concerning the future of cigarette advertising. Such happenings as those which made a travesty of the Saturday of the Centenary Test match are also of no encouragement to would-be sponsors.

The Centenary Fracas

This great jamboree, arranged to celebrate 100 years of Test cricket between England and Australia in England, had been eagerly awaited. Its counterpart, at Melbourne in 1977, had been a wonderful success. As will be clear from the account of it elsewhere in this almanack, last summer's match was ill-fated from the start. Some would say that the hours from eleven o'clock until six o'clock on the Saturday were like a nightmare. So incensed were certain members of MCC by the middle of the afternoon that play was not in progress, owing, as they thought, to the obstinacy of the umpires, that a scuffle took place on the steps of the pavilion, in which the umpires, one or two members, and the captains were involved. As a result of it, the umpires were shaken, the reputation of MCC was damaged and the occasion impaired.

Two and a half months later, following what MCC described as a "thorough inquiry" – which included taking the evidence of the umpires, the captains and a number of members, and studying a BBC film recording of the incident – Peter May, President of MCC, wrote in a letter to all members of the club that "appropriate disciplinary action" had been taken. He made the point, too, that it was no more fitting for members of a club publicly to question the decision of the umpires, let alone abuse them, than for players to do so on the field. If good is to come from a sorry affair, it will be to see that efforts are redoubled to provide the best possible covering on all first-class grounds, especially those where Test matches are staged. As many have said, it seems laughable to be able to land a man on the moon yet to have discovered no adequate way of protecting the square at Lord's.

Who Would Be an Umpire?

One way and another it was a difficult year for umpires. With such large amounts of prize-money at stake, and a levelling-out of standards in Test and other first-class cricket, the game is becoming ever more fiercely competitive and the umpire's job correspondingly more demanding. Not only that. Every decision a Test umpire makes is subjected to a slow-motion television replay. In the Jubilee Test Match which England played in Bombay on their way home from Australia in February (50 years had passed since the Board of Control for Cricket in India was officially constituted), an umpire was constrained to change a decision. Having shown his surprise at being given out to an appeal for a catch at the wicket, Taylor, the England wicket-keeper, was reprieved upon the request of the Indian captain. That this, however well intentioned, was a misguided gesture became more clear in England's second innings when the same umpire, having given Boycott out, leg before wicket, changed his own mind when the batsman stood his ground. An umpire without confidence is worse than no umpire at all.

I am opposed to the idea of neutral umpires for Test matches. By the very nature of their job all umpires are fallible, whoever they may be, and on the rare occasions that I have wondered about the integrity of an umpire it has usually been because one side or the other has been harassing him. Remember, too, that if ever neutral umpires are introduced into Test cricket, England will never again have the benefit of playing under those who by common consent are the best of all umpires – the two dozen or so, that is, who stand day in and day out in the English county game. By the John Langridges of the world, that is. After 52 years as player and umpire in first-class cricket, Langridge has gone into honourable retirement.

The Over-rate Problem

Before moving on to other matters, I do enjoin umpires to keep a close eye on over-rates, especially in Test matches. For fear of being fined, as now happens, for dropping below nineteen overs an hour, English county sides are conscious of the need to keep moving. Unfortunately the International Cricket Conference allowed their annual meeting at Lord's last August to pass without giving more than a shadowy undertaking to keep an eye on what is becoming a cause for serious concern in the Test game. Meeting as they did immediately after a Test series in which England and West Indies had seldom bowled more than fifteen overs an hour and sometimes as few as twelve, the time was ripe for taking firm action. But nothing positive was done.

The Passing of WSC

On the surface, the end of traditional cricket's acrimonious dispute with Mr Kerry Packer brought a reasonably harmonious return to normality. But at what cost to the game? Cricketers who were previously paid too little are now, in some cases, being paid more than the game can afford or they themselves are worth. Money has become the talk of the first-class dressing-rooms, with the average county cricketer feeling that Test players are getting a disproportionately large slice of the cake.

In Australia, one worrying aspect of the settlement which led to the running-down of World Series Cricket is the new structure of the first-class game there, this now being devised to accommodate commercial television. When England were in Australia in the winter of 1979-80, a tour they shared with West Indies, such was the confusion of fixtures that attendances and authenticity both suffered. The public seemed not to know what to expect next, or indeed for what trophy any given match was being played. As for the players, they were given little chance to settle down to any one type of cricket, whether one-day, four-day or five-day, all of which call for different tactics and not necessarily the same skills. It is important that before England tour Australia next, in 1982-83, they should negotiate resolutely for the itinerary they consider to be in the best interests of both countries.

Too Much Test Cricket

The reason most often given for the decline in interest in the first-class game in Australia is that it has reached the point of saturation. The same applies to association football in England. There is too much of it, just as there is now, to my mind, too much Test cricket. Between the middle of July 1979 and the middle of February 1980, a matter of seven months, India played seventeen Test matches. A series between them and West Indies, due to have taken place in March and April 1980, was cancelled simply because both countries were surfeited with Test cricket. Between December 1974 and the first week of September this year, England will have played Australia no fewer than 31 times. This is more than twice the rate at which they met until only a few years ago. In 1981, for the first time in England, Australia are playing six Test matches. We must be careful not to kill the goose that lays the golden egg.

Also for the first time in England there will be Test cricket on Sundays in 1981 – not in every Test but at Trent Bridge, Edgbaston and Old Trafford. The case for this, by those keen to make it, was strengthened by the loss of so much play on the first three days of last year's Centenary Test. Both captains expressed the view then that the Sunday should have been set aside for making up time lost. The decision now taken to implement Sunday play means that in three of this season's Test matches there will be no rest day. Thinking, as I do, that both players and public need one, and being opposed to the advancing tide of Continentalism on Sundays, this is a barrier which I would rather had not been broken down. So, no doubt, would John Player and Sons who, since their Sunday League began in 1969, have had Sunday afternoons more or less to themselves.

The Night Experiment

New to the English scene in 1980 was night cricket, played on football grounds. Though the cricket itself was of no consequence, a germ has been implanted. There are, in cricketing administration today, marketing men whose desire to bring money into the game causes them to trifle with its origins and gamble with its charm. Night cricket in Sydney, being on a genuine cricket ground, indeed a great one, can be a dazzling spectacle, not far removed from the real thing; at Stamford Bridge it smacks of gimmickry. Should it ever catch on, it may have to be given another name, which is not to dismiss it as being of no threat to the present game. I have not included in this edition of *Wisden* the scores of the three night matches played in England last summer because they were meaningless.

Middlesex Win the Championship

The most coveted prize in English cricket, the Schweppes County Championship, was won for the third time in the last five years by Middlesex, who were gallantly pursued right to the last by Surrey. When they were all fit, Daniel, van der Bijl, Selvey, Emburey and Edmonds comprised as strong a county attack as any since the Bedsers, Laker, Loader and Lock bowled for Surrey in the 1950s. With Brearley, a full-time county cricketer now that he is no longer England's captain, Barlow, Gatting, Radley and the West Indian, Roland Butcher, all averaging over 40, the Middlesex batting was good enough. van der Bijl, a giant South African who had already taken more wickets in South Africa's Currie Cup competition than anyone before him, had been signed during the winter of 1979-80 for one year's county cricket, which was something he had always wanted to have. This was when Middlesex thought that Daniel was certain to be chosen for last summer's West Indian tour of England. In the event, Daniel was overlooked by West Indies and Middlesex were left with not one but two formidable opening bowlers.

The Overseas Influence

Yet even to some of their own supporters, Middlesex's victory meant less than if it had not owed so much to overseas assistance. The extent to which these cricketers from abroad are being allowed to hinder the progress of young English talent has become an intolerable frustration to the England selectors. Time after time in 1980, Alec Bedser, in his nineteenth season as a selector and his eleventh as Chairman, went, as he hoped, to see an England candidate in action, only to spend most of his day watching someone bat or bowl who was ineligible to play for England. At different times during the season ten West Indians, four South Africans, two Pakistanis, two Australians, a Zimbabwian and a New Zealander were to be found opening the bowling in English county cricket.

It was the same in batting. There were days when the first three places in the Gloucestershire order were occupied by two Pakistanis and a South African, and when most of Derbyshire's runs were scored by a New Zealander, a South African, a 38-year-old exile from Northamptonshire and a 37-year-old Yorkshireman who had recently been under suspension for the manner in which he had left Lancashire, his previous employers. Not surprisingly, K. J. Barnett, a Derbyshire cricketer of high promise, was deprived of the opportunities which he needed and England need him to have.

There are many other examples of how counties, in trying to buy success for themselves, are impeding England's prospects. Sussex, heavily over-drawn, were in the absurd position in 1980 of employing three highly paid overseas players, of whom, in County Championship matches, they were allowed at any one time to include only two. Imran Khan and le Roux, although no doubt they helped to win Sussex a match or two, are both opening bowlers; as such they hindered the advancement of Pigott, a young Englishman who has thrown in his lot with Sussex, and hastened the retirement of Spencer. Wessels, a South African living in Australia, for whom he is now qualified to play, was Sussex's third overseas player.

The Selectors' Difficulties

There must in the circumstances be much sympathy for the England selectors. They are being hopelessly hamstrung. It is the present intention of the counties that they shall each be limited, from 1982 onwards, to one overseas player, other than those who were already registered with them, or in the process of being, in November 1978. Against the day when this happens, towards the end of last season Gloucestershire had their captain, Procter, converted into an "Englishman". Although the regulations entitled Gloucestershire to do so (Procter now has a home in England and it is ten years since he played for South Africa), their motives were purely subjective. As an "Englishman" Procter will no longer count as an overseas player when, next year, the rules of qualification are tightened.

As I write these notes, a Test and County Cricket Board working party, under the chairmanship of C. R. M. Atkinson, a former Somerset captain, is looking into the idea of introducing some system of compensation to be awarded to counties whose players are lured away by the offer of a more lucrative contract. As the doors close to players from overseas, the richer counties may be expected to look to other counties, rather than other countries, to strengthen their sides, in which case a transfer market could well develop.

Technically, once Procter had been registered as an "Englishman" there was nothing to stop him from being chosen to go with the England side to West Indies. The selectors had already picked a West Indian (Butcher) who had lived in England since he was a boy, and on merit Procter was eminently worth a place. There was, of course, a political reason for not taking him: whatever England's cricketing regulations may say, Procter is a South African, and in the West Indies South Africans are taboo. Many fine cricketers from overseas have enhanced the English county game – by way of entertainment, quality and example. But by their very numbers they have now become an embarrassment.

England's New Captain

Ian Botham's accession to the England captaincy emphasised how much Brearley, his successor, had meant in his measured way to the England side. It was Brearley's reluctance to tour any more that forced the selectors to make a change, and although Fletcher, Rose, David Lloyd, Knight, Hampshire and Boycott all had their advocates to succeed him, Brearley was known to favour Botham, who, once he had been given last summer's six Test matches, was the logical choice to take the side to the West Indies.

Botham's start in what is an increasingly taxing job was inauspicious. Suffering from a back injury which slowed him down as a bowler, and faced with leading a pedestrian England side against the West Indians, he was unable to reproduce the brilliant form that had enabled him, within a fortnight in February, to score 119 not out against Australia in Melbourne and dominate the Jubilee Test match in Bombay. Moreover, owing to a calendar in which so many days are given over to one-day cricket, Botham went from June 4 to August 3 without playing a single first-class innings for his county. It was hardly surprising that he complained of having no chance to bat himself into form for the Test matches.

Donning the Helmet

Last year was the first in which helmets, or reinforced caps, became standard wear in first-class cricket. When, as more often than not, they have a visor attached, they reduce the batsman, or short-leg fielder, to wretched anonymity. I find it sartorially and aesthetically an objectionable trend. It has, furthermore, detracted from the artistry of batting. As you would expect, old players deplore the sight of a helmeted batsman. Yet if their use saves cricketers from serious injury, they must be allowed. Had short-pitched bowling, over the years, not got so out of hand, they would not be necessary. But it has, and because of the protection which helmets afford, there may in future be more bumpers than ever. This, certainly, is something which umpires will need to watch. The game's administrators would prefer to prohibit the use of helmets in the field. Here too, though, there is the aspect of safety. The helmet, it seems, has come to stay – an unsightly adjunct to an increasingly dangerous game.

The Gillette Connection

A word of gratitude to Gillette, who were one of the pioneers of modern cricket sponsorship, from which they have now withdrawn. So smoothly did their knockout cup overcome the objections to one-day cricket that one of their reasons for giving it up was that it had come to be associated not with anything they made but almost exclusively with cricket. Their place has been taken by the National Westminster Bank. At a dinner to mark the end of the Gillette connection, Clive Lloyd was nominated as the outstanding cricketer of their eighteen years in the game.

Full Covering

As the year ended, and to the dismay of many traditionalists, the seventeen first-class counties, through the Test and County Cricket Board, voted that in 1981 pitches should be fully covered in all Championship matches. Although groundsmen are to be asked to prepare drier pitches, which show earlier signs of wear, in order to compensate spin bowlers for being deprived of the occasional "sticky dog" to bowl on, this will be difficult to implement. At times, inevitably, the weather will prevent it; at others, broken pitches will be an embarrassment to the home authorities no less than to batsmen.

When pitches were last fully covered in Championship cricket, in 1959, the experiment was soon discontinued. Now that it is to be given another trial, it is as well to keep an open mind. I cannot forbear, even so, from lamenting even a temporary loss of a part of the very heritage of English cricket – a drying pitch and a sizzling sun. Some of the great feats of batsmanship have been performed under these conditions. It is to try to make county cricket as much as possible like Test cricket, in which full covering is universally practised, that the Test and County Cricket Board have taken this important decision.

What most concerns groundsmen about it are the ill-effects that come from a strip of turf being too regularly protected from the elements. The danger of disease increases, as was seen at Headingley in 1972 when fuserium fungus so ravaged the Test pitch. However, last December's change to full covering was not recommended without much careful consideration by the Cricket Committee of the Test and County Cricket Board. It had been rejected at the TCCB's Spring Meeting, when the Cricket Committee was under the chairmanship of P. B. H. May; when it was proposed again, and carried, D. J. Insole had taken the place of May, who by then was President of MCC.

A Restriction Ended

At this same December meeting it was decided to dispense with the 100 overs first innings limitation in County Championship matches. For many reasons it was felt to be doing more harm than good to English cricket. Among them were the unreasonable pressure it placed upon middle-order batsmen, many of them the less-experienced members of a side, to hit out wildly as the 100 overs ran out; the tendency for the fielding side to revert to negative tactics in the certain knowledge that their opponents' innings had only a short time to run; and the idea that it discouraged creative captaincy. Although bonus points in Championship cricket are likewise liable to encourage a fielding side to concentrate upon saving runs rather than taking wickets, they, for the moment, are to be retained.

NORMAN PRESTON, MBE

EDITOR OF WISDEN 1951-1980

Born March 18, 1903,
died March 6, 1980

The following tribute was paid by Denis Compton to Norman Preston at Norman's Memorial Service held at St Bride's, Fleet Street, on April 10, 1980.

Throughout my cricketing career I regarded Norman Preston as one of my best friends. His jovial face, lively sense of humour and infectious laugh endeared him to all cricketers. How true it was when he was affectionately described by John Woodcock of *The Times* as the Mr Pickwick of cricket.

Norman was always a great family man and very proud of his wife Molly and three children, Brian, David and Helen.

Many here today will, like me, have their own personal memories of Norman but there will be some we all share because Norman Preston was not one to present different faces to different people. Rather, he could be described as a definite man: definite in appearance, definite in his opinions, and definite in his likes and dislikes. To those of us who were privileged to know him well he was also a man of great humanity and pride in the best sense of that word.

That pride showed itself in his pleasure at being honoured by the award of the MBE in the Queen's Jubilee Honours List in 1977 – an award he regarded as belonging as much to his beloved Almanack as to himself. Pride, too, in his profession, which he showed on receiving his MBE from the Queen when, on being asked what he did, replied: "I am a sporting reporter, Your Majesty." Sporting reporter he certainly was, with a career spanning 47 years which began when he joined the old Pardon's Cricket Reporting Agency in 1933 and took in three overseas tours as Reuters' correspondent.

The 28 editions of *Wisden Cricketers' Almanack* published under his editorship are also testimony to the truth of that statement. They cover a period which saw more changes and innovations than any other in the history of the game. Norman saw to it that *Wisden* faithfully recorded events as they occurred and never forebore to comment forthrightly whenever he thought such comment was called for.

Although cricket was perhaps his first love, this beautiful church reminds us of one of his other great joys – the sound of good choral singing. Norman always maintained that the greatest thrill he experienced on his overseas tours was not a cricketing moment but singing in the Sydney Cathedral choir one Sunday morning. I am sure many of his journalist friends will also recall that he always enjoyed a sing-song, and enlivened many a convivial evening with a rendering of the "Fishermen Of England" in his rich bass-baritone voice.

[*Courtesy of Mrs N. Preston*   [*Patrick Eagar*

Hubert and Norman Preston – between them 86 years of compiling and then editing *Wisden Cricketers' Almanack*.

Norman Preston is rightly assured of a place in cricket history, not because of prowess on the field of play, nor indeed because of the power of his pen, but because for 28 years he ensured that every detail of cricket was duly compiled, collated and published without fear or favour. He would not, I feel sure, have wanted it any other way.

A tribute by Harold Abel, who for many years was the late editor's closest adviser and assistant in the production of Wisden.

To have lived 35 years knowing Norman Preston, first as my employer, then as a close colleague, and finally, I like to think, as a trusted friend, means that his passing leaves a deep chasm. Here was a man who within half an hour could chastise you, console you and take you for a drink. To be able to forgive is one of life's great virtues – and Norman could do that. To bear a grudge was not for him. He was an extrovert, ever ready to enter a conversation, invited or uninvited. Nobody needed to be lonely in his presence, and no-one was for long.

Norman's voice was heard more than once from the choir stalls of St Paul's Cathedral. He sang better than he played sport, though in his 76 years he entered wholeheartedly into many pastimes. Towards the end of his days he bore a strong facial resemblance to his father, Hubert, known, likewise with affection, as "Deafy". Both spent most of their working days in Fleet Street as partners in the Cricket Reporting Agency (C. F. Pardon), from whence, until it was merged in 1965 with the Press Association, came the majority of *Wisden's* editors.

Hubert was in the editorial chair from 1944 until 1951, and Norman from 1952 (when *Wisden* cost twelve shillings and sixpence) until his death. The book was never far from the minds of either of them. Norman also found time to make three MCC tours as Reuters' correspondent. *Wisden's* other editors have been W. H. Knight (1864-1879), G. H. West (1880-1886), Charles F. Pardon (1887-1890), Sydney H. Pardon (1891-1925), C. Stewart Caine (1926-1933), Sydney J. Southerton (1934-1935), Wilfrid H. Brookes (1936-1939) and Haddon Whitaker (1940-1943).

CLARRIE GRIMMETT

Born in Dunedin, December 25, 1891,
died in Adelaide, May 2, 1980

By W. J. O'REILLY

Born in Dunedin in the South Island of New Zealand on Christmas Day, Clarence Victor Grimmett must have been the best Christmas present Australia ever received from that country. Going to Australia in 1914, on a "short working holiday" which lasted for 66 years, he joined the Sydney club, which had its headquarters at Rushcutters Bay. Three years in Sydney District cricket were sufficient to warn him that Arthur Mailey, another great spinner, had literally been given the green light towards the New South Wales team and all fields beyond. This, and marriage to a Victorian girl, took Grimmett to Melbourne, where he played with the South Melbourne club. During his six years in Melbourne he was given only three invitations to play for Victoria, the third of which was against South Australia when, providentially, he collected eight wickets.

It was after his visit to Sydney with the Victorians, for the first Shield match after the Great War, that I managed to see him for the first time. In Sydney, in the match against New South Wales, Ted McDonald had performed outstandingly for Victoria and was consequently the cynosure of all eyes when the Victorian team, on its way home to Melbourne, played an up-country match in the mountain city of Goulburn. Not quite all eyes, however. The attention of one pair, belonging to a thirteen-year-old boy named O'Reilly, was rivetted on a wiry little leg-spinner whose name on the local score-board was "Grummett". To me, from that day onward, "Grummett" he remained, and my own endearing name for him throughout our later long association was "Grum".

We played together for the first time in an Australian team at Adelaide against Herbie Cameron's South Africans in 1931, and for the last time in the Durban Test of 1936 when Vic Richardson's Australian side became the first ever to go through a tour undefeated – a feat paralleled by Bradman's 1948 team in England. On that 1935-36 South African tour, "Grum" set an Australian record for a Test series with 44 wickets, yet he came home to be dropped forever from the Australian side. He was shoved aside like a worn-out boot for each of the five Tests against Gubby Allen's English team in Australia in 1936-37 and he failed to gain a place in the 1938 team to England, led by Bradman.

It was illogical to assume that age was the reason for his discard. He was 47, it is true, when the touring side was chosen, yet two years later, at the age of 49, he established an Australian record of 73 wickets for a domestic first-class season. Which raises, rather pointedly, the question of "why the hell was he dropped?" By now Don Bradman was Grimmett's captain for South Australia, and also Australia's captain. As such he was an Australian selector, and Bradman, it seemed, had become inordinately impressed with the spin ability of Frank Ward, a former clubmate of his in Sydney. It was Ward who was chosen for the first three Tests against Allen's side in 1936-37 and who caught the boat for England in 1938. Bradman, it seemed, had lost faith in the best spin bowler the world has seen. "Grum's" departure was a punishing blow to me and to my plans of attack. His diagnostic type of probing spin buttressed my own methods to such a degree that my reaction to his dismissal was one of infinite loss and loneliness.

Unlike Arthur Mailey, the first of the Australian spin trilogy of the inter-wars era, Grimmett never insisted on spin as his chief means of destruction. To him it was no more than an important adjunct to unerring length and tantalising direction. Grimmett seldom beat a batsman by spin alone. Mailey often did. I cannot remember Grimmett bowling a long-hop, whereas Mailey averaged one an over. So much, in fact, did inaccuracy become a feature of Mailey's success that he himself came to believe that it was an essential ingredient. Such wantoness was anathema to Grimmett, who believed that a bowler should bowl as well as he possibly could every time he turned his arm over. And Grimmett was perhaps the best and most consistently active cricket thinker I ever met.

He loved to tell his listeners that it was he who taught Stan McCabe how to use his left hand correctly on the bat handle – and I never heard Stan deny it. The "flipper" was originated by "Grum" during that Babylonian Captivity of his, and he used it to good effect in his record-breaking last season before the Second World War. He passed it on to men like Bruce Dooland and Cecil Pepper. He seldom bowled the "wrong 'un", because he preferred not to toss the ball high. On hard, true pitches he would bowl faster than his usual pace, taunting good batsmen to get to him on the half-volley. He was a genius on direction, and his talent for preying on a batsman's weakness was unequalled. He never let a batsman off the hook; once you were under his spell you were there to stay.

Grimmett joined South Australia from Victoria in 1923, just in time to bowl his way into the final Test in Sydney against Arthur Gilligan's 1924-25 England team. In his baptismal effort he took eleven wickets. In 79 Sheffield Shield games he tallied 513 wickets, an Australian record that will probably last for ever. The most successful Shield spinner in modern times, Richie Benaud, totalled 266 wickets in 73 matches, a relatively insignificant performance. Of Grimmett's 106 Test wickets against England, nearly 70 were collected on English pitches in a land where savants say leg-spinners are ineffective. One wonders what colossal figures he would have amassed had he played all his first-class cricket in England. Had he done so, you can be sure there would not be half the present insistence on pacier finger-cutting.

It was lucky for me that I preferred to bowl downwind, an unusual trait in a spinner's character. It allowed our partnership to develop and prosper. No captain ever had to worry which bowling end was whose. We competed strongly with each other and kept a critical eye on one another's

Old bowlers in the press box. Clarrie Grimmett (left) and Bill O'Reilly, lifelong friends, at work in their retirement.

performances. In Johannesburg in 1936, all-rounder "Chud" Langton hit me clean over the top of the square-leg grandstand of the old Wanderers ground. Cackling gleefully, "Grum" left no doubt in my mind that it was the biggest hit he had ever seen. Silently I was inclined to agree. In Clarrie's next over, "Chud" clouted him straight over the sightscreen and so far into the railway marshalling yards that the ball was never returned. From that delivery, until hostilities ceased for the afternoon, I never managed to get within earshot of my bowling mate.

Social life meant little to "Grum". Not until late in his career did he discover that it was not a bad idea to relax between matches. In England in 1934 I bought him a beer in the Star Hotel in Worcester to celebrate his first ten wickets of the tour. It took him so long to sink it that I decided to wait for his return gesture till some other time on the tour. Later he told me, with obvious regret, that on previous tours he had been keeping the wrong company and had never really enjoyed a touring trip. That I thought was sad, but not half as sad as I felt when, at the very zenith of his glorious career, he was tipped out of business altogether. With "Grum" at the other end, prepared to pick me up and dust me down, I feared no batsman. Our association must have been one of cricket's greatest success stories of the twentieth century.

C. V. GRIMMETT IN FIRST-CLASS CRICKET

By MICHAEL FORDHAM

	Runs	Wickets	Average	5 wkts/ Inns	10 wkts/ Match
New Zealand					
1911-12	116	4	29.00	0	0
1912-13	65	1	65.00	0	0
1913-14	498	17	29.29	0	0
Australia					
1918-19	34	0	—	0	0
1920-21	110	1	110.00	0	0
1921-22	161	6	26.83	0	0
1922-23	50	2	25.00	0	0
1923-24	98	9	10.88	1	0
1924-25	1,300	59	22.03	8	1
1925-26	1,794	59	30.40	8	3
1926 (*in England*)	1,857	105	17.68	7	1
1926-27	1,030	30	34.33	2	0
1927-28 (*in Australia*)	1,151	42	27.40	4	2
1927-28 (*in New Zealand*)	795	47	16.91	5	1
1928-29	2,432	71	34.53	5	0
1929-30	1,943	82	23.20	9	3
1930 (*in England*)	2,427	144	16.85	15	5
1930-31	1,417	74	19.14	7	1
1931-32	1,535	77	19.93	6	1
1932-33	1,577	55	28.67	5	1
1933-34	1,441	66	21.37	7	1
1934 (*in England*)	2,159	109	19.80	10	1
1934-35	1,215	58	20.94	6	3
1935-36 (*in South Africa*)	1,362	92	14.80	9	4
1936-37	1,443	48	30.06	1	0
1937-38	845	41	20.60	2	0
1938-39	563	27	20.85	2	1
1939-40	1,654	73	22.65	9	4
1940-41	668	25	26.72	1	0
Totals	31,740	1,424	22.29	129	33

BEST BOWLING

Ten for 37　　Australians v Yorkshire at Sheffield 1930
Nine for 74　　Australians v Cambridge University at Cambridge 1934
Nine for 180　South Australia v Queensland at Adelaide 1934-35

HAT-TRICK

South Australia v Queensland at Brisbane 1928-29

Note: C. V. Grimmett is one of only two Australian bowlers who have taken more than 1,000 wickets in their first-class careers without having played county cricket in England, the other being G. Giffen (1,022 wickets).

　　In Test cricket, Grimmett took 216 wickets in 37 Test matches (average 24.21). He was the first bowler to take 200 wickets in Tests, and only four other Australian bowlers have reached this figure: R. Benaud (248 wickets in 63 Tests), G. D. McKenzie (246 wickets in 60 Tests), R. R. Lindwall (228 wickets in 61 Tests), and D. K. Lillee (214 wickets in 42 Tests).

FIFTY YEARS ON

By G. O. ALLEN

The Test match against Australia at Lord's in 1930 was my first. Now, 50 years later, presumably because I am, sadly, the only surviving member of that England team, I have been asked to record my impressions of, and draw some comparisons between, that match and the Centenary Test match against Australia at Lord's last summer.

That the former was one of the great games in cricket history and the latter was not was due partly to chance. For one thing, the weather in 1930 was perfect. So, though on the slow side, was the pitch, which had been specially prepared, this being the first ever four-day Test match at Lord's. In 1980 it rained often enough and hard enough on the first three days to have confounded even the 1930 sides from providing as much entertainment and fine cricket as I believe they did half a century ago. To that extent, Chappell and Botham and their two sides were up against it from the start. On the other hand, I am sure that in 1930, in conditions similar to those on the Saturday of the Centenary Test match, play would have started much earlier than it did. In fact, looking back to the thirties, when pitches were uncovered and there was much less covering generally, I think that play was often started too soon; but surely the pendulum has now swung too far in the opposite direction.

It must seem incredible to many who play and watch the game today that England could have made 425 in the first innings of a four-day match, as they did at Lord's in 1930, and yet have lost. In reply, Australia scored 729 for six declared. In the last two hours forty minutes on the second day, Australia went from 162 for one to 404 for two – 255 runs, that is, in 160 minutes, of which Bradman made 155. At the start of the last day England, in their second innings, were 98 for two, still 206 behind with Hobbs and Woolley out, and it needed a great innings of 121 in two and a half hours by Chapman to save his side from an innings defeat. In the end Australia, losing three wickets (including that of Bradman) for 22 runs, had a minor crisis to surmount before winning with an hour to spare.

But this was the age of the batsman, the age before the lbw law was changed, and this was a batsman's match throughout. The pitch, for the reason I have mentioned, was easy-paced, and the bowlers, the leg-spinners and White excepted, were perhaps slightly below standard, Tate by then being a little over the top.

For England the outstanding innings were those of Chapman and Duleepsinhji, though Woolley's 41 in very quick time on the first morning was a gem. Duleepsinhji's 173 in his first Test match against Australia was one of the most graceful exhibitions of batting I have ever seen: he was a superb player of spinners as he proved on this occasion. Chapman's was a fine effort, particularly the second half of it, though he played and missed

many times in his first fifty. I can vouch for this as I was in with him, and he
should have been out before scoring. I can see it now: he failed to spot
Grimmett's googly and hit a skier on the off side. Woodfull, Richardson
and Ponsford all could have caught it easily, but at the last moment, no one
having called, each left it to the other. Amidst much laughter and some
apologies all Grimmett said was "Never mind, I'll get him out next over".
When watching the Centenary match with Ponsford, I mentioned the
incident to him. He remembered it well, but to our mutual enjoyment he
was disinclined to admit to more than a minor share of the guilt.

For Australia, the first four, Woodfull, Ponsford, Bradman and Kippax,
all played fine innings, each in his own rather different style: Woodfull with
his short backlift, very sure but always looking for runs; Ponsford mainly
on the back foot or up the wicket to the spinners and a superb timer of the
ball; Kippax a very elegant stroke-player on both sides of the wicket – and
then, of course, Bradman. The best comment on Bradman's innings is
probably his own. When asked which was the best innings he ever played,
he is on record as saying: "My 254 at Lord's in 1930 because I never hit a
ball anywhere than I intended and I never lifted one off the ground until the
stroke from which I was out." Some believe he was unorthodox. Well,
perhaps he was when he was really on the rampage, but in defence and
when necessary, none was more correct. It was his early judgement of
length, his quickness of foot and his ruthless concentration which made him
the undoubted genius he was.

The Centenary Test match is a different story. As I have already said,
conditions were unfavourable from the start. Even had MCC acquired an
additional cover, and before the match the captains and umpires had been
requested by the authorities to be rather less stern in their judgement as to
fitness for play, I doubt if it would have helped greatly as it is always
difficult to make a game flow once it has been subjected to frequent
interruptions.

I hate saying it, but I do not think either looked a very good side. There
were, of course, several high-class batsmen amongst them, and in Lillee
certainly the best fast bowler in either match. Although perhaps not quite as
fast as he was, his rhythm, his ability to move the ball and vary his pace,
and his unbounded determination were a feature of the match.

For Australia, Wood played a sound first innings and Chappell two good
though for him rather subdued innings. In form, with all his strokes going,
Chappell must rank high amongst batsmen of our time. But in this match it
was Hughes who caught the eye, at least mine. Of course he took some
chances and had his moments of luck, particularly in the second innings,
but he was reluctant to be dictated to, moved his feet well, and with a
wholesome backlift was able and prepared to play all the strokes. After 50
years one's memory is hazy, but of one thing I am sure – his straight six off
Old was unquestionably the best hit in either match, indeed possibly the
most remarkable straight hit I have seen. To take two paces up the wicket
to a fast-medium bowler of Old's class and hit a flat "skimmer" on to the
top of the Pavilion at Lord's takes some beating. Goodness only knows

where it might have gone had he, to use a golfing term, taken a slightly more lofted club.

For England, the batting, with two exceptions, was below Test match standard, even after making allowances for the excellent fast attack of Lillee and Pascoe and the fact that the match took place late in the season after a difficult series against some relentless West Indian fast bowling. Boycott showed his undoubted class in two typically determined innings. Technically he is head and shoulders ahead of any other batsman in England, indeed his technique is so good it is surprising he does not tear the attack apart more often. Gower twice played some fine strokes and was beginning to look the batsman all Englishmen hope and believe he will be, only to get out to two bad shots. Unfortunately Gooch, who is now an extremely good opener and a powerful striker of the ball, failed in both innings.

So much for my impressions of the two matches; now for some comparisons. My first and foremost must be regarding the pace at which they were played, and the Centenary match is a fair example of how the game has slowed down over the span of years. I may have some regrets about the present-day game, but this is my one real criticism of it. Statistics are often boring and can be unjust, but in this instance I think they are interesting and revealing in that they provide some indication as to how much and why this state of affairs has come about.

In the 1930 match 1,601 runs were scored in 23 hours 10 minutes, that is at an average of 69 runs per hour, whereas in the Centenary match 1,023 were scored in 21 hours 7 minutes, an average of 48.4, per hour. A difference of 20 runs an hour is disturbing, to say the least; yet if one looks at the runs per 100 balls one finds very little between them, there being 53 runs in 1930 and 51.2 in 1980. If one then takes into account the importance nowadays attached by captains to containment and the present high standard of fielding, it is clear the batsmen must be exonerated.

And so, inevitably, to the over-rate. In 1930, 260 overs of pace and 245 of spin were bowled at an average of 21.50 an hour: in 1980, 210 overs of pace and 122 of spin were bowled at an average of 15.82 an hour. These figures for pace and spin suggest to me that it is not solely the predominance of fast bowling that is responsible for the loss of 5.68 overs an hour. The endless discussions between bowlers and captains, the frequent changes in field-placing – and the waiting for new batsmen to reach the crease before making some of them – waste part of the time. But it is the absurdly long run-ups of many of the fast bowlers, and even of some of the medium-paced bowlers, often coupled with a funereal walk back to their marks, that are the real cause of the trouble. For those who saw little or no cricket before World War Two, I can assure them one could count on the fingers of one hand the number of fast bowlers who ran more than 25 yards: nowadays one can count on the fingers of one hand those who do not – and some run 40 or 45 yards. Of course a few of these long-runners are a fine sight coming in, but please let us be spared their country strolls.

CENTENARY TEST GROUP AT LORD'S

Patrick Eagar

Key to Centenary Test group at Lord's.

1 F. J. Bryant (*Australian Cricket Board*), 2 T. C. J. Caldwell (*ACB*), 3 L. V. Maddocks, 4 A. N. Connolly, 5 M. H. N. Walker, 6 A. E. Moss, 7 P. E. Richardson, 8 C. R. Ingamells (*ACB*), 9 K. R. Stackpole, 10 R. A. L. Massie, 11 R. B. Simpson, 12 R. T. Simpson, 13 W. M. Lawry, 14 A. Turner, 15 R. Tattersall, 16 R. A. Gaunt, 17 M.J. McInnes (*ACB*), 18 A. W. Walsh (*ACB*), 19 J. W. Gleeson, 20 A. C. Smith, 21 G. B. Hole, 22 D. L. Richards (*ACB*), 23 D. A. Allen, 24 R. M. Prideaux, 25 H. W. H. Rigg (*ACB*), 26 R. Subba Row, 27 T. R. Veivers, 28 F. J. Titmus, 29 F. W. C. Bennett (*ACB*), 30 K. D. Mackay, 31 T. W. Cartwright, 32 R. Edwards, 33 J. T. Murray, 34 W. Watson, 35 R. M. Cowper, 36 C. S. Serjeant, 37 J. S. E. Price, 38 M. J. K. Smith, 39 J. M. Parks, 40 C. C. McDonald, 41 B. L. D'Oliveira, 42 A. S. M. Oakman, 43 J. A. Flavell, 44 I. A. Ledward (*ACB*), 45 L. J. Coldwell, 46 R. Benaud, 47 I.

R. Redpath, 48 G. R. A. Langley, 49 P. H. Edmonds, 50 G. A. R. Lock, 51 F. E. Rumsey, 52 J. H. de Courcy, 53 K. V. Andrew, 54 R. B. McCosker, 55 H. B. Taber, 56 J. H. Hampshire, 57 F. M. Misson, 58 T. W. Graveney, 59 A. K. Davidson, 60 K. D. Walters, 61 G. D. McKenzie, 62 P. J. Loader, 63 E. W. Freeman, 64 G. D. Watson, 65 G. E. Corling, 66 A. J. W. McIntyre, 67 D. B. Close, 68 G. J. Gilmour, 69 I. M. Chappell, 70 F. H. Tyson, 71 R. Illingworth, 72 D. J. Colley, 73 J. B. Statham, 74 K. Taylor, 75 P. H. Parfitt, 76 R. Appleyard, 77 P. J. Sharpe, 78 C. G. Howard (*MCC*), 79 I. J. Jones, 80 E. R. Dexter, 81 A. R. Barnes (*ACB*), 82 I. D. Craig, 83 C. S. Elliott (*TCCB*), 84 V. J. W. M. Lawrence (*MCC*), 85 K. F. Barrington, 86 I. H. Wardle, 87 W. E. Bowes, 88 J. G. Dewes, 89 A. G. Chipperfield, 90 C. J. Barnett, 91 T. G. Evans, 92 E. W. Clark, 93 J. A. Young, 94 W. Voce, 95 J. C. Laker, 96 Sir L. Hutton, 97 E. R. H. Toshack, 98 E. L. McCormick, 99 W. A. Johnston, 100 K. E. Rigg, 101 A. R. Morris, 102 D. T. Ring, 103 F. R. Brown, 104 S. J. E. Loxton, 105 K. R. Miller, 106 D. V. P. Wright, 107 A. V. Bedser, 108 K. Cranston, 109 M. G. Waite, 110 C. Washbrook, 111 C. L. Badcock, 112 N. W. D. Yardley, 113 A. L. Hassett, 114 H. E. Dollery, 115 W. A. Brown, 116 J. T. Ikin, 117 L. G. James (*MCC*), 118 W. E. Hollies; 119 J. A. Bailey (*MCC secretary*), 120 A. R. Border, 121 J. Dyson, 122 G. Dymock, 123 R. J. Bright, 124 B. M. Laird, 125 G. M. Wood, 126 G. N. Yallop, 127 K. J. Hughes, 128 R. W. Marsh, 129 L. S. Pascoe, 130 J. R. Thomson, 131 A. A. Mallett, 132 D. K. Lillee, 133 P. M. Lush (*TCCB*), 134 J. R. Stephenson (*MCC*); 135 D. B. Carr (*TCCB secretary*), 136 D. J. Constant (*umpire*), 137 P. Willey, 138 J. E. Emburey, 139 C. W. J. Athey, 140 R. D. Jackman, 141 D. L. Bairstow, 142 M. W. Gatting, 143 C. M. Old, 144 M. Hendrick, 145 G. Boycott, 146 G. A. Gooch, 147 D. I. Gower, 148 H. D. Bird (*umpire*); 149 W. J. O'Reilly, 150 L. S. Darling, 151 E. L. a'Beckett, 152 W. H. Ponsford, 153 A. Sandham, 154 R. C. Steele (*ACB*), 155 P. B. H. May, 156 G. S. Chappell, 157 S. C. Griffith (*MCC president*), 158 I. T. Botham, 159 R. J. Parish (*ACB chairman*), 160 F. G. Mann (*TCCB chairman*), 161 H. S. T. L. Hendry, 162 G. O. B. Allen, 163 R. E. S. Wyatt, 164 P. G. H. Fender.

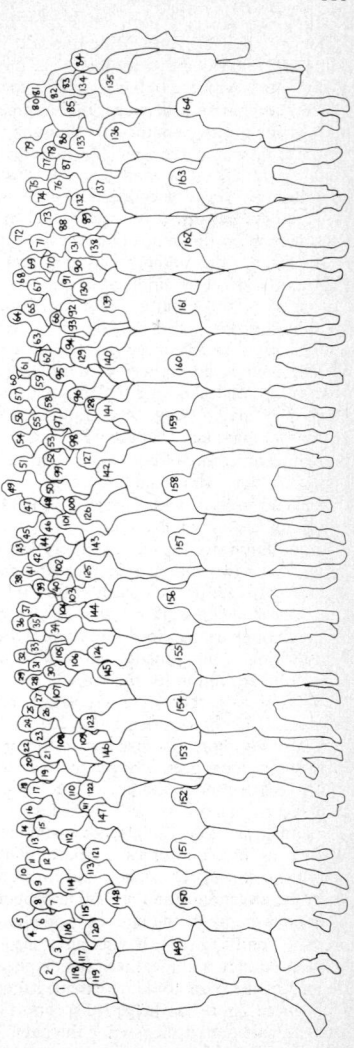

One last statistic, a sombre thought. In a 30-hour Test match, the loss of 5.68 overs and 20 runs an hour could mean the loss of as many as 170 overs and 600 runs. Put another way, the debit, in terms of the modern rate as compared with the old, is roughly two whole days' play.

The comparison between the number of paying customers and the takings for the two matches is illuminating: in 1930, 110,000 people paid £14,500 to watch the four-day match; in 1980, 84,938 over the five-day match paid £360,850 and had the weather been kinder that figure must have been in excess of £400,000. At the moment the situation is clearly very satisfactory, but might not the crunch come if the tempo is not increased, especially when the opposition is less glamorous?

As regards the fielding there can be no argument. In the 1930 match it was moderate. For England Hammond and Duleepsinhji were two fine "slippers"; I still maintain that the former was the best I have ever seen. Chapman, who made magnificent catches to dismiss Bradman in both innings, was excellent anywhere, as was Robins. Hobbs, Hendren and Woolley, who had all been of the highest class, were by then getting on in years. For Australia only Bradman and Richardson really stood out. In the Centenary match the general standard was far superior, the ground fielding and throwing being superb. The catching was not put to the test, but knowing something of both sides I am certain it, too, would have been of the highest order. The "sliding tackle" is a spectacular innovation. In the thirties, even if I had thought of it, I could barely have afforded the additional cleaning bills.

In addition to the tempo there was another fundamental difference between the two matches, namely the approach and tactics of the sides in the field. In 1930, with both teams relying heavily on a leg-spinner and slow left-armer, the theme was always likely to be attack. In the modern game, though rather less in evidence in the Centenary match, defensive field-placing, containment, call it what you will, plays an important rôle. Hence the attraction for the crowds lies more in the brilliance of the fielding and perhaps a fiercer sense of conflict engendered by the menace of the fast bowling. It is not surprising that defensive tactics have crept into cricket – they are common to most sports today. No doubt more or earlier use of them might have been advantageous in the thirties, but strange, even crazy, as it may seem now, I simply do not think that was the way either captains or players wanted to play their cricket.

I said earlier that I might have some regrets about the present-day game. Well, I do have one or two. I particularly regret the lack of variety, once one of the charms of cricket, and for much of this I blame, each in its own way, the change in the lbw law introduced way back in 1935 and the lack of pace in many of the pitches. The change in the lbw law was designed to prevent "padding-up"; it was also argued that it would help all types of bowlers equally and increase off-side play. In the event, apart from reducing the use of the pads to some extent, it has, in my opinion, done more harm than good. As it has helped disproportionally bowlers who bring the ball into the batsman, it has swung the game more towards the leg-side and has contributed in no small degree to the demise of both the leg-spinner and the slow left-armer. Then, with pitches getting slower and slower, containment was bound to become the order of the day. I, for one, do not blame the players, I simply pray for more variety. But how to restore it is the baffling question.

I regret, too, the predominance of the "forward prod" to balls short of a length: that can certainly be blamed on the lbw law. It is safer forward. But excessive forward play must restrict the batsman's range, there being so many attractive and lucrative strokes to be found off the back foot.

And my last lament: I find the incessant noise on many big-match days thoroughly irksome. I welcome the enthusiasm, the cheering and the clapping, but the banging of cans and the endless alcoholic shouting is not for me.

But I have no wish to end these thoughts on a critical note. The game has undoubtedly changed in some respects, mainly in the last 25 years, but in saying this I am not suggesting that it is not in a healthy state: it is. Sadly, circumstances conspired against the Centenary match; yet it was a happy, nostalgic occasion, wherein old rivalries were recalled and old friendships renewed. There is, after all, nothing in cricket to compare with England v Australia, the oldest of all Test match fixtures.

The following took part in the Centenary celebrations but are not included in the photograph on page 110:

W. E. Alley (*umpire*), L. E. G. Ames, G. G. Arnold, T. E. Bailey, R. W. Barber, A. Barnes (*ACB secretary*), J. M. Brearley, W. L. Budd (*umpire*), P. J. P. Burge, D. G. Clark (*MCC*), D. C. S. Compton, M. C. Cowdrey, M. H. Denness, J. H. Edrich, W. J. Edrich, J. H. W. Fingleton, L. B. Fishlock, J. Hardstaff jr, R. N. Harvey, D. W. Hookes, D. J. Insole, R. J. Inverarity, B. N. Jarman, A. P. E. Knott, J. G. Langridge (*umpire*), H. Larwood, F. S. Lee (*umpire*), P. Lever, R. R. Lindwall, D. Lloyd, B. W. Luckhurst, C. Milburn, C. A. Milton, K. J. O'Keeffe, C. H. Palmer (*Cricket Council chairman*), W. G. A. Parkhouse, P. I. Pocock, R. D. Robinson, G. R. J. Roope, W. E. Russell, Rt Rev. D. S. Sheppard, J. A. Snow, R. Swetman, D. Tallon, D. L. Underwood, C. F. Walters, J. J. Warr, R. G. D. Willis, R. A. Woolmer.

RADIO REFLECTIONS

By E. W. SWANTON

The retirement of John Arlott, who over the course of the 35 summers since the end of the war has spread over the air more words about cricket than any other man has done, or perhaps is ever likely to do, is an appropriate time to look back to the beginnings of cricket broadcasting on Sound radio and attempt some sort of sketch of its development. The first of all cricket broadcasts concerned the first match of the first New Zealand tour to England in 1927, against Essex at the old county headquarters at Leyton. Plum Warner – and who more appropriate? – gave eye-witness accounts of each day's play, while later that summer the Rev. F. H. Gillingham, the well-known cricketing parson, was in action similarly at The Oval. The very first of all sporting broadcasts had been made at Twickenham by H. B. T. Wakelam only in January, 1927. Cricket, therefore, was early in the field.

History is somewhat misty regarding the first years, for a bomb played havoc with the pre-war archives of the BBC. It is clear enough, though, that cricket was not, for a while, rated very highly as entertainment by the hierarchy. Almost up to the outbreak of war, other games, wherein the action was faster, were given wider attention. Don Bradman's first visit to England in 1930 coincided with the first coverage of Test matches, but only to the extent of periodical reports: by M. K. Foster, youngest but one of the brotherhood of seven, on the first Test, by A. C. MacLaren on the second and third, and by Aubrey Faulkner on the fourth and fifth.

An interesting sidelight on these early experiments discloses that John Snagge, a BBC staff man from the earliest Savoy Hill days, was sent down to The Oval to help Faulkner, who was unwell. According to Snagge, and not surprisingly, he struggled a bit in an unfamiliar rôle. Yet on the strength of his performance he was chosen by Gerald Cock, the first head of Outside Broadcasts, to cover the Boat Race the following year. Thus, fortuitously, he began surely the longest of all sporting assignments, for he broadcast every race from 1931 until his retirement from the job in 1980.

Thereafter things at first moved but slowly, MCC taking much longer to appreciate the evangelistic possibilities of radio than, for instance, the equally conservative Rugby Union. Hence the story of how Howard Marshall, who was to become the first professional cricket commentator, was required in the early 1930s to hustle from Lord's round the corner to a semi-basement room in Grove End Road, where he had to compete with extraneous noises including that of a child's piano lesson in a room above. However, by 1934 Marshall was at least installed inside the ground, even though he had to tell the world about Hedley Verity's famous rout of the 1934 Australians on a turning wicket from a window in the old Tavern at square leg.

Arlott, to whose researches for the BBC publication, *Armchair Cricket*, I must make due acknowledgment, recalls his youthful memories of Marshall's rich, unmistakable voice in paying tribute to him as the

[*Patrick Eagar*

John Arlott, with Keith Miller alongside him, makes his last Test match broadcast during the Centenary Test at Lord's.

innovator, "the first person to link the news-duty of the commentator with visual and human impressions". There never was a deeper, more mellifluous and attractive voice than Howard's, and when Seymour de Lotbinière became Director of Outside Broadcasts in 1935 the pair of them, along with Michael Standing, "Lobby's" deputy and himself, like Marshall, a competent club cricketer, began to explore the possibilities of the running commentary.

In the later 1930s, county cricket began to be covered in this way in addition to the Test matches, this increased activity culminating in the England-West Indies series of 1939 which was broadcast, for the first time, in its entirety ball by ball. It was then that I joined Marshall and Standing to make a commentary team of three. This comprehensive arrangement, as I recall, put something of a strain on BBC resources. It was said to have been instigated by a BBC governor who, on a winter cruise in the Caribbean, had discovered the islanders' deep fervour for the game and promised them the full treatment.

I expect I was conceited enough to think that the decision may also have owed something to my having blazed the trail the preceding winter in South Africa, where I toured with Walter Hammond's MCC side. This was the first time cricket had been broadcast in South Africa. Nor had anyone previously gone out from England to broadcast cricket home. The first reward was, in the very first Test, to find myself with a hat-trick to describe; the second was to report the longest of all Test matches. It was Tom Goddard who woke up a few at home, dozing after their Christmas dinners, by achieving the second of only three Test hat-tricks by an Englishman in this century. As to that dreary ten-day marathon at Durban, I have a memento in the form of a letter from the BBC, saying that the great Corporation had been considering the question of some further remuneration, seeing that the match fee had been based on a duration of four days, and that they thought an extra payment of 25 guineas would be a fair arrangement. In case anyone should think this an odd computation, they pointed out that there had been no play on one of the days because of rain. Careful were the BBC in those days: my first post-war contracts offered match fees plus railway vouchers (first-class) plus expenses at the rate of one pound "for each night necessarily spent away from home".

But to less frivolous matters, and the great surge of interest in cricket after the war which broadcasting of all first-class cricket on a wide scale did so much to stimulate. Where hitherto cricket had strained to keep up in the broadcast race, now it set the pace. Rex Alston had abandoned schoolmastering at Bedford in favour of the BBC, where his first-hand sporting experience of athletics, cricket and rugby football were at once utilised. In all three activities he was a key member of the broadcast team for twenty years or more. At first Alston, Standing and I formed the Test panel, and divided between ourselves – without benefit of scorer – the lengthy coverage of many county matches as well as the Lord's classics of University Match and Gentlemen and Players.

There came, too, a fresh figure on the scene, a member of the BBC staff seconded to follow the 1946 Indian team, John Arlott. It is no stretching of the truth to compare the impact made on listeners by him with that which had been made by Neville Cardus of the *Manchester Guardian* ("Cricketer") on the cricket world a quarter of a century earlier.

With both, perhaps, the facts and the technicalities of the game sometimes ran second to the characters involved and the context of the occasion, the places and the people. John Arlott, his Hampshire tones distinctly lighter than in his later days, like Cardus, had imagination, keen powers of observation and not least the gift of words. There was an element of chance in the binding of both to cricket, Cardus being sent out for a summer's fresh air after illness, and Arlott having joined the BBC the previous year not on the sports staff but as a talks and poetry producer.

In the emergence of these two at moments when interest was booming anyway, Cardus after the first war, Arlott after the second, the game had two rare strokes of luck, for each man developed his own new following. Not least, each put across a wit and humour, which helped persuade readers and audiences that cricket was a game played by flesh-and-blood characters, to be savoured and enjoyed. For 35 years until his retirement at the end of last summer John kept at it, for much of the period doubling broadcasting and journalism. Having worked alongside him for most of that time, it is for me a pleasure to add, in cricket's official chronicle, this appreciation to the many others he has received.

Marshall pursued other interests after the war, and though sometimes to be heard on major occasions – notably from Westminster Abbey at the Coronation – he did no more cricket broadcasting. Yet the technique which he had evolved, with the ever-present advice of de Lotbinière, was aimed at by us all in our own individual ways. Howard's running commentary leading up to Len Hutton's breaking of Don Bradman's record score of 334, in The Oval Test of 1938, which is re-broadcast on nostalgic occasions, may seem a stately period-piece to some of the modern school, but most of them could profit by noting how scrupulously he observed the ground-rules.

The general picture of the occasion – the field, the weather, the crowd, the personalities and attitudes of the players, the position of the game, tactical appreciations and the options open to the captains – all these and maybe other aspects less immediate invite a wide variety of comment. By the time de Lotbinière gave his celebrated "teach-in" to the foremost outside-broadcasters in 1951, all this was called "associative material". To a large degree it makes or mars the whole performance. Yet in cricket, as in all games, the focal point is the ball, and all must be subsidiary to the bowler's approach and delivery and the batsman's reaction to it. In other words, timing is all-important in commentary, and it is a cardinal sin to be late on the stroke. "The golden pause" was, I believe, first commended as one of the many attributes of the late Henry Longhurst as a television commentator on golf ("If you've nothing to say, don't say it!"); but I have always thought it also applicable to the break of a couple of seconds or more immediately before the bowler's arm comes over in the last stride and the man at the "mike", having drawn breath, reflects the speed of the ball and the nature of the stroke as he describes it all at an increased tempo to his listeners.

Nowadays, of course, the commentator of the moment has not only a statistician, perhaps Bill Frindall, on one side of him but one of the regular summarisers, Trevor Bailey, Fred Trueman or Tony Lewis maybe, on the other. If the ball bowled has had some dramatic effect, whether to the batsman's advantage or otherwise, the commentator will probably bring in one of these for his opinion, or the scorer will chip in with a relevant fact or two. Yet the man at the controls, so to speak, is still the commentator.

Marshall, as long ago as 1934, was the first man to use a scorer. At his request Lancashire lent him a young groundstaff cricketer named Arthur Wrigley for the England-Australia Test at Old Trafford – which, as England declared at 627 for nine, was a prescient move on his part. It was not, however, immediately followed up. Not until after the war (according to my memory and Michael Standing's) were scorers used, and then for a further while only for Test matches.

One important advantage the older generation of commentators had over those of today was the regular training and practice they received from broadcasting county cricket. What was then the major part of the over-all coverage of cricket gave the BBC in addition the chance of trying out new material. The modern instant reports, lasting a minute or two from county grounds, demand little knowledge of the game, and one wonders how the gaps will be filled when Brian Johnston, seemingly perennial and in his particular jovial way still a highly popular element in the team, eventually follows Arlott into retirement. Though others have made acceptable contributions – and Henry Blofeld chalked up a marked success in Australia – the only other notable addition among the younger generation who comes across as combining close knowledge of the game with facility of expression is Christopher Martin-Jenkins.

Many overseas broadcasters accompanying the touring teams have added flavour to the over-all performance, notably a succession of West Indians from Learie Constantine to the present explicit, conspicuously fair-minded Tony Cozier. But for both quality and length of service, Alan McGilvray's career at the microphone stands alone. To the listeners of every Test-playing country he stands for generous-minded, unbiased, factual common sense. At any crucial moment of an England-Australia Test, the ideal recipe, for me, is to turn on the television picture, turn off the sound, and listen to Alan.

Naturally, as an old hand, one cocks a friendly yet critical ear to the Radio 3 Test programmes, and in the most important thing of all they earn surely very high marks. For they convey the feeling that they are enjoying what they are doing, and also, in so far as they conscientiously can, that this is a game played by men who, however great the financial rewards, have still for the most part some respect, diluted maybe in certain cases, for the traditional spirit of cricket. This being so, it is a valuable if tacit sanction that the cricketers know that, if they overstep the mark, commentators and critics in whom the public have confidence will not fail to say so. To this extent, apart from all else, the broadcasters fulfil an important function. It would be an evil day for cricket if its reporting over the air were to fall into prejudiced, over-sensational hands.

One feels now and then that there is so much free, uninhibited talk that one cannot see the wood for the trees, and also that we are getting a slight overdose of statistical material. But, comparing the present with the past, consider how much has to be said about so little. Thirty or forty years ago one had to describe 120 balls an hour, sometimes more. There was little time for reminiscence and chit-chat when Ramadhin and Valentine were spinning England into knots at Lord's in 1950. Nowadays, fast bowlers are allowed to wander back interminable distances, and the ration can be 72 balls an hour, sometimes even less. No wonder Bill Frindall – a formidable repository of fact as were his forerunners, Arthur Wrigley and Roy Webber – is an essential member of the team. Too much dressing-room jargon for the ordinary listener? On the whole, yes. And there is one perpetual irritant, the regular use of the utterly superfluous word "on" before a score. This was never, until comparatively recently, part of the language of cricket. Yet on the whole, surely, the pleasure far outweighs the pain.

CRICKET IN THE PACIFIC

By SCYLD BERRY

The two epicentres of cricket in the Pacific – or so it seemed to me during the travels I was fortunately able to make after England's last two tours to Australia – lie in Fiji and Papua New Guinea; the island of Lakeba in the former and the villages along the south coast of the latter. These two countries are the only two in the region that are currently Associate Members of the International Cricket Conference, and between them they could perhaps turn out a team with a potential of good minor county standard. However, cricket is played, in some form or other, in most countries of the South Pacific, and it struck me as an interesting question why the game is so widespread and relatively popular.

The primary sport in the Pacific is usually rugby union or rugby league, because of Australia's influence, or football. But there is a fairly compelling reason why cricket comes first in Lakeba (pronounced "Lakemba"), a small island 200 miles to the east of Suva, the capital, on Fiji's main island. The Prime Minister, a native of Lakeba, banned all forms of rugby there; and he banned it because its close physical contact led to outbreaks of tribal warfare. So the islanders, 2,400 of them, all built like rugby players – though the more slender women might only make fly-halves – have long devoted their leisure energies to cricket.

Lakeba has eight villages, and each village has an "A" and a "B" team. Wednesdays are given over as devotedly to cricket as Sundays are to religion; the majority practise Methodism, the rest Catholicism, while everyone practises cricket as the original missionaries brought both bats and bibles. The island's collective fervour has its focus on the Dewar Shield, which is challenged for annually by one of the various district associations – Suva, Lautoka, etc. It is the most splendid cup I have seen: huge and silver on a platform of wood. To the great pride of Lakebans, the cup has taken up almost permanent residence in the Prime Minister's house, which stands on the fine leg boundary of the island's main ground.

Of all Lakeba's and Fiji's players, the star is Peni Dakai, thick-set, square-jawed, and in his eyes is the killer instinct that great batsmen have. He is a nephew of Bula, who was acknowledged in his day as the finest of Fijian batsmen, the maker of hundreds against provincial sides in New Zealand. Dakai also lives next to the main ground, which is of the village-green type, roughly grassed, with only the canvas-spread concrete wicket left untouched during the week. Dakai lives at mid-wicket, in a three-roomed house on stilts, and can beat a regular thud every match day on his corrugated roof.

The new ball swings violently in Lakeba, either because of the humidity or the wind off the ocean a hundred yards away. Dakai also opens the bowling and swings both ways. But it is his batting which is celebrated: not

only his mid-wicket pull but his lofted straight drive over the Prime
Minister's house and a variety of cuts. I did not see him bat during my visit
(he had hurt his leg on coral while snorkelling after fish), but in 1979 I saw
him hit a straight six in England that went off his bat like a tracer bullet. I
can believe Peter Roebuck of Somerset,who has coached in Lakeba, when
he says positively that Dakai can hit the ball as far and as hard as either Viv
Richards or Ian Botham.

His lifestyle would partly explain it. Lakeba is only starting to be
integrated into the cash economy, and most of Dakai's time, as a villager, is
taken up in subsistence farming. He goes fishing, too, for a couple of days
at a time with his spear, and grows copra, his only cash-crop which brings
him an income of a few hundred dollars a year. He also cuts down pine
trees as part of one of those community projects which characterise the
Polynesian and Melanesian lifestyle. Such work must have given him good
eyesight and immense strength of limb. For his sixes he needs but a short
backlift, which is also a help against the late, oceanic swing.

If Dakai is the champion of Fiji – and his failure to prove himself as such
during the 'mini' World Cup in England in 1979 was an immense
disappointment to him; in mitigation, he was rather a fish out of water as he
cannot speak English – then Papua New Guinea's champion is Kila Alewa.
He comes from that other epicentre; the villages, centred on Hula on the
south coast of the island, that jut into the muddy waters of the Coral Sea.
Even today Hula is four hours' drive from the capital, Port Moresby,
through thick coastal savannah along a winding track. It is easy to
understand why the first missionaries arrived by sea in the second half of
the nineteenth century.

Today the clergy maintains as strong a hold on the game in Papuan
villages as ever it did in the rural England of Cardus's imagination. The
pastor of Hula – here again most missionaries were low church, Unitarians
now – is not only captain of the village team, he also leads his flock by
opening the batting and bowling, a monopoly which no-one is going to
challenge as long as he keeps all the kit in his house. It is the same pattern
as in Lakeba: one day a week set aside for religion, another for cricket, and
another couple for community projects in lieu of rates and taxes. The
simplicity is appealing, the lifestyle ideal for exercising a cricketer.

However, because there is no employment other than as a villager or
pastor, most young men of the area, having learnt their cricket, migrate to
Port Moresby and the few other towns. But they come together again for
the few international matches that Papua New Guinea has played and form
the bulk of the side: players like Kila Alewa, a fast-medium bowler with an
action like Imran Khan's, hostile when he wants to be, Vavine Pala, his
left-arm opening partner, and Brian Amini, the first native-born to captain a
representative side – when they beat Fiji in 1977 by eight wickets.

Although organised cricket is a minority interest elsewhere in the Pacific,
five other countries were able to send teams to the South Pacific Games
held in Suva in late 1979: Tuvalu (formerly the Ellice Islands), New
Caledonia, the weakest team for having to play the game in a French

[Courtesy of P. A. Snow

The strongest Fiji team was the 1948 one which toured New Zealand with outstanding success, defeating two first-class provinces (Auckland and Wellington) and losing only narrowly to Canterbury and Otago. P. A. Snow is seen leading the side on to the field, followed by Ratu Sir Edward Cakobau (later Deputy Prime Minister, he was the son of King George II of Tonga), in a match against the Rest of Fiji at Albert Park, Suva, on Fiji's return to the Islands.

culture inimical to it, the Solomon Islands, where Australian expatriates have nurtured the game, New Hebrides and Tonga.

Papua New Guinea won the limited-overs tournament by beating the New Hebridean outsiders by nine wickets in the final. In the following months New Hebrides were otherwise engaged in becoming the independent state of Vanuatu, but several factors promise a future for cricket in the islands, apart from the fact that the secessionist Jimmy Stevens has a beard like W.G.'s. Their new President, Walter Lini, is said to encourage the game, and the two secondary schools on the main island both teach it. In consequence there are some good native batsmen, while bowling is mostly in the hands of expatriates. In New Hebrides, as elsewhere, those coming late and uncoached to the game are prone to throw.

Tonga was the surprise of the competition. For a start, few were aware that cricket is played in Tonga. But it is, if in a fairly unconventional form: the umpiring a highly subjective process, the bowling more a matter of throwing. If the canons have not been inculcated, then it is partly because there were very few British officials in Tonga in colonial days, and those who were posted there were not interested in cricket coaching. More recently, Tonga has been the victim of that disinterest which the ICC has shown all too widely. To promote cricket in Tonga it has done nothing. The first team to visit there was from the University of California, only a few years ago. Indeed, apart from New Zealand's interest in Fiji, and some generous help given by New South Wales to Papua New Guinea, the Pacific story is one of total neglect by the game's established authorities.

Given this, it is remarkable that cricket has made the headway it has in the Pacific. Compared with the state of the game in former British colonies in East and West Africa, cricket is much more popular amongst Polynesians and Melanesians than amongst African Negroes. The reason why appears to lie with those missionaries.

They came principally from the London Missionary Society, and apart from a few castaways and beachcombers they were the first white men to settle in the South Pacific; courageous men, too, for the cooking pots took a toll of them. According to their reports, they found cannibalism and inter-tribal warfare to be endemic. Frequent, indiscriminate massacring of entire villages made refinements like birth control superfluous. How were these missionaries to stop the natives butchering each other? By teaching them cricket, they decided; it was as simple as that. To quote chapter and verse of the missionaries' strategy: "We transformed their spears into wickets, their shields into cricket bats." This was written by Charles Abel, the Missionary Society's leading evangelizer in Papua New Guinea.

Facts fall in with this theory. Fiji's Prime Minister bans rugby in Lakeba because it led to tribal violence – and even tiny Lakeba has 32 tribes. The clergy of Hula and its surroundings propagate the gospel and cricket, leading the community in both. Cricket, in short, was introduced into the Pacific as a surrogate for war, and it is still capable of serving that purpose today.

Non-conventional cricket in the Pacific confirms this. There is a mass form of the game – where whole villages of a hundred or more play one another, with one ball per over, thrown not bowled, and made of wood – made familiar by a recent film on cricket in the Trobriand Islands of Papua New Guinea. It is played by men and women alike, from Kiribati (the former Gilbert Islands) to Pitcairn Island, and even in non-British colonies like Samoa. This form of the game is even more manifestly a surrogate for war. Where in the past a village would take up its spears and go raiding its neighbour, now the inhabitants go armed with bats for a festival of eating, dancing and "krikiti". Cultural imperialism it may have been on the part of those missionaries, but they certainly did a good job in imposing the peace. So the next question is: has cricket everywhere been a substitute for war?

Scyld Berry writes on cricket for The Observer.

THE HELMET

SENSIBLE ADJUNCT OR WELL-MARKETED GIMMICK?

by TREVOR BAILEY

One of cricket's many charms used to be the way it was possible to walk into a ground and instantly recognise the batsman at the crease. Apart from his style, he was unmistakable because of his build, features, headgear or hair. Who could have failed to pick out Cyril Washbrook with his cap at a jaunty angle, or Jack Robertson, who wore his with the precision of a guardsman? Then again, there were the hairstyles of Herbert Sutcliffe, black "patent-leather" glinting in the sun, complete with the straightest of partings, the blonde waves of Joe Hardstaff, Reg Simpson's dark curls, and Denis Compton's, so unlike those Brylcream advertisements, forever unruly. Today, as often as not, it is impossible to tell who is batting without first consulting a scorecard, so many players being encrusted in helmets and camouflaged by visors. This gives them a space-age image, devoid of individuality and as dull as dirty denims.

Obviously a helmet makes batting, which personally I never considered as even a vaguely dangerous occupation, less dangerous; just as wearing one in a car, or on a bicycle in traffic, would reduce the risk of injury following a road accident. However, assuming the player obeys the fundamental principle of batsmanship and keeps his eye on the ball, he should not be hit on the head by a fast bowler – provided the pitch is reasonable and the batsman competent. He is, in fact, safer than a fieldsman in any of the more suicidal bat-and-pad positions or a wicket-keeper standing up to fast-medium bowling. It is interesting that 'keepers, who have the riskiest job in cricket, have so far rejected the helmet, perhaps because increased safety fails to compensate for lack of comfort. No batsman with reasonably quick reflexes should be struck on the head, though there is always the risk of his edging a hook into his face. The latter fate is most likely to occur against very fast bowling, especially when the stroke has been attempted against a ball that is too fully pitched for hooking safely.

Although helmets rob batsmen of much of their personality, and are aesthetically unattractive, they have become almost standard equipment in first-class cricket. But are they necessary? In an effort to find the answer, I have spoken to a number of very good players who performed in the helmetless era, to discover how often they were struck on the head by fast bowling. I chose cricketers with different techniques – with intriguing results.

Reg Simpson was a tall and graceful back-foot player who never bothered to hook and probably coped better with real pace than any other

The faceless face of cricket – Kepler Wessels, a naturalised Australian, born in South Africa, now playing for Sussex.

Englishman in the post-war period. He was never hit or even looked in the slightest danger as he watched the balls fly harmlessly through to the wicket-keeper. Colin Milburn, a stocky, impulsive hooker, was also never hit. This was true, also, of two contrasting West Indians: Clyde Walcott, a big, strong, powerful hooker, with a high backlift, and Everton Weekes, small, neat and very quick-moving.

Gary Sobers never bothered with a thigh pad, so it is difficult to imagine he would have ever required a helmet. He was hit on one occasion, in England at Lord's by a medium-pacer when the ball lifted off a length. Denis Compton, another who never wore a thigh pad, was also hit only once in a long career. It happened when he changed his stroke at the last moment, against a no ball from Ray Lindwall, and the ball flew off the edge into his face. Brian Close, despite an initial movement forward, had noticeably less difficulty in coping with the genuine speed of Roberts, Holding and Daniel, when in his mid-forties, than his younger colleagues. He, too, was never hit on the head, though he did twice mis-hook medium-paced bowlers, whom he dismissed as "trundlers", into his face on dodgy pitches. My own experience, as an essentially forward player and a non-hooker, was being hit on the back of the head when I ducked to a ball from Keith Miller, which failed to rise as much as expected, and unintentionally nodding down a delivery of no more than medium-pace which rose unexpectedly in a Championship match.

It is fair to say that none of the players I have mentioned required a helmet for protection, for either physical or mental reasons, which is, of course, why they are worn. Which leads to the question, has the pace of the bowlers increased dramatically? I don't personally think so. Apart from anything else, the bowlers are now forced to release the ball farther from the batsman than when the law allowed them an enormous drag. Gordon Rorke, for example, actually broke the *popping* crease with his back foot. On the other hand, there has been a marked increase in the amount of fast, fast-medium, and medium-paced seam bowling.

Are the present-day pitches more uneven in bounce? The wickets overseas do appear to have become more receptive to seam and less helpful for batting; but, remembering the ridge at Lord's in the 1950s, this, I think, does not apply in this country. The best reason for wearing a helmet was put forward by Graham Gooch: "In first-class cricket, the helmets are now popular and I wear one all the time. I've got no qualms about it. I just feel more confident and therefore a better player when I'm wearing one. The day can't be far off when batsmen start wearing them in club cricket. If you're tempted to wear one, do so – and if anyone laughs at you, just point to the runs in the scorebook." Although the cynic might point to the runs made by Sir Donald Bradman, Gary Sobers, or Vivian Richards without one, if a helmet gives a player confidence it must be an asset to him. A helmet might have made a considerable difference to a fine county cricketer of my vintage, who regularly clocked up over 2,000 runs a season, yet was so apprehensive that he scored many fewer than he should have done against a team which contained a really quick bowler.

John Snow, who in his time has hit his share of batsmen with the bouncer, favours the helmet because it makes life easier for the members of the later order. It is also interesting that David Gower, who is a lovely mover and has lots of time to play his strokes, has, in a comparatively short career, twice been hit on the head. Once it was his own fault through his ducking into the ball; on the other occasion he mis-hooked into his face. The latter is liable to happen even to as fine a natural hooker as David; but, rather strangely in these circumstances, he scorns the use of a visor with his helmet and the extra protection it provides. One of the first times I saw protective headgear used was by Mike Brearley and Geoff Boycott in a Test match on a placid pitch against bowling of such gentle pace that they seemed much over-dressed; but presumably it gave them extra and valuable confidence.

A fascinating, somewhat ironic outcome of the helmet has been the marked increase in the number of batsmen hit on the head and in the face. This can't be put down solely to the increase in fast and medium-paced bowling. What, then, is the reason? My view is that the extra protection has meant that batsmen have become less worried and apprehensive. As a result, they are attempting to play, or hook, deliveries which previously they would have been thankful to have avoided. The outcome is that they are not moving quite so quickly, and are being hit.

Whether the helmet is a sensible adjunct to batting, like pads and gloves, or merely a well-marketed gimmick and a modern trend is a matter of opinion. Although on many occasions a helmet is unnecessary, it can hardly be condemned if it provides batsmen as successful as Gooch and Boycott with extra confidence. Less objectionable than the dirt-track crash-helmet type are those that look like caps. I would rather they were not worn in the field – but that is another issue.

WISDEN CRICKETERS' ALMANACK

In 1899, a set (1864-98) of the almanack was advertised at £10.

In 1925, a bound set (1864-1924) was advertised at 50 guineas.

At a Sotheby's sale in 1937, of the library of J. A. H. Catton, a set (1864–1936) and a further eleven duplicated volumes (unspecified) fetched £33.

Messrs Hodgson and Co. of Chancery Lane auctioned a set (1864-1953) in 1954 and the price was £145.

In 1963 the price of a set in good condition and collated as complete was £250.

Currently, the *Wisden* of 1916 is the rarest, its value being in the region of £150, though in September 1979, at a Phillips's sale, £460 was paid for the editions of 1864 and 1874 and for the Index 1864-1943 by a well-known cricketer who needed them to complete his set. – J.W.

CRICKETANA – A "BULL" MARKET

By DAVID FRITH

Not so very long ago, cricket books and ephemera were collected by enthusiasts for the pure, albeit competitive, joy of possession. The scene has changed. Public interest in cricket has risen since the early 1970s; the frailty of currency in times of economic inflation has persuaded people – not all necessarily cricket-lovers – that cricketana is a solid investment; and the obsessive nostalgia which dependably visits mankind in time of stress has done the rest.

The "business" of collecting cricket material was brisk enough in the days when Leslie Gutteridge presided over his cavern of literary treasures, extraordinarily fairly priced, at Epworth Bookshop in London's City Road. E. K. Brown of Liskeard, Cornwall, took the premier spot among dealers when Mr Gutteridge moved to Canada, and J. W. McKenzie and Martin Wood, of the younger breed, further answered and encouraged the growth in interest which accompanied cricket's latest ascendancy.

Yet it was the sudden concentrated awareness of London's auction rooms which triggered off the unprecedented boom. In September 1978, some of Phillips's estimates for over a hundred lots were doubled, even trebled. Unlike the notorious Cahn sale at Sotheby's in 1951, this was attended by a large gathering, and bidding was determined beyond mere doggedness. A. H. Burr's oil on canvas, *A Game of Cricket*, fetched top price at £7,500 (an almost identical work entitled *The Veteran Bowler* made £2,800 a year later); the charming *The Young Cricketers* (English school) £2,600; and lithographs after J. C. Anderson £50 or £60 apiece.

That these unique or rare and desirable lots should realise such high sums was no surprise. A first edition *Felix on the Bat* (1845) made £280, Denison's *Sketches of the Players* (1846) £180, and Sir Jeremiah Colman's *The Noble Game of Cricket* (1941), one of a limited edition of 150, £460, establishing positively a new era of valuation. But when a bisque figure of W. G. Grace saw bidding escalate to £440 and a WG Century of Centuries Coalport plate raised £800, when a WG commemorative handkerchief made £850 and a signed photograph of the 1909 Australian touring team made £190, there was no doubting that cricket's stock market was in a state of excitement.

There came the inevitable reaction. Seven months later, at the same saleroom, when the most historically interesting item was a mid-eighteenth century bat (£550), an original Victorian cast-iron pub table with moulded portraits of W. G. Grace on the legs fetched £140, half the figure at the previous sale (only for values to be confounded again in December when, at Sotheby's, a modern reproduction was sold for £180); a WG handkerchief made £220 – still an astonishing price, yet little more than a quarter of that at the earlier sale – and another handkerchief, The Australian Cricketers 1882, made £340. While prints and paintings, ancient and modern, fetched substantial sums, there were signs that things were settling down.

Whatever the oscillations in price in the areas of silver, art and ephemera, books held steady, with *Wisden Cricketers' Almanacks* the gold bullion. A run of 97 *Wisdens* from 1864 to 1969, lacking nine pre-1900, took bidding to £4,200. This transaction was topped a year later when Sir Pelham Warner's *Wisdens* (1864-1963) were bought for £7,800. Even the auctioneer gulped as bidding reached this unexpected peak. It should be remembered, too, that 11½ per cent had to be added as buyer's premium plus VAT.

The salerooms now filled each time a cricket auction was staged in London, for media interest had increased public awareness. It also caused one buyer to realise too late that, having confessed to a radio audience of millions that he had paid £60 for eight coloured lithographs of the 1882 Australians, he could hardly expect to conceal the fact from his wife.

Postcards, medallions, tankards and pots, salvers, magic lantern slides: they came out of the bureaux and down from the attics and found their current values according to demand. The dealers, armed with sizable budgets, proved almost unbeatable when they set their sights on books, and there were suspicions that the market was being cornered, a depressing prospect for budding collectors. But by May 1980, a WG handkerchief – admittedly perhaps less pristine than others – had slipped to £65, and a large white marble figure of a boy with a bat, which had sold for £2,000 twenty months before, was knocked down, or conceivably bought back, at £750.

Wisdens and "Graceiana" continued to be the most appealing hallmarks. Even an 1894 telegram from WG to his mother was so highly regarded as to fetch £90.

The occasional hidden gem slipped through. Alerted at the preview, a West Country buyer paid little for a darkened bat which, it transpired, bore a lengthy inscription and signature by Arthur Shrewsbury. But the feeling persisted: that prices were getting out of hand, that the frenzy for possession would create a vacuum in its wake. Absurdities such as the pair of prints (1977) which went for £16, though still available from the publisher for £5, guaranteed this backlash.

"Spy" cartoons and Chevallier Tayler chromolithographs came through in profusion; menus, signed photos, scorecards; "Plum" Warner's England blazer and a dozen caps, one of them his renowned Harlequin "lid". "Spy's" original watercolour of Tom Hayward sold for £300, while Frank Reynolds drawings went for £50 or so per pair. A stevengraph of WG made £300, and in the book department Ranji's *Jubilee Book*, the signed, limited edition, made £110. *The Laws of Cricket*, revised at the Star & Garter, Pall Mall, in 1774, proved a prize catch, and made £500 to a Northern collector. The silver cigar-box presented to Wally Hammond by the 1928-29 MCC team went for £270. A delightful little eighteenth century Bilston patch-box, decorated with a view of a match at Sevenoaks in 1782, fetched £1,250.

By now, Phillips's sales were being scheduled several times annually, and taking two or three hours to conduct. With the scope now so broad and the hammer prices having levelled slightly, there was potentially plenty for everybody, particularly among the lesser rarities. The queue at the collection counter was long. Over £30,000 changed hands at Phillips's sale of May 1980, and £18,000 in September – when a daguerreotype of a cricketer, after being dropped to the floor accidentally, made £55. Other desirable items were A. P. F. Chapman's four photo albums (£180) and a copy of *Biers & Fairfax Australian Cricketer's Guide* for 1856-57 (£240). Spasmodically, well-known names appeared in the commodity descriptions: formerly the property of Jack Hobbs ... Arthur Fielder ... J. R. Mason ... author Eric Parker ... and, by a circuitous route, John Arlott.

In the spring of 1980, Sussex County Cricket Club, severely financially embarrassed, took their cue and mounted an auction at Hove of purportedly duplicate cricketana from the club's library and museum. Some £10,000 was raised: a late eighteenth/early nineteenth century oil of Kent v Sussex, Malling (surely no duplicate) made £1,650; Tony Greig's "last" Sussex bat £200 and a boxful of his ties £22; two small Felix watercolours brought £300.

Next, Worcestershire pulled in almost £5,000 at the end of the season, auctioning donated objects which included the Benson and Hedges Gold Award medallion withheld when Somerset captain Brian Rose declared, rendering the match void. Someone thought highly enough of this oddity to pay £300. The ball used for the seventeen deliveries in that doomed match made, with arithmetical neatness, £17. Peter May's England cap fetched £38, Basil D'Oliveira's £33, and David Sheppard's Sussex cap £15. These will not have gone unnoticed by county beneficiaries of the future.

The last major sale of 1980, Sotheby's at Gleneagles, saw a most special heirloom change hands when a five-piece silver tea service presented to Mrs W. L. Murdoch by Prince Ranjitsinhji was offered to the public. With its evocative associations it seemed reasonably priced at £450 when the auctioneer's hammer descended.

The comfort for all genuine cricket-lovers whose purses have not stretched to the heavier demands comes in the knowledge that while so many people care about the preservation of the game's tangible heritage, it will remain protected. In an ideal world all worthwhile exhibits, to say nothing of a copy of every cricket book ever published, would be on permanent view to the nation and its overseas visitors, rather than scattered in private collections. But while the temptation exists to sell soon after buying, at least a kind of availability persists, given the funds. And for the poorer spectator there is at least the chance to examine the goods at auction previews before attending the sale and watching the tight-jawed purchasers in fervent competition.

Will values hold? If inflation continues to subside and if the boom in cricket's grip on the public's imagination runs into a recession, as predicted by the jeremiahs, then probably not. But the delight in handling a book first held by an *aficionado* a hundred years ago, or of placing an Edwardian Test cricketer's cap upon one's head, will never cease momentarily to paralyse an addict with ecstasy.

David Frith is the editor of Wisden Cricket Monthly.

DATES IN CRICKET HISTORY

1300   First probable reference to cricket: in the wardrobe accounts of King Edward I:
        locality Newenden, Kent.
1344(c.) Club-ball, early form of single-wicket, played, and believed to have been started in
        13th century.
1550(c.) Cricket played at "The Free School" at Guildford.
1595   G. Florio's Italian–English Dictionary mentions cricket.
1610   Reference to "Cricketing" between Weald and Upland near Chevening, Kent.
1611   A reference to cricket in John Bullokar's "England Expositor".
1622   At Boxgrove in Sussex six parishioners prosecuted for playing cricket in the
        churchyard on Sunday.
1636(c.) Reference to cricket at East Horsley, Surrey.
1646   First recorded cricket match, at Coxheath, Kent.
1647   Probable reference to cricket being played by Winchester Scholars on St Catherine's
        Hill; in a Latin Poem by Robert Matthew.
1656   "Krickett" proscribed by Cromwell's Commissioners throughout Ireland: all
        "sticks" and balls to be burnt by the common hangman.
1670(c.) John Churchill, Duke of Marlborough, played cricket at old St Paul's School.
1676   First reference to cricket abroad, played by English residents at Aleppo.
1677   The Earl of Sussex went to a "crekitt" match at ye Dicker in Sussex.
1694   2s. 6d. paid for a Wagger [sic] about the Cricket Match at Lewis [sic].
1706   First full description of a cricket match: in a Latin Poem written by William
        Goldwin, of Eton and King's, Cambridge.
1709   First "County Match": Kent v London.
1710   First reference to cricket at the University: Cambridge.
1727   Articles of Agreement governing the conduct of matches between the teams of the
        second Duke of Richmond and Mr Brodrick of Peperharow.
        First mention of cricket at Oxford University.
1729   Date of earliest surviving bat: inscribed "J. C." (John Chitty) 1729. This bat is in the
        Pavilion at The Oval.
1730   First recorded match on the Artillery Ground, Finsbury: London v Surrey. This
        ground has continued ever since to be the ground of the HAC.
1743   Picture of a match by Francis Hayman; now at Lord's.
1744   June 18. The first great match of which the full score is preserved: Kent v All-
        England on the Artillery Ground, Finsbury. This match, won by Kent by one
        wicket, was described in full by James Love in his "Cricket: a Heroic Poem" pub-
        lished the same year.
        Laws of Cricket, a revision of an earlier code, were drawn up by the London Club,
        of which Frederick Louis, Prince of Wales and father of George III, was President.
        First recorded charge for admission: 2d to the Artillery Ground.
1751   Old Etonians play the Gentlemen of England. Cricket mentioned as far north as
        Durham and Yorkshire.
        First recording of the score at the fall of each wicket.
1760   "Winchester beat Eton" in Port Meadow, Oxford.
1763   First mention of cricket in Wales; in Pembroke.
1767(c.) Foundation of the Hambledon Club: they played first on Broadhalfpenny and then
        on Windmill Down, often defeated All-England, and their great days lasted till 1796,
        though the club survived for many more years. Their great players, immortalised in
        Nyren (see 1833), evolved a new and much advanced technique.
1769   First recorded century: Minshull 107 for Duke of Dorset's XI v Wrotham.
1771   Sheffield play Nottingham.
1772   Picture of boys playing cricket at Harrow School.
1774   "Batts" advertised for sale by maker, William Staples of Sevenoaks.
1776   Earliest known score-cards, printed by Pratt, scorer to the Vine Club, Sevenoaks.
1777   First record of the bowler being credited for catches off his bowling.
1780   Dukes of Penshurst (established 1760) manufacture the first six-seamed ball
        and present it to the Prince of Wales, afterwards George IV. Farington, in his
        diary of 1811, says that the Duke family had then been making cricket balls for 250
        years.

1787   First match, Middlesex v Essex, on Thomas Lord's first ground; on the site of Dorset Square.

Formation of MCC by members of the White Conduit Club.

First mention of a county club: Oxfordshire.

1788   June 27, MCC played their first match at Lord's.

First revision of the Laws by MCC; dated May 30.

1791   Publication of the first record of match scores by Samuel Britcher: these subsequently covered the chief matches till 1805.

1794   First recorded school match, Charterhouse v Westminster at Lord's.

1796   A match between Eton and Westminster at Hounslow, played in defiance of Dr Heath, Headmaster of Eton, who flogged the whole eleven on their return: Eton lost by 66 runs.

1800   Publication of first book on technique; by Thomas Boxall.

1800?   A match between Eton and Harrow.

1803   William Pitt refers to cricket in introducing his Defence Act.

1805   Eton played Harrow at Lord's and won by an innings. Lord Byron, the poet, was in the Harrow XI.

1806   First Gentlemen v Players match at Lord's.

1807   First mention of the "straight-armed" (i.e. round-arm) bowling; by John Willes of Kent.

1809   Lord's second ground opened at "North Bank".

1810   Lowest score ever recorded in a match of importance: 6 by "The Bs" v England at Lord's.

1814   Lord's third ground opened on present site: the original turf of the first ground was transplanted at each move.

1817   First two separate centuries: 107 and 157 by William Lambert for Sussex v Epsom at Lord's.

1820   First recorded score of 200: 278 by William Ward for MCC v Norfolk at Lord's, a record for that ground for 105 years.

1821   First century in Gentlemen v Players: 113 not out by Thomas Beagley.

1822   John Willes "no-balled" for throwing; i.e. round-arm bowling.

1826   First recorded century in a school match: 146 not out by W. Meyrick for Winchester v Harrow.

1827   First University match: drawn. The captains were Charles Wordsworth, Oxford, and Herbert Jenner, Cambridge.

The three experimental matches between Sussex and England to try out the new (round-arm) bowling, now perfected by William Lillywhite and James Broadbridge of Sussex.

1828   MCC authorise the bowler to raise his hand level with the elbow.

1833   John Nyren writes his *Young Cricketer's Tutor* and *The Cricketers of My Time*: the latter is the *locus classicus* for late eighteenth century history and personalities of the game.

1835   MCC adopt a revised Code of the Laws on May 20.

1836   First North v South match: for many years recognised as the greatest match of the season.

1838   Opening of the Trent Bridge Ground, Nottingham, by William Clarke.

1841   The Duke of Wellington issues an order that a cricket ground is to be made as an adjunct to every military barracks.

1842   The Canterbury Week and "The Old Stagers" instituted.

1845   First match on The Oval.

I Zingari formed.

1846   "The All-England Eleven", organised by William Clarke, begins its great work of playing matches, against odds, all over the country. The eleven was subsequently managed by George Parr. An admirable lithograph of the team from a drawing by the famous Kent batsman, N. Felix, was published in 1847.

Last match played for the single-wicket championship; A. Mynn v N. Felix.

Fenner's Ground, Cambridge, opened: leased by CUCC from 1873: freehold purchased 1892.

The Telegraph score-board introduced at Lord's.

Score-cards first sold at Lord's.

1848   July 18, W. G. Grace born.

Edmund Hinkly (Kent) took all ten wickets v England at Lord's.

1849   First Yorkshire v Lancashire match.
1850   J. Wisden bowled all ten batsmen in one innings, North v South, at Lord's.
1851   Oxford University CC rented the Magdalen Ground, Cowley, for a University ground: they migrated to their present quarters in "The Parks" in 1881.
1852   The United All-England XI formed, in rivalry to the All-England XI. Secretaries: Wisden and Dean.
1853   First mention of a champion county (Nottinghamshire).
1854   Last of the "Public Schools Weeks" (Eton, Harrow, Winchester) at Lord's.
1850–55(c.) About this time the mowing machine began to be used on cricket grounds, but sheep continued to be used at Lord's for many more years.
1855   W. Clarke takes 476 wickets in a season.
        Bramall Lane Ground, Sheffield, opened.
1857   The Cricketers Fund Friendly Society instituted. For ten years the great match between the AEE and the UAEE was played in its support. From 1884 until his death, Lord Harris was its president.
1858   First recorded instance of hat being given to the bowler for taking three wickets with consecutive balls.
1862   In a match at The Oval, England v Surrey, Edgar Willsher of Kent was no-balled by John Lillywhite for having his hand higher than his shoulder. Willsher left the field, and the game was suspended for the day. Next day another umpire replaced Lillywhite, who refused to reconsider his view. This led to the change in the law in 1864.
        Publication of Vols 1–4 of *Scores and Biographies*, compiled by Arthur Haygarth. This work recorded the full scores of all discoverable matches from 1744 onwards.
1864   June 10, "Overhand bowling" authorised.
        W. G. Grace's first appearance in big cricket: two days before his sixteenth birthday he scored 170 and 56 not out for South Wales Club v Gentlemen of Sussex.
        First known champion county of the regular series.
        First issue of *Wisden Cricketers' Almanack*.
1865   Practice nets first used at Lord's.
1867   Culmination of long period of rivalry and ill-feeling between professionals of North and South, and of the two "All England" XIs: these two great matches abandoned in this year.
1868   Visit to England of a team of Australian aborigines, managed by Charles Lawrence.
1870   The heavy roller first used at Lord's: the great general improvement of pitches begins with this innovation.
1871   W. G. Grace's greatest year: the first batsman to reach 2,000 runs in a season (2,739): no other batsman achieved this until A. E. Stoddart and William Gunn did so in 1893. "W.G." played in three benefit matches for three of the best-known old professionals and with much, for the beneficiaries, depending on his success, he scored 189 not out, 268, 217.
1872   First experiment, at Lord's, in covering the pitch before the start of a match.
1873   First recorded instance of 1,000 runs and 100 wickets in a season; by W. G. Grace.
1876   W. G. Grace established the following records:
        (1) First score of 300 in first-class cricket: 344 for MCC v Kent at Canterbury. His next two scores were 177 for Glos v Notts and 318 for Glos v Yorks, all between August 11 and August 18.
        (2) 400 not out for All-England XI v XXII of Grimsby.
1877   First Test match: Australia beat England by 45 runs, at Melbourne (Richmond Police Paddock). Charles Bannerman scored the first Test match century (165).
1878   Visit of first Australian team to England: D. W. Gregory captain. Australian cricket established reputation by their sensational defeat in a single day and by nine wickets of a very strong MCC XI.
1880   First Test match in England: England beat Australia at The Oval by five wickets. W. G. Grace 152, W. L. Murdoch 153 not out.
1882   First Australian victory in a Test match in England, by seven runs at The Oval: a spectator died from excitement. Tradition of "The Ashes" established by "obituary notice" to English cricket in the *Sporting Times*.
1884   April 21, a completely revised Code of the Laws adopted by MCC. Omitted from the new code were the laws for settling bets.
        September 16, first use of title "Test Match", in the *Melbourne Argus*.
1884–85 First series of five Test matches in Australia. England won three.
1888–89 Present Lord's pavilion built.
1890   South African Cricket Association established.

1892	Instructions to umpires issued by MCC.

1892   Instructions to umpires issued by MCC.
1894   New Zealand Cricket Council established.
1895   First 1,000 runs in May: W. G. Grace, at the age of 47, in 22 days. He also scored his 100th century.
1898   Board of Control set up to administer Test matches played in England.
1899   First series of five Test matches in England: Australia won the only finished game at Lord's, by ten wickets.
        For the first time a single Selection Committee picked the teams for all the "Tests", hitherto chosen by ground authorities.
        First score of 300 by an Australian in England: 300 not out by Victor Trumper, then on his first tour, v Sussex at Brighton.
        Record individual score: 628 not out by A. E. J. Collins for Clark's v North Town in a junior house match at Clifton College.
1902   Easter classes for boys instituted at Lord's.
1903   Abortive agitation for wider wickets and "Timeless Tests".
        First representative Public Schools XI play MCC at Lord's.
1905   Australian Board of Control set up. Last test of a series to be played to a finish if necessary. It was not until 1912 that the necessity arose when the last Test at The Oval took four days.
1909   Imperial Cricket Conference (ICC) constituted: MCC, Australia, and South Africa the original members.
1911   Warwickshire champions: first county to be so outside those who had originated the Championship.
1912   The first and the only Triangular Tournament in England.
        First "trial matches" for the "Tests".
1926   India, New Zealand, and West Indies admitted to the Imperial Cricket Conference.
        Women's Cricket Association formed.
1930   Four-day "Test Matches" v Australia in England.
1932–33 The "body-line" controversy during the MCC tour in Australia.
1935   MCC condemn "body-line" bowling and issue instructions to umpires against its future practice.
1937   Sir Pelham Warner first cricketer to receive a knighthood.
1938   Test matches at Lord's televised for the first time.
1945   Australian Services XI tour England: the "Victory Tests".
1947   Major revision of the Laws of Cricket.
1948   First five-day Test matches in England.
1949   Election of 26 professional cricketers to Honorary Life Membership of MCC.
1952   Pakistan admitted to Imperial Cricket Conference.
1953   Imperial Cricket Memorial Gallery at Lord's opened by HRH The Duke of Edinburgh.
        Association of Cricket Umpires formed.
1956   J. C. Laker took 19 wickets in one match, England v Australia at Manchester.
1963   Distinction between amateur and professional abolished in English first-class cricket.
        Gillette Cricket Cup competition inaugurated.
1964   New drainage system laid at Lord's.
1965   Imperial Cricket Conference changes its title to International Cricket Conference and introduces Associate Membership.
1967   Cricketers' Association formed.
1968   Cricket Council formed: Test and County Cricket Board replaces Board of Control for Test matches at home and Advisory County Cricket Committee.
        Proposed MCC tour of South Africa cancelled because of non-acceptance by South African government of B. L. D'Oliveira.
1969   John Player League for Sunday cricket inaugurated.
1970   Proposed South African tour of England cancelled at request of British government following anti-apartheid protests.
1972   Benson and Hedges League Cup inaugurated.
1973   Bookmakers in operation at Trent Bridge, Lord's, The Oval, Hove, and Yorkshire grounds.
1975   First international (Prudential) World Cup single-innings tournament in England. Eight countries take part, but not South Africa. West Indies beat Australia in the final, at Lord's.
1976   Women play for first time at Lord's, August 4, England v Australia; Golden Jubilee year of the Women's Cricket Association.

1977 Kerry Packer (Australia) signed 51 of the world's leading players in opposition to the International Cricket Conference. In a High Court action that followed, Packer won on all counts; member countries of the ICC paid £250,000 in legal costs.
1977–79 Two Australian seasons of unofficial cricket (World Series Cricket) played in opposition to the official game.
1979 Kerry Packer (Channel 9) granted exclusive television rights for Test and other official matches in Australia.
1980 Laws of Cricket rewritten.
WSC disbanded. No victimisation of those who had played for Mr Packer.

EVOLUTION OF THE LAWS OF CRICKET
The Pitch

The 22 yards laid down in the laws of 1744 have never varied. The pitch may well have originated from the width of the Saxon acre-strip or the mediaeval measure of the gad = 5½ yards. It is identical with the length of the agricultural chain.

The Popping Crease

The 46 inches between the creases, laid down in 1744, represent the old English unit of the cloth yard, 45 inches, plus 2 half-inches to the middle of each crease. In 1819, the 46 inches between creases was increased to 48 inches.

The Bowling Crease

1902. The length of the bowling crease, which since 1774 had been 3 feet on either side of the wicket, was increased to 4 feet. Both creases were originally cut in the turf; whitewash was not used till the 1830s, at Lord's not till the early sixties. Since 1939, when the width of the wicket was increased from 8 to 9 inches, the bowling crease has measured 3 feet 11¼ inches either side of the stumps.

Sweeping and Rolling

1788 Originally the pitch was left untouched during a match, but in 1788 by mutual consent the pitch could be rolled, watered, covered, and mown during a match.
1788 Sawdust was authorised in the Laws.
1849 The pitch could be swept and rolled before each innings at the request of either side.
1860 The rolling between the innings to be solely at the request of the side batting next.
1883 Rolling permitted for 10 minutes before the start of play on each day.
1910 Covering the bowler's footholds and the batsmen's standing ground authorised.
1931 Period of rolling reduced to 7 minutes.

The Wicket

Year	Stumps	Height	Bails	Breadth
c. 1700	2	22 inches	1	6 inches
c. 1776	3	22 inches	1	6 inches
1785	3	22 inches	2 or 1	6 inches
1798	3	24 inches	2 or 1	7 inches
c. 1819	3	26 inches	2	7 inches
c. 1823	3	27 inches	2	8 inches
1931	3	28 inches	2	†9 inches

† *Optional till 1947.*

The Bat

No dimensions specified in original Laws, when the bat was curved and much longer in the handle.
1771 Width of bat limited to 4¼ inches.
1835 Length of bat limited to 38 inches.
1836 Dark's bats sold by Sadd of Cambridge for 8s. 6d.

1853–54   Cane handles invented by Nixon.
1880   Rubber handle-covers patented.
Early bats were very heavy: the bat with which William Ward made his record score of **278** in 1820 weighed 4lb 2oz.

The Ball

1744   Between 5 and 6 ounces.
1774   Between 5¼ and 5¾ ounces.
1838   Circumference to be between 9 and 9¼ inches.
1927   Circumference to be between 8¹³⁄₁₆ and 9 inches.

Pads

c. 1800   A player named Robinson experimented with boards strapped to his legs. He was "laughed out of his invention".
c. 1836   Pads invented by (?) H. Daubeny of Oxford.
1800   Skeleton pads advertised for sale in *Wisden*.

Gloves

c. 1827   Tubular gloves produced by Daniel Day: no doubt in reaction to the new round-arm bowling.
c. 1850   Wicket-keeping "gauntlets" first appeared.

The Over

1744   4 balls. Though nowhere mentioned in the official Laws, unofficial manuals in the early nineteenth century make it clear that 6-ball overs were customary in rural cricket.
1884   5- or 6-ball overs legalised in one-day cricket; they were already widely used.
6-ball overs first used in Australian first-class cricket.
1885   6-balls introduced to Philadelphia.
1889   5 balls introduced for two- and three-day matches.
1890   8 or 10 balls permitted in Philadelphia. Generally 8 balls used there in competitions until 1920s.
1900   6 balls introduced for two- and three-day matches.
1918   8-ball overs used in all domestic cricket in Australia henceforth, except MCC matches in 1920-21, all Tests 1928-29 to 1932-33 inclusive, and Victoria v MCC, March 1929.
1939   8 balls used experimentally in England in first-class matches.
1946   England reverted to six balls.
1947   At the request of either captain the final over of a match must be completed, even though time has been reached.

No-ball

c. 1809   "Foot over crease", the only no-ball.
1816   First attempt to legislate against "throwing"; the hand to be below the elbow.
1835   The hand not to be above the shoulder.
1864   Revised to present form.
1884   The "absolutely satisfied" clause inserted in the no-ball law.
1899   "*Either* umpire . . . shall call no-ball".
1947   The back foot, at the moment of delivery, need not be "grounded" though it must be behind the bowling crease.
1963   Experimental change of law under which the front foot must land behind the popping crease.

Declaration

1889   First authorised, but only on the third day or in a one-day match.
1900   Any time after lunch on the second day.
1906   Allowed on the first day of a two-day match.
1910   At any time on the second day of a three-day match.
1957   At any time.

Follow-on

1787	First recorded instance.
1835	Compulsory after a deficit of 100 runs.
1854-94	After a deficit of 80 runs.
1894	Compulsory after a deficit of 120 runs.
1900	Optional after a deficit of 150 runs.
1961	In abeyance in County Championship for two years.

Handled Ball

1797	First recorded.

Toss

1744	Toss confers choice of pitch and innings.
1774	Visiting side to have the choice of pitch and innings.
c. 1809	Umpires to select pitch, and toss to give choice of innings.

LBW

1744	No mention.
1774	If, *with design*, the striker prevents the ball hitting the wicket with his leg.
1788	"Design" clause omitted, and ball must pitch straight.
1795	First recorded.
c. 1821	Ball need not pitch straight, but must be "delivered straight".
1839	Reverts to 1788.
1901	Very strong move to alter law by omitting "pitch straight" clause, but two-thirds majority necessary for any alteration of Laws not secured in MCC meeting.
1937	Extended to include ball pitched on the off side of the wicket, after a two seasons' trial, 1935-36.
1970	Experimental law to include ball pitched outside off stump to which batsman, struck on part of person outside off stump, has made "no genuine attempt to play the ball with his bat". Revised in 1972 to 1937 law, but intent clause retained.

Stumped

1744	First recorded.

Scoring

1751	First recording of the score at the fall of each wicket.
1769	First known stroke-by-stroke record of a match.
1777	First recording of the bowler being credited for catches off his bowling.
1827	Wides first recorded as such.
1829	No-balls to be scored as such, and a run debited; first recorded thus, 1830.
1836	The bowler to be credited by name with the wickets caught and stumped.
1840	Bowling analysis first kept in MCC score-book.
1844	Wides to be "run for".
1848	Leg-byes first recorded as such.

Boundaries

1884	First mentioned in the Laws, though operative, with varying allowances, long before.
1910	Advisory County Cricket Committee recommends allowance of six runs for hits over the boundary, hitherto for hits out of the ground only.

GROWTH OF CRICKET OVERSEAS

Europe

1736	Crews of HM ships playing cricket at Lisbon.
1766	Horace Walpole watches cricket near Neuilly-sur-Seine.

1768	Cricket at Spa in Belgium.
1810	Crawfurd's "Light Division" play cricket at Lisbon.
1811	Colonel Maceroni forms a cricket club at Naples.
1815	June 12: a match played by the officers of the Brigade of Guards near Brussels, visited by the Duke of Wellington.
	Cricket in Vienna.
1829	An English cricket club near Paris.
1830	A good cricket ground near Geneva.
1833	St Omer v Boulogne.
1840	Calais v Dover.
1846	An English XI plays a match at Calais.
1855	Club formed in Utrecht.
1857	A cricket club at Balta Liman on the Bosporus.
1858	Berlin CC formed.
1863	Paris CC formed.
	Hamburg v Frankfurt.
1864	Match between Boulogne and Barnsley clubs.
1865	A cricket week at Hamburg.
1866	Cricket known to be played in Denmark.
	Christiana CC formed in Oslo, Norway.
1867	MCC send a team to Paris.
1892	Visit of first Dutch team to England.
1921	First tour of Free Foresters to the Netherlands.
1922	MCC visit Denmark.
1926	First Danish XI to visit England.

Australia

1803	Cricket regularly played in Sydney.
1817	First mention of cricket in Tasmania.
1830	First printed account of a match.
1832	First club formed in Hobart, Tasmania.
1835	First mention of cricket in Western Australia.
1838	Melbourne CC formed.
1839	First recorded game in South Australia.
	First recorded century in Australia – 120 by F. A. Paulett at Melbourne.
1851	First Inter-Colonial match: Tasmania v Victoria at Launceston.
1856	First match between NSW and Victoria, at Melbourne.
1861–62	First visit of an English team captained by H. H. Stephenson. This was a business speculation, financed by Messrs Spiers and Pond, the caterers, who cleared over £11,000. All matches were against odds. At the end of the tour, Charles Lawrence, the Surrey professional, stayed at Sydney as coach.
1863–64	Second English team, under George Parr: all matches against odds. William Caffyn stays as professional at Melbourne.
1873	Adelaide Oval opened.
1876–77	First Test Match: England v Australia, at Melbourne. Australia won by 45 runs. Charles Bannerman 165, the first Test match century.
1878–79	First visit of a team from New Zealand (Canterbury).
1892–93	Sheffield Shield competition instituted.
1903–04	First MCC team to visit Australia; captain P. F. Warner. England won the rubber 3-2.
1907–08	First visit of a team from a Fijian island.
1910–11	First visit of a South African team.
1930–31	First visit of a West Indian team.
1931–32	Visit of South Africans: Bradman averages 201 in Test matches.
1947–48	First visit of a team from India: lost four of five Tests.
1959–60	First visit of a team from Ceylon (National Schools).
1960–61	First "tie" in a Test – Australia v West Indies at Brisbane.
1964–65	First visit of a team from Pakistan: only Test drawn.
1977–79	World Series Cricket set up by Kerry Packer in opposition to the official game.

New Zealand

1832   First reference to cricket in the diary of Archdeacon Williams.
1841   Cricket played in the Bay of Islands.
1842   First full, recorded match, at Nelson.
        Wellington CC already in existence.
1848   Cricket clubs existing at Dunedin and Wellington.
1860   First Inter-Provincial match, Wellington v Auckland.
1864   George Parr's team visited New Zealand from Australia.
1878   First Australian team to England visited New Zealand.
1894   New Zealand Cricket Council established.
1895   First visit by a Fijian team.
1927   First New Zealand team to tour England.
1948   First visit by a Fijian representative team.
1955–56   First Test match victory; over West Indies at Auckland; captain J. R. Reid.
1977–78   First Test match victory over England, at Wellington; captain M. G. Burgess.

Pacific

1912   First visit by an Australian team to Fiji.
1956   First visit by West Indies to Fiji.
1965   Fiji elected to Associate Membership of ICC.
1970   Papua New Guinea elected to Associate Membership of ICC.
1977   First visit by Pakistan to Fiji.
1979   First visit of Fiji and Papua New Guinea to England, taking part in ICC Trophy
        competition.

Africa

1808   A match advertised to be played at Cape Town between officers of the Artillery Mess
        and officers of the Colony "for a thousand dollars a side".
1842   Cricket played at Wynberg, Cape Colony, and first known century in Africa: 110 by
        Mr Taylor for Civilians v Military.
1843   Port Elizabeth CC formed.
1843–44   Cricket played by military teams at Pietermaritzburg, Natal.
1863   First cricket club in Transvaal.
1876   "Champion Bat" competition established in Cape Colony.
1888–89   First visit of an English team; captain C. A. Smith.
1889–90   South Africa's first Test match, beaten by eight wickets by England, at Port
        Elizabeth.
        Currie Cup Tournament established.
1890   South African Cricket Association established.
        First recorded game in Zanzibar.
1894   First visit of South African team to England.
1902–03   Darling's Australian team visited South Africa on way hime from England.
1905   First MCC team, captain P. F. Warner, visits South Africa. South African cricket
        finally established in reputation by winning four out of the five Test matches. This was
        really the triumph of the "googly" on matting, as bowled by Vogler, White, Faulkner,
        and Schwarz.
1927   Formation of Kenya Kongonis CC.
1935   South Africa, under H. F. Wade, gained their first Test victory in England and won the
        rubber.
1956   First visit by a first-class team to East Africa (Pakistan Cricket Writers).
1957–58   First visit of MCC to East Africa.
1961   South Africa ceased to be a member of the Imperial Cricket Conference.

America

North America

1709 Mr William Byrd of Westover, Virginia, playing cricket with his friends.
1737 Mention of cricket in Georgia.
1742 Highland Scots celebrate St Andrew's Day in Savannah (Georgia) – founded only nine years before – by playing cricket.
1751 A match recorded between New York and a London XI, played "according to the London method"; i.e. presumably in accordance with the 1744 rules.
1785 Canadians playing in Montreal.
1838 Mexican CC in existence.
1844 First match between Canada and the USA.
      First known century scored in North America – 120 by J. Turner.
1859 First touring team to leave England (captain, George Parr) visit the USA and Canada. Their matches drew large crowds and, together with their general experiences on the tour, were well-described by their scorer, Fred Lillywhite, in the first book in the long catalogue of "touring literature".
1874 First team from USA to visit England: team of baseballers who also played cricket.
1878 The Australian team visits America on their way back from England.
1880 First team from Canada visited England: not representative and the tour terminated prematurely.
1884 First Gentlemen of Philadelphia team to visit England.
1896 Haverford College toured and played English Public Schools.
1903 Kent visit USA.
1905 First MCC team visited USA and Canada; captain E. W. Mann.
1961 United States Cricket Association founded.
1963 Revival of USA v Canada match, last played in 1912.
1965 United States elected to associate membership of ICC.
1968 Canada elected to associate membership of ICC.

South America

1806 Cricket played in Argentina.
1840 Cricket Club in Rio de Janeiro, Brazil.
1861 Buenos Aires CC established.
1891–92 First North v South of Argentina match.
1912 First MCC team to Argentina, under the captaincy of Lord Hawke.
1932 Visit of South American team to England

West Indies

1806 A meeting of St Anne's CC in Barbados.
1842 Trinidad CC already "of very long standing".
1863 Kingston CC formed in Jamaica.
1886 A West Indies team toured Canada and USA.
1887 An American team toured the West Indies.
1891 First Triangular Tournament between Barbados, Trinidad, and Demerara.
1895 First visit of an English team; captain R. S. Lucas.
1900 First West Indies team to tour England.
1911 First MCC team to visit West Indies.
1930–31 First West Indies team to tour Australia and NZ.
1950 West Indies, under J. D. Goddard, gained their first Test victory in England and won the rubber.
1954–55 First Australian team visited West Indies; became first visiting side to win Test rubber in Caribbean.
1964 First regional tournament between four West Indian countries.
1965–66 First tournament for Shell Shield.
1975 West Indies, under Clive Lloyd, win the first (Prudential) World Cup single-innings tournament.

India

1721   Cricket played by mariners of East India Co.'s ships at Cambay.
1792   Calcutta CC formed.
1804   First century in India: 102 by Robert Vansittart for Old Etonians v The Rest.
1886   Parsee team visited England.
1889–90   First English team visited India.
1911   First All-Indian team visited England.
1922   First visit by South African Indian team.
1926–27   First visit by MCC team, captain A. E. R. Gilligan.
1951–52   India gained their first Test victory over England; captain V. S. Hazare.
1970–71   India, under A. L. Wadekar, gained their first Test victory over West Indies and
          won the rubber in WI.
1971   India gained their first Test win in England and won the rubber.

Pakistan

1948–49   First visit to Pakistan by a first-class touring team: West Indies, who drew only
          representative match.
1952   Pakistan admitted to Imperial Cricket Conference.
       Pakistan visited India and played their first Test.
1954   Pakistan became the only side to win a Test on a first visit to England.

EARLY CRICKET DRESS

Eighteenth Century

Three-cornered or jockey hats, often with silver or gold lace; shirts, generally frilled; nankeen breeches, silk stockings, buckled shoes. The Hambledon Club wore sky-blue coats with buttons, engraved "C.C.". The first uniform of the MCC was in azure blue.

1800–1850

From about 1810–15 trousers began to replace breeches, though Eton and Harrow still wore the latter in 1830. Tall "beaver" hats, in black or white, became the rule. Shirts no longer frilled, but worn with rather high collars and spreading bow ties; singlets instead of shirts not uncommon. Wide braces often seen, especially on professionals. Black "Oxford" shoes universal. Belts, with metal clasps, for the waist.

Towards the end of this period the tall hat began to give place to a full flannel cap, white or chequered, or, less commonly, to a straw hat, often rather of a haymaker's shape. Short, white flannel jackets, mentioned as early as 1812, began to appear as forerunners of "the blazer"; T. Lockyer, the Surrey cricketer, is thought to have been the first to wear "a cricket coat".

1850–1880

Under the lead of I Zingari (established 1845) club cricket colours began to appear, often as ribbons round the white bowler hats which were replacing the tall and straw hats of the previous two decades. Club caps date from about 1850, but Eton may have sported their light blue caps as early as 1831 and the Rugby XI were "habited alike" in 1843. The Winchester XI first wore their blue caps in 1851 and Harrow their striped caps in 1852. The Cambridge "blue" seems to date from 1861, the Oxford "blue" certainly from 1863. Coloured shirts became common as uniform; e.g. a pattern of coloured spots, stripes, or checks on a white ground: the All-England XI wore white shirts with pink spots.

1880–1895

Coloured shirts disappeared (except at Rugby School, where light blue shirts are still retained for the first eleven). White shirts, with starched or semi-starched fronts, the rule. Ties not so common, but small bow ties in low turned-down starched collars common enough. White buckskin boots were first worn about 1882, but they only gradually superseded the old brown and brown-and-white type.

TEST CRICKETERS

FULL LIST FROM 1877 TO SEPTEMBER 2, 1980

These lists have been compiled on a home and abroad basis, appearances abroad being printed in *italics*.

Abbreviations.—E: England. A: Australia. SA: South Africa. WI: West Indies. NZ: New Zealand. In: India. P: Pakistan.

All appearances are placed in this order of seniority. Hence, any England cricketer playing against Australia in England has that achievement recorded first and the remainder of his appearances at home (if any) set down before passing to matches abroad. Although the distinction between amateur and professional was abolished in 1963, initials of English professionals before that date are still given in brackets. The figures immediately following each name represent the total number of appearances in *all* Tests.

Where the season embraces two different years, the first year is given, i.e. 1876 indicates 1876-77.

When South Africa left the British Commonwealth in 1961 they ceased membership of the International Cricket Conference. Later the rules were changed and although Pakistan have left the Commonwealth they remain members of ICC.

ENGLAND

Number of Test cricketers: 487

Abel (R.) 13: v A 1888 (3) 1896 (3) 1902 (2): *v A 1891 (3); v SA 1888 (2)*

Absolom, C. A. 1: *v A 1878*

Allen (D. A.) 39: v A 1961 (4) 1964 (1); v SA 1960 (2); v WI 1963 (2) 1966 (1); v P 1962 (4); *v A 1962 (1) 1965 (4); v SA 1964 (4); v WI 1959 (5); v NZ 1965 (3); v In 1961 (5); v P 1961 (3)*

Allen, G. O. B. 25: v A 1930 (1) 1934 (2); v WI 1933 (1); v NZ 1931 (3); v In 1936 (3); *v A 1932 (5) 1936 (5); v WI 1947 (3); v NZ 1932 (2)*

Allom, M. J. C. 5: *v SA 1930 (1); v NZ 1929 (4)*

Ames (L. E. G.) 47: v A 1934 (5) 1938 (2); v SA 1929 (1) 1935 (4); v WI 1933 (3); v NZ 1931 (3) 1937 (3); v In 1932 (1); *v A 1932 (5) 1936 (5); v SA 1938 (5); v WI 1929 (4) 1934 (4); v NZ 1932 (2)*

Amiss, D. L. 50: v A 1968 (1) 1975 (2) 1977 (2); v WI 1966 (1) 1973 (3) 1976 (1); v NZ 1973 (3); v In 1967 (2) 1971 (1) 1974 (3); v P 1967 (1) 1971 (3) 1974 (3); *v A 1974 (5) 1976 (1); v WI 1973 (5); v NZ 1974 (2); v In 1972 (3) 1976 (5); v P 1972 (3)*

Andrew (K. V.) 2: v WI 1963 (1); *v A 1954 (1)*

Appleyard (R.) 9: v A 1956 (1); v SA 1955 (1); v P 1954 (1); *v A 1954 (4); v NZ 1954 (2)*

Archer, A. G. 1: *v SA 1898*

Armitage (T.) 2: *v A 1876 (2)*

Arnold (E. G.) 10: v A 1905 (4); v SA 1907 (2); *v A 1903 (4)*

Arnold, G. G. 34: v A 1972 (3) 1975 (1); v WI 1973 (3); v NZ 1969 (1) 1973 (3); v In 1974 (2); v P 1967 (2) 1974 (3); *v A 1974 (4); v WI 1973 (3); v NZ 1974 (2); v In 1972 (4); v P 1972 (3)*

Arnold (J.) 1: v NZ 1931

Astill (W. E.) 9: *v SA 1927 (5); v WI 1929 (4)*

Athey, C. W. J. 1: v A 1980

Attewell (W.) 10: v A 1890 (1); *v A 1884 (5) 1887 (1) 1891 (3)*

Bailey, T. E. 61: v A 1953 (5) 1956 (4); v SA 1951 (2) 1955 (5); v WI 1950 (2) 1957 (4); v NZ 1949 (4) 1958 (4); v P 1954 (3); *v A 1950 (4) 1954 (5) 1958 (5); v SA 1956 (5); v WI 1953 (5); v NZ 1950 (2) 1954 (2)*

Bairstow, D. L. 3: v A 1980 (1); v WI 1980 (1); v In 1979 (1)

Bakewell (A. H.) 6: v SA 1935 (2); v WI 1933 (1); v NZ 1931 (2); *v In 1933 (1)*

Balderstone, J. C. 2: v WI 1976 (2)

Barber, R. W. 28: v A 1964 (1) 1968 (1); v SA 1960 (1) 1965 (3); v WI 1966 (2); v NZ 1965 (3); *v A 1965 (5); v SA 1964 (4); v In 1961 (5); v P 1961 (3)*

Barber (W.) 2: v SA 1935 (2)

Barlow, G. D. 3: v A 1977 (1); *v In 1976 (2)*

Barlow (R. G.) 17: v A 1882 (1) 1884 (3) 1886 (3); *v A 1881 (4) 1882 (4) 1886 (2)*

Barnes (S. F.) 27: v A 1902 (1) 1909 (3) 1912 (3); v SA 1912 (3); *v A 1901 (3) 1907 (5) 1911 (5); v SA 1913 (4)*

Barnes (W.) 21: v A 1880 (1) 1882 (1) 1884 (2) 1886 (2) 1888 (3) 1890 (2); *v A 1882 (4) 1884 (5) 1886 (1)*

Barnett (C. J.) 20: v A 1938 (3) 1948 (1); v SA 1947 (3); v WI 1933 (1); v NZ 1937 (3); v In 1936 (1); *v A 1936 (5); v In 1933 (3)*

Barratt (F.) 5: v SA 1929 (1); *v NZ 1929 (4)*

Barrington (K. F.) 82: v A 1961 (5) 1964 (5) 1968 (3); v SA 1955 (2) 1960 (4) 1965 (3); v WI 1963 (3) 1966 (2); v NZ 1965 (2); v In 1959 (5) 1967 (3); v P 1962 (4) 1967 (3); *v A 1962 (5) 1965 (5); v SA 1964 (5); v WI 1959 (5) 1967 (5); v NZ 1962 (3); v In 1961 (5) 1963 (1); v P 1961 (2)*

Barton (V. A.) 1: *v SA 1891*

Bates (W.) 15: v A 1881 (4) 1882 (4) 1884 (5) 1886 (2)

Bean (G.) 3: *v A 1891 (3)*

Bedser (A. V.) 51: v A 1948 (5) 1953 (5); v SA 1947 (3) 1951 (2) 1955 (1); v WI 1950 (3); v NZ 1949 (2); v In 1946 (3) 1952 (4); v P 1954 (2); *v A 1946 (5) 1950 (5) 1954 (1); v SA 1948 (5); v NZ 1946 (1) 1950 (2)*

Berry (R.) 2: v WI 1950 (2)

Binks, J. G. 2: *v In 1963 (2)*

Bird, M. C. 10: *v SA 1909 (5) 1913 (5)*

Birkenshaw, J. 5: *v WI 1973 (2); v In 1972 (2); v P 1972 (1)*

Bligh, Hon. I. F. W. 4: *v A 1882 (4)*

Blythe (C.) 19: v A 1905 (1) 1909 (2); v SA 1907 (3); *v A 1901 (5) 1907 (1); v SA 1905 (5) 1909 (2)*

Board (J. H.) 6: *v SA 1898 (2) 1905 (4)*

Bolus, J. B. 7: v WI 1963 (2); *v In 1963 (5)*

Booth (M. W.) 2: *v SA 1913 (2)*

Bosanquet, B. J. T. 7: v A 1905 (3); *v A 1903 (4)*

Botham, I. T. 31: v A 1977 (2) 1980 (1); v WI 1980 (5); v NZ 1978 (3); v In 1979 (4); v P 1978 (3); *v A 1978 (6) 1979 (3); v NZ 1977 (3); v In 1979 (4)*

Bowden, M. P. 2: *v SA 1888 (2)*

Bowes (W. E.) 15: v A 1934 (3) 1938 (2); v SA 1935 (4); v WI 1939 (2); v In 1932 (1) 1946 (1); *v A 1932 (1); v NZ 1932 (1)*

Bowley (E. H.) 5: v SA 1929 (2); *v NZ 1929 (3)*

Boycott, G. 94: v A 1964 (4) 1968 (3) 1972 (2) 1977 (3) 1980 (1); v SA 1965 (2); v WI 1966 (4) 1969 (3) 1973 (3) 1980 (5); v NZ 1965 (2) 1969 (3) 1973 (3) 1978 (2); v In 1967 (3) 1971 (1) 1974 (1) 1979 (4); v P 1967 (1) 1971 (2); *v A 1965 (5) 1970 (5) 1978 (6) 1979 (3); v SA 1964 (5); v WI 1967 (5) 1973 (5); v NZ 1965 (2) 1977 (3); v In 1979 (1); v P 1977 (3)*

Bradley, W. M. 2: v A 1899 (2)

Braund (L. C.) 23: v A 1902 (5); v SA 1907 (3); *v A 1901 (5) 1903 (5) 1907 (5)*

Brearley, J. M. 35: v A 1977 (5); v WI 1976 (2); v NZ 1978 (3); v In 1979 (4); v P 1978 (3); *v A 1976 (1) 1978 (6) 1979 (3); v In 1976 (5) 1979 (1); v P 1977 (3)*

Brearley, W. 4: v A 1905 (2) 1909 (1); v SA 1912 (1)

Brennan, D. V. 2: v SA 1951 (2)

Briggs (John) 33: v A 1886 (3) 1888 (3) 1893 (2) 1896 (1) 1899 (1); *v A 1884 (5) 1886 (2) 1887 (1) 1891 (3) 1894 (5) 1897 (5); v SA 1888 (2)*

Brockwell (W.) 7: v A 1893 (1) 1899 (1); *v A 1894 (5)*

Bromley-Davenport, H. R. 4: *v SA 1895 (3) 1898 (1)*

Brookes (D.) 1: *v WI 1947*

Brown (A.) 2: *v In 1961 (1); v P 1961 (1)*

Brown, D. J. 26: v A 1968 (4); v SA 1965 (2); v WI 1966 (1) 1969 (1); v In 1967 (2); *v A 1965 (4); v WI 1967 (4); v NZ 1965 (2); v P 1968 (3)*

Brown, F. R. 22: v A 1953 (1); v SA 1951 (5); v WI 1950 (1); v NZ 1931 (2) 1937 (1) 1949 (2); v In 1932 (1); *v A 1950 (5); v NZ 1932 (2) 1950 (2)*

Brown (G.) 7: v A 1921 (3); *v SA 1922 (4)*
Brown (J. T.) 8: v A 1896 (2) 1899 (1); *v A 1894 (5)*
Buckenham (C. P.) 4: *v SA 1909 (4)*
Butcher, A. R. 1: v In 1979
Butler (H. J.) 2: v SA 1947 (1); *v WI 1947 (1)*
Butt (H. R.) 3: *v SA 1895 (3)*

Calthorpe, Hon. F. S. G. 4: *v WI 1929 (4)*
Carr, A. W. 11: v A 1926 (4); v SA 1929 (2); *v SA 1922 (5)*
Carr, D. B. 2: *v In 1951 (2)*
Carr, D. W. 1: v A 1909
Cartwright, T. W. 5: v A 1964 (2); v SA 1965 (1); v NZ 1965 (1); *v SA 1964 (1)*
Chapman, A. P. F. 26: v A 1926 (4) 1930 (4); v SA 1924 (2); v WI 1928 (3); *v A 1924 (4) 1928 (4); v SA 1930 (5)*
Charlwood (H. R. J.) 2: *v A 1876 (2)*
Chatterton (W.) 1: *v SA 1891*
Christopherson, S. 1: v A 1884
Clark (E. W.) 8: v A 1934 (2); v SA 1929 (1); v WI 1933 (2); *v In 1933 (3)*
Clay, J. C. 1: v SA 1935
Close (D. B.) 22: v A 1961 (1); v SA 1955 (1); v WI 1957 (2) 1963 (5) 1966 (1) 1976 (3); v NZ 1949 (1); v In 1959 (1) 1967 (3); v P 1967 (3); *v A 1950 (1)*
Coldwell (L. J.) 7: v A 1964 (2); v P 1962 (2); *v A 1962 (2); v NZ 1962 (1)*
Compton (D. C. S.) 78: v A 1938 (4) 1948 (5) 1953 (5) 1956 (1); v SA 1947 (5) 1951 (4) 1955 (5); v WI 1939 (3) 1950 (1); v NZ 1937 (1) 1949 (4); v In 1946 (3) 1952 (2); v P 1954 (4); *v A 1946 (5) 1950 (4) 1954 (4); v SA 1948 (5) 1956 (5); v WI 1953 (5); v NZ 1946 (1) 1950 (2)*
Cook (C.) 1: v SA 1947
Cope, G. A. 3: *v P 1977(3)*
Copson (W. H.) 3: v SA 1947 (1); v WI 1939 (2)
Cornford (W. L.) 4: *v NZ 1929 (4)*
Cottam, R. M. H. 4: *v In 1972 (2); v P 1968 (2)*
Coventry, Hon. C. J. 2: *v SA 1888 (2)*
Cowdrey, M. C. 114: v A 1956 (5) 1961 (4) 1964 (3) 1968 (4); v SA 1955 (1) 1960 (5) 1965 (3); v WI 1957 (5) 1963 (2) 1966 (4); v NZ 1958 (4) 1965 (3); v In 1959 (5); v P 1962 (4) 1967 (2) 1971 (1); *v A 1954 (5) 1958 (5) 1962 (5) 1965 (4) 1970 (3) 1974 (5); v SA 1956 (5); v WI 1959 (5) 1967 (5); v NZ 1954 (2) 1958 (2) 1962 (3) 1965 (3) 1970 (1); v In 1963 (3); v P 1968 (3)*
Coxon (A.) 1: v A 1948
Cranston, J. 1: v A 1890
Cranston, K. 8: v A 1948 (1); v SA 1947 (3); *v WI 1947 (4)*
Crapp (J. F.) 7: v A 1948 (3); *v SA 1948 (4)*
Crawford, J. N. 12: v SA 1907 (2); *v A 1907 (5); v SA 1905 (5)*
Cuttell (W. R.) 2: *v SA 1898 (2)*

Dawson, E. W. 5: *v SA 1927 (1); v NZ 1929 (4)*
Dean (H.) 3: v A 1912 (2); v SA 1912 (1)
Denness, M. H. 28: v A 1975 (1); v NZ 1969 (1); v In 1974 (3); v P 1974 (3); *v A 1974 (5); v WI 1973 (5); v NZ 1974 (2); v In 1972 (5); v P 1972 (3)*
Denton (D.) 11: v A 1905 (1); *v SA 1905 (5) 1909 (5)*
Dewes, J. G. 5: v A 1948 (1); v WI 1950 (2); *v A 1950 (2)*
Dexter, E. R. 62: v A 1961 (5) 1964 (5) 1968 (2); v SA 1960 (5); v WI 1963 (5); v NZ 1958 (1) 1965 (2); v In 1959 (2); v P 1962 (5); *v A 1958 (2) 1962 (5); v SA 1964 (5); v WI 1959 (5); v NZ 1958 (2) 1962 (3); v In 1961 (5); v P 1961 (3)*
Dilley, G. R. 5: v WI 1980 (3); *v A 1979 (2)*
Dipper (A. E.) 1: v A 1921
Doggart, G. H. G. 2: v WI 1950 (2)
D'Oliveira, B. L. 44: v A 1968 (2) 1972 (5); v WI 1966 (4) 1969 (5); v NZ 1969 (3); v In 1967 (2) 1971 (3); v P 1967 (3) 1971 (3); *v A 1970 (6); v WI 1967 (5); v NZ 1970 (2); v P 1968 (3)*
Dollery (H. E.) 4: v A 1948 (2); v SA 1947 (1); v WI 1950 (1)
Dolphin (A.) 1: *v A 1920*
Douglas, J. W. H. T. 23: v A 1912 (1) 1921 (5); v SA 1924 (1); *v A 1911 (5) 1920 (5) 1924 (1); v SA 1913 (5)*

Druce, N. F. 5: *v A 1897 (5)*
Ducat (A.) 1: v A 1921
Duckworth (G.) 24: v A 1930 (5); v SA 1924 (1) 1929 (4) 1935 (1); v WI 1928 (1); v In 1936 (3); *v A 1928 (5); v SA 1930 (3); v NZ 1932 (1)*
Duleepsinhji, K. S. 12: v A 1930 (4); v SA 1929 (1); v NZ 1931 (3); *v NZ 1929 (4)*
Durston (F. J.) 1: v A 1921

Edmonds, P. H. 18: v A 1975 (2); v NZ 1978 (3); v In 1979 (4); v P 1978 (3); *v A 1978 (1); v NZ 1977 (3); v P 1977 (2)*
Edrich, J. H. 77: v A 1964 (3) 1968 (5) 1972 (5) 1975 (4); v SA 1965 (1); v WI 1963 (3) 1966 (1) 1969 (3) 1976 (2); v NZ 1965 (1) 1969 (3); v In 1967 (2) 1971 (3) 1974 (3); v P 1971 (3) 1974 (3); *v A 1965 (5) 1970 (6) 1974 (4); v WI 1967 (5); v NZ 1965 (3) 1970 (2) 1974 (2); v In 1963 (2); v P 1968 (3)*
Edrich, W. J. 39: v A 1938 (4) 1948 (5) 1953 (3); v SA 1947 (4); v WI 1950 (2); v NZ 1949 (4); v In 1946 (1); v P 1954 (1); *v A 1946 (5) 1954 (4); v SA 1938 (5); v NZ 1946 (1)*
Elliott (H.) 4: v WI 1928 (1); *v SA 1927 (1); v In 1933 (2)*
Emburey, J. E. 10: v A 1980 (1); v WI 1980 (3); v NZ 1978 (1); *v A 1978 (4); v In 1979 (1)*
Emmett (G. M.) 1: v A 1948
Emmett (T.) 7: *v A 1876 (2) 1878 (1) 1881 (4)*
Evans, A. J. 1: v A 1921
Evans (T. G.) 91: v A 1948 (5) 1953 (5) 1956 (5); v SA 1947 (5) 1951 (3) 1955 (3); v WI 1950 (3) 1957 (5); v NZ 1949 (4) 1958 (5); v In 1946 (1) 1952 (4) 1959 (2); v P 1954 (4); *v A 1946 (4) 1950 (5) 1954 (4) 1958 (3); v SA 1948 (3) 1956 (5); v WI 1947 (4) 1953 (4); v NZ 1946 (1) 1950 (2) 1954 (2)*

Fagg (A. E.) 5: v WI 1939 (1); v In 1936 (2); *v A 1936 (2)*
Fane, F. L. 14: *v A 1907 (4); v SA 1905 (5) 1909 (5)*
Farnes, K. 15: v A 1934 (2) 1938 (4); *v A 1936 (2); v SA 1938 (5); v WI 1934 (2)*
Farrimond (W.) 4: v SA 1935 (1); *v SA 1930 (2); v WI 1934 (1)*
Fender, P. G. H. 13: v A 1921 (2); v SA 1924 (2) 1929 (1); *v A 1920 (3); v SA 1922 (5)*
Ferris, J. J. 1: *v SA 1891*
Fielder (A.) 6: *v A 1903 (2) 1907 (4)*
Fishlock (L. B.) 4: v In 1936 (2) 1946 (1); *v A 1946 (1)*
Flavell (J. A.) 4: v A 1961 (2) 1964 (2)
Fletcher, K. W. R. 52: v A 1968 (1) 1972 (1) 1975 (2); v WI 1973 (3); v NZ 1969 (2) 1973 (3); v In 1971 (2) 1974 (3); v P 1974 (3); *v A 1970 (5) 1974 (5) 1976 (1); v WI 1973 (4); v NZ 1970 (1) 1974 (2); v In 1972 (5) 1976 (3); v P 1968 (3) 1972 (3)*
Flowers (W.) 8: v A 1893 (1); *v A 1884 (5) 1886 (2)*
Ford, F. G. J. 5: *v A 1894 (5)*
Foster, F. R. 11: v A 1912 (3); v SA 1912 (3); *v A 1911 (5)*
Foster, R. E. 8: v SA 1907 (3); *v A 1903 (5)*
Fothergill (A. J.) 2: *v SA 1888 (2)*
Freeman (A. P.) 12: v SA 1929 (3); v WI 1928 (3); *v A 1924 (2); v SA 1927 (4)*
Fry, C. B. 26: v A 1899 (5) 1902 (3) 1905 (4) 1909 (3) 1912 (3); v SA 1907 (3) 1912 (3); *v SA 1895 (2)*

Gatting, M. W. 7: v A 1980 (1); v WI 1980 (4); *v NZ 1977 (1); v P 1977 (1)*
Gay, L. H. 1: *v A 1894*
Geary (G.) 14: v A 1926 (2) 1930 (1) 1934 (2); v SA 1924 (1) 1929 (3); *v A 1928 (4); v SA 1927 (2)*
Gibb, P. A. 8: v In 1946 (2); *v A 1946 (1); v SA 1938 (5)*
Gifford, N. 15: v A 1964 (2) 1972 (3); v NZ 1973 (2); v In 1971 (2); v P 1971 (2); *v In 1972 (2); v P 1972 (2)*
Gilligan, A. E. R. 11: v SA 1924 (4); *v A 1924 (5); v SA 1922 (2)*
Gilligan, A. H. H. 4: *v NZ 1929 (4)*
Gimblett (H.) 3: v WI 1939 (1); v In 1936 (2)
Gladwin (C.) 8: v SA 1947 (2); v NZ 1949 (1); *v SA 1948 (5)*
Goddard (T. W. J.) 8: v A 1930 (1); v WI 1939 (2); v NZ 1937 (2); *v SA 1938 (3)*
Gooch, G. A. 26: v A 1975 (2) 1980 (1); v WI 1980 (5); v NZ 1978 (3); v In 1979 (4); v P 1978 (2); *v A 1978 (6) 1979 (2); v In 1979 (1)*

Gover (A. R.) 4: v NZ 1937 (2); v In 1936 (1) 1946 (1)

Gower, D. I. 22: v A 1980 (1); v WI 1980 (1); v NZ 1978 (3); v In 1979 (4); v P 1978 (3); *v A 1978 (6) 1979 (3); v In 1979 (1)*

Grace, E. M. 1: v A 1880

Grace, G. F. 1: v A 1880

Grace, W. G. 22: v A 1880 (1) 1882 (1) 1884 (3) 1886 (3) 1888 (3) 1890 (2) 1893 (2) 1896 (3) 1899 (1): *v A 1891 (3)*

Graveney (T. W.) 79: v A 1953 (5) 1956 (2) 1968 (5); v SA 1951 (1) 1955 (5); v WI 1957 (4) 1966 (4) 1969 (1); v NZ 1958 (4); v In 1952 (4) 1967 (3); v P 1954 (3) 1962 (4) 1967 (3); *v A 1954 (2) 1958 (5) 1962 (3); v WI 1953 (5) 1967 (5); v NZ 1954 (2) 1958 (2); v In 1951 (4); v P 1968 (3)*

Greenhough (T.) 4: v SA 1960 (1); v In 1959 (3)

Greenwood (A.) 2: *v A 1876 (2)*

Greig, A. W. 58: v A 1972 (5) 1975 (4) 1977 (5); v WI 1973 (3) 1976 (5); v NZ 1973 (3); v In 1974 (3); v P 1974 (3); *v A 1974 (6) 1976 (1); v WI 1973 (5); v NZ 1974 (2); v In 1972 (5) 1976 (5); v P 1972 (3)*

Grieve, B. A. F. 2: *v SA 1888 (2)*

Griffith, S. C. 3: *v SA 1948 (2); v WI 1947 (1)*

Gunn (G.) 15: v A 1909 (1); *v A 1907 (5) 1911 (5); v WI 1929 (4)*

Gunn (J. R.) 6: v A 1905 (1); *v A 1901 (5)*

Gunn (W.) 11: v A 1888 (2) 1890 (2) 1893 (2) 1896 (3) 1899 (1); *v A 1886 (2)*

Haig, N. E. 5: v A 1921 (1); *v WI 1929 (4)*

Haigh (S.) 11: v A 1905 (2) 1909 (1) 1912 (1); *v SA 1898 (2) 1905 (5)*

Hallows (C.) 2: v A 1921 (1); v WI 1928 (1)

Hammond, W. R. 85: v A 1930 (5) 1934 (5) 1938 (4); v SA 1929 (4) 1935 (5); v WI 1928 (3) 1933 (3) 1939 (3); v NZ 1931 (3) 1937 (3); v In 1932 (1) 1936 (2) 1946 (3); *v A 1928 (5) 1932 (5) 1936 (5) 1946 (4); v SA 1927 (5) 1930 (5) 1938 (5); v NZ 1932 (2) 1946 (1); v WI 1934 (4)*

Hampshire, J. H. 8: v A 1972 (1) 1975 (1); v WI 1969 (2); *v A 1970 (2); v NZ 1970 (2)*

Hardinge (H. T. W.) 1: v A 1921

Hardstaff (J.) 5: *v A 1907 (5)*

Hardstaff (J. Jnr) 23: v A 1938 (2) 1948 (1); v SA 1935 (1); v WI 1939 (1); v NZ 1937 (3); v In 1936 (1) 1946 (2); *v A 1936 (5) 1946 (1); v WI 1947 (3)*

Harris, Lord 4: v A 1880 (1) 1884 (2); *v A 1878 (1)*

Hartley, J. C. 2: *v SA 1905 (2)*

Hawke, Lord 5: *v SA 1895 (3) 1898 (2)*

Hayes (E. G.) 5: v A 1909 (1); v SA 1912 (1); *v SA 1905 (3)*

Hayes, F. C. 9: v WI 1973 (3) 1976 (2); *v WI 1973 (4)*

Hayward (T. W.) 35: v A 1896 (2) 1899 (5) 1902 (1) 1905 (5) 1909 (1); v SA 1907 (3); *v A 1897 (5) 1901 (5) 1903 (5); v SA 1895 (3)*

Hearne (A.) 1: *v SA 1891*

Hearne (F.) 2: *v SA 1888 (2)*

Hearne (G. G.) 1: *v SA 1891*

Hearne (J. T.) 12: v A 1896 (3) 1899 (3); *v A 1897 (5); v SA 1891 (1)*

Hearne (J. W.) 24: v A 1912 (3) 1921 (1) 1926 (1); v SA 1912 (2) 1924 (3); *v A 1911 (5) 1920 (2) 1924 (4); v SA 1913 (3)*

Hendren (E. H.) 51: v A 1921 (2) 1926 (5) 1930 (2) 1934 (4); v SA 1924 (5) 1929 (4); v WI 1928 (1); *v A 1920 (5) 1924 (5) 1928 (5); v SA 1930 (5); v WI 1929 (4) 1934 (4)*

Hendrick, M. 28: v A 1977 (3) 1980 (1); v WI 1976 (2) 1980 (2); v NZ 1978 (2); v In 1974 (3) 1979 (3); v P 1974 (2); *v A 1974 (2) 1978 (5); v NZ 1974 (1) 1977 (1)*

Heseltine, C. 2: v SA 1895 (2)

Higgs, K. 15: v A 1968 (1); v WI 1966 (5); v SA 1965 (1); v In 1967 (1); v P 1967 (3); *v A 1965 (1); v NZ 1965 (3)*

Hill (A.) 2: *v A 1876 (2)*

Hill, A. J. L. 3: *v SA 1895 (3)*

Hilton (M. J.) 4: v SA 1951 (1); v WI 1950 (1); *v In 1951 (2)*

Hirst (G. H.) 24: v A 1899 (1) 1902 (4) 1905 (3) 1909 (4); v SA 1907 (3); *v A 1897 (4) 1903 (5)*

Hitch (J. W.) 7: v A 1912 (1) 1921 (1); v SA 1912 (1); *v A 1911 (3) 1920 (1)*

Hobbs (J. B.) 61: v A 1909 (3) 1912 (3) 1921 (1) 1926 (5) 1930 (5); v SA 1912 (3) 1924 (4) 1929 (1); v WI 1928 (2); *v A 1907 (4) 1911 (5) 1920 (5) 1924 (5) 1928 (5); v SA 1909 (5) 1913 (5)*

Hobbs, R. N. S. 7: v In 1967 (3); v P 1967 (1) 1971 (1); *v WI 1967 (1); v P 1968 (1)*

Hollies (W. E.) 13: v A 1948 (1); v SA 1947 (3); v WI 1950 (2); v NZ 1949 (4); *v WI 1934 (3)*

Holmes, E. R. T. 5: v SA 1935 (1): *v WI 1934 (4)*

Holmes, (P.) 7: v A 1921 (1); v In 1932 (1); *v SA 1927 (5)*

Hone, L. 1: *v A 1878*

Hopwood (J. L.) 2: v A 1934 (2)

Hornby, A. N. 3: v A 1882 (1) 1884 (1); *v A 1878 (1)*

Horton (M. J.) 2: v In 1959 (2)

Howard, N. D. 4: *v In 1951 (4)*

Howell (H.) 5: v A 1921 (1); v SA 1924 (1); *v A 1920 (3)*

Howorth (R.) 5: v SA 1947 (1); *v WI 1947 (4)*

Humphries (J.) 3: *v A 1907 (3)*

Hunter (J.) 5: *v A 1884 (5)*

Hutchings, K. L. 7: v A 1909 (2); *v A 1907 (5)*

Hutton (L.) 79: v A 1938 (3) 1948 (4) 1953 (5); v SA 1947 (5) 1951 (5); v WI 1939 (3) 1950 (3); v NZ 1937 (3) 1949 (4); v In 1946 (3) 1952 (4); v P 1954 (2); *v A 1946 (5) 1950 (5) 1954 (5); v SA 1938 (4) 1948 (5); v WI 1947 (2) 1953 (5); v NZ 1950 (2) 1954 (2)*

Hutton, R. A. 5: v In 1971 (3); v P 1971 (2)

Iddon (J.) 5: v SA 1935 (1); *v WI 1934 (4)*

Ikin (J. T.) 18: v SA 1951 (3) 1955 (1); v In 1946 (2) 1952 (2); *v A 1946 (5); v NZ 1946 (1); v WI 1947 (4)*

Illingworth (R.) 61: v A 1961 (2) 1968 (3) 1972 (5); v SA 1960 (4); v WI 1966 (2) 1969 (3) 1973 (3); v NZ 1958 (1) 1965 (1) 1969 (3) 1973 (3); v In 1959 (2) 1967 (3) 1971 (3); v P 1962 (1) 1967 (1) 1971 (3); *v A 1962 (2) 1970 (6); v WI 1959 (5); v NZ 1962 (3) 1970 (2)*

Insole, D. J. 9: v A 1956 (1); v SA 1955 (1); v WI 1950 (1) 1957 (1); *v SA 1956 (5)*

Jackson, F. S. 20: v A 1893 (2) 1896 (3) 1899 (5) 1902 (5) 1905 (5)

Jackson (H. L.) 2: v A 1961 (1); v NZ 1949 (1)

Jameson, J. A. 4: v In 1971 (2); *v WI 1973 (2)*

Jardine, D. R. 22: v WI 1928 (2) 1933 (2); v NZ 1931 (3); v In 1932 (1); *v A 1928 (5) 1932 (5); v NZ 1932 (1); v In 1933 (3)*

Jenkins (R. O.) 9: v WI 1950 (2); v In 1952 (2); *v SA 1948 (5)*

Jessop, G. L. 18: v A 1899 (1) 1902 (4) 1905 (1) 1909 (2); v SA 1907 (3) 1912 (2); *v A 1901 (5)*

Jones, A. O. 12: v A 1899 (1) 1905 (2) 1909 (2); *v A 1901 (5) 1907 (2)*

Jones, I. J. 15: v WI 1966 (2); *v A 1965 (4); v WI 1967 (5); v NZ 1965 (3); v In 1963 (1)*

Jupp (H.) 2: *v A 1876 (2)*

Jupp, V. W. C. 8: v A 1921 (2); v WI 1928 (2); *v SA 1922 (4)*

Keeton (W. W.) 2: v A 1934 (1); v WI 1939 (1)

Kennedy (A. S.) 5: *v SA 1922 (5)*

Kenyon (D.) 8: v A 1953 (2); v SA 1955 (3); *v In 1951 (3)*

Killick, E. T. 2: v SA 1929 (2)

Kilner (R.) 9: v A 1926 (4); v SA 1924 (2): *v A 1924 (3)*

King (J. H.) 1: v A 1909

Kinneir (S.) 1: *v A 1911*

Knight (A. E.) 3: *v A 1903 (3)*

Knight (B. R.) 29: v A 1968 (2); v WI 1966 (1) 1969 (3); v NZ 1969 (2); v P 1962 (2); *v A 1962 (1) 1965 (2); v NZ 1962 (3) 1965 (2); v In 1961 (4) 1963 (5); v P 1961 (2)*

Knight, D. J. 2: v A 1921 (3)

Knott, A. P. E. 93: v A 1968 (5) 1972 (5) 1975 (4) 1977 (5); v WI 1969 (3) 1973 (3) 1976 (5) 1980 (4); v NZ 1969 (3) 1973 (3); v In 1971 (3) 1974 (3); v P 1967 (2) 1971 (3) 1974 (3); *v A 1970 (6) 1974 (6) 1976 (1); v WI 1967 (2) 1973 (5); v NZ 1970 (1) 1974 (2); v In 1972 (5) 1976 (5); v P 1968 (3) 1972 (3)*

Knox, N. A. 2: v SA 1907 (2)

Laker (J. C.) 46: v A 1948 (3) 1953 (3) 1956 (5); v SA 1951 (2) 1955 (1); v WI 1950 (1) 1957 (4); v NZ 1949 (1) 1958 (4); v In 1952 (4); v P 1954 (1); *v A 1958 (4); v SA 1956 (5); v WI 1947 (4) 1953 (4)*

Langridge (James) 8: v SA 1935 (1); v WI 1933 (2); v In 1936 (1) 1946 (1): *v In 1933 (3)*
Larkins, W. 5: v WI 1980 (3); *v A 1979 (1); v In 1979 (1)*
Larter (J. D. F.) 10: v SA 1965 (2); v NZ 1965 (1): v P 1962 (1); *v NZ 1962 (3); v In 1963 (3)*
Larwood (H.) 21: v A 1926 (2) 1930 (3); v SA 1929 (3); v WI 1928 (2); v NZ 1931 (1); *v A 1928 (5) 1932 (5)*
Leadbeater (E.) 2: *v In 1951 (2)*
Lee (H. W.) 1: *v SA 1930*
Lees (W. S.) 5: *v SA 1905 (5)*
Legge, G. B. 5: *v SA 1927 (1); v NZ 1929 (4)*
Leslie, C. F. H. 4: *v A 1882 (4)*
Lever, J. K. 18: v A 1977 (3); v WI 1980 (1); v In 1979 (1); *v A 1976 (1) 1978 (1) 1979 (1); v NZ 1977 (1); v In 1976 (5) 1979 (1); v P 1977 (3)*
Lever, P. 17: v A 1972 (1) 1975 (1); v In 1971 (1); v P 1971 (3); *v A 1970 (5) 1974 (2); v NZ 1970 (2) 1974 (2)*
Leveson Gower, H. D. G. 3: *v SA 1909 (3)*
Levett, W. H. V. 1: *v In 1933*
Lewis, A. R. 9: v NZ 1973 (1); *v In 1972 (5); v P 1972 (3)*
Leyland (M.) 41: v A 1930 (3) 1934 (5) 1938 (1); v SA 1929 (5) 1935 (4); v WI 1928 (1) 1933 (1); v In 1936 (2); *v A 1928 (1) 1932 (5) 1936 (5); v SA 1930 (5); v WI 1934 (3)*
Lilley (A. F. A.) 35: v A 1896 (3) 1899 (4) 1902 (5) 1905 (5) 1909 (5); v SA 1907 (3); *v A 1901 (5) 1903 (5)*
Lillywhite (Jas. Jnr.) 2: *v A 1876 (2)*
Lloyd, D. 9: v In 1974 (2); v P 1974 (3); *v A 1974 (4)*
Loader (P. J.) 13: v SA 1955 (1); v WI 1957 (2); v NZ 1958 (3); v P 1954 (1); *v A 1958 (2); v SA 1956 (4)*
Lock (G. A. R.) 49: v A 1953 (2) 1956 (4) 1961 (3); v SA 1955 (3); v WI 1957 (3) 1963 (3); v NZ 1958 (5); v In 1952 (2); v P 1962 (3); *v A 1958 (4); v SA 1956 (1); v WI 1953 (5) 1967 (2); v NZ 1958 (2); v In 1961 (5); v P 1961 (2)*
Lockwood (W. H.) 12: v A 1893 (2) 1899 (1) 1902 (4); *v A 1894 (5)*
Lohmann (G. A.) 18: v A 1886 (3) 1888 (3) 1890 (2) 1896 (1); *v A 1886 (2) 1887 (1) 1891 (3); v SA 1895 (3)*
Lowson (F. A.) 7: v SA 1951 (2) 1955 (1); *v In 1951 (4)*
Lucas, A. P. 5: v A 1880 (1) 1882 (1) 1884 (2); *v A 1878 (1)*
Luckhurst, B. W. 21: v A 1972 (4); v WI 1973 (2); v In 1971 (3); v P 1971 (3) *v A 1970 (5) 1974 (2); v NZ 1970 (2)*
Lyttelton, Hon. A. 4: v A 1880 (1) 1882 (1) 1884 (2)

Macaulay (G. G.) 8: v A 1926 (1); v SA 1924 (1); v WI 1933 (2); *v SA 1922 (4)*
MacBryan, J. C. W. 1: v SA 1924
McConnon (J. E.) 2: v P 1954 (2)
McGahey, C. P. 2: *v A 1901 (2)*
MacGregor, G. 8: v A 1890 (2) 1893 (3); *v A 1891 (3)*
McIntyre (A. J. W.) 3: v SA 1955 (1); v WI 1950 (1); *v A 1950 (1)*
MacKinnon, F. A. 1: *v A 1878*
MacLaren, A. C. 35: v A 1896 (2) 1899 (4) 1902 (5) 1905 (4) 1909 (5); *v A 1894 (5) 1897 (5) 1901 (5)*
McMaster, J. E. P. 1: *v SA 1888*
Makepeace (J. W. H.) 4: *v A 1920 (4)*
Mann, F. G. 7: v NZ 1949 (2); *v SA 1948 (5)*
Mann, F. T. 5: *v SA 1922 (5)*
Marriott, C. S. 1: v WI 1933
Martin (F.) 2: v A 1890 (1); *v SA 1891 (1)*
Martin, J. W. 1: v SA 1947
Mason, J. R. 5: *v A 1897 (5)*
Matthews (A. D. G.) 1: v NZ 1937
May, P. B. H. 66: v A 1953 (2) 1956 (5) 1961 (4); v SA 1951 (2) 1955 (5); v WI 1957 (5); v NZ 1958 (5); v In 1952 (4) 1959 (3); v P 1954 (4); *v A 1954 (5) 1958 (5); v SA 1956 (5); v WI 1953 (5) 1959 (3); v NZ 1954 (2) 1958 (2)*
Mead (C. P.) 17: v A 1921 (2); *v A 1911 (4) 1928 (1); v SA 1913 (5) 1922 (5)*
Mead (W.) 1: v A 1899
Midwinter (W. E.) 4: *v A 1881 (4)*
Milburn, C. 9: v A 1968 (2); v WI 1966 (4); v In 1967 (1); v P 1967 (1); *v P 1968 (1)*

Miller, A. M. 1: *v SA 1895*
Miller, G. 24: v A 1977 (2); v WI 1976 (1); v NZ 1978 (2); v In 1979 (3); v P 1978 (3); *v A 1978 (6) 1979 (1); v NZ 1977 (3); v P 1977 (3)*
Milligan, F. W. 2: *v SA 1898 (2)*
Millman (G.) 6: v P 1962 (2); *v In 1961 (2); v P 1961 (2)*
Milton (C. A.) 6: v NZ 1958 (2); v In 1959 (2); *v A 1958 (2)*
Mitchell (A.) 6: v SA 1935 (2); v In 1936 (1); *v In 1933 (3)*
Mitchell, F. 2: *v SA 1898 (2)*
Mitchell (T. B.) 5: v A 1934 (2); v SA 1935 (1); *v A 1932 (1); v NZ 1932 (1)*
Mitchell-Innes, N. S. 1: v SA 1935
Mold (A. W.) 3: v A 1893 (3)
Moon, L. J. 4: *v SA 1905 (4)*
Morley (F.) 4: v A 1880 (1); *v A 1882 (3)*
Mortimore (J. B.) 9: v A 1964 (1); v In 1959 (2); *v A 1958 (1); v NZ 1958 (2); v In 1963 (3)*
Moss (A. E.) 9: v A 1956 (1); v SA 1960 (2); v In 1959 (3); *v WI 1953 (1) 1959 (2)*
Murdoch, W. L. 1: *v SA 1891*
Murray, J. T. 21: v A 1961 (5); v WI 1966 (1); v In 1967 (3); v P 1962 (3) 1967 (1); *v A 1962 (1); v SA 1964 (1); v NZ 1962 (1) 1965 (1); v In 1961 (3); v P 1961 (1)*

Newham (W.) 1: *v A 1887*
Nichols (M. S.) 14: v A 1930 (1); v SA 1935 (4); v WI 1933 (1) 1939 (1); *v NZ 1929 (4); v In 1933 (3)*

Oakman (A. S. M.) 2: v A 1956 (2)
O'Brien, T. C. 5: v A 1884 (1) 1888 (1); *v SA 1895 (3)*
O'Connor (J.) 4: v SA 1929 (1); *v WI 1929 (3)*
Old, C. M. 43: v A 1975 (3) 1977 (2) 1980 (1); v WI 1973 (1) 1976 (2) 1980 (1); v NZ 1973 (2) 1978 (1); v In 1974 (3); v P 1974 (3) 1978 (3); *v A 1974 (2) 1976 (1) 1978 (1); v WI 1973 (4); v NZ 1974 (1) 1977 (2); v In 1972 (4) 1976 (4); v P 1972 (1) 1977 (1)*
Oldfield (N.) 1: v WI 1939

Padgett (D. E. V.) 2: v SA 1960 (2)
Paine (G. A. E.) 4: *v WI 1934 (4)*
Palairet, L. C. H. 2: v A 1902 (2)
Palmer, C. H. 1: *v WI 1953*
Palmer, K. E. 1: *v SA 1964*
Parfitt (P. H.) 37: v A 1964 (4) 1972 (3); v SA 1965 (2); v WI 1969 (1); v NZ 1965 (2); v P 1962 (5); *v A 1962 (2); v SA 1964 (5); v NZ 1962 (3) 1965 (3); v In 1961 (2) 1963 (3); v P 1961 (2)*
Parker (C. W. L.) 1: v A 1921
Parkhouse (W. G. A.) 7: v WI 1950 (2); v In 1959 (2); *v A 1950 (2); v NZ 1950 (1)*
Parkin (C. H.) 10: v A 1921 (4); v SA 1924 (1); *v A 1920 (5)*
Parks (J. H.) 1: v NZ 1937
Parks (J. M.) 46: v A 1964 (5); v SA 1960 (5) 1965 (3); v WI 1963 (4) 1966 (4); v NZ 1965 (3); v P 1954 (1); *v A 1965 (5); v SA 1964 (5); v WI 1959 (1) 1967 (3); v NZ 1965 (2); v In 1963 (5)*
Pataudi, Nawab of, 3: v A 1934 (1); *v A 1932 (2)*
Paynter (E.) 20: v A 1938 (4); v WI 1939 (2); v NZ 1931 (1) 1937 (2); v In 1932 (1); *v A 1932 (3); v SA 1938 (5); v NZ 1932 (2)*
Peate (E.) 9: v A 1882 (1) 1884 (3) 1886 (1); *v A 1881 (4)*
Peebles, I. A. R. 13: v A 1930 (2); v NZ 1931 (3); *v SA 1927 (4) 1930 (4)*
Peel (R.) 20: v A 1888 (3) 1890 (1) 1893 (1) 1896 (1); *v A 1884 (5) 1887 (1) 1891 (3) 1894 (5)*
Penn, F. 1: v A 1880
Perks (R. T. D.) 2: v WI 1939 (1); *v SA 1938 (1)*
Philipson, H. 5: *v A 1891 (1) 1894 (4)*
Pilling (R.) 8: v A 1884 (1) 1886 (1) 1888 (1); *v A 1881 (4) 1887 (1)*
Place (W.) 3: *v WI 1947 (3)*
Pocock, P. I. 17: v A 1968 (1); v WI 1976 (2) *v WI 1967 (2) 1973 (4); v In 1972 (4); v P 1968 (1) 1972 (3)*
Pollard, (R.) 4: v A 1948 (2); v In 1946 (1); *v NZ 1946 (1)*
Poole (C. J.) 3: *v In 1951 (3)*
Pope (G. H.) 1: v SA 1947

Pougher (A. D.) 1: *v SA 1891*
Price, J. S. E. 15: v A 1964 (2) 1972 (1); v In 1971 (3); v P 1971 (1); *v SA 1964 (4); v In 1963 (4)*
Price (W. F. F.) 1: v A 1938
Prideaux, R. M. 3: v A 1968 (1); *v P 1968 (2)*
Pullar (G.) 28: v A 1961 (5); v SA 1960 (3); v In 1959 (3); v P 1962 (2); *v A 1962 (4); v WI 1959 (5); v In 1961 (3); v P 1961 (3)*

Quaife (Wm) 7: v A 1899 (2); *v A 1901 (5)*

Radley, C. T. 8: v NZ 1978 (3); v P 1978 (3); *v NZ 1977 (2)*
Randall, D. W. 27: v A 1977 (5); v In 1979 (3); *v A 1976 (1) 1978 (6) 1979 (2); v NZ 1977 (3); v In 1976 (4); v P 1977 (3)*
Ranjitsinhji, K. S. 15: v A 1896 (2) 1899 (5) 1902 (3); *v A 1897 (5)*
Read, H. D. 1: v SA 1935
Read (J. M.) 17: v A 1882 (1) 1890 (2) 1893 (1); *v A 1884 (5) 1886 (2) 1887 (1) 1891 (3); v SA 1888 (2)*
Read, W. W. 18: v A 1884 (2) 1886 (3) 1888 (3) 1890 (3) 1893 (2); *v A 1882 (4) 1887 (1); v SA 1891 (1)*
Relf (A. E.) 13: v A 1909 (1); *v A 1903 (2); v SA 1905 (5) 1913 (5)*
Rhodes (H. J.) 2: v In 1959 (2)
Rhodes (W.) 58: v A 1899 (3) 1902 (5) 1905 (4) 1909 (4) 1912 (3) 1921 (1) 1926 (1); v SA 1912 (3); *v A 1903 (5) 1907 (5) 1911 (5) 1920 (5); v SA 1909 (5) 1913 (5); v WI 1929 (4)*
Richardson (D. W.) 1: v WI 1957
Richardson (P. E.) 34: v A 1956 (5); v WI 1957 (5) 1963 (1); v NZ 1958 (4); *v A 1958 (4); v SA 1956 (5); v NZ 1958 (2); v In 1961 (5); v P 1961 (3)*
Richardson (T.) 14: v A 1893 (1) 1896 (3); *v A 1894 (5) 1897 (5)*
Richmond (T. L.) 1: v A 1921
Ridgway (F.) 5: *v In 1951 (5)*
Robertson (J. D. B.) 11: v SA 1947 (1); v NZ 1949 (1); *v WI 1947 (4); v In 1951 (5)*
Robins, R. W. V. 19: v A 1930 (2); v SA 1929 (1) 1935 (3); v WI 1933 (2); v NZ 1931 (1) 1937 (3); v In 1932 (1) 1936 (2); *v A 1936 (4)*
Roope, G. R. J. 21: v A 1975 (1) 1977 (2); v WI 1973 (1); v NZ 1973 (3) 1978 (1); v P 1978 (3); *v NZ 1977 (3); v In 1972 (2); v P 1972 (2) 1977 (3)*
Root (C. F.) 3: v A 1926 (3)
Rose, B. C. 8: v WI 1980 (3); *v NZ 1977 (2); v P 1977 (3)*
Royle, V. P. F. A. 1: *v A 1878*
Rumsey, F. E. 5: v A 1964 (1); v SA 1965 (1); v NZ 1965 (3)
Russell (C. A. G.) 10: v A 1921 (2); *v A 1920 (4); v SA 1922 (4)*
Russell, W. E. 10: v SA 1965 (1); v WI 1966 (2); v P 1967 (1); *v A 1965 (1); v NZ 1965 (3); v In 1961 (1); v P 1961 (1)*

Sandham (A.) 14: v A 1921 (1); v SA 1924 (2); *v A 1924 (2); v SA 1922 (5); v WI 1929 (4)*
Schultz, S. S. 1: *v A 1878*
Scotton (W. H.) 15: v A 1884 (1) 1886 (3); *v A 1881 (4) 1884 (5) 1886 (2)*
Selby (J.) 6: *v A 1876 (2) 1881 (4)*
Selvey, M. W. W. 3: v WI 1976 (2); *v In 1976 (1)*
Shackleton (D.) 7: v SA 1951 (1); v WI 1950 (1) 1963 (4); *v In 1951 (1)*
Sharp (J.) 3: v A 1909 (3)
Sharpe (J. W.) 3: v A 1890 (1); *v A 1891 (2)*
Sharpe, P. J. 12: v A 1964 (2); v WI 1963 (3) 1969 (3); v NZ 1969 (3); *v In 1963 (1)*
Shaw (A.) 7: v A 1880 (1); *v A 1876 (2) 1881 (4)*
Sheppard, Rt. Rev. D. S. 22: v A 1956 (2); v WI 1950 (1) 1957 (2); v In 1952 (2); v P 1954 (2) 1962 (2); *v A 1950 (2) 1962 (5); v NZ 1950 (1) 1962 (3)*
Sherwin (M.) 3: v A 1888 (1); *v A 1886 (2)*
Shrewsbury (A.) 23: v A 1884 (2) 1886 (3) 1890 (2) 1893 (3); *v A 1881 (4) 1884 (5) 1886 (2) 1887 (1)*
Shuter, J. 1: v A 1888
Shuttleworth, K. 5: v P 1971 (1); *v A 1970 (2); v NZ 1970 (2)*
Simpson, R. T. 27: v A 1953 (2); v SA 1951 (3); v WI 1950 (3); v NZ 1949 (2); v In 1952 (2); v P 1954 (3); *v A 1950 (5) 1954 (1); v SA 1948 (1); v NZ 1950 (2) 1954 (2)*

Simpson-Hayward, G. H. T. 5: *v SA 1909 (5)*
Sims (J. M.) 4: v SA 1935 (1); v In 1936 (1); *v A 1936 (2)*
Sinfield (R. A.) 1: v A 1938
Smailes (T. F.) 1: v In 1946
Smith, A. C. 6: *v A 1962 (4); v NZ 1962 (2)*
Smith, C. A. 1: *v SA 1888*
Smith (C. I. J.) 5: v NZ 1937 (1); *v WI 1934 (4)*
Smith (D.) 2: v SA 1935 (2)
Smith (D. R.) 5: *v In 1961 (5)*
Smith (D. V.) 3: v WI 1957 (3)
Smith (E. J.) 11: v A 1912 (3); v SA 1912 (3); *v A 1911 (4); v SA 1913 (1)*
Smith (H.) 1: v WI 1928
Smith, M. J. K. 50: v A 1961 (1) 1972 (3); v SA 1960 (4) 1965 (3); v WI 1966 (1); v NZ
   1958 (3) 1965 (3); v In 1959 (2); *v A 1965 (5); v SA 1964 (5); v WI 1959 (5); v NZ
   1965 (3); v In 1961 (4) 1963 (5); v P 1961 (3)*
Smith (T. P. B.) 4: v In 1946 (1); *v A 1946 (2); v NZ 1946 (1)*
Smithson (G. A.) 2: *v WI 1947 (2)*
Snow, J. A. 49: v A 1968 (5) 1972 (5) 1975 (4); v SA 1965 (1); v WI 1966 (3) 1969 (3)
   1973 (1) 1976 (3); v NZ 1965 (1) 1969 (2) 1973 (3); v In 1967 (3) 1971 (2); v P 1967 (1);
   v A 1970 (6); v WI 1967 (4); v P 1968 (2)
Southerton (J.) 2: *v A 1876 (2)*
Spooner, R. H. 10: v A 1905 (2) 1909 (2) 1912 (3); v SA 1912 (3)
Spooner (R. T.) 7: v SA 1955 (1); *v In 1951 (5); v WI 1953 (1)*
Stanyforth, R. T. 4: *v SA 1927 (4)*
Staples (S. J.) 3: *v SA 1927 (3)*
Statham (J. B.) 70: v A 1953 (1) 1956 (3) 1961 (4); v SA 1951 (2) 1955 (4) 1960 (5) 1965 (1);
   v WI 1957 (3) 1963 (2); v NZ 1958 (2); v In 1959 (3); v P 1954 (4) 1962 (3); *v A 1954 (5)
   1958 (4) 1962 (5); v SA 1956 (4); v WI 1953 (4) 1959 (3); v NZ 1950 (1) 1954 (2); v In
   1951 (5)*
Steel, A. G. 13: v A 1880 (1) 1882 (1) 1884 (3) 1886 (3) 1888 (1); *v A 1882 (4)*
Steele, D. S. 8: v A 1975 (3); v WI 1976 (5)
Stevens, G. T. S. 10: v A 1926 (2); *v SA 1922 (1) 1927 (5); v WI 1929 (2)*
Stevenson, G. B. 1: *v In 1979*
Stewart (M. J.) 8: v WI 1963 (4); v P 1962 (2); *v In 1963 (2)*
Stoddart, A. E. 16: v A 1893 (3) 1896 (2); *v A 1887 (1) 1891 (3) 1894 (3) 1897 (2)*
Storer (W.) 6: v A 1899 (1); *v A 1897 (5)*
Street (G. B.) 1: *v SA 1922*
Strudwick (H.) 28: v A 1921 (2) 1926 (5); v SA 1924 (1); *v A 1911 (1) 1920 (4) 1924 (5);
   v SA 1909 (5) 1913 (5)*
Studd, C. T. 5: v A 1882 (1); *v A 1882 (4)*
Studd, G. B. 4: *v A 1882 (4)*
Subba Row, R. 13: v A 1961 (5); v SA 1960 (4); v NZ 1958 (1); v In 1959 (1); *v WI 1959 (2)*
Sugg (F. H.) 2: v A 1888 (2)
Sutcliffe (H.) 54: v A 1926 (5) 1930 (4) 1934 (4); v SA 1924 (5) 1929 (5) 1935 (2); v WI 1928
   (3) 1933 (2); v NZ 1931 (2); v In 1932 (1); *v A 1924 (5) 1928 (4) 1932 (5); v SA 1927
   (5); v NZ 1932 (2)*
Swetman (R.) 11: v In 1959 (3); *v A 1958 (2); v WI 1959 (4); v NZ 1958 (2)*

Tate (F. W.) 1: v A 1902
Tate (M. W.) 39: v A 1926 (5) 1930 (5); v SA 1924 (5) 1929 (3) 1935 (1); v WI 1928 (3);
   v NZ 1931 (1); *v A 1924 (5) 1928 (5); v SA 1930 (5); v NZ 1932 (1)*
Tattersall (R.) 16: v A 1953 (1); v SA 1951 (5); v P 1954 (1); *v A 1950 (2); v NZ 1950 (2);
   v In 1951 (5)*
Tavaré, C. J. 2: v WI 1980 (2)
Taylor (K.) 3: v A 1964 (1); v In 1959 (2)
Taylor, R. W. 26: v NZ 1978 (3); v In 1979 (3); v P 1978 (3); *v A 1978 (6) 1979 (3); v NZ
   1970 (1) 1977 (3); v In 1979 (1); v P 1977 (3)*
Tennyson, Hon. L. H. 9: v A 1921 (4); *v SA 1913 (5)*
Thompson (G. J.) 6: v A 1909 (1); *v SA 1909 (5)*
Thomson, N. I. 5: *v SA 1964 (5)*
Titmus (F. J.) 53: v A 1964 (5); v SA 1955 (2) 1965 (3); v WI 1963 (4) 1966 (3); v NZ 1965
   (3); v P 1962 (2) 1967 (2); *v A 1962 (5) 1965 (5) 1974 (4); v SA 1964 (5); v WI 1967 (2);
   v NZ 1962 (3); v In 1963 (5)*

Tolchard, R. W. 4: *v In 1976 (4)*
Townsend, C. L. 2: v A 1899 (2)
Townsend, D. C. H. 3: *v WI 1934 (3)*
Townsend (L. F.) 4: *v WI 1929 (1); v In 1933 (3)*
Tremlett (M. F.) 3: *v WI 1947 (3)*
Trott (A. E.) 2: *v SA 1898 (2)*
Trueman (F. S.) 67: v A 1953 (1) 1956 (2) 1961 (4) 1964 (4); v SA 1955 (1) 1960 (5); v WI
   1957 (5) 1963 (5); v NZ 1958 (5) 1965 (2); v In 1952 (4) 1959 (5); v P 1962 (4); *v A
   1958 (3) 1962 (5); v WI 1953 (3) 1959 (5); v NZ 1958 (2) 1962 (2)*
Tufnell, N. C. 1: *v SA 1909*
Turnbull, M. J. L. 9: v WI 1933 (2); v In 1936 (1); *v SA 1930 (5); v NZ 1929 (1)*
Tyldesley (G. E.) 14: v A 1921 (3) 1926 (1); v SA 1924 (1); v WI 1928 (3); *v A 1928 (1); v
   SA 1927 (5)*
Tyldesley (J. T.) 31: v A 1899 (2) 1902 (5) 1905 (5) 1909 (4); v S.. .... (3); *v A 1901 (5)
   1903 (5); v SA 1898 (2)*
Tyldesley (R. K.) 7: v A 1930 (2); v SA 1924 (4); *v A 1924 (1)*
Tylecote, E. F. S. 6: v A 1886 (2); *v A 1882 (4)*
Tyler (E. J.) 1: *v SA 1895*
Tyson (F. H.) 17: v A 1956 (1); v SA 1955 (1); v P 1954 (1); *v A 1954 (5) 1958 (2); v SA
   1956 (2); v NZ 1954 (2) 1958 (2)*

Ulyett (G.) 25: v A 1882 (1) 1884 (3) 1886 (3) 1888 (2) 1890 (1); *v A 1876 (2) 1878 (1)
   1881 (4) 1884 (5) 1887 (1); v SA 1888 (2)*
Underwood, D. L. 79: v A 1968 (4) 1972 (2) 1975 (4) 1977 (5); v WI 1966 (2) 1969 (2) 1973
   (3) 1976 (5) 1980 (1); v NZ 1969 (3) 1973 (1); v In 1971 (1) 1974 (3); v P 1967 (2) 1971
   (1) 1974 (3); *v A 1970 (5) 1974 (5) 1976 (1) 1979 (3); v WI 1973 (4); v NZ 1970 (2) 1974
   (2); v In 1972 (4) 1976 (5) 1979 (1); v P 1968 (3) 1972 (2)*

Valentine, B. H. 7: *v SA 1938 (5); v In 1933 (2)*
Verity (H.) 40: v A 1934 (5) 1938 (4); v SA 1935 (4); v WI 1933 (2) 1939 (1); v NZ 1931 (2)
   1937 (1); v In 1936 (3); *v A 1932 (4) 1936 (5); v SA 1938 (5); v NZ 1932 (1); v In
   1933 (3)*
Vernon, G. F. 1: *v A 1882*
Vine (J.) 2: *v A 1911 (2)*
Voce (W.) 27: v NZ 1931 (1) 1937 (1); v In 1932 (1) 1936 (1) 1946 (1); *v A 1932 (4) 1936
   (5) 1946 (2); v SA 1930 (5); v NZ 1932 (2); v WI 1929 (4)*

Waddington (A.) 2: *v A 1920 (2)*
Wainwright (E.) 5: v A 1893 (1); *v A 1897 (4)*
Walker (P. M.) 3: v SA 1960 (3)
Walters, C. F. 11: v A 1934 (5); v WI 1933 (3); *v In 1933 (3)*
Ward (A.) 7: v A 1893 (2); *v A 1894 (5)*
Ward, A. 5: v WI 1976 (1); v NZ 1969 (3); v P 1971 (1)
Wardle (J. H.) 28: v A 1953 (3) 1956 (1); v SA 1951 (2) 1955 (3); v WI 1950 (1) 1957 (1);
   v P 1954 (1); *v A 1954 (4); v SA 1956 (4); v WI 1947 (1) 1953 (2); v NZ 1954 (2)*
Warner, P. F. 15: v A 1909 (1) 1912 (1); v SA 1912 (1): *v A 1903 (5); v SA 1898 (2) 1905
   (5)*
Warr, J. J. 2: *v A 1950 (2)*
Warren (A. R.) 1: v A 1905
Washbrook (C.) 37: v A 1948 (4) 1956 (3); v SA 1947 (5); v WI 1950 (2); v NZ 1937 (1)
   1949 (2); v In 1946 (3); *v A 1946 (5) 1950 (5); v SA 1948 (5); v NZ 1946 (1) 1950 (1)*
Watkins (A. J.) 15: v A 1948 (1); v NZ 1949 (1); v In 1952 (3); *v SA 1948 (5); v In 1951 (5)*
Watson (W.) 23: v A 1953 (2) 1956 (2); v SA 1951 (5) 1955 (1); v NZ 1958 (2); v In 1952 (1);
   v A 1958 (2); v WI 1953 (5); v NZ 1958 (2)
Webbe, A. J. 1: *v A 1878*
Wellard (A. W.) 2: v A 1938 (1); v NZ 1937 (1)
Wharton (A.) 1: v NZ 1949
White, J. C. 15: v A 1921 (1) 1930 (1); v SA 1929 (1); v WI 1928 (1); *v A 1928 (5); v SA
   1930 (4)*
White (D. W.) 2: *v P 1961 (2)*
Whysall (W. W.) 4: v A 1930 (1); *v A 1924 (3)*
Wilkinson (L. L.) 3: *v SA 1938 (3)*

Willey, P. 12: v A 1980 (1); v WI 1976 (2) 1980 (5); v In 1979 (1); *v A 1979 (3)*
Willis, R. G. D. 57: v A 1977 (5); v WI 1973 (1) 1976 (2) 1980 (4); v NZ 1978 (3); v In 1974
    (1) 1979 (3); v P 1974 (1) 1978 (3); *v A 1970 (4) 1974 (5) 1976 (1) 1978 (6) 1979 (3); v
    WI 1973 (3); v NZ 1970 (1) 1977 (3); v In 1976 (5); v P 1977 (3)*
Wilson, C. E. M. 2: *v SA 1898 (2)*
Wilson, D. 6: *v NZ 1970 (1); v In 1963 (5)*
Wilson, E. R. 1: *v A 1920*
Wood (A.) 4: v A 1938 (1); v WI 1939 (3)
Wood, B. 12: v A 1972 (1) 1975 (3); v WI 1976 (1); v P 1978 (1); *v NZ 1974 (2); v In 1972
    (3); v P 1972 (1)*
Wood, G. E. C. 3: v SA 1924 (3)
Wood (H.) 4: v A 1888 (1); *v SA 1888 (2) 1891 (1)*
Wood (R.) 1: *v A 1886*
Woods, S. M. J. 3: *v SA 1895 (3)*
Woolley (F. E.) 64: v A 1909 (1) 1912 (3) 1921 (5) 1926 (5) 1930 (2) 1934 (1); v SA 1912
    (3) 1924 (5) 1929 (3); v NZ 1931 (1); v In 1932 (1); *v A 1911 (5) 1920 (5) 1924 (5);
    v SA 1909 (5) 1913 (5) 1922 (5); v NZ 1929 (4)*
Woolmer, R. A. 17: v A 1975 (2) 1977 (5); v WI 1976 (5) 1980 (2); *v A 1976 (1); v In 1976
    (2)*
Worthington (T. S.) 9: v In 1936 (2); *v A 1936 (3); v NZ 1929 (4)*
Wright, C. W. 3: *v SA 1895 (3)*
Wright (D. V. P.) 34: v A 1938 (3) 1948 (1); v SA 1947 (4); v WI 1939 (3) 1950 (1); v NZ
    1949 (1); v In 1946 (2); *v A 1946 (5) 1950 (5); v SA 1938 (3) 1948 (3); v NZ 1946 (1)
    1950 (2)*
Wyatt, R. E. S. 40: v A 1930 (1) 1934 (4); v SA 1929 (2) 1935 (5); v WI 1933 (2); v In 1936
    (1); *v A 1932 (5) 1936 (2); v SA 1927 (5) 1930 (5); v WI 1929 (2) 1934 (4); v NZ
    1932 (2)*
Wynyard, E. G. 3: v A 1896 (1); *v SA 1905 (2)*

Yardley, N. W. D. 20: v A 1948 (5); v SA 1947 (5); v WI 1950 (3); *v A 1946 (5); v SA
    1938 (1); v NZ 1946 (1)*
Young (H. I.) 2: v A 1899 (2)
Young (J. A.) 8: v A 1948 (3); v SA 1947 (1); v NZ 1949 (2); *v SA 1948 (2)*
Young, R. A. 2: *v A 1907 (2)*

AUSTRALIA

Number of Test cricketers: 308

A'Beckett, E. L. 4; v E 1928 (2); v SA 1931 (1); *v E 1930 (1)*
Alexander, G. 2: v E 1884 (1); *v E 1880 (1)*
Alexander, H. H. 1: v E 1932
Allan, F. E. 1: v E 1878
Allan, P. J. 1: v E 1965
Allen, R. C. 1: v E 1886
Andrews, T. J. E. 16: v E 1924 (3); *v E 1921 (5) 1926 (5); v SA 1921 (3)*
Archer, K. A. 5: v E 1950 (3); v WI 1951 (2)
Archer, R. G. 19: v E 1954 (4); v SA 1952 (1); *v E 1953 (3) 1956 (5); v WI 1954 (5);
    v P 1956 (1)*
Armstrong, W. W. 50: v E 1901 (4) 1903 (3) 1907 (5) 1911 (5) 1920 (5); v SA 1910 (5);
    v E 1902 (5) 1905 (5) 1909 (5) 1921 (5); v SA 1902 (3)

Badcock, C. L. 7: v E 1936 (3); *v E 1938 (4)*
Bannerman, A. C. 28: v E 1878 (1) 1881 (3) 1882 (4) 1884 (4) 1886 (1) 1887 (1) 1891 (3);
    v E 1880 (1) 1882 (1) 1884 (3) 1888 (3) 1893 (3)
Bannerman, C. 3: v E 1876 (2) 1878 (1)
Bardsley, W. 41: v E 1911 (4) 1920 (5) 1924 (3); v SA 1910 (5); *v E 1909 (5) 1912 (3)
    1921 (5) 1926 (5); v SA 1912 (3) 1921 (3)*

Barnes, S. G. 13: v E 1946 (4); v In 1947 (3); *v E 1938 (1) 1948 (4); v NZ 1945 (1)*
Barnett, B. A. 4: *v E 1938 (4)*
Barrett, J. E. 2: *v E 1890 (2)*
Beard, G. R. 3: *v P 1979 (3)*
Benaud, J. 3: v P 1972 (2); *v WI 1972 (1)*
Benaud, R. 63: v E 1954 (5) 1958 (5) 1962 (5); v SA 1952 (4) 1963 (4); v WI 1951 (1) 1960 (5); *v E 1953 (3) 1956 (5) 1961 (4); v SA 1957 (5); v WI 1954 (5); v In 1956 (3) 1959 (5); v P 1956 (1) 1959 (3)*
Blackham, J. McC. 35: v E 1876 (2) 1878 (1) 1881 (4) 1882 (4) 1884 (2) 1886 (1) 1887 (1) 1891 (3) 1894 (1); *v E 1880 (1) 1882 (1) 1884 (3) 1886 (3) 1888 (3) 1890 (2) 1893 (3)*
Blackie, D. D. 3: v E 1928 (3)
Bonnor, G. J. 17: v E 1882 (4) 1884 (3); *v E 1880 (1) 1882 (1) 1884 (3) 1886 (2) 1888 (3)*
Booth, B. C. 29: v E 1962 (5) 1965 (3); v SA 1963 (4); v P 1964 (1); *v E 1961 (2) 1964 (5); v WI 1964 (5); v In 1964 (3); v P 1964 (1)*
Border, A. R. 21: v E 1978 (3) 1979 (3); v WI 1979 (3); v P 1978 (2); *v E 1980 (1); v In 1979 (6); v P 1979 (3)*
Boyle, H. F. 12: v E 1878 (1) 1881 (4) 1882 (1) 1884 (1); *v E 1880 (1) 1882 (1) 1884 (3)*
Bradman, D. G. 52: v E 1928 (4) 1932 (4) 1936 (5) 1946 (5); v SA 1931 (5); v WI 1930 (5); v In 1947 (5); *v E 1930 (5) 1934 (5) 1938 (4) 1948 (5)*
Bright, R. J. 9: v E 1979 (1); v WI 1979 (1); *v E 1977 (3) 1980 (1); v P 1979 (3)*
Bromley, E. H. 2: v E 1932 (1): *v E 1934 (1)*
Brown, W. A. 22: v E 1936 (2); v In 1947 (3); *v E 1934 (5) 1938 (4) 1948 (2); v SA 1935 (5); v NZ 1945 (1)*
Bruce, W. 14: v E 1884 (2) 1891 (3) 1894 (4); *v E 1886 (2) 1893 (3)*
Burge, P. J. P. 42: v E 1954 (1) 1958 (1) 1962 (3) 1965 (4); v SA 1963 (5); v WI 1960 (2); *v E 1956 (3) 1961 (5) 1964 (5); v SA 1957 (1); v WI 1954 (1); v In 1956 (3) 1959 (2) 1964 (3); v P 1959 (2) 1964 (1)*
Burke, J. W. 24: v E 1950 (2) 1954 (2) 1958 (5); v WI 1951 (1): *v E 1956 (5); v SA 1957 (5); v In 1956 (3); v P 1956 (1)*
Burn, K. E. 2: *v E 1890 (2)*
Burton, F. J. 2: v E 1886 (1) 1887 (1)

Callaway, S. T. 3: v E 1891 (2) 1894 (1)
Callen, I. W. 1: v In 1977
Carkeek, W. 6: *v E 1912 (3); v SA 1912 (3)*
Carlson, P. H. 2: v E 1978 (2)
Carter, H. 28: v E 1907 (5) 1911 (5) 1920 (2); v SA 1910 (5); *v E 1909 (5) 1921 (4); v SA 1921 (2)*
Chappell, G. S. 61: v E 1970 (5) 1974 (6) 1976 (1) 1979 (3); v WI 1975 (6) 1979 (3); v NZ 1973 (3); v P 1972 (3) 1976 (3); *v E 1972 (5) 1975 (4) 1977 (5) 1980 (1); v WI 1972 (5); v NZ 1973 (3) 1976 (2); v P 1979 (3)*
Chappell, I. M. 75: v E 1965 (2) 1970 (6) 1974 (6) 1979 (2); v WI 1968 (5) 1975 (6) 1979 (1); v NZ 1973 (3); v In 1967 (4); v P 1964 (1) 1972 (3); *v E 1968 (5) 1972 (5) 1975 (4); v SA 1966 (5) 1969 (4); v WI 1972 (5); v NZ 1973 (3); v In 1969 (5)*
Charlton, P. C. 2: *v E 1890 (2)*
Chipperfield, A. G. 14: v E 1936 (3); *v E 1934 (5) 1938 (1); v SA 1935 (5)*
Clark, W. M. 10: v In 1977 (5); v P 1978 (1); *v WI 1977 (4)*
Colley, D. J. 3: *v E 1972 (3)*
Collins, H. L. 19: v E 1920 (5) 1924 (5); *v E 1921 (3) 1926 (3); v SA 1921 (3)*
Coningham, A. 1: v E 1894
Connolly, A. N. 29: v E 1965 (1) 1970 (1); v SA 1963 (3); v WI 1968 (5); v In 1967 (3); *v E 1968 (5); v SA 1969 (4); v In 1964 (2) 1969 (5)*
Cooper, B. B. 1: v E 1876
Cooper, W. H. 2: v E 1881 (1) 1884 (1)
Corling, G. E. 5: *v E 1964 (5)*
Cosier, G. J. 18: v E 1976 (1) 1978 (2); v WI 1975 (3); v In 1977 (4); v P 1976 (3); *v WI 1977 (3); v NZ 1976 (2)*
Cottam, W. J. 1: v E 1886
Cotter, A. 21: v E 1903 (2) 1907 (2) 1911 (4); v SA 1910 (5); *v E 1905 (3) 1909 (5)*
Coultard, G. 1: v E 1881
Cowper, R. M. 27: v E 1965 (4); v In 1967 (4); v P 1964 (1): *v E 1964 (1) 1968 (4); v SA 1966 (5); v WI 1964 (5); v In 1964 (2); v P 1964 (1)*

Craig, I. D. 11: v SA 1952 (1); *v E 1956* (2); *v SA 1957* (5); *v In 1956* (2); *v P 1956* (1)
Crawford, W. P. A. 4: *v E 1956* (1); *v In 1956* (3)

Darling, J. 34: v E 1894 (5) 1897 (5) 1901 (3); *v E 1896* (3) *1899* (5) *1902* (5) *1905* (5);
   v SA 1902 (3)
Darling, L. S. 12: v E 1932 (2) 1936 (1); *v E 1934* (4); *v SA 1935* (5)
Darling, W. M. 14: v E 1978 (4); v In 1977 (1); v P 1978 (1); *v WI 1977* (3); *v In 1979* (5)
Davidson, A. K. 44: v E 1954 (3) 1958 (5) 1962 (5); v WI 1960 (4); *v E 1953* (5) *1956* (2)
   1961 (5); *v SA 1957* (5); *v In 1956* (1) *1959* (5); *v P 1956* (1) *1959* (5)
Davis, I. C. 15: v E 1976 (1); v NZ 1973 (3); v P 1976 (3); *v E 1977* (3); *v NZ 1973* (3)
   1976 (2)
De Courcy, J. H. 3: *v E 1953* (3)
Dell, A. R. 2: v E 1970 (1); v NZ 1973 (1)
Donnan, H. 5: v E 1891 (2); *v E 1896* (3)
Dooland, B. 3: v E 1946 (2): v In 1947 (1)
Duff, R. A. 22: v E 1901 (4) 1903 (5); *v E 1902* (5) *1905* (5); *v SA 1902* (3)
Duncan, J. R. F. 1: v E 1970
Dymock, G. 21: v E 1974 (1) 1978 (3) 1979 (3); v WI 1979 (2); v NZ 1973 (1); v P 1978 (1);
   v NZ 1973 (2); *v In 1979* (5); *v P 1979* (3)
Dyson, J. 3: v In 1977 (3)

Eady, C. J. 2: v E 1901 (1); *v E 1896* (1)
Eastwood, K. H. 1: v E 1970
Ebeling, H. I. 1: *v E 1934*
Edwards, J. D. 3: *v E 1888* (3)
Edwards, R. 20: v E 1974 (5); v P 1972 (2); *v E 1972* (4) *1975* (4); *v WI 1972* (5)
Edwards, W. J. 3: v E 1974 (3)
Emery, S. H. 4: *v E 1912* (2); *v SA 1912* (2)
Evans, E. 6: v E 1881 (2) 1882 (1) 1884 (1); *v E 1886* (2)

Fairfax, A. G. 10: v E 1928 (1); v WI 1930 (5); *v E 1930* (4)
Favell, L. E. 19: v E 1954 (4) 1958 (2); v WI 1960 (4); *v WI 1954* (2); *v In 1959* (4); *v P 1959* (3)
Ferris, J. J. 8: v E 1886 (2) 1887 (1): *v E 1888* (3) *1890* (2)
Fingleton, J. H. W. 18: v E 1932 (3) 1936 (5); v SA 1931 (1); *v E 1938* (4); *v SA 1935* (5)
Fleetwood-Smith, L. O'B. 10: v E 1936 (3); *v E 1938* (4); *v SA 1935* (3)
Francis, B. C. 3: *v E 1972* (3)
Freeman, E. W. 11: v WI 1968 (4); v In 1967 (2); *v E 1968* (2); *v SA 1969* (2); *v In 1969* (1)
Freer, F. W. 1: v E 1946

Gannon, J. B. 3: v In 1977 (3)
Garrett, T. W. 19: v E 1876 (2) 1878 (1) 1881 (3) 1882 (3) 1884 (3) 1886 (2) 1887 (1); *v E 1882* (1) *1886* (3)
Gaunt, R. A. 3: v SA 1963 (1); *v E 1961* (1); *v SA 1957* (1)
Gehrs, D. R. A. 6: v E 1903 (1); v SA 1910 (4); *v E 1905* (1)
Giffen, G. 31: v E 1881 (3) 1882 (4) 1884 (3) 1891 (3) 1894 (5); *v E 1882* (1) *1884* (3) *1886* (3) *1893* (3) *1896* (3)
Giffen, W. F. 3: v E 1886 (1) 1891 (2)
Gilmour, G. J. 15: v E 1976 (1); v WI 1975 (5); v NZ 1973 (2); v P 1976 (3); *v E 1975* (1); *v NZ 1973* (1) *1976* (2)
Gleeson, J. W. 29: v E 1970 (5); v WI 1968 (5); v In 1967 (4); *v E 1968* (5) *1972* (3); *v SA 1969* (4); *v In 1969* (3)
Graham, H. 6: v E 1894 (2); *v E 1893* (3) *1896* (1)
Gregory, E. J. 1: v E 1876
Gregory, D. W. 3: v E 1876 (2) 1878 (1)
Gregory, J. M. 24: v E 1920 (5) 1924 (5) 1928 (1); *v E 1921* (5) *1926* (5); *v SA 1921* (3)
Gregory, R. G. 2: v E 1936 (2)
Gregory, S. E. 58: v E 1891 (1) 1894 (5) 1897 (5) 1901 (5) 1903 (4) 1907 (2) 1911 (1); *v E 1890* (2) *1893* (3) *1896* (3) *1899* (5) *1902* (5) *1905* (3) *1909* (5) *1912* (3); *v SA 1902* (3) *1912* (3)
Grimmett, C. V. 37: v E 1924 (1) 1928 (5) 1932 (3); v SA 1931 (5); v WI 1930 (5); *v E 1926* (3) *1930* (5) *1934* (5); *v SA 1935* (5)

Groube, T. U. 1: *v E 1880*

Grout, A. T. W. 51: v E 1958 (5) 1962 (2) 1965 (5); v SA 1963 (5); v WI 1960 (5); *v E 1961 (5) 1964 (5); v SA 1957 (5); v WI 1964 (5); v In 1959 (4) 1964 (1); v P 1959 (3) 1964 (1)*

Guest, C. E. J. 1: v E 1962

Hamence, R. A. 3: v E 1946 (1); v In 1947 (2)

Hammond, J. R. 5: *v WI 1972 (5)*

Harry, J. 1: v E 1894

Hartigan, R. J. 2: v E 1907 (2)

Hartkopf, A. E. V. 1: v E 1924

Harvey, M. R. 1: v E 1946

Harvey, R. N. 79: v E 1950 (5) 1954 (5) 1958 (5) 1962 (5); v SA 1952 (5); v WI 1951 (5) 1960 (4); v In 1947 (2); *v E 1948 (2) 1953 (5) 1956 (5) 1961 (5); v SA 1949 (5) 1957 (4); v WI 1954 (5); v In 1956 (3) 1959 (5); v P 1956 (1) 1959 (3)*

Hassett, A. L. 43: v E 1946 (5) 1950 (5); v SA 1952 (5); v WI 1951 (4); v In 1947 (4); *v E 1938 (4) 1948 (5) 1953 (5); v SA 1949 (5); v NZ 1945 (1)*

Hawke, N. J. N. 27: v E 1962 (1) 1965 (4); v SA 1963 (4); v In 1967 (1); v P 1964 (1); *v E 1964 (5) 1968 (2); v SA 1966 (2); v WI 1964 (5); v In 1964 (1); v P 1964 (1)*

Hazlitt, G. R. 9: v E 1907 (2) 1911 (1); *v E 1912 (3); v SA 1912 (3)*

Hendry, H. S. T. L. 11: v E 1924 (1) 1928 (4); *v E 1921 (4); v SA 1921 (2)*

Hibbert, P. A. 1: v In 1977

Higgs, J. D. 17: v E 1978 (6) 1979 (1); v WI 1977 (4); *v WI 1977 (4); v In 1979 (6)*

Hilditch, A. M. J. 9: v E 1978 (1); v P 1978 (2); *v In 1979 (6)*

Hill, C. 49: v E 1897 (5) 1901 (5) 1903 (5) 1907 (5) 1911 (5); v SA 1910 (5); *v E 1896 (3) 1899 (3) 1902 (5) 1905 (5); v SA 1902 (3)*

Hill, J. C. 3: *v E 1953 (2); v WI 1954 (1)*

Hoare, D. E. 1: v WI 1960

Hodges, J. H. 2: v E 1876 (2)

Hogg, R. M. 16: v E 1978 (6); v WI 1979 (2); v P 1978 (2); *v In 1979 (6)*

Hole, G. B. 18: v E 1950 (1) 1954 (3); v SA 1952 (4); v WI 1951 (5); *v E 1953 (5)*

Hookes, D. W. 8: v E 1976 (1); v WI 1979 (1); *v E 1977 (5); v P 1979 (1)*

Hopkins, A. J. Y. 20: v E 1901 (2) 1903 (5); *v E 1902 (5) 1905 (3) 1909 (2); v SA 1902 (3)*

Horan, T. P. 15: v E 1876 (1) 1878 (1) 1881 (4) 1882 (4) 1884 (4); *v E 1882 (1)*

Hordern, H. V. 7: v E 1911 (5); v SA 1910 (2)

Hornibrook, P. M. 6: v E 1928 (1); *v E 1930 (5)*

Howell, W. P. 18: v E 1897 (3) 1901 (4) 1903 (3); *v E 1899 (5) 1902 (1); v SA 1902 (2)*

Hughes, K. J. 27: v E 1978 (6) 1979 (3); v WI 1979 (3); v In 1977 (2); v P 1978 (2); *v E 1977 (1) 1980 (1); v In 1979 (6); v P 1979 (3)*

Hunt, W. A. 1: v SA 1931

Hurst, A. G. 12: v E 1978 (6); v NZ 1973 (1); v In 1977 (1); v P 1978 (2); *v In 1979 (2)*

Hurwood, A. 2: v WI 1930 (2)

Inverarity, R. J. 6: v WI 1968 (1); *v E 1968 (2) 1972 (3)*

Iredale, F. A. 14: v E 1894 (5) 1897 (4); *v E 1896 (2) 1899 (3)*

Ironmonger, H. 14: v E 1928 (2) 1932 (4); v SA 1931 (4); v WI 1930 (4)

Iverson, J. B. 5: v E 1950 (5)

Jackson, A. 8: v E 1928 (2); v WI 1930 (4); *v E 1930 (2)*

Jarman, B. N. 19: v E 1962 (3); v WI 1968 (4); v In 1967 (4); v P 1964 (1); *v E 1968 (4); v In 1959 (1) 1964 (2)*

Jarvis, A. H. 11: v E 1884 (3) 1894 (4); *v E 1886 (2) 1888 (2)*

Jenner, T. J. 9: v E 1970 (2) 1974 (2); v WI 1975 (1); *v WI 1972 (4)*

Jennings, C. B. 6: *v E 1912 (3); v SA 1912 (3)*

Johnson, I. W. 45: v E 1946 (4) 1950 (5) 1954 (4); v SA 1952 (1); v WI 1951 (4); v In 1947 (4); *v E 1948 (4) 1956 (5); v SA 1949 (5); v WI 1954 (5); v NZ 1945 (1); v In 1956 (2); v P 1956 (1)*

Johnson, L. J. 1: v In 1947

Johnston, W. A. 40: v E 1950 (5) 1954 (4); v SA 1952 (5); v WI 1951 (5); v In 1947 (4); *v E 1948 (5) 1953 (3); v SA 1949 (5); v WI 1954 (5)*

Jones, E. 19: v E 1894 (1) 1897 (5) 1901 (2); *v E 1896 (3) 1899 (5) 1902 (2); v SA 1902 (1)*

Jones, S. P. 12: v E 1881 (2) 1884 (4) 1886 (1) 1887 (1); *v E 1882 (1) 1886 (3)*

Joslin, L. R. 1: v In 1967

Kelleway, C. 26: v E 1911 (4) 1920 (5) 1924 (5) 1928 (1); v SA 1910 (5); *v E 1912 (3); v SA 1912 (3)*

Kelly, J. J. 36: v E 1897 (5) 1901 (5) 1903 (5); *v E 1896 (3) 1899 (5) 1902 (5) 1905 (5); v SA 1902 (3)*

Kelly, T. J. D. 2: v E 1876 (1) 1878 (1)

Kendall, T. 2: v E 1876 (2)

Kippax, A. F. 22: v E 1924 (1) 1928 (5) 1932 (1); v SA 1931 (4); v WI 1930 (5); *v E 1930 (5) 1934 (1)*

Kline, L. F. 13: v E 1958 (2); v WI 1960 (2); *v SA 1957 (5); v In 1959 (3); v P 1959 (1)*

Laird, B. M. 9: v E 1979 (2) v WI 1979 (3); *v E 1980 (1): v P 1979 (3)*

Langley, G. R. A. 26: v E 1954 (2); v SA 1952 (5); v WI 1951 (5); *v E 1953 (4) 1956 (3); v WI 1954 (4); v In 1956 (2); v P 1956 (1)*

Laughlin, T. J. 3: v E 1978 (1); *v WI 1977 (2)*

Laver, F. 15: v E 1901 (1) 1903 (1); *v E 1899 (4) 1905 (5) 1909 (4)*

Lawry, W. M. 67: v E 1962 (5) 1965 (5) 1970 (5); v SA 1963 (5); v WI 1968 (5); v In 1967 (4); v P 1964 (1); *v E 1961 (5) 1964 (5) 1968 (4); v SA 1966 (5) 1969 (4); v WI 1964 (5); v In 1964 (3) 1969 (5); v P 1964 (1)*

Lee, P. K. 2: v E 1932 (1); v SA 1931 (1)

Lillee, D. K. 42: v E 1970 (2) 1974 (6) 1976 (1) 1979 (3); v WI 1975 (5) 1979 (3); v P 1972 (3) 1976 (3); *v E 1972 (5) 1975 (4) 1980 (1): v WI 1972 (1); v NZ 1976 (2); v P 1979 (3)*

Lindwall, R. R. 61: v E 1946 (4) 1950 (5) 1954 (4) 1958 (2); v SA 1952 (4); v WI 1951 (5); v In 1947 (5); *v E 1948 (5) 1953 (5) 1956 (4); v SA 1949 (4); v WI 1954 (5); v NZ 1945 (1); v In 1956 (3) 1959 (2); v P 1956 (1) 1959 (2)*

Love, H. S. B. 1: v E 1932

Loxton, S. J. E. 12: v E 1950 (3); v In 1947 (1); *v E 1948 (3); v SA 1949 (5)*

Lyons, J. J. 14: v E 1886 (1) 1891 (3) 1894 (3) 1897 (1); *v E 1888 (1) 1890 (2) 1893 (3)*

McAlister, P. A. 8: v E 1903 (2) 1907 (4); *v E 1909 (2)*

Macartney, C. G. 35: v E 1907 (5) 1911 (1) 1920 (2); v SA 1910 (4); *v E 1909 (5) 1912 (3) 1921 (5) 1926 (5); v SA 1912 (3) 1921 (2)*

McCabe, S. J. 39: v E 1932 (5) 1936 (5); v SA 1931 (5); v WI 1930 (5); *v E 1930 (5) 1934 (5) 1938 (4); v SA 1935 (5)*

McCool, C. L. 14: v E 1946 (5); v In 1947 (3); *v SA 1949 (5) v NZ 1945 (1)*

McCormick, E. L. 12: v E 1936 (4); *v E 1938 (3); v SA 1935 (5)*

McCosker, R. B. 25: v E 1974 (3) 1976 (1) 1979 (2); v WI 1975 (4) 1979 (1); v P 1976 (3); *v E 1975 (4) 1977 (5); v NZ 1976 (2)*

McDonald, C. C. 47: v E 1954 (2) 1958 (5); v SA 1952 (5); v WI 1951 (1) 1960 (5); *v E 1956 (5) 1961 (3); v SA 1957 (5); v WI 1954 (5); v In 1956 (2) 1959 (5); v P 1956 (1) 1959 (3)*

McDonald, E. A. 11: v E 1920 (3); *v E 1921 (5); v SA 1921 (3)*

McDonnell, P. S. 19: v E 1881 (4) 1882 (3) 1884 (2) 1886 (2) 1887 (1); *v E 1880 (1) 1884 (3) 1888 (3)*

McIlwraith, J. 1: *v E 1886*

Mackay, K. D. 37: v E 1958 (5) 1962 (3); v WI 1960 (5); *v E 1956 (3) 1961 (5); v SA 1957 (5); v In 1956 (3) 1959 (5); v P 1959 (3)*

McKenzie, G. D. 60: v E 1962 (5) 1965 (4) 1970 (3); v SA 1963 (5); v WI 1968 (5); v In 1967 (2); v P 1964 (1); *v E 1961 (5) 1964 (5) 1968 (5); v SA 1966 (5) 1969 (3); v WI 1964 (5); v In 1964 (3) 1969 (5); v P 1964 (1)*

McKibbin, T. R. 5: v E 1894 (1) 1897 (2); *v E 1896 (2)*

McLaren, J. W. 1: v E 1911

Maclean, J. A. 4: v E 1978 (4)

McLeod, C. E. 17: v E 1894 (1) 1897 (5) 1901 (2) 1903 (3); *v E 1899 (1) 1905 (5)*

McLeod, R. W. 6: v E 1891 (3); *v E 1893 (3)*

McShane, P. G. 3: v E 1884 (1) 1886 (1) 1887 (1)

Maddocks, L. V. 7: v E 1954 (3); *v E 1956 (2); v WI 1954 (1); v In 1956 (1)*

Mailey, A. A. 21: v E 1920 (5) 1924 (5); *v E 1921 (3) 1926 (5); v SA 1921 (3)*

Mallett, A. A. 38: v E 1970 (2) 1974 (5) 1979 (1); v WI 1968 (1) 1975 (6) 1979 (1); v NZ 1973 (3); v P 1972 (2); *v E 1968 (1) 1972 (2) 1975 (4) 1980 (1); v SA 1969 (1); v NZ 1973 (3); v In 1969 (3)*

Malone, M. F. 1: *v E 1977*

Mann, A. L. 4: v In 1977 (4)

Marr, A. P. 1: v E 1884

Marsh, R. W. 62: v E 1970 (6) 1974 (6) 1976 (1) 1979 (3); v WI 1975 (6) 1979 (3); v NZ 1973 (3); v P 1972 (3) 1976 (3); *v E 1972 (5) 1975 (4) 1977 (5) 1980 (1); v WI 1972 (5); v NZ 1973 (3) 1976 (2); v P 1979 (3)*

Martin, J. W. 8: v SA 1963 (1); v WI 1960 (3); *v SA 1966 (1); v In 1964 (2); v P 1964 (1)*

Massie, H. H. 9: v E 1881 (4) 1882 (3) 1884 (1); *v E 1882 (1)*

Massie, R. A. L. 6: v P 1972 (2); *v E 1972 (4)*

Matthews, T. J. 8: v E 1911 (2); *v E 1912 (3); v SA 1912 (3)*

Mayne, E. R. 4: *v E 1912 (1); v SA 1912 (1) 1921 (2)*

Mayne, L. C. 6: *v SA 1969 (2); v WI 1964 (3); v In 1969 (1)*

Meckiff, I. 18: v E 1958 (4); v SA 1963 (1); v WI 1960 (2); *v SA 1957 (4); v In 1959 (5); v P 1959 (2)*

Meuleman, K. D. 1: *v NZ 1945*

Midwinter, W. E. 8: v E 1876 (2) 1882 (1) 1886 (2): *v E 1884 (3)*

Miller, K. R. 55: v E 1946 (5) 1950 (5) 1954 (4); v SA 1952 (4); v WI 1951 (5); v In 1947 (5); *v E 1948 (5) 1953 (5) 1956 (5); v SA 1949 (5); v WI 1954 (5); v NZ 1945 (1); v P 1956 (1)*

Minnett, R. B. 9: v E 1911 (5); *v E 1912 (1); v SA 1912 (3)*

Misson, F. M. 5: v WI 1960 (3); *v E 1961 (2)*

Moroney, J. R. 7: v E 1950 (1); v WI 1951 (1); *v SA 1949 (5)*

Morris, A. R. 46: v E 1946 (5) 1950 (5) 1954 (4); v SA 1952 (5); v WI 1951 (4); v In 1947 (4); *v E 1948 (5) 1953 (5); v SA 1949 (5); v WI 1954 (4)*

Morris, S. 1: v E 1884

Moses, H. 6: v E 1886 (2) 1887 (1) 1891 (2) 1894 (1)

Moss, J. K. 1: v P 1978

Moule, W. H. 1: *v E 1880*

Murdoch, W. L. 18: v E 1876 (1) 1878 (1) 1881 (4) 1882 (4) 1884 (1); *v E 1880 (1) 1882 (1) 1884 (3) 1890 (2)*

Musgrove, H. 1: v E 1884

Nagel, L. E. 1: v E 1932

Nash, L. J. 2: v E 1936 (1); v SA 1931 (1)

Nitschke, H. C. 2: v SA 1931 (2)

Noble, M. A. 42: v E 1897 (4) 1901 (5) 1903 (5) 1907 (5); *v E 1899 (5) 1902 (5) 1905 (5) 1909 (5); v SA 1902 (3)*

Noblet, G. 3: v SA 1952 (1); v WI 1951 (1); *v SA 1949 ʻ(1)*

Nothling, O. E. 1: v E 1928

O'Brien, L. P. J. 5: v E 1932 (2) 1936 (1); *v SA 1935 (2)*

O'Connor, J. D. A. 4: v E 1907 (3); *v E 1909 (1)*

Ogilvie, A. D. 5: v In 1977 (3); *v WI 1977 (2)*

O'Keeffe, K. J. 24: v E 1970 (2) 1976 (1); v NZ 1973 (3); v P 1972 (2) 1976 (3); *v E 1977 (3); v WI 1972 (5); v NZ 1973 (3) 1976 (2)*

Oldfield, W. A. S. 54: v E 1920 (3) 1924 (5) 1928 (5) 1932 (4) 1936 (5); v SA 1931 (5); v WI 1930 (5); *v E 1921 (1) 1926 (5) 1930 (5) 1934 (5); v SA 1921 (1) 1935 (5)*

O'Neill, N. C. 42: v E 1958 (5) 1962 (5); v SA 1963 (4); v WI 1960 (5); *v E 1961 (5) 1964 (4); v WI 1964 (4); v In 1959 (5) 1964 (2); v P 1959 (3)*

O'Reilly, W. J. 27: v E 1932 (5) 1936 (5); v SA 1931 (2); *v E 1934 (5) 1938 (4); v SA 1935 (5); v NZ 1945 (1)*

Oxenham, R. K. 7: v E 1928 (3); v SA 1931 (1); v WI 1930 (3)

Palmer, G. E. 17: v E 1881 (4) 1882 (4) 1884 (2); *v E 1880 (1) 1884 (3) 1886 (3)*

Park, R. L. 1: v E 1920

Pascoe, L. S. 7: v E 1979 (2); v WI 1979 (1); *v E 1977 (3) 1980 (1)*

Pellew, C. E. 10: v E 1920 (4); *v E 1921 (5); v SA 1921 (1)*

Philpott, P. I. 8: v E 1965 (3); *v WI 1964 (5)*

Ponsford, W. H. 29: v E 1924 (5) 1928 (2) 1932 (3); v SA 1931 (4); v WI 1930 (5); *v E 1926 (2) 1930 (4) 1934 (4)*

Pope, R. J. 1: v E 1884

Ransford, V. S. 20: v E 1907 (5) 1911 (5); v SA 1910 (5); *v E 1909 (5)*

Redpath, I. R. 66: v E 1965 (1) 1970 (6) 1974 (6); v SA 1963 (1); v WI 1968 (5) 1975 (6); v In 1967 (3); v P 1972 (3); *v E 1964 (5) 1968 (5); v SA 1966 (5) 1969 (4); v WI 1972 (5); v NZ 1973 (3); v In 1964 (2) 1969 (5); v P 1964 (1)*

Reedman, J. C. 1: v E 1894
Renneberg, D. A. 8: v In 1967 (3); *v SA 1966* (5)
Richardson, A. J. 9: v E 1924 (4); *v E 1926* (5)
Richardson, V. Y. 19: v E 1924 (3) 1928 (2) 1932 (5); *v E 1930* (4); *v SA 1935* (5)
Rigg, K. E. 8: v E 1936 (3); v SA 1931 (4); v WI 1930 (1)
Ring, D. T. 13: v SA 1952 (5); v WI 1951 (5); v In 1947 (1); *v E 1948* (1) *1953* (1)
Rixon, S. J. 10: v In 1977 (5); *v WI 1977* (5)
Robertson, W. R. 1: v E 1884
Robinson, R. D. 3: *v E 1977* (3)
Robinson, R. H. 1: v E 1936
Rorke, G. F. 4: v E 1958 (2); *v In 1959* (2)
Rutherford, J. W. 1: *v In 1956*
Ryder, J. 20: v E 1920 (5) 1924 (3) 1928 (5); *v E 1926* (4); *v SA 1921* (3)

Saggers, R. A. 6: *v E 1948* (1); *v SA 1949* (5)
Saunders, J. V. 14: v E 1901 (1) 1903 (2) 1907 (5); *v E 1902* (4); *v SA 1902* (5)
Scott, H. J. H. 8: v E 1884 (2); *v E 1884* (3) *1886* (3)
Sellers, R. H. D. 1: *v In 1964*
Serjeant, C. S. 12: v In 1977 (4); *v E 1977* (3); *v WI 1977* (5)
Sheahan, A. P. 31: v E 1970 (2); v WI 1968 (5); v NZ 1973 (2); v In 1967 (4); v P 1972 (2); *v E 1968* (5) *1972* (2); *v SA 1969* (4); *v In 1969* (5)
Shepherd, B. K. 9: v E 1962 (2); v SA 1963 (4); v P 1964 (1); *v WI 1964* (2)
Sievers, M. W. 3: v E 1936 (3)
Simpson, R. B. 62: v E 1958 (1) 1962 (5) 1965 (3); v SA 1963 (5); v WI 1960 (5); v In 1967 (3) 1977 (5); v P 1964 (1); *v E 1961* (5) *1964* (5); *v SA 1957* (5) *1966* (5); *v WI 1964* (5) *1977* (5); *v In 1964* (3); *v P 1964* (1)
Sincock, D. J. 3: v E 1965 (1); v P 1964 (1); *v WI 1964* (1)
Slater, K. N. 1: v E 1958
Sleep, P. R. 3: v P 1978 (1); *v In 1979* (2)
Slight, J. 1: *v E 1880*
Smith, D. B. M. 2: *v E 1912* (2)
Spofforth, F. R. 18: v E 1876 (1) 1878 (1) 1881 (1) 1882 (4) 1884 (3) 1886 (1); *v E 1882* (1) *1884* (3) *1886* (3)
Stackpole, K. R. 43: v E 1965 (2) 1970 (6); v WI 1968 (5); v NZ 1973 (3); v P 1972 (1); *v E 1972* (5); *v SA 1966* (5) *1969* (4); *v WI 1972* (4); *v NZ 1973* (3); *v In 1969* (5)
Stevens, G. B. 4: *v In 1959* (2); *v P 1959* (2)

Taber, H. B. 16: v WI 1968 (1); *v E 1968* (1); *v SA 1966* (5) *1969* (4); *v In 1969* (5)
Tallon, D. 21: v E 1946 (5) 1950 (5); v In 1947 (5); *v E 1948* (4) *1953* (1); *v NZ 1945* (1)
Taylor, J. M. 20: v E 1920 (5) 1924 (5); *v E 1921* (5) *1926* (3); *v SA 1921* (2)
Thomas, G. 8: v E 1965 (3); *v WI 1964* (5)
Thompson, N. 2: v E 1876 (2)
Thoms, G. R. 1: v WI 1951
Thomson, A. L. 4: v E 1970 (4)
Thomson, J. R. 34: v E 1974 (5) 1979 (1); v WI 1975 (6) 1979 (1); v In 1977 (5); v P 1972 (1) 1976 (1); *v E 1975* (4) *1977* (5); *v WI 1977* (5)
Thurlow, H. M. 1: v SA 1931
Toohey, P. M. 15: v E 1978 (5) 1979 (1); v WI 1979 (1); v In 1977 (5); *v WI 1977* (3)
Toshack, E. R. H. 12: v E 1946 (5); v In 1947 (2); *v E 1948* (4); *v NZ 1945* (1)
Travers, J. P. F. 1: v E 1901
Tribe, G. E. 3: v E 1946 (3)
Trott, A. E. 3: v E 1894 (3)
Trott, G. H. S. 24: v E 1891 (3) 1894 (5) 1897 (5); *v E 1888* (3) *1890* (2) *1893* (3) *1896* (3)
Trumble, H. 32: v E 1894 (1) 1897 (5) 1901 (5) 1903 (4); *v E 1890* (2) *1893* (3) *1896* (3) *1899* (5) *1902* (3); *v SA 1902* (1)
Trumble, J. W. 7: v E 1884 (4); *v E 1886* (3)
Trumper, V. T. 48: v E 1901 (5) 1903 (5) 1907 (5) 1911 (5); v SA 1910 (5); *v E 1899* (5) *1902* (5) *1905* (5) *1909* (5); *v SA 1902* (3)
Turner, A. 14: v WI 1975 (6); v P 1976 (3); *v E 1975* (3); *v NZ 1976* (2)
Turner, C. T. B. 17: v E 1886 (2) 1887 (1) 1891 (3) 1894 (3); *v E 1888* (3) *1890* (2) *1893* (3)

Veivers, T. R. 21: v E 1965 (4); v SA 1963 (3); v P 1964 (1); *v E 1964* (5); *v SA 1966* (4); *v In 1964* (3); *v P 1964* (1)

Waite, M. G. 2: v *E 1938 (2)*
Walker, M. H. N. 32: v E 1974 (6) 1976 (1); v WI 1975 (3); v NZ 1973 (1); v P 1972 (2) 1976 (2); *v E 1975 (4) 1977 (5); v WI 1972 (5); v NZ 1973 (3) 1976 (2)*
Wall, T. W. 18: v E 1928 (1) 1932 (4); v SA 1931 (3); v WI 1930 (1); *v E 1930 (5) 1934 (4)*
Walters, F. H. 1: v E 1884
Walters, K. D. 68: v E 1965 (5) 1970 (6) 1974 (6) 1976 (1); v WI 1968 (4); v NZ 1973 (3); v In 1967 (2); v P 1972 (1) 1976 (3); *v E 1968 (5) 1972 (4) 1975 (4) 1977 (5); v SA 1969 (4); v WI 1972 (5); v NZ 1973 (3) 1976 (2); v In 1969 (5)*
Ward, F. A. 4: v E 1936 (3); *v E 1938 (1)*
Watkins, J. R. 1: v P 1972
Watson, G. D. 5: *v E 1972 (2); v SA 1966 (3)*
Watson, W. 4: v E 1954 (1); *v WI 1954 (3)*
Whatmore, D. F. 7: v P 1978 (2); *v In 1979 (5)*
Whitty, W. J. 14: v E 1911 (2); v SA 1910 (5); *v E 1909 (1) 1912 (3); v SA 1912 (3)*
Wiener, J. M. 6: v E 1979 (2); v WI 1979 (2); *v P 1979 (2)*
Wilson, J. W. 1: *v In 1956*
Wood, G. M. 16: v E 1978 (6); v In 1977 (1); v P 1978 (1); *v E 1980 (1); v WI 1977 (5); v In 1979 (2)*
Woodcock, A. J. 1: v NZ 1973
Woodfull, W. M. 35: v E 1928 (5) 1932 (5); v SA 1931 (5); v WI 1930 (5); *v E 1926 (5) 1930 (5) 1934 (5)*
Woods, S. M. J. 3: *v E 1888 (3)*
Worrall, J. 11: v E 1884 (1) 1887 (1) 1894 (1) 1897 (1); *v E 1888 (3) 1899 (4)*
Wright, K. J. 10: v E 1978 (2); v P 1978 (2); *v In 1979 (6)*

Yallop, G. N. 25: v E 1978 (6); v WI 1975 (3); v In 1977 (1); v P 1978 (1); *v E 1980 (1); v WI 1977 (4); v In 1979 (6); v P 1979 (3)*
Yardley, B. 14: v E 1978 (4); v In 1977 (1); v P 1978 (1); *v WI 1977 (5); v In 1979 (3)*

SOUTH AFRICA

Number of Test cricketers: 235

Adcock, N. A. T. 26: v E 1956 (5); v A 1957 (5); v NZ 1953 (5) 1961 (2); *v E 1955 (4) 1960 (5)*
Anderson, J. H. 1: v A 1902
Ashley, W. H. 1: v E 1888

Bacher, A. 12: v A 1966 (5) 1969 (4); *v E 1965 (3)*
Balaskas, X. C. 9: v E 1930 (2) 1938 (1); v A 1935 (3); *v E 1935 (1); v NZ 1931 (2)*
Barlow, E. J. 30: v E 1964 (5); v A 1966 (5) 1969 (4); v NZ 1961 (5); *v E 1965 (3); v A 1963 (5); v NZ 1963 (3)*
Baumgartner, H. V. 1: v E 1913
Beaumont, R. 5: v E 1913 (2); *v E 1912 (1); v A 1912 (2)*
Begbie, D. W. 5: v E 1948 (3); v A 1949 (2)
Bell, A. J. 16: v E 1930 (3); *v E 1929 (3) 1935 (3); v A 1931 (5); v NZ 1931 (2)*
Bisset, M. 3: v E 1898 (2) 1909 (1)
Bissett, G. F. 4: v E 1927 (4)
Blanckenberg, J. M. 18: v E 1913 (5) 1922 (5); v A 1921 (3); *v E 1924 (5)*
Bland, K. C. 21: v E 1964 (5); v A 1966 (1); v NZ 1961 (5); *v E 1965 (3); v A 1963 (4); v NZ 1963 (3)*
Bock, E. G. 1: v A 1935
Bond, G. E. 1: v E 1938
Botten, J. T. 3: *v E 1965 (3)*
Brann, W. H. 3: v E 1922 (3)
Briscoe, A. W. 2: v E 1938 (1); v A 1935 (1)
Bromfield, H. D. 9: v E 1964 (3); v NZ 1961 (5); *v E 1965 (1)*
Brown, L. S. 2: *v A 1931 (1); v NZ 1931 (1)*
Burger, C. G. de V. 2: v A 1957 (2)
Burke, S. F. 2: v E 1964 (1); v NZ 1961 (1)
Buys, I. D. 1: v E 1922

Cameron, H. B. 26: v E 1927 (5) 1930 (5); *v E 1929 (4) 1935 (5); v A 1931 (5); v NZ 1931 (2)*
Campbell, T. 5: v E 1909 (4); *v E 1912 (1)*
Carlstein, P. R. 8: v A 1957 (1); *v E 1960 (5); v A 1963* (2)
Carter, C. P. 10: v E 1913 (2); v A 1921 (3); *v E 1912 (2) 1924* (3)
Catterall, R. H. 24: v E 1922 (5) 1927 (5) 1930 (4); *v E 1924 (5) 1929* (5)
Chapman, H. W. 2: v E 1913 (1); v A 1921 (1)
Cheetham, J. E. 24: v E 1948 (1); v A 1949 (3); v NZ 1953 (5); *v E 1951 (5) 1955 (3); v A 1952 (5); v NZ 1952* (2)
Chevalier, G. A. 1: v A 1969
Christy, J. A. J. 10: v E 1930 (1); *v E 1929 (2); v A 1931 (5); v NZ 1931* (2)
Chubb, G. W. A. 5: *v E 1951* (5)
Cochran, J. A. K. 1: v E 1930
Coen, S. K. 2: v E 1927 (2)
Commaille, J. M. M. 12: v E 1909 (5) 1927 (2); *v E 1924* (5)
Conyngham, D. P. 1: v E 1922
Cook, F. J. 1: v E 1895
Cooper, A. H. C. 1: v E 1913
Cox, J. L. 3: v E 1913 (3)
Cripps, G. 1: v E 1891
Crisp, R. J. 9: v A 1935 (4); *v E 1935* (5)
Curnow, S. H. 7: v E 1930 (3); *v A 1931* (4)

Dalton, E. L. 15: v E 1930 (1) 1938 (4); v A 1935 (1); *v E 1929 (1) 1935 (4); v A 1931 (2); v NZ 1931* (2)
Davies, E. Q. 5: v E 1938 (3); v A 1935 (2)
Dawson, O. C. 9: v E 1948 (4); *v E 1947* (5)
Deane, H. G. 17: v E 1927 (5) 1930 (2); *v E 1924 (5) 1929* (5)
Dixon, C. D. 1: v E 1913
Dower, R. R. 1: v E 1898
Draper, R. G. 2: v A 1949 (2)
Duckworth, C. A. R. 2: v E 1956 (2)
Dumbrill, R. 5: v A 1966 (2); *v E 1965* (3)
Duminy, J. P. 3: v E 1927 (2); *v E 1929 (1)*
Dunell, O. R. 2: v E 1888 (2)
Du Preez, J. H. 2: v A 1966 (2)
Du Toit, J. F. 1: v E 1891
Dyer, D. V. 3: *v E 1947* (3)

Elgie, M. K. 3: v NZ 1961 (3)
Endean, W. R. 28: v E 1956 (5); v A 1957 (5); v NZ 1953 (5); *v E 1951 (1) 1955 (5); v A 1952 (5); v NZ 1952* (2)

Farrer, W. S. 6: v NZ 1961 (3); *v NZ 1963* (3)
Faulkner, G. A. 25: v E 1905 (5) 1909 (5); *v E 1907 (3) 1912 (3) 1924 (1); v A 1910 (5) 1912* (3)
Fellows-Smith, J. P. 4: *v E 1960* (4)
Fichardt, C. G. 2: v E 1891 (1) 1895 (1)
Finlason, C. E. 1: v E 1888
Floquet, C. E. 1: v E 1909
Francis, H. H. 2: v E 1898 (2)
Francois, C. M. 5: v E 1922 (5)
Frank, C. N. 3: v A 1921 (3)
Frank, W. H. B. 1: v E 1895
Fuller, E. R. H. 7: v A 1957 (1); *v E 1955 (2); v A 1952 (2); v NZ 1952* (2)
Fullerton, G. M. 7: v A 1949 (2); *v E 1947 (2) 1951* (3)
Funston, K. J. 18: v E 1956 (3); v A 1957 (5); v NZ 1953 (3); *v A 1952 (5); v NZ 1952* (2)

Gamsy, D. 2: v A 1969 (2)
Gleeson, R. A. 1: v E 1895
Glover, G. K. 1: v E 1895
Goddard, T. L. 41: v E 1956 (5) 1964 (5); v A 1957 (5) 1966 (5) 1969 (3); *v E 1955 (5) 1960 (5); v A 1963 (5); v NZ 1963* (3)
Gordon, N. 5: v E 1938 (5)

Graham, R. 2: v E 1898 (2)
Grieveson, R. E. 2: v E 1938 (2)
Griffin, G. M. 2: *v E 1960 (2)*

Hall, A. E. 7: v E 1922 (4) 1927 (2) 1930 (1)
Hall, G. G. 1: v E 1964
Halliwell, E. A. 8: v E 1891 (1) 1895 (3) 1898 (1); v A 1902 (3)
Halse, C. G. 3: *v A 1963 (3)*
Hands, P. A. M. 7: v E 1913 (5); v A 1921 (1); *v E 1924 (1)*
Hands, R. H. M. 1: v E 1913
Hanley, M. A. 1: v E 1948
Harris, T. A. 3: v E 1948 (1); *v E 1947 (2)*
Hartigan, G. P. D. 5: v E 1913 (3); *v E 1912 (1); v A 1912 (1)*
Harvey, R. L. 2: v A 1935 (2)
Hathorn, C. M. H. 12: v E 1905 (5); v A 1902 (3); *v E 1907 (3); v A 1910 (1)*
Hearne, F. 4: v E 1891 (1) 1895 (3)
Hearne, G. A. L. 3: v E 1922 (2); *v E 1924 (1)*
Heine, P. S. 14: v E 1956 (5); v A 1957 (4); v NZ 1961 (1); *v E 1955 (4)*
Hime, C. F. W. 1: v E 1895
Hutchinson, P. 2: v E 1888 (2)

Ironside, D. E. J. 3: v NZ 1953 (3)
Irvine, B. L. 4: v A 1969 (4)

Johnson, C. L. 1: v E 1895
Jones, P. S. T. 1: v A 1902

Keith, H. J. 8: v E 1956 (3); *v E 1955 (4); v A 1952 (1)*
Kempis, G. A. 1: v E 1888
Kotze, J. J. 3: v A 1902 (2); *v E 1907 (1)*
Kuys, F. 1: v E 1898

Lance, H. R. 13: v A 1966 (5) 1969 (3); v NZ 1961 (2); *v E 1965 (3)*
Langton, A. B. C. 15: v E 1938 (5); v A 1935 (5); *v E 1935 (5)*
Lawrence, G. B. 5: v NZ 1961 (5)
Le Roux, F. le S. 1: v E 1913
Lewis, P. T. 1: v E 1913
Lindsay, D. T. 19: v E 1964 (3); v A 1966 (5) 1969 (2); *v E 1965 (3); v A 1963 (3); v NZ 1963 (3)*
Lindsay, J. D. 3: *v E 1947 (3)*
Lindsay, N. V. 1: v A 1921
Ling, W. V. S. 6: v E 1922 (3); v A 1921 (3)
Llewellyn, C. B. 15: v E 1895 (1) 1898 (1); v A 1902 (3); *v E 1912 (3); v A 1910 (5) 1912 (2)*
Lundie, E. B. 1: v E 1913

Macaulay, M. J. 1: v E 1964
McCarthy, C. N. 15: v E 1948 (5); v A 1949 (5); *v E 1951 (5)*
McGlew, D. J. 34: v E 1956 (1); v A 1957 (5); v NZ 1953 (5) 1961 (5); *v E 1951 (2) 1955 (5) 1960 (5); v A 1952 (4); v NZ 1952 (2)*
McKinnon, A. H. 8: v E 1964 (2); v A 1966 (2); v NZ 1961 (1); *v E 1960 (1) 1965 (2)*
McLean, R. A. 40: v E 1956 (5) 1964 (2); v A 1957 (4); v NZ 1953 (4) 1961 (5); *v E 1951 (3) 1955 (5) 1960 (5); v A 1952 (5); v NZ 1952 (2)*
McMillan, Q. 13: v E 1930 (5); *v E 1929 (2); v A 1931 (4); v NZ 1931 (2)*
Mann, N. B. F. 19: v E 1948 (5); v A 1949 (5); *v E 1947 (5) 1951 (4)*
Mansell, P. N. F. 13: *v E 1951 (2) 1955 (4); v A 1952 (5); v NZ 1952 (2)*
Markham, L. A. 1: v E 1948
Marx, W. F. E. 3: v A 1921 (3)
Meintjes, D. J. 2: v E 1922 (2)
Melle, M. G. 7: v A 1949 (2); *v E 1951 (1); v A 1952 (4)*
Melville, A. 11: v E 1938 (5) 1948 (1); *v E 1947 (5)*
Middleton, J. 6: v E 1895 (2) 1898 (2); v A 1902 (2)
Mills, C. 1: v E 1891
Milton, W. H. 3: v E 1888 (2) 1891 (1)

Mitchell, B. 42: v E 1930 (5) 1938 (5) 1948 (5); v A 1935 (5); *v E 1929 (5) 1935 (5) 1947 (5); v A 1931 (5); v NZ 1931* (2)
Mitchell, F. 3: *v E 1912 (1); v A 1912* (2)
Morkel, D. P. B. 16: v E 1927 (5); *v E 1929 (5); v A 1931 (5); v NZ 1931* (1)
Murray, A. R. A. 10: v NZ 1953 (4); *v A 1952 (4); v NZ 1952* (2)

Nel, J. D. 6: v A 1949 (5) 1957 (1)
Newberry, C. 4: v E 1913 (4)
Newson, E. S. 3: v E 1930 (1) 1938 (2)
Nicholson, F. 4: v A 1935 (4)
Nicolson, J. F. W. 3: v E 1927 (3)
Norton, N. O. 1: v E 1909
Nourse, A. D. 34: v E 1938 (5) 1948 (5); v A 1935 (5) 1949 (5); *v E 1935 (4) 1947 (5) 1951* (5)
Nourse, A. W. 45: v E 1905 (5) 1909 (5) 1913 (5) 1922 (5); v A 1902 (3) 1921 (3); *v E 1907 (3) 1912 (3) 1924 (5); v A 1910 (5) 1912* (3)
Nupen, E. P. 17: v E 1922 (4) 1927 (5) 1930 (3); v A 1921 (2) 1935 (1); *v E 1924* (2)

Ochse, A. E. 2: v E 1888 (2)
Ochse, A. L. 3: v E 1927 (1); *v E 1929* (2)
O'Linn, S. 7: v NZ 1961 (2); *v E 1960* (5)
Owen-Smith, H. G. 5: *v E 1929* (5)

Palm, A. W. 1: v E 1927
Parker, G. M. 2: *v E 1924* (2)
Parkin, D. C. 1: v E 1891
Partridge, J. T. 11: v E 1964 (3); *v A 1963 (5); v NZ 1963* (3)
Pearse, O. C. 3: *v A 1910* (3)
Pegler, S. J. 16: v E 1909 (1); *v E 1912 (3) 1924 (5); v A 1910 (4) 1912* (3)
Pithey, A. J. 17: v E 1956 (3) 1964 (5); *v E 1960 (2); v A 1963 (4); v NZ 1963* (3)
Pithey, D. B. 8: v A 1966 (2); *v A 1963 (3); v NZ 1963* (3)
Plimsoll, J. B. 1: *v E 1947*
Pollock, P. M. 28: v E 1964 (5); v A 1966 (5) 1969 (4); v NZ 1961 (3); *v E 1965 (3); v A 1963 (5); v NZ 1963* (3)
Pollock, R. G. 23: v E 1964 (5); v A 1966 (5) 1969 (4); *v E 1965 (3); v A 1963 (5); v NZ 1963* (1)
Poore, R. M. 3: v E 1895 (3)
Pothecary, J. E. 3: *v E 1960* (3)
Powell, A. W. 1: v E 1898
Prince, C. F. H. 1: v E 1898
Procter, M. J. 7: v A 1966 (3) 1969 (4)
Promnitz, H. L. E. 2: v E 1927 (2)

Quinn, N. A. 12: v E 1930 (1); *v E 1929 (4); v A 1931 (5); v NZ 1931* (2)

Reid, N. 1: v A 1921
Richards, A. R. 1: v E 1895
Richards, B. A. 4: v A 1969 (4)
Richards, W. H. 1: v E 1888
Robertson, J. B. 3: v A 1935 (3)
Rose-Innes, A. 2: v E 1888 (2)
Routledge, T. W. 4: v E 1891 (1) 1895 (3)
Rowan, A. M. B. 15: v E 1948 (5); *v E 1947 (5) 1951* (5)
Rowan, E. A. B. 26: v E 1938 (4) 1948 (4); v A 1935 (3) 1949 (5); *v E 1935 (5) 1951* (5)
Rowe, G. A. 5: v E 1895 (2) 1898 (2); v A 1902 (1)

Samuelson, S. V. 1: v E 1909
Schwarz, R. O. 20: v E 1905 (5) 1909 (4); *v E 1907 (3) 1912 (1); v A 1910 (5) 1912* (2)
Seccull, A. W. 1: v E 1895
Seymour, M. A. 7: v E 1964 (2); v A 1969 (1); *v A 1963* (4)
Shalders, W. A. 12: v E 1898 (1) 1905 (5); v A 1902 (3); *v E 1907* (3)
Shepstone, G. H. 2: v E 1895 (1) 1898 (1)
Sherwell, P. W. 13: v E 1905 (5); *v E 1907 (3); v A 1910* (5)

Siedle, I. J. 18: v E 1927 (1) 1930 (5) v A 1935 (5); *v E 1929 (3) 1935 (4)*
Sinclair, J. H. 25: v E 1895 (3) 1898 (2) 1905 (5) 1909 (4); v A 1902 (3); *v E 1907 (3); v A 1910 (5)*
Smith, C. J. E. 3: v A 1902 (3)
Smith, F. W. 3: v E 1888 (2) 1895 (1)
Smith, V. I. 9: v A 1949 (3) 1957 (1); *v E 1947 (4) 1955 (1)*
Snooke, S. D. 1: *v E 1907*
Snooke, S. J. 26: v E 1905 (5) 1909 (5) 1922 (3); *v E 1907 (3) 1912 (3); v A 1910 (5) 1912 (2)*
Solomon, W. R. 1: v E 1898
Stewart, R. B. 1: v E 1888
Stricker, L. A. 13: v E 1909 (4); *v E 1912 (2); v A 1910 (5) 1912 (2)*
Susskind, M. J. 5: *v E 1924 (5)*

Taberer, H. M. 1: v A 1902
Tancred, A. B. 2: v E 1888 (2)
Tancred, L. J. 14: v E 1905 (5) 1913 (1); v A 1902 (3); *v E 1907 (1) 1912 (2); v A 1912 (2)*
Tancred, V. M. 1: v E 1898
Tapscott, G. L. 1: v E 1913
Tapscott, L. E. 2: v E 1922 (2)
Tayfield, H. J. 37: v E 1956 (5); v A 1949 (5) 1957 (5); v NZ 1953 (5); *v E 1955 (5) 1960 (5); v A 1952 (5); v NZ 1952 (2)*
Taylor, A. I. 1: v E 1956
Taylor, D. 2: v E 1913 (2)
Taylor, H. W. 42: v E 1913 (5) 1922 (5) 1927 (5) 1930 (4); v A 1921 (3); *v E 1912 (3) 1924 (5) 1929 (3); v A 1912 (3) 1931 (5); v NZ 1931 (1)*
Theunissen, N. H. G. de J. 1: v E 1888
Thornton, P. G. 1: v A 1902
Tomlinson, D. S. 1: *v E 1935*
Traicos, A. J. 3: v A 1969 (3)
Trimborn, P. H. J. 4: v A 1966 (3) 1969 (1)
Tuckett, L. 9: v E 1948 (4); *v E 1947 (5)*
Tuckett, L. R. 1: v E 1913

Van der Bijl, P. G. V. 5: v E 1938 (5)
Van der Merwe, E. A. 2: v A 1935 (1); *v E 1929 (1)*
Van der Merwe, P. L. 15: v E 1964 (2); v A 1966 (5); *v E 1965 (3); v A 1963 (3); v NZ 1963 (2)*
Van Ryneveld, C. B. 19: v E 1956 (5); v A 1957 (4); v NZ 1953 (5); *v E 1951 (5)*
Varnals, G. D. 3: v E 1964 (3)
Viljoen, K. G. 27: v E 1930 (3) 1938 (4) 1948 (2); v A 1935 (4); *v E 1935 (4) 1947 (5); v A 1931 (4); v NZ 1931 (1)*
Vincent, C. L. 25: v E 1927 (5) 1930 (5); *v E 1929 (4) 1935 (4); v A 1931 (5); v NZ 1931 (2)*
Vintcent, C. H. 3: v E 1888 (2) 1891 (1)
Vogler, A. E. E. 15: v E 1905 (5) 1909 (5); *v E 1907 (3); v A 1910 (2)*

Wade, H. F. 10: v A 1935 (5); *v E 1935 (5)*
Wade, W. W. 11: v E 1938 (3) 1948 (5); v A 1949 (3)
Waite, J. H. B. 50: v E 1956 (5) 1964 (2); v A 1957 (5); v NZ 1953 (5) 1961 (5); *v E 1951 (4) 1955 (5) 1960 (5); v A 1952 (5) 1963 (4); v NZ 1952 (2) 1963 (3)*
Walter, K. A. 2: v NZ 1961 (2)
Ward, T. A. 23: v E 1913 (5) 1922 (5); v A 1921 (3); *v E 1912 (2) 1924 (5); v A 1912 (3)*
Watkins, J. C. 15: v E 1956 (2); v A 1949 (3); v NZ 1953 (3); *v A 1952 (5); v NZ 1952 (2)*
Wesley, C. 3: *v E 1960 (3)*
Westcott, R. J. 5: v A 1957 (2); v NZ 1953 (3)
White, G. C. 17: v E 1905 (5) 1909 (4); *v E 1907 (3) 1912 (2); v A 1912 (3)*
Willoughby, J. T. I. 2: v E 1895 (2)
Wimble, C. S. 1: v E 1891
Winslow, P. L. 5: v A 1949 (2); *v E 1955 (3)*
Wynne, O. E. 6: v E 1948 (3); v A 1949 (3)

Zulch, J. W. 16: v E 1909 (5) 1913 (3); v A 1921 (3); *v A 1910 (5)*

WEST INDIES

Number of Test cricketers: 173

Achong, E. 6: v E 1929 (1) 1934 (2); *v E 1933 (3)*
Alexander, F. C. M. 25: v E 1959 (5); v P 1957 (5); *v E 1957 (2); v A 1960 (5); v In 1958 (5); v P 1958 (3)*
Ali, Imtiaz 1: v In 1975
Ali, Inshan 12: v E 1973 (2); v A 1972 (3); v In 1970 (1); v P 1976 (1); v NZ 1971 (3); *v E 1973 (1); v A 1975 (1)*
Allan, D. W. 5: v A 1964 (1); v In 1961 (2); *v E 1966 (2)*
Asgarali, N. 2: *v E 1957 (2)*
Atkinson, D. St. E. 22: v E 1953 (4); v A 1954 (4); v P 1957 (1); *v E 1957 (2); v A 1951 (2); v NZ 1951 (1) 1955 (4); v In 1948 (4)*
Atkinson, E. St. E. 8: v P 1957 (3); *v In 1958 (3); v P 1958 (2)*
Austin, R. A. 2: v A 1977 (2)

Bacchus, S. F. A. F. 13: v A 1977 (2); *v E 1980 (5); v In 1978 (6)*
Baichan, L. 3: *v A 1975 (1); v P 1974 (2)*
Barrow, I. 11: v E 1929 (1) 1934 (1); *v E 1933 (3) 1939 (1); v A 1930 (5)*
Barrett, A. G. 6: v E 1973 (2); v In 1970 (2); *v In 1974 (2)*
Bartlett, E. L. 5: *v E 1928 (1); v A 1930 (4)*
Betancourt, N. 1: v E 1929
Binns, A. P. 5: v A 1954 (1); v In 1952 (1); *v NZ 1955 (3)*
Birkett, L. S. 4: *v A 1930 (4)*
Boyce, K. D. 21: v E 1973 (4); v A 1972 (4); v In 1970 (1); *v E 1973 (3); v A 1975 (4); v In 1974 (3); v P 1974 (2)*
Browne, C. R. 4: v E 1929 (2); *v E 1928 (2)*
Butcher, B. F. 44: v E 1959 (2) 1967 (5); v A 1964 (5); *v E 1963 (5) 1966 (5) 1969 (3); v A 1968 (5) v NZ 1968 (3); v In 1958 (5) 1966 (3); v P 1958 (3)*
Butler, L. 1: v A 1954
Bynoe, M. R. 4: *v In 1966 (3); v P 1958 (1)*

Camacho, G. S. 11: v E 1967 (5); v In 1970 (2); *v E 1969 (2); v A 1968 (2)*
Cameron, F. J. 5: *v In 1948 (5)*
Cameron, J. H. 2: *v E 1939 (2)*
Carew, G. M. 4: v E 1934 (1) 1947 (2); *v In 1948 (1)*
Carew, M. C. 19: v E 1967 (1); v NZ 1971 (3); v In 1970 (3); *v E 1963 (2) 1966 (1) 1969 (1); v A 1968 (5); v NZ 1968 (3)*
Challenor, G. 3: *v E 1928 (3)*
Chang, H. S. 1: *v In 1978*
Christiani, C. M. 4: v E 1934 (4)
Christiani, R. J. 22: v E 1947 (4) 1953 (1); v In 1952 (2); *v E 1950 (4); v A 1951 (5); v NZ 1951 (1); v In 1948 (5)*
Clarke, C. B. 3: *v E 1939 (3)*
Clarke, S. T. 6: v A 1977 (1); *v In 1978 (5)*
Constantine, L. N. 18: v E 1929 (3) 1934 (3); *v E 1928 (3) 1933 (1) 1939 (3); v A 1930 (5)*
Croft, C. E. H. 16: v A 1977 (2); v P 1976 (5); *v E 1980 (3); v A 1979 (3); v NZ 1979 (3)*

Da Costa, O. C. 5: v E 1929 (1) 1934 (1); *v E 1933 (3)*
Daniel, W. W. 5: v In 1975 (1); *v E 1976 (4)*
Davis, B. A. 4: v A 1964 (4)
Davis, C. A. 15: v A 1972 (2); v NZ 1971 (5); v In 1970 (4); *v E 1969 (3); v A 1968 (1)*
De Caires, F. I. 3: v E 1929 (3)
Depeiza, C. C. 5: v A 1954 (3); *v NZ 1955 (2)*
Dewdney, T. 9: v A 1954 (2); v P 1957 (3); *v E 1957 (1); v NZ 1955 (3)*
Dowe, U. G. 4: v A 1972 (1); v NZ 1971 (1); v In 1970 (2)

Edwards, R. M. 5: *v A 1968 (2); v NZ 1968 (3)*

Ferguson, W. 8: v E 1947 (4) 1953 (1); *v In 1948 (3)*
Fernandes, M. P. 2: v E 1929 (1); *v E 1928 (1)*
Findlay, T. M. 10: v A 1972 (1); v NZ 1971 (5); v In 1970 (2); *v E 1969 (2)*
Foster, M. L. C. 14: v E 1973 (1); v A 1972 (4) 1977 (1); v NZ 1971 (3); v In 1970 (2); v P 1976 (1); *v E 1969 (1) 1973 (1)*
Francis, G. N. 10: v E 1929 (1); *v E 1928 (3) 1933 (1); v A 1930 (5)*
Frederick, M. C. 1: v E 1953
Fredericks, R. C. 59: v E 1973 (5); v A 1972 (5); v NZ 1971 (5); v In 1970 (4) 1975 (4); v P 1976 (2); *v E 1969 (3) 1973 (3) 1976 (5); v A 1968 (4) 1975 (6); v NZ 1968 (3); v In 1974 (5); v P 1974 (2)*
Fuller, R. L. 1: v E 1934
Furlonge, H. A. 3: v A 1954 (1); *v NZ 1955 (2)*

Ganteaume, A. G. 1: v E 1947
Garner, J. 18: v A 1977 (2); v P 1976 (5); *v E 1980 (5); v A 1979 (3); v NZ 1979 (3)*
Gaskin, B. B. M. 2: v E 1947 (2)
Gibbs, G. L. R. 1: v A 1954
Gibbs, L. R. 79: v E 1967 (5) 1973 (5); v A 1964 (5) 1972 (5); v NZ 1971 (2); v In 1961 (5) 1970 (1); v P 1957 (4); *v E 1963 (5) 1966 (5) 1969 (3) 1973 (3); v A 1960 (3) 1968 (5) 1975 (6); v NZ 1968 (3); v In 1958 (1) 1966 (3) 1974 (5); v P 1958 (3) 1974 (2)*
Gilchrist, R. 13: v P 1957 (5); *v E 1957 (4); v In 1958 (4)*
Gladstone, G. 1: v E 1929
Goddard, J. D. C. 27: v E 1947 (4); *v E 1950 (4) 1957 (5); v A 1951 (4); v NZ 1951 (2) 1955 (3); v In 1948 (5)*
Gomes, H. A. 11: v A 1977 (3); *v E 1976 (2); v In 1978 (6)*
Gomez, G. E. 29: v E 1947 (4) 1953 (4); v In 1952 (4); *v E 1939 (2) 1950 (4); v A 1951 (5); v NZ 1951 (1); v In 1948 (5)*
Grant, G. C. 12: v E 1934 (4); *v E 1933 (3); v A 1930 (5)*
Grant, R. S. 7: v E 1934 (4); *v E 1939 (3)*
Greenidge, A. T. 6: v A 1977 (2); *v In 1978 (4)*
Greenidge, C. G. 30: v A 1977 (2); v P 1976 (5); *v E 1976 (5) 1980 (5); v A 1975 (2) 1979 (3); v NZ 1979 (3); v In 1974 (5)*
Greenidge, G. A. 5: v A 1972 (3); v NZ 1971 (2)
Grell, M. G. 1: v E 1929
Griffith, C. C. 28: v E 1959 (1) 1967 (4); v A 1964 (5); *v E 1963 (5) 1966 (5); v A 1968 (3); v NZ 1968 (2); v In 1966 (3)*
Griffith, H. C. 13: v E 1929 (3); *v E 1928 (3) 1933 (2); v A 1930 (5)*
Guillen, S. C. 5: *v A 1951 (3); v NZ 1951 (2)*

Hall, W. W. 48: v E 1959 (5) 1967 (4); v A 1964 (5); v In 1961 (5); *v E 1963 (5) 1966 (5); v A 1960 (5) 1968 (2); v NZ 1968 (1); v In 1958 (5) 1966 (3); v P 1958 (3)*
Haynes, D. L. 13: v A 1977 (2); *v E 1980 (5); v A 1979 (3); v NZ 1979 (3)*
Headley, G. A. 22: v E 1929 (4) 1934 (4) 1947 (1) 1953 (1); *v E 1933 (3) 1939 (3); v A 1930 (5); v In 1948 (1)*
Headley, R. G. A. 2: *v E 1973 (2)*
Hendriks, J. L. 20: v A 1964 (4); v In 1961 (1); *v E 1966 (3) 1969 (1); v A 1968 (5); v NZ 1968 (3); v In 1966 (3)*
Hoad, E. L. G. 4: v E 1929 (1); *v E 1928 (1) 1933 (2)*
Holder, V. A. 40: v E 1973 (1); v A 1972 (3) 1977 (3); v NZ 1971 (4); v In 1970 (3) 1975 (1); v P 1976 (1); *v E 1969 (1) 1973 (2) 1976 (4); v A 1975 (3); v In 1974 (4) 1978 (6); v P 1974 (2)*
Holding, M. A. 24: v In 1975 (4); *v E 1976 (4) 1980 (5); v A 1975 (3) 1979 (3); v NZ 1979 (3)*
Holford, D. A. J. 24: v E 1967 (4); v NZ 1971 (5); v In 1970 (1) 1975 (2); v P 1976 (1); *v E 1966 (5); v A 1968 (2); v NZ 1968 (3); v In 1966 (1)*
Holt, J. K. 17: v E 1953 (5); v A 1954 (5); *v In 1958 (5); v P 1958 (2)*
Howard, A. B. 1: v NZ 1971
Hunte, C. C. 44: v E 1959 (5); v A 1964 (5); v In 1961 (5); v P 1957 (5); *v E 1963 (5) 1966 (5); v A 1960 (5); v In 1958 (5) 1966 (3); v P 1958 (1)*
Hunte, E. A. C. 3: v E 1929 (3)
Hylton, L. G. 6: v E 1934 (4); *v E 1939 (2)*

Johnson, H. H. H. 3: v E 1947 (1); *v E 1950 (2)*
Johnson, T. F. 1: *v E 1939*

Jones, C. M. 4: v E 1929 (1) 1934 (3)
Jones, P. E. 9: v E 1947 (1); *v E 1950 (2); v A 1951 (1); v In 1948 (5)*
Julien, B. D. 24: v E 1973 (5); v In 1975 (4); v P 1976 (1); *v E 1973 (3) 1976 (2); v A 1975 (3); v In 1974 (4); v P 1974 (2)*
Jumadeen, R. R. 12: v A 1972 (1) 1977 (2); v NZ 1971 (1); v In 1975 (4); v P 1976 (1); *v E 1976 (1); v In 1978 (2)*

Kallicharran, A. I. 62: v E 1973 (5); v A 1972 (5) 1977 (5); v NZ 1971 (2); v In 1975 (4); v P 1976 (5); *v E 1973 (3) 1976 (3) 1980 (5); v A 1975 (6) 1979 (3); v NZ 1979 (3); v In 1974 (5) 1978 (6); v P 1974 (2)*
Kanhai, R. B. 79: v E 1959 (5) 1967 (5) 1973 (5); v A 1964 (5) 1972 (5); v In 1961 (5) 1970 (5); v P 1957 (5); *v E 1957 (5) 1963 (5) 1966 (5) 1973 (3); v A 1960 (5) 1968 (5); v In 1958 (5) 1966 (3); v P 1958 (3)*
Kentish, E. S. M. 2: v E 1947 (1) 1953 (1)
King, C. L. 9: v P 1976 (1); *v E 1976 (3) 1980 (1); v A 1979 (1); v NZ 1979 (3)*
King, F. M. 14: v E 1953 (3); v A 1954 (4); v In 1952 (5); v NZ 1955 (2)
King, L. A. 2: v E 1967 (1); v In 1961 (1)

Lashley, P. D. 4: *v E 1966 (2); v A 1960 (2)*
Legall, R. 4: v In 1952 (4)
Lewis, D. M. 3: v In 1970 (3)
Lloyd, C. H. 74: v E 1967 (5) 1973 (5); v A 1972 (3) 1977 (2); v NZ 1971 (2); v In 1970 (5) 1975 (4); v P 1976 (5); *v E 1969 (3) 1973 (3) 1976 (5) 1980 (4); v A 1968 (4) 1975 (6) 1979 (3); v NZ 1968 (3) 1979 (3); v In 1966 (3) 1974 (5); v P 1974 (2)*

McMorris, E. D. A. 13: v E 1959 (4); v In 1961 (4); v P 1957 (1); *v E 1963 (2) 1966 (2)*
McWatt, C. A. 6: v E 1953 (5); v A 1954 (1)
Madray, I. S. 2: v P 1957 (2)
Marshall, M. D. 7: *v E 1980 (4); v In 1978 (3)*
Marshall, N. E. 1: v A 1954
Marshall, R. E. 4: *v A 1951 (2); v NZ 1951 (2)*
Martin, F. R. 9: v E 1929 (1); *v E 1928 (3); v A 1930 (5)*
Martindale, E. A. 10: v E 1934 (4); *v E 1933 (3) 1939 (3)*
Mendonca, I. L. 2: v In 1961 (2)
Merry, C. A. 2: *v E 1933 (2)*
Miller, R. 1: v In 1952
Moodie, G. H. 1: v E 1934
Murray, D. A. 9: v A 1977 (3); *v In 1978 (6)*
Murray, D. L. 62: v E 1967 (5) 1973 (5); v A 1972 (4) 1977 (2); v In 1975 (4); v P 1976 (5); *v E 1963 (5) 1973 (3) 1976 (5) 1980 (5); v A 1975 (6) 1979 (3); v NZ 1979 (3); v In 1974 (5); v P 1974 (2)*

Neblett, J. M. 1: v E 1934
Noreiga, J. M. 4: v In 1970 (4)
Nunes, R. K. 4: v E 1929 (1); *v E 1928 (3)*
Nurse, S. M. 29: v E 1959 (1) 1967 (5); v A 1964 (5); v In 1961 (1); *v E 1966 (5); v A 1960 (3) 1968 (5); v NZ 1968 (3); v In 1966 (2)*

Padmore, A. L. 2: v In 1975 (1); *v E 1976 (1)*
Pairaudeau, B. H. 13: v E 1953 (2); v In 1952 (5); *v E 1957 (2); v NZ 1955 (4)*
Parry, D. R. 12: v A 1977 (5); *v NZ 1979 (1); v In 1978 (6)*
Passailaigue, C. C. 1: v E 1929
Phillip, N. 9: v A 1977 (3); *v In 1978 (6)*
Pierre, L. R. 1: v E 1947

Rae, A. F. 15: v In 1952 (2); *v E 1950 (4); v A 1951 (3); v NZ 1951 (1); v In 1948 (5)*
Ramadhin, S. 43: v E 1953 (5) 1959 (4); v A 1954 (4); v In 1952 (4); *v E 1950 (4) 1957 (5); v A 1951 (5) 1960 (2); v NZ 1951 (2) 1955 (4); v In 1958 (2); v P 1958 (2)*
Richards, I. V. A. 36: v A 1977 (2); v In 1975 (4); v P 1976 (5); *v E 1976 (4) 1980 (5); v A 1975 (6) 1979 (3); v In 1974 (5); v P 1974 (2)*
Rickards, K. R. 2: v E 1947 (1); *v A 1951 (1)*
Roach, C. A. 16: v E 1929 (4) 1934 (1); *v E 1928 (3) 1933 (3); v A 1930 (5)*

Roberts, A. M. E. 35: v E 1973 (1); v A 1977 (2); v In 1975 (2); v P 1976 (5); *v E 1976 (5) 1980 (3); v A 1975 (5) 1979 (3); v NZ 1979 (2); v In 1974 (5); v P 1974 (2)*
Roberts, A. T. 1: *v NZ 1955*
Rodriguez, W. V. 5: v E 1967 (1); v A 1964 (1); v In 1961 (2); *v E 1963 (1)*
Rowe, L. G. 30: v E 1973 (5); v A 1972 (3); v NZ 1971 (4); v In 1975 (4); *v E 1976 (2); v A 1975 (6) 1979 (3); v NZ 1979 (3)*

St Hill, E. L. 2: v E 1929 (2)
St Hill, W. H. 3: v E 1929 (1); *v E 1928 (2)*
Scarlett, R. G. 3: v E 1959 (3)
Scott, A. P. H. 1: v In 1952
Scott, O. C. 8: v E 1929 (1); *v E 1928 (2); v A 1930 (5)*
Sealey, B. J. 1: *v E 1933*
Sealy, J. E. D. 11: v E 1929 (2) 1934 (4); *v E 1939 (3); v A 1930 (2)*
Shepherd, J. N. 5: v In 1970 (2); *v E 1969 (3)*
Shillingford, G. C. 7: v NZ 1971 (2); v In 1970 (3); *v E 1969 (2)*
Shillingford, I. T. 4: v A 1977 (1); v P 1976 (3)
Shivnarine, S. 8: v A 1977 (3); *v In 1978 (5)*
Singh, C. K. 2: v E 1959 (2)
Small, J. A. 3: v E 1929 (1); *v E 1928 (2)*
Smith, C. W. 5: v In 1961 (1); *v A 1960 (4)*
Smith, O. G. 26: v A 1954 (4); v P 1957 (5); *v E 1957 (5); v NZ 1955 (4); v In 1958 (5); v P 1958 (3)*
Sobers, G. S. 93: v E 1953 (1) 1959 (5) 1967 (5) 1973 (4); v A 1954 (4) 1964 (5); v NZ 1971 (5); v In 1961 (5) 1970 (5); v P 1957 (5); *v E 1957 (5) 1963 (5) 1966 (5) 1969 (3) 1973 (3); v A 1960 (5) 1968 (5); v NZ 1955 (4) 1968 (3); v In 1958 (5) 1966 (3); v P 1958 (3)*
Solomon, J. S. 27: v E 1959 (2); v A 1964 (4); v In 1961 (4); *v E 1963 (5); v A 1960 (5); v In 1958 (4); v P 1958 (3)*
Stayers, S. C. 4: v In 1961 (4)
Stollmeyer, J. B. 32: v E 1947 (2) 1953 (5); v A 1954 (2); v In 1952 (5); *v E 1939 (3) 1950 (4); v A 1951 (5); v NZ 1951 (2); v In 1948 (4)*
Stollmeyer, V. H. 1: *v E 1939*

Taylor, J. 3: v P 1957 (1); *v In 1958 (1); v P 1958 (1)*
Trim, J. 4: v E 1947 (1); *v A 1951 (1); v In 1948 (2)*

Valentine, A. L. 36: v E 1953 (3); v A 1954 (3); v In 1952 (5) 1961 (2); v P 1957 (1); *v E 1950 (4) 1957 (2); v A 1951 (5) 1960 (5); v NZ 1951 (2) 1955 (4)*
Valentine, V. A. 2: *v E 1933 (2)*

Walcott, C. L. 44: v E 1947 (4) 1953 (5) 1959 (2); v A 1954 (5); v In 1952 (5); v P 1957 (4); *v E 1950 (4) 1957 (5); v A 1951 (3); v NZ 1951 (2); v In 1948 (5)*
Walcott, L. A. 1: v E 1929
Watson, C. 7: v E 1959 (5); v In 1961 (1); *v A 1960 (1)*
Weekes, E. D. 48: v E 1947 (4) 1953 (4); v A 1954 (5); v In 1952 (5); v P 1957 (5); *v E 1950 (4) 1957 (5); v A 1951 (5); v NZ 1951 (2) 1955 (4); v In 1948 (5)*
Weekes, K. H. 2: *v E 1939 (2)*
White, W. A. 2: v A 1964 (2)
Wight, C. V. 2: v E 1929 (1); *v E 1928 (1)*
Wight, G. L. 1: v In 1952
Wiles, C. A. 1: *v E 1933*
Willett, E. T. 5: v A 1972 (3); *v In 1974 (2)*
Williams, A. B. 7: v A 1977 (3); *v In 1978 (4)*
Williams, E. A. V. 4: v E 1947 (3); *v E 1939 (1)*
Wishart, K. L. 1: v E 1934
Worrell, F. M. M. 51: v E 1947 (3) 1953 (4) 1959 (4); v A 1954 (4); v In 1952 (5) 1961 (5); *v E 1950 (4) 1957 (5) 1963 (5); v A 1951 (5) 1960 (5); v NZ 1951 (2)*

NEW ZEALAND

Number of Test cricketers: 146

Alabaster, J. C. 21: v E 1962 (2); v WI 1955 (1); v In 1967 (4); *v E 1958 (2); v SA 1961 (5); v WI 1971 (2); v In 1955 (4); v P 1955 (1)*
Allcott, C. F. W. 6: v E 1929 (2); v SA 1931 (1); *v E 1931 (3)*
Anderson, R. W. 9: v E 1977 (3); *v E 1978 (3); v P 1976 (3)*
Anderson, W. M. 1: v A 1945
Andrews, B. 2: *v A 1973 (2)*

Badcock, F. T. 7: v E 1929 (3) 1932 (2); v SA 1931 (2)
Barber, R. T. 1: v WI 1955
Bartlett, G. A. 10: v E 1965 (2); v In 1967 (2); v P 1964 (1); *v SA 1961 (5)*
Barton, P. T. 7: v E 1962 (3); *v SA 1961 (4)*
Beard, D. D. 4: v WI 1951 (2) 1955 (2)
Beck, J. E. F. 8: v WI 1955 (4); *v SA 1953 (4)*
Bell, W. 2: *v SA 1953 (2)*
Bilby, G. P. 2: v E 1965 (2)
Blair, R. W. 19: v E 1954 (1) 1958 (2) 1962 (2); v SA 1952 (2) 1963 (3); v WI 1955 (2); *v E 1958 (3); v SA 1953 (4)*
Blunt, R. C. 9: v E 1929 (4); v SA 1931 (2); *v E 1931 (3)*
Bolton, B. A. 2: v E 1958 (2)
Boock, S. L. 12: v E 1977 (3); v WI 1979 (3); v P 1978 (3); *v E 1978 (3)*
Bracewell, B. P. 4: v P 1978 (1); *v E 1978 (3)*
Bradburn, W. P. 2: v SA 1963 (2)
Burgess, M. G. 47: v E 1970 (1) 1977 (3); v A 1973 (1) 1976 (2); v WI 1968 (2); v In 1967 (4) 1975 (3); v P 1972 (3) 1978 (3); *v E 1969 (2) 1973 (3) 1978 (3); v WI 1971 (5); v In 1969 (3) 1976 (3); v P 1969 (3) 1976 (3)*
Burke, C. 1: v A 1945
Burtt, T. B. 10: v E 1946 (1) 1950 (2); v SA 1952 (1); v WI 1951 (2); *v E 1949 (4)*
Butterfield, L. A. 1: v A 1945

Cairns, B. L. 17: v E 1974 (1) 1977 (1); v A 1976 (1); v WI 1979 (3); v In 1975 (1); v P 1978 (3); *v E 1978 (2); v A 1973 (1); v In 1976 (2); v P 1976 (2)*
Cameron, F. J. 19: v E 1962 (3); v SA 1963 (3); v P 1964 (3); *v E 1965 (2); v SA 1961 (5); v In 1964 (1); v P 1964 (2)*
Cave, H. B. 19: v E 1954 (2); v WI 1955 (3); *v E 1949 (4) 1958 (2); v In 1955 (5); v P 1955 (3)*
Chapple, M. E. 14: v E 1954 (1) 1965 (1); v SA 1952 (1) 1963 (3); v WI 1955 (1); *v SA 1953 (5) 1961 (2)*
Chatfield, E. J. 4: v E 1974 (1) 1977 (1); v A 1976 (2)
Cleverley, D. C. 2: v SA 1931 (1); v A 1945 (1)
Collinge, R. O. 35: v E 1970 (2) 1974 (2) 1977 (3); v A 1973 (3); v In 1967 (2) 1975 (3); v P 1964 (3) 1972 (2); *v E 1965 (3) 1969 (1) 1973 (1) 1978 (1); v In 1964 (2) 1976 (1); v P 1964 (2) 1976 (2)*
Colquhoun, I. A. 2: v E 1954 (2)
Coney, J. V. 10: v A 1973 (2); v WI 1979 (3); v P 1978 (3); *v A 1973 (2)*
Congdon, B. E. 61: v E 1965 (3) 1970 (2) 1974 (2) 1977 (3); v A 1973 (3) 1976 (2); v WI 1968 (3); v In 1967 (4) 1975 (3); v P 1964 (3) 1972 (3); *v E 1965 (3) 1969 (3) 1973 (3) 1978 (3); v A 1973 (3); v WI 1971 (5); v In 1964 (3) 1969 (3); v P 1964 (1) 1969 (3)*
Cowie, J. 9: v E 1946 (1); v A 1945 (1); *v E 1937 (3) 1949 (4)*
Cresswell, G. F. 3: v E 1950 (2); *v E 1949 (1)*
Cromb, I. B. 5: v SA 1931 (2); *v E 1931 (3)*
Cunis, R. S. 20: v E 1965 (3) 1970 (2); v SA 1963 (1); v WI 1968 (3); *v E 1969 (1); v WI 1971 (2); v In 1969 (3); v P 1969 (2)*

D'Arcy, J. W. 5: *v E 1958 (5)*
Dempster, C. S. 10: v E 1929 (4) 1932 (2); v SA 1931 (2); *v E 1931 (2)*
Dempster, E. W. 5: v SA 1952 (1); *v SA 1953 (4)*

Dick, A. E. 17: v E 1962 (3); v SA 1963 (2); v P 1964 (2); *v E 1965 (2); v SA 1961 (5); v P 1964 (3)*

Dickinson, G. R. 3: v E 1929 (2); v SA 1931 (1)

Donnelly, M. P. 7: *v E 1937 (3) 1949 (4)*

Dowling, G. T. 39: v E 1962 (3) 1970 (2); v In 1967 (4); v SA 1963 (1); v WI 1968 (3); v P 1964 (2); *v E 1965 (3) 1969 (3); v SA 1961 (4); v WI 1971 (2); v In 1964 (4) 1969 (3); v P 1964 (2) 1969 (3)*

Dunning, J. A. 4: v E 1932 (1); *v E 1937 (3)*

Edgar, B. A. 9: v WI 1979 (3); v P 1978 (3); *v E 1978 (3)*

Edwards, G. N. 5: v E 1977 (1); v A 1976 (2); *v E 1978 (2)*

Emery, R. W. G. 2: v WI 1951 (2)

Fisher, F. E. 1: v SA 1952

Foley, H. 1: v E 1929

Freeman, D. L. 2: v E 1932 (2)

Gallichan, N. 1: *v E 1937*

Gedye, S. G. 4: v SA 1963 (3); v P 1964 (1)

Guillen, S. C. 3: v WI 1955 (3)

Guy, J. W. 12: v E 1958 (2); v WI 1955 (2); *v SA 1961 (2); v In 1955 (5); v P 1955 (1)*

Hadlee, D. R. 26: v E 1974 (2) 1977 (1); v A 1973 (3) 1976 (1); v In 1975 (3); v P 1972 (2); *v E 1969 (2) 1973 (3); v A 1973 (3); v In 1969 (3); v P 1969 (3)*

Hadlee, R. J. 29: v E 1977 (3); v A 1973 (3) 1976 (2); v WI 1979 (3); v In 1975 (2); v P 1972 (1) 1978 (3); *v E 1973 (1) 1978 (3); v A 1973 (3); v In 1976 (3); v P 1976 (3)*

Hadlee, W. A. 11: v E 1946 (1) 1950 (2); v A 1945 (1); *v E 1937 (3) 1949 (4)*

Harford, N. S. 8: *v E 1958 (4); v In 1955 (2); v P 1955 (2)*

Harford, R. I. 3: v In 1967 (3)

Harris, P. G. Z. 9: v P 1964 (1); *v SA 1961 (5); v In 1955 (1); v P 1955 (2)*

Harris, R. M. 2: v E 1958(2)

Hastings, B. F. 31: v E 1974 (2); v A 1973 (3); v WI 1968 (3); v In 1975 (1); v P 1972 (3); *v E 1969 (3) 1973 (3); v A 1973 (3); v WI 1971 (5); v In 1969 (3); v P 1969 (3)*

Hayes, J. A. 15: v E 1950 (2) 1954 (1); v WI 1951 (2); *v E 1958 (4); v In 1955 (5); v P 1955 (1)*

Henderson, M. 1: v E 1929

Hough, K. W. 2: v E 1958 (2)

Howarth, G. P. 20: v E 1974 (2) 1977 (3); v A 1976 (2); v WI 1979 (3); v P 1978 (3); *v E 1978 (3); v In 1976 (2); v P 1976 (2)*

Howarth, H. J. 30: v E 1970 (2) 1974 (2); v A 1973 (3) 1976 (2); v In 1975 (3); v P 1972 (3); *v E 1969 (3) 1973 (2); v WI 1971 (5); v In 1969 (3); v P 1969 (3)*

James, K. C. 11: v E 1929 (4) 1932 (2); v SA 1931 (2); *v E 1931 (3)*

Jarvis, T. W. 13: v E 1965 (1); v P 1972 (3); *v WI 1971 (4); v In 1964 (2); v P 1964 (3)*

Kerr, J. L. 7: v E 1932 (2); v SA 1931 (1); *v E 1931 (2) 1937 (2)*

Lees, W. K. 15: v E 1977 (2); v A 1976 (1); v WI 1979 (3); v P 1978 (3); *v In 1976 (3); v P 1976 (3)*

Leggatt, I. B. 1: *v SA 1953*

Leggat, J. G. 9: v E 1954 (1); v SA 1952 (1); v WI 1951 (1) 1955 (1); *v In 1955 (3); v P 1955 (2)*

Lissette, A. F. 2: v WI 1955 (2)

Lowry, T. C. 7: v E 1929 (4); *v E 1931 (3)*

MacGibbon, A. R. 26: v E 1950 (2) 1954 (2); v SA 1952 (1); v WI 1955 (3); *v E 1958 (5); v SA 1953 (5); v In 1955 (5); v P 1955 (3)*

McEwan, P. E. 1: v WI 1979

McGirr, H. M. 2: v E 1929 (2)

McGregor, S. N. 25: v E 1954 (2) 1958 (2); v SA 1963 (3); v WI 1955 (4); v P 1964 (2); *v SA 1961 (5); v In 1955 (4); v P 1955 (3)*

McLeod, E. G. 1: v E 1929

McMahon, T. G. 5: v WI 1955 (1); *v In 1955 (3); v P 1955 (1)*
McRae, D. A. N. 1: v A 1945
Matheson, A. M. 2: v E 1929 (1); *v E 1931 (1)*
Meale, T. 2: *v E 1958 (2)*
Merritt, W. E. 6: v E 1929 (4); *v E 1931 (2)*
Meuli, E. M. 1: v SA 1952
Milburn, B. D. 3: v WI 1968 (3)
Miller, L. S. M. 13: v SA 1952 (2); v WI 1955 (3); *v E 1958 (4); v SA 1953 (4)*
Mills, J. E. 7: v E 1929 (3) 1932 (1); *v E 1931 (3)*
Moir, A. M. 17: v E 1950 (2) 1954 (2) 1958 (2); v SA 1952 (1); v WI 1951 (2) 1955 (1); *v E 1958 (2); v In 1955 (2); v P 1955 (3)*
Moloney, D. A. R. 3: *v E 1937 (3)*
Mooney, F. L. H. 14: v E 1950 (2); v SA 1952 (2); v WI 1951 (2); *v E 1949 (3); v SA 1953 (5)*
Morgan, R. W. 20: v E 1965 (2) 1970 (2); v WI 1968 (1); v P 1964 (2); *v E 1965 (3); v WI 1971 (3); v In 1964 (4); v P 1964 (3)*
Morrison, B. D. 1: v E 1962
Morrison, J. F. M. 14: v E 1974 (2); v A 1973 (3); v In 1975 (3); *v A 1973 (3); v In 1976 (1); v P 1976 (2)*
Motz, R. C. 32: v E 1962 (2) 1965 (3); v SA 1963 (2); v WI 1968 (3); v In 1967 (4); v P 1964 (5); *v E 1965 (3) 1969 (3); v SA 1961 (5); v In 1964 (3); v P 1964 (1)*
Murray, B. A. G. 13: v E 1970 (1); v In 1967 (4); *v E 1969 (2); v In 1969 (3); v P 1969 (3)*

Newman, J. 3: v E 1932 (2); v SA 1931 (1)

O'Sullivan, D. R. 11: v In 1975 (1); v P 1972 (1); *v A 1973 (3); v In 1976 (3); v P 1976 (3)*
Overton, G. W. F. 3: *v SA 1953 (3)*

Page, M. L. 14: v E 1929 (4) 1932 (2); v SA 1931 (2); *v E 1931 (3) 1937 (3)*
Parker, J. M. 33: v E 1974 (2) 1977 (3); v A 1973 (3) 1976 (2); v WI 1979 (3); v In 1975 (3); v P 1972 (1) 1978 (2); *v E 1973 (3) 1978 (2); v A 1973 (3); v In 1976 (3); v P 1976 (3)*
Parker, N. M. 3: *v In 1976 (2); v P 1976 (1)*
Petherick, P. J. 6: v A 1976 (1); *v In 1976 (3); v P 1976 (2)*
Petrie, E. C. 14: v E 1958 (2) 1965 (3); *v E 1958 (5); v In 1955 (2); v P 1955 (2)*
Playle, W. R. 8: v E 1962 (3); *v E 1958 (5)*
Pollard, V. 32: v E 1965 (3) 1970 (1); v WI 1968 (3); v In 1967 (4); v P 1972 (1); *v E 1965 (3) 1969 (3) 1973 (3); v In 1964 (4) 1969 (1); v P 1964 (3) 1969 (3)*
Poore, M. B. 14: v SA 1952 (1); *v SA 1953 (5); v In 1955 (4); v P 1955 (3)*
Puna, N. 3: v E 1965 (3)

Rabone, G. O. 12: v E 1954 (2); v SA 1952 (1); v WI 1951 (2); *v E 1949 (4); v SA 1953 (3)*
Redmond, R. E. 1: v P 1972
Reid, J. F. 1: v P 1978
Reid, J. R. 58: v E 1950 (2) 1954 (2) 1958 (2) 1962 (3); v SA 1952 (2) 1963 (3); v WI 1951 (2) 1955 (4); v P 1964 (3); *v E 1949 (2) 1958 (5) 1965 (3); v SA 1953 (5) 1961 (5); v In 1955 (5) 1964 (4); v P 1955 (3) 1964 (3)*
Roberts, A. D. G. 7: v In 1975 (2); *v In 1976 (3); v P 1976 (2)*
Roberts, A. W. 5: v E 1929 (1); v SA 1931 (2); *v E 1937 (2)*
Rowe, C. G. 1: v A 1945

Scott, R. H. 1: v E 1946
Scott, V. J. 10: v E 1946 (1) 1950 (2); v A 1945 (1); v WI 1951 (2); *v E 1949 (4)*
Shrimpton, M. J. F. 10: v E 1962 (2) 1965 (3) 1970 (2); v SA 1963 (1); *v A 1973 (2)*
Sinclair, B. W. 21: v E 1962 (3) 1965 (3); v SA 1963 (3); v In 1967 (2); v P 1964 (2); *v E 1965 (3); v In 1964 (2); v P 1964 (3)*
Sinclair, I. M. 2: v WI 1955 (2)
Smith, H. D. 1: v E 1932
Smith, F. B. 4: v E 1946 (1); v WI 1951 (1); *v E 1949 (2)*
Snedden, C. A. 1: v E 1946
Sparling, J. T. 11: v E 1958 (2) 1962 (1); v SA 1963 (2); *v E 1958 (3); v SA 1961 (3)*
Sutcliffe, B. 42: v E 1946 (1) 1950 (2) 1954 (2) 1958 (2); v SA 1952 (2); v WI 1951 (2) 1955 (2); *v E 1949 (4) 1958 (4) 1965 (1); v SA 1953 (5); v In 1955 (5) 1964 (4); v P 1955 (3) 1964 (3)*

Taylor, B. R. 30: v E 1965 (1); v WI 1968 (3); v In 1967 (3); v P 1972 (3); *v E 1965 (2) 1969 (2) 1973 (3); v WI 1971 (4); v In 1964 (3) 1969 (2); v P 1964 (3) 1969 (1)*
Taylor, D. D. 3: v E 1946 (1); v WI 1955 (2)
Thomson, K. 2: v In 1967 (2)
Tindill, E. W. T. 5: v E 1946 (1); v A 1945 (1); *v E 1937 (3)*
Troup, G. B. 6: v WI 1979 (3); v P 1978 (2); *v In 1976 (1)*
Truscott, P. B. 1: v P 1964
Turner, G. M. 39: v E 1970 (2) 1974 (2); v A 1973 (3) 1976 (2); v WI 1968 (3); v In 1975 (3); v P 1972 (3); *v E 1969 (2) 1973 (3); v A 1973 (2); v WI 1971 (5); v In 1969 (3) 1976 (3); v P 1969 (1) 1976 (2)*

Vivian, G. E. 5: *v WI 1971 (4); v In 1964 (1)*
Vivian, H. G. 7: v E 1932 (1); v SA 1931 (1); *v E 1931 (2) 1937 (3)*

Wadsworth, K. J. 33: v E 1970 (2) 1974 (2); v A 1973 (3); v In 1975 (3); v P 1972 (3); *v E 1969 (3) 1973 (3); v A 1973 (3); v WI 1971 (5); v In 1969 (3); v P 1969 (3)*
Wallace, W. M. 13: v E 1946 (1) 1950 (2); v A 1945 (1); v SA 1952 (2); *v E 1937 (3) 1949 (4)*
Ward, J. T. 8: v SA 1963 (1); v In 1967 (1); v P 1964 (1); *v E 1965 (1); v In 1964 (4)*
Watt, L. 1: v E 1954
Webb, M. G. 3: v E 1970 (1); v A 1973 (1); *v WI 1971 (1)*
Webb, P. N. 2: v WI 1979 (2)
Weir, G. L. 11: v E 1929 (3) 1932 (2); v SA 1931 (2); *v E 1931 (3) 1937 (1)*
Whitelaw, P. E. 2: v E 1932 (2)
Wright, J. G. 11: v E 1977 (3); v WI 1979 (3); v P 1978 (3); *v E 1978 (2)*

Yuile, B. W. 17: v E 1962 (2); v WI 1968 (3); v In 1967 (1); v P 1964 (3); *v E 1965 (1); v In 1964 (3) 1969 (1); v P 1964 (1) 1969 (2)*

INDIA

Number of Test cricketers: 149

Adhikari, H. R. 21: v E 1951 (3); v A 1956 (2); v WI 1948 (5) 1958 (1); v P 1952 (2); *v E 1952 (3); v A 1947 (5)*
Ali, S. Abid, 29: v E 1972 (4); v A 1969 (1); v WI 1974 (2); v NZ 1969 (3); *v E 1971 (3) 1974 (3); v A 1967 (4); v WI 1970 (5); v NZ 1967 (4)*
Ali, S. Nazir, 2: v E 1933 (1); *v E 1932 (1)*
Ali, S. Wazir, 7: v E 1933 (3); *v E 1932 (1) 1936 (3)*
Amarnath, L. 24: v E 1933 (3) 1951 (3); v WI 1948 (5); v P 1952 (5); *v E 1946 (3); v A 1947 (5)*
Amarnath, M. 26: v E 1976 (2); v A 1969 (1) 1979 (1); v WI 1978 (2); v NZ 1976 (3); *v E 1979 (2) v A 1977 (5); v WI 1975 (4); v NZ 1975 (3); v P 1978 (3)*
Amarnath, S. 8: v E 1976 (2); *v WI 1975 (2); v NZ 1975 (1); v P 1978 (3)*
Amar Singh 7: v E 1933 (3); *v E 1932 (1) 1936 (3)*
Amir Elahi 1: *v A 1947*
Apte, A. L. 1: *v E 1959*
Apte, M. L. 7: v P 1952 (2); *v WI 1952 (5)*

Baig, A. A. 10: v A 1959 (3); v WI 1966 (2); v P 1960 (3); *v E 1959 (2)*
Banerjee, S. A. 1: v WI 1948
Banerjee, S. N. 1: v WI 1948
Bedi, B. S. 67: v E 1972 (5) 1976 (5); v A 1969 (5); v WI 1966 (2) 1974 (4) 1978 (3); v NZ 1969 (3) 1976 (3); *v E 1967 (3) 1971 (3) 1974 (3) 1979 (3); v A 1967 (2) 1977 (5); v WI 1970 (5) 1975 (4); v NZ 1967 (4) 1975 (2); v P 1978 (3)*
Bhandari, P. 3: v A 1956 (1); v NZ 1955 (1); *v P 1954 (1)*
Binny, R. M. 7: v E 1979 (1); v P 1979 (6)
Borde, C. G. 55: v E 1961 (5) 1963 (5); v A 1959 (5) 1964 (3) 1969 (1); v WI 1958 (4) 1966 (3); v NZ 1964 (4); v P 1960 (5); *v E 1959 (4) 1967 (3); v A 1967 (4); v WI 1961 (5); v NZ 1967 (4)*

Chandrasekhar, B. S. 58: v E 1963 (4) 1972 (5) 1976 (5); v A 1964 (2); v WI 1966 (3) 1974
 (4) 1978 (4); v NZ 1964 (2) 1976 (3); *v E 1967 (3) 1971 (3) 1974 (2) 1979 (1); v A 1967
 (2) 1977 (5); v WI 1975 (4); v NZ 1975 (3); v P 1978 (3)*
Chauhan, C. P. S. 34: v E 1972 (2); v A 1969 (1) 1979 (6); v WI 1978 (6); v NZ 1969 (2); v P
 1979 (6); *v E 1979 (4); v A 1977 (4); v P 1978 (2)*
Chowdhury, N. R. 2: v E 1951 (1); v WI 1948 (1)
Colah, S. H. M. 2: v E 1933 (1); *v E 1932 (1)*
Contractor, N. J. 31: v E 1961 (5); v A 1956 (1) 1959 (5); v WI 1958 (5); v NZ 1955 (4); v P
 1960 (5); *v E 1959 (4); v WI 1961 (2)*

Dani, H. T. 1: v P 1952
Desai, R. B. 28: v E 1961 (4) 1963 (2); v A 1959 (3); v WI 1958 (1); v NZ 1964 (3); v P 1960
 (5); *v E 1959 (5); v A 1967 (1); v WI 1961 (3); v NZ 1967 (1)*
Dilawar Hussain 3: v E 1933 (2); *v E 1936 (1)*
Divecha, R. V. 5: v E 1951 (2); v P 1952 (1); *v E 1952 (2)*
Doshi, D. R. 13: v E 1979 (1); v A 1979 (6); v P 1979 (6)
Durani, S. A. 29: v E 1961 (5) 1963 (5) 1972 (3); v A 1959 (1) 1964 (3); v WI 1966 (1); v NZ
 1964 (3); *v WI 1961 (5) 1970 (3)*

Engineer, F. M. 46: v E 1961 (4) 1972 (5); v A 1969 (5); v WI 1966 (1) 1974 (5); v NZ 1964
 (4) 1969 (2); *v E 1967 (3) 1971 (3) 1974 (3); v A 1967 (4); v WI 1961 (3); v NZ 1967 (4)*

Gadkari, C. V. 6: *v WI 1952 (3); v P 1954 (3)*
Gaekwad, A. D. 21: v E 1976 (4); v WI 1974 (3) 1978 (5); v NZ 1976 (3); *v E 1979 (2);
 v A 1977 (1); v WI 1975 (3)*
Gaekwad, D. K. 11: v WI 1958 (1); v P 1952 (2) 1960 (1); *v E 1952 (1) 1959 (4); v WI 1952
 (2)*
Gaekwad, H. G. 1: v P 1952
Gandotra, A. 2: v A 1969 (1); v NZ 1969 (1)
Gavaskar, S. M. 63: v E 1972 (5) 1976 (5) 1979 (1); v A 1979 (6); v WI 1974 (2) 1978 (6); v
 NZ 1976 (3); v P 1979 (6); *v E 1971 (3) 1974 (3) 1979 (4); v A 1977 (5); v WI 1970 (4)
 1975 (4); v NZ 1975 (3); v P 1978 (3)*
Ghavri, K. D. 35: v E 1976 (3) 1979 (1); v A 1979 (6); v WI 1974 (3) 1978 (6); v NZ 1976
 (2); v P 1979 (6); *v E 1979 (4); v A 1977 (3); v P 1978 (1)*
Ghorpade, J. M. 8: v A 1956 (1); v WI 1958 (1); v NZ 1955 (1); *v E 1959 (3); v WI 1952 (2)*
Ghulam Ahmed 22: v E 1951 (2); v A 1956 (2); v WI 1948 (3) 1958 (2); v NZ 1955 (1); v P
 1952 (4); *v E 1952 (4); v P 1954 (4)*
Gopalan, M. J. 1: v E 1933
Gopinath, C. D. 8: v E 1951 (3); v A 1959 (1); v P 1952 (1); *v E 1952 (1); v P 1954 (2)*
Guard, G. M. 2: v A 1959 (1); v WI 1958 (1)
Guha, S. 4: v A 1969 (3); *v E 1967 (1)*
Gul Mahomed 8: v P 1952 (2); *v E 1946 (1); v A 1947 (5)*
Gupte, B. P. 3: v E 1963 (1); v NZ 1964 (1); v P 1960 (1)
Gupte, S. P. 36: v E 1951 (1) 1961 (2); v A 1956 (3); v WI 1958 (5); v NZ 1955 (5); v P 1952
 (1) 1960 (3); *v E 1959 (5); v WI 1952 (5); v P 1954 (5)*

Hafeez, A. 3: *v E 1946 (3)*
Hanumant Singh 14: v E 1963 (2); v A 1964 (3); v WI 1966 (2); v NZ 1964 (4) 1969 (1); *v E
 1967 (2)*
Hardikar, M. S. 2: v WI 1958 (2)
Hazare, V. S. 30: v E 1951 (5); v WI 1948 (3); v P 1952 (2); *v E 1946 (3) 1952 (4); v A 1947
 (5); v WI 1952 (5)*
Hindlekar, D. D. 4: *v E 1936 (1) 1946 (3)*

Ibrahim, K. C. 4: v WI 1948 (4)
Indrajitsinhji, K. S. 4: v A 1964 (3); v NZ 1969 (1)
Irani, J. K. 2: *v A 1947 (2)*

Jai, L. P. 1: v E 1933
Jaisimha, M. L. 39: v E 1961 (5) 1963 (5); v A 1959 (1) 1964 (3); v WI 1966 (2); v NZ 1964
 (4) 1969 (1); v P 1960 (4); *v E 1959 (1); v A 1967 (2); v WI 1961 (4) 1970 (3); v NZ 1967
 (4)*

Jamshedji, R. J. 1: v E 1933
Jayantilal, K. 1: *v WI 1970*
Jilani, M. Baqa 1: *v E 1936*
Joshi, P. G. 12: v E 1951 (2); v A 1959 (1); v WI 1958 (1); v P 1952 (1) 1960 (1); *v E 1959 (3); v WI 1952 (3)*

Kanitkar, H. S. 2: v WI 1974 (2)
Kapil Dev 26: v E 1979 (1); v A 1979 (6); v WI 1978 (6); v P 1979 (6); *v E 1979 (4); v P 1978 (3)*
Kardar, A. H., *see* Hafeez
Kenny, R. B. 5: v A 1959 (4); v WI 1958 (1)
Khan, M. Jahangir, 4: *v E 1932 (1) 1936 (3)*
Kirmani, S. M. H. 42: v E 1976 (5) 1979 (1); v A 1979 (6); v WI 1978 (6); v NZ 1976 (3); v P 1979 (6); *v A 1977 (5); v WI 1975 (4); v NZ 1975 (3); v P 1978 (3)*
Kischenchand, G. 5: v P 1952 (1); *v A 1947 (4)*
Kripal Singh, A. G. 14: v E 1961 (3) 1963 (2); v A 1956 (2) 1964 (1); v WI 1958 (1); v NZ 1955 (4); *v E 1959 (1)*
Krishnamurthy, P. 5: *v WI 1970 (5)*
Kulkarni, U. N. 4: *v A 1967 (3); v NZ 1967 (1)*
Kumar, V. V. 2: v E 1961 (1); v P 1960 (1)
Kunderan, B. K. 18: v E 1961 (1) 1963 (5); v A 1959 (3); v WI 1966 (2); v NZ 1964 (1); v P 1960 (2); *v E 1967 (2); v WI 1961 (2)*

Lall Singh 1: *v E 1932*

Madan Lal, S. 16: v E 1976 (2); v WI 1974 (2); v NZ 1976 (1); *v E 1974 (2); v A 1977 (2); v WI 1975 (4); v NZ 1975 (3)*
Maka, E. S. 2: v P 1952 (1); *v WI 1952 (1)*
Manjrekar, V. L. 55: v E 1951 (2) 1961 (5) 1963 (4); v A 1956 (3) 1964 (3); v WI 1958 (4); v NZ 1955 (5) 1964 (1); v P 1952 (3) 1960 (5); *v E 1952 (4) 1959 (2); v WI 1952 (4) 1961 (5); v P 1954 (5)*
Mankad, A. V. 21: v E 1976 (1); v A 1969 (5); v WI 1974 (1) 1976 (1); v NZ 1969 (2); *v E 1971 (3) 1974 (1); v A 1977 (3); v WI 1970 (3)*
Mankad, V. M. H. 44: v E 1951 (5); v A 1956 (3); v WI 1948 (5) 1958 (2); v NZ 1955 (4); v P 1952 (4); *v E 1946 (3) 1952 (3); v A 1947 (5); v WI 1952 (5); v P 1954 (5)*
Mansur Ali Khan (see Pataudi)
Mantri, M. K. 4: v E 1951 (1); *v E 1952 (2); v P 1954 (1)*
Meherhomji, K. R. 1: *v E 1936*
Mehra, V. L. 8: v E 1961 (1) 1963 (2); v NZ 1955 (2); *v WI 1961 (3)*
Merchant, V. M. 10: v E 1933 (3) 1951 (1); *v E 1936 (3) 1946 (3)*
Milkha Singh, A. G. 4: v E 1961 (1); v A 1959 (1); v P 1960 (2)
Modi, R. S. 10: v E 1951 (1); v WI 1948 (5); v P 1952 (1); *v E 1946 (3)*
Muddiah, V. M. 2: v A 1959 (1); v P 1960 (1)
Mushtaq Ali 11: v E 1933 (2) 1951 (1); v WI 1948 (3); *v E 1936 (3) 1946 (2)*

Nadkarni, R. G. 41: v E 1961 (1) 1963 (5); v A 1959 (5) 1964 (3); v WI 1958 (1) 1966 (1); v NZ 1955 (1) 1964 (4); v P 1960 (4); *v E 1959 (4); v A 1967 (3); v WI 1961 (5); v NZ 1967 (4)*
Naik, S. S. 3: v WI 1974 (2); *v E 1974 (1)*
Naoomal Jeoomal 3: v E 1933 (2); *v E 1932 (1)*
Narasimha Rao, M. V. 4: v A 1979 (2); v WI 1978 (2)
Navle, J. G. 2: v E 1933 (1); *v E 1932 (1)*
Nayudu, C. K. 7: v E 1933 (3); *v E 1932 (1) 1936 (3)*
Nayudu, C. S. 11: v E 1933 (2) 1951 (1); *v E 1936 (2) 1946 (2); v A 1947 (4)*
Nissar, Mahomed 6: v E 1933 (2); *v E 1932 (1) 1936 (3)*
Nyalchand, K. 1: v P 1952

Pai, A. M. 1: v NZ 1969
Palia, P. E. 2: *v E 1932 (1) 1936 (1)*
Parkar, R. D. 2: v E 1972 (2)
Parsana, D. D. 2: v WI 1978 (2)
Patankar, C. T. 1: v NZ 1955
Pataudi, Nawab of, 3: *v E 1946 (3)*

Pataudi, Nawab of (now Mansur Ali Khan) 46: v E 1961 (3) 1963 (5) 1972 (3); v A 1964 (3) 1969 (5); v WI 1966 (3) 1974 (4); v NZ 1964 (4) 1969 (3); *v E 1967 (3); v A 1967 (3); v WI 1961 (3); v NZ 1967 (4)*

Patel, B. P. 21: v E 1976 (5); v WI 1974 (3); v NZ 1976 (3): *v E 1974 (2); v A 1977 (2); v WI 1975 (3); v NZ 1975 (3)*

Patel, J. M. 7: v A 1956 (2) 1959 (3); v NZ 1955 (1); *v P 1954 (1)*

Patil, S. M. 3: v E 1979 (1); v P 1979 (2)

Patil, S. R. 1: v NZ 1955

Patiala, Yuvraj of, 1: v E 1933

Phadkar, D. G. 31: v E 1951 (4); v A 1956 (1); v WI 1948 (4) 1958 (1); v NZ 1955 (4); v P 1952 (2); *v E 1952 (4); v A 1947 (4); v WI 1952 (4); v P 1954 (3)*

Prasanna, E. A. S. 49: v E 1961 (1) 1972 (3) 1976 (4); v A 1969 (5); v WI 1966 (1) 1974 (5); v NZ 1969 (3); *v E 1967 (3) 1974 (2); v A 1967 (4) 1977 (4); v WI 1961 (1) 1970 (3) 1975 (1); v NZ 1967 (4) 1975 (3); v P 1978 (2)*

Punjabi, P. H. 5: *v P 1954 (5)*

Rai Singh, K. 1: *v A 1947*

Rajindernath, V. 1: v P 1952

Rajinder Pal 1: v E 1963

Ramaswami, C. 2: *v E 1936 (2)*

Ramchand, G. S. 33: v A 1956 (3) 1959 (5); v WI 1958 (3); v NZ 1955 (5); *v P 1952 (3); v E 1952 (4); v WI 1952 (5); v P 1954 (5)*

Ramji, L. 1: v E 1933

Rangachari, C. R. 4: v WI 1948 (2); *v A 1947 (2)*

Rangnekar, K. M. 3: *v A 1947 (3)*

Ranjane, V. B. 7: v E 1961 (3) 1963 (1); v A 1964 (1); v WI 1958 (1); *v WI 1961 (1)*

Reddy, B. 4: *v E 1979 (4)*

Rege, M. R. 1: v WI 1948

Roy, A. 4: v A 1969 (2); v NZ 1969 (2)

Roy, P. 43: v E 1951 (5); v A 1956 (3) 1959 (5); v WI 1958 (5); v NZ 1955 (3); v P 1952 (3) 1960 (1); *v E 1952 (4) 1959 (5); v WI 1952 (4); v P 1954 (5)*

Sardesai, D. N. 30: v E 1961 (1) 1963 (5) 1972 (1); v A 1964 (3) 1969 (1); v WI 1966 (3); v NZ 1964 (3); *v E 1967 (1) 1971 (3); v A 1967 (2); v WI 1961 (3) 1970 (5)*

Sarwate, C. T. 9: v E 1951 (1); v WI 1948 (2); *v E 1946 (1); v A 1947 (5)*

Saxena, R. C. 1: *v E 1967*

Sen, P. 14: v E 1951 (2); v WI 1948 (5); v P 1952 (2); *v E 1952 (2); v A 1947 (3)*

Sengupta, A. K. 1: v WI 1958

Sharma, P. 5: v E 1976 (2); v WI 1974 (2); *v WI 1975 (1)*

Shinde, S. G. 7: v E 1951 (3); v WI 1948 (1); *v E 1946 (1) 1952 (3)*

Shodhan, D. H. 3: v P 1952 (1); *v WI 1952 (2)*

Sohoni, S. W. 4: v E 1951 (1); *v E 1946 (2); v A 1947 (1)*

Solkar, E. D. 27: v E 1972 (5) 1976 (1); v A 1969 (4); v WI 1974 (4); v NZ 1969 (1); *v E 1971 (3) 1974 (3); v WI 1970 (5) 1975 (1)*

Sood, M. M. 1: v A 1959

Subramanya, V. 9: v WI 1966 (2); v NZ 1964 (1); *v E 1967 (2); v A 1967 (2); v NZ 1967 (2)*

Sunderram, G. 2: v NZ 1955 (2)

Surendranath, R. 11: v A 1959 (2); v WI 1958 (2); v P 1960 (2); *v E 1959 (5)*

Surti, R. F. 26: v E 1963 (1); v A 1964 (2) 1969 (1); v WI 1966 (2); v NZ 1964 (1) 1969 (2); v P 1960 (2); *v E 1967 (2); v A 1967 (4); v WI 1961 (5); v NZ 1967 (4)*

Swamy, V. N. 1: v NZ 1955

Tamhane, N. S. 21: v A 1956 (3) 1959 (1); v WI 1958 (4); v NZ 1955 (4); v P 1960 (2); *v E 1959 (2); v P 1954 (5)*

Tarapore, K. K. 1: v WI 1948

Umrigar, P. R. 59: v E 1951 (5) 1961 (4); v A 1956 (3) 1959 (3); v WI 1948 (1) 1958 (5); v NZ 1955 (5); v P 1952 (5) 1960 (5); *v E 1952 (4) 1959 (4); v WI 1952 (5) 1961 (5); v P 1954 (5)*

Vengsarkar, D. B. 36: v E 1976 (1) 1979 (1); v A 1979 (6); v WI 1978 (6); v P 1979 (5); *v E 1979 (4); v A 1977 (5); v WI 1975 (2); v NZ 1975 (3); v P 1978 (3)*

Venkataraghavan, S. 50: v E 1972 (2) 1976 (1); v A 1969 (5) 1979 (3); v WI 1966 (2) 1974
(2) 1978 (6); v NZ 1964 (4) 1969 (2) 1976 (3); *v E 1967 (1) 1971 (3) 1974 (2) 1979 (4); v
A 1977 (1); v WI 1970 (5) 1975 (3); v NZ 1975 (1)*

Viswanath, G. R. 69: v E 1972 (5) 1976 (5) 1979 (1); v A 1969 (4) 1979 (6); v WI 1974 (5)
1978 (6); v NZ 1976 (3); v P 1979 (6); *v E 1971 (3) 1974 (3) 1979 (4); v A 1977 (5); v WI
1970 (3) 1975 (4); v NZ 1975 (3); v P 1978 (3)*

Vizianagram, Maharaj Sir Vijaya 3: *v E 1936 (3)*

Wadekar, A. L. 37: v E 1972 (5); v A 1969 (5); v WI 1966 (2); v NZ 1969 (3); *v E 1967 (3)
1971 (3) 1974 (3); v A 1967 (4); v WI 1970 (5); v NZ 1967 (4)*

Yadav, N. S. 11: v E 1979 (1); v A 1979 (5); v P 1979 (5)

Yajurvindra Singh 4: v E 1976 (2); v A 1979 (1); *v E 1979 (1)*

Yashpal Sharma 16: v E 1979 (1); v A 1979 (6); v P 1979 (6); *v E 1979 (3)*

Note: Hafeez, on going later to Oxford University, took his correct name, Kardar.

PAKISTAN

Number of Test cricketers: 85

Abdul Kadir 4: v A 1964 (1); *v A 1964 (1); v NZ 1964 (2)*

Abdul Qadir 6: v E 1977 (3); *v In 1979 (3)*

Afaq Hussain 2: v E 1961 (1); *v A 1964 (1)*

Aftab Baloch 2: v WI 1974 (1); v NZ 1969 (1)

Aftab Gul 6: v E 1968 (2); v NZ 1969 (1); *v E 1971 (3)*

Agha Saadat Ali 1: v NZ 1955

Agha Zahid 1: v WI 1974

Alim-ud-Din 25: v E 1961 (2); v A 1956 (1) 1959 (1); v WI 1958 (1); v NZ 1955 (3); v In 1954
(5); *v E 1954 (3) 1962 (3); v WI 1957 (5); v In 1960 (1)*

Amir Elahi 5: *v In 1952 (5)*

Anwar Hussain 4: *v In 1952 (4)*

Anwar Khan 1: *v NZ 1978*

Arif Butt 3: *v A 1964 (1); v NZ 1964 (2)*

Asif Iqbal 58: v E 1968 (3) 1972 (3); v A 1964 (1); v WI 1974 (2); v NZ 1964 (3) 1969 (3)
1976 (3); v In 1978 (3); *v E 1967 (3) 1971 (3) 1974 (3); v A 1964 (1) 1972 (3) 1976 (3)
1978 (2); v WI 1976 (5); v NZ 1964 (3) 1972 (3) 1978 (2); v In 1979 (6)*

Asif Masood 16: v E 1968 (2) 1972 (1); v WI 1974 (2); v NZ 1969 (1); *v E 1971 (3) 1974 (3);
v A 1972 (3) 1976 (1)*

Azhar Khan 1: v A 1979

Azmat Rana 1: v A 1979

Burki, J. 25: v E 1961 (3); v A 1964 (1); v NZ 1964 (3) 1969 (1); *v E 1962 (5) 1967 (3); v A
1964 (1); v NZ 1964 (3); v In 1960 (5)*

D'Souza, A. 6: v E 1961 (2); v WI 1958 (1); *v E 1962 (3)*

Ehtesham-ud-Din 4: v A 1979 (1); *v In 1979 (3)*

Farooq Hamid 1: *v A 1964*

Farrukh Zaman 1: v NZ 1976

Fazal Mahmood 34: v E 1961 (1); v A 1956 (1) 1959 (2); v WI 1958 (3); v NZ 1955 (2); v In
1954 (4); *v E 1954 (4) 1962 (2); v WI 1957 (5); v In 1952 (5) 1960 (5)*

Ghazali, M. E. Z. 2: *v E 1954 (2)*

Ghulam Abbas 1: *v E 1967*

Gul Mahomed 1: v A 1956

Hanif Mohammad 55: v E 1961 (3) 1968 (3); v A 1956 (1) 1959 (3) 1964 (1); v WI 1958 (1);
v NZ 1955 (3) 1964 (3) 1969 (1); v In 1954 (5); *v E 1954 (4) 1962 (5) 1967 (3); v A 1964
(1); v WI 1957 (5); v NZ 1964 (3); v In 1952 (5) 1960 (5)*

Haroon Rashid 16: v E 1977 (3); v A 1979 (2); *v E 1978 (3); v A 1976 (1) 1978 (1); v WI 1976 (5); v NZ 1978 (1)*
Haseeb Ahsan 12: v E 1961 (2); v A 1959 (1); v WI 1958 (1); *v WI 1957 (3); v In 1960 (5)*

Ibadulla, K. 4: v A 1964 (1); *v E 1967 (2); v NZ 1964 (1)*
Ijaz Butt 8: v A 1959 (2); v WI 1958 (3); *v E 1962 (3)*
Imran Khan 29: v A 1979 (2); v NZ 1976 (3); v In 1978 (3); *v E 1971 (1) 1974 (3); v A 1976 (3) 1978 (2); v WI 1976 (5); v NZ 1978 (2); v In 1979 (5)*
Imtiaz Ahmed 41: v E 1961 (3); v A 1956 (1) 1959 (3); v WI 1958 (3); v NZ 1955 (3); v In 1954 (5); *v E 1954 (4) 1962 (4); v WI 1957 (5); v In 1952 (5) 1960 (5)*
Intikhab Alam 47: v E 1961 (2) 1968 (3) 1972 (3); v A 1959 (1) 1964 (1); v WI 1974 (2); v NZ 1964 (3) 1969 (3) 1976 (3); *v E 1962 (3) 1967 (3) 1971 (3) 1974 (3); v A 1964 (1) 1972 (3); v WI 1976 (1); v NZ 1964 (3) 1972 (3); v In 1960 (3)*
Iqbal Qasim 23: v E 1977 (3); v A 1979 (3); v In 1978 (3); *v E 1978 (3); v A 1976 (3); v WI 1976 (2); v In 1979 (6)*
Israr Ali 4: v A 1959 (2); *v In 1952 (2)*

Javed Akhtar 1: *v E 1962*
Javed Miandad 30: v E 1977 (3); v A 1979 (3); v NZ 1976 (3); v In 1978 (3); *v E 1978 (3); v A 1976 (3) 1978 (2); v WI 1976 (1); v NZ 1978 (3); v In 1979 (6)*

Kardar, A. H. 23: v A 1956 (1); v NZ 1955 (3); v In 1954 (5); *v E 1954 (4); v WI 1957 (5); v In 1952 (5)*
Khalid Hassan 1: *v E 1954*
Khalid Wazir 2: *v E 1954 (2)*
Khan, Majid Jahangir 53: v E 1968 (3) 1972 (3); v A 1964 (1) 1979 (3); v WI 1974 (2); v NZ 1964 (3) 1976 (3); v In 1978 (3); *v E 1967 (3) 1971 (2) 1974 (3); v A 1972 (3) 1976 (3) 1978 (2); v WI 1976 (5); v NZ 1972 (3) 1978 (2); v In 1979 (6)*
Khan Mohammad 13: v A 1956 (1); v NZ 1955 (3); v In 1954 (4); *v E 1954 (2); v WI 1957 (2); v In 1952 (1)*

Liaqat Ali 5: v E 1977 (2); v WI 1974 (1); *v E 1978 (2)*

Mahmood Hussain 27: v E 1961 (1); v WI 1958 (3); v NZ 1955 (1); v In 1954 (5); *v E 1954 (2) 1962 (3); v WI 1957 (3); v In 1952 (4) 1960 (5)*
Maqsood Ahmed 16: v NZ 1955 (2); v In 1954 (5); *v E 1954 (4); v In 1952 (5)*
Mathias, Wallis 21: v E 1961 (1); v A 1956 (1) 1959 (2); v WI 1958 (3); v NZ 1955 (1); *v E 1962 (3); v WI 1957 (5); v In 1960 (5)*
Miran Bux 2: v In 1954 (2)
Mohammad Aslam 1: *v E 1954*
Mohammad Farooq 7: v NZ 1964 (3); *v E 1962 (2); v In 1960 (2)*
Mohammad Ilyas 10: v E 1968 (2); v NZ 1964 (3); *v E 1967 (1); v A 1964 (1); v NZ 1964 (3)*
Mohammad Munaf 4: v E 1961 (2); v A 1959 (2)
Mohammad Nazir 4: v E 1972 (1); v NZ 1969 (3)
Mohsin Khan 6: v E 1977 (1); *v E 1978 (3); v A 1978 (1); v NZ 1978 (1)*
Mudassar Nazar 19: v E 1977 (3); v A 1979 (3); v In 1978 (2); *v E 1978 (3); v A 1976 (1) 1978 (1); v NZ 1978 (1); v In 1979 (5)*
Mufasir-ul-Haq 1: *v NZ 1964*
Munir Malik 3: v A 1959 (1); *v E 1962 (2)*
Mushtaq Mohammad 57: v E 1961 (3) 1968 (3) 1972 (3); v WI 1958 (1) 1974 (2); v NZ 1969 (2) 1976 (3); v In 1978 (3); *v E 1962 (5) 1967 (3) 1971 (3) 1974 (3); v A 1972 (3) 1976 (3) 1978 (2); v WI 1976 (5); v NZ 1972 (2) 1978 (3); v In 1960 (5)*

Nasim-ul-Ghani 29: v E 1961 (2); v A 1959 (2) 1964 (1); v WI 1958 (3); *v E 1962 (5) 1967 (2); v A 1964 (1) 1972 (1); v WI 1957 (5); v NZ 1964 (3); v In 1960 (4)*
Naushad Ali 6: v NZ 1964 (3); *v NZ 1964 (3)*
Nazar Mohammad 5: *v In 1952 (5)*
Niaz Ahmed 2: v E 1968 (1); *v E 1967 (1)*

Pervez Sajjad 19: v E 1968 (1) 1972 (2); v A 1964 (1); v NZ 1964 (3) 1969 (3); *v E 1971 (3); v NZ 1964 (3) 1972 (3)*

Rehman, S. F. 1: *v EI 1957*

Sadiq Mohammad 38: v E 1972 (3) 1977 (2); v WI 1974 (1); v NZ 1969 (3) 1976 (3); v In 1978 (1); *v E 1971 (3) 1974 (3) 1978 (3); v A 1972 (3) 1976 (2); v WI 1976 (5); v NZ 1972 (3); v In 1979 (3)*

Saeed Ahmed 41: v E 1961 (3) 1968 (3); v A 1959 (3) 1964 (1); v WI 1958 (3); v NZ 1964 (3); *v E 1962 (5) 1967 (3) 1971 (1); v A 1964 (1) 1972 (2); v WI 1957 (5); v NZ 1964 (3); v In 1960 (5)*

Salah-ud-Din 5: v E 1968 (1); v NZ 1964 (3) 1969 (1)

Saleem Altaf 21: v E 1972 (3); v NZ 1969 (2); v In 1978 (1); *v E 1967 (2) 1971 (2); v A 1972 (3) 1976 (2); v WI 1976 (3); v NZ 1972 (3)*

Sarfraz Nawaz 37: v E 1968 (1) 1972 (2) 1977 (2); v A 1979 (3); v WI 1974 (2); v NZ 1976 (3); v In 1978 (3); *v E 1974 (3) 1978 (2); v A 1972 (2) 1976 (2) 1978 (2); v WI 1976 (4); v NZ 1972 (3) 1978 (3)*

Shafiq Ahmed 4: v E 1977 (3); *v E 1974 (1)*

Shafqat Rana 5: v E 1968 (2); v A 1964 (1); v NZ 1969 (2)

Shahid Israr 1: v NZ 1976

Shahid Mahmood 1: *v E 1962*

Sharpe, D. 3: v A 1959 (3)

Shuja-ud-Din 19: v E 1961 (2); v A 1959 (3); v WI 1958 (3); v NZ 1955 (3); v In 1954 (5); *v E 1961 (3)*

Sikander Bakht 19: v E 1977 (2); v NZ 1976 (1); v In 1978 (2); *v E 1978 (3); v A 1978 (2); v WI 1976 (1); v NZ 1978 (3); v In 1979 (5)*

Talat Ali 10: v E 1972 (3); *v E 1978 (2); v A 1972 (1); v NZ 1972 (1) 1978 (3)*

Taslim Arif 4: v A 1979 (3); *v In 1979 (1)*

Tausif Ahmed 3: v A 1979 (3)

Waqar Hassan 21: v A 1956 (1) 1959 (1); v WI 1958 (1); v NZ 1955 (3); v In 1954 (5); *v E 1954 (4); v WI 1957 (1); v In 1952 (5)*

Wasim Bari 56: v E 1968 (3) 1972 (3) 1977 (3); v WI 1974 (2); v NZ 1969 (3) 1976 (2); v In 1978 (3); *v E 1967 (3) 1971 (3) 1974 (3) 1978 (3); v A 1972 (3) 1976 (3) 1978 (2); v WI 1976 (5); v NZ 1972 (3) 1978 (3); v In 1979 (6)*

Wasim Raja 33: v E 1972 (1) 1977 (3); v A 1979 (3); v WI 1974 (2); v NZ 1976 (1); *v E 1974 (2) 1978 (3); v A 1978 (1); v WI 1976 (5); v NZ 1972 (3) 1978 (3); v In 1979 (6)*

Wazir Mohammad 20: v A 1956 (1) 1959 (1); v WI 1958 (3); v NZ 1955 (2); v In 1954 (5); *v E 1954 (2); v WI 1957 (5); v In 1952 (1)*

Younis Ahmed 2: v NZ 1969 (2)

Zaheer Abbas 40: v E 1972 (2); v A 1979 (2); v WI 1974 (2); v NZ 1969 (1) 1976 (3); v In 1978 (3); *v E 1971 (3) 1974 (3); v A 1972 (3) 1976 (3) 1978 (2); v WI 1976 (3); v NZ 1972 (3) 1978 (2); v In 1979 (5)*

Zulfiqar Ahmed 9: v A 1956 (1); v NZ 1955 (3); *v E 1954 (2); v In 1952 (3)*

ENGLAND v REST OF THE WORLD

The following were awarded England caps for playing against the Rest of the World in England in 1970, although the five matches played are now generally considered not to have rated as full Tests: D. L. Amiss (1), G. Boycott (2), D. J. Brown (2), M. C. Cowdrey (4), M. H. Denness (1), B. L. D'Oliveira (4), J. H. Edrich (2), K. W. R. Fletcher (4), A. W. Greig (3), R. Illingworth (5), A. Jones (1), A. P. E. Knott (5), P. Lever (1), B. W. Luckhurst (5), C. M. Old (2), P. J. Sharpe (1), K. Shuttleworth (1), J. A. Snow (5), D. L. Underwood (3), A. Ward (1), D. Wilson (2).

TWO COUNTRIES

Twelve cricketers have appeared for two countries in Test matches, namely:

Amir Elahi, *India and Pakistan*.

J. J. Ferris, *Australia and England*.

S. C. Guillen, *West Indies and NZ*.

Gul Mahomed, *India and Pakistan*.

F. Hearne, *England and South Africa*.

A. H. Kardar, *India and Pakistan*.

W. E. Midwinter, *England and Australia*.

F. Mitchell, *England and South Africa*.

W. L. Murdoch, *Australia and England*.

Nawab of Pataudi, snr, *England and India*.

A. E. Trott, *Australia and England*.

S. M. J. Woods, *Australia and England*.

CRICKET RECORDS

Amended by MICHAEL FORDHAM to end of 1980 season in England

Unless stated to be of a minor character, all records apply only to first-class cricket including some performances in the distant past which have always been recognised as of exceptional merit.

* Denotes not out or an unbroken partnership.

(A), (SA), (WI), (NZ), (I), or (P) indicates either the nationality of the player, or the country in which the record was made.

INDEX

BATTING

BATTING RECORDS

INDIVIDUAL SCORES OF 300 OR MORE

499	Hanif Mohammad	Karachi v Bahawalpur at Karachi	1958-59
452*	D. G. Bradman	NSW v Queensland at Sydney	1929-30
443*	B. B. Nimbalkar	Maharashtra v Kathiawar at Poona	1948-49
437	W. H. Ponsford	Victoria v Queensland at Melbourne	1927-28
429	W. H. Ponsford	Victoria v Tasmania at Melbourne	1922-23
428	Aftab Baloch	Sind v Baluchistan at Karachi	1973-74
424	A. C. MacLaren	Lancashire v Somerset at Taunton	1895
385	B. Sutcliffe	Otago v Canterbury at Christchurch	1952-53
383	C. W. Gregory	NSW v Queensland at Brisbane	1906-07
369	D. G. Bradman	South Australia v Tasmania at Adelaide	1935-36
365*	C. Hill	South Australia v NSW at Adelaide	1900-01
365*	G. S. Sobers	West Indies v Pakistan at Kingston	1957-58
364	L. Hutton	England v Australia at The Oval	1938
359*	V. M. Merchant	Bombay v Maharashtra at Bombay	1943-44
359	R. B. Simpson	NSW v Queensland at Brisbane	1963-64
357*	R. Abel	Surrey v Somerset at The Oval	1899
357	D. G. Bradman	South Australia v Victoria at Melbourne	1935-36
356	B. A. Richards	South Australia v W. Australia at Perth	1970-71
355	B. Sutcliffe	Otago v Auckland at Dunedin	1949-50
352	W. H. Ponsford	Victoria v NSW at Melbourne	1926-27
350	Rashid Israr	Habib Bank v National Bank at Lahore	1976-77
345	C. G. Macartney	Australians v Nottinghamshire at Nottingham	1921
344*	G. A. Headley	Jamaica v Lord Tennyson's XI at Kingston	1931-32
344	W. G. Grace	MCC v Kent at Canterbury	1876
343*	P. A. Perrin	Essex v Derbyshire at Chesterfield	1904
341	G. H. Hirst	Yorkshire v Leicestershire at Leicester	1905

340*	D. G. Bradman	NSW v Victoria at Sydney	1928-29
338*	R. C. Blunt	Otago v Canterbury at Christchurch	1931-32
338	W. W. Read	Surrey v Oxford University at The Oval	1888
337*	Pervez Akhtar	Railways v Dera Ismail Khan at Lahore	1964-65
337†	Hanif Mohammad	Pakistan v West Indies at Bridgetown	1957-58
336*	W. R. Hammond	England v New Zealand at Auckland	1932-33
336	W. H. Ponsford	Victoria v South Australia at Melbourne	1927-28
334	D. G. Bradman	Australia v England at Leeds	1930
333	K. S. Duleepsinhji	Sussex v Northamptonshire at Hove	1930
332	W. H. Ashdown	Kent v Essex at Brentwood	1934
331*	J. D. B. Robertson	Middlesex v Worcestershire at Worcester	1949
325*	H. S. T. L. Hendry	Victoria v New Zealanders at Melbourne	1925-26
325	C. L. Badcock	South Australia v Victoria at Adelaide	1935-36
325	A. Sandham	England v West Indies at Kingston	1929-30
324	J. B. Stollmeyer	Trinidad v British Guiana at Port-of-Spain	1946-47
324	Waheed Mirza	Karachi Whites v Quetta at Karachi	1976-77
323	A. L. Wadekar	Bombay v Mysore at Bombay	1966-67
322	E. Paynter	Lancashire v Sussex at Hove	1937
321	W. L. Murdoch	NSW v Victoria at Sydney	1881-82
319	Gul Mahomed	Baroda v Holkar at Baroda	1946-47
318*	W. G. Grace	Gloucestershire v Yorkshire at Cheltenham	1876
317	W. R. Hammond	Gloucestershire v Nottinghamshire at Gloucester ..	1936
316*	V. S. Hazare	Maharashtra v Baroda at Poona	1939-40
316*	J. B. Hobbs	Surrey v Middlesex at Lord's	1926
316	R. H. Moore	Hampshire v Warwickshire at Bournemouth	1937
315*	T. W. Hayward	Surrey v Lancashire at The Oval	1898
315*	P. Holmes	Yorkshire v Middlesex at Lord's	1925
315*	A. F. Kippax	NSW v Queensland at Sydney	1927-28
314*	C. L. Walcott	Barbados v Trinidad at Port-of-Spain	1945-46
313	H. Sutcliffe	Yorkshire v Essex at Leyton	1932
312*	W. W. Keeton	Nottinghamshire v Middlesex at The Oval	1939
312*	J. M. Brearley	MCC Under 25 v N. Zone at Peshawar	1966-67
311	J. T. Brown	Yorkshire v Sussex at Sheffield	1897
311	R. B. Simpson	Australia v England at Manchester	1964
311	Javed Miandad	Karachi Whites v National Bank at Karachi	1974-75
310*	J. H. Edrich	England v New Zealand at Leeds	1965
310	H. Gimblett	Somerset v Sussex at Eastbourne	1948
309	V. S. Hazare	The Rest v Hindus at Bombay	1943-44
308*	F. M. M. Worrell	Barbados v Trinidad at Bridgetown	1943-44
307	M. C. Cowdrey	MCC v South Australia at Adelaide	1962-63
307	R. M. Cowper	Australia v England at Melbourne	1965-66
306*	A. Ducat	Surrey v Oxford University at The Oval	1919
306*	E. A. B. Rowan	Transvaal v Natal at Johannesburg	1939-40
305*	F. E. Woolley	MCC v Tasmania at Hobart	1911-12
305*	F. R. Foster	Warwickshire v Worcestershire at Dudley	1914
305*	W. H. Ashdown	Kent v Derbyshire at Dover	1935
304*	P. H. Tarilton	Barbados v Trinidad at Bridgetown	1919-20
304*	A. W. Nourse	Natal v Transvaal at Johannesburg	1919-20
304*	E. D. Weekes	West Indians v Cambridge University at Cambridge	1950
304	R. M. Poore	Hampshire v Somerset at Taunton	1899
304	D. G. Bradman	Australia v England at Leeds	1934
303*	W. W. Armstrong	Australians v Somerset at Bath	1905
303*	Mushtaq Mohammad	Karachi Blues v Karachi University at Karachi	1967-68
302*	P. Holmes	Yorkshire v Hampshire at Portsmouth	1920
302*	W. R. Hammond	Gloucestershire v Glamorgan at Bristol	1934
302	W. R. Hammond	Gloucestershire v Glamorgan at Newport	1939
302	L. G. Rowe	West Indies v England at Bridgetown	1973-74
301*	E. H. Hendren	Middlesex v Worcestershire at Dudley	1933
301	W. G. Grace	Gloucestershire v Sussex at Bristol	1896
300*	V. T. Trumper	Australians v Sussex at Hove	1899
300*	F. B. Watson	Lancashire v Surrey at Manchester	1928
300*	Imtiaz Ahmed	PM's XI v Commonwealth XI at Bombay	1950-51
300	J. T. Brown	Yorkshire v Derbyshire at Chesterfield	1898

| 300 | D. C. S. Compton | MCC v N.E. Transvaal at Benoni .... | 1948-49 |
| 300 | R. Subba Row | Northamptonshire v Surrey at The Oval .... | 1958 |

† *Hanif Mohammad batted for 16 hours 10 minutes – the longest innings in first-class cricket.*

HIGHEST INDIVIDUAL SCORES FOR TEAMS

For English Teams in Australia

| 307 | M. C. Cowdrey | MCC v South Australia at Adelaide .... | 1962-63 |
| 287 | R. E. Foster | England v Australia at Sydney (Highest in a Test)...... | 1903-04 |

Against Australians in England

| 364 | L. Hutton | England v Australia at The Oval .... | 1938 |
| 219 | A. Sandham | Surrey at The Oval (record for any county) .... | 1934 |

For Australian Teams in England

| 345 | C. G. Macartney | v Nottinghamshire at Nottingham .... | 1921 |
| 334 | D. G. Bradman | Australia v England at Leeds .... | 1930 |

Against English Teams in Australia

| 307 | R. M. Cowper | Australia v England at Melbourne .... | 1965-66 |
| 280 | A. J. Richardson | South Australia v MCC at Adelaide .... | 1922-23 |

For Each First-Class County

Derbyshire	......	274	G. Davidson v Lancashire at Manchester	1896
Essex	....	343*	P. A. Perrin v Derbyshire at Chesterfield	1904
Glamorgan	......	287*	D. E. Davies v Gloucestershire at Newport	1939
Gloucestershire	...	318*	W. G. Grace v Yorkshire at Cheltenham	1876
Hampshire	......	316	R. H. Moore v Warwickshire at Bournemouth	1937
Kent	....	332	W. H. Ashdown v Essex at Brentwood	1934
Lancashire	......	424	A. C. MacLaren v Somerset at Taunton	1895
Leicestershire	....	252*	S. Coe v Northamptonshire at Leicester	1914
Middlesex	....	331*	J. D. B. Robertson v Worcestershire at Worcester	1949
Northamptonshire		300	R. Subba Row v Surrey at The Oval	1958
Nottinghamshire	..	312*	W. W. Keeton v Middlesex at The Oval†	1939
Somerset	....	310	H. Gimblett v Sussex at Eastbourne	1948
Surrey	....	357*	R. Abel v Somerset at The Oval	1899
Sussex	....	333	K. S. Duleepsinhji v Northamptonshire at Hove	1930
Warwickshire	....	305*	F. R. Foster v Worcestershire at Dudley	1914
Worcestershire	....	276	F. L. Bowley v Hampshire at Dudley	1914
Yorkshire	....	341	G. H. Hirst v Leicestershire at Leicester	1905

† *On this date Eton played Harrow at Lord's.*

HIGHEST IN A MINOR COUNTY MATCH

| 323* | F. E. Lacey | Hampshire v Norfolk at Southampton .... | 1887 |

HIGHEST IN MINOR COUNTIES CHAMPIONSHIP

282	E. Garnett	Berkshire v Wiltshire at Reading	1908
254	H. E. Morgan	Glamorgan v Monmouthshire at Cardiff	1901
253*	G. J. Whittaker	Surrey II v Gloucestershire II at The Oval	1950
253	A. Booth	Lancashire II v Lincolnshire at Grimsby	1950
252	J. A. Deed	Kent II v Surrey II at The Oval (on début)	1924

HIGHEST FOR ENGLISH PUBLIC SCHOOL

| 278 | J. L. Guise | Winchester v Eton at Eton .... | 1921 |

HIGHEST IN OTHER MATCHES

628*	A. E. J. Collins, Clark's Team v North Town at Clifton College. (A Junior House match. His innings of 6 hours 50 minutes was spread over five afternoons)	1899
566	C. J. Eady, Break-o'-Day v Wellington at Hobart	1901-02
515	D. R. Havewalla, B.B. and C.I. Rly v St Xavier's at Bombay	1933-34
506*	J. C. Sharp, Melbourne GS v Geelong Coll. at Melbourne	1914-15
502*	Chaman Lal, Mehandra Coll., Patiala v Government Coll., Rupar at Patiala	1956-57
485	A. E. Stoddart, Hampstead v Stoics at Hampstead	1886
475*	Mohammad Iqbal, Muslim Model HS v Islamia HS, Sialkot at Lahore	1958-59
466*	G. T. S. Stevens, Beta v Lambda (University Coll. School House Match) at Neasden	1919
459	J. A. Prout, Wesley Coll. v Geelong Coll. at Geelong	1908-09

HUNDRED ON DEBUT IN ENGLAND

(The following list does not include instances of players who have previously appeared in first-class cricket outside England.)

107*	G. Barker	Essex v Canadians at Clacton	†1954
116*	B. L. Bisgood	Somerset v Worcestershire at Worcester	1907
107*	H. O. Bloomfield	Surrey v Northamptonshire at Northampton	1921
101	R. P. Hammond-Chambers-Borgnis	Combined Services v New Zealanders at Portsmouth ..	1937
124	G. J. Bryan	Kent v Nottinghamshire at Nottingham	†1920
100	J. F. Byrne	Warwickshire v Leicestershire at Birmingham	1897
118	A. P. F. Chapman	Cambridge University v Essex at Cambridge	1920
113	G. J. Chidgey	Free Foresters v Cambridge University at Cambridge ..	1962
100*	E. A. Clark	Middlesex v Cambridge University at Cambridge	1959
112	J. A. Claughton	Oxford University v Gloucestershire at Oxford	†1976
101*	S. H. Day	Kent v Gloucestershire at Cheltenham	†1897
		At the time, Day was a schoolboy at Malvern, aged 18	
108	E. W. Dillon	London County v Worcestershire at Crystal Palace ...	1900
215*	G. H. G. Doggart	Cambridge University v Lancashire at Cambridge	1948
137	C. H. M. Ebden	Cambridge U. v Leveson Gower's XI at Cambridge ...	1902
108	A. Fairbairn	Middlesex v Somerset at Taunton	†‡1947
123	H. Gimblett	Somerset v Essex at Frome	1935
101	P. M. Hall	Oxford University v Free Foresters at Oxford	1919
105	C. P. Hamilton	Army v Royal Air Force at The Oval	1932
156	M. N. Harbottle	Army v Oxford University at Camberley	1938
110*	A. J. Harvey-Walker	Derbyshire v Oxford University at Burton-on-Trent ..	†1971
124	P. Hearn	Kent v Warwickshire at Gillingham	1947
101	K. A. Higgs	Sussex v Worcestershire at Hove	1920
103*	A. L. Hilder	Kent v Essex at Gravesend	†1924
139*	J. E. Hill	Warwickshire v Nottinghamshire at Nottingham	1894
158*	J. H. Human	Cambridge U. v Leveson Gower's XI at Eastbourne ...	1932
146*	J. S. Johnson	Minor Counties v Indians at Wellington	1979
111*	C. F. H. Leslie	Oxford University v MCC and Ground at Oxford	1881
100*	A. W. Lilley	Essex v Nottinghamshire at Nottingham	†1978
108	A. C. MacLaren	Lancashire v Sussex at Hove	1890
124	N. Miller	Surrey v Sussex at Hove	1899
106*	W. Murray Wood	Oxford University v Gloucestershire at Oxford	1936
104	M. Nichol	Worcestershire v West Indians at Worcester	1928
101	A. H. C. Parnaby	Minor Counties v Oxford University at Oxford	1939
101	C. A. L. Payne	MCC and Ground v Derbyshire at Lord's	1905
138*	F. B. Pinch	Glamorgan v Worcestershire at Swansea	1921
124	H. C. Pretty	Surrey v Nottinghamshire at The Oval	1899
149	H. R. J. Rhys	Free Foresters v Cambridge University at Cambridge ..	1929
195*	J. Ricketts	Lancashire v Surrey at The Oval	1867
137	J. G. C. Scott	Sussex v Oxford University at Eastbourne	1907

108	D. R. Shepherd	Gloucestershire v Oxford University at Oxford	1965
135	J. K. E. Slack	Cambridge University v Middlesex at Cambridge	1954
114	F. W. Stocks	Nottinghamshire v Kent at Nottingham	1946
110	N. Taylor	Kent v Sri Lankans at Canterbury	1979
110	Hon. L. H. Tennyson	MCC and Ground v Oxford University at Lord's	†1913
103	A. H. Trevor	Sussex v Kent at Hove	†1880
125	G. S. Tuck	Royal Navy v New Zealanders at Portsmouth	1927
106	J. B. Turner	Minor Counties v Pakistan at Jesmond	1974
100*	C. T. Tyson	Yorkshire v Hampshire at Southampton	1921
102	I. D. Walker	Middlesex v Surrey at The Oval	1862
131*	R. Whitehead	Lancashire v Nottinghamshire at Manchester	1908
173	J. Whitehouse	Warwickshire v Oxford University at Oxford	1971
117*	E. R. Wilson	A. J. Webbe's XI v Cambridge University at Cambridge	1899
124	L. Winslow	Sussex v Gloucestershire at Hove	1875

† *In second innings.*

‡ *A. Fairbairn (Middlesex) in 1947 scored hundreds in the second innings of his first two matches in first-class cricket: 108 Middlesex v Somerset at Taunton, 110* Middlesex v Nottinghamshire at Nottingham.*

★   ★   ★   ★   ★

Notes: A number of players abroad have also made a hundred on a first appearance.

The highest innings on début was hit by W. F. E. Marx when he made 240 for Transvaal against Griqualand West at Johannesburg in 1920-21.

There are three instances of a cricketer making two separate hundreds on début: A. R. Morris, New South Wales, 148 and 111 against Queensland in 1940-41, N. J. Contractor, Gujerat, 152 and 102* against Baroda in 1952-53, and Aamer Malik, Lahore "A", 132* and 110* against Railways in 1979-80.

J. S. Solomon, British Guiana, scored a hundred in each of his first three innings in first-class cricket: 114* v Jamaica: 108 v Barbados in 1956-57; 121 v Pakistanis in 1957-58.

R. Watson-Smith, Border, scored 310 runs before he was dismissed in first-class cricket, including not-out centuries in his first two innings: 183* v Orange Free State and 125* v Griqualand West in 1969-70.

MOST INDIVIDUAL HUNDREDS

(35 or More)

	Hundreds Total	Abroad	100th 100		Hundreds Total	Abroad	100th 100
J. B. Hobbs	197	22	1923	T. W. Graveney ..	122	31	1964
E. H. Hendren ...	170	19	1928	G. Boycott	120	24	1977
W. R. Hammond..	167	33	1935	D. G. Bradman ..	117	41†	1947
C. P. Mead	153	8	1927	M. C. Cowdrey ...	107	27	1973
H. Sutcliffe	149	14	1932	A. Sandham	107	20	1935
F. E. Woolley	145	10	1929	T. W. Hayward ...	104	4	1913
L. Hutton	129	24	1951	J. H. Edrich	103	13	1977
W. G. Grace	124	1	1895	L. E. G. Ames ...	102	13	1950
D. C. S. Compton .	123	31	1952	G. E. Tyldesley ...	102	8	1934

J. W. Hearne 96	M. Leyland 80	J. O'Connor 72
C. B. Fry 94	B. A. Richards 79	Wm. Quaife 72
G. M. Turner 89	K. F. Barrington 76	K. S. Ranjitsinhji ... 72
W. J. Edrich 86	J. G. Langridge 76	D. Brookes 71
G. S. Sobers 86	C. Washbrook 76	Mushtaq Mohammad . 71
J. T. Tyldesley 86	D. L. Amiss 75	C. A. G. Russell ... 71
P. B. H. May 85	H. T. W. Hardinge ... 75	D. Denton 69
R. E. S. Wyatt 85	R. Abel 74	M. J. K. Smith 69
J. Hardstaff, jr 83	D. Kenyon 74	R. E. Marshall 68
R. B. Kanhai 83	Zaheer Abbas 73	R. N. Harvey 67

† *Scored outside Australia.*

P. Holmes 67	C. G. Macartney 49	Sadiq Mohammad 41
J. D. B. Robertson 67	M. J. Stewart 49	E. J. Barlow 40
Majid J. Khan 66	K. G. Suttle 49	C. G. Greenidge 40
P. A. Perrin 66	P. R. Umrigar 49	M. J. Smith 40
C. H. Lloyd 65	W. M. Woodfull 49	C. L. Walcott 40
R. T. Simpson 64	C. J. Barnett 48	D. M. Young 40
G. Gunn 62	E. G. Hayes 48	W. H. Ashdown 39
G. S. Chappell 60	B. W. Luckhurst 48	J. B. Bolus 39
G. H. Hirst 60	W. Gunn 47	W. A. Brown 39
R. B. Simpson 60	A. C. MacLaren 47	R. J. Gregory 39
P. F. Warner 60	W. H. Ponsford 47	W. R. D. Payton 39
I. M. Chappell 59	M. J. Procter 47	J. R. Reid 39
A. L. Hassett 59	J. Iddon 46	F. M. M. Worrell 39
A. Shrewsbury 59	A. R. Morris 46	F. L. Bowley 38
A. E. Fagg 58	W. W. Armstrong 45	P. J. P. Burge 38
P. H. Parfitt 58	G. L. Berry 45	J. F. Crapp 38
W. Rhodes 58	A. W. Carr 45	R. C. Fredericks 38
S. M. Gavaskar 57	C. Hill 45	V. L. Manjrekar 38
V. S. Hazare 57	N. C. O'Neill 45	A. W. Nourse 38
L. B. Fishlock 56	E. Paynter 45	N. Oldfield 38
C. A. Milton 56	I. V. A. Richards 45	Rev. J. H. Parsons 38
C. Hallows 55	Rev. D. S. Sheppard . . . 45	W. W. Read 38
Hanif Mohammad . . . 55	H. H. I. Gibbons 44	J. Sharp 38
W. Watson 55	A. Mitchell 44	L. J. Todd 38
D. J. Insole 54	P. E. Richardson 44	J. Arnold 37
W. W. Keeton 54	B. Sutcliffe 44	G. Brown 37
W. Bardsley 53	B. L. D'Oliveira 43	G. M. Emmett 37
A. E. Dipper 53	A. I. Kallicharran 43	H. W. Lee 37
G. L. Jessop 53	A. F. Kippax 43	M. A. Noble 37
James Seymour 53	J. W. H. Makepeace . . . 43	E. Oldroyd 37
E. H. Bowley 52	V. M. Merchant 43	H. S. Squires 37
D. B. Close 52	K. D. Walters 43	R. T. Virgin 37
A. Ducat 52	Asif Iqbal 42	C. J. B. Wood 37
R. G. Pollock 52	James Langridge 42	N. F. Armstrong 36
E. R. Dexter 51	H. W. Parks 42	J. M. Brearley 36
J. M. Parks 51	T. F. Shepherd 42	J. H. Hampshire 36
W. W. Whysall 51	V. T. Trumper 42	W. Place 36
G. Cox, jr 50	J. R. Gunn 41	E. D. Weekes 36
H. E. Dollery 50	M. J. Harris 41	A. L. Wadekar 36
K. S. Duleepsinhji 50	K. R. Miller 41	C. S. Dempster 35
H. Gimblett 50	A. D. Nourse 41	D. R. Jardine 35
A. Jones 50	J. H. Parks 41	C. T. Radley 35
W. M. Lawry 50	R. M. Prideaux 41	B. H. Valentine 35
F. B. Watson 50	G. Pullar 41	G. R. Viswanath 35
K. W. R. Fletcher 49	W. E. Russell 41	

Notes: W. G. Grace's previously published total of 126 hundreds included two which are not first-class.

In all cricket J. B. Hobbs hit 244 hundreds and W. G. Grace hit 221.

TWO SEPARATE HUNDREDS IN A MATCH

Seven times: W. R. Hammond.
Six times: J. B. Hobbs.
Five times: C. B. Fry.
Four times: D. G. Bradman, G. S. Chappell, J. H. Edrich, L. B. Fishlock, T. W. Graveney, H. T. W. Hardinge, E. H. Hendren, G. L. Jessop, P. A. Perrin, B. Sutcliffe, H. Sutcliffe, G. M. Turner.
Three times: L. E. G. Ames, I. M. Chappell, D. C. S. Compton, M. C. Cowdrey, D. Denton, K. S. Duleepsinhji, R. E. Foster, R. C. Fredericks, S. M. Gavaskar, W. G. Grace, G. Gunn, M. R. Hallam, Hanif Mohammad, M. J. Harris, T. W. Hayward, V. S. Hazare, L. Hutton, A. Jones, P. B. H. May, C. P. Mead, C. A. G. Russell, J. T. Tyldesley, Zaheer Abbas.

Twice: B. J. T. Bosanquet, G. Boycott, C. C. R. Dacre, G. M. Emmett, A. E. Fagg, L. E. Favell, H. Gimblett, C. G. Greenidge, C. Hallows, R. A. Hamence, A. L. Hassett, G. A. Headley, D. W. Hookes, J. H. King, A. F. Kippax, J. G. Langridge, H. W. Lee, E. Lester, C. B. Llewellyn, C. G. Macartney, R. B. McCosker, C. A. Milton, A. R. Morris, P. H. Parfitt, Nawab of Pataudi, jnr, E. Paynter, C. Pinch, R. G. Pollock, R. M. Prideaux, W. Rhodes, B. A. Richards, P. Roy, Sadiq Mohammad, Jas. Seymour, R. B. Simpson, G. S. Sobers, G. E. Tyldesley, C. L. Walcott, W. W. Whysall.

Notes: W. Lambert scored 107 and 157 for Sussex v Epsom at Lord's in 1817 and it was not until W. G. Grace made 130 and 102* for South of the Thames v North of the Thames at Canterbury in 1868 that the feat was repeated.

T. W. Hayward (Surrey) set up a unique record in 1906 when in one week – six days – he hit four successive hundreds, 144 and 100 v Nottinghamshire at Nottingham and 143 and 125 v Leicestershire at Leicester.

D. W. Hookes (South Australia) scored four successive hundreds in eleven days at Adelaide in 1976-77: 185 and 105 v Queensland (tied match) and 135 and 156 v New South Wales.

A. E. Fagg alone has scored two double hundreds in the same match: 244 and 202* for Kent v Essex at Colchester, 1938.

L. G. Rowe is alone in scoring hundreds in each innings on his first appearance in Test cricket: 214 and 100* for West Indies v New Zealand at Kingston in 1971-72.

Zaheer Abbas (Gloucestershire) set a unique record in 1976 by twice scoring a double hundred and a hundred in the same match without being dismissed: 216* and 156* v Surrey at The Oval and 230* and 104* v Kent at Canterbury. In 1977 he achieved this feat for a third time, scoring 205* and 108* v Sussex at Cheltenham.

M. R. Hallam (Leicestershire), opening the batting each time, achieved the following treble: 210* and 157 v Glamorgan at Leicester, 1959: 203* and 143* v Sussex at Worthing, 1961; 107* and 149* v Worcestershire at Leicester, 1965. In the last two matches he was on the field the whole time, as was C. J. B. Wood when he scored 107* and 117* for Leicestershire against Yorkshire at Bradford, 1911.

W. L. Foster, 140 and 172*, and R. E. Foster, 134 and 101*, for Worcestershire v Hampshire at Worcester in July 1899, were the first brothers each to score two separate hundreds in the same first-class match.

The brothers I. M. Chappell, 145 and 121, and G. S. Chappell, 247* and 133, for Australia v New Zealand at Wellington in 1973-74, became the first players on the same side each to score a hundred in each innings of a Test match.

G. Gunn, 183, and G. V. Gunn, 100*, for Nottinghamshire v Warwickshire at Birmingham in 1931, provide the only instance of father and son each hitting a century in the same innings of a first-class match.

Most Recent Instances

In 1979-80:

Aamer Malik†	132*	110*	Lahore "A" v Railways at Lahore
Asad Rauf	122	145*	Universities v Peshawar at Peshawar
Asif Iqbal	104	110*	PIA v Habib Bank at Lahore
A. R. Border	150*	153	Australia v Pakistan at Lahore
Tariq Alam	132	107	HBFC v Rawalpindi at Lahore

† *On début in first-class cricket.*

In 1980: See Features of 1980.

BATSMEN WHO HAVE SCORED 25,000 RUNS

	Career	Runs	Inns	Not Outs	Highest Inns	100s	Average
J. B. Hobbs	1905-34	61,237	1,315	106	316*	197	50.65
F. E. Woolley	1906-38	58,969	1,532	85	305*	145	40.75
E. H. Hendren	1907-38	57,611	1,300	166	301*	170	50.80
C. P. Mead	1905-36	55,061	1,340	185	280*	153	47.67
W. G. Grace	1865-1908	54,211	1,478	104	344	124	39.45
W. R. Hammond	1920-51	50,551	1,005	104	336*	167	56.10

	Career	Runs	Inns	Not Outs	Highest Inns	100s	Average
H. Sutcliffe	1919-45	50,138	1,088	123	313	149	51.95
T. W. Graveney	1948-72	47,793	1,223	159	258	122	44.91
T. W. Hayward	1893-1914	43,551	1,138	96	315*	104	41.79
M. C. Cowdrey	1950-76	42,719	1,130	134	307	107	42.89
A. Sandham	1911-38	41,284	1,000	79	325	107	44.82
L. Hutton	1934-60	40,140	814	91	364	129	55.51
M. J. K. Smith	1951-75	39,832	1,091	139	204	69	41.84
W. Rhodes	1898-1930	39,802	1,528	237	267*	58	30.83
J. H. Edrich	1956-78	39,790	979	104	310*	103	45.47
R. E. S. Wyatt	1923-57	39,404	1,141	157	232	85	40.04
D. C. S. Compton ...	1936-64	38,942	839	88	300	123	51.85
G. E. Tyldesley	1909-36	38,874	961	106	256*	102	45.46
J. T. Tyldesley	1895-1923	37,897	994	62	295*	86	40.60
G. Boycott	1962-80	37,624	782	119	261*	120	56.74
J. W. Hearne	1909-36	37,252	1,025	116	285*	96	40.98
L. E. G. Ames	1926-51	37,248	951	95	295	102	43.51
D. Kenyon	1946-67	37,002	1,159	59	259	74	33.63
W. J. Edrich	1934-58	36,965	964	92	267*	86	42.39
J. M. Parks	1949-76	36,673	1,227	172	205*	51	34.76
D. Denton	1894-1920	36,479	1,163	70	221	69	33.37
G. H. Hirst	1891-1929	36,323	1,215	151	341	60	34.13
Wm. Quaife	1894-1928	36,012	1,203	186	255*	72	35.38
R. E. Marshall	1945-72	35,725	1,053	59	228*	68	35.94
G. Gunn	1902-32	35,208	1,061	82	220	62	35.96
D. B. Close	1949-78	34,833	1,217	169	198	52	33.23
J. G. Langridge	1928-55	34,380	984	66	250*	76	37.45
C. Washbrook	1933-64	34,101	906	107	251*	76	42.67
M. Leyland	1920-48	33,659	932	101	263	80	40.50
H. T. W. Hardinge ...	1902-33	33,519	1,021	103	263*	75	36.51
R. Abel	1881-1904	32,669	994	73	357*	74	35.47
A. Jones	1957-80	32,307	1,043	63	204*	50	32.96
C. A. Milton	1948-74	32,150	1,078	125	170	56	33.73
J. D. B. Robertson ...	1937-59	31,914	897	46	331*	67	37.50
J. Hardstaff, jr	1930-55	31,847	812	94	266	83	44.35
D. L. Amiss	1960-80	31,724	825	95	262*	75	43.45
James Langridge	1924-53	31,716	1,058	157	167	42	35.20
K. F. Barrington	1953-68	31,714	831	136	256	76	45.63
G. M. Turner	1964-80	30,941	729	94	259	89	48.72
C. B. Fry	1892-1921	30,886	658	43	258*	94	50.22
D. Brookes	1934-59	30,874	925	70	257	71	36.10
Mushtaq Mohammad .	1957-80	30,777	833	103	303*	71	42.16
P. Holmes	1913-35	30,574	810	84	315*	67	42.11
R. T. Simpson	1944-63	30,546	852	55	259	64	38.32
G. L. Berry	1924-51	30,225	1,056	57	232	45	30.25
K. G. Suttle	1949-71	30,225	1,064	92	204*	49	31.09
K. W. R. Fletcher ...	1962-80	29,870	906	129	228*	50	38.44
P. A. Perrin	1896-1928	29,709	918	91	343*	66	35.92
P. F. Warner	1894-1929	29,028	875	75	244	60	36.28
J. O'Connor	1921-39	28,875	906	80	248	72	34.95
T. E. Bailey	1945-67	28,642	1,072	215	205	28	33.42
R. B. Kanhai	1955-77	28,639	663	82	256	83	49.29
G. S. Sobers	1953-74	28,315	609	93	365*	86	54.87
E. H. Bowley	1912-34	28,163	853	46	283	52	34.89
A. E. Dipper	1908-32	28,075	865	69	252*	53	35.27
D. G. Bradman	1927-49	28,067	338	43	452*	117	95.14
P. B. H. May	1948-63	27,592	618	77	285*	85	51.00
C. A. G. Russell	1908-30	27,545	719	59	273	71	41.73
E. G. Hayes	1896-1926	27,318	896	48	276	48	32.21
B. A. Richards	1964-78	27,293	543	53	356	79	55.70
A. E. Fagg	1932-57	27,291	803	46	269*	58	36.05
James Seymour	1900-26	27,238	911	62	218*	53	32.08

	Career	Runs	Inns	Not Outs	Highest Inns	100s	Average
P. H. Parfitt	1956-74	26,924	845	104	200*	58	36.33
G. L. Jessop	1894-1914	26,698	855	37	286	53	32.63
D. E. Davies	1924-54	26,566	1,033	79	287*	32	27.84
M. J. Stewart	1954-72	26,492	898	93	227*	49	32.90
A. Shrewsbury	1875-1902	26,439	811	90	267	59	36.66
P. E. Richardson.....	1949-65	26,055	794	41	185	44	34.60
J. W. H. Makepeace ..	1906-30	25,799	778	66	203	43	36.23
W. Watson	1939-64	25,670	753	109	257	55	39.86
G. Brown	1908-33	25,649	1,012	52	232*	37	26.71
G. M. Emmett	1936-59	25,602	865	50	188	37	31.41
M. H. Denness	1959-80	25,886	838	65	195	33	33.48
J. B. Bolus	1956-75	25,598	833	81	202*	39	34.03
W. E. Russell	1956-72	25,525	796	64	193	41	34.87
W. Gunn	1880-1904	25,457	846	71	273	47	32.84
C. J. Barnett	1927-54	25,389	821	45	259	48	32.71
L. B. Fishlock	1931-52	25,376	699	54	253	56	39.34
D. J. Insole	1947-63	25,237	743	72	219*	54	37.61
J. Vine	1896-1922	25,171	920	79	202	34	29.94
R. M. Prideaux	1958-75	25,136	808	75	202*	41	34.29
J. H. King	1895-1926	25,121	988	69	227*	34	27.33

Notes: W. G. Grace's career figures as published previously (54,896 – 1,493 – 105 – 126 – 39.55) included a number of matches which cannot be regarded as first-class.

K. S. Ranjitsinhji (1893-1920) had career figures of 24,692 – 500 – 62 – 285* – 72 – 56.37.

1,000 RUNS IN A SEASON

(Includes Overseas Tours and Seasons)

28 times: W. G. Grace 2,000 (5); F. E. Woolley 3,000 (1), 2,000 (12).

27 times: M. C. Cowdrey 2,000 (2); C. P. Mead 3,000 (2), 2,000 (9).

26 times: J. B. Hobbs 3,000 (1), 2,000 (16).

25 times: E. H. Hendren 3,000 (3), 2,000 (9).

24 times: Wm. Quaife 2,000 (1); H. Sutcliffe 3,000 (3), 2,000 (12).

22 times: T. W. Graveney 2,000 (7); W. R. Hammond 3,000 (3), 2,000 (9).

21 times: G. Boycott 2,000 (3); D. Denton 2,000 (5); J. H. Edrich 2,000 (6); W. Rhodes 2,000 (2).

20 times: D. B. Close; G. Gunn; T. W. Hayward 3,000 (2), 2,000 (8); A. Jones; James Langridge 2,000 (1); J. M. Parks 2,000 (3); A. Sandham 2,000 (8); M. J. K. Smith 3,000 (1), 2,000 (5); C. Washbrook 2,000 (5).

19 times: J. W. Hearne 2,000 (4); G. H. Hirst 2,000 (3); D. Kenyon 2,000 (7); G. E. Tyldesley 3,000 (1), 2,000 (5); J. T. Tyldesley 3,000 (1), 2,000 (4).

18 times: G. L. Berry 2,000 (1); H. T. W. Hardinge 2,000 (5); R. E. Marshall 2,000 (6); P. A. Perrin; R. E. S. Wyatt 2,000 (5).

17 times: L. E. G. Ames 3,000 (1), 2,000 (5); D. L. Amiss 2,000 (2); T. E. Bailey 2,000 (1); D. Brookes 2,000 (6); D. C. S. Compton 3,000 (1), 2,000 (5); L. Hutton 3,000 (1), 2,000 (8); J. G. Langridge 2,000 (11); M. Leyland 2,000 (7); K. G. Suttle 2,000 (7).

16 times: D. G. Bradman 2,000 (4); D. E. Davies 2,000 (1); K. W. R. Fletcher; E. G. Hayes 2,000 (2); C. A. Milton 2,000 (1); J. O'Connor 2,000 (4); James Seymour 2,000 (1); G. M. Turner 2,000 (2).

15 times: G. Barker; K. F. Barrington 2,000 (3); E. H. Bowley 2,000 (4); M. H. Denness; A. E. Dipper 2,000 (5); H. E. Dollery 2,000 (2); W. J. Edrich 3,000 (1), 2,000 (8); P. Holmes 2,000 (7); Mushtaq Mohammad; R. B. Nicholls 2,000 (1); P. H. Parfitt 2,000 (3); W. G. A. Parkhouse 2,000 (1); B. A. Richards 2,000 (1); J. D. B. Robertson 2,000 (9); G. S. Sobers; M. J. Stewart 2,000 (1).

Notes: F. E. Woolley reached 1,000 runs in 28 consecutive seasons (1907-1938). C. P. Mead did so 27 seasons in succession (1906-1936).

Outside England, 1,000 runs in a season has been reached most times by D. G. Bradman (in 12 seasons in Australia).

Three batsmen have scored 1,000 runs in a season in each of four different countries: G. S. Sobers in West Indies, England, India, and Australia; M. C. Cowdrey and G. Boycott in England, South Africa, West Indies, and Australia.

FOUR HUNDREDS OR MORE IN SUCCESSION

Six in succession: C. B. Fry 1901; D. G. Bradman 1938-39; M. J. Procter 1970-71.

Five in succession: E. D. Weekes 1955-56.

Four in succession: D. G. Bradman 1931-32, 1948-49; D. C. S. Compton 1946-47; N. J. Contractor 1957-58; K. S. Duleepsinhji 1931; C. B. Fry 1911; W. R. Hammond 1936-37, 1945-46; H. T. W. Hardinge 1913; T. W. Hayward 1906; J. B. Hobbs 1920, 1925; D. W. Hookes 1976-77; P. N. Kirsten 1976-77; J. G. Langridge 1949; C. G. Macartney 1921; K. S. McEwan 1977; P. B. H. May 1956-57; V. M. Merchant 1941-42; A. Mitchell 1933; Nawab of Pataudi 1931; L. G. Rowe 1971-72; P. Roy 1962-63; Sadiq Mohammad 1976; Saeed Ahmed 1961-62; H. Sutcliffe 1931, 1939; G. E. Tyldesley 1926; W. W. Whysall 1930; F. E. Woolley 1929; Zaheer Abbas 1970-71.

Hundreds in Successive Test Innings

Five: E. D. Weekes (West Indies), 141 v England in West Indies 1947-48; 128, 194, 162 and 101 in India 1948-49.

Four: J. H. W. Fingleton (Australia), 112, 108, 118 in South Africa 1935-36, and 100 v England in Australia 1936-37; A. Melville (South Africa), 103 v England in South Africa 1938-39, 189, 104* and 117 in England 1947.

MOST HUNDREDS IN A SEASON

Eighteen: D. C. S. Compton in 1947. These included six hundreds against the South Africans in which matches his average was 84.78. His aggregate for the season was 3,816, also a record.

Sixteen: J. B. Hobbs in 1925, when aged 42, played 16 three-figure innings in first-class matches. It was during this season that he exceeded the number of hundreds obtained in first-class cricket by W. G. Grace.

Fifteen: W. R. Hammond in 1938.

Fourteen: H. Sutcliffe in 1932.

Thirteen: G. Boycott in 1971, D. G. Bradman in 1938, C. B. Fry in 1901, W. R. Hammond in 1933 and 1937, T. W. Hayward in 1906, E. H. Hendren in 1923, 1927, and 1928, C. P. Mead in 1928, and H. Sutcliffe in 1928 and 1931.

FAST FIFTIES

Minutes

8†	C. C. Inman (57)	Leicestershire v Nottinghamshire at Nottingham ..	1965
11	C. I. J. Smith (66)	Middlesex v Gloucestershire at Bristol	1938
14	S. J. Pegler (50)	South Africans v Tasmania at Launceston	1910-11
14	F. T. Mann (53)	Middlesex v Nottinghamshire at Lord's	1921
14	H. B. Cameron (56)	Transvaal v Orange Free State at Johannesburg ..	1934-35
14	C. I. J. Smith (52)	Middlesex v Kent at Maidstone	1935

† *Full tosses were bowled to expedite a declaration.*

FAST HUNDREDS

Minutes

35	P. G. H. Fender (113*)	Surrey v Northamptonshire at Northampton	1920
37	C. M. Old (107)	Yorkshire v Warwickshire at Birmingham	1977
40	G. L. Jessop (101)	Gloucestershire v Yorkshire at Harrogate	1897
42	G. L. Jessop (191)	Gentlemen of South v Players of South at Hastings	1907
43	A. H. Hornby (106)	Lancashire v Somerset at Manchester	1905
44	R. N. S. Hobbs (100)	Essex v Australians at Chelmsford	1975

FAST DOUBLE HUNDREDS

Minutes

120	G. L. Jessop (286)	Gloucestershire v Sussex at Hove	1903
120	C. H. Lloyd (201*)	West Indians v Glamorgan at Swansea	1976
130	G. L. Jessop (234)	Gloucestershire v Somerset at Bristol . .:.......	1905
131	V. T. Trumper (293)	Australians v Canterbury at Christchurch	1913-14

FAST TRIPLE HUNDREDS

Minutes

181	D. C. S. Compton (300)	MCC v N.E. Transvaal at Benoni	1948-49
205	F. E. Woolley (305*)	MCC v Tasmania at Hobart	1911-12
205	C. G. Macartney (345)	Australians v Nottinghamshire at Nottingham	1921
213	D. G. Bradman (369)	South Australia v Tasmania at Adelaide	1935-36

FAST SCORING

P. G. H. Fender, for Surrey v Northamptonshire at Northampton in 1920, scored 113* out of 171 in forty-two minutes. He reached 50 in nineteen minutes and 100 in thirty-five minutes. Fender and H. A. Peach added 171 (unfinished) in forty-two minutes for the sixth wicket.

    C. M. Old scored a century in 37 minutes off 72 balls, with six 6s and twelve 4s, for Yorkshire v Warwickshire at Birmingham in 1977. His second 50 took nine minutes.

    C. I. J. Smith, in June 1938, made 69 in twenty minutes for Middlesex against Sussex at Lord's, and ten days later against Gloucestershire at Bristol he scored 66 in eighteen minutes – the first 50 coming in eleven minutes.

    E. B. Alletson, for Nottinghamshire v Sussex at Hove in 1911, scored 189 out of 227 runs obtained while at the wicket in ninety minutes. He went from 50 to 189 in thirty minutes.

    For Auckland v Otago at Dunedin in 1936-37, P. E. Whitelaw and W. N. Carson added 445 runs for the third wicket in 268 minutes – a world record.

    Worcestershire, set to make 131 in forty minutes against Nottinghamshire at Worcester in 1951, hit off the runs in thirty-five minutes for the loss of D. Kenyon's wicket. The other batsmen were G. Dews and R. O. Jenkins.

    Kent scored 219 in seventy-one minutes when beating Gloucestershire at Dover, 1937. They averaged 9 runs an over.

    H. Sutcliffe (194) and M. Leyland (45) hit 102 off six consecutive overs for Yorkshire v Essex at Scarborough, 1932.

    J. B. Hobbs (47) and J. N. Crawford (48) made 96 without loss in thirty-two minutes at The Oval, 1919, after Kent left Surrey to get 95 in forty-two minutes.

RECORD HIT

The Rev. W. Fellows, while at practice on the Christ Church ground at Oxford in 1856, drove a ball bowled by Charles Rogers 175 yards from hit to pitch.

MOST PERSONAL SIXES IN AN INNINGS

15	J. R. Reid (296)	Wellington v N. Districts at Wellington	1962-63
13	Majid J. Khan (147*)	Pakistan v Glamorgan at Swansea	1967
13	C. G. Greenidge (273*)	D. H. Robins' XI v Pakistanis at Eastbourne	1974
13	C. G. Greenidge (259)	Hampshire v Sussex at Southampton	1975
12	Gulfraz Khan (207)	Railways v Universities at Lahore	1976-77
11	C. K. Nayudu (153)	Hindus v MCC at Bombay	1926-27
11	C. J. Barnett (194)	Gloucestershire v Somerset at Bath	1934
11	R. Benaud (135)	Australians v T. N. Pearce's XI at Scarborough ..	1953

Note: W. J. Stewart (Warwickshire) hit seventeen 6s in the match v Lancashire. at Blackpool. July 29, 30, 31, 1959; ten in his first innings of 155 and seven in the second innings of 125.

MOST PERSONAL BOUNDARIES IN AN INNINGS

68	P. A. Perrin (343*)	Essex v Derbyshire at Chesterfield	1904
65	A. C. MacLaren (424)	Lancashire v Somerset at Taunton	1895
64	Hanif Mohammad (499)	Karachi v Bahawalpur at Karachi	1958-59
57	J. H. Edrich (310*)	England v New Zealand at Leeds	1965
55	C. W. Gregory (383)	NSW v Queensland at Brisbane	1906-07
54	G. H. Hirst (341)	Yorkshire v Leicestershire at Leicester	1905
53	A. W. Nourse (304*)	Natal v Transvaal at Johannesburg	1919-20
51	W. G. Grace (344)	MCC v Kent at Canterbury	1876
51	C. G. Macartney (345)	Australians v Nottinghamshire at Nottingham ...	1921
50	D. G. Bradman (369)	South Australia v Tasmania at Adelaide	1935-36
50	B. B. Nimbalkar (443*)	Maharashtra v Kathiawar at Poona	1948-49
50	J. R. Reid (296)	Wellington v N. Districts at Wellington	1962-63

Note: Boundaries include sixes.

MOST RUNS SCORED OFF ONE OVER

(All instances refer to six-ball overs)

36	G. S. Sobers	off M. A. Nash. Nottinghamshire v Glamorgan at Swansea (six 6s)	1968
34	F. C. Hayes	off M. A. Nash. Lancashire v Glamorgan at Swansea (646666)	1977
34	E. B. Alletson	off E. H. Killick. Nottinghamshire v Sussex at Hove (including two no-balls)	1911
32	C. C. Inman	off N. W. Hill. Leicestershire v Nottinghamshire at Nottingham (full tosses were provided for him to hit) ...	1965
32	C. C. Smart	off G. Hill. Glamorgan v Hampshire at Cardiff	1935
32	I. R. Redpath	off N. Rosendorff. Australians v Orange Free State at Bloemfontein	1969-70
31	A. W. Wellard	off F. E. Woolley. Somerset v Kent at Wells (including five 6s)	1938
31	M. H. Bowditch (1) and M. J. Procter (30)	off A. A. Mallett. Western Province v Australians at Cape Town (Procter hit five 6s)	1969-70
30	D. G. Bradman	off A. P. Freeman. Australians v England XI at Folkestone	1934
30	H. B. Cameron	off H. Verity. South Africans v Yorkshire at Sheffield	1935
30	D. T. Lindsay	off W. T. Greensmith. South African Fezela XI v Essex at Chelmsford (five successive 6s to win the match)	1961
30	Majid J. Khan	off R. C. Davis. Pakistanis v Glamorgan at Swansea	1967
30	A. W. Wellard	off T. R. Armstrong. Somerset v Derbyshire at Wells (five 6s off successive balls)	1936

30	D. Wilson	off R. N. S. Hobbs, Yorkshire v MCC at Scarborough	1966
30	P. L. Winslow	off J. T. Ikin, South Africans v Lancashire at Manchester .	1955
30	Zaheer Abbas	off D. Breakwell, Gloucestershire v Somerset at Taunton ..	1979

Note: The greatest number of runs scored off an eight-ball over is 34 (three 6s, four 4s) by R. M. Edwards off M. C. Carew, Governor-General's XI v West Indians at Auckland, 1968-69.

300 RUNS IN ONE DAY

345	C. G. Macartney	Australians v Nottinghamshire at Nottingham	1921
334	W. H. Ponsford	Victoria v New South Wales at Melbourne	1926-27
333	K. S. Duleepsinhji	Sussex v Northamptonshire at Hove	1930
331*	J. D. B. Robertson	Middlesex v Worcestershire at Worcester	1949
325*	B. A. Richards	S. Australia v W. Australia at Perth	1970-71
322†	E. Paynter	Lancashire v Sussex at Hove	1937
318	C. W. Gregory	New South Wales v Queensland at Brisbane	1906-07
316†	R. H. Moore	Hampshire v Warwickshire at Bournemouth	1937
315*	R. C. Blunt	Otago v Canterbury at Christchurch	1931-32
312*	J. M. Brearley	MCC Under 25 v North Zone at Peshawar	1966-67
309*	D. G. Bradman	Australia v England at Leeds	1930
307*	W. H. Ashdown	Kent v Essex at Brentwood	1934
306*	A. Ducat	Surrey v Oxford University at The Oval	1919
305*	F. R. Foster	Warwickshire v Worcestershire at Dudley	1914

† *E. Paynter's 322 and R. H. Moore's 316 were scored on the same day: July 28, 1937.*

HIGHEST PARTNERSHIPS

577	V. S. Hazare (288) and Gul Mahomed (319), fourth wicket, Baroda v Holkar at Baroda	1946-47
574*	F. M. M. Worrell (255*) and C. L. Walcott (314*), fourth wicket, Barbados v Trinidad at Port-of-Spain	1945-46
561	Waheed Mirza (324) and Mansoor Akhtar (224*), first wicket, Karachi Whites v Quetta at Karachi	1976-77
555	P. Holmes (224*) and H. Sutcliffe (313), first wicket, Yorkshire v Essex at Leyton	1932
554	J. T. Brown (300) and J. Tunnicliffe (243), first wicket, Yorkshire v Derbyshire at Chesterfield	1898
502*	F. M. M. Worrell (308*) and J. D. C. Goddard (218*), fourth wicket, Barbados v Trinidad at Bridgetown	1943-44
490	E. H. Bowley (283) and J. G. Langridge (195), first wicket, Sussex v Middlesex at Hove	1933
487*	G. A. Headley (344*) and C. C. Passailaigue (261*), sixth wicket, Jamaica v Lord Tennyson's XI at Kingston	1931-32
465*	J. A. Jameson (240*) and R. B. Kanhai (213*), second wicket, Warwickshire v Gloucestershire at Birmingham	1974
456	W. H. Ponsford (248) and E. R. Mayne (209), first wicket, Victoria v Queensland at Melbourne	1923-24
456	Khalid Irtiza (290) and Aslam Ali (236), third wicket, United Bank v Multan at Karachi	1975-76
455	B. B. Nimbalkar (443*) and K. V. Bhandarkar (205), second wicket, Maharashtra v Kathiawar at Poona	1948-49
451	D. G Bradman (244) and W. H. Ponsford (266), second wicket, Australia v England, Fifth Test, at The Oval	1934
451*	S. Desai (218*) and R. Binny (211*), first wicket, Karnataka v Kerala at Chikmagalur	1977-78

PARTNERSHIPS FOR FIRST WICKET

561	Waheed Mirza and Mansoor Akhtar, Karachi Whites v Quetta at Karachi ..	1976-77
555	P. Holmes and H. Sutcliffe, Yorkshire v Essex at Leyton	1932
554	J. T. Brown and J. Tunnicliffe, Yorkshire v Derbyshire at Chesterfield	1898
490	E. H. Bowley and J. G. Langridge, Sussex v Middlesex at Hove	1933
456	E. R. Mayne and W. H. Ponsford, Victoria v Queensland at Melbourne	1923-24
451*	S. Desai and R. Binny, Karnataka v Kerala at Chikmagalur	1977-78
428	J. B. Hobbs and A. Sandham, Surrey v Oxford University at The Oval	1926
424	J. F. W. Nicholson and I. J. Siedle, Natal v Orange Free State at Bloemfontein	1926-27
413	V. M. H. Mankad and P. Roy, India v New Zealand at Madras (world Test record)	1955-56
405	C. P. S. Chauhan and M. S. Gupte, Maharashtra v Vidarbha at Poona	1972-73
395	D. M. Young and R. B. Nicholls, Gloucestershire v Oxford University at Oxford	1962
391	A. O. Jones and A. Shrewsbury, Nottinghamshire v Gloucestershire at Bristol	1899
390	G. L. Wight and G. L. R. Gibbs, B. Guiana v Barbados at Georgetown ...	1951-52
390	B. Dudleston and J. F. Steele, Leicestershire v Derbyshire at Leicester	1979
387	G. M. Turner and T. W. Jarvis, New Zealand v West Indies at Georgetown .	1971-72
382	R. B. Simpson and W. M. Lawry, Australia v West Indies at Bridgetown ..	1964-65
380	H. Whitehead and C. J. B. Wood, Leicestershire v Worcestershire at Worcester	1906
379	R. Abel and W. Brockwell, Surrey v Hampshire at The Oval	1897
378	J. T. Brown and J. Tunnicliffe, Yorkshire v Sussex at Sheffield	1897
377*	N. F. Horner and Khalid Ibadulla, Warwickshire v Surrey at The Oval	1960
375	W. H. Ponsford and W. M. Woodfull, Victoria v New South Wales at Melbourne	1926-27
373	B. Sutcliffe and L. Watt, Otago v Auckland at Auckland	1950-51
368	A. C. MacLaren and R. H. Spooner, Lancashire v Gloucestershire at Liverpool	1903
368	E. H. Bowley and J. H. Parks, Sussex v Gloucestershire at Hove	1929
364	R. Abel and D. L. A. Jephson, Surrey v Derbyshire at The Oval	1900
361	N. Oldfield and V. Broderick, Northamptonshire v Scotland at Peterborough	1953
359	L. Hutton and C. Washbrook, England v South Africa at Johannesburg	1948-49
355	A. F. Rae and J. B. Stollmeyer, West Indies v Sussex at Hove	1950
352	T. W. Hayward and J. B. Hobbs, Surrey v Warwickshire at The Oval	1909
350*	C. Washbrook and W. Place, Lancashire v Sussex at Manchester	1947

FIRST-WICKET HUNDREDS IN BOTH INNINGS

B. Sutcliffe and D. D. Taylor, for Auckland v Canterbury in 1948-49, scored for the first wicket 220 in the first innings and 286 in the second innings. This is the only instance of two double-century opening stands in the same match.

T. W. Hayward and J. B. Hobbs in 1907 accomplished a performance without parallel by scoring over 100 together for Surrey's first wicket four times in one week; 106 and 125 v Cambridge University at The Oval, and 147 and 105 v Middlesex at Lord's.

L. Hutton and C. Washbrook, in three consecutive Test match innings which they opened together for England v Australia in 1946-47, made 138 in the second innings at Melbourne, and 137 and 100 at Adelaide. They also opened with 168 and 129 at Leeds in 1948.

J. B. Hobbs and H. Sutcliffe, in three consecutive Test match innings which they opened together for England v Australia in 1924-25, made 157 and 110 at Sydney and 283 at Melbourne. On 26 occasions – 15 times in Test matches – Hobbs and Sutcliffe took part in a three-figure first-wicket partnership. Seven of these stands exceeded 200.

G. Boycott and J. H. Edrich, in three consecutive Test match innings which they opened together for England v Australia 1970-71, made 161* in the second innings at Melbourne, and 107 and 103 at Adelaide.

In 1971 R. G. A. Headley and P. J. Stimpson of Worcestershire shared in first-wicket hundred partnerships on each of the first four occasions they opened the innings together: 125 and 147 v Northamptonshire at Worcester, 102 and 128* v Warwickshire at Birmingham.

J. B. Hobbs during his career, which extended from 1905 to 1934, helped to make 100 or more for the first wicket in first-class cricket 166 times – 15 of them in 1926, when in consecutive innings he helped to make 428, 182, 106, and 123 before a wicket fell. As many as 117 of the 166 stands were made for Surrey. In all first-class matches Hobbs and A. Sandham shared 66 first-wicket partnerships of 100 or more runs.

P. Holmes and H. Sutcliffe made 100 or more runs for the first wicket of Yorkshire on 69 occasions; J. B. Hobbs and A. Sandham for Surrey on 63; W. W. Keeton and C. B. Harris of Nottinghamshire on 46; T. W. Hayward and J. B. Hobbs of Surrey on 40; G. Gunn and W. W. Whysall of Nottinghamshire on 40; J. D. B. Robertson and S. M. Brown of Middlesex on 34; C. B. Fry and J. Vine of Sussex on 33; R. E. Marshall and J. R. Gray of Hampshire on 33; D. E. Davies and A. H. Dyson of Glamorgan on 32; and A. O. Jones and J. Iremonger of Nottinghamshire on 24.

J. Douglas and A. E. Stoddart in 1896 scored over 150 runs for the Middlesex first wicket three times within a fortnight. In 1901, J. Iremonger and A. O. Jones obtained over 100 for the Nottinghamshire first wicket four times within eight days, scoring 134 and 144* v Surrey at The Oval, 238 v Essex at Leyton, and 119 v Derbyshire at Welbeck.

J. W. Lee and F. S. Lee, brothers, for Somerset in 1934, scored over 100 runs thrice in succession in the County Championship.

W. G. Grace and A. E. Stoddart, in three consecutive innings against the Australians in 1893, made over 100 runs for each opening partnership.

C. Hallows and F. B. Watson, in consecutive innings for Lancashire in 1928, opened with 200, 202, 107, 118; reached three figures twelve times, 200 four times.

H. Sutcliffe, in the period 1919-1939 inclusive, shared in 145 first-wicket partnerships of 100 runs or more.

There were four first-wicket hundred partnerships in the match between Somerset and Cambridge University at Taunton in 1960. G. Atkinson and R. T. Virgin scored 172 and 112 for Somerset and R. M. Prideaux and A. R. Lewis 198 and 137 for Cambridge University.

Most Recent Instances

In 1979-80:
150 112 B. Whitfield and B. Plummer, Natal "B", v Eastern Province "B" at Port Elizabeth.

Note: For West Zone v Pakistanis at Pune, A. D. Gaekwad and G. Parkar made 222 for the first wicket in the first innings and A. Shroff and S. M. Patil 111 in the second innings.

In 1980: See Features of 1980.

WICKET RECORDS FOR ALL COUNTRIES

Best First-Wicket Stands

Pakistan	561	Waheed Mirza (324) and Mansoor Akhtar (224*), Karachi Whites v Quetta at Karachi	1976-77
English	555	P. Holmes (224*) and H. Sutcliffe (313), Yorkshire v Essex at Leyton	1932
Australian	456	W. H. Ponsford (248) and E. R. Mayne (209), Victoria v Queensland at Melbourne	1923-24
Indian	451*	S. Desai (218*) and R. Binny (211*), Karnataka v Kerala at Chikmagalur	1977-78
South African	424	J. F. W. Nicolson (252*) and I. J. Siedle (174), Natal v Orange Free State at Bloemfontein	1926-27
West Indian	390	G. L. Wight (262*) and G. L. R. Gibbs (216), British Guiana v Barbados at Georgetown	1951-52
New Zealand	387	G. M. Turner (259) and T. W. Jarvis (182), New Zealand v West Indies at Georgetown	1971-72

Best Second-Wicket Stands

English	465*	J. A. Jameson (240*) and R. B. Kanhai (213*), Warwickshire v Gloucestershire at Birmingham	1974
Indian	455	B. B. Nimbalkar (443*) and K. V. Bhandarkar (205), Maharashtra v Kathiawar at Poona	1948-49

Australian	451	W. H. Ponsford (266) and D. G. Bradman (244), Australia v England at The Oval	1934
West Indian	446	C. C. Hunte (260) and G. S. Sobers (365*), West Indies v Pakistan at Kingston	1957-58
Pakistan	426	Arshad Pervez (220) and Mohsin Khan (220), Habib Bank v Income Tax Dept. at Lahore	1977-78
South African	305	S. K. Coen (165) and J. M. M. Commaille (186), Orange Free State v Natal at Bloemfontein	1926-27
New Zealand	301	C. S. Dempster (180) and C. F. W. Allcott (131), New Zealanders v Warwickshire at Birmingham	1927

Best Third-Wicket Stands

Pakistan	456	Khalid Irtiza (290) and Aslam Ali (236), United Bank v Multan at Karachi	1975-76
New Zealand	445	P. E. Whitelaw (195) and W. N. Carson (290), Auckland v Otago at Dunedin	1936-37
West Indian	434	J. B. Stollmeyer (324) and G. E. Gomez (190), Trinidad v British Guiana at Port-of-Spain	1946-47
English	424*	W. J. Edrich (168*) and D. C. S. Compton (252*), Middlesex v Somerset at Lord's	1948
Indian	410	L. Amarnath (262) and R. S. Modi (156), India in England v The Rest at Calcutta	1946-47
Australian	389	W. H. Ponsford (281*) and S. J. McCabe (192), Australians v MCC at Lord's	1934
South African	341	E. J. Barlow (201) and R. G. Pollock (175), South Africa v Australia at Adelaide	1963-64

Best Fourth-Wicket Stands

Indian	577	V. S. Hazare (288) and Gul Mahomed (319), Baroda v Holkar at Baroda	1946-47
West Indian	574*	C. L. Walcott (314*) and F. M. M. Worrell (255*), Barbados v Trinidad at Port-of-Spain	1945-46
English	448	R. Abel (193) and T. W. Hayward (273), Surrey v Yorkshire at The Oval	1899
Australian	424	I. S. Lee (258) and S. O. Quin (210), Victoria v Tasmania at Melbourne	1933-34
Pakistan	350	Mushtaq Mohammad (201) and Asif Iqbal (175), Pakistan v New Zealand at Dunedin	1972-73
South African	342	E. A. B. Rowan (196) and P. J. M. Gibb (203), Transvaal v N.E. Transvaal at Johannesburg	1952-53
New Zealand	324	J. R. Reid (188*) and W. M. Wallace (197), New Zealanders v Cambridge University at Cambridge	1949

Best Fifth-Wicket Stands

Australian	405	S. G. Barnes (234) and D. G. Bradman (234), Australia v England at Sydney	1946-47
English	393	E. G. Arnold (200*) and W. B. Burns (196), Worcestershire v Warwickshire at Birmingham	1909
Indian	360	Uday Merchant (217) and M. N. Raiji (170), Bombay v Hyderabad at Bombay	1947-48
Pakistan	355	Altaf Shah (276) and Tariq Bashir (196), House Building Finance Corporation v Multan at Multan	1976-77
South African	338	R. G. Pollock (194) and A. L. Wilmot (152), Eastern Province v Natal at Port Elizabeth	1975-76
West Indian	335	B. F. Butcher (151) and C. H. Lloyd (201*), West Indians v Glamorgan at Swansea	1969
New Zealand	266	B. Sutcliffe (355) and W. S. Haig (67), Otago v Auckland at Dunedin	1949-50

Best Sixth-Wicket Stands

West Indian	...	487*	G. A. Headley (344*) and C. C. Passailaigue (261*), Jamaica v Lord Tennyson's XI at Kingston	1931-32
Australian	....	428	M. A. Noble (284) and W. W. Armstrong (172*), Australians v Sussex at Hove	1902
English	....	411	R. M. Poore (304) and E. G. Wynyard (225), Hampshire v Somerset at Taunton	1899
Indian	....	371	V. M. Merchant (359*) and R. S. Modi (168), Bombay v Maharashtra at Bombay	1943-44
Pakistan	......	353	Salah-ud-Din (256) and Zaheer Abbas (197), Karachi v East Pakistan at Karachi	1968-69
South African	..	244*	J. M. M. Commaille (132*) and A. W. Palm (106*), Western Province v Griqualand West at Johannesburg	1923-24
New Zealand	..	220	G. M. Turner (223*) and K. J. Wadsworth (78), New Zealand v West Indies at Kingston	1971-72

Best Seventh-Wicket Stands

West Indian	...	347	D. St E. Atkinson (219) and C. C. Depeiza (122), West Indies v Australia at Bridgetown	1954-55
English	....	344	K. S. Ranjitsinhji (230) and W. Newham (153), Sussex v Essex at Leyton	1902
Australian	....	335	C. W. Andrews (253) and E. C. Bensted (155), Queensland v New South Wales at Sydney	1934-35
Pakistan	......	308	Waqar Hassan (189) and Imtiaz Ahmed (209), Pakistan v New Zealand at Lahore	1955-56
South African	..	299	B. Mitchell (159) and A. Melville (153), Transvaal v Griqualand West at Kimberley	1946-47
Indian	....	274	K. C. Ibrahim (250) and K. M. Rangnekar (138), Bijapur XI v Bengal XI at Bombay	1942-43
New Zealand	..	265	J. L. Powell (164) and N. Dorreen (105*), Canterbury v Otago at Christchurch	1929-30

Best Eighth-Wicket Stands

Australian	.....	433	A. Sims (184*) and V. T. Trumper (293), An Australian XI v Canterbury at Christchurch	1913-14
English	....	292	R. Peel (210*) and Lord Hawke (166), Yorkshire v Warwickshire at Birmingham	1896
West Indian	...	255	E. A. V. Williams (131*) and E. A. Martindale (134), Barbados v Trinidad at Bridgetown	1935-36
Pakistan	......	240	Gulfraz Khan (207) and Raja Sarfraz (102), Railways v Universities at Lahore	1976-77
Indian	....	236	C. T. Sarwate (235) and R. P. Singh (88), Holkar v Delhi and District at Delhi	1949-50
South African	..	222	D. P. B. Morkel (114) and S. S. L. Steyn (261*), Western Province v Border at Cape Town	1929-30
New Zealand	..	190*	J. E. Mills (104*) and F. W. Allcott (102*), New Zealanders v Civil Service at Chiswick	1927

Best Ninth-Wicket Stands

English	....	283	A. Warren (123) and J. Chapman (165), Derbyshire v Warwickshire at Blackwell	1910
Indian	....	245	V. S. Hazare (316*) and N. D. Nagarwalla (98), Maharashtra v Baroda at Poona	1939-40
New Zealand	..	239	H. B. Cave (118) and I. B. Leggat (142*), Central Districts v Otago at Dunedin	1952-53

Australian.....	232	C. Hill (365*) and E. Walkley (53), South Australia v New South Wales at Adelaide	1900-01
South African ..	221	N. V. Lindsay (160*) and G. R. McCubbin (97), Transvaal v Rhodesia at Bulawayo	1922-23
Pakistan	190	Asif Iqbal (146) and Intikhab Alam (51), Pakistan v England at The Oval	1967
West Indian ...	155*†	A. Persaud (85) and K. C. Glasgow (102), Demerara v Berbice at Rose Hall	1976-77

† 201 runs were added for this wicket in two separate partnerships; K. C. Glasgow retired hurt and was replaced by C. E. H. Croft when 155 had been added.

Best Tenth-Wicket Stands

Australian.....	307	A. F. Kippax (260*), and J. E. H. Hooker (62), New South Wales v Victoria at Melbourne	1928-29
Indian	249	C. T. Sarwate (124*) and S. N. Banerjee (121), Indians v Surrey at The Oval	1946
English	235	F. E. Woolley (185) and A. Fielder (112*), Kent v Worcestershire at Stourbridge	1909
New Zealand ..	184	R. C. Blunt (338*) and W. Hawkesworth (21), Otago v Canterbury at Christchurch	1931-32
South African ..	174	H. R. Lance (168) and D. Mackay-Coghill (57*), Transvaal v Natal at Johannesburg	1965-66
Pakistan	146	Mahmood Ahmed (204) and Tehsin Ilyas (28*), United Bank v Railways at Lahore	1976-77
West Indian ...	138	E. L. G. Hoad (149*) and H. C. Griffith (84), West Indians v Sussex at Hove	1933

Note: All the English record wicket partnerships were made in the County Championship.

HIGHEST AGGREGATES IN A SEASON: OVER 3,000

	Season	Inns	Not Outs	Runs	Highest Inns	100s	Average
D. C. S. Compton	1947	50	8	3,816	246	18	90.85
W. J. Edrich	1947	52	8	3,539	267*	12	80.43
T. W. Hayward	1906	61	8	3,518	219	13	66.37
L. Hutton	1949	56	6	3,429	269*	12	68.58
F. E. Woolley	1928	59	4	3,352	198	12	60.94
H. Sutcliffe	1932	52	7	3,336	313	14	74.13
W. R. Hammond	1933	54	5	3,323	264	13	67.81
E. H. Hendren	1928	54	7	3,311	209*	13	70.44
R. Abel	1901	68	8	3,309	247	7	55.15
W. R. Hammond	1937	55	5	3,252	217	13	65.04
M. J. K. Smith	1959	67	11	3,245	200*	8	57.94
E. H. Hendren	1933	65	9	3,186	301*	11	56.89
C. P. Mead	1921	52	6	3,179	280*	10	69.10
T. W. Hayward	1904	63	5	3,170	203	11	54.65
K. S. Ranjitsinhji	1899	58	8	3,159	197	8	63.18
C. B. Fry	1901	43	3	3,147	244	13	78.67
K. S. Ranjitsinhji	1900	40	5	3,065	275	11	87.57
L. E. G. Ames	1933	57	5	3,058	295	9	58.80
J. T. Tyldesley	1901	60	5	3,041	221	9	55.29
C. P. Mead	1928	50	10	3,027	180	13	75.67
J. B. Hobbs	1925	48	5	3,024	266*	16	70.32
G. E. Tyldesley	1928	48	10	3,024	242	10	79.57
W. E. Alley	1961	64	11	3,019	221*	11	56.96
W. R. Hammond	1938	42	2	3,011	271	15	75.27

	Season	Inns	Not Outs	Runs	Highest Inns	100s	Average
E. H. Hendren	1923	51	12	3,010	200*	13	77.17
H. Sutcliffe	1931	42	11	3,006	230	13	96.96
J. H. Parks	1937	63	4	3,003	168	11	50.89
H. Sutcliffe	1928	44	5	3,002	228	13	76.97

Note: W. G. Grace scored 2,739 runs in 1871 – the first batsman to reach 2,000 runs in a season. He made ten hundreds and twice exceeded 200, with an average of 78.25 in all first-class matches. At the time, the over consisted of four balls.

HIGHEST AGGREGATES IN A SEASON: OVER 2,000

Since Reduction of Championship Matches in 1969

	Season	Inns	Not Outs	Runs	Highest Inns	100s	Average
Zaheer Abbas	1976	39	5	2,554	230*	11	75.11
G. Boycott	1971	30	5	2,503	233	13	100.12
G. M. Turner	1973	44	8	2,416	153*	9	67.11
G. M. Turner	1970	46	7	2,379	154*	10	61.00
J. H. Edrich	1969	39	7	2,238	181	8	69.93
M. J. Harris	1971	45	1	2,238	177	9	50.86
R. T. Virgin	1970	47	0	2,223	178	7	47.29
I. V. A. Richards	1977	35	2	2,161	241*	7	65.48
J. B. Bolus	1970	53	9	2,143	147*	2	48.70
D. L. Amiss	1976	38	6	2,110	203	8	65.92
Majid J. Khan	1972	38	4	2,074	204	8	61.00
G. Boycott	1970	42	5	2,051	260*	4	55.43
J. H. Edrich	1971	44	1	2,031	195*	6	47.23
D. L. Amiss	1978	41	3	2,030	162	7	53.42

Note: The feat was not achieved in 1974, 1975, 1979 or 1980.

HIGHEST BATTING AVERAGES IN AN ENGLISH SEASON

(Qualification: 12 innings)

	Season	Inns	Not Outs	Runs	Highest Inns	100s	Average
D. G. Bradman	1938	26	5	2,429	278	13	115.66
G. Boycott	1979	20	5	1,538	175*	6	102.53
W. A. Johnston	1953	17	16	102	28*	0	102.00
G. Boycott	1971	30	5	2,503	233	13	100.12
D. G. Bradman	1930	36	6	2,960	334	10	98.66
H. Sutcliffe	1931	42	11	3,006	230	13	96.96
R. M. Poore	1899	21	4	1,551	304	7	91.23
D. R. Jardine	1927	14	3	1,002	147	5	91.09
D. C. S. Compton	1947	50	8	3,816	246	18	90.85
D. G. Bradman	1948	31	4	2,428	187	11	89.92
K. S. Ranjitsinhji	1900	40	5	3,065	275	11	87.57
D. R. Jardine	1928	17	4	1,133	193	3	87.15
W. R. Hammond	1946	26	5	1,783	214	7	84.90
D. G. Bradman	1934	27	3	2,020	304	7	84.16
R. B. Kanhai	1975	22	9	1,073	178*	3	82.53
J. B. Hobbs	1928	38	7	2,542	200*	12	82.00
C. B. Fry	1903	40	7	2,683	234	9	81.30
W. J. Edrich	1947	52	8	3,539	267*	12	80.43
E. D. Weekes	1950	33	4	2,310	304*	7	79.65
G. E. Tyldesley	1928	48	10	3,024	242	10	79.57

	Season	Inns	Not Outs	Runs	Highest Inns	100s	Average
Nawab of Pataudi	1934	15	3	945	214*	3	78.75
A. Shrewsbury	1887	23	2	1,653	267	8	78.71
C. B. Fry	1901	43	3	3,147	244	13	78.67
W. G. Grace	1871	39	4	2,739	268	10	78.25
J. B. Hobbs	1926	41	3	2,949	316*	10	77.60
W. H. Ponsford	1934	27	4	1,784	281*	5	77.56
E. H. Hendren	1923	51	12	3,010	200*	13	77.17
H. Sutcliffe	1928	44	5	3,002	228	13	76.97
W. R. Hammond	1934	35	4	2,366	302*	8	76.32
G. S. Sobers	1970	32	9	1,742	183	7	75.73
C. P. Mead	1928	50	10	3,027	180	13	75.67
C. Hallows	1927	44	13	2,343	233*	7	75.58
W. R. Hammond	1938	42	2	3,011	271	15	75.27
Zaheer Abbas	1976	39	5	2,554	230*	11	75.11

HIGHEST AGGREGATES OUTSIDE ENGLAND

	Season	Inns	Not Outs	Runs	Highest Inns	100s	Average
In Australia							
D. G. Bradman	1928-29	24	6	1,690	340*	7	93.88
In South Africa							
J. R. Reid	1961-62	30	2	1,915	203	7	68.39
In West Indies							
E. H. Hendren	1929-30	18	5	1,765	254*	6	135.76
In New Zealand							
G. M. Turner	1975-76	20	4	1,244	177*	5	77.75
In India							
C. G. Borde	1964-65	28	3	1,604	168	6	64.16
In Pakistan							
Zaheer Abbas	1973-74	24	5	1,597	174	5	84.05

Note: In more than one country, the following aggregates of over 2,000 runs have been recorded.

	Season	Inns	Not Outs	Runs	Highest Inns	100s	Average
S. M. Gavaskar	1978-79	30	6	2,121	205	10	88.37
J. R. Reid	1961-62	36	2	2,083	203	7	61.26

1,000 RUNS IN MAY

Three batsmen have scored 1,000 runs in May, and four others – D. G. Bradman twice – have made 1,000 runs before June. Their innings-by-innings records are as follows:

	Runs	Average
W. G. Grace, May 9 to May 30, 1895 (22 days):		
13, 103, 18, 25, 288, 52, 257, 73*, 18, 169	1,016	112.88
"W.G." was within two months of completing his 47th year.		
W. R. Hammond, May 7 to May 31, 1927 (25 days):		
27, 135, 108, 128, 17, 11, 99, 187, 4, 30, 83, 7, 192, 14	1,042	74.42
Hammond scored his 1,000th run on May 28, thus equalling "W.G.'s" record of 22 days.		
C. Hallows, May 5 to May 31, 1928 (27 days):		
100, 101, 51*, 123, 101*, 22, 74, 104, 58, 34*, 232	1,000	125.00
T. W. Hayward, April 16 to May 31, 1900:		
120*, 55, 108, 131*, 55, 193, 120, 5, 6, 3, 40, 146, 92	1,074	97.63
D. G. Bradman, April 30 to May 31, 1930:		
236, 185*, 78, 9, 48*, 66, 4, 44, 252*, 32, 47*	1,001	143.00
On April 30 Bradman scored 75 not out.		

D. G. Bradman, April 30 to May 31, 1938:

258, 58, 137, 278, 2, 143, 145*, 5, 30* 1,056 150.85
Bradman scored 258 on April 30, and his 1,000th run on May 27.

W. J. Edrich, April 30 to May 31, 1938:

104, 37, 115, 63, 20*, 182, 71, 31, 53*, 45, 15, 245, 0, 9, 20* 1,010 84.16
Edrich scored 21 not out on April 30. All his runs were scored at
Lord's.

G. M. Turner, April 24 to May 31, 1973:

41, 151*, 143, 85, 7, 8, 17*, 81, 13, 53, 44, 153*, 3, 2, 66*, 30, 10*,
111 .... 1,018 78.30

1,000 RUNS IN TWO SEPARATE MONTHS

Only four batsmen, C. B. Fry, K. S. Ranjitsinhji, H. Sutcliffe, and L. Hutton, have scored over 1,000 runs in each of two months in the same season. L. Hutton, by scoring 1,294 in June 1949, made more runs in a single month than anyone else. He also made 1,050 in August 1949.

HANDLED THE BALL

J. Grundy	MCC v Kent at Lord's	1857
G. Bennett	Kent v Sussex at Hove	1872
W. H. Scotton	Smokers v Non-Smokers at East Melbourne	1886-87
C. W. Wright	Nottinghamshire v Gloucestershire at Bristol	1893
E. Jones	South Australia v Victoria at Melbourne	1894-95
A. W. Nourse	South Africans v Sussex at Hove	1907
E. T. Benson	MCC v Auckland at Auckland	1929-30
A. W. Gilbertson	Otago v Auckland at Auckland	1952-53
W. R. Endean	South Africa v England at Cape Town	1956-57
P. J. P. Burge	Queensland v New South Wales at Sydney	1958-59
Dildar Awan	Services v Lahore at Lahore	1959-60
Mahmood-ul-Hasan	Karachi University v Railways-Quetta at Karachi	1960-61
Ali Raza	Karachi Greens v Hyderabad at Karachi	1961-62
Mohammad Yusuf	Rawalpindi v Peshawar at Peshawar	1962-63
A. Rees	Glamorgan v Middlesex at Lord's	1965
Pervez Akhtar	Multan v Karachi Greens at Sahiwal	1971-72
Javaid Mirza	Railways v Punjab at Lahore	1972-73
R. G. Pollock	Eastern Province v Western Province at Cape Town	1973-74
C. I. Dey	Northern Transvaal v Orange Free State at Bloemfontein	1973-74
Nasir Valika	Karachi Whites v National Bank at Karachi	1974-75
Haji Yousuf	National Bank v Railways at Lahore	1974-75
Masood-ul-Hasan	PIA v National Bank 'B' at Lyallpur	1975-76
D. K. Pearse	Natal v Western Province at Cape Town	1978-79
A. M. J. Hilditch	Australia v Pakistan at Perth	1978-79
Musleh-ud-Din	Railways v Lahore at Lahore	1979-80

OBSTRUCTING THE FIELD

C. A. Absolom	Cambridge University v Surrey at The Oval	1868
T. Straw	Worcestershire v Warwickshire at Worcester	1899
T. Straw	Worcestershire v Warwickshire at Birmingham	1901
J. P. Whiteside	Leicestershire v Lancashire at Leicester	1901
L. Hutton	England v South Africa at The Oval	1951
J. A. Hayes	Canterbury v Central Districts at Christchurch	1954-55
D. D. Deshpande	Madhya Pradesh v Uttar Pradesh at Benares	1956-57
K. Ibadulla	Warwickshire v Hampshire at Coventry	1963
Kaiser	Dera Ismail Khan v Pakistan W.R. at Lahore	1964-65
Qasim Feroze	Bahawalpur v Universities at Lahore	1974-75
T. Quirk	Northern Transvaal v Border at East London	1978-79

Note: This method of dismissal has occurred twice in the *John Player League:*

R. W. Tolchard	Leicestershire v Middlesex at Lord's	1972
D. J. S. Taylor	Somerset v Warwickshire at Birmingham	1980

HIT THE BALL TWICE

H. E. Bull	MCC v Oxford University at Lord's	1864
H. R. J. Charlwood	Sussex v Surrey at Hove	1872
I. J. Salmon	Wellington v Hawke's Bay at Wellington	1873-74
R. G. Barlow	North v South at Lord's	1878
P. S. Wimble	Transvaal v Griqualand West at Kimberley	1892-93
G. B. Nicholls	Somerset v Gloucestershire at Bristol	1896
A. F. A. Lilley	Warwickshire v Yorkshire at Birmingham	1897
J. H. King	Leicestershire v Surrey at The Oval	1906
A. P. Binns	Jamaica v British Guiana at Georgetown	1956-57
K. Bavanna	Andhra v Mysore at Guntur	1963-64
Zaheer Abbas	PIA 'A' v Karachi Blues at Karachi	1969-70

BOWLING AND FIELDING RECORDS

FOUR WICKETS WITH CONSECUTIVE BALLS

J. Wells	Kent v Sussex at Brighton	1862
G. Ulyett	Lord Harris's XI v New South Wales at Sydney	1878-79
J. B. Hide	Sussex v MCC and Ground at Lord's	1890
F. J. Shacklock	Nottinghamshire v Somerset at Nottingham	1893
A. D. Downes	Otago v Auckland at Dunedin	1893-94
F. Martin	MCC and Ground v Derbyshire at Lord's	1895
A. W. Mold	Lancashire v Nottinghamshire at Nottingham	1895
W. Brearley†	Lancashire v Somerset at Manchester	1905
S. Haigh	MCC v Army XI at Pretoria	1905-06
A. E. Trott‡	Middlesex v Somerset at Lord's	1907
F. A. Tarrant	Middlesex v Gloucestershire at Bristol	1907
A. Drake	Yorkshire v Derbyshire at Chesterfield	1914
S. G. Smith	Northamptonshire v Warwickshire at Birmingham	1914
H. A. Peach	Surrey v Sussex at The Oval	1924
A. F. Borland	Natal v Griqualand West at Kimberley	1926-27
J. E. H. Hooker†	New South Wales v Victoria at Sydney	1928-29
R. K. Tyldesley†	Lancashire v Derbyshire at Derby	1929
R. J. Crisp	Western Province v Griqualand West at Johannesburg	1931-32
R. J. Crisp	Western Province v Natal at Durban	1933-34
A. R. Gover	Surrey v Worcestershire at Worcester	1935
W. H. Copson	Derbyshire v Warwickshire at Derby	1937
W. A. Henderson	N.E. Transvaal v Orange Free State at Bloemfontein	1937-38
F. Ridgway	Kent v Derbyshire at Folkestone	1951
A. K. Walker§	Nottinghamshire v Leicestershire at Leicester	1956
S. N. Mohol	Board of Control President's XI v Minister for Small Savings' XI at Poona	1965-66
P. I. Pocock	Surrey v Sussex at Eastbourne	1972

    † *Not all in the same innings.*
    ‡ *Trott achieved another hat-trick in the same innings of this, his benefit match.*
    § *Walker dismissed Firth with the last ball of the first innings and Lester, Tompkin and Smithson with the first three balls of the second innings, a feat without parallel.*

Notes: In their match with England at The Oval in 1863, Surrey lost four wickets in the course of a four-ball over from G. Bennett.

    Sussex lost five wickets in the course of the final (six-ball) over of their match with Surrey at Eastbourne in 1972. P. I. Pocock, who had taken three wickets in his previous over, captured four more, taking in all seven wickets with eleven balls, a feat unique in first-class matches. (The eighth wicket fell to a run out.)

    P. G. H. Fender (Surrey) took six Middlesex wickets with eleven balls (including five with seven) at Lord's in 1927.

HAT-TRICKS

Double Hat-Trick

Besides Trott's performance, which is given in the preceding section, the following instances are recorded of players having performed the hat-trick twice in the same match, Rao doing so in the same innings.

A. Shaw	Nottinghamshire v Gloucestershire at Nottingham	1884
T. J. Matthews	Australia v South Africa at Manchester	1912
C. W. L. Parker	Gloucestershire v Middlesex at Bristol	1924
R. O. Jenkins	Worcestershire v Surrey at Worcester	1949
J. S. Rao	Services v Northern Punjab at Amritsar	1963-64
Amin Lakhani	Combined XI v Indians at Multan	1978-79

Five Wickets with Six Consecutive Balls

W. H. Copson	Derbyshire v Warwickshire at Derby	1937
W. A. Henderson	N.E. Transvaal v Orange Free State at Bloemfontein	1937-38
P. I. Pocock	Surrey v Sussex at Eastbourne	1972

Most Hat-Tricks

Seven times: D. V. P. Wright.
Six times: T. W. J. Goddard, C. W. L. Parker.
Five times: S. Haigh, V. W. C. Jupp, A. E. G. Rhodes, F. A. Tarrant.
Four times: R. G. Barlow, J. T. Hearne, J. C. Laker, G. A. R. Lock, G. G. Macaulay, T. J. Matthews, M. J. Procter, T. Richardson, F. S. Truman.
Three times: W. M. Bradley, H. J. Butler, W. H. Copson, R. J. Crisp, J. W. H. T. Douglas, J. A. Flavell, A. P. Freeman, G. Giffen, K. Higgs, A. Hill, R. D. Jackman, R. O. Jenkins, A. S. Kennedy, W. H. Lockwood, E. A. McDonald, T. L. Pritchard, J. S. Rao, A. Shaw, F. R. Spofforth, J. B. Statham, M. W. Tate, H. Trumble, D. Wilson, G. A. Wilson.

Most Recent Instances

In 1979-80:

Rashid Khan	PIA v National Bank at Lahore
M. H. Toynbee	Central Districts v Northern Districts at Gisborne

In 1980: See Features of 1980.

Unusual Hat-Tricks

All 'Stumped':	by W. H. Brain off C. L. Townsend, Gloucestershire v Somerset at Cheltenham	1893
All 'Caught':	by G. J. Thompson off S. G. Smith, Northamptonshire v Warwickshire at Birmingham	1914
	by Cyril White off R. Beesly, Border v Griqualand West at Queenstown	1946-47
	by G. O. Dawkes (wicket-keeper) off H. L. Jackson, Derbyshire v Worcestershire at Kidderminster	1958
All 'LBW':	H. Fisher, Yorkshire v Somerset at Sheffield	1932
	J. A. Flavell, Worcestershire v Lancashire at Manchester ..	1963
	M. J. Procter, Gloucestershire v Essex at Westcliff	1972
	B. J. Ikin, Griqualand West v OFS at Kimberley	1973-74
	M. J. Procter, Gloucestershire v Yorkshire at Cheltenham ..	1979

TEN WICKETS IN ONE INNINGS

	O	M	R		
E. Hinkly (Kent)				v England at Lord's	1848
J. Wisden (North)				v South at Lord's	1850
V. E. Walker (England)	43	17	74	v Surrey at The Oval	1859
E. M. Grace (MCC)	32.2	7	69	v Gents of Kent at Canterbury	1862
V. E. Walker (Middlesex)	44.2		104	v Lancashire at Manchester	1865
G. Wootton (All England)				v Yorkshire at Sheffield	1865
S. E. Butler (Oxford)	24.1	11	38	v Cambridge at Lord's	1871
Jas. Lillywhite (South)	60.2	22	129	v North at Canterbury	1872
W. G. Grace (MCC)	46.1	15	92	v Kent at Canterbury	1873
A. Shaw (MCC)	36.2	8	73	v North at Lord's	1874
E. Barratt (Players)	29	11	43	v Australians at The Oval	1878
G. Giffen (Australian XI)	26	10	66	v The Rest at Sydney	1883-84
W. G. Grace (MCC)	36.2	17	49	v Oxford University at Oxford	1886
G. Burton (Middlesex)	52.3	25	59	v Surrey at The Oval	1888
†A. E. Moss (Canterbury)	21.3	10	28	v Wellington at Christchurch	1889-90
S. M. J. Woods (Cambridge U.)	31	6	69	v Thornton's XI at Cambridge	1890
T. Richardson (Surrey)	15.3	3	45	v Essex at The Oval	1894
H. Pickett (Essex)	27	11	32	v Leicestershire at Leyton	1895
E. J. Tyler (Somerset)	34.3	15	49	v Surrey at Taunton	1895
W. P. Howell (Australians)	23.2	14	28	v Surrey at The Oval	1899
C. H. G. Bland (Sussex)	25.2	0	48	v Kent at Tonbridge	1899
J. Briggs (Lancashire)	28.5	7	55	v Worcestershire at Manchester	1900
A. E. Trott (Middlesex)	14.2	5	42	v Somerset at Taunton	1900
F. Hinds (A. B. St Hill's XI)	19.1	6	36	v Trinidad at Port-of-Spain	1900-01
A. Fielder (Players)	24.5	1	90	v Gentlemen at Lord's	1906
E. G. Dennett (Gloucestershire)	19.4	7	40	v Essex at Bristol	1906
A. E. E. Vogler (E. Province)	12	2	26	v Griqualand West at Johannesburg	1906-07
C. Blythe (Kent)	16	7	30	v Northamptonshire at Northampton	1907
A. Drake (Yorkshire)	8.5	0	35	v Somerset at Weston-super-Mare	1914
F. A. Tarrant (Maharaja of Cooch Behar's XI)	35.4	4	90	v Lord Willingdon's XI at Poona	1918-19
W. Bestwick (Derbyshire)	19	2	40	v Glamorgan at Cardiff	1921
A. A. Mailey (Australians)	28.4	5	66	v Gloucestershire at Cheltenham	1921
C. W. L. Parker (Glos.)	40.3	13	79	v Somerset at Bristol	1921
T. Rushby (Surrey)	17.5	4	43	v Somerset at Taunton	1921
J. C. White (Somerset)	42.2	11	76	v Worcestershire at Worcester	1921
G. C. Collins (Kent)	19.3	4	65	v Nottinghamshire at Dover	1922
H. Howell (Warwickshire)	25.1	5	51	v Yorkshire at Birmingham	1923
A. S. Kennedy (Players)	22.4	10	37	v Gentlemen at The Oval	1927
G. O. B. Allen (Middlesex)	25.3	10	40	v Lancashire at Lord's	1929
A. P. Freeman (Kent)	42	9	131	v Lancashire at Maidstone	1929
G. Geary (Leicestershire)	16.2	8	18	v Glamorgan at Pontypridd	1929
C. V. Grimmett (Australians)	22.3	8	37	v Yorkshire at Sheffield	1930
A. P. Freeman (Kent)	30.4	8	53	v Essex at Southend	1930
H. Verity (Yorkshire)	18.4	6	36	v Warwickshire at Leeds	1931
A. P. Freeman (Kent)	36.1	9	79	v Lancashire at Manchester	1931
V. W. C. Jupp (Northants)	39	6	127	v Kent at Tunbridge Wells	1932
H. Verity (Yorkshire)	19.4	16	10	v Nottinghamshire at Leeds	1932
T. W. Wall (South Australia)	12.4	2	36	v New South Wales at Sydney	1932-33
T. B. Mitchell (Derbyshire)	19.1	4	64	v Leicestershire at Leicester	1935
J. Mercer (Glamorgan)	26	10	51	v Worcestershire at Worcester	1936
T. W. J. Goddard (Glos.)	28.4	4	113	v Worcestershire at Cheltenham	1937
T. F. Smailes (Yorkshire)	17.1	5	47	v Derbyshire at Sheffield	1939
E. A. Watts (Surrey)	24.1	8	67	v Warwickshire at Birmingham	1939
W. E. Hollies (Warwickshire)	20.4	4	49	v Nottinghamshire at Birmingham	1946

	O	M	R		
J. M. Sims (East)	18.4	2	90	v West at Kingston	1948
T. E. Bailey (Essex)	39.4	9	90	v Lancashire at Clacton	1949
J. K. R. Graveney (Glos.)	18.4	2	66	v Derbyshire at Chesterfield	1949
R. Berry (Lancashire)	36.2	9	102	v Worcestershire at Blackpool	1953
S. P. Gupte (Bombay)	24.2	7	78	v Combined XI at Bombay	1954-55
J. C. Laker (Surrey)	46	18	88	v Australians at The Oval	1956
J. C. Laker (England)	51.2	23	53	v Australia at Manchester	1956
G. A. R. Lock (Surrey)	29.1	18	54	v Kent at Blackheath	1956
K. Smales (Nottinghamshire)	41.3	20	66	v Gloucestershire at Stroud	1956
P. Chatterjee (Bengal)	19	11	20	v Assam at Jorhat	1956-57
J. D. Bannister (Warwickshire)	23.3	11	41	v Comb. Services at Birmingham	1959
A. J. G. Pearson (Cambridge University)	30.3	8	78	v Leicestershire at Loughborough	1961
N. I. Thomson (Sussex)	34.2	19	49	v Warwickshire at Worthing	1964
P. J. Allan (Queensland)	15.6	3	61	v Victoria at Melbourne	1965-66
I. J. Brayshaw (W. Australia)	17.6	4	44	v Victoria at Perth	1967-68
Shahid Mahmood (Karachi Whites)	25	5	58	v Khairpur at Karachi	1969-70

† *On début in first-class cricket.*

MOST WICKETS IN A MATCH

19-90	J. C. Laker	England v Australia at Manchester	1956
17-48	C. Blythe	Kent v Northamptonshire at Northampton	1907
17-50	C. T. B. Turner	Australians v England XI at Hastings	1888
17-54	W. P. Howell	Australians v Western Province at Cape Town	1902-03
17-56	C. W. L. Parker	Gloucestershire v Essex at Gloucester	1925
17-67	A. P. Freeman	Kent v Sussex at Hove	1922
17-89	W. G. Grace	Gloucestershire v Nottinghamshire at Cheltenham	1877
17-89	F. C. L. Matthews	Nottinghamshire v Northants at Nottingham	1923
17-91	H. Dean	Lancashire v Yorkshire at Liverpool	1913
17-91	H. Verity	Yorkshire v Essex at Leyton	1933
17-92	A. P. Freeman	Kent v Warwickshire at Folkestone	1932
17-103	W. Mycroft	Derbyshire v Hampshire at Southampton	1876
17-106	G. R. Cox	Sussex v Warwickshire at Horsham	1926
17-106	T. W. J. Goddard	Gloucestershire v Kent at Bristol	1939
17-119	W. Mead	Essex v Hampshire at Southampton	1895
17-137	W. Brearley	Lancashire v Somerset at Manchester	1905
17-159	S. F. Barnes	England v South Africa at Johannesburg	1913-14
17-201	G. Giffen	South Australia v Victoria at Adelaide	1885-86
17-212	J. C. Clay	Glamorgan v Worcestershire at Swansea	1937

Notes: H. A. Arkwright took eighteen wickets for 96 runs in a 12-a-side match for Gentlemen of MCC v Gentlemen of Kent at Canterbury in 1861.

W. Mead took seventeen wickets for 205 runs for Essex v Australians at Leyton in 1893, the year before Essex were raised to first-class status.

F. P. Fenner took seventeen wickets for Cambridge Town Club v University of Cambridge at Cambridge in 1844.

OUTSTANDING ANALYSES

(Also see Ten Wickets in One Innings)

	O	M	R	W		
H. Verity (Yorkshire)	19.4	16	10	10	v Nottinghamshire at Leeds	1932
G. Elliott (Victoria)	19	17	2	9	v Tasmania at Launceston	1857-58
Ahad Khan (Railways)	6.3	4	7	9	v Dera Ismail Khan at Lahore	1964-65
J. C. Laker (England)	14	12	2	8	v The Rest at Bradford	1950
D. Shackleton (Hampshire)	11.1	7	4	8	v Somerset at Weston-super-Mare	1955

	O	M	R	W		
E. Peate (Yorkshire)	16	11	5	8	v Surrey at Holbeck	1883
F. R. Spofforth (Australians)	8.3	6	3	7	v England XI at Birmingham ..	1884
W. A. Henderson (N.E. Transvaal)	9.3	7	4	7	v Orange Free State at Bloemfontein	1937-38
Rajinder Goel (Haryana) ...	7	4	4	7	v Jammu and Kashmir at Chandigarh	1977-78
V. I. Smith (South Africans)	4.5	3	1	6	v Derbyshire at Derby	1947
S. Cosstick (Victoria)	21.1	20	1	6	v Tasmania at Melbourne	1868-69
Israr Ali (Bahawalpur)	11	10	1	6	v Dacca U. at Bahawalpur	1957-58
A. D. Pougher (MCC)	3	3	0	5	v Australians at Lord's	1896
G. R. Cox (Sussex)	6	6	0	5	v Somerset at Weston-super-Mare	1921
R. K. Tyldesley (Lancashire).	5	5	0	5	v Leicestershire at Manchester .	1924
P. T. Mills (Gloucestershire) .	6.4	6	0	5	v Somerset at Bristol	1928

SIXTEEN OR MORE WICKETS IN A DAY

17-48	C. Blythe	Kent v Northamptonshire at Northampton	1907
17-91	H. Verity	Yorkshire v Essex at Leyton	1933
17-106	T. W. J. Goddard	Gloucestershire v Kent at Bristol	1939
16-38	T. Emmett	Yorkshire v Cambridgeshire at Hunslet	1869
16-52	J. Southerton	South v North at Lord's	1875
16-69	T. G. Wass	Nottinghamshire v Lancashire at Liverpool	1906
16-38	A. E. E. Vogler	E. Province v Griqualand West at Johannesburg ...	1906-07
16-103	T. G. Wass	Nottinghamshire v Essex at Nottingham	1908
16-83	J. C. White	Somerset v Worcestershire at Bath	1919

200 OR MORE WICKETS IN A SEASON

	Season	Overs	Maidens	Runs	Wickets	Average
A. P. Freeman ...	1928	1,976.1	423	5,489	304	18.05
A. P. Freeman ...	1933	2,039	651	4,549	298	15.26
T. Richardson ...	1895‡	1,690.1	463	4,170	290	14.37
C. T. B. Turner**	1888†	2,427.2	1,127	3,307	283	11.68
A. P. Freeman ...	1931	1,618	360	4,307	276	15.60
A. P. Freeman ...	1930	1,914.3	472	4,632	275	16.84
T. Richardson ...	1897‡	1,603.4	495	3,945	273	14.45
A. P. Freeman ...	1929	1,670.5	381	4,879	267	18.27
W. Rhodes	1900	1,553	455	3,606	261	13.81
J. T. Hearne	1896‡	2,003.1	818	3,670	257	14.28
A. P. Freeman ...	1932	1,565.5	404	4,149	253	16.39
W. Rhodes	1901	1,565	505	3,797	251	15.12
T. W. J. Goddard	1937	1,478.1	359	4,158	248	16.76
W. C. Smith	1910	1,423.3	420	3,225	247	13.05
T. Richardson ...	1896‡	1,656.2	526	4,015	246	16.32
A. E. Trott	1899‡	1,772.4	587	4,086	239	17.09
T. W. J. Goddard	1947	1,451.2	344	4,119	238	17.30
M. W. Tate	1925	1,694.3	472	3,415	228	14.97
J. T. Hearne	1898‡	1,802.2	781	3,120	222	14.05
C. W. L. Parker ..	1925	1,512.3	478	3,311	222	14.91
G. A. Lohmann ..	1890‡	1,759.1	737	2,998	220	13.62
M. W. Tate	1923	1,608.5	331	3,061	219	13.97
C. F. Root	1925	1,493.2	416	3,770	219	17.21
C. W. L. Parker ..	1931	1,320.4	386	3,125	219	14.26
H. Verity	1936	1,289.3	463	2,847	216	13.18
G. A. R. Lock ...	1955	1,408.4	497	3,109	216	14.39
C. Blythe	1909	1,273.5	343	3,128	215	14.54
E. Peate	1882†	1,853.1	868	2,466	214	11.52
A. W. Mold	1895‡	1,629	598	3,400	213	15.96

	Season	Overs	Maidens	Runs	Wickets	Average
W. Rhodes	1902	1,306.3	405	2,801	213	13.15
C. W. L. Parker . .	1926	1,739.5	556	3,920	213	18.40
J. T. Hearne	1893‡	1,741.4	667	3,492	212	16.47
A. P. Freeman . . .	1935	1,503.2	320	4,562	212	21.51
G. A. R. Lock . . .	1957	1,194.1	449	2,550	212	12.02
A. E. Trott	1900	1,547.1	363	4,923	211	23.33
G. G. Macaulay . .	1925	1,338.2	307	3,268	211	15.48
H. Verity	1935	1,279.2	453	3,032	211	14.36
J. Southerton	1870†	1,876.5	709	3,074	210	14.63
G. A. Lohmann . .	1888†	1,649.1	783	2,280	209	10.90
C. H. Parkin	1923	1,356.2	356	3,543	209	16.94
G. H. Hirst	1906	1,306.1	271	3,434	208	16.50
F. R. Spofforth . .	1884†	1,577	653	2,774	207	13.25
A. W. Mold	1894‡	1,288.3	456	2,548	207	12.30
C. W. L. Parker . .	1922	1,294.5	445	2,712	206	13.16
A. S. Kennedy . . .	1922	1,346.4	366	3,444	205	16.80
M. W. Tate	1924	1,469.5	465	2,818	205	13.74
E. A. McDonald .	1925	1,249.4	282	3,828	205	18.67
A. P. Freeman . . .	1934	1,744.4	440	4,753	205	23.18
C. W. L. Parker . .	1924	1,303.5	411	2,913	204	14.27
G. A. Lohmann . .	1889‡	1,614.1	646	2,714	202	13.43
H. Verity	1937	1,386.2	487	3,168	202	15.68
A. Shaw	1878†	2,630	1,586	2,203	201	10.96
E. G. Dennett . . .	1907	1,216.2	305	3,227	201	16.05
A. R. Gover	1937	1,219.4	191	3,816	201	18.98
C. H. Parkin	1924	1,162.5	357	2,735	200	13.67
T. W. J. Goddard .	1935	1,553	384	4,073	200	20.36
A. R. Gover	1936	1,159.2	185	3,547	200	17.73
T. W. J. Goddard .	1939§	819	139	2,973	200	14.86
R. Appleyard	1951	1,313.2	391	2,829	200	14.14

† *Indicates 4-ball overs; ‡ 5-ball overs. All others were 6-ball overs except § 8-ball overs.*
** *Exclusive of matches not reckoned as first-class.*

Notes: In four consecutive seasons (1928-31), A. P. Freeman took 1,122 wickets, and in eight consecutive seasons (1928-35), 2,090 wickets. In each of these eight seasons he took over 200 wickets.

T. Richardson took 1,005 wickets in four consecutive seasons (1894-97).

In 1896, J. T. Hearne took his 100th wicket as early as June 12. In 1931, C. W. L. Parker did the same and A. P. Freeman obtained his 100th wicket a day later.

C. T. B. Turner is the only bowler to take over 100 wickets in first-class matches in a season in Australia – 106 wickets in twelve matches, 1887-88.

100 OR MORE WICKETS IN A SEASON

Since Reduction of Championship Matches in 1969

	Season	Overs	Maidens	Runs	Wickets	Average
L. R. Gibbs	1971	1,024.1	295	2,475	131	18.89
R. D. Jackman . .	1980	745.2	220	1,864	121	15.40
A. M. E. Roberts .	1974	727.4	198	1,621	119	13.62
B. S. Bedi	1974	1,085.3	307	2,758	112	24.62
P. G. Lee	1975	799.5	193	2,067	112	18.45
D. L. Underwood .	1978	815.1	359	1,594	110	14.49
R. M. H. Cottam .	1969	989.1	252	2,294	109	21.04
M. J. Procter	1977	777.3	226	1,967	109	18.04
T. W. Cartwright .	1969	880.5	373	1,748	108	16.18
M. J. Procter	1969	639.3	160	1,623	108	15.02
P. J. Sainsbury . . .	1971	845.5	332	1,874	107	17.51
D. J. Shepherd . . .	1970	1,123.3	420	2,031	106	19.16

	Season	Overs	Maidens	Runs	Wickets	Average
J. K. Lever	1978	681.1	160	1,610	106	15.18
J. K. Lever	1979	700	166	1,834	106	17.30
D. L. Underwood	1979	799.2	334	1,575	106	14.85
N. Gifford	1970	965.5	331	2,092	105	19.92
F. J. Titmus	1970	1,106.3	320	2,804	105	26.70
B. S. Bedi	1973	864.2	307	1,884	105	17.94
T. W. Cartwright .	1971	976.4	407	1,852	104	17.80
Intikhab Alam ...	1971	1,097.4	244	2,950	104	28.36
F. J. Titmus	1971	1,065.1	341	2,355	104	22.64
D. Wilson	1969	964.1	384	1,772	102	17.37
R. N. S. Hobbs ..	1970	736	178	2,183	102	21.40
D. L. Underwood	1971	945.5	368	1,986	102	19.47
D. L. Underwood	1969	808.3	355	1,561	101	15.45
P. G. Lee	1973	740.3	181	1,901	101	18.82
Sarfraz Nawaz ..	1975	728.4	173	2,051	101	20.30
M. W. W. Selvey .	1978	743.5	199	1,929	101	19.09
D. R. Doshi	1980	962.2	268	2,700	101	26.73
I. T. Botham	1978	605.2	143	1,640	100	16.40

Note: The feat was not achieved in 1972 or 1976.

1,500 WICKETS OR MORE IN A CAREER

	Career	Wickets	Runs	Average
W. Rhodes	1898-1930	4,187	69,993	16.71
A. P. Freeman	1914-36	3,776	69,577	18.42
C. W. L. Parker	1903-35	3,278	63,821	19.46
J. T. Hearne	1888-1923	3,061	54,342	17.75
T. W. J. Goddard	1922-52	2,979	59,116	19.84
A. S. Kennedy	1907-36	2,874	61,044	21.24
D. Shackleton	1948-69	2,857	53,303	18.65
G. A. R. Lock	1946-71	2,844	54,710	19.23
F. J. Titmus	1949-80	2,827	63,221	22.36
W. G. Grace	1865-1908	2,809	50,932	18.13
M. W. Tate	1912-37	2,784	50,567	18.16
G. H. Hirst	1891-1929	2,739	51,300	18.72
C. Blythe	1899-1914	2,506	42,136	16.81
W. E. Astill	1906-39	2,431	57,781	23.76
J. C. White	1909-37	2,356	43,759	18.57
W. E. Hollies	1932-57	2,323	48,656	20.94
F. S. Trueman	1949-69	2,304	42,154	18.29
J. B. Statham	1950-68	2,260	36,995	16.36
R. T. D. Perks	1930-55	2,233	53,770	24.07
J. Briggs	1879-1900	2,221	35,390	15.93
D. J. Shepherd	1950-72	2,218	47,298	21.32
E. G. Dennett	1903-26	2,147	42,568	19.82
T. Richardson	1892-1905	2,105	38,794	18.42
T. E. Bailey	1945-67	2,082	48,170	23.13
F. E. Woolley	1906-38	2,068	41,066	19.85
G. Geary	1912-38	2,063	41,339	20.03
D. V. P. Wright	1932-57	2,056	49,305	23.98
J. Newman	1906-30	2,032	51,211	25.20
R. Illingworth	1951-78	2,031	40,485	19.93
A. Shaw	1864-97	2,021	24,496	12.13
S. Haigh	1895-1913	2,012	32,091	15.94
H. Verity	1930-39	1,956	29,146	14.90
J. C. Laker	1946-65	1,944	35,789	18.40
W. Attewell	1881-1900	1,932	29,745	15.39
D. L. Underwood	1963-80	1,926	37,519	19.48
A. V. Bedser	1939-60	1,924	39,281	20.41

	Career	Wickets	Runs	Average
W. Mead	1892-1913	1,916	36,388	18.99
A. E. Relf	1900-21	1,897	39,724	20.94
P. G. H. Fender	1910-36	1,894	47,457	25.05
J. W. H. T. Douglas	1901-30	1,893	44,159	23.32
J. H. Wardle	1946-58	1,846	35,027	18.97
G. R. Cox	1895-1928	1,843	42,138	22.86
M. S. Nichols	1924-39	1,841	39,845	21.64
J. W. Hearne	1909-36	1,839	44,927	24.43
G. G. Macaulay	1920-35	1,837	32,440	17.65
J. B. Mortimore	1950-75	1,807	41,904	23.18
G. A. Lohmann	1884-98	1,805	25,110	13.91
C. Cook	1946-64	1,782	36,578	20.52
R. Peel	1882-99	1,754	28,446	16.21
H. L. Jackson	1947-63	1,733	30,101	17.36
T. P. B. Smith	1929-52	1,697	45,193	26.63
J. Southerton	1854-79	1,680	24,257	14.43
A. E. Trott	1892-1911	1,674	35,316	21.09
A. W. Mold	1889-1901	1,673	26,012	15.54
T. G. Wass	1896-1920	1,666	34,091	20.46
V. W. C. Jupp	1909-38	1,658	38,166	23.01
C. Gladwin	1939-58	1,653	30,265	18.30
W. E. Bowes	1928-47	1,639	27,470	16.76
N. Gifford	1960-80	1,626	35,688	21.94
A. W. Wellard	1927-50	1,614	39,292	24.34
N. I. Thomson	1952-72	1,597	32,866	20.57
J. Mercer	1919-47	1,593	37,302	23.41
G. J. Thompson	1897-1922	1,591	30,060	18.89
T. Emmett	1866-88	1,582	21,147	13.36
J. M. Sims	1929-53	1,582	39,401	24.90
W. Voce	1927-52	1,558	35,961	23.08
A. R. Gover	1928-48	1,555	36,753	23.63
T. W. Cartwright	1952-77	1,536	29,357	19.11
K. Higgs	1958-80	1,530	36,132	23.61
James Langridge	1924-53	1,530	34,524	22.56
J. A. Flavell	1949-67	1,529	32,847	21.48
B. S. Bedi	1961-80	1,527	33,106	21.68
C. F. Root	1910-33	1,512	31,933	21.11
R. K. Tyldesley	1919-35	1,509	25,980	17.21
Intikhab Alam	1957-80	1,505	41,870	27.82

Note: W. G. Grace's career figures as published previously (2,876 – 51,545 – 17.92) included a number of matches which cannot be regarded as first-class.

100 WICKETS IN A SEASON EIGHT TIMES OR MORE

23 times: W. Rhodes 200 wkts (3).
20 times: D. Shackleton.
17 times: A. P. Freeman 300 wkts (1), 200 wkts (7).
16 times: T. W. J. Goddard 200 wkts (4), C. W. L. Parker 200 wkts (5), R. T. D. Perks, F. J. Titmus.
15 times: J. T. Hearne 200 wkts (3), G. H. Hirst 200 wkts (1), A. S. Kennedy 200 wkts (1).
14 times: C. Blythe 200 wkts (1), W. E. Hollies, G. A. R. Lock 200 wkts (2), M. W. Tate 200 wkts (3), J. C. White.
13 times: J. B. Statham.
12 times: J. Briggs, E. G. Dennett 200 wkts (1), C. Gladwin, D. J. Shepherd, N. I. Thomson, F. S. Trueman.
11 times: A. V. Bedser, G. Geary, S. Haigh, J. C. Laker, M. S. Nichols, A. E. Relf.
10 times: W. Attewell, R. Illingworth, H. L. Jackson, V. W. C. Jupp, G. G. Macaulay 200 wkts (1), W. Mead, T. B. Mitchell, T. Richardson 200 wkts (3), R. K. Tyldesley, J. H. Wardle, T. G. Wass, D. V. P. Wright.

9 times: W. E. Astill, T. E. Bailey, W. E. Bowes, C. Cook, W. G. Grace, R. Howorth, J. Mercer, A. W. Mold 200 wkts (2), J. Newman, C. F. Root 200 wkts (1), A. Shaw 200 wkts (1), J. Southerton 200 wkts (1), D. L. Underwood, H. Verity 200 wkts (3).

8 times: T. W. Cartwright, H. Dean, J. A. Flavell, A. R. Gover 200 wkts (2), H. Larwood, G. A. Lohmann 200 wkts (3), R. Peel, J. M. Sims, F. A. Tarrant, R. Tattersall, G. J. Thompson, G. E. Tribe, A. W. Wellard, F. E. Woolley, J. A. Young.

ALL-ROUND CRICKET

20,000 RUNS AND 2,000 WICKETS IN A CAREER

	Career	Runs	Average	Wickets	Average	'Doubles'
W. E. Astill ..	1906-39	22,726	22.54	2,431	23.76	9
T. E. Bailey ..	1945-67	28,642	33.42	2,082	23.13	8
W. G. Grace .	1865-1908	54,211	39.45	2,809	18.13	7
G. H. Hirst ..	1891-1929	36,323	34.13	2,739	18.72	14
R. Illingworth	1951-78	23,977	28.40	2,031	19.93	6
W. Rhodes ...	1898-1930	39,802	30.83	4,187	16.71	16
M. W. Tate ..	1912-37	21,717	25.01	2,784	18.16	8
F. J. Titmus ..	1949-80	21,587	23.11	2,827	22.36	8
F. E. Woolley ..	1906-38	58,969	40.75	2,068	19.85	8

THE DOUBLE

2,000 RUNS AND 200 WICKETS IN A SEASON

1906	G. H. Hirst	2,385 runs and 208 wickets

3,000 RUNS AND 100 WICKETS IN A SEASON

1937	J. H. Parks	3,003 runs and 101 wickets

2,000 RUNS AND 100 WICKETS IN A SEASON

	Season	Runs	Wickets		Season	Runs	Wickets
W. G. Grace	1876	2,622	129	F. E. Woolley	1914	2,272	125
C. L. Townsend ..	1899	2,440	101	J. W. Hearne	1920	2,148	142
G. L. Jessop	1900	2,210	104	V. W. C. Jupp ...	1921	2,169	121
G. H. Hirst	1904	2,501	132	F. E. Woolley	1921	2,101	167
G. H. Hirst	1905	2,266	110	F. E. Woolley	1922	2,022	163
W. Rhodes	1909	2,094	141	F. E. Woolley	1923	2,091	101
W. Rhodes	1911	2,261	117	L. F. Townsend ..	1933	2,268	100
F. A. Tarrant	1911	2,030	111	D. E. Davies	1937	2,012	103
J. W. Hearne	1913	2,036	124	James Langridge .	1937	2,082	101
J. W. Hearne	1914	2,116	123	T. E. Bailey	1959	2,011	100

1,000 RUNS AND 200 WICKETS IN A SEASON

	Season	Runs	Wickets		Season	Runs	Wickets
A. E. Trott	1899	1,175	239	M. W. Tate	1923	1,168	219
A. E. Trott	1900	1,337	211	M. W. Tate	1924	1,419	205
A. S. Kennedy ...	1922	1,129	205	M. W. Tate	1925	1,290	228

The double feat of scoring 1,000 runs and taking 100 wickets in one season of first-class cricket has been accomplished as follows, the last instance being by F. J. Titmus in 1967:

Sixteen times: W. Rhodes. **Fourteen times:** G. H. Hirst.
Ten times: V. W. C. Jupp. **Nine times:** W. E. Astill.
Eight times: T. E. Bailey, M. S. Nichols, A. E. Relf, F. A. Tarrant, M. W. Tate, F. J. Titmus, F. E. Woolley.
Seven times: W. G. Grace, G. E. Tribe.
Six times: P. G. H. Fender, R. Illingworth, James Langridge.
Five times: J. W. H. T. Douglas, J. W. Hearne, A. S. Kennedy, J. Newman.
Four times: E. G. Arnold, J. R. Gunn, R. Kilner, B. R. Knight.
Three times: W. W. Armstrong (Australians), L. C. Braund, G. Giffen (Australians), N. E. Haig, R. Howorth, C. B. Llewellyn, J. B. Mortimore, Ray Smith, S. G. Smith, L. F. Townsend, A. W. Wellard.
Twice: W. H. R. Andrews, F. R. Brown, D. B. Close, J. N. Crawford, D. E. Davies, B. Dooland, F. R. Foster, G. Goonesena, J. L. Hopwood, M. J. Horton, R. O. Jenkins, G. L. Jessop, W. H. Lockwood, S. H. Martin, J. H. Parks, G. H. Pope, J. S. Pressdee, R. A. Sinfield, C. T. Studd, G. J. Thompson, C. L. Townsend, A. E. Trott, A. J. Watkins, J. C. White.
Once: D. A. Allen, W. E. Alley, J. Bailey, F. Barratt, M. W. Booth, B. J. T. Bosanquet, W. Brockwell, V. Broderick, Hon. F. S. G. Calthorpe, T. W. Cartwright, H. L. Collins (Australians), L. N. Constantine (West Indians), J. A. Cuffe, W. R. Cuttell, G. Davidson, A. Drake, G. A. Faulkner (South Africans), W. Flowers, A. E. R. Gilligan, J. M. Gregory (Australians), S. Haigh, J. Hallows, T. W. Hayward, F. S. Jackson, V. E. Jackson, E. H. Killick, J. H. King, V. M. H. Mankad (Indians), J. R. Mason, B. L. Muncer, K. E. Palmer, F. A. Pearson, R. Peel, R. W. V. Robins, C. F. Root, H. L. Simms, T. F. Smailes, T. P. B. Smith, S. J. Storey, L. J. Todd, H. Trumble (Australians), J. van Geloven, J. Vine, E. Wainwright, P. M. Walker, J. E. Walsh, A. F. Wensley, W. Wooller.

Notes: L. E. G. Ames, in 1928, scored 1,919 runs and obtained 121 wickets while keeping wicket. In 1929 his aggregates were, 1,795 runs and 127 wickets, and in 1932, 2,482 runs and 100 wickets.

J. T. Murray, in 1957, scored 1,025 runs and obtained 104 wickets while keeping wicket.

Since the reduction of Championship matches in 1969, the following players have scored 1,000 runs and taken 75 wickets in a season: Mushtaq Mohammad (1969), A. W. Greig (1971), R. A. Hutton (1971), K. D. Boyce (1972) and M. J. Procter (1979).

CENTURY AND HAT-TRICK

W. G. Grace, MCC v Kent at Canterbury; 123, five for 82, and six for 47 including hat-trick (12-a-side). 1874

G. Giffen, Australians v Lancashire at Manchester; 13, 113, and six for 55 including hat-trick. 1884

W. E. Roller, Surrey v Sussex at The Oval; 204, four for 28 including hat-trick, and two for 16. (Unique instance of 200 and hat-trick) 1885

W. B. Burns, Worcestershire v Gloucestershire at Worcester; 102*, three for 56, including hat-trick, and two for 21. 1913

V. W. C. Jupp, Sussex v Essex at Colchester; 102, six for 61, including hat-trick, and six for 78. 1921

R. E. S. Wyatt, MCC v Ceylon at Colombo; 124 and five for 39 including hat-trick. 1926-27

L. N. Constantine, West Indians v Northamptonshire at Northampton; seven for 45, including hat-trick, 107 (five 6s), and six for 67. 1928

D. E. Davies, Glamorgan v Leicestershire at Leicester; 139, four for 27, and three for 31 including hat-trick. 1937

V. M. Merchant, Dr C. R. Pereira's XI v Sir Homi Mehta's XI at Bombay; 1, 142, three for 31 including hat-trick, and no wicket for 17. 1946-47

M. J. Procter, Gloucestershire v Essex at Westcliff-on-Sea; 51, 102, three for 43, and five for 30 including hat-trick (all lbw). 1972

M. J. Procter, Gloucestershire v Leicestershire at Bristol; 122, no wkt for 32 and seven for 26 including hat-trick 1979

CENTURY AND TEN WICKETS IN ONE INNINGS

V. E. Walker, England v Surrey at The Oval; ten for 74, four for 17, 20* and 108.   1859
E. M. Grace, MCC v Gentlemen of Kent at Canterbury; five for 77, ten for 69,
    and 192*.   1862
W. G. Grace, MCC v Oxford University at Oxford; two for 60, ten for 49, and 104.   1886
F. A. Tarrant, Maharaja of Cooch Behar's XI v Lord Willingdon's XI at Poona;
    ten for 90, one for 22, 182* and 8*.   1918-19

CENTURY IN EACH INNINGS AND FIVE WICKETS TWICE

G. H. Hirst, Yorkshire v Somerset at Bath; six for 70, five for 45, 111 and 117*. . . .   1906

WICKET-KEEPING RECORDS
Most Dismissals in a Career

	Catches	Stumpings	Total
J. T. Murray (1952-75)	1,270	257	1,527
H. Strudwick (1902-27)	1,215	253	1,468
R. W. Taylor (1960-80)	1,238	150	1,388
F. H. Huish (1895-1914)	952	376	1,328
D. Hunter (1889-1909)	995	372	1,327
B. Taylor (1949-73)	1,082	212	1,294
H. R. Butt (1890-1912)	971	291	1,262
J. H. Board (1891-1915)	852	354	1,206
H. Elliott (1920-47)	895	300	1,195
J. M. Parks (1949-76)	1,089	93	1,182
R. Booth (1951-70)	946	176	1,122
L. E. G. Ames (1926-51)	698	415	1,113
A. P. E. Knott (1965-80)	982	108	1,090
G. Duckworth (1923-47)	751	339	1,090
H. W. Stephenson (1948-64)	752	332	1,084
J. G. Binks (1955-75)	895	176	1,071
T. G. Evans (1939-69)	811	249	1,060
A. Long (1960-80)	922	124	1,046
G. O. Dawkes (1937-61)	896	146	1,042
W. L. Cornford (1921-47)	656	334	1,000

100 OR MORE DISMISSALS IN A SEASON

127 (79c 48s)	L. E. G. Ames, Kent	1929
121 (69c 52s)	L. E. G. Ames, Kent	1928
110 (62c 48s)	H. Yarnold, Worcestershire	1949
107 (77c 30s)	G. Duckworth, Lancashire	1928
107 (96c 11s)	J. G. Binks, Yorkshire	1960
104 (82c 22s)	J. T. Murray, Middlesex	1957
102 (70c 32s)	F. H. Huish, Kent	1913
102 (95c 7s)	J. T. Murray, Middlesex	1960
101 (85c 16s)	R. Booth, Worcestershire	1960
100 (62c 38s)	F. H. Huish, Kent	1911
100 (36c 64s)	L. E. G. Ames, Kent	1932
100 (91c 9s)	R. Booth, Worcestershire	1964

TEN OR MORE DISMISSALS IN A MATCH

12 (8c 4s)	E. Pooley	Surrey v Sussex at The Oval	1868
12 (9c 3s)	D. Tallon	Queensland v New South Wales at Sydney	1938-39
12 (9c 3s)	H. B. Taber	New South Wales v South Australia at Adelaide	1968-69
11 (all c)	A. Long	Surrey v Sussex at Hove	1964
11 (all c)	R. W. Marsh	Western Australia v Victoria at Perth	1975-76
10 (5c 5s)	H. Phillips	Sussex v Surrey at The Oval	1872
10 (2c 8s)	E. Pooley	Surrey v Kent at The Oval	1878
10 (9c 1s)	T. W. Oates	Nottinghamshire v Middlesex at Nottingham	1906
10 (1c 9s)	F. H. Huish	Kent v Surrey at The Oval	1911
10 (9c 1s)	J. C. Hubble	Kent v Gloucestershire at Cheltenham	1923
10 (8c 2s)	H. Elliott	Derbyshire v Lancashire at Manchester	1935
10 (7c 3s)	P. Corrall	Leicestershire v Sussex at Hove	1936
10 (9c 1s)	R. A. Saggers	New South Wales v Combined XI at Brisbane	1940-41
10 (all c)	A. E. Wilson	Gloucestershire v Hampshire at Portsmouth	1953
10 (7c 3s)	B. N. Jarman	South Australia v New South Wales at Adelaide ...	1961-62
10 (all c)	L. A. Johnson	Northamptonshire v Sussex at Worthing	1963
10 (all c)	R. W. Taylor	Derbyshire v Hampshire at Chesterfield	1963
10 (8c 2s)	L. A. Johnson	Northamptonshire v Warwickshire at Birmingham ...	1965
10 (9c 1s)	R. C. Jordon	Victoria v South Australia at Melbourne	1970-71
10 (all c)	R. W. Marsh†	Western Australia v South Australia at Perth	1976-77
10 (6c 4s)	Taslim Arif	National Bank v Punjab at Lahore	1978-79
10 (9c 1s)	Arif-ud-Din	United Bank v Karachi 'B' at Karachi............	1978-79
10 (all c)	R. W. Taylor	England v India at Bombay	1979-80

† *Marsh also scored a hundred (104), a unique "double".*

SEVEN OR MORE DISMISSALS IN AN INNINGS

8 (all c)	A. T. W. Grout	Queensland v Western Australia at Brisbane	1959-60
7 (4c 3s)	E. J. Smith	Warwickshire v Derbyshire at Birmingham	1926
7 (6c 1s)	W. Farrimond	Lancashire v Kent at Manchester	1930
7 (all c)	W. F. F. Price	Middlesex v Yorkshire at Lord's	1937
7 (3c 4s)	D. Tallon	Queensland v Victoria at Brisbane	1938-39
7 (all c)	R. A. Saggers	New South Wales v Combined XI at Brisbane	1940-41
7 (1c 6s)	H. Yarnold	Worcestershire v Scotland at Dundee	1951
7 (4c 3s)	J. W. Brown	Scotland v Ireland at Dublin	1957
7 (6c 1s)	N. Kirsten	Border v Rhodesia at East London	1959-60
7 (all c)	M. S. Smith	Natal v Border at East London	1959-60
7 (all c)	K. V. Andrew	Northamptonshire v Lancashire at Manchester ...	1962
7 (all c)	A. Long	Surrey v Sussex at Hove	1964
7 (all c)	R. M. Schofield	Central Districts v Wellington at Wellington	1964-65
7 (all c)	R. W. Taylor	Derbyshire v Glamorgan at Derby	1966
7 (6c 1s)	H. B. Taber	New South Wales v South Australia at Adelaide ...	1968-69
7 (6c 1s)	E. W. Jones	Glamorgan v Cambridge University at Cambridge .	1970
7 (6c 1s)	S. Benjamin	Central Zone v North Zone at Bombay	1973-74
7 (all c)	R. W. Taylor	Derbyshire v Yorkshire at Chesterfield	1975
7 (6c 1s)	Shahid Israr	Karachi Whites v Quetta at Karachi	1976-77
7 (5c 2s)	Taslim Arif	National Bank v Punjab at Lahore	1978-79
7 (all c)	Wasim Bari	Pakistan v New Zealand at Auckland	1978-79
7 (all c)	R. W. Taylor	England v India at Bombay	1979-80

WICKET-KEEPERS' HAT-TRICKS

W. H. Brain, Gloucestershire v Somerset at Cheltenham, 1893 – three stumpings off successive balls from C. L. Townsend.

G. O. Dawkes, Derbyshire v Worcestershire at Kidderminster, 1958 – three catches off successive balls from H. L. Jackson.

MOST CATCHES – EXCLUDING WICKET-KEEPERS

In a Career

1,018	F. E. Woolley (1906-38)		810	D. B. Close (1949-78)
872	W. G. Grace (1865-1908)		786	J. G. Langridge (1928-55)
830	G. A. R. Lock (1946-71)		755	E. H. Hendren (1907-38)
819	W. R. Hammond (1920-51)		755	C. A. Milton (1948-74)

In a Season

78	W. R. Hammond	1928		65	W. R. Hammond	1925
77	M. J. Stewart	1957		65	P. M. Walker	1959
73	P. M. Walker	1961		65	D. W. Richardson	1961
71	P. J. Sharpe	1962		64	J. Tunnicliffe	1904
70	J. Tunnicliffe	1901		64	K. F. Barrington	1957
69	J. G. Langridge	1955		64	G. A. R. Lock	1957
69	P. M. Walker	1960		63	K. J. Grieves	1950
65	J. Tunnicliffe	1895		63	C. A. Milton	1956

In a Match

10	W. R. Hammond	Gloucestershire v Surrey at Cheltenham	1928
8	W. B. Burns	Worcestershire v Yorkshire at Bradford	1907
8	A. H. Bakewell	Northamptonshire v Essex at Leyton	1928
8	W. R. Hammond	Gloucestershire v Worcestershire at Cheltenham	1932
8	K. J. Grieves	Lancashire v Sussex at Manchester	1951
8	C. A. Milton	Gloucestershire v Sussex at Hove	1952
8	G. A. R. Lock	Surrey v Warwickshire at The Oval	1957
8	J. M. Prodger	Kent v Gloucestershire at Cheltenham	1961
8	P. M. Walker	Glamorgan v Derbyshire at Swansea	1970
8	Javed Miandad	Habib Bank v Universities at Lahore	1977-78

In an Innings

7	M. J. Stewart	Surrey v Northamptonshire at Northampton	1957
7	A. S. Brown	Gloucestershire v Nottinghamshire at Nottingham	1966

THE SIDES

HIGHEST TOTALS

1,107	Victoria v New South Wales at Melbourne	1926-27
1,059	Victoria v Tasmania at Melbourne	1922-23
951-7 dec.	Sind v Baluchistan at Karachi	1973-74
918	New South Wales v South Australia at Sydney	1900-01
912-8 dec.	Holkar v Mysore at Indore	1945-46
910-6 dec.	Railways v Dera Ismail Khan at Lahore	1964-65
903-7 dec.	England v Australia at The Oval	1938
887	Yorkshire v Warwickshire at Birmingham	1896
849	England v West Indies at Kingston	1929-30
843	Australians v Oxford and Cambridge Universities Past and Present at Portsmouth	1893

HIGHEST FOR EACH FIRST-CLASS COUNTY

Derbyshire	645	v Hampshire at Derby	1898
Essex	692	v Somerset at Taunton	1895
Glamorgan	587-8	v Derbyshire at Cardiff	1951
Gloucestershire	653-6	v Glamorgan at Bristol	1928
Hampshire	672-7	v Somerset at Taunton	1899
Kent	803-4	v Essex at Brentwood	1934
Lancashire	801	v Somerset at Taunton	1895
Leicestershire	701-4	v Worcestershire at Worcester	1906
Middlesex	642-3	v Hampshire at Southampton	1923
Northamptonshire	557-6	v Sussex at Hove	1914
Nottinghamshire	739-7	v Leicestershire at Nottingham	1903
Somerset	675-9	v Hampshire at Bath	1924
Surrey	811	v Somerset at The Oval	1899
Sussex	705-8	v Surrey at Hastings	1902
Warwickshire	657-6	v Hampshire at Birmingham	1899
Worcestershire	633	v Warwickshire at Worcester	1906
Yorkshire	887	v Warwickshire at Birmingham	1896

LOWEST TOTALS

12	Oxford University v MCC and Ground at Oxford	†1877
12	Northamptonshire v Gloucestershire at Gloucester	1907
13	Wellington v Nelson at Nelson	1862-63
13	Auckland v Canterbury at Auckland	1877-78
13	Nottinghamshire v Yorkshire at Nottingham	1901
15	MCC v Surrey at Lord's	1839
15	Victoria v MCC at Melbourne	†1903-04
15	Northamptonshire v Yorkshire at Northampton	†1908
15	Hampshire v Warwickshire at Birmingham	1922
	(Following on, Hampshire scored 521 and won by 155 runs)	
16	MCC and Ground v Surrey at Lord's	1872
16	Derbyshire v Nottinghamshire at Nottingham	1879
16	Surrey v Nottinghamshire at The Oval	1880
16	Warwickshire v Kent at Tonbridge	1913
16	Trinidad v Barbados at Bridgetown	1941-42
16	Border v Natal at East London (first innings)	1959-60
17	Gentlemen of Kent v Gentlemen of England at Lord's	1850
17	Gloucestershire v Australians at Cheltenham	1896
18	The 'B's v England at Lord's	1831
18	Kent v Sussex at Gravesend	†1867
18	Tasmania v Victoria at Melbourne	1868-69
18	Australians v MCC and Ground at Lord's	†1896
18	Border v Natal at East London (second innings)	1959-60
19	Sussex v Surrey at Godalming	1830
19	Sussex v Nottinghamshire at Hove	†1873
19	MCC and Ground v Australians at Lord's	1878
19	Wellington v Nelson at Nelson	1885-86

† *Signifies that one man was absent.*

LOWEST TOTAL IN A MATCH

34	(16 and 18) Border v Natal at East London	1959-60
42	(27 and 15) Northamptonshire v Yorkshire at Northampton	1908

Note: Northamptonshire batted one man short in each innings.

LOWEST FOR EACH FIRST-CLASS COUNTY

Derbyshire	16	v Nottinghamshire at Nottingham	1879
Essex	30	v Yorkshire at Leyton	1901
Glamorgan	22	v Lancashire at Liverpool	1924
Gloucestershire	17	v Australians at Cheltenham	1896
Hampshire	15	v Warwickshire at Birmingham	1922
Kent	18	v Sussex at Gravesend	1867
Lancashire	25	v Derbyshire at Manchester	1871
Leicestershire	25	v Kent at Leicester	1912
Middlesex	20	v MCC at Lord's	1864
Northamptonshire	12	v Gloucestershire at Gloucester	1907
Nottinghamshire	13	v Yorkshire at Nottingham	1901
Somerset	25	v Gloucestershire at Bristol	1947
Surrey	16	v Nottinghamshire at The Oval	1880
Sussex	19	v Nottinghamshire at Hove	1873
Warwickshire	16	v Kent at Tonbridge	1913
Worcestershire	24	v Yorkshire at Huddersfield	1903
Yorkshire	23	v Hampshire at Middlesbrough	1965

HIGHEST MATCH AGGREGATES

2,376 for 38 wickets	Maharashtra v Bombay at Poona	1948-49
2,078 for 40 wickets	Bombay v Holkar at Bombay	1944-45
1,981 for 35 wickets	England v South Africa at Durban	1938-39
1,929 for 39 wickets	New South Wales v South Australia at Sydney	1925-26
1,911 for 34 wickets	New South Wales v Victoria at Sydney	1908-09
1,905 for 40 wickets	Otago v Wellington at Dunedin	1923-24

In England

1,723 for 31 wickets	England v Australia at Leeds	1948
1,601 for 29 wickets	England v Australia at Lord's	1930
1,507 for 28 wickets	England v West Indies at The Oval	1976
1,502 for 28 wickets	MCC v New Zealanders at Lord's	1927
1,499 for 31 wickets	T. N. Pearce's XI v Australians at Scarborough	1961
1,496 for 24 wickets	England v Australia at Nottingham	1938
1,494 for 37 wickets	England v Australia at The Oval	1934
1,492 for 33 wickets	Worcestershire v Oxford University at Worcester	1904
1,477 for 32 wickets	Hampshire v Oxford University at Southampton	1913
1,477 for 33 wickets	England v South Africa at The Oval	1947
1,475 for 27 wickets	Northamptonshire v Surrey at Northampton	1920

HIGHEST FOURTH INNINGS TOTALS

(Unless otherwise stated, the side making the runs won the match.)

654-5	England v South Africa at Durban	1938-39
	(After being set 696 to win. The match was left drawn on the tenth day.)	
604	Maharashtra v Bombay at Poona	1948-49
	(After being set 959 to win.)	
576-8	Trinidad v Barbados at Port-of-Spain	1945-46
	(After being set 672 to win. Match drawn on fifth day.)	

572	New South Wales v South Australia at Sydney	1907-08
	(After being set 593 to win.)	
529-9	Combined XI v South Africans at Perth	1963-64
	(After being set 579 to win. Match drawn on fourth day.)	
518	Victoria v Queensland at Brisbane	1926-27
	(After being set 753 to win.)	
507-7	Cambridge University v MCC and Ground at Lord's	1896
502-6	Middlesex v Nottinghamshire at Nottingham	1925
	(Game won by an unfinished stand of 271; a county record.)	
502-8	Players v Gentlemen at Lord's	1900
500-7	South African Universities v Western Province at Stellenbosch	1978-79

LARGEST VICTORIES

Largest Innings Victories

Inns and 851 runs:	Railways (910-6 dec.) v Dera Ismail Khan (Lahore)	1964-65
Inns and 666 runs:	Victoria (1,059) v Tasmania (Melbourne)	1922-23
Inns and 656 runs:	Victoria (1,107) v New South Wales (Melbourne)	1926-27
Inns and 605 runs:	New South Wales (918) v South Australia (Sydney)	1900-01
Inns and 579 runs:	England (903-7 dec.) v Australia (The Oval)	1938
Inns and 575 runs:	Sind (951-7 dec.) v Baluchistan (Karachi)	1973-74
Inns and 527 runs:	New South Wales (713) v South Australia (Adelaide)	1908-09
Inns and 517 runs:	Australians (675) v Nottinghamshire (Nottingham)	1921

Largest Victories by Runs Margins

685 runs:	New South Wales (235 and 761-8 dec.) v Queensland (Sydney)	1929-30
675 runs:	England (521 and 342-8 dec.) v Australia (Brisbane)	1928-29
638 runs:	New South Wales (304 and 770) v South Australia (Adelaide)	1920-21
625 runs:	Sargodha (376 and 416) v Lahore Municipal Corporation (Faisalabad)	1978-79
609 runs:	Muslim Commercial Bank (575 and 282-0 dec.) v WAPDA (Lahore) .	1977-78
571 runs:	Victoria (304 and 649) v South Australia (Adelaide)	1926-27
562 runs:	Australia (701 and 327) v England (The Oval)	1934

Victory Without Losing a Wicket

Lancashire (166-0 dec. and 66-0) beat Leicestershire by ten wickets (Manchester) .	1956
Karachi 'A' (277-0 dec.) beat Sind 'A' by an innings and 77 runs (Karachi)	1957-58
Railways (236-0 dec. and 16-0) beat Jammu and Kashmir by ten wickets (Srinagar)	1960-61
Karnataka (451-0 dec.) beat Kerala by an innings and 186 runs (Chikmagalur) ...	1977-78

TIE MATCHES IN FIRST-CLASS CRICKET

There have been 27 tie matches since the First World War.

Somerset v Sussex at Taunton	1919
The last Sussex batsman not allowed to bat under Law 45 [subsequently Law 17 and now Law 31]	
Orange Free State v Eastern Province at Bloemfontein	1925-26
(Eastern Province had two wickets to fall.)	
Essex v Somerset at Chelmsford	1926
(Although Essex had one man to go in, MCC ruled that the game should rank as a tie. The ninth wicket fell half a minute before time.)	
Gloucestershire v Australians at Bristol	1930
Victoria v MCC at Melbourne	1932-33
(Victoria's third wicket fell to the last ball of the match when one run was needed to win.)	

Worcestershire v Somerset at Kidderminster 1939
Southern Punjab v Baroda at Patiala 1945-46
Essex v Northamptonshire at Ilford 1947
Hampshire v Lancashire at Bournemouth 1947
D. G. Bradman's XI v A. L. Hassett's XI at Melbourne 1948-49
Hampshire v Kent at Southampton 1950
Sussex v Warwickshire at Hove 1952
Essex v Lancashire at Brentwood 1952
Northamptonshire v Middlesex at Peterborough 1953
Yorkshire v Leicestershire at Huddersfield 1954
Sussex v Hampshire at Eastbourne 1955
Victoria v New South Wales at Melbourne 1956-57
T. N. Pearce's XI v New Zealanders at Scarborough 1958
Essex v Gloucestershire at Leyton 1959
Australia v West Indies (First Test) at Brisbane 1960-61
Bahawalpur v Lahore 'B' at Bahawalpur 1961-62
Hampshire v Middlesex at Portsmouth 1967
England XI v England Under 25 XI at Scarborough 1968
Yorkshire v Middlesex at Bradford 1973
Sussex v Essex at Hove 1974
South Australia v Queensland at Adelaide 1976-77
Central Districts v England XI at New Plymouth 1977-78
Allied Bank v Peshawar at Peshawar 1979-80

Note: Since 1948 a tie has been recognised only when the scores are level with all the wickets down in the fourth innings. This ruling applies to all grades of cricket, and in the case of a one-day match to the second innings, provided that the match has not been brought to a further conclusion.

MATCHES BEGUN AND FINISHED IN ONE DAY

The most notable instances during the nineteenth and present centuries are:

The 'B's v England at Lord's, June 13 1831
Cambridge University v MCC and Ground at Cambridge, May 18 1837
MCC and Ground v Cambridge University at Lord's, June 19 1848
Gentlemen of Kent v Gentlemen of England at Lord's, July 1 1850
North v South at Lord's, July 15 1850
MCC and Ground v Sussex at Lord's, June 2 1856
Surrey v Sussex at The Oval, July 16 1857
Kent v England at Lord's, July 5 1858
MCC and Ground v Oxford University at Lord's, June 18 1863
North of Thames v South of Thames at Lord's, July 8 1868
MCC and Ground v Surrey at Lord's, May 14 1872
Middlesex v Oxford University at Prince's, June 18 1874
North v South at Lord's, May 17 1875
Oxford University v MCC and Ground at Oxford, May 24 1877
MCC and Ground v Australians at Lord's, May 27 1878
Oxford University v MCC and Ground at Oxford, May 28 1880
An England XI v Australians at Aston Lower Ground, Birmingham, May 26 1884
MCC and Ground v Lancashire at Lord's, May 18 1886
North v South, at Lord's, May 30 1887
Lancashire v Surrey at Manchester, August 2 1888
MCC and Ground v Nottinghamshire at Lord's, June 1 1891
Lancashire v Somerset at Manchester, August 9 1892
MCC and Ground v Sussex at Lord's, May 2 1894
Lancashire v Somerset at Manchester, July 17 1894
Yorkshire v Somerset at Huddersfield, July 19 1894
Leicestershire v Surrey at Leicester, June 10 1897
Hampshire v Yorkshire at Southampton, May 27 (H. Baldwin's benefit) 1898
Middlesex v Somerset at Lord's, May 23 (W. Flowers' benefit) 1899
Yorkshire v Worcestershire at Bradford, May 7 1900
MCC and Ground v London County at Lord's, May 20 1903

TEST MATCH RECORDS

SCORERS OF 1,500 RUNS IN TESTS

FOR ENGLAND

	Tests	Inns	Not Outs	Runs	Highest Inns	100s	Average
M. C. Cowdrey	114	188	15	7,624	182	22	44.06
W. R. Hammond	85	140	16	7,249	336*	22	58.45
G. Boycott	94	165	21	7,115	246*	19	49.40
L. Hutton	79	138	15	6,971	364	19	56.67
K. F. Barrington	82	131	15	6,806	256	20	58.67
D. C. S. Compton	78	131	15	5,807	278	17	50.06
J. B. Hobbs	61	102	7	5,410	211	15	56.94
J. H. Edrich	77	127	9	5,138	310*	12	43.54
T. W. Graveney	79	123	13	4,882	258	11	44.38
H. Sutcliffe	54	84	9	4,555	194	16	60.73
P. B. H. May	66	106	9	4,537	285*	13	46.77
E. R. Dexter	62	102	8	4,502	205	9	47.89
A. P. E. Knott	93	145	14	4,211	135	5	32.14
D. L. Amiss	50	88	10	3,612	262*	11	46.30
A. W. Greig	58	93	4	3,599	148	8	40.43
E. H. Hendren	51	83	9	3,525	205*	7	47.63
F. E. Woolley	64	98	7	3,283	154	5	36.07
K. W. R. Fletcher	52	85	11	2,975	216	7	40.20
M. Leyland	41	65	5	2,764	187	9	46.06
C. Washbrook	37	66	6	2,569	195	6	42.81
B. L. D'Oliveira	44	70	8	2,484	158	5	40.06
W. J. Edrich	39	63	2	2,440	219	6	40.00
T. G. Evans	91	133	14	2,439	104	2	20.49
L. E. G. Ames	47	72	12	2,434	149	8	40.56
W. Rhodes	58	98	21	2,325	179	2	30.19
T. E. Bailey	61	91	14	2,290	134*	1	29.74
M. J. K. Smith	50	78	6	2,278	121	3	31.63
P. E. Richardson	34	56	1	2,061	126	5	37.47
T. W. Hayward	35	60	2	1,999	137	3	34.46
G. Pullar	28	49	4	1,974	175	4	43.86
J. M. Parks	46	68	7	1,962	108*	2	32.16
A. C. MacLaren	35	61	4	1,931	140	5	33.87
P. H. Parfitt	37	52	6	1,882	131*	7	40.91
R. E. S. Wyatt	40	64	6	1,839	149	2	31.70
R. Illingworth	61	90	11	1,836	113	2	23.24
M. H. Denness	28	45	3	1,667	188	4	39.69
J. T. Tyldesley	31	55	1	1,661	138	4	30.75
J. Hardstaff jr	23	38	3	1,636	205*	4	46.74
E. Paynter	20	31	5	1,540	243	4	59.23
I. T. Botham	31	45	2	1,505	137	6	35.00

FOR AUSTRALIA

	Tests	Inns	Not Outs	Runs	Highest Inns	100s	Average
D. G. Bradman	52	80	10	6,996	334	29	99.94
R. N. Harvey	79	137	10	6,149	205	21	48.41
I. M. Chappell	75	136	10	5,345	196	14	42.42
W. M. Lawry	67	123	12	5,234	210	13	47.15
G. S. Chappell	61	109	15	5,171	247*	17	55.01
K. D. Walters	68	116	12	4,960	250	14	47.69
R. B. Simpson	62	111	7	4,869	311	10	46.81
I. R. Redpath	66	120	11	4,737	171	8	43.45
A. R. Morris	46	79	3	3,533	206	12	46.48
C. Hill	49	89	2	3,412	191	7	39.21
V. T. Trumper	48	89	8	3,163	214*	8	39.04
C. C. McDonald	47	83	4	3,106	170	5	39.31
A. L. Hassett	43	69	3	3,073	198*	10	46.56
K. R. Miller	55	87	7	2,958	147	7	36.97
W. W. Armstrong	50	84	10	2,863	159*	6	38.68
K. R. Stackpole	43	80	5	2,807	207	7	37.42
N. C. O'Neill	42	69	8	2,779	181	6	45.55
S. J. McCabe	39	62	5	2,748	232	6	48.21
R. W. Marsh	62	98	11	2,645	132	3	30.40
W. Bardsley	41	66	5	2,469	193*	6	40.47
W. M. Woodfull	35	54	4	2,300	161	7	46.00
P. J. P. Burge	42	68	8	2,290	181	4	38.16
S. E. Gregory	58	100	7	2,282	201	4	24.53
R. Benaud	63	97	7	2,201	122	3	24.45
C. G. Macartney	35	55	4	2,131	170	7	41.78
W. H. Ponsford	29	48	4	2,122	266	7	48.22
R. M. Cowper	27	46	2	2,061	307	5	46.84
M. A. Noble	42	73	7	1,997	133	1	30.25
K. J. Hughes	27	50	3	1,934	130*	4	41.14
B. C. Booth	29	48	6	1,773	169	5	42.21
A. R. Border	21	40	8	1,732	162	5	54.12
G. N. Yallop	25	47	3	1,727	172	5	39.25
J. Darling	34	60	2	1,657	178	3	28.56
R. B. McCosker	25	46	5	1,622	127	4	39.56
A. P. Sheahan	31	53	6	1,594	127	2	33.91
W. A. Brown	22	35	1	1,592	206*	4	46.82
K. D. Mackay	37	52	7	1,507	89	0	33.48
R. R. Lindwall	61	84	13	1,502	118	2	21.15

FOR SOUTH AFRICA

	Tests	Inns	Not Outs	Runs	Highest Inns	100s	Average
B. Mitchell	42	80	9	3,471	189*	8	48.88
A. D. Nourse	34	62	7	2,960	231	9	53.81
H. W. Taylor	42	76	4	2,936	176	7	40.77
E. J. Barlow	30	57	2	2,516	201	6	45.74
T. L. Goddard	41	78	5	2,516	112	1	34.46
D. J. McGlew	34	64	6	2,440	255*	7	42.06
J. H. B. Waite	50	86	7	2,405	134	4	30.44
R. G. Pollock	23	41	4	2,256	274	7	60.97
A. W. Nourse	45	83	8	2,234	111	1	29.78
R. A. McLean	40	73	3	2,120	142	5	30.28
E. A. B. Rowan	26	50	5	1,965	236	3	43.66
G. A. Faulkner	25	47	4	1,754	204	4	40.79
K. C. Bland	21	39	5	1,669	144*	3	49.08
W. R. Endean	28	52	4	1,630	162*	3	33.95
R. H. Catterall	24	43	2	1,555	120	3	37.92

FOR WEST INDIES

	Tests	Inns	Not Outs	Runs	Highest Inns	100s	Average
G. S. Sobers	93	160	21	8,032	365*	26	57.78
R. B. Kanhai	79	137	6	6,227	256	15	47.53
C. H. Lloyd	74	126	8	5,067	242*	13	42.94
E. D. Weekes	48	81	5	4,455	207	15	58.61
R. C. Fredericks	59	109	7	4,334	169	8	42.49
A. I. Kallicharran	62	103	9	4,319	187	12	45.94
F. M. M. Worrell	51	87	9	3,860	261	9	49.48
C. L. Walcott	44	74	7	3,798	220	15	56.68
I. V. A. Richards	36	57	2	3,265	291	10	59.36
C. C. Hunte	44	78	6	3,245	260	8	45.06
B. F. Butcher	44	78	6	3,104	209*	7	43.11
S. M. Nurse	29	54	1	2,523	258	6	47.60
C. G. Greenidge	30	54	3	2,212	134	5	43.37
G. A. Headley	22	40	4	2,190	270*	10	60.83
J. B. Stollmeyer	32	56	5	2,159	160	4	42.33
L. G. Rowe	30	49	2	2,047	302	7	43.55
D. L. Murray	62	96	9	1,993	91	0	22.90

FOR NEW ZEALAND

	Tests	Inns	Not Outs	Runs	Highest Inns	100s	Average
B. E. Congdon	61	114	7	3,448	176	7	32.22
J. R. Reid	58	108	5	3,431	142	6	33.31
G. M. Turner	39	70	6	2,920	259	7	45.62
B. Sutcliffe	42	76	8	2,727	230*	5	40.10
M. G. Burgess	47	86	5	2,562	119*	5	31.62
G. T. Dowling	39	77	3	2,306	239	3	31.16
B. F. Hastings	31	56	6	1,510	117*	4	30.20

FOR INDIA

	Tests	Inns	Not Outs	Runs	Highest Inns	100s	Average
S. M. Gavaskar	63	114	8	5,974	221	23	56.35
G. R. Viswanath	69	121	9	5,003	179	11	44.66
P. R. Umrigar	59	94	8	3,631	223	12	42.22
V. L. Manjrekar	55	92	10	3,209	189*	7	39.13
C. G. Borde	55	97	11	3,062	177*	5	35.60
M. A. K. Pataudi	46	83	3	2,792	203*	6	34.90
F. M. Engineer	46	87	3	2,611	121	2	31.08
P. Roy	43	79	4	2,441	173	5	32.54
V. S. Hazare	30	52	6	2,192	164*	7	47.65
A. L. Wadekar	37	71	3	2,113	143	1	31.07
V. M. H. Mankad	44	72	5	2,109	231	5	31.47
D. B. Vengsarkar	36	59	6	2,058	157*	5	38.83
M. L. Jaisimha	39	71	4	2,056	129	3	30.68
D. N. Sardesai	30	55	4	2,001	212	5	39.23
C. P. S. Chauhan	34	57	2	1,696	93	0	30.83
N. J. Contractor	31	52	1	1,611	108	1	31.58

FOR PAKISTAN

	Tests	Inns	Not Outs	Runs	Highest Inns	100s	Average
Hanif Mohammad	55	97	8	3,915	337	12	43.98
Mushtaq Mohammad	57	100	7	3,643	201	10	39.17
Asif Iqbal	58	99	7	3,575	175	11	38.85
Majid J. Khan	53	90	4	3,562	167	8	41.41
Saeed Ahmed	41	78	4	2,991	172	5	40.41
Zaheer Abbas	40	71	5	2,662	274	6	40.33
Sadiq Mohammad	38	69	2	2,493	166	5	37.20
Javed Miandad	30	51	12	2,433	206	7	62.38
Imtiaz Ahmed	41	72	1	2,079	209	3	29.28
Wasim Raja	33	54	8	1,776	117*	2	38.60

BOWLERS WITH 75 WICKETS IN TESTS

FOR ENGLAND

	Tests	Balls	Runs	Wickets	Average	5 Wkts/ Inns	10 Wkts/ match
F. S. Trueman	67	15,178	6,625	307	21.57	17	3
D. L. Underwood	79	20,159	7,141	279	25.59	16	6
J. B. Statham	70	16,032	6,261	252	24.84	9	1
A. V. Bedser	51	15,941	5,876	236	24.89	15	5
J. A. Snow	49	12,021	5,387	202	26.66	8	1
R. G. D. Willis	57	10,871	5,043	198	25.46	12	—
J. C. Laker	46	12,009	4,099	193	21.23	9	3
S. F. Barnes	27	7,873	3,106	189	16.43	24	7
G. A. R. Lock	49	13,063	4,452	174	25.58	9	3
M. W. Tate	39	12,571	4,055	155	26.16	7	1
I. T. Botham	31	7,202	3,092	153	20.20	14	3
F. J. Titmus	53	15,124	4,931	153	32.22	7	—
H. Verity	40	11,143	3,510	144	24.37	5	2
A. W. Greig	58	9,802	4,541	141	32.20	6	2
C. M. Old	43	8,258	3,796	137	27.70	4	—
T. E. Bailey	61	9,712	3,856	132	29.21	5	1
W. Rhodes	58	8,220	3,425	127	26.96	6	1
D. A. Allen	39	11,297	3,778	122	30.96	4	—
R. Illingworth	61	11,934	3,807	122	31.20	3	—
J. Briggs	33	5,332	2,094	118	17.74	9	4
G. G. Arnold	34	7,650	3,254	115	28.29	6	—
G. A. Lohmann	18	3,821	1,205	112	10.75	9	5
D. V. P. Wright	34	8,141	4,224	108	39.11	6	1
R. Peel	20	5,216	1,715	102	16.81	6	2
J. H. Wardle	28	6,597	2,080	102	20.39	5	1
C. Blythe	19	4,438	1,863	100	18.63	9	4
W. Voce	27	6,360	2,733	98	27.88	3	2
T. Richardson	14	4,485	2,220	88	25.22	11	4
W. R. Hammond	85	7,967	3,140	83	37.83	2	—
F. E. Woolley	64	6,495	2,815	83	33.91	4	1
G. O. B. Allen	25	4,392	2,379	81	29.37	5	1
M. Hendrick	28	5,606	2,027	81	25.02	—	—
D. J. Brown	26	5,098	2,237	79	28.31	2	—
H. Larwood	21	4,969	2,212	78	28.35	4	1
F. H. Tyson	17	3,452	1,411	76	18.56	4	1

FOR AUSTRALIA

	Tests	Balls	Runs	Wickets	Average	5 Wkts/ inns	10 Wkts/ match
R. Benaud	63	19,093	6,704	248	27.03	16	1
G. D. McKenzie	60	17,681	7,328	246	29.78	16	3
R. R. Lindwall	61	13,666	5,257	228	23.05	12	—
C. V. Grimmett	37	14,573	5,231	216	24.21	21	7
D. K. Lillee	42	11,251	5,169	214	24.15	15	5
A. K. Davidson	44	11,665	3,828	186	20.58	14	2
K. R. Miller	55	10,474	3,905	170	22.97	7	1
W. A. Johnston	40	11,048	3,825	160	23.90	7	—
J. R. Thomson	34	7,512	3,892	152	25.60	6	—
W. J. O'Reilly	27	10,024	3,254	144	22.59	11	3
H. Trumble	32	8,099	3,072	141	21.78	9	3
M. H. N. Walker	34	10,094	3,792	138	27.47	6	—
A. A. Mallett	38	9,990	3,940	132	29.84	6	1
M. A. Noble	42	7,109	3,027	121	25.01	9	2
I. W. Johnson	45	8,773	3,182	109	29.19	3	—
G. Giffen	31	6,325	2,791	103	27.09	7	1
A. N. Connolly	29	7,818	2,981	102	29.22	4	—
C. T. B. Turner	17	5,195	1,670	101	16.53	11	2
A. A. Mailey	21	6,117	3,358	99	33.91	6	2
F. R. Spofforth	18	4,185	1,731	94	18.41	7	4
J. W. Gleeson	29	8,857	3,367	93	36.20	3	—
N. J. N. Hawke	27	6,974	2,677	91	29.41	6	1
A. Cotter	21	4,633	2,549	89	28.64	7	—
W. W. Armstrong	50	8,052	2,923	87	33.59	3	—
J. M. Gregory	24	5,581	2,648	85	31.15	4	—
J. V. Saunders	14	3,565	1,797	79	22.74	6	—
G. Dymock	21	5,545	2,116	78	27.12	5	1
G. E. Palmer	17	4,519	1,678	78	21.51	6	2

FOR SOUTH AFRICA

	Tests	Balls	Runs	Wickets	Average	5 Wkts/ inns	10 Wkts/ match
H. J. Tayfield	37	13,568	4,405	170	25.91	14	2
T. L. Goddard	41	11,735	3,226	123	26.22	5	—
P. M. Pollock	28	6,522	2,806	116	24.18	9	1
N. A. T. Adcock	26	6,423	2,195	104	21.10	5	—
C. L. Vincent	25	5,863	2,631	84	31.32	3	—
G. A. Faulkner	25	4,227	2,180	82	26.58	4	—

FOR WEST INDIES

	Tests	Balls	Runs	Wickets	Average	5 Wkts/ inns	10 Wkts/ match
L. R. Gibbs	79	27,115	8,989	309	29.09	18	2
G. S. Sobers	93	21,599	7,999	235	34.03	6	—
W. W. Hall	48	10,415	5,066	192	26.38	9	1
A. M. E. Roberts	35	8,594	4,052	159	25.48	10	2
S. Ramadhin	43	13,939	4,577	158	28.96	10	1
A. L. Valentine	36	12,961	4,215	139	30.32	8	2
V. A. Holder	40	9,095	3,627	109	33.27	3	—
M. A. Holding	24	5,525	2,535	98	25.86	5	1
C. C. Griffith	28	5,631	2,683	94	28.54	5	—
J. Garner	18	4,465	1,790	92	19.45	1	—
C. E. H. Croft	16	3,609	1,795	77	23.31	1	—

FOR NEW ZEALAND

	Tests	Balls	Runs	Wickets	Average	5 Wkts/ inns	10 Wkts/ match
R. J. Hadlee	29	7,345	3,586	126	28.46	8	3
R. O. Collinge	35	7,689	3,393	116	29.25	3	—
B. R. Taylor	30	6,334	2,953	111	26.60	4	—
R. C. Motz	32	7,034	3,148	100	31.48	5	—
H. J. Howarth	30	8,833	3,178	86	36.95	2	—
J. R. Reid	58	7,719	2,837	85	33.37	1	—

FOR INDIA

	Tests	Balls	Runs	Wickets	Average	5 Wkts/ inns	10 Wkts/ match
B. S. Bedi	67	21,364	7,637	266	28.71	14	1
B. S. Chandrasekhar ...	58	15,963	7,199	242	29.74	16	2
E. A. S. Prasanna	49	14,353	5,742	189	30.38	10	2
V. M. H. Mankad	44	14,686	5,235	162	32.31	8	2
S. P. Gupte	36	11,284	4,402	149	29.54	12	1
S. Venkataraghavan ...	50	13,442	4,944	145	34.09	3	1
Kapil Dev	26	5,511	2,758	103	26.77	6	1
K. D. Ghavri	35	6,292	3,253	98	33.19	3	—
R. G. Nadkarni	41	9,175	2,559	88	29.07	4	1
S. A. Durani	29	6,446	2,657	75	35.42	3	1

FOR PAKISTAN

	Tests	Balls	Runs	Wickets	Average	5 Wkts/ inns	10 Wkts/ match
Fazal Mahmood	34	9,870	3,437	139	24.72	13	4
Intikhab Alam	47	10,475	4,492	125	35.93	5	2
Sarfraz Nawaz	37	9,451	3,924	122	32.16	4	1
Imran Khan	29	7,767	3,533	118	29.94	7	1
Mushtaq Mohammad ..	57	5,260	2,310	79	29.24	3	—

Note: Only G. S. Sobers (West Indies) and R. Benaud (Australia) have scored 2,000 runs and taken 200 wickets.

HUNDRED ON TEST DEBUT

C. Bannerman (165*)	Australia v England at Melbourne	1876-77
W. G. Grace (152)	England v Australia at The Oval	1880
H. Graham (107)........	Australia v England at Lord's	1893
K. S. Ranjitsinhji (154*) ..	England v Australia at Manchester	1896
P. F. Warner (132*)	England v South Africa at Johannesburg	1898-99
R. A. Duff (104)	Australia v England at Melbourne	1901-02
R. E. Foster (287)	England v Australia at Sydney	1903-04
G. Gunn (119)	England v Australia at Sydney	1907-08
R. J. Hartigan (116)	Australia v England at Adelaide	1907-08
H. L. Collins (104)	Australia v England at Sydney	1920-21
W. H. Ponsford (110) ...	Australia v England at Sydney	1924-25
A. Jackson (164)	Australia v England at Adelaide	1928-29
G. A. Headley (176)	West Indies v England at Bridgetown	1929-30
J. E. Mills (117)........	New Zealand v England at Wellington	1929-30
Nawab of Pataudi (102) ..	England v Australia at Sydney	1932-33
B. H. Valentine (136).....	England v India at Bombay	1933-34
L. Amarnath (118)	India v England at Bombay	1933-34
P. A. Gibb (106)	England v South Africa at Johannesburg	1938-39
S. C. Griffith (140)	England v West Indies at Port-of-Spain	1947-48
A. G. Ganteaume (112)...	West Indies v England at Port-of-Spain	1947-48
J. W. Burke (101*)	Australia v England at Adelaide	1950-51
P. B. H. May (138)	England v South Africa at Leeds	1951

D. H. Shodhan (110)	India v Pakistan at Calcutta	1952-53
B. H. Pairaudeau (115) . . .	West Indies v India at Port-of-Spain	1952-53
O. G. Smith (104)	West Indies v Australia at Kingston	1954-55
A. G. Kripal Singh (100*) .	India v New Zealand at Hyderabad	1955-56
C. C. Hunte (142)	West Indies v Pakistan at Bridgetown	1957-58
C. A. Milton (104*)	England v New Zealand at Leeds	1958
A. A. Baig (112)	India v England at Manchester	1959
Hanumant Singh (105) . . .	India v England at Delhi	1963-64
Khalid Ibadulla (166)	Pakistan v Australia at Karachi	1964-65
B. R. Taylor (105)	New Zealand v India at Calcutta	1964-65
K. D. Walters (155)	Australia v England at Brisbane	1965-66
J. H. Hampshire (107)	England v West Indies at Lord's	1969
G. R. Viswanath (137) . . .	India v Australia at Kanpur	1969-70
G. S. Chappell (108)	Australia v England at Perth	1970-71
†L. G. Rowe (214, 100*) . .	West Indies v New Zealand at Kingston	1971-72
A. I. Kallicharran (100*) . .	West Indies v New Zealand at Georgetown	1971-72
R. E. Redmond (107)	New Zealand v Pakistan at Auckland	1972-73
F. C. Hayes (106*)	England v West Indies at The Oval	1973
C. G. Greenidge (107)	West Indies v India at Bangalore	1974-75
L. Baichan (105*)	West Indies v Pakistan at Lahore	1974-75
G. J. Cosier (109)	Australia v West Indies at Melbourne	1975-76
S. Amarnath (124)	India v New Zealand at Auckland	1975-76
Javed Miandad (163)	Pakistan v New Zealand at Lahore	1976-77
A. B. Williams (100)	West Indies v Australia at Georgetown	1977-78

† *L. G. Rowe is the only batsman to score a hundred in each innings on début.*

300 RUNS IN FIRST TEST MATCH

314	L. G. Rowe (214, 100*)	West Indies v New Zealand at Kingston	1971-72
306	R. E. Foster (287, 19)	England v Australia at Sydney	1903-04

HUNDRED AND TEN WICKETS IN A TEST MATCH

I. T. Botham . . . . 114 and thirteen for 106 England v India at Bombay 1979-80

HUNDRED AND FIVE WICKETS IN ONE TEST INNINGS

J. H. Sinclair . . .	106 and six for 26	South Africa v England at Cape Town . .	1898-99
G. A. Faulkner . .	123 and five for 120	South Africa v England at Johannesburg	1909-10
C. Kelleway	114 and five for 33	Australia v South Africa at Manchester .	1912
J. M. Gregory . .	100 and seven for 69	Australia v England at Melbourne	1920-21
V. M. H. Mankad .	184 and five for 196	India v England at Lord's	1952
D. St E. Atkinson	219 and five for 56	West Indies v Australia at Bridgetown . .	1954-55
K. R. Miller	109 and six for 107	Australia v West Indies at Kingston	1954-55
R. Benaud	100 and five for 84	Australia v South Africa at Johannesburg	1957-58
O. G. Smith	100 and five for 90	West Indies v India at Delhi	1958-59
P. R. Umrigar . . .	172* and five for 107	India v West Indies at Port-of-Spain	1961-62
G. S. Sobers	104 and five for 63	West Indies v India at Kingston	1961-62
†B. R. Taylor . . .	105 and five for 86	New Zealand v India at Calcutta	1964-65
G. S. Sobers . . .	174 and five for 41	West Indies v England at Leeds	1966
Mushtaq Mohammad . .	201 and five for 49	Pakistan v New Zealand at Dunedin	1972-73
A. W. Greig	148 and six for 164	England v West Indies at Bridgetown . . .	1973-74
Mushtaq Mohammad . .	121 and five for 28	Pakistan v West Indies at Port-of-Spain .	1976-77
I. T. Botham . . .	103 and five for 73	England v New Zealand at Christchurch .	1977-78
I. T. Botham . . .	108 and eight for 34	England v Pakistan at Lord's	1978
I. T. Botham . . .	114 and six for 58 (1st innings), seven for 48 (2nd innings) England v India at Bombay	1979-80

† *Taylor's feat was on Test début.*

TWO SEPARATE HUNDREDS IN A TEST MATCH

Three times: S. M. Gavaskar v West Indies (1970-71), v Pakistan (1978-79), v West Indies (1978-79).

Twice in one series: C. L. Walcott v Australia (1954-55).

Twice: H. Sutcliffe v Australia (1924-25), v South Africa (1929); G. A. Headley v England (1929-30 and 1939); G. S. Chappell v New Zealand (1973-74), v West Indies (1975-76).

Once: W. Bardsley v England (1909); C. A. G. Russell v South Africa (1922-23); W. R. Hammond v Australia (1928-29); E. Paynter v South Africa (1938-39); D. C. S. Compton v Australia (1946-47); A. R. Morris v England (1946-47); A. Melville v England (1947); B. Mitchell v England (1947); D. G. Bradman v India (1947-48); V. S. Hazare v Australia (1947-48); E. D. Weekes v India (1948-49); J. Moroney v South Africa (1949-50); G. S. Sobers v Pakistan (1957-58); R. B. Kanhai v Australia (1960-61); Hanif Mohammad v England (1961-62); R. B. Simpson v Pakistan (1964-65); K. D. Walters v West Indies (1968-69); †L. G. Rowe v New Zealand (1971-72); I. M. Chappell v New Zealand (1973-74); G. M. Turner v Australia (1973-74); C. G. Greenidge v England (1976); G. P. Howarth v England (1977-78); ‡A. R. Border v Pakistan (1979-80).

  † *L. G. Rowe's two hundreds were on his Test début.*

  ‡ *A. R. Border scored 150* and 153 to become the first batsman to score 150 in each innings of a Test match.*

CENTURY AND DOUBLE-CENTURY IN SAME TEST

K. D. Walters (Australia)	242 and 103 v West Indies (Sydney)	1968-69
S. M. Gavaskar (India)	124 and 220 v West Indies (Port-of-Spain)	1970-71
†L. G. Rowe (West Indies)	214 and 100* v New Zealand (Kingston)	1971-72
G. S. Chappell (Australia)	247* and 133 v New Zealand (Wellington)	1973-74

  † *On Test début.*

MOST RUNS IN A TEST SERIES

	Tests	Inns	Not Outs	Runs	Highest Inns	100s	Average		
D. G. Bradman .	5	7	0	974	334	4	139.14	A v E	1930
W. R. Hammond	5	9	1	905	251	4	113.12	E v A	1928-29
R. N. Harvey	5	9	0	834	205	4	96.66	A v SA	1952-53
I. V. A. Richards	4	7	0	829	291	3	118.42	WI v E	1976
C. L. Walcott ...	5	10	0	827	155	5	82.70	WI v A	1954-55
G. S. Sobers ...	5	8	2	824	365*	3	137.33	WI v P	1957-58
D. G. Bradman .	5	9	0	810	270	3	90.00	A v E	1936-37
D. G. Bradman .	5	5	1	806	299*	4	201.50	A v SA	1931-32
E. D. Weekes ...	5	7	0	779	194	4	111.28	WI v I	1948-49
†S. M. Gavaskar	4	8	3	774	220	4	154.80	I v WI	1970-71
D. G. Bradman .	5	8	0	758	304	2	94.75	A v E	1934
D. C. S. Compton	5	8	0	753	208	4	94.12	E v SA	1947

  † *Gavaskar's aggregate was achieved in his first Test series.*

CARRYING BAT THROUGH TEST INNINGS

(Figures in brackets show side's total.)

A. B. Tancred	26*	(47)	South Africa v England (Cape Town)	1888-89
J. E. Barrett	67*	(176)	Australia v England (Lord's)	1890
R. Abel	132*	(307)	England v Australia (Sydney)	1891-92
P. F. Warner	132*	(237)	England v South Africa (Johannesburg)	1898-99
W. W. Armstrong .	159*	(309)	Australia v South Africa (Johannesburg)	1902-03

J. W. Zulch	43*	(103)	South Africa v England (Cape Town)	1909-10
W. Bardsley	193*	(383)	Australia v England (Lord's)	1926
W. M. Woodfull	30*	(66)‡	Australia v England (Brisbane)	1928-29
W. M. Woodfull	73*	(193)†	Australia v England (Adelaide)	1932-33
W. A. Brown	206*	(422)	Australia v England (Lord's)	1938
L. Hutton	202*	(344)	England v West Indies (The Oval)	1950
L. Hutton	156*	(272)	England v Australia (Adelaide)	1950-51
Nazar Mohammad	124*	(331)	Pakistan v India (Lucknow)	1952-53
F. M. M. Worrell	191*	(372)	West Indies v England (Nottingham)	1957
T. L. Goddard	56*	(99)	South Africa v Australia (Cape Town)	1957-58
D. J. McGlew	127*	(292)	South Africa v New Zealand (Durban)	1961-62
C. C. Hunte	60*	(131)	West Indies v Australia (Port-of-Spain)	1964-65
G. M. Turner	43*	(131)	New Zealand v England (Lord's)	1969
W. M. Lawry	49*	(107)	Australia v India (Delhi)	1969-70
W. M. Lawry	60*	(116)†	Australia v England (Sydney)	1970-71
G. M. Turner	223*	(386)	New Zealand v West Indies (Kingston)	1971-72
I. R. Redpath	159*	(346)	Australia v New Zealand (Auckland)	1973-74
G. Boycott	99*	(215)	England v Australia (Perth)	1979-80

† *One man absent.*   ‡ *Two men absent.*

Notes: G. M. Turner (223*) holds the record for the highest score by a player carrying his bat through a Test innings. He is also the youngest player to do so, being 22 years 63 days old when he first achieved the feat (1969).

D. L. Amiss (262*) batted throughout England's second innings of 432 for nine v West Indies at Kingston, 1973-74, the tenth wicket adding 40, unbroken, in fifty-three minutes.

FASTEST TEST FIFTIES

Minutes

28	J. T. Brown	England v Australia at Melbourne		1894-95
29	S. A. Durani	India v England at Kanpur		1963-64
30	E. A. V. Williams	West Indies v England at Bridgetown		1947-48
30	B. R. Taylor	New Zealand v West Indies at Auckland		1968-69
33	C. A. Roach	West Indies v England at The Oval		1933
34	C. R. Browne	West Indies v England at Georgetown		1929-30

FASTEST TEST HUNDREDS

Minutes

70	J. M. Gregory	Australia v South Africa at Johannesburg		1921-22
75	G. L. Jessop	England v Australia at The Oval		1902
78	R. Benaud	Australia v West Indies at Kingston		1954-55
80	J. H. Sinclair	South Africa v Australia at Cape Town		1902-03
86	B. R. Taylor	New Zealand v West Indies at Auckland		1968-69

FASTEST TEST DOUBLE HUNDREDS

Minutes

214	D. G. Bradman	Australia v England at Leeds		1930
223	S. J. McCabe	Australia v England at Nottingham		1938
226	V. T. Trumper	Australia v South Africa at Adelaide		1910-11
234	D. G. Bradman	Australia v England at Lord's		1930
240	W. R. Hammond	England v New Zealand at Auckland		1932-33
241	S. E. Gregory	Australia v England at Sydney		1894-95
245	D. C. S. Compton	England v Pakistan at Nottingham		1954

FASTEST TEST TRIPLE HUNDREDS

Minutes
287	W. R. Hammond .	England v New Zealand at Auckland	1932-33
336	D. G. Bradman ...	Australia v England at Leeds	1930

MOST RUNS IN A DAY BY A BATSMAN

309	D. G. Bradman ...	Australia v England at Leeds	1930
295	W. R. Hammond .	England v New Zealand at Auckland	1932-33
273	D. C. S. Compton	England v Pakistan at Nottingham	1954
271	D. G. Bradman ...	Australia v England at Leeds	1934

MOST RUNS IN A DAY (BOTH SIDES)

588	England (398 for six), India (190 for no wkt) at Manchester	1936
522	England (503 for two), South Africa (19 for no wkt) at Lord's	1924
508	England (221 for two), South Africa (287 for six) at The Oval	1935

MOST RUNS IN A DAY (ONE SIDE)

503	England (503 for two) v South Africa at Lord's	1924
494	Australia (494 for six) v South Africa at Sydney	1910-11
475	Australia (475 for two) v England at The Oval	1934
471	England (471 for eight) v India at The Oval	1936
458	Australia (458 for three) v England at Leeds	1930
455	Australia (455 for one) v England at Leeds	1934

SLOWEST INDIVIDUAL TEST BATTING

3* in 100 minutes	J. T. Murray, England v Australia at Sydney	1962-63
5 in 102 minutes	M. A. K. Pataudi, India v England at Bombay	1972-73
8 in 120 minutes	T. E. Bailey, England v South Africa at Leeds	1955
9 in 125 minutes	T. W. Jarvis, New Zealand v India at Madras	1964-65
10* in 133 minutes	T. G. Evans, England v Australia at Adelaide	1946-47
18 in 194 minutes	W. R. Playle, New Zealand v England at Leeds	1958
20 in 195 minutes	Hanif Mohammad, Pakistan v England at Lord's	1954
21 in 210 minutes	P. G. Z. Harris, New Zealand v Pakistan at Karachi	1955-56
28* in 250 minutes	J. W. Burke, Australia v England at Brisbane	1958-59
31 in 264 minutes	K. D. Mackay, Australia v England at Lord's	1956
40 in 289 minutes	H. L. Collins, Australia v England at Manchester	1921
45 in 318 minutes	Shuja-ud-Din, Pakistan v Australia at Lahore	1959-60
58 in 367 minutes	Ijaz Butt, Pakistan v Australia at Karachi	1959-60
68 in 458 minutes	T. E. Bailey, England v Australia at Brisbane	1958-59
99 in 505 minutes	M. L. Jaisimha, India v Pakistan at Kanpur	1960-61
105 in 575 minutes	D. J. McGlew, South Africa v Australia at Durban	1957-58
114 in 591 minutes	Mudassar Nazar, Pakistan v England at Lahore	1977-78
	(He took 545 minutes to reach 100)	
197* in 682 minutes	F. M. M. Worrell, West Indies v England at Bridgetown ...	1959-60
	(He took 557 minutes to reach 100)	
259 in 705 minutes	G. M. Turner, New Zealand v West Indies at Georgetown ..	1971-72
337 in 970 minutes	Hanif Mohammad, Pakistan v West Indies at Bridgetown ..	1957-58

LOWEST TEST SCORES IN FULL DAY'S PLAY

95 At Karachi, October 11, 1956. Australia 80 all out: Pakistan 15 for two (first day).
104 At Karachi, December 8, 1959. Pakistan 0 for no wicket to 104 for five v Australia (fourth day).
106 At Brisbane, December 9, 1958. England 92 for two to 198 all out v Australia (fourth day).
108 At Karachi, January 23, 1978. England 114 for one to 222 for five v Pakistan (fifth day).
     Note: Short time was played.
112 At Karachi, October 15, 1956. Australia 138 for six to 187 all out: Pakistan 63 for one (fourth day).
117 At Madras, October 19, 1956. India 117 for five v Australia (first day).
119 At Johannesburg, February 11, 1958. South Africa 7 for no wicket to 126 for two v Australia (fourth day).
120 At Calcutta, November 3, 1956. India 15 for no wicket to 135 for eight v Australia (second day).
122 At Port Elizabeth, March 4, 1957. England's last wicket fell after the first twenty minutes without addition. South Africa then made 122 for seven in five and a half hours (third day).
122 At Brisbane, December 8, 1958. Australia 156 for six to 186 all out: England 92 for two (third day).
122 At Melbourne, January 3, 1959. Australia 282 for seven to 308 all out and 9 for one; England 87 all out (fourth day).
122 At Melbourne, December 30, 1978. Australia 243 for four to 258 all out: England 107 for eight (second day).
123 At Hyderabad, January 4, 1978. England 123 for two to 191 all out: Pakistan 55 for one (third day).
124 At Dacca, November 17, 1959. Pakistan 74 for four to 134 all out: Australia 64 for one (fourth day).
124 At Kanpur, December 23, 1959. India 226 for six to 291 all out: Australia 59 for two (fourth day).
125 At Dunedin, March 11, 1955. New Zealand 125 all out v England (first day).
128 At Bridgetown, February 9, 1954. England 53 for two to 181 for nine v West Indies (third day).

In England:

151 At Lord's, August 26, 1978. England 175 for two to 289 all out: New Zealand 37 for seven (third day).
159 At Leeds, July 10, 1971. Pakistan 208 for four to 350 all out: England 17 for one (third day).

HIGHEST TEST WICKET PARTNERSHIPS

413 for 1st	V. M. H. Mankad (231) and P. Roy (173) for India v New Zealand at Madras	1955-56
451 for 2nd	W. H. Ponsford (266) and D. G. Bradman (244) for Australia v England at The Oval	1934
370 for 3rd	W. J. Edrich (189) and D. C. S. Compton (208) for England v South Africa at Lord's	1947
411 for 4th	P. B. H. May (285*) and M. C. Cowdrey (154) for England v West Indies at Birmingham	1957

405 for 5th	S. G. Barnes (234) and D. G. Bradman (234) for Australia v England at Sydney	1946-47
346 for 6th	J. H. W. Fingleton (136) and D. G. Bradman (270) for Australia v England at Melbourne	1936-37
347 for 7th	D. St E. Atkinson (219) and C. C. Depeiza (122) for West Indies v Australia at Bridgetown	1954-55
246 for 8th	L. E. G. Ames (137) and G. O. B. Allen (122) for England v New Zealand at Lord's	1931
190 for 9th	Asif Iqbal (146) and Intikhab Alam (51) for Pakistan v England at The Oval	1967
151 for 10th	B. F. Hastings (110) and R. O. Collinge (68*) for New Zealand v Pakistan at Auckland	1972-73

MOST WICKETS IN A TEST

19-90	J. C. Laker	England v Australia at Manchester	1956
17-159	S. F. Barnes	England v South Africa at Johannesburg	1913-14
16-137†	R. A. L. Massie	Australia v England at Lord's	1972
15-28	J. Briggs	England v South Africa at Cape Town	1888-89
15-45	G. A. Lohmann	England v South Africa at Port Elizabeth	1895-96
15-99	C. Blythe	England v South Africa at Leeds	1907
15-104	H. Verity	England v Australia at Lord's	1934
15-124	W. Rhodes	England v Australia at Melbourne	1903-04
14-90	F. R. Spofforth	Australia v England at The Oval	1882
14-99	A. V. Bedser	England v Australia at Nottingham	1953
14-102	W. Bates	England v Australia at Melbourne	1882-83
14-124	J. M. Patel	India v Australia at Kanpur	1959-60
14-144	S. F. Barnes	England v South Africa at Durban	1913-14
14-149	M. A. Holding	West Indies v England at The Oval	1976
14-199	C. V. Grimmett	Australia v South Africa at Adelaide	1931-32

† *On Test début.*

Notes: The best for South Africa is 13-165 by H. J. Tayfield against Australia at Melbourne, 1952-53.
 The best for New Zealand is 11-58 by R. J. Hadlee against India at Wellington, 1975-76.
 The best for Pakistan is 13-114 by Fazal Mahmood against Australia at Karachi, 1956-57.

MOST WICKETS IN A TEST INNINGS

10-53	J. C. Laker	England v Australia at Manchester	1956
9-28	G. A. Lohmann	England v South Africa at Johannesburg	1895-96
9-37	J. C. Laker	England v Australia at Manchester	1956
9-69	J. M. Patel	India v Australia at Kanpur	1959-60
9-86	Sarfraz Nawaz	Pakistan v Australia at Melbourne	1978-79
9-95	J. M. Noreiga	West Indies v India at Port-of-Spain	1970-71
9-102	S. P. Gupte	India v West Indies at Kanpur	1958-59
9-103	S. F. Barnes	England v South Africa at Johannesburg	1913-14
9-113	H. J. Tayfield	South Africa v England at Johannesburg	1956-57

9-121	A. A. Mailey	Australia v England at Melbourne	1920-21
8-7	G. A. Lohmann	England v South Africa at Port Elizabeth	1895-96
8-11	J. Briggs	England v South Africa at Cape Town	1888-89
8-29	S. F. Barnes	England v South Africa at The Oval	1912
8-29	C. E. H. Croft	West Indies v Pakistan at Port-of-Spain	1976-77
8-31	F. Laver	Australia v England at Manchester	1909
8-31	F. S. Trueman	England v India at Manchester	1952
8-34	I. T. Botham	England v Pakistan at Lord's	1978
8-35	G. A. Lohmann	England v Australia at Sydney	1886-87
8-38	L. R. Gibbs	West Indies v India at Bridgetown	1961-62
8-43†	A. E. Trott	Australia v England at Adelaide	1894-95
8-43	H. Verity	England v Australia at Lord's	1934
8-51	D. L. Underwood ..	England v Pakistan at Lord's	1974
8-52	V. M. H. Mankad ..	India v Pakistan at Delhi	1952-53
8-53	G. B. Lawrence	South Africa v New Zealand at Johannesburg ..	1961-62
8-53†	R. A. L. Massie ...	Australia v England at Lord's	1972
8-55	V. M. H. Mankad ..	India v England at Madras	1951-52
8-56	S. F. Barnes	England v South Africa at Johannesburg	1913-14
8-58	G. A. Lohmann	England v Australia at Sydney	1891-92
8-59	C. Blythe	England v South Africa at Leeds	1907
8-59	A. A. Mallett	Australia v Pakistan at Adelaide	1972-73
8-65	H. Trumble	Australia v England at The Oval	1902
8-68	W. Rhodes	England v Australia at Melbourne	1903-04
8-69	H. J. Tayfield	South Africa v England at Durban	1956-57
8-69	Sikander Bakht	Pakistan v India at Delhi	1979-80
8-70	S. J. Snooke	South Africa v England at Johannesburg	1905-06
8-71	G. D. McKenzie	Australia v West Indies at Melbourne	1968-69
8-72	S. Venkataraghavan .	India v New Zealand at Delhi	1964-65
8-76	E. A. S. Prasanna ..	India v New Zealand at Auckland	1975-76
8-79	B. S. Chandrasekhar	India v England at Delhi	1972-73
8-81	L. C. Braund	England v Australia at Melbourne	1903-04
8-84†	R. A. L. Massie ...	Australia v England at Lord's	1972
8-86	A. W. Greig	England v West Indies at Port-of-Spain	1973-74
8-92	M. A. Holding	West Indies v England at The Oval	1976
8-94	T. Richardson	England v Australia at Sydney	1897-98
8-104†	A. L. Valentine	West Indies v England at Manchester	1950
8-107	B. J. T. Bosanquet ..	England v Australia at Nottingham	1905
8-126	J. C. White	England v Australia at Adelaide	1928-29
8-143	M. H. N. Walker ...	Australia v England at Melbourne	1974-75

† *On Test début.*

Note: The best for New Zealand is 7-23 by R. J. Hadlee against India at Wellington, 1975-76.

MOST WICKETS IN A TEST SERIES

	Tests	Runs	Wkts	Average		
S. F. Barnes	4	536	49	10.93	England v South Africa	1913-14
J. C. Laker	5	442	46	9.60	England v Australia ...	1956
C. V. Grimmett	5	642	44	14.59	Australia v South Africa	1935-36
R. M. Hogg	6	527	41	12.85	Australia v England ...	1978-79
A. V. Bedser	5	682	39	17.48	England v Australia ...	1953
M. W. Tate	5	881	38	23.18	England v Australia ...	1924-25
W. J. Whitty	5	632	37	17.08	Australia v South Africa	1910-11
H. J. Tayfield	5	636	37	17.18	South Africa v England	1956-57
A. E. E. Vogler	5	783	36	21.75	South Africa v England	1909-10
A. A. Mailey	5	946	36	26.27	Australia v England ...	1920-21
G. A. Lohmann	3	203	35	5.80	England v South Africa	1895-96
B. S. Chandrasekhar	5	662	35	18.91	India v England	1972-73

TEST HAT-TRICKS

F. R. Spofforth	Australia v England at Melbourne	1878-79
W. Bates	England v Australia at Melbourne	1882-83
J. Briggs	England v Australia at Sydney	1891-92
G. A. Lohmann	England v South Africa at Port Elizabeth	1895-96
J. T. Hearne	England v Australia at Leeds	1899
H. Trumble	Australia v England at Melbourne	1901-02
H. Trumble	Australia v England at Melbourne	1903-04
T. J. Matthews† ...	} Australia v South Africa at Manchester	1912
T. J. Matthews ...		
M. J. C. Allom‡ ...	England v New Zealand at Christchurch	1929-30
T. W. Goddard	England v South Africa at Johannesburg	1938-39
P. J. Loader	England v West Indies at Leeds	1957
L. F. Kline	Australia v South Africa at Cape Town	1957-58
W. W. Hall	West Indies v Pakistan at Lahore	1958-59
G. M. Griffin	South Africa v England at Lord's	1960
L. R. Gibbs	West Indies v Australia at Adelaide	1960-61
P. J. Petherick‡ ...	New Zealand v Pakistan at Lahore	1976-77

† *T. J. Matthews did the hat-trick in each innings of the same match.*
‡ *On Test début.*

MOST BALLS BOWLED IN A TEST MATCH

S. Ramadhin (West Indies) sent down 774 balls in 129 overs against England at Birmingham, 1957. It was the most delivered by any bowler in a Test, beating H. Verity's 766 for England against South Africa at Durban, 1938-39. In this match Ramadhin also bowled the most balls (588) in any single first-class innings, including Tests. The highest number of balls bowled by one man in a first-class match is 917 by C. S. Nayudu for Holkar v Bombay, 1944-45. It should be noted that six balls were bowled to the over in the Australia v England Test series of 1928-29 and 1932-33 when the eight-ball over was otherwise in force in Australia.

WICKET-KEEPING RECORDS

Most Dismissals in a Test Career

	Tests	Caught	Stumped	Total
A. P. E. Knott (England)	93	244	19	263
R. W. Marsh (Australia)	62	217	10	227
T. G. Evans (England)	91	173	46	219
D. L. Murray (West Indies)	62	181	8	189
A. T. W. Grout (Australia)	51	163	24	187
Wasim Bari (Pakistan)	56	136	18	154
J. H. B. Waite (South Africa)	50	124	17	141
W. A. S. Oldfield (Australia)	54	78	52	130
J. M. Parks (England)†	46	103	11	114
S. M. H. Kirmani (India)	42	77	23	100

† *J. M. Parks' figures include two catches taken in three Tests in which he did not keep wicket.*

Note: K. J. Wadsworth (92c, 4s) made most dismissals for New Zealand.

Most Dismissals in a Test Series

26 (26c)	R. W. Marsh	Australia v West Indies (6 Tests)	1975-76
26 (23c 3s)	J. H. B. Waite	South Africa v New Zealand	1961-62
24 (21c 3s)	A. P. E. Knott	England v Australia (6 Tests)	1970-71
24 (24c)	D. T. Lindsay	South Africa v Australia	1966-67
24 (22c 2s)	D. L. Murray	West Indies v England	1963
23 (22c 1s)	F. C. M. Alexander	West Indies v England	1959-60
23 (21c 2s)	A. E. Dick	New Zealand v South Africa	1961-62
23 (20c 3s)	A. T. W. Grout	Australia v West Indies	1960-61
23 (22c 1s)	A. P. E. Knott	England v Australia (6 Tests)	1974-75
23 (21c 2s)	R. W. Marsh	Australia v England	1972
23 (16c 7s)	J. H. B. Waite	South Africa v New Zealand	1953-54
22 (22c)	S. J. Rixon	Australia v India	1977-78
21 (20c 1s)	A. T. W. Grout	Australia v England	1961
21 (16c 5s)	G. R. A. Langley	Australia v West Indies	1951-52
21 (13c 8s)	R. A. Saggers	Australia v South Africa	1949-50
21 (15c 6s)	H. Strudwick	England v South Africa	1913-14
20 (18c 2s)	T. G. Evans	England v South Africa	1956-57
20 (17c 3s)	A. T. W. Grout	Australia v England	1958-59
20 (16c 4s)	G. R. A. Langley	Australia v West Indies	1954-55
20 (19c 1s)	H. B. Taber	Australia v South Africa	1966-67
20 (16c 4s)	D. Tallon	Australia v England	1946-47
20 (18c 2s)	R. W. Taylor	England v Australia (6 Tests)	1978-79

Most Dismissals in a Test Innings

7 (all c)	Wasim Bari	Pakistan v New Zealand at Auckland	1978-79
7 (all c)	R. W. Taylor	England v India at Bombay	1979-80
6 (all c)	A. T. W. Grout	Australia v South Africa at Johannesburg	1957-58
6 (all c)	D. T. Lindsay	South Africa v Australia at Johannesburg	1966-67
6 (all c)	J. T. Murray	England v India at Lord's	1967
6 (5c 1s)	S. M. H. Kirmani	India v New Zealand at Christchurch	1975-76

Most Dismissals in One Test

10 (all c)	R. W. Taylor	England v India at Bombay	1979-80
9 (8c 1s)	G. R. A. Langley	Australia v England at Lord's	1956
8 (6c 2s)	L. E. G. Ames	England v West Indies at The Oval	1933
8 (6c 2s)	A. T. W. Grout	Australia v Pakistan at Lahore	1959-60
8 (all c)	A. T. W. Grout	Australia v England at Lord's	1961
8 (all c)	J. J. Kelly	Australia v England at Sydney	1901-02
8 (all c)	G. R. A. Langley	Australia v West Indies at Kingston	1954-55
8 (all c)	J. M. Parks	England v New Zealand at Christchurch	1965-66
8 (all c)	D. T. Lindsay	South Africa v Australia at Johannesburg	1966-67
8 (7c 1s)	H. B. Taber	Australia v South Africa at Johannesburg	1966-67
8 (all c)	Wasim Bari	Pakistan v England at Leeds	1971
8 (all c)	R. W. Marsh	Australia v West Indies at Melbourne	1975-76
8 (all c)	R. W. Marsh	Australia v New Zealand at Christchurch	1976-77

MOST CATCHES – EXCLUDING WICKET-KEEPERS

In a Test Career

M. C. Cowdrey (England)	120 in	114 matches
R. B. Simpson (Australia)	110 in	62 matches
W. R. Hammond (England)	110 in	85 matches
G. S. Sobers (West Indies)	110 in	93 matches
I. M. Chappell (Australia)	105 in	75 matches

In a Test Series

15	J. M. Gregory	Australia v England	1920-21
14	G. S. Chappell	Australia v England (6 Tests)	1974-75
13	R. B. Simpson	Australia v South Africa	1957-58
13	R. B. Simpson	Australia v West Indies	1960-61

In a Test Innings

5	V. Y. Richardson	Australia v South Africa at Durban	1935-36
5	Yajurvindra Singh	India v England at Bangalore	1976-77

In One Test

7	G. S. Chappell	Australia v England at Perth	1974-75
7	Yajurvindra Singh	India v England at Bangalore	1976-77
6	A. Shrewsbury	England v Australia at Sydney	1887-88
6	A. E. E. Vogler	South Africa v England at Durban	1909-10
6	F. E. Woolley	England v Australia at Sydney	1911-12
6	J. M. Gregory	Australia v England at Sydney	1920-21
6	B. Mitchell	South Africa v Australia at Melbourne	1931-32
6	V. Y. Richardson	Australia v South Africa at Durban	1935-36
6	R. N. Harvey	Australia v England at Sydney	1962-63
6	M. C. Cowdrey	England v West Indies at Lord's	1963
6	E. D. Solkar	India v West Indies at Port-of-Spain	1970-71
6	G. S. Sobers	West Indies v England at Lord's	1973
6	I. M. Chappell	Australia v New Zealand at Adelaide	1973-74
6	A. W. Greig	England v Pakistan at Leeds	1974
6	D. F. Whatmore	Australia v India at Kanpur	1979-80

SAME CAPTAIN WINNING TOSS IN ALL FIVE TESTS

Hon. F. S. Jackson, for England v Australia	1905
M. A. Noble, for Australia v England	1909
H. G. Deane, for South Africa v England	1927-28
J. D. C. Goddard, for West Indies v India	1948-49
A. L. Hassett, for Australia v England	1953
M. C. Cowdrey, for England v South Africa	1960
Nawab of Pataudi, for India v England	1963-64
G. S. Sobers, for West Indies v England	1966
G. S. Sobers, for West Indies v New Zealand	1971-72

Notes: P. B. H. May (3) and M. C. Cowdrey (2) won the toss in all five Tests for England in West Indies, 1959-60.

I. M. Chappell won the toss in five of the six Tests against England in Australia, 1974-75.

G. S. Chappell won the toss in five of the six Tests against West Indies in Australia, 1975-76.

G. N. Yallop won the toss in five of the six Tests against England in Australia, 1978-79.

HUNDREDS BY RIVAL CAPTAINS IN THE SAME TEST

J. W. H. T. Douglas (119) and H. W. Taylor (109), South Africa v England at Durban	1913-14
W. M. Woodfull (155) and A. P. F. Chapman (121), England v Australia at Lord's	1930
W. R. Hammond (240) and D. G. Bradman (102*), England v Australia at Lord's	1938
W. R. Hammond (140) and A. Melville (103), South Africa v England at Durban .	1938-39
L. Hutton (145) and A. L. Hassett (104), England v Australia at Lord's	1953
P. B. H. May (117) and D. J. McGlew (104*), England v South Africa at Manchester	1955
J. R. Reid (142) and D. J. McGlew (120), South Africa v New Zealand at Johannesburg	1961-62

R. B. Simpson (311) and E. R. Dexter (174), England v Australia at Manchester .. 1964
G. S. Sobers (113*) and M. C. Cowdrey (101), West Indies v England at Kingston 1967-68
W. M. Lawry (151) and G. S. Sobers (113), Australia v West Indies at Sydney 1968-69
G. S. Sobers (142) and B. E. Congdon (126), West Indies v New Zealand at
Bridgetown 1971-72
R. B. Kanhai (105) and I. M. Chappell (106*), West Indies v Australia at
Bridgetown 1972-73
B. E. Congdon (132) and I. M. Chappell (145 and 121), New Zealand v Australia
at Wellington 1973-74
S. M. Gavaskar (205) and A. I. Kallicharran (187), India v West Indies at Bombay 1978-79
Javed Miandad (106*) and G. S. Chappell (235), Pakistan v Australia at Faisalabad 1979-80

YOUNGEST TEST PLAYERS

Years	Days			
15	124	Mushtaq Mohammad .	Pakistan v West Indies at Lahore	1958-59
16	191	Aftab Baloch	Pakistan v New Zealand at Dacca	1969-70
16	248	Nasim-ul-Ghani	Pakistan v West Indies at Bridgetown ..	1957-58
16	352	Khalid Hassan	Pakistan v England at Nottingham	1954
17	122	J. E. D. Sealy	West Indies v England at Bridgetown ..	1929-30
17	239	I. D. Craig	Australia v South Africa at Melbourne ..	1952-53
17	245	G. S. Sobers	West Indies v England at Kingston	1953-54
17	265	V. L. Mehra	India v New Zealand at Bombay	1955-56
17	300	Hanif Mohammad	Pakistan v India at Delhi	1952-53
17	341	Intikhab Alam	Pakistan v Australia at Karachi	1959-60
18	13	A. G. Milkha Singh ...	India v Australia at Madras	1959-60
18	26	Majid Jahangir Khan .	Pakistan v Australia at Karachi	1964-65
18	31	M. R. Bynoe	West Indies v Pakistan at Lahore	1958-59
18	41	Salah-ud-Din	Pakistan v New Zealand at Rawalpindi .	1964-65
18	44	Khalid Wazir	Pakistan v England at Lord's	1954
18	105	J. B. Stollmeyer	West Indies v England at Lord's	1939
18	149	D. B. Close	England v New Zealand at Manchester ..	1949
18	173	A. T. Roberts	West Indies v New Zealand at Auckland	1955-56
18	186	Haseeb Ahsan	Pakistan v West Indies at Bridgetown ..	1957-58
18	190	Imran Khan	Pakistan v England at Birmingham	1971
18	197	D. L. Freeman	New Zealand v England at Christchurch	1932-33
18	232	T. W. Garrett	Australia v England at Melbourne	1876-77
18	242	A. P. H. Scott	West Indies v India at Kingston	1952-53
18	249	B. S. Chandrasekhar ..	India v England at Bombay	1963-64
18	260	Mohammad Ilyas	Pakistan v Australia at Melbourne	1964-65
18	267	H. G. Vivian	New Zealand v England at The Oval ...	1931
18	295	R. O. Collinge	New Zealand v Pakistan at Wellington ..	1964-65
18	312	S. Venkataraghavan ..	India v New Zealand at Madras	1964-65
18	316	B. P. Bracewell	New Zealand v England at The Oval ...	1978

OLDEST PLAYERS ON TEST DEBUT

Years	Days			
49	119	J. Southerton	England v Australia at Melbourne	1876-77
47	284	Miran Bux	Pakistan v India at Lahore	1954-55
46	253	D. D. Blackie	Australia v England at Sydney	1928-29
46	237	H. Ironmonger	Australia v England at Brisbane	1928-29
42	242	N. Betancourt	West Indies v England at Port-of-Spain .	1929-30
41	337	E. R. Wilson	England v Australia at Sydney	1920-21
41	27	R. J. D. Jamshedji ...	India v England at Bombay	1933-34
40	345	C. A. Wiles	West Indies v England at Manchester ...	1933
40	216	S. Kinneir	England v Australia at Sydney	1911-12
40	110	H. W. Lee	England v South Africa at Johannesburg	1930-31
40	56	G. W. A. Chubb	South Africa v England at Nottingham ..	1951
40	37	C. Ramaswami	India v England at Manchester	1936

OLDEST TEST PLAYERS

(Age on final day of their last Test match)

Years	Days			
52	165	W. Rhodes	England v West Indies at Kingston	1929-30
50	327	H. Ironmonger	Australia v England at Sydney	1932-33
50	320	W. G. Grace	England v Australia at Nottingham	1899
50	303	G. Gunn	England v West Indies at Kingston	1929-30
49	139	J. Southerton	England v Australia at Melbourne	1876-77
47	302	Miran Bux	Pakistan v India at Peshawar	1954-55
47	249	J. B. Hobbs	England v Australia at The Oval	1930
47	87	F. E. Woolley	England v Australia at The Oval	1934
46	309	D. D. Blackie	Australia v England at Adelaide	1928-29
46	206	A. W. Nourse	South Africa v England at The Oval	1924
46	202	H. Strudwick	England v Australia at The Oval	1926
46	41	E. H. Hendren	England v West Indies at Kingston	1934-35
45	245	G. O. B. Allen	England v West Indies at Kingston	1947-48
45	215	P. Holmes	England v India at Lord's	1932
45	140	D. B. Close	England v West Indies at Manchester	1976
44	341	E. G. Wynyard	England v South Africa at Johannesburg	1905-06
44	238	R. Abel	England v Australia at Manchester	1902
44	236	G. A. Headley	West Indies v England at Kingston	1953-54
44	105	Amir Elahi	Pakistan v India at Calcutta	1952-53

MOST CONSECUTIVE TEST APPEARANCES

85	G. S. Sobers, West Indies	Port-of-Spain 1954-55 to Port-of-Spain 1971-72
71	I. M. Chappell, Australia	Adelaide 1965-66 to Melbourne 1975-76
65	A. P. E. Knott, England	Auckland 1970-71 to The Oval 1977
65	G. R. Viswanath, India	Georgetown 1970-71 to Bombay (v England) 1979-80
61	R. B. Kanhai, West Indies	Birmingham 1957 to Sydney 1968-69
58†	A. W. Greig, England	Manchester 1972 to The Oval 1977
58†	J. R. Reid, New Zealand	Manchester 1949 to Leeds 1965
52	R. W. Marsh, Australia	Brisbane 1970-71 to The Oval 1977
52	P. B. H. May, England	The Oval 1953 to Leeds 1959
52	F. E. Woolley, England	The Oval 1909 to The Oval 1926
51	G. S. Chappell, Australia	Perth 1970-71 to The Oval 1977
49	C. G. Borde, India	Leeds 1959 to Auckland 1967-68
48†	V. T. Trumper, Australia	Nottingham 1899 to Sydney 1911-12
47	B. E. Congdon, New Zealand	Karachi 1964-65 to Wellington 1975-76
47	S. M. Gavaskar, India	Bombay 1974-75 to Bombay (v England) 1979-80
47	W. M. Lawry, Australia	Birmingham 1961 to Birmingham 1968
46	R. N. Harvey, Australia	Leeds 1948 to Calcutta 1956-57
45	Asif Iqbal, Pakistan	Karachi 1964-65 to Kingston 1976-77
45	R. C. Fredericks, West Indies	Kingston 1971-72 to Kingston 1976-77
45†	A. W. Nourse, South Africa	Johannesburg 1902-03 to The Oval 1924
44	W. W. Hall, West Indies	Bombay 1958-59 to Bridgetown 1967-68
43	E. R. Dexter, England	Manchester 1959 to The Oval 1963
42	L. R. Gibbs, West Indies	Sydney 1960-61 to Leeds 1969
42	C. C. McDonald, Australia	Adelaide 1954-55 to Leeds 1961
42†	B. Mitchell, South Africa	Birmingham 1929 to Port Elizabeth 1948-49
42†	M. A. Noble, Australia	Melbourne 1897-98 to The Oval 1909
41	P. R. Umrigar, India	Delhi 1951-52 to Manchester 1959
41	D. L. Murray, West Indies	Bridgetown 1972-73 to Bridgetown 1977-78
40	C. H. Lloyd, West Indies	Port-of-Spain 1972-73 to Bridgetown 1977-78
40	J. H. B. Waite, South Africa	Brisbane 1952-53 to Sydney 1963-64

† *Indicates complete Test career.*

SUMMARY OF ALL TEST MATCHES

To end of 1980 season in England

ENGLAND

Against	Won		Lost		Drawn		Tied		Total
Australia	79	..	92	..	69	..	0	..	240
South Africa	46	..	18	..	38	..	0	..	102
West Indies	21	..	23	..	32	..	0	..	76
New Zealand . . .	27	..	1	..	25	..	0	..	53
India	27	..	7	..	24	..	0	..	58
Pakistan	11	..	1	..	21	..	0	..	33
Totals	211	..	142	..	209	..	0	..	562

AUSTRALIA

Against	Won		Lost		Drawn		Tied		Total
England	92	..	79	..	69	..	0	..	240
South Africa	29	..	11	..	13	..	0	..	53
West Indies	25	..	12	..	11	..	1	..	49
New Zealand . . .	5	..	1	..	3	..	0	..	9
India	19	..	7	..	10	..	0	..	36
Pakistan	7	..	4	..	6	..	0	..	17
Totals	177	..	114	..	112	..	1	..	404

SOUTH AFRICA

Against	Won		Lost		Drawn		Tied		Total
England	18	..	46	..	38	..	0	..	102
Australia	11	..	29	..	13	..	0	..	53
New Zealand . . .	9	..	2	..	6	..	0	..	17
Totals	38	..	77	..	57	..	0	..	172

WEST INDIES

Against	Won		Lost		Drawn		Tied		Total
England	23	..	21	..	32	..	0	..	76
Australia	12	..	25	..	11	..	1	..	49
New Zealand . . .	5	..	3	..	9	..	0	..	17
India	17	..	5	..	21	..	0	..	43
Pakistan	6	..	4	..	5	..	0	..	15
Totals	63	..	58	..	78	..	1	..	200

NEW ZEALAND

Against	Won		Lost		Drawn		Tied		Total
England	1	..	27	..	25	..	0	..	53
Australia	1	..	5	..	3	..	0	..	9
South Africa	2	..	9	..	6	..	0	..	17
West Indies	3	..	5	..	9	..	0	..	17
India	3	..	10	..	9	..	0	..	22
Pakistan	1	..	8	..	12	..	0	..	21
Totals	11	..	64	..	64	..	0	..	139

INDIA

Against	Won		Lost		Drawn		Tied		Total
England	7	..	27	..	24	..	0	..	58
Australia	7	..	19	..	10	..	0	..	36
West Indies	5	..	17	..	21	..	0	..	43
New Zealand ...	10	..	3	..	9	..	0	..	22
Pakistan	4	..	3	..	17	..	0	..	24
Totals	33	..	69	..	81	..	0	..	183

PAKISTAN

Against	Won		Lost		Drawn		Tied		Total
England	1	..	11	..	21	..	0	..	33
Australia	4	..	7	..	6	..	0	..	17
West Indies	4	..	6	..	5	..	0	..	15
New Zealand ...	8	..	1	..	12	..	0	..	21
India	3	..	4	..	17	..	0	..	24
Totals	20	..	29	..	61	..	0	..	110

ENGLAND v AUSTRALIA

Season	England	Australia	Tests	Won by England	Won by Australia	Drawn
	Captains					
1876-77	James Lillywhite	D. W. Gregory	2	1	1	0
1878-79	Lord Harris	D. W. Gregory	1	0	1	0
1880	Lord Harris	W. L. Murdoch	1	1	0	0
1881-82	A. Shaw	W. L. Murdoch	4	0	2	2
1882	A. N. Hornby	W. L. Murdoch	1	0	1	0

THE ASHES

Season	England	Australia	Tests	Won by England	Won by Australia	Drawn
1882-83	Hon. I. F. W. Bligh	W. L. Murdoch	4*	2	2	0
1884	Lord Harris[1]	W. L. Murdoch	3	1	0	2
1884-85	A. Shrewsbury	T. Horan[2]	5	3	2	0
1886	A. G. Steel	H. J. H. Scott	3	3	0	0
1886-87	A. Shrewsbury	P. S. McDonnell	2	2	0	0
1887-88	W. W. Read	P. S. McDonnell	1	1	0	0
1888	W. G. Grace[3]	P. S. McDonnell	3	2	1	0
1890†	W. G. Grace	W. L. Murdoch	2	2	0	0
1891-92	W. G. Grace	J. McC. Blackham	3	1	2	0
1893	W. G. Grace[4]	J. McC. Blackham	3	1	0	2
1894-95	A. E. Stoddart	G. Giffen[5]	5	3	2	0
1896	W. G. Grace	G. H. S. Trott	3	2	1	0
1897-98	A. E. Stoddart[6]	G. H. S. Trott	5	1	4	0
1899	A. C. MacLaren[7]	J. Darling	5	0	1	4
1901-02	A. C. MacLaren	J. Darling[8]	5	1	4	0
1902	A. C. MacLaren	J. Darling	5	1	2	2
1903-04	P. F. Warner	M. A. Noble	5	3	2	0
1905	Hon. F. S. Jackson	J. Darling	5	2	0	3
1907-08	A. O. Jones[9]	M. A. Noble	5	1	4	0

Season	Captains England	Australia	Tests	Won by England	Won by Australia	Drawn
1909	A. C. MacLaren	M. A. Noble	5	1	2	2
1911-12	J. W. H. T. Douglas	C. Hill	5	4	1	0
1912	C. B. Fry	S. E. Gregory	3	1	0	2
1920-21	J. W. H. T. Douglas					
		W. W. Armstrong	5	0	5	0
1921	Hon. L. H. Tennyson[10]					
		W. W. Armstrong	5	0	3	2
1924-25	A. E. R. Gilligan	H. L. Collins	5	1	4	0
1926	A. W. Carr[11]	H. L. Collins[12]	5	1	0	4
1928-29	A. P. F. Chapman[13]	J. Ryder	5	4	1	0
1930	A. P. F. Chapman[14]	W. M. Woodfull	5	1	2	2
1932-33	D. R. Jardine	W. M. Woodfull	5	4	1	0
1934	R. E. S. Wyatt[15]	W. M. Woodfull	5	1	2	2
1936-37	G. O. B. Allen	D. G. Bradman	5	2	3	0
1938†	W. R. Hammond	D. G. Bradman	4	1	1	2
1946-47	W. R. Hammond[16]	D. G. Bradman	5	0	3	2
1948	N. W. D. Yardley	D. G. Bradman	5	0	4	1
1950-51	F. R. Brown	A. L. Hassett	5	1	4	0
1953	L. Hutton	A. L. Hassett	5	1	0	4
1954-55	L. Hutton	I. W. Johnson[17]	5	3	1	1
1956	P. B. H. May	I. W. Johnson	5	2	1	2
1958-59	P. B. H. May	R. Benaud	5	0	4	1
1961	P. B. H. May[18]	R. Benaud[19]	5	1	2	2
1962-63	E. R. Dexter	R. Benaud	5	1	1	3
1964	E. R. Dexter	R. B. Simpson	5	0	1	4
1965-66	M. J. K. Smith	R. B. Simpson[20]	5	1	1	3
1968	M. C. Cowdrey[21]	W. M. Lawry[22]	5	1	1	3
1970-71†	R. Illingworth	W. M. Lawry[23]	6	2	0	4
1972	R. Illingworth	I. M. Chappell	5	2	2	1
1974-75	M. H. Denness[24]	I. M. Chappell	6	1	4	1
1975	A. W. Greig[25]	I. M. Chappell	4	0	1	3
1976-77‡	A. W. Greig	G. S. Chappell	1	0	1	0
1977	J. M. Brearley	G. S. Chappell	5	3	0	2
1978-79	J. M. Brearley	G. N. Yallop	6	5	1	0
1979-80‡	J. M. Brearley	G. S. Chappell	3	0	3	0
1980‡	I. T. Botham	G. S. Chappell	1	0	0	1
In Australia			129	48	64	17
In England			111	31	28	52
Totals			240	79	92	69

 * *The Ashes were awarded in 1882-83 after a series of three matches which England won 2-1. A fourth unofficial match was played, each innings being played on a different pitch, and this was won by Australia.*
 † *The matches at Manchester in 1890 and 1938 and at Melbourne (Third Test) in 1970-71 were abandoned without a ball being bowled and are excluded.*
 ‡ *The Ashes were not at stake in these series.*

Notes: The following deputised for the official touring captain or were appointed by the home authority for only a minor proportion of the series:

[1] A. N. Hornby (First). [2] W. L. Murdoch (First), H. H. Massie (Third), J. McC. Blackham (Fourth). [3] A. G. Steel (First). [4] A. E. Stoddart (First). [5] J. McC. Blackham (First). [6] A. C. MacLaren (First, Second and Fifth). [7] W. G. Grace (First). [8] H. Trumble (Fourth and Fifth). [9] F. L. Fane (First, Second and Third). [10] J. W. H. T. Douglas (First and Second). [11] A. P. F. Chapman (Fifth). [12] W. Bardsley (Third and Fourth). [13] J. C. White (Fifth). [14] R. E. S. Wyatt (Fifth). [15] C. F. Walters (First). [16] N. W. D. Yardley (Fifth). [17] A. R. Morris (Second). [18] M. C. Cowdrey (First and Second). [19] R. N. Harvey (Second). [20] B. C. Booth (First and Third). [21] T. W. Graveney (Fourth). [22] B. N. Jarman (Fourth). [23] I. M. Chappell (Seventh). [24] J. H. Edrich (Fourth). [25] M. H. Denness (First).

HIGHEST TOTALS FOR AN INNINGS

By England			By Australia		
903-7	The Oval	1938	729-6	Lord's	1930
658-8	Nottingham	1938	701	The Oval	1934
636	Sydney	1928-29	695	The Oval	1930
627-9	Manchester	1934	659-8	Sydney	1946-47
611	Manchester	1964	656-8	Manchester	1964
			645	Brisbane	1946-47
			604	Melbourne	1936-37
			601-8	Brisbane	1954-55
			600	Melbourne	1924-25

SMALLEST TOTALS FOR AN INNINGS

By England			By Australia		
45	Sydney	1886-87	36	Birmingham	1902
52	The Oval	1948	42	Sydney	1887-88
53	Lord's	1888	44	The Oval	1896

INDIVIDUAL HUNDREDS IN THE MATCHES 1876-77–1980

For England (166)

132*	R. Abel, Sydney	1891-92	104	M. C. Cowdrey, Birmingham	1968
120	L. E. G. Ames, Lord's	1934	188	M. H. Denness, Melbourne	1974-75
185	R. W. Barber, Sydney	1965-66	180	E. R. Dexter, Birmingham	1961
134	W. Barnes, Adelaide	1884-85	174	E. R. Dexter, Manchester	1964
129	C. J. Barnett, Adelaide	1936-37	158	B. L. D'Oliveira, The Oval	1968
126	C. J. Barnett, Nottingham	1938	117	B. L. d'Oliveira, Melbourne	1970-71
132*	K. F. Barrington, Adelaide	1962-63	173†	K. S. Duleepsinhji, Lord's	1930
101	K. F. Barrington, Sydney	1962-63	120†	J. H. Edrich, Lord's	1964
256	K. F. Barrington, Manchester	1964	109	J. H. Edrich, Melbourne	1965-66
102	K. F. Barrington, Adelaide	1965-66	103	J. H. Edrich, Sydney	1965-66
115	K. F. Barrington, Melbourne	1965-66	164	J. H. Edrich, The Oval	1968
119*	I. T. Botham, Melbourne	1979-80	115*	J. H. Edrich, Perth	1970-71
113	G. Boycott, The Oval	1964	130	J. H. Edrich, Adelaide	1970-71
142*	G. Boycott, Sydney	1970-71	175	J. H. Edrich, Lord's	1975
119*	G. Boycott, Adelaide	1970-71	119	W. J. Edrich, Sydney	1946-47
107	G. Boycott, Nottingham	1977	111	W. J. Edrich, Leeds	1948
191	G. Boycott, Leeds	1977	146	K. W. R. Fletcher, Melbourne	1974-75
128*	G. Boycott, Lord's	1980	287†	R. E. Foster, Sydney	1903-04
103*	L. C. Braund, Adelaide	1901-02	144	C. B. Fry, The Oval	1905
102	L. C. Braund, Sydney	1903-04	102	D. I. Gower, Perth	1978-79
121	J. Briggs, Melbourne	1884-85	152†	W. G. Grace, The Oval	1880
140	J. T. Brown, Melbourne	1894-95	170	W. G. Grace, The Oval	1886
121	A. P. F. Chapman, Lord's	1930	111	T. W. Graveney, Sydney	1954-55
102†	D. C. S. Compton, Nottingham	1938	110	A. W. Greig, Brisbane	1974-75
147 / 103*	D. C. S. Compton, Adelaide	1946-47	119†	G. Gunn, Sydney	1907-08
			122*	G. Gunn, Sydney	1907-08
184	D. C. S. Compton, Nottingham	1948	102*	W. Gunn, Manchester	1893
145*	D. C. S. Compton, Manchester	1948	251	W. R. Hammond, Sydney	1928-29
			200	W. R. Hammond, Melbourne	1928-29
102	M. C. Cowdrey, Melbourne	1954-55	119* / 177	W. R. Hammond, Adelaide	1928-29
100*	M. C. Cowdrey, Sydney	1958-59	113	W. R. Hammond, Leeds	1930
113	M. C. Cowdrey, Melbourne	1962-63	112	W. R. Hammond, Sydney	1932-33
104	M. C. Cowdrey, Melbourne	1965-66	101	W. R. Hammond, Sydney	1932-33

231* W. R. Hammond, Sydney .	1936-37	117 J. W. H. Makepeace, Melbourne	1920-21
240 W. R. Hammond, Lord's . .	1938	
169* J. Hardstaff jr, The Oval .	1938	104 P. B. H. May, Sydney	1954-55
130 T. W. Hayward, Manchester	1899	101 P. B. H. May, Leeds	1956
		113 P. B. H. May, Melbourne . .	1958-59
137 T. W. Hayward, The Oval .	1899	182* C. P. Mead, The Oval	1921
114 J. W. Hearne, Melbourne . .	1911-12	102† Nawab of Pataudi, Sydney	1932-33
127* E. H. Hendren, Lord's	1926	216* E. Paynter, Nottingham . . .	1938
169 E. H. Hendren, Brisbane . .	1928-29	174† D. W. Randall, Melbourne	1976-77
132 E. H. Hendren, Manchester	1934	150 D. W. Randall, Sydney . . .	1978-79
126* J. B. Hobbs, Melbourne . . .	1911-12	154†* K. S. Ranjitsinhji, Manchester	1896
187 J. B. Hobbs, Adelaide	1911-12	
178 J. B. Hobbs, Melbourne . . .	1911-12	175 K. S. Ranjitsinhji, Sydney	1897-98
107 J. B. Hobbs, Lord's	1912	117 W. W. Read, The Oval	1884
122 J. B. Hobbs, Melbourne . . .	1920-21	179 W. Rhodes, Melbourne . . .	1911-12
123 J. B. Hobbs, Adelaide	1920-21	104 P. E. Richardson, Manchester	1956
115 J. B. Hobbs, Sydney	1924-25	
154 J. B. Hobbs, Melbourne . . .	1924-25	135* C. A. G. Russell, Adelaide . .	1920-21
119 J. B. Hobbs, Adelaide	1924-25	101 C. A. G. Russell, Manchester	1921
119 J. B. Hobbs, Lord's	1926	102* C. A. G. Russell, The Oval	1921
100 J. B. Hobbs, The Oval	1926	105 J. Sharp, The Oval	1909
142 J. B. Hobbs, Melbourne . . .	1928-29	113 Rev. D. S. Sheppard, Manchester	1956
126 K. L. Hutchings, Melbourne	1907-08	
		113 Rev. D. S. Sheppard, Melbourne	1962-63
100† L. Hutton, Nottingham . . .	1938	
364 L. Hutton, The Oval	1938	105* A. Shrewsbury, Melbourne	1884-85
122* L. Hutton, Sydney	1946-47	164 A. Shrewsbury, Lord's	1886
156* L. Hutton, Adelaide	1950-51	106 A. Shrewsbury, Lord's	1893
145 L. Hutton, Lord's	1953	156* R. T. Simpson, Melbourne .	1950-51
103 Hon. F. S. Jackson, The Oval	1893	135* A. G. Steel, Sydney	1882-83
		148 A. G. Steel, Lord's	1884
118 Hon. F. S. Jackson, The Oval	1899	134 A. E. Stoddart, Adelaide . .	1891-92
		173 A. E. Stoddart, Melbourne .	1894-95
128 Hon. F. S. Jackson, Manchester	1902	112† R. Subba Row, Birmingham	1961
144* Hon. F. S. Jackson, Leeds	1905	137 R. Subba Row, The Oval . .	1961
113 Hon. F. S. Jackson, Manchester	1905	115† H. Sutcliffe, Sydney	1924-25
		176 127 } H. Sutcliffe, Melbourne . . .	1924-25
104 G. L. Jessop, The Oval . . .	1902	
106* A. P. E. Knott, Adelaide . .	1974-75	143 H. Sutcliffe, Melbourne . . .	1924-25
135 A. P. E. Knott, Nottingham	1977	161 H. Sutcliffe, The Oval	1926
137† M. Leyland, Melbourne . . .	1928-29	135 H. Sutcliffe, Melbourne . . .	1928-29
109 M. Leyland, Lord's	1934	161 H. Sutcliffe, The Oval	1930
153 M. Leyland, Manchester . .	1934	194 H. Sutcliffe, Sydney	1932-33
110 M. Leyland, The Oval	1934	138 J. T. Tyldesley, Birmingham	1902
126 M. Leyland, Brisbane	1936-37	100 J. T. Tyldesley, Leeds	1905
111* M. Leyland, Melbourne . . .	1936-37	112* J. T. Tyldesley, The Oval . .	1905
187 M. Leyland, The Oval	1938	149 G. Ulyett, Melbourne	1881-82
131 B. W. Luckhurst, Perth . . .	1970-71	117 A. Ward, Sydney	1894-95
109 B. W. Luckhurst, Melbourne	1970-71	109† W. Watson, Lord's	1953
		112 C. Washbrook, Melbourne	1946-47
120 A. C. MacLaren, Melbourne	1894-95	143 C. Washbrook, Leeds	1948
		133* F. E. Woolley, Sydney	1911-12
109 A. C. MacLaren, Sydney . .	1897-98	123 F. E. Woolley, Sydney	1924-25
124 A. C. MacLaren, Adelaide . .	1897-98	149 R. A. Woolmer, The Oval . .	1975
116 A. C. MacLaren, Sydney . .	1901-02	120 R. A. Woolmer, Lord's . . .	1977
140 A. C. MacLaren, Nottingham	1905	137 R. A. Woolmer, Manchester	1977

† *Signifies hundred on first appearance in England–Australia Tests.*

Note: In consecutive innings in 1928-29, W. R. Hammond scored 251 at Sydney, 200 and 32 at Melbourne, and 119* and 177 at Adelaide.

For Australia (184)

133*	W. W. Armstrong, Melbourne	1907-08
158	W. W. Armstrong, Sydney	1920-21
121	W. W. Armstrong, Adelaide	1920-21
123*	W. W. Armstrong, Melbourne	1920-21
118	C. L. Badcock, Melbourne	1936-37
165*†	C. Bannerman, Melbourne	1876-77
136 130 }	W. Bardsley, The Oval	1909
193*	W. Bardsley, Lord's	1926
234	S. G. Barnes, Sydney	1946-47
141	S. G. Barnes, Lord's	1948
128	G. J. Bonnor, Sydney	1884-85
112	B. C. Booth, Brisbane	1962-63
103	B. C. Booth, Melbourne	1962-63
115	A. R. Border, Perth	1979-80
112	D. G. Bradman, Melbourne	1928-29
123	D. G. Bradman, Melbourne	1928-29
131	D. G. Bradman, Nottingham	1930
254	D. G. Bradman, Lord's	1930
334	D. G. Bradman, Leeds	1930
232	D. G. Bradman, The Oval	1930
103*	D. G. Bradman, Melbourne	1932-33
304	D. G. Bradman, Leeds	1934
244	D. G. Bradman, The Oval	1934
270	D. G. Bradman, Melbourne	1936-37
212	D. G. Bradman, Adelaide	1936-37
169	D. G. Bradman, Melbourne	1936-37
144*	D. G. Bradman, Nottingham	1938
102*	D. G. Bradman, Lord's	1938
103	D. G. Bradman, Leeds	1938
187	D. G. Bradman, Brisbane	1946-47
234	D. G. Bradman, Sydney	1946-47
138	D. G. Bradman, Nottingham	1948
173*	D. G. Bradman, Leeds	1948
105	W. A. Brown, Lord's	1934
133	W. A. Brown, Nottingham	1938
206*	W. A. Brown, Lord's	1938
181	P. J. P. Burge, The Oval	1961
103	P. J. P. Burge, Sydney	1962-63
160	P. J. P. Burge, Leeds	1964
120	P. J. P. Burge, Melbourne	1965-66
101*†	J. W. Burke, Adelaide	1950-51
108†	G. S. Chappell, Perth	1970-71
131	G. S. Chappell, Lord's	1972
113	G. S. Chappell, The Oval	1972
144	G. S. Chappell, Sydney	1974-75
102	G. S. Chappell, Melbourne	1974-75
112	G. S. Chappell, Manchester	1977
114	G. S. Chappell, Melbourne	1979-80
111	I. M. Chappell, Melbourne	1970-71
104	I. M. Chappell, Adelaide	1970-71
118	I. M. Chappell, The Oval	1972
192	I. M. Chappell, The Oval	1975
104†	H. L. Collins, Sydney	1920-21
162	H. L. Collins, Adelaide	1920-21
114	H. L. Collins, Sydney	1924-25

307	R. M. Cowper, Melbourne	1965-66
101	J. Darling, Sydney	1897-98
178	J. Darling, Adelaide	1897-98
160	J. Darling, Sydney	1897-98
104†	R. A. Duff, Melbourne	1901-02
146	R. A. Duff, The Oval	1905
170*	R. Edwards, Nottingham	1972
115	R. Edwards, Perth	1974-75
100	J. H. W. Fingleton, Brisbane	1936-37
136	J. H. W. Fingleton, Melbourne	1936-37
161	G. Giffen, Sydney	1894-95
107†	H. Graham, Lord's	1893
105	H. Graham, Sydney	1894-95
100	J. M. Gregory, Melbourne	1920-21
201	S. E. Gregory, Sydney	1894-95
103	S. E. Gregory, Lord's	1896
117	S. E. Gregory, The Oval	1899
112	S. E. Gregory, Adelaide	1903-04
116†	R. J. Hartigan, Adelaide	1907-08
112†	R. N. Harvey, Leeds	1948
122	R. N. Harvey, Manchester	1953
162	R. N. Harvey, Brisbane	1954-55
167	R. N. Harvey, Melbourne	1958-59
114	R. N. Harvey, Birmingham	1961
154	R. N. Harvey, Adelaide	1962-63
128	A. L. Hassett, Brisbane	1946-47
137	A. L. Hassett, Nottingham	1948
115	A. L. Hassett, Nottingham	1953
104	A. L. Hassett, Lord's	1953
112	H. S. T. L. Hendry, Sydney	1928-29
188	C. Hill, Melbourne	1897-98
135	C. Hill, Lord's	1899
119	C. Hill, Sheffield	1902
160	C. Hill, Adelaide	1907-08
124	T. P. Horan, Melbourne	1881-82
129	K. J. Hughes, Brisbane	1978-79
117	K. J. Hughes, Lord's	1980
140	F. A. Iredale, Adelaide	1894-95
108	F. A. Iredale, Manchester	1896
164†	A. Jackson, Adelaide	1928-29
147	C. Kelleway, Adelaide	1920-21
100	A. F. Kippax, Melbourne	1928-29
130	W. M. Lawry, Lord's	1961
102	W. M. Lawry, Manchester	1961
106	W. M. Lawry, Manchester	1964
166	W. M. Lawry, Brisbane	1965-66
119	W. M. Lawry, Adelaide	1965-66
108	W. M. Lawry, Melbourne	1965-66
135	W. M. Lawry, The Oval	1968
100	R. R. Lindwall, Melbourne	1946-47
134	J. J. Lyons, Sydney	1891-92
170	C. G. Macartney, Sydney	1920-21
115	C. G. Macartney, Leeds	1921
133*	C. G. Macartney, Lord's	1926
151	C. G. Macartney, Leeds	1926
109	C. G. Macartney, Manchester	1926
187*	S. J. McCabe, Sydney	1932-33
137	S. J. McCabe, Manchester	1934
112	S. J. McCabe, Melbourne	1936-37

232	S. J. McCabe, Nottingham	1938
104*	C. L. McCool, Melbourne .	1946-47
127	R. B. McCosker, The Oval	1975
107	R. B. McCosker, Nottingham	1977
170	C. C. McDonald, Adelaide	1958-59
133	C. C. McDonald, Melbourne	1958-59
147	P. S. McDonnell, Sydney . .	1881-82
103	P. S. McDonnell, The Oval	1884
124	P. S. McDonnell, Adelaide .	1884-85
112	C. E. McLeod, Melbourne .	1897-98
110*	R. W. Marsh, Melbourne . .	1976-77
141*	K. R. Miller, Adelaide . . .	1946-47
145*	K. R. Miller, Sydney	1950-51
109	K. R. Miller, Lord's	1953
155	A. R. Morris, Melbourne . .	1946-47
122 \ 124*	A. R. Morris, Adelaide . . .	1946-47
105	A. R. Morris, Lord's	1948
182	A. R. Morris, Leeds	1948
196	A. R. Morris, The Oval . . .	1948
206	A. R. Morris, Adelaide . . .	1950-51
153	A. R. Morris, Brisbane . . .	1954-55
153*	W. L. Murdoch, The Oval .	1880
211	W. L. Murdoch, The Oval .	1884
133	M. A. Noble, Sydney	1903-04
117	N. C. O'Neill, The Oval . . .	196†
100	N. C. O'Neill, Adelaide . . .	1962-63
116	C. E. Pellew, Melbourne . .	1920-21
104	C. E. Pellew, Adelaide . . .	1920-21
110†	W. H. Ponsford, Sydney . .	1924-25
128	W. H. Ponsford, Melbourne	1924-25
110	W. H. Ponsford, The Oval .	1930
181	W. H. Ponsford, Leeds . . .	1934
266	W. H. Ponsford, The Oval .	1934
143*	V. S. Ransford, Lord's	1909
171	I. R. Redpath, Perth	1970-71
105	I. R. Redpath, Sydney	1974-75
100	A. J. Richardson, Leeds . . .	1926
138	V. Y. Richardson, Melbourne	1924-25
201*	J. Ryder, Adelaide	1924-25
112	J. Ryder, Melbourne	1928-29
102	H. J. H. Scott, The Oval . .	1884
311	R. B. Simpson, Manchester	1964
225	R. B. Simpson, Adelaide . .	1965-66
207	K. R. Stackpole, Brisbane .	1970-71
136	K. R. Stackpole, Adelaide .	1970-71
114	K. R. Stackpole, Nottingham	1972
108	J. M. Taylor, Sydney	1924-25
143	G. H. S. Trott, Lord's	1896
135*	V. T. Trumper, Lord's	1899
104	V. T. Trumper, Manchester	1902
185*	V. T. Trumper, Sydney . . .	1903-04
113	V. T. Trumper, Adelaide . .	1903-04
166	V. T. Trumper, Sydney . . .	1907-08
113	V. T. Trumper, Sydney . . .	1911-12
155†	K. D. Walters, Brisbane . .	1965-66
115	K. D. Walters, Melbourne .	1965-66
112	K. D. Walters, Brisbane . . .	1970-71
103	K. D. Walters, Perth	1974-75
100	G. M. Wood, Melbourne . .	1978-79
112	G. M. Wood, Lord's	1980
141	W. M. Woodfull, Leeds . . .	1926
117	W. M. Woodfull, Manchester	1926
111	W. M. Woodfull, Sydney . .	1928-29
107	W. M. Woodfull, Melbourne	1928-29
102	W. M. Woodfull, Melbourne	1928-29
155	W. M. Woodfull, Lord's . . .	1930
102†	G. N. Yallop, Brisbane . . .	1978-79
121	G. N. Yallop, Sydney	1978-79

† *Signifies hundred on first appearance in England–Australia Tests.*

Notes: D. G. Bradman's scores in 1930 were 8 and 131 at Nottingham, 254 and 1 at Lord's, 334 at Leeds, 14 at Manchester, and 232 at The Oval.

D. G. Bradman scored a hundred in eight successive Tests against England in which he batted – three in 1936-37, three in 1938 and two in 1946-47. He was injured and unable to bat at The Oval in 1938.

W. H. Ponsford and K. D. Walters each hit centuries in their first two Tests.

C. Bannerman and H. Graham each scored their maiden century in first-class cricket in their first Test.

No right-handed batsman has obtained two 100s for Australia in a Test match against England. H. Sutcliffe, in his first two games for England, scored 59 and 115 at Sydney and 176 and 127 at Melbourne in 1924-25. In the latter match, which lasted into the seventh day, he was on the field throughout except for 86 minutes, namely 27 hours and 52 minutes.

C. Hill made 98 and 97 at Adelaide in 1901-02, and F. E. Woolley 95 and 93 at Lord's in 1921.

H. Sutcliffe in 1924-25, C. G. Macartney in 1926 and A. R. Morris in 1946-47 made three hundreds in consecutive innings.

J. B. Hobbs and H. Sutcliffe shared eleven first-wicket three-figure partnerships.

L. Hutton and C. Washbrook twice made three-figure stands in each innings, at Adelaide in 1946-47 and at Leeds in 1948.

H. Sutcliffe, during his highest score of 194, v Australia in 1932-33, took part in three stands each exceeding 100, viz. 112 with R. E. S. Wyatt for the first wicket, 188 with W. R. Hammond for the second wicket, and 123 with the Nawab of Pataudi for the third wicket. In

1903-04 R. E. Foster, in his historic innings of 287, added 192 for the fifth wicket with L. C. Braund, 115 for the ninth with A. E. Relf, and 130 for the tenth with W. Rhodes.

When L. Hutton scored 364 at The Oval in 1938 he added 382 for the second wicket with M. Leyland, 135 for the third wicket with W. R. Hammond and 215 for the sixth wicket with J. Hardstaff jr.

D. C. S. Compton and A. R. Morris at Adelaide in 1946-47 provide the only instance of a player on each side hitting two separate hundreds in a Test match.

G. S. and I. M. Chappell at The Oval in 1972 provided the first instance in Test matches of brothers each scoring hundreds in the same innings.

G. Boycott (191 at Leeds, 1977) is the only batsman to score his hundredth first-class century in a Test match.

RECORD PARTNERSHIPS FOR EACH WICKET

By England

323 for 1st	J. B. Hobbs and W. Rhodes at Melbourne	1911-12
382 for 2nd†	L. Hutton and M. Leyland at The Oval	1938
262 for 3rd	W. R. Hammond and D. R. Jardine at Adelaide	1928-29
222 for 4th	W. R. Hammond and E. Paynter at Lord's	1938
206 for 5th	E. Paynter and D. C. S. Compton at Nottingham	1938
215 for 6th {	L. Hutton and J. Hardstaff at The Oval	1938
	G. Boycott and A. P. E. Knott at Nottingham	1977
143 for 7th	F. E. Woolley and J. Vine at Sydney	1911-12
124 for 8th	E. H. Hendren and H. Larwood at Brisbane	1928-29
151 for 9th	W. H. Scotton and W. W. Read at The Oval	1884
130 for 10th†	R. E. Foster and W. Rhodes at Sydney	1903-04

By Australia

244 for 1st	R. B. Simpson and W. M. Lawry at Adelaide	1965-66
451 for 2nd†	W. H. Ponsford and D. G. Bradman at The Oval	1934
276 for 3rd	D. G. Bradman and A. L. Hassett at Brisbane	1946-47
388 for 4th†	W. H. Ponsford and D. G. Bradman at Leeds	1934
405 for 5th†	S. G. Barnes and D. G. Bradman at Sydney	1946-47
346 for 6th†	J. H. W. Fingleton and D. G. Bradman at Melbourne	1936-37
165 for 7th	C. Hill and H. Trumble at Melbourne	1897-98
243 for 8th†	R. J. Hartigan and C. Hill at Adelaide	1907-08
154 for 9th†	S. E. Gregory and J. McC. Blackham at Sydney	1894-95
127 for 10th†	J. M. Taylor and A. A. Mailey at Sydney	1924-25

† *Denotes record partnership against all countries.*

MOST RUNS IN A SERIES

England in England	562 (average 62.44)	D. C. S. Compton	1948
England in Australia	905 (average 113.12)	W. R. Hammond	1928-29
Australia in England	974 (average 139.14)	D. G. Bradman	1930
Australia in Australia	810 (average 90.00)	D. G. Bradman	1936-37

TEN WICKETS OR MORE IN A MATCH

For England (35)

13-163 (6-42, 7-121)	S. F. Barnes, Melbourne	1901-02
14-102 (7-28, 7-74)	W. Bates, Melbourne	1882-83
10-105 (5-46, 5-59)	A. V. Bedser, Melbourne	1950-51
14-99 (7-55, 7-44)	A. V. Bedser, Nottingham	1953
11-102 (6-44, 5-58)	C. Blythe, Birmingham	1909
11-176 (6-78, 5-98)	I. T. Botham, Perth	1979-80

11-74 (5-29, 6-45)	J. Briggs, Lord's	1886
12-136 (6-49, 6-87)	J. Briggs, Adelaide	1891-92
10-148 (5-34, 5-114)	J. Briggs, The Oval	1893
10-179 (5-102, 5-77)†	K. Farnes, Nottingham	1934
10-60 (6-41, 4-19)	J. T. Hearne, The Oval	1896
11-113 (5-58, 6-55)	J. C. Laker, Leeds	1956
19-90 (9-37, 10-53)	J. C. Laker, Manchester	1956
10-124 (5-96, 5-28)	H. Larwood, Sydney	1932-33
11-76 (6-48, 5-28)	W. H. Lockwood, Manchester	1902
12-104 (7-36, 5-68)	G. A. Lohmann, The Oval	1886
10-87 (8-35, 2-52)	G. A. Lohmann, Sydney	1886-87
10-142 (8-58, 2-84)	G. A. Lohmann, Sydney	1891-92
12-102 (6-50, 6-52)†	F. Martin, The Oval	1890
10-58 (5-18, 5-40)	R. Peel, Sydney	1887-88
11-68 (7-31, 4-37)	R. Peel, Manchester	1888
15-124 (7-56, 8-68)	W. Rhodes, Melbourne	1903-04
10-156 (5-49, 5-107)†	T. Richardson, Manchester	1893
11-173 (6-39, 5-134)	T. Richardson, Lord's	1896
13-244 (7-168, 6-76)	T. Richardson, Manchester	1896
10-204 (8-94, 2-110)	T. Richardson, Sydney	1897-98
11-228 (6-130, 5-98)†	M. W. Tate, Sydney	1924-25
11-88 (5-58, 6-30)	F. S. Trueman, Leeds	1961
10-130 (4-45, 6-85)	F. H. Tyson, Sydney	1954-55
10-82 (4-37, 6-45)	D. L. Underwood, Leeds	1972
11-215 (7-113, 4-102)	D. L. Underwood, Adelaide	1974-75
15-104 (7-61, 8-43)	H. Verity, Lord's	1934
10-57 (6-41, 4-16)	W. Voce, Brisbane	1936-37
13-256 (5-130, 8-126)	J. C. White, Adelaide	1928-29
10-49 (5-29, 5-20)	F. E. Woolley, The Oval	1912

For Australia (33)

10-239 (4-129, 6-110)	L. O'B. Fleetwood-Smith, Adelaide	1936-37
10-160 (4-88, 6-72)	G. Giffen, Sydney	1891-92
11-82 (5-45, 6-37)†	C. V. Grimmett, Sydney	1924-25
10-201 (5-107, 5-94)	C. V. Grimmett, Nottingham	1930
10-122 (5-65, 5-57)	R. M. Hogg, Perth	1978-79
10-66 (5-30, 5-36)	R. M. Hogg, Melbourne	1978-79
12-175 (5-85, 7-90)†	H. V. Hordern, Sydney	1911-12
10-161 (5-95, 5-66)	H. V. Hordern, Sydney	1911-12
10-164 (7-88, 3-76)	E. Jones, Lord's	1899
10-181 (5-58, 5-123)	D. K. Lillee, The Oval	1972
11-165 (6-26, 5-139)	D. K. Lillee, Melbourne	1976-77
11-138 (6-60, 5-78)	D. K. Lillee, Melbourne	1979-80
11-85 (7-58, 4-27)	C. G. Macartney, Leeds	1909
10-302 (5-160, 5-142)	A. A. Mailey, Adelaide	1920-21
13-236 (4-115, 9-121)	A. A. Mailey, Melbourne	1920-21
16-137 (8-84, 8-53)†	R. A. L. Massie, Lord's	1972
10-152 (5-72, 5-80)	K. R. Miller, Lord's	1956
13-77 (7-17, 6-60)	M. A. Noble, Melbourne	1901-02
11-103 (5-51, 6-52)	M. A. Noble, Sheffield	1902
10-129 (5-63, 5-66)	W. J. O'Reilly, Melbourne	1932-33
11-129 (4-75, 7-54)	W. J. O'Reilly, Nottingham	1934
10-122 (5-66, 5-56)	W. J. O'Reilly, Leeds	1938
11-165 (7-68, 4-97)	G. E. Palmer, Sydney	1881-82
10-126 (7-65, 3-61)	G. E. Palmer, Melbourne	1882-83
13-110 (6-48, 7-62)	F. R. Spofforth, Melbourne	1878-79
14-90 (7-46, 7-44)	F. R. Spofforth, The Oval	1882
11-117 (4-73, 7-44)	F. R. Spofforth, Sydney	1882-83
10-144 (4-54, 6-90)	F. R. Spofforth, Sydney	1884-85
12-89 (6-59, 6-30)	H. Trumble, The Oval	1896

10-128	(4-75, 6-53)	H. Trumble, Manchester	1902
12-173	(8-65, 4-108)	H. Trumble, The Oval	1902
12-87	(5-44, 7-43)	C. T. B. Turner, Sydney	1887-88
10-63	(5-27, 5-36)	C. T. B. Turner, Lord's	1888

† *Significes ten wickets or more on first appearance in England–Australia Tests.*

Note: J. Briggs, J. C. Laker, T. Richardson in 1896, R. M. Hogg, A. A. Mailey, H. Trumble and C. T. B. Turner took ten wickets or more in successive Tests. J. Briggs was omitted, however, from the England team for the first Test match in 1893.

MOST WICKETS IN A SERIES

England in England	46 (average 9.60)	J. C. Laker 1956
England in Australia	38 (average 23.18)	M. W. Tate 1924-25
Australia in England	31 (average 17.67)	D. K. Lillee 1972
Australia in Australia	41 (average 12.85)	R. M. Hogg (6 Tests) .. 1978-79

THE HAT-TRICK

For England		**For Australia**	
W. Bates at Melbourne	1882-83	F. R. Spofforth at Melbourne ...	1878-79
J. Briggs at Sydney	1891-92	H. Trumble at Melbourne	1901-02
J. T. Hearne at Leeds	1899	H. Trumble at Melbourne	1903-04

WICKET-KEEPING – MOST DISMISSALS

	Matches	Caught	Stumped	Total
†A. P. E. Knott (England)	32	91	8	99
R. W. Marsh (Australia)	31	90	7	97
†W. A. S. Oldfield (Australia) .	38	59	31	90
A. F. A. Lilley (England)	32	65	19	84
A. T. W. Grout (Australia) ..	22	69	7	76
T. G. Evans (England)	31	63	12	75

† *The number of catches by A. P. E. Knott (91) and stumpings by W. A. Oldfield (31) are respective records in England–Australia Tests.*

SCORERS OF OVER 2,000 RUNS

	Tests		Innings		Not Outs		Runs		Highest Inns		Average
D. G. Bradman	37	..	63	..	7	..	5,028	..	334	..	89.78
J. B. Hobbs	41	..	71	..	4	..	3,636	..	187	..	54.26
W. R. Hammond ...	31	..	58	..	3	..	2,852	..	251	..	51.85
H. Sutcliffe	27	..	46	..	5	..	2,741	..	194	..	66.85
C. Hill	41	..	76	..	1	..	2,660	..	188	..	35.46
J. H. Edrich	32	..	57	..	3	..	2,644	..	175	..	48.96
G. Boycott	32	..	59	..	9	..	2,553	..	191	..	51.06
M. C. Cowdrey	43	..	75	..	4	..	2,433	..	113	..	34.26
L. Hutton	27	..	49	..	6	..	2,428	..	364	..	56.46
R. N. Harvey	37	..	68	..	5	..	2,416	..	167	..	38.34
V. T. Trumper	40	..	74	..	5	..	2,263	..	185*	..	32.79
W. M. Lawry	29	..	51	..	5	..	2,233	..	166	..	48.54
G. S. Chappell	30	..	55	..	6	..	2,230	..	144	..	45.51
S. E. Gregory	52	..	92	..	7	..	2,193	..	201	..	25.80
W. W. Armstrong ..	42	..	71	..	9	..	2,172	..	158	..	35.03
I. M. Chappell	30	..	56	..	4	..	2,138	..	192	..	41.11
K. F. Barrington	23	..	39	..	6	..	2,111	..	256	..	63.96
A. R. Morris	24	..	43	..	2	..	2,080	..	206	..	50.73

BOWLERS WITH 100 WICKETS

	Tests	Balls	Runs	Wickets	5 Wkts/ Inns	Average
H. Trumble	31	.. 7,895	.. 2,945	.. 141	.. 9	.. 20.88
D. K. Lillee	22	.. 6,220	.. 2,452	.. 124	.. 9	.. 19.77
M. A. Noble	39	.. 6,845	.. 2,860	.. 115	.. 9	.. 24.86
R. R. Lindwall	29	.. 6,728	.. 2,559	.. 114	.. 6	.. 22.44
W. Rhodes	41	.. 5,791	.. 2,616	.. 109	.. 6	.. 24.00
S. F. Barnes	20	.. 5,749	.. 2,288	.. 106	.. 12	.. 21.58
C. V. Grimmett	22	.. 9,224	.. 3,439	.. 106	.. 11	.. 32.44
D. L. Underwood ...	29	.. 8,000	.. 2,770	.. 105	.. 4	.. 26.38
A. V. Bedser	21	.. 7,065	.. 2,859	.. 104	.. 7	.. 27.49
G. Giffen	31	.. 6,325	.. 2,791	.. 103	.. 7	.. 27.09
W. J. O'Reilly	19	.. 7,864	.. 2,587	.. 102	.. 8	.. 25.36
R. Peel	20	.. 5,216	.. 1,715	.. 102	.. 6	.. 16.81
C. T. B. Turner	17	.. 5,195	.. 1,670	.. 101	.. 11	.. 16.53

ENGLAND v SOUTH AFRICA

	Captains			Won by	Won by	
Season	England	South Africa	Tests	England	South Africa	Drawn
1888-89	C. A. Smith[1]	O. R. Dunell[2]	2	2	0	0
1891-92	W. W. Read	W. H. Milton	1	1	0	0
1895-96	Lord Hawke[3]	E. A. Halliwell[4]	3	3	0	0
1898-99	Lord Hawke	M. Bisset	2	2	0	0
1905-06	P. F. Warner	P. W. Sherwell	5	1	4	0
1907	R. E. Foster	P. W. Sherwell	3	1	0	2
1909-10	H. D. G. Leveson Gower[5]	S. J. Snooke	5	2	3	0
1912	C. B. Fry	F. Mitchell[6]	3	3	0	0
1913-14	J. W. H. T. Douglas	H. W. Taylor	5	4	0	1
1922-23	F. T. Mann	H. W. Taylor	5	2	1	2
1924	A. E. R. Gilligan[7]	H. W. Taylor	5	3	0	2
1927-28	R. T. Stanyforth[8]	H. G. Deane	5	2	2	1
1929	J. C. White[9]	H. G. Deane	5	2	0	3
1930-31	A. P. F. Chapman	H. G. Deane[10]	5	0	1	4
1935	R. E. S. Wyatt	H. F. Wade	5	0	1	4
1938-39	W. R. Hammond	A. Melville	5	1	0	4
1947	N. W. D. Yardley	A. Melville	5	3	0	2
1948-49	F. G. Mann	A. D. Nourse	5	2	0	3
1951	F. R. Brown	A. D. Nourse	5	3	1	1
1955	P. B. H. May	J. E. Cheetham[11]	5	3	2	0
1956-57	P. B. H. May	C. B. van Ryneveld[12]	5	2	2	1
1960	M. C. Cowdrey	D. J. McGlew	5	3	0	2
1964-65	M. J. K. Smith	T. L. Goddard	5	1	0	4
1965	M. J. K. Smith	P. L. van der Merwe	3	0	1	2
	In South Africa		58	25	13	20
	In England		44	21	5	18
	Totals		102	46	18	38

Notes: The following deputised for the official touring captain or were appointed by the home authority for only a minor proportion of the series:

[1] M. P. Bowden (Second). [2] W. H. Milton (Second). [3] Sir T. C. O'Brien (First). [4] A. R. Richards (Third). [5] F. L. Fane (Fourth and Fifth). [6] L. J. Tancred (Second and Third). [7] J. W. H. T. Douglas (Fourth). [8] G. T. S. Stevens (Fifth). [9] A. W. Carr (Fourth and Fifth). [10] E. P. Nupen (First), H. B. Cameron (Fourth and Fifth). [11] D. J. McGlew (Third and Fourth). [12] D. J. McGlew (Second).

HIGHEST TOTALS FOR AN INNINGS

By England				By South Africa		
654-5	Durban	1938-39		538	Leeds	1951
608	Johannesburg	1948-49		533	Nottingham	1947
559-9	Cape Town	1938-39		530	Durban	1938-39
554-8	Lord's	1947		521-8	Manchester	1955
551	Nottingham	1947		513-8	Cape Town	1930-31
534-6	The Oval	1935		502	Port Elizabeth	1964-65
531-2	Lord's	1924		501-7	Cape Town	1964-65
531	Johannesburg	1964-65		500	Leeds	1955

SMALLEST TOTALS FOR AN INNINGS

By England				By South Africa		
76	Leeds	1907		30	Port Elizabeth	1895-96
92	Cape Town	1898-99		30	Birmingham	1924
110	Port Elizabeth	1956-57		35	Cape Town	1898-99

INDIVIDUAL HUNDREDS IN THE MATCHES 1888-89—1965

For England (87)

120	R. Abel, Cape Town	1888-89	
148*	L. E. G. Ames, The Oval	1935	
115	L. E. G. Ames, Cape Town	1938-39	
148*	K. F. Barrington, Durban	1964-65	
121	K. F. Barrington, Johannesburg	1964-65	
117	G. Boycott, Port Elizabeth	1964-65	
104†	L. C. Braund, Lord's	1907	
208	D. C. S. Compton, Lord's	1947	
163†	D. C. S. Compton, Nottingham	1947	
115	D. C. S. Compton, Manchester	1947	
113	D. C. S. Compton, The Oval	1947	
114	D. C. S. Compton, Johannesburg	1948-49	
112	D. C. S. Compton, Nottingham	1951	
158	D. C. S. Compton, Manchester	1955	
101	M. C. Cowdrey, Cape Town	1956-57	
155	M. C. Cowdrey, The Oval	1960	
105	M. C. Cowdrey, Nottingham	1965	
104	D. Denton, Johannesburg	1909-10	
172	E. R. Dexter, Johannesburg	1964-65	
119†	J. W. H. T. Douglas, Durban	1913-14	
219	W. J. Edrich, Durban	1938-39	
191	W. J. Edrich, Manchester	1947	
189	W. J. Edrich, Lord's	1947	
143	F. L. Fane, Johannesburg	1905-06	
129	C. B. Fry, The Oval	1907	
106†	P. A. Gibb, Johannesburg	1938-39	
120	P. A. Gibb, Durban	1938-39	
138*	W. R. Hammond, Birmingham	1929	
101*	W. R. Hammond, The Oval	1929	
136*	W. R. Hammond, Durban	1930-31	
181	W. R. Hammond, Cape Town	1938-39	
120	W. R. Hammond, Durban	1938-39	
140	W. R. Hammond, Durban	1938-39	
122	T. W. Hayward, Johannesburg	1895-96	
132	E. H. Hendren, Leeds	1924	
142	E. H. Hendren, The Oval	1924	
124	A. J. L. Hill, Cape Town	1895-96	
187	J. B. Hobbs, Leeds	1909-10	
211	J. B. Hobbs, Lord's	1924	
100	L. Hutton, Leeds	1947	
158	L. Hutton, Johannesburg	1948-49	
123	L. Hutton, Johannesburg	1948-49	
100	L. Hutton, Leeds	1951	
110*	D. J. Insole, Durban	1956-57	
102	M. Leyland, Lord's	1929	
161	M. Leyland, The Oval	1935	
136*	F. G. Mann, Port Elizabeth	1948-49	
138†	P. B. H. May, Leeds	1951	
112	P. B. H. May, Lord's	1955	
117	P. B. H. May, Manchester	1955	
102	C. P. Mead, Johannesburg	1913-14	
117	C. P. Mead, Port Elizabeth	1913-14	
181	C. P. Mead, Durban	1922-23	
122*	P. H. Parfitt, Johannesburg	1964-65	
108*	J. M. Parks, Durban	1964-65	
117† 100	} E. Paynter, Johannesburg	1938-39	
243	E. Paynter, Durban	1938-39	
175	G. Pullar, The Oval	1960	

152	W. Rhodes, Johannesburg .	1913-14
117†	P. E. Richardson, Johannesburg	1956-57
108	R. W. V. Robins, Manchester	1935
140 111	} C. A. G. Russell, Durban ..	1922-23
137	R. T. Simpson, Nottingham	1951
121	M. J. K. Smith, Cape Town	1964-65
119†	R. H. Spooner, Lord's	1912
122	H. Sutcliffe, Lord's	1924
102	H. Sutcliffe, Johannesburg ..	1927-28
114	H. Sutcliffe, Birmingham ..	1929
100	H. Sutcliffe, Lord's	1929
104 109*	} H. Sutcliffe, The Oval	1929
100*	M. W. Tate, Lord's	1929

122	G. E. Tyldesley, Johannesburg	1927-28
100	G. E. Tyldesley, Durban ..	1927-28
112	J. T. Tyldesley, Cape Town	1898-99
112	B. H. Valentine, Cape Town	1938-39
132*†	P. F. Warner, Johannesburg	1898-99
195	C. Washbrook, Johannesburg	1948-49
111	A. J. Watkins, Johannesburg	1948-49
134*	H. Wood, Cape Town	1891-92
115*	F. E. Woolley, Johannesburg	1922-23
134*	F. E. Woolley, Lord's	1924
154	F. E. Woolley, Manchester	1929
113	R. E. S. Wyatt, Manchester	1929
149	R. E. S. Wyatt, Nottingham	1935

For South Africa (58)

138	E. J. Barlow, Cape Town ..	1964-65
144*	K. C. Bland, Johannesburg	1964-65
127	K. C. Bland, The Oval	1965
120	R. H. Catterall, Birmingham	1924
120	R. H. Catterall, Lord's	1924
119	R. H. Catterall, Durban ...	1927-28
117	E. L. Dalton, The Oval	1935
102	E. L. Dalton, Johannesburg	1938-39
116*	W. R. Endean, Leeds	1955
123	G. A. Faulkner, Johannesburg	1909-10
112	T. L. Goddard, Johannesburg	1964-65
102	C. M. H. Hathorn, Johannesburg	1905-06
104*	D. J. McGlew, Manchester	1955
133	D. J. McGlew, Leeds	1955
142	R. A. McLean, Lord's	1955
100	R. A. McLean, Durban	1956-57
109	R. A. McLean, Manchester	1960
103	A. Melville, Durban	1938-39
189 104*	} A. Melville, Nottingham ..	1947
117	A. Melville, Lord's	1947
123	B. Mitchell, Cape Town ...	1930-31
164*	B. Mitchell, Lord's	1935
128	B. Mitchell, The Oval	1935
109	B. Mitchell, Durban	1938-39
120 189*	} B. Mitchell, The Oval	1947
120	B. Mitchell, Cape Town ...	1948-49
120	A. D. Nourse, Cape Town .	1938-39
103	A. D. Nourse, Durban	1938-39
149	A. D. Nourse, Nottingham	1947

115	A. D. Nourse, Manchester .	1947
129*	A. D. Nourse, Johannesburg	1948-49
112	A. D. Nourse, Cape Town .	1948-49
208	A. D. Nourse, Nottingham	1951
129	H. G. Owen-Smith, Leeds .	1929
154	A. J. Pithey, Cape Town ..	1964-65
137	R. G. Pollock, Port Elizabeth	1964-65
125	R. G. Pollock, Nottingham	1965
156*	E. A. B. Rowan, Johannesburg	1948-49
236	E. A. B. Rowan, Leeds	1951
115	P. W. Sherwell, Lord's	1907
141	I. J. Siedle, Cape Town	1930-31
106	J. H. Sinclair, Cape Town .	1898-99
109	H. W. Taylor, Durban	1913-14
176	H. W. Taylor, Johannesburg	1922-23
101	H. W. Taylor, Johannesburg	1922-23
102	H. W. Taylor, Durban	1922-23
101	H. W. Taylor, Johannesburg	1927-28
121	H. W. Taylor, The Oval ...	1929
117	H. W. Taylor, Cape Town .	1930-31
125	P. G. V. van der Bijl, Durban	1938-39
124	K. G. Viljoen, Manchester .	1935
125	W. W. Wade, Port Elizabeth	1948-49
113	J. H. B. Waite, Manchester	1955
147	G. C. White, Johannesburg	1905-06
118	G. C. White, Durban	1909-10
108	P. L. Winslow, Manchester	1955

† *Signifies hundred on first appearance in England–South Africa Tests.*

Notes: P. F. Warner carried his bat through the second innings.

The highest score by a South African batsman on début is 93* by A. W. Nourse at Johannesburg in 1905-06.

P. N. F. Mansell made 90 at Leeds in 1951, the best on début in England.

RECORD PARTNERSHIP FOR EACH WICKET

By England

359 for 1st†	L. Hutton and C. Washbrook at Johannesburg	1948-49
280 for 2nd	P. A. Gibb and W. J. Edrich at Durban	1938-39
370 for 3rd†	W. J. Edrich and D. C. S. Compton at Lord's	1947
197 for 4th	W. R. Hammond and L. E. G. Ames at Cape Town	1938-39
237 for 5th	D. C. S. Compton and N. W. D. Yardley at Nottingham	1947
206* for 6th	K. F. Barrington and J. M. Parks at Durban	1964-65
115 for 7th	M. C. Bird and J. W. H. T. Douglas at Durban	1913-14
154 for 8th	C. W. Wright and H. R. Bromley-Davenport at Johannesburg	1895-96
71 for 9th	H. Wood and J. T. Hearne at Cape Town	1891-92
92 for 10th	C. A. G. Russell and A. E. R. Gilligan at Durban	1922-23

By South Africa

260 for 1st†	I. J. Siedle and B. Mitchell at Cape Town	1930-31
198 for 2nd†	E. A. B. Rowan and C. B. van Ryneveld at Leeds	1951
319 for 3rd	A. Melville and A. D. Nourse at Nottingham	1947
214 for 4th†	H. W. Taylor and H. G. Deane at The Oval	1929
157 for 5th†	A. J. Pithey and J. H. B. Waite at Johannesburg	1964-65
171 for 6th	P. L. Winslow and J. H. B. Waite at Manchester	1955
123 for 7th	H. G. Deane and E. P. Nupen at Durban	1927-28
109* for 8th	B. Mitchell and L. Tuckett at The Oval	1947
137 for 9th†	E. L. Dalton and A. B. C. Langton at The Oval	1935
103 for 10th†	H. G. Owen-Smith and A. J. Bell at Leeds	1929

† *Denotes record partnership against all countries.*

MOST RUNS IN A SERIES

England in England	753 (average 94.12)	D. C. S. Compton	1947
England in South Africa	653 (average 81.62)	E. Paynter	1938-39
South Africa in England	621 (average 69.00)	A. D. Nourse	1947
South Africa in South Africa ...	582 (average 64.66)	H. W. Taylor	1922-23

TEN WICKETS OR MORE IN A MATCH

For England (23)

11-110 (5-25, 6-85)†	S. F. Barnes, Lord's	1912
10-115 (6-52, 4-63)	S. F. Barnes, Leeds	1912
13-57 (5-28, 8-29)	S. F. Barnes, The Oval	1912
10-105 (5-57, 5-48)	S. F. Barnes, Durban	1913-14
17-159 (8-56, 9-103)	S. F. Barnes, Johannesburg	1913-14
14-144 (7-56, 7-88)	S. F. Barnes, Durban	1913-14
12-112 (7-58, 5-54)	A. V. Bedser, Manchester	1951
11-118 (6-68, 5-50)	C. Blythe, Cape Town	1905-06
15-99 (8-59, 7-40)	C. Blythe, Leeds	1907
10-104 (7-46, 3-58)	C. Blythe, Cape Town	1909-10
15-28 (7-17, 8-11)	J. Briggs, Cape Town	1888-89
13-91 (6-54, 7-37)†	J. J. Ferris, Cape Town	1891-92
10-207 (7-115, 3-92)	A. P. Freeman, Leeds	1929
12-171 (7-71, 5-100)	A. P. Freeman, Manchester	1929
12-130 (7-70, 5-60)	G. Geary, Johannesburg	1927-28
11-90 (6-7, 5-83)	A. E. R. Gilligan, Birmingham	1924
10-119 (4-64, 6-55)	J. C. Laker, The Oval	1951

15-45 (7-38, 8-7)†	G. A. Lohmann, Port Elizabeth	1895-96
12-71 (9-28, 3-43)	G. A. Lohmann, Johannesburg	1895-96
11-97 (6-63, 5-34)	J. B. Statham, Lord's	1960
12-101 (7-52, 5-49)	R. Tattersall, Lord's	1951
12-89 (5-53, 7-36)	J. H. Wardle, Cape Town	1956-57
10-175 (5-95, 5-80)	D. V. P. Wright, Lord's	1947

For South Africa (6)

11-112 (4-49, 7-63)†	A. E. Hall, Cape Town	1922-23
11-150 (5-63, 6-87)	E. P. Nupen, Johannesburg	1930-31
10-87 (5-53, 5-34)	P. M. Pollock, Nottingham	1965
12-127 (4-57, 8-70)	S. J. Snooke, Johannesburg	1905-06
13-192 (4-79, 9-113)	H. J. Tayfield, Johannesburg	1956-57
12-181 (5-87, 7-94)	A. E. E. Vogler, Johannesburg	1909-10

† *Signifies ten wickets or more on first appearance in England–South Africa Tests.*

Note: S. F. Barnes took ten wickets or more in his first five Tests v South Africa and in six of his seven Tests v South Africa. A. P. Freeman and G. A. Lohmann took ten wickets or more in successive matches.

MOST WICKETS IN A SERIES

England in England	34 (average 8.29)	S. F. Barnes	1912
England in South Africa	49 (average 10.93)	S. F. Barnes	1913-14
South Africa in England	26 (average 21.84)	H. J. Tayfield	1955
South Africa in England	26 (average 22.57)	N. A. T. Adcock	1960
South Africa in South Africa ...	37 (average 17.18)	H. J. Tayfield	1956-57

HIGHEST MATCH AGGREGATES

1,981 for 35 wickets at Durban	1938-39
1,477 for 33 wickets at The Oval	1947
1,458 for 31 wickets at Nottingham	1947

LOWEST MATCH AGGREGATES

378 for 30 wickets at The Oval	1912
382 for 30 wickets at Cape Town	1888-89

THE HAT-TRICK

For England		**For South Africa**	
G. A. Lohmann at Port Elizabeth	1895-96	G. M. Griffin at Lord's	1960
T. W. J. Goddard at Johannesburg	1938-39		

Note: At Leeds in 1947 K. Cranston finished South Africa's second innings by taking four wickets in one over of six balls for no runs, but this did not include the hat-trick.

ENGLAND v WEST INDIES

Season	England	West Indies (Captains)	Tests	Won by England	Won by West Indies	Drawn
1928	A. P. F. Chapman	R. K. Nunes	3	3	0	0
1929-30	Hon. F. S. G. Calthorpe	E. L. G. Hoad[1]	4	1	1	2
1933	D. R. Jardine[2]	G. C. Grant	3	2	0	1
1934-35	R. E. S. Wyatt	G. C. Grant	4	1	2	1
1939	W. R. Hammond	R. S. Grant	3	1	0	2
1947-48	G. O. B. Allen[3]	J. D. C. Goddard[4]	4	0	2	2
1950	N. W. D. Yardley[5]	J. D. C. Goddard	4	1	3	0
1953-54	L. Hutton	J. B. Stollmeyer	5	2	2	1
1957	P. B. H. May	J. D. C. Goddard	5	3	0	2
1959-60	P. B. H. May[6]	F. C. M. Alexander	5	1	0	4

THE WISDEN TROPHY

1963	E. R. Dexter	F. M. Worrell	5	1	3	1
1966	M. C. Cowdrey[7]	G. S. Sobers	5	1	3	1
1967-68	M. C. Cowdrey	G. S. Sobers	5	1	0	4
1969	R. Illingworth	G. S. Sobers	3	2	0	1
1973	R. Illingworth	R. B. Kanhai	3	0	2	1
1973-74	M. H. Denness	R. B. Kanhai	5	1	1	3
1976	A. W. Greig	C. H. Lloyd	5	0	3	2
1980	I. T. Botham	C. H. Lloyd[8]	5	0	1	4
	In England		44	14	15	15
	In West Indies		32	7	8	17
	Totals		76	21	23	32

Notes: The following deputised for the official touring captain or were appointed by the home authority for only a minor proportion of the series:
   [1] N. Betancourt (Second), M. P. Fernandes (Third), R. K. Nunes (Fourth). [2] R. E. S. Wyatt (Third). [3] K. Cranston (First). [4] G. A. Headley (First), G. E. Gomez (Second). [5] F. R. Brown (Fourth). [6] M. C. Cowdrey (Fourth and Fifth). [7] M. J. K. Smith (First), D. B. Close (Fifth). [8] I. V. A. Richards (Fifth).

HIGHEST TOTALS FOR AN INNINGS

By England			By West Indies		
849	Kingston	1929-30	687-8	The Oval	1976
619-6	Nottingham	1957	681-8	Port-of-Spain	1953-54
583-4	Birmingham	1957	652-8	Lord's	1973
568	Port-of-Spain	1967-68	596-8	Bridgetown	1973-74
537	Port-of-Spain	1953-54	583-9	Kingston	1973-74
527	The Oval	1966	563-8	Bridgetown	1959-60
482	Bridgetown	1959-60	558	Nottingham	1950

LOWEST TOTALS FOR AN INNINGS

By England			By West Indies		
71	Manchester	1976	86	The Oval (2nd Inns)	1957
103	Kingston	1934-35	89	The Oval (1st Inns)	1957
103	The Oval	1950	91	Birmingham	1963
107	Port-of-Spain	1934-35	97	Lord's	1933

INDIVIDUAL HUNDREDS IN THE MATCHES 1928–1980

For England (72)

105	L. E. G. Ames, Port-of-Spain	1929-30
149	L. E. G. Ames, Kingston	1929-30
126	L. E. G. Ames, Kingston	1934-35
174	D. L. Amiss, Port-of-Spain	1973-74
262*	D. L. Amiss, Kingston	1973-74
118	D. L. Amiss, Georgetown	1973-74
203	D. L. Amiss, The Oval	1976
107†	A. H. Bakewell, The Oval	1933
128†	K. F. Barrington, Bridgetown	1959-60
121	K. F. Barrington, Port-of-Spain	1959-60
143	K. F. Barrington, Port-of-Spain	1967-68
116	G. Boycott, Georgetown	1967-68
128	G. Boycott, Manchester	1969
106	G. Boycott, Lord's	1969
112	G. Boycott, Port-of-Spain	1973-74
120†	D. C. S. Compton, Lord's	1939
133	D. C. S. Compton, Port-of-Spain	1953-54
154†	M. C. Cowdrey, Birmingham	1957
152	M. C. Cowdrey, Lord's	1957
114	M. C. Cowdrey, Kingston	1959-60
119	M. C. Cowdrey, Port-of-Spain	1959-60
101	M. C. Cowdrey, Kingston	1967-68
148	M. C. Cowdrey, Port-of-Spain	1967-68
136*†	E. R. Dexter, Bridgetown	1959-60
110	E. R. Dexter, Georgetown	1959-60
146	J. H. Edrich, Bridgetown	1967-68
104	T. G. Evans, Manchester	1950
129*	K. W. R. Fletcher, Bridgetown	1973-74
123	G. A. Gooch, Lord's	1980
258	T. W. Graveney, Nottingham	1957
164	T. W. Graveney, The Oval	1957
109	T. W. Graveney, Nottingham	1966
165	T. W. Graveney, The Oval	1966
118	T. W. Graveney, Port-of-Spain	1967-68

148	A. W. Greig, Bridgetown	1973-74
121	A. W. Greig, Georgetown	1973-74
116	A. W. Greig, Leeds	1976
140†	S. C. Griffith, Port-of-Spain	1947-48
138	W. R. Hammond, The Oval	1939
107†	J. H. Hampshire, Lord's	1969
106*†	F. C. Hayes, The Oval	1973
205*	E. H. Hendren, Port-of-Spain	1929-30
123	E. H. Hendren, Georgetown	1929-30
159	J. B. Hobbs, The Oval	1928
196†	L. Hutton, Lord's	1939
165*	L. Hutton, The Oval	1939
202*	L. Hutton, The Oval	1950
169	L. Hutton, Georgetown	1953-54
205	L. Hutton, Kingston	1953-54
113	R. Illingworth, Lord's	1969
127	D. R. Jardine, Manchester	1933
116	A. P. E. Knott, Leeds	1976
135	P. B. H. May, Port-of-Spain	1953-54
285*	P. B. H. May, Birmingham	1957
104	P. B. H. May, Nottingham	1957
126*	C. Milburn, Lord's	1966
112†	J. T. Murray, The Oval	1966
101*†	J. M. Parks, Port-of-Spain	1959-60
107	W. Place, Kingston	1947-48
126	P. E. Richardson, Nottingham	1957
107	P. E. Richardson, The Oval	1957
133	J. D. B. Robertson, Port-of-Spain	1947-48
152†	A. Sandham, Bridgetown	1929-30
325	A. Sandham, Kingston	1929-30
108	M. J. K. Smith, Port-of-Spain	1959-60
106†	D. S. Steele, Nottingham	1976
100†	R. Subba Row, Georgetown	1959-60
122†	G. E. Tyldesley, Lord's	1928
114†	C. Washbrook, Lord's	1950
102	C. Washbrook, Nottingham	1950
116†	W. Watson, Kingston	1953-54
100*	P. Willey, The Oval	1980

For West Indies (77)

105	I. Barrow, Manchester	1933
133	B. F. Butcher, Lord's	1963
209*	B. F. Butcher, Nottingham	1966
107	G. M. Carew, Port-of-Spain	1947-48
103	C. A. Davis, Lord's	1969
150	R. C. Fredericks, Birmingham	1973
138	R. C. Fredericks, Lord's	1976
109	R. C. Fredericks, Leeds	1976

112†	A. G. Ganteaume, Port-of-Spain	1947-48
134 }	C. G. Greenidge, Manchester	1976
101 }		
115	C. G. Greenidge, Leeds	1976
184	D. L. Haynes, Lord's	1980
176†	G. A. Headley, Bridgetown	1929-30
114 }	G. A. Headley, Georgetown	1929-30
112 }		

223	G. A. Headley, Kingston ..	1929-30
169*	G. A. Headley, Manchester	1933
270*	G. A. Headley, Kingston ..	1934-35
106 107 }	G. A. Headley, Lord's	1939
105*	D. A. J. Holford, Lord's ...	1966
166	J. K. Holt, Bridgetown ...	1953-54
182	C. C. Hunte, Manchester ..	1963
108*	C. C. Hunte, The Oval	1963
135	C. C. Hunte, Manchester ..	1966
121	B. D. Julien, Lord's	1973
158	A. I. Kallicharran, Port-of-Spain	1973-74
119	A. I. Kallicharran, Bridgetown	1973-74
110	R. B. Kanhai, Port-of-Spain	1959-60
104	R. B. Kanhai, The Oval ...	1966
153	R. B. Kanhai, Port-of-Spain	1967-68
150	R. B. Kanhai, Georgetown	1967-68
157	R. B. Kanhai, Lord's	1973
118*	C. H. Lloyd, Port-of-Spain	1967-68
113*	C. H. Lloyd, Bridgetown ..	1967-68
132	C. H. Lloyd, The Oval	1973
101	C. H. Lloyd, Manchester ..	1980
137	S. M. Nurse, Leeds	1966
136	S. M. Nurse, Port-of-Spain	1967-68
106	A. F. Rae, Lord's	1950
109	A. F. Rae, The Oval	1950
232†	I. V. A. Richards, Nottingham	1976
135	I. V. A. Richards, Manchester	1976
291	I. V. A. Richards, The Oval	1976
145	I. V. A. Richards, Lord's ..	1980
122	C. A. Roach, Bridgetown ..	1929-30
209	C. A. Roach, Georgetown .	1929-30
120	L. G. Rowe, Kingston	1973-74
302	L. G. Rowe, Bridgetown ..	1973-74
123	L. G. Rowe, Port-of-Spain	1973-74
161†	O. G. Smith, Birmingham .	1957
168	O. G. Smith, Nottingham .	1957
226	G. S. Sobers, Bridgetown ..	1959-60
147	G. S. Sobers, Kingston	1959-60
145	G. S. Sobers, Georgetown .	1959-60
102	G. S. Sobers, Leeds	1963
161	G. S. Sobers, Manchester ..	1966
163*	G. S. Sobers, Lord's	1966
174	G. S. Sobers, Leeds	1966
113*	G. S. Sobers, Kingston	1967-68
152	G. S. Sobers, Georgetown .	1967-68
150*	G. S. Sobers, Lord's	1973
168*	C. L. Walcott, Lord's	1950
220	C. L. Walcott, Bridgetown .	1953-54
124	C. L. Walcott, Port-of-Spain	1953-54
116	C. L. Walcott, Kingston ..	1953-54
141	E. D. Weekes, Kingston	1947-48
129	E. D. Weekes, Nottingham	1950
206	E. D. Weekes, Port-of-Spain	1953-54
137	K. H. Weekes, The Oval ..	1939
131*	F. M. M. Worrell, Georgetown	1947-48
261	F. M. M. Worrell, Nottingham	1950
138	F. M. M. Worrell, The Oval	1950
167	F. M. M. Worrell, Port-of-Spain	1953-54
191*	F. M. M. Worrell, Nottingham	1957
197*	F. M. M. Worrell, Bridgetown	1959-60

† *Signifies hundred on first appearance in England–West Indies Tests. S. C. Griffith provided the only instance for England of a player hitting his maiden century in first-class cricket in his first Test.*

RECORD PARTNERSHIPS FOR EACH WICKET

By England

212 for 1st	C. Washbrook and R. T. Simpson at Nottingham	1950
266 for 2nd	P. E. Richardson and T. W. Graveney at Nottingham	1957
264 for 3rd	L. Hutton and W. R. Hammond at The Oval	1939
411 for 4th†	P. B. H. May and M. C. Cowdrey at Birmingham	1957
130* for 5th	C. Milburn and T. W. Graveney at Lord's	1966
163 for 6th	A. W. Greig and A. P. E. Knott at Bridgetown	1973-74
197 for 7th†	M. J. K. Smith and J. M. Parks at Port-of-Spain	1959-60
217 for 8th	T. W. Graveney and J. T. Murray at The Oval	1966
109 for 9th	G. A. R. Lock and P. I. Pocock at Georgetown	1967-68
128 for 10th	K. Higgs and J. A. Snow at The Oval	1966

By West Indies

206 for 1st	R. C. Fredericks and L. G. Rowe at Kingston	1973-74
249 for 2nd	L. G. Rowe and A. I. Kallicharran at Bridgetown	1973-74
338 for 3rd†	E. D. Weekes and F. M. M. Worrell at Port-of-Spain	1953-54
399 for 4th†	G. S. Sobers and F. M. M. Worrell at Bridgetown	1959-60
265 for 5th†	S. M. Nurse and G. S. Sobers at Leeds	1966
274* for 6th†	G. S. Sobers and D. A. J. Holford at Lord's	1966
155*‡ for 7th	G. S. Sobers and B. D. Julien at Lord's	1973
99 for 8th	C. A. McWatt and J. K. Holt at Georgetown	1953-54
63* for 9th	G. S. Sobers and W. W. Hall at Port-of-Spain	1967-68
55 for 10th	F. M. M. Worrell and S. Ramadhin at Nottingham	1957

† *Denotes record partnership against all countries.*

‡ *231 runs were added for this wicket in two separate partnerships; G. S. Sobers retired ill and was replaced by K. D. Boyce when 155 had been added.*

TEN WICKETS OR MORE IN A MATCH

For England (10)

11-98 (7-44, 4-54)	T. E. Bailey, Lord's	1957
10-93 (5-54, 5-39)	A. P. Freeman, Manchester	1928
13-156 (8-86, 5-70)	A. W. Greig, Port-of-Spain	1973-74
11-48 (5-28, 6-20)	G. A. R. Lock, The Oval	1957
11-96 (5-37, 6-59)†	C. S. Marriott, The Oval	1933
10-142 (4-82, 6-60)	J. A. Snow, Georgetown	1967-68
10-195 (5-105, 5-90)†	G. T. S. Stevens, Bridgetown	1929-30
11-152 (6-100, 5-52)	F. S. Trueman, Lord's	1963
12-119 (5-75, 7-44)	F. S. Trueman, Birmingham	1963
11-149 (4-79, 7-70)	W. Voce, Port-of-Spain	1929-30

For West Indies (10)

11-147 (5-70, 6-77)†	K. D. Boyce, The Oval	1973
11-229 (5-137, 6-92)	W. Ferguson, Port-of-Spain	1947-48
11-157 (5-59, 6-98)†	L. R. Gibbs, Manchester	1963
10-106 (5-37, 5-69)	L. R. Gibbs, Manchester	1966
14-149 (8-92, 6-57)	M. A. Holding, The Oval	1976
10-96 (5-41, 5-55)†	H. H. H. Johnson, Kingston	1947-48
11-152 (5-66, 6-86)	S. Ramadhin, Lord's	1950
10-123 (5-60, 5-63)	A. M. E. Roberts, Lord's	1976
11-204 (8-104, 3-100)†	A. L. Valentine, Manchester	1950
10-160 (4-121, 6-39)	A. L. Valentine, The Oval	1950

† *Signifies ten wickets or more on first appearance in England–West Indies Tests.*

Note: F. S. Trueman took ten wickets or more in successive matches.

HAT-TRICK

P. J. Loader for England at Leeds   1957

ENGLAND v NEW ZEALAND

	Captains			Won by	Won by	
Season	England	New Zealand	Tests	England	New Zealand	Drawn
1929-30	A. H. H. Gilligan	T. C. Lowry	4	1	0	3
1931	D. R. Jardine	T. C. Lowry	3	1	0	2
1932-33	D. R. Jardine[1]	M. L. Page	2	0	0	2
1937	R. W. V. Robins	M. L. Page	3	1	0	2
1946-47	W. R. Hammond	W. A. Hadlee	1	0	0	1
1949	F. G. Mann[2]	W. A. Hadlee	4	0	0	4
1950-51	F. R. Brown	W. A. Hadlee	2	1	0	1
1954-55	L. Hutton	G. O. Rabone	2	2	0	0
1958	P. B. H. May	J. R. Reid	5	4	0	1
1958-59	P. B. H. May	J. R. Reid	2	1	0	1
1962-63	E. R. Dexter	J. R. Reid	3	3	0	0
1965	M. J. K. Smith	J. R. Reid	3	3	0	0
1965-66	M. J. K. Smith	B. W. Sinclair[3]	3	0	0	3
1969	R. Illingworth	G. T. Dowling	3	2	0	1
1970-71	R. Illingworth	G. T. Dowling	2	1	0	1
1973	R. Illingworth	B. E. Congdon	3	2	0	1
1974-75	M. H. Denness	B. E. Congdon	2	1	0	1
1977-78	G. Boycott	M. G. Burgess	3	1	1	1
1978	J. M. Brearley	M. G. Burgess	3	3	0	0
	In New Zealand		26	11	1	14
	In England		27	16	0	11
	Totals		53	27	1	25

Notes: The following deputised for the official touring captain or were appointed by the home authority for only a minor proportion of the series:
[1] R. E. S. Wyatt (Second). [2] F. R. Brown (Third and Fourth). [3] M. E. Chapple (First).

HIGHEST TOTALS FOR AN INNINGS

By England				By New Zealand		
593-6	Auckland	1974-75		551-9	Lord's	1973
562-7	Auckland	1962-63		484 ..	Lord's	1949
560-8	Christchurch	1932-33		469-9	Lord's	1931
550 ..	Christchurch	1950-51		440 ..	Wellington	1929-30
548-7	Auckland	1932-33		440 ..	Nottingham	1973

LOWEST TOTALS FOR AN INNINGS

By England				By New Zealand		
64 ..	Wellington	1977-78		26 ..	Auckland	1954-55
181 ..	Christchurch	1929-30		47 ..	Lord's	1958
187 ..	Manchester	1937		65 ..	Christchurch	1970-71
190 ..	Lord's	1969		67 ..	Leeds	1958
				67 ..	Lord's	1978

INDIVIDUAL HUNDREDS IN THE MATCHES 1929-30—1978

For England (55)

122† G. O. B. Allen, Lord's	1931	216 K. W. R. Fletcher, Auckland 1974-75
137† L. E. G. Ames, Lord's	1931	111† D. I. Gower, The Oval 1978
103 L. E. G. Ames, Christchurch	1932-33	139† A. W. Greig, Nottingham .. 1973
138*† D. L. Amiss, Nottingham .	1973	100* W. R. Hammond, The Oval 1931
164* D. L. Amiss, Christchurch .	1974-75	227 W. R. Hammond, Christchurch 1932-33
134* T. E. Bailey, Christchurch .	1950-51	336* W. R. Hammond, Auckland 1932-33
126† K. F. Barrington, Auckland	1962-63	140 W. R. Hammond, Lord's .. 1937
163 K. F. Barrington, Leeds ...	1965	114† J. Hardstaff, Lord's 1937
137 K. F. Barrington, Birmingham	1965	103 J. Hardstaff, The Oval ... 1937
103 I. T. Botham, Christchurch	1977-78	100 L. Hutton, Manchester ... 1937
109 E. H. Bowley, Auckland ..	1929-30	101 L. Hutton, Leeds 1949
115 G. Boycott, Leeds	1973	206 L. Hutton, The Oval 1949
131 G. Boycott, Nottingham ...	1978	125† B. R. Knight, Auckland ... 1962-63
114 D. C. S. Compton, Leeds ..	1949	101 A. P. E. Knott, Auckland .. 1970-71
116 D. C. S. Compton, Lord's .	1949	196 G. B. Legge, Auckland ... 1929-30
128* M. C. Cowdrey, Wellington	1962-63	113* P. B. H. May, Leeds 1958
119 M. C. Cowdrey, Lord's ...	1965	101 P. B. H. May, Manchester . 1958
181 M. H. Denness, Auckland ..	1974-75	124* P. B. H. May, Auckland ... 1958-59
141 E. R. Dexter, Christchurch	1958-59	104*† C. A. Milton, Leeds 1958
100 B. L. D'Oliveira, Christchurch	1970-71	131*† P. H. Parfitt, Auckland ... 1962-63
117 K. S. Duleepsinhji, Auckland	1929-30	158 C. T. Radley, Auckland ... 1977-78
109 K. S. Duleepsinhji, The Oval	1931	100† P. E. Richardson, Birmingham 1958
310*† J. H. Edrich, Leeds	1965	121† J. D. B. Robertson, Lord's . 1949
115 J. H. Edrich, Lord's	1969	111 P. J. Sharpe, Nottingham .. 1969
155 J. H. Edrich, Nottingham ..	1969	103† R. T. Simpson, Manchester 1949
100 W. J. Edrich, The Oval ...	1949	117† H. Sutcliffe, The Oval 1931
178 K. W. R. Fletcher, Lord's .	1973	109*† H. Sutcliffe, Manchester .. 1931
		103* C. Washbrook, Leeds 1949

For New Zealand (21)

104 M. G. Burgess, Auckland .	1970-71	122 } G. P. Howarth, Auckland . 1977-78
105 M. G. Burgess, Lord's	1973	102 }
104 B. E. Congdon, Christchurch	1965-66	123 G. P. Howarth, Lord's 1978
176 B. E. Congdon, Nottingham	1973	117† J. E. Mills, Wellington 1929-30
175 B. E. Congdon, Lord's	1973	104 M. L. Page, Lord's 1931
136 C. S. Dempster, Wellington	1929-30	121 J. M. Parker, Auckland ... 1974-75
120 C. S. Dempster, Lord's ...	1931	116 V. Pollard, Nottingham ... 1973
206 M. P. Donnelly, Lord's ...	1949	105* V. Pollard, Lord's 1973
116 W. A. Hadlee, Christchurch	1946-47	100 J. R. Reid, Christchurch ... 1962-63
		114 B. W. Sinclair, Auckland .. 1965-66
		101 B. Sutcliffe, Manchester .. 1949
		116 B. Sutcliffe, Christchurch .. 1950-51

† *Signifies hundred on first appearance in England–New Zealand Tests.*

RECORD PARTNERSHIPS FOR EACH WICKET

By England

147 for 1st	L. Hutton and R. T. Simpson at The Oval	1949
369 for 2nd	J. H. Edrich and K. F. Barrington at Leeds	1965
245 for 3rd	W. R. Hammond and J. Hardstaff at Lord's	1937
266 for 4th	M. H. Denness and K. W. R. Fletcher at Auckland	1974-75
242 for 5th	W. R. Hammond and L. E. G. Ames at Christchurch	1932-33

240 for 6th†	P. H. Parfitt and B. R. Knight at Auckland	1962-63
149 for 7th	A. P. E. Knott and P. Lever at Auckland	1970-71
246 for 8th†	L. E. G. Ames and G. O. B. Allen at Lord's	1931
163* for 9th†	M. C. Cowdrey and A. C. Smith at Wellington	1962-63
59 for 10th	A. P. E. Knott and N. Gifford at Nottingham	1973

By New Zealand

276 for 1st	C. S. Dempster and J. E. Mills at Wellington	1929-30
131 for 2nd	B. Sutcliffe and J. R. Reid at Christchurch	1950-51
190 for 3rd	B. E. Congdon and B. F. Hastings at Lord's	1973
142 for 4th	M. L. Page and R. C. Blunt at Lord's	1931
177 for 5th	B. E. Congdon and V. Pollard at Nottingham	1973
117 for 6th	M. G. Burgess and V. Pollard at Lord's	1973
104 for 7th	B. Sutcliffe and V. Pollard at Birmingham	1965
104 for 8th	A. W. Roberts and D. A. R. Moloney at Lord's	1937
64 for 9th	J. Cowie and T. B. Burtt at Christchurch	1946-47
57 for 10th	F. L. H. Mooney and J. A. Cowie at Leeds	1949

† *Denotes record partnership against all countries.*

TEN WICKETS OR MORE IN A MATCH

For England (7)

11-140 (6-101, 5-39)	I. T. Botham, Lord's	1978
10-149 (5-98, 5-51)	A. W. Greig, Auckland	1974-75
11-65 (4-14, 7-51)	G. A. R. Lock, Leeds	1958
11-84 (5-31, 6-53)	G. A. R. Lock, Christchurch	1958-59
11-70 (4-38, 7-32)†	D. L. Underwood, Lord's	1969
12-101 (6-41, 6-60)	D. L. Underwood, The Oval	1969
12-97 (6-12, 6-85)	D. L. Underwood, Christchurch	1970-71

For New Zealand (2)

10-140 (4-73, 6-67)	J. Cowie, Manchester	1937
10-100 (4-74, 6-26)	R. J. Hadlee, Wellington	1977-78

† *Signifies ten wickets or more on first appearance in England–New Zealand Tests.*

Note: D. L. Underwood took twelve wickets in successive matches against New Zealand in 1969 and 1970-71.

MOST WICKETS IN A SERIES

G. A. R. Lock, 34 wickets for 7.47 in five Tests, 1958.

THE HAT-TRICK

M. J. C. Allom, in his first Test match, England v New Zealand at Christchurch in 1929-30, dismissed T. C. Lowry, K. C. James, and F. T. Badcock with consecutive balls and took four wickets in five balls.

ENGLAND v INDIA

Season	Captains England	India	Tests	Won by England	Won by India	Drawn
1932	D. R. Jardine	C. K. Nayudu	1	1	0	0
1933-34	D. R. Jardine	C. K. Nayudu	3	2	0	1
1936	G. O. B. Allen	Maharaj of Vizianagram	3	2	0	1
1946	W. R. Hammond	Nawab of Pataudi, sr	3	1	0	2
1951-52	N. D. Howard[1]	V. S. Hazare	5	1	1	3
1952	L. Hutton	V. S. Hazare	4	3	0	1
1959	P. B. H. May[2]	D. K. Gaekwad[3]	5	5	0	0
1961-62	E. R. Dexter	N. J. Contractor	5	0	2	3
1963-64	M. J. K. Smith	Nawab of Pataudi, jr	5	0	0	5
1967	D. B. Close	Nawab of Pataudi, jr	3	3	0	0
1971	R. Illingworth	A. L. Wadekar	3	0	1	2
1972-73	A. R. Lewis	A. L. Wadekar	5	1	2	2
1974	M. H. Denness	A. L. Wadekar	3	3	0	0
1976-77	A. W. Greig	B. S. Bedi	5	3	1	1
1979	J. M. Brearley	S. Venkataraghavan	4	1	0	3
1979-80	J. M. Brearley	G. R. Viswanath	1	1	0	0
	In England		29	19	1	9
	In India		29	8	6	15
	Totals		58	27	7	24

Notes: The 1932 Indian touring team was captained by the Maharaj of Porbandar but he did not play in the Test match.
   The following deputised for the official touring captain or were appointed by the home authority for only a minor proportion of the series:
   [1] D. B. Carr (Fifth). [2] M. C. Cowdrey (Fourth and Fifth). [3] P. Roy (Second).

HIGHEST TOTALS FOR AN INNINGS

By England				By India		
633-5	Birmingham	1979		510	Leeds	1967
629	Lord's	1974		485-9	Bombay	1951-52
571-8	Manchester	1936		467-8	Kanpur	1961-62
559-8	Kanpur	1963-64		466	Delhi	1961-62
550-4	Leeds	1967		463-4	Delhi	1963-64
537	Lord's	1952		457-9	Madras	1951-52
500-8	Bombay	1961-62		457-7	Madras	1963-64

LOWEST TOTALS FOR AN INNINGS

By England				By India		
101	The Oval	1971		42	Lord's	1974
134	Lord's	1936		58	Manchester	1952
159	Madras	1972-73		82	Manchester	1952
163	Calcutta (2nd Innings)	1972-73		83	Madras	1976-77
				92	Birmingham	1967
174	Calcutta (1st Innings)	1972-73		93	Lord's	1936
				96	Lord's	1979
177	Bangalore	1976-77		98	The Oval	1952

INDIVIDUAL HUNDREDS IN THE MATCHES 1932–1979-80

For England (47)

188	D. L. Amiss, Lord's	1974	148	A. W. Greig, Bombay	1972-73
179	D. L. Amiss, Delhi	1976-77	106	A. W. Greig, Lord's	1974
151*	K. F. Barrington, Bombay	1961-62	103	A. W. Greig, Calcutta	1976-77
172	K. F. Barrington, Kanpur	1961-62	167	W. R. Hammond, Manchester	
113*	K. F. Barrington, Delhi	1961-62			1936
137	I. T. Botham, Leeds	1979	217	W. R. Hammond, The Oval	1936
114	I. T. Botham, Bombay	1979-80	205*	J. Hardstaff jr, Lord's	1946
246*†	G. Boycott, Leeds	1967	150	L. Hutton, Lord's	1952
155	G. Boycott, Birmingham	1979	104	L. Hutton, Manchester	1952
125	G. Boycott, The Oval	1979	107	R. Illingworth, Manchester	1971
160	M. C. Cowdrey, Leeds	1959	127	B. R. Knight, Kanpur	1963-64
107	M. C. Cowdrey, Calcutta	1963-64	125	A. R. Lewis, Kanpur	1972-73
151	M. C. Cowdrey, Delhi	1963-64	214*	D. Lloyd, Birmingham	1974
118	M. H. Denness, Lord's	1974	101	B. W. Luckhurst, Manchester	
100	M. H. Denness, Birmingham				1971
		1974	106	P. B. H. May, Nottingham	1959
126*	E. R. Dexter, Kanpur	1961-62	121	P. H. Parfitt, Kanpur	1963-64
109†	B. L. D'Oliveira, Leeds	1967	131	G. Pullar, Manchester	1959
100*	J. H. Edrich, Manchester	1974	119	G. Pullar, Kanpur	1961-62
104	T. G. Evans, Lord's	1952	119	D. S. Sheppard, The Oval	1952
113	K. W. R. Fletcher, Bombay	1972-73	100†	M. J. K. Smith, Manchester	1959
123*	K. W. R. Fletcher, Manchester		136†	B. H. Valentine, Bombay	1933-34
		1974	102	C. F. Walters, Madras	1933-34
200*†	D. I. Gower, Birmingham	1979	137*†	A. J. Watkins, Delhi	1951-52
175†	T. W. Graveney, Bombay	1951-52	128	T. S. Worthington, The Oval	
151	T. W. Graveney, Lord's	1967			1936

For India (34)

118†	L. Amarnath, Bombay	1933-34	114	V. M. Merchant, Manchester	
112†	A. A. Baig, Manchester	1959			1936
121	F. M. Engineer, Bombay	1972-73	128	V. M. Merchant, The Oval	1946
101	S. M. Gavaskar, Manchester		154	V. M. Merchant, Delhi	1951-52
		1974	112	Mushtaq Ali, Manchester	1936
108	S. M. Gavaskar, Bombay	1976-77	122*	R. G. Nadkarni, Kanpur	1963-64
221	S. M. Gavaskar, The Oval	1979	103	Nawab of Pataudi, Madras	1961-62
105†	Hanumant Singh, Delhi	1963-64	203*	Nawab of Pataudi, Delhi	1963-64
164*	V. S. Hazare, Delhi	1951-52	148	Nawab of Pataudi, Leeds	1967
155	V. S. Hazare, Bombay	1951-52	115	D. G. Phadkar, Calcutta	1951-52
127	M. L. Jaisimha, Delhi	1961-62	140	P. Roy, Bombay	1951-52
129	M. L. Jaisimha, Calcutta	1963-64	111	P. Roy, Madras	1951-52
192	B. K. Kunderan, Madras	1963-64	130*	P. R. Umrigar, Madras	1951-52
100	B. K. Kunderan, Delhi	1963-64	118	P. R. Umrigar, Manchester	1959
133	V. L. Manjrekar, Leeds	1952	147*	P. R. Umrigar, Kanpur	1961-62
189*	V. L. Manjrekar, Delhi	1961-62	103	D. B. Vengsarkar, Lord's	1979
108	V. L. Manjrekar, Madras	1963-64	113	G. R. Viswanath, Bombay	1972-73
184	V. M. H. Mankad, Lord's	1952	113	G. R. Viswanath, Lord's	1979

† *Signifies hundred on first appearance in England–India Tests.*

RECORD PARTNERSHIPS FOR EACH WICKET

By England

159 for 1st	P. E. Richardson and G. Pullar at Bombay	1961-62
221 for 2nd	D. L. Amiss and J. H. Edrich at Lord's	1974
169 for 3rd	R. Subba Row and M. J. K. Smith at The Oval	1959
266 for 4th	W. R. Hammond and T. S. Worthington at The Oval	1936

254 for 5th†	K. W. R. Fletcher and A. W. Greig at Bombay	1972-73
171 for 6th	I. T. Botham and R. W. Taylor at Bombay	1979-80
103 for 7th	A. P. E. Knott and R. A. Hutton at The Oval	1971
168 for 8th	R. Illingworth and P. Lever at Manchester	1971
83 for 9th	K. W. R. Fletcher and N. Gifford at Madras	1972-73
57 for 10th	J. T. Murray and R. N. S. Hobbs at Birmingham	1967

By India

213 for 1st	S. M. Gavaskar and C. P. S. Chauhan at The Oval	1979
192 for 2nd	F. M. Engineer and A. L. Wadekar at Bombay	1972-73
211 for 3rd {	V. M. Merchant and V. S. Hazare at Delhi	1951-52
	V. M. H. Mankad and V. S. Hazare at Lord's	1952
222 for 4th†	V. S Hazare and V. L. Manjrekar at Leeds	1952
190* for 5th	Nawab of Pataudi and C. G. Borde at Delhi	1963-64
105 for 6th	V. S. Hazaré and D. G. Phadkar at Leeds	1952
153 for 7th	C. G. Borde and S. A. Durani at Bombay	1963-64
101 for 8th	R. G. Nadkarni and F. M. Engineer at Madras	1961-62
54 for 9th	G. S. Ramchand and S. G. Shinde at Lord's	1952
51 for 10th	R. G. Nadkarni and B. S. Chandrasekhar at Calcutta	1963-64

† *Denotes record partnership against all countries.*

TEN WICKETS OR MORE IN A MATCH

For England (6)

10-78 (5-35, 5-43)†	G. O. B. Allen, Lord's	1936
11-145 (7-49, 4-96)†	A. V. Bedser, Lord's	1946
11-93 (4-41, 7-52)	A. V. Bedser, Manchester	1946
13-106 (6-58, 7-48)	I. T. Botham, Bombay	1979-80
10-70 (7-46, 3-24)†	J. K. Lever, Delhi	1976-77
11-153 (7-49, 4-104)	H. Verity, Madras	1933-34

For India (2)

10-177 (6-105, 4-72)	S. A. Durani, Madras	1961-62
12-108 (8-55, 4-53)	V. M. H. Mankad, Madras	1951-52

† *Signifies ten wickets or more on first appearance in England–India Tests.*

Note: A. V. Bedser took eleven wickets in a match in the first two Tests of his career.

MOST WICKETS IN A SERIES

B. S. Chandrasekhar, 35 wickets for 18.91 in five Tests, 1972-73.

ENGLAND v PAKISTAN

Season	England	Captains Pakistan	Tests	Won by England	Won by Pakistan	Drawn
1954	L. Hutton[1]	A. H. Kardar	4	1	1	2
1961-62	E. R. Dexter	Imtiaz Ahmed	3	1	0	2
1962	E. R. Dexter[2]	Javed Burki	5	4	0	1
1967	D. B. Close	Hanif Mohammad	3	2	0	1
1968-69	M. C. Cowdrey	Saeed Ahmed	3	0	0	3
1971	R. Illingworth	Intikhab Alam	3	1	0	2
1972-73	A. R. Lewis	Majid J. Khan	3	0	0	3
1974	M. H. Denness	Intikhab Alam	3	0	0	3
1977-78	J. M. Brearley[3]	Wasim Bari	3	0	0	3
1978	J. M. Brearley	Wasim Bari	3	2	0	1
	In England		21	10	1	10
	In Pakistan		12	1	0	11
	Totals		33	11	1	21

Notes: [1] D. S. Sheppard captained in Second and Third Tests. [2] M. C. Cowdrey captained in Third Test. [3] G. Boycott captained in Third Test.

HIGHEST TOTALS FOR AN INNINGS

	By England				By Pakistan	
558-6	Nottingham	1954		608-7	Birmingham	1971
545 ..	The Oval	1974		600-7	The Oval	1974
544-5	Birmingham	1962		569-9	Hyderabad	1972-73
507 ..	Karachi	1961-62		445-6	Karachi	1972-73
502-7	Karachi	1968-69		422 ..	Lahore	1972-73

LOWEST TOTALS FOR AN INNINGS

	By England				By Pakistan	
130 ..	The Oval (1st Inns) ...	1954		87 ..	Lord's	1954
143 ..	The Oval (2nd Inns) ..	1954		90 ..	Manchester	1954

INDIVIDUAL HUNDREDS IN THE MATCHES 1954–1978

For England (33)

112	D. L. Amiss, Lahore	1972-73		159†	M. C. Cowdrey, Birmingham	1962
158	D. L. Amiss, Hyderabad ..	1972-73		182	M. C. Cowdrey, The Oval .	1962
183	D. L. Amiss, The Oval	1974		100	M. C. Cowdrey, Lahore ...	1968-69
139†	K. F. Barrington, Lahore ..	1961-62		205	E. R. Dexter, Karachi	1961-62
148	K. F. Barrington, Lord's ..	1967		172	E. R. Dexter, The Oval ...	1962
109*	K. F. Barrington, Nottingham	1967		114*	B. L. D'Oliveira, Dacca ...	1968-69
142	K. F. Barrington, The Oval	1967		122	K. W. R. Fletcher, The Oval	1974
100†	I. T. Botham, Birmingham .	1978		153	T. W. Graveney, Lord's ...	1962
108	I. T. Botham, Lord's	1978		114	T. W. Graveney, Nottingham	1962
121*	G. Boycott, Lord's	1971		105	T. W. Graveney, Karachi .	1968-69
112	G. Boycott, Leeds	1971		116	A. P. E. Knott, Birmingham	1971
100*	G. Boycott, Hyderabad ...	1977-78				
278	D. C. S. Compton, Nottingham	1954				

108*†	B. W. Luckhurst, Birmingham	1971	119	P. H. Parfitt, Leeds	1962
139	C. Milburn, Karachi	1968-69	101*	P. H. Parfitt, Nottingham	1962
111	P. H. Parfitt, Karachi	1961-62	165	G. Pullar, Dacca	1961-62
101*	P. H. Parfitt, Birmingham	1962	106†	C. T. Radley, Birmingham	1978
			101	R. T. Simpson, Nottingham	1954

For Pakistan (21)

109	Alim-ud-Din, Karachi	1961-62	138	Intikhab Alam, Hyderabad	1972-73
146	Asif Iqbal, The Oval	1967	114†	Mudassar Nazar, Lahore	1977-78
104*	Asif Iqbal, Birmingham	1971	100*	Mushtaq Mohammad, Nottingham	1962
102	Asif Iqbal, Lahore	1972-73	100	Mushtaq Mohammad, Birmingham	1971
138†	Javed Burki, Lahore	1961-62	157	Mushtaq Mohammad, Hyderabad	1972-73
140	Javed Burki, Dacca	1961-62	101	Nasim-ul-Ghani, Lord's	1962
101	Javed Burki, Lord's	1962	119	Sadiq Mohammad, Lahore	1972-73
111 104	Hanif Mohammad, Dacca	1961-62	274†	Zaheer Abbas, Birmingham	1971
187*	Hanif Mohammad, Lord's	1967	240	Zaheer Abbas, The Oval	1974
122†	Haroon Rashid, Lahore	1977-78			
108	Haroon Rashid, Hyderabad	1977-78			

† *Signifies hundred on first appearance in England–Pakistan Tests.*

Note: Three batsmen – Majid J. Khan, Mushtaq Mohammad, and D. L. Amiss – were dismissed for 99 at Karachi, 1972-73: the only instance in Test matches.

RECORD PARTNERSHIPS FOR EACH WICKET

By England

198 for 1st	G. Pullar and R. W. Barber at Dacca	1961-62
248 for 2nd	M. C. Cowdrey and E. R. Dexter at The Oval	1962
201 for 3rd	K. F. Barrington and T. W. Graveney at Lord's	1967
188 for 4th	E. R. Dexter and P. H. Parfitt at Karachi	1961-62
192 for 5th	D. C. S. Compton and T. E. Bailey at Nottingham	1954
153 for 6th	P. H. Parfitt and D. A. Allen at Birmingham	1962
159 for 7th	A. P. E. Knott and P. Lever at Birmingham	1971
99 for 8th	P. H. Parfitt and D. A. Allen at Leeds	1962
76 for 9th	T. W. Graveney and F. S. Trueman at Lord's	1962
55 for 10th	D. L. Underwood and P. I. Pocock at Hyderabad	1972-73

By Pakistan

122 for 1st	Hanif Mohammad and Alim-ud-Din at Dacca	1961-62
291 for 2nd†	Zaheer Abbas and Mushtaq Mohammad at Birmingham	1971
180 for 3rd	Mudassar Nazar and Haroon Rashid at Lahore	1977-78
153 for 4th	Javed Burki and Mushtaq Mohammad at Lahore	1961-62
197 for 5th	Javed Burki and Nasim-ul-Ghani at Lord's	1962
145 for 6th	Mushtaq Mohammad and Intikhab Alam at Hyderabad	1972-73
51 for 7th	Saeed Ahmed and Nasim-ul-Ghani at Nottingham	1962
130 for 8th†	Hanif Mohammad and Asif Iqbal at Lord's	1967
190 for 9th†	Asif Iqbal and Intikhab Alam at The Oval	1967
62 for 10th	Sarfraz Nawaz and Asif Masood at Leeds	1974

† *Denotes record partnership against all countries.*

TEN WICKETS OR MORE IN A MATCH

For England (1)

13-71 (5-20, 8-51)   D. L. Underwood, Lord's   1974

For Pakistan (1)

12-99 (6-53, 6-46)   Fazal Mahmood, The Oval   1954

AUSTRALIA v SOUTH AFRICA

Season	Australia (Captains)	South Africa (Captains)	Tests	Won by Australia	Won by South Africa	Drawn
1902-03 *S*	J. Darling	H. M. Taberer[1]	3	2	0	1
1910-11 *A*	C. Hill	P. W. Sherwell	5	4	1	0
1912 *E*	S. E. Gregory	F. Mitchell[2]	3	2	0	1
1921-22 *S*	H. L. Collins	H. W. Taylor	3	1	0	2
1931-32 *A*	W. M. Woodfull	H. B. Cameron	5	5	0	0
1935-36 *S*	V. Y. Richardson	H. F. Wade	5	4	0	1
1949-50 *A*	A. L. Hassett	A. D. Nourse	5	4	0	1
1952-53 *A*	A. L. Hassett	J. E. Cheetham	5	2	2	1
1957-58 *S*	I. D. Craig	C. B. van Ryneveld[3]	5	3	0	2
1963-64 *A*	R. B. Simpson[4]	T. L. Goddard	5	1	1	3
1966-67 *S*	R. B. Simpson	P. L. van der Merwe	5	1	3	1
1969-70 *S*	W. M. Lawry	A. Bacher	4	0	4	0
	In South Africa		30	15	7	8
	In Australia		20	12	4	4
	In England		3	2	0	1
	Totals		53	29	11	13

S Played in South Africa.   A Played in Australia.   E Played in England.

Notes: The following deputised for the official touring captain or were appointed by the home authority for only a minor proportion of the series:
  [1] J. H. Anderson (Second), E. A. Halliwell (Third). [2] L. J. Tancred (Third). [3] D. J. McGlew (First). [4] R. Benaud (First).

HIGHEST TOTALS FOR AN INNINGS

	By Australia				By South Africa	
578	..	Melbourne	1910-11	622-9	Durban	1969-70
554	..	Melbourne	1931-32	620 ..	Johannesburg	1966-67
549-7	..	Port Elizabeth	1949-50	595 ..	Adelaide	1963-64

SMALLEST TOTALS FOR AN INNINGS

	By Australia				By South Africa	
75	..	Durban	1949-50	36	†Melbourne	1931-32
143	..	Johannesburg	1966-67	45	†Melbourne	1931-32
147	..	Durban	1966-67	80 ..	Melbourne	1910-11
153	..	Melbourne	1931-32	85 ..	Johannesburg	1902-03

† *The aggregate of 81 (12 extras) for two innings is the smallest in Test cricket.*

INDIVIDUAL HUNDREDS IN THE MATCHES 1902-03–1969-70

For Australia (55)

159*	W. W. Armstrong, Johannesburg	1902-03
132	W. W. Armstrong, Melbourne	1910-11
132†	W. Bardsley, Sydney	1910-11
121	W. Bardsley, Manchester	1912
164	W. Bardsley, Lord's	1912
122	R. Benaud, Johannesburg	1957-58
100	R. Benaud, Johannesburg	1957-58
169†	B. C. Booth, Brisbane	1963-64
102*	B. C. Booth, Sydney	1963-64
226†	D. G. Bradman, Brisbane	1931-32
112	D. G. Bradman, Sydney	1931-32
167	D. G. Bradman, Melbourne	1931-32
299*	D. G. Bradman, Adelaide	1931-32
121	W. A. Brown, Cape Town	1935-36
189	J. W. Burke, Cape Town	1957-58
109†	A. G. Chipperfield, Durban	1935-36
203	H. L. Collins, Johannesburg	1921-22
112	J. H. W. Fingleton, Cape Town	1935-36
108	J. H. W. Fingleton, Johannesburg	1935-36
118	J. H. W. Fingleton, Durban	1935-36
119	J. M. Gregory, Johannesburg	1921-22
178	R. N. Harvey, Cape Town	1949-50
151*	R. N. Harvey, Durban	1949-50
116	R. N. Harvey, Port Elizabeth	1949-50
100	R. N. Harvey, Johannesburg	1949-50
109	R. N. Harvey, Brisbane	1952-53
190	R. N. Harvey, Sydney	1952-53
116	R. N. Harvey, Adelaide	1952-53
205	R. N. Harvey, Melbourne	1952-53
112†	A. L. Hassett, Johannesburg	1949-50
167	A. L. Hassett, Port Elizabeth	1949-50
163	A. L. Hassett, Adelaide	1952-53
142†	C. Hill, Johannesburg	1902-03
191	C. Hill, Sydney	1910-11
100	C. Hill, Melbourne	1910-11
114	C. Kelleway, Manchester	1912
102	C. Kelleway, Lord's	1912
157	W. M. Lawry, Melbourne	1963-64
101*	S. J. E. Loxton, Johannesburg	1949-50
137	C. G. Macartney, Sydney	1910-11
116	C. G. Macartney, Durban	1921-22
149	S. J. McCabe, Durban	1935-36
189*	S. J. McCabe, Johannesburg	1935-36
154	C. C. McDonald, Adelaide	1952-53
111	A. R. Morris, Johannesburg	1949-50
157	A. R. Morris, Port Elizabeth	1949-50
118 101*	J. Moroney, Johannesburg	1949-50
127†	K. E. Rigg, Sydney	1931-32
142	J. Ryder, Cape Town	1921-22
153	R. B. Simpson, Cape Town	1966-67
134	K. R. Stackpole, Cape Town	1966-67
159	V. T. Trumper, Melbourne	1910-11
214*	V. T. Trumper, Adelaide	1910-11
161	W. M. Woodfull, Melbourne	1931-32

For South Africa (36)

114†	E. J. Barlow, Brisbane	1963-64
109	E. J. Barlow, Melbourne	1963-64
201	E. J. Barlow, Adelaide	1963-64
127	E. J. Barlow, Cape Town	1969-70
110	E. J. Barlow, Johannesburg	1969-70
126	K. C. Bland, Sydney	1963-64
162*	W. R. Endean, Melbourne	1952-53
204	G. A. Faulkner, Melbourne	1910-11
115	G. A. Faulkner, Adelaide	1910-11
122*	G. A. Faulkner, Manchester	1912
152	C. N. Frank, Johannesburg	1921-22
102	B. L. Irvine, Port Elizabeth	1969-70
182	D. T. Lindsay, Johannesburg	1966-67
137	D. T. Lindsay, Durban	1966-67
131	D. T. Lindsay, Johannesburg	1966-67
108	D. J. McGlew, Johannesburg	1957-58
105	D. J. McGlew, Durban	1957-58
231	A. D. Nourse, Johannesburg	1935-36
114	A. D. Nourse, Cape Town	1949-50
111	A. W. Nourse, Johannesburg	1921-22
122	R. G. Pollock, Sydney	1963-64
175	R. G. Pollock, Adelaide	1963-64
209	R. G. Pollock, Cape Town	1966-67
105	R. G. Pollock, Port Elizabeth	1966-67
274	R. G. Pollock, Durban	1969-70
140	B. A. Richards, Durban	1969-70
126	B. A. Richards, Port Elizabeth	1969-70

143	E. A. B. Rowan, Durban ..	1949-50	115	J. H. B. Waite, Johannes-	
101	J. H. Sinclair, Johannesburg	1902-03		burg	1957-58
104	J. H. Sinclair, Cape Town .	1902-03	134	J. H. B. Waite, Durban ...	1957-58
103	S. J. Snooke, Adelaide	1910-11	105	J. W. Zulch, Adelaide ...	1910-11
111	K. G. Viljoen, Melbourne .	1931-32	150	J. W. Zulch, Sydney	1910-11

† *Signifies hundred on first appearance in Australia–South Africa Tests.*

RECORD PARTNERSHIPS FOR EACH WICKET

By Australia

233 for 1st	J. H. W. Fingleton and W. A. Brown at Cape Town	1935-36
275 for 2nd	C. C. McDonald and A. L. Hassett at Adelaide	1952-53
242 for 3rd	C. Kelleway and W. Bardsley at Lord's	1912
168 for 4th	R. N. Harvey and K. R. Miller at Sydney	1952-53
143 for 5th	W. W. Armstrong and V. T. Trumper at Melbourne	1910-11
107 for 6th	C. Kelleway and V. S. Ransford at Melbourne	1910-11
160 for 7th	R. Benaud and G. D. McKenzie at Sydney	1963-64
83 for 8th	A. G. Chipperfield and C. V. Grimmett at Durban	1935-36
78 for 9th {	D. G. Bradman and W. J. O'Reilly at Adelaide	1931-32
	K. D. Mackay and I. Meckiff at Johannesburg	1957-58
82 for 10th	V. S. Ransford and W. J. Whitty at Melbourne	1910-11

By South Africa

176 for 1st	D. J. McGlew and T. L. Goddard at Johannesburg	1957-58
173 for 2nd	L. J. Tancred and C. B. Llewellyn at Johannesburg	1902-03
341 for 3rd†	E. J. Barlow and R. G. Pollock at Adelaide	1963-64
206 for 4th	C. N. Frank and A. W. Nourse at Johannesburg	1921-22
129 for 5th	J. H. B. Waite and W. R. Endean at Johannesburg	1957-58
200 for 6th†	R. G. Pollock and H. R. Lance at Durban	1969-70
221 for 7th	D. T. Lindsay and P. L. van der Merwe at Johannesburg	1966-67
124 for 8th†	A. W. Nourse and E. A. Halliwell at Johannesburg	1902-03
85 for 9th	R. G. Pollock and P. M. Pollock at Cape Town	1966-67
53 for 10th	L. A. Stricker and S. J. Pegler at Adelaide	1910-11

† *Denotes record partnership against all countries.*

TEN WICKETS OR MORE IN A MATCH

For Australia (5)

14-199 (7-116, 7-83)	C. V. Grimmett, Adelaide	1931-32
10-88 (5-32, 5-56)	C. V. Grimmett, Cape Town	1935-36
10-110 (3-70, 7-40)	C. V. Grimmett, Johannesburg	1935-36
13-173 (7-100, 6-73)	C. V. Grimmett, Durban	1935-36
11-24 (5-6, 6-18)	H. Ironmonger, Melbourne	1931-32

For South Africa (2)

10-116 (5-43, 5-73)	C. B. Llewellyn, Johannesburg	1902-03
13-165 (6-84, 7-81)	H. J. Tayfield, Melbourne	1952-53

Note: C. V. Grimmett took ten wickets or more in three consecutive matches in 1935-36.

MOST WICKETS IN A SERIES

44, for 11.59 runs in five Tests, C. V. Grimmett, for Australia in 1935-36.
30, for 28.10 runs in five Tests, H. J. Tayfield, for South Africa in 1952-53.

HAT-TRICKS

T. J. Matthews (Australia), twice on the same afternoon in separate innings against South Africa at Manchester, 1912. A feat without parallel in Test cricket.
  L. F. Kline (Australia), Cape Town, 1957-58.

AUSTRALIA v WEST INDIES

Season	Australia	Captains West Indies	Tests	Won by A	Won by WI	Tie	Drawn
1930-31*A*	W. M. Woodfull	G. C. Grant	5	4	1	0	0
1951-52*A*	A. L. Hassett[1]	J. D. C. Goddard[2]	5	4	1	0	0
1954-55*W*	I. W. Johnson	D. S. Atkinson[3]	5	3	0	0	2
1960-61*A*	R. Benaud	F. M. Worrell	5†	2	1	1	1

THE FRANK WORRELL TROPHY

Season	Australia	Captains West Indies	Tests	Won by A	Won by WI	Tie	Drawn
1964-65*W*	R. B. Simpson	G. S. Sobers	5	1	2	0	2
1968-69*A*	W. M. Lawry	G. S. Sobers	5	3	1	0	1
1972-73*W*	I. M. Chappell	R. B. Kanhai	5	2	0	0	3
1975-76*A*	G. S. Chappell	C. H. Lloyd	6	5	1	0	0
1977-78*W*	R. B. Simpson	A. I. Kallicharran[4]	5	1	3	0	1
1979-80*A*	G. S. Chappell	C. H. Lloyd[5]	3	0	2	0	1
	In Australia		29	18	7	1	3
	In West Indies		20	7	5	0	8
	Totals		49	25	12	1	11

  † *The First Test at Brisbane resulted in a tie. This is the only instance of a Test match resulting in a tie.*

A Played in Australia.   W Played in the West Indies.
Notes: The following deputised for the official touring captain or were appointed by the home authority for only a minor proportion of the series:
  [1] A. R. Morris (Third). [2] J. B. Stollmeyer (Fifth). [3] J. B. Stollmeyer (Second and Third). [4] C. H. Lloyd (First and Second). [5] D. L. Murray (First).

HIGHEST TOTALS FOR AN INNINGS

By Australia			By West Indies		
758-8	Kingston	1954-55	616	.. Adelaide	1968-69
668	Bridgetown	1954-55	585	.. Perth	1975-76
650-6	Bridgetown	1964-65	573	.. Bridgetown	1964-65
619	Sydney	1968-69	510	.. Bridgetown	1954-55
600-9	Port-of-Spain	1954-55	453	.. Brisbane	1960-61
558	Brisbane	1930-31	448	.. Adelaide	1979-80
547	Sydney	1968-69	441	.. Brisbane	1979-80
533	Adelaide	1968-69	439	.. Georgetown	1977-78
516	Port-of-Spain	1964-65	432-6	.. Adelaide	1960-61
515-9	Kingston	1954-55	429	.. Port-of-Spain	1964-65
510	Melbourne	1968-69	428	.. Kingston	1972-73

LOWEST TOTALS FOR AN INNINGS

By Australia			By West Indies		
82	.. Adelaide	1951-52	78	.. Sydney	1951-52
90	.. Port-of-Spain	1977-78	90	.. Sydney	1930-31
94	.. Port-of-Spain	1977-78	99	.. Melbourne	1930-31

INDIVIDUAL HUNDREDS IN THE MATCHES 1930-31–1979-80

For Australia (57)

128	R. G. Archer, Kingston	1954-55	118	R. R. Lindwall, Bridgetown	1954-55
121	R. Benaud, Kingston	1954-55	109*	R. B. McCosker, Melbourne	1975-76
117	B. C. Booth, Port-of-Spain	1964-65	110	C. C. McDonald, Port-of-Spain	1954-55
223	D. G. Bradman, Brisbane	1930-31	127	C. C. McDonald, Kingston	1954-55
152	D. G. Bradman, Melbourne	1930-31	129	K. R. Miller, Sydney	1951-52
106	G. S. Chappell, Bridgetown	1972-73	147	K. R. Miller, Kingston	1954-55
123 109* }	‡G. S. Chappell, Brisbane	1975-76	137	K. R. Miller, Bridgetown	1954-55
182*	G. S. Chappell, Sydney	1975-76	109	K. R. Miller, Kingston	1954-55
124	G. S. Chappell, Brisbane	1979-80	111	A. R. Morris, Port-of-Spain	1954-55
117†	I. M. Chappell, Brisbane	1968-69	181†	N. C. O'Neill, Brisbane	1960-61
165	I. M. Chappell, Melbourne	1968-69	183	W. H. Ponsford, Sydney	1930-31
106*	I. M. Chappell, Bridgetown	1972-73	109	W. H. Ponsford, Brisbane	1930-31
109	I. M. Chappell, Georgetown	1972-73	132	I. R. Redpath, Sydney	1968-69
156	I. M. Chappell, Perth	1975-76	102	I. R. Redpath, Adelaide	1975-76
109†	G. J. Cosier, Melbourne	1975-76	103	I. R. Redpath, Adelaide	1975-76
143	R. M. Cowper, Port-of-Spain	1964-65	101	I. R. Redpath, Melbourne	1975-76
102	R. M. Cowper, Bridgetown	1964-65	124	C. S. Serjeant, Georgetown	1977-78
133	R. N. Harvey, Kingston	1954-55	201	R. B. Simpson, Bridgetown	1964-65
133	R. N. Harvey, Port-of-Spain	1954-55	142	K. R. Stackpole, Kingston	1972-73
204	R. N. Harvey, Kingston	1954-55	122	P. M. Toohey, Kingston	1977-78
132	A. L. Hassett, Sydney	1951-52	136	A. Turner, Adelaide	1975-76
102	A. L. Hassett, Melbourne	1951-52	118	K. D. Walters, Sydney	1968-69
130*†	K. J. Hughes, Brisbane	1979-80	110	K. D. Walters, Adelaide	1968-69
146†	A. F. Kippax, Adelaide	1930-31	242 103 }	K. D. Walters, Sydney	1968-69
210	W. M. Lawry, Bridgetown	1964-65	102*	K. D. Walters, Bridgetown	1972-73
105	W. M. Lawry, Brisbane	1968-69	112	K. D. Walters, Port-of-Spain	1972-73
205	W. M. Lawry, Melbourne	1968-69	126	G. M. Wood, Georgetown	1977-78
151	W. M. Lawry, Sydney	1968-69			

‡ *G. S. Chappell is the only player to score hundreds in both innings of his first Test as captain.*

For West Indies (47)

108	F. C. M. Alexander, Sydney	1960-61	129	R. B. Kanhai, Bridgetown	1964-65
219	D. S. Atkinson, Bridgetown	1954-55	121	R. B. Kanhai, Port-of-Spain	1964-65
117	B. F. Butcher, Port-of-Spain	1964-65	105	R. B. Kanhai, Bridgetown	1972-73
101	B. F. Butcher, Sydney	1968-69	129†	C. H. Lloyd, Brisbane	1968-69
118	B. F. Butcher, Adelaide	1968-69	178	C. H. Lloyd, Georgetown	1972-73
122	C. C. Depeiza, Bridgetown	1954-55	149	C. H. Lloyd, Perth	1975-76
125†	M. L. C. Foster, Kingston	1972-73	102	C. H. Lloyd, Melbourne	1975-76
169	R. C. Fredericks, Perth	1975-76	121	C. H. Lloyd, Adelaide	1979-80
101†	H. A. Gomes, Georgetown	1977-78	123*	F. R. Martin, Sydney	1930-31
115	H. A. Gomes, Kingston	1977-78	201	S. M. Nurse, Bridgetown	1964-65
102*	G. A. Headley, Brisbane	1930-31	137	S. M. Nurse, Sydney	1968-69
105	G. A. Headley, Sydney	1930-31	101	I. V. A. Richards, Adelaide	1975-76
110	C. C. Hunte, Melbourne	1960-61	140	I. V. A. Richards, Brisbane	1979-80
101	A. I. Kallicharran, Brisbane	1975-76	107	L. G. Rowe, Brisbane	1975-76
127	A. I. Kallicharran, Port-of-Spain	1977-78	104†	O. G. Smith, Kingston	1954-55
126	A. I. Kallicharran, Kingston	1977-78	132	G. S. Sobers, Brisbane	1960-61
			168	G. S. Sobers, Sydney	1960-61
106	A. I. Kallicharran, Adelaide	1979-80	110	G. S. Sobers, Adelaide	1968-69
117 115 }	R. B. Kanhai, Adelaide	1960-61	113	G. S. Sobers, Sydney	1968-69
			104	J. B. Stollmeyer, Sydney	1951-52
			108	C. L. Walcott, Kingston	1954-55

126	C. L. Walcott, Port-of-		100† A. B. Williams, George-	
110	Spain	1954-55	town	1977-78
155	C. L. Walcott, Kingston ..	1954-55	108 F. M. M. Worrell, Mel-	
110			bourne	1951-52
139	E. D. Weekes, Port-of-			
	Spain	1954-55		

† *Signifies hundred on first appearance in Australia–West Indies Tests. F. C. M. Alexander hit the only hundred of his career in a Test match.*

RECORD PARTNERSHIPS FOR EACH WICKET

By Australia

382 for 1st†	W. M. Lawry and R. B. Simpson at Bridgetown	1964-65
298 for 2nd	W. M. Lawry and I. M. Chappell at Melbourne	1968-69
295 for 3rd†	C. C. McDonald and R. N. Harvey at Kingston	1954-55
336 for 4th	W. M. Lawry and K. D. Walters at Sydney	1968-69
220 for 5th	K. R. Miller and R. G. Archer at Kingston	1954-55
206 for 6th	K. R. Miller and R. G. Archer at Bridgetown	1954-55
134 for 7th	A. K. Davidson and R. Benaud at Brisbane	1960-61
137 for 8th	R. Benaud and I. W. Johnson at Kingston	1954-55
97 for 9th	K. D. Mackay and J. W. Martin at Melbourne	1960-61
73 for 10th	J. W. Gleeson and A. N. Connolly at Sydney	1968-69

By West Indies

145 for 1st	C. C. Hunte and B. A. Davis at Bridgetown	1964-65
165 for 2nd	M. C. Carew and R. B. Kanhai at Brisbane	1968-69
242 for 3rd	C. L. Walcott and E. D. Weekes at Port-of-Spain	1954-55
198 for 4th	L. G. Rowe and A. I. Kallicharran at Brisbane	1975-76
210 for 5th	R. B. Kanhai and M. L. C. Foster at Kingston	1972-73
165 for 6th	R. B. Kanhai and D. L. Murray at Bridgetown	1972-73
347 for 7th†‡	D. St E. Atkinson and C. C. Depeiza at Bridgetown	1954-55
74 for 8th	F. C. M. Alexander and L. R. Gibbs at Sydney	1960-61
122 for 9th†	D. A. J. Holford and J. L. Hendriks at Adelaide	1968-69
56 for 10th	J. Garner and C. E. H. Croft at Brisbane	1979-80

† *Denotes record partnership against all countries.*
‡ *The 347 partnership for the 7th wicket is the highest for this wicket in first-class cricket.*

TEN WICKETS OR MORE IN A MATCH

For Australia (5)

11-222 (5-135, 6-87)†	A. K. Davidson, Brisbane	1954-55
11-183 (7-87, 4-96)†	C. V. Grimmett, Adelaide	1930-31
10-115 (6-72, 4-43)	N. J. N. Hawke, Georgetown	1964-65
11-79 (7-23, 4-56)	H. Ironmonger, Melbourne	1930-31
10-159 (8-71, 2-88)	G. D. McKenzie, Melbourne	1968-69

For West Indies (1)

10-113 (7-55, 3-58)	G. E. Gomez, Sydney	1951-52

† *Signifies ten wickets or more on first appearance in Australia–West Indies Tests.*

HAT-TRICK

L. R. Gibbs (West Indies) at Adelaide 1960-61

AUSTRALIA v NEW ZEALAND

Season	Australia	New Zealand	Tests	Won by Australia	Won by New Zealand	Drawn
	Captains					
1945-46N	W. A. Brown	W. A. Hadlee	1	1	0	0
1973-74A	I. M. Chappell	B. E. Congdon	3	2	0	1
1973-74N	I. M. Chappell	B. E. Congdon	3	1	1	1
1976-77N	G. S. Chappell	G. M. Turner	2	1	0	1
	In Australia		3	2	0	1
	In New Zealand		6	3	1	2
	Totals		9	5	1	3

A Played in Australia.   N Played in New Zealand.

HIGHEST TOTALS FOR AN INNINGS

By Australia			By New Zealand		
552 ..	Christchurch	1976-77	484 ..	Wellington	1973-74
511-6	Wellington	1973-74	357 ..	Christchurch	1976-77

LOWEST TOTALS FOR AN INNINGS

By Australia			By New Zealand		
162 ..	Sydney	1973-74	42 ⎫		
221 ..	Auckland	1973-74	54 ⎭ ..	Wellington	1945-46

INDIVIDUAL HUNDREDS IN THE MATCHES 1945-46–1976-77

For Australia (10)

247* ⎫	G. S. Chappell, Wellington	1973-74	159*	I. R. Redpath, Auckland ..	1973-74
133 ⎭			122†	K. R. Stackpole, Melbourne	1973-74
145 ⎫	I. M. Chappell, Wellington	1973-74	104*	K. D. Walters, Auckland ..	1973-74
121 ⎭			250	K. D. Walters, Christchurch	1976-77
132	R. W. Marsh, Adelaide ...	1973-74			
101	G. J. Gilmour, Christchurch	1976-77			

For New Zealand (7)

132	B. E. Congdon, Wellington	1973-74	117	J. F. M. Morrison, Sydney	1973-74
107*	B. E. Congdon, Christchurch	1976-77	108	J. M. Parker, Sydney	1973-74
101	B. F. Hastings, Wellington	1973-74	101 ⎫ 110* ⎭	G. M. Turner, Christchurch	1973-74

† *Signifies hundred on first appearance in Australia–New Zealand Tests.*

Notes: G. S. and I. M. Chappell at Wellington in 1973-74 provide the only instance in Test matches of brothers both scoring a hundred in each innings and in the same Test.

G. S. Chappell's match aggregate of 380 (247* and 133) for Australia at Wellington in 1973-74 is the record in Test matches.

RECORD PARTNERSHIPS FOR EACH WICKET

By Australia

75 for 1st	K. R. Stackpole and A. P. Sheahan at Melbourne	1973-74
141 for 2nd	I. R. Redpath and I. M. Chappell at Wellington	1973-74
264 for 3rd	I. M. Chappell and G. S. Chappell at Wellington	1973-74
106 for 4th	I. R. Redpath and I. C. Davis at Christchurch	1973-74
93 for 5th	G. S. Chappell and K. D. Walters at Christchurch	1976-77
87 for 6th	I. R. Redpath and R. W. Marsh at Auckland	1973-74
217 for 7th†	K. D. Walters and G. J. Gilmour at Christchurch	1976-77
93 for 8th	G. J. Gilmour and K. J. O'Keeffe at Auckland	1976-77
50 for 9th	K. D. Walters and D. K. Lillee at Christchurch	1976-77
48 for 10th	K. D. Walters and M. H. N. Walker at Christchurch	1976-77

By New Zealand

107 for 1st	G. M. Turner and J. M. Parker at Auckland	1973-74
108 for 2nd	G. M. Turner and J. F. Morrison at Wellington	1973-74
58 for 3rd	B. E. Congdon and J. M. Parker at Christchurch	1976-77
229 for 4th†	B. E. Congdon and B. F. Hastings at Wellington	1973-74
80 for 5th	J. M. Parker and J. V. Coney at Sydney	1973-74
105 for 6th	M. G. Burgess and R. J. Hadlee at Auckland	1976-77
66 for 7th	K. J. Wadsworth and D. R. Hadlee at Adelaide	1973-74
42 for 8th	G. N. Edwards and H. J. Howarth at Christchurch	1976-77
73 for 9th	H. J. Howarth and D. R. Hadlee at Christchurch	1976-77
47 for 10th	H. J. Howarth and M. G. Webb at Wellington	1973-74

† *Denotes record partnership against all countries.*

TEN WICKETS OR MORE IN A MATCH

For Australia (1)

11-123 (5-51, 6-72)   D. K. Lillee, Auckland 1976-77

Note: The best match figures by a New Zealand bowler are 9-166 (5-82, 4-84), R. O. Collinge at Auckland, 1973-74.

AUSTRALIA v INDIA

	Captains		Tests	Won by Australia	Won by India	Drawn
Season	Australia	India				
1947-48*A*	D. G. Bradman	L. Amarnath	5	4	0	1
1956-57*I*	I. W. Johnson[1]	P. R. Umrigar	3	2	0	1
1959-60*I*	R. Benaud	G. S. Ramchand	5	2	1	2
1964-65*I*	R. B. Simpson	Nawab of Pataudi, jr	3	1	1	1
1967-68*A*	R. B. Simpson[2]	Nawab of Pataudi, jr[3]	4	4	0	0
1969-70*I*	W. M. Lawry	Nawab of Pataudi, jr	5	3	1	1
1977-78*A*	R. B. Simpson	B. S. Bedi	5	3	2	0
1979-80*I*	K. J. Hughes	S. M. Gavaskar	6	0	2	4
	In Australia		14	11	2	1
	In India		22	8	5	9
	Totals		36	19	7	10

A Played in Australia.   I Played in India.

Notes: The following deputised for the official touring captain or were appointed by the home authority for only a minor proportion of the series:
    [1] R. R. Lindwall (Second). [2] W. M. Lawry (Third and Fourth). [3] C. G. Borde (First).

HIGHEST TOTALS FOR AN INNINGS

By Australia				By India		
674	..	Adelaide	1947-48	510-7	Delhi	1979-80
575-8		Melbourne	1947-48	458-8	Bombay	1979-80
529	..	Melbourne	1967-68	457-5	Bangalore	1979-80
523-7		Bombay	1956-57	445	.. Adelaide	1977-78
505	..	Adelaide	1977-78	402	.. Perth	1977-78

LOWEST TOTALS FOR AN INNINGS

By Australia				By India		
105	..	Kanpur	1959-60	58	.. Brisbane	1947-48
107	..	Sydney	1947-48	67	.. Melbourne	1947-48
107	..	Delhi	1969-70	98	.. Brisbane	1947-48

INDIVIDUAL HUNDREDS IN THE MATCHES 1947-48–1979-80

For Australia (32)

112	S. G. Barnes, Adelaide	1947-48
162†	A. R. Border, Madras	1979-80
185†	D. G. Bradman, Brisbane	1947-48
132 / 127*	D. G. Bradman, Melbourne	1947-48
201	D. G. Bradman, Adelaide	1947-48
161	J. W. Burke, Bombay	1956-57
151	I. M. Chappell, Melbourne	1967-68
138	I. M. Chappell, Delhi	1969-70
108	R. M. Cowper, Adelaide	1967-68
165	R. M. Cowper, Sydney	1967-68
101	L. E. Favell, Madras	1959-60
153	R. N. Harvey, Melbourne	1947-48
140	R. N. Harvey, Bombay	1956-57
114	R. N. Harvey, Delhi	1959-60
102	R. N. Harvey, Bombay	1959-60
198*	A. L. Hassett, Adelaide	1947-48
100	K. J. Hughes, Madras	1979-80
100	W. M. Lawry, Melbourne	1967-68
105	A. L. Mann, Perth	1977-78
100*	A. R. Morris, Melbourne	1947-48
163	N. C. O'Neill, Bombay	1959-60
113	N. C. O'Neill, Calcutta	1959-60
114	A. P. Sheahan, Kanpur	1969-70
103	R. B. Simpson, Adelaide	1967-68
109	R. B. Simpson, Melbourne	1967-68
176	R. B. Simpson, Perth	1977-78
100	R. B. Simpson, Adelaide	1977-78
103†	K. R. Stackpole, Bombay	1969-70
102	K. D. Walters, Madras	1969-70
121†	G. N. Yallop, Adelaide	1977-78
167	G. N. Yallop, Calcutta	1979-80

For India (21)

100	M. Amarnath, Perth	1977-78
108	N. J. Contractor, Bombay	1959-60
113†	S. M. Gavaskar, Brisbane	1977-78
127	S. M. Gavaskar, Perth	1977-78
118	S. M. Gavaskar, Melbourne	1977-78
115	S. M. Gavaskar, Delhi	1979-80
123	S. M. Gavaskar, Bombay	1979-80
145 / 116	V. S. Hazare, Adelaide	1947-48
101	M. L. Jaisimha, Brisbane	1967-68
101*	S. M. H. Kirmani, Bombay	1979-80
116	V. M. H. Mankad, Melbourne	1947-48
111	V. M. H. Mankad, Melbourne	1947-48
128*†	Nawab of Pataudi, Madras	1964-65
123	D. G. Phadkar, Adelaide	1947-48
109	G. S. Ramchand, Bombay	1956-57
112	D. B. Vengsarkar, Bangalore	1979-80
137†	G. R. Viswanath, Kanpur	1969-70
161*	G. R. Viswanath, Bangalore	1979-80
131	G. R. Viswanath, Delhi	1979-80
100*	Yashpal Sharma, Delhi	1979-80

† *Signifies hundred on first appearance in Australia–India Tests.*

RECORD PARTNERSHIPS FOR EACH WICKET

By Australia

191 for 1st	R. B. Simpson and W. M. Lawry at Melbourne	1967-68
236 for 2nd	S. G. Barnes and D. G. Bradman at Adelaide	1947-48
222 for 3rd	A. R. Border and K. J. Hughes at Madras	1979-80
159 for 4th	R. N. Harvey and S. J. E. Loxton at Melbourne	1947-48
223* for 5th	A. R. Morris and D. G. Bradman at Melbourne	1947-48
151 for 6th	T. R. Veivers and B. N. Jarman at Bombay	1964-65
64 for 7th	T. R. Veivers and J. W. Martin at Madras	1964-65
73 for 8th	T. R. Veivers and G. D. McKenzie at Madras	1964-65
87 for 9th	I. W. Johnson and W. P. A. Crawford at Madras	1956-57
52 for 10th	K. J. Wright and J. D. Higgs at Delhi	1979-80

By India

192 for 1st	S. M. Gavaskar and C. P. S. Chauhan at Bombay	1979-80
193 for 2nd	S. M. Gavaskar and M. Amarnath at Perth	1977-78
159 for 3rd	S. M. Gavaskar and G. R. Viswanath at Delhi	1979-80
159 for 4th	D. B. Vengsarkar and G. R. Viswanath at Bangalore	1979-80
109 for 5th	A. A. Baig and R. B. Kenny at Bombay	1959-60
188 for 6th	V. S. Hazare and D. G. Phadkar at Adelaide	1947-48
132 for 7th	V. S. Hazare and H. R. Adhikari at Adelaide	1947-48
127 for 8th	S. M. H. Kirmani and K. D. Ghavri at Bombay	1979-80
54 for 9th	Nawab of Pataudi, jr and R. B. Desai at Melbourne	1967-68
39 for 10th	C. G. Borde and B. S. Chandrasekhar at Calcutta	1964-65

TEN WICKETS OR MORE IN A MATCH

For Australia (7)

11-105 (6-52, 5-53)	R. Benaud, Calcutta	1956-57
12-124 (5-31, 7-93)	A. K. Davidson, Kanpur	1959-60
11-166 (5-99, 7-67)	G. Dymock, Kanpur	1979-80
10-91 (6-58, 4-33)†	G. D. McKenzie, Madras	1964-65
10-151 (7-66, 3-85)	G. D. McKenzie, Melbourne	1967-68
10-144 (5-91, 5-53)	A. A. Mallett, Madras	1964-65
11-31 (5-2, 6-29)†	E. R. H. Toshack, Brisbane	1947-48

For India (6)

10-194 (5-89, 5-105)	B. S. Bedi, Perth	1977-78
12-104 (6-52, 6-52)	B. S. Chandrasekhar, Melbourne	1977-78
10-130 (7-49, 3-81)	Ghulam Ahmed, Calcutta	1956-57
11-122 (5-31, 6-91)	R. G. Nadkarni, Madras	1964-65
14-124 (9-69, 5-55)	J. M. Patel, Kanpur	1959-60
10-174 (4-100, 6-74)	E. A. S. Prasanna, Madras	1969-70

† *Signifies ten wickets or more on first appearance in Australia–India Tests.*

AUSTRALIA v PAKISTAN

Season	Australia	Captains Pakistan	Tests	Won by Australia	Won by Pakistan	Drawn
1956-57P	I. W. Johnson	A. H. Kardar	1	0	1	0
1959-60P	R. Benaud	Fazal Mahmood[1]	3	2	0	1
1964-65P	R. B. Simpson	Hanif Mohammad	1	0	0	1
1964-65A	R. B. Simpson	Hanif Mohammad	1	0	0	1
1972-73A	I. M. Chappell	Intikhab Alam	3	3	0	0
1976-77A	G. S. Chappell	Mushtaq Mohammad	3	1	1	1
1978-79A	G. N. Yallop[2]	Mushtaq Mohammad	2	1	1	0
1979-80P	G. S. Chappell	Javed Miandad	3	0	1	2
	In Pakistan		8	2	2	4
	In Australia		9	5	2	2
	Totals		17	7	4	6

A Played in Australia.   P Played in Pakistan.

Notes: [1] Imtiaz Ahmed captained in Second Test. [2] K. J. Hughes captained in Second Test.

HIGHEST TOTALS FOR AN INNINGS

By Australia				By Pakistan		
617	..	Faisalabad	1979-80	574-8	Melbourne	1972-73
585	..	Adelaide	1972-73	466	.. Adelaide	1976-77

LOWEST TOTALS FOR AN INNINGS

By Australia				By Pakistan		
80	..	Karachi	1956-57	106	.. Sydney	1972-73

INDIVIDUAL HUNDREDS IN THE MATCHES 1956-57–1979-80

For Australia (19)

142	J. Benaud, Melbourne	1972-73	105	R. B. McCosker, Melbourne	1976-77
105†	A. R. Border, Melbourne ..	1978-79	118†	R. W. Marsh, Adelaide ...	1972-73
150* / 153	A. R. Border, Lahore	1979-80	134	N. C. O'Neill, Lahore ...	1959-60
116*	G. S. Chappell, Melbourne	1972-73	135	I. R. Redpath, Melbourne .	1972-73
121	G. S. Chappell, Melbourne	1976-77	127	A. P. Sheahan, Melbourne .	1972-73
235	G. S. Chappell, Faisalabad	1979-80	153† / 115	R. B. Simpson, Karachi ...	1964-65
196	I. M. Chappell, Adelaide ..	1972-73	107	K. D. Walters, Adelaide ...	1976-77
168	G. J. Cosier, Melbourne ..	1976-77	172	G. N. Yallop, Faisalabad ..	1979-80
105†	I. C. Davis, Adelaide	1976-77			

For Pakistan (17)

152* Asif Iqbal, Adelaide	1976-77	110* Majid J. Khan, Lahore 1979-80
120 Asif Iqbal, Sydney	1976-77	121 Mushtaq Mohammad, Sydney 1972-73
134* Asif Iqbal, Perth	1978-79	137 Sadiq Mohammad, Melbourne 1972-73
101* Hanif Mohammad, Karachi	1959-60	105 Sadiq Mohammad, Melbourne 1976-77
104 Hanif Mohammad, Melbourne	1964-65	166 Saeed Ahmed, Lahore 1959-60
166† Khalid Ibadulla, Karachi ..	1964-65	210* Taslim Arif, Faisalabad ... 1979-80
129* Javed Miandad, Perth	1978-79	101 Zaheer Abbas, Adelaide .. 1976-77
106* Javed Miandad, Faisalabad	1979-80	
158 Majid J. Khan, Melbourne .	1972-73	
108 Majid J. Khan, Melbourne .	1978-79	

† *Signifies hundred on first appearance in Australia–Pakistan Tests.*

RECORD PARTNERSHIPS FOR EACH WICKET

By Australia

134 for 1st	I. C. Davis and A. Turner at Melbourne	1976-77
233 for 2nd	A. P. Sheahan and J. Benaud at Melbourne	1972-73
179 for 3rd	K. J. Hughes and G. S. Chappell at Faisalabad	1979-80
217 for 4th	G. S. Chappell and G. N. Yallop at Faisalabad	1979-80
171 for 5th	G. S. Chappell and G. J. Cosier at Melbourne	1976-77
139 for 6th	R. M. Cowper and T. R. Veivers at Melbourne	1964-65
134 for 7th	A. R. Border and G. R. Beard at Lahore	1979-80
117 for 8th	G. J. Cosier and K. J. O'Keeffe at Melbourne	1976-77
83 for 9th	J. R. Watkins and R. A. L. Massie at Sydney	1972-73
52 for 10th	D. K. Lillee and M. H. N. Walker at Sydney	1976-77

By Pakistan

249 for 1st†	Khalid Ibadulla and Abdul Kadir at Karachi	1964-65
195 for 2nd	Sadiq Mohammad and Majid J. Khan at Melbourne	1972-73
223* for 3rd†	Taslim Arif and Javed Miandad at Faisalabad	1979-80
84 for 4th	Javed Burki and Hanif Mohammad at Melbourne	1964-65
139 for 5th	Mushtaq Mohammad and Asif Iqbal at Sydney	1972-73
115 for 6th	Asif Iqbal and Javed Miandad at Sydney	1976-77
104 for 7th	Intikhab Alam and Wasim Bari at Adelaide	1972-73
111 for 8th	Majid J. Khan and Imran Khan at Lahore	1979-80
56 for 9th	Intikhab Alam and Afaq Hussain at Melbourne	1964-65
87 for 10th	Asif Iqbal and Iqbal Qasim at Adelaide	1976-77

† *Denotes record partnership against all countries.*

TEN WICKETS OR MORE IN A MATCH

For Australia (2)

10-111 (7-87, 3-24)†	R. J. Bright, Karachi	1979-80
10-135 (6-82, 4-53)	D. K. Lillee, Melbourne	1976-77

For Pakistan (4)

13-114 (6-34, 7-80)†	Fazal Mahmood, Karachi	1956-57
12-165 (6-102, 6-63)	Imran Khan, Sydney	1976-77
11-118 (4-69, 7-49)	Iqbal Qasim, Karachi	1979-80
11-125 (2-39, 9-86)	Sarfraz Nawaz, Melbourne	1978-79

† *Signifies ten wickets or more on first appearance in Australia–Pakistan Tests.*

SOUTH AFRICA v NEW ZEALAND

Season	South Africa	New Zealand	Tests	Won by South Africa	Won by New Zealand	Drawn
	Captains					
1931-32N	H. B. Cameron	M. L. Page	2	2	0	0
1952-53N	J. E. Cheetham	W. M. Wallace	2	1	0	1
1953-54S	J. E. Cheetham	G. O. Rabone[1]	5	4	0	1
1961-62S	D. J. McGlew	J. R. Reid	5	2	2	1
1963-64N	T. L. Goddard	J. R. Reid	3	0	0	3
	In New Zealand		7	3	0	4
	In South Africa		10	6	2	2
	Totals		17	9	2	6

N Played in New Zealand.   S Played in South Africa.

Note: [1] B. Sutcliffe captained in Fourth and Fifth Tests.

HIGHEST TOTALS FOR AN INNINGS

By South Africa			By New Zealand		
524-8	Wellington	1952-53	505 ..	Cape Town	1953-54

LOWEST TOTALS FOR AN INNINGS

By South Africa			By New Zealand		
148 ..	Johannesburg	1953-54	79 ..	Johannesburg	1953-54

INDIVIDUAL HUNDREDS IN THE MATCHES 1931-32–1963-64

For South Africa (11)

122*	X. C. Balaskas, Wellington	1931-32	113	R. A. McLean, Cape Town	1961-62
103†	J. A. J. Christy, Christchurch	1931-32	101	R. A. McLean, Durban ...	1953-54
116	W. R. Endean, Auckland ..	1952-53	113†	B. Mitchell, Christchurch .	1931-32
255*†	D. J. McGlew, Wellington .	1952-53	109†	A. R. A. Murray, Wellington	1952-53
127*	D. J. McGlew, Durban ...	1961-62	101	J. H. B. Waite, Johannesburg	1961-62
120	D. J. McGlew, Johannesburg	1961-62			

For New Zealand (7)

109	P. T. Barton, Port Elizabeth	1961-62	142	J. R. Reid, Johannesburg ..	1961-62
101	P. G. Z. Harris, Cape Town	1961-62	138	B. W. Sinclair, Auckland ..	1963-64
107	G. O. Rabone, Durban ...	1953-54	100†	H. G. Vivian, Wellington ..	1931-32
135	J. R. Reid, Cape Town	1953-54			

† *Signifies hundred on first appearance in South Africa–New Zealand Tests.*

RECORD PARTNERSHIPS FOR EACH WICKET

By South Africa

196 for 1st	J. A. J. Christy and B. Mitchell at Christchurch	1931-32
76 for 2nd	J. A. J. Christy and H. B. Cameron at Wellington	1931-32
112 for 3rd	D. J. McGlew and R. A. McLean at Johannesburg	1961-62
135 for 4th	K. J. Funston and R. A. McLean at Durban	1953-54
130 for 5th	W. R. Endean and J. E. Cheetham at Auckland	1952-53
83 for 6th	K. C. Bland and D. T. Lindsay at Auckland...................	1963-64
246 for 7th†	D. J. McGlew and A. R. A. Murray at Wellington	1952-53
95 for 8th	J. E. Cheetham and H. J. Tayfield at Cape Town	1953-54
60 for 9th	P. M. Pollock and N. A. T. Adcock at Port Elizabeth	1961-62
47 for 10th	D. J. McGlew and H. D. Bromfield at Port Elizabeth	1961-62

By New Zealand

126 for 1st	G. O. Rabone and M. E. Chapple at Cape Town	1953-54
51 for 2nd	W. P. Bradburn and B. W. Sinclair at Dunedin	1963-64
94 for 3rd	M. B. Poore and B. Sutcliffe at Cape Town	1953-54
171 for 4th	B. W. Sinclair and S. N. McGregor at Auckland	1963-64
174 for 5th	J. R. Reid and J. E. F. Beck at Cape Town	1953-54
100 for 6th	H. G. Vivian and F. T. Badcock at Wellington	1931-32
84 for 7th	J. R. Reid and G. A. Bartlett at Johannesburg	1961-62
73 for 8th	P. G. Z. Harris and G. A. Bartlett at Durban	1961-62
69 for 9th	C. F. W. Allcott and I. B. Cromb at Wellington	1931-32
49* for 10th	A. E. Dick and F. J. Cameron at Cape Town	1961-62

† *Denotes record partnership against all countries.*

TEN WICKETS OR MORE IN A MATCH

For South Africa (1)

11-196 (6-128, 5-68)† S. F. Burke, Cape Town 1961-62

† *Signifies ten wickets or more on first appearance in South Africa–New Zealand Tests.*

Note: The best match figures by a New Zealand bowler are 8-180 (4-61, 4-119), J. C. Alabaster at Cape Town, 1961-62.

WEST INDIES v NEW ZEALAND

	Captains			Won by	Won by	
Season	West Indies	New Zealand	Tests	West Indies	New Zealand	Drawn
1951-52N	J. D. C. Goddard	B. Sutcliffe	2	1	0	1
1955-56N	D. St E. Atkinson	J. R. Reid[1]	4	3	1	0
1968-69N	G. S. Sobers	G. T. Dowling	3	1	1	1
1971-72W	G. S. Sobers	G. T. Dowling[2]	5	0	0	5
1979-80N	C. H. Lloyd	G. P. Howarth	3	0	1	2
	In New Zealand		12	5	3	4
	In West Indies		5	0	0	5
	Totals		17	5	3	9

N Played in New Zealand.   W Played in West Indies.

Notes: The following deputised for the official touring captain or were appointed by the home authority for only a minor proportion of the series:
   [1] H. B. Cave (First).   [2] B. E. Congdon (Third, Fourth and Fifth).

HIGHEST TOTALS FOR AN INNINGS

	By West Indies			By New Zealand	
564-8	Bridgetown	1971-72	543-3	Georgetown	1971-72
546-6	Auckland	1951-52	460 ..	Christchurch	1979-80
508-4	Kingston	1971-72	422 ..	Bridgetown	1971-72

LOWEST TOTALS FOR AN INNINGS

	By West Indies			By New Zealand	
77 ..	Auckland	1955-56	74 ..	Dunedin	1955-56

INDIVIDUAL HUNDREDS IN THE MATCHES 1951-52–1979-80

By West Indies (20)

109† M. C. Carew, Auckland ..	1968-69	258 S. M. Nurse, Christchurch .	1968-69
183 C. A. Davis, Bridgetown ..	1971-72	214† L. G. Rowe, Kingston	1971-72
163 R. C. Fredericks, Kingston	1971-72	100*	
105† D. L. Haynes, Dunedin ..	1979-80	100 L. G. Rowe, Christchurch	1979-80
122 D. L. Haynes, Christchurch	1979-80	142 G. S. Sobers, Bridgetown ..	1971-72
100*†A. I. Kallicharran, Georgetown	1971-72	152 J. B. Stollmeyer, Auckland ..	1951-52
101 A. I. Kallicharran, Port-of-Spain	1971-72	115 C. L. Walcott, Auckland ..	1951-52
100* C. L. King, Christchurch ..	1979-80	123 E. D. Weekes, Dunedin ..	1955-56
168† S. M. Nurse, Auckland ...	1968-69	103 E. D. Weekes, Christchurch	1955-56
		156 E. D. Weekes, Wellington .	1955-56
		100 F. M. M. Worrell, Auckland	1951-52

By New Zealand (12)

101 M. G. Burgess, Kingston ..	1971-72	105 B. F. Hastings, Bridgetown	1971-72
166* B. E. Congdon, Port-of-Spain	1971-72	147 G. P. Howarth, Christchurch	1979-80
126 B. E. Congdon, Bridgetown	1971-72	182 T. W. Jarvis, Georgetown .	1971-72
127 B. A. Edgar, Auckland ...	1979-80	124† B. R. Taylor, Auckland ...	1968-69
103 R. J. Hadlee, Christchurch	1979-80	223* G. M. Turner, Kingston ...	1971-72
117* B. F. Hastings, Christchurch	1968-69	259 G. M. Turner, Georgetown	1971-72

† *Signifies hundred on first appearance in West Indies–New Zealand Tests.*

Notes: E. D. Weekes in 1955-56 made three hundreds in consecutive innings.
   L. G. Rowe and A. I. Kallicharran each scored hundreds in their first two innings in Test cricket, Rowe being the only batsman to do so in his first match.

RECORD PARTNERSHIPS FOR EACH WICKET

By West Indies

225 for 1st	C. G. Greenidge and D. L. Haynes at Christchurch	1979-80
269 for 2nd	R. C. Fredericks and L. G. Rowe at Kingston	1971-72
174 for 3rd	S. M. Nurse and B. F. Butcher at Auckland	1968-69
162 for 4th	E. D. Weekes and O. G. Smith at Dunedin	1955-56
	C. G. Greenidge and A. I. Kallicharran at Christchurch	1979-80
189 for 5th	F. M. M. Worrell and C. L. Walcott at Auckland	1951-52
254 for 6th	C. A. Davis and G. S. Sobers at Bridgetown	1971-72
143 for 7th	D. St E. Atkinson and J. D. C. Goddard at Christchurch	1955-56
75 for 8th	J. D. C. Goddard and S. Ramadhin at Dunedin	1955-56
56 for 9th	D. A. J. Holford and V. A. Holder at Port-of-Spain	1971-72
31 for 10th	T. M. Findlay and G. C. Shillingford at Bridgetown	1971-72

By New Zealand

387 for 1st†	G. M. Turner and T. W. Jarvis at Georgetown	1971-72
139 for 2nd	G. M. Turner and B. E. Congdon at Port-of-Spain	1971-72
75 for 3rd	B. E. Congdon and B. F. Hastings at Christchurch	1968-69
175 for 4th	B. E. Congdon and B. F. Hastings at Bridgetown	1971-72
110 for 5th	B. F. Hastings and V. Pollard at Christchurch	1968-69
220 for 6th†	G. M. Turner and K. J. Wadsworth at Kingston	1971-72
98 for 7th	J. V. Coney and R. J. Hadlee at Christchurch	1979-80
136 for 8th†	B. E. Congdon and R. S. Cunis at Port-of-Spain	1971-72
62* for 9th	V. Pollard and R. S. Cunis at Auckland	1968-69
41 for 10th	B. E. Congdon and J. C. Alabaster at Port-of-Spain	1971-72

† *Denotes record partnership against all countries.*

TEN WICKETS OR MORE IN A MATCH

For New Zealand (2)

11-102 (5-34, 6-68)†	R. J. Hadlee, Dunedin	1979-80
10-166 (4-71, 6-95)	G. B. Troup, Auckland	1979-80

† *Signifies ten wickets or more on first appearance in West Indies–New Zealand Tests.*

Note: The best match figures by a West Indian bowler are 9-125 (5-86, 4-39), S. Ramadhin at Christchurch, 1951-52, and 9-81 (6-23, 3-58), S. Ramadhin at Dunedin, 1955-56.

WEST INDIES v INDIA

	Captains		Tests	Won by West Indies	Won by India	Drawn
Season	West Indies	India				
1948-49*I*	J. D. C. Goddard	L. Amarnath	5	1	0	4
1952-53*W*	J. B. Stollmeyer	V. S. Hazare	5	1	0	4
1958-59*I*	F. C. M. Alexander	Ghulam Ahmed[1]	5	3	0	2
1961-62*W*	F. M. M. Worrell	N. J. Contractor[2]	5	5	0	0
1966-67*I*	G. S. Sobers	Nawab of Pataudi, jr	5	2	0	1
1970-71*W*	G. S. Sobers	A. L. Wadekar	5	0	1	4
1974-75*I*	C. H. Lloyd	M. A. K. Pataudi[3]	5	3	2	0
1975-76*W*	C. H. Lloyd	B. S. Bedi	4	2	1	1
1978-79*I*	A. I. Kallicharran	S. M. Gavaskar	6	0	1	5
	In India		24	9	3	12
	In West Indies		19	8	2	9
	Totals		43	17	5	21

I Played in India. W Played in West Indies.

Notes: The following deputised for the official touring captain or were appointed by the home authority for only a minor proportion of the series:
[1] P. R. Umrigar (First), V. M. H. Mankad (Fourth), H. R. Adhikari (Fifth). [2] Nawab of Pataudi, jr (Third, Fourth and Fifth). [3] S. Venkataraghavan (Second).

HIGHEST TOTALS FOR AN INNINGS

By West Indies			By India		
644-8	Delhi	1958-59	644-7	Kanpur	1978-79
631-8	Kingston	1961-62	566-8	Delhi	1978-79
631 ..	Delhi	1948-49	454 ..	Delhi	1948-49
629-6	Bombay	1948-49	444 ..	Kingston	1952-53
614-5	Calcutta	1958-59	427 ..	Port-of-Spain	1970-71
604-6	Bombay	1974-75	424 ..	Bombay	1978-79

Cricket Records

LOWEST TOTALS FOR AN INNINGS

	By West Indies				By India	
151	..	Madras	1978-79	97†	..	Kingston	1975-76
154	..	Madras (2nd Inns) ...	1974-75	98	..	Port-of-Spain	1961-62
172	..	Delhi	1978-79	118	..	Bangalore	1974-75
192	..	Madras (1st Inns)	1974-75	124	..	Calcutta	1958-59

† *Five men absent hurt.*

INDIVIDUAL HUNDREDS IN THE MATCHES 1948-49–1978-79

For West Indies (55)

250	S. F. A. Bacchus, Kanpur .	1978-79
103	B. F. Butcher, Calcutta ...	1958-59
142	B. F. Butcher, Madras	1958-59
107†	R. J. Christiani, Delhi	1948-49
125*	C. A. Davis, Georgetown .	1970-71
105	C. A. Davis, Port-of-Spain .	1970-71
100	R. C. Fredericks, Calcutta .	1974-75
104	R. C. Fredericks, Bombay .	1974-75
101†	G. E. Gomez, Delhi	1948-49
107†	C. G. Greenidge, Bangalore	1974-75
123	J. K. Holt, Delhi	1958-59
101	C. C. Hunte, Bombay	1966-67
124†	A. I. Kallicharran, Bangalore ...	1974-75
103*	A. I. Kallicharran, Port-of-Spain ...	1975-76
187	A. I. Kallicharran, Bombay	1978-79
256	R. B. Kanhai, Calcutta ...	1958-59
138	R. B. Kanhai, Kingston ...	1961-62
139	R. B. Kanhai, Port-of-Spain	1961-62
158*	R. B. Kanhai, Kingston ...	1970-71
163	C. H. Lloyd, Bangalore ...	1974-75
242*	C. H. Lloyd, Bombay	1974-75
102	C. H. Lloyd, Bridgetown ..	1975-76
125†	E. D. A. McMorris, Kingston	1961-62
115†	B. H. Pairaudeau, Port-of-Spain	1952-53
104	A. F. Rae, Bombay	1948-49
109	A. F. Rae, Madras	1948-49
192*	I. V. A. Richards, Delhi ...	1974-75
142	I. V. A. Richards, Bridgetown	1975-76

130	I. V. A. Richards, Port-of-Spain	1975-76
177	I. V. A. Richards, Port-of-Spain	1975-76
100	O. G. Smith, Delhi	1958-59
142*†	G. S. Sobers, Bombay	1958-59
198	G. S. Sobers, Kanpur	1958-59
106*	G. S. Sobers, Calcutta ...	1958-59
153	G. S. Sobers, Kingston ...	1961-62
104	G. S. Sobers, Kingston ...	1961-62
108*	G. S. Sobers, Georgetown .	1970-71
178*	G. S. Sobers, Bridgetown ..	1970-71
132	G. S. Sobers, Port-of-Spain	1970-71
100*	J. S. Solomon, Delhi	1958-59
160	J. B. Stollmeyer, Madras ..	1948-49
104*	J. B. Stollmeyer, Port-of-Spain	1952-53
152†	C. L. Walcott, Delhi	1948-49
108	C. L. Walcott, Calcutta ...	1948-49
125	C. L. Walcott, Georgetown	1952-53
118	C. L. Walcott, Kingston ..	1952-53
128†	E. D. Weekes, Delhi	1948-49
194	E. D. Weekes, Bombay ...	1948-49
162, 101	E. D. Weekes, Calcutta ...	1948-49
207	E. D. Weekes, Port-of-Spain	1952-53
161	E. D. Weekes, Port-of-Spain	1952-53
109	E. D. Weekes, Kingston ..	1952-53
111	A. B. Williams, Calcutta ..	1978-79
237	F. M. M. Worrell, Kingston	1952-53

For India (40)

114*†	H. R. Adhikari, Delhi	1948-49
101*	M. Amarnath, Kanpur	1978-79
163*	M. L. Apte, Port-of-Spain .	1952-53
109	C. G. Borde, Delhi	1958-59
121	C. G. Borde, Bombay	1966-67
125	C. G. Borde, Madras	1966-67
104	S. A. Durani, Port-of-Spain	1961-62
109	F. M. Engineer, Madras ...	1966-67
102	A. D. Gaekwad, Kanpur ..	1978-79
116	S. M. Gavaskar, Georgetown	1970-71

117*	S. M. Gavaskar, Bridgetown	1970-71
124, 220	S. M. Gavaskar, Port-of-Spain	1970-71
156	S. M. Gavaskar, Port-of-Spain	1975-76
102	S. M. Gavaskar, Port-of-Spain	1975-76
205	S. M. Gavaskar, Bombay .	1978-79
107, 182*	S. M. Gavaskar, Calcutta .	1978-79

120	S. M. Gavaskar, Delhi	1978-79	102	E. D. Solkar, Bombay	1974-75
134*	V. S. Hazare, Bombay	1948-49	130	P. R. Umrigar, Port-of-	
122	V. S. Hazare, Bombay	1948-49		Spain	1952-53
126*	Kapil Dev, Delhi	1978-79	117	P. R. Umrigar, Kingston ..	1952-53
118	V. L. Manjrekar, Kingston	1952-53	172*	P. R. Umrigar, Port-of-	
112	R. S. Modi, Bombay	1948-49		Spain	1961-62
106†	Mushtaq Ali, Calcutta	1948-49	157*	D. B. Vengsarkar, Calcutta	1978-79
115*	B. P. Patel, Port-of-Spain ..	1975-76	109	D. B. Vengsarkar, Delhi ...	1978-79
150	P. Roy, Kingston	1952-53	139	G. R. Viswanath, Calcutta	1974-75
212	D. N. Sardesai, Kingston ..	1970-71	112	G. R. Viswanath, Port-of-	
112	D. N. Sardesai, Port-of-			Spain	1975-76
	Spain	1970-71	124	G. R. Viswanath, Madras .	1978-79
150	D. N. Sardesai, Bridgetown	1970-71	179	G. R. Viswanath, Kanpur .	1978-79

† Signifies hundred on first appearance in West Indies–India Tests.

RECORD PARTNERSHIPS FOR EACH WICKET

By West Indies

239 for 1st†	J. B. Stollmeyer and A. F. Rae at Madras	1948-49
255 for 2nd	E. D. A. McMorris and R. B. Kanhai at Kingston	1961-62
220 for 3rd	I. V. A. Richards and A. I. Kallicharran at Bridgetown	1975-76
267 for 4th	C. L. Walcott and G. E. Gomez at Delhi	1948-49
219 for 5th	E. D. Weekes and B. H. Pairaudeau at Port-of-Spain	1952-53
250 for 6th	C. H. Lloyd and D. L. Murray at Bombay	1974-75
127 for 7th	G. S. Sobers and I. L. Mendonca at Kingston	1961-62
124 for 8th†	I. V. A. Richards and K. D. Boyce at Delhi	1974-75
106 for 9th	R. J. Christiani and D. St E. Atkinson at Delhi	1948-49
98* for 10th†	F. M. M. Worrell and W. W. Hall at Port-of-Spain	1961-62

By India

153 for 1st	S. M. Gavaskar and C. P. S. Chauhan at Bombay	1978-79
344* for 2nd†	S. M. Gavaskar and D. B. Vengsarkar at Calcutta	1978-79
159 for 3rd	M. Amarnath and G. R. Viswanath at Port-of-Spain	1975-76
172 for 4th	G. R. Viswanath and A. D. Gaekwad at Kanpur	1978-79
204 for 5th†	S. M. Gavaskar and B. P. Patel at Port-of-Spain	1975-76
137 for 6th	D. N. Sardesai and E. D. Solkar at Kingston	1970-71
186 for 7th†	D. N. Sardesai and E. D. Solkar at Bridgetown	1970-71
94 for 8th	R. G. Nadkarni and F. M. Engineer at Kingston	1961-62
122 for 9th	D. N. Sardesai and E. A. S. Prasanna at Kingston	1970-71
62 for 10th	D. N. Sardesai and B. S. Bedi at Bridgetown	1970-71

† Denotes record partnership against all countries.

TEN WICKETS OR MORE IN A MATCH

For West Indies (2)

11-126 (6-50, 5-76)	W. W. Hall, Kanpur	1958-59
12-121 (7-64, 5-57)	A. M. E. Roberts, Madras	1974-75

For India (2)

11-235 (7-157, 4-78)†	B. S. Chandrasekhar, Bombay	1966-67
10-223 (9-102, 1-121)	S. P. Gupte, Kanpur	1958-59

† Signifies ten wickets or more on first appearance in West Indies–India Tests.

WEST INDIES v PAKISTAN

Season	West Indies	Captains Pakistan	Tests	Won by West Indies	Won by Pakistan	Drawn
1957-58 *W*	F. C. M. Alexander	A. H. Kardar	5	3	1	1
1958-59 *P*	F. C. M. Alexander	Fazal Mahmood	3	1	2	0
1974-75 *P*	C. H. Lloyd	Intikhab Alam	2	0	0	2
1976-77 *W*	C. H. Lloyd	Mushtaq Mohammad	5	2	1	2
	In West Indies		10	5	2	3
	In Pakistan		5	1	2	2
	Totals		15	6	4	5

P Played in Pakistan.   W Played in West Indies.

HIGHEST TOTALS FOR AN INNINGS

By West Indies			By Pakistan		
790-3	Kingston	1957-58	657-8	Bridgetown	1957-58

LOWEST TOTALS FOR AN INNINGS

By West Indies				By Pakistan		
76	..	Dacca	1958-59	104	.. Lahore	1958-59
146	..	Karachi	1958-59	106	.. Bridgetown	1957-58

INDIVIDUAL HUNDREDS IN THE MATCHES 1957-58–1976-77

For West Indies (16)

105*†	L. Baichan, Lahore	1974-75	217 R. B. Kanhai, Lahore	1958-59
120	R. C. Fredericks, Port-of-Spain	1976-77	157 C. H. Lloyd, Bridgetown ..	1976-77
100	C. G. Greenidge, Kingston	1976-77	120 I. T. Shillingford, Georgetown	1976-77
142†	C. C. Hunte, Bridgetown ..	1957-58	365* G. S. Sobers, Kingston	1957-58
260	C. C. Hunte, Kingston	1957-58	125 } G. S. Sobers, Georgetown .	1957-58
114	C. C. Hunte, Georgetown .	1957-58	109*	
101	B. D. Julien, Karachi	1974-75	145 C. L. Walcott, Georgetown	1957-58
115	A. I. Kallicharran, Karachi	1974-75	197† E. D. Weekes, Bridgetown .	1957-58

For Pakistan (13)

135	Asif Iqbal, Kingston	1976-77	121 Mushtaq Mohammad, Port-of-Spain	1976-77
337†	Hanif Mohammad, Bridgetown	1957-58	150 Saeed Ahmed, Georgetown	1957-58
103	Hanif Mohammad, Karachi	1958-59	107* Wasim Raja, Karachi	1974-75
122	Imtiaz Ahmed, Kingston ..	1957-58	117* Wasim Raja, Bridgetown .	1976-77
100	Majid J. Khan, Karachi ...	1974-75	106 Wazir Mohammad, Kingston	1957-58
167	Majid J. Khan, Georgetown	1976-77	189 Wazir Mohammad, Port-of-Spain	1957-58
123	Mushtaq Mohammad, Lahore	1974-75		

† Signifies hundred on first appearance in West Indies–Pakistan Tests.

RECORD PARTNERSHIPS FOR EACH WICKET

By West Indies

182 for 1st	R. C. Fredericks and C. G. Greenidge at Kingston	1976-77
446 for 2nd†	C. C. Hunte and G. S. Sobers at Kingston	1957-58
162 for 3rd	R. B. Kanhai and G. S. Sobers at Lahore	1958-59
188* for 4th	G. S. Sobers and C. L. Walcott at Kingston	1957-58
185 for 5th	E. D. Weekes and O. G. Smith at Bridgetown	1957-58
151 for 6th	C. H. Lloyd and D. L. Murray at Bridgetown	1976-77
70 for 7th	C. H. Lloyd and J. Garner at Bridgetown	1976-77
50 for 8th	B. D. Julien and V. A. Holder at Karachi	1974-75
46 for 9th	J. Garner and C. E. H. Croft at Port-of-Spain	1976-77
26 for 10th {	A. M. E. Roberts and C. E. H. Croft at Georgetown	1976-77
{	A. M. E. Roberts and C. E. H. Croft at Port-of-Spain	1976-77

By Pakistan

159‡ for 1st	Majid J. Khan and Zaheer Abbas at Georgetown	1976-77
178 for 2nd	Hanif Mohammad and Saeed Ahmed at Karachi	1958-59
169 for 3rd	Saeed Ahmed and Wazir Mohammad at Port-of-Spain	1957-58
154 for 4th	Wazir Mohammad and Hanif Mohammad at Port-of-Spain	1957-58
87 for 5th	Mushtaq Mohammad and Asif Iqbal at Kingston	1976-77
166 for 6th	Wazir Mohammad and A. H. Kardar at Kingston	1957-58
128 for 7th	Wasim Raja and Wasim Bari at Karachi	1974-75
73 for 8th	Imran Khan and Sarfraz Nawaz at Port-of-Spain	1976-77
73 for 9th	Wasim Raja and Sarfraz Nawaz at Bridgetown	1976-77
133 for 10th†	Wasim Raja and Wasim Bari at Bridgetown	1976-77

† *Denotes record partnership against all countries.*
‡ *219 runs were added for this wicket in two separate partnerships; Sadiq Mohammad retired hurt and was replaced by Zaheer Abbas when 60 had been added. The highest partnership by two opening batsmen is 152 by Hanif Mohammad and Imtiaz Ahmed at Bridgetown, 1957-58.*

TEN WICKETS OR MORE IN A MATCH

For Pakistan (1)

12-100 (6-34, 6-66)   Fazal Mahmood, Dacca 1958-59

Note: The best match figures by a West Indian bowler are 9-187 (5-66, 4-121), A. M. E. Roberts at Lahore, 1974-75, and 9-95 (8-29, 1-66), C. E. H. Croft at Port-of-Spain, 1976-77.

NEW ZEALAND v INDIA

	Captains			Won by	Won by	
Season	New Zealand	India	Tests	New Zealand	India	Drawn
1955-56*I*	H. B. Cave	P. R. Umrigar[1]	5	0	2	3
1964-65*I*	J. R. Reid	Nawab of Pataudi, jr	4	0	1	3
1967-68*N*	G. T. Dowling[2]	Nawab of Pataudi, jr	4	1	3	0
1969-70*I*	G. T. Dowling	Nawab of Pataudi, jr	3	1	1	1
1975-76*N*	G. M. Turner	B. S. Bedi[3]	3	1	1	1
1976-77*I*	G. M. Turner	B. S. Bedi	3	0	2	1
	In India		15	1	6	8
	In New Zealand		7	2	4	1
	Totals		22	3	10	9

I Played in India.   N Played in New Zealand.

Notes: [1] Ghulam Ahmed captained in First Test. [2] B. W. Sinclair captained in First Test. [3] S. M. Gavaskar captained in First Test.

HIGHEST TOTALS FOR AN INNINGS

	By New Zealand				By India	
502	..	Christchurch	1967-68	537-3	Madras	1955-56
462-9		Calcutta	1964-65	531-7	Delhi	1955-56
450-2		Delhi	1955-56	524-9	Kanpur	1976-77

LOWEST TOTALS FOR AN INNINGS

	By New Zealand				By India	
101	..	Auckland	1967-68	81	.. Wellington	1975-76
127	..	Bombay	1969-70	88	.. Bombay	1964-65
136	..	Bombay	1955-56	89	.. Hyderabad	1969-70

INDIVIDUAL HUNDREDS IN THE MATCHES 1955-56–1976-77

For New Zealand (13)

120	G. T. Dowling, Bombay ...	1964-65	119*	J. R. Reid, Delhi	1955-56
143	G. T. Dowling, Dunedin	1967-68	230*	B. Sutcliffe, Delhi	1955-56
239	G. T. Dowling, Christ-church	1967-68	137*†	B. Sutcliffe, Hyderabad ...	1955-56
			151*	B. Sutcliffe, Calcutta	1964-65
102†	J. W. Guy, Hyderabad ...	1955-56	105†	B. R. Taylor, Calcutta	1964-65
104	J. M. Parker, Bombay	1976-77	117	G. M. Turner, Christchurch	1975-76
120	J. R. Reid, Calcutta	1955-56	113	G. M. Turner, Kanpur	1976-77

For India (20)

124†	S. Amarnath, Auckland ...	1975-76	223	V. M. H. Mankad, Bombay	1955-56
109	C. G. Borde, Bombay	1964-65	153	Nawab of Pataudi, Calcutta	1964-65
116†	S. M. Gavaskar, Auckland	1975-76	113	Nawab of Pataudi, Delhi ..	1964-65
119	S. M. Gavaskar, Bombay .	1976-77	106*	G. S. Ramchand, Calcutta .	1955-56
100*†	A. G. Kripal Singh, Hy-derabad	1955-56	173	P. Roy, Madras	1955-56
			100	P. Roy, Calcutta	1955-56
177	V. L. Manjrekar, Delhi ...	1955-56	200*	D. N. Sardesai, Bombay ..	1964-65
118†	V. L. Manjrekar, Hydera-bad	1955-56	106	D. N. Sardesai, Delhi	1964-65
102*	V. L. Manjrekar, Madras .	1964-65	223†	P. R. Umrigar, Hyderabad	1955-56
231	V. M. H. Mankad, Madras	1955-56	103*	G. R. Viswanath, Kanpur .	1976-77
			143	A. L. Wadekar, Wellington	1967-68

† *Signifies hundred on first appearance in New Zealand–India Tests. B. R. Taylor provided the only instance for New Zealand of a player scoring his maiden century in first-class cricket in his first Test.*

RECORD PARTNERSHIPS FOR EACH WICKET

By New Zealand

126 for 1st	B. A. G. Murray and G. T. Dowling at Christchurch	1967-68
155 for 2nd	G. T. Dowling and B. E. Congdon at Dunedin	1967-68
222* for 3rd†	B. Sutcliffe and J. R. Reid at Delhi	1955-56
103 for 4th	G. T. Dowling and M. G. Burgess at Christchurch	1967-68
119 for 5th	G. T. Dowling and K. Thomson at Christchurch	1967-68
87 for 6th	J. W. Guy and A. R. MacGibbon at Hyderabad	1955-56
163 for 7th	B. Sutcliffe and B. R. Taylor at Calcutta	1964-65
81 for 8th	V. Pollard and G. E. Vivian at Calcutta	1964-65
69 for 9th	M. G. Burgess and J. C. Alabaster at Dunedin	1967-68
61 for 10th	J. T. Ward and R. O. Collinge at Madras	1964-65

By India

413 for 1st†	V. M. H. Mankad and P. Roy at Madras	1955-56
204 for 2nd	S. M. Gavaskar and S. Amarnath at Auckland	1975-76
238 for 3rd†	P. R. Umrigar and V. L. Manjrekar at Hyderabad	1955-56
171 for 4th	P. R. Umrigar and A. G. Kripal Singh at Hyderabad	1955-56
127 for 5th	V. L. Manjrekar and G. S. Ramchand at Delhi	1955-56
193* for 6th†	D. N. Sardesai and Hanumant Singh at Bombay	1964-65
116 for 7th	B. P. Patel and S. M. H. Kirmani at Wellington	1975-76
143 for 8th†	R. G. Nadkarni and F. M. Engineer at Madras	1964-65
105 for 9th	S. M. H. Kirmani and B. S. Bedi at Bombay	1976-77
57 for 10th	R. B. Desai and B. S. Bedi at Dunedin	1967-68

† *Denotes record partnership against all countries.*

TEN WICKETS OR MORE IN A MATCH

For New Zealand (1)

11-58 (4-35, 7-23)	R. J. Hadlee, Wellington	1975-76

For India (2)

11-140 (3-64, 8-76)	E. A. S. Prasanna, Auckland	1975-76
12-152 (8-72, 4-80)	S. Venkataraghavan, Delhi	1964-65

NEW ZEALAND v PAKISTAN

Season	New Zealand	Pakistan	Tests	Won by New Zealand	Won by Pakistan	Drawn
	Captains					
1955-56*P*	H. B. Cave	A. H. Kardar	3	0	2	1
1964-65*N*	J. R. Reid	Hanif Mohammad	3	0	0	3
1964-65*P*	J. R. Reid	Hanif Mohammad	3	0	2	1
1969-70*P*	G. T. Dowling	Intikhab Alam	3	1	0	2
1972-73*N*	B. E. Congdon	Intikhab Alam	3	0	1	2
1976-77*P*	G. M. Turner[1]	Mushtaq Mohammad	3	0	2	1
1978-79*N*	M. G. Burgess	Mushtaq Mohammad	3	0	1	2
	In Pakistan		12	1	6	5
	In New Zealand		9	0	2	7
	Totals		21	1	8	12

N Played in New Zealand.   P Played in Pakistan.

Note: [1] J. M. Parker captained in Third Test.

HIGHEST TOTALS FOR AN INNINGS

By New Zealand			**By Pakistan**		
482-6	Lahore	1964-65	565-9	Karachi	1976-77
468	Karachi	1976-77	561 ..	Lahore	1955-56
402	Auckland	1972-73	507-6	Dunedin	1972-73
402	Napier	1978-79	473-8	Hyderabad	1976-77

LOWEST TOTALS FOR AN INNINGS

By New Zealand			**By Pakistan**		
70 ..	Dacca	1955-56	114 ..	Lahore	1969-70
79 ..	Rawalpindi	1964-65	187 ..	Wellington	1964-65

INDIVIDUAL HUNDREDS IN THE MATCHES 1955-56–1978-79

For New Zealand (11)

119*	M. G. Burgess, Dacca	1969-70	111	S. N. McGregor, Lahore	..	1955-56
111	M. G. Burgess, Lahore	1976-77	107†	R. E. Redmond, Auckland		1972-73
129†	B. A. Edgar, Christchurch	1978-79	128	J. R. Reid, Karachi	......	1964-65
110	B. F. Hastings, Auckland	1972-73	130	B. W. Sinclair, Lahore	....	1964-65
114	G. P. Howarth, Napier	1978-79	110†	G. M. Turner, Dacca	....	1969-70
152	W. K. Lees, Karachi	1976-77				

For Pakistan (22)

175	Asif Iqbal, Dunedin	1972-73	126	Mohammad Ilyas, Karachi	1964-65
166	Asif Iqbal, Lahore	1976-77	201	Mushtaq Mohammad, Dunedin	1972-73
104	Asiq Iqbal, Napier	1978-79			
103	Hanif Mohammad, Dacca	1955-56	101	Mushtaq Mohammad, Hyderabad	1976-77
100*	Hanif Mohammad, Christchurch	1964-65	107	Mushtaq Mohammad, Karachi	1976-77
203*	Hanif Mohammad, Lahore	1964-65			
209	Imtiaz Ahmed, Lahore	1955-56	166	Sadiq Mohammad, Wellington	1972-73
163†	Javed Miandad, Lahore	1976-77			
206	Javed Miandad, Karachi	1976-77	103*	Sadiq Mohammad, Hyderabad	1976-77
160*	Javed Miandad, Christchurch	1978-79	172	Saeed Ahmed, Karachi	1964-65
110	Majid J. Khan, Auckland	1972-73	189	Waqar Hassan, Lahore	1955-56
112	Majid J. Khan, Karachi	1976-77	135	Zaheer Abbas, Auckland	1978-79
119*	Majid J. Khan, Napier	1978-79			

† *Signifies hundred on first appearance in New Zealand–Pakistan Tests.*

Note: Mushtaq and Sadiq Mohammad, at Hyderabad in 1976-77, provided the fourth instance in Test matches, after the Chappells (thrice), of brothers each scoring hundreds in the same innings.

RECORD PARTNERSHIPS FOR EACH WICKET

By New Zealand

159 for 1st	R. E. Redmond and G. M. Turner at Auckland	1972-73
195 for 2nd†	J. G. Wright and G. P. Howarth at Napier	1978-79
178 for 3rd	B. W. Sinclair and J. R. Reid at Lahore	1964-65
128 for 4th	B. F. Hastings and M. G. Burgess at Wellington	1972-73
183 for 5th†	M. G. Burgess and R. W. Anderson at Lahore	1976-77
91 for 6th	M. G. Burgess and W. K. Lees at Karachi	1976-77
186 for 7th†	W. K. Lees and R. J. Hadlee at Karachi	1976-77
100 for 8th	B. W. Yuile and D. R. Hadlee at Karachi	1969-70
96 for 9th†	M. G. Burgess and R. S. Cunis at Dacca	1969-70
151 for 10th†	B. F. Hastings and R. O. Collinge at Auckland	1972-73

By Pakistan

147 for 1st‡	Sadiq Mohammad and Majid J. Khan at Karachi	1976-77
114 for 2nd	Mohammad Ilyas and Saeed Ahmed at Rawalpindi	1964-65
171 for 3rd	Sadiq Mohammad and Majid J. Khan at Wellington	1972-73
350 for 4th†	Mushtaq Mohammad and Asif Iqbal at Dunedin	1972-73
281 for 5th†	Javed Miandad and Asif Iqbal at Lahore	1976-77
217 for 6th†	Hanif Mohammad and Majid J. Khan at Lahore	1964-65
308 for 7th†	Waqar Hassan and Imtiaz Ahmed at Lahore	1955-56
72 for 8th	Asif Iqbal and Imran Khan at Lahore	1976-77
52 for 9th	Intikhab Alam and Arif Butt at Auckland	1964-65
65 for 10th	Salah-ud-Din and Mohammad Farooq at Rawalpindi	1964-65

† *Denotes record partnership against all countries.*

‡ *In the preceding Test, at Hyderabad, of this series 164 runs were added for this wicket by Sadiq Mohammad, Majid J. Khan and Zaheer Abbas. Sadiq Mohammad retired hurt after 136 had been scored.*

TEN WICKETS OR MORE IN A MATCH

For Pakistan (3)

10-182 (5-91, 5-91)	Intikhab Alam, Dacca	1969-70
11-130 (7-52, 4-78)	Intikhab Alam, Dunedin	1972-73
11-79 (5-37, 6-42)†	Zulfiqar Ahmed, Karachi	1955-56

† *Signifies ten wickets or more on first appearance in New Zealand–Pakistan Tests.*

Note: The best match figures by a New Zealand bowler are 9-70 (4-36, 5-34), F. J. Cameron at Auckland, 1964-65.

INDIA v PAKISTAN

Season	India		Pakistan	Tests	Won by India	Won by Pakistan	Drawn
		Captains					
1952-53*I*	L. Amarnath		A. H. Kardar	5	2	1	2
1954-55*P*	V. M. H. Mankad		A. H. Kardar	5	0	0	5
1960-61*I*	N. J. Contractor		Fazal Mahmood	5	0	0	5
1978-79*P*	B. S. Bedi	Mushtaq Mohammad		3	0	2	1
1979-80*I*	S. M. Gavaskar[1]		Asif Iqbal	6	2	0	4
	In India			16	4	1	11
	In Pakistan			8	0	2	6
	Totals			24	4	3	17

I Played in India.   P Played in Pakistan.

Notes: The following deputised for the official touring captain or were appointed by the home authority for only a minor proportion of the series: [1]G. R. Viswanath (Sixth).

HIGHEST TOTALS FOR AN INNINGS

By India			By Pakistan		
539-9	Madras	1960-61	539-6	Lahore	1978-79
465 ..	Lahore	1978-79	503-8	Faisalabad	1978-79

LOWEST TOTALS FOR AN INNINGS

By India			By Pakistan		
106 ..	Lucknow	1952-53	150 ..	Delhi.............	1952-53

INDIVIDUAL HUNDREDS IN THE MATCHES 1952-53–1979-80

For India (13)

177*	C. G. Borde, Madras	1960-61	108	P. R. Umrigar, Peshawar ..	1954-55
111	S. M. Gavaskar, Karachi ..	1978-79	115	P. R. Umrigar, Kanpur ...	1960-61
137			117	P. R. Umrigar, Madras ...	1960-61
166	S. M. Gavaskar, Madras ..	1979-80	112	P. R. Umrigar, Delhi	1960-61
146*	V. S. Hazare, Bombay	1952-53	146*	D. B. Vengsarkar, Delhi ...	1979-80
110†	D. H. Shodhan, Calcutta ..	1952-53	145†	G. R. Viswanath, Faisala-	
102	P. R. Umrigar, Bombay ...	1952-53		bad	1978-79

For Pakistan (14)

103* Alim-ud-Din, Karachi	1954-55	101	Mushtaq Mohammad, Delhi	1960-61
104† Asif Iqbal, Faisalabad	1978-79	124*	Nazar Mohammad, Lucknow	1952-53
142 Hanif Mohammad, Bahawalpur	1954-55	121†	Saeed Ahmed, Bombay ...	1960-61
160 Hanif Mohammad, Bombay	1960-61	103	Saeed Ahmed, Madras	1960-61
135 Imtiaz Ahmed, Madras ...	1960-61	176†	Zaheer Abbas, Faisalabad .	1978-79
154*† Javed Miandad, Faisalabad	1978-79	235*	Zaheer Abbas, Lahore	1978-79
100 Javed Miandad, Karachi ..	1978-79			
126 Mudassar Nazar, Bangalore	1979-80			

† *Signifies hundred on first appearance in India–Pakistan Tests.*

RECORD PARTNERSHIPS FOR EACH WICKET

By India

192 for 1st	S. M. Gavaskar and C. P. S. Chauhan at Lahore	1978-79
117 for 2nd	S. M. Gavaskar and M. Amarnath at Karachi	1978-79
130* for 3rd	P. Roy and V. L. Manjrekar at Dacca	1954-55
183 for 4th	V. S. Hazare and P. R. Umrigar at Bombay	1952-53
177 for 5th	P. R. Umrigar and C. G. Borde at Madras	1960-61
82 for 6th	C. G. Borde and R. G. Nadkarni at Bombay	1960-61
95 for 7th	S. M. H. Kirmani and Kapil Dev at Bombay	1979-80
84 for 8th	K. D. Ghavri and Kapil Dev at Karachi	1978-79
149 for 9th†	P. G. Joshi and R. B. Desai at Bombay	1960-61
109 for 10th†	H. R. Adhikari and Ghulam Ahmed at Delhi	1952-53

For Pakistan

162 for 1st	Hanif Mohammad and Imtiaz Ahmed at Madras	1960-61
246 for 2nd	Hanif Mohammad and Saeed Ahmed at Bombay	1960-61
166 for 3rd	Zaheer Abbas and Asif Iqbal at Faisalabad	1978-79
255 for 4th	Zaheer Abbas and Javed Miandad at Faisalabad	1978-79
155 for 5th	Alim-ud-Din and A. H. Kardar at Karachi	1954-55
154 for 6th	Javed Miandad and Mushtaq Mohammad at Karachi	1978-79
88 for 7th	Mushtaq Mohammad and Intikhab Alam at Calcutta	1960-61
82 for 8th	Wasim Raja and Iqbal Qasim at Kanpur	1979-80
60 for 9th	Wasim Bari and Iqbal Qasim at Bangalore	1979-80
104 for 10th	Zulfiqar Ahmed and Amir Elahi at Madras	1952-53

† *Denotes record partnership against all countries.*

TEN WICKETS OR MORE IN A MATCH

For India (2)

11-146 (4-90, 7-56)	Kapil Dev, Madras	1979-80
13-131 (8-52, 5-79)†	V. M. H. Mankad, Delhi	1952-53

For Pakistan (3)

12-94 (5-52, 7-42)	Fazal Mahmood, Lucknow	1952-53
10-175 (4-135, 6-40)	Iqbal Qasim, Bombay	1979-80
11-190 (8-69, 3-121)	Sikander Bakht, Delhi	1979-80

† *Signifies ten wickets or more on first appearance in India–Pakistan Tests.*

MISCELLANEOUS

RELATIONS IN TEST CRICKET

FATHERS AND SONS

England
J. Hardstaff (5 Tests, 1907-08) and J. Hardstaff Jnr (23 Tests, 1935–1948).
Sir L. Hutton (79 Tests, 1937–1954-55) and R. A. Hutton (5 Tests, 1971).
F. T. Mann (5 Tests, 1922-23) and F. G. Mann (7 Tests, 1948-49–1949).
J. H. Parks (1 Test, 1937) and J. M. Parks (46 Tests, 1954–1967-68).
F. W. Tate (1 Test, 1902) and M. W. Tate (39 Tests, 1924–1935).
C. L. Townsend (2 Tests, 1899) and D. C. H. Townsend (3 Tests, 1934-35).

Australia
E. J. Gregory (1 Test, 1876-77) and S. E. Gregory (58 Tests, 1890–1912).

South Africa
F. Hearne (4 Tests, 1891-92–1895-96) and G. A. L. Hearne (3 Tests, 1922-23–1924).
   F. Hearne also played 2 Tests for England in 1888-89.
J. D. Lindsay (3 Tests, 1947) and D. T. Lindsay (19 Tests, 1963-64–1969-70).
A. W. Nourse (45 Tests, 1902-03–1924) and A. D. Nourse (34 Tests, 1935–1951).
L. R. Tuckett (1 Test, 1913-14) and L. Tuckett (9 Tests, 1947–1948-49).

West Indies
G. A. Headley (22 Tests, 1929-30–1953-54) and R. G. A. Headley (2 Tests, 1973).
O. C. Scott (8 Tests, 1928–1930-31) and A. P. H. Scott (1 Test, 1952-53).

New Zealand
W. M. Anderson (1 Test, 1945-46) and R. W. Anderson (9 Tests, 1976-77–1978).
W. A. Hadlee (11 Tests, 1937–1950-51) and D. R. Hadlee (26 Tests, 1969–1977-78); R. J.
   Hadlee (29 Tests, 1972-73–1979-80).
H. G. Vivian (7 Tests, 1931–1937) and G. E. Vivian (5 Tests, 1964-65–1971-72).

India
L. Amarnath (24 Tests, 1933-34–1952-53) and M. Amarnath (26 Tests, 1969-70–1979-80);
   S. Amarnath (8 Tests, 1975-76–1978-79).
D. K. Gaekwad (11 Tests, 1952–1960-61) and A. D. Gaekwad (21 Tests, 1974-75–1979).
Nawab of Pataudi (Iftikhar Ali Khan) (3 Tests, 1946) and Nawab of Pataudi (Mansur Ali
   Khan) (46 Tests, 1961-62–1974-75).
   Nawab of Pataudi Snr also played 3 Tests for England, 1932-33–1934.
V. M. H. Mankad (44 Tests, 1946–1958-59) and A. V. Mankad (22 Tests, 1969-70–1977-78).

India and Pakistan
M. Jahangir Khan (4 Tests, 1932–1936) and Majid J. Khan (53 Tests, 1964-65–1979-80).
S. Wazir Ali (7 Tests, 1932–1936) and Khalid Wazir (2 Tests, 1954).

Pakistan
Nazar Mohammad (5 Tests, 1952-53) and Mudassar Nazar (19 Tests, 1976-77–1979-80).

GRANDFATHERS AND GRANDSONS

Australia
V. Y. Richardson (19 Tests, 1924-25–1935-36) and G. S. Chappell (61 Tests, 1970-71–1980);
   I. M. Chappell (75 Tests, 1964-65–1979-80).

GREAT-GRANDFATHER AND GREAT-GRANDSON

Australia
W. H. Cooper (2 Tests, 1881-82 and 1884-85) and A. P. Sheahan (31 Tests, 1967-68–1973-74).

BROTHERS IN SAME TEST TEAM

England
E. M., G. F. and W. G. Grace: 1 Test, 1880.
C. T. and G. B. Studd: 4 Tests, 1882-83.
A. and G. G. Hearne: 1 Test, 1891-92.
    F. Hearne, their brother, played in this match for South Africa.
D. W. and P. E. Richardson: 1 Test, 1957.

Australia
E. J. and D. W. Gregory: 1 Test, 1876-77.
C. and A. C. Bannerman: 1 Test, 1878-79.
G. and W. F. Giffen: 2 Tests, 1891-92.
G. H. S. and A. E. Trott: 3 Tests, 1894-95.
I. M. and G. S. Chappell: 43 Tests, 1970-71–1979-80.

South Africa
S. J. and S. D. Snooke: 1 Test, 1907.
R. H. M. and P. A. M. Hands: 1 Test, 1913-14.
E. A. B. and A. M. B. Rowan: 9 Tests, 1948-49–1951.
P. M. and R. G. Pollock: 23 Tests, 1963-64–1969-70.
A. J. and D. B. Pithey: 5 Tests, 1963-64.

West Indies
G. C. and R. S. Grant: 4 Tests, 1934-35.
J. B. and V. H. Stollmeyer: 1 Test, 1939.
D. St E. and E. St E. Atkinson: 1 Test, 1957-58.

New Zealand
D. R. and R. J. Hadlee: 10 Tests, 1973–1977-78.
H. J. and G. P. Howarth: 4 Tests, 1974-75–1976-77.
J. M. and N. M. Parker: 3 Tests, 1976-77.

India
S. Wazir Ali and S. Nazir Ali: 2 Tests, 1932–1933-34.
L. Ramji and Amar Sinh: 1 Test, 1933-34.
C. K. and C. S. Nayudu: 4 Tests, 1933-34–1936.
A. G. Kripal Singh and A. G. Milkha Singh: 1 Test, 1961-62.
S. and M. Amarnath: 8 Tests, 1975-76–1978-79.

Pakistan
Wazir and Hanif Mohammad: 18 Tests, 1952-53–1959-60.
Wazir and Mushtaq Mohammad: 1 Test, 1958-59.
Hanif and Mushtaq Mohammad: 19 Tests, 1960-61–1969-70.
Hanif, Mushtaq and Sadiq Mohammad: 1 Test, 1969-70.
Mushtaq and Sadiq Mohammad: 26 Tests, 1969-70–1978-79.

GENTLEMEN v PLAYERS

The highest individual scores were:

266*	J. B. Hobbs	Scarborough	1925	215	W. G. Grace	The Oval . . .	1870
247	R. Abel	The Oval . . .	1901	203	T. W. Hayward	The Oval . . .	1904
241	L. Hutton	Scarborough	1953	201	L. E. G. Ames	Folkestone .	1933
232*	C. B. Fry	Lord's	1903	195	R. Abel	The Oval . . .	1899
223	C. P. Mead	Scarborough	1911	194*	E. H. Hendren	The Oval . . .	1932
217	W. G. Grace	Brighton . . .	1871				

Notes: W. G. Grace played no fewer than fifteen three-figure innings for Gentlemen v Players. On his 58th birthday – at The Oval in July 1906 – he scored 74.

J. B. Hobbs in all matches under this title scored sixteen three-figure innings, and had an aggregate of 4,052 runs with an average of 54.75.

The match, first played in 1806, has not been contested since 1962, owing to the abolition of the amateur status in first-class cricket.

There were 137 matches played at Lord's from 1806; Players won 68, Gentlemen won 41, and 28 were drawn. Individual hundreds and results since 1919 appeared in *Wisden* 1963, page 358.

LARGE ATTENDANCES

Test Series

943,000	Australia v England (5 Tests)	1936-37

In England

549,650	England v Australia (5 Tests)	1953

Test Match

350,534	Australia v England, Melbourne (Third Test)	1936-37
325,000+	India v England, Calcutta (Second Test)	1972-73

In England

158,000+	England v Australia, Leeds (Fourth Test)	1948
137,915	England v Australia, Lord's (Second Test)	1953

Test Match Day

90,800	Australia v West Indies, Melbourne (Fifth Test, 2nd day)	1960-61

Other First-Class Matches in England

80,000+	Surrey v Yorkshire, The Oval (3 days)	1906
78,792	Yorkshire v Lancashire, Leeds (3 days)	1904
76,617	Lancashire v Yorkshire, Manchester (3 days)	1926

LORD'S CRICKET GROUND

Lord's and the MCC were founded in 1787. The Club has enjoyed an uninterrupted career since that date, but there have been three grounds known as Lord's. The first (1787-1810) was situated where Dorset Square now is; the second (1809-13), at North Bank, had to be abandoned owing to the cutting of the Regent's Canal; and the third, opened in 1814, is the present one at St John's Wood. It was not until 1866 that the freehold of Lord's was secured by the MCC. The present pavilion was erected in 1890 at a cost of £21,000.

LARGEST INDIVIDUAL SCORES MADE AT LORD'S

316*	J. B. Hobbs	Surrey v Middlesex	1926
315*	P. Holmes	Yorkshire v Middlesex	1925
281*	W. H. Ponsford	Australians v MCC	1934
278	W. Ward	MCC v Norfolk (with E. H. Budd, T. Vigne and F. Ladbroke)	1820
278	D. G. Bradman	Australians v MCC	1938
277*	E. H. Hendren	Middlesex v Kent	1922

HIGHEST TOTALS OBTAINED AT LORD'S

First-Class Matches

729-6	Australia v England	1930
665	West Indians v Middlesex	1939
652-8	West Indies v England	1973
629	England v India	1974
612-8	Middlesex v Nottinghamshire	1921
610-5	Australians v Gentlemen	1948
609-8	Cambridge University v MCC and Ground	1913
608-7	Middlesex v Hampshire	1919
607	MCC and Ground v Cambridge University	1902

Minor Match

735-9	MCC and Ground v Wiltshire	1888

BIGGEST HIT AT LORD'S

The only known instance of a batsman hitting a ball over the present pavilion at Lord's occurred when A. E. Trott, appearing for MCC against Australians on July 31, August 1, 2, 1899, drove M. A. Noble so far and high that the ball struck a chimney pot and fell behind the building.

THROWING THE CRICKET BALL

140 yards 2 feet, Robert Percival, on the Durham Sands, Co. Durham Racecourse ...	1884
140 yards 9 inches, Ross Mackenzie, at Toronto	1872

Notes: W. F. Forbes, on March 16, 1876, threw 132 yards at the Eton College Sports. He was then 18 years of age.

William Yardley, while a boy at Rugby, threw 100 yards with his right hand and 78 yards with his left.

Charles Arnold, of Cambridge, once threw 112 yards with the wind and 108 against. W. H. Game, at The Oval in 1875, threw the ball 111 yards and then back the same distance. W. G. Grace threw 109 yards one way and back 105, and George Millyard 108 with the wind and 103 against. At The Oval in 1868, W. G. Grace made three successive throws of 116, 117, and 118 yards, and then threw back over 100 yards. D. G. Foster (Warwickshire) threw 133 yards, and in 1930 he made a Danish record with 120.1 metres – about 130 yards.

DATES OF FORMATION OF COUNTY CLUBS NOW FIRST-CLASS

County	First known county organisation	Original date	Present Club Reorganisation, if substantial
Derbyshire	November 4, 1870	November 4, 1870	—
Essex	By May, 1790	January 14, 1876	—
Glamorgan	1863	July 6, 1888	—
Gloucestershire	November 3, 1863	1871	—
Hampshire	April 3, 1849	August 12, 1863	July, 1879
Kent	August 6, 1842	March 1, 1859	December 6, 1870
Lancashire	January 12, 1864	January 12, 1864	—
Leicestershire	By August, 1820	March 25, 1879	—
Middlesex	December 15, 1863	December 15, 1863	—
Northamptonshire ...	1820	1820	July 31, 1878
Nottinghamshire	March/April, 1841	March/April, 1841	December 11, 1866
Somerset	October 15, 1864	August 18, 1875	—
Surrey	August 22, 1845	August 22, 1845	—
Sussex	June 16, 1836	March 1, 1839	August, 1857
Warwickshire	May, 1826	January 19, 1884	—
Worcestershire	1844	March 5, 1865	—
Yorkshire	March 7, 1861	January 8, 1863	December 10, 1891

DATES OF FORMATION OF CLUBS IN THE CURRENT MINOR COUNTIES CHAMPIONSHIP

County	First known county organisation	Present Club
Bedfordshire	May, 1847	November 3, 1899
Berkshire	By May, 1841	March 17, 1895
Buckinghamshire ...	November, 1864	January 15, 1891
Cambridgeshire	March 13, 1844	June 6, 1891
Cheshire	1819	September 29, 1908
Cornwall	1813	November 12, 1894
Cumberland	January 2, 1884	April 10, 1948
Devon	1824	November 26, 1899
Dorset	1862 *or* 1871	February 5, 1896
Durham	January 24, 1874	May 10, 1882
Hertfordshire	1838	March 8, 1876
Lincolnshire	1853	September 28, 1906
Norfolk	January 11, 1827	October 14, 1876
Northumberland	1834	December, 1895
Oxfordshire	1787	December 14, 1921
Shropshire	1819 *or* 1829	June 28, 1956
Staffordshire	November 24, 1871	November 24, 1871
Suffolk	July 27, 1864	August, 1932
Wiltshire	February 24, 1881	January, 1893

CONSTITUTION OF COUNTY CHAMPIONSHIP

There are references in the sporting press to a champion county as early as 1825, but the list is not continuous and in some years only two counties contested the title. The earliest reference in any cricket publication is from 1864, and at this time there were eight leading counties who have come to be regarded as first-class from that date – Cambridgeshire, Hampshire, Kent, Middlesex, Nottinghamshire, Surrey, Sussex and Yorkshire. The newly formed Lancashire club began playing inter-county matches in 1865, Gloucestershire in 1870 and Derbyshire in 1871, and they are therefore regarded as first-class from these respective dates. Cambridgeshire dropped out after 1871, Hampshire, who had not played inter-county matches in certain seasons, after 1885, and Derbyshire after 1887. Somerset, who had played matches against the first-class counties since 1879, were regarded as first-class from 1882 to 1885, and were admitted formally to the Championship in 1891. In 1894, Derbyshire, Essex, Leicestershire and Warwickshire were granted first-class status, but did not compete in the Championship until 1895 when Hampshire returned. Worcestershire, Northamptonshire and Glamorgan were admitted to the Championship in 1899, 1905 and 1921 respectively and are regarded as first-class from these dates.

MOST COUNTY CHAMPIONSHIP APPEARANCES

763	W. Rhodes	Yorkshire	1898-1930
707	F. E. Woolley ...	Kent	1906-38
665	C. P. Mead	Hampshire	1906-36

MOST CONSECUTIVE COUNTY CHAMPIONSHIP APPEARANCES

423	K. G. Suttle	Sussex	1954-69
412	J. G. Binks	Yorkshire	1955-69
399	J. Vine	Sussex	1899-1914
344	E. H. Killick	Sussex	1898-1912
326	C. N. Woolley ...	Northamptonshire ..	1913-31
305	A. H. Dyson	Glamorgan	1930-47
301	B. Taylor	Essex	1961-72

Notes: J. Vine made 417 consecutive appearances for Sussex in *all* first-class matches between July 1900 and September 1914.

J. G. Binks did not miss a Championship match for Yorkshire between making his début in June 1955 and retiring at the end of the 1969 season.

CHAMPION COUNTY SINCE 1864

Note: The earliest county champions were decided usually by the fewest matches lost, but in 1888 an unofficial points system was introduced. In 1890, the Championship was constituted officially. Since 1977, it has been sponsored by Schweppes.

1864	Surrey	1897	Lancashire	1946	Yorkshire
1865	Nottinghamshire	1898	Yorkshire	1947	Middlesex
1866	Middlesex	1899	Surrey	1948	Glamorgan
1867	Yorkshire	1900	Yorkshire	1949	Middlesex / Yorkshire
1868	Nottinghamshire	1901	Yorkshire		
1869	Nottinghamshire / Yorkshire	1902	Yorkshire	1950	Lancashire / Surrey
		1903	Middlesex		
1870	Yorkshire	1904	Lancashire	1951	Warwickshire
1871	Nottinghamshire	1905	Yorkshire	1952	Surrey
1872	Nottinghamshire	1906	Kent	1953	Surrey
1873	Gloucestershire / Nottinghamshire	1907	Nottinghamshire	1954	Surrey
		1908	Yorkshire	1955	Surrey
1874	Gloucestershire	1909	Kent	1956	Surrey
1875	Nottinghamshire	1910	Kent	1957	Surrey
1876	Gloucestershire	1911	Warwickshire	1958	Surrey
1877	Gloucestershire	1912	Yorkshire	1959	Yorkshire
1878	Undecided	1913	Kent	1960	Yorkshire
1879	Nottinghamshire / Lancashire	1914	Surrey	1961	Hampshire
		1919	Yorkshire	1962	Yorkshire
1880	Nottinghamshire	1920	Middlesex	1963	Yorkshire
1881	Lancashire	1921	Middlesex	1964	Worcestershire
1882	Nottinghamshire / Lancashire	1922	Yorkshire	1965	Worcestershire
		1923	Yorkshire	1966	Yorkshire
1883	Nottinghamshire	1924	Yorkshire	1967	Yorkshire
1884	Nottinghamshire	1925	Yorkshire	1968	Yorkshire
1885	Nottinghamshire	1926	Lancashire	1969	Glamorgan
1886	Nottinghamshire	1927	Lancashire	1970	Kent
1887	Surrey	1928	Lancashire	1971	Surrey
1888	Surrey	1929	Nottinghamshire	1972	Warwickshire
1889	Surrey / Lancashire / Nottinghamshire	1930	Lancashire	1973	Hampshire
		1931	Yorkshire	1974	Worcestershire
		1932	Yorkshire	1975	Leicestershire
1890	Surrey	1933	Yorkshire	1976	Middlesex
1891	Surrey	1934	Lancashire	1977	Middlesex / Kent
1892	Surrey	1935	Yorkshire		
1893	Yorkshire	1936	Derbyshire	1978	Kent
1894	Surrey	1937	Yorkshire	1979	Essex
1895	Surrey	1938	Yorkshire	1980	Middlesex
1896	Yorkshire	1939	Yorkshire		

Notes: The title has been won outright as follows: Yorkshire 31 times, Surrey 18, Nottinghamshire 12, Lancashire 8, Middlesex 7, Kent 6, Gloucestershire 3, Warwickshire 3, Worcestershire 3, Glamorgan 2, Hampshire 2, Derbyshire 1, Essex 1, Leicestershire 1.

Eight times the title has been shared as follows: Nottinghamshire 5, Lancashire 4, Middlesex 2, Surrey 2, Yorkshire 2, Gloucestershire 1 and Kent 1.

The earliest date the Championship has been won in any season since it was expanded in 1895 was August 12, 1910, by Kent.

THE MINOR COUNTIES CHAMPIONS

1895	Norfolk	1923	Buckinghamshire	1956	Kent II
	Durham	1924	Berkshire	1957	Yorkshire II
	Worcestershire	1925	Buckinghamshire	1958	Yorkshire II
1896	Worcestershire	1926	Durham	1959	Warwickshire II
1897	Worcestershire	1927	Staffordshire	1960	Lancashire II
1898	Worcestershire	1928	Berkshire	1961	Somerset II
1899	Northamptonshire	1929	Oxfordshire	1962	Warwickshire II
	Buckinghamshire	1930	Durham	1963	Cambridgeshire
1900	Glamorgan	1931	Leicestershire II	1964	Lancashire II
	Durham	1932	Buckinghamshire	1965	Somerset II
	Northamptonshire	1933	Undecided	1966	Lincolnshire
1901	Durham	1934	Lancashire II	1967	Cheshire
1902	Wiltshire	1935	Middlesex II	1968	Yorkshire II
1903	Northamptonshire	1936	Hertfordshire	1969	Buckinghamshire
1904	Northamptonshire	1937	Lancashire II	1970	Bedfordshire
1905	Norfolk	1938	Buckinghamshire	1971	Yorkshire II
1906	Staffordshire	1939	Surrey II	1972	Bedfordshire
1907	Lancashire II	1946	Suffolk	1973	Shropshire
1908	Staffordshire	1947	Yorkshire II	1974	Oxfordshire
1909	Wiltshire	1948	Lancashire II	1975	Hertfordshire
1910	Norfolk	1949	Lancashire II	1976	Durham
1911	Staffordshire	1950	Surrey II	1977	Suffolk
1912	In abeyance	1951	Kent II	1978	Devon
1913	Norfolk	1952	Buckinghamshire	1979	Suffolk
1920	Staffordshire	1953	Berkshire	1980	Durham
1921	Staffordshire	1954	Surrey II		
1922	Buckinghamshire	1955	Surrey II		

SECOND ELEVEN CHAMPIONS

1959	Gloucestershire	1967	Hampshire	1975	Surrey
1960	Northamptonshire	1968	Surrey	1976	Kent
1961	Kent	1969	Kent	1977	Yorkshire
1962	Worcestershire	1970	Kent	1978	Sussex
1963	Worcestershire	1971	Hampshire	1979	Warwickshire
1964	Lancashire	1972	Nottinghamshire	1980	Glamorgan
1965	Glamorgan	1973	Essex		
1966	Surrey	1974	Middlesex		

FEATURES OF 1980

Double Centuries

254	K. C. Wessels	Sussex v Middlesex at Hove.
228*	G. M. Turner	Worcestershire v Gloucestershire at Worcester.
228	I. T. Botham	Somerset v Gloucestershire at Taunton.
216*	A. R. Butcher	Surrey v Cambridge University at Cambridge.
213*	P. N. Kirsten	Derbyshire v Glamorgan at Derby.
209*	P. N. Kirsten	Derbyshire v Northamptonshire at Derby.
205	G. A. Gooch	Essex v Cambridge University at Cambridge.
204*	A. Jones	Glamorgan v Hampshire at Basingstoke.
204	G. D. Mendis	Sussex v Glamorgan at Eastbourne.
202*	P. N. Kirsten	Derbyshire v Essex at Chesterfield.

Century in Each Innings of a Match

124	150*	B. C. Rose	Somerset v Worcestershire at Worcester.
101	131*	J. A. Ormrod	Worcestershire v Somerset at Worcester.
131*	114*	C. E. B. Rice.	Nottinghamshire v Somerset at Nottingham.

Fastest Century; for the Lawrence Trophy

66 minutes: I. V. A. Richards (100) West Indians v Glamorgan at Swansea, June 28.

Century Before Lunch

B. C. Broad, Gloucestershire v Oxford University at Oxford (on the 1st day of the season).
G. M. Turner, Worcestershire v Warwickshire at Birmingham (1st day).
A. R. Butcher, Surrey v Glamorgan at The Oval (1st day).
J. M. Brearley, Middlesex v Glamorgan at Cardiff (3rd day).

First to 1,000 Runs

G. A. Gooch (Essex) on June 19.

Carrying Bat Through Completed Innings

K. D. Smith (120* out of 230) Warwickshire v Essex at Southend.
J. A. Ormrod (126* out of 219) Worcestershire v Hampshire at Bournemouth.
T. M. Tremlett (70* out of 182) Hampshire v Leicestershire at Southampton.

Partnerships of 250 and Over

322 (2nd wicket) W. Larkins (156) and R. G. Williams (175*), Northamptonshire v Leicestershire at Leicester – county record for the 2nd wicket.
321* (2nd wicket) J. G. Wright (166*) and P. N. Kirsten (162*), Derbyshire v Lancashire at Manchester.
310 (4th wicket) P. W. Denning (98) and I. T. Botham (228), Somerset v Gloucestershire at Taunton – county record for the 4th wicket.
270 (3rd wicket) D. W. Randall (166) and C. E. B. Rice (121*), Nottinghamshire v Yorkshire at Harrogate.
269 (2nd wicket) J. R. T. Barclay (72) and K. C. Wessels (197*), Sussex v Nottinghamshire at Eastbourne.
266 (1st wicket) A. R. Butcher (216*) and G. S. Clinton (89), Surrey v Cambridge University at Cambridge.
264 (3rd wicket) J. A. Hopkins (112) and Javed Miandad (181), Glamorgan v Warwickshire at Birmingham.
256 (4th wicket) Imran Khan (124) and C. M. Wells (135), Sussex v Glamorgan at Swansea.
254 (3rd wicket) Zaheer Abbas (173) and A. J. Hignell (100*), Gloucestershire v Somerset at Taunton.
253 (2nd wicket) J. G. Wright (117) and P. N. Kirsten (209*), Derbyshire v Northamptonshire at Derby.

First-Wicket Hundred in Both Innings of a Match

114 and 131, B. Wood and J. G. Wright, Derbyshire v Worcestershire at Worcester.
104 and 106*, D. L. Amiss and K. D. Smith, Warwickshire v Somerset at Taunton.

Note: J. M. Brearley and P. R. Downton put on 104 for the 1st wicket (1st innings) and P. R. Downton and K. P. Tomlins 109 for the 1st wicket (2nd innings) for Middlesex v Kent at Lord's.

Highest Innings Total

550 for nine declared: Sussex v Middlesex at Hove.
534 for six: Somerset v Gloucestershire at Taunton.
524 for nine: Glamorgan v Warwickshire at Birmingham.
518: West Indies v England at Lord's.

Lowest Innings Totals

54   Derbyshire v Nottinghamshire at Worksop.
58   Hampshire v Nottinghamshire at Nottingham.
60   Essex v Surrey at Chelmsford.

Hat-Tricks

M. Hendrick . . . . Derbyshire v West Indians at Derby.
S. T. Clarke. . . . . Surrey v Nottinghamshire at The Oval.
D. S. Steele. . . . . Derbyshire v Glamorgan at Derby.
R. G. Williams . . . . Northamptonshire v Gloucestershire at Northampton.

Eight Wickets or More in an Innings

Eight for 34   P. G. Lee . . . . Lancashire v Oxford University at Oxford.
Eight for 58   R. D. Jackman. . . Surrey v Lancashire at Manchester.
Eight for 57   G. B. Stevenson. . Yorkshire v Northamptonshire at Leeds.

Fourteen Wickets or More in a Match

Fourteen for 76 (seven for 16, seven for 60) M. J. Procter, Gloucestershire v Worcestershire at Cheltenham.

First to 100 Wickets

R. D. Jackman on August 18.

Eight Dismissals in Match

I. J. Gould (7 ct, 1 st), Middlesex v Somerset at Taunton.

Career Aggregates

The following career aggregates were achieved during the season:

30,000 runs   G. M. Turner.
20,000 runs   M. J. Procter.
15,000 runs   B. Wood.
10,000 runs   G. Cook, T. E. Jesty, G. W. Johnson, P. Willey.
5,000 runs   D. I. Gower, E. E. Hemmings, G. W. Humpage, A. Kennedy, P. A. Neale, P. W. G. Parker, P. M. Roebuck, J. Simmons, K. D. Smith, P. A. Todd.
75 centuries   D. L. Amiss.
1,500 wickets Intikhab Alam.
1,000 wickets J. K. Lever.
500 catches   K. W. R. Fletcher.
400 catches   C. T. Radley.
300 catches   D. L. Amiss, G. S. Chappell, D. Lloyd, M. J. Procter.

County Caps Awarded in 1980

Derbyshire . . . . S. Oldham, B. Wood.
Glamorgan . . . . N. G. Featherstone, Javed Miandad.
Hampshire . . . . N. E. J. Pocock.
Kent . . . . G. R. Dilley.
Lancashire . . . . B. W. Reidy.
Middlesex . . . . V. A. P. van der Bijl.
Nottinghamshire. . . . . M. K. Bore, K. E. Cooper, B. N. French, P. J. Hacker, E. E. Hemmings.
Somerset. . . . . S. M. Gavaskar.
Surrey . . . . S. T. Clarke, G. S. Clinton, D. M. Smith.
Sussex. G. D. Mendis, C. P. Phillipson.
Warwickshire . . . . D. R. Doshi, T. A. Lloyd.
Worcestershire . . . . A. P. Pridgeon.
Yorkshire . . . . C. W. J. Athey, J. D. Love, A. Sidebottom.

Essex, Gloucestershire, Leicestershire, and Northamptonshire did not award any new caps.

FIRST-CLASS AVERAGES, 1980

BATTING

(Qualification: 8 innings)

* *Signifies not out.*   † *Denotes a left-handed batsman.*

	Inns	Not Outs	Runs	Highest Innings	Average
A. J. Lamb (*Northamptonshire*)	39	12	1,797	152	66.55
J. Whitehouse (*Warwickshire*)	19	8	725	197	65.90
†K. C. Wessels (*Sussex*)	29	5	1,562	254	65.08
P. N. Kirsten (*Derbyshire*)	36	6	1,895	213*	63.16
G. M. Turner (*Worcestershire*)	35	4	1,817	228*	58.61
C. T. Radley (*Middlesex*)	34	8	1,491	136*	57.34
Javed Miandad (*Glamorgan*)	32	5	1,460	181	54.07
C. E. B. Rice (*Nottinghamshire*)	36	9	1,448	131*	53.62
G. Boycott (*Yorkshire*)	28	4	1,264	154*	52.66
J. H. Hampshire (*Yorkshire*)	27	8	987	124	51.94
I. V. A. Richards (*WI and Somerset*) ..	25	1	1,217	170	50.70
†B. C. Rose (*Somerset*)	26	4	1,084	150*	49.27
†J. G. Wright (*Derbyshire*)	36	5	1,504	166*	48.51
G. A. Gooch (*Essex*)	35	5	1,437	205	47.90
†C. H. Lloyd (*WI and Lancashire*)	15	2	621	116	47.76
J. M. Brearley (*Middlesex*)	33	5	1,335	134*	47.67
G. R. J. Roope (*Surrey*)	30	9	996	101	47.42
N. Russom (*Cambridge University and Somerset*)	13	8	235	79*	47.00
B. F. Davison (*Leicestershire*)	32	4	1,310	151	46.78
J. A. Ormrod (*Worcestershire*)	35	3	1,495	131*	46.71
†A. R. Butcher (*Surrey*)	41	4	1,713	216*	46.29
W. Larkins (*Northamptonshire*)	42	3	1,772	156	45.43
C. M. Wells (*Sussex*)	28	5	1,024	135	44.52
D. J. S. Taylor (*Somerset*)	26	9	743	59	43.70
J. C. Balderstone (*Leicestershire*)	39	5	1,472	158*	43.29
I. T. Botham (*Somerset*)	27	0	1,149	228	42.55
†A. Jones (*Glamorgan*)	37	4	1,393	204*	42.21
D. L. Amiss (*Warwickshire*)	42	2	1,686	117*	42.15
M. W. Gatting (*Middlesex*)	25	4	880	136	41.90
C. J. Tavaré (*Kent*)	37	5	1,339	144*	41.84
†G. D. Barlow (*Middlesex*)	32	8	1,002	128*	41.75
F. C. Hayes (*Lancashire*)	33	6	1,117	102*	41.37
†R. D. V. Knight (*Surrey*)	37	7	1,224	132	40.80
P. R. Downton (*Middlesex*)	15	2	521	90*	40.07
K. W. R. Fletcher (*Essex*)	38	4	1,349	122*	39.67
R. O. Butcher (*Middlesex*)	22	2	792	179	39.60
†C. M. Old (*Yorkshire*)	14	5	355	89	39.44
Imran Khan (*Sussex*)	28	6	863	124	39.22
Zaheer Abbas (*Gloucestershire*)	35	1	1,296	173	38.11
K. S. McEwan (*Essex*)	38	6	1,217	140*	38.03
D. W. Randall (*Nottinghamshire*)	37	1	1,361	170	37.80
†Younus Ahmed (*Worcestershire*)	33	6	1,018	121*	37.70
†G. S. Clinton (*Surrey*)	39	6	1,240	120	37.57
†J. O. D. Orders (*Oxford University*) ...	9	1	295	70*	36.87
K. D. Smith (*Warwickshire*)	45	2	1,582	140	36.79
J. D. Love (*Yorkshire*)	32	7	917	105*	36.68

	Inns	Not Outs	Runs	Highest Innings	Average
†T. A. Lloyd (*Warwickshire*)	44	5	1,423	130*	36.48
M. A. Lynch (*Surrey*)	11	3	291	92	36.37
N. G. Featherstone (*Glamorgan*)	34	6	1,015	107	36.25
E. J. O. Hemsley (*Worcestershire*)	27	4	828	76	36.00
D. R. Pringle (*Cambridge University and Essex*)	24	4	713	123	35.65
P. W. G. Parker (*Sussex*)	40	6	1,200	122*	35.29
G. D. Mendis (*Sussex*)	42	1	1,437	204	35.04
†D. M. Smith (*Surrey*)	31	9	771	104*	35.04
A. J. Hignell (*Gloucestershire*)	23	5	630	100*	35.00
M. J. Procter (*Gloucestershire*)	33	2	1,081	134*	34.87
R. W. Tolchard (*Leicestershire*)	34	8	898	109	34.53
†D. Lloyd (*Lancashire*)	30	6	827	112*	34.45
S. M. Gavaskar (*Somerset*)	23	3	686	155*	34.30
†A. Kennedy (*Lancashire*)	38	3	1,194	169*	34.11
R. G. Williams (*Northamptonshire*) . . .	41	4	1,262	175*	34.10
J. R. T. Barclay (*Sussex*)	26	3	783	119	34.04
R. G. Lumb (*Yorkshire*)	39	3	1,223	129	33.97
B. R. Hardie (*Essex*)	36	4	1,084	95	33.87
C. G. Greenidge (*WI and Hampshire*) .	24	2	744	165	33.81
G. B. Stevenson (*Yorkshire*)	29	9	668	111	33.40
R. T. Robinson (*Nottinghamshire*)	26	3	765	138	33.26
C. W. J. Athey (*Yorkshire*)	37	3	1,123	125*	33.02
P. Carrick (*Yorkshire*)	32	8	786	131*	32.75
G. W. Humpage (*Warwickshire*)	43	2	1,339	101	32.65
†D. I. Gower (*Leicestershire*)	36	1	1,142	138	32.62
B. Wood (*Derbyshire*)	30	3	880	113	32.59
†Sadiq Mohammad (*Gloucestershire*) . .	40	4	1,172	92	32.55
†A. I. Kallicharran (*WI and Warw.*) . . .	28	1	876	90	32.44
†I. J. Gould (*Middlesex*)	16	4	388	57	32.33
D. L. Bairstow (*Yorkshire*)	26	6	646	145	32.30
N. F. M. Popplewell (*Somerset*)	20	6	445	135*	31.78
C. L. Smith (*Hampshire*)	35	2	1,048	130	31.75
†P. W. Denning (*Somerset*)	34	2	1,012	184	31.62
R. A. Woolmer (*Kent*)	32	2	948	171	31.60
S. Turner (*Essex*)	28	7	662	83*	31.52
R. S. Cowan (*Oxford University*)	11	1	313	63	31.30
P. A. Neale (*Worcestershire*)	33	3	933	123	31.10
M. H. Denness (*Essex*)	30	4	805	87	30.96
T. D. Booth Jones (*Sussex*)	17	1	493	89*	30.81
V. J. Marks (*Somerset*)	32	7	765	82	30.60
†B. W. Reidy (*Lancashire*)	27	5	671	110*	30.50
N. R. Taylor (*Kent*)	17	4	396	63	30.46
Intikhab Alam (*Surrey*)	10	3	212	57*	30.28
B. Hassan (*Nottinghamshire*)	27	3	720	91	30.00
†J. W. Lloyds (*Somerset*)	16	3	388	70	29.84
A. G. E. Ealham (*Kent*)	29	2	801	145	29.66
J. F. Steele (*Leicestershire*)	37	4	979	118	29.66
J. A. Hopkins (*Glamorgan*)	39	1	1,123	112	29.55
Sarfraz Nawaz (*Northamptonshire*) . . .	16	5	324	50	29.45
†J. Birkenshaw (*Leicestershire*)	18	4	412	76	29.42
E. A. Moseley (*Glamorgan*)	16	6	294	70*	29.40
D. S. Steele (*Derbyshire*)	31	7	698	86*	29.08
†D. R. Turner (*Hampshire*)	35	3	925	115*	28.90
†R. J. Hadlee (*Nottinghamshire*)	9	1	231	68	28.87
G. Miller (*Derbyshire*)	29	5	693	78*	28.87
†D. J. Humphries (*Worcestershire*)	21	3	518	108*	28.77
G. S. le Roux (*Sussex*)	20	5	431	68*	28.73
J. D. Birch (*Nottinghamshire*)	27	5	632	105*	28.72
J. N. Shepherd (*Kent*)	23	8	428	100	28.53

	Inns	Not Outs	Runs	Highest Innings	Average
J. Simmons (*Lancashire*)	30	6	682	96	28.41
B. C. Broad (*Gloucestershire*)	35	1	961	120	28.26
†M. J. Llewellyn (*Glamorgan*)	19	5	395	69	28.21
G. Sharp (*Northamptonshire*)	28	8	562	94	28.10
G. Cook (*Northamptonshire*)	39	4	976	109	27.88
P. R. Oliver (*Warwickshire*)	35	7	772	76*	27.57
T. M. Tremlett (*Hampshire*)	30	4	717	84	27.57
C. S. Cowdrey (*Kent*)	31	3	768	87	27.42
P. A. Todd (*Nottinghamshire*)	35	3	874	71	27.31
D. P. Hughes (*Lancashire*)	21	6	405	66*	27.00
J. P. C. Mills (*Cambridge University*) ..	14	1	350	79	26.92
†T. J. Yardley (*Northamptonshire*)	31	5	685	100*	26.34
I. A. Greig (*Sussex*)	19	5	366	53	26.14
M. C. J. Nicholas (*Hampshire*)	31	1	783	112	26.10
P. M. Roebuck (*Somerset*)	37	3	885	101	26.02
A. W. Stovold (*Gloucestershire*)	39	2	958	89	25.89
D. N. Patel (*Worcestershire*)	18	4	360	74	25.71
A. M. Mubarak (*Cambridge University*)	14	0	359	105	25.64
V. A. P. van der Bijl (*Middlesex*)	16	3	331	76	25.46
†D. Breakwell (*Somerset*)	14	3	276	73*	25.09
D. A. Francis (*Glamorgan*)	14	3	276	78*	25.09
M. W. W. Selvey (*Middlesex*)	17	4	322	40*	24.76
C. J. C. Rowe (*Kent*)	24	2	539	109	24.50
†K. Sharp (*Yorkshire*)	13	1	293	100*	24.41
P. B. Clift (*Leicestershire*)	26	5	512	67	24.38
M. D. Marshall (*WI and Hampshire*) ..	22	3	462	72*	24.31
K. P. Tomlins (*Middlesex*)	8	1	169	55	24.14
†M. D. Partridge (*Gloucestershire*)	18	6	286	48	23.83
†G. Fowler (*Lancashire*)	12	1	262	106*	23.81
T. E. Jesty (*Hampshire*)	25	3	522	114*	23.72
N. E. J. Pocock (*Hampshire*)	40	3	874	66	23.62
R. J. Parks (*Hampshire*)	13	3	233	64*	23.30
A. Odendaal (*Cambridge University*) ..	14	0	325	61	23.21
J. A. Claughton (*Warwickshire*)	28	5	533	108*	23.17
T. J. Boon (*Leicestershire*)	12	1	253	53	23.00
P. Willey (*Northamptonshire*)	29	4	572	100*	22.88
†M. W. Stovold (*Gloucestershire*)	8	2	137	75*	22.83
A. M. Ferreira (*Warwickshire*)	27	4	523	90	22.73
R. D. Jackman (*Surrey*)	24	8	363	47	22.68
†M. R. Benson (*Kent*)	13	2	248	58*	22.54
N. G. Cowley (*Hampshire*)	37	3	766	80*	22.52
A. P. E. Knott (*Kent*)	28	4	540	85*	22.50
G. P. Howarth (*Surrey*)	17	2	332	66	22.13
A. Sidebottom (*Yorkshire*)	14	1	284	43	21.84
C. P. Phillipson (*Sussex*)	33	3	655	87	21.83
M. N. S. Taylor (*Hampshire*)	15	2	279	58	21.46
J. E. Emburey (*Middlesex*)	19	5	300	43*	21.42
D. A. Graveney (*Gloucestershire*)	31	7	513	119	21.37
G. A. Cope (*Yorkshire*)	12	8	85	33	21.25
R. A. B. Ezekowitz (*Oxford University*)	17	1	340	57	21.25
†W. N. Slack (*Middlesex*)	13	0	276	47	21.23
G. W. Johnson (*Kent*)	29	5	509	84	21.20
H. T. Tunnicliffe (*Nottinghamshire*) ...	17	3	296	100*	21.14
†J. Walters (*Derbyshire*)	26	4	460	72	20.90
M. S. A. McEvoy (*Essex*)	29	0	600	65	20.68
E. E. Hemmings (*Nottinghamshire*) ...	28	4	496	86	20.66
†M. J. Bailey (*Hampshire*)	9	5	82	24	20.50
†S. F. Graf (*Hampshire*)	19	5	284	57*	20.28
B. J. Lloyd (*Glamorgan*)	14	7	140	30	20.00
R. Marsden (*Oxford University*)	12	0	240	50	20.00
B. N. French (*Nottinghamshire*)	20	4	317	70*	19.81

	Inns	Not Outs	Runs	Highest Innings	Average
†N. Gifford (*Worcestershire*)	28	10	352	45	19.55
E. W. Jones (*Glamorgan*)	29	5	465	67	19.37
R. J. Boyd-Moss (*Cambridge University and Northamptonshire*) ..	23	1	426	71	19.36
†S. J. G. Doggart (*Cambridge University*)	11	2	174	43	19.33
D. C. Holliday (*Cambridge University*)	12	3	173	76*	19.22
P. H. Edmonds (*Middlesex*)	13	2	208	52	18.90
N. Phillip (*Essex*)	24	4	376	77*	18.80
†R. M. Tindall (*Northamptonshire*)	14	3	204	60*	18.54
N. E. Briers (*Leicestershire*)	26	2	444	94	18.50
I. Cockbain (*Lancashire*)	27	6	388	69*	18.47
J. J. Rogers (*Oxford University*)	12	1	203	53	18.45
C. J. Richards (*Surrey*)	20	6	258	48	18.42
†S. P. Henderson (*Worcestershire*)	8	0	147	64	18.37
†P. J. Watts (*Northamptonshire*)	15	3	220	37*	18.33
M. Olive (*Somerset*)	17	1	290	50	18.12
B. Dudleston (*Leicestershire*)	14	1	234	83	18.00
G. C. Holmes (*Glamorgan*)	28	6	393	40	17.86
S. N. Hartley (*Yorkshire*)	22	2	352	72*	17.60
D. C. Hopkins (*Warwickshire*)	18	9	156	33	17.33
K. F. Jennings (*Somerset*)	10	4	104	21*	17.33
K. J. Barnett (*Derbyshire*)	21	0	362	69	17.23
R. E. East (*Essex*)	25	4	361	47	17.19
I. S. Anderson (*Derbyshire*)	15	4	187	36	17.00
G. R. Stephenson (*Hampshire*)	23	5	304	65	16.88
†S. J. Rouse (*Warwickshire*)	21	7	233	35	16.64
†A. Long (*Sussex*)	15	5	165	31	16.50
M. F. Malone (*Lancashire*)	14	3	181	38	16.45
D. B. Pauline (*Surrey*)	11	1	162	46	16.20
M. J. Harris (*Nottinghamshire*)	20	2	289	65	16.05
C. C. Curzon (*Nottinghamshire*)	13	1	192	45	16.00
P. A. Slocombe (*Somerset*)	18	2	256	114	16.00
J. W. Southern (*Hampshire*)	25	7	282	46*	15.66
P. Bainbridge (*Gloucestershire*)	29	2	422	71	15.62
†M. A. Nash (*Glamorgan*)	24	2	342	49*	15.54
C. J. Tunnicliffe (*Derbyshire*)	24	7	264	56*	15.52
Asif Iqbal (*Kent*)	16	2	208	41	14.85
S. T. Clarke (*Surrey*)	18	1	248	55	14.58
N. Smith (*Essex*)	25	5	290	63*	14.50
R. W. Taylor (*Derbyshire*)	23	6	241	75	14.17
W. K. Watson (*Nottinghamshire*)	9	3	85	44	14.16
K. R. Pont (*Essex*)	17	2	210	36	14.00
S. N. V. Waterton (*Kent*)	9	1	110	40*	13.75
I. G. Peck (*Cambridge University and Northamptonshire*)	13	2	151	34	13.72
†J. Abrahams (*Lancashire*)	14	0	191	59	13.64
M. Hendrick (*Derbyshire*)	17	8	122	33	13.55
†B. J. R. Jones (*Worcestershire*)	17	0	227	49	13.35
H. L. Alleyne (*Worcestershire*)	19	2	225	72	13.23
J. D. Inchmore (*Worcestershire*)	21	2	251	64	13.21
J. Spencer (*Sussex*)	9	4	66	14*	13.20
C. E. Waller (*Sussex*)	17	11	79	15*	13.16
G. E. Trim (*Lancashire*)	8	0	105	31	13.12
C. Maynard (*Warwickshire*)	8	1	91	30	13.00
A. H. Wilkins (*Glamorgan*)	24	3	262	44	12.47
R. G. D. Willis (*Warwickshire*)	21	6	185	33	12.33
N. V. H. Mallett (*Oxford University*) ..	8	0	98	38	12.25
N. G. B. Cook (*Leicestershire*)	24	9	180	75	12.00
T. M. Lamb (*Northamptonshire*)	21	12	108	13*	12.00
R. E. Dexter (*Nottinghamshire*)	8	1	83	32	11.85
R. M. Carter (*Northamptonshire*).....	20	2	213	32	11.83

	Inns	Not Outs	Runs	Highest Innings	Average
†G. J. Parsons (*Leicestershire*)	13	4	106	25*	11.77
S. J. Malone (*Hampshire*)	11	5	70	20	11.66
J. K. Lever (*Essex*)	21	10	123	18*	11.18
V. A. Holder (*Worcestershire*)	8	1	78	34	11.14
H. R. Moseley (*Somerset*)	9	4	55	16	11.00
T. J. Head (*Sussex*)	8	0	87	41	10.87
A. P. Pridgeon (*Worcestershire*)	22	11	118	28*	10.72
J. M. Rice (*Hampshire*)	16	0	171	30	10.68
J. P. Durack (*Oxford University*)	13	0	136	45	10.46
G. G. Arnold (*Sussex*)	17	2	155	29*	10.33
A. J. Borrington (*Derbyshire*)	10	1	93	36	10.33
P. J. W. Allott (*Lancashire*)	11	4	72	30*	10.28
P. I. Pocock (*Surrey*)	16	6	91	20*	9.10
B. M. Brain (*Gloucestershire*)	26	5	185	37*	8.80
†R. G. L. Cheatle (*Surrey*)	10	6	35	13*	8.75
K. Stevenson (*Hampshire*)	26	8	156	25	8.66
J. L. Rawlinson (*Oxford University*)	10	0	85	19	8.50
†K. E. Cooper (*Nottinghamshire*)	15	4	93	35	8.45
P. B. Fisher (*Worcestershire*)	10	5	40	11	8.00
H. I. E. Gore (*Somerset*)	11	5	48	22*	8.00
D. L. Acfield (*Essex*)	19	8	83	26	7.54
J. P. Agnew (*Leicestershire*)	13	0	98	31	7.53
†C. H. Dredge (*Somerset*)	21	5	113	21*	7.06
M. K. Bore (*Nottinghamshire*)	16	7	63	24*	7.00
W. W. Daniel (*Middlesex*)	12	4	56	15	7.00
R. W. Hills (*Kent*)	16	4	82	12	6.83
P. J. Hacker (*Nottinghamshire*)	18	7	69	12	6.27
C. J. Ross (*Oxford University*)	13	2	64	23*	5.81
G. C. Small (*Warwickshire*)	15	4	64	16	5.81
M. C. L. MacPherson (*Oxford University*)	10	1	52	22	5.77
†C. J. Scott (*Lancashire*)	18	5	75	14	5.76
R. N. S. Hobbs (*Glamorgan*)	8	2	34	14	5.66
†I. J. Curtis (*Oxford University*)	12	7	27	9*	5.40
A. J. Brassington (*Gloucestershire*)	30	8	113	14*	5.13
†D. R. Doshi (*Warwickshire*)	23	7	81	10*	5.06
†J. H. Childs (*Gloucestershire*)	19	10	44	8*	4.88
D. L. Underwood (*Kent*)	16	6	47	11*	4.70
L. B. Taylor (*Leicestershire*)	14	8	28	8	4.66
A. A. Jones (*Glamorgan*)	14	3	50	12	4.54
S. P. Sutcliffe (*Oxford University*)	13	0	57	16	4.38
S. P. Perryman (*Warwickshire*)	8	4	16	5	4.00
†G. R. Dilley (*Kent*)	11	5	21	12*	3.50
B. J. Griffiths (*Northamptonshire*)	16	1	35	10	2.33
W. Hogg (*Lancashire*)	13	5	18	5*	2.25
S. Oldham (*Derbyshire*)	10	4	11	7	1.83

BOWLING

(Qualification: 10 wickets in 10 innings)

† Denotes a left-arm bowler.

	Overs	Maidens	Runs	Wickets	Average
R. J. Hadlee (*Nottinghamshire*)	222.1	82	410	29	14.13
V. A. P. van der Bijl (*Middlesex*)	642.3	213	1,252	85	14.72
R. D. Jackman (*Surrey*)	746.2	220	1,864	121	15.40
†J. F. Steele (*Leicestershire*)	347.5	139	704	40	17.60

	Overs	Maidens	Runs	Wickets	Average
M. D. Marshall (*WI and Hampshire*) ..	477.3	128	1,170	66	17.72
M. Hendrick (*Derbyshire*)	444.5	128	980	55	17.81
Imran Khan (*Sussex*)	402.5	109	967	54	17.90
M. J. Procter (*Gloucestershire*)	372.1	102	931	51	18.25
W. G. Merry (*Middlesex*)	96	21	300	15	20.00
J. E. Emburey (*Middlesex*)	739.2	248	1,518	75	20.24
P. J. W. Allott (*Lancashire*)	183	47	473	23	20.56
†P. J. Hacker (*Nottinghamshire*)	379.2	99	1,092	52	21.00
C. M. Old (*Yorkshire*)	503	160	1,159	55	21.07
S. T. Clarke (*Surrey*)	605.3	139	1,700	79	21.51
W. W. Daniel (*Middlesex*)	492.5	112	1,454	67	21.70
W. Hogg (*Lancashire*)	340.1	69	1,114	51	21.84
Intikhab Alam (*Surrey*)	277.2	77	792	36	22.00
C. E. B. Rice (*Nottinghamshire*)	329.4	80	859	39	22.02
E. E. Hemmings (*Nottinghamshire*) ...	622.5	171	1,700	77	22.07
†D. S. Steele (*Derbyshire*)	430	123	1,221	54	22.61
K. B. S. Jarvis (*Kent*)	384.3	86	1,209	53	22.81
G. W. Johnson (*Kent*)	351.1	95	959	42	22.83
P. B. Clift (*Leicestershire*)	551.3	172	1,282	56	22.89
A. Sidebottom (*Yorkshire*)	346.1	92	962	42	22.90
G. B. Stevenson (*Yorkshire*)	602.1	164	1,669	72	23.18
†D. L. Underwood (*Kent*)	585.1	208	1,418	61	23.24
G. R. Dilley (*Kent*)	292.5	68	861	37	23.27
†M. A. Nash (*Glamorgan*)	611.4	196	1,723	74	23.28
G. S. le Roux (*Sussex*)	281.3	84	780	33	23.63
J. R. T. Barclay (*Sussex*)	274.5	77	718	30	23.93
†A. H. Wilkins (*Glamorgan*)	393.5	86	1,245	52	23.94
†J. H. Childs (*Gloucestershire*)	373.4	98	1,034	43	24.04
G. A. Gooch (*Essex*)	144	38	367	15	24.46
†R. E. East (*Essex*)	530.2	135	1,494	61	24.49
R. D. V. Knight (*Surrey*)	307	74	838	34	24.64
†N. G. B. Cook (*Leicestershire*)	754.1	237	1,856	75	24.74
H. L. Alleyne (*Worcestershire*)	521.1	100	1,604	64	25.06
C. H. Dredge (*Somerset*)	571.2	136	1,600	63	25.39
D. L. Acfield (*Essex*)	553.5	171	1,210	47	25.74
G. Miller (*Derbyshire*)	576.2	182	1,446	56	25.82
G. G. Arnold (*Sussex*)	505.1	180	1,220	47	25.95
T. M. Lamb (*Northamptonshire*)	627	164	1,725	66	26.13
E. A. Moseley (*Glamorgan*)	430	94	1,340	51	26.27
M. F. Malone (*Lancashire*)	466	131	1,191	45	26.46
†C. J. Tunnicliffe (*Derbyshire*)	427.5	89	1,244	47	26.46
†D. R. Doshi (*Warwickshire*)	961.2	268	2,700	101	26.73
W. K. Watson (*Nottinghamshire*)	124.3	23	463	17	27.23
J. N. Shepherd (*Kent*)	473.1	118	1,220	44	27.72
R. G. D. Willis (*Warwickshire*)	457.2	118	1,366	49	27.87
P. I. Pocock (*Surrey*)	565.4	155	1,430	51	28.03
B. M. Brain (*Gloucestershire*)	525.5	104	1,609	57	28.22
J. P. Agnew (*Leicestershire*)	247.4	52	880	31	28.38
†J. K. Lever (*Essex*)	591	123	1,703	60	28.38
P. G. Lee (*Lancashire*)	193.1	56	512	18	28.44
†B. W. Reidy (*Lancashire*)	188.2	46	543	19	28.57
†R. G. L. Cheatle (*Surrey*)	257.3	86	659	23	28.65
D. R. Pringle (*Cambridge University and Essex*)	352.2	82	976	34	28.70
†N. Gifford (*Worcestershire*)	727.1	204	1,755	61	28.77
†D. A. Graveney (*Gloucestershire*)	554.4	152	1,598	55	29.05
A. M. Ferreira (*Warwickshire*)	367.4	80	1,166	40	29.15
V. A. Holder (*Worcestershire*)	161.2	26	439	15	29.26
†P. H. Edmonds (*Middlesex*)	473	143	1,125	38	29.60
H. R. Moseley (*Somerset*)	470.5	107	1,193	40	29.82

	Overs	Maidens	Runs	Wickets	Average
S. Turner (*Essex*)	481.4	94	1,343	45	29.84
K. Stevenson (*Hampshire*)	493.4	105	1,588	53	29.96
†J. W. Southern (*Hampshire*)	556.1	143	1,530	51	30.00
†C. E. Waller (*Sussex*)	480.4	128	1,292	43	30.04
G. J. Parsons (*Leicestershire*)	206	40	722	24	30.08
†M. K. Bore (*Nottinghamshire*)	389.2	126	970	32	30.31
Sarfraz Nawaz (*Northamptonshire*)	408.1	114	1,104	36	30.66
J. Birkenshaw (*Leicestershire*)	135.4	35	374	12	31.16
R. M. Carter (*Northamptonshire*)	77.2	11	312	10	31.20
S. P. Sutcliffe (*Oxford University*)	252.3	61	749	24	31.20
B. J. Griffiths (*Northamptonshire*)	564.3	143	1,612	51	31.60
A. P. Pridgeon (*Worcestershire*)	537	114	1,614	51	31.64
K. E. Cooper (*Nottinghamshire*)	353.3	92	985	31	31.77
N. G. Cowley (*Hampshire*)	458.4	125	1,271	40	31.77
J. W. Lloyds (*Somerset*)	264	55	899	28	32.10
M. W. W. Selvey (*Middlesex*)	487.3	155	1,188	37	32.10
†D. Lloyd (*Lancashire*)	167	35	515	16	32.18
†P. Carrick (*Yorkshire*)	608.5	189	1,652	51	32.39
R. W. Hills (*Kent*)	197	54	524	16	32.75
†D. P. Hughes (*Lancashire*)	336.1	96	861	26	33.11
R. G. Williams (*Northamptonshire*)	535.5	100	1,611	48	33.56
P. Bainbridge (*Gloucestershire*)	144.4	23	504	15	33.60
S. Oldham (*Derbyshire*)	460.2	102	1,381	41	33.68
T. M. Tremlett (*Hampshire*)	178.2	32	579	17	34.05
†R. J. Maru (*Middlesex*)	140.4	36	412	12	34.33
N. F. M. Popplewell (*Somerset*)	186.5	46	587	17	34.52
I. T. Botham (*Somerset*)	453.3	122	1,387	40	34.67
S. J. Malone (*Hampshire*)	140.1	27	457	13	35.15
N. Phillip (*Essex*)	412.2	59	1,412	40	35.30
J. D. Inchmore (*Worcestershire*)	419.1	67	1,419	40	35.47
G. C. Small (*Warwickshire*)	240	52	864	24	36.00
B. Wood (*Derbyshire*)	142	29	364	10	36.40
G. A. Cope (*Yorkshire*)	584.3	175	1,558	42	37.09
J. Cumbes (*Worcestershire*)	186.4	38	558	15	37.20
P. Willey (*Northamptonshire*)	447.5	123	1,056	28	37.71
J. Spencer (*Sussex*)	194	53	537	14	38.35
D. C. Hopkins (*Warwickshire*)	208.3	50	615	16	38.43
L. B. Taylor (*Leicestershire*)	385.5	83	1,164	30	38.80
A. A. Jones (*Glamorgan*)	445	76	1,604	41	39.12
H. P. Cooper (*Yorkshire*)	152	36	431	11	39.18
S. P. Perryman (*Warwickshire*)	279	64	836	21	39.80
N. C. Crawford (*Cambridge University*)	168.4	32	568	14	40.57
J. Simmons (*Lancashire*)	398.3	110	988	24	41.16
T. E. Jesty (*Hampshire*)	205.2	56	584	14	41.71
G. C. Holmes (*Glamorgan*)	149	29	522	12	43.50
K. F. Jennings (*Somerset*)	225.2	53	615	14	43.92
N. G. Featherstone (*Glamorgan*)	154	40	487	11	44.27
S. F. Graf (*Hampshire*)	313.5	72	889	20	44.45
V. J. Marks (*Somerset*)	756.1	196	2,157	46	46.89
I. A. Greig (*Sussex*)	165.3	34	518	11	47.09
†H. I. E. Gore (*Somerset*)	253.5	66	669	14	47.78
N. Russom (*Cambridge University and Somerset*)	272.3	59	864	18	48.00
C. J. Ross (*Oxford University*)	162.4	27	589	12	49.08
†D. Breakwell (*Somerset*)	330	101	910	18	50.55
D. N. Patel (*Worcestershire*)	159.4	33	519	10	51.90
M. D. Partridge (*Gloucestershire*)	161.5	36	572	11	52.00
C. C. Clifford (*Warwickshire*)	191	40	688	13	52.92
†S. J. Rouse (*Warwickshire*)	243.3	41	890	16	55.62
B. J. Lloyd (*Glamorgan*)	208.1	57	679	11	61.72

The following took 10 wickets but bowled in fewer than ten innings:

	Overs	Maidens	Runs	Wickets	Average
R. A. White (*Nottinghamshire*)	48	16	85	11	7.72
S. P. Hughes (*Middlesex*)	110.4	25	352	18	19.55
P. H. L. Wilson (*Surrey*)	104	25	246	11	22.36
F. J. Titmus (*Middlesex*)	149.2	38	313	12	26.08
K. R. Pont (*Essex*)	124.4	27	306	11	27.81
†I. J. Curtis (*Oxford University*)	228	61	592	13	45.53

FIELDING

Wicket-keepers

62 C. J. Richards (59ct, 3st)	41 {G. Sharp (38ct, 3st)
59 A. J. Brassington (45ct, 14st)	{N. Smith (39ct, 2st)
50 {D. L. Bairstow (46ct, 4st)	37 D. J. S. Taylor (33ct, 4st)
{G. W. Humpage (42ct, 8st)	32 A. Long (31ct, 1st)
49 R. W. Tolchard (43ct, 6st)	31 D. J. Humphries (28ct, 3st)
46 E. W. Jones (44ct, 2st)	29 P. R. Downton (26ct, 3st)
44 B. N. French (38ct, 6st)	27 C. C. Curzon (26ct, 1st)
43 {I. J. Gould (36ct, 7st)	24 P. B. Fisher (22ct, 2st)
{C. J. Scott (41ct, 1st)	20 G. R. Stephenson (19ct, 1st)
42 {A. P. E. Knott (39ct, 3st)	
{R. W. Taylor (35ct, 7st)	

Fieldsmen

31 G. R. J. Roope	{C. S. Cowdrey
27 {N. E. J. Pocock	22 {R. D. V. Knight
{Sadiq Mohammad	{G. Miller
26 C. W. J. Athey	{G. Cook
24 {I. T. Botham	{B. R. Hardie
{C. P. Phillipson	21 {J. A. Hopkins
{B. Wood	{T. J. Yardley
23 {K. W. R. Fletcher	{J. D. Birch
{C. J. Tavaré	20 {J. E. Emburey
	{J. Simmons

INDIVIDUAL SCORES OF 100 AND OVER

There were 187 three-figure innings in 1980, 46 fewer than in 1979. The list includes 167 hit in the County Championship and twenty in other first-class games, but not the eleven by the West Indian touring team nor the three by the Australian touring team, which can be found in their respective sections.

G. M. Turner (7)
228* Worcs. v Glos., Worcester
182* Worcs. v Derby., Worcester
168 Worcs. v Essex, Colchester
115 Worcs. v Yorks., Bradford
103* Worcs. v Kent, Worcester
101 Worcs. v Warw., Birmingham
100 Worcs. v Middx, Worcester

G. A. Gooch (6)
205 Essex v Cambridge U., Cambridge
134 Essex v Glos., Gloucester
123 England v WI, Lord's
122 Essex v Kent, Ilford
108* Essex v Glam., Swansea
108 Essex v Surrey, Chelmsford

P. N. Kirsten (6)
213* Derby. v Glam., Derby
209 Derby. v Northants, Derby
202* Derby. v Essex, Chesterfield
162* Derby. v Lancs., Manchester
116 Derby. v Sussex, Derby
101 Derby. v Somerset, Chesterfield

J. M. Brearley (5)
134* Middx v Lancs., Lord's
124* Middx v Glam., Cardiff
114 Middx v Sussex, Hove
106 Middx v Kent, Lord's
104 Middx v Kent, Canterbury

A. J. Lamb (5)
152 Northants v Leics., Leicester
149* Northants v Worcs., Northampton
117 Northants v Lancs., Southport
113* Northants v Glos., Bristol
112 Northants v Middx, Lord's

J. A. Ormrod (5)
101 } Worcs. v Somerset, Worcester
131*
126* Worcs. v Hants, Bournemouth
106 Worcs. v Warw., Birmingham
103 Worcs. v Kent, Worcester

C. T. Radley (5)
136* Middx v Yorks., Lord's
136 Middx v Surrey, Lord's
124 Middx v Cambridge U., Cambridge
119 Middx v Oxford U., Oxford
114* Middx v Worcs., Worcester

C. E. B. Rice (5)
131* } Notts. v Somerset, Nottingham
114*
121* Notts. v Yorks., Harrogate
108* Notts. v Leics., Leicester
100* Notts. v Sussex, Eastbourne

C. J. Tavaré (5)
144* Kent v Worcs., Worcester
126* Kent v Northants, Canterbury
115 MCC v Essex, Lord's
108 Kent v Leics., Leicester
100* Kent v Glam., Canterbury

R. D. V. Knight (4)
132 Surrey v Lancs., The Oval
106 Surrey v Hants, The Oval
102* Surrey v Warw., Birmingham
102 Surrey v Worcs., Worcester

W. Larkins (4)
156 Northants v Leics., Leicester
127 Northants v Glos., Northampton
105 Northants v Hants, Wellingborough
103* Northants v Glam., Cardiff

P. W. G. Parker (4)
122* Sussex v Northants, Eastbourne
117 Sussex v Kent, Tunbridge Wells
105 Sussex v Hants, Southampton
102 Sussex v Derby., Derby

G. D. Barlow (3)
128* Middx v Sussex, Lord's
119* Middx v Warw., Birmingham
100* Middx v Essex, Lord's

G. Boycott (3)
154* Yorks. v Derby., Scarborough
135 Yorks. v Lancs., Manchester
128* England v Australia, Lord's

B. C. Broad (3)
120 Glos. v Oxford U., Oxford
116 Glos. v Hants, Cheltenham
101 Glos. v Warw., Birmingham

A. R. Butcher (3)
216* Surrey v Cambridge U., Cambridge
118 Surrey v Hants, Portsmouth
107 Surrey v Glam., The Oval

Javed Miandad (3)
181 Glam. v Warw., Edgbaston
141 Glam. v Glos., Bristol
140* Glam. v Essex, Swansea

R. G. Lumb (3)
129 Yorks. v Glam., Bradford
118 Yorks. v Worcs., Bradford
101 Yorks. v Glos., Sheffield

C. L. Smith (3)
130 Hants v Kent, Bournemouth
125* Hants v Sussex, Southampton
109 Hants v Somerset, Bath

J. G. Wright (3)
166* Derby. v Lancs., Manchester
155 Derby. v Worcs., Worcester
117 Derby. v Northants., Derby

C. W. J. Athey (2)
125* Yorks. v Glos., Sheffield
114 Yorks. v Warw., Birmingham

J. C. Balderstone (2)
158* Leics. v Notts., Leicester
102 Leics. v Northants, Northampton

J. R. T. Barclay (2)
119 Sussex v Leics., Hove
115 Sussex v Glos., Hove

I. T. Botham (2)
228 Somerset v Glos., Taunton
126 Somerset v Warw., Birmingham

R. O. Butcher (2)
179 Middx v Yorks., Scarborough
153* Middx v Hants, Lord's

J. A. Claughton (2)
108* Warw. v Worcs., Worcester
103* Warw. v Somerset, Birmingham

G. Cook (2)
109 Northants v Essex, Northampton
101 Northants v Cambridge U., Cambridge

B. F. Davison (2)
151 Leics. v Sussex, Hove
150 Leics. v Essex, Leicester

M. W. Gatting (2)
136 Middx v Surrey, Lord's
110 Middx v Yorks., Lord's

S. M. Gavaskar (2)
155* Somerset v Yorks., Weston-super-Mare
138 Somerset v Surrey, The Oval

D. I. Gower (2)
138 Leics. v Hants, Southampton
100 Leics. v Derby., Burton upon Trent

J. H. Hampshire (2)
124 Yorks. v Somerset, Weston-super-Mare
101* Yorks. v Warw., Bradford

J. A. Hopkins (2)
112 Glam. v Warw., Edgbaston
105 Glam. v Lancs., Manchester

G. W. Humpage (2)
101 Warw. v Derby., Birmingham
101 Warw. v Cambridge U., Cambridge

Imran Khan (2)
124 Sussex v Glam., Swansea
114 Sussex v Hants, Hove

A. Jones (2)
204* Glam. v Hants, Basingstoke
119 Glam. v Derby., Derby

T. A. Lloyd (2)
130* Warw. v Worcs., Birmingham
121 Warw. v Worcs., Worcester

J. D. Love (2)
105* Yorks. v Lancs., Manchester
104 Yorks. v Warw., Birmingham

K. S. McEwan (2)
104* Essex v Northants, Northampton
103* Essex v Sussex, Hove

D. R. Pringle (2)
123 Cambridge U. v Notts., Cambridge
109 Cambridge U. v Middx, Cambridge

B. C. Rose (2)
124 }
150*} Somerset v Worcs., Worcester

D. W. Randall (2)
170 Notts. v Lancs., Manchester
166 Notts. v Yorks., Harrogate

K. D. Smith (2)
140 Warw. v Somerset, Birmingham
120* Warw. v Essex, Southend

J. F. Steele (2)
118 Leics. v Cambridge U., Cambridge
117 Leics. v Northants, Leicester

K. C. Wessels (2)
254 Sussex v Middx, Hove
197 Sussex v Notts., Eastbourne

R. G. Williams (2)
175* Northants v Leics., Leicester
122 Northants v WI, Milton Keynes

B. Wood (2)
113   Derby. v Warw., Birmingham
101*   Derby. v Worcs., Worcester

Younis Ahmed (2)
121*   Worcs. v Warw., Birmingham
109   Worcs. v Notts., Cleethorpes

R. A. Woolmer (2)
171   Kent v Sussex, Hove
102*   Kent v Hants, Bournemouth

Zaheer Abbas (2)
173   Glos. v Somerset, Taunton
104   Glos. v Northants, Bristol

The following 42 cricketers each played one three-figure innings:

D. L. Amiss, 117*, Warw. v Lancs., Liverpool.

D. L. Bairstow, 145, Yorks. v Middx, Scarborough; J. D. Birch, 105*, Notts. v Cambridge U., Cambridge.

P. Carrick, 131*, Yorks. v Northants, Northampton; G. S. Clinton, 120, Surrey v Northants, Northampton.

P. W. Denning, 184, Somerset v Notts., Nottingham.

A. G. E. Ealham, 145, Kent v Essex, Ilford.

N. G. Featherstone, 107, Glam. v Oxford U., Oxford; G. A. Gooch, 118, Essex v Northants, Chelmsford.

N. G. Featherstone, 107, Glam. v Oxford, Swansea; K. W. R. Fletcher, 122*, Essex v Derby., Colchester; G. Fowler, 106*, Lancs. v Notts., Manchester.

D. A. Graveney, 119, Glos. v Oxford U., Oxford.

F. C. Hayes, 102*, Lancs. v Australia, Manchester; A. J. Hignell, 100*, Glos. v Somerset, Taunton; D. J. Humphries, 108*, Worcs. v Lancs., Stourport-on-Severn.

T. E. Jesty, 114*, Hants v Somerset, Bath.

A. Kennedy, 169*, Lancs. v Derby., Manchester.

C. H. Lloyd, 101, Lancs. v Yorks., Manchester; D. Lloyd, 112*, Lancs. v Hants, Portsmouth.

G. D. Mendis, 204, Sussex v Northants, Eastbourne; A. M. Mubarak, 105, Cambridge U. v Warw., Cambridge.

P. A. Neale, 123, Worcs. v Sussex, Hove; M. C. J. Nicholas, 112, Hants v Somerset, Bournemouth.

N. F. M. Popplewell, 135, Somerset v Kent, Taunton; M. J. Procter, 134*, Glos. v Middx, Cheltenham.

B. W. Reidy, 110*, Lancs. v Worcs., Manchester; I. V. A. Richards, 170, Somerset v Glos., Bristol; R. T. Robinson, 138, Notts. v Leics., Nottingham; P. M. Roebuck, 101, Somerset v Glos., Bristol; G. R. J. Roope, 101, Surrey v Hants, The Oval; C. J. C. Rowe, 109, Kent v Hants, Bournemouth.

K. Sharp, 100*, Yorks. v Middx, Lord's; J. N. Shepherd, 100, Kent v Surrey, Maidstone; P. A. Slocombe, 114, Somerset v Oxford U., Oxford; D. M. Smith, 104*, Surrey v Leics., Leicester; G. B. Stevenson, 111, Yorks. v Derby., Chesterfield.

R. W. Tolchard, 109, Leics. v Middx, Lord's; H. T. Tunnicliffe, 100*, Notts. v Middx, Nottingham; D. R. Turner, 115*, Hants v Glam., Cardiff.

C. M. Wells, 135, Sussex v Glam., Swansea; J. Whitehouse, 197, Warw. v Glam., Edgbaston; P. Willey, 100*, England v WI, The Oval.

T. J. Yardley, 100*, Northants v Glos. Northampton.

Note. C. H. Lloyd (3) and I. V. A. Richards (4) also scored hundreds for the West Indian touring team, and these can be found in that section.

TEN WICKETS IN A MATCH

There were 23 instances of bowlers taking ten or more wickets in a match in first-class cricket in 1980. The list includes 21 in the County Championship and two in other first-class games.

R. E. East (2)
11-118   Essex v Surrey, Chelmsford
10-198   Essex v Leics., Leicester

A. Sidebottom (2)
11-64   Yorks. v Kent, Sheffield
10-30   Yorks. v Oxford U., Oxford

M. A. Nash (2)
11-130   Glam. v Glos., Bristol
10-216   Glam. v Warw., Birmingham

D. L. Underwood (2)
12-99   Kent v Essex, Folkestone
11-160   Kent v Middx, Canterbury

The following each took ten wickets in a match on one occasion:

H. Alleyne, 11-94, Worcs. v Notts., Worcester.
D. R. Doshi, 11-167, Warw. v Somerset, Taunton.
J. E. Emburey, 12-107, Middx v Notts., Lord's.
N. Gifford, 10-40, Worcs. v Lancs., Stourport-on-Severn.
E. E. Hemmings, 11-188, Notts. v Yorks., Harrogate; W. Hogg, 10-82, Lancs. v Warw.,
  Birmingham.
R. D. Jackman, 11-91, Surrey v Lancs., Manchester; G. W. Johnson, 10-111, Kent v Glos.,
  Folkestone.
J. W. Lloyds, 11-95, Somerset v Worcs., Weston-super-Mare.
D. R. Pringle, 10-101, Cambridge U. v Warw., Cambridge; M. J. Procter, 14-76, Glos. v
  Worcs., Cheltenham.
D. S. Steele, 11-174, Derby. v Notts., Worksop; G. B. Stevenson, 11-74, Yorks. v Notts.,
  Nottingham.
V. A. P. van der Bijl, 10-59, Middx v Derby., Uxbridge.
R. A. White, 10-57, Notts. v Derby., Worksop.

SIX WICKETS IN AN INNINGS

There were 74 instances of bowlers taking six or more wickets in an innings in first-class cricket in 1980. The list includes 59 in the County Championship, four by the West Indian touring side, one by the Australian touring side and ten in other first-class matches.

E. E. Hemmings (3)
7-62   Notts. v Leics., Leicester
6-37   Notts. v Kent, Nottingham
6-127   Notts. v Yorks., Harrogate

R. D. Jackman (3)
8-58   Surrey v Lancs., Manchester
6-30   Surrey v Essex, The Oval
6-53   Surrey v Lancs., The Oval

M. A. Nash (3)
7-29   Glam. v Glos., Swansea
6-72   Glam. v Glos., Bristol
6-105   Glam. v Warw., Birmingham

D. L. Underwood (3)
7-75   Kent v Middx, Canterbury
6-71 } Kent v Essex, Folkestone
6-28 }

H. Alleyne (2)
6-50   Worcs. v Notts., Worcester
6-94   Worcs. v Middx, Worcester

R. E. East (2)
6-56   Essex v Leics., Leicester
6-72   Essex v Surrey, Chelmsford

J. E. Emburey (2)
6-31 } Middx v Notts., Lord's
6-76 }

D. A. Graveney (2)
6-49   Glos. v Oxford U., Oxford
6-71   Glos. v Sussex, Bristol

M. Hendrick (2)
7-19   Derby v Hants, Chesterfield
6-50   Derby. v Leics., Burton upon Trent

M. D. Marshall (2)
7-56   WI v Worcs., Worcester
6-54   WI v Glam., Swansea

E. A. Moseley (2)
6-41   Glam. v Middx, Cardiff
6-102   Glam. v Essex, Swansea

M. J. Procter (2)
7-16 } Glos. v Worcs., Cheltenham
7-60 }

A. Sidebottom (2)
7-18   Yorks. v Oxford U., Oxford
6-30   Yorks. v Kent, Sheffield

G. B. Stevenson (2)
8-57   Yorks. v Northants, Leeds
7-48   Yorks. v Notts., Nottingham

C. J. Tunnicliffe (2)
7-36   Derby. v Essex, Chesterfield
6-41   Derby v Northants, Northampton

R. G. Williams (2)
7-73   Northants v Cambridge U., Cambridge
6-65   Northants v Glos., Northampton

The following each took six wickets in an innings on one occasion:

D. L. Acfield, 6-37, Essex v Kent, Folkestone.
B. M. Brain, 6-68, Glos. v Glam., Bristol.
P. Carrick, 6-138, Yorks. v Worcs., Bradford; J. H. Childs, 6-90, Glos. v Essex, Gloucester; S. T. Clarke, 6-73, Surrey v Somerset, The Oval; C. E. H. Croft, 6-80, WI v Yorks., Leeds.
D. R. Doshi, 6-72, Warw. v Somerset, Taunton; C. H. Dredge, 6-57, Somerset v Northants, Northampton.
N. Gifford, 6-15, Worcs. v Lancs., Stourport-on-Severn; B. J. Griffiths 7-52, Northants v Yorks., Leeds.
P. J. Hacker, 6-35, Notts. v Hants, Nottingham; W. Hogg, 6-45, Lancs. v Warw., Birmingham; M. A. Holding, 6-67, WI v England, Lord's.
Imran Khan, 6-80, Sussex v Kent, Hove; J. D. Inchmore, 6-107, Worcs. v Somerset, Weston-super-Mare.
K. B. S. Jarvis, 6-100, Kent v Glam., Canterbury.
N. J. Kemp, 6-119, Kent v Surrey, The Oval.
T. M. Lamb, 7-56, Northants v Cambridge U., Cambridge; P. G. Lee, 8-34, Lancs. v Oxford U., Oxford; G. S. le Roux, 6-84, Sussex v Essex, Hove; J. K. Lever, 6-121, Essex v Hants, Chelmsford; D. K. Lillee, 6-133, Australians v Notts., Nottingham; J. W. Lloyds, 6-61, Somerset v Worcs., Weston-super-Mare.
H. R. Moseley, 6-58, Somerset v Yorks., Weston-super-Mare.
C. M. Old, 6-44, Yorks. v Derby., Chesterfield.
D. P. Patel, 6-47, Worcs. v Oxford U., Oxford; N. Phillip, 6-47, Essex v Northants, Chelmsford; P. I. Pocock, 6-40, Surrey v Worcs., Worcester; D. R. Pringle, 6-90, Cambridge U. v Warw., Cambridge.
J. F. W. Sanderson, 6-67, Oxford U. v Middx, Oxford; Sarfraz Nawaz, 6-49, Northants v Warw., Nuneaton; D. S. Steele, 7-133, Derby. v Notts., Worksop; J. F. Steele, 7-29, Leics. v Glos., Leicester; J. W. Southern, 6-109, Hants v Australians, Southampton; S. P. Sutcliffe, 6-19, Oxford U. v Warw., Oxford.
S. Turner, 6-69, Essex v Northants, Chelmsford.
V. A. P. van der Bijl, 6-47, Middx v Sussex, Hove.
R. A. White, 6-24, Notts. v Derby., Worksop.

YOUNG CRICKETER OF THE YEAR

The following are the winners of the annual trophy awarded by the Cricket Writers Club to, in their opinion, the best Young Cricketer of the Year.

1950	R. Tattersall	1966	D. L. Underwood
1951	P. B. H. May	1967	A. W. Greig
1952	F. S. Trueman	1968	R. M. H. Cottam
1953	M. C. Cowdrey	1969	A. Ward
1954	P. J. Loader	1970	C. M. Old
1955	K. F. Barrington	1971	J. Whitehouse
1956	B. Taylor	1972	D. R. Owen-Thomas
1957	M. J. Stewart	1973	M. Hendrick
1958	A. C. D. Ingleby-Mackenzie	1974	P. H. Edmonds
1959	G. Pullar	1975	A. Kennedy
1960	D. A. Allen	1976	G. Miller
1961	P. H. Parfitt	1977	I. T. Botham
1962	P. J. Sharpe	1978	D. I. Gower
1963	G. Boycott	1979	P. W. G. Parker
1964	J. M. Brearley	1980	G. R. Dilley
1965	A. P. E. Knott		

THE WEST INDIANS IN ENGLAND, 1980

[Ken Kelly]

Back row: D. Waight (physiotherapist), D. L. Haynes, M. D. Marshall, C. L. King, M. A. Holding, J. Garner, C. E. H. Croft, D. R. Parry, S. F. A. Bacchus, C. G. Greenidge, D. A. Murray. Front row: C. L. Walcott (manager), A. I. Kallicharran, D. L. Murray, C. H. Lloyd (captain), I. V. A. Richards, L. G. Rowe, A. M. E. Roberts, C. W. Smith (assistant manager).

THE WEST INDIANS IN ENGLAND, 1980

The eleventh West Indian side to visit England, excluding those that did so in 1975 and 1979 for the Prudential Cup, were prevented by the weather from achieving a record to compare with those of some of the great Australian touring parties. Even so, they won their first five county matches and they had the better of all five Test matches, although, with rain constantly intervening, they were able to win only one of them.

Of the sixteen players, captained as in 1976 in England by Clive Lloyd, only Bacchus had not been a member, the previous winter, of the victorious West Indian side in Australia. There was, however, a change of manager. Clyde Walcott, the great West Indian batsman and manager of the 1976 side, took the place of Willie Rodriguez, whose control of the West Indian players when they visited New Zealand on their way home from Australia had left something to be desired.

As in Australia, the West Indian bowling was left almost exclusively to their formidable quintet of pacemen – Croft, Garner, Holding, Marshall and Roberts. Their only specialist spinner, Derek Parry, from the little island of Nevis, was not chosen for a Test match. As a result, the West Indian over-rate seldom topped fourteen an hour and came in for much criticism. Not that Mr Walcott, nor Lloyd for that matter, was worried by this. Their philosophy was to choose those whom they considered to be their best bowlers, rather than to concern themselves with balancing their attack or bowling more balls to the hour.

For England's batsmen there was no respite from bowlers operating off long runs and often pitching the ball fearsomely short. When, towards the end of the tour, Garner, Croft and Roberts were handicapped by injury, runs came more easily to England, and in two Test matches West Indies were denied victories they might have achieved with a full side. Nevertheless Lloyd's side remained one of the hardest to beat that can ever have visited England.

In addition to the unrelenting nature of their attack, they fielded brilliantly and batted with a blend of daring and discretion that has only recently been the case with West Indian sides. With their ever-widening experience of cricket in different parts of the world, West Indian batsmen cope much better now with the moving ball. This was clearly shown in the first Test when, in extravagantly English conditions, with the ball swinging prodigiously, West Indies gained the one decisive victory of the series. Little was it thought at the time that upon the thrilling finish at Trent Bridge would hang the destiny of the Wisden Trophy.

It must also be said that after the West Indians had blotted their copybook in New Zealand, their behaviour both on and off the field was unexceptionable. If at times their fast bowlers pitched persistently short and took too long to bowl their overs, the umpires, though empowered to intervene, never did so as if they meant it. Although much was made at one time of a supposed "feud" between Vivian Richards and England's opening bowler, Willis, the players concerned vehemently denied that there was one. Between the West Indians and the majority of sides they met there existed many friendships struck up over the years in English county cricket.

The sponsorship of Holt Lloyd Ltd, makers of motoring accessories, has vested the matches between touring teams and the counties with a new interest. The time came, a few years ago, when counties would rest their over-worked players rather than put out their full side against the touring team. Now, with sizeable sums of money to be won by the winners of each match, and a jackpot of £100,000 available to the West Indians should they win all their three-day county games, interest grew as Lloyd and his eager players started with successive victories over Worcestershire, Leicestershire, Northamptonshire, Derbyshire and Kent. As was always likely, the English climate beat them in the end – but not until mid-June, at Hove. None the less the West Indians went through the tour unbeaten except in two limited-overs matches – against Essex at Chelmsford and against England in the second of the two Prudential internationals.

The fast bowlers, the side's bodyguards, owed much to Mr Denis Waight, the physiotherapist whose searching programme of physical exercises kept them fit from the start of their Australian tour in November 1979 until most of the way through their tour of England. From his great height of 6ft 9in Joel Garner achieved an accuracy and steepness of lift which made him at once the team's most economical and effective bowler. Though a shade less rhythmical, and therefore less irresistibly fast, than in 1976, Michael Holding was still a fine performer, at his best in short spells.

Malcolm Marshall, the slightest of the fast bowlers, was capable, owing to his lissomness and sense of timing, of as much pace as any. A fine all-round fielder and a useful batsman he looks to have a bright future. After a slow start to the tour, Colin Croft secured a Test place. He and Holding took to bowling round the wicket at Boycott, a fierce tactic which not surprisingly unsettled England's chief run-getter. Until his back let him down Roberts, at 29 the oldest of the five fast men, bowled extremely effectively and with fine control.

In county matches Parry did well enough with his off-breaks to suggest that, given the chance, he would make an adequate Test bowler. The rest of the bowling was insignificant. Collis King, seldom fully fit, had a disappointing tour, and Richards, the only "spinner" in the Test side, took but a single wicket in his 68 first-class overs on the tour. It was of little encouragement to England's batsmen, present or future, to know that besides the fast bowlers in the touring party there were others playing in English county cricket, such as Daniel of Middlesex and Clarke of Surrey, who were equally effective.

If the West Indian batting lacked the depth of other years the presence of Richards, the world's greatest player, was an inspiration to the side. There seldom seemed much reason for him not to make a large and entertaining score, and his runs came so fast that he could be given, by way of a rest, a lower place in the order and still have time to make a telling contribution. It would be hard to overpraise Richards, either for the brilliance with which he bats or the spirit in which he plays the game.

In spite of missing several matches, including one Test, with an injured hand – and also pulling a hamstring – Lloyd remained a major batting force. As a captain he had the respect due to a father figure. Kallicharran, though as neat as ever, was less effective than in the past. Of the two batsmen on their first full tour of England, Faoud Bacchus and Desmond Haynes, the latter made the greater impact. In the first two Tests he displayed a fierce self-discipline, his 62 in the second innings of the first Test winning the day for West Indies and his 184 in the second Test being the highest Test score ever made by a West Indian at Lord's. Haynes is another in the unending line of vastly gifted Barbadian batsmen. Bacchus, a Guyanese, was always taking the eye in the field and batted with a confidence which was invariably exciting and occasionally disastrous. He, too, is a talented stroke-player.

After his three successive Test centuries in England in 1976, Gordon Greenidge had a comparatively poor series, while Lawrence Rowe, the maker of a treble-hundred against England at Bridgetown in 1973-74, was again dogged by injury. When Rowe returned home towards the end of the tour, Timur Mohamed, a Guyanese playing as a professional with Suffolk, joined the touring party. Deryck Murray, at 37 one of the game's most senior players, was kept in the Test side more for his knack of making useful runs at number seven than for his wicket-keeping, which was not always tidy. The ability of Garner, Holding and Roberts, as well as Marshall, to make runs meant that the Test side had no tail to speak of.

When the tour ended West Indies had lost only one of their eleven Test matches since returning to full strength after the disbanding of World Series Cricket; that by one wicket against New Zealand in Dunedin. In England in 1980 they did much to enliven a dismal summer and attracted good crowds wherever they played. – J.W.

WEST INDIAN TOUR RESULTS

Test matches – Played 5: Won 1, Drawn 4.

First-class matches – Played 16: Won 8, Drawn 8.

Wins – England, Derbyshire, Gloucestershire, Kent, Leicestershire, Northamptonshire, Worcestershire, Yorkshire.

Draws – England (4), Glamorgan, Somerset, Sussex, Warwickshire.

Non first-class matches – Played 12: Won 8, Lost 2, Drawn 2. *Wins* – England, Essex, Glamorgan, Ireland, Lavinia Duchess of Norfolk's XI, Middlesex, Oxford and Cambridge Universities, Scotland. *Losses* – England, Essex. *Draws* – Ireland, Minor Counties.

TEST MATCH AVERAGES

ENGLAND – BATTING

	Tests	Innings	Not Outs	Runs	Highest Inns	Average
B. C. Rose	3	6	1	243	70	48.60
G. Boycott	5	10	1	368	86	40.88
G. A. Gooch	5	10	0	394	123	39.40
P. Willey	5	9	2	262	100*	37.42
R. A. Woolmer	2	4	1	109	46	36.33
M. W. Gatting	4	7	0	172	56	24.57
J. E. Emburey	3	5	2	70	28*	23.33
R. G. D. Willis	4	6	3	61	24*	20.33
I. T. Botham	5	9	0	169	57	18.77
C. J. Tavaré	2	4	0	65	42	16.25
W. Larkins	3	6	0	90	33	15.00
A. P. E. Knott	4	7	0	36	9	5.14

Also batted: G. R. Dilley (3 Tests) 5, 1, 1, 0; M. Hendrick (2 Tests) 7*, 2*, 10*; D. L. Bairstow (1 Test) 40, 9*; D. I. Gower (1 Test) 20, 1; J. K. Lever (1 Test) 15, 4; C. M. Old (1 Test) 6; D. L. Underwood (1 Test) 3.

* *Signifies not out.*

BOWLING

	Overs	Maidens	Runs	Wickets	Average
J. E. Emburey	39.3	13	83	6	13.83
G. R. Dilley	74	19	183	11	16.63
R. G. D. Willis	110.1	27	407	14	29.07
I. T. Botham	131	41	385	13	29.61

Also bowled: G. Boycott 7–2–11–0; G. A. Gooch 25–7–59–3; M. Hendrick 44–11–141–2; J. K. Lever 28–4–101–1; C. M. Old 28.5–9–64–2; D. L. Underwood 29.2–7–108–1; P. Willey 43–16–111–2.

WEST INDIES – BATTING

	Tests	Innings	Not Outs	Runs	Highest Inns	Average
I. V. A. Richards	5	6	0	379	145	63.16
D. L. Haynes	5	6	0	308	184	51.33
C. H. Lloyd	4	4	0	169	101	42.25
M. A. Holding	5	6	4	61	35	30.50
A. M. E. Roberts	3	4	1	78	24	26.00
D. L. Murray	5	6	0	145	64	24.16
C. G. Greenidge	5	6	0	124	53	20.66
S. F. A. Bacchus	5	6	0	121	61	20.16
M. D. Marshall	4	5	0	90	45	18.00
A. I. Kallicharran	5	6	0	102	37	17.00
J. Garner	5	5	0	63	46	12.60

Also batted: C. E. H. Croft (3 Tests) 0, 0, 1*; C. L. King (1 Test) 12.

* *Signifies not out.*

BOWLING

	Overs	Maidens	Runs	Wickets	Average
J. Garner	212.4	73	371	26	14.26
A. M. E. Roberts	105.2	24	262	11	23.81
M. D. Marshall	172.3	42	436	15	29.06
M. A. Holding	230.5	56	632	20	31.60
C. E. H. Croft	104	25	306	9	34.00

Also bowled: S. F. A. Bacchus 1–0–3–0; C. G. Greenidge 3–2–4–0; D. L. Haynes 1–0–2–0; A. I. Kallicharran 7–1–24–0; C. L. King 12–3–32–0; C. H. Lloyd 1–0–1–C; I. V. A. Richards 36–12–85–0.

WEST INDIAN AVERAGES – FIRST-CLASS MATCHES

BATTING

	Matches	Innings	Not Outs	Runs	Highest Inns	Average
I. V. A. Richards	13	17	1	911	145	56.93
C. H. Lloyd	12	12	2	487	116	48.70
D. L. Haynes	14	22	3	874	184	46.00
A. I. Kallicharran	15	19	1	653	90	36.27
C. G. Greenidge	13	18	2	577	165	36.06
S. F. A. Bacchus	15	23	2	710	164*	33.80
D. A. Murray	6	8	2	161	49	26.83
D. L. Murray	12	14	2	315	64	26.25
M. D. Marshall	12	12	2	211	52	21.10
J. Garner	11	10	0	206	104	20.60
D. R. Parry	11	13	8	103	26*	20.60
M. A. Holding	11	11	6	99	35	19.80
A. M. E. Roberts	9	10	1	114	31	12.66
C. L. King	9	11	2	86	26*	9.55
C. E. H. Croft	9	4	3	8	7*	8.00
L. G. Rowe	3	2	0	13	13	6.50

Also batted: Timur Mohamed (1 match) 2, 45.

* *Signifies not out.*

BOWLING

	Overs	Maidens	Runs	Wickets	Average
J. Garner	351	123	683	49	13.93
M. D. Marshall	336.3	86	864	49	17.63
D. R. Parry	303.1	93	800	40	20.00
A. M. E. Roberts	234.2	57	657	27	24.33
M. A. Holding	392.1	96	1,096	44	24.90
C. E. H. Croft	230.3	54	690	25	27.60
C. L. King	98	24	301	7	43.00

Also bowled: S. F. A. Bacchus 2–0–11–0; C. G. Greenidge 6–3–6–0; D. L. Haynes 1–0–2–0; A. I. Kallicharran 15–3–55–2; C. H. Lloyd 1–0–1–0; D. A. Murray 1–0–1–0; I. V. A. Richards 68–21–177–1.

FIELDING

D. L. Murray 35 (33ct 2st), D. A. Murray 17 (16ct 1st), S. F. A. Bacchus 14, A. I. Kallicharran 14, I. V. A. Richards 13, J. Garner 8, C. H. Lloyd 7, C. G. Greenidge 6, C. L. King 4, D. L. Haynes 2, M. A. Holding 2, M. D. Marshall 2, D. R. Parry 2, L. G. Rowe 2.

HUNDREDS FOR WEST INDIANS

The following fifteen three-figure innings were played for the West Indians, eleven in first-class matches and four in matches not first-class.

I. V. A. Richards (5)
   145   v England at Lord's (Second Test)
   131   v Northamptonshire at Milton Keynes
   122† v Essex at Chelmsford
   103   v Somerset at Taunton
   100   v Glamorgan at Swansea

C. H. Lloyd (3)
   116   v Northamptonshire at Milton Keynes
   102   v Somerset at Taunton
   101   v England at Manchester (Third Test)

S. F. A. Bacchus (2)
   164* v Yorkshire at Leeds
   163† v Ireland at Dublin

J. Garner (1)
   104   v Gloucestershire at Bristol

C. G. Greenidge (1)
   165   v Leicestershire at Leicester

D. L. Haynes (1)
   184   v England at Lord's (Second Test)

A. I. Kallicharran (1)
   109† v Minor Counties at Jesmond

Timur Mohamed (1)
   119† v Minor Counties at Jesmond

   * *Signifies not out.*   † *Not first-class.*

HUNDREDS AGAINST WEST INDIANS

The following four three-figure innings were played against the West Indians, three in first-class matches and one in a match not first-class.

G. A. Gooch (1)
   123   for England at Lord's (Second Test)

Javed Miandad (1)
   101*† for Glamorgan at Swansea

P. Willey (1)
   100* for England at The Oval (Fourth Test)

R. G. Williams (1)
   122   for Northamptonshire at Milton Keynes.

   * *Signifies not out.*   † *Not first-class.*

LAVINIA, DUCHESS OF NORFOLK'S XI v WEST INDIANS

At Arundel, May 8. West Indians won by 121 runs. A true pitch and attractive surroundings provided the West Indians with an untroubled opening to their 1980 tour. Any discomfort they might have felt resulted entirely from the lowness of the temperature, for a bowling attack featuring D'Oliveira (48), Titmus (47), Higgs (43) and Wilson (42) was not designed to inhibit their stroke-makers. D'Oliveira batted as of old, but of the younger brigade Gower went for 13 while Davison, his Leicestershire captain, and Timur Mohamed, of Guyana and Suffolk, failed to score.

West Indians 243 for four (45 overs) (C. G. Greenidge 67, S. F. A. Bacchus 60, C. L. King 60 not out); Lavinia, Duchess of Norfolk's XI 122 for nine (45 overs) (B. L. D'Oliveira 55 not out).

WORCESTERSHIRE v WEST INDIANS

At Worcester, May 10, 11, 12. West Indians beat Worcestershire by seven wickets. Marshall, rated only fifth in the formidable West Indies pace battery, made the best possible start to the touring team's county programme by dismissing Worcestershire's openers in his first four deliveries. The young Barbadian later announced some pretensions as an all-rounder with an important innings of 52 before bowling Worcestershire towards defeat in their second innings, taking seven for 38 in 12.1 overs on the third morning and finishing with a personal-best return of seven for 56. Marshall's considerable pace and the well-controlled off-spin of Parry – match figures of six for 76 in 39 overs – overshadowed all else in a rather inconsistent performance by the West Indians. There was some irony in that the county's Barbadian pace pair, Alleyne and Holder, almost wrecked their fellow-countrymen's first innings until Kallicharran played an excellent face-saving innings of 89 (twelve 4s) in three and a quarter hours. Worcestershire were desperately short of resolution in their second innings, which began with an out-of-character display by Turner, who stepped back and "slogged" at almost every delivery as he made 45 in 24 balls before stepping on to his wicket. The general interpretation was that Turner's approach was linked with his strong criticism of the West Indians' conduct on their tour of his native New Zealand in the previous winter. There were also suggestions that he had asked not to be selected for the match because of a back strain. The county's cricket committee chairman, Mr Roy Booth, later interviewed Turner but an official statement was no more informative than that the club was satisfied Turner had no grievances with them.

Worcestershire

G. M. Turner c Bacchus b Marshall	17	– hit wkt b Garner 45
J. A. Ormrod c Murray b Marshall	0	– b Parry 22
B. J. R. Jones c Garner b Parry	41	– (4) lbw b Marshall 3
E. J. O. Hemsley b Parry	26	– (5) b Marshall. 23
Younis Ahmed c Murray b Croft	43	– (6) c Richards b Marshall. 1
D. N. Patel b Parry	33	– (7) not out 13
†D. J. Humphries c Murray b Garner	40	– (8) b Marshall. 0
V. A. Holder c Bacchus b Parry	12	– (9) b Marshall. 4
H. Alleyne lbw b Garner	2	– (11) c Bacchus b Parry. 8
*N. Gifford b Garner	3	– (10) c Richards b Marshall. 3
A. P. Pridgeon not out	5	– (3) c Murray b Marshall. 3
B 8, l-b 4, n-b 18	30	B 5, l-b 6, n-b 8 19

1/17 2/17 3/88 4/109 5/170   252   1/69 2/79 3/79 4/95 5/102   144
6/205 7/219 8/236 9/247   6/119 7/120 8/125 9/139

Bowling: *First Innings*—Croft 19–6–56–1; Marshall 17–3–56–2; Garner 22.1–5–55–3; Parry 24–11–55–4. *Second Innings*—Marshall 17.1–3–56–7; Croft 5–1–23–0; Garner 5–1–25–1; Parry 15–8–21–2.

West Indians

	First Innings		Second Innings	
C. G. Greenidge b Alleyne	1	– c Pridgeon b Patel	60
D. L. Haynes lbw b Alleyne	0	– c Pridgeon b Gifford	41
I. V. A. Richards b Holder	5	– (4) c and b Patel	0
S. F. A. Bacchus c Humphries b Holder	13	– (3) not out	17
A. I. Kallicharran c Ormrod b Patel	89		
*C. H. Lloyd c Humphries b Alleyne	14		
D. R. Parry lbw b Gifford	20	– (5) not out	9
†D. L. Murray c Holder b Alleyne	4		
M. D. Marshall c Gifford b Holder	52		
J. Garner c Holder b Pridgeon	37		
C. E. H. Croft not out	7		
B 9, l-b 5, w 1, n-b 9	24	L-b 4, n-b 3	7

1/1 2/7 3/7 4/42 5/94   266   1/103 2/113 3/113   (3 wkts) 134
6/135 7/152 8/172 9/238

Bowling: *First Innings*—Alleyne 20–3–83–4; Holder 23.2–5–67–3; Pridgeon 6–1–23–1; Patel 14–4–23–1; Gifford 19–5–46–1. *Second Innings*—Alleyne 3–1–19–0; Holder 6–1–15–0; Patel 15–4–53–2; Pridgeon 6–0–27–0; Gifford 4–1–13–1.

Umpires: W. E. Alley and D. O. Oslear.

LEICESTERSHIRE v WEST INDIANS

At Leicester, May 14, 15. West Indians won by an innings and 21 runs. Leicestershire, beaten in the extra half hour of the second day, were outclassed as Greenidge, Garner and Holding aired their special skills. A boundary flurry by Leicestershire's openers was an illusion, and on a pitch offering variable bounce to the fast men and spin to Parry the innings disintegrated, though Gower held on for eighteen overs. The West Indians were in soon after lunch and 120 ahead by the close, Greenidge overcoming the dual handicaps of an awkward pitch and a badly bruised knee in 275 minutes of dominance which produced one 6 and 26 4s. On the second morning Clift and Cook precipitated a collapse, but Leicestershire were deeper in trouble when Roberts followed a lightning-fast ball, which accounted for Steele, with an even swifter throw to run out Dudleston. Balderstone, Gower and Davison regained some measure of self-respect before Holding returned decisively at 5.15 to capitalise on Kallicharran's breakthrough. His extreme pace and devastating yorker brought him five for 21 in five overs, including three wickets in six balls, and the match was all over ninety minutes after he began his second spell.

Leicestershire

	First Innings		Second Innings	
B. Dudleston c Murray b Roberts	26	– run out	4
J. F. Steele c Murray b Holding	8	– b Roberts	9
J. C. Balderstone c Kallicharran b Garner	18	– b Kallicharran	43
D. I. Gower b Garner	9	– c Kallicharran b Holding	57
*B. F. Davison c Murray b Garner	0	– c Rowe b Holding	54
†R. W. Tolchard c Rowe b Parry	5	– lbw b Holding	4
T. J. Boon c King b Parry	9	– b Holding	0
P. B. Clift c sub b Garner	6	– b Holding	11
N. G. B. Cook b Garner	0	– not out	12
J. P. Agnew b Parry	6	– c Murray b Garner	10
L. B. Taylor not out	1	– lbw b Parry	4
B 1, l-b 7, n-b 3	11	B 1, l-b 1, w 1, n-b 3	6

1/34 2/36 3/66 4/66 5/71   99   1/9 2/16 3/111 4/136   214
6/74 7/80 8/80 9/97   5/140 6/140 7/164 8/186
9/204

Bowling: *First Innings*—Roberts 6–0–30–1; Holding 7–2–17–1; Garner 12–5–22–5; Parry 12–4–19–3. *Second Innings*—Roberts 13–5–48–1; Holding 14–4–57–5; Garner 14–3–46–1; Parry 20.4–4–56–1; Kallicharran 1–0–1–1.

West Indians

C. G. Greenidge c Steele b Clift	165	A. M. E. Roberts lbw b Cook	2
S. F. A. Bacchus b Steele	60	J. Garner c Tolchard b Agnew	2
*I. V. A. Richards b Steele	4	M. A. Holding b Taylor	20
L. G. Rowe b Steele	13	B 1, l-b 12, n-b 8	21
A. I. Kallicharran c Tolchard b Cook	17		
C. L. King b Cook	4	1/183 2/195 3/238 4/278	334
†D. A. Murray lbw b Clift	0	5/278 6/282 7/282	
D. R. Parry not out	26	8/286 9/294	

Bowling: Agnew 16–1–79–1; Taylor 16–2–62–1; Clift 19–8–50–2; Cook 14–1–54–3; Steele 18–7–35–3; Boon 3–1–17–0; Balderstone 7–2–16–0.

Umpires: D. J. Constant and H. D. Bird.

NORTHAMPTONSHIRE v WEST INDIES

At Milton Keynes, May 17, 18, 19. West Indians won by six wickets with nearly two hours left. This was the first time a first-class match was played at Milton Keynes, and although Saturday and Sunday saw 658 runs scored, including three centuries, on the final day the wicket had both teams struggling. The most successful bowler was the touring team's off-spinner Parry, with match figures of nine for 132. The first day was a triumph for Williams, Northamptonshire's 22-year-old batsman, who followed his century against the Indians in 1979 with 122 (one 6 and eighteen 4s) in three and threequarter hours. The second day saw brilliant stroke-play as Richards and Lloyd shared a fourth-wicket stand of 132 in 93 minutes. Richards batted for just over three hours for his 131 (one 6 and twenty 4s) while Lloyd took nearly three hours and gathered two 6s and seventeen 4s in his 116. With the wicket posing problems on the third day, Northamptonshire were dismissed for 166 and owed much to a fine half-century from Allan Lamb (one 6 and eight 4s) in eighty minutes and brave defiance from Yardley. Needing only 58 for victory the West Indians lost four wickets, but Richards skilfully mastered both the pitch and the bowling.

Northamptonshire

*G. Cook c Lloyd b Holding	1	– c Murray b Marshall	16
W. Larkins c and b Parry	40	– c Bacchus b Marshall	23
R. G. Williams lbw b Marshall	122	– c sub b Marshall	1
A. J. Lamb st Murray b Parry	19	– b Parry	58
P. Willey c sub b Holding	22	– c Richards b Parry	5
T. J. Yardley b Marshall	1	– c Murray b Parry	34
R. M. Tindall c Murray b Parry	1	– c Kallicharran b Holding	3
R. M. Carter lbw b Marshall	4	– b Parry	0
†G. Sharp c Bacchus b Parry	21	– not out	13
T. M. Lamb not out	13	– c sub b Holding	3
B. J. Griffiths lbw b Parry	0	– b Holding	0
B 1, l-b 6, n-b 9	16	B 6, w 4	10

1/1 2/82 3/126 4/195 5/213	260	1/35 2/40 3/51 4/82 5/139	166
6/214 7/220 8/240 9/260		6/142 7/146 8/147 9/154	

Bowling: *First Innings*—Roberts 11–2–40–0; Holding 16–2–65–2; Marshall 18–4–39–3; Parry 27.2–9–83–5; Richards 4–0–17–0. *Second Innings*—Roberts 10–2–40–0; Holding 13.2–1–38–3; Parry 14–1–49–4; Marshall 7–1–29–3.

West Indians

D. L. Haynes c Willey b Griffiths	4	– c Cook b Griffiths	5
S. F. A. Bacchus c Tindall b T. M. Lamb	44	– c Cook b Griffiths	7
I. V. A. Richards c and b Griffiths	131	– not out	27
A. I. Kallicharran c Yardley b Willey	13	– b Williams	14
*C. H. Lloyd c A. J. Lamb b T. M. Lamb	116	– (6) not out	4
†D. L. Murray c Tindall b T. M. Lamb	0		
D. R. Parry lbw b T. M. Lamb	0		
M. D. Marshall c Yardley b Tindall	17	– (5) b Williams	2
A. M. E. Roberts lbw b Griffiths	31		
M. A. Holding not out	1		
L. G. Rowe absent hurt	0		
B 4, l-b 5, w 2, n-b 1	12	L-b 1	1

1/16 2/110 3/126 4/258 5/259 6/259   369   1/7 2/12 3/48 4/50   (4 wkts)   60
7/306 8/367 9/369

Bowling: *First Innings*—Griffiths 18–3–69–2; T. M. Lamb 20.1–4–73–4; Willey 18–4–58–1; Williams 11–1–58–0; Tindall 11–1–60–2; Carter 7–1–39–0. *Second Innings*—Griffiths 7–1–28–2; T. M. Lamb 3–1–2–0; Willey 3–1–9–0; Williams 3–1–4–2; Tindall 3.4–1–15–0; A. J. Lamb 1–0–1–0.

Umpires: B. J. Meyer and K. E. Palmer.

MIDDLESEX v WEST INDIANS

At Lord's, May 20. Abandoned.

MIDDLESEX v WEST INDIANS

At Lord's, May 21. West Indians won by nine wickets. The Middlesex batsmen could not live up to the hopes of their supporters, and the West Indian pace quintet took a firm stranglehold. Gatting lasted for nineteen overs and Emburey initiated a response which doubled the score from 62 for seven. However, the West Indians achieved an easy victory; Haynes took the opportunity to fight his way into form and Bacchus produced the most fluent batting of the day.

Middlesex

*J. M. Brearley c D. A. Murray		V. A. P. van der Bijl c Garner b King	15
b Holding.	12	M. W. W. Selvey b Garner	15
M. J. Smith c Haynes b Roberts	4	W. W. Daniel not out	5
C. T. Radley c D. L. Murray b Roberts	0		
G. D. Barlow lbw b Marshall	6	L-b 2, n-b 1	3
M. W. Gatting c D. L. Murray b Holding	27		
†I. J. Gould b Garner	8	1/10 2/16 3/16 (49.1 overs) 124	
P. H. Edmonds c Holding b Marshall	0	4/37 5/46 6/49 7/62	
J. E. Emburey c D. L. Murray b King	29	8/103 9/103	

Bowling: Roberts 10–2–28–2; Holding 10–2–21–2; Garner 9.1–3–16–2; Marshall 10–1–32–2; King 10–2–24–2.

West Indians

C. G. Greenidge b Gatting	23
D. L. Haynes not out	52
S. F. A. Bacchus not out	46
B 2, w 1, n-b 1	4

1/53   (1 wkt, 37.2 overs) 125

A. I. Kallicharran, C. L. King, D. A. Murray, *†D. L. Murray, A. M. E. Roberts, M. D. Marshall, J. Garner and M. A. Holding did not bat.

Bowling: van der Bijl 6–1–16–0; Daniel 5–0–26–0; Emburey 10–2–18–0; Selvey 7–2–26–0; Edmonds 6–0–30–0; Gatting 3–2–4–1; Brearley 0.2–0–1–0.

Umpires: W. L. Budd and D. G. L. Evans.

ESSEX v WEST INDIANS

At Chelmsford, May 22. Essex won by five wickets. Essex became the first side to inflict defeat on the tourists in this 50 overs per side friendly. The West Indians never recovered from losing Greenidge and Richards in Pont's first over – the eighth of the match – and, making the ball swing disconcertingly, he went on to finish with four for 36, Haynes offering the only real resistance. Pont was well supported by Lever, who again demonstrated his accuracy. After a slow and somewhat uncertain start, Denness and Fletcher shared in a third-wicket partnership of 98 in nineteen overs to speed Essex to victory. Denness hit seven boundaries, three of them in one over from King to reach his half-century, while Fletcher stroked five 4s.

West Indians

C. G. Greenidge lbw b Pont	12	M. D. Marshall not out		10
D. L. Haynes c Gooch b East	46	J. Garner lbw b East		1
I. V. A. Richards b Pont	0	M. A. Holding b Lever		1
C. L. King b Lever	0	L-b 5, w 7, n-b 2		14
A. I. Kallicharran st Smith b Pont	20			
*C. H. Lloyd c Smith b Gooch	20	1/20 2/20 3/21	(45.2 overs)	149
†D. A. Murray b Pont	18	4/60 5/108 6/119 7/134		
D. R. Parry run out	7	8/139 9/148		

Bowling: Lever 7.2–1–10–2; Sainsbury 10–0–37–0; Pont 9–3–36–4; Gooch 10–1–28–1; East 9–0–24–2.

Essex

G. A. Gooch lbw b Marshall	13	K. R. Pont not out		4
M. H. Denness b Marshall	63			
K. S. McEwan b Garner	3	L-b 7, n-b 4		11
*K. W. R. Fletcher c Murray b Holding	48			
B. R. Hardie c King b Holding	11	1/18 2/27 3/125	(5 wkts, 44.1 overs)	153
M. S. A. McEvoy not out	0	4/142 5/145		

R. E. East, †N. Smith, J. K. Lever and G. E. Sainsbury did not bat.

Bowling: Holding 9–2–26–2; Marshall 10–3–15–2; Garner 7–5–7–1; King 10–0–49–0; Parry 3–0–21–0; Richards 5.1–0–24–0.

Umpires: J. G. Langridge and K. E. Palmer.

ESSEX v WEST INDIANS

At Chelmsford, May 23. West Indians won by 141 runs. Richards and Haynes dominated the touring side's innings with a partnership of 230 spanning 38 overs. Richards was particularly impressive, hitting three 6s and nine 4s during a fine exhibition of stroke-play. Haynes's effort contained one 6 and six 4s. Lever finished off the West Indians' innings by achieving the hat-trick – Lloyd, Roberts and Holding being his victims. Against a battery of fast bowlers, Essex never posed a threat, despite attractive knocks from McEwan and Fletcher.

West Indians

C. G. Greenidge c McEwan b Lever	1	A. M. E. Roberts b Lever	8
D. L. Haynes lbw b East	88	J. Garner not out	0
I. V. A. Richards c McEwan b East	122	M. A. Holding lbw b Lever	0
A. I. Kallicharran b Lever	17	B 6, l-b 11, w 14	31
C. L. King c Gooch b East	1		
*C. H. Lloyd c Pont b Lever	12	1/4 2/234 3/242	(50 overs) 290
†D. A. Murray b Sainsbury	0	4/248 5/262 6/263 7/277	
M. D. Marshall c Lilley b Pont	10	8/290 9/290	

Bowling: Lever 10–1–42–5; Sainsbury 10–0–60–1; Pont 10–0–64–1; Gooch 10–0–42–0; East 10–1–51–3.

Essex

G. A. Gooch b Roberts	21	A. W. Lilley not out	10
M. S. A. McEvoy c sub b Marshall	12	B 1, l-b 1, w 2, n-b 1	5
K. S. McEwan c Holding b Richards	50		
*K. W. R. Fletcher run out	39	1/31 2/47 3/114	(4 wkts, 50 overs) 149
B. R. Hardie not out	12	4/134	

K. R. Pont, R. E. East, †N. Smith, J. K. Lever and G. E. Sainsbury did not bat.

Bowling: Roberts 8–2–23–1; Holding 8–2–23–0; Garner 6–1–17–0; Marshall 10–0–22–1; King 10–1–43–0; Richards 5–0–12–1; Greenidge 3–1–4–0.

Umpires: J. G. Langridge and K. E. Palmer.

DERBYSHIRE v WEST INDIANS

At Chesterfield, May 24, 25, 26. West Indians won by nine wickets. Put in on a pitch on which the ball moved about, Derbyshire owed much to courageous batting by Steele (who shunned either protective helmet or cap) and Wright, whose 96 was the highest score for the county against the West Indians. Wood, in his first innings for the county, retired hurt after being struck on the head, though he resumed later; and his bowling helped Derbyshire restrict the tourists to a lead of 61 on the second day, when Hendrick finished the innings off without addition by taking the first hat-trick of his career. With the pitch still lively, however, Derbyshire had no answer to the pace of Roberts, Marshall and Garner and were bowled out a second time for just 68.

Derbyshire

B. Wood b Marshall		10 – (8) c King b Garner	9
J. G. Wright c Kallicharran b Roberts	96	– (1) b Roberts	13
P. N. Kirsten b Marshall		4 – c Kallicharran b Roberts	0
D. S. Steele c Murray b King		31 – c Murray b Roberts	7
K. J. Barnett lbw b Roberts		2 – lbw b Garner	22
A. J. Borrington lbw b Marshall		14 – (2) c Murray b Roberts	0
*G. Miller b Marshall		9 – (6) c Kallicharran b Garner	12
J. Walters b Roberts		20 – (7) b Garner	0
†R. W. Taylor c Lloyd b Parry		3 – not out	0
A. J. Mellor lbw b Parry		0 – (11) b Marshall	0
M. Hendrick not out		2 – (10) c Murray b Marshall	1
B 2, l-b 16, w 8, n-b 12	38	L-b 2, w 1, n-b 1	4

1/11 2/105 3/108 4/139 5/157   229   1/0 2/13 3/14 4/21 5/41   68
6/208 7/211 8/224 9/225   6/41 7/52 8/67 9/68

Bowling: *First Innings*—Roberts 23–7–46–3; Marshall 22–7–52–4; Garner 19–9–27–0; King 12–2–29–1; Parry 16.3–4–37–2. *Second Innings*—Roberts 8–2–28–4; Marshall 11.5–5–20–2; Garner 9–4–16–4.

West Indians

C. G. Greenidge lbw b Wood	40	– not out	0
S. F. A. Bacchus c Wright b Miller	62	– c Kirsten b Wright	5
I. V. A. Richards b Hendrick	4		
A. I. Kallicharran c Miller b Wood	88		
*C. H. Lloyd c Taylor b Walters	39		
C. L. King c Walters b Hendrick	1		
†D. L. Murray b Wood	15		
D. R. Parry not out	9	– (3) not out	4
M. D. Marshall c Kirsten b Hendrick	11		
A. M. E. Roberts c Barnett b Hendrick	0		
J. Garner c Steele b Hendrick	0		
B 8, l-b 5, w 2, n-b 6	21	N-b 2	2

1/105 2/111 3/119 4/223 5/224   290   1/7   (1 wkt) 11
6/259 7/266 8/290 9/290

Bowling: *First Innings*—Hendrick 23.4–6–59–5; Walters 21–1–70–1; Mellor 6–1–37–0; Wood 31–7–67–3; Miller 13–3–36–1. *Second Innings*—Walters 1–0–5–0; Wright 0.4–0–4–1.

Umpires: D. O. Oslear and D. J. Constant.

ENGLAND v WEST INDIES

First Prudential Trophy Match

At Leeds, May 28, 29. West Indies won by 24 runs. The match ran into a second day, rain and bad light causing delays on the first – when the gates were closed by noon. West Indies, put in by Botham who was leading England for the first time, had a hard struggle to reach 198 off their 55 overs. In poor light and on an unsound pitch only Greenidge played an innings of any length. With two for 12 in eleven overs Old, brought into the England side on the eve of the match when Willis was unfit, had most to do with pinning West Indies down. For a long time England found runs even harder to come by. When play was called off on the first day they had received 23 overs and reached only 35 for three. However, Tavaré, playing his first match at this level, batted very well next morning, in less taxing conditions, and with some spirited assistance from Botham and Bairstow he had made a good game of it by the time he ran out of partners. Tavaré was made Man of the Match. Paying attendance was 16,000, with receipts of £60,000.

West Indians

C. G. Greenidge b Botham	78	A. M. E. Roberts c Botham b Dilley	10
D. L. Haynes c Tavaré b Old	19	J. Garner run out	14
I. V. A. Richards c Gower b Gooch	7	M. A. Holding not out	0
S. F. A. Bacchus c Lever b Gooch	2	B 5, l-b 15, w 2	22
A. I. Kallicharran c Botham b Old	10		
*C. H. Lloyd c and b Lever	21	1/36 2/49 3/51 (55 overs) 198
M. D. Marshall b Botham	6	4/110 5/151 6/161 7/163
†D. L. Murray run out	9	8/178 9/197

Bowling: Dilley 11–3–41–1; Lever 11–4–36–1; Botham 11–1–45–2; Old 11–4–12–2; Gooch 7–2–30–2; Willey 4–0–12–0.

England

G. Boycott c Kallicharran b Garner	5	C. M. Old b Marshall	4
P. Willey c Richards b Marshall	7	G. R. Dilley c Haynes b Roberts	0
C. J. Tavaré not out	82	J. K. Lever run out	6
G. A. Gooch c Murray b Richards	2	L-b 4, b 3, w 2	9
D. I. Gower c Murray b Holding	12		
*I. T. Botham c Murray b Marshall	30	1/11 2/15 3/23 (51.2 overs) 174	
D. Lloyd b Greenidge	1	4/38 5/81 6/86 7/130	
†D. L. Bairstow c Garner b Holding	16	8/149 9/150	

Bowling: Holding 9–3–16–2; Roberts 11–4–30–1; Garner 9.2–0–20–1; Marshall 11–2–28–3; Richards 7–0–50–1; Greenidge 4–0–21–1.

Umpires: K. E. Palmer and B. J. Meyer.

ENGLAND v WEST INDIES

Second Prudential Trophy Match

At Lord's, May 30. England won by three wickets. Another full house (paying attendance 24,000 with receipts of £94,604) watched a thrilling day's play, played mostly in sunshine, which ended with Botham hitting the winning boundary with three balls left. As at Leeds, two days earlier, Botham won the toss and chose to field, and until he himself bowled some expensive overs late in the West Indian innings England did a good containing job. Marks, a former Oxford captain, had a useful match, bowling eleven economical overs of off-breaks and helping Botham to add 34 at an important stage of England's innings. Chasing 236 England were given a splendid start by Boycott and Willey with an opening partnership of 135 in 33 overs. When a collapse followed, with four wickets falling cheaply, it seemed that England would lose; but Botham hit about him to great effect and, amidst much excitement, England just got home. Boycott was Man of the Match. The Prudential Trophy was won by West Indies for having the higher scoring-rate in the two matches.

West Indies

C. G. Greenidge c Lever b Marks	39	M. D. Marshall b Willis	0
D. L. Haynes c Willis b Marks	50	M. A. Holding b Willis	0
S. F. A. Bacchus run out	40		
*I. V. A. Richards c Lever b Botham	26	L-b 9, n-b 2	11
A. I. Kallicharran c Willis b Old	11		
C. L. King run out	33	1/86 2/113 3/147 (9 wkts, 55 overs) 235	
A. M. E. Roberts not out	25	4/169 5/186 6/231 7/233	
J. Garner run out	0	8/233 9/235	

†D. A. Murray did not bat.

Bowling: Willis 10–1–25–2; Lever 7–1–23–0; Botham 11–2–71–1; Old 11–1–43–1; Marks 11–1–44–2; Willey 5–0–18–0.

England

P. Willey c and b Holding	56	†D. L. Bairstow run out	2
G. Boycott run out	70	J. K. Lever not out	0
C. J. Tavaré c Murray b Holding	5	L-b 22, w 4, n-b 2	28
G. A. Gooch c Bacchus b Marshall	12		
D. I. Gower c Bacchus b Roberts	12	1/135 2/143 3/156 (7 wkts, 54.3 overs) 236	
*I. T. Botham not out	42	4/160 5/178 6/212	
V. J. Marks b Holding	9	7/231	

C. M. Old and R. G. D. Willis did not bat.

Bowling: Roberts 11–3–42–1; Holding 11–0–28–3; Garner 10.3–0–41–0; Marshall 11–1–45–1; Richards 5–0–28–0; Greenidge 6–0–24–0.

Umpires: D. J. Constant and D. G. L. Evans.

KENT v WEST INDIES

At Canterbury, May 31, June 1, 2. West Indians won by five wickets. No play was possible on the first day because of rain and the Sunday afternoon was spent in both sides getting quick runs before declaring to set the scene for a finish. Kent's declaration was effected after Cowdrey had struck two 6s and six 4s in reaching 50 out of 78 in seventy minutes. Haynes achieved his half-century in ninety-four minutes with six 4s, adding 70 in fifty-one minutes with Greenidge. On the third morning Holding had Kent reeling with two quick wickets and the only resistance came from Knott, who held out for close on two hours. The tourists had their shocks, too, losing half their side for 60, but Lloyd and his vice-captain D. L. Murray steered them sensibly, and in the end comfortably, to victory.

Kent

R. A. Woolmer c Lloyd b Holding	12	– c D. A. Murray b Garner	11
C. J. C. Rowe c D. L. Murray b Croft	18	– lbw b Holding	1
C. J. Tavaré c D. L. Murray b Croft	17	– c Bacchus b Parry	8
C. S. Cowdrey not out	51	– b Holding	2
G. W. Johnson c D. A. Murray b Kallicharran	18	– c D. A. Murray b Garner	2
N. R. Taylor not out	0	– lbw b Holding	11
*†A. P. E. Knott (did not bat)	–	st D. A. Murray b Parry	30
R. W. Hills (did not bat)	–	c Lloyd b Parry	6
G. R. Dilley (did not bat)	–	lbw b Garner	4
D. L. Underwood (did not bat)	–	not out	1
K. B. S. Jarvis (did not bat)	–	c D. A. Murray b Parry	0
B 8, l-b 3, w 1, n-b 2	14	B 4, l-b 4	8

1/16 2/50 3/57   (4 wkts dec.) 130   1/3 2/23 3/26 4/31 5/31   84
4/112   6/60 7/71 8/80 9/84

Bowling: *First Innings*—Holding 6–4–3–1; Croft 12–3–38–2; Garner 7–2–16–0; Parry 14–5–43–0; Greenidge 3–1–2–0; Kallicharran 6–2–14–1. *Second Innings*—Holding 17–8–19–3; Croft 9–2–20–0; Garner 10–6–9–3; Parry 21.2–9–28–4.

West Indians

S. F. A. Bacchus c Johnson b Hills	14	– b Jarvis	4
D. L. Haynes not out	50	– lbw b Hills	16
C. G. Greenidge not out	48	– c Woolmer b Dilley	1
A. I. Kallicharran (did not bat)	–	c Cowdrey b Jarvis	6
†D. A. Murray (did not bat)	–	b Hills	11
*C. H. Lloyd (did not bat)	–	not out	33
†D. L. Murray (did not bat)	–	not out	23
N-b 1	1	L-b 6, n-b 3	9

1/43   (1 wkt dec.) 113   1/9 2/15 3/32   (5 wkts) 103
4/34 5/60

D. R. Parry, J. Garner, M. A. Holding and C. E. H. Croft did not bat.

Bowling: *First Innings*—Dilley 7–1–20–0; Jarvis 6–0–27–0; Underwood 8–3–21–0; Hills 7–1–44–1. *Second Innings*—Dilley 4–0–17–1; Jarvis 12–2–32–2; Hills 12.2–0–42–2; Underwood 4–2–3–0.

D. L. Murray kept wicket in the first innings, D. A. Murray in the second innings.

Umpires: W. E. Alley and C. T. Spencer.

ENGLAND v WEST INDIES

First Cornhill Test

At Nottingham, June 5, 6, 7, 9, 10. West Indies won by two wickets. Barely 1,000 spectators made the effort to turn up for the final morning with West Indies requiring only 99 runs for victory with eight second innings wickets in hand. But those who saw the ending were rewarded by a gripping and courageous fight-back, by England's bowlers in general and Willis in particular, that went close to presenting Botham with a startling victory in his first Test as captain.

Throughout the previous four days the bowlers on both sides had held the upper hand on a wicket that offered extravagant movement off the seam and in conditions conducive to swing bowling. On the final morning even putting bat against ball proved difficult and only Haynes batted with any degree of authority during his three hundred and five minutes, match-winning vigil. Willis's heroic bowling was rewarded with nine wickets in the match, and if one of two vital catches on the final day had been taken England might easily have won.

The bitter split in English cricket caused by the Packer affair was officially healed with Knott and Woolmer being welcomed back into the England side for the first time since they rejected their country in 1977. In all, Kent provided four of the England side. It would have been five but for the omission of Underwood from the England twelve, owing largely to the weather conditions and the need to include an extra pace bowler because of fitness doubts concerning Botham (back) and Hendrick (shoulder). Injuries to Rowe, King and Croft saw Bacchus and Marshall play their first Tests in England for West Indies.

The match missed catches affected the fortunes of both sides. Boycott, Woolmer and Botham benefited to a considerable degree on the first day after Botham had won the toss. In attempting to take one of them, Lloyd was forced to leave the field in mid-afternoon after splitting the webbing between the first and second fingers of his right hand, an injury which required two stitches and was to prove a handicap when batting. Boycott had made only 4 when he gave a chance behind. Woolmer (0) and Botham (20) also offered edges in the slip region, their escapes enabling England to reach 243 for seven by the close; a respectable figure in the conditions, especially against the movement obtained by Roberts and West Indies' slow over-rate.

In making his half-century Botham demonstrated he could cope with the responsibility of leading a Test side without losing his belligerence, while Woolmer gave the innings stability in the middle with his stay of three hours twenty minutes. Both innings began to look insignificant the following morning when West Indies started their reply. After losing Haynes in Willis's fifth over, Greenidge and Richards added 88 in only 91 minutes, a scoring-rate Bacchus helped to maintain after Knott and Hendrick had combined to dismiss Greenidge. Another large West Indies total threatened but Willis, bowling with a rhythm and aggression lacking in Australia, induced edges from the third-wicket pair to reverse the trend; it needed an unusually violent Murray – dropped when 23 – to steer his side to a 45-run lead when their innings ended an hour into the third day.

An unfortunate run out of Gooch, when he was batting well, by the agile Bacchus, and a spectacular thunderstorm interrupted England's second innings progress. Boycott and Woolmer again benefited from missed chances, and England were in a handy position at the start of the fourth day, 100 runs ahead at 145 for two. Slow progress by these two, however, enabled Richards, who had taken control in the field in Lloyd's absence, to maintain an attacking field. Only 29 more runs came off fourteen overs in the first hour on the fourth morning, a lack of progress accentuated over the next thirty-five minutes when both were dismissed along with Gower and Botham for the addition of just 9 runs against the bowling of Roberts and Garner. Boycott batted more than five hours for his 75 and Woolmer took two hundred minutes over his 29. Their departure left only Willey to produce a number of powerful blows, helping England to 252 all out, a total boosted considerably by 52 extras. The unfortunate Murray had a difficult time behind the wicket trying to cope with the movement his bowlers obtained.

West Indies were left with a target of 208 in just over eight hours, one that was never going to be easy, especially after Greenidge was caught behind with only 11 on the board. There followed, however, probably the decisive innings of the match as Richards ripped into England's bowling. In 56 minutes he scored 48 runs, striking eight boundaries with supreme arrogance, before Botham produced a leg-cutter to get him lbw shortly before the close.

Although Richards's innings eased the pressure on the rest of the batsmen, the tension returned immediately the next morning when West Indies started the final day only 99 runs from victory with eight wickets in hand. Bacchus, driving recklessly at Hendrick's opening ball, gave a catch behind and opened the way for England's bold effort to snatch victory. With Willis showing the stamina many believed he had lost, West Indies suffered casualties regularly. That they were still inching their way towards the target owed much to the resolute Haynes, who might have fallen to Willis at slip when he was 23.

Roberts, too, was dropped off Willis when West Indies needed just 13 to win. Even then their anxiety showed as Haynes, after five hours five minutes at the crease, was run out by a direct throw from Willey after being sent back. Haynes raced from the field in tears, believing he had thrown away a victory by his rashness, even though only 3 runs were required with two wickets left. Two balls later it was all over when Roberts, chancing his arm again, lifted Botham over long-on to secure victory for his side and the Man of the Match award for himself. West Indies' victory, achieved half an hour after lunch, was one of the closest winning margins in Tests between the two countries and put them one ahead in the series.

The official attendance was 50,010; takings were £153,700. – P.S.

England

G. A. Gooch c Murray b Roberts	17	– run out	27
G. Boycott c Murray b Garner	36	– b Roberts	75
C. J. Tavaré b Garner	13	– c Richards b Garner	4
R. A. Woolmer c Murray b Roberts	46	– c Murray b Roberts	29
D. I. Gower c Greenidge b Roberts	20	– lbw b Garner	1
*I. T. Botham c Richards b Garner	57	– c Richards b Roberts	4
P. Willey b Marshall	13	– b Marshall	38
†A. P. E. Knott lbw b Roberts	6	– lbw b Marshall	7
J. K. Lever c Richards b Holding	15	– c Murray b Garner	4
R. G. D. Willis b Roberts	8	– b Garner	9
M. Hendrick not out	7	– not out	2
B 7, l-b 11, w 3, n-b 4	25	B 19, l-b 13, w 10, n-b 10	52

1/27 2/72 3/74 4/114 5/204 6/208   263   1/46 2/68 3/174 4/175 5/180   252
7/228 8/246 9/254   6/183 7/218 8/237 9/248

Bowling: *First Innings*—Roberts 25–7–72–5; Holding 23.5–7–61–1; Marshall 19–3–52–1; Richards 1–0–9–0; Garner 23–9–44–3. *Second Innings*—Roberts 24–6–57–3; Holding 26–5–65–0; Marshall 24–8–44–2; Garner 34.1–20–30–4; Greenidge 3–2–4–0.

West Indies

C. G. Greenidge c Knott b Hendrick	53	– c Knott b Willis	6
D. L. Haynes c Gower b Willis	12	– run out	62
I. V. A. Richards c Knott b Willis	64	– lbw b Botham	48
S. F. A. Bacchus c Botham b Willis	30	– c Knott b Hendrick	19
A. I. Kallicharran b Botham	17	– c Knott b Willis	9
†D. L. Murray b Willis	64	– (7) c Hendrick b Willis	16
*C. H. Lloyd c Knott b Lever	9	– (6) lbw b Willis	3
M. D. Marshall c Tavaré b Gooch	20	– b Willis	7
A. M. E. Roberts lbw b Botham	21	– not out	22
J. Garner c Lever b Botham	2		
M. A. Holding not out	0	– (10) not out	0
B 1, l-b 9, w 2, n-b 4	16	L-b 8, n-b 9	17

1/19 2/107 3/151 4/165 5/208 6/227   308   1/11 2/69 3/109 4/125   (8 wkts) 209
7/265 8/306 9/308   5/129 6/165 7/180 8/205

Bowling: *First Innings*—Willis 20.1–5–82–4; Lever 20–2–76–1; Hendrick 19–4–69–1; Willey 5–3–4–0; Botham 20–6–50–3; Gooch 7–2–11–1. *Second Innings*—Willis 26–4–65–5; Lever 8–2–25–0; Hendrick 14–5–40–1; Botham 16.4–6–48–1; Gooch 2–1–2–0; Willey 2–0–12–0.

Umpires: D. J. Constant and D. O. Oslear.

OXFORD & CAMBRIDGE UNIVS v WEST INDIES

At Cambridge, June 12, 13. West Indians won by ten wickets. A dashing 86 (fifteen 4s) in two and a quarter hours by Mubarak enabled the Universities to declare at 208 for four, after they had been put in. The Sri Lankan hit 81 out of 106 before lunch, while the South African Ezekowitz stayed solidly at the other end, making only 6 in ten overs. Croft, in a wayward spell, was no balled thirteen times for overstepping. The Universities hurried to their declaration as 58 runs were added in 39 minutes by Boyd-Moss and Pringle, whose spirited 50 included nine boundaries. Although Sutcliffe's off-spin slowed the run-rate, the West Indians passed the students' total before the close and declared overnight. The next morning Croft and Roberts attacked menacingly, conceding only 15 runs in the first twelve overs, and then Parry's off-spin wrapped up the innings. Only freshman Boyd-Moss reached double figures as the Universities were bowled out for 68, the last five wickets falling for 12 runs and Parry returning figures of five for 22. Haynes and Bacchus needed only 35 minutes to score the 59 runs for victory, 40 coming in boundaries.

Oxford & Cambridge Univs

A. M. Mubarak c Greenidge b Croft	86	– c Haynes b Croft	7
J. P. C. Mills c Bacchus b Croft	5	– c D. L. Murray b Croft	4
R. A. B. Ezekowitz c Rowe b Parry	32	– run out	8
A. Odendaal c D. L. Murray b Croft	2	– c Greenidge b Parry	1
D. R. Pringle not out	50	– st D. L. Murray b Parry	7
R. J. Boyd-Moss not out	18	– lbw b Roberts	17
*†I. G. Peck (did not bat)		– c Greenidge b Parry	7
N. Russom (did not bat)		– c Bacchus b Parry	6
C. J. Ross (did not bat)		– b Parry	1
S. P. Sutcliffe (did not bat)		– b King	1
I. J. Curtis (did not bat)		– not out	0
B 3, l-b 2, n-b 10	15	B 3, l-b 2, w 1, n-b 3	9

1/16 2/121 3/123 4/150   (4 wkts dec.) 208   1/7 2/12 3/21 4/22 5/32   68
                                                             6/56 7/61 8/65 9/68

Bowling: *First Innings*—Roberts 5–0–15–0; Croft 16–3–71–3; Marshall 9–3–15–0; Parry 14–6–36–1; King 12–1–56–0. *Second Innings*—Roberts 10–6–9–1; Croft 11–4–20–2; Marshall 6–2–8–0; Parry 15–4–22–5; King 0.4–0–0–1.

West Indians

C. G. Greenidge b Russom	44		
D. L. Haynes c Pringle b Russom	32	– not out	23
S. F. A. Bacchus not out	79	– (1) not out	34
L. G. Rowe not out	53		
L-b 4, w 2, n-b 4	10	W 2	2

1/66 2/86   (2 wkts dec.) 218   (no wkt) 59

C. L. King, D. A. Murray, *†D. L. Murray, D. R. Parry, M. D. Marshall, A. M. E. Roberts and C. E. H. Croft did not bat.

Bowling: *First Innings*—Ross 8–0–57–0; Russom 10–1–41–2; Pringle 8–1–41–0; Curtis 6–0–38–0; Sutcliffe 10–2–31–0. *Second Innings*—Ross 4.5–1–42–0; Russom 3–1–9–0; Pringle 1–0–6–0.

Umpires: B. J. Meyer and P. S. G. Stevens.

SUSSEX v WEST INDIES

At Hove, June 14, 15, 16. Drawn. Sussex, aided and abetted by unfriendly weather, ended the bid of the tourists to win the Holts Product's £100,000 jackpot by winning all eleven county first-class fixtures. They had won the first five convincingly, but long hold-ups on the first and last days, plus determined work with bat and ball by the under-strength home side, ended with

Sussex 107 on in their second innings. The West Indian fast bowlers, backed up by off-spinner Parry who took four wickets, had skittled Sussex out for only 143 in the first innings, Imran Khan displaying his composure and class with 50 confident runs. Richards hit a whirlwind 55, including striking le Roux for four consecutive boundaries as the tourists took a lead of 84, but a brisk 41 by Mendis, 54 not out by Imran and 55 from Booth Jones, until a few weeks previously a teacher at Hastings, enabled Sussex to make a fight of it.

Sussex

G. D. Mendis c Kallicharran b Croft	3	– c Murray b Holding 41
T. D. Booth Jones c Murray b Croft	15	– run out 55
P. W. G. Parker c Murray b Croft	23	– c Bacchus b Parry 27
Imran Khan c Richards b Marshall	50	– not out 54
C. P. Phillipson c Richards b Marshall	1	– c Bacchus b Parry 6
I. A. Greig c Holding b Parry	22	– not out 0
G. S. le Roux b Marshall	6	
†T. J. Head c Bacchus b Parry	4	
A. C. S. Pigott b Parry	4	
G. G. Arnold b Parry	0	
*J. Spencer not out	9	
B 5, n-b 1	6	B 2, l-b 2, w 1, n-b 3 8

1/3 2/32 3/47 4/96 5/99 6/113   143   1/73 2/122 3/164   (4 wkts) 191
7/118 8/128 9/128   4/191

Bowling: *First Innings*—Holding 9–2–35–0; Croft 11–4–23–3; Marshall 15–4–40–3; Parry 6.2–1–29–4; Richards 5–3–10–0. *Second Innings*—Holding 10–1–41–1; Croft 10–0–33–0; Parry 17–7–58–2; Marshall 4–0–18–0; Richards 6–2–17–0; Kallicharran 1–0–16–0.

West Indians

D. R. Parry lbw b Imran	8	C. L. King retired hurt 26
D. L. Haynes run out	44	M. A. Holding b Pigott............. 1
S. F. A. Bacchus c Spencer b Greig	24	
*I. V. A. Richards b Arnold	55	L-b 3, w 2, n-b 5 10
L. G. Rowe lbw b Greig	0	
A. I. Kallicharran not out	43	1/9 2/59 3/114 (8 wkts dec.) 227
†D. A. Murray c Spencer b Imran	11	4/114 5/144 6/160
M. D. Marshall lbw b Arnold	5	7/169 8/227

C. E. H. Croft did not bat.

Bowling: le Roux 14–2–67–0; Imran 14–2–50–2; Pigott 9.1–0–27–1; Greig 9–1–31–2; Spencer 3–1–10–0; Arnold 8–1–32–2.

Umpires: D. J. Dennis and A. G. T. Whitehead.

ENGLAND v WEST INDIES

Second Cornhill Test

At Lord's, June 19, 20, 21, 23, 24. Drawn. A game which began with three memorable innings was submerged, as were seven Lord's Tests during the 1970s, in a waterlogged finish. The loss of more than eight hours on the last two days almost certainly saved England from going two down in the series. Richards, of course, operated on a higher plane than anyone else, and it is a measure of Gooch's skills that he was not far behind in stroke production; especially taking into account the difference in the ferocity of the respective attacks. Haynes, who beat the Lord's West Indies record of 168 not out set by his manager Clyde Walcott in 1950, showed high application, a phlegmatic temperament and a fair range of shots on the Saturday. But whereas Richards produces these innings almost at will, the two other century-makers surpassed anything they had achieved before for their countries.

West Indies adjusted their pace quartet and brought in Croft for Marshall. England, doubtless with some reluctance, dropped Gower. Gatting returned – he had last played for

England in New Zealand in 1978 – and Underwood replaced Lever for his first home Test since his two years with Packer.

England's innings had a disjointed start with a break for bad light and the loss of Boycott. This made Gooch's display even more creditable. Tavaré stood secure while Gooch played with an authority and power seldom seen from an Englishman in the last fifteen years or so. His driving was especially fruitful, he was quick to position himself to hook the short ball, and he sailed nonchalantly past his century, showing no sign that he had waited 36 Test innings to reach the mark. He made his runs out of 165 and was out fifteen minutes before tea, having batted just over three and a half hours with one 6 and seventeen 4s. At tea the virtually passive Tavaré was a mere 27. England, naturally, could not sustain Gooch's pace or command and, with Garner and Holding now posing considerable problems with their speed and control, West Indies struck back hard in the last session. Tavaré and Woolmer had to be dug out – Tavaré after almost five hours – but Gatting and Botham played loose shots, and at the close England had slipped from 165 for one to a disappointing 232 for seven.

The new ball ensured that Knott and Willey could not organise a revival on the second morning. In forty minutes batting before lunch, Greenidge introduced England to the mauling they were to encounter over the next two days by carving Willis's first three balls for 4. These blows also illustrated how sharply England's fielding had descended in one year from the athletic to the laboured. England were delighted to dismiss Greenidge in the second over after lunch, but all elation evaporated as Richards, in his first Test at Lord's, exploded into action. England seemed determined to give him few on-side scoring opportunities but, as with all the greatest batsmen, tactics and theories become irrelevant. Botham's populated off-side field was penetrated by five smooth boundaries. Richards eased past 50 and in one over from Underwood hit four 4s to all parts of the compass. Cricket appeared faintly ludicrous when, immediately after this fusillade, play halted briefly for bad light. Richards's dazzling century took just one hundred and twenty-five minutes and he went on to bat two hundred minutes, hitting 100 runs in 4s, with one 6 off Willey. His dismissal, when it came, was decidedly freakish after all that preceded it: an innocuous ball scooped to substitute Dilley at square-leg.

On any other day Haynes's 92 not out would have brought wide attention, but he earned a full share of notice on Saturday when England's bowling continued to be weakened by the absence of Hendrick with thigh trouble. Night-watchman Croft departed cheaply, but Kallicharran helped Haynes add 51 in just over an hour. The new ball accounted for Bacchus before Lloyd, stroking the ball around in his old casual fashion, contributed 56 to a stand of 107 in 88 minutes. When Haynes left after batting nearly eight and a quarter hours, with one 6 and 27 4s, England's torment was prolonged for a further hour.

Faced with forty minutes batting on the Saturday night and a deficit of 249, Gooch attacked the mountain belligerently, both then and in the half hour's play that was possible on Monday before the rain set in at mid-day. On the final day Boycott carried his overnight 13 to 49 and did enough to ensure that England would probably have forced a draw through their own efforts and without the two thunderstorms that saved them the trouble. Woolmer had joined Boycott at 12.30 p.m. and in their hour together they did more than just survive. Survival, regrettably, had been Tavaré's only aim.

Richards took the Man of the Match award. The attendance was 77,002; the receipts were £292,595. – T.C.

England

G. A. Gooch lbw b Holding	123	– b Garner	47
G. Boycott c Murray b Holding	8	– not out	49
C. J. Tavaré c Greenidge b Holding	42	– lbw b Garner	6
R. A. Woolmer c Kallicharran b Garner	15	– not out	19
M. W. Gatting b Holding	18		
*I. T. Botham lbw b Garner	8		
D. L. Underwood lbw b Garner	3		
P. Willey b Holding	4		
†A. P. E. Knott c Garner b Holding	9		
R. G. D. Willis b Garner	14		
M. Hendrick not out	10		
B 4, l-b 1, w 4, n-b 6	15	L-b 1, n-b 11	12

	269		**(2 wkts) 133**

1/20 2/165 3/190 4/219 5/220   **269**   1/71 2/96   (2 wkts) 133
6/231 7/232 8/244 9/245

Bowling: *First Innings*—Roberts 18–3–50–0; Holding 28–11–67–6; Garner 24.3–8–36–4; Croft 20–3–77–0; Richards 5–1–24–0. *Second Innings*—Roberts 13–3–24–0; Holding 15–5–51–0; Garner 15–6–21–2; Croft 8–2–24–0; Richards 1–0–1–0.

West Indies

C. G. Greenidge lbw b Botham	25	A. M. E. Roberts b Underwood	24
D. L. Haynes lbw b Botham	184	J. Garner c Gooch b Willis	15
I. V. A. Richards c sub b Willey	145	M. A. Holding not out	0
C. E. H. Croft run out	0		
A. I. Kallicharran c Knott b Willis	15	B 1, l-b 9, w 1, n-b 9	20
S. F. A. Bacchus c Gooch b Willis	0		
*C. H. Lloyd b Willey	56	1/37 2/260 3/275 4/326 5/330	518
†D. L. Murray c Tavaré b Botham	34	6/437 7/469 8/486 9/518	

Bowling: Willis 31–12–103–3; Botham 37–7–145–3; Underwood 29.2–7–108–1; Hendrick 11–2–32–0; Gooch 7–1–26–0; Willey 25–8–73–2; Boycott 7–2–11–0.

Umpires: W. E. Alley and B. J. Meyer.

IRELAND v WEST INDIANS

At Dublin, June 25. Drawn. Rain, already having reduced the match to 50 overs, again intervened during lunch, and both sides agreed to play it out as a single-innings game. After an early surprise when Greenidge was dismissed without a run scored, the West Indians had reached 105 for two at lunch, when they closed their innings. Ireland, left an hour and a half to better that total, were troubled by King and Marshall and could reach only 39 for five before the match was declared a draw.

West Indians

C. G. Greenidge c Halliday b Corlett	0
S. F. A. Bacchus c Murphy b Anderson	50
A. I. Kallicharran not out	42
C. L. King not out	9
L-b 4	4
1/0 2/85 (2 wkts dec.)	105

D. A. Murray, *†D. L. Murray, M. D. Marshall, J. Garner, A. M. E. Roberts, D. R. Parry and C. E. H. Croft did not bat.

Bowling: Corlett 5–2–3–1; Elder 6–4–3–0; Halliday 10–3–27–0; Monteith 6–1–28–0; Anderson 6–1–27–1; Reith 2–0–13–0.

Ireland

J. F. Short c Bacchus b Garner	2	R. I. Johnston c D. A. Murray b King	3
M. S. Reith not out	16	†G. F. Murphy not out	5
B. A. O'Brien b Marshall	2	B 2, w 1, n-b 6	9
I. J. Anderson c D. L. Murray			
b Marshall	2	1/3 2/9 3/15 (5 wkts)	39
D. W. Harrison c Greenidge b King	0	4/22 5/32	

*J. D. Monteith, S. C. Corlett, M. Halliday and J. W. G. Elder did not bat.

Bowling: Marshall 10–6–6–2; Garner 7–2–9–1; King 5–3–5–2; Parry 3–0–5–0; Kallicharran 2–0–3–0; D. L. Murray 1–0–1–0; Bacchus 2–1–1–0.

Umpires: N. Fitzsimons and E. Parsons.

IRELAND v WEST INDIANS

At Dublin, June 26. West Indians won by 73 runs. Bacchus provided the backbone of the West Indians' innings with a superb 163, which included seven 6s and twelve 4s. After rain had reduced the match to 30 overs, Ireland were chasing 155 but, with frequent showers interrupting their innings, they never looked like achieving the required run-rate and managed only 82 for one.

West Indians

C. G. Greenidge run out	10	A. M. E. Roberts b Corlett	16
S. F. A. Bacchus c O'Brien b Corlett	163	J. Garner not out	10
D. A. Murray c O'Brien b Halliday	27		
A. I. Kallicharran b Anderson	15	L-b 6	6
C. L. King c O'Brien b Monteith	7		
M. D. Marshall b Corlett	10	1/17 2/93 3/129 (7 wkts, 55 overs) 284	
D. R. Parry not out	20	4/154 5/179 6/246 7/264	

*†D. L. Murray and M. A. Holding did not bat.

Bowling: Corlett 11–3–67–3; Elder 5–0–24–0; Monteith 11–0–65–1; Halliday 11–1–29–1; Anderson 11–1–37–1; Johnston 6–0–56–0.

Ireland

M. S. Reith b Kallicharran	20
J. F. Short not out	31
B. A. O'Brien not out	21
B 5, l-b 2, w 3	10

1/48　　　　　(1 wkt, 30 overs) 82

I. J. Anderson, D. W. Harrison, R. I. Johnston, *J. D. Monteith, †G. F. Murphy, S. C. Corlett, M. Halliday and J. W. G. Elder did not bat.

Bowling: Roberts 4–1–6–0; Holding 6–2–7–0; Marshall 3–0–13–0; King 4–1–4–0; Parry 5–2–9–0; Kallicharran 5–0–23–1; Bacchus 3–0–10–0.

Umpires: N. Fitzsimons and E. Parsons.

GLAMORGAN v WEST INDIANS

At Swansea, June 28, 30, July 1. Drawn. The West Indian openers, put in, made an uninspiring start against the accurate Glamorgan attack. Then Richards exploded into action, hitting nine 6s and nine 4s as he reached his hundred in 24 overs, 75 runs coming in 23 minutes after tea. His magnificent performance brought the spectators to their feet in applause. Also noteworthy was his dismissal; he was stumped by Eifion Jones, who thus set a new Glamorgan wicket-keeping record of 783 dismissals. Rain ended play after less than an hour on the second day, when the West Indians added another 31 runs and declared at 327 for five. When Glamorgan replied on the third day Marshall dismissed the first six batsmen for 164, but Featherstone (two 6s and nine 4s) batted staunchly to reach his highest score for Glamorgan, averting the follow-on and possible defeat. The West Indians then had an hour's batting practice before the end.

West Indians

C. G. Greenidge c E. W. Jones b Cordle	28			
D. L. Haynes c Hopkins b Lloyd	82	– (1) not out		29
I. V. A. Richards st E. W. Jones b Lloyd	100			
A. I. Kallicharran c Lloyd b Cordle	58			
C. L. King c Featherstone b Cordle	2			
†D. A. Murray not out	37	– (2) not out		30
D. R. Parry not out	10			
L-b 3, n-b 7	10		N-b 1	1

1/50 2/187 3/229 4/236   (5 wkts dec.) 327   (no wkt) 60
5/283

*C. H. Lloyd, M. D. Marshall, J. Garner and C. E. H. Croft did not bat.

Bowling: *First Innings*—Mack 14–4–69–0; Cordle 27–4–84–3; Ontong 5–0–39–0; Lloyd 14–4–45–2; Holmes 6–0–44–0; Featherstone 6–1–36–0. *Second Innings*—Mack 5–1–15–0; Ontong 5–2–11–0; Featherstone 6–1–19–0; Miandad 5–1–14–0.

Glamorgan

A. Jones b Marshall	15	*B. J. Lloyd not out		10
J. A. Hopkins b Marshall	19	A. E. Cordle c Garner b Croft		6
R. C. Ontong c Murray b Marshall	2	A. J. Mack c Garner b Parry		6
Javed Miandad c Richards b Marshall	18			
N. G. Featherstone c Murray b Marshall	76	B 5, l-b 4, n-b 14		23
G. C. Holmes c Garner b Marshall	21			
M. J. Llewellyn b Croft	19	1/27 2/33 3/50 4/68 5/163		242
†E. W. Jones c Kallicharran b Croft	27	6/164 7/213 8/220 9/226		

Bowling: Marshall 19–5–54–6; Croft 17–4–58–3; Parry 20–4–72–1; Garner 13–4–31–0; King 1–0–4–0.

Umpires: H. D. Bird and R. S. Herman.

GLAMORGAN v WEST INDIES

At Swansea, June 29. West Indians won by five wickets. Glamorgan's commendable total was never enough to deprive the West Indians of a comfortable victory. After the home team had been put in on a placid pitch Javed Miandad provided the backbone of their innings with a dazzling unbeaten 101, reaching his century in the final over and hitting one 6 and thirteen 4s. Haynes and Bacchus (three 6s) produced an opening stand of 157 off 24 overs, against an attack severely weakened by the absence of Nash and A. A. Jones. Richards hit a glorious 6 over the rugby stand, but was dismissed for 19 attempting to make another similar hit. Although Lloyd and Kallicharran went cheaply, the target was already in view and the visitors achieved victory with 6.1 overs to spare.

Glamorgan

A. Jones c Bacchus b Croft	22	R. C. Ontong not out		21
J. A. Hopkins run out	5			
G. C. Holmes run out	12	B 5, l-b 7, w 4, n-b 1		17
Javed Miandad not out	101			
N. G. Featherstone c Richards b King	20	1/20 2/38 3/67 (5 wkts, 39 overs) 209		
M. J. Llewellyn c and b Marshall	11	4/117 5/140		

†E. W. Jones, *B. J. Lloyd, A. E. Cordle and E. A. Moseley did not bat.

Bowling: Roberts 8–0–47–0; Holding 7–0–39–0; Marshall 8–1–34–1; Croft 8–0–41–1; King 8–0–31–1.

West Indians

D. L. Haynes c E. W. Jones b Moseley	.. 71	M. D. Marshall not out	 0
S. F. A. Bacchus c Miandad b Holmes	.. 79		
I. V. A. Richards b Holmes	 19	B 5, l-b 2, w 6, n-b 2	 15
A. I. Kallicharran c Lloyd b Moseley	 2		
*C. H. Lloyd c Ontong b Holmes	 10	1/157 2/157 3/167 (5 wkts, 32.5 overs) 211	
C. L. King not out	 15	4/184 5/207	

†D. L. Murray, A. M. E. Roberts, M. A. Holding and C. E. H. Croft did not bat.

Bowling: Moseley 6.5–0–28–2; Cordle 6–0–26–0; Lloyd 7–0–40–0; Ontong 5–0–40–0; Miandad 3–0–21–0; Holmes 5–0–41–3.

Umpires: H. D. Bird and R. S. Herman.

GLOUCESTERSHIRE v WEST INDIES

At Bristol, July 2, 3, 4. West Indians won by 58 runs. Gloucestershire had the distinction of being the first side to dismiss the touring team twice. Yet the power of the West Indians' fast bowlers eventually proved decisive, and Garner not only took six wickets but also scored his maiden century. This came on the first day when the West Indians declined from 92 for three to 100 for eight against splendid bowling, on a helpful pitch, from Procter and Wilkins, the latter having a spell of three wickets in eight deliveries. Garner, using his great reach to good effect when defending, lofted the ball to untenanted areas of the outfield when he did attack. When Murray's shrewd innings ended at 229 Garner still needed 32 runs for his century; Holding provided noble support until he reached his hundred which contained three 6s and ten 4s. Sadiq called on his vast experience against the world's best fast bowlers to help Gloucestershire recover from 66 for six. He stayed three hours for his 76, Graveney chipping in with a determined half-century after helping to add 75 for the seventh wicket. Futile attempts to hit Graveney out of the ground hastened the end of the West Indians' second innings, but they seemed confident there were enough runs for a victory. Gloucestershire needed a major innings from Zaheer or Procter in order to reach their target of 257 in even time. Both started well but were dismissed just as they looked threatening; the middle order was swept aside and it took some brave hitting by Wilkins to delay the end.

West Indians

C. G. Greenidge c Zaheer b Wilkins	 42	– c Hignell b Brain 4
D. L. Haynes c and b Procter	 12	– b Bainbridge 32
S. F. A. Bacchus c Brassington b Brain	 9	– c Brassington b Broad 69
A. I. Kallicharran b Wilkins	 15	– b Wilkins 5
*C. H. Lloyd lbw b Procter	 10	– (11) c Brassington b Graveney... 0
C. L. King lbw b Procter	 0	– (5) lbw b Wilkins 2
†D. L. Murray c Procter b Brain	 64	– (6) b Broad 24
D. R. Parry lbw b Wilkins	 0	– (10) not out 1
A. M. E. Roberts c Hignell b Wilkins	 0	– (7) c Bainbridge b Graveney ... 3
J. Garner c Broad b Graveney	 104	– (8) c Procter b Graveney 0
M. A. Holding not out	 10	– (9) st Brassington b Graveney ... 6
L-b 6, n-b 6	 12	B 1, l-b 6, w 1, n-b 7 15

1/20 2/59 3/70 4/92 5/92 6/100	278
7/100 8/100 9/229	

1/8 2/69 3/76 4/78 5/139	161
6/144 7/144 8/156 9/160	

Bowling: *First Innings*—Brain 25–3–95–2; Procter 18–4–51–3; Wilkins 19–5–51–4; Bainbridge 6–2–11–0; Graveney 18.1–4–43–1; Sadiq 1–0–15–0. *Second Innings*—Brain 10–0–52–1; Procter 8–1–23–0; Wilkins 9–3–20–2; Bainbridge 7–2–25–1; Graveney 8.4–3–12–4; Broad 8–4–14–2.

Gloucestershire

B. C. Broad lbw b Roberts	2	– c Murray b Roberts	4
Sadiq Mohammad c and b King	76	– b Garner	27
Zaheer Abbas c King b Holding	0	– c Haynes b Holding	33
A. W. Stovold c Murray b Holding	7	– b Roberts	25
*M. J. Procter b Garner	7	– lbw b Roberts	28
A. J. Hignell c Greenidge b Roberts	2	– lbw b Holding	1
P. Bainbridge lbw b Garner	0	– b Holding	1
D. A. Graveney c Bacchus b King	50	– not out	15
A. H. Wilkins b King	6	– c Murray b Garner	44
†A. J. Brassington not out	8	– b Garner	0
B. M. Brain c Greenidge b King	0	– c Greenidge b Garner	12
B 8, l-b 5, w 11, n-b 1	25	B 4, l-b 3, w 1	8

1/12 2/13 3/29 4/62 5/65 6/66   183   1/46 2/71 3/112 4/113 5/119   198
7/141 8/165 9/183   6/121 7/180 8/180 9/198

Bowling: *First Innings*—Roberts 17–4–41–2; Holding 16–5–37–2; Garner 13–6–34–2; King 15–3–46–4. *Second Innings*—Roberts 11–0–44–3; Holding 17–5–55–3; Garner 14.1–5–31–4; Parry 17–1–60–0.

Umpires: R. Aspinall and D. G. L. Evans.

SOMERSET v WEST INDIANS

At Taunton, July 5, 6, 7. Drawn. In good weather, West Indians made a productive but not entirely convincing start on a pitch which showed some early wear, giving uneven bounce. Richards then played a masterly innings on his home ground, reaching 50 in 41 minutes and 100 in 118 minutes with five 6s and eleven 4s. After a slow, watchful start Lloyd also opened out entertainingly, taking 157 minutes to score his century, with four 6s and thirteen 4s, before West Indians declared at their overnight total. On a dull overcast day, play was reduced by rain and bad light to a total of one hundred and ten minutes in two spells. Croft was especially menacing and Gavaskar was laid low by a painful blow in the groin from Marshall; but he and Rose (six 4s) survived profitably. Rain prevented play on the final day.

West Indians

D. L. Haynes b Marks	53	†D. A. Murray c Gard b Dredge	20
C. G. Greenidge c Gard b Moseley	38	D. R. Parry not out	2
S. F. A. Bacchus c Marks b Dredge	46	M. D. Marshall not out	2
I. V. A. Richards c Roebuck b Popplewell	103	B 8, l-b 13, n-b 4	25
*C. H. Lloyd c Moseley b Marks	102		
C. L. King c Rose b Popplewell	9		

1/60 2/122 3/215   (7 wkts dec.) 400
4/278 5/308 6/391 7/397

A. M. E. Roberts and C. E. H. Croft did not bat.

Bowling: Moseley 22–4–71–1; Gore 21–3–90–0; Dredge 26–4–84–2; Marks 30–4–97–2; Popplewell 9–3–33–2.

Somerset

*B. C. Rose not out	41
S. M. Gavaskar not out	22
B 4, l-b 1, n-b 9	14

(no wkt) 77

P. M. Roebuck, P. W. Denning, V. J. Marks, P. A. Slocombe, N. F. M. Popplewell, C. H. Dredge, †T. Gard, H. R. Moseley and H. I. E. Gore did not bat.

Bowling: Roberts 9–3–24–0; Croft 8–3–18–0; Marshall 7–2–21–0.

Umpires: R. Julian and P. B. Wight.

ENGLAND v WEST INDIES

Third Cornhill Test

At Manchester, July 10, 11, 12, 14, 15. Drawn. More than ten and a half hours lost to bad light and rain, as well as determined batting in England's second innings, combined to produce the first post-war drawn Test against West Indies at Old Trafford. Had Willey not been missed at slip by Greenidge when 13, West Indies might have taken an unassailable lead in the series.

England dropped the two Kent batsmen Tavaré and Woolmer and replaced them with Rose and Larkins as an attacking move, while West Indies preferred Marshall to Croft in their fast bowling ranks. Rose, the Somerset captain, was thus playing under his county vice-captain Botham, the first such occurrence since, in Australia in 1936-37, G. O. B. Allen of Middlesex took the field behind R. W. V. Robins.

West Indies captain Lloyd, who enjoyed the personal triumph of making his thirteenth Test hundred on his home county ground, caused a ripple of surprise by putting England in to bat on an overcast, chilly first morning. The pitch looked to be an excellent one for batting but, by 3.52 p.m., Lloyd's decision had been fully justified. England had been bowled out for 150. Their collapse, from 126 for three, was triggered off by the departure of Gatting to Marshall. Before then, he and Rose had advanced the score by 91 in just over an hour and a half, the much-vaunted West Indies pace attack being temporarily mastered.

England lost their last seven wickets for 24 in fifty-two minutes to record their lowest home total since West Indies destroyed A. W. Greig's side for 71 and 126 on the same ground during their victorious 1976 tour. Marshall was the main force behind the decline, taking three wickets in fourteen balls including that of Rose, who had kept to his pre-match pledge of attacking the fast bowlers and made a splendidly aggressive 70. England's disappointment at surrendering a potentially commanding position was not reflected in the field, and when bad light accounted for the last ninety minutes of play West Indies were 38 for three.

The brilliant Richards, responsible for all but 6 of these runs, continued a remarkable, vendetta-like attack on Willis next morning. But a miscalculation of Botham's line cost him his wicket for a magnificent 65 when a second successive Test hundred appeared to be comfortably within his grasp. Richards's thrilling stroke-play was reserved almost exclusively for Willis, England's main strike bowler, off whom he collected 53 of his runs. Only three hours twelve minutes play was possible on the second day, when West Indies took their lead to 69 and Lloyd passed 5,000 Test runs to stand alongside Sobers and Kanhai as the only other West Indians to have achieved the distinction. For England the 21-year-old Dilley bowled with speed, heart and determination in only his third Test.

Lloyd had to wait until Monday for the hundred he fervently wanted on his last Test appearance at Old Trafford. Saturday's play again fell victim to the weather, the umpires abandoning all hope of any play at 4.45 p.m. following six inspections. On Monday Lloyd duly collected the 21 he needed for his hundred before West Indies' innings was wound up for 260 by the off-spin of Emburey, who picked up the last three wickets for 10 in 27 balls.

Facing a deficit of 110 in their second innings, England needed a rapid 350 to stand any possible chance of victory. But a slow over-rate and the limited scoring opportunities presented by the battery of West Indian fast bowlers were against such an ambitious prospect. In the event, England took a lead of 91 into the final day, Boycott showing typical steadiness with 81 not out. He had added only 5 on the last morning when Holding won an lbw verdict against him.

At 290 for six soon after lunch, England were edging towards defeat, 180 ahead with about three and a quarter hours of the match left. But Willey held on splendidly and received valuable support from Emburey. Although the final overs of Willey's innings were played out against the less regular bowlers, the first hour and a half of it was fashioned under considerable pressure, even allowing for the absence from most of the last day of Roberts, who was suffering from a back injury.

Lloyd took the £350 Man of the Match award. The total attendance was 57,426 and receipts were £170,000. – D.F.

England

G. Boycott c Garner b Roberts	5	– (2) lbw b Holding	86
G. A. Gooch lbw b Roberts	2	– (1) c Murray b Marshall	26
B. C. Rose b Marshall	70	– c Kallicharran b Holding	32
W. Larkins lbw b Garner	11	– c Murray b Marshall	33
M. W. Gatting c Richards b Marshall	33	– c Kallicharran b Garner	56
*I. T. Botham c Murray b Garner	8	– lbw b Holding	35
P. Willey b Marshall	0	– not out	62
†A. P. E. Knott run out	2	– c and b Garner	6
J. E. Emburey c Murray b Roberts	3	– not out	28
G. R. Dilley b Garner	0		
R. G. D. Willis not out	5		
L-b 4, w 3, n-b 4	11	B 5, l-b 8, w 1, n-b 13	27

1/3 2/18 3/35 4/126 5/131 6/132   150   1/32 2/86 3/181 4/217   (7 wkts) 391
7/142 8/142 9/142   5/290 6/290 7/309

Bowling: *First Innings*—Roberts 11.2–3–23–3; Holding 14–2–46–0; Garner 11–2–34–3; Marshall 12–5–36–3. *Second Innings*—Roberts 14–2–36–0; Holding 34–8–100–3; Garner 40–11–73–2; Marshall 35–5–116–2; Richards 16–6–31–0; Lloyd 1–0–1–0; Bacchus 1–0–3–0; Haynes 1–0–2–0; Kallicharran 1–0–2–0.

West Indies

C. G. Greenidge c Larkins b Dilley	0	A. M. E. Roberts c Knott b Emburey	11
D. L. Haynes c Knott b Willis	1	J. Garner lbw b Emburey	0
I. V. A. Richards b Botham	65	M. A. Holding not out	4
S. F. A. Bacchus c Botham b Dilley	0		
A. I. Kallicharran c Knott b Botham	13	B 2, l-b 13, w 3, n-b 12	30
*C. H. Lloyd c Gooch b Emburey	101		
†D. L. Murray b Botham	17	1/4 2/25 3/25 4/67 5/100	260
M. D. Marshall c Gooch b Dilley	18	6/154 7/209 8/250 9/250	

Bowling: Willis 14–1–99–1; Dilley 28–7–47–3; Botham 20–6–64–3; Emburey 10.3–1–20–3.

Umpires: H. D. Bird and K. E. Palmer.

SCOTLAND v WEST INDIANS

At Broughty Ferry, July 18. West Indians won by 80 runs. A 50-overs match was played after the scheduled two-day fixture was abandoned with only fifty-five minutes of play possible the previous day. Before the rain intervened on the 17th, Greenidge (34) and Haynes (31) had taken the West Indians to 70 for no wicket.

West Indians

C. G. Greenidge c Swan b Clark	5	M. D. Marshall c Warner b Robertson	11
D. L. Haynes st Steele b Clark	5	D. L. Murray not out	9
S. F. A. Bacchus c Bell b Robertson	11	C. E. H. Croft st Steele b Donald	3
A. I. Kallicharran b Donald	55	L-b 4, b 3	7
C. L. King c Swan b Clark	9		
†D. A. Murray run out	49	1/7 2/22 3/22 4/31 (47.4 overs)	233
*I. V. A. Richards c Hayes b Donald	69	5/112 6/120 7/210	
D. R. Parry c Steele b Donald	2	8/211 9/230	

Bowling: Robertson 12–0–42–2; Clark 7–1–33–3; Johnston 6–0–34–0; Donald 16.4–1–78–4; Moir 6–0–39–0.

Scotland

*R. G. Swan b Croft	3	D. G. Moir b Parry	19
S. K. Dharsi c D. A. Murray b King	24	†A. Steele not out	0
D. L. Bell b King	6		
D. L. Hays b Parry	17		
C. J. Warner not out	57	B 4, n-b 2	6
W. A. Donald c D. A. Murray b Parry	15		
H. G. F. Johnston c Haynes b D. L. Murray.	6	1/5 2/21 3/44 (7 wkts, 50 overs) 153 4/56 5/116 6/125 7/150	

F. Robertson and J. Clark did not bat.

Bowling: Croft 6–1–10–1; Marshall 4–2–3–0; King 10–4–23–2; Parry 19–1–64–3; Richards 8–1–33–0; D. L. Murray 3–0–14–1.

Umpires: G. Cormack and T. Bertram.

YORKSHIRE v WEST INDIES

At Leeds, July 19, 20, 21. West Indians won by 58 runs. A virtual second-team Yorkshire attack was slaughtered by the tourists, with Bacchus becoming the highest West Indian scorer in an innings against the county. Yorkshire struggled for their runs, even though the West Indians were without Marshall, who was ill, and then Croft, who had a headache. Two declarations set up an interesting last day but, with Croft back in action, the Yorkshire batsmen were always under fierce pressure. Hartley and Love made 61 in 50 minutes of cheerful defiance, but there was no real threat to the West Indians' superiority.

West Indians

C. G. Greenidge c Whiteley b Ramage	26		
D. L. Haynes c Love b Athey	47	– (1) not out	69
S. F. A. Bacchus not out	164	– (2) c Bairstow b Cooper	25
A. I. Kallicharran c Bairstow b Hartley	90		
C. L. King (did not bat)	–	(3) not out	23
B 6, l-b 8, n-b 1	15	L-b 2	2

1/42 2/131 3/342   (3 wkts dec.) 342   1/46   (1 wkt dec.) 119

*C. H. Lloyd, †D. L. Murray, D. R. Parry, M. D. Marshall, M. A. Holding and C. E. H. Croft did not bat.

Bowling: *First Innings*—Ramage 23–0–106–1; Cooper 29–8–68–0; Hartley 8.4–1–38–1; Boycott 5–1–6–0; Athey 3–0–13–1; Carrick 22–5–78–0; Whiteley 8–2–18–0. *Second Innings*—Cooper 8–0–42–1; Ramage 7–0–24–0; Carrick 6.2–1–27–0; Whiteley 8–0–24–0.

Yorkshire

G. Boycott b Parry	53	– c Bacchus b Holding	4
R. G. Lumb lbw b Croft	10	– lbw b Holding	54
C. W. J. Athey c Bacchus b Holding	19	– c Haynes b Croft	9
*J. H. Hampshire c Murray b Parry	8	– c Bacchus b King	19
J. D. Love not out	55	– c Greenidge b Croft	37
S. N. Hartley c and b Parry	13	– c Murray b Croft	51
P. Carrick not out	21	– c sub b Croft	4
†D. L. Bairstow (did not bat)	–	c Murray b Croft	2
A. Ramage (did not bat)	–	not out	14
J. P. Whiteley (did not bat)	–	lbw b Croft	1
H. P. Cooper (did not bat)	–	b Parry	1
B 6, l-b 5, n-b 4	15	B 1, l-b 5, w 2, n-b 5	13

1/33 2/66 3/94 4/111   (5 wkts dec.) 194   1/14 2/23 3/61 4/99 5/160   209
5/151   6/170 7/181 8/206 9/208

Bowling: *First Innings*—Holding 12–3–35–1; Croft 13.3–3–35–1; King 26–9–75–0; Parry 23.3–10–34–3. *Second Innings*—Holding 22–3–62–2; Croft 22–3–80–6; King 6–2–22–1; Parry 9.1–2–32–1.

Umpires: C. T. Spencer and R. Palmer.

ENGLAND v WEST INDIES

Fourth Cornhill Test

At The Oval, July 24, 25, 26, 28, 29. Drawn. Considering a complete day was lost to the weather, that only 29 wickets fell, and that West Indies averaged 12.3 overs an hour, the fourth Test was a much better match than it might have been. Its main features were Gooch's tremendous attacking 83 which inspired England's best batting of the summer, a West Indian collapse that put them in momentary danger of a follow-on, and an unbroken last-wicket stand of 117 between Willey and Willis that saved England from defeat.

How England came to be 92 for nine in their second innings after making 370 in the first is something that requires no explanation to anyone familiar with the brittleness of their batting, or with the potency of Holding, Croft and Garner. When Willey and Willis came together a West Indian victory looked likely with England only 197 ahead and with three and a half hours left. Yet they played with exemplary coolness and courage, and after a surprisingly short time showed no sign of being parted.

West Indies were badly handicapped by injuries to Croft and Garner, but Holding and Marshall were still relatively fresh when the ninth wicket fell twenty-five minutes after lunch. Willis's 24 not out equalled his highest score in 80 innings for England and followed a sequence of ten innings in which he had only once reached double figures. Sadly, because of his lost bowling form, it proved to be his last Test innings of the season.

For all that was owed to the ungainly effectiveness of Willis's lunging forward stroke, it was to Willey that England were mainly indebted for survival. Ironically, he would not even have been playing had Greenidge caught him at 13 in the Old Trafford Test a fortnight earlier – an escape which enabled him to add 62 not out to an aggregate of 90 in his ten previous innings for England. It was to his reputation as a fighter that Willey owed his continued presence in the side, and at The Oval he justified the selectors' faith in him. Arriving at 67 for six, thirty-five minutes before lunch, he showed the full face of the bat to the West Indian fast bowlers from the moment he came in. He held concentration and resolve as Botham, Knott and Dilley were briskly swept aside, resourcefully protected Willis from the strike and, when the West Indian effort faded, availed himself of a well-deserved first hundred.

England were unchanged from the side which drew at Old Trafford, with Old again twelfth man, while West Indies brought in Croft for Roberts, whose back was still not better. It proved an unlucky match for West Indies with injuries for, as well as the loss of Croft and Garner for part of England's second innings, Lloyd badly tore a hamstring chasing a leg-side hit by Emburey. Lloyd would have batted with a runner had West Indies needed him to save the follow-on, having been hastily summoned from the tourists' hotel during their collapse, but in practice he took no further part in this Test nor the fifth.

Botham won the toss for the third time in four Tests and Gooch and Boycott launched an England innings which, but for the funereal over-rate, would have been recognised for its enterprise as much as its effectiveness. It began unpromisingly when Croft, attacking Boycott round the wicket, worked a bouncer through his guard. Although Boycott took some of the weight off the ball with a forearm, it cannoned hard enough into the visor of his helmet to draw blood from his right eyebrow, and to blacken both eyes for the remainder of the match. Rose, who took his place with the score at 9, began uncertainly, but Gooch hooked, drove and cut with the authority of his century at Lord's, and his confidence was infectious.

Rose was soon straight-driving and scoring off his legs with equal assurance, and the innings was in only its 44th over when Gooch missed a back-foot stroke at Holding and was lbw for a majestic 83 after he had hammered Croft for 13 in one over. Rose was bowled by Croft at once, but Boycott, returning at the fall of Gooch's wicket, helped Gatting take England to 236 for three at close of play. On the second day Boycott was brilliantly run out by Greenidge from mid-on, and Gatting was bowled by Croft in the over before lunch. In the afternoon, Willey and Emburey batted sensibly and it was not till after tea that the innings ended. In ten and a quarter hours, West Indies had bowled only 129 overs, all but three by the fast bowlers.

After another blank Saturday, a great gulley catch by Willey gave Botham the pleasure of claiming Richards as his 150th wicket in his 29th Test. With Dilley at his fastest, West Indies collapsed to 105 for five, but Bacchus played his best innings of the series and, with confident help from Marshall, the follow-on was avoided before Garner and Croft added 64 for the eighth wicket. Even so, West Indies, 105 behind with seven hours twenty minutes left, were 100 to one with the bookmakers, Ladbrokes, before Holding and Croft cut England down to 20 for four in eighty minutes before the close.

Next day they looked like pulling off an extraordinary victory until the Willey-Willis stand. West Indies' last chance went when they had been together for forty minutes, Greenidge missing Willis low at second slip when England's lead was 216 with three hours left for play.

The official attendance was 49,287; takings were £236,000. – J.D.T.

England

G. A. Gooch lbw b Holding	83	– lbw b Holding	0
G. Boycott run out	53	– c Murray b Croft	5
B. C. Rose b Croft	50	– lbw b Garner	41
W. Larkins lbw b Garner	7	– b Holding	0
M. W. Gatting b Croft	48	– (6) c Murray b Garner	15
P. Willey c Lloyd b Holding	34	– (8) not out	100
†A. P. E. Knott c Lloyd b Marshall	3	– (9) lbw b Holding	3
*I. T. Botham lbw b Croft	9	– (7) c Greenidge b Garner	4
J. E. Emburey c Holding b Marshall	24	– (5) c Bacchus b Croft	2
G. R. Dilley b Garner	1	– c sub b Holding	1
R. G. D. Willis not out	1	– not out	24
B 7, l-b 21, w 10, n-b 19	57	L-b 6, w 1, n-b 7	14

1/155 2/157 3/182 4/269 5/303   370   1/2 2/10 3/13   (9 wkts dec.) 209
6/312 7/336 8/343 9/368   4/18 5/63 6/67 7/73
                               8/84 9/92

Bowling: *First Innings*—Holding 28–5–67–2; Croft 35–9–97–3; Marshall 29.3–6–77–2; Garner 33–8–67–2; Richards 3–1–5–0. *Second Innings*—Holding 29–7–79–4; Croft 10–6–8–2; Marshall 23–7–47–0; Garner 17–5–24–3; Richards 9–3–15–0; Kallicharran 6–1–22–0.

West Indies

C. G. Greenidge lbw b Willis	6	M. A. Holding lbw b Dilley	22
D. L. Haynes c Gooch b Dilley	7	C. E. H. Croft not out	0
I. V. A. Richards c Willey b Botham	26	*C. H. Lloyd absent hurt	0
S. F. A. Bacchus c Knott b Emburey	61		
A. I. Kallicharran c Rose b Dilley	11	L-b 12, w 1, n-b 28	41
†D. L. Murray hit wkt b Dilley	0		
M. D. Marshall c Rose b Emburey	45	1/15 2/34 3/72 4/99 5/105	265
J. Garner c Gatting b Botham	46	6/187 7/197 8/261 9/265	

Bowling: Willis 19–5–58–1; Dilley 23–6–57–4; Botham 18.2–8–47–2; Emburey 23–12–38–2; Gooch 1–0–2–0; Willey 11–5–22–0.

Umpires: B. J. Meyer and D. O. Os!ear.

MINOR COUNTIES v WEST INDIANS

At Jesmond, July 31, August 1. Drawn. A mid-afternoon storm on the second day washed out a match in which 21-year-old Timur Mohamed, called up from Suffolk by the injury-hit West Indians, upstaged their Test players. After Minor Counties had made a promising start, with Yeabsley taking two quick wickets, left-handers Timur Mohamed (one 6 and fourteen 4s) and Kallicharran put on 230 for the third wicket in 147 minutes, each scoring a century before Kippax removed them both with consecutive balls. The leg-spinner was denied a hat-trick by Richards, whose cameo innings ended when he in turn lost his wicket to Kippax. From an overnight score of 124 for three, Minor Counties were dismissed 181 behind, despite an excellent knock by Tolchard. The West Indians did not enforce the follow-on and batted into the afternoon when they declared, setting a target of 284 in three hours. Then came the rain to ruin what might have been an interesting finish.

West Indians

D. L. Haynes c Gill b Yeabsley	15	– (5) not out	5
S. F. A. Bacchus c Collyer b Yeabsley	7	– (4) st Collyer b Allin	8
Timur Mohamed c Gill b Kippax	119		
A. I. Kallicharran c Allin b Kippax	109		
C. L. King lbw b Greensword	9	– (3) c Greensword b Kippax	31
*I. V. A. Richards b Kippax	33		
†D. A. Murray not out	50		
D. R. Parry c Collyer b Collins	25	– (1) not out	54
M. D. Marshall (did not bat)		– (2) b Collins	1
B 8, l-b 3, w 4, n-b 1	16	L-b 4, w 1	5

1/10 2/36 3/266 4/266   (7 wkts dec.) 383   1/12 2/76 3/85   (3 wkts dec.) 104
5/276 6/318 7/383

D. L. Murray and M. A. Holding did not bat.

Bowling: *First Innings*—Collins 17.2–3–75–1; Yeabsley 14–2–44–2; Greensword 17–2–67–1; Kippax 16–2–97–3; Bailey 11–0–50–0; Allin 5–0–34–0. *Second Innings*—Collins 6–0–38–1; Yeabsley 5–0–28–0; Allin 3.1–0–16–1; Kippax 3–0–17–1.

Minor Counties

J. S. Johnson c Richards b Parry	30	– not out	0
J. G. Tolchard c Mohamed b Parry	86	– not out	0
P. N. Gill c D. A. Murray b King	1		
*D. Bailey lbw b King	9		
S. Greensword c Mohamed b Parry	32		
P. J. Kippax c Bacchus b Parry	8		
S. G. Plumb c D. L. Murray b Richards	15		
†F. E. Collyer st D. A. Murray b Richards	5		
B. J. Collins c King b Parry	6		
D. I. Yeabsley not out	3		
A. W. Allin st D. A. Murray b Richards	1		
B 8	8		

1/43 2/48 3/64 4/135 5/163 6/188   204   (no wkt) 0
7/194 8/194 9/200

Bowling: *First Innings*—Holding 3–0–15–0; Marshall 3–2–6–0; Parry 32–8–88–5; King 17–5–31–2; D. L. Murray 8–1–39–0; Richards 15.2–7–17–3. *Second Innings*—Holding 0.2–0–0–0.

Umpires: R. H. Duckett and P. J. Eele.

WARWICKSHIRE v WEST INDIANS

At Birmingham, August 2, 3, 4. Drawn. Warwickshire, without Amiss, became only the fourth county to avoid defeat by the touring team, after declining to go for a target of 320 in 255 minutes. Play ended fifty minutes early on the first day with the county at 11 without loss in reply to the West Indians' 315, of which Kallicharran and Richards added 125 for the fifth wicket. Warwickshire began shakily on the Sunday, losing three early wickets before Humpage and Oliver punished an under-strength attack in a robust stand of 118 off nineteen overs. Ferreira added 30, but the early momentum was not maintained and the innings closed 92 behind. The West Indians had increased their lead to 158 at the start of the last day and Richards made a spectacular 41 which included three 6s and five 4s; in seven consecutive balls from Clifford he hit 4–6–6–4–4–6–4. Smith later countered with a solid 86, hitting one 6 and twelve 4s.

West Indians

D. L. Haynes c Smith b Oliver	62	– lbw b Ferreira	20
S. F. A. Bacchus c Humpage b Small	25	– b Small	1
Timur Mohamed c Willis b Ferreira	2	– c Humpage b Small	45
C. L. King b Ferreira	4	– c Lloyd b Willis	3
A. I. Kallicharran c Humpage b Ferreira	75	– (6) lbw b Doshi	38
*I. V. A. Richards c Oliver b Small	62	– (7) st Humpage b Doshi	41
†D. L. Murray lbw b Willis	30	– (9) not out	10
D. A. Murray c and b Doshi	3	– (5) b Clifford	49
D. R. Parry run out	9	– (8) not out	5
M. D. Marshall not out	32		
A. M. E. Roberts lbw b Willis	0		
B 1, l-b 5, w 1, n-b 4	11	B 3, l-b 6, w 1, n-b 5	15

1/43 2/64 3/93 4/105 5/230 6/241   315   1/8 2/42 3/66   (7 wkts dec.) 227
7/247 8/264 9/315   4/105 5/171 6/171 7/214

Bowling: *First Innings*—Willis 11–4–37–2; Small 13–3–55–2; Ferreira 18–6–50–3; Oliver 5–0–24–1; Clifford 22–6–60–0; Doshi 31–9–78–1. *Second Innings*—Willis 9–1–25–1; Small 14–5–36–2; Ferreira 9–1–42–1; Doshi 19–4–65–2; Clifford 11–2–44–1.

Warwickshire

K. D. Smith b King	25	– c D. A. Murray b Richards	86
T. A. Lloyd b Roberts	2	– retired hurt	24
J. A. Claughton retired hurt	9		
†G. W. Humpage c D. A. Murray b Roberts	62	– (3) c D. L. Murray b Marshall	0
J. Whitehouse lbw b Marshall	4	– (4) c sub b Parry	3
P. R. Oliver b Parry	57	– (5) not out	35
A. M. Ferreira lbw b Marshall	30	– (6) not out	25
G. C. Small c D. A. Murray b Parry	1		
*R. G. D. Willis b Marshall	5		
D. R. Doshi st D. L. Murray b Parry	3		
C. C. Clifford not out	0		
B 6, l-b 7, w 4, n-b 8	25	B 1, l-b 1, w 1, n-b 4	7

1/13 2/42 3/51 4/184 5/190 6/211   223   1/43 2/67 3/133   (3 wkts) 180
7/216 8/221 9/223

Bowling: *First Innings*—Roberts 16–5–45–2; Marshall 16–5–29–3; King 15–4–59–1; Parry 17.2–5–54–3; Richards 3–1–11–0. *Second Innings*—Roberts 4–3–4–0; Marshall 11–5–19–1; King 11–1–34–0; Parry 29–8–70–1; Richards 14–3–37–1; D. A. Murray 1–0–1–0; Bacchus 1–0–8–0.

Umpires: D. J. Halfyard and A. Jepson.

ENGLAND v WEST INDIES

Fifth Cornhill Test

At Leeds, August 7, 8, 9, 11, 12. Drawn. The weather ruined the Headingley Test for the third successive year, no play at all being possible on the first and fourth days. After two virtually unbroken days of rain on the Wednesday and Thursday had created a series of small lakes on the playing area, the umpires' decision to abandon play for the day on Thursday was put over the public address system at 10.30 a.m. It was a tribute to the ground staff that play started as early as 2.45 p.m. on Friday. Richards, leading West Indies in the absence of the injured Clive Lloyd, put England in; they had thus batted first in all five matches in the series.

In less than three and a half hours England were dismissed for 143, the lowest total of the series. Although Bairstow, preferred to Knott, hit a valiant 40 at number eight, and there was an aggressive but brief innings from Botham, the rest of England's batting was inadequate.

For West Indies, the twenty-four hours delay was a boon. It allowed Croft, out since the fourth Test with damaged thigh muscles, and Garner, who had strained his bowling shoulder, time to get back into action. So worried was West Indies manager Walcott at the state of his fast bowling that on the eve of the match he made vain attempts to bring in Wayne Daniel of Middlesex and Sylvester Clarke of Surrey. However, the only change from the eleven which played at The Oval was King for Lloyd.

On the third day, thick grey cloud hung sullenly over the ground from start to stumps, creating an atmosphere straight out of *Wuthering Heights*. The England attack, spearheaded by Dilley, strove hard to turn the conditions to advantage, but the West Indian batsmen fought for survival. Greenidge and Haynes gave their side a superb start with a partnership of 83, the best opening stand of the series by West Indies. Haynes's 42 earned him the Man of the Match award on the grounds that he made his runs when conditions were at their most difficult and especially strange to him. The last-wicket partnership of 38 between Holding and Croft was the second best of the innings.

As West Indies inched towards a total of 245, Rose had to retire with a pulled thigh muscle, suffered when turning suddenly on the wet and heavy outfield, and Botham chipped a bone at the base of his right hand, attempting a slip catch. Other than Dilley, with four for 79, no bowler impressed. When England batted a second time, Boycott and Gooch survived until bad light brought Saturday's play to a premature end.

The game still remained very much alive, but a miserable day on Monday brought another abandonment, at 2.00 p.m., and destroyed any hope England might still have had of winning the match and thus saving the series. Although a full day's play was possible on Tuesday, there could now be only two results – a West Indian victory or a draw. When England's fifth wicket fell before tea with only 72 runs separating the sides the former was still a possibility. But Rose, batting with Gooch as his runner, dispatched Croft for three boundaries in one over just before tea to ease the pressure. In the final session of the match Holding soon had Willey caught at the wicket, but Bairstow stayed with Rose and before long West Indies acknowledged that they would have to take the series by their two-wicket victory in the first Test at Trent Bridge.

Garner was able to bowl only one over in England's second innings before his shoulder failed him again, but his 26 wickets at 14.26 won him the Man of the Series award from John Arlott who was covering his last Headingley Test.

The official attendance was 32,860 and receipts for the match totalled £141,000, at least £30,000 below the expected minimum. Final takings for the five Tests thus failed by £7,000 to reach the £1 million mark but, with nearly seven full playing days out of 25 sacrificed to the unpredictable climate, total receipts of £993,000 reflect the remarkable degree of interest shown in this clash for the Wisden Trophy, which England last won in 1969. – B.E.

England

G. A. Gooch c Marshall b Garner	14	– lbw b Marshall	55
G. Boycott c Kallicharran b Holding	4	– c Kallicharran b Croft	47
B. C. Rose b Croft	7	– (5) not out	43
W. Larkins c Kallicharran b Garner	9	– (3) lbw b Marshall	30
M. W. Gatting c Marshall b Croft	1	– (4) lbw b Holding	1
*I. T. Botham c Richards b Holding	37	– lbw b Marshall	7
P. Willey c Murray b Croft	1	– c Murray b Holding	10
†D. L. Bairstow lbw b Marshall	40	– not out	9
J. E. Emburey not out	13		
C. M. Old c Garner b Marshall	6		
G. R. Dilley b Garner	0		
B 3, l-b 3, w 1, n-b 4	11	B 5, l-b 11, w 2, n-b 7	25

1/9 2/27 3/28 4/34 5/52 6/59   143   1/95 2/126 3/129   (6 wkts) 227
7/89 8/131 9/140   4/162 5/174 6/203

Bowling: *First Innings*—Holding 10–4–34–2; Croft 12–3–35–3; Garner 14–4–41–3; Marshall 11–3–22–2. *Second Innings*—Holding 23–2–62–2; Croft 19–2–65–1; Garner 1–0–1–0; Marshall 19–5–42–3; King 12–3–32–0; Richards 1–1–0–0.

West Indies

C. G. Greenidge lbw b Botham	34	J. Garner c Emburey b Gooch	0
D. L. Haynes b Emburey	42	M. A. Holding b Old	35
*I. V. A. Richards b Old	31	C. E. H. Croft not out	1
S. F. A. Bacchus c and b Dilley	11		
A. I. Kallicharran c Larkins b Dilley	37	B 2, l-b 9, w 3, n-b 14	28
C. L. King c Bairstow b Gooch	12		
†D. L. Murray c Emburey b Dilley	14	1/83 2/105 3/133 4/142 5/170	245
M. D. Marshall c Bairstow b Dilley	0	6/198 7/198 8/207 9/207	

Bowling: Dilley 23–6–79–4; Old 28.5–9–64–2; Botham 19–8–31–1; Emburey 6–0–25–1; Gooch 8–3–18–2.

Umpires: W. E. Alley and K. E. Palmer.

OLD ENGLAND v OLD AUSTRALIA

At The Oval, August 27, 1980. Australia's former Test cricketers maintained their country's statistical advantage over England when they defeated Old England by seven wickets in a 50-over match. The home team was the more experienced, boasting 724 England caps to 401 Australian, but Old Australia had youth on their side, being an aggregate of 96 years the junior. The match, played at the scene of the first Test match between the two countries in England, was a feature of the Centenary celebrations to commemorate 100 years of Test cricket in England.

Old England

J. H. Edrich c Redpath b Simpson	61	†J. M. Parks not out	5
P. E. Richardson b Corling	6		
*M. C. Cowdrey st Taber b Gleeson	44	L-b 6, w 3, n-b 1	10
K. F. Barrington c Harvey b Corling	45		
M. J. K. Smith b Simpson	3	1/12 2/87 3/119 (5 wkts, 50 overs)	230
B. L. D'Oliveira not out	56	4/127 5/197	

F. J. Titmus, F. S. Trueman, G. A. R. Lock, F. H. Tyson and †T. G. Evans did not bat.

Bowling: Connolly 10–2–37–0; Misson 2–0–3–0; Corling 9–1–29–2; Gleeson 10–0–42–1; Veivers 5–0–35–0; Simpson 5–0–22–2; Cowper 5–0–31–0; Stackpole 4–0–21–0.

Old Australia

*R. B. Simpson st Evans b Titmus	75
I. R. Redpath st Evans b Titmus	27
R. M. Cowper st Parks b Lock	35
K. R. Stackpole not out	57
R. N. Harvey not out	29
B 1, l-b 7	8

1/79 2/124   (3 wkts, 39.2 overs) 231
3/158

†B. N. Jarman, G. E. Corling, T. R. Veivers, A. N. Connolly, J. W. Gleeson, F. M. Misson and †H. B. Taber did not bat.

Bowling: Trueman 6–0–24–0; Tyson 5–0–31–0; Lock 10–0–66–1; Titmus 5–0–29–2; Barrington 7–0–41–0; D'Oliveira 6.2–0–32–0.

Umpires: C. S. Elliott and J. G. Langridge.

THE AUSTRALIANS IN ENGLAND, 1980

The reason for Australia's brief visit to England in August 1980 was to play a Centenary Test match. It was 100 years since the two countries had first met in England, and although the original match was played at The Oval on September 6, 7, 8, 1880, last year's celebration was held at Lord's.

With only three weeks' cricket before the Test match, in which to become accustomed to English conditions, and with their WSC players now back in the fold, the Australians relied heavily on experience. Of their fourteen players, ten had been to England before on full tours while Allan Border, Graeme Wood and Graham Yallop were all in the Australian party for the Prudential Cup in 1979. Only John Dyson, an opening batsman from New South Wales, had not already visited England with an official Australian team.

By the end of the tour the only specialist bowler not to have passed the age of 30 was the orthodox left-arm spinner, Ray Bright. Although Dennis Lillee, who was 31, bowled beautifully, it was obvious that the Australian selectors would soon be searching for young bowling talent. Len Pascoe's five for 59 in the first innings at Lord's was in the best traditions, but the limitations of the Australian attack were revealed in the defeat by England, in the two limited-overs internationals, and by both Surrey and Nottinghamshire in two of their matches against the counties. With every English county except Yorkshire now reinforced by overseas players, these are no longer matches which touring sides are able to take in their stride. And, in spite of having played a good deal of it, limited-overs cricket is something at which the Australians have yet to excel. The weather, too, was against a side with little time to find its feet.

Yet Australia's performance in the match that mattered most, the Centenary Test, did them much credit. Whereas the occasion was memorable, the match itself was not; but for the disappointments on the field and the controversies which developed off it the Australian cricketers were blameless. They bowled, batted and fielded better than England, putting behind them the unconvincing form of their earlier matches.

Having won the toss, on an easy-paced pitch, Australia batted very well. Greg Chappell, on his second tour to England as Australia's captain and his fourth English tour in all, remains one of the best batsmen in the world and at 32 he still has a lot of runs left in him. Both Hughes and Wood scored Centenary hundreds, Hughes showing a flair that marked him as a new star in the Australian constellation, and the left-handed Wood batting with a doggedness that England first encountered when he scored 100 against them at Melbourne in 1978-79. As vice-captain of the party, Hughes had the look of Chappell's natural successor. After several low scores he ran into form in the first of the limited-overs internationals, making 73 not out after being dropped before he had scored. His other scores in the representative games were 98, 117 and 84.

As in Pakistan earlier in the year, the Australian batting averages were headed by Allan Border, a left-hander no more than 5ft 7in tall who shows an uncommon ability to accumulate large scores without compromising his attacking instincts. Comparisons have been made between Border and the great Australian batsman, Neil Harvey. Yallop, also a left-hander and, like Hughes, a former Test captain (during the WSC days), played in a much stronger Australian side against West Indies as long ago as 1975-76, and he is still only 28. He too, and also Bruce Laird, a much improved opening batsman since he was last in England in 1975, made the point at Lord's that Australia should not go short of runs in the immediate future.

The form of Jeff Thomson bore no comparison with his great days of the mid-1970s. He was left out of the Lord's match and was seldom sufficiently sure of the shoulder injury, which first set him back in 1976, to let fly with a throw-in from the deep. The two specialist spinners, Ashley Mallett and Bright, went short of wickets, and Border, who also bowls orthodox left-arm spin, was no more than plain. As a bowler at medium pace Chappell is inclined to underrate himself.

All the bowlers, except when Pascoe was finishing off England's first innings at Lord's, were overshadowed by Lillee. As in Australia in 1979-80, when he caused England such trouble, he was nothing like as fast as he used to be, but his wonderful control and ability to move the ball late more than compensated for this. Lillee showed in England last year that it is possible to be fiercely hostile without bowling either furiously fast or persistently short. With his classical action and strict attention to physical fitness he remains one of the most formidable of strike bowlers, and it was worth a visit to Lord's just to see him bowl. Rodney Marsh, the wicket-keeper, had also retained his fitness and enthusiasm remarkably successfully. He was at least two stones lighter than when in England last. The side was managed by Mr Phil Ridings, a former captain of South Australia, who was appointed Chairman of the Australian Cricket Board of Control in succession to Mr R. J. Parish soon after his return home.

AUSTRALIAN TOUR RESULTS

Test matches – Played 1: Drawn 1.

First-class matches – Played 5: Won 1, Lost 2, Drawn 2.

Win – Hampshire.

Losses – Nottinghamshire, Surrey.

Draws – England, Lancashire.

Non first-class matches – Played 3: Lost 2, Drawn 1. *Losses* – England (2). *Draw* – Young England.

FIRST-CLASS AVERAGES

BATTING

	Matches	Innings	Not Outs	Runs	Highest Inns	Average
A. R. Border	4	7	3	321	95	80.25
R. W. Marsh	5	7	4	172	56	57.33
G. S. Chappell	4	6	0	303	101	50.50
G. M. Wood	4	7	1	282	112	47.00
K. J. Hughes	5	9	1	249	117	31.12
B. M. Laird	5	9	1	240	85	30.00
D. K. Lillee	4	4	1	81	33	27.00
A. A. Mallett	4	3	1	49	30*	24.50
G. N. Yallop	5	7	1	108	45	18.00
J. Dyson	3	6	1	66	33	13.20
J. R. Thomson	3	4	0	42	33	10.50
L. S. Pascoe	4	3	1	8	6	4.00

Also batted: R. J. Bright 21; G. Dymock 37.

* *Signifies not out.*

BOWLING

	Overs	Maidens	Runs	Wickets	Average
D. K. Lillee	116.2	25	391	20	19.55
L. S. Pascoe	114.1	14	445	17	26.17
R. J. Bright	105.1	40	292	7	41.71
J. R. Thomson	68	15	265	6	44.16
A. A. Mallett	77.2	16	282	5	56.40

Also bowled: G. S. Chappell 16–4–51–2; G. Dymock 42–6–184–2.

FIELDING

R. W. Marsh 11, G. N. Yallop 5, G. S. Chappell 4, G. M. Wood 4, A. R. Border 3, K. J. Hughes 3, B. M. Laird 3, J. R. Thomson 3, R. J. Bright 1, L. S. Pascoe 1.

HUNDREDS FOR AUSTRALIANS

The following three three-figure innings were played for the Australians, all in first-class matches.

* *Signifies not out.*

G. S. Chappell (1)
   101   v Lancashire at Manchester.

K. J. Hughes (1)
   117   v England at Lord's (Centenary Test).

G. M. Wood (1)
   112   v England at Lord's (Centenary Test).

HUNDREDS AGAINST AUSTRALIANS

The following three three-figure innings were played against the Australians, two in first-class matches and one in a match not first-class.

* Signifies not out. † Not first-class.

G. Boycott (1)
128* for England at Lord's (Centenary Test).

G. A. Gooch (1)
108† for England at Birmingham.

F. C. Hayes (1)
102* for Lancashire at Manchester.

HAMPSHIRE v AUSTRALIANS

At Southampton, August 6, 7, 8. Australians won by ten wickets. The first match of their short tour provided the Australians with plenty of practice and left Chappell pleased with the form of his team. Lillee bowled with pace and control, backed up by some excellent slip catching, as the county were dismissed for 199, only Smith and Cowley batting with composure. Although Wood and Hughes went cheaply, Laird, Border and the magnificent Chappell batted with skill and enterprise as the touring team built a lead of 251. Hampshire showed more spirit in their second innings, with Turner and Pocock sharing a gritty stand of 90 for the fifth wicket before Pascoe broke through and an innings defeat seemed likely. However, Stephenson took the game into a fourth innings with a belligerent 65 from 37 balls.

Hampshire

C. L. Smith c Border b Lillee	79	– lbw b Lillee	10
T. M. Tremlett c Chappell b Lillee	0	– lbw b Pascoe	11
M. C. J. Nicholas c Yallop b Lillee	0	– c Marsh b Thomson	7
D. R. Turner c Hughes b Thomson	24	– c Border b Pascoe	69
*N. E. J. Pocock c Laird b Bright	5	– (6) b Pascoe	64
N. G. Cowley c Thomson b Bright	57	– (7) c Chappell b Pascoe	12
M. N. S. Taylor c Yallop b Pascoe	5	– (8) c Wood b Pascoe	0
S. F. Graf c Hughes b Bright	8	– (9) b Bright	18
†G. R. Stephenson c Wood b Thomson	0	– (10) c Yallop b Lillee	65
M. J. Bailey not out	6	– (5) run out	9
J. W. Southern lbw b Pascoe	1	– not out	0
B 1,l-b 4, n-b 9	14	B 4,l-b 8, w 1, n-b 5	18

1/1 2/1 3/69 4/87   199   1/22 2/24 3/50 4/77   283
5/139 6/163 7/185 8/187 9/193   5/167 6/196 7/196 8/197 9/277

Bowling: *First Innings*—Lillee 14–3–54–3; Pascoe 15.1–2–49–2; Thomson 15–3–45–2; Bright 12–6–20–3; Chappell 6–3–17–0. *Second Innings*—Lillee 14.4–3–38–2; Pascoe 22–4–94–5; Thomson 10–3–32–1; Bright 25–9–101–1.

Australians

B. M. Laird c Nicholas b Southern	85		
G. M. Wood c Nicholas b Tremlett	9	– (1) not out	25
K. J. Hughes c Pocock b Graf	0	– (2) not out	4
*G. S. Chappell b Southern	86		
G. N. Yallop b Southern	45		
A. R. Border b Tremlett	95		
†R. W. Marsh c Southern b Graf	20		
D. K. Lillee b Southern	33		
R. J. Bright b Southern	21		
J. R. Thomson b Southern	33		
L. S. Pascoe not out	1		
B 9, l-b 3, w 2, n-b 8	22	B 4	4

1/19 2/20 3/170 4/233   450   (no wkt) 33
5/282 6/359 7/361 8/410 9/443

Bowling: *First Innings*—Graf 18–3–73–2; Tremlett 18–5–57–2; Southern 40–14–109–6; Taylor 11–1–56–0; Bailey 14–2–40–0; Cowley 24–3–82–0; Smith 3–0–11–0. *Second Innings*—Nicholas 3.2–0–6–0; Turner 3–0–23–0.

Umpires: C. T. Spencer and T. W. Spencer.

SURREY v AUSTRALIANS

At The Oval, August 10, 11, 12. Surrey won by 59 runs. Surrey became the first county to defeat a touring side in 1980, as they beat the Australians for the first time since 1956, when Laker took all ten wickets in the first innings and Lock took seven in the second. After an initial slump Surrey were in command with Butcher (fifteen 4s) and Howarth putting on 123 for the third wicket. Butcher batted for one hundred and sixty minutes and hit his 1,500th run of the season. The bowlers, especially Thomson, were then treated with scant respect as Howarth and Roope took 76 runs off fifteen overs. Roope reached his half-century by despatching Mallett over square leg – the second 6 of his innings. Knight made the first of two Surrey declarations, which went some way towards answering Chappell's criticism of negative play in county cricket. The second of them, following a rain-affected second day, left the Australians to score 300 at roughly 1 a minute. With four wickets down for 43 they never looked likely to achieve that, or even to save the day. Marsh made 56 in 73 minutes, with two 6s and seven 4s, and there was some gritty resistance from Mallett and Dymock. However, the off-spin of Pocock proved to be the deciding factor and the end came with 7.3 overs remaining.

Surrey

A. R. Butcher b Chappell	88	– c Thomson b Lillee	13
G. S. Clinton c Marsh b Lillee	4	– c Marsh b Lillee	0
*R. D. V. Knight c Marsh b Lillee	0	– lbw b Dymock	32
G. P. Howarth c Chappell b Mallett	66	– c Marsh b Thomson	6
G. R. J. Roope c Yallop b Mallett	54	– not out	14
M. A. Lynch b Chappell	59	– not out	16
Intikhab Alam c Yallop b Thomson	14		
R. D. Jackman not out	32		
†C. J. Richards not out	1		
B 4, l-b 5, w 3, n-b 8	20	L-b 5, w 1	6

1/18 2/18 3/141   (7 wkts dec.) 338   1/1 2/29 3/51 4/59 (4 wkts dec.) 87
4/217 5/236 6/255 7/321

P. H. L. Wilson and P. I. Pocock did not bat.

Bowling: *First Innings*—Lillee 17–4–59–2; Thomson 15–3–67–1; Dymock 19–2–91–0; Chappell 8–1–32–2; Mallett 15–4–69–2. *Second Innings*—Lillee 7–2–11–2; Dymock 9–0–58–1; Thomson 3–0–12–1.

Australians

B. M. Laird st Richards b Knight	58	– lbw b Jackman	11
J. Dyson c Richards b Knight	23	– c Butcher b Pocock	33
K. J. Hughes lbw b Jackman	16	– lbw b Jackman	5
*G. S. Chappell c Butcher b Jackman	4	– c Lynch b Pocock	6
G. N. Yallop b Knight	0	– c Butcher b Pocock	1
A. R. Border not out	13	– c Jackman b Pocock	25
†R. W. Marsh not out	3	– lbw b Jackman	56
D. K. Lillee (did not bat)		– c Lynch b Pocock	15
A. A. Mallett (did not bat)		– not out	30
G. Dymock (did not bat)		– b Intikhab	37
J. R. Thomson (did not bat)		– b Intikhab	4
L-b 1, w 2, n-b 6	9	B 7, l-b 10	17

1/56 2/99 3/105   (5 wkts dec.) 126   1/20 2/34 3/41 4/43   240
4/106 5/115   5/77 6/123 7/155 8/166 9/232

Bowling: *First Innings*—Jackman 19.5–8–34–2; Wilson 14–2–47–0; Knight 18–4–36–3. *Second Innings*—Jackman 17–5–50–3; Wilson 4–0–16–0; Knight 6–0–26–0; Pocock 38–15–61–5; Intikhab 20.3–4–70–2; Howarth 1–1–0–0.

Umpires: D. J. Constant and B. J. Meyer.

YOUNG ENGLAND v AUSTRALIANS

At Worcester, August 14. Drawn. The match, already reduced by an earlier shower to 49 overs, ended when rain flooded the ground, with England only 17 for one in reply to the Australians' modest score of 176 for four. As a trial for potential England players this limited-overs match, on a pitch assisting the seamers, revealed little that the selectors did not already know. The pace quartet bowled steadily but failed to disturb Australian batsmen obviously short of match practice. Border played the only positive innings, striking seven 4s while making 57 before he was brilliantly run out by Marks.

Australians

G. M. Wood lbw b Pringle	23	G. N. Yallop not out	4
J. Dyson run out	28	L-b 12, w 2, n-b 7	21
*G. S. Chappell lbw b Cooper	25		
A. R. Border run out	57	1/64 2/68 3/116 (4 wkts, 49 overs) 176	
K. J. Hughes not out	18	4/158	

†R. W. Marsh, G. Dymock, D. K. Lillee, J. R. Thomson and L. S. Pascoe did not bat.

Bowling: Hogg 8–0–27–0; Parsons 8–4–15–0; Cooper 11–1–48–1; Pringle 11–2–24–1; Marks 11–1–41–0.

Young England

K. D. Smith not out	7
R. T. Robinson c Marsh b Lillee	7
D. I. Gower not out	0
B 1, w 2	3

1/17   (1 wkt, 8 overs) 17

K. J. Barnett, P. M. Roebuck, *V. J. Marks, D. R. Pringle, †I. J. Gould, W. Hogg, K. E. Cooper and G. J. Parsons did not bat.

Bowling: Lillee 4–1–8–1; Thomson 4–1–6–0.

Umpires: A. G. T. Whitehead and J. van Geloven.

LANCASHIRE v AUSTRALIANS

At Manchester, August 16, 17, 18. Drawn. A superb century by Chappell dominated the first day on a green but easy paced pitch. However, the touring captain made few friends when he walked away from the wicket without a word of explanation or apology to the opposition immediately he reached three figures. He retired to allow other batsmen to practise and Laird, with a stubborn 55 spread over 165 minutes, and Marsh, with a more aggressive half-century in an hour, enabled the Australians to declare at 296 for five. Lancashire made a good start with Lloyd and Kennedy putting on 49 in the last hour of the opening day. Major honours on the Sunday went to Hayes, whose first century in two years included three 6s. A declaration with Lancashire 44 runs behind was of no avail when rain prevented the match being continued on the last day.

Australians

B. M. Laird run out	55	– not out	0
J. Dyson c Simmons b Hogg	3	– not out	0
G. M. Wood c Fowler b Simmons	28		
*G. S. Chappell retired	101		
K. J. Hughes c Fowler b Hughes	14		
G. N. Yallop not out	26		
†R. W. Marsh not out	50		
B 12, l-b 2, n-b 5	19		

1/12 2/71 3/124   (5 wkts dec.) 296   (no wkt) 0
4/189 5/220

R. J. Bright, A. A. Mallett, G. Dymock and L. S. Pascoe did not bat.

Bowling: *First Innings*—Hogg 16–3–56–1; Malone 14.1–4–26–0; Allott 6–0–21–0; Simmons 24–4–78–1; Hughes 27–5–76–1; O'Shaughnessy 9–1–20–0. *Second Innings*—Hogg 0.5–0–0–0.

Lancashire

A. Kennedy c Marsh b Pascoe	40	D. P. Hughes c Wood b Bright	22
D. Lloyd c Marsh b Pascoe	38	P. J. W. Allott not out	4
*F. C. Hayes not out	102		
B. W. Reidy b Dymock	18	L-b 5, n-b 9	14
S. J. O'Shaughnessy lbw b Pascoe	1		
J. Simmons c Chappell b Bright	7	1/74 2/87 3/148 (7 wkts dec.) 252
†G. Fowler c Laird b Bright	6	4/150 5/157 6/201 7/236

M. F. Malone and W. Hogg did not bat.

Bowling: Pascoe 21–2–52–3; Dymock 14–4–35–1; Mallett 24–6–74–0; Bright 22.1–10–77–3.

Umpires: H. D. Bird and D. G. L. Evans.

ENGLAND v AUSTRALIA

First Prudential Trophy Match

At The Oval, August 20. England won by 23 runs. Their victory was more easily achieved than the score may suggest. Having been put in by Chappell, England were given a fine start by Boycott and Gooch, who put on 108 for the first wicket. With Athey, in his first international match, maintaining the momentum, only some good closing overs by Lillee and Pascoe kept England from passing 250 in their 55 overs. Australia, in reply, were soon in trouble, their opening pair going cheaply and Hendrick, a late replacement for Dilley, who had contracted glandular fever, reducing them to 75 for five. Only Hughes and Marsh showed any batting form for Australia. Hendrick's five for 31 earned him the Man of the Match award. The attendance was 13,500 with receipts of £61,000.

England

G. A. Gooch b Border	54	P. Willey c Yallop b Lillee		2
G. Boycott c Hughes b Lillee	99	†D. L. Bairstow not out		9
A. R. Butcher lbw b Dymock	14	B 2, l-b 8, w 3, n-b 4		17
C. W. J. Athey c Chappell b Lillee	32			
M. W. Gatting not out	17	1/108 2/140 3/212	(6 wkts, 55 overs)	248
*I. T. Botham c Yallop b Lillee	4	4/221 5/225 6/232		

R. D. Jackman, C. M. Old and M. Hendrick did not bat.

Bowling: Lillee 11–1–35–4; Thomson 11–3–25–0; Dymock 9–0–50–1; Pascoe 11–1–50–0; Border 11–2–61–1; Chappell 2–0–10–0.

Australia

B. M. Laird lbw b Gooch	15	D. K. Lillee c Willey b Hendrick		0
G. M. Wood c Athey b Jackman	4	J. R. Thomson run out		15
*G. S. Chappell c Bairstow b Hendrick	36	G. Dymock not out		14
A. R. Border b Hendrick	13	B 3, l-b 10, w 1		14
K. J. Hughes not out	73			
G. N. Yallop b Hendrick	0	1/11 2/36 3/68	(8 wkts, 55 overs)	225
†R. W. Marsh c Bairstow b Hendrick	41	4/71 5/75 6/161 7/161 8/192		

L. S. Pascoe did not bat.

Bowling: Old 9–0–43–0; Jackman 11–0–46–1; Botham 9–1–28–0; Gooch 7–0–29–1; Hendrick 11–3–31–5; Willey 8–0–34–0.

Umpires: W. E. Alley and D. G. L. Evans.

ENGLAND v AUSTRALIA

Second Prudential Trophy Match

At Birmingham, August 22. England won by 47 runs. The result was never in any doubt after they had been put in for the second time in three days – and Boycott and Gooch had given them another splendid start with an opening partnership of 154. Athey and the West Indian Roland Butcher, playing in his first representative match for England, made good half-centuries in England's 320 for eight, a record total for these Prudential Trophy matches. After 30 overs Australia were 119 for three. That they made 154 in their remaining 25 overs was due mainly to Hughes, who followed his 73 not out at The Oval with a brilliant 98, and Yallop. Gooch's 108 won him the Man of the Match award. Men of the Series were Gooch for England and Hughes for Australia. The attendance was 17,000 and the takings were £61,485.

England

G. A. Gooch b Thomson	108	J. E. Emburey not out		1
G. Boycott c Marsh b Border	78	C. M. Old not out		2
C. W. J. Athey b Pascoe	51			
R. O. Butcher c Dyson b Pascoe	52	B 4, l-b 3, w 1, n-b 4		12
M. W. Gatting run out	2			
*I. T. Botham b Pascoe	2	1/154 2/215 3/292	(8 wkts, 55 overs)	320
†D. L. Bairstow b Lillee	6	4/298 5/302 6/311		
R. D. Jackman c Marsh b Pascoe	6	7/313 8/318		

M. Hendrick did not bat.

Bowling: Thomson 11–1–69–1; Lillee 11–0–43–1; Pascoe 11–0–69–4; Bright 8–0–48–0; Chappell 11–0–65–0; Border 3–0–14–1.

Australia

B. M. Laird c Emburey b Hendrick	 36	R. J. Bright not out	....	5
J. Dyson b Hendrick	 24			
K. J. Hughes c and b Gooch	 98	B 1,l-b 9, w 1	....	11
A. R. Border run out	 26			
G. N. Yallop not out	 52	1/53 2/80 3/119	(5 wkts, 55 overs)	273
D. K. Lillee b Hendrick	 21	4/222 5/259		

*G. S. Chappell, †R. W. Marsh, J. R. Thomson and L. S. Pascoe did not bat.

Bowling: Old 11–2–44–0; Jackman 11–1–45–0; Botham 11–1–41–0; Hendrick 10–0–54–3; Emburey 8–0–51–0; Gooch 3–0–16–1; Boycott 1–0–11–0.

Umpires: H. D. Bird and D. O. Oslear.

NOTTINGHAMSHIRE v AUSTRALIANS

At Nottingham, August 23, 24, 25. Nottinghamshire won by an innings and 76 runs. They completed an emphatic victory – the biggest inflicted on the Australians by a county side this century. They began their domination after the Australians slid from 146 for two to 207 all out on the opening day against the inspired bowling of Watson and Hadlee – both overseas players. Then, after losing Todd without a run on the board, Nottinghamshire amassed a huge total at a rate of between 5 and 6 runs an over. Surprisingly no century was scored – except in the Australian bowling figures. Had it not been for Lillee, with six for 133, Australia would have been in an even sorrier position. They were 258 behind on first innings and never came to terms with the task of saving the match. Nottinghamshire collected the Holts Products Trophy for the biggest win against the Australians.

Australians

G. M. Wood b Hemmings	 76	– c Dexter b Hacker	 24
J. Dyson c French b Rice	 1	– (3) c Birch b Hadlee	 6
B. M. Laird c Dexter b Watson	 1	– (2) lbw b Watson	 0
A. R. Border lbw b Watson	 73	– (5) c French b Hemmings	 38
G. N. Yallop c French b Hadlee	 13	– (8) c French b Hadlee	 21
*K. J. Hughes c French b Hadlee	 0	– b Hacker	 9
†R. W. Marsh c Rice b Hadlee	 3	– not out	 24
D. K. Lillee not out	 15	– (9) c French b Hemmings	 18
A. A. Mallett c Dexter b Watson	 9	– (4) c Hadlee b Watson	 10
J. R. Thomson b Watson	 0	– c Randall b Hemmings	 5
L. S. Pascoe c Dexter b Watson	 6	– c French b Hadlee	 1
L-b 6, w 4	 10	B 6,l-b 10, w 9, n-b 1	 26

1/12 2/25 3/146 4/167	207	1/7 2/20 3/34 4/63	182
5/168 6/171 7/172 8/185 9/185		5/97 6/113 7/146 8/171 9/179	

Bowling: *First Innings*—Rice 10–1–46–1; Watson 15.3–3–57–5; Hacker 11–3–33–0; Hadlee 19–8–29–3; Hemmings 7–1–32–1. *Second Innings*—Hadlee 29.1–12–39–3; Watson 11–4–18–2; Hacker 16–7–26–2; Hemmings 22–3–66–3; Rice 1–0–7–0.

Nottinghamshire

P. A. Todd c Thomson b Lillee	 0	E. E. Hemmings c Marsh b Lillee	 24
R. T. Robinson lbw b Pascoe	 33	W. K. Watson c Pascoe b Lillee	 44
D. W. Randall lbw b Lillee	 12	P. J. Hacker not out	 8
*C. E. B. Rice c Marsh b Lillee	 90		
R. E. Dexter c Hughes b Thomson	 32	B 18,l-b 14, w 7, n-b 13	 52
J. D. Birch b Mallett	 57		
†B. N. French c Marsh b Lillee	 45	1/0 2/11 3/78 4/186	465
R. J. Hadlee run out	 68	5/220 6/287 7/372 8/384 9/419	

Bowling: Lillee 29.4–4–133–6; Thomson 25–6–109–1; Pascoe 21–0–118–1; Mallett 10–1–53–1.

Umpires: C. Cook and D. Shackleton.

ENGLAND v AUSTRALIA

Cornhill Centenary Test

At Lord's, August 28, 29, 30, September 1, 2. Drawn. It had been hoped that England's Centenary Test, to mark the centenary of the first Test played in England – at The Oval in 1880 – might be played in late summer sunshine with many a nostalgic reunion, some splendid fighting cricket and a finish to savour.

Over 200 former England and Australian players assembled from all over the world; it was impossible to move anywhere at Lord's without meeting the heroes of yesteryear. The welcoming parties, the dinners and the take-over by Cornhill Insurance of a London theatre for a night were all hugely successful. Sadly, however, the party in the middle was markedly less so.

After almost ten hours had been lost to rain in the first three days, the match ended in a tepid draw, with many people disappointed that England did not make a bolder bid to meet Australia's final challenge to score 370 in 350 minutes. With Boycott 128 not out and Gatting 51 not out they had reached only 244 for three at the finish.

As much as for the cricket, though, the game will be remembered for a regrettable incident, seen by millions on television on the Saturday afternoon, in which angry MCC members were involved in a momentary scuffle with umpire Constant as the umpires and captains moved into the Long Room after their fifth pitch inspection of the day. Ian Botham, the England captain, and Greg Chappell, his Australian counterpart, saw to it that matters got no worse. When play finally started at 3.45 p.m., police escorted the umpires through the Long Room and on to the field.

Two MCC members, identified by Chappell, were questioned by the Secretary, Mr J. A. Bailey, after the incident on Saturday afternoon. This was followed, on the Monday, by the following statement:

"Enquiries instituted today into the behaviour of certain MCC members towards the umpires and captains on Saturday leave no doubt that their conduct was inexcusable in any circumstances. Investigations are continuing and will be rigorously pursued with a view to identifying and disciplining the culprits. Meanwhile the club is sending to the umpires and to the captains of both sides their profound apologies that such an unhappy incident should have occurred at the headquarters of the game and on an occasion of such importance."

Fifty minutes had been lost to rain on the first day and all but an hour and a quarter on the second. On the third, the Saturday, ninety minutes' rain in the early morning left a soft area around two old uncovered pitches on the Tavern side of the ground. The ground staff, however, thought play could have started by lunch, as did a crowd of some 20,000 who were growing increasingly impatient in sunshine and breeze. Umpires Bird and Constant were the sole judges of when play should start, with one captain noticeably keener to play than the other; Australia being in the stronger position, Chappell was the more eager of the two. They conducted inspection after inspection, seemingly insensitive to the crowd's rising anger and the need for flexibility on such a special occasion. By the time the President of MCC, Mr S. C. Griffith, exerted pressure on the umpires to get the game started, the pavilion fracas had occurred. Although the authorities decided, when play did resume, that it could continue until eight o'clock that Saturday evening, it was fairly certain the light, by then, would not have been fit for play. In the event it soon rained again. An extra hour was also added to each of the last two days of the match.

On the field Australia were much the more convincing side, making a nonsense of the pre-match odds of seven to one against an Australian victory. After Chappell had won the toss Australia batted well through repeated interruptions before declaring on the Saturday evening at 385 for five. Wood contributed a battling 112, before being brilliantly stumped by Bairstow off Emburey, and Hughes graced the occasion with a highly talented and spirited 117 in which he hit three 6s and fourteen 4s, every stroke being played according to the fighting intentions of his side. Against such aggression England's bowling, with the exception of Old, looked very ordinary.

Lillee and Pascoe, with faster and more skilful bowling than their opponents', routed England for 205 on the Monday with enough time left that evening for Australia to score 106 for two, taking their lead to 286. In England's first innings Boycott, Gower and Old were the only batsmen to pass 20. Lillee, superbly controlled, removed the first four batsmen, and Pascoe finished the innings with a spell of five for 15 in 32 balls. Both bowlers took all their wickets at the Nursery End, once so infamous for its ridge. Chappell insisted that the ridge was still plainly visible and very much in play although the pitch had been shifted some four or five feet away from the Pavilion End in an effort to escape its influence.

England's first innings collapse, in which they lost their last seven wickets for 68 runs, had left Australia in a potentially winning position when the last day began. They hammered a further 83 runs in under an hour before Chappell's second declaration left England to score for almost six hours at over a run a minute. In Australia's second innings Chappell made a sound 59 and Hughes a brilliant 84. Moving into his shots with zest and certainty Hughes played the most spectacular stroke of the match when he danced down the pitch to hit the lively Old on to the top deck of the pavilion.

England did not attempt to meet Chappell's challenge. When Lillee trapped Gooch lbw for 16 and Pascoe removed Athey, to a bat-pad catch, for 1, survival became the priority. The in-form Boycott dropped anchor and Gower curbed his attacking instincts as they consolidated. When the score had reached 112 for two by three o'clock, with play possible until seven o'clock, many felt it would have been fitting if Botham had come in himself and had a fling. But the highest total England have ever made in a fourth innings to beat Australia in England is 269 for nine, at The Oval in 1902, and now they looked upon their first innings collapse as good enough reason for not risking another. Amid more boos than cheers they moved unhurriedly towards a draw. During the match the insatiable Boycott passed the Test aggregates of both Sir Leonard Hutton (6,971) and Sir Donald Bradman (6,996) and took his own Test aggregate to 7,115 runs. Boycott's second innings hundred was his sixth against Australia and his nineteenth in Tests.

The Cornhill Trophy and cheque for £500 as Man of the Match went to Hughes, and the prize-money of £4,500 was split between the sides. The official attendance was 84,938; takings were £360,850.50. – C.W.

Australia

G. M. Wood st Bairstow b Embury	112	– (2) lbw b Old	8
B. M. Laird c Bairstow b Old	24	– (1) c Bairstow b Old	6
*G. S. Chappell c Gatting b Old	47	– b Old	59
K. J. Hughes c Athey b Old	117	– lbw b Botham	84
G. N. Yallop lbw b Hendrick	2		
A. R. Border not out	56	– (5) not out	21
†R. W. Marsh not out	16		
B 1, l-b 8, n-b 2	11	B 1, l-b 8, n-b 2	11

1/64 2/150 3/260   (5 wkts dec.) 385   1/15 2/28 3/139   (4 wkts dec.) 189
4/267 5/320   4/189

D. K. Lillee, A. A. Mallett, R. J. Bright and L. S. Pascoe did not bat.

Bowling: *First Innings*—Old 35–9–91–3; Hendrick 30–6–67–1; Botham 22–2–89–0; Embury 38–9–104–1; Gooch 8–3–16–0; Willey 1–0–7–0. *Second Innings*—Old 20–6–47–3; Hendrick 15–4–53–0; Embury 9–2–35–0; Botham 9.2–1–43–1.

England

G. A. Gooch c Bright b Lillee	8	– lbw b Lillee	16
G. Boycott c Marsh b Lillee	62	– not out	128
C. W. J. Athey b Lillee	9	– c Laird b Pascoe	1
D. I. Gower b Lillee	45	– b Mallett	35
M. W. Gatting lbw b Pascoe	12	– not out	51
*I. T. Botham c Wood b Pascoe	0		
P. Willey lbw b Pascoe	5		
†D. L. Bairstow lbw b Pascoe	6		
J. E. Embury lbw b Pascoe	3		
C. M. Old not out	24		
M. Hendrick c Border b Mallett	5		
B 6, l-b 8, n-b 12	26	B 3, l-b 2, n-b 8	13

1/10 2/41 3/137 4/151   205   1/19 2/43 3/124   (3 wkts) 244
5/158 6/163 7/164 8/173 9/200

Bowling: *First Innings*—Lillee 15–4–43–4; Pascoe 18–5–59–5; Chappell 2–0–2–0; Bright 21–6–50–0; Mallett 7.2–3–25–1. *Second Innings*—Lillee 19–5–53–1; Pascoe 17–1–73–1; Bright 25–9–44–0; Mallett 21–2–61–1.

Umpires: H. D. Bird and D. J. Constant.

THE CRICKET COUNCIL, 1979-80

The Cricket Council, which first took office on October 1, 1974, consists of a President, a Chairman, the Chairman of the Council's Public Relations and Promotions Sub-Committee, fifteen representatives from its constituent bodies, and a representative each of the Minor Counties Cricket Association and the Irish and Scottish Cricket Unions. The President of the Council is also President of MCC, while the Chairman of the Council is elected annually by the Council. All cricket is thus represented at the highest administrative level.

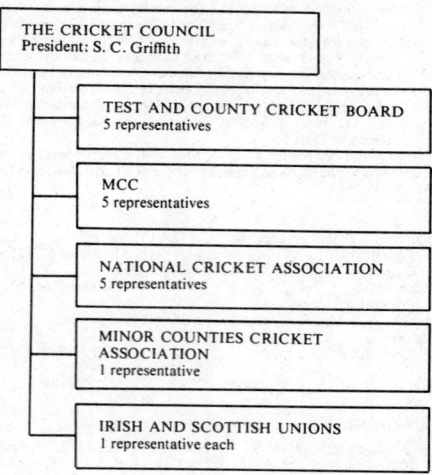

THE CRICKET COUNCIL
President: S. C. Griffith

TEST AND COUNTY CRICKET BOARD
5 representatives

MCC
5 representatives

NATIONAL CRICKET ASSOCIATION
5 representatives

MINOR COUNTIES CRICKET ASSOCIATION
1 representative

IRISH AND SCOTTISH UNIONS
1 representative each

OFFICERS AND PERSONNEL

S. C. Griffith (President), C. H. Palmer (Chairman), J. G. W. Davies (Vice-Chairman), D. B. Carr (Secretary).

TCCB: F. G. Mann (Chairman), D. B. Carr (Secretary), B. Langley (Assistant-Secretary), P. B. H. May, E. H. King, C. S. Rhoades, F. M. Turner.

MCC: S. C. Griffith (President), J. G. W. Davies (Treasurer), J. A. Bailey (Secretary), Lt-Col. L. James (Assistant-Secretary), G. O. Allen, C. G. A. Paris, D. G. Clark, W. H. Webster.

NCA: D. J. Robson (Chairman), B. J. Aspital (Secretary), J. G. Overy, F. H. Elliott, F. R. Brown, J. Lane.

MCCA: R. A. C. Forrester (Chairman).

Irish Cricket Union: D. Scott. Scottish Cricket Union: R. W. Barclay.

Public Relations and Promotions Sub-Committee: F. M. Turner (Chairman), P. M. Lush (Secretary), R. J. Roe (Promotions Officer), J. G. W. Davies, C. S. Rhoades, J. Lane, C. G. A. Paris, F. H. Elliott. *Specially co-opted member* – D. J. Insole.

THE MARYLEBONE CRICKET CLUB

Patron – HER MAJESTY THE QUEEN

President – S. C. GRIFFITH

President Designate – P. B. H. MAY

Life Vice-Presidents – CAPTAIN THE LORD CORNWALLIS, G. O. B. ALLEN

Trustees – R. AIRD, G. O. B. ALLEN, G. C. NEWMAN

Treasurer – J. G. W. DAVIES

Treasurer Designate – D. G. CLARK

Chairman of Finance – E. W. PHILLIPS

Secretary – J. A. BAILEY

(Lord's Cricket Ground, St John's Wood, NW8 8QN)

Assistant Secretaries – LT-COL. L. G. JAMES (Administration), LT-COL. J. R. STEPHENSON (Cricket), WG-CDR V. J. W. M. LAWRENCE (Chief Accountant)

Curator – S. E. A. GREEN

MCC Committee for 1979-80 – S. C. Griffith, J. G. W. Davies, E. W. Phillips, R. Aird, G. C. Newman, G. O. B. Allen, M. C. Cowdrey, C. J. Harrison, J. S. O. Haslewood, Sir Cyril Hawker, C. G. A. Paris, C. Stansfield Smith, E. W. Swanton, W. H. Webster, L. E. G. Ames, D. J. Insole, R. V. C. Robins, O. J. Wait, Lord Caccia, D. G. Clark, G. H. G. Doggart, F. G. Mann, M. E. L. Melluish, D. R. W. Silk, M. G. Crawford, C. B. Howland, A. C. D. Ingleby-Mackenzie, P. B. H. May, C. H. Palmer.

Finance and Administration

The President, at the 193rd annual meeting of the Club, mentioned that Lt-Col. J. R. Stephenson had been appointed Assistant Secretary (Cricket) and Lt-Col. L. G. James had succeeded Colonel G. C. K. Rowe in the post of Assistant Secretary (Administration). He also mentioned that Mr A. W. Flower, Secretary of Middlesex CCC and a former employee of MCC, had retired during the year. He drew members' attention to the fact that, as 1980 was the year of the Centenary Test match, the Club would be entertaining many guests, both from Australia and England, and there would be a special exhibition in the Memorial Gallery to commemorate 100 years of Test match cricket. The President also informed members that, during the winter, he and the Secretary, together with other cricket administrators, had been guests of the Board of Control for Cricket in India

360   *The Marylebone Cricket Club, 1980*

at their Jubilee Test celebrations and that he had been touched by the affection and respect shown to MCC.

Members were informed that the membership of the Club remained in a healthy state and that, on the financial side, there had been a surplus of £34,274 after taxation, which was a satisfactory result for the Club in view of the high increase in inflation over the past year.

Among notable personalities connected with the game whose deaths were reported were Admiral of the Fleet, the Earl Mountbatten of Burma, who was an MCC Honorary Life Member; Sir Hubert Ashton, ex-President MCC; R. H. Twining, ex-President and Life Vice-President MCC; B. K. Castor, ex-Secretary of Essex and Surrey, and also B. A. Barnett, J. W. Burke, Colonel R. A. W. Binny, E. W. Dawson, E. J. Gothard, N. D. Howard, E. Paynter, E. J. Smith and S. A. Block.

Griffith nominates May

P. B. H. May was nominated by S. C. Griffith to succeed him as President of MCC on October 1, 1980. Aged 50, Peter May had played for Surrey and England and captained England on many occasions. He first played for England at the age of 21 and hit a century in his first Test match, against South Africa. He had been a selector between the years 1955 and 1968 and had more recently been Chairman of the TCCB Cricket Committee as well as being a member of the MCC Committee over the years. In the history of the club, only two Presidents, the Duke of Edinburgh and the late Lord Cobham, have been appointed at a younger age.

MCC v ESSEX

At Lord's, April 23, 24, 25. Drawn. Although customary cheerless weather marked the opening of the first-class season, the pitch was a good one, the first three weeks of April having been unusually dry. Tavaré, the 25-year-old Kent batsman, took full advantage of this by scoring 84 and 115. For Essex, the champion county, victory became a possibility when, after gaining a first innings lead of 48, they took two early wickets on the second evening when MCC batted a second time. But Tavaré again shored up the MCC innings and on the last evening Essex themselves were in some danger of defeat. Denness showed that, at 39, he retained much of his former skill with the bat, and three young bowlers, Dilley, Wilson and Sainsbury (in only his second match for Essex) had their moments.

MCC

A. R. Butcher c Denness b Turner	17	– c Gooch b Sainsbury	17
R. G. Lumb lbw b Sainsbury	0	– b Sainsbury	0
C. J. Tavaré b Pont	84	– c Hardie b Fletcher	115
P. M. Roebuck c McEwan b Turner	0	– lbw b Lever	19
P. W. G. Parker lbw b Lever	32	– c Smith b Turner	1
*I. T. Botham c Smith b Lever	18	– b Lever	34
G. Miller lbw b Turner	16	– lbw b East	15
†D. L. Bairstow b Gooch	19	– c Smith b Pont	3
P. H. Edmonds not out	11	– b Gooch	20
G. R. Dilley not out	1	– not out	2
B 1, l-b 8, w 2	11	B 8, l-b 5, w 3, n-b 2	18

1/8 2/41 3/41 4/100 (8 wkts dec.) 209   1/4 2/21 3/66 (9 wkts dec.) 244
5/122 6/167 7/197 8/199   4/85 5/135 6/174 7/185
                                  8/235 9/244

P. H. L. Wilson did not bat.

Bowling: *First Innings*—Lever 16–2–48–2; Sainsbury 15–5–47–1; Turner 24–11–30–3; Pont 21–3–64–1; Gooch 3–1–9–1. *Second Innings*—Lever 17–4–53–2; Sainsbury 11–1–52–2; Turner 19–2–54–1; Pont 15–6–28–1; East 10–3–19–1; Gooch 4–2–7–1; Fletcher 2.5–0–13–1.

Essex

G. A. Gooch lbw b Dilley	44	– c Botham b Wilson 4
M. H. Denness c Bairstow b Dilley	69	– lbw b Dilley 19
K. S. McEwan c Bairstow b Wilson	1	– c Bairstow b Wilson 10
*K. W. R. Fletcher c Miller b Wilson	41	– b Edmonds 10
B. R. Hardie c Parker b Miller	23	– not out 22
K. R. Pont c Miller b Botham	9	– c Tavaré b Wilson 1
S. Turner not out	35	– not out 29
†N. Smith lbw b Dilley	9	
R. E. East not out	9	
B 2, l-b 8, w 1, n-b 11	17	B 1, l-b 3, w 2, n-b 1 7

1/98 2/107 3/144 4/189   (7 wkts dec.) 257   1/6 2/30 3/48   (5 wkts) 102
5/200 6/212 7/236   4/48 5/50

J. K. Lever and G. E. Sainsbury did not bat.

Bowling: *First Innings*—Dilley 21.5–3–83–3; Botham 26–10–51–1; Edmonds 14–1–30–0; Wilson 16–3–49–2; Butcher 3–1–11–0; Miller 10–5–16–1. *Second Innings*—Dilley 10–1–33–1; Wilson 7–1–23–3; Botham 2–0–9–0; Edmonds 10–2–22–1; Miller 2.4–0–8–0.

Umpires: J. G. Langridge and P. B. Wight.

At Lord's, May 7. MCC Young Cricketers won by seven wickets. MCC 195 for eight (M. G. Griffith 68, A. R. Wagner 34; D. Wilson three for 16); MCC Young Cricketers 198 for three (M. S. Scott 103, D. D'Oliveira 49 not out, R. J. Finney 30 not out; N. J. W. Stewart three for 54).

At Oxford, May 28, 29, 30. MCC beat Oxford University by ten wickets (See Oxford University section).

At Belfast, June 7, 8, 9. MCC lost to Ireland by 175 runs (See Other Matches, 1980).

At Lord's, August 11, 12. Drawn. MCC 85 for five dec. and 229 for five dec. (R. J. Lanchbury 117 not out); Scotland 78 for four and 170 for seven (D. L. Hays 64, D. L. Bell 53).

MCC ENGLAND HONORARY MEMBERS

D. A. Allen	T. G. Evans, CBE	J. M. Parks
L. E. G. Ames, CBE	G. Geary	G. Pullar
T. E. Bailey	T. W. Graveney, OBE	P. E. Richardson
R. W. Barber	J. Hardstaff	A. Sandham
C. J. Barnett	Sir Leonard Hutton	M. J. K. Smith, OBE
K. F. Barrington	J. T. Ikin	J. B. Statham, CBE
A. V. Bedser, OBE	R. Illingworth, CBE	F. J. Titmus, MBE
W. E. Bowes	J. C. Laker	F. S. Trueman
D. B. Close, CBE	H. Larwood	F. H. Tyson
D. C. S. Compton, CBE	G. A. R. Lock	W. Voce
M. C. Cowdrey, CBE	P. B. H. May	J. H. Wardle
E. R. Dexter	C. Milburn	C. Washbrook
B. L. D'Oliveira, OBE	J. T. Murray, MBE	W. Watson
W. J. Edrich, DFC	P. H. Parfitt	D. V. P. Wright

OTHER MATCHES AT LORD'S, 1980

May 30. Prudential Trophy. WEST INDIES beat ENGLAND by 24 runs (See West Indian tour section).

June 19, 20, 21, 23, 24. Second Cornhill Test. ENGLAND drew with WEST INDIES (See West Indian tour section).

OXFORD UNIVERSITY v CAMBRIDGE UNIVERSITY

June 28, 30, July 1. Drawn. Only four hours and ten minutes play was possible in the 136th University Match. The first and last days were washed out; on the second day Oxford scored 206 for six after being put in. Three Oxford players – Sutcliffe, Curtis and Sanderson – thus won their Blues without taking the field. Cowan, a tall footballer, made a powerful 61, hitting well off his legs, and Rogers was instrumental in giving an unfancied Oxford side a useful start. For Cambridge, Doggart, son and grandson of Cambridge Blues, took three wickets with off-breaks. In 1920, the last correspondingly wet year, there was no play on the first two days and, although a fourth was arranged, it ended without two innings having been completed.

Oxford University

R. A. B. Ezekowitz (*Capetown Univ. and Wolfson*) c Doggart b Pringle....		11
J. J. Rogers (*Sedbergh and University*) c Pringle b Crawford		49
R. S. Cowan (*Lewis GS and Magdalen*) b Doggart		61
J. O. D. Orders (*Winchester and Trinity*) b Doggart		6
S. J. Halliday (*Downside and St Benet's Hall*) c Pringle b Doggart		19
R. P. Moulding (*Haberdashers' Aske's and Christ Church*) c Odendaal b Boyd-Moss		16
*C. J. Ross (*Wellington Univ. and Magdalen*) not out...............		23
†T. E. O. Bury (*Charterhouse and St Edmund Hall*) not out		0
B 7, l-b 5, w 3, n-b 6		21
1/50 2/81 3/100	(6 wkts)	206
4/162 5/163 6/189		

S. P. Sutcliffe (*King George V, Southport and Lincoln*), I. J. Curtis (*Whitgift and Lincoln*) and J. F. W. Sanderson (*Westminster and New College*) did not bat.

Bowling: Howat 6–1–20–0; Russom 21–6–49–0; Pringle 14–2–30–1; Crawford 11–3–22–1; Doggart 23–5–54–3; Boyd-Moss 2–1–10–1.

Cambridge University

A. M. Mubarak (*Royal Coll., Colombo and Christ's*), J. P. C. Mills (*Oundle and Corpus Christi*), A. Odendaal (*Queen's Coll., Queenstown and St John's*), R. J. Boyd-Moss (*Bedford and Magdalene*), D. R. Pringle (*Felsted and Fitzwilliam*), S. J. G. Doggart (*Winchester and Magdalene*), N. Russom (*Huish's GS and St Catherine's*). *†I. G. Peck (*Bedford and Magdalene*), D. C. Holliday (*Oundle and Christ's*), N. C. Crawford (*Shrewsbury and Magdalene*) and M. G. Howat (*Abingdon and Magdalene*).

Umpires: T. W. Spencer and A. G. T. Whitehead.

OXFORD v CAMBRIDGE, RESULTS AND HUNDREDS

The University match dates back to 1827. Altogether there have been 136 official matches, Cambridge winning 52, and Oxford 45, with 39 drawn. Results since 1950:

1950	Drawn	1966	Oxford won by an innings and 9 runs
1951	Oxford won by 21 runs	1967	Drawn
1952	Drawn	1968	Drawn
1953	Cambridge won by two wickets	1969	Drawn
1954	Drawn	1970	Drawn
1955	Drawn	1971	Drawn
1956	Drawn	1972	Cambridge won by an innings and
1957	Cambridge won by an innings and		25 runs
	186 runs	1973	Drawn
1958	Cambridge won by 99 runs	1974	Drawn
1959	Oxford won by 85 runs	1975	Drawn
1960	Drawn	1976	Oxford won by ten wickets
1961	Drawn	1977	Drawn
1962	Drawn	1978	Drawn
1963	Drawn	1979	Cambridge won by an innings and
1964	Drawn		52 runs
1965	Drawn	1980	Drawn

Seventy-two three-figure innings have been played in the University matches. For those scored before 1919 see 1940 *Wisden*. Those subsequent to 1919 include the six highest, as shown here:

238*	Nawab of Pataudi	1931 Oxford		201	A. Ratcliffe	1931 Cam.
211	G. Goonesena	1957 Cam.		200	Majid J. Khan	1970 Cam.
201*	M. J. K. Smith	1954 Oxford		193	D. C. H. Townsend	1934 Oxford
170	M. Howell	1919 Oxford		116*	D. R. W. Silk	1953 Cam.
167	B. W. Hone	1932 Oxford		116	M. C. Cowdrey	1953 Oxford
158	P. M. Roebuck	1975 Cam.		115	A. W. Allen	1934 Cam.
157	D. R. Wilcox	1932 Cam.		114*	D. R. Owen-Thomas	1972 Cam.
155	F. S. Goldstein	1968 Oxford		114	J. R. Pretlove	1955 Cam.
149	J. T. Morgan	1929 Cam.		113	E. R. T. Holmes	1927 Oxford
146	R. O'Brien	1956 Cam.		113*	J. M. Brearley	1962 Cam.
146	D. R. Owen-Thomas	1971 Cam.		112*	E. D. Fursdon	1975 Oxford
145*	H. E. Webb	1948 Oxford		111*	G. W. Cook	1957 Cam.
145	D. P. Toft	1967 Oxford		109	C. H. Taylor	1923 Oxford
142	M. P. Donnelly	1946 Oxford		108	F. G. H. Chalk	1934 Oxford
136	E. T. Killick	1930 Cam.		106	Nawab of Pataudi	1929 Oxford
135	H. A. Pawson	1947 Oxford		105	E. J. Craig	1961 Cam.
131	Nawab of Pataudi	1960 Oxford		104	H. J. Enthoven	1924 Cam.
129	H. J. Enthoven	1925 Cam.		104	M. J. K. Smith	1955 Oxford
127	D. S. Sheppard	1952 Cam.		103*	A. R. Lewis	1962 Cam.
124	A. K. Judd	1927 Cam.		103*	D. R. Pringle	1979 Cam.
124	A. Ratcliffe	1932 Cam.		102*	A. P. F. Chapman	1922 Cam.
122	P. A. Gibb	1938 Cam.		101*	R. W. V. Robins	1928 Cam.
121	J. N. Grover	1937 Oxford		101	N. W. D. Yardley	1937 Cam.
119	J. M. Brearley	1964 Cam.		100	P. J. Dickinson	1939 Cam.
118	H. Ashton	1921 Cam.		100*	M. Manasseh	1964 Oxford
118	D. R. W. Silk	1954 Cam.		100	N. J. Cosh	1967 Cam.
117	M. J. K. Smith	1956 Oxford				

* Signifies not out.

Highest Totals

503	Oxford	1900		432-9	Cambridge	1936
457	Oxford	1947		431	Cambridge	1932
453-8	Oxford	1931		425	Cambridge	1938

Lowest Totals

32	Oxford................	1878		42	Oxford................	1890
39	Cambridge.............	1858		47	Cambridge.............	1838

Notes: A. P. F. Chapman and M. P. Donnelly enjoy the following distinction: Chapman scored a century at Lord's in the University match (102*, 1922); for Gentlemen v Players (160, 1922); (108, 1926); and for England v Australia (121, 1930). M. P. Donnelly scored a century at Lord's in the University match (142, 1946); for Gentlemen v Players (162*, 1947); and for New Zealand v England (206, 1949).

A. Ratcliffe's 201 for Cambridge remained a record for the match for only one day, being beaten by the Nawab of Pataudi's 238* for Oxford next day.

M. J. K. Smith (Oxford) is the only player who has scored three hundreds; 201* in 1954, 104 in 1955, and 117 in 1956. His aggregate, 477, surpassed the previous best, 457, by the Nawab of Pataudi, 1929-31.

The following players have scored two hundreds: W. Yardley (Cambridge) 100 in 1870 and 130 in 1872; H. J. Enthoven (Cambridge) 104 in 1924 and 129 in 1925; The Nawab of Pataudi (Oxford) 106 in 1929 and 238 not out in 1931; A. Ratcliffe (Cambridge) 201 in 1931 and 124 in 1932; D. R. W. Silk (Cambridge) 116 not out in 1953 and 118 in 1954; J. M. Brearley (Cambridge) 113 not out in 1962 and 119 in 1964; D. R. Owen-Thomas (Cambridge) 146 in 1971 and 114 not out in 1972.

F. C. Cobden, in the Oxford v Cambridge match in 1870, performed the hat-trick by taking the last three wickets and won an extraordinary game for Cambridge by two runs. The feat is without parallel in first-class cricket. Cobden obtained the last three Oxford wickets in each innings – a curious coincidence. Other hat-tricks, all for Cambridge, have been credited to A. G. Steel (1879), P. H. Morton (1880), J. F. Ireland (1911), and R. G. H. Lowe (1926).

S. E. Butler, in the 1871 match, took all the wickets in the Cambridge first innings. The feat is unique in University matches. He bowled 24 overs and a ball. In the follow-on he took five wickets for 57, making fifteen for 95 runs in the match.

P. R. Le Couteur scored 160 and took eleven Cambridge wickets for 66 runs in 1910 – the best all-round performance in the history of the match.

D. W. Jarrett (Oxford 1975, Cambridge 1976) and S. M. Wookey (Cambridge 1975-76, Oxford 1978) are alone in gaining cricket Blues for both Universities.

ETON v HARROW

July 12, 13. Drawn. Harrow had bowled Eton out for 90 by lunch on the second day, and forced them to follow on 140 behind. But soon after these arrears had been erased, rain dashed any hopes Harrow still had of winning the oldest of all Lord's fixtures. With 230 for nine declared, Harrow maintained their record of not having been dismissed by Eton for nine years. Sixteen-year-old Haggas batted promisingly with top score of 75. Eton's batting in their first innings never threatened the leg-spin of Horn nor the medium-paced bowling of Findlay who returned match figures of seven for 25. Eton in their second innings they showed more resolute resistance as their captain, Rawlinson, added 42 for the second wicket with Russell and 62 for the third with Birch Reynardson. When rain ended play two hours early Eton's position looked safe.

Harrow

M. L. Sealy b Rudd	2		R. C. Patrick not out		2
*C. L. Feather b Bluett..............	48		T. S. M. S. Riley-Smith c Metaxa		
J. A. G. H. Stewart b Bluett	23			b Bluett.	2
S. E. Haggas b Farquhar	75		B 5, l-b 15, w 4, n-b 5.......		29
D. J. Fowler-Watt c Metaxa b Bluett ...	28				
A. R. Dick c Metaxa b Bluett.........	0		1/6 2/68 3/108	(9 wkts dec.)	230
O. F. O. Findlay c Rawlinson b Bluett..	21		4/178 5/180 6/207 7/207		
†D. C. Crerar b Farquhar	0		8/226 9/230		

F. W. A. Horn did not bat.

Bowling: Rudd 18–5–52–1; Farquhar 15–6–24–2; Bluett 26.2–4–55–6; Blake 13–2–53–0; Butcher 3–0–17–0.

Eton

†N. A. Metaxa c Crerar b Findlay	12	– c Crerar b Findlay	10
D. C. E. Russell b Findlay	8	– c Feather b Horn	31
*H. T. Rawlinson c and b Horn	29	– lbw b Findlay	41
C. C. Birch Reynardson b Findlay	0	– not out	30
T. R. V. Robins b Horn	4	– c Dick b Findlay	6
M. J. B. Rudd lbw b Findlay	7	– not out	6
I. R. M. D. Bluett c Haggas b Horn	6		
L. T. Fenwicke-Clennell c Crerar b Horn	4		
J. L. J. Butcher b Patrick	1		
W. N. S. Blake b Patrick	0		
R. C. Farquhar not out	1		
B 4, l-b 7, w 3, n-b 4	18	B 4, l-b 5, w 3, n-b 5	17

1/27 2/31 3/32 4/44 5/61 6/82	90	1/21 2/63 3/125 (4 wkts) 141
7/83 8/88 9/89		4/131

Bowling: *First Innings*—Patrick 17.3–6–15–2; Riley-Smith 8–1–14–0; Findlay 13–8–13–4; Feather 5–2–5–0; Horn 21–11–25–4. *Second Innings*—Patrick 12–3–22–0; Riley-Smith 8–2–19–0; Findlay 9–3–12–3; Feather 10–3–27–0; Horn 14–3–34–1; Sealy 3–0–10–0.

Umpires: G. E. Loveland and A. E. D. Smith.

ETON v HARROW, RESULTS AND HUNDREDS

Of the 145 matches played Eton have won 49, Harrow 44 and 52 have been drawn. This is the generally published record, but Harrow men object strongly to the first game in 1805 being treated as a regular contest between the two schools, contending that it is no more correct to count one than the fixture of 1857 which has been rejected.

The matches played during the war years 1915-18 and 1940-45 are not reckoned as belonging to the regular series.

Results since 1950:

1950	Drawn	1966	Drawn
1951	Drawn	1967	Drawn
1952	Harrow won by seven wickets	1968	Harrow won by seven wickets
1953	Eton won by ten wickets	1969	Drawn
1954	Harrow won by nine wickets	1970	Eton won by 97 runs
1955	Eton won by 38 runs	1971	Drawn
1956	Drawn	1972	Drawn
1957	Drawn	1973	Drawn
1958	Drawn	1974	Harrow won by eight wickets
1959	Drawn	1975	Harrow won by an innings and 151 runs
1960	Harrow won by 124 runs		
1961	Harrow won by an innings and 12 runs	1976	Drawn
		1977	Eton won by six wickets
1962	Drawn	1978	Drawn
1963	Drawn	1979	Drawn
1964	Eton won by eight wickets	1980	Drawn
1965	Harrow won by 48 runs		

Forty-five three-figure innings have been played in matches between these two schools. Those since 1918:

161*	M. K. Fosh	1975 Harrow	106	D. M. Smith	1966 Eton
159	E. W. Dawson	1923 Eton	104	R. Pulbrook	1932 Harrow
158	I. S. Akers-Douglas	1928 Eton	103	L. G. Crawley	1921 Harrow
153	N. S. Hotchkin	1931 Eton	103	T. Hare	1947 Eton
151	R. M. Tindall	1976 Harrow	102*	P. H. Stewart-Brown	1923 Harrow
135	J. C. Atkinson-Clark	1930 Eton	102	R. V. C. Robins	1953 Eton
115	E. Crutchley	1939 Harrow	100	R. H. Cobbold	1923 Eton
112	A. W. Allen	1931 Eton	100*	P. V. F. Cazalet	1926 Eton
112*	T. M. H. James	1978 Harrow	100	A. N. A. Boyd	1934 Eton
111	R. A. A. Holt	1937 Harrow	100*	P. M. Studd	1935 Harrow
109	K. F. H. Hale	1929 Eton	100	S. D. D. Sainsbury	1947 Harrow
109	N. S. Hotchkin	1932 Eton	100	M. J. J. Faber	1968 Eton
107	W. N. Coles	1946 Eton			

* *Signifies not out.*

In 1904, D. C. Boles of Eton, making 183, set up a new record for the match, beating the 152 obtained for Eton in 1841 by Emilius Bayley, afterwards the Rev. Sir John Robert Laurie Emilius Bayley Laurie. M. C. Bird, Harrow, in 1907, scored 100 not out and 131, the only batsman who has made two 100s in the match. N. S. Hotchkin, Eton, played the following innings: 1931, 153; 1932, 109 and 96; 1933, 88 and 12.

July 19, 21. Benson and Hedges Cup final. NORTHAMPTONSHIRE beat ESSEX by 6 runs (See Benson and Hedges Cup section).

MCC SCHOOLS v NATIONAL ASSOCIATION OF YOUNG CRICKETERS

July 23, 24. Drawn. Batting first in warm sunshine, NAYC were restrained by an attack which was accurate but, apart from several difficult chances going to ground, rarely threatened. A scoring-rate of 2 an over improved once Settle, compact with sound strokes, reached his 50; Bailey's elegant forcing drives and good running between the wickets hastened NAYC to their declaration. Little, always looking to play his strokes, and Kent, with professional-like tucks off his legs and persuasions to third man, gave MCC Schools a sound start. Robertshaw, slow left-arm, troubled both batsmen with control and flight, keeping Little on 35 for four maiden overs. Davis declared overnight, thus depriving Little of a century at Lord's, but after inroads by Foster's pace and the slow left-arm of Spiller hopes of a result were thwarted by a sixth-wicket stand of 74 between Bailey and Settle. All Foster's wickets were caught by substitute wicket-keeper A. J. Stewart (*Tiffin*).

National Association of Young Cricketers

A. P. Sutton (*Yorkshire*) c and b Spiller	36	– (4) c Davis b Spiller 35
A. Settle (*Lancashire*) not out	76	– (7) c sub b Foster 42
S. J. Bailey (*Staffordshire*) not out	40	– (6) c sub b Foster 56
D. P. Bembridge (*Nottinghamshire*) (did not bat) .		– (1) lbw b Spiller 28
N. T. Gadsby (*Cambridgeshire*) (did not bat)		– (2) run out 7
E. P. Neal (*Hertfordshire*) (did not bat)		– (3) lbw b Spiller 12
*M. Bailey (*Suffolk*) (did not bat)		– (5) b Cunningham 7
D. M. Robertshaw (*Yorkshire*) (did not bat)		– (8) c sub b Foster 2
M. Haswell (*Gloucestershire*) (did not bat)		– (9) not out 6
†C. Metson (*Middlesex*) (did not bat)		– (10) lbw b Spiller 4
B 9, l-b 12, w 4, n-b 3	28	B 5, l-b 8, n-b 2 15

1/81   (1 wkt dec.) 180   1/15 2/50 3/69   (9 wkts dec.) 214
                                                       4/78 5/114 6/188 7/196
                                                       8/205 9/214

M. Hinchcliffe (*Berkshire*) did not bat.

Bowling: *First Innings*—Meadows 13–2–36–0; Foster 14–5–23–0; Penn 14–4–24–0; Spiller 21–5–49–1; Cunningham 6–1–20–0. *Second Innings*—Meadows 12–3–42–0; Foster 15–5–45–3; Penn 6–1–13–0; Spiller 29–5–90–4; Cunningham 8–1–9–1.

MCC Schools

G. J. Little (*Marling*) not out	94	
T. J. Kent (*Clevedon CS*) st Metson b Sutton	55	– (4) st Metson b Sutton 21
I. L. Pont (*Brentwood*) not out	14	– (3) b Robertshaw 1
P. A. N. Armstrong (*Eastbourne*) (did not bat)		– (1) b Bailey 23
*P. A. Davis (*Wellington*) (did not bat)		– (2) c and b Settle 28
E. J. Cunningham (*Marlborough*) (did not bat)		– (5) not out 5
B 4, l-b 2, w 1	7	

1/126	(1 wkt dec.) 170	1/34 2/39 3/53 (4 wkts) 78
		4/78

A. W. J. Spiller (*Yeovil College*), †P. Gill (*Grange*), C. Penn (*Dover GS*), N. A. P. Meadows (*Sedbergh*) and N. A. Foster (*Philip Morant*) did not bat.

Bowling: *First Innings*—Hinchliffe 10–3–18–0; Haswell 9–4–19–0; Robertshaw 17–6–36–0; Gadsby 4–0–20–0; Neal 4–0–22–0; M. Bailey 9–1–28–0; Sutton 6–0–20–1. *Second Innings*—Hinchliffe 4–1–10–0; Haswell 3–1–10–0; M. Bailey 6–4–3–1; Robertshaw 14–5–25–1; Sutton 5–0–14–1; Settle 6–0–8–1; Gadsby 2–0–8–0.

Umpires: A. E. Bishop and D. E. E. Collins.

July 25. Combined Services won by four wickets. NCA Young Cricketers 183 for six (55 overs) (A. Settle 60 not out, S. J. Bailey 37); Combined Services 187 for six (52.4 overs) (R. C. Moylan-Jones 38, A. Izzard 35, A. T. D. Lerwill 32 not out, M. J. Robinson 30).

August 23. John Haig Trophy final. Moseley won by nine wickets. Gosport Borough 176 for eight (45 overs) (M. Swain 49, M. Nurmohamed 45; A. Donner four for 39); Moseley 177 for one (42.1 overs) (R. B. Milne 85 not out, J. Watts 50 not out).

August 24. Samuel Whitbread National Village Championship final. Marchwiel won by 79 runs. Marchwiel (North Wales) 161 for eight (40 overs) (P. Barrett 47, R. Davis 34); Longparish (Hampshire) 82 for nine (40 overs) (J. Bell three for 23).

August 28, 29, 30, September 1, 2. Cornhill Centenary Test. ENGLAND drew with AUSTRALIA (See Australian tour section).

September 6. Gillette Cup final. MIDDLESEX beat SURREY by seven wickets (See Gillette Cup section).

HONOURS' LIST

In 1980 the following were decorated for their services to cricket:

New Year's Honours: S. Atkin (Australia) MBE (also to the Anglican Church); R. J. Halliday (Australia) MBE.

Queen's Birthday Honours: G. Boycott (England) OBE; F. R. Brown (England) CBE; R. J. Hadlee (New Zealand) MBE; J. A. Maclean (Australia) MBE; W. J. O'Reilly (Australia) OBE.

COUNTY CHAMPIONSHIP, 1980

Sponsored by Schweppes

MIDDLESEX LEAD THE WAY

The County Championship, which reflects more accurately than any other competition the true cricketing abilities of the participants, was, for the second successive season, virtually a one-horse race. Middlesex went top on June 3 and, although chased by runners-up Surrey, who on July 8 used the advantage of an extra game played to get within four points of the leaders, always looked assured of their seventh outright title win and the £9,000 prize money. Surrey retained second place from June 6, thus maintaining their previous season's improvement and winning themselves £4,000. Surrey's 67 points advantage over Nottinghamshire, whose rise from ninth to third won them £2,000, emphasised the superiority of the two leaders. Sussex, despite economic troubles, struck form in the season's second half to maintain fourth place and win £1,000.

Somerset's good August enabled them to advance from eighth to fifth, but lacking their stars for much of the time they never made a serious challenge, while Gloucestershire's advance from tenth to seventh was due mainly to three successive wins in August which took them out of the lower reaches. Derbyshire's advance of seven places to ninth came as the result of their mid-season consistency after a poor start, and although they and Glamorgan – last to thirteenth – never looked likely to break into the top flight, both counties must be grateful for comparative respectability.

Seventh in 1979, Yorkshire were among the leaders in July but declined to a discontented sixth. Northamptonshire, too, gradually lost their momentum to remain much as they were the previous season. Warwickshire showed no real improvement after early promise, while Lancashire gave little indication of escape from the slough that has enveloped their cricket of late. Leicestershire failed to check their recent steady decline and seem in need of a new stimulus.

Major declines were shown by four sides. Defending champions Essex led the field in late May but gradually drifted out of contention as their stalwarts struggled, and Worcestershire, lacking bowling penetration, plunged from second to eleventh. The biggest slump, however, was suffered by Kent – eleven places from fifth to sixteenth. Last of all, Hampshire, lacking their two West Indians, Greenidge and Marshall, for most of the season and in the throes of rebuilding, hit the bottom on May 30, waited until August 26 for their only win, and never looked likely to improve their position.

SCHWEPPES CHAMPIONSHIP TABLE

Win = 12 points	Played	Won	Lost	Drawn	Bonus points Batting	Bowling	Points
1 – Middlesex (14)	22	10	2	10	58	80	258
2 – Surrey (3)	22	10	4	8	51	74	245
3 – Nottinghamshire (9) ...	22	6	5	11	42	64	178
4 – Sussex (4)	22	4	3	15	60	60	168
5 – Somerset (8)	21	3	5	13	56	70	168
6 – Yorkshire (7)	22	4	3	15	51	64	163
7 – Gloucestershire (10) ...	21	4	5	12	39	74	161
8 – Essex (1)	22	4	3	15	48	64	160
9 – ⎰ Derbyshire (16)	20	4	3	13	47	62	157
⎱ Leicestershire (6)	22	4	2	16	45	58	157
11 – Worcestershire (2)	21	3	7	11	54	61	151
12 – Northamptonshire (11) .	22	5	4	13	41	47	148
13 – Glamorgan (17)	21	4	4	13	43	57	148
14 – Warwickshire (15)	22	3	4	15	55	54	145
15 – Lancashire (13)	20	4	3	13	26	58	132
16 – Kent (5)	22	2	8	12	36	59	119
17 – Hampshire (12)	22	1	10	11	34	56	102

1979 positions in brackets.

Under Regulation 2(c), Leicestershire and Somerset were awarded 6 points in drawn matches when the scores were level.

The following four matches were abandoned and are not included in the above table: June 14, 16, 17 – Glamorgan v Worcestershire at Swansea, Gloucestershire v Derbyshire at Bristol, Somerset v Lancashire at Bath; August 9, 11, 12 – Derbyshire v Lancashire at Buxton.

REGULATIONS FOR SCHWEPPES CHAMPIONSHIP

1. Awards

First (Middlesex)..	£9,000
Second (Surrey)..	£4,000
Third (Nottinghamshire)..	£2,000
Fourth (Sussex)...	£1,000
Winner of each match..	£150
Each bonus point	£5

2. Scoring of Points

(a) For a win, 12 points, plus any points scored in the first innings.

(b) In a tie, each side to score six points, plus any points scored in the first innings.

(c) If the scores are equal in a drawn match, the side batting in the fourth innings to score six points, plus any points scored in the first innings.

(d) **First Innings Points** (awarded only for performances **in the first 100 overs** of each first innings and retained whatever the result of the match).

    (i) A maximum of four batting points to be available as under:
        150 to 199 runs – 1 point; 200 to 249 runs – 2 points; 250 to 299 runs – 3 points; 300 runs or over – 4 points.

    (ii) A maximum of four bowling points to be available as under:
        3 to 4 wickets taken – 1 point; 5 to 6 wickets taken – 2 points; 7 to 8 wickets taken – 3 points; 9 to 10 wickets taken – 4 points.

(*e*) If play starts when less than eight hours playing time remain and a one innings match is played, no first innings points shall be scored. The side winning on the one innings to score 12 points.

(*f*) The side which has the highest aggregate of points gained at the end of the season shall be the Champion County. Should any sides in the County Championship Table be equal on points, the side with most wins will have priority.

3. Limitation of Overs in First Innings

The two first innings will be limited to a total of 200 overs, of which the side batting first will be limited to not more than 100 overs. Any partly completed over at the end of the innings of the side batting first, shall count as a full over in assessing the numbers of overs to be allowed to the side batting second.

4. Declarations

Law 14 will apply, but, in addition, a captain may also forfeit his first innings, subject to the provisions set out in Law 14.2.

COUNTY CHAMPIONSHIP – MATCH RESULTS 1864-1980

County	Years of Play	Played	Won	Lost	Tied	Drawn
Derbyshire	1871-87; 1895-1980	1,883	468	713	—	702
Essex	1895-1980	1,847	499	558	5	785
Glamorgan	1921-1980	1,381	318	484	—	579
Gloucestershire	1870-1980	2,126	647	798	1	680
Hampshire	1864-85; 1895-1980	1,956	506	697	4	749
Kent	1864-1980	2,242	845	695	2	700
Lancashire	1865-1980	2,321	902	463	3	953
Leicestershire	1895-1980	1,813	377	715	1	720
Middlesex	1864-1980	2,025	762	527	5	731
Northamptonshire	1905-1980	1,580	376	586	2	616
Nottinghamshire	1864-1980	2,154	652	573	—	929
Somerset	1882-85, 1891-1980	1,853	442	796	3	612
Surrey	1864-1980	2,400	981	523	4	892
Sussex	1864-1980	2,297	654	804	4	835
Warwickshire	1895-1980	1,826	491	535	1	799
Worcestershire	1899-1980	1,767	432	651	1	683
Yorkshire	1864-1980	2,424	1,152	386	2	884
Cambridgeshire	1864-69; 1871	19	8	8	—	3
		33,914	10,512	10,512	38	12,852

1. Counties participated in the years shown, except that there were no matches in the years 1915-18 and 1940-45; Hampshire did not play inter-county matches in 1868-69, 1871-74 and 1879; Worcestershire did not take part in the Championship in 1919.
2. Matches abandoned without a ball bowled are wholly excluded.

DERBYSHIRE

President – THE DUKE OF DEVONSHIRE

Chairman, Cricket Committee – C. S. ELLIOTT

Secretary – D. A. HARRISON
County Ground, Nottingham Road, Derby, DE2 6DA

Captain – G. MILLER

P. N. Kirsten	County Badge	J. Walters

Derbyshire's progress in 1980 could be measured by improved final placings in both the John Player League and the Schweppes County Championship, in which two more victories would have given them third place. In a dismally wet summer, bleak statistics adequately support Derbyshire's frustration. Four games which looked like being won were washed out, while no play at all was possible in two others.

There were disappointments in the Gillette Cup, with an unexpected defeat by Hampshire, and in the Benson and Hedges Cup, when the early unavailability of Mike Hendrick and the newly signed Barry Wood, as well as some curious team selection, led to performances far inferior to those of the two previous seasons.

The same handicaps contributed to a poor start in the John Player League, a competition in which early success is vital. Eventually, when the side knitted together, they achieved a succession of victories to suggest they might challenge for honours, but in the end they fell away in a manner which seemed to sum up their season: an above-average team but one that still lacked some of the ingredients of success.

Geoff Miller, in his first full season as captain, inevitably came under pressure. While striving to lead the side aggressively and positively, he could not avoid mistakes, and the fact that he was often preoccupied with his own form made his job no easier. Although his place in the batting order seemed low for a player of Test experience, this was no doubt influenced by the cares of captaincy, and his vigorous displays when opening on Sundays illustrated what the team was missing.

Yet, when everyone was fit and in form, Miller frequently welded them into an effective and competitive unit. However, the balance of the side was sometimes questionable, one reason being that Miller's bowling was only ordinary for much of the season. Although David Steele took his 100th wicket for the county in two seasons – besides doing the hat-trick – there was often a lack of top-class spin. The 100 overs regulation can be partially blamed for the limited use of Kim Barnett's leg-spin, even though there were plenty of big totals for him to bowl against and so gain experience.

The seam attack was strengthened by the arrival of Steve Oldham and there were few days when he did not make a contribution, despite having less luck than most. Colin Tunnicliffe at last broke the five-wicket barrier, achieving career-best figures in successive matches, and when Hendrick was at his best their attack looked formidable. Despite one or two match-winning performances, however, and a memorable hat-trick against the West Indians, Hendrick had days when his appetite for the game seemed diminished. This must have contributed to his decision not to make himself available for the tour of the West Indies earlier this year.

The batting was dominated by the overseas pair, Peter Kirsten and John Wright. Kirsten had one of the most prolific seasons in the county's history. His six Championship centuries equalled the record established by Leslie Townsend in 1933 and, whereas no previous Derbyshire batsman had ever made more than two double centuries in a career, Kirsten hit three in the season, all unbeaten. Having solved the problems of concentration which bedevilled him earlier, the slenderly built South African scored run after run in a manner that was both aristocratic and ruthless.

Wright's 96 against the West Indians, on a pitch generally acknowledged as "lethal", was outstandingly courageous. Although still a batsman of moods, Wright hit three Championship centuries and, with Kirsten, became the first Derbyshire player since 1971 to pass 1,500 runs in first-class matches. Wood, unable to play until early June after his move from Lancashire, made two Championship centuries, yet probably needed more cricket to do himself full justice. His attitude on and off the field was invaluable, as was his experience as Miller's deputy. Wood's arrival meant there was no place for Alan Hill, and the success of the early batting tended to restrict opportunities for the middle order or, ironically, to put them under pressure if the overseas pair were dismissed cheaply.

Bob Taylor, despite being unluckily discarded by the England selectors, was back to his impeccable best behind the stumps; he also made his highest score for the county and richly deserves his second benefit.

All things considered, a better Derbyshire emerged through the murk and rain that constituted the summer of 1980. Given a full-strength start, plus weather that allows them to display their talents under a more experienced captain, there should be enough potential for success in the short-term. But time is not on the side of certain key members and there is as yet little evidence of adequate replacements. – Michael Carey.

373

DERBYSHIRE

Derby Evening Telegraph

Back row: A. J. McLellan, I. S. Anderson, A. J. Mellor, K. G. Brooks, R. C. Wincer, J. W. Lister. *Middle row:* R. C. Beardmore (*scorer*), K. J. Barnett, J. Walters, A. J. Borrington, C. J. Tunnicliffe, A. Hill, S. Oldham, J. D. Brown (*coaching organiser*), F. Allen (*physiotherapist*). *Front row:* P. N. Kirsten, D. S. Steele, B. Wood, G. Miller (*captain*), D. A. Harrison (*secretary*), R. W. Taylor, P. E. Russell (*coach*), J. G. Wright.

DERBYSHIRE RESULTS

All First-class Matches – Played 21: Won 4, Lost 4, Drawn 13. Abandoned 2.

County Championship Matches – Played 20: Won 4, Lost 3, Drawn 13. Abandoned 2.

Bonus points – Batting 47, Bowling 62.

COUNTY CHAMPIONSHIP AVERAGES

BATTING

	Birthplace	Matches	Inns	Not Outs	Runs	Highest Inns	Avge
P. N. Kirsten	Pietermaritzburg, SA	20	34	6	1,891	213*	67.53
P. G. Newman	Leicester	3	4	3	60	29*	60.00
J. G. Wright	Darfield, NZ	19	34	5	1,395	166*	48.10
B. Wood	Ossett	16	28	3	861	113	34.44
G. Miller	Chesterfield	19	25	5	641	78*	32.05
D. S. Steele	Stoke-on-Trent	19	29	7	660	86*	30.00
J. Walters	Brampton	16	24	0	440	72	22.00
K. J. Barnett	Stoke-on-Trent	15	19	0	338	69	17.78
I. S. Anderson	Derby	13	15	4	187	36	17.00
C. J. Tunnicliffe	Derby	20	24	7	264	56*	15.52
R. W. Taylor	Stoke-on-Trent	20	21	5	238	75	14.87
M. Hendrick	Darley Dale	11	11	4	95	33	13.57
A. J. Borrington	Derby	5	8	1	79	36	11.28
A. Hill	Buxworth	2	4	0	14	7	3.50
S. Oldham	Sheffield	19	10	4	11	7	1.83

Also batted: K. G. Brooks (*Reading*) 3, 8; R. C. Wincer (*Portsmouth*) played in two matches but did not bat.

* *Signifies not out.*

BOWLING

	Overs	Maidens	Runs	Wickets	Average
M. Hendrick	332.1	101	660	47	14.04
D. S. Steele	430	123	1,221	54	22.61
G. Miller	550.4	174	1,386	54	25.66
C. J. Tunnicliffe	427.5	89	1,244	47	26.46
S. Oldham	460.2	102	1,381	41	33.68

Also bowled: I. S. Anderson 23–2–94–0; K. J. Barnett 55.3–13–230–7; P. N. Kirsten 28.5–8–90–1; P. G. Newman 40.2–7–143–4; J. Walters 13.4–0–55–0; R. C. Wincer 27–5–109–3; B. Wood 111–22–297–7.

HUNDREDS

The following eleven three-figure innings were played for Derbyshire in County Championship matches – P. N. Kirsten 213* v Glamorgan (Derby), 209* v Northamptonshire (Derby), 202* v Essex (Chesterfield), 162* v Lancashire (Manchester), 116 v Sussex (Derby), 101 v Somerset (Chesterfield); J. G. Wright 166* v Lancashire (Manchester), 155 v Worcestershire (Worcester), 117 v Northamptonshire (Derby); B. Wood 113 v Warwickshire (Birmingham), 101* v Worcestershire (Worcester).

At Manchester, April 30, May 1, 2. DERBYSHIRE drew with LANCASHIRE.

DERBYSHIRE v NORTHAMPTONSHIRE

At Derby, May 7, 8, 9. Northamptonshire won by two wickets. Northamptonshire 14 pts, Derbyshire 8 pts. A partnership of 253 between Kirsten, whose career-best unbeaten 209 included three 6s and 24 4s, and Wright, who also scored a century, put Derbyshire in command on a good pitch. A week earlier the same pair figured in an unbroken stand of 321 against Lancashire. Northamptonshire narrowly avoided the follow-on, thanks mainly tc Carter who was missed at slip. After another good innings by Wright the visitors were asked tc make 321 in 280 minutes, and with their first four batsmen all playing well, it looked an easy task. But the return of Tunnicliffe and Oldham brought a dramatic change and victory was achieved with only four balls to spare.

Derbyshire

A. Hill b T. M. Lamb	0	– lbw b T. M. Lamb	7
J. G. Wright c Sharp b Williams	117	– st Sharp b Carter	88
P. N. Kirsten not out	209	– lbw b T. M. Lamb	8
D. S. Steele not out	42	– c Cook b Willey	3
K. J. Barnett (did not bat)	–	lbw b T. M. Lamb	20
A. J. Borrington (did not bat)	–	c Sharp b Carter	0
I. S. Anderson (did not bat)	–	not out	21
*†R. W. Taylor (did not bat)	–	c A. J. Lamb b T. M. Lamb	1
C. J. Tunnicliffe (did not bat)	–	not out	17
B 1, l-b 2, n-b 1	4	B 1, l-b 6, n-b 2	9

1/0 2/253   (2 wkts) 372   1/12 2/26 3/37   (7 wkts dec.) 174
4/113 5/119 6/134 7/141

R. C. Wincer and S. Oldham did not bat.

Bonus points – Derbyshire 4.

Bowling: *First Innings*—T. M. Lamb 27–4–89–1; Booden 15–0–53–0; Larkins 8–1–36–0; Willey 29–6–82–0; Carter 6–0–31–0; Williams 15–1–77–1. *Second Innings*—T. M. Lamb 25–10–49–4; Booden 9–0–33–0; Willey 22–8–31–1; Williams 5–1–18–0; Carter 10.2–3–34–2.

Northamptonshire

W. Larkins lbw b Oldham	7	c Kirsten b Tunnicliffe	37
*G. Cook c Barnett b Tunnicliffe	1	b Wincer	48
R. G. Williams c Taylor b Tunnicliffe	1	(4) b Oldham	72
A. J. Lamb c and b Steele	73	(3) c Tunnicliffe b Oldham	97
P. Willey b Wincer	55	c Taylor b Tunnicliffe	0
T. J. Yardley c Tunnicliffe b Steele	14	lbw b Oldham	14
R. M. Tindall c Wright b Oldham	25	c Kirsten b Tunnicliffe	15
†G. Sharp c Taylor b Oldham	6	not out	22
R. M. Carter c Anderson b Barnett	26	c Wright b Oldham	0
T. M. Lamb c Taylor b Oldham	0	not out	1
C. D. Booden not out	6		
B 2, l-b 2, n-b 8	12	L-b 7, n-b 11	18

1/1 2/9 3/10 4/102   226   1/79 2/100 3/264   (8 wkts) 324
5/131 6/182 7/186 8/199 9/199   4/269 5/271 6/288
7/312 8/312

Bonus points – Northamptonshire 2, Derbyshire 4.

Bowling: *First Innings*—Oldham 25–4–75–4; Tunnicliffe 10–1–43–2; Steele 30–13–45–2; Wincer 5–0–25–1; Anderson 10–1–26–0; Barnett 0.1–0–0–1. *Second Innings*—Oldham 23.2–4–81–4; Tunnicliffe 29–4–105–3; Steele 13–1–46–0; Wincer 2–0–18–1; Anderson 4–1–10–0; Barnett 4–0–32–0; Kirsten 6–2–14–0.

Umpires: A. Jepson and C. T. Spencer.

At Chesterfield, May 24, 25, 26. DERBYSHIRE lost to WEST INDIANS by nine wickets (See West Indian tour section).

DERBYSHIRE v HAMPSHIRE

At Chesterfield, May 28, 29, 30. Derbyshire won by ten wickets. Derbyshire 18 pts, Hampshire 4 pts. With the ball moving about and bouncing unevenly, Hampshire were undermined by Hendrick who took seven for 19, following up his good performance against the West Indians on the same pitch. The visitors failed to exploit the conditions and Miller's aggressive 66 steered Derbyshire to a lead of 134. Struggling in their second innings against the spin of Steele, Hampshire were close to defeat in two days. Derbyshire needed less than half an hour on the last morning to complete their first Championship win of the season and their first over Hampshire for seventeen years.

Hampshire

J. M. Rice lbw b Hendrick	2	– c and b Steele	18
C. L. Smith c Wright b Hendrick	6	– c Taylor b Tunnicliffe	3
D. R. Turner c Tunnicliffe b Hendrick	1	– c Walters b Steele	25
T. E. Jesty b Oldham	18	– c Walters b Hendrick	0
*N. E. J. Pocock c Steele b Hendrick	18	– st Taylor b Steele	31
N. G. Cowley lbw b Tunnicliffe	7	– c Walters b Steele	0
M. N. S. Taylor c Wright b Hendrick	10	– not out	30
†G. R. Stephenson c Wright b Hendrick	0	– c Barnett b Steele	0
J. W. Southern c Miller b Hendrick	6	– lbw b Miller	0
K. Stevenson c Hendrick b Tunnicliffe	5	– c Barnett b Miller	11
S. J. Malone not out	0	– lbw b Miller	1
B 1, l-b 4, w 2, n-b 6	13	B 9, l-b 7, n-b 10	26

1/9 2/10 3/19 4/34 5/63 6/63   86
7/63 8/78 9/82

1/10 2/33 3/34 4/72 5/72   145
6/99 7/107 8/116 9/143

Bonus points – Derbyshire 4.

Bowling: *First Innings*—Hendrick 17–6–19–7; Tunnicliffe 18.3–5–36–2; Oldham 6–3–11–1; Walters 4–0–7–0. *Second Innings*—Hendrick 13–5–16–1; Tunnicliffe 5–1–16–1; Steele 17–7–52–5; Miller 19.5–9–32–3; Oldham 2–0–3–0.

Derbyshire

A. J. Borrington c Pocock b Malone	4	– not out	5
J. G. Wright c Stephenson b Taylor	26	– not out	7
P. N. Kirsten c Pocock b Stevenson	51		
D. S. Steele c Taylor b Malone	20		
K. J. Barnett c Taylor b Rice	8		
*G. Miller c Turner b Jesty	66		
J. Walters c Stephenson b Cowley	5		
†R. W. Taylor not out	17		
C. J. Tunnicliffe c Malone b Southern	11		
S. Oldham c and b Jesty	0		
M. Hendrick b Jesty	2		
L-b 5, w 3, n-b 2	10		

1/4 2/56 3/92 4/107 5/120 6/143   220
7/201 8/216 9/216

(no wkt) 12

Bonus points – Derbyshire 2, Hampshire 4.

Bowling: *First Innings*—Malone 16–4–64–2; Stevenson 16–2–56–1; Taylor 8–0–32–1; Rice 10–3–17–1; Southern 12–4–25–1; Cowley 3–1–5–1; Jesty 6.2–2–11–3. *Second Innings*—Turner 3.1–1–9–0; Cowley 2–1–3–0; Stephenson 1–1–0–0.

Umpires: D. O. Oslear and R. Julian.

At Leicester, May 31, June 2, 3. DERBYSHIRE drew with LEICESTERSHIRE.

At Birmingham, June 4, 5, 6. DERBYSHIRE drew with WARWICKSHIRE.

DERBYSHIRE v GLAMORGAN

At Derby, June 7, 9, 10. Drawn. Derbyshire 7 pts, Glamorgan 5 pts. In a remarkable display of attacking batsmanship, Kirsten made his second double century in successive months and became the first Derbyshire player ever to make three. His first was also made against Glamorgan, in 1978. Hitting 32 4s and five 6s in two hundred and thirty-one minutes, Kirsten devastated an unpretentious attack in an innings of only 68 overs. He made a century between lunch and tea, then added his final 105 runs out of 127 in eighteen overs, making 63 from the last seven overs of the innings. For Glamorgan, Alan Jones hit the 49th century of his career, but the visitors were still 85 behind. After rain on the last day, they were asked to make 227 in 150 minutes, and had reached 177 for three with eight overs left when Steele cut short their challenge by dismissing Nash, Featherstone and Holmes to achieve the hat-trick for the first time.

Derbyshire

B. Wood c A. Jones b Ontong	43	– b Lloyd	22
J. G. Wright run out	94	– not out	75
P. N. Kirsten not out	213	– c E. W. Jones b Nash	39
D. S. Steele c Hopkins b Holmes	16	– not out	1
K. J. Barnett c Nash b Holmes	3		
J. Walters not out	20		
B 4, l-b 6, n-b 3	13	L-b 3, n-b 1	4

1/83 2/191 3/259 4/275   (4 wkts) 402   1/67 2/138   (2 wkts dec.) 141

*G. Miller, I. S. Anderson, †R. W. Taylor, C. J. Tunnicliffe and S. Oldham did not bat.

Bonus points – Derbyshire 4, Glamorgan 1.

Bowling: *First Innings*—Nash 23–4–80–0; A. A. Jones 21–2–90–0; Ontong 17–3–57–1; Lloyd 15–3–64–0; Hobbs 11–2–44–0; Holmes 13–3–54–2. *Second Innings*—A. A. Jones 7–1–44–0; Nash 15.3–7–51–1; Ontong 8–2–30–0; Lloyd 4–1–11–1; Hobbs 2–1–1–0; Featherstone 1–1–0–0.

Glamorgan

A. Jones c Steele b Wood	119	– c Taylor b Miller	44
J. A. Hopkins b Miller	61	– c sub b Steele	39
R. C. Ontong c Kirsten b Steele	52	– run out	20
Javed Miandad st Taylor b Steele	28	– not out	44
N. G. Featherstone st Taylor b Steele	2	– (6) c Wood b Steele	0
G. C. Holmes not out	11	– (7) c and b Steele	0
†E. W. Jones c Walters b Steele	2	– (8) c Oldham b Steele	5
*M. A. Nash b Oldham	13	– (5) c and b Steele	35
B. J. Lloyd not out	14	– not out	0
L-b 5, n-b 10	15	L-b 3, n-b 8	11

1/152 2/228 3/266 4/271   (7 wkts) 317   1/79 2/102 3/117   (7 wkts) 198
5/275 6/278 7/296   4/177 5/177 6/177 7/193

R. N. S. Hobbs and A. A. Jones did not bat.

Bonus points – Glamorgan 4, Derbyshire 3.

Bowling: *First Innings*—Oldham 23–6–63–1; Tunnicliffe 11–3–33–0; Steele 28–6–94–4; Wood 15–1–61–1; Miller 17–6–25–1; Barnett 4–0–22–0; Anderson 4–0–22–0. *Second Innings*—Oldham 5–0–25–0; Wood 3–1–4–0; Miller 21–3–84–1; Steele 20–4–74–5.

Umpires: H. D. Bird and D. J. Dennis.

At Bristol, June 14, 16, 17. GLOUCESTERSHIRE v DERBYSHIRE. Abandoned.

At Northampton, June 18, 19, 20. DERBYSHIRE beat NORTHAMPTONSHIRE by eight wickets.

DERBYSHIRE v ESSEX

At Chesterfield, June 21, 23, 24. Drawn. Derbyshire 8 pts, Essex 1 pt. The remarkable Kirsten completed his third, unbeaten double-century of the season and, at 78, became the second batsman to 1,000 runs for the season after Gooch. He batted with measured aggression for just over six hours, hitting two 6s and nineteen 4s, and on the second morning was joined by Miller (ten 4s) to add 108 from 21 overs. Essex collapsed against the bowling of Oldham and Tunnicliffe, who had career-best figures for the second successive innings. Following on, Essex collapsed to 16 for three, and when rain arrived on the final day they were still 56 behind with seven wickets down. On resumption, there was time for only 34 deliveries before the game ended in a draw.

Derbyshire

J. G. Wright c Smith b Lever	8	*G. Miller not out		71
B. Wood lbw b Lever	0			
P. N. Kirsten not out	202	L-b 8, w 6, n-b 5		19
D. S. Steele lbw b Phillip	34			
K. J. Barnett lbw b Lever	18	1/0 2/17 3/131 4/186	(4 wkts dec.)	352

I. S. Anderson, J. Walters, †R. W. Taylor, C. J. Tunnicliffe and S. Oldham did not bat.

Bonus points – Derbyshire 4, Essex 1.

Bowling: Lever 35–6–92–3; Phillip 31.5–3–145–1; Pont 21–1–59–0; East 7–0–17–0; Acfield 5–2–20–0.

Essex

M. H. Denness c Taylor b Oldham	0 – c Miller b Tunnicliffe	2
M. S. A. McEvoy lbw b Oldham	24 – c Tunnicliffe b Steele	65
K. S. McEwan b Tunnicliffe	6 – lbw b Oldham	0
*K. W. R. Fletcher c Miller b Tunnicliffe	2 – c Taylor b Oldham	0
B. R. Hardie c Steele b Tunnicliffe	13 – c Taylor b Tunnicliffe	70
K. R. Pont c Taylor b Tunnicliffe	10 – c Kirsten b Oldham	10
N. Phillip c Taylor b Oldham	7 – c Miller b Oldham	14
R. E. East c Wood b Tunnicliffe	0 – not out	35
J. K. Lever c Taylor b Tunnicliffe	1 – not out	5
D. L. Acfield not out	2	
†N. Smith b Tunnicliffe	15	
B 1, n-b 4	5	B 3, l-b 2, n-b 11	16

1/1 2/11 3/13 4/35 5/58	85	1/8 2/16 3/16 4/113	(7 wkts) 217
6/58 7/58 8/67 9/68		5/146 6/160 7/192	

Bonus points – Derbyshire 4.

Bowling: *First Innings*—Tunnicliffe 19.1–5–36–7; Oldham 19–5–44–3. *Second Innings*—Tunnicliffe 20–6–43–2; Oldham 22.4–3–79–4; Steele 18–4–46–1; Wood 4–2–3–0; Walters 3–0–4–0; Miller 12–4–22–0; Barnett 1–0–4–0.

Umpires: P. B. Wight and T. W. Spencer.

At Dartford, June 28, 30, July 1. DERBYSHIRE drew with KENT.

DERBYSHIRE v LEICESTERSHIRE

At Burton upon Trent, July 2, 3, 4. Drawn. Derbyshire 6 pts, Leicestershire 4 pts. Overnight rain prevented any play on the final day of a hard-fought game played on a pitch where the batsmen always had to work for runs. Derbyshire's 216, after they had been put in, was at that stage the season's lowest score for a team not bowled out in 100 overs. They were indebted to a useful opening partnership, followed by a gritty innings from Steele and a more fluent one by Miller. On the second day, Gower's first Championship century since 1977 (fifteen 4s) kept his side in contention, although Hendrick took the last five wickets for 8 runs in six overs to restrict their lead.

Derbyshire

J. G. Wright c Balderstone b Steele	31	– not out		17
B. Wood c Tolchard b Clift	38	– not out		26
P. N. Kirsten c Cook b Steele	5			
D. S. Steele c Davison b Clift	47			
K. J. Barnett b Steele	12			
*G. Miller not out	51			
C. J. Tunnicliffe st Tolchard b Cook	6			
I. S. Anderson not out	6			
L-b 15, w 1, n-b 4	20	L-b 1		1

1/73 2/73 3/83 4/105	(6 wkts) 216	(no wkt) 44
5/174 6/183		

†R. W. Taylor, S. Oldham and M. Hendrick did not bat.

Bonus points – Derbyshire 2, Leicestershire 2.

Bowling: *First Innings*—Taylor 16–4–38–0; Agnew 9–2–21–0; Cook 24–6–57–1; Birkenshaw 3–0–16–0; Steele 29–14–38–3; Clift 19–9–26–2. *Second Innings*—Taylor 5–1–17–0; Clift 5–2–7–0; Agnew 3–1–8–0; Cook 2–0–11–0.

Leicestershire

J. F. Steele c Anderson b Hendrick	0	N. G. B. Cook b Hendrick		0
N. E. Briers run out	4	J. P. Agnew b Hendrick		8
J. C. Balderstone lbw b Miller	9	L. B. Taylor b Hendrick		0
D. I. Gower b Steele	100			
*B. F. Davison lbw b Tunnicliffe	36	L-b 11, n-b 4		15
†R. W. Tolchard c Miller b Hendrick	32			
J. Birkenshaw b Hendrick	12	1/0 2/7 3/28 4/83 5/179		226
P. B. Clift not out	10	6/205 7/212 8/212 9/226		

Bonus points – Leicestershire 2, Derbyshire 4.

Bowling: Hendrick 25–10–50–6; Oldham 20–4–42–0; Tunnicliffe 8–2–19–1; Miller 20–9–35–1; Steele 9–0–52–1; Wood 10–3–13–0.

Umpires: D. J. Dennis and D. Shackleton.

DERBYSHIRE v SOMERSET

At Chesterfield, July 12, 14, 15. Derbyshire won by nine wickets. Derbyshire 20 pts, Somerset 4 pts. After winning the toss Somerset batted unevenly on a pitch that gave some slow movement to seam bowling. Hendrick proved his fitness by bowling 34 overs. Derbyshire achieved a first innings lead of 109 thanks to a high-class innings by Wright – who hit thirteen 4s before falling to a brilliant stumping – and yet another century from Kirsten, who hit three 6s and eleven 4s. In the second innings Hendrick took the crucial wicket of Gavaskar and, with the ball turning slowly, Miller and Steele kept Somerset under pressure. Derbyshire were left with ninety minutes to complete their victory.

Somerset

S. M. Gavaskar c Walters b Tunnicliffe	26	– c Oldham b Hendrick	6
M. Olive c Steele b Hendrick	21	– c Miller b Steele	15
P. M. Roebuck lbw b Tunnicliffe	0	– c Taylor b Miller	33
P. W. Denning b Oldham	38	– c Taylor b Miller	5
P. A. Slocombe c Kirsten b Miller	23	– c Miller b Hendrick	2
*V. J. Marks b Hendrick	29	– c Wood b Steele	8
†D. J. S. Taylor lbw b Hendrick	28	– c Wood b Steele	48
N. F. M. Popplewell c Wood b Hendrick	3	– lbw b Miller	1
C. H. Dredge c Taylor b Hendrick	21	– c Miller b Hendrick	5
K. F. Jennings lbw b Oldham	21	– not out	17
H. R. Moseley not out	12	– c Tunnicliffe b Miller	16
L-b 6, n-b 3	9	N-b 3	3

1/41 2/41 3/60 4/108   231   1/10 2/32 3/59 4/64   159
5/128 6/149 7/155   5/64 6/114 7/117
8/189 9/202   8/121 9/142

Bonus points – Somerset 2, Derbyshire 4.

Bowling: *First Innings*—Hendrick 34–12–64–5; Tunnicliffe 24–4–64–2; Oldham 19.3–3–62–2; Miller 15–8–27–1; Wood 4–0–5–0. *Second Innings*—Hendrick 17–3–49–3; Tunnicliffe 5–2–8–0; Steele 17–5–34–3; Oldham 3–1–11–0; Miller 19.3–7–54–4.

Derbyshire

B. Wood c Taylor b Dredge	48	– not out	22
J. G. Wright st Taylor b Popplewell	72	– c Denning b Slocombe	25
P. N. Kirsten c Jennings b Dredge	101	– not out	0
D. S. Steele c Denning b Marks	38		
K. J. Barnett b Dredge	41		
*G. Miller b Dredge	19		
J. Walters c Marks b Popplewell	3		
C. J. Tunnicliffe c Marks b Dredge.	0		
†R. W. Taylor not out	2		
B 2, l-b 7, w 1, n-b 6	16	L-b 4, w 1	5

1/110 2/132 3/227 4/277   (8 wkts) 340   1/48   (1 wkt) 52
5/309 6/336 7/336 8/340

M. Hendrick and S. Oldham did not bat.

Bonus points – Derbyshire 4, Somerset 2 (Score at 100 overs: 334-5).

Bowling: *First Innings*—Moseley 23–0–53–0; Dredge 29–6–68–5; Jennings 13–2–42–0; Popplewell 15–1–78–2; Marks 21–1–81–1; Roebuck 1–0–2–0. *Second Innings*—Moseley 6–1–10–0; Dredge 3–0–13–0; Marks 6–1–8–0; Jennings 4–1–5–0; Roebuck 1.2–0–6–0; Slocombe 1–0–5–1.

Umpires: C. Cook and J. van Geloven.

At Worksop, July 23, 24, 25. DERBYSHIRE lost to NOTTINGHAMSHIRE by 89 runs.

At Worcester, July 26, 28, 29. DERBYSHIRE drew with WORCESTERSHIRE.

DERBYSHIRE v YORKSHIRE

At Chesterfield, August 2, 4, 5. Drawn. Derbyshire 4 pts, Yorkshire 6 pts. Both teams seemed capable of winning a remarkable contest on an unpredictable pitch until Derbyshire, facing defeat at the end of the second day, achieved a memorable recovery. After Old's best bowling performance of the season had plunged Derbyshire in trouble, Yorkshire were themselves reduced to 79 for seven and owed much to Stevenson's maiden century after he had been missed at 16. He batted nearly three hours, hitting eleven 4s and three 6s. Derbyshire lost half their wickets before wiping out their first innings arrears, but then Yorkshire had to wait until after lunch on the last day for their next wicket. Half-centuries from Miller, Taylor, Walters and Tunnicliffe took the home team to safety. Taylor's innings included seven 4s and was his highest for the county.

Derbyshire

J. G. Wright c Hampshire b Old	8	– c Athey b Old	0
B. Wood c Athey b Old	14	– c Hampshire b Cope	12
P. N. Kirsten c and b Cooper	20	– lbw b Stevenson	8
D. S. Steele b Old	6	– c Carrick b Stevenson	3
K. J. Barnett c Athey b Cooper	10	– c Hampshire b Cooper	7
*G. Miller c Bairstow b Old	17	– c Stevenson b Old	61
J. Walters lbw b Stevenson	20	– (8) b Carrick	72
†R. W. Taylor c Bairstow b Old	5	– (7) c and b Carrick	75
C. J. Tunnicliffe c Cooper b Carrick	9	– not out	56
M. Hendrick c Cope b Old	21	– not out	0
S. Oldham not out	2		
B 1, l-b 5, w 4, n-b 5	15	B 7, l-b 4, n-b 9	20

1/13 2/47 3/47 4/56 5/77 6/97   147   1/0 2/14 3/24   (8 wkts dec.) 314
7/109 8/118 9/122   4/32 5/53 6/148
                                             7/209 8/313

Bonus points – Yorkshire 4.

Bowling: *First Innings*—Old 21.2–8–44–6; Stevenson 16–6–29–1; Cooper 10–1–39–2; Carrick 17–6–20–1. *Second Innings*—Old 31–9–66–2; Stevenson 20–3–70–2; Cooper 10–1–41–1; Carrick 31–14–45–2; Cope 24–6–44–1; Boycott 2–0–6–0; Love 3–0–22–0.

Yorkshire

G. Boycott run out	29	G. B. Stevenson c and b Hendrick	111
R. G. Lumb c Barnett b Hendrick	2	C. M. Old c Tunnicliffe b Miller	0
C. W. J. Athey c Taylor b Hendrick	2	H. P. Cooper not out	5
*J. H. Hampshire c Taylor b Hendrick	1		
J. D. Love c Barnett b Miller	4	L-b 5, w 2, n-b 11	18
P. Carrick b Tunnicliffe	16		
G. A. Cope c Oldham b Miller	33		223
†D. L. Bairstow c Miller b Tunnicliffe	2		

1/7 2/21 3/26 4/43 5/51
6/77 7/79 8/171 9/175

Bonus points – Yorkshire 2, Derbyshire 4.

Bowling: Hendrick 35–11–52–4; Tunnicliffe 22–3–57–2; Oldham 16–5–30–0; Steele 3–1–2–0; Miller 13–5–23–3; Walters 1–0–16–0; Wood 6–2–25–0.

Umpires: K. E. Palmer and W. L. Budd.

DERBYSHIRE v LANCASHIRE

At Buxton, August 9, 11, 12. Abandoned.

DERBYSHIRE v SURREY

At Derby, August 16, 18, 19. Derbyshire won by 174 runs. Derbyshire 17 pts, Surrey 4 pts. Put in on a variable pitch, Derbyshire lost their last six wickets for only 14 runs as Jackman became the first bowler in England to reach 100 wickets for the season, with a spell of four for 3. Surrey were then bowled out in only 49 overs and owed much to an aggressive innings by Clarke (four 6s and four 4s). Kirsten held the home team's second innings together, making 74 of the last 114 added. Required to make 289 in 221 minutes the visitors were soon in trouble as they chased the win they needed to keep in touch with Middlesex, the Championship leaders. Knight carried his bat for 57 but Miller's best bowling performance of the season, well supported by Hendrick, saw Derbyshire home.

Derbyshire

J. G. Wright c Jackman b Pocock	26	– c Clinton b Pocock 57
B. Wood c Cheatle b Pocock	27	– b Clarke 37
P. N. Kirsten c Jackman b Knight	68	– not out 84
D. S. Steele c Knight b Jackman	33	– (5) c Richards b Jackman 0
*G. Miller lbw b Pocock	9	– (6) c Lynch b Knight 10
J. Walters lbw b Jackman	14	– (7) c Smith b Pocock 2
I. S. Anderson c Richards b Jackman	0	– (9) b Knight 1
†R. W. Taylor b Pocock	3	– (4) c Richards b Jackman 6
C. J. Tunnicliffe b Jackman	5	– (8) b Pocock 0
M. Hendrick b Jackman	0	– c Knight b Clarke 11
S. Oldham not out	0	– b Clarke 1
B 5, l-b 3, w 1	9	B 9, l-b 4, n-b 1 14

1/59 2/65 3/162 4/164 5/182   194   1/86 2/102 3/125 4/125   223
6/186 7/186 8/194 9/194   5/175 6/188 7/188 8/201
                                                   9/221

Bonus points – Derbyshire 1, Surrey 4.

Bowling: *First Innings*—Clarke 15–6–25–0; Jackman 26–8–43–5; Pocock 30.3–7–64–4; Cheatle 12–4–24–0; Lynch 5–0–19–0; Knight 5–0–10–1. *Second Innings*—Jackman 18–5–34–2; Clarke 16.2–5–37–3; Knight 16–3–42–2; Pocock 29–6–73–3; Cheatle 4–0–23–0.

Surrey

A. R. Butcher lbw b Hendrick	6	– b Tunnicliffe 0
G. S. Clinton lbw b Oldham	20	– c Taylor b Oldham 7
*R. D. V. Knight c Hendrick b Miller	6	– not out 57
D. M. Smith b Oldham	1	– (6) lbw b Hendrick 6
G. R. J. Roope c Kirsten b Miller	11	– c Wood b Miller 0
M. A. Lynch c Steele b Miller	7	– (4) c Anderson b Miller 6
R. D. Jackman b Hendrick	2	– c Wood b Miller 7
†C. J. Richards lbw b Steele	10	– c Wood b Miller 6
S. T. Clarke c Walters b Oldham	55	– c Walters b Miller 18
P. I. Pocock c Walters b Oldham	0	– c Taylor b Hendrick 0
R. G. L. Cheatle not out	1	– b Hendrick 0
L-b 8, n-b 2	10	B 1, l-b 1, n-b 5 7

1/10 2/21 3/30 4/43 5/58 6/61   129   1/1 2/25 3/39 4/39 5/63   114
7/61 8/112 9/128   6/74 7/87 8/108 9/110

Bonus points – Derbyshire 4.

Bowling: *First Innings*—Hendrick 14–5–16–2; Tunnicliffe 5–1–6–0; Miller 14–6–40–3; Oldham 10.5–1–41–4; Steele 5–1–16–1. *Second Innings*—Hendrick 9.1–4–11–3; Tunnicliffe 4–0–19–1; Oldham 5–3–10–1; Miller 20–6–55–5; Kirsten 4–1–7–0; Steele 6–4–5–0.

Umpires: B. J. Meyer and R. Aspinall.

At Lord's, August 20, 21, 22. DERBYSHIRE lost to MIDDLESEX by nine wickets.

At Colchester, August 23, 25, 26. DERBYSHIRE drew with ESSEX.

DERBYSHIRE v NOTTINGHAMSHIRE

At Ilkeston, August 27, 28, 29. Drawn. Derbyshire 6 pts Nottinghamshire 5 pts. Derbyshire were frustrated by the loss of the last day because of rain after they had developed a winning position. This was first-class cricket's return to a ground which was banned in 1977 and Nottinghamshire, surprisingly put in, batted without distinction. Newman impressed on his second appearance for the home county. They, too, struggled for runs but the lower order scraped together a valuable lead and a good spell by Oldham plunged Nottinghamshire into more trouble before the end of the second day.

Nottinghamshire

P. A. Todd b Newman	19	– b Steele	27
R. T. Robinson c Wright b Oldham	16	– lbw b Oldham	8
D. W. Randall lbw b Tunnicliffe	11	– c Miller b Oldham	3
*C. E. B. Rice c Kirsten b Tunnicliffe	13	– (5) not out	19
R. E. Dexter c Anderson b Tunnicliffe	5	– (4) lbw b Oldham	2
J. D. Birch c and b Miller	25	– b Steele	5
†B. N. French c Anderson b Tunnicliffe	1		
R. J. Hadlee c Tunnicliffe b Miller	1		
E. E. Hemmings c Kirsten b Newman	45		
R. A. White c Tunnicliffe b Miller	2		
P. J. Hacker not out	11	– (7) not out	0
L-b 7, n-b 5	12	B 3, l-b 1, w 1, n-b 6	11

1/37 2/39 3/54 4/67 5/68   161   1/22 2/32   (5 wkts) 75
6/70 7/74 8/127 9/131   3/43 4/52 5/74

Bonus points – Nottinghamshire 1, Derbyshire 4.

Bowling: *First Innings*—Tunnicliffe 18–3–56–4; Oldham 14–3–31–1; Newman 14.2–4–41–2; Miller 18–10–21–3. *Second Innings*—Oldham 12–0–42–3; Tunnicliffe 6–2–11–0; Miller 3–0–3–0; Steele 8–5–8–2.

Derbyshire

B. Wood lbw b Hadlee	10	C. J. Tunnicliffe c Hacker b White	17
J. G. Wright b Hacker	20	P. G. Newman not out	17
P. N. Kirsten c French b Hadlee	0	S. Oldham b Rice	7
D. S. Steele lbw b Hadlee	14	B 1, l-b 10, w 8, n-b 1	20
*G. Miller c French b Rice	25		
J. Walters lbw b Rice	12	1/33 2/33 3/34 4/61	206
I. S. Anderson b Hacker	36	5/86 6/101 7/142	
†R. W. Taylor lbw b Hemmings	28	8/172 9/193	

Bonus points – Derbyshire 2, Nottinghamshire 4 (Score at 100 overs: 201-9).

Bowling: Hadlee 39–15–59–3; Rice 25–10–44–3; Hacker 19–7–41–2; White 13–4–28–1; Hemmings 7–2–14–1.

Umpires: D. J. Halfyard and D. Shackleton.

DERBYSHIRE v SUSSEX

At Derby, August 30, September 1, 2. Drawn. Derbyshire 5 pts, Sussex 6 pts. Sussex were put in on a rain-hit first day and batted with increasing vigour; especially Wessels and Parker, whose impressive century took one hundred and forty-five minutes, with five 6s and ten 4s. When Derbyshire replied, Kirsten made his sixth century of the summer, equalling the county record, and Walters gave him good support. After more fine stroke-play by Parker, Derbyshire were set to make 233 in 167 minutes. They quickly ran into trouble against the spin of Barclay and Waller and went into the last hour with eight wickets already down. However Steele and Newman batted with much aplomb to save the game.

Sussex

J. R. T. Barclay c Taylor b Newman	15	– b Oldham	45
G. D. Mendis b Steele	63	– c Oldham b Wood	18
K. C. Wessels c sub b Kirsten	78	– c Wood b Miller	16
P. W. G. Parker c Anderson b Wood	102	– c Tunnicliffe b Wood	51
Imran Khan not out	31	– not out	20
C. M. Wells c and b Wood	0	– not out	22
C. P. Phillipson c Wright b Wood	0		
B 6, l-b 6, n-b 3	15	L-b 4, n-b 2	6

1/67 2/96 3/231 4/304   (6 wkts dec.) 304   1/34 2/54   (4 wkts dec.) 178
5/304 6/304   3/133 4/137

I. A. Greig, *†A. Long, G. G. Arnold and C. E. Waller did not bat.

Bonus points – Sussex 4, Derbyshire 2.

Bowling: *First Innings*—Oldham 26–6–69–0; Tunnicliffe 9–0–38–0; Wood 13–3–22–3; Miller 15–4–40–0; Steele 7–2–51–1; Newman 8–0–25–1; Kirsten 10–1–44–1. *Second Innings*—Oldham 15–4–54–1; Newman 3–0–18–0; Wood 21–2–61–2; Miller 7–1–30–1; Steele 3–1–9–0.

Derbyshire

J. G. Wright c sub b Barclay	20	– c Wessels b Arnold	5
B. Wood c Wessels b Imran	17	– c Phillipson b Waller	11
P. N. Kirsten c Parker b Barclay	116	– c Wells b Barclay	13
D. S. Steele c Long b Waller	7	– not out	62
J. Walters b Barclay	66	– c Parker b Barclay	0
C. J. Tunnicliffe c Parker b Barclay	1	– (9) lbw b Barclay	1
I. S. Anderson not out	5	– (6) c Waller b Barclay	10
†R. W. Taylor not out	7	– (7) c Wessels b Waller	0
*G. Miller (did not bat).		– (8) b Waller	0
P. G. Newman (did not bat)		– not out	29
L-b 6, w 1, n-b 4	11	L-b 5, n-b 1	6

1/22 2/53 3/81 4/232   (6 wkts dec.) 250   1/11 2/29 3/39   (8 wkts) 137
5/237 6/240   4/39 5/53 6/54
                                                    7/54 8/61

S. Oldham did not bat.

Bonus points – Derbyshire 3, Sussex 2.

Bowling: *First Innings*—Arnold 16–3–45–0; Imran 15–5–29–1; Barclay 24–3–85–4; Waller 26–8–62–1; Greig 7–3–18–0. *Second Innings*—Arnold 9–4–13–1; Imran 8–1–31–0; Waller 21–6–47–3; Barclay 19–6–40–4.

Umpires: R. Julian and D. O. Oslear.

At Scarborough, September 3, 4, 5. DERBYSHIRE drew with YORKSHIRE.

ESSEX

President – T. N. PEARCE, OBE

Chairman, Cricket Committee – B. TAYLOR

Secretary – P. J. EDWARDS
County Ground, New Writtle Street, Chelmsford CM2 0RW

Captain – K. W. R. FLETCHER

G. A. Gooch   County Badge   B. R. Hardie

Following their success in the previous year, Essex must count 1980 as a season of bitter disappointment. After starting it as champions, they finished eighth in the Schweppes County Championship, and only a late surge in the final weeks prevented them from finishing bottom of the John Player League. The nearest the county came to honours was in the Benson and Hedges Cup where, against Northamptonshire at Lord's, they failed, by 6 runs, to retain the trophy. The Gillette Cup also brought Essex disappointment when they succumbed to Surrey in a quarter-final which was, at one stage, theirs for the taking.

Many reasons can be put forward for the county's failure. Injury and illness repeatedly upset the balance of the team, and as early as May a virus claimed three players during the match against Somerset, with the result that the county were all out with only seven batsmen dismissed by the opposition. The shortage of players led to officials seeking the head-master's permission to play Neil Foster, then still at Philip Morant School, Colchester, in the next match. Foster received the invitation on his eighteenth birthday and found himself opening the county attack on the following day. Of a spate of injuries suffered by key players, Turner's proved the most costly. Apart from one match, the medium-paced all-rounder was unavailable throughout June when the damp, green wickets would have suited his talents.

Yet to offer illness and injury as the major factor in the county's lack of success would be to mask the real reason – namely a lack of consistency and confidence. With the exception of Graham Gooch, who passed 1,000 runs before any of his colleagues had reached 500, the batsmen found runs hard to come by. Gooch registered all his six first-class hundreds before the middle of June, his last – against West Indies at Lord's – being his first Test century. Yet the other Essex batsmen struggled to find any fluency between frequent interruptions for rain.

When, in the second half of the season, the sun started to shine, the recognised batsmen warmed to their task. Keith Fletcher, despite the burden of captaincy, finished with well over 1,300 first-class runs, and in doing so overtook P. A. Perrin as Essex's leading run-maker. Perrin achieved a first-class aggregate of 29,162 between 1896-1928; Fletcher, who made his county début in 1962, needs only another 130 runs to reach 30,000. With his obvious enthusiasm and talent, Fletcher is likely to set a much stiffer target.

Ken McEwan and Brian Hardie also completed 1,000 runs for the season, McEwan doing so with an impressive and eye-catching aggression. On Sundays, too, he was a delight to watch. In the John Player League he amassed 693 runs, hitting two centuries and the most 6s to win the sponsor's £250 award. In contrast to the South African, Hardie is a dour performer, though no less reliable, with both the ability and patience to hold an innings together. And these are qualities on which Essex may be relying increasingly, after their decision not to offer Mike Denness a new contract. The former England captain did everything asked of him and could have been expected comfortably to top 1,000 runs had he not missed several games. So why the cold shoulder? The assumption must be that it is because Essex are fortunate in having several younger players waiting in the wings and that Denness was seen as a figure blocking their progress.

In the absence of Gooch – likely to be away on regular Test duty – and Denness, Essex may have difficulty in finding an opening pair. Michael McEvoy made encouraging strides last season, failing only twice in his last 23 innings to reach double figures; but he reached fifty only twice during that time, which suggests he may need another couple of seasons to develop the concentration needed to make an impression as an opener. Hardie seems a likely candidate to open in Gooch's absence, although such a move would rob the middle order of solidarity.

The county's bowling in 1980 left much to be desired. The new-ball attack of Norbert Phillip and John Lever lacked its previous penetration, Phillip, who was particularly ill at ease with himself, managing only 40 wickets. The spin combination of Ray East and David Acfield was more impressive. East had the distinction of being the chief wicket-taker, with 61 first-class wickets, though it was Acfield who often commanded the greater respect. On his return, the redoubtable Turner proved, as usual, a willing and often effective performer. Like all the players and their supporters, however, he will be hoping for better things in 1981. – Nigel Fuller.

[*Ken Kelly*]

ESSEX

Back row: M. H. Denness, B. R. Hardie, N. Smith, K. R. Pont, A. W. Lilley, N. Phillip, G. A. Gooch, M. S. A. McEvoy. *Front row*: K. S. McEwan, J. K. Lever, K. W. R. Fletcher (*captain*), R. E. East, D. L. Acfield.

ESSEX RESULTS

All First-class Matches – Played 24: Won 4, Lost 3, Drawn 17.

County Championship Matches – Played 22: Won 4, Lost 3, Drawn 15.

Bonus points – Batting 48, Bowling 64.

COUNTY CHAMPIONSHIP AVERAGES

BATTING

	Birthplace	Matches	Inns	Not Outs	Runs	Highest Inns	Avge
G. A. Gooch	Leytonstone	11	20	5	766	134	51.06
K. S. McEwan	Bedford, SA	21	35	6	1,165	140*	40.17
K. W. R. Fletcher ...	Worcester	22	35	4	1,225	122*	39.51
B. R. Hardie	Stenhousemuir	22	33	3	1,001	95	33.36
M. H. Denness	Bellshill	16	27	3	685	87	28.54
S. Turner	Chester	17	26	5	598	83*	28.47
M. S. A. McEvoy	Jorhat, India	16	29	0	600	65	20.68
N. Phillip	Bioche, Dominica	19	23	4	376	77*	19.78
K. R. Pont	Wanstead	10	14	2	199	36	16.58
R. E. East	Manningtree	18	23	2	328	47	15.61
N. Smith	Dewsbury	19	23	5	262	63*	14.55
D. R. Pringle	Nairobi, Kenya	8	10	1	109	40*	12.11
J. K. Lever	Ilford	18	18	9	100	18*	11.11
R. Herbert	Cape Town, SA	3	4	1	29	14*	9.66
D. L. Acfield	Chelmsford	19	18	8	83	26	8.30

Also batted: N. A. Foster (*Colchester*) 8*; A. W. Lilley (*Ilford*) 9, 6; G. E. Sainsbury (*Wanstead*) 2*, 0*.

* *Signifies not out.*

BOWLING

	Overs	Maidens	Runs	Wickets	Average
R. E. East	517.2	130	1,469	60	24.48
D. L. Acfield	542.5	167	1,194	46	25.95
J. K. Lever	498	103	1,435	50	28.70
S. Turner	438.4	81	1,259	41	30.70
D. R. Pringle	111.1	25	324	10	32.40
N. Phillip	394.2	57	1,347	40	33.67

Also bowled: K. W. R. Fletcher 25.5–2–200–3; N. A. Foster 25–5–80–3; R. Herbert 36.4–3–148–3; G. A. Gooch 85–17–247–8; K. R. Pont 71.4–15–165–8; G. E. Sainsbury 31–4–90–4.

HUNDREDS

The following seven three-figure innings were played for Essex in County Championship matches – G. A. Gooch 134 v Gloucestershire (Gloucester), 122 v Kent (Ilford), 108* v Glamorgan (Swansea), 108 v Surrey (Chelmsford); K. S. McEwan 140* v Northamptonshire (Northampton), 103* v Sussex (Hove); K. W. R. Fletcher 122* v Derbyshire (Colchester).

At Lord's, April 23, 24, 25. ESSEX drew with MCC.

At Cambridge, April 26, 28, 29. ESSEX drew with CAMBRIDGE UNIVERSITY.

At Swansea, April 30, May 1, 2. ESSEX drew with GLAMORGAN.

ESSEX v SOMERSET

At Ilford, May 3, 5, 6. Drawn. Essex 4 pts, Somerset 6 pts. Essex were stricken by illness shortly after the match began. On the second day Gooch was unable to resume his innings while Pont and Phillip were also victims of a flu virus which confined them to bed. Consequently, the Essex innings closed for the loss of seven wickets and 104 adrift of Somerset's first innings, 222. Rose and Botham were largely responsible for that, and this pair, along with Marks, played attractively to record half-centuries when the visitors batted again. Rose's failure to declare much earlier was difficult to understand, considering the handicaps under which Essex were labouring; he left them a target of 402, although the champions were still without McEwan and Phillip, and Pont and Gooch had still not fully recovered. Yet it was the latter pair who saw Essex to a draw after Fletcher and Hardie had defied Somerset for the greater part of the final day with a stand of 193.

Somerset

*B. C. Rose c and b Pont	41	– b Lever	63
P. A. Slocombe c McEvoy b Phillip	13		
P. M. Roebuck lbw b Turner	29	– c Hardie b Turner	27
P. W. Denning c Smith b Turner	20	– (2) lbw b Lever	24
I. T. Botham c sub b Phillip	47	– c Lever b Turner	63
V. J. Marks b Lever	12	– (4) not out	65
D. Breakwell hit wkt b Lever	26	– (6) b Turner	11
†D. J. S. Taylor c Turner b Phillip	10	– (7) not out	21
C. H. Dredge b Phillip	0		
K. F. Jennings not out	16		
H. R. Moseley lbw b Turner	0		
L-b 5, w 2, n-b 1	8	B 5, l-b 13, w 1, n-b 4	23

1/33 2/81 3/104 4/119 5/152   222   1/87 2/96 3/137   (5 wkts dec.) 297
6/178 7/204 8/204 9/219   4/220 5/251

Bonus points – Somerset 2, Essex 4.

Bowling: *First Innings*—Lever 27–8–74–2; Turner 30.3–6–79–3; Phillip 16–1–44–4; Pont 8–3–17–1. *Second Innings*—Lever 29–4–106–2; Turner 28–3–99–3; East 23–4–69–0.

Essex

G. A. Gooch retired ill	29	– (7) not out	16
B. R. Hardie c Taylor b Moseley	22	– (3) c Taylor b Botham	95
K. S. McEwan lbw b Moseley	0		
*K. W. R. Fletcher c Breakwell b Moseley	28	– lbw b Moseley	99
M. S. A. McEvoy lbw b Botham	5	– lbw b Botham	13
S. Turner c Taylor b Botham	1		
R. E. East c Taylor b Botham	12	– (1) c and b Botham	7
†N. Smith not out	12	– (2) c Taylor b Moseley	29
J. K. Lever b Moseley	0		
K. R. Pont absent ill		– (6) not out	11
N. Phillip absent ill			
B 4, l-b 3, w 1, n-b 1	9	B 6, l-b 4, w 1	11

1/45 2/45 3/72 4/84 5/104   118   1/16 2/44 3/237   (5 wkts) 281
6/105 7/118   4/241 5/265

Bonus points – Somerset 4.

Bowling: *First Innings*—Moseley 15.5–5–39–4; Dredge 4–0–17–0; Jennings 9–2–19–0; Breakwell 1–1–0–0; Botham 8–1–34–3. *Second Innings*—Botham 39–10–129–3; Moseley 20–5–51–2; Breakwell 22–14–23–0; Marks 22–13–53–0; Dredge 10–7–11–0; Jennings 3–1–3–0.

Umpires: A. G. T. Whitehead and R. S. Herman.

ESSEX v KENT

At Ilford, May 7, 8, 9. Essex won by two wickets. Essex 18 pts, Kent 7 pts. The power and brilliance of Gooch helped Essex snatch a thrilling triumph after they were set a target of 222 in ninety minutes plus twenty overs. He reached his century in only ninety-four minutes – the quickest of the season to date – and his innings contained seventeen 4s and three 6s. Yet in the end it needed the coolness and experience of Turner and Lever to see Essex home with just seven balls to spare. Because of illness, Essex called up eighteen-year-old schoolboy Foster to partner Lever in attack, and the youngster responded by grabbing the first two wickets before Ealham and Rowe came together in a stand of 186. Smith's robust innings enabled Essex to collect maximum batting points and finish only 61 runs behind Kent's first innings. Kent's second effort was a dour affair, brightened only by Shepherd, before Ealham's declaration paved the way for an exciting finish.

Kent

R. A. Woolmer c Smith b Foster	18	– c Smith b Lever	0
C. J. C. Rowe lbw b East	98	– c and b East	35
C. J. Tavaré c Smith b Foster	2	– lbw b Lever	4
*A. G. E. Ealham c Fletcher b Foster	145	– c Gooch b Turner	19
†A. P. E. Knott c Gooch b East	39	– (6) b East	15
N. R. Taylor c Gooch b East	4	– (7) b Turner	33
J. N. Shepherd not out	40	– (8) not out	41
R. W. Hills not out	4	– (5) c McEvoy b East	6
L-b 6, w 5, n-b 1	12	L-b 5, w 1, n-b 1	7

1/39 2/41 3/227 4/297 (6 wkts) 362   1/0 2/7 3/45 (7 wkts dec.) 160
5/309 6/344   4/62 5/67 6/104 7/160

G. R. Dilley, D. L. Underwood and K. B. S. Jarvis did not bat.

Bonus points – Kent 4, Essex 2.

Bowling: *First Innings*—Lever 21–1–80–0; Foster 15–3–51–3; Turner 25–2–75–0; East 33–5–125–3; Pont 6–1–19–0. *Second Innings*—Lever 17–4–27–2; Foster 10–2–29–0; Turner 21.4–8–33–2; East 36–16–64–3.

Essex

M. S. A. McEvoy b Shepherd	5	– c Woolmer b Shepherd	4
G. A. Gooch c Woolmer b Dilley	37	– c Tavaré b Dilley	122
B. R. Hardie c Knott b Shepherd	48	– c Underwood b Jarvis	19
*K. W. R. Fletcher b Underwood	36	– b Underwood	10
K. R. Pont c Hills b Jarvis	27	– run out	0
A. W. Lilley b Shepherd	9	– (7) c Taylor b Underwood	6
S. Turner c Knott b Underwood	1	– (8) not out	28
R. E. East c Hills b Shepherd	47	– (6) c Jarvis b Underwood	0
†N. Smith not out	63	– b Underwood	9
N. A. Foster not out	8		
J. K. Lever (did not bat)		– not out	13
B 4, l-b 14, w 1, n-b 1	20	B 4, l-b 9, w 1	14

1/35 2/47 3/133 4/137 (8 wkts dec.) 301   1/4 2/81 3/152 (8 wkts) 225
5/161 6/164 7/193 8/246   4/153 5/162 6/166 7/174
                                          8/189

Bonus points – Essex 4, Kent 3.

Bowling: *First Innings*—Dilley 17–6–31–1; Shepherd 33.3–9–94–4; Jarvis 17–5–58–1; Underwood 27–9–83–2; Hills 5–2–15–0. *Second Innings*—Dilley 12–2–80–1; Shepherd 6–0–28–1; Underwood 15.5–1–77–4; Jarvis 10–0–26–1.

Umpires: A. G. T. Whitehead and R. S. Herman.

At Chelmsford, May 22. ESSEX beat WEST INDIANS by five wickets (See West Indian tour section).

At Chelmsford, May 23. ESSEX lost to WEST INDIANS by 141 runs (See West Indian tour section).

ESSEX v SURREY

At Chelmsford, May 24, 26, 27. Essex won by ten wickets. Essex 20 pts, Surrey 5 pts. This match was a personal triumph for East, the left-arm spinner returning match figures of eleven for 118. Five of his wickets came in the first innings, one in which Surrey were indebted to Smith and Butcher who scored more than two-thirds of their side's total with Smith hitting three 6s before running out of partners. Yet it was Gooch who provided the innings of the match, his century coming in two hours twenty-four minutes and containing thirteen 4s and three 6s. McEwan also batted attractively as Essex went on to earn a first innings lead of 177. Butcher batted for around four hours when Surrey went in again, but once he was out they collapsed. East finished with six for 72, figures which would have been more impressive but for Clarke who, during a brief explosive stay, hit five 6s off the spinner, one of them shattering a bar window beneath the pavilion.

Surrey

A. R. Butcher c Fletcher b East	56	– c Fletcher b East	58
G. S. Clinton lbw b Lever	0	– c sub b Lever	49
D. B. Pauline b Phillip	6	– c McEwan b East	12
*R. D. V. Knight c Fletcher b Lever	17	– lbw b Acfield	2
G. R. J. Roope c Turner b Lever	1	– (6) not out	21
D. M. Smith not out	71	– (7) lbw b Acfield	0
R. D. Jackman c Fletcher b Acfield	4	– (8) b East	0
†C. J. Richards c and b East	1	– (5) c Lever b East	7
S. T. Clarke b East	4	– c Hardie b East	32
P. I. Pocock lbw b East	0	– c Fletcher b East	0
R. G. L. Cheatle c Smith b East	4	– lbw b Acfield	1
B 2, l-b 5, w 2, n-b 1	10	B 2, l-b 3, w 5, n-b 4	14

1/2 2/10 3/44 4/46 5/122 6/147   174   1/88 2/114 3/120 4/135   196
7/148 8/154 9/162   5/144 6/145 7/150 8/189
                                   9/191

Bonus points – Surrey 1, Essex 4.

Bowling: *First Innings*—Lever 14–4–35–3; Phillip 4–1–15–1; Turner 10–2–20–0; Gooch 6–3–11–0; East 19.3–8–46–5; Acfield 18–6–37–1. *Second Innings*—Lever 11–2–25–1; Phillip 4–0–23–0; Gooch 4–1–15–0; Acfield 36.3–16–47–3; East 38–16–72–6.

Essex

G. A. Gooch lbw b Clarke	108	– not out		17
M. H. Denness c and b Knight	6	– not out		4
K. S. McEwan lbw b Jackman	83			
*K. W. R. Fletcher c Richards b Clarke	2			
B. R. Hardie c Richards b Clarke	6			
N. Phillip b Knight	28			
R. E. East c Jackman b Knight	3			
†N. Smith c Pocock b Jackman	33			
S. Turner c Richards b Jackman	11			
J. K. Lever not out	18			
D. L. Acfield c Butcher b Jackman	26			
B 10, l-b 13, w 1, n-b 3	27	N-b 2		2

1/23 2/162 3/169 4/187 5/252   351   (no wkt) 23
6/254 7/259 8/295 9/306

Bonus points – Essex 4, Surrey 4.

Bowling: *First Innings*—Clarke 30–8–66–3; Jackman 25.1–6–67–4; Knight 15–2–56–3; Pocock 20–3–101–0; Cheatle 4–0–34–0. *Second Innings*—Jackman 2.4–1–7–0; Smith 2–0–14–0.

Umpires: J. G. Langridge and K. E. Palmer.

At Gloucester, May 31, June 2, 3. ESSEX drew with GLOUCESTERSHIRE.

At The Oval, June 7, 9. ESSEX lost to SURREY by ten wickets.

ESSEX v WARWICKSHIRE

At Southend, June 14, 16, 17. Drawn. Essex 4 pts, Warwickshire 2 pts. Rain delayed the start until after lunch on the first day, the second was completely washed out, and fewer than ninety minutes of action were seen on the final day before the abandonment came. Warwickshire, who won the toss, reached 167 for three on the Saturday, thanks largely to Smith, who made 80 of those and went on to carry his bat on the final day as spinners East and Acfield took advantage of the damp wicket. Smith batted for five and a quarter hours, hitting nine 4s and a 6. Half an hour or so before lunch a heavy storm sent the players scurrying to the pavilion and they did not return.

Warwickshire

D. L. Amiss c Smith b Gooch	26	*R. G. D. Willis c Pont b Acfield		7
K. D. Smith not out	120	S. J. Rouse lbw b Acfield		0
T. A. Lloyd c Gooch b Lever	37	D. R. Doshi b East		2
J. A. Claughton b East	14			
P. R. Oliver c Hardie b East	0	B 4, l-b 3, w 1, n-b 3		11
G. W. Humpage b East	9			
†C. Maynard c Smith b Acfield	0	1/39 2/125 3/160 4/180 5/195 6/200		230
A. M. Ferreira c Fletcher b East	4	7/209 8/226 9/226		

Bonus points – Warwickshire 2, Essex 4.

Bowling: Lever 19–4–44–1; Phillip 6–0–18–0; Gooch 5–1–17–1; Acfield 33–11–65–3; East 32–9–75–5.

Essex

G. A. Gooch not out   1
M. H. Denness not out   2

(no wkt)   3

K. S. McEwan, *K. W. R. Fletcher, B. R. Hardie, K. R. Pont, N. Phillip, R. E. East, †N. Smith, J. K. Lever and D. L. Acfield did not bat.

Bowling: Willis 1–0–2–0; Ferreira 0.2–0–1–0.

Umpires: D. J. Halfyard and D. J. Constant.

ESSEX v MIDDLESEX

At Southend, June 18, 19, 20. Middlesex won by eight wickets. Middlesex 18 pts, Essex 5 pts. With runs never easy to gather on a rain-affected pitch, the tall van der Bijl proved Middlesex's major weapon, finishing with a match haul of eight for 65 from 51.3 overs. East batted with commendable discipline in both Essex innings, while career-best figures by medium-pace bowler Pont restricted Middlesex to a first innings lead of 42. Faced with a victory target of 74, Brearley guided Middlesex home with comparative ease.

Essex

M. H. Denness c Embury b van der Bijl	23	– lbw b Daniel	2
B. R. Hardie b Daniel	4	– b van der Bijl	5
K. S. McEwan b Maru	13	– b Selvey	27
*K. W. R. Fletcher lbw b van der Bijl	28	– lbw b Daniel	0
M. S. A. McEvoy b van der Bijl	2	– lbw b van der Bijl	0
K. R. Pont lbw b Daniel	36	– c Maru b Emburey	12
N. Phillip run out	7	– c Brearley b van der Bijl	11
R. E. East run out	33	– b van der Bijl	38
†N. Smith b Emburey	15	– c Maru b Daniel	0
J. K. Lever b van der Bijl	0	– c Maru b Emburey	16
D. L. Acfield not out	0	– not out	0
L-b 3	3	L-b 4	4

1/17 2/35 3/45 4/49 5/98 6/105   164   1/5 2/9 3/9 4/24 5/43   115
7/137 8/163 9/164   6/49 7/72 8/75 9/109

Bonus points – Essex 1, Middlesex 4.

Bowling: *First Innings*—van der Bijl 29–12–47–4; Selvey 10–4–18–0; Emburey 12.5–5–18–1; Daniel 14–3–37–2; Maru 21–8–41–1. *Second Innings*—van der Bijl 22.3–13–18–4; Daniel 17–4–49–3; Emburey 13–4–21–2; Selvey 9–2–15–1; Maru 1–0–8–0.

Middlesex

*J. M. Brearley c Smith b Lever	3	– not out	37
W. N. Slack b East	29	– lbw b Lever	10
C. T. Radley b Pont	39	– c Fletcher b Acfield	17
G. D. Barlow b Pont	25	– not out	8
R. O. Butcher c Smith b Pont	19		
†I. J. Gould c McEvoy b Pont	0		
J. E. Emburey lbw b Pont	1		
V. A. P. van der Bijl b East	29		
M. W. W. Selvey lbw b Phillip	23		
R. Maru lbw b East	9		
W. W. Daniel not out	13		
B 9, l-b 5, w 1, n-b 1	16	B 1, n-b 1	2

1/5 2/75 3/77 4/112 5/114 6/118   206   1/27 2/54   (2 wkts) 74
7/141 8/167 9/181

Bonus points – Middlesex 2, Essex 4.

Bowling: *First Innings*—Lever 30–13–59–1; Phillip 20.2–5–48–1; East 13–3–50–3; Acfield 2–2–0–0; Pont 20–5–33–5. *Second Innings*—Lever 10–4–23–1; Phillip 5–1–15–0; Acfield 7–3–7–1; East 3–1–8–0; Fletcher 3.5–1–19–0.

Umpires: D. J. Halfyard and D. J. Constant.

At Chesterfield, June 21, 23, 24. ESSEX drew with DERBYSHIRE.

At Nottingham, June 28, 30, July 1. ESSEX drew with NOTTINGHAMSHIRE.

ESSEX v YORKSHIRE

At Chelmsford, July 9, 10, 11. Drawn. Essex 3 pts, Yorkshire 4 pts. The loss of the opening day to the weather did not prevent a nail-biting finish after Yorkshire had been left to score 283 in 205 minutes. They lost half their side for 90 but were revived by Love, Bairstow and Carrick and helped by the insistence of Fletcher and East on tossing the ball up to keep them interested. The result was an exciting finale, with Yorkshire's last pair at the crease 10 short of victory. Stevenson and Turner both hit half-centuries in under half an hour while Fletcher, Hardie and McEwan also batted attractively.

Essex

M. H. Denness lbw b Stevenson	2	– c Sidebottom b Stevenson	3
M. S. A. McEvoy lbw b Stevenson	33	– c Athey b Carrick	12
K. S. McEwan b Ramage	2	– b Carrick	70
*K. W. R. Fletcher c Bairstow b Carrick	70	– b Cope	6
B. R. Hardie c Cope b Carrick	54	– c Ramage b Cope	30
D. R. Pringle c Athey b Cope	13	– not out	40
K. R. Pont run out	10	– b Carrick	4
S. Turner not out	5	– not out	61
R. E. East not out	4		
L-b 5, w 1, n-b 1	7	B 5,l-b 2	7

1/5 2/8 3/90   (7 wkts dec.) 200   1/4 2/38 3/49   (6 wkts dec.) 233
4/127 5/166 6/184 7/191   4/101 5/133 6/142

†N. Smith and J. K. Lever did not bat.

Bonus points – Essex 2, Yorkshire 3.

Bowling: *First Innings*—Stevenson 18–3–44–2; Ramage 6–2–16–1; Sidebottom 12–1–26–0; Cope 11.1–4–24–1; Carrick 25–4–83–2. *Second Innings*—Stevenson 7–2–14–1; Ramage 4–0–27–0; Carrick 21–3–99–3; Cope 16.5–1–81–2; Athey 2–0–5–0.

Yorkshire

P. G. Ingham b Pringle	0	– c Pont b Turner	14
R. G. Lumb c and b Fletcher	36	– c McEwan b Turner	20
C. W. J. Athey b Pringle	8	– (4) c Fletcher b East	26
*J. H. Hampshire not out	32	– (5) c McEwan b Turner	0
G. B. Stevenson b Turner	61	– (3) c Hardie b East	26
J. D. Love not out	11	– b Pringle	58
†D. L. Bairstow (did not bat)		– not out	61
P. Carrick (did not bat)		– c Turner b East	41
A. Ramage (did not bat)		– c McEvoy b East	5
A. Sidebottom (did not bat)		– c Hardie b East	9
G. A. Cope (did not bat)		– not out	3
L-b 2, n-b 1	3	B 2,l-b 4, n-b 4	10

1/2 2/14   (4 wkts dec.) 151   1/31 2/49 3/65 4/77   (9 wkts) 273
3/63 4/132   5/90 6/154 7/234 8/242
                                      9/253

Bonus points – Yorkshire 1, Essex 1.

Bowling: *First Innings*—Lever 7–0–22–0; Pringle 8.1–3–16–2; Turner 8–1–40–1; East 7–1–30–0; Fletcher 4–0–40–1. *Second Innings*—Lever 3–1–4–0; Pringle 13–3–42–1; East 31–4–121–5; Turner 13–0–39–3; Fletcher 8–0–57–0.

Umpires: W. E. Alley and R. S. Herman.

ESSEX v LEICESTERSHIRE

At Chelmsford, July 12, 14, 15. Drawn. Essex 3 pts, Leicestershire 5 pts. After the second day's play had been washed out, declarations by both captains set up an exciting finish. Chasing 161 in 100 minutes, Leicestershire seemed favourites when they needed 106 off the last twenty overs with nine wickets still in hand. But on a drying pitch they were sent spinning into trouble by Acfield, although they juggled their batting order to continue the chase until the end. East accounted for Balderstone with the first ball of the final over, but last man Cook stood firm.

Essex

M. H. Denness b Cook	53	– c Balderstone b Clift 23
M. S. A. McEwan c Birkenshaw b Parsons	11	– c Clift b Steele 16
†K. S. McEwan c Tolchard b Taylor	2	– (6) not out 5
*K. W. R. Fletcher lbw b Parsons	62	– b Clift 1
B. R. Hardie lbw b Parsons	1	– c Parsons b Cook 16
D. R. Pringle c Briers b Parsons	5	
K. R. Pont c and b Cook	34	
S. Turner c Gower b Cook	24	– (3) c Taylor b Steele 16
N. Phillip lbw b Cook	18	
R. E. East c Briers b Birkenshaw	11	
D. L. Acfield not out	5	
L-b 3, n-b 1	4	N-b 3 3

1/16 2/19 3/127 4/128   230   1/42 2/42 3/50   (5 wkts dec.) 80
5/133 6/154 7/186 8/213 9/214   4/62 5/80

Bonus points – Essex 2, Leicestershire 4.

Bowling: *First Innings*—Taylor 18–7–44–1; Parsons 18–7–38–4; Clift 20–8–51–0; Steele 5–3–5–0; Cook 25–9–43–4; Birkenshaw 13.4–1–45–1. *Second Innings*—Taylor 4–0–16–0; Parsons 2–0–9–0; Clift 7–1–22–2; Steele 5–0–26–2; Cook 0.4–0–4–1.

Leicestershire

N. E. Briers b Phillip	0	– b Acfield 30
J. F. Steele c Hardie b East	36	– (10) not out 0
J. C. Balderstone c Denness b Acfield	41	– (9) c Pringle b East 12
D. I. Gower c Denness b Acfield	25	– (2) run out 46
*B. F. Davison not out	39	– (3) lbw b East 12
†R. W. Tolchard not out	1	– (5) c Hardie b Acfield 1
J. Birkenshaw (did not bat)		– (4) b Acfield 7
P. B. Clift (did not bat)		– (6) c McEvoy b Acfield 1
L. B. Taylor (did not bat)		– (7) b Acfield 8
G. J. Parsons (did not bat)		– (8) run out 11
N. G. B. Cook (did not bat)		– not out 0
B 2, l-b 3, w 1, n-b 2	8	B 2, l-b 1 3

1/5 2/72 3/94   (4 wkts dec.) 150   1/48 2/61 3/78 4/80   (9 wkts) 131
4/139   5/92 6/106 7/108
                                   8/129 9/131

Bonus points – Leicestershire 1, Essex 1.

Bowling: *First Innings*—Phillip 8–1–28–1; Pringle 11–6–21–0; Turner 2–0–3–0; East 22.2–6–52–1; Acfield 27–9–38–2. *Second Innings*—Phillip 2–0–8–0; Pringle 1–0–7–0; Acfield 15–6–31–5; East 15–1–82–2.

Umpires: W. E. Alley and D. Shackleton.

At Leicester, July 23, 24, 25. ESSEX beat LEICESTERSHIRE by 101 runs.

At Hove, July 26, 28, 29. ESSEX drew with SUSSEX.

At Lord's, August 2, 4, 5. MIDDLESEX beat ESSEX by an innings and 4 runs.

ESSEX v HAMPSHIRE

At Chelmsford, August 9, 11, 12. Drawn. Essex 5 pts, Hampshire 5 pts. Left a target of 280 in 202 minutes, Essex were grateful to settle for a draw after reaching the final hour at 156 for six. Their victory bid was halted by spinners Cowley and Southern, despite another good performance by Denness who completed his second half-century of the match. Lever took the first six Hampshire wickets on the opening day, including those of Nicholas and Pocock who shared a century stand for the fourth wicket. Later Parks registered his maiden fifty as he and Graf figured in an unbroken eighth-wicket partnership of 119. In an attempt to make up for time lost because of poor weather, Fletcher declared 112 behind and Hampshire responded by declaring their second innings, in which Cowley hit Fletcher for three successive 6s.

Hampshire

C. L. Smith c Hardie b Lever	16	– b Phillip	14
J. M. Rice c Smith b Lever	8		
M. C. J. Nicholas c McEvoy b Lever	67	– lbw b Turner	26
D. R. Turner c Pringle b Lever	0	– c Hardie b Turner	18
*N. E. J. Pocock lbw b Lever	57	– c sub b Fletcher	29
N. G. Cowley c Acfield b Phillip	21	– b Acfield	41
T. M. Tremlett lbw b Lever	2	– not out	10
†R. J. Parks not out	64	– (2) lbw b Lever	15
S. F. Graf not out	57	– (8) not out	2
L-b 10, n-b 10	20	– L-b 7, n-b 5	12

1/24 2/34 3/34   (7 wkts) 312   1/26 2/40 3/73   (6 wkts dec.) 167
4/142 5/159 6/163 7/193   4/86 5/128 6/164

J. W. Southern and K. Stevenson did not bat.

Bonus points – Hampshire 4, Essex 3.

Bowling: *First Innings*—Lever 34–6–121–6; Phillip 20–3–50–1; Turner 29–7–80–0; Acfield 11–3–19–0; Pringle 6–1–22–0. *Second Innings*—Lever 9–2–25–1; Phillip 6–0–18–1; Acfield 14–2–47–1; Turner 8–3–14–2; Fletcher 4–0–51–1.

Essex

M. H. Denness c Pocock b Cowley	73	– run out	60
M. S. A. McEvoy c Nicholas b Southern	11	– c and b Cowley	21
K. S. McEwan b Cowley	68	– c Smith b Cowley	12
*K. W. R. Fletcher not out	29	– c sub b Southern	13
B. R. Hardie not out	11	– (6) not out	40
S. Turner (did not bat)		– (5) c sub b Southern	22
N. Phillip (did not bat)		– c Smith b Cowley	1
D. R. Pringle (did not bat)		– b Southern	0
†N. Smith (did not bat)		– not out	25
L-b 4, n-b 4	8	B 3, l-b 5, w 1, n-b 5	14

1/22 2/143 3/170   (3 wkts dec.) 200   1/57 2/88 3/112   (7 wkts) 208
                                4/118 5/155 6/156 7/158

J. K. Lever and D. L. Acfield did not bat.

Bonus points – Essex 2, Hampshire 1.

Bowling: *First Innings*—Graf 11–3–23–0; Stevenson 16–3–44–0; Southern 22–5–72–1; Tremlett 8–2–12–0; Cowley 18–5–41–2. *Second Innings*—Graf 8–0–38–0; Stevenson 5–1–17–0; Tremlett 6–0–30–0; Cowley 23–9–57–3; Southern 20–6–43–3; Smith 5–2–9–0.

Umpires: T. W. Spencer and R. Aspinall.

At Folkestone, August, 16, 18. ESSEX beat KENT by 50 runs.

At Northampton, August 20, 21, 22. ESSEX drew with NORTHAMPTONSHIRE.

ESSEX v DERBYSHIRE

At Colchester, August 23, 25, 26. Drawn. Essex 6 pts, Derbyshire 8 pts. A target of 249 in 147 minutes proved just beyond Derbyshire, who ran out of time only 13 runs short of victory. Wood and Wright gave them a good start, putting on 84 in fourteen overs, and they were still in a promising position when the last twenty overs arrived with 127 required and nine wickets standing. Yet half-centuries from Wright and Kirsten were in vain once Phillip put a sharp and decisive brake on things near the end. Fletcher provided the backbone to both Essex's innings, hitting eleven boundaries in his first innings and one 6 and fifteen 4s in his second innings hundred – the 49th of his first-class career. He took nearly three hours to reach his second 50 of the match, but his next 72 runs came in sixty-nine minutes as he shared in an unbroken stand of 190 with Hardie.

Essex

G. A. Gooch c Steele b Miller	25	– lbw b Hendrick	10
M. S. A. McEvoy c Miller b Hendrick	48	– lbw b Tunnicliffe	16
K. S. McEwan b Miller	6	– (5) c Wood b Steele	17
*K. W. R. Fletcher b Tunnicliffe	84	– not out	122
B. R. Hardie c Taylor b Hendrick	42	– (6) not out	75
S. Turner c Anderson b Oldham	9		
R. Herbert lbw b Tunnicliffe	2	– (3) c Walters b Hendrick	9
N. Phillip not out	44		
†N. Smith c Miller b Tunnicliffe	0		
J. K. Lever c Hendrick b Miller	8		
D. L. Acfield run out	9		
B 2, 1-b 7, n-b 5	14	B 5,1-b 2, n-b 7	14

1/55 2/67 3/115 4/211   291   1/26 2/28   (4 wkts dec.) 263
5/223 6/237 7/250 8/250 9/281   3/42 4/73

Bonus points – Essex 3, Derbyshire 4.

Bowling: *First Innings*—Hendrick 21–2–66–2; Tunnicliffe 21–3–59–3; Oldham 21–5–60–1; Miller 21–5–56–3; Steele 11–4–25–0; Wood 5–1–11–0. *Second Innings*—Hendrick 20–4–45–2; Tunnicliffe 17–4–46–1; Steele 24–8–58–1; Miller 20.2–5–65–0; Oldham 3–1–14–0; Anderson 2–0–21–0.

Derbyshire

B. Wood run out	27	– run out	32
J. G. Wright c Phillip b Lever	89	– c and b Acfield	66
P. N. Kirsten b Gooch	31	– b Lever	58
D. S. Steele c Fletcher b Turner	54	– (8) not out	6
*G. Miller c McEwan b Lever	13	– (4) lbw b Acfield	2
J. Walters c Acfield b Lever	39	– (5) c Herbert b Phillip	29
I. S. Anderson c McEvoy b Lever	10		
C. J. Tunnicliffe not out	23	– (6) c Fletcher b Phillip	16
†R. W. Taylor not out	4		
M. Hendrick (did not bat)		– (7) b Phillip	4
B 5, l-b 10, w 1	16	B 12, l-b 10, w 1	23

1/120 2/161 3/185   (7 wkts) 306   1/84 2/126 3/134   (7 wkts) 236
4/228 5/269 6/272 7/293   4/182 5/224 6/224 7/236

S. Oldham did not bat.

Bonus points – Derbyshire 4, Essex 3.

Bowling: *First Innings*—Lever 29–7–75–4; Phillip 14–1–55–0; Acfield 24–9–54–0; Turner 16–1–65–1; Gooch 11–5–18–1; Herbert 6–0–23–0. *Second Innings*—Lever 10–0–49–1; Turner 3–0–24–0; Acfield 16–1–75–2; Gooch 12–0–56–0; Phillip 1.5–0–9–3.

Umpires: D. G. L. Evans and A. Jepson.

ESSEX v WORCESTERSHIRE

At Colchester, August 27, 28, 29. Drawn. Essex 6 pts, Worcestershire 7 pts. Fletcher's decision to put Worcestershire in was soon regretted as Turner punished a succession of bowling changes. The New Zealander so dominated the bowling that his 168 came off just 204 balls, during the course of which he hit 98 in boundaries before being run out. Neale, Younis and Hemsley helped pile on the agony with forceful contributions. Following a resolute half-century from McEvoy, Fletcher and McEwan provided the brightest Essex batting with a stand of 98 in 21 overs before both fell to the toiling Pridgeon. After Essex declared 88 behind Lever immediately had the visitors struggling in their second innings. He claimed all five wickets to fall before rain ended play shortly after lunch, when an intriguing finish looked likely.

Worcestershire

G. M. Turner run out	168	– lbw b Lever	23
J. A. Ormrod c McEvoy b Turner	26	– b Lever	27
P. A. Neale c Herbert b Pringle	66	– lbw b Lever	4
Younis Ahmed not out	60	– c Turner b Lever	10
E. J. O. Hemsley b Lever	49	– c and b Lever	1
D. N. Patel c McEwan b Lever	0	– not out	19
†P. B. Fisher not out	2	– not out	1
L-b 10, w 1, n-b 6	17	L-b 4, w 1, n-b 1	6

1/101 2/263   (5 wkts) 388   1/30 2/36 3/55   (5 wkts) 91
3/284 4/385 5/385   4/63 5/88

H. Alleyne, *N. Gifford, A. P. Pridgeon and J. Cumbes did not bat.

Bonus points – Worcestershire 4, Essex 2.

Bowling: *First Innings*—Lever 19–4–68–2; Phillip 17–1–50–0; Turner 19–1–90–1; Pringle 18–2–69–1; Acfield 17–2–51–0; Herbert 10–0–43–0. *Second Innings*—Lever 16–6–34–5; Phillip 4–1–8–0; Turner 10–2–31–0; Pringle 4–1–12–0.

Essex

M. H. Denness c Younis b Pridgeon	21	N. Phillip lbw b Alleyne	12
M. S. A. McEvoy lbw b Cumbes	55	R. Herbert c Alleyne b Pridgeon	4
D. R. Pringle c Fisher b Cumbes	11	J. K. Lever not out	0
*K. W. R. Fletcher c Fisher b Pridgeon	75	B 1, l-b 14, w 10, n-b 3	28
†K. S. McEwan c Younis b Pridgeon	57		
B. R. Hardie c Fisher b Alleyne	25	1/31 2/54 3/135 (8 wkts dec.) 300	
S. Turner not out	12	4/233 5/256 6/265 7/284 8/295	

D. L. Acfield did not bat.

Bonus points – Essex 4, Worcestershire 3.

Bowling: Alleyne 25–5–62–2; Pridgeon 30–6–86–4; Cumbes 28–8–88–2; Gifford 13–3–36–0.

Umpires: D. G. L. Evans and A. Jepson.

At Blackpool, August 30, September 1, 2. ESSEX drew with LANCASHIRE.

ESSEX v NORTHAMPTONSHIRE

At Chelmsford, September 3, 4, 5. Drawn. Essex 7 pts, Northamptonshire 3 pts. Following several stoppages for bad light and rain, Essex were finally beaten by the weather. After bowling Northamptonshire out for 271 in their second innings, the home county were left needing 43 from thirteen overs. But before they could begin their innings, rain caused a further delay which left them with only five overs to acquire the runs. It was a target which proved beyond them, despite batsmen swinging heartily at nearly every delivery. Phillip returned his best figures of the season as the visitors were routed in their first innings; as did Turner when they batted a second time and offered greater resistance through Cook and Yardley. Essex lost their first three wickets for just 9 runs in reply to Northamptonshire's disappointing first innings but recovered splendidly to achieve a lead of 229. Hardie led the way with a fighting 95 as he completed his 1,000 runs for the season.

Northamptonshire

*G. Cook c Smith b Turner	30	– lbw b Gooch	70
W. Larkins c Gooch b Turner	7	– lbw b Gooch	18
R. G. Williams c Smith b Gooch	19	– c Hardie b Turner	28
A. J. Lamb lbw b Phillip	18	– c Acfield b Turner	28
P. Willey c East b Gooch	3	– b Gooch	3
T. J. Yardley lbw b Phillip	11	– c Pont b Turner	56
R. M. Tindall c Smith b Phillip	7	– c Smith b Phillip	1
†G. Sharp not out	19	– c Gooch b Turner	23
T. M. Lamb b Phillip	2	– lbw b Turner	5
N. A. Mallender b Phillip	0	– not out	2
B. J. Griffiths lbw b Phillip	0	– b Turner	4
L-b 4, n-b 6	10	B 4, l-b 16, n-b 13	33

1/14 2/58 3/67 4/81	126	1/65 2/117 3/149 4/168 271
5/81 6/93 7/104 8/116 9/124		5/171 6/172 7/228 8/262 9/267

Bonus points – Essex 4.

Bowling: *First Innings*—Phillip 19–7–47–6; Turner 18–4–40–2; Gooch 14–4–29–2. *Second Innings*—Phillip 14–2–64–1; Turner 36.3–9–69–6; Gooch 18–2–57–3; East 5–1–14–0; Acfield 11–3–34–0.

Essex

Essex			
G. A. Gooch b Griffiths	1	– c Sharp b T. M. Lamb	11
M. S. A. McEvoy lbw b Griffiths	2		
K. S. McEwan b T. M. Lamb	6	– (2) c Cook b Griffiths	1
*K. W. R. Fletcher lbw b Griffiths	45		
B. R. Hardie c Sharp b T. M. Lamb	95		
K. R. Pont lbw b Mallender	13	– (5) not out	1
S. Turner c Sharp b T. M. Lamb	60	– (3) c Griffiths b T. M. Lamb	2
N. Phillip lbw b Larkins	47	– (4) c Larkins b Griffiths	5
R. E. East c Williams b Willey	43		
†N. Smith not out	8	– (6) not out	1
D. L. Acfield c Yardley b Willey	1		
B 8, l-b 12, w 3, n-b 11	34	L-b 4	4

1/2 2/9 3/9 4/106   355   1/15 2/16 3/18 4/23   (4 wkts) 25
5/139 6/229 7/248 8/342 9/348

Bonus points – Essex 3, Northamptonshire 3 (Score at 100 overs: 253-7).

Bowling: *First Innings*—Griffiths 37–16–63–3; T. M. Lamb 40–10–90–3; Mallender 22–4–92–1; Willey 27.5–10–49–2; Larkins 9–2–27–1. *Second Innings*—Griffiths 2.5–0–9–2; T. M. Lamb 2–0–12–2.

Umpires: C. Cook and K. E. Palmer.

THE ASHES

The Ashes were originated in 1882 when, on August 29, Australia defeated the full strength of England on English soil for the first time. The Australians won by the narrow margin of 7 runs and the following day the *Sporting Times* printed a mock obituary notice, written by Shirley Brooks, son of an editor of *Punch*, which read:

"In affectionate remembrance of English Cricket which died at The Oval, 29th August, 1882. Deeply lamented by a large circle of sorrowing friends and acquaintances. R.I.P. N.B. The body will be cremated and the Ashes taken to Australia."

The following winter the Hon. Ivo Bligh, afterwards Lord Darnley, set out to Australia to recover these mythical Ashes. Australia won the first match by nine wickets, but England won the next two, and the real ashes came into being when some Melbourne women burnt a bail used in the third game and presented the ashes in an urn to Ivo Bligh.

When Lord Darnley died in 1927, the urn, by a bequest in his will, was given to MCC, and it held a place of honour in the Long Room at Lord's until 1953 when, with other cricket treasures, it was moved to the newly built Imperial Cricket Memorial near the pavilion. There it stands permanently, together with the velvet bag in which the urn was originally given to Lord Darnley and the score card of the 1882 match.

GLAMORGAN

President — HIS HONOUR JUDGE ROWE HARDING

Chairman — O. S. WHEATLEY

Secretary — P. B. CLIFT
6 High Street, Cardiff, CF1 1YU

Cricket Manager — T. W. CARTWRIGHT

Captain — M. A. NASH

N. G. Featherstone

County Badge

Javed Miandad

It was thought during the winter of 1979-80 that, after Glamorgan's sad and disappointing summer in 1979, things could only improve in 1980. And so they did, even though, at the end of the season, weaknesses were still highlighted. The county finished thirteenth in the Schweppes County Championship and moving away from bottom position was a comfort for all concerned; especially the new captain, Malcolm Nash, who, feeling his way cautiously, was attempting to achieve the right balance between boldness and temerity.

Of their 21 matches, Glamorgan won four and lost four with thirteen drawn; another twenty points were within their grasp and would have left them much higher in the table. In the John Player League, however, they flattered to deceive. After being at the top of the table at the end of May, they finished at the bottom, playing without resolution in many matches.

A review of the season's performances with bat and ball shows that the attack caused the greater problem. Nash and newcomer Ezra Moseley were the most effective bowlers, with 74 and 51 first-class wickets respectively, but, after these two, Glamorgan were thin on the ground. Allan Jones, in his first season with his fourth county, took 41 wickets at 39.12. Robin Hobbs, in the second year of a three-year contract, bowled 113.3 overs in the Championship and took eight wickets for 414 runs, proving an expensive luxury in an attack that required more bite. Featherstone, in his first season with Glamorgan, and young Geoffrey Holmes captured the odd wicket, but several of the younger players failed to develop as bowlers, suggesting that the county might do well to analyse its coaching system to achieve a higher return of talent. Although, in the past, much has been promised, Glamorgan still find it necessary to import players.

The batting was much better and more reliable, the first four in the averages – Javed Miandad, Alan Jones, Norman Featherstone and John Hopkins – all passing 1,000 first-class runs. It was a splendid summer for Miandad in his first season with Glamorgan after leaving Sussex; besides being the leading run-getter, with an average of 54.07, he instilled greater punch into the batting and gave it a touch of class, especially in the first half of the season.

For Alan Jones, the "veteran" of the side, it was also a splendid summer; at Basingstoke in July he scored the first double-century of his long career. This was also his fiftieth century and he achieved 1,000 runs for the twentieth consecutive season; a record of remarkable consistency. Featherstone made an impression as a useful middle-order batsman, and Hopkins, if not always as fluent as expected, opened the innings capably. The tail was a long one, but Glamorgan would still have done better had they been able to dismiss lower-order batsmen more cheaply. They allowed many sides to recover after having them in trouble.

In mitigation, South Wales was as wet as anywhere, if not wetter, during the summer of 1980 and many a finish was prevented. Only two players, Tony Cordle and Andrew Mack, did not have their contracts renewed at the end of the season, but the search goes on for bowlers who can strengthen the attack. A player of the character and stamina of D. J. Shepherd would make all the difference. – J. B. G. Thomas.

GLAMORGAN

[*Western Mail & Echo Ltd*]

Back row: D. A. Francis, A. L. Jones, N. G. Featherstone, M. J. Llewellyn, A. A. Jones, A. J. Mack, E. A. Moseley, N. J. Perry, R. C. Ontong, G. C. Holmes, M. N. Davies, T. Davies. *Front row:* T. W. Cartwright (*coach*), A. Jones, R. N. S. Hobbs, B. J. Lloyd, M. A. Nash (*captain*), J. A. Hopkins, A. E. Cordle, E. W. Jones, K. J. Lyons.

GLAMORGAN RESULTS

All First-class Matches — Played 22: Won 4, Lost 4, Drawn 14. Abandoned 1.

County Championship Matches — Played 21: Won 4, Lost 4, Drawn 13. Abandoned 1.

Bonus points — Batting 43, Bowling 57.

COUNTY CHAMPIONSHIP AVERAGES

BATTING

	Birthplace	Matches	Inns	Not Outs	Runs	Highest Inns	Avge
Javed Miandad	Karachi, Pakistan	19	31	5	1,442	181	55.46
A. Jones	Swansea	20	36	4	1,378	204*	43.06
N. G. Featherstone . .	Que Que, Rhod.	21	33	6	939	107	34.77
J. A. Hopkins	Maesteg	21	38	1	1,104	112	29.83
E. A. Moseley	Barbados, WI	14	16	6	294	70*	29.40
M. J. Llewellyn	Clydach	13	18	5	376	69	28.92
D. A. Francis	Clydach	9	14	3	276	78*	25.09
R. C. Ontong	Johannesburg, SA	4	6	1	108	52	21.60
E. W. Jones	Velindre	21	28	5	438	67	19.04
B. J. Lloyd	Neath	11	13	6	130	30	18.57
G. C. Holmes	Newcastle-on-Tyne	17	27	6	372	40	17.71
M. A. Nash	Abergavenny	18	24	2	342	49*	15.54
A. L. Jones	Alltwen	3	5	0	47	22	9.40
R. N. S. Hobbs	Chippenham	7	8	2	34	14	5.66
A. E. Cordle	Barbados, WI	4	3	1	11	6*	5.50
A. J. Mack	Aylsham	7	6	4	11	4*	5.50
A. A. Jones	Horley	16	14	3	50	12	4.54
N. J. Perry	Sutton	6	5	1	11	6	2.75

* *Signifies not out.*

BOWLING

	Overs	Maidens	Runs	Wickets	Average
M. A. Nash	611.4	196	1,723	74	23.28
E. A. Moseley	430	94	1,340	51	26.27
A. A. Jones	445	76	1,604	41	39.12
N. G. Featherstone . . .	142	38	432	11	39.27
G. C. Holmes	143	29	478	12	39.83

Also bowled: A. E. Cordle 135–52–286–5; R. N. S. Hobbs 113.3–27–414–8; Javed Miandad 29–7–118–2; B. J. Lloyd 194.1–53–634–9; A. J. Mack 79–12–278–7; R. C. Ontong 63–10–239–4; N. J. Perry 88.5–33–268–6.

HUNDREDS

The following eight three-figure innings were played for Glamorgan in County Championship matches – Javed Miandad 181 v Warwickshire (Birmingham), 141 v Gloucestershire (Bristol), 140* v Essex (Swansea); J. A. Hopkins 112 v Warwickshire (Birmingham), 105 v Lancashire (Manchester); A. Jones 204* v Hampshire (Basingstoke), 119 v Derbyshire (Derby); N. G. Featherstone 107 v Gloucestershire (Swansea).

GLAMORGAN v ESSEX

At Swansea, April 30, May 1, 2. Drawn. Glamorgan 6 pts, Essex 8 pts. In extremely cold weather the new Glamorgan signing from the West Indies, Ezra Moseley, made a good start to the season with six for 102 before Essex declared at 300 for nine. Glamorgan replied with 235 for nine on the second day thanks to a brilliant innings by Javed Miandad, in his first match since leaving Sussex. On the third day Glamorgan were all out for 241 and Essex had a merry thrash in their second innings, with Gooch hitting an undefeated 108 supported by McEwan. This left Glamorgan to score 257 in 170 minutes but, once Miandad was out in the fourth of the last twenty overs, the match subsided to a draw.

Essex

M. H. Denness c E. W. Jones b Moseley	25	
G. A. Gooch lbw b Nash	47	– (1) not out 108
K. S. McEwan c Featherstone b Moseley	13	– not out 54
*K. W. R. Fletcher c E. W. Jones b Moseley	46	
B. R. Hardie c Hopkins b Moseley	36	– (2) c E. W. Jones b Moseley..... 24
S. Turner c E. W. Jones b A. A. Jones	9	
N. Phillip not out	77	
R. E. East run out	24	
†N. Smith c A. L. Jones b Moseley	0	
J. K. Lever c Nash b Moseley	1	
D. L. Acfield not out	2	
B 1, l-b 9, n-b 10	20	B 4, l-b 1, w 1, n-b 5 11

1/58 2/90 3/98 4/164   (9 wkts dec.) 300   1/76   (1 wkt dec.) 197
5/175 6/205 7/259 8/264 9/271

Bonus points – Essex 4, Glamorgan 4.

Bowling: *First Innings*—Nash 24–4–75–1; A. A. Jones 24–2–92–1; Moseley 32–4–102–6; Lloyd 5–3–9–0; Miandad 2–0–2–0. *Second Innings*—Nash 6–1–36–0; A. A. Jones 11–2–29–0; Moseley 16–4–50–1; Lloyd 16–2–66–0; Miandad 1–0–5–0.

Glamorgan

A. Jones b Phillip	11	– b Lever 0
A. L. Jones c Smith b Lever	0	– run out 16
B. J. Lloyd c Hardie b Lever	15	
J. A. Hopkins c Hardie b Phillip	5	– (3) lbw b East 39
Javed Miandad not out	140	– (4) st Smith b East 67
N. G. Featherstone lbw b Turner	24	– (5) not out 10
G. C. Holmes c Phillip b Acfield	21	– (6) not out 1
†E. W. Jones c Phillip b Lever	9	
*M. A. Nash run out	0	
E. A. Moseley run out	0	
A. A. Jones b Phillip	0	
B 5, l-b 9, n-b 2	16	L-b 4, n-b 3............. 7

1/1 2/21 3/31 4/35 5/70   241   1/2 2/35 3/108   (4 wkts) 140
6/132 7/218 8/218 9/223   4/133

Bonus points – Glamorgan 2, Essex 4.

Bowling: *First Innings*—Lever 23–4–65–3; Phillip 16–1–52–3; Turner 9–2–22–1; East 19–3–46–0; Acfield 15–2–40–1. *Second Innings*—Lever 5–2–5–1; Phillip 4–2–7–0; Turner 2–0–8–0; East 16–2–59–2; Acfield 18–2–47–0; Fletcher 1–0–7–0.

Umpires: D. J. Constant and D. G. L. Evans.

At Bristol, May 7, 8, 9. GLAMORGAN beat GLOUCESTERSHIRE by seven wickets.

GLAMORGAN v NOTTINGHAMSHIRE

At Swansea, May 24, 26, 27. Nottinghamshire won by seven wickets. Nottinghamshire 20 pts, Glamorgan 6 pts. After a promising start with a first-wicket partnership of 113, Glamorgan collapsed to 206 all out against the attack of Rice and Hemmings. Nottinghamshire made 113 for three before resuming on the second day to score freely, with Rice dominating as they reached 345. Batting a second time, Glamorgan again collapsed and began the last day with a lead of only 11 runs at 150 for five. Rearguard action from E. W. Jones took them to 272, but Nottinghamshire achieved victory with seven wickets in hand.

Glamorgan

A. Jones lbw b Rice	84	– c Cooper b Hemmings	31
J. A. Hopkins lbw b Hemmings	61	– c Hassan b Hemmings	26
D. A. Francis c Harris b Hemmings	13	– c Hassan b Hemmings	6
Javed Miandad lbw b Hadlee	2	– lbw b Hemmings	0
N. G. Featherstone c Tunnicliffe b Hadlee	1	– c Curzon b Rice	47
G. C. Holmes not out	14	– b Bore	40
†E. W. Jones c Harris b Rice	0	– c Tunnicliffe b Bore	67
*M. A. Nash c Rice b Hemmings	11	– c Curzon b Bore	2
E. A. Moseley b Hemmings	0	– b Cooper	10
R. N. S. Hobbs c Todd b Rice	1	– c Hassan b Bore	12
A. A. Jones b Rice	0	– not out	4
B 11, l-b 8	19	B 9, l-b 11, w 1, n-b 6	27

1/113 2/139 3/141 4/163 5/184   **206**   1/44 2/61 3/65 4/78 5/144   **272**
6/184 7/203 8/203 9/204   6/208 7/210 8/235 9/257

Bonus points – Glamorgan 2, Nottinghamshire 4.

Bowling: *First Innings*—Hadlee 20–6–39–2; Rice 17.4–6–35–4; Bore 13–4–33–0; Cooper 13–4–36–0; Hemmings 22–7–44–4. *Second Innings*—Rice 27–11–61–1; Cooper 8–1–34–1; Hemmings 33–13–91–4; Bore 25.4–12–59–4.

Nottinghamshire

M. J. Harris lbw b Nash	7	– lbw b Nash	8
P. A. Todd lbw b Moseley	50	– c E. W. Jones b A. A. Jones	4
H. T. Tunnicliffe c Hopkins b Nash	52	– c Hopkins b Nash	1
J. D. Birch c E. W. Jones b A. A. Jones	12	– not out	69
K. E. Cooper c Hopkins b A. A. Jones	5		
*C. E. B. Rice c Hopkins b Nash	87		
B. Hassan lbw b Moseley	8	– (5) not out	47
†C. C. Curzon c Francis b Hobbs	45		
R. J. Hadlee c Hopkins b Nash	32		
E. E. Hemmings b A. A. Jones	25		
M. K. Bore not out	1		
B 1, l-b 9, w 9, n-b 2	21	B 4, n-b 3	7

1/33 2/94 3/106 4/126 5/147   **345**   1/8 2/12 3/21   **(3 wkts) 136**
6/168 7/273 8/280 9/343

Bonus points – Nottinghamshire 4, Glamorgan 4.

Bowling: *First Innings*—Nash 30–8–86–4; Moseley 22–1–69–2; A. A. Jones 24.4–4–85–3; Hobbs 10–2–46–1; Holmes 1–0–11–0; Featherstone 5–0–27–0. *Second Innings*—Nash 8–2–32–2; A. A. Jones 7–1–32–1; Hobbs 5.4–1–36–0; Moseley 3–0–18–0; Miandad 2–0–11–0.

Umpires: W. E. Alley and D. G. L. Evans.

At Manchester, May 28, 29, 30. GLAMORGAN drew with LANCASHIRE.

GLAMORGAN v NORTHAMPTONSHIRE

At Cardiff, May 31, June 2, 3. Drawn. In a rain-ruined match, there was no play on the first day and only eighty minutes on the second, when Northamptonshire scored 63 for two. On the third day they declared at this total and Glamorgan forfeited their first innings in an attempt to achieve a result. Thus no bonus points were earned by either side. In their second innings the visitors declared at 193 for two after a splendid innings by Larkins who hit two 6s and ten 4s. Glamorgan went for the runs at first but, at 121 for six, defeat seemed imminent until Holmes and Nash steered them to safety.

Northamptonshire

G. Cook lbw b Nash	0	– lbw b Moseley	28
W. Larkins c E. W. Jones b Nash	32	– not out	103
R. G. Williams not out	19	– c Featherstone b Lloyd	37
A. J. Lamb not out	11	– not out	12
N-b 1	1	B 1, l-b 5, n-b 7	13

1/29 2/40   (2 wkts dec.) 63   1/64 2/165   (2 wkts dec.) 193

P. Willey, T. J. Yardley, †G. Sharp, *P. J. Watts, T. M. Lamb, B. J. Griffiths and Sarfraz Nawaz did not bat.

Bowling: *First Innings*—Nash 10–4–17–2; A. A. Jones 6–2–31–0; Lloyd 5–2–12–0; Moseley 2–1–2–0. *Second Innings*—Nash 2–0–14–0; A. A. Jones 10–1–28–0; Moseley 10–2–26–1; Lloyd 18.1–3–83–1; Holmes 8–1–29–0.

Glamorgan

A. Jones (did not bat)	– c A. J. Lamb b Sarfraz	22
J. A. Hopkins (did not bat)	– c Sharp b Sarfraz	10
N. G. Featherstone (did not bat)	– b Sarfraz	16
Javed Miandad (did not bat)	– c Sharp b Willey	34
M. J. Llewellyn (did not bat)	– lbw b T. M. Lamb	5
G. C. Holmes (did not bat)	– not out	39
†E. W. Jones (did not bat)	– c Sarfraz b Willey	3
*M. A. Nash (did not bat)	– not out	49
	L-b 6, w 1, n-b 17	24

1/38 2/44 3/74   (6 wkts) 202
4/104 5/106 6/121

B. J. Lloyd, E. A. Moseley and A. A. Jones did not bat.

Bowling: Sarfraz 15–4–56–3; Griffiths 9–1–40–0; T. M. Lamb 10–4–24–1; Willey 8–1–31–2; Williams 6–0–27–0.

Glamorgan forfeited their first innings.

Umpires: C. Cook and P. S. G. Stevens.

At Derby, June 7, 9, 10. GLAMORGAN drew with DERBYSHIRE.

GLAMORGAN v WORCESTERSHIRE

At Swansea, June 14, 16, 17. Abandoned.

GLAMORGAN v WARWICKSHIRE

At Cardiff, June 18, 19, 20. Glamorgan won by four wickets. Glamorgan 16 pts, Warwickshire 4 pts. Warwickshire, put in on a damp pitch and in difficult batting conditions, could manage no more than 127, with Nash claiming four for 19. Glamorgan fared a little better and were 83 for two at the close. On the second day though, Doshi ran through their innings with five for 43, limiting their lead to 19. In their second innings Warwickshire reached 180, with 55 from Lloyd, and set the home team 162 to win. On the third day Glamorgan collected the necessary runs for the loss of six wickets, achieving their first victory at home for two years.

Warwickshire

*D. L. Amiss c E. W. Jones b A. A. Jones	30	– c Hopkins b A. A. Jones	2
K. D. Smith c Perry b Nash	10	– lbw b Cordle	9
T. A. Lloyd lbw b Nash	0	– c Miandad b A. A. Jones	55
J. A. Claughton lbw b A. A. Jones	9	– lbw b Nash	2
G. W. Humpage lbw b Cordle	0	– c Nash b A. A. Jones	20
P. R. Oliver c E. W. Jones b A. A. Jones	17	– b A. A. Jones	13
†C. Maynard c Featherstone b Perry	20	– c E. W. Jones b A. A. Jones	10
A. M. Ferreira c Holmes b Nash	29	– lbw b Cordle	32
D. C. Hopkins c Hopkins b Perry	2	– not out	22
G. C. Small not out	2	– lbw b Nash	1
D. R. Doshi c A. A. Jones b Nash	4	– c A. A. Jones b Nash	6
B 1, l-b 1, w 1, n-b 1	4	B 4, l-b 4	8
	127		**180**

1/24 2/24 3/50 4/51 5/51 6/83   127   1/2 2/26 3/31 4/85 5/102   180
7/93 8/121 9/123   6/113 7/122 8/161 9/172

Bonus points – Glamorgan 4.

Bowling: *First Innings*—Nash 13.4–6–19–4; A. A. Jones 16–4–58–3; Cordle 13–4–33–1; Perry 8–5–13–2. *Second Innings*—A. A. Jones 24–4–51–5; Cordle 25–8–57–2; Nash 12.4–7–27–3; Perry 13–2–37–0.

Glamorgan

A. Jones lbw b Ferreira	15	– c Smith b Doshi	23
J. A. Hopkins lbw b Hopkins	53	– lbw b Ferreira	21
N. G. Featherstone b Doshi	1	– b Doshi	2
Javed Miandad b Doshi	33	– b Doshi	30
M. J. Llewellyn b Doshi	7	– not out	31
G. C. Holmes c Lloyd b Doshi	2	– b Hopkins	17
*M. A. Nash b Hopkins	6	– run out	19
†E. W. Jones not out	2	– not out	0
A. E. Cordle st Maynard b Doshi	0		
N. J. Perry lbw b Hopkins	0		
A. A. Jones c Smith b Hopkins	11		
B 2, l-b 5, w 1, n-b 8	16	B 6, l-b 8, w 2, n-b 4	20
	146	(6 wkts)	**163**

1/28 2/34 3/110 4/121 5/126   146   1/40 2/53 3/73   (6 wkts) 163
6/133 7/133 8/133 9/134   4/89 5/131 6/161

Bonus points – Warwickshire 4.

Bowling: *First Innings*—Small 4–1–16–0; Ferreira 14–1–51–1; Doshi 20–6–43–5; Hopkins 9.5–3–20–4. *Second Innings*—Small 3–1–12–0; Ferreira 13–2–42–1; Doshi 15.1–1–65–3; Hopkins 5–1–24–1.

Umpires: C. Cook and D. Shackleton.

GLAMORGAN v SOMERSET

At Cardiff, June 21, 23. 24. Drawn. Glamorgan 6 pts, Somerset 3 pts. Batting first, Glamorgan achieved maximum batting points, thanks mainly to Miandad and Llewellyn who put on 127 for the third wicket. Somerset reached 12 for one before the close. On the second day rain delayed proceedings until 4.45 p.m. and then the visitors struggled against the bowling of Allan Jones and Featherstone on the rain-affected pitch. They reached 109 for five but, with no play possible on the third day, the match was abandoned as a draw.

Glamorgan

A. Jones c Jennings b Dredge	14	†E. W. Jones run out		10
J. A. Hopkins c Taylor b Dredge	24	A. E. Cordle not out		6
M. J. Llewellyn lbw b Jennings	69	L-b 16		16
Javed Miandad b Jennings	83			
N. G. Featherstone not out	42	1/21 2/66 3/193		(7 wkts) 300
G. C. Holmes lbw b Dredge	10	4/196 5/213 6/262		
*M. A. Nash run out	26	7/281		

A. A. Jones and N. J. Perry did not bat.

Bonus points – Glamorgan 4, Somerset 3.

Bowling: Moseley 24–5–68–0; Dredge 35–3–100–3; Jennings 29–4–66–2; Breakwell 7–2–25–0; Marks 5–2–25–0.

Somerset

*B. C. Rose b Featherstone	23	V. J. Marks not out		11
P. A. Slocombe c A. Jones b A. A. Jones	0			
D. Breakwell c Cordle b Featherstone	31	L-b 1		1
S. M. Gavaskar b A. A. Jones	6			
P. M. Roebuck not out	26	1/2 2/38 3/53		(5 wkts) 109
P. W. Denning lbw b Cordle	11	4/63 5/96		

†D. J. S. Taylor, K. F. Jennings, C. H. Dredge and H. R. Moseley did not bat.

Bonus points – Glamorgan 2.

Bowling: Nash 2–0–6–0; A. A. Jones 12–2–54–2; Cordle 13–8–8–1; Featherstone 13–3–32–2; Perry 3–0–8–0.

Umpires: C. Cook and D. Shackleton.

At Swansea, June 28, 30, July 1. GLAMORGAN drew with WEST INDIANS (See West Indian tour section).

At Swansea, June 29. GLAMORGAN lost to WEST INDIANS by five wickets (See West Indian tour section).

At Basingstoke, July 2, 3, 4. GLAMORGAN drew with HAMPSHIRE.

At Bradford, July 5, 7, 8. GLAMORGAN drew with YORKSHIRE.

GLAMORGAN v SUSSEX

At Swansea, July 9, 10. Sussex won by an innings and 189 runs. Sussex 20 pts, Glamorgan 3 pts. Glamorgan suffered their heaviest defeat in 31 years in a match that was completed in two days. They were dismissed for 135 in 45.5 overs before Sussex replied with 283 for three in 50 overs. Imran Khan was supreme, taking four Glamorgan wickets for 25 and then hitting an undefeated 89. On the second day Sussex proved even more formidable as Imran (five 6s and thirteen 4s) moved on to 124 and Wells scored his maiden century with four 6s and nineteen 4s, in a partnership of 256. The visitors declared at 440 for eight, setting Glamorgan a target of 306 to avoid an innings defeat. However, they managed only 116, with Imran taking four for 8 in nine overs and le Roux five for 49.

Glamorgan

A. Jones c Waller b Imran	2	– c Arnold b le Roux		3
J. A. Hopkins c Long b Imran	25	– c Mendis b Imran		6
G. C. Holmes lbw b Imran	2	– absent hurt		0
Javed Miandad c Phillipson b Imran	20	– (3) lbw b le Roux		42
N. G. Featherstone c Greig b Arnold	0	– (4) b Imran		4
M. J. Llewellyn lbw b Arnold	4	– (5) c Barclay b Imran		0
†E. W. Jones c Barclay b le Roux	36	– (6) c Barclay b le Roux		36
*B. J. Lloyd c le Roux b Arnold	16	– (7) not out		6
E. A. Moseley not out	0	– (8) c Phillipson b le Roux		6
R. N. S. Hobbs b le Roux	0	– (9) lbw b Imran		2
A. A. Jones c Greig b le Roux	12	– (10) c Phillipson b le Roux		0
L-b 6, w 1, n-b 11	18	– L-b 3, w 6, n-b 2		11

1/4 2/7 3/55 4/57 5/57 6/65   135   1/13 2/14 3/38 4/45 5/95   116
7/119 8/123 9/123   6/102 7/108 8/115 9/116

Bonus points – Sussex 4.

Bowling: *First Innings*—Imran 10–5–25–4; le Roux 16.5–7–43–3; Arnold 17–7–35–3; Greig 2–0–14–0. *Second Innings*—Imran 9–3–8–4; le Roux 12.3–3–49–5; Arnold 4–2–21–0; Waller 9–3–27–0.

Sussex

G. D. Mendis c Llewellyn b A. A. Jones	53	G. S. le Roux st E. W. Jones b Hobbs		46
J. R. T. Barclay c Miandad b Moseley	23	*†A. Long not out		8
P. W. G. Parker c A. A. Jones b Moseley	15			
Imran Khan c Llewellyn b A. A. Jones	124	B 10, l-b 4, w 10, n-b 6		30
C. M. Wells c A. A. Jones b A. A. Jones	135			
C. P. Phillipson c E. W. Jones b A. A. Jones	0	1/71 2/97 3/111	(8 wkts dec.)	440
I. A. Greig c E. W. Jones b Lloyd	6	4/367 5/367 6/384		
		7/384 8/440		

G. G. Arnold and C. E. Waller did not bat.

Bonus points – Sussex 4, Glamorgan 3.

Bowling: A. A. Jones 23–2–102–4; Moseley 23–4–111–2; Lloyd 18–4–79–1; Holmes 12–2–63–0; Hobbs 5.4–0–37–1; Featherstone 3–0–18–0.

Umpires: B. J. Meyer and P. S. G. Stevens.

GLAMORGAN v HAMPSHIRE

At Cardiff, July 12, 14, 15. Drawn. Glamorgan 3 pts, Hampshire 4 pts. With no play on the second day and a meagre ration on the third, a draw was inevitable despite Hampshire's big total, which was the highest scored by a side at Sophia Gardens ground. Turner, back in form, hit ten 4s in his undefeated 115 while Nicholas (fourteen 4s) fell 3 short of his maiden century. Play on the third day did not begin until mid-afternoon. Glamorgan declared at 72 for two after 36 overs to deprive Hampshire of a possible bowling point.

Hampshire

T. M. Tremlett b A. A. Jones	4	S. F. Graf lbw b Ontong		3
C. L. Smith lbw b Nash	22	†G. R. Stephenson not out		31
M. C. J. Nicholas b Hobbs	97			
T. E. Jesty c Miandad b Nash	27	B 6, l-b 10, w 2, n-b 7		25
D. R. Turner not out	115			
*N. E. J. Pocock run out	33	1/13 2/48 3/132	(7 wkts)	383
N. G. Cowley b A. A. Jones	26	4/198 5/259 6/327 7/334		

J. W. Southern and K. Stevenson did not bat.

Bonus points – Hampshire 4, Glamorgan 3.

Bowling: Nash 28–8–74–2; A. A. Jones 25–5–74–2; Ontong 19–0–94–1; Hobbs 16–3–62–1; Featherstone 12–0–54–0.

Glamorgan

A. Jones c Pocock b Cowley	....	26
J. A. Hopkins c and b Cowley	....	34
R. C. Ontong not out	....	1
*M. A. Nash not out	....	0
B 4, w 6, n-b 1	....	11

1/66 2/71   (2 wkts dec.)   72

D. A. Francis, Javed Miandad, N. G. Featherstone, M. J. Llewellyn, †E. W. Jones, R. N. S. Hobbs and A. A. Jones did not bat.

Bowling: Graf 2–1–3–0; Stevenson 5–2–12–0; Southern 16–6–27–0; Jesty 4–2–10–0; Cowley 9–7–9–2.

Umpires: B. J. Meyer and P. S. G. Stevens.

At Leicester, July 19, 21, 22. GLAMORGAN drew with LEICESTERSHIRE.

GLAMORGAN v LEICESTERSHIRE

At Cardiff, July 26, 28, 29. Drawn. Glamorgan 7 pts, Leicestershire 5 pts. Rain and bad light on the third day prevented a finish to an interesting match. Glamorgan elected to bat on a slow pitch and reached 271 for nine, with Hopkins, Featherstone and Llewellyn giving the innings a backbone. The second day was a lively one, with nineteen wickets falling, and Leicestershire were dismissed for 195 against the bowling of Nash and Mack. Glamorgan then collapsed to 149 for nine. They declared when play resumed at 4.30 p.m. on the third day, but with only one hour's batting time left, a tame draw was inevitable.

Glamorgan

A. Jones lbw b Clift	....	23 – c Steele b Taylor.	 4
J. A. Hopkins c Tolchard b Agnew	....	78 – c Steele b Taylor.	 0
R. C. Ontong b Steele.	....	2 – lbw b Parsons.	 6
N. G. Featherstone lbw b Clift	....	50 – b Parsons.	 3
Javed Miandad c Tolchard b Taylor	....	5 – (6) lbw b Agnew.	 32
M. J. Llewellyn not out.	....	49 – (5) b Agnew	 46
*M. A. Nash b Clift	....	29 – b Clift.	 6
†E. W. Jones c and b Taylor	....	8 – c Steele b Clift.	 6
B. J. Lloyd lbw b Parsons.	....	7 – lbw b Clift.	 30
A. J. Mack c Steele b Parsons	....	2 – not out	 3
A. A. Jones not out.	....	1 – not out	 4
B 4, l-b 7, w 1, n-b 5	....	17	B 1, l-b 1, w 7	 9

1/71 2/79 3/132 4/143   (9 wkts) 271   1/4 2/8 3/12   (9 wkts dec.) 149
5/176 6/215 7/237   4/25 5/96 6/103 7/111
8/250 9/269   8/131 9/142

Bonus points – Glamorgan 3, Leicestershire 4.

Bowling: *First Innings*—Taylor 21–5–40–2; Parsons 18–3–67–2; Agnew 14–3–49–1; Clift 26–8–49–3; Steele 11–3–19–1; Cook 10–5–30–0. *Second Innings*—Taylor 11–0–39–2; Parsons 7–1–34–2; Clift 12–4–28–3; Agnew 8–0–39–2.

Leicestershire

J. C. Balderstone c Hopkins b A. A. Jones	4	– not out	18
J. F. Steele lbw b Mack	9	– not out	22
D. I. Gower c Hopkins b Nash	41		
*B. F. Davison c Nash b Mack	9		
N. E. Briers c E. W. Jones b Ontong	12		
†R. W. Tolchard lbw b Nash	0		
P. B. Clift c Ontong b Mack	67		
G. J. Parsons c E. W. Jones b Nash	8		
J. P. Agnew b A. A. Jones	31		
N. G. B. Cook b Lloyd	2		
L. B. Taylor not out	2		
B 4, l-b 3, w 5, n-b 7	19	B 5, w 1	6

1/4 2/59 3/61 4/61 5/61 6/120   195   (no wkt) 46
7/148 8/155 9/172

Bonus points – Leicestershire 1, Glamorgan 4.

Bowling: *First Innings*—Nash 21–6–61–3; A. A. Jones 14.4–2–50–2; Mack 8–0–32–3; Ontong 6–2–23–1; Lloyd 10–6–10–1. *Second Innings*—Nash 9–4–11–0; A. A. Jones 5–1–15–0; Featherstone 6–2–13–0; Lloyd 3–2–1–0.

Umpires: K . E. Palmer and P. B. Wight.

At Canterbury, August 2, 4, 5. GLAMORGAN beat KENT by three wickets.

At The Oval, August 6, 7, 8. GLAMORGAN lost to SURREY by 104 runs.

At Worcester, August 9, 11, 12. GLAMORGAN drew with WORCESTERSHIRE.

GLAMORGAN v GLOUCESTERSHIRE

At Swansea, August 16, 18, 19. Glamorgan won by eight wickets. Glamorgan 18 pts, Gloucestershire 4 pts. Gloucestershire struggled after being put in, on a soft pitch, reaching a total of only 146, with Moseley taking four for 49. Featherstone scored his first century for Glamorgan, hitting two 6s and seven 4s in his watchful innings, and was awarded his county cap. In marked contrast was Procter's typically swashbuckling 88 (two 6s and fourteen 4s) when Gloucestershire batted again. But it was not enough to hold off Glamorgan and after Nash had taken seven wickets for 79, the home team easily scored the runs for victory.

Gloucestershire

A. W. Stovold c E. W. Jones b Moseley	9	– c Miandad b Moseley	24
B. C. Broad lbw b Nash	4	– c E. W. Jones b Nash	12
Sadiq Mohammad c and b Holmes	0	– c E. W. Jones b Holmes	12
Zaheer Abbas c Francis b Mack	46	– c Featherstone b Nash	50
*M. J. Procter c E. W. Jones b Nash	11	– b Nash	88
P. Bainbridge c E. W. Jones b Moseley	0	– (7) b Nash	12
D. A. Graveney b Moseley	0	– (8) c Hopkins b Nash	9
A. H. Wilkins c Miandad b Moseley	6	– (9) c Holmes b Nash	6
†A. J. Brassington c Perry b Mack	6	– (6) lbw b Nash	0
B. M. Brain not out	37	– b Moseley	0
J. H. Childs c Nash b Perry	7	– not out	4
B 9, l-b 5, n-b 3	17	B 1, l-b 8, w 3, n-b 7	19

1/17 2/17 3/33 4/54   146   1/37 2/44 3/84 4/184   236
5/65 6/65 7/75 8/94 9/107   5/186 6/213 7/223 8/227 9/228

Bonus points – Glamorgan 4.

Bowling: *First Innings*—Nash 24–10–43–2; Moseley 20–6–49–4; Holmes 4–0–16–1; Mack 6–1–17–2; Perry 5.5–3–4–1. *Second Innings*—Nash 24.5–5–79–7; Moseley 24–5–77–2; Mack 10–1–27–0; Perry 6–4–21–0; Holmes 2–0–13–1.

Glamorgan

A. Jones c Bainbridge b Brain	20	– b Bainbridge................ 42
J. A. Hopkins c Graveney b Procter..........	6	– not out 64
G. C. Holmes lbw b Wilkins..................	1	
Javed Miandad c Stovold b Brain.............	27	– not out 47
N. G. Featherstone b Bainbridge 107		
D. A. Francis b Wilkins..................	21	– (3) c Sadiq b Childs 16
*M. A. Nash c Procter b Brain................	1	
†E. W. Jones c and b Brain	9	
E. A. Moseley c Sadiq b Bainbridge........	10	
N. J. Perry b Bainbridge.....................	0	
A. J. Mack not out	4	
L-b 5, w 1........................	6	B' 1, l-b 1............. 2

1/14 2/19 3/52 4/61   212   1/79 2/104   (2 wkts) 171
5/132 6/134 7/164 8/195 9/197

Bonus points – Glamorgan 2, Gloucestershire 4.

Bowling: *First Innings*—Brain 43–12–76–4; Procter 12–5–24–1; Wilkins 26–6–68–2; Bainbridge 8.5–2–17–3; Graveney 6–0–21–0. *Second Innings*—Brain 11–4–26–0; Procter 5–2–4–0; Graveney 5–1–19–0; Childs 7–0–26–1; Wilkins 8–1–35–0; Bainbridge 11–4–25–1; Stovold 3–0–18–0; Sadiq 2.5–0–16–0.

Umpires: W. L. Budd and D. J. Constant.

At Birmingham, August 23, 25, 26. GLAMORGAN drew with WARWICKSHIRE.

At Taunton, August 27, 28, 29. GLAMORGAN drew with SOMERSET.

GLAMORGAN v MIDDLESEX

At Cardiff, August 30, September 1, 2. Middlesex won by 72 runs. Middlesex 17 pts, Glamorgan 4 pts. Victory, in a tense finish, brought Middlesex the Championship title outright for the seventh time, with one game remaining. Wet conditions restricted play to an hour on Saturday, when Middlesex were put in. They reached a first innings total of only 163, struggling against the hostile pace of Moseley, who recorded a career-best six for 41. However, Glamorgan failed against the variable bounce and Middlesex began their second innings 23 ahead. The pitch had dried out and Brearley, who had reached 11 the previous evening, made the most of conditions, achieving an unbeaten 124 on the last morning, with a century before lunch. His lunchtime declaration left Glamorgan to score 235 in four hours. Despite a gallant innings from Holmes, who defied the Middlesex bowlers for two hours and put on 52 for the sixth wicket with Moseley, van der Bijl broke through and Middlesex swept to victory with eight overs to spare.

Middlesex

*J. M. Brearley c E. W. Jones b Moseley	3 – not out .124	
†P. R. Downton c E. W. Jones b Moseley	3 – c A. L. Jones b Holmes	46
C. T. Radley c Perry b Nash	40 – not out	22
G. D. Barlow c Hopkins b Moseley	2	
M. W. W. Selvey c Hopkins b Nash.	22	
R. O. Butcher b Moseley	14	
W. N. Slack c Hopkins b Moseley	4	
P. H. Edmonds lbw b Nash	21	
V. A. P. van der Bijl c Featherstone b Moseley . . .	40	
W. W. Daniel b Nash.	0	
S. P. Hughes not out.	0	
B 2, l-b 5, n-b 7	14	B 5, l-b 5, w 2, n-b 7 19

1/3 2/12 3/15 4/53　　　　　　　　　　　163　　1/34　　　　　　　(1 wkt dec.) 211
5/70 6/76 7/114 8/127 9/127

Bonus points – Middlesex 1, Glamorgan 4.

Bowling: *First Innings*—Nash 27–7–102–4; Moseley 22–9–41–6; Holmes 5–2–6–0. *Second Innings*—Nash 10–1–53–0; Moseley 17–3–57–0; Holmes 10–2–18–1; Mack 4–0–19–0; Perry 6–1–45–0.

Glamorgan

J. A. Hopkins b van der Bijl	40 – c Barlow b Hughes.	18
A. L. Jones lbw b Daniel	0 – b Hughes	9
D. A. Francis b Daniel	5 – b Selvey	22
N. G. Featherstone c Edmonds b Hughes	17 – c Butcher b Hughes	5
M. J. Llewellyn b van der Bijl.	12 – lbw b Daniel.	18
G. C. Holmes b van der Bijl	28 – c Butcher b Daniel	33
E. A. Moseley c Downton b Hughes	10 – b van der Bijl	28
†E. W. Jones b Hughes	0 – c Radley b Daniel.	7
*M. A. Nash c Butcher b Hughes.	9 – c Brearley b Edmonds	1
N. J. Perry not out	3 – c Downton b Edmonds.	2
A. J. Mack b van der Bijl	0 – not out	2
B 10, w 1, n-b 5	16	L-b 6, n-b 11.	17

1/6 2/20 3/45 4/72　　　　　　　　　　140　　1/28 2/33 3/42 4/75　　　　　　162
5/85 6/99 7/99 8/111 9/140　　　　　　　　5/84 6/136 7/145 8/154 9/157

Bonus points – Middlesex 4.

Bowling: *First Innings*—van der Bijl 19.3–6–40–4; Daniel 12–2–40–2; Hughes 14–5–36–4; Edmonds 2–1–5–0; Selvey 4–2–3–0. *Second Innings*—van der Bijl 15–5–28–1; Daniel 17–2–71–3; Hughes 11–3–29–3; Selvey 8–4–8–1; Edmonds 8–3–9–2.

Umpires: R. Palmer and A. G. T. Whitehead.

GLOUCESTERSHIRE

Patron – THE DUKE OF BEAUFORT

President – T. L. ROBINSON

Chairman, Cricket Committee – B. G. STONES

Secretary/Cricket Manager – A. S. BROWN
County Ground, Nevil Road, Bristol BS7 9EJ

Captain – M. J. PROCTER

| B. C. Broad | County Badge | A. J. Hignell |

Gloucestershire's improvement in the Schweppes County Championship from tenth to seventh, modest as it was, seemed out of the question at the start of August when they entered the Cheltenham Festival without a win in competitive three-day matches. Furthermore, they had failed to progress beyond the group stages of the Benson and Hedges Cup – numbering Minor Counties among their three defeats – and had fallen at the first hurdle in the Gillette Cup. True, Gloucestershire's programme was badly interfered with by the weather, but the rain was sometimes an ally.

Consequently, interest in the opening match of the Festival against Hampshire surrounded the likelihood that it would decide which of the two counties finished with the wooden spoon. In the event Gloucestershire won handsomely, and followed this victory by beating Worcestershire and champions-elect Middlesex, also at the Festival. Before the end of the season they accounted for Kent on an untrustworthy pitch at Folkestone and so 1980 finished on an optimistic note.

Worries about the strength of the bowling appeared completely justified during the dry days of May. Turner of Worcestershire and Botham both took double-centuries off a struggling attack and Somerset's 534 for six at Taunton was a record for 100 overs in the Championship.

With the change in the weather the bowlers did well enough, and bowling bonus points eventually totalled 74, a number beaten by only Middlesex and Surrey. However, the batsmen found run-getting a struggle. Compared with nineteen Championship centuries in 1979, there were only six. Sadiq Mohammad, who hit eight the previous season, failed to reach three figures once and had to work hard for his 1,000 runs. Zaheer's aggregate was also down, although he played some fine innings, notably a match-saving 173 against Somerset and a match-winning 98 against Kent at Folkestone.

Chris Broad, a tall, elegant, left-handed opener, confirmed all the good opinions of 1979 and just missed 1,000 runs in his first full season. Although he was often dismissed cheaply, he appeared to learn quickly and fully deserved his two Championship hundreds in addition to one before lunch against Oxford University. Andrew Stovold dodged about between opener and number four and passed 50 on six occasions but could not manage a century. Philip Bainbridge, although proving his worth as a seam bowler, did not advance as a batsman as quickly as had been hoped, but he held a middle-order position for most of the season in preference to David Partridge. Alastair Hignell began well and finished with a respectable average, despite suffering injuries early in the season and later.

Before the season Gloucestershire signed two additional pace bowlers in David Surridge, the Cambridge Blue from Hertfordshire, and the Glamorgan left-armer Alan Wilkins. Unhappily, Surridge went down with a back injury early on and took no part in the Championship. But Wilkins proved a useful recruit, the sort of first-change bowler Gloucestershire had lacked for several seasons. Brian Brain, in his 40th year maintaining pace and fitness to a remarkable degree, was capable of troubling the best batsmen with the new ball, while John Childs again looked a more likely wicket-taker than Graveney, the other left-arm spinner.

All the bowlers had reason to be grateful to Andy Brassington behind the stumps. His shortcomings as a batsman may deny him the opportunity of international cricket, but he had a fine season, showing rare agility and enthusiasm. Thought should be given to including him for the limited-overs games, at the risk of weakening the batting, for had he been included at The Oval, Surrey might well have been beaten in the Gillette Cup.

And so to Mike Procter, who has dominated Gloucestershire cricket for a decade. Injuries prevented him from bowling at his fastest on many occasions, and there were whispers around the counties that he was in decline. His batting and bowling figures were ordinary by his own high standards until he suddenly exploded, at Cheltenham. Against Worcestershire, with a mixture of pace and spin, he took fourteen wickets, the outstanding bowling performance of the season. In addition, he made over 100 runs in a low-scoring game. Then, against Middlesex, he played one of his finest innings, an unbeaten 134 which had all present united in their praise of a magnificent display against the best bowling attack in the Championship. He further cheered the county's supporters by announcing his desire to finish his playing career as a Gloucestershire cricketer, so ending the rumours of his leaving. – G.W.

GLOUCESTERSHIRE

[Press Association

Back row: A. J. Hignell, B. Avery (*scorer*), A. H. Wilkins, I. Broome, S. J. Windaybank, A. J. Wright, M. D. Partridge, D. Surridge, B. C. Broad, J. H. Childs, A. J. Brassington, P. Bainbridge, M. W. Stovold. *Front row:* A. W. Stovold, B. M. Brain, J. K. R. Graveney (*chairman*), M. J. Procter (*captain*), A. S. Brown (*secretary/manager*), D. A. Graveney, G. Wiltshire.

GLOUCESTERSHIRE RESULTS

All First-class Matches – Played 23: Won 5, Lost 6, Drawn 12. Abandoned 1.

County Championship Matches – Played 21: Won 4, Lost 5, Drawn 12. Abandoned 1.

Bonus points – Batting 39, Bowling 74.

COUNTY CHAMPIONSHIP AVERAGES

BATTING

	Birthplace	Matches	Inns	Not Outs	Runs	Highest Inns	Avge
Zaheer Abbas	*Sialkot, Pakistan*	19	33	1	1,263	173	39.46
M. J. Procter	*Durban, SA*	18	31	2	1,046	134*	36.06
A. J. Hignell	*Cambridge*	13	20	4	564	100*	35.25
Sadiq Mohammad	*Junagadh, India*	21	38	4	1,069	92	31.44
B. C. Broad	*Bristol*	18	32	1	835	116	26.93
A. W. Stovold	*Bristol*	21	37	2	926	89	26.45
M. D. Partridge	*Birdlip*	10	17	5	251	48	20.91
P. Bainbridge	*Stoke-on-Trent*	15	25	2	347	71	15.08
D. A. Graveney	*Bristol*	19	28	6	329	55	14.95
A. H. Wilkins	*Cardiff*	17	22	3	212	32	11.15
M. W. Stovold	*Bristol*	4	6	0	58	36	9.66
B. M. Brain	*Worcester*	20	24	5	173	37*	9.10
A. J. Brassington	*Bagnall, Staffs*	21	27	7	103	14*	5.15
J. H. Childs	*Plymouth*	15	19	10	44	8*	4.88

* *Signifies not out.*

BOWLING

	Overs	Maidens	Runs	Wickets	Average
M. J. Procter	346.1	97	857	48	17.85
J. H. Childs	373.4	98	1,034	43	24.04
B. M. Brain	471.5	93	1,428	53	26.94
A. H. Wilkins	348.3	72	1,135	42	27.02
D. A. Graveney	496.5	125	1,486	44	33.77
P. Bainbridge	122.4	17	450	13	34.61

Also bowled: B. C. Broad 20–4–95–1; M. D. Partridge 143.5–26–544–8; Sadiq Mohammad 53.5–3–237–1; A. W. Stovold 4.4–0–24–0; Zaheer Abbas 11–3–46–2.

HUNDREDS

The following six three-figure innings were played for Gloucestershire in County Championship matches – B. C. Broad 116 v Hampshire (Cheltenham), 101 v Warwickshire (Birmingham); Zaheer Abbas 173 v Somerset (Taunton), 104 v Northamptonshire (Bristol); A. J. Hignell 100* v Somerset (Taunton); M. J. Procter 134* v Middlesex (Cheltenham).

At Oxford, April 23, 24, 25. GLOUCESTERSHIRE beat OXFORD UNIVERSITY by 342 runs.

At Worcester, April 30, May 1, 2. GLOUCESTERSHIRE drew with WORCESTERSHIRE.

GLOUCESTERSHIRE v NORTHAMPTONSHIRE

At Bristol, May 3, 5, 6. Northamptonshire won by eight wickets. Northamptonshire 18 pts, Gloucestershire 7 pts. Gloucestershire were in control until the final afternoon when Williams and Allan Lamb took their county to victory with an unbroken third-wicket partnership of 216 in 178 minutes, the win coming with 29 balls to spare. Procter had set Northamptonshire a target of 308 in 281 minutes. Zaheer (fourteen boundaries) and Stovold provided the backbone of Gloucestershire's first innings with a third-wicket stand of 166. Procter made an early breach in Northamptonshire's first innings and, despite a defiant half-century by Yardley, the visitors conceded a first innings advantage of 79 after Graveney had steadily worked his way through. Few thought Procter over-generous when he declared the Gloucestershire second innings, having plundered an unbeaten 88 in eighty-four minutes against opponents who provided him with 1979's fastest century. However, Willey and Larkins built a solid foundation and, after an early escape, Williams gave fine support to Lamb, who hit eleven 4s and one 6 in a splendid display of attacking batsmanship. Hignell, fielding at short leg without a helmet, was taken to hospital with a broken nose on the second day after being hit by Tim Lamb and took no further part.

Gloucestershire

B. C. Broad c T. M. Lamb b Griffiths	5	– lbw b T. M. Lamb	6
Sadiq Mohammad c Sharp b Griffiths	0	– c Sharp b Willey	61
Zaheer Abbas b Williams	104	– c Yardley b T. M. Lamb	5
A. W. Stovold c Sharp b Willey	89	– b T. M. Lamb	51
*M. J. Procter c T. M. Lamb b Willey	36	– not out	88
A. J. Hignell not out	30		
M. D. Partridge c Watts b Carter	4	– (6) not out	4
D. A. Graveney lbw b Carter	6		
†A. J. Brassington c Sharp b Carter	0		
B. M. Brain b Carter	1		
J. H. Childs c Sharp b Willey	0		
L-b 7, n-b 5	12	B 4, l-b 4, w 1, n-b 4	13

1/3 2/6 3/172 4/233 5/254 287 1/10 2/32 3/118 (4 wkts dec.) 228
6/266 7/277 8/280 9/284 4/158

Bonus points – Gloucestershire 3, Northamptonshire 4.

Bowling: *First Innings*—Griffiths 20–4–57–2; T. M. Lamb 20–4–74–0; Larkins 3–0–24–0; Willey 21.3–3–48–3; Carter 12–3–27–4; Williams 15–2–45–1.*Second Innings*—Griffiths 16–4–37–0; T. M. Lamb 20–7–62–3; Carter 2–0–18–0; Willey 20–6–51–1; Williams 17–5–47–0.

Northamptonshire

P. Willey c Brassington b Procter	8	– c Graveney b Childs	49
W. Larkins c Brassington b Procter	12	– b Childs	41
R. G. Williams c Brassington b Procter	4	– not out	80
A. J. Lamb c Brassington b Brain	43	– not out	113
T. J. Yardley c Procter b Graveney	51		
†G. Sharp c Broad b Graveney	20		
R. M. Tindall st Brassington b Graveney	11		
R. M. Carter c Procter b Graveney	6		
*P. J. Watts b Brain	32		
T. M. Lamb not out	12		
B. J. Griffiths c Childs b Graveney	1		
B 1, l-b 3, n-b 4	8	B 13, l-b 11, n-b 3	27

1/18 2/25 3/32 4/97 5/135   **208**   1/89 2/94   (2 wkts) **310**
6/148 7/154 8/165 9/199

Bonus points – Northamptonshire 2, Gloucestershire 4.

Bowling: *First Innings*—Procter 17–3–47–3; Brain 27–10–53–2; Partridge 8–3–17–0; Childs 7–2–9–0; Graveney 28.2–5–74–5. *Second Innings*—Brain 13–3–56–0; Procter 11–1–32–0; Graveney 27–6–83–0; Childs 29–5–108–2; Stovold 0.1–0–4–0.

Umpires: D. J. Halfyard and J. van Geloven.

GLOUCESTERSHIRE v GLAMORGAN

At Bristol, May 7, 8, 9. Glamorgan won by seven wickets. Glamorgan 16 pts, Gloucestershire 5 pts. Glamorgan's first Championship victory since August 1978 was celebrated with champagne in the dressing-room at the expense of their captain Nash, who took eleven wickets in the match. Eighteen wickets fell on the first day and another fourteen on the second as inconsistent bounce helped the pace bowlers. With Procter unable to bowl, because of a strained shoulder, and Brain, destroyer of Glamorgan's first innings (including four wickets in nine balls), breaking down after six overs, Gloucestershire again lost the upper hand in the fourth innings. Javed Miandad thrashed secondary seam bowling with rare gusto and, with the spinners ineffective, he reached his century in one hundred and forty-six minutes just before the close of the second day; only ninety minutes were needed on the third as Featherstone took charge to finish the match.

Gloucestershire

B. C. Broad c E. W. Jones b Moseley	16	– b A. A. Jones	26
Sadiq Mohammad c A. A. Jones b Moseley	56	– b Moseley	4
Zaheer Abbas c Featherstone b A. A. Jones	7	– b Nash	93
A. W. Stovold c E. W. Jones b A. A. Jones	9	– c Lloyd b Moseley	9
*M. J. Procter c A. L. Jones b Nash	20	– b Nash	41
P. Bainbridge b Nash	1	– c sub b Nash	4
D. A. Graveney c Featherstone b Moseley	3	– (8) lbw b Nash	4
M. D. Partridge not out	36	– (7) c E. W. Jones b Nash	2
†A. J. Brassington lbw b Nash	9	– b A. A. Jones	0
B. M. Brain b Nash	15	– not out	15
J. H. Childs b Nash	0	– c Holmes b Nash	4
B 3, l-b 2, w 1, n-b 5	11	B 2, l-b 8, w 5, n-b 3	18

1/24 2/39 3/61 4/85 5/91   **180**   1/14 2/58 3/78 4/143 5/155   **220**
6/107 7/119 8/146 9/180   6/175 7/194 8/201 9/201

Bonus points – Gloucestershire 1, Glamorgan 4.

Bowling: *First Innings*—Nash 22.5–7–58–5; Moseley 19–2–54–3; A. A. Jones 19–3–57–2. *Second Innings*—Nash 23.2–9–72–6; Moseley 14–1–63–2; A. A. Jones 15–4–46–2; Holmes 6–1–21–0.

Glamorgan

A. Jones c Brassington b Procter	3	– b Bainbridge 30
A. L. Jones lbw b Brain	22	
J. A. Hopkins lbw b Brain	5	– (2) c Brassington b Brain 4
Javed Miandad c Brassington b Brain	33	– (3) b Partridge 141
N. G. Featherstone lbw b Brain	0	– (4) not out 73
G. C. Holmes b Brain	0	– (5) not out 21
†E. W. Jones c Brassington b Partridge	8	
*M. A. Nash c Stovold b Brain	30	
B. J. Lloyd not out	4	
E. A. Moseley lbw b Partridge	3	
A. A. Jones b Partridge	4	
B 6, l-b 1, w 2, n-b 4	13	L-b 4, n-b 3 7

1/6 2/17 3/68 4/68 5/69　　　　　125　　1/13 2/72 3/213　　　(3 wkts) 276
6/70 7/106 8/110 9/119

Bonus points – Gloucestershire 4.

Bowling: *First Innings*—Procter 6–1–19–1; Brain 18–3–68–6; Partridge 12.4–3–25–3. *Second Innings*—Brain 6.2–1–21–1; Partridge 22.4–4–87–1; Bainbridge 17–2–73–1; Childs 7–0–31–0; Broad 5–1–13–0; Graveney 8–1–43–0; Stovold 0.3–0–1–0.

Umpires: D. J. Halfyard and J. van Geloven.

At Taunton, May 24, 26, 27. GLOUCESTERSHIRE drew with SOMERSET.

At Leicester, May 28, 29, 30. GLOUCESTERSHIRE drew with LEICESTERSHIRE.

GLOUCESTERSHIRE v ESSEX

At Gloucester, May 31, June 2, 3. Drawn. Gloucestershire 6 pts, Essex 8 pts. The loss of the first day to rain and the absence of a more challenging declaration by Gloucestershire on the Monday turned the match into a struggle for bonus points. None the less, there were some notable individual performances. After Gloucestershire had begun well Pringle, on leave from Cambridge, captured the first three wickets for 9 runs in seventeen deliveries. Gooch launched the Essex reply in thrilling style with his fifth century in twelve first-class innings, his 134 (two 6s and eighteen 4s) coming in just under three hours as he and Denness put on 197 for the first wicket. After lunch on the third day, Childs took full advantage of a turning pitch to take six consecutive wickets as Essex pressed on to a lead of 115. When Gloucestershire batted again with two and a half hours remaining, Sadiq ensured that the Essex spinners were never in a position to emulate Childs.

Gloucestershire

A. W. Stovold c Smith b Pringle	60	– (2) c Gooch b East 10
Sadiq Mohammad c Smith b Pringle	25	– (1) not out 55
Zaheer Abbas c Gooch b Pringle	9	– b East 2
A. J. Hignell lbw b Lever	44	– not out 18
*M. J. Procter b Lever	13	
M. W. Stovold b Phillip	11	
M. D. Partridge b Lever	28	
D. A. Graveney not out	11	
†A. J. Brassington c Hardie b Lever	0	
B. M. Brain c McEwan b East	11	
J. H. Childs not out	0	
B 2, l-b 2, w 1, n-b 3	8	B 2, l-b 1 3

1/83 2/96 3/97 4/114　　　(9 wkts dec.) 220　　1/24 2/40　　　(2 wkts) 88
5/138 6/185 7/200 8/200 9/213

Bonus points – Gloucestershire 2, Essex 4.

Bowling: *First Innings*—Lever 24–2–83–4; Phillip 16–2–55–1; Pringle 10–1–34–3; Acfield 13–2–25–0; East 7–3–15–1. *Second Innings*—Lever 4–3–5–0; Phillip 2–0–2–0; Pringle 3–0–8–0; East 18–2–50–2; Acfield 17–8–20–0.

Essex

M. H. Denness st Brassington b Childs	87	†N. Smith b Childs	4
G. A. Gooch st Brassington b Procter	134	D. R. Pringle lbw b Brain	22
K. S. McEwan c Brassington b Graveney	22	J. K. Lever not out	8
*K. W. R. Fletcher b Childs	8	L-b 6, w 2	8
B. R. Hardie b Childs	34		
N. Phillip st Brassington b Childs	0	1/197 2/235 3/252 4/261 (9 wkts dec.)	335
R. E. East b Childs	8	5/261 6/281 7/289 8/310 9/335	

D. L. Acfield did not bat.

Bonus points – Essex 4, Gloucestershire 4.

Bowling: Brain 19.4–4–55–1; Procter 15–4–39–1; Partridge 3–0–14–0; Graveney 33–6–129–1; Childs 23–3–90–6.

Umpires: R. S. Herman and A. Jepson.

At Northampton, June 7, 9, 10. GLOUCESTERSHIRE lost to NORTHAMPTONSHIRE by six wickets.

GLOUCESTERSHIRE v DERBYSHIRE

At Bristol, June 14, 16, 17. Abandoned.

GLOUCESTERSHIRE v LANCASHIRE

At Bristol, June 18, 19, 20. Drawn. Gloucestershire 5 pts, Lancashire 4 pts. Bowlers dominated the match until the final afternoon when Kennedy seemed to be leading Lancashire towards victory. Both sides recorded their lowest Championship totals of the season in the first innings. Hughes commanded such respect that he bowled thirteen consecutive maiden overs – coming within sight of Horace Hazell's record of 105 successive scoreless balls – and but for Stovold Gloucestershire would not have managed a batting point. Lancashire fared even worse, with Brain the main destroyer, although Simmons again showed his fighting qualities before Procter finished the innings with off-breaks. Gloucestershire's collapse on the final morning, following another good effort by Stovold, was checked by Graveney and Wilkins before Malone finished the innings off with the new ball. With Kennedy in splendid form Lancashire needed 96 from the last eighty minutes when the rain came, and after an interruption of twenty minutes there was time for only three more overs before the conclusive downpour.

Gloucestershire

B. C. Broad c Kennedy b Malone	26	– lbw b Hughes	34
Sadiq Mohammad c Hayes b Malone	41	– c Fowler b Allott	4
Zaheer Abbas c Scott b Simmons	1	– c Scott b Malone	17
A. W. Stovold not out	43	– c Scott b Malone	49
*M. J. Procter b Reidy	21	– c Scott b Hughes	8
A. J. Hignell lbw b Reidy	3	– c Simmons b Malone	15
P. Bainbridge lbw b Reidy	1	– c Scott b Hughes	5
D. A. Graveney c Scott b Allott	1	– c Simmons b Malone	17
A. H. Wilkins c Cockbain b Hughes	1	– c Lloyd b Hughes	21
†A. J. Brassington c Kennedy b Allott	2	– not out	14
B. M. Brain b Reidy	13	– b Malone	7
L-b 2	2	B 1, l-b 7, n-b 1	9

1/68 2/69 3/69 4/103 5/109 6/113	155	1/10 2/35 3/85 4/97 5/130
7/119 8/120 9/135		6/139 7/139 8/176 9/188

200

Bonus points – Gloucestershire 1, Lancashire 4.

Bowling: *First Innings*—Malone 19–6–45–2; Allott 18–4–47–2; Reidy 15.2–4–31–4; Simmons 9–5–19–1; Hughes 18–14–11–1. *Second Innings*—Malone 26.3–7–57–5; Allott 13–4–18–1; Simmons 23–7–27–0; Hughes 34–14–58–4; Reidy 5–2–19–0; Lloyd 9–3–12–0.

Lancashire

D. Lloyd lbw b Brain	2		
A. Kennedy c Brassington b Wilkins	17	– (1) not out	73
I. Cockbain c Graveney b Brain	2	– lbw b Wilkins	15
*F. C. Hayes lbw b Procter	28	– lbw b Wilkins	1
B. W. Reidy c Brassington b Wilkins	19	– not out	4
G. Fowler lbw b Brain	20	– (2) c Hignell b Procter	31
J. Simmons not out	42		
D. P. Hughes lbw b Brain	2		
P. J. W. Allott c Brassington b Wilkins	0		
†C. J. Scott c Brassington b Procter	9		
M. F. Malone c Hignell b Procter	0		
B 1, w 1	2	L-b 2	2

1/6 2/15 3/41 4/57 5/85 6/105   143   1/78 2/115 3/117   (3 wkts) 126
7/107 8/108 9/143

Bonus points – Gloucestershire 4.

Bowling: *First Innings*—Brain 20–2–46–4; Procter 14–3–35–3; Wilkins 15–2–51–3; Graveney 2–0–9–0. *Second Innings*—Brain 6–1–14–0; Procter 14–3–40–1; Wilkins 10–2–30–2; Bainbridge 6–2–18–0; Graveney 2–0–11–0; Zaheer 1–0–1–0; Sadiq 4–0–10–0.

Umpires: K. E. Palmer and R. S. Herman.

At Bournemouth, June 21, 23, 24. GLOUCESTERSHIRE drew with HAMPSHIRE.

At Guildford, June 28, 30, July 1. GLOUCESTERSHIRE drew with SURREY.

At Bristol, July 2, 3, 4. GLOUCESTERSHIRE lost to WEST INDIANS by 58 runs (see West Indian tour section).

GLOUCESTERSHIRE v NOTTINGHAMSHIRE

At Bristol, July 5, 7, 8. Drawn. Gloucestershire 4 pts, Nottinghamshire 7 pts. Rain took six hours from the playing time and robbed Nottinghamshire of deserved victory. After they had been put in the innings galloped along at 4 an over before the hard-hitting Rice was fifth out at 206, with three batsmen scoring half-centuries. Gloucestershire replied with 72 for one on Saturday but weekend rain freshened the pitch, helping Hacker to a career-best performance as the last nine wickets tumbled before lunch on Monday. Rain prevented Nottinghamshire from building on their advantage until the following morning when, with Graveney obtaining turn and lift on a drying surface, they did well to make 138 in two hours for the loss of six wickets. Gloucestershire made a dismal start in their quest for 270 against Hacker and Cooper, losing four wickets for 6 runs. They were 78 for six with over two hours remaining but rain permitted only seven more overs and, although another two wickets fell, Hignell and Brassington held out.

Nottinghamshire

B. Hassan lbw b Wilkins	50	– c Wilkins b Graveney	28
R. T. Robinson c Stovold b Procter	0	– c Brassington b Graveney	15
D. W. Randall c Zaheer b Wilkins	58	– st Brassington b Graveney	35
*C. E. B. Rice c Bainbridge b Graveney	74	– c Broad b Zaheer	8
J. D. Birch lbw b Brain	11	– c Procter b Graveney	5
M. J. Harris c Sadiq b Procter	23	– not out	6
†B. N. French lbw b Wilkins	1	– (8) not out	29
E. E. Hemmings c Wilkins b Graveney	39	– (7) b Procter.	5
P. J. Hacker c Brassington b Brain.	0		
K. E. Cooper c Bainbridge b Procter	6		
M. K. Bore not out	2		
B 2, l-b 4, n-b 5	11	B 4, l-b 2, n-b 1	7

1/2 2/104 3/135 4/174 5/206   **275**   1/47 2/68 3/77   (6 wkts dec.) **138**
6/214 7/263 8/263 9/268   4/95 5/98 6/107

Bonus points – Nottinghamshire 3, Gloucestershire 4.

Bowling: *First Innings*—Brain 16–2–70–2; Procter 15.3–6–37–3; Wilkins 23–5–62–3; Bainbridge 3–0–17–0; Graveney 24–8–78–2. *Second Innings*—Brain 7–1–20–0; Procter 12–4–26–1; Graveney 14–2–52–4; Zaheer 3–0–28–1; Wilkins 1–0–5–0.

Gloucestershire

B. C. Broad lbw b Cooper	28	– c French b Hacker	0
Sadiq Mohammad c French b Hacker	1	– c French b Cooper	5
Zaheer Abbas c French b Hacker	55	– c Birch b Hacker	1
A. W. Stovold c Hassan b Hacker	0	– c Birch b Cooper	0
*M. J. Procter c Harris b Hacker	9	– c Hassan b Hemmings	37
A. J. Hignell c French b Hacker	4	– not out	38
P. Bainbridge c French b Cooper	13	– c Hassan b Hemmings	0
D. A. Graveney c Rice b Bore	6	– b Hemmings	0
A. H. Wilkins c and b Hemmings	12	– c Randall b Bore.	7
†A. J. Brassington not out	4	– not out	0
B. M. Brain c Randall b Hemmings	8		
L-b 3, n-b 1	4	L-b 1	1

1/7 2/78 3/82 4/92 5/100 6/104   **144**   1/0 2/6 3/6 4/6 5/78   (8 wkts) **89**
7/117 8/121 9/136   6/78 7/78 8/87

Bonus points – Nottinghamshire 4.

Bowling: *First Innings*—Hacker 17–8–46–5; Cooper 24–8–50–2; Hemmings 13–7–17–2; Bore 15–4–27–1. *Second Innings*—Hacker 7–1–27–2; Cooper 5–2–14–2; Hemmings 10–2–35–3; Bore 8.5–2–12–1.

Umpires: W. E. Alley and R. Aspinall.

GLOUCESTERSHIRE v SUSSEX

At Bristol, July 12, 14, 15. Sussex won by two wickets. Sussex 17 pts, Gloucestershire 4 pts. Big hitting by le Roux finally settled an enthralling match. Sixteen wickets fell on the first day for 213 runs and Gloucestershire would not have reached three figures had not Broad battled away for three hours against Imran, le Roux and Arnold. Sussex did little better against Brain and Procter until Wells put bat to ball firmly and on Monday Greig's 50 gained them a valuable lead of 66. Gloucestershire lost only two wickets clearing the arrears but Zaheer went soon afterwards to a fine tumbling catch by Greig. The final day began with Gloucestershire only 9 ahead but Procter (one 6 and fourteen 4s) gave a masterly display, with useful support from Hignell and Bainbridge. Sussex, left to score 169 in three and a half hours, found themselves 110 for six with only ten overs remaining, all six wickets having fallen to Graveney whose father Ken took ten for 66 against Derbyshire in 1949. However, the turning ball did not bother le Roux who, with a flurry of 4s and 6s, won the match for Sussex with ten balls to spare.

Gloucestershire

B. C. Broad c Barclay b Arnold	32	– (2) c Long b le Roux	0
Sadiq Mohammad c Long b Imran	0	– (1) lbw b Waller	20
Zaheer Abbas c Parker b le Roux	17	– c Greig b Barclay	47
A. W. Stovold lbw b le Roux	3	– c Waller b Barclay	1
*M. J. Procter c Parker b le Roux	10	– (6) b Barclay	75
A. J. Hignell lbw b le Roux	0	– (7) c Phillipson b Barclay	29
P. Bainbridge c Long b Arnold	17	– (8) c Long b Waller	26
D. A. Graveney not out	8	– (9) c Phillipson b Waller	8
A. H. Wilkins c Long b Arnold	0	– (10) not out	11
†A. J. Brassington c Mendis b Imran	4	– (5) c Long b Imran	5
B. M. Brain c Long b Arnold	0	– lbw b Waller	0
B 1, l-b 1, w 2, n-b 6	10	B 6, l-b 5, n-b 1	12

1/0 2/21 3/33 4/51 5/51 6/81   101   1/0 2/50 3/70 4/70   234
7/88 8/88 9/99   5/80 6/137 7/193
8/209 9/234

Bonus points – Sussex 4.

Bowling: *First Innings*—Imran 15–4–25–2; le Roux 17–6–29–4; Arnold 17–11–18–4; Greig 6–1–19–0. *Second Innings*—Imran 17–3–67–1; le Roux 2–0–8–1; Arnold 11–3–32–0; Waller 20.4–6–62–4; Barclay 25–11–53–4.

Sussex

J. R. T. Barclay b Procter	5	– (2) c Stovold b Graveney	30
G. D. Mendis lbw b Brain	16	– (1) c Sadiq b Graveney	19
P. W. G. Parker c Brassington b Brain	16	– c Zaheer b Graveney	4
Imran Khan lbw b Procter	12	– st Brassington b Graveney	1
C. M. Wells c Broad b Brain	43	– c Zaheer b Graveney	44
C. P. Phillipson c Sadiq b Procter	1	– c Stovold b Graveney	9
I. A. Greig not out	50	– b Wilkins	1
G. S. le Roux c Stovold b Procter	0	– not out	39
*†A. Long c Brassington b Wilkins	11	– c Brassington b Wilkins	9
G. G. Arnold c Sadiq b Procter	1	– not out	12
C. E. Waller c Sadiq b Graveney	6		
B 1, l-b 1, n-b 4	6	L-b 3, n-b 1	4

1/8 2/31 3/40 4/71 5/75 6/107   167   1/25 2/29 3/30 4/86 (8 wkts) 172
7/112 8/141 9/142   5/104 6/106 7/121 8/139

Bonus points – Sussex 1, Gloucestershire 4.

Bowling: *First Innings*—Brain 15–3–48–3; Procter 26–4–81–5; Wilkins 12–1–28–1; Graveney 5–4–4–1. *Second Innings*—Brain 15–7–26–0; Wilkins 17.2–4–50–2; Graveney 23–7–71–6; Procter 5–1–21–0.

Umpires: D. J. Constant and D. O. Oslear.

At Sheffield, July 26, 28, 29. GLOUCESTERSHIRE drew with YORKSHIRE.

GLOUCESTERSHIRE v HAMPSHIRE

At Cheltenham, August 2, 4, 5. Gloucestershire won by 197 runs. Gloucestershire 20 pts, Hampshire 5 pts. Gloucestershire's first win of the season was accomplished with over two hours to spare, Hampshire generally batting like a team reconciled to bottom place in the table. An opening partnership of 151 between Broad (one 6 and twenty 4s) and Sadiq gave Gloucestershire the control they never relinquished, although after Broad's second Championship century no-one played Cowley with any assurance. Then Wilkins used helpful conditions with intelligence to gain Gloucestershire a first innings lead of 125. Sadiq led the way as they increased it to 300, and Procter's declaration left Hampshire four hours to score the runs. They were never a threat against the spin of Graveney and Childs, and the last three wickets went in six balls for no runs.

Gloucestershire

B. C. Broad c Turner b Malone 116	– b Cowley	30
Sadiq Mohammad b Cowley 52	– not out	90
Zaheer Abbas c Pocock b Graf 23	– c Pocock b Tremlett	25
A. W. Stovold lbw b Cowley 45	– (5) not out	13
*M. J. Procter c Pocock b Graf 2	– (4) c Cowley b Tremlett	1
P. Bainbridge c and b Rice 7		
D. A. Graveney c Pocock b Malone. 26		
A. H. Wilkins c sub b Cowley 3		
†A. J. Brassington run out 0		
B. M. Brain not out. 5		
J. H. Childs c Graf b Cowley 0		
B 3, l-b 5, w 5, n-b 11 24	B 1, l-b 7, w 2, n-b 6	16

1/152 2/205 3/217 4/220 5/244   303   1/56 2/117 3/119   (3 wkts dec.) 175
6/282 7/297 8/297 9/298

Bonus points – Gloucestershire 4, Hampshire 4.

Bowling: *First Innings*—Graf 16.5–5–42–2; Stevenson 9–2–56–0; Malone 17.1–2–42–2; Rice 12–2–39–1; Nicholas 3–0–20–0; Tremlett 5–0–21–0; Cowley 29.3–11–58–4; Smith 1–0–1–0. *Second Innings*—Graf 12–3–31–0; Stevenson 7–1–24–0; Cowley 16–3–58–1; Tremlett 11.3–1–46–2.

Hampshire

J. M. Rice c Brassington b Brain 25	– (2) b Procter.	11
C. L. Smith lbw b Procter. 13	– (1) c Brassington b Graveney. . . .	0
M. C. J. Nicholas c Graveney b Wilkins 32	– c Procter b Graveney.	17
D. R. Turner c Sadiq b Wilkins 21	– c Wilkins b Childs	24
*N. E. J. Pocock b Wilkins. 15	– b Childs	7
N. G. Cowley c Brassington b Wilkins 9	– c Brassington b Graveney	22
T. M. Tremlett c Brassington b Wilkins 11	– c Procter b Graveney	8
S. F. Graf run out 0	– not out	8
†G. R. Stephenson c Bainbridge b Brain 3	– c sub b Graveney	0
K. Stevenson c Sadiq b Procter 25	– lbw b Childs	0
S. J. Malone not out 6	– absent ill	0
B 9, w 1, n-b 8 18	B 1, l-b 5.	6

1/41 2/43 3/100 4/119 5/122 6/131   178   1/11 2/11 3/48 4/60 5/65   103
7/137 8/145 9/157   6/92 7/103 8/103 9/103

Bonus points – Hampshire 1, Gloucestershire 4.

Bowling: *First Innings*—Brain 17–2–42–2; Procter 16.2–7–26–2; Graveney 17–7–23–0; Childs 3–0–3–0; Bainbridge 4–1–16–0; Wilkins 20–6–50–5. *Second Innings*—Wilkins 4–2–7–0; Procter 10–5–28–1; Graveney 15–8–24–5; Childs 8.2–0–38–3.

Umpires: D. J. Dennis and J. G. Langridge.

GLOUCESTERSHIRE v WORCESTERSHIRE

At Cheltenham, August 6, 7, 8. Gloucestershire won by 96 runs. Gloucestershire 17 pts, Worcestershire 4 pts. After a relatively quiet season Procter exploded into life with a vengeance, taking fourteen wickets to record the best Championship bowling performance of the season. He was not idle with the bat either; his powerfully-hit 73 took Gloucestershire to a respectable total after they had been put in. No-one else could cope with the bowling of Inchmore and Pridgeon, ably assisted by wicket-keeper Fisher, who took five catches on his début following his move from Middlesex. Worcestershire ended the first day at 84 for one but totalled only 111 after Procter's spell of seven wickets for 9 runs the following morning. It was a mixture of pace and off-spin which brought him his second innings haul of seven for 60 as Worcestershire were defeated, despite a defiant half-century from Ormrod.

Gloucestershire

B. C. Broad c Fisher b Holder	9	– c and b Inchmore		5
Sadiq Mohammad c Fisher b Inchmore	5	– c Younis b Holder		12
Zaheer Abbas c Younis b Inchmore	0	– c Fisher b Pridgeon		34
A. W. Stovold c Fisher b Inchmore	32	– c Fisher b Pridgeon		7
*M. J. Procter c Fisher b Inchmore	73	– c Neale b Pridgeon		35
P. Bainbridge c Younis b Inchmore	2	– c Turner b Gifford		18
D. A. Graveney c Fisher b Pridgeon	15	– c Holder b Inchmore		42
A. H. Wilkins c Gifford b Pridgeon	3	– c Turner b Gifford		0
†A. J. Brassington c Gifford b Pridgeon	2	– b Inchmore		2
B. M. Brain c Gifford b Pridgeon	23	– c Henderson b Inchmore		0
J. H. Childs not out	1	– not out		6
L-b 6, w 3, n-b 4	13	L-b 2, w 5, n-b 9		16

1/8 2/8 3/27 4/111 5/121 6/134   178   1/21 2/23 3/41 4/86   177
7/137 8/143 9/172   5/110 6/126 7/126
                                          8/134 9/134

Bonus points – Gloucestershire 1, Worcestershire 4.

Bowling: *First Innings*—Holder 13–3–52–1; Inchmore 20–3–62–5; Gifford 2–0–5–0; Pridgeon 16.2–3–46–4. *Second Innings*—Holder 16–2–41–1; Inchmore 17.5–4–59–4; Pridgeon 12–1–42–3; Gifford 15–7–19–2.

Worcestershire

G. M. Turner c Sadiq b Procter	57	– c Brassington b Procter		0
J. A. Ormrod c Sadiq b Bainbridge	26	– c Sadiq b Childs		53
P. A. Neale c Brassington b Procter	0	– c Childs b Procter		1
Younis Ahmed b Wilkins	9	– c Brain b Procter		15
B. J. R. Jones c Brassington b Procter	1	– c Graveney b Procter		0
S. P. Henderson c and b Procter	7	– c Brassington b Procter		38
†P. B. Fisher c Sadiq b Wilkins	0	– c Bainbridge b Procter		2
J. D. Inchmore b Procter	4	– st Brassington b Childs		9
V. A. Holder not out	5	– c Brassington b Childs		1
*N. Gifford c Sadiq b Procter	0	– not out		13
A. P. Pridgeon b Procter	0	– c Wilkins b Procter		10
L-b 2	2	B 3, l-b 1, w 1, n-b 1		6

1/72 2/84 3/85 4/93 5/97 6/97   111   1/1 2/9 3/29 4/29 5/105   148
7/102 8/111 9/111   6/111 7/111 8/112 9/137

Bonus points – Gloucestershire 4.

Bowling: *First Innings*—Brain 10–2–29–0; Procter 15.5–7–16–7; Wilkins 19–4–52–2; Bainbridge 2–0–12–1. *Second Innings*—Procter 27.3–9–60–7; Wilkins 9–1–35–0; Graveney 10–2–19–0; Childs 13–4–28–3.

Umpires: J. G. Langridge and D. J. Dennis.

GLOUCESTERSHIRE v MIDDLESEX

At Cheltenham, August 9, 11, 12. Gloucestershire won by six wickets. Gloucestershire 16 pts, Middlesex 6 pts. The champions elect had a grip on this match until the final afternoon, when a remarkable innings by Procter won the match for Gloucestershire, who had narrowly averted the follow-on. Middlesex were put in on a damp pitch and did well to reach 220. At the close, van der Bijl, fully exploiting the conditions, had reduced Gloucestershire to 37 for five. However, Broad stood firm and, with Graveney and Wilkins making valuable contributions, Middlesex's lead was restricted to 111. Stoppages for rain reduced Middlesex's second innings batting time but Brearley's declaration, leaving the opposition 270 in 285 minutes, looked reasonable. Zaheer batted briskly for a while yet, with three down for 65, Gloucestershire looked a beaten side. Then entered Procter to play one of his finest innings, making the formidable Middlesex attack look almost ordinary. He gave one chance, at 58 when Brearley missed him at second slip off Daniel, but otherwise it was a virtuoso display, full of cultured drives and cuts. Sadiq and Bainbridge played the supporting rôles as Procter finished the match with more than an hour to spare, scoring his only century of the season but one of the best ever seen on the College ground.

Middlesex

*J. M. Brearley lbw b Brain	5	– lbw b Wilkins	54
†P. R. Downton c Bainbridge b Procter	44	– lbw b Graveney	16
C. T. Radley c Bainbridge b Brain	17	– (4) not out	21
R. O. Butcher st Brassington b Childs	35	– (5) c Broad b Wilkins	15
G. D. Barlow c Wilkins b Brain	47	– (3) c Bainbridge b Wilkins	18
K. P. Tomlins c Sadiq b Brain	34	– not out	20
V. A. P. van der Bijl c Procter b Childs	3		
M. W. W. Selvey lbw b Wilkins	21		
R. Maru c Sadiq b Brain	1		
F. J. Titmus lbw b Procter	4		
W. W. Daniel not out	0		
L-b 8, n-b 1	9	B 4, l-b 7, n-b 3	14

1/11 2/33 3/92 4/111 5/189 6/190   220   1/44 2/86   (4 wkts dec.) 158
7/192 8/199 9/220   3/99 4/121

Bonus points – Middlesex 2, Gloucestershire 4.

Bowling: *First Innings*—Brain 18–6–46–5; Procter 16.1–5–40–2; Wilkins 10–4–22–1; Bainbridge 2–0–6–0; Graveney 22–12–36–0; Childs 23–10–61–2. *Second Innings*—Brain 12–0–55–0; Procter 4–1–12–0; Wilkins 8–2–31–3; Graveney 12–5–19–1; Childs 11–4–27–0.

Gloucestershire

B. C. Broad c Downton b Titmus	36	– c Maru b Titmus	11
Sadiq Mohammad c Titmus b van der Bijl	6	– (3) b Daniel	37
Zaheer Abbas c Radley b Daniel	1	– (4) c Radley b Daniel	37
A. W. Stovold b van der Bijl	1	– (2) c Radley b van der Bijl	10
*M. J. Procter b van der Bijl	4	– not out	134
†A. J. Brassington lbw b van der Bijl	2		
P. Bainbridge c Downton b Daniel	1	– (6) not out	32
D. A. Graveney c Downton b Daniel	18		
A. H. Wilkins b Daniel	23		
B. M. Brain not out	8		
J. H. Childs c Downton b Daniel	4		
L-b 2, w 1, n-b 2	5	L-b 2, w 1, n-b 7	10

1/12 2/13 3/16 4/30 5/36 6/41   109   1/15 2/24 3/65   (4 wkts) 271
7/63 8/96 9/101   4/172

Bonus points – Middlesex 4.

Bowling: *First Innings*—van der Bijl 19–1–45–4; Daniel 15.4–5–32–5; Titmus 12–3–25–1; Maru 1–0–2–0. *Second Innings*—van der Bijl 16–1–70–1; Daniel 16–3–61–2; Titmus 14–2–43–1; Maru 2–0–22–0; Selvey 9–0–36–0; Tomlins 2–0–21–0; Brearley 0.4–0–8–0.

Umpires: D. G. L. Evans and R. Palmer.

At Swansea, August 16, 18, 19. GLOUCESTERSHIRE lost to GLAMORGAN by eight wickets.

At Folkestone, August 20, 21, 22. GLOUCESTERSHIRE beat KENT by 55 runs.

GLOUCESTERSHIRE v SOMERSET

At Bristol, August 23, 25, 26. Drawn. Gloucestershire 8 pts, Somerset 14 pts. Somerset took six extra points as the team batting last in a match in which the scores finished level. Championship regulations and The Laws of Cricket were required reading at the end. Roebuck, needing a single off the last ball, attempted a run with the bails off and the ball in Brassington's gloves. But umpire Palmer had already called "over" to finish the match after rejecting Gloucestershire's appeals for lbw. This was one of the best West Country derby games for many years. Gloucestershire struggled against Dredge but still reached a substantial total. However, Somerset took control thanks to a third-wicket partnership of 239 in 51 overs between Roebuck and Richards, who hit three 6s – all off Graveney – and 26 4s. With Stovold and Sadiq adding 138 and Procter attempting the season's fastest century (84 in 48 minutes), Gloucestershire looked like saving the game with ease. But the later batsmen were swept aside by Marks, and Somerset needed 201 in 38 overs. When Richards, unwell, was caught first ball they were in trouble at 140 for six before Roebuck and Popplewell took them to the brink of victory.

Gloucestershire

A. W. Stovold b Popplewell	37	– c and b Lloyds	80
B. C. Broad run out	0	– c Popplewell b Gore	3
Sadiq Mohammad b Dredge	43	– c Popplewell b Lloyds	92
Zaheer Abbas c Popplewell b Dredge	5	– absent hurt	0
*M. J. Procter c Botham b Dredge	57	– (4) st Gard b Marks	84
M. D. Partridge c Olive b Botham	48	– (5) c Olive b Marks	15
D. A. Graveney c Richards b Dredge	55	– (6) c Botham b Marks	10
A. H. Wilkins c Botham b Popplewell	32	– (7) b Marks	15
†A. J. Brassington b Popplewell	12	– (8) b Marks	0
B. M. Brain c Gard b Dredge	4	– (9) b Lloyds	1
J. H. Childs not out	1	– (10) not out	0
B 1, l-b 8, w 1, n-b 5	15	B 4, l-b 6, n-b 7	17

1/6 2/69 3/74 4/112 5/161 6/224 309   1/14 2/152 3/272 4/276 317
7/274 8/290 9/299   5/300 6/313 7/316 8/317
                                       9/317

Bonus points – Gloucestershire 4, Somerset 4.

Bowling: *First Innings*—Gore 12–3–34–0; Dredge 32–6–95–5; Popplewell 23.5–5–54–3; Richards 6–0–24–0; Botham 14–5–55–1; Marks 9–2–32–0. *Second Innings*—Gore 13–2–48–1; Dredge 10–0–47–0; Marks 30–11–77–5; Lloyds 29.2–11–77–3; Popplewell 8–1–51–0.

Somerset

M. Olive c Brassington b Brain	1	– c Sadiq b Childs	21
J. W. Lloyds c Brassington b Brain	33	– c Childs b Graveney	64
I. V. A. Richards c Brain b Childs	170	– (7) c sub b Graveney	0
P. M. Roebuck st Brassington b Childs	101	– (6) not out	37
P. W. Denning c Procter b Wilkins	4	– (4) run out	1
*I. T. Botham c Childs b Wilkins	18	– (5) c sub b Graveney	13
V. J. Marks c Brassington b Childs	29	– (3) st Brassington b Graveney	32
N. F. M. Popplewell st Brassington b Childs	19	– b Brain	25
†T. Gard b Procter	22		
C. H. Dredge not out	13	– (9) not out	1
H. I. E. Gore b Procter	4		
B 9, n-b 3	12	L-b 6	6

1/4 2/61 3/300 4/311 5/333 6/342   426   1/70 2/96 3/104   (7 wkts) 200
7/371 8/390 9/419   4/119 5/140 6/140 7/197

Bonus points – Somerset 4, Gloucestershire 4 (Score at 100 overs: 422-9).

Bowling: *First Innings*—Brain 20–1–91–2; Wilkins 24–5–94–2; Procter 2.5–0–13–2; Partridge 6–0–43–0; Graveney 23–2–103–0; Childs 25–6–70–4. *Second Innings*—Brain 8–2–32–1; Wilkins 4–0–24–0; Childs 15–0–73–1; Procter 2–0–12–0; Graveney 9–0–53–4.

Umpires: K. E. Palmer and C. T. Spencer.

At Birmingham, August 27, 28, 29. GLOUCESTERSHIRE drew with WARWICKSHIRE.

At Hove, September 3, 4, 5. GLOUCESTERSHIRE drew with SUSSEX.

GLOUCESTERSHIRE RETAIN HOLTS PRODUCTS TROPHY

Gloucestershire, who won the Holts Products Trophy in 1979 when they defeated the Indian touring side, were again awarded the trophy and £1,200 in 1980 for the best performance by a county against the West Indians. Gloucestershire were the only team to dismiss the touring side in both innings and might have beaten them but for a maiden century by J. Garner, batting at number ten. West Indians won by 58 runs.

The individual awards of £600 went to R. G. Williams, whose 122 for Northamptonshire was the only first-class hundred for a county against the West Indians, and to M. Hendrick, whose five for 59 for Derbyshire against the West Indians included the first hat-trick of his career. A. J. Brassington (Gloucestershire) and G. W. Humpage (Warwickshire) shared the wicket-keepers' award.

UMPIRES FOR 1981

TEST MATCH UMPIRES

D. G. L. Evans, a former Glamorgan wicket-keeper, was named in the panel of seven umpires to officiate in the six-Test series between England and Australia in 1981. He will join the six umpires who stood in Test matches in 1980: W. E. Alley, H. D. Bird, D. J. Constant, B. J. Meyer, D. O. Oslear and K. E. Palmer. For the three Prudential Trophy matches, A. G. T. Whitehead joins Alley, Constant, Meyer and Palmer.

FIRST-CLASS UMPIRES

Three new umpires were added to the first-class list for 1981: B. Leadbeater, formerly of Yorkshire, D. R. Shepherd, formerly of Gloucestershire, and, promoted from the Minor Counties list, P. J. Eele, formerly of Somerset. J. G. Langridge and T. W. Spencer retired, the former after a career covering 52 years in first-class cricket, as player and umpire.

The full list: W. E. Alley, R. Aspinall, H. D. Bird, W. L. Budd, D. J. Constant, C. Cook, P. J. Eele, D. G. L. Evans, D. J. Halfyard, R. S. Herman, A. Jepson, R. Julian, B. Leadbeater, B. J. Meyer, D. O. Oslear, K. E. Palmer, R. Palmer, D. Shackleton, D. R. Shepherd, C. T. Spencer, P. S. G. Stevens, J. van Geloven, A. G. T. Whitehead, P. B. Wight.

HAMPSHIRE

President — R. AIRD, MC, GD

Chairman, Cricket Committee — C. J. KNOTT

Secretary — A. K. JAMES
Northlands Road, Southampton SO9 2TY

Captain — N. E. J. POCOCK

N. E. J. Pocock   County Badge   C. L. Smith

If 1979 was a bad season for Hampshire, 1980 represented an even greater decline. They gained only one win in the Schweppes County Championship, thus suffering their worst season since 1905 when they also finished bottom of the table. Their record in the Benson and Hedges Cup, in which they lost all four group matches for the second year in succession, was also dismal. Eleventh position in the John Player League was one place lower than in 1979, though the Gillette Cup at least saw a splendid victory over Derbyshire before defeat by Yorkshire.

That Hampshire would have a difficult season was obvious. They were still suffering from the departure of Richards, Gilliat and Roberts, and in addition, Gordon Greenidge and Malcolm Marshall, their two Test players, were on tour for most of the summer with the West Indians. The absence of their two best players was always likely to make rebuilding a more than usually difficult task and so it proved, particularly as injury and loss of form had also to be faced.

Falling into one or other category, and in some cases both, were John Rice, David Turner and Trevor Jesty, three players Hampshire needed to be at the top of their form. Especially as the county's problems were increased when, on the eve of the season, opening batsman David Rock announced his retirement. Rice, Turner and Jesty were all out of form early in the season, and just when he was running into form in July, Jesty was forced to undergo a cartilage operation.

The two most experienced members of the side, wicket-keeper Bob Stephenson and all-rounder Mike Taylor, both announced their retirement at the end of the season, during which they were omitted to help hasten the rebuilding process. As a result Nick Pocock, the new captain, was forced to lead a side which, like himself, was largely inexperienced.

There were, however, some good omens, notably the advance made by Mark Nicholas, Tim Tremlett and Bob Parks, and the promise shown by Chris Smith, a young South African who will, by qualification, become an "Englishman" early in 1983. Hopes that Turner and Jesty would take the pressure off their less experienced colleagues were unfulfilled, Turner scoring a mere 147 runs in his first nine Championship innings and Jesty 150 in his first eleven.

Smith, though never having done the job before, was successfully converted into an opening batsman and was the only Hampshire player to score 1,000 runs in first-class cricket. Tremlett, his opening partner for much of a season which saw fifteen different combinations used, played with considerable resolution and achieved career-best figures with both bat and ball. He made a major contribution to Hampshire's only Championship win, over Worcestershire at Bournemouth. Nicholas, a confident young man, possessed a wide range of attacking shots with a particular liking for strokes through mid-wicket. He scored a maiden century, narrowly missed two others and, had he been included in the side earlier, would almost certainly have scored 1,000 runs. Parks, son of J. M., the former England wicket-keeper, may well prove a worthy successor to Stephenson. He is neat and agile behind the stumps and a useful batsman.

Inconsistent batting was again a major problem in all four competitions and there were times when a more determined approach was required. This was particularly noticeable towards the end of the season when several players seemed to be feeling the effects of continuous pressure. However, the presence of Greenidge and Marshall in 1981 should mean that Hampshire can anticipate better fortunes. Jesty will be fit, and the younger players will be better for having been thrown in at the deep end in 1980. – Brian Hayward.

433

HAMPSHIRE

[*Press Association*

Back row: S. N. C. Massey, M. C. J. Nicholas, C. L. Smith, M. J. Bailey, D. J. Rock, T. M. Tremlett, S. J. Malone, V. P. Terry, R. R. Savage, R. J. Parks, P. Sainsbury (*coach*). *Front row*: N. G. Cowley, J. W. Southern, J. M. Rice, G. R. Stephenson, N. E. J. Pocock (*captain*), T. E. Jesty, C. G. Greenidge, M. N. S. Taylor, K. Stevenson.

HAMPSHIRE RESULTS

All First-class Matches – Played 24: Won 2, Lost 11, Drawn 11.

County Championship Matches – Played 22: Won 1, Lost 10, Drawn 11.

Bonus points – Batting 34, Bowling 56.

COUNTY CHAMPIONSHIP AVERAGES

BATTING

	Birthplace	Matches	Inns	Not Outs	Runs	Highest Inns	Avge
C. L. Smith	Durban, SA	18	31	1	917	130	30.56
T. M. Tremlett	Wellington, Som.	16	28	4	706	84	29.41
M. D. Marshall	Barbados, WI	5	10	1	251	72*	27.88
C. G. Greenidge	Barbados, WI	3	6	0	167	65	27.83
M. C. J. Nicholas	London	17	29	1	776	112	27.71
M. N. S. Taylor	Amersham	8	12	2	268	58	26.80
D. R. Turner	Chippenham	18	32	3	772	115*	26.62
T. E. Jesty	Gosport	15	23	2	494	114*	23.52
R. J. Parks	Cuckfield	7	13	3	233	64*	23.30
M. J. Bailey	Cheltenham	4	7	4	67	24	22.33
N. E. J. Pocock	Maracaibo, Venezuela	22	37	3	739	61*	21.73
N. G. Cowley	Shaftesbury	21	33	3	584	80*	19.46
S. F. Graf	Melbourne, Aust.	13	16	5	214	57*	19.45
G. R. Stephenson	Derby	15	20	5	238	47	15.86
V. P. Terry	Osnabruck, WG	3	6	0	87	31	14.50
J. W. Southern	King's Cross	20	22	5	245	46*	14.41
S. J. Malone	Chelmsford	7	11	5	70	20	11.66
J. M. Rice	Chandler's Ford	8	14	0	128	25	9.14
K. Stevenson	Derby	22	25	7	151	25	8.38

* *Signifies not out.*

BOWLING

	Overs	Maidens	Runs	Wickets	Average
M. D. Marshall	141	42	306	17	18.00
K. Stevenson	450.4	88	1,494	48	31.12
N. G. Cowley	391.4	110	1,098	35	31.37
T. M. Tremlett	160.2	27	522	15	34.80
J. W. Southern	470.4	111	1,363	39	34.94
S. J. Malone	140.1	27	457	13	35.15
T. E. Jesty	196.2	51	567	14	40.50
S. F. Graf	265.5	55	772	16	48.25

Also bowled: M. J. Bailey 69–12–240–5; M. C. J. Nicholas 13–0–61–0; N. E. J. Pocock 1–0–8–0; J. M. Rice 90–18–263–3; C. L. Smith 16–4–30–0; G. R. Stephenson 1–1–0–0; M. N. S. Taylor 67.5–11–185–7; D. R. Turner 4.1–1–10–0.

HUNDREDS

The following six three-figure innings were played for Hampshire in County Championship matches – C. L. Smith 130 v Kent (Bournemouth), 125* v Sussex (Southampton), 109 v Somerset (Bath); T. E. Jesty 114* v Somerset (Bath); M. C. J. Nicholas 112 v Somerset (Bournemouth); D. R. Turner 115* v Glamorgan (Cardiff).

At The Oval, April 30, May 1, 2. HAMPSHIRE drew with SURREY.

HAMPSHIRE v WARWICKSHIRE

At Southampton, May 3, 5, 6. Warwickshire won by 159 runs. Warwickshire 19 pts, Hampshire 6 pts. Stevenson rocked Warwickshire at the start of their first innings by taking the wickets of Amiss and Claughton at a personal cost of 8 runs, but Smith, in partnerships of 74 and 45 with Lloyd and Oliver respectively, repaired the damage. Humpage and Oliver added 80 for the fifth wicket but the last five wickets fell for 30 with Taylor taking four of them. There was less solidity about Hampshire's batting and only Smith, Taylor and Graf came out with much credit. Warwickshire were soon building on their lead of 53, and their declaration left Hampshire a target of 302 in 264 minutes. It was way beyond them, and after Willis and Ferreira had made the initial breakthrough, Doshi destroyed the middle order. Willis ended the innings with two wickets in two deliveries.

Warwickshire

D. L. Amiss c Rice b Stevenson	3	– b Cowley	85
K. D. Smith c Stephenson b Jesty	79	– c and b Graf	73
J. A. Claughton c Stephenson b Stevenson	1	– c Taylor b Cowley	35
T. A. Lloyd run out	37	– c Pocock b Cowley	10
P. R. Oliver c Graf b Taylor	47	– lbw b Cowley	4
†G. W. Humpage c Graf b Cowley	46	– b Stevenson	23
A. M. Ferreira c Cowley b Graf	24	– not out	26
G. C. Small lbw b Taylor	0		
*R. G. D. Willis c Graf b Taylor	2		
D. R. Doshi not out	7		
S. P. Perryman c Stephenson b Taylor	1		
B 4, l-b 3	7	B 5, l-b 4, w 1, n-b 2	12

1/13 2/17 3/91 4/136 5/216   254   1/166 2/166 3/191 (6 wkts dec.) 248
6/224 7/235 8/239 9/253   4/212 5/224 6/248

Bonus points – Warwickshire 3, Hampshire 4.

    Bowling: *First Innings*—Graf 18–3–43–1; Stevenson 16–2–34–2; Rice 13–4–25–0; Taylor 16.5–4–46–4; Jesty 11–4–31–1; Bailey 3–0–13–0; Cowley 19–4–55–1. *Second Innings*—Graf 19–6–49–1; Stevenson 15–2–82–1; Rice 9–3–32–0; Jesty 8–2–26–0; Cowley 16–4–47–4.

Hampshire

J. M. Rice run out	16	– c Humpage b Willis	2
N. G. Cowley c Humpage b Willis	7	– c Oliver b Doshi	21
†G. R. Stephenson c Amiss b Ferreira	8	– (9) c Oliver b Willis	29
C. L. Smith c Humpage b Ferreira	37	– (3) c Humpage b Ferreira	19
T. E. Jesty b Small	17	– (4) c Perryman b Doshi	22
D. R. Turner lbw b Doshi	12	– (5) c Amiss b Doshi	10
*N. E. J. Pocock c Humpage b Ferreira	3	– (6) b Small	1
M. N. S. Taylor c Doshi b Perryman	48	– (7) c Ferreira b Small	19
S. F. Graf c Oliver b Perryman	25	– (8) b Doshi	14
M. J. Bailey b Small	1	– not out	0
K. Stevenson not out	0	– b Willis	0
L-b 16, w 1, n-b 10	27	L-b 1, n-b 4	5

1/30 2/42 3/44 4/75 5/107   201   1/2 2/45 3/52 4/79 5/80   142
6/122 7/129 8/184 9/197   6/80 7/111 8/121 9/142

Bonus points – Hampshire 2, Warwickshire 4.

    Bowling: *First Innings*—Willis 23–11–43–1; Small 13–2–29–2; Ferreira 24–10–37–3; Doshi 18–4–35–1; Perryman 13.2–3–30–2. *Second Innings*—Willis 10.3–3–24–3; Small 14–4–66–2; Doshi 18–8–36–4; Ferreira 9–5–11–1; Oliver 1–1–0–0.

Umpires: W. L. Budd and R. Palmer.

At Oxford, May 7, 8, 9. HAMPSHIRE beat OXFORD UNIVERSITY by 86 runs.

HAMPSHIRE v KENT

At Bournemouth, May 24, 26, 27. Kent won by ten wickets. Kent 19 pts, Hampshire 5 pts. Smith, a South African pressed into service as an opener, provided the substance to Hampshire's first innings by scoring his maiden first-class century in England. He shared in good stands with Pocock and Cowley before being fifth out, having hit twenty 4s in making 130 in four and threequarter hours. Hampshire gained an early success when Woolmer played on to Stevenson, but they had to wait a long time for their next as Rowe and Tavaré added 188 in 63 overs. Rowe batted just over four hours for his 109. When the Kent innings closed a draw seemed likely, but Hampshire slumped to 71 for seven before Taylor and Southern staged a recovery. Kent, batting again, were not tested by the target of 164 in 150 minutes, and won with almost six overs to spare, thanks principally to Woolmer whose unbeaten 102 took him 135 minutes and contained fifteen 4s.

Hampshire

J. M. Rice c Knott b Dilley	1	– b Dilley	4
C. L. Smith c Hills b Underwood	130	– c Cowdrey b Dilley	11
D. R. Turner c Tavaré b Underwood	17	– c Tavaré b Shepherd	3
T. E. Jesty c Woolmer b Hills	17	– c Woolmer b Shepherd	15
*N. E. J. Pocock b Dilley	26	– c Hills b Shepherd	9
N. G. Cowley c Cowdrey b Dilley	33	– c Knott b Dilley	1
M. N. S. Taylor b Dilley	13	– c Hills b Cowdrey	58
†G. R. Stephenson b Dilley	0	– c Knott b Shepherd	12
J. W. Southern not out	27	– c and b Cowdrey	36
K. Stevenson not out	6	– not out	16
S. J. Malone (did not bat)		– b Cowdrey	9
B 8, l-b 5, w 2, n-b 2	17	B 1, l-b 3, w 3	7

1/16 2/65 3/94 4/136	(8 wkts) 287	1/11 2/18 3/20 4/38 5/41	181
5/233 6/242 7/242 8/255		6/47 7/71 8/153 9/156	

Bonus points – Hampshire 3, Kent 3.

Bowling: *First Innings*—Dilley 27–5–94–5; Shepherd 20–6–50–0; Hills 23–6–46–1; Underwood 23–7–57–2; Johnson 7–0–23–0. *Second Innings*—Dilley 29–6–86–3; Shepherd 28–11–36–4; Hills 11–2–31–0; Underwood 4–3–4–0; Cowdrey 7.1–2–17–3.

Kent

R. A. Woolmer b Stevenson	25	– not out	102
C. J. C. Rowe c Cowley b Rice	109	– not out	57
C. J. Tavaré lbw b Malone	98		
*A. G. E. Ealham c Cowley b Malone	6		
C. S. Cowdrey b Taylor	34		
†A. P. E. Knott c Stephenson b Stevenson	17		
G. W. Johnson not out	0		
J. N. Shepherd not out	3		
B 2, l-b 10, w 1	13	B 2, l-b 2, w 1	5

1/42 2/230 3/244 4/253	(6 wkts) 305	(no wkt) 164
5/301 6/301		

G. R. Dilley, R. W. Hills and D. L. Underwood did not bat.

Bonus points – Kent 4, Hampshire 2.

Bowling: *First Innings*—Malone 22–3–63–2; Stevenson 24–8–64–2; Jesty 12–2–38–0; Taylor 15–4–27–1; Southern 9–2–28–0; Cowley 8–2–32–0; Rice 10–1–40–1. *Second Innings*—Stevenson 4–0–22–0; Malone 9–0–30–0; Jesty 6–1–27–0; Southern 12–3–42–0; Cowley 2.3–1–12–0; Rice 9–2–26–0.

Umpires: D. J. Dennis and P. B. Wight.

At Chesterfield, May 28, 29, 30. HAMPSHIRE lost to DERBYSHIRE by ten wickets.

HAMPSHIRE v SUSSEX

At Southampton, June 4, 5, 6. Drawn. Hampshire 3 pts, Sussex 8 pts. The initiative was with Sussex for all but the final innings when Hampshire, with more enterprise, might have gone close to winning. Sussex dominated the early play through Wessels, Booth Jones and Parker, who took advantage of being dropped twice to score his first century of the season. He batted 185 minutes for his 105, hitting a 6 and sixteen 4s. Arnold and Alan Willows, a nineteen-year-old slow left-arm bowler making his début, soon had Hampshire in trouble and only Cowley batted with authority. Sussex did not enforce the follow-on and Wessels again played attractively before the declaration left Hampshire to score 345 in six and a half hours. At 95 for one they were up with the clock at lunch, but the loss of Turner and Jesty saw a premature putting-up of the shutters. Smith and Pocock, in fact, put on an unbroken 111 in 51 overs and the chase should not have been called off while they were in. Smith took fourteen overs to go from 96 to his century and in all he batted for nearly six hours for his undefeated 125 (nineteen 4s).

Sussex

K. C. Wessels b Jesty	53	– c Jesty b Cowley	95
T. D. Booth Jones c Pocock b Southern	76	– b Stevenson	14
G. D. Mendis lbw b Jesty	2	– st Parks b Southern	45
P. W. G. Parker c Smith b Southern	105	– not out	14
C. P. Phillipson c Parks b Stevenson	35	– st Parks b Southern	0
C. M. Wells not out	26		
G. S. le Roux not out	12		
L-b 9, w 2, n-b 2	13	B 1, l-b 2, w 1, n-b 2	6

1/92 2/112 3/171   (5 wkts) 322   1/35 2/158   (4 wkts dec.) 174
4/264 5/296   3/162 4/174

*†A. Long, G. G. Arnold, J. Spencer and A. Willows did not bat.

Bonus points – Sussex 4, Hampshire 2.

Bowling: *First Innings*—Malone 7–0–46–0; Stevenson 18–3–64–1; Jesty 20–7–46–2; Taylor 13–0–44–0; Southern 28–6–73–2; Cowley 14–4–36–0. *Second Innings*—Malone 7–1–20–0; Stevenson 10–1–32–1; Rice 10–1–32–0; Jesty 7–0–24–0; Southern 6.1–0–32–2; Cowley 6–1–28–1.

Hampshire

J. M. Rice lbw b Arnold	1	– c Phillipson b le Roux	22
C. L. Smith b Arnold	13	– not out	125
D. R. Turner b le Roux	0	– b Willows	19
T. E. Jesty c Long b Arnold	22	– b Arnold	7
*N. E. J. Pocock b le Roux	2	– not out	33
N. G. Cowley not out	62		
M. N. S. Taylor c Parker b Arnold	15		
†R. J. Parks b Willows	0		
J. W. Southern c Wessels b Willows	15		
K. Stevenson lbw b Willows	2		
S. J. Malone lbw b Willows	15		
B 2, l-b 1, w 1, n-b 1	5	B 4, l-b 5, n-b 8	17

1/6 2/9 3/20 4/41 5/43 6/69   152   1/61 2/97 3/112   (3 wkts) 223
7/74 8/104 9/114

Bonus points – Hampshire 1, Sussex 4.

Bowling: *First Innings*—le Roux 25–8–69–2; Arnold 20–9–43–4; Spencer 5–3–2–0; Willows 13.2–4–33–4. *Second Innings*—le Roux 20–8–38–1; Arnold 24–11–40–1; Wells 13–2–32–0; Willows 33–11–55–1; Spencer 11–2–34–0; Wessels 3–0–7–0.

Umpires: C. Cook and A. G. T. Whitehead.

At Tunbridge Wells, June 14, 16, 17. HAMPSHIRE drew with KENT.

At Bath, June 18, 19, 20. HAMPSHIRE drew with SOMERSET.

HAMPSHIRE v GLOUCESTERSHIRE

At Bournemouth, June 21, 23, 24. Drawn. Hampshire 4 pts, Gloucestershire 4 pts. Rain prevented any play on the third day and restricted play on the first to just one hour forty-nine minutes and 30.3 overs. In that time Gloucestershire lost half their wickets for 110 and, on the second day, a spell of three for 6 by Southern hastened the fall of the remaining five. Hampshire also struggled on the rain-affected wicket against Procter, bowling off-spin, and Childs.

Gloucestershire

B. C. Broad lbw b Stevenson	19	†A. J. Brassington	
Sadiq Mohammad lbw b Graf	10	c Stephenson b Southern	3
Zaheer Abbas c Pocock b Stevenson	3	B. M. Brain lbw b Cowley	1
A. W. Stovold c Stephenson b Jesty	37	J. H. Childs not out	1
*M. J. Procter c Stephenson b Southern	28	B 1, l-b 10, w 2, n-b 3	16
A. J. Hignell c Stephenson b Jesty	17		
P. Bainbridge st Stephenson b Southern	38	1/31 2/38 3/55 4/102 5/110 6/131	175
A. H. Wilkins c Cowley b Southern	2	7/134 8/165 9/172	

Bonus points – Gloucestershire 1, Hampshire 4.

Bowling: Graf 16–4–47–1; Stevenson 13–3–41–2; Southern 16.3–11–23–4; Jesty 11–4–32–2; Cowley 8–1–16–1.

Hampshire

C. L. Smith c Sadiq b Childs	17	S. F. Graf not out	9
T. M. Tremlett c Hignell b Procter	21	†G. R. Stephenson not out	0
M. C. J. Nicholas c and b Procter	9		
T. E. Jesty lbw b Procter	15	B 3, l-b 4, n-b 1	8
*N. E. J. Pocock c Hignell b Procter	4		
N. G. Cowley c and b Childs	36	1/35 2/49 3/51 4/63 (7 wkts) 132	
M. N. S. Taylor lbw b Childs	13	5/76 6/122 7/129	

J. W. Southern and K. Stevenson did not bat.

Bonus points – Gloucestershire 3.

Bowling: Brain 9–2–17–0; Procter 25–10–51–4; Childs 31–13–56–3.

Umpires: J. G. Langridge and R. Palmer.

HAMPSHIRE v YORKSHIRE

At Southampton, June 28, 30, July 1. Drawn. Hampshire 3 pts, Yorkshire 6 pts. This match was ruined by rain, which completely washed out play on the first day. When the game did get under way, Hampshire struck quickly with Graf trapping Boycott leg before, but Athey was missed behind the wicket at 9. Hampshire paid for that mistake as Athey went on to make 71. However, it was the Yorkshire captain who played the best innings, dominating a fourth-wicket partnership with Love that put on 92 in 58 minutes. After rain had delayed the start on the third day by ninety minutes, Yorkshire declared at their overnight total. Turner propped up Hampshire with a gritty knock and Stephenson hit out boldly, swinging Cope for two 6s before Pocock declared just before the end to deny Yorkshire the chance of a fourth bowling point.

Yorkshire

G. Boycott lbw b Graf	4	G. B. Stevenson c Tremlett b Southern	13
R. G. Lumb c Pocock b Stevenson	13	†D. L. Bairstow not out	10
C. W. J. Athey c Nicholas b Tremlett	71		
*J. H. Hampshire c Stephenson b Stevenson.	74	B 2, l-b 7, w 2, n-b 1	12
J. D. Love c Stevenson b Southern	37	1/8 2/61 3/105 (6 wkts dec.)	263
P. Carrick not out	29	4/197 5/215 6/229	

C. M. Old, A. Sidebottom and G. A. Cope did not bat.

Bonus points – Yorkshire 3, Hampshire 2.

Bowling: Graf 19–6–51–1; Stevenson 26–8–66–2; Jesty 14–2–58–0; Tremlett 11–4–25–1; Nicholas 2–0–2–0; Southern 9–1–49–2.

Hampshire

T. M. Tremlett b Cope	33	S. F. Graf c Bairstow b Cope	7
C. L. Smith c Carrick b Old	3	†G. R. Stephenson not out	29
M. C. J. Nicholas c Old b Carrick	4	J. W. Southern not out	0
T. E. Jesty c Athey b Cope	1	B 5, l-b 4.	9
D. R. Turner c Boycott b Cope	44		
*N. E. J. Pocock c Old b Carrick	10	1/3 2/17 3/18 4/58 (8 wkts dec.)	166
N. G. Cowley c Old b Carrick	26	5/75 6/118 7/127 8/137	

K. Stevenson did not bat.

Bonus points – Hampshire 1, Yorkshire 3.

Bowling: Old 5–3–5–1; Stevenson 7–1–12–0; Cope 36–17–69–4; Carrick 32.5–13–67–3; Athey 1–0–4–0.

Umpires: C. Cook and D. G. L. Evans.

HAMPSHIRE v GLAMORGAN

At Basingstoke, July 2, 3, 4. Drawn. Hampshire 5 pts, Glamorgan 5 pts. In a high-scoring match Glamorgan, set a target of 239 for victory in 150 minutes, were in some trouble at 75 for four soon after the start of the final twenty overs. Then a sharp shower took the players off the field for twenty minutes and a draw became inevitable. The pattern for run-making was set early in the game by Smith, Nicholas – unluckily run out when in sight of his first Championship century – and Turner, who was unbeaten on 97 and shared a fifth-wicket partnership of 129 with Pocock. Glamorgan scored even more freely, the highlight of their innings being a career-best double century by Alan Jones, who batted five and a quarter hours and hit three 6s and 23 4s. It was the fiftieth three-figure innings of his career, the highest by a Glamorgan player against Hampshire and the highest at the ground. Glamorgan led by 105 but Tremlett – with a career-best 84 – Smith, Pocock and Cowley batted freely before the declaration. Pocock and Cowley shared an unbroken sixth-wicket partnership of 134 in ninety minutes.

Hampshire

T. M. Tremlett c Lloyd b A. A. Jones.	0	– c Holmes b Lloyd	84
C. L. Smith b Moseley	60	– c Cordle b Lloyd	68
M. C. J. Nicholas run out	89	– c E. W. Jones b A. A. Jones	8
T. E. Jesty b Lloyd	6	– b Lloyd	9
D. R. Turner not out.	97	– c Miandad b Lloyd	18
*N. E. J. Pocock not out.	43	– not out	61
N. G. Cowley (did not bat).		– not out	80
L-b 5, w 1	6	B 4, l-b 7, n-b 4	15

1/6 2/117 3/128 4/172	(4 wkts dec.) 301	1/110 2/141 (5 wkts dec.)	343
		3/170 4/181 5/209	

S. F. Graf, †G. R. Stephenson, J. W. Southern and K. Stevenson did not bat.

Bonus points – Hampshire 4, Glamorgan 1.

Bowling: *First Innings*—A. A. Jones 22.5–4–69–1; Moseley 23–3–70–1; Cordle 21–8–42–0; Holmes 11–2–37–0; Lloyd 22–6–77–1. *Second Innings*—A. A. Jones 18–2–73–1; Moseley 17–4–52–0; Cordle 20–9–29–0; Lloyd 38–8–95–4; Featherstone 6–1–27–0; Miandad 8–2–52–0.

Glamorgan

A. Jones not out	204	– c Pocock b Graf	21
J. A. Hopkins run out	30	– c and b Stevenson	7
*B. J. Lloyd c Turner b Southern	29		
Javed Miandad c Smith b Jesty	82	– (3) not out	45
G. C. Holmes c Nicholas b Jesty	3	– (4) c Pocock b Southern	13
N. G. Featherstone not out	49	– (5) c Pocock b Cowley	0
M. J. Llewellyn (did not bat)	–	(6) not out	14
L-b 6, n-b 3	9	– L-b 4	4

1/60 2/134 3/272 4/281   (4 wkts) 406   1/32 2/32 3/58 4/75   (4 wkts) 104

†E. W. Jones, A. E. Cordle, E. A. Moseley and A. A. Jones did not bat.

Bonus points – Glamorgan 4, Hampshire 1.

Bowling: *First Innings*—Graf 17–1–53–0; Stevenson 9–0–40–0; Southern 28–5–118–1; Tremlett 9–0–44–0; Cowley 20–4–88–0; Jesty 16–1–53–2; Smith 1–0–1–0. *Second Innings*—Graf 9–3–22–1; Stevenson 9–0–27–1; Southern 8–1–27–1; Cowley 7–2–24–1.

Umpires: D. J. Halfyard and A. G. T. Whitehead.

At Hove, July 5, 7, 8. HAMPSHIRE drew with SUSSEX.

At Lord's, July 9, 10, 11. HAMPSHIRE lost to MIDDLESEX by five wickets.

At Cardiff, July 12, 14, 15. HAMPSHIRE drew with GLAMORGAN.

HAMPSHIRE v SURREY

At Portsmouth, July 23, 24, 25. Surrey won by eight wickets. Surrey 20 pts, Hampshire 3 pts. Hampshire, who elected to bat, never recovered from losing three wickets for 20 and were always troubled by the bowling of Jackman and Clarke, who took nine wickets between them in the first innings. Turner and Smith were the only batsmen to show confidence, but batting looked altogether an easier exercise when Butcher and Clinton took Surrey to 89 without loss by the close. Butcher went on to complete his century and Smith and Roope batted well for Surrey to establish a first innings lead of 192. Hampshire, starting the third day at 65 for two, batted with spirit and stretched their opponents more than had seemed likely. Jesty was the principal contributor. Surrey, left to score 75 in 100 minutes, got home with thirteen overs to spare for the loss of two wickets.

Hampshire

T. M. Tremlett lbw b Jackman	1	c Richards b Clarke	19
C. L. Smith c Richards b Jackman	46	c Smith b Jackman	37
M. C. J. Nicholas lbw b Clarke	1	c Butcher b Clarke	1
T. E. Jesty c Richards b Jackman	4	c Smith b Knight	62
D. R. Turner c Pocock b Cheatle	77	c Roope b Cheatle	21
*N. E. J. Pocock b Clarke	16	c Clarke b Pocock	30
N. G. Cowley lbw b Clarke	0	c Knight b Cheatle	22
S. F. Graf lbw b Jackman	21	lbw b Jackman	21
†G. R. Stephenson b Clarke	10	c Richards b Jackman	31
J. W. Southern not out	2	b Clarke	10
K. Stevenson b Clarke	0	not out	3
B 5, l-b 4, w 1, n-b 3	13	B 1, l-b 3, n-b 5	9

1/2 2/3 3/20 4/86 5/118 6/121   193   1/26 2/28 3/79 4/137   266
7/179 8/183 9/193   5/149 6/191 7/201
    8/221 9/246

Bonus points – Hampshire 1, Surrey 4.

Bowling: *First Innings*—Clarke 21.3–3–49–5; Jackman 24–11–48–4; Knight 10–4–27–0; Pocock 19–5–45–0; Cheatle 6–2–11–1. *Second Innings*—Clarke 19–4–81–3; Jackman 23.3–8–68–3; Cheatle 19–6–36–2; Pocock 17–4–45–1; Knight 7–2–27–1.

Surrey

A. R. Butcher lbw b Stevenson	118	c Turner b Tremlett	25
G. S. Clinton c Stevenson b Graf	35	c Southern b Stevenson	1
*R. D. V. Knight c Pocock b Jesty	21	not out	33
D. M. Smith c Pocock b Tremlett	60	not out	10
G. R. J. Roope c Graf b Tremlett	50		
G. P. Howarth c and b Cowley	3		
R. D. Jackman c Smith b Stevenson	18		
†C. J. Richards not out	27		
S. T. Clarke c Jesty b Stevenson	6		
P. I. Pocock c Graf b Stevenson	8		
R. G. L. Cheatle not out	9		
B 4, l-b 22, n-b 4	30	L-b 7	7

1/102 2/155 3/198 4/298 5/314   (9 wkts) 385   1/2 2/32   (2 wkts) 76
6/314 7/342 8/351 9/362

Bonus points – Surrey 4, Hampshire 2 (Score at 100 overs: 314-5).

Bowling: *First Innings*—Graf 27–5–75–1; Stevenson 26–2–98–4; Cowley 22–8–63–1; Jesty 14–6–30–1; Tremlett 22–2–69–2; Southern 8–2–20–0. *Second Innings*—Graf 3–0–18–0; Stevenson 5–1–28–1; Cowley 3.4–1–11–0; Tremlett 5–0–11–1; Turner 1–0–1–0.

Umpires: P. S. G. Stevens and D. J. Constant.

HAMPSHIRE v LANCASHIRE

At Portsmouth, July 26, 28, 29. Lancashire won by 146 runs. Lancashire 18 pts, Hampshire 4 pts. Hampshire's bowlers built an early advantage which was quickly surrendered. Lancashire, put in, scored 50 off the first ten overs, but the seamers caused problems on a green pitch and, after Stevenson had taken five wickets, the total was restricted to 212, with Hayes the main contributor. Hampshire were soon in trouble at 13 for three in the absence of Jesty, who later underwent a cartilage operation. Nicholas, Turner and Pocock led a partial recovery, but the last six wickets fell for only 19 runs. Lancashire, 86 ahead, soon stretched their lead, with Lloyd (one 6 and eleven 4s) completing his first century of the season. The visitors batted five overs into the third day before declaring and asking Hampshire to score 315 in 330 minutes. It was way beyond them and wickets were soon falling at regular intervals. Indeed, it was left to eighth-wicket pair Southern and Stevenson to produce the highest stand of the innings.

Lancashire

D. Lloyd b Stevenson	34	– not out	112
A. Kennedy c Southern b Stevenson	31	– c Cowley b Malone	49
I. Cockbain c Pocock b Malone	0	– c and b Southern	32
*F. C. Hayes lbw b Jesty	61	– c Pocock b Malone	16
B. W. Reidy b Tremlett	22	– not out	10
J. Simmons c Stephenson b Malone	1		
D. P. Hughes c Smith b Malone	0		
M. F. Malone lbw b Stevenson	33		
†C. J. Scott c Stephenson b Stevenson	7		
P. J. W. Allott not out	4		
W. Hogg c Turner b Stevenson	0		
B 1, l-b 15, w 2, n-b 1	19	B 1, l-b 5, w 1, n-b 2	9

1/50 2/53 3/78 4/144 5/151   212   1/97 2/164 3/211   (3 wkts dec.) 228
6/151 7/186 8/208 9/208

Bonus points – Lancashire 2, Hampshire 4.

Bowling: *First Innings*—Malone 24–8–56–3; Stevenson 25.2–6–86–5; Jesty 18–9–25–1; Tremlett 8–5–26–1. *Second Innings*—Stevenson 15–3–44–0; Malone 12–3–42–2; Tremlett 10–2–25–0; Nicholas 4–0–22–0; Southern 11–2–43–1; Cowley 19–5–43–0.

Hampshire

T. M. Tremlett c Scott b Hogg	0	– c Kennedy b Hogg	11
C. L. Smith c Scott b Malone	4	– c Simmons b Allott	19
†G. R. Stephenson c Scott b Hogg	2	– (7) c Hughes b Allott	19
M. C. J. Nicholas lbw b Allott	33	– (3) lbw b Hogg	2
D. R. Turner c Reidy b Allott	28	– (4) c Lloyd b Simmons	20
*N. E. J. Pocock c Hughes b Hogg	29	– (5) c Simmons b Lloyd	11
N. G. Cowley b Hogg	4	– (6) lbw b Hogg	30
J. W. Southern c Kennedy b Allott	0	– c Reidy b Simmons	28
K. Stevenson not out	13	– c Hughes b Simmons	13
S. J. Malone b Allott	2	– not out	0
T. E. Jesty absent hurt	0	– absent hurt	0
L-b 2, w 1, n-b 8	11	B 3, l-b 6, w 2, n-b 4	15

1/2 2/9 3/13 4/58 5/107 6/107   126   1/23 2/25 3/56 4/60 5/97   168
7/107 8/111 9/126   6/116 7/126 8/167 9/168

Bonus points – Lancashire 4.

Bowling: *First Innings*—Hogg 13–5–32–4; Malone 12–4–15–1; Allott 11–3–30–4; Simmons 6–0–23–0; Hughes 4–1–15–0. *Second Innings*—Hogg 13–0–55–3; Malone 7–1–16–0; Allott 6–2–20–2; Simmons 9.3–2–26–3; Hughes 5–2–19–0; Lloyd 13–5–17–1.

Umpires: D. J. Constant and P. S. G. Stevens.

At Cheltenham, August 2, 4, 5. HAMPSHIRE lost to GLOUCESTERSHIRE by 197 runs.

At Southampton, August 6, 7, 8. HAMPSHIRE lost to AUSTRALIANS by ten wickets (See Australian tour section).

At Chelmsford, August 9, 11, 12. HAMPSHIRE drew with ESSEX.

At Wellingborough, August 16, 18, 19. HAMPSHIRE lost to NORTHAMPTONSHIRE by eight wickets.

HAMPSHIRE v SOMERSET

At Bournemouth, August 20, 21, 22. Drawn. Hampshire 6 pts, Somerset 7 pts. When Somerset slumped to 71 for five in their second innings, Hampshire seemed in with a chance of registering their first Championship win of the season. But they were thwarted by Marks and Popplewell in an unbroken partnership of 76 in two hours. Marks, captaining Somerset in the absence of Rose (injured) and Botham (on international duty), had earlier caused problems with his off-spin in a first innings which was notable for a maiden Championship century by Nicholas. Particularly strong on the leg side, Nicholas reached his century in one hundred and sixty-eight minutes and hit two 6s and twelve 4s. The dismissal of Richards for 22 gave Hampshire reason to hope for a substantial lead, but Roebuck batted solidly and Somerset ended their first innings only 14 in arrears. Tremlett gave Hampshire a good start in their second innings, but six wickets had fallen for 141 before Marshall and Parks shared a seventh-wicket partnership of 116 in 107 minutes.

Hampshire

C. G. Greenidge c Lloyds b Popplewell	33	– (6) c Roebuck b Dredge	7
T. M. Tremlett c Taylor b Marks	16	– (1) lbw b Dredge	50
M. C. J. Nicholas b Marks	112	– c Olive b Popplewell	44
D. R. Turner b Lloyds	11	– c and b Lloyds	22
*N. E. J. Pocock c Dredge b Marks	11	– c and b Lloyds	12
N. G. Cowley c Olive b Lloyds	4	– (2) c Slocombe b Dredge	1
M. D. Marshall c Popplewell b Marks	31	– b Popplewell	67
†R. J. Parks not out	13	– c Denning b Richards	53
J. W. Southern c Slocombe b Marks	20	– b Richards	1
K. Stevenson c Gore b Lloyds	14	– (11) c Gore b Richards	0
M. J. Bailey not out	7	– (10) not out	7
B 2, l-b 11, w 1, n-b 1	15	B 4, l-b 8, n-b 2	14

1/46 2/68 3/93 4/128   (9 wkts) 294   1/1 2/70 3/114 4/127   278
5/147 6/224 7/229 8/261   5/141 6/141 7/257
9/279   8/263 9/275

Bonus points – Hampshire 3, Somerset 4.

Bowling: *First Innings*—Gore 11–5–20–0; Dredge 16–4–29–0; Popplewell 10–4–30–1; Lloyds 32–6–113–3; Marks 31–7–87–5. *Second Innings*—Gore 15–6–32–0; Dredge 20–7–48–3; Richards 7–2–12–3; Marks 24–8–61–0; Popplewell 10–2–41–2; Lloyds 19–1–70–2.

Somerset

M. Olive c Stevenson b Cowley	46	– b Southern	12
P. A. Slocombe c Parks b Marshall	6	– b Stevenson	1
I. V. A. Richards c Tremlett b Southern	22	– lbw b Stevenson	0
P. M. Roebuck c Nicholas b Southern	81	– st Parks b Southern	28
P. W. Denning c Bailey b Cowley	21	– b Southern	8
*V. J. Marks c Parks b Marshall	43	– not out	50
N. F. M. Popplewell not out	19	– not out	38
†D. J. S. Taylor lbw b Marshall	16		
J. W. Lloyds not out	2		
B 4, l-b 11, n-b 9	24	B 1, l-b 6, w 1, n-b 2	10

1/22 2/49 3/118 4/167 5/239   (7 wkts) 280   1/4 2/8 3/29   (5 wkts) 147
6/243 7/269   4/37 5/71

C. H. Dredge and H. I. E. Gore did not bat.

Bonus points – Somerset 3, Hampshire 3.

Bowling: *First Innings*—Marshall 19–7–34–3; Stevenson 7–4–12–0; Southern 38–10–92–2; Bailey 20–2–77–0; Cowley 16–2–41–2. *Second Innings*—Marshall 12–3–27–0; Stevenson 4–2–2–2; Southern 23–6–38–3; Bailey 11–1–36–0; Pocock 1–0–8–0; Cowley 9–1–26–0.

Umpires: D. J. Dennis and P. S. G. Stevens.

HAMPSHIRE v WORCESTERSHIRE

At Bournemouth, August 23, 25, 26. Hampshire won by four wickets. Hampshire 18 pts, Worcestershire 6 pts. Hampshire's only Championship victory of the summer was gained with nearly two hours to spare. Worcestershire had looked in a strong position in the first innings when Ormrod and Neale put on 123 for the second wicket, but Neale's dismissal signalled a collapse. Hampshire also had their batting problems, but Tremlett again reached his half-century and useful knocks by Terry, Parks and Bailey helped Hampshire to a lead of 17. Worcestershire soon lost Ormrod, but Turner and Neale progressed well until Marshall tore a hole in the batting with a devastating spell in which he took five wickets for 3 runs in 28 balls. Hampshire needed to score only 139 for victory and the calm assurance of Tremlett saw them to a long-awaited success. Hampshire's side included seven uncapped players.

Worcestershire

G. M. Turner c Pocock b Stevenson	12	– c Smith b Stevenson 53
J. A. Ormrod not out	126	– c Marshall b Stevenson 2
P. A. Neale c Parks b Marshall	56	– st Parks b Southern 40
Younis Ahmed b Marshall	0	– c Smith b Marshall 23
E. J. O. Hemsley c Pocock b Marshall	0	– st Parks b Southern 0
D. N. Patel b Stevenson	0	– b Marshall 9
†P. B. Fisher c Marshall b Stevenson	0	– not out 10
J. D. Inchmore lbw b Stevenson	0	– lbw b Marshall 2
H. Alleyne c Southern b Stevenson	1	– b Marshall 0
*N. Gifford lbw b Tremlett	11	– b Marshall 0
A. P. Pridgeon b Marshall	1	– c Marshall b Southern 7
L-b 8, n-b 4	12	B 1, l-b 3, w 1, n-b 4 9

1/16 2/139 3/139 4/145 5/146   219   1/6 2/94 3/111 4/111   155
6/164 7/164 8/172 9/192   5/131 6/132 7/134 8/140
                                 9/140

Bonus points – Worcestershire 2, Hampshire 4.

Bowling: *First Innings*—Marshall 28–9–53–4; Stevenson 23–5–66–5; Tremlett 19–3–52–1; Southern 12–1–27–0; Bailey 2–0–9–0. *Second Innings*—Marshall 19–4–39–5; Stevenson 10–2–39–2; Tremlett 3–0–16–0; Southern 20.4–6–52–3.

Hampshire

C. L. Smith b Alleyne	15	– c Fisher b Alleyne 17
T. M. Tremlett c Fisher b Pridgeon	76	– not out 67
M. C. J. Nicholas lbw b Alleyne	0	– c Fisher b Alleyne 7
D. R. Turner c Fisher b Pridgeon	10	– b Gifford 1
*N. E. J. Pocock b Pridgeon	0	– b Gifford 20
V. P. Terry lbw b Alleyne	31	– c Fisher b Gifford............ 6
M. D. Marshall c Turner b Alleyne	4	– c Turner b Hemsley 10
†R. J. Parks c Fisher b Alleyne	31	– not out 6
J. W. Southern c Gifford b Pridgeon	5	
M. J. Bailey not out	21	
K. Stevenson c Patel b Gifford	11	
B 17, l-b 6, w 5, n-b 4	32	B 3, l-b 1, w 4 8

1/36 2/36 3/52 4/52 5/104 6/108   236   1/48 2/60 3/61   (6 wkts) 142
7/165 8/180 9/198   4/99 5/119 6/136

Bonus points – Hampshire 2, Worcestershire 4.

Bowling: *First Innings*—Alleyne 29–8–72–5; Inchmore 17–0–54–0; Pridgeon 20–8–29–4; Gifford 26.4–10–41–1; Patel 1–0–8–0. *Second Innings*—Alleyne 12–2–37–2; Pridgeon 11–4–22–0; Gifford 24–6–42–3; Patel 6–2–15–0; Hemsley 6.2–0–18–1.

Umpires: D. J. Dennis and P. B. Wight.

At Nottingham, August 30, September 1. HAMPSHIRE lost to NOTTINGHAMSHIRE by an innings and 22 runs.

HAMPSHIRE v LEICESTERSHIRE

At Southampton, September 3, 4. Leicestershire won by an innings and 34 runs. Leicestershire 20 pts, Hampshire 4 pts. Hampshire completed a disappointing season by losing in two days. With neither Greenidge nor Smith available, they sent in Parks as Tremlett's partner to form the fifteenth opening combination used in the season. Parks soon fell to Agnew, but Tremlett provided the backbone with a determined display which saw him carry his bat for 70. Leicestershire, despite losing Dudleston and Boon cheaply, had no trouble building a substantial lead, thanks principally to Gower and Tolchard who added 119 runs for the fifth wicket in 34 overs. Gower, missed twice, batted just over three and threequarter hours, hitting 21 4s in his top score of the season. Hampshire needed 151 to make Leicestershire bat again, but they succumbed feebly.

Hampshire

T. M. Tremlett not out	70	– c Cook b Agnew	4
†R. J. Parks c Balderstone b Agnew	5	– (8) c Tolchard b Agnew	11
M. C. J. Nicholas c Gower b Taylor	17	– (2) c Tolchard b Agnew	2
D. R. Turner b Clift	1	– (7) b Cook	32
*N. E. J. Pocock b Clift	1	– (3) c Tolchard b Agnew	2
N. G. Cowley b Agnew	18	– (4) c Tolchard b Parsons	18
V. P. Terry c Dudleston b Cook	23	– (5) b Clift	27
M. D. Marshall lbw b Cook	13	– (6) c Gower b Taylor	3
J. W. Southern c Gower b Taylor	8	– c Tolchard b Taylor	10
K. Stevenson c Gower b Taylor	14	– c Tolchard b Taylor	0
S. J. Malone b Clift	1	– not out	3
L-b 3, n-b 8	11	L-b 1, n-b 4	5

1/16 2/39 3/40 4/50 5/81 6/116   182   1/4 2/6 3/23 4/39 5/56   117
7/142 8/155 9/179   6/64 7/85 8/99 9/99

Bonus points – Hampshire 1, Leicestershire 4.

Bowling: *First Innings*—Agnew 9–2–32–2; Parsons 9–1–36–0; Clift 11.2–4–25–3; Taylor 16–2–51–3; Cook 16–6–27–2; Balderstone 2–2–0–0. *Second Innings*—Agnew 10–3–36–4; Parsons 7–3–27–1; Taylor 9–1–35–3; Clift 8–4–9–1; Cook 3.2–1–5–1.

Leicestershire

J. C. Balderstone b Cowley	32	N. G. B. Cook b Cowley	0
B. Dudleston lbw b Stevenson	5	J. P. Agnew b Stevenson	16
T. J. Boon c Marshall b Malone	12	L. B. Taylor not out	0
D. I. Gower c and b Southern	138		
N. E. Briers c Pocock b Southern	20	B 10, l-b 11, w 1, n-b 2	24
*†R. W. Tolchard lbw b Cowley	74		
P. B. Clift c Southern b Cowley	0	1/22 2/37 3/113 4/169 5/288	333
G. J. Parsons lbw b Stevenson	12	6/297 7/310 8/310 9/332	

Bonus points – Leicestershire 4, Hampshire 3 (Score at 100 overs: 313-8).

Bowling: Marshall 18–8–50–0; Stevenson 17.2–6–39–3; Malone 12–1–52–1; Southern 34–5–97–2; Cowley 26–7–71–4.

Umpires: W. E. Alley and A. G. T. Whitehead.

KENT

Patron — HRH THE DUKE OF KENT

President — V. COLLINS

Chairman, Cricket Committee — A. H. PHEBEY

Secretary — M. D. FENNER
St Lawrence Ground, Old Dover Road, Canterbury

Cricket Manager — J. C. T. PAGE

Captain — 1980 A. G. E. EALHAM; 1981 ASIF IQBAL

| C. S. Cowdrey | County Badge | A. P. E. Knott |

For an unseemly length of time before the end of the 1980 season, the record book was being investigated to reveal how long it had been since Kent had endured such an unsuccessful summer. It was found to be 1956, this being the last time they had finished sixteenth in the Championship; but not since 1897 had they won only two Championship matches.

They slumped also to a worst-ever eleventh position in the John Player League table, fell at the first hurdle in the Gillette Cup, and failed to qualify for the knockout stages of the Benson and Hedges Cup. It was a poor way to start the 1980s for a side which had dominated all spheres of cricket throughout the previous decade.

So what went wrong? There were Test calls again, but they grew progressively less demanding as Woolmer, Tavaré, Underwood and finally Knott were discarded by England. By then injuries had complicated matters. Kevin Jarvis, who had bowled more impressively than most, missed four games late in the season, while Guy Spelman, one of the younger players seeking to establish himself in the side, broke down on July

28 and did not play again. With these two fast bowlers out of action, it did not help that Graham Dilley, recalled to the England squad for the second Test, did not bowl in a first-class county game after July 5. John Shepherd, plagued by niggling injuries but missing only four Championship matches, battled away to alleviate the obvious deficiencies in attack.

These were accentuated by the fact that Derek Underwood, frustrated by a lack of bowling and a general shortage of cricket in the first half of the season, could not get among the wickets as has been his regular custom. He and Kent were equally relieved when the tide turned so favourably that in the last six matches he captured two-thirds of his season's tally. At the same time Graham Johnson's off-breaks, if not his bat, began to reap greater success.

Yet there was more to the decline. It had been decided, before the end of May, to embark on a policy of giving unestablished and young players the best possible chance to develop. A period of transformation, inevitable in sport, was to begin, with senior players left out of the side from time to time. That was the plan, and it was Asif Iqbal who was side-lined most. Thus the best side was not always selected and a certain amount of confusion and frustration was caused.

That better results did not materialise should not reflect against the young players, nor those seeking to establish themselves. Everything was done to accommodate them, and this meant that Knott and Shepherd, both proven run-makers, found themselves batting frequently at numbers eight and nine, which are not their true positions. In hindsight, it might have been better to have picked the team on merit. In the event, the batting followed a go-stop-go pattern.

It began well. By the end of the third game Woolmer, Rowe, Tavaré and Alan Ealham had all scored centuries. Then came a faltering period. Bob Woolmer and Chris Tavaré, dropped by England, had their problems, and Tavaré toiled through eight innings before he passed the half-century mark again, after which he hit a purple patch. Woolmer went nine innings after the second Test before he reached 50. For him it was a frustrating summer; whenever he went to the wicket he looked in majestic form, only to be dismissed so often in the 20s and 30s. Charles Rowe started in fine form, but as his fortunes waned he lost his place for seven matches, while Chris Cowdrey, although maintaining his first team place, lacked consistency.

Of the young players to be introduced, Stuart Waterton had the more settled and therefore the more rewarding experience; he deputised very promisingly for Alan Knott and showed ability with the bat. Neil Taylor and the left-handed Mark Benson both had batting opportunities and did enough to suggest that they will challenge for regular places.

Some two months after the season ended, Ealham's frustrations were climaxed by the decision to relieve him of the captaincy and reinstate Asif, captain for one season in 1977 and the 1981 beneficiary. This was Kent's fourth captaincy change since 1972. Ealham, who will play on – he takes a benefit in 1982 – could feel understandably disappointed. The traumas of the 1980 season were never wholly attributable to him. – Dudley Moore.

KENT

[*Fisk-Moore, Canterbury*]

Back row: C. Lewis (*scorer*), M. R. Benson, C. J. C. Rowe, N. J. Kemp, C. S. Cowdrey, G. R. Dilley, K. B. S. Jarvis, G. D. Spelman, R. W. Hills, C. J. Tavaré, N. R. Taylor, D. Aslett, B. W. Luckhurst, J. C. T. Page (*manager*). *Front row:* D. Nicholls, G. W. Johnson, J. N. Shepherd, A. G. E. Ealham (*captain*), D. L. Underwood, Asif Iqbal, A. P. E. Knott, R. A. Woolmer.

KENT RESULTS

All First-class Matches – Played 23: Won 2, Lost 9, Drawn 12.

County Championship Matches – Played 22: Won 2, Lost 8, Drawn 12.

Bonus points – Batting 36, Bowling 59.

COUNTY CHAMPIONSHIP AVERAGES

BATTING

	Birthplace	Matches	Inns	Not Outs	Runs	Highest Inns	Avge
C. J. Tavaré	Orpington	18	29	5	1,050	144*	43.75
R. A. Woolmer	Kanpur, India	16	26	1	816	171	32.64
N. R. Taylor	Orpington	9	15	3	385	63	32.08
A. G. E. Ealham	Ashford	20	29	2	801	145	29.66
A. P. E. Knott	Belvedere	15	20	4	474	85*	29.62
J. N. Shepherd	Barbados, WI	20	23	8	428	100	28.53
C. S. Cowdrey	Farnborough	20	29	2	715	87	26.48
C. J. C. Rowe	Hong Kong	14	22	2	520	109	26.00
M. R. Benson	Shoreham, Sussex	9	13	2	248	58*	22.54
G. W. Johnson	Beckenham	20	27	5	489	84	22.22
Asif Iqbal	Hyderabad, India	9	16	2	208	41	14.85
S. N. V. Waterton ...	Dartford	7	9	1	110	40*	13.75
G. R. Dilley	Dartford	8	4	3	12	12*	12.00
N. J. Kemp	Bromley	5	5	0	48	23	9.60
R. W. Hills	Borough Green	10	15	4	76	12	6.90
D. L. Underwood ...	Bromley	19	14	5	43	11*	4.77
K. B. S. Jarvis	Dartford	17	10	4	12	4	2.00
G. D. Spelman	Westminster	6	7	1	9	4	1.50

* *Signifies not out.*

BOWLING

	Overs	Maidens	Runs	Wickets	Average
D. L. Underwood	543.5	196	1,286	60	21.43
K. B. S. Jarvis	366.3	84	1,150	51	22.54
G. W. Johnson	351.1	95	959	42	22.83
G. R. Dilley	176	44	525	21	25.00
J. N. Shepherd	473.1	118	1,220	44	27.72
R. W. Hills	177.4	53	438	13	33.69

Also bowled: Asif Iqbal 7–3–13–0; C. S. Cowdrey 53.3–8–188–6; A. G. E. Ealham 5–0–42–0; N. J. Kemp 82.3–5–348–7; A. P. E. Knott 1–0–5–1; C. J. C. Rowe 48–12–132–4; G. D. Spelman 98.1–23–291–7; C. J. Tavaré 14.3–2–71–0; N. R. Taylor 9–2–20–0; R. A. Woolmer 54–15–154–5.

HUNDREDS

The following nine three-figure innings were played for Kent in County Championship matches – C. J. Tavaré 144* v Worcestershire (Worcester), 126* v Northamptonshire (Canterbury), 108 v Leicestershire (Leicester), 100* v Glamorgan (Canterbury); R. A. Woolmer 171 v Sussex (Hove), 102* v Hampshire (Bournemouth); A. G. E. Ealham 145 v Essex (Ilford); C. J. C. Rowe 109 v Hampshire (Bournemouth); J. N. Shepherd 100 v Surrey (Maidstone).

KENT v NORTHAMPTONSHIRE

At Canterbury, April 30, May 1, 2. Drawn. Kent 5 pts, Northamptonshire 5 pts. Kent made a bad start when play began at 1.40, but they prospered as Woolmer and Tavaré added 80 for the second wicket and on the second morning Tavaré (thirteen 4s) and Johnson took their stand to 82 off 31 overs. Larkins and Cook gave Northamptonshire a fine start, scoring 106 in 41 overs, and although Jarvis had a lethal spell of four for 20 in 6.5 overs, Allan Lamb provided first-class entertainment with two 6s and nine 4s in his unbeaten innings. Woolmer again displayed good form and with Ealham and Knott adding 81 in fifty-three minutes, Northamptonshire were set 222 to win in 140 minutes. Already without the injured Sarfraz and with Cook retiring hurt, it was a target they did not attempt.

Kent

R. A. Woolmer c Sharp b T. M. Lamb	50	– c Sharp b Williams	79
C. J. C. Rowe c Sharp b Griffiths	0	– st Sharp b Carter	30
C. J. Tavaré not out	126	– c Yardley b Griffiths	10
Asif Iqbal c Sarfraz b T. M. Lamb	2	– (7) not out	8
*A. G. E. Ealham c and b Willey	22	– (4) c Yardley b T. M. Lamb	71
†A. P. E. Knott lbw b Griffiths	3	– (5) b T. M. Lamb	30
G. W. Johnson c Sharp b Sarfraz	37	– (6) not out	1
J. N. Shepherd not out	2		
L-b 2, n-b 9	11	B 4, l-b 5, w 1, n-b 3	13

1/13 2/93 3/101   (6 wkts dec.) 255   1/60 2/109 3/152   (5 wkts dec.) 242
4/144 5/149 6/231   4/233 5/233

G. R. Dilley, D. L. Underwood and K. B. S. Jarvis did not bat.

Bonus points – Kent 3, Northamptonshire 2.

Bowling: *First Innings*—Sarfraz 27–4–74–1; Griffiths 21–5–53–2; T. M. Lamb 25–6–65–2; Carter 4–0–21–0; Willey 16–3–31–1. *Second Innings*—Sarfraz 4–2–5–0; Griffiths 15–3–45–1; T. M. Lamb 12.2–3–32–2; Carter 7–1–29–1; Willey 19–4–59–0; Williams 18–2–59–1.

Northamptonshire

*G. Cook b Jarvis	87	– retired hurt	7
W. Larkins c Tavaré b Johnson	58	– c Johnson b Rowe	25
R. G. Williams run out	8	– c Johnson b Dilley	2
A. J. Lamb not out	88	– not out	23
P. Willey b Jarvis	5	– not out	1
T. J. Yardley c Tavaré b Jarvis	14		
R. M. Carter c Woolmer b Jarvis	0		
†G. Sharp not out	4		
L-b 3, n-b 9	12	L-b 7, n-b 1	8

1/106 2/120 3/203   (6 wkts dec.) 276   1/18 2/63   (2 wkts) 66
4/211 5/241 6/252

Sarfraz Nawaz, T. M. Lamb and B. J. Griffiths did not bat.

Bonus points – Northamptonshire 3, Kent 2.

Bowling: *First Innings*—Dilley 13–2–48–0; Shepherd 17–4–40–0; Jarvis 19–3–81–4; Underwood 15–7–54–0; Johnson 17–6–41–1. *Second Innings*—Dilley 6–1–12–1; Shepherd 6–3–6–0; Jarvis 2–1–3–0; Underwood 4–2–7–0; Johnson 5–2–8–0; Rowe 7–1–20–1; Woolmer 5–4–2–0.

Umpires: J. G. Langridge and D. J. Dennis.

At Ilford, May 7, 8, 9. KENT lost to ESSEX by two wickets.

At Bournemouth, May 24, 26, 27. KENT beat HAMPSHIRE by ten wickets.

At Hove, May 28, 29, 30. KENT drew with SUSSEX.

At Canterbury, May 31, June 1, 2. KENT lost to WEST INDIANS by five wickets (See West Indian tour section).

At Sheffield, June 4, 5, 6. KENT lost to YORKSHIRE by two wickets.

KENT v HAMPSHIRE

At Tunbridge Wells, June 14, 16, 17. Drawn. Kent 4 pts, Hampshire 2 pts. After two hours thirty-five minutes play had been lost, Hampshire struggled against an accurate attack spearheaded by Dilley and Jarvis. Pocock and Jesty added 73 off 23 overs and there was late resistance from Taylor and Graf who stayed thirteen overs for the seventh wicket. Jarvis quickly polished off the Hampshire innings on the second morning, and after Kent had begun badly rain held up play for more than five hours. In the last hour and a half Kent had their problems against a persistent attack in which Graf proved his return to fitness. Only one over was bowled on the third morning before the weather again intervened and ended the match.

Hampshire

J. M. Rice c Shepherd b Dilley	2	†G. R. Stephenson c Knott b Jarvis	16
C. L. Smith c Knott b Dilley	8	J. W. Southern c Shepherd b Jarvis	3
M. C. J. Nicholas c Dilley b Jarvis	7	K. Stevenson not out	0
T. E. Jesty c Knott b Underwood	26		
*N. E. J. Pocock c Knott b Dilley	48	B 1, l-b 5, w 6, n-b 9	21
N. G. Cowley c Knott b Jarvis	9		
M. N. S. Taylor c Johnson b Shepherd	18	1/2 2/14 3/26 4/103 5/104 6/122	179
S. F. Graf c Tavaré b Johnson	21	7/157 8/157 9/179	

Bonus points – Hampshire 1, Kent 4.

Bowling: Dilley 14–3–39–3; Jarvis 12.5–3–36–4; Shepherd 13–2–39–1; Woolmer 5–1–21–0; Underwood 14–6–14–1; Johnson 7–3–9–1.

Kent

R. A. Woolmer c Stephenson b Graf	5	G. W. Johnson not out	10
C. J. C. Rowe c Stephenson b Jesty	23		
C. J. Tavaré not out	22	B 1, l-b 1, w 1	3
C. S. Cowdrey c Smith b Jesty	4		
*A. G. E. Ealham c Jesty b Graf	0	1/11 2/47 3/51 4/52 (4 wkts)	67

†A. P. E. Knott, J. N. Shepherd, G. R. Dilley, D. L. Underwood and K. B. S. Jarvis did not bat.

Bonus points – Hampshire 1.

Bowling: Graf 16–6–24–2; Stevenson 11–4–17–0; Jesty 8–1–19–2; Southern 1–0–4–0.

Umpires: W. L. Budd and A. Jepson.

KENT v SUSSEX

At Tunbridge Wells, June 18, 19, 20. Drawn. Kent 6 pts, Sussex 3 pts. Sussex, put in to bat, floundered on a wicket that helped the bowlers, although Phillipson provided resistance for three hours. Kent crawled along in reply, Taylor batting 245 minutes (65 overs) for his 47, but fortunately Cowdrey had few misgivings about the Sussex attack and hit ten 4s in an entertaining stay. Sussex again started badly, but Mendis and Parker pulled them round by adding 105 in two hours and that was followed by a belligerent consolidation as Parker and Imran thrashed 131 in an hour and a half. Imran hit four 6s and seven 4s and Parker reached his century in 200 minutes with one 6 and twelve 4s. Jarvis hit back for Kent, taking three for 6 in five overs, and the eventual declaration left Kent 225 to win in two and a half hours. With Asif a flu victim, and able to bat only in an emergency, Kent never attempted to meet the challenge.

Sussex

G. D. Mendis c Rowe b Shepherd	5	– c Waterton b Spelman 43
T. D. Booth Jones c Shepherd b Spelman	10	– lbw b Jarvis 0
P. W. G. Parker c Waterton b Shepherd	21	– c Rowe b Johnson 117
Imran Khan c Cowdrey b Jarvis	10	– c Waterton b Jarvis 75
C. P. Phillipson c Cowdrey b Johnson	38	– b Jarvis 8
C. M. Wells b Jarvis	16	– c Spelman b Johnson 6
I. A. Greig c Cowdrey b Johnson	1	– c and b Spelman 32
G. S. le Roux c Waterton b Spelman	7	– b Jarvis 0
*†A. Long b Jarvis	13	– not out 11
G. G. Arnold lbw b Jarvis	1	
C. E. Waller not out	7	
B 1, l-b 3, w 2, n-b 7	13	B 1, l-b 7, n-b 5 13

1/15 2/34 3/45 4/57 5/81 6/87   142   1/1 2/106 3/237   (8 wkts dec.) 305
7/101 8/130 9/131   4/252 5/253 6/259
                                                7/262 8/305

Bonus points – Kent 4.

Bowling: *First Innings*—Jarvis 22.4–12–21–4; Spelman 24–13–27–2; Shepherd 21–8–33–2; Johnson 25–8–48–2. *Second Innings*—Jarvis 20–3–71–4; Spelman 22.3–4–73–2; Shepherd 17–5–39–0; Johnson 29–9–99–2; Rowe 3–1–10–0.

Kent

C. J. C. Rowe lbw b Imran	0	– c Phillipson b Arnold 2
N. R. Taylor c le Roux b Wells	47	– not out 41
M. Benson c Long b Arnold	28	– run out 2
Asif Iqbal c Phillipson b Arnold	4	
*A. G. E. Ealham c Long b Imran	25	
C. S. Cowdrey b le Roux	83	– (4) not out 27
G. W. Johnson c Parker b Waller	8	
J. N. Shepherd lbw b Greig	7	
†S. N. V. Waterton run out	4	
G. D. Spelman not out	2	
K. B. S. Jarvis c Parker b le Roux	0	
B 1, l-b 3, w 6, n-b 5	15	L-b 1, n-b 2 3

1/3 2/57 3/77 4/115 5/121 6/153   223   1/8 2/12   (2 wkts) 75
7/180 8/221 9/221

Bonus points – Kent 2, Sussex 3 (Score at 100 overs: 210-7).

Bowling: *First Innings*—Imran 21–8–44–2; le Roux 21.1–5–53–2; Arnold 23–10–32–2; Greig 16–6–35–1; Waller 15–5–28–1; Wells 7–1–16–1. *Second Innings*—Imran 3–0–5–0; le Roux 5–2–9–0; Arnold 10–3–22–1; Waller 9–3–34–0; Greig 2.3–1–2–0.

Umpires: W. L. Budd and A. Jepson.

At Manchester, June 21, 23, 24. KENT drew with LANCASHIRE.

KENT v DERBYSHIRE

At Dartford, June 28, 30, July 1. Drawn. Kent 1 pt, Derbyshire 3 pts. The first day was washed out by rain and on the second day Kent laboured against a persistent attack in which the slow left-arm spin of Steele caused most problems. Tavaré and Ealham added 44 off nine overs for the fourth wicket, Ealham reaching 51 out of 74 in seventy minutes with a 6 and seven 4s. Just when it seemed Kent might recover they lost four wickets for 16 runs in fifteen overs. Rain intervened at the tea interval and completely washed out play on the final day.

Kent

R. A. Woolmer c Miller b Hendrick	 2	J. N. Shepherd c Anderson b Steele	 2
C. J. C. Rowe c Oldham b Steele	 21	G. R. Dilley not out	 12
C. J. Tavaré c Wright b Steele	 42	D. L. Underwood not out	 4
C. S. Cowdrey lbw b Hendrick	 7	B 3, l-b 1, w 1, n-b 6	 11
*A. G. E. Ealham b Steele	 64		
†A. P. E. Knott c Taylor b Oldham	 7	1/9 2/56 3/69 4/113	(8 wkts) 175
G. W. Johnson c Miller b Steele	 3	5/143 6/150 7/152 8/159	

K. B. S. Jarvis did not bat.

Bonus points – Kent 1, Derbyshire 3.

Bowling: Hendrick 20–6–57–2; Tunnicliffe 10–2–35–0; Oldham 18–9–27–1; Steele 27–10–45–5.

Derbyshire

B. Wood, J. G. Wright, P. N. Kirsten, D. S. Steele, K. J. Barnett, *G. Miller, I. S. Anderson, C. J. Tunnicliffe, †R. W. Taylor, M. Hendrick, S. Oldham.

Umpires: J. G. Langridge and D. Shackleton.

KENT v LEICESTERSHIRE

At Maidstone, July 5, 7, 8. Drawn. Kent 4 pts, Leicestershire 3 pts. After an early shock, Leicestershire recovered thanks initially to Balderstone and Gower. Then Davison (sixteen 4s) held the rest of the innings together, standing firm as three wickets fell for 10 runs in eight overs, and had steered his side to their third bonus point when he was dismissed 10 short of his century. Kent made a dismal start, losing two wickets cheaply before the close, and the match was never resumed because of rain.

Leicestershire

J. F. Steele c Tavaré b Jarvis	 17	J. P. Agnew c Knott b Dilley	 1
N. E. Briers c Shepherd b Jarvis	 1	G. J. Parsons c Knott b Shepherd	 14
J. C. Balderstone c Dilley b Woolmer	... 64	L. B. Taylor not out	 0
D. I. Gower b Dilley	 38	B 1, l-b 10, w 2, n-b 7	 20
*B. F. Davison c Knott b Jarvis	 90		
†R. W. Tolchard lbw b Dilley	 0	1/2 2/68 3/113 4/142	254
J. Birkenshaw c Tavaré b Jarvis	 9	5/152 6/205 7/207	
N. G. B. Cook c Dilley b Jarvis	 0	8/215 9/250	

Bonus points – Leicestershire 3, Kent 4.

Bowling: Dilley 22–5–46–3; Jarvis 20–3–63–5; Shepherd 20.3–5–49–1; Underwood 18–6–49–0; Woolmer 10–2–25–1; Johnson 1–0–2–0.

Kent

R. A. Woolmer lbw b Agnew	 7
C. J. C. Rowe c Tolchard b Taylor	 3
G. R. Dilley not out	 0
C. J. Tavaré not out	 0
W 3, n-b 3	 6

1/15 2/15   (2 wkts) 16

C. S. Cowdrey, *A. G. E. Ealham, †A. P. E. Knott, G. W. Johnson, J. N. Shepherd, D. L. Underwood and K. B. S. Jarvis did not bat.

Bowling: Taylor 8–5–6–1; Agnew 4–4–0–1; Parsons 4–2–4–0.

Umpires: D. J. Constant and D. J. Halfyard.

KENT v SURREY

At Maidstone, July 9, 10, 11. Drawn. Terrible weather ruled out play until five o'clock on the second day when a one-innings match was started. Kent, put in, were in trouble with half the side dismissed for 77 before Shepherd rescued them, hitting his century out of 131 in one hundred and fourteen minutes with two 6s and nine 4s. He and Waterton added 121 in 31 overs. With Kent's declaration leaving the visitors just under two and a half hours to score the runs, Butcher and Clinton made a good start by scoring 117 in 105 minutes. Needing 77 off the last ten overs, Surrey lost wickets trying to reach the target, which eventually became unattainable.

Kent

R. A. Woolmer c Knight b Jackman	....	33
C. J. C. Rowe c Knight b Pocock	....	14
C. J. Tavaré c Clarke b Jackman	......	5
C. S. Cowdrey c Smith b Pocock	......	18
*A. G. E. Ealham c Knight b Pocock	...	1
G. W. Johnson c Butcher b Pocock	.....	0
J. N. Shepherd c Knight b Pocock	......	100

†S. N. V. Waterton not out	....	40
G. D. Spelman lbw b Clarke	....	0
B 5, l-b 5, w 1	....	11
1/39 2/57 3/68	(8 wkts dec.)	222
4/69 5/77 6/88 7/209		
8/222		

D. L. Underwood and K. B. S. Jarvis did not bat.

Bowling: Clarke 20–4–37–1; Jackman 26–10–54–2; Knight 1–0–6–0; Pocock 28–8–73–5; Intikhab 7–1–20–0; Cheatle 6–1–21–0.

Surrey

A. R. Butcher c Tavaré b Shepherd	.....	60
G. S. Clinton c Ealham b Jarvis	.....	70
Intikhab Alam c Shepherd b Jarvis	.....	7
*R. D. V. Knight c sub b Jarvis	....	17
D. M. Smith st Waterton b Johnson	....	2
G. R. J. Roope c Cowdrey b Jarvis	.....	24

S. T. Clarke c Tavaré b Spelman	....	9
R. D. Jackman not out	....	8
L-b 11, n-b 1	....	12
1/117 2/144 3/146	(7 wkts)	209
4/152 5/184 6/198 7/209		

†C. J. Richards, P. I. Pocock and R. G. L. Cheatle did not bat.

Bowling: Jarvis 10–0–42–4; Spelman 8.5–1–34–1; Underwood 9–3–32–0; Shepherd 9–0–44–1; Johnson 7–0–33–1; Rowe 1–0–12–0.

Umpires: D. J. Constant and D. J. Halfyard.

At Nottingham, July 12, 14. KENT lost to NOTTINGHAMSHIRE by an innings and 1 run.

At Taunton, July 23, 24, 25. KENT lost to SOMERSET by six wickets.

At Lord's, July 26, 28, 29. KENT drew with MIDDLESEX.

KENT v GLAMORGAN

At Canterbury, August 2, 4, 5. Glamorgan won by three wickets. Glamorgan 18 pts, Kent 8 pts. Tavaré dominated a second-wicket stand of 137 in 46 overs with Johnson (eight 4s) after Kent had elected to bat. Jarvis then had Glamorgan in trouble with three for 21 in seven overs. Their rescuers were E. W. Jones and Moseley who added 99 off 28 overs, but after an interruption through rain Jarvis wrapped up the innings. Tavaré again led the Kent innings, hitting an unbeaten century in three hours with his second 50 coming in even time. Glamorgan, left to score 242 in 150 minutes, were given a good start by A. Jones, and Ealham kept them interested with an expensive five-overs spell. Glamorgan readily accepted the challenge and Francis (one 6 and eleven 4s) steered them to victory with seven balls to spare.

Kent

R. A. Woolmer b A. A. Jones	27	– c E. W. Jones b Nash	20
G. W. Johnson b Featherstone	84	– c Miandad b Hobbs	18
C. J. Tavaré b Nash	87	– not out	100
Asif Iqbal b Nash	41	– c E. W. Jones b Nash	1
*A. G. E. Ealham c Hopkins b Nash	0	– c E. W. Jones b Hobbs	5
C. S. Cowdrey c E. W. Jones b Moseley	1	– c and b Featherstone	11
M. Benson c Nash b Featherstone	11	– lbw b Featherstone	14
†A. P. E. Knott not out	33	– not out	28
J. N. Shepherd not out	8		
B 2, l-b 2, n-b 5	9	B 4, l-b 5	9

1/34 2/171 3/236 4/236	(7 wkts) 301	1/39 2/51 3/52 (6 wkts dec.) 206
5/246 6/246 7/280		4/67 5/90 6/120

D. L. Underwood and K. B. S. Jarvis did not bat.

Bonus points – Kent 4, Glamorgan 3.

Bowling: *First Innings*—Nash 35–10–103–3; A. A. Jones 16–5–46–1; Moseley 21–6–56–1; Hobbs 5–0–27–0; Featherstone 23–6–60–2. *Second Innings*—A. A. Jones 11–6–30–0; Moseley 6–0–26–0; Nash 13–6–28–2; Hobbs 30.1–11–58–2; Featherstone 20–8–55–2.

Glamorgan

A. Jones c Tavaré b Jarvis	7	– st Knott b Johnson	71
J. A. Hopkins b Jarvis	9	– c Cowdrey b Johnson	24
D. A. Francis b Jarvis	2	– (4) not out	78
Javed Miandad b Jarvis	37	– (3) c Underwood b Johnson	0
N. G. Featherstone run out	51	– (7) lbw b Johnson	7
M. J. Llewellyn c Tavaré b Woolmer	13	– b Underwood	17
*M. A. Nash c Woolmer b Shepherd	9	– (5) b Johnson	25
†E. W. Jones b Johnson	55	– b Underwood	0
E. A. Moseley not out	70	– not out	1
R. N. S. Hobbs lbw b Jarvis	0		
A. A. Jones b Jarvis	6		
L-b 2, n-b 5	7	B 7, l-b 7, n-b 5	19

1/8 2/17 3/27 4/78 5/115 6/130	266	1/55 2/55 3/138 (7 wkts) 242
7/136 8/235 9/240		4/170 5/220 6/239 7/241

Bonus points – Glamorgan 3, Kent 4.

Bowling: *First Innings*—Jarvis 28–5–100–6; Shepherd 12–2–40–1; Underwood 21–6–53–0; Johnson 8–3–23–1; Woolmer 10–0–43–1. *Second Innings*—Jarvis 6–2–28–0; Shepherd 3–1–12–0; Johnson 19–3–98–5; Underwood 16.5–1–43–2; Ealham 5–0–42–0.

Umpires: R. Aspinall and D. G. L. Evans.

KENT v WARWICKSHIRE

At Canterbury, August 6, 7, 8. Kent won by 163 runs. Kent 20 pts, Warwickshire 5 pts. Woolmer and Tavaré gave Kent a good start with a second-wicket stand of 120 off 40 overs, and Cowdrey took advantage of a spin-dominated attack to hit eleven 4s in his two hours' stay. Amiss and Humpage offered Warwickshire's main resistance with 75 off 26 overs but the last seven wickets fell for 45 runs. Tavaré passed the half-century mark for the fourth successive first-class innings before Kent's declaration left Warwickshire two hundred and eighty-five minutes to score 339. They were never in the hunt and at 155 for seven, with twenty overs to go, it looked all over. However, Willis resisted for eighty minutes and the last-wicket pair were in their eighth over of defiance when Doshi was caught at silly point off the final ball of the match.

Kent

R. A. Woolmer c Oliver b Clifford	81	– c Whitehouse b Small......... 39
G. W. Johnson c Oliver b Willis	5	– (5) b Ferreira 18
C. J. Tavaré c Lloyd b Doshi	55	– b Doshi.................. 62
C. S. Cowdrey b Clifford	87	– lbw b Ferreira.............. 0
*A. G. E. Ealham c Willis b Doshi	36	– (7) not out 26
M. Benson c Lloyd b Clifford	12	– (2) run out 38
†A. P. E. Knott b Doshi	13	– (8) not out 33
J. N. Shepherd not out	9	
R. W. Hills not out	6	– c Humpage b Ferreira 9
L-b 15, n-b 6..........	21	B 4, l-b 5, w 1, n-b 6..... 16

1/18 2/138 3/164 4/232 5/266   (7 wkts) 325   1/71 2/106 3/114   (6 wkts dec.) 241
6/303 7/309   4/169 5/170 6/187

D. L. Underwood and K. B. S. Jarvis did not bat.

Bonus points – Kent 4, Warwickshire 3.

Bowling: *First Innings*—Willis 13–4–31–1; Small 8–2–20–0; Doshi 37–8–125–3; Ferreira 13–5–27–0; Clifford 29–7–101–3. *Second Innings*—Small 13–5–45–1; Willis 12–2–41–0; Ferreira 19–6–63–3; Doshi 12–1–44–1; Clifford 11–5–28–0; Oliver 2–1–4–0.

Warwickshire

D. L. Amiss c Woolmer b Hills	56	– c Ealham b Underwood 44
K. D. Smith c Knott b Jarvis	11	– c sub b Johnson 17
T. A. Lloyd c Tavaré b Hills	0	– b Woolmer b Underwood 3
†G. W. Humpage b Johnson	76	– c Benson b Johnson 23
J. Whitehouse b Underwood	27	– c Ealham b Johnson 15
P. R. Oliver c Tavaré b Underwood	4	– c Tavaré b Underwood 0
A. M. Ferreira c sub b Johnson	4	– b Underwood 16
*R. G. D. Willis c Shepherd b Underwood	13	– c Cowdrey b Shepherd........ 11
G. C. Small not out	9	– lbw b Hills 2
D. R. Doshi b Johnson	8	– c Hills b Johnson 4
C. C. Clifford b Johnson	0	– not out 1
B 6, l-b 3, n-b 11..........	20	B 9, l-b 11, w 1, n-b 18... 39

1/35 2/37 3/112 4/183 5/187 6/195   228   1/49 2/75 3/84 4/110 5/127   175
7/196 8/219 9/227   6/137 7/155 8/164 9/164

Bonus points – Warwickshire 2, Kent 4.

Bowling: *First Innings*—Jarvis 7.2–1–25–1; Shepherd 15–5–35–0; Hills 13.4–4–32–2; Underwood 34–15–53–3; Johnson 21.2–6–49–4; Woolmer 7–4–14–0. *Second Innings*—Shepherd 10–4–16–1; Hills 10–3–36–1; Underwood 39–29–26–4; Johnson 37–16–58–4.

Umpires: R. Aspinall and D. G. L. Evans.

At Leicester, August 9, 11, 12. KENT drew with LEICESTERSHIRE.

KENT v ESSEX

At Folkestone, August 16, 18. Essex won by 50 runs. Essex 16 pts, Kent 4 pts. On a wicket which saw the ball lift and turn, 40 wickets crashed, mainly to the spinners, for 362 runs in just over nine hours of play. Top score for the match was Turner's 35, out of 41, in Essex's first innings when Underwood swept to his best figures of the match. Acfield performed even more economically, bowling Essex to a lead of 42 runs as Kent's last six wickets tumbled for 14 runs in seven overs, and on the second day Underwood, again well supported by Shepherd, bettered his first innings figures to return a match analysis of twelve for 99. Yet there was no stopping Essex and, after the medium pace of Turner and Pringle had done early damage, Acfield and East spun Kent to defeat. The wicket was reported to Lord's by the umpires, and a new wicket hurriedly prepared further down the square for the Gloucestershire match.

Essex

Batsman	1st innings		2nd innings	
G. A. Gooch c Knott b Shepherd	0	– b Shepherd	0
M. S. A. McEvoy c Johnson b Underwood	19	– c Taylor b Shepherd	3
K. S. McEwan c Tavaré b Underwood	15	– b Underwood	30
*K. W. R. Fletcher c Johnson b Underwood	30	– c Taylor b Shepherd	18
B. R. Hardie b Shepherd	1	– b Underwood	6
D. R. Pringle lbw b Shepherd	2	– c Cowdrey b Underwood	0
S. Turner lbw b Underwood	35	– lbw b Underwood	9
R. E. East lbw b Johnson	17	– run out	0
†N. Smith c Hills b Underwood	5	– c Kemp b Underwood	1
J. K. Lever not out	1	– b Underwood	4
D. L. Acfield b Underwood	1	– not out	3
B 1, l-b 2, n-b 1	4	L-b 1, w 1	2

1/0 2/17 3/56 4/57 5/59 6/100   130   1/4 2/5 3/41 4/55 5/55   76
7/113 8/127 9/127   6/58 7/58 8/59 9/69

Bonus points – Kent 4.

Bowling: *First Innings*—Shepherd 14–4–30–3; Underwood 24.1–7–71–6; Johnson 11–0–25–1. *Second Innings*—Shepherd 12–2–31–3; Underwood 7.2–1–28–6; Kemp 4–0–15–0.

Kent

Batsman	1st innings		2nd innings	
G. W. Johnson lbw b Lever	0	– c Fletcher b Turner	10
N. R. Taylor c Acfield	10	– c Hardie b Pringle	0
C. J. Tavaré c Gooch b East	33	– b Turner	4
Asif Iqbal b Pringle	11	– (5) c Smith b East	15
*A. G. E. Ealham lbw b Acfield	2	– (6) c Smith b East	11
C. S. Cowdrey lbw b Acfield	9	– (4) c McEvoy b Acfield	8
†A. P. E. Knott lbw b Acfield	2	– lbw b East	0
J. N. Shepherd c McEwan b East	2	– c McEwan b East	0
R. W. Hills c Fletcher b Acfield	2	– not out	5
N. J. Kemp b Acfield	6	– b Acfield	1
D. L. Underwood not out	10	– lbw b Acfield	0
B 7, l-b 1, n-b 2	10	B 5, l-b 7, n-b 2	14

1/0 2/14 3/33 4/42 5/74 6/76   88   1/7 2/14 3/20 4/32 5/55   68
7/76 8/80 9/81   6/57 7/62 8/63 9/68

Bonus points – Essex 4.

Bowling: *First Innings*—Lever 5–3–4–1; Pringle 11–2–26–1; Acfield 18.4–4–37–6; East 9–5–11–2. *Second Innings*—Pringle 5–2–3–1; Turner 14–5–16–2; Acfield 14.3–6–23–3; East 7–3–12–4.

Umpires: C. Cook and P. B. Wight.

KENT v GLOUCESTERSHIRE

At Folkestone, August 20, 21, 22. Gloucestershire won by 55 runs. Gloucestershire 18 pts, Kent 5 pts. A third-wicket stand of 72 off 30 overs by Sadiq and Zaheer followed by a sound innings from Bainbridge paved the way for the only total of over 200 in the week. As in the previous match, batting first was all important for, although the wicket was not as spiteful as in the Essex game, it always helped the bowlers. Tavaré resisted for two and a half hours as the left-arm spin of Childs and Graveney set up a first innings lead of 44. Gloucestershire slumped to 76 for seven before Graveney joined Zaheer to put on 69 in 80 minutes. Zaheer (one 6 and twelve 4s) scored his 98 out of 136 in 161 minutes with easily the most entertaining and skilled batting of the week. Kent were encouraged by a seventh-wicket stand of 53 in 49 minutes by Cowdrey and Knott, but ironically it was the pace of Brain and the seam of Wilkins which finally sent them to defeat.

Gloucestershire

A. W. Stovold b Shepherd	17	– c Tavaré b Underwood	5
B. C. Broad b Underwood	7	– lbw b Shepherd	2
Sadiq Mohammad c Ealham b Johnson	39	– lbw b Shepherd	2
Zaheer Abbas c Rowe b Johnson	46	– b Johnson	98
P. Bainbridge b Rowe	45	– c Hills b Underwood	6
A. J. Hignell b Underwood	1	– lbw b Johnson	1
D. A. Graveney lbw b Johnson	0	– (9) c Knott b Underwood	29
A. H. Wilkins c Hills b Johnson	4	– lbw b Johnson	1
†A. J. Brassington not out	13	– (10) lbw b Johnson	0
*B. M. Brain c Rowe b Johnson	14	– (7) c Knott b Johnson	2
J. H. Childs b Underwood	0	– not out	7
B 1, l-b 6, w 2, n-b 11	20	L-b 3, w 1, n-b 2	6

1/27 2/29 3/101 4/125 5/134 6/135   206   1/7 2/9 3/23 4/53 5/54   159
7/139 8/185 9/206   6/69 7/76 8/145 9/151

Bonus points – Gloucestershire 2, Kent 4.

Bowling: *First Innings*—Shepherd 15–6–23–1; Hills 10–3–15–0; Underwood 36.1–18–57–3; Johnson 26–9–70–5; Rowe 10–2–21–1. *Second Innings*—Shepherd 12–2–22–2; Hills 5–2–13–0; Underwood 22.1–4–58–3; Johnson 18–4–41–5; Rowe 10–3–19–0.

Kent

R. A. Woolmer lbw b Childs	17	– b Graveney	14
G. W. Johnson run out	13	– c Stovold b Childs	5
C. J. Tavaré run out	34	– lbw b Childs	7
Asif Iqbal b Childs	3	– lbw b Brain	24
R. W. Hills c Stovold b Childs	0	– (10) not out	0
*A. G. E. Ealham c and b Graveney	13	– (5) c Hignell b Childs	6
C. S. Cowdrey c Brain b Graveney	10	– (6) lbw b Wilkins	46
C. J. C. Rowe c Childs b Graveney	25	– (7) lbw b Childs	6
†A. P. E. Knott b Childs	24	– (8) c Brassington b Wilkins	28
J. N. Shepherd b Childs	16	– (9) c sub b Brain	2
D. L. Underwood not out	0	– (11) c Stovold b Brain	0
B 3, l-b 4	7	B 4, l-b 5, w 1	10

1/25 2/35 3/38 4/42 5/63 6/75   162   1/14 2/27 3/35 4/49 5/63   148
7/115 8/122 9/161   6/88 7/141 8/148 9/148

Bonus points – Kent 1, Gloucestershire 4.

Bowling: *First Innings*—Brain 4–1–7–0; Wilkins 2–0–9–0; Graveney 39–14–78–3; Childs 39.1–14–61–5. *Second Innings*—Brain 14.5–2–24–3; Bainbridge 3–0–4–0; Childs 25–6–65–4; Graveney 19–5–42–1; Wilkins 1–1–3–2.

Umpires: C. Cook and P. B. Wight.

At The Oval, August 23, 25, 26. KENT lost to SURREY by nine wickets.

At Worcester, August 30, September 1, 2. KENT drew with WORCESTERSHIRE.

KENT v MIDDLESEX

At Canterbury, September 3, 4, 5. Drawn. Kent 6 pts, Middlesex 5 pts. In a match dominated by spin bowlers Middlesex struggled until Barlow (seven 4s) and Gatting added 73 off sixteen overs for the fifth wicket. Kent fared even worse, slumping to 107 for seven before Knott came in to hit eight 4s in a stay of two and a half hours, steering his team to an unexpected lead. Brearley (eleven 4s) batted brilliantly over four hours when Middlesex faltered in their second innings as Underwood took seven wickets for 77 runs, his best innings return for the season. Kent, needing 204 in 165 minutes, were again toiling against the spin of Edmonds and Emburey when bad light and rain brought an all-too-familiar end to an interesting contest.

Middlesex

*J. M. Brearley b Jarvis	18	– c Taylor b Underwood	104
†P. R. Downton b Underwood	35	– lbw b Underwood	1
C. T. Radley c Taylor b Underwood	12	– b Underwood	9
G. D. Barlow st Knott b Johnson	71	– b Underwood	4
R. O. Butcher b Underwood	8	– (6) c Benson b Underwood	37
M. W. Gatting b Underwood	36	– (5) b Johnson	6
P. H. Edmonds c Cowdrey b Johnson	9	– c Taylor b Jarvis	6
J. E. Emburey c Cowdrey b Johnson	20	– c Cowdrey b Underwood	17
V. A. P. van der Bijl c Cowdrey b Johnson	5	– not out	8
M. W. W. Selvey not out	13	– lbw b Underwood	1
S. P. Hughes b Johnson	0		
B 4, l-b 5, n-b 6	15	B 2, l-b 3, n-b 17	22

1/30 2/64 3/75 4/83 5/156 6/184   242 1/10 2/43 3/51 (9 wkts dec.) 215
7/211 8/225 9/229   4/73 5/142 6/168 7/197
                      8/211 9/215

Bonus points – Middlesex 2, Kent 4.

Bowling: *First Innings*—Jarvis 7–2–16–1; Kemp 9–1–38–0; Underwood 36–11–85–4; Johnson 28.5–8–88–5. *Second Innings*—Jarvis 22–3–68–1; Kemp 2–0–3–0; Underwood 38–11–75–7; Johnson 18–3–47–1.

Kent

R. A. Woolmer c Downton b Edmonds	21	– c Downton b Edmonds	8
N. R. Taylor c Downton b Edmonds	16	– c Emburey b Edmonds	27
C. J. Tavaré c Hughes b Emburey	1	– c Brearley b Edmonds	5
C. S. Cowdrey c Hughes b Edmonds	26	– b Emburey	8
Asif Iqbal st Downton b Emburey	26	– not out	16
M. Benson b Emburey	5	– not out	1
N. J. Kemp st Downton b Edmonds	6		
G. W. Johnson c Butcher b Edmonds	42		
*†A. P. E. Knott not out	85		
D. L. Underwood c Butcher b Emburey	4		
K. B. S. Jarvis b Emburey	0		
B 8, l-b 12, n-b 2	22	L-b 6, w 1	7

1/39 2/40 3/50 4/74 5/96 6/105   254 1/15 2/29 3/50 (4 wkts) 72
7/107 8/219 9/230   4/64

Bonus points – Kent 2, Middlesex 3 (Score at 100 overs: 227-8).

Bowling: *First Innings*—Selvey 5–1–7–0; Hughes 7–3–12–0; Edmonds 51–18–94–5; Emburey 45.2–10–105–5; van der Bijl 3–1–10–0; Radley 1–0–4–0. *Second Innings*—van der Bijl 3–3–0–0; Selvey 2–0–3–0; Emburey 16–2–29–1; Edmonds 15–5–33–3.

Umpires: R. Palmer and D. Shackleton.

LANCASHIRE

Patron – HM THE QUEEN

President – W. D. CRUMBLEHULME

Secretary – C. D. HASSELL
County Cricket Ground, Old Trafford, Manchester M16 0PX

Cricket Manager – J. D. BOND

Captain – F. C. HAYES (1980), C. H. LLOYD (1981)

| G. Fowler | County Badge | A. Kennedy |

With the arrival of Jack Bond as the club's first-ever cricket manager, Lancashire's main task in 1980 was to rebuild a side that had failed to win major honours since the early seventies. In the event the team's fifteenth position in the Schweppes County Championship and thirteenth placing in the John Player League, plus an early dismissal from the Gillette Cup, served to stress the magnitude of the task facing the new manager. Bond promised no cricketing "miracles" and produced none. He was badly handicapped by the defection of Barry Wood to Derbyshire and the absence of Clive Lloyd with the West Indian touring team, factors that cost Lancashire a lot of runs and reduced the ranks of experienced batsmen to two – the captain, Frank Hayes, and David Lloyd, who shared a heavy burden. Although Andrew Kennedy had his best season for some years and topped 1,000 runs, as did Hayes, it was always obvious the side lacked depth when it came to scoring.

Bernard Reidy began the season in great style – he was awarded a county cap in May – but injury and illness handicapped this hard-hitting batsman and useful seam bowler and too much responsibility had to be placed on young newcomers. Ian Cockbain and Graeme Fowler showed promising form at times, but John Abrahams faded disappointingly. Hopes that the long-serving Harry Pilling could make a telling comeback to first-class cricket were not realised. Geoff Trim also failed to make an impact, but a nineteen-year-old from Bolton, Steve O'Shaughnessy, who has the makings of an excellent all-rounder, was given every chance late in a season that saw bad weather, a spate of injuries, and illness combine to off-set a good start when all the Benson and Hedges Cup group matches were won impressively in pleasant sunshine and on fast pitches.

The bowling, like the batting, lacked experience. Willie Hogg suffered an attack of glandular fever before the season commenced and was slow to find form once he recovered. A bowler of genuine pace Hogg was usually posing problems, and a lack of control in harnessing line to length, plus a tendency to bowl no balls, did not prevent him from picking up more than 50 wickets for the first time. Australian Mick Malone, who had shown such good form when introduced into the side at the end of 1979, returned to Old Trafford handicapped by a strained side and he also suffered from recurring trouble with his bowling elbow. Consequently he was never the force expected, and with Bob Ratcliffe out of action, for almost the whole summer with one injury after another, Lancashire had problems both with the old ball and the new. Peter Lee failed to find form, and although spinners Jack Simmons and David Hughes remained steady, neither was accurate nor consistent enough to take command. Indeed, Lancashire were so worried about their shortcomings in attack that they signed South African all-rounder Neal Radford from a Lancashire League club in readiness for 1981.

Chris Scott was proving himself an excellent wicket-keeper when he fractured a thumb against Sussex and missed the last month of the season. As in 1979 Lancashire appeared to suffer more than most counties with injuries, only Kennedy coming through the campaign without damage. The eventual reappearance of Clive Lloyd, who takes over the captaincy from Hayes in 1981, illustrated how seriously Lancashire's lack of experienced batting has been felt. His return in time to hit a century in the Roses game at Old Trafford earned Lancashire their first Championship victory over the ancient foe for eight years; but by then support in general and gate receipts in particular had dwindled to a low ebb. Much remains to be done, but manager Bond has faith in his youngsters and pleads for time to allow them to develop. While having a free hand to continue with the rebuilding process, he warns that time and patience are essential priorities before Lancashire become bouyant and successful again. – John Kay.

LANCASHIRE

[*Press Association*]

Back row: G. E. Trim, I. Cockbain, M. F. Malone, P. J. W. Allott, G. Fowler, S. J. O'Shaughnessy. *Middle row:* J. Bond (*manager*), D. Hayes, C. J. Scott, A. Kennedy, J. Abrahams, B. W. Reidy, J. Savage (*coach*). *Front row:* D. P. Hughes, H. Pilling, J. Simmons, F. C. Hayes (*captain*), D. Lloyd, R. M. Ratcliffe, P. G. Lee.

LANCASHIRE RESULTS

All First-class Matches – Played 22: Won 5, Lost 3, Drawn 14. Abandoned 2.

County Championship Matches – Played 20: Won 4, Lost 3, Drawn 13. Abandoned 2.

Bonus points – Batting 26, Bowling 58.

COUNTY CHAMPIONSHIP AVERAGES

BATTING

	Birthplace	Matches	Inns	Not Outs	Runs	Highest Inns	Avge
C. H. Lloyd	*Guyana, WI*	2	3	0	134	101	44.66
F. C. Hayes	*Preston*	19	31	4	1,013	94*	37.51
D. Lloyd	*Accrington*	17	28	5	752	112*	32.69
A. Kennedy	*Blackburn*	20	35	2	1,071	169*	32.45
B. W. Reidy	*Whalley*	15	26	5	653	110*	31.09
J. Simmons	*Clayton-le-Moors*	20	29	6	675	96	29.34
D. P. Hughes	*Newton-le-Willows*	16	19	6	350	66*	26.92
G. Fowler	*Accrington*	8	10	1	228	106*	25.33
S. J. O'Shaughnessy ..	*Bury*	2	3	1	40	28	20.00
I. Cockbain	*Bootle*	17	27	6	388	69*	18.47
N. V. Radford	*Luanshya, N. Rhod.*	3	6	0	100	34	16.66
M. F. Malone	*Perth, WA*	15	14	3	181	38	16.45
H. Pilling	*Ashton-under-Lyne*	3	6	1	80	56*	16.00
J. Abrahams	*Cape Town, SA*	8	13	0	181	59	13.92
G. E. Trim	*Openshaw*	5	8	0	105	31	13.12
R. M. Ratcliffe	*Accrington*	4	3	0	38	26	12.66
P. J. W. Allott	*Altrincham*	10	10	3	68	30*	9.71
C. J. Scott	*Swinton*	16	18	5	75	14	5.76
W. Hogg	*Ulverston*	14	13	5	18	5*	2.25
P. G. Lee	*Arthingworth*	6	3	1	0	0*	0.00

* Signifies not out.

BOWLING

	Overs	Maidens	Runs	Wickets	Average
P. J. W. Allott	177	47	452	23	19.65
W. Hogg	323.2	66	1,058	50	21.16
M. F. Malone	451.5	127	1,165	45	25.88
B. W. Reidy	188.2	46	543	19	28.57
D. P. Hughes	266.1	74	720	22	32.72
D. Lloyd	136.2	26	454	12	37.83
J. Simmons..........	374.3	106	910	23	39.56
P. G. Lee	153.1	43	446	10	44.60

Also bowled: J. Abrahams 4–1–14–0; A. Kennedy 45–9–180–4; S. J. O'Shaughnessy 15–4–41–1; N. V. Radford 32.5–6–150–2; R. M. Ratcliffe 88.1–30–238–2.

HUNDREDS

The following five three-figure innings were played for Lancashire in County Championship matches – G. Fowler 106* v Nottinghamshire (Manchester); A. Kennedy 169* v Derbyshire (Manchester); C. H. Lloyd 101 v Yorkshire (Manchester); D. Lloyd 112* v Hampshire (Portsmouth); B. W. Reidy 110* v Worcestershire (Manchester).

LANCASHIRE v DERBYSHIRE

At Manchester, April 30, May 1, 2. Drawn. Lancashire 7 pts, Derbyshire 3 pts. After the driest April in years Old Trafford provided a hard and fast pitch for its opening match and batsmen enjoyed themselves immensely in an encounter which produced 1,077 runs for the fall of sixteen wickets. After winning the toss Derbyshire totalled 248 for seven, with Barnett producing a highly promising 57 and Miller a defiant 78. Lancashire replied with 326 for four, owing most to Kennedy, who hit one 6 and 26 4s in an unbeaten 169, and with Hayes giving excellent support the home side gained a lead of 78 runs. Wright (twenty boundaries) and Kirsten (three 6s and twenty 4s) added 321 runs for Derbyshire's second wicket in majestic manner before the declaration left Lancashire to hit 263 runs in 155 minutes. Kennedy again batted superbly but the home side were still 100 runs short, with six overs and six wickets in hand, when the inevitable was realised.

Derbyshire

J. G. Wright c Lloyd b Lee	2	– not out	166
A. Hill c Scott b Malone	2	– c Scott b Lee	5
P. N. Kirsten c Scott b Lee	31	– not out	162
D. S. Steele c Simmons b Lee	1		
K. J. Barnett lbw b Lee	57		
A. J. Borrington c Pilling b Simmons	36		
*G. Miller not out	78		
†R. W. Taylor run out	25		
C. J. Tunnicliffe not out	10		
L-b 6	6	L-b 4, n-b 3	7

1/6 2/7 3/73 4/108 5/108   (7 wkts) 248   1/19   (1 wkt dec.) 340
6/148 7/225

R. C. Wincer and S. Oldham did not bat.

Bonus points – Derbyshire 2, Lancashire 3.

Bowling: *First Innings*—Malone 31–9–71–1; Lee 30–9–70–4; Ratcliffe 25–9–58–0; Lloyd 1–0–9–0; Simmons 13–3–34–1. *Second Innings*—Malone 16–6–35–0; Lee 17–5–58–1; Ratcliffe 8–2–35–0; Kennedy 11–1–52–0; Lloyd 14–1–58–0; Simmons 25–2–95–0.

Lancashire

A. Kennedy not out	169	– b Miller	73
G. E. Trim c Tunnicliffe b Miller	9	– b Barnett	10
H. Pilling c Taylor b Wincer	16	– not out	56
*F. C. Hayes b Oldham	72	– c Hill b Oldham	3
D. Lloyd c Barnett b Steele	28	– (6) not out	2
J. Simmons not out	17	– (5) lbw b Oldham	0
L-b 4, n-b 11	15	B 9, l-b 4, n-b 6	19

1/35 2/79 3/216 4/292   (4 wkts) 326   1/33 2/135 3/148   (4 wkts) 163
                                 4/149

I. Cockbain, R. M. Ratcliffe, †C. J. Scott, M. F. Malone and P. G. Lee did not bat.

Bonus points – Lancashire 4, Derbyshire 1.

Bowling: *First Innings*—Oldham 23–8–62–1; Tunnicliffe 18–4–75–0; Miller 24–13–50–1; Steele 15–2–58–1; Wincer 20–5–66–1. *Second Innings*—Oldham 9–1–23–2; Tunnicliffe 3–0–10–0; Barnett 11–1–50–1; Steele 9–3–24–0; Miller 13–6–26–1; Kirsten 3–1–11–0.

Umpires: R. Julian and R. Aspinall.

At Lord's, May 3, 5, 6. LANCASHIRE drew with MIDDLESEX.

LANCASHIRE v WORCESTERSHIRE

At Manchester, May 7, 8, 9. Lancashire won by four wickets. Lancashire 16 pts, Worcestershire 5 pts. On a pitch of variable pace and bounce batsmen struggled on the first two days, the best cricket coming on the third when Lancashire, set to hit 262 runs in four and threequarter hours, lost their first six batsmen for 90. However, an unbeaten partnership of 175 between Reidy (eighteen boundaries) and Simmons took them to victory. After winning the toss Worcestershire were dismissed for 163, Malone taking five for 64; but Lancashire found that total beyond them as Pridgeon took five for 50. In their second innings Hemsley and Ormrod scored half-centuries for Worcestershire while Lloyd enjoyed a return of four for 39 and Malone's four for 69 took his match figures to nine for 133 for £225 in sponsorship money.

Worcestershire

J. A. Ormrod c Cockbain b Malone	5	– c Kennedy b Lloyd	61
G. M. Turner c Cockbain b Malone	0	– c Cockbain b Malone	7
B. J. R. Jones c Simmons b Malone	19	– c Cockbain b Malone	17
E. J. O. Hemsley c Scott b Reidy	29	– run out	76
Younis Ahmed c Scott b Ratcliffe	27	– c Scott b Malone	24
D. N. Patel lbw b Reidy	4	– c Scott b Lloyd	4
†D. J. Humphries b Reidy	47	– lbw b Lloyd	6
J. D. Inchmore c Hayes b Malone	9	– c Trim b Lloyd	0
H. Alleyne lbw b Malone	0	– (10) lbw b Simmons	22
*N. Gifford not out	18	– (9) lbw b Malone	10
A. P. Pridgeon b Ratcliffe	4	– not out	0
L-b 4	4	B 1, l-b 1, n-b 5	7

1/0 2/7 3/36 4/79 5/81	163	1/12 2/58 3/167 4/167 5/173 234
6/87 7/102 8/102 9/147		6/187 7/187 8/205 9/226

Bonus points – Worcestershire 1, Lancashire 4.

Bowling: *First Innings*—Malone 26–10–64–5; Reidy 21–9–43–3; Ratcliffe 19.1–7–48–2; Simmons 8–4–4–0. *Second Innings*—Malone 27–6–69–4; Reidy 10–2–29–0; Ratcliffe 13–5–30–0; Simmons 16.2–5–39–1; Kennedy 6–0–21–0; Lloyd 17–7–39–4.

Lancashire

A. Kennedy b Alleyne	14	– c Ormrod b Gifford	39
G. E. Trim c Hemsley b Pridgeon	31	– b Humphries b Gifford	23
H. Pilling b Alleyne	0	– c Hemsley b Alleyne	1
*F. C. Hayes c Humphries b Pridgeon	10	– c Turner b Pridgeon	5
R. M. Ratcliffe b Alleyne	7		
D. Lloyd c Younis b Inchmore	11	– (5) st Humphries b Gifford	12
I. Cockbain lbw b Pridgeon	11	– (6) b Pridgeon	4
B. W. Reidy lbw b Pridgeon	4	– (7) not out	110
J. Simmons c Ormrod c Pridgeon	10	– (8) not out	53
†C. J. Scott not out	6		
M. F. Malone c Humphries b Inchmore	9		
B 4, l-b 8, w 1, n-b 10	23	B 2, l-b 10, w 1, n-b 5	18

1/19 2/21 3/44 4/65 5/87	136	1/62 2/63 3/67 (6 wkts) 265
6/90 7/95 8/110 9/121		4/85 5/85 6/90

Bonus points – Worcestershire 4.

Bowling: *First Innings*—Alleyne 17–6–38–3; Inchmore 17.4–7–23–2; Pridgeon 29–11–50–5; Gifford 3–2–2–0. *Second Innings*—Alleyne 24–6–81–1; Inchmore 13–1–53–0; Pridgeon 13–6–23–2; Gifford 29–8–68–3; Patel 5–0–22–0.

Umpires: R. Aspinall and D. G. L. Evans.

At Leeds, May 24, 26, 27. LANCASHIRE drew with YORKSHIRE.

LANCASHIRE v GLAMORGAN

At Manchester, May 28, 29, 30. Drawn. Lancashire 6 pts, Glamorgan 5 pts. Glamorgan, electing to bat, had to battle hard for their total of 222 after rain had delayed the start until after lunch. The visitors owed most to Hopkins (one 6 and sixteen 4s), who batted for almost four and a half hours to reach 105. In reply, Lancashire were troubled by the left-arm seam bowling of Nash. Half the home side had gone at 91 but Simmons stayed two and a half hours to hit a superb 95 before close of play, putting on an unbroken 78 for the ninth wicket with Malone. Simmons hit one 6 and fifteen 4s but, when rain again intervened on the last day, Lancashire declared, leaving him 5 runs short of his century.

Glamorgan

A. Jones c Simmons b Hogg	10	– b Hughes	47
J. A. Hopkins lbw b Malone	105	– b Simmons	11
D. A. Francis retired hurt	2		
Javed Miandad lbw b Reidy	9	– (3) c Kennedy b Hughes	82
N. G. Featherstone lbw b Reidy	7	– (4) not out	37
G. C. Holmes c Simmons b Hogg	29	– (5) c Abrahams b Hughes	11
†E. W. Jones c Scott b Hogg	0	– (6) not out	22
*M. A. Nash c Scott b Malone	16		
B. J. Lloyd b Malone	0		
E. A. Moseley not out	29		
A. A. Jones c Scott b Malone	0		
B 4, l-b 2, w 1, n-b 8	15	B 2, l-b 1	3

1/26 2/49 3/61 4/144 5/144 6/165   222   1/16 2/111   (4 wkts) 213
7/169 8/218 9/222   3/158 4/178

Bonus points – Glamorgan 2, Lancashire 4.

Bowling: *First Innings*—Malone 22.1–10–48–4; Hogg 19–2–60–3; Reidy 15–4–46–2; Hughes 16–3–35–0; Simmons 10–5–18–0. *Second Innings*—Malone 10–6–13–0; Reidy 10–1–35–0; Hughes 24–5–70–3; Simmons 22–4–60–1; Kennedy 11–5–18–0; Abrahams 4–1–14–0.

Lancashire

A. Kennedy lbw b Nash	16	D. P. Hughes b A. A. Jones	3
G. E. Trim lbw b Nash	20	†C. J. Scott lbw b Nash	1
J. Abrahams c Hopkins b Nash	4	M. F. Malone not out	18
*F. C. Hayes c Nash b Moseley	28	B 5, l-b 9, w 2, n-b 4	20
B. W. Reidy b Moseley	14		
I. Cockbain lbw b A. A. Jones	2	1/23 2/38 3/51 4/89 (8 wkts dec.) 221	
J. Simmons not out	95	5/91 6/124 7/134 8/143	

W. Hogg did not bat.

Bonus points – Lancashire 2, Glamorgan 3.

Bowling: Nash 35–17–58–4; A. A. Jones 19–4–52–2; Moseley 20–6–60–2; Lloyd 6–5–8–0; Holmes 4–2–7–0; Miandad 3–1–16–0.

Umpires: J. van Geloven and T. W. Spencer.

LANCASHIRE v WARWICKSHIRE

At Liverpool, May 31, June 2, 3. Drawn. Lancashire 2 pts, Warwickshire 4 pts. With no play possible on the first day and only three hours on the second, the final day produced three declarations and a thrilling finish as Lancashire failed by 2 runs to reach a target of 221 in two hours. When Warwickshire elected to take first use of a good batting pitch, Amiss saw his side to 192 for two before rain caused an early adjournment. On the final day Warwickshire batted on for half an hour before declaring, Amiss hitting one 6 and seventeen 4s after being missed at 41 and 113. Lancashire lost their first four batsmen for 55, and were saved from following on by Reidy who hit two 6s and eleven 4s in an unbeaten 84. Warwickshire hammered 122 for four in fifty minutes before setting the final challenge. Lancashire, given a good start with a half-century opening partnership, were always in with a chance, requiring 117 from the last twenty overs and 65 from the last ten. However, Hayes, needing 11 from the last over, failed by 2 runs in a glorious finale.

Warwickshire

D. L. Amiss not out	117	– c Hughes b Kennedy	18
K. D. Smith c Scott b Malone	33		
T. A. Lloyd c Simmons b Hughes	2	– (6) not out	2
J. A. Claughton c and b Hughes	43	– (3) st Scott b Kennedy	8
P. R. Oliver c Hughes b Malone	1		
†G. W. Humpage not out	16	– (2) b Malone	39
A. M. Ferreira (did not bat)		– (4) b Kennedy	27
S. J. Rouse (did not bat)		– (5) not out	24
L-b 2, w 4, n-b 2	8	L-b 3, n-b 1	4

1/60 2/123 3/219	(4 wkts dec.) 250	1/46 2/64 (4 wkts dec.) 122
4/224		3/72 4/117

G. C. Small, *R. G. D. Willis and D. R. Doshi did not bat.

Bonus points – Warwickshire 3, Lancashire 1.

Bowling: *First Innings*—Hogg 18–4–42–0; Malone 15–1–60–2; Reidy 8–1–40–0; Hughes 17.1–2–77–2; Simmons 7–0–23–0. *Second Innings*—Malone 6–1–31–1; Kennedy 8–1–58–3; Hughes 2–0–29–0.

Lancashire

A. Kennedy c Amiss b Ferreira	27	– c Ferreira b Oliver	52
G. E. Trim c Oliver b Rouse	0		
J. Abrahams c Humpage b Willis	3	– (2) c Claughton b Small	17
*F. C. Hayes c Oliver b Ferreira	22	– (4) not out	58
B. W. Reidy not out	84	– (3) c Small b Oliver	31
I. Cockbain not out	13	– (5) c Claughton b Doshi	9
J. Simmons (did not bat)		– (6) b Rouse	21
D. P. Hughes (did not bat)		– (7) c Willis b Rouse	4
M. F. Malone (did not bat)		– (8) run out	5
†C. J. Scott (did not bat)		– (9) run out	0
L-b 2, n-b 1	3	B 1, l-b 8, w 2, n-b 11	22

1/2 2/21 3/50 4/55	(4 wkts dec.) 152	1/50 2/104 (8 wkts) 219
		3/124 4/168 5/198 6/204
		7/210 8/218

W. Hogg did not bat.

Bonus points – Lancashire 1, Warwickshire 1.

Bowling: *First Innings*—Willis 8–2–32–1; Rouse 7–2–22–1; Doshi 17–5–50–0; Ferreira 6–1–23–2; Oliver 4–0–22–0. *Second Innings*—Willis 6–0–19–0; Rouse 4–0–25–2; Doshi 14–2–55–1; Small 4–0–30–1; Oliver 9–0–68–2.

Umpires: D. J. Dennis and T. W. Spencer.

At Oxford, June 4, 5, 6. LANCASHIRE beat OXFORD UNIVERSITY by ten wickets.

LANCASHIRE v NOTTINGHAMSHIRE

At Manchester, June 7, 9, 10. Lancashire won by five wickets. Lancashire 18 pts, Nottinghamshire 7 pts. A superb 170 by Randall was the corner-stone of Nottinghamshire's innings. Rice's decision to bat first on an easy-paced wicket proved correct as Randall dominated the day's play, hitting a 6 and 21 4s in a display marred only by a very difficult chance when 15 and an easier one when 138. Lancashire, 48 for one at close of play, slumped to 95 for six on the Monday to Bore and Hemmings and were rescued by Fowler, a 23-year-old left-hander playing in only his second Championship match. He batted delightfully to register his maiden century and Lancashire finished only 41 runs behind. No play was possible until after tea on the third day when the captains decided to go on even though the umpires were dubious about conditions. A sporting Nottinghamshire declaration at their overnight score of 156 for six set Lancashire to make 198 in seventy minutes plus 20 overs which, with Lloyd and Reidy leading the way, they accomplished with eleven balls to spare.

Nottinghamshire

P. A. Todd lbw b Reidy	20	– c Lloyd b Hughes	69
B. Hassan lbw b Lee	3	– lbw b Reidy	2
D. W. Randall b Simmons	170	– c Scott b Simmons	19
*C. E. B. Rice c Hughes b Simmons	30	– (5) c sub b Simmons	6
H. T. Tunnicliffe b Lee	6	– (4) c sub b Simmons	4
J. D. Birch b Hughes	31	– not out	37
†C. C. Curzon st Scott b Lloyd	15	– c Hughes b Simmons	0
K. S. Mackintosh b Simmons	1	– not out	13
E. E. Hemmings not out	13		
M. K. Bore b Lloyd	0		
K. E. Cooper c Reidy b Simmons	5		
B 5, l-b 6	11	L-b 6	6

1/8 2/47 3/105 4/173 5/236   305   1/20 2/91 3/100   (6 wkts dec.) 156
6/267 7/268 8/294 9/299   4/100 5/113 6/119

Bonus points – Nottinghamshire 4, Lancashire 4.

Bowling: *First Innings*—Malone 15–3–34–0; Lee 20–1–83–2; Reidy 13–3–47–1; Hughes 15–2–49–1; Simmons 19–6–48–4; Lloyd 13.2–0–33–2. *Second Innings*—Lee 4–0–26–0; Reidy 5–0–18–1; Hughes 14–4–41–1; Simmons 19–6–43–4; Lloyd 4–2–22–0.

Lancashire

A. Kennedy c Curzon b Bore	18	– lbw b Hemmings	25
D. Lloyd st Curzon b Hemmings	33	– not out	80
J. Abrahams c Curzon b Hemmings	2	– (5) c Curzon b Bore	10
B. W. Reidy c Birch b Bore	9	– c Birch b Bore	52
I. Cockbain lbw b Hemmings	14	– (7) not out	12
*J. Simmons c Rice b Bore	4	– (3) c Hassan b Cooper	12
G. Fowler not out	106	– (6) c Rice b Bore	6
D. P. Hughes c Rice b Bore	50		
†C. J. Scott run out	1		
M. F. Malone not out	20		
L-b 5, n-b 2	7	L-b 4	4

1/34 2/52 3/57 4/70 5/74   (8 wkts) 264   1/58 2/81 3/148   (5 wkts) 199
6/95 7/192 8/213   4/167 5/177

P. G. Lee did not bat.

Bonus points – Lancashire 2, Nottinghamshire 3 (Score at 100 overs: 230-8).

Bowling: *First Innings*—Cooper 23–6–57–0; Mackintosh 11–4–21–0; Bore 34–13–82–4; Hemmings 36–15–97–3. *Second Innings*—Cooper 11–0–63–1; Mackintosh 4–0–29–0; Bore 12.1–1–60–3; Hemmings 12–0–43–1.

Umpires: B. J. Meyer and K. E. Palmer.

At Bath, June 14, 16, 17. SOMERSET v LANCASHIRE. Abandoned.

At Bristol, June 18, 19, 20. LANCASHIRE drew with GLOUCESTERSHIRE.

LANCASHIRE v KENT

At Manchester, June 21, 23, 24. Drawn. Only ninety-five minutes cricket was possible over three days. After winning the toss, Kent drearily scored 27 runs from 25 overs in the seventy-five minutes play after tea on the first day and added another 13 in 7.1 overs on the second. The third day was completely washed out.

Kent

C. J. C. Rowe not out	....	26
N. R. Taylor not out	....	13
L-b 1	....	1

(no wkt) 40

M. Benson, C. S. Cowdrey, *A. G. E. Ealham, G. W. Johnson, †S. N. V. Waterton, J. N. Shepherd, G. R. Dilley, G. D. Spelman and K. B. S. Jarvis did not bat.

Bowling: Malone 13–6–11–0; Allott 6–2–12–0; Hughes 10–5–14–0; Simmons 3.1–1–2–0.

Lancashire

A. Kennedy, D. Lloyd, I. Cockbain, *F. C. Hayes, G. Fowler, J. Simmons, D. P. Hughes, R. M. Ratcliffe, †C. J. Scott, P. J. W. Allott, M. F. Malone.

Umpires: R. Julian and J. van Geloven.

LANCASHIRE v SURREY

At Manchester, June 25, 26, 27. Drawn. Surrey 4 pts. There was no play on the first day and thunderstorms delayed the start until after lunch on the second when Lancashire were dismissed cheaply after being put in. The seam bowling of Jackman, who returned his best figures in England, eight for 58, and Knight, who bowled nineteen overs for only 13 runs and two wickets, was too much for all but Cockbain, Hayes and Simmons. Surrey reached 25 for the loss of Butcher before the close, and declared 52 runs behind on the third day. Lancashire slumped to 10 for three but Abrahams played a stubborn defensive innings and saved the game with assistance from Hayes and Radford. Knight's captaincy was a leading feature in a game where his team were always playing the more positive cricket.

Lancashire

A. Kennedy lbw b Jackman	6	– (2) c Roope b Jackman	4
D. Lloyd b Knight	19	– (1) b Clarke	0
I. Cockbain lbw b Jackman	41	– b Clarke	2
*F. C. Hayes c Richards b Jackman	33	– c Knight b Clarke	18
J. Abrahams c Roope b Jackman	0	– c Roope b Pocock	59
J. Simmons c Roope b Jackman	23	– c Clarke b Jackman	10
D. P. Hughes c Knight b Jackman	4	– b Jackman	7
N. Radford b Jackman	0	– b Intikhab	33
†C. J. Scott b Knight	5	– b Intikhab	14
M. F. Malone c Richards b Jackman	0	– (11) not out	8
W. Hogg not out	0	– (10) c Smith b Pocock	5
B 8, l-b 6, n-b 1	15	L-b 6, n-b 3	9

1/21 2/43 3/98 4/106 5/107 6/119   146   1/0 2/10 3/10 4/40 5/60   169
7/119 8/142 9/146   6/72 7/112 8/156 9/158

Bonus points – Surrey 4.

Bowling: *First Innings*—Clarke 9–0–40–0; Jackman 25.4–7–58–8; Knight 19–12–13–2; Pocock 6–1–20–0. *Second Innings*—Clarke 14–3–36–3; Jackman 13–3–33–3; Pocock 21–8–44–2; Intikhab 17–5–47–2.

Surrey

A. R. Butcher c Lloyd b Hogg 2
G. S. Clinton not out 45
*R. D. V. Knight lbw b Hogg. 16
D. M. Smith not out 25
       N-b 6 6

1/2 2/44   (2 wkts dec.) 94

G. R. J. Roope, D. B. Pauline, Intikhab Alam, †C. J. Richards, R. D. Jackman, S. T. Clarke and P. I. Pocock did not bat.

  Bowling: Hogg 11–1–32–2; Malone 10–1–30–0; Simmons 2–1–1–0; Radford 7.5–3–25–0.

        Umpires: J. van Geloven and R. Julian.

At Leicester, June 28, 30, July 1. LANCASHIRE drew with LEICESTERSHIRE.

At Birmingham, July 5, 7, 8. LANCASHIRE drew with WARWICKSHIRE.

At Stourport-on-Severn, July 12, 14, 15. LANCASHIRE lost to WORCESTERSHIRE by an innings and 153 runs.

LANCASHIRE v NORTHAMPTONSHIRE

At Southport, July 23, 24, 25. Drawn. Lancashire 5 pts, Northamptonshire 4 pts. Northamptonshire elected to bat on a green and grassy pitch and, with the pace bowlers enjoying tremendous lift and movement, they were all out before tea in the face of impressive returns by Hogg and Malone. Lancashire were also in trouble, losing their first four wickets for 32 runs. However, Hayes and Simmons reshaped the innings and, with Malone and Hogg adding 30 for the last wicket, the home side achieved a first innings lead of 106 as the pitch gradually eased. Allan Lamb dominated Northamptonshire's second innings with an aggressive century, and on the last morning wicket-keeper Sharp was within sight of his first century in twelve years of Championship cricket. Set a target of 278 in four hours, Lancashire were in disarray when six batsmen had fallen for 86. But Hayes played a superb innings and, with sound support from Radford and Malone – who hit off-spinner Williams for four 6s – he rallied his side to within sight of victory before falling at 235 with six overs to go. Scott and Hogg then wisely settled for a draw.

Northamptonshire

G. Cook c Hughes b Hogg.	9	– c Reidy b Malone.	2
R. M. Carter c Cockbain b Malone	5	– c Kennedy b Hogg	15
R. G. Williams c Hughes b Malone	16	– c Lloyd b Hogg	47
A. J. Lamb c Radford b Hogg	9	– lbw b Malone	117
R. J. Boyd-Moss c Cockbain b Malone	2	– b Hughes	12
T. J. Yardley c Simmons b Hogg	14	– c Scott b Simmons	5
†G. Sharp c Kennedy b Hogg	4	– c Scott b Hughes	94
*P. J. Watts not out	27	– c Hayes b Reidy	7
Sarfraz Nawaz c Scott b Malone	1	– c Radford b Hogg	50
T. M. Lamb c Simmons b Radford.	0	– not out	9
B. J. Griffiths lbw b Hogg.	1	– b Hogg.	0
L-b 1	1	B 9, l-b 5, w 3, n-b 8	25

1/10 2/14 3/39 4/41 5/43 6/56   89   1/8 2/73 3/84 4/144 5/167   383
7/61 8/62 9/80   6/263 7/301 8/374 9/380

                 Bonus points – Lancashire 4.

  Bowling: *First Innings*—Hogg 17.3–4–39–5; Malone 15–5–43–4; Radford 2–1–6–1. *Second Innings*—Hogg 28.5–8–97–4; Malone 28–11–68–2; Radford 10–1–63–0; Reidy 19–4–52–1; Hughes 11–2–38–2; Simmons 16–7–40–1.

Lancashire

A. Kennedy c T. M. Lamb b Sarfraz	35	1 – c Cook b T. M. Lamb	35
D. Lloyd c Carter b Griffiths	11	– c Sharp b Sarfraz	1
I. Cockbain c Watts b Griffiths	0	– c Cook b Williams	25
*F. C. Hayes c A. J. Lamb b Griffiths	57	– c Yardley b T. M. Lamb	87
B. W. Reidy b Griffiths	8	– c Sharp b Williams	7
J. Simmons c A. J. Lamb b Sarfraz	61	– c A. J. Lamb b Williams	0
D. P. Hughes c Carter b Griffiths	6	– c Sharp b T. M. Lamb	1
N. Radford b Sarfraz	1	– c Watts b Williams	34
†C. J. Scott c Sharp b Sarfraz	0	– (10) not out	7
M. F. Malone b Sarfraz	38	– (9) lbw b T. M. Lamb	38
W. Hogg not out	4	– not out	1
L-b 3, n-b 5	8	B 4, n-b 2	6

1/11 2/11 3/17 4/32 5/129 6/141   195   1/2 2/61 3/65 4/81   (9 wkts) 242
7/144 8/144 9/165   5/81 6/86 7/155
                                          8/220 9/235

Bonus points – Lancashire 1, Northamptonshire 4.

Bowling: *First Innings*—Sarfraz 21.2–6–62–5; Griffiths 24–4–100–5; T. M. Lamb 6–2–14–0; Williams 5–1–11–0. *Second Innings*—Sarfraz 16–5–49–1; Griffiths 12–1–58–0; T. M. Lamb 19–6–56–4; Williams 26–10–73–4.

Umpires: A. Jepson and R. Aspinall.

At Portsmouth, July 26, 28, 29. LANCASHIRE beat HAMPSHIRE by 146 runs.

LANCASHIRE v SUSSEX

At Manchester, August 2, 4, 5. Sussex won by 98 runs. Sussex 19 pts, Lancashire 5 pts. After electing to bat on an easy-paced pitch, Sussex were given a great start by Mendis (eight 4s) and Barclay (six boundaries) who put on 142 before Hogg broke through after lunch. Despite a minor collapse to 201 for five at tea, Sussex reached a substantial total, then dismissed Kennedy without a run scored in the last quarter of an hour. On the Monday Lancashire were caught on a drying pitch, and lost Scott with a fractured thumb as they collapsed to 58 for five. Simmons and Hughes averted the follow-on but the home team trailed by 141 on the first innings. Sussex added 93 runs for the loss of three wickets before close of play and when rain delayed the start on the last day for an hour and a quarter they declared, setting Lancashire a target of 235 runs in 285 minutes. While the effects of the roller were wearing off Kennedy and Cockbain scored 45 quick runs, but after lunch Arnold dominated with clever seam bowling which brought him figures of five for 29 and took his team to victory with an hour and a half to spare.

Sussex

J. R. T. Barclay c Scott b Hogg	54	– c Hayes b Allott	10
G. D. Mendis c Reidy b Hogg	85	– c and b Hogg	0
P. W. G. Parker b Malone	11	– not out	32
Imran Khan c Kennedy b Malone	11	– c sub b Allott	17
C. M. Wells c Hogg b Simmons	1	– not out	23
C. P. Phillipson c Simmons b Hogg	36		
I. A. Greig c Simmons b Hughes	37		
G. S. le Roux b Hughes	30		
*†A. Long not out	13		
G. G. Arnold c Hughes b Hogg	0		
C. E. Waller not out	5		
B 3, l-b 5, w 1, n-b 7	16	B 2, l-b 2, w 1, n-b 6	11

1/142 2/154 3/173 4/174   (9 wkts) 299   1/0 2/26 3/57   (3 wkts dec.) 93
5/176 6/230 7/268 8/286 9/289

Bonus points – Sussex 3, Lancashire 4.

Bowling: *First Innings*—Hogg 17–3–82–4; Malone 23–2–56–2; Allott 12–2–31–0; Simmons 21–7–29–1; Hughes 27–6–85–2. *Second Innings*—Hogg 7–3–22–1; Malone 11–4–19–0; Allott 11–5–26–2; Simmons 4–2–11–0; Hughes 1–0–4–0.

Lancashire

A. Kennedy b Imran	0	– c Phillipson b Arnold	33
I. Cockbain c Imran b le Roux	8	– lbw b Arnold	10
†C. J. Scott retired hurt	1	– (11) absent hurt	0
*F. C. Hayes c Long b Waller	12	– (3) b Arnold	18
B. W. Reidy c Greig b Arnold	14	– (4) c Barclay b Waller	14
G. Fowler c Mendis b Waller	10	– (5) c Parker b Barclay	15
J. Simmons b Arnold	58	– (6) run out	19
D. P. Hughes not out	33	– (7) not out	15
M. F. Malone c Greig b le Roux	3	– (8) c Phillipson b Arnold	6
P. J. W. Allott b Imran	7	– (9) c le Roux b Barclay	5
W. Hogg c Greig b Waller	0	– (10) b Arnold	0
L-b 8, w 1, n-b 3	12	L-b 1	1

1/0 2/22 3/22 4/36 5/58 6/133	**158**	1/42 2/43 3/76 4/76 5/102
7/138 8/155 9/158		6/111 7/124 8/135 9/136

136

Bonus points – Lancashire 1, Sussex 4.

Bowling: *First Innings*—Imran 20–10–33–2; le Roux 14–6–32–2; Waller 22–6–56–3; Arnold 9–1–25–2. *Second Innings*—Imran 9–1–32–0; le Roux 5–2–17–0; Waller 8–3–15–1; Arnold 16.3–7–29–5; Barclay 15–2–42–2.

Umpires: W. E. Alley and H. D. Bird.

At Nottingham, August 6, 7, 8. LANCASHIRE drew with NOTTINGHAMSHIRE.

At Buxton, August 9, 11, 12. DERBYSHIRE v LANCASHIRE. Abandoned.

At Manchester, August 16, 18, 19. LANCASHIRE drew with AUSTRALIANS (See Australian tour section).

LANCASHIRE v YORKSHIRE

At Manchester, August 23, 25, 26. Lancashire won by three wickets. Lancashire 19 pts, Yorkshire 6 pts. Three days of superb cricket in glorious weather brought Lancashire their first Championship victory over their ancient rivals in eight years. The winning runs came with just two balls to spare in an exciting finish. After winning the toss Yorkshire made the most of a perfect pitch with Boycott hitting his ninth Roses century to equal Herbert Sutcliffe's record against Lancashire. Athey and Lumb also batted with power and panache. Lancashire replied with tremendous spirit as Hayes, Kennedy and Reidy took them to within 36 runs of Yorkshire. The visitors then galloped to 265 for five, thanks to a century from Love and an aggressive innings from Hampshire, whose brave declaration at lunch left Lancashire to hit 302 runs in two hundred and fifty minutes. Clive Lloyd hammered out his fourth Roses century with sound support from David Lloyd and Reidy, although it was left to nineteen-year-old O'Shaughnessy to win the match. Coming to the wicket with the scores level and four balls remaining, he calmly played his first delivery back to the bowler and hit the next for 4, leaving Yorkshire to ponder over two dropped catches that gave Clive Lloyd reprieves at 68 and 70.

Yorkshire

G. Boycott c and b D. Lloyd	135	– c D. Lloyd b Hogg	3
R. G. Lumb c Fowler b Hogg	67	– c Hughes b O'Shaughnessy	10
C. W. J. Athey c Hayes b Malone	71	– c Hayes b Hogg	30
J. D. Love b Simmons	12	– not out	105
*J. H. Hampshire not out	8	– c Fowler b Simmons	89
P. Carrick run out	2	– b Malone	5
G. B. Stevenson c Reidy b Malone	26	– not out	10
†D. L. Bairstow b Malone	5		
B 2, l-b 12, n-b 6	20	B 1, l-b 5, n-b 7	13

1/178 2/241 3/272 4/327	(7 wkts) 346	1/6 2/38 3/65 (5 wkts dec.) 265
5/333 6/335 7/346		4/242 5/251

G. A. Cope, C. M. Old and A. Sidebottom did not bat.

Bonus points – Yorkshire 4, Lancashire 3.

Bowling: *First Innings*—Hogg 18–2–61–1; Malone 22–5–68–3; Reidy 20–5–54–0; Simmons 17–3–66–1; Hughes 5–0–27–0; O'Shaughnessy 11–4–25–0; D. Lloyd 7–1–25–1. *Second Innings*—Hogg 11–0–43–2; Malone 8–2–36–1; O'Shaughnessy 4–0–16–1; Hughes 8–2–18–0; Simmons 21–4–75–1; D. Lloyd 10–2–35–0; Reidy 5–0–29–0.

Lancashire

A. Kennedy c Boycott b Carrick	55	– c Boycott b Old	13
D. Lloyd lbw b Stevenson	17	– c Carrick b Cope	61
D. P. Hughes b Cope	18	– (8) not out	2
*F. C. Hayes not out	94	– (3) c Bairstow b Carrick	8
C. H. Lloyd run out	0	– (5) b Sidebottom	101
B. W. Reidy b Stevenson	75	– (5) b Stevenson	60
J. Simmons not out	29	– (6) lbw b Stevenson	11
†G. Fowler (did not bat)		– (7) c and b Sidebottom	12
S. J. O'Shaughnessy (did not bat)		– not out	4
B 3, l-b 12, w 2, n-b 5	22	B 14, l-b 13, w 1, n-b 5	33

1/24 2/93 3/120 4/120 5/256	(5 wkts) 310	1/40 2/91 3/125 (7 wkts) 305
		4/243 5/275 6/290 7/301

M. F. Malone and W. Hogg did not bat.

Bonus points – Lancashire 4, Yorkshire 2.

Bowling: *First Innings*—Old 15–6–40–0; Stevenson 20–5–68–2; Cope 22–7–62–1; Sidebottom 15–3–43–0; Carrick 28–8–75–1. *Second Innings*—Old 14–2–43–1; Stevenson 8–1–33–2; Sidebottom 15.4–1–63–2; Carrick 15–2–61–1; Cope 20–4–72–1.

Umpires: R. Aspinall and D. J. Halfyard.

LANCASHIRE v ESSEX

At Blackpool, August 30, September 1, 2. Drawn. Lancashire 6 pts, Essex 6 pts. With the first day washed out there was no sense of urgency to suggest a positive result. Lancashire dawdled through 89 overs for their total, Hayes leading the way with five boundaries and Acfield bowling his off-spinners effectively. The pitch was encouraging spin on the last day and Essex saved the follow-on with only three men out; yet Fletcher did not consider a declaration justified and allowed the innings to go the full course. In the face of some excellent spin bowling from Hughes, who returned his best figures of the season, Essex finished 18 runs behind. Lancashire batted briskly for the last two hours with Kennedy collecting one 6 and twelve 4s in his innings, but the draw was inevitable.

Lancashire

A. Kennedy c Herbert b Phillip	21	– c McEvoy b Herbert	92
D. Lloyd c McEwan b Lever	4	– b Herbert	18
*F. C. Hayes lbw b Acfield	41		
C. H. Lloyd c Lever b Turner	33		
B. W. Reidy c and b Turner	25		
†G. Fowler b Acfield	13		
J. Simmons c Hardie b Lever	29	– (4) not out	1
S. J. O'Shaughnessy lbw b Acfield	8	– (3) c Pringle b Herbert	28
D. P. Hughes c McEwan b Phillip	32		
P. J. W. Allott not out	30		
W. Hogg lbw b Acfield	0		
B 1, l-b 5, n-b 2	8	B 5, l-b 5, w 1, n-b 2	13

1/4 2/38 3/80 4/114 5/134 6/163   244   1/35 2/148 3/152   (3 wkts) 152
7/181 8/181 9/235

Bonus points – Lancashire 2, Essex 4.

Bowling: *First Innings*—Lever 21–2–61–2; Phillip 12–2–32–2; Turner 19–6–53–2; Acfield 31.4–10–72–4; Herbert 5–0–18–0. *Second Innings*—Lever 1–0–1–0; Phillip 3–0–14–0; Turner 3–0–8–0; Acfield 12–3–39–0; Herbert 15.4–3–64–3; Pringle 4–1–13–0.

Essex

M. H. Denness c Hughes b Allott	45	N. Phillip c Simmons b D. Lloyd	12
M. S. A. McEvoy lbw b Simmons	34	R. Herbert not out	14
†K. S. McEwan b Hughes	46	J. K. Lever c Kennedy b Hughes	10
*K. W. R. Fletcher c C. H. Lloyd b Simmons	9	D. L. Acfield st Fowler b Simmons	1
B. R. Hardie c C. H. Lloyd b Hughes	31	B 2, l-b 3, n-b 7	12
D. R. Pringle b Hughes	2	1/79 2/95 3/125 4/155 5/159	226
S. Turner st Fowler b Hughes	10	6/175 7/200 8/200 9/221	

Bonus points – Essex 2, Lancashire 4.

Bowling: Hogg 13–3–58–0; Allott 19–7–40–1; Hughes 24–8–40–5; Simmons 26.3–5–61–3; D. Lloyd 6–1–15–1.

Umpires: R. S. Herman and C. T. Spencer.

At The Oval, September 3, 4, 5. LANCASHIRE lost to SURREY by an innings and 110 runs.

A BRITISH STANDARD CRICKET BALL

In 1981, for the first time, cricket balls used in first-class matches have to meet certain specifications. These have been drawn up with the support of the Cricket Council and the British Sports and Allied Industries Federation, and cover weight, circumference, hardness, height of bounce, width of seam, height of external stitching and resistance to wear. Also specified are "maximum permissible changes in shape" during and at the end of tests involving impact and abrasion. The ball, to be known as the BS 5993, will be in four categories – for use by men, women and juniors, and in first-class cricket (Grade 1). Until now, although the Laws have prescribed a ball's weight and circumference, its essential characteristics have not been standardised.

LEICESTERSHIRE

President – W. BENTLEY, MBE

Chairman, Cricket Committee – J. J. PALMER

Secretary/Cricket Manager – F. M. TURNER
County Cricket Ground, Grace Road, Leicester LE2 8AD

Captain – B. F. DAVISON

| N. G. B. Cook | County Badge | J. F. Steele |

The sun shone too late in the season for Leicestershire. But briefly, during the few later weeks when there was warmth in the air and the pitches rolled out fast and true, they showed the sort of form that indicated their depth of talent. From a stuttering run that included thirteen consecutive drawn games and two defeats, their fortunes improved so dramatically that from their last six matches they took no fewer than 81 points – more than half their final total in the Schweppes County Championship. They won four games; the first against the champions-elect Middlesex at Lord's by an innings, and another against their old foes, Northamptonshire, in perhaps the best game of the season.

In the end Leicestershire's tenth position, four places lower than the previous season, was as good a return as could be expected in a summer when rain cost them many lost hours and eleven complete days of county cricket. For Brian Davison, leading the county for the first time, the final weeks were a bonus, while Leicestershire's involvement in the John Player League was an extra plus that existed until the penultimate game, when they lost to Warwickshire. Their performances in the other limited-overs competitions were as damp and colourless as the weather. They failed again to qualify for the knockout rounds of the Benson and Hedges Cup, and their interest in the Gillette Cup went no further than a comprehensive defeat by Essex in the second round.

It took Leicestershire a long time to find a balanced side. Their two young pace bowlers, Jonathan Agnew and Gordon Parsons, played secondary rôles early in the season but finished as the first-choice new-ball attack. Agnew, in particular, benefited from the confidence placed in him; having overcome his earlier back worries he began to bowl very fast, though there were problems with his run-up. Leslie Taylor, the other new-ball bowler, was not quite as effective as in previous years, but in the John Player League he took three wickets in a match on four occasions.

The form of Paddy Clift, a genuine all-rounder, gave cause for most satisfaction. He was always dependable, during one golden spell capturing 23 wickets in five matches and scoring nearly 250 runs. Left-arm spinner Nick Cook continued to make excellent progress, his 75 first-class wickets speaking much for his ability and future prospects. When the ball was turning he was ably supported by John Steele, who statistically was Leicestershire's best bowler, finishing fifth in the first-class averages. As usual Steele gave excellent support to his captain, and even if he was not as consistent as in other years, there was a period near the end of July when he headed the national batting averages. In the end, in spite of scoring two centuries, he failed by 21 to score 1,000 first-class runs for the season.

It was no coincidence that Leicestershire's fortunes improved with the revival of David Gower. His relegation from the England team proved not only a bonus to his county but something of a relief to the player himself, for it enabled him to readjust in the quieter backwaters of county cricket. The sparkling strokes and easy timing were still there, but they were brought under control. He grafted more for his runs, and with two centuries he enjoyed his best, and longest, season for Leicestershire. His reward was to be recalled by England.

Davison, like many others, had trouble putting together big innings as interruptions by rain made concentration difficult. Even so, he returned two scores of 150 or more and managed over 1,300 first-class runs for the season, a fair return in view of his extra responsibilities. Yet how he must have despaired at the prospects of victory when a run of thirteen consecutive drawn games ended with defeat at home, by Essex, at the end of July. A further draw, at Cardiff, followed by another defeat, this time at Trent Bridge, did little to refute suggestions that Leicestershire could be heading for their worst season for a decade. Then everything began to go right. Agnew and Parsons produced their best form in harness; Cook sampled the delights of a Lord's pitch that turned; Roger Tolchard hit form with the bat and scored a century; and Leicestershire recorded their first win of the campaign, an innings victory over Middlesex inside two days.

They were brought back to earth when rain washed out two days of play against Kent, leaving both sides without a point from what became a one-innings match, but they took off again, defeating Somerset by 157 runs. Next came an exciting win by three wickets over Northamptonshire, with nine balls to spare after more than 1,300 runs had been scored in the match, and finally Hampshire were crushed, also in two days – a splendid climax to a season that had started so unpromisingly. – P.J.

LEICESTERSHIRE

Back row: M. Schepens, R. A. Cobb, G. J. Parsons, P. B. Clift, N. E. Briers, D. I. Gower, L. B. Taylor, J. P. Agnew, P. Booth, N. G. B. Cook, T. J. Boon, D. J. Barlow, I. P. Butcher, M. A. Garnham, D. A. Wenlock, D. J. Munden. *Front row*: K. Shuttleworth, J. F. Steele, R. W. Tolchard, C. H. Palmer (*chair-man*), B. F. Davison (*captain*), W. Bentley (*president*), K. Higgs, F. M. Turner (*secretary/manager*) J. Birkenshaw, J. C. Balderstone, B. Dudleston.

LEICESTERSHIRE RESULTS

All First-class Matches – Played 25: Won 4, Lost 3, Drawn 18.

County Championship Matches – Played 22: Won 4, Lost 2, Drawn 16.

Bonus points – Batting 45, Bowling 58.

COUNTY CHAMPIONSHIP AVERAGES

BATTING

	Birthplace	Matches	Inns	Not Outs	Runs	Highest Inns	Avge
B. F. Davison	Bulawayo, Rhod.	19	29	3	1,165	151	44.80
J. C. Balderstone	Huddersfield	22	36	5	1,375	158*	44.35
R. W. Tolchard	Torquay	22	32	8	889	109	37.04
D. I. Gower	Tunbridge Wells	19	29	1	929	138	33.17
J. Birkenshaw	Rothwell	14	18	4	412	76	29.42
J. F. Steele	Stafford	20	34	4	844	117	28.13
P. B.Clift	Salisbury, Rhod.	19	23	5	494	67	27.44
T. J. Boon	Doncaster	5	9	1	211	53	26.37
P. Booth	Shipley	4	3	1	49	41*	24.50
N. E. Briers	Leicester	17	25	2	438	94	19.04
B. Dudleston	Bebington	7	12	1	204	83	18.54
D. A. Wenlock	Leicester	3	5	3	30	13*	15.00
G. J. Parsons	Slough	14	13	4	106	25*	11.77
N. G. B. Cook	Leicester	22	21	8	152	75	11.69
J. P. Agnew	Macclesfield	13	10	0	80	31	8.00
L. B. Taylor	Earl Shilton	16	12	7	23	8	4.60

Also batted: K. Higgs (*Sandyford*) 7*, 2*; M. Schepens (*Barrow-upon-Soar*) 8, 0; K. Shuttleworth (*St Helens*) 0, 6.

* *Signifies not out.*

BOWLING

	Overs	Maidens	Runs	Wickets	Average
J. F. Steele	311.5	123	650	36	18.05
P. B. Clift	491.3	148	1,162	47	24.72
N. G. B. Cook	692.1	210	1,730	69	25.07
J. P. Agnew	209.4	42	756	30	25.20
G. J. Parsons	206	40	722	24	30.08
J. Birkenshaw	135.4	35	374	12	31.16
L. B. Taylor	346.3	72	1,051	29	36.24

Also bowled: J. C. Balderstone 108.4–27–330–7; P. Booth 71–19–217–5; N. E. Briers 9–1–26–0; B. F. Davison 8–1–38–0; B. Dudleston 9–4–11–2; D. I. Gower 1–0–1–0; K. Higgs 96.5–30–222–6; K. Shuttleworth 42–7–122–1; D. A. Wenlock 17.5–1–68–2.

HUNDREDS

The following eight three-figure innings were played for Leicestershire in County Championship matches – J. C. Balderstone 158* v Nottinghamshire (Leicester), 102 v Northamptonshire (Northampton); B. F. Davison 151 v Sussex (Hove), 150 v Essex (Leicester); D. I. Gower 138 v Hampshire (Southampton), 100 v Derbyshire (Burton upon Trent); J. F. Steele 117 v Northamptonshire (Leicester); R. W. Tolchard 109 v Middlesex (Lord's).

At Cambridge, April 23, 24, 25. LEICESTERSHIRE drew with CAMBRIDGE UNIVERSITY.

LEICESTERSHIRE v YORKSHIRE

At Leicester, April 30, May 1, 2. Drawn. Leicestershire 5 pts, Yorkshire 3 pts. Rain prevented play until the second day when Leicestershire, put in, were helped to three bonus points in under 74 overs by a purposeful innings from Balderstone. Yorkshire's cause was helped by Old luckily running out Gower by deflecting a drive on to the stumps. Despite two declarations on the final day there was little chance of a definite result. Yorkshire made no effort to score 269 in 145 minutes, Boycott and Lumb using the time for batting practice.

Leicestershire

J. F. Steele c and b Carrick	53	– (2) c Stevenson b Sidebottom ... 19
N. E. Briers lbw b Old	3	– (1) b Old	7
J. C. Balderstone b Cope	92	– c Bairstow b Sidebottom	26
D. I. Gower run out	34	– lbw b Stevenson	13
*B. F. Davison run out	7	– not out	46
†R. W. Tolchard not out	35	– lbw b Carrick	15
P. B. Clift not out	21	– run out	26
J. Birkenshaw (did not bat)		– not out	0
B 1, l-b 1, n-b 10	12	B 2, l-b 14, n-b 1	17

1/13 2/78 3/172   (5 wkts dec.) 257   1/11 2/58 3/68   (6 wkts dec.) 169
4/180 5/206   4/74 5/129 6/162

J. P. Agnew, N. G. B. Cook and K. Higgs did not bat.

Bonus points – Leicestershire 3, Yorkshire 2.

Bowling: *First Innings*—Old 16–4–32–1; Stevenson 17–0–79–0; Sidebottom 14–3–29–0; Carrick 12–3–48–1; Cope 14.5–2–57–1. *Second Innings*—Old 7–2–16–1; Stevenson 11–2–37–1; Sidebottom 8–4–16–2; Cope 12–4–35–0; Carrick 10–0–48–1.

Yorkshire

G. Boycott c Tolchard b Cook	31	– (2) not out	57
R. G. Lumb c Davison b Birkenshaw	56	– (1) not out	45
C. M. Old c Davison b Birkenshaw	38		
C. W. J. Athey c Balderstone b Birkenshaw	0		
*J. H. Hampshire not out	21		
K. Sharp c Tolchard b Birkenshaw	0		
P. Carrick not out	8		
L-b 2, n-b 2	4	B 8, w 1	9

1/75 2/110 3/110   (5 wkts dec.) 158   (no wkt) 111
4/145 5/145

†D. L. Bairstow, A. Sidebottom, G. B. Stevenson and G. A. Cope did not bat.

Bonus points – Yorkshire 1, Leicestershire 2.

Bowling: *First Innings*—Higgs 11–5–12–0; Agnew 4–0–11–0; Clift 6–2–13–0; Cook 21–3–71–1; Steele 7–3–13–0; Birkenshaw 11–2–34–4. *Second Innings*—Agnew 5–1–10–0; Higgs 5–1–14–0; Cook 16–8–19–0; Birkenshaw 10–1–41–0; Balderstone 6–1–18–0.

Umpires: K. E. Palmer and T. W. Spencer.

At Hove, May 3, 5, 6. LEICESTERSHIRE drew with SUSSEX.

At Leicester, May 14, 15, 16. LEICESTERSHIRE lost to WEST INDIANS by an innings and 24 runs (See West Indian tour section).

At Northampton, May 24, 26, 27. LEICESTERSHIRE drew with NORTHAMPTON-
SHIRE.

LEICESTERSHIRE v GLOUCESTERSHIRE

At Leicester, May 28, 29, 30. Drawn. Leicestershire 6 pts, Gloucestershire 5 pts. Rain limited
play to 60 overs on the first day, when Leicestershire were rocked by a spell of three for 3 in
eight balls from Brain. It was left to Boon and a battling knock of two and a half hours by Clift
to achieve a second batting point. Gloucestershire made a promising start, but as the drying
pitch produced turn and uneven bounce they collapsed against the left-arm spin of Steele
(seven for 29), leaving Leicestershire a lead of 27. This was built on by Tolchard, Briers and
Birkenshaw until Gloucestershire were set 252 in 170 minutes – a target that proved well
outside their scope. When Procter failed for the second time in the match, defeat seemed likely
as they slumped from 40 for no wicket to 89 for seven, with Steele and Birkenshaw posing
problems.

Leicestershire

B. Dudleston lbw b Brain	1			
J. F. Steele c Sadiq b Brain	19	– (1) lbw b Brain	0
*J. C. Balderstone b Brain	20	– (2) c Procter b Sadiq	35
N. E. Briers c Brassington b Brain	0	– (3) lbw b Graveney	54
†R. W. Tolchard lbw b Partridge	15	– (5) not out	61
T. J. Boon c Brassington b Childs	44	– (6) not out	27
P. B. Clift c Sadiq b Childs	51		
J. Birkenshaw c Brassington b Brain	32	– (4) c Hignell b Graveney	41
P. Booth b Graveney	0		
N. G. B. Cook c Sadiq b Childs	14		
G. J. Parsons not out	0		
B 1, l-b 4, n-b 5	10	L-b 2, n-b 4	6

1/7 2/45 3/46 4/49 5/83   206   1/0 2/79   (4 wkts dec.) 224
6/128 7/192 8/192 9/198   3/120 4/137

Bonus points – Leicestershire 2, Gloucestershire 4.

Bowling: *First Innings*—Brain 29–9–70–5; Procter 14–1–32–0; Partridge 15–4–47–1;
Childs 23–10–41–3; Graveney 3–1–6–1. *Second Innings*—Brain 6–2–16–1; Procter
2–0–9–0; Graveney 30–6–79–2; Childs 15–2–58–0; Sadiq 15–2–56–1.

Gloucestershire

A. W. Stovold b Clift	33	– lbw b Steele	36
Sadiq Mohammad c Steele b Birkenshaw	39	– b Parsons	15
Zaheer Abbas c Balderstone b Steele	35	– run out	6
A. J. Hignell c Cook b Clift	34	– lbw b Steele	3
*M. J. Procter b Steele	0	– lbw b Birkenshaw	3
M. W. Stovold lbw b Steele	0	– hit wkt b Birkenshaw	8
M. D. Partridge c Briers b Steele	11	– c sub b Cook	13
D. A. Graveney c sub b Steele	5	– not out	2
†A. J. Brassington not out	7	– not out	0
B. M. Brain c Tolchard b Steele	0		
J. H. Childs b Steele	1		
B 8, l-b 2, n-b 4	14	L-b 1, n-b 4	5

1/52 2/106 3/118 4/118 5/118   179   1/40 2/59 3/64   (7 wkts) 91
6/146 7/164 8/176 9/177   4/65 5/74 6/87 7/89

Bonus points – Gloucestershire 4, Leicestershire 4.

Bowling: *First Innings*—Booth 6–1–16–0; Parsons 3–0–10–0; Cook 25–6–50–0; Clift
17–8–28–2; Birkenshaw 12–3–29–1; Steele 24.2–14–29–7; Balderstone 1–0–3–0. *Second
Innings*—Booth 5–0–21–0; Parsons 8–1–24–1; Steele 17–9–16–2; Cook 11.4–6–10–1;
Birkenshaw 9–7–3–2; Clift 2–1–8–0; Balderstone 3–1–4–0.

Umpires: W. L. Budd and J. G. Langridge.

LEICESTERSHIRE v DERBYSHIRE

At Leicester, May 31, June 2, 3. Drawn. Leicestershire 10 pts, Derbyshire 3 pts. Leicestershire failed by 1 run to achieve victory, but gained six extra points for levelling the scores. Both captains made every effort to produce a positive result after the first day had been reduced to 22 overs. Hendrick dominated the early part of the game, finishing top scorer in Derbyshire's innings and then taking four wickets. Excellent spin bowling by Cook and Steele set up a possible Leicestershire victory and a total of 199 in 135 minutes did not look beyond them. A stand of 63 in nine overs by Balderstone and Gower appeared to swing the match and only 1 run was needed off the last over. With Gower at the non-striker's end, Boon faced a crowded close field, and some commendable leg-spin bowling from Barnett; the single eluded him, and he was run out off the last ball of the match.

Derbyshire

A. J. Borrington lbw b Parsons	15	– c Birkenshaw b Cook	17
J. G. Wright lbw b Taylor	26	– b and b Parsons	0
P. N. Kirsten c Tolchard b Cook	21	– c Tolchard b Parsons	0
D. S. Steele lbw b Cook	16	– c Steele b Parsons	14
K. J. Barnett c Steele b Cook	2	– lbw b Cook	17
*G. Miller c Balderstone b Parsons	7	– c and b Cook	17
J. Walters b Cook	22	– c Booth b Steele	18
†R. W. Taylor c Tolchard b Taylor	31	– st Tolchard b Steele	15
C. J. Tunnicliffe c Birkenshaw b Booth	10	– c Tolchard b Steele	9
M. Hendrick c Gower b Taylor	33	– not out	6
S. Oldham not out	0	– c Birkenshaw b Steele	1
L-b 6, w 1, n-b 8	15	B 1, n-b 3	4

1/38 2/53 3/80 4/87 5/94 6/100   198   1/0 2/0 3/26 4/39 5/68   118
7/132 8/145 9/183   6/69 7/95 8/109 9/112

Bonus points – Derbyshire 1, Leicestershire 4.

Bowling: *First Innings*—Taylor 27.4–10–66–3; Booth 20–7–53–1; Parsons 11–3–21–2; Cook 30–14–43–4. *Second Innings*—Taylor 13–6–22–0; Parsons 8–1–47–3; Cook 10–5–15–3; Steele 9.2–5–13–4; Birkenshaw 8–1–17–0.

Leicestershire

J. F. Steele c Taylor b Hendrick	5	– b Steele	30
N. E. Briers c Oldham b Hendrick	5	– c Oldham b Steele	13
*J. C. Balderstone c Taylor b Miller	5	– c and b Miller	61
D. I. Gower c Hendrick b Miller	10	– (5) not out	35
T. J. Boon c Walters b Hendrick	2	– (7) run out	3
†R. W. Tolchard not out	62	– c Walters b Barnett	6
J. Birkenshaw c Tunnicliffe b Hendrick	15	– (4) c and b Hendrick	43
N. G. B. Cook not out	7		
L-b 4, n-b 3	7	L-b 3, n-b 4	7

1/6 2/12 3/22 4/25 5/43   (6 wkts dec.) 118   1/39 2/53 3/115   (6 wkts) 198
6/89   4/178 5/190 6/198

P. Booth, G. J. Parsons and L. B. Taylor did not bat.

Bonus points – Derbyshire 2.

Bowling: *First Innings*—Hendrick 21–8–35–4; Tunnicliffe 4–2–5–0; Miller 21–4–39–2; Oldham 4–2–17–0; Steele 1–0–15–0. *Second Innings*—Hendrick 10–2–35–1; Tunnicliffe 4–0–31–0; Miller 18–0–79–1; Steele 9–2–34–2; Barnett 4–1–12–1.

Umpires: W. L. Budd and D. J. Halfyard.

LEICESTERSHIRE v NOTTINGHAMSHIRE

At Leicester, June 4, 5, 6. Drawn. Leicestershire 7 pts, Nottinghamshire 6 pts. Rice, with support from Randall, Birch and Hemmings, provided the backbone to Nottinghamshire's first innings, his stand of 102 in 28 overs with Birch (four 6s in his 45) putting them on course for maximum batting points. On the second day Leicestershire, owing much to an excellent unbeaten 158 from Balderstone and Rice's inability to bowl because of a strained back, matched their opponents. Balderstone found willing partners in first Tolchard, dropped at 38, and then Birkenshaw; their unbroken stand of 102 in the final sixteen overs left Leicestershire with a 6-run lead. Randall gave a timely reminder to the England selectors with a fine array of strokes in Nottinghamshire's second innings and Leicestershire were left 229 to win. However, with the wicket taking spin, they lost half their wickets for 53. Birkenshaw kept them on course before becoming one of Hemmings' seven victims with 30 needed from six overs. Cook and Parsons went in quick succession, leaving Booth, who had taken part in a seventh-wicket stand of 93, and Taylor to play out the last four overs.

Nottinghamshire

P. A. Todd b Cook	53	– lbw b Parsons	12
B. Hassan c and b Taylor	12	– c Davison b Steele	44
D. W. Randall lbw b Taylor	36	– c Parsons b Taylor	92
*C. E. B. Rice not out	108	– lbw b Taylor	26
H. T. Tunnicliffe c Tolchard b Taylor	16	– (6) c Birkenshaw b Cook	0
J. D. Birch c Steele b Birkenshaw	45	– (7) lbw b Cook	19
†C. C. Curzon c and b Cook	14	– (8) c Parsons b Steele	6
K. S. Mackintosh b Cook	0	– (9) not out	16
E. E. Hemmings b Taylor	21	– (10) c Tolchard b Taylor	7
K. E. Cooper not out	6	– (5) c Balderstone b Cook	10
M. K. Bore (did not bat)		– c Tolchard b Taylor	0
B 4, l-b 9, n-b 7	20	B 1, n-b 1	2

1/37 2/78 3/120 4/141 5/243   (8 wkts) 331   1/17 2/108 3/169 4/183 5/184   234
6/274 7/274 8/305   6/185 7/202 8/219 9/234

Bonus points – Nottinghamshire 4, Leicestershire 3.

Bowling: *First Innings*—Taylor 20–2–64–4; Parsons 9–0–45–0; Booth 10–2–42–0; Steele 19–4–45–0; Cook 29–4–85–3; Birkenshaw 13–2–30–1. *Second Innings*—Taylor 16.2–2–59–4; Parsons 5–0–26–1; Cook 23–6–59–3; Booth 6–0–20–0; Steele 16–5–54–2; Birkenshaw 2–0–14–0.

Leicestershire

J. F. Steele lbw b Mackintosh	34	– c Birch b Cooper	42
N. E. Briers c Curzon b Cooper	8	– c Curzon b Mackintosh	7
J. C. Balderstone not out	158	– lbw b Hemmings	25
M. Schepens b Tunnicliffe	8	– c Curzon b Hemmings	0
*B. F. Davison c Curzon b Hemmings	11	– c Hassan b Hemmings	0
†R. W. Tolchard c Curzon b Bore	51	– c Randall b Hemmings	0
J. Birkenshaw not out	52	– b Hemmings	76
P. Booth (did not bat)		– not out	41
N. G. B. Cook (did not bat)		– c Tunnicliffe b Hemmings	5
G. J. Parsons (did not bat)		– c and b Hemmings	0
L. B. Taylor (did not bat)		– not out	4
L-b 10, w 1, n-b 4	15	B 6, l-b 2, n-b 4	12

1/13 2/75 3/94 4/109 5/235   (5 wkts) 337   1/19 2/50 3/50 4/51   (9 wkts) 212
                                                     5/53 6/106 7/199 8/207
                                                     9/207

Bonus points – Leicestershire 4, Nottinghamshire 2.

Bowling: *First Innings*—Cooper 20–4–51–1; Mackintosh 13–2–28–1; Bore 33–6–115–1; Hemmings 23–1–102–1; Tunnicliffe 11–3–26–1. *Second Innings*—Cooper 15–3–38–1; Mackintosh 9–1–33–1; Hemmings 28–11–62–7; Bore 27–9–67–0.

Umpires: D. J. Halfyard and R. Julian.

At Oxford, June 14, 16, 17. LEICESTERSHIRE drew with OXFORD UNIVERSITY.

LEICESTERSHIRE v SURREY

At Leicester, June 18, 19, 20. Drawn. Leicestershire 3 pts, Surrey 8 pts. Surrey were indebted to Smith and Roope for their maximum batting points. After the first 70 overs had produced only 155, they put on an unbeaten 184, of which 100 came off the final seventeen overs with Smith (two 6s and thirteen 4s) reaching his century in one hundred and fifty-one minutes. Jackman kept Surrey on top with four wickets which included his 1,000th for the county. Steele, Gower and Birkenshaw all looked set but were dismissed playing rash strokes, and Leicestershire finished 78 behind. Roope reached another large unbeaten score before Surrey set Leicestershire 284 in 255 minutes. The home team were never in the hunt and Surrey hoped for a win. However, seven interruptions through rain reduced the time by ninety-five minutes, and with stubborn batting by Balderstone and Tolchard, the chance was lost.

Surrey

A. R. Butcher lbw b Taylor	6	– lbw b Shuttleworth 20
G. S. Clinton c Davison b Steele	31	– c Shuttleworth b Clift 0
D. B. Pauline b Cook	46	– c Clift b Cook 27
*R. D. V. Knight c Birkenshaw b Cook	9	– b Cook 20
D. M. Smith not out	104	– b Cook 21
G. R. J. Roope not out	87	– not out 56
Intikhab Alam (did not bat)		– c Shuttleworth b Cook 36
R. D. Jackman (did not bat)		– not out 23
L-b 15, n-b 5	20	B 1, l-b 1 2

1/16 2/65 3/96 4/119   (4 wkts) 303   1/0 2/36 3/65   (6 wkts dec.) 205
4/78 5/104 6/172

†C. J. Richards, S. T. Clarke and P. I. Pocock did not bat.

Bonus points – Surrey 4, Leicestershire 1.

Bowling: *First Innings*—Taylor 21–5–70–1; Clift 22–8–53–0; Shuttleworth 12–2–33–0; Steele 15–6–41–1; Cook 22–7–66–2; Birkenshaw 8–2–20–0. *Second Innings*—Taylor 9–4–16–0; Clift 12–2–32–1; Cook 32–8–98–4; Shuttleworth 21–4–57–1.

Leicestershire

B. Dudleston b Clarke	3	– c Richards b Jackman 1
J. F. Steele c Smith b Jackman	62	– c and b Jackman 4
J. C. Balderstone lbw b Jackman	28	– not out 65
D. I. Gower lbw b Intikhab	43	– lbw b Jackman 23
*B. F. Davison c Pocock b Jackman	2	– lbw b Jackman 5
†R. W. Tolchard c Richards b Clarke	12	– not out 45
J. Birkenshaw c Richards b Jackman	42	
P. B. Clift c Clarke b Intikhab	7	
K. Shuttleworth b Intikhab	0	
N. G. B. Cook b Pocock	5	
L. B. Taylor not out	4	
B 2, l-b 13, n-b 2	17	B 1, l-b 3, n-b 8 12

1/4 2/78 3/121 4/125 5/163 6/177   225   1/4 2/13 3/49   (4 wkts) 155
7/214 8/214 9/214   4/66

Bonus points – Leicestershire 2, Surrey 4.

Bowling: *First Innings*—Clarke 22–3–50–2; Jackman 24–9–50–4; Pocock 16.4–5–50–1; Intikhab 24–9–58–3. *Second Innings*—Clarke 14–3–37–0; Jackman 17–5–41–4; Intikhab 8–1–34–0; Pocock 8–0–31–0; Smith 2–2–0–0.

Umpires: T. W. Spencer and A. G. T. Whitehead.

At Worcester, June 21, 23, 24. LEICESTERSHIRE drew with WORCESTERSHIRE.

LEICESTERSHIRE v LANCASHIRE

At Leicester, June 28, 30, July 1. Drawn. Only 39 overs were possible in three days. Rain washed out the first and third days and there was play only before lunch on the second. During that time Lloyd made rapid runs; after being dropped by Davison at slip he hit some splendid boundaries before being caught at long-on.

Lancashire

D. Lloyd c Clift b Steele 46
A. Kennedy c Steele b Agnew 19
I. Cockbain not out 29
*F. C. Hayes not out 7
            L-b 3, n-b 1 4

1/40 2/52   (2 wkts) 105

J. Abrahams, J. Simmons, D. P. Hughes, P. J. W. Allott, †C. J. Scott, W. Hogg and P. G. Lee did not bat.

Bowling: Taylor 10–4–15–0; Agnew 7–1–22–1; Clift 11–1–26–0; Steele 7–2–34–1; Cook 3–3–0–0; Birkenshaw 1–0–4–0.

Leicestershire

N. E. Briers, J. F. Steele, J. C. Balderstone, D. I. Gower, *B. F. Davison, †R. W. Tolchard, J. Birkinshaw, P. B. Clift, N. G. B. Cook, J. P. Agnew and L. B. Taylor.

Umpires: D. J. Dennis and A. Jepson.

At Burton upon Trent, July 2, 3, 4. LEICESTERSHIRE drew with DERBYSHIRE.

At Maidstone, July 5, 7, 8. LEICESTERSHIRE drew with KENT.

At Chelmsford, July 12, 14, 15. LEICESTERSHIRE drew with ESSEX.

LEICESTERSHIRE v GLAMORGAN

At Leicester, July 19, 21, 22. Drawn. Leicestershire 3 pts, Glamorgan 2 pts. The loss of the first day's play through rain and dreary batting during Glamorgan's first innings were unlikely forerunners of the tension that followed, as Leicestershire's ninth-wicket pair – Parsons and Cook – batted out the last eight overs for a draw. A five-hour knock of 93 by Alan Jones was the cornerstone of Glamorgan's first innings after they had been put in. Leicestershire's spinners bowled tightly and Steele was on a hat-trick at one stage, dismissing Llewellyn and Nash in successive deliveries. Both captains made every effort to gain a definite result, with Davison declaring Leicestershire's first innings closed at their overnight 38 for one, and Nash closing Glamorgan's at 135 for one – Jones again being the main contributor. This left Leicestershire to score 307 in four hours but it became an uphill struggle once Steele and Balderstone were parted after scoring 54 for the first wicket in under an hour. Balderstone made 74 in 127 minutes but he received little support, and Cook and Parsons were left to save the game after three wickets had fallen in the first twelve of the final twenty overs.

Glamorgan

A. Jones st Tolchard b Steele	93	– not out	71
J. A. Hopkins c Balderstone b Parsons	13	– st Tolchard b Steele	48
R. C. Ontong b Cook	27		
Javed Miandad c Tolchard b Cook	16	– (3) not out	10
N. G. Featherstone c Cook b Taylor	24		
M. J. Llewellyn c Tolchard b Steele	1		
*M. A. Nash c Tolchard b Steele	0		
†E. W. Jones c Parsons b Steele	21		
B. J. Lloyd not out	3		
B 4, l-b 3, w 1, n-b 3	11	L-b 1, w 1, n-b 4	6

1/28 2/86 3/105 4/160   (8 wkts dec.) 209   1/123   (1 wkt dec.) 135
5/173 6/173 7/202 8/209

A. J. Mack and A. A. Jones did not bat.

Bonus points – Glamorgan 2, Leicestershire 3.

Bowling: *First Innings*—Taylor 14–2–39–1; Parsons 16–8–25–1; Clift 14–4–33–0; Cook 19–5–38–2; Birkenshaw 15–5–37–0; Steele 16.1–6–26–4. *Second Innings*—Taylor 6–0–24–0; Clift 13–5–29–0; Cook 9–1–41–0; Balderstone 4–0–22–0; Steele 6–3–13–1.

Leicestershire

J. F. Steele not out	8	– c Lloyd b Mack	35
D. I. Gower lbw b Nash	7	– (3) b Mack	0
J. C. Balderstone not out	18	– (2) b A. A. Jones	74
N. E. Briers (did not bat)		– lbw b Miandad	24
*B. F. Davison (did not bat)		– c E. W. Jones b Ontong	10
†R. W. Tolchard (did not bat)		– b A. A. Jones	13
J. Birkenshaw (did not bat)		– c Nash b Miandad	12
G. J. Parsons (did not bat)		– not out	25
P. B. Clift (did not bat)		– lbw b A. A. Jones	4
N. G. B. Cook (did not bat)		– not out	5
B 4, w 1	5	B 1, l-b 6, w 3, n-b 5	15

1/15   (1 wkt dec.) 38   1/54 2/58 3/122 4/149   (8 wkts) 217
5/156 6/182 7/182 8/192

L. B. Taylor did not bat.

Bowling: *First Innings*—Nash 6–3–16–1; A. A. Jones 3–0–13–0; Mack 3–2–4–0. *Second Innings*—Nash 12–4–26–0; A. A. Jones 18.5–6–64–3; Mack 6–1–24–2; Ontong 13–3–35–1; Lloyd 10–5–28–0; Miandad 10–3–25–2.

Umpires: A. Jepson and T. W. Spencer.

LEICESTERSHIRE v ESSEX

At Leicester, July 23, 24, 25. Essex won by 101 runs. Essex 18 pts, Leicestershire 6 pts. This encounter was played on the pitch used for the previous Championship match, and it held up well at the start with both sides gaining maximum batting points. Essex were indebted to powerful displays from Denness, McEwan and Fletcher who, dropped twice at 16, fell 4 short of his hundred. Davison boldly dominated the Leicestershire innings, helping it from 74 for two to 305 for five before declaring 7 behind. He swept, pulled and hooked well, taking full advantage of being dropped at 20 to hit four 6s, seven 4s and a 5. East bore the brunt of the attack, bowling a gruelling unchanged spell of 46.2 overs, yet claiming four wickets. The pitch began to break up when Essex batted a second time but, with Turner holding the innings together after being dropped twice, they set Leicestershire a target of 256 in 200 minutes. This time, however, the spin of East and Acfield proved too much for the home team. East exploited a rough patch and four wickets tumbled for 9 runs in thirty-five minutes spanning tea. Acfield provided excellent support, although Essex were held up by Clift, who batted with dour resistance for an hour until he was last out.

Essex

M. S. A. McEvoy b Taylor	27 – b Agnew	16
M. H. Denness c Steele b Agnew	57 – c and b Balderstone	18
K. S. McEwan run out	70 – c Gower b Cook	34
*K. W. R. Fletcher b Cook	96 – c Birkenshaw b Taylor	25
B. R. Hardie c Balderstone b Steele	14 – c Gower b Balderstone	0
S. Turner c Davison b Taylor	32 – (7) not out	83
N. Phillip not out	0 – (8) b Cook	8
R. E. East (did not bat)	– (6) b Cook	15
†N. Smith (did not bat)	– c Gower b Cook	4
J. K. Lever (did not bat)	– b Cook	1
D. L. Acfield (did not bat)	– c Davison b Birkenshaw	18
B 1, l-b 13, w 1, n-b 1	16	B 16, l-b 7, n-b 3	26

1/60 2/111 3/187   (6 wkts dec.) 312   1/30 2/59 3/73 4/78 5/115   248
4/218 5/312 6/312   6/135 7/175 8/191 9/199

Bonus points – Essex 4, Leicestershire 2.

Bowling: *First Innings*—Taylor 23.3–2–83–2; Agnew 17–3–46–1; Clift 20–5–45–0; Cook 27–4–81–1; Steele 12–3–41–1. *Second Innings*—Taylor 10–2–34–1; Agnew 8–0–40–1; Cook 43–14–105–5; Balderstone 24–10–34–2; Clift 8–5–5–0; Birkenshaw 1–0–4–1.

Leicestershire

J. F. Steele c sub b East	25 – lbw b East	34
J. C. Balderstone c McEvoy b East	42 – c Fletcher b Turner	12
D. I. Gower c sub b East	10 – c Hardie b East	16
*B. F. Davison c Denness b East	150 – c McEwan b Acfield	28
N. E. Briers b Acfield	32 – c McEwan b East	20
†R. W. Tolchard not out	23 – b East	1
J. Birkenshaw (did not bat)	– c sub b East	1
P. B. Clift (did not bat)	– c Hardie b East	36
J. P. Agnew (did not bat)	– c McEvoy b Acfield	0
N. G. B. Cook (did not bat)	– b Acfield	0
L. B. Taylor (did not bat)	– not out	0
B 4, l-b 16, n-b 3	23	L-b 5, w 1	6

1/69 2/74 3/86 4/198   (5 wkts dec.) 305   1/15 2/41 3/90 4/94   154
5/305   5/97 6/99 7/137
                                                    8/154 9/154

Bonus points – Leicestershire 4, Essex 2.

Bowling: *First Innings*—Lever 6–1–18–0; Phillip 19–4–70–0; Turner 1–0–3–0; East 46.2–8–142–4; Acfield 27–12–49–1. *Second Innings*—Phillip 4–0–23–0; Turner 3–0–14–1; East 28.1–9–56–6; Acfield 28–13–55–3.

Umpires: D. J. Dennis and D. Shackleton.

At Cardiff, July 26, 28, 29. LEICESTERSHIRE drew with GLAMORGAN.

At Nottingham, August 2, 4, 5. LEICESTERSHIRE lost to NOTTINGHAMSHIRE by nine wickets.

At Lord's, August 6, 7, 8. LEICESTERSHIRE beat MIDDLESEX by an innings and 100 runs.

LEICESTERSHIRE v KENT

At Leicester, August 9, 11, 12. Drawn. After the first two days had been washed out by rain both sides played for 12 Championship points, but there was little hope of a positive result. Kent, put in, scored well and were indebted to a century from Tavaré, who was joined by Taylor in a partnership of 171. Leicestershire were given 145 minutes to score 264 runs, but lost Steele early. They were always in with a chance while Gower was at the crease, but he was run out following a superb piece of fielding by Cowdrey, who hit the stumps directly. Leicestershire lost only three wickets but finished nearly 100 runs short, with Balderstone having played well for his unbeaten 74.

Kent

R. A. Woolmer c Tolchard b Agnew 0	G. W. Johnson not out.............. 33	
N. R. Taylor c Steele b Agnew 63	L-b 5, n-b 2 7	
C. J. Tavaré c Parsons b Clift 108		
C. S. Cowdrey not out 52	1/0 2/171 3/175 (3 wkts dec.) 263	

M. Benson, *†A. P. E. Knott, J. N. Shepherd, N. J. Kemp, R. W. Hills and D. L. Underwood did not bat.

Bowling: Agnew 12–3–40–2; Parsons 8–0–41–0; Taylor 14–1–67–0; Clift 15–3–61–1; Cook 6–2–27–0; Steele 4–0–20–0.

Leicestershire

J. F. Steele c Tavaré b Kemp 2	N. E. Briers not out 23	
J. C. Balderstone not out 74	B 4, l-b 1, n-b 1............. 6	
D. I. Gower run out 35		
*B. F. Davison c Knott b Woolmer 25	1/14 2/68 3/115 (3 wkts) 165	

†R. W. Tolchard, P. B. Clift, G. J. Parsons, J. P. Agnew, N. G. B. Cook and L. B. Taylor did not bat.

Bowling: Kemp 10–0–58–1; Shepherd 11–4–43–0; Hills 5–0–19–0; Woolmer 2–0–8–1; Johnson 4–0–8–0; Tavaré 2–0–23–0.

Umpires: W. L. Budd and D. O. Oslear.

At Taunton, August 16, 18, 19. LEICESTERSHIRE beat SOMERSET by 157 runs.

LEICESTERSHIRE v NORTHAMPTONSHIRE

At Leicester, August 23, 25, 26. Leicestershire won by three wickets. Leicestershire 15 pts, Northamptonshire 7 pts. On probably the best batting pitch of the season at Grace Road, 1,354 runs were scored for the loss of only 23 wickets. After acting-captain Cook had been dismissed with only 1 run on the board, Larkins and Williams ensured that Northamptonshire gained maximum batting points and their opponents no bowling points. They set a record second-wicket stand for the county of 322 with 49 boundaries; and Williams's 175 was the best of his career. In reply, Leicestershire were unable to match the excellence of this batting, but Steele made a solid century and dominated a third-wicket stand of 170 with Boon. Northamptonshire built on their first innings lead of 40, the brilliant Lamb making his runs in almost even time. Leicestershire were set 381 in 330 minutes and, with Cook maintaining an aggressive field, the excitement rose as Gower, dropped at 13, made 84 in 128 minutes with seventeen 4s. His innings gave Leicestershire the impetus they needed and, after consolidating knocks from Steele and the middle order, Wenlock and Cook negotiated the final deliveries for a thrilling victory with nine balls remaining.

Northamptonshire

*G. Cook c Tolchard b Agnew	0	– c Tolchard b Agnew	4
W. Larkins c and b Steele	156	– c and b Clift	68
R. G. Williams not out	175	– c Steele b Parsons	4
A. J. Lamb not out	3	– c Gower b Balderstone	152
P. Willey (did not bat)		– b Cook	73
T. J. Yardley (did not bat)		– c Agnew b Balderstone	20
†G. Sharp (did not bat)		– b Cook	5
Sarfraz Nawaz (did not bat)		– not out	2
N. A. Mallender (did not bat)		– not out	2
L-b 1, w 1	2	B 4, l-b 2, w 3, n-b 1	10

1/1 2/323   (2 wkts) 336   1/20 2/25 3/132   (7 wkts dec.) 340
4/264 5/320 6/329 7/337

B. J. Griffiths and T. M. Lamb did not bat.

Bonus points – Northamptonshire 4.

Bowling: *First Innings*—Agnew 5–1–22–1; Parsons 4–1–26–0; Clift 20–4–52–0; Cook 23–6–68–0; Steele 17–6–40–1; Wenlock 6–0–27–0; Balderstone 17–1–61–0; Davison 8–1–38–0. *Second Innings*—Agnew 10–0–64–1; Parsons 6–0–31–1; Wenlock 4–0–18–0; Clift 14–1–54–1; Cook 24–3–120–2; Steele 5–1–26–0; Balderstone 9–2–17–2.

Leicestershire

J. C. Balderstone c Cook b Sarfraz	11	– c Sarfraz b Griffiths	0
J. F. Steele b Williams	117	– c Sarfraz b Williams	70
D. I. Gower c Sarfraz b Griffiths	16	– c Sharp b Willey	83
T. J. Boon c T. M. Lamb b Williams	53	– c Cook b Willey	42
*B. F. Davison c Yardley b Willey	8	– b Willey	42
†R. W. Tolchard run out	21	– c Larkins b Williams	67
P. B. Clift not out	33	– c Sarfraz b Williams	30
D. A. Wenlock run out	0	– not out	9
G. J. Parsons not out	8		
N. G. B. Cook (did not bat)		– (9) not out	4
B 4, l-b 8, w 2, n-b 15	29	B 14, l-b 17, w 1, n-b 3	35

1/21 2/45 3/215 4/232   (7 wkts) 296   1/2 2/146 3/199 4/263   (7 wkts) 382
5/232 6/279 7/279   5/266 6/354 7/369

J. P. Agnew did not bat.

Bonus points – Leicestershire 3, Northamptonshire 3.

Bowling: *First Innings*—Sarfraz 20–4–58–1; Griffiths 9–1–26–1; T. M. Lamb 15–2–37–0; Willey 29–8–71–1; Williams 17–2–51–2; Mallender 10–2–24–0. *Second Innings*—Sarfraz 8–0–29–0; Griffiths 16–3–61–1; Mallender 4–1–17–0; Williams 36–3–129–3; Willey 39.3–7–111–3.

Umpires: J. van Geloven and R. Palmer.

LEICESTERSHIRE v WARWICKSHIRE

At Leicester, August 30, September 1, 2. Drawn. Leicestershire 7 pts, Warwickshire 5 pts. Seven interruptions for rain on the first day prevented a positive result. An opening century partnership by Balderstone and Dudleston set Leicestershire on their way to maximum batting points. Humpage and Kallicharran dominated Warwickshire's reply with 52 in twelve overs, but Leicestershire's spinners proved difficult to play, especially Cook who took five of the eight wickets to fall before Warwickshire declared. Davison hit a fine 80 and set a target of 298 in just over three hours. Although Warwickshire started promisingly, with Amiss and Smith scoring 102 in less than an hour, Cook again proved troublesome and, once Lloyd and Humpage had been dismissed in successive deliveries, Warwickshire were content to play out for a draw.

Leicestershire

J. C. Balderstone c Humpage b Hopkins	50	– (2) b Hopkins	62
B. Dudleston b Hopkins	50	– (1) b Perryman	8
T. J. Boon b Doshi	17	– st Humpage b Doshi	11
*B. F. Davison b Perryman	62	– c Perryman b Hopkins	80
N. E. Briers b Doshi	40	– c Perryman b Hopkins	6
†R. W. Tolchard not out	34	– c sub b Doshi	16
P. B. Clift b Doshi	21	– c Smith b Doshi	25
D. A. Wenlock not out	7	– not out	13
G. J. Parsons (did not bat)		– not out	5
B 2, l-b 7, w 2, n-b 18	29	B 5, l-b 5, n-b 1	11

1/104 2/112 3/165 4/244   (6 wkts dec.) 310   1/19 2/72 3/160   (7 wkts dec.) 237
5/244 6/290   4/171 5/178 6/208
                                                  7/226

N. G. B. Cook and L. B. Taylor did not bat.

Bonus points – Leicestershire 4, Warwickshire 2.

Bowling: *First Innings*—Rouse 23–4–71–0; Hopkins 15–5–57–2; Perryman 26–7–52–1; Doshi 33.2–13–92–3; Kallicharran 2–0–9–0. *Second Innings*—Perryman 12–0–41–1; Hopkins 15–1–68–3; Doshi 21.4–3–101–3; Oliver 3–0–16–0.

Warwickshire

*D. L. Amiss lbw b Clift	34	– b Cook	58
K. D. Smith c and b Cook	40	– lbw b Balderstone	42
T. A. Lloyd c Balderstone b Clift	4	– b Cook	21
†G. W. Humpage c and b Cook	40	– b Balderstone	15
A. I. Kallicharran b Cook	52	– c Tolchard b Cook	39
J. Whitehouse c Wenlock b Cook	34	– c Davison b Cook	6
P. R. Oliver not out	21	– not out	30
S. J. Rouse c and b Balderstone	12	– not out	2
D. R. Doshi c Briers b Cook	4		
D. C. Hopkins not out	6		
L-b 3	3	B 8, l-b 4, n-b 1	13

1/61 2/75 3/79 4/131 5/202   (8 wkts dec.) 250   1/102 2/108 3/139   (6 wkts) 226
6/207 7/230 8/235   4/139 5/146 6/207

S. P. Perryman did not bat.

Bonus points – Warwickshire 3, Leicestershire 3.

Bowling: *First Innings*—Taylor 8–0–20–0; Parsons 6–0–21–0; Clift 16–5–58–2; Cook 29–12–81–5; Balderstone 14.4–2–67–1. *Second Innings*—Taylor 5–0–28–0; Parsons 3–0–11–0; Cook 30–11–86–4; Balderstone 16–3–62–2; Clift 12.5–3–23–0; Dudleston 2–1–3–0.

Umpires: R. Aspinall and P. S. G. Stevens.

At Southampton, September 3, 4. LEICESTERSHIRE beat HAMPSHIRE by an innings and 34 runs.

MIDDLESEX

Patron — HRH THE DUKE OF EDINBURGH

President — W. H. WEBSTER, CBE

Chairman, Cricket Committee — F. G. MANN, DSO, MC

Secretary — A. J. BURRIDGE
Lord's Cricket Ground, St John's Wood, London NW8 8QN

Captain — J. M. BREARLEY, OBE

R. O. Butcher

County Badge

P. R. Downton

Observers who believed that Middlesex's fourteenth place in 1979 was a freakishly false one were vindicated when Brearley's team clinched the Schweppes County Championship on September 2, four years to the day after their 1976 triumph. Having resisted Surrey's persistent challenge, they denied them again four days later by beating them in the Gillette Cup final, and next day Middlesex finished third in the John Player League. Having also reached the semi-finals of the Benson and Hedges Cup, they could look back on the most successful year by any county in the nine seasons that have offered four trophies. The previous best record was their own in 1977.

Although it was probable that the generation moulded by Mike Brearley would improve substantially on 1979's performance, they still required an assortment of new players to clinch 1980's rewards. Paramount among them was Vintcent van der Bijl, to whom Brearley referred as "the biggest single factor behind our success". He was initially recruited as a replacement for Daniel, who was expected to be chosen for the West Indian team in England. When West Indies decided to do without Daniel, Middlesex were left with one of the most dangerous attacks in their history.

John Emburey and Phil Edmonds did not play a full county season, but van der Bijl surpassed even the high expectations aroused by his South

African record. He brought the ball down from around nine feet, more swiftly than many opponents imagined, moved it, made it lift, and bowled unerringly straight. A measure of his stump-riveting line was that 49 of his 85 Championship victims were bowled or lbw, and he had seventeen more caught behind. In eighteen of van der Bijl's twenty Championship matches Middlesex took full bowling points, and he also contained batsmen in limited-overs games, besides wafting 6s with a nonchalant half-swing. He and Middlesex parted with considerable regret.

Two other newcomers contributed usefully in the second half of the season. In contrast to van der Bijl's brief stay, both Simon Hughes and Paul Downton promise years more service. Hughes's wicket to win the Essex match was of paramount importance and Brearley called him "the best fast-bowling prospect in England". An unexpected bonus was Downton's emergence as an opening batsman, his assurance and stroke-play making him sometimes indistinguishable from Brearley. His success was important, Mike Smith, Roland Butcher and Wilfred Slack having opened with only modest results. Sadly, Downton's arrival persuaded the admirable Ian Gould that his wicket-keeping future lay elsewhere.

After being dropped from a number of matches, Butcher shrugged off the disappointment in astonishing fashion. There was no hint of what lay in store when he began his second innings against Hampshire at Lord's, but with a succession of breathtaking shots he made a match-winning 153 and went on to produce similar strokes against Yorkshire and Essex. These outstanding innings won him a place in England's Prudential Trophy side, followed by a trip back to his birthplace as an England player.

The feats of the newcomers and Butcher's rise to eminence, complemented the efforts of the regulars. Clive Radley and Mike Gatting enjoyed simultaneous purple patches with centuries in consecutive games in June. England duty meant that Gatting's later appearances were spasmodic, but Radley, Brearley and Graham Barlow made ample runs. The most welcome of Barlow's several big scores was his 97 against Nottinghamshire which revived the side when they were struggling at 86 for six after two successive defeats. Brearley ended a fine season with three centuries and a 67 in the last four matches. It is no coincidence that Middlesex's outright Championship titles have come either side of his spell as England's captain. Both as captain and batsman he is vital to the side.

Edmond's summer was ruined by a knee injury and he showed great fortitude in playing a month after the required operation. Emburey, as artistic in the longer game as he is restrictive in one-day cricket, became England's premier spinner. His highlight came when he destroyed Nottinghamshire with twelve wickets in a day. When these two were away, Middlesex played seventeen-year-old Rajesh Maru or Fred Titmus (48), both of whom collected a dozen useful wickets. Daniel thrived with the extra pace-bowling support and Mike Selvey relished a rare new-ball chance by wrecking Essex's strong batting. – Terry Cooper.

MIDDLESEX

|Bill Smith

Back row: J. Miller (*physiotherapist*), D. Bennett (*coach*), K. P. Tomlins, W. G. Merry, V. A. P. van der Bijl, M. W. W. Selvey, K. D. James, W. N. Slack, R. P. G. Ellis, R. O. Butcher, R. J. Maru, H. Sharpe (*scorer*). *Front row:* I. J. Gould, J. E. Emburey, M. J. Smith, P. H. Edmonds, J. M. Brearley (*captain*), C. T. Radley, G. D. Barlow, M. W. Gatting.

MIDDLESEX RESULTS

All First-class Matches – Played 24: Won 10, Lost 2, Drawn 12.

County Championship Matches – Played 22: Won 10, Lost 2, Drawn 10.

Bonus points – Batting 58, Bowling 80.

COUNTY CHAMPIONSHIP AVERAGES

BATTING

	Birthplace	Matches	Inns	Not Outs	Runs	Highest Inns	Avge
C. T. Radley	Hertford	22	32	8	1,248	136*	52.00
M. W. Gatting	Kingsbury	13	15	3	602	136	50.16
J. M. Brearley	Harrow	22	32	5	1,282	134*	47.48
G. D. Barlow	Folkestone	22	30	8	952	128*	43.27
R. O. Butcher	Barbados, WI	15	21	2	792	179	41.68
P. R. Downton	Farnborough	9	15	2	521	90*	40.07
I. J. Gould	Slough	13	14	4	295	57	29.50
K. P. Tomlins	Kingston-upon-Thames	5	7	1	160	55	26.66
V. A. P. van der Bijl . .	Cape Town, SA	20	16	3	331	76	25.46
M. W. W. Selvey	Chiswick	19	15	4	254	40*	23.09
J. E. Emburey	Peckham	15	11	3	183	43*	22.87
W. N. Slack	St Vincent, WI	8	11	0	230	47	20.90
P. H. Edmonds	Lusaka, N. Rhod.	14	10	1	157	52	17.44
M. J. Smith	Enfield	4	5	0	83	24	16.60
F. J. Titmus	St Pancras	5	6	3	23	10*	7.66
W. W. Daniel	Barbados, WI	19	12	4	56	15	7.00
R. J. Maru	Nairobi, Kenya	8	6	0	40	13	6.66
S. P. Hughes	Kingston-upon-Thames	5	4	2	0	0*	0.00

W. G. Merry (*Newbury*) played in four matches but did not bat.

* Signifies not out.

BOWLING

	Overs	Maidens	Runs	Wickets	Average
V. A. P. van der Bijl . . .	642.3	213	1,252	85	14.72
W. G. Merry	69	15	218	14	15.57
S. P. Hughes	110.4	25	352	18	19.55
J. E. Emburey	594	196	1,202	61	19.70
W. W. Daniel	492.5	112	1,454	67	21.70
F. J. Titmus	149.2	38	313	12	26.08
P. H. Edmonds	386	118	930	34	27.35
R. J. Maru	127.4	33	373	12	31.08
M. W. W. Selvey	413.3	127	1,013	26	38.96

Also bowled: G. D. Barlow 8–0–31–2; J. M. Brearley 15.4–3–65–0; M. W. Gatting 33.4–5–107–4; C. T. Radley 5.3–0–19–1; K. P. Tomlins 31–8–103–0.

HUNDREDS

The following fifteen three-figure innings were played for Middlesex in County Championship matches – J. M. Brearley 134* v Lancashire (Lord's), 124* v Glamorgan (Cardiff), 114 v Sussex (Hove), 106 v Kent (Lord's), 104 v Kent (Canterbury); G. D. Barlow 128* v Sussex (Lord's), 119* v Warwickshire (Birmingham), 100* v Essex (Lord's); C. T. Radley 136* v Yorkshire (Lord's), 136 v Surrey (Lord's), 114* v Worcestershire (Worcester); R. O. Butcher 179 v Yorkshire (Scarborough), 153* v Hampshire (Lord's); M. W. Gatting 136 v Surrey, (Lord's), 110 v Yorkshire (Lord's).

At Nottingham, April 30, May 1, 2. MIDDLESEX drew with NOTTINGHAMSHIRE.

MIDDLESEX v LANCASHIRE

At Lord's, May 3, 5, 6. Drawn. Middlesex 7 pts, Lancashire 2 pts. The South African van der Bijl introduced himself to Middlesex followers with a remarkably accurate, productive display at the heart of a dominant performance by the pace attack. Lloyd seldom middled the ball but fought with customary defiance. Brearley, on the field throughout the match, had trouble maintaining a personal rate of more than 1 an over, but his partners proved more assertive. His stand with Gatting lasted 40 overs and provided the substance of the innings, but Malone's control was largely responsible for Middlesex falling short of maximum points. Lancashire looked beaten at 88 for five at 12.30 on the last day, but Cockbain organised resistance by the later batsmen with an assurance astonishing in only his third first-class innings. His 195-minute vigil meant that Lancashire did not really need the rain in the final hour to save the match.

Lancashire

A. Kennedy c Gould b Selvey	12	– c Brearley b Daniel 0
G. E. Trim c Gould b van der Bijl	7	– c Brearley b Daniel 5
H. Pilling lbw b Daniel	7	– c Gould b Daniel 0
*F. C. Hayes c Emburey b van der Bijl	21	– c Gatting b Emburey 56
D. Lloyd not out	64	– lbw b Emburey 15
I. Cockbain lbw b van der Bijl	3	– not out 69
J. Simmons c Edmonds b Emburey	15	– b Daniel 10
R. M. Ratcliffe c Gould b van der Bijl	5	– c Gatting b Emburey 26
†C. J. Scott b Daniel	4	– not out 11
M. F. Malone lbw b Gatting	3	
P. G. Lee c Gould b Gatting	0	
L-b 6, w 1, n-b 4	11	B 8, l-b 5, w 1, n-b 5 19

1/9 2/27 3/27 4/65 5/77   152   1/0 2/0 3/29   (7 wkts) 211
6/107 7/114 8/132 9/152   4/87 5/88 6/102 7/169

Bonus points – Lancashire 1, Middlesex 4.

Bowling: *First Innings*—van der Bijl 28–13–36–4; Daniel 22–7–42–2; Selvey 25–7–42–1; Gatting 4.4–1–3–2; Emburey 10–4–18–1. *Second Innings*—Daniel 28.4–10–53–4; van der Bijl 22–7–46–0; Selvey 15–3–32–0; Emburey 27–11–44–3; Gatting 1–1–0–0; Edmonds 9–4–17–0.

Middlesex

*J. M. Brearley not out	134	†I. J. Gould not out	47
M. J. Smith b Malone	24		
C. T. Radley lbw b Kennedy	23	L-b 12, n-b 3	15
G. D. Barlow c Kennedy b Malone	21		
M. W. Gatting c Cockbain b Malone	51	1/45 2/91 3/120 4/242 (4 wkts)	315

P. H. Edmonds, J. E. Emburey, V. A. P. van der Bijl, W. W. Daniel and M. W. W. Selvey did not bat.

Bonus points – Middlesex 3, Lancashire 1 (Score at 100 overs: 256-4).

Bowling: Malone 34–12–90–3; Lee 29–6–79–0; Ratcliffe 23–7–67–0; Kennedy 8–2–27–1; Simmons 16–4–37–0.

Umpires: W. E. Alley and P. S. G. Stevens.

At Cambridge, May 7, 8, 9. MIDDLESEX drew with CAMBRIDGE UNIVERSITY.

At Lord's, May 20. MIDDLESEX v WEST INDIANS. Abandoned.

At Lord's, May 21. MIDDLESEX lost to WEST INDIANS by nine wickets (See West Indian tour section).

MIDDLESEX v SUSSEX

At Lord's, May 24, 26, 27. Middlesex won by an innings and 5 runs. Middlesex 20 pts, Sussex 2 pts. After a promising start, Sussex declined disappointingly as Middlesex's hostile pace trio exerted an increasingly secure grip, although Wells played with fluent assurance. Long, cracked on the head by Daniel, took no further part in the match (Mendis kept wicket efficiently) and Sussex received a second injury blow in their second innings when, for the third time, Graves broke a finger batting against Middlesex; he was struck twice on the right hand, first by Daniel then by van der Bijl. Parker fought for three and a half hours, but Middlesex had won by tea. The Middlesex innings accelerated sharply after a torpid start, despite an attack that lacked menace. The first 87 took 36 overs, but Radley and Barlow put on 136 off 41 overs for the third wicket. Radley was run out by a typically slick throw from Parker, but Barlow continued to a chanceless and powerful 128.

Sussex

G. D. Mendis lbw b van der Bijl	10	– (2) c Brearley b van der Bijl	0
K. C. Wessels c Radley b van der Bijl	32	– (1) c Gatting b Daniel	17
P. W. G. Parker b Daniel	15	– (4) c Gould b Selvey	43
P. J. Graves lbw b Daniel	8	– (5) c Gatting b van der Bijl	13
C. P. Phillipson b Selvey	8	– (6) c Gatting b Selvey	30
C. M. Wells b Selvey	49	– (7) c Radley b Emburey	0
G. S. le Roux c Barlow b van der Bijl	14	– (8) c Emburey b van der Bijl	11
*†A. Long retired hurt	14	– (11) absent hurt	0
G. G. Arnold c Smith b Selvey	2	– run out	0
J. Spencer not out	14	– (3) b Daniel	9
C. E. Waller b Daniel	10	– (10) not out	0
L-b 14, w 1, n-b 4	19	L-b 7, n-b 16	23

1/22 2/43 3/67 4/72 5/86 6/130   195   1/1 2/29 3/30 4/86 5/132   146
7/149 8/156 9/195   6/133 7/145 8/145 9/146

Bonus points – Sussex 1, Middlesex 4.

Bowling: *First Innings*—van der Bijl 29–9–44–3; Selvey 32–11–64–3; Emburey 12–5–18–0; Daniel 21.3–7–38–3; Gatting 4–1–12–0. *Second Innings*—van der Bijl 18–6–30–3; Daniel 14.2–7–19–2; Selvey 19.1–5–47–2; Emburey 14.4–5–17–1; Edmonds 5–1–10–0.

Middlesex

*J. M. Brearley lbw b le Roux	42	†I. J. Gould not out	8
M. J. Smith c Wessels b Spencer	18		
C. T. Radley run out	97	B 3, l-b 14, w 1, n-b 3	21
G. D. Barlow not out	128		
M. W. Gatting c Wessels b Arnold	32	1/44 2/87 3/223 4/307	(4 wkts) 346

P. H. Edmonds, J. E. Emburey, V. A. P. van der Bijl, M. W. W. Selvey and W. W. Daniel did not bat.

Bonus points – Middlesex 4, Sussex 1.

Bowling: le Roux 22–2–80–1; Arnold 24–4–61–1; Spencer 14–3–46–1; Waller 19–5–51–0; Wells 15–2–64–0; Phillipson 7–0–23–0.

Umpires: R. Aspinall and H. D. Bird.

At Worcester, May 28, 29, 30. MIDDLESEX drew with WORCESTERSHIRE.

At Taunton, May 31, June 2, 3. MIDDLESEX beat SOMERSET by seven wickets.

MIDDLESEX v SURREY

At Lord's, June 4, 5, 6. Middlesex won by an innings and 58 runs. Middlesex 20 pts, Surrey 2 pts. Surrey failed to overcome the difficulties of a slow pitch and the control of the Middlesex bowlers. Although the openers stayed until after lunch, their progress had been so laboured that Clarke was promoted to speed the run-rate, but to no avail, and the innings subsided after Clinton was run out. At 53 for three in the first over of the second morning Middlesex were faring worse, but Radley and Gatting transformed the mood of the match in an attractive partnership of 248. Radley, in an innings of five and a quarter hours, explored the off side resourcefully; Gatting – batting an hour and threequarters less – supplied the substance of their fourth-wicket stand. He drove fiercely for many of his eighteen 4s and skilfully carved Pocock through the covers. Edmonds, Gould and van der Bijl further demoralised Surrey during the bonus overs. The visitors were 51 for two after the first over of the third day. Butcher and Knight fought resolutely past lunch but after the interval the spinners, achieving a fraction more turn, effected a breakthrough. Despite resistance from Roope, Smith and Jackman, the game was over before the final hour.

Surrey

A. R. Butcher st Gould b Emburey	55	– c Gatting b Edmonds	71
G. S. Clinton run out	33	– c Brearley b Emburey	16
S. T. Clarke lbw b van der Bijl	0	– (9) st Gould b Edmonds	4
G. P. Howarth c Gould b van der Bijl	5	– b Daniel	0
*R. D. V. Knight c Gould b Daniel	8	– lbw b Emburey	53
G. R. J. Roope b Merry	15	– c Edmonds c Emburey	33
D. M. Smith b Emburey	1	– c Gould b Emburey	15
R. D. Jackman c Barlow b Daniel	4	– c van der Bijl b Edmonds	8
†C. J. Richards c Gould b Edmonds	15	– (3) c Gould b Emburey	14
P. I. Pocock not out	11	– c Brearley b Edmonds	4
R. G. L. Cheatle b Emburey	1	– not out	0
B 5, l-b 6, n-b 5	16	B 12, n-b 1	13

1/95 2/96 3/98 4/108 5/122   164   1/50 2/51 3/145 4/145 5/176   231
6/125 7/131 8/142 9/157   6/209 7/209 8/217 9/221

Bonus points – Surrey 1, Middlesex 4.

Bowling: *First Innings*—van der Bijl 18–5–30–2; Daniel 12–2–19–2; Merry 7–2–15–1; Emburey 26.5–9–42–3; Gatting 2–0–11–0; Edmonds 12–2–31–1. *Second Innings*—van der Bijl 12–3–17–0; Daniel 11–0–48–1; Emburey 47.5–22–73–5; Merry 2–0–11–0; Edmonds 41–16–68–4; Brearley 2–1–1–0.

Middlesex

*J. M. Brearley c Knight b Jackman	....	6	V. A. P. van der Bijl b Knight	29
R. O. Butcher lbw b Clarke		0	W. W. Daniel not out	1
C. T. Radley c Smith b Pocock 136				
G. D. Barlow c Roope b Pocock		11	B 5, l-b 15, w 1, n-b 6	27
M. W. Gatting run out		136		
P. H. Edmonds b Pocock		52	1/1 2/23 3/53 4/301 (8 wkts dec.) 453	
†I. J. Gould c Knight b Clarke		55	5/327 6/408 7/451 8/453	

J. E. Emburey and W. G. Merry did not bat.

Bonus points – Middlesex 4, Surrey 1 (Score at 100 overs: 301-4).

Bowling: Clarke 21.2–5–84–2; Jackman 22–3–63–1; Knight 20–1–55–1; Pocock 38–7–140–3; Cheatle 19–6–84–0.

Umpires: W. L. Budd and J. van Geloven.

MIDDLESEX v YORKSHIRE

At Lord's, June 7, 9, 10. Drawn. Middlesex 6 pts, Yorkshire 6 pts. Middlesex put Yorkshire in, dismissed Lumb for his third successive duck, and retained control until Carrick joined Sharp, who had toiled through 40 overs for 31. Together they changed the shape of the day with a brisk stand of 165 as Carrick struck ten 4s and one 6 and Sharp reached his maiden century. Old shrewdly declared and took two wickets on the first evening. Middlesex lost two more batsmen on the second morning before Radley and Gatting again revived the innings with 177 in only 38 overs, Gatting playing the major rôle with seventeen 4s in his 107-minute century. After an early declaration Middlesex took only one wicket on the second evening and the game remained evenly poised, with Athey, Love and Carrick playing pleasantly, until two hours of rain killed the chance of a result.

Yorkshire

R. G. Lumb c Gatting b van der Bijl	0	– c Butcher b Edmonds	34
C. W. J. Athey c Gould b Daniel	43	– c Emburey b Daniel	65
S. N. Hartley c Radley b Merry	19	– c Gould b Edmonds	6
J. D. Love c Radley b Merry	31	– not out	39
K. Sharp not out	100	– st Gould b Emburey	1
P. Carrick b Emburey	73	– st Gould b Edmonds	22
G. B. Stevenson c Barlow b Emburey	3		
†D. L. Bairstow not out	10	– (7) c Gatting b Emburey	14
*C. M. Old (did not bat)		– (8) not out	6
B 10, l-b 13, n-b 12	35	B 2, l-b 13, w 1, n-b 1 ...	17

1/2 2/40 3/93 4/125	(6 wkts dec.) 314	1/79 2/97 3/124	(6 wkts) 204
5/290 6/296		4/131 5/160 6/193	

A. Sidebottom and G. A. Cope did not bat.

Bonus points – Yorkshire 4, Middlesex 2.

Bowling: *First Innings*—van der Bijl 22–7–66–1; Daniel 17–2–61–1; Edmonds 16–5–30–0; Merry 12–1–51–2; Gatting 7–0–25–0; Emburey 22–8–46–2. *Second Innings*—Daniel 8–0–30–1; van der Bijl 12–6–24–0; Merry 6–3–7–0; Edmonds 30–9–64–3; Emburey 31–8–60–2; Radley 1–0–2–0.

Middlesex

*J. M. Brearley c Sharp b Old	26	†I. J. Gould not out	22
R. O. Butcher c Hartley b Old	11		
J. E. Emburey c Sharp b Old	2	B 2, l-b 6, n-b 8	16
C. T. Radley not out	136		
G. D. Barlow c Bairstow b Stevenson	5	1/20 2/22 3/66 4/86 (5 wkts dec.)	328
M. W. Gatting c Athey b Cope	110	5/263	

P. H. Edmonds, V. A. P. van der Bijl, W. G. Merry and W. W. Daniel did not bat.

Bonus points – Middlesex 4, Yorkshire 2.

Bowling: Old 19–3–72–3; Stevenson 20–4–61–1; Sidebottom 16–3–50–0; Cope 12–2–40–1; Carrick 15–1–60–0; Athey 3–0–29–0.

Umpires: W. L. Budd and J. van Geloven.

At The Oval, June 14, 16, 17. MIDDLESEX drew with SURREY.

At Southend, June 18, 19, 20. MIDDLESEX beat ESSEX by eight wickets.

At Oxford, June 21, 23, 24. MIDDLESEX drew with OXFORD UNIVERSITY.

At Birmingham, June 28, 30, July 1. MIDDLESEX drew with WARWICKSHIRE.

MIDDLESEX v NORTHAMPTONSHIRE

At Lord's, July 5, 7, 8. Drawn. Middlesex 5 pts, Northamptonshire 3 pts. Middlesex played three spinners on a pitch affording noticeable turn. When Larkins went at 65 it appeared that Middlesex had control, but Allan Lamb played with the ease and power few batsmen can match. Watts and Sarfraz lent loyal and skilled support and Northamptonshire reached a satisfactory total. On the second morning Cook was sent to hospital after receiving a blow behind the right ear from Slack, while fielding at short leg. Slack and Radley made pleasant progress, but Middlesex were tending to slow down when rain ended the game just after lunch.

Northamptonshire

G. Cook c Maru b Emburey	3	Sarfraz Nawaz c Gould b Edmonds	21
W. Larkins c Maru b Emburey	35	T. M. Lamb not out	2
R. G. Williams c Gatting b van der Bijl	8	B. J. Griffiths b Daniel	0
A. J. Lamb c Gould b Emburey	112		
P. Willey run out	11	B 11, l-b 10, n-b 1	22
T. J. Yardley b Maru	4		
†G. Sharp b Edmonds	8	1/22 2/35 3/61 4/92 5/97 6/139	248
*P. J. Watts c Brearley b Edmonds	22	7/209 8/243 9/247	

Bonus points – Northamptonshire 2, Middlesex 4.

Bowling: Daniel 15.3–4–40–1; van der Bijl 15–6–28–1; Emburey 26–8–78–3; Edmonds 25–9–58–3; Maru 7–0–22–1.

Middlesex

*J. M. Brearley lbw b Griffiths	19	G. D. Barlow not out	10
W. N. Slack lbw b Sarfraz	47	L-b 11, n-b 3	14
C. T. Radley not out	74		
M. W. Gatting run out	1	1/39 2/104 3/105 (3 wkts)	165

†I. J. Gould, P. H. Edmonds, J. E. Emburey, V. A. P. van der Bijl, R. Maru and W. W. Daniel did not bat.

Bonus points – Middlesex 1, Northamptonshire 1.

Bowling: Sarfraz 14–3–36–1; Griffiths 16–6–38–1; Willey 23–10–47–0; Williams 12–1–24–0; T. M. Lamb 3–1–6–0.

Umpires: D. J. Dennis and R. S. Herman.

MIDDLESEX v HAMPSHIRE

At Lord's, July 9, 10, 11. Middlesex won by five wickets. Middlesex 15 pts, Hampshire 3 pts. The first day was lost and Hampshire, put in on the second morning, batted soundly on a bland pitch. Jesty was the most enterprising, while Turner and Pocock had bright moments. Three wickets to van der Bijl in the 72nd over preceded a declaration. Brearley was struck on the forehead by Graf, who led a useful breakthrough that saw Middlesex struggling. Tremlett played attractively as Hampshire worked towards the third declaration, when Middlesex were set 296 in 220 minutes. The target looked unreachable as the home county lumbered to 54 for three. But Radley set them on the right path with an assault on Cowley, and Butcher produced a display of unusual violence to win the match. He hit Southern for two 6s and a 4 in one over, then savaged Stevenson and Jesty. His daring never outstripped his skill in a memorable innings which took just one hundred and forty-four minutes, was the highest of his career until he surpassed it two weeks later, and contained nine 6s and eight 4s.

Hampshire

T. M. Tremlett c Gould b Daniel	1	– not out	74
C. L. Smith c Gould b Selvey	24	– c Barlow b Maru	33
M. C. J. Nicholas c Gould b Daniel	26	– st Gould b Barlow	48
T. E. Jesty lbw b van der Bijl	55	– not out	7
D. R. Turner b van der Bijl	44		
*N. E. J. Pocock b van der Bijl	40		
N. G. Cowley c Daniel b van der Bijl	13		
S. F. Graf lbw b van der Bijl	1		
†G. R. Stephenson not out	0		
L-b 6, n-b 5	11	L-b 3, n-b 2	5

1/5 2/44 3/74 4/118   (8 wkts dec.) 215   1/57 2/139   (2 wkts dec.) 167
5/197 6/214 7/215 8/215

J. W. Southern and K. Stevenson did not bat.

Bonus points – Hampshire 2, Middlesex 3.

Bowling: *First Innings*—van der Bijl 20–4–40–5; Daniel 13–2–54–2; Selvey 22–8–56–1; Edmonds 6–0–18–0; Maru 10–1–29–0; Brearley 1–0–7–0. *Second Innings*—Daniel 6–1–18–0; van der Bijl 7–3–21–0; Maru 16–2–69–1; Selvey 9–1–44–0; Barlow 4–0–10–1.

Middlesex

*J. M. Brearley retired hurt	12	– b Southern	14
W. N. Slack b Stevenson	3	– lbw b Stevenson	18
C. T. Radley lbw b Graf	30	– c and b Graf	75
G. D. Barlow lbw b Graf	2	– c and b Southern	5
R. O. Butcher b Tremlett		– not out	153
†I. J. Gould not out	17	– c Stevenson b Tremlett	16
V. A. P. van der Bijl not out	7	– not out	4
B 1, l-b 3, w 1, n-b 3	8	L-b 10, n-b 1	11

1/12 2/22 3/47 4/70   (4 wkts dec.) 87   1/30 2/38 3/54   (5 wkts) 296
                                               4/231 5/291

P. H. Edmonds, M. W. W. Selvey, R. Maru and W. W. Daniel did not bat.

Bonus points – Hampshire 1.

Bowling: *First Innings*—Graf 12–2–32–2; Stevenson 10–3–18–1; Tremlett 5–0–18–1; Jesty 6–1–11–0. *Second Innings*—Graf 16–2–75–1; Stevenson 16–1–87–1; Southern 7–0–37–2; Cowley 5–0–32–0; Jesty 10–1–48–0; Tremlett 1–0–6–1.

Umpires: W. L. Budd and J. G. Langridge.

At Scarborough, July 23, 24, 25. MIDDLESEX beat YORKSHIRE by eight wickets.

MIDDLESEX v KENT

At Lord's, July 26, 28, 29. Drawn. Middlesex 8 pts, Kent 4 pts. With the first day lost, Middlesex's basic ambition became the accumulation of full bonus points, which they achieved. Downton, playing his first game for Middlesex and against his old county, surpassed anything he had achieved with the bat before in first-class cricket and played as easily as Brearley during their 59-overs stand. Eight 4s from van der Bijl sped Middlesex towards 300. On the last day Middlesex entertained hopes of making Kent follow on, but the main bowlers failed to break through from 115 for four and Brearley delivered seventeen looping full-tosses to induce some indiscretion – a tactic he was to employ without success on other occasions later in the summer. Hughes, who ended Taylor's 39 overs of toil, was another newcomer who impressed for Middlesex.

Middlesex

*J. M. Brearley b Jarvis	106		
†P. R. Downton c Shepherd b Underwood	64	– (1) not out	46
C. T. Radley c Waterton b Shepherd	13		
G. D. Barlow not out	39		
V. A. P. van der Bijl b Jarvis	46		
R. O. Butcher not out	9		
K. P. Tomlins (did not bat).		– (2) run out	55
B 1, l-b 4, w 1, n-b 17	23	B 3, l-b 2, w 3	8

1/160 2/197 3/219   (4 wkts dec.) 300   1/109   (1 wkt) 109
4/265

S. P. Hughes, M. W. W. Selvey, R. Maru and W. W. Daniel did not bat.

Bonus points – Middlesex 4, Kent 1.

Bowling: *First Innings*—Jarvis 24–4–79–2; Spelman 5.5–2–18–0; Shepherd 17–1–47–1; Underwood 20.1–6–61–1; Johnson 12–2–29–0; Cowdrey 9.2–0–43–0. *Second Innings*—Shepherd 5–0–14–0; Cowdrey 8–1–28–0; Tavaré 11–2–39–0; Taylor 9–2–20–0.

Kent

N. R. Taylor c Downton b Hughes	34	D. L. Underwood b Hughes	7
G. W. Johnson run out	2	K. B. S. Jarvis c Butcher b Hughes	0
C. J. Tavaré c Butcher b van der Bijl	23	G. D. Spelman b Maru	0
C. S. Cowdrey lbw b Daniel	44		
*A. G. E. Ealham c Downton b Hughes	41	B 2, l-b 6, n-b 2	10
M. Benson not out	58		
†S. N. V. Waterton lbw b Daniel	3	1/5 2/51 3/88 4/115 5/162	258
J. N. Shepherd c Butcher b Maru	36	6/178 7/229 8/237 9/237	

Bonus points – Kent 3, Middlesex 4.

Bowling: Daniel 16–3–37–2; van der Bijl 10–4–9–1; Hughes 23–6–82–4; Tomlins 7–2–15–0; Selvey 12–5–32–0; Maru 17.1–7–50–2; Brearley 4–0–23–0.

Umpires: H. D. Bird and C. Cook.

MIDDLESEX v ESSEX

At Lord's, August 2, 4, 5. Middlesex won by an innings and 4 runs. Middlesex 20 pts, Essex 2 pts. Selvey relished a rare chance to use the new ball, taking four for 29 in his opening two-hour spell on a damp pitch and in a humid atmosphere. Hughes collected two wickets in his first thirteen balls and, despite a few blows from Phillip, Middlesex were batting by mid-afternoon and were well ahead at the close. After Downton had dominated the first evening, Butcher (two 6s) commanded the second morning, before Barlow, held back through injury, turned the screw. On the last day the main Essex batsmen organised such effective resistance in their second innings that they reached tea at 219 for three. Fletcher and Hardie departed late, but, with Emburey out of action after being hit on the nose by a shot from Turner, and bad light reducing play by seven overs, Essex looked safe again at 261 for six. The light improved, however, and Daniel returned with the new ball to take four for 11 in 25 balls. With only three overs left and 4 runs wanted for a draw Hughes dramatically yorked Acfield to give Middlesex an unexpected but crucial victory.

Essex

G. A. Gooch c Butcher b Selvey	5	– c Daniel b Emburey	38
M. S. A. McEvoy lbw b Selvey	22	– lbw b Emburey	41
K. S. McEwan c Downton b Selvey	0	– b Emburey	70
B. R. Hardie lbw b Hughes	2	– (5) c Downton b Daniel	32
*K. W. R. Fletcher c Butcher b Selvey	16	– (4) c Emburey b Maru	49
S. Turner c Downton b Hughes	2	– c Selvey b Daniel	18
N. Phillip c Hughes b Emburey	51	– c Radley b Hughes	1
R. E. East lbw b Emburey	8	– b Daniel	1
†N. Smith b Selvey	4	– b Daniel	21
J. K. Lever not out	6	– not out	7
D. L. Acfield c Brearley b Daniel	7	– b Hughes	0
L-b 4, n-b 1	5	B 1, l-b 6, w 3, n-b 2	12

1/8 2/14 3/29 4/29 5/35 6/73   128   1/81 2/105 3/193 4/226   290
7/108 8/115 9/115   5/247 6/255 7/261
                                  8/282 9/283

Bonus points – Middlesex 4.

Bowling: *First Innings*—Selvey 21–6–42–5; Daniel 7.1–1–28–1; Hughes 11–3–40–2; Emburey 12–6–13–2; Maru 1–1–0–0. *Second Innings*—Daniel 24–4–74–4; Selvey 14–7–26–0; Hughes 20.4–3–65–2; Emburey 33–13–55–3; Maru 18–5–39–1; Brearley 3–1–6–0; Radley 3–0–13–0.

Middlesex

*J. M. Brearley lbw b Turner	19	J. E. Emburey c Smith b Lever	24
†P. R. Downton c Smith b Phillip	67	M. W. W. Selvey not out	40
C. T. Radley c East b Acfield	12		
M. W. Gatting c Smith b East	45	L-b 10, w 1, n-b 8	19
R. O. Butcher c Phillip b Acfield	83		
R. Maru c Fletcher b Acfield	13	1/61 2/86 3/153 (7 wkts dec.) 422
G. D. Barlow not out	100	4/159 5/199 6/288 7/346

W. W. Daniel and S. P. Hughes did not bat.

Bonus points – Middlesex 4, Essex 2.

Bowling: Lever 33–4–133–1; Phillip 25–4–72–1; Acfield 32–8–90–3; Turner 22–2–66–1; East 12–5–30–1; Gooch 4–1–12–0.

Umpires: D. Shackleton and P. B. Wight.

MIDDLESEX v LEICESTERSHIRE

At Lord's, August 6, 7. Leicestershire won by an innings and 100 runs. Leicestershire 20 pts, Middlesex 3 pts. Leicestershire's young pace bowlers collected an early wicket each, but Middlesex had no cause for real alarm until Butcher's reckless running eliminated Radley and himself. The accuracy of Clift and Parsons ensured that there would be no recovery. The first morning having virtually settled the match, it remained only for Davison and Tolchard to make substantial scores on the easing pitch after the capture of four wickets had raised false hopes for Middlesex. Davison, often at his best at Lord's, had made his handsome 98 by the last over of the first day, and Tolchard, 65 overnight, masterminded the 113 runs added for the last five wickets. Middlesex were in no condition after that to make a fight of it. Brearley could not bat until number ten because of a back injury and Selvey was struck on the nose by a mis-hook. Agnew's speed accounted for openers Downton and Tomlins and, after a brief challenge, both Butcher and Barlow lost patience against Cook, who hurried through the later batsmen to end the game in the extra half hour of the second day. It was Leicestershire's first win and Middlesex's first defeat of the season.

Middlesex

*J. M. Brearley lbw b Agnew	18	– (10) not out	15
†P. R. Downton c Tolchard b Parsons	10	– (1) b Agnew	13
C. T. Radley run out	0	– lbw b Clift	9
G. D. Barlow c Tolchard b Clift	7	– (5) c Balderstone b Cook	56
R. O. Butcher run out	23	– (4) c Parsons b Cook	27
K. P. Tomlins c Gower b Parsons	1	– (2) lbw b Agnew	0
M. W. W. Selvey c Agnew b Parsons	0	– (8) c Agnew b Wenlock	20
F. J. Titmus lbw b Agnew	2	– (7) c Balderstone b Cook	0
R. Maru b Clift	4	– (6) c Davison b Cook	11
W. W. Daniel b Agnew	15	– (9) b Cook	5
S. P. Hughes not out	0	– c Agnew b Wenlock	0
L-b 2, n-b 5	7	B 4, l-b 2, n-b 2	8

1/29 2/31 3/33 4/61 5/61 6/62   87   1/0 2/19 3/43 4/58 5/134   164
7/64 8/68 9/81   6/134 7/141 8/145 9/161

Bonus points – Leicestershire 4.

Bowling: *First Innings*—Agnew 10.2–0–46–3; Parsons 12–3–25–3; Clift 8–5–9–2. *Second Innings*—Agnew 10–2–34–2; Parsons 11–4–33–0; Clift 16–2–49–1; Cook 14–6–17–5; Wenlock 7.5–1–23–2.

Leicestershire

J. C. Balderstone c Downton b Hughes	33	G. J. Parsons c Tomlins b Maru	11
J. F. Steele c Titmus b Selvey	5	J. P. Agnew b Hughes	20
D. I. Gower lbw b Hughes	6	N. G. B. Cook not out	6
*B. F. Davison b Selvey	98		
N. E. Briers lbw b Daniel	18	B 3, l-b 10, w 3, n-b 4	20
†R. W. Tolchard c Downton b Daniel	109		
P. B. Clift run out	24	1/27 2/40 3/57 4/93 5/238	351
D. A. Wenlock b Titmus	1	6/279 7/287 8/302 9/337	

Bonus points – Leicestershire 4, Middlesex 3 (Score at 100 overs: 329-8).

Bowling: Daniel 23.4–5–80–2; Selvey 22–5–63–2; Hughes 24–2–88–3; Maru 10–1–29–1; Titmus 23–7–34–1; Tomlins 6–1–26–0; Brearley 3–1–11–0.

Umpires: D. O. Oslear and P. B. Wight.

At Cheltenham, August 9, 11, 12. MIDDLESEX lost to GLOUCESTERSHIRE by six wickets.

MIDDLESEX v NOTTINGHAMSHIRE

At Lord's, August 16, 18, 19. Middlesex won by an innings and 17 runs. Middlesex 19 pts, Nottinghamshire 4 pts. With two successive defeats behind them, Middlesex were put in on a damp pitch and were reduced, mainly by Rice, to 86 for six. At this critical time Barlow and van der Bijl transformed the match and, possibly, the result of the Championship. Their stand of 152 began with grinding defence but, as the pitch eased, they branched out, van der Bijl lofting the ball judiciously and Barlow driving and running productively. Emburey delivered 52.5 of the 84 overs of spin bowled on the second day as Nottinghamshire gradually surrendered. He exploited every fraction of help as the ball turned occasionally and slowly. Nottinghamshire followed on and were virtually beaten in two days, the match ending after ten minutes' play on the final day.

Middlesex

*J. M. Brearley b Watson	0	M. W. W. Selvey b Watson	29
†P. R. Downton c French b Rice	1	W. W. Daniel c Randall b Hacker	10
C. T. Radley b Rice	54	F. J. Titmus not out	0
M. W. Gatting b Hemmings	9		
R. O. Butcher c Randall b Watson	2	L-b 1, w 1, n-b 1	3
G. D. Barlow st French b Hacker	97		
J. E. Emburey lbw b Rice	3	1/2 2/8 3/34 4/37 5/80	284
V. A. P. van der Bijl lbw b Watson	76	6/86 7/238 8/264 9/280	

Bonus points – Middlesex 3, Nottinghamshire 4.

Bowling: Rice 16–4–41–3; Watson 20–5–53–4; Hacker 11.2–0–37–2; Hemmings 32–6–87–1; Bore 19–4–63–0.

Nottinghamshire

P. A. Todd run out	14	– c Selvey b Emburey	23
R. T. Robinson c Radley b Emburey	9	– c Radley b Emburey	31
D. W. Randall b van der Bijl	12	– lbw b van der Bijl	49
*C. E. B. Rice lbw b van der Bijl	12	– b Emburey	4
M. J. Harris st Downton b Emburey	6	– c Radley b Emburey	6
†B. N. French lbw b Emburey	6	– c Butcher b Titmus	24
B. Hassan not out	1	– c Downton b Emburey	14
E. E. Hemmings c Emburey b Titmus	1	– c Gatting b Emburey	11
W. K. Watson b Emburey	1	– not out	7
P. J. Hacker lbw b Emburey	0	– lbw b van der Bijl	1
M. K. Bore c Downton b Emburey	0	– lbw b Daniel	1
B 5, l-b 4, n-b 2	11	B 1, l-b 9, w 1, n-b 1	12

1/25 2/41 3/55 4/64 5/74	84	1/44 2/76 3/86	183
6/75 7/83 8/84 9/84		4/121 5/129 6/158 7/168	
		8/173 9/175	

Bonus points – Middlesex 4.

Bowling: *First Innings*—Daniel 3–2–10–0; van der Bijl 13–4–20–2; Emburey 21.5–8–31–6; Titmus 7–3–7–1; Selvey 5–3–5–0. *Second Innings*—Daniel 9.3–4–20–1; van der Bijl 13–5–20–2; Emburey 37–10–76–6; Titmus 27–8–40–1; Selvey 5–1–11–0; Brearley 1–0–4–0.

Umpires: A. Jepson and J. G. Langridge.

MIDDLESEX v DERBYSHIRE

At Uxbridge, August 20, 21, 22. Middlesex won by nine wickets. Middlesex 17 pts, Derbyshire 6 pts. Centenary Test preparations forced Middlesex away from Lord's for only the third time since World War Two. However, the Uxbridge pitch proved adequate and the crowds were large. Steele, pushing and deflecting, and Kirsten, artistic and fluent, held up Middlesex for 47 overs while adding 141. But when van der Bijl hit Kirsten's off stump the innings fell apart, five batsmen failing to score. Middlesex lost their openers on the first evening, and Miller bowled splendidly on the second day when the pitch accepted some spin. When Derbyshire batted again, 56 ahead, Wood survived for four hours before Titmus beat his drive. On the third day van der Bijl wrapped up Derbyshire's last four wickets in seven overs, achieving match figures of ten for 59. Brearley and Downton made Middlesex's target of 199 appear an easy one and, when Brearley left, Downton developed his range of shots to take Middlesex home in style.

Derbyshire

B. Wood c Downton b van der Bijl	20	– (2) b Titmus	58
A. J. Borrington lbw b van der Bijl	2	– (1) b Daniel	0
P. N. Kirsten b van der Bijl	92	– lbw b Daniel	22
D. S. Steele not out	86	– b Edmonds	14
*G. Miller c Downton b Titmus	0	– lbw b van der Bijl	17
J. Walters lbw b van der Bijl	0	– run out	1
I. S. Anderson lbw b van der Bijl	0	– b van der Bijl	12
†R. W. Taylor run out	0	– b van der Bijl	2
C. J. Tunnicliffe c Tomlins b Titmus	1	– b van der Bijl	0
P. G. Newman c and b Edmonds	8	– not out	6
S. Oldham lbw b Titmus	0	– b van der Bijl	0
B 5, l-b 2, n-b 4	11	L-b 8, n-b 2	10

1/9 2/44 3/185 4/190 5/191 6/191   220   1/0 2/40 3/69 4/96 5/109   142
7/195 8/196 9/213   6/123 7/125 8/125 9/142

Bonus points – Derbyshire 2, Middlesex 4.

Bowling: *First Innings*—Daniel 10–3–24–0; van der Bijl 23–8–34–5; Selvey 16–6–31–0; Titmus 21.5–5–55–3; Edmonds 14–1–50–1; Tomlins 5–1–15–0. *Second Innings*—van der Bijl 23–13–25–5; Daniel 9–2–27–2; Edmonds 32–13–61–1; Titmus 7–1–19–1.

Middlesex

*J. M. Brearley c Steele b Miller	7	– c Taylor b Newman	67
†P. R. Downton c Taylor b Tunnicliffe	18	– not out	90
C. T. Radley c Tunnicliffe b Miller	26	– not out	22
M. W. W. Selvey lbw b Steele	30		
G. D. Barlow lbw b Miller	17		
K. P. Tomlins c Taylor b Tunnicliffe	1		
W. N. Slack c Newman b Steele	38		
V. A. P. van der Bijl c and b Miller	1		
P. H. Edmonds c and b Miller	0		
F. J. Titmus not out	10		
W. W. Daniel b Steele	1		
L-b 5, n-b 10	15	B 3, l-b 8, n-b 9	20

1/29 2/29 3/74 4/109 5/110 6/124   164   1/138   (1 wkt) 199
7/126 8/126 9/162

Bonus points – Middlesex 1, Derbyshire 4.

Bowling: *First Innings*—Newman 8–1–38–0; Oldham 6–2–14–0; Miller 25–8–52–5; Tunnicliffe 17–7–19–2; Steele 14.2–6–26–3. *Second Innings*—Oldham 7–2–19–0; Tunnicliffe 10–5–24–0; Miller 21–7–59–0; Newman 7–2–21–1; Steele 12–4–27–0; Anderson 3–0–15–0; Kirsten 3.5–1–14–0.

Umpires: J. G. Langridge and W. L. Budd.

At Hove, August 23, 25, 26. MIDDLESEX drew with SUSSEX.

At Cardiff, August 30, September 1, 2. MIDDLESEX beat GLAMORGAN by 72 runs.

At Canterbury, September 3, 4, 5. MIDDLESEX drew with KENT.

NORTHAMPTONSHIRE

President – H. W. WRIGHT

Chairman, Cricket Committee – A. P. ARNOLD

Secretary – K. C. TURNER
County Ground, Wantage Road, Northampton NN1 4TJ

Captain – P. J. WATTS (1980), G. COOK (1981)

| P. J. Watts | County Badge | R. G. Williams |

The highlight of Northamptonshire's 1980 season was, without question, their victory at Lord's where they won the Benson and Hedges Cup for the first time. And in so doing continued their successful Cup run of recent years. In 1976 they gained their first-ever major trophy when they won the Gillette Cup, and in 1979 they were again finalists, losing to Somerset.

They reached the knockout stages of the Benson and Hedges Cup with good wins over all four opponents in the group matches, and then followed keenly contested ties in which they demonstrated their fighting qualities as they disposed of Nottinghamshire, Middlesex, and finally Essex at Lord's.

Claiming one of the four major trophies was a fitting climax to the long career of their captain, Jim Watts, who retired in August after three spells with the county, the first of them beginning in 1957. Having trained as a school-teacher, he returned for the last time in 1978 to stabilise the club after the upheaval caused by the departure of four leading players in 1977, among them the previous captain, Mushtaq Mohammad. The captaincy has been passed to the opening batsman, Geoff Cook. Middlesbrough-born, Cook joined Northamptonshire in 1971 and had been Watts's deputy for the previous three seasons. He also has the experience of several winters playing in South Africa for Eastern Province.

In finishing sixth equal in the John Player League, Northamptonshire might feel some disappointment, having appeared likely champions until the end of July. Four wins from their last six games would have put them alongside Warwickshire's final, winning points tally of 46, but a batting slump produced five defeats and undid the earlier successes.

Indeed, the season's early results were probably the most successful in Northamptonshire's history, sixteen wins being notched by the end of June: six each in the Benson and Hedges Cup and in the John Player League, three in the County Championship, and one over Cambridge University. Two of the Championship wins were achieved by meeting targets of over 300 in the fourth innings. But July was less fruitful, and it was August before two more Championship wins came along. With thirteen of their Championship matches affected by rain, Watts was prepared to sacrifice bonus points in an attempt to obtain a definite result, but his enterprise found little reward. Altogether five Championship matches were won, and only last-wicket defiance by Lancashire and Essex prevented two more wins which would have given Northamptonshire fourth place instead of twelfth. Significantly, bonus points dropped from 117 in 1979 to 88.

The county began the season in the belief, of their supporters, that they had the best first five batsmen in the country, but as the summer progressed disappointingly, only three lived up to their reputations. Wayne Larkins, Allan Lamb and Richard Williams enjoyed splendid seasons, Lamb having his best yet with 1,797 runs in first-class matches at an average of 66.55. His many large scores featured five first-class hundreds, and the delight his batting gave contributed to his inclusion as one of the Almanack's Five Cricketers. He won the Gold Award in the Benson and Hedges Cup final.

Larkins was in fine, aggressive county form with 1,682 first-class runs and an average of over 50, hitting four hundreds and passing fifty in eight innings. He and Williams shared a second-wicket stand of 322 against Leicestershire in August, a record for the county. Williams, 23, continued his encouraging progress; in all competitions he totalled around 2,000 runs and took more than 60 wickets. He hit a career-best 175 not out against Leicestershire, had a best-ever return of seven for 73 against Cambridge University, and did the hat-trick against Gloucestershire.

The disappointments were Cook and Peter Willey, who fell below their best form. Willey, owing to England calls, played in only twelve Championship matches for the county, scoring a mere 278 runs at 18.53 and taking only 26 wickets with his off-spin – nine of these in a match-winning effort against Hampshire. Fortunately the middle-order batting of Jim Yardley, wicket-keeper George Sharp and Sarfraz Nawaz proved satisfactory. Sharp three times only narrowly missed his maiden century, while Yardley hit his first hundred for Northamptonshire.

With the ball, the fast-medium combination of Jim Griffiths, Sarfraz and Tim Lamb was an effective attacking force. Lamb showed the benefits of a winter in Australian cricket, enjoying his best season for Northamptonshire with 66 first-class wickets, and Griffiths again reached the 50 mark. Sarfraz, though hindered at times by injuries, bowled economically and was a commanding figure in the Benson and Hedges Cup matches at Lord's, both in the semi-final and the final. – Fred Speakman.

NORTHAMPTONSHIRE

Patrick Eagar

Back row: A. J. Lamb. T. M. Lamb, Sarfraz Nawaz, B. J. Griffiths. T. J. Yardley, W. Larkins, R. M. Carter, R. G. Williams. *Front row*: G. Sharp. P. Willey.
P. J. Watts (*captain*), G. Cook.

NORTHAMPTONSHIRE RESULTS

All First-class Matches – Played 24: Won 6, Lost 5, Drawn 13.

County Championship Matches – Played 22: Won 5, Lost 4, Drawn 13.

Bonus points – Batting 41, Bowling 47.

COUNTY CHAMPIONSHIP AVERAGES

BATTING

	Birthplace	Matches	Inns	Not Outs	Runs	Highest Inns	Avge
A. J. Lamb	*Langebaanweg, SA*	22	37	12	1,720	152	68.80
W. Larkins	*Roxton*	18	32	3	1,511	156	52.10
R. G. Williams	*Bangor*	22	37	3	1,061	175*	31.20
Sarfraz Nawaz	*Lahore, Pakistan*	17	16	5	324	50	29.45
G. Sharp	*West Hartlepool*	22	26	7	528	94	27.78
G. Cook	*Middlesbrough*	20	35	4	810	109	26.12
T. J. Yardley	*Chaddesley Corbett*	22	28	4	600	100*	25.00
P. Willey	*Sedgefield*	12	17	2	278	73	18.53
P. J. Watts	*Henlow*	14	15	3	220	37*	18.33
R. M. Tindall	*Harrow-on-the-Hill*	6	10	1	119	48	13.22
R. M. Carter	*King's Lynn*	11	16	2	177	32	12.64
R. J. Boyd-Moss	*Hatton, Ceylon*	7	10	1	106	56	11.77
T. M. Lamb	*Hartford*	22	19	11	92	12*	11.50
B. J. Griffiths	*Wellingborough*	21	14	1	35	10	2.69
N. A. Mallender	*Kirk Sandall*	4	6	3	4	2*	1.33

Also batted: C. D. Booden (*Newport Pagnell*) 6*; I. G. Peck (*Great Staughton*) 4.

* *Signifies not out.*

BOWLING

	Overs	Maidens	Runs	Wickets	Average
R. M. Carter	65.2	10	255	10	25.50
T. M. Lamb	564.3	148	1,560	53	29.43
Sarfraz Nawaz	408.1	114	1,104	36	30.66
B. J. Griffiths	539.3	139	1,515	47	32.23
P. Willey	382.5	102	871	25	34.84
R. G. Williams	481	91	1,430	39	36.66

Also bowled: C. D. Booden 24–0–86–0; R. J. Boyd-Moss 37–4–130–1; G. Cook 3–0–11–0; A. J. Lamb 4–0–26–1; W. Larkins 42–3–181–2; N. A. Mallender 81.4–14–302–6; G. Sharp 13–2–47–1; R. M. Tindall 11–0–59–0; P. J. Watts 8–0–54–0; T. J. Yardley 3–0–14–0.

HUNDREDS

The following twelve three-figure innings were played for Northamptonshire in County Championship matches – A. J. Lamb 152 v Leicestershire (Leicester), 149* v Worcestershire (Northampton), 117 v Lancashire (Southport), 113* v Gloucestershire (Bristol), 112 v Middlesex (Lord's); W. Larkins 156 v Leicestershire (Leicester), 127 v Gloucestershire (Northampton), 105 v Hampshire (Wellingborough), 103* v Glamorgan (Cardiff); G. Cook 109 v Essex (Northampton); R. G. Williams 175* v Leicestershire (Leicester); T. J. Yardley 100* v Gloucestershire (Northampton).

At Canterbury, April 30, May 1, 2. NORTHAMPTONSHIRE drew with KENT.

At Bristol, May 3, 5, 6. NORTHAMPTONSHIRE beat GLOUCESTERSHIRE by eight wickets.

At Derby, May 7, 8, 9. NORTHAMPTONSHIRE beat DERBYSHIRE by two wickets.

At Milton Keynes, May 17, 18, 19. NORTHAMPTONSHIRE lost to WEST INDIANS by six wickets (See West Indian tour section).

NORTHAMPTONSHIRE v LEICESTERSHIRE

At Northampton, May 24, 26, 27. Drawn. Northamptonshire 6 pts, Leicestershire 4 pts. A tense finish found Northamptonshire struggling desperately to avoid defeat in mediocre light as the umpires conferred four times without calling a halt. On the first day, the visitors had no answer to the pace of Sarfraz, Griffiths and Tim Lamb. But after their first innings deficit of 100 Dudleston (nine 4s) began the reply with a determined 83. An excellent century by Balderstone (twelve 4s) took 202 minutes and Davison (one 6 and eight 4s) accelerated towards the declaration with 60 in 80 minutes. Apart from Larkins (thirteen 4s) and Sarfraz (six 4s) Northamptonshire also found runs difficult. Facing a target of 249 in 145 minutes they collapsed against keen bowling until Willey, Watts and finally Sharp and Tim Lamb averted defeat.

Leicestershire

B. Dudleston lbw b Griffiths	4	– c Sharp b T. M. Lamb	83
J. F. Steele lbw b T. M. Lamb	21	– c A. J. Lamb b Willey	47
J. C. Balderstone c Cook b Sarfraz	5	– c Williams b A. J. Lamb	102
D. I. Gower lbw b T. M. Lamb	0	– lbw b T. M. Lamb	0
*B. F. Davison b Sarfraz	3	– (6) c Griffiths b Williams	60
†R. W. Tolchard b T. M. Lamb	32	– (5) b Sarfraz	16
P. B. Clift lbw b Griffiths	11	– not out	8
J. Birkenshaw c Watts b Griffiths	23	– not out	11
P. Booth c Watts b Griffiths	8		
N. G. B. Cook c Sarfraz b T. M. Lamb	3		
K. Higgs not out	2		
B 5, w 2, n-b 7	14	B 2, l-b 7, w 2, n-b 10	21

1/22 2/37 3/37 4/37 5/43 6/84 7/93   **126**   1/115 2/161   (6 wkts dec.) **348**
8/118 9/119   3/161 4/231 5/324 6/329

Bonus points – Northamptonshire 4.

Bowling: *First Innings*—Sarfraz 18–9–18–2; Griffiths 23–9–48–4; T. M. Lamb 21–11–27–4; Watts 3–0–17–0; Willey 3–1–2–0. *Second Innings*—Sarfraz 22–6–44–1; Griffiths 19–3–74–0; T. M. Lamb 26–6–73–2; Willey 23–5–50–1; Larkins 11–0–41–0; A. J. Lamb 4–0–26–1; Williams 4–1–19–1.

Northamptonshire

G. Cook lbw b Clift	3	– c Davison b Booth	4
W. Larkins lbw b Clift	91	– lbw b Higgs	5
R. G. Williams c Cook b Higgs	2	– c Cook b Dudleston	6
A. J. Lamb b Clift	20	– b Dudleston	13
P. Willey c Balderstone b Booth	18	– c Cook b Clift	21
T. J. Yardley c Cook b Booth	6	– c Davison b Cook	1
*P. J. Watts c Clift b Booth	2	– c Davison b Clift	25
†G. Sharp c Tolchard b Higgs	17	– not out	7
Sarfraz Nawaz b Clift	32	– c Balderstone b Cook	5
T. M. Lamb not out	10	– not out	2
B. J. Griffiths b Higgs	10		
L-b 13, n-b 2	15	B 1,l-b 2, n-b 1	4

1/18 2/21 3/57 4/110 5/123 6/139   226   1/9 2/9 3/25 4/34   (8 wkts) 93
7/168 8/174 9/215   5/35 6/73 7/80 8/91

Bonus points – Northamptonshire 2, Leicestershire 4.

Bowling: *First Innings*—Higgs 33.5–12–80–3; Booth 18–6–49–3; Clift 33–17–74–4; Cook 5–4–1–0; Steele 6–3–7–0. *Second Innings*—Higgs 9–3–13–1; Booth 6–3–16–1; Cook 12–6–16–2; Dudleston 7–3–8–2; Birkenshaw 4–2–5–0; Clift 9.5–2–31–2; Balderstone 2–2–0–0.

Umpires: R. Palmer and D. J. Halfyard.

NORTHAMPTONSHIRE v YORKSHIRE

At Northampton, May 28, 29, 30. Drawn. Northamptonshire 2 pts, Yorkshire 7 pts. In a rain-affected match Northamptonshire's Richard Williams destroyed a Yorkshire victory bid. The visitors declared with a first innings lead of 200, hoping to bowl Northamptonshire out cheaply for a second time, but Williams battled against them for three hours, hitting one 6 and twelve 4s in his 93. Cook and Larkins gave Northamptonshire a useful start in their fight back, and Allan Lamb helped Williams put on 113 for the third wicket. In their first innings Northamptonshire had slumped against the pace of Stevenson and the spin of Carrick. It was a fine all-round match for Carrick, who hit a career-best 131 not out in 230 minutes with one 6 and fourteen 4s; his spirited batting earned Yorkshire their lead.

Northamptonshire

G. Cook c Coverdale b Stevenson	6	– b Cope	36
W Larkins lbw b Stevenson	25	– c Lumb b Cope	24
R. G. Williams c Coverdale b Stevenson	9	– b Athey	93
A. J. Lamb st Coverdale b Carrick	41	– not out	40
T. J. Yardley b Sidebottom	19	– not out	4
*P. J. Watts c Hartley b Stevenson	3		
†G. Sharp c Coverdale b Cope	3		
R. M. Carter c Sidebottom b Carrick	11		
Sarfraz Nawaz c Stevenson b Carrick	0		
T. M. Lamb not out	12		
B. J. Griffiths c Love b Cope	0		
B 1,l-b 2, w 1, n-b 7	11	B 4, l-b 8, n-b 5	17

1/22 2/41 3/42 4/87 5/94 6/103   140   1/46 2/95 3/208   (3 wkts) 214
7/121 8/123 9/136

Bonus points – Yorkshire 4.

Bowling: *First Innings*—Stevenson 22–6–51–4; Cooper 11–4–31–0; Cope 13.1–4–19–2; Sidebottom 10–5–17–1; Carrick 8–4–11–3. *Second Innings*—Stevenson 13–7–22–0; Cooper 6–2–16–0; Carrick 28–10–58–0; Cope 20–8–48–2; Sidebottom 7–4–9–0; Athey 8–2–26–1; Sharp 6–1–18–0.

Yorkshire

*R. G. Lumb c T. M. Lamb b Sharp	4	S. N. Hartley b Griffiths	12
C. W. J. Athey lbw b T. M. Lamb	36	H. P. Cooper b Griffiths	3
K. Sharp lbw b T. M. Lamb	40	G. A. Cope not out	0
J. D. Love c A. J. Lamb b Williams	47	B 5, l-b 12, w 1, n-b 7	25
P. Carrick not out	131		
†S. P. Coverdale c Watts b Griffiths	18	1/30 2/50 3/127 4/152 (9 wkts dec.) 340	
G. B. Stevenson c Yardley b Sarfraz	1	5/213 6/230 7/299 8/323	
A. Sidebottom c Griffiths b Sarfraz	23	9/334	

Bonus points – Yorkshire 3, Northamptonshire 2 (Score at 100 overs: 265-6).

Bowling: Sarfraz 27–9–71–2; Griffiths 27–8–63–3; Williams 24–5–75–1; Sharp 13–2–47–1; T. M. Lamb 24–6–59–2.

Umpires: D. J. Halfyard and R. Palmer.

At Cardiff, May 31, June 2, 3. NORTHAMPTONSHIRE drew with GLAMORGAN.

At Cambridge, June 4, 5, 6. NORTHAMPTONSHIRE beat CAMBRIDGE UNIVERSITY by 34 runs.

NORTHAMPTONSHIRE v GLOUCESTERSHIRE

At Northampton, June 7, 9, 10. Northamptonshire won by six wickets. Northamptonshire 19 pts, Gloucestershire 7 pts. This game swung considerably, for after Gloucestershire had scored prolifically on the first day they lost all ten second innings wickets on the final morning. This left Northamptonshire with a target of 223 in the afternoon and evening sessions and they won comfortably with Larkins hitting twenty 4s in his 127. However, the last day really belonged to Williams, who did the hat-trick after earlier being on a hat-trick when he dismissed Sadiq and Stovold with successive balls. The first day produced brilliant batting by Zaheer, Hignell and Bainbridge, and Zaheer again passed the 70 mark in the second innings. After their early free-scoring Gloucestershire looked strongly placed on the second day when they dismissed the first four home batsmen for 115. But Yardley led the recovery with an unbeaten century, his first in five seasons at Northampton since leaving Worcestershire. He hit fourteen 4s in a stay of three hours and shared a century fifth-wicket stand with Tindall.

Gloucestershire

Sadiq Mohammad b T. M. Lamb	31	– c Watts b Williams	32
B. C. Broad c Yardley b Sarfraz	28	– c A. J. Lamb b Sarfraz	18
Zaheer Abbas c and b Sarfraz	79	– c Sharp b T. M. Lamb	75
A. W. Stovold b Sarfraz	6	– c Cook b Williams	0
*A. J. Hignell b Griffiths	89	– c Sharp b T. M. Lamb	30
P. Bainbridge b Sarfraz	71	– c Yardley b Williams	0
M. D. Partridge c A. J. Lamb b Sarfraz	13	– c Yardley b Williams	0
D. A. Graveney not out	9	– c Cook b Williams	0
A. H. Wilkins (did not bat)		– run out	15
†A. J. Brassington (did not bat)		– c Sharp b Williams	1
J. H. Childs (did not bat)		– not out	0
B 4, l-b 5, n-b 7	16	B 1, l-b 2, n-b 8	11

1/35 2/82 3/119 4/162 (7 wkts dec.) 342   1/46 2/64 3/64 4/140 5/146   182
5/309 6/329 7/342   6/146 7/146 8/181 9/182

Bonus points – Gloucestershire 4, Northamptonshire 3.

Bowling: *First Innings*—Sarfraz 25–6–65–5; Griffiths 22–5–77–1; T. M. Lamb 17–5–54–1; Williams 27–5–82–0; Tindall 6–0–30–0; Watts 2–0–18–0. *Second Innings*—Sarfraz 19–6–46–1; Griffiths 10–4–17–0; Williams 29.5–9–65–6; T. M. Lamb 9–5–14–2; Tindall 5–0–29–0.

Northamptonshire

G. Cook b Wilkins	19	– c and b Graveney 11
W. Larkins c Brassington b Childs	49	– c Wilkins b Zaheer 127
R. G. Williams lbw b Wilkins	15	– c and b Childs 37
A. J. Lamb c Wilkins b Broad	12	– c Partridge b Childs 36
T. J. Yardley not out	100	– not out 1
R. M. Tindall b Bainbridge	48	– not out 10
†G. Sharp c Hignell b Childs	16	
*P. J. Watts b Childs	4	
Sarfraz Nawaz not out	22	
L-b 11, n-b 6	17	L-b 3 3

1/38 2/60 3/92 4/115   (7 wkts dec.) 302   1/63 2/136 3/201   (4 wkts) 225
5/219 6/257 7/263   4/212

T. M. Lamb and B. J. Griffiths did not bat.

Bonus points – Northamptonshire 4, Gloucestershire 3.

Bowling: *First Innings*—Wilkins 22–7–61–2; Partridge 13–4–38–0; Graveney 18–5–50–0; Bainbridge 13–2–36–1; Broad 5–1–18–1; Childs 23–6–59–3; Sadiq 6–0–23–0. *Second Innings*—Wilkins 4–0–14–0; Partridge 6–2–17–0; Childs 18.1–3–71–2; Graveney 11–1–37–1; Bainbridge 5–0–18–0; Sadiq 4–1–23–0; Broad 2–0–25–0; Zaheer 7–3–17–1.

Umpires: T. W. Spencer and W. E. Alley.

NORTHAMPTONSHIRE v NOTTINGHAMSHIRE

At Northampton, June 14, 16, 17. Drawn. Nottinghamshire 1 pt. Only a brief period of play on the second afternoon was possible. The heavy rainstorms saturated the square and Larkins did well to score 47 with a 6 and five 4s in such difficult conditions. With the hope of getting a result Watts declared his first innings, but he was thwarted when the final day, like the first, was totally washed out.

Northamptonshire

G. Cook run out	11	P. Willey not out	6
W. Larkins c Hemmings b Tunnicliffe	47	B 1, w 1	2
R. G. Williams c Rice b Cooper	0		
A. J. Lamb not out	20	1/28 2/32 3/78 (3 wkts dec.) 86	

T. J. Yardley, *P. J. Watts, †G. Sharp, Sarfraz Nawaz, T. M. Lamb and B. J. Griffiths did not bat.

Bonus points – Nottinghamshire 1.

Bowling: Cooper 7–3–27–1; Hacker 9–2–30–0; Hemmings 9.1–5–12–0; Tunnicliffe 7–0–15–1.

Nottinghamshire

P. A. Todd not out	13
B. Hassan not out	15
L-b 2, n-b 2	4

(no wkt) 32

D. W. Randall, *C. E. B. Rice, H. T. Tunnicliffe, J. D. Birch, †C. C. Curzon, P. J. Hacker, E. E. Hemmings, M. E. Allbrook and K. E. Cooper did not bat.

Bowling: Sarfraz 5–0–15–0; Griffiths 4–0–13–0.

Umpires: D. G. L. Evans and P. S. G. Stevens.

NORTHAMPTONSHIRE v DERBYSHIRE

At Northampton, June 18, 19, 20. Derbyshire won by eight wickets. Derbyshire 17 pts, Northamptonshire 6 pts. Derbyshire imposed Northamptonshire's first Championship defeat of the season in decisive fashion after the game swung their way on the second evening. Their pace bowlers, Tunnicliffe and Oldham, reduced Northamptonshire to 83 for six and carried on the next morning to provide Derbyshire with a final target of 154 in 196 minutes. Tunnicliffe finished with career-best figures of six for 41; Oldham took the other four wickets. Wright and Wood comfortably scored 127 for the first wicket, both playing fine innings to give Derbyshire a clear-cut win. On the opening day Allan Lamb had hit 93 in three hours (four 6s and ten 4s) and a profitable stand of 79 between Watts and Sharp allowed the former to declare on obtaining maximum bonus points. Derbyshire's first innings was remarkable for Wood playing only one scoring shot in seventy-nine minutes.

Northamptonshire

G. Cook c Walters b Oldham	17	– c Taylor b Tunnicliffe		2
W. Larkins lbw b Oldham	32	– c Walters b Oldham		18
R. G. Williams c Tunnicliffe b Steele	41	– lbw b Tunnicliffe		23
A. J. Lamb c Walters b Tunnicliffe	93	– c Wood b Oldham		21
T. J. Yardley b Miller	17	– c Taylor b Oldham		10
R. M. Tindall c Steele b Miller	1	– c Steele b Tunnicliffe		1
†G. Sharp not out	42	– c Wood b Oldham		4
*P. J. Watts not out	37	– c Walters b Tunnicliffe		6
Sarfraz Nawaz (did not bat)		– c Steele b Tunnicliffe		9
T. M. Lamb (did not bat)		– b Tunnicliffe		12
B. J. Griffiths (did not bat)		– not out		0
B 4, l-b 4, n-b 12	20	B 1, l-b 2, n-b 9		12

1/34 2/59 3/132 4/192   (6 wkts dec.) 300   1/10 2/36 3/53 4/76 5/77   118
5/208 6/221   6/83 7/93 8/94 9/113

Bonus points – Northamptonshire 4, Derbyshire 2.

Bowling: *First Innings*—Tunnicliffe 18–3–68–1; Oldham 21–1–81–2; Steele 31.1–11–70–1; Wood 5–1–16–0; Miller 23–13–45–2. *Second Innings*—Tunnicliffe 17.1–3–41–6; Oldham 18–4–55–4; Walters 1–0–5–0; Steele 1–0–4–0; Miller 2–1–1–0; Barnett 1–1–0–0.

Derbyshire

B. Wood c Sharp b Griffiths	4	– c Sharp b Williams		59
J. G. Wright c Yardley b Griffiths	4	– not out		81
P. N. Kirsten lbw b Williams	67	– c Sharp b Williams		6
D. S. Steele c Cook b Williams	32	– not out		1
K. J. Barnett b Williams	69			
*G. Miller c Sharp b T. M. Lamb	14			
I. S. Anderson not out	19			
J. Walters not out	33			
B 8, l-b 8, w 1, n-b 6	23	L-b 1, n-b 6		7

1/7 2/36 3/117 4/146   (6 wkts) 265   1/127 2/137   (2 wkts) 154
5/189 6/221

†R. W. Taylor, C. J. Tunnicliffe and S. Oldham did not bat.

Bonus points – Derbyshire 3, Northamptonshire 2 (Score at 100 overs: 263-6).

Bowling: *First Innings*—Sarfraz 20–8–58–0; Griffiths 23–9–43–2; T. M. Lamb 28–6–69–1; Williams 30–6–72–3. *Second Innings*—Sarfraz 11–2–31–0; Griffiths 11–1–45–0; T. M. Lamb 12–2–37–0; Williams 10.2–2–31–2; Cook 2–0–3–0.

Umpires: D. G. L. Evans and P. S. G. Stevens.

At Nuneaton, June 21, 23, 24. NORTHAMPTONSHIRE drew with WARWICKSHIRE.

NORTHAMPTONSHIRE v WORCESTERSHIRE

At Northampton, June 28, 30, July 1. Drawn. Northamptonshire 4 pts, Worcestershire 3 pts. South African Allan Lamb dominated a rain-spoiled match of only 88 overs with the last day blank. His masterly unbeaten 149 included 24 excellent 4s, and he had the frustration of the game being abandoned when only 18 short of his 1,000 runs by the end of June. When play began after lunch Larkins and Cook hit 30 off the first four overs, Larkins attacking freely for his half-century in ninety-three minutes and completing his 1,000 runs for the season.

Northamptonshire

G. Cook c Younis b Cumbes	17	*P. J. Watts c Younis b Alleyne	23
W. Larkins c Inchmore b Pridgeon	78	Sarfraz Nawaz not out	14
R. G. Williams c Humphries b Cumbes	9		
A. J. Lamb not out	149	B 3, l-b 6, n-b 13	22
P. Willey lbw b Cumbes	6		
T. J. Yardley c Ormrod b Cumbes	0	1/63 2/79 3/147 4/172 5/173 (7 wkts) 340	
†G. Sharp b Inchmore	22	6/223 7/276	

T. M. Lamb and B. J. Griffiths did not bat.

Bonus points – Northamptonshire 4, Worcestershire 3.

Bowling: Alleyne 21–5–79–1; Pridgeon 19–2–71–1; Inchmore 18–5–44–1; Cumbes 30–3–124–4.

Worcestershire

*G. M. Turner, J. A. Ormrod, P. A. Neale, E. J. O. Hemsley, Younis Ahmed, D. N. Patel, †D. J. Humphries, J. D. Inchmore, H. Alleyne, A. P. Pridgeon, J. Cumbes.

Umpires: R. Julian and C. T. Spencer.

At Lord's July 5, 7, 8. NORTHAMPTONSHIRE drew with MIDDLESEX.

NORTHAMPTONSHIRE v WARWICKSHIRE

At Northampton, July 9, 10, 11. Drawn. Northamptonshire 3 pts, Warwickshire 3 pts. After rain had prevented play on the first day, full bonus points were sacrificed as both teams declared their first innings. Finally Warwickshire set the home county the high target of 269 in 150 minutes but, after Northamptonshire's opening pair had scored 56 in eighteen overs, more rain put an end to the game. It was a successful match for Warwickshire opener David Smith who shared an opening stand of 100 with Amiss and in 220 minutes hit two 6s and eight 4s. His second innings half-century included another seven boundaries. Williams was Northamptonshire's most successful bowler in the first innings, taking four wickets – two in consecutive balls – despite being hit for four 6s. Northamptonshire declared 96 behind after Allan Lamb (seven 4s) hit an unbeaten 37 in eighteen minutes. Before Warwickshire's cautious second innings declaration, Smith was helped by aggressive batting from Humpage, whose 83 included thirteen 4s.

Warwickshire

*D. L. Amiss c Sharp b Sarfraz	43	– c Sharp b Sarfraz	5
K. D. Smith c and b Williams	90	– c Sarfraz b T. M. Lamb	59
T. A. Lloyd c Watts b Sarfraz	5	– run out	7
†G. W. Humpage c Yardley b Williams	13	– not out	83
J. A. Claughton b Williams	0	– not out	15
P. R. Oliver c Sharp b T. M. Lamb	3		
A. M. Ferreira c Yardley b Williams	11		
D. C. Hopkins not out	9		
G. C. Small lbw b Griffiths	16		
B 2, l-b 3, n-b 5	10	L-b 1, n-b 2	3

1/100 2/121 3/146   (8 wkts dec.) 200   1/9 2/31 3/128   (3 wkts dec.) 172
4/146 5/155 6/165 7/177 8/200

D. R. Doshi and S. P. Perryman did not bat.

Bonus points – Warwickshire 2, Northamptonshire 3.

Bowling: *First Innings*—Sarfraz 21–9–37–2; Griffiths 14.4–4–33–1; T. M. Lamb 19–9–30–1; Carter 4–1–7–0; Williams 26–6–83–4. *Second Innings*—Sarfraz 7–2–7–1; Griffiths 5–1–14–0; Williams 16–2–61–0; T. M. Lamb 15–2–71–1; Cook 1–0–8–0; Yardley 1–0–8–0.

Northamptonshire

G. Cook c Claughton b Doshi	36	– not out	34
R. M. Carter c Humpage b Ferreira	20	– not out	14
R. G. Williams b Doshi	5		
A. J. Lamb not out	37		
R. J. Boyd-Moss not out	0		
L-b 4, w 2	6	L-b 4, w 2, n-b 2	8

1/60 2/62 3/92   (3 wkts dec.) 104   (no wkt) 56

T. J. Yardley, †G. Sharp, *P. J. Watts, Sarfraz Nawaz, T. M. Lamb and B. J. Griffiths did not bat.

Bonus points – Warwickshire 1.

Bowling: *First Innings*—Small 7–4–15–0; Hopkins 9–3–11–0; Doshi 12–4–20–2; Perryman 5–0–18–0; Ferreira 3.2–0–34–1. *Second Innings*—Small 4–1–4–0; Hopkins 2–0–4–0; Doshi 7–2–20–0; Lloyd 5–1–20–0.

Umpires: D. G. L. Evans and D. O. Oslear.

At Southport, July 23, 24, 25. NORTHAMPTONSHIRE drew with LANCASHIRE.

NORTHAMPTONSHIRE v SURREY

At Northampton, August 2, 4, 5. Surrey won by an innings and 31 runs. Surrey 19 pts, Northamptonshire 2 pts. Although Surrey won decisively Northamptonshire had made a brave fight on the last day. The damage was done on the first morning when the home county were dismissed cheaply in 29.4 overs. Surrey went on to build up a mammoth lead of 313 after Clinton had set them on the way with his first century of the season. Northamptonshire lost four second innings wickets for 47 but were rallied on the final day by bold hitting from Williams, Yardley, Sharp (one 6 and ten 4s) and Sarfraz. Batting with a runner, the injured Williams hit a brisk half-century in eighty-eight minutes with nine fours. Despite the fight-back Surrey won comfortably soon after tea with Clarke, Pocock and Cheatle each taking three wickets.

Northamptonshire

R. M. Carter c Knight b Jackman	6	– lbw b Clarke	1
W. Larkins b Clarke	6	– c Lynch b Pocock	18
R. G. Williams b Jackman	10	– (6) c Butcher b Pocock	52
A. J. Lamb c Richards b Clarke	15	– (3) b Clarke	8
P. Willey lbw b Jackman	6	– (4) c Richards b Clarke	12
T. J. Yardley b Knight	30	– (5) c Knight b Cheatle	62
†G. Sharp c Roope b Jackman	1	– c Roope b Cheatle	87
*P. J. Watts not out	20	– c Roope b Pocock	7
Sarfraz Nawaz lbw b Knight	0	– c Lynch b Jackman	21
T. M. Lamb b Knight	3	– not out	4
B. J. Griffiths c Richards b Knight	0	– c Roope b Cheatle	0
N-b 4	4	B 4, l-b 5, w 1	10

1/12 2/12 3/26 4/40　　　　　　　　101　　1/3 2/19 3/43 4/47　　　　　　　282
5/44 6/46 7/87 8/87 9/93　　　　　　　　5/146 6/164 7/190 8/248 9/282

Bonus points – Surrey 4.

Bowling: *First Innings*—Clarke 11–1–49–2; Jackman 11–4–39–4; Knight 5.4–2–9–4; Pocock 2–2–0–0. *Second Innings*—Clarke 17–1–77–3; Jackman 18–8–43–1; Knight 1–0–12–0; Pocock 34–11–97–3; Cheatle 15.3–2–43–3.

Surrey

A. R. Butcher run out	3	†C. J. Richards not out	31
G. S. Clinton c Sharp b Griffiths	120	S. T. Clarke b T. M. Lamb	26
G. P. Howarth c Yardley b T. M. Lamb	19	P. I. Pocock not out	12
*R. D. V. Knight lbw b Willey	49	B 1, l-b 16, w 1, n-b 7	25
G. R. J. Roope c Sharp b Griffiths	53		
M. A. Lynch c Watts b Sarfraz	29	1/5 2/44 3/148　　　(8 wkts dec.)	414
R. D. Jackman c Sarfraz b Larkins	47	4/250 5/265 6/306 7/363 8/399	

R. G. L. Cheatle did not bat.

Bonus points – Surrey 3, Northamptonshire 2 (Score at 100 overs: 276-5).

Bowling: Sarfraz 27–8–84–1; Griffiths 32–6–85–2; T. M. Lamb 25–4–87–2; Willey 34–8–80–1; Larkins 11–0–53–1.

Umpires: D. O. Oslear and R. Palmer.

At Eastbourne, August 6, 7, 8. NORTHAMPTONSHIRE lost to SUSSEX by eight wickets.

NORTHAMPTONSHIRE v SOMERSET

At Northampton, August 9, 11, 12. Drawn. Northamptonshire 5 pts, Somerset 5 pts. Rain interfered badly, delaying the start until 2.30 p.m. on the first day and completely washing out the second, although the final day produced entertaining cricket. Three pace bowlers dominated the game; on the first day Griffiths captured four wickets with lively bowling and on the final morning Tim Lamb took the four remaining wickets for 13 runs in 8.2 overs with a season's best return of five for 47 in the innings. These performances were eclipsed by Dredge, who took four wickets for 11 in four overs, finishing with a career-best analysis of six for 57. Somerset quickly lost their opening pair in the first innings but were rallied by a fighting half-century from Denning, well supported by Marks and Popplewell. Northamptonshire fought back from 50 for five with hectic hitting by Williams and Sarfraz who made a succession of hard boundary shots.

Somerset

M. Olive c Williams b Griffiths	7	– not out	9
S. M. Gavaskar c Cook b Sarfraz	9		
P. M. Roebuck lbw b Griffiths	14		
P. W. Denning c Carter b T. M. Lamb	52		
*V. J. Marks c Sarfraz b Griffiths	30		
N. F. M. Popplewell c T. M. Lamb b Griffiths	22		
†D. J. S. Taylor lbw b T. M. Lamb	8		
J. W. Lloyds c Cook b T. M. Lamb	21	– (2) st Sharp b Carter	20
C. H. Dredge c Sarfraz b T. M. Lamb	7		
H. I. E. Gore c Sarfraz b T. M. Lamb	7	– (3) not out	8
H. R. Moseley not out	6		
B 6, 1-b 3, w 2, n-b 2	13		

1/17 2/21 3/59 4/107   196   1/26   (1 wkt) 37
5/132 6/137 7/173 8/183 9/184

Bonus points – Somerset 1, Northamptonshire 4.

Bowling: *First Innings*—Sarfraz 14–4–36–1; Griffiths 25–8–57–4; T. M. Lamb 22.2–6–47–5; Williams 15–2–43–0. *Second Innings*—Griffiths 3–2–5–0; T. M. Lamb 2–0–9–0; Carter 5–0–17–1; Boyd-Moss 3–3–0–0; Yardley 2–0–6–0.

Northamptonshire

*G. Cook b Dredge	26	Sarfraz Nawaz c Taylor b Dredge	38
R. M. Carter b Dredge	6	T. M. Lamb not out	9
R. J. Boyd-Moss lbw b Dredge	0	B. J. Griffiths c Popplewell b Lloyds	10
A. J. Lamb c Popplewell b Dredge	6		
T. J. Yardley b Lloyds	7	B 2, 1-b 3, n-b 1	6
I. G. Peck c Gavaskar b Dredge	4		
R. G. Williams c Lloyds b Gore	39	1/17 2/25 3/41 4/42	163
†G. Sharp c Taylor b Moseley	12	5/50 6/92 7/94 8/118 9/150	

Bonus points – Northamptonshire 1, Somerset 4.

Bowling: Moseley 15–4–29–1; Gore 11–2–36–1; Dredge 20–7–57–6; Lloyds 7.5–1–20–2; Popplewell 4–0–15–0.

Umpires: A. Jepson and C. T. Spencer.

NORTHAMPTONSHIRE v HAMPSHIRE

At Wellingborough, August 16, 18, 19. Northamptonshire won by eight wickets. Northamptonshire 20 pts, Hampshire 4 pts. On a rain-affected wicket Northamptonshire outplayed a Hampshire side strengthened by the return of their West Indian players Marshall and Greenidge. Play began after an early lunch on the first day when Hampshire were dismissed cheaply before tea by the off-spinners Williams and Willey, despite a fighting stand by Marshall and Southern. Northamptonshire gained maximum batting points thanks to a fine century from Larkins (two 6s and twelve 4s) and lusty hitting by Sharp and Sarfraz. Bailey persevered in the Hampshire attack and was rewarded with five wickets. The visitors again struggled against Willey, who achieved his season's best analysis of nine for 128. They were eight wickets down when the extra half-hour was taken on the second evening but Marshall hit his best score for Hampshire and, ably supported by Bailey, took the game into the third morning.

Hampshire

C. G. Greenidge b Williams	15	– c Sarfraz b Williams	28
T. M. Tremlett b Williams	17	– lbw b Willey	6
M. C. J. Nicholas c Cook b Williams	15	– lbw b Willey	11
D. R. Turner c Sharp b Williams	6	– lbw b Willey	43
*N. E. J. Pocock c Cook b Willey	9	– b Boyd-Moss	9
N. G. Cowley c Yardley b Willey	6	– b Willey	11
†R. J. Parks c Yardley b Willey	3	– c Larkins b Williams	16
M. D. Marshall c and b Williams	29	– not out	72
J. W. Southern b Willey	8	– c Sharp b Willey	1
M. J. Bailey run out		– c Sharp b T. M. Lamb	24
K. Stevenson not out	2	– lbw b T. M. Lamb	13
B 4, l-b 5	9	B 5, l-b 8	13

1/28 2/33 3/45 4/64   119   1/26 2/46 3/56 4/77   247
5/64 6/73 7/74 8/106 9/109   5/100 6/125 7/135 8/143 9/213

Bonus points – Northamptonshire 4.

Bowling: *First Innings*—Sarfraz 7–3–10–0; Griffiths 4–2–7–0; Willey 21–5–43–4; Williams 18.5–2–50–5. *Second Innings*—Sarfraz 3–2–12–0; T. M. Lamb 8.5–3–21–2; Williams 32–10–61–2; Willey 47–17–85–5; Boyd-Moss 17–1–43–1; Griffiths 2–1–12–0.

Northamptonshire

*G. Cook c Parks b Marshall	0	– not out	20
W. Larkins c Parks b Southern	105	– c and b Stevenson	5
R. G. Williams b Bailey	33	– c Tremlett b Stevenson	0
A. J. Lamb c Turner b Bailey	15	– not out	32
P. Willey lbw b Bailey	1		
T. M. Lamb c Parks b Southern	1		
T. J. Yardley b Bailey	1		
R. J. Boyd-Moss c Stevenson b Bailey	0		
†G. Sharp not out	81		
Sarfraz Nawaz c Stevenson b Cowley	29		
B. J. Griffiths b Marshall	9		
B 13, l-b 8, w 1, n-b 4	26	B 3, l-b 4, n-b 2	9

1/1 2/74 3/100 4/114   301   1/11 2/13   (2 wkts) 66
5/131 6/136 7/142 8/216 9/268

Bonus points – Northamptonshire 4, Hampshire 4.

Bowling: *First Innings*—Marshall 15–3–39–2; Stevenson 3–1–6–0; Southern 27–6–98–2; Cowley 18–4–43–1; Bailey 28–7–89–5. *Second Innings*—Marshall 9–3–15–0; Stevenson 6–3–7–2; Bailey 5–2–16–0; Southern 3–0–19–0.

Umpires: R. Julian and T. W. Spencer.

NORTHAMPTONSHIRE v ESSEX

At Northampton, August 20, 21, 22. Drawn. Northamptonshire 4 pts, Essex 7 pts. On a batsmen's wicket this was a big-scoring match until the final evening session when Essex collapsed, leaving their tenth-wicket pair, Lever and Acfield, to survive the last 22 balls. Northamptonshire began the game with their best opening stand for fourteen years – 216 from Cook and Larkins. Cook hit his first Championship century of the season with eleven 4s and Larkins, with twelve boundaries, was only 2 short of his hundred, but the home innings petered out later against Turner and Phillip. Essex also produced a double-century stand with McEwan and Fletcher unbeaten in a third-wicket partnership of 202 after a good opening innings by Denness. Northamptonshire had lost three wickets by the second evening, but were rallied by a fifth-wicket stand of 101 in 85 minutes from Yardley and Cambridge Blue Boyd-Moss, who hit his first Championship half-century. Set to make 241 in 153 minutes. Essex seemed settled for a draw after losing four wickets but the game came to life in the final twenty overs. The 19-year-old pace bowler Mallender – on his Championship début – took three wickets in four overs, Griffiths took another two, and Essex had to struggle to avoid defeat.

Northamptonshire

*G. Cook c McEwan b Acfield	109	– lbw b Acfield 29
W. Larkins c Smith b Turner	98	– c Fletcher b East 26
R. G. Williams c Smith b Turner	2	– b East 19
A. J. Lamb c McEwan b Phillip	48	– c McEvoy b Acfield 37
R. J. Boyd-Moss lbw b Turner	2	– c East b Lever 56
T. J. Yardley b Phillip	19	– b Lever 48
R. M. Carter lbw b Phillip	9	– lbw b Lever. 6
†G. Sharp not out	11	– b Acfield 7
N. A. Mallender not out	0	– st Smith b Acfield........ 0
T. M. Lamb (did not bat)		– not out 2
B 1, l-b 6, n-b 9	16	– B 7, l-b 10 17

1/216 2/217 3/224   (7 wkts) 314   1/37 2/78 3/78   (9 wkts dec.) 247
4/226 5/269 6/295 7/306   4/122 5/223 6/234
                                           7/243 8/243 9/247

B. J. Griffiths did not bat.

Bonus points – Northamptonshire 4, Essex 3.

Bowling: *First Innings*—Lever 13–2–45–0; Phillip 17–1–99–3; Turner 29–10–57–3; East 8–1–39–0; Acfield 33–9–58–1. *Second Innings*—Lever 15–3–33–3; Phillip 11–2–31–0; East 36–8–96–2; Turner 12–2–21–0; Acfield 26.3–10–49–4.

Essex

M. H. Denness c T. M. Lamb b Williams	67	– lbw b Griffiths 4
M. S. A. McEvoy c Larkins b T. M. Lamb	27	– b Griffiths............... 22
K. S. McEwan not out	140	– c Boyd-Moss b T. M. Lamb.. 16
*K. W. R. Fletcher not out	81	– c Larkins b Williams 14
B. R. Hardie (did not bat)		– b Mallender 37
S. Turner (did not bat)		– c Cook b Mallender 12
N. Phillip (did not bat)		– b Mallender 10
R. E. East (did not bat)		– b Griffiths............... 8
†N. Smith (did not bat)		– c Boyd-Moss b Griffiths.... 4
J. K. Lever (did not bat)		– not out 1
D. L. Acfield (did not bat)		– not out 0
L-b 4, n-b 2	6	B 1, l-b 15................ 16

1/83 2/119   (2 wkts) 321   1/6 2/25 3/53 4/73   (9 wkts) 144
                                      5/117 6/128 7/132 8/139 9/144

Bonus points – Essex 4.

Bowling: *First Innings*—Griffiths 22–3–66–0; T. M. Lamb 24–6–68–1; Williams 32–5–82–1; Mallender 15–2–67–0; Boyd-Moss 7–0–32–0. *Second Innings*—Griffiths 14–6–44–3; T. M. Lamb 8–2–22–1; Williams 14–4–33–1; Mallender 12–3–29–3.

Umpires: R. Julian and A. G. T. Whitehead.

At Leicester, August 23, 25, 26. NORTHAMPTONSHIRE lost to LEICESTERSHIRE by three wickets.

At Leeds, August 30, September 1, 2. NORTHAMPTONSHIRE beat YORKSHIRE by eight wickets.

At Chelmsford, September 3, 4, 5. NORTHAMPTONSHIRE drew with ESSEX.

NOTTINGHAMSHIRE

President – DR J. COCHRANE, FRCOG

Chairman, Cricket Committee – J. R. HEATLEY

Chief Executive – P. G. CARLING
County Cricket Ground, Trent Bridge, Nottingham NG2 6AG

Cricket Manager – K. A. TAYLOR

Captain – C. E. B. RICE

P. J. Hacker   County Badge   E. E. Hemmings

The overall improvement in Nottinghamshire's cricket in 1980 could not fail to be recognised, even if the majority of their limited-overs performances left something to be desired. Finishing third in the Schweppes County Championship – their highest final position since last winning the title in 1929 – brought considerable, if far from total, satisfaction.

The ironies of the season were plentiful. Not least was the widely held belief that the side was better equipped for an assault on the limited-overs competitions. Yet, having qualified for the Benson and Hedges Cup quarter-finals, they were depressingly swept aside by the eventual winners, Northamptonshire. Middlesex, also eventual winners, brought an abrupt end to their Gillette Cup aspirations after Durham had come uncomfortably near to forcing another memorable victory over a first-class county. And only a final flourish lifted Nottinghamshire away from the foot of the John Player League after they had struggled for much of the summer to come to terms with the demands of a competition in which they were confident of doing well.

Throughout the season, however, Nottinghamshire overcame what could have been a crippling sequence of injuries to retain their interest in the Championship. There was more irony in the fact that they maintained their lofty position in the table in spite of the absence of Hadlee and Rice for a large part of the season. On the occasions when these two were able to operate together, they justified their reputation as one of the most hostile pace combinations in the country.

Richard Hadlee, particularly, was plagued by injury, which led to an admission by the New Zealand star that he found it difficult to absorb the physical demands of all-the-year cricket. But when in action, more often than not off a shortened run, Hadlee showed that he is undoubtedly a world-class bowler. Clive Rice, too, overcame the problems of injury, as well as the pressures of captaincy, to reveal his enormous value with the ball in addition to his considerable stature as a batsman.

With Hadlee and Rice out of the firing line for lengthy periods, the responsibility and much of the credit for Championship achievement rested among others. After several summers of promise, Peter Hacker emerged not only as a bowler capable of holding down a regular place but one possessing match-winning credentials. A succession of career-best figures, culminating in his six for 35 against Hampshire, emphasised the progress he made after reducing his run-up and his pace in order to concentrate more on accuracy and movement. Hacker and Kevin Cooper – both capped, along with wicket-keeper Bruce French at the end of the season – deserved enormous credit for the way they deputised for Hadlee and Rice and then supported them on their return.

Nottinghamshire's strength was, without question, their bowling. In addition to the battery of seamers, Eddie Hemmings bowled with a consistency reflected in an all-matches tally of 77 wickets that matched anything he achieved in his twelve years at Edgbaston. His professionalism also showed through in his batting. Hemmings's spin partner, Mike Bore, also looked set for a prolific season until injuries forced him out of the reckoning.

Had Nottinghamshire been able to make more runs to support the unstinting efforts of their bowlers, they might have been in a position to make a lasting challenge to Middlesex and Surrey who alone finished above them. But apart from Rice, again the outstanding stroke-maker, and Derek Randall, who just lacked the consistency to stake a fresh claim with England, the batting lacked substance. Paul Todd had a disappointing season and Mike Harris's loss of form was a severe blow. Basharat Hassan and John Birch played useful and entertaining innings without making regular contributions and it was understandable that youth was given a chance.

The hope must be that more players of the calibre of Tim Robinson can be unearthed. He has remarkable composure and the extra time for playing his strokes that is the hallmark of class. It was no surprise that he highlighted a season of high individual promise by scoring a maiden century against Leicestershire.

Robinson's arrival in the first team is indicative of the changes being made at Trent Bridge under the positive leadership of Rice and the thoughtful guidance of manager Ken Taylor. With commercial activities continuing to flourish under the umbrella of chief executive Philip Carling, there is every hope that further success on the field will follow. – John Lawson.

NOTTINGHAMSHIRE

|Press Association

Back row: M. K. Bore, P. J. Hacker, W. K. Watson, K. Saxelby, J. D. Birch, K. E. Cooper, R. T. Robinson, N.l. Weightman. *Middle row:* C. C. Curzon, E. E. Hemmings, M. E. Allbrook, H. T. Tunnicliffe, G. Lyas (*physiotherapist*), N. Nanan, R. E. Dexter, K. S. Mackintosh, B. N. French. *Front row:* P. A. Todd, B. Hassan, R. J. Hadlee, C. E. B. Rice (*captain*), K. Taylor (*manager*), M. J. Harris, R. A. White, D. W. Randall.

NOTTINGHAMSHIRE RESULTS

All First-class Matches – Played 24: Won 8, Lost 5, Drawn 11.

County Championship Matches – Played 22: Won 6, Lost 5, Drawn 11.

Bonus points – Batting 42, Bowling 64.

COUNTY CHAMPIONSHIP AVERAGES

BATTING

	Birthplace	Matches	Inns	Not Outs	Runs	Highest Inns	Avge
C. E. B. Rice	Johannesburg, SA	22	35	9	1,358	131*	52.23
D. W. Randall	Retford	21	36	1	1,349	170	38.54
R. T. Robinson	Sutton-in-Ashfield	13	23	3	672	138	33.60
B. Hassan	Nairobi, Kenya	16	27	3	720	91	30.00
P. A. Todd	Morton	17	32	2	785	71	26.16
H. T. Tunnicliffe	Derby	9	15	3	281	100*	23.41
R. J. Hadlee	Christchurch, NZ	7	8	1	163	44*	23.28
E. E. Hemmings	Leamington Spa	22	26	4	459	86	20.86
J. D. Birch	Nottingham	16	24	4	400	69*	20.00
B. N. French	Warsop	13	18	4	257	70*	18.35
M. J. Harris	St Just-in-Roseland	11	18	2	266	65	16.62
K. S. Mackintosh ...	Surbiton	3	4	2	30	16*	15.00
C. C. Curzon	Lenton	9	12	1	160	45	14.54
R. E. Dexter	Nottingham	4	7	1	51	30*	8.50
K. E. Cooper	Hucknall	15	15	4	93	35	8.45
W. K. Watson	Port Elizabeth, SA	5	8	3	41	13	8.20
M. K. Bore	Hull	16	16	7	63	24*	7.00
N. Nanan	Trinidad, WI	2	4	0	26	11	6.50
P. J. Hacker	Nottingham	15	16	5	59	12	5.36

Also batted: M. E. Allbrook (*Frimley*) 0*; K. Saxelby (*Worksop*) 0, 15; R. A. White (*Fulham*) 2, 6, 2.

* *Signifies not out.*

BOWLING

	Overs	Maidens	Runs	Wickets	Average
R. A. White	48	16	85	11	7.72
R. J. Hadlee	174	62	342	23	14.86
P. J. Hacker	314.2	73	964	48	20.08
C. E. B. Rice	318.4	79	806	38	21.21
E. E. Hemmings	564.5	157	1,539	72	21.37
M. K. Bore	389.2	126	970	32	30.31
K. E. Cooper	353.3	92	985	31	31.77
W. K. Watson	98	16	388	10	38.80

Also bowled: M. E. Allbrook 15–2–57–1; K. S. Mackintosh 44–8–131–2; D. W. Randall 5–0–23–0; R. T. Robinson 6–0–47–1; K. Saxelby 21–2–79–1; H. T. Tunnicliffe 52–19–104–4.

HUNDREDS

The following nine three-figure innings were played for Nottinghamshire in County Championship matches – C. E. B. Rice 131* and 114* v Somerset (Nottingham), 121* v Yorkshire (Harrogate), 108* v Leicestershire (Leicester), 100* v Sussex (Eastbourne); D. W. Randall 170 v Lancashire (Manchester), 166 v Yorkshire (Harrogate); R. T. Robinson 138 v Leicestershire (Nottingham); H. T. Tunnicliffe 100* v Middlesex (Nottingham).

NOTTINGHAMSHIRE v MIDDLESEX

At Nottingham, April 30, May 1, 2. Drawn. Nottinghamshire 5 pts, Middlesex 6 pts. Only seventy-five minutes play were possible on the opening day and, although a draw was always inevitable, there were some notable performances. Daniel and South African van der Bijl, making his début in English cricket, each picked up four wickets as Nottinghamshire were bowled out cheaply. Rice went one better with five wickets but the home team's satisfaction came from the performances of Tunnicliffe, Cooper and Curzon. Curzon took five catches and Cooper claimed four wickets. When Nottinghamshire batted for a second time, with no chance of a positive result, Tunnicliffe recorded his maiden first-class century, hitting eleven boundaries.

Nottinghamshire

M. J. Harris c Gould b Daniel	9	– b Daniel	0
P. A. Todd b Daniel	20	– c and b Emburey	71
D. W. Randall c Barlow b Daniel	13	– b Daniel	8
*C. E. B. Rice c Barlow b Daniel	19	– (6) not out	1
H. T. Tunnicliffe b van der Bijl	33	– (4) not out	100
N. Nanan b Selvey	11	– (5) lbw b van der Bijl	10
†C. C. Curzon c Gould b van der Bijl	0		
R. J. Hadlee c and b Emburey	42		
E. E. Hemmings lbw b van der Bijl	0		
K. E. Cooper b van der Bijl	3		
M. K. Bore not out	5		
B 1, l-b 4, n-b 4	9	L-b 1, w 4, n-b 4	9

1/30 2/35 3/60 4/65 5/97   164   1/0 2/22 3/151   (4 wkts) 199
6/98 7/142 8/142 9/150   4/195

Bonus points – Nottinghamshire 1, Middlesex 4.

Bowling: *First Innings*—Daniel 18–4–58–4; van der Bijl 28–8–62–4; Selvey 18–8–34–1; Edmonds 2–1–1–0; Emburey 1.4–1–0–1. *Second Innings*—Daniel 12–3–41–2; van der Bijl 13.1–4–28–1; Selvey 12–4–10–0; Edmonds 19–4–64–0; Gatting 4–0–12–0; Emburey 18–4–35–1.

Middlesex

*J. M. Brearley c Curzon b Cooper	21	V. A. P. van der Bijl b Rice	20
M. J. Smith c Curzon b Rice	22	M. W. W. Selvey not out	17
C. T. Radley c Curzon b Cooper	10	W. W. Daniel c Curzon b Rice	6
G. D. Barlow lbw b Hadlee	7		
M. W. Gatting c Curzon b Cooper	0		
†I. J. Gould c Curzon b Rice	57	B 3, l-b 13, n-b 1	17
P. H. Edmonds b Cooper	14		
J. E. Emburey c Hemmings b Rice	13	1/35 2/51 3/67 4/67 5/71	204
		6/108 7/137 8/181 9/184	

Bonus points – Middlesex 2, Nottinghamshire 4.

Bowling: Hadlee 17–4–43–1; Rice 21–5–64–5; Cooper 29–4–80–4.

Umpires: D. O. Oslear and H. D. Bird.

NOTTINGHAMSHIRE v YORKSHIRE

At Nottingham, May 7, 8, 9. Yorkshire won by an innings and 47 runs. Yorkshire 19 pts, Nottinghamshire 3 pts. Fine bowling by Stevenson inspired Yorkshire's comfortable victory; he finished with match figures of eleven for 74 after a remarkable spell in the first innings when he took five wickets from thirteen deliveries without conceding a run. Only Randall defied Yorkshire who led by 170 on the first innings, Carrick top scoring with 84 after coming in as night-watchman. Nottinghamshire collapsed to the bowling of Stevenson and Old and, although last pair Cooper and Bore both registered their best scores for the county in a last-wicket stand of 56, an innings defeat was inevitable.

Nottinghamshire

P. A. Todd c Boycott b Stevenson	11	– c Old b Stevenson		9
M. J. Harris c Athey b Stevenson	4	– c Athey b Stevenson		1
D. W. Randall c Lumb b Stevenson	8	– lbw b Old		8
*C. E. B. Rice c Boycott b Sidebottom	31	– (5) c Athey b Old		8
H. T. Tunnicliffe c Sharp b Old	14	– (4) c Athey b Old		0
N. Nanan c Athey b Ramage	0	– lbw b Stevenson		5
†C. C. Curzon c Bairstow b Stevenson	17	– c Boycott b Old		0
E. E. Hemmings b Stevenson	0	– c Bairstow b Stevenson		11
W. K. Watson not out	0	– c Bairstow b Sidebottom		13
K. E. Cooper c Old b Stevenson	1	– c Carrick b Boycott		35
M. K. Bore b Stevenson	0	– not out		24
L-b 8, n-b 4	12	B 1, l-b 2, n-b 6		9

1/13 2/30 3/75 4/105 5/108   162   1/2 2/17 3/19 4/24   123
6/159 7/159 8/160 9/162   5/29 6/29 7/36 8/44 9/67

Bonus points – Nottinghamshire 1, Yorkshire 4.

Bowling: *First Innings*—Old 14–4–45–1; Stevenson 18.5–3–48–7; Sidebottom 12–3–37–1; Ramage 9–3–17–1; Boycott 4–1–3–0. *Second Innings*—Old 19–3–59–4; Stevenson 22–9–26–4; Ramage 5–2–6–0; Sidebottom 7–1–19–1; Boycott 2–1–4–1.

Yorkshire

G. Boycott b Bore	24	G. B. Stevenson b Cooper	1
R. G. Lumb c Curzon b Hemmings	49	C. M. Old c Curzon b Bore	27
C. W. J. Athey c Hemmings b Watson	27	A. Ramage not out	1
P. Carrick c Curzon b Hemmings	84		
*J. H. Hampshire c Rice b Hemmings	35	L-b 7, w 1	8
K. Sharp c Curzon b Bore	41		
†D. L. Bairstow c Bore	28	1/72 2/78 3/118 4/186 5/253	332
A. Sidebottom b Bore	7	6/273 7/290 8/290 9/328	

Bonus points – Yorkshire 3, Nottinghamshire 2 (Score at 100 overs: 253-5).

Bowling: Rice 24–5–54–0; Watson 17–4–68–1; Cooper 33–9–76–2; Bore 35–13–73–4; Hemmings 19–4–53–3.

Umpires: D. J. Dennis and B. J. Meyer.

At Swansea, May 24, 26, 27. NOTTINGHAMSHIRE beat GLAMORGAN by seven wickets.

NOTTINGHAMSHIRE v WARWICKSHIRE

At Nottingham, May 28, 29, 30. Drawn. Nottinghamshire 4 pts, Warwickshire 7 pts. In another game badly affected by the weather, Warwickshire ran out of time after enforcing the follow-on. A spirited 89 by Humpage was the backbone of Warwickshire's first innings and, on a helpful pitch, left-arm spinner Doshi, with support from Ferreira and Rouse, bowled out his former county for 86. However, Nottinghamshire resisted the attack when they batted again and ruled out any chance of a second successive innings defeat at Trent Bridge.

Warwickshire

*D. L. Amiss c Tunnicliffe b Rice	4	G. C. Small not out	5
K. D. Smith c Curzon b Rice	30	D. R. Doshi c Tunnicliffe b Hemmings	1
T. A. Lloyd c Birch b Bore	14	S. P. Perryman not out	2
J. A. Claughton c Curzon b Cooper	34	B 10, l-b 6, w 4, n-b 3	23
P. R. Oliver c Hemmings b Rice	25		
†G. W. Humpage b Rice	89	(9 wkts) 252	
A. M. Ferreira c Curzon b Cooper	15		
S. J. Rouse c Saxelby b Hemmings	10		

1/4 2/35 3/66 4/112 5/152 6/195 7/244 8/244 9/246

Bonus points – Warwickshire 3, Nottinghamshire 4.

Bowling: Rice 25–9–55–4; Saxelby 15–1–50–0; Bore 27–9–58–1; Cooper 18–4–46–2; Hemmings 13–7–20–2.

Nottinghamshire

P. A. Todd c Amiss b Rouse	4	– c sub b Doshi	52
B. Hassan lbw b Ferreira	18	– c Rouse b Ferreira	35
D. W. Randall c Lloyd b Rouse	6	– c Humpage b Oliver	31
*C. E. B. Rice c Ferreira b Rouse	0		
H. T. Tunnicliffe c Humpage b Ferreira	15	– (4) not out	20
J. D. Birch c Smith b Doshi	1		
†C. C. Curzon c sub b Doshi	0	– (5) not out	14
K. Saxelby c Smith b Doshi	0		
E. E. Hemmings lbw b Ferreira	11		
K. E. Cooper c Lloyd b Doshi	8		
M. K. Bore not out	1		
B 8, l-b 10, n-b 4	22	B 2, l-b 4, w 1, n-b 3	10

1/5 2/25 3/27 4/58 5/59 6/59 7/60 8/61 9/82   86   1/72 2/121 3/129   (3 wkts) 162

Bonus points – Warwickshire 4.

Bowling: *First Innings*—Small 3–0–7–0; Rouse 9–0–26–3; Doshi 15.1–6–20–4; Ferreira 10–4–11–3. *Second Innings*—Rouse 13–6–32–0; Ferreira 14–4–32–1; Small 4–1–16–0; Doshi 20–7–32–1; Oliver 6–0–25–1; Lloyd 3–0–15–0.

Umpires: H. D. Bird and R. S. Herman.

At The Oval, May 31, June 2, 3. NOTTINGHAMSHIRE beat SURREY by 38 runs.

At Leicester, June 4, 5, 6. NOTTINGHAMSHIRE drew with LEICESTERSHIRE.

At Manchester, June 7, 9, 10. NOTTINGHAMSHIRE lost to LANCASHIRE by five wickets.

At Northampton, June 14, 16, 17. NOTTINGHAMSHIRE drew with NORTHAMPTON-SHIRE.

At Cambridge, June 18, 19, 20. NOTTINGHAMSHIRE beat CAMBRIDGE UNIVER-SITY by seven wickets.

At Harrogate, June 21, 23, 24. NOTTINGHAMSHIRE lost to YORKSHIRE by 27 runs.

NOTTINGHAMSHIRE v ESSEX

At Nottingham, June 28, 30, July 1. Drawn. Rain washed out the entire opening day's play and much of the second too, leaving captains Rice and Fletcher to attempt to manufacture an exciting finish. Despite their enterprise – Nottinghamshire forfeited their first innings – the home side were left with a demanding target of 206 in 145 minutes. Robinson and Hassan began well, but the fall of three wickets for 16 in the first seven of the last twenty overs virtually ruled out any chance of a positive result.

Essex

M. H. Denness c Mackintosh b Hacker	13	– not out 24
G. A. Gooch c Hassan b Hacker	49	– st French b Robinson 8
K. S. McEwan not out	39	– not out 54
*K. W. R. Fletcher not out	11	
L-b 2, w 2	4	L-b 2, n-b 1 3

1/61 2/68	(2 wkts dec.) 116	1/16 (1 wkt dec.) 89

B. R. Hardie, K. R. Pont, N. Phillip, R. E. East, †N. Smith, J. K. Lever and D. L. Acfield did not bat.

Bowling: *First Innings*—Hacker 12–5–32–2; Cooper 12–3–45–0; Mackintosh 7–1–20–0; Bore 8–3–15–0. *Second Innings*—Bore 5–1–8–0; Hemmings 3–0–8–0; Robinson 6–0–47–1; Randall 5–0–23–0.

Nottinghamshire

B. Hassan (did not bat)	– c Smith b Gooch 42
R. T. Robinson (did not bat)	– not out 42
D. W. Randall (did not bat)	– c Lever b Phillip 3
*C. E. B. Rice (did not bat)	– c Gooch b East 3
J. D. Birch (did not bat)	– not out 6
	L-b 3, w 4 7

1/80 2/85 3/96	(3 wkts) 103

K. S. Mackintosh, P. J. Hacker, †B. N. French, E. E. Hemmings, M. K. Bore and K. E. Cooper did not bat.

Bowling: Lever 8–1–19–0; Phillip 7–1–33–1; Gooch 11–0–32–1; East 3–1–7–1; Acfield 3–0–5–0.

Nottinghamshire forfeited their first innings.

Umpires: D. O. Oslear and P. S. G. Stevens.

At Bristol, July 5, 7, 8. NOTTINGHAMSHIRE drew with GLOUCESTERSHIRE.

NOTTINGHAMSHIRE v SOMERSET

At Nottingham, July 9, 10, 11. Drawn. Nottinghamshire 6 pts, Somerset 7 pts. Both sides were considerably weakened – Somerset by Test calls and Nottinghamshire by injuries – but, although the game ended disappointingly, it produced some intriguing cricket. Nottinghamshire captain Rice made the most of the amiable pitch, hitting two centuries, and the dashing stroke-play of Randall as well as the calm assurance of Robinson, who hit a career-best 92, were other pleasing features of the home county's batting. Somerset's outstanding performer was Denning (three 6s and eighteen 4s) who, with his side in some trouble, produced a superb career-best 184 in four hours seven minutes to give the visitors a first innings lead. When Nottinghamshire set Somerset a target of 266 in eighty minutes plus the statutory twenty overs, a draw was inevitable.

Nottinghamshire

B. Hassan c Taylor b Dredge	4	– c Taylor b Moseley	0
R. T. Robinson c Dredge b Moseley	35	– c Roebuck b Marks	92
D. W. Randall b Moseley	63	– c Gavaskar b Breakwell	86
*C. E. B. Rice not out	131	– not out	114
J. D. Birch lbw b Dredge	4	– not out	15
M. J. Harris c Roebuck b Breakwell	19		
†B. N. French b Moseley	0		
E. E. Hemmings lbw b Moseley	15		
W. K. Watson lbw b Dredge	6		
P. J. Hacker not out	7		
B 2, 1-b 20, w 1, n-b 5	28	B 1, 1-b 4, n-b 3	8

1/5 2/92 3/127 4/141　　　　　(8 wkts dec.) 312　1/0 2/129　　　(3 wkts dec.) 315
5/216 6/219 7/247 8/274　　　　　　　　　　　　　　3/267

M. K. Bore did not bat.

Bonus points – Nottinghamshire 4, Somerset 3.

Bowling: *First Innings*—Moseley 30–6–65–4; Dredge 26–3–83–3; Popplewell 30–6–78–0; Marks 5–0–23–0; Breakwell 8–1–35–1. *Second Innings*—Moseley 12–2–29–1; Dredge 8–3–30–0; Popplewell 3–0–14–0; Marks 28–7–98–1; Breakwell 28–4–106–1; Gavaskar 4–0–19–0; Roebuck 1–0–5–0; Slocombe 1–0–6–0.

Somerset

S. M. Gavaskar c French b Watson	3	– c Randall b Hacker	0
M. Olive c Robinson b Bore	6		
P. M. Roebuck c French b Hacker	2	– not out	34
P. W. Denning c Hassan b Hemmings	184	– (2) c Hemmings b Hacker	34
P. A. Slocombe c Harris b Watson	4	– not out	3
*V. J. Marks c Robinson b Watson	82	– (4) c Hemmings b Hacker	11
†D. J. S. Taylor not out	57		
N. F. M. Popplewell not out	18		
L-b 3, n-b 3	6	L-b 2	2

1/3 2/7 3/62 4/67　　　　　　(6 wkts dec.) 362　1/0 2/61 3/79　　　(3 wkts) 84
5/232 6/319

D. Breakwell, C. H. Dredge and H. R. Moseley did not bat.

Bonus points – Somerset 4, Nottinghamshire 2.

Bowling: *First Innings*—Hacker 20–2–88–1; Watson 21–3–86–3; Bore 27–7–73–1; Hemmings 25.3–5–109–1. *Second Innings*—Hacker 9.3–1–33–3; Watson 5–0–40–0; Bore 4–0–9–0.

Umpires: R. Julian and T. W. Spencer.

NOTTINGHAMSHIRE v KENT

At Nottingham, July 12, 14. Nottinghamshire won by an innings and 1 run. Nottinghamshire 18 pts, Kent 2 pts. Nottinghamshire strengthened their position as rising Championship contenders with an emphatic two-day victory on a rain-affected wicket. Kent, however, contributed to their own downfall on the opening day when they were bowled out for just 67 with the wicket behaving normally. Cooper took five for 31 as all ten wickets fell for the addition of 33 runs; only Woolmer reached double figures. Hassan and Rice did much to put Nottinghamshire in a strong position and, after a rain storm had saturated the pitch, Rice declared 150 ahead. With Hacker taking the first three wickets and Hemmings reaping six for 37, Kent failed to make Nottinghamshire bat again.

Kent

R. A. Woolmer c Birch b Hacker	25	– c Randall b Hacker	0
G. W. Johnson lbw b Cooper	9	– c Harris b Hacker	9
C. J. Tavaré lbw b Hacker	2	– c Hassan b Hacker	2
Asif Iqbal lbw b Hacker	2	– c French b Cooper	7
*A. G. E. Ealham b Cooper	0	– c Cooper b Hemmings	27
C. S. Cowdrey c Birch b Cooper	3	– c Birch b Hemmings	54
†S. N. V. Waterton lbw b Bore	8	– c Hassan b Hemmings	36
R. W. Hills c Randall b Cooper	9	– c French b Hemmings	3
G. D. Spelman b Bore	4	– c Robinson b Hemmings	0
D. L. Underwood c Birch b Cooper	0	– c Randall b Hemmings	8
K. B. S. Jarvis not out	2	– not out	1
L-b 3, n-b 2	5	L-b 2	2

1/34 2/34 3/35 4/36 5/36	67	1/0 2/2 3/13 4/31	149
6/42 7/50 8/61 9/65		5/64 6/109 7/114	
		8/132 9/148	

Bonus points – Nottinghamshire 4.

Bowling: *First Innings*—Hacker 15–6–20–3; Cooper 20–6–31–5; Bore 5.2–1–11–2. *Second Innings*—Hacker 7–0–36–3; Cooper 10–2–32–1; Hemmings 12.5–4–37–6; Rice 9–0–42–0.

Nottinghamshire

R. T. Robinson c Johnson b Spelman	11	†B. N. French not out	20
B. Hassan lbw b Hills	63		
D. W. Randall c Waterton b Spelman	26	N-b 3	3
*C. E. B. Rice c Waterton b Woolmer	59		
J. D. Birch b Woolmer	25	1/34 2/84 3/107	(5 wkts dec.) 217
M. J. Harris not out	10	4/178 5/189	

E. E. Hemmings, K. E. Cooper, P. J. Hacker and M. K. Bore did not bat.

Bonus points – Nottinghamshire 2, Kent 2.

Bowling: Jarvis 17–3–69–0; Spelman 19–1–76–2; Hills 12–4–39–1; Woolmer 7–3–12–2; Underwood 11–6–18–0.

Umpires: A. Jepson and T. W. Spencer.

NOTTINGHAMSHIRE v DERBYSHIRE

At Worksop, July 23, 24, 25. Nottinghamshire won by 89 runs. Nottinghamshire 16 pts, Derbyshire 6 pts. Nottinghamshire swept to a dramatic victory in a match it once seemed they would lose by an innings. The pitch showed signs of taking spin on the opening day, when Steele and Tunnicliffe took four wickets apiece to dismiss Nottinghamshire cheaply. Kirsten batted with his customary composure as Derbyshire built up a healthy first innings lead of 118. Nottinghamshire were soon in trouble a second time but Rice, Harris and Hemmings batted with skill and concentration to leave Derbyshire a target of 144. Then 43-year-old off-spinner White, who had not played for two seasons after stepping down to captain the Second XI, turned the game Nottinghamshire's way. Following his four for 33 in the first innings, White took six for 24 in the second as Derbyshire were bowled out for just 54.

Nottinghamshire

B. Hassan c Wood b Tunnicliffe	6	– c Wood b Steele	1
R. T. Robinson c Steele b Tunnicliffe	12	– c Hendrick b Steele	19
D. W. Randall c Taylor b Tunnicliffe	5	– c Wood b Steele	4
*C. E. B. Rice c Taylor b Tunnicliffe	0	– st Taylor b Miller	80
J. D. Birch c Kirsten b Steele	18	– c and b Steele	6
M. J. Harris st Taylor b Steele	6	– c sub b Steele	65
†B. N. French b Hendrick	18	– c Hendrick b Steele	5
E. E. Hemmings c Barnett b Steele	39	– not out	46
R. A. White c Wood b Hendrick	2	– c Steele b Miller	6
W. K. Watson not out	0	– c Tunnicliffe b Steele	10
P. J. Hacker b Steele	2	– c sub b Miller	6
B 5, l-b 3, n-b 2	10	B 1, l-b 5, n-b 7	13

1/11 2/23 3/23 4/24 5/47 6/57   **118**   1/3 2/13 3/50 4/68 5/160   **261**
7/104 8/116 9/116   6/169 7/221 8/227 9/241

Bonus points – Derbyshire 4.

Bowling: First Innings—Hendrick 15–3–32–2; Tunnicliffe 13–5–19–4; Steele 12.3–2–41–4; Miller 5–1–16–0. *Second Innings*—Hendrick 12–7–16–0; Tunnicliffe 2–1–2–0; Steele 37–9–133–7; Miller 33–2–97–3; Barnett 1–1–0–0.

Derbyshire

B. Wood b Hacker	18	– c French b Hemmings	14
J. G. Wright c Birch b Watson	4	– c Hassan b Hemmings	0
P. N. Kirsten c Randall b Hacker	75	– c Birch b Hemmings	2
D. S. Steele c Rice b White	23	– (5) lbw b White	6
K. J. Barnett c Randall b White	17	– (7) c Harris b White	0
*G. Miller c Robinson b White	40	– (8) b White	10
I. S. Anderson c Hassan b Hemmings	1	– (4) lbw b White	12
†R. W. Taylor c Hassan b White	3	– (10) c White b Hemmings	0
J. Walters c Rice b Hemmings	17	– b White	0
C. J. Tunnicliffe c Birch b Hemmings	20	– (6) b White	2
M. Hendrick not out	0	– not out	0
B 11, l-b 2, w 5	18	B 1, l-b 7	8

1/9 2/80 3/107 4/140 5/149   **236**   1/3 2/5 3/28 4/37 5/43   **54**
6/156 7/163 8/214 9/236   6/43 7/53 8/53 9/54

Bonus points – Derbyshire 2, Nottinghamshire 4.

Bowling: First Innings—Hacker 13–3–42–2; Watson 11–2–38–1; Rice 7–4–16–0; Hemmings 36.5–10–89–3; White 18–5–33–4. *Second Innings*—Hacker 2–0–2–0; Watson 2–1–1–0; Hemmings 17.2–6–19–4; White 17–7–24–6.

Umpires: R. S. Herman and C. T. Spencer.

NOTTINGHAMSHIRE v LEICESTERSHIRE

At Nottingham, August 2, 4, 5. Nottinghamshire won by nine wickets. Nottinghamshire 19 pts, Leicestershire 5 pts. With Hadlee and Rice in full flight for the first time in the season, Nottinghamshire comfortably completed their third successive victory. It was set up when Leicestershire were bowled out for 179 in the first innings – a total that owed much to Briers. Then Robinson scored his maiden first-class century, which included 21 boundaries and took Nottinghamshire to a lead of 92. Leicestershire fared little better in their second innings, although Tolchard and Clift threatened to deny Nottinghamshire until Rice removed them both, leaving the home side to score just 79. With Randall in a hurry, Nottinghamshire raced to an emphatic victory before rain could intervene.

Leicestershire

J. F. Steele c Rice b Hadlee	1	– c Hacker b Hadlee	15
J. C. Balderstone c Hadlee b Rice	1	– c Todd b Hadlee	27
D. I. Gower c Rice b Hadlee	3	– c Harris b Hemmings	27
*B. F. Davison c French b Rice	23	– lbw b Hacker	26
N. E. Briers lbw b Cooper	94	– (6) c Hassan b Hemmings	0
†R. W. Tolchard c Hadlee b Cooper	2	– (7) c Randall b Rice	28
P. B. Clift c French b Hadlee	34	– (8) c Harris b Rice	22
G. J. Parsons c French b Hacker	4	– (9) st French b Hemmings	7
J. P. Agnew c Hassan b Hemmings	2	– (5) b Hadlee	0
N. G. B. Cook c Harris b Hemmings	2	– not out	2
L. B. Taylor not out	0	– c Hadlee b Rice	2
B 3, l-b 5, w 2, n-b 3	13	B 6, l-b 7, w 1	14

1/5 2/9 3/14 4/38 5/60 6/123   179   1/31 2/56 3/97 4/99 5/99   170
7/136 8/165 9/175   6/99 7/158 8/165 9/167

Bonus points – Leicestershire 1, Nottinghamshire 4.

Bowling: *First Innings*—Hadlee 11–5–23–3; Rice 12–3–57–2; Cooper 14.3–4–38–2; Hacker 14–3–47–1; Hemmings 4–3–1–2. *Second Innings*—Hadlee 18–6–40–3; Rice 17.5–6–27–3; Cooper 7–2–22–0; Hemmings 27–9–60–3; Hacker 4–0–7–1.

Nottinghamshire

P. A. Todd b Agnew	4	– c Steele b Agnew	13
R. T. Robinson lbw b Clift	138	– not out	19
D. W. Randall c Tolchard b Clift	43	– not out	44
B. Hassan c Briers b Clift	4		
*C. E. B. Rice b Clift	1		
M. J. Harris c and b Clift	52		
†B. N. French c Tolchard b Parsons	1		
R. J. Hadlee c and b Parsons	0		
E. E. Hemmings c Davison b Parsons	2		
P. J. Hacker b Agnew	5		
K. E. Cooper not out	14		
L-b 2, w 1, n-b 4	7	L-b 4	4

1/25 2/105 3/109 4/111 5/247 6/248   271   1/15   (1 wkt)   80
7/248 8/250 9/250

Bonus points – Nottinghamshire 3, Leicestershire 4.

Bowling: *First Innings*—Taylor 11–1–40–0; Agnew 13.2–3–51–2; Cook 17–3–38–0; Parsons 16–2–49–3; Clift 24–5–43–5; Steele 10–6–17–0; Briers 9–1–26–0. *Second Innings*—Parsons 2–0–5–0; Agnew 7–1–29–1; Cook 8.4–2–31–0; Balderstone 2–0–10–0; Gower 1–0–1–0.

Umpires: R. S. Herman and J. van Geloven.

NOTTINGHAMSHIRE v LANCASHIRE

At Nottingham, August 6, 7, 8. Drawn. Nottinghamshire 2 pts, Lancashire 4 pts. Despite a series of enterprising declarations on the final day, Nottinghamshire's sequence of Championship victories came to an end when the game finished as a draw. All three days were heavily affected by rain with ten hours lost, and Lancashire's target of 204 in 145 minutes was always out of reach. Earlier, Nottinghamshire had picked up two batting points, thanks to Randall and Hadlee, while Lancashire were indebted to Hogg and Malone for their four bowling points.

Nottinghamshire

P. A. Todd c Fowler b Malone	26	– not out	24
R. T. Robinson c Reidy b Hogg	10	– not out	25
D. W. Randall c Cockbain b Allott	50		
*C. E. B. Rice c Reidy b Malone	2		
B. Hassan c Simmons b Hogg	35		
M. J. Harris b Allott	6		
†B. N. French c Fowler b Hogg	13		
R. J. Hadlee not out	44		
E. E. Hemmings run out	3		
P. J. Hacker c Cockbain b Malone	1		
K. E. Cooper not out	0		
B 4, l-b 2, w 2, n-b 4	12	L-b 4, w 1, n-b 2	7

1/20 2/76 3/94 4/94 5/104   (9 wkts dec.) 202   (no wkt dec.) 56
6/131 7/167 8/171 9/193

Bonus points – Nottinghamshire 2, Lancashire 4.

Bowling: *First Innings*—Hogg 18.5–4–80–3; Malone 24–4–71–3; Allott 12–2–39–2. *Second Innings*—Hogg 6–1–25–0; Malone 6–1–24–0.

Lancashire

D. Lloyd not out	19	– b Cooper	23
A. Kennedy c French b Hacker	19	– c French b Rice	10
I. Cockbain not out	7	– c and b Hemmings	3
*F. C. Hayes (did not bat)		– not out	45
B. W. Reidy (did not bat)		– not out	5
B 4, l-b 5, w 1	10	B 1, l-b 5, w 1	7

1/36   (1 wkt dec.) 55   1/12 2/25 3/75   (3 wkts) 93

†G. Fowler, J. Simmons, D. P. Hughes, P. J. W. Allott, M. F. Malone and W. Hogg did not bat.

Bowling: *First Innings*—Hadlee 4–2–6–0; Rice 5–3–10–0; Hacker 5–3–9–1; Cooper 4–0–20–0. *Second Innings*—Hadlee 4–4–0–0; Rice 9–2–20–1; Hemmings 11–2–39–1; Cooper 8–3–16–1; Hacker 3–0–11–0.

Umpires: R. S. Herman and J. van Geloven.

At Eastbourne, August 9, 11, 12. NOTTINGHAMSHIRE drew with SUSSEX.

At Lord's, August 16, 18, 19. NOTTINGHAMSHIRE lost to MIDDLESEX by an innings and 17 runs.

NOTTINGHAMSHIRE v WORCESTERSHIRE

At Cleethorpes, August 20, 21, 22. Worcestershire won by two wickets. Worcestershire 16 pts, Nottinghamshire 8 pts. A game that seemed to be heading Nottinghamshire's way suddenly tilted towards Worcestershire on the final day, when they completed a thrilling victory off the final ball. On the first day the home team had reached a substantial total, with wicket-keeper French making a career-best 70 not out. When Worcestershire were dismissed 80 behind, after losing their last six wickets for 29, Nottinghamshire strengthened their position before declaring. The visitors were set 308 in 254 minutes and, with three wickets down for 34, their hopes of even saving the match looked bleak. But Younis, with good fortune – he was dropped four times – and considerable help from Hemsley and Patel, swung the game Worcestershire's way. He hit fourteen boundaries in his match-winning innings.

Nottinghamshire

P. A. Todd b Pridgeon	23	– c Turner b Inchmore	7
R. T. Robinson lbw b Gifford	26	– st Fisher b Gifford	37
D. W. Randall lbw b Alleyne	58	– c Pridgeon b Gifford	36
*C. E. B. Rice c Turner b Inchmore	63	– lbw b Alleyne	40
J. D. Birch c Younis b Inchmore	13	– (6) c Pridgeon b Gifford	21
R. E. Dexter not out	30	– (5) lbw b Pridgeon	14
†B. N. French not out	70	– not out	41
E. E. Hemmings (did not bat)		– run out	1
W. K. Watson (did not bat)		– b Gifford	4
P. J. Hacker (did not bat)		– not out	2
B 1, l-b 12, w 3, n-b 9	25	B 4, l-b 8, w 2, n-b 10	24

1/48 2/69 3/167 4/188 5/195　　　(5 wkts) 308　　1/11 2/86 3/109　　(8 wkts dec.) 227
　　　　　　　　　　　　　　　　　　　　　　　4/146 5/152 6/197
　　　　　　　　　　　　　　　　　　　　　　　7/198 8/216

M. K. Bore did not bat.

Bonus points – Nottinghamshire 4, Worcestershire 2.

Bowling: *First Innings*—Alleyne 23–3–85–1; Inchmore 21–6–64–2; Pridgeon 25–8–49–1; Gifford 31–8–85–1. *Second Innings*—Alleyne 17–1–60–1; Inchmore 9–0–39–1; Pridgeon 21–2–65–1; Gifford 14–2–39–4.

Worcestershire

G. M. Turner c Robinson b Hacker	51	– c Randall b Hacker	18
J. A. Ormrod lbw b Rice	0	– c Birch b Rice	0
J. D. Inchmore hit wkt b Rice	10	– (8) lbw b Rice	9
P. A. Neale c French b Hacker	7	– (3) c Dexter b Hacker	0
Younis Ahmed st French b Bore	66	– (4) c Robinson b Hemmings	109
E. J. O. Hemsley c Rice b Bore	34	– (5) c Randall b Bore	60
D. N. Patel b Hemmings	1	– (6) st French b Hemmings	52
†P. B. Fisher c Dexter b Hemmings	5	– (10) not out	9
H. Alleyne c Todd b Bore	1	– c sub b Watson	17
*N. Gifford not out	4	– (7) not out	10
A. P. Pridgeon c Dexter b Hacker	11		
B 1, l-b 7	8	B 1, l-b 20, w 1, n-b 2	24

1/6 2/22 3/98 4/101 5/199 6/206　　　　228　　1/3 2/8 3/34 4/144　　(8 wkts) 308
7/206 8/207 9/215　　　　　　　　　　　　　　　5/246 6/250 7/263 8/290

Bonus points – Worcestershire 2, Nottinghamshire 4.

Bowling: *First Innings*—Watson 15–1–50–0; Rice 12–5–17–2; Hemmings 29–10–70–2; Bore 16–7–29–3; Hacker 11.3–0–54–3. *Second Innings*—Rice 17–1–46–2; Hacker 25–7–82–2; Watson 7–0–52–1; Bore 7–1–31–1; Hemmings 19–3–73–2.

Umpires: R. Palmer and D. Shackleton.

At Ilkeston, August 27, 28, 29. NOTTINGHAMSHIRE drew with DERBYSHIRE.

NOTTINGHAMSHIRE v HAMPSHIRE

At Nottingham, August 30, September 1. Nottinghamshire won by an innings and 22 runs. Nottinghamshire 17 pts, Hampshire 4 pts. Nottinghamshire, needing victory to take them towards third place in the table, trounced Hampshire with more than a day to spare. Pocock elected to bat first on a green, moist pitch and must have regretted his decision as Hacker again improved his career-best figures with a return of six for 35. Nottinghamshire looked to have wasted an opportunity when they slid from 110 for one to 180 all out, but then Hampshire's batting crumbled against the pace and hostility of Rice and Hadlee, who took five wickets each. Deeper embarrassment was saved by Malone and Southern, who doubled the score after Hampshire had lost nine wickets for 29.

Hampshire

T. M. Tremlett b Hadlee	13	– lbw b Rice	0
C. L. Smith c Todd b Rice	4	– c Birch b Hadlee	5
M. C. J. Nicholas lbw b Hacker	18	– lbw b Rice	6
D. R. Turner c French b Hacker	3	– c French b Rice	0
*N. E. J. Pocock b Hadlee	4	– b Hadlee	7
N. G. Cowley c French b Hadlee	0	– lbw b Hadlee	0
M. D. Marshall c Hemmings b Hacker	19	– (8) b Rice	3
†R. J. Parks c Birch b Hacker	11	– (7) c French b Hadlee	5
J. W. Southern b Hacker	8	– not out	11
K. Stevenson b Hacker	0	– b Hadlee	0
S. J. Malone not out	13	– c Robinson b Rice	20
L-b 3, w 2, n-b 2	7	L-b 1	1
	100		58

1/15 2/25 3/34 4/40 5/40 6/49 7/70
8/81 9/81

1/3 2/5 3/12 4/19 5/19
6/24 7/27 8/29 9/29

Bonus points – Nottinghamshire 4.

Bowling: *First Innings*—Hadlee 18–5–43–3; Rice 5–1–15–1; Hacker 13–3–35–6. *Second Innings*—Hadlee 13–5–32–5; Rice 12.1–6–25–5.

Nottinghamshire

P. A. Todd c Parks b Marshall	59	
R. T. Robinson c Pocock b Malone	19	
D. W. Randall lbw b Stevenson	17	
*C. E. B. Rice c Parks b Marshall	19	
R. E. Dexter c Pocock b Marshall	0	
J. D. Birch b Tremlett	26	
†B. N. French c Parks b Tremlett	2	
R. J. Hadlee c Parks b Tremlett	0	

E. E. Hemmings not out	10
P. J. Hacker lbw b Tremlett	0
M. K. Bore c Parks b Tremlett	10
B 11, l-b 5, w 1, n-b 1	18
	180

1/49 2/110 3/110 4/112
5/134 6/147 7/159
8/164 9/164

Bonus points – Nottinghamshire 1, Hampshire 4.

Bowling: Marshall 21–5–49–3; Malone 14–5–42–1; Stevenson 12–1–41–1; Tremlett 9.5–1–30–5.

Umpires: K. E. Palmer and J. van Geloven.

At Worcester, September 3, 4, 5. NOTTINGHAMSHIRE drew with WORCESTERSHIRE.

THE WRIGLEY CRICKET CRUSADE

In conjunction with the National Cricket Association and the English Schools Cricket Association, the Wrigley Company have launched a new sponsorship with the objectives of:

(a) Providing more children with the opportunity to play cricket.
(b) Increasing interest in the game.
(c) Raising the overall standard throughout the country.

The scheme is aimed mainly at State schools, especially primary schools, where facilities for playing cricket are limited. Soft Ball Cricket is to be encouraged to overcome the difficulty of preparing pitches good enough to make cricket with a hard ball an enjoyable game, and to preclude the need for expensive equipment.

In 1981, schools taking part in the Wrigley Soft Ball Team Cricket Tournament for primary schools will be restricted to sixteen areas, chosen by the ESCA. The final will be staged on a Test ground between eight schools.

SOMERSET

President – C. R. M. ATKINSON

Chairman, Cricket Committee – R. C. KERSLAKE

Secretary – D. G. SEWARD
County Cricket Ground, St James's Street, Taunton

Captain – B. C. ROSE

N. F. M. Popplewell

County Badge

S. M. Gavaskar

Considering all things, Somerset enjoyed another remarkably successful season after the triumphs of 1979. The absence for much of the year of Garner and Richards (with the West Indian touring side) and of Botham was expected. However, further serious setbacks occurred during the year. The captain, Brian Rose, was ill for two vital Benson and Hedges Cup games, was picked for three Tests and then suffered two injuries. Ian Botham, the vice-captain, was bedevilled by severe back trouble; and Joel Garner, when he did return in August, was not completely fit. It was a traditional Somerset paradox that, while these circumstances suggested that any success would be in the shorter competitions, the county advanced to fourth in the Schweppes County Championship and emerged as runners-up in the John Player League.

Originally, the year was seen as one in which to test the younger players, and this was eventually achieved. As temporary measures, however, one-year contracts were given to two overseas players. Sunil Gavaskar, regarded as a "star" substitute for Richards, began with several marvellous innings, when the sun was shining, and endured a miserable spell when the rain began – apart from a few important Sunday efforts – before ending with a fine 155 not out against Yorkshire. Hugh Gore, a left-arm opening medium-pacer from Antigua, was signed to cover possible injuries to Hallam Moseley and Colin Dredge. In the event Gore was away with muscle injuries more often than those he was to augment, but he did put in some useful spells.

With certain exceptions the regular players produced figures in accordance with their known capabilities. Among those who disappointed was Phil Slocombe, though despite a wretched year with the bat he fielded as brilliantly as ever – as did the rest of the team for most of the season. Dennis Breakwell and Keith Jennings, after some useful occasional efforts, could not hold a place later in the year, while Vic Marks found his wickets costing him a good deal more in the Championship. However, everyone, at various times, had something of importance to offer, especially on Sundays.

Rose made hundreds in both innings against Worcestershire and Botham produced several exciting performances, including a memorable 228 against Gloucestershire. The latter put in some steady Sunday spells later in the season, but his back ailment often upset the balance of the side. Dredge, a sound, hard-working professional, improved in control, subtlety, and stamina with splendid bowling results all season. Derek Taylor's batting and wicket-keeping seem to improve with each passing year and Moseley managed, remarkably, almost to fill the large gap left by Garner on Sundays. Viv Richards returned after the West Indian tour to play two inimitable match-winning Sunday innings.

The real bonuses came in the development of Popplewell, Lloyds and Olive, at last given extended trials. Nigel Popplewell, a lively, engaging optimist, made a maiden century and always had plenty to offer, reminding observers of many of the attributes that Botham first brought to the game. Jeremy Lloyds, emerging suddenly with eleven wickets in a match, spun and flighted his off-breaks most encouragingly, and given the chance to open the innings he responded with four successive fifties. After a long sojourn in the Second Eleven, Martin Olive did enough to suggest a future as a sound opening batsman.

If equal fourth place in the Championship was rather misleading – only two teams won fewer matches; only three lost more – bonus points kept them well up, and victory over John Player League champions Warwickshire on the last day of the season rounded off a resounding retort to the season's various setbacks. In an abominable year the retirement for health reasons of the head groundsman, and the new pavilion development at Taunton, conspired to make pitch arrangements more difficult than usual. None the less the harassed staff worked hard in depressing circumstances.

Membership subscriptions raised an astonishing £100,000 – in 1978 the new "record" was £45,000 – and the amalgamation of the promotional interests of players and club was a major step forward. Indeed, and the ageing observer mentions it with the guilty feeling of one offering hostages to misfortune, there are many signs that Somerset's prospects have seldom been brighter. – Eric Hill.

SOMERSET

[*Press Association*]

Back row: P. A. Slocombe, M. Olive, V. J. Marks, P. M. Roebuck, C. H. Dredge, K. F. Jennings, J. W. Lloyds, T. Gard, N. F. M. Popplewell. *Front row*: P. W. Denning, H. R. Moseley, I. T. Botham, B. C. Rose (*captain*), D. J. S. Taylor, P. J. Robinson, D. Breakwell.

SOMERSET RESULTS

All First-class Matches – Played 23: Won 4, Lost 5, Drawn 14. Abandoned 1.

County Championship Matches – Played 21: Won 3, Lost 5, Drawn 13. Abandoned 1.

Bonus points – Batting 56, Bowling 70.

COUNTY CHAMPIONSHIP AVERAGES

BATTING

	Birthplace	Matches	Inns	Not Outs	Runs	Highest Inns	Avge
I. T. Botham	Heswall	10	14	0	875	228	62.50
B. C. Rose	Dartford	12	17	2	793	150*	52.86
D. J. S. Taylor	Amersham	19	24	7	709	59	41.70
I. V. A. Richards	Antigua, WI	4	8	0	306	170	38.25
N. F. M. Popplewell ..	Chislehurst	12	18	5	433	135*	33.30
S. M. Gavaskar	Bombay, India	14	22	2	664	155*	33.20
V. J. Marks	Middle Chinnock	20	30	7	721	82	31.34
P. W. Denning	Chewton Mendip	21	33	2	952	184	30.70
J. W. Lloyds	Penang, Malaya	11	16	3	388	70	29.84
P. M. Roebuck	Oxford	20	33	3	807	101	26.90
D. Breakwell	Brierley Hill	11	12	3	233	73*	25.88
M. Olive	Watford	9	17	1	290	50	18.12
K. F. Jennings	Wellington	10	9	4	88	21*	17.60
H. R. Moseley	Barbados, WI	15	9	4	55	16	11.00
P. A. Slocombe	Weston-super-Mare	11	17	2	142	38	9.46
H. I. E. Gore	Antigua, WI	10	11	5	48	22*	8.00
C. H. Dredge	Frome	19	21	5	113	21*	7.06

Also batted: T. Gard (*West Lambrook*) 22, 19; N. Russom (*Finchley*) 9.

* *Signifies not out.*

BOWLING

	Overs	Maidens	Runs	Wickets	Average
C. H. Dredge	545.2	132	1,516	61	24.85
H. R. Moseley	419.5	94	1,063	39	27.25
J. W. Lloyds	264	55	899	28	32.10
I. T. Botham	224	55	736	18	40.88
H. I. E. Gore	232.5	63	579	14	41.35
N. F. M. Popplewell ...	161.5	34	534	12	44.50
K. F. Jennings	215.2	49	596	13	45.84
V. J. Marks	687.3	176	1,981	40	49.52
D. Breakwell	279	83	825	13	63.46

Also bowled: P. W. Denning 1.5–0–8–0; S. M. Gavaskar 15.2–2–69–0; I. V. A. Richards 30–2–110–3; P. M. Roebuck 24.2–2–113–2; B. C. Rose 5–0–25–0; N. Russom 19–7–54–0; P. A. Slocombe 3–0–18–2; D. J. S. Taylor 2–1–1–0.

HUNDREDS

The following ten three-figure innings were played for Somerset in County Championship matches – I. T. Botham 228 v Gloucestershire (Taunton), 126 v Warwickshire (Birmingham); S. M. Gavaskar 155* v Yorkshire (Weston-super-Mare), 138 v Surrey (The Oval); B. C. Rose 124 and 150* v Worcestershire (Worcester); P. W. Denning 184 v Nottinghamshire (Nottingham); N. F. M. Popplewell 135* v Kent (Taunton); I. V. A. Richards 170 v Gloucestershire (Bristol); P. M. Roebuck 101 v Gloucestershire (Bristol).

At Oxford, April 26, 28, 29. SOMERSET beat OXFORD UNIVERSITY by 98 runs.

SOMERSET v SUSSEX

At Taunton, April 30, May 1, 2. Drawn. Somerset 5 pts, Sussex 6 pts. Rain ruined the match after the first storm had stopped play with Sussex 43 for one. Barclay and Parker (nine 4s) sustained the innings as Dredge achieved career-best figures. Rose (one 6 and seven 4s) gave Somerset a fine start, but a considerable deficit looked likely until Taylor (two 6s) restricted the lead to 17. However, after many interruptions on the first two days, the last was totally washed out.

Sussex

K. C. Wessels c Denning b Botham	14	– not out	2
J. R. T. Barclay c Moseley b Botham	33	– not out	0
G. D. Mendis c Roebuck b Moseley	14		
P. W. G. Parker c Roebuck b Dredge	60		
P. J. Graves c Popplewell b Marks	14		
C. P. Phillipson c Botham b Dredge	1		
A. C. S. Pigott c Roebuck b Marks	17		
G. S. le Roux c Denning b Dredge	21		
*†A. Long lbw b Dredge	13		
G. G. Arnold c Denning b Dredge	11		
C. E. Waller not out	1		
L-b 1	1		

1/24 2/51 3/67 4/111 5/112   200   (no wkt) 2
6/145 7/165 8/188 9/189

Bonus points – Sussex 2, Somerset 4.

Bowling: *First Innings*—Botham 17–2–33–2; Moseley 19–6–39–1; Dredge 20.1–5–46–5; Marks 21–7–60–2; Breakwell 12–6–21–0. *Second Innings*—Moseley 2–1–2–0; Dredge 1–1–0–0.

Somerset

*B. C. Rose b Pigott	61	N. F. M. Popplewell c Long b Waller	4
P. A. Slocombe c Long b Arnold	11	C. H. Dredge c Wessels b Arnold	6
P. M. Roebuck c Graves b Barclay	14	H. R. Moseley not out	0
P. W. Denning c Long b Pigott	21		
I. T. Botham c Long b Waller	10	L-b 1, n-b 1	2
V. J. Marks c Wessels b Waller	21		
D. Breakwell c Phillipson b Barclay	2	1/34 2/63 3/107 4/108 5/124	183
†D. J. S. Taylor c Phillipson b Barclay	31	6/141 7/141 8/148 9/182	

Bonus points – Somerset 1, Sussex 4.

Bowling: le Roux 7–0–33–0; Arnold 13.4–3–37–2; Barclay 22–9–29–3; Waller 17–7–55–3; Pigott 5–0–27–2.

Umpires: W. L. Budd and C. Cook.

At Ilford, May 3, 5, 6. SOMERSET drew with ESSEX.

At Birmingham, May 7, 8, 9. SOMERSET drew with WARWICKSHIRE.

SOMERSET v GLOUCESTERSHIRE

At Taunton, May 24, 26, 27. Drawn. Somerset 8 pts, Gloucestershire 4 pts. After a delightful innings by Gavaskar, an astonishing attacking effort by Botham dominated the game. Missed only twice when 140 and 195, he hit ten 6s and 27 4s in 48 overs, reaching 100 in 107 minutes and finally batting 184 minutes for his 228. His fourth-wicket stand of 310 with Denning, who batted determinedly for 75 overs, was a record for the county. Gloucestershire never handled the seam attack well, although Zaheer and Hignell reduced the deficit to 295. After overnight rain the pitch offered sharp turn for a while on the final day, but as it eased completely Zaheer, with a superb 173 (two 6s and 24 4s) in 95 overs, and Hignell, with an unbeaten hundred, saved the side comfortably, adding 254 in three and a half hours. The final irrelevant phase included all eleven Somerset players bowling, and Botham keeping wicket.

Somerset

*B. C. Rose c Sadiq b Brain	32	†D. J. S. Taylor not out	57
S. M. Gavaskar c Sadiq b Wilkins	75	D. Breakwell not out	22
P. A. Slocombe lbw b Brain	0	L-b 18, n-b 4	22
P. W. Denning c and b Graveney	98		
I. T. Botham c Sadiq b Procter	228	1/78 2/78 3/119 4/429	(6 wkts) 534
V. J. Marks lbw b Procter	0	5/429 6/486	

H. R. Moseley, C. H. Dredge and K. F. Jennings did not bat.

Bonus points – Somerset 4, Gloucestershire 2.

Bowling: Procter 24–5–81–2; Brain 21–0–134–2; Wilkins 18–4–112–1; Partridge 21–2–104–0; Graveney 16–4–81–1.

Gloucestershire

A. W. Stovold c Marks b Dredge	32	– c Botham b Dredge	14
Sadiq Mohammad c Dredge b Moseley	4	– b Breakwell	55
Zaheer Abbas run out	62	– c and b Jennings	173
A. J. Hignell c Taylor b Dredge	80	– not out	100
*M. J. Procter c and b Jennings	23	– (6) c Marks b Slocombe	32
M. W. Stovold c Botham b Jennings	2	– (5) lbw b Jennings	1
M. D. Partridge b Jennings	15	– not out	3
D. A. Graveney c Taylor b Jennings	1		
†A. J. Brassington c Rose b Moseley	3		
A. H. Wilkins c Taylor b Moseley	7		
B. M. Brain not out	0		
L-b 6, w 1, n-b 3	10	B 3, l-b 10, n-b 3	16
1/12 2/82 3/112 4/142 5/159 6/184	239	1/33 2/92 3/346	(5 wkts) 394
7/204 8/231 9/237		4/356 5/390	

Bonus points – Gloucestershire 2, Somerset 4.

Bowling: *First Innings*—Moseley 21–3–66–3; Dredge 21–5–51–2; Jennings 25–9–87–4; Marks 14–5–25–0. *Second Innings*—Moseley 10–1–35–0; Dredge 17–4–58–1; Marks 31–13–66–0; Botham 15–4–57–0; Breakwell 16–6–39–1; Jennings 15–4–59–2; Gavaskar 7–2–29–0; Rose 5–0–25–0; Slocombe 1–0–7–1; Denning 1–0–2–0; Taylor 2–1–1–0.

Umpires: D. Shackleton and P. S. G. Stevens.

At The Oval, May 28, 29, 30. SOMERSET lost to SURREY by eight wickets.

SOMERSET v MIDDLESEX

At Taunton, May 31, June 1, 2. Middlesex won by seven wickets. Middlesex 19 pts, Somerset 6 pts. In cold windy weather, Somerset's innings was founded on a fine partnership of 121 between Botham (four 6s and eight 4s) and Denning. After inroads by Edmonds, Marks and Dredge then added 63 in an unbroken partnership. Botham broke through on a humid Monday morning, but Brearley, Barlow (eleven 4s) and Gatting (fourteen 4s) revived the Middlesex innings. Somerset, 23 for no wicket overnight, collapsed on a wearing pitch before van der Bijl and Merry, who achieved his best figures. In seven lively overs Botham hit four 6s, three of them off successive Emburey deliveries. Middlesex easily achieved their target of 130 in 194 minutes, thanks to a steady innings from Radley.

Somerset

*B. C. Rose c Gould b Edmonds	28	– c Brearley b Emburey	14
S. M. Gavaskar run out	14	– c Gould b van der Bijl	8
P. M. Roebuck c Gould b Merry	29	– c Gould b van der Bijl	2
P. W. Denning b van der Bijl	40	– b Merry	19
I. T. Botham c and b Edmonds	89	– c Radley b Merry	31
V. J. Marks not out	52	– c Gould b Merry	0
J. W. Lloyds b Edmonds	0	– c Selvey b Merry	11
†D. J. S. Taylor lbw b Merry	7	– c Edmonds b Emburey	27
K. F. Jennings c Gould b Edmonds	1	– st Gould b Edmonds	0
C. H. Dredge not out	21	– not out	9
H. I. E. Gore (did not bat)		– c Gould b van der Bijl	1
B 11, l-b 6, w 1, n-b 2	20	B 2, l-b 2, w 1, n-b 1	6

1/42 2/54 3/91 4/212 (8 wkts dec.) 301   1/23 2/23 3/28 4/71 5/71 128
5/216 6/217 7/236 8/238   6/76 7/98 8/109 9/127

Bonus points – Somerset 4, Middlesex 3.

Bowling: *First Innings*—van der Bijl 21–9–44–1; Selvey 9.2–0–57–0; Merry 12–2–48–2; Emburey 20–6–61–0; Edmonds 25–5–71–4. *Second Innings*—van der Bijl 19–8–31–3; Selvey 6–2–14–0; Emburey 19–10–42–2; Edmonds 7–4–11–1; Merry 7–1–24–4.

Middlesex

*J. M. Brearley c and b Jennings	98	– c Taylor b Jennings	25
R. O. Butcher c and b Botham	6	– c Jennings b Marks	14
C. T. Radley lbw b Botham	0	– not out	44
G. D. Barlow c Jennings b Marks	72	– c Botham b Lloyds	27
M. W. Gatting not out	81	– not out	14
†I. J. Gould c Botham b Dredge	12		
P. H. Edmonds not out	21		
B 3, l-b 6, n-b 1	10	B 1, l-b 4, n-b 1	6

1/13 2/17 3/154 (5 wkts dec.) 300   1/19 2/55 3/105 (3 wkts) 130
4/218 5/251

J. E. Emburey, M. W. W. Selvey, V. A. P. van der Bijl and W. G. Merry did not bat.

Bonus points – Middlesex 4, Somerset 2.

Bowling: *First Innings*—Botham 18–5–71–2; Gore 13–3–40–0; Jennings 27.2–8–60–1; Dredge 11–1–47–1; Marks 25–4–68–1; Lloyds 1–0–4–0. *Second Innings*—Botham 7–1–21–0; Gore 3–1–3–0; Marks 11–3–32–1; Jennings 7–0–21–1; Dredge 4–0–20–0; Lloyds 4.5–0–20–1; Gavaskar 1–0–7–0.

Umpires: D. Shackleton and A. G. T. Whitehead.

At Worcester, June 4, 5, 6. SOMERSET beat WORCESTERSHIRE by eight wickets.

SOMERSET v LANCASHIRE

At Bath, June 14, 16, 17. Abandoned.

SOMERSET v HAMPSHIRE

At Bath, June 18, 19, 20. Drawn. Somerset 6 pts, Hampshire 6 pts. Play did not begin until 2.40. Tremlett, with a career-best 81 (two 6s and eleven 4s) in 70 overs, and Smith, batting 83 overs for his 109 (three 6s and ten 4s), put on 174 for the first wicket, and later Pocock and Nicholas ensured Hampshire took full batting points for the first time in the season. Rose led a crisp reply on a slow, turning pitch until Southern took three for 1 in six balls. Taylor prevented a further decline with two 6s and five 4s in 31 overs, benefiting from two missed chances. Hampshire's initial response to Somerset's declaration was slow, but Jesty's superb 114 not out (three 6s and eighteen 4s) in 28 overs – including the fastest century of the season so far in seventy-nine minutes – and an enterprising innings by Nicholas allowed Pocock to set Somerset 265 in 186 minutes. Rose and Roebuck put on 62 in an hour for the second wicket, but a slump against Cowley to 92 for five with an hour and a half to go suggested a Hampshire victory. However, Roebuck, Marks and Taylor, the latter defending for the last forty minutes, saved the game.

Hampshire

T. M. Tremlett c Moseley b Jennings	81	– lbw b Breakwell 24
C. L. Smith c Roebuck b Breakwell	109	– c Denning b Marks 22
T. E. Jesty c Jennings b Breakwell	10	– (4) not out 114
M. C. J. Nicholas run out	30	– (3) not out 46
*N. E. J. Pocock c Breakwell b Marks	54	
N. G. Cowley run out	4	
M. N. S. Taylor c Jennings b Marks	2	
S. F. Graf not out	4	
†G. R. Stephenson not out	1	
B 4, l-b 4, n-b 3	11	B 10, l-b 1 11

1/174 2/208 3/212 4/275   (7 wkts) 306 1/42 2/54   (2 wkts dec.) 217
5/292 6/301 7/304

K. Stevenson and J. W. Southern did not bat.

Bonus points – Hampshire 4, Somerset 3.

Bowling: *First Innings*—Moseley 20–7–49–0; Gore 12–4–26–0; Jennings 15–4–49–1; Marks 31–4–81–2; Breakwell 22–5–90–2. *Second Innings*—Moseley 2–2–0–0; Jennings 2–0–5–0; Breakwell 28–11–84–1; Marks 25–3–92–1; Roebuck 5–1–25–0.

Somerset

*B. C. Rose c Jesty b Southern	83	– c sub b Cowley 34
S. M. Gavaskar c Nicholas b Southern	36	– c sub b Stevenson 4
P. M. Roebuck c Southern b Cowley	28	– c Stevenson b Southern 49
P. W. Denning not out	35	– c Nicholas b Cowley 11
P. A. Slocombe c Stephenson b Southern	0	– (6) lbw b Southern 0
V. J. Marks c Nicholas b Southern	4	– (7) not out 51
†D. J. S. Taylor c Southern b Cowley	55	– (8) not out 7
D. Breakwell not out	10	– (5) c Tremlett b Cowley 5
L-b 5, n-b 3	8	B 2, l-b 2, n-b 1 5

1/108 2/153 3/153 4/153 (6 wkts dec.) 259 1/4 2/66 3/79   (6 wkts) 168
5/161 6/241   4/91 5/92 6/135

K. F. Jennings, H. R. Moseley and H. I. E. Gore did not bat.

Bonus points – Somerset 3, Hampshire 2.

Bowling: *First Innings*—Graf 5–2–9–0; Stevenson 6–1–19–0; Southern 32.2–6–108–4; Tremlett 8–2–24–0; Jesty 10–4–21–0; Cowley 23–8–61–2; Smith 6–2–9–0. *Second Innings*—Stevenson 4–0–12–1; Tremlett 3–0–10–0; Southern 30–6–83–2; Cowley 26–9–48–3; Smith 3–0–10–0.

Umpires: H. D. Bird and D. O. Oslear.

At Cardiff, June 21, 23, 24. SOMERSET drew with GLAMORGAN.

At Hove, June 28, 30, July 1. SOMERSET drew with SUSSEX.

At Taunton, July 5, 6, 7. SOMERSET drew with WEST INDIANS (See West Indian tour section).

At Nottingham, July 9, 10, 11. SOMERSET drew with NOTTINGHAMSHIRE.

At Chesterfield, July 12, 14, 15. SOMERSET lost to DERBYSHIRE by nine wickets.

SOMERSET v KENT

At Taunton, July 23, 24, 25. Somerset won by six wickets with seventeen balls to spare. Somerset 20 pts, Kent 5 pts. Although the Kent batsmen gained a good start, only Shepherd (two 6s and six 4s) could build on it in the face of a steady attack. Underwood's spell of four for 18 in his first eleven overs caused a Somerset collapse, the only resistance coming from Denning until a maiden century by Popplewell brought about a remarkable recovery. Popplewell's enthusiastic and aggressive stroke-play produced a century in 141 minutes, with two 6s and seventeen 4s, as he put on 64 with Taylor and was joined by Breakwell in an unbroken stand of 179 for the eighth wicket. With a deficit of 160 on a slow, turning pitch Kent slumped to 55 for three against Moseley before a fine stand of 124 between Ealham (twelve 4s) and a dogged Johnson seemed to have saved them. However, Dredge and Lloyds broke through, Kent collapsed, and Somerset needed 75 in 70 minutes. Shepherd reduced them to 17 for three, aided by a superb boundary catch by Jarvis, but Denning played twelve important overs and Marks (three boundaries) successfully completed his first victory as captain.

Kent

R. A. Woolmer st Taylor b Popplewell	23	– c Taylor b Moseley	10
G. W. Johnson c Denning b Dredge	20	– b Lloyds	57
C. J. Tavaré c Taylor b Moseley	16	– b Moseley	4
C. S. Cowdrey b Dredge	0	– c Denning b Moseley	18
*A. G. E. Ealham b Marks	34	– c Gavaskar b Dredge	82
N. R. Taylor c Taylor b Breakwell	28	– not out	27
†S. N. V. Waterton c Taylor b Dredge	13	– b Dredge	1
J. N. Shepherd b Popplewell	60	– c and b Marks	19
G. D. Spelman b Marks	3	– b Moseley	0
D. L. Underwood b Marks	1	– c Taylor b Moseley	3
K. B. S. Jarvis not out	0	– b Dredge	3
B 4,1-b 10, n-b 4	18	B 6,1-b 2, n-b 2	10

1/44 2/56 3/56 4/104   216   1/24 2/30 3/55 4/179   234
5/108 6/136 7/179 8/214 9/215   5/179 6/182 7/207 8/208 9/215

Bonus points – Kent 2, Somerset 4.

Bowling: *First Innings*—Moseley 21–7–35–1; Dredge 22–5–68–3; Popplewell 18–7–28–2; Marks 27.1–14–48–3; Breakwell 7–2–19–1. *Second Innings*—Moseley 22–5–59–5; Dredge 22.3–6–53–3; Marks 29–15–41–1; Breakwell 13–9–14–0; Popplewell 3–0–11–0; Lloyds 20–10–46–1.

Somerset

S. M. Gavaskar c Johnson b Jarvis	17	– b Shepherd	6
M. Olive b Underwood	22	– c Taylor b Shepherd	10
P. M. Roebuck lbw b Underwood	2	– c Jarvis b Shepherd	0
C. H. Dredge b Jarvis	1		
P. W. Denning c Tavaré b Johnson	58	– (4) c Waterton b Shepherd	20
*V. J. Marks b Underwood	5	– (5) not out	35
J. W. Lloyds c and b Underwood	3	– (6) not out	5
†D. J. S. Taylor lbw b Underwood	32		
N. F. M. Popplewell not out	135		
D. Breakwell not out	73		
B 5, l-b 11, w 2, n-b 10	28	L-b 2	2

1/30 2/34 3/38 4/72   (8 wkts) 376   1/11 2/11 3/17 4/60   (4 wkts) 78
5/94 6/106 7/133 8/197

H. R. Moseley did not bat.

Bonus points – Somerset 4, Kent 3 (Score at 100 overs: 340-8).

Bowling: *First Innings*—Jarvis 21–4–65–2; Spelman 18–2–63–0; Shepherd 15–0–73–0; Underwood 36–9–104–5; Johnson 14–4–43–1. *Second Innings*—Jarvis 1–0–9–0; Shepherd 10–0–37–4; Underwood 9.1–2–30–0.

Umpires: H. D. Bird and K. E. Palmer.

SOMERSET v WORCESTERSHIRE

At Weston-super-Mare, August 2, 4, 5. Somerset won by ten wickets. Somerset 20 pts, Worcestershire 6 pts. On a slow, variable pitch Neale, dropped before scoring, hit thirteen 4s in 56 overs to redress a poor start; but off-spinner Lloyds, who had previously taken only two Championship wickets, then caused a remarkable collapse, with only Holder extending the innings. Somerset began well thanks to Gavaskar and Roebuck who added 86 in 28 overs, but they slumped to 147 for five before Botham (five 6s and ten 4s) played a magnificent attacking innings lasting only eighty minutes and 24 overs. The tail supported him well to give Somerset a lead of 96. Once again Lloyds created havoc – ending with match figures of eleven for 95 – but a wet ball and some determined tailend resistance prolonged the innings. Somerset needed only 41 but, when extra time on the second day was interrupted by rain, were required to return on the final day.

Worcestershire

G. M. Turner lbw b Moseley	11	– c Gavaskar b Botham	10
J. A. Ormrod c Popplewell b Dredge	14	– c Popplewell b Lloyds	29
P. A. Neale c Popplewell b Lloyds	93	– c Taylor b Lloyds	11
S. P. Henderson b Popplewell	27	– c Moseley b Lloyds	0
Younis Ahmed lbw b Marks	25	– st Taylor b Lloyds	0
T. S. Curtis c Botham b Lloyds	2	– c Botham b Lloyds	13
†D. J. Humphries c Popplewell b Lloyds	5	– b Moseley	16
J. D. Inchmore c Botham b Lloyds	1	– (10) b Dredge	29
V. A. Holder c Denning b Lloyds	34	– b Botham b Dredge	9
*N. Gifford b Lloyds	5	– (8) b Moseley	11
A. P. Pridgeon not out	0	– not out	3
L-b 3, n-b 2	5	L-b 2, n-b 3	5

1/15 2/27 3/102 4/175   222   1/14 2/35 3/35 4/37   136
5/177 6/177 7/178 8/183 9/222   5/60 6/65 7/87 8/92 9/129

Bonus points – Worcestershire 2, Somerset 4.

Bowling: *First Innings*—Botham 13–3–18–0; Moseley 11–4–28–1; Dredge 5–1–28–1; Popplewell 8–1–46–1; Marks 21–6–36–1; Lloyds 20–5–61–6. *Second Innings*—Botham 10–3–33–1; Moseley 13–4–28–2; Lloyds 12–5–34–5; Marks 11–5–13–0; Dredge 8–2–23–2.

Somerset

*B. C. Rose c Humphries b Holder	16	– not out	19
S. M. Gavaskar b Inchmore	34	– not out	17
P. M. Roebuck c Humphries b Inchmore	56		
P. W. Denning c Humphries b Holder	6		
C. H. Dredge run out	0		
I. T. Botham c Holder b Inchmore	94		
V. J. Marks b Gifford	14		
†D. J. S. Taylor b Inchmore	25		
N. F. M. Popplewell lbw b Inchmore	6		
J. W. Lloyds not out	26		
H. R. Moseley b Inchmore	13		
L-b 7, w 3, n-b 18	28	L-b 7, w 1	8

1/27 2/113 3/126 4/129	318	(no wkt) 44
5/147 6/220 7/258 8/270 9/278		

Bonus points – Somerset 4, Worcestershire 4.

Bowling: *First Innings*—Holder 19–2–46–2; Inchmore 25.3–2–107–6; Pridgeon 12–1–60–0; Gifford 26–9–65–1; Younis 2–0–12–0. *Second Innings*—Holder 3–0–5–0; Inchmore 2–0–3–0; Pridgeon 1–0–6–0; Neale 3–1–6–0; Henderson 2.4–0–16–0.

Umpires: D. J. Constant and R. Julian.

SOMERSET v YORKSHIRE

At Weston-super-Mare, August 6, 7, 8. Drawn. Somerset 7 pts, Yorkshire 4 pts. Gavaskar dominated Somerset's innings, hitting his highest score for the county with three 6s and twenty 4s. He began briskly, slowed against some steady spells, then opened out splendidly after being recalled by Constant at 80, having "walked" for an attempted catch. Hampshire's superb innings (sixteen 4s) was important for Yorkshire. He led a third-wicket partnership of 67 with Love then, after a devastating spell of five for 13 in 26 balls by Moseley, received dogged support from the tail. As the unreliable pitch gave more help to the spinners, Carrick and Cope gradually reduced Somerset, the only resistance coming from Olive with a determined maiden 50. Yorkshire, needing 213 in 205 minutes, lost three wickets for 36 in an hour before Hartley (two 6s and four 4s) and Athey gave them a glimpse of victory. When Athey was out, however, the requirement was 94 from fourteen overs, and after a further nine overs in poor light both sides gave up.

Somerset

M. Olive c Carrick b Dennis	7	– c Lumb b Carrick	50
S. M. Gavaskar not out	155	– c Hartley b Dennis	14
P. M. Roebuck c Coverdale b Sidebottom	32	– b Sidebottom	11
P. W. Denning b Sidebottom	2	– c Athey b Cope	20
*V. J. Marks b Cooper	28	– b Sidebottom	13
N. F. M. Popplewell c Sidebottom b Cooper	12	– b Cope	1
†D. J. S. Taylor not out	32	– c Athey b Carrick	4
J. W. Lloyds (did not bat)		– c Dennis b Cope	9
C. H. Dredge (did not bat)		– not out	1
H. R. Moseley (did not bat)		– c Dennis b Carrick	6
H. I. E. Gore (did not bat)		– b Carrick	1
L-b 4, n-b 4	8	B 9, l-b 5, w 1	15

1/36 2/114 3/120	(5 wkts) 276	1/19 2/39 3/68 4/97	145
4/166 5/183		5/100 6/120 7/136 8/136 9/144	

Bonus points – Somerset 3, Yorkshire 2.

Bowling: *First Innings*—Cooper 22–6–57–2; Dennis 15–0–58–1; Sidebottom 17–6–52–2; Cope 17–2–54–0; Carrick 29–11–47–0. *Second Innings*—Sidebottom 15–4–38–2; Dennis 5–2–16–1; Carrick 23.4–11–27–4; Cope 27–11–49–3.

Yorkshire

R. G. Lumb c Taylor b Gore	9	– lbw b Moseley	5
C. W. J. Athey c Taylor b Moseley	18	– b Marks	40
J. D. Love c Denning b Moseley	15	– lbw b Moseley	6
*J. H. Hampshire c Marks b Dredge	124	– lbw b Gore	14
S. N. Hartley b Moseley	0	– not out	72
P. Carrick c Popplewell b Moseley	9	– not out	15
A. Sidebottom c Dredge b Moseley	5		
G. A. Cope c Popplewell b Moseley	0		
†S. P. Coverdale c Taylor b Dredge	8		
H. P. Cooper lbw b Marks	11		
S. J. Dennis not out	1		
B 1,1-b 3, w 2, n-b 3	9	B 2,1-b 9, n-b 1	12

1/22 2/30 3/97 4/97   209   1/6 2/18 3/36 4/119   (4 wkts) 164
5/107 6/113 7/114 8/133 9/191

Bonus points – Yorkshire 2, Somerset 4.

Bowling: *First Innings*—Moseley 23–6–58–6; Gore 19–5–47–1; Dredge 19.1–8–27–2; Lloyds 5–0–28–0; Popplewell 4–0–13–0; Marks 7–2–27–1. *Second Innings*—Moseley 12–3–21–2; Gore 12–4–34–1; Dredge 15–4–32–0; Lloyds 8–1–29–0; Marks 10–3–36–1.

Umpires: D. J. Constant and R. Julian.

At Northampton, August 9, 11, 12. SOMERSET drew with NORTHAMPTONSHIRE.

SOMERSET v LEICESTERSHIRE

At Taunton, August 16, 18, 19. Leicestershire won by 157 runs. Leicestershire 19 pts, Somerset 7 pts. Gower, dropped at 57, hit thirteen 4s in a delightful innings which took his side to 170 for two before Dredge, with three wickets in eight balls, altered the situation. However Clift (ten 4s) rescued the innings with Tolchard his best assistant. Richards (twelve 4s) steered Somerset to 126 for three, but Clift caused a slump to 139 for seven, taking four for 4 in 23 balls. Botham then led the recovery and Taylor, with seven 4s, helped put on 117 for the last two wickets. Balderstone (two 6s and ten 4s) gave Leicestershire a positive start in their second innings. Steele played usefully and Cook, sent in as night-watchman, excelled as he reached his highest score with one 6 and ten 4s. Somerset needed 302 in 225 minutes and, after Denning and Richards had gone, Botham attacked furiously. However, Cook's spell of four for 6 in 27 balls was decisive and Leicestershire achieved victory with ninety minutes to spare.

Leicestershire

J. F. Steele lbw b Gore	4	– c Richards b Dredge	66
J. C. Balderstone b Gore	33	– b Marks	87
D. I. Gower c Richards b Dredge	94	– (4) c Popplewell b Marks	2
*B. F. Davison b Dredge	42	– (5) not out	72
N. E. Briers lbw b Dredge	0	– (6) not out	17
†R. W. Tolchard c Richards b Gore	25		
P. B. Clift c Richards b Dredge	59		
G. J. Parsons b Popplewell	1		
J. P. Agnew c Roebuck b Gore	1		
N. G. B. Cook not out	3	– (3) c Dredge b Marks	75
L. B. Taylor b Dredge	0		
L-b 2, n-b 3	5	B 2,1-b 7, n-b 1	10

1/5 2/100 3/170 4/170   267   1/139 2/192 (4 wkts dec.) 329
5/177 6/234 7/235 8/243 9/267   3/201 4/276

Bonus points – Leicestershire 3, Somerset 4.

Bowling: *First Innings*—Gore 22–8–42–4; Dredge 19.3–4–50–5; Popplewell 17–5–57–1; Richards 7–0–28–0; Marks 11–3–30–0; Lloyds 12–1–55–0. *Second Innings*—Gore 15–2–44–0; Dredge 24–6–56–1; Marks 21–2–90–3; Lloyds 25–5–72–0; Roebuck 5–0–32–0; Botham 2–0–25–0.

Somerset

M. Olive c Clift b Taylor	15	– (9) lbw b Cook		1
P. M. Roebuck c Tolchard b Agnew	4	– (1) st Tolchard b Cook		32
I. V. A. Richards c Parsons b Clift	75	– c Davison b Agnew		25
C. H. Dredge b Cook	1	– (10) c Davison b Clift		9
P. W. Denning c Tolchard b Clift	31	– (2) c Clift b Agnew		2
*I. T. Botham c Balderstone b Clift	41	– (4) c Clift b Cook		24
V. J. Marks lbw b Clift	0	– (5) c Gower b Cook		0
J. W. Lloyds lbw b Clift	1	– (7) b Clift		19
N. F. M. Popplewell c Tolchard b Agnew	32	– (6) c Clift b Cook		1
†D. J. S. Taylor b Cook	59	– (8) c Tolchard b Clift		26
H. I. E. Gore not out	22	– not out		4
B 9, l-b 3, n-b 2	14	B 1		1

1/6 2/66 3/73 4/126   **295**   1/2 2/34 3/76 4/78   **144**
5/133 6/137 7/139 8/178 9/238   5/82 6/88 7/116 8/131 9/131

Bonus points – Somerset 3, Leicestershire 4 (Score at 100 overs: 292-9).

Bowling: *First Innings*—Agnew 12–2–56–2; Parsons 10–0–39–0; Taylor 11–2–36–1; Cook 36.1–10–83–2; Steele 12–5–18–0; Clift 20–5–49–5; Balderstone 1–1–0–0. *Second Innings*—Agnew 4–0–25–2; Parsons 3–0–28–0; Taylor 2–0–21–0; Cook 19–6–30–5; Steele 8–2–15–0; Clift 9.3–2–24–3.

Umpires: W. E. Alley and P. S. G. Stevens.

At Bournemouth, August 20, 21, 22. SOMERSET drew with HAMPSHIRE.

At Bristol, August 23, 25, 26. SOMERSET drew with GLOUCESTERSHIRE.

SOMERSET v GLAMORGAN

At Taunton, August 27, 28, 29. Drawn. Somerset 4 pts, Glamorgan 8 pts. Glamorgan made a poor start on a slow pitch but recovered thanks to a third-wicket partnership of 129 by Francis and Featherstone (two 6s and twelve 4s), who had been dropped when 8. After another slump, Moseley (seven 4s) and Eifion Jones added 99 in 29 overs. On a turning pitch, Featherstone caused a Somerset collapse to 112 for seven, only Lloyds (nine 4s) offering any resistance. However Popplewell, hitting nine 4s in a splendidly paced innings, averted the follow-on with fine support from Gard. Alan Jones and Featherstone usefully increased Glamorgan's lead but rain prevented any play on the final day.

Glamorgan

A. Jones c Gavaskar b Marks	18	– c Dredge b Lloyds	58
J. A. Hopkins b Dredge	2	– lbw b Marks	22
D. A. Francis c and b Marks	52	– b Lloyds	13
N. G. Featherstone c Popplewell b Dredge	89	– not out	36
M. J. Llewellyn run out	27	– not out	4
G. C. Holmes c Gard b Dredge	6		
E. A. Moseley not out	53		
†E. W. Jones not out	45		
B 4, 1-b 4, n-b 2	10	B 8, 1-b 6	14

1/11 2/25 3/154   (6 wkts) 302   1/46 2/65 3/122   (3 wkts) 147
4/188 5/203 6/203

*M. A. Nash, N. J. Perry and A. J. Mack did not bat.

Bonus points – Glamorgan 4, Somerset 2.

Bowling: *First Innings*—Dredge 29–13–54–3; Russom 17–6–52–0; Marks 29–8–107–2; Lloyds 17–2–61–0; Popplewell 8–2–18–0. *Second Innings*—Dredge 9–4–12–0; Russom 2–1–2–0; Marks 24–5–62–1; Lloyds 17–3–57–2.

Somerset

*B. C. Rose c Perry b Featherstone	20	N. Russom c Holmes b Perry	9
J. W. Lloyds b Featherstone	50	†T. Gard lbw b Nash	19
S. M. Gavaskar c Perry b Featherstone	4	C. H. Dredge c Perry b Nash	1
P. M. Roebuck b Nash	8		
P. W. Denning b Featherstone	10	B 6, 1-b 4, n-b 3	13
P. A. Slocombe c Moseley b Perry	10		
V. J. Marks c Hopkins b Featherstone	5	1/43 2/47 3/56 4/79	228
N. F. M. Popplewell not out	79	5/106 6/112 7/112 8/138 9/216	

Bonus points – Somerset 2, Glamorgan 4.

Bowling: Nash 21.4–8–41–3; Moseley 6–0–33–0; Featherstone 28–6–90–5; Perry 19–6–51–2.

Umpires: D. J. Dennis and B. J. Meyer.

SOMERSET v WARWICKSHIRE

At Taunton, September 3, 4, 5. Warwickshire won by ten wickets. Warwickshire 20 pts, Somerset 8 pts. An excellent start by Lloyds and Olive, followed by a slump against Doshi, prefaced a recovery led by Botham (two 6s and twelve 4s) and supported by Marks, Taylor and Popplewell. Warwickshire's reply followed similar lines, with Amiss and Smith leading the way before Lloyd, Whitehouse and Ferreira (two 6s and thirteen 4s) revived the innings. Somerset received another fine start from their openers, Lloyds making his fourth successive Championship 50, but then Doshi and Perryman caused a collapse. Heavy rain on the final morning delayed play for three hours before Ferreira and Doshi, making full use of a drying pitch, destroyed the last half of the batting; only Marks and Taylor could make any progress. Doshi's splendid match figures of eleven for 167 took him past 100 wickets for the season. Warwickshire easily scored the 104 runs needed for victory in just over an hour.

Somerset

M. Olive b Ferreira	28	– c Rouse b Doshi	19
J. W. Lloyds lbw b Doshi	70	– c Rouse b Doshi	54
I. V. A. Richards st Humpage b Doshi	14	– c and b Perryman	0
P. M. Roebuck c Humpage b Doshi	5	– lbw b Perryman	10
P. W. Denning c Smith b Doshi	6	– b Ferreira	3
*I. T. Botham b Lloyd	70	– b Doshi	21
V. J. Marks c Humpage b Ferreira	37	– c Ferreira b Doshi	45
N. F. M. Popplewell c Humpage b Ferreira	16	– lbw b Ferreira	2
†D. J. S. Taylor lbw b Doshi	33	– not out	14
C. H. Dredge lbw b Ferreira	6	– c Ferreira b Doshi	0
H. I. E. Gore not out	0	– c Amiss b Doshi	0
B 4, l-b 8, n-b 4	16	B 4, l-b 6, n-b 2	12

1/76 2/103 3/122 4/130　　　　　　301　　1/75 2/76 3/88 4/90　　　　　　180
5/137 6/213 7/250 8/255 9/301　　　　　5/115 6/121 7/133 8/180 9/180

Bonus points – Somerset 4, Warwickshire 4.

Bowling: *First Innings*—Botham 3–1–14–0; Hopkins 13–3–39–0; Perryman 13–2–39–0; Doshi 41–11–95–5; Ferreira 20.4–5–75–4; Lloyd 6–1–23–1. *Second Innings*—Rouse 2–1–2–0; Hopkins 7–1–21–0; Doshi 26.3–7–72–6; Ferreira 14–1–41–2; Perryman 7–2–32–2.

Warwickshire

*D. L. Amiss c Richards b Marks	52	– not out	51
K. D. Smith c Lloyds b Dredge	52	– not out	51
†G. W. Humpage b Dredge	11		
T. A. Lloyd c Popplewell b Lloyds	47		
J. Whitehouse c Popplewell b Lloyds	41		
P. R. Oliver c Taylor b Lloyds	32		
A. M. Ferreira b Dredge	90		
S. J. Rouse c Roebuck b Marks	4		
D. C. Hopkins b Marks	31		
S. P. Perryman c Popplewell b Marks	5		
D. R. Doshi not out	2		
L-b 11	11	B 4	4

1/104 2/116 3/123 4/198　　　　　　378　　(no wkt) 106
5/217 6/280 7/303 8/366 9/375

Bonus points – Warwickshire 4, Somerset 4.

Bowling: *First Innings*—Botham 6–0–21–0; Gore 14–3–28–0; Marks 30.2–3–122–4; Lloyds 21–3–94–3; Dredge 18–1–77–3; Richards 5–0–25–0. *Second Innings*—Dredge 2–0–10–0; Gore 1–0–5–0; Marks 5–0–26–0; Lloyds 5–1–24–0; Richards 5–0–21–0; Botham 5–2–10–0; Denning 0.5–0–6–0.

Umpires: J. G. Langridge and R. S. Herman.

SURREY

Patron – HM THE QUEEN

President – A. R. GOVER

Chairman, Cricket Committee – R. SUBBA ROW

Secretary – I. F. B. SCOTT-BROWNE
Kennington Oval, London, SE11 5SS

Cricket Manager – M. J. STEWART

Captain – R. D. V. KNIGHT

G. S. Clinton   County Badge   M. J. Stewart

Finishing runners-up seldom satisfies. Winning is the thing. Yet perhaps two seconds could be said to add up to one first for Surrey who, in chasing Middlesex home in the Schweppes County Championship and going down to them in the final of the Gillette Cup, at least played second fiddle to a very good side. Indeed, Surrey could consider themselves well above the remaining fifteen counties; Nottinghamshire, third in the Championship, being the proverbial mile away, 67 points adrift. They were the only worthwhile challengers to Middlesex from midway through the season, and early in August, when just four points separated the two sides, Surrey had a real chance. But Middlesex had two games in hand and these cushioned them in their run-up to success by a final margin of thirteen points.

Surrey, in fact, ended their Championship programme with six wins from eight games, four of them with maximum points, the other two with nineteen. This augured well for 1981. But almost as if to underline that they were the masters in 1980, Middlesex, who had already beaten Surrey in the Championship, the John Player League and the Benson and Hedges Cup, completed the grand slam in the season's finale, the Gillette Cup final at Lord's.

However, Surrey also had their firsts. Roger Knight, who played several fine innings, hit the first Championship century of the season, and Robin Jackman became the first of only two bowlers to complete 100 wickets – on August 18. There was also a first against the touring teams, Surrey beating the season's second visitors, the Australians, in their second game.

Jackman bowled with a bigger heart than ever, thankful that he had a fully fit Clarke at the other end to "soften them up" in the manner of modern West Indians. Jackman took part in every three-day match bar one, when he was required by England for one of the two Prudential Trophy matches against Australia. He was also named in England's party for the Centenary Test which followed, but he again missed out on winning a first cap. Of the 26 limited-overs games played by Surrey he missed only three. Throughout the season his effort never wavered. Fifteen times he took four or more wickets in a Championship innings, with eight for 58 against Lancashire at Old Trafford a new best performance for him in England. A final average of 15.40 from 121 wickets left him fourth in the national averages and only his age, 35, can have prevented the selectors from sending him to the West Indies in the winter.

Sylvester Clarke's first-class average of 21.51 for 79 wickets further illustrated the power of this opening attack. He took the season's first Championship hat-trick, dismissing the considerable Nottinghamshire trio of Todd, Randall and Rice. Giles Cheatle began his first season at The Oval well, but as the pitches became firmer so Intikhab Alam was restored with leg-breaks and googlies in support of Pat Pocock's off spin. Hugh Wilson fell away after promising much in 1979, but another of the younger school, "Jack" Richards, kept wicket well enough to suggest an international future.

Alan Butcher had a fine season with the bat, as to a lesser degree did his opening partner, Grahame Clinton; but too often in the early part of the season insufficient advantage was taken of good beginnings. Geoff Howarth, the incumbent New Zealand captain, dropped down to the Second Eleven to recover his touch, and having achieved that he found his way back barred because Surrey were already fielding their overseas limit of two players in Clarke and Intikhab. Butcher hit his first double-hundred, against Cambridge University, and throughout the country his aggregate of 1,713 runs was bettered by only four batsmen, Allan Lamb, Kirsten, Glenn Turner and Larkins. Reward for Butcher came by way of an appearance in one of the Prudential Trophy matches but, like Jackman, he did not play in a Test and missed out on the winter tour to the West Indies, England leaving out for the third year running without a Surrey man.

Team manager Mickey Stewart was again busy behind the scenes, not least with a floodlit game on the football pitch at Stamford Bridge. Although Surrey were prevented by the extension of a Gillette tie from playing in this night game they continued as backers, along with Chelsea, and came away with a profit upwards of £15,000, which pleased the accountants. Whether the true supporters who supply the bread and butter looked upon this addition to the calendar as jam or poison was another matter. – Harold Abel.

[Press Association

SURREY

Back row: M. J. Bamber, I. R. Payne, G. Monkhouse, P. H. L. Wilson, D. J. Thomas, R. G. L. Cheatle, D. B. Pauline, A. Needham, G. S. Clinton, D. Gibson (*coach*). *Front row:* D. M. Smith, G. P. Howarth, R. D. Jackman, P. I. Pocock, R. D. V. Knight (*captain*), M. J. Stewart (*manager*), G. R. J. Roope, Intikhab Alam, A. R. Butcher, C. J. Richards.

SURREY RESULTS

All First-class Matches – Played 24: Won 12, Lost 4, Drawn 8.

County Championship Matches – Played 22: Won 10, Lost 4, Drawn 8.

Bonus points – Batting 51, Bowling 74.

COUNTY CHAMPIONSHIP AVERAGES

BATTING

	Birthplace	Matches	Inns	Not Outs	Runs	Highest Inns	Avge
G. R. J. Roope	Fareham	21	28	8	928	101	46.40
R. D. V. Knight	Streatham	22	35	7	1,192	132	42.57
A. R. Butcher	Croydon	21	36	3	1,362	118	41.27
G. S. Clinton	Sidcup	22	36	6	1,147	120	38.23
D. M. Smith	Balham	21	31	9	771	104*	35.04
Intikhab Alam	Hoshiarpur, India	10	9	3	198	57*	33.00
M. A. Lynch	Guyana, WI	7	9	2	216	92	30.85
R. D. Jackman	Simla, India	21	22	7	317	47	21.13
C. J. Richards	Penzance	22	18	4	253	48	18.07
D. B. Pauline	Aberdeen	8	11	1	162	46	16.20
G. P. Howarth	Auckland, NZ	9	14	1	206	66	15.84
S. T. Clarke	Barbados, WI	20	18	1	248	55	14.58
R. G. L. Cheatle	London	13	10	6	35	13*	8.75
P. I. Pocock	Bangor	21	15	5	71	14	7.10

Also batted: D. J. Thomas (*Solihull*) 43; P. H. L. Wilson (*Guildford*) played in two matches but did not bat.

* *Signifies not out.*

BOWLING

	Overs	Maidens	Runs	Wickets	Average
R. D. Jackman	686.3	197	1,713	114	15.02
Intikhab Alam	256.5	73	722	34	21.23
S. T. Clarke	579.3	130	1,661	77	21.57
R. D. V. Knight	268	67	726	30	24.20
P. I. Pocock	496.3	129	1,314	43	30.55
R. G. L. Cheatle	197.3	64	528	16	33.00

Also bowled: A. R. Butcher 23–6–54–1; G. S. Clinton 8–0–77–2; G. P. Howarth 19–1–102–1; M. A. Lynch 7–2–19–0; D. B. Pauline 3–0–5–0; G. R. J. Roope 12–1–51–1; D. M. Smith 65–15–197–4; D. J. Thomas 54.1–15–129–9; P. H. L. Wilson 63–19–111–6.

HUNDREDS

The following nine three-figure innings were played for Surrey in County Championship matches – R. D. V. Knight 132 v Lancashire (The Oval), 106 v Hampshire (The Oval), 102* v Warwickshire (Birmingham), 102 v Worcestershire (Worcester); A. R. Butcher 118 v Hampshire (Portsmouth), 107 v Glamorgan (The Oval); G. S. Clinton 120 v Northamptonshire (Northampton); G. R. J. Roope 101 v Hampshire (The Oval); D. M. Smith 104* v Leicestershire (Leicester).

SURREY v HAMPSHIRE

At The Oval, April 30, May 1, 2. Drawn. Surrey 8 pts, Hampshire 2 pts. After rain delayed the start by two hours thirty-five minutes, Surrey slumped to 16 for two, at which point a close of play total of 202 for three was far from the minds of the dozen paying spectators. But Knight, 93, and Roope, 72, produced the transformation on one of Surrey's new pitches, which looked well up to standard. Their stand grew to 168 in 55 overs, with Knight completing the first Championship century of 1980 ten minutes into the second day. Taking three and three quarter hours it included nine 4s and was slightly less boisterous than Roope's in three and a half hours with one 6 and eight 4s. Jackman, the old hand, and Cheatle, the newcomer, whose first wicket for Surrey was that of Greenidge, helped produce the follow-on, and though Stephenson and Southern showed admirable spirit, when Hampshire were still 12 runs short of saving an innings defeat with two wickets left it seemed Surrey would scamper home. Eventually they wanted 82 in fourteen overs, but the impetus was missing and they finished 15 runs short. Roope, who was beginning his benefit season, recalled that he also opened the 1979 Championship with a century. It proved to be his last!

Surrey

A. R. Butcher c Cowley b Taylor	....	30	– c Rice b Stevenson	25
G. S. Clinton lbw b Stevenson	....	2	– run out	1
G. P. Howarth c Stephenson b Stevenson	......	0	– b Graf	7
*R. D. V. Knight c Southern b Graf	....	106	– run out	0
G. R. J. Roope c Rice b Southern	....	101	– not out	14
D. M. Smith not out	....	35	– c Stephenson b Graf	12
R. D. Jackman not out	....	24		
B 5, l-b 6, w 1		12	B 1, l-b 7	8

1/14 2/16 3/56 4/224   (5 wkts) 310   1/5 2/32 3/32 4/43   (5 wkts) 67
5/273   5/67

†C. J. Richards, P. I. Pocock, R. G. L. Cheatle and P. H. L. Wilson did not bat.

Bonus points – Surrey 4, Hampshire 2.

Bowling: *First Innings*—Graf 21–0–68–1; Stevenson 20–4–59–2; Taylor 15–3–36–1; Jesty 5–0–24–0; Rice 17–2–52–0; Southern 13–3–33–1; Cowley 9–3–26–0. *Second Innings*—Stevenson 7–0–29–1; Graf 7–0–30–2.

Hampshire

C. G. Greenidge b Cheatle	....	65	– lbw b Jackman	19
J. M. Rice lbw b Jackman	....	6	– c Richards b Wilson	10
N. G. Cowley c Jackman b Knight	....	15	– c Knight b Cheatle	29
T. E. Jesty c Roope b Jackman	....	6	– c Roope b Jackman	0
*N. E. J. Pocock c Richards b Jackman	......	6	– b Smith	33
V. P. Terry lbw b Cheatle	....	0	– c Roope b Smith	0
M. N. S. Taylor not out	....	18	– c Cheatle b Wilson	24
S. F. Graf c Richards b Wilson	....	11	– c Howarth b Jackman	8
†G. R. Stephenson b Wilson	....	0	– c Richards b Knight	47
J. W. Southern c Richards b Jackman	....	0	– not out	46
K. Stevenson lbw b Jackman	....	0	– c Cheatle b Jackman	3
B 6, l-b 11, w 3, n-b 2		22	B 8, l-b 13, n-b 2	23

1/32 2/71 3/97 4/115 5/115   149   1/24 2/35 3/35 4/106 5/108   242
6/119 7/139 8/141 9/149   6/108 7/137 8/149 9/214

Bonus points – Surrey 4.

Bowling: *First Innings*—Jackman 22–7–52–5; Wilson 18–5–31–2; Pocock 23–8–26–0; Knight 5–2–5–1; Cheatle 7–2–13–2. *Second Innings*—Jackman 21.1–3–55–4; Wilson 18–5–38–2; Smith 20–6–51–2; Knight 10–2–25–1; Pocock 21–9–34–0; Cheatle 9–4–16–1.

Umpires: W. E. Alley and C. T. Spencer.

At Cambridge, May 3, 5, 6. SURREY beat CAMBRIDGE UNIVERSITY by nine wickets.

SURREY v SUSSEX

At The Oval, May 7, 8, 9. Surrey won by nine wickets. Surrey 20 pts, Sussex 5 pts. In contrast
to the previous home match, Knight changed his batting order and sent in Howarth with
Butcher when Surrey faced a challenging target, 109 in sixty-five minutes. And with a
partnership of 87 they guided their side home in nineteen overs, which left two in hand. Victory
was made possible by Cheatle some two months after his move from Hove to The Oval. With
Mendis and Parker seemingly saving Sussex, Cheatle parted them, and between that wicket
and his fifth conceded only 9 runs. Sounder batting all round had given Surrey the edge earlier,
though the highest innings came from a Sussex man, Graves, whose fighting 98 in four hours
thirty-eight minutes ended when he was brilliantly thrown out by Howarth from square leg.
Two diving gulley catches by Smith in the space of three deliveries from Jackman had reduced
Sussex to 16 for two at the start of the first day. At the start of the second, Imran Khan gave
Surrey a boost. Their first 20 runs came from 13 byes, 6 wides and 1 no ball, all but 1 of them
accountable to the Pakistan fast bowler as he found lots of pace but little length or direction.
Only Butcher bettered the final extras total as Surrey went on to collect maximum bonus
points.

Sussex

K. C. Wessels c Smith b Jackman	13	– lbw b Jackman	2
G. D. Mendis c Richards b Jackman	34	– (3) c Jackman b Cheatle	44
P. W. G. Parker c Smith b Jackman	0	– (4) b Cheatle	42
P. J. Graves run out	98	– (5) lbw b Jackman	18
Imran Khan c Jackman b Wilson	12	– (6) c Butcher b Cheatle	4
J. R. T. Barclay c Richards b Pocock	0	– (2) lbw b Wilson	3
C. P. Phillipson lbw b Pocock	33	– c Richards b Butcher	2
*†A. Long b Smith	31	– c Knight b Cheatle	3
G. G. Arnold run out	4	– c Roope b Cheatle	18
J. Spencer not out	7	– c Richards b Jackman	3
C. E. Waller not out	2	– not out	0
B 1, l-b 4, w 1, n-b 10	16	B 3, l-b 8, w 2, n-b 8	21

1/16 2/16 3/77 4/92   (9 wkts) 250   1/8 2/8 3/102 4/107 5/121   160
5/92 6/187 7/221 8/234 9/246   6/125 7/128 8/154 9/158

Bonus points – Sussex 3, Surrey 4.

Bowling: First Innings—Jackman 19–10–36–3; Wilson 18–6–33–1; Smith 21–3–67–1;
Knight 6–2–10–0; Cheatle 12–7–14–0; Pocock 24–5–74–2. *Second Innings*—Jackman
19–9–34–3; Wilson 9–3–9–1; Smith 5–0–19–0; Knight 7–4–9–0; Cheatle 32–22–28–5;
Butcher 18–4–37–1; Pocock 2–1–3–0.

Surrey

A. R. Butcher c Long b Spencer	68	– lbw b Waller	40
G. S. Clinton lbw b Imran	36		
G. P. Howarth c Wessels b Spencer	16	– (2) not out	43
*R. D. V. Knight c Long b Spencer	26	– (3) not out	18
G. R. J. Roope b Spencer	22		
D. M. Smith b Spencer	18		
R. D. Jackman not out	36		
†C. J. Richards not out	34		
B 26, l-b 5, w 8, n-b 7	46	B 4, l-b 3, w 1	8

1/107 2/148 3/163   (6 wkts dec.) 302   1/87   (1 wkt) 109
4/203 5/220 6/243

R. G. L. Cheatle, P. I. Pocock and P. H. L. Wilson did not bat.

Bonus points – Surrey 4, Sussex 2.

Bowling: *First Innings*—Imran 22.5–6–48–1; Arnold 20–5–60–0; Spencer 36–11–97–5; Barclay 14–2–38–0; Waller 6–2–13–0. *Second Innings*—Imran 4–0–13–0; Arnold 6–0–36–0; Spencer 3–0–21–0; Barclay 3–0–23–0; Waller 3–0–8–1.

Umpires: K. E. Palmer and D. Shackleton.

At Chelmsford, May 24, 26, 27. SURREY lost to ESSEX by ten wickets.

SURREY v SOMERSET

At The Oval, May 28, 29, 30. Surrey won by eight wickets. Surrey 19 pts, Somerset 4 pts. Although Gavaskar did his best to deny Surrey victory with a century, they had thirteen overs to spare after chasing a modest 114 in two and a half hours. The early play went very much Surrey's way, with Butcher and Clinton helping to put them 58 runs ahead at the close of the first day with a possible 107 overs in hand. That their lead was kept to 171 was largely through the efforts of Somerset's new left-arm opening bowler, Gore, who in his first match of any kind for them took five for 66. He had arrived in England from Antigua a few days earlier. Gavaskar's 138 in two hours fifty minutes included seventeen 4s and contained one or two cover drives that reminded Surrey supporters of Peter May. However, support for him was limited, and another substantial opening stand between Butcher and Clinton put Surrey on the path to victory.

Somerset

*B. C. Rose c Howarth b Knight	25	– c Pocock b Knight	41
S. M. Gavaskar c Richards b Clarke	15	– b Jackman	138
P. A. Slocombe b Clarke	1	– b Clarke	3
P. M. Roebuck c Smith b Knight	0	– b Clarke	7
P. W. Denning c Clinton b Clarke	46	– c Smith b Clarke	2
†D. J. S. Taylor c Richards b Jackman	16	– b Clarke	45
D. Breakwell b Jackman	0	– b Jackman	24
K. F. Jennings c Richards b Jackman	3	– b Clarke	2
C. H. Dredge b Jackman	1	– c Richards b Jackman	9
H. I. E. Gore not out	0	– b Clarke	1
H. R. Moseley b Jackman	0	– not out	2
B 10, l-b 5, w 3, n-b 3	21	B 3, l-b 3, w 2, n-b 2	10

1/49 2/51 3/56 4/56 5/96 6/98   128   1/83 2/94 3/117 4/119 5/239   284
7/116 8/128 9/128   6/243 7/245 8/279 9/282

Bonus points – Surrey 4.

Bowling: *First Innings*—Clarke 15–4–35–3; Jackman 16.5–6–31–5; Knight 9–2–33–2; Smith 3–0–8–0. *Second Innings*—Clarke 31–6–73–6; Jackman 32.4–7–97–3; Knight 20–5–68–1; Pocock 4–0–21–0; Smith 2–0–11–0; Cheatle 3–2–4–0.

Surrey

A. R. Butcher b Gore	92	– c Slocombe b Roebuck 57
G. S. Clinton c Jennings b Gore	83	– not out 33
G. P. Howarth c Taylor b Gore	15	– c Gore b Roebuck 4
*R. D. V. Knight c Rose b Moseley	11	– not out 17
G. R. J. Roope b Moseley	6	
D. M. Smith c Taylor b Moseley	10	
R. D. Jackman c Jennings b Dredge	17	
†C. J. Richards b Jennings	7	
S. T. Clarke c Taylor b Gore	36	
P. I. Pocock lbw b Gore	0	
R. G. L. Cheatle not out	4	
L-b 17, w 1	18	L-b 3 3

1/152 2/196 3/203 4/218 5/222 6/237   299   1/86 2/94   (2 wkts) 114
7/246 8/274 9/274

Bonus points – Surrey 3, Somerset 4.

Bowling: *First Innings*—Moseley 27–6–73–3; Gore 31.5–10–66–5; Dredge 20–2–82–1; Jennings 14–5–37–1; Breakwell 6–0–23–0. *Second Innings*—Moseley 5–0–20–0; Gore 6–1–12–0; Dredge 2–0–11–0; Breakwell 12–5–17–0; Roebuck 11–1–43–2; Gavaskar 2.2–0–8–0.

Umpires: R. Aspinall and P. B. Wight.

SURREY v NOTTINGHAMSHIRE

At The Oval, May 31, June 2, 3. Nottinghamshire won by 38 runs. Nottinghamshire 14 pts, Surrey 3 pts. Not even the first hat-trick of the 1980 Championship, by Clarke at 6.15 on Monday, could bring Surrey victory. They had put Nottinghamshire in after a blank Saturday, but both sides were merely jockeying for position and waiting for Tuesday. With Nottinghamshire 15 for no wicket after two declarations, Clarke had Todd brilliantly caught by Cheatle in the slips, dismissed Randall leg before, without his playing a stroke, and yorked Rice. In the next over play finished because of bad light. Clarke went on to take two in three balls the next morning – and so the first five wickets for 25 – but Hassan played through this, as he had done the hat-trick, and was last out, having batted just over three hours. Surrey, left to score 170 in roughly three hours, "froze" against some useful, but by no means deadly, bowling by Bore and Hemmings, with the pitch giving only a modicum of assistance. Pocock was caught off the last ball of the game after he and Cheatle had played through three overs surrounded by fieldsmen.

Nottinghamshire

P. A. Todd c Jackman b Knight	17	– c Cheatle b Clarke 8
B. Hassan b Cheatle	79	– c Clarke b Jackman 91
D. W. Randall c Jackman b Clarke	53	– lbw b Clarke 0
*C. E. B. Rice not out	16	– b Clarke 0
H. T. Tunnicliffe not out	9	– b Clarke 11
J. D. Birch (did not bat)		– c Butcher b Clarke 0
†C. C. Curzon (did not bat)		– b Pocock 28
E. E. Hemmings (did not bat)		– run out 22
K. Saxelby (did not bat)		– lbw b Pocock 15
K. E. Cooper (did not bat)		– c Roope b Pocock 0
M. K. Bore (did not bat)		– not out 0
B 8, w 1, n-b 2	11	B 5, l-b 4, n-b 1 10

1/36 2/151 3/160   (3 wkts dec.) 185   1/15 2/15 3/15 4/55 5/55   185
                                               6/113 7/155 8/183 9/185

Bonus points – Nottinghamshire 1, Surrey 1.

Bowling: *First Innings*—Clarke 12–0–58–1; Jackman 11–0–38–0; Knight 7–2–23–1; Cheatle 15–4–43–1; Pocock 5–2–12–0. *Second Innings*—Clarke 16–3–64–5; Jackman 10.5–1–33–1; Cheatle 13–0–49–0; Pocock 9–0–29–3.

Surrey

A. R. Butcher c Todd b Bore	44	– c Curzon b Cooper	12
G. S. Clinton c Curzon b Saxelby	0	– lbw b Rice	4
G. P. Howarth lbw b Bore	64	– c and b Bore	27
*R. D. V. Knight not out	65	– b Hemmings	17
G. R. J. Roope lbw b Hemmings	0	– c and b Bore	1
D. M. Smith not out	9	– b Bore	36
R. D. Jackman (did not bat)		– b Bore	2
†C. J. Richards (did not bat)		– c Birch b Hemmings	2
S. T. Clarke (did not bat)		– b Hemmings	2
P. I. Pocock (did not bat)		– c Todd b Hemmings	14
R. G. L. Cheatle (did not bat)		– not out	2
B 11, l-b 6, w 2	19	B 6, l-b 5, n-b 1	12

1/5 2/85 3/154   (4 wkts dec.) 201   1/18 2/18 3/58 4/65 5/70   131
4/169   6/72 7/83 8/85 9/125

Bonus points – Surrey 2, Nottinghamshire 1.

Bowling: *First Innings*—Rice 4–1–21–0; Saxelby 6–1–29–1; Cooper 6–1–19–0; Bore 18–4–57–2; Hemmings 14.3–1–56–1. *Second Innings*—Rice 11–4–22–1; Cooper 5–0–25–1; Bore 18–7–24–4; Hemmings 19–4–48–4.

Umpires: R. Aspinall and P. B. Wight.

At Lord's, June 4, 5, 6. SURREY lost to MIDDLESEX by an innings and 58 runs.

SURREY v ESSEX

At The Oval, June 7, 9. Surrey won by ten wickets. Surrey 19 pts, Essex 6 pts. The dismissal of Essex in two hours for 60 – the lowest first-class total of the season to date – came about on the second day through a very fickle wicket. With the ball flying through at shoulder height or skidding along towards the shin, Jackman took six for 30 and Clarke four for 29. There was no need to call on any other bowlers. The demise of the Essex batsmen emphasised the value of 36 in two hours forty-eight minutes by nineteen-year-old Aberdeen-born Pauline, brought in for the out-of-form Roope, during the morning on the Monday. Richards, however, hit 48 in half that time. Intikhab, with his leg-breaks, was the most successful bowler on the Saturday, though even he found Turner a handful as the Essex all-rounder struck six 6s while scoring 76.

Essex

M. H. Denness c Smith b Jackman	8	– b Clarke	3
B. R. Hardie c Richards b Clarke	40	– c Smith b Jackman	0
K. S. McEwan lbw b Smith	36	– c Richards b Jackman	17
*K. W. R. Fletcher c Richards b Jackman	22	– b Jackman	19
K. R. Pont b Intikhab	19	– c Smith b Jackman	12
S. Turner c and b Jackman	76	– c Richards b Clarke	1
N. Phillip lbw b Intikhab	1	– b Clarke	0
R. E. East lbw b Knight	7	– c Lynch b Jackman	5
†N. Smith lbw b Intikhab	3	– b Jackman	0
D. L. Acfield c Knight b Intikhab	5	– b Clarke	2
G. E. Sainsbury not out	2	– not out	0
B 4, l-b 10, w 4	18	L-b 1	1

1/17 2/91 3/91 4/120 5/180 6/186   237   1/2 2/8 3/30 4/39 5/40   60
7/195 8/198 9/208   6/40 7/51 8/51 9/60

Bonus points – Essex 2, Surrey 4.

Bowling: *First Innings*—Clarke 16–4–57–1; Jackman 23.2–5–67–3; Knight 10–1–27–1; Smith 6–1–23–1; Intikhab 13–4–45–4. *Second Innings*—Clarke 15.1–4–29–4; Jackman 15–3–30–6.

Surrey

A. R. Butcher c Smith b Phillip	0	– not out		5
G. S. Clinton c Fletcher b Pont	36	– not out		7
M. A. Lynch c Hardie b Sainsbury	11			
*R. D. V. Knight lbw b Sainsbury	55			
D. M. Smith c Smith b Phillip	23			
D. B. Pauline c Denness b Sainsbury	36			
Intikhab Alam c Pont b Phillip	21			
R. D. Jackman c Fletcher b Phillip	23			
†C. J. Richards c Fletcher b Pont	48			
S. T. Clarke b Sainsbury	2			
P. I. Pocock not out	8			
B 7, l-b 6, w 5, n-b 4	22	W 1		1

1/0 2/25 3/78 4/127 5/137 6/168   285   (no wkt) 13
7/212 8/239 9/247

Bonus points – Surrey 3, Essex 4 (Score at 100 overs: 273-9).

Bowling: *First Innings*—Phillip 31–7–80–4; Sainsbury 30–4–85–4; Turner 6–0–15–0; Acfield 8–2–17–0; Pont 16.4–5–37–2; East 11–2–29–0. *Second Innings*—Phillip 1.2–0–7–0; Sainsbury 1–0–5–0.

Umpires: D. Shackleton and C. T. Spencer.

SURREY v MIDDLESEX

At The Oval, June 14, 16, 17. Drawn. Surrey 4 pts, Middlesex 5 pts. A masterly 91 (eleven 4s) in three hours thirty-six minutes by a clean-shaven Brearley enabled Middlesex to make something of a rain-affected match. It was Tuesday before Surrey resumed their first innings at 87 for six in reply to 232, so there was never any chance of a result. However, Brearley was in the picture again, forfeiting his second innings and leaving Surrey to score 113 in eight overs, an apparent retaliation by the Middlesex captain for the fact that Knight did not make an earlier declaration following the loss of four and a half hours through rain. Knight described Brearley's action as "a touch of pique". Van der Bijl looked a very awkward customer while taking five for 34, though both he and Daniel bowled their full quota of short-pitched balls.

Middlesex

*J. M. Brearley b Intikhab	91	V. A. P. van der Bijl b Intikhab	1
W. N. Slack lbw b Jackman	28	M. W. W. Selvey c Pauline b Intikhab	5
C. T. Radley c Richards b Clarke	17	W. W. Daniel b Intikhab	4
G. D. Barlow c Richards b Clarke	0		
M. W. Gatting c Richards b Clarke	7	B 5, l-b 6, w 1	12
†I. J. Gould lbw b Clarke	6		
P. H. Edmonds c Pocock b Jackman	34	1/46 2/84 3/84 4/107 5/118 6/193 232
J. E. Emburey not out	27	7/198 8/200 9/226

Bonus points – Middlesex 2, Surrey 4.

Bowling: Clarke 23–6–76–4; Jackman 22–4–68–2; Knight 15–3–54–0; Intikhab 8.2–1–22–4.

Middlesex forfeited their second innings.

Surrey

A. R. Butcher lbw b van der Bijl	19	– (3) not out	0
G. S. Clinton retired hurt	1		
D. B. Pauline b van der Bijl	0	– (4) not out	0
*R. D. V. Knight c Gould b van der Bijl	13		
D. M. Smith lbw b van der Bijl	6		
G. R. J. Roope c Gould b van der Bijl	10		
Intikhab Alam c van der Bijl b Daniel	25		
R. D. Jackman not out	22	– (1) lbw b Edmonds	0
†C. J. Richards c Brearley b Emburey	12	– (2) lbw b Emburey	1
S. T. Clarke b Edmonds	1		
P. I. Pocock not out	0		
B 2, l-b 2, w 1, n-b 6	11	B 4	4

1/3 2/34 3/35 4/46 5/76   (8 wkts dec.) 120   1/1 2/1   (2 wkts) 5
6/84 7/114 8/115

Bonus points – Middlesex 3.

Bowling: *First Innings*—van der Bijl 17–6–34–5; Daniel 14–3–44–1; Selvey 5–2–10–0; Emburey 10–2–14–1; Edmonds 5–2–7–1. *Second Innings*—van der Bijl 1–1–0–0; Edmonds 3–2–1–1; Emburey 2.5–2–0–1.

Umpires: W. E. Alley and B. J. Meyer.

At Leicester, June 18, 19, 20. SURREY drew with LEICESTERSHIRE.

At Manchester, June 25, 26, 27. SURREY drew with LANCASHIRE.

SURREY v GLOUCESTERSHIRE

At Guildford, June 28, 30, July 1. Drawn. Surrrey 4 pts, Gloucestershire 2 pts. Jackman left his mark on a rain-ruined match in which the last day was washed out completely. By taking five for 41 after Gloucestershire had been put in, he completed a remarkable record. Prior to this match, Gloucestershire were the only county against whom he had not taken five or more wickets in an innings. Moreover, having ended their innings with two wickets in two balls, he would have been on a hat-trick had they batted a second time. Surrey found run-making equally hazardous, particularly when Procter went round the wicket. He claimed both Clinton and Howarth leg-before with deliveries that straightened.

Gloucestershire

B. C. Broad run out	6		†A. J. Brassington b Clarke	2
Sadiq Mohammad c Richards b Jackman	4		B. M. Brain b Jackman	0
Zaheer Abbas c Cheatle b Knight	40		J. H. Childs b Jackman	0
A. W. Stovold c Cheatle b Jackman	4			
*M. J. Procter lbw b Cheatle	16		B 12, l-b 7, w 4	23
A. J. Hignell lbw b Jackman	10			
P. Bainbridge b Clarke	32		1/6 2/16 3/20 4/79 5/79 6/98	157
A. H. Wilkins not out	20		7/148 8/152 9/157	

Bonus points – Gloucestershire 1, Surrey 4.

Bowling: Clarke 23–6–55–2; Jackman 25.5–9–41–5; Knight 9–6–9–1; Cheatle 6–1–18–1; Pocock 6–1–11–0.

Surrey

A. R. Butcher not out	49	D. M. Smith not out	1
G. S. Clinton lbw b Procter	11	L-b 6, n-b 3	9
G. P. Howarth lbw b Procter	0		
*R. D. V. Knight c Broad b Wilkins	10	1/43 2/47 3/78	(3 wkts) 80

G. R. J. Roope, R. G. L. Cheatle, R. D. Jackman, †C. J. Richards, S. T. Clarke and P. I. Pocock did not bat.

Bonus points – Gloucestershire 1.

Bowling: Brain 5–0–23–0; Procter 13–4–30–2; Wilkins 8.1–1–18–1.

Umpires: D. J. Constant and R. Palmer.

At Worcester, July 5, 7, 8. SURREY beat WORCESTERSHIRE by nine wickets.

At Maidstone, July 9, 10, 11. SURREY drew with KENT.

SURREY v YORKSHIRE

At The Oval, July 12, 14, 15. Drawn. Surrey 4 pts, Yorkshire 5 pts. There was much encouragement for seam bowlers on the first day, but Smith, using his height to keep down the lifting ball, hit seven 4s in a fine 44 before playing on off the inside edge. Surrey were all out by tea; then Yorkshire lost three wickets for 77. On a pudding pitch after a blank Monday, the early play on Tuesday was concentrated on winning bonus points. Pocock took a return catch off his second delivery to dispose of Love and suggest a tricky time ahead for batsmen, but even he extracted insufficient turn to satisfy the array of fielders waiting for the bat-pad catch. The rain returned after lunch, limiting the third day to 30 overs.

Surrey

A. R. Butcher c Carrick b Sidebottom	33	†C. J. Richards lbw b Sidebottom	8
G. S. Clinton lbw b Ramage	17	S. T. Clarke b Old	4
*R. D. V. Knight c Bairstow		P. I. Pocock c Love b Old	7
b Sidebottom	18	R. G. L. Cheatle not out	13
D. M. Smith b Stevenson	44	L-b 5, n-b 4	9
G. R. J. Roope lbw b Sidebottom	0		
D. B. Pauline c Lumb b Old	17	1/38 2/69 3/74 4/74	175
R. D. Jackman b Old	5	5/134 6/141 7/149 8/155 9/155	

Bonus points – Surrey 1, Yorkshire 4.

Bowling: Old 14.5–4–48–4; Stevenson 18–5–55–1; Ramage 12–3–29–1; Sidebottom 15–3–31–4; Carrick 1–0–3–0.

Yorkshire

P. G. Ingham c Roope b Jackman	26	†D. L. Bairstow not out	10
R. G. Lumb lbw b Jackman	1	G. B. Stevenson c Butcher b Pocock	6
C. W. J. Athey c Richards b Clarke	31	B 2, l-b 2, n-b 1	5
*J. H. Hampshire lbw b Jackman	61		
J. D. Love c and b Pocock	12	1/9 2/55 3/67 4/96	(7 wkts) 194
P. Carrick b Pocock	42	5/178 6/184 7/194	

C. M. Old, A. Sidebottom and A. Ramage did not bat.

Bonus points – Yorkshire 1, Surrey 3.

Bowling: Clarke 15–3–42–1; Jackman 21–5–45–3; Knight 6–1–12–0; Smith 4–3–4–0; Pocock 9.4–1–45–3; Cheatle 6–0–22–0; Pauline 3–0–5–0; Butcher 2–0–14–0.

Umpires: D. J. Halfyard and R. Julian.

At Portsmouth, July 23, 24, 25. SURREY beat HAMPSHIRE by eight wickets.

At Birmingham, July 26, 28, 29. SURREY drew with WARWICKSHIRE.

At Northampton, August 2, 4, 5. SURREY beat NORTHAMPTONSHIRE by an innings and 31 runs.

SURREY v GLAMORGAN

At The Oval, August 6, 7, 8. Surrey won by 104 runs. Surrey 20 pts, Glamorgan 7 pts. Butcher set Surrey off on the right road with a three-figure innings which ended to the last ball before lunch. He hit one 6 and seventeen 4s, putting on 142 with Clinton in the first 32 overs. Their assault was followed by another from Roope, who took his 75 off only 79 balls. The total should have been larger but later batsmen managed only 30 off the last seventeen overs. Glamorgan replied adequately without Francis, who retired after taking a blow on the head facing Clarke, and on a very reasonable batting surface it began to look doubtful whether Surrey could force a win. But leg-spinner Intikhab, in the side for such an occasion, took five for 83 in 30 overs on the last day to bring a victory which took Surrey to within four points of Middlesex at the top of the table. Glamorgan's leading batsmen had fallen to pace when facing a target of 321 in about five hours, Alan Jones, Miandad and Featherstone managing only 18 between them. However, Francis recovered from his injury to lead a fight-back which kept the game going until 5.30 p.m. With Jackman out of action with a bruised instep, wicket-keeper Jones and Moseley worried Surrey, putting on 62 for the eighth wicket, but the persevering Intikhab had the final say.

Surrey

A. R. Butcher c Featherstone b Holmes	107	– c sub b A. A. Jones	38
G. S. Clinton lbw b Holmes	49	– c Nash b Moseley	8
*R. D. V. Knight lbw b Holmes	55	– lbw b Moseley	2
D. M. Smith c Hopkins b Holmes	9	– lbw b Hobbs	46
G. R. J. Roope c E. W. Jones b Holmes	75	– c Hobbs b A. A. Jones	20
M. A. Lynch c E. W. Jones b Moseley	5	– not out	55
Intikhab Alam b Moseley	10	– not out	29
R. D. Jackman b Holmes	21		
†C. J. Richards not out	13		
S. T. Clarke c E. W. Jones b Nash	4		
P. I. Pocock lbw b Nash	1		
B 9, l-b 11, n-b 6	26	B 2, l-b 8, w 1, n-b 4	15

1/142 2/179 3/211 4/257   375   1/27 2/34 3/70   (5 wkts dec.) 213
5/278 6/313 7/333 8/365 9/370   4/120 5/124

Bonus points – Surrey 4, Glamorgan 4.

Bowling: *First Innings*—Nash 25.4–6–74–2; A. A. Jones 15–0–84–0; Moseley 23–7–78–3; Featherstone 1–0–8–0; Holmes 24–6–86–5; Hobbs 6–0–19–0. *Second Innings*—Nash 12.3–4–27–0; A. A. Jones 16–1–81–2; Moseley 13–2–61–2; Holmes 7–1–23–0; Hobbs 3–1–6–1.

Glamorgan

A. Jones b Intikhab	58	– c Richards b Clarke 8
J. A. Hopkins b Clarke.	1	– lbw b Jackman 22
D. A. Francis retired hurt.	2	– (6) c Richards b Intikhab 41
Javed Miandad c Richards b Clarke.	90	– (3) c Jackman b Clarke 5
N. G. Featherstone b Intikhab	61	– (4) c Butcher b Jackman 5
G. C. Holmes lbw b Clarke	0	– (5) c Butcher b Intikhab 17
*M. A. Nash c Lynch b Pocock	16	– c Pocock b Intikhab 21
†E. W. Jones lbw b Jackman	10	– b Intikhab 59
E. A. Moseley b Clarke	17	– b Intikhab 26
R. N. S. Hobbs not out.	1	– not out 4
A. A. Jones b Clarke	0	– b Pocock 1
B 1, l-b 6, n-b 5	12	B 2, l-b 4, n-b 1 7

1/1 2/106 3/188 4/188	268	1/26 2/32 3/38 4/51	216
5/224 6/241 7/256 8/268 9/268		5/86 6/116 7/128 8/190 9/213	

Bonus points – Glamorgan 3, Surrey 4.

Bowling: *First Innings*—Clarke 23.1–6–79–5; Jackman 17–4–56–1; Intikhab 16–3–48–2; Knight 5–1–20–0; Roope 5–0–19–0; Pocock 11–0–34–1. *Second Innings*—Jackman 11–3–32–2; Clarke 16–1–45–2; Intikhab 30–14–83–5; Knight 4–2–8–0; Pocock 21.4–7–41–1; Lynch 1–1–0–0.

Umpires: W. L. Budd and D. Shackleton.

At The Oval, August 9, 10, 11. SURREY beat AUSTRALIANS by 52 runs (See Australian tour section).

At Derby, August 16, 18, 19. SURREY lost to DERBYSHIRE by 174 runs.

At Hove, August 20, 21, 22. SURREY beat SUSSEX by 145 runs.

SURREY v KENT

At The Oval, August 23, 25, 26. Surrey won by nine wickets. Surrey 19 pts, Kent 4 pts. Best Championship scores by Lynch and Thomas enabled Surrey to finish a hectic first day 83 ahead with four wickets in hand after they had dismissed Kent in 50 overs. Yet at 43 for five before tea, the home team had appeared to be struggling. Lynch played particularly well as he and Thomas steadied things with a stand of 87; his innings was worthy of a century. Intikhab's unbeaten 57 also helped Surrey lengthen their first innings lead to 160, and Jackman increased the prospects of a two-day win by dismissing Rowe, Woolmer and Cowdrey at a personal cost of 11 runs. Then Tavaré and Ealham took the strain against an attack temporarily weakened by the absence of Clarke, suffering from a leg injury. The young left-hander Benson scored a useful half-century and took the game into a third day, although Surrey won soon after lunch.

Kent

R. A. Woolmer c Butcher b Jackman	17	– lbw b Jackman	22
C. J. C. Rowe b Thomas	7	– c Richards b Jackman	6
C. J. Tavaré c Roope b Jackman	8	– c Richards b Thomas	38
C. S. Cowdrey lbw b Clarke	18	– c Clinton b Jackman	0
*A. G. E. Ealham c Clarke b Thomas	7	– b Thomas	53
M. Benson b Knight	3	– c Roope b Jackman	53
†A. P. E. Knott b Clarke	16	– lbw b Intikhab	10
J. N. Shepherd c Butcher b Knight	1	– c Butcher b Thomas	30
R. W. Hills c Richards b Thomas	10	– c Roope b Jackman	8
N. J. Kemp c Richards b Jackman	12	– c Richards b Thomas	23
D. L. Underwood not out	0	– not out	11
B 1, l-b 3, n-b 4	8	B 10, l-b 3, w 1, n-b 4	18

1/25 2/27 3/44 4/60   107   1/18 2/33 3/39 4/109   272
5/65 6/65 7/67 8/87 9/107   5/121 6/163 7/211 8/229 9/248

Bonus points – Surrey 4.

Bowling: *First Innings*—Clarke 15–7–14–2; Jackman 17–3–55–3; Thomas 9.3–3–20–3; Knight 8–4–10–2. *Second Innings*—Clarke 14–7–27–0; Jackman 37–9–98–5; Thomas 20.4–6–44–4; Intikhab 27–6–85–1.

Surrey

A. R. Butcher c Tavaré b Shepherd	4	– st Woolmer b Knott	53
G. S. Clinton b Kemp	4	– not out	50
*R. D. V. Knight b Kemp	20		
D. M. Smith c Knott b Shepherd	6	– (3) not out	5
G. R. J. Roope c Hills b Kemp	3		
M. A. Lynch b Kemp	92		
D. J. Thomas c Underwood b Hills	43		
Intikhab Alam not out	57		
R. D. Jackman lbw b Kemp	0		
†C. J. Richards c Knott b Shepherd	5		
S. T. Clarke c Rowe b Kemp	21		
L-b 9, w 1, n-b 2	12	L-b 1, w 2, n-b 4	7

1/8 2/8 3/35 4/39 5/43   267   1/110   (1 wkt) 115
6/124 7/211 8/211 9/236

Bonus points – Surrey 3, Kent 4.

Bowling: *First Innings*—Shepherd 24–5–75–3; Kemp 24.3–2–119–6; Hills 8–1–32–1; Woolmer 8–1–29–0; Underwood 1–1–0–0. *Second Innings*—Shepherd 8–2–27–0; Kemp 7–0–24–0; Hills 8–2–24–0; Rowe 8–2–19–0; Tavaré 1.3–0–9–0; Knott 1–0–5–1.

Umpires: P. S. G. Stevens and A. G. T. Whitehead.

SURREY v LANCASHIRE

At The Oval, September 3, 4. Surrey won by an innings and 110 runs. Surrey 20 pts, Lancashire 2 pts. The knowledge that they could do no better than second in the Championship did not deter Surrey from a virile performance which brought victory inside two days. Put in by Lancashire, they accumulated on the fortune of Clinton, who was already on his way for just a single when wicket-keeper Fowler dropped the easiest of catches. After Butcher had already tormented the bowlers, Clinton, Knight and Roope laid in as well to move the total to 387. Lancashire were then reduced to 51 for six in the last eighty minutes of the first day, mainly by the fast bowling of Clarke, and when they followed on 289 behind it was fittingly Jackman who put them to flight. He took four wickets in his opening spell and then finished the match with two successive balls. It was the eighth time in the season that he had taken five wickets or more in a Championship innings. It was also fitting that the best batting should come from Knight, whose 132 in under three hours contained six 6s and eight 4s for he led his side with much imagination. Adding to the first day's entertainment was a team of sky-divers, who descended – one of them across the road in Archbishop Tenison's Grammar School – in connection with Roope's benefit.

Surrey

A. R. Butcher lbw b Radford	66	Intikhab Alam b Lloyd	1
G. S. Clinton c Abrahams b Simmons	85	S. T. Clarke not out	8
*R. D. V. Knight c Reidy b Lloyd	132	B 6, l-b 25, n-b 2	33
D. M. Smith b Lloyd	14		
G. R. J. Roope not out	47	1/111 2/200 3/243 (6 wkts)	387
M. A. Lynch lbw b Hughes	1	4/360 5/372 6/373	

R. D. Jackman, †C. J. Richards and P. I. Pocock did not bat.

Bonus points – Surrey 4, Lancashire 2.

Bowling: Hogg 9–2–40–0; Radford 13–1–56–1; Allott 4–0–12–0; Simmons 30–7–70–1; Lloyd 33–3–131–3; Hughes 11–0–45–1.

Lancashire

A. Kennedy c Richards b Clarke	16	– (2) b Jackman	3	
D. Lloyd b Jackman	1	– (1) c Jackman b Intikhab	22	
*F. C. Hayes b Clarke	15	– c Richards b Jackman	66	
B. W. Reidy b Clarke	0	– b Jackman	8	
J. Abrahams run out	0	– lbw b Jackman	0	
†G. Fowler b Intikhab	9	– b Jackman	6	
J. Simmons c Intikhab b Jackman	8	– b Intikhab	35	
N. Radford c Richards b Clarke	15	– c Butcher b Intikhab	17	
P. J. W. Allott b Intikhab	1	– (10) not out	7	
D. P. Hughes not out	25	– (9) b Intikhab	3	
W. Hogg c Lynch b Intikhab	2	– b Jackman	0	
B 4, w 1, n-b 1	6	B 3, w 1, n-b 8	12	

1/7 2/32 3/37 4/37 5/40   98   1/21 2/32 3/47 4/53 5/70   179
6/51 7/57 8/60 9/79   6/120 7/145 8/163 9/179

Bonus points – Surrey 4.

Bowling: *First Innings*—Clarke 14–2–43–4; Jackman 13–8–21–2; Pocock 4–3–1–0; Intikhab 12.3–0–27–3. *Second Innings*—Clarke 14–3–48–0; Jackman 14.5–1–53–6; Intikhab 20–7–51–4; Pocock 8–2–12–0; Lynch 1–1–0–0; Knight 3–0–3–0.

Umpires: C. T. Spencer and P. S. G. Stevens.

SUSSEX

President – S. CAMA

Chairman, Cricket Committee – A. CROLE-REES

Secretary – R. G. STEVENS
County Ground, Eaton Road, Hove BN3 3AN

Captain – A. LONG (1980), J. R. T. BARCLAY (1981)

| C. M. Wells | County Badge | Imran Khan |

It is generally felt that Sussex gets the best of the weather, but if it is any consolation to other counties the alleged 1980 summer was as depressingly damp and dismal on the south coast as elsewhere. Climate apart, though, the Sussex season was not a bad one, either from a playing point of view or from the equally important one of fund-raising. Sussex were fourth in the Schweppes County Championship for the second successive season, besides reaching the quarter-finals of the Benson and Hedges Cup and the semi-finals of the Gillette Cup, in which they were knocked out by the eventual winners, Middlesex. The Sussex Young Cricketers won the Cambridge Festival competition, and the Under 25 side triumphed in their competition. It is many a year since so many young hopefuls were poised in the wings at the Hove County Ground.

This is an encouraging sign for the future, even if the three overseas players did take the batting and bowling honours in the averages. Kepler Wessels returned a batting average of 65.08 in the Championship and Imran Khan topped the bowling averages with 54 wickets in all matches (17.90) ahead of Garth le Roux in second place. Wessels was injured for a time, thus easing the problem of which two from the three to select, but he was in magnificent form later in the season, his memorable 254 against champions Middlesex being an object lesson in concentration and wise selection of the right ball to punish. On the fast Hove wicket Imran and le

Roux were a hostile pair, and Geoff Arnold revealed much of his old skill and control while sending down more overs than any other Sussex bowler.

The Sussex haul of 60 batting bonus points was the highest by any county. A young man who played a notable part in this was twenty-year-old Colin Wells, a Sussex-born lad from Newhaven. Usually, each season, a young star emerges with most clubs, and Wells's team-mates did not nickname him "Bomber" for nothing. He gave the ball a terrific whack, hitting numerous 6s over mid-wicket and passing 1,000 runs in his first full season. Long before the end of the summer critics were rating him as a youngster with Test potential, particularly as he also bowls at a useful medium-pace and he fields smartly.

Gehan Mendis somewhat belatedly received his county cap. This consistent player, with a liking for playing the quicker bowlers, joined the talented band of batsmen who have scored double-centuries when he hit 204 of Sussex's 482 for three against Northamptonshire at the Saffrons. Paul Parker had a rather disappointing season, although remaining among the "fringe" of Test hopefuls.

A new name appeared in county scorebooks when Tim Booth Jones, a batsman in his late twenties, played one sound innings after another and achieved the step-up from club cricket with Hastings Priory to the first-class game with commendable determination and skill. He went tantalisingly close to scoring a maiden century against Cambridge University, play being washed out when he was 89 not out at Hastings, where he has proved the scourge of opposing club bowlers over the years. There were useful contributions from Paul Phillipson, who was awarded his county cap in his tenth season with Sussex, and Ian Greig, younger brother of Tony, who was down from Cambridge and batted, bowled and fielded with obvious enthusiasm.

After a praiseworthy career which started with Surrey, Arnold Long is retiring from the game and is succeeded as captain by the conscientious John Barclay, whose vice-captain will be Parker. Long's thoughtful captaincy served Sussex well. Peter Graves and John Spencer are also departing after loyal and sound service. After the season had ended it was surprising to learn that the club intended to discontinue the policy of engaging a cricket manager and that Tony Buss would therefore be ending his career with the club which extended over 25 years as player, coach and manager.

The county's chief executive, Roy Stevens, considers that the overdraft, which has been a fearsome burden for several exacting years, will be written off in the not-too-distant future. A new lottery and a football pool are helping to pay bills and the President's appeal should be generously supported. Moreover, the newly formed Supporters' Club is tackling the question of increasing the membership, and of making greater and more profitable use of the amenities at the County Ground. – Jack Arlidge.

SUSSEX

[Bill Smith

Back row: G. D. Mendis, P. W. G. Parker, Imran Khan, G. S. le Roux, I. A. Greig, T. D. Booth Jones, C. M. Wells. *Front row:* J. Spencer, C. E. Waller, A. Long (*captain*), J. R. T. Barclay, G. G. Arnold, C. P. Phillipson.

SUSSEX RESULTS

All First-class Matches – Played 23: Won 4, Lost 3, Drawn 16.

County Championship Matches – Played 22: Won 4, Lost 3, Drawn 15.

Bonus points – Batting 60, Bowling 60.

COUNTY CHAMPIONSHIP AVERAGES

BATTING

	Birthplace	Matches	Inns	Not Outs	Runs	Highest Inns	Avge
K. C. Wessels	Bloemfontein, SA	15	29	5	1,562	254	65.08
C. M. Wells	Newhaven	19	27	5	991	135	45.04
P. W. G. Parker	Bulawayo, Rhod.	20	36	6	1,117	122*	37.23
Imran Khan	Lahore, Pakistan	16	26	5	759	124	36.14
G. D. Mendis	Colombo	22	39	1	1,326	204	34.89
J. R. T. Barclay	Bonn, W. Germany	16	26	3	783	119	34.04
G. S. le Roux	Cape Town, SA	13	19	5	425	68*	30.35
P. J. Graves	Hove	4	7	0	206	98	29.42
I. A. Greig	Queenstown, SA	14	16	3	336	53	25.84
C. P. Phillipson	Brindaban, India	21	30	3	648	87	24.00
T. D. Booth Jones	Dover	8	14	0	334	76	23.85
A. Long	Cheam	16	15	5	165	31	16.50
C. E. Waller	Guildford	19	17	11	79	15*	13.16
A. C. S. Pigott	London	4	6	2	48	17	12.00
T. J. Head	Hammersmith	6	7	0	83	41	11.85
J. Spencer	Brighton	6	8	3	57	14*	11.40
G. G. Arnold	Earlsfield	19	16	2	155	29*	11.07

Also batted: J. R. P. Heath (*Turner's Hill*) 0; A. Willows (*Portslade*) 1.

* *Signifies not out.*

BOWLING

	Overs	Maidens	Runs	Wickets	Average
Imran Khan	388.5	107	917	52	17.63
G. S. le Roux	252.3	76	686	30	22.86
J. R. T. Barclay	274.5	77	718	30	23.93
G. G. Arnold	488.1	171	1,184	43	27.53
C. E. Waller	472.1	124	1,275	39	32.69
J. Spencer	182	47	519	13	39.92

Also bowled: I. A. Greig 152.3–32–477–9; P. W. G. Parker 1–0–12–0; C. P. Phillipson 42–5–142–1; A. C. S. Pigott 53–4–223–6; C. M. Wells 226–39–733–9; K. C. Wessels 3–0–7–0; A. Willows 82.2–26–203–8.

HUNDREDS

The following twelve three-figure innings were played for Sussex in County Championship matches – P. W. G. Parker 122* v Northamptonshire (Eastbourne), 117 v Kent (Tunbridge Wells), 105 v Hampshire (Southampton), 102 v Derbyshire (Derby); J. R. T. Barclay 119 v Leicestershire (Hove), 115 v Gloucestershire (Hove); Imran Khan 124 v Glamorgan (Swansea), 114 v Hampshire (Hove); K. C. Wessels 254 v Middlesex (Hove), 197* v Nottinghamshire (Eastbourne); G. D. Mendis 204 v Northamptonshire (Eastbourne); C. M. Wells 135 v Glamorgan (Swansea).

At Taunton, April 30, May 1, 2. SUSSEX drew with SOMERSET.

SUSSEX v LEICESTERSHIRE

At Hove, May 3, 5, 6. Drawn. Sussex 7 pts, Leicestershire 7 pts. In a biting north-east wind which kept the number of spectators down to small shivering groups, two notable centuries were scored. The first came from Barclay, whose opening stand of 143 with Wessels gave Sussex an impressive start; the second from Davison, the new Leicestershire captain, included twenty boundaries. Although the match petered out in a tame draw, le Roux had time to show his skill as a batsman, as well as a fast bowler of hostile pace, while Agnew and Cook bowled promisingly for Leicestershire.

Sussex

K. C. Wessels c Higgs b Steele	96	– c Agnew b Birkenshaw 76
J. R. T. Barclay c Higgs b Clift	119	
G. D. Mendis c Tolchard b Agnew	0	– (2) c Tolchard b Higgs 15
P. W. G. Parker c Davison b Steele	5	– (3) st Tolchard b Cook 17
P. J. Graves c Birkenshaw b Cook	12	– (4) lbw b Cook 43
G. S. le Roux b Cook	8	– (7) not out 68
C. P. Phillipson c Tolchard b Clift	14	– (5) c Steele b Cook 22
A. C. S. Pigott not out	2	– (6) c Tolchard b Higgs 9
*†A. Long b Cook	3	
L-b 3	3	B 3, l-b 6, n-b 4 13

1/143 2/158 3/173 4/203 　(8 wkts) 262　　1/58 2/95 3/122　(6 wkts dec.) 263
5/225 6/257 7/257 8/262　　　　　　　　4/149 5/173 6/263

G. G. Arnold and C. E. Waller did not bat.

Bonus points – Sussex 3, Leicestershire 3.

Bowling: *First Innings*—Agnew 14–5–33–1; Higgs 21–4–68–0; Clift 22–3–56–2; Cook 23–6–67–3; Birkenshaw 2–0–13–0; Steele 18–8–22–2. *Second Innings*—Agnew 14–5–42–0; Higgs 17–5–35–2; Cook 31.4–11–69–3; Birkenshaw 13–6–37–1; Clift 12–3–27–0; Steele 7–4–8–0; Balderstone 7–2–32–0.

Leicestershire

B. Dudleston c sub b le Roux	10	– not out 19
J. F. Steele b Arnold	2	– not out 14
J. C. Balderstone lbw b Waller	40	
D. I. Gower lbw b Arnold	0	
*B. F. Davison c Parker b Phillipson	151	
†R. W. Tolchard not out	77	
P. B. Clift c Phillipson b Waller	1	
J. Birkenshaw c sub b Waller	0	
N. G. B. Cook b Waller	11	
J. P. Agnew b le Roux	1	
K. Higgs not out	7	
B 4, l-b 6, w 2, n-b 10	22	B 2, n-b 3 5

1/2 2/22 3/23 4/125 　　(9 wkts) 322　　　　　　(no wkt) 38
5/265 6/267 7/267 8/308 9/311

Bonus points – Leicestershire 4, Sussex 4.

Bowling: *First Innings*—le Roux 26–8–69–2; Arnold 19–6–66–2; Pigott 7–0–29–0; Phillipson 12–1–36–1; Waller 36–8–100–4. *Second Innings*—le Roux 4–0–7–0; Arnold 8–2–20–0; Phillipson 5–2–6–0.

Umpires: K. E. Palmer and D. Shackleton.

At The Oval, May 7, 8, 9. SUSSEX lost to SURREY by nine wickets.

At Lord's, May 24, 26, 27. SUSSEX lost to MIDDLESEX by 5 runs.

SUSSEX v KENT

At Hove, May 28, 29, 30. Drawn. Sussex 3 pts, Kent 8 pts. A career-best 171 from Woolmer and an exciting last-day revival by Sussex were the features of an interesting match. Woolmer's disciplined innings, with one 6 and 21 4s, gave Kent a substantial first innings lead. Booth Jones, making his début for Sussex, recovered from a first innings duck to launch the Sussex fight-back with a competent 51. All-rounder Wells was their top scorer with 87 (one 6 and thirteen 4s) and Imran completed a classy all-round display with 82 runs and a fiery six for 80. Kent used eight bowlers on an easy-paced pitch with Underwood conceding only 17 runs in 21 overs.

Sussex

K. C. Wessels c Knott b Shepherd	29	– b Shepherd	20
T. D. Booth Jones c Knott b Jarvis	0	– c Woolmer b Hills	51
G. D. Mendis c Johnson b Hills	30	– c Woolmer b Hills	9
P. W. G. Parker c Knott b Cowdrey	22	– b Hills	1
Imran Khan c Cowdrey b Hills	1	– c Knott b Jarvis	82
C. P. Phillipson c Knott b Shepherd	26	– c and b Johnson	64
C. M. Wells c Knott b Jarvis	34	– b Underwood	87
†T. J. Head c Cowdrey b Hills	16	– c and b Cowdrey	41
G. G. Arnold b Jarvis	15	– b Rowe	18
*J. Spencer c Hills b Cowdrey	8	– not out	9
C. E. Waller not out	0	– c Woolmer b Rowe	12
L-b 4, w 1, n-b 3	8	B 4, l-b 7, n-b 3	14

1/3 2/59 3/66 4/68 5/96 6/139   189   1/31 2/40 3/46 4/164 5/167   408
7/163 8/163 9/189   6/300 7/324 8/363 9/383

Bonus points – Sussex 1, Kent 4.

Bowling: *First Innings*—Jarvis 17.4–5–46–3; Shepherd 18–3–47–2; Hills 22–11–27–3; Cowdrey 13–2–46–2; Underwood 5–2–15–0. *Second Innings*—Jarvis 28–7–81–1; Shepherd 30–7–84–1; Hills 25–6–70–3; Cowdrey 16–3–54–1; Underwood 21–17–17–1; Asif 7–3–13–0; Johnson 18–5–44–1; Rowe 9–3–31–2.

Kent

R. A. Woolmer b Imran	171	R. W. Hills c Head b Imran	0
C. J. C. Rowe b Wells	30	D. L. Underwood lbw b Spencer	4
G. W. Johnson c Booth Jones b Waller	45	K. B. S. Jarvis b Imran	4
Asif Iqbal c Head b Imran	0		
*A. G. E. Ealham not out	27	B 3, l-b 10, w 2, n-b 6	21
C. S. Cowdrey c Head b Imran	5		
†A. P. E. Knott c and b Wells	23	1/70 2/195 3/196 4/228 5/282 6/311	330
J. N. Shepherd c Parker b Imran	0	7/311 8/312 9/317	

Bonus points – Kent 4, Sussex 2 (Score at 100 overs: 311-5).

Bowling: Imran 29.1–8–80–6; Arnold 23–7–62–0; Spencer 17–4–46–1; Wells 16–2–53–2; Waller 21–5–68–1.

Umpires: C. T. Spencer and A. G. T. Whitehead.

At Middlesbrough, May 31, June 2, 3. SUSSEX drew with YORKSHIRE.

At Southampton, June 4, 5, 6. SUSSEX drew with HAMPSHIRE.

SUSSEX v WORCESTERSHIRE

At Hove, June 7, 9, 10. Drawn. Sussex 6 pts, Worcestershire 8 pts. The steady attack of Pridgeon and Cumbes, who claimed seven of the wickets between them, restricted Sussex to a first innings of 258, and then Neale's century, during which Humphries joined him in a stand of 151 off 31 overs, took the visitors to a first innings lead of 116. Rain on the final day left only two hours of play. Worcestershire made a bid to bowl their rivals out quickly, but gave up after half of the last twenty overs had been bowled and only three wickets had fallen. They were foiled by Wessels, with a disciplined 50 not out, and Parker, who displayed cool confidence to deny any breakthrough.

Sussex

K. C. Wessels c Humphries b Pridgeon	15	– not out ... 50
T. D. Booth Jones c Humphries b Pridgeon	35	– c Younis b Inchmore ... 1
G. D. Mendis c Humphries b Pridgeon	27	– c Hemsley b Inchmore ... 0
P. W. G. Parker c Neale b Cumbes	9	– (5) not out ... 22
Imran Khan c Patel b Pridgeon	34	– (4) c Pridgeon b Inchmore ... 9
C. P. Phillipson not out	56	
C. M. Wells c Younis b Inchmore	32	
A. C. S. Pigott run out	11	
*†A. Long lbw b Cumbes	11	
G. G. Arnold b Cumbes	2	
A. Willows lbw b Inchmore	1	
B 5, l-b 9, w 2, n-b 9	25	L-b 5, n-b 9 ... 14

1/20 2/66 3/84 4/122 5/141 6/199   258   1/11 2/11 3/57   (3 wkts) 96
7/240 8/250 9/252

Bonus points – Sussex 3, Worcestershire 4.

Bowling: *First Innings*—Inchmore 21.1–5–78–2; Pridgeon 30–4–74–4; Cumbes 17–6–35–3; Gifford 24–9–46–0. *Second Innings*—Inchmore 11–2–37–3; Pridgeon 9–3–28–0; Gifford 2–0–4–0; Cumbes 5.1–3–13–0.

Worcestershire

G. M. Turner c Wessels b Imran	11	J. D. Inchmore not out ... 10
J. A. Ormrod b Imran	47	*N. Gifford c Wessels b Pigott ... 2
J. Cumbes b Willows	43	A. P. Pridgeon not out ... 0
P. A. Neale c Wells b Pigott	123	
E. J. O. Hemsley b Imran	4	L-b 8, w 4, n-b 13 ... 25
Younis Ahmed c Booth Jones b Imran	2	
D. N. Patel c Phillipson b Pigott	22	1/16 2/95 3/127 4/141 (9 wkts dec.) 374
†D. J. Humphries c Arnold b Pigott	85	5/143 6/187 7/338 8/363 9/372

Bonus points – Worcestershire 4, Sussex 3 (Score at 100 overs: 348-7).

Bowling: Imran 27.2–7–65–4; Arnold 22–5–65–0; Pigott 19–4–65–4; Wells 20–2–69–0; Willows 9–1–37–1; Phillipson 8–0–48–0.

Umpires: D. J. Halfyard and J. G. Langridge.

At Tunbridge Wells, June 18, 19, 20. SUSSEX drew with KENT.

SUSSEX v CAMBRIDGE UNIVERSITY

At Hastings, June 21, 23, 24. Drawn. Play was possible only on the first day, the ground being waterlogged after heavy rain on the Sunday and later showers making it impossible to resume. Having won the toss, the University batted first and by mid-afternoon were bundled out for only 69, a total the Sussex opening batsmen, Mendis and Booth Jones, comfortably passed before the tea interval. Booth Jones was 89 not out at close of play, within hailing distance of his maiden first-class century, and it must have been tantalising to see this chance washed out. For Cambridge, Mills "dropped anchor" for ninety-five minutes to make 12 before being sixth out.

Cambridge University

A. M. Mubarak c Head b le Roux	4	D. C. Holliday c Head b Waller	10
J. P. C. Mills lbw b Arnold	12	N. C. Crawford not out	7
A. Odendaal c Wells b le Roux	0	M. G. Howat c Head b Waller	0
R. J. Boyd-Moss lbw b Spencer	7		
D. R. Pringle c Greig b le Roux	3	B 1,l-b 1, w 1	3
S. J. G. Doggart b Arnold	4		
*†I. G. Peck c Arnold b Waller	19	1/7 2/7 3/20 4/25 5/29 6/36	69
N. Russom lbw b Waller	0	7/43 8/56 9/63	

Bowling: le Roux 15–6–27–3; Arnold 9–8–4–2; Spencer 9–5–8–1; Greig 4–1–10–0; Waller 8.3–4–17–4.

Sussex

G. D. Mendis run out	67	I. A. Greig not out	8
T. D. Booth Jones not out	89		
A. M. Green lbw b Pringle	0	B 1,l-b 4, w 1, n-b 6	12
C. P. Phillipson lbw b Pringle	0		
C. M. Wells c Peck b Pringle	33	1/120 2/120 3/120 4/181 (4 wkts) 209

G. S. le Roux, †T. J. Head, G. G. Arnold, *J. Spencer and C. E. Waller did not bat.

Bowling: Howat 9–1–37–0; Russom 13–2–59–0; Crawford 5–3–14–0; Pringle 19–4–65–3; Doggart 9–2–22–0.

Umpires: D. J. Halfyard and A. Jepson.

SUSSEX v SOMERSET

At Hove, June 28, 30, July 1. Drawn. Sussex 4 pts, Somerset 2 pts. Play was possible only on the first day, the other days being spent in wicket inspections, covers being wheeled on and off, and with the old enemy triumphing in the end. Wells, a twenty-year-old from Newhaven, was confidently advancing towards a maiden century when persistent rain sent the players in with eighty minutes remaining. He and Greig, with a workmanlike 53, dealt with Botham and company in spirited style while adding 131 off 24 overs, Wells having struck eleven 4s and a couple of hefty 6s in his unbeaten 89.

Sussex

G. D. Mendis c and b Botham	60	I. A. Greig c Botham b Marks	53
T. D. Booth Jones c Taylor b Dredge	46	G. S. le Roux not out	0
C. P. Phillipson hit wkt b Botham	29	L-b 4, n-b 3	7
Imran Khan c Moseley b Botham	24		
C. M. Wells not out	89	1/90 2/119 3/153 4/174 5/305 (5 wkts) 308

J. R. T. Barclay, *†A. Long, G. G. Arnold and C. E. Waller did not bat.

Bonus points – Sussex 4, Somerset 2.

Bowling: Botham 25–6–93–3; Moseley 17–3–69–0; Dredge 23–8–60–1; Marks 5–0–15–1; Jennings 20–3–45–0; Breakwell 2–0–19–0.

Somerset

*B. C. Rose, S. M. Gavaskar, P. M. Roebuck, P. W. Denning, I. T. Botham, V. J. Marks, D. Breakwell, †D. J. S. Taylor, K. F. Jennings, C. H. Dredge, H. R. Moseley.

Umpires: W. E. Alley and W. L. Budd.

SUSSEX v HAMPSHIRE

At Hove, July 5, 7, 8. Drawn. Sussex 6 pts, Hampshire 2 pts. The unsporting cricket weather of June continued into this July fixture and the match was abandoned as a draw at lunch on the third day, dashing Sussex's hopes of a first Championship victory of the season. An interesting first day saw Sussex pile on a useful total then snap up three Hampshire wickets for only 45 before the close. Imran hit a delightful century with one 6 and sixteen 4s then sent back Tremlett and Nicholas, to leave Hampshire in serious trouble. Only eighty minutes of play were possible on the second day when Hampshire lost two more wickets for 72 with Turner holding out defiantly.

Sussex

G. D. Mendis c Cowley b Stevenson	 19	I. A. Greig run out	....	10
T. D. Booth Jones b Stevenson	 9	*J. R. T. Barclay not out	....	1
C. P. Phillipson c Stephenson				
b Stevenson.	87	L-b 14, w 10, n-b 7	....	31
Imran Khan c Turner b Cowley	114			
C. M. Wells c Smith b Stevenson	 72	1/33 2/40 3/240 4/315	(6 wkts)	398
G. S. le Roux not out	 55	5/351 6/386		

†T. J. Head, G. G. Arnold and C. E. Waller did not bat.

Bonus points – Sussex 4, Hampshire 2.

Bowling: Graf 11–3–39–0; Stevenson 21–1–104–4; Tremlett 16–5–57–0; Jesty 10–2–33–0; Southern 24–8–53–0; Nicholas 4–0–17–0; Cowley 14–2–64–1.

Hampshire

T. M. Tremlett c Mendis b Imran	 3	N. G. Cowley not out	....	8
C. L. Smith b le Roux	 17			
M. C. J. Nicholas c Head b Imran	 1	B 1, l-b 1, n-b 8	....	10
T. E. Jesty lbw b Arnold	 34			
D. R. Turner not out	 29	1/8 2/14 3/22	(5 wkts)	117
*N. E. J. Pocock b Arnold	 15	4/79 5/104		

S. F. Graf, †G. R. Stephenson, J. W. Southern and K. Stevenson did not bat.

Bonus points – Sussex 2.

Bowling: Imran 11–1–52–2; le Roux 6–3–16–1; Waller 6–2–14–0; Arnold 8–3–19–2; Barclay 4–1–6–0.

Umpires: R. Palmer and B. J. Meyer.

At Swansea, July 9, 10. SUSSEX beat GLAMORGAN by an innings and 189 runs.

At Bristol, July 12, 14, 15. SUSSEX beat GLOUCESTERSHIRE by two wickets.

SUSSEX v ESSEX

At Hove, July 26, 28, 29. Drawn. Sussex 7 pts, Essex 7 pts. In a sporting match which held the interest throughout, Sussex fought for their target of 277 until last-wicket pair Arnold and Waller came together at 234 with six overs remaining. They pluckily survived after Arnold had dealt robustly with a number of deliveries, and Essex, having earlier bowled themselves into a commanding position, were foiled. Turner for Essex and le Roux for Sussex produced fine bowling spells in the first innings, extracting pace and lift from a fast wicket.

Essex

M. H. Denness b Imran	6	– st Long b Waller	54
M. S. A. McEvoy c Phillipson b le Roux	15	– lbw b Greig	31
K. S. McEwan c Long b le Roux	31	– not out	103
*K. W. R. Fletcher b Imran	57	– c Long b Greig	12
B. R. Hardie c Waller b le Roux	73		
D. R. Pringle c Long b le Roux	14		
S. Turner c Barclay b le Roux	43	– (5) c sub b Greig	16
N. Phillip c Parker b le Roux	11	– (6) not out	11
R. E. East c Arnold b Waller	2		
†N. Smith c and b Waller	6		
D. L. Acfield not out	1		
B 1, l-b 8, n-b 21	30	B 4, l-b 6, n-b 10	20

1/14 2/24 3/90 4/181 5/221   289   1/47 2/153 3/193   (4 wkts dec.) 247
6/230 7/262 8/281 9/287   4/233

Bonus points – Essex 3, Sussex 4.

Bowling: *First Innings*—Imran 23–5–63–2; le Roux 26–4–84–6; Arnold 15–5–78–0; Wells 10–2–25–0; Waller 3–0–9–2. *Second Innings*—Imran 5–1–15–0; le Roux 2–0–7–0; Greig 20–0–74–3; Arnold 10–2–24–0; Wells 11–2–40–0; Waller 16–0–67–1.

Sussex

G. D. Mendis c Smith b Phillip	23	– c East b Turner	78
J. R. T. Barclay lbw b Turner	18	– c Smith b Phillip	12
Imran Khan c Turner b Pringle	26	– c McEwan b Phillip	27
C. M. Wells c Smith b Turner	26	– (5) b Acfield	2
C. P. Phillipson b Turner	4	– (6) c and b East	68
I. A. Greig c McEvoy b Turner	3	– (8) c Denness b Fletcher	10
G. S. le Roux c Fletcher b Phillip	46	– c Phillip b Turner	0
P. W. G. Parker c and b Turner	34	– (4) lbw b Acfield	1
*†A. Long not out	13	– c Fletcher b East	10
G. G. Arnold c Pringle b Phillip	23	– not out	29
C. E. Waller not out	15	– not out	4
B 1, l-b 3, n-b 25	29	L-b 5, w 1, n-b 7	13

1/35 2/58 3/71 4/82   (9 wkts dec.) 260   1/25 2/78 3/79 4/81   (9 wkts) 254
5/95 6/122 7/188 8/205   5/178 6/178 7/205 8/220
9/242   9/234

Bonus points – Sussex 3, Essex 4.

Bowling: *First Innings*—Phillip 24–3–86–3; Pringle 17–3–51–1; Turner 25–5–94–5. *Second Innings*—Phillip 9–1–39–2; Turner 16–0–81–2; Acfield 9–1–43–2; East 12–3–52–2; Fletcher 5–1–26–1.

Umpires: J. G. Langridge and R. Palmer.

At Manchester, August 2, 4, 5. SUSSEX beat LANCASHIRE by 98 runs.

SUSSEX v NORTHAMPTONSHIRE

At Hove, August 6, 7, 8. Sussex won by eight wickets. Sussex 19 pts, Northamptonshire 4 pts. On an easy-paced batting wicket a total of 1,093 runs was scored for the loss of only 22 wickets. During this run-feast Mendis gave his side a commanding start, featuring in partnerships of 52 with Barclay, 209 with Wessels and 197 with Parker. In reply the visitors tackled their mammoth task in spirited fashion, but even their sizeable total left them 185 in arrears and following on. Imran touched his Test-class form with match figures of seven for 58 and Sussex, despite a sound 92 by Williams and some vigorous hitting by Sarfraz, were left to score just 65 for victory.

Sussex

G. D. Mendis c and b T. M. Lamb.............204	– c Yardley b Sarfraz	14
*J. R. T. Barclay lbw b T. M. Lamb........... 26	– c Boyd-Moss b Sarfraz........	4
K. C. Wessels c Watts b T. M. Lamb........... 97	– not out	20
P. W. G. Parker not out.....................122	– not out	19
Imran Khan not out 4		
L-b 17, w 1, n-b 11................. 29	B 1, l-b 1, n-b 6........	8

1/52 2/261 3/458   (3 wkts) 482   1/21 2/22   (2 wkts) 65

C. M. Wells, C. P. Phillipson, I. A. Greig, †T. J. Head, G. G. Arnold and A. Willows did not bat.

Bonus points – Sussex 4, Northamptonshire 1.

Bowling: *First Innings*—Sarfraz 25–3–117–0; Griffiths 17–2–82–0; T. M. Lamb 28–4–100–3; Carter 2–0–20–0; Watts 3–0–19–0; Boyd-Moss 10–0–55–0; Williams 15–1–60–0. *Second Innings*—Griffiths 8–1–22–0; Sarfraz 7.5–1–35–2.

Northamptonshire

G. Cook c Phillipson b Barclay 85	– c Phillipson b Arnold	1
R. G. Williams c Parker b Arnold 39	– b Barclay	92
R. J. Boyd-Moss c Arnold b Willows........... 34	– lbw b Arnold	0
A. J. Lamb b Imran....................... 49	– c Head b Imran	42
T. J. Yardley lbw b Imran.................. 0	– c Phillipson b Imran..........	28
R. M. Carter not out...................... 20	– c Head b Greig	32
†G. Sharp c Head b Imran.................. 8	– c Greig b Imran	5
*P. J. Watts b Imran...................... 4	– c Head b Barclay	1
Sarfraz Nawaz not out..................... 44	– not out	36
T. M. Lamb (did not bat)	– c Barclay b Willows..........	0
B. J. Griffiths (did not bat)	– c Greig b Barclay...........	0
B 6, l-b 7, n-b 1................. 14	L-b 3, w 3, n-b 6........	12

1/46 2/143 3/216 4/218 5/218   (7 wkts) 297   1/2 2/2 3/95 4/170 5/176   249
6/226 7/230   6/188 7/189 8/245 9/246

Bonus points – Northamptonshire 3, Sussex 3.

Bowling: *First Innings*—Imran 20–7–36–4; Arnold 24–13–48–1; Greig 13–4–31–0; Barclay 23–3–103–1; Willows 20–7–65–1. *Second Innings*—Imran 16–3–22–3; Arnold 18–4–65–2; Greig 13–2–56–1; Barclay 18.5–4–70–3; Willows 7–3–13–1; Wells 5–2–11–0.

Umpires: D. J. Halfyard and P. S. G. Stevens.

SUSSEX v NOTTINGHAMSHIRE

At Eastbourne, August 9, 11, 12. Drawn. Sussex 8 pts, Nottinghamshire 2 pts. A brilliant fighting innings by their captain saved Nottinghamshire from an innings defeat after Sussex had taken a first innings lead of 156, and when stumps were drawn with nine of the final twenty overs bowled, the visitors were 132 runs ahead with Rice unbeaten for his century (one 6 and thirteen 4s). Wessels had batted superbly for Sussex as he and Barclay amassed 269. Imran managed to extract some pace from the friendly Saffrons pitch and followed his five for 11 in the first innings with three for 50 in the second. However, there was no shifting Rice.

Nottinghamshire

P. A. Todd lbw b Arnold	9	– c Mendis b Waller	51
R. T. Robinson c Long b Arnold	11	– b Arnold	28
D. W. Randall lbw b Arnold	31	– c Long b Imran	31
*C. E. B. Rice c Barclay b Wells	49	– (5) not out	100
B. Hassan b Imran	17	– (4) b Waller	1
M. J. Harris b Arnold	18	– c Phillipson b Imran	20
†B. N. French c Long b Imran	4	– c Long b Imran	8
E. E. Hemmings lbw b Imran	0	– c Parker b Wells	22
P. J. Hacker not out	1	– lbw b Wells	0
K. E. Cooper c Phillipson b Imran	0	– (11) not out	0
M. K. Bore lbw b Imran	0	– (10) b Barclay	1
L-b 8, w 1, n-b 6	15	B 7, l-b 7, n-b 12	26

1/13 2/38 3/59 4/101 5/132   155   1/57 2/115 3/124   (9 wkts) 288
6/150 7/150 8/150 9/155   4/126 5/192 6/219 7/251
                                       8/252 9/285

Bonus points – Nottinghamshire 1, Sussex 4.

Bowling: *First Innings*—Imran 13.3–5–11–5; Arnold 19–5–53–4; Greig 8–1–36–0; Wells 16–5–39–1; Waller 1–0–1–0. *Second Innings*—Imran 21–5–50–3; Arnold 15–8–21–1; Waller 24–4–93–2; Barclay 25–11–42–1; Wells 11–0–56–2.

Sussex

G. D. Mendis lbw b Hacker	11	Imran Khan not out	5
J. R. T. Barclay c Harris b Hacker	72	L-b 13, w 2, n-b 2	17
K. C. Wessels not out	197		
P. W. G. Parker c French b Hacker	9	1/13 2/282 3/298	(3 wkts dec.) 311

C. M. Wells, C. P. Phillipson, I. A. Greig, *†A. Long, G. G. Arnold and C. E. Waller did not bat.

Bonus points – Sussex 4, Nottinghamshire 1.

Bowling: Rice 17–1–58–0; Hacker 25–4–70–3; Cooper 18–5–78–0; Bore 23.2–10–45–0; Hemmings 13–3–43–0.

Umpires: D. J. Halfyard and P. S. G. Stevens.

At Birmingham, August 16, 18, 19. SUSSEX drew with WARWICKSHIRE.

SUSSEX v SURREY

At Hove, August 20, 21, 22. Surrey won by 145 runs. Surrey 20 pts, Sussex 2 pts. Surrey took command from the first day after being sent in on a friendly wicket. They achieved a first innings lead of 149 and finally set the home side the daunting task of scoring 401 for victory in five and a half hours. Knight displayed his all-round ability with two assured innings and some vital wickets. Sussex, who were third in the Championship table immediately behind Surrey, made a determined effort to chase the target but fell behind the clock despite a vigorous 74 for the fifth wicket by Wessels and Wells. Intikhab's spin and guile earned him three wickets, and Sussex's hopes of second place at the end of the season were severely dented.

Surrey

D. B. Pauline c Greig b Spencer	4	– c and b Greig	2
G. S. Clinton c Wessels b Waller	56	– c Mendis b Waller	46
*R. D. V. Knight b Spencer	65	– b Wells	48
D. M. Smith c and b Spencer	82	– not out	64
G. R. J. Roope not out	75	– not out	79
M. A. Lynch not out	10		
L-b 1, n-b 8	9	B 4, l-b 5, n-b 3	12

1/5 2/118 3/148 4/286   (4 wkts dec.) 301   1/3 2/95 3/103   (3 wkts dec.) 251

Intikhab Alam, D. J. Thomas, †C. J. Richards, P. I. Pocock and S. T. Clarke did not bat.

Bonus points – Surrey 4, Sussex 1.

Bowling: *First Innings*—Imran 9–3–15–0; Spencer 30–6–100–3; Greig 16–2–36–0; Wells 19–2–65–0; Waller 25.4–4–76–1. *Second Innings*—Spencer 17–3–57–0; Greig 18–1–67–1; Waller 17–1–58–1; Wells 18–5–57–1.

Sussex

G. D. Mendis c Richards b Thomas	1	– c Clarke b Thomas	30
*J. R. T. Barclay c Knight b Clarke	4	– c Richards b Knight	9
K. C. Wessels c Roope b Knight	22	– c sub b Intikhab	56
P. W. G. Parker run out	22	– c Richards b Knight	6
Imran Khan not out	55	– c Smith b Clarke	11
C. M. Wells lbw b Knight	0	– c Clarke b Intikhab	64
C. P. Phillipson c and b Knight	4	– c Roope b Intikhab	19
I. A. Greig c Richards b Clarke	17	– not out	27
†T. J. Head c Roope b Intikhab	7	– c Roope b Clarke	2
C. E. Waller b Clarke	0	– lbw b Clarke	7
J. Spencer run out	5	– lbw b Knight	2
B 1, l-b 3, n-b 11	15	B 5, l-b 13, w 1, n-b 3	22

1/7 2/7 3/53 4/58 5/62 6/70   152   1/38 2/51 3/59 4/79 5/153   255
7/103 8/118 9/120   6/212 7/217 8/222 9/232

Bonus points – Sussex 1, Surrey 4.

Bowling: *First Innings*—Clarke 18.1–5–41–3; Thomas 13–2–47–1; Knight 15–3–32–3; Intikhab 2–1–6–1; Pocock 1–0–11–0. *Second Innings*—Clarke 24–6–85–3; Thomas 11–4–18–1; Knight 15.3–1–39–3; Intikhab 32–9–91–3.

Umpires: C. T. Spencer and R. S. Herman.

SUSSEX v MIDDLESEX

At Hove, August 23, 25, 26. Drawn. Sussex 2 pts, Middlesex 8 pts. Middlesex needed a win to make certain of the Championship title and for two days they were right on course. Put in on a good batting wicket they reached a substantial total, thanks mainly to Brearley who hit seventeen 4s. An innings defeat looked likely when Sussex were tumbled out for 172 as van der Bijl, extracting lift, took six for 47. Following on, the home team lost two wickets before wiping out the deficit, but by then Wessels was firmly established. His disciplined defence and accurate eye for the right ball to punish finally took him to his double-century, scored in six hours with three 6s and 29 4s. Middlesex may have felt that a declaration could have been made at tea but Sussex batted on.

Middlesex

*J. M. Brearley st Head b Barclay	114	G. D. Barlow not out	11
†P. R. Downton b Greig	67		
C. T. Radley c Walker b Barclay	38	L-b 4, n-b 6	10
M. W. Gatting not out	49		
R. O. Butcher st Head b Barclay	71	1/144 2/217 3/223 4/341 (4 wkts) 360

P. H. Edmonds, J. E. Embury, W. W. Daniel, M. W. W. Selvey and V. A. P. van der Bijl did not bat.

Bonus points – Middlesex 4, Sussex 1.

Bowling: le Roux 13–8–24–0; Pigott 22–0–102–0; Greig 11–4–49–1; Wells 25–6–56–0; Waller 12–4–35–0; Barclay 17–0–84–3.

Sussex

G. C. Mendis lbw b Selvey	22	– lbw b van der Bijl	21
*J. R. T. Barclay c Downton b van der Bijl	28	– c Downton b van der Bijl	44
K. C. Wessels c Downton b Daniel	28	– c Embury b Gatting	254
P. W. G. Parker c Downton b van der Bijl	4	– c Downton b Daniel	17
T. D. Booth Jones c Brearley b van der Bijl	23	– c Brearley b van der Bijl	9
C. M. Wells c Brearley b van der Bijl	17	– c Embury b Edmonds	97
I. A. Greig c Radley b Selvey	6	– b Gatting	18
G. S. le Roux c Brearley b Selvey	8	– c Embury b Barlow	50
†T. J. Head c Downton b van der Bijl	4	– c Embury b Radley	13
C. E. Waller not out	9		
A. C. S. Pigott lbw b van der Bijl	9	– (10) not out	0
B 2, l-b 4, w 1, n-b 7	14	B 10, l-b 2, w 1, n-b 14	27

1/32 2/79 3/91 4/98 5/131	172
6/140 7/142 8/151 9/155	

1/44 2/144 3/192 (9 wkts dec.) 550
4/220 5/436 6/483 7/486
8/548 9/550

Bonus points – Sussex 1, Middlesex 4.

Bowling: *First Innings*—Daniel 15–1–53–1; van der Bijl 24.2–6–47–6; Embury 5–0–15–0; Selvey 21–9–38–3; Gatting 1–0–5–0. *Second Innings*—Daniel 16–3–68–1; Selvey 12–0–66–0; van der Bijl 22–5–46–3; Edmonds 34–6–155–1; Embury 36–4–128–0; Gatting 10–2–39–2; Barlow 4–0–21–1; Radley 0.3–0–0–1.

Umpires: R. S. Herman and B. J. Meyer.

At Derby, August 30, September 1, 2. SUSSEX drew with DERBYSHIRE.

SUSSEX v GLOUCESTERSHIRE

At Hove, September 3, 4, 5. Drawn. Sussex 6 pts, Gloucestershire 7 pts. The last match of such a wet summer ended appropriately – washed out! No play was possible on the last day, the County Ground being awash with pools of various sizes after a torrential downpour. Sussex had batted well in their first innings, Barclay steadily building an innings of 115 (thirteen 4s) in two hundred and seventy-four minutes and the promising Wells, with 50 of his 65 runs in boundaries, completing 1,000 runs in his first full season. In the persevering Gloucestershire attack Wilkins took five wickets for 76. After the visitors had declared 103 behind, Andrew Stovold having hit a stubborn 85, the second day was considerably brightened by Mendis and Wessels racing to a century stand in seventy minutes.

Sussex

G. D. Mendis c Wilkins b Bainbridge	44	– not out	81
J. R. T. Barclay c and b Partridge	115	– b Brain	7
K. C. Wessels b Partridge	35	– not out	53
P. W. G. Parker b Wilkins	33		
Imran Khan c Sadiq b Childs	16		
C. M. Wells c Sadiq b Wilkins	65		
C. P. Phillipson lbw b Wilkins	2		
I. A. Greig not out	26		
*†A. Long c Brassington b Wilkins	2		
G. G. Arnold c Broad b Wilkins	1		
C. E. Waller b Partridge	1		
B 1, l-b 6, w 1, n-b 5	13	L-b 6	6

1/58 2/105 3/179 4/214 5/313   353   1/43   (1 wkt) 147
6/316 7/325 8/336 9/346

Bonus points – Sussex 4, Gloucestershire 4.

Bowling: *First Innings*—Brain 12–3–34–0; Wilkins 24–3–76–5; Bainbridge 10–0–59–1; Partridge 20.3–3–66–3; Graveney 9–1–46–0; Childs 16–4–34–1; Broad 6–2–25–0. *Second Innings*—Brain 15–0–51–1; Wilkins 4–0–26–0; Bainbridge 8–0–44–0; Broad 2–0–14–0; Childs 1–0–6–0.

Gloucestershire

A. W. Stovold b Waller	85	D. A. Graveney not out	1
B. C. Broad b Greig	65	A. H. Wilkins not out	1
P. Bainbridge b Waller	0	B 1, l-b 5, w 8, n-b 5	19
Sadiq Mohammad c Greig b Waller	22		
M. W. Stovold b Imran	36	1/133 2/134 3/183 4/190 (6 wkts dec.) 250	
M. D. Partridge c Long b Imran	21	5/243 6/248	

†A. J. Brassington, *B. M. Brain and J. H. Childs did not bat.

Bonus points – Gloucestershire 3, Sussex 2.

Bowling: Imran 25–5–71–2; Arnold 23–6–52–0; Barclay 10–2–19–0; Waller 28–8–41–3; Wells 5–1–18–0; Greig 9–2–30–1.

Umpires: D. G. L. Evans and R. Julian.

CRICKETERS' SALARIES IN 1981

County cricketers are to receive a 12.5 per cent pay rise in 1981 following negotiations between the Cricketers' Association and the Test and County Cricket Board. Basic salaries of capped players, exclusive of sponsors' prize-money, go up by £600 from £4,850 to £5,450. If a player is capped during the 1981 season, his salary for the remainder of the year will be £5,000. Thereafter he will be paid at the full rate of a capped player.

Other increases agreed for non-capped players are: aged up to seventeen, from £1,700 to £1,950; aged up to eighteen, £2,000 to £2,250; aged up to nineteen, £2,300 to £2,575; aged up to twenty, £2,500 to £2,900, and aged up to twenty-one, £2,850 to £3,250.

WARWICKSHIRE

President — LORD AYLESFORD

Chairman, Cricket Committee — R. E. HITCHCOCK

Secretary — A. C. SMITH
County Ground, Edgbaston, Birmingham B5 7QU

Cricket Manager — D. J. BROWN

Captain — R. G. D. WILLIS

| D. R. Doshi | County Badge | R. G. D. Willis |

Having undergone a wretched season in 1979, Warwickshire staged a partial recovery by winning the John Player League in 1980. But in the Schweppes County Championship early hopes were not realised and the team finished only fourteenth; an improvement of just one place. They made no real mark in the Benson and Hedges Cup and the Gillette Cup.

The season began with a new look, Willis replacing Whitehouse as captain, and David Brown, the county's former England pace bowler, taking over as team manager. The Warwickshire Supporters' Association offered tempting cash prizes — £5,000 for winning the Championship, £5,000 for the John Player League and £5,000 for the Gillette Cup, plus an additional £5,000 for winning all three competitions.

A promising start was made in the Championship, despite the absence of Alvin Kallicharran, on duty with the West Indian touring team. There was an early win over Hampshire at Southampton, another over Worcestershire at Worcester, and in the first home game — a draw with Somerset — there were centuries by both David Smith and John Claughton, as well as a sound, unbeaten 75 by Phil Oliver. Such promise was not maintained. As the weather deteriorated, the proportion of drawn matches increased, so that by the time the campaign closed, with victory over Somerset at Taunton, the team had shifted a long way off course.

Warwickshire were seldom wanting for runs. As was expected of him, Dennis Amiss played a major part, totalling 1,626 in the Championship. David Smith had an excellent season, Andy Lloyd came to the fore as a rapidly improving batsman and Geoff Humpage again made his presence felt. John Whitehouse, relieved of the burden of captaincy, returned in the second half of the season to show the form which had once made him an England prospect, finishing second in the first-class averages with 725 runs at 65.90. His match-saving 197 not out in the draw with Glamorgan was especially memorable.

Anton Ferreira demonstrated that he is no mean performer with the bat when the occasion demands, as well as making steady progress with the ball. But the most striking success among the bowlers was that of Dilip Doshi, recruited at the start of the season after achieving only modest success with Nottinghamshire. Doshi's high-class spin was invariably treated with respect and, when he wound up the season with a match return of eleven for 167 against Somerset, he became the first Warwickshire bowler to capture 100 wickets in a season since Gibbs did so in 1971. Together with Lloyd, Doshi was awarded his county cap before the last match of the season.

Despite Doshi's performance the Championship bowling averages tell their own story with the Indian in 49th place, Willis 53rd and Ferreira 64th. A promising start was made by Gladstone Small, an eighteen-year-old fast bowler, but, with Bob Willis getting no younger and increasingly prone to run-up and injury problems, Warwickshire are in urgent need of a genuine fast bowler.

On the brighter side, the team's success in the John Player League yielded strikingly improved rewards at the turnstiles. From their eight Sunday home matches, watched by 46,000 people, they took nearly £29,500, compared with £8,430 in the previous summer. A home defeat by Northamptonshire in their second Benson and Hedges match quickly damaged their hopes of progress in that competition, and they met with only moderate success in the Gillette Cup, despite starting with two relatively easy home draws. But in the John Player League they came up with a startling transformation.

Anxious to improve on their position at the bottom of the table, Brown and Willis worked hard on fitness and the tactical side of the game, with positive results. The fielding was often brilliant, particularly from Oliver, Claughton, and Lloyd. Amiss sparkled with the bat, and by the end of June Warwickshire had taken an eight points' lead over their nearest challengers, Middlesex, who were beaten at Edgbaston by five wickets, thanks to an aggressive century from Humpage. Defeats by Worcestershire and Nottinghamshire temporarily halted their progress, but they soon re-captured their flair. As the competition neared its climax, they called in the help of Snow, the former Sussex and England bowler, and after an exciting tied match against Kent they clinched the title at Leicester. A crowd of 11,000 turned up for the last home Sunday match against Somerset. – Geoff Beane.

WARWICKSHIRE

Ken Kelly

Back row: A. Oakman (*coach*), D. R. Doshi, T. A. Lloyd, G. C. Small, C. Maynard, J. A. Snow, D. C. Hopkins, A. M. Ferreira, D. Smith, P. R. Oliver, J. A. Claughton, C. Grove (*scorer*). *Front row:* S. P. Perryman, J. Whitehouse, A. I. Kallicharran, D. Brown (*cricket manager*), R. G. D. Willis (*captain*), D. L. Amiss, S. J. Rouse, G. W. Humpage.

WARWICKSHIRE RESULTS

All First-class Matches – Played 25: Won 4, Lost 5, Drawn 16.

County Championship Matches – Played 22: Won 3, Lost 4, Drawn 15.

Bonus points – Batting 55, Bowling 54.

COUNTY CHAMPIONSHIP AVERAGES

BATTING

	Birthplace	Matches	Inns	Not Outs	Runs	Highest Inns	Avge
J. Whitehouse	Nuneaton	9	17	8	718	197	79.77
D. L. Amiss	Birmingham	22	40	2	1,626	117*	42.78
T. A. Lloyd	Oswestry	22	38	4	1,273	130*	37.44
K. D. Smith	Jesmond	22	39	2	1,343	140	36.29
G. W. Humpage	Birmingham	22	37	2	1,125	101	32.14
A. I. Kallicharran	Guyana, WI	5	9	0	223	52	24.77
J. A. Claughton	Leeds	13	23	4	466	108*	24.52
P. R. Oliver	West Bromwich	19	29	5	534	75*	22.25
A. M. Ferreira	Pretoria, SA	17	23	3	443	90	22.15
S. J. Rouse	Merthyr Tydfil	13	17	7	217	35	21.70
D. C. Hopkins	Birmingham	10	14	7	106	31	15.14
R. G. D. Willis	Sunderland	13	13	3	119	33	11.90
C. Maynard	Haslemere	5	6	1	46	20	9.20
G. C. Small	Barbados, WI	13	12	4	58	16	7.25
S. P. Perryman	Birmingham	11	7	4	16	5	5.33
D. R. Doshi	Rajkot, India	22	19	6	65	8	5.00
C. C. Clifford	Hoveringham	4	3	1	7	6	3.50

* Signifies not out.

BOWLING

	Overs	Maidens	Runs	Wickets	Average
D. R. Doshi	828.2	227	2,402	87	27.60
A. M. Ferreira	320.4	70	1,002	36	27.83
R. G. D. Willis	302.5	78	856	27	31.70
D. C. Hopkins	167.3	38	516	14	36.85
G. C. Small	188	41	684	16	42.75
C. C. Clifford	158	32	584	12	48.66
S. P. Perryman	250.5	51	804	16	50.25
S. J. Rouse	214.3	35	805	15	53.66

Also bowled: G. W. Humpage 7–3–13–2; A. I. Kallicharran 11–2–51–0; T. A. Lloyd 14–2–58–1; P. R. Oliver 87–12–412–7; J. Whitehouse 1.3–0–12–0.

HUNDREDS

The following nine three-figure innings were played for Warwickshire in County Championship matches – J. A. Claughton 108* v Worcestershire (Worcester), 103* v Somerset (Birmingham); T. A. Lloyd 130* v Worcestershire (Birmingham), 121 v Worcestershire (Worcester); K. D. Smith 140 v Somerset (Birmingham), 120* v Essex (Southend); D. L. Amiss 117* v Lancashire (Liverpool); G. W. Humpage 101 v Derbyshire (Birmingham); J. Whitehouse 197 v Glamorgan (Birmingham).

At Oxford, April 30, May 1, 2. WARWICKSHIRE beat OXFORD UNIVERSITY by 85 runs.

At Southampton, May 3, 5, 6. WARWICKSHIRE beat HAMPSHIRE by 159 runs.

WARWICKSHIRE v SOMERSET

At Birmingham, May 7, 8, 9. Drawn. Warwickshire 7 pts, Somerset 7 pts. Warwickshire took maximum batting points, but when Somerset countered with 306 for eight on the second day a draw was already in sight. Botham's adventurous 126 took just 109 minutes, 100 of his runs coming in boundaries; he reached his 50 with three successive 4s off Willis and scored 119 in eighty minutes after lunch. On the final day Warwickshire were not prepared to take risks: Smith scored a career-best 140 and Oxford Blue Claughton was unbeaten with 103 in his fourth Championship match. Somerset, set an impossible target of 339 in eighty-five minutes, merely played out time.

Warwickshire

D. L. Amiss b Moseley	56	– run out	29
K. D. Smith lbw b Dredge	34	– lbw b Botham	140
J. A. Claughton b Botham	7	– not out	103
T. A. Lloyd lbw b Botham	50	– not out	49
P. R. Oliver not out	75		
†G. W. Humpage c Botham b Moseley	32		
A. M. Ferreira b Breakwell	21		
D. C. Hopkins c Botham b Dredge	0		
G. C. Small not out	6		
B 5, l-b 9	14	B 4, l-b 4, w 1	9

1/70 2/91 3/128 4/177   (7 wkts) 314   1/80 2/225   (2 wkts dec.) 330
5/221 6/258 7/302

*R. G. D. Willis and D. R. Doshi did not bat.

Bonus points – Warwickshire 4, Somerset 3.

Bowling: *First Innings*—Botham 22–6–61–2; Moseley 26–4–92–2; Dredge 20–6–53–2; Jennings 21–6–56–0; Marks 1–0–1–0; Breakwell 10–0–37–1. *Second Innings*—Botham 23–7–75–1; Moseley 5–0–10–0; Marks 45–6–151–0; Breakwell 28–7–85–0.

Somerset

*B. C. Rose c Amiss b Willis	19		
P. A. Slocombe b Doshi	38	– (3) not out	27
P. M. Roebuck c Amiss b Willis	1	– (1) lbw b Oliver	20
P. W. Denning c Amiss b Ferreira	19		
I. T. Botham c Oliver b Doshi	126		
V. J. Marks b Small	0		
D. Breakwell c Willis b Ferreira	14		
†D. J. S. Taylor not out	51		
C. H. Dredge c Humpage b Ferreira	0	– (2) lbw b Doshi	1
K. F. Jennings not out	21	– (4) not out	7
B 5, l-b 3, n-b 9	17	W 1	1

1/30 2/33 3/64   (8 wkts dec.) 306   1/6 2/31   (2 wkts) 56
4/178 5/179 6/227 7/234 8/238

H. R. Moseley did not bat.

Bonus points – Somerset 4, Warwickshire 3.

Bowling: *First Innings*—Willis 22–6–59–2; Small 11–1–68–1; Ferreira 22–8–71–3; Doshi 21–6–59–2; Hopkins 8.4–2–32–0. *Second Innings*—Hopkins 6–1–21–0; Doshi 9–4–15–1; Oliver 5–2–19–1.

Umpires: C. Cook and P. B. Wight.

At Worcester, May 24, 26, 27. WARWICKSHIRE beat WORCESTERSHIRE by seven wickets.

At Nottingham, May 28, 29, 30. WARWICKSHIRE drew with NOTTINGHAMSHIRE.

At Liverpool, May 31, June 2, 3. WARWICKSHIRE drew with LANCASHIRE.

WARWICKSHIRE v DERBYSHIRE

At Birmingham, June 4, 5, 6. Drawn. Warwickshire 7 pts, Derbyshire 7 pts. Warwickshire, having been set a target of 278 in 178 minutes, were hard pressed to save the game in an exciting final over. Miller, the Derbyshire captain, was on a hat-trick when the last batsman, Doshi, came in and succeeded in fending off the last ball of the over. The feature of the first day was a century by Wood on his return to Championship cricket following his break with Lancashire. Humpage countered with a robust 101 in Warwickshire's reply before Amiss declared 27 runs in arrears. The threat of rain hampered Derbyshire's second innings and they lost their first four wickets for 91 going for a declaration. Warwickshire, after a sound start by Amiss and Smith, lost six batsmen in the last hour as they tried to accelerate against the off-spin of Miller and the leg-spin of teenager Barnett.

Derbyshire

B. Wood c Humpage b Ferreira	113	– c Smith b Hopkins	48
J. G. Wright c Humpage b Small	0	– c Oliver b Ferreira	17
P. N. Kirsten b Doshi	91	– c Humpage b Hopkins	20
K. J. Barnett c Smith b Doshi	18	– c Humpage b Hopkins	1
*G. Miller not out	50	– (7) c Lloyd b Doshi	26
I. S. Anderson c Humpage b Hopkins	21	– (5) lbw b Rouse	33
J. Walters run out	0	– (6) b Doshi	42
K. G. Brooks c Small b Doshi	3	– c Humpage b Small	8
C. J. Tunnicliffe not out	1	– (10) not out	24
†R. W. Taylor (did not bat)		– (9) not out	2
B 2, l-b 13, w 1, n-b 14	30	B 6, l-b 4, w 8, n-b 11	29

1/1 2/170 3/238 4/250   (7 wkts) 327   1/39 2/79 3/85   (8 wkts dec.) 250
5/313 6/317 7/324   4/91 5/174 6/190
                                                              7/218 8/218

S. Oldham did not bat.

Bonus points – Derbyshire 4, Warwickshire 3.

Bowling: *First Innings*—Rouse 14–3–46–0; Small 11–1–43–1; Ferreira 17–2–58–1; Doshi 41–9–101–3; Hopkins 17–2–49–1. *Second Innings*—Rouse 15–4–48–1; Small 13–3–26–1; Doshi 34–10–77–2; Ferreira 13–2–52–1; Hopkins 12–5–16–3; Oliver 1–0–2–0.

Warwickshire

*D. L. Amiss c Miller b Tunnicliffe	29	– run out	49
K. D. Smith lbw b Tunnicliffe	5	– c Brooks b Miller	17
T. A. Lloyd c Taylor b Wood	69	– (4) b Barnett	21
J. A. Claughton lbw b Oldham	1	– (5) c Kirsten b Miller	20
P. R. Oliver c Barnett b Tunnicliffe	4	– (6) c Brooks b Barnett	4
†G. W. Humpage c Wood b Miller	101	– (3) c Wood b Barnett	6
A. M. Ferreira run out	60	– c Wood b Barnett	4
S. J. Rouse not out	7	– not out	23
D. C. Hopkins not out	1	– c Wood b Miller	3
G. C. Small (did not bat)		– lbw b Miller	0
D. R. Doshi (did not bat)		– not out	0
B 5, l-b 6, n-b 12	23	B 4, l-b 5, w 1, n-b 2	12

1/10 2/69 3/76 4/88   (7 wkts dec.) 300   1/48 2/70 3/80 4/106   (9 wkts) 159
5/149 6/291 7/294   5/113 6/121 7/141 8/159
                                      9/159

Bonus points – Warwickshire 4, Derbyshire 3.

Bowling: *First Innings*—Oldham 24–3–77–1; Tunnicliffe 22–3–68–3; Miller 21–6–52–1; Barnett 1–0–8–0; Wood 14–2–49–1; Walters 4.4–0–23–0. *Second Innings*—Oldham 6–3–4–0; Tunnicliffe 8–1–23–0; Miller 25–13–44–4; Barnett 22–7–76–4; Kirsten 2–2–0–0.

Umpires: W. E. Alley and R. Palmer.

At Cambridge, June 7, 9, 10. WARWICKSHIRE drew with CAMBRIDGE UNIVERSITY.

At Southend, June 14, 16, 17. WARWICKSHIRE drew with ESSEX.

At Cardiff, June 18, 19, 20. WARWICKSHIRE lost to GLAMORGAN by four wickets.

WARWICKSHIRE v NORTHAMPTONSHIRE

At Nuneaton, June 21, 23, 24. Drawn. Warwickshire 2 pts, Northamptonshire 4 pts. The weather was an easy winner at the Colliery Ground where not a ball was bowled on the final day. Warwickshire, electing to bat first, scored a somewhat pedestrian 206 for five off 81 overs on a rain-affected first day, Amiss leading the way. Rain again held up the start on the Monday before Sarfraz finished off the Warwickshire innings, taking five for 3 in three overs. Northamptonshire, off to a sound start, had scored 81 without loss by the close, but had no chance to improve their bonus points.

Warwickshire

*D. L. Amiss b Griffiths	67	D. C. Hopkins c Cook b Sarfraz	3
K. D. Smith run out	12	G. C. Small c Griffiths b Sarfraz	2
T. A. Lloyd c Sharp b Sarfraz	45	D. R. Doshi not out	0
J. A. Claughton c Williams b Sarfraz	39		
G. W. Humpage c Williams b Carter	30	B 1, l-b 6, w 1, n-b 6	14
A. M. Ferreira c Yardley b Carter	6		
†C. Maynard b Sarfraz	16	1/34 2/119 3/153 4/190 5/196	235
S. J. Rouse c Watts b Sarfraz	1	6/227 7/228 8/229 9/234	

Bonus points – Warwickshire 2, Northamptonshire 4.

Bowling: Sarfraz 23.4–8–49–6; Griffiths 27–9–43–1; T. M. Lamb 23–5–49–0; Carter 13–2–51–2; Williams 8–1–29–0.

Northamptonshire

G. Cook not out	....	29
W. Larkins not out	....	35
B 1, l-b 10, w 2, n-b 4	....	17

(no wkt) 81

R. G. Williams, A. J. Lamb, T. J. Yardley, R. M. Carter, †G. Sharp, *P. J. Watts, Sarfraz Nawaz, T. M. Lamb and B. J. Griffiths did not bat.

Bowling: Small 4–2–16–0; Rouse 2–0–19–0; Doshi 1–0–8–0; Ferreira 7.2–2–19–0; Hopkins 7–6–2–0.

Umpires: D. J. Constant and D. J. Dennis.

WARWICKSHIRE v MIDDLESEX

At Birmingham, June 28, 30, July 1. Drawn. Warwickshire 4 pts, Middlesex 7 pts. Despite the earnest endeavours of the captains to contrive a finish, the weather won another victory, although at one stage Warwickshire were in danger of defeat at 70 for six with seven overs left. Rain marred all three days play. On the first, when nearly three hours were lost, Warwickshire held the Championship leaders to 167 for five, but Barlow, 50 not out, went on to reach 119 (eighteen 4s), still unbeaten. After Middlesex's declaration Warwickshire had trouble with Emburey's spin and were 136 for seven when Brearley offered to forfeit his second innings – should Warwickshire avoid the follow-on – if the tea interval could be foregone. Willis agreed – provided the Warwickshire innings could be closed immediately – and thus gained an extra ten minutes in which to attack a target of 166 in what turned out to be 31 overs. However, when Humpage was bowled in the seventh of the last twenty overs, Warwickshire gave up the chase.

Middlesex

*J. M. Brearley lbw b Willis	....	17	M. W. W. Selvey b Doshi	....	2
W. N. Slack c Maynard b Willis	....	24	R. J. Maru b Doshi	....	2
C. T. Radley c Maynard b Willis	......	9	W. W. Daniel not out	....	1
M. W. Gatting lbw b Rouse	....	25			
G. D. Barlow not out	....	119	B 1, l-b 5, w 6, n-b 19	....	31
†I. J. Gould lbw b Rouse	....	10			
J. E. Emburey c Lloyd b Doshi	....	17	1/47 2/48 3/68 4/103	(9 wkts dec.) 301
V. A. P. van der Bijl c Humpage b Doshi	44	5/125 6/184 7/272 8/286 9/296	

Bonus points – Middlesex 4, Warwickshire 4.

Bowling: Willis 24–5–75–3; Rouse 19–3–58–2; Hopkins 18–2–63–0; Ferreira 11–1–34–0; Doshi 12.4–4–40–4.

Middlesex forfeited their second innings.

Warwickshire

D. L. Amiss c Emburey b van der Bijl	....	38	– c Gatting b Maru	....	18
K. D. Smith b Daniel	....	6	– c Slack b Emburey	....	15
T. A. Lloyd c Gatting b Maru	....	51	– (5) c Gould b Emburey	....	1
J. A. Claughton c Gatting b Daniel	....	4	– (3) c Gatting b Emburey	....	15
G. W. Humpage b Daniel	....	6	– (4) b Maru	....	12
A. M. Ferreira b Maru	....	8	– b Emburey	....	2
S. J. Rouse c van der Bijl b Maru	....	20	– lbw b Emburey	....	0
D. C. Hopkins not out	....	0	– not out	....	4
*R. G. D. Willis not out	....	0			
†C. Maynard absent hurt	....		– (9) not out	....	0
B 1, w 1, n-b 1	....	3	L-b 3, w 1, n-b 5	....	9

1/14 2/80 3/99 4/105   (7 wkts dec.) 136   1/38 2/39 3/65 4/66   (7 wkts) 76
5/111 6/125 7/136   5/69 6/69 7/74

D. R. Doshi did not bat.

Bonus points – Middlesex 3.

Bowling: *First Innings*—van der Bijl 9–5–11–1; Emburey 26–15–34–0; Daniel 14–5–35–3; Maru 13.3–7–29–3; Selvey 5–1–24–0. *Second Innings*—Daniel 4–3–4–0; van der Bijl 3–0–8–0; Emburey 11.4–5–22–5; Maru 10–1–33–2.

Umpires: B. J. Meyer and J. van Geloven.

WARWICKSHIRE v LANCASHIRE

At Birmingham, July 5, 7, 8. Drawn. Warwickshire 3 pts, Lancashire 8 pts. Lancashire, batting on a wicket which had escaped the weekend rain, had much the better of things although they were denied a win. Warwickshire fell victim to some fine bowling by Hogg on the first day and his six for 45 restricted them to a modest 175. Lancashire were always able to bat with more freedom. Kennedy and Hayes gave them a good start, then Simmons scored 96 in under three hours, sharing with Hughes in a fifth-wicket stand of 106 in sixty-five minutes. Warwickshire were 165 in arrears when they batted again and lost Amiss to the second delivery of the innings. Smith and Lloyd took the score to 131 but Hogg had claimed three more wickets before the innings closed at 214, just 49 ahead. However, by that time only two overs were available to the visitors.

Warwickshire

D. L. Amiss lbw b Hogg	42	– c Scott b Hogg	0
K. D. Smith c Lloyd b Hogg	39	– c Scott b Allott	64
T. A. Lloyd b Hogg	1	– c Hughes b Hogg	60
J. A. Claughton c Scott b Allott	2	– c Scott b Hogg	0
†G. W. Humpage b Allott	16	– c Simmons b Allott	11
P. R. Oliver b Lee	15	– run out	15
A. M. Ferreira b Allott	0	– c Scott b Hogg	19
S. J. Rouse not out	30	– b Allott	10
D. C. Hopkins lbw b Hogg	3	– not out	3
*R. G. D. Willis c Simmons b Hogg	2	– c Scott b Lee	6
D. R. Doshi b Hogg	6	– c and b Lee	0
B 2, l-b 5, w 3, n-b 9	19	B 3, l-b 10, w 2, n-b 11	26

1/82 2/86 3/91 4/111 5/125 6/127   175   1/0 2/131 3/133 4/143   214
7/127 8/160 9/162   5/153 6/171 7/194
                                                          8/201 9/210

Bonus points – Warwickshire 1, Lancashire 4.

Bowling: *First Innings*—Hogg 25.1–7–45–6; Lee 16–9–31–1; Allott 23–4–55–3; Reidy 9–1–25–0. *Second Innings*—Hogg 24–9–37–4; Lee 22.1–9–45–2; Allott 22–9–35–3; Hughes 14–3–28–0; Reidy 8–1–23–0; Simmons 10–7–12–0; Lloyd 1–0–8–0.

Lancashire

A. Kennedy c Willis b Doshi	68	P. J. W. Allott lbw b Ferreira	4
I. Cockbain c Smith b Doshi	18	†C. J. Scott not out	5
*F. C. Hayes c Humpage b Doshi	53	B 5, l-b 12, w 2, n-b 11	30
B. W. Reidy lbw b Willis	0		
J. Simmons b Ferreira	96	1/93 2/109 3/109 (6 wkts)	340
D. P. Hughes not out	66	4/210 5/316 6/320	

D. Lloyd, W. Hogg and P. G. Lee did not bat.

Bonus points – Lancashire 4, Warwickshire 2 (Score at 100 overs: 320-5).

Bowling: Willis 28–9–63–1; Rouse 16.3–1–53–0; Hopkins 13–3–37–0; Ferreira 14–2–49–2; Doshi 34–11–93–3; Oliver 5–1–15–0.

Umpires: K. E. Palmer and C. T. Spencer.

At Northampton, July 9, 10, 11. WARWICKSHIRE drew with NORTHAMPTONSHIRE.

WARWICKSHIRE v WORCESTERSHIRE

At Birmingham, July 23, 24, 25. Worcestershire won by 96 runs. Worcestershire 17 pts, Warwickshire 8 pts. The return of fine weather inspired a high-scoring match which was given a notable send-off by Turner with a century before lunch – his eighth against Warwickshire. The spinners Doshi and Clifford shared the wickets as Worcestershire pressed on to 324 for nine before declaring. Lloyd made a century for Warwickshire, hitting fifteen 4s in his career-best 130, and former captain Whitehouse made a pleasing return with a half-century before Amiss declared 24 behind. Worcestershire created their winning position by declaring at 330 for five, after two more centuries had been reached by Ormrod and Younis. Left to score 355 in 260 minutes, Warwickshire were given a sound start by Amiss but, once he was out leg before to Alleyne for 99, their innings collapsed well short of the target.

Worcestershire

G. M. Turner st Humpage b Doshi	101	– c Amiss b Small	42
J. A. Ormrod c Oliver b Doshi	55	– b Clifford	106
P. A. Neale c Humpage b Doshi	0	– b Small	4
E. J. O. Hemsley c Humpage b Clifford	17	– lbw b Clifford	18
Younis Ahmed c Oliver b Doshi	13	– not out	121
T. S. Curtis not out	59	– lbw b Doshi	9
†D. J. Humphries c Humpage b Clifford	15	– not out	25
J. D. Inchmore c Ferreira b Clifford	13		
H. Alleyne b Clifford	1		
*N. Gifford b Doshi	27		
A. P. Pridgeon not out	8		
B 1, l-b 9, w 4, n-b 1	15	B 1, n-b 4	5

1/140 2/150 3/169 4/191   (9 wkts) 324   1/48 2/53 3/99   (5 wkts dec.) 330
5/193 6/218 7/232 8/233 9/314   4/274 5/301

Bonus points – Worcestershire 4, Warwickshire 4.

Bowling: *First Innings*—Small 11–3–42–0; Hopkins 5–0–31–0; Oliver 2–0–12–0; Ferreira 10–1–38–0; Doshi 33–10–76–5; Clifford 39–12–110–4. *Second Innings*—Small 8–2–34–2; Hopkins 5–0–21–0; Ferreira 5–0–23–0; Clifford 35–5–133–2; Doshi 35–4–114–1.

Warwickshire

*D. L. Amiss b Alleyne	49	– lbw b Alleyne	99
K. D. Smith c Hemsley b Alleyne	49	– c Younis b Alleyne	10
T. A. Lloyd not out	130	c Ormrod b Inchmore	19
†G. W. Humpage c Inchmore b Gifford	31	– b Inchmore	49
J. Whitehouse not out	50	– c Pridgeon b Gifford	16
A. M. Ferreira (did not bat)		– run out	3
P. R. Oliver (did not bat)		– b Gifford	20
D. C. Hopkins (did not bat)		– c Alleyne b Gifford	0
G. C. Small (did not bat)		– lbw b Alleyne	7
C. C. Clifford (did not bat)		– b Alleyne	6
D. R. Doshi (did not bat)		– not out	7
B 21, l-b 3, w 3, n-b 10	37	L-b 5, w 3, n-b 14	22

1/6 2/114 3/185   (3 wkts dec.) 300   1/29 2/55 3/143 4/193 5/206   258
                                              6/229 7/230 8/239 9/249

Bonus points – Warwickshire 4, Worcestershire 1.

Bowling: *First Innings*—Alleyne 22.5–6–66–2; Pridgeon 19–3–54–0; Gifford 33–4–71–1; Inchmore 12–2–46–0; Younis 5–0–26–0. *Second Innings*—Alleyne 19.2–5–63–4; Inchmore 17–2–62–2; Gifford 23–5–70–3; Pridgeon 7–1–41–0.

Umpires: W. L. Budd and D. G. L. Evans.

WARWICKSHIRE v SURREY

At Birmingham, July 26, 28, 29. Drawn. Warwickshire 4 pts, Surrey 2 pts. Rain severely curtailed the first day's play, when Warwickshire reached 137 for one, but a full second day and an agreement between the captains ensured an entertaining finish. Warwickshire declared at 300 for four, and Surrey declared before the start of the final day 89 behind, after Knight and Clinton had added 202 for the second wicket. Batting again, Warwickshire punished Surrey's second-line bowlers for 274 in 115 minutes and set a target of 364 in 240 minutes. After Butcher's 98 (two 6s and fourteen 4s) Surrey began their last twenty overs requiring a further 157. Clifford sent back Smith, Howarth and Richards and, with Doshi removing Clarke, Surrey slumped to 268 for eight before they were seen to safety by Jackman and Pocock.

Warwickshire

*D. L. Amiss b Jackman	50	– b Clinton	27
K. D. Smith c Knight b Jackman	62	– c Knight b Roope	60
T. A. Lloyd c Cheatle b Pocock	75		
†G. W. Humpage lbw b Pocock	74	– (3) c Roope b Clinton	54
J. Whitehouse not out	12	– (4) not out	79
J. A. Claughton not out	3	– (5) c Roope b Howarth	2
A. M. Ferreira (did not bat)		– (6) not out	36
B 6, l-b 4, w 6, n-b 8	24	B 9, l-b 4, n-b 3	16

1/106 2/146 3/263   (4 wkts dec.) 300   1/36 2/119 3/178   (4 wkts dec.) 274
4/292   4/193

S. J. Rouse, G. C. Small, C. C. Clifford and D. R. Doshi did not bat.

Bonus points – Warwickshire 4, Surrey 1.

Bowling: *First Innings*—Clarke 20–4–54–0; Jackman 25–8–62–2; Knight 7–0–26–0; Pocock 29–8–80–2; Cheatle 9–1–45–0; Howarth 3–1–9–0. *Second Innings*—Roope 7–1–32–1; Knight 6.5–0–56–0; Clinton 8–0–77–2; Howarth 16–0–93–1.

Surrey

A. R. Butcher b Small	2	– st Humpage b Doshi	98
G. S. Clinton c Small b Ferreira	92	– b Ferreira	18
*R. D. V. Knight not out	102	– lbw b Ferreira	1
G. R. J. Roope not out	1	– c Humpage b Doshi	54
D. M. Smith (did not bat)		– c Claughton b Clifford	26
G. P. Howarth (did not bat)		– lbw b Clifford	3
R. D. Jackman (did not bat)		– not out	46
S. T. Clarke (did not bat)		– c Ferreira b Doshi	16
†C. J. Richards (did not bat)		– st Humpage b Clifford	12
P. I. Pocock (did not bat)		– not out	6
B 2, l-b 10, n-b 2	14	B 3, l-b 7, w 2, n-b 3	15

1/2 2/204   (2 wkts dec.) 211   1/57 2/62 3/154 4/207 (8 wkts) 295
                                                5/207 6/218 7/247 8/268

R. G. L. Cheatle did not bat.

Bonus points – Surrey 2.

Bowling: *First Innings*—Small 6–3–13–1; Rouse 7–1–25–0; Doshi 23–3–87–0; Ferreira 9–1–19–1; Clifford 16–1–53–0. *Second Innings*—Small 5–2–12–0; Rouse 12–1–56–0; Doshi 28.5–9–69–3; Ferreira 8–1–32–2; Clifford 20–2–111–3.

Umpires: W. L. Budd and D. G. L. Evans.

At Birmingham, August 2, 3, 4. WARWICKSHIRE drew with WEST INDIANS (See West Indian tour section).

At Canterbury, August 6, 7, 8. WARWICKSHIRE lost to KENT by 163 runs.

WARWICKSHIRE v YORKSHIRE

At Birmingham, August 9, 11, 12. Yorkshire won by eight wickets. Yorkshire 14 pts, Warwickshire 3 pts. Although no play was possible on the Monday, a high peak of entertainment was reached on the final day when three declarations were made and 460 runs scored, including two Yorkshire centuries. Overnight rain delayed the start on the opening day until 2.30 p.m. and Warwickshire batted stubbornly to reach 235 off 76 overs. They batted on for ten minutes before declaring on the last day and Yorkshire, in turn, declared 146 behind. The second Warwickshire innings lasted only seventy minutes and left Yorkshire to score 243 in 160 minutes. The injured Lumb was out of action but Love joined Athey in an entertaining match-winning stand. Athey hit sixteen 4s and Love's first Championship century included two 6s and eleven 4s.

Warwickshire

D. L. Amiss c Carrick b Stevenson	8	– c Athey b Carrick	31
K. D. Smith c Hampshire b Stevenson	35	– c Dennis b Cope	25
T. A. Lloyd b Cooper	28	– st Coverdale b Cope	15
†G. W. Humpage b Cooper	33	– st Coverdale b Carrick	4
J. Whitehouse not out	79	– not out	12
P. R. Oliver lbw b Cope	35		
A. M. Ferreira c Cooper b Carrick	24		
*R. G. D. Willis not out	1		
B 1, l-b 5, n-b 2	8	B 2, l-b 7	9

1/9 2/70 3/76 4/121   (6 wkts dec.) 251   1/44 2/68 3/72   (4 wkts dec.) 96
5/172 6/236   4/96

C. C. Clifford, D. R. Doshi and S. P. Perryman did not bat.

Bonus points – Warwickshire 3, Yorkshire 2.

Bowling: *First Innings*—Stevenson 20–2–80–2; Dennis 10–2–28–0; Cooper 17–7–24–2; Carrick 17.5–4–50–1; Hartley 4–0–25–0; Cope 10–3–36–1. *Second Innings*—Stevenson 3–3–0–0; Dennis 3–1–8–0; Carrick 10–2–40–2; Cope 9.2–0–39–2.

Yorkshire

R. G. Lumb retired hurt	10		
C. W. J. Athey not out	58	– b Willis	114
J. D. Love c Willis b Doshi	0	– (1) c and b Doshi	104
*J. H. Hampshire not out	35	– (3) not out	5
G. B. Stevenson (did not bat)		– (4) not out	9
L-b 1, n-b 1	2	L-b 6, n-b 6	12

1/20   (1 wkt dec.) 105   1/224 2/235   (2 wkts) 244

S. N. Hartley, P. Carrick, †S. P. Coverdale, G. A. Cope, H. P. Cooper and S. J. Dennis did not bat.

Bowling: *First Innings*—Willis 4–0–7–0; Ferreira 5–1–9–0; Perryman 4–3–2–0; Doshi 7–1–41–1; Clifford 4–0–32–0; Whitehouse 1.3–0–12–0. *Second Innings*—Willis 15.1–2–63–1; Ferreira 9–0–53–0; Doshi 15–1–72–1; Perryman 7–1–28–0; Clifford 4–0–16–0.

Umpires: H. D. Bird and R. S. Herman.

WARWICKSHIRE v SUSSEX

At Coventry, August 16, 18, 19. Drawn. Warwickshire 6 pts, Sussex 8 pts. Whitehouse, batting nearly four hours, saved Warwickshire from defeat on an awkward, turning pitch after his side had been set to score 328 in 310 minutes and had lost half their wickets for 74. Mendis missed a century by only 1 run on the first day when Sussex accumulated a useful total. Warwickshire ran into trouble against the spin of Barclay and Waller after Amiss and Lloyd had put on 86 for the second wicket and they ended their first innings 97 behind. Mendis again batted well and Barclay was undefeated when he declared on the last day. Arnold, who finished with four for 23 off 23 overs, appeared to have set up a Sussex win but Whitehouse and Oliver resisted for 44 overs on a pitch which had crusted as it dried out.

Sussex

G. D. Mendis c Humpage b Perryman	99	– c Humpage b Willis	45
*J. R. T. Barclay c Kallicharran b Perryman	20	– not out	86
K. C. Wessels c Humpage b Oliver	36	– b Willis	0
P. W. G. Parker b Small	74	– lbw b Willis	43
C. M. Wells c Willis b Doshi	4	– c and b Perryman	1
C. P. Phillipson c Smith b Doshi	4	– not out	43
I. A. Greig b Willis	39		
G. S. le Roux c Whitehouse b Willis	10		
†T. J. Head b Willis	0		
G. G. Arnold run out	18		
C. E. Waller not out	0		
L-b 9, w 2	11	L-b 9, w 1, n-b 2	12

1/81 2/154 3/164 4/181 5/196 6/286   315   1/70 2/70   (4 wkts dec.) 230
7/287 8/287 9/308   3/145 4/148

Bonus points – Sussex 4, Warwickshire 4.

Bowling: *First Innings*—Willis 15–3–41–3; Small 11–0–53–1; Doshi 35–10–96–2; Perryman 32–8–92–2; Kallicharran 1–0–10–0; Oliver 6–4–12–1. *Second Innings*—Willis 16.1–3–65–3; Small 4–1–16–0; Doshi 16–2–78–0; Perryman 8.5–1–28–1; Oliver 5–0–31–0.

Warwickshire

D. L. Amiss c Barclay b Waller	39	– c Phillipson b Arnold	10
K. D. Smith lbw b Arnold	0	– lbw b Arnold	13
T. A. Lloyd c Parker b Barclay	82	– lbw b Arnold	0
†G. W. Humpage b Barclay	6	– (5) c Wells b Waller	9
A. I. Kallicharran st Head b Barclay	37	– (4) c Head b Arnold	29
J. Whitehouse c Wessels b Barclay	12	– not out	61
P. R. Oliver st Head b Waller	2	– run out	25
*R. G. D. Willis c Arnold b Barclay	10	– c Head b Greig	4
G. C. Small c sub b Waller	8		
D. R. Doshi c sub b Waller	5	– (9) not out	1
S. P. Perryman not out	2		
B 4, l-b 6, n-b 5	15	B 1, l-b 4, w 1, n-b 5	11

1/7 2/93 3/108 4/160 5/189 6/190   218   1/17 2/17 3/26 4/44   (7 wkts) 163
7/195 8/207 9/211   5/74 6/137 7/152

Bonus points – Warwickshire 2, Sussex 4.

Bowling: *First Innings*—le Roux 8–4–19–0; Arnold 21–8–39–1; Barclay 26–4–58–5; Wells 9–2–26–0; Waller 27–6–61–4. *Second Innings*—Arnold 23–14–23–4; Wells 4–1–10–0; Waller 43.5–21–71–1; Barclay 29–19–26–0; Greig 11–5–10–1; Parker 1–0–12–0.

Umpires: R. Palmer and D. Shackleton.

At Bradford, August 20, 21, 22. WARWICKSHIRE drew with YORKSHIRE.

WARWICKSHIRE v GLAMORGAN

At Birmingham, August 23, 25, 26. Drawn. Warwickshire 3 pts, Glamorgan 8 pts. After Glamorgan had put together a daunting total on the second day and had taken five Warwickshire wickets for 98, the home county began the last day facing an innings defeat. But they found the batsman they so badly needed in Whitehouse, whose career-best 197 included 39 boundaries. After he was out the last pair Willis and Perryman stayed together for another forty-five minutes before Willis closed the innings with thirty minutes left. The Glamorgan batting featured a dashing 181 in even time by Miandad, with three 6s and 27 4s. Hopkins (seventeen 4s) took nearly five hours over his second century of the season but Featherstone was more severe on the Warwickshire attack, scoring his 84 in 89 minutes with two 6s and twelve 4s.

Warwickshire

D. L. Amiss c E. W. Jones b Nash	76	– c E. W. Jones b Moseley 28
K. D. Smith lbw b Nash	0	– c E. W. Jones b Moseley 1
T. A. Lloyd b Nash	12	– c E. W. Jones b Nash 1
A. I. Kallicharran b Nash	36	– lbw b Nash 12
†G. W. Humpage b Moseley	8	– b Nash 0
J. Whitehouse b Nash	22	– (7) b Perry 197
P. R. Oliver lbw b Nash	4	– (6) c Hopkins b Moseley 69
S. J. Rouse not out	20	– c Perry b Nash 35
*R. G. D. Willis b Moseley	33	– not out 9
D. R. Doshi b Moseley	0	– c and b Moseley 0
S. P. Perryman b Moseley	1	– not out 4
B 6, l-b 10, n-b 7	23	B 10, l-b 20, w 5, n-b 11 .. 46

1/1 2/28 3/96 4/113 5/165 6/173   235   1/14 2/17 3/44   (9 wkts dec.) 402
7/180 8/225 9/231   4/44 5/57 6/208 7/373
    8/389 9/389

Bonus points – Warwickshire 2, Glamorgan 4.

Bowling: *First Innings*—Nash 35–12–105–6; Moseley 16–5–38–4; Mack 12–3–49–0; Perry 1–0–1–0; Featherstone 14–6–19–0. *Second Innings*—Nash 46–20–111–4; Moseley 35–15–70–4; Miandad 3–1–7–0; Featherstone 10–5–29–0; Holmes 5–2–6–0; Mack 15–4–45–0; Perry 27–12–88–1.

Glamorgan

A. Jones b Willis	49	E. A. Moseley not out 31
J. A. Hopkins c Humpage b Rouse	112	N. J. Perry run out 6
D. A. Francis b Oliver	3	A. J. Mack not out 0
Javed Miandad lbw b Rouse	181	B 2, l-b 16, w 2, n-b 11 31
N. G. Featherstone b Willis	84	
G. C. Holmes c Humpage b Willis	8	1/77 2/96 3/360 4/367 (9 wkts) 524
*M. A. Nash b Perryman	4	5/418 6/435 7/483
†E. W. Jones c Humpage b Willis	15	8/492 9/519

Bonus points – Glamorgan 4, Warwickshire 1 (Score at 100 overs: 410-4).

Bowling: Willis 36–11–87–4; Rouse 15–2–78–2; Perryman 33–3–134–1; Oliver 12–2–65–1; Doshi 20–4–97–0; Kallicharran 6–0–32–0.

Umpires: R. Julian and D. O. Oslear.

WARWICKSHIRE v GLOUCESTERSHIRE

At Birmingham, August 27, 28, 29. Drawn. Warwickshire 5 pts, Gloucestershire 8 pts. The breaking of the fine spell of weather washed out the last day, leaving the match in an interesting position after Warwickshire had been committed to another salvage effort to avoid defeat. Two features of the first day were Broad's century and Humpage's achievement in taking his first two Championship wickets for 13 in seven overs. Warwickshire's top scorer Smith had to retire for half an hour with a bruised elbow after being struck by a ball from Brain.

Gloucestershire

A. W. Stovold b Humpage	59	– c Maynard b Rouse	9
B. C. Broad c Oliver b Humpage	101	– b Doshi	14
Sadiq Mohammad c Lloyd b Rouse	19	– not out	59
*M. J. Procter lbw b Doshi	52	– c sub b Doshi	44
P. Bainbridge b Doshi	3	– b Doshi	10
M. D. Partridge c Perryman b Doshi	6	– not out	0
D. A. Graveney c Humpage b Perryman	1		
A. H. Wilkins c Smith b Rouse	22		
B. M. Brain b Doshi	8		
†A. J. Brassington not out	9		
J. H. Childs not out	8		
B 4, l-b 2, w 3, n-b 14	23	B 1, l-b 4, n-b 2	7

1/76 2/169 3/250 4/251 5/257   (9 wkts) 311   1/21 2/32 3/120   (4 wkts) 143
6/262 7/262 8/274 9/295   4/136

Bonus points – Gloucestershire 4, Warwickshire 4.

Bowling: *First Innings*—Willis 13–1–38–0; Rouse 19–1–85–2; Perryman 24–4–90–1; Oliver 5–0–23–0; Doshi 32–18–39–4; Humpage 7–3–13–2. *Second Innings*—Rouse 13–3–50–1; Perryman 10–1–28–0; Doshi 21–11–58–3; Kallicharran 2–2–0–0.

Warwickshire

D. L. Amiss b Bainbridge	34	*R. G. D. Willis c Stovold b Bainbridge	21
K. D. Smith lbw b Wilkins	56	D. R. Doshi b Bainbridge	8
T. A. Lloyd b Bainbridge	7	S. P. Perryman not out	1
A. I. Kallicharran lbw b Brain	5	L-b 1, n-b 5	6
G. W. Humpage c Partridge b Brain	2		
P. R. Oliver c Procter b Wilkins	25	1/64 2/81 3/84 4/89	182
†C. Maynard b Brain	0	5/96 6/133 7/136	
S. J. Rouse b Wilkins	17	8/173 9/173	

Bonus points – Warwickshire 1, Gloucestershire 4.

Bowling: Brain 18–4–45–3; Wilkins 21–4–64–3; Bainbridge 11.5–2–48–4; Childs 11–6–19–0.

Umpires: K. E. Palmer and A. G. T. Whitehead.

At Leicester, August 30, September 1, 2. WARWICKSHIRE drew with LEICESTERSHIRE.

At Taunton, September 3, 4, 5. WARWICKSHIRE beat SOMERSET by ten wickets.

WORCESTERSHIRE

President — THE REV. PREBENDARY W. R. CHIGNELL

Chairman, Cricket Committee — R. BOOTH

Secretary — M. D. VOCKINS
County Ground, New Road, Worcester WR2 4QQ

Captain — N. GIFFORD, MBE (1980), G. M. TURNER (1981)

H. L. Alleyne

County Badge

G. M. Turner

In 1980 Worcestershire dropped nine places in the Schweppes County Championship and five in the John Player League compared with 1979. However, the decline in these competitions was countered by an improvement in the Benson and Hedges Cup, in which they had the worst of the weather in losing to Essex in the semi-final, and in the Gillette Cup, in which they were beaten by the eventual winners, Middlesex, in the quarter-final. In common with most counties, Worcestershire suffered from the interference of bad weather which dogged them to the last day of the season, when the loss of four hours play denied them a likely victory over Nottinghamshire.

Their captain, Norman Gifford, retired after ten seasons during which he led Worcestershire to the Championship title in 1974 and the John Player League title in 1971. Gifford will continue to play under the captaincy of Glenn Turner in 1981.

Batting, as in 1979, was Worcestershire's strength. There is no more dependable opening combination in county cricket than Turner's imaginative stroke-play and Alan Ormrod's studious efficiency. At times, Turner played to a level reached only by a few, and it is doubtful if any batsman played a better innings than his 122 in the Benson and Hedges Cup quarter-final at Old Trafford in June. The New Zealander scored ten centuries in all cricket during the season, seven of these in the Championship. He finished the summer with 89 first-class hundreds and it can be only a matter of time before he emulates Sir Donald Bradman to become the second overseas-born player ever to score a century of centuries. Ormrod supported Turner with five centuries in the Championship, including two in the match against Somerset. His unflappable temperament enabled him to follow a "pair" against Nottinghamshire with 126 in his next innings, against Hampshire.

Although Philip Neale was not as consistent in the Championship as in 1979, he played well enough to prompt a suggestion by his captain that he should be considered for future representative honours. He made a wise choice by insisting to his winter employers, Lincoln City Football Club, that cricket must take preference when the seasons overlap. Ted Hemsley, also free from dual interest since finishing his soccer career with Doncaster Rovers in 1979, enjoyed a successful first half to the season, but lost his place briefly in August when Worcestershire introduced Stephen Henderson, a left-hander who graduated from Durham University, and Tim Curtis, a right-hand batsman who will continue his studies at Durham in 1981. In the last match of the season, Worcester-born opening batsman Martin Weston made his Championship début. Younis Ahmed did not repeat his outstanding form of 1979, when he was second in the national averages. He had scored only 500 first-class runs by the end of July, but made 50 or more in five of his last ten innings during the better weather of August. He is such an attacking player that firm, dry pitches are essential to his performance.

The pitches, usually slow and lifeless at New Road, were also a handicap to Worcestershire's pace bowlers. John Inchmore delivered some of his better performances away from Worcester, being, like Barbadian newcomer Hartley Alleyne, frustrated by the lack of bounce. Alleyne was undeniably quick and, as he learned more about the virtues of line and length on English pitches, he finished the season on a high note by taking eleven for 94 against Nottinghamshire, hitting the stumps six times. In all, he took 64 first-class wickets and promises to be an excellent successor to Vanburn Holder. Paul Pridgeon, though not aspiring to the hostility of either Alleyne or Inchmore, was invaluable as the third seamer, often bowling into the wind and being asked to operate as the stock bowler for as many as 30 overs in an innings. Pridgeon amply deserved the award of a county cap after nine seasons with the club.

Yet Worcestershire are aware that their bowling resources are slender. Holder, able to play only infrequently because of the overseas registration restrictions, is not re-engaged for 1981, although he may continue to appear on a match basis if required. The county have given a contract to Martyn Saunders, a local fast-medium bowler who played in three Championship matches, showed a willingness to attack the stumps, and took five wickets against Kent. Jimmy Cumbes did not play as regularly as he would have wished in 1980 and, with Saunders, will be competing with Pridgeon for the third seamer's place in 1981.

At the age of 40 Gifford remains one of the most effective and skilful slow bowlers in England. His wish is that Worcestershire should find another slow left-arm spinner in time for him to teach the newcomer the tricks of the trade out in the middle. His county also look for a return to form by Dipak Patel, who, after a winter playing in Australia and New Zealand, lost his confidence as a batsman and off-break bowler. Worcestershire's attack was unbalanced without Patel as a second spinner.

One area where Worcestershire gained in strength was in wicket-keeping. Paul Fisher, the former Oxford Blue, was signed from Middlesex in August and played so impressively, with 24 dismissals in seven Championship matches, that he resigned his post as a schoolmaster at Marlborough College to join the county staff for 1981. The arrival of Fisher, although a disappointment to David Humphries, could be the competitive factor to bring out the best in both of them. Humphries has the edge in batting – he scored a century against Lancashire in July – and at his best there would be little to choose between his and Fisher's wicket-keeping qualities.

Off the field, Worcestershire's season was notable for the county taking a benefit themselves, rather than awarding one to a player. The money was necessary to reduce a considerable financial liability and it is to be hoped that 1981 will begin with fewer economic worries. To this end, a Championship match was taken to a new venue, Stourport-on-Severn, where the Parsons Chain company guaranteed a sizeable sponsorship. The fixture will be repeated in 1981 and a further break from New Road comes with the scheduling of a three-day game at Stourbridge for the first time in twenty years. – Michael Beddow.

[Ken Kelly

WORCESTERSHIRE

Back row: P. A. Neale, D. N. Patel, J. Cumbes, A. P. Pridgeon, H. L. Alleyne, Younis Ahmed, D. J. Humphries, J. W. Sewter (scorer). Front row: J. D. Inchmore, G. M. Turner, N. Gifford (captain), J. A. Ormrod, E. J. O. Hemsley.

WORCESTERSHIRE RESULTS

All First-class Matches – Played 23: Won 3, Lost 8, Drawn 12. Abandoned 1.

County Championship Matches – Played 21: Won 3, Lost 7, Drawn 11. Abandoned 1.

Bonus points – Batting 54, Bowling 61.

COUNTY CHAMPIONSHIP AVERAGES

BATTING

	Birthplace	Matches	Inns	Not Outs	Runs	Highest Inns	Avge
G. M. Turner	Dunedin, NZ	20	33	4	1,755	228*	60.51
J. A. Ormrod	Ramsbottom	20	32	2	1,378	131*	45.93
Younis Ahmed	Jullundur, India	20	31	6	974	121*	38.96
E. J. O. Hemsley	Norton	16	24	3	744	76	35.42
P. A. Neale	Scunthorpe	19	31	2	889	123	30.65
D. J. Humphries	Alveley	14	19	3	478	108*	29.87
J. Cumbes	East Didsbury	7	5	3	55	43	27.50
N. Gifford	Ulverston	20	26	10	346	45	21.62
T. S. Curtis	Chislehurst	3	5	1	85	59*	21.25
D. N. Patel	Nairobi, Kenya	11	15	2	246	74	18.92
S. P. Henderson	Oxford	6	8	0	147	64	18.37
H. L. Alleyne	Barbados, WI	16	17	2	215	72	14.33
J. D. Inchmore	Ashington	16	21	2	251	64	13.21
V. A. Holder	Barbados, WI	4	6	1	62	34	12.40
A. P. Pridgeon	Wall Heath	19	20	10	110	28*	11.00
B. J. R. Jones	Shrewsbury	8	13	0	129	30	9.92
P. B. Fisher	Edmonton	7	10	5	40	11	8.00

Also batted: B. L. D'Oliveira (*Cape Town, SA*) 21, 16; M. Saunders (*Worcester*) 0, 12; M. J. Weston (*Worcester*) 3.

* *Signifies not out.*

BOWLING

	Overs	Maidens	Runs	Wickets	Average
H. L. Alleyne	498.1	96	1,502	60	25.03
V. A. Holder	116	17	324	11	29.45
N. Gifford	685.1	191	1,656	56	29.57
A. P. Pridgeon	519	112	1,545	50	30.90
J. Cumbes	168.4	32	521	15	34.73
J. D. Inchmore	419.1	67	1,419	40	35.47

Also bowled: B. L. D'Oliveira 2–0–12–0; E. J. O. Hemsley 12.2–1–35–1; S. P. Henderson 2.4–0–16–0; P. A. Neale 3–1–6–0; J. A. Ormrod 0.3–0–0–0; D. N. Patel 101.3–10–396–1; M. Saunders 51–9–212–6; Younis Ahmed 19–1–95–1.

HUNDREDS

The following sixteen three-figure innings were played for Worcestershire in County Championship matches – G. M. Turner 228* v Gloucestershire (Worcester), 182* v Derbyshire (Worcester), 168 v Essex (Colchester), 115 v Yorkshire (Bradford), 103* v Kent (Worcester), 101 v Warwickshire (Birmingham), 100 v Middlesex (Worcester); J. A. Ormrod 101 and 131* v Somerset (Worcester), 126* v Hampshire (Bournemouth), 106 v Warwickshire (Birmingham), 103 v Kent (Worcester); Younis Ahmed 121* v Warwickshire (Birmingham), 109 v Nottinghamshire (Cleethorpes); D. J. Humphries 108* v Lancashire (Stourport-on-Severn); P. A. Neale 123 v Sussex (Hove).

WORCESTERSHIRE v GLOUCESTERSHIRE

At Worcester, April 30, May 1, 2. Drawn. Worcestershire 6 pts, Gloucestershire 5 pts. Bad weather restricted playing time by more than a third, but the New Road pitch remained easy-paced throughout and the conditions were fully exploited by Turner, whose unbeaten 228 (nine 6s and eighteen 4s) was his highest score for Worcestershire. He was joined by Hemsley in a third-wicket stand of 184 in 165 minutes. Gloucestershire, with a fine send-off by left-hander Broad, also batted in comfort, although their momentum was severely stifled by 40-year-old Gifford, who took two wickets for 2 runs from 8.3 overs.

Gloucestershire

B. C. Broad c Humphries b Inchmore	62	– (2) not out	35
Sadiq Mohammad c Humphries b Alleyne	30	– (1) not out	21
Zaheer Abbas c Inchmore b Gifford	33		
A. W. Stovold b Alleyne	1		
*M. J. Procter c and b Gifford	1		
A. J. Hignell c Gifford b Inchmore	18		
M. D. Partridge not out	32		
D. A. Graveney not out	42		
B 6, l-b 12, w 5, n-b 8	31	B 5, n-b 1	6

1/65 2/135 3/136 4/139   (6 wkts. dec.) 250   (no wkt) 62
5/155 6/168

A. H. Wilkins, †A. J. Brassington and B. M. Brain did not bat.

Bonus points – Gloucestershire 3, Worcestershire 2.

Bowling: First Innings—Alleyne 25–5–58–2; Inchmore 25–3–87–2; Cumbes 14–4–49–0; Gifford 23–13–14–2; Patel 0.4–0–11–0. *Second Innings*—Alleyne 2–0–6–0; Inchmore 2–0–5–0; Patel 10–1–26–0; Cumbes 7.3–3–16–0; Ormrod 0.3–0–0–0; Gifford 2–1–3–0.

Worcestershire

G. M. Turner not out	228	†D. J. Humphries not out	36
J. A. Ormrod c Brassington b Brain	2		
B. J. R. Jones c Procter b Graveney	13	L-b 6, n-b 1	7
E. J. O. Hemsley c Procter b Wilkins	61		
Younis Ahmed b Graveney	1	1/6 2/36 3/220 4/241 (5 wkts. dec.) 361	
D. N. Patel lbw b Graveney	13	5/287	

J. D. Inchmore, H. Alleyne, *N. Gifford and J. Cumbes did not bat.

Bonus points – Worcestershire 4, Gloucestershire 2.

Bowling: Procter 11–3–20–0; Brain 17–2–65–1; Wilkins 18–3–81–1; Graveney 26–4–102–3; Partridge 16–1–86–0.

Umpires: A. Jepson and B. J. Meyer.

At Manchester, May 7, 8, 9. WORCESTERSHIRE lost to LANCASHIRE by four wickets.

At Worcester, May 10, 11, 12. WORCESTERSHIRE lost to WEST INDIANS by seven
wickets (See West Indian tour section).

WORCESTERSHIRE v WARWICKSHIRE

At Worcester, May 24, 26, 27. Warwickshire beat Worcestershire by seven wickets.
Warwickshire 19 pts, Worcestershire 6 pts. Willis, proving to be an imaginative leader in his
first season as Warwickshire captain, declared his first innings 110 behind, and Gifford
responded by leaving a target of 335 at approximately 4 per over. Amiss gave Warwickshire
an ideal start with 81 in a second-wicket stand of 139 with Lloyd, whose career-best 121
included thirteen 4s, after he had scored an unbeaten 90 in the first innings. Claughton (two 6s
and fifteen 4s) reached his century in 142 minutes, and Warwickshire won comfortably with a
partnership of 181 by their two youngest batsmen. Worcestershire also had batting success on
a good wicket, Turner scoring 95 out of 143 in 118 minutes and Hemsley completing two
half-centuries. Less fortunate was Patel, who spent a night in hospital after being struck in the
face by a no ball from Small.

Worcestershire

G. M. Turner lbw b Ferreira	95	– b Ferreira	25
J. A. Ormrod c Lloyd b Ferreira	30	– b Small	1
P. A. Neale c Amiss b Ferreira	2	– c Smith b Doshi	20
D. N. Patel b Willis	74	– retired hurt	7
E. J. O. Hemsley b Perryman	53	– not out	56
B. J. R. Jones lbw b Perryman	4	– c Claughton b Doshi	1
†D. J. Humphries c Amiss b Willis	16	– c Ferreira b Small	10
H. Alleyne lbw b Perryman	25	– c Humpage b Small	28
*N. Gifford c Ferreira b Willis	5	– st Humpage b Doshi	19
A. P. Pridgeon not out	28	– c Perryman b Doshi	17
J. Cumbes not out	1	– not out	6
B 11, l-b 3, n-b 13	27	B 4, l-b 4, w 10, n-b 17	34

1/143 2/146 3/147 4/274   (9 wkts) 360   1/24 2/52 3/100   (8 wkts dec.) 224
5/280 6/280 7/318 8/322 9/342   4/111 5/140 6/176
                                                           7/195 8/212

Bonus points – Worcestershire 4, Warwickshire 4.

Bowling: *First Innings*—Willis 28–7–74–3; Small 15–2–59–0; Ferreira 19–4–61–3;
Perryman 19–5–74–3; Doshi 19–5–65–0. *Second Innings*—Willis 4–0–28–0; Small
12–0–42–3; Ferreira 11–1–36–1; Doshi 20–7–59–4; Perryman 7–4–16–0; Oliver 2–0–9–0.

Warwickshire

D. L. Amiss c Hemsley b Gifford	36	– b Gifford	81
K. D. Smith c Hemsley b Alleyne	29	– c Neale b Alleyne	1
T. A. Lloyd not out	90	– c and b Gifford	121
J. A. Claughton c Ormrod b Cumbes	1	– not out	108
P. R. Oliver c Patel b Alleyne	12	– not out	3
†G. W. Humpage b Alleyne	43		
A. M. Ferreira not out	2		
B 12, l-b 24, n-b 1	37	B 4, l-b 14, w 1, n-b 3	22

1/72 2/97 3/102   (5 wkts dec.) 250   1/3 2/142 3/323   (3 wkts) 336
4/146 5/248

G. C. Small, *R. G. D. Willis, S. P. Perryman and D. R. Doshi did not bat.

Bonus points – Warwickshire 3, Worcestershire 2.

Bowling: *First Innings*—Alleyne 24–3–71–3; Pridgeon 7–2–21–0; Gifford 31–11–57–1;
Cumbes 15–2–39–1; Patel 11–1–25–0. *Second Innings*—Alleyne 23.3–3–95–1; Pridgeon
16–1–73–0; Gifford 27–5–102–2; Cumbes 12–0–44–0.

Umpires: C. Cook and A. Jepson.

WORCESTERSHIRE v MIDDLESEX

At Worcester, May 28, 29, 30. Drawn. Worcestershire 4 pts, Middlesex 7 pts. Rain and bad light reduced the first day by half, but both captains acted positively to produce an exciting finish. Worcestershire, challenged to make 275 in 210 minutes, were clear favourites after an opening stand of 123 between Turner and Ormrod. But Turner was pinned down, largely by van der Bijl, as he approached the 83rd century of his career, and his last 15 runs came in singles. When he departed Worcestershire subsided quickly, and defeat was averted only by the ninth pair, Gifford and Alleyne, who survived seven overs together. It was the second time he had let the match slip. On the final morning, Middlesex, in trouble against a career-best performance by Alleyne of six for 94, recovered from 136 for eight with an unbroken partnership of 89 by Emburey and Selvey.

Middlesex

*J. M. Brearley lbw b Pridgeon	21	– lbw b Alleyne		6
M. J. Smith c Humphries b Alleyne	7	– b Alleyne		12
C. T. Radley not out	114	– run out		48
G. D. Barlow c and b Inchmore	5	– lbw b Alleyne		0
R. O. Butcher lbw b Inchmore	50	– c Humphries b Alleyne		28
†I. J. Gould hit wkt b Inchmore	0	– c Turner b Alleyne		30
P. H. Edmonds b Inchmore	0	– lbw b Alleyne		0
J. E. Emburey not out	16	– not out		43
V. A. P. van der Bijl (did not bat)		– c Humphries b Pridgeon		3
M. W. W. Selvey (did not bat)		– not out		31
B 5, l-b 14, w 4, n-b 16	39	B 8, l-b 12, n-b 4		24

1/26 2/72 3/114 4/200   (6 wkts dec.) 252   1/17 2/31 3/31   (8 wkts dec.) 225
5/210 6/212   4/70 5/125 6/125
                                                    7/130 8/136

W. G. Merry did not bat.

Bonus points – Middlesex 3, Worcestershire 2.

Bowling: *First Innings*—Alleyne 18.1–3–66–1; Inchmore 23–3–91–4; Pridgeon 19–4–56–1; *Second Innings*—Alleyne 22–2–94–6; Inchmore 10–1–44–0; Pridgeon 16–6–38–1; Gifford 5–1–13–0; D'Oliveira 2–0–12–0.

Worcestershire

G. M. Turner c Gould b Merry	51	– c Barlow b Merry		100
J. A. Ormrod b Edmonds	18	– c Gould b van der Bijl		45
P. A. Neale c Emburey b Selvey	1	– (4) lbw b van der Bijl		24
Younis Ahmed c Gould b Merry	16	– (3) c Gould b van der Bijl		3
B. J. R. Jones st Gould b Edmonds	30	– c van der Bijl b Merry		16
B. L. D'Oliveira b Emburey	16	– (7) c van der Bijl b Emburey		16
†D. J. Humphries b Edmonds	0	– (6) c Butcher b Merry		4
J. D. Inchmore not out	27	– c Radley b Emburey		4
H. Alleyne c Barlow b Emburey	1	– not out		11
*N. Gifford b van der Bijl	16	– not out		6
A. P. Pridgeon not out	2			
B 9, l-b 9, n-b 2	20	B 4, n-b 1		5

1/67 2/79 3/91 4/136   (9 wkts dec.) 203   1/123 2/135 3/169   (8 wkts) 234
5/140 6/152 7/152 8/158 9/197   4/185 5/197 6/197 7/213
                                                    8/222

Bonus points – Worcestershire 2, Middlesex 4.

Bowling: *First Innings*—van der Bijl 14–4–26–1; Selvey 11–2–55–1; Emburey 16.4–5–38–2; Merry 11–4–20–2; Edmonds 19–7–44–3. *Second Innings*—van der Bijl 20–3–73–3; Selvey 4–0–17–0; Emburey 18.5–4–69–2; Merry 12–2–42–3; Edmonds 6–0–28–0.

Umpires: C. Cook and A. Jepson.

At Oxford, May 31, June 2, 3. WORCESTERSHIRE drew with OXFORD UNIVERSITY.

WORCESTERSHIRE v SOMERSET

At Worcester, June 4, 5, 6. Somerset won by eight wickets. Somerset 19 pts, Worcestershire 6 pts. More than 250 overs were bowled by spinners and two batsmen each scored two centuries – Ormrod for Worcestershire and Rose for Somerset – in a match which produced 1,183 runs. Ormrod faced 503 balls in nine hours to make his aggregate of 232. Rose scored at a similar pace in the first innings, but adjusted to increased demands with an unbeaten 150 (eighteen 4s) in three and a half hours when Somerset clinched victory by scoring 291 at 4.77 runs per over. Smart running for singles was the feature of his partnership of 153 with Roebuck, and then he was joined by Denning in a positive sprint, the last 119 runs coming from 18.5 overs in 59 minutes. Despite such dominance by the bat, the match also featured some sustained spin bowling, notably by Breakwell and Gifford in the first innings.

Worcestershire

G. M. Turner lbw b Gore	7	– c Roebuck b Breakwell	4
J. A. Ormrod c Denning b Breakwell	101	– not out	131
P. A. Neale b Jennings	10	– c Denning b Marks	33
E. J. O. Hemsley lbw b Moseley	19	– c and b Marks	67
Younis Ahmed c Taylor b Breakwell	74	– not out	25
D. N. Patel c Taylor b Breakwell	25		
†D. J. Humphries c Lloyds b Marks	42		
J. D. Inchmore st Taylor b Breakwell	13		
H. Alleyne not out	23		
*N. Gifford not out	0		
L-b 3, n-b 6	9	L-b 7, n-b 1	8

1/8 2/29 3/84 4/205 5/230   (8 wkts) 323   1/19 2/93 3/210   (3 wkts dec.) 268
6/285 7/299 8/301

A. P. Pridgeon did not bat.

Bonus points – Worcestershire 4, Somerset 3.

Bowling: *First Innings*—Moseley 15–2–29–1; Gore 20–4–58–1; Jennings 10–0–38–1; Marks 30–7–109–1; Breakwell 25–5–80–4. *Second Innings*—Moseley 3–2–6–0; Gore 2–0–4–0; Marks 42–6–98–2; Breakwell 32–5–108–1; Jennings 1–0–4–0; Gavaskar 1–0–6–0; Lloyds 8–0–34–0.

Somerset

S. M. Gavaskar st Humphries b Gifford	66	– b Inchmore	11
*B. C. Rose c Pridgeon b Gifford	124	– not out	150
P. M. Roebuck c Alleyne b Gifford	30	– b Gifford	55
P. W. Denning c and b Gifford	41	– not out	60
D. Breakwell c Alleyne b Patel	13		
V. J. Marks not out	9		
B 1, l-b 12, n-b 5	18	B 4, l-b 4, n-b 7	15

1/148 2/222 3/243   (5 wkts dec.) 301   1/19 9/172   (2 wkts) 291
4/272 5/301

†D. J. S. Taylor, J. W. Lloyds, H. R. Moseley, K. F. Jennings and H. I. E. Gore did not bat.

Bonus points – Somerset 4, Worcestershire 2.

Bowling: *First Innings*—Alleyne 5–1–22–0; Inchmore 8–0–23–0; Gifford 42.2–11–92–4; Patel 39–6–125–1; Pridgeon 5–1–21–0. *Second Innings*—Alleyne 5–0–24–0; Inchmore 13–1–58–1; Gifford 23–3–79–1; Patel 13.5–0–89–0; Pridgeon 6–0–26–0.

Umpires: R. S. Herman and K. E. Palmer.

At Hove, June 7, 9, 10. WORCESTERSHIRE drew with SUSSEX.

At Swansea, June 14, 16, 17. GLAMORGAN v WORCESTERSHIRE. Abandoned.

At Bradford, June 18, 19 20. WORCESTERSHIRE drew with YORKSHIRE.

WORCESTERSHIRE v LEICESTERSHIRE

At Worcester, June 21, 23, 24. Drawn. Worcestershire 8 pts, Leicestershire 3 pts. Turner and Ormrod took the initiative for Worcestershire with an opening stand of 127, Turner, as usual, setting the pace with 70 in less than two hours and his partner playing the more solid rôle with 74 in three and a half hours. Leicestershire regained some control during a sustained spell of spin bowling by Steele before Hemsley, after losing five partners for 52, was joined by Gifford in an unbroken stand of 69. Worcestershire's score doubled in value when weekend rain affected the pitch and Leicestershire, apart from a polished innings by Gower, offered little resistance as the seamers enforced the follow-on. Gower, absent from the England team for the first time in two years, welcomed the opportunity to rediscover his form in county cricket and, together with Birkenshaw, held off the threat of Gifford until a thunderstorm at lunch on the third day allowed Leicestershire to escape.

Worcestershire

G. M. Turner c Taylor b Birkenshaw ... 70	J. D. Inchmore c Davison b Steele 6	
J. A. Ormrod c Dudleston b Steele 74	*N. Gifford not out 22	
P. A. Neale c Taylor b Steele 34		
E. J. O. Hemsley not out 67	B 3, l-b 9, w 1, n-b 9 22	
Younis Ahmed b Clift 6		
D. N. Patel c Taylor b Clift 0	1/127 2/184 3/199 4/212 (7 wkts) 305	
†D. J. Humphries c Gower b Steele 4	5/212 6/222 7/236	

H. Alleyne and J. Cumbes did not bat.

Bonus points – Worcestershire 4, Leicestershire 3.

Bowling: Taylor 17–4–61–0; Clift 26–7–63–2; Shuttleworth 9–1–32–0; Cook 12–1–38–0; Birkenshaw 10–3–25–1; Steele 26–8–64–4.

Leicestershire

B. Dudleston b Alleyne 9	– c Hemsley b Alleyne 11
J. C. Balderstone c Gifford b Cumbes 7	– (4) c Patel b Gifford 2
D. I. Gower b Alleyne 37	– (5) c Turner b Gifford 47
*B. F. Davison b Inchmore 13	– (6) c Patel b Gifford 22
†R. W. Tolchard c Turner b Cumbes 0	– (7) c Turner b Gifford 15
J. Birkenshaw c Ormrod b Cumbes 5	– (8) not out 31
P. B. Clift lbw b Alleyne 2	– (9) not out 1
J. F. Steele c Patel b Gifford 3	– (2) c Gifford b Alleyne 23
K. Shuttleworth c Humphries b Alleyne 6	
N. G. B. Cook not out 4	– (3) c Humphries b Gifford 4
L. B. Taylor run out 5	
L-b 7, w 1, n-b 10 18	L-b 7, n-b 1 8

1/18 2/25 3/44 4/51 5/59 6/82   109   1/25 2/40 3/40   (7 wkts) 164
7/85 8/95 9/100   4/43 5/67 6/107 7/156

Bonus points – Worcestershire 4.

Bowling: *First Innings*—Alleyne 18–6–28–4; Inchmore 13–6–18–1; Cumbes 10–1–32–3; Gifford 10.1–6–13–1. *Second Innings*—Alleyne 16–3–40–2; Inchmore 9–0–29–0; Gifford 25–7–53–5; Patel 3–0–19–0; Cumbes 7–2–15–0.

Umpires: H. D. Bird and D. O. Oslear.

At Northampton, June 28, 30, July 1. WORCESTERSHIRE drew with NORTHAMPTONSHIRE.

WORCESTERSHIRE v SURREY

At Worcester, July 5, 7, 8. Surrey won by nine wickets. Surrey 20 pts, Worcestershire 3 pts. Knight (ten 4s) scored his second Championship century of the season and was well supported by Clinton and Roope as Surrey built a match-winning total before the pitch began to favour their bowlers. As Gifford was to remark later, the match was really decided by the toss. Jackman and Clarke broke the back of Worcestershire's batting on Saturday evening, taking four wickets for 22 runs, and on Monday the home side were in trouble as Pocock exploited ideal spinning conditions. He emerged with match figures of nine for 97 and Worcestershire would have been beaten in two days but for two half-centuries by Younis and the determined efforts of Gifford, who batted for 76 overs in the match. His last-wicket stand of 38 with Cumbes occupied nineteen overs and forced Surrey to bat again for their fourth Championship victory of the summer.

Surrey

A. R. Butcher lbw b Pridgeon	25	– c Hemsley b Inchmore	13
G. S. Clinton c Turner b Gifford	77	– not out	6
*R. D. V. Knight c Younis b Cumbes	102	– not out	1
D. M. Smith c Younis b Gifford	9		
G. R. J. Roope run out	69		
D. B. Pauline b Cumbes	12		
Intikhab Alam not out	12		
R. D. Jackman not out	0		
B 4, l-b 15, w 4, n-b 3	26	W 3, n-b 2	5

1/71 2/152 3/172 4/293   (6 wkts) 332   1/15   (1 wkt) 25
5/314 6/327

†C. J. Richards, S. T. Clarke and P. I. Pocock did not bat.

Bonus points – Surrey 4, Worcestershire 2.

Bowling: *First Innings*—Alleyne 14–1–51–0; Inchmore 14–0–44–0; Pridgeon 14–2–63–1; Gifford 35–5–82–2; Cumbes 23–0–66–2. *Second Innings*—Alleyne 2.4–0–13–0; Inchmore 2–0–7–1.

Worcestershire

G. M. Turner c Pocock b Jackman	26	– (2) lbw b Jackman	10
B. J. R. Jones lbw b Jackman	0	– (1) c Richards b Clarke	16
P. A. Neale lbw b Jackman	0	– c Butcher b Pocock	19
E. J. O. Hemsley b Jackman	8	– c Richards b Pocock	7
J. Cumbes b Clarke	0	– (11) not out	5
Younis Ahmed c Butcher b Pocock	61	– (5) st Richards b Pocock	54
†D. J. Humphries c Richards b Pocock	12	– (6) c Smith b Pocock	0
J. D. Inchmore b Intikhab	33	– (7) b Pocock	4
H. Alleyne b Pocock	0	– (8) st Richards b Intikhab	4
*N. Gifford b Clarke	22	– (9) b Clarke	45
A. P. Pridgeon not out	2	– (10) c Roope b Pocock	6
L-b 4, n-b 2	6	B 6, l-b 8, w 1, n-b 1	16

1/0 2/4 3/15 4/16 5/36 6/79   170   1/23 2/37 3/57 4/60 5/64   186
7/118 8/119 9/146   6/70 7/75 8/126 9/148

Bonus points – Worcestershire 1, Surrey 4.

Bowling: *First Innings*—Clarke 15.1–5–42–2; Jackman 10–3–34–4; Pocock 18–5–57–3; Intikhab 13–4–31–1. *Second Innings*—Clarke 9.4–2–26–2; Jackman 6–1–27–1; Pocock 31–10–40–6; Intikhab 27–8–74–1; Butcher 3–2–3–0.

Umpires: C. Cook and A. G. T. Whitehead.

WORCESTERSHIRE v LANCASHIRE

At Stourport-on-Severn, July 12, 14, 15. Worcestershire won by an innings and 153 runs. Worcestershire 20 pts, Lancashire 4 pts. In the first County Championship fixture played at the Chain Wire sports ground, Hogg celebrated his 25th birthday by taking three for 21 before lunch on the first day. On a good batting wicket Humphries became the first century-maker at the new venue and led Worcestershire to their highest total of the season. He was assisted by career-best scores from Henderson (thirteen boundaries) and Alleyne (five 6s and six 4s) during a stand of 146 in 96 minutes. Humphries struck eighteen 4s to reach his century from 114 deliveries. Heavy rain over the weekend prevented play on Monday, and created a spiteful wicket on which Lancashire were dismissed twice in under four and a half hours on the third day. Gifford turned the ball prodigiously in his best performance for nearly six years, taking six for 15 before lunch and emerging with a match return of ten for 40.

Worcestershire

G. M. Turner b Allott	43	*N. Gifford b Reidy		0
J. A. Ormrod c Scott b Hogg	6	A. P. Pridgeon lbw b Reidy		2
P. A. Neale c Kennedy b Hogg	59	M. Saunders lbw b Reidy		0
E. J. O. Hemsley c Scott b Hogg	17			
Younis Ahmed c Scott b Hogg	0	B 1, l-b 5, n-b 10		16
S. P. Henderson c Scott b Allott	64			
†D. J. Humphries not out	108	1/19 2/67 3/105 4/105		387
H. Alleyne b Allott	72	5/150 6/222 7/368 8/375 9/387		

Bonus points – Worcestershire 4, Lancashire 4.

Bowling: Hogg 24–3–105–4; Lee 15–3–54–0; Allott 20–3–87–3; Simmons 21–9–47–0; Reidy 8–2–28–3; Lloyd 8–1–50–0.

Lancashire

D. Lloyd c Henderson b Gifford	41	– b Alleyne	11
A. Kennedy c Humphries b Pridgeon	35	– c Hemsley b Alleyne	16
I. Cockbain lbw b Alleyne	2	– retired hurt	0
*F. C. Hayes c Ormrod b Pridgeon	23	– c Turner b Saunders	4
B. W. Reidy c Hemsley b Pridgeon	5	– b Gifford	40
J. Abrahams c Humphries b Gifford	1	– c Humphries b Alleyne	16
J. Simmons c Turner b Gifford	4	– lbw b Gifford	0
†C. J. Scott c Hemsley b Gifford	1	– c Hemsley b Gifford	2
P. J. W. Allott st Humphries b Gifford	9	– b Gifford	1
W. Hogg not out	0	– b Alleyne	1
P. G. Lee c Ormrod b Gifford	0	– not out	0
L-b 4, w 1, n-b 8	13	L-b 5, n-b 4	9

1/66 2/77 3/102 4/118   134   1/29 2/34 3/34 4/88   100
5/119 6/124 7/124 8/124 9/127   5/88 6/98 7/98 8/100 9/100

Bonus points – Worcestershire 4.

Bowling: *First Innings*—Alleyne 14–1–45–1; Pridgeon 13–3–40–3; Saunders 2–0–16–0; Gifford 18–13–15–6; Hemsley 2–0–5–0. *Second Innings*—Alleyne 11.2–2–35–4; Saunders 5–0–24–1; Gifford 9–3–25–4; Pridgeon 3–0–7–0.

Umpires: C. T. Spencer and P. B. Wight.

At Birmingham, July 23, 24, 25. WORCESTERSHIRE beat WARWICKSHIRE by 96 runs.

WORCESTERSHIRE v DERBYSHIRE

At Worcester, July 26, 28, 29. Drawn. Worcestershire 5 pts, Derbyshire 3 pts. After the loss of more than four hours play on the first day, batsmen dominated the match until a thunderstorm denied Derbyshire victory when they required 55 from eleven overs to reach a target of 252 in 145 minutes. New Zealand Test players Turner (three 6s and 23 4s) and Wright (one 6 and 25 4s) each scored a century and both made more than 200 runs in the match. Worcestershire faltered in their second innings against Hendrick and Miller until Turner, batting at number 6, and the hard-hitting Humphries averted a crisis. Gifford's declaration – based on 6 runs an over – was severe because of the absence through injury of his quickest bowler Alleyne; but Wood took Derbyshire to the brink of victory with his second hundred for his new county, reaching 101 not out in 123 minutes with three 6s and ten 4s.

Worcestershire

G. M. Turner not out 182	– (6) not out	50
J. A. Ormrod b Hendrick 53	– (1) c Wood b Hendrick	0
P. A. Neale not out 54	– run out	14
E. J. O. Hemsley (did not bat)	– (2) c Taylor b Hendrick	20
Younis Ahmed (did not bat)	– (4) b Miller	25
T. S. Curtis (did not bat).	– (5) c Wood b Miller	2
†D. J. Humphries (did not bat).	– c Barnett b Steele	46
J. D. Inchmore (did not bat).	– b Miller.	0
*N. Gifford (did not bat)	– st Taylor b Steele	28
A. P. Pridgeon (did not bat)	– not out	7
L-b 3, n-b 9........................ 12	B 10, n-b 2	12

1/165   (1 wkt dec.) 301   1/0 2/17 3/42   (8 wkts dec.) 204
                                                        4/55 5/72 6/149 7/151
                                                        8/196

H. Alleyne did not bat.

Bonus points – Worcestershire 4.

Bowling: *First Innings*—Tunnicliffe 16–2–56–0; Oldham 12–3–48–0; Hendrick 19–2–52–1; Wood 5–1–20–0; Miller 17–3–60–0; Barnett 5.2–1–33–0; Steele 7–1–20–0. *Second Innings*—Hendrick 17–9–24–2; Tunnicliffe 4–0–34–0; Steele 7–0–32–2; Miller 23–7–60–3; Oldham 5–1–42–0.

Derbyshire

B. Wood c Humphries b Gifford 26	– not out 101
J. G. Wright c Humphries b Pridgeon 155	– c Humphries b Pridgeon........ 50
P. N. Kirsten c Ormrod b Younis............. 27	– c Humphries b Pridgeon....... 17
D. S. Steele not out....................... 14	
K. J. Barnett c Humphries b Pridgeon 1	
J. Walters not out........................ 10	
*G. Miller (did not bat).....................	– (4) not out 7
L-b 9, n-b 12....................... 21	B 6, l-b 3, n-b 9......... 18

1/114 2/191   (4 wkts dec.) 254   1/131 2/182   (2 wkts) 193
3/229 4/232

†R. W. Taylor, C. J. Tunnicliffe, M. Hendrick and S. Oldham did not bat.

Bonus points – Derbyshire 3, Worcestershire 1.

Bowling: *First Innings*—Alleyne 6–1–15–0; Inchmore 13–1–58–0; Pridgeon 14–2–53–2; Gifford 28–7–70–1; Younis 7–1–37–1. *Second Innings*—Pridgeon 11–0–58–2; Inchmore 9–1–49–0; Gifford 10–1–68–0.

Umpires: W. E. Alley and J. van Geloven.

At Weston-super-Mare, August 2, 4, 5. WORCESTERSHIRE lost to SOMERSET by ten wickets.

At Cheltenham, August 6, 7, 8. WORCESTERSHIRE lost to GLOUCESTERSHIRE by 96 runs.

WORCESTERSHIRE v GLAMORGAN

At Worcester, August 9, 11, 12. Drawn. Worcestershire 3 pts, Glamorgan 2 pts. Nearly all the action of this rain-marred match was packed into a final day of three declarations. Gifford closed Worcestershire's innings 149 behind, then Nash's declaration, after an opening partnership of 105 by Alan Jones and Hopkins, left the home county to score 255 in 200 minutes. Ormrod (ten 4s) featured in brisk stands with Neale and Younis, taking Worcestershire to 200 for two with ten overs remaining. Moseley then swung the pendulum dramatically, taking three wickets including that of Ormrod. Younis batted on strongly, with scant support, reaching the last over with 9 runs wanted. Inchmore and Holder were bowled by Nash going for big hits and Gifford came in to face the final ball. Needing 4, he swung it to long leg where Alan Jones dived to stop the ball inches from the boundary, saving Glamorgan from defeat and leaving Worcestershire 2 runs short of success.

Glamorgan

A. Jones lbw b Holder	28	– not out 57
J. A. Hopkins c Fisher b Holder	22	– st Fisher b Gifford 40
G. C. Holmes b Inchmore	4	
Javed Miandad lbw b Gifford	74	
N. G. Featherstone lbw b Inchmore	33	
M. J. Llewellyn lbw b Inchmore	6	
*M. A. Nash b Holder	14	
†E. W. Jones not out	2	
B. J. Lloyd not out	2	
B 13, l-b 7, w 1, n-b 12	33	L-b 3, n-b 5 8

1/52 2/59 3/70   (7 wkts dec.) 218   1/105   (1 wkt dec.) 105
4/170 5/192 6/192 7/215

A. J. Mack and E. A. Moseley did not bat.

Bonus points – Glamorgan 2, Worcestershire 3.

Bowling: *First Innings*—Holder 22–3–47–3; Inchmore 27–7–65–3; Pridgeon 18–7–37–0; Gifford 18–8–36–1. *Second Innings*—Holder 11–2–42–0; Inchmore 5–0–23–0; Gifford 6–0–32–1.

Worcestershire

G. M. Turner lbw b Moseley	27	– lbw b Nash 22
J. A. Ormrod b Moseley	7	– c Featherstone b Moseley 76
P. A. Neale not out	10	– c E. W. Jones b Holmes 45
Younis Ahmed not out	18	– c Holmes b Moseley 77
B. J. R. Jones (did not bat)		– c Holmes b Moseley 4
S. P. Henderson (did not bat)		– b Moseley 6
J. D. Inchmore (did not bat)		– b Nash 4
V. A. Holder (did not bat)		– b Nash 0
*N. Gifford (did not bat)		– not out 2
L-b 2, n-b 5	7	B 4, l-b 12, n-b 1 17

1/26 2/42   (2 wkts dec.) 69   1/36 2/110 3/202   (7 wkts) 253
                                      4/212 5/246 6/251 7/251

†P. B. Fisher and A. P. Pridgeon did not bat.

Bowling: *First Innings*—Nash 5–1–16–0; Moseley 7–2–10–2; Mack 6–0–31–0; Lloyd 2–0–5–0. *Second Innings*—Nash 28–5–122–3; Moseley 19–2–67–3; Mack 9–0–30–0; Holmes 5–0–11–1; Lloyd 4–2–6–0.

Umpires: J. G. Langridge and A. G. T. Whitehead.

At Cleethorpes, August 20, 21, 22. WORCESTERSHIRE beat NOTTINGHAMSHIRE by two wickets.

At Bournemouth, August 23, 25, 26. WORCESTERSHIRE lost to HAMPSHIRE by four wickets.

At Colchester, August 27, 28, 29. WORCESTERSHIRE drew with ESSEX.

WORCESTERSHIRE v KENT

At Worcester, August 30, September 1, 2. Drawn. Worcestershire 3 pts, Kent 3 pts. After a seriously curtailed first day, both captains made early declarations in their first innings. Turner scored his 89th first-class century, hitting thirteen 4s in one hundred and ninety minutes, and Tavaré also batted well for a century (one 6 and twenty 4s) as Kent added 182 in 115 minutes on the final morning. Worcestershire's target of 309 in 235 minutes was reasonable on an easy-paced pitch and, until tea, it seemed they would achieve a comfortable victory. Turner and Ormrod set off at a rare gallop, scoring 64 in eleven overs, and Neale joined Ormrod to put on 104. However, with only 108 required from the last twenty overs, Worcestershire slipped behind the scoring-rate once Johnson bowled Ormrod (thirteen 4s) for 103. Underwood took four for 25 in the final phase, leaving Younis to save Worcestershire from unexpected defeat.

Kent

C. J. C. Rowe lbw b Pridgeon	0	– c Younis b Alleyne	3
M. Benson lbw b Alleyne	11	– b Saunders	12
C. J. Tavaré c Hemsley b Pridgeon	10	– not out	144
C. S. Cowdrey b Saunders	42	– c Younis b Saunders	20
*A. G. E. Ealham c Younis b Saunders	25	– b Alleyne	29
G. W. Johnson not out	39	– b Gifford	5
†A. P. E. Knott c Fisher b Saunders	49	– c Henderson b Gifford	19
J. N. Shepherd not out	15	– not out	21
L-b 1, w 3, n-b 5	9	B 8, l-b 9, n-b 6	23

1/4 2/21 3/30   (6 wkts. dec.) 200   1/6 2/45 3/95   (6 wkts. dec.) 276
4/93 5/100 6/173   4/161 5/178 6/230

N. J. Kemp, D. L. Underwood and K. B. S. Jarvis did not bat.

Bonus points – Kent 2, Worcestershire 2.

Bowling: *First Innings*—Alleyne 19.1–4–52–1; Pridgeon 19–3–53–2; Saunders 14–4–47–3; Gifford 14–2–39–0. *Second Innings*—Alleyne 17–2–50–2; Pridgeon 14–3–53–0; Saunders 11–1–46–2; Hemsley 4–1–12–0; Gifford 20–1–92–2.

Worcestershire

G. M. Turner not out	103	– c Knott b Jarvis	33
J. A. Ormrod c Cowdrey b Underwood	21	– b Johnson	103
P. A. Neale b Rowe b Johnson	16	– c Knott b Shepherd	51
Younis Ahmed st Knott b Underwood	6	– not out	53
E. J. O. Hemsley not out	18	– b Underwood	5
H. Alleyne (did not bat)		– b Underwood	0
S. P. Henderson (did not bat)		– c Kemp b Underwood	3
*N. Gifford (did not bat)		– b Underwood	1
†P. B. Fisher (did not bat)		– not out	0
N-b 4	4	L-b 5, w 1, n-b 5	11

1/75 2/122 3/137   (3 wkts. dec.) 168   1/64 2/168 3/218   (7 wkts) 260
4/227 5/237 6/251 7/256

A. P. Pridgeon and M. Saunders did not bat.

Bonus points – Worcestershire 1, Kent 1.

Bowling: *First Innings*—Jarvis 7–0–37–0; Kemp 12–0–29–0; Underwood 15–2–58–2; Johnson 9–2–40–1. *Second Innings*—Jarvis 12–1–60–1; Kemp 14–2–62–0; Underwood 19–6–57–4; Shepherd 15–4–37–1; Johnson 9–2–33–1.

Umpires: D. J. Dennis and B. J. Meyer.

WORCESTERSHIRE v NOTTINGHAMSHIRE

At Worcester, September 3, 4, 5. Drawn. Worcestershire 7 pts, Nottinghamshire 6 pts. Alleyne, bowling fast and straight, took four for 3 in 31 balls as Nottinghamshire collapsed to 18 for five on the first morning; but the pitch was not to blame. Robinson and French began a recovery with a stand of 71 and Hemmings batted without difficulty to make a career-best 86. Worcestershire based their reply on a sound innings by Ormrod, who was out only 8 runs short of a second successive century. Five wickets then fell for 32 before Gifford, on his last appearance as county captain, and Saunders put on 46 for the last wicket. Nottinghamshire were again disturbed by Alleyne's pace as he took the first five wickets, but a delay of four hours because of rain on the last day, combined with an unbeaten 82 by Rice, allowed them to escape defeat. Alleyne achieved two career-best performances – six for 50 in the second innings and eleven for 94 in the match.

Nottinghamshire

P. A. Todd c Fisher b Alleyne	5	–	b Alleyne	50
R. T. Robinson c and b Gifford	63	–	b Alleyne	6
D. W. Randall b Alleyne	2	–	c Fisher b Alleyne	0
*C. E. B. Rice c Henderson b Pridgeon	5	–	(5) not out	82
R. E. Dexter c Fisher b Alleyne	0	–	(4) b Alleyne	0
J. D. Birch b Alleyne	0	–	b Alleyne	2
†B. N. French c Ormrod b Pridgeon	15	–	(8) b Gifford	0
R. J. Hadlee c Henderson b Pridgeon	20	–	(9) c Weston b Pridgeon	24
E. E. Hemmings c Henderson b Alleyne	86	–	(10) not out	3
P. J. Hacker c Fisher b Pridgeon	12			
M. K. Bore not out	9	–	(7) c Ormrod b Alleyne	9
L-b 6, n-b 1	7		B 2,1-b 3, n-b 3	8

1/8 2/12 3/17 4/18   224   1/9 2/13 3/21 4/80   (8 wkts) 184
5/18 6/89 7/99 8/118 9/185   5/89 6/123 7/132 8/160

Bonus points – Nottinghamshire 2, Worcestershire 4.

Bowling: *First Innings*—Alleyne 21.1–8–44–5; Pridgeon 24–5–82–4; Saunders 10–3–30–0; Younis 5–0–20–0; Gifford 18–4–41–1. *Second Innings*—Alleyne 24–4–50–6; Pridgeon 19–6–31–1; Saunders 9–1–49–0; Gifford 17–7–46–1.

Worcestershire

J. A. Ormrod c French b Hacker	92	*N. Gifford not out 34
M. J. Weston lbw b Hadlee	3	A. P. Pridgeon run out 0
P. A. Neale c Rice b Hacker	16	M. Saunders run out 12
Younis Ahmed c French b Rice	45	
E. J. O. Hemsley lbw b Hadlee	58	L-b 8, w 5, n-b 7 20
S. P. Henderson b Hacker	2	
†P. B. Fisher lbw b Hadlee	11	1/12 2/46 3/127 4/224 302
H. Alleyne c French b Hacker	9	5/230 6/232 7/252 8/256 9/256

Bonus points – Worcestershire 3, Nottinghamshire 4 (Score at 100 overs: 260-9).

Bowling: Hadlee 30–10–57–3; Rice 25–2–76–1; Hacker 35–7–108–4; Hemmings 6–2–13–0; Bore 12–5–28–0.

Umpires: W. L. Budd and D. J. Dennis.

YORKSHIRE

Patron – HRH THE DUCHESS OF KENT

President – SIR KENNETH PARKINSON

Chairman, Cricket Committee – M. G. CRAWFORD

Secretary – J. LISTER
Headingley Cricket Ground, Leeds LS6 3BU

Cricket Manager – R. ILLINGWORTH, CBE

Captain – J. H. HAMPSHIRE (1980), C. M. OLD (1981)

P. Carrick   County Badge   C. M. Old

Another disappointing season for Yorkshire was followed by the resignation of their captain, John Hampshire, who will be replaced in 1981 by Chris Old. Richard Lumb has been appointed vice-captain to cover for Old's possible absence on Test duty.

A measure of the confusion which has clouded the county's prospects during several years of political intrigue can be gained from the fact that Lumb made it clear he did not want to become captain. His attitude is understandable. With two former captains, Boycott and Hampshire, remaining in the dressing-room, the likelihood of complications is obvious. Old thus comes into an uneasy inheritance.

Unfortunately the appointment of Ray Illingworth as team manager has not solved as many problems as had been expected, partly because no real discipline has been imposed. This point was underlined by the rumbling of discontent from other players after Geoff Boycott, Hampshire and Old had been made special cases with regard to their contracts. County chairman Michael Crawford has promised that, in future, all contracts will be discussed at the same time – though he might more profitably have told the players to concentrate on getting better results on the field. Too many of the county's promising youngsters have grown up to accept standards that would not have been countenanced in happier times.

There are, however, other reasons for Yorkshire's plight. The county made a major contribution to England's cause and were without the compensation of overseas talent. Yet they again betrayed their own abilities with some indifferent application, while Hampshire's captaincy provided a negative lead.

The main area of concern was the bowling, which was weakened by the problems of off-spinner Geoff Cope, whose disappearance from the first-class scene became inevitable after another unfavourable report on his action. Both he and left-arm spinner Phil Carrick were disappointing, but even more serious was the erratic nature of the seamers' contribution. After a poor start, Old recovered his form to become an automatic England choice; but the support was variable.

Graham Stevenson was the leading wicket-taker, looking extremely hostile at times, but he lost enthusiasm too quickly and in 29 out of 37 innings he failed to take more than two wickets. Arnie Sidebottom, despite much hard work in the nets, continued to be "called" for overstepping, and his performance was affected by the inevitable uncertainty. Alan Ramage showed most promise after a disastrous time in the Benson and Hedges Cup group matches, but just as he was combining his above average pace with the necessary accuracy he returned to soccer training. With Ramage's availability thus limited, the progress of Simon Dennis, a nineteen-year-old left-arm seamer from Scarborough and the nephew of Sir Leonard Hutton, will be closely watched. He is certain to be needed, particularly as Howard Cooper has not been re-engaged.

On a brighter note, the batting was adequate, with the strength being in its depth. Lumb was solidly reliable, Hampshire scored readily, and Bill Athey made a welcome advance, particularly in the John Player League where his stroke-play was more often in evidence. Jim Love also had some splendid moments and, like Athey and Sidebottom, was awarded his county cap. Against Derbyshire, Yorkshire had a full complement of capped players for the first time since 1968.

Disappointments came from the absence of Kevin Sharp, who was obliged to rest, suffering from nervous tension, and the fact that Neil Hartley fell short of expectations. He never came to grips with his batting, although maintaining a high standard in the field and proving a useful support bowler in the John Player League.

David Bairstow received a well-deserved chance as England's wicket-keeper, continuing to hold many remarkable catches standing back. He also had the distinction of making the highest score by a Yorkshire wicket-keeper with 145 against Middlesex at Scarborough. Bairstow shows the competitive spirit that is needed throughout the side if things are to improve.
– John Callaghan.

614

YORKSHIRE

[Press Association

Back row: H. P. Cooper, K. Sharp, J. D. Love, C. W. J. Athey. *Middle row:* G. B. Stevenson, P. Carrick, A. Sidebottom, R. G. Lumb, J. P. Whiteley, C. Johnson. *Front row:* D. L. Bairstow, G. Boycott, J. H. Hampshire (*manager*), R. Illingworth (*captain*), C. M. Old, G. A. Cope.

YORKSHIRE RESULTS

All First-class Matches – Played 24: Won 5 , Lost 4, Drawn 15.

County Championship Matches – Played 22: Won 4, Lost 3, Drawn 15.

Bonus points – Batting 51, Bowling 64.

COUNTY CHAMPIONSHIP AVERAGES

BATTING

	Birthplace	Matches	Inns	Not Outs	Runs	Highest Inns	Avge
J. H. Hampshire	Thurnscoe	16	24	8	954	124	59.62
G. Boycott	Fitzwilliam	9	13	2	572	154*	52.00
C. M. Old	Middlesbrough	15	12	4	325	89	40.62
C. W. J. Athey	Middlesbrough	20	32	3	1,068	125*	36.82
R. G. Lumb	Doncaster	21	34	3	1,107	129	35.70
D. L. Bairstow	Bradford	17	19	4	523	145	34.86
J. D. Love	Leeds	19	30	6	825	105*	34.37
P. Carrick	Armley	22	30	7	761	131*	33.08
G. B. Stevenson	Ackworth	21	28	8	620	111	31.00
P. G. Ingham	Sheffield	4	7	0	197	64	28.14
K. Sharp	Leeds	9	13	1	293	100*	24.41
A. Sidebottom	Barnsley	19	13	1	268	43	22.33
G. A. Cope	Leeds	20	12	8	85	33	21.25
S. N. Hartley	Shipley	12	19	2	288	72*	16.94
H. P. Cooper	Bradford	6	6	2	56	23	14.00
S. P. Coverdale	York	5	3	0	31	18	10.33

Also batted: S. J. Dennis (*Scarborough*) 1*, 0; A. Ramage (*Guisborough*) 1*, 5.

* Signifies not out.

BOWLING

	Overs	Maidens	Runs	Wickets	Average
C. M. Old	395.1	117	943	46	20.50
G. B. Stevenson	568.1	146	1,615	67	24.10
A. Sidebottom	320.1	76	932	32	29.12
P. Carrick	555.3	165	1,521	50	30.42
H. P. Cooper	115	28	321	10	32.10
G. A. Cope	560.3	165	1,523	41	37.14

Also bowled: C. W. J. Athey 15–2–69–1; G. Boycott 28–7–55–2; S. J. Dennis 70–10–237–6; S. N. Hartley 24–2–112–4; J. D. Love 3–0–22–0; A. Ramage 36–10–95–3; K. Sharp 6–1–19–0.

HUNDREDS

The following fifteen three-figure innings were played for Yorkshire in County Championship matches – R. G. Lumb 129 v Glamorgan (Bradford), 118 v Worcestershire (Bradford), 101 v Gloucestershire (Sheffield); C. W. J. Athey 125* v Gloucestershire (Sheffield), 114 v Warwickshire (Birmingham); G. Boycott 154* v Derbyshire (Scarborough), 135 v Lancashire (Manchester); J. H. Hampshire 124 v Somerset (Weston-super-Mare), 101* v Warwickshire (Bradford); J. D. Love 105* v Lancashire (Manchester), 104 v Warwickshire (Birmingham); D. L. Bairstow 145 v Middlesex (Scarborough); P. Carrick 131* v. Northamptonshire (Northampton); K. Sharp 100* v Middlesex (Lord's); G. B. Stevenson 111 v Derbyshire (Chesterfield).

At Leicester, April 30, May 1, 2. YORKSHIRE drew with LEICESTERSHIRE.

At Oxford, May 3, 5, 6. YORKSHIRE beat OXFORD UNIVERSITY by an innings and 71 runs.

At Nottingham, May 7, 8, 9. YORKSHIRE beat NOTTINGHAMSHIRE by 47 runs.

YORKSHIRE v LANCASHIRE

At Leeds, May 24, 26, 27. Drawn. Yorkshire 7 pts, Lancashire 6 pts. Lancashire, put in on a pitch of uneven bounce, were reduced to 94 for five with Lloyd retired hurt before scoring, but Cockbain, on his Roses début, retrieved the situation in partnership with the determined Hughes. Yorkshire, in command after Carrick and Bairstow had made 104 in ninety-three minutes, missed five chances in the second innings – seven in the match – and Abrahams' application saved Lancashire any embarrassment. Rain on the second day cut too much time out of the match. Hampshire broke his finger while batting and took no further part in the game.

Lancashire

A. Kennedy c Bairstow b Old	7	– b Stevenson	3
D. Lloyd st Bairstow b Cope	36	– b Old	29
J. Abrahams c Bairstow b Sidebottom	15	– c Stevenson b Carrick	54
*F. C. Hayes c Hampshire b Boycott	26	– c Lumb b Cope	25
B. W. Reidy c Bairstow b Old	33	– c Old b Stevenson	0
I. Cockbain b Boycott b Stevenson	57	– c sub b Stevenson	2
J. Simmons lbw b Old	0	– b Stevenson	11
D. P. Hughes c Bairstow b Stevenson	40	– not out	39
†C. J. Scott b Stevenson	0	– c Bairstow b Stevenson	1
M. F. Malone c Bairstow b Stevenson	0		
W. Hogg not out	5		
B 2, l-b 12, w 1	15	B 3, l-b 14, n-b 1	18

1/7 2/42 3/77 4/90 5/94 6/191   234   1/36 2/38 3/88   (8 wkts) 182
7/191 8/192 9/195   4/91 5/93 6/128 7/153 8/182

Bonus points – Lancashire 2, Yorkshire 4.

Bowling: First Innings—Old 21–8–34–3; Stevenson 30–12–70–4; Sidebottom 18–6–48–1; Boycott 9–3–17–1; Cope 15.4–6–38–1; Carrick 4–0–12–0. *Second Innings*—Old 18–5–40–1; Stevenson 28.1–11–71–5; Cope 21–11–35–1; Carrick 8–3–18–1.

Yorkshire

G. Boycott c Scott b Hogg	12	A. Sidebottom c Simmons b Malone	18
R. G. Lumb lbw b Hogg	0	C. M. Old not out	6
C. W. J. Athey lbw b Reidy	15	G. B. Stevenson b Malone	10
G. A. Cope c Simmons b Reidy	19		
K. Sharp c Scott b Hogg	0	B 1, l-b 1, w 1, n-b 15	18
*J. H. Hampshire c Hughes b Reidy	35		
P. Carrick c Hughes b Hogg	63	1/1 2/30 3/30 4/35 5/86 6/97	257
†D. L. Bairstow c Lloyd b Reidy	61	7/201 8/232 9/247	

Bonus points – Yorkshire 3, Lancashire 4.

Bowling: Hogg 30–5–103–4; Malone 25.1–4–91–2; Reidy 17–7–24–4; Kennedy 1–0–4–0; Hughes 6–1–17–0.

Umpires: B. J. Meyer and R. Julian.

At Northampton, May 28, 29, 30. YORKSHIRE drew with NORTHAMPTONSHIRE.

YORKSHIRE v SUSSEX

At Middlesbrough, May 31, June 2, 3. Drawn. Yorkshire 5 pts, Sussex 4 pts. On a slow wicket, Yorkshire were restricted by rain on the first day and then by steady bowling with Imran providing the only hostile spells. Boycott was painfully cautious, but Sussex did little better, although Wessels produced some quality strokes. Despite attacking innings from Carrick and Old on the last day, the acting captain had little scope for a declaration, finally setting 250 in 145 minutes. Wessels and Jones started purposefully but, with the ball turning a little, a draw was inevitable.

Yorkshire

G. Boycott lbw b Wells	85	– c Phillipson b Imran	3
C. W. J. Athey c Waller b Imran	5	– run out	16
J. D. Love b Waller	26	– c Long b Spencer	6
K. Sharp b Imran	22	– c Long b Spencer	6
S. N. Hartley c Phillipson b Waller	42	– c Long b Wells	4
P. Carrick not out	13	– c Wells b Spencer	87
G. B. Stevenson not out	16	– (9) not out	17
†D. L. Bairstow (did not bat)	–	(7) c Long b Imran	19
*C. M. Old (did not bat)	–	(8) not out	74
B 1, l-b 1, n-b 5	7	B 4, l-b 1, w 1, n-b 3	9

1/7 2/57 3/104   (5 wkts dec.) 216   1/4 2/17 3/25   (7 wkts dec.) 241
4/172 5/193   4/35 5/35 6/86 7/193

A. Sidebottom and G. A. Cope did not bat.

Bonus points – Yorkshire 2, Sussex 2.

Bowling: *First Innings*—Imran 17–6–27–2; Spencer 24–12–26–0; Wells 16–1–67–1; Waller 27–5–89–2. *Second Innings*—Imran 18–5–50–2; Spencer 25–3–90–3; Wells 6–1–29–1; Waller 9–2–34–0; Phillipson 10–2–29–0.

Sussex

K. C. Wessels c Bairstow b Carrick	92	– c Athey b Carrick	64
T. D. Booth Jones c Athey b Stevenson	12	– c Sidebottom b Carrick	48
G. D. Mendis c Athey b Carrick	16	– (4) c Boycott b Carrick	26
C. P. Phillipson lbw b Sidebottom	3	– (6) not out	2
Imran Khan c Bairstow b Carrick	33	– (3) st Bairstow b Cope	1
C. M. Wells not out	36		
J. R. Heath b Carrick	0		
P. W. G. Parker c Bairstow b Carrick	8	– (5) not out	1
B 4, l-b 1, n-b 3	8	L-b 2, n-b 2	4

1/29 2/68 3/81   (7 wkts dec.) 208   1/99 2/106 3/132   (4 wkts) 146
4/133 5/164 6/164 7/208   4/144

*†A. Long, J. Spencer and C. E. Waller did not bat.

Bonus points – Sussex 2, Yorkshire 3.

Bowling: *First Innings*—Old 11–2–26–0; Stevenson 16–3–50–1; Sidebottom 13–3–42–1; Cope 5–0–19–0; Carrick 20.1–7–63–5. *Second Innings*—Old 4–1–10–0; Stevenson 6–2–14–0; Sidebottom 4–0–19–0; Carrick 12–1–59–3; Cope 10–2–40–1.

Umpires: R. Julian and R. Palmer.

YORKSHIRE v KENT

At Sheffield, June 4, 5, 6. Yorkshire won by two wickets. Yorkshire 17 pts, Kent 4 pts. A pitch of uneven bounce unsettled Kent, although there was aggressive defiance from Cowdrey. Sidebottom achieved exceptional lift at times, as did Dilley and Jarvis in their turn when Yorkshire were in serious trouble until Old, Stevenson and Sidebottom gave them a vital lead. Taylor used up four and a half hours in the second innings, but again Sidebottom proved almost unplayable. Although Yorkshire had plenty of time at their disposal, batting was never easy. Love held them together over two and half patient, chanceless hours, but Dilley was guilty of some rather wide bowling at a crucial time. The admirable Shepherd did not deserve to be on the losing side.

Kent

C. J. C. Rowe c Bairstow b Stevenson	11	c Love b Stevenson	12
N. R. Taylor b Sidebottom	7	c Bairstow b Sidebottom	35
G. W. Johnson c Bairstow b Sidebottom	0	b Old	16
Asif Iqbal c Sharp b Old	8	c and b Carrick	40
*A. G. E. Ealham b Cope	18	c Sidebottom b Cope	6
C. S. Cowdrey c Love b Sidebottom	47	c Love b Cope	33
†S. N. V. Waterton lbw b Sidebottom	1	c Love b Sidebottom	4
J. N. Shepherd c Stevenson b Cope	14	c Bairstow b Sidebottom	0
R. W. Hills c Lumb b Sidebottom	2	c Bairstow b Sidebottom	12
G. R. Dilley not out	0	c Athey b Sidebottom	0
K. B. S. Jarvis c Bairstow b Sidebottom	0	not out	2
B 2, l-b 4, n-b 4	10	L-b 6, n-b 4	10
	118		170

1/21 2/21 3/25 4/35 5/76 6/85
7/102 8/118 9/118

1/19 2/50 3/96 4/103 5/141
6/152 7/152 8/157 9/157

Bonus points – Yorkshire 4.

Bowling: *First Innings*—Old 11–4–17–1; Stevenson 13–7–19–1; Sidebottom 14–6–30–6; Carrick 6–2–13–0; Cope 7–0–29–2. *Second Innings*—Old 17–8–22–1; Stevenson 16–3–48–1; Sidebottom 20–8–34–5; Cope 20–9–23–2; Carrick 25–12–33–1.

Yorkshire

R. G. Lumb c Shepherd b Dilley	0	c Waterton b Jarvis	3
C. W. J. Athey c Cowdrey b Jarvis	5	c Taylor b Jarvis	10
S. N. Hartley b Jarvis	1	c Waterton b Jarvis	9
J. D. Love c Cowdrey b Dilley	0	not out	40
K. Sharp lbw b Shepherd	18	c Dilley b Shepherd	0
P. Carrick lbw b Shepherd	9	b Dilley	1
†D. L. Bairstow b Shepherd	4	c Rowe b Hills	24
*C. M. Old c Waterton b Shepherd	61	c Ealham b Dilley	5
A. Sidebottom c Cowdrey b Jarvis	20	c Rowe b Shepherd	19
G. B. Stevenson c Taylor b Shepherd	26	not out	5
G. A. Cope not out	3		
B 7, l-b 5, w 2, n-b 9	23	B 1, l-b 2	3
	170	(8 wkts)	119

1/2 2/11 3/12 4/12 5/27 6/35
7/62 8/116 9/160

1/10 2/13 3/24 (8 wkts)
4/25 5/36 6/69 7/80 8/114

Bonus points – Yorkshire 1, Kent 4.

Bowling: *First Innings*—Dilley 19–6–44–2; Jarvis 20–10–33–3; Shepherd 19.2–7–40–5; Hills 14–4–30–0. *Second Innings*—Dilley 17–8–45–2; Jarvis 15–7–33–3; Shepherd 16.5–6–29–2; Hills 6–3–9–1.

Umpires: H. D. Bird and D. J. Dennis.

At Lord's, June 7, 9, 10. YORKSHIRE drew with MIDDLESEX.

YORKSHIRE v WORCESTERSHIRE

At Bradford, June 18, 19, 20. Drawn. Yorkshire 7 pts, Worcestershire 8 pts. Yorkshire, electing to bat on a slow pitch, made a very poor show, throwing away wickets with a series of careless strokes, although the admirable Holder and the lively Pridgeon earned much credit for bowling straight and keeping the ball well up. Old and then Stevenson, with six 6s, helped Lumb to turn the tide. Turner was brilliant, leading Worcestershire's reply with style, but Yorkshire's spinners had worked their way into a useful position when Inchmore slogged seven 6s in a blistering half-century. The issue was neatly balanced as Lumb and Athey scored steadily in the second innings, but rain washed out the last day. In all the match contained nineteen 6s.

Yorkshire

*R. G. Lumb c Gifford b Pridgeon	118	– not out	51
C. W. J. Athey b Holder	0	– not out	45
S. N. Hartley b Pridgeon	6		
J. D. Love c Humphries b Pridgeon	1		
K. Sharp c Patel b Holder	13		
P. Carrick c Ormrod b Holder	7		
†D. L. Bairstow lbw b Gifford	19		
C. M. Old b Gifford	89		
A. Sidebottom lbw b Holder	0		
G. B. Stevenson b Pridgeon	62		
G. A. Cope not out	1		
L-b 10, n-b 8	18	L-b 4, n-b 1	5

1/1 2/18 3/20 4/35 5/49 6/77   334   (no wkt) 101
7/238 8/239 9/333

Bonus points – Yorkshire 4, Worcestershire 4.

Bowling: *First Innings*—Holder 26–4–77–4; Inchmore 19–3–73–0; Pridgeon 23.4–2–86–4; Gifford 21–4–66–2; Patel 2–0–14–0. *Second Innings*—Holder 6–1–14–0; Inchmore 5–2–14–0; Pridgeon 3–2–1–0; Gifford 17–5–25–0; Patel 10–0–42–0.

Worcestershire

G. M. Turner c Old b Carrick	115	V. A. Holder c Stevenson b Carrick	13
J. A. Ormrod run out	41	*N. Gifford not out	35
P. A. Neale c Love b Carrick	46	A. P. Pridgeon not out	2
Younis Ahmed c Lumb b Carrick	6		
D. N. Patel b Carrick	19	B 9, l-b 3, n-b 1	13
B. J. R. Jones c Hartley b Carrick	8		
†D. J. Humphries lbw b Cope	1	1/98 2/202 3/212 4/215	(9 wkts) 363
J. D. Inchmore b Cope	64	5/240 6/241 7/311 8/313 9/338	

Bonus points – Worcestershire 4, Yorkshire 3 (Score at 100 overs: 317-8).

Bowling: Old 13–4–25–0; Stevenson 18–6–55–0; Sidebottom 6–0–40–0; Carrick 36–9–138–6; Cope 35–9–92–2.

Umpires: R. Aspinall and C. T. Spencer.

YORKSHIRE v NOTTINGHAMSHIRE

At Harrogate, June 21, 23, 24. Yorkshire won by 27 runs with three balls remaining. Yorkshire 14 pts, Nottinghamshire 8 pts. Yorkshire, having batted badly against a weakened attack on another slow pitch, were duly punished when Randall, after a hesitant start, and the more confident Rice slaughtered their bowling. Despite patient resistance from Lumb, Yorkshire were in trouble when their sixth second innings wicket fell for a lead of only 78. Bairstow led spirited late-order resistance, however, and Nottinghamshire were left to make 191 in 135 minutes. Off-spinner Hemmings had been their outstanding bowler, and now Yorkshire's spinners had the last word after an inspiring burst from Old. They steadily outwitted the Nottinghamshire batsmen, who committed various forms of cricketing suicide to lose a match they had dominated for two and a half days.

Yorkshire

*R. G. Lumb lbw b Cooper	11	– c Curzon b Hacker	97
C. W. J. Athey c Tunnicliffe b Cooper	6	– c Curzon b Cooper	52
S. N. Hartley b Hacker	0	– b Cooper	0
J. D. Love c Todd b Hemmings	40	– c Birch b Hemmings	4
K. Sharp c Hassan b Hemmings	28	– c sub b Hemmings	24
P. Carrick b Hemmings	22	– b Hemmings	6
†D. L. Bairstow c Rice b Tunnicliffe	35	– c Tunnicliffe b Hemmings	48
C. M. Old c Rice b Hemmings	0	– c sub b Hemmings	8
A. Sidebottom c Hacker b Hemmings	43	– b Hemmings	32
G. B. Stevenson c Hassan b Tunnicliffe	16	– b Allbrook	26
G. A. Cope not out	0	– not out	4
B 2, l-b 10	12	B 4, l-b 9, w 1, n-b 2	16

1/15 2/18 3/20 4/76 5/111 6/113   213   1/114 2/114 3/119 4/171   317
7/113 8/177 9/197   5/182 6/205 7/234
                                                   8/273 9/302

Bonus points – Yorkshire 2, Nottinghamshire 4.

Bowling: *First Innings*—Cooper 22–11–32–2; Hacker 21–7–40–1; Tunnicliffe 22–11–43–2; Hemmings 25.3–9–61–5; Allbrook 4–0–25–0. *Second Innings*—Hacker 16–4–67–1; Cooper 21–6–55–2; Hemmings 40.1–6–127–6; Tunnicliffe 12–5–20–0; Allbrook 11–2–32–1.

Nottinghamshire

P. A. Todd b Old	5	– b Stevenson	13
B. Hassan b Cope	45	– c Athey b Carrick	55
D. W. Randall c Bairstow b Sidebottom	166	– lbw b Old	0
*C. E. B. Rice not out	121	– (5) c Stevenson b Old	27
J. D. Birch (did not bat)	–	(4) b Old	4
H. T. Tunnicliffe (did not bat)	–	lbw b Old	0
†C. C. Curzon (did not bat)	–	c Old b Carrick	21
E. E. Hemmings (did not bat)	–	lbw b Cope	17
P. J. Hacker (did not bat)	–	b Cope	11
K. E. Cooper (did not bat)	–	b Carrick	0
M. E. Allbrook (did not bat)	–	not out	0
L-b 3	3	B 6, l-b 8, w 1	15

1/18 2/70 3/340   (3 wkts dec.) 340   1/17 2/22 3/47 4/95 5/95   163
                                              6/124 7/149 8/162 9/163

Bonus points – Nottinghamshire 4 (Score at 100 overs: 339-2).

Bowling: *First Innings*—Old 26–8–75–1; Stevenson 17–6–50–0; Carrick 20–5–76–0; Cope 30–3–88–1; Sidebottom 6.3–0–42–1; Athey 1–0–6–0. *Second Innings*—Old 14–2–38–4; Stevenson 5–1–22–1; Sidebottom 2–0–11–0; Cope 11.3–3–47–2; Carrick 5–0–30–3.

Umpires: R. Aspinall and C. T. Spencer.

At Southampton, June 28, 30, July 1. YORKSHIRE drew with HAMPSHIRE.

YORKSHIRE v GLAMORGAN

At Bradford, July 5, 7, 8. Drawn. Yorkshire 8 pts, Glamorgan 3 pts. Batting first on a slow pitch Yorkshire scored steadily against an attack in which only leg-spinner Hobbs was occasionally dangerous. Century-maker Lumb was missed twice, at 32 and 97, but Athey played the most impressive innings. Yorkshire bowled a poor line, being sustained only by Old, as Llewellyn played doggedly to hold the Glamorgan innings together. Hampshire eventually set the visitors a target of 300 in four hours, which Glamorgan showed no interest in, and rain on the last afternoon made the draw inevitable.

Yorkshire

G. Boycott c E. W. Jones b Hobbs	11	– c Lloyd b A. A. Jones	24
R. G. Lumb c Llewellyn b A. A. Jones	129	– c A. A. Jones b Cordle	70
C. W. J. Athey c Llewellyn b Holmes	74	– c A. Jones b Hobbs	34
*J. H. Hampshire not out	61	– (7) not out	21
G. B. Stevenson not out	21	– (6) c Holmes b A. A. Jones	15
J. D. Love (did not bat)		– (4) not out	42
P. Carrick (did not bat)		– (5) c E. W. Jones b A. A. Jones	4
B 12, l-b 9	21	L-b 3	3

1/16 2/153 3/291   (3 wkts dec.) 317   1/45 2/118 3/147   (5 wkts dec.) 213
                                                         4/153 5/179

†D. L. Bairstow, C. M. Old, A. Sidebottom and G. A. Cope did not bat.

Bonus points – Yorkshire 4, Glamorgan 1.

Bowling: First Innings—A. A. Jones 15–2–48–1; Cordle 21–9–50–0; Hobbs 15–5–47–1; Lloyd 18–2–80–0; Holmes 25–5–71–1. *Second Innings*—A. A. Jones 26–4–106–3; Cordle 22–6–67–1; Holmes 1–0–6–0; Hobbs 4–1–31–1.

Glamorgan

A. Jones c Boycott b Stevenson	26	– not out	36
J. A. Hopkins b Old	5	– c Athey b Cope	12
G. C. Holmes c Bairstow b Sidebottom	36	– not out	5
Javed Miandad c Stevenson b Old	3		
N. G. Featherstone c Bairstow b Stevenson	52		
M. J. Llewellyn not out	53		
†E. W. Jones b Old	1		
*B. J. Lloyd c Bairstow b Old	4		
A. E. Cordle run out	5		
R. N. S. Hobbs b Old	14		
A. A. Jones run out	7		
B 1, l-b 7, n-b 17	25	L-b 2, w 2	4

1/35 2/35 3/38 4/121   231   1/51   (1 wkt) 57
5/171 6/180 7/190 8/202 9/220

Bonus points – Glamorgan 2, Yorkshire 4.

Bowling: First Innings—Old 24–8–68–5; Stevenson 22.4–5–56–2; Sidebottom 19–5–42–1; Boycott 11–2–25–0; Carrick 3–1–15–0. *Second Innings*—Old 6–2–12–0; Stevenson 4–0–23–0; Sidebottom 7–1–11–0; Cope 5–2–7–1.

Umpires: H. D. Bird and D. O. Oslear.

At Chelmsford, July 9, 10, 11. YORKSHIRE drew with ESSEX.

At The Oval, July 12, 14, 15. YORKSHIRE drew with SURREY.

At Leeds, July 19, 20, 21. YORKSHIRE lost to WEST INDIANS by 58 runs (See West Indian tour section).

YORKSHIRE v MIDDLESEX

At Scarborough, July 23, 24, 25. Middlesex won by eight wickets. Middlesex 20 pts, Yorkshire 4 pts. Deprived of Old, England's twelfth man in the fourth Test, Yorkshire gave a dreadful bowling performance, surrendering completely as Butcher launched a magnificent attack in which he made 179 in 177 minutes with 21 4s and eight 6s. Pathetic batting against the superb bowling of van der Bijl and the constant threat of Daniel's pace added to Yorkshire's problems before Sidebottom showed both character and ability in his innings. When Yorkshire followed-on Bairstow (21 4s) gave a brilliant display to reach a career-best 145; also the highest score achieved by a Yorkshire wicket-keeper. Yet it could not save the match and Middlesex strolled to victory.

Middlesex

*J. M. Brearley lbw b Sidebottom	28 – c and b Cope	28
W. N. Slack b Cooper	3 – c and b Carrick	26
C. T. Radley c Bairstow b Stevenson	65 – not out	19
G. D. Barlow b Hartley	14 – not out	24
R. O. Butcher c Carrick b Cooper	179	
K. P. Tomlins c Sidebottom b Stevenson	49	
V. A. P. van der Bijl b Cooper	15	
†I. J. Gould c Hampshire b Stevenson	15	
M. W. W. Selvey b Stevenson	0	
W. W. Daniel b Stevenson	0	
F. J. Titmus not out	7	
B 2, l-b 6, w 1, n-b 7	16	L-b 2, n-b 2	4

1/25 2/47 3/64 4/206   391   1/58 2/58   (2 wkts) 101
5/338 6/357 7/373 8/374 9/374

Bonus points – Middlesex 4, Yorkshire 4.

Bowling: *First Innings*—Stevenson 24–4–84–5; Cooper 26–5–77–3; Sidebottom 18–2–74–1; Hartley 12–2–47–1; Cope 15–3–61–0; Carrick 4–1–32–0. *Second Innings*—Stevenson 5–1–16–0; Cooper 10–2–24–0; Cope 16–6–30–1; Carrick 10–4–27–1.

Yorkshire

R. G. Lumb lbw b Selvey	0 – c Brearley b Daniel	13
C. W. J. Athey lbw b van der Bijl	16 – c Gould b van der Bijl	9
J. D. Love b Selvey	0 – lbw b van der Bijl	18
G. A. Cope c Brearley b van der Bijl	17 – (11) not out	2
*J. H. Hampshire b Selvey	10 – (4) c Butcher b Daniel	67
S. N. Hartley b Daniel	2 – (5) b van der Bijl	7
P. Carrick c Radley b Daniel	1 – (6) c Butcher b Titmus	22
†D. L. Bairstow c and b Daniel	11 – (7) lbw b Daniel	145
G. B. Stevenson b Selvey	2 – c Radley b Daniel	11
A. Sidebottom not out	26 – (8) c Butcher b Selvey	42
H. P. Cooper lbw b Titmus	23 – (10) c Radley b Titmus	13
B 1, l-b 5, n-b 4	10	B 6, l-b 4, n-b 11	21

1/0 2/4 3/28 4/40   118   1/21 2/45 3/46 4/76   370
5/48 6/48 7/51 8/67 9/69   5/86 6/165 7/181 8/309 9/368

Bonus points – Middlesex 4.

Bowling: *First Innings*—Selvey 20–9–39–4; van der Bijl 13–3–36–2; Daniel 11–2–25–3; Titmus 6.3–2–8–1. *Second Innings*—Daniel 24.5–3–114–4; van der Bijl 26–6–58–3; Selvey 26–9–64–1; Titmus 32–7–82–2; Tomlins 11–4–26–0; Brearley 1–0–5–0.

Umpires: T. W. Spencer and R. Julian.

YORKSHIRE v GLOUCESTERSHIRE

At Sheffield, July 26, 28, 29. Drawn. Yorkshire 2 pts, Gloucestershire 5 pts. Rain prevented any play on the first day and altogether eight and a half hours were lost. Yorkshire again batted badly after being put in on a slow pitch and their bowling was of a similar standard, although Old had a lot of bad luck. Sadiq and Broad scored freely before Gloucestershire declared, but there was no hope of a result. Lumb and Athey both scored centuries against bored bowling and indifferent fielding.

Yorkshire

R. G. Lumb lbw b Wilkins	15	– st Brassington b Graveney	101
C. W. J. Athey c Sadiq b Brain	14	– not out	125
J. D. Love c Brassington b Brain	31		
*J. H. Hampshire lbw b Bainbridge	9		
S. N. Hartley c Hignell b Graveney	47		
P. Carrick b Brain	6	– (3) not out	4
†D. L. Bairstow lbw b Brain	0		
G. B. Stevenson b Graveney	14		
C. M. Old not out	11		
H. P. Cooper not out	1		
W 1, n-b 4	5	B 7, l-b 2, w 2, n-b 2	13

1/33 2/33 3/51 4/111   (8 wkts dec.) 153   1/225   (1 wkt dec.) 243
5/127 6/127 7/132 8/142

G. A. Cope did not bat.

Bonus points – Yorkshire 1, Gloucestershire 3.

Bowling: *First Innings*—Brain 15–2–50–4; Procter 5–1–12–0; Wilkins 9–3–17–1; Bainbridge 11–1–35–1; Graveney 11.3–3–34–2. *Second Innings*—Brain 4–0–18–0; Procter 5–2–10–0; Bainbridge 7–0–22–0; Wilkins 5–1–10–0; Graveney 23–5–60–1; Sadiq 22–0–109–0; Stovold 1–0–1–0.

Gloucestershire

Sadiq Mohammad c Hampshire b Stevenson	66	P. Bainbridge not out	3
B. C. Broad st Bairstow b Hartley	79		
Zaheer Abbas not out	34	B 1, l-b 1, w 1, n-b 7	10
*M. J. Procter c Carrick b Hartley	0	1/126 2/162 (4 wkts dec.) 201	
A. W. Stovold c Old b Hartley	9	3/162 4/184	

A. J. Hignell, D. A. Graveney, A. H. Wilkins, †A. J. Brassington and B. M. Brain did not bat.

Bonus points – Gloucestershire 2, Yorkshire 1.

Bowling: Old 16–2–43–0; Stevenson 16–3–50–1; Cooper 3–0–12–0; Cope 9–1–41–0; Carrick 1–0–5–0; Hartley 8–0–40–3.

Umpires: T. W. Spencer and A. G. T. Whitehead.

At Chesterfield, August 2, 4, 5. YORKSHIRE drew with DERBYSHIRE.

At Weston-super-Mare, August 6, 7, 8. YORKSHIRE drew with SOMERSET.

At Birmingham, August 9, 11, 12. YORKSHIRE beat WARWICKSHIRE by eight wickets.

YORKSHIRE v WARWICKSHIRE

At Bradford, August 20, 21, 22. Drawn. Yorkshire 6 pts, Warwickshire 5 pts. Yorkshire made a hesitant start on a slow wicket before Hampshire accelerated the innings. He took fifteen overs to score 10, but eventually reached his unbeaten 101 in 145 minutes with one 6 and fourteen 4s. Despite a rain-affected pitch, Warwickshire were never threatened, with Amiss and Lloyd standing firm against some indifferent Yorkshire bowling, particularly from the spinners. Runs again came easily for Yorkshire, who set a target of 275 in 210 minutes. After Dennis, the nephew of Sir Len Hutton, had taken two wickets in his opening over Warwickshire gave up the chase and played for a draw.

Yorkshire

R. G. Lumb c Humpage b Oliver	68	– c Humpage b Perryman	19
P. G. Ingham lbw b Rouse	59	– c Lloyd b Doshi	34
J. D. Love c Whitehouse b Doshi	9	– c Perryman b Doshi	63
*J. H. Hampshire not out	101	– st Humpage b Doshi	64
G. B. Stevenson c Humpage b Willis	22	– (7) not out	0
S. N. Hartley c Smith b Doshi	40	– (5) c Willis b Doshi	12
P. Carrick b Perryman	1	– (6) not out	9
B 1, l-b 8, n-b 3	12	L-b 6, n-b 5	11

1/86 2/113 3/181 (6 wkts dec.) 312 1/41 2/65 3/187 (5 wkts dec.) 212
4/216 5/295 6/312 4/188 5/207

A. Sidebottom, †S. P. Coverdale, S. J. Dennis and G. A. Cope did not bat.

Bonus points – Yorkshire 4, Warwickshire 2.

Bowling: *First Innings*—Willis 17–7–45–1; Rouse 14–0–81–1; Perryman 20.4–6–65–1; Doshi 24–6–62–2; Oliver 11–1–47–1. *Second Innings*—Rouse 7–2–14–0; Willis 7–2–19–0; Doshi 19–3–91–4; Perryman 9–1–35–1; Oliver 8–0–42–0.

Warwickshire

D. L. Amiss run out	75	– lbw b Sidebottom	27
K. D. Smith c Stevenson b Dennis	0	– c Stevenson b Dennis	0
T. A. Lloyd b Cope	72	– c Hampshire b Dennis	0
A. I. Kallicharran c Love b Carrick	8	– b Stevenson	5
†G. W. Humpage c Coverdale b Stevenson	44	– c Coverdale b Cope	51
J. Whitehouse not out	37	– not out	18
P. R. Oliver c Hartley b Stevenson	0	– not out	29
S. J. Rouse not out	2		
L-b 10, n-b 2	12	L-b 4	4

1/2 2/133 3/146 (6 wkts dec.) 250 1/12 2/12 3/27 (5 wkts) 134
4/204 5/210 6/224 4/46 5/93

*R. G. D. Willis, S. P. Perryman and D. R. Doshi did not bat.

Bonus points – Warwickshire 3, Yorkshire 2.

Bowling: *First Innings*—Stevenson 18–6–39–2; Dennis 6–2–14–1; Cope 42–20–91–1; Sidebottom 6–1–25–0; Carrick 26–5–69–1. *Second Innings*—Stevenson 10.2–1–40–1; Dennis 12–3–38–2; Sidebottom 6–1–16–1; Carrick 17–10–14–0; Cope 13–6–22–1.

Umpires: R. Aspinall and J. van Geloven.

At Manchester, August 23, 25, 26. YORKSHIRE lost to LANCASHIRE by three wickets.

YORKSHIRE v NORTHAMPTONSHIRE

At Leeds, August 30, September 1, 2. Northamptonshire won by eight wickets. Northamptonshire 15 pts, Yorkshire 5 pts. After the first day had been lost to rain, both sides declared at 200 in their first innings. Stevenson, in with a chance of taking all ten wickets after a hostile performance, went off the field for ten minutes to change his shirt and subsequently returned to the attack without success. Larkins and Allan Lamb were in fine form for Northamptonshire, before Griffiths, moving the ball a little off the seam, destroyed Yorkshire's spineless second innings. Only Stevenson and Sidebottom offered any resistance, and the visitors scored their winning runs from only 21 overs in a style that put Yorkshire to shame.

Yorkshire

R. G. Lumb lbw b T. M. Lamb	25	– c Cook b Mallender	3
P. G. Ingham c Larkins b Williams	64	– b Griffiths	0
J. D. Love not out	64	– lbw b Griffiths	0
*J. H. Hampshire b Mallender	27	– (5) b Griffiths	6
S. N. Hartley not out	3	– (4) b Griffiths	6
P. Carrick (did not bat)		– lbw b Griffiths	5
A. Sidebottom (did not bat)		– c Sharp b Griffiths	24
G. B. Stevenson (did not bat)		– b T. M. Lamb	52
†S. P. Coverdale (did not bat)		– c A. J. Lamb b Griffiths	5
G. A. Cope (did not bat)		– not out	3
S. J. Dennis (did not bat)		– lbw b T. M. Lamb	0
L-b 3, n-b 14	17	B 1, n-b 4	5

1/78 2/112 3/175   (3 wkts dec.) 200   1/3 2/3 3/5 4/14   109
                                                        5/21 6/22 7/89 8/94 9/108

Bonus points – Yorkshire 2, Northamptonshire 1.

Bowling: *First Innings*—Griffiths 14–4–26–0; Mallender 10.4–1–47–1; T. M. Lamb 18–4–87–1; Williams 6–1–23–1. *Second Innings*—Griffiths 15–3–52–7; Mallender 8–1–26–1; T. M. Lamb 10–3–26–2; Williams 1–1–0–0.

Northamptonshire

*G. Cook lbw b Stevenson	4	– c Coverdale b Dennis	22
W. Larkins c Carrick b Stevenson	63	– not out	60
R. G. Williams b Stevenson	1	– c Hartley b Carrick	14
A. J. Lamb c Coverdale b Stevenson	76	– not out	11
R. J. Boyd-Moss lbw b Stevenson	0		
T. J. Yardley not out	44		
R. M. Tindall b Stevenson	0		
†G. Sharp c Coverdale b Stevenson	0		
N. A. Mallender b Stevenson	0		
T. M. Lamb not out	6		
L-b 1, n-b 5	6	W 1, n-b 4	5

1/10 2/14 3/130   (8 wkts dec.) 200   1/68 2/96   (2 wkts) 112
4/136 5/143 6/154 7/159 8/159

B. J. Griffiths did not bat.

Bonus points – Northamptonshire 2, Yorkshire 3.

Bowling: *First Innings*—Stevenson 20.1–7–57–8; Dennis 11–0–38–0; Sidebottom 6–0–21–0; Carrick 4–0–21–0; Cope 15–3–57–0. *Second Innings*—Stevenson 6–0–37–0; Dennis 8–0–37–1; Sidebottom 4–0–27–0; Carrick 3–0–6–1.

Umpires: C. Cook and A. Jepson.

YORKSHIRE v DERBYSHIRE

At Scarborough, September 3, 4, 5. Drawn. Yorkshire 8 pts, Derbyshire 2 pts. Boycott, missed three times, dominated the first day after Yorkshire had elected to bat on a pitch giving some help to the spinners. He was also given not out to a confident appeal for a catch at the wicket when 32, and this decision seemed to upset Derbyshire who thereafter offered little resistance. Their batting was unproductive while Old bowled superbly in difficult circumstances. Forced to follow on, Derbyshire again struggled, although Steele and Barnett showed welcome application. Stevenson bowled effectively but with rain reducing play to only nine overs on the last day, Yorkshire were denied victory.

Yorkshire

G. Boycott not out	154	†D. L. Bairstow b Steele	17
R. G. Lumb c and b Steele	23	G. B. Stevenson not out	38
C. W. J. Athey b Miller	2	B 2, l-b 10, n-b 14.	26
J. D. Love c Wood b Miller	0		
*J. H. Hampshire st Taylor b Steele	54	1/57 2/60 3/60	(6 wkts) 338
P. Carrick run out	24	4/151 5/216 6/282	

C. M. Old, A. Sidebottom and G. A. Cope did not bat.

Bonus points – Yorkshire 4, Derbyshire 2.

Bowling: Hendrick 13–2–21–0; Tunnicliffe 10–2–39–0; Oldham 16–2–65–0; Miller 24–2–94–2; Steele 28–7–75–3; Barnett 3–0–11–0; Wood 6–3–7–0.

Derbyshire

B. Wood c Old b Carrick	11	– c Bairstow b Stevenson	3
J. G. Wright c Bairstow b Old	24	– c Bairstow b Stevenson	15
J. Walters lbw b Cope	5	– (7) not out	10
P. N. Kirsten c Bairstow b Old	8	– (3) lbw b Stevenson	24
D. S. Steele c Athey b Old	18	– (4) c and b Carrick	49
K. J. Barnett c Hampshire b Cope	1	– (5) b Stevenson	36
*G. Miller c Athey b Cope	7	– (6) b Old	24
†R. W. Taylor b Old	12	– lbw b Old	0
C. J. Tunnicliffe b Stevenson	20	– not out	5
M. Hendrick c Old b Carrick	18		
S. Oldham not out	0		
B 5, l-b 5, n-b 2	12	L-b 7, w 1, n-b 6	14
1/22 2/35 3/48 4/61	136	1/10 2/47 3/54	(7 wkts) 180
5/62 6/74 7/80 8/107 9/136		4/126 5/165 6/165 7/165	

Bonus points – Yorkshire 4.

Bowling: *First Innings*—Old 20.2–7–34–4; Stevenson 10–3–20–1; Carrick 10–4–12–2; Cope 18–4–52–3; Sidebottom 2–1–6–0. *Second Innings*—Old 17.4–8–29–2; Stevenson 22–3–65–4; Sidebottom 5–1–14–0; Cope 7–2–22–0; Carrick 17–5–36–1.

Umpires: T. W. Spencer and J. van Geloven.

THE UNIVERSITIES IN 1980

OXFORD

Captain – C. J. ROSS
(Wellington University and Magdalen)

Secretary – R. MARSDEN
(Merchant Taylors', Northwood, and Christ Church)

Captain for 1981 – R. P. MOULDING
(Haberdashers' Aske's and Christ Church)

Secretary – S. P. SUTCLIFFE
(King George V School, Southport, and Lincoln)

Much of what was written about Oxford's poor performance in 1979
retained its relevance in 1980 when, for the fourth successive year, not a
single first-class match was won, and only rain prevented an even worse
record. The decision by two of the counties – Gloucestershire and Somerset
– to bat a second time, rather than to enforce the follow-on, also lessened
the margin of those defeats.

An unusually large number of Blues were in residence, but supporters
saw few of them in action and, for most of the season, Ross had to rely on
relatively inexperienced players. As examinations and injuries took a heavy
toll, the only Blue to play regularly was Steven Wookey, who had missed
the previous season with a mysterious elbow injury. He toiled hard without
ever regaining his form, and it was no surprise when he was omitted from
the University Match.

There was a general weakness in all aspects of the game and Broad's
century before lunch for Gloucestershire on the first day of the season was
the first of many records and personal best performances by visiting
players. Bowlers also profited, and Lee's return of eight for 34 for
Lancashire was the best in the Parks.

Few batsmen showed any consistency, and a lack of determination was
reflected in frequent collapses. Johnathan Orders, before he temporarily
retired to prepare for Schools, and soccer Blue Ralph Cowan played some
good innings. Simon Halliday looked useful in non-first-class games, yet he
never showed the same confidence against the counties. The South African
Alan Ezekowitz made two half-centuries against Warwickshire but tended
to lose his wicket as soon as he looked to have played himself in. His
opening partner, Phil Durack, never made the most of an extended trial and
eventually lost his place to Bob Marsden, whom many considered unlucky
to miss his Blue.

The pace attack was a disappointment. John Knight at times failed to pitch on the playing strip and his lack of control cost him a place at Lord's. John Ross and Nick Mallett, the University rugby captain, caused batsmen few problems, and the only success was John Sanderson, whose line, length and movement off the pitch made his opponents work for runs. His six for 67 against Middlesex earned him a deserved Blue. It was as well for Oxford that they possessed two useful slow bowlers, each in his first season. Off-spinner Simon Sutcliffe made an immediate impact and Ian Curtis, a slow left-arm bowler who pushed the ball through faster, also earned respect. Sutcliffe, the leading wicket-taker, was quickly snapped up by Warwickshire against whom he had taken six for 19.

Oxford's fielding and catching fell far short of what is expected from a University side and the standard of wicket-keeping was an additional worry which was never satisfactorily resolved. – Paton Fenton.

OXFORD UNIVERSITY RESULTS

First-class matches – Played 10: Lost 6, Drawn 4.

All matches – Played 12: Lost 8, Drawn 4.

BATTING

	Matches	Innings	Not Outs	Runs	Highest Inns	Average
J. O. D. Orders	5	9	1	295	70*	36.87
R. S. Cowan	7	11	1	313	63	31.30
D. C. G. Foster	4	6	1	124	67	24.80
S. J. Halliday	5	7	1	135	37	22.50
R. A. B. Ezekowitz . . .	10	17	1	340	57	21.25
R. Marsden	7	12	0	240	50	20.00
J. J. Rogers	7	12	1	203	53	18.45
N. V. H. Mallett	4	8	0	98	38	12.25
T. E. O. Bury	3	4	1	32	22	10.66
S. M. Wookey	3	3	1	21	10*	10.50
J. P. Durack	7	13	0	136	45	10.46
R. P. Moulding	3	5	0	47	24	9.40
J. L. Rawlinson	5	10	0	85	19	8.50
C. J. Ross	8	13	2	64	23*	5.81
M. C. L. Macpherson . .	5	10	1	52	22	5.77
I. J. Curtis	9	12	7	27	9*	5.40
J. F. W. Sanderson	5	5	2	16	9	5.33
S. P. Sutcliffe	10	13	0	57	16	4.38

Played in two matches: P. N. Huxford 4. Played in one match: J. M. Knight 4, 0.

* *Signifies not out.*

BOWLING

	Overs	Maidens	Runs	Wickets	Average
J. F. W. Sanderson	84	25	216	8	27.00
S. P. Sutcliffe	252.3	61	749	24	31.20
I. J. Curtis	228	61	592	13	45.53
N. V. H. Mallett	94	11	386	8	48.25
C. J. Ross	162.4	27	589	12	49.08

Also bowled: R. S. Cowan 24–3–84–2; J. P. Durack 8.4–1–32–0; J. M. Knight 21–3–108–1; J. O. D. Orders 18–3–80–1; S. M. Wookey 40–8–108–2.

OXFORD UNIVERSITY v GLOUCESTERSHIRE

At Oxford, April 23, 24, 25. Gloucestershire won by 342 runs. Gloucestershire, electing to bat, ravaged Oxford's bowlers in both innings. Broad (nineteen 4s) made a spectacular start to the season with a century before lunch as the county raced to 319 for three declared. Oxford were shot out for 79, but the follow-on was not enforced and Graveney scored his maiden century in the second innings before Gloucestershire again declared. Left to score 501, the Dark Blues lost their first seven wickets for 63 before Orders found a useful partner in Mallett. Together they added 82 in seventy minutes, helping the University to a total of 158. Graveney followed his 119 by taking six for 49.

Gloucestershire

S. J. Windaybank b Orders	20	– (3) hit wkt b Sutcliffe	43
B. C. Broad b Knight	120		
M. W. Stovold not out	75	– (6) not out	4
P. Bainbridge c MacPherson b Mallett	25	– (1) b Ross	49
A. J. Hignell not out	63		
M. D. Partridge (did not bat)		– (4) not out	35
D. A. Graveney (did not bat)		– (2) c Durack b Sutcliffe	119
†A. J. Brassington (did not bat)		– (5) c sub b Sutcliffe	2
B 4, w 2, n-b 10	16	L-b 6, w 2	8

1/92 2/187 3/243   (3 wkts dec.) 319   1/116 2/181 3/247 (4 wkts dec.) 260
4/254

*B. M. Brain, A. H. Wilkins and D. Surridge did not bat.

Bowling: *First Innings*—Ross 18–4–74–0; Knight 17–3–77–1; Mallett 13–0–53–1; Orders 7–0–44–1; Sutcliffe 25–6–55–0. *Second Innings*—Knight 4–0–31–0; Mallett 9–0–51–0; Sutcliffe 31–9–92–3; Ross 19–2–69–1; Orders 6–2–9–0.

Oxford University

J. P. Durack c Brassington b Surridge	2	– lbw b Surridge	0
R. A. B. Ezekowitz lbw b Wilkins	10	– c Windaybank b Bainbridge	18
J. L. Rawlinson lbw b Wilkins	10	– lbw b Graveney	7
*C. J. Ross c Brassington b Wilkins	0	– (10) c Brassington b Brain	5
J. O. D. Orders b Partridge	19	– (4) not out	70
J. J. Rogers lbw b Surridge	19	– (5) c Hignell b Graveney	2
R. P. Moulding b Surridge	0	– (6) c Bainbridge b Graveney	1
†M. C. L. MacPherson not out	1	– (7) c Bainbridge b Graveney	0
J. M. Knight b Partridge	4	– (8) lbw b Graveney	0
N. V. H. Mallett lbw b Partridge	0	– (9) c Brassington b Graveney	38
S. P. Sutcliffe b Wilkins	5	– b Hignell	1
B 4, n-b 5	9	B 6, l-b 6, w 1, n-b 3	16

1/8 2/27 3/27 4/28 5/67 6/67   79   1/5 2/26 3/30 4/51 5/55   158
7/67 8/71 9/72   6/63 7/63 8/145 9/154

Bowling: *First Innings*—Brain 7–5–8–0; Surridge 17–9–24–3; Partridge 12–7–18–3; Wilkins 10.2–5–12–4; Graveney 11–7–8–0. *Second Innings*—Brain 12–3–26–1; Surridge 4–2–9–1; Bainbridge 9–2–18–1; Graveney 25–13–49–6; Wilkins 7–1–27–0; Partridge 6–3–10–0; Hignell 2–1–3–1.

Umpires: P. S. G. Stevens and A. G. T. Whitehead.

OXFORD UNIVERSITY v SOMERSET

At Oxford, April 26, 28, 29. Somerset won by 98 runs. Somerset quickly recovered from losing Rose at 7 as Slocombe, who went on to score 114, and former Oxford captain Marks put on 106 for the second wicket. Later Denning and Botham thrashed 87 in 38 minutes before Rose declared at 343 for seven. Rogers, Durack and Orders batted well for the University, who were dismissed for 172 but were not asked to follow on. Somerset declared their second innings, setting the University to score 294 on the third day. Although Rose gave his spinners most of the bowling – Botham purveying gentle off-breaks – the University were never in the hunt and, despite the efforts of Durack and Orders once more, the innings ended shortly after tea.

Somerset

*B. C. Rose lbw b Mallett	5	– c MacPherson b Ross	2
P. A. Slocombe c Rogers b Sutcliffe	114		
V. J. Marks b Mallett	43	– (7) c Ezekowitz b Sutcliffe	1
P. M. Roebuck c Ezekowitz b Curtis	19	– (3) c Orders b Sutcliffe	40
P. W. Denning c Orders b Curtis	60		
I. T. Botham c Ross b Curtis	53		
D. Breakwell run out	19	– (2) c Curtis b Mallett	24
†D. J. S. Taylor not out	12	– (5) not out	22
N. F. M. Popplewell not out	2	– (6) lbw b Curtis	10
K. F. Jennings (did not bat)	–	– (4) lbw b Sutcliffe	16
B 5, l-b 2, n-b 9	16	B 4, l-b 2, n-b 1	7

1/7 2/113 3/154   (7 wkts dec.) 343   1/2 2/43 3/87   (6 wkts dec.) 122
4/220 5/307 6/324 7/336   4/90 5/119 6/122

H. R. Moseley did not bat.

Bowling: *First Innings*—Ross 13–1–69–0; Mallett 15–1–62–2; Orders 5–1–27–0; Curtis 29–7–106–3; Sutcliffe 18–7–63–1. *Second Innings*—Ross 8–2–37–1; Mallett 10–2–37–1; Curtis 8–3–23–1; Sutcliffe 6–2–18–3.

Oxford University

J. P. Durack c and b Botham	36	– b Breakwell	45
R. A. B. Ezekowitz b Popplewell	4	– c Jennings b Popplewell	2
J. L. Rawlinson c Marks b Popplewell	6	– b Jennings	12
J. O. D. Orders c Taylor b Marks	32	– b Botham	42
J. J. Rogers lbw b Botham	53	– lbw b Breakwell	15
R. P. Moulding lbw b Marks	6	– c Botham b Breakwell	24
†M. C. L. MacPherson c Botham b Breakwell	0	– b Botham	0
N. V. H. Mallett b Breakwell	0	– lbw b Botham	27
*C. J. Ross lbw b Botham	7	– not out	5
S. P. Sutcliffe c Marks b Botham	16	– c Jennings b Marks	4
I. J. Curtis not out	0	– c Rose b Marks	0
L-b 10, w 2	12	B 13, l-b 6	19

1/18 2/26 3/80 4/92 5/105   172   1/9 2/50 3/76 4/104 5/146   195
6/118 7/118 8/135 9/163   6/146 7/184 8/184 9/195

Bowling: *First Innings*—Botham 25.1–10–38–4; Moseley 19–5–40–0; Jennings 6–4–6–0; Popplewell 10–5–13–2; Breakwell 21–8–29–2; Marks 18–7–34–2. *Second Innings*—Moseley 10–4–19–0; Popplewell 6–4–7–1; Breakwell 30–10–56–3; Marks 20.4–9–45–2; Jennings 4–0–13–1; Botham 14–3–36–3.

Umpires: J. van Geloven and P. B. Wight.

OXFORD UNIVERSITY v WARWICKSHIRE

At Oxford, April 30, May 1, 2. Warwickshire won by 85 runs. Personal-best performances by Ezekowitz, Cowan and Sutcliffe failed to save Oxford University from defeat. Sutcliffe, who later joined Warwickshire, took six for 19 as the county were dismissed for a modest 195, before the Dark Blues struggled to 130, with Ezekowitz and Cowan adding 86 for the fifth wicket. Mallett then took four wickets as Warwickshire slumped to 56 for four, but Oliver led a recovery with a punishing unbeaten 76, and the visitors declared 258 ahead. Ezekowitz and Cowan both completed half-centuries before the University were dismissed for 173, eight batsmen falling to lbw decisions.

Warwickshire

D. L. Amiss c Ezekowitz b Ross	20	– c and b Mallett	40
K. D. Smith c MacPherson b Sutcliffe	84	– lbw b Mallett	10
J. A. Claughton c Ezekowitz b Curtis	5	– lbw b Mallett	0
T. A. Lloyd lbw b Curtis	36	– c Rawlinson b Mallett	5
P. R. Oliver c Marsden b Curtis	14	– not out	76
†G. W. Humpage c Ezekowitz b Sutcliffe	11	– b Sutcliffe	30
S. J. Rouse c Rogers b Sutcliffe	0	– st MacPherson b Sutcliffe	16
D. C. Hopkins not out	4	– b Ross	7
*R. G. D. Willis c Marsden b Sutcliffe	0		
D. R. Doshi c Rogers b Sutcliffe	2		
S. P. Perryman c MacPherson b Sutcliffe	0		
B 1, l-b 5, w 1, n-b 12	19	B 2, l-b 5, n-b 2	9

1/43 2/63 3/152 4/176 5/176   195   1/24 2/44 3/55   (7 wkts dec.) 193
6/176 7/193 8/193 9/195   4/56 5/102 6/138 7/193

Bowling: *First Innings*—Ross 17–1–51–1; Mallett 12–1–50–0; Curtis 27–9–56–3; Sutcliffe 12.3–4–19–6. *Second Innings*—Ross 4.4–0–20–1; Mallett 14–3–44–4; Curtis 25–6–65–0; Sutcliffe 22–10–55–2.

Oxford University

J. P. Durack lbw b Willis	6	– lbw b Willis	14
R. A. B. Ezekowitz b Perryman	57	– lbw b Hopkins	53
J. L. Rawlinson lbw b Rouse	2	– lbw b Perryman	14
R. Marsden b Perryman	4	– b Doshi	14
J. J. Rogers lbw b Doshi	2	– lbw b Oliver	2
R. S. Cowan b Willis	39	– not out	55
†M. C. L. MacPherson lbw b Perryman	7	– lbw b Hopkins	3
N. V. H. Mallett c Humpage b Perryman	1	– lbw b Doshi	1
*C. J. Ross c Rouse b Doshi	2	– lbw b Doshi	1
S. P. Sutcliffe b Doshi	0	– b Willis	2
I. J. Curtis not out	0	– lbw b Willis	0
L-b 10	10	B 6, l-b 6, w 1, n-b 1	14

1/7 2/12 3/19 4/21 5/107   130   1/18 2/48 3/79 4/92 5/124   173
6/126 7/127 8/130 9/130   6/134 7/135 8/166 9/173

Bowling: *First Innings*—Rouse 13–4–18–1; Willis 16–5–25–2; Perryman 17.1–7–20–4; Doshi 19–4–37–3; Oliver 3–1–6–0; Hopkins 4–1–14–0. *Second Innings*—Rouse 4–0–18–0; Willis 8.2–3–16–3; Perryman 11–6–12–1; Hopkins 15–4–36–2; Doshi 23–8–35–3; Oliver 12–2–42–1.

Umpires: J. van Geloven and P. B. Wight.

OXFORD UNIVERSITY v YORKSHIRE

At Oxford, May 3, 4, 5. Yorkshire won by an innings and 71 runs. Oxford batted ineptly in both innings and suffered their heaviest defeat of the season. Boycott and Lumb gave Yorkshire an excellent start with 133 for the first wicket, then Bairstow and Stevenson put on an unbroken 69 before the county declared. Stevenson took five for 25 as Oxford were shot out for 81, and Sidebottom claimed three for 12. Sidebottom was virtually unplayable when the University followed on, and in 15.2 overs he returned his best-ever figures of seven for 18.

Yorkshire

G. Boycott c Ezekowitz b Sutcliffe	77	A. Sidebottom run out	16
R. G. Lumb c MacPherson b Curtis	52	G. B. Stevenson not out	48
C. W. J. Athey c Rawlinson b Sutcliffe	17	B 2, l-b 6	8
*J. H. Hampshire c Ezekowitz b Sutcliffe	6		
S. N. Hartley b Sutcliffe	0	1/133 2/133 3/147 (6 wkts dec.) 268
†D. L. Bairstow not out	44	4/147 5/160 6/199

P. Carrick, C. M. Old and G. A. Cope did not bat.

Bowling: Ross 17–3–50–0; Sanderson 13–4–20–0; Curtis 38–12–89–1; Sutcliffe 27–6–101–4.

Oxford University

J. P. Durack lbw b Stevenson	14	– lbw b Sidebottom	6
R. A. B. Ezekowitz c Bairstow b Stevenson	12	– c Athey b Cope	15
J. L. Rawlinson c Boycott b Stevenson	0	– c Hartley b Carrick	14
R. Marsden c Boycott b Stevenson	0	– c Bairstow b Sidebottom	38
J. J. Rogers lbw b Boycott	14	– lbw b Old	17
R. S. Cowan lbw b Sidebottom	10	– c Hampshire b Sidebottom	4
†M. C. L. MacPherson b Stevenson	10	– c Boycott b Sidebottom	0
*C. J. Ross c Boycott b Sidebottom	0	– b Sidebottom	1
S. P. Sutcliffe c Athey b Boycott	0	– c Stevenson b Sidebottom	0
I. J. Curtis not out	6	– c Hampshire b Sidebottom	2
J. F. W. Sanderson c Hampshire b Sidebottom	4	– not out	2
B 2, l-b 8, n-b 1	11	B 5, l-b 10, n-b 2	17

1/28 2/28 3/28 4/31 5/47   81   1/12 2/43 3/52 4/105 5/107   116
6/63 7/70 8/70 9/70   6/108 7/111 8/111 9/113

Bowling: *First Innings*—Old 6–3–9–0; Stevenson 17–8–25–5; Carrick 8–6–5–0; Cope 5–2–9–0; Sidebottom 10.4–8–12–3; Boycott 10.4–4–10–2. *Second Innings*—Old 8–6–5–1; Stevenson 17–10–29–0; Carrick 17–12–21–1; Cope 19–8–26–1; Sidebottom 15.2–8–18–7; Boycott 1–1–0–0; Hartley 2–2–0–0.

Umpires: D. J. Constant and M. J. Kitchen.

OXFORD UNIVERSITY v HAMPSHIRE

At Oxford, May 7, 8, 9. Hampshire won by 86 runs. Hampshire, put in, were able to declare at 365 for nine after Cowley, Pocock and Turner had reached half-centuries. Oxford made a positive reply with 228, Ezekowitz and Marsden adding 85 for the second wicket and Orders hitting 57. After a bold innings by Cowley, Hampshire declared at lunch, 241 ahead. Orders and Cowan made useful contributions, but hopes of a draw disappeared after tea when the last six wickets fell for only 53 runs.

Hampshire

J. M. Rice c Orders b Cowan	30	– c MacPherson b Ross	13
N. G. Cowley b Ross	65	– c MacPherson b Ross	48
C. L. Smith c MacPherson b Sutcliffe	20	– not out	22
T. E. Jesty c Rawlinson b Ross	10	– not out	18
D. R. Turner c Marsden b Curtis	60		
*N. E. J. Pocock c and b Ross	66		
M. N. S. Taylor run out	6		
S. F. Graf c Orders b Curtis	44		
†G. R. Stephenson b Ross	1		
J. W. Southern not out	36		
K. Stevenson not out	5		
B 4, l-b 13, w 5	22	L-b 3	3

1/92 2/113 3/129 4/135   (9 wkts dec.) 365   1/40 2/77   (2 wkts dec.) 104
5/249 6/279 7/281 8/286 9/344

Bowling: *First Innings*—Ross 29–9–76–4; Mallett 16–3–66–0; Curtis 29–5–89–2; Cowan 15–2–44–1; Sutcliffe 17–1–68–1. *Second Innings*—Ross 12–2–50–2; Mallett 5–1–23–0; Sutcliffe 7–0–28–0.

Oxford University

J. P. Durack c Jesty b Graf	4	– c sub b Stevenson 0
R. A. B. Ezekowitz c Pocock b Southern	36	– lbw b Taylor 11
R. Marsden c Rice b Southern	44	– lbw b Taylor 6
J. O. D. Orders lbw b Stevenson	57	– b Cowley 43
R. S. Cowan c Graf b Cowley	7	– lbw b Cowley 34
J. L. Rawlinson b Cowley	19	– lbw b Stevenson 1
†M. C. L. MacPherson c Pocock b Southern	22	– c Smith b Stevenson 9
N. V. H. Mallett c Rice b Southern	6	– b Cowley 25
S. P. Sutcliffe b Graf	0	– (10) c Cowley b Southern 8
*C. J. Ross c sub b Southern	7	– (9) lbw b Stevenson 2
I. J. Curtis not out	9	– not out 0
B 7, l-b 8, w 2	17	B 7, l-b 9 16

1/4 2/89 3/108 4/131 5/164   228   1/0 2/15 3/30 4/88 5/102   155
6/199 7/210 8/211 9/218   6/116 7/116 8/119 9/155

Bowling: *First Innings*—Graf 27–12–43–2; Stevenson 26–12–48–1; Jesty 9–5–17–0; Southern 32.1–13–42–5; Taylor 4–3–1–0; Cowley 23–7–40–2; Smith 4–2–14–0; Rice 4–2–6–0. *Second Innings*—Graf 3–2–1–0; Stevenson 17–5–46–4; Southern 13.2–5–16–1; Taylor 7–2–19–2; Cowley 20–5–51–3; Smith 3–1–6–0.

Umpires: D. J. Constant and M. J. Kitchen.

OXFORD UNIVERSITY v FREE FORESTERS

At Oxford, May 24, 26, 27 (Not first-class). Free Foresters won by 56 runs. Free Foresters 254 (M. G. M. Groves 106; J. F. W. Sanderson four for 71, S. P. Sutcliffe four for 75) and 157 for eight dec. (D. R. Worsley 53, R. M. K. Gracey 50; J. F. W. Sanderson four for 73); Oxford University 168 (S. J. Halliday 65) and 187 (S. J. Halliday 95).

OXFORD UNIVERSITY v MCC

At Oxford, May 28, 29, 30 (Not first-class). MCC won by ten wickets. An unbroken sixth-wicket partnership of 107 by Mence and Ellison laid the foundations for MCC's win. Oxford University 167 (S. J. Halliday 70) and 127 (N. J. W. Stewart five for 28); MCC 267 for five dec. (R. M. Ellison 67 not out, M. D. Mence 62 not out, R. J. Lanchbury 59, G. J. Saville 53) and 30 for no wkt.

OXFORD UNIVERSITY v WORCESTERSHIRE

At Oxford, May 31, June 2, 3. Drawn. Rain prevented any play on the first day, and on the second Ormrod and Jones put on 92 for the first wicket after Worcestershire had been put in. Ormrod, who had survived three stumping chances and two dropped catches, looked set for a century and was just 5 runs short when Gifford declared. Oxford also began promisingly as Ezekowitz and Marsden opened with 77, but the spinners dashed their hopes of a first innings lead. Patel captured six wickets for 47 while Gifford kept the pressure on at the other end. Patel followed his bowling success with an unbeaten 68 in Worcestershire's second innings.

Worcestershire

B. J. R. Jones c Durack b Curtis	49	– (2) c Durack b Wookey 5
J. A. Ormrod not out	95	
P. A. Neale c Cowan b Curtis	35	– (4) not out 9
E. J. O. Hemsley not out	35	
M. J. Weston (did not bat)		– (1) lbw b Cowan 22
D. N. Patel (did not bat)		– (3) not out 68
B 13, l-b 2, w 3	18	L-b 1, w 3, n-b 4 8

1/92 2/171   (2 wkts dec.) 232   1/5 2/88   (2 wkts) 112

†D. J. Humphries, V. A. Holder, *N. Gifford, A. P. Pridgeon and J. Cumbes did not bat.

Bowling: *First Innings*—Wookey 8–0–27–0; Sanderson 13–3–44–0; Curtis 30–8–57–2; Sutcliffe 25–3–86–0. *Second Innings*—Wookey 8–2–28–1; Sanderson 6–2–13–0; Sutcliffe 15–5–18–0; Cowan 9–1–40–1; Durack 4–1–5–0.

Oxford University

R. A. B. Ezekowitz b Holder	36	S. P. Sutcliffe c Weston b Gifford	2
*R. Marsden c Neale b Patel	50	I. J. Curtis b Patel	9
D. C. G. Foster c Hemsley b Patel	25	J. F. W. Sanderson not out	0
S. J. Halliday b Patel	17		
R. S. Cowan c Pridgeon b Patel	1	B 5, l-b 5, n-b 7	17
J. P. Durack c Patel b Gifford	5		
S. M. Wookey b Gifford	9	1/77 2/103 3/137 4/140 5/141	193
†T. E. O. Bury b Patel	22	6/150 7/155 8/160 9/186	

Bowling: Holder 16–3–33–1; Pridgeon 6–1–19–0; Cumbes 18–6–37–0; Patel 29.1–15–47–6; Gifford 19–7–40–3.

Umpires: D. G. L. Evans and B. J. Meyer.

OXFORD UNIVERSITY v LANCASHIRE

At Oxford, June 4, 5, 6. Lancashire won by ten wickets. The unpredictability of Oxford's batting was highlighted in this match when their highest total was followed by their lowest. Ezekowitz and Marsden gave them a sound start before Cowan and Foster hit career-best scores, enabling Oxford to declare. O'Shaughnessy, who was making his début, compiled an unbeaten half-century for Lancashire who also declared, 24 behind. The University's second innings provided Lee with career-best figures of eight for 34, the best by any bowler in the season. After the Dark Blues had been shot out for 64, Lloyd and Kennedy easily scored 89 runs for victory.

Oxford University

R. A. B. Ezekowitz c Scott b Lloyd	48	– lbw b Lee	2
*R. Marsden b Hughes b Kennedy	28	– c K. A. Hayes b Lee	5
R. S. Cowan run out	63	– b Lee	5
S. J. Halliday c and b Lloyd	14	– c and b Hughes	3
D. C. G. Foster c Scott b Lloyd	67	– (6) c O'Shaughnessy b Hughes	14
J. P. Durack b Hughes	4	– (7) c O'Shaughnessy b Lee	0
S. M. Wookey not out	10	– (5) c Abrahams b Lee	2
I. J. Curtis lbw b Lloyd	0	– (10) not out	1
†P. N. Huxford (did not bat)		– (8) b Lee	4
S. P. Sutcliffe (did not bat)		– (9) b Lee	11
J. F. W. Sanderson (did not bat)		– c Scott b Lee	9
B 4, L-b 7, n-b 1	12	B 2, l-b 5, w 1	8

1/54 2/99 3/121 4/176	(7 wkts dec.) 246	1/2 2/8 3/15 4/15 5/19 64
5/198 6/239 7/246		6/19 7/30 8/46 9/52

Bowling: *First Innings*—Lee 15–4–32–0; Radford 15–4–26–0; O'Shaughnessy 3–1–9–0; Kennedy 12–3–25–1; Hughes 26–9–47–1; Lloyd 30.4–9–61–4; Abrahams 10–4–34–0. *Second Innings*—Lee 25–9–34–8; Radford 1–1–0–0; Kennedy 6–5–4–0; Hughes 17–8–18–2.

Lancashire

A. Kennedy lbw b Wookey	32	– (2) not out	51
K. A. Hayes b Sanderson	27		
J. Abrahams b Sutcliffe	10		
G. Fowler c Wookey b Sutcliffe	28		
S. J. O'Shaughnessy not out	50		
D. P. Hughes hit wkt b Sutcliffe	33		
N. Radford b Sanderson	15		
*F. C. Hayes not out	2		
D. Lloyd (did not bat)		– (1) not out	37
B 14, l-b 9, w 1, n-b 1	25	W 1	1

1/49 2/75 3/92   (6 wkts dec.) 222   (no wkt) 89
4/138 5/188 6/218

†C. J. Scott and P. G. Lee did not bat.

Bowling: *First Innings*—Wookey 18–5–29–1; Sanderson 20–9–35–2; Sutcliffe 27–6–70–3; Curtis 30–9–63–0. *Second Innings*—Wookey 6–1–24–0; Sanderson 10–3–37–0; Durack 4.4–0–27–0.

Umpires: D. G. L. Evans and B. J. Meyer.

OXFORD UNIVERSITY v LEICESTERSHIRE

At Oxford, June 14, 16, 17. Drawn. Rain washed out the first and third days, and restricted play to two and a half hours on the second, when Oxford reached 89 for four, after being put in. Wenlock, on his début, was punished by Cowan, Oxford's top scorer.

Oxford University

R. A. B. Ezekowitz lbw b Cook	18	J. J. Rogers not out	1
R. Marsden c Garnham b Clift	17		
R. S. Cowan lbw b Clift	34	B 3, l-b 2, w 1	6
S. J. Halliday b Clift	9		
D. C. G. Foster not out	4	1/23 2/64 3/75 4/88 (4 wkts) 89	

S. M. Wookey, †P. N. Huxford, S. P. Sutcliffe, I. J. Curtis and *C. J. Ross did not bat.

Bowling: Taylor 11–7–16–0; Shuttleworth 10–2–18–0; Cook 9–5–11–1; Wenlock 10–3–21–0; Clift 8–1–17–3.

Leicestershire

R. A. Cobb, I. P. Butcher, T. J. Boon, *D. I. Gower, N. E. Briers, †M. A. Garnham, P. B. Clift, D. A. Wenlock, N. G. B. Cook, K. Shuttleworth, L. B. Taylor.

Umpires: J. G. Langridge and D. R. Shepherd.

OXFORD UNIVERSITY v MIDDLESEX

At Oxford, June 21, 23, 24. Drawn. Rain restricted play on the third day to three overs, saving Oxford from a possible innings defeat. James and Emburey troubled the University, whose cause was worsened by three run outs. In reply to Oxford's 133, Middlesex lost three wickets for 70 before Radley, who hit his fifth century of the season, was joined by Gould to steady the innings after a stand of 75 in an hour. Despite fine bowling by Sanderson, who finished with career-best figures of six for 67, Middlesex accumulated 296, and when play was abandoned soon after lunch on the third day, Oxford were struggling at 92 for six.

Oxford University

R. A. B. Ezekowitz run out	2	– (8) not out	5
R. Marsden lbw b James	9	– (1) c Maru b Selvey	25
D. C. G. Foster c Barlow b James	6	– c Maru b Selvey	8
J. O. D. Orders lbw b Emburey	26	– lbw b Selvey	0
J. J. Rogers lbw b Emburey	22	– (2) lbw b Cowans	7
S. J. Halliday b James	37	– (5) not out	36
*C. J. Ross b Emburey	7	– lbw b James	4
†T. E. O. Bury run out	9	– (6) b Selvey	1
S. P. Sutcliffe run out	8		
I. J. Curtis not out	0		
J. F. W. Sanderson lbw b Emburey	1		
L-b 4, w 1, n-b 1	6	B 1, l-b 4, w 1	6

1/11 2/14 3/18 4/65 5/66 6/76　　　133　　1/17 2/41 3/41　　(6 wkts) 92
7/106 8/131 9/132　　　　　　　　　　　4/42 5/44 6/71

Bowling: *First Innings*—Cowans 5–1–10–0; James 8–3–14–3; Selvey 17–6–37–0; Emburey 21.5–10–27–4; Maru 13–3–39–0. *Second Innings*—Cowans 11–3–32–1; Selvey 16–7–37–4; James 7–3–15–1; Emburey 2–1–2–0.

Middlesex

M. J. Smith c Bury b Sanderson	0	K. D. James b Sanderson	16
W. N. Slack b Sanderson	18	R. Maru not out	9
*C. T. Radley c Sanderson b Sutcliffe	119	N. G. Cowans c Halliday b Sanderson	1
G. D. Barlow c Bury b Sanderson	18		
†I. J. Gould c Halliday b Curtis	41	B 6, l-b 6, w 3, n-b 1	16
J. E. Emburey c Halliday b Ross	20		
K. P. Tomlins lbw b Ross	9	1/0 2/50 3/70 4/145 5/199	296
M. W. W. Selvey c Sutcliffe b Sanderson	29	6/241 7/241 8/281 9/288	

Bowling: Sanderson 22–4–67–6; Ross 25–3–93–2; Curtis 12–2–44–1; Sutcliffe 20–2–76–1.

Umpires: K. E. Palmer and D. R. Shepherd.

At Lord's, June 28, 30, July 1. OXFORD UNIVERSITY drew with CAMBRIDGE UNIVERSITY (See Other Matches at Lord's).

CAMBRIDGE

Captain – I. G. PECK
(Bedford and Magdalene)

Secretary – D. C. HOLLIDAY
(Oundle and Christ's)

Captain in 1981 – I. G. PECK　　　　Secretary – J. P. C. MILLS
(Bedford and Magdalene)　　　　　　(Oundle and Corpus Christi)

In one of the wettest summers of recent years, Cambridge University found an oasis of sun at Fenner's, although April showers disrupted the opening matches. However, the weather changed with a vengence at the end of June, and the University Match was badly affected, with play possible only on the second day; a disappointing situation as Cambridge had travelled to London with high hopes of gaining a second successive victory over Oxford.

Their strength lay in the all-round skills of Derek Pringle and the side's ability to make runs right down the order. Pringle hit two centuries and for much of the Fenner's term enjoyed the unusual distinction, for an undergraduate, of figuring amongst the leaders of both first-class batting and bowling averages.

In terms of runs scored, he was followed by Aziz Mubarak, whose new-found consistency earned him a maiden century in his third season at Cambridge. The Sri Lankan's opening partner was the reliable Peter Mills, who twice shared in century stands and displayed great reluctance to surrender his wicket – a quality his colleagues did not always emulate. Of the freshmen, Robin Boyd-Moss, who later played for Northamptonshire, showed an ability to score consistently while going for his shots.

Although the runs came regularly, enabling captain Ian Peck to declare against county teams, the University found the wickets of first-class batsmen harder to claim. Pringle was the most successful bowler, while Neil Russom, a player highly rated by Somerset, toiled honestly with the new ball on unhelpful pitches.

Much interest was taken in the performance of Simon Doggart – son of the 1950 captain G. H. G. Doggart and grandson of the 1921 and 1922 Blue, A. G. – in his first season out of schools cricket. Although he found wickets hard to come by, he bowled his off-spinners tidily and showed that his batting could boost the middle-order in the coming seasons.

The team, which fielded well, was one of the happiest of recent years and much of the credit for this must go to Peck, who led his men with intelligence and confidence despite his own indifferent form with the bat. He was fortunate to have the help of coach Brian Taylor, the former Essex captain, whose influence was considerable following the retirement of Cyril Coote, groundsman and mentor to successive generations of Cambridge cricketers. – David Hallett.

CAMBRIDGE UNIVERSITY RESULTS

First-class matches – Played 9: Lost 3, Drawn 6.

All matches – Played 18: Won 3, Lost 5, Drawn 10.

BATTING

	Matches	Innings	Not Outs	Runs	Highest Inns	Average
N. Russom	9	12	8	226	79*	56.50
D. R. Pringle	9	14	3	604	123	54.90
J. P. C. Mills	9	14	1	350	79	26.92
A. M. Mubarak	9	14	0	359	105	25.64
R. J. Boyd-Moss	9	13	0	320	71	24.61

	Matches	Innings	Not Outs	Runs	Highest Inns	Average
A. Odendaal	9	14	0	325	61	23.21
S. J. G. Doggart	9	11	2	174	43	19.33
D. C. Holliday	9	12	3	173	76*	19.22
I. G. Peck	9	12	2	147	34	14.70
N. C. Crawford	8	7	1	84	28	14.00
M. G. Howat	9	6	0	61	32	10.16

Played in one match: P. D. Hemsley 12*.

* Signifies not out.

BOWLING

	Overs	Maidens	Runs	Wickets	Average
D. R. Pringle	241.1	57	652	24	27.16
N. C. Crawford	168.4	32	568	14	40.57
S. J. G. Doggart	153	43	392	9	43.55
N. Russom	253.3	52	810	18	45.00
M. G. Howat	185.2	34	679	8	84.87

Also bowled: R. J. Boyd-Moss 37–5–145–2; P. D. Hemsley 11–1–53–1; D. C. Holliday 37.5–9–123–1.

CAMBRIDGE UNIVERSITY v LEICESTERSHIRE

At Cambridge, April 23, 24, 25. Drawn. After rain had restricted play on the first day, the Cambridge innings lasted well into the second. On a slow, docile wicket, Mubarak fell just 8 short of his maiden century, while Odendaal, a South African making his début in England, made a valuable contribution. When Leicestershire replied, Steele scored a patient hundred and Davison's unbeaten 91 included fifteen boundaries. Their declaration, 132 ahead, could have troubled the University, but careful batting made sure there were few alarms.

Cambridge University

A. M. Mubarak b Balderstone	92	– lbw b Steele	9
J. P. C. Mills b Clift	14	– not out	33
*†I. G. Peck c Garnham b Clift	0	– c Clift b Cook	15
A. Odendaal c Gower b Davison	61	– run out	5
D. R. Pringle not out	26	– not out	13
R. J. Boyd-Moss c Gower b Cook	24		
D. C. Holliday lbw b Clift	4		
N. C. Crawford c Davison b Clift	0		
N. Russom not out	0		
B 11, l-b 12, w 1, n-b 7	31	B 3, n-b 1	4

1/36 2/36 3/181   (7 wkts dec.) 252   1/17 2/40 3/59   (3 wkts) 79
4/200 5/232 6/237 7/241

S. J. G. Doggart and M. G. Howat did not bat.

Bowling: *First Innings*—Agnew 19–7–42–0; Taylor 12.2–2–35–0; Cook 33–19–39–1; Clift 28–12–45–4; Steele 8–6–5–0; Boon 7–2–24–0; Balderstone 5–2–13–1; Davison 5.4–1–18–1. *Second Innings*—Agnew 3–2–3–0; Boon 3–2–9–0; Steele 10–3–14–1; Balderstone 9–6–9–0; Clift 5–3–8–0; Cook 6–2–22–1; Briers 4–1–10–0; Gower 1–1–0–0.

Leicestershire

J. F. Steele c Odendaal b Doggart	118	N. G. B. Cook c Holliday b Russom	16
N. E. Briers c Pringle b Russom	6	J. P. Agnew c Pringle b Russom	2
J. C. Balderstone b Pringle	36	L. B. Taylor absent hurt	0
D. I. Gower c Mubarak b Russom	46		
T. J. Boon c and b Doggart	33	B 1,l-b 11, w 3, n-b 6	21
*B. F. Davison not out	91		
P. B. Clift c and b Howat	1	1/10 2/89 3/163 4/233	384
†M. A. Garnham lbw b Pringle	14	5/252 6/259 7/312 8/371 9/384	

Bowling: Howat 19–4–68–1; Russom 24–6–84–4; Crawford 21–4–67–0; Pringle 30–9–82–2; Boyd-Moss 9–2–21–0; Doggart 16–6–41–2.

Umpires: H. D. Bird and W. E. Alley.

CAMBRIDGE UNIVERSITY v ESSEX

At Cambridge, April 26, 28, 29. Drawn. Cambridge scored runs right down the order, led by Pringle who made 75 against his county colleagues. Rain having restricted play on the first day, the University's innings lasted until late on the second evening, Lever taking five wickets in four spells. Essex batted for the rest of the match with Gooch (four 6s and 36 4s) scoring a double century in ten minutes under four hours. The first wicket realised 224, with Denness contributing 32 before he retired hurt at the close of the second day, and Fletcher joined Gooch to add 114 for the second wicket in 96 minutes.

Cambridge University

A. M. Mubarak c Gooch b Lever	2	N. Russom c Smith b Lever	18
J. P. C. Mills c Smith b Pont	36	S. J. G. Doggart not out	37
*†I. G. Peck c Hardie b Lever	34	M. G. Howat c Smith b Fletcher	0
A. Odendaal c Fletcher b Lever	14		
D. R. Pringle b Lever	75	B 6,l-b 6, n-b 1	13
R. J. Boyd-Moss c Smith b Gooch	37		
D. C. Holliday c Smith b Acfield	2	1/28 2/48 3/77 4/101	277
N. C. Crawford c Denness b Gooch	9	5/164 6/168 7/180 8/227 9/274	

Bowling: Lever 32–10–66–5; Phillip 18–2–65–0; Pont 17–3–49–1; Gooch 19–8–29–2; East 3–2–6–0; Fletcher 4.4–0–33–1; Acfield 11–4–16–1.

Essex

M. H. Denness retired hurt	32	R. E. East not out	24
G. A. Gooch c Odendaal b Russom	205	D. L. Acfield c Peck b Crawford	0
K. S. McEwan b Howat	41	J. K. Lever not out	4
*K. W. R. Fletcher c and b Russom	73		
K. R. Pont c Doggart b Holliday	1	L-b 5, n-b 13, w 4	22
B. R. Hardie c Boyd-Moss b Crawford	38		
N. Phillip b Russom	0	1/224 2/338 3/353 (8 wkts) 459	
†N. Smith c Pringle b Crawford	19	4/394 5/394 6/425 7/434 8/438	

Bowling: Howat 28–5–113–1; Russom 20–5–74–3; Pringle 12–3–27–0; Crawford 23–5–88–3; Doggart 13–2–51–0; Boyd-Moss 8–1–44–0; Holliday 14–3–40–1.

Umpires: H. D. Bird and W. E. Alley.

CAMBRIDGE UNIVERSITY v SUFFOLK

At Cambridge, May 1, 2. Drawn. Cambridge University 200 for five dec. (D. C. Holliday 83 not out) and 230 for four dec. (A. M. Mubarak 61, R. J. Boyd-Moss 57 not out); Suffolk 191 for eight dec. (J. P. Stuck 74) and 209 for eight.

CAMBRIDGE UNIVERSITY v SURREY

At Cambridge, May 3, 5, 6. Surrey won by nine wickets. Mubarak played the major rôle in a century opening partnership with Mills, who took more than two hours over his 24, before runs from the middle order enabled the University to declare at the close of the first day. On a fast and true Fenner's wicket, Butcher made an unbeaten double-century in five and a half hours, hitting one 6 and 30 4s. He put on 266 for the first wicket with Clinton and 136 for the second with Howarth, taking Surrey to their declaration 150 ahead. On the final day Cambridge fell to spinners Cheatle and Pocock, leaving the visitors to score just 38 for victory.

Cambridge University

A. M. Mubarak c and b Cheatle	72	– c Roope b Smith	10
J. P. C. Mills c Smith b Clarke	24	– c Howarth b Cheatle	33
R. J. Boyd-Moss lbw b Clarke	2	– (6) c Roope b Cheatle	28
A. Odendaal c Pocock b Cheatle	32	– c Butcher b Cheatle	21
D. R. Pringle run out	37	– c Roope b Pocock	17
D. C. Holliday c Jackman b Knight	0	– (7) c Roope b Cheatle	13
*†I. G. Peck not out	16	– (3) lbw b Jackman	6
S. J. G. Doggart b Jackman	43	– c Smith b Pocock	9
N. Russom not out	0	– c Knight b Cheatle	18
P. D. Hemsley (did not bat)		– not out	12
M. G. Howat (did not bat)		– c Roope b Pocock	13
B 9, l-b 16, w 1	26	B 3, l-b 1, w 1, n-b 2	7

1/104 2/120 3/120	(7 wkts dec.) 252	1/20 2/34 3/71 4/77 187
4/185 5/193 6/193 7/251		5/119 6/119 7/140 8/150 9/170

Bowling: *First Innings*—Clarke 26–9–39–2; Jackman 11–5–35–1; Knight 15–3–50–1; Pocock 14–6–20–0; Cheatle 27–9–53–2; Smith 19–6–29–0. *Second Innings*—Jackman 12–5–32–1; Smith 9–4–19–1; Cheatle 33–13–78–5; Roope 5–2–12–0; Butcher 2–0–4–0; Pocock 17.1–5–35–3.

Surrey

A. R. Butcher not out	216		
G. S. Clinton lbw b Pringle	89		
G. P. Howarth not out	54		
P. I. Pocock (did not bat)		– (1) not out	20
R. D. Jackman (did not bat)		– (2) c Howat b Hemsley	14
†C. J. Richards (did not bat)		– (3) not out	4
B 5, l-b 18, n-b 20	43	B 1	1

1/266	(1 wkt dec.) 402	1/23	(1 wkt) 39

*R. D. V. Knight, G. R. J. Roope, D. M. Smith, S. T. Clarke and R. G. L. Cheatle did not bat.

Bowling: *First Innings*—Howat 20–3–79–0; Russom 23–5–75–0; Pringle 20–6–65–1; Doggart 15–6–37–0; Hemsley 8–0–49–0; Boyd-Moss 6–0–27–0; Holliday 7–1–27–0. *Second Innings*—Howat 3–0–18–0; Hemsley 3–1–4–1; Holliday 1.5–0–16–0.

Umpires: D. O. Oslear and T. W. Spencer.

CAMBRIDGE UNIVERSITY v CRYPTICS

At Cambridge, May 4. Cryptics won by five wickets. Cambridge University 176 (I. R. H. Simpkin 55); Cryptics 177 for five (C. M. B. Williams 62).

CAMBRIDGE UNIVERSITY v MIDDLESEX

At Cambridge, May 7, 8, 9. Drawn. After Selvey had taken the first two Cambridge wickets for no score in his first over, Pringle led a recovery, scoring a century (fourteen 4s) and putting on 148 for the fifth wicket with Boyd-Moss. Cambridge prospered further by adding 70 for the last two wickets in the final hour. Middlesex built solidly on Brearley's half-century; century-maker Radley batted for nearly three and a half hours and Gould contributed a half-century in even time before the county were dismissed early on the third morning. Selvey again had the University in early trouble but Mills, Odendaal and Crawford (one 6 and four 4s) took them safely to a draw.

Cambridge University

A. M. Mubarak b Selvey	0	– lbw b Selvey	2
J. P. C. Mills c Gould b Merry	7	– b Emburey	52
*†I. G. Peck lbw b Selvey	0	– c Emburey b Selvey	0
A. Odendaal c Gatting b Selvey	20	– c Emburey b Gatting	44
D. R. Pringle lbw b Edmonds	109	– b Edmonds	8
R. J. Boyd-Moss lbw b Gatting	71	– lbw b Emburey	3
D. C. Holliday b Edmonds	35	– b Emburey	11
S. J. G. Doggart b Selvey	17	– not out	9
N. C. Crawford c Radley b Selvey	15	– b Radley	28
N. Russom not out	23	– not out	0
M. G. Howat c Emburey b Radley	32		
B 8, l-b 13, n-b 11	32	L-b 1, w 2, n-b 3	6

1/0 2/0 3/18 4/61   361   1/11 2/13 3/90   (8 wkts) 163
5/209 6/239 7/275 8/291 9/319   4/110 5/110 6/115 7/132 8/161

Bowling: *First Innings*—Selvey 32–10–86–5; Merry 20–5–54–1; Edmonds 30–5–89–2; Gatting 18–3–63–1; Emburey 12–3–28–0; Brearley 1–0–5–0; Radley 0.3–0–4–1. *Second Innings*—Selvey 9–5–15–2; Merry 7–1–28–0; Edmonds 33–17–54–1; Emburey 23–14–37–3; Gatting 10–1–22–1; Radley 2–2–0–1; Gould 2–1–1–0.

Middlesex

W. N. Slack c Peck b Howat	28	J. E. Emburey b Pringle	24
*J. M. Brearley c Pringle b Crawford	53	M. W. W. Selvey c Odendaal b Crawford	39
C. T. Radley c Mills b Howat	124	W. G. Merry not out	6
G. D. Barlow c Howat b Russom	32		
M. W. Gatting lbw b Pringle	43	B 8, l-b 12, n-b 7	27
R. O. Butcher c and b Boyd-Moss	0		
†I. J. Gould c Odendaal b Russom	52	1/52 2/119 3/185 4/285	448
P. H. Edmonds c Pringle b Russom	20	5/287 6/316 7/366 8/386 9/424	

Bowling: Howat 17–3–61–2; Russom 39–2–145–3; Crawford 19.4–4–53–2; Pringle 36–6–100–2; Holliday 2–1–4–0; Doggart 8–1–29–0; Boyd-Moss 8–0–29–1.

Umpires: D. O. Oslear and T. W. Spencer.

CAMBRIDGE UNIVERSITY v DURHAM UNIVERSITY

At Cambridge, May 10. Drawn. Durham University 239 for nine (R. Dyer 87); Cambridge University 170 for seven (T. D. W. Edwards 74 not out; S. P. Hughes five for 68).

CAMBRIDGE UNIVERSITY v NORFOLK

At Cambridge, May 12. Drawn. Cambridge University 184 for eight dec. (A. J. Murley 56; S. J. Starling five for 35); Norfolk 170 for eight (N. D. Cook 60, N. Witherden 53 not out).

CAMBRIDGE UNIVERSITY v CLUB CRICKET CONFERENCE

At Cambridge, May 16. Club Cricket Conference won by eight wickets. Cambridge University 252 for six dec. (A. J. Murley 80, T. D. W. Edwards 58); Club Cricket Conference 255 for two (J. R. Kilbee 119, M. E. Gear 96).

CAMBRIDGE UNIVERSITY v CAMBRIDGESHIRE

At Cambridge, May 17, Cambridge University won by nine wickets. Cambridgeshire 241 for nine dec. (M. Stephenson 62, N. Gadsby 54; D. C. Holliday five for 81); Cambridge University 244 for one (I. R. H. Simpkin 115, A. J. Murley 108 not out).

CAMBRIDGE UNIVERSITY v NORTHAMPTONSHIRE

At Cambridge, June 4, 5, 6. Northamptonshire won by 34 runs. Cook and Larkins put on 119 for the first wicket before lunch, and Cook reached his hundred in another century partnership – with Williams – before Yardley took his team to the declaration. Cambridge had lost both openers by the close and, on the second day, Tim Lamb breached their middle order with a career-best performance before Pringle and Russom rescued the innings with a partnership of 129 for the eighth wicket. Northamptonshire batted enterprisingly before declaring at lunch on the third day. Set to score 294 in four hours, Cambridge made a brave attempt, with Pringle hitting nine 4s in his 63; but the task was beyond them as Williams returned career-best figures of seven for 73.

Northamptonshire

*G. Cook b Crawford	101 –	(5) b Crawford 48
W. Larkins c Doggart b Howat	71 –	(1) c Doggart b Russom 37
R. G. Williams c Holliday b Pringle	65 –	(6) not out 13
†T. J. Yardley not out	50	
D. J. Wild b Doggart	0 –	(3) c and b Howat 22
R. M. Carter c Peck b Pringle	2 –	(2) c Russom b Pringle 30
R. M. Tindall not out	21 –	(4) not out 60
B 5, l-b 3, n-b 5	13	B 5, l-b 10, n-b 4 19

1/119 2/223 3/260   (5 wkts dec.) 323   1/43 2/84 3/112   (4 wkts dec.) 229
4/262 5/267   4/190

G. Forster, T. M. Lamb, N. A. Mallender and C. D. Booden did not bat.

Bowling: *First Innings*—Howat 14.4–2–74–1; Russom 15–2–42–0; Pringle 23–6–59–2; Crawford 16–2–64–1; Doggart 21–7–43–1; Boyd-Moss 4–1–14–0; Holliday 2–0–14–0. *Second Innings*—Howat 16–2–62–1; Russom 12–2–23–1; Pringle 11–5–18–1; Crawford 17–3–60–1; Doggart 15–4–47–0.

Cambridge University

A. M. Mubarak lbw b Lamb	5 –	lbw b Lamb 21
J. P. C. Mills b Mallender	8 –	lbw b Williams 24
A. Odendaal c Yardley b Lamb	18 –	c Wild b Williams 24
R. J. Boyd-Moss c Cook b Lamb	12 –	c Cook b Williams 1
D. R. Pringle b Forster	80 –	c Booden b Lamb 63
S. J. G. Doggart b Lamb	0 –	b Williams 43
*†I. G. Peck lbw b Lamb	1 –	not out 30
D. C. Holliday b Lamb	0 –	c Forster b Williams 3
N. Russom not out	79 –	c Larkins b Williams 18
N. C. Crawford c Mallender b Forster	17 –	c Williams b Forster 8
M. G. Howat b Lamb	16 –	lbw b Williams 0
B 14, l-b 8, n-b 1	23	B 11, l-b 13 24

1/9 2/26 3/43 4/48   259   1/42 2/70 3/72 4/91   259
5/48 6/54 7/59 8/188 9/216   5/171 6/207 7/215 8/247 9/259

Bowling: *First Innings*—Lamb 25.2–9–56–7; Mallender 22–6–61–1; Booden 10–1–25–0; Williams 13–1–46–0; Carter 5–1–18–0; Forster 10–1–30–2. *Second Innings*—Lamb 14–2–34–2; Mallender 11–1–30–0; Williams 27.5–6–73–7; Forster 20–4–70–1; Tindall 7–0–28–0.

Umpires: R. Aspinall and K. Goodwin.

CAMBRIDGE UNIVERSITY v WARWICKSHIRE

At Cambridge, June 7, 9, 10. Drawn. A maiden century by Mubarak highlighted an opening partnership, with Mills, of 189. Cambridge retained control as Boyd-Moss scored a half-century, enabling the University to declare before the close. Warwickshire survived without loss until the second morning when their innings disintegrated from 94 for two to 142 all out, with Pringle taking four cheap wickets. Following on 172 behind, Warwickshire struggled until Humpage (one 6 and seventeen 4s) took them to a respectable total with his second century in a week. Night-watchman Hopkins stayed stubbornly until after lunch, by which time the University's hopes of victory were disappearing, despite the performance of Pringle who took ten wickets in the match. They squandered wickets in an attempt to win the game, but lacked the experience to succeed.

Cambridge University

A. M. Mubarak st Maynard b Humpage	105	– b Small		6
J. P. C. Mills b Small	79	– c Lloyd b Doshi		24
A. Odendaal c Ferreira b Doshi	23	– b Small		16
R. J. Boyd-Moss b Doshi	53	– st Maynard b Doshi		20
D. R. Pringle not out	37	– c Oliver b Small		9
S. J. G. Doggart (did not bat)		– lbw b Doshi		1
N. Russom (did not bat)		– not out		4
D. C. Holliday (did not bat)		– not out		10
B 1, l-b 7, w 7, n-b 2	17	B 2, l-b 10, w 4		16

1/189 2/204 (4 wkts dec.) 314 1/23 2/50 3/60 (6 wkts) 106
3/238 4/314 4/72 5/89 6/92

*†I. G. Peck, N. C. Crawford and M. G. Howat did not bat.

Bowling: *First Innings*—Rouse 6–0–31–0; Ferreira 20–3–72–0; Small 11–0–44–1; Doshi 30–15–56–2; Oliver 10–3–24–0; Hopkins 22–7–49–0; Humpage 5–1–21–1. *Second Innings*—Rouse 6–2–18–0; Small 14–2–45–3; Doshi 11–1–27–3; Lloyd 1–1–0–0.

Warwickshire

K. D. Smith c sub b Russom	31	– c Pringle b Howat		3
*J. A. Claughton lbw b Howat	7	– (3) b Doggart		46
P. R. Oliver c sub b Crawford	26	– (4) b Pringle		30
†C. Maynard c Mills b Russom	30	– (7) c sub b Pringle		15
A. M. Ferreira c sub b Pringle	25	– (9) c sub b Pringle		0
G. W. Humpage c Crawford b Pringle	10	– c Boyd-Moss b Russom		101
T. A. Lloyd c and b Crawford	4	– (2) c Odendaal b Doggart		79
S. J. Rouse run out	0	– c Mubarak b Pringle		0
D. C. Hopkins not out	6	– (5) lbw b Pringle		33
G. C. Small lbw b Pringle	0	– c Doggart b Pringle		5
D. R. Doshi c Mills b Pringle	1	– not out		10
L-b 2	2	L-b 10, n-b 2		12

1/35 2/39 3/94 4/100 142 1/10 2/125 3/138 4/169 334
5/118 6/135 7/135 8/136 9/136 5/254 6/295 7/298 8/299 9/315

Bowling: *First Innings*—Howat 11–4–29–1; Russom 22–4–66–2; Pringle 9.1–5–11–4; Crawford 11–3–34–2; Doggart 1–1–0–0. *Second Innings*—Howat 16–6–43–1; Russom 38.3–10–97–1; Pringle 36–9–90–6; Crawford 14–3–39–0; Doggart 16–6–31–2; Holliday 11–4–22–0.

Umpires: R. Aspinall and K. Goodwin.

CAMBRIDGE UNIVERSITY v QUIDNUNCS

At Cambridge, June 8. Cambridge University won by six wickets. Quidnuncs 216 for five dec. (P. D. Briggs 112 not out, P. J. Hayes 53); Cambridge University 218 for four (R. J. Boyd-Moss 84 not out, A. M. Mubarak 61).

CAMBRIDGE UNIVERSITY v COMBINED SERVICES

At Cambridge, June 15, 16, 17. (Not first-class.) Drawn. Cambridge University 291 for six dec. (J. P. C. Mills 79) and 216 for six dec. (C. F. E. Goldie 59, K. I. Hodgson 54); Combined Services 241 (L. M. L. Barnwell 95) and 142 for six.

CAMBRIDGE UNIVERSITY v NOTTINGHAMSHIRE

At Cambridge, June 18, 19, 20. Nottinghamshire won by seven wickets. A second century of the season by Pringle and another half-century from Boyd-Moss enabled Cambridge to declare before the end of the first day. Birch, with support from the middle order, helped Nottinghamshire get within 30 of their opponents' total before declaring themselves. Batting again, Cambridge slipped to 48 for five and two more wickets fell quickly on the final morning. However, from 71 for six Cambridge recovered to 204 without further loss, both Holliday and Russom making career-best scores. Cambridge's second declaration was in vain as Birch, with a belligerent maiden century which included five 6s and nine 4s guided Nottinghamshire to an unlikely victory.

Cambridge University

A. M. Mubarak c Hemmings b Tunnicliffe	25	– lbw b Hacker	6
J. P. C. Mills c Todd b Mackintosh	4	– c Harris b Mackintosh	0
A. Odendaal lbw b Birch	20	– b Tunnicliffe	27
R. J. Boyd-Moss c Birch b Tunnicliffe	51	– lbw b Hacker	11
D. R. Pringle st French b Hemmings	123	– lbw b Tunnicliffe	4
S. J. G. Doggart c French b Tunnicliffe	8	– c Allbrook b Mackintosh	3
*†I. G. Peck c French b Mackintosh	4	– c French b Mackintosh	4
N. Russom not out	1	– not out	65
D. C. Holliday not out	9	– not out	76
L-b 7, w 2, n-b 2	11	L-b 5, n-b 3	8

1/18 2/44 3/73   (7 wkts dec.) 274   1/6 2/6 3/33   (7 wkts dec.) 204
4/161 5/208 6/255 7/265   4/39 5/48 6/56 7/61

N. C. Crawford and M. G. Howat did not bat.

Bowling: *First Innings*—Hacker 17–7–35–0; Mackintosh 20–3–74–2; Tunnicliffe 22–5–55–3; Birch 4–0–24–1; Hemmings 15–6–26–1; Allbrook 16–1–49–0. *Second Innings*—Hacker 21–9–34–2; Mackintosh 14–4–36–3; Hemmings 14–4–37–0; Tunnicliffe 11–3–28–2; Harris 11–4–36–0; Allbrook 9–4–25–0.

Nottinghamshire

*M. J. Harris c Mubarak b Russom	22	– c Holliday b Russom	1
R. T. Robinson c Pringle b Russom	10	– c Mubarak b Pringle	50
H. T. Tunnicliffe c Peck b Russom	0	– c Mubarak b Crawford	15
J. D. Birch c and b Pringle	70	– not out	105
C. C. Curzon lbw b Crawford	32		
P. A. Todd b Crawford	42	– (5) not out	47
†B. N. French c Boyd-Moss b Doggart	15		
K. S. Mackintosh not out	16		
E. E. Hemmings c Peck b Crawford	13		
P. J. Hacker not out	2		
L-b 7, w 2, n-b 11	20	B 5, l-b 8, n-b 6	19

1/34 2/34 3/43 4/142   (8 wkts dec.) 242   1/11 2/61 3/104   (3 wkts) 237
5/146 6/206 7/208 8/224

M. E. Allbrook did not bat.

Bowling: *First Innings*—Howat 13–3–35–0; Russom 15–5–43–3; Pringle 18–2–46–1; Doggart 16–3–37–1; Crawford 19–1–61–3. *Second Innings*—Howat 12.4–0–40–0; Russom 11–3–53–1; Pringle 13–0–59–1; Crawford 12–1–66–1.

Umpires: J. G. Langridge and P. B. Wight.

At Hastings, June 21, 23, 24. CAMBRIDGE UNIVERSITY drew with SUSSEX.

At Guildford, June 25, 26, 27. (Not first-class.) CAMBRIDGE UNIVERSITY beat D. H. ROBINS' XI by 8 runs (See Other Matches, 1980).

At Lord's, June 28, 30, July 1. CAMBRIDGE UNIVERSITY drew with OXFORD UNIVERSITY (See Other Matches at Lord's).

UAU CHAMPIONSHIP, 1980

Quarter-finals
Liverpool beat London School of Economics by 39 runs. Liverpool 127 (J. Atkinson 54); London School of Economics 88.
  Loughborough beat Lancaster by nine wickets. Lancaster 104; Loughborough 105 for one (T. Robery 63).
  Leicester beat Bangor by eight wickets. Bangor 93 (G. Phoseby four for 28); Leicester 94 for two.
  Exeter beat Durham by three wickets. Durham 102; Exeter 103 for seven.

Semi-finals
Liverpool beat Leicester by 46 runs. Liverpool 180 for seven (60 overs); Leicester 134 (P. Harris 51).
  Exeter beat Loughborough by three wickets. Loughborough 157 (T. J. Beisiegel five for 49); Exeter 159 for seven (P. R. Downton 62).

Final
Exeter beat Liverpool by eight wickets. Liverpool 174 for seven (60 overs) (R. Davies 42 not out); Exeter 178 for two (B. F. Green 63 not out, R. M. Ellison 54 not out).

WHITBREAD SCHOLARSHIPS

The Whitbread Brewery Scholarships, first awarded in 1976, were instituted to help young cricketers further their experience by playing for a season in Australia. Scholarships have been awarded to the following:

1976-77: C. W. J. Athey (Yorkshire), I. T. Botham (Somerset), M. W. Gatting (Middlesex), G. B. Stevenson (Yorkshire).
1977-78: C. S. Cowdrey (Kent), J. E. Emburey (Middlesex), J. A. Hopkins (Glamorgan), J. D. Love (Yorkshire).
1978-79: J. P. Agnew (Leicestershire), M. W. Gatting (Middlesex), W. Larkins (Northamptonshire), C. J. Tavaré (Kent).
1979-80: K. J. Barnett (Derbyshire), D. N. Patel (Worcestershire), A. C. S. Pigott (Sussex), R. G. Williams (Northamptonshire).
1980-81: N. G. B. Cook (Leicestershire), W. Hogg (Lancashire), D. M. Smith (Surrey).

LIST OF BLUES

From 1919-1980

Blues prior to 1919 are omitted, except some of special interest for personal or family reasons.

OXFORD

Aamer Hameed (Govt Coll., Punjab Univ.) 1979
Abell, G. E. B. (Marlborough) 1924, 1926-27
Allan, J. M. (Edinburgh Academy) 1953-56
Allerton, J. W. O. (Stowe) 1969
Allison, A. D. F. (Greenmore) 1970
Altham, H. S. (Repton) 1911-12
Arenhold, J. A. (Diocesan Coll., SA) 1954

Baig, A. A. (Osmania Univ.) 1959-62
Baig, M. A. (Osmania Univ.) 1962-64
Bailey, J. A. (Christ's Hospital) (Capt. in 1958) 1956-58
Ballance, T. G. L. (Uppingham) 1935, 1937
Barber, A. T. (Shrewsbury) (Capt. in 1929) 1927-29
Barker, A. H. (Charterhouse) 1964-65, 1967
Barlow, E. A. (Shrewsbury) 1932-34
Barnard, F. H. (Charterhouse) 1922, 1924
Barnes, R. G. (Harrow) 1906-07
Bartlett, J. N. (Chichester) 1946, 1951
Barton, M. R. (Winchester) 1936-37
Bell, G. F. (Repton) 1919
Belle, B. H. (Forest School) 1936
Benn, A. (Harrow) 1935
Benson, E. T. (Blundell's) 1928-29
Bettington, R. H. B. (The King's School, Parramatta) (Capt. in 1923) 1920-23
Bickmore, A. F. (Clifton) 1920-21
Bird, W. S. (Malvern) (Capt. in 1906) 1904-06
Birrell, H. B. (St Andrews, South Africa) 1953-54
Blagg, P.H. (Shrewsbury) 1939
Blaikie, K. G. (Maritzburg) 1924
Blake, P. D. S. (Eton) (Capt. in 1952) 1950-52
Bloy, N. C. F. (Dover) 1946-47
Bonham-Carter, M. (Winchester) 1902
Boobbyer, B. (Uppingham) 1949-52
Bosanquet, B. J. T. (Eton) 1898-1900
Botton, N. D. (City of Bath) 1974
Bowman, R. (Fettes) 1957
Bradshaw, W. H. (Malvern) 1930-31
Brett, P. J. (Winchester) 1929
Brettell, D. N. (Cheltenham) 1977
Brooke, R. H. J. (St Edward's, Oxford) 1932
Brooks, R. A. (Quintin) 1967
Bruce, C. N. (later Lord Aberdare) (Winchester) 1907-08
Burchnall, R. L. (Winchester) 1970-71

Bury, T. E. O. (Charterhouse) 1980
Burki, J. (Punjab Univ.) 1958-60
Burton, M. St J. (Umtali) (Capt. in 1970) 1969-71
Bush, J. E. (Magdalen Coll. Sch.) 1952
Butterworth, R. E. C. (Harrow) 1927
Campbell, A. N. (Berkhamsted) 1970)
Campbell, I. P. (Canford) 1949-50
Campbell, I. P. F. (Repton) (Capt. in 1913) 1911-13
Cantlay, C. P. T. (Radley) 1975
Carr, D. B. (Repton) (Capt. in 1950) 1949-51
Carroll, P. R. (Sydney Univ.) 1971
Cazalet, P. V. F. (Eton) 1927
Chalk, F. G. H. (Uppingham) (Capt. in 1934) 1931-34
Chesterton, G. H. (Malvern) 1949
Claughton, J. A. (King Edward's, Birmingham) (Capt. in 1978) 1976-79
Clements, S. M. (Ipswich) (Capt. in 1979) 1976, 1979
Clube, S. V. M. (St John's, Leatherhead) 1956
Corlett, S. C. (Worksop) 1971-72
Corran, A. J. (Gresham's) 1958-60
Coutts, I. D. F. (Dulwich) 1952
Cowan, R. S. (Lewes GS) 1980
Cowdrey, M. C. (Tonbridge) (Capt. in 1954) 1952-54
Coxon, A. J. (Harrow CS) 1952
Crawley, A. M. (Harrow) 1927-30
Crutchley, G. E. V. (Harrow) 1912
Curtis, I. J. (Whitgift) 1980
Cushing, V. G. B. (KCS Wimbledon) 1973
Cuthbertson, J. L. (Rugby) 1962-63

Darwall-Smith, R. F. H. (Charterhouse) 1935-38
Davidson, W. W. (Brighton) 1947-48
Davis, F. J. (Blundell's) 1963
Delisle, G. P. S. (Stonyhurst) 1955-56
de Saram, F. C. (Royal College, Colombo) 1934-35
Dillon, E. W. (Rugby) 1901-02
Divecha, R. V. (Bombay Univ.) 1950-51
Dixon, E. J. H. (St Edward's, Oxford) (Capt. in 1939) 1937-39
Donnelly, M. P. (Canterbury Univ., NZ) (Capt. in 1947) 1946-47

Khan, Imran (Worcester RGS), (Capt. in 1974) 1973-75
Kimpton, R. C. M. (Melbourne Univ.) 1935, 1937-38
Kingsley, P. G. T. (Winchester) (Capt. in 1930) 1928-30
Kinkead-Weekes, R. (Eton) 1972
Knight, D. J. (Malvern) 1914, 1919
Knight, J. M. (Oundle) 1979
Knight, N. S. (Uppingham) 1934
Knott, C. H. (Tonbridge) (Capt. in 1924) 1922-24
Knott, F. H. (Tonbridge) (Capt. in 1914) 1912-14
Knox, F. P. (Dulwich) (Capt. in 1901) 1899-1901

Lamb, T. M. (Shrewsbury) 1973-74
Lee, R. J. (Sydney Univ.) 1972-74
Legard, A. R. (Winchester) 1932, 1935
Legge, G. B. (Malvern) (Capt. in 1926) 1925-26
L'Estrange, M. L. (Sydney Univ.) 1977, 1979
Leveson Gower, H. D. G. (Winchester) (Capt. in 1896) 1893-96
Lewis, D. J. (Cape Town Univ.) 1951
Lindsay, W. O'B. (Harrow) 1931
Lloyd, M. F. D. (Magdalen Coll. Sch., Oxford) 1974
Lomas, J. M. (Charterhouse) 1938-39
Lowe, J. C. M. (Uppingham) 1907-09
Lowndes, W. G. L. F. (Eton) 1921
Lyon, B. H. (Rugby) 1922-23
Lyon, G. W. F. (Brighton) 1925

McBride, W. N. (Westminster) 1926
McCanlis, M. A. (Cranleigh) (Capt. in 1928) 1926-28
Macindoe, D. H. (Eton) (Capt. in 1946) 1937-39, 1946
McIntosh, R. I. F. (Uppingham) 1927-28
M'Iver, C. D. (Forest School) 1903-04
McKinna, G. H. (Manchester GS) 1953
Majendie, N. L. (Winchester) 1962-63
Mallett, A. W. H. (Dulwich) 1947-48
Manasseh, M. (Epsom) 1964
Marie, G. V. (Univ. of Western Australia) 1978 (Capt. in 1979, but injury prevented him playing v Cambridge)
Marks, V. J. (Blundell's) (Capt. in 1976-77) 1975-78
Marshall, J. C. (Rugby) 1953
Marsham, A. J. B. (Eton) 1939
Marsham, C. D. B. (Private) (Capt. in 1857-58) 1854-58
Marsham, C. H. B. (Eton) (Capt. in 1902) 1900-02
Marsham, C. J. B. (Private) 1851
Marsham, R. H. B. (Private) 1856
Marsland, G. P. (Rossall) 1954
Martin, J. D. (Magdalen Coll. Sch.) (Capt. in 1965) 1962-63, 1965
Matthews, M. H. (Westminster) 1936-37

Maudsley, R. H. (Malvern) 1946-47
May, B. (Prince Edward's, Salisbury, Rhodesia) (Capt. in 1971) 1970-72
Mayhew, J. F. N. (Eton) 1930
Melville, A. (Michaelhouse, SA) (Capt. in 1931-32) 1930-33
Melville, C. D. (Michaelhouse, SA) 1957
Metcalfe, S. G. (Leeds GS) 1956
Millener, D. J. (Auckland Univ.) 1969-70
Minns, R. E. F. (King's, Canterbury) 1962-63
Mitchell, W. M. (Dulwich) 1951-52
Mitchell-Innes, N. S. (Sedbergh) (Capt. in 1936) 1934-37
Monro, R. W. (Harrow) 1860
Moore, D. N. (Shrewsbury) (Capt. in 1931, when he did not play v Cambridge owing to illness) 1930
Morgan, A. H. (Hastings GS) 1969
Morrill, N. D. (Sandown GS and Millfield) 1979
Moulding, R. P. (Haberdashers' Aske's) 1978-80
Mountford, P. N. G. (Bromsgrove) 1963
Murray-Wood, W. (Mill Hill) 1936

Naumann, F. C. G. (Malvern) 1914, 1919
Neate, F. W. (St Paul's) 1961-62
Neser, V. H. (South African College, Cape Town) 1921
Newman, G. C. (Eton) 1926-27
Newton-Thompson, J. O. (Diocesan College, Rondebosch, SA) 1946
Niven, R. A. (Berkhamsted) 1968-69, 1973
Nunn, J. A. (Sherborne) 1926-27

O'Brien, T. C. (St Charles' College, Notting Hill) 1884-85
Oldfield, P. C. (Repton) 1932-33
Orders, J. O. D. (Winchester) 1978-80
Owen-Smith, H. G. (Diocesan College, SA) 1931-33

Palairet, L. C. H. (Repton) (Capt. in 1892-93) 1890-93
Palairet, R. C. N. (Repton) 1893-94
Pathmanathan, G. (Royal College, Colombo) 1975-78
Pataudi, Nawab of (Chief's College, Lahore) 1929-31
Pataudi, Nawab of (Winchester) (Capt. in 1961 when he did not play v Cambridge owing to a car accident and 1963) 1960, 1963
Patten, M. (Winchester) 1922-23
Paver, R. G. L. (King's, Canterbury) 1973-74
Pawson, A. C. (Winchester) 1903
Pawson, A. G. (Winchester) (Capt. in 1910) 1908-11
Pawson, H. A. (Winchester) (Capt. in 1948) 1947-48
Pearce, J. P. (Ampleforth) 1979

Pearse, G. V. (Maritzburg College, Natal) 1919
Peebles, I. A. R. (Glasgow Academy) 1930
Pershke, W. J. (Uppingham) 1938
Pether, S. (Magdalen Coll. Sch.) 1939
Phillips, J. B. (King's, Canterbury) 1955
Piachaud, J. D. (St Thomas's College, Colombo) 1958-61
Pithey, D. B. (Univ. of Capetown) 1961-62
Porter, S. R. (Peers, Littlemore) 1973
Potter, I. C. (King's, Canterbury) 1961-62
Potts, H. J. (Stand GS) 1950
Price, V. R. (Bishop's Stortford) (Capt. in 1921) 1919-22
Proud, R. B. (Winchester) 1939
Pycroft, J. (Bath) 1836

Raikes, D. C. G. (Shrewsbury) 1931
Raikes, G. B. (Shrewsbury) 1894-95
Raikes, T. B. (Winchester) 1922-24
Randolph, B. M. (Charterhouse) 1855-56
Raybould, J. G. (Leeds GS) 1959
Richardson, J. V. (Uppingham) 1925
Ridley, G. N. S. (Milton, Bulawayo, Rhodesia) (Capt. in 1967) 1965-68
Ridley, R. M. (Clifton) 1968-70
Robertson-Glasgow, R. C. (Charterhouse) 1920-23
Robinson, G. A. (Preston Cath. Coll.) 1971
Robinson, H. B. (North Shore College, Vancouver) 1947-48
Rogers, J. J. (Sedbergh) 1979-80
Ross, C. J. (Wanganui and Wellington Univ., NZ) (Capt. in 1980) 1978-80
Royle, Vernon (Rossall) 1875-76
Rucker, C. E. S. (Charterhouse) 1914
Rucker, P. W. (Charterhouse) 1919
Rudd, C. R. D. (Eton) 1949
Rumbold, J. S. (St Andrew's College, NZ) 1946

Sabine, P. N. B. (Marlborough) 1963
Sale, R. (Repton) 1910
Sale, R. (Repton) 1939, 1946
Sanderson, J. F. W. (Westminster) 1980
Saunders, C. J. (Lancing) 1964
Savage, R. Le Q. (Marlborough) 1976-78
Sayer, D. M. (Maidstone GS) 1958-60
Scott, K. B. (Winchester) 1937
Scott, M. D. (Winchester) 1957
Scott, R. S. G. (Winchester) 1931
Seamer, J. W. (Marlborough) 1934-36
Sinclair, E. H. (Winchester) 1924
Singleton, A. P. (Shrewsbury) (Capt. in 1937) 1934-37
Siviter, K. (Liverpool Coll.) 1976
Skeet, C. H. L. (St Paul's) 1920
Skene, D. (Sedbergh) 1928
Smith, A. C. (King Edward's, Birmingham) (Capt. in 1959-60) 1958-60
Smith, G. O. (Charterhouse) 1895-96
Smith, M. J. K. (Stamford) (Capt. in 1956) 1954-56

Stainton, R. G. (Malvern) 1933
Stallibrass, M. J. D. (Lancing) 1974
Stanning, J. (Winchester) 1939
Stephenson, J. S. (Shrewsbury) 1925-26
Stevens, G. T. S. (UCS) (Capt. in 1922) 1920-23
Stewart-Brown, P. H. (Harrow) 1925-26
Sutcliffe, S. P. (King George V, Southport) 1980
Sutton, M. A. (Ampleforth) 1946

Tavaré, C. J. (Sevenoaks) 1975-77
Taylor, C. H. (Westminster) 1923-26
Thackeray, P. R. (St Edward's, Oxford) 1974
Thomas, R. J. A. (Radley) 1965
Tindall, R. G. (Winchester) 1933-34
Toft, D. P. (Tonbridge) 1966-67
Topham, R. D. M. (Shrewsbury) 1976
Townsend, D. C. H. (Winchester) 1933-34
Travers, B. H. (Sydney Univ.) 1946, 1948
Tuff, F. N. (Malvern) 1910
Twining, R. H. (Eton) (Capt. in 1912) 1910-13

Van der Bijl, P. G. (Diocesan Coll., SA) 1932
Van Ryneveld, C. B. (Diocesan Coll., SA) (Capt. in 1949) 1948-50

Wagstaffe, M. C. (Rossall) 1972
Waldock, F. A. (Uppingham) 1919-20
Walford, M. M. (Rugby) 1936, 1938
Walker, D. F. (Uppingham) (Capt. in 1935) 1933-35
Waller, G. W. (Hurstpierpoint) 1974
Walsh, D. R. (Marlborough) 1967-69
Walshe, A. P. (Milton, Rhodesia) 1953, 1955-56
Walton, A. C. (Radley) (Capt. in 1957) 1955-57
Ward, H. P. (Shrewsbury) 1919, 1921
Ward, J. M. (Newcastle-u-Lyme) 1971-73
Warner, P. F. (Rugby) 1895-96
Watson, A. G. M. (St Lawrence) 1965-66, 1968
Webb, H. E. (Winchester) 1948
Webbe, A. J. (Harrow) (Capt. in 1877-78) 1875-78
Wellings, E. M. (Cheltenham) 1929, 1931
Westley, S. A. (Lancaster RGS) 1968-69
Wheatley, G. A. (Uppingham) 1946
Whitcombe, P. A. (Winchester) 1947-49
Whitcombe, P. J. (Worcester GS) 1951-52
Whitehouse, P. M. (Marlborough) 1938
Wiley, W. G. E. (Diocesan Coll. Rondebosch, SA) 1952
Williams, C. C. P. (Westminster) (Capt. in 1955) 1953-55
Wilson, P. R. B. (Milton, Rhodesia) 1968, 1970
Wilson, R. W. (Warwick) 1957

Wingfield Digby, A. R. (Sherborne) 1971, 1975-77

Winn, C. E. (King's College School, Wimbledon) 1948-51

Woodcock, R. G. (Worcester RGS) 1957-58

Wookey, S. M. (Malvern and Cambridge Univ.) 1978

Wordsworth, Chas. (Harrow) (Capt. both years, First Oxford Capt.) 1827, 1829

Worsley, D. R. (Bolton) (Capt. in 1964) 1961-64

Wrigley, M. H. (Harrow) 1949

Young, D. E. (KCS, Wimbledon) 1938

CAMBRIDGE

Acfield, D. L. (Brentwood) 1967-68

Aers, D. R. (Tonbridge) 1967

Aird, R. (Eton) 1923

Alexander, F. C. M. (Wolmer's Coll., Jamaica) 1952-53

Allbrook, M. E. (Tonbridge) 1975-78

Allen, A. W. (Eton) 1933-34

Allen, B. O. (Clifton), 1933

Allen, G. O. (Eton) 1922-23

Allom, M. J. C. (Wellington) 1927-28

Ashton, C. T. (Winchester) (Capt. in 1923) 1921-23

Ashton, G. (Winchester) (Capt. in 1921) 1919-21

Ashton, H. (Winchester) (Capt. in 1922) 1920-22

Atkins, G. (Challenors) 1960

Austin, H. M. (Melbourne) 1924

Aworth, C. J. (Tiffin), (Capt. in 1975) 1973-75

Bagnell, H. F. (Harrow) 1923

Bailey, T. E. (Dulwich) 1947-48

Baker, R. K. (Brentwood) 1973-74

Bannister, C. S. (Caterham) 1976

Barber, R. W. (Ruthin) 1956-57

Barford, M. T. (Eastbourne) 1970-71

Bartlett, H. T. (Dulwich) (Capt. in 1936) 1934-36

Beaumont, D. J. (Bridgford GS) 1978

Benke, A. F. (Cheltenham) 1962

Bennett, B. (Welbeck) 1979

Bennett, C. T. (Harrow) (Capt. in 1925) 1923, 1925

Bernard, J. R. (Clifton) 1958-60

Bhatia, A. N. (Doon, India) 1969

Blake, J. P. (Aldenham) 1939

Bligh, Ivo F. W. (Lord Darnley) (Eton) (Capt. in 1881) 1878-81

Block, S. A. (Marlborough) 1929

Blofeld, H. C. (Eton) 1959

Blundell, E. D. (Waitaki, NZ) 1928-29

Bodkin, P. E. (Bradfield) (Capt. in 1946) 1946

Boyd-Moss, R. J. (Bedford) 1980

Brearley, J. M. (City of London) (Capt. in 1963-64) 1961-64

Brocklebank, J. M. (Eton) 1936

Brodhurst, A. H. (Malvern) 1939

Brodie, J. B. (Union HS, SA) 1960

Brodrick, P. D. (Royal GS, Newcastle) 1961

Bromley, R. C. (Christchurch, NZ) 1970

Brooker, M. E. W. (Burnley GS) 1976

Brooke-Taylor, G. P. (Cheltenham) 1919-20

Brown, F. R. (Leys) 1930-31

Browne, F. B. R. (Aldro School and Eastbourne Coll.) 1922

Bryan, J. L. (Rugby) 1921

Burnett, A. C. (Lancing) 1949

Burnup, C. J. (Malvern) 1896-98

Bushby, M. H. (Dulwich) (Capt. in 1954) 1952-54

Butterworth, H. R. W. (Rydal Mount) 1929

Calthorpe, F. S. G. (Repton) 1912-14, 1919

Cameron, J. H. (Taunton) 1935-37

Cangley, B. G. (Felsted) 1947

Carling, P. G. (Kingston GS) 1968, 1970

Carris, B. D. (Harrow) 1938-39

Carris, H. E. (Mill Hill) 1930

Cawston, E. (Lancing) 1932

Chambers, R. E. J. (Forest) 1966

Chapman, A. P. F. (Oakham and Uppingham) 1920-22

Christopherson, J. C. (Uppingham) 1931

Close, P. A. (Haileybury) 1965

Cobbold, P. W. (Eton) 1896

Cobbold, R. H. (Eton) 1927

Cobden, F. C. (Harrow) 1870-72

Cockett, J. A. (Aldenham) 1951

Coghlan, T. B. L. (Rugby) 1960

Colbeck, L. G. (Marlborough) 1905-06

Collins, D. C. (Wellington Coll. NZ) 1910-11

Comber, J. T. H. (Marlborough) 1931-33

Conradi, E. R. (Oundle) 1946

Cook, G. W. (Dulwich) 1957-58

Cooper, N. H. C. (St Brendans, Bristol and East Anglia Univ.) 1979

Cosh, N. J. (Dulwich) 1966-68

Cottrell, G. A. (Kingston GS) (Capt. in 1968) 1966-68

Cottrell, P. R. (Chislehurst and Sidcup GS) 1979

Coverdale, S. P. (St Peter's, York) 1974-77

Craig, E. J. (Charterhouse) 1961-63

Crawford, N. C. (Shrewsbury) 1979-80

Crawley, E. (Harrow) 1887-89

Crawley, L. G. (Harrow) 1923-25

Croft, P. D. (Gresham's) 1955
Crookes, D. V. (Michaelhouse, SA) 1953
Cumberlege, B. S. (Durham) 1913

Daniell, J. (Clifton) 1899-1901
Daniels, D. M. (Rutlish) 1964-65
Datta, P. B. (Asutosh Coll., Calcutta) 1947
Davies, G. B. (Rossall) 1913-14
Davies, J. G. W. (Tonbridge) 1933-34
Dawson, E. W. (Eton) (Capt. in 1927) 1924-27
Day, S. H. (Malvern) (Capt. in 1901) 1899-1902
Dewes, A. R. (Dulwich) 1978
Dewes, J. G. (Aldenham) 1948-50
Dexter, E. R. (Radley) (Capt. in 1958) 1956-58
Dickinson, D. C. (Clifton) 1953
Dickinson, P. J. (KCS, Wimbledon) 1939
Doggart, A. G. (Bishop's Stortford) 1921-22
Doggart, G. H. G. (Winchester) (Capt. in 1950) 1948-50
Doggart, S. J. G. (Winchester) 1980
Douglas-Pennant, S. (Eton) 1959
Downes, K. D. (Rydal) 1939
Duleepsinhji, K. S. (Cheltenham) 1925-26, 1928

Edmonds, P. H. (Cranbrook) (Capt. in 1973) 1971-73
Elgood, B. C. (Bradfield) 1948
Enthoven, H. J. (Harrow) (Capt. in 1926) 1923-26
Estcourt, N. S. D. (Plumtree, Southern Rhodesia) 1954
Evans, R. G. (King Edward, Bury St Edmunds) 1921

Fabian, A. H. (Highgate) 1929-31
Fairbairn, G. A. (Church of England GS, Geelong) 1913-14, 1919
Falcon, M. (Harrow) (Capt. in 1910) 1908-11
Farnes, K. (Royal Liberty School, Romford) 1931-33
Fiddian-Green, C. A. (Leys) 1921-22
Field, M. N. (Bablake) 1974
Fitzgerald, J. F. (St Brendan's) 1968
Ford, A. F. J. (Repton) 1878-81
Ford, F. G. J. (Repton) (Capt. in 1889) 1887-90
Ford, W. J. (Repton) 1873
Fosh, M. K. (Harrow) 1977-78
Francis, T. E. S. (Tonbridge) 1925
Franklin, W. B. (Repton) 1912
Fraser, T. W. (Jeppe, SA) 1937
Fry, K. R. B. (Cheltenham) 1904

Gardiner, S. J. (St Andrew's, Bloemfontein) 1978
Gibb, P. A. (St Edward's, Oxford) 1935-38
Gibson, C. H. (Eton) 1920-21
Gillespie, D. W. (Uppingham) 1939

Gilligan, A. E. R. (Dulwich) 1919-20
Goodfellow, A. (Marlborough) 1961-62
Goonesena, G. (Royal Coll., Colombo) (Capt. in 1957) 1954-57
Grace, W. G., junr (Clifton) 1895-96
Grant, G. C. (Trinidad) 1929-30
Grant, R. S. (Trinidad) 1933
Green, D. J. (Burton GS) (Capt. in 1959) 1957-59
Greig, I. A. (Queen's Coll., SA) (Capt. in 1979) 1977-79
Grierson, H. (Bedford) 1911
Griffith, M. G. (Marlborough) 1963-65
Griffith, S. C. (Dulwich) 1935
Griffiths, W. H. (Charterhouse) 1946-48
Grimshaw, J. W. T. (King William's Coll., Isle of Man) 1934-35

Hadingham, A. W. G. (St Paul's) 1932
Hadley, R. J. (Sanfields) 1971-73
Hall, J. E. (Ardingly) 1969
Hall, P. J. (Geelong) 1949
Harbinson, W. K. (Marlborough) 1929
Harvey, J. R. W. (Marlborough) 1965
Hawke, M. B. (Lord) (Eton) (Capt. in 1885) 1822-83, 1885
Hayes, P. J. (Brighton) 1974-77
Hays, D. L. (Highgate) 1966, 1968
Hayward, W. I. D. (St Peter's Coll., Adelaide) 1950-51, 1953
Haywood, D. C. (Nottingham HS) 1968
Hazelrigg, A. G. (Eton) (Capt. in 1932) 1930-32
Hewan, G. E. (Marlborough) 1938
Hignell, A. J. (Denstone) (Capt. in 1977-78) 1975-78
Hill-Wood, W. W. (Eton) 1922
Hobson, B. S. (Taunton) 1946
Hodson, P. R. (Q.E. Wakefield) 1972-73
Holliday, D. C. (Oundle) 1979-80
Hopley, G. W. V. (Harrow) 1912
Hotchkin, N. S. (Eton) 1935
Howat, M. G. (Abingdon) 1977, 1980
Howland, C. B. (Dulwich) (Capt. in 1960) 1958-60
Hughes, G. (Cardiff HS) 1965
Human, J. H. (Repton) (Capt. in 1934) 1932-34
Human, R. H. C. (Repton) 1930-31
Hunt, R. G. (Aldenham) 1937
Hurd, A. (Chigwell) 1958-60
Hutton, R. A. (Repton) 1962-64

Insole, D. J. (Monoux, Walthamstow) (Capt. in 1949) 1947-49
Irvine, L. G. (Taunton) 1926-27

Jackson, E. J. W. (Winchester) 1974-76
Jackson, F. S. (Harrow) (Capt. in 1892-93) 1890-93
Jagger, S. T. (Malvern) 1925-26
James, R. M. (St John's, Leatherhead) 1956-58

Jameson, T. E. N. (Taunton) 1970
Jarrett, D. W. (Wellington and Oxford Univ.) 1976
Jefferson, R. I. (Winchester) 1961
Jenner, Herbert (Eton) (Capt. in 1827, First Cambridge Capt.) 1827
Jephson, D. L. A. (Manor House, Clapham) 1890-92
Jessop, G. L. (Cheltenham GS) (Capt. in 1899) 1896-99
Johnson, P. D. (Nottingham HS) 1970-72
Johnstone, C. P. (Rugby) 1919-20
Jones, A. O. (Bedford Modern) 1893
Jorden, A. M. (Monmouth) (Capt. in 1969-70) 1968-70
Judd, A. K. (St Paul's) 1927

Kaye, M. A. C. P. (Harrow) 1938
Kelland, P. A. (Repton) 1950
Kemp-Welch, G. D. (Charterhouse) (Capt. in 1931) 1929-31
Kendall, M. P. (Gillingham HS) 1972
Kenny, C. J. M. (Ampleforth) 1952
Kerslake, R. C. (Kingswood) 1963-64
Khan, Jahangir (Lahore) 1933-36
Khan, Majid Jahangir (Lahore) (Capt. in 1971-72) 1970-72
Khanna, B. C. (Lahore) 1937
Killick, E. T. (St Paul's) 1928-30
King, F. (Dulwich) 1934
Kirby, D. (St Peter's, York) (Capt. in 1961) 1959-61
Kirkman, M. C. (Dulwich) 1963
Knight, R. D. V. (Dulwich) 1967-70
Knightley-Smith, W. (Highgate) 1953

Lacey, F. E. (Sherborne) 1882
Lacy-Scott, D. G. (Marlborough) 1946
Lagden, R. B. (Marlborough) 1912-14
Langley, J. D. A. (Stowe) 1938
Lawrence, A. S. (Harrow) 1933
Lewis, A. R. (Neath GS) (Capt. in 1962) 1960-62
Lewis, L. K. (Taunton) 1953
Littlewood, D. J. (Enfield GS) 1978
Lockhart, J. H. B. (Sedbergh) 1909-10
Longfield, T. C. (Aldenham) 1927-28
Longrigg, E. F. (Rugby) 1927-28
Lowe, R. G. H. (Westminster) 1925-27
Lowry, T. C. (Christ's College, NZ) (Capt. in 1924) 1923-24
Lumsden, V. R. (Munro College, Jamaica) 1953-55
Lyon, M. D. (Rugby) 1921-22
Lyttelton, 4th Lord (Eton) 1838
Lyttelton, Alfred (Eton) (Capt. in 1879) 1876-79
Lyttelton, C. F. (Eton) 1908-09
Lyttelton, C. G. (Lord Cobham) (Eton) 1861-64
Lyttelton, Edward (Eton) (Capt. in 1878) 1875-78
Lyttelton, G. W. S. (Eton) 1866-67

McAdam, K. P. W. J. (Millfield) 1965-66
MacBryan, J. C. W. (Exeter) 1920
McCarthy, C. N. (Pietermaritzburg Coll., SA) 1952
McDowall, J. I. (Rugby) 1969
MacGregor, G. (Uppingham) (Capt. in 1891) 1888-91
Machin, R. S. (Lancing) 1927
Mackinnon, F. A. (Harrow) 1870
McLachlan, A. A. (St. Peter's, Adelaide) 1964-65
McLachlan, I. M. (St Peter's Adelaide) 1957-58
Malalasekera, V. P. (RC, Colombo) 1966-67
Mann, E. W. (Harrow) (Capt. in 1905) 1903-05
Mann, F. G. (Eton) 1938-39
Mann, F. T. (Malvern) 1909-11
Mann, J. E. F. (Geelong) 1924
Mansfield, J. W. (Winchester) 1883-84
Marlar, R. G. (Harrow) (Capt. in 1953) 1951-53
Marriott, C. S. (St Columba's) 1920-21
Mathews, K. P. A. (Felsted) 1951
May, P. B. H. (Charterhouse) 1950-52
Melluish, M. E. L. (Rossall) (Capt. in 1956) 1954-56
Meyer, R. J. O. (Haileybury) 1924-26
Miller, M. E. (Prince Henry GS) 1963
Mills, J. M. (Oundle) (Capt. in 1948) 1946-48
Mills, J. P. C. (Oundle) 1979-80
Mischler, N. M. (St Paul's) 1946-47
Mitchell, F. (St Peter's, York) (Capt. in 1896) 1894-97
Morgan, J. T. (Charterhouse) (Capt. in 1930) 1928-30
Morgan, M. N. (Marlborough) 1954
Morris, R. J. (Blundell's) 1949
Morrison, J. S. F. (Charterhouse) (Capt. in 1919) 1912, 1914, 1919
Moses, G. (Cwmtawe) 1974
Moylan, A. C. D. (Clifton) 1927
Mubarak, A. M. (Royal Coll., Colombo) 1978-80
Murray, D. L. (Queen's RC, Trinidad) (Capt. in 1966) 1965-66
Murrills, T. J. (Leys), (Capt. in 1976) 1973-74, 1976

Naumann, J. H. (Malvern) 1913, 1919
Nelson, R. P. (St George's, Harpenden) 1936
Nevin, M. R. S. (Winchester) 1969
Norris, D. W. (Harrow) 1967-68

O'Brien, R. (Wellington) 1955-56
Odendaal, A. (Queen's Coll., SA) 1980
Owen-Thomas, D. R. (KCS Wimbledon) 1969-72

Palfreman, A. B. (Nottingham) 1966
Parker, G. W. (Crypt, Gloucester) (Capt. in 1935) 1934-35

Parker, P. W. G. (Collyer's GS) 1976-78
Parry, D. M. (Merchant Taylors') 1931
Parsons, A. B. D. (Brighton) 1954-55
Partridge, N. E. (Malvern) 1920
Paull, R. K. (Millfield) 1967
Pawle, J. H. (Harrow) 1936-37
Payne, A. U. (St Edmund's, Canterbury) 1925
Payne, M. W. (Wellington) (Capt. in 1907) 1904-07
Payton, W. E. G. (Nottingham HS) 1937
Pearman, H. (King Alfred's) 1969
Pearson, A. J. G. (Downside) 1961-63
Peck, I. G. (Bedford) (Capt. in 1980) 1980
Pelham, A. G. (Eton) 1934
Pepper, J. (Leys) 1946-48
Pieris, P. I. (St Thomas, Colombo) 1957-58
Ponniah, C. E. M. (St Thomas, Colombo) 1967-69
Ponsonby, F. G. B. (Lord Bessborough) (Harrow) 1836
Popplewell, N. F. M. (Radley) 1977-79
Popplewell, O. B. (Charterhouse) 1949-51
Powell, A. G. (Charterhouse) 1934
Pretlove, J. F. (Alleyn's) 1954-56
Prideaux, R. M. (Tonbridge) 1958-60
Pritchard, G. C. (King's, Canterbury) 1964
Pringle, D. R. (Felsted) 1979-80
Pryer, B. J. K. (City of London) 1948
Pyemont, C. P. (Marlborough) 1967

Ranjitsinhji, K. S. (Rajkumar Coll., India) 1893
Ratcliffe, A. (Rydal School) 1930-32
Reddy, N. S. K. (Doon School, Doura Dun, India) 1959-61
Rees-Davies, W. R. (Eton) 1938
Riddell, V. H. (Clifton) 1926
Rimell, A. G. J. (Charterhouse) 1949-50
Robins, R. W. V. (Highgate) 1926-28
Roebuck, P. M. (Millfield) 1975-77
Roopnaraine, R. (Queen's RC, BG) 1965-66
Rose, M. H. (Pocklington) 1963-64
Ross, N. P. G. (Marlborough) 1969
Rotherham, G. A. (Rugby) 1919
Rought-Rought, D. C. (Private) 1937
Rought-Rought, R. C. (Private) 1930, 1932
Roundell, J. (Winchester) 1973
Russell, D. P. (West Park, St Helens) 1974-75
Russell, S. G. (Tiffin) (Capt. in 1967) 1965-67
Russom, N. (Huish's GS) 1980

Seabrook, F. J. (Haileybury) (Capt. in 1928) 1926-28
Seager, G. (Peterhouse, Rhodesia) 1971
Selvey, M. W. W. (Battersea GS) 1971
Shelmerdine, G. O. (Cheltenham) 1922
Sheppard, D. S. (Sherborne) (Capt. in 1952) 1950-52
Sherwell, N. B. (Tonbridge) 1923-25

Shirley, W. R. (Eton) 1924
Shirreff, A. C. (Dulwich) 1939
Short, R. L. (Denstone) 1969
Shuttleworth, G. M. (Queen Elizabeth GS) 1946-48
Silk, D. R. W. (Christ's Hospital) (Capt. in 1955) 1953-55
Singh, S. (Khalsa and Punjab U.) 1955-56
Sinker, N. D. (Winchester) 1966
Slack, J. K. E. (UCS) 1954
Smith, C. S. (William Hulme's GS) 1954-57
Smith, D. J. (Stockport GS) 1955-56
Smyth, R. I. (Sedbergh) 1973-75
Snowden, W. (Merchant Taylors', Crosby) (Capt. in 1974) 1972-75
Spencer, J. (Brighton and Hove GS) 1970-72
Steele, H. K. (King's Coll., NZ) 1971-72
Stevenson, M. H. (Rydal) 1949-52
Studd, C. T. (Eton) (Capt. in 1883) 1880-83
Studd, G. B. (Eton) (Capt. in 1882) 1879-82
Studd, J. E. K. (Eton) (Capt. in 1884) 1881-84
Studd, P. M. (Harrow) (Capt. in 1939) 1937-39
Studd, R. A. (Eton) 1895
Subba Row, R. (Whitgift) 1951-53
Surridge, D. (Richard Hale and Southampton Univ.) 1979
Swift, B. T. (St Peter's, Adelaide) 1957

Taylor, C. R. V. (Birkenhead) 1971-73
Thompson, J. R. (Tonbridge) 1938-39
Thompson, R. H. (Bexhill) 1961-62
Thwaites, I. G. (Eastbourne Coll.) 1964
Tindall, M. (Harrow) (Capt. in 1937) 1935-37
Tomlinson, W. J. V. (Felsted) 1923
Tordoff, G. G. (Normanton GS) 1952
Trapnell, B. M. W. (UCS) 1946
Tufnell, N. C. (Eton) 1909-10
Turnbull, M. J. (Downside) (Capt. in 1929) 1926, 1928-29

Urquhart, J. R. (King Edward VI School, Chelmsford) 1948

Valentine, B. H. (Repton) 1929

Wait, O. J. (Dulwich), 1949, 1951
Warr, J. J. (Ealing County GS) (Capt. in 1951) 1949-52
Watts, H. E. (Downside) 1947
Webster, J. (Bradford GS) 1939
Webster, W. H. (Highgate) 1932
Weedon, M. J. H. (Harrow) 1962
Wells, T. U. (King's Coll., NZ) 1950
Wheatley, O. S. (King Edward's, Birmingham) 1957-58
Wheelhouse, A. (Nottingham HS) 1959
White, A. F. T. (Uppingham) 1936
White, A. H. (Geelong) 1924

White, R. C. (Hilton, SA) (Capt. in 1965) 1962-65
Wilcox, D. R. (Dulwich) (Capt. in 1933) 1931-33
Wild, J. V. (Taunton) 1938
Wilenkin, B. C. G. (Harrow) 1956
Wilkin, C. L. (St Kitts GS) 1970
Willard, M. J. L. (Judd) 1959-61
Willatt, G. L. (Repton) (Capt. in 1947) 1946-47
Wilson, G. (Harrow) 1919
Windows, A. R. (Clifton) 1962-64
Winlaw, R. de W. K. (Winchester) 1932-34

Wood, G. E. C. (Cheltenham) (Capt. in 1920) 1914, 1919-20
Wookey, S. M. (Malvern) 1975-76
Wooller, W. (Rydal) 1935-36
Wright, C. C. G. (Tonbridge), 1907-08
Wright, P. A. (Wellingborough) 1922-24
Wright, S. (Mill Hill) 1973
Wykes, N. G. (Oundle) 1928

Yardley, N. W. D. (St Peter's, York) (Capt. in 1938) 1935-38
Young, R. A. (Repton) (Capt. in 1908) 1905-08

I ZINGARI RESULTS, 1980

Matches 29 – Won 8, Lost 5, Drawn 11. Abandoned 5.

May 10	Honourable Artillery Company	Won by six wickets
May 11	Staff College	Lost by six wickets
May 17	Royal Engineers	Won by seven wickets
May 18	Royal Artillery	Won by two wickets
May 24	Eton Ramblers	Lost by four wickets
May 24	Harrow School	Drawn
May 25	Royal Military Academy	Lost by seven wickets
June 7	Charterhouse School	Drawn
June 7	Hurlingham CC	Lost by 43 runs
June 8	Lord Porchester's XI	Drawn
June 14	P. L. B. Stoddart's XI	Won by 36 runs
June 17	Winchester College	Drawn
June 21	Guards Brigade CC	Won by two wickets
June 22	Lavinia, Duchess of Norfolk's XI	Won by seven wickets
June 28	Green Jackets Club	Abandoned
June 29	Old Wykehamists	Drawn
July 5	Eton College 1st XI	Drawn
July 5	Eton College 2nd XI (XXII)	Drawn
July 6	J. H. Pawle's XI	Drawn
July 13	London New Zealand CC	Drawn
July 19	Bradfield Waifs	Abandoned
July 19	Gentlemen of Leicestershire	Abandoned
July 20	Captain R. H. Hawkins' XI	Abandoned
July 27	Royal Armoured Corps	Won by 38 runs
August 2	South Wales Hunt's XI	Drawn
August 10	R. Leigh Pemberton's XI	Lost by nine wickets
August 30	Hampshire Hogs	Abandoned
September 7	Rickling Green CC	Won by four wickets
September 13	J. H. Weatherley's XI	Drawn

OTHER MATCHES, 1980

At Belfast, June 7, 8, 9 (not first-class). Ireland won by 175 runs. Ireland 256 for eight dec. (R. I. Johnstone 72; R. LeQ. Savage five for 71) and 178 for five dec. (B. A. O'Brien 54, I. J. Anderson 51 not out); MCC 166 (R. J. Lanchbury 57) and 93 (J. W. E. Elder six for 43, J. D. Monteith four for 42).

At Guildford, June 25, 26, 27 (not first-class). Cambridge University won by 8 runs. Cambridge University 257 for eight dec. (A. M. Mubarak 74, J. P. C. Mills 72; F. J. Titmus three for 37) and 325 for seven dec. (J. P. C. Mills 89, S. J. G. Doggart 63, A. M. Mubarak 61, D. R. Pringle 54; I. A. Greig three for 80); D. H. Robins' XI 323 for four dec. (C. L. Smith 131, G. D. Mendis 88, T. E. Jesty 55 not out) and 251 (T. E. Jesty 88, C. L. Smith 60, I. A. Greig 45; M. G. Howat five for 61, N. Russom three for 79).

THE TILCON TROPHY

Rain again affected the Tilcon Trophy matches at the Harrogate Festival, causing the first match to be abandoned in the fifteenth over and interrupting the other two. In the final, Kent, without Asif, Knott, Tavaré, Underwood and Woolmer, were completely outplayed by Glamorgan, who profited from the all-round performance of Holmes, adventurously promoted to number three in the order when Glamorgan were put in to bat.

June 25. Kent won on the toss of a coin. Kent 19 for one when rain stopped play. Derbyshire did not bat.

June 26. Glamorgan won by ten wickets after the match was reduced to 34 overs with a target of 143 runs. Yorkshire 176 for four (42 overs) (C. W. J. Athey 94, P. G. Ingham 31 not out); Glamorgan 146 for no wkt (30.5 overs) (J. A. Hopkins 76 not out, A. Jones 61 not out). *Man of the Match*: C. W. J. Athey.

June 27. Final. Glamorgan won by 54 runs. Glamorgan 276 for four (55 overs) (G. C. Holmes 87 not out, Javed Miandad 68, N. G. Featherstone 61, A. Jones 38); Kent 222 (48.4 overs) (A. G. E. Ealham 59, M. Benson 34; E. A. Moseley four for 22, G. C. Holmes four for 60). *Man of the Match*: G. C. Holmes.

At Rathmines, Dublin, July 27, 28, 29 (not first-class). Drawn. Ireland 288 for six dec. (I. J. Anderson 105 not out, J. F. Short 54, M. F. Cohen 43; H. Slade three for 55, G. P. Ellis three for 76) and 224 for seven dec. (B. A. O'Brien 70, I. J. Anderson 47, J. D. Monteith 33 not out); Wales 330 for seven dec. (W. Harries 79, G. P. Ellis 67, J. Bell 55 not out, D. Samuel 46, D. A. Jones 41; J. W. E. Elder three for 62, M. Halliday three for 97) and 76 for three (G. P. Ellis 33).

SCOTLAND v IRELAND

At Coatbridge, August 16, 17, 18. Drawn. The loss, on the second day, of more than four hours play ruined what promised to be an interesting struggle. Scotland, put in on a damp wicket, recovered from an unpromising start, thanks to an immaculately controlled innings from Racionzer. They then collapsed to 132 for six before Warner and Moir added 79 for the seventh wicket. Runs were difficult to come by and the Scots took 131.5 overs to complete their innings, leaving Ireland to face only two overs before the close. Rain and bad light restricted play to just 42 overs on the Sunday, when Ireland took their total to 103 for two. The visitors were quickly dismissed on the final day but Scotland were struggling at 36 for four at lunch as tight bowling held them in check. Their declaration left Ireland seventy-two minutes plus twenty overs to score 184. Clark claimed two early wickets but Short and Anderson steered Ireland safely to a draw.

Scotland

T. B. Racionzer c Corlett b Monteith	61	– c Bushe b Corlett	20
R. G. Swan b Elder	5	– c Short b Corlett	0
D. L. Bell c Short b Halliday	39	– not out	17
D. L. Hays c Cohen b Monteith	14	– b Corlett	8
C. J. Warner c and b Halliday	48	– lbw b Corlett	3
W. A. Donald c Bushe b Halliday	0		
†A. Steele lbw b Monteith	4		
D. G. Moir c Harpur b Monteith	44	– lbw b Corlett	26
*G. F. Goddard not out	14		
F. Robertson b Halliday	0		
J. Clark lbw b Monteith	15		
B 2,1-b 2, n-b 4	8	B 1,1-b 1	2

1/16 2/108 3/114 4/127   **252**   1/5 2/17 3/32   (5 wkts dec.) **76**
5/127 6/132 7/211 8/227 9/229   4/36 5/76

Bowling: *First Innings*—Corlett 17–6–32–0; Elder 20–7–36–1; Monteith 42.5–15–81–5; Halliday 39–19–66–4; Reith 3–1–8–0; Anderson 10–2–21–0. *Second Innings*—Corlett 13.3–4–32–5; Elder 13–1–42–0.

Ireland

J. F. Short c Hays b Robertson	1	– not out	44
M. S. Reith c Warner b Moir	59	– b Clark	4
B. A. O'Brien lbw b Clark	33	– c Moir b Clark	3
I. J. Anderson c Bell b Clark	13	– not out	22
T. Harpur c Warner b Moir	4		
*J. D. Monteith b Clark	6		
M. F. Cohen c Swan b Clark	0		
S. C. Corlett run out	13		
M. Halliday b Moir	0		
J. W. G. Elder c Goddard b Moir	6		
†E. A. Bushe not out	0		
L-b 8, w 1, n-b 1	10	B 2,1-b 1, n-b 1	4

1/5 2/93 3/112 4/115   **145**   1/22 2/28   (2 wkts) **77**
5/125 6/125 7/131 8/131 9/141

Bowling: *First Innings*—Goddard 12–1–31–0; Robertson 12–3–32–1; Clark 19–8–29–4; Moir 22–7–43–4; *Second Innings*—Goddard 8–2–13–0; Robertson 5–0–12–0; Clark 9–2–13–2; Moir 12–2–35–0.

Umpires: T. W. Kerr and W. B. Smith.

THE FENNER TROPHY

The Scarborough Festival was dealt a double blow in 1980, first with the decision of J. H. Fenner Ltd, the Hull engineering firm, to withdraw their sponsorship after the 1981 competition, and then with the abandonment after lunch of the final, between Hampshire and Leicestershire, because of rain.

August 27. Hampshire won by 72 runs. Hampshire 201 (50 overs) (M. C. J. Nicholas 94, C. L. Smith 45; P. Carrick three for 28); Yorkshire 129 (38.5 overs) (R. G. Lumb 50; N. G. Cowley four for 17). *Man of the Match*: M. C. J. Nicholas.

August 28. Leicestershire won by 107 runs. Leicestershire 160 (50 overs) (P. B. Clift 38, T. J. Boon 37; C. M. Wells three for 47); Sussex 53 (16.4 overs) (J. P. Agnew five for 23, P. B. Clift three for 0). *Man of the Match*: J. P. Agnew.

August 29. Final. No result. Leicestershire 135 for five (33 overs) (B. Dudleston 39, B. F. Davison 39). Hampshire did not bat.

GILLETTE CUP, 1980

The eighteenth and last Gillette Cup – the same competition will be sponsored in 1981 by the National Westminster Bank – was won for the second time in four years by Middlesex. They received £6,500 as well as the Cup, which has been presented to Lord's. Surrey, who had won a thrilling quarter-final against Essex, took £3,000 as runners-up. The losing semi-finalists won £1,500 each, the losing quarter-finalists £750 each. One of the reasons Gillette gave for ending their sponsorship of this, the original limited-overs competition, was that it had come to be identified not so much with razor blades, or any of their many other products, but with cricket.

FIRST ROUND

DEVON v CORNWALL

At Exeter, July 2. Devon won by 145 runs. Devon convincingly won this contest between West-Country rivals in spite of an unpromising start when Jeff Tolchard was dismissed by the fourth ball of the game. A score of 110 for one off 40 overs was few enough to make Green's 53 in fifteen overs an important contribution. When Cornwall batted Yeabsley struck in his second over, having their chief hope Dunstan caught at slip cheaply. Goulding hurried through the middle order and two run outs sent Cornwall to swift defeat, with only Wilcock giving the innings some substance. Wallen was named Man of the Match for his impressive century.

Devon

*B. L. Matthews b Toseland	32	E. Picton not out	2
†J. G. Tolchard b Johns	4		
G. Wallen c Willetts b Trenwith	104	B 1, l-b 7, w 4, n-b 10	22
B. C. Green c Wilcock b Trenwith	54		
R. F. Harriott c Coombe b Trenwith	11	1/5 2/120 (5 wkts, 60 overs) 229	
R. C. Tolchard not out	0	3/202 4/224 5/226	

A. W. Allin, D. I. Yeabsley, M. J. Goulding and I. C. Roberts did not bat.

Bowling: Johns 12–1–41–1; Machin 12–4–23–0; Trenwith 12–3–51–3; Toseland 12–2–44–1; Coombe 12–1–48–0.

Cornwall

E. G. Wilcock b Goulding	43	D. A. Toseland c Green b Goulding	1
F. T. Willetts c J. G. Tolchard b Yeabsley	1	P. I. Johns c Green b Goulding	0
*M. S. T. Dunstan c Matthews b Yeabsley	1	M. O. Trenwith not out	14
		†W. J. Lawry absent ill	0
C. J. Trudgeon run out	9		
N. G. Cock b Goulding	5	B 2, l-b 5, w 3	10
A. Machin b Goulding	0	1/2 2/5 3/24 4/50 (37.1 overs) 84	
P. A. Coombe run out	0	5/50 6/53 7/61 8/61 9/84	

Bowling: Roberts 7–1–11–0; Yeabsley 9–5–15–2; Goulding 10.1–4–21–5; Allin 7–4–19–0; Green 4–2–8–0.

Umpires: K. E. Palmer and R. Palmer.

MIDDLESEX v IRELAND

At Lord's, July 2. Middlesex won by five wickets. Ireland's previous experiences of Lord's ensured that they would not be overawed, and their performance in their first competitive game was highly creditable. Off-spinner Halliday took them to a position from which they might have reached victory against a side with less depth of batting than their opponents. Bowling an attacking line and length, he seriously embarrassed the county when he removed Brearley – who had taken twenty overs to score his 11 – Gatting and Butcher within eleven deliveries. In Ireland's innings the Middlesex new-ball bowlers each made an early strike, but Anderson and Short bravely added 68 in 24 overs. Gatting dismissed both and a static spell of 21 runs in seventeen overs followed. The innings cascaded from 99 for five to 102 when van der Bijl proved too penetrative for the lower order, taking four wickets with eleven balls. The Man of the Match award went to van der Bijl who was dropped making the winning hit.

Ireland

J. F. Short c Barlow b Gatting	33	†G. S. Murphy b Daniel	0
M. S. Reith b Daniel	0	M. Halliday lbw b van der Bijl	0
B. A. O'Brien c Brearley b van der Bijl	1	A. J. Hughes b van der Bijl	0
I. J. Anderson b Gatting	37		
D. W. Harrison b van der Bijl	11	L-b 2, w 2, n-b 2	6
I. J. Johnstone c Gould b Selvey	13		
*J. D. Monteith c Gould b van der Bijl	0	1/5 2/7 3/75 4/78 (51.4 overs) 102	
S. C. Corlett not out	1	5/99 6/99 7/100 8/101 9/102	

Bowling: Daniel 8–1–16–2; van der Bijl 10.4–5–12–5; Emburey 12–5–21–0; Selvey 7–0–16–1; Slack 4–0–17–0; Gatting 10–2–14–2.

Middlesex

*J. M. Brearley lbw b Halliday	11	V. A. P. van der Bijl not out	25
W. N. Slack lbw b Corlett	12		
C. T. Radley c O'Brien b Halliday	1	B 12, l-b 1	13
G. D. Barlow not out	39		
M. W. Gatting b Halliday	2	1/17 2/18 (5 wkts, 38.3 overs) 103	
R. O. Butcher c Reith b Halliday	0	3/57 4/65 5/67	

†I. J. Gould, J. E. Emburey, M. W. W. Selvey and W. W. Daniel did not bat.

Bowling: Corlett 5–2–13–1; Hughes 3–1–5–0; Halliday 12–3–22–4; Monteith 11.3–4–32–0; Anderson 7–1–18–0.

Umpires: C. T. Spencer and T. W. Spencer.

NOTTINGHAMSHIRE v DURHAM

At Nottingham, July 2, 3. Nottinghamshire won by four wickets. Durham came close to victory, with Nottinghamshire having to lean heavily on the experience and expertise of Harris to save the match. Durham's innings owed much to Man of the Match Wasim Raja whose 53 took just 59 minutes and included two 6s and five 4s. He shared a thrilling third-wicket stand of 82 with Atkinson but then the Durham innings fell away. When Nottinghamshire replied, the visitors hit back as leg-spinner Kippax took the wickets of Hassan and Randall in quick succession, before rain and bad light took the game into a second day. Again the Durham bowlers responded to the challenge and Nottinghamshire were in some trouble, needing 85 off the last sixteen overs with five wickets down. However, a quick-fire 25 by Hadlee and an innings of calm assurance and character by Harris saw their side to victory in the penultimate over.

Durham

S. R. Atkinson lbw b Cooper	47	†R. A. D. Mercer c Hemmings b Hacker	19
P. W. Romaines c Hassan b Hadlee	0	S. A. B. Daniels not out	2
P. J. Kippax c b Cooper	5	J. S. Wilkinson b Hacker	1
Wasim Raja c Hemmings b Hadlee	53		
*N. A. Riddell b Hacker	9	L-b 13, w 1, n-b 2	16
P. C. Birtwisle b Bore	15		
P. J. Crane c Cooper b Hacker	17	1/2 2/21 3/103 4/125 (59.1 overs) 186
B. L. Cairns lbw b Bore	2	5/131 6/152 7/154 8/181 9/183

Bowling: Hadlee 12–3–30–2; Hacker 11.1–2–30–4; Cooper 12–3–33–2; Hemmings 12–2–45–0; Bore 12–5–32–2.

Nottinghamshire

†B. Hassan c Atkinson b Kippax	16	R. J. Hadlee c Birtwisle b Wasim	25
R. T. Robinson st Mercer b Kippax	30	E. E. Hemmings not out	18
D. W. Randall b Kippax	0	L-b 4, n-b 2	6
*C. E. B. Rice c Cairns b Wasim	48		
J. D. Birch c and b Cairns	2	1/29 2/29 3/74 (6 wkts, 58.5 overs) 187
M. J. Harris not out	42	4/89 5/102 6/150

K. E. Cooper, P. J. Hacker and M. K. Bore did not bat.

Bowling: Wilkinson 11.5–4–38–0; Cairns 11–3–36–1; Kippax 12–3–25–3; Daniels 12–3–32–0; Wasim 12–1–50–2.

Umpires: D. O. Oslear and P. S. G. Stevens.

SOMERSET v WORCESTERSHIRE

At Taunton, July 2. Worcestershire won by two wickets. Somerset were put in on a dry pitch and in cloudy conditions which gave increasing help to the bowlers. They started well through Rose, Denning and Roebuck but lost their last eight wickets in 21 overs for 48 runs. After Ormrod had sustained a badly cut eyebrow while facing Botham, Worcestershire also collapsed, mainly against Gore, to 78 for six. Man of the Match Humphries led a recovery with one 6 and seven 4s and with Alleyne added a vital 46 in thirteen overs before Botham dismissed them both. Ormrod bravely returned at the fall of the seventh wicket and dominated the final decisive partnership with Pridgeon, achieving victory with four balls to spare.

Somerset

*B. C. Rose lbw b Pridgeon	38	K. F. Jennings b Alleyne	1
S. M. Gavaskar c Turner b Inchmore	15	H. R. Moseley lbw b Pridgeon	0
P. W. Denning b Younis	35	H. I. E. Gore not out	0
P. M. Roebuck lbw b Alleyne	34		
I. T. Botham c Humphries b Alleyne	3	B 1, l-b 11, w 8, n-b 4	24
V. J. Marks c Turner b Cumbes	2		
†D. J. S. Taylor c Turner b Cumbes	1	1/57 2/83 3/117 4/126 (49.1 overs) 165
D. Breakwell lbw b Pridgeon	12	5/140 6/142 7/162 8/165 9/165

Bowling: Alleyne 10–1–27–3; Inchmore 9–0–35–1; Pridgeon 9.1–3–25–3; Younis 12–1–27–1; Cumbes 9–2–27–2.

Worcestershire

*G. M. Turner b Gore 7	J. D. Inchmore run out. 9
J. A. Ormrod not out 22	H. Alleyne c Moseley b Botham. 19
P. A. Neale lbw b Gore 9	A. P. Pridgeon not out 13
E. J. O. Hemsley c Taylor b Gore 5	B 4, l-b 12, w 3 19
Younis Ahmed c Jennings b Marks 13	
D. N. Patel b Botham. 1	1/18 2/24 3/31 (8 wkts, 59.2 overs) 168
†D. J. Humphries lbw b Botham 51	4/33 5/59 6/78 7/124 8/131

J. Cumbes did not bat.

Bowling: Botham 12–5–21–3; Moseley 12–3–36–0; Gore 12–3–19–3; Jennings 10–3–35–0; Marks 8.2–3–21–1; Breakwell 5–0–17–0.

Umpires: R. S. Herman and C. Cook.

SURREY v NORTHAMPTONSHIRE

At The Oval, July 2. Surrey won by seven wickets. Man of the Match Jackman tore the heart out of the Northamptonshire batting with six for 32, taking the wickets of Larkins and Williams with successive deliveries. Clarke bowled at a sizzling pace in support and with such accuracy that his first seven overs cost only 2 runs. The visitors were 28 for six after being put in but Sarfraz effected a revival which carried the total to 142. Surrey achieved victory with only three wickets down and seven overs to spare, although only Smith (eight 4s) played with any authority.

Northamptonshire

G. Cook b Clarke. 4	Sarfraz Nawaz not out. 39
W. Larkins lbw b Jackman 5	T. M. Lamb st Richards b Cheatle. 12
R. G. Williams c Lynch b Jackman 0	B. J. Griffiths st Richards b Cheatle. 1
A. J. Lamb lbw b Jackman. 8	
P. Willey c Richards b Jackman 3	L-b 6, w 2, n-b 1 9
T. J. Yardley c Knight b Jackman 4	
†G. Sharp c Richards b Jackman 28	1/10 2/10 3/12 4/20 (59.5 overs) 141
*P. J. Watts c Roope b Knight. 28	5/27 6/28 7/81 8/88 9/139

Bowling: Clarke 12–7–9–1; Jackman 12–3–32–6; Knight 12–4–24–1; Pocock 12–0–21–0; Smith 6–0–32–0; Cheatle 5.5–0–14–2.

Surrey

A. R. Butcher c Willey b T. M. Lamb . . . 16	G. R. J. Roope not out. 7
G. S. Clinton lbw b Griffiths 19	B 2, l-b 2, w 1, n-b 3 8
*R. D. V. Knight c A. J. Lamb b Sarfraz. 34	
D. M. Smith not out 59	1/28 2/43 3/129 (3 wkts, 43 overs) 143

M. A. Lynch, R. D. Jackman, †C. J. Richards, S. T. Clarke, P. I. Pocock and R. G. L. Cheatle did not bat.

Bowling: Sarfraz 12–0–51–1; Griffiths 11–1–27–1; T. M. Lamb 5–0–20–1; Watts 4–0–10–0; Willey 5–3–5–0; Williams 5–1–14–0; A. J. Lamb 1–0–8–0.

Umpires: H. D. Bird and R. Julian.

SUSSEX v SUFFOLK

At Hove, July 2. Sussex won by eight wickets. For the third successive year Sussex defeated Suffolk at Hove in this competition, despite brave efforts by the Minor County. Sent in to bat on a drying wicket, the visitors reached a commendable total after their two overseas players Timur Mohamed and Done had come together at 25 for three to score 120 off 30 overs.

However, later batsmen failed to consolidate, and serious fielding lapses when Sussex batted helped the home county to recover from an uncertain opening. Imran Khan was partnered by Phillipson in a match-winning stand of 126, and was nominated Man of the Match for his flamboyant innings, a beautifully judged catch to send back Timur, and his economical bowling.

Suffolk

P. C. Rice b le Roux	6	B. Mayes not out	13
A. G. Warrington c Waller b le Roux	1	†S. A. Westley c Long b le Roux	3
Timur Mohamed c Imran b Greig	85	K. Bishop not out	3
S. M. Clements b Barclay	2	B 2, l-b 5, w 4, n-b 7	18
R. P. Done b Arnold	53		
R. J. Robinson b Greig	0	1/6 2/20 3/25 (8 wkts, 60 overs) 185	
*P. H. Jones b Arnold	1	4/145 5/147 6/148 7/164 8/178	

C. Rutterford did not bat.

Bowling: Imran 11–6–9–0; le Roux 12–1–27–3; Barclay 7–1–26–1; Arnold 10–1–32–2; Greig 12–0–49–2; Waller 8–2–24–0.

Sussex

G. D. Mendis c Westley b Clements	33
T. D. Booth Jones c Westley b Done	1
C. P. Phillipson not out	70
Imran Khan not out	63
L-b 16, w 1, n-b 2	19

1/4 2/60 (2 wkts, 49.1 overs) 186

C. M. Wells, I. A. Greig, J. R. T. Barclay, G. S. le Roux, *†A. Long, G. G. Arnold and C. E. Waller did not bat.

Bowling: Rutterford 8.1–4–17–0; Done 12–3–45–1; Robinson 4–0–20–0; Jones 12–1–24–0; Clements 12–0–55–1; Mayes 1–0–6–0.

Umpires: W. E. Alley and W. L. Budd.

WARWICKSHIRE v OXFORDSHIRE

At Birmingham, July 2. Warwickshire won by 134 runs. Put in on an easy-paced wicket Warwickshire marched to a formidable 314 for six, their highest score in the competition, and the main threat to their progress into the next round was a two-hour stoppage through rain when Oxfordshire were 55 for three off 25 overs. There was spirited resistance from the visitors' captain and opening batsman Nurton, who reached an undefeated 67 in the gathering gloom as the innings closed. Amiss was named Man of the Match.

Warwickshire

D. L. Amiss b Gallop	82	A. M. Ferreira c Busby b Collis	14
K. D. Smith b Bradbury	46	S. J. Rouse not out	4
T. A. Lloyd run out	63	L-b 10, w 5, n-b 4	19
J. A. Claughton c Bradbury b Gallop	23		
†G. W. Humpage st Crossley b Busby	31	1/101 2/168 3/209 (6 wkts, 60 overs) 314	
P. R. Oliver not out	32	4/258 5/262 6/305	

D. C. Hopkins, *R. G. D. Willis and D. R. Doshi did not bat.

Bowling: Busby 12–0–49–1; Beckett 10–0–57–0; Collis 12–0–56–1; Bradbury 10–1–55–1; Densham 4–0–16–0; Gallop 12–0–62–2.

Oxfordshire

*M. D. Nurton not out	67	P. L. Bradbury lbw b Doshi	22
P. J. Densham c Humpage b Rouse	10	R. N. Busby b Willis	22
P. J. Garner c Ferreira b Willis	3	D. A. Gallop not out	19
C. J. Clements c Willis b Hopkins	5	B 4, l-b 3, w 1, n-b 7	15
M. D. Thomas lbw b Doshi	15		
B. A. Collis c Smith b Doshi	0	1/18 2/32 3/44 (8 wkts, 60 overs) 180
†A. Crossley lbw b Hopkins	2	4/79 5/79 6/82 7/115 8/140

D. Beckett did not bat.

Bowling: Willis 12–2–38–2; Rouse 11–3–23–1; Hopkins 12–3–23–2; Ferreira 12–5–24–0; Doshi 12–2–52–3; Claughton 1–0–5–0.

Umpires: B. J. Meyer and J. van Geloven.

SECOND ROUND

DERBYSHIRE v HAMPSHIRE

At Derby, July 16. Hampshire won by four wickets. A fine innings by Man of the Match Jesty, whose 118 made out of 195 was his highest score in one-day cricket, took Hampshire to a well-deserved win. The last-minute withdrawal of Hendrick through injury seemed to upset Derbyshire and, despite some late aggression by Miller, their total did not look adequate. Hampshire also struggled at first, with even Jesty playing and missing a good deal. He and Pocock added 141 in 36 overs, and when Jesty reached three figures out of 148 he joined the select band of batsmen who have made hundreds in all three one-day competitions.

Derbyshire

B. Wood c Stephenson b Graf	49	C. J. Tunnicliffe c Malone b Stevenson	1
J. G. Wright b Graf	12	†R. W. Taylor not out	0
P. N. Kirsten c Stephenson b Stevenson	29		
D. S. Steele b Malone	17	L-b 16, w 6	22
K. J. Barnett lbw b Graf	0		
*G. Miller c Nicholas b Stevenson	58	1/26 2/99 3/107 (8 wkts, 60 overs) 215
I. S. Anderson b Malone	6	4/108 5/135 6/147 7/209
J. Walters not out	21	8/212

S. Oldham did not bat.

Bowling: Graf 12–3–44–3; Stevenson 12–1–46–3; Malone 12–4–40–2; Jesty 12–3–29–0; Tremlett 12–1–34–0.

Hampshire

T. M. Tremlett c Miller b Tunnicliffe	3	N. G. Cowley run out	3
C. L. Smith c Steele b Oldham	3	†G. R. Stephenson not out	0
M. C. J. Nicholas c Steele b Walters	9	L-b 4, w 1	5
T. E. Jesty c Anderson b Oldham	118		
D. R. Turner c Kirsten b Wood	2	1/6 2/7 3/50 (6 wkts, 57.5 overs) 216
*N. E. J. Pocock not out	73	4/61 5/202 6/212

S. F. Graf, S. J. Malone and K. Stevenson did not bat.

Bowling: Tunnicliffe 12–1–37–1; Oldham 11.5–1–49–2; Wood 12–1–38–1; Walters 10–0–36–1; Miller 6–0–24–0; Steele 6–0–27–0.

Umpires: C. Cook and A. G. T. Whitehead.

LEICESTERSHIRE v ESSEX

At Leicester, July 16. Essex won by 113 runs. Leicestershire gambled on putting Essex in and suffered accordingly. They gained some hope when Denness was out early but Man of the Match McEwan celebrated his 28th birthday by scoring 119 (ten 4s and four 6s) off 130 balls. He received firm support from Gooch in a stand of 86, and from Hardie in a fourth-wicket stand of 120 in only eighteen overs, and in becoming Essex's top scorer in the competition he virtually put the game out of Leicestershire's grasp. Gower attempted to match the tempo with 14 off three balls from Gooch but Leicestershire struggled and, once Turner had broken through the early batting, wickets tumbled at regular intervals.

Essex

G. A. Gooch c Garnham b Higgs	52	N. Phillip not out	25
M. H. Denness c Higgs b Parsons	8	R. E. East not out	9
K. S. McEwan c Steele b Briers	119		
*K. W. R. Fletcher b Clift	5	B 1, l-b 5, w 4, n-b 5	15
B. R. Hardie c Parsons b Briers	65		
K. R. Pont run out	0	1/25 2/111 3/132 (7 wkts, 60 overs) 310
S. Turner b Clift	12	4/252 5/252 6/266 7/279

†N. Smith and J. K. Lever did not bat.

Bowling: Taylor 12–2–45–0; Parsons 12–1–50–1; Clift 12–1–61–2; Steele 8–0–51–0; Higgs 12–0–59–1; Briers 4–0–29–2.

Leicestershire

D. I. Gower c Gooch b Turner	39	G. J. Parsons run out	22
N. E. Briers c Gooch b Turner	8	L. B. Taylor st Smith b East	5
J. C. Balderstone run out	2	K. Higgs not out	0
*B. F. Davison c East b Pont	43		
R. W. Tolchard c McEwan b Gooch	8	B 4, l-b 11, w 2, n-b 5	22
†M. A. Garnham b Gooch	25		
J. F. Steele c Hardie b Lever	7	1/30 2/35 3/73 4/90 (52.2 overs) 197
P. B. Clift c Hardie b Pont	16	5/128 6/146 7/155 8/178 9/194

Bowling: Lever 10–3–27–1; Phillip 7–2–13–0; Turner 11–2–25–2; Gooch 12–1–56–2; Pont 12–0–54–2; East 0.2–0–0–1.

Umpires: R. Aspinall and D. G. L. Evans.

NOTTINGHAMSHIRE v MIDDLESEX

At Nottingham, July 16. Middlesex won by four wickets. Although Nottinghamshire made Middlesex fight harder than once seemed likely, a superb unbeaten 95 by Gatting assured the visitors of victory. Nottinghamshire again failed to capitalise on the promising start of 74 in 23 overs from the first-wicket pair, Todd and Robinson, and half the side were out for the addition of only another 46 as Selvey, van der Bijl and Emburey made inroads. Only a half-century partnership between Birch and Harris enabled a reasonable target to be set. Nottinghamshire struck quickly by removing Radley, but Brearley and Gatting added 90 for the second wicket to put Middlesex on course. Butcher also provided useful support for Gatting, who was named Man of the Match after steering Middlesex to victory with more than two overs to spare.

Nottinghamshire

P. A. Todd c Barlow b Selvey	41	E. E. Hemmings b Daniel	6
R. T. Robinson lbw b Selvey	32	W. K. Watson not out	2
†B. Hassan c Gould b van der Bijl	14		
D. W. Randall c Daniel b Emburey	9	L-b 7, w 8, n-b 4	19
*C. E. B. Rice c Brearley b van der Bijl	11		
J. D. Birch not out	29	1/74 2/79 3/98 (7 wkts, 60 overs) 190
M. J. Harris c Barlow b Hughes	27	4/104 5/120 6/176 7/188

P. J. Hacker and K. E. Cooper did not bat.

Bowling: Daniel 12–3–45–1; Hughes 12–1–46–1; van der Bijl 12–2–27–2; Selvey 12–3–27–2; Emburey 12–2–26–1.

Middlesex

C. T. Radley c Harris b Watson	5	V. A. P. van der Bijl c and b Hemmings	3
*J. M. Brearley c Cooper	49	J. E. Emburey not out	1
M. W. Gatting not out	95	L-b 3, w 5, n-b 1	9
G. D. Barlow lbw b Cooper	0		
R. O. Butcher c sub b Hacker	32	1/17 2/107 3/107 (6 wkts, 57.4 overs) 194
†I. J. Gould c Robinson b Watson	0	4/167 5/173 6/180

S. P. Hughes, M. W. W. Selvey and W. W. Daniel did not bat.

Bowling: Hacker 12–1–36–1; Watson 12–4–31–2; Rice 10.4–0–47–0; Cooper 12–5–17–2; Hemmings 11–0–54–1.

Umpires: A. Jepson and J. van Geloven.

WORCESTERSHIRE v LANCASHIRE

At Worcester, July 16. Worcestershire won by 39 runs, making their highest-ever total in the competition after a second-wicket stand of 115 in 25 overs. Lancashire missed two chances – Hayes dropped Turner at mid-on when the New Zealander had made only 7 and wicket-keeper Scott missed a first-ball edge from Neale – both off Radford. Turner's fourth Gillette Cup century included nine 4s, all scored during his first 50, and won him the Man of the Match award. Lancashire failed to gain ground in a slow second-wicket partnership of 79 in 27 overs between Kennedy and Hayes. The pressure became too much for the later batsmen and all hope went with Hayes's dismissal during Gifford's fine containing spell of one for 29.

Worcestershire

G. M. Turner c Simmons b Radford	115	H. Alleyne not out	5
J. A. Ormrod lbw b Radford	24	*N. Gifford run out	4
P. A. Neale c Hughes b Simmons	51	A. P. Pridgeon not out	9
Younis Ahmed c Scott b Hogg	13	B 1, l-b 6, w 2, n-b 5	14
E. J. O. Hemsley b Radford	5		
S. P. Henderson b Allott	17	1/41 2/156 3/181 (9 wkts, 60 overs) 265
†D. J. Humphries b Reidy	0	4/204 5/227 6/229 7/246
J. D. Inchmore c Scott b Allott	8	8/247 9/251

Bowling: Hogg 12–1–46–1; Radford 12–2–52–3; Hughes 4–1–24–0; Allott 8–0–38–2; Simmons 12–1–40–1; Reidy 12–0–51–1.

Lancashire

A. Kennedy c Gifford b Younis	34	P. J. W. Allott not out	19
D. K. Beckett c Turner b Inchmore	1	†C. J. Scott c and b Pridgeon	4
*F. C. Hayes c Pridgeon b Gifford	63	W. Hogg not out	4
B. W. Reidy lbw b Alleyne	7	B 2, l-b 18, w 2, n-b 14	36
D. Lloyd b Inchmore	22		
J. Simmons b Pridgeon	15	1/14 2/93 3/109 (9 wkts, 60 overs) 226	
D. P. Hughes run out	13	4/154 5/157 6/183 7/193	
N. V. Radford b Pridgeon	8	8/202 9/212	

Bowling: Alleyne 12–4–32–1; Inchmore 12–1–44–2; Younis 12–1–44–1; Gifford 12–2–29–1; Pridgeon 12–2–41–3.

Umpires: P. B. Wight and D. J. Constant.

SURREY v GLOUCESTERSHIRE

At The Oval, July 16. Surrey won by 8 runs. The match was largely a contest between the two captains, and was won by Knight – formerly of Gloucestershire – who was named Man of the Match. Jackman joined Knight in a stand of 66 in thirteen overs when Surrey seemed on the verge of collapse after a promising opening partnership of 71 between Butcher and Clinton. Gloucestershire lost half their side for 66, but Procter led a recovery with useful assistance from Partridge and Graveney. However, the final requirement of 19 off the last over from Clarke was beyond them.

Surrey

A. R. Butcher c Stovold b Bainbridge	34	D. J. Thomas not out	10
G. S. Clinton c Sadiq b Bainbridge	24	S. T. Clarke lbw b Brain	0
*R. D. V. Knight b Brain	59	P. I. Pocock run out	1
D. M. Smith run out	11	B 6, l-b 18, w 5, n-b 1	30
G. R. J. Roope b Graveney	0		
M. A. Lynch c Stovold b Graveney	0	1/71 2/72 3/105 (60 overs) 200	
R. D. Jackman lbw b Procter	31	4/107 5/117 6/183 7/183	
†C. J. Richards c Stovold b Procter	0	8/184 9/185	

Bowling: Brain 12–2–45–2; Procter 12–4–35–2; Partridge 6–0–17–0; Wilkins 10–1–35–0; Bainbridge 8–2–22–2; Graveney 12–3–16–2.

Gloucestershire

Sadiq Mohammad c Richards b Knight	8	M. D. Partridge b Jackman	20
B. C. Broad lbw b Jackman	1	A. H. Wilkins b Jackman	0
†A. W. Stovold c Jackman b Knight	23	B. M. Brain not out	2
Zaheer Abbas c Richards b Jackman	1	B 2, l-b 13, w 5, n-b 2	22
*M. J. Procter c Butcher b Thomas	52		
A. J. Hignell b Knight	0	1/5 2/30 3/31 (9 wkts, 60 overs) 192	
P. Bainbridge c sub b Thomas	20	4/66 5/66 6/112 7/129	
D. A. Graveney not out	43	8/180 9/180	

Bowling: Jackman 12–3–26–4; Clarke 12–1–36–0; Knight 12–3–40–3; Thomas 12–2–36–2; Pocock 12–2–32–0.

Umpires: D. J. Halfyard and R. S. Herman.

SUSSEX v GLAMORGAN

At Hove, July 16. Sussex won by 104 runs. After being put in they set Glamorgan 259 runs to win and bowled them out for 154 in 48.3 overs. The highlight was a superb innings from Mendis, who hit one 6 and twelve 4s in his 119 to win the Man of the Match award. He was joined by Parker in a second-wicket stand of 132 off 32 overs, and the Sussex total might have been a really formidable one but for a middle-order collapse, when six wickets fell for 45. Apart from a determined first-wicket partnership of 52 between Alan Jones and Hopkins, and a dogged 31 from Ontong, Glamorgan offered little resistance to a strong Sussex attack in which Imran again bowled impressively.

Sussex

G. D. Mendis c Nash b A. A. Jones	119	I. A. Greig c Miandad b A. A. Jones	7
J. R. T. Barclay b Nash	18	*†A. Long not out	5
P. W. G. Parker c Nash b Ontong	67		
Imran Khan c Ontong b Lloyd	0	B 2, l-b 13, w 2, n-b 2	19
C. M. Wells run out	2		
C. P. Phillipson not out	16	1/62 2/197 3/197 (7 wkts, 60 overs) 258	
G. S. le Roux c Lloyd b A. A. Jones	5	4/224 5/224 6/229 7/242	

G. G. Arnold and J. Spencer did not bat.

Bowling: Nash 12–3–36–1; A. A. Jones 12–1–49–3; Ontong 12–1–47–1; Cordle 12–0–60–0; Lloyd 12–1–47–1.

Glamorgan

A. Jones c Long b Spencer	24	A. E. Cordle c Arnold b le Roux	9
J. A. Hopkins c Barclay b Spencer	27	B. J. Lloyd run out	1
R. C. Ontong b Imran	31	A. A. Jones not out	0
Javed Miandad lbw b Imran	18	B 1, l-b 4, w 2, n-b 3	10
N. G. Featherstone c Parker b Barclay	21		
M. J. Llewellyn c Mendis b Imran	1	1/52 2/57 3/106 (48.3 overs) 154	
*M. A. Nash b Barclay	0	4/114 5/120 6/121 7/140	
†E. W. Jones c Long b le Roux	12	8/146 9/147	

Bowling: Imran 8–1–19–3; le Roux 9.3–2–26–2; Spencer 12–0–40–2; Arnold 12–1–28–0; Barclay 7–1–31–2.

Umpires: D. J. Dennis and D. Shackleton.

WARWICKSHIRE v DEVON

At Birmingham, July 16. Warwickshire won by seven wickets. Warwickshire achieved their expected victory to reach the quarter-finals, Lloyd seeing them home comfortably with fifteen 4s in his 81. Devon chose to bat but lost their first two wickets for only 5 runs. The innings was revived by Green, an Australian student who had captained Young Australia, but the visitors reached only a modest total. Green also captured Amiss's wicket while bowling twelve overs at a cost of only 34 and earned himself the Man of the Match award.

Devon

†J. G. Tolchard lbw b Willis	10	M. C. Wagstaffe c Small b Willis	3
*B. L. Matthews b Hopkins	3	A. W. Allin c Claughton b Oliver	2
R. C. Tolchard lbw b Small	0	D. I. Yeabsley not out	1
B. C. Green b Doshi	59	L-b 2, w 7, n-b 9	18
G. Wallen lbw b Doshi	18		
E. Picton b Doshi	2	1/4 2/5 3/43 (8 wkts, 60 overs) 143	
R. F. Harriott not out	27	4/94 5/98 6/109 7/136 8/139	

M. J. Goulding did not bat.

Bowling: Willis 12–3–17–2; Small 12–3–27–1; Hopkins 9–4–17–1; Ferreira 4–1–18–0; Doshi 12–5–27–3; Oliver 11–2–19–1.

Warwickshire

D. L. Amiss b Green	38	J. A. Claughton not out	0
K. D. Smith lbw b Goulding	5	B 4, l-b 2	6
T. A. Lloyd run out	81		
†G. W. Humpage not out	17	1/7 2/86 3/143 (3 wkts, 43.2 overs)	147

P. R. Oliver, A. M. Ferreira, D. C. Hopkins, G. C. Small, *R. G. D. Willis and D. R. Doshi did not bat.

Bowling: Goulding 10–3–44–1; Yeabsley 9.2–3–25–0; Green 12–0–34–1; Allin 12–2–38–0.

Umpires: D. O. Oslear and R. Palmer.

YORKSHIRE v KENT

At Leeds, July 16. Yorkshire won by 46 runs. They were indebted for their victory to Athey and Sidebottom, both of whom were awarded their county caps between innings. Yorkshire were troubled by Dilley after being put in and made a slow start, taking twelve overs to reach 29. Boycott and Athey then accelerated, taking their second-wicket stand to 202, with Man of the Match Athey scoring a sparkling century. When Kent replied, Sidebottom captured two quick wickets before Woolmer and Asif came together in a magnificent stand of 94. As the runs flowed Kent had a real chance of victory, but then Asif, Ealham and Woolmer were removed in quick succession and, despite an enterprising innings from Knott, the massive Yorkshire total was out of reach.

Yorkshire

G. Boycott b Woolmer	87	†D. L. Bairstow not out	18
R. G. Lumb run out	1	P. Carrick not out	19
C. W. J. Athey b Jarvis	115	L-b 6, w 4, n-b 6	16
G. B. Stevenson c Dilley b Woolmer	9		
*J. H. Hampshire c Cowdrey b Jarvis	3	1/4 2/206 3/221 (6 wkts, 60 overs)	279
J. D. Love c Knott b Jarvis	11	4/229 5/240 6/248	

C. M. Old, A. Sidebottom and A. Ramage did not bat.

Bowling: Dilley 12–2–51–0; Jarvis 12–0–59–3; Woolmer 10–1–54–2; Hills 12–1–28–0; Underwood 8–1–44–0; Asif 6–0–27–0.

Kent

R. A. Woolmer b Sidebottom	91	G. R. Dilley c Bairstow b Old	4
G. W. Johnson lbw b Sidebottom	6	D. L. Underwood c Hampshire b Old	0
C. J. Tavaré b Sidebottom	4	K. B. S. Jarvis b Sidebottom	4
Asif Iqbal c Old b Stevenson	35	B 1, l-b 8, w 13, n-b 4	26
*A. G. E. Ealham run out	2		
C. S. Cowdrey b Old	14	1/37 2/49 3/143 (56 overs)	233
†A. P. E. Knott not out	40	4/150 5/170 6/174 7/210	
R. W. Hills c Stevenson b Boycott	7	8/218 9/218	

Bowling: Old 10–2–28–3; Stevenson 12–1–43–1; Sidebottom 10–0–35–4; Ramage 12–1–48–0; Boycott 12–0–53–1.

Umpires: B. J. Meyer and C. T. Spencer.

QUARTER-FINALS

ESSEX v SURREY

At Chelmsford, July 30. Surrey won, by virtue of having lost fewer wickets, with both scores level. An amazing finish saw East run out off the penultimate ball when seeking the winning run. After a disastrous start, with four men back in the pavilion for just 35 in fifteen overs, Essex launched a recovery through Hardie and Pont to take the score into three figures. Pont and Turner then departed in quick succession before the resolute Hardie found another sound partner in Phillip. Between them they took Essex to within sight of victory with only 11 required from five overs, and four wickets left. Then came the dramatic climax. Hardie became Man of the Match Jackman's fifth victim, Phillip was run out, Smith was bowled, and finally the run out of East left Essex in a state of disbelief. Earlier, Clinton had batted with sense and authority, receiving good support from Smith as Surrey overcame the loss of two quick wickets to reach what proved to be a winning score.

Surrey

A. R. Butcher c Denness b Gooch	8	R. D. Jackman not out	26
G. S. Clinton c McEwan b East	58	S. T. Clarke not out	11
*R. D. V. Knight lbw b Lever	2		
G. P. Howarth c Fletcher b Gooch	19	B 3, l-b 10	13
D. M. Smith c Phillip b East	37		
G. R. J. Roope c Hardie b Lever	4	1/14 2/19 3/58 (7 wkts, 60 overs) 195	
D. J. Thomas b Lever	17	4/131 5/136 6/148 7/176	

†C. J. Richards and P. I. Pocock did not bat.

Bowling: Lever 12–4–26–3; Phillip 12–0–48–0; Gooch 12–1–44–2; Turner 12–1–36–0; East 12–1–28–2.

Essex

G. A. Gooch b Jackman	11	R. E. East run out	4
M. H. Denness c Thomas b Jackman	1	†N. Smith b Clarke	1
K. S. McEwan lbw b Jackman	2	J. K. Lever not out	1
*K. W. R. Fletcher b Knight	9		
B. R. Hardie c Butcher b Jackman	70	B 6, l-b 6, w 2, n-b 4	18
K. R. Pont c Richards b Knight	29		
S. Turner c and b Jackman	4	1/7 2/18 3/19 4/35 (59.5 overs) 195	
N. Phillip run out	45	5/100 6/108 7/185 8/191 9/193	

Bowling: Jackman 12–4–22–5; Clarke 12–1–47–1; Knight 12–3–35–2; Thomas 11.5–0–56–0; Pocock 12–5–17–0.

Umpires: H. D. Bird and A. G. T. Whitehead.

HAMPSHIRE v YORKSHIRE

At Southampton, July 30. Yorkshire won by seven wickets. Although the visitors achieved a comfortable victory, there were moments when Hampshire had hopes of success and a place in the semi-final. Having been put in, they began well with Rice, Nicholas and Turner making useful contributions. Yet they lacked acceleration and command in the absence of Jesty, who was recovering from a cartilage operation. A target of 197 seemed unlikely to cause Yorkshire undue difficulty, but Lumb and Boycott were soon dismissed, leaving the visitors struggling at 9 for two. Hampshire was run out at 55 for three after 22 overs, but Man of the Match Athey and Love applied themselves in an unbroken partnership of 142, taking Yorkshire to victory with 5.1 overs to spare.

Hampshire

J. M. Rice c Old b Ramage	29	†G. R. Stephenson c Hartley b Ramage	4
C. L. Smith c Bairstow b Sidebottom	9	K. Stevenson c Hartley b Stevenson	13
M. C. J. Nicholas st Bairstow b Boycott	28	S. J. Malone not out	7
D. R. Turner c and b Stevenson	53	L-b 20, w 1	21
*N. E. J. Pocock run out	4		
N. G. Cowley b Ramage	16	1/39 2/51 3/113 (58 overs) 196	
T. M. Tremlett lbw b Stevenson	5	4/126 5/151 6/156 7/169	
S. F. Graf b Old	7	8/174 9/176	

Bowling: Old 11–1–32–1; Stevenson 11–3–32–3; Sidebottom 12–0–35–1; Ramage 12–1–33–3; Boycott 9–2–33–1; Hartley 3–0–10–0.

Yorkshire

G. Boycott lbw b Stevenson	7	J. D. Love not out	61
R. G. Lumb c Stephenson b Graf	0	B 4, l-b 9, w 5, n-b 5	23
C. W. J. Athey not out	93		
*J. H. Hampshire run out	13	1/5 2/9 3/55 (3 wkts, 54.5 overs)	197

S. N. Hartley, †D. L. Bairstow, C. M. Old, G. B. Stevenson, A. Sidebottom and A. Ramage did not bat.

Bowling: Graf 9–1–31–1; Stevenson 12–1–27–1; Malone 11.5–2–42–0; Rice 11–3–40–0; Tremlett 5–0–14–0; Cowley 6–1–20–0.

Umpires: D. J. Constant and J. G. Langridge.

SUSSEX v WARWICKSHIRE

At Hove, July 30. Sussex won by nine wickets to go through to the semi-finals for the tenth time. Man of the Match Mendis batted with tremendous zest and ability, hitting one 6 and 22 4s in his thrilling innings. Barclay proved an able opening partner for Mendis and the score had mounted to 157 before Barclay, batting unselfishly, was bowled by Small. There were 10.5 overs remaining when Parker struck the winning boundary among the jubilant Sussex followers. Morning conditions helped the Sussex pace bowlers, after Warwickshire had elected to bat; only Smith and Whitehouse looked at all confident as Warwickshire were restricted to 210 for eight. The wicket was easier in the afternoon sunshine, suiting Mendis's relentless thirst for runs.

Warwickshire

D. L. Amiss c Long b Imran	6	G. C. Small run out	9
K. D. Smith c Phillipson b le Roux	64	*R. G. D. Willis not out	1
T. A. Lloyd c Barclay b Spencer	15		
†G. W. Humpage c and b Spencer	2	B 6, l-b 16, w 4, n-b 3	29
J. Whitehouse c Parker b Greig	46		
P. R. Oliver c Phillipson b Arnold	14	1/13 2/57 3/61 (8 wkts, 60 overs)	210
J. A. Snow b le Roux	13	4/125 5/161 6/164 7/188	
S. J. Rouse not out	11	8/204	

D. R. Doshi did not bat.

Bowling: Imran 12–3–29–1; le Roux 12–1–28–2; Arnold 11–0–39–1; Spencer 12–2–26–2; Barclay 4–1–19–0; Greig 9–0–40–1.

Sussex

G. D. Mendis not out	141	
J. R. T. Barclay b Small	33	
P. W. G. Parker not out	22	
B 4, l-b 6, w 2, n-b 6	18	
1/157 (1 wkt, 49.1 overs)	214	

Imran Khan, C. M. Wells, C. P. Phillipson, I. A. Greig, G. S. le Roux, *†A. Long, G. G. Arnold and J. Spencer did not bat.

Bowling: Willis 5–1–27–0; Rouse 12–1–44–0; Snow 8–3–33–0; Doshi 12–3–19–0; Small 9–0–51–1; Oliver 3–0–18–0; Amiss 0.1–0–4–0.

Umpires: R. Julian and K. E. Palmer.

WORCESTERSHIRE v MIDDLESEX

At Worcester, July 30. Middlesex won by ten wickets. The match was effectively decided in the space of ten overs during which Worcestershire tumbled from 49 for no wicket to 59 for five. Hughes, a fast-medium bowler from Durham University on only his third first-team appearance, included the menacing Turner in his haul of three for 5 in 30 balls and was named Man of the Match. Embury, turning the ball considerably on a disappointing wicket, took two wickets cheaply and also held two catches. Middlesex were never in danger as Brearley and Radley completed an overwhelming victory with 15.1 overs in hand.

Worcestershire

G. M. Turner c Downton b Hughes	32	J. D. Inchmore c sub b Selvey	9
J. A. Ormrod b Hughes	15	*N. Gifford not out	5
Younis Ahmed c Brearley b Embury	0	A. P. Pridgeon c Embury b Daniel	0
P. A. Neale b Embury	3		
E. J. O. Hemsley c Embury b Hughes	2	B 4, l-b 7, w 7, n-b 1	19
D. N. Patel c Barlow b Selvey	15		
†D. J. Humphries b Daniel	26	1/49 2/53 3/55 4/59 (54.2 overs)	126
V. A. Holder b Daniel	0	5/59 6/105 7/105 8/105 9/126	

Bowling: Daniel 10.2–2–24–3; van der Bijl 8–3–20–0; Embury 12–5–22–2; Hughes 12–5–23–3; Selvey 8–3–8–2; Gatting 4–2–10–0.

Middlesex

C. T. Radley not out	64
*J. M. Brearley not out	46
L-b 9, w 2, n-b 6	17
(no wkt, 44.5 overs)	127

†P. R. Downton, M. W. Gatting, R. O. Butcher, G. D. Barlow, J. E. Embury, V. A. P. van der Bijl, M. W. W. Selvey, W. W. Daniel and S. P. Hughes did not bat.

Bowling: Holder 12–4–16–0; Inchmore 7–3–13–0; Gifford 11–3–19–0; Pridgeon 8–2–26–0; Patel 6.5–1–36–0.

Umpires: W. L. Budd and P. B. Wight.

SEMI-FINALS

SURREY v YORKSHIRE

At The Oval, August 13, 14. Surrey won by four wickets. Winning the toss gave Surrey a big advantage in a match spread over two days because of the weather. Yorkshire batted first on the newly laid pitch and in poor light – which was criticised by Yorkshire manager Ray Illingworth – and were shot out for 135 in 53.5 overs. Surrey batted in much more tolerable conditions on the second day, needing 2.75 runs an over. Clinton laid the foundation and Lynch revived the innings after the loss of three for 9 had left the score looking inadequate at 85 for five. In the end, however, Surrey achieved a comfortable victory. The first day's play centred around the hostile bowling of Clarke, who sent down enough bouncers to bring a warning from umpire Spencer. His first over, officially a maiden, was wild enough to cost 10 runs from an assortment of extras. He had two catches dropped in the slips yet took four for 38 including the all-important wicket of Boycott in his second over. Going round the wicket, Clarke hit Boycott on the shoulder with a lifter and then dismissed him leg-before next ball. Two leg-byes accrued when he hit Athey on the helmet and he finally incensed some of the crowd by bouncing at the Yorkshire number eleven. The end of Clarke's furious spell gave Yorkshire no respite as Knight, relieving him, took a wicket in each of his first three overs, finishing with three for 20 in twelve overs, and received the Man of the Match award.

Yorkshire

G. Boycott lbw b Clarke	5	C. M. Old b Clarke	10
C. W. J. Athey lbw b Knight	15	A. Sidebottom not out	12
J. D. Love b Clarke	4	H. P. Cooper c Howarth b Clarke	0
*J. H. Hampshire c Roope b Knight	3		
S. N. Hartley c Thomas b Roope	23	B 9, l-b 5, w 6, n-b 4	24
P. Carrick c Roope b Knight			
†D. L. Bairstow c Richards b Jackman	26	1/17 2/23 3/45 4/52 (53.5 overs) 135	
G. B. Stevenson c Lynch b Pocock	13	5/54 6/92 7/111 8/112 9/128	

Bowling: Jackman 12–3–23–1; Clarke 11.5–1–38–4; Knight 12–3–20–3; Thomas 9–3–11–0; Roope 6–2–9–1; Pocock 3–0–10–1.

Surrey

A. R. Butcher b Sidebottom	19	D. J. Thomas c Bairstow b Stevenson	13
G. S. Clinton lbw b Old	33	R. D. Jackman not out	12
*R. D. V. Knight b Sidebottom	1	L-b 3, w 1, n-b 12	16
G. P. Howarth c Bairstow b Sidebottom	17		
G. R. J. Roope c and b Old	0	1/26 2/35 3/74 (6 wkts, 47.5 overs) 136	
M. A. Lynch not out	25	4/74 5/83 6/109	

†C. J. Richards, S. T. Clarke and P. I. Pocock did not bat.

Bowling: Old 12–7–11–2; Stevenson 12–1–32–1; Sidebottom 9.5–1–37–3; Cooper 7–1–21–0; Hartley 2–0–8–0; Boycott 5–1–11–0.

Umpires: W. E. Alley and T. W. Spencer.

SUSSEX v MIDDLESEX

At Hove, August 13, 14. Middlesex won by 64 runs. The match went into a second day after overnight rain had caused a late start. Middlesex, put in, reeled from three mighty blows by Arnold who made full use of the overcast conditions to dismiss Brearley, Radley and Butcher for only 4 runs off nineteen balls. The visitors began the second day at 90 for four and despite useful contributions from Gatting, Emburey and van der Bijl their total did not look too formidable for Sussex. However, Daniel, bowling at a torrid pace down the slope, bowled Barclay in his first over, then Mendis and Parker quickly followed, having scored only 4 runs between them. Sussex never recovered and, in his second thrilling spell, Daniel took three more wickets as the last five crashed for only 18. He finished with six for 15 off ten overs and received the Man of the Match award.

Middlesex

*J. M. Brearley lbw b Arnold	13	M. W. W. Selvey b Greig	11
†P. R. Downton c Phillipson b le Roux	10	W. W. Daniel not out	1
C. T. Radley c Phillipson b Arnold	13	S. P. Hughes lbw b Imran	6
M. W. Gatting c Phillipson b le Roux	32	B 4, l-b 10, w 5, n-b 3	22
R. O. Butcher lbw b Arnold	0		
G. D. Barlow c Long b Spencer	20	1/24 2/38 3/51 (60 overs) 179	
J. E. Emburey c Long b le Roux	26	4/57 5/91 6/117 7/158	
V. A. P. van der Bijl c le Roux b Greig	25	8/160 9/170	

Bowling: Imran 12–1–31–1; le Roux 12–0–40–3; Arnold 12–3–17–3; Wells 9–2–27–0; Spencer 12–2–33–1; Greig 3–0–9–2.

Sussex

J. R. T. Barclay b Daniel	0		*†A. Long lbw b Daniel		2
G. D. Mendis b Daniel	3		G. G. Arnold not out		2
P. W. G. Parker c van der Bijl b Daniel	1		J. Spencer b Hughes		0
Imran Khan c Downton b van der Bijl	20				
C. M. Wells run out	23		B 3, w 17, n-b 7		27
C. P. Phillipson hit wkt b Daniel	15				
I. A. Greig c Barlow b Selvey	17		1/1 2/9 3/18 4/58 (49.2 overs) 115		
G. S. le Roux b Daniel	5		5/69 6/97 7/109 8/111 9/114		

Bowling: Daniel 10–2–15–6; van der Bijl 9–4–9–1; Hughes 7.2–1–14–1; Selvey 9–3–28–1; Emburey 12–5–16–0; Gatting 2–1–6–0.

Umpires: P. B. Wight and A. Jepson.

FINAL

MIDDLESEX v SURREY

At Lord's, September 6. Middlesex won by seven wickets, completing the major double of Schweppes Championship and Gillette Cup. Gillette's good fortune with the weather held until the end of their sponsorship, the game being played in sunshine on a slow low-bouncing pitch. Unlike many recent finals it was, therefore, a bowlers' match. Only Brearley could accumulate without stress, until Butcher arrived to play the sort of vintage Caribbean strokes that became the hallmark of Gillette Cup finals.

Brearley put Surrey in, and although the lack of malice in the pitch allowed no breakthrough, the opening bowlers conceded only 21 runs in their first eleven overs. Against a strong attack Surrey were obliged to attempt an assault on the excellently controlled bowling of Selvey. His first 6.3 overs brought him the wickets of both openers at a cost of 10 runs and, with Brearley shrewdly bowling him out, he finished with figures for 17. Hughes also made two strikes after lunch, leaving Surrey almost without hope at 123 for five in the 48th over. A muscular stand, however, between the previously passive Smith and Intikhab revived the innings and the match. Hughes was the chief sufferer as these two clubbed a series of boundaries in an electrifying partnership of 62 in eight overs. When Daniel and van der Bijl were reunited Smith and Intikhab were caught on the boundary and the momentum faded.

The Middlesex start was even slower than Surrey's, but they had less need to hurry. They were 57 for two at tea, Downton and Radley having gone in an attempt to accelerate; but a stabilising stand of 64 in sixteen overs between Brearley and Gatting ensured that Middlesex maintained their control. The third-wicket pair showed a steadiness and composure rare in limited-overs cricket, and, when it looked as though Middlesex might have trouble with the light, Butcher brought the match to an unexpectedly early conclusion. He wafted Knight for two on-side 6s, and when Jackman returned to the attack he too was flicked into the Tavern. Five sparkling 4s gave adjudicator Ian Botham extra cause to praise Butcher's effort as "one of the most exciting Gillette Cup innings I have seen", before giving the Man of the Match award to Brearley.

The official attendance was 22,971; takings were £142,242.50.

Surrey

A. R. Butcher b Selvey	29		R. D. Jackman b Daniel		5
G. S. Clinton c Radley b Selvey	13		S. T. Clarke not out		3
*R. D. V. Knight c and b Emburey	15		†C. J. Richards run out		0
D. M. Smith c van der Bijl b Daniel	50		B 1, l-b 5, w 1, n-b 7		14
G. R. J. Roope b Hughes	35				
M. A. Lynch c Butcher b Hughes	3		1/26 2/52 3/59 (60 overs) 201		
Intikhab Alam c Butcher b van der Bijl	34		4/109 5/123 6/185 7/186		
D. J. Thomas b Hughes	4		8/195 9/201		

Bowling: Daniel 12–3–33–2; van der Bijl 12–0–32–1; Selvey 12–5–17–2; Hughes 11–0–60–3; Emburey 12–2–34–1; Gatting 1–0–11–0.

Middlesex

*J. M. Brearley not out...............	96	R. O. Butcher not out...............	50
†P. R. Downton c Clarke b Knight.....	13	B 3, l-b 11................	14
C. T. Radley c and b Thomas.........	5		
M. W. Gatting b Jackman............	24	1/44 2/57 3/121 (3 wkts, 53.5 overs)	202

G. D. Barlow, S. P. Hughes, J. E. Emburey, V. A. P. van der Bijl, M. W. W. Selvey and W. W. Daniel did not bat.

Bowling: Jackman 11–1–31–1; Clarke 8.5–1–29–0; Knight 10–2–38–1; Thomas 12–0–38–1; Intikhab 12–0–52–0.

Umpires: H. D. Bird and J. G. Langridge.

GILLETTE CUP RECORDS

Batting

Highest individual scores: 177, C. G. Greenidge, Hampshire v Glamorgan at Southampton, 1975; 146, G. Boycott, Yorkshire v Surrey at Lord's, 1965; 145, P. W. Denning, Somerset v Glamorgan at Cardiff, 1978; 143 not out, B. L. Reed, Hampshire v Buckinghamshire at Chesham, 1970; 141 not out, G. D. Mendis, Sussex v Warwickshire at Hove, 1980; 140, R. E. Marshall, Hampshire v Bedfordshire at Goldington, 1968; 139 not out, I. V. A. Richards, Somerset v Warwickshire at Taunton, 1978; 132, G. Robinson, Lincolnshire v Northumberland at Jesmond, 1971. (93 centuries were scored in this competition.)

Fastest hundred: R. E. Marshall in 77 minutes at Goldington, 1968.

Highest innings total: 371 for four wickets off 60 overs, Hampshire v Glamorgan at Southampton, 1975; 330 for four off 60 overs, Somerset v Glamorgan at Cardiff, 1978; 327 for seven off 60 overs, Gloucestershire v Berkshire at Reading, 1966; 326 for six off 60 overs, Leicestershire v Worcestershire at Leicester, 1979; 321 for four off 60 overs, Hampshire v Bedfordshire at Goldington, 1968; 317 for four off 60 overs, Yorkshire v Surrey (in the final) at Lord's, 1965.

Highest innings total by a minor county: 229 for five off 60 overs, Devon v Cornwall at Exeter, 1980.

Highest totals by a side batting second: 297 for four off 57.1 overs, Somerset v Warwickshire at Taunton, 1978; 287 for six off 59 overs, Warwickshire v Glamorgan at Birmingham, 1976; 287 off 60 overs, Essex v Somerset at Taunton, 1978; 282 for nine off 60 overs, Leicestershire v Gloucestershire at Leicester, 1975. Somerset's 297 for four v Warwickshire at Taunton, 1978 was the highest by a side batting second and winning the match.

Highest innings by a side batting first and losing: 292 for five off 60 overs, Warwickshire v Somerset at Taunton, 1978.

Lowest innings in the final at Lord's: 118 off 60 overs, Lancashire v Kent, 1974.

Lowest completed innings totals: 41 of 20 overs, Cambridgeshire v Buckinghamshire at Cambridge, 1972; 41 off 19.4 overs, Middlesex v Essex at Westcliff, 1972; 41 off 36.1 overs, Shropshire v Essex at Wellington, 1974.

Lowest total by a side batting first and winning: 98 off 56.2 overs, Worcestershire v Durham at Chester-le-Street, 1968.

Shortest innings: 10.1 overs (60 for one), Worcestershire v Lancashire at Worcester, 1963.

Matches re-arranged on a limited number of overs are excluded from the above.

Record partnerships for each wicket

227 for 1st	R. E. Marshall and B. L. Reed, Hampshire v Bedfordshire at Goldington	1968
223 for 2nd	M. J. Smith and C. T. Radley, Middlesex v Hampshire at Lord's	1977
160 for 3rd	B. Wood and F. C. Hayes, Lancashire v Warwickshire at Birmingham	1976
234* for 4th	D. Lloyd and C. H. Lloyd, Lancashire v Gloucestershire at Manchester	1978
141 for 5th	T. E. Jesty and N. E. J. Pocock, Hampshire v Derbyshire at Derby	1980
105 for 6th	G. S. Sobers and R. A. White, Nottinghamshire v Worcestershire at Worcester	1974
107 for 7th	D. R. Shepherd and D. A. Graveney, Gloucestershire v Surrey at Bristol	1973
69 for 8th	S. J. Rouse and D. J. Brown, Warwickshire v Middlesex at Lord's	1977
87 for 9th	M. A. Nash and A. E. Cordle, Glamorgan v Lincolnshire at Swansea ..	1974
45 for 10th	A. T. Castell and D. W. White, Hampshire v Lancashire at Manchester	1970

Bowling

Hat-tricks: J. D. F. Larter, Northamptonshire v Sussex at Northampton, 1963; D. A. D. Sydenham, Surrey v Cheshire at Hoylake, 1964; R. N. S. Hobbs, Essex v Middlesex at Lord's, 1968; N. M. McVicker, Warwickshire v Lincolnshire at Birmingham, 1971.

Four wickets in five balls: D. A. D. Sydenham, Surrey v Cheshire at Hoylake, 1964.

Three wickets in four balls: J. D. Bannister, Warwickshire v Somerset at Birmingham, 1966.

Best analyses: seven for 15, A. L. Dixon, Kent v Surrey at The Oval, 1967; seven for 30, P. J. Sainsbury, Hampshire v Norfolk at Southampton, 1965; seven for 33, R. D. Jackman, Surrey v Yorkshire at Harrogate, 1970; six for 14, R. D. Healey, Devon v Hertfordshire at Stevenage, 1969; six for 14, J. A. Flavell, Worcestershire v Lancashire at Worcester, 1963; six for 15, F. S. Trueman, Yorkshire v Somerset at Taunton, 1965; six for 15, W. W. Daniel, Middlesex v Sussex at Hove, 1980; six for 18, T. J. P. Eyre, Derbyshire v Sussex at Chesterfield, 1969.

Results

Largest victories in runs: Leicestershire by 214 runs v Staffordshire at Longton, 1975; Sussex by 200 runs v Durham at Hove, 1964; Surrey by 184 runs v Derbyshire at The Oval, 1967; Buckinghamshire by 183 runs v Cambridgeshire at Cambridge, 1972; and in the final by 175 runs, Yorkshire v Surrey at Lord's, 1965.

Quickest finishes: both at 2.20 p.m. Worcestershire beat Lancashire by nine wickets at Worcester, 1963; Essex beat Middlesex by eight wickets at Westcliff, 1972.

Scores level: Nottinghamshire 215, Somerset 215 for nine at Taunton, 1964; Surrey 196, Sussex 196 for eight at The Oval, 1970; Somerset 287 for six, Essex 287 at Taunton, 1978; Surrey 195 for seven, Essex 195 at Chelmsford, 1980. Under the rules the side which lost fewer wickets won.

Minor Counties: Durham became the first minor county to defeat a first-class county when they beat Yorkshire at Harrogate by five wickets in 1973. Lincolnshire became the second when they beat Glamorgan at Swansea by six wickets in 1974 and Hertfordshire the first minor county to reach the third round when they beat Essex at Hitchin by 33 runs in 1976. Cumberland is the only minor county that did not appear in the competition.

PAST WINNERS

1963   SUSSEX beat Worcestershire by 14 runs.
1964   SUSSEX beat Warwickshire by eight wickets.
1965   YORKSHIRE beat Surrey by 175 runs.
1966   WARWICKSHIRE beat Worcestershire by five wickets.
1967   KENT beat Somerset by 32 runs.
1968   WARWICKSHIRE beat Sussex by four wickets.
1969   YORKSHIRE beat Derbyshire by 69 runs.
1970   LANCASHIRE beat Sussex by six wickets.
1971   LANCASHIRE beat Kent by 24 runs.
1972   LANCASHIRE beat Warwickshire by four wickets.
1973   GLOUCESTERSHIRE beat Sussex by 40 runs.
1974   KENT beat Lancashire by four wickets.
1975   LANCASHIRE beat Middlesex by seven wickets.
1976   NORTHAMPTONSHIRE beat Lancashire by four wickets.
1977   MIDDLESEX beat Glamorgan by five wickets.
1978   SUSSEX beat Somerset by five wickets.
1979   SOMERSET beat Northamptonshire by 45 runs.
1980   MIDDLESEX beat Surrey by seven wickets.

GILLETTE CUP RULES

The Playing Conditions for first-class matches in the United Kingdom will apply except where specified below.

Duration of Matches

The matches will consist of one innings per side and each innings will be limited to 60 overs. The matches are intended to be completed in one day, but three days (four days if Sunday play is scheduled) will be allocated in case of weather interference.

Matches scheduled to start on Saturday, but not completed on that day, may be continued or, if necessary, started on the Sunday during the hours of 2.00 p.m. to 7.00 p.m. Umpires may order extra time until 7.30 p.m. on the Sunday if, in their opinion, a finish can be obtained that day.

Hours of Play

Normal hours will be 10.30 a.m. to 7.30 p.m. The umpires may order extra time if, in their opinion, a finish can be obtained on any day or in order to give the team batting second an opportunity to complete twenty overs. The captains of the two teams in the final will be warned that heavy shadows may move across the pitch towards the end of the day and that no appeal against the light will be considered in such circumstances.

In the event of the Cup Final starting not less than 30 minutes nor more than 90 minutes late, owing to the weather or the state of the ground, each innings shall be limited to 50 overs. If, however, the start of play is delayed for more than 90 minutes, the 60 over limit shall apply.

Intervals

Lunch	12.45 p.m. – 1.25 p.m. This may be varied if, owing to the weather or state of the ground, an alteration has been agreed upon by the captains or ordered by the umpires.
Between innings . . .	10 minutes.
Tea	20 minutes.

1. In an uninterrupted match, the tea interval will be taken at 4.00 p.m. or after 25 overs of the innings of the side batting second, whichever is the later.

2. In a match where the start is delayed or play is suspended for such a length of time as to make it impracticable to adopt 1 above, owing to the unlikelihood of completing the match on that day, the tea interval will be taken at 4.00 p.m., except in the following circumstances:

(a) If nine wickets are then down or no more than six overs of an innings remain to be bowled, the tea interval will be taken at the end of the innings, or after 30 minutes play, whichever is the earlier.

(b) If, between the hours of 3.15 p.m. and 4.00 p.m., play is suspended (this includes a suspension which may be in progress at 3.15 p.m.) the tea interval of twenty minutes will then be taken.

Note: The timing of any interval may be delayed for a maximum of fifteen minutes on the second or third day of a match, if the umpires consider that a finish can be obtained within that time.

Covering of the Pitch

The pitch will be completely covered in the event of rain.

Limitation of Overs by Any One Bowler

In a 60 over match no bowler may bowl more than twelve overs in an innings. In a match where the start is delayed and the innings of both teams is restricted from the start to less than 60 overs, no bowler may bowl more than one fifth of the total overs allowed, except that where the total overs is not divisible by five, an additional over shall be allowed to the minimum number of bowlers necessary to make up the balance – e.g. in a 33 overs match, three bowlers may bowl a maximum of seven overs and no other bowler more than six overs. In the event of a bowler breaking down and being unable to complete an over, the remaining balls will be bowled by another bowler. Such part of an over will count as a full over only in so far as each bowler's limit is concerned.

The number of overs bowled by each individual bowler shall be indicated on the scoreboard, from the commencement of an innings.

Law 14 – Declarations

Law 14 will not apply in this competition. The captain of the batting side may not declare his innings closed at any time during the course of a match.

Law 24.1 – No Ball – Mode of Delivery

Law 24.1 will apply in this competition, except that no bowler may deliver the ball underarm.

Law 25.1 – Wide Ball – Judging a Wide

Umpires are instructed to apply a very strict and consistent interpretation in regard to this Law in order to prevent negative bowling wide of the wicket or over the batsman's head.

The following criteria should be adopted as a guide to umpires:

1. If the ball passes either side of the wicket sufficiently wide to make it virtually impossible for the striker to play a "normal cricket stroke" both from where he is standing and from where he should normally be standing at the crease, the umpire should call and signal "Wide".

2. If the ball passes over head height of the striker standing upright at the crease, the umpire should call and signal "Wide".

Note: The above provisions do not apply if the striker makes contact with the ball, or if it passes below head height between the striker and the wicket.

The Result

1. A Tie

In the event of a tie, the following will apply:

   (a) The side losing the lesser number of wickets shall be the winner.

   (b) If both sides are all out, the side with the higher overall scoring-rate shall be the winner.

   (c) If the result cannot be decided by (a) or (b), the winner shall be the side with the higher score (i) after 30 overs, or if still equal (ii) after 20 overs, of if still equal (iii) after 10 overs.

2. Unfinished Match

If a match remains unfinished after three days (four days if Sunday play is scheduled) the winner will be the side which has scored the faster in runs per over throughout the innings, provided that at least twenty overs have been bowled at the side batting second. If the scoring-rate is the same, the side losing the lesser number of wickets in the first twenty overs of each innings will be the winner.

If, however, at any time on the third day (fourth day if Sunday play is scheduled), the umpires are satisfied that there is insufficient time remaining to achieve a definite result or where applicable, for the team batting second to complete its 60 overs, they shall order a new match to be started, allowing an equal number of overs per side (minimum 10 overs each side) bearing in mind the time remaining for play until 7.30 p.m.

In the event of no result being obtained within this rule and the captains are unable to reach agreement on an alternative method of achieving a result to the match, it shall be decided by the toss of a coin.

BENSON AND HEDGES CUP, 1980

Northamptonshire, whose only previous success was winning the Gillette Cup in 1976, returned to Lord's for the second successive season to win the Benson and Hedges Cup by 6 runs from Essex in a tense finish. They lost the Gillette Cup final to Somerset in 1979. In addition to the Benson and Hedges Gold Cup, which they hold for one year, Northamptonshire received £7,500 in prize-money. Essex received £3,000 as runners-up.

The losing semi-finalists, Middlesex and Worcestershire, each received £1,750, while Nottinghamshire, Lancashire, Surrey and Sussex, the losing quarter-finalists, received £850 each. The winners of the 40 group matches each took £300.

Allan Lamb, winner of the Gold Award in the final, received £250. The Gold Award winners in the semi-finals each received £150; in the quarter-finals £100 each; and in the group matches £50 each.

Total prize-money for the competition was £32,350, an increase of £5,170 over 1979. Benson and Hedges had increased their total sponsorship to the TCCB for 1980 from £130,000 to £160,000.

FINAL GROUP TABLES

Group A	Played	Won	Lost	No Result	Points
LANCASHIRE	4	4	0	0	8
NOTTINGHAMSHIRE	4	3	1	0	6
Leicestershire	4	2	2	0	4
Derbyshire	4	1	3	0	2
Scotland	4	0	4	0	0
Group B					
NORTHAMPTONSHIRE	4	4	0	0	8
WORCESTERSHIRE	4	3	1	0	6
Warwickshire	4	2	2	0	4
Yorkshire	4	1	3	0	2
Oxford & Cambridge Univs	4	0	4	0	0
Group C					
ESSEX	4	3	1	0	6
SUSSEX	4	3	1	0	6
Glamorgan	4	2	2	0	4
Gloucestershire	4	1	3	0	2
Minor Counties	4	1	3	0	2
Group D					
MIDDLESEX	4	4	0	0	8
SURREY	4	3	1	0	6
Somerset	4	2	2	0	4
Kent	4	1	3	0	2
Hampshire	4	0	4	0	0

The top two counties in each group qualified for the quarter-finals.
Where two or more teams finished with the same number of points, the position in the group was determined by their bowlers' striking-rate.

BOWLERS' STRIKING-RATES

Group A	Balls	Wickets	Striking-Rate
LANCASHIRE	1,227	36	34.08
NOTTINGHAMSHIRE	1,274	33	38.60
Leicestershire	1,318	33	39.93
Derbyshire	1,292	24	53.83
Scotland	944	9	104.88
Group B			
NORTHAMPTONSHIRE	1,315	36	36.52
WORCESTERSHIRE	1,320	31	42.58
Warwickshire	1,286	19	67.68
Yorkshire	1,313	31	42.35
Oxford & Cambridge Univs	1,131	15	75.40
Group C			
ESSEX	1,288	31	41.54
SUSSEX	1,313	31	42.35
Glamorgan	1,174	24	48.91
Gloucestershire	1,314	31	42.38
Minor Counties	1,061	20	53.05
Group D			
MIDDLESEX	1,271	36	35.30
SURREY	1,252	29	43.17
Somerset	1,282	29	44.20
Kent	1,241	24	51.70
Hampshire	1,271	30	42.36

GROUP A

DERBYSHIRE v LANCASHIRE

At Chesterfield, May 17. Lancashire won by 33 runs. Lancashire, put in, were in early trouble, but Lloyd and Reidy, with 184 in 32 overs, set a new fourth wicket record for the competition of 184 unbeaten and took them to a total too formidable for Derbyshire. Reidy's wonderfully clean hitting (six 6s and eight 4s) was largely responsible for 120 runs coming from the last 14 overs and won him the Gold Award. Derbyshire's hopes depended on the in-form Wright, but after he fell in the 39th over their chances receded.

Lancashire

A. Kennedy c Kirsten b Tunnicliffe 10	B. W. Reidy not out 109	
D. Lloyd not out 100	L-b 6, n-b 4 10	
J. Abrahams c Miller b Wincer 18		
*F. C. Hayes c Taylor b Miller 2	1/17 2/54 3/65 (3 wkts, 55 overs) 249	

G. Fowler, J. Simmons, D. P. Hughes, †C. J. Scott, M. F. Malone and W. Hogg did not bat.

Bowling: Oldham 10–1–35–0; Tunnicliffe 10–2–58–1; Miller 11–6–25–1; Wincer 8–2–39–1; Steele 9–1–43–0; Kirsten 7–0–39–0.

Derbyshire

A. J. Borrington c Simmons b Hogg	7	†R. W. Taylor run out	1
J. G. Wright c Fowler b Reidy	70	R. C. Wincer c Hayes b Kennedy	0
P. N. Kirsten b Simmons	36	S. Oldham b Malone	2
D. S. Steele lbw b Reidy	22		
K. J. Barnett b Kennedy	30	L-b 6, w 4, n-b 3	13
C. J. Tunnicliffe c Simmons b Hogg	7		
*G. Miller c Fowler b Malone	26	1/13 2/91 3/139 4/144 (53 overs) 216
K. G. Brooks not out	2	5/155 6/210 7/210 8/211 9/211

Bowling: Malone 10–1–31–2; Hogg 9–2–38–2; Reidy 11–0–44–2; Hughes 11–0–42–0; Simmons 11–0–47–1; Kennedy 1–0–1–2.

Umpires: T. W. Spencer and J. van Geloven.

DERBYSHIRE v LEICESTERSHIRE

At Derby, May 22. Leicestershire won by 14 runs. Neither side could qualify for the quarter-finals, but the occasion was given some meaning by the return of Hendrick after his injury in Australia and an excellent unbeaten century by Gower, who took the Gold Award. His innings gave Leicestershire respectability after they had struggled against the moving ball. Derbyshire, at 149 for two, appeared to have the game won, but with the dismissal of Wright, their innings disintegrated.

Leicestershire

B. Dudleston lbw b Tunnicliffe	3	N. E. Briers c Barnett b Steele	11
J. F. Steele b Tunnicliffe	1	P. B. Clift not out	18
T. J. Boon c Taylor b Hendrick	1	B 1, l-b 8, w 2, n-b 5	16
D. I. Gower not out	114		
*B. F. Davison c Kirsten b Steele	24	1/4 2/5 3/11 (6 wkts, 55 overs) 202
†R. W. Tolchard b Hendrick	14	4/80 5/116 6/141

K. Higgs, P. Booth and D. A. Wenlock did not bat.

Bowling: Hendrick 11–5–22–2; Tunnicliffe 5–1–11–2; Russell 11–1–64–0; Walters 2–0–15–0; Miller 11–2–30–0; Steele 11–3–27–2; Kirsten 4–0–17–0.

Derbyshire

J. G. Wright c Boon b Higgs	77	C. J. Tunnicliffe run out	3
A. J. Borrington c Dudleston b Booth	6	M. Hendrick not out	2
P. N. Kirsten b Higgs	52	P. E. Russell b Clift	0
D. S. Steele lbw b Wenlock	5		
K. J. Barnett b Clift	14	L-b 7, w 2, n-b 6	15
*G. Miller c Booth b Wenlock	1		
J. Walters run out	8	1/17 2/124 3/149 4/150 (54.4 overs) 188
†R. W. Taylor b Higgs	5	5/152 6/170 7/182 8/185 9/188

Bowling: Higgs 11–1–24–3; Booth 11–1–48–1; Wenlock 9–3–24–2; Clift 10.4–0–39–2; Steele 11–1–35–0; Briers 2–0–3–0.

Umpires: D. O. Oslear and B. J. Meyer.

LANCASHIRE v NOTTINGHAMSHIRE

At Manchester, May 14. Lancashire won by 113 runs. A perfect cricketing day and a winning toss gave Lancashire an advantage they never relinquished, as Kennedy and Lloyd built a solid base for victory with an opening partnership of 164 from 41 overs. Although Lancashire grew careless after lunch, losing five men in the last fifteen overs, they reached a formidable total with Kennedy hitting fourteen boundaries and Lloyd eight. Nottinghamshire struggled through thirteen overs for 36 before losing three wickets for no further score. Their innings disintegrated under the attack of Hughes, Simmons and notably Lloyd, who received the Gold Award.

Lancashire

A. Kennedy c Curzon b Rice	91	J. Simmons not out	12
D. Lloyd c Rice b Cooper	65		
B. W. Reidy c Rice b Cooper	10	B 2, l-b 5, w 3	10
*F. C. Hayes not out	29		
G. Fowler b Hadlee	1	1/164 2/166	(5 wkts, 55 overs) 232
J. Abrahams b Hadlee	14	3/180 4/183 5/219	

D. P. Hughes, †C. J. Scott, M. F. Malone and W. Hogg did not bat.

Bowling: Hadlee 11–2–32–2; Rice 11–1–51–1; Cooper 11–3–46–2; Bore 11–1–30–0; Hemmings 4–0–24–0; Tunnicliffe 7–0–39–0.

Nottinghamshire

M. J. Harris b Hughes	10	E. E. Hemmings b Simmons	5
P. A. Todd b Reidy	18	K. E. Cooper b Lloyd	0
H. T. Tunnicliffe b Hughes	27	M. K. Bore lbw b Lloyd	4
*C. E. B. Rice c Fowler b Hughes	0		
D. W. Randall lbw b Simmons	18	B 7, l-b 2, w 4, n-b 3	16
B. Hassan not out	14		
†C. Curzon b Lloyd	0	1/36 2/36 3/36 4/81	(41.3 overs) 119
R. J. Hadlee b Lloyd	7	5/83 6/83 7/99 8/106 9/111	

Bowling: Malone 5–1–7–0; Hogg 5–1–9–0; Reidy 6–1–14–1; Hughes 11–4–27–3; Simmons 10–2–29–2; Lloyd 4.3–1–17–4.

Umpires: A. Jepson and P. S. G. Stevens.

LANCASHIRE v SCOTLAND

At Manchester, May 22. Lancashire won by 61 runs. Lancashire, put in, were never in danger after Kennedy's and Lloyd's opening partnership of 121 runs from 34 overs. Lloyd added three wickets to his century to win his second Gold Award of the season. Scotland took some hope from an aggressive opening innings by Racionzer, but the spin of Lloyd, Hughes and Simmons contained their batsmen until Moir's final flourish with two 6s in his hard-hit 44. Lancashire's success gave them a maximum eight points to head their qualifying group.

Lancashire

A. Kennedy c and b Johnston	38	B. W. Reidy not out	12
D. Lloyd run out	113	B 3, l-b 3, w 1	7
J. Abrahams b Johnston	0		
*F. C. Hayes not out	43	1/121 2/125 3/176	(3 wkts, 55 overs) 213

I. Cockbain, J. Simmons, D. P. Hughes, †C. J. Scott, M. F. Malone and W. Hogg did not bat.

Bowling: Smith 5–1–9–0; Clark 7–2–32–0; Donald 7–0–25–0; Black 4–0–17–0; Moir 10–0–54–0; Goddard 11–1–26–0; Johnston 11–0–43–2.

Scotland

T. B. Racionzer b Hughes	30	*G. F. Goddard c Kennedy b Lloyd	6
W. A. Donald c Cockbain b Hughes	4	H. K. More not out	1
R. G. Swan c Scott b Simmons	2	J. Clark not out	3
†B. K. Kunderan c Malone b Hughes	6	B 5, l-b 9, w 1	15
H. G. F. Johnston st Scott b Lloyd	19		
T. M. Black c Malone b Lloyd	22	1/35 2/39 3/43 4/59	(8 wkts, 55 overs) 152
D. G. Moir b Hogg	44	5/94 6/98 7/129 8/149	

G. M. Smith did not bat.

Bowling: Hogg 11–1–45–1; Malone 11–6–24–0; Simmons 11–4–26–1; Hughes 11–3–19–3; Lloyd 11–4–23–3.

Umpires: R. Aspinal and H. D. Bird.

LEICESTERSHIRE v NOTTINGHAMSHIRE

At Leicester, May 17. Nottinghamshire won by 63 runs. Hassan's sparkling innings, with one 6 and nine 4s, put Nottinghamshire in a commanding position, which was built on by Rice, Randall and Hadlee. Bore rammed home the advantage with some splendid seam bowling as he took the first four Leicestershire wickets. Clift made a defiant 91 but, when Gold Award winner Bore returned to the attack, Leicestershire's resistance folded.

Nottinghamshire

P. A. Todd b Steele	24	K. Saxelby not out	1
B. Hassan c Steele b Taylor	90		
H. T. Tunnicliffe c Dudleston b Taylor	29	L-b 3, w 1, n-b 2	6
*C. E. B. Rice run out	51		
D. W. Randall run out	30	1/38 2/105 (6 wkts, 55 overs) 255	
R. J. Hadlee c Briers b Clift	24	3/175 4/226 5/254 6/255	

M. J. Harris, M. K. Bore, †C. C. Curzon and K. E. Cooper did not bat.

Bowling: Higgs 11–2–66–0; Taylor 11–1–43–2; Clift 11–2–60–1; Steele 11–2–42–1; Cook 11–3–38–0.

Leicestershire

B. Dudleston lbw b Bore	3	N. G. B. Cook c Rice b Hadlee	3
N. E. Briers c and b Bore	11	K. Higgs lbw b Hadlee	1
J. C. Balderstone b Bore	9	L. B. Taylor not out	0
D. I. Gower c and b Bore	8		
*B. F. Davison b Bore	5	L-b 15, n-b 5	20
†R. W. Tolchard c Curzon b Saxelby	24		
P. B. Clift c Curzon b Rice	91	1/18 2/30 3/37 4/52 (54.1 overs) 192	
J. F. Steele b Bore	17	5/100 6/153 7/169 8/174 9/192	

Bowling: Hadlee 11–3–23–2; Rice 10.1–1–32–1; Bore 11–4–22–6; Cooper 11–1–49–0; Saxelby 11–1–46–1.

Umpires: H. D. Bird and D. J. Constant.

LEICESTERSHIRE v LANCASHIRE

At Leicester, May 20, 21. Lancashire won by 3 runs. When rain forced the match into a second day Lancashire had batted for only thirteen minutes and had lost David Lloyd. Two more wickets fell cheaply when play resumed, but Reidy's entertaining 63 in even time helped Lancashire to a respectable total, and won him the Gold Award. Later, his accurate spell put the brake on Leicestershire's innings when they appeared well on target after Dudleston, Steele and Gower had given them a good start. Hostile bowling from Hogg further hindered Leicestershire, and two run outs, as Gower tried to increase the tempo, proved decisive.

Lancashire

A. Kennedy b Wenlock	10	†C. J. Scott b Clift	18
D. Lloyd hit wkt b Booth	6	M. F. Malone c Gower b Higgs	3
J. Abrahams c Dudleston b Booth	47	W. Hogg not out	0
*F. C. Hayes c Higgs b Wenlock	1	L-b 4, n-b 2	6
B. W. Reidy c Steele b Clift	63		
G. Fowler c Davison b Clift	7	1/7 2/26 3/30 4/121 (55 overs) 184	
J. Simmons c Steele b Higgs	23	5/133 6/141 7/141 8/177 9/184	
D. P. Hughes lbw b Clift	0		

Bowling: Higgs 11–1–30–2; Booth 11–3–29–2; Wenlock 11–1–39–2; Clift 11–4–32–4; Briers 3–0–25–0; Steele 6–0–21–0; Birkenshaw 2–0–2–0.

Leicestershire

N. E. Briers hit wkt b Hogg	7	J. Birkenshaw b Hogg		1
B. Dudleston c Scott b Hogg	43	D. A. Wenlock run out		15
J. F. Steele c Abrahams b Simmons	41	P. Booth not out		0
D. I. Gower not out	41	B 2, l-b 9, w 3, n-b 7		21
*B. F. Davison c and b Hughes	4			
†R. W. Tolchard run out	7	1/15 2/99 3/103 (8 wkts, 55 overs) 181		
P. B. Clift c Lloyd b Reidy	1	4/128 5/148 6/150 7/151 8/180		

K. Higgs did not bat.

Bowling: Hogg 11–3–23–3; Malone 11–3–31–0; Reidy 9–1–36–1; Hughes 11–1–40–1; Simmons 11–5–21–1; Kennedy 2–0–9–0.

Umpires: R. Aspinall and B. J. Meyer.

NOTTINGHAMSHIRE v DERBYSHIRE

At Nottingham, May 10. Nottinghamshire won by 103 runs. West Indian batsman Nanan marked his first appearance in the Benson and Hedges Cup with an innings of 93 that took Nottinghamshire to their highest total in the competition. Tunnicliffe and Rice both added considerable support as the Derbyshire bowling suffered. In reply, only Steele looked like mastering the Nottinghamshire attack, in which the pace and penetration of Hadlee were too much for Derbyshire. Nanan received the Gold Award but was unable to collect it after being sent home to nurse a back injury.

Nottinghamshire

P. A. Todd lbw b Oldham	6	B. Hassan not out		5
N. Nanan run out	93			
H. T. Tunnicliffe run out	54	L-b 10, w 2, n-b 3		15
*C. E. B. Rice not out	79			
D. W. Randall c Borrington b Tunnicliffe	10	1/10 2/114 (5 wkts, 55 overs) 269		
R. J. Hadlee b Kirsten	7	3/213 4/240 5/258		

†C. C. Curzon, K. Saxelby, M. K. Bore and K. E. Cooper did not bat.

Bowling: Oldham 8–0–49–1; Wincer 11–1–42–0; Tunnicliffe 11–2–38–1; Miller 11–2–44–0; Steele 2–0–16–0; Brooks 9–0–51–0; Kirsten 3–0–14–1.

Derbyshire

K. G. Brooks c Curzon b Rice	10	C. J. Tunnicliffe c Rice b Hadlee		1
J. G. Wright c Rice b Bore	31	R. C. Wincer run out		1
P. N. Kirsten c Curzon b Hadlee	1	S. Oldham not out		0
D. S. Steele c Cooper b Hadlee	71			
K. J. Barnett c sub b Cooper	34	L-b 3, w 4		7
A. J. Borrington c Curzon b Saxelby	0			
*G. Miller b Saxelby	1	1/15 2/16 3/50 4/131 (48.1 overs) 166		
†R. W. Taylor c Tunnicliffe b Hadlee	9	5/131 6/139 7/164 8/165 9/165		

Bowling: Hadlee 7.1–3–13–4; Rice 8–1–13–1; Cooper 11–1–46–1; Saxelby 11–0–46–2; Bore 11–1–41–1.

Umpires: D. J. Dennis and B. J. Meyer.

NOTTINGHAMSHIRE v SCOTLAND

At Nottingham, May 20. Nottinghamshire won by six wickets. Nottinghamshire needed to beat Scotland and bowl them out to be certain of qualifying for the quarter-finals, but they found neither of those targets easy. Despite a hostile spell by Gold Award winner Hadlee

Scotland showed resilience and character as they denied Nottinghamshire their first objective of bowling the opposition out, the main resistance coming from Black. Scotland's opening bowlers responded to the challenge as Robertson and Clark picked up two early wickets each and, with Nottinghamshire precariously positioned on 63 for four, it needed an unbeaten fifth-wicket partnership of 80 between Randall and Birch to see them to victory.

Scotland

T. B. Racionzer b Hadlee	4	D. G. Moir c Hassan b Hadlee	17
H. K. More retired hurt	16	F. Robertson not out	3
R. G. Swan lbw b Hadlee	3	J. Clark not out	0
†B. K. Kunderan c Randall b Rice	9		
W. A. Donald b Bore	2	B 5, l-b 11, w 7, n-b 4	27
H. G. F. Johnston b Cooper	20		
T. M. Black b Hadlee	38	1/10 2/18 3/35 (8 wkts, 55 overs) 141
*G. F. Goddard b Saxelby	2	4/45 5/87 6/109 7/123 8/140

Bowling: Hadlee 11–2–20–4; Rice 11–3–23–1; Bore 11–5–11–1; Cooper 11–2–37–1; Saxelby 11–2–23–1.

Nottinghamshire

P. A. Todd lbw b Robertson	35	J. D. Birch not out	47
B. Hassan lbw b Robertson	0	B 1, l-b 9, w 1, n-b 6	17
H. T. Tunnicliffe c Johnston b Clark	14		
*C. E. B. Rice b Clark	0	1/15 2/46 3/51 (4 wkts, 27.4 overs) 143
D. W. Randall not out	30	4/63	

†C. C. Curzon, R. J. Hadlee, K. Saxelby, M. K. Bore and K. E. Cooper did not bat.

Bowling: Robertson 11–1–49–2; Clark 9–2–21–2; Donald 3–0–23–0; Moir 3–0–16–0; Goddard 1.4–0–17–0.

Umpires: D. O. Oslear and J. van Geloven.

SCOTLAND v LEICESTERSHIRE

At Glasgow, May 10. Leicestershire won by eight wickets. Scotland encountered the classic dilemma of non-first-class batsmen against top bowling. Staying in was difficult enough, but quick scoring seemed impossible. The fifth-wicket partnership between Swan and Donald proved useful and hard hitting lower down the order gave the Scots a creditable total. It was never enough, though and Leicestershire meandered to their target. Swan received the Gold Award.

Scotland

T. B. Racionzer c Clift b Birkenshaw	15	J. E. Ker not out	8
H. K. More b Birkenshaw	15	*G. F. Goddard not out	3
†B. K. Kunderan b Steele	16		
R. G. Swan c Steele b Clift	40	L-b 7, n-b 1	8
D. G. Moir b Steele	2		
W. A. Donald st Tolchard b Balderstone	22	1/30 2/31 3/58 (7 wkts, 55 overs) 146
H. G. F. Johnston c Davison b Higgs	17	4/62 5/112 6/116 7/139

F. Robertson and G. M. Smith did not bat.

Bowling: Higgs 7–1–21–1; Taylor 6–3–9–0; Agnew 3–1–5–0; Steele 11–2–17–2; Birkenshaw 11–4–21–2; Clift 10–1–41–1; Balderstone 7–0–24–1.

Leicestershire

B. Dudleston not out	54
J. F. Steele c and b Robertson	47
J. C. Balderstone c Donald b Johnston . .	20
D. I. Gower not out	8
B 8, l-b 5, w 2, n-b 4	19

1/92 2/128   (2 wkts, 47.4 overs) 148

*B. F. Davison, †R. W. Tolchard, P. B. Clift, J. Birkenshaw, K. Higgs, J. P. Agnew and L. B. Taylor did not bat.

Bowling: Robertson 8–1–24–1; Smith 5–2–7–0; Goddard 10–1–24–0; Moir 9–0–21–0; Donald 3–1–9–0; Ker 2–0–9–0; Johnston 10.4–1–35–1.

Umpires: P. S. G. Stevens and R. Julian.

SCOTLAND v DERBYSHIRE

At Glasgow, May 14. Derbyshire won by ten wickets. Lacking experience of limited-overs cricket at the highest level Scotland were unable to withstand the sharp seam bowling, restrictive spin and efficient fielding of their opponents. Johnston hit five 4s in his 28, but Derbyshire were home after only 27 overs. As their openers strolled to victory, making 63 from ten overs, Wright led the way; his second 6 ended the match, and he took the Gold Award.

Scotland

T. B. Racionzer c Kirsten b Tunnicliffe . .	3	D. G. Moir lbw b Miller	14
S. K. Dharsi c Steele b Tunnicliffe	0	J. Clark run out	18
R. G. Swan c Tunnicliffe b Wincer	16	G. M. Smith not out	0
†B. K. Kunderan c Taylor b Tunnicliffe .	15		
W. A. Donald c Taylor b Steele	4	L-b 4, w 1, n-b 6	11
H. G. F. Johnston lbw b Oldham	28		
J. E. Ker lbw b Miller	6	1/3 2/4 3/27 4/40 (50.2 overs) 116
*G. F. Goddard c Miller b Oldham	1	5/49 6/63 7/74 8/81 9/114	

Bowling: Oldham 11–3–20–2; Tunnicliffe 11–1–22–3; Wincer 11–4–33–1; Miller 9.2–3–19–2; Steele 8–5–11–1.

Derbyshire

J. G. Wright not out	82
A. J. Borrington not out	37
L-b 2	2

(no wkt, 27 overs) 121

K. G. Brooks, P. N. Kirsten, D. S. Steele, K. J. Barnett, C. J. Tunnicliffe, *G. Miller, †R. W. Taylor, R. C. Wincer and S. Oldham did not bat.

Bowling: Clark 5–1–18–0; Smith 2–0–19–0; Ker 2–0–20–0; Goddard 9–1–30–0; Moir 7–2–19–0; Johnston 2–0–13–0.

Umpires: C. T. Spencer and B. J. Meyer.

GROUP B

NORTHAMPTONSHIRE v OXFORD & CAMBRIDGE UNIVS

At Northampton, May 10. Northamptonshire won by 69 runs as both teams struggled for runs and two bowlers achieved main success. Russom took five wickets – including those of Cook and Allan Lamb in three balls – and won the Gold Award. Opening batsman Larkins did the hat-trick, dismissing Boyd-Moss, Mallett and Russom when tried as sixth bowler. The Universities did well to restrict the home side to just over 200 but never looked capable of achieving it themselves. For Northamptonshire Williams hit seven 4s; Boyd-Moss, who is on the Northamptonshire staff, hit five 4s for the Universities.

Northamptonshire

*G. Cook b Russom	29	R. M. Tindall b Russom	9
W. Larkins c Boyd-Moss b Ross	17	R. M. Carter not out	8
R. G. Williams b Curtis	57	T. M. Lamb not out	10
A. J. Lamb c Ezekowitz b Russom	0	B 1, l-b 7, w 1, n-b 7	16
P. Willey c Mills b Pringle	28		
T. J. Yardley b Russom	19	1/28 2/81 3/81 (8 wkts, 55 overs) 203
†G. Sharp b Russom	10	4/132 5/138 6/165 7/182 8/185

B. J. Griffiths did not bat.

Bowling: Ross 11–0–53–1; Mallett 11–0–47–0; Russom 11–0–40–5; Curtis 11–1–33–1; Pringle 11–4–14–1.

Oxford & Cambridge Univs

A. M. Mubarak lbw b Griffiths	0	N. Russom b Larkins	0
R. A. B. Ezekowitz lbw b Carter	4	*C. J. Ross lbw b Larkins	6
J. P. C. Mills c Sharp b T. M. Lamb	0	I. J. Curtis not out	12
R. J. Boyd-Moss c Carter b Larkins	58	B 13, l-b 10, n-b 5	28
D. R. Pringle run out	11		
R. S. Cowan lbw b Willey	1	1/1 2/4 3/22 4/71 (9 wkts, 55 overs) 134
†I. G. Peck not out	14	5/80 6/106 7/106 8/106 9/118
N. V. H. Mallett lbw b Larkins	0	

Bowling: Griffiths 9–3–13–1; T. M. Lamb 6–4–6–1; Willey 11–3–16–1; Carter 7–1–20–1; Williams 11–7–14–0; Larkins 11–0–37–4.

Umpires: C. Cook and C. T. Spencer.

NORTHAMPTONSHIRE v WORCESTERSHIRE

At Northampton, May 20, 21. Northamptonshire won by 5 runs in a thrilling finish. Williams batted well for Northamptonshire after a steady start from Cook and Larkins when the home side were put in to bat. Younis and Inchmore each took four wickets and made the later batsmen struggle. Worcestershire began the final over needing 6 runs from their last pair, but Turner hit the first ball from Griffiths straight to Yardley at deep mid-on. Turner batted throughout the innings, hitting five 4s and winning the Gold Award. Only Hemsley gave useful support, the remaining nine Worcestershire batsmen totalling only 34. Northamptonshire fielded brilliantly and bowled accurately with five bowlers taking two wickets each.

Northamptonshire

G. Cook st Humphries b Younis	19	Sarfraz Nawaz b Inchmore	2
W. Larkins c Turner b Inchmore	23	T. M. Lamb not out	6
R. G. Williams c Neale b Younis	33	B. J. Griffiths not out	5
A. J. Lamb c Hemsley b Younis	9		
P. Willey c Humphries b Inchmore	18	B 3, l-b 9, w 9, n-b 3	24
T. J. Yardley b Inchmore b Younis	11		
*P. J. Watts c Ormrod b Inchmore	10	1/46 2/70 3/85 4/98 (9 wkts, 55 overs) 169
†G. Sharp c Inchmore b Gifford	9	5/112 6/135 7/147 8/150 9/156

Bowling: Alleyne 11–3–25–0; Pridgeon 11–1–33–0; Inchmore 11–1–28–4; Younis 11–0–37–4; Gifford 11–5–22–1.

Worcestershire

G. M. Turner c Yardley b Griffiths	97	*N. Gifford b Sarfraz	9
J. A. Ormrod lbw b Griffiths	6	H. Alleyne b T. M. Lamb	3
P. A. Neale lbw b T. M. Lamb	1	A. P. Pridgeon not out	1
E. J. O. Hemsley b Sarfraz	23		
Younis Ahmed lbw b Watts	5	L-b 5, w 5	10
D. N. Patel c Yardley b Willey	1		
†D. J. Humphries c Willey b Watts	4	1/33 2/34 3/96 4/105 (54.1 overs) 164
J. D. Inchmore c Sharp b Willey	4	5/112 6/119 7/126 8/157 9/162

Bowling: Sarfraz 11–3–30–2; Griffiths 10.1–1–23–2; T. M. Lamb 10–1–27–2; Larkins 3–0–13–0; Watts 9–0–35–2; Willey 11–0–26–2.

Umpires: H. D. Bird and D. Shackleton.

OXFORD & CAMBRIDGE UNIVS v WORCESTERSHIRE

At Cambridge, May 14. Worcestershire won by seven wickets. Inchmore's early burst of three for 5 won him the Gold Award and justified Gifford's decision to field first. Pringle and Peck gave substance to the Universities' innings with their sixth-wicket stand of 71, and Russom and Mallett added a brisk 25 in the final six overs. Turner dominated an opening stand of 50 in 12.3 overs and Jones batted with confidence to take Worcestershire to their comfortable win.

Oxford and Cambridge Univs

J. P. C. Mills c Humphries b Inchmore	13	†I. G. Peck b Patel	31
R. A. B. Ezekowitz c Humphries b Alleyne	1	N. Russom not out	16
A. M. Mubarak c Humphries b Inchmore	13	N. V. H. Mallett not out	10
R. J. Boyd-Moss c Hemsley b Gifford	0	L-b 11, w 1, n-b 3	15
D. R. Pringle c Gifford b Inchmore	51	1/8 2/31 3/32 (7 wkts, 55 overs) 150
R. S. Cowan c Hemsley b Inchmore	0	4/34 5/34 6/105 7/123

*C. J. Ross and I. J. Curtis did not bat.

Bowling: Alleyne 11–4–13–1; Pridgeon 11–2–27–0; Inchmore 11–2–21–4; Gifford 10–1–21–1; Patel 10–0–42–1; Younis 2–0–11–0.

Worcestershire

G. M. Turner c Boyd-Moss b Curtis	31	Younis Ahmed not out	16
J. A. Ormrod b Pringle	15	B 7, l-b 8, n-b 1	18
B. J. R. Jones not out	44		
E. J. O. Hemsley c Peck b Mallett	28	1/50 2/50 3/116 (3 wkts, 43.3 overs) 152

D. N. Patel, †D. J. Humphries, H. Alleyne, J. D. Inchmore, *N. Gifford and A. P. Pridgeon did not bat.

Bowling: Ross 4–0–17–0; Mallett 10–2–28–1; Pringle 11–3–21–1; Curtis 11–3–18–1; Russom 7–1–46–0; Ezekowitz 0.3–0–4–0.

Umpires: D. O. Oslear and D. J. Dennis.

OXFORD & CAMBRIDGE UNIVS v YORKSHIRE

At Oxford, May 20, 21. Yorkshire won by nine wickets. Orders and Odendaal had embarked on their recovery stand when rain, which restricted play to the afternoon session, returned at tea. Resuming at 78 for three, they carried their attractive partnership past the century mark. But the target was nowhere near enough to test Yorkshire, despite the early capture of Lumb's wicket. Curtis managed to trouble Boycott, but Athey, who took the Gold Award, had few problems.

Oxford & Cambridge Univs

R. A. B. Ezekowitz b Old	2	S. P. Sutcliffe not out	7
A. M. Mubarak lbw b Sidebottom	13	M. G. Howat not out	0
J. P. C. Mills c Bairstow b Cooper	3		
A. Odendaal b Cooper	41	B 4, l-b 7, w 3	14
J. O. D. Orders st Bairstow b Boycott	63		
R. J. Boyd-Moss run out	6	1/13 2/19 3/21 (7 wkts, 55 overs) 150
†I. G. Peck c Bairstow b Stevenson	1	4/124 5/140 6/141 7/144

*C. J. Ross and I. J. Curtis did not bat.

Bowling: Old 11–5–12–1; Stevenson 11–5–18–1; Sidebottom 11–2–31–1; Cooper 11–1–43–2; Boycott 7–0–20–1; Athey 4–0–12–0.

Yorkshire

G. Boycott not out	69
R. G. Lumb b Ross	0
C. W. J. Athey not out	74
B 5, w 3	8

1/3   (1 wkt, 39.3 overs) 151

*J. H. Hampshire, K. Sharp, P. Carrick, †D. L. Bairstow, A. Sidebottom, C. M. Old, G. B. Stevenson and H. P. Cooper did not bat.

Bowling: Ross 6–1–16–1; Howat 6–0–25–0; Curtis 11–3–28–0; Sutcliffe 11–1–49–0; Orders 5.3–0–25–0.

Umpires: D. J. Constant and K. E. Palmer.

WARWICKSHIRE v NORTHAMPTONSHIRE

At Birmingham, May 14. Northamptonshire won by six wickets. Warwickshire, put in, lost a quick wicket to Sarfraz before Amiss and Lloyd raised their hopes with a stand of 97. But once past 50 Amiss lost patience and the innings never recovered, with Tim Lamb taking three wickets in successive overs. Willis struck an early blow when Northamptonshire batted, but the match-winning stand followed when Willey joined Larkins, who scored a magnificent century and won the Gold Award.

Warwickshire

D. L. Amiss c Griffiths b Williams	52	*R. G. D. Willis c T. M. Lamb b Griffiths	7
K. D. Smith c Sharp b Sarfraz	8	D. R. Doshi not out	1
T. A. Lloyd lbw b T. M. Lamb	47	S. P. Perryman not out	1
J. A. Claughton c Sharp b T. M. Lamb	7	B 1, l-b 10, w 11, n-b 3	25
P. R. Oliver b T. M. Lamb	10		
†G. W. Humpage b Griffiths	12	1/17 2/114 3/132 (9 wkts, 55 overs) 202
A. M. Ferreira c A. J. Lamb b Sarfraz	29	4/137 5/146 6/171 7/189
G. C. Small c Cook b Sarfraz	3	8/197 9/200

Bowling: Sarfraz 11–1–30–3; Griffiths 11–1–23–2; T. M. Lamb 11–0–54–3; Willey 11–2–30–0; Williams 11–0–40–1.

Northamptonshire

*G. Cook b Willis	4	T. J. Yardley not out	1
W. Larkins b Willis	108	L-b 4, w 2, n-b 9	15
R. G. Williams b Doshi	9		
A. J. Lamb c Smith b Oliver	3	1/19 2/69 (4 wkts, 52.3 overs) 206
P. Willey not out	66	3/76 4/201

†G. Sharp, R. M. Carter, Sarfraz Nawaz, T. M. Lamb and B. J. Griffiths did not bat.

Bowling: Willis 11–4–26–2; Small 6.3–0–41–0; Perryman 7–3–25–0; Ferreira 6–0–45–0; Doshi 11–6–14–1; Oliver 11–1–40–1.

Umpires: D. G. L. Evans and R. Aspinall.

WARWICKSHIRE v OXFORD & CAMBRIDGE UNIVS

At Birmingham, May 17. Warwickshire won by seven wickets, with 4.3 overs to spare. Odendaal's 74, which won him the Gold Award, gave the Universities' total respectability, but Amiss was again in form when the county began their reply. He and Smith took Warwickshire halfway to their target, and the result looked inevitable thereafter, although Sutcliffe conceded only 11 runs off his eleven overs.

Oxford & Cambridge Univs

A. M. Mubarak c Oliver b Willis	0	*†I. G. Peck not out	17
R. A. B. Ezekowitz b Ferreira	26	N. Russom not out	2
A. Odendaal c Humpage b Small	74	B 3, l-b 5, w 8, n-b 4	20
R. J. Boyd-Moss run out	11		—
D. R. Pringle b Small	16	1/5 2/101 3/124	(6 wkts, 55 overs) 166
R. S. Cowan b Perryman	0	4/134 5/135 6/159	

N. V. H. Mallett, I. J. Curtis and S. P. Sutcliffe did not bat.

Bowling: Willis 11–5–19–1; Small 9–4–11–2; Perryman 9–3–25–1; Ferreira 11–4–26–1; Doshi 11–1–39–0; Oliver 4–0–26–0.

Warwickshire

D. L. Amiss b Pringle	50	P. R. Oliver not out	17
K. D. Smith b Pringle	24	B 2, l-b 5, w 1	8
T. A. Lloyd not out	33		—
J. A. Claughton run out	35	1/69 2/84 3/144	(3 wkts, 50.3 overs) 167

†G. W. Humpage, A. M. Ferreira, *R. G. D. Willis, G. C. Small, S. P. Perryman and D. R. Doshi did not bat.

Bowling: Mallett 5–0–36–0; Russom 9–1–34–0; Pringle 11–1–36–2; Sutcliffe 11–6–11–0; Curtis 9.3–1–22–0; Boyd-Moss 5–1–20–0.

Umpires: D. O. Oslear and P. S. G. Stevens.

WORCESTERSHIRE v YORKSHIRE

At Worcester, May 17. Worcestershire won by four wickets. For the second time Yorkshire were beaten after making a record score for the county in the competition. Boycott dominated their innings with 142 (one 6 and fourteen 4s) out of 251 and was involved in four half-century partnerships. Moreover, it was not until the arrival of Old, with an unbeaten 41 in nine overs, that Boycott's scoring-rate was eclipsed. Yorkshire's all-seam attack was overwhelmed by a second-wicket partnership of 166 in 31 overs between Younis and Ormrod. Younis's best-ever limited-overs score of 115 won him the Gold Award and took Worcestershire to within 7 runs of victory.

Yorkshire

G. Boycott c Hemsley b Alleyne	142	C. M. Old not out	41
R. G. Lumb c Humphries b Patel	16	G. B. Stevenson not out	12
C. W. J. Athey lbw b Gifford	19	B 1, l-b 7, w 6, n-b 4	18
*J. H. Hampshire c Alleyne b Patel	0		—
K. Sharp b Inchmore	21	1/58 2/117 3/118	(6 wkts, 55 overs) 269
†D. L. Bairstow b Patel	0	4/185 5/195 6/251	

H. P. Cooper, A. Ramage and A. Sidebottom did not bat.

Bowling: Alleyne 11–1–51–1; Inchmore 11–2–32–1; Pridgeon 11–1–48–0; Patel 11–1–42–3; Gifford 11–0–78–1.

Worcestershire

G. M. Turner lbw b Stevenson	17	B. J. R. Jones not out		5
J. A. Ormrod c Sharp b Old	74	J. D. Inchmore not out		1
Younis Ahmed c Hampshire b Cooper	115	L-b 6, w 2, n-b 10		18
E. J. O. Hemsley c Athey b Old	0			
D. N. Patel b Stevenson	13	1/34 2/200 3/200	(6 wkts, 54 overs)	270
†D. J. Humphries c Athey b Cooper	27	4/231 5/263 6/268		

*N. Gifford, H. Alleyne and A. P. Pridgeon did not bat.

Bowling: Old 11–1–57–2; Stevenson 10–1–38–2; Sidebottom 11–0–40–0; Ramage 9–0–53–0; Boycott 5–0–25–0; Cooper 8–1–39–2.

Umpires: R. S. Herman and R. Julian.

WORCESTERSHIRE v WARWICKSHIRE

At Worcester, May 22, 23. Worcestershire won by five wickets and qualified for the quarter-finals. For Warwickshire, Smith hit nine boundaries in his 84, but the bowling of Inchmore again proved a decisive factor for Worcestershire. Willis dismissed Turner in the second over of an excellent opening spell and Worcestershire, held up by bad light, required a further 173 from 34 overs on the second day. The result turned on an innings of 45 out of 79 in twelve overs by Younis and a dropped catch on the square leg boundary when Gold Award winner Hemsley was on 57. Hemsley hit twelve boundaries in a personal-best limited-overs performance as he led Worcestershire home with nineteen balls in hand.

Warwickshire

D. L. Amiss lbw b Pridgeon	10	G. C. Small not out		8
K. D. Smith c Alleyne b Younis	84	*R. G. D. Willis c Gifford b Inchmore		6
T. A. Lloyd lbw b Inchmore	12	D. R. Doshi not out		0
J. A. Claughton run out	37	B 2, l-b 16, w 4, n-b 4		26
P. R. Oliver c Humphries b Alleyne	5			
G. W. Humpage b Inchmore	25	1/16 2/50 3/147	(9 wkts, 55 overs)	227
A. M. Ferreira b Inchmore	13	4/161 5/183 6/208 7/213		
†C. Maynard c Humphries b Alleyne	1	8/214 9/223		

Bowling: Alleyne 11–1–38–2; Inchmore 11–3–31–4; Pridgeon 11–0–58–1; Gifford 11–2–39–0; Younis 11–0–35–1.

Worcestershire

G. M. Turner c Maynard b Willis	0	D. N. Patel not out		7
J. A. Ormrod b Ferreira	4			
P. A. Neale b Humpage	24	B 4, l-b 12, w 5, n-b 12		33
E. J. O. Hemsley not out	95			
Younis Ahmed c Maynard b Willis	45	1/11 2/14 3/79	(5 wkts, 51.5 overs)	228
†D. J. Humphries b Humpage	20	4/158 5/198		

J. D. Inchmore, *N. Gifford, H. Alleyne and A. P. Pridgeon did not bat.

Bowling: Willis 10–4–29–2; Small 9.5–3–27–0; Ferreira 11–2–49–1; Doshi 11–1–47–0; Humpage 10–1–43–2.

Umpires: C. Cook and R. Palmer.

YORKSHIRE v WARWICKSHIRE

At Leeds, May 10. Warwickshire won by one wicket with a ball to spare. Yorkshire, put in, scored a substantial total, with some brilliant batting from Hampshire, who took the Gold Award. Their defensive fielding, however, allowed Smith and Claughton to pick up many easy singles. Doshi, hitting five successive 2s from Old in the last over, fashioned a thrilling victory for Warwickshire, who had appeared well beaten.

Yorkshire

G. Boycott run out	40	†D. L. Bairstow not out	31
R. G. Lumb run out	35	B 3, l-b 9, w 1	13
C. W. J. Athey c Ferreira b Small	19		
K. Sharp c Maynard b Small	45	1/70 2/99 3/99 (4 wkts, 55 overs) 268	
*J. H. Hampshire not out	85	4/168	

A. Sidebottom, C. M. Old, G. B. Stevenson, H. P. Cooper and A. Ramage did not bat.

Bowling: Willis 11–1–27–0; Small 9–1–53–2; Humpage 11–0–51–0; Ferreira 11–2–31–0; Doshi 11–1–58–0; Oliver 2–0–35–0.

Warwickshire

D. L. Amiss b Boycott	27	G. C. Small b Cooper	0
K. D. Smith b Ramage	65	R. G. D. Willis c Hampshire b Old	11
T. A. Lloyd lbw b Ramage	11	D. R. Doshi not out	19
J. A. Claughton c Bairstow b Old	52		
P. R. Oliver b Ramage	12	L-b 12, n-b 5	17
G. W. Humpage c Bairstow b Sidebottom	15	1/71 2/100 3/134 (9 wkts, 54.5 overs) 269	
A. M. Ferreira b Cooper	23	4/156 5/180 6/215	
†C. Maynard not out	17	7/227 8/227 9/246	

Bowling: Old 10.5–1–47–2; Stevenson 8–2–26–0; Sidebottom 11–0–47–1; Ramage 11–0–63–3; Cooper 11–1–53–2; Boycott 3–0–16–1.

Umpires: H. D. Bird and T. W. Spencer.

YORKSHIRE v NORTHAMPTONSHIRE

At Bradford, May 22. Northamptonshire won by 2 runs. After Northamptonshire were put in on a green pitch, Williams made the most of some inaccurate Yorkshire bowling and won the Gold Award. Boycott's early departure upset Yorkshire, although the patient Lumb held the innings together. With 10 needed from the last over, and the injured Ramage unable to bat, Yorkshire just failed in an exciting finish.

Northamptonshire

G. Cook c Lumb b Ramage	16	Sarfraz Nawaz not out	2
W. Larkins c Sidebottom b Old	19	T. M. Lamb b Stevenson	1
R. G. Williams c Athey b Cooper	83		
A. J. Lamb b Cooper	29	B 5, l-b 3, w 2	10
P. Willey c Bairstow b Sidebottom	23		
T. J. Yardley b Old	11	1/26 2/49 3/148 (9 wkts, 55 overs) 205	
*P. J. Watts c Bairstow b Stevenson	9	4/149 5/190 6/194	
†G. Sharp c Bairstow b Stevenson	2	7/202 8/203 9/205	

B. J. Griffiths did not bat.

Bowling: Old 11–4–38–2; Stevenson 11–4–13–3; Sidebottom 11–0–48–1; Boycott 7–1–23–0; Cooper 11–0–54–2; Ramage 4–1–19–1.

Yorkshire

G. Boycott c Sharp b Sarfraz	0	G. B. Stevenson b Sarfraz	5
R. G. Lumb c Watts b Griffiths	90	A. Sidebottom not out	15
C. W. J. Athey run out	29	H. P. Cooper not out	2
K. Sharp b Watts	0	L-b 9, w 1	10
*J. H. Hampshire c and b Watts	8		
†D. L. Bairstow c Williams b Griffiths	27	1/2 2/61 3/63 4/86 (8 wkts, 55 overs) 203
C. M. Old c A. J. Lamb b T. M. Lamb	17	5/134 6/168 7/179 8/193

A. Ramage did not bat.

Bowling: Sarfraz 11–2–35–2; Griffiths 11–2–23–2; T. M. Lamb 9–3–37–1; Larkins 3–0–19–0; Willey 11–0–29–0; Watts 10–0–50–2.

Umpires: J. van Geloven and T. W. Spencer.

GROUP C

ESSEX v SUSSEX

At Chelmsford, May 10. Essex won by four wickets. The title holders were in trouble at 100 for four in the 30th over, but a masterful 61 from Fletcher saw them to victory and won him the Gold Award. Cautious at first, he produced some thrilling strokes and found a superb partner in Turner, their fifth-wicket stand producing 78 in fourteen overs. Sussex, put in, were given a fine start by Wessels and Barclay, who put on 124 before they were separated in the 39th over on the stroke of lunch. Yet the visitors could not maintain the scoring-rate, mainly because of the accuracy of Lever and East.

Sussex

K. C. Wessels c Lever b Turner	71	A. C. S. Pigott not out	1
J. R. T. Barclay b Phillip	80		
G. D. Mendis c McEwan b Phillip	13	L-b 5, w 2, n-b 2	9
P. W. G. Parker c Gooch b Lever	8		
Imran Khan c Smith b Lever	18	1/124 2/147 (6 wkts, 55 overs) 217
P. J. Graves run out	16	3/163 4/189 5/210
C. P. Phillipson not out	1	6/215

*†A. Long, G. G. Arnold and J. Spencer did not bat.

Bowling: Lever 11–4–29–2; Phillip 9–0–55–2; Turner 11–1–35–1; Gooch 11–0–33–0; Acfield 5–0–32–0; East 8–2–24–0.

Essex

G. A. Gooch b Pigott	29	N. Phillip not out	27
B. R. Hardie c Long b Pigott	22	R. E. East not out	10
K. S. McEwan b Spencer	13	B 2, l-b 5, w 1	8
A. W. Lilley c Parker b Spencer	15		
*K. W. R. Fletcher b Pigott	61	1/44 2/51 3/68 (6 wkts, 53.5 overs) 220
S. Turner c Graves b Imran	35	4/100 5/178 6/184

D. L. Acfield, †N. Smith and J. K. Lever did not bat.

Bowling: Imran 11–3–29–1; Arnold 11–2–64–0; Pigott 11–0–47–3; Spencer 11–3–28–2; Phillipson 4–0–18–0; Barclay 5.3–0–26–0.

Umpires: W. L. Budd and A. G. T. Whitehead.

ESSEX v GLAMORGAN

At Chelmsford, May 20, 21. Essex won by five wickets. Gold Award winner Fletcher took his team into the quarter-finals with a stylish unbeaten 54 and a third-wicket partnership of 70 in seventeen overs with McEwan. After rain had washed out play completely on the Tuesday, Lever gave Essex an excellent start by removing Alan Jones with the second ball of the match. Francis quickly followed and, although Hopkins and Miandad inspired a brief recovery, Pont removed them both, whereupon Glamorgan's innings collapsed.

Glamorgan

A. Jones lbw b Lever	0	E. A. Moseley lbw b Turner	1	
J. A. Hopkins c Denness b Pont	28	A. J. Mack not out	3	
D. A. Francis b Phillip	0	A. A. Jones c Pont b Lever	14	
Javed Miandad c Smith b Pont	43	B 5, l-b 11, w 3	19	
N. G. Featherstone c Smith b Phillip	29			
G. C. Holmes c Fletcher b Pont	4	1/0 2/7 3/66 4/91	(53 overs) 147	
*M. A. Nash b Phillip	4	5/101 6/116 7/127		
†E. W. Jones lbw b Phillip	2	8/128 9/129		

Bowling: Lever 10–4–7–2; Phillip 11–3–32–4; Turner 10–1–32–1; Gooch 11–0–40–0; Pont 11–2–17–3.

Essex

G. A. Gooch b Nash	16	S. Turner not out	15	
M. H. Denness c A. Jones b Holmes	11			
K. S. McEwan c E. W. Jones b Mack	45	B 5, n-b 3	8	
*K. W. R. Fletcher not out	54			
B. R. Hardie b Mack	0	1/19 2/47 3/117	(5 wkts, 38 overs) 149	
K. R. Pont c Miandad b A. A. Jones	0	4/117 5/120		

N. Phillip, R. E. East, †N. Smith and J. K. Lever did not bat.

Bowling: Nash 6–1–23–1; Moseley 8–1–29–0; A. A. Jones 11–0–49–1; Holmes 5–2–14–1; Featherstone 2–0–3–0; Mack 6–1–23–2.

Umpires: C. T. Spencer and A. Jepson.

GLAMORGAN v MINOR COUNTIES

At Swansea, May 17. Glamorgan won by ten wickets. The visitors, put in on an easy-paced pitch, totalled 175 for nine, with a fine knock by Timur Mohamed. Glamorgan replied with their highest partnership for any wicket in this tournament as Gold Award winner Hopkins and Alan Jones produced an unbroken stand of 176. Minor Counties' left-arm spinner Tony Allin formerly played for Glamorgan, but was unsuccessful in this match, his nine overs costing 42 runs.

Minor Counties

J. G. Tolchard c Francis b Nash	31	D. I. Yeabsley b A. A. Jones	9	
J. S. Johnson b Moseley	0	D. C. Wing not out	2	
Timur Mohamed c Francis b A. A. Jones	63	B. G. Collins not out	10	
*D. Bailey c Miandad b Holmes	0	B 6, l-b 13, w 1, n-b 2	22	
P. D. Johnson b Holmes	0			
S. G. Plumb run out	11	1/0 2/75 3/84	(9 wkts, 55 overs) 175	
†F. E. Collyer c Francis b A. A. Jones	24	4/89 5/115 6/121 7/132		
A. W. Allin b Moseley	3	8/159 9/173		

Bowling: Nash 11–2–37–1; Moseley 11–0–31–2; A. A. Jones 11–2–37–3; Holmes 11–3–21–2; Mack 11–2–27–0.

Glamorgan

A. Jones not out......................	61
J. A. Hopkins not out................	103
B 4, l-b 5, w 1, n-b 2.........	12

(no wkt, 42.5 overs) 176

D. A. Francis, Javed Miandad, N. G. Featherstone, G. C. Holmes, *M. A. Nash, †E. W. Jones, E. A. Moseley, A. J. Mack and A. A. Jones did not bat.

Bowling: Collins 8–1–23–0; Wing 8–2–25–0; Yeabsley 9–0–35–0; Allin 9–1–42–0; Bailey 6.5–1–30–0; Plumb 2–0–9–0.

Umpires: D. Shackleton and A. G. T. Whitehead.

GLAMORGAN v SUSSEX

At Cardiff, May 22, 23. Sussex won by eight wickets. Glamorgan struggled after being asked to bat on a wicket of uneven bounce. Javed Miandad and Francis initiated a recovery with a stand of 69, but once their partnership was broken the innings collapsed. Gold Award winner Mendis and Parker gave Sussex an encouraging start with a second-wicket partnership of 100, and when play ended at 7.45 p.m., an hour having been lost because of bad light, the visitors needed 38 runs off fourteen overs. Mendis (four 4s) and Imran (one 6 and five 4s) easily achieved victory the next morning, taking Sussex into the quarter-finals.

Glamorgan

A. Jones c Graves b Wells............	20	A. E. Cordle c Parker b Arnold........	8
J. A. Hopkins b Imran................	2	E. A. Moseley not out	3
D. A. Francis c Spencer b Phillipson....	48	A. A. Jones not out	9
Javed Miandad c Long b Waller	33	L-b 6, w 6	12
N. G. Featherstone lbw b Phillipson	16		
G. C. Holmes c Wessels b Arnold	20	1/6 2/33 3/102 (9 wkts, 55 overs) 185	
*M. A. Nash c Wessels b Phillipson.....	13	4/129 5/134 6/156 7/162	
†E. W. Jones c Waller b Arnold........	1	8/173 9/173	

Bowling: Imran 11–2–28–1; Arnold 11–3–23–3; Wells 7–0–26–1; Spencer 11–2–33–0; Phillipson 8–0–38–3; Waller 7–0–25–1.

Sussex

K. C. Wessels lbw b Nash	15	
G. D. Mendis not out................	61	
P. W. G. Parker b Cordle............	44	
Imran Khan not out.................	48	
B 5, L-b 9, w 6, n-b 1........	21	

1/31 2/131 (2 wkts, 47.4 overs) 189

P. J. Graves, C. P. Phillipson, C. M. Wells, *†A. Long, G. G. Arnold, J. Spencer and C. E. Waller did not bat.

Bowling: Nash 11–4–29–1; Moseley 8–1–23–0; A. A. Jones 8–0–19–0; Cordle 11–1–30–1; Holmes 4–0–26–0; Featherstone 5.4–0–41–0.

Umpires: R. S. Herman and P. B. Wight.

GLOUCESTERSHIRE v GLAMORGAN

At Bristol, May 10. Glamorgan won by 1 run. Gloucestershire's makeshift attack, with Brain absent and Procter unable to bowl, limited Glamorgan to 228 for eight. Gloucestershire suffered a mid-innings collapse, but Procter and Partridge swung the match again, and victory seemed within reach until Procter was bowled, with 14 runs still required. In an exciting finish, Wilkins, formerly of Glamorgan, needed 3 runs off the last ball, but managed only a single. A. A. Jones received the Gold Award.

Glamorgan

A. Jones c and b Bainbridge	25
J. A. Hopkins c Bainbridge b Graveney	31
D. A. Francis c Wilkins b Graveney	39
Javed Miandad c A. W. Stovold b Broad	32
N. G. Featherstone run out	32
G. C. Holmes c Surridge b Wilkins	30
*M. A. Nash c Procter b Surridge	14
†E. W. Jones b Surridge	2

A. A. Jones did not bat.

E. A. Moseley not out 7
A. J. Mack not out 0

B 2, 1-b 7, w 3, n-b 4 16
———
1/54 2/66 3/129   (8 wkts, 55 overs) 228
4/145 5/184 6/209
7/220 8/222

Bowling: Wilkins 11–2–39–1; Surridge 8–0–42–2; Bainbridge 11–3–27–1; Graveney 11–1–47–2; Partridge 6–1–31–0; Broad 8–2–26–1.

Gloucestershire

B. C. Broad c Hopkins b A. A. Jones	10
Sadiq Mohammad b A. A. Jones	22
Zaheer Abbas c Francis b Nash	31
†A. W. Stovold c Miandad b Mack	46
*M. J. Procter b Moseley	50
M. W. Stovold c Hopkins b Nash	6
P. Bainbridge lbw b Nash	3
M. D. Partridge st E. W. Jones b Holmes	14

D. Surridge did not bat.

D. A. Graveney not out 11
A. H. Wilkins not out 5

B 15, 1-b 5, w 5, n-b 4 29
———
1/29 2/42 3/119   (8 wkts, 55 overs) 227
4/127 5/137 6/143 7/196
8/215

Bowling: Nash 11–1–38–3; Moseley 11–3–22–1; A. A. Jones; 11–1–44–2; Holmes 8–0–45–1; Mack 11–2–28–1; Featherstone 1–0–7–0; Miandad 2–0–14–0.

Umpires: D. J. Halfyard and J. van Geloven.

GLOUCESTERSHIRE v ESSEX

At Bristol, May 17. Gloucestershire won by five wickets, a victory which looked improbable when Gooch was blazing away before lunch, hitting nine 4s and a 6 in his 62. When he departed, Essex lost the initiative, although Hardie and Pont had a good stand before the last six wickets went for 32 in six overs to Wilkins and Procter. Gold Award winner Andy Stovold played the crucial innings for Gloucestershire, putting on 57 for the fifth wicket with his brother Martin, and Bainbridge also batted sensibly. Essex did their cause no good by bowling thirteen no balls, equivalent to giving the opposition more than two extra overs.

Essex

G. A. Gooch b Bainbridge	62
M. H. Denness c M. W. Stovold b Bainbridge	16
K. S. McEwan c A. W. Stovold b Partridge	6
*K. W. R. Fletcher lbw b Partridge	1
B. R. Hardie b Wilkins	53
K. R. Pont c Broad b Wilkins	44
S. Turner b Procter	7

N. Phillip b Wilkins 5
R. E. East lbw b Procter 1
†N. Smith b Wilkins 6
J. K. Lever not out 3
B 4, 1-b 12, w 4 20
———
1/69 2/84 3/90 4/104   (54 overs) 224
5/192 6/197 7/209 8/211
9/216

Bowling: Procter 10–0–26–2; Wilkins 10–1–55–4; Bainbridge 10–1–43–2; Partridge 11–3–32–2; Graveney 11–1–33–0; Broad 2–0–15–0.

Gloucestershire

B. C. Broad c Gooch b Lever	11	P. Bainbridge not out	16
Sadiq Mohammad c East b Pont	28		
Zaheer Abbas b Turner	12	L-b 23, w 4, n-b 13	40
†A. W. Stovold not out	73		
*M. J. Procter c Smith b Pont	13	1/13 2/28 (5 wkts, 54 overs) 225	
M. W. Stovold b Gooch	32	3/96 4/116 5/173	

M. D. Partridge, D. A. Graveney, A. H. Wilkins and S. J. Windaybank did not bat.

Bowling: Lever 11–2–33–1; Phillip 11–1–45–0; Turner 11–3–27–1; Gooch 10–1–32–1; Pont 7–0–33–2; East 4–0–15–0.

Umpires: D. G. L. Evans and R. Palmer.

MINOR COUNTIES v ESSEX

At Watford, May 14. Essex won by nine wickets. Minor Counties' cause was undermined within nine overs by Phillip's pace and Lever's swing. Tolchard and Cairns called on their first-class experience to repair the innings against the change bowlers, adding 86 in 27 overs as Tolchard worked steadfastly for 51 overs. Essex plundered 57 from their first eight overs as Gooch, the Gold Award winner, and McEwan matched each other's stroke-play – Gooch thrashing three 6s – and the game ended before tea.

Minor Counties

J. G. Tolchard b Lever	54	R. L. Johns c Turner b East	2
R. V. Lewis c McEwan b Phillip	4	D. I. Yeabsley not out	4
Timur Mohamed b Phillip	0	B. G. Collins b Lever	6
*D. Bailey b Phillip	2	L-b 11, w 6, n-b 5	22
P. D. Johnson lbw b Lever	1		
S. Greensword b Gooch b Lever	1	1/8 2/12 3/14 4/15 (52.4 overs) 157	
B. L. Cairns c Denness b East	43	5/17 6/103 7/138	
†F. E. Collyer lbw b Turner	18	8/143 9/151	

Bowling: Lever 10.4–2–24–4; Phillip 10–2–22–3; Pont 5–0–24–0; Turner 11–2–24–1; Gooch 6–0–19–0; East 10–3–22–2.

Essex

G. A. Gooch not out	77
M. H. Denness b Cairns	25
K. S. McEwan not out	40
B 2, l-b 7, w 7	16

1/57   (1 wkt, 24 overs) 158

*K. W. R. Fletcher, B. R. Hardie, K. R. Pont, S. Turner, N. Phillip, R. E. East, †N. Smith and J. K. Lever did not bat.

Bowling: Cairns 8–2–38–1; Collins 7–2–33–0; Yeabsley 4–0–24–0; Greensword 3–0–21–0; Johns 2–0–26–0.

Umpires: R. Palmer and P. B. Wight.

MINOR COUNTIES v GLOUCESTERSHIRE

At Chippenham, May 22. Minor Counties won by 3 runs. The decision to combine the talents of Minor Counties after eight years was handsomely vindicated when they finally broke through to beat a first-class county. Their innings was heavily under-pinned by Tolchard and Cairns, who was the chief beneficiary as Gloucestershire spilled three chances; he was dropped on 5. Gloucestershire, already behind the required rate, fell into serious trouble when Procter was caught on the boundary 4 runs after his third-wicket stand of 62 with Zaheer had ended. They needed 50 from the last six overs, reduced to 10 from the last. Bainbridge, required to bat with a broken finger, was bowled off stump as he swung in search of the winning boundary off the last ball. Cairns won the Gold Award.

Minor Counties

J. S. Johnson c Graveney b Surridge	22	B. G. Collins b Wilkins	0
J. G. Tolchard st Stovold b Graveney	35	A. W. Allin not out	3
Timur Mohamed c Sadiq b Surridge	20		
*D. Bailey c Sadiq b Partridge	23	L-b 13, w 2, n-b 1	16
B. L. Cairns b Procter	54		
P. D. Johnson run out	4	1/45 2/80 3/87 (8 wkts, 55 overs) 212	
S. Greensword not out	22	4/123 5/149 6/183 7/206	
†F. E. Collyer c A. W. Stovold b Wilkins	13	8/209	

D. I. Yeabsley did not bat.

Bowling: Wilkins 11–2–35–2; Procter 11–2–39–1; Surridge 11–1–32–2; Bainbridge 7–2–21–0; Partridge 10–0–49–1; Graveney 4–1–17–1; Broad 1–0–3–0.

Gloucestershire

B. C. Broad c Cairns b Yeabsley	7	A. H. Wilkins lbw b Cairns	27
Sadiq Mohammad c P. D. Johnson b Yeabsley	42	D. Surridge run out	0
		P. Bainbridge b Collins	2
Zaheer Abbas c Collyer b Collins	26		
*M. J. Procter c P. D. Johnson b Cairns	45	B 1, l-b 12, w 3	16
†A. W. Stovold c P. D. Johnson b Allin	15		
M. W. Stovold c Tolchard b Allin	5	1/44 2/60 3/122 4/126 (55 overs) 209	
D. A. Graveney c and b Allin	2	5/146 6/151 7/151 8/202	
M. D. Partridge not out	22	9/205	

Bowling: Collins 11–2–38–2; Cairns 11–0–35–2; Greensword 11–2–32–0; Yeabsley 11–0–49–2; Allin 10–1–37–3; Bailey 1–0–2–0.

Umpires: W. E. Alley and A. G. T. Whitehead.

SUSSEX v GLOUCESTERSHIRE

At Hove, May 14. Sussex won by 9 runs. When Zaheer and Broad were progressing attractively towards a second-wicket stand of 97, the target of 238 appeared to be within Gloucestershire's reach. But, despite a stubborn 61 not out by Andrew Stovold, Gloucestershire fell behind the run-rate, and still needed 17 off the final over. Stovold and Graveney could manage only 7. The Gold Award was deservedly won by Mendis, who hit a dozen forceful 4s in his 109 and, with Imran, delighted spectators with a purposeful third-wicket partnership of 146 off 32 overs. Brain had a splendid bowling spell at the start of the Sussex innings, conceding only 9 runs from his eleven overs.

Sussex

G. D. Mendis c Graveney b Wilkins	109	A. C. S. Pigott not out	4
K. C. Wessels c Sadiq b Brain	11		
P. W. G. Parker lbw b Wilkins	4	B 16, l-b 10, w 10	36
Imran Khan c M. W. Stovold b Procter	55		
P. J. Graves b Procter	4	1/38 2/45 3/191 (5 wkts, 55 overs) 238	
C. P. Phillipson not out	15	4/200 5/228	

*†A. Long, G. G. Arnold, J. Spencer and C. E. Waller did not bat.

Bowling: Procter 11–1–48–2; Brain 11–6–9–1; Wilkins 10–0–55–2; Bainbridge 7–1–34–0; Partridge 11–2–34–0; Broad 5–0–22–0.

Gloucestershire

B. C. Broad c Long b Spencer	40	M. D. Partridge c and b Pigott	5
Sadiq Mohammad c Graves b Arnold	4	D. A. Graveney not out	9
Zaheer Abbas c Imran b Waller	60		
*M. J. Procter c Parker b Imran	1	B 2, 1-b 14, n-b 2	18
†A. W. Stovold not out	61		
M. W. Stovold c Long b Pigott	19	1/10 2/107 3/108 (7 wkts, 55 overs) 229
P. Bainbridge b Pigott	12	4/111 5/178 6/200 7/210

A. H. Wilkins and B. M. Brain did not bat.

Bowling: Imran 11–2–35–1; Arnold 11–2–35–1; Pigott 11–0–62–3; Spencer 11–0–41–1; Waller 11–0–38–1.

Umpires: W. L. Budd and J. G. Langridge.

SUSSEX v MINOR COUNTIES

At Hove, May 20, 21. Sussex won by 30 runs. Minor Counties fought bravely throughout and at one time looked to be heading for a shock victory. Yeabsley quickly sent back Wessels and Parker, and a steady attack restricted the run-rate until Gold Award winner Imran Khan and Graves came together to plunder 76 off eight hectic overs. Mendis, Imran and Graves scored all but 33 of the Sussex total. The visitors recovered from the early loss of Tolchard as Lewis and Timur Mohamed added 61 off fifteen overs. Bailey scored a determined 66 (nine 4s) and only when he was fifth out at 170 did Sussex start to take control.

Sussex

K. C. Wessels b Yeabsley	16	*†A. Long run out	0
G. D. Mendis c Johnson b Bailey	69	G. G. Arnold b Collins	4
P. W. G. Parker b Yeabsley	1	C. E. Waller not out	0
Imran Khan c Johnson b Cairns	68	L-b 4, w 3	7
P. J. Graves not out	67		
C. P. Phillipson c and b Cairns	5	1/38 2/46 3/114 (9 wkts, 55 overs) 237
C. M. Wells run out	0	4/190 5/208 6/215 7/220
A. C. S. Pigott b Collins	0	8/223 9/231

Bowling: Collins 11–1–65–2; Cairns 11–4–40–2; Greensword 11–3–38–0; Yeabsley 11–0–28–2; Allin 9–0–46–0; Bailey 2–0–13–1.

Minor Counties

J. G. Tolchard c Wells b Imran	10	†F. E. Collyer b Arnold	3
R. V. Lewis lbw b Wells	31	B. G. Collins not out	16
Timur Mohamed b Wells	29		
*D. Bailey c Long b Arnold	66	B 8, w 6, n-b 2	16
P. D. Johnson c Long b Imran	9		
S. Greensword not out	27	1/15 2/76 3/87 4/128 (7 wkts, 55 overs) 207
B. L. Cairns b Pigott	0	5/170 6/172 7/177

A. W. Allin and D. I. Yeabsley did not bat.

Bowling: Imran 11–3–24–2; Arnold 11–1–33–2; Pigott 8–0–49–1; Wells 11–3–36–2; Waller 9–1–31–0; Phillipson 5–0–18–0.

Umpires: D. J. Dennis and R. S. Herman.

GROUP D

HAMPSHIRE v MIDDLESEX

At Southampton, May 14. Middlesex won by seven wickets. Hampshire lost two wickets for 4 in the first four overs but an impressive innings by Jesty and useful contributions from Taylor and Stephenson gave them a respectable total. Middlesex made an equally disastrous start, losing Brearley and Slack for 7 and Radley at 36. Then Barlow and Gatting took them to a comfortable victory with an unbeaten fourth-wicket partnership of 166 – a record for the competition, which was broken three days later by Lloyd and Reidy for Lancashire. Gold Award winner Barlow hit one 6 and ten 4s and Gatting hit eleven 4s.

Hampshire

C. L. Smith c Gould b Daniel.........	3	†G. R. Stephenson b Daniel..........	32
N. G. Cowley c Brearley b van der Bijl ..	0	J. W. Southern not out..............	8
D. R. Turner c Gould b Edmonds	19	K. Stevenson run out	2
T. E. Jesty c Gatting b James..........	67		
*N. E. J. Pocock run out	6	B 1, l-b 8, n-b 5.............	14
V. P. Terry c Gould b Edmonds........	7		
M. N. S. Taylor b Gatting	38	1/2 2/4 3/62 4/80 5/93 (55 overs) 199	
S. F. Graf c Gatting b James	3	6/134 7/143 8/168 9/196	

Bowling: van der Bijl 11–4–20–1; Daniel 11–1–45–2; James 6–0–32–2; Emburey 11–2–24–0; Edmonds 11–1–40–2; Gatting 5–0–24–1.

Middlesex

*J. M. Brearley c Stephenson b Graf	1	M. W. Gatting not out	83
W. N. Slack b Stevenson	3	B 4, l-b 6, w 3, n-b 1.........	14
C. T. Radley lbw b Taylor	12		
G. D. Barlow not out	89	1/5 2/7 3/36 (3 wkts, 48.3 overs) 202	

†I. J. Gould, P. H. Edmonds, J. E. Emburey, V. A. P. van der Bijl, W. W. Daniel and K. D. James did not bat.

Bowling: Graf 11–4–24–1; Stevenson 11–1–43–1; Taylor 4–0–22–1; Jesty 7–0–21–0; Southern 8.3–0–41–0; Cowley 7–0–37–0.

Umpires: W. E. Alley and K. E. Palmer.

HAMPSHIRE v SOMERSET

At Bournemouth, May 22. Somerset won by 55 runs. Hampshire became the first first-class county to lose all four of their zonal games in successive seasons. They started the match well as lively bowling from Stevenson and Malone reduced the visitors to 23 for three in six overs. However, Somerset's fortunes were revived by Gold Award winner Marks, Botham and Taylor. With Botham unable to bowl because of a back injury, a total of 204 should not have been beyond Hampshire but Nicholas, Cowley and Jesty all fell for 19 in the first ten overs. Pocock and Taylor added 52 in fourteen overs for the sixth wicket, but once they were parted the end was not long delayed. Dredge's figures of 7.3–0–10–4 were the best for Somerset in the competition.

Somerset

*B. C. Rose b Malone	13	K. F. Jennings b Stevenson	6
S. M. Gavaskar b Stevenson	0	C. H. Dredge b Stevenson	2
P. W. Denning b Stevenson	6	H. R. Moseley b Malone	5
I. T. Botham b Southern.............	33	B 9, l-b 12, w 4	25
V. J. Marks not out	81		
†D. J. S. Taylor c Nicholas b Cowley ...	28	1/8 2/16 3/23 4/75 (54.5 overs) 204	
G. I. Burgess c Stevenson b Cowley.....	4	5/140 6/158 7/159	
D. Breakwell lbw b Jesty	1	8/179 9/193	

Bowling: Malone 10.5–2–32–2; Stevenson 9–0–38–4; Taylor 5–0–14–0; Jesty 11–0–35–1; Southern 9–1–38–1; Cowley 10–2–22–2.

Hampshire

N. G. Cowley lbw b Moseley	7	J. W. Southern b Dredge		14
M. C. J. Nicholas c Taylor b Moseley	0	K. Stevenson not out		2
C. L. Smith run out	23	S. J. Malone c Gavaskar b Dredge		0
T. E. Jesty c Taylor b Dredge	1	B 1, l-b 9, w 1, n-b 3		14
D. R. Turner c and b Marks	25			
*N. E. J. Pocock b Dredge	41	1/1 2/14 3/19 4/50	(49.3 overs)	149
M. N. S. Taylor c Rose b Jennings	20	5/66 6/118 7/121 8/136		
†G. R. Stephenson run out	2	9/149		

Bowling: Moseley 8–1–22–2; Dredge 7.3–0–10–4; Burgess 11–1–37–0; Marks 11–4–26–1; Breakwell 6–0–26–0; Jennings 6–1–14–1.

Umpires: W. L. Budd and D. J. Constant.

KENT v SOMERSET

At Canterbury, May 10. Somerset won by nine wickets. This was a crushing defeat for Kent, who made a respectable total after being put in and making a shaky start. Ealham hit his half-century in fifty-seven minutes with a 6 and seven 4s, and Cowdrey reached his in even time with seven boundaries. Rose and Gavaskar – making his début for Somerset – set a new first-wicket record for the competition, adding 241 in 44 overs. Gavaskar batted one hundred and sixty minutes and hit twelve 4s, while Rose's unbeaten innings contained seven 6s and eleven 4s. He hit the off-spinner Rowe for two 6s in one over and four in succession in the next, hastening victory with 11.4 overs to spare, and taking the Gold Award.

Kent

R. A. Woolmer c and b Dredge	20	R. W. Hills b Moseley		5
C. J. C. Rowe b Moseley	4	G. R. Dilley not out		2
C. J. Tavaré c Taylor b Jennings	16			
Asif Iqbal c Breakwell b Marks	46	B 2, l-b 5, w 3		10
*A. G. E. Ealham st Taylor b Breakwell	51			
†A. P. E. Knott c Denning b Moseley	29	1/15 2/35 3/53	(7 wkts, 55 overs)	242
C. S. Cowdrey not out	59	4/144 5/154 6/206 7/229		

D. L. Underwood and K. B. S. Jarvis did not bat.

Bowling: Botham 11–1–48–0; Moseley 11–1–48–3; Dredge 8–1–36–1; Jennings 11–4–34–1; Breakwell 9–0–51–1; Marks 5–1–15–1.

Somerset

S. M. Gavaskar c sub b Hills	90		
*B. C. Rose not out	137		
P. A. Slocombe not out	4		
L-b 10, w 3, n-b 1	14		
1/241		(1 wkt, 43.2 overs)	245

P. W. Denning, I. T. Botham, V. J. Marks, †D. J. S. Taylor, D. Breakwell, K. F. Jennings, C. H. Dredge and H. R. Moseley did not bat.

Bowling: Dilley 8–3–24–0; Jarvis 8–0–43–0; Woolmer 6–0–30–0; Hills 4.2–0–23–1; Underwood 11–1–39–0; Cowdrey 4–0–33–0; Rowe 2–0–39–0.

Umpires: D. J. Constant and K. E. Palmer.

KENT v HAMPSHIRE

At Canterbury, May 20, 21. Kent won by 1 run. Tavaré and Asif retrieved Kent's fortunes with a third-wicket stand of 56 off twelve overs, and Ealham and Tavaré added 75 off eighteen overs. Tavaré hit two 6s over the square leg boundary and ten 4s, many of them fine off-side drives. Dilley shocked Hampshire with two early wickets in six balls, but Smith and

Jesty, who won the Gold Award, pulled them round before rain interrupted play. On the next morning they took their stand to 134, off 36 overs, but once they were out Hampshire again faltered. Turner tried in vain to steer them home but Shepherd struck twice for Kent. Although the target was finally narrowed to 2 to level the scores off the last ball, Hampshire managed only a single and Kent won a game they thought was lost.

Kent

R. A. Woolmer b Jesty	19	G. R. Dilley not out	13
G. W. Johnson lbw b Malone	3	D. L. Underwood run out	2
C. J. Tavaré c Nicholas b Cowley	87		
Asif Iqbal lbw b Jesty	24	L-b 6, w 3, n-b 1	10
*A. G. E. Ealham c Taylor b Stevenson	38		
†A. P. E. Knott run out	13	1/10 2/33 3/89 (9 wkts, 55 overs) 212	
C. S. Cowdrey run out	1	4/164 5/178 6/179 7/186	
J. N. Shepherd b Malone	2	8/206 9/212	

K. B. S. Jarvis did not bat.

Bowling: Malone 11–2–35–2; Stevenson 11–2–29–1; Taylor 7–0–31–0; Jesty 11–0–38–2; Southern 10–3–39–0; Cowley 5–0–30–1.

Hampshire

M. C. J. Nicholas b Dilley	3	M. N. S. Taylor run out	1
N. G. Cowley b Dilley	3	J. W. Southern not out	4
C. L. Smith b Johnson	48	B 4, l-b 8, w 8, n-b 9	29
T. E. Jesty b Underwood	74		
D. R. Turner b Shepherd	27	1/6 2/13 3/147 (8 wkts, 55 overs) 211	
*N. E. J. Pocock c Johnson b Shepherd	13	4/155 5/195 6/206	
†G. R. Stephenson b Dilley	9	7/206 8/211	

K. Stevenson and S. J. Malone did not bat.

Bowling: Dilley 11–2–29–3; Shepherd 11–1–40–2; Jarvis 9–2–34–0; Asif 5–1–26–0; Woolmer 4–0–17–0; Underwood 11–2–22–1; Johnson 4–1–14–1.

Umpires: J. G. Langridge and R. Palmer.

MIDDLESEX v SURREY

At Lord's, May 10. Middlesex won by eight wickets. Surrey were virtually runless against the new ball, van der Bijl conceding just three singles in his first eight overs. Howarth, nine overs on 0, initiated a recovery against uncharacteristically inaccurate spin bowling. Emburey atoned by disposing of Howarth and Knight in successive overs and Daniel returned with three wickets in one over. Middlesex were well on their way when Radley joined Brearley – the Gold Award winner – in a match-winning stand of 139 in 27 overs. Brearley's unbeaten century was his second of the week at Lord's.

Surrey

A. R. Butcher b Daniel	1	†C. J. Richards not out	16
G. S. Clinton c Gatting b Emburey	16	P. I. Pocock not out	0
G. P. Howarth c Brearley b Emburey	61		
*R. D. V. Knight c Selvey b Emburey	32	B 6, l-b 18, w 2	26
G. R. J. Roope c Gould b Daniel	19		
D. M. Smith c Radley b Daniel	27	1/6 2/47 3/127 (8 wkts, 55 overs) 211	
S. T. Clarke c Barlow b Gatting	13	4/134 5/175 6/176 7/176	
R. D. Jackman b Daniel	0	8/208	

P. H. L. Wilson did not bat.

Bowling: van der Bijl 11–5–13–0; Daniel 11–2–28–4; Edmonds 5–0–24–0; Selvey 11–1–49–0; Gatting 6–1–23–1; Emburey 11–1–48–3.

Middlesex

M. J. Smith c Smith b Knight	26
*J. M. Brearley not out	100
C. T. Radley b Clarke	68
G. D. Barlow not out	11
B 4, l-b 5, w 1	10

1/59 2/198   (2 wkts, 48.2 overs) 215

M. W. Gatting, †I. J. Gould, P. H. Edmonds, J. E. Emburey, V. A. P. van der Bijl, M. W. W. Selvey and W. W. Daniel did not bat.

Bowling: Clarke 10–0–34–1; Jackman 11–3–39–0; Knight 8–0–38–1; Wilson 8–0–40–0; Pocock 11–1–50–0; Clinton 2–0–4–0.

Umpires: R. S. Herman and J. G. Langridge.

MIDDLESEX v KENT

At Lord's, May 22. Middlesex won by 80 runs. Middlesex, put in, made an excellent start, but Asif undermined the innings when, as sixth bowler, he swept through the main batting for his best return in the competition. Middlesex needed the insurance given them by a stand of 48 in six overs between Emburey and van der Bijl. The South African made sure of the Gold Award with yet another restrictive spell and a smooth pick-up and throw to run out Ealham. Tavaré clinched his place in the Prudential Trophy squad by withstanding Daniel's pace.

Middlesex

M. J. Smith c Rowe b Shepherd	17	J. E. Emburey not out ... 17
*J. M. Brearley c Johnson b Asif	47	V. A. P. van der Bijl run out ... 29
C. T. Radley c and b Asif	37	L-b 14, w 2 ... 16
G. D. Barlow c Tavaré b Asif	20	
M. W. Gatting b Underwood	16	1/28 2/99 3/108 (8 wkts, 55 overs) 213
†I. J. Gould c Rowe b Asif	5	4/138 5/149 6/153 7/165
P. H. Edmonds c Underwood b Asif	9	8/213

M. W. W. Selvey and W. W. Daniel did not bat.

Bowling: Dilley 11–2–42–0; Shepherd 11–2–46–1; Jarvis 6–0–19–0; Underwood 11–2–22–1; Johnson 5–0–26–0; Asif 11–0–42–5.

Kent

G. W. Johnson c Radley b Emburey	15	G. R. Dilley b Daniel ... 0
C. J. C. Rowe c Gould b van der Bijl	1	D. L. Underwood not out ... 3
C. J. Tavaré b Gatting	46	K. B. S. Jarvis b Emburey ... 1
C. S. Cowdrey c and b Gatting	10	
*A. G. E. Ealham run out	0	B 2, l-b 8, w 1, n-b 1 ... 12
Asif Iqbal lbw b Emburey	31	
†A. P. E. Knott c Gould b Gatting	12	1/1 2/55 3/78 4/79 5/80 (46.5 overs) 133
J. N. Shepherd c Edmonds b Daniel	2	6/108 7/127 8/127 9/131

Bowling: van der Bijl 7–5–10–1; Daniel 8–1–17–2; Selvey 4–1–14–0; Emburey 9.5–1–35–3; Edmonds 11–1–26–0; Gatting 7–0–19–3.

Umpires: R. Julian and C. T. Spencer.

SOMERSET v MIDDLESEX

At Taunton, May 17. Middlesex won by 1 run in a palpitating finish as Somerset's final pair just failed to score the 10 needed from the last five balls. Middlesex recovered superbly from a bad start as Barlow hit fifteen 4s and Gatting hit fourteen in a fourth-wicket stand of 163 in 30 overs. Somerset were without Rose, who was ill, and injury had prevented Botham from bowling, but, led by Gavaskar, they were soon in hot pursuit of the vast total. Gavaskar, given excellent help by Denning and Slocombe, hit three 6s and twelve 4s in a superb innings, but once Edmonds dismissed him at 217 Somerset were always just too far behind. Taylor and Popplewell – the latter escaping a disputed run out because umpire Wight was unsighted – strove well against the seamers, but the task of scoring 17 off the last three overs and 11 off the last was beyond them. Edmonds won the Gold Award.

Middlesex

*J. M. Brearley c Denning b Dredge	6	P. H. Edmonds c Denning b Moseley	32
M. J. Smith c Botham b Jennings	13	J. E. Emburey not out	5
C. T. Radley lbw b Dredge	0	B 4, l-b 21, w 5, n-b 1	31
G. D. Barlow c Slocombe b Moseley	93		
M. W. Gatting not out	95	1/11 2/11 3/45 (6 wkts, 55 overs)	282
†I. J. Gould c Denning b Moseley	7	4/208 5/218 6/264	

V. A. P. van der Bijl, M. W. W. Selvey and W. W. Daniel did not bat.

Bowling: Moseley 11–2–39–3; Dredge 11–0–59–2; Popplewell 8–1–42–0; Jennings 11–2–39–1; Breakwell 7–1–31–0; Marks 7–0–41–0.

Somerset

S. M. Gavaskar st Gould b Edmonds	123	K. F. Jennings run out	0
P. W. Denning c Daniel b Edmonds	42	C. H. Dredge not out	3
P. A. Slocombe c Emburey b Edmonds	42		
*I. T. Botham c Edmonds b Selvey	3	B 3, l-b 6, w 3, n-b 8	20
D. Breakwell c Daniel b Edmonds	4		
V. J. Marks c Radley b Daniel	10	1/120 2/217 3/220 (8 wkts, 55 overs)	281
†D. J. S. Taylor run out	21	4/227 5/229 6/254	
N. F. M. Popplewell not out	13	7/268 8/273	

H. R. Moseley did not bat.

Bowling: Daniel 11–3–44–1; van der Bijl 11–1–42–0; Emburey 11–0–49–0; Selvey 8–0–64–1; Edmonds 11–0–45–4; Gatting 3–0–17–0.

Umpires: P. B. Wight and D. J. Halfyard.

SOMERSET v SURREY

At Taunton, May 20, 21. Surrey won by four wickets. Somerset were put in on a fresh pitch and slumped to 55 for four as Jackman struck firmly, but they recovered well through Marks (eight 4s), Taylor, Burgess and Breakwell (two 6s in four lively overs). Rain delayed Surrey's innings until the second day when they met early trouble from Dredge before Knight and Butcher, missed at 3 and 35, put together the decisive partnership of 119 in 33 overs. Butcher hit eight 4s in 41 overs and, although three wickets fell quickly, Jackman, the Gold Award winner, safely achieved the target of 10 from the last seventeen balls.

Somerset

S. M. Gavaskar run out	12	D. Breakwell not out	29
P. W. Denning c Smith b Jackman	4	K. F. Jennings not out	2
P. A. Slocombe lbw b Jackman	12		
*I. T. Botham c Smith b Jackman	15	B 8, l-b 10, w 1	19
V. J. Marks b Clarke	62		
†D. J. S. Taylor b Clarke	31	1/4 2/28 3/30 4/55 (7 wkts, 55 overs)	215
G. I. Burgess c Howarth b Knight	29	5/126 6/170 7/192	

C. H. Dredge and H. R. Moseley did not bat.

Bowling: Clarke 11–1–45–2; Jackman 11–3–20–3; Smith 5–0–27–0; Pocock 11–3–26–0; Cheatle 11–1–45–0; Knight 6–0–33–1.

Surrey

A. R. Butcher b Marks	72	G. R. J. Roope not out	3
G. S. Clinton c Botham b Dredge	1	R. D. Jackman not out	9
G. P. Howarth lbw b Dredge	21	L-b 11, w 4, n-b 4	19
*R. D. V. Knight c Slocombe b Moseley	68		
D. M. Smith c and b Dredge	22	1/4 2/30 3/149　(6 wkts, 54.1 overs) 216	
S. T. Clarke c Taylor b Dredge	1	4/196 5/198 6/206	

†C. J. Richards, P. I. Pocock and R. G. L. Cheatle did not bat.

Bowling: Moseley 11–1–42–1; Dredge 11–2–34–4; Jennings 8.1–0–30–0; Burgess 11–1–38–0; Marks 11–0–44–1; Breakwell 2–0–9–0.

Umpires: W. E. Alley and D. J. Halfyard.

SURREY v KENT

At The Oval, May 15. Surrey won by three wickets. The only county to put their match back 24 hours because of the TUC Day of Action, Surrey were rewarded with a fair crowd and a victory. Kent, choosing to bat on a good pitch, lost Woolmer fifth ball to Gold Award winner Clarke who went on to take five for 23 and knocked in the final nail by hitting three 6s, the last of which ended the match. He also broke the one substantial Kent partnership – 98 in 22 overs between Tavaré and Asif – and this was followed by a post-lunch collapse in which seven wickets fell for 31 runs in nine overs. Tavaré (fourteen 4s) fell 5 runs short of his third century of the summer. Surrey stuttered with similar uncertainty after an opening partnership of 69 but were sustained by the stubborn qualities of Clinton, who almost invariably does well against his former county.

Kent

R. A. Woolmer lbw b Clarke	0	G. R. Dilley lbw b Clarke	0
C. J. C. Rowe b Pocock	17	D. L. Underwood hit wkt b Clarke	3
C. J. Tavaré c Richards b Smith	95	K. B. S. Jarvis not out	11
Asif Iqbal c Howarth b Clarke	41	B 1, l-b 9, w 7	17
*A. G. E. Ealham c Clarke b Smith	8		
†A. P. E. Knott c Richards b Clarke	0	1/0 2/59 3/157 4/171　(51.1 overs) 199	
C. S. Cowdrey c Clarke b Smith	16	5/173 6/186 7/191	
J. N. Shepherd c and b Smith	2	8/194 9/198	

Bowling: Clarke 10.1–1–23–5; Thomas 7–1–43–0; Smith 9–2–29–4; Pocock 11–2–30–1; Cheatle 11–0–36–0; Knight 3–0–21–0.

Surrey

A. R. Butcher c Shepherd b Underwood	34	S. T. Clarke not out	29
G. S. Clinton b Dilley	62	†C. J. Richards not out	5
G. P. Howarth c Asif b Underwood	13	B 4, l-b 12, w 4, n-b 1	21
*R. D. V. Knight c Tavaré b Jarvis	11		
G. R. J. Roope lbw b Jarvis	1	1/69 2/95 3/121　(7 wkts, 53.3 overs) 201	
D. M. Smith lbw b Woolmer	10	4/129 5/143 6/160	
D. J. Thomas b Woolmer	15	7/171	

P. I. Pocock and R. G. L. Cheatle did not bat.

Bowling: Dilley 11–3–25–1; Shepherd 7.3–0–25–0; Jarvis 10–1–47–2; Underwood 11–0–42–2; Woolmer 6–1–18–2; Asif 8–0–23–0.

Umpires: R. Julian and D. Shackleton.

SURREY v HAMPSHIRE

At The Oval, May 17. Surrey won by two wickets and again scraped home with nine deliveries in hand. Runs were hard to come by on a good pitch and twelve out of 21 batsmen had departed in single figures before Smith achieved the top score of 45 not out for which he received the Gold Award. At 109 for seven Surrey looked in some trouble but, with Graf out of action with a strained back, Smith, helped by Richards in an eighth-wicket stand of 42, was able to guide his side home.

Hampshire

J. M. Rice lbw b Clarke	8	S. F. Graf not out	25
M. C. J. Nicholas c Howarth b Smith	8	†G. R. Stephenson c Richards b Smith	8
C. L. Smith st Richards b Cheatle	30	S. J. Malone b Clarke	0
T. E. Jesty run out	5	B 3, l-b 8, w 5, n-b 1	17
D. R. Turner c Jackman b Cheatle	25		
*N. E. J. Pocock c and b Cheatle	0	1/14 2/24 3/45 4/80 (54.1 overs) 167	
N. G. Cowley c Butcher b Clarke	40	5/80 6/91 7/94	
M. N. S. Taylor lbw b Pocock	1	8/155 9/165	

Bowling: Clarke 10.1–3–22–3; Jackman 11–2–36–0; Smith 11–1–49–2; Cheatle 11–2–26–3; Pocock 11–3–17–1.

Surrey

A. R. Butcher c Stephenson b Nicholas	30	†C. J. Richards lbw b Jesty	17
G. S. Clinton c Stephenson b Graf	2	P. I. Pocock not out	8
G. P. Howarth b Malone	2		
*R. D. V. Knight c Stephenson b Jesty	40	B 3, l-b 10, w 10, n-b 1	24
G. R. J. Roope c Pocock b Nicholas	0		
D. M. Smith not out	45	1/6 2/9 3/65 4/67 (8 wkts, 53.3 overs) 168	
R. D. Jackman c Rice b Nicholas	0	5/101 6/108 7/109	
S. T. Clarke b Jesty	0	8/151	

Bowling: Graf 3–0–7–1; Malone 11–2–30–1; Taylor 11–1–36–0; Cowley 4.3–1–7–0; Nicholas 11–1–29–3; Jesty 11–1–27–3; Pocock 2–0–8–0.

Umpires: C. Cook and A. Jepson.

QUARTER-FINALS

ESSEX v SURREY

At Chelmsford, June 11. Essex won by 86 runs. Gooch and Denness scored 74 in sixteen overs after their team had been put in. Knight dismissed them both in the space of seven deliveries, but McEwan and Fletcher recaptured the initiative with a partnership of 96 in 24 overs. McEwan, the Gold Award winner, went on to score 46 out of a stand of 69 in eight overs with Hardie, and was finally caught on the square leg boundary, having hit two 6s and eleven 4s in one hundred and sixteen minutes. When Surrey replied Turner broke down with a calf muscle injury after bowling just four deliveries, but the home county still had enough resources to win with ease.

Essex

G. A. Gooch b Knight	43	S. Turner not out	5
M. H. Denness lbw b Knight	18		
K. S. McEwan c Howarth b Smith	95	B 4, l-b 12, w 6	22
*K. W. R. Fletcher b Jackman	46		
B. R. Hardie not out	37	1/74 2/75 (5 wkts, 55 overs) 270	
K. R. Pont b Clarke	4	3/171 4/240 5/256	

N. Phillip, R. E. East †N. Smith and J. K. Lever did not bat.

Bowling: Clarke 11–3–37–1; Jackman 11–1–41–1; Wilson 7–1–43–0; Knight 11–1–40–2; Pocock 11–1–50–0; Smith 4–0–37–1.

Surrey

A. R. Butcher c Smith b Pont	32	S. T. Clarke not out	1
G. S. Clinton c McEwan b Gooch	23	P. I. Pocock c Phillip b Pont	3
G. P. Howarth run out	42	P. H. L. Wilson b Pont	0
*R. D. V. Knight c Gooch b East	11		
D. M. Smith lbw b Phillip	13	B 1, l-b 15, w 6	22
M. A. Lynch lbw b Gooch	1		
R. D. Jackman c Hardie b Lever	32	1/52 2/97 3/118 4/131 (48 overs) 184
†C. J. Richards b Lever	4	5/134 6/144 7/180 8/181 9/184

Bowling: Lever 7–1–30–2; Phillip 9–0–31–1; Gooch 11–1–33–2; East 11–0–41–1; Pont 9.2–0–26–3; Turner 0.4–0–1–0.

Umpires: R. Julian and J. G. Langridge.

LANCASHIRE v WORCESTERSHIRE

At Manchester, June 11, 12. Worcestershire won by 45 runs. No play was possible on the first day because of rain. Gold Award winner Turner gave Worcestershire a decisive start with 72 out of 98 from the first sixteen overs possible in the hour before lunch, going on to score 122 in one hundred and thirty minutes (one 6 and thirteen 4s). The New Zealander and Neale, who batted for one hundred and sixty minutes for his 128 (thirteen 4s), continued to dominate the attack with a second-wicket partnership of 191, after Neale had been dropped at the wicket when 54. Facing the biggest total ever hit against them in one-day cricket Lancashire lost their first three batsmen for 56, but Abrahams and Hughes made useful scores and Cockbain and Simmons produced half-centuries without seriously threatening the visitors' total – a new record for Worcestershire in the competition.

Worcestershire

G. M. Turner b Reidy	122	†D. J. Humphries not out	5
J. A. Ormrod c Simmons b Hogg	2		
P. A. Neale c Cockbain b Simmons	128	B 1, l-b 4, n-b 2	7
E. J. O. Hemsley c Hughes b Reidy	8		
Younis Ahmed c Hayes b Malone	37	1/31 2/222 (5 wkts, 55 overs) 314
D. N. Patel not out	5	3/238 4/294 5/305

J. D. Inchmore, H. Alleyne, *N. Gifford and A. P. Pridgeon did not bat.

Bowling: Hogg 11–0–70–1; Malone 9–0–56–1; Reidy 11–0–70–2; Hughes 11–0–41–0; Simmons 10–0–53–1; Lloyd 3–0–17–0.

Lancashire

A. Kennedy c Humphries b Alleyne	11	M. F. Malone b Younis	2
D. Lloyd b Alleyne	4	†C. J. Scott not out	5
J. Abrahams b Patel	42	W. Hogg b Alleyne	0
*F. C. Hayes b Inchmore	19		
B. W. Reidy c Pridgeon b Patel	25	B 1, l-b 7, w 4, n-b 2	14
I. Cockbain c Turner b Younis	53		
J. Simmons c Inchmore b Gifford	53	1/4 2/22 3/56 4/100 (54.2 overs) 269
D. P. Hughes c Patel b Pridgeon	41	5/107 6/200 7/240 8/249 9/269

Bowling: Alleyne 10.2–1–39–3; Inchmore 11–0–47–1; Pridgeon 11–1–49–1; Patel 7–0–48–2; Gifford 11–0–55–1; Younis 4–0–17–2.

Umpires: C. Cook and A. Jepson.

MIDDLESEX v SUSSEX

At Lord's, June 11. Middlesex won by 29 runs. The match had an extraordinary start and an even more unusual finish. Imran was involved both times. In the morning he swung the ball so extravagantly that he bowled eight wides in his first five overs and eleven of the final count of nineteen. The extras conceded by Sussex were higher than their margin of defeat. Eight hours later, as Daniel produced some characteristically explosive bowling to clinch Middlesex's win, there was plenty of stuff whistling round the batsmen's heads and Imran protested to umpire van Geloven when Pigott was hit on the arm. (Daniel had broken Wessels's hand with an earlier lifter.) Immediately Brearley came in to give his view and, almost incredibly, he and Imran appeared on the point of grappling. The intervention of van Geloven prevented an unsavoury incident from degenerating. Imran said "When I bowl bumpers at tailenders, I am warned. Daniel bowled five, so I objected." In his report van Geloven stated that he had never heard such bad language, on or off the field, as Imran's. The TCCB asked each county to inquire and to take action. Over a month later the Board's Disciplinary Committee stated that the matter was ended, as they were satisfied with the reprimand Sussex delivered to Imran and with Middlesex's expression of regret that Brearley had become involved. Otherwise, the sides produced excellent cricket. Brearley and Radley were improving an almost static Middlesex start when Wells ran through their main batting. At 133 for seven it needed all Emburey's ability to nudge the ball about and van der Bijl's powerful hitting to work the score up to 195. Sussex, in reply, were only 48 for one from 30 overs, but Mendis and Parker attacked Edmonds successfully and Gatting had to be pressed into service. Gatting took the important wicket of Parker, Radley athletically ran out Mendis, and Daniel's hostility proved too much for Sussex's middle order. Emburey received the Gold Award.

Middlesex

M. J. Smith c Phillipson b Imran	0		V. A. P. van der Bijl c Long b Arnold	30
*J. M. Brearley c Long b Wells	32		M. W. W. Selvey lbw b Arnold	1
C. T. Radley c Pigott b Wells	28		W. W. Daniel b Imran	1
G. D. Barlow c Imran b Wells	0			
M. W. Gatting c Imran b Wells	15		B 4, l-b 13, w 19, n-b 2	38
†I. J. Gould c Wessels b Phillipson	10			
P. H. Edmonds c Long b Imran	6		1/7 2/75 3/77 4/93	(54.5 overs) 195
J. E. Emburey not out	34		5/99 6/108 7/133 8/179 9/184	

Bowling: Imran 10.5–4–12–3; Arnold 11–5–35–2; Spencer 11–1–41–0; Pigott 6–0–25–0; Wells 11–7–21–4; Phillipson 5–0–23–1.

Sussex

K. C. Wessels retired hurt	10		*†A. Long c Daniel b Gatting	2
T. D. Booth Jones lbw b Selvey	3		G. G. Arnold c Emburey b Gatting	0
G. D. Mendis run out	43		J. Spencer not out	0
P. W. G. Parker b Gatting	59			
Imran Khan c Radley b van der Bijl	23		B 1, l-b 6, w 5, n-b 7	19
C. P. Phillipson c Smith b Daniel	4			
C. M. Wells c Gould b Daniel	2		1/20 2/112 3/146 4/152	(53.3 overs) 166
A. C. S. Pigott c Gould b Daniel	1		5/157 6/159 7/165 8/166 9/166	

Bowling: van der Bijl 10–2–28–1; Daniel 11–2–21–3; Selvey 11–1–25–1; Emburey 11–3–15–0; Edmonds 3–0–22–0; Gatting 7.3–0–36–3.

Umpires: J. van Geloven and P. B. Wight.

NORTHAMPTONSHIRE v NOTTINGHAMSHIRE

At Northampton, June 11. Northamptonshire won by seven wickets. Electing to bat, Nottinghamshire were restricted to a total of only 143 by the seam bowling of Tim Lamb and Sarfraz. Lamb received the Gold Award for fiery bowling that produced five successive maidens, including four wickets. In reply, Northamptonshire soon lost Larkins but then Cook (seven 4s) and Williams (one 6 and six 4s) put on 108 in 35 overs, despite mediocre light, and victory was achieved with 7.5 overs to spare.

Nottinghamshire

P. A. Todd run out	18	E. E. Hemmings c Williams b Sarfraz	1
B. Hassan c Sharp b T. M. Lamb	10	K. E. Cooper b Sarfraz	2
H. T. Tunnicliffe c Cook b T. M. Lamb	13	M. K. Bore not out	0
*C. E. B. Rice b T. M. Lamb	3		
D. W. Randall c T. M. Lamb b Griffiths	48	B 1, l-b 7, n-b 2	10
J. D. Birch b T. M. Lamb	1		
†C. C. Curzon lbw b Willey	15	1/27 2/43 3/46 4/49 (51.1 overs) 143	
R. J. Hadlee b Sarfraz	22	5/57 6/80 7/115 8/119 9/136	

Bowling: Sarfraz 9–3–22–3; Griffiths 8.1–1–24–1; Watts 11–1–33–0; T. M. Lamb 11–6–11–4; Willey 9–1–34–1; Larkins 3–0–9–0.

Northamptonshire

G. Cook c and b Tunnicliffe	66	P. Willey not out	5
W. Larkins c Rice b Hadlee	1	B 2, w 1, n-b 8	11
R. G. Williams b Hadlee	59		
A. J. Lamb not out	3	1/16 2/124 3/128 (3 wkts, 47.1 overs) 145	

T. J. Yardley, *P. J. Watts, †G. Sharp, Sarfraz Nawaz, T. M. Lamb and B. J. Griffiths did not bat.

Bowling: Hadlee 11–2–24–2; Cooper 8–1–21–0; Hemmings 9–2–28–0; Bore 11–3–23–0; Tunnicliffe 8.1–1–38–1.

Umpires: W. E. Alley and T. W. Spencer.

SEMI-FINALS

MIDDLESEX v NORTHAMPTONSHIRE

At Lord's, June 25, 26. Northamptonshire won by 11 runs. An excellent match, played on the Test pitch, began an hour late with Larkins ferociously driving Daniel. This helped his side to a highly promising position by lunch but they were pegged back to 72 for one at halfway. Williams had problems at first, and the innings declined as Larkins and Lamb went during a fine spell from Embury. Then Williams sorted himself out and began hitting the ball with certainty to make 73 of the last 144, helped by a valuable knock from Sharp. When Middlesex batted Brearley was out immediately and Sarfraz produced two beautiful balls that moved off the pitch to unseat Radley and Barlow. Gatting and Slack buckled down to repair the damage and had all but done so when Williams, getting turn, picked up Slack and Butcher late on the first day. Middlesex began a gripping second morning wanting 79 from fourteen overs. Northamptonshire resumed with five overs of spin, to which van der Bijl reacted by hitting both Williams and Willey far over the leg boundary before being held just inside it. Gatting and Gould had added 20 in three overs when Sarfraz returned to take three wickets in ten deliveries, including Embury's and Gatting's in his last over. Northamptonshire, therefore, slipped home after twice looking losers and Williams received the Gold Award.

Northamptonshire

G. Cook c Gatting b Selvey	17	*P. J. Watts b Gatting	2
W. Larkins c Barlow b Emburey	62	Sarfraz Nawaz c and b Gatting	1
R. G. Williams not out	73		
A. J. Lamb c Daniel b Emburey	1	B 9, l-b 5, w 3, n-b 7	24
P. Willey run out	4		
T. J. Yardley b Daniel	7	1/62 2/136 3/142 (8 wkts, 55 overs) 206	
†G. Sharp b Gatting	15	4/152 5/172 6/198 7/204 8/206	

T. M. Lamb and B. J. Griffiths did not bat.

Bowling: Daniel 11–2–44–1; van der Bijl 11–3–21–0; Selvey 11–3–27–1; Gatting 11–0–68–3; Emburey 11–2–22–2.

Middlesex

*J. M. Brearley lbw b Griffiths	0
W. N. Slack st Sharp b Williams	42
C. T. Radley c Sharp b Sarfraz	13
G. D. Barlow lbw b Sarfraz	0
M. W. Gatting b Sarfraz	91
R. O. Butcher c Watts b Williams	6
V. A. P. van der Bijl c Yardley b Willey . .	18
†I. J. Gould b Sarfraz	8

J. E. Emburey c Sharp b Sarfraz	1
M. W. W. Selvey c Sarfraz b Griffiths . . .	2
W. W. Daniel not out	0
L-b 12, w 1, n-b 1	14
1/1 2/16 3/16 4/114 (53.4 overs) 195	
5/128 6/165 7/185 8/191 9/193	

Bowling: Sarfraz 11–4–21–5; Griffiths 10.4–2–25–2; Watts 7–1–30–0; T. M. Lamb 11–1–31–0; Willey 9–0–50–1; Williams 5–0–24–2.

Umpires: W. L. Budd and A. G. T. Whitehead.

WORCESTERSHIRE v ESSEX

At Worcester, June 25, 26, 27. Essex won by eight wickets and thus qualified for the final for the second successive year. The weather allowed Worcestershire to face only fifteen overs in the first two days, when they lost Turner in the first over. On the third day, the pitch played very easily and Ormrod and Younis increased the pace with a fourth-wicket stand of 68 in thirteen overs. Worcestershire lost six wickets for 58 in the last eleven overs and a target of 237 was comfortably within Essex's reach after a partnership of 136 in 29 overs between Gooch and Denness. Gold Award winner Gooch continued his outstanding form with nine 4s in one hundred and thirteen minutes, leaving McEwan and Fletcher to take their team to victory with four overs in hand.

Worcestershire

G. M. Turner c McEwan b Lever	4
J. A. Ormrod run out	70
P. A. Neale lbw b Pont	29
E. J. O. Hemsley b Gooch	24
Younis Ahmed c McEwan b East	43
†D. J. Humphries b Acfield	3
J. D. Inchmore not out	14
H. Alleyne run out	10

*N. Gifford c Gooch b Phillip	13
A. P. Pridgeon b Lever	3
J. Cumbes not out	3
L-b 15, w 4, n-b 1	20
1/4 2/64 3/110 (9 wkts, 55 overs) 236	
4/178 5/187 6/190 7/201	
8/223 9/232	

Bowling: Lever 9–0–46–2; Phillip 10–0–43–1; Gooch 11–1–30–1; Pont 7–2–18–1; East 10–0–43–1; Acfield 8–0–36–1.

Essex

M. H. Denness run out	66
G. A. Gooch lbw b Alleyne	81
K. S. McEwan not out	65
*K. W. R. Fletcher not out	16
L-b 6, w 1, n-b 5	12
1/136 2/186 (2 wkts, 51 overs) 240	

B. R. Hardie, K. R. Pont, N. Phillip, R. E. East, †N. Smith, J. K. Lever and D. L. Acfield did not bat.

Bowling: Alleyne 11–3–48–1; Inchmore 9–1–45–0; Pridgeon 9–1–32–0; Cumbes 11–0–57–0; Gifford 11–1–46–0.

Umpires: D. G. L. Evans and K. E. Palmer.

FINAL

ESSEX v NORTHAMPTONSHIRE

At Lord's, July 19, 21. Northamptonshire won by 6 runs. The ninth final of the Benson and Hedges Cup, played on Monday after heavy rain had prevented any play on Saturday, produced an enthralling finish of fluctuating fortunes. Essex, at 198 for seven, required 12 to win off the final over, by Sarfraz. But Smith, instead of pushing for a single to give the hard-hitting Phillip the strike, aimed for glory and was bowled by the second ball. East ran a single off the third, Phillip hit 2 from the next, and 8 were needed from the last two balls, for in the event of tied scores Essex would win on fewer wickets lost. However, Phillip missed the next ball and his 2 off the final delivery sufficed only to send the jubilant Northamptonshire supporters swarming over the boundary.

Northamptonshire, having won the toss, found run-getting made difficult by a combination of Lever, whose first six overs cost only 7 runs, the slow outfield and the shrewdly set field. Denness, running back at long-on, held a fine catch to remove Larkins in their fifteenth over, Williams was caught at slip playing to leg, and in the twenty-third over Cook, aiming to run the ball through gulley, gave Gooch an easy catch at slip. All three wickets fell to Pont.

When Willey went to an injudicious pull to square leg in the last over before lunch – the 35th – and Gooch dismissed Yardley in the 36th, Northamptonshire were heavily dependent on Allan Lamb, as they were in the previous year's Gillette Cup final. He rose to the occasion magnificently with a match-winning innings of beautifully executed strokes, refreshing footwork and well-judged running between the wickets. A square cut off Phillip pushed Fletcher on to the defensive, and he approached his 50 with a 6 over mid-wicket off Lever. Watts, who after the match announced his retirement from cricket, played a true captain's innings and their 50 partnership arrived in the 50th over at 186 for six. Four runs later McEwan added the run out of Watts to his two catches, and in the 52nd over Hardie capped a keen display by Essex in the field with a marvellous diving catch at long-on to dismiss Lamb for 72.

Essex, needing 3.81 runs an over, began comfortably with Gooch moving into his strokes with such intent that he soon outscored Denness. When McEwan joined Gooch, their command of the bowling made the Northamptonshire total look inadequate and a repeat of their partnership in the 1979 final was in the offing. The Essex 100 came in the 31st over, but two overs later Gooch, having faced only nine balls in seven overs, struck out at Tim Lamb and was caught second attempt by Allan Lamb at mid-on. In the 36th over McEwan gave himself room to cut once too often and was bowled by Willey's quicker ball. Two wickets had fallen in ten minutes. Fletcher struggled to get going, and Essex fell further behind when Hardie played on to Watts.

At the Nursery End Watts had replaced the off-spin of Willey with the more extravagant turn of Williams and – after two possible stumpings were missed – was rewarded for his adventurous captaincy when Williams bowled Pont in the 44th over. Turner struck lustily, but the return of Sarfraz to bowl the 50th over saw Essex still needing 50 runs. Phillip, launching a counter-attack that realised 30 off two overs from Griffiths, gave Essex hope and produced the thrilling climax. Sarfraz, with three for 23 off his eleven overs, bowled with spirit and intelligence to put him in the running for the Gold Award, but Ken Barrington's eventual choice was Allan Lamb.

Because all tickets had been sold well in advance of the final, and as these were valid for Monday's play, the gates were officially closed at lunch, even though the attendance of 23,263 did not fill the ground to capacity. The takings were £144,472.50.

Northamptonshire

G. Cook c Gooch b Pont	29	Sarfraz Nawaz not out	10
W. Larkins c Denness b Pont	18	T. M. Lamb lbw b Turner	4
R. G. Williams c McEwan b Pont	15	B. J. Griffiths b Turner	0
A. J. Lamb c Hardie b Phillip	72		
P. Willey c McEwan b Turner	15	B 1, l-b 8, w 4, n-b 3	16
T. J. Yardley c Smith b Gooch	0		
†G. Sharp c Fletcher b Pont	8	1/36 2/61 3/78 4/110 (54.5 overs) 209	
*P. J. Watts run out	22	5/110 6/131 7/190 8/193 9/209	

Bowling: Lever 11–3–38–0; Phillip 11–1–38–1; Turner 10.5–2–33–3; Pont 11–1–60–4; Gooch 11–0–24–1.

Essex

M. H. Denness b Willey	14		†N. Smith b Sarfraz	2
G. A. Gooch c A. J. Lamb b T. M. Lamb	60		R. E. East not out	1
K. S. McEwan b Willey	38			
*K. W. R. Fletcher b Sarfraz	29		B 1, l-b 5, w 3	9
B. R. Hardie b Watts	0			
K. R. Pont b Williams	2		1/52 2/112 3/118 (8 wkts, 55 overs) 203
S. Turner c Watts b Sarfraz	16		4/121 5/129 6/160 7/180
N. Phillip not out	32		8/198

J. K. Lever did not bat.

Bowling: Sarfraz 11–3–23–3; Griffiths 7–0–46–0; Watts 8–1–30–1; T. M. Lamb 11–0–42–1; Willey 11–1–34–2; Williams 7–0–19–1.

Umpires: B. J. Meyer and D. J. Constant.

RECORDS

Highest individual scores: 173* C. G. Greenidge, Hampshire v Minor Counties (South), Amersham, 1973; 158* B. F. Davison, Leicestershire v Warwickshire, Coventry, 1972. 76 hundreds have been scored in the competition.

Highest totals in 55 overs: 350 for three, Essex v Oxford & Cambridge Univs, Chelmsford, 1979; 327 for four, Leicestershire v Warwickshire, Coventry, 1972; 321 for one, Hampshire v Minor Counties (South), Amersham, 1973.

Lowest totals: 61 in 26 overs, Sussex v Middlesex, Hove, 1978; 62 in 26.5 overs, Gloucestershire v Hampshire, Bristol, 1975; 63 in 37.4 overs, Minor Counties (East) v Sussex, Eastbourne, 1978.

Best bowling: Seven for 12, W. W. Daniel, Middlesex v Minor Counties (East), Ipswich, 1978; six for 8, N. Gifford, Worcestershire v Minor Counties (South), High Wycombe, 1979; six for 13, M. J. Procter, Gloucestershire v Hampshire, 1977.

Hat-tricks: G. D. McKenzie, Leicestershire v Worcestershire, Worcester, 1972; K. Higgs, Leicestershire v Surrey in the final, Lord's, 1974; A. A. Jones, Middlesex v Essex, Lord's, 1977; M. J. Procter, Gloucestershire v Hampshire, Southampton, 1977; W. Larkins, Northamptonshire v Oxford & Cambridge Univs, Northampton, 1980.

Record partnerships for each wicket

241 for 1st	S. M. Gavaskar and B. C. Rose, Somerset v Kent at Canterbury	1980
285* for 2nd	C. G. Greenidge and D. R. Turner, Hampshire v Minor Counties (South) at Amersham	1973
227 for 3rd	M. E. Norman and B. F. Davison, Leicestershire v Warwickshire at Coventry	1972
227 for 3rd	D. Lloyd and F. C. Hayes, Lancashire v Minor Counties (North) at Manchester	1973
184* for 4th	D. Lloyd and B. W. Reidy, Lancashire v Derbyshire at Chesterfield	1980
134 for 5th	M. Maslin and D. N. F. Slade, Minor Counties (East) v Nottinghamshire at Nottingham	1976
114 for 6th	Majid J. Khan and G. P. Ellis, Glamorgan v Gloucestershire at Bristol	1975
102 for 7th	E. W. Jones and M. A. Nash, Glamorgan v Hampshire at Swansea	1976
109 for 8th	R. E. East and N. Smith, Essex v Northamptonshire at Chelmsford	1977
81 for 9th	J. N. Shepherd and D. L. Underwood, Kent v Middlesex at Lord's	1975
61 for 10th	J. M. Rice and A. M. E. Roberts, Hampshire v Gloucestershire at Bristol	1975

WINNERS 1972-80

1972 LEICESTERSHIRE beat Yorkshire by five wickets.
1973 KENT beat Worcestershire by 39 runs.
1974 SURREY beat Leicestershire by 27 runs.
1975 LEICESTERSHIRE beat Middlesex by five wickets.
1976 KENT beat Worcestershire by 43 runs.
1977 GLOUCESTERSHIRE beat Kent by 64 runs.
1978 KENT beat Derbyshire by six wickets.
1979 ESSEX beat Surrey by 35 runs.
1980 NORTHAMPTONSHIRE beat Essex by 6 runs.

WINS BY OXFORD AND CAMBRIDGE UNIVERSITIES

1973 OXFORD beat Northamptonshire at Northampton by two wickets.
1975 OXFORD & CAMBRIDGE beat Worcestershire at Cambridge by 66 runs.
1975 OXFORD & CAMBRIDGE beat Northamptonshire at Oxford by three wickets.
1976 OXFORD & CAMBRIDGE beat Yorkshire at Barnsley by seven wickets.

BENSON AND HEDGES CUP RULES

The Playing Conditions for first-class matches in the United Kingdom will apply, with the following exceptions.

Duration of Matches

The matches will consist of one innings per side, each innings being limited to 55 overs. All matches will be completed in one day, if possible, but three days (four days if Sunday play is scheduled) will be allocated in case of weather interference. Matches scheduled to start on Saturday, but not completed on that day, may be continued or, if necessary, started on the Sunday.

Hours of Play

Normal hours will be 11 a.m. to 7.30 p.m. (start at 2.00 p.m. on Sundays). The umpires may order extra time if they consider a finish can be obtained on any day, or in order to give the team batting second an opportunity to complete twenty overs.

Intervals

    Lunch . . . . .1.15 p.m.–1.55 p.m.
    Between innings. . . . . .10 minutes.
    Tea (20 minutes) . . . . .To be taken at 4.30 p.m., except in the following circumstances:

    (a) If nine wickets are then down or no more than six overs of an innings remain to be bowled, the tea interval will be taken at the end of the innings, or after thirty minutes play, whichever is the earlier.

    (b) If the team batting second commences its innings before 3.00 p.m., tea will be taken after one and a half hours of that innings, provided there is no interruption.

    (c) If, between the hours of 3.45 p.m. and 4.30 p.m., an innings closes or play is suspended (this includes a suspension which may be in progress at 3.45 p.m.), the tea interval of twenty minutes (to include the interval between innings) will then be taken.

Note: The timing of any interval may be delayed for a maximum of fifteen minutes on the second or third day of a match, if the umpires consider a finish can be obtained within that time.

Covering of the Pitch

The pitch will be fully covered in the event of rain.

Limitation of Overs by any one bowler

In a 55 overs match no bowler may bowl more than eleven overs in an innings. In a match in which the start is delayed and the innings of both teams is restricted from the start to fewer than 55 overs, no bowler may bowl more than one fifth of the total overs allowed, except that where the total overs is not divisible by five, an additional over shall be allowed to the minimum number of bowlers necessary to make up the balance – e.g. in a 33 overs match, three bowlers may bowl a maximum of seven overs and no other bowler more than six overs.

In the event of a bowler breaking down and being unable to complete an over, the remaining balls will be bowled by another bowler. Such part of an over will count as a full over only in so far as each bowler's limit is concerned.

The number of overs bowled by each individual bowler shall be indicated on the score-board, from the commencement of an innings.

Declarations

Law 14 will not apply in this competition. The captain of the batting side may not declare his innings closed at any time during the course of a match.

Mode of Delivery

Law 24.1 applies, except that no bowler may deliver the ball underarm.

The Result

(a) *Unfinished Match*

If a match remains unfinished after three days (four days if Sunday play is scheduled), the winner will be the side which has scored the faster in runs per over throughout the innings, provided that at least twenty overs have been bowled at the side batting second. If the scoring-rate is the same, the side losing the lesser number of wickets in the first twenty overs of each innings will be the winner.

If, however, at any time on the third day (fourth day if Sunday play is scheduled), the umpires are satisfied that there is insufficient time remaining to achieve a definite result or, where applicable, for the team batting second to complete its 55 overs, they shall order a new match to be started, allowing an equal number of overs per side (minimum ten overs each side) bearing in mind the time remaining for play until 7.30 p.m.

If it is impossible to achieve a result in a group league match, it shall be declared "No result".

In the event of no result being obtained within this rule in a knockout match, and the captains are unable to reach agreement on an alternative method of achieving a result to the match, it shall be decided by the toss of a coin.

(b) *A Tie*

In the event of a tie, the following shall apply:

(a) The side taking the greater number of wickets shall be the winner.
(b) If both sides are all out, the side with the higher overall scoring-rate shall be the winner.
(c) If the result cannot be decided by (a) or (b), the winner shall be the side with the higher score (i) after thirty overs, or if still equal (ii) after twenty overs, or if still equal (iii) after ten overs.

Points Scoring System for Group League Matches

(a) The team winning the match to score three points.

(b) In a "No result" match, each team to score one point.

(c) In the event of two or more teams in any group having an equal number of points, their positions in the table shall be based on the faster rate of taking wickets in all group league matches (to be calculated by total balls bowled, divided by wickets taken).

JOHN PLAYER LEAGUE, 1980

WARWICKSHIRE'S REMARKABLE TRANSFORMATION

Warwickshire put two lean years behind them in 1980 to win the John Player League for the first time. In 1979 they had finished bottom of the table, with only two wins, and the year before they were sixteenth. In 1980, rediscovering form and confidence under the new leadership of David Brown, the manager, and captain Bob Willis, they were a fit and enthusiastic side, always prepared to fight determinedly. The change of mood at Edgbaston was also reflected at the turnstiles, with some 46,000 spectators attending the eight home games.

Warwickshire began the season in title-contending style, going eight games without defeat until neighbouring Worcestershire upset them on July 6. This month brought two more defeats and saw the introduction to the side of the former England fast bowler, John Snow. August passed without a loss, although there was a tied match with Kent, and the title, plus the John Player Trophy and £6,500 in prize-money, was ensured on the penultimate Sunday with victory over Leicestershire, then second in the table.

The defending champions, Somerset, were slow to start, stuttered in mid-season, but finished strongly with four successive wins – including the defeat of champions Warwickshire – to collect £3,000 as runners-up. Middlesex, having won the County Championship during the previous week and the Gillette Cup the day before, beat Hampshire on the last Sunday to take third place and £1,650. Throughout June, the Londoners had led the League with Warwickshire but their challenge fell away in mid-season as Northamptonshire, Derbyshire and Leicestershire in turn took up the chase.

FINAL TABLE

		Played	Won	Lost	Tied	No result	Points	6s	4 wkts
1	Warwickshire (17)	16	11	4	1	0	46	23	2
2	Somerset (1)	16	11	5	0	0	44	32	0
3	Middlesex (4)	16	10	5	0	1	42	22	3
4	Leicestershire (6)	16	9	6	0	1	38	12	1
5	Surrey (12)	16	8	6	0	2	36	21	2
6	⎰ Derbyshire (7)	16	8	7	0	1	34	14	1
	Northamptonshire (12) ..	16	8	7	0	1	34	15	4
	⎱ Worcestershire (3)......	16	8	7	0	1	34	26	1
9	Sussex (12)	16	6	6	0	4	32	25	0
10	Gloucestershire (8)	16	7	8	0	1	30	21	1
11	⎰ Hampshire (10)	16	6	8	0	2	28	17	5
	⎱ Kent (2).............	16	6	8	1	1	28	13	2
13	Lancashire (10)	16	6	9	0	1	26	44	0
14	⎰ Essex (6)	16	6	10	0	0	24	37	4
	Nottinghamshire (8)	16	6	10	0	0	24	20	3
	⎱ Yorkshire (4)	16	6	10	0	0	24	28	1
17	Glamorgan (12)	16	4	10	0	2	20	26	1

1979 positions in brackets.

CHAMPIONS: 1969-80

1969	Lancashire	1975	Hampshire
1970	Lancashire	1976	Kent
1971	Worcestershire	1977	Leicestershire
1972	Kent	1978	Hampshire
1973	Kent	1979	Somerset
1974	Leicestershire	1980	Warwickshire

DISTRIBUTION OF PRIZE-MONEY

The total prize-money was £30,940.

£6,500 and John Player Trophy: WARWICKSHIRE
£3,000 to runners-up: SOMERSET
£1,650 to third placing: MIDDLESEX
£140 each match to the winners – shared if tied or no result: 126 wins, 1 tie, 9 no results.

Batting award: £250 to K. S. McEwan (Essex) who hit seventeen 6s in the season.

Other leading six-hitters:

11 – I. T. Botham (Somerset), M. J. Procter (Gloucestershire).
10 – S. M. Gavaskar (Somerset), A. Kennedy (Lancashire), P. W. G. Parker (Sussex), G. M. Turner (Worcestershire).
 9 – J. D. Birch (Nottinghamshire), J. A. Hopkins (Glamorgan), Zaheer Abbas (Gloucestershire).
 8 – T. E. Jesty (Hampshire), B. W. Reidy (Lancashire).
 7 – R. O. Butcher (Middlesex), J. D. Love (Yorkshire).
 6 – D. Lloyd (Lancashire), J. A. Claughton (Warwickshire), F. C. Hayes (Lancashire).
 5 – H. A. Alleyne (Worcestershire), D. L. Amiss (Warwickshire), D. L. Bairstow (Yorkshire), N. E. Briers (Leicestershire), P. N. Kirsten (Derbyshire), A. W. Lilley (Essex), Sarfraz Nawaz (Northamptonshire), D. J. Thomas (Surrey), B. Wood (Derbyshire).

Fastest televised fifty (£250)

39 balls – I. V. A. Richards, Somerset v Warwickshire at Birmingham, September 7.

Bowling award: £250, shared by W. W. Daniel, R. J. Hadlee and R. G. Williams, who each took four or more wickets twice.

Bowlers to take four or more wickets on one occasion were: H. L. Alleyne (Worcestershire), P. Bainbridge (Gloucestershire), R. G. L. Cheatle (Surrey), N. G. Cowley (Hampshire), G. R. Dilley (Kent), R. E. East (Essex), B. J. Griffiths (Northamptonshire), P. J. Hacker (Nottinghamshire), R. D. Jackman (Surrey), G. W. Johnson (Kent), A. A. Jones (Glamorgan), J. K. Lever (Essex), S. J. Malone (Hampshire), P. G. Newman (Derbyshire), N. Phillip (Essex), C. M. Old (Yorkshire), J. M. Rice (Hampshire), M. W. W. Selvey (Middlesex), G. C. Small (Warwickshire), J. A. Snow (Warwickshire), J. F. Steele (Leicestershire), M. N. S. Taylor (Hampshire), T. M. Tremlett (Hampshire), S. Turner (Essex), P. Willey (Northamptonshire).

DERBYSHIRE

DERBYSHIRE v SURREY

At Derby, May 4. Surrey won by eight wickets. Kirsten's brilliant innings of 60 in nineteen overs was not enough to give Derbyshire a substantial total on a good pitch and although Surrey still needed to make 121 from 23 overs, Knight and Smith saw them home with some high-class stroke-play. Knight, missed off Tunnicliffe at 3, hit eight 4s and Smith hit nine as they knocked off the runs with two overs in hand.

Derbyshire

A. Hill c Smith b Knight	28	*G. Miller not out	1
J. G. Wright c Howarth b Wilson	26		
P. N. Kirsten c sub b Wilson	60	B 5, l-b 12	17
D. S. Steele run out	15		
K. J. Barnett not out	22	1/52 2/72 3/113　　(5 wkts, 40 overs) 181	
A. J. Borrington c Richards b Wilson	12	4/152 5/174	

†R. W. Taylor, C. J. Tunnicliffe, S. Oldham and R. C. Wincer did not bat.

Bowling: Jackman 8–2–28–0; Clarke 8–1–30–0; Wilson 7–0–23–3; Knight 6–0–26–1; Pocock 8–0–43–0; Smith 3–1–14–0.

Surrey

A. R. Butcher c Taylor b Wincer	27
G. P. Howarth b Tunnicliffe	6
*R. D. V. Knight not out	77
D. M. Smith not out	60
B 1, l-b 8, n-b 3	12

1/11 2/61　　　(2 wkts, 37.5 overs) 182

G. R. J. Roope, R. D. Jackman, G. S. Clinton, S. T. Clarke, †C. J. Richards, P. I. Pocock and P. H. L. Wilson did not bat.

Bowling: Tunnicliffe 8–3–22–1; Oldham 8–1–35–0; Miller 8–1–27–0; Wincer 8–0–40–1; Kirsten 2.5–0–23–0; Steele 3–0–23–0.

Umpires: D. O. Oslear and T. W. Spencer.

At Nottingham, May 18. DERBYSHIRE lost to NOTTINGHAMSHIRE by 13 runs.

At Leicester, June 1. DERBYSHIRE lost to LEICESTERSHIRE by four wickets.

DERBYSHIRE v GLAMORGAN

At Derby, June 8. Derbyshire won by two wickets. Glamorgan, put in, made only 44 in the first 21 overs as Wood bowled accurately on his first Sunday appearance for Derbyshire. Stroke-play was not always easy on a slow pitch but Javed Miandad batted with discipline and restraint. Derbyshire appeared to be coasting to victory, although the loss of three quick wickets in the middle order caused some concern until Barnett and Tunnicliffe made the last 36 runs from the final five overs.

Glamorgan

A. Jones b Tunnicliffe	5	*M. A. Nash c Brooks b Oldham	18
J. A. Hopkins c Taylor b Oldham	0	†E. W. Jones not out	2
R. C. Ontong c Kirsten b Wood	20	A. E. Cordle not out	0
Javed Miandad b Tunnicliffe	82	L-b 3, w 1, n-b 5	9
N. G. Featherstone c Tunnicliffe b Kirsten	12	1/1 2/18 3/44 4/88 (7 wkts, 40 overs) 151
G. C. Holmes st Taylor b Walters	3	5/107 6/140 7/151

B. J. Lloyd and A. A. Jones did not bat.

Bowling: Oldham 7–3–16–2; Tunnicliffe 8–0–38–2; Miller 8–0–25–0; Wood 8–3–17–1; Walters 5–0–28–1; Kirsten 4–0–18–1.

Derbyshire

B. Wood c Hopkins b Nash	4	K. G. Brooks b Lloyd	3
J. G. Wright c E. W. Jones b A. A. Jones	0	†R. W. Taylor lbw b A. A. Jones	17
P. N. Kirsten b Lloyd b Nash	19	C. J. Tunnicliffe not out	13
D. S. Steele b Cordle	40	L-b 11, w 3	14
K. J. Barnett not out	44	
*G. Miller c E. W. Jones b Lloyd	0	1/5 2/7 3/46 4/71 (8 wkts, 39.4 overs) 154
J. Walters c Cordle b Lloyd	0	5/72 6/78 7/84 8/116

S. Oldham did not bat.

Bowling: Nash 8–2–23–2; A. A. Jones 8–1–39–2; Ontong 6.4–0–24–0; Lloyd 8–1–22–3; Cordle 8–1–19–1; Holmes 1–0–13–0.

Umpires: H. D. Bird and D. J. Dennis.

DERBYSHIRE v ESSEX

At Chesterfield, June 22. Derbyshire won by 2 runs. In a remarkable finish, Essex lost their last six wickets for 9 runs in seven overs after Fletcher's masterful half-century appeared to have the match won. Derbyshire struggled to 148 on a sluggish pitch then Essex lost two early wickets and, after a stoppage, were required to make 110 in 29 overs. Against bowling hampered by a wet ball, Fletcher and Pont added 70 in thirteen overs before Fletcher's dismissal prompted a collapse. When the last over began 3 were needed from the last pair but Miller bowled Sainsbury with the fourth ball.

Derbyshire

J. G. Wright run out	26	*G. Miller c Smith b East	2
K. G. Brooks c Smith b Sainsbury	7	†R. W. Taylor b Lever	4
P. N. Kirsten lbw b Sainsbury	2	S. Oldham not out	1
J. Walters c Hardie b East	25	L-b 8, w 4	12
D. S. Steele b McEwan b Lever	19	
B. Wood b East	21	1/28 2/34 3/45 (9 wkts, 39 overs) 148
K. J. Barnett c Fletcher b East	11	4/80 5/90 6/107 7/120
C. J. Tunnicliffe not out	18	8/122 9/145

Bowling: Phillip 7–1–22–0; Sainsbury 8–1–24–2; Acfield 8–0–27–0; Lever 8–0–30–2; Pont 3–0–10–0; East 5–0–23–4.

Essex

M. H. Denness lbw b Tunnicliffe	2	J. K. Lever c Kirsten c Steele	1
†N. Smith c Steele b Oldham	2	D. L. Acfield not out	2
K. S. McEwan c Taylor b Oldham	1	G. E. Sainsbury b Miller	0
*K. W. R. Fletcher b Wood	56	B 3, l-b 9, w 1, n-b 5	18
B. R. Hardie lbw b Tunnicliffe	4	
K. R. Pont b Steele	16	1/3 2/8 3/8 4/28 (28.4 overs) 107
N. Phillip b Steele	5	5/98 6/102 7/103 8/103 9/107
R. E. East c Steele b Wood	0	

Bowling: Oldham 8–1–28–2; Tunnicliffe 8–0–26–2; Wood 8–0–25–2; Steele 4–2–10–3; Miller 0.4–0–0–1.

Umpires: T. W. Spencer and P. B. Wight.

At Canterbury, June 29. DERBYSHIRE beat KENT by eight wickets.

At Lord's, July 6. DERBYSHIRE beat MIDDLESEX by eight wickets.

DERBYSHIRE v SOMERSET

At Chesterfield, July 13. Derbyshire won by seven wickets. A fine innings by Miller took Derbyshire to victory in the 37th over. He made his 84 off 98 balls, hitting thirteen 4s and one 6 in his highest John Player League score since the 44 he achieved on his first appearance in 1973. Somerset could not adapt to a slow pitch and several of their batsmen fell trying to hit accurate bowling over the top.

Somerset

S. M. Gavaskar c Tunnicliffe b Steele ... 14	N. F. M. Popplewell not out 11
†D. J. S. Taylor b Hendrick 32	C. H. Dredge c and b Hendrick 2
P. W. Denning c Hendrick b Oldham ... 25	L-b 9, w 3, n-b 1 13
P. M. Roebuck c Barnett b Steele 22	
*V. J. Marks c Kirsten b Steele 4	1/31 2/73 3/80　　(8 wkts, 40 overs) 150
D. Breakwell b Hendrick 19	4/106 5/107 6/124 7/147
P. A. Slocombe c Taylor b Tunnicliffe ... 8	8/150

K. F. Jennings and H. R. Moseley did not bat.

Bowling: Tunnicliffe 8–0–32–1; Oldham 8–1–27–1; Steele 8–1–32–3; Wood 8–2–22–0; Hendrick 8–1–24–3.

Derbyshire

*G. Miller c Popplewell b Dredge 84	K. J. Barnett not out 4
J. G. Wright b Dredge 2	B 2, l-b 5, w 2 9
P. N. Kirsten b Moseley 4	
D. S. Steele not out 48	1/13 2/18 3/134　　(3 wkts, 37 overs) 151

B. Wood, J. Walters, †R. W. Taylor, C. J. Tunnicliffe, S. Oldham and M. Hendrick did not bat.

Bowling: Moseley 8–0–28–1; Dredge 8–0–29–2; Popplewell 5–0–21–0; Marks 7–0–25–0; Jennings 6–1–22–0; Breakwell 3–0–17–0.

Umpires: C. Cook and J. van Geloven.

At Northampton, July 20. NORTHAMPTONSHIRE v DERBYSHIRE. No result.

DERBYSHIRE v WARWICKSHIRE

At Derby, July 27. Derbyshire won by six wickets. Put in, Warwickshire never came to terms with a slow pitch which made stroke-play hazardous. Although Lloyd effectively played the anchor rôle, attempts to accelerate at the other end invariably led to dismissal. Derbyshire were always in touch with their task, especially while Kirsten and Steele were together, adding 48 in nine overs. After both had been dismissed in the same over, Barnett and Wood saw their side home, helped by wayward bowling in the final stages.

Warwickshire

*D. L. Amiss c Oldham b Hendrick..... 12	S. J. Rouse c Tunnicliffe b Oldham 4
T. A. Lloyd not out 58	J. A. Snow not out 6
K. D. Smith c Steele b Wood........ 2	
†G. W. Humpage c Miller b Hendrick... 17	B 2, l-b 12, w 2, n-b 1........ 17
J. A. Claughton c Miller b Wood....... 12	
P. R. Oliver c Wood b Miller 11	1/22 2/25 3/56 (7 wkts, 38 overs) 144
A. M. Ferreira c Wright b Oldham 5	4/84 5/106 6/116 7/137

G. C. Small and D. R. Doshi did not bat.

Bowling: Oldham 7–0–16–2; Tunnicliffe 8–0–30–0; Hendrick 7–0–13–2; Wood 8–1–23–2; Walters 2–0–20–0; Steele 3–1–15–0; Miller 3–0–10–1.

Derbyshire

*G. Miller c Humpage b Small........ 0	B. Wood not out................. 13
J. G. Wright c Humpage b Ferreira 32	B 5, w 4 9
P. N. Kirsten c Small b Doshi 50	
D. S. Steele c Ferreira b Doshi........ 26	1/8 2/67 (4 wkts, 37.2 overs) 147
K. J. Barnett not out............... 17	3/114 4/115

J. Walters, †R. W. Taylor, C. J. Tunnicliffe, M. Hendrick and S. Oldham did not bat.

Bowling: Small 8–2–21–1; Rouse 7.2–0–23–0; Snow 7–0–33–0; Doshi 8–1–30–2; Ferreira 7–1–31–1.

Umpires: W. L. Budd and D. G. L. Evans.

At Leeds, August 3. DERBYSHIRE lost to YORKSHIRE by four wickets.

DERBYSHIRE v LANCASHIRE

At Buxton, August 10. Lancashire won by 6 runs. County cricket's return to Buxton produced a crowd in excess of 4,000, but a pitch that was not conducive to stroke-play led to a low-scoring game. Lancashire owed much to Hayes and Lloyd, who was dropped at 3, while the turning-point in Derbyshire's innings came with the dismissal of Wright and Kirsten in Reidy's first over.

Lancashire

A. Kennedy c Wright b Wood 23	†G. Fowler not out................. 8
J. Simmons b Oldham 3	M. F. Malone not out............... 10
*F. C. Hayes c and b Wood........... 34	
D. Lloyd b Hendrick 35	B 3, l-b 15, w 2, n-b 1........ 21
B. W. Reidy c and b Tunnicliffe........ 0	
S. J. O'Shaughnessy c Kirsten	1/14 2/58 3/91 (7 wkts, 40 overs) 148
b Tunnicliffe. 1	4/97 5/100 6/116
D. P. Hughes b Malone.............. 13	7/132

N. Radford and P. J. W. Allott did not bat.

Bowling: Tunnicliffe 8–1–25–2; Oldham 8–0–37–2; Hendrick 8–2–18–1; Miller 8–0–29–0; Wood 8–3–18–2.

Derbyshire

*G. Miller b Radford 8	C. J. Tunnicliffe b Radford........... 0
J. G. Wright c O'Shaughnessy b Reidy .. 18	†R. W. Taylor b Malone 7
P. N. Kirsten c Fowler b Reidy 23	L-b 3 3
D. S. Steele b Allott 14	
K. J. Barnett not out............... 48	1/15 2/47 3/50 (8 wkts, 40 overs) 142
B. Wood b O'Shaughnessy............ 13	4/81 5/104 6/120 7/123
J. Walters run out................. 8	8/142

M. Hendrick and S. Oldham did not bat.

Bowling: Radford 8–2–26–2; Malone 8–0–29–1; Allott 8–2–17–1; Simmons 2–0–14–0; Reidy 8–0–33–2; O'Shaughnessy 6–0–20–1.

Umpires: C. Cook and D. Shackleton.

At Worcester, August 17. DERBYSHIRE beat WORCESTERSHIRE by five wickets.

At Southampton, August 24. DERBYSHIRE lost to HAMPSHIRE by 5 runs.

DERBYSHIRE v SUSSEX

At Derby, August 31. Sussex won by 75 runs. An excellent unbeaten 73 by Wessels laid the foundation for a comfortable Sussex win after they had been put in. He made his runs out of 93, with twelve 4s, on a pitch which none found straightforward, even though Derbyshire were without Miller, Hendrick and Tunnicliffe.

Sussex

G. D. Mendis c Borrington b Newman . .	2	G. G. Arnold c Steele b Newman		0
K. C. Wessels c and b Kirsten	73	J. Spencer run out		1
P. W. G. Parker c and b Steele	26	C. E. Waller not out		2
Imran Khan not out	51	B 3, l-b 4, w 3, n-b 1		11
T. D. Booth Jones c Kirsten b Wood	3			
C. P. Phillipson c Kirsten b Newman	21	1/2 2/93 3/115	(9 wkts, 40 overs)	194
J. R. T. Barclay b Newman	3	4/121 5/168 6/179 7/182		
*†A. Long b Oldham	1	8/183 9/191		

Bowling: Newman 8–0–30–4; Oldham 8–1–50–1; Kirsten 8–0–28–1; Wood 8–1–50–1; Steele 8–0–25–1.

Derbyshire

J. G. Wright c Phillipson b Imran	1	†R. W. Taylor c Parker b Spencer		7
A. J. Borrington c Booth Jones b Arnold .	15	P. G. Newman not out		6
P. N. Kirsten c Spencer b Imran	1	S. Oldham c Long b Phillipson		9
D. S. Steele c Wessels b Barclay	33	B 1, n-b 2		3
K. J. Barnett run out	12			
*B. Wood c Arnold b Barclay	9	1/7 2/9 3/37 4/62	(36.5 overs)	119
J. Walters c Parker b Spencer	4	5/72 6/75 7/84		
I. S. Anderson c Mendis b Spencer	19	8/104 9/104		

Bowling: Arnold 8–1–16–1; Imran 4–1–10–2; Waller 8–1–30–0; Spencer 8–0–36–3; Barclay 8–0–22–2; Phillipson 0.5–0–2–1.

Umpires: R. Julian and D. O. Oslear.

DERBYSHIRE v GLOUCESTERSHIRE

At Chesterfield, September 7. Derbyshire won by six wickets. Although Andy Stovold played a solid anchor rôle, Gloucestershire did not bat consistently enough to set their opponents a substantial target on a mild pitch. Miller, opening, also carried his bat and shared in a partnership of 84 in twenty overs with Kirsten after Wright had gone first ball.

Gloucestershire

B. C. Broad b Wood	9	A. J. Hignell run out		22
†A. W. Stovold not out	62	D. A. Graveney not out		6
*M. J. Procter st Taylor b Wood	8	L-b 7, n-b 3		10
Sadiq Mohammad c Steele b Miller	15			
P. Bainbridge b Newman	10	1/24 2/38 3/55	(6 wkts, 40 overs)	154
M. W. Stovold b Newman	12	4/75 5/101 6/139		

M. D. Partridge, A. H. Wilkins and B. M. Brain did not bat.

Bowling: Tunnicliffe 8–1–28–0; Oldham 8–0–24–0; Miller 8–1–30–1; Wood 8–1–21–2; Newman 8–0–41–2.

Derbyshire

*G. Miller not out	67	B. Wood not out		12
J. G. Wright c Broad b Brain	0	B 2, l-b 12, w 2, n-b 1		17
P. N. Kirsten c Broad b Graveney	44			
D. S. Steele st A. W. Stovold b Graveney	1	1/0 2/84 3/87	(4 wkts, 35.3 overs)	155
K. J. Barnett b Bainbridge	14	4/117		

J. Walters, †R. W. Taylor, C. J. Tunnicliffe, S. Oldham and P. G. Newman did not bat.

Bowling: Brain 6–2–19–1; Procter 5–1–16–0; Bainbridge 5–0–22–1; Wilkins 8–0–28–0; Graveney 7–1–34–2; Partridge 4–0–15–0; Hignell 0.3–0–4–0.

Umpires: P. S. G. Stevens and J. van Geloven.

ESSEX

ESSEX v SOMERSET

At Ilford, May 4. Somerset won by five wickets. Rose scored his first century in the competition, hitting fifteen boundaries as he dominated an opening stand of 99 in seventeen overs with Denning. Following such a great start, the titleholders were able to coast to victory with nearly two overs to spare after they had been set what looked a formidable target. McEwan had provided the backbone of the Essex innings with batting full of grace and authority.

Essex

G. A. Gooch c Taylor b Garner	10	R. E. East not out		7
A. W. Lilley c Taylor b Botham	10	†N. Smith not out		1
K. S. McEwan run out	75			
*K. W. R. Fletcher b Dredge	34	B 2, l-b 7, w 5		14
B. R. Hardie b Richards	15			
S. Turner c Richards b Botham	23	1/21 2/21 3/110	(7 wkts, 40 overs)	214
N. Phillip c Dredge b Garner	25	4/143 5/164 6/205 7/210		

J. K. Lever and D. L. Acfield did not bat.

Bowling: Garner 8–2–26–2; Botham 8–0–42–2; Jennings 8–0–37–0; Dredge 8–0–40–1; Breakwell 2–0–14–0; Richards 6–0–41–1.

Somerset

*B. C. Rose not out	112	D. Breakwell not out		7
P. W. Denning c Hardie b Phillip	28			
I. V. A. Richards lbw b Turner	23	L-b 11, w 8		19
P. M. Roebuck c Hardie b Lever	15			
I. T. Botham c and b Acfield	4	1/99 2/151	(5 wkts, 38.1 overs)	217
V. J. Marks b Lever	9	3/181 4/190 5/199		

†D. J. S. Taylor, C. H. Dredge, K. F. Jennings and J. Garner did not bat.

Bowling: Lever 7.1–1–34–2; Phillip 8–0–48–1; Acfield 8–0–38–1; Turner 8–0–41–1; East 7–0–37–0.

Umpires: R. S. Herman and A. G. T. Whitehead.

At Swansea, May 18. ESSEX lost to GLAMORGAN by eight wickets.

ESSEX v SURREY

At Chelmsford, May 25. Essex won by 40 runs. Surrey never came to terms with an accurate pace and seam attack after Phillip had dismissed both Butcher and Knight in the eighth over. Essex's total was built on two substantial stands. McEwan and Pont put on 55 in thirteen overs for the fifth wicket after early inroads by Jackman; then Smith and Lever, coming together with the home county in trouble at 114 for eight, added 56 in eight overs.

Essex

G. A. Gooch c Richards b Jackman	28	†N. Smith c Richards b Clarke	44
A. W. Lilley lbw b Jackman	8	J. K. Lever not out	9
K. S. McEwan c Roope b Knight	29	D. L. Acfield not out	1
*K. W. R. Fletcher c Smith b Jackman	0	B 2, l-b 8, w 1, n-b 1	12
B. R. Hardie lbw b Jackman	4		
K. R. Pont b Pocock	36	1/39 2/42 3/42 (9 wkts, 40 overs) 173
N. Phillip lbw b Clarke	2	4/52 5/107 6/113 7/114
R. E. East c Butcher b Clarke	0	8/114 9/170

Bowling: Jackman 8–2–16–4; Clarke 8–1–48–3; Thomas 5–0–28–0; Knight 8–1–31–1; Smith 3–0–13–0; Pocock 8–2–25–1.

Surrey

A. R. Butcher lbw b Phillip	9	S. T. Clarke c Hardie b Pont	0
G. R. J. Roope lbw b Gooch	15	†C. J. Richards not out	23
*R. D. V. Knight lbw b Phillip	0	P. I. Pocock not out	19
D. M. Smith c Lilley b Pont	23	L-b 8, w 7	15
G. S. Clinton lbw b Acfield	6		
D. J. Thomas lbw b Acfield	6	1/19 2/19 3/32 (8 wkts 40 overs) 133
R. D. Jackman b Lever	17	4/64 5/70 6/73 7/74 8/101

R. G. L. Cheatle did not bat.

Bowling: Lever 8–1–30–1; Phillip 7–1–21–2; Gooch 8–1–16–1; Pont 8–2–23–2; Acfield 8–1–24–2; Hardie 1–0–4–0.

Umpires: J. G. Langridge and K. E. Palmer.

At Gloucester, June 1. ESSEX lost to GLOUCESTERSHIRE by 32 runs.

ESSEX v WARWICKSHIRE

At Southend, June 15. Warwickshire won by 5 runs. When play finally started at 5.15 p.m. rain had reduced the match to eleven overs. After being put in, Warwickshire lost Lloyd and Claughton in Phillip's first over but intelligent striking from Humpage left Essex to score around 8 an over for victory. Ferreira removed Gooch and Hardie with successive balls before Essex had reached double figures. McEwan and Fletcher batted well, but once they were out the visitors regained control.

Warwickshire

D. L. Amiss st Smith b East	12	P. R. Oliver not out	1
T. A. Lloyd b Phillip	2		
J. A. Claughton c Pont b Phillip	2	B 2, l-b 4, w 2	8
G. W. Humpage not out	41		
†C. Maynard b Lever	18	1/6 2/9 3/41 4/77 (4 wkts, 11 overs) 84

A. M. Ferreira, S. J. Rouse, *R. G. D. Willis, G. C. Small and D. R. Doshi did not bat.

Bowling: Lever 3–0–20–1; Phillip 2–0–13–2; Gooch 2–0–10–0; East 2–0–17–1; Pont 2–0–16–0.

Essex

G. A. Gooch c Maynard b Ferreira	 1	†N. Smith run out	 14
B. R. Hardie c Lloyd b Ferreira	 8	M. S. A. McEvoy not out	 1
K. S. McEwan c Amiss b Doshi	 15	R. E. East not out	 6
*K. W. R. Fletcher c Claughton b Small	. 20	L-b 5, w 2	 7
K. R. Pont c and b Willis	 3		
A. W. Lilley run out	 0	1/9 2/9 3/31	(8 wkts, 11 overs) 79
N. Phillip run out	 4	4/47 5/49 6/55 7/55 8/71	

J. K. Lever did not bat.

Bowling: Willis 3–0–17–1; Ferreira 2–0–7–2; Doshi 2–0–18–1; Small 2–0–13–1; Rouse 2–0–17–0.

Umpires: D. J. Constant and D. J. Halfyard.

At Chesterfield, June 22. ESSEX lost to DERBYSHIRE by 2 runs.

ESSEX v NOTTINGHAMSHIRE

At Chelmsford, June 29. Nottinghamshire won by 18 runs. After losing their first three wickets for 21, Essex found the modest Nottinghamshire total beyond them. McEwan and Hardie did their best with a stand of 66 in nineteen overs but paceman Hacker emerged as the match-winner, returning figures of six for 16 – his best in the competition. Nottinghamshire, put in, took 22 overs to hoist the 50 before Rice dominated an unbroken fifth-wicket stand which produced 54 in ten overs.

Nottinghamshire

R. T. Robinson b East	 33	M. J. Harris not out	 12
†B. Hassan c Smith b Pont	 22	B 1, l-b 8, w 3, n-b 2	 14
J. D. Birch c Fletcher b Pont	 25		
*C. E. B. Rice not out	 45	1/39 2/87	(4 wkts, 40 overs) 155
D. W. Randall b Gooch	 4	3/92 4/101	

M. K. Bore, R. J. Hadlee, E. E. Hemmings, P. J. Hacker and K. E. Cooper did not bat.

Bowling: Lever 8–0–33–0; Phillip 8–0–28–0; Gooch 8–3–19–1; Acfield 5–1–16–0; Pont 6–0–23–2; East 5–1–22–1.

Essex

G. A. Gooch c Hadlee b Hacker	 0	†N. Smith b Hacker	 2
M. S. A. McEvoy b Hacker	 4	J. K. Lever b Hacker	 12
K. S. McEwan c Robinson b Cooper	 55	D. L. Acfield not out	 1
*K. W. R. Fletcher c Hadlee b Cooper	.. 1		
B. R. Hardie c Rice b Bore	 26	B 1, l-b 7, w 2, n-b 1	 11
K. R. Pont b Hacker	 19		
N. Phillip c Robinson b Bore	 4	1/2 2/12 3/21 4/87	(39.3 overs) 137
R. E. East c Hemmings b Hacker	 2	5/99 6/106 7/120 8/121 9/130	

Bowling: Hadlee 8–1–28–0; Hacker 7.3–1–16–6; Cooper 8–0–30–2; Hemmings 8–0–26–0; Bore 8–0–26–2.

Umpires: T. W. Spencer and A. G. T. Whitehead.

At Leeds, July 6. ESSEX lost to YORKSHIRE by seven wickets.

ESSEX v LEICESTERSHIRE

At Chelmsford, July 13. Leicestershire won by nine wickets: Essex's heaviest defeat in the competition. Put in, their batsmen struggled through a combination of poor strokes and accurate bowling. Only an eighth-wicket partnership of 52 in nine overs between Lilley and Phillip gave them any respectability. When Leicestershire replied, Briers and Gower were soon scoring freely, Gower hitting the game's only 6 as well as five 4s.

Essex

S. Turner c and b Steele	26	N. Phillip b Taylor	25
M. S. A. McEvoy c Steele b Parsons	15	R. Herbert not out	1
†K. S. McEwan c Steele b Parsons	6	G. E. Sainsbury b Clift	0
*K. W. R. Fletcher run out	15		
B. R. Hardie c Gower b Higgs	11	L-b 13, w 2	15
K. R. Pont b Higgs	18		
A. W. Lilley run out	23	1/28 2/40 3/54 4/68 (38.2 overs) 155	
D. R. Pringle b Clift	0	5/94 6/99 7/100 8/152 9/152	

Bowling: Taylor 7–0–38–1; Parsons 8–1–22–2; Steele 8–0–22–1; Higgs 8–1–29–2; Clift 7.2–1–29–2.

Leicestershire

N. E. Briers not out	66
D. I. Gower c Lilley b Pringle	66
J. C. Balderstone not out	7
L-b 13, n-b 5	18

1/138   (1 wkt, 36.1 overs) 157

*B. F. Davison, R. W. Tolchard, †M. A. Garnham, J. F. Steele, P. B. Clift, G. J. Parsons, L. B. Taylor and K. Higgs did not bat.

Bowling: Phillip 4–1–7–0; Sainsbury 8–0–20–0; Turner 7–1–26–0; Herbert 7–0–38–0; Pont 4–0–20–0; Pringle 6.1–0–28–1.

Umpires: W. E. Alley and D. Shackleton.

At Hastings, July 27. ESSEX lost to SUSSEX by 8 runs.

At Lord's, August 3. ESSEX beat MIDDLESEX by 57 runs.

ESSEX v HAMPSHIRE

At Chelmsford, August 10. Hampshire won by seven wickets. Indifferent strokes as well as the agility of Parks behind the stumps led to Essex's demise on an easy-paced pitch. Making his League début, Parks established a Hampshire wicket-keeping record in the competition with five dismissals, including two stumpings. Smith, Nicholas and Turner all batted soundly as Hampshire gained a comfortable victory.

Essex

†N. Smith c Parks b Stevenson	14	D. R. Pringle c Parks b Graf	6
S. Turner lbw b Stevenson	9	J. K. Lever c Nicholas b Stevenson	6
K. S. McEwan st Parks b Tremlett	10	D. L. Acfield not out	5
*K. W. R. Fletcher st Parks b Cowley	17		
N. Phillip b Rice	2	L-b 4, w 4, n-b 2	10
B. R. Hardie c Parks b Graf	26		
A. W. Lilley b Tremlett	31	1/12 2/26 3/51 4/54 (39 overs) 137	
K. R. Pont c Turner b Tremlett	1	5/64 6/113 7/115 8/122 9/125	

Bowling: Stevenson 8–0–22–3; Graf 7–1–24–2; Tremlett 8–3–25–3; Rice 8–1–25–1; Cowley 8–3–31–1.

Hampshire

J. M. Rice c and b Turner	10	N. G. Cowley not out	13
C. L. Smith lbw b Acfield	35	L-b 4, w 4	8
M. C. J. Nicholas b Phillip	47		
D. R. Turner not out	25	1/23 2/67 3/116 (3 wkts, 37.2 overs) 138	

*N. E. J. Pocock, T. M. Tremlett, †R. J. Parks, S. F. Graf, J. W. Southern and K. Stevenson did not bat.

Bowling: Lever 8–1–23–0; Phillip 7–0–33–1; Turner 8–1–9–1; Acfield 8–0–27–1; Pont 2.2–0–18–0; Pringle 4–0–20–0.

Umpires: R. Aspinall and T. W. Spencer.

At Folkestone, August 17. ESSEX beat KENT by 13 runs.

ESSEX v WORCESTERSHIRE

At Colchester, August 24. Essex won by 30 runs. After Alleyne had removed Gooch and Hardie in his opening two overs, McEwan (four 6s) dominated the stage to roar to his second John Player League century of the summer. Against a varied and accurate attack, backed up by keen fielding, Worcestershire never threatened their opponents, despite a brave attempt from Neale.

Essex

G. A. Gooch c Humphries b Alleyne	8	K. R. Pont not out	15
B. R. Hardie c Humphries b Alleyne	0		
†K. S. McEwan not out	129	L-b 9, w 5	14
A. W. Lilley b Cumbes	5		
N. Phillip c and b Pridgeon	36	1/1 2/9 3/30 (5 wkts, 40 overs) 231	
S. Turner b Cumbes	24	4/101 5/173	

*K. W. R. Fletcher, D. R. Pringle, D. L. Acfield and J. K. Lever did not bat.

Bowling: Alleyne 8–0–38–2; Pridgeon 8–0–37–1; Cumbes 8–0–46–2; Gifford 8–0–46–0; Younis 6–0–39–0; Hemsley 2–0–11–0.

Worcestershire

J. A. Ormrod lbw b Gooch	21	*N. Gifford b Lever	2
G. M. Turner c Pringle b Acfield	25	A. P. Pridgeon not out	2
H. Alleyne c Phillip b Acfield	0	J. Cumbes b Phillip	0
Younis Ahmed c McEwan b Gooch	39		
P. A. Neale b Phillip	64	B 1, l-b 6, w 3, n-b 1	11
E. J. O. Hemsley c Pont b Pringle	19		
D. N. Patel b Phillip	17	1/36 2/37 3/65 4/103 (39.2 overs) 201	
†D. J. Humphries b Pringle	1	5/136 6/176 7/183 8/195 9/201	

Bowling: Lever 5–1–13–1; Phillip 6.2–0–20–3; Acfield 8–0–30–2; Gooch 8–0–38–2; Turner 4–0–29–0; Pringle 7–0–46–2; Pont 1–0–14–0.

Umpires: D. G. L. Evans and A. Jepson.

At Lancashire, August 31. ESSEX beat LANCASHIRE by 24 runs.

ESSEX v NORTHAMPTONSHIRE

At Chelmsford, September 7. Essex won by 91 runs. McEwan hit his sixth half-century of the season as he guided Essex to an overwhelming victory. In the process, he hit three more 6s to win the John Player League prize of £250 for the batsman hitting the most throughout the summer. His 79 came off 77 deliveries and he received great support from Lilley (60 from 61 balls) as they added 140 in 22 overs for the third wicket. Northamptonshire always struggled. East destroyed the middle order and paved the way for Phillip to return and register his best John Player League figures. Fittingly, a brilliant catch by McEwan ended the visitors' reply.

Essex

*G. A. Gooch c Willey b Griffiths	4	K. R. Pont b Griffiths	19
†N. Smith b Griffiths	4	B. R. Hardie not out	4
K. S. McEwan c Yardley b Williams	79	L-b 19	19
A. W. Lilley c Cook b Mallender	60		
N. Phillip c Mallender b Griffiths	36	1/5 2/12 3/152 (7 wkts, 40 overs) 240
S. Turner c Willey b T. M. Lamb	15	4/170 5/209 6/222 7/240

R. E. East, J. K. Lever and D. L. Acfield did not bat.

Bowling: Sarfraz 8–1–13–0; Griffiths 8–1–35–4; T. M. Lamb 8–0–59–1; Willey 8–0–52–0; Williams 5–0–42–1; Mallender 3–0–20–1.

Northamptonshire

W. Larkins b Phillip	8	T. M. Lamb c McEwan b Hardie	9
P. Willey c Lever b Acfield	37	N. A. Mallender b Phillip	1
A. J. Lamb lbw b Turner	13	B. J. Griffiths not out	7
*G. Cook b East	13		
R. G. Williams b East	17	B 2, l-b 11, n-b 3	16
T. J. Yardley b East	8		
Sarfraz Nawaz c Smith b Phillip	6	1/14 2/58 3/65 4/89 (38.5 overs) 149
†G. Sharp b Phillip	14	5/105 6/110 7/127 8/128 9/134

Bowling: Lever 4–0–20–0; Phillip 6–0–19–4; Acfield 8–0–21–1; Turner 8–0–23–1; East 8–1–35–3; Gooch 2–0–4–0; McEwan 2–0–7–0; Hardie 0.5–0–4–1.

Umpires: H. D. Bird and W. L. Budd.

GLAMORGAN

At Manchester, May 11. GLAMORGAN beat LANCASHIRE by 41 runs.

GLAMORGAN v ESSEX

At Swansea, May 18. Glamorgan won by eight wickets. Fletcher, with a fine 77 and a display of remarkable footwork, was superbly supported by McEwan as they attacked the support bowlers, after Essex had been put in. The target of 218 was considerable by Glamorgan's standards, but Jones and Hopkins sent them away with an opening stand of 138, a record partnership for any Glamorgan wicket in this tournament. Javed Miandad's swift scoring then brought victory with two balls to spare.

Essex

G. A. Gooch c A. Jones b Nash	19	S. Turner c Featherstone b Mack	5
A. W. Lilley b Nash	1	N. Phillip not out	3
K. S. McEwan c A. A. Jones b Holmes	74	†N. Smith not out	3
*K. W. R. Fletcher c Francis		B 1, l-b 5, w 5, n-b 2	13
b A. A. Jones	77		
B. R. Hardie c Miandad b Holmes	1	1/15 2/30 3/156 (7 wkts, 40 overs)	217
K. R. Pont b Mack	21	4/159 5/196 6/211 7/212	

R. E. East and J. K. Lever did not bat.

Bowling: Nash 8–2–25–2; A. A. Jones 8–1–38–1; Mack 8–1–30–2; Ontong 8–1–53–0; Holmes 8–0–58–2.

Glamorgan

A. Jones not out	82	
J. A. Hopkins run out	65	
Javed Miandad st Smith b Turner	30	
R. C. Ontong not out	14	
B 9, l-b 17, w 3, n-b 1	30	

1/138 2/185 (2 wkts, 39.4 overs) 221

N. G. Featherstone, D. A. Francis, G. C. Holmes, *M. A. Nash, †E. W. Jones, A. J. Mack and A. A. Jones did not bat.

Bowling: Lever 8–3–23–0; Phillip 4–1–22–0; Turner 8–1–34–1; Gooch 8–0–40–0; Pont 8–0–40–0; East 3.4–0–32–0.

Umpires: D. Shackleton and A. G. T. Whitehead.

GLAMORGAN v NOTTINGHAMSHIRE

At Swansea, May 25. Glamorgan won by 46 runs. Glamorgan were put in and Javed Miandad batted with authority and enterprise as Featherstone provided staunch support. Nash, swinging his left-arm deliveries awkwardly, took the first three Nottinghamshire wickets and Holmes, who held three excellent catches at point, took three for 17. This success enabled Glamorgan briefly to head the John Player League table.

Glamorgan

A. Jones c Birch b Hemmings	24	*M. A. Nash c Hassan b Bore	1
J. A. Hopkins lbw b Rice	24	†E. W. Jones not out	13
R. C. Ontong b Rice	5		
Javed Miandad not out	62	B 4, l-b 10, w 3, n-b 1	18
N. G. Featherstone c Birch b Cooper	46		
D. A. Francis run out	0	1/55 2/61 3/61 (7 wkts, 40 overs)	195
G. C. Holmes b Rice	2	4/147 5/154 6/161 7/162	

A. E. Cordle and A. A. Jones did not bat.

Bowling: Cooper 8–0–40–1; Bore 8–0–41–1; Rice 8–1–26–3; Hemmings 8–1–24–1; Saxelby 8–0–46–0.

Nottinghamshire

P. A. Todd c Ontong b Nash	1	K. Saxelby b Holmes	8
B. Hassan c Holmes b Cordle	30	K. E. Cooper b Holmes	0
*C. E. B. Rice b Nash	19	M. K. Bore c Holmes b A. A. Jones	2
J. D. Birch lbw b Nash	0		
D. W. Randall b Holmes	37	B 1, l-b 10, w 4	15
H. T. Tunnicliffe c Holmes b Cordle	5		
†C. C. Curzon lbw b Cordle	1	1/4 2/33 3/33 4/92 (35.1 overs)	149
E. E. Hemmings not out	31	5/101 6/103 7/106 8/121 9/133	

Bowling: Nash 8–0–25–3; A. A. Jones 5.1–1–22–1; Holmes 8–1–17–3; Ontong 8–0–39–0; Cordle 6–1–31–3.

Umpires: W. E. Alley and D. G. L. Evans.

GLAMORGAN v NORTHAMPTONSHIRE

At Cardiff, June 1. Northamptonshire won by seven wickets. Glamorgan collapsed after being put in on a drying pitch and ended their sequence of three victories. The first four wickets fell for 20 runs before Featherstone and Holmes effected a partial recovery with a stand worth 46. Northamptonshire also experienced difficulties with two wickets going at 19, but Cook scored a defiant 62 and Williams helped him in an unbroken stand of 115.

Glamorgan

A. Jones run out	8	†E. W. Jones not out	16
J. A. Hopkins b Griffiths	3	A. E. Cordle not out	13
R. C. Ontong c Cook b Sarfraz	3		
Javed Miandad c Cook b Sarfraz	1	L-b 4, w 1, n-b 5	10
N. G. Featherstone b Willey	29		
G. C. Holmes c A. J. Lamb b Griffiths	37	1/9 2/17 3/18 4/20 (7 wkts, 40 overs) 139	
*M. A. Nash b Willey	19	5/66 6/98 7/109	

B. J. Lloyd and A. A. Jones did not bat.

Bowling: Sarfraz 8–4–16–2; Willey 4–1–15–2; Griffiths 8–1–28–2; T. M. Lamb 8–0–22–0; Watts 8–3–22–0; Larkins 4–0–26–0.

Northamptonshire

P. Willey c E. W. Jones b Cordle	17	R. G. Williams not out	46
W. Larkins b Nash	7	L-b 5, w 3	8
A. J. Lamb lbw b Nash	0		
G. Cook not out	62	1/19 2/19 3/25 (3 wkts, 36.2 overs) 140	

T. J. Yardley, †G. Sharp, *P. J. Watts, Sarfraz Nawaz, T. M. Lamb and B. J. Griffiths did not bat.

Bowling: Nash 8–1–16–2; A. A. Jones 6.2–0–32–0; Cordle 6–1–19–1; Lloyd 8–0–17–0; Ontong 4–0–20–0; Holmes 4–0–28–0.

Umpires: C. Cook and P. S. G. Stevens.

At Derby, June 8. GLAMORGAN lost to DERBYSHIRE by two wickets.

GLAMORGAN v YORKSHIRE

At Swansea, June 15. Glamorgan won on faster scoring-rate. With rain proving a serious handicap, the match was reduced to 25 and later to eighteen overs. Yorkshire, put in, found the home catchers on their toes with some notable performances, and then Hopkins (three 6s) dominated with an unbeaten 50, achieving victory with nine balls remaining.

Yorkshire

K. Sharp lbw b Nash	0	G. Boycott not out	19
C. W. J. Athey c and b Lloyd	10	P. Carrick run out	29
J. D. Love c Cordle b Lloyd	25	*C. M. Old not out	3
†D. L. Bairstow c A. Jones b A. A. Jones	22	L-b 7, w 2	9
S. N. Hartley c A. Jones b A. A. Jones	21		
G. B. Stevenson c E. W. Jones b A. A. Jones	1	1/0 2/16 3/43 (7 wkts, 25 overs) 139 4/81 5/84 6/89 7/134	

A. Sidebottom and A. Ramage did not bat.

Bowling: Nash 5–1–19–1; Holmes 5–0–27–0; Lloyd 5–0–25–2; Cordle 5–0–33–0; A. A. Jones 5–0–26–3.

Glamorgan

A. Jones c Carrick b Ramage	4	G. C. Holmes b Stevenson	4
J. A. Hopkins not out	50	†E. W. Jones not out	1
Javed Miandad c Athey b Old	4	L-b 13, w 1	14
M. J. Llewellyn c Bairstow b Old	8		
N. G. Featherstone lbw b Stevenson	3	1/7 2/26 3/39 (6 wkts, 16. 3 overs) 101	
*M. A. Nash b Sidebottom	13	4/54 5/78 6/95	

A. E. Cordle, B. J. Lloyd and A. A. Jones did not bat.

Bowling: Old 5–0–21–2; Ramage 4–0–25–1; Stevenson 4–0–24–2; Sidebottom 3.3–0–17–1.

Umpires: R. Palmer and P. B. Wight.

At Bath, June 22. GLAMORGAN lost to SOMERSET by six wickets.

GLAMORGAN v HAMPSHIRE

At Cardiff, July 13. No result.

At The Oval, July 20. SURREY v GLAMORGAN No result.

GLAMORGAN v LEICESTERSHIRE

At Ebbw Vale, July 27. Leicestershire won by eight wickets. Javed Miandad was unwell, and looked hopelessly out of touch when his team were put in to endure the tricky pitch at its worst. Clift took three for 21 as only Ontong and Hopkins gave Glamorgan's innings reprieve from complete disintegration. Briers then scored an excellent unbeaten 80 to steer Leicestershire to victory.

Glamorgan

A. Jones c Briers b Clift	17	†E. W. Jones c Garnham b Clift	3
J. A. Hopkins b Higgs	35	B. J. Lloyd not out	9
Javed Miandad c Tolchard b Higgs	14		
N. G. Featherstone lbw b Briers	2	B 7, l-b 7, w 6	20
M. J. Llewellyn b Briers	12		
R. C. Ontong not out	37	1/33 2/75 3/80 (7 wkts, 39 overs) 159	
*M. A. Nash c Briers b Clift	10	4/82 5/108 6/130 7/143	

A. J. Mack and A. A. Jones did not bat.

Bowling: Taylor 8–0–33–0; Parsons 8–0–29–0; Clift 7–1–21–3; Higgs 8–2–22–2; Briers 8–0–34–2.

Leicestershire

N. E. Briers not out	80
D. I. Gower c Llewellyn b Nash	15
J. C. Balderstone st E. W. Jones b Lloyd	35
*B. F. Davison not out	14
B 2, l-b 3, w 7, n-b 4	16

1/36 2/108 (2 wkts, 34.1 overs) 160

R. W. Tolchard, †M. A. Garnham, J. F. Steele, P. B. Clift, G. J. Parsons, L. B. Taylor and K. Higgs did not bat.

Bowling: Nash 8–1–26–1; A. A. Jones 5.1–2–11–0; Mack 8–2–24–0; Lloyd 8–0–48–1; Ontong 5–0–35–0.

Umpires: K. E. Palmer and P. B. Wight.

At Canterbury, August 3. GLAMORGAN lost to KENT by 55 runs.

At Worcester, August 10. GLAMORGAN lost to WORCESTERSHIRE by seven wickets.

GLAMORGAN v GLOUCESTERSHIRE

At Swansea, August 17. Gloucestershire won on faster scoring-rate. Zaheer Abbas, dropped at 57, hit three 6s and seven 4s in his century, after Gloucestershire had been put in. Glamorgan again batted badly with three top-order batsmen being run out. Broad's throw from deep cover to hit the stumps and run out Javed Miandad was particularly praiseworthy.

Gloucestershire

Zaheer Abbas c A. A. Jones b Nash	103	A. J. Hignell not out	10
B. C. Broad b Moseley	20	D. A. Graveney b Moseley	2
†A. W. Stovold c E. W. Jones		M. D. Partridge not out	1
b A. A. Jones	18		
*M. J. Procter b Holmes	13	B 4, l-b 5, n-b 3	12
P. Bainbridge b A. A. Jones	5		
M. W. Stovold c E. W. Jones		1/45 2/92 3/133 (7 wkts, 40 overs) 184	
b A. A. Jones	0	4/154 5/154 6/181 7/183	

A. H. Wilkins and B. M. Brain did not bat.

Bowling: Moseley 8–1–23–2; Nash 8–3–23–1 A. A. Jones 8–1–43–3; Holmes 8–0–48–1; Mack 8–1–35–0.

Glamorgan

A. Jones lbw b Brain	11	†E. W. Jones b Bainbridge	8
J. A. Hopkins run out	19	E. A. Moseley not out	4
D. A. Francis b Wilkins	22	A. J. Mack not out	1
Javed Miandad run out	25	L-b 12	12
N. G. Featherstone run out	4		
G. C. Holmes c Bainbridge b Partridge	12	1/24 2/53 3/61 (8 wkts, 33.4 overs) 122	
*M. A. Nash b Partridge	4	4/70 5/102 6/106 7/107 8/118	

A. A. Jones did not bat.

Bowling: Brain 5–0–21–1; Procter 5–1–11–0; Wilkins 8–1–28–1; Partridge 8–0–25–2; Bainbridge 7.4–1–25–1.

Umpires: W. L. Budd and D. J. Constant.

At Birmingham, August 24. GLAMORGAN lost to WARWICKSHIRE by four wickets.

GLAMORGAN v MIDDLESEX

At Cardiff, August 31. Middlesex won by 11 runs. Middlesex owed much to Radley after being put in on a difficult, drying pitch, with the ball lifting spitefully. Mack returned his best League figures but Glamorgan's batting suffered in the absence of Javed Miandad and the injured Alan Jones, although they came surprisingly close to their target.

Middlesex

*J. M. Brearley c E. W. Jones b Mack	14	V. A. P. van der Bijl c Llewellyn b Nash	0
C. T. Radley c Nash b Holmes	48	†P. R. Downton b Mack	2
G. D. Barlow c Mack b Holmes	13	B 3, l-b 6, w 3, n-b 3	15
R. O. Butcher lbw b Holmes	33		
W. N. Slack not out	26	1/29 2/48 3/113 (8 wkts, 40 overs) 172	
P. H. Edmonds c Ontong b Nash	7	4/119 5/136 6/162 7/164	
M. W. W. Selvey c Holmes b Mack	14	8/172	

W. G. Merry and W. W. Daniel did not bat.

Bowling: Nash 8–0–36–2; Mack 8–2–24–3; Lloyd 8–0–37–0; Holmes 8–0–36–3; Ontong 8–2–24–0.

Glamorgan

A. L. Jones run out	27	†E. W. Jones b Daniel	1
J. A. Hopkins b Daniel	18	B. J. Lloyd not out	7
D. A. Francis st Downton b Edmonds	9	A. J. Mack not out	0
N. G. Featherstone b Edmonds	6	L-b 8, w 5, n-b 4	17
M. J. Llewellyn run out	37		
R. C. Ontong st Downton b Edmonds	24	1/18 2/44 3/56 (9 wkts, 40 overs) 161	
G. C. Holmes c Radley b van der Bijl	12	4/73 5/112 6/142 7/147	
*M. A. Nash run out	3	8/149 9/156	

Bowling: Selvey 8–0–45–0; van der Bijl 8–1–19–1; Edmonds 8–2–26–3; Daniel 8–3–17–2; Merry 8–1–37–0.

Umpires: R. Palmer and A. G. T. Whitehead.

At Hove, September 7. GLAMORGAN lost to SUSSEX by five wickets.

GLOUCESTERSHIRE

GLOUCESTERSHIRE v NORTHAMPTONSHIRE

At Bristol, May 4. Northamptonshire won by 14 runs after being put in on a day of high winds. All-rounder Richard Williams made a major contribution, hitting his 51 in even time (six 4s) and putting on 75 for the fifth wicket with Sharp. While Procter and Hignell were together Gloucestershire's hopes were high, but once Procter had gone the innings subsided. Williams bowled Hignell and then snuffed out further resistance with his accurate off-breaks.

Northamptonshire

P. Willey c Stovold b Brain	10	*P. J. Watts not out	2
W. Larkins c Sadiq b Brain	16		
A. J. Lamb c Procter b Partridge	28	B 4, l-b 11, w 6	21
T. J. Yardley c Hignell b Partridge	17		
R. G. Williams c Graveney b Procter	51	1/19 2/47 3/76 (5 wkts, 40 overs) 186	
†G. Sharp not out	41	4/106 5/181	

R. M. Tindall, R. M. Carter, T. M. Lamb and B. J. Griffiths did not bat.

Bowling: Brain 8–3–12–2; Wilkins 8–0–40–0; Surridge 8–0–45–0; Partridge 8–2–21–2; Procter 7–0–41–1; Broad 1–0–6–0.

Gloucestershire

Zaheer Abbas c A. J. Lamb b Watts	....	38
Sadiq Mohammad b Watts	....	17
†A. W. Stovold lbw b Watts	....	2
*M. J. Procter c Willey b Carter	......	46
A. J. Hignell b Williams	....	38
D. A. Graveney run out	....	0
B. C. Broad b Williams	....	4
M. D. Partridge c and b Williams	......	8

A. H. Wilkins b Williams	....	1
D. Surridge not out	....	0
B. M. Brain not out	....	3
B 1, l-b 9, w 4, n-b 1	....	15

1/43 2/55 3/60   (9 wkts, 40 overs) 172
4/140 5/141 6/156 7/164
8/169 9/169

Bowling: Griffiths 8–1–29–0; T. M. Lamb 7–1–27–0; Willey 8–1–33–0; Watts 8–1–26–3; Williams 6–0–28–4; Carter 3–0–14–1.

Umpires: D. J. Halfyard and J. van Geloven.

At Leicester, May 18. GLOUCESTERSHIRE lost to LEICESTERSHIRE by 78 runs.

At Manchester, May 25. GLOUCESTERSHIRE lost to LANCASHIRE by eight wickets.

GLOUCESTERSHIRE v ESSEX

At Gloucester, June 1. Gloucestershire won by 32 runs. A third-wicket partnership of 104 between Sadiq and Procter was the cornerstone of a Gloucestershire total which proved more than adequate on a pitch giving seam bowlers every encouragement. Lever and Phillip permitted only 32 runs between them. Essex fared even worse. Only when McEwan and Phillip were going well in a sixth-wicket partnership which produced 44 in six overs were the County champions a serious threat, and when both fell to catches in the deep the Essex challenge quickly fizzled out.

Gloucestershire

Zaheer Abbas b Lever	....	0
Sadiq Mohammad c Fletcher b Lever	...	54
†A. W. Stovold c Smith b Phillip	....	1
*M. J. Procter run out	....	51
A. J. Hignell b Lever	....	15
M. W. Stovold b Phillip	....	1
M. D. Partridge not out	....	4

D. A. Graveney lbw b Lever	....	0
D. Surridge b Gooch	....	4
A. H. Wilkins not out	....	3
B 3, l-b 8, w 6	....	17

1/0 2/1 3/105   (8 wkts, 39 overs) 150
4/133 5/136 6/140 7/140 8/146

B. M. Brain did not bat.

Bowling: Lever 8–1–18–4; Phillip 8–3–14–2; Pringle 8–1–26–0; Gooch 8–0–42–1; Pont 7–1–33–0.

Essex

G. A. Gooch b Surridge	....	18
A. W. Lilley c A. W. Stovold b Wilkins	.	8
K. S. McEwan c Hignell b Partridge	....	23
*K. W. R. Fletcher b Partridge	....	3
B. R. Hardie c A. W. Stovold b Wilkins..	0
K. R. Pont run out	....	1
N. Phillip c Surridge b Brain	....	32
D. R. Pringle c A. W. Stovold b Brain...	4

†N. Smith run out	....	14
R. E. East not out	....	7
J. K. Lever b Procter	....	0
L-b 8	....	8

1/28 2/28 3/31 4/32   (36 overs) 118
5/36 6/80 7/96 8/99 9/117

Bowling: Brain 6–2–12–2; Procter 7–1–23–1; Surridge 8–1–32–1; Wilkins 8–1–17–2; Partridge 7–1–26–2.

Umpires: R. S. Herman and A. Jepson.

At Canterbury, June 8. GLOUCESTERSHIRE lost to KENT by five wickets.

GLOUCESTERSHIRE v WORCESTERSHIRE

At Bristol, June 15. Gloucestershire won by 2 runs. Worcestershire, recovering from 86 for six, started the last over needing 9 runs with two wickets in hand. But Neale and Gifford, who had put on 68 in ten overs, both perished in the final over, bowled by Wilkins, and Gloucestershire scrambled home. Neale was run out off the fifth ball and then Gifford lost his middle stump. Gloucestershire's total was built around Zaheer's superbly paced unbeaten 112 which included one 6 and five 4s, while Procter contributed a forceful 58 to a third-wicket partnership of 107 in thirteen overs.

Gloucestershire

Zaheer Abbas not out	112	A. J. Hignell not out	4
Sadiq Mohammad c Humphries b Inchmore.	3	L-b 4, w 3, n-b 2	9
†A. W. Stovold b Gifford	27		
*M. J. Procter c Pridgeon b Holder	58	1/11 2/78 3/185 (3 wkts, 40 overs)	213

P. Bainbridge, M. D. Partridge, D. A. Graveney, B. C. Broad, A. H. Wilkins and B. M. Brain did not bat.

Bowling: Holder 8–1–45–1; Inchmore 8–0–30–1; Younis 8–0–41–0; Pridgeon 8–0–24–0; Gifford 8–0–64–1.

Worcestershire

G. M. Turner c Stovold b Brain	14	V. A. Holder b Partridge	13
J. A. Ormrod run out	17	*N. Gifford b Wilkins.	12
Younis Ahmed b Wilkins	1	A. P. Pridgeon not out	0
E. J. O. Hemsley c Hignell b Bainbridge	5		
P. A. Neale run out	84	B 1, l-b 17, w 5	23
D. N. Patel c Hignell b Bainbridge	3		
†D. J. Humphries c Brain b Partridge	15	1/35 2/36 3/36 4/49 (40 overs)	211
J. D. Inchmore b Partridge	24	5/63 6/86 7/123 8/143 9/211	

Bowling: Brain 8–1–20–1; Procter 8–1–30–0; Wilkins 8–1–31–2; Bainbridge 8–0–49–2; Partridge 8–1–58–3.

Umpires: H. D. Bird and K. E. Palmer.

At Guildford, June 29. GLOUCESTERSHIRE beat SURREY by 41 runs.

GLOUCESTERSHIRE v NOTTINGHAMSHIRE

At Bristol, July 6. Gloucestershire won by five wickets. Gloucestershire's fourth win in five matches came with three balls to spare after a shower early in the innings had reduced the target to 171 from 36 overs. Nottinghamshire had batted consistently, Rice and Birch rounding off their innings with a vigorous partnership of 98 after Rice was missed when 15. A typically polished 79 by Zaheer led Gloucestershire's reply and, when his wicket fell, they had reached 132 for two. But Nottinghamshire's tight out-cricket kept home supporters in suspense until Hignell and Graveney finished the task.

Nottinghamshire

†B. Hassan lbw b Wilkins	20	J. D. Birch not out	38
R. T. Robinson b Bainbridge	25	B 1, l-b 12, w 8	21
D. W. Randall lbw b Wilkins	24		
*C. E. B. Rice not out	60	1/42 2/62 3/90 (3 wkts, 40 overs)	188

M. J. Harris, W. K. Watson, E. E. Hemmings, K. E. Cooper, P. J. Hacker and M. K. Bore did not bat.

Bowling: Brain 8–3–25–0; Procter 8–0–26–0; Bainbridge 8–0–31–1; Wilkins 8–1–40–2; Partridge 8–0–45–0.

Gloucestershire

Zaheer Abbas c Robinson b Watson	79	D. A. Graveney not out		3
B. C. Broad lbw b Hemmings	16·			
†A. W. Stovold b Bore	34	B 5, l-b 4, w 7		16
*M. J. Procter c Randall b Watson	10			
A. J. Hignell not out	5	1/68 2/132 3/136	(5 wkts, 35.3 overs)	171
P. Bainbridge run out	8	4/148 5/165		

M. W. Stovold, M. D. Partridge, A. H. Wilkins and B. M. Brain did not bat.

Bowling: Hacker 7.3–1–28–0; Watson 8–1–42–2; Cooper 8–0–43–0; Hemmings 4–0–22–1; Bore 8–0–20–1.

Umpires: W. E. Alley and R. Aspinall.

GLOUCESTERSHIRE v SUSSEX

At Moreton-in-Marsh, July 13. No result. Rain prevented Sussex starting their reply to Gloucestershire's total of 200 for eight – a formidable score on a damp pitch. When Procter came in his side were struggling at 46 for three in seventeen overs, after being put in; but he revived the innings, hitting four 6s and adding 92 in thirteen overs with Hignell. Bainbridge then carried on the assault until the weather had the final word.

Gloucestershire

Zaheer Abbas c Mendis b le Roux	21	M. D. Partridge b Barclay		0
B. C. Broad c Long b Arnold	5	A. H. Wilkins not out		1
†A. W. Stovold b Waller	16			
*M. J. Procter c Long b Greig	79	L-b 4, w 2, n-b 2		8
A. J. Hignell c Wells b le Roux	26			
P. Bainbridge c Long b le Roux	35	1/9 2/44 3/46	(8 wkts, 40 overs)	200
Sadiq Mohammad c Long b Barclay	5	4/138 5/174 6/194		
D. A. Graveney not out	4	7/198 8/198		

B. M. Brain did not bat.

Bowling: Arnold 8–3–16–1; Imran 8–0–32–0; Waller 8–1–37–1; le Roux 8–0–44–3; Greig 6–0–47–1; Barclay 2–0–16–2.

Sussex

G. D. Mendis, J. R. T. Barclay, P. W. G. Parker, Imran Khan, C. P. Phillipson, C. M. Wells, I. A. Greig, C. E. Waller, G. S. le Roux, *†A. Long, G. G. Arnold.

Umpires: D. J. Constant and D. O. Oslear.

At Birmingham, July 20. GLOUCESTERSHIRE lost to WARWICKSHIRE by 1 run.

At Hull, July 27. GLOUCESTERSHIRE lost to YORKSHIRE by six wickets.

GLOUCESTERSHIRE v HAMPSHIRE

At Cheltenham, August 3. Gloucestershire won by two wickets. Two showers reduced Gloucestershire's target to 173, following a moderate batting effort from Hampshire. After a fine opening stand by Zaheer and Broad the home team were given a scare by seam bowler Mike Taylor, playing only because of injuries to other bowlers, but they scrambled home thanks to a partnership of 30 runs in five overs from Martin Stovold and Partridge.

Hampshire

J. M. Rice b Brain	63	†G. R. Stephenson not out	12
C. L. Smith run out	0	S. F. Graf not out	0
M. C. J. Nicholas c Broad b Bainbridge	19		
D. R. Turner lbw b Graveney	12	L-b 13, n-b 1	14
*N. E. J. Pocock c Brain b Bainbridge	4		
N. G. Cowley c Zaheer b Partridge	29	1/0 2/38 3/55 (8 wkts, 40 overs) 182	
M. N. S. Taylor run out	1	4/70 5/125 6/127 7/159	
T. M. Tremlett c Brain b Procter	28	8/176	

K. Stevenson did not bat.

Bowling: Brain 8–1–29–1; Procter 8–0–32–1; Bainbridge 8–0–28–2; Wilkins 8–0–37–0; Graveney 3–0–24–1; Partridge 5–0–18–1.

Gloucestershire

Zaheer Abbas b Tremlett	46	M. D. Partridge c Pocock b Taylor	16
B. C. Broad b Taylor	36	A. H. Wilkins not out	1
A. W. Stovold lbw b Rice	4		
*M. J. Procter c Stephenson b Taylor	16	L-b 8, w 7, n-b 2	17
P. Bainbridge c Rice b Tremlett	3		
†M. W. Stovold not out	21	1/76 2/83 3/97 (8 wkts, 37.2 overs) 173	
A. J. Wright c Stephenson b Taylor	7	4/111 5/113 6/126	
D. A. Graveney c Stephenson b Graf	6	7/137 8/167	

B. M. Brain did not bat.

Bowling: Stevenson 2–0–8–0; Graf 8–0–36–1; Rice 8–1–30–1; Tremlett 7.2–0–38–2; Cowley 4–0–12–0; Taylor 8–0–32–4.

Umpires: D. J. Dennis and J. G. Langridge.

GLOUCESTERSHIRE v MIDDLESEX

At Cheltenham, August 10. Gloucestershire won by 55 runs. A superb innings by Zaheer, and Procter's skilful bowling changes, brought about Middlesex's third successive defeat in the competition. Zaheer, dropped twice, held the innings together with a typically assured display after his team had been put in. From the moment he claimed his rival captain Brearley, Procter appeared to have the game under control and no-one threatened the sizeable Gloucestershire innings, thanks to the medium pace of Bainbridge and Partridge,

Gloucestershire

Zaheer Abbas not out	81	D. A. Graveney c Downton b Merry	11
B. C. Broad c Brearley b Tomlins	25	M. D. Partridge b Daniel	5
*M. J. Procter c Brearley b Selvey	18	L-b 11, w 2, n-b 2	15
P. Bainbridge c Slack b Selvey	6		
M. W. Stovold run out	13	1/48 2/81 3/90 (8 wkts, 39 overs) 183	
A. J. Knight c Daniel b van der Bijl	8	4/109 5/137 6/138	
†A. W. Stovold b van der Bijl	1	7/159 8/183	

A. H. Wilkins and B. M. Brain did not bat.

Bowling: van der Bijl 8–1–28–2; Selvey 8–0–25–2; Merry 8–2–48–1; Tomlins 7–0–31–1; Daniel 8–0–36–1.

Middlesex

C. T. Radley b Wilkins	27	W. N. Slack b Bainbridge	16
*J. M. Brearley c A. W. Stovold b Procter	8	M. W. W. Selvey c Partridge b Wilkins	6
†P. R. Downton b Graveney	12	W. W. Daniel b Bainbridge	0
G. D. Barlow c Graveney b Bainbridge	3	W. G. Merry b Partridge	5
R. O. Butcher lbw b Partridge	18	B 2, l-b 12	14
V. A. P. van der Bijl c Broad b Bainbridge	3		
K. P. Tomlins not out	16		

1/16 2/48 3/50 (31.5 overs) 128
4/52 5/66 6/76 7/109
8/116 9/118

Bowling: Brain 4–0–11–0; Procter 5–0–16–1; Wilkins 8–0–30–2; Graveney 2–0–6–1; Bainbridge 8–1–27–4; Partridge 4.5–0–24–2.

Umpires: D. G. L. Evans and R. Palmer.

At Swansea, August 17. GLOUCESTERSHIRE beat GLAMORGAN on faster scoring-rate.

GLOUCESTERSHIRE v SOMERSET

At Bristol, August 24. Somerset won by one wicket. There was drama from the second ball when Zaheer collided with his opening partner Broad and had to go to hospital with a serious shoulder injury. Procter was stricken by back trouble after a hard-hit 57, so Gloucestershire had two substitutes in the field when Somerset batted. Rose and Richards went cheaply but Botham, Roebuck, Marks and Popplewell all made useful contributions. However, wickets fell in each of the last four overs, and the scores were level until Moseley struck Brain's last ball to the boundary.

Gloucestershire

Zaheer Abbas retired hurt	1	M. D. Partridge lbw b Garner	0
B. C. Broad b Marks	54	A. H. Wilkins not out	6
†A. W. Stovold c Popplewell b Dredge	3	B. M. Brain not out	1
*M. J. Procter b Popplewell	57	L-b 15, w 1	16
P. Bainbridge c Roebuck b Marks	9		
M. W. Stovold b Garner	27	1/11 2/118 3/133 (8 wkts, 39 overs) 179
A. J. Hignell c Taylor b Marks	1	4/139 5/143 6/160
D. A. Graveney b Garner	4	7/160 8/177

Bowling: Botham 7–0–19–0; Dredge 4–1–17–1; Moseley 8–0–45–0; Garner 8–0–36–3; Popplewell 7–0–27–1; Marks 5–0–19–3.

Somerset

P. W. Denning c Broad b Bainbridge	18	J. Garner c Hignell b Brain	0
*B. C. Rose c and b Graveney	9	†D. J. S. Taylor not out	6
I. V. A. Richards c M. W. Stovold b Bainbridge	0	C. H. Dredge lbw b Brain	0
I. T. Botham c Broad b Partridge	22	H. R. Moseley not out	4
P. M. Roebuck c M. W. Stovold b Wilkins	47	B 2, l-b 14, w 2, n-b 1	19
N. F. M. Popplewell c Broad b Partridge	27	1/24 2/27 3/56 (9 wkts, 39 overs) 183
V. J. Marks c Hignell b Brain	31	4/62 5/116 6/167 7/168
		8/176 9/179

Bowling: Brain 8–1–28–3; Wilkins 6–0–23–1; Bainbridge 8–0–38–2; Graveney 8–0–31–1; Partridge 6–0–27–2; Broad 3–0–17–0.

Umpires: K. E. Palmer and C. T. Spencer.

At Chesterfield, September 7. GLOUCESTERSHIRE lost to DERBYSHIRE by six wickets.

HAMPSHIRE

HAMPSHIRE v WARWICKSHIRE

At Southampton, May 4. Warwickshire won by eight wickets. Hampshire, put in, made a good start, reaching 70 for one in the seventeenth over. However, the position changed when Humpage removed Greenidge and Doshi broke the middle batting with a spell of three for 9 in three overs. Warwickshire were given a tremendous start by Amiss and Kallicharran, and after the loss of Kallicharran and Lloyd, Claughton helped Amiss (one 6 and six 4s) steer Warwickshire to victory.

Hampshire

C. G. Greenidge c Oliver b Humpage ... 38	M. N. S. Taylor b Willis 0
J. M. Rice c Oliver b Humpage 14	S. F. Graf c Amiss b Willis 2
D. R. Turner b Doshi 36	†G. R. Stephenson not out 6
T. E. Jesty c Amiss b Doshi 3	B 1, l-b 7, w 3 11
*N. E. J. Pocock c Oliver b Doshi 7	
N. G. Cowley not out 49	1/33 2/70 3/90 (8 wkts, 40 overs) 181
V. P. Terry c Maynard b Willis 15	4/99 5/104 6/140 7/151 8/161

K. Stevenson did not bat.

Bowling: Willis 8-0-29-3; Small 8-0-34-0; Perryman 8-1-29-0; Humpage 8-0-36-2; Doshi 8-1-42-3.

Warwickshire

D. L. Amiss not out 82
A. I. Kallicharran c Graf b Cowley 54
T. A. Lloyd run out 2
J. A. Claughton not out 37
B 1, l-b 2, w 4 7

1/99 2/104   (2 wkts, 36.2 overs) 182

P. R. Oliver, G. W. Humpage, †C. Maynard, G. C. Small, *R. G. D. Willis, D. R. Doshi and S. P. Perryman did not bat.

Bowling: Stevenson 6.2-0-33-0; Graf 8-0-30-0; Jesty 5-0-21-0; Taylor 6-0-34-0; Rice 4-0-23-0; Cowley 7-0-34-1.

Umpires: W. L. Budd and R. Palmer.

At The Oval, May 18. HAMPSHIRE lost to SURREY by 1 run.

HAMPSHIRE v KENT

At Bournemouth, May 25. Hampshire won by five wickets. Their first win of the season in any competition was achieved by tight bowling, keen fielding and sensible batting. After restricting Kent to 160 they were given a solid foundation by Smith, who drove and cut powerfully to reach 58 in 21 overs before Jesty took over the major rôle. He was caught at long-leg going for the winning hit, but Taylor took his side to a safe victory.

738 *John Player League, 1980*

Kent

G. W. Johnson b Jesty	20	R. W. Hills lbw b Stevenson	7
C. J. C. Rowe c and b Cowley	24	G. R. Dilley b Stevenson	4
C. J. Tavaré c Malone b Jesty	22	D. L. Underwood c Rice b Taylor	2
Asif Iqbal c Turner b Taylor	28	K. B. S. Jarvis b Malone	0
*A. G. E. Ealham c Stephenson		B 1, l-b 8, w 5	14
b Cowley	0		
C. S. Cowdrey c Stephenson b Stevenson	9	1/50 2/50 3/103 (40 overs) 160	
†A. P. E. Knott not out	30	4/103 5/104 6/121 7/131 8/139 9/154	

Bowling: Stevenson 8–1–28–3; Malone 8–1–23–1; Cowley 8–0–32–2; Jesty 8–2–31–2; Taylor 8–0–32–2.

Hampshire

J. M. Rice c Asif b Hills	8	M. N. S. Taylor not out	4
C. L. Smith c Dilley b Johnson	58		
D. R. Turner st Knott b Johnson	8	L-b 15, w 2	17
T. E. Jesty c Hills b Dilley	51		
*N. E. J. Pocock run out	15	1/43 2/86 3/90 (5 wkts, 37 overs) 164	
N. G. Cowley not out	3	4/122 5/158	

M. C. J. Nicholas, †G. R. Stephenson, K. Stevenson and S. J. Malone did not bat.

Bowling: Dilley 6–1–30–1; Jarvis 6–0–31–0; Asif 5–0–18–0; Hills 4–0–20–1; Underwood 8–3–18–0; Johnson 8–1–30–2.

Umpires: D. J. Dennis and P. B. Wight.

HAMPSHIRE v WORCESTERSHIRE

At Southampton, June 1. Worcestershire won by four wickets. After Malone had removed Ormrod and Turner for 18, Younis Ahmed revived Worcestershire's innings, scoring 79 from 82 deliveries with one 6 and nine 4s. Earlier, Rice and Turner had batted productively for Hampshire, sharing a stand of 84 at 4 an over; Jesty then increased the scoring-rate and his dismissal was a vital blow for Worcestershire.

Hampshire

J. M. Rice b Patel	52	M. N. S. Taylor not out	0
C. L. Smith run out	4	M. C. J. Nicholas not out	2
D. R. Turner b Patel	30		
T. E. Jesty c Patel b Alleyne	43		
*N. E. J. Pocock run out	22	B 5, l-b 20, w 2, n-b 3	30
N. G. Cowley c Turner b Inchmore	5		
†G. R. Stephenson c Humphries		1/14 2/98 3/113 (7 wkts, 40 overs) 188	
b Inchmore	0	4/166 5/185 6/186 7/186	

K. Stevenson and S. J. Malone did not bat.

Bowling: Alleyne 8–0–40–1; Inchmore 8–2–31–2; Patel 8–0–44–2; Pridgeon 8–1–27–0; Gifford 8–1–16–0.

Worcestershire

J. A. Ormrod c Stephenson b Malone	8	†D. J. Humphries not out	11
G. M. Turner c and b Malone	4	J. D. Inchmore not out	8
Younis Ahmed b Jesty	79	L-b 8, w 5	13
E. J. O. Hemsley b Jesty	17		
P. A. Neale b Malone	28	1/13 2/18 3/84 (6 wkts, 39 overs) 190	
D. N. Patel run out	22	4/141 5/159 6/175	

H. Alleyne, *N. Gifford and A. P. Pridgeon did not bat.

Bowling: Malone 8–1–24–3; Stevenson 7–0–29–0; Rice 8–0–37–0; Cowley 5–0–22–0; Jesty 7–0–45–2; Taylor 4–0–20–0.

Umpires: D. G. L. Evans and B. J. Meyer.

At Leicester, June 8. HAMPSHIRE beat LEICESTERSHIRE by six wickets.

HAMPSHIRE v YORKSHIRE

At Basingstoke, June 29. Yorkshire won by 10 runs. Put in on a wicket which encouraged seam bowling, Yorkshire owed much to Athey who, like Boycott, fell to Malone, who took four wickets in a John Player League match for the first time. Smith and Rice gave Hampshire a useful start, and the innings was gathering momentum when Rice was needlessly run out. Jesty and Turner added 23 in four overs, but Stevenson removed them both at the start of his second spell. Old finished the match with three wickets in 21 deliveries.

Yorkshire

G. Boycott c and b Malone	2	P. Carrick not out	21
*J. H. Hampshire c Stephenson b Rice	26	C. M. Old run out	11
C. W. J. Athey c Cowley b Malone	57		
J. D. Love b Cowley	21	L-b 3, w 6, n-b 2	11
G. B. Stevenson b Rice	11		
†D. L. Bairstow b Malone	14	1/10 2/53 3/93 (8 wkts, 40 overs) 177	
S. N. Hartley c Jesty b Malone	3	4/108 5/139 6/140 7/146 8/177	

P. G. Ingham and A. Sidebottom did not bat.

Bowling: Malone 8–0–39–4; Graf 8–2–24–0; Jesty 8–1–16–0; Stevenson 4–0–30–0; Rice 8–0–39–2; Cowley 4–0–18–1.

Hampshire

J. M. Rice run out	17	†G. R. Stephenson b Old	11
C. L. Smith b Sidebottom	25	K. Stevenson not out	7
D. R. Turner c Bairstow b Stevenson	12	S. J. Malone lbw b Old	1
T. E. Jesty c Bairstow b Stevenson	18		
*N. E. J. Pocock c Hampshire b Hartley	6	L-b 19, w 7, n-b 2	28
N. G. Cowley c and b Sidebottom	24		
M. C. J. Nicholas c Carrick b Stevenson	16	1/42 2/53 3/86 4/95 (39.3 overs) 167	
S. F. Graf c Hampshire b Old	2	5/103 6/135 7/139 8/158 9/160	

Bowling: Old 7.3–3–15–3; Stevenson 8–1–30–3; Sidebottom 8–1–34–2; Boycott 8–2–21–0; Hartley 8–0–39–1.

Umpires: C. Cook and D. G. L. Evans.

At Hove, July 6. SUSSEX v HAMPSHIRE. No result.

At Cardiff, July 13. GLAMORGAN v HAMPSHIRE. No result.

HAMPSHIRE v SOMERSET

At Portsmouth, July 20. Hampshire won by 81 runs. Jesty took Hampshire to a comfortable victory with an exhilarating 96 off 45 balls, in a match reduced to twenty overs after a wet square and outfield had delayed the start. Hampshire, put in, were 14 for two when Jesty came in to dominate a third-wicket stand of 120 in ten overs with Smith. He raced to his 50 in 31 deliveries and hit Botham for two leg-side 6s in one over before being brilliantly caught by England's captain as he tried to complete his century. He batted just forty minutes and scored 80 of his runs in boundaries (six 6s and eleven 4s). Somerset were soon in trouble against the Hampshire bowlers, defending such a high score, and the only question to be answered was the margin of victory.

Hampshire

M. C. J. Nicholas run out	3	T. M. Tremlett not out		1
C. L. Smith c Popplewell b Botham	34	S. F. Graf not out		1
D. R. Turner c Botham b Moseley	4			
T. E. Jesty c Botham b Jennings	96	B 1, l-b 7, w 2		10
*N. E. J. Pocock b Botham	5			—
N. G. Cowley c Dredge b Botham	14	1/4 2/14 3/134 (7 wkts, 20 overs) 168		
†G. R. Stephenson b Dredge	0	4/142 5/156 6/160 7/166		

S. J. Malone and K. Stevenson did not bat.

Bowling: Moseley 4–0–12–1; Dredge 4–0–19–1; Popplewell 2–0–28–0; Marks 2–0–26–0; Jennings 4–0–41–1; Botham 4–0–32–3.

Somerset

*B. C. Rose c Stephenson b Stevenson	1	†D. J. S. Taylor not out		10
S. M. Gavaskar c Malone b Stevenson	1	C. H. Dredge not out		0
P. W. Denning b Jesty	10			
I. T. Botham lbw b Graf	0	L-b 10, w 9		19
P. M. Roebuck b Malone	10			—
V. J. Marks c Pocock b Jesty	7	1/3 2/4 3/7 4/25 (7 wkts, 20 overs) 87		
N. F. M. Popplewell c Nicholas b Graf	29	5/27 6/56 7/87		

H. R. Moseley and K. F. Jennings did not bat.

Bowling: Graf 4–0–12–2; Stevenson 4–0–13–2; Malone 4–0–10–1; Tremlett 4–1–13–0; Jesty 4–0–20–2.

Umpires: D. J. Dennis and D. G. L. Evans.

HAMPSHIRE v LANCASHIRE

At Southampton, July 27. Lancashire won by four wickets. Hampshire were given a good start by Rice – replacing the injured Jesty – and Smith (33 from 33 balls). However, Allott pinned them down, and when Turner went the innings began to lose momentum. Hampshire's cause looked bright when Lancashire were reduced to 17 for two by Graf, but Kennedy and O'Shaughnessy gave the innings substance. Fowler finished the match with a six off Cowley, taking Lancashire home with five balls to spare.

Hampshire

J. M. Rice c and b Allott	11	K. Stevenson c Lloyd b Hughes		0
C. L. Smith c Fowler b Allott	33	S. J. Malone not out		0
M. C. J. Nicholas b Reidy	14			
D. R. Turner b Reidy	21			
*N. E. J. Pocock not out	35			
N. G. Cowley c Fowler b O'Shaughnessy	7	B 2, l-b 16, w 10, n-b 2		30
T. M. Tremlett b O'Shaughnessy	3			—
S. F. Graf b Hughes	9	1/34 2/67 3/77 (9 wkts, 39 overs) 165		
†G. R. Stephenson c Hogg		4/112 5/133 6/139 7/155		
b O'Shaughnessy	2	8/160 9/164		

Bowling: Hogg 5–0–28–0; Malone 5–1–13–0; Allott 8–1–19–2; Reidy 8–0–31–2; Hughes 7–0–21–2; O'Shaughnessy 6–0–23–3.

Lancashire

A. Kennedy c Rice b Tremlett	43	D. P. Hughes b Graf		1
D. K. Beckett lbw b Graf	0	†G. Fowler not out		12
*F. C. Hayes b Graf	7	B 1, l-b 9, w 5, n-b 1		16
B. W. Reidy run out	16			—
S. J. O'Shaughnessy lbw b Cowley	38	1/1 2/17 3/61 (6 wkts, 38.1 overs) 166		
D. Lloyd not out	33	4/76 5/142 6/144		

M. F. Malone, P. J. W. Allott and W. Hogg did not bat.

Bowling: Graf 8–1–26–3; Stevenson 8–0–22–0; Malone 4–0–26–0; Rice 8–1–19–0; Tremlett 7–1–32–1; Cowley 3.1–0–25–1.

Umpires: P. S. G. Stevens and D. J. Constant.

At Cheltenham, August 3. HAMPSHIRE lost to GLOUCESTERSHIRE by two wickets.

At Chelmsford, August 10. HAMPSHIRE beat ESSEX by seven wickets.

At Wellingborough, August 17. HAMPSHIRE beat NORTHAMPTONSHIRE by three wickets.

HAMPSHIRE v DERBYSHIRE

At Southampton, August 24. Hampshire won by 5 runs. Chasing 232 after putting Hampshire in, Derbyshire needed 90 runs from the last ten overs, and that they came so close was due to Wood's unbeaten 90, made off 69 balls. The substance of Hampshire's highest John Player League score of the season was the second-wicket 108 in fifteen overs by Nicholas (62 off 56 balls) and Turner.

Hampshire

C. G. Greenidge lbw b Miller	30	V. P. Terry b Kirsten	19
D. R. Turner c Steele b Tunnicliffe	67		
M. C. J. Nicholas c Taylor b Hendrick	62	B 1, l-b 7, n-b 3	11
*N. E. J. Pocock b Tunnicliffe	17		
N. G. Cowley b Kirsten	22	1/44 2/152 3/169 (6 wkts, 39 overs)	231
M. D. Marshall not out	3	4/205 5/207 6/231	

T. M. Tremlett, †R. J. Parks, K. Stevenson and S. J. Malone did not bat.

Bowling: Hendrick 8–0–23–1; Tunnicliffe 8–0–43–2; Miller 8–1–33–1; Oldham 8–0–58–0; Wood 3–0–30–0; Kirsten 4–0–33–2.

Derbyshire

J. G. Wright b Stevenson	8	†R. W. Taylor run out	22
*G. Miller b Marshall	2	C. J. Tunnicliffe run out	2
P. N. Kirsten b Cowley	41	M. Hendrick not out	2
D. S. Steele lbw b Malone	31	B 5, l-b 10, w 6	21
A. J. Borrington lbw b Cowley	0		
B. Wood not out	90	1/13 2/24 3/73 (8 wkts, 39 overs)	226
J. Walters c Pocock b Malone	7	4/73 5/129 6/151 7/190 8/193	

S. Oldham did not bat.

Bowling: Marshall 8–3–28–1; Stevenson 7–0–56–1; Cowley 8–0–37–2; Malone 8–0–35–2; Tremlett 8–0–49–0.

Umpires: D. J. Dennis and P. B. Wight.

At Nottingham, August 31. HAMPSHIRE lost to NOTTINGHAMSHIRE by 16 runs.

HAMPSHIRE v MIDDLESEX

At Bournemouth, September 7. Middlesex won by five wickets. As in the previous day's Gillette Cup final, Brearley and Butcher set up Middlesex's victory, scoring 68 in fourteen overs before Butcher was caught on the square leg boundary. After two more wickets had fallen for 24, Gatting and Edmonds saw Middlesex home. Hampshire's total owed much to Smith's 66, his best John Player League score.

Hampshire

C. L. Smith c Edmonds b Daniel	66	K. Stevenson b van der Bijl	0
D. R. Turner b Selvey	0	*N. E. J. Pocock not out	4
M. C. J. Nicholas c Brearley b Emburey	27		
T. E. Jesty b Edmonds	3	B 3, 1-b 9, w 4	16
N. G. Cowley b Selvey	29		
V. P. Terry b van der Bijl	19	1/3 2/48 3/59 (7 wkts, 40 overs)	181
T. M. Tremlett not out	17	4/121 5/141 6/177 7/177	

†R. J. Parks and S. J. Malone did not bat.

Bowling: van der Bijl 8–0–35–2; Selvey 8–0–27–2; Emburey 8–0–33–1; Edmonds 8–1–23–1; Daniel 8–0–47–1.

Middlesex

*J. M. Brearley c Nicholas b Tremlett	50	P. H. Edmonds not out	31
C. T. Radley b Malone	6		
G. D. Barlow st Parks b Jesty	17	B 1, 1-b 9, w 1	11
R. O. Butcher c Terry b Tremlett	46		
M. W. Gatting not out	24	1/11 2/49 3/117 (5 wkts, 38.4 overs)	185
V. A. P. van der Bijl c Turner b Jesty	0	4/135 5/141	

†P. R. Downton, J. E. Emburey, M. W. W. Selvey and W. W. Daniel did not bat.

Bowling: Stevenson 8–0–19–0; Malone 7–1–26–1; Jesty 7.4–0–58–2; Cowley 8–1–26–0; Tremlett 8–0–45–2.

Umpires: D. J. Constant and A. G. T. Whitehead.

KENT

At Nottingham, May 4. KENT beat NOTTINGHAMSHIRE by 20 runs.

KENT v SOMERSET

At Canterbury, May 11. Kent won by 13 runs. Rowe was the sheet anchor of the Kent innings, recording his highest score in the competition. Somerset made a disastrous start but Gavaskar and Botham steadied them with a third-wicket stand of 75 off thirteen overs until Asif removed them both in successive overs. Slocombe and Breakwell resisted bravely before Shepherd struck decisively and Kent cruised home.

Kent

R. A. Woolmer c Taylor b Moseley	7	G. R. Dilley b Botham	0
C. J. C. Rowe run out	81	D. L. Underwood not out	2
C. J. Tavaré b Moseley	30		
Asif Iqbal run out	39	L-b 6, w 4	10
*A. G. E. Ealham not out	49		
C. S. Cowdrey b Dredge	0	1/11 2/55 3/134 (8 wkts, 40 overs)	218
†A. P. E. Knott c Botham b Dredge	0	4/214 5/214 6/214 7/216	
J. N. Shepherd b Botham	0	8/217	

K. B. S. Jarvis did not bat.

Bowling: Botham 8–0–49–2; Moseley 8–0–36–2; Marks 8–0–39–0; Jennings 8–0–52–0; Dredge 8–0–32–2.

Somerset

*B. C. Rose b Dilley	2	K. F. Jennings run out		11
S. M. Gavaskar c Knott b Asif	40	C. H. Dredge b Dilley		3
V. J. Marks b Dilley	0	H. R. Moseley not out		1
I. T. Botham c Tavaré b Asif	37	L-b 21, w 6		27
P. A. Slocombe c and b Shepherd	27			
P. W. Denning c Woolmer b Jarvis	5	1/7 2/15 3/90 4/92	(39.5 overs)	205
D. Breakwell b Shepherd	41	5/104 6/175 7/183 8/193		
†D. J. S. Taylor c Knott b Shepherd	11	9/198		

Bowling: Dilley 8–1–20–3; Shepherd 7.5–0–46–3; Jarvis 8–1–35–1; Asif 8–1–34–2; Underwood 7–0–29–0; Cowdrey 1–0–14–0.

Umpires: D. J. Constant and K. E. Palmer.

At Bournemouth, May 25. KENT lost to HAMPSHIRE by five wickets.

KENT v GLOUCESTERSHIRE

At Canterbury, June 8. Kent won by five wickets. Gloucestershire, put in, made a disastrous start as Dilley took two for 16 in his first six overs. Zaheer (seven 4s) and Hignell added 50 off fourteen overs but Dilley returned to remove Zaheer and Wilkins off successive balls. Kent themselves struggled until Ealham and Cowdrey set them on the road to victory, adding 60 off twelve overs. Cowdrey reached his 50 in sixty-two minutes with eight 4s.

Gloucestershire

B. C. Broad run out	0	A. H. Wilkins lbw b Dilley		0
Sadiq Mohammad c and b Dilley	4	I. Broome not out		0
Zaheer Abbas b Dilley	68			
†A. W. Stovold c Asif b Dilley	10	L-b 2, w 1, n-b 2		5
*A. J. Hignell c Rowe b Jarvis	24			
M. D. Partridge c Nicholls b Jarvis	1	1/4 2/13 3/25	(8 wkts, 39 overs)	140
P. Bainbridge st Nicholls b Underwood	8	4/75 5/79 6/95 7/130		
D. A. Graveney not out	20	8/130		

J. H. Childs did not bat.

Bowling: Dilley 8–3–20–4; Shepherd 7–1–25–0; Hills 8–1–30–0; Jarvis 8–0–32–2; Underwood 8–1–28–1.

Kent

G. W. Johnson b Bainbridge	22	†D. Nicholls not out		0
C. J. C. Rowe c Stovold b Partridge	15			
Asif Iqbal c Sadiq b Broad	5	B 1, l-b 8, w 3, n-b 1		13
*A. G. E. Ealham lbw b Broad	21			
C. S. Cowdrey b Wilkins	52	1/40 2/48 3/48	(5 wkts, 37.4 overs)	141
J. N. Shepherd not out	13	4/108 5/137		

R. W. Hills, G. R. Dilley, D. L. Underwood and K. B. S. Jarvis did not bat.

Bowling: Wilkins 7–2–15–1; Broome 7–0–38–0; Partridge 7.4–0–31–1; Bainbridge 8–1–23–1; Broad 8–4–21–2.

Umpires: C. T. Spencer and D. Shackleton.

At Manchester, June 22. KENT lost to LANCASHIRE by seven wickets.

KENT v DERBYSHIRE

At Canterbury, June 29. Derbyshire won by eight wickets. Put in, Kent's batsmen laboured against an accurate seam attack. Tavaré was the exception but lacked support until Knott assisted in adding 33 off nine overs. Then Shepherd and Dilley added an aggressive 37 off six overs. Wright, who in 1976 had played for Kent's second eleven, and Miller gave Derbyshire a good start. Later Steele provided the perfect foil for Wright, who hit one 6 and ten 4s in an innings of 112 minutes, his partnership with Steele adding 77 off nineteen overs.

Kent

R. A. Woolmer b Oldham	1	G. R. Dilley lbw b Miller	17
G. W. Johnson lbw b Tunnicliffe	1	D. L. Underwood not out	3
C. J. Tavaré c Taylor b Miller	42		
C. S. Cowdrey c Taylor b Tunnicliffe	1	L-b 8, w 1, n-b 2	11
*A. G. E. Ealham b Wood	9		
Asif Iqbal c Taylor b Hendrick	7	1/1 2/7 3/14 (8 wkts, 40 overs) 133	
†A. P. E. Knott c Taylor b Hendrick	13	4/30 5/41 6/74 7/92	
J. N. Shepherd not out	28	8/129	

K. B. S. Jarvis did not bat.

Bowling: Tunnicliffe 8–3–10–2; Oldham 8–0–29–1; Wood 8–0–29–1; Hendrick 8–3–14–2; Miller 8–0–40–2.

Derbyshire

J. G. Wright not out	88
*G. Miller run out	23
P. N. Kirsten c Jarvis b Underwood	1
D. S. Steele not out	17
L-b 3, w 4	7

1/56 2/59   (2 wkts, 36.2 overs) 136

B. Wood, K. J. Barnett, J. Walters, C. J. Tunnicliffe, †R. W. Taylor, M. Hendrick and S. Oldham did not bat.

Bowling: Dilley 6.2–1–20–0; Shepherd 8–1–23–0; Woolmer 4–0–19–0; Jarvis 5–0–19–0; Underwood 8–2–19–1; Johnson 5–0–29–0.

Umpires: J. G. Langridge and D. Shackleton.

KENT v LEICESTERSHIRE

At Maidstone, July 6. Leicestershire won on faster scoring-rate. Kent, put in, struggled throughout their innings and then in the field as the weather caused continual reductions in the number of overs allowed to their opponents. Gower took his side to above the required run-rate and interruptions reduced Leicestershire's target to 72 off twenty overs. They were never in trouble and, when bad light stopped play after 11.4 overs, their scoring-rate was easily enough for victory.

Kent

G. W. Johnson c Steele b Higgs	42	†A. P. E. Knott c and b Taylor	12
M. Benson c Garnham b Taylor	0	J. N. Shepherd not out	2
C. J. Tavaré c Clift b Parsons	2	L-b 8, n-b 3	11
C. S. Cowdrey b Steele	16		
*A. G. E. Ealham b Higgs	0	1/6 2/19 3/48 (6 wkts, 34 overs) 121	
Asif Iqbal not out	36	4/49 5/80 6/109	

G. R. Dilley, D. L. Underwood and K. B. S. Jarvis did not bat.

Bowling: Taylor 6–1–21–2; Parsons 8–1–25–1; Clift 5–1–13–0; Steele 7–2–21–1; Higgs 8–0–30–2.

Leicestershire

N. E. Briers not out	. . . .	18
D. I. Gower lbw b Shepherd	. . . .	25
J. C. Balderstone not out	. . . .	6
L-b 4, w 2, n-b 1	. . . .	7

1/30   (1 wkt, 11.4 overs) 56

*B. F. Davison, R. W. Tolchard, †M. A. Garnham, J. F. Steele, P. B. Clift, G. J. Parsons, L. B. Taylor and K. Higgs did not bat.

Bowling: Dilley 6–0–25–0; Shepherd 4–0–20–1; Jarvis 1.4–0–4–0.

Umpires: D. J. Constant and D. J. Halfyard.

At Luton, July 13. KENT lost to NORTHAMPTONSHIRE by four wickets.

KENT v SUSSEX

At Maidstone, July 20. No result.

At Lord's, July 27. KENT beat MIDDLESEX by 13 runs.

KENT v GLAMORGAN

At Canterbury, August 3. Kent won by 55 runs. A Kent record fourth-wicket stand for the competition was the main feature of their innings as Tavaré and Ealham added 146 off eighteen overs. Tavaré hit one 6 and thirteen 4s in his run-a-minute innings and Ealham struck one 6 and seven 4s in his stay of just over an hour. Alan Jones (four 4s) gave Glamorgan a good start but they could not maintain the scoring-rate and, with ten overs to go, still wanted 110.

Kent

R. A. Woolmer b Nash	. . . .	0	J. N. Shepherd not out	13
G. W. Johnson st E. W. Jones b Nash	. . .	8	B 4, l-b 7, w 7	18
C. J. Tavaré b Moseley	. . . .	110		
C. S. Cowdrey run out	. . . .	25	1/2 2/27 3/78 (4 wkts, 40 overs) 255	
*A. G. E. Ealham not out	. . . .	81	4/224	

M. Benson, †A. P. E. Knott, G. R. Dilley, D. L. Underwood and K. B. S. Jarvis did not bat.

Bowling: Nash 8–3–25–2; A. A. Jones 8–1–56–0; Mack 8–0–44–0; Lloyd 6–0–42–0; Moseley 8–1–45–1; Featherstone 2–0–25–0.

Glamorgan

A. Jones st Knott b Underwood	. . . .	59	E. A. Moseley c Shepherd b Dilley	. . . . . .	7
J. A. Hopkins c Jarvis b Underwood	. . . .	29	A. J. Mack not out	2
Javed Miandad c Knott b Woolmer	. . . . .	8	A. A. Jones not out	7
N. G. Featherstone b Woolmer	. . . .	33	L-b 16, w 6, n-b 3	25
M. J. Llewellyn c Knott b Jarvis	. . . .	2		
*M. A. Nash c Woolmer b Shepherd	. . .	19	1/85 2/96 3/126 (9 wkts, 40 overs) 200	
†E. W. Jones c Knott b Dilley	. . . .	4	4/141 5/165 6/171 7/177	
B. J. Lloyd st Knott b Ealham	. . . .	5	8/190 9/192	

Bowling: Dilley 8–0–29–2; Shepherd 7–1–40–1; Jarvis 8–0–27–1; Underwood 8–0–33–2; Woolmer 8–0–38–2; Ealham 1–0–8–1.

Umpires: R. Aspinall and D. G. L. Evans.

At Birmingham, August 10. KENT tied with WARWICKSHIRE.

KENT v ESSEX

At Folkestone, August 17. Essex won by 13 runs. Essex, put in after the match had been reduced to ten overs, were indebted to a last-over assault by Turner who scored 18 of the 21 conceded by Hills. The home team seemed to be in control at 42 for two in the sixth over, but when Essex turned on the pressure the Kent challenge petered out.

Essex

G. A. Gooch c Knott b Asif	18	B. R. Hardie not out	10
†N. Smith c Hills b Shepherd	9		
K. S. McEwan c Underwood b Hills	6	B 1, l-b 2, w 1	4
S. Turner not out	26		
N. Phillip st Knott b Underwood	2	1/13 2/23 3/35 (5 wkts, 10 overs) 80
K. R. Pont b Asif	5	4/39 5/50

*K. W. R. Fletcher, D. R. Pringle, J. K. Lever and M. S. A. McEvoy did not bat.

Bowling: Shepherd 2–0–7–1; Kemp 2–0–10–0; Hills 2–0–30–1; Asif 2–0–16–2; Underwood 2–0–13–1.

Kent

G. W. Johnson run out	18	J. N. Shepherd not out	1
C. J. Tavaré c Smith b Phillip	8	L-b 3, w 1, n-b 2	6
Asif Iqbal not out	26		
*A. G. E. Ealham c McEvoy b Lever	8	1/15 2/42 3/65 (3 wkts, 10 overs) 67

C. J. C. Rowe, C. S. Cowdrey, †A. P. E. Knott, R. W. Hills, N. J. Kemp and D. L. Underwood did not bat.

Bowling: Phillip 2–0–6–1; Turner 2–0–14–0; Gooch 2–0–15–0; Pringle 2–0–14–0; Lever 2–0–12–1.

Umpires: P. B. Wight and C. Cook.

At The Oval, August 24. KENT lost to SURREY by three wickets.

At Worcester, August 31. KENT lost to WORCESTERSHIRE by four wickets.

KENT v YORKSHIRE

At Canterbury, September 7. Kent won by 10 runs. Woolmer and Johnson (nine 4s) gave Kent a great start with 81 off the first sixteen overs, and then Johnson and Tavaré added 73 in thirteen overs. Yorkshire, after a sound start, lost four wickets for 16 in four overs, and it needed Old's 49 in forty-four minutes, including two huge 6s, to make a fight of it.

Kent

R. A. Woolmer c Stevenson b Cooper . . .	33	C. S. Cowdrey not out	3
G. W. Johnson c Old b Carrick	87		
C. J. Tavaré c Sharp b Carrick	33	L-b 7, w 2, n-b 1	10
†D. Nicholls c Coverdale b Sidebottom . .	34		
Asif Iqbal c Stevenson b Sidebottom	17	1/81 2/154 3/169 (5 wkts, 40 overs) 219
*A. G. E. Ealham not out	2	4/210 5/216

M. Benson, N. J. Kemp, D. L. Underwood and J. N. Shepherd did not bat.

Bowling: Old 7–1–30–0; Stevenson 8–1–37–0; Sidebottom 8–0–42–2; Cooper 8–1–41–1; Hartley 4–0–32–0; Carrick 5–0–27–2.

Yorkshire

P. G. Ingham b Johnson	47	A. Sidebottom not out 15
C. W. J. Athey c Shepherd b Underwood	47	†S. P. Coverdale not out 0
J. D. Love c Ealham b Johnson	2	
G. B. Stevenson c Johnson b Woolmer	15	B 2, l-b 11, w 4 17
K. Sharp c Tavaré b Underwood	0	
C. M. Old c Woolmer b Shepherd	49	1/97 2/99 3/112 (8 wkts, 40 overs) 209
S. N. Hartley c Ealham b Shepherd	10	4/113 5/138 6/172 7/185
P. Carrick c and b Shepherd	7	8/201

H. P. Cooper did not bat.

Bowling: Kemp 7–1–29–0; Shepherd 8–1–28–3; Woolmer 7–0–41–1; Asif 4–0–15–0; Johnson 6–0–26–2; Underwood 8–0–53–2.

Umpires: W. E. Alley and J. G. Langridge.

LANCASHIRE

At Lord's, May 4. LANCASHIRE lost to MIDDLESEX by 7 runs.

LANCASHIRE v GLAMORGAN

At Manchester, May 11. Glamorgan won by 41 runs after winning the toss and batting first on an excellent pitch. Alan Jones and Hopkins set them off with 82 from sixteen overs, and Javed Miandad later added a splendid 69. Kennedy gave Lancashire a good start, with three boundaries in an over from Moseley, but was foolishly run out at 16 and Lancashire lost their first five wickets for 54. Reidy (four 6s) and Fowler put on 88 in nine hectic overs but A. A. Jones came back to ensure Glamorgan's victory.

Glamorgan

A. Jones run out	44	G. C. Holmes not out 8
J. A. Hopkins b Simmons	63	†E. W. Jones not out 6
D. A. Francis run out	0	B 1, l-b 9, w 2 12
Javed Miandad run out	69	
N. G. Featherstone c Hayes b Simmons	9	1/82 2/82 (6 wkts, 40 overs) 222
*M. A. Nash b Malone	11	3/152 4/168 5/195 6/216

E. A. Moseley, A. J. Mack and A. A. Jones did not bat.

Bowling: Hogg 8–1–27–0; Malone 8–0–44–1; Simmons 8–0–38–2; Hughes 5–0–33–0; Reidy 7–0–46–0; Kennedy 4–0–22–0.

Lancashire

A. Kennedy run out	13	D. P. Hughes c E. W. Jones b Mack	0
H. Pilling c Miandad b Nash	8	M. F. Malone b A. A. Jones	2
I. Cockbain lbw b Nash	2	W. Hogg not out	2
*F. C. Hayes run out	4	L-b 9, w 5, n-b 2	16
D. Lloyd c E. W. Jones b A. A. Jones	12	
B. W. Reidy b A. A. Jones	74	1/16 2/19 3/23 (34.3 overs) 181
†G. Fowler run out	34	4/28 5/54 6/142 7/175
J. Simmons lbw b A. A. Jones	14	8/176 9/178

Bowling: Nash 8–4–8–2; Moseley 6–0–36–0; Holmes 8–1–37–0; A. A. Jones 5.3–0–32–4; Mack 7–1–52–1.

Umpires: D. J. Dennis and B. J. Meyer.

LANCASHIRE v GLOUCESTERSHIRE

At Manchester, May 25. Lancashire won by eight wickets. Gloucestershire, put in on an unpredictable pitch, were always struggling for runs against the spin of Lloyd and Hughes. Lancashire made a slow start, scoring only 16 from eleven overs, but their innings revived when Lloyd and Hayes joined together in an unbeaten partnership of 154; Lloyd struck one 6 and fourteen 4s, Hayes one 6 and five 4s. The winning hit came after 120 had been hit off nineteen overs.

Gloucestershire

Sadiq Mohammad c Hayes b Hughes ...	37	M. D. Partridge not out	11
Zaheer Abbas b Hughes..............	14	D. A. Graveney not out	5
†A. W. Stovold b Lloyd..............	20	B 2, l-b 6, w 3, n-b 1	12
*M. J. Procter c Reidy b Simmons	37		
M. W. Stovold b Lloyd..............	11	1/31 2/66 (6 wkts, 40 overs) 166	
A. J. Hignell b Lloyd	19	3/115 4/115 5/140 6/155	

A. H. Wilkins, D. Surridge and B. M. Brain did not bat.

Bowling: Hogg 4–1–15–0; Malone 8–2–20–0; Hughes 8–0–28–2; Reidy 6–0–33–0; Simmons 8–0–35–1; Lloyd 6–1–23–3.

Lancashire

A. Kennedy c Partridge b Brain........	0		
D. Lloyd not out	90		
J. Abrahams b Wilkins...............	5		
*F. C. Hayes not out	67		
B 6, w 1, n-b 1	8		

1/1 2/16   (2 wkts, 39 overs) 170

B. W. Reidy, I. Cockbain, †G. Fowler, J. Simmons, D. P. Hughes, M. F. Malone and W. Hogg did not bat.

Bowling: Brain 8–2–21–1; Procter 8–4–13–0; Wilkins 7–0–29–1; Partridge 8–0–43–0; Graveney 5–0–35–0; Surridge 3–0–21–0.

Umpires: R. Julian and B. J. Meyer.

LANCASHIRE v WARWICKSHIRE

At Liverpool, June 1. Warwickshire won by eight wickets. Lancashire's batsmen struggled after being put in, although the pitch presented no real difficulties. Warwickshire bowled admirably and fielded with tremendous energy from a deep defensive cordon. For Warwickshire Amiss and Lloyd put together an opening partnership of 107 in 27 overs, Amiss hitting two 6s and Lloyd eight 4s as they steered their side to victory.

Lancashire

A. Kennedy c and b Willis	5	D. P. Hughes run out	13
*F. C. Hayes b Small................	16	M. F. Malone not out...............	4
J. Abrahams c Rouse b Doshi	32		
B. W. Reidy b Small................	24	B 1, l-b 16, w 3, n-b 3........	23
I. Cockbain b Ferreira	34		
†G. Fowler b Doshi	5	1/18 2/34 3/76 (9 wkts, 40 overs) 173	
J. Simmons c Small b Ferreira	16	4/103 5/115 6/146 7/151	
S. J. O'Shaughnessy b Ferreira	1	8/155 9/173	

W. Hogg did not bat.

Bowling: Willis 8–1–34–1; Rouse 8–4–9–0; Small 8–0–27–2; Doshi 8–0–39–2; Ferreira 8–0–41–3.

Warwickshire

D. L. Amiss b Reidy 64
T. A. Lloyd not out 74
J. A. Claughton c Hughes b Reidy 6
P. R. Oliver not out 27
       L-b 3, w 2, n-b 1 6

1/107 2/115   (2 wkts, 38 overs) 177

G. W. Humpage, †C. Maynard, A. M. Ferreira, *R. G. D. Willis, G. C. Small, D. R. Doshi and S. J. Rouse did not bat.

Bowling: Hogg 7–1–26–0; Malone 7–0–36–0; Hughes 5–0–25–0; Reidy 8–0–29–2; Simmons 8–0–37–0; Kennedy 3–0–18–0.

Umpires: D. J. Dennis and T. W. Spencer.

At Tring, June 8. LANCASHIRE lost to NORTHAMPTONSHIRE by seven wickets.

At Bath, June 15. LANCASHIRE lost to SOMERSET by five wickets.

LANCASHIRE v KENT

At Manchester, June 22. Lancashire won by seven wickets. Rain reduced the match to twelve overs a side and Lancashire achieved victory when Shepherd bowled a no ball off what should have been the final delivery of the match. Kent, put in, were restricted to a modest total against a fielding cordon that included seven men on the boundary. Lancashire, propelled by Kennedy, required 4 runs from the last over, and when Fowler was run out Simmons had to hit a single from the last ball. He drove it to Cowdrey at mid-off and was comfortably "caught" until the fieldsmen realised umpire van Geloven had called a no ball.

Kent

G. W. Johnson lbw b Malone 18
C. J. C. Rowe b Hughes 9
C. S. Cowdrey not out 25
*A. G. E. Ealham not out 21
      L-b 6 6

1/30 2/34   (2 wkts, 12 overs) 79

G. R. Dilley, J. N. Shepherd, †D. Nicholls, M. Benson, R. W. Hills, K. B. S. Jarvis and G. D. Spelman did not bat.

Bowling: Radford 2–0–11–0; Allott 2–0–11–0; Malone 3–0–23–1; Hughes 3–0–13–1; Simmons 2–0–15–0.

Lancashire

A. Kennedy not out 36
*F. C. Hayes b Dilley 19
D. Lloyd b Jarvis 9
†G. Fowler run out 4
J. Simmons not out 0
      B 2, l-b 7, w 2, n-b 1 12

1/33 2/57 3/79   (3 wkts, 11.5 overs) 80

J. Abrahams, N. Radford, I. Cockbain, D. P. Hughes, M. F. Malone and P. J. W. Allott did not bat.

Bowling: Dilley 3–0–10–1; Spelman 2–0–18–0; Hills 2–0–14–0; Jarvis 2–0–13–1; Shepherd 2.5–0–13–0.

Umpires: R. Julian and J. van Geloven.

At Leicester, June 29. LANCASHIRE beat LEICESTERSHIRE by five wickets.

LANCASHIRE v SURREY

At Manchester, July 6. Surrey won by six wickets. Put in on a pitch of variable pace, Lancashire failed to make the most of an opening partnership of 58 off fourteen overs from Hayes and Kennedy. Cheatle and Pocock undermined the innings, although Reidy hit three 6s. Lancashire's modest total and some slip-shod bowling by their pace attack never seriously threatened Surrey, and when Roope took 14 runs in one over from Allott, the result was never in doubt.

Lancashire

A. Kennedy c Roope b Pocock	39	N. Radford b Clarke	3
*F. C. Hayes c Roope b Knight	26	P. J. W. Allott c Richards b Clarke	11
I. Cockbain c Lynch b Cheatle	4		
B. W. Reidy c Jackman b Cheatle	28	L-b 6, w 4	10
J. Abrahams c Richards b Cheatle	5		
J. Simmons c Smith b Cheatle	15	1/58 2/73 3/84 (9 wkts, 40 overs) 155	
†G. Fowler b Knight	2	4/103 5/109 6/125 7/126	
D. P. Hughes not out	12	8/131 9/155	

W. Hogg did not bat.

Bowling: Jackman 8–0–43–0; Clarke 8–3–19–2; Knight 8–0–28–2; Pocock 8–2–21–1; Cheatle 8–0–34–4.

Surrey

A. R. Butcher b Hogg	5	M. A. Lynch not out	4
G. S. Clinton b Simmons	29	B 2, l-b 7, w 10	19
*R. D. V. Knight b Allott	21		
D. M. Smith c Cockbain b Hogg	31	1/18 2/53 3/71 (4 wkts, 38.1 overs) 157	
G. R. J. Roope not out	48	4/148	

S. T. Clarke, R. D. Jackman, †C. J. Richards, P. I. Pocock and R. G. L. Cheatle did not bat.

Bowling: Hogg 7.1–1–23–2; Radford 7–2–25–0; Simmons 8–0–15–1; Allott 8–0–41–1; Hughes 8–1–34–0.

Umpires: K. E. Palmer and C. T. Spencer.

At Worcester, July 13. WORCESTERSHIRE v LANCASHIRE. No result.

At Southampton, July 27. LANCASHIRE beat HAMPSHIRE by four wickets.

LANCASHIRE v SUSSEX

At Manchester, August 3. Sussex won on faster scoring-rate. Although Kennedy batted soundly and hit three 6s Lancashire never scored fast enough after being put in on an easy-paced pitch. Not until Simmons was in was the tempo increased, 74 coming from the last nine overs. Sussex lost two wickets before a heavy shower reduced their target to 152 from 34 overs. Malone soon removed Imran, but Lancashire's hopes faded as Mendis and Wells raced along. At 125 for five rain again intervened, but Sussex had done enough to win the match with a scoring-rate of 4.80 against Lancashire's 4.48.

Lancashire

A. Kennedy c Barclay b Imran	74	D. P. Hughes b Imran	3
D. K. Beckett c Mendis b Imran	11	N. Radford not out.	1
*F. C. Hayes c Barclay b Greig	31	B 6, l-b 2, w 2	10
B. W. Reidy c Imran b Greig	4		
S. J. O'Shaughnessy c Arnold b Spencer .	8	1/15 2/64 3/70 (7 wkts, 39 overs) 174
†G. Fowler b Spencer	0	4/89 5/92 6/145
J. Simmons not out.	32	7/166

P. J. W. Allott and M. F. Malone did not bat.

Bowling: Arnold 8–3–12–0; Imran 7–0–37–3; le Roux 8–0–56–0; Greig 8–0–22–2; Spencer 8–0–37–2.

Sussex

G. D. Mendis not out.	57	I. A. Greig not out	1
J. R. T. Barclay c Fowler b Radford	2		
P. W. G. Parker c Reidy b Radford	0	L-b 5, w 1	6
Imran Khan c Fowler b Malone.	6		
C. M. Wells b Malone	53	1/21 2/21 3/28 (5 wkts, 26 overs) 125
C. P. Phillipson c Fowler b Radford	0	4/121 5/122

G. S. le Roux, *†A. Long, G. G. Arnold and J. Spencer did not bat.

Bowling: Radford 7–0–28–3; Malone 7–1–13–2; O'Shaughnessy 2–0–12–0; Allott 2–0–21–0; Reidy 4–0–22–0; Simmons 4–0–23–0.

Umpires: W. E. Alley and H. D. Bird.

At Buxton, August 10. LANCASHIRE beat DERBYSHIRE by 6 runs.

LANCASHIRE v YORKSHIRE

At Manchester, August 24. Lancashire won by 1 run. All the excitement was reserved for the last half hour. Lancashire, put in, were restricted to a modest total, only for Yorkshire to collapse remarkably following the dismissal of Boycott for 50 (one 6) with 63 required from the last eight overs. Yorkshire needed their last man, Dennis, to hit 3 off the last ball but he failed and was run out going for a second run to tie the scores. Lancashire was indebted to Hayes and D. Lloyd, who added 70 runs in fourteen overs for the fourth wicket, and to the bowling of Allott and teenager O'Shaughnessy.

Lancashire

A. Kennedy c Love b Sidebottom	20	†G. Fowler not out.	6
J. Simmons c Bairstow b Sidebottom.	16	S. J. O'Shaughnessy not out.	0
*F. C. Hayes b Hartley	40		
C. H. Lloyd c and b Hartley	8	B 2, l-b 7, w 4, n-b 3	16
D. Lloyd c Hartley b Old	49		
B. W. Reidy b Old	7	1/33 2/42 3/60 (7 wkts, 40 overs) 162
D. P. Hughes c Hampshire b Old.	0	4/130 5/153 6/153 7/160

M. F. Malone and P. J. W. Allott did not bat.

Bowling: Old 8–4–20–3; Dennis 8–0–39–0; Sidebottom 8–0–28–2; Stevenson 8–4–17–0; Hartley 8–0–42–2.

Yorkshire

G. Boycott c Allott b O'Shaughnessy	... 50	P. G. Ingham run out		13
*J. H. Hampshire c Reidy		A. Sidebottom not out		0
b O'Shaughnessy.	8	S. J. Dennis run out		1
C. W. J. Athey b O'Shaughnessy	45			
G. B. Stevenson b Simmons	2	L-b 6, w 2		8
J. D. Love c Reidy b Allott	21			
S. N. Hartley b Allott	8	1/16 2/99 3/104 4/110	(40 overs)	161
†D. L. Bairstow c Fowler b Malone	0	5/138 6/139 7/143		
C. M. Old b Allott	5	8/158 9/160		

Bowling: Malone 8–2–21–1; Allott 8–2–20–3; O'Shaughnessy 8–0–44–3; Reidy 8–0–31–0; Simmons 8–0–37–1.

Umpires: R. Aspinall and D. J. Halfyard.

LANCASHIRE v ESSEX

At Manchester, August 31. Essex won by 24 runs. Lancashire elected to field but performed well below par, allowing Essex to reach a substantial total. Hardie laid the foundation and McEwan, Lilley and Turner all hit well. Simmons was the most effective home bowler and he also proved their best batsman in his new rôle as opener. Lancashire were going well until they lost three wickets in the course of three balls at 127 and, with 73 runs needed from the last nine overs, there was no recovery.

Essex

B. R. Hardie c Simmons b Malone	72	K. R. Pont not out		2
M. H. Denness c O'Shaughnessy b Allott	7			
†K. S. McEwan c C. H. Lloyd b Reidy	33	L-b 13, n-b 2		15
A. W. Lilley c Malone b Simmons	31			
N. Phillip b Simmons	0	1/21 2/74 3/128	(5 wkts, 40 overs)	199
S. Turner not out	39	4/128 5/177		

*K. W. R. Fletcher, D. R. Pringle, J. K. Lever and D. L. Acfield did not bat.

Bowling: Malone 8–1–45–1; Allott 8–2–24–1; O'Shaughnessy 4–0–16–0; Reidy 6–0–35–1; Simmons 8–0–32–2; Hughes 6–0–32–0.

Lancashire

A. Kennedy lbw b Acfield	24	D. P. Hughes c Pringle b Phillip		2
J. Simmons c Hardie b Pont	65	M. F. Malone not out		0
*F. C. Hayes c Lilley b Acfield	7	L-b 13, n-b 1		14
C. H. Lloyd c and b Turner	20			
B. W. Reidy c Lever b Pont	0	1/48 2/82 3/127	(7 wkts, 40 overs)	175
D. Lloyd not out	24	4/127 5/127 6/168		
†G. Fowler c Pont b Lever	19	7/174		

S. J. O'Shaughnessy and P. J. W. Allott did not bat.

Bowling: Lever 8–0–37–1; Phillip 8–0–36–1; Acfield 8–2–22–2; Turner 8–2–21–1; Pringle 6–0–35–0; Pont 2–0–10–2.

Umpires: R. S. Herman and C. T. Spencer.

At Nottingham, September 7. LANCASHIRE lost to NOTTINGHAMSHIRE by six wickets.

LEICESTERSHIRE

At Hove, May 4. LEICESTERSHIRE beat SUSSEX by three wickets.

LEICESTERSHIRE v GLOUCESTERSHIRE

At Leicester, May 18. Leicestershire won by 78 runs. After the early dismissal of Dudleston, Briers and Gower put on 41 for the second wicket, the stand coming to an end when Gower gave himself out, caught behind. Gloucestershire were unable to make much headway after Booth struck early blows dismissing Zaheer and Sadiq. The Stovold brothers were run out and from then on the visitors were unable to master some accurate seam and spin bowling.

Leicestershire

B. Dudleston lbw b Wilkins	7	J. F. Steele run out	23
N. E. Briers st A. W. Stovold b Graveney	30	D. A. Wenlock not out	6
D. I. Gower c A. W. Stovold b Partridge	26	P. Booth not out	2
*B. F. Davison c A. W. Stovold b Broad	25		
†R. W. Tolchard c A. W. Stovold b Wilkins	34	B 4, l-b 17, w 1, n-b 3	25
P. B. Clift b Broad	2	1/20 2/61 3/87 (8 wkts, 40 overs)	204
T. J. Boon run out	24	4/108 5/120 6/167 7/176 8/202	

K. Higgs did not bat.

Bowling: Wilkins 7–3–25–2; Procter 8–0–36–0; Partridge 6–0–30–1; Bainbridge 6–0–26–0; Graveney 8–0–42–1; Broad 5–0–20–2.

Gloucestershire

Zaheer Abbas c Davison b Booth	18	M. D. Partridge c Briers b Steele	7
Sadiq Mohammad c Tolchard b Booth	4	D. A. Graveney not out	6
*M. J. Procter c Gower b Wenlock	15	A. H. Wilkins run out	2
†A. W. Stovold run out	34		
M. W. Stovold run out	1	B 4, l-b 4, w 3, n-b 1	12
P. Bainbridge c Tolchard b Clift	14		
B. C. Broad lbw b Wenlock	0	1/18 2/25 3/67 4/72 (36 overs)	126
S. J. Windaybank b Clift	13	5/75 6/77 7/99 8/110 9/113	

Bowling: Higgs 4–0–20–0; Booth 8–0–34–2; Wenlock 8–2–25–2; Briers 5–0–12–0; Steele 6–0–13–1; Clift 5–0–10–2.

Umpires: H. D. Bird and D. J. Constant.

LEICESTERSHIRE v DERBYSHIRE

At Leicester, June 1. Leicestershire won by four wickets. Kirsten provided the backbone of Derbyshire's innings, his 90 minutes at the crease producing three 6s and seven 4s. A first-wicket stand of 92 between Birkenshaw and Briers (five 4s and two 6s) provided the platform for Gower to build on with help from Tolchard and Butcher. Gower completed the match with a straight drive to the boundary off the last ball, 22 runs having come off the final three overs.

Derbyshire

A. J. Borrington run out	0	C. J. Tunnicliffe b Higgs	7
J. G. Wright c Tolchard b Taylor	10	†R. W. Taylor run out	2
P. N. Kirsten lbw b Higgs	89	M. Hendrick not out	2
D. S. Steele c and b Booth	26	L-b 2, w 2, n-b 2	6
K. J. Barnett b Taylor	18		
*G. Miller c Butcher b Taylor	4	1/1 2/25 3/96 (8 wkts, 40 overs) 175	
J. Walters not out	11	4/138 5/151 6/158 7/169 8/173	

S. Oldham did not bat.

Bowling: Higgs 8–1–29–2; Taylor 8–0–34–3; Steele 8–1–17–0; Booth 8–0–45–1; Wenlock 8–0–44–0.

Leicestershire

J. Birkenshaw c Kirsten b Walters	34	J. F. Steele run out	1
N. E. Briers b Oldham	51	D. A. Wenlock not out	0
D. I. Gower not out	49	L-b 10, w 3, n-b 5	18
†R. W. Tolchard lbw b Hendrick	11		
T. J. Boon c Taylor b Kirsten	0	1/92 2/95 3/129 (6 wkts, 40 overs) 179	
I. P. Butcher b Kirsten	15	4/135 5/171 6/173	

P. Booth, L. B. Taylor and *K. Higgs did not bat.

Bowling: Hendrick 8–2–20–1; Tunnicliffe 8–0–16–0; Miller 4–0–32–0; Oldham 8–0–24–1; Walters 8–0–38–1; Kirsten 4–0–31–2.

Umpires: W. L. Budd and D. J. Halfyard.

LEICESTERSHIRE v HAMPSHIRE

At Leicester, June 8. Hampshire won by six wickets. Leicestershire, put in, lost three early wickets before Briers and Tolchard led their recovery with 122 in 25 overs. A second-wicket stand of 102 by Smith and Turner provided the basis of the visitors' success. They were both dismissed by Higgs in one over, but Hampshire had enough in hand for a comfortable victory.

Leicestershire

J. Birkenshaw c Stephenson b Graf	2	J. F. Steele not out	15
N. E. Briers b Graf	79	D. A. Wenlock not out	5
B. Dudleston c Turner b Rice	5	B 3, l-b 15, w 2, n-b 1	21
*B. F. Davison lbw b Stevenson	1		
†R. W. Tolchard b Malone	37	1/7 2/15 3/16 (6 wkts, 40 overs) 170	
T. J. Boon b Graf	5	4/138 5/144 6/150	

L. B. Taylor, P. Booth and K. Higgs did not bat.

Bowling: Malone 8–2–27–1; Graf 8–1–24–3; Stevenson 8–0–30–1; Rice 8–0–26–1; Jesty 4–0–19–0; Taylor 4–0–23–0.

Hampshire

J. M. Rice c and b Taylor	10	N. G. Cowley not out	8
C. L. Smith c Tolchard b Higgs	55	B 1, l-b 11, w 1, n-b 2	15
D. R. Turner b Higgs	57		
T. E. Jesty not out	22	1/30 2/132 (4 wkts, 37.1 overs) 173	
*N. E. J. Pocock b Wenlock	6	3/133 4/146	

S. F. Graf, M. N. S. Taylor, †G. R. Stephenson , K. Stevenson and S. J. Malone did not bat.

Bowling: Higgs 7–0–28–2; Taylor 7.1–1–33–1; Steele 8–1–17–0; Booth 6–0–35–0; Wenlock 6–0–28–1; Birkenshaw 3–0–17–0.

Umpires: R. Aspinall and R. Julian.

At Worcester, June 22. LEICESTERSHIRE lost to WORCESTERSHIRE by eight wickets.

LEICESTERSHIRE v LANCASHIRE

At Leicester, June 29. Lancashire won by five wickets. A dropped catch by Davison, early in Kennedy's innings, was costly for Leicestershire who were beaten with only two balls to spare. Kennedy took advantage of his "life" by dominating Lancashire's chase for runs and, with Lloyd (two 6s), put on 93 for the second wicket. Leicestershire's innings had been given a brisk start by Briers and Gower, but Davison was not at his best and their final total proved just too low.

Leicestershire

N. E. Briers b Lee	25	P. B. Clift b Allott		9
D. I. Gower c Hogg b Allott	18	J. F. Steele run out		12
R. W. Tolchard lbw b Allott	5	B 1, l-b 9, w 3, n-b 2		15
*B. F. Davison c Kennedy b Simmons	35			
†M. A. Garnham b Simmons	24	1/43 2/52 3/68	(7 wkts, 40 overs)	165
T. J. Boon not out	22	4/111 5/123 6/148 7/165		

D. A. Wenlock, L. B. Taylor and K. Higgs did not bat.

Bowling: Hogg 7–1–24–0; Lee 8–2–23–1; Allott 8–2–27–3; Hughes 6–0–31–0; Simmons 8–0–31–2; Kennedy 3–0–14–0.

Lancashire

A. Kennedy c Gower b Clift	62	D. P. Hughes not out		3
*F. C. Hayes c Garnham b Taylor	3			
D. Lloyd c Tolchard b Steele	43	B 6, l-b 7, w 1, n-b 3		17
I. Cockbain b Steele	10			
J. Abrahams not out	23	1/11 2/104 3/122	(5 wkts, 39.4 overs)	166
J. Simmons c Gower b Taylor	5	4/137 5/159		

†C. J. Scott, W. Hogg, P. J. W. Allott and P. G. Lee did not bat.

Bowling: Higgs 8–1–29–0; Taylor 7.4–0–28–2; Wenlock 8–0–37–0; Clift 7–0–22–1; Steele 8–0–33–2; Briers 1–1–0–0.

Umpires: D. J. Dennis and A. Jepson.

At Maidstone, July 6. LEICESTERSHIRE beat KENT on faster scoring-rate.

At Chelmsford, July 13. LEICESTERSHIRE beat ESSEX by nine wickets.

LEICESTERSHIRE v MIDDLESEX

At Leicester, July 20. No result.

At Ebbw Vale, July 27. LEICESTERSHIRE beat GLAMORGAN by eight wickets.

At Trent Bridge, August 3, LEICESTERSHIRE beat NOTTINGHAMSHIRE by 12 runs.

LEICESTERSHIRE v YORKSHIRE

At Leicester, August 10. Leicestershire won by five wickets. A rain-affected pitch made scoring difficult. Parsons struck the first blow by bowling Hampshire, but the player to make most inroads was Steele, whose spin took four wickets. Although Leicestershire lost three cheap wickets, a partnership of 44 between Davison and Tolchard eased them home with more than seven overs to spare.

Yorkshire

P. G. Ingham b Briers	28	†S. P. Coverdale b Higgs	1
*J. H. Hampshire b Parsons	4	H. P. Cooper c Garnham b Clift	0
C. W. J. Athey c Gower b Steele	11	S. J. Dennis not out	4
J. D. Love b Steele	21		
G. B. Stevenson b Steele	4	L-b 10, w 3, n-b 1	14
S. N. Hartley b Steele	0		
P. Carrick b Higgs	19	1/27 2/46 3/55 4/67 (37.5 overs) 108	
A. Sidebottom run out	2	5/77 6/84 7/101 8/103 9/104	

Bowling: Taylor 4–0–9–0; Parsons 8–2–21–1; Clift 7–0–10–1; Steele 8–0–32–4; Briers 4–1–9–1; Higgs 6.5–0–13–2.

Leicestershire

D. I. Gower b Sidebottom	19	J. F. Steele not out	0
N. E. Briers c Coverdale b Sidebottom	8		
J. C. Balderstone run out	5	L-b 10, w 4, n-b 3	17
*B. F. Davison run out	27		
R. W. Tolchard not out	19	1/16 2/33 (5 wkts, 32.3 overs) 111	
†M. A. Garnham b Cooper	16	3/39 4/83 5/103	

P. B. Clift, G. J. Parsons, L. B. Taylor and K. Higgs did not bat.

Bowling: Stevenson 6.2–2–23–0; Dennis 8–1–20–0; Sidebottom 8–3–27–2; Cooper 8–2–21–1; Hartley 2–0–3–0.

Umpires: W. L. Budd and D. O. Oslear.

At Taunton, August 17. LEICESTERSHIRE lost to SOMERSET by 41 runs.

LEICESTERSHIRE v NORTHAMPTONSHIRE

At Leicester, August 24. Leicestershire won by 17 runs. Davison provided the corner-stone of Leicestershire's innings and an unbeaten seventh-wicket stand of 52 between Clift and Steele accelerated the scoring at the right time. Allan Lamb and Williams looked capable of seeing Northamptonshire home but, once Lamb was run out, tight bowling and slick fielding put a brake on the tempo.

Leicestershire

D. I. Gower lbw b Sarfraz	11	P. B. Clift not out	26
N. E. Briers b Willey	31	J. F. Steele not out	28
J. C. Balderstone c Williams b T. M. Lamb	14	L-b 22	22
*B. F. Davison c Watts b Willey	43		
R. W. Tolchard c Cook b Willey	18	1/26 2/59 3/69 (6 wkts, 40 overs) 201	
†M. A. Garnham b Willey	8	4/128 5/143 6/149	

G. J. Parsons, L. B. Taylor and D. A. Wenlock did not bat.

Bowling: Sarfraz 8–4–15–1; Griffiths 8–0–27–0; Watts 4–0–25–0; T. M. Lamb 6–0–43–1; Willey 8–0–38–4; Williams 6–0–31–0.

Northamptonshire

W. Larkins lbw b Wenlock	6	†G. Sharp b Taylor	0
P. Willey c Garnham b Taylor	17	*P. J. Watts b Clift	23
A. J. Lamb run out	37	T. M. Lamb not out	2
R. G. Williams c Steele b Taylor	42	B 1,l-b 7, w 1, n-b 3	12
G. Cook c Taylor b Steele	16		
T. J. Yardley c Garnham b Clift	1	1/24 2/45 3/88 (8 wkts, 40 overs) 184	
Sarfraz Nawaz not out	28	4/120 5/121 6/137 7/137 8/181	

B. J. Griffiths did not bat.

Bowling: Taylor 8–0–40–3; Parsons 8–2–13–0; Wenlock 8–0–39–1; Steele 8–0–47–1; Clift 8–1–33–2.

Umpires: R. Palmer and J. van Geloven.

LEICESTERSHIRE v WARWICKSHIRE

At Leicester, August 31. Warwickshire won by six wickets, and took the John Player League title. With Snow dismissing Dudleston and Davison in successive overs, Leicestershire slipped to 55 for four, but wicket-keepers Tolchard and Garnham improved the position with a fifth-wicket stand of 65 in fourteen overs and quick running by Tolchard helped add another 60 in the last ten. However Leicestershire's total proved inadequate as Lloyd and Kallicharran paced Warwickshire's reply perfectly. Humpage was out with the totals level, and it was left to Oliver to score the winning run with two overs remaining.

Leicestershire

B. Dudleston lbw b Snow	20	G. J. Parsons c Humpage b Small	4
N. E. Briers c Maynard b Small	0	L. B. Taylor not out	0
J. C. Balderstone c Maynard b Ferreira	19	K. Higgs not out	2
*B. F. Davison b Snow	2	B 9, l-b 14, w 2, n-b 5	30
R. W. Tolchard b Small	59		
†M. A. Garnham c Small b Oliver	27	1/1 2/40 3/46 (9 wkts, 40 overs) 180
P. B. Clift run out	12	4/55 5/120 6/143 7/153
J. F. Steele c Maynard b Willis	5	8/178 9/178

Bowling: Willis 8–1–25–1; Small 8–2–42–3; Ferreira 8–1–18–1; Snow 8–0–27–2; Oliver 8–0–38–1.

Warwickshire

D. L. Amiss c Dudleston b Parsons	18	P. R. Oliver not out	1
T. A. Lloyd b Higgs	46	L-b 3, w 1, n-b 1	5
A. I. Kallicharran lbw b Clift	36		
G. W. Humpage b Clift	47	1/46 2/88 (4 wkts, 38 overs) 181
J. Whitehouse not out	28	3/114 4/180

†C. Maynard, J. A. Snow, *R. G. D. Willis, G. C. Small and A. M. Ferreira did not bat.

Bowling: Taylor 7–0–43–0; Parsons 8–1–16–1; Steele 8–0–31–0; Higgs 8–0–46–1; Clift 7–0–40–2.

Umpires: R. Aspinall and P. S. G. Stevens.

At The Oval, September 7. LEICESTERSHIRE lost to SURREY by five wickets.

MIDDLESEX

MIDDLESEX v LANCASHIRE

At Lord's, May 4. Middlesex won by 7 runs. Both sides produced excellent batting and the result hinged on the difference in fielding; Middlesex were efficient whereas Lancashire were clumsy and laboured. Barlow commanded his second-wicket stand with Radley of 129 in 27 overs. Kennedy and Pilling were playing beautifully at a speed verging on the required rate until Pilling's run out and a fine return catch by Gatting turned the game.

Middlesex

*J. M. Brearley lbw b Malone	0	†I. J. Gould b Lee	23
C. T. Radley c Lloyd b Kennedy	77	L-b 5, w 1...............	6
G. D. Barlow c Simmons b Kennedy....	76		
M. W. Gatting not out	26	1/0 2/129 3/162 (5 wkts, 40 overs) 221	
R. O. Butcher lbw b Lee.............	13	4/179	

P. H. Edmonds, J. E. Emburey, V. A. P. van der Bijl, M. W. W. Selvey and W. W. Daniel did not bat.

Bowling: Malone 8–2–28–1; Lee 8–0–44–2; Ratcliffe 8–1–44–0; Simmons 4–0–22–0; Hughes 8–0–55–0; Kennedy 4–0–22–2.

Lancashire

A. Kennedy c and b Gatting	72	D. P. Hughes not out	6
H. Pilling run out	46		
*F. C. Hayes st Gould b Gatting	7	B 4, l-b 6, w 1.............	11
D. Lloyd not out	37		
I. Cockbain c Brearley b Gatting	21	1/122 2/129 (5 wkts, 40 overs) 214	
J. Simmons b Daniel	14	3/136 4/174 5/208	

R. M. Ratcliffe, †G. Fowler, M. F. Malone and P. G. Lee did not bat.

Bowling: van der Bijl 8–0–37–0; Selvey 5–1–32–0; Edmonds 3–0–18–0; Emburey 8–1–41–0; Daniel 8–1–32–1; Gatting 8–0–43–3.

Umpires: W. E. Alley and P. S. G. Stevens.

At Worcester, May 18. MIDDLESEX beat WORCESTERSHIRE by nine wickets.

MIDDLESEX v NORTHAMPTONSHIRE

At Lord's, May 25. Middlesex won by seven wickets. Even the fluent Northamptonshire batsmen could make little headway against van der Bijl and Gatting, who each conceded just 15 from their overs. A measure of the Middlesex accuracy was that the off stump was hit four times. Gatting then celebrated his selection for the Prudential Trophy squad with an exhilarating 71 which took his team to victory.

Northamptonshire

W. Larkins b van der Bijl	20	Sarfraz Nawaz not out..............	3
P. Willey b Selvey	4	T. M. Lamb lbw b Selvey...........	0
A. J. Lamb b Daniel	13	B. J. Griffiths b Daniel..............	1
G. Cook c Gould b Daniel	32	B 2, l-b 9, w 1, n-b 2.........	14
R. G. Williams c Barlow b Emburey	16		
T. J. Yardley b Gatting.	16	1/9 2/41 3/45 4/68 (38.3 overs) 134	
†G. Sharp run out	7	5/104 6/111 7/124 8/131	
*P. J. Watts c Brearley b Selvey........	8	9/133	

Bowling: Selvey 7–0–38–3; van der Bijl 8–2–15–1; Daniel 7.3–1–27–3; Gatting 8–2–15–1; Emburey 8–1–25–1.

Middlesex

*J. M. Brearley run out	43	R. O. Butcher not out..............	5
C. T. Radley b Griffiths	7	B 1, l-b 5, n-b 4............	10
G. D. Barlow lbw b Griffiths	0		
M. W. Gatting not out	71	1/20 2/26 3/122 (3 wkts, 35.1 overs) 136	

†I. J. Gould, P. H. Edmonds, V. A. P. van der Bijl, M. W. W. Selvey, J. E. Emburey and W. W. Daniel did not bat.

Bowling; Sarfraz 7–1–28–0; Griffiths 7.1–4–16–2; T. M. Lamb 8–1–27–0; Willey 8–1–27–0; Watts 3–0–12–0; Williams 2–0–16–0.

Umpires: R. Aspinall and H. D. Bird.

At Taunton, June 1. MIDDLESEX beat SOMERSET by 122 runs.

MIDDLESEX v YORKSHIRE

At Lord's, June 8. Middlesex won by three wickets. Although Yorkshire batted consistently and soundly, their running was poor and they failed to achieve an adequate total. However, their crisp fielding sent Middlesex slipping from the comfortable position of 128 for three, when Brearley was out after an effortless knock. Athey and Bairstow took marvellous catches but van der Bijl settled the game with a 6 and a 4 off Stevenson in the 37th over and another 4 in the 39th.

Yorkshire

R. G. Lumb b van der Bijl	64	†D. L. Bairstow not out	9
C. W. J. Athey c Emburey b Gatting	39	B 1, l-b 4, w 2, n-b 1	8
J. D. Love c Gould b Daniel	21		
K. Sharp b Daniel	36	1/77 2/113 (4 wkts, 39 overs) 187	
S. N. Hartley not out	10	3/166 4/166	

P. Carrick, *C. M. Old, A. Sidebottom, G. B. Stevenson and A. Ramage did not bat.

Bowling: Selvey 8–2–23–0; van der Bijl 8–0–40–1; Daniel 8–0–46–2; Emburey 8–1–34–0; Gatting 6–0–27–1; Edmonds 1–0–9–0.

Middlesex

*J. M. Brearley c and b Athey	63	V. A. P. van der Bijl not out	21
C. T. Radley b Stevenson	0	J. E. Emburey not out	1
G. D. Barlow c Bairstow b Sidebottom	26		
M. W. Gatting c Bairstow b Sidebottom	46	B 4, l-b 9, w 4	17
R. O. Butcher c Old b Athey	2		
†I. J. Gould c Athey b Sidebottom	6	1/3 2/58 3/128 (7 wkts, 38.4 overs) 190	
P. H. Edmonds c Old b Stevenson	8	4/136 5/149 6/160 7/167	

M. W. W. Selvey and W. W. Daniel did not bat.

Bowling: Stevenson 7.4–0–41–2; Old 8–0–22–0; Sidebottom 8–1–38–3; Ramage 3–0–22–0; Carrick 5–0–20–0; Athey 7–0–30–2.

Umpires: W. L. Budd and J. van Geloven.

MIDDLESEX v SURREY

At Lord's, June 15. Middlesex won by ten wickets. Surrey, put in, gave a dreadful display and Middlesex did not have to work particularly hard for their wickets. After Daniel had wrapped up the innings with three wickets in fifteen balls during his second spell, Brearley and Radley strolled to an early success.

Surrey

A. R. Butcher c Gould b Selvey	6	S. T. Clarke b Daniel	1
G. P. Howarth run out	13	P. I. Pocock b Daniel	1
*R. D. V. Knight c Gould b van der Bijl	3	R. G. L. Cheatle not out	2
D. M. Smith b Gatting	12	B 4, l-b 5, w 1, n-b 1	11
G. S. Clinton c Edmonds b Daniel	9		
M. A. Lynch c Butcher b Gatting	9	1/16 2/21 3/26 (32.3 overs) 85	
R. D. Jackman st Gould b Emburey	15	4/44 5/58 6/65 7/80	
†C. J. Richards c Brearley b Daniel	3	8/82 9/82	

Bowling: Selvey 8–2–16–1; van der Bijl 7–2–12–1; Daniel 5.3–0–20–4; Emburey 8–2–17–1; Gatting 4–0–9–2.

Middlesex

*J. M. Brearley not out.............. 40
C. T. Radley not out 40
      L-b 3, w 3................ 6

        (no wkt, 24.5 overs) 86

G. D. Barlow, M. W. Gatting, R. O. Butcher, †I. J. Gould, P. H. Edmonds, J. E. Emburey, V. A. P. van der Bijl, M. W. W. Selvey and W. W. Daniel did not bat.

  Bowling: Jackman 8–0–14–0; Clarke 7.5–1–20–0; Pocock 3–0–15–0; Knight 3–0–15–0; Cheatle 3–0–16–0.

        Umpires: W. E. Alley and B. J. Meyer.

At Birmingham, June 29. MIDDLESEX lost to WARWICKSHIRE by five wickets.

MIDDLESEX v DERBYSHIRE

At Lord's, July 6. Derbyshire won by eight wickets. Rain around five o'clock turned the match into a mathematical issue which worked in Derbyshire's favour. They were 50 off twelve overs when the first rain fell, and the Middlesex scoring-rate was then the faster. A brief spell of play – only five balls – brought Derbyshire 13 runs and took them ahead by a fraction of a run. At the second resumption they needed 11 from thirteen balls and although Miller and Kirsten were out to successive deliveries, playing reckless shots, Wood calmly scored the necessary runs. Gatting had steered Middlesex away from a hesitant start, batting through from the tenth over.

Middlesex

C. T. Radley c Kirsten b Miller 15
*J. M. Brearley c Taylor b Oldham 2
G. D. Barlow c Kirsten b Miller........ 25
M. W. Gatting not out 82
R. O. Butcher lbw b Wood............ 2
V. A. P. van der Bijl b Tunnicliffe 40

†I. J. Gould not out 5

     B 1, l-b 8, w 3, n-b 2 14

1/2 2/30 3/95   (5 wkts, 38 overs) 185
4/99 5/167

K. P. Tomlins, J. E. Emburey, M. W. W. Selvey and W. W. Daniel did not bat.

  Bowling: Tunnicliffe 7–1–28–1; Oldham 7–0–37–1; Wood 8–0–44–1; Miller 8–1–37–2; Hendrick 8–1–25–0.

Derbyshire

*G. Miller c Gould b Daniel........... 20
J. G. Wright not out................. 40
P. N. Kirsten lbw b Daniel........... 0
B. Wood not out.................... 6
    B 3, l-b 3, w 2.............. 8

1/66 2/66   (2 wkts, 14.2 overs) 74

D. S. Steele, K. J. Barnett, A. J. Borrington, †R. W. Taylor, C. J. Tunnicliffe, S. Oldham and M. Hendrick did not bat.

  Bowling: Selvey 6–0–19–0; van der Bijl 6.2–0–32–0; Emburey 1–0–11–0; Daniel 1–0–4–2.

        Umpires: D. J. Dennis and R. S. Herman.

At Leicester, July 20. LEICESTERSHIRE v MIDDLESEX. No result.

MIDDLESEX v KENT

At Lord's, July 27. Kent won by 13 runs. Middlesex put Kent in and were optimistic when Woolmer departed at 111 for five, after batting bravely with strained abdomen muscles. However, the visitors' innings was taken to a useful total by Ealham's crisp hitting in an unbroken stand of 66 from eight overs with Cowdrey. Middlesex progressed encouragingly to 78 for three, but subsided on a drying pitch to the spin of Johnson, who was helped when Nicholls stumped Selvey and Tomlins in the same over. A last-wicket stand of 45 in seven overs between Daniel and van der Bijl, in which both batsmen hit two 6s, had reduced Middlesex's target to 14 from nine balls when van der Bijl edged Jarvis to Nicholls.

Kent

R. A. Woolmer c Slack b Maru	52	C. S. Cowdrey not out	18
G. W. Johnson c Gould b van der Bijl	39		
C. J. Tavaré b Maru	5	L-b 7, n-b 2	9
†D. Nicholls b Tomlins	5		
Asif Iqbal c Brearley b Daniel	3	1/61 2/68 3/93 (5 wkts, 40 overs) 177	
*A. G. E. Ealham not out	46	4/101 5/111	

J. N. Shepherd, D. L. Underwood, G. D. Spelman and K. B. S. Jarvis did not bat.

Bowling: Selvey 8–0–36–0; van der Bijl 8–1–24–1; Tomlins 8–1–34–1; Maru 8–0–41–2; Daniel 8–1–33–1.

Middlesex

*J. M. Brearley c Shepherd b Jarvis	10	K. P. Tomlins st Nicholls b Johnson	0
C. T. Radley c Underwood b Shepherd	19	W. W. Daniel c Ealham b Johnson	14
G. D. Barlow b Underwood	25	R. J. Maru not out	3
R. O. Butcher c Nicholls b Asif	1	B 7, l-b 7, n-b 3	17
†I. J. Gould b Johnson	17		
W. N. Slack c Ealham b Johnson	10	1/21 2/36 3/37 (38.4 overs) 164	
V. A. P. van der Bijl c Nicholls b Jarvis	47	4/78 5/81 6/95 7/97	
M. W. W. Selvey st Nicholls b Johnson	1	8/97 9/119	

Bowling: Jarvis 6.4–1–25–2; Spelman 7–0–27–0; Shepherd 5–0–15–1; Asif 5–1–19–1; Underwood 8–3–35–2; Johnson 7–1–26–4.

Umpires: H. D. Bird and C. Cook.

MIDDLESEX v ESSEX

At Lord's, August 3. Essex won by 57 runs. Essex established a John Player League record for Lord's with their total of 255 for five. Their new opening partnership of Gooch (three 6s) and Smith proved successful with a stand of 116 in seventeen overs. Fletcher and Phillip then maintained the pace, and the Middlesex start of 79 from fifteen overs was inadequate against such a total. Turner collected wickets from reckless batsmen and, when the gamble of promoting Daniel had failed, Middlesex had no answer to Fletcher's field-setting.

Essex

G. A. Gooch c Butcher b Gatting	86	K. R. Pont not out	1
†N. Smith c Butcher b Daniel	60		
K. S. McEwan st Downton b Selvey	14	B 5, l-b 9, w 6	20
*K. W. R. Fletcher not out	34		
N. Phillip c Emburey b Tomlins	32	1/116 2/156 (5 wkts, 38 overs) 255	
B. R. Hardie b Hughes	8	3/189 4/237 5/254	

D. R. Pringle, S. Turner, J. K. Lever and D. L. Acfield did not bat.

Bowling: Daniel 8–0–39–1; Selvey 8–0–32–1; Hughes 7–1–54–1; Gatting 6–0–48–1; Emburey 8–0–46–0; Tomlins 1–0–16–1.

Middlesex

C. T. Radley b Lever	81	†P. R. Downton b Lever		12
*J. M. Brearley st Smith b Turner	44	M. W. W. Selvey c Lever b Pringle		4
M. W. Gatting b Turner	16	S. P. Hughes not out		0
R. O. Butcher c and b Gooch	2	L-b 10, w 6		16
I. J. Gould c Acfield b Pont	10			
W. W. Daniel b Turner	0	1/79 2/113 3/118	(35.1 overs)	198
J. E. Emburey c Gooch b Turner	5	4/135 5/136 6/152 7/175		
K. P. Tomlins run out	8	8/183 9/198		

Bowling: Lever 7–1–26–2; Phillip 4–0–20–0; Gooch 8–0–45–1; Acfield 2–0–20–0; Turner 7–0–33–4; Pont 5–0–29–1; Pringle 2.1–0–9–1.

Umpires: D. Shackleton and P. B. Wight.

At Cheltenham, August 10. MIDDLESEX lost to GLOUCESTERSHIRE by 55 runs.

MIDDLESEX v NOTTINGHAMSHIRE

At Lord's, August 17. Middlesex won on faster scoring-rate. The highlight of Middlesex's win was Butcher's crisp innings during which he reached 50 off 38 balls. Nottinghamshire's target was reduced to 158 in 32 overs by bad light, but after Randall had been run out they had nothing to offer.

Middlesex

*J. M. Brearley lbw b Watson	14	W. N. Slack b Watson		2
C. T. Radley c Randall b Rice	38	J. E. Emburey not out		4
G. D. Barlow c Watson b Hemmings	41	B 5, l-b 3, w 1		9
M. W. Gatting b Hacker	8			
R. O. Butcher not out	64	1/22 2/85 3/103	(6 wkts, 38 overs)	187
V. A. P. van der Bijl b Watson	7	4/104 5/128 6/154		

†P. R. Downton, W. W. Daniel and W. G. Merry did not bat.

Bowling: Watson 8–0–30–3; Hacker 8–0–32–1; Bore 8–0–37–0; Hemmings 6–0–30–1; Rice 8–0–49–1.

Nottinghamshire

D. W. Randall run out	27	E. E. Hemmings not out		16
R. T. Robinson c Downton b van der Bijl	2			
*C. E. B. Rice b Emburey	3	L-b 9, w 3		12
J. D. Birch run out	6			
P. A. Todd b Merry	8	1/4 2/19 3/45	(5 wkts, 32 overs)	101
M. J. Harris not out	27	4/48 5/62		

†B. Hassan, W. K. Watson, P. J. Hacker and M. K. Bore did not bat.

Bowling: van der Bijl 6–1–7–1; Daniel 5–0–13–0; Emburey 8–0–22–1; Merry 8–0–22–1; Slack 3–0–15–0; Gatting 2–0–10–0.

Umpires: A. Jepson and J. G. Langridge.

At Hove, August 24. MIDDLESEX beat SUSSEX by 21 runs.

At Cardiff, August 31. MIDDLESEX beat GLAMORGAN by 11 runs.

At Bournemouth, September 7. MIDDLESEX beat HAMPSHIRE by five wickets.

NORTHAMPTONSHIRE

At Bristol, May 4. NORTHAMPTONSHIRE beat GLOUCESTERSHIRE by 14 runs.

NORTHAMPTONSHIRE v SUSSEX

At Northampton, May 11. Northamptonshire won by nine wickets after only 27.4 overs. A brave seventh-wicket stand of 46 by Wells and Pigott was not enough to give Sussex a reasonable total against accurate bowling. For Northamptonshire Willey hit nine 4s and Larkins hit twelve, in a first-wicket stand of 117. The game was watched by many cricket notabilities after Northamptonshire's £130,000 new pavilion had been opened by TCCB chairman George Mann.

Sussex

G. D. Mendis c Sharp b T. M. Lamb	0	C. M. Wells not	34
K. C. Wessels c Cook b Willey	11	A. C. S. Pigott not out	16
P. W. G. Parker c Cook b Larkins	4	B 1, l-b 8, w 2	11
Imran Khan c Williams b Willey	17		
P. J. Graves c Griffiths b Williams	21	1/2 2/14 3/24	(6 wkts, 40 overs) 123
C. P. Phillipson b Larkins	9	4/53 5/71 6/77	

*†A. Long, J. Spencer and C. E. Waller did not bat.

Bowling: Griffiths 8–2–22–0; T. M. Lamb 8–1–26–1; Willey 8–1–15–2; Larkins 8–1–23–2; Williams 8–1–26–1.

Northamptonshire

P. Willey not out	53
W. Larkins c Imran b Wells	61
A. J. Lamb not out	7
W 2, n-b 1	3

1/117 (1 wkt, 27.4 overs) 124

*G. Cook, R. G. Williams, T. J. Yardley, R. M. Tindall, R. M. Carter, †G. Sharp, T. M. Lamb and B. J. Griffiths did not bat.

Bowling: Spencer 5–0–21–0; Imran 4–0–13–0; Waller 8–2–25–0; Pigott 6–0–38–0; Wells 4.4–1–24–1.

Umpires: C. Cook and C. T. Spencer.

At Lord's, May 25. NORTHAMPTONSHIRE lost to MIDDLESEX by seven wickets.

At Cardiff, June 1. NORTHAMPTONSHIRE beat GLAMORGAN by seven wickets.

NORTHAMPTONSHIRE v LANCASHIRE

At Tring, June 8. Northamptonshire won by seven wickets in a 35 overs game after rain delayed the start. Cook was the outstanding batsman with a fine 55 (one 6 and eight 4s), he and Larkins getting the innings off to a brisk start with 40 from the first six overs. Lancashire had promised a useful total with an opening stand of 35 by Kennedy and Lloyd but they lost momentum against the accuracy of Watts and Tim Lamb until late hitting by Simmons and Abrahams took them to 132 for eight.

Lancashire

A. Kennedy c Larkins b Watts	22	J. Abrahams b Sarfraz	26
D. Lloyd c Larkins b T. M. Lamb	18	R. M. Ratcliffe not out	2
B. W. Reidy b Watts	1	P. J. W. Allott not out	3
†G. Fowler b T. M. Lamb	6	L-b 3, w 1, n-b 1	5
*J. Simmons c T. M. Lamb b Larkins	22		
D. P. Hughes c Sharp b Larkins	12	1/35 2/37 3/47 (8 wkts, 35 overs) 132	
I. Cockbain c Sarfraz b Griffiths	15	4/49 5/79 6/85 7/113 8/129	

P. G. Lee did not bat.

Bowling: Sarfraz 7–1–27–1; Griffiths 7–0–29–1; Watts 7–1–14–2; T. M. Lamb 7–2–20–2; Larkins 4–0–27–2; Carter 3–0–10–0.

Northamptonshire

G. Cook b Hughes	55	T. J. Yardley not out	8
W. Larkins b Reidy	24	L-b 8	8
A. J. Lamb lbw b Allott	13		
R. G. Williams not out	25	1/40 2/90 3/103 (3 wkts, 31.5 overs) 133	

*P. J. Watts, †G. Sharp, R. M. Carter, Sarfraz Nawaz, T. M. Lamb and B. J. Griffiths did not bat.

Bowling: Lee 3–0–15–0; Reidy 3–0–24–1; Ratcliffe 2–0–23–0; Allott 7–1–17–1; Simmons 7–1–13–0; Hughes 5.5–0–19–1; Lloyd 4–0–14–0.

Umpires: W. E. Alley and T. W. Spencer.

At Worksop, June 15. NORTHAMPTONSHIRE beat NOTTINGHAMSHIRE by 2 runs.

At Nuneaton, June 22. NORTHAMPTONSHIRE lost to WARWICKSHIRE by 26 runs.

NORTHAMPTONSHIRE v WORCESTERSHIRE

At Northampton, June 29. Northamptonshire won by seven wickets for their sixth John Player League victory in eight games. Hemsley, acting as Worcestershire's captain, elected to bat and saw his team dismissed for 99 in 33.5 overs as the home seam attack made the most of a helpful pitch. After losing half their batsmen for 47 Worcestershire rallied through a stand of 34 by Patel and Humphries, but then Larkins produced a final slump by taking three wickets in five balls. Northamptonshire began slowly, losing Cook, Willey and Larkins for 40, but good batting by Allan Lamb and Williams saw the home county to their target with an unbroken stand of 62.

Worcestershire

J. A. Ormrod b Sarfraz	7	H. Alleyne c T. M. Lamb b Larkins	0
P. A. Neale lbw b Watts	13	J. Cumbes not out	1
Younis Ahmed c Cook b Griffiths	6	A. P. Pridgeon run out	3
*E. J. O. Hemsley b T. M. Lamb	5		
B. J. R. Jones b Watts	5	B 2, l-b 8, w 1	11
D. N. Patel c Willey b Larkins	22		
†D. J. Humphries lbw b Willey	21	1/16 2/25 3/32 (33.5 overs) 99	
J. D. Inchmore lbw b Larkins	5	4/32 5/47 6/81 7/95 8/95 9/95	

Bowling: Sarfraz 5–0–17–1; Griffiths 5.5–1–11–1; T. M. Lamb 8–2–13–1; Watts 8–2–17–2; Larkins 4–0–18–3; Willey 3–0–12–1.

Northamptonshire

W. Larkins c Humphries b Pridgeon	18	R. G. Williams not out	31
P. Willey c Humphries b Alleyne	2	L-b 1, w 3, n-b 1	5
A. J. Lamb not out	36		
G. Cook c Jones b Cumbes	10	1/22 2/24 3/40 (3 wkts, 32.5 overs)	102

T. J. Yardley, *P. J. Watts, †G. Sharp, Sarfraz Nawaz, T. M. Lamb and B. J. Griffiths did not bat.

Bowling: Alleyne 6–1–11–1; Pridgeon 6.5–0–33–1; Cumbes 8–3–12–1; Inchmore 8–1–29–0; Younis 4–0–12–0.

Umpires: R. Julian and C. T. Spencer.

NORTHAMPTONSHIRE v KENT

At Luton, July 13. Northamptonshire won by four wickets with one ball to spare in an exciting finish. Victory seemed unlikely when they needed 21 from the final two overs, and 14 from the last; but Sarfraz hammered a 4 and a 6 from Spelman's fourth and fifth balls. Earlier Northamptonshire were contained by accurate bowling from Underwood and Kent seemed to have control, despite useful batting by Cook and Yardley. The 19-year-old Spelman bowled capably and took three wickets before falling victim to Sarfraz's last onslaught. On a slow wicket Kent had also found run-getting difficult but were boosted by Asif, Cowdrey and Nicholls.

Kent

R. A. Woolmer b Sarfraz	2	†D. Nicholls not out	31
G. W. Johnson b T. M. Lamb	16	R. W. Hills not out	10
C. J. Tavaré b Watts	13	B 4, l-b 7, n-b 2	13
Asif Iqbal b T. M. Lamb	28		
*A. G. E. Ealham c Sharp b Carter	3	1/5 2/22 3/46 (6 wkts, 40 overs)	138
C. S. Cowdrey c Boyd-Moss b Sarfraz	22	4/58 5/76 6/123	

D. L. Underwood, G. D. Spelman and K. B. S. Jarvis did not bat.

Bowling: Sarfraz 8–2–19–2; Griffiths 8–0–20–0; T. M. Lamb 8–0–31–2; Watts 8–0–29–1; Carter 8–1–26–1.

Northamptonshire

G. Cook c Woolmer b Underwood	31	Sarfraz Nawaz not out	19
†G. Sharp b Spelman	12	R. J. Boyd-Moss not out	9
A. J. Lamb c Ealham b Hills	16	B 3, l-b 2, w 2	7
R. G. Williams run out	14		
T. J. Yardley b Spelman	31	1/25 2/61 3/62 (6 wkts, 39.5 overs)	139
*P. J. Watts c Woolmer b Spelman	0	4/109 5/116 6/116	

R. M. Carter, T. M. Lamb and B. J. Griffiths did not bat.

Bowling: Jarvis 5–1–18–0; Spelman 7.5–1–30–3; Woolmer 7–0–30–0; Hills 5–0–20–1; Underwood 8–3–9–1; Johnson 7–0–25–0.

Umpires: D. J. Dennis and R. S. Herman.

NORTHAMPTONSHIRE v DERBYSHIRE

At Northampton, July 20. No result.

NORTHAMPTONSHIRE v SURREY

At Northampton, August 3. Surrey won by seven wickets with only two balls remaining. In the absence through injury of Cook and Williams, Northamptonshire lost three wickets to Knight for 51 in nineteen overs. However, the aggressive Sarfraz then hit two 6s and three 4s in his highest John Player League score and was aided in a fifth-wicket stand of 62 in fourteen overs by Boyd-Moss. Surrey were guided to success by Butcher, batting throughout the innings, with useful assistance from Knight and Roope. They cut their victory bid fine – 51 were needed off the last eight overs – but Lynch hit the winning boundary off the fourth ball of the final over.

Northamptonshire

W. Larkins st Richards b Knight	15	†G. Sharp not out	12
P. Willey c Butcher b Knight	28	*P. J. Watts run out	11
A. J. Lamb c Richards b Knight	0	L-b 8, w 2	10
R. J. Boyd-Moss run out	26		
T. J. Yardley b Cheatle	1	1/44 2/44 3/51　　(7 wkts, 40 overs) 152	
Sarfraz Nawaz c Richards b Clarke	49	4/57 5/119 6/133 7/152	

R. M. Carter, T. M. Lamb and B. J. Griffiths did not bat.

Bowling: Clarke 8–2–38–1; Jackman 8–1–21–0; Knight 8–2–38–3; Pocock 8–2–23–0; Cheatle 8–1–22–1.

Surrey

A. R. Butcher not out	87	M. A. Lynch not out	8
G. S. Clinton b Griffiths	3	L-b 7, w 1, n-b 1	9
*R. D. V. Knight c and b Willey	29		
G. R. J. Roope c Carter b Sarfraz	19	1/10 2/68 3/133　　(3 wkts, 39.4 overs) 155	

G. P. Howarth, R. D. Jackman, S. T. Clarke, †C. J. Richards, P. I. Pocock and R. G. L. Cheatle did not bat.

Bowling: Sarfraz 8–0–28–1; Griffiths 8–2–25–1; T. M. Lamb 8–1–32–0; Willey 8–2–23–1; Watts 7.4–1–38–0.

Umpires: D. O. Oslear and R. Palmer.

NORTHAMPTONSHIRE v SOMERSET

At Northampton, August 10. Northamptonshire won by five wickets. After putting Somerset in, the home county were encouraged by the early success of Sarfraz and Griffiths. Breakwell and Popplewell then boosted Somerset with a vigorous sixth-wicket stand of 60. Facing a modest target, Northamptonshire began slowly, losing three wickets for 39 before Yardley launched a fierce attack and put on 93 for the fourth wicket with Allan Lamb. Yardley reached his half-century in forty-one minutes and after his dismissal Lamb saw his side to victory.

Somerset

S. M. Gavaskar b Sarfraz	0	†D. J. S. Taylor c Williams b Sarfraz	11
P. W. Denning c Sharp b Griffiths	8	C. H. Dredge not out	10
P. M. Roebuck lbw b Griffiths	2	H. R. Moseley not out	4
P. A. Slocombe b Sarfraz	6		
*V. J. Marks c Sharp b T. M. Lamb	11	L-b 8	8
N. F. M. Popplewell c Carter b T. M. Lamb	47	1/0 2/3 3/16 4/18　　(8 wkts, 40 overs) 146	
D. Breakwell b Griffiths	39	5/49 6/109 7/129 8/137	

H. I. E. Gore did not bat.

Bowling: Sarfraz 8–0–19–3; Griffiths 8–0–29–3; T. M. Lamb 8–1–22–2; Watts 8–0–27–0; Carter 4–0–21–0; Williams 4–1–20–0.

Northamptonshire

G. Cook c Slocombe b Moseley	4	†G. Sharp not out		4
R. G. Williams c Taylor b Gore	7			
A. J. Lamb not out	68	L-b 2, n-b 1		3
R. J. Boyd-Moss st Taylor b Popplewell	9			
T. J. Yardley c and b Dredge	53	1/6 2/23	(5 wkts, 38.3 overs)	149
Sarfraz Nawaz run out	1	3/39 4/132 5/138		

*P. J. Watts, R. M. Carter, T. M. Lamb and B. J. Griffiths did not bat.

Bowling: Moseley 8–0–23–1; Gore 8–0–22–1; Dredge 7.3–0–29–1; Marks 8–1–31–0; Popplewell 7–0–41–1.

Umpires: A. Jepson and C. T. Spencer.

NORTHAMPTONSHIRE v HAMPSHIRE

At Wellingborough, August 17. Hampshire won by three wickets. Northamptonshire, put in on a rain-affected wicket, were restricted to accurate bowling from Marshall. Only Williams, Allan Lamb and Watts offered much resistance. Greenidge gave the visitors early batting encouragement, and following a brief slump, Pocock and Nicholas rallied their side with enterprising batting.

Northamptonshire

W. Larkins b Tremlett	5	*P. J. Watts c Terry b Tremlett		14
P. Willey lbw b Marshall	3	T. M. Lamb not out		3
A. J. Lamb c Parks b Taylor	23	B. J. Griffiths b Tremlett		1
G. Cook run out	4			
R. G. Williams b Tremlett	47	B 3, l-b 5, w 1, n-b 1		10
T. J. Yardley c Parks b Cowley	1			
Sarfraz Nawaz b Southern	1	1/8 2/8 3/23 4/59	(40 overs)	114
†G. Sharp c Parks b Taylor	2	5/62 6/66 7/83 8/107 9/112		

Bowling: Marshall 8–4–7–1; Tremlett 8–1–24–4; Cowley 8–2–18–1; Southern 8–2–18–1; Taylor 8–0–37–2.

Hampshire

C. G. Greenidge lbw b T. M. Lamb	23	†R. J. Parks not out		0
D. R. Turner c Yardley b Sarfraz	9	M. D. Marshall not out		4
T. M. Tremlett lbw b T. M. Lamb	8			
M. C. J. Nicholas b Willey	22	L-b 9, n-b 6		15
*N. E. J. Pocock c Sharp b Griffiths	30			
N. G. Cowley b Willey	6	1/4 2/41 3/58	(7 wkts, 37.3 overs)	117
M. N. S. Taylor c Cook b Watts	0	4/92 5/108 6/113 7/113		

V. P. Terry and J. W. Southern did not bat.

Bowling: Sarfraz 8–2–19–1; Griffiths 3–0–17–1; T. M. Lamb 8–2–22–2; Williams 8–3–18–0; Willey 8–3–13–2; Watts 2.3–0–13–1.

Umpires: R. Julian and T. W. Spencer.

At Leicester, August 24. NORTHAMPTONSHIRE lost to LEICESTERSHIRE by 17 runs.

At Scarborough, August 31. NORTHAMPTONSHIRE lost to YORKSHIRE by two wickets.

At Chelmsford, September 7. NORTHAMPTONSHIRE lost to ESSEX by 91 runs.

NOTTINGHAMSHIRE

NOTTINGHAMSHIRE v KENT

At Nottingham, May 4. Kent won by 20 runs. Woolmer was Kent's match-winner, scoring his first century in the competition and taking two useful wickets. His unbeaten 112, coming in 27 overs with one 6 and eight 4s, inspired Kent to a substantial total. Rice and Randall led a spirited reply but Nottinghamshire were always struggling and Kent achieved a comfortable victory.

Kent

R. A. Woolmer not out	112	*A. G. E. Ealham not out	3
C. J. C. Rowe c Curzon b Bore	0	L-b 9, w 1, n-b 1	11
C. J. Tavaré c Todd b Cooper	33		
Asif Iqbal c Randall b Hadlee	57	1/1 2/86 3/196 (3 wkts, 40 overs) 216	

C. S. Cowdrey, K. B. S. Jarvis, J. N. Shepherd, †A. P. E. Knott, G. R. Dilley and D. L. Underwood did not bat.

Bowling: Bore 8–1–29–1; Cooper 8–1–30–1; Hemmings 6–0–43–0; Tunnicliffe 2–0–11–0; Hadlee 8–0–49–1; Rice 8–0–43–0.

Nottinghamshire

P. A. Todd lbw b Shepherd	7	E. E. Hemmings run out	5
N. Nanan c Knott b Cowdrey	23	K. E. Cooper c and b Dilley	6
*C. E. B. Rice b Woolmer	52	M. K. Bore not out	1
H. T. Tunnicliffe run out	9	L-b 12	12
D. W. Randall c Ealham b Dilley	45		
B. Hassan c Ealham b Woolmer	5	1/17 2/42 3/72 (9 wkts, 40 overs) 196	
†C. C. Curzon not out	28	4/118 5/130 6/163	
R. J. Hadlee c Rowe b Shepherd	3	7/166 8/177 9/189	

Bowling: Dilley 8–0–33–2; Shepherd 8–0–33–2; Jarvis 6–0–36–0; Cowdrey 4–0–18–1; Woolmer 6–0–26–2; Underwood 8–0–38–0.

Umpires: R. Julian and C. T. Spencer.

NOTTINGHAMSHIRE v DERBYSHIRE

At Nottingham, May 18. Nottinghamshire won by 13 runs. Rice led Nottinghamshire to their first Sunday win of the season with an all-round display of aggressive batting and penetrative bowling. The home team were given a superb start by Rice and Birch (three 6s), but their innings fell away. While Borrington was in, Derbyshire looked capable of victory but Rice rejoined the attack, capturing three wickets in five balls, to tilt the game back Nottinghamshire's way.

Nottinghamshire

B. Hassan c Barnett b Tunnicliffe	5	†C. C. Curzon not out	17
J. D. Birch b Wincer	53	K. Saxelby not out	1
*C. E. B. Rice b Russell	52	L-b 13, w 3, n-b 2	18
H. T. Tunnicliffe c Kirsten b Wincer	2		
D. W. Randall st Taylor b Miller	18	1/14 2/77 3/88 (7 wkts, 39 overs) 188	
P. A. Todd b Russell	6	4/138 5/142 6/154	
R. J. Hadlee c Borrington b Tunnicliffe	16	7/181	

K. E. Cooper and M. K. Bore did not bat.

Bowling: Tunnicliffe 8–2–27–2; Wincer 8–0–33–2; Russell 8–1–44–2; Kirsten 7–1–28–0; Miller 8–0–38–1.

Derbyshire

A. J. Borrington run out	64	K. G. Brooks b Rice	1
J. G. Wright c Curzon b Cooper	21	†R. W. Taylor not out	3
P. N. Kirsten c Tunnicliffe b Saxelby	9	B 1, l-b 7, w 5, n-b 1	14
D. S. Steele b Hadlee	40		
K. J. Barnett not out	6	1/59 2/70 3/144 (7 wkts, 39 overs) 175
*G. Miller lbw b Rice	17	4/147 5/168 6/168
C. J. Tunnicliffe b Rice	0	7/170

P. E. Russell and R. C. Wincer did not bat.

Bowling: Hadlee 8–0–28–1; Bore 7–1–23–0; Cooper 8–0–36–1; Rice 8–0–37–3; Saxelby 4–0–19–1; Tunnicliffe 4–0–18–0.

Umpires: T. W. Spencer and J. van Geloven.

At Swansea, May 25. NOTTINGHAMSHIRE lost to GLAMORGAN by 46 runs.

At The Oval, June 1. NOTTINGHAMSHIRE lost to SURREY by four wickets.

NOTTINGHAMSHIRE v NORTHAMPTONSHIRE

At Worksop, June 15. Northamptonshire won by 2 runs. In a match restricted to 37 overs, Northamptonshire edged to victory by denying Nottinghamshire's final pair. Put in to bat, the visitors struggled for runs against an attack inspired by left-arm seamer Hacker – playing his first game of the season – and their total of 138 looked surmountable. Todd gave Nottinghamshire a useful start in their reply but, apart from Birch and Hemmings, the middle order failed to provide the runs needed to top the Northamptonshire score.

Northamptonshire

P. Willey c Hassan b Hacker	6	*P. J. Watts c Birch b Hacker	0
W. Larkins c Birch b Cooper	5	Sarfraz Nawaz not out	10
A. J. Lamb b Hemmings	33	T. M. Lamb not out	4
G. Cook run out	24	L-b 11, w 2, n-b 1	14
R. G. Williams c Cooper b Hemmings	16		
T. J. Yardley b Cooper	20	1/7 2/12 3/65 4/87 (8 wkts, 37 overs) 138
†G. Sharp b Hacker	6	5/98 6/122 7/122 8/127

B. J. Griffiths did not bat.

Bowling: Cooper 8–1–40–2; Hacker 8–3–10–3; Mackintosh 5–0–26–0; Hemmings 8–0–30–2; Tunnicliffe 8–1–18–0.

Nottinghamshire

P. A. Todd b Willey	31	E. E. Hemmings run out	19
R. T. Robinson lbw b Watts	15	P. J. Hacker not out	2
D. W. Randall b T. M. Lamb	5	K. E. Cooper not out	0
*C. E. B. Rice c Watts b T. M. Lamb	2	L-b 11, w 5, n-b 3	19
J. D. Birch b T. M. Lamb	22		
†B. Hassan c Willey b Williams	1	1/33 2/42 3/46 (9 wkts, 37 overs) 136
H. T. Tunnicliffe b Sarfraz	12	4/76 5/86 6/88 7/110
K. S. Mackintosh c Watts b Griffiths	8	8/116 9/136

Bowling: Sarfraz 8–1–23–1; Griffiths 8–0–36–1; T. M. Lamb 8–2–26–3; Watts 8–1–19–1; Willey 3–0–9–1; Williams 2–1–4–1.

Umpires: D. G. L. Evans and P. S. G. Stevens.

At Scarborough, June 22. NOTTINGHAMSHIRE lost to YORKSHIRE by four wickets.

At Chelmsford, June 29. NOTTINGHAMSHIRE beat ESSEX by 18 runs.

At Bristol, July 6. NOTTINGHAMSHIRE lost to GLOUCESTERSHIRE by five wickets.

NOTTINGHAMSHIRE v WARWICKSHIRE

At Nottingham, July 13. Nottinghamshire won by 77 runs. John Player League leaders Warwickshire suffered their second successive defeat when they were outplayed by a Nottinghamshire side which produced one of their best one-day batting displays of the season. Hassan took one hundred and twenty-four minutes to score his unbeaten 100, with six boundaries, and figured in partnerships of 71 with Robinson, 103 with Randall and 58 with Rice. Warwickshire were soon in trouble against the bowling of Hacker and, despite spirited resistance from Hopkins, there was little question of Warwickshire approaching Nottinghamshire's total.

Nottinghamshire

R. T. Robinson lbw b Hopkins		29
†B. Hassan not out		100
D. W. Randall c Oliver b Ferreira		51
*C. E. B. Rice not out		31
L-b 16, w 5		21

1/71 2/174   (2 wkts, 40 overs) 232

J. D. Birch, M. J. Harris, W. K. Watson, E. E. Hemmings, K. E. Cooper, P. J. Hacker and M. K. Bore did not bat.

Bowling: Small 8–0–38–0; Rouse 8–0–45–0; Ferreira 8–0–46–1; Doshi 8–0–36–0; Hopkins 8–1–46–1.

Warwickshire

*D. L. Amiss c and b Hacker	2	D. C. Hopkins not out		35
T. A. Lloyd b Hacker	3	G. C. Small c Randall b Watson		17
J. A. Claughton lbw b Watson	23	D. R. Doshi run out		6
G. W. Humpage c Hassan b Hacker	5	B 1, l-b 7, w 8		16
P. R. Oliver b Rice	21			
†C. Maynard c and b Bore	22	1/2 2/9 3/19 4/44	(33.4 overs)	155
A. M. Ferreira c Robinson b Rice	2	5/74 6/76 7/83 8/109		
S. J. Rouse c Robinson b Rice	3	9/145		

Bowling: Hacker 6–1–31–3; Watson 8–0–29–2; Cooper 7–0–23–0; Rice 5.4–1–12–3; Hemmings 5–1–38–0; Bore 2–0–6–1.

Umpires: A. Jepson and T. W. Spencer.

NOTTINGHAMSHIRE v WORCESTERSHIRE

At Nottingham, July 20. Worcestershire won by 18 runs. In a match restricted by rain to ten overs, Worcestershire's total of 74 for seven proved too much for Nottinghamshire. Hemsley was Worcestershire's chief contributor with the bat before he became one of three run out victims in the pursuit of quick runs. In their bid to match the asking-rate Nottinghamshire lost wickets at regular intervals and only South African Watson gave any hope against an attack spearheaded by Alleyne.

Worcestershire

G. M. Turner c Todd b Mackintosh	....	9	J. D. Inchmore not out.............	6
Younis Ahmed b Mackintosh.........		7	H. Alleyne run out.................	0
P. A. Neale c Todd b Hacker.........		8	B 3, l-b 4, w 4.............	11
E. J. O. Hemsley run out		18		
S. P. Henderson c Mackintosh b Cooper .		6	1/13 2/24 3/34 (7 wkts, 10 overs)	74
†D. J. Humphries run out		9	4/50 5/65 6/69 7/74	

*N. Gifford, A. P. Pridgeon and J. Cumbes did not bat.

Bowling: Hacker 2–0–13–1; Mackintosh 2–0–11–2; Hemmings 2–0–8–0; Cooper 2–0–14–1; Watson 2–0–17–0.

Nottinghamshire

P. A. Todd b Inchmore	8	K. S. Mackintosh b Alleyne...........	0
†B. Hassan c Turner b Gifford	8	P. J. Hacker b Alleyne...........	0
D. W. Randall lbw b Inchmore	0		
*C. E. B. Rice run out	2	B 1, l-b 7, w 3.............	11
J. D. Birch b Gifford	0		
E. E. Hemmings b Gifford	6	1/15 2/20 3/20 (9 wkts, 10 overs)	56
R. T. Robinson not out	4	4/22 5/30 6/34 7/56	
W. K. Watson b Alleyne	17	8/56 9/56	

K. E. Cooper did not bat.

Bowling: Pridgeon 2–0–10–0; Inchmore 2–0–6–2; Gifford 2–1–7–3; Alleyne 2–0–12–3; Cumbes 2–0–10–0.

Umpires: R. Aspinall and B. J. Meyer.

At Taunton, July 27. NOTTINGHAMSHIRE lost to SOMERSET by eight wickets.

NOTTINGHAMSHIRE v LEICESTERSHIRE

At Nottingham, August 3. Leicestershire won by 12 runs. Leicestershire moved into second place in the table with a hard-earned victory that would have been more convincing but for the all-round talents of Hadlee. They owed much to a splendid innings from Balderstone, who shared a flowing partnership of 64 in twelve overs with Davison. In reply, Hassan and Robinson gave Nottinghamshire an encouraging start but the batting collapsed, leaving Hadlee to threaten Leicestershire's bid with a belligerent innings which included two 6s.

Leicestershire

N. E. Briers st Hassan b Hemmings.....	14	J. F. Steele b Hadlee.............	14
D. I. Gower c Rice b Hadlee	4	P. B. Clift not out.................	1
J. C. Balderstone b Hadlee...........	75	B 1, l-b 10, w 4.............	15
*B. F. Davison b Hacker.............	31		
R. W. Tolchard b Hadlee.............	22	1/8 2/39 3/103 (6 wkts, 39 overs)	193
†M. A. Garnham not out	17	4/152 5/169 6/191	

G. J. Parsons, L. B. Taylor and K. Higgs did not bat.

Bowling: Hadlee 8–2–31–4; Hacker 8–3–29–1; Cooper 8–1–44–0; Hemmings 8–0–31–1; Rice 7–0–43–0.

Nottinghamshire

†B. Hassan c Parsons b Steele.........	36	R. E. Dexter b Taylor.............	3
R. T. Robinson run out	28	P. J. Hacker not out.............	1
*C. E. B. Rice c Garnham b Clift.......	21	K. E. Cooper b Clift.............	4
J. D. Birch run out	16	L-b 7	7
D. W. Randall c Garnham b Higgs	4		
M. J. Harris lbw b Clift	5	1/54 2/75 3/101 4/107 (39 overs)	181
R. J. Hadlee c and b Taylor...........	47	5/111 6/125 7/162	
E. E. Hemmings c Tolchard b Taylor ...	9	8/174 9/176	

Bowling: Taylor 8–0–40–3; Parsons 7–0–38–0; Steele 8–0–26–1; Higgs 8–0–28–1; Clift 8–0–42–3.

Umpires: R. S. Herman and J. van Geloven.

At Eastbourne, August 10. NOTTINGHAMSHIRE beat SUSSEX by 60 runs.

At Lord's, August 17. NOTTINGHAMSHIRE lost to MIDDLESEX on faster scoring-rate.

NOTTINGHAMSHIRE v HAMPSHIRE

At Nottingham, August 31. Nottinghamshire won by 16 runs. Nottinghamshire completed their fifth John Player League win of the season in a match of fluctuating fortunes. Hampshire, without the injured Marshall, contained the home batsmen to 175 and although Robinson and Rice then Birch and Randall shared half-century stands, it was left to Hadlee and Hemmings to give the total some substance. Hampshire's hopes rested with Nicholas but he fell to Hacker, and with the return of Rice, who took four wickets, and Hadlee their prospects faded fast.

Nottinghamshire

B. Hassan c Parks b Stevenson	0
R. T. Robinson c Parks b Cowley	25
*C. E. B. Rice c Turner b Cowley	33
J. D. Birch c Southern b Tremlett	27
D. W. Randall c Parks b Nicholas	23
N. I. Weightman lbw b Stevenson	2
†B. N. French run out	1
R. J. Hadlee lbw b Stevenson	21
E. E. Hemmings c Terry b Malone	17
P. J. Hacker not out	2
M. K. Bore run out	0
L-b 16, w 8	24

1/1 2/52 3/72 4/127 (40 overs) 175
5/127 6/132 7/145
8/161 9/174

Bowling: Stevenson 8–2–25–3; Malone 8–2–32–1; Cowley 8–0–27–2; Tremlett 8–1–27–1; Nicholas 8–0–40–1.

Hampshire

C. L. Smith c Rice b Hadlee	3
T. M. Tremlett b Rice	12
M. C. J. Nicholas c Hemmings b Hacker	44
D. R. Turner b Bore	18
*N. E. J. Pocock c Hemmings b Hacker	4
N. G. Cowley b Hadlee	22
V. P. Terry b Rice	11
†R. J. Parks not out	9
J. W. Southern b Rice	3
K. Stevenson run out	7
S. J. Malone b Rice	1
B 7, l-b 13, w 3, n-b 2	25

1/11 2/39 3/83 4/97 5/102 (38 overs) 159
6/137 7/143 8/148 9/157

Bowling: Hadlee 7–1–20–2; Hacker 8–1–37–2; Rice 7–2–15–4; Hemmings 8–0–36–0; Bore 8–0–26–1.

Umpires: K. E. Palmer and J. van Geloven.

NOTTINGHAMSHIRE v LANCASHIRE

At Nottingham, September 7. Nottinghamshire won by six wickets. Hadlee ended his three-year career with Nottinghamshire in sensational style by taking six for 12 as Lancashire were swept aside. It was the best bowling by any Nottinghamshire player in the competition and the most impressive figures in the John Player League during the season. Only Abrahams prevented Lancashire from total collapse as Bore supported Hadlee with three for 8. Hassan and Birch shared a second-wicket partnership of 80, taking Nottinghamshire towards their target with time and wickets to spare.

Lancashire

A. Kennedy b Hadlee	4	D. P. Hughes b Hadlee	2
J. Simmons c French b Hadlee	5	P. J. W. Allott b Hadlee	2
*F. C. Hayes c Rice b Bore	10	W. Hogg b Hadlee	0
D. Lloyd c Randall b Bore	22	B 2, l-b 8, w 2, n-b 1	13
B. W. Reidy b Hemmings	9		
J. Abrahams not out	37	1/13 2/13 3/46 4/49 (39.4 overs) 114	
†G. Fowler b Bore	0	5/63 6/66 7/91	
S. J. O'Shaughnessy c French b Hadlee	10	8/106 9/114	

Bowling: Hadlee 7.4–1–12–6; Hacker 8–0–27–0; Rice 8–1–30–0; Hemmings 8–1–24–1; Bore 8–2–8–3.

Nottinghamshire

B. Hassan c Lloyd b Hughes	35	D. W. Randall not out	4
R. T. Robinson c Abrahams b Hogg	8	B 3, l-b 7, w 5. n-b 2	17
J. D. Birch c Abrahams b Simmons	44		
N. I. Weightman lbw b Simmons	0	1/17 2/97 3/97 (4 wkts, 34 overs) 118	
*C. E. B. Rice not out	10	4/108	

†B. N. French, R. J. Hadlee, E. E. Hemmings, P. J. Hacker and M. K. Bore did not bat.

Bowling: Hogg 8–2–29–1; Allott 8–0–19–0; Reidy 2–0–5–0; Simmons 8–4–8–2; O'Shaughnessy 4–0–28–0; Lloyd 2–0–5–0; Hughes 2–0–7–1.

Umpires: D. O. Oslear and P. B. Wight.

SOMERSET

At Ilford, May 4. SOMERSET beat ESSEX by five wickets.

At Canterbury, May 11. SOMERSET lost to KENT by 13 runs.

SOMERSET v YORKSHIRE

At Taunton, May 18. Somerset won by seven wickets. Yorkshire, put in, fared poorly on a variable pitch, after brilliant fielding by Slocombe had accounted for both openers. Athey, Old and Bairstow made useful contributions but some fine boundary catches were taken and the Somerset bowlers never lost their grip. Denning with Gavaskar, who was capped before the match, gave Somerset a sound start leaving the way clear for Botham, on the day he was appointed England's Prudential Trophy captain, to take his team to victory.

Yorkshire

G. Boycott run out	3	G. B. Stevenson b Dredge	3
*J. H. Hampshire run out	8	A. Sidebottom not out	6
C. W. J. Athey c Denning b Jennings	34	H. P. Cooper not out	4
K. Sharp c Botham b Burgess	7		
J. D. Love c Slocombe b Marks	1	B 2, l-b 10, w 1	13
†D. L. Bairstow b Moseley	51		
C. M. Old c Breakwell b Dredge	23	1/6 2/23 3/34 (9 wkts, 40 overs) 158	
P. Carrick c Jennings b Moseley	5	4/39 5/86 6/125 7/137 8/144 9/144	

Bowling: Moseley 8–1–24–2; Dredge 8–0–37–2; Burgess 8–0–43–1; Marks 8–0–22–1; Jennings 8–1–19–1.

Somerset

S. M. Gavaskar c Bairstow b Cooper....	36	V. J. Marks not out	14
P. W. Denning b Sidebottom	59	B 4, l-b 4, w 4.............	12
P. A. Slocombe c Hampshire b Carrick..	17		
*I. T. Botham not out................	21	1/62 2/100 3/139 (3 wkts, 37.3 overs) 159	

D. Breakwell, †D. J. S. Taylor, G. I. Burgess, K. F. Jennings, C. H. Dredge and H. R. Moseley did not bat.

Bowling: Old 8–0–36–0; Stevenson 7–1–34–0; Cooper 6.3–0–30–1; Sidebottom 8–1–28–1; Carrick 8–1–19–1.

Umpires: D. J. Halfyard and P. B. Wight.

SOMERSET v MIDDLESEX

At Taunton, June 1. Middlesex won by 122 runs. After his team were put in on a dry pitch, Brearley scored a fine maiden John Player League century (eight 4s), reaching his 100 in the final over, after an escape at 73. Selvey's opening burst of four for 13 virtually decided the match, with a superb boundary catch by Emburey dismissing Gavaskar. Thereafter only Denning and Taylor could offer any resistance.

Middlesex

*J. M. Brearley not out..............	109	P. H. Edmonds b Dredge............	52
C. T. Radley c Rose b Botham........	6	V. A. P. van der Bijl not out........	3
G. D. Barlow c Marks c Moseley ...	33	L-b 13, w 1, n-b 3..........	17
M. W. Gatting c Roebuck b Jennings ...	10		
R. O. Butcher c Dredge b Jennings	8	1/30 2/77 3/104 (6 wkts, 40 overs) 241	
†I. J. Gould c Burgess b Dredge	3	4/118 5/128 6/213	

J. E. Emburey, M. W. W. Selvey and W. G. Merry did not bat.

Bowling: Botham 8–0–70–1; Moseley 8–0–34–1; Marks 8–0–37–0; Jennings 8–0–39–2; Dredge 8–0–44–2.

Somerset

*B. C. Rose c and b van der Bijl....	4	K. F. Jennings not out	10
S. M. Gavaskar c Emburey b Selvey ...	4	C. H. Dredge b Edmonds...........	0
P. W. Denning b Edmonds............	45	H. R. Moseley c Gatting b Brearley.....	2
I. T. Botham b Selvey................	0		
P. M. Roebuck lbw b Selvey	2		
V. J. Marks c Emburey b Selvey	2	B 4, l-b 9, w 1..........	14
G. I. Burgess b Edmonds	11		
†D. J. S. Taylor c van der Bijl b Emburey.	25	1/9 2/16 3/19 4/25 (35.3 overs) 119 5/29 6/77 7/80 8/114 9/116	

Bowling: Selvey 8–2–13–4; van der Bijl 8–0–24–1; Merry 4–0–13–0; Gatting 4–1–13–0; Edmonds 6–0–27–3; Emburey 5–0–13–1; Brearley 3–0–2–1.

Umpires: D. Shackleton and A. G. T. Whitehead.

SOMERSET v LANCASHIRE

At Bath, June 15. Somerset won by five wickets. Put in Lancashire recovered excellently from a slow start caused largely by the accurate bowling of Gore on his Sunday début. Hayes, hitting four 6s and six 4s in 25 overs, retained the impetus provided by Lloyd, and lively assistance from Reidy and Cockbain brought swift half-century stands. Rose led the reply with early help from Gavaskar and Denning. Botham, missed at 18, hit three 6s in a vital partnership of 80 in nine overs, and when he departed Rose (three 6s and four 4s) continued aggressively. He was out trying to reach his century with the scores level in the 39th over.

Lancashire

A. Kennedy c Taylor b Moseley	3	J. Simmons not out	2
D. Lloyd run out	39		
J. Abrahams c Rose b Marks	9	B 4, l-b 15, w 1	20
*F. C. Hayes not out	84		
B. W. Reidy c Marks b Botham	30	1/9 2/32 (5 wkts, 40 overs) 204	
I. Cockbain b Moseley	17	3/70 4/127 5/184	

D. P. Hughes, †C. J. Scott, M. F. Malone and P. J. W. Allott did not bat.

Bowling: Moseley 8–1–36–2; Gore 8–3–7–0; Marks 8–0–39–1; Jennings 8–0–38–0; Botham 8–0–64–1.

Somerset

*B. C. Rose c Lloyd b Malone	98	V. J. Marks not out	1
S. M. Gavaskar c Scott b Reidy	20		
P. W. Denning c Kennedy b Simmons	21	L-b 16, w 2	18
I. T. Botham c Scott b Reidy	38		
D. Breakwell run out	9	1/45 2/88 (5 wkts, 39.1 overs) 205	
P. M. Roebuck not out	0	3/168 4/204 5/204	

†D. J. S. Taylor, K. F. Jennings, H. R. Moseley and H. I. E. Gore did not bat.

Bowling: Malone 8–2–19–1; Allott 7.1–0–33–0; Hughes 8–0–26–0; Reidy 8–0–52–2; Simmons 8–0–57–1.

Umpires: D. O. Oslear and R. S. Herman.

SOMERSET v GLAMORGAN

At Bath, June 22. Somerset won by six wickets. A storm just before the start and another after an hour's play reduced the match to 30 overs. Glamorgan, put in, were struggling until Hopkins led a recovery with two 6s and three 4s in 23 overs, despite a thigh strain suffered early in his innings. Featherstone helped him add 42 in nine overs and a lively seven overs from Nash sustained the tail. In fine weather, Gavaskar's remarkable hitting steered Somerset home as he hit five 6s and one 4 in 21 overs. With Denning he put on 47 in seven overs before Roebuck (five 4s) joined him in a decisive third-wicket stand of 57 in nine overs.

Glamorgan

A. Jones c Breakwell b Moseley	18	A. E. Cordle run out	11
J. A. Hopkins b Moseley	45	B. J. Lloyd not out	4
M. J. Llewellyn c Taylor b Moseley	0	A. A. Jones run out	0
Javed Miandad c Taylor b Dredge	3		
N. G. Featherstone c Denning b Jennings	12	L-b 7, w 5	12
G. C. Holmes run out	9		
*M. A. Nash c Marks b Dredge	29	1/23 2/23 3/30 (30 overs) 155	
†E. W. Jones b Jennings	12	4/72 5/86 6/116 7/136 8/143 9/155	

Bowling: Moseley 8–0–29–3; Dredge 8–0–41–2; Jennings 7–0–41–1; Popplewell 7–2–32–0.

Somerset

*B. C. Rose b Nash	7	D. Breakwell not out	14
S. M. Gavaskar c Lloyd b A. A. Jones	54	L-b 5, n-b 1	6
P. W. Denning c Nash b Lloyd	26		
P. M. Roebuck not out	45	1/13 2/60 (4 wkts, 27.2 overs) 157	
V. J. Marks c and b Lloyd	5	3/117 4/123	

N. F. M. Popplewell, †D. J. S. Taylor, K. F. Jennings, C. H. Dredge and H. R. Moseley did not bat.

Bowling: Nash 6–0–28–1; A. A. Jones 8–0–51–1; Lloyd 8–1–20–2; Cordle 4–0–39–0; Featherstone 1.2–0–13–0.

Umpires: C. Cook and D. Shackleton.

At Hove, June 29. SOMERSET beat SUSSEX by three wickets.

At Chesterfield, July 13. SOMERSET lost to DERBYSHIRE by seven wickets.

At Portsmouth, July 20. SOMERSET lost to HAMPSHIRE by 81 runs.

SOMERSET v NOTTINGHAMSHIRE

At Taunton, July 27. Somerset won by eight wickets. After a good start of 52 in fifteen overs and a powerful 40 in nine overs from Rice (one 6 and five 4s), Nottinghamshire's innings fell away to accurate bowling, a brilliant run out by Denning and good catches. In reply, Denning – missed when 0, 10 and 11 – led Somerset's victory bid, hitting nine 4s as he made 70 out of 100 in 24 overs. Gavaskar, after a slow start, improved as the innings proceeded and, with help from Roebuck and Marks, steered Somerset home.

Nottinghamshire

†B. Hassan c Dredge b Marks	30	W. K. Watson c Gavaskar b Moseley	8
R. T. Robinson lbw b Marks	26	P. J. Hacker b Dredge	1
D. W. Randall run out	7	K. E. Cooper not out	0
*C. E. B. Rice b Jennings	40	B 5, l-b 10, w 2, n-b 2	19
J. D. Birch c Marks b Jennings	3		
M. J. Harris c Taylor b Moseley	20	1/52 2/67 3/109 (39.5 overs) 170
H. T. Tunnicliffe b Dredge	3	4/116 5/129 6/134 7/159
E. E. Hemmings c Lloyds b Moseley	13	8/159 9/162

Bowling: Moseley 7.5–0–34–3; Popplewell 8–1–22–0; Marks 8–0–38–2; Jennings 8–0–36–2; Dredge 8–2–21–2.

Somerset

S. M. Gavaskar not out 57
P. W. Denning c Rice b Cooper 70
P. M. Roebuck c Hassan b Rice 22
*V. J. Marks not out................. 14
L-b 7, w 3, n-b 1............ 11

1/100 2/148   (2 wkts, 37.4 overs) 174

N. F. M. Popplewell, D. Breakwell, J. W. Lloyds, †D. J. S. Taylor, K. F. Jennings, C. H. Dredge and H. R. Moseley did not bat.

Bowling: Hacker 8–1–23–0; Watson 6.4–2–29–0; Rice 7–0–22–1; Hemmings 4–0–29–0; Cooper 8–0–34–1; Tunnicliffe 4–0–26–0.

Umpires: D. J. Halfyard and D. Shackleton.

SOMERSET v WORCESTERSHIRE

At Weston-super-Mare, August 3. Somerset won by eight wickets in a match restricted to 26 overs. Before heavy rain delayed the game Worcestershire, put in, reached 104 for four thanks mainly to Turner who hit two 6s and two 4s in twenty overs. Somerset encountered initial difficulties against a demanding attack, but when Rose was out the requirement was 48 from eleven overs. Denning kept the momentum going until, in a typical burst of fierce striking, Botham hit three 6s and two 4s in twenty minutes, taking his team to victory with 33 balls to spare.

Worcestershire

J. A. Ormrod c Denning b Marks	16	T. S. Curtis not out	0
G. M. Turner c Gore b Marks	53	L-b 2	2
Younis Ahmed c and b Dredge	15		
P. A. Neale lbw b Moseley	14	1/64 2/77	(4 wkts, 26 overs) 104
S. P. Henderson not out	4	3/98 4/104	

†D. J. Humphries, J. D. Inchmore, V. A. Holder, *N. Gifford and A. P. Pridgeon did not bat.

Bowling: Botham 4–0–10–0; Gore 4–0–13–0; Moseley 3–0–20–1; Marks 8–0–35–2; Breakwell 6–0–21–0; Dredge 1–0–3–1.

Somerset

*B. C. Rose b Holder	15
S. M. Gavaskar lbw b Inchmore	20
P. W. Denning not out	28
I. T. Botham not out	33
L-b 7, n-b 2	9

1/29 2/57   (2 wkts, 20.3 overs) 105

P. M. Roebuck, V. J. Marks, D. Breakwell, †D. J. S. Taylor, C. H. Dredge, H. R. Moseley and H. I. E. Gore did not bat.

Bowling: Holder 8–2–22–1; Inchmore 6–0–26–1; Gifford 4–0–17–0; Pridgeon 2.3–0–31–0.

Umpires: D. J. Constant and R. Julian.

At Northampton, August 10. SOMERSET lost to NORTHAMPTONSHIRE by five wickets.

SOMERSET v LEICESTERSHIRE

At Taunton, August 17. Somerset won by 41 runs. A splendidly controlled innings by Richards (one 6 and nine 4s) dominated Somerset's innings after they were put in on a slow pitch with a very slow outfield. Marks joined him to add 103 in eighteen overs against a Leicestershire attack weakened by the breakdown of Higgs after just one over. Popplewell and Moseley took early wickets but Gower (one 6 and four 4s) made a fine early challenge. However, after he was fourth out, steady bowling and tight fielding put the target well beyond the reach of the later batsmen.

Somerset

P. W. Denning c Tolchard b Clift	16	J. W. Lloyds not out	4
P. M. Roebuck b Parsons	3	N. F. M. Popplewell not out	5
I. V. A. Richards c Garnham b Taylor	113	B 1, l-b 6, w 1	8
*I. T. Botham c Tolchard b Steele	22		
V. J. Marks c Tolchard b Taylor	32	1/4 2/47 3/88	(6 wkts, 39 overs) 205
J. Garner c Gower b Taylor	2	4/191 5/193 6/197	

†D. J. S. Taylor, C. H. Dredge and H. R. Moseley did not bat.

Bowling: Taylor 8–0–45–3; Parsons 8–0–48–1; Higgs 1–0–3–0; Briers 6–0–38–0; Clift 8–0–33–1; Steele 8–0–30–1.

Leicestershire

N. E. Briers lbw b Popplewell	7	G. J. Parsons b Dredge		3
D. I. Gower b Moseley	56	J. F. Steele not out		19
J. C. Balderstone b Popplewell	4	L. B. Taylor not out		15
*B. F. Davison b Moseley	1	L-b 10, w 1, n-b 1		12
R. W. Tolchard b Marks	9			
†M. A. Garnham c and b Marks	17	1/31 2/41 3/44	(8 wkts, 39 overs)	164
P. B. Clift b Garner	21	4/81 5/87 6/125 7/129 8/129		

K. Higgs did not bat.

Bowling: Moseley 8–0–39–2; Dredge 7–0–16–1; Popplewell 7–0–32–2; Marks 8–0–21–2; Garner 8–1–33–1; Denning 1–0–11–0.

Umpires: W. E. Alley and P. S. G. Stevens.

At Bristol, August 24. SOMERSET beat GLOUCESTERSHIRE by one wicket.

SOMERSET v SURREY

At Taunton, August 31. Somerset won by 73 runs. Put in, Somerset fared poorly until Marks and Popplewell, each making his highest John Player League score, added an exciting 114 in seventeen overs with thrilling running and fine strokes. As the pitch dried, giving more help to the bowlers, Dredge and Moseley made deep inroads into the Surrey innings, Dredge finishing with a remarkable three for 8. Lynch struck out boldly for fourteen overs and Jackman helped him add 38 for the seventh wicket, but Somerset's win was never in doubt.

Somerset

*B. C. Rose c Richards b Clarke	10	J. W. Lloyds b Clarke		2
P. W. Denning c Pocock b Jackman	17	†D. J. S. Taylor not out		2
I. V. A. Richards c Howarth b Thomas	24			
P. M. Roebuck st Richards b Jackman	12	B 2, l-b 12, w 3		17
V. J. Marks not out	71			
N. F. M. Popplewell run out	55	1/23 2/43 3/63	(7 wkts, 39 overs)	212
J. Garner b Clarke	2	4/74 5/188 6/196 7/210		

C. H. Dredge and H. R. Moseley did not bat.

Bowling: Jackman 8–1–34–2; Clarke 8–1–42–3; Knight 7–0–40–0; Thomas 8–0–37–1; Pocock 8–0–42–0.

Surrey

A. R. Butcher c Denning b Dredge	8	S. T. Clarke not out		16
G. P. Howarth b Dredge	0	†C. J. Richards b Dredge		12
*R. D. V. Knight c and b Moseley	11	P. I. Pocock run out		1
D. M. Smith c Popplewell b Marks	16			
G. R. J. Roope c Roebuck b Moseley	7	B 1, l-b 2, w 4, n-b 2		9
M. A. Lynch c Dredge b Popplewell	36			
D. J. Thomas c Dredge b Moseley	11	1/3 2/14 3/31 4/39	(38 overs)	139
R. D. Jackman st Taylor b Popplewell	12	5/54 6/68 7/106 8/114 9/133		

Bowling: Garner 7–2–25–0; Dredge 8–2–8–3; Moseley 8–0–36–3; Popplewell 8–0–32–2; Marks 7–1–29–1.

Umpires: D. G. L. Evans and D. Shackleton.

At Birmingham, September 7. SOMERSET beat WARWICKSHIRE by 26 runs.

SURREY

At Derby, May 4. SURREY beat DERBYSHIRE by eight wickets.

SURREY v HAMPSHIRE

At The Oval, May 18. Surrey won by 1 run. Following the loss of Howarth and Knight for 5, Surrey were indebted to Smith, who played the leading part with 87 not out and to Clarke, whose innings included two 6s over long-on; their unbroken sixth-wicket stand added 55 off seven overs. Hampshire's innings was even more a one-man affair, the extras of 27 coming next to 109 from Turner, whose century in ten minutes under two hours included three 6s. He was seventh out with 13 runs needed off the last fifteen balls and Hampshire's tailenders just failed to achieve victory.

Surrey

A. R. Butcher c Terry b Taylor	33	S. T. Clarke not out	34
G. R. Howarth c Cowley b Stevenson	0		
*R. D. V. Knight lbw b Malone	1	B 2, l-b 11, w 3	16
D. M. Smith not out	87		
G. R. J. Roope b Taylor	2	1/1 2/5	(5 wkts, 40 overs) 194
G. S. Clinton c Jesty b Stevenson	21	3/84 4/88 5/139	

R. D. Jackman, †C. J. Richards, P. I. Pocock and R. G. L. Cheatle did not bat.

Bowling: Stevenson 8–2–32–2; Malone 8–0–38–1; Jesty 8–0–42–0; Taylor 8–1–31–2; Cowley 8–0–35–0.

Hampshire

N. G. Cowley c Richards b Jackman	3	†G. R. Stevenson not out	8
C. L. Smith lbw b Jackman	9	K. Stevenson run out	1
D. R. Turner c Knight b Clarke	109	S. J. Malone not out	1
T. E. Jesty c Clinton b Knight	0	B 8, l-b 10, w 9	27
*N. E. J. Pocock c sub b Cheatle	6		
M. C. J. Nicholas run out	12	1/15 2/22 3/23	(9 wkts, 40 overs) 193
M. N. S. Taylor c Howarth b Knight	16	4/70 5/116 6/160 7/182	
V. P. Terry b Butcher b Clarke	1	8/183 9/186	

Bowling: Jackman 8–1–20–2; Clarke 8–0–32–2; Knight 8–0–43–2; Cheatle 8–0–38–1; Pocock 8–0–33–0.

Umpires: C. Cook and A. Jepson.

At Chelmsford, May 25. SURREY lost to ESSEX by 40 runs.

SURREY v NOTTINGHAMSHIRE

At The Oval, June 1. Surrey won by four wickets. Despite their indifferent bowling and poor batting at the start of their innings, Surrey got home with one ball to spare, thanks to a fine innings by Clinton whose unbeaten 79 included four 6s and five 4s. When Jackman joined him the requirement was 88 off eleven overs; running between the wickets well, the pair reduced it to 25 off two overs and, with 16 taken off Bore, 9 off the last. The first ball of that, bowled by Rice, was slashed for 6 over the third-man boundary by Clinton, though it counted only after Bore sportingly admitted he took the "catch" with his foot on the rope. There was more confusion slightly later when the players went to walk off with the board showing the required 187. The umpires were undecided whether that total was correct, and in fact a no ball in the penultimate over was not recorded until the last had begun.

Nottinghamshire

P. A. Todd lbw b Jackman	23	K. Saxelby run out	1
B. Hassan lbw b Knight	10	K. E. Cooper not out	0
*C. E. B. Rice run out	13		
J. D. Birch not out	69	L-b 9, w 11, n-b 1	21
D. W. Randall c and b Cheatle	13		
H. T. Tunnicliffe b Pocock	15	1/34 2/46 3/80 (8 wkts, 37 overs) 186	
†C. C. Curzon b Clarke	3	4/99 5/129 6/138	
E. E. Hemmings run out	18	7/170 8/183	

M. K. Bore did not bat.

Bowling: Jackman 8–4–18–1; Clarke 6–0–24–1; Knight 4–0–18–1; Smith 5–0–25–0; Pocock 8–0–38–1; Cheatle 6–0–42–1.

Surrey

A. R. Butcher c Hassan b Cooper	18	S. T. Clarke lbw b Cooper	1
G. P. Howarth c Hassan b Cooper	4	R. D. Jackman not out	25
*R. D. V. Knight c Randall b Hemmings	19	L-b 4, w 3, n-b 1	8
D. M. Smith b Saxelby	18		
G. R. J. Roope lbw b Hemmings	15	1/21 2/26 (6 wkts, 36.5 overs) 187	
G. S. Clinton not out	79	3/59 4/71 5/87 6/99	

†C. J. Richards, P. I. Pocock and R. G. L. Cheatle did not bat.

Bowling: Cooper 7–0–21–3; Bore 8–0–55–0; Hemmings 8–2–29–2; Rice 7.5–0–43–0; Saxelby 6–0–31–1.

Umpires: R. Aspinall and P. B. Wight.

At Birmingham, June 8. SURREY lost to WARWICKSHIRE by 16 runs.

At Lord's, June 15. SURREY lost to MIDDLESEX by ten wickets.

SURREY v SUSSEX

At The Oval, June 22. No result.

SURREY v GLOUCESTERSHIRE

At Guildford, June 29. Gloucestershire won by 41 runs. Bowlers prospered on a slow, rain-affected wicket. Bainbridge gave an excellent all-round performance, sharing top score with Procter after Gloucestershire had been put in, and taking the wickets of Knight, Roope and Clinton for 16 in eight overs. Clarke took three catches in the covers, all of them off the bowling of Knight.

Gloucestershire

Zaheer Abbas lbw b Jackman	8	A. H. Wilkins c Clarke b Knight	9
B. C. Broad c Knight b Cheatle	21	B. M. Brain b Clarke	0
A. W. Stovold b Pocock	12	†A. J. Brassington not out	2
*M. J. Procter c Smith b Cheatle	23	B 4, l-b 7, w 6, n-b 1	18
A. J. Hignell lbw b Pocock	4		
P. Bainbridge c Clarke b Knight	23	1/25 2/45 3/68 4/75 (38.4 overs) 133	
Sadiq Mohammad c Knight b Clarke	8	5/79 6/108 7/111	
D. A. Graveney c Clarke b Knight	5	8/128 9/129	

Bowling: Jackman 8–2–20–1; Clarke 7–0–20–2; Knight 7.4–0–17–3; Pocock 8–0–20–2; Cheatle 8–0–38–2.

Surrey

A. R. Butcher lbw b Brain	8	S. T. Clarke lbw b Brain	6
G. P. Howarth b Brain	2	P. I. Pocock not out	1
*R. D. V. Knight b Bainbridge	16	R. G. L. Cheatle c Brassington b Procter	0
D. M. Smith b Wilkins	12	B 2, l-b 10, n-b 1	13
G. R. J. Roope b Bainbridge	14		
G. S. Clinton c Stovold b Bainbridge	4	1/1 2/17 3/38 4/58 (34.5 overs)	92
R. D. Jackman run out	16	5/63 6/70 7/81	
†C. J. Richards b Wilkins	0	8/90 9/91	

Bowling: Brain 8–2–19–3; Procter 5.5–2–10–1; Wilkins 5–0–17–2; Bainbridge 8–3–16–3; Graveney 8–2–17–0.

Umpires: D. J. Constant and R. Palmer.

At Manchester, July 6. SURREY beat LANCASHIRE by six wickets.

SURREY v YORKSHIRE

G. R. J. Roope's Benefit Match

At The Oval, July 13. Surrey won on faster scoring-rate. In a rain-affected match, Surrey reached 66 for four off twelve overs to beat Yorkshire, who had batted adventurously to achieve 208 for six in their full quota after being put in. Athey put on 75 with Hampshire and 79 with Love, who completed a punishing 75 (four 6s and two 4s) in sixty-six minutes. Surrey's scoring-rate was 5.5 an over against 5.2. They struck out at Yorkshire's pace bowlers, Roope hitting a bright 31.

Yorkshire

*J. H. Hampshire c Roope b Cheatle	36	S. N. Hartley not out	0
C. W. J. Athey c Butcher b Clarke	61		
G. B. Stevenson b Cheatle	2	B 2, l-b 14, w 2, n-b 2	20
J. D. Love c Cheatle b Knight	75		
K. Sharp c and b Cheatle	0	1/79 2/83 3/158 (6 wkts, 40 overs)	208
†D. L. Bairstow c Roope b Knight	14	4/166 5/204 6/208	

C. M. Old, P. Carrick, A. Sidebottom and A. Ramage did not bat.

Bowling: Thomas 8–1–20–0; Clarke 8–1–24–1; Knight 8–0–54–2; Pocock 8–0–35–0; Cheatle 8–1–55–3.

Surrey

A. R. Butcher c Athey b Old	0	†C. J. Richards not out	1
G. S. Clinton b Stevenson	12		
*R. D. V. Knight b Stevenson	9	L-b 2, w 3	5
D. M. Smith not out	8		
G. R. J. Roope b Hartley	31	1/1 2/13 3/24 4/65 (4 wkts, 12 overs)	66

M. A. Lynch, S. T. Clarke, P. I. Pocock, R. G. L. Cheatle and D. A. Thomas did not bat.

Bowling: Old 6–0–32–1; Stevenson 4–1–23–2; Ramage 1–0–4–0; Hartley 1–0–2–1.

Umpires: D. J. Halfyard and R. Julian.

SURREY v GLAMORGAN

At The Oval, July 20. No result.

782 *John Player League, 1980*

At Worcester, July 27. SURREY lost to WORCESTERSHIRE by five wickets.

At Northampton, August 3. SURREY beat NORTHAMPTONSHIRE by seven wickets.

SURREY v KENT

At The Oval, August 24. Surrey won by three wickets after stuttering towards the modest target at 3.2 runs an over. Roope acknowledged a collection of £350 for his benefit by steadying the innings after half the side had gone for 61. His disciplined effort lasted 25 overs and made all the difference. Knott, Kent's highest scorer, worried the home team by taking catches to account for Butcher, Clinton and Knight early on.

Kent

R. A. Woolmer c Smith b Clarke	17	C. J. C. Rowe not out 16
G. W. Johnson run out	2	N. J. Kemp run out 11
C. J. Tavaré lbw b Jackman	2	R. W. Hills not out 2
Asif Iqbal c Smith b Jackman	5	B 2, l-b 1, w 3 6
C. S. Cowdrey c Clinton b Cheatle	19	
J. N. Shepherd c Cheatle b Thomas	4	1/17 2/19 3/21 (9 wkts, 38 overs) 123
*†A. P. E. Knott c Richards b Clarke	31	4/26 5/38 6/69 7/92
M. Benson b Roope	8	8/94 9/115

Bowling: Jackman 8–2–20–2; Clarke 8–2–26–2; Knight 7–1–18–0; Thomas 4–0–16–1; Cheatle 4–1–17–1; Roope 7–1–20–1.

Surrey

A. R. Butcher c Knott b Kemp	0	R. D. Jackman b Woolmer 3
G. S. Clinton c Knott b Shepherd	13	S. T. Clarke not out 11
*R. D. V. Knight c Knott b Shepherd	4	
D. M. Smith c Woolmer b Shepherd	24	L-b 8, w 1 9
G. R. J. Roope not out	32	
M. A. Lynch c and b Woolmer	12	1/0 2/5 3/20 4/46 (7 wkts, 33.2 overs) 127
D. J. Thomas c Knott b Woolmer	19	5/61 6/94 7/112

†C. J. Richards and R. G. L. Cheatle did not bat.

Bowling: Kemp 7–2–24–1; Shepherd 8–1–26–3; Asif 2–0–7–0; Cowdrey 2–0–9–0; Woolmer 8–2–16–3; Hills 6.2–0–36–0.

Umpires: P. S. G. Stevens and A. G. T. Whitehead.

At Taunton, August 31. SURREY lost to SOMERSET by 73 runs.

SURREY v LEICESTERSHIRE

At The Oval, September 7. Surrey won by five wickets. Perhaps in reaction to the previous day's defeat in the Gillette Cup final they looked a little shaky until Smith and Thomas joined forces at 94 for four. Thomas needed only 35 balls for his 56, which included two 6s and five 4s. Leicestershire were well served by Tolchard with the bat and Parsons with the ball. They had been on the heels of the leaders, Warwickshire, for most of August but this defeat left them in fourth place.

Leicestershire

D. I. Gower lbw b Jackman	0	P. B. Clift not out		9
N. E. Briers c Smith b Knight	16	D. A. Wenlock not out		9
J. C. Balderstone c and b Knight	19	L-b 17		17
*B. F. Davison b Thomas	33			
R. W. Tolchard run out	42	1/0 2/36 3/45 4/84	(6 wkts, 40 overs)	173
†M. A. Garnham c Thomas b Jackman	28	5/139 6/156		

G. J. Parsons, N. G. B. Cook and L. B. Taylor did not bat.

Bowling: Jackman 8–3–16–2; Clarke 8–1–33–0; Knight 8–0–47–2; Pocock 8–0–29–0; Thomas 8–1–31–1.

Surrey

A. R. Butcher c Garnham b Parsons	6	S. T. Clarke not out		3
*R. D. V. Knight c Clift b Parsons	18			
M. A. Lynch c Balderstone b Parsons	15	B 6, l-b 2		8
D. M. Smith run out	51			
G. R. J. Roope c and b Wenlock	18	1/15 2/34 3/44	(5 wkts, 38 overs)	175
D. J. Thomas not out	56	4/94 5/158		

G. S. Clinton, R. D. Jackman, †C. J. Richards and P. I. Pocock did not bat.

Bowling: Taylor 7–0–39–0; Parsons 8–0–27–3; Cook 8–2–24–0; Wenlock 8–0–44–1; Clift 7–0–33–0.

Umpires: C. Cook and B. J. Meyer.

SUSSEX

SUSSEX v LEICESTERSHIRE

At Hove, May 4. Leicestershire won by three wickets. Imran Khan, in splendid form, hit the two first 6s of the season in his entertaining innings, after Sussex had been put in. Gower's 55 for Leicestershire included nine elegant 4s, and a keen north-east wind was forgotten for a time as the Sussex total seemed to shrink before his flashing bat. Needing 6 runs to win when the last over started, the visitors reached their target with three balls remaining giving a tight finish to a match which had earlier appeared comfortably in their grasp.

Sussex

K. C. Wessels lbw b Cook	10	A. C. S. Pigott not out		0
G. D. Mendis c Higgs b Wenlock	37			
P. W. G. Parker b Cook	12	B 1, l-b 9, w 5		15
Imran Khan c Gower b Higgs	64			
P. J. Graves b Higgs	36	1/54 2/56	(5 wkts, 40 overs)	190
C. P. Phillipson not out	16	3/72 4/160 5/188		

G. G. Arnold, *†A. Long, J. Spencer and C. E. Waller did not bat.

Bowling: Booth 6–0–23–0; Higgs 8–1–35–2; Wenlock 8–1–27–1; Boon 2–0–14–0; Cook 8–2–33–2; Steele 8–0–43–0.

Leicestershire

B. Dudleston c Phillipson b Spencer	31	D. A. Wenlock c Long b Imran		11
N. E. Briers b Arnold	25	P. Booth not out		14
D. I. Gower c Phillipson b Waller	55	B 2, l-b 8, w 1, n-b 4		15
T. J. Boon b Imran	12			
†R. W. Tolchard not out	16	1/46 2/103	(7 wkts, 39.3 overs)	193
*B. F. Davison st Long b Waller	5	3/133 4/133 5/142		
J. F. Steele c and b Waller	9	6/152 7/167		

N. G. B. Cook and K. Higgs did not bat.

Bowling: Arnold 8–1–34–1; Imran 7.3–0–33–2; Waller 8–3–22–3; Spencer 6–0–44–1; Pigott 8–0–31–0; Phillipson 2–0–14–0.

Umpires: K. E. Palmer and D. Shackleton.

At Northampton, May 11. SUSSEX lost to NORTHAMPTONSHIRE by nine wickets.

At Birmingham, May 18, SUSSEX lost to WARWICKSHIRE by nine wickets.

At Middlesbrough, June 1. SUSSEX beat YORKSHIRE by three wickets.

SUSSEX v WORCESTERSHIRE

At Horsham, June 8. Sussex won by 32 runs in a magnificent match. They achieved their highest score to date in the competition (bettered only by Worcestershire in 1975), with Parker hammering a thrilling century that included six 6s, one over the adjoining tennis courts. Turner played an equally memorable innings for Worcestershire, hitting seven 6s. With only five overs remaining the visitors still needed 44, but when Turner was last out, caught in the deep in the 37th over, only 11 more runs had been scored.

Sussex

G. D. Mendis c Turner b Pridgeon		64
T. D. Booth Jones run out		30
P. W. G. Parker not out		106
Imran Khan c Ormrod b Younis		73
C. P. Phillipson c Inchmore b Holder		1
B 1, l-b 12, w 2, n-b 4		19

1/79 2/126   (4 wkts, 40 overs) 293
3/282 4/293

C. M. Wells, G. S. le Roux, A. C. S. Pigott, *†A. Long, G. G. Arnold and J. Spencer did not bat.

Bowling: Holder 7–0–37–1; Inchmore 4–0–40–0; Pridgeon 8–0–58–1; Patel 8–0–35–0; Gifford 8–0–59–0; Younis 5–0–45–1.

Worcestershire

G. M. Turner c Pigott b le Roux	147	V. A. Holder c Pigott b Spencer ... 16
J. A. Ormrod b Pigott	21	*N. Gifford c Long b Imran ... 4
Younis Ahmed run out	15	A. P. Pridgeon not out ... 0
E. J. O. Hemsley lbw b Pigott	5	L-b 5, w 4, n-b 1 ... 10
P. A. Neale lbw b Imran	15	
D. N. Patel b Wells	5	1/45 2/73 3/89 (36.2 overs) 261
†D. J. Humphries c le Roux b Arnold	13	4/149 5/158 6/185 7/200
J. D. Inchmore c Pigott b Spencer	10	8/228 9/251

Bowling: le Roux 6.2–0–36–1; Arnold 6–0–46–1; Pigott 7–0–42–2; Spencer 8–0–60–2; Imran 7–0–47–2; Wells 2–0–20–1.

Umpires: D. J. Halfyard and J. G. Langridge.

At The Oval, June 22. SURREY v SUSSEX. No result.

SUSSEX v SOMERSET

At Hove, June 29. Somerset won by three wickets. A crowd of nearly 5,000 watched Botham give a demonstration of his all-round power with two wickets, two catches, a swift run out and a swashbuckling 26. Despite useful contributions from Phillipson and Wells, Sussex's total was never enough as Somerset skipper Rose eased his side towards victory.

Sussex

G. D. Mendis c Taylor b Botham	0	*†A Long c Botham b Moseley	7
T. D. Booth Jones lbw b Jennings	27	G. G. Arnold c Jennings b Moseley	12
I. A. Greig lbw b Marks	21	J. Spencer not out	0
Imran Khan c Dredge b Marks	4		
C. P. Phillipson c Denning b Jennings	34	B 2, l-b 5, w 2	9
C. M. Wells c Botham b Moseley	36		
G. S. le Roux run out	10	1/0 2/42 3/51 4/59 (39.5 overs) 162	
J. R. T. Barclay c Moseley b Botham	2	5/120 6/133 7/140 8/145 9/162	

Bowling: Botham 8–2–21–2; Moseley 7.5–1–31–3; Marks 8–1–25–2; Jennings 8–1–31–2; Dredge 8–0–45–0.

Somerset

S. M. Gavaskar c and b Arnold	16	†D. J. S. Taylor not out	8
*B. C. Rose c Long b le Roux	47	C. H. Dredge not out	1
P. W. Denning c Barclay b Arnold	16		
I. T. Botham c sub b Barclay	26	L-b 11, w 10, n-b 1	22
P. M. Roebuck b Imran	22		
V. J. Marks c Long b le Roux	4	1/35 2/58 3/88 (7 wkts, 37.2 overs) 165	
D. Breakwell run out	0	4/143 5/147 6/153 7/157	

K. F. Jennings and H. R. Moseley did not bat.

Bowling: Imran 8–0–21–1; le Roux 8–2–21–2; Arnold 5.2–0–43–2; Barclay 8–0–26–1; Greig 8–1–32–0.

Umpires: W. E. Alley and W. L. Budd.

SUSSEX v HAMPSHIRE

At Hove, July 6. No result. Rain reduced the Sussex innings to 32 overs and then washed out hopes of a Hampshire reply. Mendis set a purposeful example, racing to 50 in forty minutes, and was fifth out for an attractive 70 off 21 overs. He was joined in a second-wicket thrash of 59 in seven overs by Phillipson who received his county cap before the start after ten years with the club. Twelve wides were bowled, eight of them in Malone's first over which yielded 13 runs.

Sussex

G. D. Mendis c Stephenson b Malone	70	G. S. le Roux c Pocock b Cowley	9
T. D. Booth Jones b Stevenson	12	†T. J. Head not out	6
C. P. Phillipson b Jesty	21	A. C. S. Pigott not out	1
Imran Khan run out	2	L-b 15, w 12	27
C. M. Wells c Smith b Cowley	0		
I. A. Greig b Cowley	12	1/55 2/114 3/120 (9 wkts, 32 overs) 200	
J. R. Heath st Stephenson b Cowley	33	4/120 5/134 6/146 7/168	
*J. R. T. Barclay b Stevenson	7	8/191 9/194	

Bowling: Malone 8–0–41–1; Graf 6–1–28–0; Stevenson 6–0–30–2; Jesty 4–0–28–1; Cowley 8–0–46–4.

Hampshire

C. L. Smith, T. M. Tremlett, D. R. Turner, T. E. Jesty, *N. E. J. Pocock, N. G. Cowley, M. C. J. Nicholas, S. F. Graf, G. R. Stephenson, K. Stevenson, S. J. Malone.

Umpires: B. J. Meyer and R. Palmer.

At Moreton-in-Marsh, July 13. GLOUCESTERSHIRE v SUSSEX. No result.

At Maidstone, July 20. KENT v SUSSEX. No result.

SUSSEX v ESSEX

At Hastings, July 27. Sussex won by 8 runs. In an entertaining match Sussex mounted what appeared to be a formidable total of 267 for five off 39 overs, thanks mainly to the in-form Parker and Wells. McEwan followed with a sparkling 136 which threatened to snatch victory for Essex and included six prodigious 6s that had spectators scattering. But with his dismissal by fellow South African Greig went Essex's serious challenge, and the task of hitting 15 runs off the last over proved too much for the tailenders.

Sussex

G. D. Mendis c Herbert b Pringle	27	I. A. Greig not out	30
J. R. T. Barclay b Herbert	40		
P. W. G. Parker c Pringle b Pont	73	B 5, l-b 6, w 2, n-b 4	17
Imran Khan c Pringle b Pont	6		
C. M. Wells not out	65	1/4 2/114 3/152 (5 wkts, 39 overs) 267	
C. P. Phillipson c Hardie b Pringle	9	4/186 5/212	

G. S. le Roux, *†A. Long, G. G. Arnold and J. Spencer did not bat.

Bowling: Phillip 8–0–51–0; Pringle 8–0–47–2; Herbert 8–0–57–1; Turner 7–0–51–0; Pont 8–0–44–2.

Essex

M. H. Denness lbw b Arnold	14	D. R. Pringle not out	19
†N. Smith b Arnold	7	M. S. A. McEvoy not out	8
K. S. McEwan b Greig	136		
N. Phillip c and b le Roux	13	B 5, l-b 2, w 3, n-b 2	12
*K. W. R. Fletcher b le Roux	17		
B. R. Hardie c Mendis b Wells	19	1/28 2/37 3/79 (8 wkts, 39 overs) 259	
K. R. Pont c Arnold b Wells	2	4/113 5/172 6/180	
S. Turner c Wells b le Roux	12	7/230 8/234	

R. Herbert did not bat.

Bowling: Arnold 8–1–35–2; Imran 8–0–44–0; Barclay 2–0–24–0; le Roux 8–0–38–3; Spencer 5–0–44–0; Wells 5–0–43–2; Greig 3–0–19–1.

Umpires: J. G. Langridge and R. Palmer.

At Manchester, August 3. SUSSEX beat LANCASHIRE on faster scoring-rate.

SUSSEX v NOTTINGHAMSHIRE

At Eastbourne, August 10. Nottinghamshire won by 60 runs. A splendid innings by Rice enabled the visitors to reach 206 for seven on an easy-paced wicket. Sussex struggled against the Nottinghamshire attack and, after the first five wickets had fallen for 45, only a useful knock by Phillipson and an eighth-wicket stand of 46 by Barclay and Head gave their total any respectability.

Nottinghamshire

†B. Hassan c Head b Wells	22	E. E. Hemmings b le Roux		9
R. T. Robinson b Arnold	23	M. J. Harris not out		6
*C. E. B. Rice not out	93			
J. D. Birch c le Roux b Spencer	22	B 1, l-b 11, w 2, n-b 2		16
D. W. Randall c Wessels b Greig	14			
P. A. Todd b Greig	0	1/43 2/59 3/117	(7 wkts, 40 overs)	206
R. J. Hadlee c Head b le Roux	1	4/155 5/155 6/156 7/183		

P. J. Hacker and M. K. Bore did not bat.

Bowling: Arnold 8–1–32–1; le Roux 8–0–24–2; Wells 8–0–36–1; Spencer 8–0–48–1; Greig 8–0–50–2.

Sussex

G. D. Mendis lbw b Hadlee	2	†T. J. Head c Bore b Rice		24
K. C. Wessels b Hadlee	15	G. G. Arnold b Rice		0
P. W. G. Parker c Harris b Hacker	5	J. Spencer not out		5
C. M. Wells b Bore	10	B 2, l-b 14, w 11, n-b 1		28
C. P. Phillipson b Hacker	26			
I. A. Greig lbw b Bore	0	1/8 2/17 3/29 4/43	(34.1 overs)	146
G. S. le Roux c Rice b Hemmings	5	5/45 6/66 7/93		
*J. R. T. Barclay run out	30	8/139 9/139		

Bowling: Hadlee 5–1–19–2; Hacker 8–0–36–2; Hemmings 8–1–17–1; Bore 8–2–24–2; Rice 5.1–0–22–2.

Umpires: D. J. Halfyard and P. S. G. Stevens.

SUSSEX v MIDDLESEX

At Hove, August 24. Middlesex won by 21 runs. Sussex fought gamely with a weakened side, but the target of 227 was always beyond them. Although aggressive knocks by Mendis, Parker and Wessels gave them a promising start, the middle-order batsmen could not maintain the drive. On a beautiful batting wicket, Radley had laid the foundation for Middlesex with an entertaining innings which included ten boundaries and received typical support from Gatting and Butcher.

Middlesex

*J. M. Brearley run out	4	J. E. Emburey not out		14
C. T. Radley c Mendis b Pigott	93	M. W. W. Selvey not out		9
G. D. Barlow c Parker b Greig	17	B 1, l-b 2, w 1, n-b 1		5
M. W. Gatting c and b Waller	34			
R. O. Butcher c and b Pigott	33	1/19 2/68 3/118	(6 wkts, 40 overs)	226
V. A. P. van der Bijl b Pigott	17	4/180 5/190 6/214		

†P. R. Downton, W. G. Merry and W. W. Daniel did not bat.

Bowling: Pigott 8–1–29–3; Spencer 8–0–55–0; Barclay 4–0–22–0; Greig 8–0–45–1; Waller 8–0–42–1; Wells 4–0–28–0.

Sussex

G. D. Mendis b Emburey	22	A. C. S. Pigott run out		1
K. C. Wessels c van der Bijl b Selvey	28	C. E. Waller c Brearley b Gatting		11
P. W. G. Parker c van der Bijl b Merry	27	J. Spencer not out		2
C. M. Wells c Downton b Merry	6	B 3, l-b 12, n-b 3		18
C. P. Phillipson c Downton b Merry	15			
I. A. Greig b Daniel	30	1/37 2/79 3/92	(9 wkts, 40 overs)	205
*J. R. T. Barclay not out	40	4/95 5/127 6/158 7/175		
†T. J. Head run out	5	8/178 9/197		

Bowling: Selvey 8–1–27–1; van der Bijl 7–0–41–0; Emburey 8–2–38–1; Daniel 8–0–38–1; Merry 8–0–35–3; Gatting 1–0–8–1.

Umpires: R. S. Herman and B. J. Meyer.

At Derby, August 31. SUSSEX beat DERBYSHIRE by 75 runs.

SUSSEX v GLAMORGAN

At Hove, September 7. Sussex won by five wickets. Javed Miandad, who had been with Sussex the previous season, played orthodox and cheeky shots as he hit one 6 and eight 4s in his entertaining innings. Glamorgan's total looked a testing target, but Mendis took 13 runs off the first over, Wessels and Wells kept the run-rate racing along, and an unbroken partnership of 53 off the last ten overs from Phillipson and Greig took Sussex to victory with one over to spare.

Glamorgan

J. A. Hopkins run out	26	M. J. Llewellyn not out	25
D. A. Francis b Arnold	11	B 5, l-b 8, w 1, n-b 3	17
Javed Miandad not out	95		
N. G. Featherstone c Parker b Barclay	40	1/23 2/68 3/158 (3 wkts, 40 overs)	214

B. J. Lloyd, G. C. Holmes, *M. A. Nash, †E. W. Jones, E. A. Moseley and A. J. Mack did not bat.

Bowling: Arnold 8–0–33–1; Imran 8–1–31–0; Greig 6–1–24–0; Waller 6–0–36–0; Barclay 8–0–41–1; Wells 4–0–32–0.

Sussex

G. D. Mendis c Jones b Moseley	19	I. A. Greig not out	26
K. C. Wessels c Jones b Moseley	40		
P. W. G. Parker c Jones b Holmes	21	B 8, l-b 9, w 3, n-b 2	22
Imran Khan c Hopkins b Holmes	7		
C. M. Wells c Featherstone b Lloyd	42	1/28 2/81 3/89 (5 wkts, 39 overs)	218
C. P. Phillipson not out	41	4/96 5/165	

*J. R. T. Barclay, †T. J. Head, G. G. Arnold and C. E. Waller did not bat.

Bowling: Mack 7–0–48–0; Moseley 8–0–44–2; Nash 8–2–30–0; Lloyd 8–0–41–1; Holmes 8–3–33–2.

Umpires: R. Palmer and C. T. Spencer.

WARWICKSHIRE

At Southampton, May 4. WARWICKSHIRE beat HAMPSHIRE by eight wickets.

At Huddersfield, May 11. WARWICKSHIRE beat YORKSHIRE by five wickets.

WARWICKSHIRE v SUSSEX

At Birmingham, May 18. Warwickshire won by nine wickets. After Sussex were put in, only Imran Khan and le Roux were able to achieve reasonable scores against the Warwickshire bowling as Small took three for 9 in 40 balls and Doshi took two for 13 in eight overs. Facing a modest total, Warwickshire achieved their third League victory with ease, thanks mainly to Amiss, whose unbeaten 94 included fifteen 4s and who became the first Warwickshire player to score 4,000 runs in the competition.

Sussex

G. D. Mendis c Claughton b Small	1	*†A. Long not out	13
P. J. Graves c Maynard b Willis	9	J. Spencer c Small b Ferreira	0
P. W. G. Parker c Ferreira b Small	12	C. E. Waller b Small	6
Imran Khan c Amiss b Humpage	33	L-b 7, w 6	13
C. P. Phillipson b Doshi	12		
C. M. Wells run out	0	1/15 2/19 3/48	(37.4 overs) 133
G. S. le Roux c Maynard b Ferreira	34	4/75 5/77 6/80 7/90	
A. C. S. Pigott lbw b Doshi	0	8/124 9/125	

Bowling: Willis 7–1–40–1; Small 6.4–2–9–3; Ferreira 8–1–32–2; Humpage 8–0–26–1; Doshi 8–2–13–2.

Warwickshire

D. L. Amiss not out	94		
K. D. Smith lbw b Spencer	13		
T. A. Lloyd not out	24		
B 1, l-b 2, w 2, n-b 1	6		
1/40	(1 wkt, 32.5 overs) 137		

J. A. Claughton, P. R. Oliver, G. W. Humpage, A. M. Ferreira, †C. Maynard, G. C. Small, *R. G. D. Willis and D. R. Doshi did not bat.

Bowling: Imran 5–1–23–0; le Roux 6–0–23–0; Spencer 8–3–18–1; Waller 4–0–21–0; Wells 6–1–24–0; Pigott 3.5–0–22–0.

Umpires: D. O. Oslear and P. S. G. Stevens.

At Liverpool, June 1. WARWICKSHIRE beat LANCASHIRE by eight wickets.

WARWICKSHIRE v SURREY

At Birmingham, June 8. Warwickshire won by 16 runs. They maintained their winning sequence thanks mainly to a career-best five for 29 by their teenage pace bowler, Small. Warwickshire, put in, had reached only 170 after losing five wickets for 88. Small gave his side a flying start by dismissing Butcher and Knight in three balls when Surrey began their reply. Roope led a recovery but Small claimed two more wickets and led Warwickshire to victory.

Warwickshire

*D. L. Amiss c Knight b Cheatle	42	D. C. Hopkins b Clarke	1
T. A. Lloyd c and b Pocock	30	G. C. Small b Clarke	0
J. A. Claughton c Pocock b Cheatle	8	D. R. Doshi run out	3
P. R. Oliver c and b Cheatle	1	B 1, l-b 10, w 8	19
G. W. Humpage b Pocock	0		
†C. Maynard c Cheatle b Clarke	17	1/60 2/86 3/87 4/88	(37.5 overs) 170
S. J. Rouse not out	38	5/88 6/134 7/162	
A. M. Ferreira b Smith	11	8/165 9/165	

Bowling: Jackman 8–1–26–0; Clarke 7–0–27–3; Pocock 8–0–23–2; Cheatle 8–1–33–3; Smith 4.5–0–22–1; Roope 2–0–20–0.

Surrey

A. R. Butcher lbw b Small	4	†C. J. Richards not out	12
G. P. Howarth b Doshi	23	P. I. Pocock b Small	0
*R. D. V. Knight c Maynard b Small	0	R. G. L. Cheatle not out	0
D. M. Smith c Doshi b Ferreira	28	B 6, l-b 14, w 6, n-b 5	31
G. R. J. Roope lbw b Small	32		
G. S. Clinton run out	0	1/14 2/14 3/57	(9 wkts, 38 overs) 154
S. T. Clarke c Claughton b Humpage	3	4/85 5/86 6/95 7/134	
R. D. Jackman c and b Small	21	8/154 9/154	

Bowling: Rouse 8–1–27–0; Small 8–3–29–5; Ferreira 7–1–20–1; Doshi 8–3–15–1; Hopkins 3–0–17–0; Humpage 4–0–15–1.

Umpires: B. J. Meyer and K. E. Palmer.

At Southend, June 15. WARWICKSHIRE beat ESSEX by 5 runs.

WARWICKSHIRE v NORTHAMPTONSHIRE

At Nuneaton, June 22. Warwickshire won by 26 runs. Amiss laid the foundations of Warwickshire's total, which always looked too much for the visitors in a match reduced by rain to 37 overs. He put on 140 for the first wicket with Lloyd, who went on to reach 80. When Northamptonshire batted, Small removed both Cook and Larkins in three balls in his first over. Lamb and Williams led a recovery but Doshi bowled eight economical overs and a target of 71 off seven overs was too much for Northamptonshire.

Warwickshire

*D. L. Amiss c Cook b T. M. Lamb	81	P. R. Oliver not out	0
T. A. Lloyd b Griffiths	80		
J. A. Claughton c Williams b Watts	22	B 1, l-b 9, w 1, n-b 2	13
G. W. Humpage c Cook b Sarfraz	29		
A. M. Ferreira lbw b Griffiths	0	1/140 2/181	(5 wkts, 37 overs) 234
†C. Maynard not out	9	3/200 4/200 5/229	

S. J. Rouse, D. C. Hopkins, G. C. Small and D. R. Doshi did not bat.

Bowling: Sarfraz 8–0–49–1; Griffiths 8–0–45–2; Watts 7–0–36–1; T. M. Lamb 8–0–45–1; Williams 6–0–46–0.

Northamptonshire

G. Cook b Small	1	*P. J. Watts not out	24
W. Larkins lbw b Small	0	R. M. Carter not out	3
A. J. Lamb lbw b Hopkins	48		
R. G. Williams c Maynard b Rouse	69	B 2, l-b 13, w 7	22
T. J. Yardley b Hopkins	7		
†G. Sharp c Amiss b Small	29	1/2 2/3 3/91	(7 wkts, 37 overs) 208
Sarfraz Nawaz c Hopkins b Rouse	5	4/113 5/170 6/170 7/186	

T. M. Lamb and B. J. Griffiths did not bat.

Bowling: Small 8–0–42–3; Rouse 6–0–27–2; Ferreira 5–0–35–0; Doshi 8–2–23–0; Hopkins 8–0–40–2; Humpage 2–0–19–0.

Umpires: D. J. Constant and D. J. Dennis.

WARWICKSHIRE v MIDDLESEX

At Birmingham, June 29. Warwickshire won by five wickets. Warwickshire extended their lead at the top of the table to eight points with a victory over second-placed Middlesex. Middlesex, put in, built their healthy total around an unbeaten 94 by Barlow (nine 4s and one 6) and an attractive 53 from Brearley. Warwickshire began shakily, losing their first three wickets for only 37, before Humpage pulled the innings round with an unbeaten 108 which included fifteen 4s and one 6. Middlesex were punished with 73 off eight overs and Warwickshire reached their target with three overs to spare.

Middlesex

*J. M. Brearley b Doshi	53	V. A. P. van der Bijl not out	3
C. T. Radley c Rouse b Willis	1		
G. D. Barlow not out	94	L-b 10, w 2, n-b 1	13
M. W. Gatting b Doshi	5		
†I. J. Gould b Ferreira	12	1/5 2/94 3/102	(5 wkts, 40 overs) 216
R. O. Butcher run out	35	4/125 5/198	

J. E. Embury, K. D. James, M. W. W. Selvey and W. W. Daniel did not bat.

Bowling: Willis 8–1–30–1; Rouse 8–0–52–0; Small 8–1–36–0; Ferriera 8–0–45–1; Doshi 8–0–40–2.

Warwickshire

D. L. Amiss b Selvey	12	A. M. Ferreira not out	30
T. A. Lloyd run out	7		
J. A. Claughton lbw b Daniel	0	L-b 17, w 1, n-b 3	21
†G. W. Humpage not out	108		
P. R. Oliver run out	15	1/26 2/29	(5 wkts, 36.5 overs) 217
K. D. Smith c Brearley b James	24	3/37 4/88 5/126	

S. J. Rouse, *R. G. D. Willis, G. C. Small and D. R. Doshi did not bat.

Bowling: Selvey 7.5–1–38–1; Daniel 8–1–16–1; van der Bijl 7–1–33–0; Emburey 7–0–55–0; James 4–0–31–1; Gatting 3–0–23–0.

Umpires: B. J. Meyer and J. van Geloven.

At Worcester, July 6. WARWICKSHIRE lost to WORCESTERSHIRE by 15 runs.

At Nottingham, July 13. WARWICKSHIRE lost to NOTTINGHAMSHIRE by 77 runs.

WARWICKSHIRE v GLOUCESTERSHIRE

At Birmingham, July 20. Warwickshire won by 1 run. Defending a total of 150 for eight, Warwickshire atoned for two successive defeats with an exciting victory in the final over from which Gloucestershire required 6 to win. The first three balls produced singles; Willis bowled Procter with the fourth; Graveney missed the fifth but off-drove the last to Doshi at long-off and was run out. In an attempt to recover their former fire Warwickshire introduced Snow, the former England and Sussex bowler.

Warwickshire

D. L. Amiss c M. W. Stovold b Procter . .	3
T. A. Lloyd lbw b Wilkins	25
K. D. Smith b Bainbridge	28
†G. W. Humpage b Bainbridge	2
J. A. Claughton st A. W. Stovold	
b Graveney .	6
P. R. Oliver b Procter	28
A. M. Ferreira c A. W. Stovold	
b Partridge .	18

J. A. Snow not out	13
G. C. Small c M. W. Stovold b Brain	1
*R. G. D. Willis not out	12
B 1, l-b 10, w 3	14
	——
1/4 2/58 3/60 4/61 (8 wkts, 32 overs) 150	
5/69 6/113 7/127 8/128	

D. R. Doshi did not bat.

Bowling: Brain 7–0–29–1; Procter 7–2–24–2; Bainbridge 6–0–27–2; Wilkins 6–0–30–1; Graveney 3–0–19–1; Partridge 3–0–7–1.

Gloucestershire

B. C. Broad c Claughton b Ferreira	39
A. J. Hignell c Willis b Small	8
†A. W. Stovold b Doshi	6
*M. J. Procter b Willis	44
P. Bainbridge b Ferreira	23
M. W. Stovold not out	13

D. A. Graveney run out	1
B 1, l-b 8, w 4, n-b 2	15
1/39 2/58 3/68 (6 wkts, 32 overs) 149	
4/106 5/148 6/149	

S. J. Windaybank, M. D. Partridge, A. H. Wilkins and B. M. Brain did not bat.

Bowling: Willis 7–0–32–1; Small 6–0–24–1; Snow 6–1–27–0; Doshi 7–0–28–1; Ferreira 6–1–23–2.

Umpires: R. Julian and P. S. G. Stevens.

At Derby, July 27. WARWICKSHIRE lost to DERBYSHIRE by six wickets.

WARWICKSHIRE v KENT

At Birmingham, August 10. Tied. Having been defeated off the final ball in their Championship match against Kent two days earlier, Warwickshire just failed to snatch victory and thus became involved in the first John Player League tie for five years. They paced their reply well, with Lloyd (nine 4s) always looking confident, but it all went wrong in the final over when only 2 runs were needed. Ferreira was out to the first ball and Lloyd managed only a single off the next four before being run out off Shepherd's final delivery.

Kent

G. W. Johnson b Small	1
R. A. Woolmer b Doshi	69
C. J. Tavaré b Willis	2
C. S. Cowdrey c Smith b Ferreira	19
*A. G. E. Ealham b Snow	8
M. Benson c Humpage b Ferreira	10
†A. P. E. Knott run out	31

J. N. Shepherd not out	20
N. J. Kemp b Small	5
R. W. Hills not out	0
L-b 10, w 2, n-b 3	15
1/7 2/13 3/58 4/85 (8 wkts, 40 overs) 180	
5/105 6/111 7/158 8/176	

D. L. Underwood did not bat.

Bowling: Willis 8–2–29–1; Small 8–1–28–2; Snow 8–0–34–1; Ferreira 8–2–18–2; Doshi 6–0–42–1; Oliver 2–0–14–0.

Warwickshire

D. L. Amiss c Ealham b Shepherd	1	A. M. Ferreira c Tavaré b Shepherd	23
T. A. Lloyd run out	90	J. A. Snow not out	0
K. D. Smith lbw b Woolmer	9	B 1,l-b 15, w 1, n-b 3	20
†G. W. Humpage b Underwood	19		
P. R. Oliver st Knott b Johnson	2	1/1 2/35 3/97 (7 wkts, 40 overs) 180
J. Whitehouse c and b Underwood	16	4/106 5/128 6/179 7/180

*R. G. D. Willis, G. C. Small and D. R. Doshi did not bat.

Bowling: Kemp 5–1–17–0; Shepherd 8–1–31–2; Hills 7–2–31–0; Woolmer 4–0–15–1; Underwood 8–1–34–2; Johnson 8–0–32–1.

Umpires: H. D. Bird and R. S. Herman.

WARWICKSHIRE v GLAMORGAN

At Birmingham, August 24. Warwickshire won by four wickets. In reply to Glamorgan's healthy total, the home team lost their key batsmen, Amiss and Humpage, without scoring. That they remained top of the table owed much to Whitehouse and Lloyd, Whitehouse hitting 21 of 22 runs taken off an over from Featherstone. With 52 needed off the last eight overs, Maynard and Ferreira saw them through with eight balls to spare. For Glamorgan, Francis scored his first John Player League century after being dropped at 10 and 32.

Glamorgan

A. Jones st Maynard b Ferreira	55	N. G. Featherstone not out	0
J. A. Hopkins lbw b Snow	18	B 2,l-b 17, w 1, n-b 1	21
D. A. Francis not out	101		
Javed Miandad run out	34	1/38 2/135 3/214 (4 wkts, 40 overs) 235
*M. A. Nash c Oliver b Small	6	4/234

G. C. Holmes, †E. W. Jones, E. A. Moseley, A. J. Mack and A. A. Jones did not bat.

Bowling: Willis 8–1–36–0; Small 6–0–37–1; Snow 8–0–51–1; Humpage 3–0–18–0; Ferreira 8–0–35–1; Oliver 7–0–37–0.

Warwickshire

D. L. Amiss c E. W. Jones b Moseley	0	†C. Maynard not out	22
T. A. Lloyd b Featherstone	51	A. M. Ferreira not out	37
A. I. Kallicharran lbw b Nash	20		
G. W. Humpage c E. W. Jones		B 1,l-b 10, w 7, n-b 2	20
b A. A. Jones	0		
J. Whitehouse c E. W. Jones b Moseley	77	1/3 2/53 3/54 (6 wkts, 38.4 overs) 237
P. R. Oliver c Hopkins b Featherstone	10	4/98 5/144 6/184

J. A. Snow, *R. G. D. Willis and G. C. Small did not bat.

Bowling: Nash 8–2–34–1; Moseley 7–1–29–2; A. A. Jones 7.4–0–53–1; Mack 8–0–45–0; Featherstone 7–1–52–2; Holmes 1–0–4–0.

Umpires: R. Julian and D. O. Oslear.

At Leicester, August 31. WARWICKSHIRE beat LEICESTERSHIRE by six wickets.

WARWICKSHIRE v SOMERSET

At Birmingham, September 7. Somerset won by 26 runs. Having won the John Player League title at Leicester, Warwickshire disappointed a crowd of 11,000 by failing to match Somerset's total on a good batting pitch. They lost Amiss to Garner's first ball, were 43 for three after twelve overs and, despite a promising stand of 53 between Kallicharran and Whitehouse, fell short of their target. Snow had earlier registered his best performance for Warwickshire with four for 32, but the highlight of the Somerset innings was Richards's 89 (two 6s and three 4s). Taylor was given out "obstructing the field" after kicking the ball away when Willis attempted to run him out.

Somerset

P. W. Denning c Lloyd b Snow	35	J. Garner not out	1
J. W. Lloyds c Amiss b Snow	29	C. H. Dredge not out	2
I. V. A. Richards run out	89		
*I. T. Botham c Kallicharran b Snow	7	L-b 5, w 4	9
P. M. Roebuck lbw b Doshi	6		
V. J. Marks b Snow	7	1/67 2/69 3/81 (8 wkts, 40 overs) 215	
N. F. M. Popplewell run out	17	4/89 5/144 6/190 7/209	
†D. J. S. Taylor obstructing the field	13	8/213	

H. R. Moseley did not bat.

Bowling: Willis 8–0–53–0; Small 8–0–47–0; Doshi 8–1–29–1; Snow 8–0–32–4; Kallicharran 8–0–45–0.

Warwickshire

D. L. Amiss c Botham b Garner	0	*R. G. D. Willis run out	4
T. A. Lloyd run out	9	G. C. Small not out	4
A. I. Kallicharran c Botham b Dredge	38		
G. W. Humpage b Moseley	11	L-b 12, w 1, n-b 1	14
J. Whitehouse c Denning b Moseley	42		
P. R. Oliver c Taylor b Dredge	22	1/0 2/26 3/43 (8 wkts, 40 overs) 189	
†C. Maynard run out	20	4/96 5/110 6/146 7/160	
J. A. Snow not out	25	8/174	

D. R. Doshi did not bat.

Bowling: Garner 7–0–35–1; Botham 8–2–22–0; Marks 8–0–39–0; Moseley 8–0–40–2; Popplewell 2–0–13–0; Dredge 7–1–26–2.

Umpires: R. Aspinall and A. Jepson.

WORCESTERSHIRE

At Bradford, May 4. WORCESTERSHIRE beat YORKSHIRE by seven wickets.

WORCESTERSHIRE v MIDDLESEX

At Worcester, May 18. Middlesex won by nine wickets. For Worcestershire Turner batted impeccably, becoming the first player to complete 5,000 runs in the League. But van der Bijl made a significant breakthrough with two wickets in four balls, and after Turner's was one of two wickets taken in three deliveries by Edmonds, Worcestershire were exposed to a devastating final burst by Daniel, who took a wicket in each of his last four overs. In reply Middlesex were only 4 runs short of victory when Brearley was dismissed for 65 to end his opening stand with Radley of 129 in 31 overs.

Worcestershire

G. M. Turner st Gould b Edmonds	54	H. Alleyne lbw b Daniel	0
J. A. Ormrod b Selvey	6	*N. Gifford not out	3
Younis Ahmed c Gould b van der Bijl	2	A. P. Pridgeon b Daniel	0
E. J. O. Hemsley b van der Bijl	0	B 8, l-b 6	14
D. N. Patel c and b Gatting	13		
B. J. R. Jones c Gould b Daniel	22	1/19 2/24 3/24 4/68 (36 overs) 132	
†D. J. Humphries b Edmonds	0	5/102 6/102 7/126	
J. D. Inchmore c Gould b Daniel	18	8/126 9/130	

Bowling: Daniel 6–1–12–4; van der Bijl 8–1–18–2; Selvey 4–0–22–1; Emburey 8–2–27–0; Gatting 6–0–17–1; Edmonds 4–0–22–2.

Middlesex

*J. M. Brearley c Hemsley b Gifford	....	65
C. T. Radley not out	....	59
G. D. Barlow not out	....	0
B 2, l-b 3, w 1, n-b 3	....	9

1/129   (1 wkt, 31.1 overs) 133

R. O. Butcher, M. W. Gatting, †I. J. Gould, P. H. Edmonds, J. E. Emburey, V. A. P. van der Bijl, M. W. W. Selvey and W. W. Daniel did not bat.

Bowling: Alleyne 8–0–29–0; Inchmore 5–0–16–0; Patel 7–0–22–0; Pridgeon 3–0–20–0; Gifford 5–2–15–1; Younis 3.1–0–22–0.

Umpires: R. S. Herman and R. Julian.

At Southampton, June 1. WORCESTERSHIRE beat HAMPSHIRE by four wickets.

At Horsham, June 8. WORCESTERSHIRE lost to SUSSEX by 32 runs.

At Bristol, June 15. WORCESTERSHIRE lost to GLOUCESTERSHIRE by 2 runs.

WORCESTERSHIRE v LEICESTERSHIRE

At Worcester, June 22. Worcestershire won by eight wickets after rain had reduced their target to a comfortable 54 in twelve overs. Leicestershire originally held the advantage during an opening stand of 84 in eighteen overs by Briers and Gower, but the intervention of the weather heavily favoured the home county.

Leicestershire

D. I. Gower st Humphries b Gifford	....	38
N. E. Briers b Gifford	....	39
†R. W. Tolchard not out	....	12
*B. F. Davison not out	....	9
B 1, l-b 7, w 1, n-b 5	....	14

1/84 2/93   (2 wkts, 25 overs) 112

P. B. Clift, M. A. Garnham, D. A. Wenlock, T. J. Boon, J. F. Steele, L. B. Taylor and K. Higgs did not bat.

Bowling: Alleyne 4–0–15–0; Inchmore 4–1–18–0; Pridgeon 4–0–26–0; Gifford 8–3–16–2; Cumbes 5–0–23–0.

Worcestershire

J. A. Ormrod c Garnham b Taylor	7
G. M. Turner run out	4
Younis Ahmed not out	18
E. J. O. Hemsley not out	21
L-b 4, n-b 1	5

1/11 2/13   (2 wkts, 10.4 overs)   55

P. A. Neale, †D. J. Humphries, H. Alleyne, J. D. Inchmore, *N. Gifford, A. P. Pridgeon and J. Cumbes did not bat.

Bowling: Higgs 4–0–21–0; Taylor 4–0–17–1; Clift 2.4–0–12–0.

Umpires: H. D. Bird and D. O. Oslear.

At Northampton, June 29. WORCESTERSHIRE lost to NORTHAMPTONSHIRE by seven wickets.

WORCESTERSHIRE v WARWICKSHIRE

At Worcester, July 6. Worcestershire won by 15 runs and halted their local rivals' run of eight consecutive victories – the best start by any county in the twelve seasons of the Sunday competition. Warwickshire's outstanding form attracted a crowd of 6,500 who paid £6,390, almost double Worcestershire's cash record for a John Player League fixture. Warwickshire's defeat was signposted by Turner's typically audacious innings of 48 (seven 4s) in 46 balls. Younis followed with 50 in sixty-three minutes, and although Doshi dismissed the two top scorers in a fine spell of three for 32, Worcestershire's total of 209 proved sufficient. Warwickshire started slowly, managing only 30 runs in ten overs, and victory was always unlikely, despite Amiss's 88 which took his Sunday total to 506 in only nine innings. Claughton joined him in a second-wicket stand of 96 and Ferreira, dropped twice, made 31 in a punishing partnership of 73 in eleven overs; but Worcestershire, with Neale saving countless runs in the deep, were more effective in the field than Warwickshire.

Worcestershire

G. M. Turner st Maynard b Doshi	48	*N. Gifford b Rouse	4
P. A. Neale c Oliver b Small	15	A. P. Pridgeon not out	1
Younis Ahmed c Rouse b Doshi	50	J. Cumbes c Amiss b Rouse	2
H. Alleyne c Maynard b Doshi	18	L-b 8, w 1, n-b 3	12
E. J. O. Hemsley run out	11		
S. P. Henderson b Ferreira	28	1/50 2/76 3/114 4/142 (40 overs) 209
†D. J. Humphries b Ferreira	5	5/151 6/174 7/200
J. D. Inchmore b Ferreira	15	8/203 9/207

Bowling: Willis 8–0–33–0; Rouse 8–0–44–2; Small 8–1–49–1; Doshi 8–0–32–3; Ferreira 8–0–39–3.

Warwickshire

D. L. Amiss run out	88	G. C. Small c Neale b Inchmore	0
T. A. Lloyd c Humphries b Alleyne	1	*R. G. D. Willis not out	0
J. A. Claughton run out	32		
G. W. Humpage lbw b Gifford	0	B 1, l-b 15, w 8, n-b 4	28
P. R. Oliver c Turner b Cumbes	10		
S. J. Rouse b Gifford	2	1/6 2/102 3/102 (8 wkts, 40 overs) 194
A. M. Ferreira c Younis b Alleyne	31	4/113 5/118 6/191
†C. Maynard not out	2	7/192 8/193

D. R. Doshi did not bat.

Bowling: Alleyne 8–1–30–2; Inchmore 8–1–19–1; Pridgeon 8–1–26–0; Cumbes 8–0–64–1; Gifford 8–0–27–2.

Umpires: A. G. T. Whitehead and P. S. G. Stevens.

WORCESTERSHIRE v LANCASHIRE

At Worcester, July 13. No result. Rain denied Worcestershire a likely victory after an excellent bowling performance by Alleyne, who took two wickets with his first ten balls and returned his best League figures. Lancashire lost half their side for 78, Lloyd's 60 receiving little support other than useful innings by Reidy and Simmons.

Lancashire

A. Kennedy c Neale b Alleyne	0	†G. Fowler b Alleyne	3
*F. C. Hayes c Humphries b Alleyne	1	N. Radford not out	6
D. Lloyd st Humphries b Younis	60	P. J. W. Allott not out	2
B. W. Reidy b Cumbes	23	L-b 16, n-b 1	17
I. Cockbain run out	9		
J. Abrahams c Turner b Pridgeon	0	1/0 2/7 3/54 4/77 (8 wkts, 39 overs) 148
J. Simmons c Gifford b Alleyne	27	5/78 6/124 7/140 8/140

W. Hogg did not bat.

Bowling: Alleyne 8–0–24–4; Inchmore 7–1–15–0; Cumbes 8–2–22–1; Pridgeon 8–0–29–1; Gifford 6–1–34–0; Younis 2–0–7–1.

Worcestershire

G. M. Turner, P. A. Neale, E. J. O. Hemsley, Younis Ahmed, S. P. Henderson, †D. J. Humphries, H. Alleyne, J. D. Inchmore, *N. Gifford, A. P. Pridgeon, J. Cumbes.

Umpires: C. T. Spencer and P. B. Wight.

At Nottingham, July 20. WORCESTERSHIRE beat NOTTINGHAMSHIRE by 18 runs.

WORCESTERSHIRE v SURREY

At Worcester, July 27. Worcestershire won by five wickets. After an opening partnership of 91 between Howarth and Clinton, Surrey slipped to 118 for five but Thomas took them to a sizeable total, hitting two 6s and five 4s in half an hour. However, it was not enough to withstand yet another assault by their former team-mate, Younis. He completed his fifth half-century in seven innings against Surrey and became only the third batsman to score 1,000 runs for two counties in the John Player League. Neale then finalised a comfortable Worcestershire win with fifteen balls to spare.

Surrey

G. P. Howarth b Gifford	55	S. T. Clarke b Inchmore	7
G. S. Clinton st Humphries b Gifford	34	P. I. Pocock not out	1
*R. D. V. Knight run out	5	R. G. L. Cheatle not out	0
D. M. Smith run out	0	B 15, n-b 2	17
G. R. J. Roope c Pridgeon b Inchmore	26		
M. A. Lynch lbw b Pridgeon	2	1/91 2/100 3/102 (9 wkts, 39 overs) 202
D. J. Thomas c Humphries b Inchmore	55	4/111 5/118 6/185 7/191
†C. J. Richards b Alleyne	0	8/200 9/201

Bowling: Alleyne 7–0–40–1; Inchmore 8–0–48–3; Younis 8–0–39–0; Pridgeon 8–0–29–1; Gifford 8–1–29–2.

Worcestershire

G. M. Turner c Lynch b Knight	21	T. S. Curtis not out	5
J. A. Ormrod b Pocock	37		
Younis Ahmed b Thomas	56	B 1, l-b 6, w 5	12
E. J. O. Hemsley b Richards b Pocock	9		
H. Alleyne b Cheatle	15	1/45 2/90 3/110 (5 wkts, 36.3 overs) 204	
P. A. Neale not out	49	4/125 5/180	

†D. J. Humphries, J. D. Inchmore, *N. Gifford and A. P. Pridgeon did not bat.

Bowling: Clarke 6.3–0–42–0; Thomas 8–0–38–1; Knight 6–0–31–1; Cheatle 8–0–42–1; Pocock 8–0–39–2.

Umpires: W. E. Alley and J. van Geloven.

At Weston-super-Mare, August 3. WORCESTERSHIRE lost to SOMERSET by eight wickets.

WORCESTERSHIRE v GLAMORGAN

At Worcester, August 10. Worcestershire won by seven wickets. Glamorgan never looked like gaining their first-ever Sunday League win in Worcestershire as the home pace bowlers, with seam and swing, whisked out their first six batsmen for 63 runs. Worcestershire's new wicket-keeper Fisher, with two catches and two stumpings (one standing up to Cumbes), took his total of dismissals to eleven in three innings. Nash's economical two for 8 in Worcestershire's reply included Turner's wicket off the first ball, but Ormrod and Neale found no serious hazards and Glamorgan's 88 was passed in the 29th over.

Glamorgan

A. Jones lbw b Holder	8	B. J. Lloyd b Gifford	14
J. A. Hopkins c Fisher b Inchmore	1	E. A. Moseley not out	7
G. C. Holmes lbw b Holder	2	A. J. Mack st Fisher b Cumbes	0
Javed Miandad b Cumbes	14		
N. G. Featherstone c Ormrod b Gifford	22	L-b 6	6
M. J. Llewellyn c Fisher b Pridgeon	7		
*M. A. Nash b Pridgeon	5	1/4 2/13 3/20 4/32 (34.2 overs) 88	
†E. W. Jones st Fisher b Gifford	2	5/47 6/63 7/67 8/68 9/87	

Bowling: Holder 6–1–11–2; Inchmore 6–2–7–1; Pridgeon 8–1–23–2; Cumbes 7.2–0–23–2; Gifford 7–0–18–3.

Worcestershire

G. M. Turner c E. W. Jones b Nash	0	S. P. Henderson not out	15
J. A. Ormrod run out	24	B 3, l-b 3, w 5 n-b 2	13
Younis Ahmed lbw b Nash	3		
P. A. Neale not out	36	1/0 2/17 3/59 (3 wkts, 28.5 overs) 91	

†P. B. Fisher, J. D. Inchmore, V. A. Holder, *N. Gifford, A. P. Pridgeon and J. Cumbes did not bat.

Bowling: Nash 6–3–8–2; Moseley 5–0–14–0; Holmes 4–1–11–0; Mack 4–0–11–0; Lloyd 7–2–23–0; Miandad 2.5–0–11–0.

Umpires: J. G. Langridge and A. G. T. Whitehead.

WORCESTERSHIRE v DERBYSHIRE

At Worcester, August 17. Derbyshire won by five wickets. Ormrod and Turner – dropped at cover in the opening over – gave Worcestershire a promising start with 87 in 23 overs; but the pitch always assisted the seamers and the innings subsided against excellent bowling by

Hendrick and Wood. Although Pridgeon achieved similar success for Worcestershire, the visitors were taken to victory by Wright, who batted throughout with seven 4s in his unbeaten 92. He was joined in a match-winning partnership of 81 by Barnett, who made only 12 in 22 overs.

Worcestershire

G. M. Turner c Miller b Wood	49	V. A. Holder run out		3
J. A. Ormrod c Miller b Hendrick	35	†P. B. Fisher not out		0
Younis Ahmed st Taylor b Wood	10	L-b 7, w 4, n-b 1		12
P. A. Neale not out	36			
S. P. Henderson b Tunnicliffe	13	1/87 2/95 3/111	(6 wkts, 40 overs)	158
J. D. Inchmore b Tunnicliffe	0	4/141 5/147 6/157		

*N. Gifford, A. P. Pridgeon and J. Cumbes did not bat.

Bowling: Tunnicliffe 8–1–41–2; Hendrick 8–1–23–1; Oldham 8–0–28–0; Miller 8–0–30–0; Wood 8–1–24–2.

Derbyshire

J. G. Wright not out	92	J. Walters not out		4
*G. Miller c Turner b Holder	8			
P. N. Kirsten lbw b Pridgeon	4	B 4, l-b 18, w 1, n-b 2		25
D. S. Steele c Henderson b Pridgeon	7			
K. J. Barnett lbw b Holder	12	1/24 2/36 3/53	(5 wkts, 39.1 overs)	159
B. Wood b Gifford	7	4/134 5/149		

†R. W. Taylor, C. J. Tunnicliffe, M. Hendrick and S. Oldham did not bat.

Bowling: Holder 8–0–27–2; Inchmore 8–1–36–0; Pridgeon 8–3–24–2; Cumbes 8–2–15–0; Gifford 7.1–0–32–1.

Umpires: R. Palmer and D. Shackleton.

At Colchester, August 24. WORCESTERSHIRE lost to ESSEX by 30 runs.

WORCESTERSHIRE v KENT

At Worcester, August 31. Worcestershire won by four wickets. The pitch, dusting on a spinner's length but dark and damp in the middle, played tricks for all types of bowling. Kent were given a good start by Benson and Johnson but then had considerable problems in reaching 140 for eight. The ball popped and turned for Gifford and did much the same for the two Kent spinners, Underwood and Johnson, who seemed to have the game won when Worcestershire were 69 for five. Johnson had taken two for 3 in six overs but was then hit for two 6s by Alleyne and another – the winning hit – by Hemsley off the first ball of the last over.

Kent

M. Benson b Gifford	29	N. J. Kemp b Gifford		3
G. W. Johnson run out	24	R. W. Hills not out		6
C. J. Tavaré b Cumbes	5	D. L. Underwood not out		1
C. S. Cowdrey c Henderson b Hemsley	14	B 4, l-b 9, w 2		15
*A. G. E. Ealham b Alleyne	27			
J. N. Shepherd c Neale b Alleyne	14	1/57 2/57 3/72	(8 wkts, 40 overs)	140
†A. P. E. Knott c Fisher b Pridgeon	2	4/79 5/108 6/110 7/129 8/137		

K. B. S. Jarvis did not bat.

Bowling: Alleyne 8–1–24–2; Pridgeon 8–0–26–1; Hemsley 8–0–35–1; Cumbes 8–1–22–1; Gifford 8–2–18–2.

Worcestershire

J. A. Ormrod c Knott b Underwood 6	H. Alleyne c Shepherd b Underwood.... 32
G. M. Turner c Underwood b Jarvis 21	*N. Gifford not out 6
Younis Ahmed c Cowdrey b Kemp 2	B 3, l-b 11, n-b 2........... 16
S. P. Henderson st Knott b Johnson 8	
P. A. Neale c Tavaré b Johnson........ 22	1/25 2/29 3/29 (6 wkts, 39.1 overs) 146
E. J. O. Hemsley not out 33	4/62 5/69 6/132

†P. B. Fisher, A. P. Pridgeon and J. Cumbes did not bat.

Bowling: Jarvis 7–0–33–1; Shepherd 4–1–7–0; Kemp 8–1–17–1; Underwood 8–0–31–2; Johnson 7.1–4–21–2; Hills 5–0–21–0.

Umpires: D. J. Dennis and B. J. Meyer.

YORKSHIRE

YORKSHIRE v WORCESTERSHIRE

At Bradford, May 4. Worcestershire won by seven wickets. Yorkshire, put in, were handicapped by a slow opening stand of 87 in 23 overs by Boycott and Hampshire, and although Athey and Love repaired some of the damage, Worcestershire were never in trouble. The winners always had something in hand as Younis, driving fluently on either side of the wicket, made the most of some poor bowling.

Yorkshire

G. Boycott c Humphries b Inchmore.... 66	S. N. Hartley not out 2
*J. H. Hampshire b Gifford 44	C. M. Old not out................... 1
C. W. J. Athey b Alleyne 33	L-b 9, w 1............... 10
J. D. Love b Alleyne................. 19	
†D. L. Bairstow b Gifford 16	1/87 2/128 3/163 (6 wkts, 40 overs) 191
G. B. Stevenson b Alleyne 0	4/178 5/178 6/188

A. Ramage, A. Sidebottom and H. P. Cooper did not bat.

Bowling: Alleyne 8–0–26–3; Inchmore 8–0–23–1; Pridgeon 8–0–42–0; Younis 8–0–34–0; Gifford 8–0–56–2.

Worcestershire

J. A. Ormrod lbw b Ramage 42	D. N. Patel not out................. 12
G. M. Turner c Hampshire b Old....... 2	
Younis Ahmed not out............... 98	B 8, l-b 4, w 1, n-b 2......... 15
E. J. O. Hemsley c Bairstow	
b Sidebottom. 26	1/4 2/111 (3 wkts, 38.1 overs) 195

B. J. R. Jones, †D. J. Humphries, J. D. Inchmore, H. Alleyne, *N. Gifford and A. P. Pridgeon did not bat.

Bowling: Old 8–0–30–1; Stevenson 7.1–1–25–0; Sidebottom 8–0–33–1; Ramage 8–0–49–1; Cooper 7–0–43–0.

Umpires: R. Aspinall and A. Jepson.

YORKSHIRE v WARWICKSHIRE

At Huddersfield, May 11. Warwickshire won by five wickets. Boycott, in good form, had to retire after losing two contact lenses on the field and, despite a good stand between Athey and Bairstow, Yorkshire failed to score sufficient runs after being sent in on a good pitch with a fast outfield. Furthermore their bowling was again dreadful, and Claughton and Lloyd scored freely as the field was spread farther and wider.

Yorkshire

G. Boycott retired not out	37	P. Carrick not out	2
*J. H. Hampshire c Lloyd b Humpage	27	A. Sidebottom run out	0
C. W. J. Athey b Willis	50		
K. Sharp c Willis b Doshi	9	B 2, l-b 19, n-b 1	22
J. D. Love c and b Doshi	8		
†D. L. Bairstow c Amiss b Small	55	1/61 2/87 3/109 (8 wkts, 40 overs) 223	
C. M. Old c Maynard b Willis	9	4/189 5/205 6/212 7/222	
G. B. Stevenson c Claughton b Small	4	8/223	

H. P. Cooper did not bat.

Bowling: Willis 8–1–31–2; Small 8–0–53–2; Ferriera 8–1–23–0; Humpage 6–0–36–1; Doshi 8–1–38–2; Oliver 2–0–20–0.

Warwickshire

D. L. Amiss b Boycott	31	A. M. Ferreira not out	23
K. D. Smith lbw b Sidebottom	17		
T. A. Lloyd run out	55	B 1, l-b 14, w 2, n-b 3	20
J. A. Claughton c Hampshire b Cooper	65		
P. R. Oliver st Bairstow b Carrick	0	1/46 2/57 (5 wkts, 37.3 overs) 225	
G. W. Humpage not out	14	3/182 4/185 5/185	

†C. Maynard, G. C. Small, *R. G. D. Willis and D. R. Doshi did not bat.

Bowling: Old 8–0–35–0; Stevenson 6.3–0–47–0; Sidebottom 5–1–34–1; Boycott 6–0–29–1; Cooper 7–0–33–1; Carrick 5–1–27–1.

Umpires: H. D. Bird and T. W. Spencer.

At Taunton, May 18. YORKSHIRE lost to SOMERSET by seven wickets.

YORKSHIRE v SUSSEX

At Middlesbrough, June 1. Sussex won by three wickets. Yorkshire's fourth successive defeat made this their worst start in the competition. Sent in, Yorkshire were given a useful start by Boycott and Athey, who made 93 from nineteen overs in a match reduced by rain to 28 overs. Steady Sussex bowling then brought about a collapse. Old bowled his overs straight through, which exposed the bowling in the later stages of the innings, and Sussex were allowed to recover from 98 for six, thanks to some splendid batting by Phillipson.

Yorkshire

G. Boycott c Mendis b Imran	38	*C. M. Old run out	6
C. W. J. Athey b Waller	50	P. Carrick not out	2
J. D. Love c Heath b le Roux	0	B 1, l-b 8, w 2	11
K. Sharp run out	15		
S. N. Hartley not out	16	1/93 2/93 3/111 (6 wkts, 28 overs) 138	
†D. L. Bairstow c Long b Imran	0	4/111 5/112 6/126	

G. B. Stevenson, A. Sidebottom and H. P. Cooper did not bat.

Bowling: le Roux 8–0–30–1; Wells 4–0–25–0; Imran 8–0–30–2; Spencer 6–1–29–0; Waller 2–0–13–1.

Sussex

T. D. Booth Jones c Old b Sidebottom...	24	*†A. Long b Cooper	14
G. D. Mendis lbw b Old	15	J. R. Heath not out	4
P. W. G. Parker c Athey b Stevenson ...	31		
Imran Khan run out	13	L-b 10, w 2	12
C. P. Phillipson not out	25		
G. S. le Roux c Boycott b Stevenson ...	0	1/30 2/56 3/92 (7 wkts, 27.2 overs) 139	
C. M. Wells c Bairstow b Sidebottom ..	1	4/94 5/94 6/98 7/135	

J. Spencer and C. E. Waller did not bat.

Bowling: Old 8–0–22–1; Stevenson 8–0–43–2; Sidebottom 8–0–24–2; Cooper 3.2–0–38–1.

Umpires: R. Julian and R. Palmer.

At Lord's, June 8. YORKSHIRE lost to MIDDLESEX by three wickets.

At Swansea, June 15. YORKSHIRE lost to GLAMORGAN on faster scoring-rate.

YORKSHIRE v NOTTINGHAMSHIRE

At Scarborough, June 22. Yorkshire won by four wickets. After Yorkshire had won the toss for the first time, a return to form by Old and Stevenson made the going difficult for the Nottinghamshire batsmen. Randall and Rice looked threatening until they were dismissed by Hartley, who was bowling for the first time in the competition. Rain reduced Yorkshire's target to 122 from 32 overs and Bairstow took them to victory with a typically robust and professional innings.

Nottinghamshire

P. A. Todd c Bairstow b Old	4	P. J. Hacker lbw b Old	0
R. T. Robinson b Old................	0	K. E. Cooper b Old	3
D. W. Randall c Carrick b Hartley	48	M. K. Bore not out................	10
*C. E. B. Rice c Ingham b Hartley	25		
J. D. Birch c Carrick b Hartley	27	L-b 15, w 2	17
H. T. Tunnicliffe b Stevenson	1		
†B. Hassan not out	16	1/4 2/5 3/69 (9 wkts, 40 overs) 152	
E. E. Hemmings c Bairstow		4/116 5/118 6/122 7/125	
b Sidebottom.	1	8/128 9/132	

Bowling: Old 8–1–26–4; Stevenson 8–1–14–1; Sidebottom 8–0–25–1; Athey 8–0–39–0; Hartley 8–1–31–3.

Yorkshire

J. D. Love st Hassan b Hemmings	28	*C. M. Old b Hacker	0
C. W. J. Athey run out	31	P. G. Ingham not out...............	11
G. B. Stevenson c Robinson b Hemmings	6	B 1, l-b 5, w 1, n-b 1	8
†D. L. Bairstow not out..............	25		
S. N. Hartley c Robinson b Hemmmings.	3	1/54 2/68 3/71 (6 wkts, 30.2 overs) 123	
P. Carrick c and b Hacker	11	4/99 5/99 6/100	

K. Sharp, A. Sidebottom and M. D. Moxon did not bat.

Bowling: Cooper 7–1–24–0; Hacker 7.2–1–42–2; Hemmmings 8–1–27–3; Bore 8–1–22–0.

Umpires: R. Aspinall and C. T. Spencer.

At Basingstoke, June 29. YORKSHIRE beat HAMPSHIRE by 10 runs.

YORKSHIRE v ESSEX

At Leeds, July 6. Yorkshire won by seven wickets. Essex, put in on a seaming pitch, never looked like accumulating sufficient runs, with Hartley proving his value as a utility bowler. Gooch was the only obstacle to Yorkshire's progress. Essex were as subdued with the ball as they had been with the bat, and Ingham and Hampshire set the home county on the way to victory with 98 in 21 overs.

Essex

G. A. Gooch b Hartley	65	R. Herbert c Stevenson b Old	8
M. S. A. McEvoy c Sharp b Hartley	7	†N. Smith not out	2
K. S. McEwan c Ingham b Hartley	8		
*K. W. R. Fletcher b Sidebottom	3	B 1, l-b 7, w 5, n-b 4	17
B. R. Hardie run out	7		
K. R. Pont not out	37	1/29 2/42 3/54 (8 wkts, 39 overs) 156	
D. R. Pringle b Stevenson	1	4/91 5/115 6/122 7/129	
N. Phillip b Carrick	1	8/150	

G. E. Sainsbury did not bat.

Bowling: Old 7–0–22–1; Stevenson 8–0–21–1; Sidebottom 8–0–26–1; Hartley 8–0–32–3; Carrick 6–1–25–1; Athey 2–0–13–0.

Yorkshire

P. G. Ingham not out	53	K. Sharp not out	4
*J. H. Hampshire c Hardie b Herbert	66	L-b 9, w 6	15
C. W. J. Athey run out	13		
J. D. Love c McEvoy b Gooch	6	1/98 2/119 3/142 (3 wkts, 37.5 overs) 157	

S. N. Hartley, P. Carrick, †D. L. Bairstow, C. M. Old, G. B. Stevenson and A. Sidebottom did not bat.

Bowling: Sainsbury 4–1–18–0; Herbert 4–0–24–1; Phillip 6.5–0–30–0; Gooch 8–0–23–1; Pringle 8–2–28–0; Pont 7–1–19–0.

Umpires: H. D. Bird and D. O. Oslear.

At The Oval, July 13. YORKSHIRE lost to SURREY on faster scoring-rate.

YORKSHIRE v GLOUCESTERSHIRE

At Hull, July 27. Yorkshire won by six wickets. Gloucestershire, put in, were indebted to a third-wicket partnership of 100 in thirteen overs by Zaheer (two 6s and six 4s) and Procter. Ingham again batted well for Yorkshire, who made the most of some moderate bowling on an easy-paced pitch where only Bainbridge threatened the batsmen.

Gloucestershire

Zaheer Abbas not out	104	M. W. Stovold not out	9
B. C. Broad c and b Cope	17	B 7, l-b 9, w 2, n-b 1	19
P. Bainbridge c Bairstow b Cope	13		
M. J. Procter run out	61	1/40 2/80 (4 wkts, 40 overs) 232	
†A. W. Stovold b Old	9	3/180 4/214	

A. J. Hignell, M. D. Partridge, D. A. Graveney, A. H. Wilkins and B. M. Brain did not bat.

Bowling: Old 8–1–35–1; Stevenson 8–0–45–0; Cooper 8–0–41–0; Cope 8–1–35–2; Carrick 6–0–42–0; Hartley 2–0–15–0.

Yorkshire

P. G. Ingham not out	87	S. N. Hartley not out	30
C. W. J. Athey b Bainbridge	38	B 2, l-b 10, w 5, n-b 4	21
*C. M. Old b Wilkins	18		—
J. D. Love st A. W. Stovold b Graveney	2	1/99 2/118	(4 wkts, 38 overs) 233
G. B. Stevenson b Procter	37	3/131 4/194	

M. Moxon, P. Carrick, †D. L. Bairstow, H. P. Cooper and G. A. Cope did not bat.

Bowling: Procter 7–0–50–1; Brain 8–0–38–0; Bainbridge 8–0–25–1; Wilkins 7–0–42–1; Graveney 4–0–29–1; Partridge 2–0–13–0; Broad 2–0–15–0.

Umpires: T. W. Spencer and A. G. T. Whitehead.

YORKSHIRE v DERBYSHIRE

At Leeds, August 3. Yorkshire won by four wickets, their innings being reduced to 37 overs in a rain-affected match. On a pitch that allowed some movement off the seam, Stevenson followed an economical bowling spell with a career-best John Player League innings that proved decisive in a low-scoring match. Derbyshire, whose bowling tactics were not easy to follow, suffered a major setback when Old brilliantly ran out the prolific Kirsten.

Derbyshire

*G. Miller c Bairstow b Old	7	C. J. Tunnicliffe b Old	5
J. G. Wright c Cope b Stevenson	8	M. Hendrick b Old	13
P. N. Kirsten run out	48	S. Oldham not out	1
D. S. Steele b Boycott	11	B 2, l-b 7, w 3, n-b 1	13
K. J. Barnett b Hartley	7		—
B. Wood b Hartley	1	1/15 2/15 3/48	(9 wkts, 40 overs) 145
J. Walters run out	14	4/87 5/89 6/94 7/115	
†R. W. Taylor not out	17	8/120 9/138	

Bowling: Old 8–1–32–3; Stevenson 8–0–20–1; Hartley 8–0–24–2; Boycott 8–0–31–1; Cooper 8–0–25–0.

Yorkshire

P. G. Ingham lbw b Oldham	6	†D. L. Bairstow not out	13
G. Boycott b Wood	11	P. Carrick not out	9
C. W. J. Athey c and b Wood	15	L-b 7, w 2, n-b 1	10
J. D. Love c Taylor b Hendrick	1		—
S. N. Hartley b Miller	30	1/9 2/28 3/29	(6 wkts, 36 overs) 138
G. B. Stevenson c Barnett b Oldham	43	4/40 5/102 6/127	

*C. M. Old, H. P. Cooper and G. A. Cope did not bat.

Bowling: Tunnicliffe 7–1–23–0; Oldham 8–0–34–2; Hendrick 8–1–15–1; Wood 8–0–22–2; Miller 5–0–34–1.

Umpires: W. L. Budd and K. E. Palmer.

At Leicester, August 10. YORKSHIRE lost to LEICESTERSHIRE by five wickets.

At Manchester, August 24. YORKSHIRE lost to LANCASHIRE by 1 run.

YORKSHIRE v NORTHAMPTONSHIRE

At Scarborough, August 31. Yorkshire won by two wickets. On a slightly seaming pitch, Northamptonshire struggled against accurate bowling before sixth-wicket pair Boyd-Moss and Sarfraz – who hit a League best 59 not out – added 74 from nineteen overs. In reply Yorkshire were in trouble at 94 for seven until Sidebottom and Coverdale turned the tide with some excellent running between the wickets.

Northamptonshire

W. Larkins lbw b Stevenson	17	†G. Sharp b Stevenson ... 3
*G. Cook c Stevenson b Dennis	7	N. A. Mallender not out ... 1
A. J. Lamb b Cooper	7	
R. G. Williams c Coverdale b Cooper	10	L-b 5, w 5, n-b 2 ... 12
T. J. Yardley c Hampshire b Sidebottom	1	
R. J. Boyd-Moss c Cooper b Stevenson	34	1/25 2/33 3/35 (7 wkts, 40 overs) 151
Sarfraz Nawaz not out	59	4/39 5/51 6/125 7/140

T. M. Lamb and B. J. Griffiths did not bat.

Bowling: Stevenson 8–2–19–3; Dennis 8–1–22–1; Cooper 8–4–18–2; Sidebottom 8–0–29–1; Hartley 6–0–40–0; Carrick 2–0–11–0.

Yorkshire

R. G. Lumb c Sharp b Griffiths	11	A. Sidebottom c Larkins b Griffiths ... 31
*J. H. Hampshire c Williams b Griffiths	1	†S. P. Coverdale not out ... 17
J. D. Love b Mallender	24	H. P. Cooper not out ... 4
P. G. Ingham c Larkins b Williams	41	B 2, l-b 10, w 6, n-b 2 ... 20
G. B. Stevenson c and b Williams	1	
S. N. Hartley c Mallender b Williams	2	1/6 2/22 3/56 (8 wkts, 39.1 overs) 155
P. Carrick c Boyd-Moss b Williams	3	4/63 5/76 6/80 7/94 8/137

S. J. Dennis did not bat.

Bowling: Sarfraz 8–3–27–0; Griffiths 7.1–0–28–3; T. M. Lamb 8–0–30–0; Mallender 8–0–28–1; Williams 8–1–22–4.

Umpires: C. Cook and A. Jepson.

At Canterbury, September 7. YORKSHIRE lost to KENT by 9 runs.

JOHN PLAYER LEAGUE RECORDS

Batting

Highest score: 163* C. G. Greenidge – Hampshire v Warwickshire (Birmingham) 1979. (150 hundreds have been scored in this League.)

Most runs in a season: 814 C. E. B. Rice (Nottinghamshire) 1977.

Most sixes in an innings: 10 C. G. Greenidge – Hampshire v Warwickshire (Birmingham) 1979.

Most sixes by a team in an innings: 14 Leicestershire v Somerset (Frome) 1970.

Most sixes in a season: 26 – I. V. A. Richards (Somerset) 1977.

Highest total: 307 for four, Worcestershire v Derbyshire (Worcester) 1975.

Highest total – batting second: 261 for eight, Warwickshire v Nottinghamshire (Birmingham) 1976; 261 Worcestershire v Sussex (Horsham) 1980.

Highest match aggregate: 554 Sussex (293 for four) v Worcestershire (261) (Horsham) 1980.

Lowest total: 23 Middlesex v Yorkshire (Leeds) 1974.

Shortest complete innings: 16 overs, Northamptonshire 59 v Middlesex (Tring) 1974.

Shortest match: 2 hr 13 min (40.3 overs), Essex v Northamptonshire (Ilford) 1971.

Biggest victories: 190 runs, Kent beat Northamptonshire (Brackley) 1973.
There have been sixteen instances of victory by ten wickets – by Derbyshire, Essex, Glamorgan, Hampshire, Leicestershire (twice), Middlesex (twice), Somerset, Surrey (twice), Warwickshire (twice), Worcestershire and Yorkshire (twice).

Ties: Nottinghamshire v Kent (Nottingham) 1969 in match reduced to 20 overs.
Gloucestershire v Hampshire (Bristol) 1972.
Gloucestershire v Northamptonshire (Bristol) 1972.
Surrey v Worcestershire (Byfleet) 1973.
Middlesex v Lancashire (Lord's) 1974.
Sussex v Leicestershire (Hove) 1974.
Lancashire v Worcestershire (Manchester) 1975.
Somerset v Glamorgan (Taunton) 1975.
Warwickshire v Kent (Birmingham) 1980.

Record Partnerships for each Wicket

218 for 1st	A. R. Butcher and G. P. Howarth, Surrey v Gloucestershire at The Oval	1976
179 for 2nd	B. W. Luckhurst and M. H. Denness, Kent v Somerset at Canterbury	1973
182 for 3rd	H. Pilling and C. H. Lloyd, Lancashire v Somerset at Manchester	1970
175* for 4th	M. J. K. Smith and D. L. Amiss, Warwickshire v Yorkshire at Birmingham	1970
163 for 5th	A. G. E. Ealham and B. D. Julien, Kent v Leicestershire at Leicester	1977
121 for 6th	C. P. Wilkins and A. J. Borrington, Derbyshire v Warwickshire at Chesterfield	1972
96* for 7th	R. Illingworth and J. Birkenshaw, Leicestershire v Somerset at Leicester	1971
95* for 8th	D. Breakwell and K. F. Jennings, Somerset v Nottinghamshire at Nottingham	1976
86 for 9th	D. P. Hughes and P. Lever, Lancashire v Essex at Leyton	1973
57 for 10th	D. A. Graveney and J. B. Mortimore, Gloucestershire v Lancashire at Tewkesbury	1973

Bowling

Best analyses: eight for 26, K. D. Boyce, Essex v Lancashire at Manchester, 1971; seven for 15, R. A. Hutton, Yorkshire v Worcestershire at Leeds, 1969; seven for 39, A. Hodgson, Northamptonshire v Somerset at Northampton, 1976; six for 6, R. W. Hooker, Middlesex v Surrey at Lord's, 1969; six for 7, M. Hendrick, Derbyshire v Nottinghamshire at Nottingham, 1972.

Four wickets in four balls: A. Ward, Derbyshire v Sussex at Derby, 1970.

Hat-tricks: A. Ward, Derbyshire v Sussex at Derby, 1970; R. Palmer, Somerset v Gloucestershire at Bristol, 1970; K. D. Boyce, Essex v Somerset at Westcliff, 1971; G. D. McKenzie, Leicestershire v Essex at Leicester, 1972; R. G. D. Willis, Warwickshire v Yorkshire at Birmingham, 1973; W. Blenkiron, Warwickshire v Derbyshire at Buxton, 1974; A. Buss, Sussex v Worcestershire at Hastings, 1974; J. M. Rice, Hampshire v Northamptonshire at Southampton, 1975; M. A. Nash, Glamorgan v Worcestershire at Worcester, 1975; A. Hodgson, Northamptonshire v Somerset at Northampton, 1976; A. E. Cordle, Glamorgan v Hampshire at Portsmouth, 1979; C. J. Tunnicliffe, Derbyshire v Worcestershire at Derby, 1979.

Most economical analysis: 8–8–0–0; B. A. Langford, Somerset v Essex at Yeovil, 1969.

Most expensive analysis: 8–0–79–1; R. E. East, Essex v Glamorgan at Swansea, 1969.

Most wickets in a season: 34 R. J. Clapp (Somerset) 1974.

RULES OF THE JOHN PLAYER LEAGUE

(As applied in 1980)

Hours of Play

All matches shall commence at 2.00 p.m., with a tea interval of twenty minutes at 4.10 p.m., or between innings, whichever is the earlier. The duration and time of the tea interval can be varied in the case of an interrupted match. Close of play shall normally be at 6.40 p.m., but play may continue after that time if, in the opinion of the umpires, the overs remaining to be bowled can be completed by 7.00 p.m.

Length of Innings

(i) In an uninterrupted match:
    (a) Each team shall bat for 40 overs unless all out earlier.
    (b) In the possible event of the team fielding first failing to bowl 40 overs by 4.10 p.m., the over in progress shall be completed and the innings of the team batting second shall be limited to the same number of overs as the innings of the team batting first. See Note 1.
    (c) If the team batting first is all out and its last wicket falls within two minutes of the scheduled time for the tea interval, the innings of the side batting second shall be limited to the same number of overs as the innings of the team batting first (the over in which the last wicket falls to count as a complete over).

(ii) In matches where the start is delayed or play is suspended:
    (a) The object shall always be to rearrange the number of overs so that both teams have the opportunity of batting for the same number of overs (minimum ten overs each team). The calculation of the number of overs to be bowled shall be based on an average rate of eighteen overs per hour (one over per $3\frac{1}{3}$ minutes or part thereof) in the time remaining before close of play at 6.40 p.m. See Note 2.
    (b) If the number of overs of the side batting first is reduced, no fixed time will be specified for the close of their innings.
    (c) If, owing to a suspension of play during the innings of the team batting second, it is not possible for that team to have the opportunity of batting for the same number of overs as the team batting first, they will bat for a number of overs to be calculated as in (ii) (a).
    (d) In the event of a suspension occurring in the middle of an over, the full number of overs to be bowled in the time remaining will be calculated as in (ii) (a), any balls remaining to be bowled in the over during which play was suspended being added.
    (e) The team batting second shall not bat for a greater number of overs than the first team, unless the latter has been all out in fewer than the agreed number of overs.

Note 1: All teams are normally required to bowl at an average rate of twenty overs per hour. It is appreciated, however, that in certain exceptional circumstances it may not be possible to attain this average, and a short additional period for each innings is allowed in the Hours of Play. If, at 6.40 p.m. more than three overs remain to be bowled, play may continue as allowed in Hours of Play, but the matter will be referred to the Discipline Committee.

If the umpires report that a team fielding first has failed to bowl its full quota of overs on account of unnecessary "time wasting", the matter will also be referred to the Discipline Committee.

Note 2: Umpires will notify the home authority of the time of resumption of play, following any delay or suspension, immediately they have reached a decision. The home authority will provide a representative who will be responsible for assisting umpires in calculating the revised number of overs to be played in the match and for notifying the decision of the umpires immediately to all concerned.

The Result

(i) A result can be achieved only if both teams have batted for at least ten overs, unless one team has been all out in less than ten overs or unless the team batting second scores enough runs to win in fewer than 10 overs. All other matches in which one or both teams have not had an opportunity of batting for a minimum of ten overs shall be declared "No Result" matches.

(ii) In matches in which both teams have had an opportunity of batting for the agreed number of overs (i.e. 40 overs each, in an uninterrupted match, or a lesser number of overs in an interrupted match) the team scoring the higher number of runs shall be the winner. If the scores are equal, the result shall be a "Tie" and no account shall be taken of the number of wickets which have fallen.

(iii) If the team batting second have not had the opportunity to complete the agreed number of overs, and have neither been all out nor have passed their opponent's score, the following shall apply:

    (a) If the match is abandoned before 6.40 p.m., the result shall be decided on the average run-rate throughout both innings.

    (b) If, due to suspension of play, the number of overs in the innings of the side batting second has to be revised, the target score shall be calculated by multiplying the reduced number of overs by the average runs per over scored by the side batting first.

(iv) In the event of the team batting first being all out in less than their full quota of overs, the calculation of their average run-rate shall be based on the full quota of overs to which they would have been entitled and not on the number of overs in which they were dismissed.

Number of Overs per Bowler

If a match starts as a 40 overs match, no bowler may bowl more than eight overs in an innings and this allowance shall not be reduced even though the total overs may subsequently be restricted owing to weather interference. If, however, the start of a match is delayed and the overs of both teams are restricted to fewer than 40 overs, no bowler may bowl more than one fifth of the total overs allowed, except that where the total overs is not divisible by five, an additional over shall be allowed to the minimum number of bowlers necessary to make up the balance – e.g. in a 33 overs match, three bowlers may bowl a maximum of seven overs and no other bowler more than six overs. In a match where the innings of either or both teams is reduced after the start of the match, the maximum number of overs allowed per bowler shall remain as at the start of the match.

    In the event of a bowler breaking down and being unable to complete an over, the remaining balls will be bowled by another bowler. Such part of an over will count as a full over only in so far as each bowler's limit is concerned.

    The number of overs bowled by each individual bowler shall be indicated on the scoreboard, from the commencement of an innings.

Limitation of the Bowler's Run-up

The bowler's run-up, including his preliminary approach, shall be limited to fifteen yards, to be measured from the wicket. A white line will mark the maximum distance allowed.

Covering of the Pitch

The pitch shall be fully covered in the event of rain.

Law 14 – Declarations

Law 14 will not apply in this competition. The captain of the batting side may not declare his innings closed at any time during the course of a match.

Law 24.1 – No Ball – Mode of Delivery

Law 24.1 will apply in this competition, except that no bowler may deliver the ball underarm.

Law 25.1 – Wide Ball – Judging a Wide

Umpires are instructed to apply a very strict and consistent interpretation in regard to this Law in order to prevent negative bowling wide of the wicket or over the batsman's head.

    The following criteria should be adopted as a guide to umpires:

(i) If the ball passes either side of the wicket sufficiently wide to make it virtually impossible for the striker to play a "normal cricket stroke" both from where he is standing and from where he should normally be standing at the crease, the umpire should call and signal "Wide".

(ii) If the ball passes over head height of the striker standing upright at the crease, the umpire should call and signal "Wide".

Note: The above provisions do not apply if the striker makes contact with the ball, or if it passes below head height between the striker and the wicket.

Other Playing Conditions

Except as specified in these Playing Conditions, the Playing Conditions for first-class matches in the United Kingdom will apply.

Scoring of Points

(i) The team winning the match to score four points.

(ii) In the event of a "Tie", each team to score two points.

(iii) In a "No Result" match, each team to score two points.

(iv) In the event of two or more teams finishing with an equal number of points for any of the first three places, their final positions will be decided by:
    (a) The most wins or, if still equal
    (b) The most away wins or, if still equal
    (c) The higher run-rate throughout the season.

MINOR COUNTIES CHAMPIONSHIP, 1980

Bedfordshire had a poor season, achieving only two wins, although on two other occasions victory seemed within reach. Apart from A. Durose's return of seven for 104 against Suffolk, the bowling was disappointing and the batting unreliable; M. G. Stedman's maiden century, also against Suffolk, was the only hundred scored for the county in 1980.

Injury and illness hampered the improved form of **Berkshire**, who won two of their first three matches, defeating Buckinghamshire and Dorset, before losing the next four. Captain G. E. J. Child excelled behind the stumps, but otherwise too many catches were dropped and the batting was often careless. The bowling depended heavily on P. J. Lewington as well as J. H. Jones, who returned seven for 29 against Dorset.

With key players often unavailable, **Buckinghamshire** called on 25 players during the season. Yet a strong team spirit was maintained under the new captain, D. E. Smith. They finished lower in the table than at any time since 1966 and had to wait until August before achieving their only win (against Bedfordshire), followed by an exciting tied match with Norfolk. S. A. Mehar and A. W. Lyon performed creditably in a weak attack, Mehar returning twelve for 58 against Hertfordshire at High Wycombe. Newcomer R. G. Humphrey scored a century against Hertfordshire in his first match for the county, and all-rounder K. I. Hodgson, a Cambridge undergraduate, made a useful contribution.

Cambridgeshire, with no wins, dropped further down the table. D. C. Collard was the most successful bowler, taking twelve for 65 against Hertfordshire, while N. T. Gadsby, playing his first full season, showed considerable ability as an opening batsman.

After their disappointment in the previous season, **Cheshire** made a spectacular recovery in 1980, moving sixteen places up the table to fourth, to qualify for the NatWest Bank Trophy in 1981. Their success came from good all-round team-work and fine fielding. Pakistan Test player Mudassar Nazar brought stability to the batting, as did experienced players J. A. Sutton and D. Bailey. Slow left-armer T. J. Taylor excelled in his first full season and was well supported by pace bowler I. J. Gemmell.

Cornwall's position near the bottom of the table was a disappointment, for their batsmen had performed well. The burden of the attack was again borne by M. O. Trenwith and D. A. Toseland, who lacked adequate support.

Cumberland, at the foot of the table for the third time in succession, had their worst season since they first competed in 1956. A weak middle order failed to support openers L. Baichan and R. Entwistle, while D. Lupton was the only bowler to find form.

Devon began the season in style, defeating Berkshire by ten wickets with A. W. Allin returning match figures of fourteen for 89. However, they won only two more matches. The batting, led by R. C. Tolchard, often lacked aggression, and the fielding was inconsistent. A. W. Allin and D. I. Yeabsley were the leading wicket-takers in an attack that often failed to bowl out opponents.

Needing one more win to qualify for the NatWest Trophy in 1981, **Dorset** failed by 10 runs to beat Somerset II in their last match. Yet they had an otherwise satisfactory season. In a strong batting line-up, R. V. Lewis, in his first year as captain, scored 799 runs, while all-rounder R. J. Murrills batted consistently and bowled his leg-spinners tidily. Apart from J. F. Blackburn, who fielded brilliantly, the catching was generally mediocre. The attack relied heavily on C. W. Allen (slow left-arm) who took 40 wickets, nearly three times as many as the next highest total.

Durham had an outstanding season, setting new records and winning the Minor Counties Championship for the seventh time, having been runners-up for the three previous years. They ended the season unbeaten in 45 consecutive Minor Counties matches, one more than the earlier record set by Surrey II in 1953-56. In addition, they won seven of their ten matches – a feat which was last achieved in 1911. S. Greensword had a memorable season, scoring 868 runs and capturing 21 wickets to become the fourteenth bowler to take 200 wickets for

Durham. He also became the first Durham batsman to score four centuries in a season, and the first to hit two hundreds in a match (against Staffordshire at Brewood). Greensword was on the field for all of this match, and is believed to be the first Durham player to achieve this distinction. Wasim Raja again scored prolifically, as did the new captain, N. A. Riddell, who maintained an excellent team spirit. B. L. Cairns, who took eleven for 84 against Cumberland, headed the Minor Counties bowling averages, and on four occasions he took six wickets in an innings. He received strong support from P. J. Kippax, Greensword and Wasim Raja.

Runners-up **Hertfordshire** enjoyed a successful season in which they won six of their ten matches. Many of the experienced players were regularly available, with a significant contribution coming from P. E. McEwan, who later toured with the New Zealanders to Australia. R. L. Johns and J. D. W. Wright led the bowling, taking 40 wickets each, and A. R. Garofall made a valuable all-round contribution.

Lancashire Second Eleven had a disappointing season, although there were encouraging individual performances. G. Fowler made a century against Cumberland and I. Cockbain hit one against Shropshire. Slow left-arm bowler B. Thorpe scored 81 not out against Cumberland.

Lincolnshire also had a poor season. In the absence of experienced middle-order batsmen, the scoring-rate tended to be slow in the first innings, despite the outstanding form of G. Robinson and P. D. Johnson. D. Marshall (slow left-arm) performed consistently, but the bowling lacked penetration and the fielding fell below its usual high standard, although G. Draper kept wicket efficiently.

When their last match, against Buckinghamshire, was tied, **Norfolk** failed by 0.2 of a point to qualify for the NatWest Bank Trophy in 1980. Although T. Barnes took ten wickets in a match against Lincolnshire and E. Wright took seven for 39 against Cambridgeshire, the bowling and fielding failed to match the high standard of the side's batting, which was led by captain P. J. Sharpe, S. G. Plumb and F. L. Q. Handley.

Northumberland, strengthened by the engagement of Mushtaq Mohammad as professional, were disappointed that they moved up only one place to twelfth position. Nevertheless, they recorded three decisive victories, defeating Lancashire II by an innings and 91 runs and by 102 runs, and Cumberland by six wickets. K. Pearson, with 956 runs, was outstanding and was unfortunate to miss the last match and the opportunity to take his aggregate to 1,000 runs. The side lacked support for the opening batsmen and bowlers.

Oxfordshire, in sixth position, qualified for the NatWest Bank Trophy in 1981. Their strength lay in the fielding, which was outstanding. The only century for the county was hit against Dorset by A. Townsley, who headed the batting averages, while P. J. Garner, who scored the most runs, missed his century by 1 run in the match against Devon. S. R. Porter was the leading wicket-taker and twice took six wickets in an innings – both against Dorset.

Indifferent batting handicapped **Shropshire,** who often failed to clinch victory after being in a winning position. J. S. Johnson led the batting with an average of 65.75. B. Perry took ten for 85 against Cheshire and headed the averages, although D. S. de Silva took the most wickets, including seven for 73 in an innings against Staffordshire.

Somerset II moved sixteen places up the table in 1980, finishing in third position, with four wins. Outstanding performances were achieved by two young players; Cambridge Blue N. Russom excelled with both bat and ball, while R. L. Ollis scored the most runs in a side in which six batsmen averaged more than 50.

Another disappointing season for **Staffordshire** left them in sixteenth position. The batting depended on G. S. Warner, P. A. Marshall and P. N. Gill, who scored 144 against Lincolnshire. Leading bowlers were R. Boothroyd, R. W. Flower and F. D. Stephenson, who was disappointing in his first season. A. Griffiths was again in excellent form behind the stumps.

Champions in 1979, **Suffolk** slipped to fifth place in 1980. In the absence of the injured R. E. Cunnell and R. P. Done, the side were indebted to nineteen-year-old Queenslander M. G. Maranta, whose all-round contribution was notable. R. F. Howlett and A. G. Warrington were the only batsmen to score 500 runs, and Timur Mohamed was disappointing by his usual high standards. Opening bowler C. Rutterford was outstanding; he took 35 wickets, and his unbeaten 53 against Bedfordshire, when he batted at number ten, took his team to an unexpected victory.

Wiltshire slipped to nineteenth position in the Championship, with only one win – by 163 runs against Berkshire – when P. Thorn scored the county's only century. I. Sinfield headed the batting, K. Emery, in his first full season, was the main wicket-taker, and R. G. Meale gave a good, consistent performance behind the stumps.

MINOR COUNTIES CHAMPIONSHIP, 1980

	Played	Won	Lost	Won 1st Inns	Lost 1st Inns	Tied	No Result	Points	Average Points
Durham NW	10	7	0	0	2	0	1	74	7.40
Hertfordshire NW	10	6	1*	2	1	0	0	70	7.00
Somerset II	8	4	0	2	0	0	2	50	6.25
Cheshire NW	10	4	1	3	1	0	1	52	5.20
Suffolk NW	10	4	2	3	1	0	0	50	5.00
Oxfordshire NW	10	3	1*	4	1	0	1	48	4.80
Norfolk	10	3	2*	2	2	1	0	46	4.60
Devon	10	3	1	1	3	0	2	40	4.00
Berkshire	10	3	5*ᵀ	1	1	0	0	39	3.90
Dorset	10	2	3†ᵀ	2	1	0	2	39	3.90
Shropshire	10	2	4†	2	0	0	2	36	3.60
Northumberland	12	3	3	2	3	0	1	41	3.41
Lancashire II	8	2	4*	0	1	0	1	26	3.25
Lincolnshire	10	1	1	4	3	0	1	27	2.70
Buckinghamshire	12	1	4†	2	3	1	1	32	2.66
Staffordshire	10	1	3*	3	2	0	1	26	2.60
Bedfordshire	10	2	4	0	3	0	1	25	2.50
Cornwall	8	1	3	2	1	0	1	19	2.37
Wiltshire	8	1	3*	0	4	0	0	17	2.12
Cambridgeshire	10	0	4	3	3	0	0	12	1.20
Cumberland	8	0	4	0	2	0	2	6	0.75

* *Signifies 1st innings lead in* ONE *match lost.*
† *Signifies 1st innings lead in* TWO *matches lost.*
ᵀ *Signifies* TIE *on 1st innings in* ONE *match lost.*
ᴺᵂ *Signifies qualified for NatWest Bank Trophy in 1981.*

CHALLENGE MATCH – DURHAM v HERTFORDSHIRE

At Durham City, September 13, 14, 15. Drawn. Hertfordshire, the challengers, elected to take first use of an excellent batting wicket. Following Dindar's early dismissal, Osman and Ottley made steady progress until the second innings score fell to 80. Thereafter wickets fell regularly, five to the leg-spin of Kippax. Atkinson and Romaines gave Durham a brisk start, but the scoring-rate slowed until Birtwisle joined Riddell to add 142 for the sixth wicket. Riddell, missed before he scored, hit seven 6s and thirteen 4s in his 139 – his highest score for Durham – and Birtwisle, missed before he reached 30, hit two 6s and ten 4s in his 75. When Riddell was eventually bowled by Collins, he declared 178 ahead. Hertfordshire had reached 55 for two in their second innings when play was abandoned early because of bad light, and rain prevented any play on the third day. There being no definite result, Durham became champion county under Rule 16 which states: "If the two top counties shall not have played each other, the second county shall have the right to challenge the first to a three-day match, which shall decide the Championship, and shall be played on a ground chosen by the challenged county. If no result shall have been attained in this match, the Championship shall be decided as if there had been no challenge. A lead on the first innings, or a tie, shall not be a 'result' within the meaning of this Rule."

Hertfordshire

W. M. Osman c Romaines b Greensword	38	– c Atkinson b Cairns		2
A. Dindar c Atkinson b Cairns	6	– not out		24
D. G. Ottley b Kippax	57	– b Johnston		22
R. H. Pomphrey lbw b Cairns	1	– not out		1
E. P. Neal lbw b Kippax	0			
A. R. Garofall not out	54			
*†F. E. Collyer c Birtwisle b Kippax	0			
T. S. Smith b Kippax	12			
J. D. W. Wright c Crane b Cairns	19			
B. G. Collins lbw b Johnston	5			
R. J. Hailey b Kippax	2			
L-b 5, n-b 3	8	L-b 1, n-b 5		6

1/17 2/80 3/98 4/99   202   1/6 2/54   (2 wkts) 55
5/106 6/118 7/139 8/168 9/186

Bowling: *First Innings*—Cairns 29–10–82–3; Johnston 21–4–40–1; Greensword 10–2–30–1; Kippax 21.2–12–27–5; Crane 5–2–15–0. *Second Innings*—Cairns 10–3–22–1; Johnston 10–1–27–1.

Durham

S. R. Atkinson c Collyer b Collins	42	B. L. Cairns b Garofall		0
P. W. Romaines b Smith	34	C. Thomas c Collyer b Collins		15
S. Greensword b Smith	27	†R. A. D. Mercer not out		11
P. J. Kippax b Hailey	9	B 6, l-b 7		13
P. J. Crane c Garofall b Hailey	15			
*N. A. Riddell b Collins	139	1/69 2/82 3/101 4/123 (9 wkts dec.) 380		
P. C. Birtwisle c Collyer b Collins	75	5/149 6/291 7/302 8/347 9/380		

J. Johnson did not bat.

Bowling: Collins 29.1–5–115–4; Wright 9–1–47–0; Garofall 12–0–54–1; Hailey 32–16–68–2; Smith 30–9–83–2.

Umpires: R. H. Duckett and S. Levison.

*In the averages that follow, * against a score signifies not out, * against a name signifies the captain, and † signifies wicket-keeper.*

BEDFORDSHIRE

Secretary – G. L. B. AUGUST, 24 Furzefield, Putnoe, Bedford

Matches 10: Won – Cambridgeshire, Shropshire. Lost – Buckinghamshire, Hertfordshire, Shropshire, Suffolk. Lost on first innings – Cambridgeshire, Hertfordshire, Suffolk. No result – Buckinghamshire.

Batting Averages

	Innings	Not Outs	Runs	Highest Inns	Average
M. G. Stedman	10	1	316	104	35.11
M. E. Gear	12	1	339	70	30.81
J. Kettleborough	7	2	142	35*	28.40
E. Benjamin	18	3	405	85*	27.00
M. Morgan	14	1	250	52	19.23
†P. G. M. August	11	6	92	21*	18.40
A. D. Curtis	9	1	127	37	15.87

Batting Averages – *continued*

	Innings	Not Outs	Runs	Highest Inns	Average
D. M. Daniels	16	1	234	43*	15.60
A. Durose	10	2	117	28	14.62
*K. V. Jones	17	1	222	44	13.87
S. Lines	10	0	124	37	12.40
K. Gentle	5	1	41	24*	10.25

Also batted: S. E. Blott, D. P. Clarke, P. R. Harris, R. Loft, A. Patel, P. Walker.

Bowling Averages

	Overs	Maidens	Runs	Wickets	Average
R. Loft	46.5	10	141	7	20.14
K. V. Jones	121	22	366	16	22.87
E. Benjamin	148.3	37	456	16	28.50
A. Durose	147.4	27	461	16	28.80
S. E. Blott	126.1	29	379	13	29.15
P. Walker	221.2	46	676	21	32.19

Also bowled: D. P. Clarke 27–5–110–3; M. E. Gear 7–0–64–1; J. Kettleborough 10–0–47–1; M. Morgan 7–0–39–1.

BERKSHIRE

Secretary – C. F. V. MARTIN, Paradise Cottage, Paradise Road,
Henley-on-Thames, Oxon, RG9 1UB

Matches 10: Won – Buckinghamshire, Dorset, Wiltshire. Lost – Devon, Dorset, Oxfordshire (twice), Wiltshire. Won on first innings – Devon. Lost on first innings – Buckinghamshire.

Batting Averages

	Innings	Not Outs	Runs	Highest Inns	Average
S. Burrow	18	7	300	53*	27.27
J. F. Harvey	20	0	481	80	24.05
N. Phillips	14	0	326	73	23.28
G. P. Knight	20	1	430	84	22.63
R. A. C. Sears	19	0	412	53	21.68
R. Latchman	10	2	153	50*	19.12
M. Simmons	16	0	243	61	15.18
*†G. E. J. Child	15	5	122	23*	12.20

Also batted: A. Applethwaite, A. R. Day, N. Gray, P. Hartridge, D. Johnston, J. H. Jones, S. Kingston, P. J. Lewington, D. Liston, M. D. Mence, M. G. Richardson, N. J. W. Stewart.

Bowling Averages

	Overs	Maidens	Runs	Wickets	Average
P. J. Lewington	350.4	90	872	44	19.81
D. Liston	51	12	179	9	19.89
J. H. Jones	257.4	45	815	32	25.46
S. Burrow	129.1	23	459	9	51.00

Also bowled: A. Applethwaite 19–2–85–4; G. E. J. Child 0.5–0–1–0; P. Hartridge 29–8–74–2; S. Kingston 12–2–38–0; M. D. Mence 36–7–99–3; N. Phillips 4–0–22–1; M. G. Richardson 45–8–170–6; M. Simmons 9–1–49–1; N. J. W. Stewart 52–5–96–2.

BUCKINGHAMSHIRE

Secretary – P. M. M. SLATTER, FIB,
The White Cottage, Framewood Road, Stoke Poges SL2 4QR

Matches 12: Won – Bedfordshire. Lost – Berkshire, Hertfordshire (twice), Suffolk. Won on first innings – Berkshire, Norfolk. Lost on first innings – Oxfordshire (twice), Suffolk. Tied – Norfolk. No result – Bedfordshire.

Batting Averages

	Innings	Not Outs	Runs	Highest Inns	Average
J. B. Turner	16	2	559	117	39.92
M. E. Milton	14	0	454	94	32.42
K. I. Hodgson	14	5	290	67*	32.22
J. K. S. Edwards	11	0	344	75	31.27
N. G. Hames	18	6	370	51*	30.83
†R. G. Humphrey	8	0	228	106	28.50
K. H. Macleay	16	2	332	69	23.71
S. A. Mehar	14	4	221	54	22.10
*D. E. Smith	19	0	404	55	21.26
G. K. Robertson	7	2	106	28	21.20
P. Dolphin	6	0	115	49	19.16
†T. E. Perkins	7	2	78	33*	15.60
L. Ainge	9	1	123	36	15.37

Also batted: P. D. M. Ashton, R. R. Bailey, M. W. Blair, C. A. Connor, R. J. Dell, R. L. Lawson, A. W. Lyon, S. P. Ridge, D. J. Smith. †B. W. Poll and †V. A. Flynn each played in one match and kept wicket but did not bat.

Bowling Averages

	Overs	Maidens	Runs	Wickets	Average
S. A. Mehar	242.2	61	628	33	19.03
A. W. Lyon	258.3	59	655	30	21.83
K. H. Macleay	134	32	422	13	32.46
G. K. Robertson	131.4	19	477	13	36.69

Also bowled: R. R. Bailey 98.2–21–301–7; M. W. Blair 57–11–174–4; C. A. Connor 79–16–302–6; K. I. Hodgson 76–20–278–6; R. L. Lawson 4–0–11–0; M. E. Milton 25.1–9–49–3; S. P. Ridge 22.3–6–86–4; D. J. Smith 92–24–275–6.

CAMBRIDGESHIRE

Secretary – P. W. GOODEN,
The Redlands, Oakington Road, Cottenham, Cambridgeshire

Matches 10: Lost – Bedfordshire, Norfolk, Suffolk (twice). Won on first innings – Bedfordshire, Hertfordshire, Lincolnshire. Lost on first innings – Hertfordshire, Lincolnshire, Norfolk.

Batting Averages

	Innings	Not Outs	Runs	Highest Inns	Average
P. Mills	7	1	206	101*	34.33
†A. M. Ponder	16	3	432	111	33.23
N. T. Gadsby	18	0	473	114	26.27
R. L. Armitage	15	3	312	104*	26.00
P. Malkin	14	3	237	74	21.54
D. H. Baker	16	2	262	49	18.71
A. Jordan	7	0	117	44	16.71
D. C. Holliday	9	1	127	61	15.87
A. Shippey	8	0	126	45	15.75
T. Howarth	10	2	86	28	10.75

Also batted: M. Brooker, M. Brown, J. Carter, P. Clayton, D. C. Collard, S. Cracknell, B. King, J. Jacklin, H. Mumford, I. Parker, D. Parry, M. Saggers, D. Smallwood, M. Stephenson, D. Wing. P. Tingey did not bat.

Bowling Averages

	Overs	Maidens	Runs	Wickets	Average
S. Cracknell	58.2	8	193	12	16.08
D. C. Collard	244.4	64	767	33	23.24
R. L. Armitage	197	36	579	18	32.16

Also bowled: D. H. Baker 1–1–0–0; M. Brooker 44–10–121–1; M. Brown 16–5–39–0; J. Carter 33–3–130–5; N. T. Gadsby 2–0–23–0; T. Howarth 24–3–89–2; D. C. Holliday 38–3–106–4; B. King 8.2–1–40–3; J. Jacklin 21–4–78–2; A. Jordan 85.2–18–259–4; P. Malkin 11.1–1–45–2; H. Mumford 21–3–76–2; I. Parker 14–3–32–1; D. Parry 31–6–144–3; D. Smallwood 3–0–7–0; P. Tingey 12–2–51–0; D. Wing 52–11–164–4.

CHESHIRE

Secretary – J. B. PICKUP
2 Castle Street, Northwich, Cheshire CW8 1AB

Matches 10: Won – Lancashire II, Northumberland, Shropshire, Staffordshire. Lost – Lancashire II. Won on first innings – Durham (twice), Staffordshire. Lost on first innings – Shropshire. No result – Northumberland.

Batting Averages

	Innings	Not Outs	Runs	Highest Inns	Average
Mudassar Nazar	9	2	417	114	59.57
D. Bailey	10	0	317	83	31.70
*J. A. Sutton	16	0	418	65	26.12
I. Cowap	15	4	276	78	25.09
R. M. O. Cooke	15	2	286	74	22.00
P. A. Tipton	16	0	287	67	17.93
P. J. Dunkley	7	1	106	63	17.66
I. J. Gemmell	9	1	94	32	11.75
N. T. O'Brien	16	1	157	23	10.46
G. M. Taylor	12	2	103	33	10.30

Also batted: N. D. Barker, †K. J. McCullagh, S. L. Milner, T. J. Taylor. N. R. Halsall played in one match but did not bat.

Bowling Averages

	Overs	Maidens	Runs	Wickets	Average
T. J. Taylor	261.2	82	652	41	15.90
R. M. O. Cooke	90	28	279	15	18.60
I. J. Gemmell	165	28	557	27	20.62
D. Bailey	48.4	6	163	7	23.28
J. A. Sutton	145.5	66	300	12	25.00

Also bowled: I. Cowap 10–0–68–0; N. R. Halsall 6.5–1–40–1; S. L. Milner 15–2–52–0; Mudassar Nazar 80.2–30–156–3; N. T. O'Brien 77–17–210–3; P. A. Tipton 8–1–24–0.

CORNWALL

Secretary – T. D. MENEER, Falbridge, Penvale Cross, Penryn

Matches 8: Won – Dorset. Lost – Somerset II, Dorset, Devon. Won on first innings – Wiltshire (twice). Lost on first innings – Devon. No result – Somerset II.

Batting Averages

	Innings	Not Outs	Runs	Highest Inns	Average
*M. S. T. Dunstan	8	1	313	102	52.16
N. G. Cock	7	1	209	62	34.83
T. J. Angove	12	2	324	72*	32.40
E. G. Willcock	11	0	332	129	30.18
F. T. Willetts	14	2	352	57	29.33
C. J. Trudgeon	14	1	378	68	29.07
J. F. Rowe	13	3	217	50	21.70

Also batted: M. Bryant, P. A. Coombe, P. I. Johns, †W. J. Lawry, A. Machin, V. K. Meneer, D. A. Toseland, M. O. Trenwith, A. H. Watts.

Bowling Averages

	Overs	Maidens	Runs	Wickets	Average
M. O. Trenwith	226.1	56	647	34	19.02
D. A. Toseland	240.2	62	597	27	22.11
A. H. Watts	147	37	362	10	36.20

Also bowled: T. J. Angove 3–0–20–0; M. Bryant 56–8–198–4; N. G. Cock 3–0–20–0; P. A. Coombe 35–8–115–2; M. S. T. Dunstan 18–2–63–2; P. I. Johns 61.3–12–247–4; W. J. Lawry 1–0–5–0; A. Machin 9–1–33–1; V. K. Meneer 18–3–55–2; C. J. Trudgeon 0.4–0–5–0; E. G. Willcock 2.1–0–6–0; F. T. Willetts 10–1–46–0.

CUMBERLAND

Secretary – N. WISE, 18 Banklands, Workington

Matches 8: Lost – Durham (twice), Lancashire II, Northumberland. Lost on first innings – Lincolnshire, Northumberland. No result – Lancashire II, Lincolnshire.

Batting Averages

	Innings	Not Outs	Runs	Highest Inns	Average
L. Baichan	7	0	302	97	43.14
R. Entwistle	10	0	346	63	34.60
A. Wilson	10	1	167	35*	18.55
*J. Moyes	8	1	120	51	17.14
A. White	7	0	120	32	17.14
K. Oliver	6	0	100	33	16.66
D. L. Ash	6	1	81	27	16.20
†N. Boustead	7	1	87	23	14.50
M. Woods	8	0	111	34	13.87
A. Sharp	9	2	97	32*	13.85
D. Walters	7	0	84	35	12.00
M. Dugdale	6	1	53	15	10.60
M. Saunders	6	0	63	29	10.50

Also batted: M. Battersby, T. Coughlan, J. Elleray, S. Gill, D. Lupton, E. Mays, G. McMeekin, D. Musgrave, D. Nelson, K. Smaple, J. Wainscott.

Bowling Averages

	Overs	Maidens	Runs	Wickets	Average
D. Lupton	138.3	27	401	13	30.84
K. Oliver	74	11	252	6	42.00
A. Sharp	118	22	405	7	57.85

Also bowled: D. L. Ash 41.2–11–159–4; M. Battersby 8–1–31–2; J. Elleray 31–14–84–2; I. Lucas 3–1–10–0; E. Mays 17.1–6–42–1; D. Musgrave 2–0–10–0; D. Nelson 48–12–128–4; J. Wainscott 11–1–67–2; M. Woods 29.1–10–96–1.

DEVON

Secretary – REV. K. J. WARREN,
The Rectory, Whitestone, Exeter, EX4 2JT

Matches 10: Won – Berkshire, Cornwall, Oxfordshire. Lost – Somerset II. Won on first innings – Cornwall. Lost on first innings – Berkshire, Dorset, Somerset II. No result – Dorset, Oxfordshire.

Batting Averages

	Innings	Not Outs	Runs	Highest Inns	Average
R. C. Tolchard	17	6	581	71	52.81
J. G. Tolchard	15	1	478	65	34.14
G. Wallen	17	0	459	83	27.00
R. F. Harriott	16	3	285	94	21.92
C. Wallen	11	3	159	32	19.87
*B. L. Matthews	11	0	213	53	19.36
†R. M. Oliver	9	4	85	30*	17.00
A. W. Allin	6	2	65	23*	16.25

Also batted: R. K. Benton, P. Considine, †O. G. R. Evans, B. C. Green, M. J. Goulding, M. B. Kershaw, I. C. Roberts, R. J. Tolliday, M. C. Wagstaffe, D. I. Yeabsley.

Bowling Averages

	Overs	Maidens	Runs	Wickets	Average
A. W. Allin	168.4	49	473	32	14.78
D. I. Yeabsley	231.1	55	560	26	21.53
P. Considine	66	7	239	10	23.90
M. J. Goulding	227.4	32	707	18	39.27

Also bowled: R. K. Benton 41.5–5–147–2; B. C. Green 47–16–161–5; R. F. Harriott 6.3–0–40–2; M. B. Kershaw 3–0–15–0; I. C. Roberts 34–2–145–3; J. G. Tolchard 1–0–5–0; M. C. Wagstaffe 55.2–13–178–4; G. Wallen 10–0–45–0.

DORSET

Secretary – D. J. W. BRIDGE,
Long Acre, Tinney's Lane, Sherborne, Dorset

Matches 10: Won – Berkshire, Cornwall. Lost – Berkshire, Cornwall, Oxfordshire. Won on first innings – Devon, Oxfordshire. Lost on first innings – Somerset II. No result – Devon, Somerset II.

Batting Averages

	Innings	Not Outs	Runs	Highest Inns	Average
†T. J. Murrills	6	1	239	78*	47.80
*R. V. Lewis	18	0	799	104	44.38
D. R. Hayward	9	4	191	50*	38.20
D. Baty	12	1	350	52	31.81
G. B. Evans	15	1	398	83	28.42
C. A. Graham	14	2	308	102	25.66
J. F. Blackburn	13	4	165	40*	18.33
†V. B. Lewis	18	1	289	45	17.00

Also batted: C. W. Allen, D. C. Brooks, A. Evans, A. J. Foot, A. S. Hodgson, A. Jarvis, R. J. Murrills, R. G. H. Pullen, R. J. Swatridge, A. R. Wingfield Digby, †M. R. Wiseman.

Bowling Averages

	Overs	Maidens	Runs	Wickets	Average
R. J. Murrills	37	9	111	7	15.85
C. W. Allen	244.1	52	792	40	19.80
A. S. Hodgson	64	12	227	8	28.37
A. R. Wingfield Digby	95	14	347	10	34.70
A. Evans	190.3	49	502	14	35.85
D. R. Hayward	102.2	26	326	9	36.22

Also bowled: D. Baty 3.2–0–20–1; J. F. Blackburn 44–3–137–3; D. C. Brooks 9–8–26–0; G. B. Evans 35–4–134–0; C. A. Graham 5–0–20–0; R. V. Lewis 32–3–156–2; R. G. H. Pullen 9–2–36–1; R. J. Swatridge 75.4–22–230–3.

DURHAM

Secretary – J. ILEY,
Roselea, Springwell Avenue, Durham City DH1 4LY

Matches 10: Won – Cumberland (twice), Northumberland (twice), Shropshire, Staffordshire (twice). Lost on first innings – Cheshire (twice). No result – Shropshire.

Batting Averages

	Innings	Not Outs	Runs	Highest Inns	Average
Wasim Raja	11	4	438	94	62.57
S. Greensword	18	4	868	141*	62.00
*N. A. Riddell	15	3	597	139	49.75
P. W. Romaines	9	2	264	73*	37.71
P. J. Crane	9	5	135	64	33.75
P. C. Birtwisle	12	3	269	75	29.88
P. J. Kippax	7	3	81	36	20.25
B. L. Cairns	8	1	139	47	19.85
S. R. Atkinson	15	0	294	42	19.60
C. Thomas	7	1	82	33	13.66

Also batted: G. Hurst, A. Maitra, †R. A. D. Mercer, D. D. Parsana, S. M. Stokoe, M. C. Thomas, J. S. Wilkinson. S. A. B. Daniels, J. Johnston, P. K. Shivalkar and I. A. Wishart did not bat.

Bowling Averages

	Overs	Maidens	Runs	Wickets	Average
B. L. Cairns	294.2	92	711	56	12.69
Wasim Raja	90	33	199	14	14.21
P. J. Kippax	139.2	50	308	20	15.40
S. Greensword	194.5	64	459	21	21.85
J. Johnston	122	27	304	13	23.38
S. A. B. Daniels	128	28	348	13	26.76

Also bowled: P. J. Crane 30–5–94–2; D. D. Parsana 60–13–173–2; P. K. Shivalkar 55–23–127–4; C. Thomas 3–0–8–0; J. S. Wilkinson 62–23–126–2; I. A. Wishart 10–1–30–1.

HERTFORDSHIRE

Secretary – C. O. HARRISON,
147A High Street, Waltham Cross, Hertfordshire

Matches 10: Won – Bedfordshire, Buckinghamshire (twice), Norfolk, Suffolk (twice). Lost – Norfolk. Won on first innings – Bedfordshire, Cambridgeshire. Lost on first innings – Cambridgeshire.

Batting Averages

	Innings	Not Outs	Runs	Highest Inns	Average
P. E. McEwan	19	2	836	127*	49.17
D. G. Ottley	18	2	612	111*	38.25
A. R. Garofall	11	3	266	61	33.25
W. M. Osman	20	0	564	84	28.20
R. H. Pomphrey	21	4	466	98	27.41
R. L. Johns	8	3	106	39*	21.20
A. Dindar	10	2	158	63*	19.75
N. Wright	13	4	175	39	19.44
P. Neal	6	0	116	61	19.33
*†F. E. Collyer	14	4	172	43*	17.20

Bowling Averages

	Overs	Maidens	Runs	Wickets	Average
J. D. W. Wright	78	26	214	16	13.37
R. L. Johns	233	76	576	40	14.40
A. R. Garofall	193.4	54	492	30	16.40
P. E. McEwan	61.1	17	141	8	17.62
B. G. Collins	300.3	103	731	40	18.27
R. J. Hailey	214.2	81	585	24	24.37
S. Cradock	63.1	16	199	7	28.42

Also bowled: P. Neal 6–0–24–2; D. G. Ottley 13–2–50–1; T. S. Smith 30–9–83–2.

LANCASHIRE SECOND ELEVEN

Secretary – C. D. HASSELL, Old Trafford, Manchester M16 0PX

*Matches 8: Won – Cheshire, Cumberland. Lost – Cheshire, Northumberland (twice),
Shropshire. Lost on first innings – Shropshire. No result – Cumberland.*

Batting Averages

	Innings	Not Outs	Runs	Highest Inns	Average
†G. Fowler	7	2	336	137	67.20
I. Cockbain	4	0	181	121	45.25
J. Abrahams	6	0	160	59	26.66
D. K. Beckett	8	0	192	62	24.00
S. J. O'Shaughnessy	10	1	182	62	20.22
B. Thorpe	6	1	97	81*	19.40
P. J. W. Allott	5	1	60	26	15.00
*H. Pilling	9	2	82	25	11.71
M. Watkinson	4	0	44	22	11.00

Also batted: M. Aspin, R. Berry, K. Boden, N. Fairbrother, I. Folley, †W. Fowler, J.
Hartley, K. Hayes, I. Herbert, W. Hogg, W. Joyce, P. G. Lee, M. F. Malone, N. V. Radford,
R. M. Ratcliffe, S. Sharp, †J. Stanworth, M. Tracy, G. E. Trim, †M. Wallwork, R. Watson.

Bowling Averages

	Overs	Maidens	Runs	Wickets	Average
W. Hogg	80.1	26	200	15	13.33
B. Thorpe	45.5	10	154	9	17.11
P. G. Lee	166	58	350	20	17.50
J. Abrahams	57	11	196	11	17.81
R. M. Ratcliffe	125.2	26	308	16	19.25
S. J. O'Shaughnessy	46	9	158	6	26.33
P. J. W. Allott	79	21	237	7	33.85

Also bowled: K. Boden 16–1–40–0; I. Cockbain 1–0–4–0; I. Folley 3–0–12–0; J. Hartley
37–7–109–6; I. Herbert 19–0–71–6; M. F. Malone 15–2–47–0; N. V. Radford 26–8–47–4;
M. Tracy 36.5–6–148–5; R. Watson 6–1–25–0.

LINCOLNSHIRE

Secretary – C. H. WARMAN,
22 Charles Avenue, Grimsby, South Humberside

Matches 10: Won – Norfolk. Lost – Norfolk. Won on first innings – Cambridgeshire, Cumberland, Northumberland (twice). Lost on first innings – Cambridgeshire, Staffordshire (twice). No result – Cumberland.

Batting Averages

	Innings	Not Outs	Runs	Highest Inns	Average
P. D. Johnson	11	4	477	151*	68.14
*G. Robinson	19	1	815	116	45.27
C. Wicks	6	1	169	56*	33.80
H. Pougher	15	2	355	90	27.30
M. J. Birmingham	17	5	287	52*	23.91
J. G. Franks	9	4	119	38*	23.80
P. S. Ramm	6	2	68	32*	17.00
T. F. Nicholls	9	1	130	29	16.25
D. Marshall	10	2	126	41*	15.75
J. C. Munton	17	1	249	63	15.56

Also batted: S. K. Adlard, C. S. Barker, †R. G. Draper, M. Maslin, H. Stroud, G. J. Wilson. P. L. Tillison did not bat.

Bowling Averages

	Overs	Maidens	Runs	Wickets	Average
J. A. Williams	121.2	35	307	20	15.35
D. Marshall	269.3	57	732	38	19.26
G. J. Wilson	164	43	474	22	21.54
T. F. Nicholls	211	51	636	21	30.28
C. S. Barker	173.5	34	533	15	35.53

Also bowled: S. K. Adlard 52.4–4–208–2; M. J. Birmingham 1–0–5–0; M. Maslin 7–1–26–1; G. Robinson 5.4–0–32–0; P. L. Tillison 22–3–68–0.

NORFOLK

Secretary – D. J. M. ARMSTRONG,
Thorpe Cottage, Mill Common, Ridlington, North Walsham NR28 9TY

Matches 10: Won – Cambridgeshire, Hertfordshire, Lincolnshire. Lost – Hertfordshire, Lincolnshire. Won on first innings – Cambridgeshire, Suffolk. Lost on first innings – Buckinghamshire, Suffolk. Tied – Buckinghamshire.

Batting Averages

	Innings	Not Outs	Runs	Highest Inns	Average
*P. J. Sharpe	15	5	557	86*	55.70
S. G. Plumb	16	2	674	123*	48.14
F. L. Q. Handley	18	0	691	107	38.38
D. G. Pilch	15	7	248	61*	31.00
R. D. Huggins	17	0	517	94	30.41
†D. E. Mattocks	11	6	113	30*	22.60
J. Barrett	8	3	108	44*	21.60
N. D. Cook	17	3	293	37*	20.92
R. L. Bradford	12	1	186	46	16.90

Also batted: T. H. Barnes, M. J. Dunn, W. J. Elliott, R. F. Innes, B. J. Leigh, S. J. Starling, E. Wright. B. L. Battelley and B. A. Meigh did not bat.

Bowling Averages

	Overs	Maidens	Runs	Wickets	Average
T. H. Barnes	313.1	80	810	40	20.25
E. Wright	253.5	37	876	36	24.33
B. A. Meigh	115	18	424	15	28.26
D. G. Pilch	130.1	17	467	16	29.18
S. G. Plumb	217.2	39	776	19	40.84

Also bowled: J. Barrett 18–1–82–4; B. L. Battelley 31–5–133–4; W. J. Elliott 12–2–51–1; R. F. Innes 80–10–299–4; S. J. Starling 50–13–146–6.

NORTHUMBERLAND

Secretary – R. W. SMITHSON,
Osborne Avenue, Jesmond, Newcastle upon Tyne NE2 1JS

Matches 12: Won – Cumberland, Lancashire II (twice). Lost – Cheshire, Durham (twice). Won on first innings – Cumberland, Staffordshire. Lost on first innings – Lincolnshire (twice), Staffordshire. No result – Cheshire.

Batting Averages

	Innings	Not Outs	Runs	Highest Inns	Average
K. Pearson	19	1	956	120	53.11
A. S. Thompson	19	3	679	101*	42.43
Mushtaq Mohammad	18	1	695	107	40.88
*M. Youll	18	1	485	85	28.52
M. E. Younger	16	3	329	64*	25.30
J. Thewlis	17	6	172	57	15.63
J. R. Purvis	12	5	91	42*	13.00

Also batted: J. S. Charleton, †K. Corby, G. J. Dodds, J. N. Graham, P. C. Graham, K. Norton, †W. G. Robson. †J. J. Cross and P. H. Twizell did not bat.

Bowling Averages

	Overs	Maidens	Runs	Wickets	Average
Mushtaq Mohammad	281.5	65	855	46	18.58
J. N. Graham	267.3	85	637	31	20.54
P. C. Graham	185	36	563	25	22.52
M. E. Younger	116	33	311	11	28.27
J. R. Purvis	91.4	15	318	11	28.90
K. Norton	135.5	51	375	12	31.25
G. J. Dodds	75	13	239	6	39.83

Also bowled: P. H. Twizell 38.5–6–158–1.

OXFORDSHIRE

Secretary – J. E. O. SMITH,
2 The Green, Horton-cum-Studley, Oxfordshire

Matches 10: Won – Berkshire (twice), Dorset. Lost – Devon. Won on first innings – Buckinghamshire (twice), Wiltshire (twice). Lost on first innings – Dorset. No result – Devon.

Batting Averages

	Innings	Not Outs	Runs	Highest Inns	Average
A. Townsley	9	2	320	113*	45.71
P. J. Garner	19	1	581	99	32.27
*M. D. Nurton	17	3	431	79*	30.78
P. J. Densham	7	0	178	85	25.42
M. D. Thomas	14	4	228	48*	22.80
S. R. Porter	13	5	151	30*	18.87
†A. Crossley	14	2	219	69	18.25
B. A. Collis	16	4	211	74*	17.58
P. Badger	7	1	93	34	15.50
C. Clements	17	2	202	50	13.46

Also batted: D. Beckett, P. L. Bradbury, R. N. Busby, P. Fowler, D. A. Gallop, G. Hobbins, B. A. Jeffries.

Bowling Averages

	Overs	Maidens	Runs	Wickets	Average
S. R. Porter	270.3	68	711	46	15.45
K. Arnold	45	12	110	7	15.71
R. N. Busby	201.2	54	500	28	17.85
G. Hobbins	41	4	155	7	22.14
P. J. Garner	63	18	179	7	25.57
P. Badger	110	30	318	11	28.90
B. A. Collis	106	18	322	11	29.27
D. A. Gallop	106	18	322	11	29.27

Also bowled: D. Beckett 24–3–76–2; P. L. Bradbury 72–19–190–3; B. A. Jeffries 17–5–21–0; M. D. Nurton 7–2–14–0; A. Townsley 16–3–61–1.

SHROPSHIRE

Secretary – H. BOTFIELD, 1 The Crescent, Much Wenlock

Matches 10: Won – Bedfordshire, Lancashire II. Lost – Bedfordshire, Cheshire, Durham, Staffordshire. Won on first innings – Cheshire, Lancashire. No result – Durham, Staffordshire.

Batting Averages

	Innings	Not Outs	Runs	Highest Inns	Average
J. S. Johnson	11	3	526	86	65.75
C. N. Boyns	12	1	323	89	29.36
M. R. Thornycroft	17	2	410	73	27.33
J. P. Dawson	4	0	81	43	20.25
D. S. de Silva	15	1	241	50	17.21

Batting Averages – *continued*

	Innings	Not Outs	Runs	Highest Inns	Average
M. A. Meman	15	2	217	39	16.69
*†G. R. Cass	15	4	183	60*	16.63
S. C. Gale	11	3	128	48	16.00
J. Foster	11	0	155	34	14.09
J. A. Smith	8	3	63	30*	12.60
B. Perry	9	2	78	21	11.14

Also batted: A. S. Barnard, C. R. Hemsley, S. J. Mason, P. L. Ranells.

Bowling Averages

	Overs	Maidens	Runs	Wickets	Average
B. Perry	99.1	33	248	15	16.53
D. S. de Silva	319.1	94	843	47	17.93
M. A. Meman	231	86	456	22	20.72
C. N. Boyns	71	19	198	8	24.75
J. A. Smith	205.4	40	556	19	29.26

Also bowled: A. S. Barnard 69.5–14–252–6; J. P. Dawson 16–7–27–7; C. R. Hemsley 6–2–18–0; P. L. Ranells 54–16–166–4.

SOMERSET SECOND ELEVEN

Secretary – D. G. SEWARD, County Cricket Ground, Taunton

Matches 8: Won – Cornwall, Devon, Wiltshire (twice). Won on first innings – Devon, Dorset. No result – Cornwall, Dorset.

Batting Averages

	Innings	Not Outs	Runs	Highest Inns	Average
P. A. Slocombe	6	3	435	109	145.00
N. Russom	8	5	417	116	139.00
M. Olive	4	2	178	75	89.00
D. Breakwell	5	2	227	92	75.66
R. L. Ollis	11	3	436	116*	54.50
A. W. J. Spiller	5	0	137	74	27.40
†T. Gard	6	0	116	40	19.33
M. J. Kitchen	5	1	62	23	15.50

Also batted: G. I. Burgess, A. J. H. Dunning, G. J. Hall, K. F. Jennings, J. W. Lloyds, G. V. Palmer, *P. J. Robinson. †G. S. Joyce, S. Palfrey and R. Sully did not bat.

Bowling Averages

	Overs	Maidens	Runs	Wickets	Average
G. I. Burgess	28	13	52	6	8.66
G. J. Hall	130.2	27	414	22	18.81
P. J. Robinson	49.2	18	152	8	19.00
N. Russom	170	40	465	22	21.13
K. F. Jennings	171	41	451	18	25.05
M. R. Davis	85.1	18	213	6	35.50

Also bowled: D. Breakwell 79–21–209–4; M. J. Kitchen 1–0–6–0; S. Palfrey 30–6–107–1; G. V. Palmer 22.3–6–58–0; P. A. Slocombe 8–3–17–0; A. W. J. Spiller 58–6–200–5; R. Sully 14–7–19–3.

STAFFORDSHIRE

Secretary – L. W. HANCOCK,
4 Kingsland Avenue, Oakhill, Stoke-on-Trent ST4 5LA

Matches 10: Won – Shropshire. Lost – Cheshire, Durham (twice). Won on first innings – Lincolnshire (twice), Northumberland. Lost on first innings – Cheshire, Northumberland. No result – Shropshire.

Batting Averages

	Innings	Not Outs	Runs	Highest Inns	Average
P. N. Gill	16	2	602	144	43.00
G. S. Warner	12	1	473	105	43.00
P. A. Marshall	13	2	380	90*	34.54
N. J. Archer	14	3	273	51	24.81
*D. A. Hancock	14	1	275	57	21.15
N. Hodgkinson	12	4	168	52	21.00
N. D. Croft	5	0	93	68	18.60
R. W. Flower	8	3	89	42	17.80
F. D. Stephenson	14	0	246	46	17.57
S. Bailey	4	0	66	36	16.50

Also batted: R. P. Archer, R. Bailey, R. Boothroyd, S. Brookes, D. Cartledge, †A. Griffiths, R. I. James, J. D. Moore, D. G. Nicholls, A. Webster, J. S. Williamson.

Bowling Averages

	Overs	Maidens	Runs	Wickets	Average
D. G. Nicholls	54	10	197	10	19.70
R. Boothroyd	217.4	60	508	24	21.16
R. W. Flower	241.5	58	732	29	25.24
F. D. Stephenson	201.2	31	664	26	25.53
R. I. James	85	14	258	8	32.25

Also bowled: R. P. Archer 18–3–80–1; S. Brookes 23–5–98–3; D. Cartledge 17–3–49–1; P. N. Gill 2.1–0–12–0; D. A. Hancock 1–0–5–0; N. Hodgkinson 1–0–3–0; P. A. Marshall 12.3–2–49–0; G. S. Warner 1–0–1–0; A. Webster 28–4–78–2.

SUFFOLK

Secretary – A. E. D. GARNETT,
Redgate House, Wherstead, Ipswich

Matches 10: Won – Bedfordshire, Buckinghamshire, Cambridgeshire (twice). Lost – Hertfordshire (twice). Won on first innings – Bedfordshire, Buckinghamshire, Norfolk. Lost on first innings – Norfolk.

Batting Averages

	Innings	Not Outs	Runs	Highest Inns	Average
C. Rutterford	10	6	175	57	43.75
R. F. Howlett	18	3	540	87	36.00
M. G. Maranta	10	3	229	67	32.71
A. G. Warrington	20	2	580	64	32.22

Batting Averages – *continued*

	Innings	Not Outs	Runs	Highest Inns	Average
Timur Mohamed	15	0	483	118	32.20
*P. H. Jones	16	3	388	54*	29.84
P. C. Rice	19	3	408	76	25.50
†S. A. Westley	15	3	256	60*	21.33
R. J. Robinson	15	4	207	35	18.81

Also batted: M. D. Bailey, M. L. Clinch, R. P. Done, C. G. Graham, B. Mayes.

Bowling Averages

	Overs	Maidens	Runs	Wickets	Average
M. G. Maranta	135	22	413	22	18.77
R. J. Robinson	181.5	32	567	23	24.65
C. Rutterford	332	85	886	35	25.31
P. H. Jones	254	60	751	24	31.29
C. G. Graham	137	22	433	12	36.08

Also bowled: M. D. Bailey 48–10–155–1; R. P. Done 40–8–95–3; B. Mayes 8–1–33–0; P. C. Rice 1–0–4–0; Timur Mohamed 19–3–86–2; A. G. Warrington 1–0–3–0.

WILTSHIRE

Secretary – J. C. GREENWOOD, 35 Rowden Hill, Chippenham

Matches 8: Won – Berkshire. Lost – Berkshire, Somerset II (twice). Lost on first innings – Cornwall (twice), Oxfordshire (twice).

Batting Averages

	Innings	Not Outs	Runs	Highest Inns	Average
I. Sinfield	16	1	475	74*	31.66
*B. H. White	14	1	381	90*	29.30
R. C. Cooper	6	0	168	56	28.00
K. Emery	13	5	169	37*	21.12
P. Meehan	12	0	249	56	20.75
P. Thorn	14	0	284	129*	20.28
J. Galley	6	0	117	54	19.50
R. Summers	12	1	210	36*	19.09
J. Newman	6	2	73	32	18.25
M. B. Mills	7	0	118	39	16.85
R. J. Gulliver	8	3	80	14	16.00
†R. G. Meale	15	5	121	23	12.10

Also batted: P. Askew, K. W. Lovegrove, A. J. Spencer, R. Wilson. R. Maisey did not bat.

Bowling Averages

	Overs	Maidens	Runs	Wickets	Average
K. Emery	166.4	43	429	26	16.50
R. J. Gulliver	159	46	469	22	21.31
A. J. Spencer	134.3	28	420	18	23.33
P. Meehan	73.5	29	206	8	25.75
R. C. Cooper	54	8	185	6	30.83
P. Thorn	93	21	313	10	31.30

Also bowled: P. Askew 4–1–8–0; K. W. Lovegrove 1–0–1–0; R. Maisey 40–14–84–3; B. H. White 13–3–31–2; R. Wilson 18.2–3–64–3.

MINOR COUNTIES AVERAGES – 1980

BATTING

(Qualification: 8 innings, average 25.00)

	Innings	Not Outs	Runs	Highest Innings	Average
N. Russom (*Somerset II*)	8	5	417	116	139.00
P. D. Johnson (*Lincolnshire*)	11	4	477	151*	68.14
J. S. Johnson (*Shropshire*)	11	3	526	86	65.75
Wasim Raja (*Durham*)	11	4	438	94	62.57
S. Greensword (*Durham*)	18	4	868	141*	62.00
Mudassar Nazar (*Cheshire*)	9	2	417	114	59.57
P. J. Sharpe (*Norfolk*)	15	5	557	86*	55.70
R. L. Ollis (*Somerset II*)	11	3	436	116*	54.50
K. Pearson (*Northumberland*)	19	1	956	120	53.11
R. C. Tolchard (*Devon*)	17	6	581	71	52.81
M. S. T. Dunstan (*Cornwall*)	8	2	313	102	52.16
N. A. Riddell (*Durham*)	15	3	597	139	49.75
P. E. McEwan (*Hertfordshire*)	19	2	836	127*	49.17
S. G. Plumb (*Norfolk*)	16	2	674	123*	48.14
A. Townsley (*Oxfordshire*)	9	2	320	113*	45.71
G. Robinson (*Lincolnshire*)	19	1	815	116	45.27
R. V. Lewis (*Dorset*)	18	0	799	104	44.38
C. Rutterford (*Suffolk*)	10	6	175	57	43.75
P. N. Gill (*Staffordshire*)	16	2	602	144	43.00
G. S. Warner (*Staffordshire*)	12	1	473	105	43.00
A. S. Thompson (*Northumberland*)	19	3	679	101*	42.43
Mushtaq Mohammad (*Northumberland*)	18	1	695	107	40.88
J. B. Turner (*Buckinghamshire*)	16	2	559	117	39.92
F. L. Q. Handley (*Norfolk*)	18	0	691	107	38.38
D. G. Ottley (*Hertfordshire*)	18	2	612	111*	38.25
D. R. Hayward (*Dorset*)	9	4	191	50*	38.20
P. W. Romaines (*Durham*)	9	2	264	73*	37.71
R. F. Howlett (*Suffolk*)	18	3	540	87	36.00
M. G. Stedman (*Bedfordshire*)	10	1	316	104	35.11
R. Entwistle (*Cumberland*)	10	0	346	63	34.60
P. A. Marshall (*Staffordshire*)	13	2	380	90*	34.54
J. G. Tolchard (*Devon*)	15	1	478	65	34.14
P. J. Crane (*Durham*)	9	5	135	64	33.75
A. R. Garofall (*Hertfordshire*)	11	3	266	61	33.25
A. M. Ponder (*Cambridgeshire*)	16	3	432	111	33.23
M. G. Maranta (*Suffolk*)	10	3	229	67	32.71
M. E. Milton (*Buckinghamshire*)	14	0	454	94	32.42
T. J. Angove (*Cornwall*)	12	2	324	72*	32.40
P. J. Garner (*Oxfordshire*)	19	1	581	99	32.27
K. I. Hodgson (*Buckinghamshire*)	14	5	290	67*	32.22
A. G. Warrington (*Suffolk*)	20	2	580	64	32.22
Timur Mohamed (*Suffolk*)	15	0	483	118	32.20
D. Baty (*Dorset*)	12	1	350	52	31.81
D. Bailey (*Cheshire*)	10	0	317	83	31.70
I. Sinfield (*Wiltshire*)	16	1	475	74*	31.66
J. K. S. Edwards (*Buckinghamshire*)	11	0	344	75	31.27
D. G. Pilch (*Norfolk*)	15	7	248	61*	31.00
N. G. Hames (*Buckinghamshire*)	18	6	370	51*	30.83
M. E. Gear (*Bedfordshire*)	12	1	339	70	30.81
M. D. Nurton (*Oxfordshire*)	17	3	431	79*	30.78
R. D. Huggins (*Norfolk*)	17	0	517	94	30.41
E. G. Willcock (*Cornwall*)	11	0	332	129	30.18

Batting Averages *– continued*

	Innings	Not Outs	Runs	Highest Innings	Average
P. C. Birtwisle (*Durham*)	12	3	269	75	29.88
P. H. Jones (*Suffolk*)	16	3	388	54*	29.84
C. N. Boyns (*Shropshire*)	12	1	323	89	29.36
F. T. Willetts (*Cornwall*)	14	2	352	57	29.33
B. H. White (*Wiltshire*)	14	1	381	90*	29.30
C. J. Trudgeon (*Cornwall*)	14	1	378	68	29.07
M. Youll (*Northumberland*)	18	1	485	85	28.52
R. G. Humphrey (*Buckinghamshire*) ...	8	0	228	106	28.50
G. B. Evans (*Dorset*)	15	1	398	83	28.42
W. M. Osman (*Hertfordshire*)	20	0	564	84	28.20
R. H. Pomphrey (*Hertfordshire*)	21	4	466	98	27.41
M. R. Thornycroft (*Shropshire*)	17	2	410	73	27.33
H. Pougher (*Lincolnshire*)	15	2	355	90	27.30
S. Burrow (*Berkshire*)	18	7	300	53*	27.27
E. Benjamin (*Bedfordshire*)	18	3	405	85*	27.00
G. Wallen (*Devon*)	17	0	459	85	27.00
N. T. Gadsby (*Cambridgeshire*)	18	0	473	114	26.27
J. A. Sutton (*Cheshire*)	16	0	418	65	26.12
R. L. Armitage (*Cambridgeshire*)	15	3	312	104*	26.00
C. A. Graham (*Dorset*)	14	2	308	102	25.66
P. C. Rice (*Suffolk*)	19	3	408	76	25.50
M. E. Younger (*Northumberland*)	16	3	329	64*	25.30
I. Cowap (*Cheshire*)	15	4	276	78	25.09

BOWLING

(Qualification: 20 wickets, average 24.00)

	Overs	Maidens	Runs	Wickets	Average
B. L. Cairns (*Durham*)	294.2	92	711	56	12.69
R. L. Johns (*Hertfordshire*)	233	76	576	40	14.40
A. W. Allin (*Devon*)	168.4	49	473	32	14.78
J. A. Williams (*Lincolnshire*)	121.2	35	307	20	15.35
P. J. Kippax (*Durham*)	139.2	50	308	20	15.40
S. R. Porter (*Oxfordshire*)	270.3	68	711	46	15.45
T. J. Taylor (*Cheshire*)	261.2	82	652	41	15.90
A. R. Garofall (*Hertfordshire*)	193.4	54	492	30	16.40
K. Emery (*Wiltshire*)	166.4	43	429	26	16.50
P. G. Lee (*Lancashire II*)	166	58	350	20	17.50
R. N. Busby (*Oxfordshire*)	201.2	54	500	28	17.85
D. S. de Silva (*Shropshire*)	319.1	94	843	47	17.93
B. G. Collins (*Hertfordshire*)	300.3	103	731	40	18.27
Mushtaq Mohammad (*Northumberland*)	281.5	65	855	46	18.58
M. G. Maranta (*Suffolk*)	135	22	413	22	18.77
G. J. Hall (*Somerset II*)	130.2	27	414	22	18.81
M. O. Trenwith (*Cornwall*)	226.1	56	647	34	19.02
S. A. Mehar (*Buckinghamshire*)	242.2	61	628	33	19.03
D. Marshall (*Lincolnshire*)	269.3	57	732	38	19.26
C. W. Allen (*Dorset*)	244.1	52	792	40	19.80
P. J. Lewington (*Berkshire*)	350.4	90	872	44	19.81
T. H. Barnes (*Norfolk*)	313.1	80	810	40	20.25
J. N. Graham (*Northumberland*)	267.3	85	637	31	20.54
I. J. Gemmell (*Cheshire*)	165	28	557	27	20.62

Bowling Averages – *continued*

	Overs	Maidens	Runs	Wickets	Average
M. A. Meman (*Shropshire*)	231	86	456	22	20.72
N. Russom (*Somerset II*)	170	40	465	22	21.13
R. Boothroyd (*Staffordshire*)	217.4	60	508	24	21.16
R. J. Gulliver (*Wiltshire*)	159	46	469	22	21.31
D. I. Yeabsley (*Devon*)	231.1	55	560	26	21.53
G. J. Wilson (*Lincolnshire*)	164	43	474	22	21.54
A. W. Lyon (*Buckinghamshire*)	258.3	59	655	30	21.83
S. Greensword (*Durham*)	194.5	64	459	21	21.85
D. A. Toseland (*Cornwall*)	240.2	62	597	27	22.11
P. C. Graham (*Northumberland*)	185	36	563	25	22.52
D. C. Collard (*Cambridgeshire*)	244.4	64	767	33	23.24

CRICKET ASSOCIATIONS AND SOCIETIES

AUSTRALIAN CRICKET SOCIETY: *Secretary* A. G. Moore, 7 Aintree Avenue, East Doncaster, Victoria 3109, Australia.

BLACKLEY CRICKET SOCIETY: *Secretary* D. Butterfield, 7 Bayswater Terrace, West Yorkshire, HX3 0NB.

BOSTON CRICKET LOVERS' SOCIETY: *Secretary* L. A. Brooks, 7 Tawney Street, Boston, Lincolnshire.

CAMBRIDGE UNIVERSITY CRICKET SOCIETY: *Secretary* D. A. Elliott, Emmanuel College, Cambridge, CB2 3AP.

CHESTERFIELD CRICKET LOVERS' SOCIETY: *Secretary* B. Holling, 24 Woodland Way, Old Tupton, Chesterfield, Derbyshire.

COUNCIL OF CRICKET SOCIETIES, THE *Secretary* P. T. Roberts, 21 Hadrian Close, Lodge Park, Witham, Essex, CM8 1XA.

CRICKET SOCIETY, THE *Secretary* E. C. R. Rice, 11 Clive Court, Babington Road, London SW16 6AL.

CRICKET STATISTICIANS, ASSOCIATION OF: *Secretary* P. Wynne-Thomas, Mill House Farm, Haughton, Retford, Nottinghamshire. *Publicity* R. W. S. Miller, 16 Greendykes Road, Dundee, DD4 7NA.

ESSEX CRICKET SOCIETY: *Secretary* P. T. Roberts, 21 Hadrian Close, Lodge Park, Witham, Essex, CM8 1XA.

FYLDE COAST CRICKET SOCIETY: *Secretary* S. Kennedy, 36 Torquay Avenue, Marton, Blackpool, Lancashire.

HAMPSHIRE CRICKET SOCIETY: *Secretary* F. Bailey, 7 Lightfoot Grove, Basingstoke, Hampshire.

HEAVY WOOLLEN CRICKET SOCIETY: *Secretary* G. S. Cooper, 27 Milford Grove, Gomersal, Cleckheaton, West Yorkshire.

LANCASHIRE AND CHESHIRE CRICKET SOCIETY: *Secretary* H. W. Pardoe, Crantock, 117a Barlow Moor Road, Didsbury, Manchester, M20 8TS.

LIMITED-OVERS INFORMATION GROUP: *Secretary* T. Allcock, 57 Low Road, Rivelin, Sheffield, S6 5FY.

LINCOLNSHIRE CRICKET LOVERS' SOCIETY: *Secretary* C. Kennedy, ACP, 26 Eastwood Avenue, Grimsby, South Humberside, DN34 5BE.

NORTHERN CRICKET SOCIETY: *Secretary* R. Marsh, 113 Cross Gate Lane, Leeds, Yorkshire, LS15 7PJ.

NOTTINGHAM CRICKET SOCIETY: *Secretary* G. Blagdurn, 2 Inham Circus, Chilwell, Beeston, Nottinghamshire, NG9 4FN.

OXFORD UNIVERSITY CRICKET SOCIETY: *Secretary* Huw Richards, Corpus Christi College, Oxford.

ROTHERHAM CRICKET SOCIETY: *Secretary* J. A. R. Atkin, 15 Gallow Tree Road, Rotherham, South Yorkshire, S65 3EE.

SCOTLAND, CRICKET SOCIETY OF: *Secretary* A. J. Robertson, 19 Barlae Avenue, Eaglesham, Glasgow, G76 0DA.

SOMERSET WYVERNS: SOUTH – *Secretary* A. H. Riley, 14a Hart Road, Thundersley, Benfleet, Essex. NORTH – *Secretary* A. H. Coulson, 33 Whingate Grove, Leeds 12, Yorkshire.

STOURBRIDGE AND DISTRICT CRICKET SOCIETY: *Secretary* A. E. Lavender, 15 Richard Road, Walsall, WS5 3QW.

SUSSEX CRICKET SOCIETY: *Secretary* A. A. Dumbrell, 6 Southdown Avenue, Brighton, East Sussex, BN1 6EG.

SYDNEY BARNES CRICKET SOCIETY: *Secretary* J. D. Scholfield, 331 Turnhurst Road, Packmoor, Stoke-on-Trent, S77 4LA.

TODMORDEN CRICKET SOCIETY: *Secretary* J. Clayton, 76 Oak Avenue, Todmorden, Lancashire.

WALES, CRICKET SOCIETY OF: *Secretary* M. A. Hook, 8 Regina Terrace, Victoria Park, Cardiff, South Glamorgan, CF5 1DJ.

WEST LANCASHIRE CRICKET SOCIETY: *Secretary* D. H. Stringfellow, 36 Cardigan Road, Southport, Merseyside, PR8 4SF.

WOMBWELL CRICKET LOVERS' SOCIETY: *Secretary* J. Sokell, 42 Woodstock Road, Barnsley, South Yorkshire, S75 1DX.

ZIMBABWE, CRICKET SOCIETY OF: *Secretary* L. G. Morgenrood, 10 Elsworth Avenue, Balgravie, Salisbury, Zimbabwe.

SECOND ELEVEN CHAMPIONSHIP, 1980

Derbyshire were undefeated but managed only one win, although in three of the drawn games they were in a winning position when rain intervened, and they gained more bonus points than in 1979. Their strength lay in the batting, with the established batsmen doing well. J. W. Lister scored a fine double-century against Northamptonshire at Heanor and young players B. G. Cooper and C. M. Smailes both gave encouraging performances. The bowling was disappointing but P. G. Newman, formerly with Leicestershire, showed promise as a fast bowler. R. C. Wincer took nine for 71 against Leicestershire at Derby.

Essex had a disappointing season with no wins. Until N. Foster joined the side in July, G. E. Sainsbury was the mainstay of the pace attack with 30 wickets and a return of six for 72 against Surrey at Chelmsford. A. W. Lilley hit three centuries and led the batting, his 628 runs being 256 more than the next highest aggregate. R. Herbert, C. Gladwin and R. J. Leiper all played useful innings, Leiper looking a good prospect in his first season out of Schools cricket.

Glamorgan won the Championship for the first time since 1965. A. L. Jones was their most prolific batsman, with 878 runs at 48.77, while the bowling was headed by B. J. Lloyd, whose 21 wickets at 12.09 included a return of seven for 51 against Worcestershire at Hereford.

With only one win and three losses, **Gloucestershire** dropped three places to thirteenth position. M. Bowyer headed the batting averages, although M. W. Stovold scored the most runs. Sadiq Mohammad, in his only appearance, scored 152 and 93 against Leicestershire at Bristol and A. J. Hignell scored an unbeaten 98 against Warwickshire, also at Bristol. M. D. Partridge and J. H. Childs were the most successful bowlers with 23 wickets each; Partridge took seven for 32 in an innings against Somerset at Street, while Childs returned match figures of eight for 73 against Warwickshire at Bedworth.

Hampshire, with a strong batting line-up, moved up to fourth place. J. M. Rice and D. R. Turner made valuable contributions in their few appearances and wicket-keeper R. J. Parks was a consistent opener. R. E. Hayward impressed in his first season for the county, after two seasons with Buckinghamshire. Excellent bowling figures were recorded by S. N. C. Massey, seven for 49 against Essex at Southampton and six for 63 against Sussex at Hove; M. J. Bailey, nine for 88 against Gloucestershire at Bournemouth; and M. C. J. Nicholas, nine for 104 against Essex at Chelmsford.

Runners-up **Kent** were unbeaten, with five wins, and led the table for much of the season, until three drawn games left them in second place. Young players M. R. Benson and N. R. Taylor headed the batting averages, and four centuries were scored for the side. L. J. Wood, still at college and playing during the vacation, was the most successful bowler and took eleven for 101 against Surrey at Norbury. S. N. V. Waterton showed promise as a wicket-keeper-batsman and successfully deputised for A. P. E. Knott in the First Eleven.

In a season of little achievement, no **Lancashire** player was outstanding. G. E. Trim made their only century – 122 against Yorkshire – and sixteen-year-old R. Watson scored 54 not out on his début against Derbyshire at Old Trafford. Two experienced players, P. G. Lee, with 32 wickets, and R. M. Ratcliffe, with 24, bore the brunt of the bowling.

A young **Leicestershire** side had an improved season, with T. J. Boon and M. A. Garnham giving outstanding performances. Boon scored the most runs, his total of 648 including one century, and he returned nine for 103 in the match against Warwickshire at Nuneaton. Garnham, a brilliant wicket-keeper with 28 catches and four stumpings, also proved to be an able batsman. The leading wicket-taker, G. J. Parsons, bowled his way into the first team, as did J. P. Agnew, whose fourteen wickets for the Second Eleven included a return of six for 17 in the one-day victory over Worcestershire at Hinckley.

Although **Middlesex** dropped five places to seventh, they were encouraged by the promise shown by their younger players. S. P. Hughes, who headed the bowling averages, took seven for 41 against Warwickshire at Harefield, and seventeen-year-old R. J. Maru's 51 wickets included a return of six for 57 against Leicestershire at Hornsey. The batting was often inconsistent, although W. N. Slack played productively when he was available and hit a double-century against Hampshire at Southampton – the second Middlesex player to do so in Second Eleven cricket since World War Two. The other was R. O. Butcher in 1978.

Northamptonshire had a disappointing season, finishing at the bottom of the table, with no wins. There were no outstanding performances, although the 1979 England Schools all-rounder, N. A. Mallender, in his first season, headed both the batting and bowling averages.

Nottinghamshire, affected by injuries, were unable to establish a regular team, but promise was shown by some of the new young players. In his first full season, N. I. Weightman scored 683 runs and took eight wickets. Of the regular players, M. E. Allbrook took 37 wickets and K. Saxelby took 26. N. Nanan's four innings brought a total of 202 runs. Yet results were poor, with one win, one loss and fourteen drawn games.

Somerset, who finished in the middle of the table, found their resources strained at the beginning of the season and youngers players benefited from the extra practice. J. W. Lloyds, who headed the batting averages with 506 runs at 50.60, also took 24 wickets, including a return of six in an innings against Warwickshire at Solihull. N. F. M. Popplewell and M. Olive provided valuable support with the bat, and captain P. J. Robinson's 29 wickets included seven wickets in an innings against Glamorgan at Bristol.

Surrey, with four wins, four losses and four draws, had an encouraging season, with a well-balanced side, although advantages gained by good bowling performances were sometimes lost through inconsistent batting. G. Monkhouse, who joined the staff after two seasons with Cumberland, took 31 wickets, including a return of nine for 44 against Sussex at Cranleigh. Intikhab Alam, who captained the side at the beginning of the season, took six for 32 in an innings against Essex at Chelmsford. D. B. Pauline headed the batting with more than 500 runs, and I. R. Payne scored attractively in the second half of the season.

Sussex were often without their leading players who were promoted for county matches owing to injuries of senior players, and a middle-of-the-table position did not reflect the team's potential. However, there were some encouraging performances from the younger players, although no centuries were scored for the side in 1980. T. J. Head topped the batting averages and performed well behind the stumps, and J. R. P. Heath scored the most runs. The attack relied mainly on leading wicket-taker C. D. B. Fletcher, as well as A. C. S. Pigott and A. Willows.

Champions in 1979, **Warwickshire** took third place in 1980. Spin bowlers C. C. Clifford, G. J. Lord and D. M. Smith all performed well, Clifford's 72 wickets including eleven for 88 against Glamorgan at Edgbaston and six for 52 in an innings against Nottinghamshire at Newark. Lord took six for 27 in an innings and scored a century in the same match – against Leicestershire at Hinckley. M. A. Din, who led both the batting and bowling averages, returned nine for 63 against Taunton at Somerset, and S. P. Perryman took six for 66 in an innings against Yorkshire at Scarborough. The batting was often inconsistent, although nine centuries were hit for the side, three coming from G. P. Thomas and two from captain R. N. Abberley. J. Whitehouse also contributed much at the beginning of the season.

Worcestershire, with only one win, dropped to fourteenth place. The most consistent form came from players with First Eleven experience; although an encouraging number of young, local players are coming into the Second Eleven, few, as yet, have achieved consistency or prominence. Four players hit centuries for the side, and R. Harrison scored most runs. M. Saunders, who made his First Eleven début in 1980, took the most wickets, followed by J. Cumbes, who took six Glamorgan wickets for 62 at Hereford. W. R. Thomas returned seven for 72 against Yorkshire at Harrogate, but otherwise his bowling tended to be expensive.

An experienced **Yorkshire** side had another successful season, with five wins and only two defeats. Top-scorer S. N. Hartley's 598 runs at 49.83 included three centuries, the only other hundred hit for the side coming from M. D. Moxon. J. P. Whiteley's 52 wickets included a return of seven for 53 against Warwickshire at Edgbaston, while A. Ramage took ten wickets in a match on one occasion and N. C. Crawford took six for 78 against Warwickshire at Scarborough.

SECOND ELEVEN CHAMPIONSHIP FINAL TABLE

	Played	Won	Lost	Drawn	Bonus Points Batting	Bonus Points Bowling	Points	Average
Glamorgan	11	5	2	4	33	40	133	12.09
Kent	10	5	0	5	22	34	116	11.60
Warwickshire	17	6	6	5	42	61	175	10.29
Hampshire	11	3	1	7	30	37	103	9.36
Yorkshire	14	5	2	7	28	38	126	9.00
Surrey	12	4	4	4	17	39	104	8.66
Middlesex	12	3	3	6	23	43	102	8.50
Leicestershire	15	4	2	9	31	39	118	7.86
Somerset	8	1	3	4	15	29	56	7.00
Sussex	12	2	2	8	24	34	82	6.83
Lancashire	11	1	2	8	26	33	71	6.45
Derbyshire	10	1	0	9	25	27	64	6.40
Gloucestershire ...	12	1	3	8	21	35	68	5.66
Worcestershire	13	1	6	6	23	35	70	5.38
Nottinghamshire ..	16	1	1	14	32	39	83	5.18
Essex	8	0	4	4	18	23	41	5.12
Northamptonshire .	8	0	2	6	12	24	36	4.50

The following were abandoned without a ball being bowled: August 4, 5, 6 – Lancashire v Warwickshire; August 6, 7, 8 – Glamorgan v Yorkshire.

In the averages that follow, * against a score signifies not out, * against a name signifies the captain and † signifies wicket-keeper.

DERBYSHIRE SECOND ELEVEN

Matches 10: Won – Northamptonshire. Drawn – Lancashire (twice), Leicestershire (twice), Northamptonshire, Nottinghamshire (twice), Yorkshire (twice).

Batting Averages

	Innings	Not Outs	Runs	Highest Inns	Average
A. J. Borrington	7	2	277	120	55.40
J. W. Lister	14	1	538	209	41.38
A. Hill	13	1	454	98	37.83
M. Johnson	6	1	162	58*	32.40
K. G. Brooks	9	0	226	72	25.11
C. M. Smailes	13	0	288	43	22.15
†A. J. McLellan	11	0	227	71	20.63
P. G. Newman	6	2	73	35	18.25
N. D. Sulley	4	0	60	29	15.00
A. Watts	6	2	42	12*	10.50

Also batted: I. S. Anderson, S. Bailey, K. J. Barnett, D. Blank, I. V. Chipchase, B. G. Cooper, S. Daniels, M. Hendrick, M. Hodgkinson, A. J. Mellor, B. Mellor, R. Merriman, *P. E. Russell, J. Walters, R. C. Wincer, B. Wood. G. Maynard and P. Reeves did not bat.

Bowling Averages

	Overs	Maidens	Runs	Wickets	Average
I. S. Anderson	32	8	97	7	13.85
K. J. Barnett	77.3	33	166	9	18.44
R. C. Wincer	139.3	36	378	17	22.23
A. Watts	87.5	27	231	9	25.66
M. Johnson	112.2	35	262	9	29.11
A. J. Mellor	345.1	123	795	26	30.57
K. G. Brooks	114	44	260	7	37.14

Also bowled: D. Blank 49–18–136–3; I. V. Chipchase 6–2–20–1; M. Hendrick 46–12–88–4; A. Hill 5–3–13–0; G. Maynard 15–2–75–0; P. G. Newman 119.3–26–400–9; P. Reeves 9–2–25–0; P. E. Russell 93–30–190–2; C. M. Smailes 40.3–8–142–4; J. Walters 8–0–24–0; B. Wood 18–4–47–3.

ESSEX SECOND ELEVEN

Matches 8: Lost – Kent, Hampshire, Surrey, Sussex. Drawn – Kent, Hampshire, Surrey, Sussex.

Batting Averages

	Innings	Not Outs	Runs	Highest Inns	Average
A. W. Lilley	13	0	628	133	48.30
K. R. Pont	6	1	192	66*	38.40
R. Herbert	12	0	372	112	31.00
R. J. Leiper	13	1	357	63	29.75
C. Gladwin	13	0	328	61	25.23
M. S. A. McEvoy	10	1	197	63	21.88
*B. Taylor	5	1	73	28	18.25
M. Gouldstone	5	0	80	24	16.00
†R. Andrews	6	1	75	24	15.00
N. A. Foster	4	0	43	40	10.75

Also batted: M. Brown, D. Collier, N. H. C. Cooper, R. E. East, T. Foley, G. Hughes, S. Lines, E. Lowe, J. Nicholls, M. Pether, D. R. Pringle, P. Prichard, G. E. Sainsbury, G. J. Saville, T. S. Smith, C. Stone, S. Turner, M. S. Webber.

Bowling Averages

	Overs	Maidens	Runs	Wickets	Average
M. S. A. McEvoy	69.3	25	141	6	23.50
G. E. Sainsbury	260.3	60	810	30	27.00
N. A. Foster	96	21	305	11	27.72
R. Herbert	212.5	61	590	16	36.87

Also bowled: M. Brown 25–5–84–0; D. Collier 24–6–79–4; N. H. C. Cooper 18–1–77–1; T. Foley 77–23–188–4; G. Hughes 7–3–25–0; A. W. Lilley 23.2–7–64–3; K. R. Pont 71.2–21–152–5; D. R. Pringle 4–0–24–3; T. S. Smith 46–22–95–4; C. Stone 11–2–46–1; S. Turner 17.2–3–42–3.

GLAMORGAN SECOND ELEVEN

Matches 11: Won – Hampshire, Somerset, Warwickshire, Worcestershire (twice). Lost – Middlesex, Yorkshire. Drawn – Gloucestershire (twice) Somerset, Warwickshire. Abandoned – Yorkshire.

Batting Averages

	Innings	Not Outs	Runs	Highest Inns	Average
M. Cohen	6	2	344	135	86.00
A. L. Jones	18	0	878	135	48.77
D. A. Francis	11	0	420	131	38.18
G. C. Holmes	5	1	149	42*	37.25
R. C. Ontong	17	1	583	171	36.43
M. J. Llewellyn	9	0	325	125	36.11
*K. J. Lyons	10	2	208	50*	26.00
M. N. Davies	21	1	485	88	24.25
B. J. Lloyd	7	1	127	46	21.16
†T. Davies	16	5	229	59*	20.81
R. N. S. Hobbs	7	2	75	45	15.00
A. E. Cordle	7	2	74	19	14.80
E. A. Moseley	6	1	60	27	12.00

Also batted: G. Bray, A. G. Davies, J. Derrick, J. During, P. Harris, K. Punter, A. J. Mack, G. Martin, B. McBride, P. J. Mir, H. Morris, N. J. Perry, R. Richardson, J. G. Thomas, M. Williams.

Bowling Averages

	Overs	Maidens	Runs	Wickets	Average
B. J. Lloyd	135	40	254	21	12.09
R. N. S. Hobbs	118	46	229	16	14.31
E. A. Moseley	71	18	192	13	14.76
A. E. Cordle	140	33	348	22	15.81
R. C. Ontong	200	60	425	23	18.47
N. J. Perry	289	93	690	25	27.60
A. J. Mack	141	36	355	12	29.58

Also bowled: J. During 31–6–95–1; G. C. Holmes 30–9–90–4; P. Lawler 7–3–25–0; M. J. Llewellyn 11–1–46–0; K. J. Lyons 11–2–35–0; M. Mansell 40–10–128–4; G. Martin 40–17–84–2; P. J. Mir 44–18–72–7; K. Punter 21–7–68–0; J. G. Thomas 8–1–20–1; M. Williams 1–1–0–0.

GLOUCESTERSHIRE SECOND ELEVEN

Matches 12: Won – Warwickshire. Lost – Kent, Leicestershire, Somerset. Drawn – Glamorgan (twice), Hampshire (twice), Leicestershire, Warwickshire, Worcestershire (twice).

Batting Averages

	Innings	Not Outs	Runs	Highest Inns	Average
M. Bowyer	7	2	272	89*	54.40
B. C. Broad	6	0	240	88	40.00
P. Bainbridge	4	0	133	73	33.25
M. W. Stovold	13	1	397	103*	33.08
R. Broughton	4	0	131	125	32.75
S. J. Windaybank	17	2	383	100	25.53
†A. J. Wright	18	5	339	77*	22.60
A. Marsh	6	0	101	39	16.83
M. D. Partridge	10	1	151	94	16.77
J. H. Childs	8	2	86	34	14.33
I. Broome	10	5	71	35*	14.20
†R. Russell	6	2	47	26	11.75

Also batted: K. Arnold, M. Bailey, A. J. Brassington, J. Brooks, C. Connor, E. Cunningham, A. E. Davies, P. Dicks, D. A. Graveney, M. Haswell, N. Hennessy, A. J. Hignell, D. Lawrence, G. Little, D. Marsden, Sadiq Mohammad, L. Nicholls, R. B. Nicholls, I. L. Pont, N. Price, P. Roebuck, D. Simpkins, D. Surridge, A. H. Wilkins.

Bowling Averages

	Overs	Maidens	Runs	Wickets	Average
D. A. Graveney	51.5	26	68	6	11.33
M. D. Partridge	194.5	53	472	23	20.52
D. Surridge	52	12	138	6	23.00
J. H. Childs	304	128	564	23	24.52
D. Lawrence	114.4	25	411	14	29.35
I. Broome	224	46	689	21	32.80

Also bowled: K. Arnold 23–3–89–0; P. Bainbridge 41–9–117–1; B. M. Brain 40.2–13–119–4; B. C. Broad 20.1–4–68–5; C. Connor 20–4–55–0; E. Cunningham 9–1–43–1; P. Dicks 26–4–83–0; M. Haswell 15–3–55–1; D. Marsden 22–4–65–1; A. Marsh 107–22–370–9; Sadiq Mohammad 14–5–47–0; L. Nicholls 23–6–57–3; R. B. Nicholls 32.4–6–81–4; I. L. Pont 7–1–39–0; N. Price 27–3–111–4; P. Roebuck 11–2–35–1; D. Simpkins 58–14–187–1; M. W. Stovold 23–2–78–2; A. H. Wilkins 56–20–135–5; A. J. Wright 11–1–58–2.

HAMPSHIRE SECOND ELEVEN

Matches 11: Won – Essex, Somerset, Surrey. Lost – Glamorgan. Drawn – Essex, Gloucestershire (twice), Kent, Middlesex, Sussex (twice).

Batting Averages

	Innings	Not Outs	Runs	Highest Inns	Average
J. M. Rice	7	1	396	94*	66.00
D. R. Turner	5	1	199	98	49.75
†R. J. Parks	15	2	501	135	38.53
M. N. S. Taylor	6	2	151	47*	37.75
J. Hardy	12	5	216	58*	30.85
R. E. Hayward	20	3	467	85	27.47
T. M. Tremlett	5	0	115	76	23.00
S. M. Clements	18	0	413	62	22.94
V. P. Terry	17	2	318	56	21.20
T. D. W. Edwards	14	1	253	64	19.46
M. J. Bailey	12	3	170	31	18.88
M. C. J. Nicholas	5	0	91	25	18.20
S. N. C. Massey	10	2	107	26	13.37
R. R. Savage	9	1	105	35	13.12

Also batted: G. Edwards, K. C. Finch, S. F. Graf, P. Green, R. Keeble, S. J. Malone, T. Morton, N. Moseley, S. J. J. Poland, C. L. Smith, J. W. Southern.

Bowling Averages

	Overs	Maidens	Runs	Wickets	Average
T. M. Tremlett	97.3	30	184	12	15.33
S. F. Graf	58.3	19	115	7	16.42
S. N. C. Massey	323.1	98	728	40	18.20
M. C. J. Nicholas	72.2	18	200	10	20.00
J. M. Rice	122	45	219	10	21.90
M. J. Bailey	319.4	110	770	35	22.00
M. N. S. Taylor	63.1	18	153	6	25.50
S. J. Malone	160.4	45	423	14	30.21
S. M. Clements	134.3	35	404	13	31.07

Also bowled: G. Downham 43–6–164–5; T. D. W. Edwards 3–2–4–1; R. E. Hayward 92–23–250–6; R. Keeble 12–2–37–1; N. Meadows 32–4–94–1; G. Oliver 8.2–1–45–0; S. J. J. Poland 106–20–324–2; R. R. Savage 2–1–5–0; C. L. Smith 24–12–54–1; J. W. Southern 14–4–37–1; V. P. Terry 4–1–8–0.

KENT SECOND ELEVEN

Matches 10: Won – Essex, Gloucestershire, Middlesex, Surrey (twice). Drawn – Essex, Hampshire, Middlesex, Sussex (twice).

Batting Averages

	Innings	Not Outs	Runs	Highest Inns	Average
N. R. Taylor	8	2	266	73*	44.33
M. R. Benson	13	1	489	170	40.75
D. Nicholls	7	2	178	112*	35.60
R. M. Ellison	8	1	240	118	34.28
E. Baptiste	15	6	272	50*	30.22
C. J. C. Rowe	5	1	120	73	30.00
R. W. Hills	9	3	176	53	29.33
D. G. Aslett	17	1	412	76	25.75
L. Potter	11	0	276	90	25.09
N. J. Kemp	15	1	283	77	20.21
S. G. Hinks	10	0	182	80	18.20
N. A. Felton	9	0	152	43	16.88
†S. N. V. Waterton	8	1	102	33*	14.57

Also batted: C. S. Cowdrey, G. W. Johnson, *B. W. Luckhurst, K. McClean, J. Skinner, G. D. Spelman, L. J. Wood.

Bowling Averages

	Overs	Maidens	Runs	Wickets	Average
C. J. C. Rowe	142	54	217	24	9.04
L. J. Wood	196.1	57	509	31	16.41
D. G. Aslett	78.2	20	225	13	17.30
G. D. Spelman	44	12	120	6	20.00
N. J. Kemp	219.3	61	574	24	23.91
J. Skinner	58	15	196	8	24.50
R. W. Hills	126.4	38	312	10	31.20
E. Baptiste	212.4	50	637	20	31.85

Also bowled: R. M. Ellison 31–9–67–3; J. Freeman 9–5–17–1; S. G. Hinks 15–3–53–3; G. W. Johnson 19–6–39–3; L. Potter 26–7–66–4; N. R. Taylor 61.1–13–176–5.

LANCASHIRE SECOND ELEVEN

Matches 11: Won – Leicestershire. Lost – Warwickshire, Yorkshire. Drawn – Derbyshire (twice), Leicestershire, Northamptonshire (twice), Nottinghamshire (twice), Yorkshire. Abandoned – Warwickshire.

Batting Averages

	Innings	Not Outs	Runs	Highest Inns	Average
J. Abrahams	6	2	271	83	67.75
*H. Pilling	13	4	321	64*	35.66
†G. E. Trim	16	3	426	122	32.76
I. Cockbain	5	0	160	50	32.00
B. Thorpe	7	1	170	86	28.33
M. Tracy	4	0	106	38	26.50
†G. Fowler	8	1	178	97	25.42
R. M. Ratcliffe	8	3	123	36	24.60
D. K. Beckett	8	3	196	68	24.50
K. Hayes	12	2	158	50	15.80
S. J. O'Shaughnessy	12	1	150	50*	13.63
J. Hartley	4	0	40	15	10.00

Also batted: P. J. W. Allott, R. Berry, P. Davies, I. Folley, P. Gill, F. C. Hayes, I. Herbert, D. P. Hughes, P. Iddon, A. Kennedy, P. G. Lee, D. Lloyd, D. Makinson, G. Marsh, J. Monks, R. Pienaar, N. V. Radford, R. Savage, J. Simmons, J. Stanworth, D. Varey, R. Watson, J. Whitehead. S. Crawley, W. Fowler, C. J. Scott, S. Sharp and M. Wallwork did not bat.

Bowling Averages

	Overs	Maidens	Runs	Wickets	Average
P. G. Lee	246.4	72	607	32	18.96
P. J. W. Allott	77.5	21	197	10	19.70
R. M. Ratcliffe	213.1	58	485	24	20.20
P. Iddon	50.1	11	195	8	24.37
J. Abrahams	90	23	221	8	27.62

Also bowled: I. Bedford 6–0–21–1; I. Folley 4–0–20–2; J. Hartley 33–9–144–1; I. Herbert 4–0–23–1; W. Hogg 29–9–74–2; D. P. Hughes 39–17–58–4; D. Makinson 14–3–60–0; K. McMahon 16–3–37–0; J. Monks 15–3–67–0; S. J. O'Shaughnessy 60.3–7–253–6; R. Pienaar 16–3–51–3; N. V. Radford 10–2–30–1; R. Savage 53–13–166–0; B. Thorpe 22–2–99–1; M. Tracy 60–16–184–2; G. E. Trim 7–3–11–0; R. Watson 21.2–5–69–2.

LEICESTERSHIRE SECOND ELEVEN

Matches 15: Won – Gloucestershire, Middlesex, Northamptonshire, Worcestershire. Lost – Lancashire, Warwickshire. Drawn – Derbyshire (twice), Gloucestershire, Lancashire, Northamptonshire, Nottinghamshire (twice), Warwickshire, Worcestershire.

Batting Averages

	Innings	Not Outs	Runs	Highest Inns	Average
N. E. Briers	9	1	429	114	53.62
K. Shuttleworth	9	6	160	47*	53.33
T. J. Boon	17	3	648	139*	46.28
B. Dudleston	14	2	435	143	36.25

Batting Averages – *continued*

	Innings	Not Outs	Runs	Highest Inns	Average
D. J. Munden	21	4	523	64	30.76
I. P. Butcher	23	2	606	126	28.85
R. A. Cobb	23	2	465	91	22.14
†M. A. Garnham	24	3	457	80*	21.76
M. Schepens	21	1	422	70	21.10
D. A. Wenlock	13	2	144	29	13.09
P. Booth	14	3	128	41	11.63

Also batted: J. P. Agnew, C. Balderstone, D. J. Barlow, T. Brown, N. G. B. Cook, P. Gordon, A. Greasley, *K. Higgs, N. Lashkari, G. J. Parsons, J. Potts, E. Roberts, L. B. Taylor.

Bowling Averages

	Overs	Maidens	Runs	Wickets	Average
K. Higgs	106.2	39	182	17	10.70
D. J. Munden	41	11	108	8	13.50
J. P. Agnew	115.3	37	238	14	17.00
G. J. Parsons	238.2	64	601	31	19.38
T. J. Boon	70	13	217	10	21.70
D. A. Wenlock	224.3	57	554	25	22.16
N. G. B. Cook	97	28	259	10	25.90
P. Booth	245.3	55	607	23	26.39
B. Dudleston	170.1	51	400	15	26.66
K. Shuttleworth	226	73	493	15	32.86
D. J. Barlow	307.2	82	797	18	44.27

Also bowled: C. Balderstone 11–2–36–1; C. Broadby 1–1–0–0; N. E. Briers 14–3–45–1; I. P. Butcher 20–5–73–0; P. Gordon 14.2–4–39–0; A. Greasley 47.3–16–107–2; J. Potts 27–6–53–1; E. Roberts 6–0–28–0; L. B. Taylor 16.3–4–56–1.

MIDDLESEX SECOND ELEVEN

Matches 12: Won – Glamorgan, Warwickshire (twice). Lost – Kent, Leicestershire, Sussex. Drawn – Hampshire, Kent, Surrey (twice), Sussex, Yorkshire.

Batting Averages

	Innings	Not Outs	Runs	Highest Inns	Average
A. G. Smith	8	1	374	83	53.42
*W. N. Slack	16	2	708	202*	50.57
R. O. Butcher	4	0	177	62	44.25
†P. R. Downton	4	0	169	69*	42.25
†I. J. Gould	5	0	149	75	29.80
R. E. P. Ellis	22	2	536	168*	26.80
M. Cohen	7	0	160	54	22.85
K. P. Tomlins	14	2	274	56	22.83
K. D. James	18	3	304	50*	20.26
N. G. Cowans	13	2	220	52	20.00
M. S. Scott	18	2	296	48	18.50
†C. E. F. Goldie	7	0	129	49	18.42
*M. J. Smith	16	0	285	54	17.81
†C. P. Metson	8	3	77	21	15.40
W. G. Merry	11	5	89	30*	14.83
R. J. Maru	18	1	247	36	14.52
C. F. W. Sergeant	6	1	67	25	13.40
P. E. McEwan	6	0	74	25	12.33
K. Brown	9	2	86	27	12.28

Also batted: J. Allan, *D. Bennett, P. A. Brooks, K. Clarke, P. H. Edmonds, J. W. Edrich, S. P. Gatting, S. P. Hughes, J. Leppard, S. J. Lines, P. Maru, M. A. Murfin, M. O'Neill, C. Rose, F. Stevenson, A. Taylor, P. Ward, P. Waterman, M. S. Webber, J. Whittaker, S. M. N. Zaidi.

Bowling Averages

	Overs	Maidens	Runs	Wickets	Average
S. P. Hughes	139.4	34	374	29	12.89
P. A. Brooks	128	65	197	14	14.07
R. J. Maru	398.3	148	959	51	18.80
W. G. Merry	285	67	756	27	28.00
N. G. Cowans	203	50	594	21	28.28
K. D. James	248	64	621	20	31.05

Also bowled: R. O. Butcher 1–0–2–0; P. H. Edmonds 29–8–65–2; R. E. Ellis 16.2–4–63–0; P. E. McEwan 4–1–23–0; M. A. Murfin 45.4–11–141–4; M. O'Neill 4–0–9–0; C. F. W. Sergeant 40.3–7–150–5; W. N. Slack 16–4–40–1; M. J. Smith 10–4–35–0; F. Stevenson 18–3–51–5; K. P. Tomlins 104–31–241–7; P. Ward 12–1–20–0; S. M. N. Zaidi 7–1–19–0.

NORTHAMPTONSHIRE SECOND ELEVEN

Matches 8: Lost – Derbyshire, Leicestershire. Drawn – Derbyshire, Lancashire (twice), Leicestershire, Nottinghamshire (twice).

Batting Averages

	Innings	Not Outs	Runs	Highest Inns	Average
N. A. Mallender	9	3	342	99	57.00
R. J. Bailey	10	1	272	46	30.22
D. J. Capel	9	0	231	92	25.66
R. M. Carter	6	1	122	43	24.40
R. M. Tindall	10	0	234	56	23.40
D. J. Wild	10	2	158	48	19.75
G. Forster	10	2	143	55*	17.87

Also batted: R. Benjamin, C. D. Booden, R. J. Boyd-Moss, R. M. Cooper, †R. J. Doughty, D. E. East, D. C. N. Eland, N. J. Gadsby, M. J. Grimley, R. Illingworth, S. J. Lines, K. G. McMahon, N. A. P. Meadows, E. P. Neal, A. S. Pearson, I. G. Peck, D. Priestley, †N. Priestley, B. L. Reynolds, R. Swann, R. G. Williams.

Bowling Averages

	Overs	Maidens	Runs	Wickets	Average
N. A. Mallender	159	40	383	15	25.53
D. J. Wild	62	10	188	7	26.85
C. D. Booden	111	24	329	11	29.90
D. C. N. Eland	119.2	25	358	11	32.54
G. Forster	159.4	43	429	12	35.75

Also bowled: R. Benjamin 8–0–38–0; R. J. Boyd-Moss 18–4–30–2; D. J. Capel 18–2–68–2; R. M. Carter 35.2–4–115–2; R. M. Cooper 18–4–44–0; N. J. Gadsby 3–0–19–0; R. Illingworth 4–0–10–1; N. A. P. Meadows 16–3–64–3; K. G. McMahon 15–0–99–0; E. P. Neal 14–2–43–0; D. Priestley 27–8–98–2; R. Swann 23–4–89–1; R. M. Tindall 55–14–186–5; R. G. Williams 41.5–17–50–5.

NOTTINGHAMSHIRE SECOND ELEVEN

Matches 16: Won – Warwickshire. Lost – Warwickshire. Drawn – Derbyshire (twice), Lancashire (twice), Leicestershire (twice), Northamptonshire (twice), Surrey, Sussex (twice), Worcestershire, Yorkshire (twice).

Batting Averages

	Innings	Not Outs	Runs	Highest Inns	Average
M. J. Harris	7	5	164	64*	82.00
R. T. Robinson	9	2	413	104*	59.00
*R. A. White	8	4	216	82	54.00
P. H. Williams	8	2	284	101	47.33
P. A. Todd	5	0	207	136	41.40
M. E. Allbrook	10	7	111	51*	37.00
B. Hassan	3	0	99	80	33.00
H. T. Tunnicliffe	11	0	350	123	31.81
†B. N. French	11	1	305	61	30.50
K. S. Mackintosh	17	4	388	99	29.84
N. I. Weightman	23	0	683	131	29.69
R. E. Dexter	11	1	290	48	29.00
M. A. Fell	11	1	271	79	27.10
†C. C. Curzon	11	1	223	56	22.30
K. Saxelby	8	1	150	54	21.42
P. J. Hacker	10	3	125	26	17.85
J. D. Birch	8	1	112	44*	16.00
D. E. Coote	3	0	42	31	14.00
M. K. Bore	3	0	36	19	12.00

Also batted: S. Ambrose, G. Bramley, P. G. Carling, K. E. Cooper, E. E. Hemmings, N. J. B. Illingworth, M. R. Jackson, N. K. James, N. Nanan, S. Ogrizovic, R. A. Pick, N. A. Stent, D. J. Walker, W. K. Watson, P. G. Wright. A. F. D. Ellison did not bat.

Bowling Averages

	Overs	Maidens	Runs	Wickets	Average
W. K. Watson	75.4	21	188	13	14.46
N. J. B. Illingworth	90	26	226	12	18.83
N. I. Weightman	63.1	25	159	8	19.87
*R. A. White	128.4	34	281	13	21.61
K. Saxelby	212.3	45	584	26	22.46
K. E. Cooper	98.4	30	222	8	27.75
P. J. Hacker	150.3	44	371	13	28.53
M. E. Allbrook	421.3	109	1,081	37	29.21
M. K. Bore	105	35	251	7	35.85
K. S. Mackintosh	224.5	56	656	16	41.00

Also bowled: S. Ambrose 27–3–104–1; M. A. Fell 55–16–112–5; M. J. Harris 20–4–53–1; B. Hassan 1–0–5–0; E. E. Hemmings 1–1–0–0; M. R. Jackson 23–1–98–1; N. K. James 13–2–48–0; P. A. Todd 1–0–2–0; H. T. Tunnicliffe 75–29–122–5; D. J. Walker 8–2–23–1; P. H. Williams 12–7–15–0; P. G. Wright 4.4–1–10–1.

SOMERSET SECOND ELEVEN

Matches 8: Won – Gloucestershire. Lost – Glamorgan, Hampshire, Warwickshire. Drawn – Glamorgan, Warwickshire, Worcestershire (twice).

Batting Averages

	Innings	Not Outs	Runs	Highest Inns	Average
J. W. Lloyds	11	1	506	126	50.60
P. A. Slocombe	10	2	317	82	39.62
N. F. M. Popplewell	12	3	353	65	39.22
M. Olive	15	0	513	126	34.20
*P. J. Robinson	10	2	189	60	23.62
†T. Gard	14	3	254	79*	23.09
R. J. Ollis	11	0	180	70	16.36
J. H. N. Wilson	8	0	81	24	10.12

Also batted: A. Parsons, D. Breakwell, A. R. A. Cooper, G. E. Cunningham, J. O. Curran, M. R. Davis, P. Dickenson, C. H. Dredge, D. R. Gurr, K. F. Jennings, M. J. Kitchen, J. Miles, C. Muggeridge, K. O'Keefe, S. Palfrey, N. R. Parsloe, S. Patil, N. Russom, M. Smith, A. W. J. Spiller, R. Talbot, S. Thorne, J. Woods.

Bowling Averages

	Overs	Maidens	Runs	Wickets	Average
P. J. Robinson	214.1	75	525	29	18.10
A. R. A. Cooper	33	6	124	6	20.66
J. W. Lloyds	213.4	52	649	24	27.04
N. F. M. Popplewell	197	64	573	16	35.81
N. Russom	67	19	215	6	35.83

Also bowled: D. Breakwell 41–14–56–0; J. O. Curran 28–8–76–4; M. R. Davis 58–15–165–0; C. H. Dredge 34–9–74–2; D. R. Gurr 17–4–44–2; G. J. Hall 26–12–57–2; K. F. Jennings 21–4–76–0; J. Miles 21–2–75–4; C. Muggeridge 22–1–87–2; K. O'Keefe 16–3–45–1; S. Palfrey 20–4–81–3; N. R. Parsloe 22.2–3–76–0; S. Patil 37–19–75–1; P. A. Slocombe 37–9–94–3; M. Smith 10–1–46–1; A. W. J. Spiller 4–2–20–0; R. Talbot 13–2–59–0; J. Woods 11–1–72–0.

SURREY SECOND ELEVEN

Matches 12: Won – Essex, Sussex (twice), Yorkshire. Lost – Hampshire, Kent (twice), Yorkshire. Drawn – Essex, Middlesex (twice), Nottinghamshire.

Batting Averages

	Innings	Not Outs	Runs	Highest Inns	Average
D. B. Pauline	14	2	541	166*	45.08
D. J. Thomas	8	3	208	51	41.60
M. A. Lynch	12	1	401	112	36.45
R. J. Peers	11	3	271	78*	33.87
†S. S. Surridge	14	6	244	46*	30.50
I. R. Payne	16	2	406	72	29.00
*Intikhab Alam	9	2	190	69	27.14
G. P. Howarth	10	0	265	60	26.50
M. J. Bamber	19	1	470	76	26.11
M. S. Butcher	12	1	160	41	14.54
G. Monkhouse	13	0	171	39	13.15
P. H. L. Wilson	10	0	104	39	10.40

Also batted: R. G. L. Cheatle, G. S. Clinton, I. J. Curtis, †A. Davies, T. P. Dodd, N. J. Falkner, *D. Gibson, R. A. Milne, A. Needham, C. H. O'Keefe, A. Stewart, N. M. Stewart, E. Tull.

Bowling Averages

	Overs	Maidens	Runs	Wickets	Average
I. R. Payne	88	34	153	12	12.75
Intikhab Alam	241.1	87	465	32	14.53
G. Monkhouse	220	68	511	31	16.48
R. G. L. Cheatle	80	29	195	10	19.50
P. H. L. Wilson	192.3	57	495	25	19.80
I. J. Curtis	96.5	33	211	10	21.10
D. J. Thomas	210.4	60	517	20	25.85
A. Needham	288	91	641	22	29.13

Also bowled: G. S. Clinton 16–3–59–1; T. P. Dodd 3–1–8–0; G. P. Howarth 18–8–32–2; M. A. Lynch 25–7–56–3; R. A. Milne 12–2–33–1; C. H. O'Keefe 5–1–22–2; D. B. Pauline 23–6–49–2; E. Tull 9–2–27–0.

SUSSEX SECOND ELEVEN

Matches 12: Won – Essex, Middlesex. Lost – Surrey (twice). Drawn – Essex, Hampshire (twice), Kent (twice), Middlesex, Nottinghamshire (twice).

Batting Averages

	Innings	Not Outs	Runs	Highest Inns	Average
†T. J. Head	16	3	421	83	32.38
J. R. P. Heath	18	1	529	67	31.11
*A. C. S. Pigott	17	2	426	89	28.40
T. D. Booth Jones	9	1	208	54	26.00
A. M. Green	22	2	468	89	23.40
S. J. G. Doggart	6	1	107	48	21.40
P. Harris	7	0	148	69	21.14
A. P. Wells	14	2	198	52	15.23

Also batted: J. R. T. Barclay, A. Beer, R. S. Cowan, M. R. Donald, S. Farrell, C. D. B. Fletcher, D. P. Grammer, I. A. Greig, J. J. Groome, P. Hayes, R. Haynes, A. Jones, N. Lemon, G. S. le Roux, S. Lishman, P. W. G. Parker, C. P. Phillipson, P. Price, M. Smallwood, D. J. Smith, J. Spencer, G. Sprenger, A. Stewart, S. J. Storey, C. E. Waller, C. M. Wells, K. C. Wessels, A. Westbury, A. Willows.

Bowling Averages

	Overs	Maidens	Runs	Wickets	Average
C. E. Waller	75	34	123	7	17.57
C. D. B. Fletcher	309	83	859	36	23.86
J. Spencer	145.4	45	329	13	25.30
A. C. S. Pigott	294.3	53	886	34	26.05
A. Willows	297.3	92	833	30	27.76
J. R. P. Heath	71	23	205	6	34.16
S. J. G. Doggart	94.1	30	243	7	34.71

Also bowled: J. R. T. Barclay 49.2–21–99–4; M. R. Donald 15–4–54–0; S. Farrell 19–2–71–1; I. A. Greig 60–24–134–5; P. Hayes 7–1–14–0; R. Haynes 5–0–22–0; A. Jones 28–3–126–1; G. S. le Roux 15–5–50–2; S. Lishman 11–2–28–1; P. Price 12–4–32–2; A. P. Wells 24–4–84–4; C. M. Wells 27.1–6–88–0; A. Westbury 24–5–85–1.

WARWICKSHIRE SECOND ELEVEN

Matches 17: Won – Lancashire, Leicestershire, Nottinghamshire, Somerset, Worcestershire (twice). Lost – Glamorgan, Gloucestershire, Middlesex (twice), Nottinghamshire, Yorkshire. Drawn – Glamorgan, Gloucestershire, Leicestershire, Somerset, Yorkshire. Abandoned – Lancashire.

Batting Averages

	Innings	Not Outs	Runs	Highest Inns	Average
M. A. Din	6	1	258	83	51.60
S. J. Rouse	9	2	324	123	46.28
†C. Maynard	12	1	465	113	42.27
J. Whitehouse	19	1	741	116	41.16
*R. N. Abberley	28	5	853	115	37.08
G. A. Tedstone	10	1	265	83*	29.44
G. P. Thomas	27	1	740	126	28.46
A. Sam	29	0	737	80	25.41
D. Marsh	7	1	136	55	22.66
G. J. Lord	22	1	456	117	21.71
R. H. I. B. Dyer	12	0	225	49	18.75
D. C. Hopkins	11	2	153	32*	17.00
R. A. Smith	11	0	155	41	14.09
S. P. Perryman	11	4	88	27	12.57
D. M. Smith	12	4	93	29	11.62

Also batted: A. Barnard, N. J. Bulpitt, J. A. Claughton, C. C. Clifford, A. M. Ferreira, T. D. Harris, P. Henney, K. R. Maguire, A. S. M. Oakman, T. O'Donnell, P. R. Oliver, K. Parrish, I. L. Pont, G. C. Small, P. Smith, S. P. Sutcliffe, H. Twizell, S. H. Wootton.

Bowling Averages

	Overs	Maidens	Runs	Wickets	Average
M. A. Din	45	6	156	13	12.00
A. M. Ferreira	61	14	114	8	14.25
C. C. Clifford	571	204	1,162	72	16.13
D. C. Hopkins	262	65	591	36	16.41
D. M. Smith	223	78	526	27	19.48
T. O'Donnell	87	17	232	11	21.09
S. P. Perryman	221	64	510	22	23.18
K. R. Maguire	178	38	557	18	30.94
G. J. Lord	225	61	578	18	32.11
S. J. Rouse	143	33	394	12	32.83

Also bowled: R. N. Abberley 6–2–7–0; A. Barnard 18–4–43–3; N. J. Bulpitt 21–1–88–1; R. H. I. B. Dyer 2–0–17–0; D. Marsh 54–18–127–3; P. R. Oliver 22–4–57–4; K. Parrish 12–2–31–0; I. L. Pont 5–1–34–0; C. A. Sam 3–2–2–1; G. C. Small 61–13–174–2; P. Smith 11–3–27–0; R. A. Smith 82–23–214–3; S. P. Sutcliffe 142–36–373–9; G. P. Thomas 3.1–0–22–0; H. Twizell 21–6–47–2; J. Whitehouse 1–0–1–0.

WORCESTERSHIRE SECOND ELEVEN

Matches 13: Won – Yorkshire. Lost – Glamorgan (twice), Leicestershire, Warwickshire (twice), Yorkshire. Drawn – Gloucestershire (twice), Leicestershire, Somerset (twice), Nottinghamshire.

Batting Averages

	Innings	Not Outs	Runs	Highest Inns	Average
S. P. Henderson	10	1	420	80	46.66
*B. L. D'Oliveira	6	2	169	120*	42.25
T. S. Curtis	13	1	501	136*	41.75
R. Harrison	22	2	745	108	37.25
M. J. Weston	20	2	635	110*	35.27
V. A. Holder	15	4	247	62*	22.45
B. J. R. Jones	11	1	224	64	22.40
W. R. Thomas	14	4	222	73	22.20
†S. Walker	9	1	156	51*	19.50
J. Cumbes	8	1	113	49	16.14
J. B. R. Jones	19	2	206	28	12.11

Also batted: R. Broughton, D. Dolan, D. D'Oliveira, †P. B. Fisher, E. J. O. Hemsley, †D. J. Humphries, P. A. Neale, R. Palmer, M. J. Reid, J. Roe, M. Scott, G. Toogood, A. Warner, S. Watkins.

Bowling Averages

	Overs	Maidens	Runs	Wickets	Average
A. Warner	78	20	184	9	20.44
M. Saunders	147	25	482	22	21.90
D. N. Patel	144	45	366	15	24.40
R. Harrison	74.3	16	237	8	29.62
J. Cumbes	280.2	78	596	20	29.80
J. B. R. Jones	77.4	14	234	7	33.42
V. A. Holder	261	59	643	18	35.72
W. R. Thomas	150.4	19	497	11	45.18

Also bowled: H. L. Alleyne 21–4–36–3; B. L. D'Oliveira 82–28–176–3; R. Palmer 25–3–86–2; J. Roe 26–6–106–0.

YORKSHIRE SECOND ELEVEN

Matches 14: Won – Glamorgan, Lancashire, Surrey, Warwickshire, Worcestershire. Lost – Surrey, Worcestershire. Drawn – Derbyshire (twice), Lancashire, Middlesex, Nottinghamshire (twice), Warwickshire. Abandoned – Glamorgan.

Batting Averages

	Innings	Not Outs	Runs	Highest Inns	Average
K. Sharp	7	1	338	89	56.33
S. N. Hartley	12	0	598	173	49.83
*C. Johnson	20	8	545	85*	45.41
P. G. Ingham	16	1	553	82	36.86
H. P. Cooper	7	3	123	33	30.75
M. D. Moxon	21	4	470	112*	27.64
P. B. Woodliffe	12	1	255	76	23.18
M. Brearley	11	1	222	75	22.20
†S. P. Coverdale	13	6	135	34	19.28
J. P. Whiteley	11	3	138	51*	17.25
A. P. Sutton	8	0	92	28	11.50
†S. J. Rhodes	5	0	54	26	10.80
N. C. Crawford	5	0	51	25	10.20

Also batted: A. P. Arundell, G. Cardall, P. Carrick, S. J. Dennis, J. H. Hampshire, P. J. Hartley, R. J. Heritage, C. Lethbridge, N. Lloyd, J. D. Love, A. A. Metcalfe, A. Ramage, P. Robinson, K. Tighe. C. Austin and R. G. Lumb did not bat.

Bowling Averages

	Overs	Maidens	Runs	Wickets	Average
A. Ramage	98	35	225	15	15.00
R. J. Heritage	160	51	499	22	22.68
H. P. Cooper	294	109	574	25	22.96
J. P. Whiteley	535	197	1,303	52	25.05
N. C. Crawford	77	14	243	8	30.37
S. J. Dennis	233	53	711	13	54.69

Also bowled: A. P. Arundell 73–17–218–5; G. Austin 9–1–29–0; P. Carrick 68–28–107–5; P. J. Hartley 87–19–303–3; S. N. Hartley 37–6–150–2; P. G. Ingham 1–1–0–0; C. Lethbridge 9.2–2–41–2; J. D. Love 14–5–24–0; M. D. Moxon 19–8–59–1; P. Robinson 4–1–9–0; K. Tighe 37–12–105–1; P. B. Woodliffe 36–20–83–4.

WARWICK UNDER 25 COMPETITION, 1980

By A. H. WIGGETT

Zone A: Yorkshire repeated their previous year's success and again qualified for the semi-finals, a total of sixteen points from their six zonal matches giving them a two-point lead over Lancashire and Nottinghamshire. Lancashire were runners-up by virtue of one away win. Yorkshire's sole defeat was at Nottingham, where the home county won an exciting game by 2 runs. Heavy rain caused the "Roses" fixture at York to be abandoned, but Yorkshire were successful in the return match at Haslingden. After Lancashire's home game against Nottinghamshire had also been called off without a ball being bowled, the return ended in a tie, both counties scoring 147 runs. The luckless Derbyshire finished bottom once more, although they improved on their 1979 record by winning their low-scoring, home game against Nottinghamshire by two wickets.

Zone B: Middlesex, starting splendidly, won their first four matches and so built up an almost unassailable lead by the end of June. Two early victories over the much-fancied Leicestershire side gave them confidence, and despite losing their final game to Essex they finished comfortable zonal winners – by four points over Northamptonshire, non-participants in the previous year's competition, who finished strongly to record two good wins over Essex. Leicestershire never quite realised their potential, although able to call on such highly promising players as Boon, Parsons and wicket-keeper Garnham, all of whom had experience at first-class level. They did, however, record good wins over Essex (twice) and Northamptonshire. Essex won just one group match, but to their credit this victory, by 21 runs at Chelmsford, was against group winners Middlesex. R. J. Leiper, with a sound 74, helped Essex set Middlesex a target of 250, which they narrowly failed to achieve.

Zone C: Sussex won this group by virtue of a greater number of away wins. As Kent finished level with Sussex on points, their fixture at Tunbridge Wells in June was, in retrospect, crucial. In this, Sussex, put in to bat, scored 204 for five in 40 overs, A. M. Green hitting 57. Despite a sound 41 by M. Benson, Kent managed only 178. Sussex also won both matches against Surrey, Green again playing a prominent part with an innings of 69 at Horsham. Kent were twice successful against Hampshire, at Canterbury and Southampton; at The Oval their game against Surrey was abandoned without a ball being bowled. Of Hampshire's two matches against Sussex the first, at Arundel, was abandoned; in the second, which Hampshire won by 45 runs at Southampton, the South African, C. L. Smith, made 62 and M. C. J. Nicholas 77 out of Hampshire's 212 for three. Surrey, who never played to their potential, finished with only one win to their credit, this by six wickets at Southampton where I. R. Payne scored 61 out of a total of 145 for four wickets.

Zone D: This group was badly affected by the weather, no fewer than five of the twelve matches finishing with no result. Gloucestershire were particularly hard hit, two of their first four games being abandoned and a third restricted to only seven overs. Not surprisingly, they were the only county of the sixteen who failed to record a win. Warwickshire were unbeaten and this, together with three "no results", made them clear winners of the group. By beating Glamorgan at Edgbaston and Chepstow they were able to end the Welsh county's challenge. The young Glamorgan side, coached by former county player Kevin Lyons, recorded two good wins over Worcestershire and also came out best in a tight finish against Gloucestershire at Pontardulais. Worcestershire were restricted to a single victory over Gloucestershire, M. Weston scoring a sound 54 in their 50-run victory.

Semi-final: *Warwickshire v Yorkshire; at Birmingham, August 17.* Warwickshire won by six wickets. Yorkshire scored 182 for three, owing much to an unbroken partnership of 130 between J. D. Love (63 not out) and M. Moxon (58 not out). Warwickshire, taking no risks, were steered home by some excellent batting from R. I. Dyer (87) and T. A. Lloyd (61).

Semi-final: *Sussex v Middlesex; at Hove, August 18.* Sussex won by 44 runs. Rain prevented play on the seventeenth, but fine, dry conditions prevailed the following day and an enjoyable game was played without interruption. Sussex, having been put in, scored 172 for nine in their

40 overs, A. M. Green making 42 and A. P. Wells 34. For Middlesex, Connor took three for 22 and K. D. James three for 30. Middlesex found scoring difficult against tight bowling and were dismissed for 128 in 37.1 overs, the wickets, except for two run outs, being shared by five Sussex bowlers.

FINAL

SUSSEX v WARWICKSHIRE

At Birmingham, August 31. Sussex won by virtue of losing the fewer wickets. The appalling weather, which caused the cancellation of the 1979 final and seriously disrupted many matches in 1980, relented sufficiently to allow Warwickshire and Sussex to enjoy one of the closest contests in the history of this popular competition. Sussex, captained by I. A. Greig, the 1979 Cambridge captain, won the toss and elected to bat on a good wicket and in bright sunshine. A sound 74 by the consistent Green and 61 from the promising all-rounder, Wells, ensured a reasonable Sussex score, le Roux, with an unbeaten 45, helping it along to 246 for five. In reply, Warwickshire reached 91 before losing a wicket with Din and Thomas both batting well. That they equalled Sussex's total was also due to good innings of 69 by Lord, a former England Schools representative, and 53 by Wootton.

Sussex

J. R. P. Heath c Thomas b Barnard	10	S. J. G. Doggart not out 4
†T. J. Head b Lord.................	20	
A. M. Green c Thomas b Barnard	74	B 2, l-b 3, w 9, n-b 2......... 16
C. M. Wells b Bulpitt	61	
*I. A. Greig b Din	16	1/34 2/44 3/136 (5 wkts, 40 overs) 246
G. S. le Roux not out	45	4/166 5/216

A. C. S. Pigott, A. P. Wells, C. D. B. Fletcher and A. Willows did not bat.

Bowling: Hopkins 8–0–51–0; Barnard 8–0–59–2; Lord 8–1–23–1; Bulpitt 8–0–37–1; Moseley 4–0–33–0; Din 4–0–27–1.

Warwickshire

*G. P. Thomas c le Roux b Greig	28	†G. A. Tedstone not out 2
M. A. Din c Head b Pigott............	57	D. C. Hopkins not out 1
M. Moseley run out	4	
G. J. Lord lbw b le Roux	69	B 1, l-b 12, w 9, n-b 2........ 24
S. H. Wootton run out	53	
N. J. Bulpitt b le Roux	7	1/91 2/95 3/104 (7 wkts, 40 overs) 246
M. Wright run out	1	4/226 5/242 6/242 7/244

D. Marsh and A. Barnard did not bat.

Bowling: Fletcher 7–0–48–0; le Roux 8–0–28–2; Willows 4–0–18–0; Doggart 3–0–18–0; Pigott 3–0–21–1; Greig 8–1–32–1; Wells 7–0–57–0.

Umpires: D. J. Halfyard and P. B. Wight.

THE LANCASHIRE LEAGUES, 1980

By JOHN KAY

It says much for the unquenchable optimism of the major Lancashire leagues that, in one of the wettest seasons of recent years, they took bold and decisive steps aimed at raising the standard of and recreating interest in their game. The Lancashire League went boldly in search of the best possible professionals, and the Central Lancashire League accepted two new clubs into membership for the 1981 season.

In recent years it has been evident that the Lancashire League's reputation for tempting the best cricketers in the world has been on the wane. But before June was out Haslingden had announced the engagement of Andy Roberts; Rishton, a small village club in fierce competition with small towns and bigger ones, recruited Michael Holding; and Nelson signed Kapil Dev; all at fees far greater than those paid in the past. These three signings have undoubtedly set their clubs back the better part of £10,000 each but, as ever, officials are not disclosing what it costs to boast "only the best are good enough for us!" It remains to be seen whether such enterprise pays off.

In the Central Lancashire League, where professionalism was always on a more modest scale, the introduction of Hyde and Norden, from the neighbouring Lancashire and Cheshire League, has been undertaken in the belief that new faces are essential. But with finance an ever-worrying factor it has to be at club rather than individual level. Fourteen clubs strong since the 1930s, the Central Lancashire League have at last opened their doors to new teams and the experiment will be watched and judged with great interest. One thing is certain. Neither league can be accused of standing still and yielding to the temptation to cut their losses at a time when gate receipts were declining. These are difficult days in league cricket, but enthusiasm and optimism remain high.

East Lancashire were the team that mattered most in 1980. The Alexandra Meadows side won the Lancashire League title and the Worsley Cup in impressive manner – their first double for fourteen years – and their Championship haul of 97 points was a record. A well-balanced side, they had in South African Peter Swart, the former Glamorgan all-rounder, the most successful professional in the league. Bacup, with another South African all-rounder in Neal Radford, kept up the pressure for the league title in magnificent style for most of the season, but their challenge petered out towards the end.

Only one professional hit more than a thousand runs in the Lancashire League, and Madan Lal's contribution of 1,067 runs and 72 wickets ensured Enfield of a top-four position without ever really threatening to press the two leading clubs. Australian Brendan McArdle, recommended to Rishton by Frank Tyson, had an enjoyable first season of league cricket but did not draw the crowds as expected and Rishton signed Holding for 1981 in the hope of attracting more spectators. Several amateurs challenged the professionals with outstanding and consistent returns and two of them, Trevor Jones of Burnley and John Howarth of Lowerhouse, appear as professionals with Ribblesdale and Bolton League appointments in 1981.

In the Central Lancashire League, Royton won the Championship and Crompton the Wood Cup in a season which saw Middleton and Crompton fiercely contest the title for most of the campaign. Royton had in West Indian Franklyn Stephenson the only bowler to capture 100 wickets, and he also hammered out 621 runs to give great all-round value to his club throughout a rainy season. Two batsmen, both West Indians, topped 1,000 runs, but neither Rohan Kanhai at Crompton nor Jim Allen at Werneth could contribute much with the ball – and that is vital in league cricket. Several amateurs outpaced the professionals in the run-race, and Milnrow's Stuart Wales was unlucky not to reach the thousand mark. He finished at 945 for an average of 45 and was well clear of his unpaid rivals. Dave Mellor of Ashton and Dennis Walters of Crompton set the League Committee a problem when both finished with 64 wickets to tie for the trophy that goes to the most successful amateur bowler.

LANCASHIRE LEAGUE

	P	W	L	NR	Pts	Professional	Runs	Avge	Wkts	Avge
East Lancs ...	26	22	3	1	97	P. D. Swart	926	48.73	81	12.12
Bacup	26	17	6	3*	83	N. V. Radford ...	709	33.75	77	13.71
Rawtenstall ..	26	16	8	2	74	G. Ross	507	28.16	65	12.93
Enfield	26	15	8	3*	70	S. Madan Lal ...	1,067	76.21	72	15.89
Lowerhouse ..	26	15	10	1	69	M. Amarnath ...	580	29.00	68	14.95
Rishton	26	14	10	2	61	B. McArdle	978	51.47	72	18.30
Ramsbottom ..	26	11	14	1	53	K. D. Ghavri ...	663	27.62	72	15.56
Burnley	26	11	13	2	51	G. Hayes	503	15.15	57	18.59
Accrington ...	26	9	14	3*	44	Mohsin Khan	944	47.20	57	20.77
Colne	26	9	14	3	43	D. Halliwell ...	369	26.50	69	12.96
Haslingden ...	26	9	15	2	41	S. Jones	475	20.65	44	24.86
Todmorden ...	26	7	16	3*	39	Aftab Baloch ...	710	25.43	41	16.34
Church	26	8	16	2	36	J. During	445	22.25	50	26.46
Nelson	26	4	20	2	24	D. Parker	411	18.71	66	17.85

* *Includes tied game.*

CENTRAL LANCASHIRE LEAGUE

	P	W	L	NR	Pts	Professional	Runs	Avge	Wkts	Avge
Royton	26	15	4	7	72	F. Stephenson ...	621	32.68	100	11.99
Middleton ...	26	15	8	3	67	J. Williams	130	14.44	80	14.57
Crompton	26	14	5	7	59	R. B. Kanhai ...	1,123	74.86	–	–
Werneth	26	11	9	6*	52	J. C. Allen	1,142	67.17	7	47.28
Ashton	26	10	11	5	51	C. Kuhn	527	20.26	54	18.29
Oldham	26	11	8	7*	51	J. Maguire	49	4.90	74	15.72
Heywood	26	10	10	6	48	R. H. Cooke ...	734	43.17	32	13.84
Milnrow	26	11	10	5	48	R. Sutcliffe	415	19.76	82	17.12
Castleton M. ..	26	9	12	5	46	D. Schofield	668	33.40	82	13.65
Stockport	26	8	11	7	43	N. Phillips	623	25.95	70	15.44
Radcliffe	26	7	14	7	36	H. Pilling	552	34.50	14	26.71
Walsden	26	8	12	6	36	L. Fernando ...	419	17.45	–	–
Littleborough ..	26	6	11	9	35	R. Graham	49	4.08	56	18.23
Rochdale	26	3	18	5	20	A. Panchasara ...	781	35.50	24	27.25

* *Includes tied game.*

SCHOOLS CRICKET IN 1980

In a summer when cricket was badly disrupted by poor weather, the English Schools Cricket Association considered themselves fortunate to get through their programme of Regional matches without interference. The games at Eastbourne, however, did suffer from the rain. The allocated wicket at The Saffrons was not considered suitable for a two-day game but, with the co-operation of the ground authorities and the umpires, two one-day games were played on different pitches.

More discouraging than the inclement weather, though, was the evidence from coaching courses and the Regional matches that the standard of schools players was not as high as in recent years. Although N. J. Falkner, T. J. Kent and G. J. Little all played good innings, the batting, overall, lacked consistency and real class. The team's strength lay in its bowling, with the seamers sound and economical. The two principal spinners, A. W. J. Spiller and E. J. Cunningham, also gave little away but the slow pitches restricted their striking-rate. The fielding, with wicket-keeper P. Gill and Spiller being notable exceptions, rarely lived up to the standard expected from schools teams and at times was little above ordinary. P. A. Davis, despite failing to bat to his full potential, led the side well in a difficult year, being particularly successful with his bowling changes.

In the representative matches, the English Schools beat the Welsh Schools by ten wickets and drew with the Scottish CU Colts and Irish Schools. The latter match, at the County Ground, Bristol, was the first ever fixture between the English and Irish Schools and featured a century by Little in England's slowly built innings of 162 for seven declared. The Irish, playing six of their national Youth team which contested the final of the 1979 International Youth Tournament, declared at 136 for six, but rain on the second day foiled their enterprise. The highlight of the victory over the Welsh Schools was the bowling of C. Penn. On as first change, he took seven for 12 in twelve overs as the Welsh were bundled out for 65 in their first innings, in which Gill took five catches.

HMC SOUTHERN SCHOOLS v THE REST

At College Field, Eastbourne, July 19, 20. Drawn. Attempts to play a limited-overs match, following a day of no play on the Saturday, were thwarted when rain after lunch on the Sunday prevented The Rest from beginning their innings.

HMC Southern Schools

P. B. Taylor (*Canford*) c Davies b Richardson. 18	I. L. Pont (*Brentwood*) not out 48
P. A. N. Armstrong (*Eastbourne*) c Davies b Crawley . 55	E. J. Cunningham (*Marlborough*) not out. 30
D. M. Elworthy (*Taunton*) c Meadows b Wood. 25	B 4, l-b 6, w 3, n-b 2 15
	1/24 2/107 3/107 (3 wkts, 50 overs) 191

*C. R. Trembath (*Clifton*), A. J. Taylor (*John Lyon*), A. J. Stewart (*Tiffin*), †N. A. Badat (*Queen's, Taunton*), T. A. Cotterell (*Downside*) and A. R. Crocker (*Winchester*) did not bat.

Bowling: Meadows 10–1–42–0; Pollock 10–3–26–0; Richardson 10–3–19–1; Crawley 10–3–22–1; Wood 10–1–67–1.

The Rest

J. J. Whitaker (*Uppingham*), J. D. Sutton (*Edinburgh Acad.*), R. J. Orr (*Fettes*), A. R. J. Barnard (*Rugby*), S. T. Crawley (*Birkenhead*), *A. J. Pollock (*Shrewsbury*), W. R. Holdsworth (*Sedbergh*), N. G. B. Richardson (*Repton*), †A. G. Davies (*Monmouth*), N. A. P. Meadows (*Sedbergh*), D. G. C. Wood (*Pocklington*).

Umpires: V. Bruce and J. R. Cave.

HMC SCHOOLS v ESCA

At The Saffrons, July 21. Drawn, after the start of play was delayed until 1.30 p.m.

ESCA 149 for eight dec. (T. J. Kent 47, G. Toogood 29; N. A. P. Meadows three for 19, C. R. Trembath two for 26, E. J. Cunningham two for 49); HMC Schools 106 for five (J. D. Sutton 24, I. L. Pont 24; N. A. Foster two for 18).

At The Saffrons, July 22. Drawn. As on the previous day, batting was never easy and the bowlers generally held the upper hand. The ESCA fielded the same side, while the HMC Schools brought in Armstrong for Badat.

HMC Schools

J. J. Whitaker (*Uppingham*) b Penn 9	I. L. Pont (*Brentwood*) st Gill b Spiller . . 18
P. A. N. Armstrong (*Eastbourne*) b Williams. 25	J. D. Sutton (*Edinburgh Acad.*) not out. . 10
D. M. Elworthy (*Taunton*) lbw b Penn . . . 2	
A. J. Taylor (*John Lyon*) b Toogood . . 0	
†A. J. Stewart (*Tiffin*) c Little b Penn . . . 30	L-b 5, n-b 4 9
*C. R. Trembath (*Clifton*) b Penn 8	
E. J. Cunningham (*Marlborough*) not out. 59	1/25 2/39 3/41 4/45 (7 wkts dec.) 170
	5/75 6/82 7/117

A. R. Crocker (*Winchester*) and N. A. P. Meadows (*Sedbergh*) did not bat.

Bowling: Foster 9–2–23–0; Williams 12–5–26–1; Penn 18–6–24–4; Toogood 15–4–44–1; Spiller 12–5–44–1.

ESCA

G. J. Little (*Marling and Glos.*) b Meadows. 17	P. Dicks (*Cleve and Glos.*) b Cunningham. 1
T. J. Kent (*Clevedon CS and Avon*) b Trembath. 19	A. W. J. Spiller (*Yeovil and Somerset*) b Meadows. 14
G. Toogood (*N. Bromsgrove HS and Worcs.*) b Meadows . 1	N. Williams (*Acland Burghley and London*) not out. 10
I. Robson (*New College and Durham*) b Meadows. 2	B 12, l-b 2, w 1, n-b 7 22
*P. A. Davis (*Wellington and Wirral*) not out. 18	1/37 2/41 3/47 (6 wkts) 104
	4/50 5/51 6/88

†P. Gill (*Grange and Lancs.*), C. Penn (*Dover GS and Kent*) and N. A. Foster (*Philip Morant and Essex*) did not bat.

Bowling: Meadows 15–5–33–4; Crocker 7–2–17–0; Trembath 8–3–14–1; Cunningham 5–3–9–1; Pont 4–1–9–0.

Umpires: V. Bruce and J. R. Cave.

Details of the match between MCC Schools and the National Association of Young Cricketers may be found in Other Matches at Lord's, 1980.

Reports from the Schools

Abingdon's strength lay in their bowling as promising off-spinner R. I. McCreery (40 wickets), as well as seam bowlers W. K. Mellor and S. J. Minter, successfully exploited the damp wickets. MCC were among four clubs defeated. Tight fielding and resilient batting offset some wayward bowling to give **Alleyn's School** their most successful season for some years, their only defeat being by Emanuel. Opening batsmen S. Banfield and left-hander J. Lyne were well supported by the captain, W. Manhood, who hit four fifties. Fast-medium bowler R. Cowland returned eight for 14 v Royal Russell. With ten of the First XI available in 1981, prospects are good. **Allhallows**, in a transitional year, built their side around M. J. Davies, an all-rounder who was ably supported by wicket-keeper-batsman S. R. Dryden and fast-medium bowler M. W. R. Luff. **Ampleforth's** fine all-round performance featured splendid batting, with J. P. Barrett – also a fine slip – scoring two centuries and A. C. Calder-Smith batting powerfully at number six. D. H. Harrison excelled behind the stumps while opening bowler S. D. Lawson and off-spinner M. C. T. Low bowled efficiently.

Bablake remain undefeated by a school since 1978, their only defeat being by an Old Boys XI. Opener C. L. Flick scored two centuries and fourteen-year-old D. A. Thorne achieved a magnificent unbeaten 134. Opening bat and fast-medium bowler W. P. Matthews scored most runs and took most wickets. The school retained the Warwickshire and Birmingham Senior Schools knockout trophy. A tour of Denmark followed a successful domestic season for **Bancroft's School.** Highlights included C. R. Thomas's record aggregate of 647 runs, and the promising all-round showing of opening bowler S. W. Grant and off-spinner I. P. Debnam. **Barnard Castle,** with good wins over St Bees, Whitehaven GS, Stockport GS, and William Hulme's GS, and only one loss – v Ashville – were indebted to valuable contributions with bat and ball from left-handed batsmen R. Andrew (right-arm medium) and A. Frater (right-arm medium-fast). **Bedford School's** batting was dominated by H. D. Ferguson, who hit an unbeaten 125 v Stowe. Not only schoolboys were troubled by the inswing of S. P. Clayton, who was well supported by N. J. Cowell, I. T. Osborne and some tidy, aggressive fielding. Schools beaten were The Leys, Oundle, Bedford Modern, Uppingham and Repton.

Defeated by only two schools – Denstone and Bedford – **Bedford Modern** recorded wins over St Albans, Kimbolton, The Perse, Oakham, Bishop Vesey's, and RGS Worcester. A. Fordham captained the victorious U. 15 XI at Lord's; his opening partner, A. K. G. Jones, topped 800 runs. **Berkhamsted** struggled until captain M. J. Parsons (right-arm medium) took over the new-ball attack. He also hit 78 in 42 minutes in their only school win, v Magdalen College School, although the batting was mainly in the hands of P. J. Allen and B. G. Evans. **Bethany School's** only defeat was by Wellingborough. Batting averages were headed by fast-medium bowler J. Hancock, who hit 50 in 21 minutes v St Edmund's, Canterbury, and played for Kent Schools U. 19. Left-hander N. Kimber strengthened the middle order and J. Blunden provided solid all-round support.

A young **Birkenhead** side remained unbeaten by a school, despite missed chances and an attack which lacked penetration, apart from the promising off-spin of R. C. A. Thorn. S. T. Crawley hit 170 in two hours v Stonyhurst (ten 6s and fifteen 4s) and 101 in 80 minutes v Liverpool College. **Bishop's Stortford College** beat The Perse, Chigwell, Aldenham, and Kimbolton but, weakened by examinations, lost to Sherborne, Queen's Taunton, and Taunton school during a West Country tour. Their strength lay in depth of batting, although the bowling was tighter than previously, with off-spinner R. E. Jackson topping the averages. **Bloxham's** inexperienced side, with an attack generally lacking penetration, were indebted to the leg-spin of P. A. D. Farrar for their two wins. A young **Blundell's** side relied for runs on their captain, left-hander H. Morris, who made five fifties. He was well supported by off-spinner P. D. Langdon, who three times took five or more wickets in an innings. S. A. Watts (right-arm fast-medium) took six for 21 v Sidmouth. M. T. G. Laimbeer scored a century in 83 minutes for **Bradfield College,** whose wins included Westminster, Canford, and Wellington.

Bradford GS, with a young side, recorded eight wins. Their fielding was accurate, with G. M. Fitzpatrick a fine slip, and wicket-keeper S. G. P. Hewitt claiming 39 victims as well as batting productively. The attack was spear-headed by left-arm paceman J. D. Thompson, while C. J. Hewitt, in his first season, claimed 30 wickets with his off-spinners. **Brentwood's** season was dominated by their captain, I. L. Pont, who took 35 per cent of the wickets and scored 33 per cent of the runs, his total of 858 setting a new record. He represented MCC Schools at Lord's. Bowlers N. Hanworth and J. Hollington both showed promise. With a strong all-round side, **Brighton** were unbeaten by a school, their most notable victory being over Epsom when captain C. J. Edmonds scored 96 not out in an hour. Medium-pace bowlers D. R. Thomson and J. A. St J. Withers led a tight attack. A young **Bryanston** side beat Taunton, Dauntsey's, and Monkton Combe, losing to only one school – **Canford,** whose other wins included King's Taunton and MCC. Canford's bowling was poor, although J. W. R. Edwards took six for 21 v MCC, and they owed much to their captain, P. B. Taylor, as well as outstanding fielder N. M. C. Fleming.

Highlights for **Charterhouse** included seven fifties by left-handed batsman C. E. G. Allen, 124 before lunch v Westminster by captain G. P. Bristowe, and seven for 37 v Bradfield by slow right-arm off-spinner J. B. D. North. **Cheltenham College** had a disappointing season, with R. H. B. Johnson and R. M. Tucker holding most innings together at five and six. The return after injury of off-spinner A. D. Marsh strengthened the side after half-term. Accurate bowling highlighted a successful season for **Cheltenham Grammar School,** whose splendid batting performance was led by A. White. Rebuilding their side, **Christ College, Brecon,** were encouraged by the powerful batting of N. C. Hanson, and a return of eight for 31 v St David's University from P. G. Chambers (slow left-arm).

Christ's Hospital, whose only win was v Cranleigh, depended mainly on captain N. Konig and all-rounder P. Cunliffe. **Clifton** beat Tonbridge, Eastbourne, Downside, Blundell's, and Colston's, losing to Taunton and Winchester. They were indebted to productive batting from M. W. Bailey as well as excellent returns by their opening bowlers, each of whom did the hat-trick; N. R. Gillespie v Downside and C. R. Trembath v Winchester. A successful tour of Holland for **Colfe's School** followed a rewarding season, which included wins v Emanuel, Chigwell, Haberdashers' Aske's (Hatcham) and Trinity Croydon (by seven wickets). Strong batting featured outstanding performances by A. Caswall and captain N. Tarrant, while the bowling was led by A. Rodgers and R. Mirza, who took his 150th wicket for the First XI. Fourteen-year-old W. M. Smith led **Colston's School's** batting, with 639 runs, as they recorded wins v Monmouth, King Edward's Bath, Cotham GS, and Bristol Cathedral School. In a mediocre season, **Cranbrook's** only noteworthy performance was a first-ever win v Incogniti CC.

Dauntsey's strong and varied attack was led by R. S. Spencer (right-arm medium), who returned eight for 14 v Kingswood, seven for 62 v Dean Close and three for 5 v Marlborough. They overcame inexperienced batting to beat Wycliffe, Marlborough, KES Bath, and Kingswood, with only one school defeat – by Bryanston. The school has introduced cricket for girls in the younger age group. A win v Malvern was the highlight for **Dean Close** in a season when poor catching prevented more wins. M. P. A. Crawshaw was top-scorer, while leg-spinner T. Jackson recorded nine for 50 v Bloxham. A young but successful **Denstone** side featured prolific batting, excellent fielding and a tight attack, with A. D. Coley (right-arm medium) taking seven for 40 v Ellesmere. In addition, left-arm spinner J. P. D. Cadman took eight for 64 v Bedford Modern and his five for 11 v King's, Tynemouth, included the hat-trick. **Dover College's** most notable victory was v Sutton Valence, when I. A. C. Syer hit 50 in under half an hour. In another game he hit four consecutive 6s. Apart from the performance of captain J. G. Ryeland, the bowling was weak and the fielding inconsistent.

In a transitional year, **Downside** were indebted to captain T. A. Cotterell (slow left-arm), who took seven for 66 v Free Foresters, and wicket-keeper-batsman M. J. Poland whose 561 runs were twice as many as the next highest aggregate. An experienced **Dulwich College** batting side often disappointed, and only W. K. Jarrett (right-arm medium) gave penetration to an attack without an experienced spinner. A young **Durham** team beat Scarborough, St Bees, RGS Newcastle, and Durham Pilgrims. P. C. Shaw and J. R. Thompson scored well; the attack, led by captain M. R. Fletcher (right-arm fast), was nicely balanced by spinners N. P. Tubbs and J. C. McKenna.

In a season of rebuilding **Eastbourne College** achieved good wins v Christ's Hospital and King's Canterbury, when N. B. Chapple (right-arm fast-medium) took seven for 25. R. D. Montgomerie was a successful all-rounder and captain P. A. N. Armstrong played for MCC Schools at Lord's. **Edinburgh Academy** were unbeaten in Scotland, their only loss being to Pocklington. Outstanding batsman J. D. Sutton scored three centuries and sixteen-year-old C. D. Fraser-Darling (two centuries) fell just four wickets short of the double of 500 runs and 50 wickets. **Elizabeth College, Guernsey,** recorded four school victories: v Victoria College (twice) with all-rounder D. J. Mechem (right-arm medium) taking five for 15 and captain C. J. Guilbert (right-arm slow-medium) taking four for 12, v Hampton with all-rounder J. R. Ravenscroft (right-arm medium) taking seven for 52, and v King Edward's, Witley, when A. G. Tapp (slow left-arm) took four for 17.

Ellesmere's strength lay in the batting of captain R. E. J. Watt, who passed 90 three times in five innings, and fourteen-year-old G. L. Home. Weakness of bowling prevented greater success. A young **Eltham College** side, ably led by all-rounder N. I. Holcombe, was restricted by a weak middle order who often failed to complement the advantage won by a tight attack. R. A. Mellors returned nine for 32 and M. J. Wright eight for 38, both v Haberdashers' Aske's, while M. R. Surguy and fifteen-year-old M. J. Holcombe made useful contributions with bat and ball. **Emanuel** were indebted to a powerful batting side for their twenty wins, which included those v Tiffin, Kingston GS, KCS Wimbledon, and Reigate GS. They also won the

London Schools knockout trophy for the third year. J. C. Waite scored 1,056 runs, with two hundreds and seven fifties, as well as taking 34 wickets.

A highlight for **Epsom College** was a stand of 184 v Old Epsomians by J. M. Paulus and N. L. Porter. The bowling was led by newcomers M. J. Morris (right-arm medium) and off-spinner R. M. C. Williams. **Eton** were undefeated and recorded wins v Charterhouse and St Paul's. The batting was led by C. C. Birch Reynardson and D. C. E. Russell and the bowling by M. J. B. Rudd (right-arm fast-medium). **Exeter School** were indebted for their strong attack to P. Sykes (medium-fast) and P. Bates (slow left-arm), both of whom were selected for the Devon U. 19 team. However, the batting often failed to fulfil its potential.

Felsted, undefeated by a British school for the fifth time in six years, beat Ipswich, Bedford, Eastbourne, and Tonbridge. Attacking batsman R. N. R. Vartan scored six fifties in his last seven matches, and was well supported by promising wicket-keeper M. W. C. Olley. I. P. Mason (medium) took three wickets or more on eight occasions and B. H. Pinkerton (slow left-arm) gave little away. With brilliant fielding and strong batting, **Fettes** were unbeaten, recording wins v St Bees, Glenalmond, Strathallan, Merchiston, and The Leys. Their bowling was erratic, although R. J. Orr (fast-medium) returned five for 22 v St Bees, six for 18 v Glenalmond, four for 11 v Strathallan and eight for 37 v Headmaster's XI, while C. I. McCrostie's off-spin claimed five for 15 v Merchiston and six for 23 v The Leys. A young **Forest School** side – eight were under sixteen – enjoyed a successful season with all-rounder J. Crossley (right-arm fast-medium) heading both batting and bowling averages. He hit his maiden century v City of London, when he shared in a partnership of 136 with his brother I. Crossley, and took nine for 58 v MCC.

Giggleswick, ably led by all-rounder G. J. Hartley (right-arm medium-fast), enjoyed a better season than they expected.

Unbeaten by a school for the fourth year, **Haberdashers' Aske's,** Elstree, lost only to MCC. Prolific batting by R. G. Price, M. C. Wilcock, N. Colverd and captain C. R. Churchman provided sufficient runs for an attack which improved towards the end of the season. All-rounder N. M. M. Andrews effectively led **Hampton** to victory over thirteen schools, including St Paul's, Emanuel, Tiffin, and Enfield. Highlights included an opening stand of 230 v St Benedict's by K. M. Wood and C. B. Dennis-Baker, and four wickets in four balls by T. Lambert v Tiffin. Again undefeated by a school, **Harrow** beat Wellington, Winchester, and St Edward's. Above-average bowling featured O. F. O. Findlay (right-arm fast-medium) and, in a solid batting side, S. E. Haggas scored a century v Wellington in his first match. With no wins, a young **Highgate** XI failed to fulfil their promise.

Hipperholme GS had a frustrating season, often narrowly avoiding victory, although they beat King's Macclesfield and Giggleswick. Apart from opening pair C. A. Heppenstall and R. S. Butterworth, the batting was inconsistent. Slow bowlers A. Furness (off-spin) and M. J. Hopwood (left-arm) took most wickets. **Hurstpierpoint** were encouraged by the performances of their captain, the hard-hitting left-hander, H. K. Bellamy, promising opening bat M. N. J. Rose, and right-arm off-spinner S. M. A. West, who took eight for 18 v Seaford College.

Wins over The Perse and MCC encouraged **Kimbolton,** although they often fell short of expectations. J. S. Chambers headed the batting, while S. C. Render showed promise as an all-rounder. **King Edward's School, Birmingham,** were hampered for half the season by the absence through injury of all-rounder S. E. Fletcher. While C. D. Jenkins (medium) capably led the attack and the fielding was sound, the batting was often slow. A win v MCC brought some satisfaction. A young **King Edward VI College, Stourbridge,** side included a number of attacking batsmen, notably D. Scriven, who hit 96 in 78 minutes with two 6s and seventeen 4s. Leg-spinner D. Glover and left-arm seamer P. N. Shillingford bowled effectively on wickets often affected by the wet summer. With a weak batting side, **King Edward VI School, Southampton,** were indebted for their nine wins to a hostile attack, led by captain G. P. J. Staples and D. M. M. Horne.

King Edward VII School, Lytham, had decisive wins v Burnley GS and St Mary's, Crosby, In a young team G. F. H. McDonnell was outstanding, both in the field and with the bat. The batting of **King Henry VIII School, Coventry,** was ably led by wicket-keeper-captain A. Savage, but, apart from promising newcomer C. J. J. Harrison (right-arm medium), their bowling lacked pace. **King's College, Taunton,** beat King's School Bruton, Plymouth College,

Monmouth, Blundell's, Downsde, and MCC. The attack featured three seam bowlers: S. C. Hunter (right-arm fast), who took seven wickets v Queen's Taunton and v King's Bruton, N. K. Gane (right-arm fast-medium) and fourteen-year-old all-rounder R. J. Harden (left-arm medium) who took seven wickets v Monmouth. Batting was adequate but unspectacular and the fielding tidy. **King's College School, Wimbledon,** were indebted for a successful season to strong all-round performances from captain K. R. Thompson, wicket-keeper M. A. Staniland, R. I. Alikhan and A. M. Bredin, whose slow left-arm spin was especially pleasing.

Slow and inconsistent scoring hampered **King's School, Bruton.** Their fielding was alert, with P. F. McIntyre excelling in the slips, and the captain, S. E. Birks, impressed with his slow bowling in an attack which gave little away. In a successful season, **King's School, Canterbury,** beat Highgate, Dulwich, and KCS Wimbledon, their only defeat being by Eastbourne College. C. P. Smith scored 189 not out v Dulwich, with six 6s and 27 4s, reaching 100 in 76 minutes and 150 in 105 minutes. M. F. Nicholson took eight for 20 v St Lawrence College, Ramsgate. **The King's School, Chester,** lost only to Aldenham, and might have won more matches had their bowling been more penetrative. With a record eleven school wins, **King's School, Macclesfield,** defeated William Hulme's GS, Stockport GS, Solihull, and Nottingham HS. They were ably led by all-rounder N. A. Kennington (off-breaks) whose fielding was exceptional. Wicket-keeper P. Moores had more stumpings than catches, reflecting a refreshing use of three spin bowlers, and opener N. D. Smedley led the batting with 801 runs at 44.50.

A young **King William's College** side owed much to the all-round skills of captain P. N. Luft, a strong, attacking batsman and right-arm medium-fast bowler. In an improved season, **Kingston GS** defeated St Paul's, St George's Weybridge, and MCC. R. J. Purchase headed the batting, with useful support from P. W. Ramussen and left-hander C. J. Cookman. Leading bowlers were I. C. P. Cranston (medium-fast) and leg-spinner R. D. S. Blackford, who took seven for 45 v St Benedict's, Ealing. **Kingswood's** strong batting side was built around W. P. Mason, G. D. Opie and wicket-keeper S. A. Gynes. Opening bowler T. J. Rawson (right-arm medium) took seven for 31 (all bowled) v King Edward's, Bath.

Lancing College recorded only one school win – v Ardingly, when M. P. Rudge did the hat-trick. The off-spin of fourteen-year-old C. S. Mays was promising, while captain M. C. Calvert-Lee and brothers P. R. and S. R. Nash batted consistently. On a tour of Holland the side was undefeated, with right-arm seamer N. S. Tudball leading the bowling. For **Leeds GS** the highlight of a disappointing season, with only three wins, was a tie v QEGS, Wakefield, whose last eight wickets fell for 17. Leading wicket-takers were captain M. D. Sims (slow left-arm) and S. A. Gray (slow right-arm). Undefeated **Leighton Park School** fielded a strong batting side, with opening bat G. J. Nienow averaging 50.75. C. D. S. Houston bowled with pace and penetration and V. Aluvihare took six for 22 v Bearwood, who were bowled out for 53. Other wins were v Reading Bluecoat and Shiplake. Keen fielding by **Liverpool College** was not adequately supported. Apart from the opening attack of M. B. Jenkins and T. F. Groom, the bowling lacked variety, and the batting was weak. There were wins v Rydal School and King William's College.

The strength of the **Lord Wandsworth College** XI lay in its batting, led by openers T. J. Coulson (captain) and sixteen-year-old S. Bentley. Apart from T. R. Jermyn (off-spin) the bowlers rarely dominated and best performances came when the school batted second. Again unbeaten by a school, **Lord Williams's School** beat RGS High Wycombe, Magdalen College School, St George's Harpenden, and MCC. A strong opening attack featured right-arm fast bowlers G. Porter and S. D. Thomson, who took seven for 29 v MCC. Only captain N. Yeomans batted with any confidence on the slow wickets. A young **Loretto** side had a disappointing season, depending heavily on R. S. Macaskill to score runs. Captain A. A. M. Macbeath bowled economically, taking six for 15 v George Watson's in the school's only win and three for 3 v Heriots. He was well supported by C. R. Marks.

Magdalen College School flourished under the captaincy of batsman P. S. Morris, with wins v Pangbourne, The Perse, Bloxnam, St Bartholomew's, Bearwood, and Oratory. Their strength lay in the fast bowling of S. P. Hazell and S. C. Shorter, with six sides being bowled out for around 50. **Malvern's** successful season featured a record opening stand of 245 v Repton between M. E. Fordham and left-hander R. C. W. Mason. With 799 runs at 79.9, Fordham achieved both record aggregate and average. The team went on tour to Barbados at the end of term. In a season of exciting finishes, **Manchester GS** defeated Leeds GS, Bradford GS,

Highgate, and Dulwich College. The attack was well balanced, with fast bowlers D. Postlethwaite and M. J. Frost (six for 26 v Bolton GS) supported by left-arm M. P. Lawrence and off-spinner R. J. Clark. A. Milnes took five for 16 v QEGS, Blackburn, and totalled 325 runs.

In their best season for many years, **Marlborough** defeated Rugby, Radley, Cheltenham and Haileybury. Captain E. J. Cunningham, absent through injury until half-term, gave a fine all-round performance and represented MCC Schools. The standard of fielding was high. J. Mylne excelling behind the stumps with R. Hampel and M. R. C. Swallow were impressive outfielders. **Merchant Taylors', Crosby**, had a disappointing season, with injuries to key players. C. N. Hughes D'Aeth bowled with maturity, taking seven for 33 v MCC. **Merchant Taylors', Northwood**, took their strength from a productive batting side, with openers S, P. Ducat and J. P. Hoskins proving most effective. The attack was affected by injuries, although M. D. J. Ingram troubled opponents. A three-week tour of Canada was embarked on in August.

Merchiston Castle School's outstanding batsman was captain-wicket-keeper R. A. Young, in his fifth year in the XI. The bowling was led by D. Robinson (left-arm slow) and M. G. Robertson (right-arm fast-medium). **Mill Hill's** captain, C. I. Quirk, was handicapped by injury, but held some splendid catches and led his team to victory v Oundle, St Paul's, and Nottingham HS. Sixteen-year-old P. H. Wickenden scored heavily; T. A. J. Dawson bowled his off-breaks with increasing confidence. **Millfield** had one of their best-ever seasons, with three prolific batsmen P. G. Roebuck (left-hand), A. J. H. Dunning and S. J. Illingworth invariably giving them a good start. Fifteen-year-old off-spinner P. A. C. Bail was an outstanding prospect; captain J. O. Curran (right-arm fast) and A. R. Welch (right-arm medium-fast) were the leading wicket-takers.

Milton Abbey's one defeat by a school – Portsmouth GS – was in the last match of a successful season, for which they were indebted to J. M. D. Boswell whose accurate fast-medium bowling took a record 66 wickets and brought him a return of eight for 17 v King's School, Bruton. The batting was inconsistent, although G. H. Acheson-Gray was a powerful striker and R. D. T. Clive played some promising innings. A young **Monkton Combe** side gained valuable experience, with fifteen-year-old A. R. C Batterham (left-arm fast) claiming 38 wickets. **Monmouth's** young side was built around their captain A. G. Davies, who has appeared for Glamorgan Second XI and whose unbeaten 144 v Kingswood established a school record. The attack lacked penetration, but with ten of the team returning in 1981, prospects are good.

Norwich School's only victory was v King's Lynn School, when A. E. Duffield took seven for 48. Fourteen-year-old S. P. Bowling (fast) showed great potential in a modest attack; with more confidence the batting could have been more productive. **Nottingham HS** played some positive cricket, with excellent all-round performances from captain S. J. Turrill and P. A. J. Gregory contributing to their seven wins.

A careless approach by the potentially strong **Oakham** side was responsible for a disappointing season. **Oundle**, rebuilding their side, achieved a notable win v St Edward's, Oxford. An accurate attack was led by the captain M. N. Forbes (medium), but the batting was always uncertain.

The Perse School achieved wins v St Edmund's College, Chigwell, The Leys, and Kimbolton, but lost to Bishop's Stortford College, Bedford Modern, and Magdalen College School. **Plymouth College** had a successful season, with twelve wins. A. Seymour (slow left-arm) took 70 wickets and also headed the batting averages. I. T. Waldock kept wicket splendidly, and R. Wood was an effective captain. **Pocklington's** sixteen wins included those v Ampleforth, St Peter's York, Ashville College, Edinburgh Academy, and MCC. An accurate attack featured T. de L. Edmunds (left-arm medium), D. C. G. Wood (leg-spin) and captain A. E. C. Shanks (right-arm medium), who also headed the batting averages.

Unbeaten in 32 matches over two years, **Queen's College, Taunton**, lost their only game of the season to Plymouth College, with good wins v King's Taunton, Bishop's Stortford, Wellington, and King's Bruton. The wicket-keeping of N. Badat was outstanding.

A strong **Radley** attack was led by captain J. A. N. Wootten, whose off-spin took 49 wickets. Six of the eight schools played were bowled out, and wins were achieved v Bradfield, Malvern, St Edward's, and Stowe, the only defeat being by Marlborough. Highlights in a disappointing season for **Ratcliffe College** included the consistent bowling of N. Evans (left-arm medium-fast) and A. MacDiarmid's seven for 41 v The Gentlemen of Leicestershire. However, the batting lacked confidence. **Reading School** ended a mediocre season with wins v Douai and MCC. Outstanding wicket-keeper G. D. Beckett achieved ten stumpings and eight catches, as well as making a decisive contribution with the bat. All-rounder H. K. Mason opened the batting effectively and took seven for 42 v St Bartholomew's, Newbury. A. G. Brown (also a left-arm leg-spinner) bowled with increasing confidence and took four for 9 v Abingdon. The batting of **Reed's School** was led by P. E. E. Farenden and captain M. A. Rowland, who was selected for Sussex Second XI. Yet early promise was not fulfilled and the bowling tended to be expensive.

Reigate GS, defeated only by RGS Colchester and Emanuel, owed much to captain N. J. Falkner whose 1,139 runs at 67.00 included four hundreds and seven fifties. He was well supported by all-rounders J. C. Perkins and C. D. Jones as well as fast bowler A. M. Babington. The team toured the Channel Islands in July. **Repton,** with wins v Shrewsbury and Worksop, benefited from the all-round ability of captain N. G. B. Richardson, who led the bowling for the third season. Fifteen-year-old left-hander S. W. Lovell had an outstanding first season with the bat. A young **Rossall** side, which defeated Sedbergh and Manchester GS, depended heavily on captain A. C. Jones, who batted prolifically. D. J. Hanson did the hat-trick v Arnold. **Royal Grammar School, Newcastle,** featured a strong batting side, with W. G. Wake, M. R. Thompson and A. G. Wilson playing for the Northumberland U. 19 side. With the bowlers lacking pace and experience, the number of wins was small. **Rydal School** were encouraged by the all-round performances of captain A. C. Rhodes (left-arm fast-medium) and T. C. N. Aughton, an opening right-hand bat and finger spinner who turned the ball both ways and who played for Welsh Schoolboys v MCC.

St Albans School improved towards the end of the season, with wins v Luton VI Form College and Bancroft's. The productive batting of A. J. Dent, T. R. Lovejoy and A. G. Lynes was well supported in depth, while accurate fielding and bowling were enhanced by the consistent wicket-keeping of N. J. Baker. The experienced batsmen of **St Dunstan's** were affected by examinations and illness, leaving a young team in which C. M. Denny and A. M. Ford showed promise. There was a good win v Surrey Young Cricketers. Prospects look good for **St Edmund's** with seven of their unbeaten side returning in 1981. Leading wicket-taker was K. A. Rumbelow, who took eight for 16 v Dover College. For **St Edward's School,** highlights included impressive batting performances by captain J. A. Lyons, N. A. Friend and P. R. J. Smith, while right-arm seam bowler N. H. M. Arkell took 21 wickets.

In an exciting season, with many close finishes, **St George's College** were indebted to punishing batsman D. A. Close and fifteen-year-old D. Hamer (medium-pace in-swinger) who took 34 wickets. **St John's School** was unbeaten by a school, their most notable victory being v St George's, Weybridge. The fielding was outstanding and captain A. G. K. Hooper gave an excellent all-round performance with 32 wickets (slow left-arm) and 295 runs; he and C. J. Presley both hit centuries v Surrey Young Cricketers. The side could have won more matches with another opening bowler of pace. All-rounder S. J. Billings ably led **St Lawrence College** for the second year. P. J. Laslett, batting at number eight, hit the school's first century for fourteen years.

The backbone of **St Peter's School** were C. J. Stubbs and A. M. Precious, who formed a left-arm opening attack and were also the leading batsmen. Captain M. W. Johnston (slow left-arm) was the leading wicket-taker. With a record ten wins, **Sedbergh School** defeated Ampleforth, Durham, Pocklington, Sherborne, Canford, William Hulme's GS, and RGS Newcastle. The fielding was excellent and the attack was led by outstanding fast bowler N. A. P. Meadows, whose 54 wickets set a school record and who played for MCC Schools. He received balanced and varied support from J. M. B. Daniels (medium), P. Rogers (off-spin) and J. L. O'B. Robinson (leg-spin). Captain W. R. Holdsworth had a fine season with the bat. A strong **Sevenoaks** side achieved easy wins over Ardingly and King's, Rochester. M. I. Dickenson batted reliably and kept wicket exceptionally, with eleven stumpings and nine catches in nine matches. P. Durdant-Hollamby showed class as an all-rounder, and P. N. Colman bowled left-arm orthodox and chinamen with remarkable control.

Sherborne's one defeat – to Sedbergh – came off the last ball after eight wickets had fallen for 12 runs in eight overs. J. F. Blackburn was an outstanding captain and capable all-rounder, while J. M. P. C. Turner was a consistent opening bat. The quality of the fielding was high. **Simon Langton GS** were unbeaten for the first time, their most memorable win being v Plymouth College during a tour in Devon. The steady attack was led by left-arm seamer F. Barrett and off-spinner A. Castle, with a best return of eight for 48. In a strong batting line-up, D. Simmonds received strong support from A. Wood. With eight players returning, prospects for 1981 are good. For **Sir Roger Manwood's School**, captain A. J. Curwen was the only batsman of note. Their opponents rarely mastered the right-arm off-spin of M. G. Norris who took eight for 11 v Duke of York's School; D. G. Chisholm (right-arm fast) took six for 20 in the win v St Lawrence, Ramsgate.

Solihull had a disappointing season, owing mainly to the failure of their leading batsmen. Of the bowlers, only N. J. Wheelwright (right-arm fast-medium) showed any consistency, and they were unable to bowl other sides out. **Stockport GS** won v Marple Hall, William Hulme's GS, and Cheadle Hulme, but were beaten by King's Macclesfield, King Edward's Lytham, and Arnold. Their middle order often failed to capitalise on a sound start from openers S. J. Hornby and A. E. Sawer. M. A. Beesley (right-arm fast) topped the bowling averages and P. D. Carroll (off-spin) took four for 1 v Marple Hall.

A young and promising **Strathallan** side were ably led by C. A. MacLeod, in his second year as captain. Outstanding performer for **Sutton Valence School** was M. T. Russell-Vick (right-arm medium) who topped both the batting and bowling averages and was selected for the HMC Schools (South) U. 15. He was well supported by R. J. Bedford (right-arm medium out-swing), while captain J. B. Hitchens was competent both with the bat and behind the stumps.

In a season of contrasts, **Taunton School** had good wins v Clifton, Downside, and Bishop's Stortford, but disappointing defeats v Bryanston and Blundell's. Their captain D. M. Elworthy, who hit a century v Downside, was selected for the Public Schools XI. A successful **Tiffin** side, with twelve wins, was indebted to captain-wicket-keeper A. J. Stewart, whose 782 runs included two centuries. N. D. Hicks gave him useful support. Spinners dominated the attack, with right-arm leg-spinner M. S. G. Robins and off-spinner S. P. Clews heading the averages. They won the Surrey Schools knockout trophy, beating Beverley School in the final.

Tonbridge School tailed off towards the end of the season after a promising start with wins v Christ's Hospital and Haileybury. Two fifteen-year-olds showed promise – G. R. Cowdrey with the bat and M. P. Hickson as an all-rounder. For **Trent College**, bowling honours were shared by J. C. Harris (right-arm fast), I. Lane (off-spin) and all-rounders M. R. Dodson and N. C. Green (both right-arm fast-medium). The batting, often brittle, relied heavily on captain D. N. Wood. **Trinity's** bowling lacked penetration, although J. R. Glynne-Jones (fast-medium) took 55 wickets. Outstanding wicket-keeper S. N. Perry set two school records, claiming 45 victims in the season and seven in an innings. The batting was prolific with J. E. Vigar hitting three centuries and M. L. Jones scoring two. In their Centenary Year, **Truro School** lost to only one school side. The highlight of the season was right-arm seamer M. E. Barlow's performance v The Past Captains XI, when he took four wickets in four balls.

A young **University College School** side showed considerable promise, the most encouraging performance coming from thirteen-year-old H. Sharp who hit 65 not out v Mill Hill and took seven for 21 v Abingdon. Generally the bowling lacked penetration and the batting tended to be brittle, although M. Furness played some useful innings. J. Brenner was the school's best wicket-keeper for many years. Careless fielding and uneconomical bowling denied **Uppingham** a win, despite the outstanding batting performances of captain J. J. Whitaker, whose 747 runs surpassed by 25 the previous record set in 1893. He hit three centuries, reaching a hundred before lunch v MCC.

Warwick School were unbeaten, but managed only one school win – v Dean Close. In the absence of a good slow bowler, the attack lacked variety, all four main bowlers bowling right-arm medium pace. The batting, led by R. A. Horner, had depth but lacked consistency. With an inexperienced side, **Wellington, Berkshire**, could not adapt to the soft wickets, defeating Charterhouse but losing to Harrow, Winchester, Bradfield, and Stowe. S. P. Loup was the steadiest bowler. Inconsistent batting and the absence of a competent spinner contributed to a disappointing season for **Westminster**, although captain S. M. Beadle played some determined innings, and both G. A. C. Davies and R. S. Rutnagur showed promise as all-rounders. Weak batting caused a young **Whitgift** side often to be bowled out cheaply, but their strength lay in a tight attack, featuring G. J. McEwan (right-arm fast) and sixteen-year-old R. D. Ronald (slow left-arm).

Though beating Sutton Valence, **William Hulme's GS** suffered defeats by Shrewsbury, Sedbergh, and St Peter's York. A fragile middle order failed to support solid foundations laid by openers S. P. Dickinson and A. P. Laker as well as captain D. B. Wright. Left-arm seamer P. A. Cotterill led the attack, and young leg-spinner N. R. Fairfax showed promise late in the season. **Winchester's** strong point was their bowling; of the four schools to be defeated – Clifton, Wellington, Charterhouse, and Eastbourne – three were bowled out for less than 100. Opening bowlers A. R. Crocker (right-arm medium-fast) and M. B. H. Wheeler (right-arm fast-medium) took 89 wickets between them, Wheeler taking six for 13 v Clifton. Crocker played for the second successive year for the Southern Schools and the Public Schools.

In the absence of a penetrative opening bowler, **Woodhouse Grove School** had only a moderate season. D. A. and J. M. Robinson (both right-arm fast-medium) were the mainstays of the attack and were supported by S. Cockerill (left-arm fast-medium) and S. A. J. Kippax (leg-breaks and googlies). S. N. Driver and D. A. Robinson dominated the batting with the promising I. W. Stott, who came into the side halfway through the season. Indifferent batting restricted **Worksop College**, where S. N. Waddington – right-arm fast-medium and a useful bat – showed himelf to be a fine prospect. After being outplayed in their first four matches, **Wycliffe College** staged a dramatic recovery and were unbeaten in their last ten encounters. The transformation came with a spectacular return to form by the captain, F. J. Hemming-Allen, who became the first Wycliffe batsman ever to top 500 runs in a season.

THE SCHOOLS

(Qualification: Batting 100 runs; Bowling 10 wickets)

* On name indicates captain.   ** On figures indicates not out.*

ABINGDON SCHOOL

Played 15: Won 7, Lost 3, Drawn 5. Abandoned 3

Master i/c: N. H. Payne

BATTING	Innings		Not Outs		Runs		Highest Inns		Average
*G. P. Lanham	15	..	1	..	321	..	59	..	22.92
N. G. Rice	14	..	1	..	254	..	48	..	19.53
A. C. Newman	13	..	4	..	175	..	40*	..	19.44
S. J. Minter	9	..	2	..	138	..	61	..	19.71
M. B. Willett	14	..	0	..	238	..	52	..	17.00
C. C. Newmark	10	..	1	..	112	..	30	..	12.44
D. H. Phillips	13	..	4	..	111	..	24	..	12.33
A. S. J. Patchett	15	..	1	..	152	..	35	..	10.85
G. D. Harper	14	..	0	..	145	..	32	..	10.35

BOWLING	Overs		Maidens		Runs		Wickets		Average
S. J. Minter	139.4	..	57	..	250	..	25	..	10.00
R. I. McCreery	164.4	..	34	..	444	..	40	..	11.10
W. K. Mellor	219.4	..	81	..	432	..	34	..	12.70
D. H. Phillips	91.4	..	19	..	255	..	13	..	19.61

ALDENHAM SCHOOL

Played 13: Won 4, Lost 2, Drawn 7

Master i/c: P. K. Smith   Cricket professional: F. J. Titmus

BATTING	Innings		Not Outs		Runs		Highest Inns		Average
*T. P. J. Dodd	11	..	3	..	443	..	120*	..	55.37
C. M. J. Dodd	7	..	4	..	110	..	51	..	36.36
M. N. Harrison	13	..	1	..	265	..	47	..	22.08
D. C. Coombs	12	..	1	..	183	..	45	..	16.63
J. P. Flindall	11	..	2	..	118	..	32	..	13.11
J. G. D. Bateson	13	..	0	..	135	..	34	..	10.38

BOWLING	Overs		Maidens		Runs		Wickets		Average
C. H. W. Ewer	73	..	24	..	166	..	15	..	11.06
J. G. D. Bateson	95	..	20	..	286	..	19	..	15.05
T. P. J. Dodd	175	..	52	..	412	..	27	..	15.25
N. J. H. Probert	94	..	24	..	248	..	14	..	17.71

ALLEYN'S SCHOOL

Played 16: Won 5, Lost 1, Drawn 10

Master i/c: Mr C. Page/Mr J. Nash

BATTING	Innings		Not Outs		Runs		Highest Inns		Average
*W. Manhood	14	..	1	..	388	..	73*	..	29.84
D. Woollatt	10	..	5	..	149	..	29	..	29.80
J. Lyne	14	..	0	..	358	..	80	..	25.57
B. Lane	14	..	0	..	323	..	84	..	23.07
S. Harmer	9	..	3	..	109	..	37	..	18.16
S. Banfield	14	..	0	..	231	..	58	..	16.50
F. Sims	11	..	4	..	100	..	30*	..	14.28

BOWLING	Overs		Maidens		Runs		Wickets		Average
R. Cowland	152.4	..	50	..	365	..	28	..	13.03
W. Manhood	72	..	18	..	204	..	12	..	17.00
W. Postlethwaite	78.4	..	18	..	200	..	11	..	18.18
S. McGlone	126.1	..	30	..	431	..	23	..	18.73
J. Cadman	145	..	34	..	409	..	20	..	20.45

ALLHALLOWS SCHOOL

Played 16: Won 4, Lost 4, Drawn 8. Abandoned 2

Master i/c: G. B. Jones   Cricket professional: R. M. H. Cottam

BATTING	Innings		Not Outs		Runs		Highest Inns		Average
S. R. Dryden	14	..	0	..	348	..	64	..	24.85
*M. J. Davies	13	..	0	..	242	..	49	..	18.61
D. A. S. Chapman	14	..	0	..	255	..	66	..	18.21
R. M. Bess	8	..	1	..	107	..	34	..	15.28
P. M. Zealey	14	..	1	..	140	..	34	..	10.76

BOWLING	Overs		Maidens		Runs		Wickets		Average
M. W. R. Luff	204.2	..	75	..	406	..	41	..	9.90
M. J. Davies	161.2	..	60	..	362	..	29	..	12.48
D. A. S. Chapman	93	..	28	..	259	..	17	..	15.23

AMPLEFORTH COLLEGE

Played 16: Won 6, Lost 3, Drawn 7

Master i/c: Dom Felix Stephens O.S.B.

BATTING	Innings		Not Outs		Runs		Highest Inns		Average
J. P. Barrett	17	..	4	..	529	..	125*	..	40.69
A. C. Calder-Smith	14	..	5	..	317	..	54*	..	35.22
D. R. O'Kelly	17	..	3	..	396	..	71	..	28.28
Hon. P. B. Fitzherbert.	17	..	3	..	336	..	77	..	24.00
D. H. Harrison	17	..	0	..	287	..	59	..	16.88
G. A. Codrington	12	..	2	..	138	..	44*	..	13.80
S. D. Lawson.	15	..	1	..	188	..	33	..	13.42
P. Ainscough.	9	..	1	..	107	..	56*	..	13.37

BOWLING	Overs		Maidens		Runs		Wickets		Average
S. D. Lawson.	174	..	66	..	327	..	27	..	12.11
P. Krasinski.	139	..	47	..	282	..	20	..	14.10
P. Crayton.	84.2	..	19	..	254	..	16	..	15.87
D. R. O'Kelly	121.5	..	34	..	351	..	19	..	18.47
M. C. T. Low	190.5	..	53	..	599	..	29	..	20.65
J. P. Barrett	79	..	15	..	254	..	10	..	25.40

ASHVILLE COLLEGE, HARROGATE

Played 17: Won 9, Lost 2, Drawn 6

Master i/c: J. M. Bromley

BATTING	Innings		Not Outs		Runs		Highest Inns		Average
*W. R. Stead.	14	..	4	..	595	..	94	..	59.50
C. R. L. Booth.	11	..	3	..	315	..	75*	..	39.37
J. D. Kirtley	15	..	2	..	396	..	86	..	30.46
J. M. Peasgood	9	..	1	..	123	..	63	..	15.37
S. D. Luery	14	..	0	..	213	..	43	..	15.21
S. P. Longbottom	16	..	0	..	230	..	39	..	14.37
M. J. S. Ramsey	13	..	1	..	138	..	31*	..	11.50

BOWLING	Overs		Maidens		Runs		Wickets		Average
M. J. S. Ramsey	102.3	..	40	..	231	..	22	..	10.50
M. W. H. Jones	61	..	15	..	145	..	12	..	12.08
M. M. Homer	182.3	..	52	..	448	..	36	..	12.44
N. R. N. Timms	120.2	..	42	..	276	..	22	..	12.54
J. D. Kirtley	147	..	26	..	507	..	33	..	15.36
I. D. Hopper	52	..	4	..	192	..	10	..	19.20

BABLAKE SCHOOL, COVENTRY

Played 22: Won 11, Lost 1, Drawn 10. Abandoned 4

Master i/c: R. A. Fewtrell

BATTING	Innings		Not Outs		Runs		Highest Inns		Average
C. L. Flick.	17	..	6	..	575	..	119*	..	52.27
W. P. Matthews.	19	..	3	..	791	..	86*	..	49.43
D. A. Thorne.	16	..	4	..	560	..	134*	..	46.66
D. R. Blower.	11	..	5	..	202	..	42*	..	33.66
R. Clift	14	..	4	..	315	..	74*	..	31.50

BOWLING	Overs		Maidens		Runs		Wickets		Average
R. Clift	124.1	..	43	..	269	..	27	..	9.96
D. A. Thorne	99.4	..	32	..	242	..	24	..	10.08
W. P. Matthews	182.1	..	46	..	454	..	39	..	11.64
A. Patel	120	..	38	..	265	..	17	..	15.58
L. Paul	63.2	..	12	..	192	..	11	..	17.45

BANCROFT'S SCHOOL

Played 22: Won 6, Lost 5, Drawn 11. Abandoned 2

Master i/c: J. G. Bromfield

BATTING	Innings		Not Outs		Runs		Highest Inns		Average
C. R. Thomas	21	..	4	..	647	..	92	..	38.05
S. W. Gant	12	..	6	..	188	..	51	..	31.33
I. P. Debnam	18	..	2	..	420	..	79	..	26.25
D. R. Johnstone	6	..	1	..	106	..	46	..	21.20
S. Winman	20	..	1	..	334	..	107*	..	17.57
M. G. De Jode	13	..	1	..	179	..	53	..	14.91
M. L. De Jode	13	..	5	..	115	..	27*	..	14.37
D. T. J. Clark	17	..	0	..	235	..	34	..	13.82
K. Bagger	12	..	1	..	129	..	36	..	11.72
*W. N. Giles	19	..	2	..	190	..	27	..	11.17

BOWLING	Overs		Maidens		Runs		Wickets		Average
S. W. Gant	152.3	..	47	..	382	..	29	..	13.17
I. P. Debnam	86.4	..	17	..	277	..	19	..	14.57
M. L. De Jode	218.3	..	53	..	607	..	33	..	18.39
S. Allen	198.3	..	48	..	572	..	26	..	22.00
M. F. Wilkinson	151	..	27	..	488	..	19	..	25.68

BARNARD CASTLE SCHOOL

Played 13: Won 8, Lost 1, Drawn 4

Master i/c: S. A. Cranville

BATTING	Innings		Not Outs		Runs		Highest Inns		Average
R. Andrew	13	..	3	..	483	..	91	..	48.30
*A. Frater	8	..	1	..	198	..	56	..	28.28
R. Kent	12	..	1	..	269	..	69	..	24.45
N. Grant	12	..	2	..	169	..	28*	..	16.90

BOWLING	Overs		Maidens		Runs		Wickets		Average
A. Frater	112.3	..	47	..	182	..	19	..	9.57
R. Andrew	103.5	..	30	..	218	..	19	..	11.47
M. Coates	163.1	..	61	..	308	..	26	..	11.84
R. Kent	115.2	..	24	..	355	..	29	..	12.24

BEDFORD SCHOOL

Played 18: Won 6, Lost 4, Drawn 8

BATTING	Innings		Not Outs		Runs		Highest Inns		Average
*H. D. Ferguson	19	..	3	..	712	..	125*	..	44.50
S. M. Smith	18	..	5	..	332	..	101*	..	25.53
S. A. Nutt	17	..	3	..	321	..	50	..	22.92
R. A. Millard	19	..	1	..	361	..	85	..	20.05
G. M. Gass	17	..	1	..	229	..	67	..	14.31
R. C. Williams	16	..	2	..	186	..	45	..	13.28

BOWLING	Overs		Maidens		Runs		Wickets		Average
S. P. Clayton............	251	..	66	..	616	..	41	..	15.02
S. M. Smith.............	71	..	12	..	240	..	15	..	16.00
I. T. Osborne...........	188	..	31	..	503	..	27	..	18.62
N. J. Cowell............	243	..	51	..	651	..	33	..	19.72

BEDFORD MODERN SCHOOL

Played 22: Won 8, Lost 4, Drawn 10. Abandoned 3

Master i/c: A. D. Curtis

BATTING	Innings		Not Outs		Runs		Highest Inns		Average
A. K. G. Jones..........	23	..	1	..	801	..	106*	..	36.40
A. Fordham	23	..	1	..	546	..	100	..	24.81
*D. F. Griffin	23	..	1	..	478	..	88	..	21.72
A. D. Tyler	15	..	6	..	194	..	35*	..	21.55
J. D. Sturt-Scobie	17	..	5	..	195	..	48*	..	16.25
P. S. Day..............	8	..	0	..	123	..	89	..	15.37
J. Hotham	20	..	2	..	252	..	45	..	14.00
A. P. Oakley	19	..	5	..	164	..	41	..	11.71
D. M. Hurley...........	16	..	2	..	115	..	15	..	8.21

BOWLING	Overs		Maidens		Runs		Wickets		Average
A. K. G. Jones..........	236.2	..	86	..	536	..	36	..	14.88
D. F. Fishwick	122	..	16	..	449	..	29	..	15.48
J. D. Sturt-Scobie	124.1	..	29	..	419	..	24	..	17.45
A. P. Oakley	152.3	..	32	..	427	..	20	..	21.35
D. F. Griffin	206.5	..	43	..	679	..	25	..	27.16
D. Lawson.............	221.2	..	53	..	568	..	19	..	29.89

BERKHAMSTED SCHOOL

Played 11: Won 4, Lost 1, Drawn 6. Abandoned 6

Master i/c: F. J. Davis   Cricket professional: M. Herring

BATTING	Innings		Not Outs		Runs		Highest Inns		Average
P. J. Allen	11	..	0	..	493	..	95	..	44.81
J. R. Neal	5	..	2	..	133	..	76	..	44.33
B. G. Evans............	11	..	3	..	342	..	70	..	42.75
G. Thrale.............	10	..	5	..	123	..	26	..	24.60
R. M. Hudson	10	..	5	..	112	..	27	..	22.40
S. Bullough	9	..	0	..	196	..	69	..	21.77
*M. J. Parsons..........	11	..	0	..	237	..	78	..	21.54

BOWLING	Overs		Maidens		Runs		Wickets		Average
M. J. Parsons	141	..	37	..	383	..	20	..	19.15

BIRKENHEAD SCHOOL

Played 20: Won 6, Lost 2, Drawn 12

Master i/c: M. H. Bowyer

BATTING	Innings		Not Outs		Runs		Highest Inns		Average
M. P. Gamet	19	..	4	..	644	..	104*	..	42.93
S. T. Crawley	20	..	2	..	745	..	170	..	41.38
*E. J. N. Cook...........	18	..	2	..	442	..	67	..	27.62
M. J. Cowdrill..........	12	..	0	..	255	..	60	..	21.25
S. M. Holroyd..........	15	..	2	..	170	..	48	..	13.07
G. D. Fletcher	14	..	3	..	140	..	40	..	12.72
A. G. Duncan	16	..	4	..	125	..	23*	..	10.41

BOWLING	Overs		Maidens		Runs		Wickets		Average
P. T. Brady	76	..	25	..	163	..	14	..	11.64
K. W. Jones	52	..	19	..	117	..	10	..	11.70
R. C. A. Thorn	180.1	..	41	..	525	..	35	..	15.00
M. McGowan	117	..	39	..	257	..	15	..	17.13
S. T. Crawley	174.4	..	52	..	399	..	21	..	19.00
G. D. Fletcher	89	..	18	..	240	..	11	..	21.81

BISHOP'S STORTFORD COLLEGE

Played 13: Won 5, Lost 3, Drawn 5. Abandoned 6

Master i/c: D. A. Hopper   Cricket professional: E. G. Witherden

BATTING	Innings		Not Outs		Runs		Highest Inns		Average
*R. L. W. Triggs	12	..	1	..	345	..	79*	..	31.36
N. P. Purkiss	13	..	3	..	296	..	100*	..	29.60
G. M. Lane	12	..	2	..	262	..	74	..	26.20
S. A. James	8	..	1	..	177	..	32	..	25.28
M. I. Thompson	12	..	1	..	262	..	80	..	23.81
P. N. R. Wacey	8	..	1	..	163	..	44	..	23.28

BOWLING	Overs		Maidens		Runs		Wickets		Average
R. E. Jackson	137.5	..	35	..	457	..	32	..	14.28
P. N. R. Wacey	111.5	..	39	..	249	..	17	..	14.64
J. S. Pryke	80.1	..	28	..	201	..	13	..	15.46
R. S. Banks	127	..	28	..	344	..	14	..	24.57

BLOXHAM SCHOOL

Played 12: Won 2, Lost 4, Drawn 6. Abandoned 1

Master i/c: M. J. Tideswell

BATTING	Innings		Not Outs		Runs		Highest Inns		Average
T. J. Abraham	12	..	3	..	288	..	55	..	32.00
R. P. Clee	12	..	1	..	193	..	59*	..	17.54
M. A. N. Thompson	12	..	0	..	196	..	58	..	16.33
M. Bury	11	..	2	..	146	..	29	..	16.22
G. A. Russell	12	..	0	..	102	..	41	..	8.50

BOWLING	Overs		Maidens		Runs		Wickets		Average
P. A. D. Farrar	196.4	..	63	..	460	..	33	..	13.93
J. J. R. Vasey	45	..	11	..	151	..	10	..	15.10
B. R. Desai	54.3	..	9	..	213	..	10	..	21.30

BLUNDELL'S SCHOOL

Played 13: Won 2, Lost 5, Drawn 6

Master i/c: E. D. Fursdon   Cricket professional: E. Steele

BATTING	Innings		Not Outs		Runs		Highest Inns		Average
*H. Morris	13	..	3	..	467	..	81*	..	46.70
P. D. Langdon	13	..	0	..	335	..	62	..	25.76
R. A. Eustace	13	..	1	..	215	..	60*	..	17.91
P. S. Selley	13	..	0	..	202	..	66	..	15.53
M. G. Beard	11	..	0	..	126	..	28	..	11.45
J. M. McKinnel	12	..	1	..	106	..	24	..	9.63

BOWLING	Overs		Maidens		Runs		Wickets		Average
P. D. Langdon	121	..	25	..	397	..	26	..	15.26
S. A. Watts	145	..	41	..	366	..	22	..	16.63
R. J. Taverner	139	..	38	..	372	..	17	..	21.88
C. G. Faye	96	..	22	..	283	..	10	..	28.30

BRADFIELD COLLEGE

Played 15: Won 4, Lost 6, Drawn 5. Abandoned 1

Master i/c: R. A. Brooks   Cricket professional: J. F. Harvey

BATTING	Innings		Not Outs		Runs		Highest Inns		Average
M. J. Gent	15	..	2	..	463	..	86	..	35.61
N. J. Straker	13	..	2	..	326	..	72	..	29.63
M. T. G. Laimbeer	15	..	2	..	269	..	102	..	20.69
P. R. C. Came	13	..	0	..	253	..	55	..	19.46
R. S. C. Blumire	13	..	2	..	211	..	48	..	19.18
*E. J. G. Bryans	11	..	3	..	150	..	58*	..	18.75
A. D. Johnston	14	..	1	..	192	..	62	..	14.76

BOWLING	Overs		Maidens		Runs		Wickets		Average
R. J. Tyler	41	..	7	..	162	..	10	..	16.20
J. J. Davies	205	..	68	..	559	..	26	..	21.50
E. J. G. Bryans	163	..	28	..	481	..	18	..	26.72
M. T. G. Laimbeer	155	..	25	..	482	..	17	..	28.35

BRADFORD GRAMMAR SCHOOL

Played 23: Won 8, Lost 3, Drawn 12. Abandoned 2

Master i/c: A. G. Smith

BATTING	Innings		Not Outs		Runs		Highest Inns		Average
A. A. Metcalfe	19	..	4	..	491	..	111*	..	32.73
*T. S. O'Brien	21	..	8	..	400	..	58	..	30.76
S. G. P. Hewitt	22	..	1	..	436	..	89	..	20.76
G. M. Fitzpatrick	20	..	2	..	304	..	49	..	16.88
R. A. Sunderland	17	..	3	..	225	..	50*	..	16.07
N. C. Fraser	19	..	1	..	240	..	41	..	13.33
I. M. Nolan	15	..	0	..	195	..	33	..	13.00
C. J. Hewitt	13	..	4	..	113	..	28*	..	12.55

BOWLING	Overs		Maidens		Runs		Wickets		Average
C. J. Hewitt	136	..	32	..	380	..	30	..	12.66
J. D. Thompson	297.3	..	92	..	711	..	49	..	14.51
G. T. N. Isbecque	149.4	..	49	..	361	..	24	..	15.04
A. A. Metcalfe	70	..	14	..	231	..	15	..	15.40
T. S. O'Brien	147.3	..	39	..	452	..	28	..	16.14
P. J. Higgins	135	..	31	..	387	..	18	..	21.50

BRENTWOOD SCHOOL

Played 16: Won 4, Lost 5, Drawn 7. Abandoned 3

Master i/c: A. G. Guyver   Cricket professional: K. C. Preston

BATTING	Innings		Not Outs		Runs		Highest Inns		Average
*I. L. Pont.............	17	..	3	..	858	..	137	..	61.28
S. Ashdown..........	14	..	2	..	325	..	91*	..	27.08
S. Robson	10	..	2	..	192	..	113	..	24.00
A. Marshall..........	15	..	2	..	295	..	82	..	22.69
M. Wedge	7	..	0	..	127	..	47	..	18.14
D. Eyres	10	..	1	..	115	..	41	..	12.77

BOWLING	Overs		Maidens		Runs		Wickets		Average
J. Hollington	193	..	61	..	461	..	37	..	12.45
N. Hanworth..........	155.5	..	46	..	449	..	29	..	15.48
I. L. Pont.............	221.4	..	62	..	648	..	40	..	16.20

BRIGHTON COLLEGE

Played 15: Won 11, Lost 1, Drawn 3. Abandoned 2

Master i/c: P. J. Hayes

BATTING	Innings		Not Outs		Runs		Highest Inns		Average
*C. J. Edmonds..........	15	..	3	..	437	..	96*	..	36.41
M. Simmonds	15	..	2	..	469	..	82	..	36.07
N. J. Lenham..........	14	..	5	..	294	..	104*	..	32.66
G. A. Cordery..........	14	..	3	..	239	..	55	..	21.72
S. C. B. Withers.......	9	..	1	..	131	..	50	..	16.37
J. A. St J. Withers	11	..	0	..	178	..	56	..	16.18
D. R. Thompson	12	..	2	..	156	..	53*	..	15.60

BOWLING	Overs		Maidens		Runs		Wickets		Average
D. R. Thompson	181.1	..	66	..	346	..	35	..	9.88
J. A. St J. Withers	170.5	..	57	..	304	..	29	..	10.48
G. A. Cordery..........	62	..	15	..	118	..	11	..	10.72
C. J. Hall..............	133	..	35	..	290	..	24	..	12.08
J. E. F. Jackson.........	115.5	..	33	..	238	..	18	..	13.22

BRYANSTON SCHOOL

Played 13: Won 3, Lost 3, Drawn 7

Master i/c: I. J. Brackley

BATTING	Innings		Not Outs		Runs		Highest Inns		Average
*J. J. A. Hewlett.......	8	..	0	..	209	..	73	..	26.12
M. Lovell Smith.	10	..	3	..	113	..	54	..	16.14
M. B. Hersov..........	10	..	1	..	145	..	53	..	16.11
G. A. Locke	12	..	0	..	192	..	49	..	16.00
P. A. A. Schreiber........	11	..	1	..	143	..	47	..	14.30
D. J. Ticehurst.	12	..	0	..	150	..	35	..	12.50

BOWLING	Overs		Maidens		Runs		Wickets		Average
J. L. Warner	45.3	..	10	..	128	..	11	..	11.63
D. J. Ticehurst.........	161.1	..	56	..	375	..	26	..	14.42
M. B. Hersov..........	54	..	13	..	182	..	10	..	18.20
E. G. Brookes.........	107.5	..	35	..	290	..	11	..	26.36

CANFORD SCHOOL

Played 14: Won 5, Lost 4, Drawn 5. Abandoned 2

Master i/c: H. A. Jarvis

BATTING	Innings		Not Outs		Runs		Highest Inns		Average
*P. B. Taylor	14	..	3	..	568	..	84	..	51.63
A. J. Vye	14	..	1	..	374	..	74	..	28.76
G. P. Daubeney	12	..	3	..	172	..	39	..	19.11
N. J. V. Atkinson	11	..	1	..	166	..	48	..	16.60
P. E. C. Bromley	14	..	1	..	205	..	39	..	15.76
J. A. Attenborough	12	..	0	..	179	..	43	..	14.91

BOWLING	Overs		Maidens		Runs		Wickets		Average
S. D. Drury	116.3	..	29	..	288	..	20	..	14.40
J. W. R. Edwards	133.4	..	36	..	355	..	20	..	17.75
A. G. Nicholson	129	..	28	..	387	..	16	..	24.18
J. A. Attenborough	105.4	..	18	..	350	..	12	..	29.16

CHARTERHOUSE

Played 17: Won 3, Lost 5, Drawn 9. Abandoned 2

Master i/c: A. S. Morrison   Cricket professional: R. V. Lewis

BATTING	Innings		Not Outs		Runs		Highest Inns		Average
C. E. G. Allen	18	..	2	..	536	..	103*	..	33.50
*G. P. Bristowe	18	..	2	..	487	..	109*	..	30.43
W. R. Bristowe	20	..	0	..	570	..	124	..	28.50
C. W. H. May	15	..	3	..	325	..	65	..	27.08
A. C. Davis	19	..	2	..	442	..	86	..	26.00
P. E. L. Ettinger	10	..	3	..	160	..	54	..	22.85
J. B. D. North	18	..	3	..	261	..	51	..	17.40

BOWLING	Overs		Maidens		Runs		Wickets		Average
J. B. D. North	227.2	..	42	..	715	..	38	..	18.81
T. P. R. Maddison	135	..	27	..	335	..	12	..	27.91
A. J. Lathwood	150.1	..	34	..	479	..	15	..	31.93
S. C. Toombs	175	..	30	..	573	..	17	..	33.70
A. C. Davis	108	..	15	..	392	..	10	..	39.20

CHELTENHAM COLLEGE

Played 15: Won 1, Lost 8, Drawn 6. Abandoned 2

Master i/c: R. W. Hosen   Cricket professional: G. A. Edrich

BATTING	Innings		Not Outs		Runs		Highest Inns		Average
R. H. B. Johnson	14	..	2	..	324	..	71	..	27.00
S. J. G. Dyer	10	..	3	..	174	..	62*	..	24.85
D. I. Wilson	14	..	1	..	319	..	112	..	24.53
R. M. Tucker	14	..	2	..	280	..	66	..	23.33
*S. W. Davies	14	..	0	..	265	..	69	..	18.92
A. D. Marsh	9	..	1	..	142	..	31	..	17.75
S. A. J. Davies	11	..	3	..	121	..	24*	..	15.12
P. M. Salter	15	..	2	..	143	..	39	..	11.00

BOWLING	Overs		Maidens		Runs		Wickets		Average
S. A. J. Davies	165.1	..	28	..	595	..	29	..	20.51
A. D. Marsh	152.5	..	38	..	455	..	20	..	22.75
S. W. Davies	193.4	..	46	..	582	..	25	..	23.28

CHELTENHAM GRAMMAR SCHOOL

Played 18: Won 10, Lost 3, Drawn 5

Master i/c: D. A. Smith   Cricket professional: C. J. Sinclair

BATTING	Innings		Not Outs		Runs		Highest Inns		Average
A. White	16	..	2	..	721	..	122*	..	51.50
C. White	11	..	7	..	190	..	33*	..	47.50
J. Cropper	16	..	2	..	379	..	62	..	27.07
A. Drake	18	..	0	..	313	..	59	..	17.38
*M. Breddy	9	..	1	..	139	..	34	..	17.37

BOWLING	Overs		Maidens		Runs		Wickets		Average
K. Morris	67.3	..	13	..	118	..	14	..	8.42
C. White	89.1	..	24	..	268	..	26	..	10.30
T. Stephens	141.3	..	29	..	415	..	33	..	12.57
N. Clay	90.2	..	28	..	212	..	16	..	13.25
G. Snell	84	..	33	..	211	..	13	..	16.23
S. Kentfield	141	..	44	..	336	..	20	..	16.80

CHIGWELL SCHOOL

Played 14: Won 1, Lost 7, Drawn 6. Abandoned 4

Master i/c: D. N. Morrison

BATTING	Innings		Not Outs		Runs		Highest Inns		Average
*M. M. Thompson	14	..	1	..	283	..	76	..	21.76
J. M. W. Yates	12	..	0	..	207	..	58	..	17.25
A. J. Muir-Taylor	14	..	0	..	157	..	31	..	11.21
A. C. Rughani	14	..	0	..	134	..	37	..	9.57
M. E. F. Deakin	13	..	2	..	103	..	28*	..	9.36
D. A. Leiper	14	..	0	..	125	..	21	..	8.92
D. Black	13	..	1	..	104	..	22	..	8.66

BOWLING	Overs		Maidens		Runs		Wickets		Average
A. J. Muir-Taylor	187.3	..	41	..	513	..	28	..	18.32
D. A. Leiper	160	..	20	..	661	..	33	..	20.03
A. C. Rughani	112.3	..	17	..	410	..	15	..	27.33

CHRIST COLLEGE, BRECON

Played 13: Won 4, Lost 6, Drawn 3. Abandoned 4

Master i/c: C. W. Kleiser

BATTING	Innings		Not Outs		Runs		Highest Inns		Average
N. C. Hanson	13	..	1	..	376	..	82	..	31.33
C. R. Williams	9	..	1	..	163	..	49	..	20.37
*S. A. Brown	13	..	1	..	181	..	40	..	15.08
J. D. Isaac	10	..	0	..	149	..	34	..	14.90
D. J. James	13	..	0	..	182	..	50	..	14.00

BOWLING	Overs		Maidens		Runs		Wickets		Average
P. G. Chambers	194	..	70	..	432	..	41	..	10.53
S. W. Harvey	59.5	..	23	..	155	..	14	..	11.07
S. A. Brown	127.4	..	36	..	325	..	19	..	17.10

CHRIST'S HOSPITAL

Played 10: Won 1, Lost 3, Drawn 6. Abandoned 5

Master i/c: J. E. Denison   Cricket professional: D. W. White

BATTING	Innings		Not Outs		Runs		Highest Inns		Average
*N. Konig	9	..	0	..	277	..	88	..	30.77
D. James	8	..	2	..	131	..	55	..	21.83
R. Charlesworth	8	..	0	..	163	..	37	..	20.37
P. Cunliffe	9	..	0	..	133	..	68	..	14.77

BOWLING	Overs		Maidens		Runs		Wickets		Average
P. Cunliffe	131.5	..	39	..	326	..	26	..	12.53
B. Roxburgh	77	..	16	..	257	..	15	..	17.13
J. Maxwell	95.1	..	19	..	302	..	17	..	17.76
M. Scott	96	..	13	..	337	..	11	..	30.63

CITY OF LONDON SCHOOL

Played 14: Won 3, Lost 4, Drawn 7. Abandoned 4

Master i/c: A. V. McL. Murray   Cricket professional: L. M. Smith

BATTING	Innings		Not Outs		Runs		Highest Inns		Average
*M. Gigney	13	..	3	..	445	..	74*	..	44.50
S. C. Hylson-Smith	13	..	2	..	247	..	44	..	22.45
N. P. Bretton	8	..	3	..	101	..	33	..	20.20
P. A. Townson	13	..	1	..	189	..	74	..	15.75
S. Manuel	10	..	1	..	137	..	46*	..	15.22
B. Webb	12	..	0	..	140	..	37	..	11.66

BOWLING	Overs		Maidens		Runs		Wickets		Average
G. D. L. Rolt	159.3	..	35	..	438	..	22	..	19.90
E. D. Kessler	84	..	21	..	241	..	10	..	24.10
M. Gigney	97	..	15	..	338	..	14	..	24.14
P. A. Townson	74.4	..	7	..	315	..	12	..	26.25
W. M. Tebbit	110.1	..	16	..	429	..	16	..	26.81

CLIFTON COLLEGE

Played 16: Won 6, Lost 4, Drawn 6. Abandoned 1

Master i/c: D. C. Henderson   Cricket professional: F. J. Andrew

BATTING	Innings		Not Outs		Runs		Highest Inns		Average
M. W. Bailey	16	..	3	..	444	..	104	..	34.15
J. E. Brooks	17	..	3	..	345	..	79*	..	24.64
P. F. Andrew	16	..	1	..	291	..	55	..	19.40
*C. R. Trembath	15	..	1	..	262	..	46	..	18.71
N. R. Gillespie	12	..	1	..	157	..	64	..	14.27
C. P. R. S. Manners	11	..	1	..	120	..	36	..	12.00
R. S. Burns-Cox	11	..	0	..	115	..	33	..	10.45
J. C. de L. Wright	14	..	1	..	134	..	44	..	10.30
D. R. Brown	12	..	2	..	102	..	21*	..	10.20

BOWLING	Overs		Maidens		Runs		Wickets		Average
C. R. Trembath	276	..	69	..	632	..	52	..	12.15
N. R. Gillespie	276	..	79	..	609	..	46	..	13.23
J. C. de L. Wright	92	..	27	..	217	..	15	..	14.46
P. F. Andrew	162	..	51	..	334	..	15	..	22.26

COLFE'S SCHOOL

Played 16: Won 6, Lost 3, Drawn 7

Master i/c: M. L. Taylor

BATTING	Innings		Not Outs		Runs		Highest Inns		Average
A. Caswall.	12	..	2	..	494	..	70	..	49.40
*N. Tarrant.	16	..	1	..	447	..	82	..	29.80
A. Fisher	13	..	5	..	203	..	67*	..	25.37
R. Thomas	14	..	4	..	195	..	48	..	19.50
G. Mockeridge	12	..	1	..	197	..	79	..	17.90

BOWLING	Overs		Maidens		Runs		Wickets		Average
A. Rodgers	203	..	57	..	436	..	37	..	11.78
R. Mirza	173	..	42	..	501	..	41	..	12.21
R. Thomas	103	..	18	..	288	..	15	..	19.20

COLSTON'S SCHOOL

Played 18: Won 5, Lost 3, Drawn 10. Abandoned 1

Master i/c: M. P. B. Tayler   Cricket professional: R. A. Sinfield

BATTING	Innings		Not Outs		Runs		Highest Inns		Average
W. M. Smith	18	..	1	..	639	..	91	..	37.58
G. O. Q. Clarke.	18	..	0	..	544	..	79	..	30.22
*M. M. Wyatt	18	..	1	..	462	..	100*	..	27.17
N. Parnell	18	..	5	..	299	..	42	..	23.00
D. B. Pigott	16	..	8	..	106	..	23	..	13.25
J. Mitchell	13	..	1	..	122	..	12	..	10.16

BOWLING	Overs		Maidens		Runs		Wickets		Average
D. B. Pigott	173.3	..	40	..	419	..	36	..	11.63
D. G. L. Mathias.	147	..	29	..	452	..	30	..	15.06
N. Parnell	53	..	10	..	185	..	12	..	15.41
J. Mitchell	113	..	28	..	338	..	21	..	16.09
J. McDonnell.	84	..	11	..	307	..	10	..	30.70

CRANBROOK SCHOOL

Played 14: Won 3, Lost 2, Drawn 9. Abandoned 6

Master i/c: T. J. Allen

BATTING	Innings		Not Outs		Runs		Highest Inns		Average
C. A. Pugh	12	..	2	..	239	..	63*	..	23.90
S. M. Shaw	14	..	2	..	274	..	58	..	22.83
T. H. T. Dunn	14	..	1	..	289	..	69	..	22.23
C. M. Llewelyn	10	..	4	..	133	..	39*	..	22.16
*N. P. Brown.	13	..	3	..	175	..	31*	..	17.50
R. J. Coleman	14	..	1	..	222	..	54*	..	17.07
C. G. Edwards	11	..	3	..	127	..	28*	..	15.87

BOWLING	Overs		Maidens		Runs		Wickets		Average
C. G. Edwards	103	..	28	..	303	..	23	..	13.17
C. M. Llewelyn	151	..	39	..	388	..	22	..	17.63
J. S. P. Clifford	165	..	36	..	488	..	19	..	25.68

DAUNTSEY'S SCHOOL

Played 14: Won 6, Lost 3, Drawn 5. Abandoned 1

Master i/c: M. K. F. Johnson   Cricket professional: P. Hough

BATTING	Innings		Not Outs		Runs		Highest Inns		Average
M. Omar	14	..	2	..	370	..	53	..	30.83
*A. B. Leng	13	..	3	..	245	..	51	..	24.50
A. S. Robinson	12	..	2	..	231	..	58*	..	23.10
N. Gallow	10	..	1	..	120	..	23	..	13.33
R. Baker	13	..	0	..	114	..	34	..	8.76

BOWLING	Overs		Maidens		Runs		Wickets		Average
A. B. Leng	93.2	..	25	..	199	..	23	..	8.65
R. S. Spencer	164.4	..	32	..	389	..	36	..	10.80
N. Gallow	137	..	40	..	295	..	23	..	12.82
S. Hassall	101.1	..	25	..	259	..	19	..	13.63
M. Omar	111.4	..	32	..	329	..	18	..	18.27

DEAN CLOSE SCHOOL

Played 16: Won 3, Lost 6, Drawn 7. Abandoned 1

Master i/c: C. M. Kenyon   Cricket professional: W. E. Jones

BATTING	Innings		Not Outs		Runs		Highest Inns		Average
N. R. Newport Black	6	..	0	..	179	..	71	..	29.83
M. P. A. Crawshaw	14	..	3	..	325	..	86*	..	29.54
C. Dyer	15	..	0	..	322	..	54	..	21.46
*K. S. Wood	13	..	3	..	207	..	36	..	20.70
C. Rhodes	12	..	2	..	190	..	41*	..	19.00
S. J. Weare	14	..	3	..	207	..	36	..	18.81
T. Jackson	13	..	1	..	209	..	46	..	17.41
G. Tredgett	11	..	0	..	144	..	29	..	13.09

BOWLING	Overs		Maidens		Runs		Wickets		Average
A. R. Godwin	157	..	43	..	343	..	22	..	15.59
T. Jackson	169.2	..	26	..	503	..	30	..	16.76
K. S. Wood	139.1	..	38	..	350	..	20	..	17.50
S. J. Weare	102.4	..	20	..	330	..	15	..	22.00

DENSTONE COLLEGE

Played 18: Won 8, Lost 5, Drawn 5. Abandoned 4

Master i/c: D. J. Dexter   Cricket professional: H. J. Rhodes

BATTING	Innings		Not Outs		Runs		Highest Inns		Average
A. J. Everall	18	..	4	..	487	..	100*	..	34.78
S. A. Roy	8	..	4	..	100	..	34	..	25.00
A. J. Little	15	..	6	..	221	..	37*	..	24.55
C. M. Smith	17	..	6	..	240	..	44*	..	21.81
J. E. Whiting	8	..	1	..	137	..	44	..	19.57
M. J. Smith	17	..	1	..	264	..	40*	..	16.50
*T. J. Marlow	16	..	0	..	190	..	33	..	11.87
P. A. Gordon	18	..	2	..	188	..	39	..	11.75
M. N. Aris	12	..	1	..	107	..	36	..	9.72

BOWLING	Overs		Maidens		Runs		Wickets		Average
J. P. D. Cadman	193.2	..	54	..	442	..	39	..	11.33
M. N. Aris...............	101.1	..	29	..	198	..	12	..	16.50
A. D. Coley.............	248.2	..	75	..	614	..	37	..	16.59
A. J. Little.............	130.4	..	37	..	319	..	17	..	18.76
M. J. Smith	134.5	..	34	..	324	..	16	..	20.25

DOUAI SCHOOL

Played 15: Won 3, Lost 1, Drawn 11. Abandoned 2

Master i/c: J. Shaw

BATTING	Innings		Not Outs		Runs		Highest Inns		Average
R. A. Keeble	14	..	3	..	476	..	100	..	43.27
C. F. B. Rudd	13	..	3	..	370	..	101*	..	37.00
A. Bush	14	..	3	..	278	..	53*	..	25.27
D. A. Joyce	11	..	3	..	194	..	38	..	24.25
*C. Whitworth	14	..	1	..	224	..	63	..	17.23

BOWLING	Overs		Maidens		Runs		Wickets		Average
R. A. Keeble	237	..	87	..	532	..	42	..	12.66
C. F. B. Rudd	139	..	33	..	421	..	30	..	14.03
J. Darby	127	..	40	..	309	..	20	..	15.45

DOVER COLLEGE

Played 14: Won 5, Lost 4, Drawn 5

Master i/c: A. Beatson

BATTING	Innings		Not Outs		Runs		Highest Inns		Average
I. A. C. Syer	14	..	0	..	407	..	71	..	29.07
A. L. G. Carpenter	6	..	1	..	102	..	40	..	20.40
*J. G. Ryeland...........	11	..	2	..	170	..	47	..	18.88
M. B. Coupland..........	13	..	2	..	196	..	38	..	17.81
J. T. P. Boorman	12	..	2	..	153	..	51	..	15.30
J. J. Corbett............	13	..	0	..	149	..	61	..	11.46
D. S. Monro	12	..	2	..	110	..	29	..	11.00

BOWLING	Overs		Maidens		Runs		Wickets		Average
J. G. Ryeland	182.2	..	43	..	449	..	30	..	14.96
S. V. Devalia............	153.4	..	42	..	448	..	22	..	20.36

DOWNSIDE SCHOOL

Played 13: Won 2, Lost 4, Drawn 7. Abandoned 1

Master i/c: D. Baty   Cricket professional: D. R. Shepherd

BATTING	Innings		Not Outs		Runs		Highest Inns		Average
M. J. Poland	12	..	1	..	561	..	138*	..	51.00
*T. A. Cotterell..........	11	..	3	..	216	..	33	..	27.00
D. F. B. Sheridan	12	..	2	..	251	..	102*	..	25.10
J. A. Smith	11	..	0	..	172	..	42	..	15.63
N. J. S. Jenkins	9	..	1	..	129	..	51	..	16.12
S. C. Vyvyan............	12	..	1	..	131	..	52	..	10.91

BOWLING	Overs		Maidens		Runs		Wickets		Average
T. A. Cotterell...........	217.1	..	41	..	647	..	41	..	15.78
J. A. Woolford	151.5	..	35	..	476	..	13	..	36.61

DULWICH COLLEGE

Played 14: Won 2, Lost 4, Drawn 8. Abandoned 1

Master i/c: M. C. Wagstaffe   Cricket professional: W. A. Smith

BATTING	Innings		Not Outs		Runs		Highest Inns		Average
N. M. K. Robinson	12	..	2	..	414	..	102	..	41.40
S. B. Howland	13	..	1	..	438	..	99	..	36.50
J. J. Beere	13	..	1	..	421	..	82	..	35.08
P. G. Sudell	10	..	2	..	257	..	68*	..	32.12
W. K. Jarrett	13	..	1	..	227	..	50	..	18.91
S. W. Bowling	12	..	2	..	188	..	45	..	18.80

BOWLING	Overs		Maidens		Runs		Wickets		Average
W. K. Jarrett	155	..	40	..	391	..	22	..	17.77
S. Edwards	97.3	..	24	..	276	..	11	..	25.09
D. R. Cuming	120.4	..	23	..	378	..	13	..	29.07
N. M. K. Robinson	161.2	..	40	..	501	..	16	..	31.31

DURHAM SCHOOL

Played 17: Won 4, Lost 6, Drawn 7

Master i/c: W. J. R. Allen

BATTING	Innings		Not Outs		Runs		Highest Inns		Average
P. C. Shaw	18	..	1	..	418	..	66*	..	24.58
J. M. Thompson	16	..	2	..	333	..	90	..	23.78
J. N. Stankley	15	..	1	..	286	..	63*	..	20.42
G. Lea-Swain	14	..	8	..	118	..	29	..	19.66
S. J. Ibbitson	18	..	0	..	312	..	47	..	17.33
N. P. Tubbs	16	..	0	..	213	..	51	..	13.31
D. M. Shaw	18	..	1	..	165	..	36	..	9.70
*M. R. Fletcher	18	..	0	..	138	..	42	..	7.66

BOWLING	Overs		Maidens		Runs		Wickets		Average
M. R. Fletcher	205	..	49	..	653	..	38	..	17.18
J. C. McKenna	111	..	44	..	401	..	22	..	18.22
N. P. Tubbs	158	..	35	..	549	..	21	..	26.14
J. M. Thompson	183	..	43	..	592	..	22	..	26.90
J. N. Stankley	75	..	15	..	276	..	10	..	27.60

EASTBOURNE COLLEGE

Played 18: Won 5, Lost 6, Drawn 7

Master i/c: N. L. Wheeler   Cricket professional: A. E. James

BATTING	Innings		Not Outs		Runs		Highest Inns		Average
S. J. D. Yorke	17	..	0	..	426	..	90	..	25.05
J. P. Payne	17	..	1	..	374	..	89	..	23.37
R. D. Montgomerie	18	..	1	..	355	..	66	..	20.88
*P. A. N. Armstrong	17	..	1	..	331	..	49	..	20.68
R. R. C. Bairamian	15	..	5	..	162	..	48	..	16.20
J. R. Prentis	10	..	0	..	133	..	34	..	13.30
A. C. Head	17	..	0	..	224	..	40	..	13.17

BOWLING	Overs		Maidens		Runs		Wickets		Average
N. B. Chapple	187.5	..	65	..	460	..	35	..	13.14
R. D. Montgomerie	221.2	..	62	..	604	..	31	..	19.48
D. Gordon	145.1	..	36	..	429	..	21	..	20.42

THE EDINBURGH ACADEMY

Played 17: Won 8, Lost 1, Drawn 8

Master i/c: A. R. Dyer

BATTING	Innings		Not Outs		Runs		Highest Inns		Average
J. D. Sutton............	18	..	3	..	794	..	117*	..	52.93
C. D. Fraser-Darling......	17	..	3	..	693	..	130	..	49.50
*T. J. B. Scott...........	16	..	5	..	229	..	48	..	20.81
A. C. C. Kennedy........	18	..	0	..	370	..	58	..	20.55
K. A. J. Coughtrie........	13	..	5	..	135	..	31*	..	16.87
C. N. R. Yule	12	..	0	..	137	..	23	..	11.41
G. M. Henderson	12	..	2	..	105	..	20	..	10.50

BOWLING	Overs		Maidens		Runs		Wickets		Average
C. D. Fraser-Darling......	311.1	..	104	..	674	..	46	..	14.65
A. M. Russell	143.2	..	28	..	435	..	24	..	18.12
C. N. R. Yule	243.3	..	68	..	634	..	34	..	18.64
T. J. B. Scott	202	..	53	..	516	..	26	..	19.84

ELIZABETH COLLEGE, GUERNSEY

Played 15: Won 6, Lost 4, Drawn 5. Abandoned 2

Master i/c: P. L. Le Cocq

BATTING	Innings		Not Outs		Runs		Highest Inns		Average
D. J. Mechem	15	..	1	..	321	..	56	..	22.92
*C. J. Guilbert..........	15	..	1	..	312	..	47	..	22.28
J. R. Ravenscroft........	14	..	3	..	218	..	41	..	19.81
P. G. Roussel	13	..	1	..	210	..	36	..	17.50
S. C. Toynton	15	..	0	..	208	..	44	..	13.86
N. W. Belton	11	..	3	..	101	..	38*	..	12.62

BOWLING	Overs		Maidens		Runs		Wickets		Average
A. G. Tapp	154.4	..	36	..	365	..	34	..	10.73
B. McL. Spittal	75.3	..	17	..	229	..	19	..	12.05
J. R. Ravenscroft........	175.2	..	44	..	425	..	32	..	13.28
D. J. Mechem	153	..	45	..	429	..	32	..	13.40

ELLESMERE COLLEGE

Played 15: Won 2, Lost 1, Drawn 12. Abandoned 3

Master i/c: R. F. Taylor   Cricket professional: R. K. Sethi

BATTING	Innings		Not Outs		Runs		Highest Inns		Average
*R. E. J. Watt	14	..	2	..	454	..	95	..	37.83
G. L. Home.............	15	..	2	..	389	..	60	..	29.92
A. I. Crow..............	12	..	5	..	178	..	38	..	25.42

BOWLING	Overs		Maidens		Runs		Wickets		Average
G. J. Young.............	86.1	..	23	..	189	..	15	..	12.60
C. I. Hill	76	..	17	..	202	..	12	..	16.83
R. E. J. Watt	228	..	68	..	570	..	30	..	19.00
M. J. Talbot............	141	..	21	..	496	..	17	..	29.17

ELTHAM COLLEGE

Played 21: Won 6, Lost 5, Drawn 10. Abandoned 5

Master i/c: P. C. McCartney

BATTING	Innings		Not Outs		Runs		Highest Inns		Average
*N. I. Holcombe	19	..	1	..	493	..	68	..	27.38
M. R. Surguy	14	..	3	..	287	..	56	..	26.09
M. J. Holcombe	16	..	1	..	338	..	50	..	22.53
N. S. Comber	17	..	1	..	180	..	38	..	11.25
D. J. Hill	13	..	2	..	107	..	26	..	9.72

BOWLING	Overs		Maidens		Runs		Wickets		Average
R. A. Mellors	131	..	48	..	265	..	20	..	13.25
M. J. Holcombe	85	..	13	..	306	..	22	..	13.90
N. I. Holcombe	137.2	..	30	..	449	..	32	..	14.03
M. J. Wright	102.1	..	26	..	266	..	18	..	14.77
M. W. D. Watkins	86	..	19	..	220	..	13	..	16.92
M. R. Surguy	182	..	60	..	344	..	20	..	17.20

EMANUEL SCHOOL

Played 26: Won 20, Lost 3, Drawn 3. Abandoned 5

Master i/c: M. J. Stewart

BATTING	Innings		Not Outs		Runs		Highest Inns		Average
J. C. Waite	26	..	7	..	1,056	..	154	..	55.57
D. I. K. Blyth	18	..	2	..	372	..	69*	..	23.25
K. R. Agutter	23	..	3	..	450	..	74	..	22.50
P. A. Young	9	..	3	..	107	..	23*	..	17.83
G. J. Henderson	12	..	6	..	105	..	54*	..	17.50
P. B. Campbell	23	..	3	..	318	..	79*	..	15.90
M. S. Farooqi	15	..	8	..	107	..	32	..	15.28
R. C. Looker	20	..	3	..	250	..	32	..	14.70
M. L. Bradley	15	..	1	..	202	..	31	..	14.42
N. P. Carrick	20	..	2	..	217	..	47	..	12.05
A. Tinker	23	..	3	..	226	..	33	..	11.30

BOWLING	Overs		Maidens		Runs		Wickets		Average
P. B. Campbell	31.4	..	7	..	91	..	12	..	7.58
J. C. Waite	164	..	56	..	340	..	34	..	10.00
P. A. Young	176.1	..	55	..	416	..	38	..	10.94
G. J. Henderson	236	..	71	..	555	..	46	..	12.06
M. S. Farooqi	165	..	40	..	482	..	33	..	14.60
R. C. Looker	187.2	..	57	..	473	..	26	..	18.19

EPSOM COLLEGE

Played 10: Won 2, Lost 1, Drawn 7. Abandoned 5

Master i/c: J. T. J. Houlson

BATTING	Innings		Not Outs		Runs		Highest Inns		Average
J. M. Paulus	11	..	2	..	322	..	128*	..	35.77
M. J. Morris	8	..	4	..	141	..	30*	..	35.25
N. L. Porter	11	..	1	..	350	..	94	..	35.00
M. C. Humphrys	10	..	1	..	223	..	73	..	24.77
P. M. Starns	10	..	2	..	184	..	38	..	23.00
*M. A. Fahmy	10	..	1	..	197	..	46	..	21.88
J. R. Ansell	10	..	1	..	194	..	38	..	21.55

BOWLING	Overs		Maidens		Runs		Wickets		Average
M. J. Morris	123.3	..	30	..	344	..	21	..	16.38
R. M. C. Williams	136.2	..	40	..	386	..	22	..	17.54

ETON COLLEGE

Played 12: Won 3, Lost 0, Drawn 9. Abandoned 4

Master i/c: P. R. Thackeray   Cricket professional: V. H. D. Cannings

BATTING	Innings		Not Outs		Runs		Highest Inns		Average
C. C. Birch Reynardson . . .	15	..	5	..	483	..	101*	..	48.30
D. C. E. Russell.	16	..	5	..	519	..	111*	..	47.18
*H. T. Rawlinson	16	..	0	..	441	..	74	..	27.56
N. A. Metaxa	8	..	1	..	178	..	47	..	25.42
I. R. M. D. Bluett	7	..	2	..	116	..	33*	..	23.20
T. R. V. Robins.	15	..	3	..	241	..	62*	..	20.08
M. J. B. Rudd	10	..	3	..	108	..	30	..	15.42

BOWLING	Overs		Maidens		Runs		Wickets		Average
M. J. B. Rudd	241.3	..	68	..	549	..	39	..	14.07
I. R. M. D. Bluett	143.1	..	33	..	395	..	26	..	15.19
A. G. Morrison	113.5	..	19	..	359	..	17	..	21.11
W. N. S. Blake.	137	..	42	..	385	..	15	..	25.66

EXETER SCHOOL

Played 17: Won 2, Lost 5, Drawn 10

Master i/c: T. J. Huxtable   Cricket professional: T. J. Dewes

BATTING	Innings		Not Outs		Runs		Highest Inns		Average
D. Cox	15	..	1	..	287	..	49	..	20.50
A. C Stone.	17	..	2	..	294	..	42	..	19.60
P. A. Hodgson.	17	..	1	..	294	..	52*	..	18.37
T. J. Buckley	13	..	4	..	161	..	44*	..	17.88
M. J. Davies	13	..	0	..	168	..	33	..	12.92
P. A. Clarke	10	..	1	..	115	..	52	..	12.77
N. Robjohns	14	..	0	..	161	..	26	..	11.50

BOWLING	Overs		Maidens		Runs		Wickets		Average
P. C. D. Sykes.	226	..	83	..	393	..	40	..	9.82
*P. Bates	179	..	35	..	570	..	42	..	13.57

FELSTED SCHOOL

Played 15: Won 5, Lost 1, Drawn 9. Abandoned 3

Master i/c: J. A. Cockett   Cricket professional: G. O. Barker

BATTING	Innings		Not Outs		Runs		Highest Inns		Average
R. N. R. Vartan.	14	..	0	..	541	..	76	..	38.64
M. W. C. Olley	14	..	3	..	384	..	78	..	34.90
*N. C. Anns	14	..	1	..	342	..	46	..	26.30
R. F. Rothwell.	13	..	4	..	186	..	42	..	20.66
S. H. J. Ruffell.	11	..	0	..	201	..	50	..	18.27
A. B. Mitchell	9	..	1	..	153	..	41	..	17.00

BOWLING	Overs		Maidens		Runs		Wickets		Average
I. P. Mason	204	..	64	..	506	..	33	..	15.33
B. H. Pinkerton	222	..	74	..	516	..	32	..	16.12
R. N. R. Vartan	164	..	48	..	443	..	20	..	22.15
R. P. S. Martin	92	..	22	..	278	..	10	..	27.80

FETTES COLLEGE

Played 18: Won 7, Lost 0, Drawn 11

Master i/c: C. H. Carruthers   Cricket professional: P. Clifford

BATTING	Innings		Not Outs		Runs		Highest Inns		Average
M. J. M. Stewart	15	..	3	..	521	..	82	..	43.41
*R. J. Orr	19	..	2	..	611	..	92*	..	35.94
C. A. Evans	16	..	5	..	375	..	68*	..	34.09
J. P. Kennedy	19	..	1	..	402	..	53*	..	22.33
D. R. L. Brown	16	..	3	..	265	..	42	..	20.38
A. S. Mackenzie	18	..	0	..	274	..	68	..	15.22
H. D. Desai	15	..	3	..	142	..	23*	..	11.83
G. J. M. Robb	13	..	1	..	113	..	26	..	9.41

BOWLING	Overs		Maidens		Runs		Wickets		Average
R. J. Orr	198.4	..	62	..	411	..	40	..	10.27
C. I. McCrostie	257	..	102	..	505	..	38	..	13.28
N. I. S. Jones	103	..	24	..	262	..	13	..	20.15
D. R. L. Brown	91.3	..	22	..	244	..	12	..	20.33
H. D. Desai	161	..	38	..	479	..	16	..	29.93

FOREST SCHOOL

Played 13: Won 5, Lost 3, Drawn 5. Abandoned 3

Master i/c: M. Surridge   Cricket professional: W. B. Morris

BATTING	Innings		Not Outs		Runs		Highest Inns		Average
J. Crossley	12	..	4	..	399	..	124*	..	49.87
I. Crossley	11	..	2	..	322	..	67	..	35.77
K. P. Hayden	9	..	3	..	157	..	36	..	26.16
C. Shokoya	12	..	2	..	259	..	64*	..	25.90
M. Hussain	10	..	0	..	119	..	31	..	11.90

BOWLING	Overs		Maidens		Runs		Wickets		Average
J. Crossley	161	..	58	..	369	..	24	..	15.37
*P. M. Andriesz	47	..	10	..	196	..	11	..	17.81
N. Munton	78	..	21	..	251	..	13	..	19.30
I. Crossley	121	..	25	..	435	..	21	..	20.71
M. Hussain	86	..	22	..	278	..	13	..	21.38

FRAMLINGHAM COLLEGE

Played 10: Won 6, Lost 1, Drawn 3. Abandoned 8

Master i/c: S. A. Westley   Cricket professional: C. Rutterford

BATTING	Innings		Not Outs		Runs		Highest Inns		Average
T. R. Smart	10	..	4	..	319	..	122*	..	53.16
C. S. Pritchard	10	..	1	..	439	..	102*	..	48.77
C. G. S. Pattinson	6	..	2	..	154	..	41*	..	38.50
G. S. Cowell	5	..	1	..	146	..	78	..	36.50
P. M. G. Moore	8	..	0	..	239	..	62	..	29.87
W. F. Schwier	7	..	1	..	108	..	49	..	18.00
J. G. Allen	8	..	0	..	113	..	45	..	14.12
M. Beale	9	..	0	..	105	..	30	..	11.66

BOWLING	Overs		Maidens		Runs		Wickets		Average
P. M. Hunter	70	..	18	..	185	..	15	..	12.33
J. R. Davies	82.5	..	17	..	306	..	17	..	18.00
G. S. Cowell	85	..	12	..	293	..	13	..	22.53
P. M. G. Moore	112.5	..	15	..	399	..	16	..	24.93

GIGGLESWICK SCHOOL

Played 14: Won 4, Lost 4, Drawn 6. Abandoned 1

Master i/c: J. Mayall

BATTING	Innings		Not Outs		Runs		Highest Inns		Average
*G. J. Hartley	14	..	3	..	427	..	68	..	38.81
J. B. Parker	14	..	1	..	375	..	78	..	28.84
J. B. Newsome	12	..	4	..	185	..	57*	..	23.12
V. Patel	12	..	2	..	164	..	32*	..	16.40
A. J. Manduell	14	..	0	..	210	..	33	..	15.00
M. J. Duckworth	14	..	0	..	136	..	27	..	9.71

BOWLING	Overs		Maidens		Runs		Wickets		Average
G. J. Hartley	121.2	..	21	..	342	..	27	..	12.66
J. B. Newsome	157.4	..	46	..	318	..	23	..	13.82
J. Obank	78.4	..	7	..	334	..	17	..	19.64
I. J. Wood	141	..	33	..	365	..	16	..	22.81

GORDONSTOUN SCHOOL

Played 12: Won 4, Lost 4, Drawn 4

Master i/c: P. S. Larkman

BATTING	Innings		Not Outs		Runs		Highest Inns		Average
T. R. Sparkes	12	..	0	..	300	..	68	..	25.00
*R. A. H. Jones	12	..	2	..	229	..	89*	..	22.90
S. H. B. Willis	10	..	2	..	140	..	75	..	17.50
G. Alireza	11	..	0	..	109	..	46	..	9.90

BOWLING	Overs		Maidens		Runs		Wickets		Average
G. Alireza	70.1	..	6	..	306	..	29	..	10.55
S. H. B. Willis	53	..	11	..	196	..	17	..	11.52
N. Tomlinson	71	..	10	..	210	..	15	..	14.00
D. J. P. Doughty	87	..	17	..	284	..	12	..	23.66

HABERDASHERS' ASKE'S SCHOOL

Played 17: Won 5, Lost 1, Drawn 11. Abandoned 2

Master i/c: D. I. Yeabsley

BATTING	Innings		Not Outs		Runs		Highest Inns		Average
R. G. Price	17	..	3	..	485	..	105*	..	34.64
M. C. Wilcock	14	..	3	..	339	..	91	..	30.81
N. Colverd	16	..	1	..	388	..	63	..	25.86
*C. R. Churchman	16	..	2	..	357	..	63	..	25.50
M. J. Bailey	12	..	1	..	193	..	41*	..	17.54
T. R. Downes	15	..	4	..	178	..	49*	..	16.18
A. Charles	13	..	1	..	141	..	35	..	11.75

BOWLING	Overs		Maidens		Runs		Wickets		Average
S. Hart................	106	..	17	..	420	..	21	..	20.00
N. J. Churchman........	123	..	40	..	364	..	16	..	22.75
R. Woolerton	200	..	59	..	521	..	21	..	24.80
R. H. Smith.............	179.5	..	51	..	433	..	17	..	25.47

HAILEYBURY COLLEGE

Played 14: Won 1, Lost 3, Drawn 10. Abandoned 2

Master i/c: R. B. Westley   Cricket professional: P. M. Ellis

BATTING	Innings		Not Outs		Runs		Highest Inns		Average
N. D. L. Medd.........	15	..	2	..	441	..	92	..	33.92
*A. J. Miller.............	16	..	2	..	464	..	121*	..	33.14
M. J. Churchill	9	..	3	..	132	..	29*	..	22.00
I. C. West	15	..	2	..	260	..	38	..	20.00
H. C. Bridgewater.......	12	..	3	..	138	..	43	..	15.33
A. Gohar...............	9	..	1	..	114	..	47	..	14.25
S. D. Lamble...........	14	..	1	..	158	..	31	..	12.15

BOWLING	Overs		Maidens		Runs		Wickets		Average
C. P. L. Thompson	286	..	96	..	621	..	43	..	14.44
H. C. Bridgewater........	154	..	42	..	409	..	22	..	18.59
N. D. L. Medd...........	239	..	57	..	582	..	23	..	25.30

HAMPTON SCHOOL

Played 22: Won 14, Lost 3, Drawn 5

Master i/c: M. Franzkowiak

BATTING	Innings		Not Outs		Runs		Highest Inns		Average
J. E. C. Poulter	19	..	5	..	840	..	88*	..	60.00
C. B. Dennis-Baker.......	20	..	4	..	466	..	95	..	29.12
K. M. Wood	18	..	1	..	366	..	123*	..	21.52
*N. M. M. Andrews	15	..	4	..	221	..	36	..	20.09
E. M. Turnill	17	..	5	..	230	..	42	..	19.16
N. J. Gray..............	17	..	1	..	124	..	45	..	7.75

BOWLING	Overs		Maidens		Runs		Wickets		Average
S. Pearse	141	..	48	..	329	..	37	..	8.89
N. M. M. Andrews	119.3	..	27	..	422	..	35	..	12.05
T. Lambert	207.4	..	48	..	533	..	43	..	12.39
J. E. C. Poulter	115.4	..	29	..	373	..	22	..	16.95
D. A. Jennings...........	87	..	24	..	228	..	13	..	17.53
T. R. Eastaugh	107	..	26	..	283	..	13	..	21.76

HARROW SCHOOL

Played 13: Won 4, Lost 2, Drawn 7. Abandoned 2

Master i/c: G. M. Attenborough   Cricket professional: P. Davis

BATTING	Innings		Not Outs		Runs		Highest Inns		Average
J. A. G. H. Stewart	14	..	3	..	438	..	103*	..	39.81
S. E. Haggas	14	..	3	..	423	..	103	..	38.45
M. L. Sealy	14	..	3	..	408	..	96	..	37.09
D. J. Fowler-Watt........	9	..	2	..	218	..	51*	..	31.14
*C. L. Feather..........	12	..	0	..	280	..	65	..	23.33
O. F. O. Findlay	9	..	1	..	108	..	30	..	13.50

BOWLING	Overs		Maidens		Runs		Wickets		Average
O. F. O. Findlay	152	..	57	..	268	..	32	..	8.37
T. S. M. S. Riley-Smith	132	..	36	..	274	..	23	..	11.91
F. W. A. Horn.	176	..	58	..	421	..	25	..	16.84
R. C. Patrick	184	..	54	..	380	..	21	..	18.09

HIGHGATE SCHOOL

Played 12: Won 0, Lost 7, Drawn 4, Tied 1. Abandoned 2

Master i/c: P. D. Barker   Cricket professional: B. L. Muncer

BATTING	Innings		Not Outs		Runs		Highest Inns		Average
*G. Tufnell	11	..	1	..	204	..	86*	..	20.40
R. Kenny	12	..	1	..	205	..	54	..	18.63
M. Sleigh	12	..	0	..	162	..	47	..	13.50
P. Mason	8	..	0	..	108	..	45	..	13.50
G. Jacobs	11	..	0	..	137	..	37	..	12.45
K. Kenny	11	..	0	..	132	..	46	..	12.00

BOWLING	Overs		Maidens		Runs		Wickets		Average
G. Jacobs	61	..	15	..	151	..	11	..	13.72
K. Kenny	88.5	..	16	..	303	..	19	..	15.94
J. Maher	118	..	22	..	306	..	17	..	18.00
A. Fawden.	98.3	..	18	..	334	..	18	..	18.55

HIPPERHOLME GRAMMAR SCHOOL

Played 17: Won 5, Lost 8, Drawn 4. Abandoned 1

Master i/c: J. M. Edwards

BATTING	Innings		Not Outs		Runs		Highest Inns		Average
*C. A. Heppenstall	17	..	2	..	463	..	69	..	30.86
R. S. Butterworth	17	..	1	..	390	..	68*	..	24.37
I. D. Hartley	14	..	2	..	161	..	27	..	13.41
A. Furness.	15	..	0	..	198	..	41	..	13.20
A. M. Butterworth.	13	..	3	..	115	..	34*	..	11.50
M. J. Best	15	..	0	..	154	..	57	..	10.26

BOWLING	Overs		Maidens		Runs		Wickets		Average
M. J. Hopwood	53.3	..	12	..	132	..	16	..	8.25
N. R. Bolton	165.3	..	38	..	437	..	38	..	11.50
A. Furness.	180.4	..	31	..	589	..	41	..	14.36
C. A. Heppenstall	51	..	9	..	189	..	11	..	17.18
I. D. Hartley	186.3	..	40	..	466	..	22	..	21.18

HURSTPIERPOINT COLLEGE

Played 9: Won 1, Lost 3, Drawn 5. Abandoned 4

Master i/c: M. J. Mance   Cricket professional: D. J. Semmence

BATTING	Innings		Not Outs		Runs		Highest Inns		Average
M. N. J. Rose	9	..	2	..	380	..	104*	..	54.28
*H. K. Ballamy	9	..	0	..	201	..	68	..	22.33
S. J. Foulds	9	..	1	..	147	..	42*	..	18.37
J. M. Rannie	10	..	1	..	139	..	40	..	15.44

BOWLING	Overs		Maidens		Runs		Wickets		Average
S. M. A. West	135	..	42	..	289	..	21	..	13.76
M. J. V. Goodall	64	..	17	..	174	..	10	..	17.40
S. J. Foulds	77	..	14	..	251	..	12	..	20.91
M. N. J. Rose	76.4	..	19	..	224	..	10	..	22.40
J. P. Edwards	74	..	14	..	292	..	10	..	29.20

KENT COLLEGE

Played 16: Won 3, Lost 3, Drawn 10. Abandoned 1

Master i/c: A. J. Frost

BATTING	Innings		Not Outs		Runs		Highest Inns		Average
N. J. Dyde	14	..	3	..	300	..	59	..	27.27
A. I. Gardiner	13	..	2	..	182	..	54	..	16.54
A. R. K. Pierson	14	..	3	..	131	..	34	..	11.90
J. P. C. D. Virgo	14	..	0	..	152	..	30	..	10.85
*G. P. Mortenson	14	..	0	..	150	..	34	..	10.71
N. J. Scambler	12	..	0	..	116	..	42	..	9.66
D. J. Eades	14	..	1	..	112	..	31	..	8.61

BOWLING	Overs		Maidens		Runs		Wickets		Average
A. I. Gardiner	111	..	31	..	283	..	25	..	11.32
D. J. Eades	119.5	..	31	..	289	..	23	..	12.56
D. A. Lloyd	82.5	..	16	..	249	..	13	..	19.15
S. J. Pascoe	156	..	32	..	426	..	22	..	19.36

KIMBOLTON SCHOOL

Played 15: Won 5, Lost 3, Drawn 7. Abandoned 5

Master i/c: I. J. Burton   Cricket professional: J. W. Hart

BATTING	Innings		Not Outs		Runs		Highest Inns		Average
J. S. Chambers	14	..	1	..	369	..	56	..	28.38
S. C. Render	12	..	4	..	203	..	36	..	25.37
C. S. Stokes	12	..	0	..	224	..	62	..	18.66
A. C. Whitman	11	..	3	..	133	..	33*	..	16.62
R. B. W. Edrich	14	..	0	..	213	..	37	..	15.21
*J. B. Hunter	11	..	0	..	152	..	47	..	13.81
S. J. Chown	10	..	1	..	117	..	27	..	13.00

BOWLING	Overs		Maidens		Runs		Wickets		Average
S. C. Render	99	..	33	..	208	..	19	..	10.94
J. B. Hunter	105	..	32	..	285	..	20	..	14.25
P. J. Chaplin	147	..	45	..	374	..	20	..	18.70
J. S. Chambers	78.2	..	10	..	292	..	15	..	19.46
D. W. Merrikin	81.3	..	6	..	217	..	10	..	21.70

KING EDWARD'S SCHOOL, BIRMINGHAM

Played 20: Won 3, Lost 7, Drawn 10. Abandoned 3

Master i/c: D. H. Benson

BATTING	Innings		Not Outs		Runs		Highest Inns		Average
S. E. Fletcher.	10	..	1	..	249	..	55	..	27.66
J. D. Sheehy	16	..	4	..	297	..	44	..	24.75
P. J. Campbell.	18	..	1	..	417	..	61	..	24.52
R. H. Benson.	20	..	1	..	456	..	99*	..	24.00
P. J. Gawthorpe	15	..	3	..	229	..	37	..	19.08
P. F. Daniell	20	..	1	..	302	..	51	..	15.89
J. M. Platt	16	..	1	..	201	..	53	..	13.40

BOWLING	Overs		Maidens		Runs		Wickets		Average
C. D. Jenkins.	270.3	..	88	..	639	..	40	..	15.97
G. W. Carr	104.2	..	24	..	302	..	18	..	16.77
S. E. Fletcher.	111	..	38	..	230	..	13	..	17.69
T. G. Haslam	191	..	52	..	502	..	28	..	17.92
E. A. Dent.	90.3	..	24	..	239	..	11	..	21.72

KING EDWARD VI COLLEGE, STOURBRIDGE

Played 13: Won 2, Lost 1, Drawn 10. Abandoned 7

Master i/c: M. L. Ryan

BATTING	Innings		Not Outs		Runs		Highest Inns		Average
D. Scriven	12	..	1	..	352	..	96	..	32.00
*D. G. Hill.	11	..	3	..	214	..	110*	..	26.75
J. H. Jones.	11	..	4	..	175	..	46*	..	25.00
M. D. Anderson	9	..	3	..	120	..	42*	..	20.00
R. D. Allen	12	..	0	..	220	..	53	..	18.33
N. J. Hooper	11	..	2	..	106	..	24	..	11.77

BOWLING	Overs		Maidens		Runs		Wickets		Average
P. N. Shillingford.	115.5	..	28	..	297	..	20	..	14.85
D. Glover	106	..	23	..	344	..	20	..	17.20
D. A. Price	112	..	25	..	280	..	13	..	21.53
P. M. Jones	95	..	23	..	246	..	11	..	22.36

KING EDWARD VI, SOUTHAMPTON

Played 20: Won 9, Lost 9, Drawn 2

Master i/c: M. H. May

BATTING	Innings		Not Outs		Runs		Highest Inns		Average
R. C. Corless.	14	..	2	..	242	..	49	..	20.16
T. L. A. Morgan	19	..	1	..	335	..	53	..	18.61
A. W. Gilbert	14	..	0	..	245	..	71	..	17.50
S. R. Cootes	20	..	0	..	334	..	44	..	16.70
R. P. May	20	..	0	..	297	..	66	..	14.85
M. P. Board.	14	..	2	..	144	..	69	..	12.00

BOWLING	Overs		Maidens		Runs		Wickets		Average
T. L. A. Morgan	57.4	..	15	..	186	..	20	..	9.30
D. M. M. Horne	197.5	..	40	..	538	..	46	..	11.69
*G. P. J. Staples	155.4	..	34	..	443	..	32	..	13.84
S. R. Cootes	75.3	..	25	..	207	..	14	..	14.78
J. R. Abraham.	50	..	11	..	189	..	11	..	17.18

KING EDWARD VII SCHOOL, LYTHAM

Played 14: Won 6, Lost 4, Drawn 4. Abandoned 1

Master i/c: J. Liggett

BATTING	Innings		Not Outs		Runs		Highest Inns		Average
G. F. H. McDonnell	11	..	2	..	307	..	85*	..	34.11
J. D. Brewster	13	..	4	..	298	..	62*	..	33.11
*D. R. Cartmell	12	..	2	..	235	..	46	..	23.50
P. J. Hargreaves	14	..	1	..	139	..	40	..	10.69

BOWLING	Overs		Maidens		Runs		Wickets		Average
P. M. Holdsworth	81.4	..	19	..	192	..	17	..	11.29
C. D. Jakeman	177	..	53	..	385	..	33	..	11.66
D. R. Cartmell	93.1	..	18	..	202	..	17	..	11.88

KING HENRY VIII, COVENTRY

Played 18: Won 5, Lost 5, Drawn 8. Abandoned 5

Master i/c: G. P. C. Courtois

BATTING	Innings		Not Outs		Runs		Highest Inns		Average
*A. Savage	17	..	0	..	497	..	96	..	29.23
N. J. Ball	15	..	6	..	183	..	57*	..	20.33
S. M. Jamieson	17	..	3	..	276	..	58	..	19.71
R. N. Wallbridge	14	..	3	..	201	..	45*	..	18.27
M. S. Baker	18	..	1	..	297	..	83*	..	17.47
C. R. Mills	18	..	3	..	232	..	57	..	15.46
J. E. Ball	12	..	1	..	112	..	34	..	10.18

BOWLING	Overs		Maidens		Runs		Wickets		Average
N. J. Ball	53.5	..	16	..	142	..	15	..	9.46
D. M. Harrott	89.2	..	23	..	262	..	21	..	12.47
S. M. Jamieson	112	..	34	..	324	..	19	..	17.05
C. J. J. Harrison	156	..	51	..	469	..	27	..	17.37
I. L. Robertson	71.4	..	17	..	229	..	12	..	19.08
J. E. Ball	75.3	..	11	..	284	..	14	..	20.28
I. D. Forth	71	..	17	..	229	..	11	..	20.81

KING'S COLLEGE, TAUNTON

Played 15: Won 8, Lost 4, Drawn 3. Abandoned 2

Master i/c: P. A. Dossett   Cricket professional: R. E. Marshall

BATTING	Innings		Not Outs		Runs		Highest Inns		Average
N. D. Everest	9	..	5	..	120	..	31	..	30.00
R. J. Harden	14	..	2	..	352	..	58	..	29.33
S. C. Hunter	14	..	2	..	310	..	83	..	25.83
D. J. Blanchard	10	..	2	..	167	..	74	..	20.87
N. K. Gane	15	..	2	..	230	..	41	..	17.69
M. A. Burdge	10	..	1	..	153	..	58	..	17.00
*R. P. Twose	15	..	1	..	222	..	44	..	15.85
C. J. Rew	11	..	2	..	138	..	31	..	15.33
C. W. Cole	13	..	0	..	191	..	72	..	14.69

BOWLING	Overs		Maidens		Runs		Wickets		Average
R. J. Harden	129.1	..	44	..	290	..	25	..	11.60
S. C. Hunter	178.2	..	46	..	511	..	32	..	15.96
N. K. Gane	145.1	..	46	..	363	..	22	..	16.50
P. J. Norman	110	..	27	..	369	..	12	..	30.75

KING'S COLLEGE SCHOOL, WIMBLEDON

Played 19: Won 8, Lost 3, Drawn 7, Tied 1. Abandoned 3

BATTING	Innings		Not Outs		Runs		Highest Inns		Average
M. A. Staniland	17	..	2	..	425	..	74	..	28.33
*K. R. Thompson	18	..	0	..	487	..	87	..	27.05
A. M. Bredin	18	..	1	..	416	..	102*	..	24.47
R. I. Alikhan	18	..	0	..	436	..	104	..	24.22
N. J. Moritz	14	..	4	..	162	..	33*	..	16.20
P. J. Morse	10	..	2	..	113	..	44	..	14.12
S. W. J. Silvester	11	..	3	..	109	..	34	..	13.62
A. J. Le Roux	12	..	1	..	124	..	43	..	11.27

BOWLING	Overs		Maidens		Runs		Wickets		Average
K. R. Thompson	141.1	..	32	..	401	..	28	..	14.32
R. I. Alikhan	174.4	..	47	..	463	..	30	..	15.43
A. M. Bredin	262.4	..	81	..	698	..	36	..	19.38
N. J. Moritz	112	..	38	..	278	..	10	..	27.80
J. D. Lamb	100	..	29	..	279	..	10	..	27.90

KING'S SCHOOL, BRUTON

Played 13: Won 2, Lost 5, Drawn 6. Abandoned 4

Master i/c: A. S. Linney

BATTING	Innings		Not Outs		Runs		Highest Inns		Average
M. R. Langham	12	..	1	..	186	..	55	..	16.90
*S. E. Birks	13	..	0	..	214	..	83	..	16.46
J. M. Ryall	13	..	0	..	214	..	52	..	16.46
P. M. Trounson	13	..	0	..	202	..	53	..	15.53
R. Rigiani	13	..	0	..	187	..	62	..	14.38

BOWLING	Overs		Maidens		Runs		Wickets		Average
P. F. McIntyre	84	..	23	..	226	..	16	..	14.12
S. E Birks	116.4	..	39	..	439	..	28	..	15.67
C. G. Weir	82	..	22	..	249	..	14	..	17.78
S. T. Harvey	61.2	..	14	..	202	..	11	..	18.36

KING'S SCHOOL, CANTERBURY

Played 12: Won 3, Lost 1, Drawn 8. Abandoned 3

Master i/c: A. W. Dyer   Cricket professional: D. V. P. Wright

BATTING	Innings		Not Outs		Runs		Highest Inns		Average
C. P. Smith	13	..	2	..	442	..	189*	..	40.18
M. F. Nicholson	8	..	4	..	110	..	53*	..	27.50
*M. A. Smith	11	..	1	..	274	..	88*	..	27.40
J. T. Underwood	11	..	1	..	234	..	59	..	23.40
D. M. Jones	12	..	2	..	196	..	50*	..	19.60
H. M. Robertson	12	..	2	..	170	..	52	..	17.00
F. W. Searle	8	..	2	..	101	..	53	..	16.83

BOWLING	Overs		Maidens		Runs		Wickets		Average
M. F. Nicholson	143.2	..	54	..	270	..	24	..	11.25
M. J. Pawley	191.4	..	39	..	443	..	34	..	13.02
P. J. Cranston-Smith	81.3	..	24	..	211	..	15	..	14.06
M. A. Smith	97.2	..	20	..	303	..	10	..	30.30

KING'S SCHOOL, CHESTER

Played 16: Won 4, Lost 2, Drawn 10. Abandoned 1

BATTING	Innings		Not Outs		Runs		Highest Inns		Average
A. S. Myers............	14	..	0	..	455	..	106	..	32.50
J. J. Brummitt	16	..	2	..	262	..	45	..	18.71
J. H. Jordan...........	13	..	0	..	231	..	42	..	17.76
R. M. Hurleston	16	..	2	..	240	..	50*	..	17.14
R. St J. V. Fisher	15	..	0	..	240	..	75	..	16.00
R. J. Ferris	10	..	2	..	120	..	36	..	15.00
M. D. Barber............	12	..	0	..	174	..	59	..	14.50

BOWLING	Overs		Maidens		Runs		Wickets		Average
S. E. Phillips	114	..	20	..	347	..	20	..	17.35
D. N. Boothroyd.........	137	..	40	..	362	..	19	..	19.05
C. N. Hudson	155.3	..	30	..	477	..	25	..	19.08
M. D. Barber............	103.3	..	24	..	299	..	15	..	19.93

KING'S SCHOOL, MACCLESFIELD

Played 25: Won 13, Lost 3, Drawn 9. Abandoned 3

Master i/c: I. A. Wilson

BATTING	Innings		Not Outs		Runs		Highest Inns		Average
N. D. Smedley...........	24	..	6	..	801	..	86	..	44.50
*N. A. Kennington	23	..	6	..	537	..	79*	..	31.58
P. Moores	19	..	4	..	370	..	56*	..	24.66
S. Moores	14	..	2	..	257	..	67	..	21.41
G. Duffy	16	..	1	..	318	..	56	..	21.20
A. P. Mannion	14	..	3	..	215	..	40	..	19.54
D. A. Hadfield...........	13	..	2	..	109	..	22	..	9.90

BOWLING	Overs		Maidens		Runs		Wickets		Average
N. A. Kennington	144	..	49	..	343	..	29	..	11.82
B. S. Greening...........	72	..	17	..	183	..	14	..	13.07
G. Duffy	135.5	..	44	..	299	..	22	..	13.59
C. D. Burgess	176.4	..	60	..	434	..	27	..	16.07
M. P. Mannion	141.5	..	43	..	321	..	19	..	16.89
J. McAlpine..............	84	..	17	..	284	..	16	..	17.75
D. A. Colclough	129	..	46	..	332	..	17	..	19.52
S. Moores	191.2	..	56	..	544	..	23	..	23.65

KING'S SCHOOL, ROCHESTER

Played 16: Won 4, Lost 6, Drawn 6. Abandoned 5

Master i/c: J. S. Irvine

BATTING	Innings		Not Outs		Runs		Highest Inns		Average
*J. A. Cornett	16	..	3	..	418	..	76*	..	32.15
J. D. Maas	15	..	1	..	250	..	62	..	17.85
N. C. Mullarkey	16	..	0	..	264	..	61	..	16.50
D. J. Raye	15	..	3	..	187	..	70	..	15.58
A. P. Baker	14	..	0	..	193	..	54	..	13.78
M. Fairbank	11	..	3	..	101	..	20*	..	12.62
D. Farnworth	14	..	2	..	122	..	26*	..	10.16

BOWLING	Overs		Maidens		Runs		Wickets		Average
M. Fairbank	246	..	75	..	552	..	39	..	14.15
J. A. Cornett	250.1	..	76	..	637	..	36	..	17.69
N. C. Mullarkey	111	..	29	..	323	..	11	..	29.36

KING'S SCHOOL, WORCESTER

Played 14: Won 2, Lost 3, Drawn 9. Abandoned 3

Master i/c: P. Petherbridge

BATTING	Innings		Not Outs		Runs		Highest Inns		Average
M. Foard	12	..	4	..	201	..	103*	..	25.12
*P. M. Wood	13	..	2	..	259	..	95	..	23.54
M. Thompson	13	..	1	..	265	..	63	..	22.08
C. Preston	7	..	1	..	120	..	53	..	20.00
J. Spicer	10	..	0	..	171	..	36	..	17.10
A. Revil	8	..	2	..	100	..	48*	..	16.66
S. Preece	12	..	4	..	126	..	23	..	15.75
D. Hudson	13	..	1	..	184	..	35	..	15.33
N. Hales	14	..	0	..	140	..	35	..	10.00

BOWLING	Overs		Maidens		Runs		Wickets		Average
S. Fleming	145	..	46	..	390	..	21	..	18.57
D. Hudson	101.1	..	15	..	394	..	15	..	26.26
C. Preston	113	..	23	..	424	..	16	..	26.50
D. Allen	116.3	..	15	..	520	..	12	..	43.33

KING WILLIAM'S COLLEGE, ISLE OF MAN

Played 18: Won 3, Lost 5, Drawn 10

Master i/c: A. Q. Bashforth　　　　　　　　　　Cricket professional: D. Mark

BATTING	Innings		Not Outs		Runs		Highest Inns		Average
*P. N. Luft	19	..	3	..	526	..	105	..	32.87
D. W. Kinrade	19	..	1	..	326	..	54	..	18.11
A. T. J. Bruce	17	..	1	..	232	..	41	..	14.50
S. C. Watson	20	..	2	..	250	..	41	..	13.88
N. A. R. Watson	13	..	1	..	124	..	27	..	10.33
T. H. Luft	14	..	1	..	129	..	45*	..	9.92
T. S. Glover	16	..	2	..	103	..	19	..	7.35

BOWLING	Overs		Maidens		Runs		Wickets		Average
P. N. Luft	289.3	..	81	..	627	..	49	..	12.79
N. A. R. Watson	175	..	38	..	498	..	23	..	21.65
C. S. Marriott	198.3	..	49	..	523	..	24	..	21.79
R. M. Phillips	112	..	34	..	327	..	15	..	21.80

KINGSTON GRAMMAR SCHOOL

Played 15: Won 4, Lost 5, Drawn 6. Abandoned 3

Master i/c: R. J. Sturgeon

BATTING	Innings		Not Outs		Runs		Highest Inns		Average
R. J. Purchase	15	..	1	..	432	..	91	..	30.85
P. W. Rasmussen	15	..	3	..	355	..	51*	..	29.58
C. J. Cookman	15	..	1	..	324	..	77	..	23.14
*M. P. Williams	14	..	2	..	226	..	36	..	18.83
D. N. Francis	12	..	3	..	149	..	43*	..	16.55
P. G. Eastwood	12	..	1	..	178	..	62	..	16.18
I. C. P. Cranston	13	..	2	..	111	..	19	..	10.09
R. J. McIntyre	13	..	0	..	121	..	35	..	9.30

BOWLING	Overs		Maidens		Runs		Wickets		Average
R. D. S. Blackford	142.5	..	37	..	498	..	29	..	17.17
I. C. P. Cranston	201.3	..	50	..	534	..	30	..	17.80
R. J. Purchase	99.2	..	25	..	297	..	13	..	22.84
M. Webster	187	..	57	..	517	..	16	..	32.31

KINGSWOOD SCHOOL

Played 13: Won 3, Lost 3, Drawn 7. Abandoned 3

Master i/c: R. J. Lewis

BATTING	Innings		Not Outs		Runs		Highest Inns		Average
W. P. Mason	13	..	1	..	301	..	59	..	25.08
S. A. Gynes	11	..	3	..	198	..	53	..	24.75
G. D. Opie	13	..	0	..	303	..	61	..	23.30
J. M. Grieves-Smith	13	..	1	..	133	..	38	..	11.08
R. W. Ward	13	..	0	..	103	..	26	..	7.92

BOWLING	Overs		Maidens		Runs		Wickets		Average
T. J. Rawson	123	..	35	..	290	..	25	..	11.60
S. D. Walkland	116	..	19	..	341	..	28	..	12.17
S. M. Harris	57	..	7	..	144	..	10	..	14.40

LANCING COLLEGE

Played 13: Won 2, Lost 3, Drawn 8. Abandoned 4

Master i/c: E. A. Evans-Jones   Cricket professional: D. V. Smith

BATTING	Innings		Not Outs		Runs		Highest Inns		Average
P. R. Nash	12	..	4	..	283	..	43	..	35.37
*M. C. Calvert-Lee	13	..	1	..	350	..	111	..	29.16
S. R. Nash	13	..	1	..	286	..	69	..	23.83
P. J. D'Anger	12	..	1	..	208	..	38	..	18.90
M. J. Beard	13	..	1	..	219	..	54*	..	18.25

BOWLING	Overs		Maidens		Runs		Wickets		Average
M. P. Rudge	110.2	..	35	..	227	..	17	..	13.35
N. C. Andrews	77	..	22	..	180	..	13	..	13.84
C. S. Mays	181	..	44	..	461	..	31	..	14.87
N. S. Tudball	141.2	..	27	..	479	..	22	..	21.77
G. C. Trevithick	83	..	29	..	219	..	10	..	21.90

LEEDS GRAMMAR SCHOOL

Played 19: Won 3, Lost 7, Drawn 8, Tied 1

BATTING	Innings		Not Outs		Runs		Highest Inns		Average
S. S. Hardaker	19	..	1	..	434	..	52	..	24.11
R. M. W. Sugden	19	..	3	..	356	..	64*	..	22.25
D. H. Innes	18	..	0	..	324	..	62	..	18.00
C. E. R. Stewart	18	..	0	..	289	..	46	..	16.05
M. Hardaker	18	..	1	..	262	..	47	..	15.41
S. A. Gray	18	..	1	..	238	..	34	..	14.00
J. K. Bowman	16	..	0	..	187	..	26	..	11.68
J. E. Cook	11	..	2	..	102	..	33	..	11.33

BOWLING	Overs		Maidens		Runs		Wickets		Average
*M. D. Sims	142.5	..	21	..	536	..	31	..	17.29
A. M. R. Jones	126.5	..	31	..	407	..	19	..	21.42
S. A. Gray	102	..	13	..	471	..	20	..	23.55
N. J. Pridmore	91	..	21	..	267	..	11	..	24.27
C. E. R. Stewart	95.5	..	24	..	374	..	15	..	24.93
J. K. Bowman	133	..	35	..	370	..	13	..	28.46

LEIGHTON PARK SCHOOL

Played 10: Won 7, Lost 0, Drawn 3. Abandoned 2

Master i/c: G. C. Shaw

BATTING	Innings		Not Outs		Runs		Highest Inns		Average
G. J. Nienow	10	..	2	..	406	..	87*	..	50.75
A. G. McMeeking	9	..	0	..	171	..	43	..	19.00
*J. R. Wills	9	..	2	..	126	..	38	..	18.00

BOWLING	Overs		Maidens		Runs		Wickets		Average
J. R. Wills	25.1	..	4	..	81	..	11	..	7.36
M. S. Preston	73.2	..	26	..	177	..	13	..	13.61
C. D. S. Houston	93.1	..	30	..	219	..	15	..	14.60
J. J. Huggins	62.3	..	17	..	166	..	11	..	15.09
G. J. Nienow	92.2	..	27	..	231	..	15	..	15.40

LIVERPOOL COLLEGE

Played 12: Won 4, Lost 8, Drawn 0. Abandoned 1

Master i/c: J. R. H. Robertson

BATTING	Innings		Not Outs		Runs		Highest Inns		Average
L. G. Stokes	14	..	2	..	250	..	87*	..	20.83
R. Llewellyn	14	..	3	..	172	..	50	..	15.63
*G. C. Fuller	13	..	1	..	155	..	41	..	12.91
C. A. Morgan	12	..	0	..	154	..	42	..	12.83
M. D. Williams	13	..	1	..	140	..	41	..	11.66

BOWLING	Overs		Maidens		Runs		Wickets		Average
M. B. Jenkins	140.2	..	31	..	450	..	28	..	16.07
T. F. Groom	140.2	..	28	..	393	..	24	..	16.37

LLANDOVERY COLLEGE

Played 16: Won 2, Lost 5, Drawn 9

Master i/c: T. G. Marks

BATTING	Innings		Not Outs		Runs		Highest Inns		Average
J. D. Owen	16	..	2	..	389	..	58	..	27.78
M. J. Thomas	17	..	2	..	359	..	55	..	23.93
S. W. Edwards	8	..	0	..	119	..	42	..	14.87
P. A. Howells	12	..	1	..	158	..	47	..	14.36
I. D. McGregor	14	..	3	..	147	..	30	..	13.36
R. B. V. Rees	8	..	0	..	104	..	32	..	13.00
*A. Hathaway	15	..	0	..	177	..	38	..	11.80
D. A. Williams	12	..	2	..	101	..	32	..	10.10

BOWLING	Overs		Maidens		Runs		Wickets		Average
J. D. Owen	171	..	48	..	450	..	43	..	10.46
M. J. Thomas	66	..	17	..	160	..	13	..	12.30
D. H. Thomas	47	..	6	..	167	..	10	..	16.70
P. A. Howells	155	..	38	..	431	..	22	..	19.59

LORD WANDSWORTH COLLEGE

Played 7: Won 2, Lost 0, Drawn 5. Abandoned 2

Master i/c: A. Dyson

BATTING	Innings		Not Outs		Runs		Highest Inns		Average
*T. J. Coulson	8	..	3	..	416	..	150*	..	83.20
M. R. Jermyn	3	..	1	..	127	..	56	..	63.50
S. Bentley	9	..	0	..	338	..	96	..	37.55
T. R. Jermyn	6	..	2	..	106	..	44	..	26.50
S. Jefferson	5	..	0	..	130	..	64	..	26.00

BOWLING	Overs		Maidens		Runs		Wickets		Average
T. R. Jermyn	64	..	8	..	225	..	21	..	10.71
R. O'Hare	98	..	29	..	294	..	15	..	19.60

LORD WILLIAMS'S SCHOOL

Played 15: Won 8, Lost 1, Drawn 6

Master i/c: G. M. D. Howat

BATTING	Innings		Not Outs		Runs		Highest Inns		Average
N. Yeomans	11	..	2	..	345	..	77	..	38.33
A. S. M. Collins	16	..	5	..	249	..	56*	..	22.63
M. R. Fairn	9	..	0	..	173	..	54	..	19.22
D. A. A. Cryer	15	..	0	..	220	..	46	..	14.66
S. G. Lambert	11	..	2	..	117	..	40	..	13.00

BOWLING	Overs		Maidens		Runs		Wickets		Average
G. Porter	80	..	22	..	179	..	26	..	6.88
P. E. Robertson	60.5	..	14	..	120	..	15	..	8.00
S. D. Thomson	92	..	24	..	200	..	23	..	8.69
M. N. Lougher	54	..	8	..	171	..	15	..	11.40
A. S. M. Collins	123.5	..	37	..	326	..	26	..	12.53

LORETTO SCHOOL

Played 13: Won 1, Lost 1, Drawn 11

Master i/c: R. G. Selley   Cricket professional: T. Sellwood

BATTING	Innings		Not Outs		Runs		Highest Inns		Average
R. S. Macaskill	10	..	2	..	414	..	126*	..	51.75
*A. A. M. Macbeath	11	..	2	..	269	..	83*	..	29.88
P. J. Ledingham	11	..	1	..	228	..	39*	..	22.80
C. R. Marks	9	..	3	..	118	..	31*	..	19.66
D. J. M. Orr	11	..	1	..	185	..	46	..	18.50

BOWLING	Overs		Maidens		Runs		Wickets		Average
C. R. Marks	110	..	24	..	329	..	20	..	16.45
P. J. Ledingham	132.5	..	29	..	388	..	23	..	16.86
A. A. M. Macbeath	151	..	50	..	351	..	19	..	18.47

MAGDALEN COLLEGE SCHOOL

Played 15: Won 8, Lost 4, Drawn 3. Abandoned 3

Master i/c: E. P. L. Sandbach   Cricket professional: D. Beckett

BATTING	Innings		Not Outs		Runs		Highest Inns		Average
*P. S. Morris............	15	..	4	..	479	..	68	..	43.54
B. G. M. Prior...........	15	..	2	..	334	..	57	..	25.69
M. R. A. Barrow.........	12	..	2	..	168	..	44	..	16.80
N. S. Dykes	11	..	1	..	150	..	32	..	15.00

BOWLING	Overs		Maidens		Runs		Wickets		Average
S. P. Hazell	184.5	..	69	..	332	..	45	..	7.37
S. C. Shorter	140.5	..	50	..	254	..	27	..	9.40
N. S. Dykes	118	..	34	..	321	..	26	..	12.34

MALVERN COLLEGE

Played 14: Won 6, Lost 3, Drawn 5. Abandoned 2

Master i/c: A. R. Duff   Cricket professional: G. D. Morton

BATTING	Innings		Not Outs		Runs		Highest Inns		Average
M. E. Fordham	13	..	3	..	799	..	154*	..	79.90
N. Dowdall	9	..	1	..	273	..	59	..	34.12
R. C. W. Mason	13	..	0	..	422	..	105	..	32.46
*R. R. Simpson..........	14	..	4	..	308	..	50	..	30.80
G. E. Davies	11	..	1	..	148	..	36*	..	14.80

BOWLING	Overs		Maidens		Runs		Wickets		Average
J. R. N. Ashworth	182.2	..	56	..	487	..	30	..	16.23
R. C. W. Mason	68.5	..	13	..	230	..	11	..	20.90
G. E. Davies	116.4	..	34	..	310	..	12	..	25.83
J. A. V. Grimshaw........	149.3	..	44	..	470	..	18	..	26.11

MANCHESTER GRAMMAR SCHOOL

Played 17: Won 7, Lost 3, Drawn 7. Abandoned 5

Master i/c: D. Moss

BATTING	Innings		Not Outs		Runs		Highest Inns		Average
S. L. Jones	9	..	5	..	145	..	69*	..	36.25
J. M. Salthouse	16	..	2	..	356	..	54*	..	25.42
I. M. Paul	16	..	0	..	372	..	62	..	23.25
A. Milnes	16	..	1	..	325	..	84	..	21.66
*G. P. W. Roberts	16	..	1	..	263	..	57	..	17.53
J. M. Binns	12	..	2	..	174	..	42	..	17.40

BOWLING	Overs		Maidens		Runs		Wickets		Average
R. J. Clark	64.4	..	14	..	187	..	14	..	13.35
D. Postlethwaite	196.5	..	66	..	461	..	32	..	14.40
M. J. Frost	178.3	..	52	..	438	..	30	..	14.60
M. P. Lawrence	216	..	58	..	560	..	28	..	20.00

MARLBOROUGH COLLEGE

Played 13: Won 6, Lost 1, Drawn 6. Abandoned 2

Master i/c: R. D. Lane   Cricket professional: P. B. Fisher

BATTING	Innings		Not Outs		Runs		Highest Inns		Average
*E. J. Cunningham	9	..	3	..	307	..	55	..	51.16
A. P. Frome	14	..	0	..	397	..	101	..	28.35
R. Hampel	9	..	1	..	223	..	63*	..	27.87
A. J. Naylor	13	..	3	..	235	..	83*	..	23.50
J. Worlidge	9	..	1	..	155	..	69	..	19.37
J. Mylne	10	..	3	..	134	..	40*	..	19.14
O. Hitchcock	10	..	1	..	116	..	60*	..	12.88

BOWLING	Overs		Maidens		Runs		Wickets		Average
E. J. Cunningham	112	..	40	..	196	..	21	..	9.33
A. Holderness	130	..	37	..	334	..	23	..	14.52
A. J. Naylor	171	..	33	..	506	..	30	..	16.86
M. R. C. Swallow	143	..	43	..	397	..	18	..	22.05

MERCHANT TAYLORS' SCHOOL, CROSBY

Played 15: Won 1, Lost 4, Drawn 10. Abandoned 1

Master i/c: J. A. Pearman   Cricket professional: L. B. P. Adams

BATTING	Innings		Not Outs		Runs		Highest Inns		Average
T. J. Bostock	12	..	3	..	302	..	96*	..	33.55
P. S. Cass	14	..	2	..	208	..	44	..	17.33
D. J. Standring	13	..	2	..	189	..	51*	..	17.18
G. Clarke	12	..	2	..	140	..	30	..	14.00
*R. G. Squires	11	..	2	..	124	..	37	..	13.77
R. A. Saundry	12	..	1	..	117	..	22*	..	10.63

BOWLING	Overs		Maidens		Runs		Wickets		Average
C. N. Hughes D'Aeth	219	..	83	..	484	..	52	..	9.30
T. J. Bostock	180	..	41	..	498	..	22	..	22.63
P. S. Cass	123	..	32	..	385	..	12	..	32.08

MERCHANT TAYLORS' SCHOOL, NORTHWOOD

Played 14: Won 4, Lost 2, Drawn 8. Abandoned 3

Master i/c: R. B. Hawkey

BATTING	Innings		Not Outs		Runs		Highest Inns		Average
J. P. Hoskins	13	..	2	..	389	..	64*	..	35.36
S. P. Ducat	14	..	2	..	384	..	67*	..	32.00
N. G. Smith	14	..	2	..	361	..	75	..	30.08
M. D. J. Ingram	11	..	1	..	216	..	69	..	21.60
N. D. Eckert	14	..	2	..	256	..	69*	..	21.33
S. R. Burrows	6	..	0	..	127	..	56	..	21.16
R. M. F. Stewart	8	..	1	..	114	..	42	..	16.28

BOWLING	Overs		Maidens		Runs		Wickets		Average
J. W. Walter	59	..	21	..	118	..	13	..	9.07
M. D. J. Ingram	177.4	..	50	..	450	..	32	..	14.06
J. G. Page	118.5	..	34	..	250	..	15	..	16.66
A. J. Lazar	102	..	20	..	332	..	15	..	22.13
N. G. Smith	110.2	..	31	..	307	..	13	..	23.61

MERCHISTON CASTLE SCHOOL

Played 15: Won 4, Lost 5, Drawn 6

Master i/c: M. C. L. Gill   Cricket professional: D. Carter

BATTING	Innings		Not Outs		Runs		Highest Inns		Average
*R. A. Young	18	..	1	..	538	..	102*	..	31.64
I. G. Carson	13	..	1	..	309	..	57	..	25.75
M. V. Townsend	18	..	1	..	392	..	84	..	23.05
P. K. Young	15	..	2	..	254	..	59*	..	19.53
A. J. Young	18	..	2	..	260	..	36	..	16.25
D. A. McCorquodale	15	..	5	..	146	..	35*	..	14.60
D. G. Arnot	15	..	0	..	189	..	40	..	12.60
A. P. Cunningham	14	..	2	..	109	..	31*	..	9.08

BOWLING	Overs		Maidens		Runs		Wickets		Average
D. Robinson	193.4	..	55	..	467	..	38	..	12.28
M. G. Robertson	165.4	..	54	..	459	..	36	..	12.75
G. D. Lobban	110	..	19	..	362	..	22	..	16.45
D. G. Arnot	101.4	..	25	..	295	..	17	..	17.35
D. A. McCorquodale	144	..	49	..	340	..	12	..	28.33

MILL HILL SCHOOL

Played 18: Won 5, Lost 5, Drawn 8. Abandoned 2

Master i/c: C. Dean   Cricket professional: C. Stone

BATTING	Innings		Not Outs		Runs		Highest Inns		Average
P. H. Wickenden	18	..	0	..	442	..	96	..	24.55
S. C. McF. Harley	17	..	4	..	290	..	71	..	22.30
S. P. H. Thomas	14	..	5	..	195	..	37	..	21.66
J. C. J. Culverhouse	18	..	1	..	365	..	71	..	21.47
I. K. Nyamekye	15	..	2	..	265	..	63*	..	20.38
K. Walli	14	..	2	..	233	..	42	..	19.41
S. S. Brijnath	11	..	3	..	125	..	30	..	15.62
P. A. Robin	12	..	3	..	135	..	52*	..	15.00
*C. I. Quirk	14	..	1	..	186	..	39	..	14.30

BOWLING	Overs		Maidens		Runs		Wickets		Average
T. A. J. Dawson	316.5	..	98	..	760	..	52	..	14.61
S. C. Greenslade	311.4	..	101	..	724	..	45	..	16.08
G. R. W. Hawley	97	..	27	..	257	..	10	..	25.70
J. C. J. Culverhouse	128.4	..	27	..	388	..	12	..	32.33

MILLFIELD SCHOOL

Played 16: Won 7, Lost 1, Drawn 8. Abandoned 3

Master i/c: F. N. Fenner   Cricket professional: G. Wilson

BATTING	Innings		Not Outs		Runs		Highest Inns		Average
P. G. Roebuck	15	..	4	..	613	..	100*	..	55.72
A. J. H. Dunning	19	..	2	..	604	..	94	..	35.52
M. R. Lintin	5	..	2	..	106	..	54*	..	35.33
S. J. Illingworth	17	..	0	..	428	..	80	..	25.17
*J. O. Curran	14	..	3	..	248	..	40	..	22.54
G. A. Sloan	11	..	4	..	130	..	30*	..	18.57
P. A. Moore	10	..	1	..	147	..	66	..	16.33
S. R. Thorne	11	..	2	..	141	..	46	..	15.66
P. C. Tucker	10	..	0	..	154	..	39	..	15.40

BOWLING	Overs		Maidens		Runs		Wickets		Average
P. A. C. Bail	114.4	..	33	..	310	..	19	..	16.31
A. J. H. Dunning	70.3	..	18	..	212	..	12	..	17.66
A. R. Welch	146.5	..	45	..	428	..	24	..	17.83
J. O. Curran	218	..	54	..	673	..	35	..	19.22
S. J. G. Hutchinson	87	..	23	..	288	..	10	..	28.80

MILTON ABBEY SCHOOL

Played 19: Won 8, Lost 5, Drawn 6

Master i/c: S. T. Smail

BATTING	Innings		Not Outs		Runs		Highest Inns		Average
*G. H. Acheson-Gray	16	..	6	..	368	..	100*	..	36.80
A. D. H. Geffen	11	..	2	..	236	..	46*	..	26.22
G. M. Cookman	14	..	5	..	233	..	51	..	25.88
M. F. Vernon	6	..	0	..	152	..	98	..	25.33
R. D. T. Clive	19	..	2	..	406	..	90	..	23.89
A. W. S. Robertson	7	..	0	..	104	..	51	..	14.85
C. M. Campbell	12	..	2	..	147	..	35	..	14.70
J. S. Dobree	14	..	0	..	180	..	50	..	12.85

BOWLING	Overs		Maidens		Runs		Wickets		Average
J. M. D. Boswell	226	..	78	..	504	..	66	..	7.63
C. M. Campbell	39	..	11	..	86	..	10	..	8.60
P. O. Farrer	46	..	10	..	143	..	10	..	14.30
J. Egerton-Warburton	156	..	60	..	331	..	23	..	14.39
G. M. Cookman	91	..	11	..	317	..	20	..	15.85
G. H. Acheson-Gray	71	..	18	..	215	..	11	..	19.54

MONKTON COMBE SCHOOL

Played 14: Won 4, Lost 4, Drawn 6. Abandoned 2

Master i/c: P. C. Sibley

BATTING	Innings		Not Outs		Runs		Highest Inns		Average
*P. M. B. Salmon	15	..	1	..	320	..	77	..	22.85
A. G. Lea	10	..	2	..	150	..	38	..	18.75
A. R. C. Batterham	12	..	3	..	138	..	24	..	15.33
R. A. Falkingham	12	..	1	..	153	..	75	..	13.90
J. B. East	13	..	2	..	147	..	44	..	13.36
T. R. Perry	12	..	0	..	130	..	36	..	10.83

BOWLING	Overs		Maidens		Runs		Wickets		Average
P. M. B. Salmon	123	..	39	..	292	..	22	..	13.27
A. R. C. Batterham	213	..	61	..	509	..	38	..	13.39
D. A. A. Dean	178	..	34	..	509	..	22	..	23.13

MONMOUTH SCHOOL

Played 15: Won 5, Lost 4, Drawn 6. Abandoned 2

Master i/c: P. D. R. Anthony   Cricket professional: G. I. Burgess

BATTING	Innings		Not Outs		Runs		Highest Inns		Average
A. G. Davies	13	..	4	..	517	..	144*	..	57.44
K. G. Lewis	10	..	2	..	250	..	68	..	31.25
G. T. Powell	13	..	2	..	286	..	89	..	26.00
R. A. Williams	11	..	0	..	228	..	68	..	20.72
L. J. J. Watts	11	..	2	..	143	..	30	..	15.88

BOWLING	Overs		Maidens		Runs		Wickets		Average
N. J. Ayres	128.3	..	29	..	367	..	25	..	14.68
P. H. Watts	172.1	..	40	..	474	..	26	..	18.23
S. M. Smith	77	..	17	..	227	..	12	..	18.91
C. L. Richards	135.4	..	25	..	397	..	20	..	19.85
L. J. J. Watts	114.3	..	23	..	329	..	16	..	20.56

NORWICH SCHOOL

Played 13: Won 1, Lost 6, Drawn 6. Abandoned 2

Master i/c: P. J. Henderson

BATTING	Innings		Not Outs		Runs		Highest Inns		Average
A. D. Baxter	12	..	3	..	253	..	53	..	28.11
C. J. Lamb	12	..	2	..	236	..	78*	..	23.60
M. C. Nicholls	10	..	1	..	179	..	43*	..	19.88
*S. M. Embleton-Smith	11	..	0	..	194	..	99	..	17.63
S. M. Quinton	10	..	1	..	157	..	42*	..	17.44
D. R. Glasbey	12	..	2	..	160	..	32	..	16.00
S. W. Abel	11	..	0	..	163	..	48	..	14.81

BOWLING	Overs		Maidens		Runs		Wickets		Average
S. P. Bowling	88.1	..	16	..	295	..	19	..	15.52
A. I. Duffield	108.2	..	21	..	342	..	20	..	17.10
N. J. Kedar	66	..	2	..	304	..	10	..	30.40

NOTTINGHAM HIGH SCHOOL

Played 25: Won 7, Lost 3, Drawn 15. Abandoned 4

Master i/c: J. E. Sadler   Cricket professional: K. J. Poole

BATTING	Innings		Not Outs		Runs		Highest Inns		Average
N. C. Lucy	7	..	5	..	123	..	50*	..	61.50
*S. J. Turrill	19	..	3	..	646	..	97	..	40.37
M. A. Briggs	12	..	2	..	309	..	90*	..	30.90
P. A. J. Gregory	24	..	3	..	647	..	51*	..	30.80
H. Burton	25	..	4	..	515	..	63*	..	24.52
M. D. Hardy	8	..	1	..	126	..	28*	..	18.00
R. Poole	19	..	4	..	264	..	54*	..	17.60
R. J. Briggs	17	..	5	..	183	..	33	..	15.25
D. A. James	13	..	1	..	128	..	18	..	10.66

BOWLING	Overs		Maidens		Runs		Wickets		Average
S. J. Turrill	310	..	104	..	695	..	48	..	14.47
P. A. J. Gregory	401.1	..	120	..	959	..	54	..	17.75
R. Phillipson	55.5	..	10	..	203	..	10	..	20.30
R. P. Rhodes	238.4	..	71	..	616	..	25	..	24.64

OAKHAM SCHOOL

Played 16: Won 3, Lost 3, Drawn 10. Abandoned 8

Master i/c: V. G. B. Cushing

BATTING	Innings		Not Outs		Runs		Highest Inns		Average
M. J. Turney	16	..	3	..	447	..	92*	..	34.38
A. Mitchell	10	..	6	..	119	..	39	..	29.75
P. J. M. Davies	14	..	1	..	355	..	57	..	27.30
*D. M. Kingham	15	..	1	..	312	..	53	..	22.28
D. M. Shaw	16	..	1	..	308	..	67	..	20.53
T. Hopper	15	..	5	..	202	..	43	..	20.20
I. J. Thorpe	8	..	1	..	120	..	34	..	17.14
M. Leaney	9	..	2	..	106	..	39*	..	15.14

BOWLING	Overs		Maidens		Runs		Wickets		Average
J. Patrick	79	..	23	..	179	..	21	..	8.52
P. Hulme	126	..	32	..	316	..	20	..	15.80
S. Wood	115	..	31	..	289	..	17	..	17.00
D. M. Shaw	169.3	..	55	..	449	..	25	..	17.96
D. M. Kingham	281.2	..	76	..	747	..	32	..	23.34

OUNDLE SCHOOL

Played 13: Won 2, Lost 3, Drawn 8. Abandoned 4

Master i/c: R. J. Firth   Cricket professional: A. J. Watkins

BATTING	Innings		Not Outs		Runs		Highest Inns		Average
J. D. O. Massey	13	..	2	..	357	..	81*	..	32.45
R. H. Covell	11	..	1	..	218	..	66	..	21.80
A. M. W. Waters	11	..	2	..	170	..	33	..	18.88
R. E. Johnson	13	..	0	..	244	..	60	..	18.76
P. A. Williamson	13	..	1	..	187	..	43	..	15.58
G. W. Beresford	12	..	0	..	187	..	64	..	15.58
D. W. S. Pimblett	12	..	2	..	139	..	29	..	13.90

BOWLING	Overs		Maidens		Runs		Wickets		Average
*M. N. Forbes	197	..	59	..	482	..	35	..	13.77
A. M. W. Waters	140	..	23	..	397	..	21	..	18.90
J. A. Wightman	75	..	11	..	293	..	12	..	24.41
R. L. Farr	157	..	33	..	494	..	17	..	29.05

THE PERSE SCHOOL

Played 15: Won 5, Lost 3, Drawn 7

Master i/c: A. W. Billinghurst

BATTING	Innings		Not Outs		Runs		Highest Inns		Average
*A. D. Cuthill	14	..	6	..	428	..	94*	..	53.50
D. H. Larcombe	14	..	2	..	343	..	83	..	28.58
P. D. Johnston	15	..	0	..	351	..	69	..	23.40
J. H. Richards	7	..	1	..	122	..	47	..	20.33
A. R. Wass	15	..	1	..	264	..	35	..	18.85
M. A. P. Hall	11	..	4	..	128	..	31	..	18.28
P. W. Sterland	15	..	0	..	185	..	43	..	12.33

BOWLING	Overs		Maidens		Runs		Wickets		Average
J. H. Richards	164.5	..	45	..	408	..	29	..	14.06
M. A. P. Hall	188	..	48	..	505	..	33	..	15.30
P. D. Johnston	141	..	46	..	369	..	18	..	20.50

PLYMOUTH COLLEGE

Played 19: Won 12, Lost 4, Drawn 3

Master i/c: T. J. Stevens

BATTING	Innings		Not Outs		Runs		Highest Inns		Average
A. Seymour	15	..	3	..	342	..	87	..	28.50
I. T. Waldock	12	..	6	..	169	..	42	..	28.16
S. M. Chipman	19	..	2	..	468	..	84	..	27.52
J. D. Back	19	..	3	..	375	..	48	..	23.43
M. Tall	12	..	2	..	224	..	69*	..	22.40
G. J. Goodman	19	..	1	..	363	..	56*	..	20.16
R. Seymour	15	..	5	..	182	..	40	..	18.20
*R. Wood	19	..	0	..	249	..	59	..	13.10

BOWLING	Overs		Maidens		Runs		Wickets		Average
A. Seymour	206.5	..	57	..	591	..	70	..	8.44
J. M. L. Duffield	105.3	..	24	..	312	..	26	..	12.00
D. S. Azam	150.1	..	27	..	475	..	32	..	14.84
P. J. Bailey	66	..	20	..	175	..	10	..	17.50

POCKLINGTON SCHOOL

Played 25: Won 16, Lost 3, Drawn 6. Abandoned 1

Master i/c: D. Nuttall

BATTING	Innings		Not Outs		Runs		Highest Inns		Average
*A. E. C. Shanks	24	..	1	..	609	..	88*	..	26.47
P. R. East	22	..	4	..	444	..	54	..	24.66
M. J. Brown	25	..	4	..	492	..	75	..	23.42
P. M. Walker	19	..	5	..	316	..	61	..	22.57
T. A. Crockatt	11	..	4	..	143	..	31	..	20.42
M. N. Townend	20	..	3	..	325	..	47	..	19.11
D. C. G. Wood	23	..	2	..	378	..	56	..	18.00
J. M. White	20	..	5	..	270	..	50	..	18.00
I. A. Crockatt	25	..	1	..	377	..	64	..	15.70

BOWLING	Overs		Maidens		Runs		Wickets		Average
T. de L. Edmunds	260.2	..	96	..	515	..	45	..	11.44
P. R. East	163.1	..	61	..	317	..	27	..	11.74
D. C. G. Wood	240	..	52	..	684	..	53	..	12.90
A. E. C. Shanks	247.2	..	64	..	602	..	46	..	13.08
C. Anderson	186.5	..	60	..	424	..	24	..	17.66

QUEEN ELIZABETH GRAMMAR SCHOOL

Played 13: Won 2, Lost 2, Drawn 8, Tied 1. Abandoned 2

Master i/c: C. W. Furniss   Cricket professional: T. Hyland

BATTING	Innings		Not Outs		Runs		Highest Inns		Average
J. S. Young	13	..	6	..	264	..	63*	..	37.71
*I. G. Shackleton	13	..	0	..	265	..	46	..	20.38
P. H. D. Eastland	13	..	1	..	244	..	48	..	20.33
M. Adams	13	..	0	..	236	..	44	..	18.15

BOWLING	Overs		Maidens		Runs		Wickets		Average
A. Chapman	209	..	73	..	457	..	34	..	13.44
J. S. Young	145	..	34	..	382	..	28	..	13.64
M. Froggett	57	..	8	..	186	..	11	..	16.90
S. Atkinson	97	..	29	..	237	..	12	..	19.75

QUEEN'S COLLEGE, TAUNTON

Played 13: Won 4, Lost 1, Drawn 8. Abandoned 4

Master i/c: J. Davies

BATTING	Innings		Not Outs		Runs		Highest Inns		Average
*J. R. Greenhow	13	..	3	..	530	..	105*	..	53.00
R. W. Fletcher	7	..	3	..	143	..	51	..	35.73
G. Palmer	13	..	2	..	348	..	120*	..	31.63
N. A. Badat	13	..	0	..	309	..	56	..	23.76
R. Brunt	10	..	3	..	143	..	36	..	20.42
R. Parsons	13	..	3	..	196	..	70*	..	19.60

BOWLING	Overs		Maidens		Runs		Wickets		Average
J. R. Greenhow	46	..	6	..	152	..	14	..	10.85
R. W. Fletcher	59.4	..	20	..	157	..	11	..	14.27
G. Palmer	159.1	..	59	..	417	..	25	..	16.68
R. Parsons	188.4	..	39	..	598	..	30	..	19.93
R. Brunt	119	..	39	..	306	..	10	..	30.60

Schools Cricket in 1980

RADLEY COLLEGE

Played 16: Won 5, Lost 4, Drawn 7. Abandoned 2

Master i/c: C. H. Hirst   Cricket professional: A. G. Robinson

BATTING	Innings		Not Outs		Runs		Highest Inns		Average
T. G. Reeve............	7	..	1	..	182	..	82*	..	30.33
P. Rogers-Coltman.......	13	..	5	..	242	..	67*	..	30.25
D. B. D. Christopherson ...	16	..	3	..	369	..	73	..	28.38
B. G. D. Hooper.........	14	..	0	..	342	..	54	..	24.42
E. H. G. Lowe..........	14	..	2	..	280	..	55*	..	23.33
J. P. Allen	16	..	1	..	335	..	44*	..	22.33
D. R. C. Gale	13	..	2	..	214	..	35	..	19.45
M. J. W. Rushton	11	..	4	..	126	..	39	..	18.00
J. J. Chaffer..........	15	..	0	..	231	..	65	..	15.40
G. P. R. Norton.........	10	..	1	..	101	..	22	..	11.22

BOWLING	Overs		Maidens		Runs		Wickets		Average
D. R. C. Gale	99.5	..	7	..	348	..	27	..	12.88
M. J. W. Rushton	136	..	44	..	352	..	23	..	15.30
*J. A. N. Wootten........	253.2	..	63	..	794	..	49	..	16.20

RATCLIFFE COLLEGE

Played 15: Won 2, Lost 9, Drawn 4. Abandoned 4

Master i/c: C. W. Swan

BATTING	Innings		Not Outs		Runs		Highest Inns		Average
D. Hearne..............	15	..	1	..	254	..	69*	..	18.14
A. Simpson	11	..	3	..	122	..	36	..	15.25
R. Wilson	15	..	1	..	190	..	40	..	13.57
N. Evans	12	..	1	..	127	..	21	..	11.54
A. MacDiarmid...........	15	..	0	..	169	..	39	..	11.26

BOWLING	Overs		Maidens		Runs		Wickets		Average
N. Evans	181	..	46	..	489	..	36	..	13.58
A. MacDiarmid...........	149.2	..	29	..	447	..	30	..	14.90
*P. Digby	112	..	35	..	302	..	16	..	18.87

READING SCHOOL

Played 13: Won 2, Lost 4, Drawn 7. Abandoned 1

Master i/c: R. G. Owen   Cricket professional: A. Dindar

BATTING	Innings		Not Outs		Runs		Highest Inns		Average
E. D. Beckett...........	13	..	1	..	391	..	86*	..	32.58
N. P. Brownlow..........	5	..	0	..	127	..	53	..	25.40
H. K. Mason	13	..	0	..	295	..	52	..	22.69
J. M. Salmon...........	13	..	1	..	269	..	75	..	22.41
*P. D. C. Gibson	9	..	2	..	130	..	42	..	18.57
R. K. Purslow	12	..	4	..	144	..	28	..	18.00
E. L. Weekes	8	..	1	..	122	..	33	..	17.42

BOWLING	Overs		Maidens		Runs		Wickets		Average
H. K. Mason	128	..	35	..	369	..	29	..	12.72
A. G. Brown	75	..	14	..	212	..	15	..	14.13
P. D. C. Gibson.........	87	..	18	..	235	..	15	..	15.66
A. F. M. Simpkins........	88	..	17	..	250	..	12	..	20.83

REED'S SCHOOL

Played 14: Won 4, Lost 3, Drawn 7. Abandoned 4

Master i/c: G. R. Martin

BATTING	Innings		Not Outs		Runs		Highest Inns		Average
R. S. Kanwal............	10	..	6	..	230	..	63*	..	57.50
*M. A. Rowland.........	13	..	3	..	411	..	59	..	41.10
P. E. E. Farenden........	13	..	0	..	475	..	89	..	36.53
M. D. Morris............	10	..	1	..	178	..	50*	..	19.77
P. J. McDuell...........	13	..	1	..	152	..	39	..	12.66
N. R. Gurney	12	..	4	..	100	..	44	..	12.50

BOWLING	Overs		Maidens		Runs		Wickets		Average
M. R. Dunn.............	59	..	12	..	157	..	14	..	11.21
J. A. Nichols...........	31.4	..	6	..	126	..	11	..	11.45
P. J. McDuell	120	..	32	..	304	..	20	..	15.20
P. D. F. Engelen	155	..	48	..	397	..	22	..	18.04
R. S. Kanwal...........	98.3	..	21	..	291	..	16	..	18.18

REIGATE GRAMMAR SCHOOL

Played 21: Won 12, Lost 3, Drawn 6. Abandoned 2

Master i/c: D. C. R. Jones

BATTING	Innings		Not Outs		Runs		Highest Inns		Average
*N. J. Falkner	21	..	4	..	1,139	..	125	..	67.00
R. J. Neal	17	..	6	..	288	..	55*	..	26.18
J. C. Perkins	18	..	3	..	313	..	75	..	20.86
C. D. Jones	19	..	1	..	367	..	75	..	20.39
J. F. Bramhall	17	..	0	..	313	..	57	..	18.41
P. N. J. Downman........	14	..	5	..	145	..	26*	..	16.11

BOWLING	Overs		Maidens		Runs		Wickets		Average
A. M. Babington	201.5	..	69	..	395	..	44	..	8.97
P. W. Gritton	122	..	29	..	355	..	30	..	11.83
M. P. G. Boden	155.5	..	48	..	336	..	26	..	12.92
J. C. Perkins	185.1	..	50	..	448	..	31	..	14.45
C. D. Jones	110	..	30	..	291	..	17	..	17.11

REPTON SCHOOL

Played 15: Won 4, Lost 1, Drawn 10. Abandoned 2

Master i/c: J. F. M. Walker   Cricket professional: E. Marsh

BATTING	Innings		Not Outs		Runs		Highest Inns		Average
S. W. Lovell............	16	..	4	..	583	..	103*	..	48.58
*N. G. B. Richardson	13	..	2	..	409	..	71	..	37.18
J. D. Carr	16	..	3	..	398	..	53*	..	30.61
J. S. Frost	11	..	3	..	212	..	56*	..	26.50
M. H. Cross	16	..	1	..	330	..	63*	..	22.00
C. J. C. Hays...........	10	..	1	..	165	..	47	..	18.33

BOWLING	Overs		Maidens		Runs		Wickets		Average
N. G. B. Richardson	187	..	46	..	576	..	38	..	15.15
J. S. Frost	223	..	64	..	605	..	33	..	18.33
J. M. Proctor...........	158	..	32	..	521	..	18	..	28.94
N. C. F. Nicholson	101	..	20	..	444	..	11	..	40.36

ROSSALL SCHOOL

Played 12: Won 4, Lost 2, Drawn 6

Master i/c: M. O. Bennett

BATTING	Innings		Not Outs		Runs		Highest Inns		Average
*A. C. Jones	13	..	2	..	344	..	119*	..	31.27
M. J. Winterbottom	12	..	2	..	233	..	53*	..	23.30
R. Kanhai	11	..	4	..	155	..	34*	..	22.14
I. Cartwright	13	..	1	..	191	..	56*	..	15.91
A. J. Higgin	13	..	1	..	164	..	30	..	13.66

BOWLING	Overs		Maidens		Runs		Wickets		Average
A. C. Jones	114	..	36	..	202	..	19	..	10.63
J. Turner	136	..	39	..	338	..	27	..	12.51
D. J. Hannon	132	..	28	..	299	..	21	..	14.23
A. J. Higgin	130	..	22	..	402	..	17	..	23.64

ROYAL GRAMMAR SCHOOL, NEWCASTLE

Played 17: Won 2, Lost 6, Drawn 9. Abandoned 2

Master i/c: D. W. Smith

BATTING	Innings		Not Outs		Runs		Highest Inns		Average
D. D. Lumley	16	..	7	..	353	..	50	..	39.22
*W. G. Wake	15	..	1	..	453	..	66*	..	32.35
M. R. Thompson	17	..	1	..	385	..	86	..	24.06
J. M. Webb	15	..	3	..	280	..	57*	..	23.33
S. G. Bell	16	..	1	..	266	..	36	..	17.73
A. G. Wilson	15	..	2	..	147	..	25*	..	11.30

BOWLING	Overs		Maidens		Runs		Wickets		Average
D. W. Gladstone	97.2	..	26	..	239	..	15	..	15.93
G. W. Anderson	153.5	..	52	..	377	..	23	..	16.39
D. D. Lumley	187	..	50	..	521	..	20	..	26.05
R. Jordan	117.4	..	24	..	427	..	16	..	26.68
W. G. Wake	88	..	16	..	290	..	10	..	29.00

RYDAL SCHOOL

Played 18: Won 1, Lost 8, Drawn 9. Abandoned 1

Master i/c: D. H. Crook   Cricket professional: R. C. W. Pitman

BATTING	Innings		Not Outs		Runs		Highest Inns		Average
T. C. N. Aughton	18	..	1	..	400	..	93	..	23.52
*A. C. Rhodes	15	..	2	..	267	..	68*	..	20.53
R. C. Bradley	14	..	3	..	143	..	28*	..	13.00
N. C. Rhodes	17	..	3	..	179	..	52*	..	12.78
D. M. Cole	13	..	0	..	153	..	59	..	11.76
P. T. A. Johnson	14	..	0	..	160	..	46	..	11.42

BOWLING	Overs		Maidens		Runs		Wickets		Average
A. C. Rhodes	283.4	..	82	..	631	..	43	..	14.67
T. C. N. Aughton	162	..	33	..	573	..	27	..	21.22
P. D. Schofield	92	..	30	..	268	..	12	..	22.33
S. Holmes	121.4	..	26	..	363	..	13	..	27.92

ST ALBANS SCHOOL

Played 17: Won 5, Lost 4, Drawn 8. Abandoned 2

Master i/c: N. J. Pritchard

BATTING	Innings		Not Outs		Runs		Highest Inns		Average
A. G. Lynes.............	16	..	4	..	371	..	84*	..	30.91
*T. R. Lovejoy	15	..	1	..	341	..	81	..	24.35
A. J. Dent	12	..	1	..	264	..	56	..	24.00
A. P. Latham............	12	..	5	..	150	..	52	..	21.42
J.-P. Rodgers...........	14	..	3	..	225	..	34	..	20.45
R. J. Loader	15	..	3	..	186	..	49*	..	15.50
N. V. K. Baylis	9	..	1	..	122	..	26	..	15.25

BOWLING	Overs		Maidens		Runs		Wickets		Average
T. R. Lovejoy	111	..	24	..	312	..	27	..	11.55
A. P. Latham...........	171.4	..	43	..	463	..	27	..	17.14
I. N. M. Jones	160	..	38	..	452	..	23	..	19.65
A. J. Dent	127.5	..	30	..	330	..	16	..	20.62
D. R. A. Hopkins	91	..	18	..	314	..	14	..	22.42

ST DUNSTAN'S COLLEGE

Played 13: Won 2, Lost 4, Drawn 7

Master i/c: P. W. Baldwin

BATTING	Innings		Not Outs		Runs		Highest Inns		Average
C. M. Denny...........	12	..	3	..	292	..	71*	..	32.44
B. J. Wood	10	..	2	..	172	..	43	..	21.50
A. M. Ford	12	..	1	..	230	..	70*	..	20.90
A. J. C. Denny	12	..	0	..	199	..	50	..	16.58
C. N. Tooley	13	..	0	..	172	..	40	..	13.23
T. W. F. Nash	9	..	0	..	113	..	41	..	12.55

BOWLING	Overs		Maidens		Runs		Wickets		Average
A. C. Ashworth.........	156	..	47	..	437	..	29	..	15.06
M. J. Blake	147.4	..	52	..	333	..	21	..	15.85
T. Bennett	143	..	46	..	400	..	20	..	20.00
T. W. F. Nash...........	83	..	28	..	219	..	10	..	21.90

ST EDMUND'S SCHOOL

Played 14: Won 5, Lost 0, Drawn 9. Abandoned 5

Master i/c: D. Knight   Cricket professional: D. V. P. Wright

BATTING	Innings		Not Outs		Runs		Highest Inns		Average
R. Walton	8	..	2	..	269	..	105*	..	44.83
I. Hitchcock	10	..	3	..	266	..	71	..	38.00
M. S. Jordan	13	..	1	..	360	..	85	..	30.00
*I. C. Hopper	12	..	4	..	230	..	41	..	28.75
A. J. Ritchie	13	..	0	..	294	..	102	..	22.61
S. E. Hull	8	..	1	..	129	..	55	..	18.42
C. C. E. Robin.	10	..	2	..	130	..	52*	..	16.25

BOWLING	Overs		Maidens		Runs		Wickets		Average
K. A. Rumbelow.........	174.1	..	55	..	414	..	36	..	11.50
S. E. Hull	146.5	..	51	..	386	..	28	..	13.78
H. T. Mount	74	..	21	..	201	..	14	..	14.35
I. C. Hopper	70	..	18	..	253	..	15	..	16.86

ST EDWARD'S SCHOOL

Played 11: Won 1, Lost 3, Drawn 7. Abandoned 3

Master i/c: P. G. Badger   Cricket professional: B. R. Edrich

BATTING	Innings		Not Outs		Runs		Highest Inns		Average
*J. A. Lyons	11	..	3	..	400	..	107*	..	50.00
N. A. Friend	9	..	1	..	288	..	100*	..	36.00
P. R. J. Smith	11	..	1	..	319	..	102*	..	31.90
S. J. H. Smith	6	..	1	..	154	..	75*	..	30.80
N. J. Gates	10	..	1	..	171	..	76	..	19.00
T. J. Rogers	11	..	2	..	123	..	31	..	13.66

BOWLING	Overs		Maidens		Runs		Wickets		Average
T. J. Rogers	92.4	..	24	..	250	..	13	..	19.23
N. H. M. Arkell	160	..	37	..	406	..	21	..	19.33
N. A. Friend	114	..	24	..	277	..	14	..	19.78

ST GEORGE'S COLLEGE

Played 15: Won 4, Lost 7, Drawn 4. Abandoned 2

Master i/c: B. O'Gorman

BATTING	Innings		Not Outs		Runs		Highest Inns		Average
D. A. Close	15	..	2	..	554	..	104	..	42.61
*D. J. Hayward	14	..	0	..	382	..	83	..	27.28
M. Buckley	11	..	3	..	201	..	49*	..	25.12
R. P. Moore	12	..	1	..	252	..	63	..	22.90
J. Talbot	14	..	1	..	243	..	102	..	18.69
N. Habib	14	..	0	..	236	..	72	..	16.85
D. Hamer	12	..	2	..	127	..	30*	..	12.70
R. Triay	10	..	0	..	120	..	52	..	12.00
S. Willis	14	..	2	..	134	..	40	..	11.16

BOWLING	Overs		Maidens		Runs		Wickets		Average
D. Hamer	188.4	..	36	..	642	..	34	..	18.88
P. Bodenham	96.4	..	27	..	378	..	15	..	25.20
M. Buckley	142.3	..	30	..	461	..	19	..	24.26

ST JOHN'S SCHOOL

Played 11: Won 4, Lost 1, Drawn 6. Abandoned 3

Master i/c: M. E. C. Comer   Cricket professional: E. Shepperd

BATTING	Innings		Not Outs		Runs		Highest Inns		Average
C. J. Presley	10	..	1	..	276	..	102*	..	30.66
*A. G. K. Hooper	11	..	1	..	295	..	110	..	29.50
D. J. Glasscock	11	..	2	..	227	..	55	..	25.22
P. A. Sidwell	7	..	2	..	112	..	42*	..	22.40
G. J. Marks	11	..	0	..	242	..	74	..	22.00
S. G. Anthony	10	..	0	..	164	..	44	..	16.40
N. I. Presley	10	..	3	..	101	..	39*	..	14.42

BOWLING	Overs		Maidens		Runs		Wickets		Average
A. G. K. Hooper	187	..	57	..	513	..	32	..	16.03
P. A. Sidwell	75.2	..	24	..	184	..	10	..	18.40
G. F. Harries	132	..	32	..	342	..	16	..	21.37
M. T. Sibley	125	..	41	..	371	..	14	..	26.50

ST LAWRENCE COLLEGE

Played 11: Won 3, Lost 3, Drawn 5. Abandoned 5

Master i/c: N. O. S. Jones

BATTING	Innings		Not Outs		Runs		Highest Inns		Average
*S. J. Billings	11	..	1	..	343	..	91	..	34.30
T. M. H. Dodd	7	..	2	..	156	..	50*	..	31.20
D. I. Ray	10	..	2	..	191	..	78*	..	23.87
P. J. Laslett	9	..	2	..	155	..	102*	..	22.14
A. J. Billings	11	..	1	..	179	..	46	..	17.90
P. S. Bailey	11	..	0	..	101	..	26	..	9.18

BOWLING	Overs		Maidens		Runs		Wickets		Average
S. J. Billings	127.3	..	48	..	247	..	24	..	10.29
J. J. Marchant	110	..	28	..	333	..	21	..	15.85
D. R. Joyce	97.2	..	24	..	230	..	12	..	19.16

ST PAUL'S SCHOOL

Played 17: Won 2, Lost 7, Drawn 8. Abandoned 3

Master i/c: G. Hughes   Cricket professional: E. W. Whitfield

BATTING	Innings		Not Outs		Runs		Highest Inns		Average
*K. B. McCray	16	..	1	..	511	..	120*	..	34.06
J. Withers Green	17	..	1	..	367	..	66	..	22.93
J. R. W. Beasley	17	..	5	..	253	..	60*	..	21.08
M. A. Colato	17	..	0	..	339	..	71	..	19.94
J. E. Boulton	17	..	0	..	335	..	52	..	19.70
R. W. D. Hampton	12	..	0	..	184	..	44	..	15.33
A. J. Duncan	14	..	3	..	110	..	26*	..	10.00
R. M. Chester	16	..	0	..	116	..	32	..	7.25

BOWLING	Overs		Maidens		Runs		Wickets		Average
D. R. Easton	183.4	..	35	..	562	..	23	..	24.43
R. M. Chester	154.5	..	18	..	620	..	24	..	25.83
J. M. Harrison	153.4	..	30	..	550	..	17	..	32.35
M. M. Burton	157	..	40	..	432	..	11	..	39.27

ST PETER'S SCHOOL

Played 17: Won 6, Lost 2, Drawn 9. Abandoned 2

Master i/c: D. Kirby   Cricket professional: K. J. Mohan

BATTING	Innings		Not Outs		Runs		Highest Inns		Average
C. J. Stubbs	14	..	5	..	312	..	106*	..	34.66
J. R. Dodman	11	..	7	..	120	..	26*	..	30.00
A. M. Precious	14	..	2	..	347	..	51	..	28.91
S. P. Burdass	10	..	4	..	110	..	36*	..	18.33
N. J. Chapman	15	..	3	..	217	..	84*	..	18.08
I. D. Hindhaugh	18	..	2	..	286	..	48	..	17.87
D. M. Noyes	18	..	3	..	267	..	50	..	17.80
A. J. N. Simpson	16	..	0	..	243	..	48	..	15.18
E. F. J. Wright	16	..	1	..	173	..	35	..	11.53

BOWLING	Overs		Maidens		Runs		Wickets		Average
A. M. Precious	199.4	..	78	..	413	..	30	..	13.76
C. J. Stubbs	211	..	58	..	527	..	33	..	15.96
*M. W. Johnston	187	..	44	..	617	..	35	..	17.62
A. J. N. Simpson	78.3	..	15	..	289	..	12	..	24.08
R. J. Kirby	83	..	20	..	289	..	11	..	26.27

SEDBERGH SCHOOL

Played 16: Won 10, Lost 1, Drawn 5. Abandoned 1

Master i/c: J. O. Morris

BATTING	Innings		Not Outs		Runs		Highest Inns		Average
N. A. P. Meadows........	14	..	5	..	323	..	67	..	35.88
*W. R. Holdsworth.......	16	..	0	..	450	..	79	..	28.12
C. D. Oliver.............	15	..	2	..	360	..	85*	..	27.69
A. W. A. Scott..........	15	..	5	..	201	..	34	..	20.10
J. W. Edgar.............	16	..	1	..	290	..	62*	..	19.33

BOWLING	Overs		Maidens		Runs		Wickets		Average
J. M. B. Daniels.........	208	..	94	..	303	..	27	..	11.22
N. A. P. Meadows........	298	..	97	..	641	..	54	..	11.87
P. Rogers..............	128	..	40	..	285	..	20	..	14.25
J. L. O'B. Robinson.......	102	..	25	..	291	..	20	..	14.55
C. D. Oliver.............	103	..	27	..	269	..	12	..	22.41

SEVENOAKS SCHOOL

Played 9: Won 3, Lost 0, Drawn 6. Abandoned 5

Master i/c: I. J. B. Walker

BATTING	Innings		Not Outs		Runs		Highest Inns		Average
M. I. Dickenson	9	..	2	..	241	..	57	..	34.42
P. Durdant-Hollamby.....	9	..	2	..	223	..	69	..	31.85
L. R. Munasinghe........	6	..	0	..	145	..	46	..	24.16
J. T. L. Piggott	8	..	3	..	116	..	27	..	23.20

BOWLING	Overs		Maidens		Runs		Wickets		Average
P. N. Colman	128.2	..	53	..	243	..	28	..	8.67
P. Durdant-Hollamby.....	91	..	27	..	174	..	16	..	10.87
R. P. L. Styles...........	64	..	11	..	219	..	16	..	13.68
J. M. P. Cotton	64	..	24	..	149	..	10	..	14.90

SHERBORNE SCHOOL

Played 17: Won 7, Lost 2, Drawn 8

Master i/c: D. F. Gibbs   Cricket professional: R. W. Clarke

BATTING	Innings		Not Outs		Runs		Highest Inns		Average
J. M. P. C. Turner	17	..	3	..	625	..	79	..	44.64
*J. F. Blackburn	15	..	4	..	382	..	94*	..	34.72
W. J. Rydon	16	..	2	..	371	..	58	..	26.50
M. M. Webb	17	..	0	..	385	..	67	..	22.64
J. S. W. Lund	11	..	2	..	159	..	57*	..	17.66
A. C. Quinlan	12	..	3	..	136	..	33	..	15.11

BOWLING	Overs		Maidens		Runs		Wickets		Average
W. J. Rydon	156.3	..	54	..	331	..	32	..	10.34
J. F. Blackburn	214.5	..	50	..	418	..	32	..	13.06
P. E. J. Sanderson	164	..	47	..	442	..	26	..	17.00
A. I. C. Wilson	136	..	36	..	328	..	18	..	18.22
A. C. Quinlan	131.4	..	28	..	411	..	17	..	24.17

SIMON LANGTON GRAMMAR SCHOOL, CANTERBURY

Played 24: Won 12, Lost 0, Drawn 12. Abandoned 4

Master i/c: R. F. Harriott

BATTING	Innings		Not Outs		Runs		Highest Inns		Average
D. Simmonds	20	..	0	..	597	..	66	..	29.85
A. Wood	23	..	1	..	453	..	73	..	20.59
*N. Williams	19	..	1	..	315	..	63	..	17.50
S. Newlyn	19	..	2	..	255	..	49*	..	15.00
T. Bowell	15	..	3	..	171	..	39	..	14.25
J. Atkinson	17	..	0	..	242	..	48	..	14.23
F. Barrett	20	..	6	..	181	..	36	..	12.92
C. Baker	17	..	5	..	149	..	32	..	12.41

BOWLING	Overs		Maidens		Runs		Wickets		Average
A. Castle	294	..	71	..	772	..	66	..	11.69
J. Richards	171.2	..	43	..	394	..	30	..	13.13
F. Barrett	280.4	..	51	..	855	..	47	..	18.19
S. Newlyn	122	..	24	..	413	..	19	..	21.73
A. Davies	111.4	..	36	..	285	..	11	..	25.90

SIR ROGER MANWOOD'S SCHOOL, SANDWICH

Played 8: Won 2, Lost 4, Drawn 2. Abandoned 3

Master i/c: P. W. Kullman

BATTING	Innings		Not Outs		Runs		Highest Inns		Average
*A. J. Curwen	8	..	0	..	160	..	94	..	20.00

BOWLING	Overs		Maidens		Runs		Wickets		Average
M. G. Norris	83.4	..	21	..	191	..	24	..	7.95
D. G. Chisholm	96.1	..	31	..	180	..	20	..	9.00
P. Millard	77.3	..	21	..	225	..	15	..	15.00

SOLIHULL SCHOOL

Played 21: Won 2, Lost 6, Drawn 13. Abandoned 2

BATTING	Innings		Not Outs		Runs		Highest Inns		Average
R. J. Hamilton	20	..	4	..	474	..	72	..	29.62
R. J. Packwood	20	..	1	..	456	..	64	..	24.00
*J. D. M. Kinsey	20	..	1	..	363	..	72	..	19.10
J. M. Robinson	14	..	3	..	206	..	39	..	18.72
S. N. Lawley	16	..	2	..	181	..	54	..	12.92
T. S. Yapp	14	..	2	..	118	..	21*	..	9.83
C. R. Holden	18	..	0	..	170	..	35	..	9.44

BOWLING	Overs		Maidens		Runs		Wickets		Average
S. N. Lawley	65	..	9	..	275	..	16	..	17.18
N. J. Wheelwright	280	..	74	..	780	..	40	..	19.50
A. J. Watson	234	..	44	..	832	..	32	..	26.00
J. D. M. Kinsey	197	..	41	..	667	..	23	..	29.00
N. J. Bellingham	109	..	20	..	395	..	13	..	30.38

STOCKPORT GRAMMAR SCHOOL

Played 15: Won 3, Lost 4, Drawn 8. Abandoned 1

Master i/c: L. P. Kynaston

Cricket professional: Duleep Mendis

BATTING	Innings		Not Outs		Runs		Highest Inns		Average
S. J. Hornby	13	..	1	..	289	..	69*	..	24.08
N. J. Sinclair	13	..	4	..	164	..	31*	..	18.22
P. D. Carroll	12	..	0	..	214	..	42	..	17.83
A. E. Sawer	11	..	1	..	173	..	52*	..	17.30
R. J. Nicholson	10	..	2	..	136	..	49*	..	17.07
A. Wickremeratne	11	..	1	..	160	..	101*	..	16.00
A. R. Wood	12	..	4	..	124	..	37	..	15.50
*A. D. Reeman	11	..	2	..	118	..	29	..	13.11
I. R. Burns	10	..	0	..	129	..	36	..	12.90
M. Woodhead	11	..	1	..	126	..	76	..	12.60

BOWLING	Overs		Maidens		Runs		Wickets		Average
M. A. Beesley	135.5	..	42	..	317	..	21	..	15.09
A. D. Reeman	66	..	20	..	207	..	13	..	15.92
A. R. Wood	83.4	..	21	..	242	..	15	..	16.13
P. D. Carroll	79	..	20	..	257	..	15	..	17.13
A. R. King	112	..	36	..	263	..	12	..	21.91

STOWE SCHOOL

Played 18: Won 4, Lost 5, Drawn 9

Master i/c: L. E. Weston

Cricket professional: C. Oakes

BATTING	Innings		Not Outs		Runs		Highest Inns		Average
*F. E. J. Law	18	..	2	..	550	..	88	..	34.37
T. A. Lester	18	..	1	..	441	..	75	..	29.94
M. C. Turner	12	..	4	..	184	..	35	..	23.00
A. R. J. Mackinnon	14	..	3	..	246	..	54*	..	22.36
P. A. Marshall	16	..	0	..	323	..	62	..	20.18
W. J. Lord	7	..	1	..	119	..	41*	..	19.83
A. B. Mclellan	17	..	3	..	212	..	48	..	15.14
C. A. Wadsworth	12	..	0	..	144	..	59	..	12.00

BOWLING	Overs		Maidens		Runs		Wickets		Average
C. A. Wadsworth	253.2	..	58	..	705	..	34	..	20.73
T. A. Lester	246.4	..	63	..	738	..	32	..	23.06
P. N. Taylor	109	..	21	..	319	..	13	..	24.53
H. A. H. Merewether	138	..	24	..	371	..	14	..	26.50
F. E. J. Law	84.5	..	9	..	367	..	12	..	30.58

STRATHALLAN SCHOOL

Played 12: Won 3, Lost 1, Drawn 8. Abandoned 1

Master i/c: R. N. Johnson

BATTING	Innings		Not Outs		Runs		Highest Inns		Average
M. J. de G. Allingham	10	..	3	..	334	..	71*	..	47.71
J. A. R. Coleman	9	..	2	..	153	..	29*	..	21.85
G. S. B. Corbett	11	..	2	..	169	..	43*	..	18.77
*C. A. MacLeod	10	..	2	..	132	..	20*	..	16.50
R. C. Inglis	9	..	1	..	130	..	33*	..	16.25
S. R. Watt	9	..	0	..	130	..	43	..	14.44

BOWLING	Overs		Maidens		Runs		Wickets		Average
C. A. MacLeod	175	..	21	..	306	..	26	..	11.76
A. O. Shepherd	47	..	5	..	147	..	10	..	14.70
M. J. de G. Allingham.....	75	..	13	..	201	..	10	..	20.10
J. A. R. Coleman.	102.2	..	20	..	285	..	11	..	25.90

SUTTON VALENCE SCHOOL

Played 18: Won 3, Lost 3, Drawn 12

Master i/c: A. N. Grierson Rickford

BATTING	Innings		Not Outs		Runs		Highest Inns		Average
M. T. Russell-Vick	17	..	1	..	448	..	86	..	28.00
*J. B. Hichens	17	..	3	..	331	..	53*	..	23.64
A. R. Shaw	17	..	4	..	292	..	51	..	22.46
P. G. G. Brice	17	..	0	..	298	..	80	..	17.52
R. J. Bedford............	16	..	5	..	180	..	54	..	16.36
B. R. Rafuse	16	..	3	..	180	..	68	..	13.84
A. K. Charlton	16	..	4	..	136	..	23	..	11.33

BOWLING	Overs		Maidens		Runs		Wickets		Average
M. T. Russell-Vick	152	..	36	..	315	..	26	..	12.11
B. R. Rafuse	67	..	9	..	232	..	14	..	16.57
R. J. Bedford	173	..	42	..	516	..	27	..	19.11
J. P. M. Dismorr	83	..	20	..	294	..	15	..	19.60
J. D. L. Goss............	150	..	41	..	396	..	18	..	22.00
A. R. Shaw	128	..	25	..	412	..	15	..	27.46

TAUNTON SCHOOL

Played 10: Won 3, Lost 2, Drawn 5. Abandoned 3

Master i/c: R. P. Smith   Cricket professional: J. A. Jameson

BATTING	Innings		Not Outs		Runs		Highest Inns		Average
*D. M. Elworthy	10	..	0	..	506	..	108	..	50.60
S. J. Button	10	..	2	..	187	..	58*	..	23.37
A. J. Blake..............	10	..	0	..	230	..	55	..	23.00
J. P. Horne	10	..	1	..	200	..	49	..	22.22

BOWLING	Overs		Maidens		Runs		Wickets		Average
R. C. Grant	152.2	..	39	..	443	..	36	..	12.30
J. T. Adam	64	..	11	..	171	..	13	..	13.15
T. J. Leahy	124.3	..	30	..	331	..	23	..	14.39

TIFFIN SCHOOL

Played 22: Won 12, Lost 3, Drawn 7. Abandoned 1

Master i/c: M. J. Williams

BATTING	Innings		Not Outs		Runs		Highest Inns		Average
*A. J. Stewart	17	..	3	..	782	..	128*	..	55.85
N. D. Hicks.............	18	..	2	..	501	..	76	..	31.31
M. A. Feltham...........	15	..	1	..	404	..	87	..	28.85
J. M. Green	16	..	0	..	445	..	81	..	27.81
P. R. C. Robinson........	15	..	5	..	267	..	39	..	26.70
P. Shepherd.............	11	..	3	..	170	..	62*	..	21.25
S. P. Clews.............	16	..	5	..	221	..	52	..	20.09

BOWLING	Overs		Maidens		Runs		Wickets		Average
M. S. G. Robins	118.3	..	25	..	399	..	37	..	10.78
S. P. Clews	249.3	..	83	..	568	..	38	..	14.94
A. W. Griffin	82.2	..	26	..	206	..	13	..	15.84
M. A. Feltham	158.3	..	34	..	466	..	27	..	17.25
J. S. Holmes	114.4	..	29	..	282	..	16	..	17.62
P. R. C. Robinson	142	..	48	..	387	..	13	..	29.76

TONBRIDGE SCHOOL

Played 15: Won 4, Lost 3, Drawn 8. Abandoned 2

Master i/c: D. R. Walsh   Cricket professional: T. W. Higginson

BATTING	Innings		Not Outs		Runs		Highest Inns		Average
G. R. Cowdrey	15	..	0	..	446	..	87	..	29.73
R. M. P. T. Morgan	15	..	1	..	369	..	122*	..	26.35
M. P. Hickson	12	..	6	..	155	..	52*	..	25.83
H. C. I. Betts	15	..	1	..	284	..	87*	..	20.28
H. S. Ward	15	..	1	..	266	..	64*	..	19.00
C. C. Ellison	13	..	3	..	189	..	57	..	18.90
J. R. Allbrook	15	..	3	..	190	..	52	..	15.83
*J. M. W. Sale	15	..	0	..	219	..	53	..	14.60

BOWLING	Overs		Maidens		Runs		Wickets		Average
C. C. Ellison	161	..	32	..	421	..	28	..	15.03
M. P. Hickson	176	..	32	..	473	..	26	..	18.19
A. N. Wanniaratchy	82	..	23	..	234	..	12	..	19.50
T. J. Hyde	81	..	19	..	226	..	10	..	22.60

TRENT COLLEGE

Played 11: Won 3, Lost 2, Drawn 6. Abandoned 4

Master i/c: M. F. Sayer   Cricket professional: A. V. Pope

BATTING	Innings		Not Outs		Runs		Highest Inns		Average
*D. N. Wood	10	..	1	..	263	..	62	..	29.22
M. R. Dodson	10	..	1	..	160	..	38	..	17.77
N. C. Green	8	..	0	..	124	..	39	..	15.50
P. Burge	8	..	3	..	116	..	50*	..	23.20

BOWLING	Overs		Maidens		Runs		Wickets		Average
J. C. Harris	131	..	30	..	336	..	20	..	16.80
M. R. Dodson	84	..	27	..	202	..	15	..	13.46
I. Lane	91	..	20	..	270	..	16	..	16.87
N. C. Green	80	..	14	..	289	..	18	..	16.05

TRINTY SCHOOL

Played 28: Won 7, Lost 4, Drawn 17. Abandoned 3

Master i/c: B. Widger

BATTING	Innings		Not Outs		Runs		Highest Inns		Average
J. E. Vigar	28	..	1	..	913	..	146	..	33.81
*M. L. Jones	27	..	1	..	815	..	137	..	31.34
S. N. Perry	25	..	3	..	509	..	59	..	23.13
P. R. Gardner	28	..	5	..	414	..	53*	..	18.00
C. J. Hall	26	..	0	..	359	..	69	..	13.80
M. B. Martin	14	..	3	..	146	..	25	..	13.27
S. R. M. Ricca	22	..	8	..	176	..	50*	..	12.57
J. R. Glynne-Jones	24	..	3	..	241	..	42*	..	11.47
P. I. Chambers	17	..	7	..	107	..	27	..	10.70

BOWLING	Overs		Maidens		Runs		Wickets		Average
N. A. Jones	230.4	..	67	..	520	..	36	..	14.44
P. I. Chambers	182.5	..	46	..	485	..	32	..	15.15
J. R. Glynne-Jones	370.4	..	99	..	910	..	55	..	16.54
T. P. Firth	283.5	..	57	..	868	..	42	..	20.66
M. B. Martin	206	..	36	..	626	..	26	..	24.07

TRURO SCHOOL

Played 14: Won 8, Lost 2, Drawn 4. Abandoned 2

Master i/c: A. J. D. Aldwinckle

BATTING	Innings		Not Outs		Runs		Highest Inns		Average
N. R. E. Illsley	11	..	2	..	183	..	50*	..	20.33
P. S. Kerkin	12	..	0	..	237	..	41	..	19.75
D. A. V. Morton	9	..	3	..	108	..	27*	..	18.00
*T. M. Chatterton	13	..	1	..	139	..	34	..	11.58
C. J. Kerkin	12	..	2	..	107	..	33*	..	10.70

BOWLING	Overs		Maidens		Runs		Wickets		Average
N. R. E. Illsley	45.2	..	17	..	92	..	15	..	6.13
M. E. Barlow	81.1	..	21	..	191	..	25	..	7.64
T. J. Manhire	128.4	..	37	..	247	..	26	..	9.50
A. R. Mitchell	103	..	29	..	220	..	22	..	10.00

UNIVERSITY COLLEGE SCHOOL, HAMPSTEAD

Played 10: Won 2, Lost 2, Drawn 6. Abandoned 2

Master i/c: T. Roberts   Cricket professional: W. Jones

BATTING	Innings		Not Outs		Runs		Highest Inns		Average
M. Furness	10	..	1	..	274	..	76	..	30.44
N. Santcross	10	..	0	..	230	..	86	..	23.00
*L. Stitcher	10	..	0	..	168	..	49	..	16.80

BOWLING	Overs		Maidens		Runs		Wickets		Average
R. Clipson	148.5	..	42	..	377	..	17	..	22.17
R. Portlock	73	..	14	..	243	..	10	..	24.30
L. Stitcher	61.3	..	16	..	229	..	10	..	22.90

UPPINGHAM SCHOOL

Played 10: Won 0, Lost 2, Drawn 8. Abandoned 3

Master i/c: G. A. Wheatley   Cricket professional: M. R. Hallam

BATTING	Innings		Not Outs		Runs		Highest Inns		Average
*J. J. Whitaker	12	..	1	..	747	..	121	..	67.90
S. G. W. Dunkley	12	..	4	..	329	..	100*	..	41.12
J. P. Green	10	..	3	..	212	..	82	..	30.28
J. C. Muncey	9	..	3	..	160	..	28	..	26.66
C. N. Agnew	8	..	1	..	115	..	46	..	16.42
R. S. Leppington	12	..	0	..	192	..	74	..	16.00
T. J. Preston-Jones	12	..	1	..	136	..	28	..	12.36

BOWLING	Overs		Maidens		Runs		Wickets		Average
C. N. Agnew	179	..	52	..	481	..	27	..	17.81
M. L. Roberts	118	..	37	..	330	..	15	..	22.00
K. Rothero	88	..	24	..	300	..	11	..	27.27
S. G. W. Dunkley	131	..	29	..	445	..	15	..	29.66

VICTORIA COLLEGE, JERSEY

Played 19: Won 7, Lost 7, Drawn 5

Master i/c: D. A. R. Ferguson   Cricket professional: G. J. Whittaker

BATTING	Innings		Not Outs		Runs		Highest Inns		Average
D. A. Oliver	9	..	4	..	126	..	53	..	25.20
*D. V. Pallot	19	..	1	..	372	..	38	..	20.66
M. Broxup	19	..	0	..	392	..	65	..	20.63
W. Jenner	11	..	1	..	178	..	52	..	17.80
N. J. Dodds	18	..	2	..	259	..	62	..	16.18
R .H. R. Boddy	19	..	2	..	254	..	75	..	14.94
R. W. Sugden	16	..	1	..	180	..	53*	..	12.00
D. J. B. Le Brocq	11	..	2	..	103	..	25*	..	11.44
M. C. Layzell	14	..	3	..	122	..	39	..	11.09

BOWLING	Overs		Maidens		Runs		Wickets		Average
M. C. Layzell	103.4	..	16	..	468	..	35	..	13.37
G. A. Holmes	145	..	38	..	362	..	25	..	14.48
P. R. B. Le Brocq	143.3	..	31	..	364	..	24	..	15.16
M. Broxup	101.4	..	21	..	342	..	20	..	17.10
R. H. R. Boddy	173	..	37	..	481	..	26	..	18.50
G. Omissi	56.5	..	12	..	276	..	11	..	25.09

WARWICK SCHOOL

Played 12: Won 2, Lost 0, Drawn 10. Abandoned 2

Master i/c: I. B. Moffatt   Cricket professional: N. Horner

BATTING	Innings		Not Outs		Runs		Highest Inns		Average
R. A. Horner	9	..	3	..	268	..	52*	..	44.66
M. A. Walter	10	..	2	..	200	..	53	..	25.00
A. C. Nunn	10	..	2	..	161	..	50*	..	20.12
D. A. Hinton	12	..	0	..	193	..	44	..	16.08
J. C. Ball	11	..	0	..	167	..	61	..	15.18
J. E. Clark	10	..	2	..	116	..	29	..	14.50
D. I. Lammie	10	..	2	..	107	..	51	..	13.37

BOWLING	Overs		Maidens		Runs		Wickets		Average
A. C. Nunn	105	..	23	..	298	..	16	..	18.62
J. E. Clark	136	..	28	..	409	..	20	..	20.45
*C. P. Willford	140	..	36	..	424	..	19	..	22.31
C. J. Guyver	77	..	11	..	281	..	10	..	28.10

WELLINGTON COLLEGE, BERKSHIRE

Played 12: Won 2, Lost 4, Drawn 6. Abandoned 5

Master i/c: D. J. Mordaunt   Cricket professional: P. J. Lewington

BATTING	Innings		Not Outs		Runs		Highest Inns		Average
M. G. Milliken-Smith	16	..	2	..	414	..	69	..	29.57
R. C. Crombie	14	..	1	..	341	..	58	..	26.23
*P. S. Lascelles	13	..	2	..	266	..	59	..	24.18
T. R. Sale	12	..	1	..	203	..	46	..	18.45
C. M. J. Bickford-Smith	11	..	2	..	117	..	23	..	13.00
R. C. Fedrick	14	..	0	..	176	..	61	..	12.57
M. C. Rogerson	12	..	2	..	104	..	24	..	10.40

BOWLING	Overs		Maidens		Runs		Wickets		Average
C. M. J. Bickford-Smith	122	..	59	..	211	..	18	..	11.72
S. P. Loup	147.3	..	64	..	273	..	18	..	15.16
R. C. Fedrick	114.5	..	22	..	364	..	22	..	16.54
A. E. Robertson	154.4	..	39	..	429	..	24	..	17.87

WESTMINSTER SCHOOL

Played 12: Won 1, Lost 7, Drawn 4

Master i/c: J. S. Baxter   Cricket professional: R. W. Gilson

BATTING	Innings		Not Outs		Runs		Highest Inns		Average
*S. M. Beadle	12	..	2	..	266	..	52*	..	26.60
S. Coles	12	..	1	..	178	..	72*	..	16.18
J. P. Warburg	12	..	0	..	175	..	34	..	14.58
M. J. Byam-Shaw	9	..	0	..	120	..	45	..	13.33
G. A. C. Davies	10	..	2	..	100	..	27	..	12.50
R. S. Rutnagur	12	..	1	..	130	..	29*	..	11.81

BOWLING	Overs		Maidens		Runs		Wickets		Average
R. S. Rutnagur	110.3	..	22	..	344	..	19	..	18.10
G. A. C. Davies	176.3	..	44	..	517	..	28	..	18.46
A. C. Beard	70.2	..	12	..	239	..	11	..	21.72
P. J. J. Wilson	76	..	6	..	358	..	15	..	23.86

WHITGIFT SCHOOL

Played 17: Won 5, Lost 5, Drawn 7. Abandoned 2

Master i/c: P. C. Fladgate   Cricket professional: D. G. W. Fletcher

BATTING	Innings		Not Outs		Runs		Highest Inns		Average
A. D. Vokes	7	..	2	..	146	..	95*	..	29.20
J. C. Carnes	16	..	1	..	366	..	86	..	24.40
M. J. Goodin	11	..	1	..	242	..	39	..	24.20
S. D. W. Horner	15	..	0	..	276	..	59	..	18.40
*P. H. D. Regan	17	..	2	..	219	..	48*	..	14.60
R. J. Ward	11	..	1	..	141	..	37	..	14.10
M. A. Lenton	15	..	2	..	158	..	26*	..	12.15
C. A. Marsh	17	..	1	..	154	..	32	..	9.62
N. W. A. Mann	17	..	0	..	130	..	31	..	7.64

BOWLING	Overs		Maidens		Runs		Wickets		Average
R. D. Ronald............	175	..	55	..	477	..	33	..	14.45
G. J. McEwan...........	209	..	53	..	503	..	30	..	16.76
R. J. Ward.............	58.3	..	13	..	231	..	11	..	21.00
J. M. Riches	121.4	..	24	..	473	..	16	..	29.56
P. H. D. Regan	160.3	..	42	..	414	..	14	..	29.57

WILLIAM HULME'S GRAMMAR SCHOOL

Played 21: Won 2, Lost 8, Drawn 11. Abandoned 1

Master i/c: I. J. Shaw

BATTING	Innings		Not Outs		Runs		Highest Inns		Average
S. P. Dickinson	21	..	1	..	657	..	94	..	32.85
A. P. Laker	19	..	5	..	369	..	85*	..	26.35
*D. B. Wright	21	..	0	..	420	..	90	..	20.00
R. P. Thornton	20	..	3	..	301	..	59*	..	17.70
N. M. Shaw	17	..	5	..	156	..	33	..	13.00
D. K. Smythe	17	..	1	..	192	..	45	..	12.00

BOWLING	Overs		Maidens		Runs		Wickets		Average
N. M. Shaw	93	..	30	..	225	..	16	..	14.06
A. D. Brown	123	..	33	..	294	..	20	..	14.70
P. A. Cotterill	251	..	70	..	711	..	48	..	14.81
G. L. Robinson	115	..	32	..	341	..	15	..	22.73

WINCHESTER COLLEGE

Played 15: Won 6, Lost 4, Drawn 5. Abandoned 2

Master i/c: J. F. X. Miller   Cricket professional: V. Broderick

BATTING	Innings		Not Outs		Runs		Highest Inns		Average
K. Storey...............	15	..	7	..	313	..	57	..	39.12
A. S. Hoare	16	..	1	..	395	..	93	..	26.33
P. M. McWhinnie	17	..	0	..	336	..	69	..	19.76
C. H. Myrtle	16	..	2	..	219	..	47	..	15.64
J. P. Medd	17	..	1	..	215	..	62	..	13.43
*A. R. Crocker	14	..	4	..	106	..	38*	..	10.60
J. M. Crocker	12	..	2	..	106	..	22	..	10.60

BOWLING	Overs		Maidens		Runs		Wickets		Average
M. B. H. Wheeler	261.5	..	78	..	653	..	49	..	13.32
M. J. Harford	96.1	..	28	..	281	..	15	..	18.73
A. R. Crocker...........	258.3	..	56	..	765	..	40	..	19.12
J. M. Crocker	84.3	..	19	..	256	..	13	..	19.69

WOODHOUSE GROVE SCHOOL

Played 14: Won 4, Lost 3, Drawn 7. Abandoned 1

Master i/c: J. F. Clay   Cricket professional: P. J. Kippax

BATTING	Innings		Not Outs		Runs		Highest Inns		Average
*D. A. Robinson.........	14	..	2	..	434	..	78	..	36.16
S. N. Driver............	14	..	0	..	347	..	87	..	24.78
I. W. Stott	9	..	3	..	119	..	44*	..	19.83
S. A. J. Kippax	12	..	3	..	164	..	55*	..	18.22
R. H. Simpson..........	12	..	0	..	136	..	36	..	11.33
P. N. Smith	10	..	0	..	103	..	43	..	10.30
S. A. Hill	12	..	1	..	101	..	39	..	9.18

BOWLING	Overs		Maidens		Runs		Wickets		Average
D. A. Robinson	111.2	..	31	..	287	..	21	..	13.66
S. Cockerill	74	..	16	..	223	..	14	..	15.92
J. M. Robinson	171.2	..	54	..	400	..	24	..	16.66
S. A. J. Kippax	88	..	16	..	350	..	20	..	17.50

WORKSOP COLLEGE

Played 12: Won 2, Lost 6, Drawn 4. Abandoned 1

Master i/c: N. S. Broadbent   Cricket professional: H. Newton

BATTING	Innings		Not Outs		Runs		Highest Inns		Average
A. P. Brookes	10	..	1	..	170	..	38	..	18.88
R. J. Wall	11	..	1	..	178	..	38	..	17.80
P. J. Wheeler	11	..	0	..	173	..	41	..	15.72
N. R. Cooke	12	..	0	..	179	..	58	..	14.91
S. N. Waddington	11	..	1	..	106	..	26	..	10.60

BOWLING	Overs		Maidens		Runs		Wickets		Average
S. N. Waddington	137.5	..	22	..	387	..	25	..	15.48
R. J. Wall	141	..	39	..	373	..	23	..	16.21
D. A. Smeaton	93	..	28	..	218	..	13	..	16.76

WREKIN COLLEGE

Played 17: Won 5, Lost 3, Drawn 9. Abandoned 1

Master i/c: E. C. Gower

BATTING	Innings		Not Outs		Runs		Highest Inns		Average
P. F. Hewitt	18	..	3	..	448	..	51*	..	29.86
*M. S. Bird	17	..	0	..	386	..	66	..	22.70
H. C. Dutton	13	..	5	..	181	..	35*	..	22.62
H. N. Sainsbury	16	..	4	..	239	..	41*	..	19.91
H. P. Taylor	15	..	5	..	196	..	38*	..	19.60
P. A. Stamp	14	..	0	..	269	..	44	..	19.21
J. R. MacKenzie	18	..	3	..	225	..	60	..	15.00
C. S. Joyner	13	..	2	..	130	..	30*	..	11.81
A. G. L. Beckett	13	..	1	..	123	..	37	..	10.25

BOWLING	Overs		Maidens		Runs		Wickets		Average
H. C. Dutton	228	..	59	..	647	..	35	..	18.48
A. C. Stubbs	209	..	56	..	587	..	29	..	20.24
J. R. MacKenzie	246	..	66	..	661	..	31	..	21.32
A. G. L. Beckett	180	..	38	..	493	..	18	..	27.38

WYCLIFFE COLLEGE

Played 14: Won 3, Lost 3, Drawn 8

Master i/c: P. J. C. Desprès

BATTING	Innings		Not Outs		Runs		Highest Inns		Average
*F. J. Hemming-Allen	14	..	1	..	513	..	117*	..	39.46
N. L. Smith	12	..	5	..	149	..	36*	..	21.28
T. G. Hale	13	..	1	..	198	..	58	..	16.50
A. P. Sims	14	..	0	..	187	..	45	..	13.35
D. W. Nicholls	14	..	3	..	101	..	18*	..	9.18
R. P. Ninnes	11	..	0	..	100	..	30	..	9.09

BOWLING	Overs		Maidens		Runs		Wickets		Average
A. C. Jones	140	..	36	..	330	..	25	..	13.20
A. W. Rowley	131.5	..	41	..	269	..	19	..	14.15
B. Hobill	149	..	39	..	300	..	18	..	16.66
D. W. Nicholls	84	..	20	..	225	..	13	..	17.30

WYGGESTON AND QUEEN ELIZABETH I
SIXTH FORM COLLEGE, LEICESTER

Played 10: Won 3, Lost 4, Drawn 3. Abandoned 2

Master i/c: A. Hirst/G. Wells

BATTING	Innings		Not Outs		Runs		Highest Inns		Average
A. Nicholls	7	..	0	..	192	..	56	..	27.42
*J. Waterfield	8	..	1	..	182	..	51	..	26.00

BOWLING	Overs		Maidens		Runs		Wickets		Average
J. Hubbard	53.4	..	16	..	121	..	13	..	9.30
A. Nicholls	43	..	9	..	156	..	11	..	14.18

The following schools provided averages too late to be included alphabetically.

CRANLEIGH SCHOOL

Master i/c: A. J. Corran

BATTING	Innings		Not Outs		Runs		Highest Inns		Average
J. G. Bennett	6	..	1	..	231	..	101*	..	46.20
M. J. Littleton	6	..	2	..	110	..	38*	..	27.50
D. A. Cardwell	7	..	0	..	146	..	75	..	20.85

BOWLING	Overs		Maidens		Runs		Wickets		Average
A. C. Gibb	50.5	..	16	..	115	..	12	..	9.58
M. W. D. Chetwode	62.3	..	21	..	155	..	10	..	15.50
P. J. L. Rollings	84	..	21	..	208	..	12	..	17.33
*A. D. Staples	75	..	18	..	246	..	10	..	24.60

SHREWSBURY SCHOOL

Played 24: Won 10, Lost 1, Drawn 13. Abandoned 1

Master i/c: C. M. B. Williams

BATTING	Innings		Not Outs		Runs		Highest Inns		Average
D. J. Saunders	24	..	3	..	756	..	108	..	36.00
*A. J. Pollock	24	..	1	..	807	..	116	..	35.08
G. R. T. Bishop	19	..	2	..	508	..	100*	..	29.88
J. C. C. Pettegree	22	..	4	..	499	..	83*	..	27.72
D. M. L. Heppard	17	..	7	..	243	..	43	..	24.30
R. G. W. Marsh	20	..	1	..	436	..	62	..	22.94

BOWLING	Overs		Maidens		Runs		Wickets		Average
M. C. B. McFarland	256.3	..	81	..	539	..	39	..	13.82
G. P. J. Bowden	269.3	..	71	..	627	..	43	..	14.58
R. M. White	98	..	28	..	266	..	18	..	14.77
A. J. Pollock	213	..	60	..	545	..	36	..	15.13
R. G. W. Marsh	298	..	73	..	873	..	54	..	16.16

IRISH CRICKET IN 1980

By DEREK SCOTT

Ireland began the 1980 season with a sequence of fifteen matches without defeat behind them, and this was extended to sixteen when MCC were rather easily beaten in a three-day match at Ormeau, Belfast. It was MCC's first defeat in Ireland since 1961.

A pitch damp from pre-match rain caused Ireland problems until the innings prospered during a sixth-wicket stand of 108 between R. I. Johnston (72) and J. D. Monteith (46). MCC replied with 166, and then Ireland declared at 178 for five, with B. A. O'Brien and I. Anderson both passing 50. MCC collapsed for 93 as J. W. G. Elder reaped a return of six for 43, five of them for 7 runs in one spell of 43 balls. The match, the only one of 1980 not held up by rain, was sponsored by Humphreys, Hollywood & Majury.

The West Indians visited Dublin for two 55 overs matches, sponsored by Rothmans with support from Aer Lingus, immediately after the Lord's Test. Rain ruined both games at Castle Avenue, the first so badly that it was agreed to call it a "draw". The West Indians made 105 for two in 35 overs (Bacchus 50) to which Ireland replied with 39 for five in 30 overs. Marshall was very hostile in gloomy conditions and only M. S. Reith prevented a complete rout. In the second match, the touring side raced to 284 for seven in 55 overs, with Bacchus hitting 163. At lunch, after 45 overs, he was 104; in the next seven overs he made 59, including seven 6s, three of them in one over from S. C. Corlett. In ten overs after lunch 109 runs were hit. Rain allowed Ireland only 30 overs off which they scored 82 for one, and so the match was lost by 73 runs on scoring-rate. For J. D. Monteith, it was his first defeat in seventeen matches as captain. The Rothman's Men of the Match awards went to Bacchus for the West Indians, on both days, and to M. S. Reith and M. Halliday for Ireland. Halliday, an off-spinner, bowled extremely well on both days, conceding 56 runs and taking one wicket in 21 overs.

In seeking a batsman-wicket-keeper for one-day cricket Ireland brought in a new cap, G. F. Murphy, for these matches, and he continued for the Gillette Cup first round tie against Middlesex at Lord's. A sunny day greeted the Irish in their first-ever competitive match, although the start was delayed by fifty minutes owing to a wet ground. Monteith won the toss and batted, feeling that this was the way to win the match, but despite the efforts of J. F. Short and I. Anderson, they were dismissed for 102. Van der Bijl finished with five for 12 as Ireland crashed from 99 for four and were left with eight overs in hand. Halliday, coming on for the eighth over and dismissing Radley with his first ball, took four for 22 in his twelve overs, and at 67 for five Middlesex must have felt some apprehension before van der Bijl struck out and won the match for them. A. J. Hughes winged his way through the night from Dublin to play in place of Elder, who became ill in London, and once again Aer Lingus were benefactors to the Irish team.

The season ended with two three-day matches. For the first, against Wales at Rathmines, Dublin, M. F. Cohen was brought in to win his first cap and an older cap, T. Harpur, restored. Out went R. I. Johnston and D. W. Harrison, and E. A. Bushe came back as wicket-keeper. The Welsh, despite injury to two players, had their best match since the series was renewed in 1971. Ireland declared at 288 for six, with Short making 54 and Anderson scoring his seventh century for Ireland; his first in Dublin. It was his eighteenth score of over 50 – beating S. F. Bergin's record – and he also became the first to score 3,000 runs for Ireland, in his 65th match. Wales took 119 overs to pass Ireland's total by 42, five of their batsmen making 41 or more, but with time already lost, a better match might have resulted had Wales declared sooner. The eventual Welsh target was 183 in about 34 overs, and they had reached 76 for three in sixteen overs when rain ended the match.

Rain was again the enemy at Coatbridge where the annual match against Scotland was drawn. For match details see Other Matches, 1980.

In the six matches, I. Anderson averaged 56.20 for his 281 runs, J. F. Short 31.57 for 221 runs, and B. A. O'Brien 27.75 for 222 runs. Five bowlers took all the wickets, S. C. Corlett having the lowest average, 20.46, and taking the most wickets, fifteen.

The Schools Match against Wales at Cardiff in August was almost entirely washed out. There followed an inaugural match against England at Bristol in which the Irish more than held their own.

After a nine-year gap Ulster Town regained the Guinness Cup, an inter-provincial tournament, in a close finish which involved three of the six teams. C. J. Harte was their leading batsman while S. C. Corlett and J. W. G. Elder took 28 wickets between them. A similar competition at Under 19 level, for the Esso Cup, was won by Ulster Country. The Leinster Under 15 team prevented a complete Northern domination by winning their tournament for the second successive year.

The two great club teams of the 1970s, Waringstown in the North and Phoenix in Dublin, won nothing in 1980. Phoenix, celebrating their 150th anniversary, ceded the John Player Knockout Cup to Pembroke after five successive wins. The Tyler League went to Malahide, by one point from Phoenix, while The Wiggins-Teape League was shared by Leinster and Clontarf, the fourth successive year in which the latter club has either won or shared this League.

In the Northern Union, Lisburn captured the League and North of Ireland Cricket Club took the Cup. Limavady won the Cup in the North-West when Sion Mills did not arrive to finish the two-innings final, for which the winners had imported Kapil Dev. Donemana won the League. In Munster, the Bank of Ireland-sponsored Cup and League were both won by Wanderers.

Highlights of 1981 will be the visits of Middlesex and Gloucestershire (in the NatWest Trophy) on successive Saturdays to Dublin. There will be a ten-day tour of England in August, while the Under 19 team will be in Denmark for the two-yearly International Youth Tournament.

SCOTTISH CRICKET IN 1980

By WATSON BLAIR

The acceptance by the Scottish Cricket Union of the offer to include Scotland in the Benson and Hedges Cup, albeit for a trial period of two seasons, was a milestone in Scotland's cricketing history. The appointment of Brian Close, the former England, Yorkshire and Somerset captain, as Scotland's team manager was a clear indication that the SCU was determined to make the best of the opportunity to participate in a national competition, and pre-season training was followed by two one-day matches in April against Worcestershire. Close had, by that time, reduced the 22-man squad to fifteen.

The first match saw Worcestershire score 239 for four off 55 overs, to which the Scots replied spiritedly with 187 for four: R. G. Swan 56, T. B. Racionzer 42, and S. K. Dharsi 37. The county again batted first in the second match, played under John Player League rules, and with Younis hitting 89 off 84 balls they reached 217 for seven. Bad light marred Scotland's innings, which began promisingly with 40 runs scored in ten overs, and they were all out for 137: Racionzer 40 and W. A. Donald 66.

As expected the Scots were beaten by Leicestershire, Derbyshire, Nottinghamshire and Lancashire during the initial stages of the Benson and Hedges Cup in May, but they were certainly not disgraced. R. G. Swan received the Gold Award for his fine 40 against Leicestershire at Titwood. With Brian Close again acting as mentor in 1981, Scotland can be expected to provide stiffer opposition and so ensure continuation in the competition. This would certainly encourage cricket in Scotland.

During the season Scotland introduced four new players to international cricket: D. G. Moir and D. L. Hays (both Aberdeenshire), S. K. Dharsi (Fifeshire) and G. M. Smith (West of Scotland).

However, the four-match programme suffered badly from interference by rain, with every match being affected. Before Scotland's match against the Netherlands in Glasgow, on June 27, 28, 29, the Dutch visitors had played two limited-over matches against the East and South Districts at Edinburgh and encountered the North and West Districts at Perth. In Glasgow, the Dutch began disastrously, losing three wickets to J. Clark in four overs for only 3 runs. However, opener D. Bekedam featured in three successive half-century stands and the Dutch recovered to close at 172. Bekedam's patient 86 took three and threequarter hours and included nine 4s. When Scotland batted, the Dutch lost their opening bowler, R. Van Weelde, after only three overs and Racionzer and Dharsi saw Scotland to 33 without loss by the close of play. Rain and bad light ruined the second day's play, and Racionzer had to wait until the final day to register his fourth century (125) for Scotland; rain having flooded the pitch when he was 98 not out. Aggressive batting by C. J. Warner and Donald enabled Scotland to declare at 272 for four, but the Dutch thwarted the Scottish bowling by holding out until the eleventh over of the last twenty, scoring 164 for seven in the process.

The two-day match against the West Indian tourists at Frothill, Broughty Ferry was another damp squib, and after the first day's play was abandoned it was agreed that the second day's play be substituted by a 50-overs match. Details may be seen in the West Indian tour section of this almanack. The Forfarshire club, in their centenary year, are to be congratulated on the excellent arrangements provided for the visit by the touring side.

The bi-annual visit to Lord's on August 11, 12 was another disappointment. MCC declared at tea when 85 for five, two hours having been lost to rain, and in seventy minutes, thanks to Swan and D. L. Hays, Scotland reached 78 for four at the close. The Scots then closed their innings, and with R. J. Lanchbury racing to an unbeaten 117, MCC declared at 229 for five, setting Scotland to score 237 in just over three hours. A fine third-wicket stand of 93 by D. L. Bell and Hays kept the Scots up with the clock, but once they were separated Scotland's prospects of winning at Lord's for the first time receded and at 170 for seven they settled for a draw.

The loss of four hours' play on the second day of the annual international against Ireland at Langloan, Coatbridge, on August 16, 17, 18 resulted in yet another rain-affected draw. Scotland were unable to press home the advantage of a first innings lead of 107 and Ireland had little difficulty in playing out time. During the match G. F. Goddard, the Scottish captain, became only the third Scottish international to achieve the coveted double of 1,000 runs and 100 wickets for Scotland. J. M. Allan and D. Barr were the other two.

Although, yet again, the season ended with Scotland failing to win a match, the "B" side had an excellent summer. In June, under the captaincy of J. Clark, they trounced the Central Lancashire League by nine wickets at Royton – for the second successive year – and followed this with a seven-wicket victory at Selkirk over a strong Durham county side which included four professionals. Scotland's Young Cricketers (Under 19 and Under 16) showed up well against their counterparts from the Welsh and English schools, drawing all four of their matches. D. Wilson, the NCA coach in Scotland, can take much credit for the fine performances of the young players.

The hard wickets which prevailed in May gave way to wet, dismal conditions and the domestic programme was adversely affected. The North retained their Inter-District Championship title after a somewhat disappointing series. In the Shish Mahal Cup, now accepted as the Scottish Cup of cricket, Stenhousemuir easily beat West of Scotland in the replayed final at Hamilton Crescent. The original final, a fortnight earlier, had been abandoned during West of Scotland's innings.

Heriot's FP successfully retained the Ryden and Partners East League championship, finishing unbeaten with 207 points (94%) followed by Watsonians, Carlton and Stenhousemuir. Watsonians defeated Stenhousemuir in the final of the Masterton Trophy.

Individual honours went to W. D. G. Loudon (Edinburgh Acads), who again scored the fastest league 50 of the season, and to T. M. Alderman, Watsonian's Western Australian professional, who won the Bill Green Trophy for the most wickets (43): D. J. M. Ramsay (Royal High) returned the best bowling figures, nine for 48 against Edinburgh Acads, while his team-mate, R. B. Crawford, registered the highest individual innings, 116 not out against Stenhousemuir. The former Middlesex player, T. Selwood (Stenhousemuir), scored 714 runs (avge 71.40), including four centuries, and captured 30 wickets for 371 runs.

A special Sportsmanship Award of £25, taking into account punctuality, turn-out, compliance with umpires' decisions, appeal behaviour, avoidance of delays, language, sociability and general attitude, was won by Royal High with 94 per cent.

Aberdeenshire again won the Beneagles Scottish Counties competition followed by Perthshire, Forfarshire, and West Lothian. The last-named, however, overcame Aberdeenshire to win the Beneagles Quaich knockout competition. P. Clifford, Clackmannanshire's Australian professional, topped the batting averages with 733 runs, including three centuries, while D. L. Hays (Aberdeenshire), the former Cambridge Blue, finished as top amateur with 370 runs from six completed innings. D. Carter, the West Indian professional with Fifeshire, was again to the fore, taking 50 wickets for 510 runs.

Clydesdale carried all before them in the D. M. Hall and Son Western Union championships, winning the first, second and third XI competitions. Ferguslie, who supplied the top two amateurs in batting and bowling (D. Heaton, 491 runs, and D. F. Forrest, 33 wickets) were runners-up, closely followed by Drumpellier and Poloc. Professionals played a leading part in the Union. W. R. Scarff (Greenock), from Western Australia, led the batting averages with 639 runs, including two centuries, while O. Henry (Poloc), from Transvaal, captured 33 wickets for 349 runs and also hit 666 runs. K. J. Hagdorn, another Western Australian, claimed 56 wickets for 757 runs in his final season with West of Scotland.

Selkirk won both the Blacklock Farries Border League and the Border Knockout Cup, with two clubs, Hawick & Wilton and Kelso, sharing second place. The Abbey Life Glasgow and District League title was won by Prestwick, who also won the Cup final from East Kilbride. Altogether it was a very successful season for the Ayrshire club, as they won the Reserve Division and were finalists in the Rowan Charity Cup, which they lost to Clydesdale, the Western Union champions. Meigle won the Grasshopper Strathmore Union with Strathmore as runners-up, and completed the double by defeating Strathmore in the final of the Three Counties Cup.

A. M. Zuill, the Stenhousemuir captain, took his aggregate of runs for the club to 21,996 at the end of the season, a new record for a Scottish club. The previous holder was the late John Kerr, who amassed 21,558 runs for Greenock. Zuill, a member of the SCU committee, played fifteen times for Scotland between 1962 and 1979 and, with several playing years ahead of him, should establish an almost unassailable aggregate of runs.

ENGLAND v REST OF THE WORLD

In 1970, owing to the cancellation of the South African tour to England, a series of matches was arranged, with the trappings of a full Test series, between England and the Rest of the World. It was played for the Guinness Trophy.

Captains				
England	*Rest*	*Matches*	*Won by England*	*Won by Rest*
R. Illingworth	G. S. Sobers	5	1	4

HIGHEST TOTALS FOR AN INNINGS

By England	**By Rest of the World**
409 at Birmingham	563-9 at Birmingham

LOWEST TOTALS FOR AN INNINGS

By England	**By Rest of the World**
127 at Lord's	276 at Nottingham

INDIVIDUAL HUNDREDS IN THE MATCHES

For England (3)

157 G. Boycott, The Oval	113* B. W. Luckhurst, Nottingham
110 B. L. D'Oliveira, Birmingham	

For Rest of the World (8)

119 E. J. Barlow, Lord's	101 C. H. Lloyd, Birmingham
142 E. J. Barlow, Nottingham	114 R. G. Pollock, The Oval
100 R. B. Kanhai, The Oval	183 G. S. Sobers, Lord's
114* C. H. Lloyd, Nottingham	114 G. S. Sobers, Leeds.

HAT-TRICK AND FOUR WICKETS IN FIVE BALLS

E. J. Barlow (Rest of the World), Leeds.

APPEARANCES FOR REST OF THE WORLD

E. J. Barlow (5), F. M. Engineer (2), L. R. Gibbs (4), Intikhab Alam (5), R. B. Kanhai (5), C. H. Lloyd (5), G. D. McKenzie (3), D. L. Murray (3), Mushtaq Mohammad (2), P. M. Pollock (1), R. G. Pollock (5), M. J. Procter (5), B. A. Richards (5), G. S. Sobers (5).

Note: A list of those players who appeared for England in these matches may be found on page 177.

ENGLAND IN AUSTRALIA AND INDIA, 1979-80

By PETER SMITH

Forty-eight hours before England's cricketers flew out of Melbourne for the last time, Alec Bedser was asked by the Australian authorities to present his considered view of the experimental twin-tour programme, the first product of the marriage between the Australian Cricket Board and World Series Cricket which had taken place some nine months earlier. He gave it a definite "thumbs down". It was a strictly personal view, sought not in his capacity as England's tour manager or as chairman of England's selectors but from a man who has had the closest possible association with the game through four decades. He received majority support from those who had the best interests of cricket at heart, particularly Australian cricket below Test level. This had been swamped by the accent on Test and one-day internationals, neatly parcelled to present a cricketing package suitable for maximum exploitation on television.

Privately, at least, the Australian players agreed with Bedser. With a programme of six Test matches – three each against England and West Indies – plus the triangular one-day competition for the Benson and Hedges World Series Cup, the Australian players became very much a touring side inside their own country. So anxious was their captain Greg Chappell to rejoin a family he had hardly seen for two months that he was flying home to Brisbane within an hour of bringing the final Test against England in Melbourne to a swift and victorious conclusion.

England's cricketers were just as unhappy with the complicated programme of matches that brought a constant switch from one-day to five-day cricket with few three-day matches in between. It could be claimed that England's verdict was coloured by their three-nil series defeat in the Tests, but Clive Lloyd, West Indies' captain, was just as critical immediately after his side's two-nil series win – their first in Australia at the sixth attempt – and their victory in the World Series Cup.

It was not only the match programme but the whole atmosphere that the England players found disagreeable. Their captain, Brearley, was the subject of a disgraceful campaign wherever he went, and a large section of the Melbourne crowd was so abusive that the Australian team manager, John Edwards, was moved to issue a statement in which he said they made him ashamed to be an Australian. The childish behaviour of Lillee during the aluminium bat affair during the first Test in Perth and his baiting of Brearley during a one-day international in Sydney proved as distasteful to them as the treatment they received from the crowd in the early night games under the Sydney floodlights when they became the target of an assortment of missiles.

The show-business style presentation of the one-day matches by the marketing company advising the Australian Cricket Board succeeded in appealing to a "new" public, but the loutish, drunken behaviour of many of the newcomers posed additional headaches for the ground authorities. Both in Melbourne and Sydney costly extra security measures were taken, along with a restriction on the amount of alcohol sold inside the grounds or taken in. This improved the behaviour but not the language.

In losing the actual Test series against this background it could be said that England achieved all that was expected of them when they arrived in Australia. For the first time for three years, the Australians had available their full complement of players, with Lillee and Thomson, destroyers of England in two previous series, on hand to team up with Hogg, who had taken 41 Test wickets against England the previous winter. Greg Chappell was back to provide the leadership and batting expertise missing twelve months earlier, and there were half a dozen others rich in Test experience. The availability of these players promised to provide England with their toughest opposition since Brearley assumed the captaincy in 1977. Against more modest bowling attacks, England's batting had proved brittle in the in-between years. Against Australia it failed to function as a unit, even though Thomson was seldom fit to take part and Hogg disappeared from the series, losing both his confidence and fitness after a severe mauling from West Indies.

There were pockets of resistance in each Test match, such as Boycott's unbeaten 99 in the second innings in the first Test in Perth when trying to save the game, Gower's unbeaten 98 in the second innings of the second Test in Sydney, Gooch's 99 in the first innings of the final Test in Melbourne and Botham's 119 not out in the second innings to delay Australia's victory. Brearley, too, offered stern resistance in every Test; but Lillee proved that, at 30, he was still a match-winning bowler, even if he had lost that explosive edge. He took 23 wickets in the series, eleven of them in the final Test in Melbourne when he cut his pace and produced a mixture of leg- and off-cutters which drew the highest praise from Brearley.

Apart from the batting failures, the England bowling lacked penetration after Hendrick was forced to return home with a shoulder injury received in his first spell in the opening match of the tour. His bowling was greatly missed. England were relying on his accuracy in the one-day games and each of the Test wickets encountered would have helped him, particularly the one in Perth. His absence – plus that of his Derbyshire colleague Miller, who was also forced to return home, and of Old, who had asked not to be considered – affected England's close-catching potential. Overall England's fielding slipped from the high match-winning standard reached in recent years.

With problems in all departments, Brearley was not as positive as he might have been in countering them. He is not a captain for laying down the law. The England sides under his command have been happy sides, and he seemed reluctant to risk spoiling that harmony by remonstrating with his batsmen even when they continued to display a lack of discipline and sense of responsibility. In fairness, Brearley was also burdened at the start of the tour with additional tasks that should have been no part of his brief and that led directly to his unpopularity with sections of the Australian crowd. Communication difficulties with the Australian Board resulted in England and West Indies arriving with the playing conditions still to be finalised. Renewed pressure was put on Brearley to accept conditions already rejected by the Test and County Cricket Board, namely the wearing of coloured stripes on shirts, flannels and sweaters, using a white ball in day-time matches, and restrictive fielding circles – as used in World Series Cricket – for the one-day internationals. As the spokesman outlining England's objections to conditions which seemed designed principally for television, Brearley was portrayed as a "whingeing Pom", which was grossly unfair. It must be hoped that no future captain is ever landed with such a burden.

Part of England's batting problems stemmed from the pre-tour idea of turning Randall into an opening batsman; a move inspired by his performance for Nottinghamshire late in the season when he scored a double century and century against Middlesex. Taking into consideration the need to score quickly at the start in the one-day competitions and the desire to fit him into the Test side, the idea appeared to have its merits when Randall, having spent three weeks playing for a club side in Perth, scored 97 opening the innings against Queensland in the first match of the tour. But from that moment on, his form slumped alarmingly. A double failure when opening in the first Test at Perth resulted in his being dropped down the order for the second Test, and he eventually lost his place in the one-day side as well. Randall finished the tour a confused figure, having lost his way in attempting to apply various technical theories to counter the Australian bowlers.

Gower was another disappointment. After topping the averages in Australia twelve months earlier, the Leicestershire left-hander was regarded as the key middle-order batsman, but only in the later stages of his innings of 98 in the Sydney Test did he rediscover his true touch and timing. Still only 22, perhaps too much was expected of him. Nobody would wish to curb his attacking bent, but the tour management was entitled to demand a more responsible selection of strokes than those that resulted in his dismissal when England were already deep in trouble.

In the absence of Miller, Willey played a key rôle in England's one-day challenge, both as a tidy off-spinner and number three batsman. But he found the rôle beyond him when it came to the Test matches, managing only 35 runs in his six innings. His Northamptonshire colleague Larkins was perhaps unfortunate. Taken along as the third opening batsman, he was left in the cold for long periods by the move to turn Randall into an opener, and he was desperately short of practice when called into the side for the final Test.

With Botham having a lean time with the bat until his final innings in Australia and his one-man exhibition of all his talents in the Jubilee Test against India, it was left to Boycott and, later, Gooch to carry the batting along with Brearley's acts of resistance lower down the order. Being left out of England's first one-day international wounded Boycott's pride, and in response he produced two of the finest innings of the tour. It is doubtful whether he has ever played better than when scoring a century in England's third one-day international, making 105 in 46 overs against Australia, or when a week later, at Perth, he showed his other side with a six hours thirty-five minutes occupation of the crease for 99 not out in a brave attempt to earn England a draw in the first Test.

Neck and finger injuries hampered Boycott in mid-tour, just at the time when Gooch was finding his feet. Surprisingly left out of the first Test team when England used both off-spinning all-rounders, Miller and Willey, plus the left-arm spin of Underwood on a wicket which helped seam bowlers, Gooch worked hard on his technique against the faster bowlers in the nets. He finished the tour a more complete batsman than at the start and missed his maiden Test century, in Melbourne, only by running himself out.

The absence of Hendrick was further highlighted by the decline of Willis as a strike bowler. So unlucky at Perth, by the end of the tour he had surrendered the use of the new ball. This in turn left Botham carrying a heavy burden, and he performed heroically as both new ball and stock bowler. His performance in the first Test was staggering, bowling 80.5 overs and claiming eleven for 176. He surpassed it, though, with thirteen wickets in the Jubilee Test in Bombay, plus a century, as he continued to rewrite the records. Botham finished as England's leading wicket-taker in the series, followed by Underwood, in spite of the latter having difficulty finding his rhythm through a lack of regular bowling. The bonus was the emergence of Underwood's Kent colleague, Dilley. Unable to get a regular place in the Kent side at the start of the 1979 summer, Dilley won a place in the Test team and, at times, looked faster than anybody on either side.

Lever, a model tourist, waited patiently for his chance and took it well in the final Test in Australia and again in Bombay where he bowled without any luck. Replacements Emburey and Stevenson – for Miller and Hendrick – did well enough in their fleeting appearances, and England could not have been served better by their two wicket-keepers. Bairstow was used in the one-day matches, while Taylor was reserved for the Tests and finished the tour in Bombay by setting a new world Test record of ten catches in the match.

At the end of the tour Brearley and Greg Chappell were in agreement that the final margin was as misleading as England's 5-1 series win had been twelve months earlier. The sides were evenly matched, the experience of Chappell and Lillee, the improvement of Hughes, and the winning of the toss in the second Test being the vital factors. The Australians were indeed fortunate to have Greg Chappell back, and the return of his elder brother Ian, surprising as it was after twice being in trouble for incidents involving umpires when leading South Australia, also added much steel to the Australian batting.

Lillee was again the leading influence in the attack, discovering a new rôle with his cutters which could keep him in the Australian side for two or three seasons yet. Additionally, Australia overcame the loss of Thomson and Hogg by utilising the left-arm medium pace of Dymock. He was their outstanding bowler in the first Test and a constant threat throughout the series, building on his fine tour of India just prior to England's visit.

Perhaps the hardest task undertaken by Greg Chappell was raising his side twice to take on England immediately following crushing defeats by West Indies. He said each time it was not a problem because he was always confident of beating England, an attitude which was reflected in his own batting.

ENGLAND TOUR RESULTS

In Australia

Test matches – Played 3: Lost 3.

First-class matches – Played 8: Won 3, Lost 3, Drawn 2.

Wins – Tasmania, Queensland, New South Wales.

Losses – Australia (3).

Draws – Queensland, South Australia.

Non first-class matches – Played 12: Won 7, Lost 4, Drawn 1. *Wins* – Northern New South Wales (2), West Indies, Australia (4). *Losses* – West Indies (4). *Draw* – Combined Universities.

In India

Test match – Played 1: Won 1.

TEST MATCH AVERAGES

AUSTRALIA – BATTING

	Tests	Innings	Not Outs	Runs	Highest Inns	Average
G. S. Chappell	3	6	2	317	114	79.25
I. M. Chappell	2	4	1	152	75	50.66
A. R. Border	3	5	1	199	115	49.75
K. J. Hughes	3	5	0	183	99	36.60
B. M. Laird	2	4	0	132	74	33.00
J. M. Wiener	2	4	0	104	58	26.00
R. B. McCosker	2	4	0	77	41	19.25
R. W. Marsh	3	4	0	70	42	17.50
G. Dymock	3	4	1	48	20*	16.00
D. K. Lillee	3	4	0	50	19	12.50
L. S. Pascoe	2	2	2	11	10*	–

Played in one Test: R. J. Bright 17, 12; J. D. Higgs 2; A. A. Mallett 25; J. R. Thomson 1*, 8; P. M. Toohey 19, 3.

Signifies not out.

BOWLING

	Overs	Maidens	Runs	Wickets	Average
G. Dymock	130.3	40	260	17	15.29
G. S. Chappell	42	21	66	4	16.50
D. K. Lillee	155.1	41	388	23	16.86
L. S. Pascoe	93.5	17	241	10	24.10
J. R. Thomson	32	6	100	3	33.33

Also bowled: R. J. Bright 25–11–36–1; A. A. Mallett 49–10–149–1; A. R. Border 6–0–23–0; J. D. Higgs 1–0–3–0; J. M. Wiener 8–3–22–0.

ENGLAND – BATTING†

	Tests	Innings	Not Outs	Runs	Highest Inns	Average
G. A. Gooch	2	4	0	172	99	43.00
G. R. Dilley	2	4	2	80	38*	40.00
I. T. Botham	3	6	1	187	119*	37.40
G. Boycott	3	6	1	176	99*	35.20
J. M. Brearley	3	6	1	171	64	34.20
D. I. Gower	3	6	1	152	98*	30.40
R. W. Taylor	3	6	0	102	32	17.00
D. L. Underwood	3	6	0	71	43	11.83
D. W. Randall	2	4	0	26	25	6.50
P. Willey	3	6	0	35	12	5.83
R. G. D. Willis	3	6	0	21	11	3.50

Played in one Test: W. Larkins 25, 3; J. K. Lever 22, 12; G. Miller 25, 8.

* *Signifies not out.* † *Test matches v Australia only.*

BOWLING†

	Overs	Maidens	Runs	Wickets	Average
I. T. Botham	173.1	62	371	19	19.52
D. L. Underwood	160.2	48	405	13	31.15
J. K. Lever	60.4	18	129	4	32.25
G. R. Dilley	53	5	143	3	47.66
R. G. D. Willis	98	26	224	3	74.66

Also bowled: G. A. Gooch 19–6–36–2; G. Miller 21–2–66–0; P. Willey 19–2–56–0.

† *Test matches v Australia only.*

ENGLAND TEAM AVERAGES – FIRST-CLASS MATCHES

(Includes 1 Test match v India)

BATTING

	Matches	Innings	Not Outs	Runs	Highest Inns	Average
G. A. Gooch	7	14	3	639	115	58.09
G. Boycott	8	15	4	599	110	54.45
G. Miller	4	6	2	203	71	50.75
I. T. Botham	6	10	1	331	119*	36.77
G. R. Dilley	5	6	3	101	38*	33.66
G. B. Stevenson	4	5	2	91	33	30.33
J. M. Brearley	7	11	1	302	81	30.20
P. Willey	6	12	3	269	101*	29.88
D. I. Gower	9	15	2	354	98*	27.23
D. W. Randall	6	10	0	250	97	25.00
R. W. Taylor	8	11	1	227	47*	22.70
W. Larkins	6	10	1	190	90	21.11
J. E. Emburey	3	4	0	71	50	17.75
J. K. Lever	7	7	2	75	22	15.00
D. L. Underwood	6	8	0	88	43	11.00
R. G. D. Willis	4	6	0	21	11	3.50

Also batted: D. L. Bairstow 1, 12; M. Hendrick 1.

* *Signifies not out.*

BOWLING

	Overs	Maidens	Runs	Wickets	Average
I. T. Botham	242	81	532	34	15.64
D. L. Underwood	260.1	81	609	25	24.36
G. B. Stevenson	87	13	307	11	27.90
G. R. Dilley	88.1	11	243	7	34.71
J. K. Lever	236	55	622	16	38.87
J. E. Emburey	111.2	25	282	7	40.28
P. Willey	111	17	332	7	47.42
G. Miller	106	20	268	5	53.60

Also bowled: G. A. Gooch 45–13–113–3; R. G. D. Willis 113–30–252–3; G. Boycott 4–0–19–0; M. Hendrick 4–1–14–0; W. Larkins 6–0–15–0.

FIELDING

R. W. Taylor 30 (29 ct, 1 st), G. A. Gooch 9, D. I. Gower 6, I. T. Botham 5, J. M. Brearley 5, D. L. Underwood, 5, J. K. Lever 4, G. Boycott 3, W. Larkins 3, G. Miller 3, D. W. Randall 3, P. Willey 3, D. L. Bairstow 2, G. R. Dilley 2, J. E. Emburey 2.

HUNDREDS FOR ENGLAND

The following eight three-figure innings were played for the England team during the tour, two of which were not first-class.

G. Boycott (3)
    110 v South Australia at Adelaide
    †105 v Australia at Sydney (B & H World Series Cup)
    101* v Tasmania at Hobart

I. T. Botham (2)
    119* v Australia at Melbourne (Third Test)
    114 v India at Bombay

G. A. Gooch (2)
    †124 v Combined Universities at Adelaide
    115 v Queensland at Brisbane

P. Willey (1)
    101* v Queensland at Brisbane

    * *Signifies not out.*   † *Not first-class.*

HUNDREDS AGAINST ENGLAND

The following two three-figure innings were played against the England team during the tour.

A. R. Border (1)
    115 for Australia at Perth (First Test)

G. S. Chappell (1)
    114 for Australia at Melbourne (Third Test)

QUEENSLAND v AN ENGLAND XI

At Brisbane, November 12, 13, 14. Drawn. England emerged from their first match of the tour better than anticipated after heavy rain had washed out all but one full practice session in Sydney. On a green wicket offering movement and bounce, they scored a psychological victory over Thomson, who was limited to one wicket after openly boasting of the havoc he would cause. On the debit side was the shoulder injury to Hendrick, who was forced out of the attack after bowling only four overs and later returned home. The move to make Randall an opening batsman proved successful. He held England's first innings together with 97 after they had been put in and made to struggle against the medium pace of Rackemann, playing only his second first-class match. Dilley bowled impressively in his first outing in Australia.

An England XI

D. W. Randall c Madders b Rackemann	97	– c Chappell b Thomson 7
G. Boycott c Chappell b Schuller	11	– c Madders b Schuller 20
D. I. Gower c Chappell b Schuller	2	– c Thomson b Schuller......... 50
G. A. Gooch c Kent b Rackemann	11	– c Thomson b Rackemann 9
P. Willey lbw b Cosier	1	– not out 57
*J. M. Brearley c Cosier b Rackemann	16	– c Kent b Rackemann 5
G. Miller c Broad b Rackemann	16	– not out 57
†D. L. Bairstow c Thomson b Carlson	1	
G. R. Dilley not out	4	
J. K. Lever c Madders b Rackemann	0	
M. Hendrick b Broad	1	
B 1, l-b 3, w 7, n-b 5	16	B 6, l-b 6, w 6, n-b 3 21

1/46 2/53 3/84 4/96 5/154	**176**	1/16 2/77 (5 wkts dec.) **226**
6/159 7/170 8/175 9/175		3/99 4/101 5/117

Bowling: First Innings—Thomson 8–1–26–0; Rackemann 14–7–25–5; Schuller 12–2–39–2; Carlson 11.2–1–38–1; Cosier 10–2–17–1; Hohns 4–0–15–0; Broad 1.3–1–0–1. *Second Innings*—Thomson 18–6–46–1; Rackemann 18–8–35–2; Schuller 18–4–54–2; Cosier 10–2–20–0; Hohns 19–6–46–0; Broad 1–1–0–0; Chappell 6–3–4–0.

Queensland

K. C. Wessels c Gooch b Lever	2	
W. R. Broad c Willey b Dilley	6	– not out 34
M. F. Kent c and b Miller	58	– (1) c Gooch b Dilley 12
*G. S. Chappell c Bairstow b Dilley	12	– (3) not out 49
G. J. Cosier c Gooch b Lever	43	
P. H. Carlson c Gooch b Dilley	2	
T. V. Hohns run out	62	
†G. J. Madders c Lever b Willey	19	
D. C. Schuller not out	2	
C. G. Rackemann c Brearley b Miller	3	
B 3, l-b 1, w 1, n-b 5	10	L-b 2 2

1/3 2/15 3/45 4/102 5/113	(9 wkts dec.) **219**	1/14 (1 wkt) **97**
6/140 7/208 8/214 9/219		

J. R. Thomson did not bat.

Bowling: First Innings—Lever 18–6–43–2; Dilley 15–3–40–3; Hendrick 4–1–14–0; Gooch 8–3–16–0; Miller 21–5–47–2; Willey 12–1–30–1; Boycott 4–0–19–0. *Second Innings*—Lever 6–1–14–0; Dilley 3.1–0–16–1; Gooch 4–0–26–0; Miller 7–0–22–0; Willey 7–0–17–0.

Umpires: C. E. Harvey and R. Willmott.

NORTHERN NEW SOUTH WALES v AN ENGLAND XI

At Newcastle, November 17. An England XI won by nine wickets. At the request of the Australian authorities England experimented with a white ball for their two 50 overs matches against Northern New South Wales. Boycott and Larkins found it much to their liking with 120 for the first wicket to set up a comfortable victory.

Northern New South Wales 133 (48 overs) (C. Beatty 67; G. R. Dilley three for 22, D. L. Underwood three for 30); An England XI 136 for one (43 overs) (G. Boycott 78, W. Larkins 38 not out).

NORTHERN NEW SOUTH WALES v AN ENGLAND XI

At Newcastle, November 18. An England XI won by 32 runs. Half-centuries by Larkins and Brearley, who put on 105 together for the second wicket, were the feature of England's innings in the second Newcastle match. As on the previous day, Underwood's left-arm bowling posed too many problems for the local side.

An England XI 213 for seven (W. Larkins 51, J. M. Brearley 67); Northern New South Wales 181 for seven (G. G. Geise 58 not out, C. J. Evans 32; D. L. Underwood three for 17).

COMBINED UNIVERSITIES v AN ENGLAND XI

At Adelaide, November 22, 23, 24, 25 (Not first-class). Drawn. England had an embarrassing first two and half days against the students in their final match before the start of the triangular one-day international series. None more so than Boycott, who was felled by a rising delivery from the Universities' opening bowler, Clough, soon after the start of the second innings and forced to go off, an incident keenly noted by the Australian and West Indian fast bowlers. The Universities' batsmen experienced their own difficulties against the varied pace and flighted deliveries of Underwood. England atoned for their first innings failure when they batted a second time. Gooch made the first century of the tour in three hours twenty-three minutes, Botham a spirited 76 in ninety-four minutes and Taylor an unbeaten 66 before England called a halt to their much-needed batting practice. Wellham, batting almost four hours, scored 95 in the Universities' second innings, being out in the final over attempting to reach his century.

An England XI 179 (D. W. Randall 61; G. Kirkwood five for 52) and 411 for eight dec. (G. A. Gooch 124, I. T. Botham 76, R. W. Taylor 66 not out, G. Boycott 41, J. K. Lever 37, P. Willey 34; G. Kirkwood four for 96); Combined Universities 168 (C. Beatty 53, G. Kirkwood 37; D. L. Underwood eight for 41) and 227 for five (D. B. Wellham 95, P. J. Davies 57, C. Beatty 35; D. L. Underwood three for 50).

At Sydney, November 28. ENGLAND beat WEST INDIES by 2 runs (See Benson and Hedges World Series Cup section).

TASMANIA v AN ENGLAND XI

At Hobart, November 30, December 1, 2. An England XI won by 100 runs. Only two balls remained when Underwood took the final wicket to complete another outstanding match. Part of the credit belonged to the Tasmania captain, Davison of Rhodesia and Leicestershire, for a sporting declaration in his first innings after gale-force winds and rain had washed out most of the second day. He also helped by asking England to bat on a good wicket, Boycott responding with his first century of the tour and so enabling Willis to declare with the innings five and a half hours old. Davison's declaration at the start of the third day initiated feverish activity. After Gooch and Gower had scored freely, Willis responded by setting Tasmania to make 279 in 240 minutes, but Underwood, making full use of a strong wind, made sure they had no hope of reaching their target by taking seven for 66.

An England XI

G. Boycott not out	101		
W. Larkins st Woolley b Goodman	21	– (3) not out	8
D. W. Randall c Goodman b Campbell	34		
G. A. Gooch c Hadlee b Campbell	51	– (1) not out	70
D. I. Gower (did not bat)		– (2) b Campbell	53
L-b 4, n-b 3	7	L-b 2, w 1, n-b 1	4

1/37 2/126 3/214   (3 wkts dec.) 214   1/102   (1 wkt dec.) 135

G. Miller, †R. W. Taylor, G. R. Dilley, D. L. Underwood, J. K. Lever and *R. G. D. Willis did not bat.

Bowling: *First Innings*—Hadlee 13–6–17–0; Blizzard 17–5–49–0; Wilson 11–2–25–0; Goodman 23–7–59–1; Campbell 16.3–1–57–2. *Second Innings*—Hadlee 5–1–16–0; Blizzard 5–1–21–0; Wilson 7–0–31–0; Goodman 5–1–37–0; Campbell 4.5–0–26–1.

Tasmania

G. W. Goodman not out	28	– run out	8
R. L. Knight c Dilley b Underwood	22	– (3) c Lever b Underwood	74
B. M. Campbell lbw b Underwood	9	– (8) c Gower b Miller	0
D. A. Smith c Taylor b Underwood	2	– (2) c Larkins b Underwood	0
D. C. Boon not out	6	– (4) c Gower b Underwood	35
*B. F. Davison (did not bat)		– (5) lbw b Underwood	15
†R. D. Woolley (did not bat)		– (6) c Miller b Underwood	24
T. W. Docking (did not bat)		– (7) c sub b Underwood	0
R. J. Hadlee (did not bat)		– c Gooch b Underwood	14
G. J. Wilson (did not bat)		– b Miller	0
P. A. Blizzard (did not bat)		– not out	2
L-b 1, n-b 3	4	L-b 3, n-b 3	6

1/34 2/59 3/64   (3 wkts dec.) 71   1/47 2/48 3/91 4/125   178
                                          5/136 6/136 7/138
                                          8/167 9/168

Bowling: *First Innings*—Dilley 10–2–24–0; Lever 8–3–17–0; Willis 8–2–15–0; Underwood 15.1–11–11–3. *Second Innings*—Dilley 7–1–20–0; Lever 1–0–1–0; Willis 7–2–13–0; Underwood 30.4–12–66–7; Miller 30–5–72–2.

Umpires: A. Jones and R. Marshall.

SOUTH AUSTRALIA v AN ENGLAND XI

At Adelaide, December 4, 5, 6. Drawn. England's second match at Adelaide coincided with the return of Ian Chappell after his three-week suspension following an incident involving an umpire when leading South Australia in their first match of the season. And his reappearance saw his involvement in another umpiring incident as he disputed a decision while batting in South Australia's first innings. This time he was given a suspended sentence. Unfortunately the action of the former Australian captain overshadowed the better features of the match, including Boycott's second century in successive games and the 117th of his career, which equalled the number scored by Sir Donald Bradman on Bradman's home ground. Brearley shared the opening responsibilities with Boycott and their 174-run partnership put down the foundation of the innings. On a typical Adelaide wicket, even three declarations never looked like producing a result.

An England XI

G. Boycott c and b Sleep	110	– (8) not out	63
*J. M. Brearley c Nash b Sleep	81		
P. Willey not out	32	– (1) c Robertson b Prior	13
G. Miller not out	26	– (7) c Darling b Sleep	71
W. Larkins (did not bat)		– (2) c sub b Mallett	19
D. I. Gower (did not bat)		– (3) lbw b Sleep	27
†D. L. Bairstow (did not bat)		– (4) lbw b Prior	12
†R. W. Taylor (did not bat)		– (5) c Nash b Mallett	0
I. T. Botham (did not bat)		– (6) lbw b Prior	4
G. B. Stevenson (did not bat)		– (9) not out	15
L-b 2, n-b 1	3	B 3	3

1/174 2/199   (2 wkts. dec.) 252   1/16 2/54 3/64   (7 wkts. dec.) 227
4/72 5/76 6/76 7/207

J. K. Lever did not bat.

Bowling: *First Innings*—Prior 11–2–34–0; McLellan 17–2–61–0; Hammond 11–2–15–0; Attenborough 6–0–30–0; Sleep 26–7–82–2; Chappell 1–1–0–0; Mallett 12–3–27–0. *Second Innings*—Prior 13–3–27–3; McLellan 9–4–24–0; Hammond 10–2–27–0; Attenborough 12–2–39–0; Sleep 22.5–8–62–2; Mallett 22–7–45–2.

South Australia

W. M. Darling lbw b Miller	45	– not out	75
J. E. Nash hit wkt b Botham	48	– c Taylor b Lever	0
*I. M. Chappell c Bairstow b Botham	0	– b Stevenson	19
J. J. Crowe not out	78	– b Willey	55
P. R. Sleep c Boycott b Stevenson	29	– not out	30
J. R. Hammond not out	17		
L-b 9	9	L-b 1, n-b 1	2

1/93 2/93 3/93 4/153   (4 wkts. dec.) 226   1/1 2/41 3/112   (3 wkts.) 181

†T. J. Robertson, G. R. Attenborough, R. McLellan, A. A. Mallett and W. Prior did not bat.

Bowling: *First Innings*—Lever 22–7–44–0; Botham 16–4–43–2; Stevenson 13–2–41–1; Miller 21–7–42–1; Willey 11–4–36–0; Larkins 4–0–11–0. *Second Innings*—Lever 11–0–53–1; Botham 4–1–12–0; Stevenson 10–2–31–1; Miller 6–1–19–0; Willey 16–0–60–1; Larkins 2–0–4–0.

Bairstow kept wicket in the first innings, Taylor in the second innings.

Umpires: G. McLeod and M. G. O'Connell.

At Melbourne, December 8. ENGLAND beat AUSTRALIA by three wickets.

At Sydney, December 11. ENGLAND beat AUSTRALIA by 72 runs (See Benson and Hedges World Series Cup section).

AUSTRALIA v ENGLAND

First Test Match

At Perth, December 14, 15, 16, 18, 19. Australia won by 138 runs. It was unfortunate that Australia's victory at the end of an enthralling match was soured by Lillee's unsavoury behaviour in seeking to use an aluminium bat in the first innings despite objections from Brearley, the umpires and his own captain. He caused play to be held up for ten minutes before being persuaded by Chappell to exchange it for the traditional willow. The incident served only to blacken Lillee's reputation and damage the image of the game as well as, eventually, the reputation of the Australian authorities because of their reluctance to take effective disciplinary action.

Lillee's behaviour also partly overshadowed other individual performances more in keeping with the spirit of the game, notably the bowling of Botham and Dymock, the batting of Hughes and Border, and Boycott's gallant attempt to save England on the final day.

Although only once before had an England captain won a Test in Australia when asking the opposition to bat first – at Melbourne in 1912 – Brearley opted for that course now to support the decision to go into the match with two off-spinning all-rounders, plus Underwood who was making his first Test appearance in Perth. Brearley must have been reasonably content with his decision when Australia's first innings closed at 244. It was built in the main around Hughes, who made 99 in almost four hours and defied the remarkable bowling effort of Botham, being used as both strike and stock bowler. In 35 overs Botham took six wickets. But any feelings of satisfaction Brearley held were soon swept away as Randall and Boycott went without scoring and the first six England wickets fell for only 90 runs. Brearley rescued the situation himself, batting stubbornly for four hours ten minutes in making 64 and producing one of his best innings for his country. Dilley, on his first Test début, gave him fine support, batting nearly three and a half hours for his 38 not out, and Australia's lead was limited to 16.

By the end of the third day, however, Australia appeared to be in a strong position, 174 ahead with eight second innings wickets in hand, after Wiener, with a half-century in his first Test, and Laird had opened with a stand of 91. But another marathon bowling stint by Botham, refreshed after the rest day, changed the situation dramatically, and Australia owed much to Border for their eventual lead of 353 with an innings of 115 in six hours twenty-four minutes. He was repeatedly in trouble against Botham early on but survived to pass 1,000 runs in Tests in eleven days short of a year. Botham, with five wickets in the innings, ended with match figures of eleven for 176 from 80 overs and five balls.

Only sixty-five minutes remained of the fourth day when England started their second innings, but it was time enough for Randall's second failure before bad light stopped play. Worse was to follow on the final day, most of the wounds self-inflicted by lack of application as England lost wickets regularly while Chappell switched his attack intelligently and Dymock responded with accurate seam bowling. Only Boycott showed the technique and determination needed to survive and he was still unbeaten, 1 short of his century, when England's last man, Willis, became Dymock's sixth victim with 14.4 of the last twenty overs left.

Australia

J. M. Wiener run out	11	– c Randall b Underwood	58
B. M. Laird lbw b Botham	0	– c Taylor b Underwood	33
A. R. Border lbw b Botham	4	– c Taylor b Willis	115
*G. S. Chappell c Boycott b Botham	19	– st Taylor b Underwood	43
K. J. Hughes c Brearley b Underwood	99	– c Miller b Botham	4
P. M. Toohey c Underwood b Dilley	19	– c Taylor b Botham	3
†R. W. Marsh c Taylor b Dilley	42	– c Gower b Botham	4
R. J. Bright c Taylor b Botham	17	– lbw b Botham	12
D. K. Lillee c Taylor b Botham	18	– c Willey b Dilley	19
G. Dymock b Botham	5	– not out	20
J. R. Thomson not out	1	– b Botham	8
B 4, l-b 3, n-b 2	9	B 4, l-b 5, w 2, n-b 7	18

1/2 2/17 3/20 4/88 5/127   244   1/91 2/100 3/168 4/183   337
6/186 7/219 8/219 9/243   5/191 6/204 7/225
                                                      8/303 9/323

Bowling: *First Innings*—Dilley 18–1–47–2; Botham 35–9–78–6; Willis 23–7–47–0; Underwood 13–4–33–1; Miller 11–2–30–0. *Second Innings*—Dilley 18–3–50–1; Botham 45.5–14–98–5; Willis 26–7–52–1; Underwood 41–14–82–3; Miller 10–0–36–0; Willey 1–0–1–0.

England

	First Innings		Second Innings	
D. W. Randall	c Hughes b Lillee	0	lbw b Dymock	1
G. Boycott	lbw b Lillee	0	not out	99
P. Willey	c Chappell b Dymock	9	lbw b Dymock	12
D. I. Gower	c Marsh b Lillee	17	c Thomson b Dymock	23
G. Miller	c Hughes b Thomson	25	c Chappell b Thomson	8
*J. M. Brearley	c Marsh b Lillee	64	(7) c Marsh b Bright	11
I. T. Botham	c Toohey b Thomson	15	(6) c Marsh b Lillee	18
†R. W. Taylor	b Chappell	14	b Lillee	15
G. R. Dilley	not out	38	c Marsh b Dymock	16
D. L. Underwood	lbw b Dymock	13	c Wiener b Dymock	0
R. G. D. Willis	b Dymock	11	c Chappell b Dymock	0
	L-b 7, n-b 15	22	L-b 3, w 1, n-b 8	12

1/1 2/12 3/14 4/41 5/74   228   1/8 2/26 3/64 4/75 5/115   215
6/90 7/123 8/185 9/203   6/141 7/182 8/211 9/211

Bowling: *First Innings*—Lillee 28–11–73–4; Dymock 29.1–14–52–3; Chappell 11–6–5–1; Thomson 21–3–70–2; Bright 2–0–6–0. *Second Innings*—Lillee 23–5–74–2; Dymock 17.2–4–34–6; Chappell 6–4–6–0; Thomson 11–3–30–1; Bright 23–11–30–1; Wiener 8–3–22–0; Border 2–0–7–0.

Umpires: M. G. O'Connell and D. G. Weser.

At Brisbane, December 23. ENGLAND lost to WEST INDIES by nine wickets.

At Sydney, December 26. ENGLAND beat AUSTRALIA by four wickets (See Benson and Hedges World Series Cup section).

QUEENSLAND v AN ENGLAND XI

At Brisbane, December 28, 29, 30, 31. An England XI won by 138 runs. Two fine innings by Gooch, seeking to regain his Test place, and a good all-round performance from Willey enabled Botham to emerge successfully from his first experience of captaincy since his school days. After Randall failed again as an opener, Gooch took charge for four hours, making 115, and a final flourish from Emburey, in his first game since joining the party as Miller's replacement, enabled England to make 324. After a weakened Queensland side was bowled out for 237, Gooch (53) and then Willey, with his first century of the tour, enabled Botham to declare. Queensland never looked like making the 362 needed once Botham turned to Emburey and Willey, who responded with three wickets each.

An England XI

	First Innings		Second Innings	
D. W. Randall	c Langley b Rackemann	0	c Phillips b Balcam	42
W. Larkins	c Langley b Schuller	5	c Phillips b Schuller	19
G. A. Gooch	c sub b Rackemann	115	c Morgan b Cosier	53
P. Willey	c Phillips b Rackemann	30	not out	101
*I. T. Botham	c Parker b Hohns	21	c Langley b Hohns	5
D. I. Gower	c Phillips b Schuller	3	b Hohns	13
†R. W. Taylor	c Hohns b Cosier	32	b Cosier	3
J. E. Emburey	b Schuller	50	c Langley b Hohns	5
G. B. Stevenson	c Langley b Balcam	33	b Cosier	0
G. R. Dilley	c Phillips b Balcam	17		
J. K. Lever	not out	4	(10) not out	16
	B 4, l-b 4, w 1, n-b 5	14	B 6, l-b 3, w 2, n-b 6	17

1/0 2/6 3/83 4/120 5/148   324   1/54 2/77   (8 wkts dec.) 274
6/194 7/253 8/283 9/311   3/169 4/178 5/214 6/225
                                          7/236 8/237

Bowling: *First Innings*—Rackemann 22–5–72–3; Schuller 27–3–74–3; Balcam 9.4–1–41–2; Cosier 8–3–14–1; Hohns 32–8–87–1; Broad 5–1–22–0. *Second Innings*—Rackemann 9–1–35–0; Schuller 7–0–31–1; Balcam 8–1–54–1; Cosier 19–1–43–3; Hohns 26–3–94–3; Broad 1–1–0–0.

Queensland

*G. J. Cosier run out	13	– c Randall b Stevenson	3
M. G. Morgan c Taylor b Lever	50	– c Gooch b Lever	28
A. D. Ogilvie b Gooch	5	– b Emburey	42
T. V. Hohns b Emburey	1	– (6) c Emburey b Willey	10
J. N. Langley c Taylor b Lever	5	– (4) c Larkins b Willey	16
W. R. Broad c Randall b Emburey	53	– (5) c Botham b Emburey	45
A. D. Parker not out	52	– b Willey	9
†R. B. Phillips c Taylor b Stevenson	12	– c Gower b Emburey	29
D. C. Schuller c Botham b Emburey	36	– c Emburey b Lever	25
L. F. Balcam b Willey	1	– absent hurt	0
C. G. Rackemann c Taylor b Willey	5	– (10) not out	4
N-b 4	4	B 10, l-b 2	12

1/19 2/30 3/35 4/67 5/89 6/138   237   1/14 2/41 3/83 4/113 5/140   223
7/163 8/212 9/221   6/154 7/162 8/201 9/223

Bowling: *First Innings*—Lever 15–3–39–2; Stevenson 14–4–43–1; Gooch 4–2–6–1; Emburey 28–7–80–3; Willey 15–1–65–2. *Second Innings*—Lever 12–5–25–2; Stevenson 4–0–29–1; Emburey 39.2–11–89–3; Willey 31–9–68–3.

Umpires: R. Willmott and M. W. Johnson.

AUSTRALIA v ENGLAND

Second Test Match

At Sydney, January 4, 5, 6, 8. Australia won by six wickets with a day to spare. A decision to give the Sydney groundstaff the day off to celebrate the New Year virtually decided the outcome of the second Test and the three-match series. The pitch was late exposed to a violent thunderstorm, and further rain over the following two days resulted in it still being damp and patchy when the match began three hours fifty minutes late.

Winning the toss almost guaranteed victory. Chappell, who protested that conditions were not fit, won it, and although the pitch was never as spiteful as many imagined, England were bundled out in 43 overs, a strange selection of strokes by the middle-order batsmen helping their downfall. Even so, it is doubtful whether Australia would have matched England's 123 if England's bowlers had been given first use of the pitch.

Brearley wasted little time introducing Underwood into his attack on the second day – he was on after only four overs – but once again it was Botham who proved the more effective as Australia inched to a 22-run lead. For this modest advantage they were heavily indebted to Ian Chappell, recalled to Test cricket after a three-year absence to add experience to the batting, who demonstrated his undoubted class during his one hundred and five minutes stay.

By the close on the second day England were in trouble once more, having lost three wickets for 59 and been forced to send in Underwood as night-watchman. He took this rôle so seriously that he turned it into a day-time occupation next day, surviving until after lunch and falling to a catch at short leg only 2 runs short of his highest Test score. Brearley and Randall proved effective partners for Underwood before Gower took over to boost England's hopes of squaring the series. Gower lived dangerously during his first half-century, going for his strokes but missing as often as he connected. Once he reached his 50, though, almost immediately everything clicked and for the last hundred minutes of his innings he again looked one of the most talented batsmen in the world. Like Boycott in Perth, Gower was denied his century, being 98 when Willis was last out.

Australia, requiring 216 to clinch the series, were 191 short with all second innings wickets intact when the rest day started. England were convinced both Wiener and McCosker should have been given out during the last thirty-five minutes of the third day and they suffered a further disappointment on the fourth when Greg Chappell, then 32, survived a concerted appeal for a catch behind off Dilley. A wicket at that stage and England would have been well in the hunt. Both openers, plus Ian Chappell, had fallen and Greg Chappell and Hughes were still struggling to impose their authority. The not out verdict by umpire Bailhache proved the turning-point, for the Australian captain and his vice-captain added 105 in 137 minutes to put victory in sight. Chappell, having secured it, was offered a long hop by Botham for the winning runs, and a chance to reach his century with a 6, but he managed only a 4.

England

G. A. Gooch b Lillee	18	– c G. S. Chappell b Dymock	4
G. Boycott b Dymock	8	– c McCosker b Pascoe	18
D. W. Randall c G. S. Chappell b Lillee	0	– (6) c Marsh b G. S. Chappell	25
P. Willey c Wiener b Dymock	8	– (3) b Pascoe	3
*J. M. Brearley c Pascoe b Dymock	7	– (4) c Marsh b Pascoe	19
D. I. Gower b G. S. Chappell	3	– (7) not out	98
I. T. Botham c G. S. Chappell b Pascoe	27	– (8) c Wiener b G. S. Chappell	0
†R. W. Taylor c Marsh b Lillee	10	– (9) b Lillee	8
G. R. Dilley not out	22	– (10) b Dymock	4
R. G. D. Willis c Wiener b Dymock	3	– (11) c G. S. Chappell b Lillee	1
D. L. Underwood c Border b Lillee	12	– (5) c Border b Dymock	43
N-b 5	5	B 1, l-b 10, w 1, n-b 2	14

1/10 2/13 3/31 4/38 5/41   123   1/6 2/21 3/29 4/77 5/105   237
6/74 7/75 8/90 9/98   6/156 7/174 8/211 9/218

Bowling: *First Innings*—Lillee 13.3–4–40–4; Dymock 17–6–42–4; Pascoe 9–4–14–1; G. S. Chappell 4–1–19–1; Higgs 1–0–3–0. *Second Innings*—Lillee 24.3–6–63–2; Dymock 28–8–48–3; Pascoe 23–3–76–3; G. S. Chappell 21–10–36–2.

Australia

R. B. McCosker c Gower b Willis	1	– (2) c Taylor b Underwood	41
J. M. Wiener run out	22	– (1) b Underwood	13
I. M. Chappell c Brearley b Gooch	42	– c Botham b Underwood	9
*G. S. Chappell c Taylor b Underwood	3	– not out	98
K. J. Hughes c Taylor b Botham	18	– c Dilley b Willis	47
A. R. Border c Gooch b Botham	15	– not out	2
†R. W. Marsh c Underwood b Gooch	7		
D. K. Lillee c Brearley b Botham	5		
G. Dymock c Taylor b Botham	4		
L. S. Pascoe not out	10		
J. D. Higgs b Underwood	2		
B 2, l-b 12, w 2	16	L-b 8, w 1	9

1/18 2/52 3/71 4/92 5/100   145   1/31 2/51 3/98   (4 wkts) 219
6/114 7/121 8/129 9/132   4/203

Bowling: *First Innings*—Botham 17–7–29–4; Willis 11–3–30–1; Underwood 13.2–3–39–2; Dilley 5–1–13–0; Willey 1–0–2–0; Gooch 11–4–16–2. *Second Innings*—Botham 23.3–12–43–0; Willis 12–2–26–1; Underwood 26–6–71–3; Dilley 12–0–33–0; Willey 4–0–17–0; Gooch 8–2–20–0.

Umpires: R. C. Bailhache and W. J. Copeland.

At Melbourne, January 12. ENGLAND v WEST INDIES. Abandoned.

At Sydney, January 14. ENGLAND beat AUSTRALIA by two wickets.

At Adelaide, January 16. ENGLAND lost to WEST INDIES by 107 runs.

At Melbourne, January 20. ENGLAND lost to WEST INDIES by 2 runs.

At Sydney, January 22. ENGLAND lost to WEST INDIES by eight wickets (See Benson and Hedges World Series Cup section).

NEW SOUTH WALES v AN ENGLAND XI

At Canberra, January 27, 28, 29. An England XI won by eight wickets. Two declarations by Walters set up a thrilling finish and allowed England their third first-class win of the tour after being set 253 to win in one hundred and forty-five minutes plus 20 overs. They were sporting gestures by the former Test player after England had been on the defensive for the best part of the match. Sound batting by former Australian vice-captain Hilditch and Trevor Chappell, the youngest of the Chappell brothers, gave Walters the chance to make his second declaration with only two wickets down. On a good batting surface England always looked like winning the race, with Larkins leading the way in one of his rare tour appearances and doing enough to remind the selectors of his presence. A final asault by Gooch and Gower clinched victory with sixteen balls left.

New South Wales

A. M. J. Hilditch c Underwood b Stevenson	21	– c Taylor b Underwood	78
J. Dyson b Stevenson	5	– b Stevenson	45
T. M. Chappell c Taylor b Stevenson	6	– not out	70
I. C. Davis c Gooch b Stevenson	2	– not out	37
P. M. Toohey c Taylor b Underwood	38		
*K. D. Walters b Lever	62		
G. R. Beard c sub b Emburey	27		
†S. J. Rixon not out	31		
G. F. Lawson not out	17		
B 1, l-b 1, w 1	3	L-b 8, n-b 5	13

1/10 2/28 3/36   (7 wkts dec.) 212   1/112 2/162   (2 wkts dec.) 243
4/37 5/99 6/154 7/182

R. P. Done and R. G. Holland did not bat.

Bowling: *First Innings*—Lever 18–4–42–1; Stevenson 15–2–44–4; Gooch 4–0–15–0; Underwood 23–4–49–1; Embury 20–0–59–1. *Second Innings*—Lever 21–3–68–0; Stevenson 12–1–47–1; Gooch 2–0–11–0; Underwood 24–5–50–1; Embury 24–7–54–0.

An England XI

G. A. Gooch b Beard	28	– (3) not out	73
G. Boycott c Rixon b Lawson	2	– (1) c Toohey b Beard	51
W. Larkins c Hilditch b Lawson	0	– (2) c Toohey b Done	90
D. I. Gower c Rixon b Done	3	– not out	35
*J. M. Brearley c Beard b Done	24		
D. W. Randall c and b Beard	44		
†R. W. Taylor not out	47		
J. E. Embury c Toohey b Holland	8		
G. B. Stevenson b Holland	16		
J. K. Lever b Holland	0		
D. L. Underwood b Lawson	16		
B 2, l-b 4, n-b 9	15	L-b 4, n-b 1	5

1/7 2/10 3/26 4/53 5/89   203   1/124 2/169   (2 wkts) 254
6/126 7/143 8/165 9/165

Bowling: *First Innings*—Lawson 15.5–3–55–3; Done 13–5–24–2; Beard 20–8–40–2; Holland 24–8–62–3; Chappell 4–2–7–0. *Second Innings*—Lawson 7–1–17–0; Done 13–1–67–1; Beard 19–2–65–1; Holland 17–3–76–0; Chappell 2–0–6–0; Walters 3–1–14–0; Toohey 0.2–0–4–0.

Umpires: A. S. Ward and R. G. Harris.

AUSTRALIA v ENGLAND

Third Test Match

At Melbourne, February 1, 2, 3, 5, 6. Australia won by eight wickets. A fine innings of 99 by Gooch enabled England to start their first innings with a bang on their last appearance in Australia. And a remarkable second innings century by Botham, with only the tail end batsmen for support, allowed them to finish with a captivating flourish. In between, however, events were largely dictated by Lillee bowling a mixture of leg- and off-cutters which presented Australia with a clean sweep in the series.

England looked to have every chance of ending the tour on a high note when Brearley, having won the toss, elected to bat and Gooch and Boycott produced England's highest opening partnership since they scored 111 together against New Zealand at Trent Bridge in 1978. When Boycott went at 116, Larkins, on his Test début, helped Gooch take the score to 170 before the all-too-familiar middle-order collapse began. Five wickets fell for the addition of 22 runs, including that of Gooch who ran himself out in the final over before tea going for the single that would have brought him his maiden Test century. Once again England were indebted to a defiant unbeaten innings from Brearley – he batted for close on four hours – while Lillee, with six wickets, caused the damage at the other end.

England's total of 306 was their best of the series but Australia had little difficulty building a useful lead of 171. With the exception of Hughes, all their leading batsmen were among the runs. Laird, a gritty, determined opening batsman, and Ian Chappell put on 127 for the second wicket; Greg Chappell and Border added 126 for the fifth, the Australian captain spending the rest day on 99 and needing 1 run to complete his sixteenth Test century and second of the summer. The third delivery on the fourth morning saw him duly reach it after two hundred and fifty-four minutes at the crease, during which time he suffered both a leg injury and a stomach upset. Lever, playing his first Test of the series, was England's most successful bowler, putting in one memorable stint when he bowled for more than two hours without a break.

Although the wicket was offering help to the bowler capable of cutting the ball, there seemed no reason why England, with sensible batting and application, should not make it tight for Australia. Yet within two and a half hours England were 88 for five and Australia appeared set for an innings victory. Botham's entrance changed the picture. He soon lost Brearley, but with the help of Taylor – 32 in an hour and a half – and Lever – 12 in 106 minutes – the England all-rounder showed the Australians how well he could bat by scoring a century in exactly two hundred minutes.

Left to make 103 to win in just under two and a half hours, Australia set about their task cautiously, determined not to repeat England's mistakes. Even so they lost both their opening batsmen in the first hour and a half and still required another 61 when Greg Chappell joined his elder brother. In another fifty-three minutes it was all over, Greg Chappell having helped himself to 40 of those runs as he batted with supreme arrogance.

England

G. A. Gooch run out	99	– b Mallett	51
G. Boycott c Mallett b Dymock	44	– b Lillee	7
W. Larkins c G. S. Chappell b Pascoe	25	– lbw b Pascoe	3
D. I. Gower lbw b Lillee	0	– b Lillee	11
P. Willey lbw b Pascoe	1	– c Marsh b Lillee	2
I. T. Botham c Marsh b Lillee	8	– (7) not out	119
*J. M. Brearley not out	60	– (6) c Border b Pascoe	10
†R. W. Taylor b Lillee	23	– c Border b Lillee	32
D. L. Underwood c I. M. Chappell b Lillee	3	– b Pascoe	0
J. K. Lever b Lillee	22	– c Marsh b Lillee	12
R. G. D. Willis c G. S. Chappell b Lillee	4	– c G. S. Chappell b Pascoe	2
B 1, l-b 2, n-b 14	17	B 2, l-b 12, n-b 10	24
	306		**273**

1/116 2/170 3/175 4/177 5/177   1/25 2/46 3/64 4/67 5/88
6/192 7/238 8/242 9/296   6/92 7/178 8/179 9/268

Bowling: *First Innings*—Lillee 33.1–9–60–6; Dymock 28–6–54–1; Mallett 35–9–104–0; Pascoe 32–7–71–2. *Second Innings*—Lillee 33–6–78–5; Dymock 11–2–30–0; Mallett 14–1–45–1; Pascoe 29.5–3–80–4; Border 4–0–16–0.

Australia

R. B. McCosker c Botham b Underwood	33	– lbw b Botham	2
B. M. Laird c Gower b Underwood	74	– c Boycott b Underwood	25
I. M. Chappell c and b Underwood	75	– not out	26
K. J. Hughes c Underwood b Botham	15		
A. R. Border c and b Lever	63		
*G. S. Chappell c Larkins b Lever	114	– (4) not out	40
†R. W. Marsh c Botham b Lever	17		
D. K. Lillee c Willey b Lever	8		
G. Dymock b Botham	19		
A. A. Mallett lbw b Botham	25		
L. S. Pascoe not out	1		
B 13, l-b 12, w 1, n-b 7	33	L-b 8, n-b 2	10

1/52 2/179 3/196 4/219 5/345   477   1/20 2/42   (2 wkts) 103
6/411 7/421 8/432 9/465

Bowling: *First Innings*—Lever 53–15–111–4; Botham 39.5–15–105–3; Willis 21–4–61–0; Underwood 53–19–131–3; Willey 13–2–36–0. *Second Innings*—Lever 7.4–3–18–0; Botham 12–5–18–1; Willis 5–3–8–0; Underwood 14–2–49–1.

Umpires: R. C. Bailhache and P. M. Cronin.

INDIA v ENGLAND

Golden Jubilee Test

At Bombay, February 15, 17, 18, 19. England won by ten wickets with a day to spare. With the rival sides fatigued, both mentally and physically, at the end of an arduous season, the Test match to celebrate the Golden Jubilee of the Board of Control for Cricket in India produced poor cricket. But it was redeemed by an extraordinary all-round performance by Botham, whose versatility was in full bloom. There was hardly a session on which he did not bring his influence to bear, performing the unprecedented feat of scoring a century and capturing thirteen wickets in a Test. Taylor, the England wicket-keeper, also established a new world Test record by taking ten catches in the match.

To England, after the Test series in Australia, this success, even if inspired by one man, brought welcome relief. But for India, the defeat ended an unbeaten run of fifteen Test matches, four of which they had won.

With the pitch uncharacteristically grassy, England were at no disadvantage from losing the toss; even less so as an overcast sky was a further aid to swing and cut on the opening morning. The Indians, jaded after playing sixteen Tests in the past seven months, could not summon the application and discipline needed to combat these conditions and were bowled out in less than a day for 242, Botham taking six for 58 and Taylor taking seven catches. India would have fared even worse but for gallant resistance from the lower order of their batting.

Batting as indifferently as they did in Australia, England at 58 for five looked most unlikely to match India's score, let alone build on the advantage created by their bowlers. But they were only 13 runs behind when they lost their next wicket two hours twenty minutes later. Botham, batting for 206 minutes and hitting 17 4s, scored 114 in an innings which was responsible and yet not lacking in enterprise. His stand of 171 with Taylor was England's best-ever sixth-wicket partnership against India. Taylor remained entrenched until the third day was more than an hour old and altogether scored 43 in a stay of four and a half hours. Yet their stand could have been cut short at only 85 when umpire Hanumantha Rao upheld an appeal against Taylor for a catch behind the wicket, off Kapil Dev. Taylor hesitated and protested at the decision. Viswanath, the Indian captain, who was fielding at first slip, was as certain as the batsman that there had been no contact and persuaded the umpire to rescind his verdict.

Even on the third day there was sufficient bounce and movement off the seam to trouble the Indian batsmen. Showing little spirit, India were only 2 runs ahead with half their second-innings wickets gone, and but for an innings of 45 not out by Kapil Dev, who batted in the forthright manner of Botham, the match might not have gone into the fourth day.

The recent history of Test pitches at the Wankhede Stadium – earlier in the season both Australia and Pakistan were beaten in four days, with spinners causing the havoc – prompted England to equip themselves with two specialist spinners in Underwood and Emburey. In the event Underwood bowled only seven overs and Emburey none at all. Of the ten wickets captured by the Indians, their opening bowlers, Ghavri and Kapil Dev, took five and three wickets, respectively. – D. R.

India

S. M. Gavaskar c Taylor b Botham	49	– c Taylor b Botham	24
R. M. Binny run out	15	– lbw b Botham	0
D. B. Vengsarkar c Taylor b Stevenson	34	– lbw b Lever	10
*G. R. Viswanath b Lever	11	– c Taylor b Botham	5
S. M. Patil c Taylor b Botham	30	– lbw b Botham	0
Yashpal Sharma lbw b Botham	21	– lbw b Botham	27
Kapil Dev c Taylor b Botham	0	– (8) not out	45
†S. M. H. Kirmani not out	40	– (7) c Gooch b Botham	0
K. D. Ghavri c Taylor b Stevenson	11	– c Brearley b Lever	5
S. Yadav c Taylor b Botham	8	– c Taylor b Botham	15
D. R. Doshi c Taylor b Botham	6	– c and b Lever	0
B 5, l-b 3, n-b 9	17	B 4, l-b 8, w 1, n-b 5	18

1/56 2/102 3/108 4/135 5/160   242   1/4 2/22 3/31 4/31 5/56   149
6/160 7/181 8/197 9/223   6/68 7/102 8/115 9/148

Bowling: *First Innings*—Lever 23–3–82–1; Botham 22.5–7–58–6; Stevenson 14–1–59–2; Underwood 6–1–23–0; Gooch 4–2–3–0. *Second Innings*—Lever 20.1–2–65–3; Botham 26–7–48–7; Stevenson 5–1–13–0; Underwood 1–0–5–0.

England

G. A. Gooch c Kirmani b Ghavri	8	– not out	49
G. Boycott c Kirmani b Binny	22	– not out	43
W. Larkins lbw b Ghavri	0		
D. I. Gower lbw b Kapil Dev	16		
*J. M. Brearley lbw b Kapil Dev	5		
I. T. Botham lbw b Ghavri	114		
†R. W. Taylor lbw b Kapil Dev	43		
J. E. Emburey c Binny b Ghavri	8		
J. K. Lever b Doshi	21		
G. B. Stevenson not out	27		
D. L. Underwood b Ghavri	1		
B 8, l-b 9, n-b 14	31	B 3, l-b 1, n-b 2	6

1/21 2/21 3/45 4/57 5/58   296   (no wkt) 98
6/229 7/245 8/262 9/283

Bowling: *First Innings*—Kapil Dev 29–8–64–3; Ghavri 20.1–5–52–5; Binny 19–3–70–1; Doshi 23–6–57–1; Yadav 6–2–22–0. *Second Innings*—Kapil Dev 8–2–21–0; Ghavri 5–0–12–0; Doshi 6–1–12–0; Yadav 6–0–31–0; Patil 3–0–8–0; Gavaskar 1–0–4–0; Viswanath 0.3–0–4–0.

Umpires: J. D. Ghosh and S. N. Hanumantha Rao.

THE WEST INDIANS IN AUSTRALIA, 1979-80

By TONY COZIER

West Indies achieved an historic and satisfying triumph over Australia in their three-match series that formed part of an unusual and revolutionary season for that country in 1979-80. In five previous tours of Australia, West Indies had always been the losers, defeat often so great as to amount to humiliation. This time they were not to be denied, converting their clear superiority over Australia into massive victories in the last two Tests after the first had been drawn.

The result was especially pleasing as this team included nine of those who had endured the 5-1 drubbing four years earlier, captain Lloyd and vice-captain Deryck Murray among them. However, they were well prepared, all but six of the party having been members of the World Series Cricket West Indies squad which had played in Australia over the two previous seasons.

Not only did West Indies retain the Worrell Trophy by securing the Test series; they also confirmed their standing as the game's most efficient limited-overs combination by defeating England in the finals of the limited-overs Benson and Hedges World Series Cup. The large proportion of the major honours – and the prize money – was theirs. Vivian Richards was voted the outstanding player of both the Test and limited-overs series, and Gordon Greenidge the player of the limited-overs finals. The team's winnings amounted to $A86,000.

West Indies' success was based principally on the magnificent batting of Richards and on their quartet of fast bowlers – Roberts, Holding, Garner and Croft – who maintained persistent pressure on opposing batsmen and were well supported by safe-handed close-catching. In addition, an intensive physical fitness schedule paid dividends in reducing injuries to a minimum.

Few individuals have so dominated a season as Richards did this one. Statistics help tell some of the story. In the Tests, he scored 140 at Brisbane, 96 at Melbourne, and 76 and 74 at Adelaide. In the World Series Cup, his sequence was 9, 153 not out, 62, 85 not out, 88, 23 and 65. Outside the Tests he batted in only two first-class innings, scoring 79 and 127. He gathered his runs with the command and range of strokes of the truly great batsmen, scoring freely against bowling of every type. That he was suffering at the time from groin and back trouble so acute that he was often forced to limp painfully emphasised the extraordinary nature of his performance.

The batting of his team-mates suffered by comparison. None of them could find consistent form although Lloyd, at the end of a season troubled by injury and self-doubt, contributed a vital and typically belligerent century on the first day of the final Test. Greenidge improved steadily from an uncertain beginning and played two sterling innings in the one-day finals, while Kallicharran chose the very last opportunity to register his only significant score of the series, a century in the second innings of the final Test. In the field, Lloyd always had at his disposal an almost irresistible form of attack, he and his co-selectors adhering rigidly to a policy of pace to the exclusion of spin.

Whereas West Indies possessed a stronger, fitter and better prepared team than they had four years earlier, the Australians were nothing like the force they were then. Greg Chappell, reinstated as captain, and Lillee, slower but shrewder, remained their outstanding individuals. Yet too much depended on these two, and the strain told. Chappell, after batting with all his old authority in the first Test, fell three times in his last four innings to the bouncer. His vice-captain, Hughes, played freely in the second innings at Brisbane and Melbourne, but the only batsman who scored with any consistency was the diminutive Western Australian opener, Laird. In his first Test series, Laird showed determination and courage, passing 50 in four of his six innings.

Perhaps Australia's biggest disappointments were in the lack of support for Lillee, the failure of Marsh's batting, and the lack of an adequate all-rounder. There were well-founded local hopes that, with Lillee and Thomson now joined by Hogg, the pace of the West Indians would be matched ball for ball. Instead, Thomson, troubled by injury, was not half the menace he had been, and Hogg was also reduced by injury, a disheartening blow following his exploits of the previous season against England. It was left to the veteran left-armer Dymock to fill the gap, which he tried nobly to do. Australia might have turned more to spin, but in the event the three spinners used, Bright, Higgs and Mallett, each played in only a single Test against West Indies.

Arranged as it was with the emphasis on the Tests and limited-overs internationals, the tour offered little opportunity for the reserve players, whose cricketing education suffered as a result. It was this aspect of the experimental, triangular international arrangement which caused most concern, although there was a body of opinion that the format of this exceptional season would be the prototype of future international cricket. As to this, only time will tell.

WEST INDIAN TOUR RESULTS

Test matches – Played 3: Won 2, Drawn 1.

First-class matches – Played 7: Won 5, Lost 1, Drawn 1.

Wins – Australia (2), South Australia, Tasmania, Tasmania Invitation XI.

Loss – Western Australia.

Draw – Australia.

Non first-class matches – Played 14: Won 8, Lost 4, Drawn 2. Abandoned 1. *Wins* – Australia (1), ACT and District, England (4), Queensland Country XI, Western Australia. *Losses* – Australia (3), England (1). *Draws* – Geelong and District, Victoria Country XI.

TEST MATCH AVERAGES

AUSTRALIA – BATTING

	Tests	Innings	Not Outs	Runs	Highest Inns	Average
B. M. Laird	3	6	0	340	92	56.66
K. J. Hughes	3	6	1	252	130*	50.40
G. S. Chappell	3	6	0	270	124	45.00
A. R. Border	3	6	0	118	54	19.66
J. M. Wiener	2	4	0	75	40	18.75
R. W. Marsh	3	6	1	57	23*	11.40
R. M. Hogg	2	3	0	33	14	11.00
G. Dymock	2	4	0	36	17	9.00
D. K. Lillee	3	5	0	28	16	5.60

Played in one Test: R. J. Bright 13, 2*; I. M. Chappell 2, 4; J. D. Higgs 0*, 0*;
D. W. Hookes 43, 37; A. A. Mallett 0, 12; R. B. McCosker 14, 33; L. S. Pascoe 5*, 5;
J. R. Thomson 0*; P. M. Toohey 10, 7.

* Signifies not out.

BOWLING

	Overs	Maidens	Runs	Wickets	Average
J. R. Thomson	27	6	93	4	23.25
G. Dymock	92.5	16	289	11	26.27
D. K. Lillee	120.1	24	365	12	30.41
J. D. Higgs	34.4	4	122	3	40.66
A. A. Mallett	65	12	211	4	52.75
L. S. Pascoe	40.3	4	183	3	61.00

Also bowled: A. R. Border 9–3–29–1; R. J. Bright 36–12–105–1; G. S. Chappell
17–4–28–1; R. M. Hogg 36–8–125–2; D. W. Hookes 5–2–15–0; K. J. Hughes 1–1–0–0;
P. M. Toohey 0.2–0–4–0.

WEST INDIES – BATTING

	Tests	Innings	Not Outs	Runs	Highest Inns	Average
I. V. A. Richards	3	4	0	386	140	96.50
C. H. Lloyd	2	3	0	201	121	67.00
A. I. Kallicharran	3	5	1	202	106	50.50
J. Garner	3	4	1	106	60	35.33
C. G. Greenidge	3	6	1	173	76	34.60
L. G. Rowe	3	5	0	162	50	32.40
D. L. Haynes	3	6	1	139	42	27.80
A. M. E. Roberts	3	4	0	78	54	19.50
D. L. Murray	3	4	0	77	28	19.25
C. E. H. Croft	3	4	2	15	12	7.50
M. A. Holding	3	4	1	22	11	7.33

Played in one Test: C. L. King 0, 8*.

* Signifies not out.

BOWLING

	Overs	Maidens	Runs	Wickets	Average
J. Garner	127.4	34	301	14	21.50
M. A. Holding	111	24	319	14	22.78
C. E. H. Croft	121.3	20	378	16	23.62
A. M. E. Roberts	112	20	296	11	26.90

Also bowled: C. L. King 27–7–63–1; A. I. Kallicharran 18–0–32–0; I. V. A. Richards 2–0–7–0.

WEST INDIAN AVERAGES – FIRST-CLASS MATCHES IN AUSTRALIA AND NEW ZEALAND

BATTING

	Matches	Innings	Not Outs	Runs	Highest Inns	Average
I. V. A. Richards	5	6	0	592	140	98.66
A. I. Kallicharran	11	20	2	773	138	42.94
H. A. Gomes	5	9	3	254	137*	42.33
D. L. Haynes	11	22	2	733	122	36.65
C. G. Greenidge	11	21	1	718	116	35.90
C. L. King	9	18	3	527	100*	35.13
L. G. Rowe	11	19	0	597	100	31.42
D. L. Murray	10	15	4	323	103	29.36
C. H. Lloyd	9	15	0	418	121	27.86
A. M. E. Roberts	8	9	2	167	54	23.85
D. R. Parry	6	8	1	152	41	21.71
J. Garner	11	15	3	204	60	17.00
M. D. Marshall	4	6	2	59	23*	14.75
D. A. Murray	3	5	0	63	23	12.60
M. A. Holding	8	12	2	57	16*	5.70
C. E. H. Croft	10	11	5	29	12	4.83

* *Signifies not out.*

BOWLING

	Overs	Maidens	Runs	Wickets	Average
J. Garner	377.3	89	929	51	18.21
M. D. Marshall	107	29	293	14	20.92
C. E. H. Croft	343	58	1,014	40	25.35
M. A. Holding	260	59	704	26	27.07
C. L. King	133	38	351	11	31.90
A. M. E. Roberts	250.3	47	688	21	32.76
D. R. Parry	210.4	40	659	20	32.95

Also bowled: H. A. Gomes 24–5–71–2; A. I. Kallicharran 41–7–81–4; I. V. A. Richards 5–1–9–0; L. G. Rowe 5–2–4–0.

FIELDING

D. L. Murray 30 (29ct 1st), C. G. Greenidge 18, J. Garner 10, D. L. Haynes 10, A. I. Kallicharran 9, C. H. Lloyd 7, I. V. A. Richards 6, D. A. Murray 5, L. G. Rowe 4, M. A. Holding 3, C. L. King 3, A. M. E. Roberts 3, M. D. Marshall 2, H. A. Gomes 1.

HUNDREDS FOR WEST INDIANS

The following thirteen three-figure innings were played for the West Indians in first-class matches in Australia and New Zealand.

   * *Signifies not out.*

A. I. Kallicharran (3)
   138   v Tasmania at Launceston
   123   v Invitation XI at Devonport
   106   v Australia at Adelaide (Third Test)

D. L. Haynes (2)
   122   v New Zealand at Christchurch (Second Test)
   105   v New Zealand at Dunedin (First Test)

I. V. A. Richards (2)
   140   v Australia at Brisbane (First Test)
   127   v Invitation XI at Devonport

H. A. Gomes (1)
   137*   v Tasmania at Launceston

C. G. Greenidge (1)
   116   v Northern Districts at Hamilton

C. L. King (1)
   100*   v New Zealand at Christchurch (Second Test)

C. H. Lloyd (1)
   121   v Australia at Adelaide (Third Test)

D. L. Murray (1)
   103   v South Australia at Adelaide

L. G. Rowe (1)
   100   v New Zealand at Christchurch (Second Test)

One three-figure innings was played for the West Indians in a non first-class match: 153* by I. V. A. Richards v Australia at Melbourne.

HUNDREDS AGAINST WEST INDIANS

The following seven three-figure innings were played against the West Indians in first-class matches in Australia and New Zealand.

   * *Signifies not out.*

G. S. Chappell (1)
   124   for Australia at Brisbane (First Test)

B. A. Edgar (1)
   127   for New Zealand at Auckland (Third Test)

R. J. Hadlee (1)
103   for New Zealand at Christchurch (Second Test)

G. P. Howarth (1)
147   for New Zealand at Christchurch (Second Test)

K. J. Hughes (1)
130*   for Australia at Brisbane (First Test)

R. S. Langer (1)
137   for Western Australia at Perth

K. S. McEwan (1)
112   for Western Australia at Perth

GEELONG AND DISTRICT v WEST INDIANS

At Geelong, November 11, 12, 13 (not first class). Drawn. The West Indians' first match, designed primarily to provide them with match practice, was largely spoiled by rain. The District team had the satisfaction of gaining a narrow first innings lead, while the best performances for the visitors came from two of their younger players: Haynes, with two half-centuries, and Marshall, who claimed five wickets.

West Indians 224 (D. L. Haynes 64, C. H. Lloyd 39, L. G. Rowe 37; D. Beams three for 46, A. Scott three for 82) and 132 for three (D. L. Haynes 59, H. A. Gomes 30 not out); Geelong and District 227 (P. Caulfield 68, P. Marshall 48; M. D. Marshall five for 62, C. E. H. Croft four for 49).

SOUTH AUSTRALIA v WEST INDIANS

At Adelaide, November 16, 17, 18. West Indians won by nine wickets. Weak South Australian batting provided little resistance against varied West Indian bowling. Darling held their first innings together after the first three wickets had fallen for 6, and former Test player Hammond and wicket-keeper Robertson contributed important runs in the lower order. The highlights of the West Indian innings were the bowling of Hogg, who confirmed his place in the Australian Test team with six well-deserved wickets, and the batting of Murray, whose first century in West Indian colours included ten 4s. Murray's dismissal, to the hook shot, was a replica of that of three earlier batsmen. When South Australia batted a second time, Hookes displayed characteristic flair while Robertson again played solidly; but the West Indians were left to score only 39 to win.

South Australia

J. E. Nash c Richards b Holding	0	– c Richards b Garner	7
D. Rolfe c Garner b Holding	0	– c Lloyd b Garner	13
W. M. Darling b Garner	88	– c Holding b Roberts	1
*D. W. Hookes run out	3	– c Garner b Parry	67
R. Zadow c Richards b Holding	19	– c Murray b Roberts	31
P. R. Sleep lbw b Holding	2	– b Garner	12
J. R. Hammond c Murray b Garner	38	– c Murray b King	28
†T. J. Robertson c Haynes b Parry	23	– not out	40
A. A. Mallett b Garner	9	– c Lloyd b Parry	4
R. M. Hogg c Roberts b Garner	14	– c Murray b Roberts	18
W. Prior not out	0	– lbw b Roberts	0
L-b 2, n-b 4	6	L-b 8, n-b 4	12

1/0 2/1 3/6 4/81 5/85 6/134   202   1/12 2/17 3/33 4/110 5/125   233
7/171 8/182 9/198   6/144 7/191 8/200 9/233

Bowling: First Innings—Roberts 16–4–37–0; Holding 14–5–27–4; Garner 22.3–3–73–4; Parry 21–3–43–1; King 9–3–16–0. *Second Innings*—Roberts 10.3–2–25–4; Holding 15–3–61–0; Garner 12–1–45–3; King 7–2–11–1; Parry 27–4–79–2.

West Indians

C. G. Greenidge c Robertson b Hammond	45	– b Hammond	9
D. L. Haynes c Zadow b Hogg	58	– not out	18
L. G. Rowe c Zadow b Prior	31		
I. V. A. Richards c Hogg b Sleep	79		
*C. H. Lloyd c sub b Hogg	11		
C. L. King c Hammond b Hogg	1	– (3) not out	15
†D. L. Murray c Hammond b Hogg	103		
D. R. Parry lbw b Hogg	31		
A. M. E. Roberts c Robertson b Hogg	11		
J. Garner not out	14		
M. A. Holding c Zadow b Mallett	2		
L-b 8, n-b 3	11		

1/73 2/113 3/156 4/182 5/184   397   1/15   (1 wkt) 42
6/259 7/338 8/369 9/394

Bowling: *First Innings*—Hogg 27–1–95–6; Hammond 18–3–52–1; Mallett 21.3–8–50–1; Sleep 13–1–62–1; Hookes 3–0–15–0; Prior 27–5–112–1. *Second Innings*—Hammond 3–0–14–1; Prior 5–0–19–0; Mallett 2–0–5–0; Nash 0.4–0–4–0.

Umpires: A. R. Crafter and M. G. O'Connell.

TASMANIA INVITATION XI v WEST INDIANS

At Devonport, November 23, 24, 25. West Indians won by 260 runs. Darling and Sleep of South Australia and Cosier of Queensland were brought across from the mainland, but the Invitation team was severely affected by the absence of Tasmania's leading players, who were involved in a McDonald's Cup match in Melbourne. Richards and Kallicharran enjoyed themselves in a third-wicket partnership of 241 before both were stumped off Campbell, and the last eight wickets fell for 72. The Invitation batsmen could find no answer to the West Indian fast bowling and fell 230 in arrears, seven of them caught either by the wicket-keeper or in the slips. Anxious to have more batting practice, Lloyd declined to enforce the follow-on, Gomes, Kallicharran and King using the opportunity to good effect. Knight again batted purposefully for the Invitation team, putting on 73 for the first wicket with Cosier. However, when Garner dismissed them both the resistance was effectively over and the West Indians accomplished their victory with time to spare.

West Indians

C. G. Greenidge c and b Whitney	24	– c Bell b Blizzard	25
D. L. Haynes b Blizzard	22	– c Howard b Whitney	14
I. V. A. Richards st Bell b Campbell	127		
A. I. Kallicharran st Bell b Campbell	123	– (6) not out	38
*C. H. Lloyd c Bell b Cosier	4	– (4) c Darling b Blizzard	13
H. A. Gomes c and b Allenby	19	– (3) not out	64
C. L. King b Blizzard	21	– (5) c Howard b Campbell	41
†D. L. Murray c and b Sleep	0		
M. D. Marshall b Sleep	1		
J. Garner not out	24		
C. E. H. Croft lbw b Sleep	0		
L-b 1, w 1, n-b 7	9	L-b 1, n-b 6	7

1/37 2/61 3/302 4/307 5/307   374   1/30 2/54   (4 wkts dec.) 202
6/343 7/348 8/348 9/349   3/71 4/130

Bowling: *First Innings*—Whitney 13–0–67–1; Blizzard 16–1–65–2; Allenby 5–1–15–1; Campbell 26–2–83–2; Broadby 10–2–59–0; Sleep 9.5–4–46–3; Cosier 7–2–30–1. *Second Innings*—Whitney 19–5–58–1; Blizzard 11–4–32–2; Campbell 9–0–38–1; Broadby 12–3–28–0; Sleep 3–0–16–0; Cosier 5–0–23–0.

Tasmania Invitation XI

W. M. Darling c Kallicharran b Garner	1	– (6) c Murray b King	15
R. L. Knight c Greenidge b Garner	33	– b Garner	57
N. Allenby b Croft	19	– lbw b Garner	6
G. J. Cosier c Murray b Marshall	12	– (1) c Greenidge b Garner	49
*S. J. Howard c Greenidge b King	24	– c Greenidge b Marshall	1
P. R. Sleep c Murray b Croft	21	– (4) b Croft	4
†J. C. Bell c Murray b Croft	6	– c Greenidge b Garner	1
B. Campbell b Croft	0	– c Haynes b Kallicharran	21
P. Blizzard lbw b King	1	– lbw b King	5
C. Broadby not out	6	– c Murray b Marshall	1
G. R. Whitney b Richards b Croft	4	– not out	0
B 2, l-b 3, n-b 12	17	B 6, l-b 1, n-b 5	12

1/1 2/49 3/68 4/81 5/114   144   1/73 2/83 3/100 4/103   172
6/129 7/130 8/131 9/135   5/139 6/144 7/145 8/156
                                                    9/164

Bowling: *First Innings*—Croft 19.3–6–49–5; Garner 11–3–30–2; Marshall 12–4–25–1; King 13–6–22–2; Richards 2–1–1–0. *Second Innings*—Croft 13–2–53–1; Garner 14–1–59–4; Marshall 13–3–32–2; King 6–3–9–2; Richards 1–0–1–0; Kallicharran 3.2–0–6–1.

Umpires: L. Cox and R. Marshall.

At Sydney, November 27. WEST INDIES lost to AUSTRALIA by five wickets (See Benson and Hedges World Series Cup).

At Sydney, November 28. WEST INDIES lost to ENGLAND by 2 runs (See Benson and Hedges World Series Cup).

AUSTRALIA v WEST INDIES

First Test Match

At Brisbane, December 1, 2, 3, 4, 5. Drawn. West Indies held sway almost throughout the match but were denied victory by steady Australian batting in the second innings, a pitch which remained placid throughout, a crucial dropped catch, and their own lack of a specialist spinner.

The first Australian Test team since the demise of World Series Cricket included eight former Packer players and was again led by Chappell, reinstated as captain by the Board in place of Hughes, who was named as his deputy. Murray, in his 52nd Test, led West Indies for the first time as Lloyd was recouperating from a knee operation. He sent Australia in and, while Laird and Chappell were adding 130 for the third wicket, it appeared that he and his team would regret that decision. Chappell was in his best form, stroking the ball confidently for two and a half hours before hooking Roberts hard and straight to King at square leg. That dismissal, soon followed by Hughes's, put a brake on the Australian scoring, and West Indies had also removed the stubborn Laird when poor light halted play an hour early at 229 for five. In his first Test, Laird had batted with tenacity for five hours, his ten boundaries coming mainly from deflections. Just 8 short of a century, he pushed at a delivery from Garner which cut away from him and was given out caught behind the wicket after long deliberation by the umpire.

Australia's innings was at the crossroads when play resumed on the second day, but once Hookes had been caught at mid-wicket batting was a struggle. That their total of 268 was unsatisfactory was given due emphasis when West Indies ended the day well placed at 233 for three. Greenidge, badly dropped by Thomson from a top-edged hook off Lillee when 3, and Haynes provided them with a fine start which Richards built on in dominant fashion, well supported by Kallicharran in a century stand for the third wicket.

On the third day, Richards and Rowe provided West Indies with their second successive century partnership, and a substantial lead seemed certain when 300 was passed with only three wickets down. However, the second new ball initiated a collapse in which six wickets fell for 68. Among the victims was Richards, well caught by the tumbling Marsh for 140. Spread over five and a half hours, it was his tenth Test century and included every shot in the book among the twenty boundaries. When Garner was joined by last man Croft, the West Indian lead was 117; when the innings ended eighty-one minutes later, it was 173. Garner lifted three huge 6s off the left-arm spin of Bright, Border and Hookes in recording his then highest first-class score of 60. The last-wicket partnership of 56 was a West Indian record against Australia, Croft's contribution being 2.

With more than two days remaining, Australia faced a considerable task to save the match. Although their openers survived the third day, McCosker and Border were again early victims and Australia looked a second time to Laird and Chappell to lead the recovery. Laird took several body blows in the early overs and Chappell needed some time to find his touch of the first innings. In one particularly tense period, Garner and Holding delivered five consecutive maidens during which Chappell, then 21, was dropped by Kallicharran at first slip off Holding; a decisive miss. By the time Laird was caught at point the West Indian lead had been erased after a partnership of 124.

At the end of the fourth day Chappell was 97 and Australia, at 240 for three, were well on the way to saving the match. The Australian captain reached his fifteenth Test century early on the final day and, despite his loss, Australia were 320 for four at lunch; 147 ahead with the match as good as saved. Chappell's innings lasted six and a quarter hours, and Hughes capitalised on it with a far more carefree century. When Chappell surprisingly declared late in the day, thus giving West Indies a meaningless threequarters of an hour's batting, Hughes was still unbeaten. Never afraid to play his shots, he used the hook to best effect and it accounted for ten of his seventeen boundaries. Chappell was named as Man of the Match.

Australia

B. M. Laird c Murray b Garner	92	– c sub b Garner	75
R. B. McCosker c Kallicharran b Croft	14	– b Holding	33
A. R. Border c Murray b Garner	1	– c Richards b Garner	7
*G. S. Chappell c King b Roberts	74	– b Croft	124
K. J. Hughes b Croft	3	– not out	130
D. W. Hookes c Holding b Croft	43	– b Roberts	37
†R. W. Marsh c Murray b Garner	3	– c Kallicharran b King	19
R. J. Bright b Holding	13	– not out	2
D. K. Lillee lbw b Garner	0		
R. M. Hogg b Roberts	8		
J. R. Thomson not out	0		
B 1, l-b 4, n-b 12	17	B 2, l-b 11, w 2, n-b 6	21

1/19 2/26 3/156 4/174 5/228   268   1/40 2/55   (6 wkts dec.) 448
6/242 7/246 8/252 9/268   3/179 4/297 5/371 6/442

Bowling: *First Innings*—Roberts 18.1–5–50–2; Holding 16–3–53–1; Croft 25–6–80–3; Garner 22–5–55–4; King 5–1–13–0. *Second Innings*—Roberts 27–5–70–1; Holding 30–4–94–1; Croft 28–3–106–1; Garner 41–13–75–2; King 22–6–50–1; Kallicharran 18–0–32–0.

West Indies

D. L. Haynes c Marsh b Thomson	42	– lbw b Hogg	4
C. G. Greenidge c Marsh b Lillee	34	– c McCosker b Thomson	0
I. V. A. Richards c Marsh b Lillee	140		
A. I. Kallicharran c Marsh b Thomson	38	– not out	10
L. G. Rowe b Chappell	50	– (3) b Hogg	3
C. L. King c Marsh b Lillee	0	– (5) not out	8
*†D. L. Murray c McCosker b Thomson	21		
A. M. E. Roberts run out	7		
J. Garner lbw b Lillee	60		
M. A. Holding b Bright	11		
C. E. H. Croft not out	2		
B 5, l-b 3, n-b 28	36	B 5, w 1, n-b 9	15
	441	(3 wkts)	**40**

1/68 2/83 3/198 4/317 5/317   441   1/2 2/15   (3 wkts) 40
6/341 7/365 8/366 9/385   3/16

Bowling: First Innings—Lillee 29.2–8–104–4; Hogg 25–6–55–0; Thomson 24–4–90–3; Chappell 12–2–25–1; Bright 32–9–97–1; Border 5–1–19–0; Hookes 5–2–15–0. *Second Innings*—Lillee 2–0–3–0; Hogg 5–2–11–2; Thomson 3–2–3–1; Bright 4–3–8–0.

Umpires: R. C. Bailhache and A. R. Crafter.

At Melbourne, December 9. WEST INDIES beat AUSTRALIA by 80 runs (See Benson and Hedges World Series Cup).

VICTORIAN COUNTRY XI v WEST INDIANS

At Yea, December 11. Drawn. West Indians 329 for three dec. (L. G. Rowe 97, C. G. Greenidge 77, D. L. Haynes 74, H. A. Gomes 55 not out); Victorian Country XI 133 for eight (M. James 31 not out, N. Byrne 30 not out; D. R. Parry four for 21).

TASMANIA v WEST INDIES

At Launceston, December 14, 15, 16, 17. West Indians won by an innings and 61 runs. As they did three weeks earlier, the West Indians again outplayed their opponents. The island-state lost their first five wickets for 39, and owed a respectable first innings total to an excellent performance by teen-ager Boon. The West Indians responded with their highest total ever against a state side, Kallicharran repeating his earlier century at Devonport and Gomes continuing his good form with his first hundred of the tour. Rowe also batted freely, but the most important performance for the West Indians was that of their captain, Lloyd, who marked his return to the game with a confident 77. Tasmania, 332 behind, again lost their first five wickets cheaply – all to Garner – but the West Indians then relaxed and Woolley took the opportunity to score an impressive 93.

Tasmania

G. W. Goodman c D. L. Murray b Roberts	9	– lbw b Garner	6
R. Jeffery c Greenidge b Croft	5	– b Garner	22
D. A. Smith c Greenidge b Croft	0	– (4) b Garner	21
R. L. Knight c D. L. Murray b Croft	14	– (3) lbw b Garner	27
*B. F. Davison c Greenidge b Roberts	5	– b Garner	3
D. C. Boon st D. L. Murray b Parry	78	– c D. A. Murray b Croft	28
†R. D. Woolley c Greenidge b Parry	34	– c D. A. Murray b Roberts	93
B. Campbell c D. L. Murray b Croft	32	– c Garner b Parry	30
R. J. Hadlee b Parry	17	– not out	10
G. Wilson b Croft	0	– c Garner b Parry	0
N. J. Majewski not out	7	– c Greenidge b Parry	4
B 5, l-b 3, n-b 4	12	B 2, l-b 9, n-b 16	27
	213		**271**

1/15 2/15 3/20 4/27 5/39   213   1/27 2/32 3/83 4/87 5/94   271
6/109 7/174 8/193 9/193   6/154 7/249 8/259 9/259

Bowling: *First Innings*—Roberts 14–4–47–2; Croft 20–2–65–5; Garner 7–1–23–0; Parry 20.5–6–66–3. *Second Innings*—Roberts 16–2–48–1; Croft 19–2–62–1; Garner 18–3–43–5; Parry 29.1–7–74–3; Gomes 2–0–15–0; Kallicharran 3–1–2–0.

West Indians

C. G. Greenidge c Boon b Hadlee	32	†D. L. Murray not out	44
L. G. Rowe c Woolley b Goodman	82		
A. I. Kallicharran st Woolley b Campbell	138	B 4, l-b 14, w 1, n-b 3	22
*C. H. Lloyd c and b Campbell	77		
H. A. Gomes not out	137	1/68 2/156 3/293 (5 wkts dec.) 545	
†D. A. Murray c Woolley b Wilson	13	4/376 5/423	

A. M. E. Roberts, D. R. Parry, J. Garner and C. E. H. Croft did not bat.

Bowling: Hadlee 24–1–83–1; Majewski 26–1–127–0; Wilson 21–2–74–1; Goodman 24–2–83–1; Campbell 19–2–94–2; Jeffery 12–1–62–0.

Umpires: J. Hay and G. Summers.

D. L. Murray kept wicket in first innings, D. A. Murray in second.

QUEENSLAND COUNTRY XI v WEST INDIANS

At Toowoomba, December 19. West Indians won by four wickets and batted on. An untrustworthy pitch spoiled the match, although for one man it will always remain memorable; the Country team's opening bowler, Charles, dismissed both Greenidge and Richards for ducks.

Queensland Country XI 96 (J. James 34; M. A. Holding three for 11, H. A. Gomes three for 16); West Indians 124 for seven (C. L. King 56; P. Charles three for 43).

At Sydney, December 21. WEST INDIES lost to AUSTRALIA by 7 runs (See Benson and Hedges World Series Cup).

At Brisbane, December 23. WEST INDIES beat ENGLAND by nine wickets (See Benson and Hedges World Series Cup).

AUSTRALIA v WEST INDIES

Second Test Match

At Melbourne, December 29, 30, 31, January 1. West Indies won by ten wickets. In winning with a day to spare, they emphatically overcame their jinx at the Melbourne Cricket Ground where they had lost every one of their previous seven Tests. They took a grip on the match from the start, bowling Australia out for 156 and replying with 103 for one off eighteen overs by the close on the first day. The scoreboard was an accurate indicator of the balance; although only one Australian batsman in the first innings and two in the second scored more than 25, eight of the first nine West Indians passed that figure.

Electing to bat, Australia lost only one wicket before lunch. This was a result mainly of wayward West Indian bowling and it was left to Garner, belatedly introduced into the attack, to show what could be done on a pitch offering generous and unpredictable bounce. He trapped Test débutant Wiener lbw, had Border caught in the slips and induced Chappell to hook unsuccessfully. Holding and Croft shared the final six wickets – four of them caught in the slips – and Australia, having passed 100 with three wickets down, were all out for 156 less than half an hour after tea.

West Indies made a spectacular reply, Greenidge taking 8 off Lillee's first over and Haynes 16 off Hogg's first. Yet it was Richards who provided most of the fireworks, coming in after Haynes had been caught at slip. In fifty minutes he raced to 45 not out off 36 balls, with a memorable 6 off Hogg and five 4s. Australia did well on the second day to contain the West Indian batsmen, despite the loss of Hogg who retired with an injured back after bowling only two overs. Lillee, mostly at reduced pace, and the left-arm Dymock shared one end while Higgs bowled his leg-spin for 29 consecutive overs without being dominated.

Rain caused the loss of almost an hour in mid-afternoon and West Indies ended play at 336 for seven with a firm, but not irreversible, hold on the match. Without achieving the heights of the previous afternoon, Richards reached 96 before offering a lazy drive to a ball from Dymock well up to him and was caught at extra-cover. Five more wickets fell, leaving Roberts and Garner to resume on the third day. They carried their eighth-wicket partnership to a valuable 70 and Roberts reached his first Test half-century. As they had done in the first Test, Australia began their second innings with a sizeable deficit: 241 this time, with more than two and a half days remaining. Laird led the fight with the same courage and dedication he had shown at Brisbane, battling against the agony of a badly bruised left hand sustained when hit by Holding in the seventh over of the innings. He continued bravely on the fourth day when Australia resumed at 167 for three. Yet, despite pain-killing injections administered on the field, it was obviously asking too much of him to resist bowling of the pace which West Indies had at their disposal and he was caught in the gully, after four hours and twenty minutes of defiance. Hughes then carried the Australian standard as wickets fell and after his departure Dymock and Hogg saved Australia from the indignity of an innings defeat. West Indies needed only 22 to take a lead in the series and these Greenidge and Haynes had made well before tea on the fourth day. Richards was named as Man of the Match.

Australia

J. M. Wiener lbw b Garner	40	– c Murray b Croft	24
B. M. Laird c Lloyd b Holding	16	– c Garner b Holding	69
A. R. Border c Richards b Garner	17	– lbw b Holding	15
*G. S. Chappell c Murray b Garner	19	– c Murray b Roberts	22
K. J. Hughes c Rowe b Holding	4	– lbw b Roberts	70
P. M. Toohey c Roberts b Holding	10	– c Murray b Croft	7
†R. W. Marsh c Kallicharran b Holding	0	– b Croft	7
D. K. Lillee c Lloyd b Croft	12	– c and b Roberts	0
G. Dymock c Kallicharran b Croft	7	– c Lloyd b Garner	17
R. M. Hogg c Greenidge b Croft	14	– c Holding b Garner	11
J. D. Higgs not out	0	– not out	0
B 9, l-b 4, w 2, n-b 2	17	B 2, l-b 10, n-b 5	17

1/38 2/69 3/97 4/108 5/112   156   1/43 2/88 3/121 4/187 5/205   259
6/118 7/123 8/133 9/143   6/228 7/228 8/233 9/258

Bowling: *First Innings*—Roberts 14–1–39–0; Holding 14–3–40–4; Croft 13.3–4–27–3; Garner 15–7–33–3. *Second Innings*—Roberts 21–1–64–3; Holding 23–7–61–2; Croft 22–2–61–3; Garner 20.4–2–56–2.

West Indies

C. G. Greenidge c Higgs b Dymock	48	– not out	9
D. L. Haynes c Hughes b Lillee	29	– not out	9
I. V. A. Richards c Toohey b Dymock	96		
A. I. Kallicharran c Laird b Higgs	39		
L. G. Rowe b Lillee	26		
*C. H. Lloyd c Marsh b Dymock	40		
†D. L. Murray b Dymock	24		
A. M. E. Roberts lbw b Lillee	54		
J. Garner c Dymock b Higgs	29		
M. A. Holding not out	1		
C. E. H. Croft lbw b Higgs	0		
L-b 4, n-b 7	11	L-b 4	4

1/46 2/156 3/215 4/226 5/250   397   (no wkt) 22
6/305 7/320 8/390 9/396

Bowling: *First Innings*—Lillee 36–7–96–3; Hogg 6–0–59–0; Dymock 31–2–106–4; Higgs 34.4–4–122–3; Chappell 5–2–3–0. *Second Innings*—Lillee 3–0–9–0; Dymock 3–0–5–0; Hughes 1–1–0–0; Toohey 0.2–0–4–0.

Umpires: A. R. Crafter and C. E. Harvey.

WESTERN AUSTRALIA v WEST INDIES

At Perth, January 5, 6, 7. Western Australia won by eight wickets with more than a day to spare. This was an embarrassing defeat for the West Indians, especially as the state were without Hughes, Lillee and Marsh on duty in the second Test against England. Batting first, the touring team faltered against the swing bowling of Alderman and Malone who claimed nine wickets between them. The West Indians made a spirited effort to retrieve the position, capturing the first three Western Australian wickets cheaply, but the left-handed Langer and South African McEwan punished some loose bowling in a fourth-wicket partnership of 207 made in under three hours, each scoring a century. Though dismissing them both, Parry conceded more than 5 runs an over in his 26 overs. The West Indians faced a deficit of 227 when Mann declared the state's innings and, when six wickets fell for 103, a huge defeat was likely. However, King mounted a typical counter-attack to register his highest score of the tour and, with Murray, Garner and Parry providing useful support, ensured that Western Australia had to bat again.

West Indians

L. G. Rowe c Mann b Alderman	3	– c Wright b Michael	11
D. L. Haynes c Wright b Malone	27	– c Wright b Michael	20
*C. H. Lloyd c Wright b Alderman	9	– (6) b Malone	0
H. A. Gomes c Shipperd b Malone	2	– c Wright b Michael	3
A. I. Kallicharran c Mann b Michael	13	– (3) b Malone	40
C. L. King b Malone	28	– (7) b Alderman	92
†D. A. Murray c Wright b Alderman	15	– (8) c and b Mann	23
D. R. Parry c Wright b Alderman	32	– (9) b Mann	41
J. Garner b Alderman	4	– (10) c O'Neil b Mann	39
M. D. Marshall not out	23	– (5) c Malone b Alderman	15
C. E. H. Croft b Malone	0	– not out	7
L-b 3, n-b 10	13	B 6, l-b 7, w 2, n-b 7	22

1/3 2/26 3/30 4/56 5/86   169   1/30 2/50 3/63 4/98 5/98   313
6/86 7/121 8/136 9/165   6/103 7/172 8/253 9/276

Bowling: *First Innings*—Michael 12–3–39–1; Alderman 18–7–47–5; Malone 14.2–4–48–4; Wood 2–0–15–0; Mann 9–6–7–0. *Second Innings*—Michael 14–2–75–3; Alderman 24–5–86–3; Malone 25–11–49–2; Mann 21–4–81–2.

Western Australia

G. Shipperd c Garner b Croft	0	– run out	44
G. M. Wood c Murray b Marshall	18	– c Kallicharran b Marshall	22
R. S. Langer b Parry	137	– not out	12
C. S. Serjeant c Murray b Marshall	20	– not out	1
K. S. McEwan c Gomes b Parry	112		
M. D. O'Neil c Murray b Marshall	24		
*A. L. Mann not out	56		
†K. J. Wright not out	1		
B 5, l-b 1, w 5, n-b 17	28	L-b 1, n-b 7	8

1/0 2/32 3/79   (6 wkts dec.) 396   1/52 2/78   (2 wkts) 87
4/286 5/317 6/392

M. F. Malone, T. M. Alderman and C. A. Michael did not bat.

Bowling: *First Innings*—Croft 20–3–62–1; Marshall 18–3–66–3; Garner 13–0–49–0; Parry 26–3–132–2; King 11–0–59–0. *Second Innings*—Croft 4–1–19–0; Marshall 9–4–21–1; Garner 5–0–18–0; Parry 2.4–0–5–0; King 6–1–16–0.

Umpires: J. D'Arcy Evans and D. G. Weser.

WESTERN AUSTRALIA v WEST INDIANS

At Perth, January 8. West Indians won by four wickets. Organised to fill the day lost as a result of the early finish to the first-class game, this limited-overs encounter produced exciting cricket and a close finish, the West Indians winning in the last over.

Western Australia 223 for eight (50 overs) (R. S. Langer 47, G. M. Wood 43, C. S. Serjeant 36); West Indians 224 for six (49.1 overs) (A. I. Kallicharran 77, D. L. Haynes 60, C. G. Greenidge 51; G. D. Porter four for 49).

At Melbourne, January 12. ENGLAND v WEST INDIES. No result. (See Benson and Hedges World Series Cup).

AUSTRALIAN CAPITAL TERRITORY AND DISTRICT v WEST INDIANS

At Canberra, January 14. West Indians won by 121 runs.

West Indians 261 for four (50 overs) (L. G. Rowe 88 not out, C. G. Greenidge 57, D. L. Haynes 50); ACT and District 140 for nine (50 overs) (A. M. E. Roberts three for 16, J. Garner three for 18).

At Adelaide, January 16. WEST INDIES beat ENGLAND by 107 runs (See Benson and Hedges World Series Cup).

At Sydney, January 18. WEST INDIES lost to AUSTRALIA by 9 runs (See Benson and Hedges World Series Cup).

At Melbourne, January 20. WEST INDIES beat ENGLAND by 2 runs (See Benson and Hedges World Series Cup).

At Sydney, January 22. WEST INDIES beat ENGLAND by eight wickets (See Benson and Hedges World Series Cup).

AUSTRALIA v WEST INDIES

Third Test Match

At Adelaide, January 26, 27, 28, 29, 30. West Indies won by 408 runs. West Indies needed only a draw to clinch their first series in Australia; instead they so outplayed their dispirited opponents that their victory was one of the most overwhelming in Tests between the two countries. As usual, their formula for success was consistent batting, irresistible fast bowling and athletically alert fielding.

Put in, West Indies were given a flying start by Richards after Greenidge had fallen an early victim to Lillee. Batting with his accustomed flair, Richards hit thirteen boundaries before the first interval, when West Indies were 115 for one. His dismissal on resumption brought a dramatic transformation in fortunes. Experienced off-spinner Mallett, playing his first Test in four years, accounted for Haynes and Kallicharran, leaving Lloyd and Rowe engaged in a desperate partnership to prevent a collapse. After an uncertain start they added 113 in under two hours, Lloyd finding his best form and taking charge in robust fashion. Dropped at 69 and 87 off Dymock, he scored 94 of his 121 runs in the final session, hitting seventeen 4s in just over three hours. He fell to Lillee in the day's final over, which also accounted for Roberts, leaving West Indies 303 for eight. The innings ended less than a quarter of an hour into the second day but, although the total was West Indies' lowest of the series, it proved well beyond Australia's capabilities.

By lunch, Australia were 26 for three, and they never recovered. The two most crucial wickets were those of the Chappell brothers to successive deliveries from Roberts, both steeply rising bouncers. Laird once more batted resolutely for his fourth half-century of the series, with useful support from Hughes and Border, who was Australia's top scorer. When Australia were all out early on the third morning, 125 behind, West Indies set about relentlessly building on their advantage.

Greenidge, dropped behind off Dymock when 9, put on 48 with Haynes and 136 with Richards to set the foundations of another huge West Indian total. His 76, ended when Mallett deceived him in flight, was his first half-century in nine Test innings in Australia; Richards's innings, ended immediately before tea during an experimental over from Border, produced his seventh successive fifty in Tests in Australia. However, their dismissal brought no respite as Kallicharran, Rowe and Lloyd all batted freely, Kallicharran ending a disappointing series with his twelfth Test century which included thirteen boundaries.

With time on his side, and mindful of past indignities suffered by West Indian teams in Australia, Lloyd let the innings run its course. When it was over, threequarters of an hour after lunch on the fourth day, Australia faced an academic target of 573. None of their batsmen seemed to have the will to make a fight of it and they were a miserable 131 for seven at stumps. Again it was Laird who defied the fast bowling longest, but West Indies needed only nine overs on the final morning to formalise their victory, retain the Worrell Trophy, and collect a cheque of $A24,000 for the accumulated prize-money for the victory. Lloyd, in almost certainly his last Test in Australia, was voted Man of the Match and Richards the Player of the Series.

West Indies

C. G. Greenidge lbw b Lillee	76	6 – st Marsh b Mallett	76
D. L. Haynes c Lillee b Mallett	28	– c Marsh b Pascoe	27
I. V. A. Richards c Marsh b Lillee	76	– b Border	74
A. I. Kallicharran c I. Chappell b Mallett	9	– b Mallett	106
L. G. Rowe c Lillee b Dymock	40	– c Marsh b Dymock	43
*C. H. Lloyd lbw b Lillee	121	– (7) c Marsh b Dymock	40
†D. L. Murray c Marsh b Dymock	4	– (8) c G. Chappell b Dymock	28
A. M. E. Roberts b Lillee	9	– (9) c Laird b Dymock	8
J. Garner c Hughes b Lillee	16	– (10) not out	1
M. A. Holding b Pascoe	9	– (11) lbw b Dymock	1
C. E. H. Croft not out	1	– (6) c Border b Pascoe	12
B 2, n-b 7	9	B 1, l-b 10, n-b 21	32
	328		448

1/11 2/115 3/115 4/126 5/239 6/252   328   1/48 2/184 3/213 4/299 5/331   448
7/300 8/303 9/326   6/398 7/417 8/443 9/446

Bowling: *First Innings*—Lillee 24–3–78–5; Dymock 25–7–74–2; Pascoe 15.3–1–90–1; Mallett 27–5–77–2. *Second Innings*—Lillee 26–6–75–0; Dymock 33.5–7–104–5; Pascoe 25–3–93–2; Mallett 38–7–134–2; Border 4–2–10–1.

Australia

J. M. Wiener c Haynes b Holding	3	– c Murray b Roberts	8
B. M. Laird c Garner b Croft	52	– lbw b Garner	36
I. M. Chappell c Greenidge b Roberts	2	– c Murray b Holding	4
*G. S. Chappell c Garner b Roberts	0	– lbw b Croft	31
K. J. Hughes c Lloyd b Croft	34	– lbw b Garner	11
A. R. Border b Roberts	54	– c Greenidge b Roberts	24
†R. W. Marsh c Murray b Croft	5	– not out	23
D. K. Lillee c Haynes b Holding	16	– c Kallicharran b Croft	0
G. Dymock c Rowe b Croft	10	– c Richards b Holding	2
A. A. Mallett c Rowe b Garner	0	– b Holding	12
L. S. Pascoe not out	5	– b Holding	5
B 1, l-b 14, n-b 7	22	L-b 2, w 2, n-b 5	9
	203		165

1/23 2/26 3/26 4/83 5/110 6/127   203   1/12 2/21 3/71 4/83 5/98   165
7/165 8/188 9/189   6/130 7/131 8/135 9/159

Bowling: *First Innings*—Roberts 16.5–3–43–3; Holding 15–5–31–2; Garner 18–4–43–1; Richards 2–0–7–0; Croft 22–4–57–4. *Second Innings*—Roberts 15–5–30–2; Holding 13–2–40–4; Garner 11–3–39–2; Croft 11–1–47–2.

Umpires: M. G. O'Connell and M. W. Johnson.

THE WEST INDIANS IN NEW ZEALAND, 1979-80

By R. T. BRITTENDEN

New Zealand's first victory in a Test rubber at home should have been a happy occasion, but the New Zealand cricket public, which had looked forward keenly to the West Indians' visit, was glad to see the back of them. New Zealand won the first Test by the narrowest of margins, and drew the remaining two. Yet the West Indians lost more than a Test series. Their reputation for sportsmanship went too. There were several extremely unsavoury incidents on the field in the first two Tests, and the situation was not improved by the extravagant statements made by their harassed manager, Willie Rodriguez.

There could be some sympathy for the West Indians, coming to New Zealand after a particularly demanding tour of Australia and having to do without Richards, because of injury. Their main complaint in New Zealand was about the umpiring, and in retrospect there is little doubt that if both sides suffered from difficult, debatable decisions, more went against West Indies than against New Zealand. Both Mr Rodriguez and the captain, Lloyd, said there should be neutral umpires in Test matches. Such complaints by touring teams are by no means uncommon; they have been made in every cricketing country for years. But Mr Rodriguez, after stating at a press conference in Christchurch that he did not think the umpiring was biased, only incompetent, claimed after his departure that the West Indians had had to get batsmen out nine times before getting a decision. And his allegations went well beyond the bounds of acceptable comment when he claimed the West Indians were "set up"; that there was "no way we could win a Test"; that New Zealand were celebrating 50 years in Tests and were "determined to do something about it". This thinly veiled suggestion that there had been collaboration between the New Zealand administration and its umpires was highly insulting to men of integrity.

On the field, the West Indian players behaved in an extraordinary fashion. In the first Test Holding, having had an appeal disallowed, kicked the stumps out of the ground at the batsman's end. When West Indies lost the match, Greenidge showed similar ill-temper as he left the field. At Christchurch in the second Test, Croft, after being no balled, flicked off the bails as he walked back, and a little later ran in very close to the umpire, F. R. Goodall — so close that the batsman could not see him — and shouldered Goodall heavily. It was the height of discourtesy when Goodall, wishing on two occasions to speak to Lloyd about Croft's behaviour, had to walk all the way to the West Indian captain, standing deep in the slips. Lloyd took not a step to meet him.

It was in this match that the West Indians refused to take the field after tea on the third day, saying they would not continue unless umpire Goodall was removed. They were finally persuaded to continue twelve minutes late. That evening they emptied their dressing-room and there was a distinct prospect that the tour would end there and then. Following protracted negotiations with the New Zealand Board of Control it was agreed to continue the match and the rest of the tour. The Board made clear its feeling that Croft, after his attack on Goodall, should not be considered for the Auckland Test, but in the event he did play.

The Auckland Test, the last of the series, produced yet another extraordinary situation. Four senior members of the West Indian team booked flights home which would have required their leaving the ground soon after lunch on the last day of the Test. However, they were dissuaded from this dramatic action after representations from the New Zealand Board.

The West Indians, being badly led and managed, were the author of their own misfortunes. For a side described as the best in the world, and the strongest since the 1948 Australians, this was singularly disappointing. It was extraordinary that New Zealand, held in scant regard by the West Indians and everyone else, actually deserved their narrow victory, for they played better cricket and played as a team, whereas the West Indians sulked or stormed in turn.

The West Indian bowlers persistently dropped the ball far too short when there was movement off the seam. They seemed intent on bouncing the New Zealanders out. And when the New Zealand bowlers used a fuller length, the touring batsmen got themselves out trying to cut or hook. In the simplest terms, they failed to adapt to changed conditions. Their outstanding batsman was Haynes, who had the technique and the temperament to counter good, steady bowling when conditions were helpful for seam bowlers – as they were at the start of each Test. The others showed flashes of ability, but lacked discipline. Garner was the best of the bowlers. The fielding was very patchy, a good many catches being dropped.

Howarth and Edgar played some fine innings for New Zealand, and Richard Hadlee, the Man of the Series, bowled most effectively. New Zealand's success was attributable largely, however, to the advance made by the left-arm bowler, Troup, who was sharper of pace, more accurate and more durable than previously. Except for one bad hour at Auckland, New Zealand's fielding was excellent.

TEST MATCH AVERAGES

NEW ZEALAND – BATTING

	Tests	Innings	Not Outs	Runs	Highest Inns	Average
B. A. Edgar	3	5	1	241	127	60.25
G. P. Howarth	3	5	0	239	147	47.80
J. V. Coney	3	5	2	140	80	46.66
R. J. Hadlee	3	4	0	178	103	44.50
J. G. Wright	3	5	0	83	23	16.60
B. L. Cairns	3	4	0	51	30	12.75

	Tests	Innings	Not Outs	Runs	Highest Inns	Average
W. K. Lees	3	4	0	44	23	11.00
G. B. Troup	3	4	2	20	13*	10.00
J. M. Parker	3	5	0	48	42	9.60
S. L. Boock	3	4	2	8	6	4.00
P. N. Webb	2	3	0	11	5	3.66

Played in one Test: P. E. McEwan 5, 21.

* Signifies not out.

BOWLING

	Overs	Maidens	Runs	Wickets	Average
R. J. Hadlee	161.3	50	361	19	19.00
G. B. Troup	162.1	49	371	18	20.61
B. L. Cairns	150	47	419	12	34.91
S. L. Boock	50	12	150	2	75.00

Also bowled: J. V. Coney 32–4–104–1; G. P. Howarth 5–0–32–1.

WEST INDIES – BATTING

	Tests	Innings	Not Outs	Runs	Highest Inns	Average
A. M. E. Roberts	2	3	2	78	35*	78.00
D. L. Haynes	3	6	0	339	122	56.50
C. G. Greenidge	3	6	0	274	97	45.66
C. L. King	3	6	1	187	100*	37.40
L. G. Rowe	3	6	0	179	100	29.83
A. I. Kallicharran	3	6	0	146	75	24.33
C. H. Lloyd	3	6	0	103	42	17.16
D. L. Murray	3	6	1	66	30	13.20
M. A. Holding	3	5	1	28	16*	7.00
C. E. H. Croft	3	4	2	7	6	3.50
J. Garner	3	5	0	12	7	2.40

Played in one Test: D. R. Parry 17, 1.

* Signifies not out.

BOWLING

	Overs	Maidens	Runs	Wickets	Average
A. I. Kallicharran	10.4	5	16	3	5.33
J. Garner	122.1	34	235	14	16.78
C. E. H. Croft	103	18	265	10	26.50
M. A. Holding	94	21	236	7	33.71
A. M. E. Roberts	72	14	196	3	65.33

Also bowled: C. L. King 12–1–74–0; D. R. Parry 22–6–63–2; L. G. Rowe 5–2–4–0.

Note: Tour averages for the West Indian tour of Australia and New Zealand may be found under "West Indians in Australia, 1979-80".

AUCKLAND XI v WEST INDIANS

At Auckland, February 2. West Indians won by 59 runs. The tourists were always in control in this 50 overs opening match, with David Murray batting particularly well. Of the Auckland players, only opener Webb made much progress.

West Indians 196 for nine (D. A. Murray 61, D. L. Haynes 37); Auckland XI 137 (P. N. Webb 39; D. R. Parry five for 34, M. D. Marshall three for 19).

NORTHERN DISTRICTS v WEST INDIANS

At Hamilton, February 3, 4, 5. Drawn. Given 80 minutes to score 153 for victory, the West Indians lost eight wickets and were 21 short when an entertaining game ended. On a good batting pitch, four contenders for the New Zealand team batted pleasantly and profitably for Northern Districts, Wright, Howarth and Roberts scoring half-centuries and Parker a convincing 39. The West Indians passed the home score easily and declared when 100 runs ahead. Greenidge, driving and hooking powerfully, scored a century in three hours and Rowe made his runs at a similarly brisk pace. But it was King who did most to thrust home his side's advantage, his 88 including three 6s and thirteen 4s. When Northern Districts batted again, Wright gave another sound display, as did Roberts, and Fowler added brisk runs before a second declaration. The West Indians made a valiant effort to knock off the runs before turning to defence for the last half-dozen overs.

Northern Districts

J. G. Wright c Haynes b King	68	– b King		84
J. G. Gibson c Haynes b Parry	25	– b Croft		6
*G. P. Howarth retired hurt	57	– b Parry		9
J. M. Parker c Greenidge b King	39	– b Gomes		26
A. D. G. Roberts not out	50	– not out		54
†M. J. Wright b King	0	– c Haynes b Parry		0
C. W. Dickeson b Parry	1	– lbw b Parry		0
W. G. Fowler b Parry	6	– c Kallicharran b Gomes		40
S. R. Gillespie b Parry	5			
S. J. Scott not out	10	– (9) not out		17
B 4, l-b 6, n-b 6	16	B 5, l-b 10, n-b 1		16

1/50 2/131 3/222   (7 wkts dec.) 277   1/15 2/44 3/100   (7 wkts dec.) 252
4/234 5/241 6/247 7/267   4/149 5/152 6/154 7/218

K. Treiber did not bat.

Bowling: *First Innings*—Roberts 10–1–39–0; Croft 14–3–39–0; Marshall 14–3–39–0; Parry 33–4–103–4; King 24–9–41–3. *Second Innings*—Croft 9–1–22–1; Marshall 8–1–27–0; Parry 28–7–85–3; King 12–4–21–1; Gomes 22–5–56–2; Kallicharran 6–1–25–0.

West Indians

C. G. Greenidge b Treiber	116	– c Parker b Gillespie		10
D. L. Haynes c Treiber b Gillespie	26	– b Treiber		9
L. G. Rowe c Parker b Treiber	74	– st M. J. Wright b Dickeson		39
A. I. Kallicharran b Treiber	29	– (5) st M. J. Wright b Howarth		26
H. A. Gomes c Dickeson b Gillespie	7	– (8) not out		1
C. L. King c Dickeson b Scott	88	– (4) c Treiber b Fowler		13
*†D. L. Murray not out	19	– (10) not out		14
D. R. Parry (did not bat)		– (6) b Howarth		13
M. D. Marshall (did not bat)		– (7) c Howarth b Dickeson		7
A. M. E. Roberts (did not bat)		– (9) c J. G. Wright b Howarth		0
B 7, l-b 11	18			

1/71 2/226 3/236   (6 wkts dec.) 377   1/17 2/19 3/36   (8 wkts) 132
4/263 5/289 6/377   4/97 5/97 6/106 7/118 8/118

C. E. H. Croft did not bat.

Bowling: First Innings—Gillespie 25–8–70–2; Treiber 19–4–81–3; Dickeson 17–7–50–0;
Scott 16–0–79–1; Roberts 8–2–35–0; Fowler 12–2–33–0; Howarth 5–0–11–0. *Second
Innings*—Gillespie 3–0–18–1; Treiber 2–0–16–1; Dickeson 6–3–13–2; Roberts 2–0–11–0;
Fowler 4–0–27–1; Howarth 7–1–40–3; Parker 1–0–7–0.

Umpires: J. B. R. Hastie and B. A. Brickwell.

NEW ZEALAND v WEST INDIES

One-day International

At Christchurch, February 6. New Zealand won by one wicket. New Zealand's unexpected
victory, acclaimed by a wildly excited crowd, provided them with much encouragement for the
coming Test series, but West Indies must have been disappointed to lose a game they seemed
to have under control until the last half-hour. During New Zealand's late charge, their fielding
fell away badly under pressure. Greenidge and Haynes batted with authority in an opening
stand of 81 while the pitch held considerable life, and Greenidge went on to make his century
from only 135 deliveries. New Zealand's bowlers were generally accurate and their fielding
quite brilliant, but the task of scoring a shade more than 4 runs an over seemed likely to be
beyond their batsmen. When the sixth wicket fell at 80, the scoreboard may have induced the
West Indians to relax, and if so they made a fatal mistake. Lees started a spectacular recovery
by hitting 6s from successive balls off the off-spinner, Parry, and with Coney, a tall
right-hander, he added 54 in 34 minutes from ten overs. With ten wickets left, the target was still
68, but Hadlee responded to the urging of the crowd, making 41 from 33 balls. Six overs
yielded 44 runs and Coney was there to make the winning hit, a fierce lofted straight drive off
Holding, with only two balls left.

West Indies 203 for seven (50 overs) (C. G. Greenidge 103); New Zealand 207 for nine
(49.4 overs) (J. V. Coney 53 not out, R. J. Hadlee 41; D. L. Parry three for 47).

NEW ZEALAND v WEST INDIES

First Test Match

At Dunedin, February 8, 9, 10, 12, 13. New Zealand won by one wicket. Clear evidence of an
inability to adjust to New Zealand conditions was given by West Indies' batting on the first
day. Lloyd, having won the toss, made a questionable decision in batting first, for the ball often
kept rather low and there was sharp movement off the pitch. Only Haynes saw the need to
get on to the front foot as much as possible, and against the pace attack he batted several
inches outside his crease. He was in for all the three and a half hours of an innings which
yielded only 140. Four West Indian batsmen, with their partiality for playing back, were lbw to
balls cutting in to them. Others lost their wickets trying to hook or cut in conditions which
made such shots extremely risky. The first three wickets fell in Hadlee's first thirteen balls, for
4 runs, and after Haynes and Lloyd had fought it out for one hundred and twelve minutes there
was little resistance.

The West Indian bowlers were as much at fault as their batsmen as New Zealand built up a
lead of 109. They bowled much too short, unlike the New Zealanders who had made the most
of the conditions by keeping the ball up. The New Zealand batsmen took a physical
hammering, but they showed considerable determination in grafting for their runs. Edgar was
in almost five hours for his 65, Howarth just over two hours for 33, but their stand of 67 was
followed by a swift decline against fiercely hostile bowling until the late-order batsmen again
came to the rescue. Cairns, a powerful hitter, took three 6s in an over from Parry which
brought him 20 runs, and Hadlee had nine 4s in his 51; their eighth-wicket partnership of 54
took just 34 minutes and swung the game New Zealand's way.

There were only seventy minutes of play on the third day, which left West Indies 18 for one,
and the fourth was dominated by Haynes and Hadlee. At 29 for four West Indies were in dire
straits, but there were stands of 87 between Haynes and King and 64 between Haynes and

Deryck Murray. The West Indian tail failed, however, and New Zealand were left needing only 104 to win. By lunch, under intense pressure, they had fought to 33 for two. About twenty minutes before lunch, Parker was given not out when Holding appealed for a catch by the wicket-keeper, which prompted Holding to demolish the stumps at the batsman's end with a full swing of the right foot. In the afternoon West Indies seemed to have the game won. Howarth was third out at 40, and fifteen minutes later New Zealand were 44 for six. Webb went at 54, but once more there was strong resistance from the tailenders. Hadlee and Cairns added 19 with Hadlee playing some fine forcing strokes; Cairns and Troup put on 27 with determination much more of a factor than finesse. At tea it was 95 for eight.

Only 1 run had been added after tea when Holding beat Cairns, but the ball touched the off stump without dislodging a bail. When Cairns was out at 100, Boock, whose best Test score was 8, saw out the last five balls of Holding's over. Garner bowled the final over. The first ball produced a bye. Boock, the non-striker, tried to make it 2 runs and turning back was almost run out. Second ball, he survived an appeal for lbw. He kept the next two out and then squeezed 2 runs backward of point to level the scores. The last ball went from his pads to backward square and the batsmen ran the leg-bye, Parry's return to the non-striker's end going wildly astray. It was the narrowest of victories, but well-earned. Hadlee, with eleven wickets for the match and a Test record of seven leg-before decisions, took his Test tally to 118, two ahead of New Zealand's previous record-holder, Richard Collinge.

West Indies

C. G. Greenidge c Cairns b Hadlee	2	– lbw b Hadlee	3
D. L. Haynes c and b Cairns	55	– c Webb b Troup	105
L. G. Rowe lbw b Hadlee	1	– lbw b Hadlee	12
A. I. Kallicharran lbw b Hadlee	0	– c Cairns b Troup	0
*C. H. Lloyd lbw b Hadlee	24	– c Lees b Hadlee	5
C. L. King c Coney b Troup	14	– c Boock b Cairns	41
†D. L. Murray c Edgar b Troup	6	– lbw b Hadlee	30
D. R. Parry b Boock	17	– c and b Hadlee	1
J. Garner c Howarth b Cairns	0	– b Hadlee	2
M. A. Holding lbw b Hadlee	4	– c Cairns b Troup	3
C. E. H. Croft not out	0	– not out	1
L-b 8, n-b 9	17	L-b 4, n-b 5	9

1/3 2/4 3/4 4/72   140   1/4 2/21 3/24 4/29   212
5/91 6/105 7/124 8/125 9/136   5/116 6/180 7/186 8/188 9/209

Bowling: *First Innings*—Hadlee 20–9–34–5; Troup 17–6–26–2; Cairns 15–5–32–2; Boock 13–4–31–1. *Second Innings*—Hadlee 36–13–68–6; Troup 36.4–13–57–3; Cairns 25–10–63–1; Boock 11–4–15–0.

New Zealand

J. G. Wright b Holding	21	– b Holding	11
B. A. Edgar lbw b Parry	65	– c Greenidge b Holding	6
*G. P. Howarth c Murray b Croft	33	– c Greenidge b Croft	11
J. M. Parker b Croft	0	– c Murray b Garner	5
P. N. Webb lbw b Parry	5	– (6) lbw b Garner	5
J. V. Coney b Holding	8	– (5) lbw b Croft	2
†W. K. Lees run out	18	– lbw b Garner	0
R. J. Hadlee c Lloyd b Garner	51	– b Garner	17
B. L. Cairns b Croft	30	– c Murray b Holding	19
G. B. Troup c Greenidge b Croft	0	– not out	7
S. L. Boock not out	0	– not out	2
B 5, l-b 2, n-b 11	18	B 7, l-b 5, n-b 7	19

1/42 2/109 3/110 4/133   249   1/15 2/28 3/40 4/44   (9 wkts) 104
5/145 6/159 7/168 8/222 9/236   5/44 6/44 7/54 8/73 9/100

Bowling: *First Innings*—Holding 22–5–50–2; Croft 25–3–64–4; Garner 25.5–8–51–1; King 1–0–3–0; Parry 22–6–63–2. *Second Innings*—Holding 16–7–24–3; Croft 11–2–25–2; Garner 23–6–36–4.

Umpires: F. R. Goodall and J. B. R. Hastie.

CENTRAL DISTRICTS v WEST INDIANS

At New Plymouth, February 15. West Indians won by ten wickets. A startling mid-order collapse took the home team from 99 for three to 104 for nine in this 45 overs game. Greenidge and Haynes had little trouble knocking off the runs with twelve overs to spare.

Central Districts 130 (G. N. Edwards 33; A. M. E. Roberts four for 20); West Indians 134 for no wkt (C. G. Greenidge 66 not out, D. L. Haynes 62 not out).

WELLINGTON v WEST INDIANS

At Lower Hutt, February 16, 17, 18. West Indians lost by six wickets. This game was played on a sub-standard pitch, with sharp movement off the seam, but a side reputed to be the world's best played poorly. There were many careless strokes as the West Indians were bundled out for 102. Marshall and Garner were mainly responsible for Wellington making only 93. Haynes attacked vigorously in the tourists' second innings, and Wellington's task of making 153 seemed very difficult. However, a courageous innings by Coney took Wellington to their first win over an overseas team for 45 years. Chatfield, an occasional Test player, had the remarkable match figures of thirteen for 86.

West Indians

C. G. Greenidge c Newdick b Chatfield	4	– c Morrison b Chatfield	6
D. L. Haynes c Gray b Chatfield	3	– c Vance b Chatfield	58
L. G. Rowe b Cater	15	– b Chatfield	1
H. A. Gomes c Morrison b Cater	13	– c Gray b Cater	8
*A. I. Kallicharran c and b Chatfield	13	– b Chatfield	5
†D. A. Murray lbw b Cater	1	– c Coney b Cater	11
C. L. King b Chatfield	27	– c Reid b Cater	6
D. R. Parry not out	1	– c Vance b Chatfield	16
M. D. Marshall b Chatfield	0	– not out	13
J. Garner c Morrison b Chatfield	2	– lbw b Chatfield	3
M. A. Holding c Coney b Cater	5	– c Reid b Chatfield	0
B 6, l-b 11, n-b 1	18	B 6, l-b 9, n-b 1	16

1/7 2/12 3/35 4/41　　　　　　　　102　　1/23 2/53 3/83 4/91　　　　　　　143
5/49 6/88 7/93 8/93 9/97　　　　　　　　　　5/95 6/102 7/119 8/135 9/143

Bowling: *First Innings*—Taylor 12–4–16–0; Chatfield 18–7–33–6; Cater 13.3–3–35–4. *Second Innings*—Taylor 8–2–20–0; Chatfield 17.4–6–53–7; Cater 12–2–54–3.

Wellington

B. A. Edgar c Garner b Marshall	14	– b Marshall	14
G. A. Newdick c Garner b Holding	2	– c and b Marshall	8
†R. H. Vance c Murray b Marshall	14	– c Murray b King	21
J. V. Coney lbw b Garner	15	– not out	69
*J. F. M. Morrison c King b Marshall	16	– hit wkt b Garner	16
R. B. Reid b Marshall	0	– not out	14
A. M. Wilson lbw b Garner	8		
E. J. Gray lbw b Marshall	0		
B. R. Taylor c Marshall b Garner	10		
S. R. Cater not out	4		
E. J. Chatfield b Garner	0		
B 4, l-b 4, n-b 2	10	B 5, l-b 7, n-b 1	13

1/19 2/19 3/49 4/65　　　　　　　　93　　1/17 2/39 3/56 4/118　　(4 wkts) 155
5/65 6/78 7/78 8/86 9/93

Bowling: *First Innings*—Holding 6–2–15–1; Marshall 16–3–43–5; Garner 10–2–25–4. *Second Innings*—Holding 20–4–46–0; Marshall 17–6–40–2; Garner 15.1–5–28–1; King 6–2–19–1; Parry 1–0–9–0.

Umpires: W. R. C. Gardiner and D. A. Kinsella.

NEW ZEALAND v WEST INDIES

Second Test Match

At Christchurch, February 22, 23, 24, 26, 27. Drawn. Sent in on a pitch which yielded some early bounce and movement, West Indies lost three wickets for 28, but when rain ended play for the day just before tea Greenidge and Kallicharran had advanced the score to 166. With Hadlee suffering from an ankle injury, New Zealand's attack was not sharp. Play was not resumed until 1.00 p.m. on the second day, and Greenidge and Kallicharran proceeded quite comfortably to 190, their stand of 162 equalling West Indies' fourth-wicket record against New Zealand. However, Greenidge's departure preceded some ill-disciplined batting. Kallicharran, Murray, Lloyd and Garner all went to wild attempts to hit across the line of the ball, and on a good batting surface the last seven wickets fell for 38. It was an incredible display. New Zealand batted, without loss, for seven overs before play ended ninety minutes early.

After losing Wright to the first ball of the third day, and Webb three runs later, New Zealand took control. Batting for almost six hours, Howarth made his fifth Test century and there was sound support from Parker and Coney. New Zealand had six wickets in hand when they passed West Indies' score, and the bowling became very ordinary as Hadlee hit his first Test century in only 115 minutes and from 92 deliveries (eleven 4s and two 6s).

West Indies batted again, just after tea on the fourth day, facing a deficit of 232, and in perfect conditions they prospered. Greenidge and Haynes put on 225 for the first wicket, only 14 short of West Indies' opening record against all countries, before Greenidge was out in the 90s for the second time. Haynes hit his second century of the series, Rowe reached three figures in three hours, and King helped himself to a century in little more than two hours of inconsequential cricket.

West Indies

C. G. Greenidge c Boock b Troup	91	– c Lees b Troup	97
D. L. Haynes c Parker b Hadlee	0	– c Cairns b Coney	122
L. G. Rowe lbw b Cairns	11	– c Boock b Howarth	100
C. L. King c Cairns	0	– (6) not out	100
A. I. Kallicharran c Wright b Cairns	75	– (4) c Lees b Troup	0
*C. H. Lloyd c Howarth b Cairns	14	– (5) b Boock	7
†D. L. Murray c Webb b Cairns	6	– not out	1
J. Garner c sub b Cairns	0		
C. E. H. Croft b Hadlee	0		
A. M. E. Roberts not out	17		
M. A. Holding lbw b Hadlee	0		
B 1, l-b 9, n-b 4	14	B 5, l-b 8, w 1, n-b 6	20

1/1 2/28 3/28 4/190	228	1/225 2/233 3/234	(5 wkts) 447
5/190 6/210 7/210 8/214 9/224		4/268 5/436	

Bowling: *First Innings*—Hadlee 23.3–5–58–3; Troup 21–7–38–1; Cairns 32–8–65–6; Coney 13–2–33–0. *Second Innings*—Hadlee 22–7–64–0; Troup 27–7–84–2; Cairns 28–8–107–0; Coney 19–2–71–1; Boock 18–3–69–1; Howarth 5–0–32–1.

New Zealand

J. G. Wright b Croft	5	B. L. Cairns run out	1
B. A. Edgar c Murray b Holding	21	G. B. Troup not out	13
P. N. Webb b Roberts	1	S. L. Boock c and b Kallicharran	6
*G. P. Howarth b Holding	147		
J. M. Parker b Garner	42	B 18, l-b 6, n-b 14	38
J. V. Coney c King b Roberts	80		
†W. K. Lees c Rowe b Garner	3	1/15 2/18 3/53 4/175	460
R. J. Hadlee b Kallicharran	103	5/267 6/292 7/390 8/404 9/448	

Bowling: Roberts 29–6–82–2; Holding 29–5–97–2; Garner 28–4–75–2; Croft 24–3–78–1; King 9–0–70–0; Kallicharran 6.4–1–16–2; Rowe 5–2–4–0.

Umpires: F. R. Goodall and S. J. Woodward.

NEW ZEALAND v WEST INDIES

Third Test Match

At Auckland, February 29, March 1, 2, 3, 4, 5. Drawn. Howarth again sent West Indies in after winning the toss and again the seamers had assistance, although the bounce was modest. McEwan, in his first Test, took a splendid catch at slip to dismiss Greenidge, and until lunch the batsmen were defeated regularly. Rowe struggled for three hours over 50, but passed 2,000 runs in Tests. Ninety minutes of play were lost through rain as West Indies struggled to 146 for five. On the second day the game did not resume until 2.30, and West Indies reached 220 only with the aid of some bad lapses in New Zealand's fielding. The next day was washed out and the rest day became the third day. By the end of it New Zealand were 239 for four, mainly through the conscientious batting of Edgar who was in for seven and a quarter hours for his 127. Howarth and Coney also batted stubbornly, but this time the tail collapsed and New Zealand led by only 85. Garner, the first West Indian bowler to appreciate the value of keeping the ball up, took five for 13 in his last spell. By the end of the fourth day West Indies were 36 ahead, with Haynes and Rowe out, but on the final day there was little prospect of a finish. Troup, with his best display in Tests, took ten wickets in the match, and West Indies could not score fast enough to make a practical declaration. New Zealand were left 154 minutes to score 180, and although there were two early run-outs the game petered to a close, bad light ending it twenty minutes early.

West Indies

C. G. Greenidge c McEwan b Hadlee	7	– c Lees b Cairns	74
D. L. Haynes c Edgar b Cairns	9	– b Troup	48
L. G. Rowe run out	50	– c Lees b Troup	5
A. I. Kallicharran c Cairns b Troup	25	– lbw b Troup	25
*C. H. Lloyd b Wright b Troup	11	– c Lees b Troup	42
C. L. King c Troup b Hadlee	23	– c Howarth b Troup	9
†D. L. Murray c Lees b Hadlee	16	– lbw b Cairns	7
A. M. E. Roberts not out	35	– c McEwan b Troup	26
J. Garner b Troup	3	– b Hadlee	7
M. A. Holding lbw b Hadlee	5	– not out	16
C. E. H. Croft b Troup	6		
B 1, l-b 7, n-b 1	9	B 1, l-b 2, n-b 2	5

1/10 2/36 3/116 4/116   220   1/86 2/92 3/137   (9 wkts dec.) 264
5/116 6/167 7/169 8/178 9/197   4/147 5/169 6/193
                                                        7/228 8/239 9/264

Bowling: *First Innings*—Hadlee 31–8–75–4; Troup 31.2–11–71–4; Cairns 20–9–56–1; Boock 2–0–9–0. *Second Innings*—Hadlee 29–8–62–1; Troup 29.1–5–95–6; Cairns 30–7–76–2; Boock 6–1–26–0.

New Zealand

J. G. Wright c Greenidge b Croft	23	– c Haynes b Kallicharran	23
B. A. Edgar b Roberts	127	– (5) not out	22
*G. P. Howarth c Haynes b Croft	47	– (2) run out	1
P. E. McEwan c Murray b Croft	5	– (3) b Garner	21
J. M. Parker lbw b Garner	0	– (4) run out	1
J. V. Coney not out	49	– not out	1
†W. K. Lees b Garner	23		
R. J. Hadlee c Murray b Garner	7		
B. L. Cairns c Murray b Garner	1		
G. B. Troup b Garner	0		
S. L. Boock lbw b Garner	0		
B 4, l-b 8, n-b 11	23	L-b 3, n-b 1	4

1/75 2/171 3/185 4/186   305   1/4 2/30 3/32 4/71   (4 wkts) 73
5/241 6/277 7/299 8/303 9/303

Bowling: *First Innings*—Roberts 34–6–90–1; Holding 33–3–54–0; Croft 33–6–81–3; Garner 36.2–15–56–6; King 2–1–1–0. *Second Innings*—Roberts 9–2–24–0; Holding 4–1–11–0; Croft 10–4–17–0; Garner 9–1–17–1; Kallicharran 4–4–0–1.

Umpires: W. R. C. Gardiner and J. B. R. Hastie.

THE AUSTRALIANS IN INDIA, 1979-80

By DICKY RUTNAGUR

The Australians' third full tour of India was of historic interest on two counts. It was Australia's final campaign before the compromise between the Australian Cricket Board of Control and World Series Cricket took effect, and it was important from their opponents' viewpoint because India won a series (2-0) against Australia for the first time. The two countries had previously contested seven rubbers over 31 years, during which India had won only five Tests to Australia's nineteen, with six drawn.

In terms of results, Australia had a poor tour. They completed it without a single win and, as well as their two losses in the series of six Tests, they were beaten by East Zone, possibly the weakest side they encountered. But to put this defeat in perspective, it must be mentioned that the tourists brought it on themselves with two declarations which were intended to finish the match in two days.

The result of the Test series was not unexpected, for the Australians were relatively inexperienced, ten of the party of fifteen never having toured before. Moreover, they were all new to conditions on the Indian sub-continent. They did have some early advantage in that India had just returned from a long and strenuous tour of England and had had no time at all to acclimatise before going into the first Test. Furthermore, India themselves were in the throes of rebuilding their side.

The main Australian gain of the tour was the tremendous advance made by two batsmen, Hughes and Border. Between the first Test and the last there was a marked development in Hughes's technique of playing spin bowling, and happily the heavy burden of captaincy had no adverse effect on his batting. The duties of captaincy might have weighed more heavily had the team management not been so superbly handled by Bob Merriman of Geelong.

The fact that Hughes's twelve innings in the series produced only one century is no reflection on his consistency. He passed the half-century mark in every Test but one and could certainly have made more runs had he not batted as positively and purposefully as he did. Border, whose Test aggregate – like Hughes's – also exceeded 500, started the series more strongly than he finished it. But as his form declined, another left-hander, Yallop, came into his own.

The most experienced player in the side, Yallop was at his best when batting conditions were most difficult. In the last two Tests, he opened the innings and filled the rôle with distinction. If he did not make an earlier impact on the series it was partly because, more than once, he was dismissed in unfortunate ways.

A major weakness of the Australian batting was its fragility at the top of the order. Wood and Darling took turns to open with Hilditch before Yallop moved up the order, and even his promotion did not remedy the situation. The best Australian opening partnership in the entire series was one of 32.

Yet this was not Australia's only weakness, nor the most prominent. It was the lack of depth to their bowling and their generally poor out-cricket that put them at such a disadvantage. On the few occasions when their bowlers rose to any heights, they were let down by the fielders, with many more slip chances going down than were held.

Fitness problems also were acute. Hurst injured his back quite early on the tour and, finding his injury unresponsive to treatment, went home after the third Test. Yardley, whose all-round ability served the Australians well in a couple of Tests, was prone to accident and illness. He was missed especially in the final Test at Bombay, where the ball turned quite extravagantly.

Hogg, who had taken a record 41 wickets in Australia's previous series, against England, was a major disappointment. In the early days of the tour he could not find his rhythm and was frequently no balled for over-stepping. This difficulty, as well as the lack of pace in the pitches, seemed to demoralise him and he roused himself only in the third and fourth Tests.

Leg-spinner Higgs had a brilliant first Test, in which he severely pressed the Indian batsmen and took seven wickets for 143 runs. But he was mastered thereafter. Easily the outstanding bowler was the veteran Dymock, always industrious, brave and thoughtful, returning match figures of twelve for 166 in the third Test. Yet this was a Test in which Australia were soundly beaten.

The series marked the end of an era in Indian cricket as, for the first time in eleven years, India took the field without any of their three great contemporary spinners, Chandrasekhar, Bedi and Prasanna. Venkataraghavan also lost his place after the first two Tests.

Bedi's mantle fell on 31-year-old Doshi, new to Test cricket but highly experienced after ten years in first-class cricket, both at home and in England. The new off-spinner was Yadav, of Hyderabad, still in his early 20s. Taking 27 and 24 wickets respectively, Doshi and Yadav played prominent parts in India's success. But the main wicket-taker, with 28 victims, was pace bowler Kapil Dev, who showed how much he had benefited from the tour of England.

India's most prolific batsman was Viswanath, who made 518 runs, including two centuries. Only he accumulated more runs than Gavaskar, who looked in want of a rest after the England tour yet aggregated 425 with two hundreds. Chauhan was a loyal and stubborn opening partner for Gavaskar and was in the forefront in the third Test, at Kanpur. India, who were behind on the first innings and 48 for two in the second, might have been in desperate trouble without Chauhan's marathon innings of six and a half hours for 84 runs. In the first innings, too, when the pitch was lively, he batted for five hours, giving India a fine start, which the later batsmen did not exploit.

In the middle order, Vengsarkar and Yashpal Sharma both made many valuable contributions and were capable of playing long innings. Yet there were indications that Yashpal, whose back foot made an initial movement away from the leg stump, would have been less successful against an attack with a fuller complement of fast bowlers. The return of Kirmani, omitted from the England tour, gave the side great strength. As wicket-keeper, he was in peak form and was never found wanting with the bat when runs were needed.

To suit Australia's convenience, the tour was scheduled for an unusually early time in the season, when the monsoons had not quite receded. The first two Test matches, played in September, were both drastically affected by the weather and it was fortunate that the others were free of interference. The Indian Board would be unfair to the paying public if, in future, they arranged tours starting any earlier than mid-November.

AUSTRALIANS TOUR RESULTS

Test matches – Played 6: Lost 2, Drawn 4.

First-class matches – Played 11: Lost 3, Drawn 8.

Losses – India (2), East Zone.

Draws – India (4), North Zone, South Zone, Central Zone, West Zone.

TEST MATCH AVERAGES

INDIA – BATTING

	Tests	Innings	Not Outs	Runs	Highest Inns	Average
G. R. Viswanath	6	8	1	518	161*	74.00
S. M. H. Kirmani	6	7	2	285	101*	57.00
S. M. Gavaskar.	6	8	0	425	123	53.12
Yashpal Sharma	6	8	2	304	100*	50.66
C. P. S. Chauhan	6	8	0	380	84	47.50
D. B. Vengsarkar	6	8	0	372	112	46.50
K. D. Ghavri.	6	6	2	148	86	37.00
Kapil Dev	6	7	1	212	83	35.33
M. V. Narasimha Rao .	2	3	1	35	20*	17.50
N. S. Yadav	5	4	1	18	18	6.00
S. Venkataraghavan . . .	3	3	1	9	4*	4.50
D. R. Doshi.	6	4	1	3	3	1.00

Played in one Test: M. Amarnath 2; Yajurvindra Singh 15.

* *Signifies not out.*

BOWLING

	Overs	Maidens	Runs	Wickets	Average
Kapil Dev	223.1	53	625	28	22.32
D. R. Doshi.	306.2	87	630	27	23.33
N. S. Yadav	234.3	63	577	24	24.04
K. D. Ghavri.	201.4	48	556	11	50.54
S. Venkataraghavan . . .	146	44	308	6	51.33

Also bowled: M. Amarnath 7–2–12–0; C. P. S. Chauhan 9–1–22–1; S. M. Gavaskar 4–1–10–0; M. V. Narasimha Rao 39–4–120–2; G. R. Viswanath 3.3–0–11–1; Yajurvindra Singh 9–1–29–0.

AUSTRALIA – BATTING

	Tests	Innings	Not Outs	Runs	Highest Inns	Average
K. J. Hughes.........	6	12	2	594	100	59.40
A. R. Border.........	6	12	0	521	162	43.41
B. Yardley..........	3	5	1	154	61*	38.50
G. N. Yallop.........	6	12	1	423	167	38.45
A. M. J. Hilditch......	6	12	0	313	85	26.08
K. J. Wright.........	6	11	4	156	55*	22.28
D. F. Whatmore......	5	10	0	220	77	22.00
P. R. Sleep	2	4	0	85	64	21.25
G. M. Wood	2	4	0	83	33	20.75
W. M. Darling........	5	9	1	158	59	19.75
G. Dymock..........	5	9	2	103	31*	14.71
R. M. Hogg.........	6	10	2	54	19	6.75
J. D. Higgs.........	6	9	3	36	11	6.00
A. G. Hurst..........	2	2	0	0	0	0.00

* Signifies not out.

BOWLING

	Overs	Maidens	Runs	Wickets	Average
G. Dymock..........	212.4	46	580	24	24.16
B. Yardley..........	159	49	381	10	38.10
J. D. Higgs	227.3	62	702	14	50.14
R. M. Hogg.........	194.2	39	591	11	53.72

Also bowled: A. R. Border 52–16–110–3; A. G. Hurst 52–11–144–0; P. R. Sleep 41–8–145–0; D. F. Whatmore 5–2–11–0; G. N. Yallop 16–2–62–1.

AUSTRALIAN AVERAGES – FIRST-CLASS MATCHES

BATTING

	Matches	Innings	Not Outs	Runs	Highest Inns	Average
K. J. Hughes.........	10	19	3	858	126	53.62
G. N. Yallop.........	10	19	4	729	167	48.60
A. R. Border.........	10	19	0	749	162	39.42
B. Yardley..........	5	8	2	173	61*	28.83
A. M. J. Hilditch......	10	19	1	507	85	26.16
W. M. Darling........	9	13	1	304	82	25.33
D. F. Whatmore......	9	17	0	411	77	24.17
K. J. Wright	10	17	6	252	55*	22.90
G. Dymock..........	8	10	2	156	53	19.50
P. R. Sleep	6	10	1	175	64	19.44
G. D. Porter	4	5	3	30	13	15.00
G. M. Wood	6	10	0	138	33	13.80
R. M. Hogg.........	9	13	3	94	22	9.40
J. D. Higgs	10	11	3	43	11	5.37
A. G. Hurst..........	4	3	1	6	6*	3.00

Played in one match: G. F. Lawson 3.

* Signifies not out.

BOWLING

	Overs	Maidens	Runs	Wickets	Average
G. Dymock..........	287.4	67	738	32	23.06
A. R. Border.........	87.2	20	207	7	29.57
P. R. Sleep	132.1	24	442	14	31.57
B. Yardley...........	230	71	555	17	32.64
J. D. Higgs	347	109	953	29	32.86
A. G. Hurst..........	91.4	26	224	6	37.33
R. M. Hogg..........	248.2	54	747	20	37.35

Also bowled: G. F. Lawson 15–9–23–3; G. D. Porter 78–22–193–1; D. F. Whatmore 10.1–4–25–3; G. M. Wood 14–3–31–4; G. N. Yallop 41–3–146–1.

FIELDING

K. J. Wright 23 (20ct, 3st), D. F. Whatmore 20, A. M. J. Hilditch 9, K. J. Hughes 9, G. N. Yallop 7 (6ct, 1st); A. R. Border 5, R. M. Hogg 4, G. D. Porter 4, W. M. Darling 2, G. M. Wood 2, J. D. Higgs 1, A. G. Hurst 1, G. F. Lawson 1, P. R. Sleep 1, B. Yardley 1.

HUNDREDS FOR AUSTRALIANS

The following five three-figure innings were played for the Australians.

A, R. Border (2)
  162   v India at Madras (First Test)
  113   v South Zone at Hyderabad

K. J. Hughes (2)
  126   v West Zone at Ahmedabad
  100   v India at Madras (First Test)

G.N. Yallop (1)
  167   v India at Calcutta (Fifth Test)

HUNDREDS AGAINST AUSTRALIANS

The following seven three-figure innings were played against the Australians.

S. M. Gavaskar (2)
  123   for India at Bombay (Sixth Test)
  115   for India at Delhi (Fourth Test)

G. R. Viswanath (2)
  161* for India at Bangalore (Second Test)
  131   for India at Delhi (Fourth Test)

S. M. H. Kirmani (1)
  101* for India at Bombay (Sixth Test)

D. B. Vengsarkar (1)
  112   for India at Bangalore (Second Test)

Yashpal Sharma (1)
  100* for India at Delhi (Fourth Test)

  * *Signifies not out.*

NORTH ZONE v AUSTRALIANS

At Srinagar, September 1, 2, 3. Drawn. With the Indian team still on tour in England, North Zone were well below full strength. Yet they held their own, thanks to the shrewd bowling of veteran left-arm spinner Goel and fine batting by Arun Lal, whose 99 brought him into contention for a Test place. After winning the toss, the Australians enjoyed the best of a pitch that deteriorated quickly. Although this was their opening fixture of the tour, and one of only two matches before the first Test, they batted positively and scored 363 on the first day. When North Zone replied Hurst and Dymock made early strikes and the Australians gained a first innings lead of 113 runs. However, with only five hours left, a draw was inevitable.

Australians

A. M. J. Hilditch b Goel	71	– c Arun Lal b Valson 35
W. M. Darling c Kumar b Goel	34	
A. R. Border b Kumar	12	– (2) b Valson 16
*K. J. Hughes c sub b Goel	70	– (6) b Goel 21
G. N. Yallop c Handa b Kumar	83	– (7) not out 4
D. F. Whatmore c Malhotra b Chopra	1	– (3) c Chaddha b Kumar 33
†K. J. Wright c Chopra b Goel	8	– (5) c Arun Lal b Goel 0
B. Yardley st Vedraj b Kumar	4	– (4) c Azad b Goel 13
G. Dymock b Goel	53	
J. D. Higgs c Chopra b Goel	7	
A. G. Hurst not out	6	
B 2, l-b 5, n-b 7	14	B 13, l-b 6, n-b 6 25

1/75 2/103 3/152 4/233 5/238   363   1/51 2/75 3/97   (6 wkts dec.) 147
6/254 7/260 8/330 9/350   4/101 5/137 6/147

Bowling: *First Innings*—Valson 8-2-31-0; Chaddha 6-2-16-0; Goel 34-6-104-6; Kumar 25-2-102-3; Chopra 23-3-96-1. *Second Innings*—Valson 13-3-41-2; Chaddha 4-0-9-0; Goel 20.4-8-43-3; Kumar 12-2-29-1.

North Zone

†Vedraj c Hughes b Hurst	0	– lbw b Yardley 6
R. Handa b Hurst	14	– not out 39
A. Malhotra lbw b Yardley	22	– c Hilditch b Yardley 9
S. Arun Lal b Dymock	99	
*S. Amarnath lbw b Dymock	2	
R. Chaddha b Dymock	0	
D. Chopra c Whatmore b Dymock	54	– (4) not out 13
Kirti Azad b Hurst	19	
Umesh Kumar c Wright b Hurst	0	
S. Valson not out	1	
R. Goel c Yallop b Hurst	0	
B 14, l-b 10, n-b 15	39	B 9 9

1/5 2/42 3/72 4/79 5/83 6/221   250   1/15 2/35   (2 wkts) 76
7/248 8/248 9/250

Bowling: *First Innings*—Hurst 19.4-9-33-5; Dymock 25-12-25-4; Yardley 25-8-60-1; Higgs 19-8-34-0; Border 9-1-33-0; Yallop 8-0-26-0. *Second Innings*—Yardley 12-3-38-2; Higgs 6-2-8-0; Yallop 6-0-21-0.

Umpires: Swaroop Kishen and K. B. Ramaswamy.

SOUTH ZONE v AUSTRALIANS

At Hyderabad, September 6, 7, 8. Drawn. The Australians had much the better of this unfinished game and it is likely they would have won had rain not prevented play after tea on the second day and delayed the start on the third. On a pitch giving only slightly variable bounce Hogg and leg-spinner Sleep did most damage as South Zone collapsed for 196.

While the Australians built a substantial lead, Border, making the first century of the tour, Yallop and Wright showed themselves ready for the first Test. The home side's batting was very brittle although Srinivasan and Sivaramakrishnan played with flourish when South Zone batted again. At the end they were just 41 runs ahead with only four wickets standing, but they would have been in deeper trouble had Hogg not lost his effectiveness after being no balled several times for over-stepping.

South Zone

V. Sivaramakrishnan c Wright b Wood	7	– (5) c Hughes b Sleep	32
S. B. Jung lbw b Hogg	14	– lbw b Sleep	23
V. Mohan Raj c Yallop b Hogg	6	– (6) not out	16
T. E. Srinivasan c Hilditch b Hogg	30	– c Hilditch b Higgs	34
R. M. Binny c Hogg b Sleep	53	– (1) c Wright b Hogg	0
M. V. Narasimha Rao c Porter b Sleep	1		
*†S. M. H. Kirmani c Porter b Higgs	32		
A. V. Jayaprakash c Wright b Sleep	10	– (3) c Hilditch b Higgs	18
P. Jyoti Prasad lbw b Higgs	11		
J. Kishore not out	7	– (8) not out	15
N. S. Yadav b Higgs	4	– (7) run out	0
L-b 4, w 3, n-b 14	21	B 6, n-b 7	13

1/24 2/32 3/57 4/82 5/84 6/145   196   1/0 2/43 3/52   (6 wkts) 151
7/172 8/185 9/185   4/110 5/125 6/128

Bowling: *First Innings*—Hogg 16–7–37–3; Porter 17–7–31–0; Wood 5–1–9–1; Higgs 24.1–8–48–3; Yallop 1–0–3–0; Sleep 16–4–47–3. *Second Innings*—Hogg 10–1–36–1; Porter 6–3–10–0; Higgs 16–8–29–2; Sleep 17–2–52–2; Border 2–0–11–0.

Australians

A. M. J. Hilditch c Kirmani b Binny	3	†K. J. Wright not out	52
G. M. Wood b Prasad	10	R. M. Hogg c Yadav b Binny	22
A. R. Border b Yadav	113	G. D. Porter not out	1
*K. J. Hughes c Sivaramakrishnan b Narasimha Rao.	26	B 3, l-b 10, w 1, n-b 9	23
G. N. Yallop c Prasad b Narasimha Rao.	56	1/4 2/19 3/85 4/215 (7 wkts dec.) 306	
P. R. Sleep c and b Narasimha Rao	0	5/216 6/229 7/284	

J. D. Higgs and W. M. Darling did not bat.

Bowling: Binny 12–2–26–2; Prasad 8–3–17–1; Narasimha Rao 32–6–97–3; Yadav 28–3–74–1; Kishore 9–0–54–0; Jayaprakash 2.2–0–15–0.

Umpires: M. V. Gothaskar and P. R. Punjabi.

INDIA v AUSTRALIA

First Test Match

At Madras, September 11, 12, 14, 15, 16. Drawn. Although rain seriously disrupted play on the last two days, a decisive result already looked unlikely after both sides, helped by dropped catches, had raised substantial first innings totals. Ironically, the Australians were better acclimatised than the home side, having practised in these conditions for almost a week, with two pre-Test matches. The Indians, however, had just returned from England, the Test match starting only a week after the end of the epic fifth Test at The Oval. Besides being travel-weary, they had to adjust hurriedly to vast differences in weather, light and pitch conditions.

To the Indians, therefore, losing the toss was not a big disadvantage. Australia batted for over eight hours to score 390, with most of the runs coming from a record third-wicket partnership of 222 between Border and Hughes.

Australia would have had to struggle harder had Ghavri bowled a straighter line in conditions favourable to swing bowling. Furthermore, the important partnership between Border and Hughes could have been broken quite early for, before he had scored, Border was put down at backward short-leg – ironically, by Yajurvindra Singh, an outstanding close-fielder. Border made India pay heavily for this lapse, hitting one 6 and 24 4s in just under seven hours. He was eventually out in a most unfortunate manner. Backing up at the non-striker's end, he was caught out of his ground when a furious straight drive by Yallop was deflected by the bowler on to the stumps.

Hughes played responsibly for his century, which occupied two hundred and seventy-one minutes. He, too, had an escape when he was 65. The innings declined sharply after the dissolution of this partnership, the last seven wickets falling for only 72 runs. The havoc was wrought by left-arm spinner Doshi who, playing in his maiden Test, took six wickets for 103.

Although India scored 425 in reply, the size of their total belied the struggle that went into its making. The innings was marked by several crises and the Indian batting never got into top gear. The only batsmen to achieve any freedom were Gavaskar, who made 50 after surviving a confident appeal for lbw at 20, and Kapil Dev, who scored 83 off 73 balls.

The presence of Hogg in the Australian attack presumably influenced the preparation of a pitch slower than usual at Chepauk. As it was the Indians were hardly disconcerted by Hogg who, apart from being unable to achieve any pace, had immense trouble in keeping his front foot behind the popping crease. The bowler to test the Indian batting was Higgs, who was remarkably tidy for a leg-spinner and took seven wickets for 143, suffering only at the hands of Kapil Dev.

When batting a second time, Australia were again sustained by Border. He and Hilditch added 101 for the second wicket before Australia were put under heavy stress by the spin of Doshi and Venkataraghavan. Tailenders Dymock and Hogg came together twenty minutes after lunch to rescue the innings at 175 for seven. Both were dropped early in their innings but, with rain having the final word, these errors amounted to little, although they might have proved crucial had the contest not been interrupted.

Australia

A. M. J. Hilditch c Venkataraghavan b Kapil Dev.	4	– lbw b Doshi 55
G. M. Wood lbw b Doshi	33	– c Chauhan b Kapil Dev 2
A. R. Border run out	162	– b Venkataraghavan 50
*K. J. Hughes c Venkataraghavan b Doshi	100	– lbw b Venkataraghavan 36
G. N. Yallop c Yajurvindra b Doshi.	18	– run out 2
D. F. Whatmore c Venkataraghavan b Doshi	20	– c Chauhan b Doshi 8
†K. J. Wright b Venkataraghavan	20	– b Venkataraghavan 5
G. Dymock lbw b Kapil Dev	16	– not out 28
R. M. Hogg c Kapil Dev b Doshi.	3	– not out 8
A. G. Hurst c Kirmani b Doshi	0	
J. D. Higgs not out	1	
B 1, l-b 7, w 1, n-b 4	13	B 11, l-b 4, n-b 3 18

1/8 2/75 3/297 4/318 5/339 6/352   390   1/2 2/103 3/123   (7 wkts) 212
7/369 8/375 9/376   4/127 5/146 6/156 7/175

Bowling: *First Innings*—Kapil Dev 25.4–3–95–2; Ghavri 20–4–49–0; Yajurvindra 9–1–29–0; Venkataraghavan 46–16–101–1; Doshi 43–10–103–6. *Second Innings*—Kapil Dev 9–3–30–1; Ghavri 17.4–8–23–0; Venkataraghavan 45–10–77–3; Doshi 42–15–64–2.

India

*S. M. Gavaskar c Wood b Hogg	50	K. D. Ghavri not out 23
C. P. S. Chauhan c Wright b Higgs	26	S. Venkataraghavan lbw b Higgs 4
†S. M. H. Kirmani b Border b Hogg	57	D. R. Doshi c Hogg b Higgs 3
G. R. Viswanath c Hughes b Higgs	17	
D. B. Vengsarkar c Whatmore b Higgs . .	65	B 2, l-b 5, n-b 23 30
Yashpal Sharma lbw b Higgs.	52	
Yajurvindra Singh c Wright b Yallop. . . .	15	1/80 2/89 3/122 4/221 5/240 425
Kapil Dev c Hurst b Higgs.	83	6/281 7/371 8/394 9/417

Bowling: First Innings—Kapil Dev 25.4–3–95–2; Ghavri 20–4–49–0; Yajurvindra 9–1–29–0; Venkataraghavan 46–16–101–1; Doshi 43–10–103–6. Second Innings—Kapil Dev 9–3–30–1; Ghavri 17.4–8–23–0; Venkataraghavan 45–10–77–3; Doshi 42–15–64–2.

Bowling: Hogg 22–1–85–2; Hurst 23–8–51–0; Higgs 41.3–12–143–7; Dymock 24–6–65–0; Border 14–4–30–0; Yallop 6–1–21–1.

Umpires: Swaroop Kishen and M. V. Gothaskar.

INDIA v AUSTRALIA

Second Test Match

At Bangalore, September 19, 20, 22, 23, 24. Drawn. This Test, like the first, was drastically affected by rain, making a draw unavoidable. What play was possible, however, emphasised that the home side held the edge over the touring side.

Australia, with one change in their side, elected to bat first again on a slow pitch. Although there were useful contributions from Hilditch and all-rounder Yardley they once more relied heavily on Border and Hughes for their total.

The home team started indifferently when they replied after tea on the second day, but they were steadied by a record fourth-wicket partnership against Australia of 159 between Vengsarkar and Viswanath, both of whom scored centuries. With Vengsarkar circumspect and Viswanath below his best, runs came ponderously even though the Australian bowling was by no means testing. With rain lopping off much of the third day's play, it was not until halfway through the last morning that Gavaskar was able to declare 124 ahead.

On the slow pitch the main Australian bowling weapon was the off-spin of Yardley, who took four wickets for 107. The pace bowlers were quite innocuous. Hogg could not work up speed, and at the start of the Indian innings again had trouble landing his front foot in the right place. After being no balled seven times in five overs delivered from different ends, Hogg lost his temper on the second evening and kicked down the stumps. The incident would have fouled the atmosphere had Hughes not taken prompt action, tendering an immediate apology to the umpire and persuading Hogg to express his regret at the end of the day's play.

Australia, batting again with four and a half hours left, were in desperate trouble at 77 for three when rain interfered decisively. All the wickets fell to off-spinner Yadav, who returned match figures of seven for 81 in his first Test.

Australia

A. M. J. Hilditch c sub b Yadav	62	– lbw b Yadav	3
W. M. Darling b Kapil Dev	7		
A. R. Border c Yadav b Doshi	44	– b Yadav	19
*K. J. Hughes c Ghavri b Kapil Dev	86	– not out	13
G. N. Yallop c Viswanath b Yadav	12	– not out	6
B. Yardley c and b Ghavri	47		
G. M. Wood c Kirmani b Ghavri	18	– (2) c Viswanath b Yadav	30
†K. J. Wright not out	16		
R. M. Hogg lbw b Venkataraghavan	19		
J. D. Higgs lbw b Yadav	1		
A. G. Hurst b Yadav	0		
B 5, l-b 6, n-b 10	21	L-b 5, n-b 1	6

1/21 2/99 3/137 4/159 5/258   333   1/13 2/53 3/62   (3 wkts) 77
6/294 7/294 8/332 9/333

Bowling: *First Innings*—Kapil Dev 25–4–89–2; Ghavri 19–5–68–2; Doshi 28–6–63–1; Venkataraghavan 20–6–43–1; Yadav 22.5–6–49–4. *Second Innings*—Kapil Dev 3–2–1–0; Ghavri 3–1–9–0; Doshi 8–4–11–0; Venkataraghavan 8–2–18–0; Yadav 15.4–4–32–3.

India

*S. M. Gavaskar c Hilditch b Yardley	10	Kapil Dev not out	38
C. P. S. Chauhan c Hilditch b Yardley	31		
D. B. Vengsarkar lbw b Yardley	112	B 12, l-b 8, w 1, n-b 17	38
†S. M. H. Kirmani st Wright b Higgs	30		
G. R. Viswanath not out	161	1/22 2/61 3/120 (5 wkts dec.) 457
Yashpal Sharma c Border b Yardley	37	4/279 5/372	

N. S. Yadav, K. D. Ghavri, S. Venkataraghavan and D. R. Doshi did not bat.

Bowling: Hogg 32–6–118–0; Hurst 29–3–93–0; Yardley 44–16–107–4; Higgs 37–9–95–1; Yallop 2–0–6–0.

Umpires: K. B. Ramaswamy and P. R. Punjabi.

CENTRAL ZONE v AUSTRALIANS

At Nagpur, September 27, 28, 29. Drawn. A slow pitch made for painstaking batting by both sides. Central Zone owed much to Parthasarathy Sharma, a habitual maker of big scores against touring sides. Sleep took five wickets for 71 runs with his leg-spin and further pressed his claims for a Test place by scoring 61 not out in Australia's reply. Darling, who had missed the first Test through injury and failed in the second, found his form with an impressive 82 (ten 4s) and Whatmore was also seen to advantage with an innings of 60. Central Zone might have been in trouble had the Australians held all their chances; as it was, they batted on until tea before making a token declaration.

Central Zone

†V. Chopra c Darling b Yardley	26	– c Wright b Hogg	0
V. Telang lbw b Hogg	8	– c Wright b Sleep	71
A. Bhanot c Whatmore b Dymock	9	– lbw b Yardley	79
*P. Sharma c Porter b Sleep	96		
Mohammad Shahid retired hurt	4		
A. Deshpande c Yallop b Sleep	32	– (4) c Hilditch b Yardley	18
V. Mathur lbw b Sleep	24	– (5) not out	8
A. Mathur c Wright b Sleep	7		
G. Sharma c Wood b Yardley	2	– (6) b Whatmore	21
R. S. Hans c and b Sleep	7		
S. Shastri not out	0		
B 2, l-b 4, n-b 23	29	N-b 2	2

1/21 2/54 3/56 4/171 5/209 6/220   244   1/0 2/115 3/168   (5 wkts dec.) 199
7/223 8/243 9/244   4/169 5/199

Bowling: *First Innings*—Hogg 9–1–39–1; Dymock 19–5–35–1; Porter 10–2–29–0; Yardley 19–9–29–2; Sleep 19.1–2–71–5; Yallop 3–1–12–0. *Second Innings*—Hogg 6–2–15–1; Dymock 7–0–27–0; Porter 10–0–36–0; Yardley 15–2–47–2; Sleep 16–4–45–1; Yallop 7–0–22–0; Whatmore 1.4–0–5–1.

Australians

*A. M. J. Hilditch c Chopra b Deshpande	7	– not out	40
W. M. Darling c and b G. Sharma	82		
G. N. Yallop lbw b Hans	21	– (2) not out	40
D. F. Whatmore lbw b P. Sharma	60		
G. M. Wood b Shastri	13		
P. R. Sleep not out	61		
G. D. Porter run out	10		
†K. J. Wright b G. Sharma	6		
B. Yardley not out	2		
B 1, l-b 2, n-b 9	12	B 1, l-b 2	3

1/19 2/62 3/165 4/186   (7 wkts dec.) 274   (no wkt) 83
5/196 6/248 7/271

R. M. Hogg and G. Dymock did not bat.

Bowling: *First Innings*—A. Mathur 9–2–24–0; Hans 32–8–70–1; Shastri 19–5–54–1; Deshpande 8–2–15–1; P. Sharma 6–0–15–1; G. Sharma 29.1–3–76–2; V. Mathur 1–0–8–0. *Second Innings*—A. Mathur 4–1–7–0; Hans 8–1–11–0; Deshpande 5–0–25–0; G. Sharma 10–1–32–0; Telang 1–0–5–0.

Umpires: B. N. Hanumantha Rao and Mohammad Ghouse.

INDIA v AUSTRALIA

Third Test Match

At Kanpur, October 2, 3, 4, 6, 7. India won by 153 runs. The wide margin was surprising after Australia had the better of the first three days' play. Needing 279 in 312 m.nutes, the touring side were bowled out for 125 on a pitch that had been grassy and fast but which became unpredictable in bounce towards the end. The Australian batsmen could not cope with its whims. However, had they held their catches in India's second innings, the final target would have been less oppressive.

India won the toss for the first time in the series and reached 231 for five at the end of an eventful opening day. First use of the newly laid pitch seemed a mixed blessing, for it had pace and bounce to encourage Hogg, while Dymock found the heavy, humid atmosphere useful to swing. Nevertheless, Gavaskar and Chauhan gave India an encouraging start with a partnership of 114. Gavaskar played and missed often, being beaten four times by Hogg in one over alone before settling down to play a handsome innings. Chauhan survived an easy chance in the slips within twenty minutes of the start and went on to bat five hours for his 58. It was a dour, tedious innings, but it proved vital to his team's success.

Although India passed 200 with only one wicket lost, the initiative at the end of the day lay with Australia, thanks to Hogg's aggressive bowling, and a brilliant, low catch by Hughes at mid-off. Hogg removed Vengsarkar, Chauhan and Yashpal in fourteen balls as India lost four wickets for 30 runs in the last half hour. These setbacks were all the more serious because the new ball was due immediately on the following morning.

Thanks to Viswanath, last out for 44, India added another 40 runs before Hogg and Dymock completed the destruction. However, he could have prolonged the resistance had he made more active efforts to farm the bowling. He took a single off the first ball of the over in which Dymock removed Ghavri and Yadav with successive balls, and later Venkataraghavan was left similarly exposed.

Australia started their reply without opener Darling who had jarred his shoulder badly in a fall while fielding. India's collapse had provided ample evidence that the pitch still offered much to pace bowlers, but the home bowlers could not harness it with Kapil Dev, for once, bowling a poor line. Australia still made a stuttering start and their innings was without stability until Hughes and Yallop, coming together at 75 for three, put on 93 for the fourth wicket. Hughes looked set for a big score when, towards the end of the second day, he was bowled by a beautiful ball from Yadav. Yallop, with 89, atoned for his cheap dismissals in the previous Tests. He was in full cry when he lost his footing while driving Kapil Dev and trod on his wicket. The innings would then have petered out had the injured Darling, batting at number eight, not come to the rescue with a brave 59.

When India batted again Australia remained in control until they had captured the second wicket at 48. Then Chauhan, batting steadfastly, and Viswanath revived the innings and Kirmani, Ghavri and Yadav sustained the recovery. The ball turned from the start of their innings and it was only because Australia's spin resources were restricted to Yardley that India were able to raise a sizeable score.

The clock was in Australia's favour but there was no question of their getting the runs. Although surviving for five hours should not have been an impossible task, the Australian batsmen were undermined by the pitch's uneven bounce.

India

*S. M. Gavaskar lbw b Dymock	76	– c Whatmore b Yardley	12
C. P. S. Chauhan c and b Hogg	58	– c Yardley b Dymock	84
D. B. Vengsarkar lbw b Hogg	52	– c Whatmore b Dymock	20
G. R. Viswanath c sub b Dymock	44	– c Whatmore b Yardley	52
Yashpal Sharma b Hogg	0	– c Wright b Dymock	0
Kapil Dev c Hughes b Border	5	– b Dymock	10
†S. M. H. Kirmani c Whatmore b Hogg	4	– b Dymock	45
K. D. Ghavri c Whatmore b Dymock	5	– c sub b Hogg	25
N. S. Yadav lbw b Dymock	0	– c Whatmore b Dymock	18
S. Venkataraghavan c Border b Dymock	1	– not out	4
D. R. Doshi not out	0	– b Dymock	0
B 5, l-b 6, n-b 15	26	B 11, l-b 9, n-b 21	41

1/114 2/201 3/206 4/214 5/231   271   1/24 2/48 3/161 4/163 5/177   311
6/239 7/246 8/246 9/256   6/256 7/261 8/302 9/311

Bowling: *First Innings*—Dymock 35–7–99–5; Hogg 26–3–66–4; Yardley 26–6–54–0; Higgs 7–4–23–0; Border 3–2–3–1. *Second Innings*—Dymock 28.4–5–67–7; Hogg 19–4–49–1; Yardley 40–15–82–2; Higgs 22–7–68–0; Border 2–1–4–0.

Australia

A. M. J. Hilditch c Chauhan b Ghavri	1	– b Doshi	23
B. Yardley c Yashpal b Ghavri	29	– (8) lbw b Kapil Dev	5
A. R. Border c Viswanath b Venkataraghavan	24	– (6) b Yadav	8
*K. J. Hughes b Yadav	50	– lbw b Kapil Dev	1
G. N. Yallop hit wkt b Kapil Dev	89	– (3) c Kirmani b Ghavri	15
†K. J. Wright lbw b Kapil Dev	6	– (7) b Yadav	11
D. F. Whatmore c Gavaskar b Doshi	14	– (5) b Yadav	33
W. M. Darling c Kirmani b Ghavri	59	– (2) lbw b Kapil Dev	4
G. Dymock run out	11	– st Kirmani b Yadav	6
R. M. Hogg b Yadav	10	– lbw b Kapil Dev	6
J. D. Higgs not out	3	– not out	8
L-b 2, n-b 6	8	B 1, l-b 2, n-b 2	5

1/1 2/51 3/75 4/168 5/175 6/192   304   1/13 2/32 3/37 4/49 5/74   125
7/246 8/263 9/294   6/93 7/104 8/106 9/113

Bowling: *First Innings*—Kapil Dev 27–5–78–2; Ghavri 23.3–5–65–3; Venkataraghavan 18–6–56–1; Doshi 16–5–32–1; Yadav 25–3–65–2. *Second Innings*—Kapil Dev 16.2–5–30–4; Ghavri 11–0–28–1; Venkataraghavan 9–4–13–0; Doshi 12–5–14–1; Yadav 12–0–35–4.

Umpires: B. N. Hanumantha Rao and Mohammad Ghouse.

WEST ZONE v AUSTRALIANS

At Ahmedabad, October 9, 10, 11. Drawn. Even with a scratch attack, the Australians pushed West Zone to the brink of defeat. The home side were also below strength with their two main batsmen, Gavaskar and Vengsarkar, resting between Test matches. Hughes made a delightful 126, reaching his century in three hours, while Australia scored 263 for seven on the first day and declared. West Zone replied adequately, after struggling at 77 for five following an opening stand of 58. Australia hurried to a second innings score of 143 for nine and again declared, leaving their opponents 135 minutes to make 190. West Zone soon ran into trouble and finished with only three wickets in hand and their target nowhere in sight.

Australians

G. M. Wood c Z. Parkar b Parsana	17	– (2) c Z. Parkar b Yajurvindra	5
A. M. J. Hilditch c Gaekwad b Jadeja	18	– (1) lbw b Parsana	20
A. R. Border b Yajurvindra	24	– b Yajurvindra	0
*K. J. Hughes b Jadeja	126	– (9) not out	10
D. F. Whatmore c Hazare b Parsana	7	– (4) c Gaekwad b Joshi	41
W. M. Darling c Gaekwad b Parsana	27	– (5) b Parsana	3
P. R. Sleep b Yajurvindra	12	– (6) c Gaekwad b Parsana	11
G. D. Porter not out	3	– c Gaekwad b Parsana	13
†K. J. Wright not out	9	– (7) c Gunjal b Joshi	21
J. D. Higgs (did not bat)	–	– b Joshi	0
B 5, l-b 9, w 1, n-b 5	20	B 9, l-b 6, n-b 4	19

1/17 2/57 3/74 4/87   (7 wkts dec.) 263   1/17 2/19 3/49   (9 wkts dec.) 143
5/161 6/241 7/250   4/57 5/85 6/94 7/128
                                         8/142 9/143

A. G. Hurst did not bat.

Bowling: *First Innings*—Jadeja 23–3–60–2; Parsana 28–4–70–3; Patil 5–1–11–0; Yajurvindra 11–2–28–2; Joshi 22–2–52–0; Gunjal 2–0–15–0; Gaekwad 3–0–6–0; Bhalekar 1–0–1–0. *Second Innings*—Jadeja 8–2–16–0; Parsana 35–13–65–4; Yajurvindra 10–3–13–2; Joshi 18.3–9–25–3; Gaekwad 2–0–5–0.

West Zone

*A. D. Gaekwad c Whatmore b Wood	35	– (8) not out	0
G. Parkar c Wright b Wood	20	– (1) c Whatmore b Border	11
Yajurvindra Singh b Wood	4	– (2) c Hilditch b Higgs	17
R. B. Bhalekar c Wright b Higgs	6	– (3) c Whatmore b Border	4
S. M. Patil c Border b Sleep	44	– lbw b Higgs	23
M. D. Gunjal c Whatmore b Higgs	0	– b Whatmore	17
R. V. Hazare c Darling b Sleep	33	– (9) not out	13
D. D. Parsana b Sleep	13	– (5) b Border	0
R. Jadeja c Hughes b Hurst	10		
†Z. Parkar not out	29	– (7) c Whatmore b Higgs	5
U. C. Joshi c Whatmore b Higgs	11		
B 6, l-b 2, w 1, n-b 3	12	B 1, l-b 2, w 2	5

1/58 2/63 3/66 4/74 5/77 6/142   217   1/19 2/27 3/45   (7 wkts) 95
7/162 8/163 9/178   4/46 5/64 6/76 7/82

Bowling: *First Innings*—Hurst 15–5–33–1; Porter 10–3–31–0; Wood 7–2–18–3; Higgs 25.2–9–63–3; Sleep 17–3–52–3; Border 3–0–8–0. *Second Innings*—Hurst 5–1–14–0; Porter 4–2–2–0; Higgs 13–8–22–3; Sleep 3–1–15–0; Border 14–1–32–3; Whatmore 2–1–5–1.

Umpires: D. N. Dotiwalla and J. D. Ghosh.

INDIA v AUSTRALIA

Fourth Test Match

At Delhi, October 13, 14, 16, 17, 18. Drawn. Although often in danger Australia, following on 212 behind, comfortably averted defeat. It was curious that they should have been in such difficulty, for it was the one contest in the series in which Hogg bowled at his fastest and at his best, even if the fact is not reflected in his figures. The fortunes of both sides were affected by dropped catches.

India lost some advantage by taking more than ten hours over their first innings, despite the accumulation of a solid 267 for three on the first day, with Gavaskar scoring his 21st Test century and Viswanath well on the way to his eleventh. Gavaskar, who was out to the last ball of the day, started badly and had two lucky escapes, his first at only 13 when Hilditch put him down at second slip.

Viswanath's was the key innings. He scored 45 of the 72 added in the last ninety minutes on the first day and provided the momentum on the second morning as Yashpal, who had bagged a pair in the previous Test, was totally inhibited, taking 200 minutes to reach 50. With the second new ball, Hogg was intensely hostile and, had Viswanath surrendered, the innings would have fallen apart. Safely past his 50, Yashpal participated in the furious onslaught preparatory to the declaration, which was made as soon as he had reached his maiden Test century on his seventh appearance.

The footsore Australians must have been grateful that the rest day followed. Yet their innings, begun late on the second day, would not have lasted through the third but for Whatmore's gallant 77, scored from 91 balls and including fourteen 4s. Australia could not save the follow-on, but a defiant last-wicket stand between Wright and Higgs, lasting eighty-seven minutes, bought Australia valuable time which later proved crucial.

India's outstanding bowler was Kapil Dev who, aided by high-class wicket-keeping from Kirmani, took five for 82. Kapil Dev was magnificently supported by Hyderabad spinners Yadav and Narasimha Rao.

The pitch had eased by the fourth morning when Australia began their second innings. Yet despite a second-wicket stand of 127 between Hilditch and Border, they were in grave peril until lunch on the last day, when they were rescued by Whatmore and Sleep. Australia finished with a big total of 413, but would have been in dire straits had Whatmore not been allowed two escapes. He was dropped at silly point when only 10 and soon afterwards luckily avoided being run out.

India

*S. M. Gavaskar lbw b Higgs	115	†S. M. H. Kirmani b Dymock 35
C. P. S. Chauhan c Whatmore b Dymock	19	K. D. Ghavri not out 8
D. B. Vengsarkar st Wright b Higgs	26	
G. R. Viswanath st Wright b Higgs	131	B 6, l-b 12, n-b 24 42
Yashpal Sharma not out	100	
Kapil Dev c Whatmore b Dymock	29	1/38 2/108 3/267 (7 wkts dec.) 510
M. V. Narasimha Rao c Wright b Dymock	5	4/338 5/395 6/415
		7/467

N. S. Yadav and D. R. Doshi did not bat.

Bowling: Dymock 42.2–8–135–4; Hogg 33–8–91–0; Yallop 5–0–21–0; Border 4–2–5–0; Higgs 47–11–150–3; Sleep 13–1–66–0.

Australia

A. M. J. Hilditch c Kirmani b Yadav	29	– c Kirmani b Ghavri	85
W. M. Darling c Kirmani b Kapil Dev	19	– c Kirmani b Kapil Dev	7
A. R. Border c Narasimha Rao b Kapil Dev	24	– c Narasimha Rao b Ghavri	46
*K. J. Hughes c Kirmani b Kapil Dev	18	– c and b Ghavri	40
D. F. Whatmore lbw b Yadav	77	– (6) lbw b Kapil Dev	54
P. R. Sleep c Chauhan b Narasimha Rao	17	– (7) c sub b Chauhan	64
G. N. Yallop c Chauhan b Narasimha Rao	21	– (5) b Doshi	25
†K. J. Wright not out	55	– b Yadav	15
G. Dymock c Kirmani b Kapil Dev	0	– not out	31
R. M. Hogg b Kapil Dev	0	– run out	0
J. D. Higgs lbw b Doshi	11	– c Vengsarkar b Viswanath	7
B 4, l-b 4, n-b 19	27	B 13, l-b 9, w 1, n-b 16	39

1/32 2/72 3/93 4/116 5/160 6/225   298   1/20 2/147 3/156 4/205   413
7/228 8/242 9/246   5/242 6/318 7/344 8/395 9/395

Bowling: *First Innings*—Ghavri 22–8–58–0; Kapil Dev 32–7–82–5; Doshi 13.3–5–29–1; Yadav 27–10–56–2; Narasimha Rao 12–1–46–2. *Second Innings*—Ghavri 30–8–74–3; Kapil Dev 20–7–48–2; Doshi 34–11–69–1; Yadav 36–10–101–1; Narasimha Rao 19–3–50–0; Gavaskar 4–1–10–0; Chauhan 5–1–11–1; Viswanath 3.3–0–11–1.

Umpires: K. B. Ramaswamy and P. R. Punjabi.

EAST ZONE v AUSTRALIANS

At Cuttack, October 21, 22, 23. East Zone won by four wickets, this being the only win scored against the touring side outside the Test series. The Australians, fearful of injuries on an awkward, underprepared pitch, tried to finish off the match in two days by declaring both innings. Their lead of 34 runs on the first was not insignificant considering the conditions, and their second declaration left East Zone 154 to win. However, with the Australian bowling less effective in the second innings, the determination of East Zone opener Das and the skill of former Test batsman Saxena saw the zone home.

Australians

G. M. Wood b Porel	5	– lbw b Porel	5
†G. N. Yallop not out	81	– b Sinha	21
A. R. Border b Porel	19	– b Porel	44
*K. J. Hughes lbw b Sinha	8	– c Saxena b Porel	3
D. F. Whatmore c Ghose b Paramjit	30	– run out	19
P. R. Sleep st Ghose b Paramjit	1	– b Porel	5
R. M. Hogg not out	5	– c Bharadwaj b Paramjit	13
G. D. Porter (did not bat)		– not out	3
G. F. Lawson (did not bat)		– b Bhattacharjee	3
B 6, l-b 2, n-b 3	11	L-b 2, n-b 1	3

1/16 2/50 3/74 4/122   (5 wkts dec.) 160   1/5 2/58 3/69   (8 wkts dec.) 119
5/136   4/78 5/94 6/94
                                              7/110 8/119

G. Dymock and J. D. Higgs did not bat.

Bowling: *First Innings*—Sinha 13–5–38–1; Porel 12–1–43–2; Bhattacharjee 14–1–44–0; Paramjit 6–0–24–2. *Second Innings*—Sinha 5–0–36–1; Porel 10–0–47–4; Bhattacharjee 2.4–0–5–1; Paramjit 8–1–28–1.

East Zone

*R. Panda c Porter b Dymock	1	– c Hughes b Lawson	1
S. Das lbw b Hogg	0	– not out	62
H. Gidwani st Yallop b Higgs	31	– c Yallop b Dymock	29
M. Dalvi c Yallop b Lawson	3	– lbw b Porter	19
R. Saxena lbw b Lawson	0	– (6) lbw b Higgs	21
A. Bharadwaj c Lawson b Higgs	1	– (5) lbw b Dymock	0
†P. Ghose b Whatmore	7	– c Yallop b Higgs	0
A. Bhattacharjee b Hogg	55	– not out	14
Paramjit Singh c Sleep b Border	14		
A. Sinha b Hogg	0		
S. Porel not out	2		
B 2, l-b 5, w 1, n-b 4	12	B 6, l-b 2, n-b 2	10

1/2 2/10 3/17 4/17 5/27 6/50   126   1/5 2/49 3/76   (6 wkts) 156
7/69 8/124 9/124   4/81 5/139 6/141

Bowling: *First Innings*—Hogg 5–2–4–3; Lawson 8–7–1–2; Dymock 7–2–16–1; Higgs 11–3–42–2; Porter 11–2–29–0; Border 2.2–0–3–1; Whatmore 1–1–0–1; Sleep 3–0–15–0; Wood 2–0–4–0. *Second Innings*—Hogg 8–2–25–0; Lawson 7–2–22–1; Dymock 17–2–55–2; Higgs 5–1–5–2; Porter 10–3–25–1; Border 5–2–10–0; Whatmore 0.3–0–4–0.

Umpires: B. Gangulli and P. D. Reporter.

INDIA v AUSTRALIA

Fifth Test Match

At Calcutta, October 26, 27, 28, 30, 31. Drawn. Although Australia, batting first, put up their biggest total of the series, and gained a first innings lead of 95, they were eventually in danger of losing after their challenging declaration in the second innings left India to score 247 runs in 245 minutes.

For the first three days the pitch was miserably slow, giving the bowlers no hope and compelling the batsmen to play with circumspection. Australia lost Hilditch in the first over but their later application and patience were rewarded. Yallop proved to be a successful opener with a sound 167 in eight and a half hours during which he put on 97 for the second wicket with Border and 206 for the third with Hughes. Kapil Dev took the first four wickets and Doshi troubled the lower half of the batting order, although Australia were encouraged by an aggressive 61 not out in an hour and a half from Yardley.

Despite the early dismissal of Gavaskar, India replied with 347, thanks principally to Vengsarkar and Viswanath, who played his best innings of the series. India might have closed the gap further had Vengsarkar not been compelled to retire injured at tea on the third day with the score 169 for two. He resumed at 290 for five shortly before lunch on the fourth day, but made no further impact. Although Australia's pace bowlers were given no encouragement, Yardley bowled his off-breaks superbly and economically.

In their second innings Australia were soon in trouble and, at 81 for five at the start of the last day, were in danger of losing. But the resolute Hughes struck out boldly and Australia declared after adding 70 in 72 minutes.

Although the ball had turned on the fourth day – a factor in Hughes's declaration – the heavy roller produced a calmer pitch on the final day. Lacking in bounce, it was of little use to the wrist-spin of Higgs, and Australia's only finger-spinner, Yardley, failed to reproduce his form of the Indian first innings.

India started well, reaching 52 in 73 minutes. But, following Gavaskar's departure to a brilliant slip catch by Hilditch, they lost Vengsarkar and Viswanath in close succession and were thrown off course, foiled by superb bowling from Dymock. Yashpal strove to keep India's victory bid alive, but Narasimha Rao could not get going.

Australia

A. M. J. Hilditch c Kirmani b Kapil Dev	0	– b Ghavri	29
G. N. Yallop c Gavaskar b Yadav	167	– lbw b Kapil Dev	4
A. R. Border lbw b Kapil Dev	54	– st Kirmani b Doshi	6
*K. J. Hughes lbw b Kapil Dev	92	– not out	64
D. F. Whatmore b Kapil Dev	4	– c Vengsarkar b Doshi	4
W. M. Darling st Kirmani b Doshi	39	– c Gavaskar b Yadav	7
B. Yardley not out	61	– c Narasimha Rao b Yadav	12
†K. J. Wright lbw b Doshi	0	– not out	12
G. Dymock lbw b Doshi	3		
R. M. Hogg c Yashpal b Doshi	0		
J. D. Higgs lbw b Kapil Dev	1		
B 7, l-b 7, n-b 7	21	B 9, l-b 4	13

1/0 2/97 3/303 4/311 5/347 6/396   442   1/21 2/39 3/53   (6 wkts dec.) 151
7/396 8/418 9/426   4/62 5/81 6/115

Bowling: *First Innings*—Kapil Dev 32–9–74–5; Ghavri 24–3–85–0; Yadav 42–8–135–1; Narasimha Rao 8–0–24–0; Doshi 43–10–92–4; Chauhan 4–0–11–0. *Second Innings*—Kapil Dev 11–3–33–1; Ghavri 13.3–5–39–1; Yadav 11–6–16–2; Doshi 22–6–50–2.

India

*S. M. Gavaskar lbw b Hogg	14	– c Hilditch b Dymock	25
C. P. S. Chauhan c Border b Higgs	39	– c Wright b Dymock	50
D. B. Vengsarkar c Hughes b Yardley	89	– c Wright b Dymock	2
G. R. Viswanath c Wright b Yardley	96	– lbw b Dymock	7
Yashpal Sharma c Wright b Hogg	22	– not out	85
M. V. Narasimha Rao run out	10	– not out	20
†S. M. H. Kirmani not out	13		
Kapil Dev c Hughes b Dymock	30		
K. D. Ghavri c Wright b Yardley	1		
N. S. Yadav c Wright b Yardley	0		
D. R. Doshi b Dymock	0		
B 12, l-b 9, w 4, n-b 8	33	B 4, l-b 7	11

1/15 2/132 3/256 4/290 5/290   347   1/52 2/54 3/70 4/123   (4 wkts) 200
6/305 7/341 8/342 9/346

Bowling: *First Innings*—Dymock 26.4–8–56–2; Hogg 26–2–103–2; Yardley 42–11–91–4; Higgs 28–12–56–1; Border 2–0–8–0; Yallop 1–1–0–0. *Second Innings*—Dymock 25–7–63–4; Hogg 8.2–1–26–0; Yardley 13–1–47–0; Higgs 16–3–51–0; Yallop 1–0–2–0.

Umpires: Swaroop Kishen and B. N. Hanumantha Rao.

INDIA v AUSTRALIA

Sixth Test Match

At Bombay, November 3, 4, 6, 7. India won by an innings and 100 runs with a day to spare. With the pitch grassless and threatening to take spin, Australia, already at a disadvantage when Yardley was ruled out of the match by injury, had the further misfortune to lose the toss; and to add to their problems Yallop and Higgs contracted stomach trouble on the first day.

After the first two days it became apparent that Australia could not win this match, and that India had thus won the series. Batting until half an hour before the close on the second day, India declared at 458 for eight. A score of such proportions had looked likely when they made 231 for three on the first day, with Gavaskar scoring his second century of the series. Their fortunes declined temporarily on the second morning but they were restored by an eighth-wicket partnership of 127 from Kirmani and Ghavri. Kirmani, who had gone in as night-watchman, scored his maiden Test century in five hours, and Ghavri made his best-ever Test score of 86.

The difficulties that the pitch would pose the Australians were indicated by Border's left-arm spin claiming two of the three wickets that fell on the first day. Higgs's illness restricted him to only a few overs on the opening day, but on the second he took two important wickets cheaply and the Australians regained more ground when Hogg removed Yashpal and Amarnath in quick succession by exploiting their weakness against the fast, short-pitched ball.

The rest day fell between the second and third days, and when the contest was resumed the pitch favoured the spinners. Doshi and Yadav wrecked the Australian innings in just over four hours, the last eight wickets falling in less than two hours after lunch. Yallop's 60, with five 4s, was the only contribution of note.

The Australians were upset by two umpiring decisions during this innings. Hilditch was aggrieved at being given run out and Hughes was even less pleased to be given out caught at silly point. There was a red patch on his shirt-sleeve to provide evidence that justice had not been done.

Following on, Australia were 60 for two at the end of the third day. On the fourth India gained no further ground until twenty minutes before lunch as Border and Hughes produced a gallant third-wicket stand of 132. Once they were parted, Kapil Dev and Doshi quickly ran through the rest of Australia's demoralised batting, although Hughes's 80, made in 108 minutes, was one of the finest innings played against Indian bowling in recent times.

India

*S. M. Gavaskar c Hughes b Border 123	K. D. Ghavri c sub b Dymock......... 86
C. P. S. Chauhan b Dymock 73	N. S. Yadav not out 0
D. B. Vengsarkar c Whatmore b Border . 6	
G. R. Viswanath c and b Higgs 10	B 3, l-b 12, n-b 17.......... 32
†S. M. H. Kirmani not out...........101	
Yashpal Sharma c Whatmore b Hogg ... 8	1/192 2/222 3/231 (8 wkts dec.) 458
M. Amarnath hit wkt b Hogg.......... 2	4/240 5/272 6/281 7/327
Kapil Dev c Whatmore b Higgs........ 17	8/454

D. R. Doshi did not bat.

Bowling: Dymock 31–5–95–2; Hogg 28–14–53–2; Higgs 29–4–116–2; Border 27–7–60–2; Sleep 28–7–79–0; Whatmore 5–2–11–0; Yallop 1–0–12–0.

Australia

A. M. J. Hilditch run out	13 – b Kapil Dev	9
G. N. Yallop c Kapil Dev b Yadav............	60 – c Amarnath b Ghavri..........	4
A. R. Border c Vengsarkar b Yadav..........	23 – b Doshi.................	61
*K. J. Hughes c Vengsarkar b Doshi..........	14 – c Ghavri b Kapil Dev..........	80
D. F. Whatmore lbw b Doshi..............	6 – lbw b Kapil Dev	0
W. M. Darling c sub b Yadav..............	16 – retired hurt	0
P. R. Sleep b Yadav	1 – c Kapil Dev b Doshi..........	3
†K. J. Wright not out	11 – lbw b Doshi	5
G. Dymock c Chauhan b Doshi.............	1 – c Viswanath b Yadav..........	7
R. M. Hogg c Amarnath b Doshi.............	5 – not out	3
J. D. Higgs b Doshi	0 – b Kapil Dev	4
B 1, l-b 2, n-b 7..........	10	L-b 12, n-b 10......... 22

1/28 2/77 3/110 4/118 5/124 6/125   160   1/11 2/17 3/149 4/154   198
7/144 8/145 9/158   5/159 6/176 7/183 8/187 9/198

Bowling: *First Innings*—Kapil Dev 9–0–26–0; Ghavri 8–1–30–0; Doshi 19.5–4–43–5; Yadav 21–7–40–4; Amarnath 5–1–11–0. *Second Innings*—Kapil Dev 14.1–5–39–4; Ghavri 10–0–28–1; Doshi 25–6–60–3; Yadav 22–9–48–1; Amarnath 2–1–1–0.

Umpires: Mohammad Ghouse and J. D. Ghosh.

TEST MATCH GROUNDS

In Chronological Sequence

	City and Ground	*Date of First Test*	*Match*
1.	Melbourne, Melbourne Cricket Ground	March 15, 1877	Australia v England
2.	London, Kennington Oval	September 6, 1880	England v Australia
3.	Sydney, Sydney Cricket Ground (No. 1)	February 17, 1882	Australia v England
4.	Manchester, Old Trafford	July 11, 1884	England v Australia

This match was due to have started on July 10, but rain prevented any play.

5.	London, Lord's	July 21, 1884	England v Australia
6.	Adelaide, Adelaide Oval	December 12, 1884	Australia v England
7.	Port Elizabeth, St George's Park	March 12, 1889	South Africa v England
8.	Cape Town, Newlands	March 25, 1889	South Africa v England
9.	Johannesburg, Old Wanderers*	March 2, 1896	South Africa v England
10.	Nottingham, Trent Bridge	June 1, 1899	England v Australia
11.	Leeds, Headingley	June 29, 1899	England v Australia
12.	Birmingham, Edgbaston	May 29, 1902	England v Australia
13.	Sheffield, Bramall Lane*	July 3, 1902	England v Australia
14.	Durban, Lord's*	January 1, 1910	South Africa v England

City and Ground	Date of First Test	Match
15. Durban, Kingsmead	January 18, 1923	South Africa v England
16. Brisbane, Exhibition Ground*	November 30, 1928	Australia v England
17. Christchurch, Lancaster Park	January 10, 1930	New Zealand v England
18. Bridgetown, Kensington Oval	January 11, 1930	West Indies v England
19. Wellington, Basin Reserve	January 24, 1930	New Zealand v England
20. Port-of-Spain, Queen's Park Oval	February 1, 1930	West Indies v England
21. Auckland, Eden Park	February 17, 1930	New Zealand v England

This match was due to have started on February 14, but rain prevented any play on the first two days.

22. Georgetown, Bourda	February 21, 1930	West Indies v England
23. Kingston, Sabina Park	April 3, 1930	West Indies v England
24. Brisbane, Woolloongabba	November 27, 1931	Australia v South Africa
25. Bombay, Gymkhana Ground*	December 15, 1933	India v England
26. Calcutta, Eden Gardens	January 5, 1934	India v England
27. Madras, Chepauk	February 10, 1934	India v England
28. Delhi, Feroz Shah Kotla	November 10, 1948	India v West Indies
29. Bombay, Brabourne Stadium*	December 9, 1948	India v West Indies
30. Johannesburg, Ellis Park*	December 27, 1948	South Africa v England
31. Kanpur, Green Park (Modi Stadium)	January 12, 1952	India v England
32. Lucknow, University Ground*	October 25, 1952	India v Pakistan
33. Dacca, Dacca Stadium*	January 1, 1955	Pakistan v India
34. Bahawalpur, Dring Stadium*	January 15, 1955	Pakistan v India
35. Lahore, Lawrence Gardens (Bagh-I-Jinnah)*	January 29, 1955	Pakistan v India
36. Peshawar, Gymkhana Ground*	February 13, 1955	Pakistan v India
37. Karachi, National Stadium	February 26, 1955	Pakistan v India
38. Dunedin, Carisbrook	March 11, 1955	New Zealand v England
39. Hyderabad, Fateh Maidan (Lal Bahadur Stadium)*	November 19, 1955	India v New Zealand
40. Madras, Corporation Stadium*	January 6, 1956	India v New Zealand
41. Johannesburg, New Wanderers	December 24, 1956	South Africa v England
42. Lahore, Gaddafi Stadium	November 21, 1959	Pakistan v Australia
43. Rawalpindi, Rawalpindi Club Ground*	March 27, 1965	Pakistan v New Zealand
44. Nagpur, Vidarbha Cricket Association Ground*	October 3, 1969	India v New Zealand
45. Perth, Western Australian Cricket Association Ground	December 11, 1970	Australia v England
46. Hyderabad, Niaz Stadium	March 16, 1973	Pakistan v England
47. Bangalore, Karnataka Cricket Association Ground	November 22, 1974	India v West Indies
48. Bombay, Wankhede Stadium	January 23, 1975	India v West Indies
49. Faisalabad, Iqbal Park	October 16, 1978	Pakistan v India
50. Napier, McLean Park	February 16, 1979	New Zealand v Pakistan

* Denotes no longer used for Test matches. In some instances the ground is no longer in existence.

THE AUSTRALIANS IN PAKISTAN, 1979-80

By GHULAM MUSTAFA KHAN

Australia's cricketers followed their intensive domestic season with a tour of Pakistan which at one time appeared as if it might not eventuate because of financial problems. Eventually the guarantee was improved from A$94,000 to A$150,000, but in the process the tour was cut from eight matches to five – three Tests and two three-day matches – the same number played by Pakistan on their tour to Australia in 1976-77.

For Pakistan, their 1-0 victory in the series was some compensation after their series defeat in India, and it provided Javed Miandad with a happy success in his first series as captain. The previous captain, Asif Iqbal, had announced his retirement from Test cricket after the tour to India, and following severe criticism in the press of Pakistan's performances there, the chairman of the BCCP, Lt-General (Ret.) K. M. Azhar Khan, resigned. In February, the government appointed Air Marshal (Ret.) M. Nur Khan as president of the BCCP and he immediately made Mushtaq Mohammad manager of the Pakistan team. Mushtaq had originally been recalled to captain the team against Australia.

AUSTRALIAN TOUR RESULTS

Test matches – Played 3: Lost 1, Drawn 2.

First-class matches – Played 5: Lost 1, Drawn 4.

Losses – Pakistan.

Draws – Pakistan (2), BCCP President's XI, Punjab Governor's XI.

TEST MATCH AVERAGES

PAKISTAN – BATTING

	Tests	Innings	Not Outs	Runs	Highest Inns	Average
Majid J. Khan	3	2	1	199	110*	199.00
Taslim Arif	3	4	1	307	210*	102.33
Javed Miandad	3	4	1	181	106*	60.33
Mudassar Nazar	3	2	0	88	59	44.00
Wasim Raja	3	3	1	67	55	33.50
Imran Khan	2	2	0	65	56	32.50
Zaheer Abbas	2	3	1	45	19	22.50
Iqbal Qasim	3	2	1	19	14*	19.00
Haroon Rashid	2	3	0	37	21	12.33
Sarfraz Nawaz	3	2	0	22	17	11.00
Tauseef Ahmad	3	1	0	0	–	

Played in one Test: Azmat Rana 49; Azhar Khan 14; Ehtesham-ud-Din did not bat.

* *Signifies not out.*

BOWLING

	Overs	Maidens	Runs	Wickets	Average
Imran Khan	56	14	144	6	24.00
Tauseef Ahmad	144.2	29	356	12	29.66
Iqbal Qasim	201	63	475	16	29.68
Wasim Raja	59	10	198	4	49.50
Sarfraz Nawaz	111	30	255	2	127.50

Also bowled: Azhar Khan 3–1–2–1; Ehtesham-ud-Din 18–2–59–1; Javed Miandad 9–0–35–0; Majid J. Khan 36–6–105–0; Mudassar Nazar 12–1–46–0; Taslim Arif 5–0–28–0.

AUSTRALIA – BATTING

	Tests	Innings	Not Outs	Runs	Highest Inns	Average
A. R. Border	3	5	2	395	153	131.66
G. S. Chappell	3	5	0	381	235	76.20
G. N. Yallop	3	5	0	237	172	47.40
K. J. Hughes	3	5	0	182	88	36.40
J. M. Wiener	2	3	0	102	93	34.00
G. R. Beard	3	5	0	114	49	22.80
B. M. Laird	3	5	0	109	63	21.80
R. W. Marsh	3	5	1	106	71	21.20
R. J. Bright	3	5	2	56	26*	18.66
D. K. Lillee	3	4	2	18	12*	9.00
G. Dymock	3	3	1	3	3	1.50

Played in one Test: D. W. Hookes 0, 0.

BOWLING

	Overs	Maidens	Runs	Wickets	Average
R. J. Bright	146.5	45	354	15	23.60
G. S. Chappell	34	9	74	3	24.66
D. K. Lillee	102	19	303	3	101.00

Also bowled: G. R. Beard 43.1–17–109–1; A. R. Border 3–2–3–0; G. Dymock 51–13–129–1; K. J. Hughes 8–1–19–0; B. M. Laird 2–1–3–0; R. W. Marsh 10–1–51–0; J. M. Wiener 1–1–19–0; G. N. Yallop 5–0–29–0.

AUSTRALIAN AVERAGES – FIRST-CLASS MATCHES

BATTING

	Matches	Innings	Not Outs	Runs	Highest Inns	Average
A. R. Border	5	9	3	674	178	112.33
G. S. Chappell	3	5	0	381	235	76.20
G. N. Yallop	4	6	0	283	172	47.16
J. M. Wiener	4	7	0	189	93	27.00
G. R. Beard	5	9	1	206	64*	25.75
R. W. Marsh	5	8	0	201	71	25.12
K. J. Hughes	5	9	0	220	88	24.44
B. M. Laird	5	9	0	202	67	22.44
R. J. Bright	5	9	2	129	52	18.42
G. Dymock	4	5	1	44	27	11.00
G. F. Lawson	2	3	1	19	4	9.50
D. K. Lillee	3	4	2	18	12*	9.00
M. F. Malone	2	3	2	3	1*	3.00
D. W. Hookes	3	6	0	10	5	1.66

* *Signifies not out.*

BOWLING

	Overs	Maidens	Runs	Wickets	Average
G. F. Lawson	41	15	107	6	17.83
R. J. Bright	230.2	72	558	29	19.24
G. S. Chappell	34	9	74	3	24.66
G. Dymock	71	17	188	4	47.00
G. R. Beard	84.1	32	214	4	53.50
D. K. Lillee	102	19	303	3	101.00

Also bowled: A. R. Border 8–4–31–0; K. J. Hughes 10–2–24–0; B. M. Laird 2–1–3–0; M. F. Malone 35–11–123–1; R. W. Marsh 12–2–55–0; J. M. Wiener 5–1–19–0; G. N. Yallop 5–0–29–0.

FIELDING

R. W. Marsh 9 (7ct, 2st), A. R. Border 7, D. W. Hookes 4, G. S. Chappell 3, R. J. Bright 3, B. M. Laird 2, G. F. Lawson 2, G. N. Yallop 1, G. R. Beard 1, K. J. Hughes 1, D. K. Lillee 1, M. F. Malone 1.

HUNDREDS FOR AUSTRALIANS

The following five three-figure innings were played for the Australians during the tour.

* Signifies not out.

A. R. Border (3)
178   v Punjab Governor's XI at Multan
150*
153 } v Pakistan at Lahore (Third Test)

G. S. Chappell (1)
235   v Pakistan at Faisalabad (Second Test)

G. N. Yallop (1)
172   v Pakistan at Faisalabad (Second Test)

HUNDREDS AGAINST AUSTRALIANS

The following four three-figure innings were played against the Australians.

* Signifies not out.

Azhar Khan (1)
100   for Punjab Governor's XI at Multan

Javed Miandad (1)
106* for Pakistan at Faisalabad (Second Test)

Majid J. Khan (1)
110* for Pakistan at Lahore (Third Test)

Taslim Arif (1)
210* for Pakistan at Faisalabad (Second Test)

BCCP PRESIDENT'S XI v AUSTRALIANS

At Rawalpindi, February 22, 23, 24. Drawn. The groundstaff had worked impressively to overcome the effects of a heavy downpour, and the match started only half an hour late on the first day, when the Australians slumped from 210 for five to a total of 223. When the President's XI replied, Rana's hard-hit 82 included thirteen 4s. The visitors' second innings began badly, the first two wickets falling for 26, until Laird, Border and Beard led a recovery, enabling Hughes to declare 217 ahead. The home team struggled against the brilliant bowling of Bright, who returned match figures of eleven for 122, but the last pair survived 35 deliveries to save the match.

Australians

	First Innings		Second Innings	
B. M. Laird	c Aftab b Ehtesham	9	c Talat b Riaz	67
J. M. Wiener	c Taslim b Hassan	46	lbw b Ehtesham	2
*K. J. Hughes	b Tariq	5	b Aftab	12
A. R. Border	c Azmat b Aftab	35	not out	46
G. N. Yallop	c Taslim b Tariq	46		
D. W. Hookes	c Taslim b Aftab	5	c Azmat b Aftab	3
†R. W. Marsh	c Mohsin b Tariq	52		
G. R. Beard	run out	2	not out	64
R. J. Bright	c Talat b Aftab	1	b Aftab	0
M. F. Malone	b Aftab	1		
G. F. Lawson	not out	1		
	B 4, l-b 6, n-b 10	20	B 2, l-b 4, n-b 3	9

1/18 2/26 3/94 4/112   223   1/11 2/26 3/132   (5 wkts dec.) 203
5/120 6/210 7/220 8/221 9/221   4/144 5/144

Bowling: *First Innings*—Ehtesham 13–3–34–1; Tariq 12–3–32–3; Riaz 14–1–46–0; Aftab 24.2–7–51–4; Iqbal 4–0–28–0; Hassan 10–3–12–1. *Second Innings*—Ehtesham 7–3–10–1; Tariq 5–1–16–0; Riaz 10–1–35–1; Aftab 18–3–70–3; Iqbal 4–1–16–0; Hassan 14–1–47–0.

BCCP President's XI

	First Innings		Second Innings	
†Taslim Arif	c Border b Lawson	4	c Marsh b Bright	11
Rizwanuzzman	b Bright	29	c and b Beard	25
Mohsin Khan	c Laird b Malone	20	lbw b Bright	2
Talat Mirza	lbw b Bright	6	b Bright	1
Azmat Rana	st Marsh b Bright	82	c Hughes b Bright	17
*Aftab Baloch	c Hughes b Bright	13	c Laird b Beard	1
Hassan Jamil	c Lawson b Bright	40	c Bright b Beard	6
Iqbal Sikandar	not out	0	c Hookes b Bright	0
Mohammad Riaz	(did not bat)		b Bright	0
Tariq Wahab	(did not bat)		not out	0
Ehtesam-ud-Din	(did not bat)		not out	0
	B 8, l-b 5, n-b 2	15	B 4, l-b 7 w 4, n-b 3	18

1/4 2/36 3/47   (7 wkts dec.) 209   1/27 2/32 3/56 4/60   (9 wkts) 81
4/119 5/147 6/200 7/209   5/70 6/75 7/75 8/81 9/81

Bowling: *First Innings*—Lawson 9–4–14–1; Malone 17–8–36–1; Bright 33.3–9–93–5; Beard 15–4–41–0; Border 3–1–10–0. *Second Innings*—Lawson 8–4–11–0; Malone 3–1–10–0; Bright 20–8–29–6; Beard 15–11–13–3.

Umpires: Khyzar Hayat and Javed Akhtar.

PAKISTAN v AUSTRALIA

First Test Match

At Karachi, February 27, 28, 29, March 2. Pakistan won by seven wickets in a match dominated by the spin bowlers. Off-spinner Tauseef Ahmad – on his Test début – and Iqbal Qasim made Australia struggle for their total of 225, after the visitors had elected to bat on a turning pitch. Their innings was given some respectability by Hughes, who batted three and threequarter hours for his 85, hitting one 6 and twelve 4s. Pakistan were in early trouble against Bright, but Taslim Arif and Javed Miandad initiated a recovery and, with Majid Khan hitting nine 4s in his four and a half hour stay, the home team achieved a promising total. On the third day Australia again had no answer to the spin of Qasim and Tauseef, ending the day only 23 ahead, having lost six wickets for 90. Despite a confident innings from Border, they were spun out for 140 on the fourth day, leaving Pakistan to score 73 for victory. Bright, again bowling effectively, took three wickets before the target was reached. Both Bright and Iqbal Qasim achieved career-best performances; Bright's match aggregate was ten for 111 and Iqbal Qasim returned figures of eleven for 118.

Australia

B. M. Laird lbw b Imran	6	– c Miandad b Qasim	23
G. N. Yallop c Taslim b Tauseef	12	– c Majid b Qasim	16
K. J. Hughes c Majid b Tauseef	85	– st Taslim b Tauseef	8
*G. S. Chappell st Taslim b Qasim	20	– c Taslim b Tauseef	13
D. W. Hookes c Majid b Qasim	0	– lbw b Qasim	0
A. R. Border lbw b Qasim	30	– not out	58
†R. W. Marsh c Haroon b Tauseef	13	– c Mudassar b Qasim	1
G. R. Beard b Imran	9	– b Qasim	4
R. J. Bright c Majid b Qasim	15	– c Majid b Qasim	0
D. K. Lillee not out	12	– lbw b Qasim	5
G. Dymock c Raja b Tauseef	3	– b Tauseef	0
B 8, l-b 9, n-b 3	20	B 4, l-b 5, w 1, n-b 2	12

1/8 2/39 3/93 4/93   225   1/38 2/51 3/55 4/59   140
5/161 6/177 7/181 8/199 9/216   5/89 6/90 7/106 8/108 9/139

Bowling: *First Innings*—Imran 16–4–28–2; Sarfraz 13–4–20–0; Mudassar 2–0–6–0; Qasim 30–11–69–4; Tauseef 30.2–9–64–4; Majid 2–0–13–0; Raja 2–0–5–0. *Second Innings*—Sarfraz 7–2–7–0; Mudassar 2–0–4–0; Qasim 42–22–49–7; Tauseef 34–11–62–3; Majid 1–1–0–0; Raja 4–1–6–0.

Pakistan

†Taslim Arif c Marsh b Bright	58	– b Bright	8
Haroon Rashid b Bright	6	– b Bright	10
Zaheer Abbas c Lillee b Bright	8	– not out	18
*Javed Miandad c Border b Chappell	40	– b Bright	21
Wasim Raja c sub b Chappell	0	– not out	12
Majid J. Khan c Border b Bright	89		
Mudassar Nazar c Border b Bright	29		
Imran Khan c Border b Chappell	9		
Sarfraz Nawaz c Chappell b Bright	17		
Iqbal Qasim not out	14		
Tauseef Ahmad b Bright	0		
L-b 12, n-b 10	22	L-b 3, n-b 4	7

1/34 2/44 3/120 4/121   292   1/17 2/26 3/60   (3 wkts) 76
5/134 6/210 7/238 8/266 9/292

Bowling: *First Innings*—Lillee 28–4–76–0; Dymock 5–2–5–0; Bright 46.5–17–87–7; Beard 17–8–39–0; Chappell 20–3–49–3; Yallop 2–0–14–0. *Second Innings*—Lillee 11–2–22–0; Dymock 2–0–9–0; Bright 11–5–24–3; Beard 1.1–0–14–0.

Umpires: Shakoor Rana and Mahboob Shah.

PAKISTAN v AUSTRALIA

Second Test Match

At Faisalabad, March 6, 7, 8, 10, 11. Drawn. Rain washed out the first day and delayed the start on the second by sixty-five minutes. The artificial methods used to restore the pitch produced a perfect batting strip on which new records were set as 999 runs were scored for the loss of just twelve wickets. For only the second time in Test history a whole side bowled; the other occasion was England v Australia at The Oval in 1884. Chappell, batting for seven hours and twenty-one minutes, scored his seventeenth Test century and shared in two record-breaking partnerships for Australia v Pakistan. With Hughes he put on 179 for the third wicket, then stayed to add 217 for the fourth with Yallop, who batted nearly eight and a half hours for his 172. Taslim Arif and Javed Miandad also set a new third-wicket record of 223 unbroken for Pakistan v Australia. Taslim, in only his third Test, batted for seven and a quarter hours, with twenty 4s, to score his unbeaten 210, remaining on the field throughout the match. Australia's 617 was their highest score against Pakistan and the first total of over 600 in a Test match in Pakistan. Yet they made an unpromising start, losing their first wicket for 1 – when Laird was out for 0 – and their second for 21; but once Hughes and Chappell came together, the runs piled up. Pakistan made a spirited reply, scoring their 382 in 435 minutes, although the game was already committed to a draw.

Australia

J. M. Wiener b Ehtesham	5	R. J. Bright b Raja	5	
B. M. Laird c Taslim b Sarfraz	0	D. K. Lillee lbw b Raja	0	
K. J. Hughes c Ehtesham b Tauseef	88	G. Dymock not out	0	
*G. S. Chappell lbw b Sarfraz	235			
G. N. Yallop b Raja	172	B 11, l-b 10, n-b 3	24	
A. R. Border run out	4			
†R. W. Marsh lbw b Tauseef	71	1/1 2/21 3/200 4/417	617	
G. R. Beard c Sarfraz b Tauseef	13	5/434 6/561 7/585 8/592 9/612		

Bowling: Sarfraz 49–13–119–2; Ehtesham 18–2–59–1; Qasim 56–11–156–0; Tauseef 34–3–77–3; Raja 30–6–100–3; Majid 22–2–66–0; Miandad 3–0–16–0.

Pakistan

†Taslim Arif not out	210
Haroon Rashid lbw b Dymock	21
Zaheer Abbas run out	19
*Javed Miandad not out	106
B 7, l-b 4, n-b 15	26

1/87 2/159   (2 wkts) 382

Mudassar Nazar, Majid J. Khan, Wasim Raja, Sarfraz Nawaz, Ehtesham-ud-Din, Tauseef Ahmad and Iqbal Qasim did not bat.

Bowling: Lillee 21–4–91–0; Dymock 20–5–49–1; Bright 33–9–71–0; Border 3–2–3–0; Beard 15–4–30–0; Hughes 8–1–19–0; Laird 2–1–3–0; Chappell 6–3–5–0; Wiener 5–1–19–0; Marsh 10–1–51–0; Yallop 3–0–15–0.

Umpires: Javed Akhtar and Khalid Aziz.

PUNJAB GOVERNOR'S XI v AUSTRALIANS

At Multan, March 13, 14, 15. Drawn. At close of play on the first day, a crowd of nearly 15,000 had seen the home team reach 86 for no wicket, after the Australians had been dismissed for 213. The next day Azhar Khan hit one 6 and seventeen 4s in his fluent hundred and, with useful assistance from Shafiq and Sultan Rana, took his team to a lead of 110. The visitors lost half their wickets for 36, and defeat seemed imminent, but Border (27 4s) stood fast. He put on 105 for the seventh wicket with Marsh, and 97 for the ninth wicket with Dymock, leaving the Governor's XI to score 193 in two hours – a target which was beyond them.

Australians

J. M. Wiener c Yousaf b Mohi-ud-Din	35	– lbw b Rashid	4
B. M. Laird c Azhar b Mohi-ud-Din	7	– c Rizwanuzzman b Mohi-ud-Din	10
D. W. Hookes c Sultan b Lakhani	2	– c Salim b Rashid	0
A. R. Border b Lakhani	20	– c Lakhani b Azhar	178
R. J. Bright c and b Ilyas	52	– c Tariq b Ilyas	20
*K. J. Hughes c Shafiq b Lakhani	17	– b Lakhani	4
†R. W. Marsh c Yousaf b Ilyas	4	– c Rizwanuzzman b Azhar	39
G. R. Beard b Lakhani	25	– c sub b Lakhani	1
G. F. Lawson c Rashid b Ilyas	14	– lbw b Rashid	4
G. Dymock c sub b Ilyas	15	– lbw b Rizwanuzzman	26
M. F. Malone not out	1	– not out	1
B 13, l-b 5, n-b 3	21	B 5, l-b 4, w 1, n-b 5	15

1/24 2/47 3/51 4/88   213   1/18 2/18 3/18 4/32   302
5/112 6/129 7/160 8/184 9/199   5/36 6/87 7/192 8/197 9/294

Bowling: *First Innings*—Mohi-ud-Din 11–3–42–2; Rashid 12–6–24–0; Lakhani 20–2–64–4; Ilyas 21.1–6–62–4. *Second Innings*—Mohi-ud-Din 5–1–17–1; Rashid 23–6–50–3; Lakhani 30–13–74–2; Ilyas 28–12–56–1; Tariq 4–0–20–0; Azhar 7.2–2–22–2; Sultan 6–0–26–0; Shafiq 4–0–20–0; Rizwanuzzman 3–1–2–1.

Punjab Governor's XI

*Shafiq Ahmad c and b Bright	66		
Rizwanuzzman c Hookes b Bright	27	– c Hookes b Lawson	0
Sultan Rana c and b Bright	53		
Azhar Khan c Marsh b Lawson	100		
Tariq Alam c Border b Lawson	23		
Bashir Kardar c Malone b Dymock	4	– not out	18
†Salim Yousaf c Marsh b Lawson	22	– not out	58
Rashid Khan lbw b Dymock	1		
Ilyas Khan lbw b Lawson	2		
Mohi-ud-Din c Lawson b Dymock	4		
Amin Lakhani not out	0		
B 5, l-b 3, n-b 13	21	B 6, l-b 5, n-b 1	12

1/86 2/120 3/203 4/284   323   1/0   (1 wkt) 88
5/285 6/289 7/299 8/305 9/313

Bowling: *First Innings*—Lawson 19–7–46–4; Dymock 20–4–59–3; Malone 10–1–46–0; Bright 30–10–82–3; Beard 11–0–51–0; *Second Innings*—Lawson 5–0–36–1; Malone 5–1–31–0; Hughes 2–1–5–0; Marsh 2–1–4–0.

Umpires: Amanullah Khan and Shakoor Rana.

PAKISTAN v AUSTRALIA

Third Test Match

At Lahore, March 18, 19, 21, 22, 23. Drawn. For the third time in the series Australia won the toss, electing to bat on a perfect wicket. And once again, new records were established. Chappell scored his 5,000th Test run in this, his sixtieth Test, becoming the fifth Australian to do so. With Wiener he added 83 for the third wicket in 82 minutes. Australia were 239 for six overnight, and the next day Border achieved his fourth Test century, hitting two 6s and sixteen 4s. On the fourth day he hit yet another hundred in just under three and a half hours, with five 6s and sixteen 4s, taking his total to five centuries in twenty Tests. He was joined by Beard to put on 134 for the seventh wicket – another record for Australia v Pakistan Tests. When Chappell declared on the second afternoon, the Australians had reached a total of 407. By evening on the third day, Pakistan were still 183 behind at 224 for five, but Majid Khan's unbeaten 110 (fourteen 4s) revived the innings and, with useful contributions from Wasim

Raja and Imran Khan, Javed Miandad was able to declare 13 runs ahead. Majid and Imran had added 111 for the eighth wicket, setting a new record for Pakistan v Australia. Lillee's three wickets were his first in Pakistan. When Australia replied, ten of the Pakistan team bowled, Miandad keeping wicket while Taslim Arif took his turn. Imran took two quick wickets, but the Australians batted with determination and the game ended in a draw, leaving Pakistan a 1-0 victory in the series.

Australia

J. M. Wiener lbw b Qasim	93	– c Mudassar b Imran	4
B. M. Laird b Tauseef	17	– c Taslim b Tauseef	63
K. J. Hughes b Qasim	1	– c Qasim b Imran	0
*G. S. Chappell lbw b Imran	56	– b Qasim	57
G. N. Yallop lbw b Qasim	3	– c and b Raja	34
A. R. Border not out	150	– st Miandad b Azhar	153
†R. W. Marsh b Qasim	8	– run out	13
G. R. Beard lbw b Imran	39	– c sub b Taslim	49
R. J. Bright not out	26	– not out	10
D. K. Lillee (did not bat)		– not out	1
B 4, l-b 6, n-b 4	14	L-b 4, n-b 3.	7

1/50 2/53 3/136   (7 wkts dec.) 407   1/4 2/7 3/115 4/149   (8 wkts) 391
4/153 5/204 6/218 7/298   5/192 6/223 7/357 8/390

G. Dymock did not bat.

Bowling: *First Innings*—Imran 28–7–86–2; Sarfraz 28–6–67–0; Mudassar 6–1–16–0; Qasim 39–10–90–4; Tauseef 21–3–81–1; Raja 14–3–45–0; Azhar 2–1–1–0; Miandad 2–0–5–0; Majid 2–0–2–0. *Second Innings*—Imran 12–3–30–2; Sarfraz 14–5–42–0; Mudassar 2–0–20–0; Qasim 34–8–111–1; Tauseef 26–3–72–1; Raja 9–1–42–1; Azhar 1–0–1–1; Miandad 4–0–14–0; Majid 9–3–24–0; Taslim 5–0–28–1.

Pakistan

Mudassar Nazar c Yallop b Lillee	59	Azhar Khan b Bright	14
†Taslim Arif c Marsh b Bright	31	Imran Khan c Chappell b Bright	56
Iqbal Qasim c Marsh b Lillee	5	Sarfraz Nawaz st Marsh b Bright	5
Azmat Rana c Chappell b Beard	49	L-b 4, w 1, n-b 17	22
*Javed Miandad c Marsh b Bright	14		
Wasim Raja c Border b Lillee	55	1/37 2/53 3/133 4/161 (9 wkts dec.) 420
Majid J. Khan not out	110	5/177 6/270 7/299 8/410 9/420

Tauseef Ahmad did not bat.

Bowling: Lillee 42–9–114–3; Dymock 24–6–66–0; Bright 56–14–172–5; Beard 10–5–26–1; Chappell 8–3–20–0.

Umpires: Amanullah Khan and Khyzar Hayat.

THE PAKISTANIS IN INDIA, 1979-80

By DICKY RUTNAGUR

Much the same Pakistan side that had totally outplayed India at home a year earlier, and won the series 2-0, went down by the same margin in a tense, controversial rubber of six Tests. The result could have been 3-0 for India, after a brave second innings recovery, were close to winning the second Test. However, Pakistan dominated the "dead" final Test, which was drawn.

The marked turn of fortunes in a year was wrought by several factors, of which India's advantage of playing at home was the least significant. The most prominent reason for India's ascendancy was the development as an opening bowler of Kapil Dev who, with 32 wickets, was the leading wicket-taker of the series for either side. And with an abundant infusion of new players, India were stronger than twelve months earlier, much of the added strength coming from greater mobility in the field and superior catching.

Although his approach was cautious, Gavaskar marshalled his forces well. He stayed in command until the series was clinched in the fifth Test and then relinquished the captaincy as he was not available for the forthcoming tour of the West Indies. (This was cancelled at the last minute because of the unavailability of players on both sides.) Viswanath captained India in the final test.

India selected their sides for the six Tests from only twelve players and fielded the same eleven for the first four. As the series immediately followed the one against Australia which, in turn, was so closely preceded by the England tour, many of the players had been together for over six months and team spirit and morale were therefore high.

With Pakistan, the opposite was true. For reasons which were never clear, but which undoubtedly stemmed from a clash of personalities, the Pakistanis toured without Sarfraz Nawaz, their main wicket-taker against India in the previous series. There was also a very apparent division of loyalties within the party. Discipline was low, with the players distracted by commercial and social interests. However, the Pakistanis, whose only win on tour was against a weak East Zone side, would not come to terms with their shortcomings. Instead, they looked elsewhere for the cause of their failures. They alleged bias on the part of the umpires and in Bombay, during the third Test, they accused the ground authorities of doctoring the pitch after the match had started. After a stormy fourth Test, in which Sikander Bakht kicked down the stumps after having an appeal disallowed, Asif Iqbal talked of calling off the rest of the tour. Although such an action would have had severe repercussions, both at political level and in the cricket world, the Indian players would not, they said, have been too sorry. The atmosphere on the field had been soured and standards of conduct had dropped to deplorable levels.

Pakistan seldom batted to anywhere near their full potential, and their bowling was always inadequate. The handicap of Sarfraz's absence was accentuated by a persistent injury to Imran Khan, who had damaged a muscle alongside the rib box. The injury made itself manifest during a torrid opening spell in the second Test, which Pakistan nearly lost but might well have won had Imran not broken down. Favourable conditions helped Sikander Bakht take eight wickets in India's first innings and were tailor-made for Imran. Still unfit, Imran was a passenger in the third Test and missed the fourth, when conditions again suited pace bowling.

Only two Pakistani batsmen, Javed Miandad and Wasim Raja, were at all consistent. Playing always in a positive, challenging manner, Raja was prone to lose his wicket through reckless shots, and yet he topped Pakistan's Test aggregates and averages with 450 runs (average 56.25). Only Gavaskar, with 529 runs for India, scored more runs in the series. For all that, when Majid Khan's lack of form necessitated a reshuffle of the batting order, Raja was dropped down rather than promoted and was less able to give Pakistan full benefit of his rich form. Miandad invariably looked to have the measure of the bowling, but quite often got himself out when looking well set. Too often he was leg-before coming across to hit the ball through mid-wicket.

In the 1978-79 series in Pakistan, India were unable to bowl Pakistan out even once in three Tests. This time they did so seven times in eleven innings, each time for totals under 300 and twice for less than 200. Apart from Raja and Miandad, not one batsman averaged even 30. The most notable failure was Zaheer Abbas who, a year earlier, had made scores against India of 176, 96, 235 not out, 34 not out and 42. In India, a 40 in the first Test and 50 in the second were followed by 2, 11, 5, 0 and 15 and he lost his place for the final Test.

Majid and Asif Iqbal were almost as disappointing. Majid, always vulnerable outside the off stump, had only one score of more than 20 in the first four Tests. Asif's form, after 55 and 64 in the first two Tests, declined with the fortunes of his side. Mudassar Nazar made a typically dogged 126 in the first Test – Pakistan's only century of the series – and then faded away. Imran never really buckled down to the task of scoring runs. Some purpose was served by bringing Sadiq Mohammad in to open after the third Test, and reserve wicket-keeper Taslim Arif rose to the occasion in the final Test by scoring 90 and 46 on his début.

Despite his affliction, Imran took nineteen wickets in the series, at 19.21, figures which stress the difference his full fitness would have made. Sikander Bakht, despite missing the first Test, did the most damage with 24 wickets in five Tests. A lot was asked of him in Imran's absence, which is why his form tapered away after the fourth Test. But until then Sikander took at least five wickets in the first innings of his three Tests and had a haul of eleven wickets in the second Test.

Ehtesham-ud-Din, the third seamer, was not a bowler of any pace but always very accurate. If there was any help in the conditions, his sure aim always brought results. The spinners were disappointing. Iqbal Qasim shone only at Bombay, on a powdering pitch, and Abdul Qadir, the leg-spinner, had only two wickets to show for his three appearances. The fielding varied in quality but Wasim Bari, behind the wicket, was as sound as ever.

Several in the Indian ranks, too, did not play to potential. This was understandable for, in the five months prior, they were engaged in the Prudential Cup, the tour of England, including four Tests, and a series of six Tests against Australia. There was an unmistakable mark of staleness about their performance. Chauhan had a poor series, and by his standards Viswanath was quite undistinguished. Gavaskar made his quota of runs, but without looking his best. Nevertheless, the Indians played with character and determination and the sum of moderate contributions sufficed to meet the challenge. Among the bowlers, Kapil Dev was outstanding. Next in order of merit came Doshi, the left-arm spinner, but the other three main bowlers all paid a high price for their wickets. Ghavri looked tired; Binny, playing in his first series, bowled the isolated good spell, but lacked the experience to bowl economically on slow wickets; off-spinner Yadav's line was not always exact, although he did suffer from Gavaskar giving him little scope to gather confidence.

For all that the Pakistanis' comments on the umpiring were in bad taste, there was no doubt that it was deficient in standards. It had been remarked on adversely by the Australians as well. The Indian Board must take steps to improve it and one way would be to induce former first-class players to take up umpiring. As elsewhere, umpiring in India is no longer a financially unattractive occupation.

PAKISTANIS TOUR RESULTS

Test matches – Played 6: Lost 2, Drawn 4.

First-class matches – Played 12: Won 1, Lost 2, Drawn 9.

Win – East Zone.

Losses – India (2).

Draws – Board President's XI, Central Zone, India (4), North Zone, South Zone, West Zone.

TEST MATCH AVERAGES

INDIA – BATTING

	Tests	Innings	Not Outs	Runs	Highest Inns	Average
S. M. Gavaskar	6	11	1	529	166	52.90
D. B. Vengsarkar	5	8	2	316	146*	52.66
Yashpal Sharma	6	9	1	314	62	39.25
S. M. Patil	2	3	0	108	62	36.00
Kapil Dev	6	9	0	278	84	30.88
G. R. Viswanath	6	10	1	228	73	25.33

	Tests	Innings	Not Outs	Runs	Highest Inns	Average
K. D. Ghavri	6	8	2	138	45*	23.00
C. P. S. Chauhan	6	11	1	226	61	22.60
N. S. Yadav	5	7	3	81	29*	20.25
S. M. H. Kirmani	6	9	1	148	41	18.50
R. M. Binny	6	9	1	143	46	17.87
D. R. Doshi	6	8	1	58	20	8.28

Signifies not out.

BOWLING

	Overs	Maidens	Runs	Wickets	Average
Kapil Dev	211.5	53	566	32	17.68
D. R. Doshi	250.3	78	504	18	28.00
R. M. Binny	120.5	21	399	11	36.26
K. D. Ghavri	182.3	33	616	15	41.06
N. S. Yadav	108.4	17	342	8	42.75

Also bowled: S. M. Gavaskar 1–0–8–0; G. R. Viswanath 3–1–6–0.

PAKISTAN – BATTING

	Tests	Innings	Not Outs	Runs	Highest Inns	Average
Wasim Raja	6	10	2	450	97	56.25
Javed Miandad	6	11	1	421	76	42.10
Asif Iqbal	6	10	1	267	64	29.66
Mudassar Nazar	5	9	0	231	126	25.66
Imran Khan	5	8	1	154	34	22.00
Sadiq Mohammad	3	5	0	106	47	21.20
Majid J. Khan	6	11	0	223	56	20.27
Zaheer Abbas	5	9	1	157	50	19.62
Abdul Qadir	3	5	1	72	29*	18.00
Iqbal Qasim	6	8	3	87	32	17.40
Wasim Bari	6	9	2	117	49*	16.71
Sikander Bakht	5	7	2	18	6	3.60
Ehtesham-ud-Din	3	1	0	2	2	2.00

Played in one Test: Taslim Arif 90, 46.

Signifies not out.

BOWLING

	Overs	Maidens	Runs	Wickets	Average
Imran Khan	152.2	38	365	19	19.21
Ehtesham-ud-Din	124.4	34	270	14	19.28
Sikander Bakht	211.3	47	641	24	26.70
Iqbal Qasim	241.5	80	568	17	33.41
Majid J. Khan	71	21	181	3	60.33
Mudassar Nazar	78	20	205	3	68.33

Also bowled: Abdul Qadir 60–17–173–2; Asif Iqbal 36.2–15–72–2; Sadiq Mohammad 0.5–0–4–0; Wasim Raja 23–5–88–1.

PAKISTANI AVERAGES – FIRST-CLASS MATCHES

BATTING

	Matches	Innings	Not Outs	Runs	Highest Inns	Average
Taslim Arif	4	7	2	430	116*	86.00
Javed Miandad	11	18	6	693	110*	57.75
Wasim Raja	11	16	4	577	97	48.08
Majid J. Khan	11	19	2	735	156	43.23
Mudassar Nazar	9	13	1	468	133	39.00
Zaheer Abbas	9	16	2	521	114	37.21
Asif Iqbal	8	14	2	378	64	31.50
Imran Khan	8	10	1	255	74	28.33
Sadiq Mohammad	9	15	0	378	88	25.20
Wasim Bari	10	13	4	177	49*	19.66
Iqbal Qasim	11	10	5	91	32	18.20
Abdul Qadir	7	6	1	73	29*	14.60
Talat Mirza	3	5	1	29	22	7.25
Sikander Bakht	9	7	2	18	6	3.60
Ehtesham-ud-Din	7	1	0	2	2	2.00

Played in two matches: Abdur Raqib did not bat; Mohsin Khan 4, 13.

Played in one match: Aslam Sanjrani 11.

* *Signifies not out.*

BOWLING

	Overs	Maidens	Runs	Wickets	Average
Imran Khan	209.5	57	537	28	19.17
Ehtesham-ud-Din	176.4	48	461	20	23.05
Sikander Bakht	266.1	65	807	31	26.03
Iqbal Qasim	319	95	787	27	29.14
Majid J. Khan	87	28	213	7	30.42
Wasim Raja	68	12	233	7	33.28
Abdur Raqib	59	11	197	5	39.40
Abdul Qadir	117	31	359	7	51.28
Mudassar Nazar	103	29	281	5	56.20

Also bowled: Asif Iqbal 38.2–15–93–2; Aslam Sanjrani 17–3–59–1; Javed Miandad 15–1–57–2; Mohsin Khan 1–0–2–0; Sadiq Mohammad 12.5–1–50–0; Talat Mirza 4–0–11–0; Wasim Bari 3–0–11–1; Zaheer Abbas 3–1–12–0.

FIELDING

Wasim Bari 25 (17ct 8st), Javed Miandad 10, Iqbal Qasim 9, Taslim Arif 8 (6ct 2st), Abdul Qadir 5, Majid J. Khan 5, Sadiq Mohammad 5, Asif Iqbal 4, Mudassar Nazar 4, Abdur Raqib 3, Wasim Raja 3, Sikander Bakht 2, Zaheer Abbas 2, Ehtesham-ud-Din 1, Imran Khan 1, Talat Mirza 1.

HUNDREDS FOR PAKISTANIS

The following nine three-figure innings were played for the Pakistanis in first-class matches.

  * *Signifies not out.*

Javed Miandad (2)
    110* v Central Zone at Jaipur
    100* v South Zone at Hyderabad

Majid J. Khan (2)
    156   v West Zone at Pune
    101   v East Zone at Gauhati

Mudassar Nazar (2)
    133   v East Zone at Gauhati
    126   v India at Bangalore (First Test)

Taslim Arif (2)
    116* v South Zone at Hyderabad
    101   v West Zone at Pune

Zaheer Abbas (1)
    114   v West Zone at Pune

HUNDREDS AGAINST PAKISTANIS

The following five three-figure innings were played against the Pakistanis in first-class matches.

  * *Signifies not out.*

A. D. Gaekwad (1)
    119   for West Zone at Pune

S. M. Gavaskar (1)
    166   for India at Madras (Fifth Test)

G. Parkar (1)
    117   for West Zone at Pune

T. E. Srinivasan (1)
    108   for South Zone at Hyderabad

D. B. Vengsarkar (1)
    146* for India at New Delhi (Second Test)

CENTRAL ZONE v PAKISTANIS

At Jaipur, November 11, 12, 13. Drawn. Although Central Zone declared 33 behind the Pakistanis, the match had a tame end with the touring side using their second innings only to provide practice for those who had not batted for any length of time in the first. Finally, Asif Iqbal left Central Zone the unrealistic target of 318 in ninety minutes. On a slow pitch the match was dominated by the bat, and all the Pakistani batsmen likely to play in the first Test played major innings, Miandad taking three and a half hours for his unbeaten 110. The only bowlers to enjoy any measure of success were Wasim Raja with leg-breaks, and Central Zone's left-arm spinner, Shastri.

Pakistanis

Majid J. Khan c Shastri b G. Sharma	55	– lbw b Shastri	48
Sadiq Mohammad lbw b P. Sharma	6	– lbw b Hans	18
Zaheer Abbas c K. Mathur b Shastri	68	– c and b Shastri	44
Javed Miandad not out	110		
Wasim Raja run out	42	– (7) not out	23
*Asif Iqbal not out	16	– (4) c V. Mathur b Hans	61
Imran Khan (did not bat)		– (5) st Vedraj b Shastri	74
†Wasim Bari (did not bat)		– (6) not out	9
B 1, l-b 2, n-b 3	6	B 1, l-b 3, n-b 3	7

1/40 2/68 3/193 4/281   (4 wkts dec.) 303   1/21 2/104   (5 wkts dec.) 284
3/121 4/226 5/251

Abdul Qadir, Iqbal Qasim and Sikander Bakht did not bat.

Bowling: *First Innings*—Deshpande 4–1–21–0; V. Mathur 3–1–7–0; P. Sharma 18–4–44–1; Hans 24.2–1–82–0; G. Sharma 17–0–86–1; Shastri 13–0–57–1. *Second Innings*—Deshpande 3–2–3–0; V. Mathur 9–1–30–0; P. Sharma 1–0–6–0; Hans 19–3–91–2; G. Sharma 27–7–71–0; Shastri 27–6–76–3.

Central Zone

K. Mathur c Bari b Imran	1	– lbw b Raja	17
V. Telang c Miandad b Qadir	66	– c Raja b Qadir	38
A. Bhanot c Bari b Miandad	58		
*P. Sharma c Qadir b Raja	70		
A. Deshpande c Miandad b Raja	1	– (4) st Bari b Raja	1
Sanjiva Rao run out	1	– (3) not out	2
V. Mathur st Bari b Qasim	30	– (5) not out	3
†Vedraj lbw b Raja	33		
G. Sharma not out	0		
B 1, l-b 5, n-b 4	10	L-b 3, w 1	4

1/4 2/89 3/180 4/181   (8 wkts dec.) 270   1/56 2/57 3/59   (3 wkts) 65
5/193 6/212 7/270 8/270

R. S. Hans and S. Shastri did not bat.

Bowling: *First Innings*—Imran 15–4–53–1; Sikander 10–1–34–0; Qadir 18–4–45–1; Qasim 20.3–3–52–1; Majid 5–3–4–0; Raja 18–3–38–3; Miandad 8–1–30–1; Zaheer 1–0–4–0. *Second Innings*—Imran 5–0–11–0; Sikander 5–1–14–0; Qadir 5–2–16–1; Qasim 4–1–4–0; Majid 5–2–11–0; Raja 3–1–4–2; Sadiq 1–0–1–0.

Umpires: Swaroop Kishen and P. R. Punjabi.

BOARD PRESIDENT'S XI v PAKISTANIS

At Baroda, November 16, 17, 18. Drawn. Rain delayed the start by an hour and threequarters and left the second and third days totally blank. The home side consisted of Test trialists and Yog Raj, a pace bowler from Haryana, took the opportunity provided by a responsive pitch to capture three good Pakistani wickets for 29 runs.

Pakistanis

Talat Mirza c Reddy b Yog Raj	0	†Wasim Bari c Gaekwad b Shukla	17
Sadiq Mohammad c Gaekwad b Bhattacharjee.	0	Abdul Qadir c Gaekwad b Shukla	1
*Majid J. Khan b Yog Raj	58	Iqbal Qasim not out	2
Javed Miandad c Reddy b Yog Raj	0	B 5, l-b 2, n-b 7.	14
Wasim Raja c Yashpal b Patil	23		
Mudassar Nazar not out	76	1/0 2/18 3/52 4/114 (7 wkts) 191
		5/154 6/155 7/165

Ehtesham-ud-Din and Sikander Bakht did not bat.

Bowling: Yog Raj 15–4–29–3; Binny 8–2–30–0; Patil 8–3–19–1; Bhattacharjee 16–2–44–1; Shukla 15–2–55–2.

Board President's XI

*A. D. Gaekwad, †B. Reddy, S. B. Jung, R. M. Binny, Yashpal Sharma, S. M. Patil, Yog Raj Singh, A. Bhattacharjee, R. Shukla, B. P. Patel, S. Arun Lal.

Umpires: Mohammad Ghouse and M. V. Gothaskar.

INDIA v PAKISTAN

First Test Match

At Bangalore, November 21, 22, 24, 25, 26. Drawn. Although the ball turned from as early as the first day, both sides topped 400 in the first innings. Pakistan's 431 for nine declared reflected the depth of their batting, with Mudassar Nazar taking more than seven hours to score 126, made off 337 balls. The Indians paid heavily for letting him off with their only lapse during almost ten hours in the field. Mudassar, flicking Kapil Dev off his legs, was dropped when only 17 and the total 62 for one.

Good bowling by Doshi limited Pakistan to 256 for four on the first day, and it was already apparent that India should have played a third spinner, as indeed Pakistan did. Moreover, they might have contained Pakistan more effectively had Gavaskar not delayed the use of spin until the seventeenth over, for the damp pitch held potential for the spinners. Doshi struck in only his second over, dismissing Zaheer Abbas, the scourge of the Indian bowling in the previous series.

India, in an hour's batting at the end of the second day, soon lost Chauhan, and the next day they were in some peril when Gavaskar, after a slow, sturdy 88 in four hours twenty minutes, was third out at 164. The innings, however, was then established by a century partnership between Viswanath, batting with authority and flair, and Yashpal Sharma. Viswanath's was the one wicket to fall on the fourth day, when play was limited by poor weather to only forty-two minutes, and India continued on into the last day. Although the last four wickets went down for just 6 runs, India finished only 15 runs behind Pakistan. Binny, making his Test début, scored 46 and atoned for some very loose bowling earlier in the match.

Although the pitch was slow, Imran Khan was Pakistan's most incisive bowler, despite the lack of adequate support with the new ball. In the prevailing conditions, Ehtesham-ud-Din did not look the part of an opening Test bowler. With the pitch turning, it was surprising that Iqbal Qasim went without a wicket, but Majid Khan's off-breaks proved useful in dealing with the lower order.

Pakistan, starting their second innings midway between lunch and tea, lost both openers at 41 and then had to bat with care to avoid further problems against the spin of Doshi and Yadav.

Pakistan

Majid J. Khan c Kirmani b Ghavri	1	– st Kirmani b Doshi	19
Mudassar Nazar c Doshi b Yadav	126	– c Kapil Dev b Yadav	17
Zaheer Abbas st Kirmani b Doshi	40	– not out	31
Javed Miandad lbw b Doshi	76	– not out	30
Wasim Raja lbw b Kapil Dev	36		
*Asif Iqbal c and b Doshi	55		
Imran Khan c Viswanath b Yadav	6		
†Wasim Bari not out	49		
Abdul Qadir lbw b Kapil Dev	8		
Iqbal Qasim run out	20		
B 1, l-b 6, n-b 7	14	B 4, n-b 7	11

1/5 2/62 3/196 4/256   (9 wkts dec.) 431   1/41 2/41   (2 wkts) 108
5/334 6/345 7/348 8/371 9/431

Ehtesham-ud-Din did not bat.

Bowling: *First Innings*—Kapil Dev 24–4–67–2; Ghavri 24–3–83–1; Binny 10–1–49–0; Doshi 52.3–20–102–3; Yadav 39–5–116–2. *Second Innings*—Kapil Dev 4–2–6–0; Ghavri 8–3–30–0; Binny 3–2–1–0; Doshi 12–3–26–1; Yadav 11–2–20–1; Viswanath 3–1–6–0; Gavaskar 1–0–8–0.

India

*S. M. Gavaskar c Miandad b Qadir ...	88	Kapil Dev b Majid	38
C. P. S. Chauhan c Majid b Imran.....	13	K. D. Ghavri b Majid..............	2
G. R. Viswanath c Bari		N. S. Yadav not out	1
b Ehtesham-ud-Din.	73	D. R. Doshi b Imran	0
D. B. Vengsarkar b Imran	33		
Yashpal Sharma c Miandad b Majid	62	B 13, l-b 10...............	23
R. M. Binny c Ehtesham-ud-Din b Imran	46		
†S. M. H. Kirmani c Qasim		1/17 2/122 3/164 4/266 5/307	416
b Ehtesham-ud-Din .	37	6/347 7/410 8/414 9/415	

Bowling: Imran 28.4–12–53–4; Ehtesham-ud-Din 18–2–52–2; Qasim 41–17–75–0; Majid 28–9–55–3; Qadir 35–8–114–1; Raja 8–2–30–0; Mudassar 6–1–14–0.

Umpires: Swaroop Kishen and M. V. Gothaskar.

NORTH ZONE v PAKISTANIS

At Amritsar, November 29, 30, December 2. Drawn. Rain reduced play to two days, but the rival captains made up for lost time with a series of declarations and provided entertainment for a large crowd from both sides of the border, which had been thrown open. Bedi, making his only appearance against the tourists, closed North Zone's innings at 191 for seven, which included a polished 43 by Test candidate Arun Lal and a less impressive 42 from Surinder Amarnath. The zone's seamers then captured three wickets for 60 before the close, but the next morning Pakistan moved on to 120 without further loss and declared. Going for quick runs in their second innings, North Zone ran into trouble and were 38 for six before the collapse was halted by all-rounders Shukla and Yog Raj. Bedi's second declaration set the touring side a target of 214 in 130 minutes, but once they lost early wickets they could not mount a serious challenge.

North Zone

V. Sunderam b Mudassar................	10	– lbw b Ehtesham-ud-Din	4
S. Arun Lal c and b Raqib	43	– run out	19
S. Amarnath b Raqib	42	– c Taslim b Sikander	4
M. Amarnath c Arif b Qadir	1	– not out	41
†S. C. Khanna b Qadir.................	8	– lbw b Sikander	0
S. Madan Lal b Raqib	25	– c Sadiq b Sikander	0
D. Chopra c Qadir b Raqib	21	– c Raqib b Ehtesham-ud-Din.....	5
R. Shukla not out	28	– st Taslim b Raqib............	33
Yog Raj Singh not out	0	– not out	28
B 1, l-b 3, n-b 9..........	13	B 1, n-b 7	8

1/33 2/101 3/104	(7 wkts dec.) 191	1/25 2/25	(7 wkts dec.) 142
4/110 5/117 6/142 7/171		3/29 4/29 5/31 6/38 7/98	

*B. S. Bedi and S. Valson did not bat.

Bowling: *First Innings*—Sikander 15–6–44–0; Ehtesham-ud-Din 7–2–19–0; Mudassar 8–3–25–1; Raqib 24–7–68–4; Qadir 13–5–22–2. *Second Innings*—Sikander 12–4–46–3; Ehtesham-ud-Din 10–3–27–2; Mudassar 6–3–13–0; Raqib 8–1–26–1; Qadir 4–2–10–0; Sadiq 4–0–12–0.

Pakistanis

Sadiq Mohammad lbw b Valson	13 – (2) c Madan Lal b Valson	1
Talat Mirza b Yog Raj	5 – (4) lbw b Valson	0
*Majid J. Khan not out	67 – (6) not out	19
Javed Miandad b Madan Lal	10 – (7) not out	1
Wasim Raja not out	11 – c Madan Lal b Valson	16
†Taslim Arif (did not bat)	– (1) lbw b Yog Raj	12
Mudassar Nazar (did not bat)	– (3) c and b M. Amarnath	17
B 8, l-b 3, n-b 3	14	B 1, l-b 1, n-b 7	9

1/11 2/45 3/60   (3 wkts dec.) 120   1/15 2/17 3/17   (5 wkts) 75
                                                    4/39 5/66

Abdul Qadir, Abdur Raqib, Sikander Bakht and Ehtesham-ud-Din did not bat.

Bowling: *First Innings*—Yog Raj 9–1–45–1; Valson 11–4–38–1; Madan Lal 4–1–12–1; Bedi 2–0–10–0; Shukla 1–0–1–0; Chopra 1–0–0–0. *Second Innings*—Yog Raj 9–4–22–1; Valson 8–1–27–3; Madan Lal 3–1–11–0; Shukla 1–0–0–0; M. Amarnath 4–2–6–1.

Umpires: K. B. Ramaswamy and B. N. Hanumantha Rao.

INDIA v PAKISTAN

Second Test Match

At New Delhi, December 4, 5, 6, 8, 9. Drawn. A venue notorious for producing some of the dullest Test matches was this time the scene of a fascinating encounter in which fortunes shifted many times as it moved to a gripping finish. India, heavily outplayed for most of the match, went to within 26 runs of winning and missed out only because they were not bold and imaginative enough to take their opportunities. Pakistan suffered from Imran Khan breaking down just as he looked like inflicting heavy damage on the Indian batting.

Pakistan, having won the toss for the second consecutive Test, batted on a pitch which had sweated under cover and was dampened further by a roller that picked up moisture on its passage across a dew-laden outfield. Consequently they had a disastrous morning, losing Majid, Mudassar and Zaheer for 36 runs to Kapil Dev, whose opening spell was quite menacing. Miandad was fourth out with less than 100 on the board.

The absence of a third seam bowler of experience in India's attack facilitated Pakistan's recovery as Asif Iqbal and Wasim Raja put on 127 without being separated by the close. However, the second new ball, taken early on the second day, and a policy of trying to force the pace straight away saw the Pakistan innings come to grief. Asif was caught from a reckless slash and Raja, needing only 3 for his century, was lbw playing off his legs. The last six wickets produced only 53 runs of which 30 were scored by Imran.

Pakistan retaliated strongly when India batted, despite being deprived of the services of Imran. The loss was emphasised by the speed and hostility with which he had bowled his first two overs before lunch, making Gavaskar fight hard for survival. Sikander Bakht, however, rose to the occasion. Bowling unchanged from the start of the innings, twenty-two minutes before lunch, until bad light stopped play seven minutes ahead of schedule, he took eight wickets for 69 and effected the fall of a ninth by inadvertently deflecting the ball on to the stumps while stopping a straight drive to run out Viswanath, the non-striker. Although India batted very poorly, finishing the day at 126 for nine, Sikander deserved great credit for exploiting their errors through his unerring direction on or just outside the off stump.

India's innings would not have survived the second day had Doshi, the last man, not stayed in for the last forty-five minutes with Yashpal Sharma in what turned out to be the highest partnership of the innings. Pakistan, with a first innings lead of 147 and almost three full days remaining once Doshi was caught, could afford to spend some time over their second innings. To some extent, caution was forced on them by another poor start – 68 for 3 – but Asif and Wasim Raja, uncharacteristically sedate this time, dug in once more and had Pakistan in a strong position at stumps: 197 for four with a lead of 344 runs. This was a formidable advantage, especially as Doshi had shown towards the end of the day that the ball was turning.

On the fourth day Pakistan once more collapsed quite dramatically, losing their six remaining wickets in one hour forty minutes for only another 45 runs. Asif, Raja and Imran all gave their wickets away with wanton shots.

India were left with 550 minutes to make 390 runs for victory, and at the close they had scored 117 for two wickets, one of them Gavaskar's. Vengsarkar remained unbeaten with 32, but the manner in which he obtained these runs did not suggest he would play a leading rôle in an Indian victory. On the final day, Viswanath started in commanding mood, promising to give the innings both solidity and impetus, but at 34, in a total of 154, he was beaten by an unplayable ball from Iqbal Qasim, one which pitched on the leg stump and hit the off. This, however, was Pakistan's only gain during the morning. Sikander, who had taken the first two wickets on the previous day to achieve ten wickets in a Test, now showed the strain of his first innings efforts and bowled less accurately.

Vengsarkar's progress, such as it was, was funereal. He scored only 17 runs before lunch and maintained this pace for quite a portion of the afternoon. In the first hour after lunch only 31 runs were added, and if the rate improved thereafter it owed much to the efforts of Yashpal. India's target in the ninety minutes after tea was 139, and at last Vengsarkar began to assert himself. There was a setback when, just before the start of the final twenty overs, Yashpal was caught and bowled by the admirable Sikander, a vital blow which contributed in no small measure to Pakistan escaping defeat. India needed 114 from the final twenty overs and were kept in touch by a hectic 21 from Kapil Dev. But Vengsarkar, who took seven hours seventeen minutes to reach his century and batted eight hours forty-seven minutes for his 146 not out, was too late in mounting a whole-hearted assault.

Pakistan

Majid J. Khan b Kapil Dev	0	– c Kirmani b Binny	40
Mudassar Nazar c Chauhan b Kapil Dev	18	– c Kirmani b Kapil Dev	12
Zaheer Abbas b Kapil Dev	3	– c Kirmani b Binny	50
Javed Miandad lbw b Ghavri	34	– run out	0
Wasim Raja lbw b Kapil Dev	97	– c Kapil Dev b Doshi	61
*Asif Iqbal c Vengsarkar b Ghavri	64	– c Kirmani b Kapil Dev	38
Imran Khan lbw b Binny	30	– c Chauhan b Doshi	2
†Wasim Bari b Kapil Dev	9	– b Ghavri	5
Abdul Qadir b Binny	9	– c Vengsarkar b Kapil Dev	11
Iqbal Qasim run out	2	– not out	5
Sikander Bakht not out	1	– lbw b Kapil Dev	6
L-b 2, n-b 4	6	B 6, l-b 4, n-b 2	12
	273		**242**

1/3 2/13 3/36 4/90 5/220 6/224
7/250 8/270 9/271

1/39 2/68 3/68 4/143 5/201
6/209 7/210 8/230 9/232

Bowling: *First Innings*—Kapil Dev 23.5–8–58–5; Ghavri 21–4–58–2; Binny 10–3–32–2; Doshi 17–3–51–0; Yadav 20–2–68–0. *Second Innings*—Kapil Dev 22.5–6–63–4; Ghavri 17–4–59–1; Binny 17–3–56–2; Doshi 19–6–31–2; Yadav 5–0–21–0.

India

*S. M. Gavaskar c Bari b Sikander	31	– c Bari b Sikander	21
C. P. S. Chauhan c Bari b Sikander	11	– lbw b Sikander	40
D. B. Vengsarkar c Miandad b Sikander	1	– not out	146
G. R. Viswanath run out	4	– b Qasim	34
Yashpal Sharma not out	28	– c and b Sikander	60
R. M. Binny lbw b Sikander	1	– (7) c Qadir b Asif	10
†S. M. H. Kirmani b Sikander	5	– (8) not out	11
Kapil Dev b Sikander	15	– (6) lbw b Mudassar	21
K. D. Ghavri lbw b Sikander	0		
N. S. Yadav c Qadir b Sikander	4		
D. R. Doshi c Miandad b Asif	10		
B 2, l-b 5, n-b 9	16	B 2, l-b 5, w 1, n-b 13	21
	126	(6 wkts)	**364**

1/19 2/35 3/46 4/52 5/56 6/70
7/87 8/87 9/94

1/37 2/92 3/154
4/276 5/308 6/343

Bowling: *First Innings*——Imran 7.3–4–11–0; Sikander 21–3–69–8; Asif 6.2–4–3–1; Majid 1–0–12–0; Qasim 3–0–7–0; Mudassar 3–0–8–0. *Second Innings*——Imran 1–0–2–0; Sikander 38–7–121–3; Asif 20–7–46–1; Majid 4–2–8–0; Qasim 21–5–87–1; Mudassar 30–8–61–1; Qadir 11–3–16–0; Raja 2–1–2–0.

Umpires: Mohammad Ghouse and P. R. Punjabi.

WEST ZONE v PAKISTANIS

At Pune, December 11, 12, 13. Drawn. Despite three declarations, the two teams came nowhere near settling this contest. Nevertheless, scintillating batting from both sides compensated the crowd for a tame finish, even if the abundance of runs and the limited success of the bowlers were to be expected on a pitch so easy and true in bounce. The tone was set by a century opening partnership for the Pakistanis by Taslim Arif, who hit the first of five hundreds recorded in the match, and Sadiq Mohammad. The other Pakistani hundreds, by Zaheer and Majid, must have been most satisfying in view of their moderate records in the first two Tests. West Zone began with a mammoth opening stand between Test reject Gaekwad and the diminutive Bombay batsman, Parkar. But the most significant performance, from the viewpoint of the Indian selectors, was Patil's. An exciting, volatile player, he hit 68 off 67 balls in the first innings and 71, off 63, in the second.

Pakistanis

Taslim Arif c N. Parsana b Yajurvindra	101	– (6) not out	62
Sadiq Mohammad lbw b D. D. Parsana	67	– (3) lbw b Jadeja	32
Zaheer Abbas c Patil b D. D. Parsana	114	– (5) c Patil b D. D. Parsana	28
*Majid J. Khan run out	8	– (1) c Bhalekar b Hazare	156
Wasim Raja c Patil b D. D. Parsana	12		
Talat Mirza not out		– (2) c and b Yajurvindra	22
†Wasim Bari not out	0	– (4) c Gaekwad b Yajurvindra	34
Aslam Sanjrani (did not bat)		– (7) lbw b Parkar	11
N-b 6	6	L-b 1, n-b 7	8

1/129 2/255 3/273 4/305 5/310   (5 wkts dec.) 310   1/41 2/111 3/174   (6 wkts dec.) 353
                                              4/224 5/310 6/353

Ehtesham-ud-Din, Iqbal Qasim and Abdur Raqib did not bat.

Bowling: *First Innings*——Jadeja 9–1–32–0; D. D. Parsana 30–5–102–3; Yajurvindra 14–1–55–1; Patil 4–1–10–0; N. Parsana 16–2–78–0; Gunjal 1–0–5–0; Gaekwad 7–1–22–0. *Second Innings*——Jadeja 13–2–43–1; D. D. Parsana 18–4–34–1; Yajurvindra 16–0–74–2; Patil 3–1–8–0; N. Parsana 26–2–104–0; Gaekwad 1–0–4–0; Hazare 10–0–73–1; Parkar 2.5–0–5–1.

West Zone

*A. D. Gaekwad st Taslim b Qasim	119		
G. Parkar run out	117		
Yajurvindra Singh not out	33		
S. M. Patil c Talat b Bari	68	– (2) st Bari b Aslam	71
R. B. Bhalekar not out	3		
†A. Shroff (did not bat)		– (1) not out	39
R. V. Hazare (did not bat)		– (3) not out	14
L-b 3, n-b 1	4	B 5, l-b 3, n-b 1	9

1/222 2/224 3/333   (3 wkts dec.) 344   1/111   (1 wkt) 133

R. Jadeja, D. D. Parsana, N. Parsana and M. D. Gunjal did not bat.

Bowling: *First Innings*——Ehtesham-ud-Din 15–2–72–0; Raja 18–2–86–0; Aslam 7–2–18–0; Raqib 22–2–82–0; Qasim 12–0–67–1; Bari 3–0–11–1; Sadiq 2–0–4–0. *Second Innings*——Ehtesham-ud-Din 5–2–22–0; Aslam 10–1–41–1; Raqib 5–1–21–0; Sadiq 5–1–29–0; Talat 4–0–11–0.

Umpires: J. D. Ghosh and G. D. Pandit.

INDIA v PAKISTAN

Third Test Match

At Bombay, December 16, 17, 18, 20. India won by 131 runs with a day to spare. The pitch was the same one on which India, only six weeks earlier, had beaten Australia in four days. This time it was even more dry and bare, and in the circumstances, winning the toss took India a long way towards winning the match.

The pitch presented problems from the first day, the ball not only turning but also coming off at varying heights and speeds. India's first reverse, the dismissal of Gavaskar, was caused by a ball that stopped. His opening partner, Chauhan, also went cheaply. That India were 232 for six at the end of the opening day owed much to a stand of 80 for the third wicket between Vengsarkar and Viswanath and the undefeated partnership of 78 between Kirmani and Kapil Dev, who batted aggressively against a tiring attack. Even on the first day, spin provided the most potent bowling and Iqbal Qasim took four for 96.

Although Kirmani and Kapil Dev did not make a substantial addition on the second day, they remained for forty-four minutes, in which time the second new ball had lost its shine. Ghavri and Yadav then put on 67 for the ninth wicket and the Pakistanis were so frustrated at being held up by the tail that Sikander Bakht frequently peppered numbers ten and eleven with bumpers.

Pakistan, beginning their reply to India's 334 shortly after lunch, were 112 for six at the close. Even before the spinners established their stranglehold, Binny, a seamer, had taken the first three wickets and Pakistan's batsmen were already in a state of panic. The next morning the four remaining wickets put on 61, proving that conditions, even if difficult, were not as impossible as the earlier batting suggested. Wasim Bari stayed in for an hour and twenty-four minutes and Abdul Qadir, who remained not out with 29, for almost the whole of the morning.

India themselves collapsed quite ignominiously in their second innings – from 117 for three at the end of the third day to 160 all out, Iqbal Qasim taking six for 40. However, India's formidable first innings lead of 161 stood them in good stead, for Pakistan were now 321 in arrears and, to save the match, had to bat for nine hours forty minutes. It was a daunting task on a pitch now at its most spiteful. Again the initial damage was done by pace before Doshi or Yadav was brought on and Ghavri turned to bowling spin.

The ball before Mudassar fell lbw to Ghavri got up and hit him in the face, whereas Zaheer was bowled by one that kept low. Pakistan were routed for 190 in three and a half hours and only Miandad, keen of eye and quick on his feet, was equal to the challenge. He not only survived for two hours nineteen minutes, but exploited the gaps left by aggressive field-placing to score 64, with seven 4s. Coming in at 32 for two, he was eighth out at 178.

For a while Miandad was overshadowed by Asif who, batting resourcefully, scored 26 out of a stand of 36 before falling to a vicious ball from Doshi which lifted as it turned. Although India made steady progress towards victory, they could not have felt totally assured until Miandad was out, leg-before playing forward to Doshi. Considering that the ball was turning so readily, he might have been unfortunate to be given out.

India

*S. M. Gavaskar c Qadir b Sikander	4	– c Zaheer b Qasim	48
C. P. S. Chauhan c Bari b Imran	5	– b Mudassar	0
D. B. Vengsarkar c Majid b Qasim	58	– c Bari b Sikander	45
G. R. Viswanath c and b Qasim	47	– lbw b Qadir	9
Yashpal Sharma b Qasim	3	– c Majid b Qasim	16
R. M. Binny c Bari b Qasim	0	– (8) c and b Sikander	0
†S. M. H. Kirmani c Asif b Sikander	41	– (6) c Asif b Qasim	15
Kapil Dev c Raja b Sikander	69	– (7) c Bari b Qasim	3
K. D. Ghavri c Asif b Sikander	36	– c Bari b Qasim	1
N. S. Yadav not out	29	– st Bari b Qasim	1
D. R. Doshi c Bari b Sikander	9	– not out	1
B 10, l-b 10, w 2, n-b 11	33	B 9, l-b 7, n-b 5	21

1/13 2/31 3/111 4/129 5/129 6/154   334   1/5 2/78 3/97 4/132 5/146   160
7/249 8/250 9/317   6/154 7/156 8/157 9/157

Bowling: *First Innings*—Imran 15–7–35–1; Sikander 22.1–5–55–5; Qasim 44–15–135–4; Majid 23–8–52–0; Qadir 3–1–16–0; Mudassar 5–0–7–0; Asif 2–1–1–0. *Second Innings*—Sikander 17–6–30–2; Mudassar 8–3–18–1; Qasim 28.5–14–40–6; Majid 4–1–14–0; Qadir 11–5–27–1; Raja 1–0–10–0.

Pakistan

Majid J. Khan c Kirmani b Binny	5	– lbw b Ghavri	7
Mudassar Nazar c Gavaskar b Doshi	25	– lbw b Ghavri	13
Zaheer Abbas b Binny	2	– b Kapil Dev	11
Javed Miandad lbw b Binny	16	– lbw b Doshi	64
Wasim Raja c Viswanath b Doshi	24	– c Vengsarkar b Ghavri	4
*Asif Iqbal c and b Yadav	14	– c Viswanath b Doshi	26
Imran Khan c Gavaskar b Doshi	15	– c Gavaskar b Ghavri	19
†Wasim Bari b Yadav	23	– lbw b Doshi	3
Abdul Qadir not out	29	– c Binny b Yadav	15
Iqbal Qasim c Kirmani b Yadav	0	– c Vengsarkar b Yadav	6
Sikander Bakht lbw b Kapil Dev	3	– not out	1
B 1, l-b 2, n-b 14	17	B 2, l-b 11, n-b 8	21
	173		**190**

1/11 2/15 3/53 4/57 5/83 6/106 7/116 8/146 9/146

1/16 2/32 3/41 4/48 5/84 6/145 7/161 8/178 9/189

Bowling: *First Innings*—Kapil Dev 14.3–4–23–1; Ghavri 7–2–17–0; Binny 12–1–53–3; Doshi 27–8–52–3; Yadav 8–4–11–3. *Second Innings*—Kapil Dev 6–1–26–1; Ghavri 18–4–63–4; Doshi 19–4–42–3; Binny 2–1–2–0; Yadav 6.4–0–36–2.

Umpires: B. N. Hanumantha Rao and K. B. Ramaswamy.

INDIA v PAKISTAN

Fourth Test Match

At Kanpur, December 25, 26, 27, 29, 30. Drawn. A violent overnight storm ruled out play on the last day but made no difference to the outcome. However, a decisive result had seemed more than probable when a green pitch claimed fifteen wickets on the first two days.

The pitch, even by English standards, was so grassy and green; so much so that Pakistan made a last-minute change in their side, leaving out left-arm spinner Abdur Raqib and including Ehtesham-ud-Din, who was not even in the squad of thirteen announced on the eve of the match. In view of these conditions, Pakistan were much the weaker for the absence of Imran Khan, whose injury had become more troublesome.

It was cloudy on the first morning, which made it all the more surprising that India elected to bat. They came to regret this decision, losing four wickets for only 17 and being saved by bad light from being bowled out on the first day. Play closed an hour and a quarter early with the score 112 for eight, five of which were taken by Sikander and three by Ehtesham-ud-Din, who completed India's rout on the following morning. English balls were used in this Test, their higher seam being a further aid to the pace bowlers in getting purchase from the grassy pitch. India would have been in a worse plight had Binny, who made 29, not been dropped at second slip, by Zaheer, when he was 12. However, they owed their recovery to Ghavri, who made 45 not out with courageous support from Yadav and Doshi.

Pakistan, in reply, scarcely fared better and finished the day at 124 for five. The only batsman to establish himself was Sadiq Mohammad, playing his first Test in the series. On the third day, Pakistan lost two more wickets for the addition of just 8 runs and yet came back to take a useful lead of 87, thanks to a magnificent innings by Wasim Raja that was skilful, bold and attractive. He was in for three hours forty-nine minutes and hit one 6 and ten 4s in his unbeaten 94. Iqbal Qasim kept him company for two hours for the eighth wicket before succumbing to the second new ball. The last two batsmen, Sikander and Ehtesham-ud-Din, scored no more than 6 between them but they each stayed for half an hour and the last two wickets produced 35 invaluable runs. Raja's innings drew such admiration that Binny, immediately after bowling the last man, ran up to apologise to Raja for depriving him of his century.

Gavaskar and Chauhan, India's openers, comfortably batted through the two hours that remained and wiped off all but 8 runs of Pakistan's lead. Next morning, batting with much greater circumspection, they added another 46. Gavaskar, having made 81, fell to a rousing catch by Mudassar at square leg, but Pakistan captured only one more wicket during the day, that of Chauhan twenty-five minutes before tea. Chauhan and Vengsarkar, both in an exercise of self-denial, put on only 43 runs in about 100 minutes, but it must be mentioned that Pakistan bowled only 19.4 overs during their stand with the rate dropping to ten overs per hour at one stage. In view of this, there was little regret when bad light again stopped play shortly after tea and when the clouds that cast this gloom produced enough rain to wipe out the last day's play.

India

*S. M. Gavaskar b Sikander	2	– c Mudassar b Ehtesham-ud-Din	81
C. P. S. Chauhan c Zaheer b Sikander	6	– c Sadiq b Raja	61
D. B. Vengsarkar c Bari b Sikander	0	– not out	16
G. R. Viswanath c Mudassar b Ehtesham-ud-Din	2	– not out	17
Yashpal Sharma c Bari b Ehtesham-ud-Din	16		
R. M. Binny b Sikander	29		
†S. M. H. Kirmani b Ehtesham-ud-Din	0		
Kapil Dev c Mudassar b Sikander	2		
K. D. Ghavri not out	45		
N. S. Yadav c Majid b Ehtesham-ud-Din	25		
D. R. Doshi c Bari b Ehtesham-ud-Din	20		
B 1, l-b 1, n-b 13	15	B 4, l-b 1, n-b 13	18

1/4 2/4 3/11 4/17 5/58 6/67   162   1/125 2/168   (2 wkts) 193
7/69 8/69 9/117

Bowling: *First Innings*—Sikander 24–9–56–5; Ehtesham-ud-Din 26.4–11–47–5; Mudassar 10–0–22–0; Asif 8–3–22–0. *Second Innings*—Sikander 23.2–5–63–0; Ehtesham-ud-Din 26–9–40–1; Qasim 16–7–28–0; Mudassar 3–1–19–0; Raja 9–2–25–1.

Pakistan

Mudassar Nazar c Kirmani b Kapil Dev	6	Iqbal Qasim b Kapil Dev	32
Sadiq Mohammad c Kirmani b Ghavri	47	Sikander Bakht c Kirmani b Kapil Dev	4
Zaheer Abbas c Gavaskar b Kapil Dev	5	Ehtesham-ud-Din b Binny	2
Javed Miandad lbw b Kapil Dev	8		
Majid J. Khan lbw b Kapil Dev	19	L-b 11, n-b 10	21
*Asif Iqbal c Viswanath b Doshi	11		
Wasim Raja not out	94	1/12 2/35 3/63 4/92 5/108	249
†Wasim Bari b Binny	0	6/131 7/132 8/214 9/226	

Bowling: Kapil Dev 28–5–63–6; Ghavri 21–5–42–1; Binny 18.5–2–76–2; Doshi 17–8–26–1; Yadav 5–1–21–0.

Umpires: Swaroop Kishen and Mohammad Ghouse.

EAST ZONE v PAKISTANIS

At Gauhati, January 10, 11. Pakistanis won by an innings and 219 runs with more than a day to spare. East Zone, replying to Pakistan's 361 for three declared, were bowled out twice on the second day in three hours forty minutes. East Zone, the only side to beat the Australians outside the Tests a few weeks earlier, thus became the only team to lose to the Pakistanis. That the pitch had little to do with their débâcle was shown by the Pakistani batting, which featured centuries by Mudassar and Majid.

Pakistanis

Mudassar Nazar b Paramjit	133	Javed Miandad not out	37
Sadiq Mohammad c Nagesh b Porel	18	B 2, l-b 2, n-b 4	8
*Majid J. Khan c S. Das b Nandi	101		
Zaheer Abbas not out	64	1/37 2/242 3/271 (3 wkts dec.)	361

Mohsin Khan, Wasim Raja, Imran Khan, †Wasim Bari, Iqbal Qasim and Sikander Bakht did not bat.

Bowling: K. Das 11–0–48–0; Porel 24–3–75–1; Paramjit 35–5–85–1; Bhattacharjee 15–1–65–0; Nagesh 5–0–30–0; U. B. Banerjee 2–0–12–0; Nandi 7–0–38–1.

East Zone

P. Nandi c Bari b Sikander	10	– absent hurt	0
†S. Das b Sikander	0	– (1) st Bari b Qasim	32
M. Dalvi c Bari b Sikander	6	– c Sadiq b Imran	8
*Raju Mukherjee b Raja	12	– b Imran	0
U. B. Banerjee b Imran	9	– b Qasim	0
Nagesh Singh st Bari b Qasim	1	– b Majid	12
S. Banerjee not out	10	– (2) c Qasim b Majid	4
A. Bhattacharjee b Imran	0	– (7) b Majid	0
K. Das st Bari b Qasim	1	– (8) c Sadiq b Majid	0
Paramjit Singh c Majid b Qasim	2	– (9) b Qasim	11
S. Porel b Sikander	11	– (10) not out	1
B 4	4	B 1, l-b 1, w 6	8

1/2 2/17 3/20 4/37 5/42 6/42   66   1/10 2/21 3/23 4/24 5/61   76
7/42 8/49 9/51   6/61 7/61 8/75 9/76

Bowling: *First Innings*—Imran 7–3–12–2; Sikander 5.4–1–12–4; Mudassar 2–0–9–0; Raja 6–1–17–1; Qasim 9–4–12–3. *Second Innings*—Imran 8–5–10–2; Sikander 7–5–16–0; Qasim 9.4–1–25–3; Majid 6–2–17–4.

Umpires: R. D. Gupta and I. Ramana Rao.

INDIA v PAKISTAN

Fifth Test Match

At Madras, January 15, 16, 17, 19, 20. India won by ten wickets. Two men shaped this decisive Indian victory – Gavaskar, with an innings of 166, the longest played in a Test match by an Indian (593 minutes), and Kapil Dev, with an outstanding all-round performance. He took eleven wickets in the match, including seven for 56 (the best figures of his Test career) in the second innings, and contributed a boisterous 84 to India's total of 430. The great-hearted bowling of Kapil Dev minimised India's self-imposed disadvantage of going into the match with only four bowlers, off-spinner Yadav having been left out.

The ball bounced more at one end than the other, but otherwise the Chepauk pitch was a better batting surface than in any recent Test on this ground. Pakistan, bowled out for 272, frittered away the advantage of winning the toss, although their batsmen did give the impression of playing with more discipline than in the previous Tests. Majid Khan ended his run of poor scores but was run out when he and Miandad looked set to enjoy a substantial partnership. Miandad batted extremely well, preventing the bowling from getting on top by running singles and 2s. Asif, too, promised much until Ghavri induced a snick with a beautiful ball, slanted across from over the wicket.

India were batting before the second morning was an hour old, and although never in deep distress, they also lost wickets regularly. At the end of the day they were 161 for four, with Gavaskar on 92. Next day, he and Sharma, the other overnight batsman, put on a century partnership which lasted until an hour after lunch, and following the dismissal in close succession of Sharma and Kirmani, he played a completely passive rôle while the flamboyant Kapil Dev hammered the tired attack.

India's innings stretched well into the morning of the fourth day, and at lunch, when Pakistan were 24 for two only thirty-eight minutes after the start of their second innings, it looked as if the match and the series would be decided before the day was out. Both Sadiq and Mudassar had fallen to loose shots, and in less than another hour, Pakistan were 58 for five. Zaheer failed yet again, out like Mudassar, glancing Kapil Dev, who took the first three wickets. Kapil Dev and Ghavri dared Majid Khan to hook, which he did profitably a couple of times before skying Ghavri to long leg. Going round the wicket, Kapil Dev had Asif caught from a square-cut, and it was only when Wasim Raja joined Miandad that resistance was at last forthcoming. Raja batted with the same abandon as the batsmen who had come to grief, but with more luck. Miandad was more discreet and built up his innings over three hours.

Pakistan still had three wickets in hand at the start of the last day and they did not concede them without a struggle. But India were left to get only 76 in the last innings, with three and threequarter hours available, and did so without loss to take a winning 2-0 lead in the series.

Pakistan

Mudassar Nazar c Kirmani b Kapil Dev	6	– c Vengsarkar b Kapil Dev 8
Sadiq Mohammad c Kirmani b Kapil Dev	46	– c Binny b Kapil Dev 0
Majid J. Khan run out	56	– c Patil b Ghavri 11
Zaheer Abbas c Kirmani b Kapil Dev	0	– c Chauhan b Kapil Dev 15
Javed Miandad c Vengsarkar b Kapil Dev	45	– c Kirmani b Doshi 52
*Asif Iqbal c Kirmani b Ghavri	34	– c Kirmani b Kapil Dev 5
Wasim Raja c Kapil Dev b Doshi	15	– c Viswanath b Doshi 57
Imran Khan run out	34	– c Doshi b Kapil Dev 29
†Wasim Bari c Binny b Ghavri	13	– lbw b Kapil Dev 15
Iqbal Qasim not out	3	– not out 19
Sikander Bakht c Vengsarkar b Ghavri	1	– b Kapil Dev 2
L-b 3, n-b 16	19	L-b 3, n-b 17 20

1/33 2/79 3/80 4/151 5/187   272   1/1 2/17 3/33 4/36 5/58   233
6/215 7/225 8/226 9/268   6/147 7/171 8/197 9/229

Bowling: *First Innings*—Kapil Dev 19–5–90–4; Ghavri 18.4–3–73–3; Binny 10–1–42–0; Doshi 26–6–48–1. *Second Innings*—Kapil Dev 23.4–7–56–7; Ghavri 14–0–82–1; Binny 13–2–33–0; Doshi 16–3–42–2.

India

*S. M. Gavaskar c Qasim b Imran	166	– not out 29
C. P. S. Chauhan c Qasim b Mudassar	5	– not out 46
D. B. Vengsarkar c Miandad b Imran	17	
G. R. Viswanath c Mudassar b Qasim	16	
S. M. Patil c Miandad b Sikander	15	
Yashpal Sharma b Qasim	46	
†S. M. H. Kirmani b Imran	2	
Kapil Dev lbw b Imran	84	
R. M. Binny not out	42	
K. D. Ghavri b Qasim	1	
D. R. Doshi c Miandad b Imran	9	
B 1, l-b 2, n-b 24	27	N-b 3 3

1/30 2/88 3/135 4/160 5/265 6/279   430   (no wkt) 78
7/339 8/412 9/413

Bowling: *First Innings*—Imran 38.2–6–114–5; Sikander 32–5–105–1; Mudassar 16–3–54–1; Qasim 37–13–81–3; Raja 2–0–19–0; Majid 9–1–30–0. *Second Innings*—Imran 5–1–20–0; Sikander 6–0–37–0; Mudassar 2–0–2–0; Qasim 4–1–12–0; Sadiq 0.5–0–4–0.

Umpires: Swaroop Kishen and M. V. Gothaskar.

SOUTH ZONE v PAKISTANIS

At Hyderabad, January 25, 26, 27. Drawn. Although they had scored runs briskly in the first innings, South Zone found a target of 240 in 150 minutes well beyond their scope. The touring side's batting was as undistinguished as in the Test match just lost, but honour was salvaged by the reserve wicket-keeper, Taslim Arif, and Miandad. Both scored unbeaten centuries and together put on 180. The Pakistanis would have been in trouble, though, had Taslim Arif not been dropped from an easy chance to mid-wicket when only 17. South Zone, after a disastrous start, declared their innings on almost even terms thanks to a delightful third-wicket partnership of 186 between Srinkanth and Srinivasan, whose 108 included two 6s and seventeen 4s. Batting practice, rather than a positive result, was the main consideration in the Pakistanis' second innings.

Pakistanis

†Taslim Arif not out	116	– c Venkataraghavan b Bharatkumar	3
Sadiq Mohammad run out	29	– c Patel b Narasimha Rao	88
Mohsin Khan c Venkataraghavan b Bharatkumar	4	– c Reddy b Kishore	13
Zaheer Abbas b Venkataraghavan	11	– c Sivaramakrishnan b Vasudevan	35
*Asif Iqbal c Narasimha Rao b Venkataraghavan	26	– (7) c sub b Narasimha Rao	8
Javed Miandad not out	100	– (8) not out	14
Imran Khan (did not bat)		– (5) b Vasudevan	27
Mudassar Nazar (did not bat)		– not out	11
Iqbal Qasim (did not bat)		– not out	2
L-b 4, n-b 3	7	L-b 12, n-b 3	15

1/43 2/54 (4 wkts dec.) 293   1/12 2/35 3/97 (7 wkts dec.) 216
3/75 4/113   4/137 5/169 6/190 7/203

Abdul Qadir and Ehtesham-ud-Din did not bat.

Bowling: *First Innings*—Bharatkumar 18–4–97–1; Kishore 9.3–3–26–0; Venkataraghavan 20–6–49–2; Vasudevan 25–6–69–0; Narasimha Rao 9–1–45–0. *Second Innings*—Bharatkumar 18–3–42–1; Kishore 7–1–28–1; Venkataraghavan 12–4–35–0; Vasudevan 19–2–51–3; Narasimha Rao 12–0–45–2.

South Zone

V. Sivaramakrishnan c Qasim b Imran	6	– lbw b Ehtesham-ud-Din	2
K. Srinkanth b Qasim	90	– (3) c Imran b Qadir	37
S. B. Jung c Taslim b Ehtesham-ud-Din	0	– (2) c Taslim b Mudassar	20
T. E. Srinivasan b Ehtesham-ud-Din	108	– b Miandad	17
B. P. Patel b Imran	35		
M. V. Narasimha Rao c Taslim b Ehtesham-ud-Din	4	– (5) b Qasim	20
J. Kishore not out	7	– (6) not out	27
†B. Reddy lbw b Imran	0	– (7) not out	3
S. Vasudevan c Taslim b Imran	0		
B 4, l-b 4, n-b 12	20	B 8, l-b 3, n-b 1, w 3	15

1/10 2/11 3/197 (8 wkts dec.) 270   1/11 2/65 3/77 (5 wkts) 141
4/231 5/237 6/268 7/268 8/270   4/109 5/128

K. Bharatkumar and *S. Venkataraghavan did not bat.

Bowling: *First Innings*—Imran 18.3–4–80–4; Ehtesham-ud-Din 11–3–47–3; Qasim 15–5–29–1; Mudassar 4–1–14–0; Javed 5–0–21–0; Qadir 10–1–59–0. *Second Innings*—Imran 4–3–6–0; Ehtesham-ud-Din 4–2–4–1; Qasim 7–1–30–1; Mudassar 5–2–15–1; Miandad 2–0–6–1; Qadir 7–0–34–1; Zaheer 2–1–8–0; Mohsin 1–0–2–0; Asif 2–0–21–0.

Umpires: M. Mukherjee and M. Y. Gupte.

INDIA v PAKISTAN

Sixth Test Match

At Calcutta, January 29, 30, 31, February 2, 3. Drawn. Pakistan's first innings declaration, with a deficit of 59 runs, followed by an exciting and volatile spell of fast bowling from Imran Khan, sustained interest in the match until the last hour. Pakistan, who had already conceded a winning lead in the series to India, were placed to win this Test at various stages, but eventually had to go on the defensive to save themselves from a third defeat.

Viswanath, captaining India for the first time, won the toss – a considerable advantage as the pitch did not look too well prepared. It was slow, with an uneven bounce, and there was an area at one end from which the ball tended to lift abruptly.

Although Pakistan's totals in the series had not exceeded 300 since the first Test, the two changes they made in their side involved the sacrifice of a batsman to accommodate an extra bowler. They replaced Mudassar Nazar, their only century-maker of the series, with the reserve wicket-keeper, Taslim Arif (playing him as a batsman) and recalled Ehtesham-ud-Din, the seam bowler, at the expense of Zaheer Abbas.

The first day went well for Pakistan, with Imran, now fully fit, bowling with much fire, and Ehtesham-ud-Din, accurate and thoughtful, making good use of conditions favourable to swing. The first four Indian wickets fell for only 99 runs, and Pakistan would have struck more deeply had Sikander, hitherto Pakistan's most successful bowler, not gone off the boil. India recovered to end the opening day at 205 for five, thanks to a partnership of 88 between Gavaskar and Patil, playing in his second Test. If not thoroughly organised in defence, Patil batted in exciting fashion to make 62, having reached his half-century off only 79 balls. At 35 he gave a return chance to Sikander, the missing of which proved a considerable reverse to Pakistan.

Pakistan put down three more chances on the following day, two of them fairly easy ones in the slips by Majid. The dogged Yashpal Sharma and Kirmani maintained the recovery begun on the first day, and in spite of Imran's magnificent bowling India achieved a total of 331.

Notwithstanding the early loss of Sadiq Mohammad's wicket, Pakistan looked every bit like matching India by scoring 263 for four at the end of the third day. Taslim, playing in his maiden Test, batted stoically for seven hours for his 90 and shared partnerships of 92 with Majid and of 73 each with Miandad and Wasim Raja. Majid played with uncharacteristic caution to bat for three hours, but from the manner in which Miandad played, India got off lightly by dismissing him for only 50. Wasim Raja again proved a difficult obstacle. Taslim, dropped at gulley when he was only 4, seemed chastened by this escape for a long time, but he chanced his arm against the second new ball and was narrowly deprived of a century on début.

Asif declared after only ten minutes on the fourth day, and less than three hours later Pakistan looked set for a brilliant triumph, having reduced India to 92 for six in their second innings. Imran had taken four of the wickets – the first three in an opening spell of eight overs. India's distress was to some extent brought about by Gavaskar's inability to open the innings because of a throat infection, but even when he came in at 48 for four he could not check the collapse.

There were signs of Pakistan's advance being halted while Gavaskar and young Patil, once more in fluent form, were together. Then Patil, at 31, got himself run out. However, the depth of India's batting again stood them in good stead. Yashpal, Kapil Dev and Ghavri batted for a total of four hours thirty-nine minutes and collectively produced 88 runs. Nor were numbers ten and eleven easily subdued. Though Yadav and Doshi jointly contributed only 9 runs, they extended the innings long enough to give India a chance of survival. Doshi, the last man, stayed with Ghavri for an hour, having faced a good few bumpers from Imran in this time. Ghavri was missed at gulley, off Imran, a slip that opened up an escape route for India.

Pakistan were left to make 265 runs in 280 minutes. Their task was more difficult than at once seemed apparent, for the pitch was worn and quite slow in pace, making free stroke-play difficult. India bowled superbly in defence of their position, although it must be said that their over-rate was on the mean side. They bowled thirteen in seventy minutes before lunch and twelve in the first hour after the break. At the end of it, Pakistan were 70 for two. The only time Pakistan speeded up their scoring significantly was when Miandad and Asif put on 42 for the fifth wicket from eight overs. They were still together when the last hour began, with 143 wanted from twenty overs, but Asif was run out in the fifth of these and Miandad gave Doshi a return catch two overs later. With 103 still wanted, Pakistan now gave up the chase, and although India moved on to the attack in an effort to take the last four wickets, Imran and Wasim Bari easily held them at bay.

India

S. M. Gavaskar c Qasim b Imran	44	– (6) c Miandad b Imran	15
C. P. S. Chauhan lbw b Ehtesham-ud-Din	18	– (1) lbw b Ehtesham-ud-Din	21
R. M. Binny lbw b Imran	15	– (2) c Raja b Imran	0
*G. R. Viswanath b Ehtesham-ud-Din	13	– b Imran	13
S. M. Patil b Imran	62	– run out	31
Yashpal Sharma c Bari b Imran	62	– (7) b Ehtesham-ud-Din	21
Kapil Dev st Bari b Qasim	16	– (8) b Qasim	30
†S. M. H. Kirmani c Qasim b Ehtesham-ud-Din	37	– (3) c Sadiq b Imran	0
K. D. Ghavri run out	16	– not out	37
N. S. Yadav not out	18	– c and b Qasim	3
D. R. Doshi b Ehtesham-ud-Din	3	– c Asif b Imran	6
B 3, l-b 9, n-b 15	27	B 9, l-b 3, n-b 16	28

1/48 2/72 3/91 4/99 5/187 6/218   331   1/7 2/10 3/33 4/48 5/88   205
7/252 8/292 9/307   6/92 7/135 8/162 9/172

Bowling: *First Innings*—Imran 33–5–67–4; Sikander 22–5–87–0; Ehtesham-ud-Din 35–7–87–4; Qasim 17–3–53–1; Majid 2–0–10–0. *Second Innings*—Imran 23.5–3–63–5; Sikander 6–2–18–0; Ehtesham-ud-Din 19–5–44–2; Qasim 21–5–50–2; Raja 1–0–2–0.

Pakistan

Taslim Arif c Chauhan b Kapil Dev	90	– c and b Binny	46
Sadiq Mohammad lbw b Kapil Dev	5	– b Ghavri	8
Majid J. Khan c Kirmani b Binny	54	– b Doshi	11
Javed Miandad lbw b Ghavri	50	– c and b Doshi	46
Wasim Raja not out	50	– run out	12
*Asif Iqbal not out	5	– run out	15
Imran Khan (did not bat)	– not out	19
†Wasim Bari (did not bat)	– not out	0
B 1, l-b 8, n-b 9	18	B 12, l-b 8, n-b 2	22

1/20 2/112 3/185   (4 wkts dec.) 272   1/24 2/58 3/86   (6 wkts) 179
4/258   4/111 5/153 6/162

Iqbal Qasim, Sikander Bakht and Ehtesham-ud-Din did not bat.

Bowling: *First Innings*—Kapil Dev 26–4–65–2; Ghavri 21.5–3–77–1; Doshi 25–12–38–0; Binny 17–3–35–1; Yadav 10–0–39–0. *Second Innings*—Kapil Dev 20–7–49–0; Ghavri 11–2–32–1; Doshi 20–5–46–2; Binny 8–2–20–1; Yadav 4–3–10–0.

Umpires: K. B. Ramaswamy and P. R. Punjabi.

DERRICK ROBINS UNDER 23 TOUR TO AUSTRALIA AND NEW ZEALAND, 1979-80

A party of fifteen players, under the managership of Bernard Simmons and the captaincy of Christopher Cowdrey, visited Australia and New Zealand in February and March 1980. Several of the players joined the touring party in Australia, where they were playing on a Whitbread scholarship or private contract. The full party was D. H. Robins, chairman, L. E. G. Ames, vice-chairman, B. Simmons, manager, H. C. Blofeld, PRO, C. S. Cowdrey (Kent), captain, C. W. J. Athey (Yorkshire), vice-captain, K. J. Barnett (Derbyshire), N. G. B. Cook (Leicestershire), K. E. Cooper (Nottinghamshire), A. L. Jones (Glamorgan), C. Maynard (Warwickshire), W. G. Merry (Middlesex), G. J. Parsons (Leicestershire), D. N. Patel (Worcestershire), A. C. S. Pigott (Sussex), C. J. Richards (Surrey), G. C. Small (Warwickshire), K. Sharp (Yorkshire), R. G. Williams (Northamptonshire).

Of the sixteen matches, eight were won, two lost and six drawn. Rain brought an early close to the matches against Canterbury Minor Association and the first-class fixture against Northern Districts. A welcome feature was the strength and success of the team's spin bowlers, and few opposing teams could combat the combination of the off-spin of Patel and Williams and the left-arm spin of Cook. Patel and Williams also batted well, as did Athey, Barnett, Cowdrey and Sharp. For the match against Young New Zealand – "the best game seen in Auckland all season", said the *New Zealand Herald* – the New Zealand Cricket Council called the Robins XI a "Young England XI".

In the wake of the acrimony caused by aspects of the West Indian tour, the English touring side did much to restore faith in cricket in New Zealand.

At Sydney, February 17 (50 overs). Derrick Robins XI won by five wickets. NSW Colts Invitation XI 98 for nine (C. W. J. Athey five for 14); Derrick Robins XI 100 for five.

At Sydney, February 18, 19. Drawn. Derrick Robins XI 169 (D. N. Patel 52) and 155 for seven dec.; NSW Colts XI 93 for eight dec. (N. G. B. Cook five for 17) and 220 for eight (R. G. Williams four for 52).

At Devonport, February 24, 25. Drawn. North-Western Tasmanian CA XI 223 for six dec. and 125 for four dec.; Derrick Robins XI 129 for seven dec. and 125 for eight.

At Launceston, February 27 (55 overs). Derrick Robins XI won by 95 runs. Derrick Robins XI 241 (C. W. J. Athey 56); North Tasmanian CA XI 146 (N. G. B. Cook three for 12).

At Launceston, February 28 (50 overs). North Tasmanian CA XI won by nine wickets. Derrick Robins XI 102; North Tasmanian CA XI 104 for one.

At Hobart, March 4, 5. Drawn. Derrick Robins XI 256 for five dec. (K. Sharp 102 not out, K. J. Barnett 61) and 140 for four dec. (C. S. Cowdrey 50 not out); Tasmanian CA XI 163 for seven dec. (G. J. Parsons four for 29) and 136 for six (B. F. Davison 87 not out).

At Alexandra, March 8, 9. Otago Minor Association won by seven wickets. Derrick Robins XI 171 for nine dec. and 146 for five dec.; Otago Minor Association 85 (K. E. Cooper six for 32) and 234 for three (J. Blakely 124 not out).

At Ashburton, March 11, 12. Drawn. Derrick Robins XI 173 (C. S. Cowdrey 60 not out). Canterbury Minor Association did not bat.

At Blenheim, March 14 (50 overs). Derrick Robins XI won by 43 runs. Derrick Robins XI 181 for eight dec.; Marlborough XI 138.

At Nelson, March 15, 16. Derrick Robins XI won by five wickets. Nelson XI 147 for nine (R. G. Williams three for 23) and 274 for five dec. (G. N. Edwards 144 not out, M. H. Toynbee 65); Derrick Robins XI 184 for seven (C. W. J. Athey 69) and 238 for five (C. W. J. Athey 73).

At Palmerston North, March 18 (50 overs). Derrick Robins XI won by ten wickets. Manawatu XI 122; Derrick Robins XI 123 for no wkt. (K. Sharp 69 not out, C. W. J. Athey 49 not out).

At Napier, March 19, 20. Derrick Robins XI won by six wickets. Derrick Robins XI 232 for five dec. (K. J. Barnett 81, R. G. Williams 52 not out) and 106 for four; Combined Hawke's Bay/Wairarapa XI 108 (K. J. Barnett three for 21, A. C. S. Pigott three for 31) and 228 (Thompson 77; D. N. Patel four for 54, K. J. Barnett three for 63).

NORTHERN DISTRICTS v DERRICK ROBINS XI

At Hamilton, March 22, 23, 24. Drawn. Rain washed out play on the third day. Northern Districts, after a reasonable start, were troubled by Patel and wickets fell regularly until the declaration. Robins' XI did well to lead the strong Shell Trophy winners on the first innings with Yorkshiremen Sharp and Athey putting on 123 for the first wicket. Sharp went on to a slow but solid century.

Northern Districts

J. G. Gibson b Cook	28	– b Barnett	65
†M. J. Wright c Williams b Patel	46	– c Cowdrey b Pigott	5
C. M. Kuggeleijn c and b Patel	34	– c and b Cook	50
J. M. Parker lbw b Cook	12	– not out	60
D. J. White lbw b Cook	7	– not out	37
A. D. G. Roberts not out	36		
*G. P. Howarth b Patel	4		
W. P. Flower c Cook b Patel	27		
C. W. Dickeson st Richards b Barnett	7		
S. J. Scott b Patel	9		
R. J. Griffiths not out	4		
L-b 3, w 1	4	B 8, w 1	9

1/51 2/105 3/114 4/126   (9 wkts dec.) 218   1/18 2/122 3/126   (3 wkts) 226
5/139 6/146 7/176 8/190 9/211

Bowling: *First Innings*—Pigott 5–1–15–0; Small 6–2–26–0; Athey 9–1–17–0; Cook 36–13–61–3; Patel 35–13–69–5; Barnett 11–2–26–1. *Second Innings*—Pigott 5.3–1–16–1; Small 10–3–24–0; Athey 3–1–7–0; Cook 33–15–56–1; Patel 11–2–50–0; Barnett 17–5–27–1; Williams 14–6–25–0; Cowdrey 3–0–12–0.

Derrick Robins XI

C. W. J. Athey lbw b White	47	A. C. S. Pigott run out	2
K. Sharp st Wright b Dickeson	106	†C. J. Richards c White b Dickeson	19
R. G. Williams lbw b Dickeson	21	N. G. B. Cook not out	0
K. J. Barnett run out	13	B 5, l-b 12, w 1	18
D. N. Patel c White b Flower	17		
*C. S. Cowdrey c Roberts b Dickeson	18	1/123 2/149 3/194	(8 wkts dec.) 318
C. Maynard not out	57	4/201 5/227 6/247 7/256 8/316	

Bowling: Griffiths 7–0–26–0; Scott 11–0–46–0; Dickeson 39–9–92–4; White 11–2–35–1; Howarth 14–8–12–0; Flower 7–1–32–1; Wright 5–1–12–0; Kuggeleijn 6–0–45–0.

At Ngatea, March 25, 26. Derrick Robins XI won by an innings and 54 runs. Thames Valley Invitation XI 172 (K. Puna 77 not out; N. G. B. Cook four for 61) and 95 (R. G. Williams five for 34, N. G. B. Cook three for 14); Derrick Robins XI 321 (R. G. Williams 157 not out, C. Maynard 50 not out).

YOUNG NEW ZEALAND v DERRICK ROBINS XI

At Auckland, March 28, 29, 30. Drawn. Patel took honours on the first day, contributing 105 to the Robins XI total of 223. In a fine spell of seam bowling Snedden took five wickets, then going in as night-watchman he batted into the next day for 69 – an excellent all-round performance. Lower down the order wicket-keeper Smith helped the Young New Zealand total, which at one stage did not look like reaching 200, to 301 for eight. Athey scored the second century of the match before Cowdrey declared, leaving Young New Zealand 223 to win at a rate of about 5 an over. Not discouraged by this stiff declaration they set about the chase with some lusty hitting and Rutherford and Blair put on 83 in an hour. With their departure, and the fall of another wicket, the team settled for a draw.

Derrick Robins XI

K. Sharp c and b Robertson	5	– c Rutherford b Gillespie	82
C. W. J. Athey run out	32	– b Snedden	116
R. G. Williams c Smith b Snedden	8	– c Smith b Gillespie	15
D. N. Patel c Gillespie b Crowe	105	– c Smith b Gillespie	54
*C. S. Cowdrey c Gillespie b Snedden	6	– not out	9
C. Maynard b Snedden	0		
K. J. Barnett c Smith b Snedden	36		
†C. J. Richards c Smith b Snedden	5		
A. C. S. Pigott b Crowe	7		
N. G. B. Cook st Smith b Brown	4		
W. G. Merry not out	0		
B 2, l-b 6, n-b 7	15	B 3, l-b 12, n-b 9	24

1/21 2/32 3/57 4/89		223	1/173 2/201 (4 wkts dec.) 300
5/89 6/161 7/175 8/218 9/223			3/290 4/300

Bowling: *First Innings*—Snedden 25–10–41–5; Robertson 20–5–73–1; Brown 11–3–13–1; Gillespie 19–5–67–0; Crowe 4–1–14–2. *Second Innings*—Snedden 17–2–73–1; Robertson 7–1–49–0; Brown 7–3–16–0; Gillespie 24.5–2–107–3; Crowe 14–3–31–0.

Young New Zealand

J. A. Rutherford c Richards b Merry	12	– c Cowdrey b Cook	75
M. D. Crowe lbw b Pigott	47	– lbw b Merry	8
M. C. Snedden c Sharp b Patel	69		
*M. H. Toynbee c Pigott b Merry	20	– c Richards b Merry	0
P. N. Webb c Sharp b Cook	2	– not out	13
B. R. Blair c Athey b Patel	0	– c Patel b Barnett	45
A. Jones not out	43	– not out	4
V. R. Brown c Athey b Cook	0		
†I. D. Smith c Williams b Cowdrey	72	– c Patel b Cook	0
S. R. Gillespie not out	17	– run out	11
B 8, l-b 7, n-b 4	19	B 1, l-b 2, n-b 1	4

1/18 2/90 3/156   (8 wkts dec.) 301   1/15 2/23 3/106   (6 wkts) 160
4/157 5/157 6/159 7/163 8/276   4/108 5/127

Bowling: *First Innings*—Merry 36–9–92–2; Pigott 18–3–51–1; Cook 8–0–37–2; Athey 9–1–33–0; Barnett 5–0–16–0; Williams 1–0–1–0; Patel 10–4–29–2; Cowdrey 3–0–23–1. *Second Innings*—Merry 8–3–15–2; Pigott 4–0–20–0; Cook 10–4–22–2; Barnett 19–4–70–1; Patel 6–1–29–0.

Umpires: D. Bindon and W. R. C. Gardiner.

BENSON AND HEDGES WORLD SERIES CUP, 1979-80

For the second time in the space of eight months, West Indies proved themselves the outstanding limited-overs side in cricket when they won the triangular Benson and Hedges World Series Cup in Australia by beating England twice in the best-of-three final. Their victory, in the end, was as emphatic as it had been the previous June at Lord's when the same eleven players defeated England in the final of the World Cup.

West Indies stumbled in the first of the final matches, in Melbourne, two run outs almost certainly costing England their chance of victory. England finished 2 runs short. That scare behind them West Indies quickly made sure the third scheduled final match would be unnecessary by over-whelming England in the second final at Sydney two days later. Here Greenidge and Richards made light of the task of scoring the 209 runs their side required to capture the first prize of £16,000.

The outcome of the triangular tournament, in which each side played the other four times in a qualifying round with the two most successful teams going into the final, was largely a battle between West Indies' heavy artillery and England's professional, limited-overs expertise based on containment and the ability to frustrate batsmen. The West Indian fire-power, usually supplied by Greenidge and Richards, generally won the day. Strangely, however, West Indies encountered difficulties whenever they came across the Australians, who bowled for wickets instead of adopting the run-saving line and length approach of England. Lloyd's team, having lost three of their four qualifying matches against Australia, all at Sydney, had had to rely on beating England to reach the finals.

Winning the limited-overs competition gave Lloyd as much pleasure as taking the Test series against Australia, although for different reasons. He felt their triumph confirmed he was leading the best side to emerge from the Caribbean, not only for their ability but also for their determination to fight back when events had gone against them. This has not often been a feature of West Indies' sides on tour. Events certainly went against them at the start of the tournament, when they were beaten in their first two games on successive nights under the Sydney floodlights. They lost the first match against Australia by five wickets and were beaten off the last ball – with every England fielder on the boundary including wicket-keeper Bairstow – the following night by England. With their own difficulties against the Australians, West Indies had to rely on England beating Australia and so clearing the way for West Indies to reach the finals. England did not let them down, winning all their four games against Australia to top the final qualifying table with eleven points.

The failure of the Australians to qualify for the finals was a major disappointment for the home crowd, the Channel Nine television company for which the competition had been specially tailored, and the Australian cricket authorities who were relying on an Australia-West Indies final to attract the crowds and help pay the costs of staging a twin tour. Yet the Australians had everything in their favour, especially in being able to select from any player in the country – unlike the World Cup in England for which every side is limited to a squad of fourteen players. It meant the Australians were able to call on in-form players in the event of injury.

In the event the Australian selectors used their advantage unwisely, calling on twenty players and seeming unable to make up their minds as to the most suitable type of bowlers for the competition. In addition their captain, Greg Chappell, made it clear he disliked such a defensive form of cricket. He attempted to win his matches without resorting to negative bowling or spreading his fielders around the boundary, and his inexperience in playing the limited-overs game showed at vital moments when he had fielders in positions where they could not prevent a single or stop a boundary.

Reaching the final was a notable achievement by the England players. Only one of them, Underwood, had previous experience of playing under floodlights and special practice sessions had to be arranged to allow the rest of the party to sample the different conditions, especially the awkward period when the natural light fades and the artificial lights are still unable to make an impression.

Throughout the series Willey played a leading rôle for England. Boycott played a magnificent innings of 105 in Sydney and only Richards of the West Indians scored more runs in the competition. Richards played two more innings than Boycott, the latter not having been considered for England's first match because the selectors thought his approach too slow. His performances in the one-day games were a revelation. Although Underwood was eventually dropped from the one-day internationals after suffering against the West Indies batsmen, off-spinners Willey, Miller (before his injury) and Emburey played their part in England's run. So, too, did wicket-keeper Bairstow, who played some important innings when the pressure was on. Brearley's overall leadership and tactical appreciation often made the difference between winning and losing.

AUSTRALIA v WEST INDIES

At Sydney, November 27. Australia won by five wickets. A masterly innings by Chappell, after surviving a confident appeal for a catch behind off his first ball, determined the outcome of the first floodlit match under the auspices of the Australian Cricket Board. The batting had been undistinguished until he took control with an elegant display, Hughes providing him with excellent support in a fourth-wicket stand of 92.

West Indies

C. G. Greenidge b Lillee	5		J. Garner run out		5
D. L. Haynes b Border	29		M. A. Holding c McCosker b Pascoe		2
I. V. A. Richards lbw b Lillee	9		C. E. H. Croft not out		0
A. I. Kallicharran c and b Border	49				
*C. H. Lloyd c Marsh b Border	16		L-b 3, n-b 3		6
C. L. King b Pascoe	29				
†D. L. Murray b Pascoe	27		1/6 2/18 3/89 4/112 (49.3 overs) 193		
A. M. E. Roberts b Pascoe	16		5/117 6/164 7/177 8/187 9/193		

Bowling: Lillee 6–2–10–2; Pascoe 9.3–1–29–4; Bright 5–0–26–0; Hogg 10–0–49–0; Border 10–0–36–3; Chappell 9–0–37–0.

Australia

B. M. Laird b Croft	20	†R. W. Marsh not out		18
R. B. McCosker lbw b Holding	1			
A. R. Border c Murray b Croft	17	L-b 14		14
*G. S. Chappell not out	74			
K. J. Hughes b Richards	52	1/1 2/37 3/52	(5 wkts, 47.1 overs)	196
D. W. Hookes b Richards	0	4/144 5/144		

R. J. Bright, D. K. Lillee, L. S. Pascoe and R. M. Hogg did not bat.

Bowling: Roberts 9–1–35–0; Holding 8.1–2–28–1; Croft 10–0–30–2; Garner 10–2–42–0; Richards 10–0–47–2.

Umpires: R. Harris and C. E. Harvey.

ENGLAND v WEST INDIES

At Sydney, November 28. England won by 2 runs. A fine opening partnership between Randall and Brearley, who put on 79 in 23 overs, plus support from Gower and Willey built England's total in their first game under floodlights. Rain reduced West Indies' target to 199 off 47 overs. Greenidge, Rowe and Kallicharran put down a firm foundation, but a collapse left Croft, the last batsman, needing to score 3 to win off the final ball. He was bowled by Botham as all the England fielders including Bairstow were pushed back to the boundary.

England

D. W. Randall c Parry b Garner	49	G. Miller b Roberts		4
*J. M. Brearley c Greenidge b Parry	25	G. R. Dilley run out		1
D. I. Gower b Croft	44	B 4, l-b 13		17
G. A. Gooch c and b Parry	2			
P. Willey not out	58	1/79 2/88 3/91	(8 wkts, 50 overs)	211
I. T. Botham b Garner	11	4/160 5/195 6/195 7/210		
†D. L. Bairstow c Murray b Garner	0	8/211		

D. L. Underwood and R. G. D. Willis did not bat.

Bowling: Roberts 9–0–37–1; Holding 9–0–47–0; Croft 10–0–34–1; Garner 10–0–31–3; Parry 10–0–35–2; Kallicharran 2–0–10–0.

West Indies

C. G. Greenidge c Willis b Miller	42	J. Garner not out		8
D. L. Haynes b Dilley	4	M. A. Holding c Gower b Underwood		0
L. G. Rowe lbw b Willis	60	C. E. H. Croft b Botham		3
A. I. Kallicharran run out	44			
*C. H. Lloyd c Brearley b Willis	4	B 1, l-b 7		8
†D. L. Murray c Gower b Underwood	3			
D. R. Parry b Underwood	4	1/19 2/68 3/132	(47 overs)	196
A. M. E. Roberts c Randall		4/143 5/144 6/155 7/177		
b Underwood.	16	8/185 9/186		

Bowling: Dilley 6–2–21–1; Botham 7–1–26–1; Underwood 10–0–44–4; Miller 10–0–33–1; Willey 8–0–29–0; Willis 6–0–35–2.

Umpires: A. Watson and C. E. Harvey.

ENGLAND v AUSTRALIA

At Melbourne, December 8. England won by three wickets. Australian captain Greg Chappell held his side together with a fighting 92 off 116 balls after their first two wickets had fallen for only 15 runs. Boycott, restored to England's limited-overs side at the last moment, and Randall gave their side a good start before a middle-order collapse saw England lose four wickets for 14 inside five overs. With Australia scenting victory, Bairstow joined Brearley in a seventh-wicket stand of 22 to steer England home with an over to spare.

Australia

J. M. Wiener b Botham	7	D. K. Lillee not out	13
B. M. Laird lbw b Dilley	7	R. M. Hogg c Brearley b Underwood	1
A. R. Border c Willey b Dilley	29		
*G. S. Chappell c Gooch b Willey	92	B 1, l-b 5, n-b 2	8
K. J. Hughes st Bairstow b Gooch	23		
K. D. Walters c Randall b Gooch	12	1/15 2/15 3/73 (9 wkts, 50 overs) 207
†R. W. Marsh c Bairstow b Willey	14	4/114 5/145 6/184 7/193
R. J. Bright c Gooch b Willey	1	8/193 9/207

J. R. Thomson did not bat.

Bowling: Dilley 10–1–30–2; Botham 9–2–27–1; Willis 7–0–28–0; Gooch 6–0–32–2; Underwood 10–0–49–1; Willey 8–0–33–3.

England

D. W. Randall lbw b Bright	28	†D. L. Bairstow not out	15
G. Boycott c Lillee b Hogg	68	G. R. Dilley not out	0
P. Willey c Marsh b Hogg	37		
D. I. Gower c Marsh b Lillee	17	L-b 3, n-b 3	6
G. A. Gooch run out	1		
I. T. Botham c Walters b Hogg	10	1/71 2/134 3/137 (7 wkts, 49 overs) 209
*J. M. Brearley c Marsh b Lillee	27	4/138 5/148 6/183 7/203

D. L. Underwood and R. G. D. Willis did not bat.

Bowling: Lillee 10–1–36–2; Hogg 10–2–26–3; Thomson 10–1–49–0; Chappell 8–0–40–0; Bright 9–1–40–1; Walters 2–0–12–0.

Umpires: R. A. French and W. Copeland.

AUSTRALIA v WEST INDIES

At Melbourne, December 9. West Indies won by 80 runs. This match will remain in the memory of a crowd of almost 40,000 and thousands of others who watched it on television for Richards's exceptional batsmanship. Given pain-killing injections to ease a back injury, and hobbling throughout his innings, he launched a furious assault on every bowler, scoring 153 not out from 131 balls with one 6 and sixteen 4s. Haynes, who played his best innings of the season, was completely overshadowed in their partnership of 205. Australia, left with a virtually impossible task, never looked likely to get on terms.

West Indies

C. G. Greenidge c Marsh b Lillee	11
D. L. Haynes c Marsh b Thomson	80
I. V. A. Richards not out	153
A. I. Kallicharran not out	16
B 1, l-b 10	11

1/28 2/233   (2 wkts, 48 overs) 271

L. G. Rowe, C. L. King, *†D. L. Murray, A. M. E. Roberts, M. A. Holding, J. Garner and D. R. Parry did not bat.

Bowling: Lillee 10–1–48–1; Hogg 10–1–50–0; Chappell 4–0–24–0; Thomson 8–0–43–1; Bright 6–0–29–0; Hookes 1–0–10–0; Border 7–0–40–0; Wiener 2–0–16–0.

Australia

B. M. Laird b Holding	7	D. K. Lillee b King	19
J. M. Wiener c and b Parry	27	R. M. Hogg not out	3
A. R. Border run out	44		
*G. S. Chappell c Richards b King	31	B 1, l-b 6	7
K. J. Hughes b Holding	12		
D. W. Hookes c Murray b Roberts	9	1/16 2/54 3/102 (8 wkts, 48 overs) 191
†R. W. Marsh c Rowe b Roberts	13	4/119 5/128 6/147 7/151
R. J. Bright not out	19	8/185

J. R. Thomson did not bat.

Bowling: Roberts 8–1–33–2; Holding 10–2–29–2; Garner 10–1–26–0; King 10–0–40–2; Parry 10–0–56–1.

Umpires: K. Carmody and R. Whitehead.

ENGLAND v AUSTRALIA

At Sydney, December 11. England won by 72 runs. A magnificent century by Boycott, supported by Randall and Willey, gave England their easiest victory of the tournament. Hitting seven 4s in all, Boycott scored his runs off 124 balls, often being prepared to chance his arm in an innings out of character with his usual approach. Losing half their side for only 39, Australia never threatened to reach their target, though Laughlin added a measure of respectability as England relaxed in the field.

England

D. W. Randall run out	42	†D. L. Bairstow c sub b Lillee	18
G. Boycott b Lillee	105	*J. M. Brearley not out	2
P. Willey c Walker b Chappell	64	L-b 6, w 1, n-b 3	10
D. I. Gower c Wiener b Lillee	7		
G. A. Gooch b Thomson	11	1/78 2/196 3/220 (7 wkts, 49 overs) 264
I. T. Botham c Walters b Lillee	5	4/236 5/242 6/245 7/264

D. L. Underwood, G. R. Dilley and R. G. D. Willis did not bat.

Bowling: Lillee 10–0–56–4; Thomson 9–0–53–1; Walker 10–1–30–0; Laughlin 8–0–39–0; Border 4–0–24–0; Chappell 5–0–28–1; Walters 3–0–24–0.

Australia

J. M. Wiener st Bairstow b Willey	14	D. K. Lillee b Botham	14
W. M. Darling c Randall b Willis	20	J. R. Thomson run out	0
A. R. Border b Willey	1	M. H. N. Walker not out	9
*G. S. Chappell run out	0	L-b 10, w 2, n-b 1	13
K. J. Hughes c Bairstow b Willis	1		
K. D. Walters c Bairstow b Botham	34	1/33 2/36 3/36 (47.2 overs) 192
†R. W. Marsh b Dilley	12	4/38 5/39 6/63 7/115
T. J. Laughlin c Gooch b Randall	74	8/146 9/147

Bowling: Dilley 9–0–29–1; Botham 10–1–36–2; Willis 10–1–32–2; Willey 5–0–18–2; Underwood 6–1–29–0; Gooch 7–0–33–0; Randall 0.2–0–2–1.

Umpires: J. Collins and R. Stevens.

AUSTRALIA v WEST INDIES

At Sydney, December 21. Australia won by 7 runs. Making his return to the Australian team in this night match Ian Chappell provided the momentum to their innings after the early batting had been pegged down. However, West Indies appeared to be heading for certain victory as Richards's continued brilliance saw them pass 100 with only two wickets down. Once he had fallen, however, the match underwent a dramatic transformation as the last seven wickets fell for 45 to provide Australia with a narrow victory.

Australia

J. M. Wiener c Lloyd b Holding	7	†R. W. Marsh run out	33
B. M. Laird c Rowe b Roberts	1	D. K. Lillee not out	12
A. R. Border c Murray b Garner	17	L-b 4, n-b 2	6
*G. S. Chappell c Lloyd b Richards	24		—
K. J. Hughes c Roberts b King	13	1/1 2/11 3/28 (6 wkts, 50 overs)	176
I. M. Chappell not out	63	4/44 5/94 6/160	

G. Dymock, L. S. Pascoe and R. M. Hogg did not bat.

Bowling: Roberts 10–1–28–1; Holding 10–1–33–1; King 10–0–38–1; Garner 10–2–34–1; Richards 8–0–35–1; Lloyd 2–0–2–0.

West Indies

C. G. Greenidge c Marsh b Lillee	33	A. M. E. Roberts lbw b Pascoe	8
D. L. Haynes c I. M. Chappell b Lillee	0	J. Garner c G. S. Chappell b Lillee	2
I. V. A. Richards c Hogg b Dymock	62	M. A. Holding b Lillee	0
A. I. Kallicharran b Pascoe	19	L-b 8, n-b 6	14
L. G. Rowe c Border b G. S. Chappell	5		—
*C. H. Lloyd c Wiener b Dymock	0	1/7 2/74 3/112 (42.5 overs)	169
C. L. King c Marsh b G. S. Chappell	9	4/124 5/126 6/139 7/144	
†D. L. Murray not out	17	8/158 9/169	

Bowling: Lillee 8.5–0–28–4; Pascoe 10–1–38–2; Hogg 10–3–47–0; Dymock 10–1–28–2; G. S. Chappell 4–0–14–2.

Umpires: R. A. French and A. Watson.

ENGLAND v WEST INDIES

At Brisbane, December 23. West Indies won by nine wickets. Boycott again proved England's most effective batsman after Randall went first ball. He shared in stands of 70 in nineteen overs with Willey and 97 in twenty overs with Gower as England scored a challenging 217 for eight. Once Richards joined Greenidge, however, the result was never in doubt. Richards hit two 6s and ten 4s in his brilliant 85 scored out of 109 for the second wicket off just 77 deliveries. Greenidge allowed his partner most of the strike as West Indies won with 3.1 overs to spare.

England

D. W. Randall c Lloyd b Roberts	0	*J. M. Brearley not out	9
G. Boycott c sub b Holding	68	G. R. Dilley b Garner	0
P. Willey run out	34	L-b 8, w 5, n-b 1	14
D. I. Gower c Holding b Roberts	59		—
G. A. Gooch b Garner	17	1/0 2/70 3/167 (8 wkts, 50 overs)	217
I. T. Botham lbw b Holding	4	4/174 5/191 6/205 7/209	
†D. L. Bairstow c Lloyd b Roberts	12	8/217	

D. L. Underwood and R. G. D. Willis did not bat.

Bowling: Roberts 10–3–26–3; Holding 10–1–44–2; Garner 10–0–37–2; Richards 10–0–44–0; King 10–0–52–0.

West Indies

C. G. Greenidge not out.............. 85
D. L. Haynes c Underwood b Gooch.... 41
I. V. A. Richards not out 85
               L-b 4, n-b 3 7

1/109   (1 wkt, 46.5 overs) 218

L. G. Rowe, A. I. Kallicharran, *C. H. Lloyd, C. L. King, †D. L. Murray, A. M. E. Roberts, M. A. Holding and J. Garner did not bat.

Bowling: Botham 10–1–39–0; Dilley 8–1–25–0; Willis 10–2–27–0; Underwood 9–0–43–0; Willey 6–0–39–0; Gooch 3.5–0–38–1.

Umpires: C. E. Harvey and M. W. Johnson.

ENGLAND v AUSTRALIA

At Sydney, December 6. England won by four wickets. After the Chappell brothers had dominated the Australian innings, Boycott made sure of England's victory with another outstanding performance. His unbeaten 86 was made against the background noise of a speedway meeting and a giant firework display in the adjoining Sydney Showground. Willey joined in a second-wicket stand of 111 in 25 overs before a collapse saw five wickets go down for the addition of 27. Bairstow joined Boycott to secure victory with eleven balls to spare in a match reduced to 47 overs per side.

Australia

B. M. Laird b Botham 6	†R. W. Marsh c Bairstow b Dilley...... 10
J. M. Wiener c Bairstow b Botham 2	D. K. Lillee not out 2
A. R. Border c Gower b Gooch 22	B 3, l-b 10, n-b 4............. 17
*G. S. Chappell run out 52	
K. J. Hughes b Willis 23	1/5 2/21 3/50 (6 wkts, 47 overs) 194
I. M. Chappell not out 60	4/109 5/133 6/179

R. M. Hogg, G. Dymock and L. S. Pascoe did not bat.

Bowling: Dilley 10–1–32–1; Botham 9–1–33–2; Willis 10–1–38–1; Underwood 10–2–36–0; Gooch 8–0–38–1.

England

G. A. Gooch lbw b Hogg 29	*J. M. Brearley c Marsh b Hogg 0
G. Boycott not out 86	†D. L. Bairstow not out 7
P. Willey b Pascoe 51	L-b 1, w 1, n-b 11........... 13
D. I. Gower c Marsh b Hogg 2	
D. W. Randall c G. S. Chappell b Pascoe 1	1/41 2/152 3/157 (6 wkts, 45.1 overs) 195
I. T. Botham lbw b Hogg 6	4/170 5/179 6/179

G. R. Dilley, D. L. Underwood and R. G. D. Willis did not bat.

Bowling: Lillee 10–0–47–0; Pascoe 10–2–28–2; Hogg 10–0–46–4; Dymock 10–1–38–0; G. S. Chappell 5.1–0–23–0.

Umpires: P. M. Cronin and R. Isherwood.

ENGLAND v WEST INDIES

At Melbourne, January 12. No result; match abandoned without a ball being bowled.

ENGLAND v AUSTRALIA

At Sydney, January 14. England won by two wickets. Playing his first match for England, Stevenson, the Yorkshire all-rounder, sparked a remarkable Australian collapse which saw their last seven wickets fall for only 15 runs. He took four of the wickets and claimed a fifth with a direct throw for a run out. Stevenson then completed a fine all-round performance by hitting the winning run after joining Bairstow when eight wickets had fallen and his side were still 35 runs away from victory with six overs left.

Australia

J. M. Wiener st Bairstow b Emburey	33	G. Dymock run out	0
R. B. McCosker c Brearley b Willey	41	J. R. Thomson not out	3
I. M. Chappell c Randall b Emburey	8	L. S. Pascoe b Stevenson	5
*G. S. Chappell c Randall b Stevenson	34	L-b 1, w 3, n-b 1	5
K. J. Hughes c Larkins b Lever	34		
A. R. Border c Bairstow b Lever	0		(48.4 overs) 163
†R. W. Marsh c Bairstow b Stevenson	0	1/74 2/82 3/89	
D. K. Lillee lbw b Stevenson	0	4/148 5/149 6/150 7/150	
		8/152 9/155	

Bowling: Lever 9–1–11–2; Botham 7–0–33–0; Gooch 3–0–13–0; Stevenson 9.4–0–33–4; Emburey 10–1–33–2; Willey 10–0–35–1.

England

G. A. Gooch c McCosker b Pascoe	69	J. E. Emburey c G. S. Chappell	
W. Larkins c Thomson b Lillee	5	b Dymock	18
P. Willey lbw b Lillee	0	G. B. Stevenson not out	28
D. I. Gower c Marsh b Lillee	3	L-b 5, w 1, n-b 9	15
*J. M. Brearley b G. S. Chappell	5		
D. W. Randall c Pascoe b G. S. Chappell	0	1/31 2/31 3/40	(8 wkts, 48.5 overs) 164
I. T. Botham b Lillee	0	4/51 5/56 6/71 7/105	
†D. L. Bairstow not out	21	8/129	

J. K. Lever did not bat.

Bowling: Thomson 9.5–0–46–0; Dymock 9–1–30–1; Lillee 10–6–12–4; Pascoe 10–0–38–1; G. S. Chappell 10–3–23–2.

Umpires: R. Isherwood and R. Whitehead.

ENGLAND v WEST INDIES

At Adelaide, January 16. West Indies won by 107 runs. England suffered another crushing defeat from the side they were to meet in the final. Good batting, led by Richards, Greenidge and Kallicharran, carried West Indies to a formidable 246 for five in ideal conditions before a capacity Adelaide crowd. With the first limited-overs final only four days away England displayed their worst batting of the competition, submitting meekly against Roberts, who became the first bowler to take five wickets in an innings in the tournament.

West Indies

C. G. Greenidge c Emburey b Willey	50	A. M. E. Roberts not out	0
D. L. Haynes c Gooch b Stevenson	26		
I. V. A. Richards b Botham	88	B 1, l-b 4, n-b 1	6
A. I. Kallicharran c and b Botham	57		
C. L. King run out	12	1/58 2/115 3/224	(5 wkts, 50 overs) 246
J. Garner not out	7	4/227 5/245	

*C. H. Lloyd, †D. L. Murray, M. A. Holding and L. G. Rowe did not bat.

Bowling: Lever 10–1–54–0; Botham 10–0–35–2; Gooch 2–0–22–0; Stevenson 8–1–53–1; Emburey 10–0–39–0; Willey 10–1–37–1.

England

G. A. Gooch b King	20	G. B. Stevenson b Roberts	1
*J. M. Brearley c Murray b Roberts	0	J. E. Emburey c Murray b Roberts	1
P. Willey c Lloyd b King	5	J. K. Lever b Garner	11
W. Larkins c Lloyd b King	24	L-b 2, w 1, n-b 1	4
D. I. Gower c sub b King	12		
D. W. Randall b Roberts	16	1/5 2/24 3/31	(42.5 overs) 139
I. T. Botham c Haynes b Roberts	22	4/52 5/68 6/98 7/100	
†D. L. Bairstow not out	23	8/105 9/109	

Bowling: Roberts 10–5–22–5; Holding 7–0–16–0; King 9–3–23–4; Garner 7.5–3–9–1; Richards 7–0–46–0; Kallicharran 2–0–19–0.

Umpires: P. M. Cronin and R. Duperouzel.

AUSTRALIA v WEST INDIES

At Sydney, January 18. Australia won by 9 runs. With the finalists already decided, this last match in the preliminary round, played under floodlights, was of merely academic interest and both teams introduced several new players. McCosker and Wiener gave Australia their only century opening stand of the competition, but Yallop's 11 was the highest of the remaining nine batsmen. Murray, Kallicharran and Lloyd all batted well for West Indies, but their last seven wickets fell for 47 to give Australia their third victory in four matches against West Indies in the tournament.

Australia

J. M. Wiener c Gomes b Parry	50	G. Dymock not out	4
R. B. McCosker c Lloyd b Holding	95	M. H. N. Walker run out	5
K. J. Hughes b Parry	4	L. S. Pascoe b Holding	0
*G. S. Chappell c and b Parry	2	B 1, l-b 10, w 1	12
G. N. Yallop b Roberts	11		
D. F. Whatmore c Murray b Holding	2	1/103 2/124 3/134	(48.3 overs) 190
†R. W. Marsh c Lloyd b Roberts	5	4/161 5/166 6/177 7/177	
D. K. Lillee c Murray b Holding	0	8/177 9/190	

Bowling: Holding 9.3–2–17–4; Croft 10–0–22–0; King 9–0–40–0; Roberts 10–0–38–2; Parry 10–0–61–3.

West Indies

L. G. Rowe lbw b Dymock	3	A. M. E. Roberts c Marsh b Lillee	2
D. L. Haynes c Marsh b Lillee	1	M. A. Holding c and b Pascoe	8
A. I. Kallicharran lbw b Chappell	66	C. E. H. Croft c Lillee b Chappell	8
†D. A. Murray c Chappell b Pascoe	35	B 3, n-b 8	11
*C. H. Lloyd not out	34		
C. L. King lbw b Walker	0	1/4 2/8 3/91	(49.1 overs) 181
H. A. Gomes lbw b Lillee	4	4/134 5/135 6/140 7/152	
D. R. Parry b Pascoe	9	8/157 9/166	

Bowling: Lillee 10–3–17–3; Dymock 10–2–18–1; Walker 10–2–46–1; Pascoe 10–0–34–3; Chappell 7.1–0–37–2; Wiener 2–0–18–0.

Umpires: K. Carmody and A. Watson.

QUALIFYING TABLE

	Played	Won	Lost	No Result	Points
England	8	5	2	1	11
West Indies	8	3	4	1	7
Australia	8	3	5	0	6

FINAL MATCHES

ENGLAND v WEST INDIES

First Final Match

At Melbourne, January 20. West Indies won by 2 runs. Three dropped catches and two run outs cost England the chance of beating the odds-on favourites and gaining a measure of revenge for their World Cup final defeat at Lord's eight months earlier. All three top-scoring West Indian batsmen were dropped early in their innings after Brearley had won the toss. Greenidge went on to make 80 in 42 overs after being dropped when 6, Kallicharran had scored 25 when he was put down, and King was only 5 when he survived a chance before going on to make 31 off 27 deliveries and see his side to 215 for eight.

Boycott and Willey repaired the damage with a stand of 61 in eighteen overs, following the early loss of Gooch, and England appeared to be pacing their effort nicely as the Northamptonshire pair Willey and Larkins added 56 in eleven overs for the fourth wicket. Then tragedy struck as both were run out in the space of five overs. Larkins's dismissal brought Brearley to the wicket and the captain tried bravely to snatch victory, partnered first by Botham and then by Bairstow. But the task of scoring 15 off the final over from Holding, 4 off the final delivery, proved just beyond him.

West Indies

C. G. Greenidge c Larkins b Botham	80	J. Garner run out	3
D. L. Haynes c Bairstow b Willis	9	M. A. Holding not out	5
I. V. A. Richards c Bairstow b Dilley	23		
A. I. Kallicharran b Botham	42	L-b 11, w 1, n-b 1	13
*C. H. Lloyd b Botham	4		
C. L. King not out	31	1/17 2/66 3/161 (8 wkts, 50 overs) 215	
†D. L. Murray c Bairstow b Dilley	4	4/168 5/168 6/181 7/183	
A. M. E. Roberts run out	1	8/197	

C. E. H. Croft did not bat.

Bowling: Willis 10–1–51–1; Botham 10–2–33–3; Emburey 10–0–31–0; Dilley 10–0–39–2; Willey 10–0–48–0.

England

G. A. Gooch c King b Holding	9	*J. M. Brearley not out	25
G. Boycott c Greenidge b Roberts	35	†D. L. Bairstow run out	4
P. Willey run out	51	B 12, l-b 12, w 1, n-b 1	26
D. I. Gower c Holding b Roberts	10		
W. Larkins run out	34	1/13 2/74 3/96 (7 wkts, 50 overs) 213	
I. T. Botham c Lloyd b Roberts	19	4/152 5/164 6/190 7/213	

J. E. Emburey, G. R. Dilley and R. G. D. Willis did not bat.

Bowling: Roberts 10–1–30–3; Holding 10–1–43–1; Garner 10–1–27–0; Croft 10–1–23–0; King 4–0–30–0; Richards 6–1–34–0.

Umpires: R. C. Bailhache and C. E. Harvey.

ENGLAND v WEST INDIES

Second Final Match

At Sydney, January 22. West Indies won by eight wickets. Greenidge and Richards, two batsmen who had haunted England throughout the series, made sure a third play-off match was unnecessary when they swept their side to a conclusive victory in the second game with fifteen balls to spare. Deciding to bat first this time, England were only 12 runs short of achieving what Lloyd, West Indies captain, believed would be a winning score on a pitch helping the seam bowlers. Once again Boycott was England's highest-scoring batsman, staying 33 overs for his 63 runs, sharing in an opening partnership of 40 with Gooch in twelve overs, and helping Gower to add 64 in twelve overs for the third wicket. A late surge by Botham, 37 off 39 balls, enabled England to reach 208 for eight and set West Indies a reasonable target.

Greenidge dominated the England bowlers right from the start as West Indies raced to 48 without loss from the first ten overs. Haynes was out in the fifteenth over, but Richards assumed command to ensure England did not get the breakthrough they desperately wanted. Together Greenidge and Richards put on 119 for the second wicket in 27 overs before Richards was caught, by which time victory was in sight. Greenidge was voted Man of the Match and Richards Man of the Series.

England

G. A. Gooch lbw b Garner	23	*J. M. Brearley run out		4
G. Boycott c Greenidge b Roberts	63	J. E. Emburey run out		6
P. Willey b Garner	3	B 1, l-b 11, n-b 1		13
D. I. Gower c Murray b Holding	27			
W. Larkins b Croft	14	1/40 2/54 3/118	(8 wkts, 50 overs)	208
I. T. Botham c King b Roberts	37	4/126 5/155 6/188 7/194		
†D. L. Bairstow not out	18	8/208		

G. R. Dilley and R. G. D. Willis did not bat.

Bowling: Roberts 10–3–31–2; Holding 10–1–34–1; Croft 10–3–29–1; Garner 10–0–44–2; Richards 3–0–19–0; King 7–1–38–0.

West Indies

C. G. Greenidge not out	98	
D. L. Haynes lbw b Botham	17	
I. V. A. Richards c Botham b Willey	65	
A. I. Kallicharran not out	8	
B 5, l-b 10, w 5, n-b 1	21	

1/61 2/180   (2 wkts, 47.3 overs) 209

*C. H. Lloyd, C. L. King, †D. L. Murray, M. A. Holding, A. M. E. Roberts, J. Garner and C. E. H. Croft did not bat.

Bowling: Willis 10–0–35–0; Dilley 7–0–37–0; Botham 10–1–28–1; Emburey 9.3–0–48–0; Willey 10–2–35–1; Gooch 1–0–5–0.

Umpires: A. R. Crafter and M. G. O'Connell.

OVERSEAS CRICKET, 1979-80

CRICKET IN AUSTRALIA, 1979-80

By PETER McFARLINE

Victoria won the Sheffield Shield for the second consecutive season, in a thrilling climax. When the last match of the competition began, between South Australia and Victoria in Adelaide, New South Wales led the table, three points ahead of South Australia and seven ahead of Victoria. At the completion of the first innings, South Australia had secured nine bonus points and Victoria six; enough, it seemed, to guarantee the home side success. But in an amazing comeback on the last afternoon, leg-spinner Higgs spun out the South Australians for 160, giving Victoria victory by 83 runs – and the Shield.

It was the first time since 1933-34 that the Victorians had secured consecutive wins – and it was a victory achieved by combined effort rather than the outstanding work of individuals. They had looked in a hopeless position in the first half of the competition, winning only one of their first four matches while first Queensland then New South Wales established big leads. But Victoria finished very strongly, winning their last five matches while Queensland, New South Wales and finally South Australia faltered.

The season, the first after the amalgamation of the Australian Cricket Board and World Series Cricket, proved a financial disaster. Despite the return to the fold of most of the country's best players, losses suffered by the various state associations totalled more than £125,000. Leading administrators sought vainly to find a formula that would bring the crowds back. The introduction of the six-ball over in the 1979-80 season did not bring the faster over-rate that was hoped for. In addition, a packed itinerary meant that several of the better-known players were rarely available for their states. Kim Hughes, of Western Australia, did not play in a single Shield match, owing to the late return of the Australian side from the 1979 tour of India and a heavy schedule of international commitments. The New South Wales left-handed batsman, Allan Border, was available only once, but still left his mark, scoring the only double-century of the season, against Queensland. The ACB revised its itinerary for the 1980-81 summer, making sure that the Test men need miss only two of the nine matches each state is committed to play. The Board also decided to experiment with a series of three-day Shield matches, using extended playing hours, in an effort to attract spectators.

The matter of player behaviour also had an adverse effect on attendances. South Australian captain Ian Chappell was twice disciplined by the Board following umpires' reports. He received a three-week suspension for abusive language in the game against Tasmania in

Devonport early in the season, and later a suspended sentence for alleged misconduct in South Australia's game against the touring Englishmen. Before the 1980-81 season began, the players themselves drew up a code of behaviour which the Board agreed should be administered by the cricketers. Thus, for the first time in sporting history, the matter of player conduct was given solely to the participants. But the over-riding cause of poor attendances could be traced directly to the saturation of international cricket in Australia. With joint tours now a fact of life, and twenty limited-overs internationals scheduled for each season, it became apparent that Australian cricket-lovers had decided, rightly or wrongly, that the Sheffield Shield was scarcely worthy of their attention or money.

While attendances kept falling, the incentives to be successful in the Shield rose dramatically. The Victorians carried off a total of £35,000 in prize-money, sponsorship and incentives for their success in the Shield and the limited-overs competition, the McDonald's Cup. They fielded eleven current or former internationals during the season, yet were not rated a particularly strong side at the start of the competition. In the event, it was the ability of all their players to contribute when needed which provided the basis of their success. Left-hander Jeff Moss was again the batting star, scoring 711 runs at 50.78 and winning, for the second year in a row, a £5,000 batting bonus from the team's sponsors. Diminutive right-hander John Scholes headed the averages, however, after a three-year absence from first-class cricket. He hit 464 runs at 66.28, including match-winning knocks of 65 and 58 not out in the last game. In addition, there were useful contributions from all the other batsmen. Trevor Laughlin, the hard-hitting left-hander, scored heavily in the latter part of the season after a miserable start and Graham Yallop and Julien Wiener contributed, although international duty restricted their appearances. In the bowling, Victoria were best served by Higgs and veteran medium-pacer Max Walker. Higgs, with 38 wickets at 18.65, returned career-best figures, twelve for 99, against Western Australia. Walker, in a season that most had expected to be his last, finished with 43 wickets at 23.74 – a tally bettered only by South Australians Geoff Attenborough (44) and Ashley Mallett (45). There were also handy contributions by all-rounder Shaun Graf and paceman John Leehane.

South Australia once again relied on the attributes of Ian Chappell and the bowling of stalwart medium-pacer Geoff Attenborough and the veteran off-spinner, Ashley Mallett. Despite his problems with authority, Chappell was the country's leading run-scorer with 713 runs at 47.53. He hit 112 in the first innings of the deciding match against Victoria, and when he was dismissed for 32 in the second innings, the batting collapsed. Their only other consistent scorers were the Test players of the previous season, Rick Darling and Peter Sleep. Opener John Nash topped 500 runs but was inconsistent. Attenborough and Mallett bowled with good control throughout the season, but there was a lack of support. Medium-pacer Jeff Hammond's 20 wickets cost 31.45 each and Wayne Prior's speed allowed 40.36 runs for just 22 wickets.

New South Wales, the former power of Australian cricket, who have not won the Shield since 1965-66, failed again despite their normal early promise. After an early victory against Western Australia, when Trevor Chappell and Ross Edwards added 174 for the third wicket on the fourth afternoon, the team tended to cave in under pressure. In one of the season's decisive games Victorian tailender John Leehane hit the last ball of the match, from leg-spinner Bob Holland, into the Melbourne sightscreen to beat New South Wales and set his side on their winning run. Although the side missed regular appearances from Border, it boasted some heavy scorers in Peter Toohey (620 runs at 56.36), John Dyson (679 runs at 45.26) and Trevor Chappell (674 runs at 42.12). But bowling was the side's main weakness. Only fast bowler Geoff Lawson proved effective throughout the season, finishing with 31 wickets at 20.67.

Queensland, yet to win the Shield, began their assault in fine fashion with victories over Victoria and Western Australia. Thereafter, the side lost momentum, especially when Greg Chappell was away on Test duty. The captain played only three matches, scoring 418 runs at 104.50. Only South African import Kepler Wessels, 621 runs at 38.81, achieved any sort of consistency. Fast bowler Jeff Thomson finished with the impressive figures of 33 wickets at 19.21, but missed three matches with injury.

Western Australia were the disappointment of the competition, winning only one of their nine matches, and that against Tasmania. The team fell apart after a decade of power in the Shield, probably owing to the regular absence of their Test players, Hughes, Lillee and Marsh. Opener Graeme Wood, who was omitted for the first three matches, eventually topped the averages but the heaviest scorers were South African Ken McEwan (591 runs at 36.93) and newcomer Greg Shipperd (536 runs at 41.23). Another newcomer, Colin Penter, scored a century in his first match against New South Wales but failed thereafter. Of the bowlers, pacemen Mick Malone (32 wickets) and Terry Alderman (34 wickets) were an effective spearhead, although both paid dearly for success.

Tasmania, in their third season in the competition on a limited basis, failed to win any of their five games. Their imported captain, Brian Davison of Leicestershire and Rhodesia, hit a superb century against Victoria but failed to sustain his form, scoring only 335 runs at 37.22. Openers Rob Jeffery and Gary Goodman established a record opening stand, of 182 against Queensland, but failed in other games. Another to disappoint was the New Zealand Test bowler, Richard Hadlee, whose twelve wickets cost 30.08 each. The Tasmanians, hoping for full status in the competition, will have to improve their results before the other states vote them in.

The Sheffield Shield match reports which follow were written by Brian Osborne.

SHEFFIELD SHIELD, 1979-80

	P	W	D	L	Batting Pts	Bowling Pts	Match Pts	Total Pts
Victoria	9	6	2	1	34	36	60	130
South Australia	9	4	2	3	43	38	40	121
New South Wales.....	9	4	3	2	45	33	40	118
Queensland	9	3	3	3	37	33	30	100
Western Australia	9	1	2	6	33	38	10	81
Tasmania............	5	0	2	3	34.2	32.4	0	66.6

Note: Tasmania's points multiplied by 9, divided by 5.

SHEFFIELD SHIELD AVERAGES, 1979-80

BATTING

(Qualification: 300 runs)

	Matches	Innings	Not Outs	Runs	Highest Inns	Average
G. S. Chappell (*Qld*) ..	3	5	1	418	185	104.50
J. W. Scholes (*Vic*) ...	5	8	1	464	126	66.28
P. M. Toohey (*NSW*) .	7	14	3	620	111	56.36
J. K. Moss (*Vic*)	9	14	0	711	132	50.78
K. D. Walters (*NSW*) .	8	15	4	535	83	48.63
I. M. Chappell (*SA*) ...	8	15	0	713	158	47.53
J. Dyson (*NSW*)	8	15	0	679	99	45.26
G. M. Wood (*WA*) ...	5	9	1	350	67	43.75
T. M. Chappell (*NSW*)	9	17	1	674	150	42.12
P. R. Sleep (*SA*)	7	13	3	416	104	41.60
G. Shipperd (*WA*)	7	14	1	536	106	41.23
R. Edwards (*NSW*) ...	5	10	2	324	91	40.50
R. F. Jeffery (*Tas*) ..	5	9	0	353	198	39.22
R. D. Woolley (*Tas*) ..	5	9	1	312	61*	39.00
K. C. Wessels (*Qld*) ...	9	17	1	621	93	38.81
T. J. Laughlin (*Vic*) ...	9	14	3	419	73*	38.09
B. F. Davison (*Tas*) ..	5	9	0	335	138	37.22
K. S. McEwan (*WA*) ..	9	17	1	591	177	36.93
R. B. McCosker (*NSW*)	8	15	1	516	123	36.85
K. J. Wright (*WA*) ...	7	11	2	321	88*	35.66
R. D. Robinson (*Vic*) .	9	12	2	352	103*	35.20
D. F. Whatmore (*Vic*) .	7	13	2	383	88	34.81
S. J. Rixon (*NSW*)	9	14	5	301	101*	33.44
W. M. Darling (*SA*) ...	7	13	1	397	134	33.08
J. E. Nash (*SA*)	9	18	1	554	134	32.58
G. J. Cosier (*Qld*)	9	16	1	460	81*	30.66
P. H. Carlson (*Qld*) ...	9	14	0	413	84	29.50
J. J. Crowe (*SA*)	7	13	2	320	109*	29.09
R. J. Inverarity (*SA*) ..	7	14	0	365	58	26.07
M. F. Kent (*Qld*)	8	15	1	338	79	24.14
T. V. Hohns (*Qld*)	9	15	2	312	60	24.00

* *Signifies not out.*

BOWLING

(Qualification: 15 wickets)

	Overs	Maidens	Runs	Wickets	Average
J. D. Higgs (*Vic*)	269.3	67	709	38	18.65
J. R. Thomson (*Qld*) ..	217.4	53	634	33	19.21
G. R. Beard (*NSW*) ...	252.4	104	405	20	20.25
G. F. Lawson (*NSW*) ..	223	49	641	31	20.67
G. R. Attenborough (*SA*)	351.1	102	974	44	22.13
A. A. Mallett (*SA*)....	417.1	126	1,013	45	22.51
M. H. N. Walker (*Vic*)	426.4	114	1,021	43	23.74
L. S. Pascoe (*NSW*) ..	232	59	646	27	23.92
P. H. Carlson (*Qld*) ...	271.4	68	671	26	25.80
S. F. Graf (*Vic*)	196	46	474	17	27.88
R. G. Holland (*NSW*) .	197.1	39	624	22	28.36
M. F. Malone (*WA*)...	388.1	123	920	32	28.75
J. F. Leehane (*Vic*) ...	197.3	33	597	20	29.85
T. M. Alderman (*WA*) .	356	87	1,047	34	30.79
J. R. Hammond (*SA*) .	265.4	78	629	20	31.45
C. G. Rackemann (*Qld*)	207	51	550	17	32.35
A. L. Mann (*WA*) ...	246.1	49	724	22	32.90
D. W. Hourn (*NSW*)..	192.3	36	607	16	37.93
W. Prior (*SA*)	299	57	888	22	40.36
D. C. Schuller (*Qld*) ..	236.1	55	649	16	40.56

QUEENSLAND v VICTORIA

At Brisbane, October 26, 27, 28, 29. Queensland won by an innings and 5 runs. Queensland 22 pts, Victoria 6 pts. The home side opened the season with a most convincing win over the Shield holders after Victoria had failed to take advantage of favourable batting conditions and early erratic bowling. Queensland's sound team effort was highlighted by a beautifully controlled century from Chappell, which included two 6s and fourteen 4s and took Queensland to a lead of 173. By the time heavy overcast conditions had concluded the third day's play thirty-five minutes early, Thomson's fiery pace had left Victoria still 42 runs behind with only six wickets in hand. On the final morning he quickly took his match aggregate to ten for 142 as Victoria's innings collapsed.

Victoria

J. M. Wiener run out....................	41	– c Madders b Thomson	12
R. G. Matthews b Schuller	17	– lbw b Thomson...............	9
J. W. Scholes c Cosier b Thomson.............	17	– b Thomson	54
M. D. Taylor c Cosier b Chappell	1	– b Schuller	8
J. K. Moss b Carlson	21	– c Madders b Thomson	25
*T. J. Laughlin c Madders b Thomson.........	9	– c and b Chappell	15
†R. D. Robinson c and b Hohns	26	– c Cosier b Schuller	20
R. J. Bright lbw b Thomson.................	39	– b Thomson...................	7
I. W. Callen not out	24	– c Hohns b Thomson...........	0
M. H. N. Walker c Kent b Hohns	8	– b Thomson	0
J. F. Leehane c Schuller b Hohns	3	– not out	6
B 7, l-b 8, w 4, n-b 9	28	B 2, l-b 1, w 2, n-b 7	12

1/32 2/67 3/75 4/105 5/114 6/132	234	1/25 2/35 3/49 4/95 5/131	168
7/188 8/196 9/216		6/133 7/144 8/145 9/145	

Bowling: *First Innings*—Thomson 23–3–84–3; Schuller 22–8–40–1; Carlson 19–7–29–1; Cosier 5–0–12–0; Chappell 10–2–13–1; Hohns 8.4–2–28–3. *Second Innings*—Thomson 25–10–58–7; Schuller 13.1–4–43–2; Carlson 9–2–16–0; Chappell 10–7–4–1; Hohns 15–5–35–0.

Queensland

K. C. Wessels c Bright b Laughlin	56	D. C. Schuller c Robinson b Walker	8
W. R. Broad c Wiener b Walker	23	†G. J. Madders not out	20
M. F. Kent c Matthews b Walker	1	J. R. Thomson c Robinson b Walker	2
*G. S. Chappell c Matthews b Walker	185		
J. N. Langley c Robinson b Callen	24	B 1, l-b 6 w 2, n-b 14	23
G. J. Cosier c sub b Leehane	21		
P. H. Carlson c Robinson b Leehane	16	1/47 2/55 3/126 4/233 5/285	407
T. V. Hohns c Robinson b Laughlin	28	6/335 7/340 8/358 9/396	

Bowling: Walker 35.4–9–92–5; Leehane 30–3–101–2; Callen 17–1–60–1; Bright 31–4–88–0; Laughlin 15–3–33–2; Wiener 1–0–10–0.

Umpires: C. E. Harvey and M. W. Johnson.

NEW SOUTH WALES v WESTERN AUSTRALIA

At Sydney, October 27, 28, 29, 30. New South Wales won by five wickets. New South Wales 16 pts, Western Australia 14 pts. Slow batting by Western Australia in their second innings handed the initiative to New South Wales who, until then, had produced indifferent cricket. The home team were taken to victory with splendid innings from Trevor Chappell and veteran Test batsman Edwards – both representing the state for the first time. Chappell hit sixteen 4s in his maiden first-class century, achieved seven years after his début with South Australia. After electing to bat, Western Australia lost two wickets in Pascoe's opening over before Laird stabilised the innings. Newcomer Penter batted brightly after being dropped at 9 and 16 and, with Rodney Marsh also hitting vigorously, 380 runs were scored for the loss of six wickets on the opening day. When New South Wales replied, Lillee brought about a collapse alleviated only by Rixon's 72 and valuable help from O'Keeffe and Hourn. Surprisingly, Marsh did not enforce the follow-on and, with one hundred and seventy-five minutes batting time remaining on the third day, Western Australia scored only 101 runs, thus losing their early advantage and leaving the home side to win a most entertaining game.

Western Australia

B. M. Laird c Walters b Hourn	117	– c Chappell b Hourn	41
G. R. Marsh c McCosker b Pascoe	0	– lbw b Gilmour	0
M. D. O'Neill b Pascoe	0	– run out	52
C. S. Serjeant c Gilmour b Hourn	25	– lbw b Walters	4
K. S. McEwan c McCosker b O'Keeffe	23	– c Chappell b Pascoe	17
*†R. W. Marsh c Gilmour b O'Keeffe	73	– c Johnston b Pascoe	0
C. E. Penter c Pascoe b Hourn	112	– c and b Hourn	9
A. L. Mann not out	52	– not out	5
M. F. Malone run out	0	– c Chappell b Hourn	6
D. K. Lillee run out	1		
T. M. Alderman lbw b Pascoe	0		
L-b 3, w 3, n-b 22	28	B 3, l-b 2, n-b 9	14

1/1 2/1 3/69 4/155 5/185 6/295   431   1/4 2/69 3/85   (8 wkts dec.) 148
7/427 8/427 9/428   4/122 5/125 6/126
                                             7/140 8/148

Bowling: *First Innings*—Pascoe 31.4–5–105–3; Gilmour 28–4–93–0; Walters 7–1–30–0; Hourn 21–5–71–3; O'Keeffe 26–5–104–2. *Second Innings*—Pascoe 21–6–37–1; Gilmour 6–2–11–1; Walters 9–5–16–1; Hourn 22.3–4–67–4; O'Keeffe 1–0–3–0.

New South Wales

*R. B. McCosker run out	33	st R. W. Marsh b Mann	29
T. M. Chappell b Lillee	12	c G. R. Marsh b Mann	150
D. A. H. Johnston c Laird b Lillee	3	lbw b Mann	17
R. Edwards c Mann b Lillee	25	c Mann b Penter	91
P. M. Toohey b Malone	11	(6) not out	21
K. D. Walters lbw b Malone	27	(7) not out	0
G. J. Gilmour c O'Neill b Mann	15	(5) c Lillee b Mann	7
K. J. O'Keeffe run out	20		
†S. J. Rixon not out	72		
L. S. Pascoe c Penter b Mann	2		
D. W. Hourn b Malone	27		
L-b 4, n-b 10	14	B 2, l-b 4	6

1/39 2/49 3/54 4/82 5/99   261   1/46 2/104 3/278   (5 wkts) 321
6/132 7/141 8/217 9/226   4/285 5/317

Bowling: *First Innings*—Lillee 31–7–84–3; Malone 32.4–11–76–3; Alderman 13–5–25–0; Mann 21–5–52–2; Penter 6–2–10–0. *Second Innings*—Lillee 22–4–74–1; Malone 13–1–43–0; Alderman 8–2–34–0; Mann 25–2–83–3; Penter 17.1–1–81–1; O'Neill 1–1–0–0.

Umpires: A. Drake and R. G. Harris.

QUEENSLAND v WESTERN AUSTRALIA

At Brisbane, November 2, 3, 4, 5. Queensland won by 46 runs. Queensland 17 pts, Western Australia 5 pts. In conditions most suitable for seam bowling, both sides scored only 668 runs from the four completed innings. Queensland, put in, were fortunate to reach 206 on the opening day, with six catches put down, and were indebted mainly to Carlson whose 47 off 52 deliveries included eight 4s. Seventeen wickets fell on the second day when Thomson, bowling at top speed, and Chappell left Western Australia 43 runs in arrears, despite a fighting innings from Rodney Marsh. Queensland struggled to a total of 151, leaving their opponents a target of 195, and again owed much to Carlson for his 44. He then proceeded to take four for 11 in four overs, supported by Thomson's speed on the final morning, completed a magnificent spell of seam bowling which accounted for seven leading batsmen. For Western Australia, Malone bowled unchanged throughout both Queensland innings to achieve match figures of eight for 108 from 65.1 overs.

Queensland

K. C. Wessels c R. W. Marsh b Malone	14	c Malone b Lillee	0
W. R. Broad c R. W. Marsh b Lillee	2	c R. W. Marsh b Malone	13
M. F. Kent c R. W. Marsh b Lillee	0	lbw b Malone	9
*G. S. Chappell b Alderman	24	c McEwan b Lillee	0
J. N. Langley b Lillee	14	lbw b Lillee	15
G. J. Cosier c Serjeant b Malone	24	lbw b Alderman	27
P. H. Carlson b Malone	47	c Serjeant b Lillee	44
T. V. Hohns c R. W. Marsh b Malone	31	lbw b Malone	10
†G. J. Madders not out	18	not out	15
J. R. Thomson c R. W. Marsh b Alderman	0	b Lillee	4
C. G. Rackemann c R. W. Marsh b Malone	16	b Lillee	0
L-b 6, n-b 10	16	B 1, l-b 4, n-b 9	14

1/8 2/8 3/45 4/49 5/89   206   1/0 2/13 3/23 4/29 5/52   151
6/93 7/161 8/184 9/185   6/84 7/115 8/144 9/150

Bowling: *First Innings*—Lillee 18–3–57–3; Malone 38.1–17–83–5; Alderman 21–10–50–2. *Second Innings*—Lillee 22.3–4–94–6; Malone 27–7–25–3; Alderman 5–1–18–1.

Western Australia

B. M. Laird c Langley b Thomson	4	– b Carlson 23
G. R. Marsh c Hohns b Chappell	18	– c Broad b Carlson 18
M. D. O'Neill b Thomson	14	– lbw b Carlson 0
C. S. Serjeant c Langley b Thomson	0	– b Carlson 17
K. S. McEwan lbw b Chappell	20	– b Thomson 15
*†R. W. Marsh c Madders b Thomson	62	– c Madders b Carlson 36
C. E. Penter c Langley b Chappell	0	– c Madders b Carlson 2
A. L. Mann lbw b Chappell	20	– b Carlson 17
M. F. Malone b Thomson	5	– b Thomson 3
D. K. Lillee c Madders b Thomson	0	– lbw b Thomson 0
T. M. Alderman not out	3	– not out 2
B 9, l-b 1, w 4, n-b 3	17	B 5, l-b 4, n-b 6 15

1/27 2/41 3/41 4/54 5/90 6/90   163   1/35 2/35 3/44 4/68 5/90   148
7/133 8/152 9/152   6/103 7/137 8/142 9/142

Bowling: *First Innings*—Thomson 15.1–4–51–6; Rackemann 17–6–40–0; Chappell 16–4–42–4; Carlson 4–0–13–0. *Second Innings*—Thomson 23–7–54–3; Rackemann 10–3–28–0; Chappell 3–0–9–0; Carlson 27.5–9–42–7.

Umpires: C. E. Harvey and M. W. Johnson.

TASMANIA v SOUTH AUSTRALIA

At Devonport, November 3, 4, 5, 6. Drawn. Tasmania 6 pts, South Australia 12 pts. Tasmania lost four wickets for 60 before Boon and Smith revived the innings on the opening day, when bad light restricted play to three hours. The partnership continued to 158 – breaking an 80-year-old Tasmanian record: Smith defending as Boon forced the pace to reach 90 in three hours seven minutes with twelve 4s. When South Australia replied, Hookes was aided by dropped catches, but Rolfe, Causby and Zadow batted with ease against the limited attack. In their second innings Tasmania again collapsed, to 23 for three, but Smith and Boon once more stood firm and useful innings from Docking and Campbell ensured South Australia would bat again. Following incidents in this match, Ian Chappell was suspended by the Australian Cricket Board from playing first-class cricket for twenty-one days.

Tasmania

R. F. Jeffery c Nash b Attenborough	18	– c Nash b Prior 17
G. W. Goodman c Rolfe b Attenborough	1	– c Rolfe b Hammond 1
D. A. Smith b Mallett	85	– b Chappell 68
*B. F. Davison c Robertson b Hammond	1	– lbw b Prior 1
†R. D. Woolley b Hammond	16	– (6) c Hammond b Hookes 30
D. C. Boon lbw b Prior	90	– (4) c Rolfe b Prior 23
T. W. Docking c Rolfe b Mallett	0	– (5) b Chappell 45
R. J. Hadlee c Robertson b Prior	4	– c Causby b Mallett 17
B. M. Campbell not out	13	– not out 52
G. J. Wilson c Prior b Mallett	10	– st Robertson b Mallett 11
N. J. Majewski c Rolfe b Mallett	0	– c Rolfe b Mallett.......... 3
L-b 10, n-b 1	11	B 8, l-b 7, n-b 2 17

1/14 2/23 3/28 4/60 5/218   249   1/18 2/18 3/23 4/66 5/131   285
6/218 7/218 8/222 9/246   6/182 7/211 8/213 9/261

Bowling: *First Innings*—Prior 26–4–76–2; Attenborough 26–10–61–2; Hammond 21–7–45–2; Hookes 4–0–16–0; Mallett 25.5–8–40–4. *Second Innings*—Prior 24–4–78–3; Attenborough 13–7–19–0; Hammond 19–7–31–1; Hookes 6–1–18–1; Mallett 35.1–14–60–3; Chappell 32–9–62–2.

South Australia

J. E. Nash c Woolley b Jeffery	18	– not out	42
D. J. Rolfe b Wilson	83		
*I. M. Chappell c Hadlee b Wilson	24	– c Hadlee b Jeffery	6
D. W. Hookes lbw b Hadlee	88	– (2) run out	9
B. L. Causby c Davison b Majewski	66		
R. J. Zadow not out	74		
J. R. Hammond c Docking b Hadlee	23	– (4) not out	1
†T. J. Robertson c Goodman b Majewski	42		
A. A. Mallett not out	8		
B 8, l-b 6, w 3, n-b 14	31	B 1, l-b 1	2

1/40 2/73 3/214 4/261   (7 wkts dec.) 457   1/44 2/51   (2 wkts) 60
5/324 6/372 7/438

W. Prior and G. R. Attenborough did not bat.

Bowling: *First Innings*—Hadlee 27–3–78–2; Wilson 23–0–98–2; Jeffery 22–2–66–1; Majewski 25–5–76–2; Goodman 7–2–35–0; Campbell 20–3–73–0. *Second Innings*—Hadlee 5–0–31–0; Jeffery 4–0–27–1.

Umpires: R. Marshall and J. Stevens.

NEW SOUTH WALES v VICTORIA

At Sydney, November 3, 4, 5, 6. Drawn. New South Wales 5 pts, Victoria 9 pts. New South Wales were struggling at 61 for four after being sent in on a grassy wicket under a cloudy sky. Then followed a century partnership between veteran pair Edwards and Walters and eventually a satisfactory 273 was obtained. When Victoria batted Hibbert took five and a half hours over his century, at one stage remaining on 27 for seventy minutes, and there were solid contributions from Scholes – recalled after four years' absence from first-class cricket – and Moss, who was dropped three times. Bad light closed play at 5.00 p.m. and, with a further one hundred and six minutes lost through rain, the match drifted to a draw.

New South Wales

*R. B. McCosker c Moss b Walker	9	– b Wiener	9
J. Dyson b Walker	9	– c Robinson b Walker	55
T. M. Chappell c Laughlin b Ross	13	– c Robinson b Bright	14
P. M. Toohey c Laughlin b Ross	28	– c Laughlin b Ross	57
R. Edwards c Walker b Bright	53	– run out	19
K. D. Walters c Ross b Laughlin	83	– run out	10
K. J. O'Keeffe run out	16		
†S. J. Rixon lbw b Laughlin	22		
R. P. Done c Robinson b Walker	13		
L. S. Pascoe c Scholes b Ross	26		
D. W. Hourn not out	0		
L-b 1	1	B 1, l-b 7	8

1/11 2/22 3/58 4/61 5/162   273   1/18 2/46   (4 wkts) 172
6/202 7/230 8/233 9/259   3/114 4/152

Bowling: *First Innings*—Walker 33–13–79–3; Ross 21.1–3–82–3; Graf 11–2–38–0; Laughlin 14–4–19–2; Bright 23–6–54–1. *Second Innings*—Walker 20–3–43–1; Ross 19–4–44–1; Graf 10–1–26–0; Laughlin 1–0–1–0; Bright 20–13–13–1; Wiener 14–4–36–1; Scholes 1–0–1–0.

Victoria

J. M. Wiener c O'Keeffe b Pascoe	31	S. F. Graf c Done b O'Keeffe	3
P. A. Hibbert c McCosker b Done	119	M. H. N. Walker not out	0
J. W. Scholes c Toohey b Hourn	85		
J. K. Moss c Done b O'Keeffe	72	L-b 6, n-b 20	26
R. G. Matthews c McCosker b Pascoe	1		
*T. J. Laughlin c Rixon b Hourn	27	1/69 2/243 3/289 (8 wkts dec.)	416
†R. D. Robinson c Toohey b O'Keeffe	17	4/304 5/352 6/366	
R. J. Bright not out	35	6/392 8/407	

G. T. Ross did not bat.

Bowling: Pascoe 34–15–66–2; Done 24–4–98–1; Walters 8–4–10–0; Hourn 40–13–96–2; O'Keeffe 50–11–120–3.

Umpires: D. Frede and A. Watson.

SOUTH AUSTRALIA v NEW SOUTH WALES

At Adelaide, November 30, December 1, 2, 3. South Australia won by 27 runs. South Australia 19 pts, New South Wales 7 pts. Darling's diving catch at point to end a vintage Walters innings (two 6s and eight 4s) precipitated New South Wales's collapse, five wickets tumbling for 11 runs as South Australia swept to victory in a game of fluctuating fortunes. Attenborough, left-arm fast-medium, took four wickets for no runs in seven balls as Beard desperately sought to hold the strike. Earlier, sound batting had given South Australia a first innings lead of 61, New South Wales relying heavily on Hourn's spin in the absence of Pascoe, who injured his shoulder while fielding. Beard bowled his off-spinners resourcefully in both innings. New South Wales were set 294 to win in 309 minutes, after Nash had struck out for a fine 73. Three early wickets fell for 3 runs but Walters and Beard added 141 before Attenborough and Mallett finished off the innings.

South Australia

W. M. Darling c Hilditch b Hourn	42	– b Lawson	10
J. E. Nash b Lawson	37	– c Walters b Beard	73
*R. J. Inverarity c Rixon b Walters	48	– lbw b Lawson	3
B. L. Causby c Beard b Hourn	80	– b Lawson	2
P. R. Sleep c Rixon b Walters	1	– (6) c Rixon b Beard	6
R. J. Zadow c Lawson b Hourn	2	– (5) lbw b Beard	49
J. R. Hammond run out	17	– not out	48
†T. J. Robertson lbw b Beard	48	– b Lawson	19
A. A. Mallett lbw b Hourn	4	– b Lawson	1
G. R. Attenborough not out	15	– c Chappell b Lawson	1
W. Prior c Edwards b Beard	0	– c Dyson b Beard	1
B 3, l-b 6, n-b 2	31	B 4, l-b 6, n-b 9	19

1/73 2/95 3/176 4/188 5/191	325	1/41 2/55 3/58 4/116 5/127	232
6/229 7/275 8/293 9/321		6/166 7/202 8/208 9/223	

Bowling: *First Innings*—Pascoe 6–0–15–0; Lawson 19–3–52–1; Beard 41.3–15–63–2; Hourn 32–1–105–4; Walters 17–3–59–2. *Second Innings*—Lawson 28–4–85–5; Beard 28.1–12–40–4; Hourn 18–3–60–1; Walters 12–7–21–0; Chappell 5–0–7–0.

New South Wales

J. Dyson b Prior	81	– c Prior b Sleep	26
A. M. J. Hilditch c Zadow b Prior	10	– b Sleep	21
T. M. Chappell lbw b Prior	26	– c Attenborough b Mallett	24
P. M. Toohey c Zadow b Attenborough	22	– c Prior b Mallett	42
*R. Edwards c and b Mallett	12	– c Inverarity b Mallett	0
K. D. Walters c Inverarity b Attenborough	43	– c Darling b Attenborough	80
G. R. Beard lbw b Prior	13	– not out	68
†S. J. Rixon c Prior b Mallett	14	– c Robertson b Attenborough	0
G. F. Lawson c Sleep b Mallett	37	– c Inverarity b Attenborough	1
D. W. Hourn b Sleep	0	– b Attenborough	0
L. S. Pascoe not out	0	– b Mallett	0
B 1, l-b 3, n-b 2	6	B 3, l-b 1	4

1/15 2/47 3/85 4/108   264   1/42 2/61 3/111 4/113 5/114   266
5/183 6/206 7/215 8/249 9/249   6/255 7/255 8/257 9/257

Bowling: *First Innings*—Prior 24–7–53–4; Attenborough 13–1–50–2; Mallett 30.3–13–75–3; Hammond 13–3–28–0; Sleep 19–6–52–1. *Second Innings*—Prior 16–3–32–0; Attenborough 7–2–27–4; Mallett 35.1–10–91–4; Hammond 12–1–26–0; Sleep 21–3–81–2; Inverarity 2–0–5–0.

Umpires: P. M. Cronin and B. E. Martin.

VICTORIA v WESTERN AUSTRALIA

At Melbourne, November 30, December 1, 2, 3. Victoria won by six wickets. Victoria 18 pts, Western Australia 6 pts. A career-best aggregate of twelve for 99 by leg-spinner Higgs on a slow MCG pitch highlighted a comfortable win for Victoria. Shipperd, replacing Laird who was on Test duty, defended with much concentration as he put together more than half the Western Australian total, bravely taking a buffeting from the fast bowling of Ross. He was last man out at 106, his only worthwhile support coming from Serjeant in a stand of 67. Victoria were soon in trouble at 25 for four, but a fine 75 from wicket-keeper Robinson took them to a first innings lead of 56. Western Australia again collapsed, from an opening partnership of 62 to 99 for seven, and it was only dropped catches which took the match into the fourth day.

Western Australia

*R. I. Charlesworth c Robinson b Ross	10	– c Robinson b Higgs	39
G. Shipperd run out	106	– lbw b Graf	32
G. R. Marsh lbw b Ross	1	– c Robinson b Higgs	0
C. S. Serjeant c and b Higgs	31	– c Robinson b Graf	17
K. S. McEwan c Laughlin b Higgs	0	– lbw b Graf	1
A. L. Mann c and b Higgs	0	– c Wiener b Higgs	0
B. Yardley c Whatmore b Walker	11	– st Robinson b Higgs	2
†K. J. Wright c Laughlin b Ross	5	– c Walker b Higgs	43
M. F. Malone c Yallop b Higgs	11	– c Whatmore b Higgs	22
T. M. Alderman c Yallop b Higgs	6	– c Walker b Higgs	10
C. A. Michael not out	0	– not out	1
B 11, n-b 3	14	B 5, l-b 5, w 4, n-b 1	15

1/34 2/36 3/103 4/103 5/103   195   1/62 2/66 3/84 4/86 5/89   182
6/126 7/140 8/181 9/192   6/95 7/99 8/162 9/177

Bowling: *First Innings*—Walker 20.4–4–50–1; Ross 21–10–42–3; Graf 16–7–26–0; Higgs 27–6–50–5; Laughlin 1–0–2–0; Wiener 10–5–11–0. *Second Innings*—Walker 19–6–43–0; Ross 15–4–27–0; Graf 15–4–24–3; Higgs 39–18–49–7; Laughlin 1–0–4–0; Wiener 8–3–7–0; Yallop 2–0–13–0.

Victoria

J. M. Wiener c Michael b Mann	50	– c sub b Michael 15
P. A. Hibbert c Shipperd b Yardley	1	– c Wright b Alderman 3
D. F. Whatmore c Shipperd b Mann	58	– not out 70
*G. N. Yallop c Wright b Malone	0	– lbw b Michael 2
J. K. Moss c Wright b Malone	8	– c Mann b Yardley 4
T. J. Laughlin c and b Mann	4	– not out 25
†R. D. Robinson c Malone b Michael	75	
S. F. Graf c Marsh b Mann	5	
M. H. N. Walker c Charlesworth b Yardley	15	
G. T. Ross c Marsh b Yardley	18	
J. D. Higgs not out	3	
B 2, l-b 5, w 1, n-b 6	14	B 4, l-b 7 11

1/8 2/102 3/105 4/120 5/126 6/132   **251**   1/14 2/36   (4 wkts) **130**
7/144 8/173 9/228   3/42 4/59

Bowling: *First Innings*—Alderman 13–1–41–0; Malone 23–6–58–2; Yardley 30–7–69–3; Michael 6.4–2–14–1; Mann 33–13–55–4. *Second Innings*—Alderman 6–0–22–1; Malone 12–3–15–0; Yardley 13–0–49–1; Michael 6–0–20–2; Mann 3–0–13–0.

Umpires: K. Carmody and R. Isherwood.

TASMANIA v QUEENSLAND

At Hobart, December 8, 9, 10, 11. Drawn. Tasmania 13 pts, Queensland 5 pts. Rain washed out the third day's play and prevented Tasmania achieving a likely win. Sent in, they had no trouble in reaching 327 for two on the first day and were 505 when they declared at tea on the second. Former Sydney players Jeffery and Goodman (sixteen 4s) put on a record 194 for the first wicket, and the captain Davison helped Jeffrey add a further 142 for the third. Queensland reached 90 for the loss of Wessels at the close but collapsed to Hadlee's pace and Campbell's spin on the fourth day and, 246 behind, were asked to follow on. Only Cosier, top-scorer in each innings, batted with any distinction.

Tasmania

G. W. Goodman c Cosier b Hohns	94	R. J. Hadlee c Ogilvie b Hohns 4
R. F. Jeffery b Schuller	198	G. J. Wilson c and b Hohns 1
D. A. Smith lbw b Dymock	5	P. A. Blizzard not out 13
*B. F. Davison c Ogilvie b Rackemann	73	B 12, l-b 14, n-b 17 43
D. C. Boon c Phillips b Rackemann	8	
†R. D. Woolley not out	60	1/182 2/237 3/379 (9 wkts dec.) **505**
T. W. Docking b Schuller	6	4/415 5/415 6/446 7/446
B. M. Campbell lbw b Schuller	0	8/466 9/476

Bowling: Rackemann 27–4–80–2; Dymock 29–5–109–1; Schuller 33–5–93–3; Carlson 15–1–58–0; Francke 13–2–38–0; Cosier 2–0–9–0; Hohns 27–7–75–3.

Queensland

K. C. Wessels lbw b Hadlee	41	– c Woolley b Wilson 12
*G. J. Cosier c Wilson b Campbell	78	– not out 81
†R. B. Phillips c Blizzard b Hadlee	20	
A. D. Ogilvie lbw b Hadlee	39	– (3) lbw b Wilson 0
M. F. Kent lbw b Hadlee	7	– (4) c Woolley b Boon 19
T. V. Hohns b Hadlee	15	– not out 14
P. H. Carlson st Woolley b Campbell	1	
G. Dymock st Woolley b Campbell	11	
F. M. Francke lbw b Goodman	5	
D. C. Schuller c Boon b Campbell	25	
C. G. Rackemann not out	1	
L-b 10, n-b 6	16	B 5, l-b 1, n-b 4 10

1/88 2/130 3/175 4/186 5/201   **259**   1/32 2/52 3/112   (3 wkts) **136**
6/202 7/216 8/223 9/254

Bowling: *First Innings*—Hadlee 28.2–7–55–5; Wilson 12–1–42–0; Jeffery 1–0–14–0; Blizzard 9–3–31–0; Davison 3–0–13–0; Campbell 31–15–59–4; Goodman 13–5–29–1. *Second Innings*—Wilson 9–2–23–2; Jeffery 6–1–29–0; Blizzard 5–1–35–0; Goodman 8–1–15–0; Boon 4–0–19–1; Smith 2–1–5–0; Docking 1–1–0–0.

Umpires: A. Jones and A. Powell.

WESTERN AUSTRALIA v NEW SOUTH WALES

At Perth, December 8, 9, 10, 11. Drawn. Western Australia 8 pts, New South Wales 11 pts. The draw seemed inevitable after high-scoring first innings accounted for nearly two-thirds of the playing time. New South Wales reached 314 for five on the first day, thanks mainly to a chanceless 123 from McCosker and a dashing 95 from Toohey, who went on to 111 in three hours. Lower-order batsmen helped McEwan restore the Western Australian innings after half the side was out for 153, Mann top scoring with nine 4s in his 67. The visitors opened with 73 but collapsed to 143 for six on the final day – this in spite of missed catches – before Rixon and Beard put together 167 runs in 175 minutes. McCosker's declaration after tea gave no opportunity for any result other than a tame draw.

New South Wales

A. M. J. Hilditch c Wright b Alderman	8	– b Alderman 47
J. Dyson c Serjeant b Yardley	28	– run out 36
*R. B. McCosker c Wright b Alderman	123	– c Wright b Alderman 0
T. M. Chappell c Charlesworth b Alderman	34	– c McEwan b Alderman 0
P. M. Toohey c Wright b Malone	111	– c McEwan b Alderman 29
R. Edwards run out	14	– c Shipperd b Malone 22
G. R. Beard c Wright b Michael	14	– (8) not out 69
†S. J. Rixon c Wright b Alderman	9	– (7) not out 101
G. F. Lawson c Serjeant b Malone	5	
R. P. Done c Wood b Michael	13	
D. W. Hourn not out	8	
B 1, l-b 6, w 2, n-b 7	16	L-b 1, n-b 5 6

1/11 2/94 3/157 4/295 5/312　　　　　383　　1/73 2/73 3/79　　(6 wkts dec.) 310
6/330 7/345 8/352 9/373　　　　　　　　　　　4/96 5/133 6/143

Bowling: *First Innings*—Alderman 35–7–83–4; Malone 41–6–123–2; Michael 14.2–2–39–2; Wood 8–0–26–0; Yardley 21–2–76–1; Mann 3–0–20–0. *Second Innings*—Alderman 23–7–77–4; Malone 25.1–11–58–1; Michael 16–3–54–0; Yardley 25–5–62–0; Mann 12–1–53–0.

Western Australia

G. M. Wood lbw b Done	36	– not out 34
G. Shipperd c Rixon b Done	8	– c McCosker b Hourn 18
K. S. McEwan c Edwards b Beard	60	– not out 4
C. S. Serjeant c Hilditch b Lawson	9	
B. Yardley c and b Lawson	20	
*R. I. Charlesworth c McCosker b Done	46	
A. L. Mann c Done b Beard	67	
†K. J. Wright c Rixon b Done	31	
M. F. Malone not out	17	
T. M. Alderman not out	26	
B 1, l-b 4, w 1, n-b 9	15	W 1 1

1/46 2/49 3/69 4/93　　(8 wkts dec.) 335　　1/52　　　(1 wkt) 57
5/153 6/216 7/274 8/289

C. A. Michael did not bat.

Bowling: *First Innings*—Lawson 31–10–77–2; Done 26–6–93–4; Beard 29–10–62–2; Hourn 26–4–88–0. *Second Innings*—Done 11–2–29–0; Beard 8–6–7–0; Hourn 7–3–9–1; Chappell 4–2–11–0; Toohey 1–1–0–0.

Umpires: P. McConnell and D. G. Weser.

VICTORIA v SOUTH AUSTRALIA

At Melbourne, December 14, 15, 16, 17. Drawn. Victoria 2 pts, South Australia 11 pts. Victoria fought their way back from a first innings deficit of 195 to a commendable draw, having set South Australia a reasonable target after following on. Capitalising on an opening stand of 104 from Nash and Darling, Chappell batted with style for his 82 and put on 148 for the third wicket with Crowe, whose century included sixteen 4s. Five Victorian batsmen fell to the finger spin of Mallett and the first innings folded at 158. In the follow-on, Matthews occupied the crease for six and a half hours to reach a painstaking century, but Moss accelerated on the final day and, with Scholes, added 94 runs in 108 minutes to enable a declaration. South Australia needed 4.5 runs per over to win but, after they lost their first four wickets in twenty-nine minutes to the opening attack of Walker and Graf, they elected to settle for a draw.

South Australia

J. E. Nash lbw b Graf	68	– c and b Walker	28
W. M. Darling c Robinson b Higgs	43	– c Robinson b Graf	19
*I. M. Chappell c Walker b Cox	82	– b Higgs	26
J. J. Crowe not out	109	– b Graf	7
R. J. Inverarity c Scholes b Cox	3	– b Walker	0
P. R. Sleep not out	32	– not out	34
J. R. Hammond (did not bat)	–	– not out	6
B 4, l-b 12	16	B 4, l-b 4	8

1/104 2/128 3/276 4/288   (4 wkts dec.) 353   1/38 2/52 3/60   (5 wkts) 128
4/60 5/119

†T. J. Robertson, G. R. Attenborough, A. A. Mallett and W. Prior did not bat.

Bowling: *First Innings*—Walker 37–6–90–0; Graf 26–9–68–1; Laughlin 9–0–42–0; Higgs 23–6–85–1; Cox 16–3–52–2. *Second Innings*—Walker 12–0–47–2; Graf 18–3–39–2; Higgs 9–2–26–1; Cox 4–1–8–0.

Victoria

R. G. Matthews c Crowe b Mallett	19	– b Mallett	124
*G. N. Yallop c Chappell b Prior	0	– c Crowe b Mallett	49
D. F. Whatmore c Chappell b Attenborough	13	– c Prior b Sleep	22
J. K. Moss b Attenborough	35	– b Attenborough	132
J. W. Scholes b Attenborough	7	– lbw b Attenborough	52
T. J. Laughlin c Inverarity b Mallett	37	– b Hammond	1
†R. D. Robinson c Inverarity b Mallett	16	– st Chappell b Hammond	7
P. J. Cox lbw b Mallett	3	– c Sleep b Attenborough	0
S. F. Graf c Prior b Mallett	19	– not out	0
M. H. N. Walker c Crowe b Inverarity	3		
J. D. Higgs not out	3		
L-b 3	3	B 12, L-b 14, w 1, n-b 2	29

1/5 2/26 3/47 4/66 5/85 6/110   158   1/78 2/120 3/305 (8 wkts dec.) 416
7/122 8/133 9/142   4/399 5/404 6/408
7/413 8/416

Bowling: *First Innings*—Prior 7–1–23–1; Attenborough 22–9–37–3; Mallett 23–3–73–5; Sleep 1–0–2–0; Inverarity 5–1–20–1. *Second Innings*—Prior 23–4–86–0; Attenborough 32–9–73–3; Mallett 38–7–102–2; Sleep 25–4–74–1; Hammond 44.1–20–52–2.

Chappell kept wicket during Victoria's second innings when Robertson was hurt.

Umpires: R. C. Bailhache and R. Whitehead.

NEW SOUTH WALES v QUEENSLAND

At Lismore, December 15, 16, 17, 18. New South Wales won by four wickets. New South Wales 17 pts, Queensland 8 pts. The first Sheffield Shield match played outside a mainland state capital – at the delightful Oakes Oval, Lismore – was keenly contested but the result, unfortunately, was influenced by the effect of heavy rain on the wicket both before and during the match. The first day's play was restricted to two and a half hours, during which Queensland reached 105 for two after being put in. Wessels went on to 85 the next day with some excellent stroke-play, but the last eight batsmen added only 61 as they fell to the aggressive bounce extracted by Lawson. Sound batting by Edwards and a fine innings from Walters left New South Wales only 27 in arrears. With searing heat producing sizeable cracks at both ends of the pitch, Cosier pushed the score along to 43 in six overs and Wessels again batted well, but the last eight wickets fell for 69. Chappell hit 40 in 69 minutes as New South Wales chased a target of 206, but it was another fine innings from Edwards – batting with a torn hamstring – which brought victory. Walters joined A. F. Kippax as the second New South Wales player to score more than 5,000 runs in the Sheffield Shield, his match total taking his aggregate to 5,023.

Queensland

K. C. Wessels b Holland	85	– b Beard	45
*G. J. Cosier c Edwards b Lawson	43	– lbw b Lawson	34
A. D. Ogilvie lbw b Lawson	0	– b Holland	1
M. F. Kent c Edwards b Holland	34	– lbw b Chappell	31
W. R. Broad st Rixon b Holland	6	– st Rixon b Beard	11
T. V. Hohns not out	30	– lbw b Chappell	4
P. H. Carlson b Lawson	0	– b Beard	4
†R. B. Phillips c McCosker b Lawson	8	– not out	13
D. C. Schuller b Lawson	4	– c and b Beard	15
C. G. Rackemann b Pascoe	1	– c Lawson b Beard	2
J. N. Maguire b Pascoe	4	– lbw b Pascoe	3
B 4, l-b 1, w 2, n-b 5	12	B 8, l-b 5, n-b 2	15

1/100 2/100 3/166 4/177 5/190   227   1/47 2/48 3/109 4/117 5/131   178
6/191 7/207 8/215 9/220   6/131 7/138 8/160 9/168

Bowling: *First Innings*—Pascoe 18.1–6–37–2; Lawson 23–7–75–5; Beard 26–9–42–0; Walters 3–0–10–0; Holland 17–2–51–3. *Second Innings*—Pascoe 5.3–0–24–1; Lawson 14–3–44–1; Beard 20–10–33–5; Holland 5–0–37–1; Chappell 10–3–25–2.

New South Wales

*R. B. McCosker c Phillips b Maguire	10	– c Phillips b Cosier	32
J. Dyson c Broad b Carlson	13	– c Ogilvie b Schuller	27
R. Edwards c Ogilvie b Carlson	35	– not out	53
D. A. H. Johnston c Phillips b Carlson	9	– lbw b Broad	0
K. D. Walters lbw b Hohns	83	– c Phillips b Broad	14
T. M. Chappell c Ogilvie b Rackemann	12	– lbw b Broad	40
†S. J. Rixon lbw b Schuller	8	– lbw b Cosier	25
G. R. Beard c Phillips b Schuller	5	– not out	9
G. F. Lawson run out	3		
R. G. Holland c Phillips b Schuller	3		
L. S. Pascoe not out	11		
L-b 5, w 1, n-b 2	8	L-b 6	6

1/20 2/28 3/55 4/84 5/118   200   1/54 2/74 3/109   (6 wkts) 206
6/136 7/142 8/159 9/172   4/109 5/142 6/193

Bowling: *First Innings*—Rackemann 19–3–59–1; Schuller 18–2–47–3; Carlson 29–8–61–3; Maguire 6–3–13–1; Hohns 2.5–0–11–1; Cosier 3–2–1–0. *Second Innings*—Rackemann 12–2–30–0; Schuller 16–4–41–1; Carlson 16–5–34–0; Maguire 3–0–10–0; Hohns 9–1–36–0; Cosier 12–1–29–2; Broad 11–1–20–3.

Umpires: A. S. Ward and A. Watson.

WESTERN AUSTRALIA v TASMANIA

At Perth, December 21, 22, 23, 24. Western Australia won by seven wickets. Western Australia 17 pts, Tasmania 8 pts. After pressing closely for three days, Tasmania fell away with a series of fielding errors, in torrid heat conditions, leaving the home state to achieve an easy win. A fighting innings by Knight, who reached his maiden first-class century, was well supported by Goodman, Boon and Davison. Keen bowling and fielding left Western Australia trailing by 18 runs on the first innings, despite sound batting from Penter and Wright. Although Mann's shrewd captaincy contained more promising Tasmanian batting, Western Australia still had to score 273 in their last innings for victory. The four top-scorers were all missed early in their innings, and strange bowling changes by Davison unnecessarily opened up the scoring-rate during the final twenty overs, when Tasmania had every opportunity to force a draw.

Tasmania

G. W. Goodman c Alderman b Porter	37	– c and b Malone	4
R. F. Jeffery c and b Malone	6	– c Wright b Alderman	34
R. L. Knight not out	114	– c Wright b Alderman	47
D. J. Smith c Serjeant b Porter	5	– b Malone	43
D. C. Boon c Wright b Penter	39	– c Wood b Mann	2
*B. F. Davison c Malone b Alderman	41	– c Penter b Malone	16
†R. D. Woolley b Alderman	10	– c Penter b Wood	52
B. M. Campbell c Wright b Malone	12	– c Wright b Mann	2
R. J. Hadlee c Wood b Alderman	3	– c Wright b Malone	31
N. J. Majewski c Wright b Alderman	0	– st Wright b Mann	15
G. J. Wilson c Porter b Malone	0	– not out	0
B 2, l-b 7, w 1, n-b 1	11	L-b 4	4

1/15 2/56 3/68 4/161 5/212 6/233   278   1/5 2/81 3/88 4/93 5/118   250
7/256 8/261 9/267   6/193 7/203 8/203 9/231

Bowling: *First Innings*—Alderman 37–15–69–4; Malone 40.3–13–84–3; Porter 21–8–45–2; Mann 13–5–36–0; Penter 13–6–33–1. *Second Innings*—Alderman 29–6–70–2; Malone 14.1–3–30–4; Porter 16–9–21–0; Mann 28–7–64–3; Penter 7–2–28–0; O'Neill 5–1–23–0; Wood 6–1–10–1.

Western Australia

G. M. Wood c Majewski b Wilson	15	– lbw b Hadlee	67
G. Shipperd c Woolley b Majewski	34	– lbw b Wilson	57
K. S. McEwan c Woolley b Wilson	3	– c Woolley b Wilson	16
C. S. Serjeant b Majewski	20	– not out	63
M. D. O'Neill lbw b Jeffery	16	– not out	52
C. E. Penter run out	57		
*A. L. Mann c Hadlee b Jeffery	6		
†K. J. Wright c Jeffery b Hadlee	51		
G. D. Porter c Woolley b Jeffery	10		
M. F. Malone c Boon b Jeffery	20		
T. M. Alderman not out	1		
B 6, l-b 3, w 2, n-b 12	23	B 1, l-b 14, n-b 3	18

1/33 2/51 3/71 4/74 5/106   256   1/130 2/149   (3 wkts) 273
6/112 7/224 8/226 9/251   3/151

Bowling: *First Innings*—Hadlee 21–5–66–1; Wilson 15–5–41–2; Majewski 13–2–50–2; Jeffery 13.2–5–37–4; Campbell 10–0–39–0. *Second Innings*—Hadlee 17–2–73–1; Wilson 16–4–37–2; Majewski 11–1–43–0; Jeffery 17–2–50–0; Campbell 8.5–1–37–0; Goodman 3–0–15–0.

Umpires: G. Duperouzel and P. McConnell.

VICTORIA v NEW SOUTH WALES

At Melbourne, December 21, 22, 23, 24. Victoria won by one wicket. Victoria 15 pts, New South Wales 6 pts. Victoria brought off a sensational win when, with 3 runs required, Leehane drove leg-spinner Holland for a boundary off the last ball of the match. The exciting finish reversed the first day's tedium when New South Wales painfully scored 217 for five at a rate of barely 2 an over. The first 100 had taken 226 minutes and only the confident stroke-play of Davis provided any relief before Walker and Higgs quickly finished off the innings. Victoria found Lawson's speed disconcerting as they proceeded to 162 for four by the close, but Moss benefited from a dropped catch off Lawson at 48 to hold the innings together. Despite another valuable innings from Dyson when New South Wales batted again, Victoria were left with a run-rate of less than 1 a minute when McCosker declared in the first session of the final day. Whatmore and Broad put together 100 in 116 minutes, and it was only after the fifth wicket fell at 182 that there were any doubts about the outcome as Lawson and Beard snatched three quick wickets.

New South Wales

*R. B. McCosker c Higgs b Leehane	4	– c Bright b Laughlin	20
J. Dyson b Higgs	46	– lbw b Walker	71
T. M. Chappell c Robinson b Higgs	73	– c Laughlin b Higgs	34
I. C. Davis c Walker b Higgs	46	– run out	9
P. M. Toohey lbw b Higgs	18	– c and b Higgs	21
K. D. Walters c Whatmore b Walker	24	– not out	34
†S. J. Rixon c Laughlin b Leehane	0	– b Higgs	25
G. R. Beard lbw b Walker	25	– (9) c Moss b Higgs	0
G. F. Lawson b Walker	2	– (8) c Whatmore b Walker	4
R. P. Done b Walker	9	– c Laughlin b Walker	4
R. G. Holland not out	1	– not out	0
B 4, l-b 8, w 1	13	B 4, l-b 7, n-b 1	12

1/4 2/113 3/160 4/185 5/217   261   1/30 2/85 3/127   (9 wkts dec.) 234
6/218 7/232 8/234 9/258   4/160 5/162 6/205 7/214
                                            8/217 9/233

Bowling: *First Innings*—Leehane 30–4–72–2; Walker 46.4–21–67–4; Laughlin 5–2–11–0; Bright 14–7–19–0; Higgs 28–5–79–4. *Second Innings*—Leehane 4–0–21–0; Walker 27–6–58–3; Laughlin 12–0–38–1; Bright 12–1–27–0; Higgs 27–3–78–4.

Victoria

R. G. Matthews c Davis b Lawson	9	– c Rixon b Lawson	0
D. J. Broad c Rixon b Lawson	3	– c Done b Beard	37
D. F. Whatmore lbw b Done	18	– c Beard b Holland	88
*G. N. Yallop c Done b Holland	51	– (5) b Lawson	22
J. K. Moss c Lawson b Chappell	80	– (6) lbw b Holland	23
T. J. Laughlin b Beard	30	– (7) not out	25
†R. D. Robinson b Lawson	8	– (4) b Holland	4
R. J. Bright c Rixon b Beard	3	– c Lawson b Beard	16
M. H. N. Walker c and b Lawson	17	– b Lawson	14
J. D. Higgs not out	8	– c Davis b Lawson	1
J. F. Leehane b Holland	3	– not out	4
B 2, l-b 4, n-b 14	20	B 2, l-b 7, n-b 4	13

1/13 2/17 3/49 4/125 5/190   250   1/0 2/100 3/115   (9 wkts) 247
6/212 7/218 8/230 9/243   4/146 5/182 6/182 7/212
                                            8/235 9/241

Bowling: *First Innings*—Lawson 27–8–75–4; Done 15–4–25–1; Beard 36–19–49–2; Walters 10–2–23–0; Holland 13.2–2–39–2; Chappell 8–1–19–1. *Second Innings*—Lawson 18–3–47–4; Done 15–1–45–0; Beard 15–0–45–2; Holland 28–1–97–3.

Umpires: K. Carmody and W. Copeland.

SOUTH AUSTRALIA v WESTERN AUSTRALIA

At Adelaide, December 28, 29, 30, 31. South Australia won by 52 runs. South Australia 25 pts, Western Australia 4 pts. The brilliant opening day's batting of South Australia received a standing ovation from the holiday crowd. Chappell's astute leadership and a sensational collapse by Western Australia produced an absorbing win with six overs to spare, despite the loss of two and a half hours on the second day and all but twenty-three minutes of the third day. Nash and Darling opened with a sound century stand in oppressive heat and Chappell matched Nash's aggression as they added 107 in 87 minutes. The South Australian captain batted for three hours fifty-seven minutes to reach his 154, with one 6 and twenty 4s, off 168 balls. Crowe helped him put on a further 129 in 106 minutes as the score rose to 365 at the close. High winds, bad light and rain interrupted Wester Australia's first innings, notable only for McEwan's competent 80 and some early help from opener Wood. Chappell's daring declaration after only fifteen minutes provided ample opportunity for Western Australia and, at 157 for two, success seemed imminent. However, once Sleep broke the run-a-minute partnership of 89 by Shipperd and Serjeant, his leg-spin and Attenborough's medium pace disposed of the last eight wickets for 33.

South Australia

W. M. Darling c Wright b Malone	50	– not out	10
J. E. Nash c Serjeant b Yardley	134	– b Alderman	0
*I. M. Chappell b Malone	154		
J. J. Crowe c Yardley b Penter	31		
D. W. Hookes not out	32		
J. R. Hammond not out	7		
P. R. Sleep (did not bat)		– (3) not out	12
L-b 4, n-b 11	15	N-b 1	1

1/124 2/231 3/360 4/398　　(4 wkts dec.) 423　1/1　　(1 wkt dec.) 23

†T. J. Robertson, A. A. Mallett, G. R. Attenborough and W. Prior did not bat.

Bowling: *First Innings*—Alderman 27–3–99–0; Malone 34–2–121–2; Wood 6–1–20–0; Yardley 16–0–86–1; Mann 8–2–37–0; O'Neill 3–0–19–0; Penter 6–1–26–1. *Second Innings*—Alderman 2–0–3–1; Malone 2–0–19–0.

Western Australia

G. M. Wood c Sleep b Prior	36	– c Prior b Attenborough	24
G. Shipperd c Crowe b Attenborough	0	– st Robertson b Sleep	69
K. S. McEwan b Prior	80	– c Prior b Mallett	23
C. S. Serjeant lbw b Prior	10	– lbw b Sleep	48
M. D. O'Neill run out	10	– c Robertson b Attenborough	1
C. E. Penter lbw b Prior	2	– not out	8
B. Yardley c Robertson b Attenborough	25	– b Sleep	0
*A. L. Mann b Mallett	16	– b Attenborough	1
†K. J. Wright b Mallett	8	– c Robertson b Attenborough	2
M. F. Malone c Robertson b Attenborough	4	– c Robertson b Attenborough	0
T. M. Alderman not out	0	– lbw b Sleep	5
B 7, l-b 4, w 2	13	B 2, l-b 6, n-b 1	9

1/4 2/73 3/124 4/144 5/150　　204　1/37 2/68 3/157 4/172 5/176　190
6/150 7/188 8/194 9/202　　　　6/176 7/181 8/183 9/183

Bowling: *First Innings*—Prior 27–9–85–4; Attenborough 18.4–4–60–3; Mallett 21–10–31–2; Sleep 5–4–6–0; Hammond 4–0–9–0. *Second Innings*—Prior 13–1–49–0; Attenborough 17–3–40–5; Mallett 12–1–50–1; Sleep 9.4–2–26–4; Hammond 4–1–16–0.

Umpires: B. E. Martin and M. G. O'Connell.

TASMANIA v NEW SOUTH WALES

At Launceston, December 29, 30, 31, January 1. New South Wales won by an innings and 55 runs. New South Wales 22 pts, Tasmania 4 pts. Tasmania were thoroughly outclassed in a game which emphasised their bowling and fielding deficiencies as well as their inexperience of batting at first-class level. A second-wicket stand of 234 by Chappell and Dyson was notable for splendid running between the wickets and ended when Chappell's helmet fell on the stumps! McCosker and Davis both added effortless centuries, and a partnership of 190 runs in 168 minutes. Tasmania collapsed to 43 for five before a fighting stand of 114 between Boon and Woolley gave respectability to an innings wrecked by Lawson's fiery speed and ended by Holland's spin. The same two batsmen provided substance in the follow-on, as did opener Jeffery and some belated hitting from Hadlee, who earlier had produced some first-class bowling.

New South Wales

A. M. J. Hilditch c Woolley b Wilson	4	†S. J. Rixon lbw b Hadlee	1	
J. Dyson c Campbell b Wilson	99	G. R. Beard not out	0	
T. M. Chappell hit wkt b Majewski	144	B 14, l-b 19, n-b 4	37	
I. C. Davis c Davison b Hadlee	112			
*R. B. McCosker not out	115	1/7 2/234 3/289	(6 wkts dec.) 517	
K. D. Walters b Hadlee	5	4/479 5/489 6/501		

G. F. Lawson, L. S. Pascoe and R. G. Holland did not bat.

Bowling: Hadlee 33–11–58–3; Wilson 25–3–95–2; Majewski 23–3–88–1; Jeffery 16–2–81–0; Goodman 25–5–101–0; Campbell 8–1–24–0; Boon 2–0–18–0; Davison 4–0–15–0.

Tasmania

G. W. Goodman b Holland	12	– lbw b Lawson	20	
R. F. Jeffery lbw b Pascoe	13	– c Davis b Lawson	43	
R. L. Knight c McCosker b Holland	2	– c McCosker b Holland	9	
D. A. Smith b Lawson	1	– c Chappell b Holland	10	
D. C. Boon lbw b Lawson	61	– b Holland	32	
*B. F. Davison c Rixon b Lawson	0	– c Davis b Chappell	27	
†R. D. Woolley c Rixon b Lawson	61	– c Dyson b Pascoe	37	
B. M. Campbell c McCosker b Holland	1	– lbw b Pascoe	0	
R. J. Hadlee not out	27	– not out	33	
G. J. Wilson c Rixon b Holland	0	– (11) c and b Pascoe	10	
N. J. Majewski c Rixon b Beard	21	– (10) c Holland b Pascoe	8	
B 3, l-b 2, w 1, n-b 7	13	B 2, l-b 6, w 1, n-b 12	21	

1/17 2/25 3/28 4/38 5/43 6/157 212   1/57 2/80 3/80 4/122 5/134 250
7/160 8/160 9/167   6/196 7/196 8/197 9/207

Bowling: *First Innings*—Pascoe 20–3–64–1; Lawson 19–6–39–4; Beard 11–4–14–1; Holland 28–7–82–4. *Second Innings*—Pascoe 20.2–7–64–4; Lawson 14–3–43–2; Beard 16–5–23–0; Holland 26–9–84–3; Walters 2–0–15–0; Chappell 2–2–0–1.

Umpires: J. Stevens and G. Summers.

QUEENSLAND v NEW SOUTH WALES

At Brisbane, January 19, 20, 21, 22. Drawn. Queensland 7 pts, New South Wales 14 pts. A batsman's wicket left no opportunity for either side to win a contest vital to their Shield aspirations, especially after three inches of rain during a storm on the second day had cost two and a half hours play. The visitors lost two wickets for 30 and Dyson laboured for almost three and threequarter hours over his 70, enabling Chappell to maintain an attacking field. Border hit the only double century of the season in his one appearance for New South Wales. He led a partnership of 160 with Toohey in 98 minutes and his second century took only 86 minutes – half the time devoted to his first 100 runs. A disciplined 169 from Chappell, achieved in nearly seven and a half hours, steered Queensland out of early trouble. Useful support from newcomer Parker, together with Carlson, Phillips and Dymock, enabled a declaration; but the match drifted to a slow draw after New South Wales's belated second innings declaration left Queensland with a target of 238 in the final session of play. At the end of Queensland's first innings Pascoe, in an ill-tempered display after a number of no balls, bowled a series of nasty deliveries at Dymock, whom Chappell then protected from the strike while ignoring easy runs.

New South Wales

*R. B. McCosker c Carlson b Schuller	1	– lbw b Carlson	11
J. Dyson run out	70	– run out	45
T. M. Chappell c Phillips b Rackemann	6	– not out	76
A. R. Border c Phillips b Rackemann	200	– c Phillips b Schuller	6
P. M. Toohey not out	100	– c Wessels b Cosier	26
K. D. Walters b Carlson	16	– run out	9
†S. J. Rixon not out	8	– not out	0
L-b 3	3	L-b 1, n-b 1	2

1/8 2/30 3/166 4/326   (5 wkts dec.) 404   1/22 2/73 3/83   (5 wkts dec.) 175
5/372   4/147 5/175

G. R. Beard, G. F. Lawson, L. S. Pascoe and R. G. Holland did not bat.

Bowling: *First Innings*—Schuller 13.1–1–60–1; Dymock 19–3–72–0; Rackemann 21–4–57–2; Hohns 8–2–46–0; Carlson 17–2–57–1; Cosier 8–1–25–0; Chappell 10–0–59–0; Broad 4–0–25–0. *Second Innings*—Schuller 13–3–31–1; Dymock 11–2–31–0; Rackemann 8–1–37–0; Carlson 16–4–37–1; Cosier 12–3–14–1; Broad 4–0–13–0.

Queensland

G. J. Cosier c Border b Lawson	3	– lbw b Lawson	7
K. C. Wessels c Holland b Pascoe	13	– c McCosker b Lawson	11
W. R. Broad b Beard	4	– c Beard b Border	44
*G. S. Chappell c Holland b Beard	169	– not out	40
A. D. Parker c Beard b Chappell	37	– not out	8
P. H. Carlson b Pascoe	29		
T. V. Hohns b Pascoe	0		
†R. B. Phillips c Border b Chappell	28		
G. Dymock not out	28		
D. C. Schuller not out	0		
B 4, l-b 5, w 1, n-b 21	31	L-b 1, n-b 2	3

1/20 2/20 3/46 4/136   (8 wkts dec.) 342   1/18 2/32 3/96   (3 wkts) 113
5/199 6/203 7/259 8/337

C. G. Rackemann did not bat.

Bowling: *First Innings*—Pascoe 28–5–82–3; Lawson 23–2–82–1; Beard 22–14–27–2; Holland 26–6–71–0; Chappell 8–2–12–2; Border 6–2–12–0; Walters 9–1–25–0. *Second Innings*—Pascoe 9–2–22–0; Lawson 7–0–22–2; Holland 9–2–50–0; Chappell 2–2–0–0; Border 7–3–16–1; Dyson 1–1–0–0.

Umpires: T. H. Warwick and M. W. Johnson.

WESTERN AUSTRALIA v SOUTH AUSTRALIA

At Perth, January 19, 20, 21, 22. South Australia won by 154 runs. South Australia 19 pts, Western Australia 6 pts. Western Australia's inability to press home early opportunities allowed the visitors gradually to take charge. Former Western Australia captain Inverarity bolstered the South Australian innings from 51 for four with a stubborn partnership of 86 with Crowe. Both scored 58, as did wicket-keeper Robertson, who featured in an eighth-wicket stand of 79 with Mallett before the last three wickets fell at 257. In reply, Porter and McEwan batted patiently for almost three hours against steady bowling, but South Australia retained a lead of 66, and openers Nash and Darling increased it with a brisk 76 off nineteen overs before the close of the second day. Nash and Chappell (twelve 4s) were missed five times as they set the pace with 101 for the second wicket, followed by effective hitting from Hookes. Western Australia lost two wickets before the close and, despite fighting innings from Wood and Shipperd, they never appeared likely to achieve the target of 392 against a diversified attack. The match was marred by unpleasantness when Langer was run out after it was believed the ball was "dead".

South Australia

J. E. Nash c Wood b Alderman	2	– c Shipperd b Malone	69
W. M. Darling c Wright b Alderman	20	– lbw b Mann	50
*I. M. Chappell c Malone b Alderman	0	– b Malone	66
J. J. Crowe lbw b Malone	58	– c Wright b Porter	23
D. W. Hookes c Malone b Porter	12	– c Shipperd b Porter	52
R. J. Inverarity lbw b Alderman	58	– b Porter	17
J. R. Hammond c Wood b Mann	15	– lbw b Alderman	10
†T. J. Robertson b Malone	58	– c Wright b Porter	11
A. A. Mallett c Laird b Mann	23	– not out	4
G. R. Attenborough b Malone	0	– not out	6
W. Prior not out	0		
L-b 11	11	B 10, l-b 7, n-b 1	18

1/6 2/6 3/29 4/51 5/137 6/171   257   1/81 2/182 3/195   (8 wkts dec.) 326
7/178 8/257 9/257   4/221 5/290 6/298
                                               7/314 8/318

Bowling: *First Innings*—Alderman 19–3–76–4; Malone 28–16–47–3; Porter 16–2–60–1; Mann 25.1–5–63–2. *Second Innings*—Alderman 29–6–83–1; Malone 25–6–74–2; Porter 32–5–112–4; Mann 10–0–39–1.

Western Australia

G. M. Wood lbw b Hammond	10	– c Robertson b Hammond	66
B. M. Laird lbw b Attenborough	0	– lbw b Attenborough	0
R. S. Langer c Hookes b Mallett	21	– run out	24
G. D. Porter c Crowe b Prior	53	– (9) c Hookes b Mallett	0
C. S. Serjeant c Robertson b Prior	4	– (4) c Robertson b Prior	5
K. S. McEwan c Inverarity b Hammond	46	– (5) lbw b Attenborough	7
G. Shipperd c Robertson b Prior	20	– (6) lbw b Inverarity	71
*A. L. Mann c Attenborough b Hammond	25	– (7) c Inverarity b Hammond	12
†K. J. Wright not out	0	– (8) c Crowe b Mallett	36
M. F. Malone b Hammond	5	– c and b Inverarity	2
T. M. Alderman c Robertson b Hammond	0	– not out	6
L-b 3, w 1, n-b 3	7	L-b 7, n-b 2	9

1/1 2/25 3/36 4/43 5/121 6/155   191   1/0 2/49 3/72 4/100 5/108   238
7/186 8/186 9/191   6/138 7/212 8/218 9/223

Bowling: *First Innings*—Attenborough 22–7–48–1; Hammond 29.4–6–84–5; Mallett 11–5–18–1; Prior 19–7–34–3. *Second Innings*—Attenborough 17–5–57–2; Hammond 19–4–53–2; Mallett 15–3–53–2; Prior 13–2–39–1; Inverarity 5.2–1–14–2; Chappell 3–0–13–0.

Umpires: P. McConnell and D. G. Weser.

WESTERN AUSTRALIA v VICTORIA

At Perth, January 26, 27, 28, 29. Victoria won by eight wickets. Victoria 20 pts, Western Australia 10 pts. Western Australia's dramatic third-day collapse – when their second innings ended after only 42.3 overs in under three hours – changed the course of this previously even struggle. Opener Wood was an early absentee, with a badly bruised hand struck by a rising ball from Leehane, but he returned at the fall of the fifth wicket to stave up the Western Australian first innings; often batting one-handed and in great pain, he hit nine 4s in an innings lasting three and a quarter hours, adding 112 for the sixth wicket with Wright. In reply Broad and Yallop both scored well and all-rounder Graf hit an undefeated 58, taking his side to within 1 run of the Western Australian total. Victoria's best bowler Walker initiated the Western Australian collapse and, with a stand of 114 by new opener Broad and Whatmore for Victoria, they won with eight wickets and four hours in hand.

Western Australia

G. M. Wood c Broad b Hibbert	62	– absent hurt		0
G. Shipperd lbw b Leehane	10	– (1) c Broad b Walker		3
R. S. Langer c Whatmore b Walker	1	– (2) c Robinson b Leehane		5
M. D. O'Neill run out	29	– c Broad b Walker		15
K. S. McEwan c and b Bright	46	– run out		53
C. E. Penter c Leehane b Bright	10	– c Bright b Graf		14
†K. J. Wright c Robinson b Leehane	57	– c Bright b Graf		0
G. D. Porter b Leehane	15	– (3) c Robinson b Walker		0
*A. L. Mann c Robinson b Walker	19	– (8) c Walker b Bright		7
M. F. Malone not out	12	– (9) run out		38
T. M. Alderman b Walker	10	– (10) not out		2
B 3, l-b 3, w 4, n-b 11	21	B 5, l-b 7, n-b 3		15

1/24 2/43 3/71 4/114 5/121　　　　　292　　1/2 2/13 3/13 4/35 5/92　　　　152
6/233 7/233 8/261 9/277　　　　　　　　　6/103 7/103 8/135 9/152

Bowling: *First Innings*—Leehane 28–5–86–3; Walker 28.4–7–87–3; Laughlin 6.1–4–10–0; Graf 17–4–45–0; Bright 12.5–2–35–2; Hibbert 7–1–8–1. *Second Innings*—Leehane 11.3–2–45–1; Walker 9–3–29–3; Graf 10–1–31–2; Bright 12–3–32–1.

Victoria

P. A. Hibbert c Wright b Malone	11	– lbw b Alderman		0
D. J. Broad c and b Mann	73	– not out		69
D. F. Whatmore run out	1	– c Porter b Penter		61
*G. N. Yallop st Wright b Mann	55	– not out		22
J. K. Moss c Porter b Langer	30			
T. J. Laughlin c Porter b Mann	4			
†R. D. Robinson c Porter b Alderman	18			
R. J. Bright c Wright b Porter	23			
S. F. Graf not out	58			
M. H. N. Walker c Langer b Mann	2			
J. F. Leehane b Malone	3			
B 4, l-b 5, n-b 4	13	L-b 3, n-b 1		4

1/17 2/21 3/117 4/166 5/180　　　　291　　1/0 2/114　　　　(2 wkts) 156
6/209 7/225 8/252 9/260

Bowling: *First Innings*—Alderman 21–7–78–1; Malone 21.3–10–36–2; Porter 25–4–57–1; Mann 26–2–79–4; Langer 4–1–22–1; O'Neill 5–1–6–0. *Second Innings*—Alderman 14–3–35–1; Malone 11–0–28–0; Porter 6–3–10–0; Mann 2–0–19–0; Langer 3–0–8–0; O'Neill 4–1–10–0; Penter 15–5–34–1; McEwan 0.3–0–8–0.

Umpires: J. D'Arcy Evans and D. G. Weser.

VICTORIA v QUEENSLAND

At Melbourne, February 8, 9, 10, 11. Victoria won by nine wickets. Victoria 21 pts, Queensland 8 pts. After forfeiting the advantage of an early Queensland batting collapse by mising six catches and two stumping chances, Victoria benefited from the visitors' poor second innings batting to win handsomely in a late run to hold the Shield. Although still troubled by a finger broken in the Lismore game Kent batted strongly for 61, yet Queensland collapsed to 135 for six as he and Carlson fell within four balls to the leg-spin of Higgs. Wicket-keeper Phillips hit a brave if fortuitous 85 in three hours before being run out off the last ball of the first day. After a delay of thirty-three minutes because of rain, Victoria took five and a half hours to score 237 on a splendid batting surface, but the next day Moss and Laughlin added

164 in 193 minutes for the fifth wicket. Carlson took all six wickets which fell before Victoria declared 119 ahead. The pace attack of Walker and Leehane left Queensland with only four wickets remaining and still 35 runs in arrears at the close, although a spirited stand of 47 for the last wicket by Thomson and Francke on the final day required Victoria to bat again for victory.

Queensland

K. C. Wessels c Broad b Leehane	2	– b Leehane	1
*G. J. Cosier lbw b Leehane	0	– lbw b Leehane	12
W. R. Broad c Whatmore b Leehane	16	– lbw b Walker	17
M. F. Kent c and b Higgs	61	– lbw b Leehane	1
T. V. Hohns b Laughlin	14	– c Whatmore b Walker	11
P. H. Carlson c Leehane b Higgs	38	– (8) c and b Walker	19
A. D. Parker c Laughlin b Higgs	40	– (6) lbw b Walker	24
D. C. Schuller c Moss b Higgs	25	– (9) run out	3
†R. B. Phillips run out	85	– (7) c Bright b Walker	4
F. M. Francke c Walker b Leehane	5	– not out	23
J. R. Thomson not out	10	– c Moss b Higgs	23
B 4, l-b 5, n-b 1	10	L-b 8	8

1/1 2/9 3/28 4/68 5/135   **306**   1/3 2/34 3/35 4/40 5/52   **146**
6/135 7/222 8/256 9/274   6/62 7/92 8/99 9/99

Bowling: *First Innings*—Leehane 28.3–5–87–4; Walker 16–1–56–0; Laughlin 10–3–25–1; Bright 17–4–38–0; Higgs 28–3–90–4. *Second Innings*—Leehane 19–6–49–3; Walker 27–8–73–5; Higgs 8.1–2–16–1.

Victoria

J. M. Wiener lbw b Carlson	49	– not out	7
D. J. Broad c Phillips b Carlson	75	– lbw b Thomson	7
D. F. Whatmore c and b Carlson	0	– not out	13
*G. N. Yallop c Hohns b Carlson	65		
J. K. Moss c Phillips b Carlson	110		
T. J. Laughlin c Broad b Carlson	68		
†R. D. Robinson not out	26		
R. J. Bright not out	12		
L-b 10, w 3, n-b 7	20	N-b 1	1

1/64 2/64 3/196 4/201   (6 wkts dec.) **425**   1/9   (1 wkt) **28**
5/365 6/398

M. H. N. Walker, J. F. Leehane and J. D. Higgs did not bat.

Bowling: *First Innings*—Thomson 31–6–96–0; Schuller 30–7–81–0; Carlson 37–9–101–6; Cosier 5–0–16–0; Francke 20–5–68–0; Broad 14–2–43–0. *Second Innings*—Thomson 4–0–15–1; Schuller 3–0–12–0.

Umpires: R. French and R. Whitehead.

SOUTH AUSTRALIA v QUEENSLAND

At Adelaide, February 15, 16, 17. Queensland won by nine wickets. Queensland 19 pts, South Australia 5 pts. Beaten within three days, South Australia were outplayed from the first morning when the pace attack of Thomson and Schuller initiated a collapse which medium-pacer Carlson finished off with four economical wickets, including that of Inverarity who had taken nearly two hours over his 15. Wessels and Carlson put Queensland 17 ahead by stumps and next morning Carlson showed his best batting form of the summer. South Australia lost five wickets for 75 before the close but, on the third morning, Darling and Sleep took their overnight partnership to 148. Darling's 134 was his first century at the Adelaide Oval. Wessels and Kent finished the match with a dashing 75 runs, of which Kent contributed 40 in 55 minutes of power-laden hitting.

South Australia

W. M. Darling c Parker b Thomson	6	– c Cosier b Schuller	134
J. E. Nash c Phillips b Schuller	14	– c Parker b Rackemann	8
R. J. Inverarity c Phillips b Carlson	15	– b Thomson	6
J. J. Crowe c Schuller b Thomson	1	– lbw b Thomson	0
*I. M. Chappell c Thomson b Rackemann	26	– c and b Carlson	10
B. L. Causby c Carlson b Rackemann	0	– c Phillips b Carlson	8
P. R. Sleep c Phillips b Carlson	0	– b Rackemann	77
J. R. Hammond c Schuller b Rackemann	1	– lbw b Rackemann	12
†T. J. Robertson b Carlson	10	– c Phillips b Hohns	6
G. R. Attenborough not out	17	– b Thomson	11
W. Prior c Cosier b Carlson	4	– not out	10
L-b 4, n-b 10	14	L-b 1, w 1, n-b 7	9
	108		291

1/21 2/23 3/26 4/62 5/62
6/65 7/66 8/79 9/90

1/35 2/50 3/50 4/65 5/75
6/223 7/253 8/270 9/270

Bowling: *First Innings*—Thomson 6–2–21–2; Schuller 6–2–14–1; Rackemann 9–1–33–3; Carlson 9.5–3–23–4; Cosier 1–0–3–0. *Second Innings*—Thomson 21.3–5–78–3; Schuller 16–5–47–1; Rackemann 24–5–64–3; Carlson 19–6–48–2; Cosier 5–2–7–0; Hohns 9–2–29–1; Broad 2–0–9–0.

Queensland

K. C. Wessels c Robertson b Prior	63	– not out	60
W. R. Broad c Causby b Prior	0	– c Hammond b Sleep	35
M. F. Kent c Sleep b Attenborough	17	– not out	40
*G. J. Cosier c Sleep b Attenborough	12		
T. V. Hohns lbw b Attenborough	7		
P. H. Carlson c Crowe b Sleep	84		
A. D. Parker c Inverarity b Attenborough	20		
†R. B. Phillips c Robertson b Sleep	20		
D. C. Schuller c Darling b Prior	3		
J. R. Thomson not out	29		
C. G. Rackemann lbw b Chappell	1		
L-b 7, n-b 1	8	L-b 1	1
	264	1/61 (1 wkt)	136

1/1 2/41 3/62 4/76 5/131
6/164 7/216 8/221 9/235

Bowling: *First Innings*—Prior 26–3–89–3; Attenborough 29–6–81–4; Hammond 22–6–44–0; Sleep 20–6–38–2; Chappell 1.4–0–4–1. *Second Innings*—Prior 6–0–23–0; Attenborough 4–1–15–0; Hammond 7–2–15–0; Sleep 12–1–60–1; Inverarity 3–0–17–0; Causby 1–0–4–0; Nash 0.2–0–1–0.

Umpires: A. R. Crafter and B. E. Martin.

VICTORIA v TASMANIA

At Melbourne, February 15, 16, 17. Victoria won by an innings and 119 runs. Victoria 20 pts, Tasmania 6 pts. Victoria moved to the top of the Shield table with an easy three-day win. Tasmanian captain Davison belatedly found his form with a commanding innings of 138 which accounted for all but 90 of their disappointing first innings total. Coming to the crease at 16 for three, he hit one 6 and fifteen 4s in just over five hours' batting. Victoria were struggling at 76 for three when Moss came in to play a sound innings, and the recalled Scholes completed a fine century on the second day. Wicket-keeper Robinson contributed an undefeated 103 before Whatmore declared 228 ahead. Davison and Woolley added 61 for the fifth wicket after another initial collapse but thereafter Tasmania batted pathetically, losing their last six wickets for 4 runs in half an hour. The outstanding bowler was Victoria's Tasmanian-born Walker, with a match aggregate of nine for 94 from some splendidly controlled pace bowling.

Tasmania

G. W. Goodman c Robinson b Leehane	3	– lbw b Walker	5
R. F. Jeffery c Moss b Leehane	9	– c Moss b Leehane	15
R. L. Knight c Robinson b Walker	27	– lbw b Graf	8
D. C. Boon b Walker	1	– b Walker	0
*B. F. Davison c Scholes b Walker	138	– c Scholes b Walker	38
†R. D. Woolley c Broad b Laughlin	11	– c Whatmore b Higgs	35
S. Saunders c and b Higgs	2	– lbw b Higgs	0
P. A. Blizzard c Scholes b Graf	6	– lbw b Higgs	3
M. B. Scholes c Graf b Walker	23	– lbw b Walker	0
G. J. Wilson c Robinson b Walker	0	– not out	0
C. J. Broadby not out	2	– b Higgs	0
B 1, l-b 5	6	L-b 4	4

1/6 2/15 3/16 4/81 5/144   228   1/13 2/21 3/26 4/44 5/105   109
6/155 7/168 8/215 9/219   6/105 7/108 8/109 9/109

Bowling: *First Innings*—Leehane 16–4–42–2; Walker 24–7–58–5; Graf 18–5–31–1; Higgs 29–8–76–1; Laughlin 10–4–15–1. *Second Innings*—Leehane 9–3–26–1; Walker 16–5–36–4; Graf 8–1–25–1; Higgs 6.1–2–18–4.

Victoria

G. M. Watts c Woolley b Scholes	2	M. H. N. Walker run out	1
D. J. Broad c Blizzard b Scholes	8	J. F. Leehane not out	4
*D. F. Whatmore b Broadby	30		
J. K. Moss b Scholes	72	B 4, l-b 11, n-b 10	25
J. W. Scholes c Knight b Scholes	126		
T. J. Laughlin c Woolley b Scholes	50	1/5 2/12 3/76 (8 wkts dec.) 456	
†R. D. Robinson not out	103	4/154 5/274 6/349	
S. F. Graf st Woolley b Saunders	35	7/439 8/448	

J. D. Higgs did not bat.

Bowling: Wilson 28–3–94–0; Scholes 30–3–86–5; Blizzard 20–3–72–0; Jeffery 6–2–18–0; Broadby 41–11–87–1; Saunders 20–3–68–1; Goodman 2–1–6–0.

Umpires: R. A. French and R. Isherwood.

NEW SOUTH WALES v SOUTH AUSTRALIA

At Sydney, February 23, 24, 25, 26. New South Wales won by 98 runs. New South Wales 20 pts, South Australia 9 pts. Sensational fast bowling by Pascoe brought unexpected success to the home state in a match marred by unpleasant conduct and alleged intimidation. New South Wales captain McCosker and coach Peter Philpott later submitted written complaints to the Australian Cricket Board concerning the conduct of some South Australian players. Toohey and Walters in two hours overcame a slow start and the loss of four early wickets with a brilliant unbroken stand of 166 which allowed McCosker to declare to preserve the balance of bonus points. Nash and Darling fell without addition to South Australia's overnight score of 15 but Chappell – although involved in several incidents with Pascoe and Walters – produced a delightful range of strokes in his 158. Inverarity helped him stabilise the innings with a stand of 191 in three and threequarter hours, and the visitors went 81 ahead before removing five New South Wales wickets before the close of play. South Australia needed only 167 to win with ample time available, but Pascoe, bowling with great hostility on a dead pitch, removed seven batsmen for 18 runs – a Sheffield Shield performance ranking only just behind the outstanding feats of Miller, Ironmonger and Fleetwood-Smith.

New South Wales

	First Innings		Second Innings	
*R. B. McCosker	c Robertson b Attenborough	82	c Sleep b Mallett	38
J. Dyson	c Nash b Mallett	30	c Robertson b Attenborough	43
T. M. Chappell	c Sleep b Attenborough	13	c Inverarity b Mallett	3
I. C. Davis	c Crowe b Mallett	1	c Hammond b Inverarity	43
P. M. Toohey	not out	100	c and b Inverarity	34
K. D. Walters	not out	72	c Chappell b Mallett	35
G. J. Gilmour	(did not bat)		c Mallett b Hammond	24
†S. J. Rixon	(did not bat)		not out	16
L. S. Pascoe	(did not bat)		b Hammond	0
R. G. Holland	(did not bat)		c Attenborough b Hammond	6
D. W. Hourn	(did not bat)		b Mallett	0
	L-b 3, n-b 1	4	L-b 6	6

1/98 2/125 3/126 4/136   (4 wkts dec.) 302   1/60 2/72 3/93 4/160 5/171   248
6/221 7/227 8/230 9/248

Bowling: *First Innings*—Prior 16-5-40-0; Attenborough 19-4-62-2; Hammond 16-2-60-0; Mallett 34-11-87-2; Inverarity 1-1-0-0. *Second Innings*—Prior 11-1-29-0; Attenborough 25-7-62-1; Hammond 9-3-12-3; Mallett 39.2-14-73-4; Inverarity 29-8-66-2.

South Australia

	First Innings		Second Innings	
J. E. Nash	c Rixon b Gilmour	8	c McCosker b Holland	11
W. M. Darling	c Rixon b Pascoe	6	lbw b Pascoe	7
*I. M. Chappell	c Davis b Pascoe	158	c Holland b Pascoe	0
R. J. Inverarity	c Davis b Walters	53	b Pascoe	7
J. J. Crowe	st Rixon b Holland	20	c Toohey b Holland	0
P. R. Sleep	c McCosker b Hourn	16	run out	24
J. R. Hammond	c McCosker b Holland	19	lbw b Pascoe	1
†T. J. Robertson	not out	52	b Pascoe	0
G. R. Attenborough	c Hourn b Holland	24	b Pascoe	16
A. A. Mallett	c Toohey b Pascoe	6	not out	0
W. Prior	lbw b Holland	0	b Pascoe	0
	B 3, l-b 6, n-b 12	21	N-b 3	3

1/15 2/15 3/206 4/246 5/265   383   1/11 2/12 3/28 4/28 5/28   69
6/273 7/306 8/372 9/383   6/33 7/33 8/65 9/69

Bowling: *First Innings*—Pascoe 26-4-112-3; Gilmour 17-4-44-1; Holland 33.5-7-94-4; Walters 12-3-25-1; Hourn 22-3-87-1; Chappell 1-1-0-0. *Second Innings*—Pascoe 12.3-6-18-7; Gilmour 6-2-5-0; Holland 11-3-19-2; Hourn 4-0-24-0.

Umpires: R. G. Harris and A. S. Ward.

WESTERN AUSTRALIA v QUEENSLAND

At Perth, February 23, 24, 25, 26. Drawn. Western Australia 11 pts, Queensland 9 pts. Bowlers struggled on an easy-paced wicket and, with 1,306 runs scored in the first three innings for the loss of only 25 wickets, there was little likelihood of a definite result. Broad opened brightly before being brilliantly caught by McEwan; Wessels played solidly yet attractively for 93 in three and a half hours. Pace bowler Alderman maintained good line and length to claim six of the nine wickets to fall. In reply Shipperd and Langer, batting fluently, put together a record shield partnership for Western Australia of 204 for the second wicket. McEwan followed with an effortless display for 177, his partnership with Wright adding 178 in 142 minutes. Queensland lost two wickets before the close but sound batting on the final day put a draw beyond doubt, Kent hitting an entertaining 79 off 83 balls.

Queensland

W. R. Broad c McEwan b Alderman	33	– b Porter	14
K. C. Wessels c O'Neill b Alderman	93	– b Alderman	7
M. F. Kent b Porter	9	– b Penter	79
*G. J. Cosier c Wright b O'Neill	54	– (5) c Penter b Alderman	12
T. V. Hohns c Marsh b Alderman	57	– (6) c Watson b Mann	60
P. H. Carlson c and b Mann	39	– (7) lbw b Mann	38
A. D. Parker lbw b Alderman	44	– (8) lbw b Watson	44
†R. B. Phillips not out	13	– (4) c Wright b Watson	59
D. C. Schuller c Wright b Alderman	5	– c Penter b Porter	37
J. R. Thomson b Alderman	2	– not out	40
C. G. Rackemann not out	2	– b Porter	3
B 3, l-b 4, n-b 2	9	B 1, l-b 3, w 3, n-b 3	10

1/50 2/68 3/177 4/201   (9 wkts dec.) 330   1/21 2/33 3/140 4/172 5/186   403
5/271 6/304 7/309 8/319 9/321   6/254 7/291 8/344 9/370

Bowling: *First Innings*—Alderman 24–4–80–6; Watson 13–3–61–0; Porter 29–7–76–1; Mann 18–5–43–1; O'Neill 5–0–29–1; Penter 11–2–32–0. *Second Innings*—Alderman 30–7–104–2; Watson 17–1–74–2; Porter 22.2–3–78–3; Mann 19–2–68–2; Penter 18–4–66–1; Langer 1–0–3–0.

Western Australia

G. Shipperd c Schuller b Hohns	104	– not out	4
G. R. Marsh c Phillips b Thomson	2	– not out	7
R. S. Langer c Wessels b Rackemann	102		
M. D. O'Neill c Cosier b Rackemann	51		
K. S. McEwan c Broad b Carlson	177		
C. E. Penter c Kent b Rackemann	0		
†K. J. Wright not out	88		
*A. L. Mann not out	10		
B 10, l-b 9, w 3, n-b 17	39	W 1	1

1/17 2/221 3/231 4/351   (6 wkts dec.) 573   (no wkt) 12
5/369 6/547

T. M. Alderman, G. G. Watson and G. D. Porter did not bat.

Bowling: *First Innings*—Thomson 28–4–91–1; Schuller 20–3–80–0; Rackemann 25–9–69–3; Carlson 33–6–114–1; Cosier 20–2–64–0; Hohns 29–6–106–1; Broad 4–2–10–0. *Second Innings*—Cosier 2–1–1–0; Broad 2–0–4–0; Kent 1–0–3–0; Parker 1–0–3–0; Wessels 1–1–0–0.

Umpires: P. McConnell and D. G. Weser.

QUEENSLAND v SOUTH AUSTRALIA

At Brisbane, February 29, March 1, 2, 3. South Australia won by six wickets. South Australia 15 pts. Queensland 5 pts. Batting first, Queensland were comfortably placed at 109 for three at lunch but a collapse followed Cosier's dismissal, with Attenborough the chief destroyer. Thomson bowled with much hostility as South Australia slumped to 28 for four and, despite resistance from Inverarity and Sleep, he took all six wickets to fall on the first day. Sleep carried on to 91 and the South Australian innings closed 10 ahead. Queensland again began well with a fine 89 from Wessels but the last five wickets fell for only 27 runs. Inverarity, deputising for the injured Darling, opening with 52 and his stand with Nash put South Australia well on the way to the victory which boosted their Shield prospects.

Queensland

K. C. Wessels b Mallett	29	– c Robertson b Mallett	89
W. R. Broad c Robertson b Attenborough	17	– c Crowe b Attenborough	24
M. F. Kent b Hammond	30	– c Nash b Attenborough	0
*G. J. Cosier c Robertson b Attenborough	43	– b Mallett	9
T. V. Hohns c Crowe b Attenborough	8	– c Robertson b Attenborough	23
P. H. Carlson b Mallett	15	– c Robertson b Attenborough	39
A. D. Parker c Nash b Attenborough	0	– c and b Mallett	0
†R. B. Phillips c Robertson b Mallett	10	– c Prior b Mallett	3
D. C. Schuller c Inverarity b Attenborough	0	– c Prior b Mallett	5
J. R. Thomson c Inverarity b Attenborough	9	– not out	19
C. G. Rackemann not out	0	– c Robertson b Attenborough	0
N-b 1	1	B 4, l-b 2, w 1, n-b 4	11

1/35 2/67 3/93 4/124 5/127   **162**   1/46 2/46 3/65 4/133 5/195   **222**
6/130 7/147 8/152 9/162   6/195 7/196 8/202 9/207

Bowling: *First Innings*—Prior 6–1–24–0; Attenborough 18–6–57–6; Hammond 7–3–12–1; Mallett 19.2–3–68–3. *Second Innings*—Prior 9–0–32–0; Attenborough 34.3–13–84–5; Mallett 36–12–67–5; Sleep 12–3–28–0.

South Australia

W. M. Darling c Phillips b Thomson	0		
J. E. Nash c Phillips b Thomson	0	– (1) c Kent b Hohns	34
*I. M. Chappell c Cosier b Thomson	0	– c and b Hohns	17
R. J. Inverarity lbw b Thomson	45	– (2) lbw b Thomson	52
J. J. Crowe c Phillips b Thomson	3	– (4) not out	61
P. R. Sleep c Phillips b Schuller	91	– (5) b Rackemann	19
G. R. Attenborough c Phillips b Thomson	0		
J. R. Hammond b Rackemann	6	– (6) not out	11
†T. J. Robertson c Cosier b Rackemann	2		
A. A. Mallett lbw b Schuller	11		
W. Prior not out	0		
B 1, l-b 4, n-b 9	14	B 6, l-b 2, n-b 11	19

1/2 2/3 3/4 4/28 5/97   **172**   1/76 2/103 3/141   (4 wkts) **213**
6/97 7/151 8/152 9/165   4/180

Bowling: *First Innings*—Thomson 21–4–45–6; Rackemann 20–6–43–2; Carlson 13–5–17–0; Schuller 18.5–5–32–2; Cosier 5–1–14–0; Hohns 2–1–7–0. *Second Innings*—Thomson 20–8–41–1; Rackemann 15–5–37–1; Carlson 7–1–21–0; Schuller 14–6–28–0; Cosier 6–1–20–0; Hohns 17–2–47–2.

Umpires: C. E. Harvey and M. W. Johnson.

SOUTH AUSTRALIA v VICTORIA

At Adelaide, March, 7, 8, 9, 10. Victoria won by 83 runs. Victoria 19 pts, South Australia 6 pts. With little more than two hours remaining on the final afternoon of the season, Victoria won this absorbing match which determined the outcome of the Sheffield Shield. When the visitors were asked to bat first, Matthews scored a painstaking century in nearly five and a half hours and contributed only 12 to his partnership with Moss of 125, which lifted Victoria to 258 for five on the first day. Laughlin and Scholes batted aggressively before the declaration. Chappell overcame the early loss of both openers with a masterly century before being run out, and Sleep made amends for any misunderstanding by ensuring the vital bonus points which kept South Australia ahead in the Shield placings with 104, including ten 4s, in four hours. Needing an outright win to overtake South Australia, Victoria hit out lustily, Laughlin scoring 51 in an hour and Scholes again passing 50. An overnight declaration set South Australia a target of 243, which Inverarity and Chappell had comfortably reduced by

90 in even time at lunch. But Higgs – without a wicket from 25 overs in the first innings – now produced an amazing spell in which he captured five wickets, including Chappell's in the first over after lunch, for 9 runs off 36 balls. Graf and Walker were effective foils to Higgs' leg-spin as the South Australian batting was swept aside and the Sheffield Shield retained by Victoria.

Victoria

R. G. Matthews b Attenborough	112		
D. J. Broad c Robertson b Hammond	18	– (3) c Attenborough b Hammond	2
*D. F. Whatmore c Sleep b Mallett	3	– (2) run out	6
J. K. Moss c and b Hammond	85	– c Inverarity b Prior	14
J. W. Scholes c Zadow b Mallett	65	– not out	58
T. J. Laughlin not out	73	– c Crowe b Mallett	51
†R. D. Robinson (did not bat)		– (1) b Hammond	32
S. F. Graf (did not bat)		– (7) c Prior b Mallett	15
B 1, l-b 5, n-b 3	9	L-b 4	4

1/59 2/78 3/203   (5 wkts dec.) 365   1/36 2/38 3/43   (6 wkts dec.) 182
4/235 5/365   4/69 5/147 6/182

M. H. N. Walker, J. F. Leehane and J. D. Higgs did not bat.

Bowling: *First Innings*—Prior 18–5–41–0; Attenborough 31–5–122–1; Mallett 35.2–12–101–2; Hammond 24–10–77–2; Sleep 2–0–15–0. *Second Innings*—Prior 15–0–55–1; Attenborough 3–0–19–0; Mallett 4.3–0–24–2; Hammond 15–3–65–2; Inverarity 2–0–15–0.

South Australia

J. E. Nash c Graf b Leehane	2	– c Broad b Graf	6
R. J. Inverarity c Whatmore b Walker	0	– c Broad b Higgs	58
*I. M. Chappell run out	112	– c Robinson b Higgs	32
J. J. Crowe c Whatmore b Walker	7	– st Robinson b Higgs	0
R. J. Zadow c Robinson b Walker	43	– c Broad b Walker	18
P. R. Sleep b Leehane	104	– b Higgs	0
J. R. Hammond b Graf	13	– c Robinson b Higgs	8
†T. J. Robertson c Broad b Graf	0	– c Whatmore b Higgs	15
G. R. Attenborough c Scholes b Graf	8	– (10) b Graf	3
A. A. Mallett lbw b Graf	0	– (9) b Graf	15
W. Prior not out	9	– not out	0
L-b 6	6	L-b 5	5

1/0 2/6 3/46 4/135 5/189   304   1/20 2/90 3/101 4/102 5/108   160
6/229 7/235 8/251 9/251   6/118 7/130 8/152 9/160

Bowling: *First Innings*—Leehane 16.3–1–42–2; Walker 40–9–93–3; Graf 32–8–71–4; Higgs 25–5–85–0; Laughlin 5–2–7–0. *Second Innings*—Leehane 6–0–26–0; Walker 15–6–20–1; Graf 15–1–50–3; Higgs 20.1–7–57–6; Laughlin 3–1–2–0.

Umpires: P. M. Cronin and A. R. Crafter.

SHEFFIELD SHIELD WINNERS

1892-93	Victoria	1901-02	New South Wales
1893-94	South Australia	1902-03	New South Wales
1894-95	Victoria	1903-04	New South Wales
1895-96	New South Wales	1904-05	New South Wales
1896-97	New South Wales	1905-06	New South Wales
1897-98	Victoria	1906-07	New South Wales
1898-99	Victoria	1907-08	Victoria
1899-1900	New South Wales	1908-09	New South Wales
1900-01	Victoria	1909-10	South Australia

1910-11	New South Wales	1949-50	New South Wales
1911-12	New South Wales	1950-51	Victoria
1912-13	South Australia	1951-52	New South Wales
1913-14	New South Wales	1952-53	South Australia
1914-15	Victoria	1953-54	New South Wales
1915-19	No competition	1954-55	New South Wales
1919-20	New South Wales	1955-56	New South Wales
1920-21	New South Wales	1956-57	New South Wales
1921-22	Victoria	1957-58	New South Wales
1922-23	New South Wales	1958-59	New South Wales
1923-24	Victoria	1959-60	New South Wales
1924-25	Victoria	1960-61	New South Wales
1925-26	New South Wales	1961-62	New South Wales
1926-27	South Australia	1962-63	Victoria
1927-28	Victoria	1963-64	South Australia
1928-29	New South Wales	1964-65	New South Wales
1929-30	Victoria	1965-66	New South Wales
1930-31	Victoria	1966-67	Victoria
1931-32	New South Wales	1967-68	Western Australia
1932-33	New South Wales	1968-69	South Australia
1933-34	Victoria	1969-70	Victoria
1934-35	Victoria	1970-71	South Australia
1935-36	South Australia	1971-72	Western Australia
1936-37	Victoria	1972-73	Western Australia
1937-38	New South Wales	1973-74	Victoria
1938-39	South Australia	1974-75	Western Australia
1939-40	New South Wales	1975-76	South Australia
1940-46	No competition	1976-77	Western Australia
1946-47	Victoria	1977-78	Western Australia
1947-48	Western Australia	1978-79	Victoria
1948-49	New South Wales	1979-80	Victoria

New South Wales have won the Shield 36 times, Victoria 24, South Australia 11, Western Australia 7, Queensland 0, Tasmania 0.

CRICKET IN SOUTH AFRICA, 1979-80

By PETER SICHEL

Transvaal were again dominant, convincingly winning both major competitions. They had the material and could put it all together when necessary to achieve the success they deserved. Their ability was best illustrated against Western Province at Newlands where, chasing a total of 378, they were in trouble at 72 for five, having lost both R. G. Pollock and C. E. B. Rice. However, splendid hundreds from H. B. Fotheringham and A. J. Kourie took them to 451 and saved the match. The side played in a positive and professional manner, splendidly led by their popular and able captain, D. D. Dyer.

Although falling short of his previous year's success, Pollock nevertheless made his runs with power, grace and authority. Rice had an outstanding season with both bat and ball, clearly demonstrating his world-class capabilities. Fotheringham and K. A. McKenzie were fine strikers of the ball and, with wicket-keeper-batsman R. W. Jennings and all-rounder Kourie, made major contributions to a team that would perform creditably at international level.

Runners-up in both competitions were Western Province, who did not perform to their true potential. With E. J. Barlow back in command, much was expected from a side full of ability. Barlow himself was often the key figure, either with bat or ball, and his captaincy was always positive — striving for outright victory at the risk of defeat rather than settling for a colourless draw. A. J. Lamb was the outstanding batsman in this side, passing 50 on seven occasions. But his innings were most notable for the delight he gave spectators with his magnificent stroke-play. P. N. Kirsten also played some fine innings, but failed to produce a century. L. Seeff demonstrated a fine technique, and was rewarded with a hundred against Transvaal. Of the bowlers, both G. S. le Roux and leg-spinner D. L. Hobson failed to produce their best form, although le Roux did bowl with fire in Salisbury and Port Elizabeth late in the season. P. D. Swart and S. D. Bruce revealed glimpses of their ability, while G. Pfuhl, in his farewell season, again showed his class.

Natal fell away after an encouraging start and eventually finished a disappointing third. There were, however, some attractive individual performances, notably from P. H. Williams and the evergreen C. P. Wilkins, who had probably his best season. A. Barrow played well, while "Tich" Smith had his moments. Once again V. A. P. van der Bijl bowled magnificently and his ability to make runs lower down the order was of enormous value. M. J. Procter, too, performed consistently well in his 25th consecutive season.

Eastern Province at times looked a very good side, particularly when defeating Natal at Port Elizabeth; yet their batsmen were too often inconsistent and their bowling lacked penetration. After his outstanding 1978-79 season, W. K. Watson suffered mid-season injuries which took the edge off his bowling. A. L. Wilmot was their best batsman, playing several innings of considerable merit. D. J. Brickett again demonstrated his value as an all-rounder, with highly creditable performances throughout the season. I. Foulkes, from Border, adjusted admirably to the higher standards demanded by the Currie Cup competition.

Zimbabwe-Rhodesia struggled for most of their last season in a South African domestic competition. They were without B. F. Davison who was assisting Tasmania in the Sheffield Shield; S. D. Robertson, their stylish left-hander, was out through injury for most of the season, and J. G. Heron, their backbone for several years, suffered a complete reversal of form. However, their captain D. A. G. Fletcher had a fine season and led the side with distinction.

Recently promoted Northern Transvaal struggled to adjust to the sterner competition but, despite finishing bottom of the table, were in no way disgraced. The side showed spirit and will almost certainly improve. Individually, players such as R. C. Ontong, P. D. de Vaal and A. H. Jordaan played well, ably supported by wicket-keeper T. Quirk and W. F. Morris, who bowled his off-breaks with accuracy and guile.

All in all, this proved to be a thoroughly interesting season, again demonstrating the high standard of cricket in the Republic. Many would agree that, given the opportunity, South Africa would perform with distinction against any of the Test-playing countries of the world.

SAB CURRIE CUP, 1979-80

	Played	Won	Lost	Drawn	Bonus points Batting	Bowling	Total points*
Transvaal (1)	8	6 (5)	0 (0)	2 (3)	38 (28)	33 (37)	131 (115)
Western Province (2) ...	8	4 (3)	1 (3)	3 (2)	34 (19)	32 (28)	*103 (77)
Natal (3)	8	3 (2)	3 (2)	2 (4)	24 (14)	33 (30)	*81 (69)
Eastern Province (5)	8	3 (1)	3 (5)	2 (2)	19 (13)	30 (23)	*76 (46)
Zimbabwe-Rhodesia (4) .	8	1 (1)	3 (2)	4 (5)	11 (8)	35 (34)	56 (52)
Northern Transvaal	8	0	6	2	7	30	*34

* 6 points were deducted from Natal and 3 each from Western Province, Eastern Province and Northern Transvaal for their slow over-rates.

(1978-79 figures in parentheses.)

CASTLE BOWL, 1979-80

	Played	Won	Lost	Drawn	Bonus points Batting	Bowling	Total points
Natal "B"	6	5	0	1	20	27	97
Western Province "B"	6	5	1	0	6	29	85
Border	6	3	2	1	7	25	62
Orange Free State	6	2	3	1	11	29	60
Transvaal "B"	6	2	2	2	17	22	59
Zimbabwe-Rhodesia "B" ..	6	1	2	3	11	20	41
Eastern Province "B"	6	0	4	2	16	21	37
Griqualand West	6	0	4	2	9	25	34

CURRIE CUP WINNERS

Winners	Year	Winners	Year
Transvaal	1889-90	Transvaal	1926-27
Griqualand West	1890-91	Transvaal	1929-30
Western Province	1892-93	Western Province	1931-32
Western Province	1893-94	Natal	1933-34
Transvaal	1894-95	Transvaal	1934-35
Western Province	1896-97	Natal	1936-37
Western Province	1897-98	Natal/Transvaal (Tied)	1937-38
Transvaal	1902-03	Natal	1946-47
Transvaal	1903-04	Natal	1947-48
Transvaal	1904-05	Transvaal	1950-51
Transvaal	1906-07	Natal	1951-52
Western Province	1908-09	Western Province	1952-53
Natal	1910-11	Natal	1954-55
Natal	1912-13	Western Province	1955-56
Western Province	1920-21	Transvaal	1958-59
Transvaal/Natal/W. Prov. (Tied)	1921-22	Natal	1959-60
Transvaal	1923-24	Natal	1960-61
Transvaal	1925-26	Natal	1962-63

Winners	Year	Winners	Year
Natal	1963-64	Transvaal	1972-73
Natal/Transvaal (Tied)	1965-66	Natal	1973-74
Natal	1966-67	Western Province	1974-75
Natal	1967-68	Natal	1975-76
Transvaal	1968-69	Natal	1976-77
Transvaal/W. Province (Tied)	1969-70	Western Province	1977-78
Transvaal	1970-71	Transvaal	1978-79
Transvaal	1971-72	Transvaal	1979-80

FIRST-CLASS AVERAGES, 1979-80

BATTING

(Qualification: 400 runs, average 30.00)

	Matches	Innings	Not Outs	Runs	Highest Innings	Average
R. G. Pollock (*Transvaal*)	9	13	2	739	168	67.18
B. J. Whitfield (*Natal "B"*)	5	9	2	444	145*	63.42
A. J. Lamb (*W. Province*)	8	13	2	594	99	54.00
C. E. B. Rice (*Transvaal*)	9	13	3	530	121*	53.00
C. P. Wilkins (*Natal*)	8	14	0	692	150	49.42
K. A. McKenzie (*Transvaal*)	8	11	2	425	91	47.22
P. N. Kirsten (*W. Province*)	8	14	2	551	93	45.91
D. R. Turner (*Natal "B"*)	6	11	1	443	82*	44.30
H. R. Fotheringham (*Transvaal*)	9	13	2	476	166	43.27
R. J. East (*Orange Free State*)	6	11	0	453	108	41.18
A. L. Wilmot (*Eastern Province*)	8	15	3	474	89*	39.50
G. C. Wallace (*Zim.-Rhod.*)	6	12	1	427	111	38.81
D. C. McKenna (*Border*)	6	11	0	412	77	37.45
R. M. Bentley (*Zim.-Rhod.*)	8	16	0	578	122	36.12
T. W. Dunk (*Zim.-Rhod.*)	7	14	1	446	98*	34.30
P. H. Williams (*Natal*)	8	14	1	446	118*	34.30
A. J. S. Smith (*Natal*)	8	14	1	420	150*	32.30
L. Seeff (*W. Province*)	9	16	1	468	114	31.20
M. J. Procter (*Natal*)	8	14	0	420	110	30.00

* *Signifies not out.*

BOWLING

(Qualification: 20 wickets, Average 30.00)

	Overs	Maidens	Runs	Wickets	Average
C. E. B. Rice (*Transvaal*)	256	99	506	43	11.76
V. A. P. van der Bijl (*Natal*)	278.3	94	503	37	13.59
J. During (*W. Province "B"*)	221.3	80	343	25	13.72
E. Schmidt (*OFS*)	153	31	403	27	14.92
E. S. Gordon (*W. Province "B"*)	164.4	43	367	24	15.29
G. E. McMillan (*Transvaal*)	254	66	583	38	15.34
I. Ebrahim (*Natal "B"*)	289	99	601	39	15.41
O. Henry (*W. Province "B"*)	192	78	341	21	16.23
E. J. Barlow (*W. Province*)	178	51	411	25	16.44

	Overs	Maidens	Runs	Wickets	Average
R. W. Hanley (*Transvaal*)	154.1	36	365	22	16.59
G. L. Ackermann (*OFS*)	186	49	482	29	16.62
G. D. Boucher (*Border*)	140.5	29	402	24	16.75
G. L. Hayes (*Border*)	181.4	54	413	24	17.20
G. S. le Roux (*W. Province*)	243.2	71	621	36	17.25
M. J. Procter (*Natal*)	300.4	80	870	45	19.33
W. F. Morris (*N. Transvaal*)	159.4	39	470	24	19.58
D. J. Brickett (*E. Province*)	208.1	61	493	25	19.72
M. K. van Vuuren (*E. Province*) ...	297.2	66	836	40	20.90
P. D. Swart (*W. Province*)	192	46	444	21	21.14
D. R. Neilson (*Transvaal*)	224	72	509	23	22.13
K. R. Cooper (*Natal*)	179	43	510	21	24.28
P. H. L. Wilson (*N. Transvaal*) ..	182.1	44	495	20	24.75
I. R. Tayfield (*Natal "B"*)	239.3	78	590	23	25.65
R. L. S. Armitage (*E. Province*) ...	229.5	65	633	24	26.37
R. H. Kaschula (*Zim.-Rhod.*)	311.2	89	852	32	26.62
A. J. Kourie (*Transvaal*)	292.3	85	745	27	27.59
V. R. Hogg (*Zim.-Rhod.*)	215	65	554	20	27.70
J. D. Ogilvie (*E. Province*)	304.2	69	863	31	27.83
R. Engelbrecht (*Griqualand West*) .	211	60	606	21	28.85
D. L. Hobson (*W. Province*)	278.5	77	754	26	29.00
P. B. Clift (*Zim.-Rhod.*)	323	86	862	29	29.72

SAB CURRIE CUP, 1979-80

At Police Ground, Salisbury, October 26, 27, 28. Zimbabwe-Rhodesia won by three wickets. Northern Transvaal 267 (R. C. Ontong 60, H. W. Raath 51 not out) and 239; Zimbabwe-Rhodesia 224 (T. W. Dunk 51; H. W. Raath four for 34) and 284 for seven (R. D. Brown 89, D. A. G. Fletcher 68). *Zimbabwe-Rhodesia 16 pts, Northern Transvaal 7 pts.*

At Queen's Ground, Bulawayo, November 3, 4, 5. Transvaal won by 84 runs. Transvaal 292 for nine dec. (K. A. McKenzie 79, A. J. Kourie 53, R. G. Pollock 40; R. H. Kaschula four for 75, D. A. G. Fletcher four for 82) and 209 for five dec. (R. V. Jennings 70, D. D. Dyer 58, R. G. Pollock 41 not out); Zimbabwe-Rhodesia 225 (R. D. Brown 68) and 192 (J. G. Heron 59; R. W. Hanley six for 52). *Transvaal 18 pts, Zimbabwe-Rhodesia 7 pts.*

At Berea Park, Pretoria, November 16, 17, 19. Transvaal won by nine wickets. Transvaal 276 (H. R. Fotheringham 78, R. V. Jennings 55; W. F. Morris five for 78, P. D. de Vaal four for 89) and 61 for one; Northern Transvaal 79 (C. E. B. Rice four for 6) and 255 (K. D. Dawson 83, P. D. de Vaal 70 not out; A. A. During four for 77). *Transvaal 19 pts, Northern Transvaal 4 pts.*

At Kingsmead, Durban, November 24, 25, 26. Natal won by four wickets. Western Province 163 (L. Seeff 46; K. R. Cooper four for 46) and 223 (S. D. Bruce 60, P. N. Kirsten 49, A. J. Lamb 40; V. A. P. van der Bijl five for 44, K. R. Cooper four for 56); Natal 197 (C. P. Wilkins 50; E. J. Barlow five for 51, P. D. Swart four for 46) and 191 for six (A. Barrow 111 not out; E. J. Barlow four for 32). *Natal 16 pts, Western Province 5 pts.*

At Berea Park, Pretoria, December 7, 8, 10. Natal won by an innings and 97 runs. Northern Transvaal 161 (R. C. Ontong 63; M. J. Procter four for 65) and 205 (G. W. Jones 45, P. D. de Vaal 41; J. S. Muil six for 58); Natal 463 for eight dec. (A. J. S. Smith 150 not out, P. H. Williams 118, C. P. Wilkins 67; W. F. Morris seven for 110). *Natal 18 pts, Northern Transvaal 3 pts.*

At The Wanderers, Johannesburg, December 15, 17, 18. Transvaal won by six wickets. Natal 298 (A. Barrow 75, M. J. Procter 58, V. A. P. van der Bijl 55) and 100 (C. E. B. Rice six for 15); Transvaal 227 (C. E. B. Rice 95, R. V. Jennings 52; V. A. P. van der Bijl four for 64) and 175 for four (R. G. Pollock 93 not out). *Transvaal 16 pts, Natal 6 pts.*

At Newlands, Cape Town, December 15, 17, 18. Western Province won by seven wickets. Eastern Province 217 (K. W. Gradwell 48, R. L. S. Armitage 40; P. D. Swart four for 43) and 269 (A. L. Wilmot 86, D. J. Brickett 72); Western Province 307 for nine dec. (E. J. Barlow 136, A. J. Lamb 75) and 184 for three (L. Seeff 94). *Western Province 18 pts, Eastern Province 4 pts.*

At Newlands, Cape Town, December 26, 27, 28. Western Province won by an innings and 84 runs. Western Province 352 for eight dec. (P. N. Kirsten 93, G. S. le Roux 70 not out, A. J. Lamb 51, S. D. Bruce 49); Northern Transvaal 152 (P. D. Swart four for 8) and 116 (G. S. le Roux five for 32). *Western Province 23 pts, Northern Transvaal 4 pts.*

At St George's Park, Port Elizabeth, December 26, 27, 28. Eastern Province won by one wicket. Natal 350 for eight dec. (C. P. Wilkins 132, M. J. Procter 110; D. J. Brickett six for 71) and 128 (D. J. Brickett four for 32); Eastern Province 238 (R. L. S. Armitage 75, I. Foulkes 45; V. A. P. van der Bijl five for 37) and 241 for nine (R. G. Fensham 51; M. J. Procter four for 44, V. A. P. van der Bijl four for 60). *Eastern Province 14 pts, Natal 9 pts.*

At The Wanderers, Johannesburg, December 26, 27, 28. Transvaal won by an innings and 34 runs. Zimbabwe-Rhodesia 121 and 183 (R. M. Bentley 51); Transvaal 338 for seven dec. (H. R. Fotheringham 127, D. D. Dyer 50, R. G. Pollock 47, G. E. McMillan 40 not out). *Transvaal 20 pts, Zimbabwe-Rhodesia 4 pts.*

At Newlands, Cape Town, December 31, January 1, 2. Drawn. Western Province 378 for eight dec. (L. Seeff 114, A. J. Lamb 95, G. S. le Roux 56 not out; N. Minnaar four for 71) and 198 for two (P. N. Kirsten 83 not out, A. J. Lamb 50 not out); Transvaal 451 (H. R. Fotheringham 166, A. J. Kourie 127 not out, K. A. McKenzie 57; D. L. Hobson four for 129). *Western Province 9 pts, Transvaal 5 pts.*

At Kingsmead, Durban, January 1, 2, 3. Drawn. Natal 332 (V. A. P. van der Bijl 87, A. J. S. Smith 60, P. H. Williams 46; R. D. Jackman four for 62) and 161 for six dec.; Zimbabwe-Rhodesia 234 (R. M. Bentley 79, P. B. Clift 51; M. J. Procter five for 65) and 198 for eight (R. M. Bentley 74). *Natal 8 pts, Zimbabwe-Rhodesia 5 pts.*

At St George's Park, Port Elizabeth, January 1, 2, 3. Drawn. Northern Transvaal 266 (E. Muntingh 72, R. C. Ontong 70; R. L. S. Armitage four for 47) and 337 (A. H. Jordaan 122, K. G. Motley 97); Eastern Province 397 for six dec. (G. Cook 172, I. Foulkes 101, A. L. Wilmot 45). *Eastern Province 13 pts, Northern Transvaal 5 pts.*

At Berea Park, Pretoria, January 18, 19, 21. Eastern Province won by five wickets. Northern Transvaal 71 (D. J. Brickett five for 17) and 194 (K. G. Motley 50; W. K. Watson five for 48); Eastern Province 186 for seven dec. (G. Cook 56) and 69 for five. *Eastern Province 17 pts, Northern Transvaal 5 pts.*

At Kingsmead, Durban, January 26, 27, 28. Natal won by an innings and 101 runs. Natal 337 for eight dec. (C. P. Wilkins 83, P. H. Williams 61, A. Barrow 58, M. J. Procter 40; G. W. Jones four for 69); Northern Transvaal 76 (M. J. Procter seven for 29) and 160. *Natal 22 pts, Northern Transvaal 4 pts.*

At Police Ground, Salisbury, January 26, 27, 28. Western Province won by nine wickets. Zimbabwe-Rhodesia 186 (R. M. Bentley 60; G. S. le Roux four for 49) and 177 (E. J. Barlow four for 25); Western Province 330 (L. Seeff 71, A. J. Lamb 54, P. D. Swart 52) and 34 for one. *Western Province 22 pts, Zimbabwe-Rhodesia 6 pts.*

At St George's Park, Port Elizabeth, February 1, 2, 4. Drawn. Zimbabwe-Rhodesia 254 (R. M. Bentley 122, D. A. G. Fletcher 79 not out; D. J. Brickett four for 38) and 206 (T. W. Dunk 40); Eastern Province 219 (R. L. S. Armitage 82, I. Foulkes 49) and 183 for eight (A. L. Wilmot 40). *Zimbabwe-Rhodesia 8 pts, Eastern Province 6 pts.*

At The Wanderers, Johannesburg, February 1, 2, 4. Drawn. Transvaal 314 for six dec. (C. E. B. Rice 121 not out, K. A. McKenzie 60, A. J. Kourie 46) and 231 for five dec. (S. J. Cook 68, R. V. Jennings 42); Western Province 246 (P. N. Kirsten 69, P. D. Swart 61) and 167 for nine (A. J. Lamb 64; C. E. B. Rice four for 29). *Transvaal 9 pts, Western Province 6 pts.*

At Berea Park, Pretoria, February 8, 9, 11. Drawn. Zimbabwe-Rhodesia 277 for eight dec. (T. W. Dunk 90, D. A. G. Fletcher 54; P. H. L. Wilson five for 36) and 264 for eight dec. (S. D. Robertson 55, J. A. Carse 44, T. W. Dunk 43; W. F. Morris six for 105); Northern Transvaal 320 for seven dec. (A. H. Jordaan 70, A. M. Ferreira 68, P. D. de Vaal 64) and 86 for eight (R. H. Kaschula four for 24, P. B. Clift four for 56). *Northern Transvaal 5 pts, Zimbabwe-Rhodesia 4 pts.*

At Kingsmead, Durban, February 9, 10, 11. Transvaal won by ten wickets. Transvaal 362 for seven dec. (R. G. Pollock 168, C. E. B. Rice 110; M. J. Procter four for 115) and 32 for no wkt; Natal 150 (A. Barrow 55; A. J. Kourie four for 38) and 243 (C. P. Wilkins 58, V. A. P. van der Bijl 50, M. J. Procter 45; A. J. Kourie five for 88). *Transvaal 23 pts, Natal 3 pts.*

At St George's Park, Port Elizabeth, February 22, 23, 25. Western Province won by six wickets. Eastern Province 285 (A. L. Wilmot 89 not out, I. Foulkes 67, G. Cook 47) and 144 (G. S. le Roux six for 33); Western Province 219 for five dec. (P. D. Swart 68 not out, P. N. Kirsten 57, H. M. Ackerman 51 not out) and 211 for four (A. J. Lamb 99). *Western Province 15 pts, Eastern Province 5 pts.*

At The Wanderers, Johannesburg, March 7, 8. Transvaal won by an innings and 197 runs. Eastern Province 94 (C. E. B. Rice six for 28) and 46; Transvaal 337 (R. G. Pollock 157, K. A. McKenzie 91; M. K. van Vuuren four for 94, J. D. Ogilvie five for 119). *Transvaal 21 pts, Eastern Province 5 pts.*

At Newlands, Cape Town, March 7, 8, 9. Drawn. Natal 146 (D. L. Hobson four for 37) and 235 for six (C. P. Wilkins 150); Western Province 227 (E. J. Barlow 51, P. N. Kirsten 41). *Western Province 8 pts, Natal 5 pts.*

At Police Ground, Salisbury, March 15, 16, 17. Eastern Province won by seven wickets. Zimbabwe-Rhodesia 261 (T. W. Dunk 98 not out, D. A. G. Fletcher 41; R. L. S. Armitage five for 41) and 76 (R. L. S. Armitage five for 25, J. D. Ogilvie four for 28); Eastern Province 201 (D. J. Brickett 58 not out; P. B. Clift four for 75) and 137 for three (K. P. Reid 52 not out, A. L. Wilmot 47 not out). *Eastern Province 15 pts, Zimbabwe-Rhodesia 6 pts.*

SAB CASTLE BOWL, 1979-80

At The Wanderers, Johannesburg, November 2, 3, 5. Transvaal "B" won by three wickets. Orange Free State 173 (T. A. Lloyd 79 not out; N. Minnaar five for 61) and 174 (R. A. le Roux 69); Transvaal "B" 221 (M. S. Venter 53; G. L. Ackermann four for 48) and 127 for seven (A. H. Drake 41 not out; G. L. Ackermann four for 27). *Transvaal "B" 17 pts, Orange Free State 3 pts.*

At The Wanderers, Johannesburg, November 17, 19, 20. Transvaal "B" won by 145 runs. Transvaal "B" 369 for nine dec. (G. E. McMillan 91, N. Minnaar 78, R. F. Pienaar 58) and 159 for eight dec. (L. J. Barnard 51 not out); Eastern Province "B" 210 (J. W. Furstenburg 57; G. E. McMillan four for 49) and 173 (R. J. B. Whyte 41). *Transvaal "B" 22 pts, Eastern Province "B" 5 pts.*

At Constantia, Cape Town, November 17, 19, 20. Natal "B" won by 95 runs. Natal "B" 226 (K. D. Verdoorn 74, B. J. Whitfield 61; E. S. Gordon four for 55) and 114 (J. During four for 21); Western Province "B" 94 (E. Hodkinson four for 35, M. Thompson five for 36) and 161 (M. Thompson four for 48). *Natal "B" 18 pts, Western Province "B" 5 pts.*

At The Ramblers, Bloemfontein, November 23, 24, 26. Drawn. Natal "B" 262 (K. D. Verdoorn 91, D. R. Turner 44; E. Schmidt five for 47) and 331 for five dec. (D. R. Turner 82 not out, F. B. Hill 67, N. P. Daniels 55, B. J. Whitfield 55, K. D. Verdoorn 45); Orange Free State 337 (R. J. East 103, D. P. le Roux 94, G. L. Ackermann 40 not out) and 155 for seven. *Orange Free State 9 pts, Natal "B" 7 pts.*

At de Beers Ground, Kimberley, November 22, 23, 24. Drawn. Eastern Province "B" 225 (G. S. Cowley 113; K. McLaren four for 34) and 253 for two dec. (J. W. Furstenburg 127 not out, K. W. Gradwell 102); Griqualand West 232 (D. Nicholson 41, A. P. Beukes 40) and 228 for eight dec. (D. N. Martin 59, M. J. D. Doherty 55, A. P. Beukes 40; M. K. van Vuuren four for 54). *Eastern Province "B" 7 pts, Griqualand West 7 pts.*

At Newlands, Cape Town, November 22, 23, 24. Western Province "B" won by 153 runs. Western Province "B" 164 (J. D. du Toit 52; I. A. Greig five for 60) and 254 (A. Green 47, A. P. Kuiper 46); Border 116 (A. P. Kuiper four for 7) and 149 (O. Henry four for 35). *Western Province "B" 15 pts, Border 5 pts.*

At Triangle, November 17, 18, 19. Drawn. Zimbabwe-Rhodesia "B" 259 (E. F. Parker 82, G. E. Peckover 52, M. M. Benkenstein 47) and 182 for seven dec. (G. C. Wallace 47, A. J. McCallum 40); Border 282 (M. J. McGill 59, D. C. McKenna 51, I. D. Harty 42) and 79 for nine (T. D. Coughlan five for 16). *Border 4 pts, Zimbabwe-Rhodesia "B" 3 pts.*

At East London, December 8, 9, 10. Border won by an innings and 72 runs. Border 442 for seven dec. (G. L. Hayes 167 not out, G. W. Nelson 59, D. C. McKenna 56, I. D. Harty 44; R. Engelbrecht five for 118); Griqualand West 131 (A. P. Beukes 72; G. L. Hayes six for 27) and 239 (S. Turner 46, G. Ricketts 41). *Border 18 pts, Griqualand West 3 pts.*

At Pinetown, December 13, 14, 15. Natal "B" won by an innings and 58 runs. Natal "B" 405 for eight dec. (C. L. Smith 106 not out, D. Bestall 88, I. R. Tayfield 74, D. R. Turner 66); Griqualand West 203 (A. P. Beukes 88, P. C. Middleton 53; I Ebrahim four for 81) and 144 (P. C. Middleton 46; I. Ebrahim seven for 50). *Natal "B" 17 pts, Griqualand West 5 pts.*

At St George's Park, Port Elizabeth, December 15, 17, 18. Western Province "B" won by six wickets. Eastern Province "B" 275 for nine dec. (K. P. Reid 109; S. A. Jones five for 47) and 194 (R. G. Fensham 65; J. During four for 48); Western Province "B" 262 (R. A. Drummond 99, P. M. Thompson 44; M. Collins four for 71) and 210 for four (J. Ackermann 63, A. Green 49). *Western Province "B" 17 pts, Eastern Province "B" 7 pts.*

At The Ramblers, Bloemfontein, December 26, 27, 28. Orange Free State won by eight wickets. Eastern Province "B" 163 (B. de-K. Robey 75; E. Schmidt four for 38) and 310 (D. Elliott 98, D. G. W. Alers 65, D. H. Howell 60; W. T. Strydom four for 40); Orange Free State 284 (D. P. le Roux 112, R. J. East 67) and 190 for two (R. A. le Roux 84, T. A. Lloyd 76 not out). *Orange Free State 19 pts, Eastern Province "B" 4 pts.*

At Kingsmead, Durban, December 26, 27, 28. Natal "B" won by 49 runs. Natal "B" 159 (N. P. Daniels 47; G. D. Boucher four for 30) and 270 for three dec. (C. L. Smith 103 not out, B. Plummer 64, D. R. Turner 61 not out); Border 144 (D. C. McKenna 59; I. Ebrahim four for 17) and 236 (R. A. Stretch 47; I. Ebrahim four for 58). *Natal "B" 15 pts, Border 5 pts.*

At East London, January 1, 2, 3. Border won by one wicket. Border 389 (R. A. Stretch 88, D. C. McKenna 77, G. L. Hayes 42, I. D. Harty 40) and 127 for nine (G. E. McMillan six for 33); Transvaal "B" 235 (G. E. McMillan 54, G. Taliadoris 41) and 280 (N. E. Wright 76, N. T. Day 50; K. Weakley four for 61). *Border 18 pts, Transvaal "B" 3 pts.*

At Pietermaritzburg, January 18, 19, 20. Natal "B" won by six wickets. Zimbabwe-Rhodesia "B" 194 (A. J. McCallum 106 not out) and 201 (E. F. Parker 76 not out, M. M. Benkenstein 44; I. Ault seven for 52); Natal "B" 282 (D. R. Turner 69, C. L. Smith 57; C. B. Jonker four for 55) and 116 for four wickets. *Natal "B" 17 pts, Zimbabwe-Rhodesia "B" 4 pts.*

At The Wanderers, Johannesburg, January 19, 21, 22. Western Province "B" won by 15 runs. Western Province "B" 217 (R. A. Drummond 71; K. J. Kerr four for 38) and 113 (N. V. Radford five for 47); Transvaal "B" 157 (N. E. Wright 43) and 158 (N. T. Day 67; E. S. Gordon six for 56). *Western Province "B" 17 pts, Transvaal "B" 4 pts.*

At de Beers Ground, Kimberley, January 24, 25, 26. Western Province "B" won by 138 runs. Western Province "B" 223 (H. M. Ackerman 114; A. P. Beukes four for 44) and 202 for seven dec. (T. A. Clarke 43); Griqualand West 178 (J. Reyneke 46) and 109 (E. S. Gordon four for 35). *Western Province "B" 15 pts, Griqualand West 5 pts.*

At The Ramblers, Bloemfontein, January 26, 28, 29. Orange Free State won by 132 runs. Orange Free State 227 for eight dec. (T. A. Lloyd 68, R. A. le Roux 57) and 285 for four dec. (R. J. East 108, R. A. le Roux 80 not out, E. Schmidt 60 not out); Zimbabwe-Rhodesia "B" 225 for eight dec. (G. C. Wallace 111; R. A. le Roux four for 52) and 155 (E. Schmidt four for 38). *Orange Free State 15 pts, Zimbabwe-Rhodesia "B" 5 pts.*

At Constantia, Cape Town, February 2, 4, 5. Western Province "B" won by nine wickets. Orange Free State 92 and 150 (L. H. Coetzee 44; J. During five for 29); Western Province "B" 196 (H. M. Ackerman 69, E. Halvorsen 44; E. Schmidt five for 33) and 49 for one. *Western Province "B" 16 pts, Orange Free State 5 pts.*

At Kemsley Park, Port Elizabeth, February 28, 29, March 1. Natal "B" won by seven wickets. Eastern Province "B" 231 for eight dec. (G. S. Cowley 40) and 322 (G. S. Cowley 67, D. Emslie 63 not out, R. G. Fensham 46, T. B. Reid 41; I. Ebrahim six for 118); Natal "B" 300 for three dec. (B. J. Whitfield 145 not out, B. Plummer 73, D. R. Turner 52) and 254 for three (B. J. Whitfield 100 not out, B. Plummer 61, N. P. Daniels 59 not out). *Natal "B" 20 pts, Eastern Province "B" 6 pts.*

At Queen's Ground, Bulawayo, March 15, 16, 17. Drawn. Zimbabwe-Rhodesia "B" 314 (J. G. Heron 77, F. de Grandhomme 60; K. J. Kerr four for 65) and 230 for five dec. (G. C. Wallace 79 not out, J. Meyer 48, E. F. Parker 46); Transvaal "B" 258 for five dec. (N. T. Day 111 not out, R. F. Pienaar 59) and 71 for one. *Transvaal "B" 7 pts, Zimbabwe-Rhodesia "B" 5 pts.*

At Queen's Ground, Bulawayo, March 22, 23, 24. Zimbabwe-Rhodesia "B" won by four wickets. Griqualand West 226 (M. J. D. Doherty 101; V. R. Hogg four for 32) and 205; Zimbabwe-Rhodesia "B" 209 (J. G. Heron 58; G. K. Funston five for 46) and 224 for six (E. F. Parker 58 not out, J. Meyer 55, D. L. Houghton 41). *Zimbabwe-Rhodesia "B" 15 pts, Griqualand West 6 pts.*

FIRST-CLASS MATCH

At The Wanderers, Johannesburg, December 4, 5, 6. Drawn. Transvaal 306 for five dec. (R. G. Pollock 80, R. F. Pienaar 63, A. J. Kourie 40) and 187 for five dec. (C. E. B. Rice 83 not out); South African Universities 257 (A. J. Pycroft 55; G. E. McMillan four for 49) and 114 for four.

CRICKET IN THE WEST INDIES, 1979-80

By TONY COZIER

Barbados retained the Shell Shield in 1980 for the fifth consecutive time and, in doing so, created a record by winning all four matches outright.

That was an accomplishment in itself, but the manner in which it was done was even more remarkable. Guyana and Jamaica were both beaten inside three days, the Combined Islands by lunch on the fourth day and Trinidad-Tobago, in the closest of their matches, with over an hour to spare. No team totalled over 300 in any single innings against the champions; yet Barbados, in four completed innings, passed 300 once, 400 twice and 500 once, the 555 in the decisive match against the Combined

Islands being the fourth highest total in the fourteen seasons of the tournament. No opposition had an answer to Barbados's strong suit of fast bowlers (Clarke, Daniel, Garner and Marshall); no attack could restrain batting which stretched from top to bottom.

Under a new points-scoring system, based on that used in Australia, bonuses were provided for quick scoring and wicket-taking over the first 100 overs of a first innings. Barbados scored heavily in both respects, gaining the maximum number of bowling points. At the same time they suffered under a scheme by which penalty points were deducted for teams failing to reach a match average of sixteen overs per hour.

Only the Combined Islands posed any threat to Barbados's dominance. They led at the halfway stage of the competition, after victories over Jamaica and Guyana, but their threat evaporated as they were held to a draw by Trinidad-Tobago and then heavily beaten by Barbados in their final match.

As is to be expected, the majority of the outstanding performances came from Barbadian players. Their formidable fast bowlers shared 60 wickets between them in Shell Shield matches, with Daniel claiming a career-best seven for 95 in the second innings against Guyana – a match in which he delivered 48 no balls! Marshall took six for 38 against Trinidad-Tobago and Garner, rested from the first two games after his arduous tour of Australia, took six for 37 against Jamaica. In addition, their Test batsmen, Haynes and King, each averaged over 50, while even those at the bottom of the order – Marshall, Garner, Daniel and Clarke – all recorded their highest first-class scores.

Barbados's most impressive batting, however, came from two as yet unestablished players: left-hander Thelston Payne and right-hander Emerson Trotman. The former, in only his second Shield season, followed separate half-centuries against Trinidad-Tobago with a dazzling 140 against the Combined Islands, against whom the aggressive Trotman registered the season's highest score of 158 not out.

Not that all the individual honours went to Barbados. Trinidadians H. A. Gomes and Gabriel batted as consistently as they had done the previous season, and Gomes's omission from the team to tour England caused howls of protest in his native island. Gabriel was the only batsman with two centuries in the Shield and his 444 was the highest aggregate. Along with Gabriel and Gomes, the left-handed Jamaican Chang was the only other player with more than 300 runs in Shield matches.

While the strength of the champions' attack lay in speed, the most successful bowlers among the other teams were spinners. Parry, of the Combined Islands, who created a Shield record by taking fifteen wickets in the match against Jamaica, finished with 25 all told, one more than Trinidadian off-spinner Nanan. Nanan, however, claimed more wickets, 30, in all first-class matches. Yet another off-spinner provided the most encouraging performance of the season. Roger Harper, the tall Guyanese schoolboy, just turned seventeen, delivered his off-spin from a high action with variation and control to take seventeen wickets.

After two seasons in the doldrums, with public interest being drained by the loss of leading players to World Series Cricket, the Shield was revitalised. The scheduled Indian tour was cancelled so that there was no counter-attraction, and the majority of those engaged in the tour of Australia and New Zealand answered the Board's plea to return home for the competition. The result was increased enthusiasm and, generally speaking, large crowds.

In view of their dominance of the Shield, it was surprising that Barbados should have been beaten – by Trinidad-Tobago and the Leeward Islands – in both their matches in the limited-overs Geddes, Grant-Harrison Line Tournament. Guyana qualified for the final from one group and the Leewards from the other, but the final itself, won convincingly by Guyana, was spoiled by the absence of the leading players who departed for the tour of England on the day of the match.

FIRST- CLASS AVERAGES

BATTING

(Qualification: average 35.00)

	Matches	Innings	Not Outs	Runs	Highest Inns	Average
E. N. Trotman (*B*)	3	3	1	255	158*	127.50
T. R. O. Payne (*B*) ...	4	6	2	290	140	72.50
H. A. Gomes (*T-T*) ...	4	8	1	384	116*	54.85
S. I. Williams (*LI*)	2	4	0	208	127	52.00
D. L. Haynes (*B*).....	4	6	1	256	73	51.20
C. L. King (*B*)	4	5	0	254	117	50.80
E. E. Lewis (*CI*)......	4	8	1	336	158	48.00
M. D. Marshall (*B*) ...	4	4	1	142	55	47.33
R. S. Gabriel (*T-T*) ...	5	10	0	452	129	45.20
H. S. Chang (*J*)	4	8	0	358	132	44.75
S. F. A. Bacchus (*G*) ..	4	5	0	222	81	44.40
T. Cuffy (*T-T*)	5	9	3	259	82	43.16
P. J. Dujon (*J*)	3	6	2	166	63*	41.50
J. Garner (*B*)	2	2	0	79	67	39.50
M. R. Pydanna (*G*) ...	5	8	1	267	117*	38.14
I. T. Shillingford (*CI*)...	5	9	1	300	67	37.50
K. R. Bainey (*T-T*) ...	5	9	0	328	80	36.44
S. Shivnarine (*G*)	5	8	1	252	87	36.00
R. C. Fredericks (*G*) ...	5	7	0	249	90	35.57
L. G. Rowe (*J*).......	2	4	0	141	94	35.25

* *Signifies not out.*

BOWLING

(Qualification: 10 wickets)

	Overs	Maidens	Runs	Wickets	Average
M. D. Marshall (*B*) ...	105.3	29	273	18	15.16
J. Garner (*B*)	65.5	19	218	13	16.76
Inshan Ali (*T-T*)	55.3	11	190	10	19.00
R. Nanan (*T-T*)	237.1	75	578	30	19.26
Imtiaz Ali (*T-T*)	117.1	29	336	17	19.76
C. E. H. Croft (*G*)	102.3	18	385	19	20.26
D. R. Parry (*CI*)	231	68	537	25	21.48
W. W. Daniel (*B*)	75.5	10	326	15	21.73
C. U. Thompson (*J*) ..	102.2	16	375	15	25.00
R. A. Harper (*G*)	208	52	463	17	27.23
N. Phillip (*CI*)	96.1	23	304	11	27.63

SHELL SHIELD

	Played	Won	Lost	Drawn	Bonus Points Batting	Bowling	Total Points
Barbados	4	4	0	0	27	20	102
Combined Islands	4	2	1	1	18	16	68
Trinidad-Tobago	4	1	1	2	17	18	64
Guyana	4	0	2	2	15	17	41
Jamaica	4	0	3	1	8	18	28

Penalty points deducted and incorporated in the table: Barbados 9, Guyana 1.

SHELL SHIELD

At Bourda, Georgetown, March 21, 22, 23. Barbados won by ten wickets. Guyana 145 (L. Baichan 40; W. W. Daniel three for 50) and 226 (M. R. Pydanna 61; W. W. Daniel seven for 95); Barbados 340 (C. L. King 96, D. L. Haynes 62, E. N. Trotman 56, R. L. Skeete 49; C. E. H. Croft six for 123, R. F. Joseph three for 65) and 32 for no wkt. *Barbados 24 pts, Guyana 4 pts.*

At Sabina Park, Kingston, March 21, 22, 23. Combined Islands won by six wickets. Jamaica 159 (H. S. Chang 50; D. R. Parry six for 25) and 246 (H. S. Chang 42, A. B. Williams 38; D. R. Parry nine for 76); Combined Islands 239 (J. C. Allen 62, I. T. Shillingford 54, V. A. Eddy 46 not out; C. U. Thompson six for 74) and 167 for four (E. E. Lewis 51, J. C. Allen 42). *Combined Islands 24 pts, Jamaica 5 pts.*

At Queen's Park Oval, Port-of-Spain, March 29, 30, 31, April 1. Barbados won by five wickets. Barbados 410 for nine dec. (A. T. Greenidge 101, T. R. O. Payne 74, D. L. Haynes 73, A. L. Padmore 50, M. D. Marshall 41 not out; R. R. Jumadeen four for 114, R. Nanan three for 126) and 104 for five (T. R. O. Payne 51 not out); Trinidad-Tobago 259 (H. A. Gomes 68, R. S. Gabriel 43; M. D. Marshall six for 38) and 251 (D. L. Murray 50, H. A. Gomes 46, R. S. Gabriel 40; A. L. Padmore three for 48, T. F. Foster three for 60). *Barbados 22 pts, Trinidad-Tobago 6 pts.*

At Jarrett Park, Montego Bay, March 29, 30, 31, April 1. Drawn. Guyana 377 (Timur Mohamed 110, R. C. Fredericks 50, R. A. Harper 38; M. A. Holding three for 61, R. A. Austin three for 92) and 328 for nine dec. (M. R. Pydanna 117 not out, T. R. Etwaroo 57); Jamaica 327 (E. H. Mattis 132, P. J. Dujon 47 not out, R. A. Austin 41; R. A. Harper five for 95, C. E. H. Croft four for 46) and 277 for nine (L. G. Rowe 94, H. S. Chang 47; R. A. Harper four for 70, D. I. Kallicharran four for 86). *Guyana 19 pts, Jamaica 12 pts.*

At Grove Park, Nevis, April 5, 6, 7, 8. Combined Islands won by 76 runs. Combined Islands 345 (I. V. A. Richards 78, N. Phillip 44, I. T. Shillingford 38, I. Cadette 37 not out; S. Shivnarine three for 30, R. A. Harper three for 63, C. E. H. Croft three for 74) and 280 (I. V. A. Richards 47, V. A. Eddy 43; D. I. Kallicharran three for 47, R. A. Harper three for 102); Guyana 267 (S. Shivnarine 62, T. R. Etwaroo 50, D. A. Hewitt 43; D. R. Parry four for 86) and 282 (S. Shivnarine 87, S. F. A. Bacchus 41; I. V. A. Richards three for 30, A. M. E. Roberts three for 43, N. Phillip three for 85). *Combined Islands 28 pts, Guyana 9 pts.*

At Queen's Park Oval, Port-of-Spain, April 5, 6, 7, 8. Trinidad-Tobago won by five wickets. Jamaica 216 (A. B. Williams 72, P. J. Dujon 63 not out; R. Nanan five for 71, Imtiaz Ali four for 61) and 214 (A. U. Campbell 48 not out, A. B. Williams 37; R. Nanan six for 66); Trinidad-Tobago 223 (Imtiaz Ali 48 not out; R. A. Austin seven for 54) and 208 for five (R. S. Gabriel 69, K. R. Bainey 47; R. A. Austin three for 55). *Trinidad-Tobago 23 pts, Jamaica 7 pts.*

At Kensington Oval, Bridgetown, April 11, 12, 13. Barbados won by an innings and 6 runs. Jamaica 155 (H. S. Chang 50; J. Garner six for 37, S. T. Clarke three for 51) and 295 (H. S. Chang 132, A. B. Williams 34; M. D. Marshall four for 38); Barbados 456 (C. L. King 117, J. Garner 67, W. W. Daniel 53 not out, E. N. Trotman 41, M. D. Marshall 41; C. U. Thompson five for 124, J. Williams three for 91). *Barbados 26 pts, Jamaica 4 pts.*

At Arnos Vale, St Vincent, April 11, 12, 13, 14. Drawn. Trinidad-Tobago 319 (H. A. Gomes 116 not out, K. R. Bainey 80; N. Phillip five for 47) and 278 for six dec. (R. S. Gabriel 129, H. A. Gomes 70; D. R. Parry four for 103); Combined Islands 283 (J. C. Allen 91, I. V. A. Richards 36; R. Nanan six for 92) and 64 for no wkt (E. E. Lewis 40 not out). *Trinidad-Tobago 17 pts, Combined Islands 9 pts.*

At Kensington Oval, Bridgetown, April 25, 26, 27, 28. Barbados won by an innings and 18 runs. Combined Islands 257 (A. L. Kelly 60, D. R. Parry 55; S. T. Clarke four for 53, J. Garner four for 76) and 279 (I. T. Shillingford 67, U. V. C. Lawrence 40; S. T. Clarke three for 54); Barbados 555 (E. N. Trotman 158 not out, T. R. O. Payne 140, D. L. Haynes 69, M. D. Marshall 55, S. T. Clarke 36). *Barbados 30 pts, Combined Islands 7 pts.*

At Albion, Guyana, April 25, 26, 27, 28. Drawn. Trinidad-Tobago 327 (R. S. Gabriel 103, T. Cuffy 82, R. Nanan 38; D. I. Kallicharran four for 54) and 50 for one; Guyana 275 (R. C. Fredericks 90, S. F. A. Bacchus 62, S. Shivnarine 75; R. R. Jumadeen five for 57). *Trinidad-Tobago 18 pts, Guyana 9 pts.*

OTHER FIRST-CLASS MATCHES

SHELL SHIELD PRELIMINARY

At Recreation Ground, St. John's, Antigua, March 11, 12, 13, 14. Leeward Islands won by 36 runs. Leeward Islands 303 (E. E. Lewis 158, A. L. Kelly 38; T. Kentish three for 69) and 278 (S. I. Williams 127; W. W. Davis three for 57, L. Paul three for 72); Windward Islands 335 (L. C. Sebastian 78, N. Phillip 63, W. W. Davis 60, M. Warner 45; J. B. Harris four for 74) and 210 (L. C. Sebastian 66, I. T. Shillingford 41; U. V. C. Lawrence four for 51, E. T. Willett three for 58).

BEAUMONT CUP

At Guaracara Park, Pointe-a-Pierre, Trinidad, March 21, 22, 23. South-Central won by seven wickets. North-East 152 (A. Rajah 59; R. Nanan four for 63, Inshan Ali three for 26) and 198 (S. A. Gomes 56, K. G. d'Heurieux 43; Inshan Ali three for 54); South-Central 213 (T. Cuffy 63 not out, K. R. Bainey 55; Imtiaz Ali seven for 66, H. Joseph three for 63) and 138 for three (A. L. Logie 42, B. W. McLeod 36 not out).

JONES CUP

At Bourda, Georgetown, Guyana, October 20, 21, 22. Abandoned. Berbice 76 for four (M. R. Pydanna 42; C. E. H. Croft three for 28) v Demerara.

CRICKET IN NEW ZEALAND, 1979-80

By C. R. BUTTERY

In a season marred by bad weather the Shell Trophy was won by Northern Districts, closely followed by Wellington. Under the capable leadership of G. P. Howarth, Northern Districts gained three outright wins and, thanks to their strong batting line-up, went through the season undefeated. Even so their winning margin was only two points and the final positions could have been reversed had not the Wellington team suffered from more than their share of bad weather. The series was limited to only one round, in which each side played seven games, and the six-ball over was re-introduced after giving way for several seasons to the eight-ball over.

The other sides, apart from Otago, never looked like overtaking the two leaders. After getting away to a slow start Otago won their fifth and sixth games to put them into second position with everything depending on their final game with Canterbury. However they were outplayed and managed only three points for the match which dropped them to fourth place. Canterbury, with several inexperienced players in the side, did well to reach third place. Central Districts and Auckland each won only one game. Better things had been expected from Auckland, who finished last despite having four international players in the side.

The series was not without its moments of excitement, for there were several tense finishes. Auckland beat Canterbury with only three balls of the final over remaining, Canterbury scraped home with a narrow 3-run victory against Central Districts, and Northern Districts obtained a nail-biting one wicket win against Central Districts, also in the last over of the match.

A number of outstanding individual performances were recorded. In a fine spell of bowling for Wellington against Central Districts E. J. Chatfield took eight for 24 in the first innings and followed this with four of the six wickets to fall in the second innings. B. L. Cairns, renowned as a lusty hitter, excelled himself against Wellington and scored the fastest century ever recorded in New Zealand first-class cricket. It came in only fifty-two minutes from 45 balls. Cairns was finally dismissed for 110, 98 of which were scored in boundaries. P. E. McEwan, the 26-year-old from Canterbury, was undoubtedly the batsman of the series. After two indifferent seasons he blossomed forth to finish the season with 551 runs including two centuries. M. D. Crowe, a 17-year-old Auckland schoolboy, showed promise in scoring 51 on his first-class début.

The rule penalising any side failing to maintain a bowling rate of at least eighteen overs an hour was the subject of unfavourable comment by the players. It caused captains to persist with a spin attack when conditions favoured pace and we also saw the unusual sight of fielders racing to get into position at the end of each over in an effort to save time. After incurring two penalty points in their game against Otago, Auckland had the dubious distinction of finishing it with a total of minus one point. It is no coincidence that Otago, whose attack was based mainly on spin, were the only team to finish the competition free of any penalties.

LEADING AVERAGES (Shell Series games only)

BATTING

(Qualification: 5 complete innings; average 30.00)

	Innings	Not Outs	Runs	Highest Inns	Average
B. A. Edgar (*Wellington*)	12	2	529	152*	52.90
J. M. Parker (*Northern Districts*)	13	3	502	100	50.20
P. E. McEwan (*Canterbury*)	13	1	551	113	45.92
W. L. Blair (*Otago*)	13	2	466	82*	42.36
A. D. G. Roberts (*Northern Districts*) .	13	3	414	128*	41.40
G. N. Edwards (*Central Districts*)	13	0	513	131	39.46
J. G. Wright (*Northern Districts*)	14	0	542	97	38.71
M. H. Toynbee (*Northern Districts*)	13	4	340	78	37.78
J. F. Reid (*Auckland*)	14	1	475	77	36.54
G. P. Howarth (*Northern Districts*) ...	14	1	459	151	35.30
E. J. Gray (*Wellington*)	9	3	193	63*	32.16
J. F. M. Morrison (*Wellington*)	11	2	283	71*	31.44
B. R. Blair (*Otago*)	13	1	377	93	31.42
R. B. Reid (*Wellington*)	9	3	186	88	31.00
B. D. Ritchie (*Canterbury*)	11	4	211	45*	30.14

* *Signifies not out.*

BOWLING

(Qualification: 20 wickets)

	Runs	Wickets	Average
E. J. Chatfield (*Wellington*)	444	36	12.33
C. W. Dickeson (*Northern Districts*)	600	33	18.18
S. L. Boock (*Otago*)	725	36	20.14
S. R. Gillespie (*Northern Districts*)	610	30	20.33
D. R. Hadlee (*Canterbury*)	567	27	21.00
J. G. Bracewell (*Otago*)	801	37	21.65
L. W. Stott (*Auckland*)	572	24	23.83
D. W. Stead (*Canterbury*)	508	20	25.40
D. R. O'Sullivan (*Central Districts*)	896	34	26.35
E. J. Gray (*Wellington*)	610	23	26.52

SHELL TROPHY

	Played	Won	Lost	Drawn	Bonus points Batting	Bowling	Penalties	Total
Northern Districts ..	7	3	0	4	18	20	1	73
Wellington	7	3	1	3	11	26	2	71
Canterbury	7	2	2	3	14	23	2	59
Otago	7	2	4	1	12	21	0	57
Central Districts	7	1	5	1	16	23	1	50
Auckland	7	1	0	6	11	21	6	38

Outright win = 12 points.

At Eden Park, Auckland, December 27, 28, 29. Drawn. Auckland 239 (J. R. Wiltshire 61; D. C. Aberhart five for 48) and 124 for three dec. (J. F. Reid 37 not out); Central Districts 123 (L. W. Stott four for 39) and 120 for eight (M. H. Toynbee 44 not out). *Auckland 6 pts, Central Districts 4 pts.*

At Hutt Recreation Ground, Wellington, December 27, 28, 29. Drawn (second and third days lost through rain). Canterbury 107 (E. J. Chatfield four for 36); Wellington 17 for one. *Wellington 3 pts.*

At Carisbrook, Dunedin, December 27, 28, 29. Northern Districts won by six wickets. Otago 231 (B. R. Blair 53; S. R. Gillespie three for 62) and 142 (W. L. Blair 55 not out; S. R. Gillespie five for 40); Northern Districts 220 (J. G. Wright 80; S. L. Boock six for 81) and 157 for four. *Northern Districts 17 pts, Otago 6 pts.*

At Maidstone Park, Upper Hutt, December 31, January 1, 2. Wellington won by an innings and 45 runs. Wellington 216 (B. R. Taylor 63, E. J. Gray 55; D. R. O'Sullivan five for 53, D. C. Aberhart four for 52); Central Districts 50 (J. V. Coney six for 17, B. R. Taylor three for 12) and 121 (J. F. M. Morrison three for 2, E. J. Gray three for 30). *Wellington 18 pts, Central Districts 3 pts.*

At Molyneux Park, Alexandra, December 31, January 1, 2. Drawn. Otago 325 for four dec. (G. M. Turner 136, W. L. Blair 82 not out); Auckland 135 (P. N. Webb 57; J. G. Bracewell five for 16) and 164 for six (J. G. Bracewell three for 65). *Otago 8 pts, Auckland minus 1 pt.*

At Lancaster Park, Christchurch, December 31, January 1, 2. Drawn. Northern Districts 237 (A. D. G. Roberts 83 not out) and 285 (J. G. Wright 73, J. M. Parker 71; V. R. Brown four for 60); Canterbury 319 (P. E. McEwan 111, D. W. Stead 57; S. J. Scott five for 50) and 160 for six (D. S. Rathie 39 not out). *Northern Districts 5 pts, Canterbury 8 pts.*

At Fitzherbert Park, Palmerston North, January 4, 5, 6. Central Districts won by nine wickets. Otago 176 (G. M. Turner 42; D. R. O'Sullivan four for 40) and 157 (I. A. Rutherford 44; D. R. O'Sullivan six for 40); Central Districts 306 (R. A. Pierce 65, G. H. Langridge 62, R. W. Anderson 55; S. L. Boock six for 103) and 28 for one. *Central Districts 18 pts, Otago 3 pts.*

At Lancaster Park, Christchurch, January 4, 5, 6. Auckland won by four wickets. Canterbury 171 (M. C. Snedden three for 30, J. M. McIntyre three for 50) and 208 (P. E. McEwan 76; J. M. McIntyre four for 20); Auckland 185 (J. F. Reid 58) and 195 for six (P. N. Webb 49). *Auckland 17 pts, Canterbury 5 pts.*

At Seddon Park, Hamilton, January 4, 5, 6. Northern Districts won by seven wickets. Wellington 191 for six dec. (J. V. Coney 74 not out; C. W. Dickeson four for 51) and 278 (B. A. Edgar 48, J. F. M. Morrison 47; C. W. Dickeson seven for 91); Northern Districts 300 for eight dec. (G. P. Howarth 151, J. M. Parker 51; E. J. Gray three for 96) and 171 for three (J. G. Gibson 60, J. G. Wright 55; E. J. Gray three for 59). *Northern Districts 18 pts, Wellington 4 pts.*

At Eden Park, Auckland, January 8, 9, 10. Drawn. Auckland 206 (J. F. Reid 64, R. C. Hooton 51; S. J. Scott five for 21) and 294 (P. N. Webb 68; C. W. Dickeson four for 69); Northern Districts 306 for nine dec. (J. G. Wright 78, G. P. Howarth 78; J. A. Cushen three for 44) and 175 for four (M. J. Wright 96 not out). *Northern Districts 7 pts, Auckland 3 pts.*

At Hutt Recreation Ground, Wellington, January 8, 9, 10. Wellington won by 124 runs. Wellington 209 (B. A. Edgar 103; S. L. Boock five for 42, J. G. Bracewell five for 48) and 266 (E. J. Gray 63 not out, B. A. Edgar 55; J. G. Bracewell five for 120); Otago 173 (B. L. Cairns 110; B. R. Taylor five for 61) and 178 (E. J. Chatfield four for 51, E. J. Gray four for 70). *Wellington 17 pts, Otago 5 pts.*

At McLean Park, Napier, January 8, 9, 10. Canterbury won by 3 runs. Canterbury 252 (C. L. Bull 76, D. W. Stead 59) and 302 (P. E. McEwan 87; D. R. O'Sullivan five for 108); Central Districts 341 for seven dec. (R. W. Anderson 91) and 210 (G. H. Langridge 62; D. W. Stead five for 65). *Canterbury 18 pts, Central Districts 8 pts.*

At Eden Park, Auckland, January 12, 13, 14. Drawn. Auckland 198 (I. Gould 54; E. J. Chatfield four for 51, J. V. Coney four for 55) and 219 (J. F. Reid 77; E. J. Chatfield three for 41); Wellington 200 for seven dec. (G. A. Newdick 65; L. W. Stott six for 68) and 174 for three. *Auckland 4 pts, Wellington 6 pts.*

At Lancaster Park, Christchurch, January 12, 13, 14. Otago won by two wickets. Canterbury 303 for five dec. (P. E. McEwan 113, C. L. Bull 76) and 253 for nine dec. (D. Dempsey 106; B. L. Cairns three for 88); Otago 266 (B. R. Blair 57; T. E. Jesty three for 41, D. R. Hadlee three for 55) and 294 for eight (B. R. Blair 93, W. L. Blair 73; D. W. Stead four for 35). *Otago 17 pts, Canterbury 7 pts.*

At Harry Barker Reserve, Gisborne, January 12, 13, 14. Northern Districts won by one wicket. Central Districts 350 for six dec. (G. N. Edwards 131, R. A. Pierce 94) and 274 (G. N. Edwards 77, M. H. Toynbee 54; S. R. Gillespie three for 48); Northern Districts 311 for six dec. (J. M. Parker 100, M. J. Wright 70, A. D. G. Roberts 60; D. C. Aberhart three for 77) and 317 for nine (A. D. G. Roberts 128 not out, M. H. Toynbee four for 100). *Northern Districts 18 pts, Central Districts 7 pts.*

At Eden Park, Auckland, January 19, 20, 21. Drawn. Auckland 252 (M. D. Crowe 51; D. W. Stead four for 73) and 207 for four dec. (A. E. W. Parsons 116 not out); Canterbury 118 (D. W. Stead 42; G. B. Troup six for 48) and 47 for one. *Auckland 4 pts, Canterbury 4 pts.*

At Carisbrook, Dunedin, January 19, 20, 21. Otago won by five wickets. Central Districts 172 for six dec. (A. M. Jones 45; J. G. Bracewell three for 59) and 157 (J. G. Bracewell seven for 78); Otago 166 for seven dec. (G. M. Turner 59; M. H. Toynbee four for 48) and 164 for five (I. A. Rutherford 57). *Otago 15 pts, Central Districts 4 pts.*

At Hutt Recreation Ground, Wellington, January 19, 20, 21. Drawn. Wellington 167 for four dec. (G. A. Newdick 48) and 154 (R. B. Reid 44; C. W. Dickeson four for 32); Northern Districts 95 (E. J. Chatfield eight for 24) and 100 for six (E. J. Chatfield four for 15). *Wellington 5 pts, Northern Districts 1 pt.*

At Pukekura Park, New Plymouth, January 27, 28, 29. Wellington won by seven wickets. Central Districts 300 for seven dec. (G. N. Edwards 100, M. H. Toynbee 78; E. J. Gray three for 108) and 255 for nine dec. (W. J. Hodgson 50; E. J. Gray three for 85); Wellington 273 for six dec. (R. H. Vance 96, R. B. Reid 88; D. R. O'Sullivan four for 84) and 284 for three (B. A. Edgar 152 not out). *Wellington 18 pts, Central Districts 6 pts.*

At Tauranga Domain, January 27, 28, 29. Drawn. Northern Districts 257 for eight dec. (J. G. Gibson 88) and 252 for six dec. (J. G. Wright 97; J. M. McIntyre three for 56, L. J. Rewcastle three for 69); Auckland 201 (J. R. Wiltshire 69; C. W. Dickeson five for 23) and 185 for eight (J. F. Reid 74; S. R. Gillespie five for 30). *Northern Districts 7 pts, Auckland 5 pts.*

At Logan Park, Dunedin, January 27, 28, 29. Canterbury won by 44 runs. Canterbury 244 for eight dec. (V. R. Brown 75, D. J. Rathie 55; B. L. Cairns four for 68) and 105 (G. B. Thomson four for 39); Otago 127 (T. E. Jesty four for 52) and 178 (W. L. Blair 74; D. R. Hadlee four for 28). *Canterbury 17 pts, Otago 3 pts.*

CRICKET IN INDIA, 1979-80

By P. N. SUNDARESAN

The Golden Jubilee celebrations of the Board of Control for Cricket in India, held in mid-February at Bombay, marked the climax of a busy cricket season in which twelve Test matches were played, as well as the usual heavy domestic programme. Besides the assemblage of over 100 cricketers, who had donned the country's colours in 182 Tests, the celebrations were marked by a Golden Jubilee Test between India and England, India, under its new captain G. R. Viswanath, lost the match mainly because of the sterling performance of Botham. England's effervescent all-rounder scored 114 runs and took thirteen wickets for 106 runs.

Mr M. Chinnaswamy, president of the Indian Board, presented silver salvers to Indian Test players and to umpires who had officiated in Tests. He also hosted a dinner at the Ashoka Hotel, Bombay, when the Indian Board was felicitated by Mr S. C. Griffith, Chairman of the International Cricket Conference, and other representatives of overseas federations.

The knockout stage of the Ranji Trophy was played after the Jubilee celebrations. B. S. Bedi, who had been left out of the Tests against Australia and Pakistan, had the satisfaction of leading Delhi to a thumping victory over Bombay in the final, to retain the trophy. This must have given Bedi profound satisfaction, the Delhi and District Cricket Association having dropped him from the captaincy of the State team but being forced to reverse their decision at the unanimous demand of the players. Delhi's success was followed by the formation of the Delhi State Cricket Association by the players, backed by some important personages. Though the apparent intention of the new body was to work in conjunction with the DDCA, only the future will unfold the significance of the move.

All the players who had been discarded from the Indian team during the season played vital rôles in Delhi's triumph in the final. Surinder Amarnath scored an excellent 77, while his brother Mohinder carried Delhi's batting on his shoulders, scoring 191 runs in a fighting tenure of eight and a half hours at the crease. In a clinching spell reminiscent of his best days Bedi broke the back of Bombay's first innings, dismissing Vengsarkar, who had touched excellent form, R. V. Mankad and S. Kshirsagar. Bombay did not recover and produced only 245 runs in reply to Delhi's tall score of 547. When Bombay batted again Bedi maintained his form to take five wickets and play the leading rôle in dismissing them for 239 runs. His match aggregate was eight for 134. Apart from claiming six wickets for the match, young Kirti Azad scored a dashing 102 for Delhi. He is a bright Test prospect. For Bombay, Gavaskar played a fighting knock in the second innings and not until his dismissal did his side accept defeat. Ravi Shastri, a left-arm spinner, impressed with his ability to stand up to hard work.

Of the earlier matches in the knockout, Haryana's victories over Uttar Pradesh and Karnataka deserve mention. In both, Haryana trailed on the first innings and, in both, Kapil Dev and left-arm spinner Rajinder Goel put their side on the road to victory by dismissing their opponents in their second innings for low scores. However, Haryana were beaten by Bombay in the semi-final, a low-scoring match, mainly because of the penetrative bowling of left-arm spinner P. K. Shivalkar.

D. B. Vengsarkar of Bombay was the outstanding batsman of the Championship with a total of 763 runs, though there were others who registered a better average. Vengsarkar gathered two double centuries – 210 v Baroda and 203 v Bihar. The best individual effort was A. Malhotra's 224 not out for Haryana against Jammu and Kashmir. And his tally for the competition fell only 39 short of Vengsarkar's. B. P. Patel of Karnataka won the L. P. Jai prize for the fastest century in the Championship. In scoring 157 runs against Haryana he reached his 100 in 157 minutes, and took 231 minutes for his 157 with one 6 and twenty-three 4s.

Rajinder Goel was the outstanding bowler with 44 wickets, and played a leading part in Haryana's progress to the semi-final. Madan Lal, who was India's opening bowler until the arrival of Kapil Dev, put in the best bowling performance in an innings, with nine for 31 against Haryana in the North Zone league; his figures for the match were thirteen for 64, also the best in the Championship for the season.

At the end of Karnataka's last match of the season, leg-spinner B. S. Chandrasekhar announced his retirement from first-class cricket. It proved an emotional farewell as he was in tears when he told his association about it. Chandrasekhar rose from the junior ranks to make his début in Test cricket in 1963-64. In 58 Tests he took 242 wickets and holds the Indian record of 35 wickets in a series (against England in 1972-73). He played sixteen years for his state, one more than his Test span, and reaped 436 wickets for 8,358 runs; in the Duleep Trophy his tally was 97 wickets for 2,241 runs in 23 matches. A lovable character, Chandrasekhar was a favourite of the crowd wherever he played. His retirement removes from the world scene a bowler who fascinated everyone with his unorthodox art.

Although the Irani Cup match between Delhi (the Ranji Trophy champions) and the Rest of India, scheduled to be played at Jullundur, was washed out and the trophy had to be shared, North Zone retained the Duleep Trophy for the zonal tournament. They won outright both their semi-final and final matches against Central and West respectively. Madan Lal displayed excellent form with bat and ball in the final, scoring an unbeaten century and taking eight wickets for 142 runs.

The Wills Trophy limited-overs tournament, sponsored by the Indian Tobacco Company, was not played.

FIRST-CLASS AVERAGES, 1979-80

BATTING

(Qualification: 500 runs)

	Innings	Not Outs	Runs	Highest Inns	100s	Average
B. P. Patel (*Karnataka*)	12	2	832	163	3	83.20
D. B. Vengsarkar (*Bombay*)	28	2	1,495	210	4	57.50
P. Sharma (*Rajasthan*)	12	0	648	127	3	54.00
A. Malhotra (*Haryana*)	17	2	790	224	2	52.66
R. B. Bhalekar (*Maharashtra*)	15	3	621	143	1	51.75
S. M. Gavaskar (*Bombay*)	32	2	1,518	166	4	50.60
M. Amarnath (*Delhi*)	17	1	777	191	1	48.56
S. Madan Lal (*Delhi*)	16	5	517	143*	2	47.00
Kirti Azad (*Delhi*)	11	0	516	130	2	46.90
S. M. Patil (*Bombay*)	18	1	796	210	1	46.82
G. R. Viswanath (*Karnataka*)	25	2	1,051	161*	3	45.69
Yashpal Sharma (*Punjab*)	20	3	756	100*	1	44.47
T. E. Srinivasan (*Tamilnadu*)	13	0	561	148	2	43.15
M. V. Narasimha Rao (*Hyderabad*)	16	3	560	159	3	43.07
Arun Lal (*Delhi*)	17	1	598	99	0	37.37
Kapil Dev (*Haryana*)	24	3	768	193	1	36.57
S. M. H. Kirmani (*Karnataka*)	24	5	586	101*	1	30.84
C. P. S. Chauhan (*Delhi*)	26	1	732	84	0	29.28

* *Signifies not out.*

BOWLING

(Qualification: 25 wickets)

	Overs	Maidens	Runs	Wickets	Average
S. Madan Lal (*Delhi*)	314.4	82	768	53	14.49
S. Valson (*Delhi*)	193.2	51	544	36	15.11
R. Goel (*Haryana*)	403.0	123	894	54	16.55
P. K. Shivalkar (*Bombay*)	334.5	104	630	38	16.57
Kapil Dev (*Haryana*)	588.5	138	1,581	79	20.01
D. D. Parsana (*Gujarat*)	303.5	101	644	27	23.85
S. Venkataraghavan (*Tamilnadu*) ..	449.1	148	857	35	24.48
S. Porel (*Bengal*)	218.0	28	702	28	25.07
B. S. Chandrasekhar (*Karnataka*) ..	290.0	62	777	30	25.90
N. Parsana (*Saurashtra*)	240.4	62	682	25	27.28
D. R. Doshi (*Bengal*)	695.4	199	1,395	49	28.46
N. S. Yadav (*Hyderabad*)	450.1	107	1,198	41	29.21
K. D. Ghavri (*Bombay*)	556.2	118	1,663	47	35.38

Note: Matches taken into account are Tests against Australia, Pakistan and England, Ranji Trophy and Duleep Trophy matches, and matches played by touring teams against the five zones and other teams.

RANJI TROPHY, 1979-80

Central Zone

At Bilaspur, November 17, 18, 19. Drawn. Madhya Pradesh 324 (S. Saxena 66, S. M. Jagdale 61, Mahmood Hasan 60; P. Kashyap four for 69, K. Fakih three for 99) and 223 for six (S. Saxena 108 not out, A. Gupta 57); Railways 391 (M. I. Ansari 162, N. P. Singh 59, Avashpal 41; A. Patel five for 82, Gopal Rao three for 37). *Railways 5 pts, Madhya Pradesh 3 pts.*

At Durg, November 23, 24, 25. Drawn. Madhya Pradesh 285 (S. Rao 65; R. S. Hans six for 100) and 249 for nine dec. (Gopal Rao 63 not out, S. Rao 53; Rafiullah three for 55); Uttar Pradesh 263 (A. Mathur 62, K. Juneja 61; P. Banerjee four for 54, A. Patel four for 82) and 0 for no wicket. *Madhya Pradesh 5 pts, Uttar Pradesh 3 pts.*

At Nagpur, November 23, 24, 25. Drawn. Railways 438 (Avashpal 157, M. I. Ansari 90, P. Kashyap 51, N. P. Singh 40; A. Bhagwat six for 79) and 233 for seven (Avashpal 44, N. P. Singh 41; A. Chitaley three for 46); Vidarbha 351 (A. P. Deshpande 164 not out, S. Phadkar 51; N. P. Singh four for 77, K. Fakih three for 102). *Railways 5 pts, Vidarbha 3 pts.*

At Agra, November 30, December 1, 2. Drawn. Rajasthan 276 (P. Sharma 127, P. Arya 48; Gopal Sharma four for 53, A. Mathur three for 53) and 111 for four (K. Mathur 51 not out); Uttar Pradesh 380 for eight dec. (A. Bamby 145, Gopal Sharma 101 not out, V. Chopra 78; K. R. Gattani four for 95). *Uttar Pradesh 5 pts, Rajasthan 3 pts.*

At Nagpur, November 30, December 1, 2. Drawn. Vidarbha 97 (P. Banerjee four for 28) and 301 for four (V. Telang 91, A. P. Deshpande 59 not out, P. Sahasrabudhe 50, J. Rathod 42); Madhya Pradesh 207 for nine dec. (Mahmood Hasan 58 not out; A. Bhagwat three for 47). *Madhya Pradesh 5 pts, Vidarbha 3 pts.*

At Delhi, December 12, 13, 14. Drawn. Railways 160 (R. Vats 62; Gopal Sharma five for 55), A. Mathur three for 19) and 285 for five dec. (R. Vats 82, P. Hansraj 70, N. P. Singh 63, C. M. Gupte 40); Uttar Pradesh 271 (Gopal Sharma 53, Rafiullah 49, A. Bamby 43; Aslam Ali seven for 77) and 35 for one. *Uttar Pradesh 5 pts, Railways 3 pts.*

At Ajmer, December 12, 13, 14. Rajasthan won by nine wickets. Vidarbha 241 (S. Phadkar 74, P. Sahasrabudhe 56, V. Telang 48) and 133 (S. Joshi five for 37, K. R. Gattani three for 42); Rajasthan 348 (Suresh Shastri 103, P. Arya 60, V. Mathur 45, S. Joshi 41 not out; A. Wankhede five for 111) and 28 for one. *Rajasthan 8 pts.*

At Delhi, December 16, 17, 18. Rajasthan won by 14 runs. Rajasthan 174 (P. Arya 50, T. Chatterjee 49; K. Fakih three for 15, R. Vats three for 55) and 154 (Bhanu Pratap Singh 48 not out; Aslam Ali four for 33, P. Kashyap three for 33); Railways 190 (M. I. Ansari 40; P. Sharma five for 69) and 124 (P. Sharma five for 47, Suresh Shastri four for 43). *Rajasthan 8 pts.*

At Jaipur, December 28, 29, 30. Drawn. Madhya Pradesh 269 (S. Rao 57, A. M. Jagdale 45; P. Sharma four for 92; K. R. Gattani three for 53) and 153 for three (S. Rao 50, S. Saxena 47); Rajasthan 306 (P. Sharma 111, K. Mathur 52; P. Banerjee three for 31, A. M. Jagdale three for 82). *Rajasthan 5 pts, Madhya Pradesh 3 pts.*

At Bareilly, January 29, 30, 31. Drawn. Uttar Pradesh 281 (Gopal Sharma 90; A. P. Deshpande three for 74, H. Wasu three for 102) and 131 for one dec. (K. Juneja 60 not out, A. Bhanot 43 not out); Vidarbha 96 (Gopal Sharma four for 27, A. Mathur three for 17) and 147 for four (S. Hadoo 43 not out). *Uttar Pradesh 5 pts, Vidarbha 3 pts.*

Rajasthan 24 pts, Uttar Pradesh 18, Madhya Pradesh 16, Railways 13, Vidarbha 9. Rajasthan and Uttar Pradesh qualified for the knockout stage.

East Zone

At Cuttack, November 22, 23, 24. Orissa won by seven wickets. Assam 105 (Paramjit Singh six for 33) and 138 (Paramjit Singh five for 39); Orissa 164 (R. Panda 44, K. Dubey 40; N. Singh six for 51) and 80 for three (K. Dubey 50). *Orissa 8 pts.*

At Cuttack, November 27, 28, 29. Drawn. Bengal 277 (Palash Nandy 80, U. Banerjee 57, Pranab Nandy 41; S. Sahu three for 42, S. Hussain three for 59, Randhir Singh three for 67) and 176 for five dec. (M. Dalvi 56, U. Banerjee 51 not out); Orissa 211 (K. Dubey 62, S. Pathak 42; S. Porel five for 63) and 102 for nine (B. Burman three for 14). *Bengal 5 pts, Orissa 3 pts.*

At Digwadi, November 27, 28, 29. Bihar won by an innings and 162 runs. Assam 90 (S. Sinha six for 35) and 103 (Venkatram three for 42); Bihar 355 for three dec. (H. Gidwani 101 retired hurt, Subrata Das 79, V. Joseph 59, R. Mukherjee 50 not out). *Bihar 9 pts, including 1 bonus point.*

At Calcutta, December 2, 3, 4. Bengal won by an innings and 11 runs. Bengal 255 for six dec. (M. Dalvi 70; P. Ghosh 44, Riazul Haque three for 88); Assam 101 (A. Goswamy 43; A. Bhattacharjee three for 19, Hyder Ali three for 34) and 143 (Gautam Das 63 not out; A. Bhattacharjee three for 18). *Bengal 8 pts.*

At Rourkela, December 2, 3, 4. Drawn. Orissa 174 (G. Patnaik 40; A. Sinha six for 45) and 329 (S. Pathak 176, Paramjit Singh 43 not out; A. Sinha three for 74); Bihar 258 (R. Saxena 87, H. Gidwani 64; Randhir Singh five for 65, Paramjit Singh three for 38) and 64 for one. *Bihar 5 pts, Orissa 3 pts.*

At Dhanbad, December 15, 16, 17. Drawn. Bihar 348 (R. Saxena 107; R. Mukherjee 70; S. Porel five for 94); Bengal 382 for five (Palash Nandy 132, M. Dalvi 126 not out, Raju Mukherjee 50). *Bengal 5 pts, Bihar 3 pts.*

Bengal 18 pts, Bihar 17, Orissa 14, Assam 0. Bengal and Bihar qualified for the knockout stage.

North Zone

At Amritsar, November 1, 2, 3. Punjab won by an innings and 124 runs. Punjab 354 (R. Handa 98, Y. Dutta 78, A. Sharma 78, D. Chopra 43; Ravikant four for 70); Jammu and Kashmir 84 for nine dec. (R. S. Ghai four for 21, A. Minna three for 13) and 146 (A. Minna five for 34, Umesh Kumar three for 27). *Punjab 8 pts.*

At Bhiwani, November 5, 6, 7. Haryana won by an innings and 190 runs. Haryana 423 for two dec. (A. Malhotra 224 not out, Premchand 100 not out, Sarabjit Singh 84); Jammu and Kashmir 115 (Ashok Singh 48; Yog Raj seven for 36, S. Talwar three for 20) and 118 (R. Amarnath three for 18). *Haryana 9 pts, including 1 bonus point.*

At Delhi, November 9, 10, 11. Delhi won by an innings and 100 runs. Delhi 360 for five dec. (S. C. Khanna 104 not out, M. Amarnath 76, S. Madan Lal 58 not out, Arun Lal 55); Jammu and Kashmir 189 (Maqbool Shah 57, Nirmal Singh 45; S. Valson five for 43) and 71 (R. Shukla three for 24). *Delhi 9 pts, including 1 bonus point.*

At Delhi, November 13, 14. Services won by an innings and 71 runs. Services 306 for eight dec. (P. Sur 80, Sudhakar Rao 76, V. Chavan 51; Pradeep four for 67); Jammu and Kashmir 77 (J. S. Bakshi six for 25) and 158 (Maqbool Shah 46 not out; Muralidharan three for 25, G. S. Shaktawat three for 37). *Services 8 pts.*

At Patiala, November 13, 14, 15. Drawn. Punjab 214 (D. Chopra 106 not out; Balram seven for 71) and 120 for no wicket (R. Handa 63 not out, S. Khanna 51 not out); Delhi 232 for seven dec. (S. C. Khanna 61, S. Amarnath 53, M. Amarnath 51; R. S. Ghai five for 50) and 15 for no wicket. *Delhi 5 pts, Punjab 3 pts.*

At Delhi, December 11, 12, 13. Delhi won by an innings and 32 runs. Services 132 (B. S. Bedi six for 32) and 227 (Chandrasekhar 51, P. Sur 48, B. Ghosh 41; S. Madan Lal four for 31); Delhi 391 for six dec. (S. Madan Lal 136, Kirti Azad 130, V. Sunderam 54; Ajay Jha five for 119). *Delhi 9 pts, including 1 bonus point.*

At Chandigarh, December 11, 12, 13. Drawn. Haryana 361 (Kapil Dev 193, Premchand 41; Satish Kumar four for 63; R. S. Ghai three for 88) and 182 for five dec. (R. Chadda 54 not out); Punjab 318 (Yashpal Sharma 90, Y. Dutta 90, D. Chopra 73; R. Goel four for 82, Kapil Dev three for 88). *Haryana 5 pts, Punjab 3 pts.*

At Rohtak, December 15, 16, 17. Drawn. Haryana 360 (A. Malhotra 119, Sarabjit Singh 83, R. Amarnath 77; Chandrasekhar three for 31, Ajay Jha three for 69) and 120 for five dec. (Sarabjit Singh 47; R. K. Ohri three for 10); Services 341 (Ajay Jha 78, V. Chavan 62, G. S. Shaktawat 59 not out, R. K. Ohri 59; Yog Raj three for 58, R. Goel five for 99) and 21 for two. *Haryana 5 pts, Services 3 pts.*

At Delhi, December 27, 28, 29. Delhi won by eight wickets. Haryana 109 (A. Malhotra 42; S. Madan Lal nine for 31) and 148 (A. Malhotra 43; S. Madan Lal four for 33, Balram three for 41); Delhi 203 (Arun Lal 50; R. Goel eight for 87) and 58 for two. *Delhi 8 pts.*

At Chandigarh, December 27, 28, 29. Drawn. Punjab 91 (G. S. Shaktawat eight for 41) and 126 for three; Services 270 (Chander Vijay 66, R. K. Ohri 52, V. Chavan 44; A. Razdan four for 56). *Services 5 pts, Punjab 3 pts.*

Delhi 31 pts, Haryana 19, Punjab 17, Services 16, Jammu and Kashmir 0. Delhi and Haryana qualified for the knockout stage.

South Zone

At Quilon, November 3, 4, 5. Drawn. Andhra 210 (K. B. Ramamurthy 89; Chandrakant three for 38, T. S. Mahadevan four for 53); Kerala 215 for eight (O. K. Ramdas 41; D. Meher Baba five for 80). *Kerala 5 pts, Andhra 3 pts.*

At Nizamabad, November 10, 11, 12. Hyderabad won by 10 wickets. Andhra 180 (Arshad Ayub three for 37, N. S. Yadav three for 48) and 108 (N. S. Yadav four for 28, M. V. Narasimha Rao four for 53); Hyderabad 244 (M. V. Narasimha Rao 134; D. Meher Baba four for 78) and 47 for no wicket. *Hyderabad 8 pts.*

At Shimoga, November 10, 11, 12. Drawn. Karnataka 392 for six dec. (G. R. Viswanath 151, B. P. Patel 78, S. Desai 46; P. T. Godwin three for 112) and 165 for two dec. (B. P. Patel 61; S. Ramesh three for 70); Kerala 332 (A. Satyendran 128 not out, R. Thomas 70; B. S. Chandrasekhar five for 86) and 156 for four (A. Satyendran 65 not out, R. Thomas 43; B. S. Chandrasekhar three for 49). *Karnataka 6 pts, including 1 bonus point, Kerala 3 pts.*

At Guntur, November 16, 17, 18. Drawn. Andhra 229 (V. Chamundeswarnath 48, J. K. Ghia 42, V. Janakiram 42; S. Vasudevan five for 62, S. Venkataraghavan three for 74); Tamilnadu 134 for eight (T. E. Srinivasan 44; D. Meher Baba three for 50). *Andhra 2 pts, Tamilnadu 2 pts.*

At Bangalore, November 30, December 1, 2. Drawn. Tamilnadu 213 (T. E. Srinivasan 75; B. S. Chandrasekhar five for 83, Vijayakrishna four for 37) and 284 (S. Venkataraghavan 60, V. Sivaramakrishnan 40; B. Vijayakrishna three for 79, B. S. Chandrasekhar three for 87); Karnataka 327 (R. Binny 141, B. P. Patel 40; K. Bharatkumar three for 37, S. Venkataraghavan three for 113). *Karnataka 5 pts, Tamilnadu 3 pts.*

At Madras, December 13, 14, 15. Tamilnadu won by an innings and 31 runs. Kerala 77 (S. Venkataraghavan six for 25) and 114 (K. Jayaram 43; S. Venkataraghavan three for 21, M. Santoshkumar three for 31); Tamilnadu 222 (A. Bharat Reddy 86, K. Srikanth 41; S. Ramesh four for 48, T. S. Mahadevan four for 57). *Tamilnadu 9 pts, including 1 bonus point.*

At Hyderabad, December 13, 14, 15. Drawn. Karnataka 237 (B. Vijayakrishna 77; K. Sainath three for 31, V. Ramnarayan three for 50) and 247 for two dec. (B. P. Patel 108 not out); Hyderabad 147 (V. Mohanraj 46; S. Shanbal six for 49) and 192 for four (V. Mohanraj 86 not out, Saad Bin Jung 57). *Karnataka 5 pts, Hyderabad 3 pts.*

At Madras, December 26, 27, 28. Drawn. Hyderabad 368 (Saad Bin Jung 136, Vijay Paul 53; S. Vasudevan six for 119) and 106 (S. Vasudevan five for 39, S. Venkataraghavan four for 22); Tamilnadu 300 (V. Sivaramakrishnan 92, K. Srikanth 66, P. S. Moses 45; Arshan Ayub five for 82, V. Ramnarayan three for 81) and 91 for three. *Hyderabad 5 pts, Tamilnadu 3 pts.*

At Vijayawada, December 27, 28, 29. Drawn. Andhra 179 (K. Chandrasekhar Rao 47; B. S. Chandrasekhar four for 64, Raghuram Bhatt three for 18) and 327 for six (J. K. Ghiya 106 not out, D. Meher Baba 71, K. Chandrasekhar Rao 49 not out); Karnataka 280 for seven dec. (R. Sudhakar Rao 54, A. V. Jayaprakash 53, B. P. Patel 53, M. R. Srinivasaprasad 47; J. K. Ghiya three for 76) and 51 for two. *Karnataka 5 pts, Andhra 3 pts.*

At Palghat, December 30, 31, January 1. Hyderabad won by an innings and 152 runs. Kerala 168 (M. V. Narasimha Rao six for 59) and 80 (K. Sainath seven for 30); Hyderabad 400 for nine dec. (M. V. Narasimha Rao 159, K. Sainath 108 not out, P. Jyotiprasad 48; S. Ramesh four for 66, T. S. Mahadevan three for 150). *Hyderabad 9 pts, including 1 bonus point.*

Hyderabad 25 pts, Karnataka 21, Tamilnadu 17, Andhra 8, Kerala 8. Hyderabad and Karnataka qualified for the knockout stage.

West Zone

At Jamnagar, November 10, 11, 12. Drawn. Gujarat 234 (J. C. Desai 58; A. Thakrar four for 79) and 203 for eight (N. Shrimali 61; M. Rajdev six for 45); Saurashtra 201 (N. Parsana 97 not out, K. Chauhan 54; J. Pandya five for 93, A. N. Joshi three for 61). *Saurashtra 5 pts, Gujarat 3 pts.*

At Kolhapur, November 11, 12, 13. Drawn. Maharashtra 443 for six dec. (R. B. Bhalekar 123, R. G. Borde 61 not out, S. F. Saldana 61, M. D. Gunjal 57, V. K. Sharma 47, P. M. Salgoankar 41 not out; C. R. Mohite four for 111); Baroda 430 (S. I. Dudha 116 not out, R. Y. Deshmukh 111, C. R. Mohite 42; N. Khaniwale six for 136). *Maharashtra 5 pts, Baroda 3 pts.*

At Bombay, November 30, December 1, 2. Drawn. Bombay 440 for six dec. (S. M. Gavaskar 153, S. V. Nayak 100 not out, S. M. Patil 46, G. Parkar 41) and 59 for no wicket (S. M. Patil 52 not out); Maharashtra 354 (S. F. Saldana 102, R. B. Bhalekar 81, R. G. Borde 43; P. K. Shivalkar three for 89). *Bombay 5 pts, Maharashtra 3 pts.*

At Baroda, November 30, December 1, 2. Drawn. Baroda 271 (A. D. Gaekwad 87, N. Y. Satham 77; P. Zaveri three for 39, D. D. Parsana three for 74) and 184 for five (N. Y. Satham 43 not out); Gujarat 210 (D. D. Parsana 95, A. Shroff 44; N. Y. Satham four for 38, D. V. Pardeshi four for 40). *Baroda 5 pts, Gujarat 3 pts.*

At Satara, December 28, 29, 30. Drawn. Saurashtra 400 (Yajurvindra Singh 214, D. Nanavati 45, N. Parsana 41, M. Chauhan 41; P. M. Salgoankar three for 87); Maharashtra 230 (R. B. Bhalekar 60; A. Thakrar three for 63, N. Parsana three for 76) and 115 for one (R. B. Bhalekar 60 not out, V. K. Sharma 54 not out). *Saurashtra 5 pts, Maharashtra 3 pts.*

At Bombay, January 8, 9, 10. Bombay won by eight wickets. Saurashtra 257 (Yajurvindra Singh 54, D. Nanavati 48, J. Bakrania 42, A. Patel 41 not out; R. V. Kulkarni four for 60) and 144 (A. Zarapkar four for 22, P. K. Shivalkar three for 43); Bombay 330 for five dec. (S. M. Patil 210, G. Parkar 40) and 72 for two. *Bombay 9 pts, including 1 bonus point.*

At Bulsar, February 9, 10, 11. Drawn. Bombay 180 (D. B. Vengsarkar 51, S. M. Patil 49; J. Pandya four for 35, U. C. Joshi three for 40) and 308 for eight dec. (D. B. Vengsarkar 79, K. D. Ghavri 59 not out, S. M. Gavaskar 55, S. V. Nayak 47; N. Amin four for 52); Gujarat

171 (P. Desai 45 not out; P. K. Shivalkar four for 38, A. Zarapkar three for 18) and 89 for five (P. K. Shivalkar four for 22). *Bombay 5 pts, Gujarat 3 pts.*

At Baroda, February 23, 24, 25. Drawn. Baroda 160 (V. Wadkar 56, K. D. Ghavri five for 44) and 106 for two; Bombay 543 for nine dec. (D. B. Vengsarkar 210, A. Zarapkar 95, S. M. Gavaskar 81, Z. Parkar 42 not out, R. Jadeja 42; V. Wadkar three for 112). *Bombay 5 pts, Baroda 3 pts.*

At Gondal, February 9, 10, 11. Drawn. Baroda 201 (J. A. Mehta 50, C. R. Mohite 49; N. Parsana six for 54) and 194 for seven dec. (A. D. Gaekwad 48, S. B. Kulkarni 44; N. Parsana five for 54); Saurashtra 170 (A. Patel 63, K. Chauhan 52; D. V. Pardeshi three for 42) and 38 for five. *Baroda 5 pts, Saurashtra 3 pts.*

At Nadiad, February 23, 24, 25. Maharashtra won by 57 runs. Maharashtra 204 (V. B. Shetty 52, V. K. Sharma 51; J. Pandya four for 41, A. N. Joshi three for 25) and 219 for eight dec. (S. F. Saldana 75); Gujarat 124 (S. Gudge five for 46, P. M. Salgoankar four for 31) and 242 (A. Shroff 62, A. M. Mehta 55, N. Amin 43; N. Khanivale four for 38). *Maharashtra 8 pts.*

Bombay 24 pts, Maharashtra 19, Baroda 16, Saurashtra 13, Gujarat 9. Bombay and Maharashtra qualified for the knockout stage.

RANJI TROPHY KNOCKOUT STAGES

At Calcutta, February 29, March 1, 2, 3. Drawn. Bengal were declared the winners on the toss of a coin as no decision could be obtained on first innings scores of the rain-affected match. Bengal 333 for six dec. (Palas Nandy 116, U. Banerjee 63 not out, Raju Mukherjee 58, P. Ghose 46; Arshad Ayub three for 51); Hyderabad 245 for five (M. V. Narasimha Rao 107 not out, Arshad Ayub 81 not out).

At Kanpur, February 29, March 1, 2, 3. Haryana won by seven wickets. Uttar Pradesh 265 (A. Mathur 65, V. Chopra 62, K. Juneja 58; Kapil Dev three for 70, R. Goel three for 86) and 117 (Kapil Dev five for 59, R. Goel three for 45); Haryana 226 (A. Malhotra 70, R. Amarnath 50; R. S. Hans five for 99, Gopal Sharma three for 64) and 157 for three (Sarabjit Singh 64, A. Malhotra 48 not out).

Quarter-Finals

At Jamshedpur, March 14, 15, 16, 17. Drawn. Bombay declared winners by virtue of their first innings lead. Bihar 190 (Subrata Das 50; Ravi Shastri three for 17) and 425 for seven dec. (H. Gidwani 164, R. Saxena 87, R. Mukherjee 47, V. Joseph 42; P. K. Shivalkar three for 75); Bombay 437 (D. B. Vengsarkar 203, Z. Parkar 60, S. M. Patil 50, R. V. Kulkarni 43; M. R. Bhalla three for 90, Jodh Singh three for 97) and 53 for one.

At Calcutta, March 14, 15, 16, 17. Delhi won by 66 runs. Delhi 337 (Arun Lal 78, Kirti Azad 60, M. Amarnath 59; B. Burman three for 94) and 239 for seven dec. (Arun Lal 60, S. Amarnath 41); Bengal 156 (S. Valson five for 62) and 354 (Raju Mukherjee 79, U. Banerjee 48, Pranab Nandy 45, D. R. Doshi 44, B. Burman 41; S. Madan Lal four for 74).

At Jaipur, March 14, 15, 16, 17. Drawn. Maharashtra declared winners by virtue of their first innings lead. Maharashtra 352 (R. B. Bhalekar 101, S. F. Saldana 53; V. Mathur three for 33, Suresh Shastri three for 63) and 254 for six dec. (M. D. Gunjal 107 not out, V. K. Sharma 88; P. Arya three for 49); Rajasthan 239 (P. Sharma 120, K. Mathur 58; N. Khaniwale five for 66) and 66 for two.

At Bangalore, March 14, 15, 16, 17. Haryana won by five wickets. Karnataka 320 (B. P. Patel 157, G. R. Viswanath 44, M. R. Srinivasaprasad 41; S. Talwar four for 84, R. Goel four for 107) and 167 (R. Goel five for 55, Kapil Dev three for 34); Haryana 232 (R. Amarnath 62, A. Rajiv 55, A. Malhotra 55; B. Vijayakrishna three for 56, B. S. Chandrasekhar three for 57) and 258 for five (R. Amarnath 84 not out, A. Malhotra 78).

Semi-Finals

At Delhi, March 28, 29, 30, 31. Delhi won by 114 runs. Delhi 229 (Kirti Azad 71; S. Torvi three for 61, P. M. Salgoankar three for 94) and 167 (P. M. Salgoankar five for 53, S. Torvi three for 54); Maharashtra 223 (R. B. Bhalekar 47, M. D. Gunjal 45; S. Madan Lal six for 68) and 59 (S. Madan Lal four for 19, S. Valson three for 24).

At Rohtak, March 28, 29, 30, 31. Bombay won by 114 runs. Bombay 143 (S. Talwar four for 42, R. Goel three for 44) and 150 (D. B. Vengsarkar 76, K. D. Ghavri 61; S. Talwar five for 63, R. Goel four for 61); Haryana 68 (P. K. Shivalkar five for 27, K. D. Ghavri three for 23) and 111 (R. Chadda 45; P. K. Shivalkar four for 30).

Final

At Delhi, April 11, 12, 13, 15, 16. Delhi won by 240 runs. Delhi 547 (M. Amarnath 191, Kirti Azad 102, S. Amarnath 77, V. Sunderam 58; P. K. Shivalkar five for 125) and 177 (S. C. Khanna 44; Ravi Shastri six for 61); Bombay 245 (D. B. Vengsarkar 81, R. D. Parkar 77, S. M. Gavaskar 44; Kirti Azad three for 55, R. Shukla three for 65, B. S. Bedi three for 74) and 239 (S. M. Gavaskar 93, S. V. Nayak 46; B. S. Bedi five for 60, Kirti Azad three for 64).

DULEEP TROPHY CHAMPIONSHIP, 1979-80

At Calcutta, December 7, 8, 9, 10. Drawn. South Zone declared winners by virtue of their first innings lead. South Zone 539 for seven dec. (B. P. Patel 163, T. E. Srinivasan 149, V. Sivaramakrishnan 78, J. K. Ghiya 54 not out, A. Bharat Reddy 40; Paramjit Singh three for 148) and 122 for two (R. Sudhakar Rao 48 not out); East Zone 435 (U. Banerjee 165 not out, Raju Mukherjee 70, H. Gidwani 52; S. Venkataraghavan five for 79).

Semi-Finals

At Bangalore, December 21, 22, 23. West Zone won by an innings and 15 runs. South Zone 147 (A. Zarapkar four for 33; D. D. Parsana four for 44) and 135 (B. P. Patel 41 not out; D. D. Parsana four for 24, R. Jadeja three for 45); West Zone 297 (R. Jadeja 63, S. F. Saldana 60, A. D. Gaekwad 49, D. D. Parsana 46 not out; S. Venkataraghavan three for 88).

At Indore, December 21, 22, 23, 24. North Zone won by ten wickets. Central Zone 197 (A. P. Deshpande 70 not out, Vedraj 49; S. Valson four for 27, Umesh Kumar four for 43) and 287 (Vedraj 67, A. Bhanot 61, P. Sharma 58, Gopal Sharma 42; S. Madan Lal three for 110); North Zone 395 (D. Chopra 87, S. Amarnath 75, R. Shukla 65, S. C. Khanna 62 M. Amarnath 40; A. Patel four for 62) and 90 for no wicket (Arun Lal 58 not out).

Final

At Bombay, January 20, 21, 22, 23. North Zone won by 104 runs. North Zone 165 (R. Shukla 41; Yajurvindra Singh four for 32, R. Jadeja three for 63) and 345 for seven dec. (S. Madan Lal 143 not out, R. Shukla 57 not out, M. Amarnath 50; N. Parsana three for 86); West Zone 271 (A. D. Gaekwad 56, D. D. Parsana 54; S. Madan Lal four for 81, S. Valson three for 78) and 135 (S. Madan Lal four for 61, M. Amarnath three for 16, S. Valson three for 36).

IRANI CUP MATCH, 1979-80

Ranji Trophy Champions (Delhi) v Rest of India

At Jullundur, February 2, 3, 4, 5. Abandoned because of rain. According to convention Delhi and Rest of India were declared joint winners.

CRICKET IN PAKISTAN, 1979-80

By GHULAM MUSTAFA KHAN

Having taken a back seat to the Banks in recent years, PIA returned to dominance in 1979-80 by claiming both major trophies: the Invitation and, after an interval of ten years, the Quaid-e-Azam. With the leading Pakistani players scheduled to be on tour in India during the Quaid-e-Azam Trophy competition, the Invitation Trophy Tournament was the only major competition to benefit from the presence of the Pakistan test players. It also took on extra significance as players sought to attract the attention of the national selectors, who later announced a squad of 28 to attend a training camp prior to the selection of the touring team.

For the third year in succession, Habib Bank and PIA contested the final of the Invitation Trophy, having shared it in 1978-79 after heavy rain had effected the abandonment of that seasons's final. This time PIA emerged as comfortable winners, thanks to Asif Iqbal who celebrated his appointment as Pakistan's captain with an unbeaten century in each innings.

PIA had looked somewhat less convincing, though, in their decisive group match against National Bank; the most entertaining game of the tournament. After a dramatic collapse to 86 for nine against the seam bowling of Ehtesham-ud-Din, they were rescued by a last-wicket stand of 114 between Wasim Bari and Iqbal Sikandar. Imran Khan then produced a devastating spell to leave the Bank in arrears on the first innings, but PIA's batting was again disappointing and National Bank were left requiring 219 to win. At 118 for one at stumps with a day to play, they looked well set, but overnight rain on the uncovered wicket – in keeping with the rules – produced conditions which Imran exploited to the full, taking six wickets for the second time in the match as National Bank failed by 19 runs. Ehtesham's first innings return of eight for 45 was the best in the tournament.

Highlight of the Quaid-e-Azam Trophy competition was the performance of seventeen-year-old Aamer Malik who, for Lahore "A" against Railways, marked his first-class début with a century in each innings, thus emulating A. R. Morris of Australia and N. J. Contractor of India. To commemorate the feat he was awarded a bat.

Concluded before the arrival of the Australia touring team, the Quaid-e-Azam Trophy, under its new format, was decided on points won in a final triangular league. National Bank required a win over PIA in the last match to retain the Trophy but, needing one more wicket, they were frustrated by Mushtaq Mohammad. Soon to be appointed manager of the test team, Mushtaq batted over five hours for his unbeaten hundred (eleven 4s) in PIA's second innings. The Airline's other hero against National Bank was Rashid Khan, whose match figures of twelve for 167 included the hat-trick. Rashid finished the competition as its leading wicket-taker and won the Kangaroo Trophy, donated by the Australian government to the best fast bowler in the national championship.

INVITATION TROPHY AVERAGES, 1979-80

BATTING

	Matches	Innings	Not Outs	Runs	Highest Inns	Average
Asif Iqbal (*PIA*)	3	4	1	233	110*	77.66
Sultan Rana (*Habib Bank*)	4	5	2	227	119*	75.66
Shafiq Ahmad (*National Bank*) .	3	5	1	280	202*	70.00
Mohammad Sabir (*Railways*) ...	2	4	0	247	114	61.75
Saleem Pervez (*National Bank*) .	3	6	1	306	80	61.20
Mudassar Nazar (*United Bank*) .	3	5	1	230	100	57.50
Javed Miandad (*Habib Bank*) ...	4	5	0	268	91	53.60
Talat Mirza (*Lahore*)	3	6	0	321	114	53.50
Zaheer Abbas (*PIA*)	4	7	0	369	170	52.71
Mansoor Akhtar (*United Bank*) .	3	5	1	175	77	43.75
Ijaz Fakih (*MCB*)	2	4	0	149	77	37.25
Siddiq Akbar (*Railways*)	3	6	1	185	71*	37.00
Khalid Masood (*Railways*)	3	6	0	202	76	33.66
Mushtaq Mohammad (*PIA*)	4	7	2	156	47*	31.20
Tehseen Javed (*Habib Bank*)....	4	5	0	152	67	30.40
Mohsin Khan (*Habib Bank*)	4	6	1	150	57	30.00
Taslim Arif (*National Bank*)	3	6	1	150	51	30.00
Mohammad Saeed (*Railways*) ..	3	6	0	156	59	26.00
Feroze Najamuddin (*Karachi*) ..	3	6	0	154	50	25.66

BOWLING

	Overs	Maidens	Runs	Wickets	Average
Ehtesham-ud-Din (*National Bank*)	62	18	145	15	9.66
Imran Khan (*PIA*)	125.5	36	268	26	10.30
Amin Lakhani (*United Bank*).....	75.4	26	110	10	11.00
Abdul Qadir (*Habib Bank*)	167	41	343	28	12.25
Aslam Kureshi (*Habib Bank*).....	73.1	23	182	14	13.00
Sikander Bakht (*United Bank*) ...	60.2	11	156	11	14.18
Naeem Ahmad (*PIA*)	94.1	20	237	16	14.81
Anwar Khan (*National Bank*)	82	24	178	12	14.83
Mohi-ud-Din (*Karachi*)	63	9	147	9	16.33
Ijaz Ahmad (*Lahore*)	146.3	45	296	18	16.44
Iqbal Qasim (*National Bank*)	137.3	39	315	19	16.57
Abdur Raqeeb (*Habib Bank*)	144.3	37	336	19	17.68
Ilyas Khan (*MCB*)	76	9	200	9	22.22
Mohammad Nazir (*Railways*)	106.5	25	265	11	24.09
Iqbal Sikandar (*PIA*)	111.3	21	347	12	28.91

INVITATION TROPHY TOURNAMENT, 1979-80

The competition was played on a league basis with two groups; one consisting of PIA, National Bank, Lahore and Railways, the other of United Bank, Habib Bank, Muslim Commercial Bank and Karachi. The group winners then played in the Final.

At Moghalpura Institute, Lahore, September 25, 26, 27, 28. National Bank won by seven wickets. Lahore 87 (Iqbal Qasim four for 17) and 215 (Salim Malik 58; Iqbal Qasim five for 69); National Bank 223 (Saleem Pervez 41, Wasim Raja 41; Ijaz Ahmad six for 61) and 81 for three.

At National Stadium, Karachi, September 25, 26, 27, 28. United Bank won by ten wickets. United Bank 240 for eight (Mudassar Nazar 100, Mansoor Akhtar 77; Akbar Najamuddin four for 59) and 73 for no wkt (Mudassar Nazar 40 not out); Karachi 84 (Sikander Bakht five for 28) and 228 (Khalid Alvi 74).

At Moghalpura Institute, Lahore, September 30, October 1, 2, 3. National Bank won by ten wickets. Railways 211 (Khalid Masood 48; Iqbal Qasim six for 78) and 222 (Siddiq Akbar 71 not out, Saeed Ahmad 59; Iqbal Qasim four for 83); National Bank 345 for three (Shafiq Ahmad 202 not out, Taslim Arif 51, Saleem Pervez 48) and 89 for no wicket (Saleem Pervez 59 not out).

At Bagh-e-Jinnah, Lahore, September 30, October 1, 2, 3. PIA won by seven wickets. Lahore 254 for eight (Talat Mirza 85, Ijaz Ahmad 56 not out, Nasir Abbas 44) and 142 (Talat Mirza 64; Naeem Ahmad seven for 31); PIA 196 (Zaheer Abbas 57, Rizwanuzzman 51; Ijaz Ahmad four for 56) and 206 for three (Zaheer Abbas 111).

At National Stadium, Karachi, September 30, October 1, 2, 3. Habib Bank won by an innings and 26 runs. Habib Bank 257 for six (Sultan Rana 66 not out, Agha Zahid 63, Javed Miandad 46); MCB 73 (Abdur Raqeeb four for 25, Abdul Qadir four for 28) and 158 (Ejaz Fakih 42; Abdul Qadir five for 37).

At Gaddafi Stadium, Lahore, October 5, 6, 7. PIA won by ten wickets. Railways 175 (Saeed Ahmad 47; Imran Khan five for 31) and 165 (Khalid Masood 47; Iqbal Sikandar four for 47); PIA 324 for six (Zaheer Abbas 170, Majid J. Khan 40) and 20 for no wkt.

At Karachi Gymkhana, Karachi, October 6, 7, 8, 9. United Bank won by an innings and 30 runs. MCB 64 (Amin Lakhani five for 21) and 162 (Ejaz Fakih 77); United Bank 256 for seven (Shahid Pervez 78, Haroon Rashid 64, Mansoor Akhtar 44; Ilyas Khan six for 87).

At National Stadium, Karachi, October 5, 6, 7, 8. Habib Bank won by ten wickets. Karachi 132 (Kamal Najamuddin 50; Abdul Qadir seven for 53) and 156 (Kamal Najamuddin 42; Abdur Raqeeb five for 48, Abdul Qadir four for 54); Habib Bank 245 for nine (Tehseen Javed 67, Mohsin Khan 57) and 44 for no wkt.

At Moghalpura Institute, Lahore, October 10, 11, 12, 13. Railways won on first innings result owing to rain on fourth day. Railways 303 (Mohammad Sabir 114, Khalid Masood 76) and 223 (Mohammad Sabir 85; Ijaz Ahmad four for 45); Lahore 253 (Talat Mirza 114, Saadat Ali 47; Mohammad Nazir six for 63) and 58 for three.

At Gaddafi Stadium, Lahore, October 10, 11, 12, 13. PIA won by 19 runs. PIA 200 (Iqbal Sikandar 76, Wasim Bari 45 not out; Ehtesham-ud-Din eight for 45) and 172 (Mushtaq Mohammad 47; Anwar Khan five for 49); National Bank 154 (Saleem Pervez 50, Maqsood 41 not out; Imran Khan six for 49) and 199 (Saleem Pervez 80; Imran Khan six for 56).

At National Stadium, Karachi, October 10, 11, 12, 13. Habib Bank won by nine wickets. United Bank 100 (Mudassar Nazar 36; Aslam Kureshi seven for 36) and 118 (Aslam Kureshi four for 33); Habib Bank 201 (Javed Miandad 50) and 18 for one.

At National Stadium, Karachi, October 16, 17, 18. Karachi won by 164 runs. MCB 127 (Mohi-ud-Din five for 38) and 77 (Fahim-ud-Din three for 10); Karachi 227 (Tariq Khan 47, G. Abbas 42; Anjum Nasir four for 44) and 141 (Fahim-ud-Din 42; Kamal Najamuddin 33; Zaigham Burki five for 42).

Final: At Gaddafi Stadium, Lahore, October 17, 18, 19, 20, 21, 22. PIA won by five wickets. Habib Bank 268 for eight dec. (Sultan Rana 119 not out, Javed Miandad 42; Imran Khan four for 36) and 303 (Javed Miandad 91, Mohsin Khan 50; Hassan Jamil four for 50); PIA 253 for eight dec. (Asif Iqbal 104 not out; Abdul Qadir three for 69) and 315 for five (Asif Iqbal 110 not out, Imran Khan 77, Majid J. Khan 47).

QUAID-E-AZAM TROPHY PRELIMINARY MATCHES AND PATRON'S TROPHY, 1979-80

In 1979-80, the national championship of Pakistan was played to an entirely different line from that of previous years. The tournament was called the preliminary round of the Quaid-e-Azam Trophy, and the winner was awarded the Patron's Trophy.

Twenty teams were placed in four groups of five as follows:

Group A: Rawalpindi, Peshawar, Defence Services, Allied Bank, Pakistan Universities.
Group B: Lahore "B", HBFC, Sargodha, WAPDA, Pakistan Inter. Board.
Group C: Multan, Bahawalpur, IDBP, Sukkur, Quetta.
Group D: Karachi "B", State Bank, Hyderabad, Pakistan PWD, PSPC.

There were three new entrants in the tournament–IDBP, State Bank, and Pakistan Inter. Board – but before the start of the competition three teams – Multan, Sukkur, and Pakistan Inter. Board – withdrew.

The tournament was contested on a league basis, with the four group winners then playing a knock-out round. In addition, however, the four group winners qualified for the main Quaid-e-Azam Trophy.

Group A

At Services Ground, Peshawar, December 2, 3, 4. Drawn: Universities won on points. Universities 255 for eight (Asad Rauf 122; Maazaullah Khan five for 66) and 253 for one dec. (Asad Rauf 145 not out, Masud Anwar 83 not out); Peshawar 251 for eight (Maqsood Kundi 68, Farooq Beg 49; Khalid Niazi five for 88, Arshad Khan four for 32) and 101 for six.

At Rawalpindi Club, Rawalpindi, December 2, 3, 4. Drawn: Rawalpindi won on points. Allied Bank 152 (Suleman Qazilbash 38; Mohammad Riaz four for 46) and 288 for nine dec. (Athar Ali Khan 111, Suleman Qazilbash 52; Mohammad Riaz four for 82); Rawalpindi 200 for eight (Mohammad Riaz 65, Salim Asghar 50; Shoib Habib three for 82) and 72 for two (Tariq Javed 36 not out).

At Services Ground, Peshawar, December 6, 7, 8. Drawn: Allied Bank won on points. Universities 282 for eight (Nasir Abbas 115, Asad Rauf 69, Ashraf Ali 43; Mazhar Alvi three for 43) and 225 (Naseer Chughtai 61, Raja Afaq 57; Shoib Habib three for 44); Allied Bank 253 for six (Suleman Qazilbash 100, Iqtidar Ali 89) and 144 for eight (Mohi-ud-Din 52; Nasir Abbas three for 21).

At Rawalpindi Club, Rawalpindi, December 6, 7, 8. Rawalpindi won by an innings and 104 runs. Rawalpindi 323 for eight (Rizwanul Islam 126, Tariq Javed 95; Iqbal Awan three for 95); Combined Services 154 (Zafar 31, Mohammad Riaz six for 44) and 65 (Iqbal Kashmiri 34, Mohammad Sabir five for 14).

At Services Ground, Peshawar, December 10, 11, 12. Tied. Peshawar 139 (Maazaullah Khan 34) and 188 (Farrukh Zaman 51 not out; Tauqeer Haider five for 36); Allied Bank 240 (Tahir Nisar 68, Suleman Qazilbash 41, Babar Sattar four for 44, Ishtiaq Ahmad four for 64) and 87 (Khurshid Akhtar five for 28).

At Rawalpindi Club, Rawalpindi, December 10, 11, 12. Universities won by 164 runs. Universities 246 (Arshad Khan 49, Jamil Zaidi 45; Taqqi three for 32) and 201 for six dec. (Naseer Chughtai 60, Asad Rauf 41); Combined Services 128 (Naseer Chughtai three for 17) and 155 (Naushad Ali 53, Athar Khan three for 18).

At Services Ground, Peshawar, December 14, 15, 16. Peshawar won by four wickets. Combined Services 200 (Khurshid Akhtar six for 64) and 146 (Khalid Khokhar 37; Maazaullah Khan four for 57); Peshawar 234 for nine (Farooq Beg 52, Khalid Beg 43, Zaidi four for 64) and 118 for six (Maazaullah Khan 34 not out; Iqbal Awan five for 42).

At Rawalpindi Club, Rawalpindi, December 14, 15, 16. Rawalpindi won by 162 runs. Rawalpindi 211 for eight (Munir Ahmad 67; Raja Afaq four for 50) and 284 for eight dec. (Tariq Javed 132 not out, Munir Ahmad 58; Khalid Niazi six for 89); Universities 189 for eight (Nasir Abbas 52, Qaisar Hussain 44; Rizwan Khatib three for 41) and 144 (Arshad Khan 39; Mohammad Sabir five for 24).

At PAF Ground, Peshawar, December 18, 19, 20. Allied Bank won by three wickets. Combined Services 299 for five (Tariq 128, Tathir Abbas 62, Naushad Ali 43 not out; Shoib Habib three for 72) and 188 (Khalid Khokhar 54; Tahir Nisar four for 51); Allied Bank 269 (Iqtidar Ali 113 not out, Taqqi three for 40) and 222 for seven (Iqtidar Ali 91; Iqbal Awan five for 52).

At Rawalpindi Club, Rawalpindi, December 18, 19, 20. Drawn; Rawalpindi won on points. Rawalpindi 229 (Rizwanul Islam 32; Khurshid Akhtar seven for 87) and 375 (Tariq Javed 170, Mohammad Riaz 63; Ishtiaq Ahmad three for 77); Peshawar 131.

Group winner: Rawalpindi.

Group B

At Gymkhana Ground, Faisalabad, December 2, 3, 4. Drawn: Sargodha won on points. WAPDA 312 for nine (Ishrat Butt 140 not out, Zahid Hussain 41; Tahir three for 73) and 238 (Shuja-ud-Din 59, Zahid Hussain 48; Waqar five for 97); Sargodha 274 for four (Tariq Cheema 114, Mushtaq Mohammad 108) and 8 for two.

At Gymkhana Ground, Faisalabad, December 6, 7, 8. Drawn: HBFC won on points. HBFC 306 for three (Tariq Alam 105 not out, Pervez Akhtar 84, Javed Sadiq 56 not out, Rais Ahmad 50) and 155 for three (Asif Nazir 50 not out); Sargodha 219 for eight (Sajjad Khan 53 not out, Mushtaq Mohammad 49; Salim-ud-Din five for 53).

At Sialkot, December 11, 12, 13. Drawn; HBFC won on points. HBFC 219 for eight (Nurul Qamar 47, Javed Sadiq 46 not out; Javed Shah three for 62) and 234 for eight (Tariq Alam 91, Rifat Alam 53; Hafiz Ramzan three for 65); Lahore "B" 141 (Ziaur Rehman 41 not out; Asif Nazir six for 33) and 240 (Hafiz Ramzan 118; Rifat Alam four for 73).

At Gaddafi Stadium, Lahore, December 15, 16, 17. HBFC won by an innings and 26 runs. WADPA 220 for eight (Zahid 89; Rifat Alam three for 56) and 122 (Tahir Hussain 43; Rifat Alam six for 44, Irshad Ahmad four for 62); HBFC 368 for seven (Tariq Alam 128 not out, Pervez Akhtar 60, Javed Sadiq 62; Shahzad three for 99).

At Faisalabad Stadium, December 15, 16, 17. Sargodha won by nine wickets. Lahore "B" 95 (Zia 37; Shakeel seven for 56) and 155 (Tahir six for 47); Sargodha 140 (Shakeel 32; Khurshid five for 57) and 113 for one (Tariq Cheema 56 not out).

At Sialkot, December 19, 20, 21. Drawn: WAPDA won on points. Lahore "B" 157 (Shahid Tanwir 36; Arshad Khan six for 43) and 223 (Mansoor Khan 77, Shafaat 49; Imran five for 80, Arshad Khan four for 48); WAPDA 358 for seven (Tahir Hussain 160, Ishrat Butt 112; Sohail Salimi four for 67) and 23 for no wkt.

Group winner: HBFC.

Group C

At Bahawalpur, December 2, 3, 4. Drawn: IDBP won on points. Bahawalpur 196 (Naseer Ahmad 62; Kahlid Mahmood three for 45) and 271 for seven (A. Rahim 76, Zafar Afghan 52, Qasim Shera 54, Shahzad Soomro 43 not out; Shahid Mahboob four for 75); IDBP 287 for eight (Iqbal Chippa 88, Anwar Miandad 46, Ghaffar Ali Khan 43; A. Sami three for 84).

At Bahawalpur, December 6, 7, 8. Drawn: IDBP won on points. Quetta 148 (Asif Baluch 34; Iqbal Chippa six for 44) and 97 (Shahid Mahboob three for 12); IDBP 283 (Jalal-ud-Din 60 not out, Tahir Rashid 53, Ghaffar Ali Khan 52; Riaz Zaidi three for 68).

At Bahawalpur, December 11, 12, 13. Bahawalpur won by seven wickets. Quetta 270 (Asif Baluch 61, Ijaz Yousuf 57 not out, Qamar Mehdi 42; Farooq Shera seven for 37) and 203 (Qamar Mehdi 103; Zulfiqar five for 45); Bahawalpur 301 (A. Rahim 69, Qasim Shera 63, Naseer Ahmad 55; Asif Baluch four for 74) and 176 for three (A. Rahim 80).

Group winner: IDBP.

Group D

At National Stadium, Karachi, December 2, 3, 4. Karachi "B" won by 48 runs. Karachi "B" 215 for eight (Shahid Alam 54, Ahmad Rashid 52 not out; Ali Furrukh three for 62) and 132 (Tauseef Ahmad three for 27); PWD 183 for seven (Nasir Ismail 44; Shahid Iqbal three for 53) and 116 (Tauseef Ahmad 30 not out; Arif Khan three for 19).

At Karachi Gymkhana, December 2, 3, 4. PSPC won by 100 runs. PSPC 154 (Aftab Ansari 36 not out; Abdul Rehman seven for 36) and 192 (Izharul Haq 44; Afzal Chowhan five for 68); Hyderabad 68 for eight dec. (Nasir Bashir five for 21) and 178 (Abid Ali 44, A. Tawab 42; Nasir Bashir four for 68).

At National Stadium, Karachi, December 6, 7, 8. Drawn: Hyderabad won on points. Hyderabad 204 for eight (A. Tawab 51; Nurul Aarfeen four for 45) and 202 for eight dec. (Afzal Chaudhry 102; Amjad Hamid four for 64); State Bank 150 for eight (Mohammad Javed 46; Younis Haroon three for 37) and 199 for eight (Kalim Ijaz 51).

At Karachi Gymkhana, Karachi, December 9, 10, 11. Drawn: PWD won on points. PWD 210 for eight (Tahsin Ahmad 44; Nasir Bashir three for 73) and 166 for nine dec. (Riasat Ali 44; Nasir Bashir four for 43); PSPC 200 for eight (Khalid Ghori 65, Izharul Haq 45; Riasat Ali four for 60) and 33 for no wkt.

At National Stadium, Karachi, December 10, 11, 12. Drawn: Karachi "B" won on points. Hyderabad 234 for eight (Abid Ali 76, Ghulam Ali 55) and 213 (A. Tawab 58, Abdul Rehman 48; Nadim Siddiqui six for 29); Karachi "B" 259 (Shahid Alam 107, Nihal Ansari 60; Abdul Rehman five for 101).

At National Stadium, Karachi, December 14, 16, 17. Karachi won by 167 runs. Karachi "B" 256 (Zahid Baluch 75, Abdur Rashid 66; Amjad Hamid five for 102) and 167 for seven dec. (Nadim Siddiqui 99; Amjad Hamid three for 62); State Bank 133 (Shahid Iqbal five for 33) and 123 (Moeen 53; Nadim Siddiqui three for 5).

At Karachi Gymkhana, Karachi, December 16, 17, 18. Drawn: PWD won on points. Hyderabad 123 (Shaukat Zaman 33; Masroor Hussain three for 14) and 172 (Afzal Chaudhry 72, Ghulam Ali 42; Tauseef Ahmad six for 52); PWD 296 (Wasim Ahmad 82, Tauseef Ahmad 43; Rehman Nizami five for 83).

At National Stadium, Karachi, December 18, 19, 20. PSPC won by ten wickets. State Bank 148 (Mohammad Javed 34) and 110 (Nurul Aarfeen 42; Nasir Baluch four for 42); PSPC 252 (Akram Khan 44; Arif Siddiqui six for 85) and 7 for no wkt.

At Karachi Gymkhana, Karachi, December 20, 21, 22. PWD won by ten wickets. PWD 225 (Naeemul Haq 53, Riasat Ali 41; Arif Siddiqui three for 88) and 24 for no wkt; State Bank 63 (Tauseef Ahmad seven for 25) and 185 (Yaseen 68; Tauseef Ahmad four for 51).

At National Stadium, Karachi, December 22, 23, 24. PSPC won by 11 runs. Karachi "B" 196 (Shahid Alam 92; Nasir Bashir three for 70) and 215 (Nihal Ansari 82, Ahmad Rashid 40; Akram Khan four for 39); PSPC 259 for eight (Akram Khan 100, Farooq Ahmad 54, Rafiq Godil 44; Shahid Iqbal three for 96) and 163 (Khalid Abbasi 34; Shahid Iqbal five for 42).

Group winner: PSPC.

Semi-Finals

At Gaddafi Stadium, Lahore, December 25, 26, 27. HBFC won on first innings lead. HBFC 254 for eight (Tariq Alam 132, Rais Ahmad 87; Raja Sarfraz three for 29) and 368 (Tariq Alam 107, Aftab Ahmad 64, Rifat Alam 53; Mohammad Sabir five for 115); Rawalpindi 178 for eight (Mohammad Riaz 68, Tariq Javed 50; Tariq Alam three for 2) and 100 for two (Mohammad Riaz 59).

At National Stadium, Karachi, December 27, 28, 29. IDBP won by an innings and 4 runs. PSPC 50 (Shahid Mahboob six for 22) and 134 (Farooq Ahmad 47; Jalal-ud-Din four for 27, Iqbal Chippa four for 31); IDBP 188 (Tahir Rashid, 62, Adnan Butt 40; Nasir Bashir four for 72).

Final

At National Stadium, Karachi, January 1, 2, 3, 4. IDBP won by seven wickets. HBFC 190 (Javed Sadiq 67, Pervez Akhtar 54; Jalal-ud-Din four for 44) and 150 (Aftab Ahmad 41; Shahid Mahboob three for 23); IDBP 246 (Shaukat Mirza 114; Rifat Alam three for 35) and 91 for three (Saghir Abbas 43).

FRIENDLY MATCHES, 1979-80

At Gaddafi Stadium, Lahore, October 15, 16, 17. North Zone won by 167 runs. North Zone 206 (Salim Malik 62; Jehanzeb four for 45) and 131 for three dec. (Waqar Malik 75); South Zone 59 (Qamar Zaidi three for 10) and 111 (Athar Ali Khan 56).

At Bahawalpur, December 19, 20, 21. Bahawalpur won by 19 runs. Bahawalpur 347 for four dec. (Naseer Ahmad 170, Shahzad Soomro 112 not out) and 101 for three dec. (Farooq Shera 50 not out, Naseer Ahmad 40); Multan 207 (Javed Ilyas 56, Shahid Butt 44; Farooq Shera five for 58) and 222 (Javed Ilyas 55 not out, Aftab Butt 50; Qasim Shera four for 40).

QUAID-E-AZAM TROPHY, 1979-80

The competition was contested on a league basis with three groups. The winners of each group then met in a triangular league with the Trophy decided on points. Of the four teams who qualified from the preliminary matches, PSPC withdrew, reducing the participants from twelve to eleven.

Note: First innings closed at 85 overs.

Group A

At National Stadium, Karachi, January 6, 7. Drawn; match abandoned after an hour's play on second day when one of the umpires took ill. MCB 190 (Zaigham Burki 53; Mohi-ud-Din four for 71); Karachi "A" 101 for eight (Zaigham Burki seven for 26). *MCB 11 pts, Karachi "A" 10 pts.*

At Karachi Gymkhana, January 6, 7, 8, 9. PIA won by eight wickets. HBFC 205 for five (Rais Ahmad 103 not out, Aftab Ahmad 41; Iqbal Sikandar five for 75) and 109 (Iqbal Sikandar five for 50); PIA 189 (Rizwanuzzman 45; Tariq Alam four for 40) and 127 for two (Rashid Israr 61 not out). *PIA 15 pts, HBFC 6 pts.*

At National Stadium, Karachi, January 11, 12, 13, 14. PIA won by seven wickets. Karachi "A" 231 for nine (Kamal Najamuddin 45; Iqbal Sikandar five for 81) and 240 (Feroze Najamuddin 91; Rashid Khan five for 54); PIA 311 for two (Aftab Baloch 151 not out, Rizwanuzzman 139 not out) and 162 for three (Shoaib Hanif 53, Mushtaq Mohammad 42). *PIA 20 pts, Karachi "A" 2 pts.*

At Karachi Gymkhana, Karachi, January 13, 14, 15, 16. MCB won by nine wickets. HBFC 223 (Tariq Alam 79) and 165 (Tariq Alam 60; Anjam Nasir five for 44, Ejaz Fakih four for 54); MCB 260 (Azmat Rana 55, Babar Basharat 55 not out; Kazim Mehdi five for 92) and 131 for one (Asif Ali 61 not out). *MCB 19 pts, HBFC 6 pts.*

At National Stadium, Karachi, January 17, 18, 19, 20. Karachi "A" won by 128 runs. Karachi "A" 250 for eight (Kamal Najamuddin 91, Afzal Ahmad 50; Asif Nazir four for 83) and 251 for nine dec. (Feroze Najamuddin 98; Kazim Mehdi five for 46); HBFC 133 (Asif Nazir 49; Mohi-ud-Din five for 52) and 240 (Tariq Alam 91; Farid Ahmad four for 43). *Karachi "A" 19 pts, HBFC 3 pts.*

At National Stadium, Karachi, January 22, 23, 24, 25. PIA won by eight wickets. MCB 188 (Azmat Rana 79; Rashid Khan four for 19) and 219 (Azmat Rana 115); PIA 201 for seven (Mushtaq Mohammad 51, Shoaib Hanif 45; Ejaz Fakih five for 78) and 207 for two (Rizwanuzzman 78, Shoaib Hanif 54, Mushtaq Mohammad 42 not out). *PIA 18 pts, MCB 4 pts.*

Group winner: PIA.

Group B

At MCC Ground, Multan, January 6, 7, 8. National Bank won by 21 runs. National Bank 309 (Ali Zia 83, Saleem Pervez 81, Ijaz Ahmad 57 not out; Tariq Wahab four for 69) and 90 (Tariq Wahab four for 55); United Bank 201 (Nasir Valika 50; Iqbal Butt eight for 78) and 177 (Arif-ud-Din 47; Munaf four for 51). *National Bank 20 pts, United Bank 6 pts.*

At PCA Ground, Lahore, January 12, 13, 14, 15. IDBP won by one wicket. United Bank 240 (Nasir Shah 105; Jalal-ud-Din five for 86) and 228 (Kamal Merchant 47, Waheed Mirza 46; Iqbal Chippa five for 47); IDBP 202 (Shaukat Mirza 47; Khurshid Akhtar five for 62) and 268 for nine (Shaukat Mirza 84; Amin Lakhani three for 52). *IDBP 18 pts, United Bank 6 pts.*

At Railway Stadium, Lahore, January 17, 18, 19, 20. National Bank won by 106 runs. National Bank 268 (Mohammad Shafiq 55, Mohammad Jamil 45; Anwar Miandad three for 65) and 263 (Mohammad Shafiq 80, Mohammad Jamil 54, Shafiq Ahmad 50; Jalal-ud-Din four for 65); IDBP 218 (Salim Yousaf 51; Iqbal Butt five for 53) and 207 (Anwar Miandad 60 not out; Iqbal Butt four for 46). *National Bank 19 pts, IDBP 6 pts.*

Group winner: National Bank.

Group C

At Faisalabad Gymkhana, Faisalabad, January 6, 7, 8. Railways won by six wickets. Rawalpindi 113 (Mohammad Nazir five for 16; Azhar Chaudhry five for 38) and 328 (Mohammad Riaz 72, Azmat Ali 72, Mahfooz Ali 41); Railways 232 for six (Gulfraz Khan 105 not out, Siddiq Akbar 78; Rizwan Khatib four for 60) and 210 for four (Siddiq Akbar 103 not out, Saeed Ahmad 71; Rizwan Khatib three for 45). *Railways 18 pts, Rawalpindi 2 pts.*

At Gaddafi Stadium, Lahore, January 11, 12, 13, 14. Lahore "A" won by 229 runs. Lahore "A" 302 for three (Aamer Malik 132 not out, Salim Malik 110) and 286 for five dec. (Aamer Malik 118, Dilshad Butt 96); Railways 182 (Sarfraz Nawaz five for 51) and 177 (Gulfraz Khan 62, Saeed Ahmad 41; Mubarik Ali four for 71). *Lahore "A" 20 pts, Railways 2 pts.*

At Faisalabad Gymkhana, Faisalabad, January 11, 12, 13, 14. Habib Bank won by 248 runs. Habib Bank 271 for seven (Azhar Khan 66 not out, Agha Zahid 65, Arshad Pervez 60; Rizwanuzzman three for 86) and 308 for eight dec. (Azhar Khan 113, Arshad Pervez 109; Mohammad Riaz four for 57); Rawalpindi 173 (Tariq Javed 48, Mohammad Riaz 45; Jamshed Hussain four for 28) and 158 (Chaudhry Yasin 39; Aslam Kureshi four for 26). *Habib Bank 13 pts, Rawalpindi 10 pts.*

At Gaddafi Stadium, Lahore, January 17, 18, 19, 20. Drawn. Lahore "A" 228 for nine (Talat Mirza 87, Salim Malik 54; Agha Zahid five for 24) and 366 (Salim Malik 87, Talat Mirza 76, Shahzad Maqbool 46 not out; Azhar Khan five for 108); Habib Bank 364 for four (Azhar Khan 101 not out, Agha Zahid 87, Tehseen Javed 82, Sultan Rana 66) and 93 for no wkt (Agha Zahid 68 not out). *Habib Bank 14 pts, Lahore "A" 9 pts.*

At Gaddafi Stadium, Lahore, January 21, 22, 23, 24. Habib Bank won by 301 runs. Habib Bank 258 (Noman Shabbir 50, Agha Zahid 48; Inayatullah three for 98) and 286 for seven dec. (Tehseen Javed 83, Azhar Khan 69; Mosleh-ud-Din six for 93); Railways 147 (Jamshed Hussain six for 44) and 96 (Jamshed Hussain five for 33) *Habib Bank 19 pts, Railways 4 pts.*

At PCA Ground, Lahore, January 21. Lahore "A" won on walk-over from Rawalpindi. *Lahore "A" 12 pts.*

Group winner: Habib Bank.

Final Round

At Gaddafi Stadium, Lahore, January 28, 29, 30, 31. Drawn. Habib Bank 271 for eight (Tehseen Javed 80, Azhar Khan 54, Agha Zahid 42) and 365 (Agha Zahid 108, Azhar Khan 49; Anwar Khan four for 79); National Bank 233 for five (Mohammad Arshad 56 not out, Maqsood Ahmad 52 not out, Ijaz Ahmad 47) and 77 for one (Ijaz Ahmad 34 not out). *Habib Bank 11 pts, National Bank 11 pts.*

At Gaddafi Stadium, Lahore, February 2, 3, 4, 5. Drawn. PIA 277 for seven (Hassan Jamil 97, Shahid Mohammad 94; Jamshed Hussain three for 65) and 311 for nine dec. (Rizwanuzzman 120; Jamshed Hussain four for 66); Habib Bank 242 (Azhar Khan 86, Arshad Pervez 64; Naeem Ahmad five for 60) and 157 for two (Agha Zahid 62, Tehseen Javed 52 not out). *PIA 13 pts, Habib Bank 11 pts.*

At Gaddafi Stadium, Lahore, February 7, 8, 9, 10. Drawn. National Bank 275 (Wasim Raja 75, Shafiq Ahmad 67, Maqsood Ahmad 54, Mohammad Shafiq 45; Rashid Khan seven for 96) and 252 for eight dec. (Wasim Raja 72, Mohammad Shafiq 63, Anwar Khan 55 not out; Rashid Khan five for 71); PIA 272 for eight (Hassan Jamil 46, Shoaib Hanif 41; Anwar Khan four for 80) and 182 for nine (Mushtaq Mohammad 103 not out; Anwar Khan four for 45). *PIA 13 pts, National Bank 12 pts.*

Final points: PIA 26, National Bank 23, Habib Bank 22.

CRICKET IN CANADA, 1980

by KENNETH R. BULLOCK

After participation in the ICC Trophy and second Prudential World Cup of 1979, Canada saw the 1980 season as one of consolidation. The feature events of the season began in June with the fourth annual Under 17 tournament in Vancouver, which was immediately followed by an Under 18 training camp. The purpose of both events was to provide a continuing opportunity for young cricketers to reach national level and attain selection for the fourth International Youth Festival team to visit Denmark in 1981. British Columbia, Ontario, Alberta and combined British Columbia-Manitoba competed in the Under 17 round-robin, with Ontario retaining the championship.

In July, the first Under 25 national tournament was held at Ridley College in St Catherines, Ontario, with British Columbia, Ontario, Quebec and the Prairies participating. Ontario easily defeated the Prairies in the final after winning all their qualifying matches in the round-robin tournament. However, O. Dipchand and R. Manoosingh of the Prairies enjoyed an impressive tournament, and were chosen to play for Canada against the USA in September. Dipchand, H. Drakes of Quebec, and Trevor Hart of British Columbia won the awards for top batsman, bowler, and fielder respectively. Chris Chappell, captain of Ontario, and Martin Stead, captain of British Columbia, the only two players at the tournament who had played in the 1979 World Cup squad, both had an excellent week.

At the conclusion of this tournament a Canada Under 25 side played a 50-over match against Bermuda Under 23 and won comfortably by 55 runs, Canada scoring 177 for six and Bermuda 122 for nine. A feature of the Canadian innings was a stand of 102 by C. Chappell (81) and M. Prashad (45). The Bermuda Under 23 team played several more matches in Ontario, and a Bermuda senior side also made a tour of Ontario to honour the 100th anniversary of the Ontario Cricket Association.

In the 35th Atholstan Trophy match, Ontario easily defeated Quebec at Upper Canada College, Toronto. In the John Ross Robertson Tournament for the national club championship, the Toronto Cricket, Skating and Curling Club travelled to Calgary to defeat Caribe Cricket Club to regain the trophy.

Canada completed the season by gaining a major victory over the USA at Forest Park, St Louis, Missouri, by 136 runs, thus retaining the K. Auty Trophy. The Canadian side was the youngest ever fielded, and their performance gave further support to the whole concept of younger players at national level.

Coaching on a national scale was continued in 1980 with two professional coaches working in Canada from early April until early August. Ted Whitfield, the former Northamptonshire and Surrey county cricketer, returned for his third season to coach at both national tournaments and at the cricket summer school in Vancouver. Rob Wood from Beeston, Nottinghamshire, a certified UK coach, came to Canada for his first coaching visit, spending time at both national tournaments and coaching in various cities across Canada. The National Coaching Committee published a Level 2 Technical Coaching Manual.

The Canadian Cricket Association held its semi-annual meeting in Toronto in April and its Annual General Meeting in Montreal in October, when Mr Jack Kyle of Vancouver was re-elected president for 1981 for his third year in office. At this meeting it was announced that a new National Officiating Committee had been established and that plans were being formulated to form the Canadian Association of Cricket Umpires. An application had been made to the federal government in Ottawa for funding for a full-time Executive Director. Should this be approved, it will be the first time the Canadian Cricket Association will have a full-time employee.

Cricket continued to grow throughout Canada, but particularly in the Victoria and District and Toronto and District leagues. Again, as in 1979, high school activity continued to expand in Toronto. A total of 217 clubs played at the senior level in twelve leagues, while 62 junior clubs played in eight leagues.

CANADA v UNITED STATES

At Forest Park, St Louis, Missouri, August 30, 31, September 1. Canada won by 136 runs. The 61st match between the two countries provided Canada with only their second victory in the United States since the resumption of the series in 1963. Coincidentally, the other win was also in St Louis, in 1964. Canada won the toss and, batting first, lost three wickets for 66 by lunch. Dennis and Seeblack added 56 for the fourth wicket, but the remainder of the order offered little resistance against the fine bowling of Mercurius and Khan. In reply, the United States batted well to score 79 for three by the close of play and seemed set to dominate the match. After an early setback when a wicket was lost with only 1 run added, a spirited stand of 44 by Small and Malik took the home side past Canada's total with five wickets remaining. However, Manoosingh's off-spin routed the tail and the USA innings ended at 153, a lead of only 32. The Canadian batting struck form in the second innings, scoring 273 for eight at a run a minute after an opening stand of 77 in 78 minutes by McKenzie and Dipchand had paved the way. Jones and Seeblack continued the onslaught. The declaration yielded a quick wicket before the close of the second day, leaving the United States needing 229 to win on the last day. The task was beyond them, and it took Canada three hours to wrap up the innings, only Bent offering any opposition.

Canada

†M. McKenzie b Khan	2	– (2) c Mitchell b Adler	37
C. Chappell run out	16	– (4) b Mitchell	12
O. Dipchand c Bent b Mercurius	2	– (1) b Mercurius	52
F. Dennis c Malik b Khan	45	– (6) c Mathews b Khan	18
T. Seeblack c and b Mercurius	33	– not out	72
D. Jones lbw b Mercurius	3	– (3) b Mitchell	53
*J. Vaughan b Khan	1	– b Mitchell	0
S. Deare c Ahmed b Mercurius	11	– c Malik b Khan	7
C. Henry b Mercurius	0	– run out	2
R. Manoosingh c Ahmed b Mercurius	3	– not out	8
F. Macdonald not out	2		
B 2, w 1	3	B 4, l-b 8	12

1/2 2/10 3/44 4/100   121   1/77 2/123 3/151   (8 wkts dec.) 273
5/100 6/103 7/111 8/115 9/116   4/163 5/198 6/206
                                             7/221 8/243

Bowling: *First Innings*—Khan 19–3–40–3; Mercurius 16.2–4–37–6; Small 2–0–13–0; Mitchell 5–0–23–0; Ahmed 2–0–5–0. *Second Innings*—Khan 20–4–63–2; Mercurius 15–2–59–1; Ahmed 4–0–22–0; Slocombe 10–2–31–0; Adler 3–1–7–1; Mitchell 17–1–79–3.

USA

S. Ahmed lbw b Jones	25	– (2) c Manoosingh b Vaughan	2
J. Slocombe b Jones	29	– (6) c McKenzie b Deare	4
C. Adler c Deare b Jones	8	– (8) c McKenzie b Vaughan	8
J. Mercurius b Jones	9	– (9) c Deare b Chappell	0
†N. Malik st McKenzie b Manoosingh	18	– (10) b Vaughan	3
D. Small c Seeblack b Manoosingh	20	– (11) not out	3
*K. Khan c Macdonald b Deare	30	– b Chappell	14
H. Mathews st McKenzie b Manoosingh	2	– (5) b Jones	0
C. Facey c Jones b Manoosingh	1	– (1) c McKenzie b Jones	18
F. Bent c Dipchand b Manoosingh	0	– (4) b Chappell	45
K. Mitchell not out	0	– (3) retired hurt	0
B 6, l-b 1, w 2, n-b 2	11	B 5, l-b 3	8

1/44 2/60 3/75 4/80   153   1/3 2/49 3/49 4/66   105
5/124 6/138 7/152 8/152 9/153   5/81 6/96 7/96 8/101 9/104

Bowling: *First Innings*—Vaughan 13–4–27–0; Henry 3–1–11–0; Deare 13–3–34–1; Jones 18–6–37–4; Macdonald 7–1–19–0; Manoosingh 11.4–3–14–5. *Second Innings*—Vaughan 12.1–2–31–3; Jones 7–3–17–2; Deare 6–3–10–1; Chappell 10–4–9–3; Henry 4–2–14–0; Manoosingh 7–1–15–0; Macdonald 3–2–1–0.

CRICKET IN SRI LANKA, 1979-80

By GERRY VAIDYASEKERA

With no major touring side visiting Sri Lanka in 1979-80, interest on the island was concentrated on club cricket, and on the performances of the Sri Lankan players after their visit to England, where they won the 1979 ICC Trophy and were victorious over India in the Prudential (World) Cup. Soon after his return, Anura Tennekoon, captain of the touring party, announced his retirement from first-class cricket. In a distinguished career, he led Sri Lanka to victories over Malaysia, MCC, West Indies, India, and Pakistan, and scored hundreds against the first four of these plus Bangladesh.

A high standard was achieved throughout the club season. The P. Saravanamuttu Trophy, Sri Lanka's principal competition, was won for the first time by Colombo CC. The oldest club on the island, formed in 1863, they won the trophy with a record 112.425 points. Nondescripts, whom Colombo's captain Michael Tissera had once led to Championship honours, were runners-up.

The Raheman Hathy Trophy was won by Nomads, with the runners-up being Kandy, whose captain, Mahes Gunatilleka, hit the fastest century of the season (83 minutes). Sinhalese Sports Club clinched the Donovan Andrée Trophy, and were runners-up in the Daily News Trophy to Galle CC, who won the trophy after an interval of seventeen years. The coveted Robert Senanayaka Trophy for three-day cricket went to the Cricket Board's Rest XI, who beat the Mercantile Cricket Association on the first innings in a match severely curtailed by heavy rain.

Confidence in Sri Lanka's cricket future was shown to be warranted by the number of excellent performances in schools cricket, with 1,000 runs or 50 wickets for the season being achieved by several players. The 101st match between Royal College and St Thomas's College – a three-day fixture – was drawn, and St Peter's College beat Nalanda Vidyala to win the inaugural Horlick's Trophy limited-overs competition for schools. However, there was disappointment over the cancellation of the proposed Sri Lankan schoolboys' tour of Australia in 1981, although it was hoped that a tour of England might be arranged instead.

WOMEN'S CRICKET, 1980

by NETTA RHEINBERG

The welcome announcement at the Women's Cricket Association AGM, held at Lord's on January 12, 1980, that the Co-operative Insurance Society of Manchester – the generous sponsors of the 1979 West Indians' tour of England – had agreed to sponsor the Junior Development programme for at least three years provided the opening for the comprehensive and ambitious junior programme. It was made clear, however, that the sponsorship did not mean that cricket for juniors would be provided free. The policy was one of helping the Association to help itself.

Four two-day residential courses at Chesterfield, Guildford, Luton and Waterlooville were held during February for specially nominated school-girls and junior players and were followed by a National Junior six-a-side tournament at Morden, Surrey, for which there was an entry of 24 teams. This was won by Surrey "A", who received the Mary Duggan Trophy, while Yorkshire "C" were runners-up. A residential coaching week, at Oakham School in July, was attended by 39 players, of whom 28 were juniors, selected by their areas. This course, re-introduced after a gap of three years, was most successful and it is hoped it will be continued.

For these and many other junior events, teams were selected to play in first-class games. Young England played Junior England at the Colts Ground, Edgbaston, on September 13, the Junior XI winning by six wickets, and the following day Young England faced the Rest at Mitchell & Butler's Ground, Birmingham, the match being drawn.

There is no doubt that these varied junior activities will yield dividends for the future. To crown the 1980 season a Young England team was selected for a six and a half weeks tour of India, beginning in January 1981. The age limit being under 25, the five three-day "Test" matches were classed as unofficial. Jill Powell (East Anglia) captained the team, which also included her twin, Jane, who plays for Yorkshire. Other team members were Julie Pritchard (vice-captain), Janet Tedstone (West Midlands); Angela Bainbridge, June Edney (Kent); Jeanette Brittin, Helen Stother, Elaine Wulcko (Sussex); Jill Hirst, Carole Hodges (Lancashire and Cheshire); Denise Leary, Wendy Watson (East Midlands); Maggie Peear (East Anglia); and Sarah Potter (West).

Anne Sanders (Middlesex), the tour manager, is a former England player who holds the MCC Advanced Coaching Certificate and has, since her retirement from first-class cricket, done much coaching. Norma Whitehorn (Surrey) the assistant manager, was Hon. Treasurer of the Association for many years, remains its Hon. Financial Adviser, and has been Hon. Secretary and President of the International Women's Cricket Council. Gill Brent (Yorkshire) toured as the team's physiotherapist.

There were two main matches of the season; firstly a one-day game at Worksop, on June 15, between An England XI and The Rest. As the start was delayed because of poor weather, the number of overs was reduced from 55 to 45; and The Rest won a low-scoring match by seven wickets. The other was a three-day match between An England XI and The Rest, scheduled for July 19, 20, 21 at Canterbury, but no play was possible on the Saturday and what there was on Sunday was badly curtailed. The match was drawn. In both games Sue Goatman captained An England XI and Megan Lear, The Rest.

Although, at the outset, there was not full support for the introduction of the Area Championship, this new venture was carried through smoothly despite the bad weather. All matches were limited-overs games. Middlesex reached the final by beating Thames Valley and Surrey, while their opponents, West Midlands, disposed of The West and Yorkshire. The final, played at St Helens, was won by Middlesex by 8 runs.

The annual National Club Knockout was won for the second year running by Gunnersbury, with Somerset Wanderers runners-up for the third year in succession. An exciting finish produced a tie on the last ball, both teams scoring 129 runs, but Gunnersbury were declared the winners, having lost only six wickets to Somerset Wanderers' nine.

The rules for this competition have been reconsidered by a working party and, from experience gained in the last years, some alterations have been recommended. Intriguing among them is the following: "If the match is rained off, the result to be decided by the toss of a coin. If the team captains are not agreeable to the toss of a coin, both teams are knocked out of the competition!"

Summarised Results

Area Final: at St Helen's, Merseyside, September 7. Middlesex won by 8 runs. Middlesex 144 for nine (55 overs) (J. Green 34, G. Hullah 34; M. Weaver three for 28); West Midlands 136 (54.3 overs) (J. Pritchard 67).

National Club Knockout Final: at Hervines Park, Amersham, September 6. Gunnersbury won on fewer wickets lost. Somerset Wanderers 129 for nine (40 overs); Gunnersbury WCC 129 for six (40 overs).

Young England v Junior England: at Colts Ground, Edgbaston, September 13. Junior England won by six wickets. Young England 179 for four dec. (Jane Powell 54 not out, C. Hodges 54); Junior England 180 for four (S. Lister 76, L. Cooke 68; C. Hodges three for 46).

Young England v The Rest: at Mitchell & Butler's Ground, Birmingham, September 14. Drawn. The Rest 142 for seven dec. (J. Court 51, M. Lear 36; C. Hodges three for 32); Young England 125 for five (C. Hodges 45 not out, J. Edney 32).

An England XI v The Rest: at St Lawrence Ground, Canterbury, July 19, 20, 21. Drawn. An England XI 208 for five dec. (C. Watmough 108 not out, J. Edney 50 not out); The Rest 105 for six (J. Court 36, E. Bakewell 31).

An England XI v The Rest: at Shireoaks, Worksop, June 15. The Rest won by seven wickets. An England XI 86 (45 overs); The Rest 87 for three (37.1 overs).

BIRTHS AND DEATHS OF CRICKETERS

The qualifications are as follows:

1. All players who have appeared in a Test match.

2. Players who have appeared in 50 or more first-class matches during their career and did not die prior to 1970. Owing to the difficulty in obtaining records from India and Pakistan, these countries are not included under this qualification.

3. Players who appeared in fifteen or more first-class matches in the 1980 English season.

4. English county captains, county caps and captains of Oxford and Cambridge Universities who did not die prior to 1970.

5. Oxford and Cambridge Blues of the last ten years. Earlier Blues may be found in previous *Wisdens*.

6. All players chosen as *Wisden* Cricketers of the Year, including the Public Schoolboys chosen for the 1918 and 1919 Almanacks. Cricketers of the Year are identified by the italic notation *CY* and year of appearance.

7. Players or personalities not otherwise qualified who are of sufficient fame or interest to merit inclusion.

Although the country is given for most overseas players, it is not done so for England players. There is a full list of Test Cricketers from page 141.

Robert W. Brooke
November, 1980

Aamer Hameed (Oxford U.) b Oct. 18, 1954

Abberley, R. N. (Warw.) b April 22, 1944

A'Beckett, E. L. (Australia) b Aug. 11, 1907

Abdul Kadir (Pakistan) b May 5, 1944

Abdul Qadir Khan (Pakistan) b Sept. 15, 1955

Abel, R. (Surrey; *CY 1890*) b Nov. 30, 1857, d Dec. 10, 1936

Abell, Sir G. E. B. (Oxford U., Worcs. and N. India) b June 22, 1904

Aberdare, 3rd Lord (*see* Bruce, Hon. C. N.)

Abid Ali, S. (India) b Sept. 9, 1941

Abrahams, J. (Lancs.) b July 21, 1952

Absolom, C. A. (Camb. U. and Kent) b June 7, 1846, d July 30, 1889

Acfield D. L. (Camb. U. and Essex) b July 24, 1947

Achong, E. (W. Indies) b Feb. 16, 1904

Ackerman, H. M. (Border, NE Transvaal, Northants, Natal and W. Province) b April 28, 1947

Adams, P. W. (Cheltenham and Sussex; *CY 1919*) b 1900, d Feb. 28, 1962

A'Court, D. G. (Glos.) b July 27, 1937

Adcock, N. A. T. (S. Africa; *CY 1961*) b March 8, 1931

Adhikari, Col. H. R. (India) b July 31, 1919

Afaq Hussain (Pakistan) b Dec. 31, 1939

Aftab Baloch (Pakistan) b April 1, 1953

Aftab Gul (Pakistan) b March 31, 1946

Agha Saadat Ali (Pakistan) b June 21, 1929

Agha Zahid (Pakistan) b Jan. 7, 1953

Agnew, J. P. (Leics.) b April 4, 1960

Ainsworth, Lt-Cdr M. L. Y. (Worcs.) b May 13, 1922, d Aug. 28, 1978

Aird, R. (Camb. U. and Hants; Sec. MCC 1953-62, Pres. MCC 1968-69) b May 4, 1902

Aitchison, Rev. J. K. (Scotland) b May 26, 1920

Alabaster, G. D. (Canterbury, N. Districts and Otago) b Dec. 10, 1933

Alabaster, J. C. (N. Zealand) b July 11, 1930

Alcock, C. W. (Sec. Surrey CCC 1872-1907, Editor *Cricket* 1882-1907) b Dec. 2, 1842, d Feb. 26, 1907

Alderman, A. E. (Derby.) b Oct. 30, 1907

Aldridge, K. J. (Worcs. and Tasmania) b March 13, 1935

Alexander, F. C. M. (Camb. U. and W. Indies) b Nov. 2, 1928

Alexander, G. (Australia) b April 22, 1851, d Nov. 6, 1930

Alexander, H. H. (Australia) b June 9, 1905

Alim-ud-Din (Pakistan) b Dec. 15, 1930

Allan, D. W. (W. Indies) b Nov. 5, 1937

Allan, F. E. (Australia) b Dec. 2, 1849, d Feb. 9, 1917

Allan, J. M. (Oxford U., Kent, Warw. and Scotland) b April 2, 1932

Allan, P. J. (Australia) b Dec. 31, 1935

Allbrook, M. E. (Camb. U., Kent and Notts.) b Nov. 15, 1954

Allcott, C. F. W. (N. Zealand) b Oct. 7, 1896, d Nov. 21, 1973

Allen, A. W. (Camb. U. and Northants) b Dec. 22, 1912

Allen, B. O. (Camb. U. and Glos.) b Oct. 13, 1911

Allen, D. A. (Glos.) b Oct. 29, 1935

Allen, G. O. B. (Camb. U. and Middx; Pres. MCC 1963-64) b Sydney July 31, 1902

Allen, M. H. J. (Northants and Derby.) b Jan. 7, 1933

Allen, R. C. (Australia) b July 2, 1858, d May 2, 1952

Alletson, E. B. (Notts.) b March 6, 1884, d July 5, 1963

Alley, W. E. (NSW and Somerset; *CY 1962*) b Feb. 3, 1919

Alleyne, H. L. (Barbados and Worcs.) b Feb. 28, 1957

Allom, M. J. C. (Camb. U. and Surrey; Pres. MCC 1969-70) b March 23, 1906

Altham, H. S. (Oxford U., Surrey and Hants; Pres. MCC 1959-60) b Nov. 30, 1888, d March 11, 1965

Amarnath, M. B. (India) b Sept. 24, 1950

Amarnath, N. B. ("Lala") (India) b Sept. 11, 1911

Amarnath, S. B. (India) b Dec. 30, 1948

Amar Singh, L. (India) b Dec. 4, 1910, d May 20, 1940

Ames, L. E. G. (Kent; *CY 1929*) b Dec. 3, 1905

Amir Elahi (India and Pakistan) b Sept. 1, 1908, d Dec. 28, 1980

Amiss, D. L. (Warw.; *CY 1975*) b April 7, 1943

Anderson, J. H. (S. Africa) b April 26, 1874, d March 11, 1926

Anderson, R. W. (N. Zealand) b Oct. 2, 1948

Anderson, W. McD. (N. Zealand) b Oct. 8, 1919, d Dec. 21, 1979

Andrew, K. V. (Northants) b Dec. 15, 1929

Andrews, B. (N. Zealand) b April 4, 1945

Andrews, T. J. E. (Australia) b Aug. 26, 1890, d Jan. 28, 1970

Andrews, W. H. R. (Somerset) b April 14, 1908

Angell, F. L. (Somerset) b June 29, 1922

Anwar Hussain (Pakistan) b July 16, 1920

Anwar Khan (Pakistan) b Dec. 24, 1955

Appleyard, R. (Yorks.; *CY 1952*) b June 27, 1924

Apte, A. L. (India) b Sept. 29, 1934

Apte, M. L. (India) b Oct. 5, 1932

Archer, A. G. (Worcs.) b Dec. 6, 1871, d July 15, 1935

Archer, K. A. (Australia) b Jan. 18, 1928

Archer, R. G. (Australia) b Oct. 25, 1933

Arif Butt (Pakistan) b May 17, 1944

Arlott, John, (Writer and Broadcaster) b Feb. 25, 1914

Armitage, T. (Yorks.) b April 25, 1848, d Sept. 21, 1922

Armstrong, N. F. (Leics.) b Dec. 22, 1892

Armstrong, T. R. (Derby.) b Oct. 13, 1909

Armstrong, W. W. (Australia; *CY 1903*) b May 22, 1879, d July 13, 1947

Arnold, E. G. (Worcs.) b Nov. 7, 1876, d Oct. 25, 1942

Arnold, G. G. (Surrey and Sussex; *CY 1972*) b Sept. 3, 1944

Arnold, J. (Hants) b Nov. 30, 1907

Arnold, P. (Canterbury and Northants) b Oct. 16, 1926

Arnott, T. (Glam.) b Feb. 16, 1902, d Feb. 2, 1975

Asgarali, N. (W. Indies) b Dec. 12, 1922

Ashdown, W. H. (Kent) b Dec. 27, 1898, d Sept. 15, 1979

Ashley, W. H. (S. Africa) b Feb. 10, 1862, d July 14, 1930

Ashton, Sqdn-Ldr C. T. (Camb. U. and Essex) b Feb. 19, 1901, d Oct. 31, 1942

Ashton, G. (Camb. U. and Worcs.) b Sept. 27, 1896

Ashton, Sir H. (Camb. U. and Essex; *CY 1922*; Pres. MCC 1960-61) b Feb. 13, 1898, d June 17, 1979

Asif Iqbal (Kent and Pakistan; *CY 1968*) b June 6, 1943

Asif Masood, S. (Pakistan) b Jan. 23, 1946

Aspinall, R. (Yorks.) b Nov. 27, 1918

Astill, W. E. (Leics.; *CY 1933*) b March 1, 1888, d Feb. 10, 1948

Athey, C. W. J. (Yorks.) b Sept. 27, 1957

Atkinson, C. R. M. (Somerset) b July 23, 1931

Atkinson, D. St E. (W. Indies) b Aug. 9, 1926

Atkinson, E. St E. (W. Indies) b Nov. 6, 1927

Atkinson, G. (Somerset and Lancs.) b March 29, 1938

Atkinson, T. (Notts.) b Sept. 27, 1930

Attenborough, G. R. (S. Australia) b Jan. 17, 1951

Attewell, W. (Notts.; *CY 1892*) b June 12, 1861, d June 11, 1927

Austin, Sir H. B. G. (Barbados) b July 15, 1877, d July 27, 1943

Austin, R. A. (W. Indies) b Sept. 5, 1954

Avery, A. V. (Essex) b Dec. 19, 1914

Aworth, C. J. (Camb. U. and Surrey) b Feb. 19, 1953

Aylward, J. (Hants and All-England) b 1741, d Dec. 27, 1827

Azhar Khan (Pakistan) b Sept. 7, 1955

Azmat Rana (Pakistan) b Nov. 3, 1951

Bacchus, S. F. A. (W. Indies) b Jan. 31, 1954

Bacher, Dr A. (S. Africa) b May 24, 1942

Badcock, C. L. (Australia) b April 10, 1914

Badcock, F. T. (N. Zealand) b Aug. 9, 1898

Baggallay, R. R. C. (Derby.) b May 4, 1884, d Dec. 12, 1975

Bagnall, H. F. (Camb. U. and Northants) b Feb. 18, 1904, d Sept. 2, 1974

Baichan, L. (W. Indies) b May 12, 1946

Baig, A. A. (Oxford U., Somerset and India) b March 19, 1939

Bailey, D. (Durham, Lancs. and Cheshire) b Sept. 9, 1944

Bailey, Sir Derrick (D. T. L.) (Glos.) b August 5, 1918

Bailey, J. (Hants) b April 6, 1908

Bailey, J. A. (Essex and Oxford U.; Sec. MCC 1974-) b June 22, 1930

Bailey, T. E. (Essex and Camb. U.; *CY 1950*) b Dec. 3, 1923

Bainbridge, P. (Glos.) b April 16, 1958

Bairstow, D. L. (Yorks. and Griqualand W.) b Sept. 1, 1951

Baker, C. S. (Warw.) b Jan. 5, 1883, d Dec. 16, 1976

Baker, R. K. (Camb. U. and Essex) b April 28, 1952

Baker, R. P. (Surrey) b April 9, 1954

Bakewell, A. H. (Northants; *CY 1934*) b Nov. 2, 1908

Balaskas, X. C. B. (S. Africa) b Oct. 15, 1910

Balderstone, J. C. (Yorks. and Leics.) b Nov. 16, 1940

Baldry, D. O. (Middx and Hants) b Dec. 26, 1931

Banerjee, S. A. (India) b Nov. 1, 1919

Banerjee, S. N. (India) b Oct. 3, 1913, d Oct. 14, 1980

Bannerman, A. C. (Australia) b March 21, 1859, d Sept. 19, 1924

Bannerman, Charles (Australia) b Woolwich, Kent July 23, 1851, d Aug. 20, 1930

Bannister, C. S. (Camb. U.) b May 22, 1956

Bannister, J. D. (Warw.) b Aug. 23, 1930

Barber, A. T. (Oxford U. and Yorks.) b June 17, 1905

Barber, R. T. (N. Zealand) b June 23, 1925

Barber, R. W. (Lancs., Camb. U. and Warw.; *CY 1967*) b Sept. 26, 1935

Barber, W. (Yorks.) b April 18, 1901, d Sept. 10, 1968

Barclay, J. R. T. (Sussex and Orange Free State) b Jan. 22, 1954

Bardsley, W. (Australia; *CY 1910*) b Dec. 7, 1882, d Jan. 20, 1954

Barford, M. T. (Camb. U.) b June 7, 1950

Baring, A. E. G. (Hants) b Jan. 21, 1910

Barker, G. (Essex) b July 6, 1931

Barling, H. T. (Surrey) b Sept. 1, 1906

Barlow, A. (Lancs.) b Aug. 31, 1915

Barlow, E. A. (Oxford U. and Lancs.) b Feb. 24, 1912, d June 27, 1980

Barlow, E. J. (Derby. and S. Africa) b Aug. 12, 1940

Barlow, G. D. (Middx) b March 26, 1950

Barlow, R. G. (Lancs.) b May 28, 1851, d July 31, 1919

Barnard, H. M. (Hants) b July 18, 1933

Barnes, A. R. (Sec. Australian Cricket Board, 1960-) b Sept. 12, 1916

Barnes, S. F. (Warw. and Lancs.; *CY 1910*) b April 19, 1873, d Dec. 26, 1967

Barnes, S. G. (Australia) b June 5, 1916, d Dec. 16, 1973

Barnes, W. (Notts.; *CY 1890*) b May 27, 1852, d March 24, 1899

Barnett, B. A. (Australia) b May 23, 1908, d June 29, 1979

Barnett, C. J. (Glos.; *CY 1937*) b July 3, 1910

Barnett, K. J. (Derby.) b July 17, 1960

Barnwell, C. J. P. (Somerset) b June 23, 1914

Baroda, Maharaja of (Manager, India in England, 1959) b April 2, 1930

Barratt, Fred (Notts.) b April 12, 1894, d Jan. 29, 1947

Barratt, R. J. (Leics.) b May 3, 1942

Barrett, A. G. (W. Indies) b Jan. 4, 1944

Barrett, J. E. (Australia) b Oct. 15, 1866, d Feb. 9, 1916

Barrick, D. W. (Northants) b April 28, 1926

Barrington, K. F. (Surrey; *CY 1960*) b Nov. 24, 1930

Barron, W. (Lancs. and Northants) b Oct. 26, 1917

Barrow, I. (W. Indies) b Jan. 6, 1911, d April 2, 1979

Bartholomew, P. C. S. (Trinidad) b Oct. 9, 1939

Bartlett, E. L. (W. Indies) b March 18, 1906, d Dec. 21, 1976

Bartlett, G. A. (N. Zealand) b Feb. 3, 1941

Bartlett, H. T. (Camb. U., Surrey and Sussex; *CY 1939*) b Oct. 7, 1914

Barton, M. R. (Oxford U. and Surrey) b Oct. 14, 1914

Barton, P. T. (N. Zealand) b Oct. 9, 1935

Barton, V. A. (Kent and Hants) b Oct. 6, 1867, d March 23, 1906

Bates, D. L. (Sussex) b May 10, 1933

Bates, L. T. A. (Warw.) b March 20, 1895, d March 11, 1971

Bates, W. (Yorks.) b Nov. 19, 1855, d Jan. 8, 1900

Bath, B. F. (Transvaal) b Jan. 16, 1947

Baumgartner, H. V. (S. Africa) b Nov. 17, 1883, d April 8, 1938

Baxter, A. D. (Devon, Lancs., Middx and Scotland) b Jan. 20, 1910

Bean, G. (Notts. and Sussex) b March 7, 1864, d March 16, 1923

Bear, M. J. (Essex and Canterbury) b Feb. 23, 1934

Beard, D. D. (N. Zealand) b Jan. 14, 1920

Booth, F. S. (Lancs.) b Feb. 12, 1907, d Jan. 21, 1980

Booth, M. W. (Yorks.; *CY 1914*) b Dec. 10, 1886, d July 1, 1916

Booth, P. (Leics.) b Nov. 2, 1952

Booth, R. (Yorks. and Worcs.) b Oct. 1, 1926

Borde, C. G. (India) b July 21, 1934

Border, A. R. (Glos. and Australia) b July 27, 1955

Bore, M. K. (Yorks. and Notts.) b June 2, 1947

Borrington, A. J. (Derby.) b Dec. 8, 1948

Bosanquet, B. J. T. (Oxford U. and Middx; *CY 1905*) b Oct. 13, 1877, d Oct. 12, 1936

Boshier, B. S. (Leics.) b March 6, 1932

Botham, I. T. (Somerset; *CY 1978*) b Nov. 24, 1955

Botten, J. T. (S. Africa) b June 21, 1938

Botton, N. D. (Oxford U.) b June 21, 1954

Boucher, J. C. (Ireland) b Dec. 22, 1910

Bourne, W. A. (Barbados and Warw.) b Nov. 15, 1952

Bowden, M. P. (Surrey and Transvaal) b Nov. 1, 1865, d Feb. 19, 1892

Bowditch, M. H. (W. Province) b Aug. 30, 1945

Bowes, W. E. (Yorks.; *CY 1932*) b July 25, 1908

Bowles, J. J. (Worcs.) b April 3, 1890, d Nov. 1971

Bowley, E. H. (Sussex and Auckland; *CY 1930*) b June 6, 1890, d July 9, 1974

Bowley, F. L. (Worcs.) b Nov. 9, 1873, d May 31, 1943

Bowman, R. (Oxford U. and Lancs.) b Jan. 26, 1934

Box, T. (Sussex) b Feb. 7, 1808, d July 12, 1876

Boyce, K. D. (Essex and W. Indies; *CY 1974*) b Oct. 11, 1943

Boycott, G. (Yorks. and N. Transvaal; *CY 1965*) b Oct. 21, 1940

Boyd-Moss, R. J. (Camb. U. and Northants) b Dec. 16, 1959

Boyes, G. S. (Hants) b March 31, 1899, d Feb. 11, 1973

Boyle, H. F. (Australia) b Dec. 10, 1847, d Nov. 21, 1907

Bracewell, B. P. (N. Zealand) b Sept. 14, 1959

Bradburn, W. P. (N. Zealand) b Nov. 24, 1938

Bradley, W. M. (Kent) b Jan. 2, 1875, d June 19, 1944

Bradman, Sir D. G. (Australia; *CY 1931*) b Aug. 27, 1908

Bradshaw, J. C. (Leics.) b Jan. 25, 1902

Brain, B. M. (Worcs. and Glos.) b Sept. 13, 1940

Brann, W. H. (S. Africa) b April 4, 1899, d Sept. 22, 1953

Brassington, A. J. (Glos.) b Aug. 9, 1954

Bratchford, J. D. (Queensland) b Feb. 2, 1929

Braund, L. C. (Surrey and Somerset; *CY 1902*) b Oct. 18, 1875, d Dec. 22, 1955

Bray, C. (Essex) b April 6, 1898

Brayshaw, I. J. (W. Australia) b Jan. 14, 1942

Brazier, A. F. (Surrey and Kent) b Dec. 7, 1924

Breakwell, D. (Northants and Somerset) b July 2, 1948

Brearley, J. M. (Camb. U. and Middx; *CY 1977*) b April 28, 1942

Brearley, W. (Lancs.; *CY 1909*) b March 11, 1876, d Jan. 30, 1937

Brennan, D. V. (Yorks.) b Feb. 10, 1920

Brettell, D. N. (Oxford U.) b March 10, 1956

Brickett, D. J. (E. Province) b Dec. 9, 1950

Bridge, W. B. (Warw.) b May 29, 1938

Bridger, Rev. J. R. (Hants) b April 8, 1920

Brierley, T. L. (Glam. and Lancs.) b June 15, 1910

Briers, N. E. (Leics.) b Jan. 15, 1955

Briggs, John (Lancs.; *CY 1889*) b Oct. 3, 1862, d Jan. 11, 1902

Bright, R. J. (Australia) b July 13, 1954

Briscoe, A. W. (S. Africa) b Feb. 6, 1911, d April 22, 1941

Broad, B. C. (Glos.) b Sept. 29, 1957

Broadbent, R. G. (Worcs.) b June 21, 1924

Brocklebank, Sir J. M. Bt (Camb. U. and Lancs.) b Sept. 3, 1915, d Sept. 13, 1974

Brocklehurst, B. G. (Somerset) b Feb. 18, 1922

Brockwell, W. (Kimberley and Surrey; *CY 1895*) b Jan. 21, 1865, d July 1, 1935

Broderick, V. (Northants) b Aug. 17, 1920

Brodhurst, A. H. (Camb. U. and Glos.) b July 21, 1916

Bromfield, H. D. (S. Africa) b June 26, 1932

Bromley, E. H. (Australia) b Sept. 2, 1912, d Feb. 1, 1967

Bromley-Davenport, H. R. (Camb. U., Cheshire and Middx) b Aug. 18, 1870, d May 23, 1954

Brooker, M. E. W. (Camb. U.) b March 24, 1954

Brookes, D. (Northants; *CY 1957*) b Oct. 29, 1915

Brookes, W. H. (Editor of *Wisden* 1936-39) b Dec. 5, 1894, d May 28, 1955

Brooks, E. W. J. (Surrey) b July 6, 1898, d Feb. 10, 1960

Brown, A. (Kent) b Oct. 17, 1935

Brown, A. S. (Glos.) b June 24, 1936

Brown, D. J. (Warw.) b Jan. 30, 1942

Brown, D. W. J. (Glos.) b Feb. 26, 1942

Brown, E. (Warw.) b Nov. 27, 1911

Brown, F. R. (Camb. U., Surrey and Northants; *CY 1933*; Pres. MCC 1971-72) b Lima, Peru Dec. 16, 1910

Brown, George (Sussex and England) b April 27, 1783, d June 25, 1857

Brown, G. (Hants) b Oct. 6, 1887, d Dec. 3, 1964

Brown, J. (Scotland) b Sept. 24, 1931

Brown, J. T. (Yorks.; *CY 1895*) b Aug. 20, 1869, d Nov. 4, 1904

Brown, L. S. (S. Africa) b Nov. 24, 1910

Brown, S. M. (Middx) b Dec. 8, 1917

Brown, W. A. (Australia; *CY 1939*) b July 31, 1912

Brown, W. C. (Northants) b Nov. 13, 1900

Browne, C. R. (W. Indies) b Oct. 8, 1890, d Jan. 12, 1964

Browne, Canon F. B. R. (Camb. U. and Sussex) b July 28, 1899, d March 11, 1970

Bruce, Hon. C. N. (3rd Lord Aberdare) (Oxford U. and Middx) b Aug. 2, 1885, d Oct. 4, 1957

Bruce, W. (Australia) b May 22, 1864, d Aug. 3, 1925

Bruyns, A. (W. Province and Natal) b Sept. 19, 1946

Bryan, Brig. G. J. (Kent) b Dec. 29, 1902

Bryan, J. L. (Camb. U. and Kent; *CY 1922*) b May 26, 1896

Bryan, R. T. (Kent) b July 30, 1898, d July 27, 1970

Buckenham, C. P. (Essex) b Jan. 16, 1876, d Feb. 23, 1937

Buckingham, J. (Warw.) b Jan. 21, 1903

Budd, E. H. (Middx and All-England) b Feb. 23, 1785, d March 29, 1875

Budd, W. L. (Hants) b Oct. 25, 1913

Buggins, B. L. (W. Australia) b Jan. 29, 1935

Bull, D. F. E. (Queensland) b Aug. 13, 1935

Bull, F. G. (Essex; *CY 1898*) b April 2, 1876, d Sept. 16, 1910

Buller, J. S. (Yorks. and Worcs.) b Aug. 23, 1909, d Aug. 7, 1970

Burchnall, R. L. (Oxford U.) b Aug. 8, 1948

Burden, M. D. (Hants) b Oct. 4, 1930

Burge, P. J. P. (Australia; *CY 1965*) b May 17, 1932

Burger, C. G. de V. (S. Africa) b July 12, 1935

Burgess, G. I. (Somerset) b May 5, 1943

Burgess, M. G. (N. Zealand) b July 17, 1944

Burke, C. (N. Zealand) b March 22, 1914

Burke, J. W. (Australia; *CY 1957*) b June 12, 1930, d Feb. 2, 1979

Burke, S. F. (S. Africa) b March 11, 1934

Burki, Javed (Oxford U. and Pakistan) b May 8, 1938

Burn, K. E. (Australia) b Sept. 17, 1863, d July 20, 1956

Burnet, J. R. (Yorks.) b Oct. 11, 1918

Burnup, C. J. (Camb. U. and Kent; *CY 1903*) b Nov. 21, 1875, d April 5, 1960

Burrough, H. D. (Somerset) b Feb. 6, 1909

Burrow, B. W. (Griqualand W.) b Feb. 8, 1940

Burton, D. C. F. (Yorks.) b Sept. 13, 1887, d Sept. 24, 1971

Burton, F. J. (Australia) b 1866, d Aug. 25, 1929

Burton, M. St J. W. (Oxford U. and E. Province) b Feb. 14, 1944

Burtt, J. W. (C. Districts) b June 11, 1944

Burtt, T. B. (N. Zealand) b Jan. 22, 1915

Bury, T. E. O. (Oxford U.) b May 14, 1958

Buse, H. T. F. (Somerset) b Aug. 5, 1910

Bushby, M. H. (Camb. U.) b July 29, 1931

Buss, A. (Sussex) b Sept. 1, 1939

Buss, M. A. (Sussex and Orange Free State) b Jan. 24, 1944

Buswell, J. E. (Northants) b July 3, 1909

Butcher, A. R. (Surrey) b Jan. 7, 1954

Butcher, B. F. (W. Indies; *CY 1970*) b Sept. 3, 1933

Butcher, R. O. (Middx and Barbados) b Oct. 14, 1953

Butler, H. J. (Notts.) b March 12, 1913

Butler, L. C. (Wellington) b Sept. 2, 1934

Butler, L. S. (W. Indies) b Feb. 9, 1929

Butt, H. R. (Sussex) b Dec. 27, 1865, d Dec. 21, 1928

Butterfield, L. A. (N. Zealand) b Aug. 29, 1913

Buxton, I. R. (Derby.) b April 17, 1938

Buys, I. D. (S. Africa) b Feb. 3, 1895

Bynoe, M. R. (W. Indies) b Feb. 21, 1941

Caesar, Julius (Surrey and All-England) b March 25, 1830, d March 6, 1878

Caffyn, W. (Surrey and NSW) b Feb. 2, 1828, d Aug. 28, 1919

Caine, C. Stewart (Editor of *Wisden* 1926-33) b Oct. 28, 1861, d April 15, 1933

Cairns, B. L. (N. Zealand) b Oct. 10, 1949

Calder, H. L. (Cranleigh; *CY 1918*) b 1900

Callaway, S. T. (Australia) b Feb. 6, 1868, d Nov. 25, 1923

Callen, I. W. (Australia) b May 2, 1955

Calthorpe, Hon. F. S. Gough- (Camb. U., Sussex and Warw.) b May 27, 1892, d Nov. 19, 1935

Camacho, G. S. (W. Indies) b Oct. 15, 1945

Cameron, F. J. (W. Indies) b June 22, 1923

Cameron, F. J. (N. Zealand) b June 1, 1932

Cameron, H. B. (S. Africa; *CY 1936*) b July 5, 1905, d Nov. 2, 1935

Cameron, J. H. (Camb. U., Somerset and W. Indies) b April 8, 1914

Campbell, K. O. (Otago) b March 20, 1943

Campbell, T. (S. Africa) b Feb. 9, 1882, d Oct. 5, 1924

Cannings, V. H. D. (Warw. and Hants) b April 3, 1919

Caple, R. G. (Middx and Hants) b Dec. 8, 1939

Cardus, Sir Neville (Cricket Writer) b April 2, 1889, d Feb. 27, 1975

Carew, G. McD. (W. Indies) b 1910, d Dec. 9, 1974

Carew, M. C. (W. Indies) b Sept. 15, 1937
Carkeek, W. (Australia) b Oct. 17, 1878, d Feb. 20, 1937
Carlson, P. H. (Australia) b Aug. 8, 1951
Carlstein, P. R. (S. Africa) b Oct. 28, 1938
Carmody, D. K. (NSW and W. Australia) b Feb. 16, 1919, d Oct. 21, 1977
Carpenter, D. (Glos.) b Sept. 12, 1935
Carpenter, R. (Cambs. and Utd England XI) b Nov. 18, 1830, d July 13, 1901
Carr, A. W. (Notts.; *CY 1923*) b May 21, 1893, d Feb. 7, 1963
Carr, D. B. (Oxford U. and Derby.; *CY 1960*; Sec. TCCB 1974-   ) b Dec. 28, 1926
Carr, D. W. (Kent; *CY 1910*) b March 17, 1872, d March 23, 1950
Carrick, P. (Yorks. and E. Province) b July 16, 1952
Carrigan, A. H. (Queensland) b Aug. 26, 1917
Carrington, E. (Derby.) b March 25, 1914
Carroll, P. R. (Oxford U.) b Nov. 7, 1941
Carter, C. P. (S. Africa) b April 23, 1881, d Nov. 8, 1952
Carter, H. (Australia) b Halifax, Yorks. March 15, 1878, d June 8, 1948
Carter, R. G. (Warw.) b April 14, 1933
Carter, R. G. M. (Worcs.) b July 11, 1937
Carter, W. (Derby.) b May 14, 1896, d Nov. 1, 1975
Cartwright, H. (Derby.) b May 12, 1951
Cartwright, T. W. (Warw., Somerset and Glam.) b July 22, 1935
Carty, R. A. (Hants) b July 28, 1922
Cass, G. R. (Essex and Worcs.) b April 23, 1940
Castell, A. T. (Hants) b Aug. 6, 1943
Castle, F. (Somerset) b April 9, 1909
Catt, A. W. (Kent and W. Province) b Oct. 2, 1933
Catterall, R. H. (S. Africa; *CY 1925*) b July 10, 1900, d Jan. 2, 1961
Causby, J. P. (S. Australia) b Oct. 27, 1942
Cave, H. B. (N. Zealand) b Oct. 10, 1922
Chadwick, D. (W. Australia) b March 29, 1941
Challenor, G. (W. Indies) b June 28, 1888, d July 30, 1947
Chandrasekhar, B. S. (India; *CY 1972*) b May 18, 1945
Chang, H. S. (W. Indies) b July 22, 1952
Chaplin, H. P. (Sussex) b March 1, 1883, d March 6, 1970
Chapman, A. P. F. (Uppingham, Camb. U. and Kent; *CY 1919*) b Sept. 3, 1900, d Sept. 16, 1961
Chapman, H. W. (S. Africa) b June 30, 1890, d Dec. 1, 1941
Chapman, T. A. (Leics. and Rhodesia) b May 14, 1919, d Feb. 19, 1979
Chappell, G. S. (Somerset and Australia; *CY 1973*) b Aug. 7, 1948

Chappell, I. M. (Lancs. and Australia; *CY 1976*) b Sept. 26, 1943
Chapple, M. E. (N. Zealand) b July 25, 1930
Charlton, P. C. (Australia) b April 9, 1867, d Sept. 30, 1954
Charlwood, H. R. J. (Sussex) b Dec. 19, 1846, d June 6, 1888
Chatfield, E. J. (N. Zealand) b July 3, 1950
Chatterton, W. (Derby.) b Dec. 27, 1861, d March 19, 1913
Chauhan, C. P. S. (India) b July 21, 1947
Cheatle, R. G. L. (Sussex and Surrey) b July 31, 1953
Cheetham, J. E. (S. Africa) b May 26, 1920, d Aug. 21, 1980
Chester, F. (Worcs.; Umpire) b Jan. 20, 1895, d April 8, 1957
Chesterton, G. H. (Oxford U. and Worcs.) b July 15, 1922
Chevalier, G. A. (S. Africa) b March 9, 1937
Childs, J. H. (Glos.) b Aug. 15, 1951
Childs-Clarke, A. W. (Middx and Northants) b May 13, 1905, d Feb. 19, 1980
Chipperfield, A. G. (Australia) b Nov. 17, 1905
Chisholm, R. H. E. (Scotland) b May 22, 1927
Chowdhury, N. R. (India) b May 23, 1923
Christiani, C. M. (W. Indies) b Oct. 28, 1913, d April 4, 1938
Christiani, R. J. (W. Indies) b July 19, 1920
Christopherson, S. (Kent; Pres. MCC 1939-45) b Nov. 11, 1861, d April 6, 1949
Christy, J. A. J. (S. Africa) b Dec. 12, 1904, d Feb. 1, 1971
Chubb, G. W. A. (S. Africa) b April 12, 1911
Clark, D. G. (Kent; Pres. MCC 1977-78) b Jan. 27, 1919
Clark, E. A. (Middx) b April 15, 1937
Clark, E. W. (Northants) b Aug. 9, 1902
Clark, L. S. (Essex) b March 6, 1914
Clark, T. H. (Surrey) b Oct. 4, 1924
Clark, W. M. (Australia) b Sept. 19, 1953
Clarke, Dr C. B. (Northants, Essex and W. Indies) b April 7, 1918
Clarke, R. W. (Northants) b April 22, 1924
Clarke, S. T. (Barbados, Surrey and W. Indies) b Dec. 11, 1954
Clarke, William (Notts.; founded All-England XI and Trent Bridge ground) b Dec. 24, 1798, d Aug. 25, 1856
Clarkson, J. A. (Yorks. and Somerset) b Sept. 5, 1939
Claughton, J. A. (Oxford U. and Warw.) b Sept. 17, 1956
Clay, J. C. (Glam.) b March 18, 1898, d Aug. 12, 1973
Clay, J. D. (Notts.) b Oct. 15, 1924
Clayton, G. (Lancs. and Somerset) b Feb. 3, 1938
Clements, S. M. (Oxford U.) b April 19, 1956

Cleverley, D. C. (N. Zealand) b Dec. 23, 1909

Clift, Patrick B. (Rhodesia and Leics.) b July 14, 1953

Clift, Philip B. (Glam.) b Sept. 3, 1919

Clinton, G. S. (Kent, Surrey and Zimbabwe-Rhodesia) b May 5, 1953

Close, D. B. (Yorks. and Somerset; *CY 1964*) b Feb. 24, 1931

Cobden, F. C. (Camb. U.) b Oct. 14, 1849, d Dec. 7, 1932

Cobham, 10th Visct (Hon. C. J. Lyttelton) (Worcs.; Pres. MCC 1954) b Aug. 8, 1909, d March 20, 1977

Cochrane, J. A. K. (S. Africa) b July 15, 1909

Cockbain, I. (Lancs.) b April 19, 1958

Coen, S. K. (S. Africa) b Oct. 14, 1902, d Jan. 28, 1967

Colah, S. M. H. (India) b Sept. 22, 1902, d Sept. 11, 1950

Colchin, Robert ("Long Robin") (Kent and All-England) b Nov. 1713, d April 1750

Coldwell, L. J. (Worcs.) b Jan. 10, 1933

Coleman, C. A. R. (Leics.) b July 7, 1906, d June 14, 1978

Colley, D. J. (Australia) b March 15, 1947

Collin, T. (Warw.) b April 17, 1911

Collinge, R. O. (N. Zealand) b April 2, 1946

Collins, H. L. (Australia) b Jan. 21, 1889, d May 28, 1959

Collins, R. (Lancs.) b March 10, 1934

Colquhoun, I. A. (N. Zealand) b June 8, 1924

Comber, J. T. H. (Camb. U.) b Feb. 26, 1911, d May 3, 1976

Commaille, J. M. M. (S. Africa) b Feb. 21, 1883, d July 27, 1956

Compton, D. C. S. (Middx; *CY 1939*) b May 23, 1918

Compton, L. H. (Middx) b Sept. 12, 1912

Coney, J. V. (N. Zealand) b June 21, 1952

Congdon, B. E. (N. Zealand; *CY 1974*) b Feb. 11, 1938

Coningham, A. (Australia) b July 4, 1866, d June 1939

Connolly, A. N. (Middx and Australia) b June 29, 1939

Constable, B. (Surrey) b Feb. 19, 1921

Constant, D. J. (Kent and Leics.) b Nov. 9, 1941

Constantine, Lord L. N. (W. Indies; *CY 1940*) b Sept. 21, 1902, d July 1, 1971

Constantine, L. S. (Trinidad) b May 25, 1874, d Jan. 5, 1942

Contractor, N. J. (India) b March 7, 1934

Conyngham, D. P. (S. Africa) b May 10, 1897

Cook, C. (Glos.) b Aug. 23, 1921

Cook, F. J. (S. Africa) b 1870, assumed dead

Cook, G. (Northants and E. Province) b Oct. 9, 1951

Cook, G. G. (Queensland) b June 29, 1910

Cook, G. W. (Camb. U. and Kent) b Feb. 9, 1936

Cook, N. G. B. (Leics.) b June 17, 1956

Cook, S. J. (Transvaal) b July 31, 1953

Cook, T. E. (Sussex) b Feb. 5, 1901, d Jan. 15, 1950

Coope, M. (Somerset) b Nov. 28, 1917, d July 5, 1974

Cooper, A. H. C. (S. Africa) b Sept. 2, 1893, d July 18, 1963

Cooper, B. B. (Middx, Kent and Australia) b March 15, 1844, d Aug. 7, 1914

Cooper, F. S. Ashley- (Cricket Historian) b March 17, 1877, d Jan. 31, 1932

Cooper, G. C. (Sussex) b Sept. 2, 1936

Cooper, H. P. (Yorks. and N. Transvaal) b April 17, 1949

Cooper, K. E. (Notts.) b Dec. 27, 1957

Cooper, N. H. C. (Glos. and Camb. U.) b Oct. 14, 1953

Cooper, W. H. (Australia) b Sept. 11, 1849, d April 5, 1939

Cope, G. A. (Yorks.) b Feb. 23, 1947

Copson, W. H. (Derby.; *CY 1937*) b April 27, 1908, d Sept. 14, 1971

Cordle, A. E. (Glam.) b Sept. 21, 1940

Corling, G. E. (Australia) b July 13, 1941

Cornford, J. H. (Sussex) b Dec. 9, 1911

Cornford, W. L. (Sussex) b Dec. 25, 1900, d Feb. 6, 1963

Corlett, S. C. (Oxford U.) b Jan. 18, 1950

Cornwallis, Capt. Hon. W. S. (2nd Lord Cornwallis) (Kent) b March 14, 1892

Corrall, P. (Leics.) b July 16, 1906

Corran, A. J. (Oxford U. and Notts.) b Nov. 25, 1936

Cosier, G. J. (Australia) b April 25, 1953

Cottam, J. T. (Australia) b Sept. 5, 1867, d Jan. 30, 1897

Cottam, R. M. H. (Hants and Northants) b Oct. 16, 1944

Cotter, A. (Australia) b Dec. 3, 1883, d Oct. 30, 1917

Cotton, J. (Notts. and Leics.) b Nov. 7, 1940

Cottrell, G. A. (Camb. U.) b March 23, 1945

Cottrell, P. R. (Camb. U.) b May 22, 1957

Coulson, S. S. (Leics.) b Oct. 17, 1898

Coulthard, G. (Australia) b Aug. 1, 1856, d Oct. 22, 1883

Coventry, Hon. C. J. (Worcs.) b Feb. 26, 1867, d June 2, 1929

Coverdale, S. P. (Camb. U. and Yorks.) b Nov. 20, 1954

Cowan, M. J. (Yorks.) b June 10, 1933

Cowan, R. S. (Oxford U.) b March 30, 1960

Cowdrey, C. S. (Kent) b Oct. 20, 1957

Cowdrey, M. C. (Oxford U. and Kent; *CY 1956*) b Dec. 24, 1932

Cowie, J. (N. Zealand) b March 30, 1912

Cowley, N. G. (Hants) b March 1, 1953

Cowper, R. M. (Australia) b Oct. 5, 1940

Cox, A. L. (Northants) b July 22, 1908

Cox, G. jnr (Sussex) b Aug. 23, 1911

Cox, G. R. (Sussex) b Nov. 29, 1873, d March 24, 1949

Cox, J. L. (S. Africa) b June 28, 1886, d July 4, 1971

Coxon, A. (Yorks.) b Jan. 18, 1916

Crabtree, H. P. (Essex) b April 30, 1906

Craig, E. J. (Camb. U. and Lancs.) b March 26, 1942

Craig, I. D. (Australia) b June 12, 1935

Cranfield, L. M. (Glos.) b Aug. 29, 1909

Cranmer, P. (Warw.) b Sept. 10, 1914

Cranston, J. (Glos.) b Jan. 9, 1859, d Dec. 10, 1904

Cranston, K. (Lancs.) b Oct. 20, 1917

Crapp, J. F. (Glos.) b Oct. 14, 1912

Crawford, J. N. (Surrey and S. Australia; *CY 1907*) b Dec. 1, 1886, d May 2, 1963

Crawford, N. C. (Camb. U.) b Nov. 26, 1958

Crawford, W. P. A. (Australia) b Aug. 3, 1933

Crawley, A. M. (Oxford U. and Kent; Pres. MCC 1972-73) b April 10, 1908

Crawley, L. G. (Camb. U., Worcs. and Essex) b July 26, 1903

Cray, S. J. (Essex) b May 29, 1921

Creese, W. L. C. (Hants) b Dec. 28, 1907, d March 9, 1974

Cresswell, G. F. (N. Zealand) b March 22, 1915, d Jan. 10, 1966

Cripps, G. (S. Africa) b Oct. 19, 1865, d July 27, 1943

Crisp, R. J. (Worcs. and S. Africa) b May 28, 1911

Croft, C. E. H. (Lancs. and W. Indies) b March 15, 1953

Cromb, I. B. (N. Zealand) b June 25, 1905

Crookes, N. S. (Natal) b Nov. 15, 1935

Cross, G. F. (Leics.) b Nov. 15, 1943

Crump, B. S. (Northants) b April 25, 1938

Crush, E. (Kent) b April 25, 1917

Cumbes, J. (Lancs., Surrey and Worcs.) b May 4, 1944

Cunis, R. S. (N. Zealand) b Jan. 5, 1941

Cunningham, K. G. (S. Australia) b July 26, 1939

Curnow, S. H. (S. Africa) b Dec. 16, 1907

Curtis, I. J. (Oxford U.) b May 13, 1959

Cushing, V. G. B. (Oxford U.) b Jan. 17, 1950

Cuthbertson, G. B. (Middx, Sussex and Northants) b March 28, 1901

Cutmore, J. A. (Essex) b Dec. 28, 1898

Cuttell, W. R. (Lancs.; *CY 1898*) b Sept. 13, 1864, d Dec. 9, 1929

Da Costa, O. C. (W. Indies) b Sept. 11, 1907, d Oct. 1, 1936

Dacre, C. C. R. (Auckland and Glos.) b May 15, 1899, d Nov. 2, 1975

Daer, A. G. (Essex) b Nov. 22, 1906

Daft, Richard (Notts. and All-England) b Nov. 2, 1835, d July 18, 1900

Dakin, G. F. (E. Province) b Aug. 13, 1935

Dalmeny, Lord (6th Earl of Rosebery) (Middx and Surrey) b Jan. 8, 1882, d May 30, 1974

Dalton, E. L. (S. Africa) b Dec. 2, 1906

Dani, H. T. (India) b May 24, 1933

Daniel, W. W. (Middx and W. Indies) b Jan. 16, 1956

Dansie, H. N. (S. Australia) b July 2, 1928

D'Arcy, J. W. (N. Zealand) b April 23, 1936

Dare, R. (Hants) b Nov. 26, 1921

Darling, J. (Australia; *CY 1900*) b Nov. 21, 1870, d Jan. 2, 1946

Darling, L. S. (Australia) b Aug. 14, 1909

Darling, W. M. (Australia) b May 1, 1957

Darnley, 8th Earl of (Hon. Ivo Bligh) (Camb. U. and Kent; Pres. MCC 1900) b March 13, 1859, d April 10, 1927

Davey, J. (Glos.) b Sept. 4, 1944

Davidson, A. K. (Australia; *CY 1962*) b June 14, 1929

Davies, Dai (Glam.) b Aug. 26, 1896, d July 16, 1976

Davies, Emrys (Glam.) b June 27, 1904, d Nov. 10, 1975

Davies, E. Q. (S. Africa) b Aug. 26, 1909, d Nov. 11, 1976

Davies, G. R. (NSW) b July 22, 1946

Davies, H. D. (Glam.) b July 23, 1932

Davies, H. G. (Glam.) b April 23, 1913

Davies, J. G. W. (Camb. U. and Kent) b Sept. 10, 1911

Davis, B. A. (Glam. and W. Indies) b May 2, 1940

Davis, C. A. (W. Indies) b Jan. 1, 1944

Davis, E. E. (Northants) b March 8, 1922

Davis, I. C. (Australia) b June 25, 1953

Davis, P. C. (Northants) b May 24, 1915

Davis, R. C. (Glam.) b Jan. 1, 1946

Davison, B. F. (Rhodesia, Leics. and Tasmania) b Dec. 21, 1946

Davison, I. (Notts.) b Oct. 4, 1937

Dawkes, G. O. (Leics. and Derby.) b July 19, 1920

Dawson, E. W. (Camb. U. and Leics.) b Feb. 13, 1904, d June 4, 1979

Dawson, O. C. (S. Africa) b Sept. 1, 1919

Day, A. P. (Kent; *CY 1910*) b April 10, 1885, d Jan. 22, 1969

Day, H. L. V. (Hants) b Aug. 12, 1898, d June 15, 1972

Dean, H. (Lancs.) b Aug. 13, 1884, d March 12, 1957

Deane, H. G. (S. Africa) b July 21, 1895, d Oct. 21, 1939

De Caires, F. I. (W. Indies) b May 12, 1909, d Feb. 2, 1959

De Courcey, J. H. (Australia) b April 18, 1927

Deed, J. A. (Kent) b Sept. 12, 1901, d Oct. 19, 1980

Delisle, G. P. S. (Middx and Oxford U.) b Dec. 25, 1934

Dell, A. R. (Australia) b Aug. 10, 1947

Dempster, C. S. (Leics., Warw. and N. Zealand; *CY 1932*) b Nov. 15, 1903, d Feb. 14, 1974

Dempster, E. W. (N. Zealand) b Jan. 25, 1925

Denness, M. H. (Scotland, Kent and Essex; *CY 1975*) b Dec. 1, 1940

Dennett, E. G. (Glos.) b April 27, 1880, d Sept. 14, 1937

Denning, P. W. (Somerset) b Dec. 16, 1949

Dennis, F. (Yorks.) b June 11, 1907

Denton, D. (Yorks.; *CY 1906*) b July 4, 1874, d Feb. 17, 1950

Denton, J. S. (Northants) b Nov. 2, 1890, d April 9, 1971

Denton, W. H. (Northants) b Nov. 2, 1890, d April 23, 1979

Depeiaza, C. C. (W. Indies) b Oct. 10, 1927

Desai, R. B. (India) b June 29, 1939

De Saram, F..C. (Oxford U. and Ceylon) b Sept, 1912

De Vaal, P. D. (Transvaal) b Dec. 3, 1945

Devereux, L. N. (Middx, Worcs. and Glam.) b Oct. 20, 1931

Dewdney, C. T. (W. Indies) b Oct. 23, 1933

Dewes, A. R. (Camb. U.) b June 2, 1957

Dewes, J. G. (Camb. U. and Middx) b Oct. 11, 1926

Dews, G. (Worcs.) b June 5, 1921

Dexter, E. R. (Camb. U. and Sussex; *CY 1961*) b May 15, 1935

Dick, A. E. (N. Zealand) b Oct. 10, 1936

Dickinson, G. R. (N. Zealand) b March 11, 1903

Dilley, G. R. (Kent) b May 18, 1959

Diment, R. A. (Glos. and Leics.) b Feb. 9, 1927

Dipper, A. E. (Glos.) b Nov. 9, 1885, d Nov. 7, 1945

Divecha, R. V. (Oxford U., Northants and India) b Oct. 18, 1927

Diver, A. J. D. (Cambs., Middx, Notts. and All-England) b June 6, 1824, d March 25, 1876

Dixon, A. L. (Kent) b Nov. 27, 1933

Dixon, C. D. (S. Africa) b Feb. 12, 1891, d Sept. 9, 1969

Dodds, T. C. (Essex) b May 29, 1919

Doggart, A. G. (Camb. U., Durham and Middx) b June 2, 1897, d June 7, 1963

Doggart, G. H. G. (Camb. U. and Sussex) b July 18, 1925

Doggart, S. J. G. (Camb. U.) b Feb. 8, 1961

Doherty, M. J. D. (Griqualand W.) b March 14, 1947

D'Oliveira, B. L. (Worcs.; *CY 1967*) b Oct. 4, 1931

Dollery, H. E. (Warw. and Wellington; *CY 1952*) b Oct. 14, 1914

Dollery, K. R. (Queensland, Auckland, Tasmania and Warw.) b Dec. 9, 1924

Dolphin, A. (Yorks.) b Dec. 24, 1885, d Oct. 24, 1942

Donnan, H. (Australia) b Nov. 12, 1864, d Aug. 13, 1956

Donnelly, M. P. (Middx, Warw., Oxford U. and N. Zealand; *CY 1948*) b Oct. 17, 1917

Dooland, B. (Notts. and Australia; *CY 1955*) b Nov. 1, 1923, d Sept. 8, 1980

Dorrinton, W. (Kent and All-England) b April 29, 1809, d Nov. 8, 1848

Dorset, 3rd Duke of (Kent) b March 24, 1745, d July 19, 1799

Doshi, D. R. (Notts., Warw. and India) b Dec. 22, 1947

Douglas, J. W. H. T. (Essex; *CY 1915*) b Sept. 3, 1882, d Dec. 19, 1930

Dovey, R. R. (Kent) b July 18, 1920, d Dec. 27, 1974

Dowding, A. L. (Oxford U.) b April 4, 1929

Dowe, U. G. (W. Indies) b March 29, 1949

Dower, R. R. (S. Africa) b June 4, 1876, d Sept. 15, 1964

Dowling, D. F. (Border, NE Transvaal and Natal) b July 25, 1914

Dowling, G. T. (N. Zealand) b March 4, 1937

Downton, P. R. (Kent and Middx) b April 4, 1957

Draper, E. J. (E. Province and Griqualand W.) b Sept. 27, 1934

Draper, R. G. (S. Africa) b Dec. 24, 1926

Dredge, C. H. (Somerset) b Aug. 4, 1954

Druce, N. F. (Camb. U. and Surrey; *CY 1898*) b Jan. 1, 1875, d Oct. 27, 1954

Drybrough, C. D. (Oxford U. and Middx) b Aug. 31, 1938

D'Souza, Antao (Pakistan) b Jan. 1, 1938

Ducat, A. (Surrey; *CY 1920*) b Feb. 16, 1886, d July 23, 1942

Duckworth, C. A. R. (S. Africa) b March 22, 1933

Duckworth, G. (Lancs.; *CY 1929*) b May 9, 1901, d Jan. 5, 1966

Dudleston, B. (Leics. and Rhodesia) b July 16, 1945

Duff, A. R. (Oxford U. and Worcs.) b Jan. 12, 1938

Duff, R. A. (Australia) b Aug. 17, 1878, d Dec. 13, 1911

Duleepsinhji, K. S. (Camb. U. and Sussex; *CY 1930*) b June 13, 1905, d Dec. 5, 1959

Dumbrill, R. (S. Africa) b London Nov. 19, 1938

Duminy, J. P. (Oxford U. and S. Africa) b Dec. 16, 1897, d Jan. 31, 1980

Duncan, J. R. F. (Australia) b March 25, 1944

Dunell, O. R. (S. Africa) b July 15, 1856, d Oct. 21, 1929

Dunning, B. (N. Districts) b March 20, 1940

Dunning, J. A. (Oxford U. and N. Zealand) b Feb. 6, 1903, d June 24, 1971

Du Preez, J. H. (S. Africa) b Nov. 14, 1942

Durani, S. A. (India) b Dec. 11, 1934

Durose, A. J. (Northants) b Oct. 10, 1944

Durston, F. J. (Middx) b July 11, 1893, d April 8, 1965

Du Toit, J. F. (S. Africa) b April 5, 1868, d July 10, 1909

Dye, J. C. J. (Kent, Northants and E. Province) b July 24, 1942

Dyer, D. D. (Natal and Transvaal) b Dec. 3, 1946

Dyer, D. V. (S. Africa) b April 2, 1914

Dymock, G. (Australia) b July 21, 1946

Dyson, A. H. (Glam.) b July 10, 1905, d June 7, 1978

Dyson, J. (Lancs.) b July 8, 1934

Dyson, John (Australia) b June 11, 1954

Eady, C. J. (Australia) b Oct. 29, 1870, d Dec. 20, 1945

Eagar, E. D. R. (Oxford U., Glos. and Hants) b Dec. 8, 1917, d Sept. 13, 1977

Eagar, M. A. (Oxford U. and Glos.) b March 20, 1934

Eaglestone, J. T. (Middx and Glam.) b July 24, 1923

Ealham, A. G. E. (Kent) b Aug. 30, 1944

East, R. E. (Essex) b June 20, 1947

Eastman, G. F. (Essex) b April 7, 1903

Eastman, L. C. (Essex and Otago) b June 3, 1897, d April 17, 1941

Eastwood, K. H. (Australia) b Nov. 23, 1935

Ebeling, H. I. (Australia) b Jan. 1, 1905, d Jan. 12, 1980

Edgar, B. A. (N. Zealand) b Nov. 23, 1956

Edmeades, B. E. A. (Essex) b Sept. 17, 1941

Edmonds, P. H. (Camb. U., Middx and E. Province) b March 8, 1951

Edmonds, R. B. (Warw.) b March 2, 1941

Edrich, B. R. (Kent and Glam.) b Aug. 18, 1922

Edrich, E. H. (Lancs.) b March 27, 1914

Edrich, G. A. (Lancs.) b July 13, 1918

Edrich, J. H. (Surrey; *CY 1966*) b June 21, 1937

Edrich, W. J. (Middx; *CY 1940*) b March 26, 1916

Edwards, F. (Surrey) b May 23, 1885, d July 10, 1970

Edwards, G. N. (N. Zealand) b May 27, 1955

Edwards, J. D. (Australia) b June 12, 1862, d July 31, 1911

Edwards, M. J. (Camb. U. and Surrey) b March 1, 1940

Edwards, R. (Australia) b Dec. 1, 1942

Edwards, R. M. (W. Indies) b March 3, 1940

Edwards, W. J. (Australia) b Dec. 23, 1949

Eele, P. J. (Somerset) b Jan. 27, 1935

Eggar, J. D. (Oxford U., Hants and Derby.) b Dec. 1, 1916

Ehtesham-ud-Din (Pakistan) b Sept. 4, 1950

Elgie, M. K. (S. Africa) b March 6, 1933

Elliott, C. S. (Derby.) b April 24, 1912

Elliott, H. (Derby.) b Nov. 2, 1891, d Feb. 2, 1976

Ellis, G. P. (Glam.) b May 24, 1950

Ellis, J. L. (Victoria) b May 9, 1890, d July 26, 1974

Elms, R. B. (Kent and Hants) b April 5, 1949

Emburey, J. E. (Middx) b Aug. 20, 1952

Emery, R. W. G. (N. Zealand) b March 28, 1915

Emery, S. H. (Australia) b Oct. 16, 1886, d Jan. 7, 1967

Emmett, G. M. (Glos.) b Dec. 2, 1912, d Dec. 18, 1976

Emmett, T. (Yorks.) b Sept. 3, 1841, d June 29, 1904

Endean, W. R. (S. Africa) b May 31, 1924

Engineer, F. M. (Lancs. and India) b Feb. 25, 1938

Enthoven, H. J. (Camb. U. and Middx) b June 4, 1903, d June 29, 1975

Evans, A. J. (Oxford U., Hants and Kent) b May 1, 1889, d Sept. 18, 1960

Evans, D. G. L. (Glam.) b July 27, 1933

Evans, E. (Australia) b March 6, 1849, d July 2, 1921

Evans, G. (Oxford U., Glam. and Leics.) b Aug. 13, 1915

Evans, J. B. (Glam.) b Nov. 9, 1936

Evans, T. G. (Kent; *CY 1951*) b Aug. 18, 1920

Evans, V. J. (Essex) b March 4, 1912, d March 28, 1975

Every, T. (Glam.) b Dec. 19, 1909

Eyre, T. J. P. (Derby.) b Oct. 17, 1939

Ezekowitz, R. A. B. (Oxford U.) b Jan. 19, 1954

Faber, M. J. J. (Oxford U. and Sussex) b Aug. 15, 1950

Fagg, A. E. (Kent) b June 18, 1915, d Sept. 13, 1977

Fairbairn, A. (Middx) b Jan. 25, 1923

Fairbairn, G. A. (Camb. U. and Middx) b June 26, 1892, d Nov. 5, 1973

Fairfax, A. G. (Australia) b June 16, 1906, d May 17, 1955

Fairservice, C. (Kent and Middx) b Aug. 21, 1909

Fairservice, W. J. (Kent) b May 16, 1881, d June 26, 1971

Falcon, M. (Camb. U.) b July 21, 1888, d Feb. 27, 1976

Fallows, J. A. (Lancs.) b July 25, 1907, d Jan. 20, 1974

Fane, F. L. (Oxford U. and Essex) b April 27, 1875, d Nov. 27, 1960

Fantham, W. E. (Warw.) b May 14, 1918

Farnes, K. (Camb. U. and Essex; *CY 1939*) b July 8, 1911, d Oct. 20, 1941

Farooq Hamid (Pakistan) b March 3, 1945

Farrer, W. S. (S. Africa) b Dec. 8, 1936

Farrimond, W. (Lancs.) b May 23, 1903, d Nov. 14, 1979

Farrukh Zaman (Pakistan) b April 2, 1956

Faulkner, G. A. (S. Africa) b Dec. 17, 1881, d Sept. 10, 1930

Favell, L. E. (Australia) b Oct. 6, 1929

Fazal Mahmood (Pakistan; *CY 1955*) b Feb. 18, 1927

Fearnley, C. D. (Worcs.) b April 12, 1940

Featherstone, N. G. (Transvaal, Middx and Glam.) b Aug. 20, 1949

'Felix', N. (Wanostrocht) (Kent, Surrey and All-England) b Oct. 4, 1804, d Sept. 3, 1876

Fellows-Smith, J. P. (Oxford U., Northants and S. Africa) b Feb. 3, 1932

Fender, P. G. H. (Sussex and Surrey; *CY 1915*) b Aug. 22, 1892

Fenley, S. (Surrey and Hants) b Jan. 4, 1896, d Sept. 2, 1972

Fenner, D. (Border) b March 27, 1929

Ferguson, W. (W. Indies) b Dec. 14, 1917, d Feb. 23, 1961

Fernandes, M. P. (W. Indies) b Aug. 12, 1897

Ferrandi, J. H. (W. Province) b April 3, 1930

Ferreira, A. M. (N. Transvaal and Warw.) b April 13, 1955

Ferris, J. J. (Glos., Australia and England; *CY 1889*) b May 21, 1867, d Nov. 21, 1900

Fichardt, C. G. (S. Africa) b March 20, 1870, d May 30, 1923

Fiddian-Green, C. A. F. (Camb. U., Warw. and Worcs.) b Dec. 22, 1898, d Sept. 5, 1976

Fiddling, K. (Yorks. and Northants) b Oct. 13, 1917

Field, M. N. (Camb. U. and Warw.) b March 23, 1950

Fielder, A. (Kent; *CY 1907*) b July 19, 1877, d Aug. 30, 1949

Findlay, T. M. (W. Indies) b Oct. 19, 1943

Findlay, W. (Oxford U. and Lancs.; Sec. Surrey CCC, Sec. MCC 1926-36) b June 22, 1880, d June 19, 1953

Fingleton, J. H. W. (Australia) b April 28, 1908

Finlason, C. E. (S. Africa) b Feb. 19, 1860, d July 31, 1917

Firth, J. (Yorks. and Leics.) b June 27, 1918

Firth, Rev. Canon J. D'E. E. (Winchester, Oxford U. and Notts.; *CY 1918*) b Jan. 21, 1900, d Sept. 21, 1957

Fisher, B. (Queensland) b Jan. 20, 1934, d April 1980

Fisher, F. E. (N. Zealand) b July 28, 1924

Fisher, P. B. (Oxford U., Middx and Worcs.) b Dec. 19, 1954

Fishlock, L. B. (Surrey; *CY 1947*) b Jan. 2, 1907

Fitzroy-Newdegate, Cdr Hon. J. M. (Northants) b March 20, 1897, d May 7, 1976

Flanagan, J. P. D. (Transvaal) b Sept. 20, 1947

Flavell, J. A. (Worcs.; *CY 1965*) b May 15, 1929

Fleetwood-Smith, L. O'B. (Australia) b March 30, 1910, d March 16, 1971

Fletcher, D. A. G. (Rhodesia, Zimbabwe) b Sept. 27, 1948

Fletcher, D. G. W. (Surrey) b July 6, 1924

Fletcher, K. W. R. (Essex; *CY 1974*) b May 20, 1944

Floquet, C. E. (S. Africa) b Nov. 3, 1884, d Nov. 22, 1963

Flowers, W. (Notts.) b Dec. 7, 1856, d Nov. 1, 1926

Foat, J. C. (Glos.) b Nov. 21, 1952

Foley, H. (N. Zealand) b Jan. 28, 1906, d Oct. 16, 1948

Foord, C. W. (Yorks.) b June 11, 1924

Forbes, C. (Notts.) b Aug. 9, 1936

Ford, D. A. (NSW) b Dec. 12, 1930

Ford, F. G. J. (Camb. U. and Middx) b Dec. 14, 1866, d Feb. 7, 1940

Ford, N. M. (Oxford U., Derby. and Middx) b Nov. 18, 1906

Ford, R. G. (Glos.) b March 3, 1907

Foreman, D. J. (W. Province and Sussex) b Feb. 1, 1933

Fosh, M. K. (Camb. U. and Essex) b Sept. 26, 1957

Foster, D. G. (Warw.) b March 19, 1907, d Oct. 13, 1980

Foster, F. R. (Warw.; *CY 1912*) b Jan. 31, 1889, d May 3, 1958

Foster, G. N. (Oxford U., Worcs. and Kent) b Oct. 16, 1884, d Aug. 11, 1971

Foster, H. K. (Oxford U. and Worcs.; *CY 1911*) b Oct. 30, 1873, d June 23, 1950

Foster, M. K. (Worcs.) b Jan. 1, 1889, d Dec. 3, 1940

Foster, M. L. C. (W. Indies) b May 9, 1943

Foster, P. G. (Kent) b Oct. 9, 1916

Foster, R. E. (Oxford U. and Worcs; *CY 1901*) b April 16, 1878, d May 13, 1914

Fothergill, A. J. (Somerset) b Aug. 26, 1854, d Aug. 1, 1932

Fotheringham, H. R. (Natal and Transvaal) b April 4, 1953

Fowler, A. J. B. (Middx) b April 1, 1891, d May 7, 1977

Francis, B. C. (Essex and Australia) b Feb. 18, 1948

Francis, D. A. (Glam.) b Nov. 29, 1953

Francis, G. N. (W. Indies) b Dec. 7, 1897, d Jan. 12, 1942

Francis, H. H. (S. Africa) b May 26, 1868, d Jan. 7, 1936

Francke, F. M. (Sri Lanka and Queensland) b March 29, 1941

Francois, C. M. (S. Africa) b June 20, 1897, d May 26, 1944

Frank, C. N. (S. Africa) b Jan. 27, 1891, d Dec. 26, 1961

Frank, W. H. B. (S. Africa) b Nov. 23, 1872, d Feb. 16, 1945

Franklin, H. W. F. (Oxford U., Surrey and Essex) b June 30, 1901

Frederick, M. C. (Derby. and W. Indies) b May 6, 1927

Fredericks, R. C. (Glam. and W. Indies; *CY 1974*) b Nov. 11, 1942

Freeman, A. P. (Kent; *CY 1923*) b May 17, 1888, d Jan. 28, 1965

Freeman, D. L. (N. Zealand) b Sept. 8, 1914

Freeman, E. W. (Australia) b July 13, 1944

Freer, F. W. (Australia) b Dec. 4, 1915

French, B. N. (Notts.) b Aug. 13, 1959

Frost, G. (Notts.) b Jan. 15, 1947

Fry, C. A. (Oxford U., Hants and Northants) b Jan. 14, 1940

Fry, C. B. (Oxford U., Surrey, Sussex and Hants; *CY 1895*) b April 25, 1872, d Sept. 7, 1956

Fuller, E. R. H. (S. Africa) b Aug. 2, 1931

Fuller, R. L. (W. Indies) b Jan. 30, 1913

Fullerton, G. M. (S. Africa) b Dec. 8, 1913

Funston, G. K. (NE Transvaal and Griqualand W.) b Nov. 2, 1948

Funston, K. J. (S. Africa) b Dec. 3, 1925

Furlonge, H. A. (W. Indies) b June 19, 1934

Fursdon, E. D. (Oxford U.) b Dec. 20, 1952

Gabriel, R. S. (Trinidad) b June 5, 1952

Gadkari, C. V. (India) b Feb. 3, 1928

Gaekwad, A. D. (India) b Sept. 23, 1952

Gaekwad, D. K. (India) b Oct. 27, 1928

Gaekwad, H. G. (India) b Aug. 29, 1923

Gale, R. A. (Middx) b Dec. 10, 1933

Gallichan, N. (N. Zealand) b June 3, 1906, d March 25, 1969

Gamsy, D. (S. Africa) b Feb. 17, 1940

Gandotra, A. (India) b Nov. 24, 1948

Gannon, J. B. (Australia) b Feb. 2, 1947

Ganteaume, A. G. (W. Indies) b Jan. 22, 1921

Gardiner, H. A. B. (Rhodesia) b Jan. 3, 1944

Gardiner, S. J. C. (Camb. U.) b March 19, 1947

Gardner, F. C. (Warw.) b June 4, 1922, d Jan. 13, 1979

Gardner, L. R. (Leics.) b Feb. 23, 1934

Garland-Wells, H. M. (Oxford U. and Surrey) b Nov. 14, 1907

Garlick, R. G. (Lancs. and Northants) b April 11, 1917

Garner, J. (Somerset and W. Indies; *CY 1980*) b Dec. 16, 1952

Garrett, T. W. (Australia) b July 26, 1858, d Aug. 6, 1943

Gaskin, B. M. (Manager, W. Indies in England, 1963) b March 21, 1908, d May 2, 1979

Gatting, M. W. (Middx) b June 6, 1957

Gaunt, R. A. (Australia) b Feb. 26, 1934

Gavaskar, S. M. (Somerset and India; *CY 1980*) b July 10, 1949

Gay, L. H. (Camb. U., Hants and Somerset) b March 24, 1871, d Nov. 1, 1949

Geary, A. C. T. (Surrey) b Sept. 11, 1900

Geary, G. (Leics.; *CY 1927*) b July 9, 1893

Gedye, S. G. (N. Zealand) b May 2, 1929

Gehrs, D. R. A. (Australia) b Nov. 29, 1880, d June 25, 1953

Ghavri, K. D. (India) b Feb. 28, 1951

Ghazali, Mohammad E. Z. (Pakistan) b June 15, 1924

Ghorpade, J. M. (India) b Oct. 2, 1930, d March 29, 1978

Ghulam Abbas (Pakistan) b May 1, 1947

Ghulam Ahmed (India) b July 4, 1922

Gibb, P. A. (Camb. U., Scotland, Yorks. and Essex) b July 11, 1913, d Dec. 7, 1977

Gibbons, H. H. I. (Worcs.) b Oct. 10, 1904, d Feb. 16, 1973

Gibbs, G. L. (W. Indies) b Dec. 27, 1925, d Feb. 21, 1979

Gibbs, L. R. (Warw., S. Australia and W. Indies; *CY 1972*) b Sept. 29, 1934

Gibbs, P. J. K. (Oxford U. and Derby.) b Aug. 17, 1944

Gibson, C. H. (Eton, Camb. U. and Sussex; *CY 1918*) b Aug. 23, 1900, d Dec. 31, 1976

Gibson, D. (Surrey) b May 1, 1936

Giffen, G. (Australia; *CY 1894*) b March 27, 1859, d Nov. 29, 1927

Giffen, W. F. (Australia) b Sept. 10, 1863, d June 29, 1949

Gifford, N. (Worcs.; *CY 1975*) b March 30, 1940

Gilchrist, R. (W. Indies) b June 28, 1934

Giles, R. J. (Notts.) b Oct. 17, 1919

Gill, A. (Notts.) b Aug. 4, 1940

Gilhouley, K. (Yorks. and Notts.) b Aug. 8, 1934

Gilliat, R. M. C. (Oxford U. and Hants) b May 20, 1944

Gilligan, A. E. R. (Camb. U., Surrey and Sussex; *CY 1924*; Pres. MCC 1967-68) b Dec. 23, 1894, d Sept. 5, 1976

Gilligan, A. H. H. (Sussex) b June 29, 1896, d May 5, 1978

Gilligan, F. W. (Oxford U. and Essex) b Sept. 20, 1893, d May 4, 1960

Gilmour, G. J. (Australia) b June 26, 1951

Gimblett, H. (Somerset; *CY 1953*) b Oct. 19, 1914, d March 30, 1978

Gladstone, G. (W. Indies) (*see* Marais, G. G.)

Gladwin, C. (Derby.) b April 3, 1916

Gleeson, J. W. (Australia) b March 14, 1938

Gleeson, R. A. (S. Africa) b Dec. 6, 1873, d Sept. 27, 1919

Glover, G. K. (S. Africa) b May 13, 1870, d Nov. 15, 1938

Glover, T. R. (Oxford U.) b Nov. 26, 1951

Goddard, J. D. C. (W. Indies) b April 21, 1919

Goddard, G. F. (Scotland) b May 19, 1938

Goddard, T. L. (S. Africa) b Aug. 1, 1931

Goddard, T. W. J. (Glos.; *CY 1938*) b Oct. 1, 1900, d May 22, 1966

Goldstein, F. S. (Oxford U., Northants, Transvaal and W. Province) b Oct. 14, 1944

Gomes, H. A. (Middx and W. Indies) b July 13, 1953

Gomes, S. A. (Trinidad) b Oct. 18, 1950

Gomez, G. E. (W. Indies) b Oct. 10, 1919

Gooch, G. A. (Essex; *CY 1980*) b July 23, 1953

Goodway, C. C. (Warw.) b July 10, 1909

Goodwin, K. (Lancs.) b June 25, 1938

Goodwin, T. J. (Leics.) b Jan. 22, 1929

Goonesena, G. (Ceylon, Notts., Camb. U. and NSW) b Feb. 16, 1931

Gopalan, M. J. (India) b June 6, 1909

Gopinath, C. D. (India) b March 1, 1930

Gordon, N. (S. Africa) b Aug. 6, 1911

Gore, A. C. (Eton and Army; *CY 1919*) b May 14, 1900

Gothard, E. J. (Derby.) b Oct. 1, 1904, d Jan. 17, 1979

Gould, I. J. (Middx) b Aug. 19, 1957

Gover, A. R. (Surrey; *CY 1937*) b Feb. 29, 1908

Gower, D. I. (Leics.; *CY 1979*) b April 1, 1957

Grace, Dr Alfred b May 17, 1840, d May 24, 1916

Grace, Dr Alfred H. (Glos.) b March 10, 1866, d Sept. 16, 1929

Grace, C. B. (Clifton) b March 1882, d June 6, 1938

Grace, Dr E. M. (Glos.) b Nov. 28, 1841, d May 20, 1911

Grace, Dr Edgar M. (MCC) (son of E. M. Grace) b Oct. 6, 1886, d Nov. 24, 1974

Grace, G. F. (Glos.) b Dec. 13, 1850, d Sept. 22, 1880

Grace, Dr Henry (Glos.) b Jan. 31, 1833, d Nov. 15, 1895

Grace, Dr H. M. (father of W. G., E. M. and G. F.) b Feb. 21, 1808, d Dec. 23, 1871

Grace, Mrs H. M. (mother of W. G., E. M. and G. F.) b July 18, 1812, d July 25, 1884

Grace, Dr W. G. (Glos.; *CY 1896*) b July 18, 1848, d Oct. 23, 1915

Grace, W. G. jnr (Camb. U. and Glos.) b July 6, 1874, d March 2, 1905

Graf, S. F. (Victoria and Hants) b May 19, 1957

Graham, H. (Australia) b Nov. 29, 1870, d Feb. 7, 1911

Graham, J. N. (Kent) b May 8, 1943

Graham, R. (S. Africa) b Sept. 16, 1877, d April 21, 1946

Grant, G. C. (Camb. U., Rhodesia and W. Indies) b May 9, 1907, d Oct. 26, 1978

Grant, R. S. (Camb. U. and W. Indies) b Dec. 15, 1909, d Oct. 18, 1977

Graveney, D. A. (Glos.) b Jan. 21, 1953

Graveney, J. K. R. (Glos.) b Dec. 16, 1924

Graveney, T. W. (Glos., Worcs. and Queensland; *CY 1953*) b June 16, 1927

Graves, P. J. (Sussex and Orange Free State) b May 19, 1946

Gray, J. R. (Hants) b May 19, 1926

Gray, L. H. (Middx) b Dec. 16, 1915

Greasley, D. G. (Northants) b Jan. 20, 1926

Green, D. J. (Derby. and Camb. U.) b Dec. 18, 1935

Green, D. M. (Oxford U., Lancs. and Glos.; *CY 1969*) b Nov. 10, 1939

Green, Brig. M. A. (Glos. and Essex; Manager MCC in S. Africa 1948-49, MCC in Australia 1950-51) b Oct. 3, 1891, d Dec. 28, 1971

Greenhough, T. (Lancs.) b Nov. 9, 1931

Greenidge, A. T. (W. Indies) b Aug. 20, 1956

Greenidge, C. G. (Hants and W. Indies; *CY 1977*) b May 1, 1951

Greenidge, G. A. (Sussex and W. Indies) b May 26, 1948

Greensmith, W. T. (Essex) b Aug. 16, 1930

Greenwood, A. (Yorks.) b Aug. 20, 1847, d Feb. 12, 1889

Greenwood, H. W. (Sussex and Northants) b Sept. 4, 1909

Greenwood, P. (Lancs.) b Sept. 11, 1924

Greetham, C. M. H. (Somerset) b Aug. 28, 1936

Gregory, David W. (Australia; first Australian captain) b April 15, 1845, d Aug. 4, 1919

Gregory, E. J. (Australia) b May 29, 1839, d April 22, 1899

Gregory, J. M. (Australia; *CY 1922*) b Aug. 14, 1895, d Aug. 7, 1973

Gregory, R. G. (Australia) b Feb. 26, 1916, d June 10, 1942

Gregory, R. J. (Surrey) b Aug. 26, 1902, d Oct. 6, 1973

Gregory, S. E. (Australia; *CY 1897*) b April 14, 1870, d July 31, 1929

Greig, A. W. (Border, E. Province and Sussex; *CY 1975*) b Oct. 6, 1946

Greig, I. A. (Camb. U., Border and Sussex) b Dec. 8, 1955

Grell, M. G. (W. Indies) b Dec. 18, 1899, d Jan. 11, 1976

Greswell, W. T. (Somerset and Ceylon) b Oct. 15, 1889, d Feb. 12, 1971

Grieve, B. A. F. (England) b May 28, 1864, d Nov. 19, 1917

Grieves, K. J. (NSW and Lancs.) b Aug. 27, 1925

Grieveson, R. E. (S. Africa) b Aug. 24, 1909

Griffin, G. M. (S. Africa) b June 12, 1939

Griffith, C. C. (W. Indies; *CY 1964*) b Dec. 14, 1938

Griffith, G. ("Ben") (Surrey and Utd England XI) b Dec. 20, 1833, d May 3, 1879

Griffith, H. C. (W. Indies) b Dec. 1, 1893, d March 18, 1980

Griffith, K. (Worcs.) b Jan. 17, 1950

Griffith, M. G. (Camb. U. and Sussex) b Nov. 25, 1943

Griffith, S. C. (Camb. U., Surrey and Sussex; Sec. MCC 1962-74; Pres. MCC 1979-80) b June 16, 1914

Griffiths, B. J. (Northants) b June 13, 1949

Griffiths, Sir W. H. (Camb. U. and Glam.) b Sept. 26, 1923

Grimmett, C. V. (Wellington and Australia; *CY 1931*) b Dec. 25, 1891, d May 2, 1980

Grimshaw, H. (Northants) b May 5, 1911

Gripper, R. A. (Rhodesia) b July 7, 1938

Groube, T. U. (Australia) b Sept. 2, 1857, d Aug. 5, 1927

Grout, A. T. W. (Australia) b March 30, 1927, d Nov. 9, 1968

Grove, C. W. (Warw. and Worcs.) b Dec. 16, 1912

Grover, J. N. (Oxford U.) b Oct. 15, 1915

Groves, B. S. (Border and Natal) b March 1, 1947

Groves, M. G. M. (Oxford U., Somerset and W. Province) b Jan. 14, 1943

Grundy, J. (Notts. and Utd England XI) b March 5, 1824, d Nov. 24, 1873

Guard, G. M. (India) b Dec. 12, 1925, d March 13, 1978

Guest, C. E. J. (Australia) b Oct. 7, 1937

Guha, S. (India) b Jan. 31, 1946

Guillen, S. C. (W. Indies and N. Zealand) b Sept. 24, 1924

Guise, J. L. (Oxford U. and Middx) b Nov. 25, 1903

Gul Mahomed (Pakistan and India) b Oct. 15, 1921

Gunn, G. (Notts.; *CY 1914*) b June 13, 1879, d June 28, 1958

Gunn, J. R. (Notts.; *CY 1904*) b July 19, 1876, d Aug. 21, 1963

Gunn, T. (Sussex) b Sept. 27, 1935

Gunn, William (Notts.; *CY 1890*) b Dec. 4, 1858, d Jan. 29, 1921

Gupte, B. P. (India) b Aug. 30, 1934

Gupte, S. P. (India) b Dec. 11, 1929

Gurr, D. R. (Oxford U. and Somerset) b March 27, 1956

Guy, J. W. (Northants and N. Zealand) b Aug. 29, 1934

Hacker, P. J. (Notts. and Orange Free State) b July 16, 1952

Hadlee, B. G. (Canterbury) b Dec. 14, 1941

Hadlee, D. R. (N. Zealand) b Jan. 6, 1948

Hadlee, R. J. (Notts. and N. Zealand) b July 3, 1951

Hadlee, W. A. (N. Zealand) b June 4, 1915

Hadley, R. J. (Camb. U. and Glam.) b Oct. 22, 1951

Hafeez, A. (*see* Kardar)

Haig, N. E. (Middx) b Dec. 12, 1887, d Oct. 27, 1966

Haigh, S. (Yorks.; *CY 1901*) b March 19, 1871, d Feb. 27, 1921

Halfyard, D. J. (Kent and Notts.) b April 3, 1931

Hall, A. E. (S. Africa) b Jan. 23, 1896, d Jan. 1, 1964

Hall, G. G. (S. Africa) b May 24, 1938

Hall, I. W. (Derby.) b Dec. 27, 1939

Hall, Louis (Yorks.; *CY 1890*) b Nov. 1, 1852, d Nov. 19, 1915

Hall, T. A. (Derby. and Somerset) b Aug. 19, 1930

Hall, W. W. (Queensland and W. Indies) b Sept. 12, 1937

Hallam, A. W. (Lancs. and Notts.; *CY 1908*) b Nov. 12, 1869, d July 24, 1940

Hallam, M. R. (Leics.) b Sept. 10, 1931

Halliday, S. J. (Oxford U.) b July 13, 1960

Halliwell, E. A. (Middx and S. Africa; *CY 1905*) b Sept. 7, 1864, d Oct. 2, 1919

Hallows, C. (Lancs.; *CY 1928*) b April 4, 1895, d Nov. 10, 1972

Hallows, J. (Lancs.; *CY 1905*) b Nov. 14, 1873, d May 20, 1910

Halse, C. G. (S. Africa) b Feb. 28, 1935

Hamblin, G. B. (Oxford U.) b April 14, 1952

Hamence, R. A. (Australia) b Nov. 25, 1915

Hamer, A. (Yorks. and Derby.) b Dec. 8, 1916

Hamilton, A. C. (Oxford U.) b Sept. 23, 1953

Hammond, H. E. (Sussex) b Nov. 7, 1907

Hammond, J. R. (Australia) b April 19, 1950

Hammond, W. R. (Glos.; *CY 1928*) b June 19, 1903, d July 2, 1965

Hampshire, J. H. (Yorks. and Tasmania) b Feb. 10, 1941

Hands, P. A. M. (S. Africa) b March 18, 1890, d April 27, 1951

Hands, R. H. M. (S. Africa) b July 26, 1888, d April 20, 1918

Hands, W. C. (Warw.) b Dec. 20, 1886, d Aug. 31, 1974

Hanif Mohammad (Pakistan; *CY 1968*) b Dec. 21, 1934

Hanley, M. A. (S. Africa) b Nov. 10, 1918

Hanley, R. W. (E. Province, Orange Free State and Transvaal) b Jan. 29, 1952

Hanumant Singh (India) b March 29, 1939

Hardie, B. R. (Scotland and Essex) b Jan. 14, 1950

Hardikar, M. S. (India) b Feb. 8, 1936

Hardinge, H. T. W. (Kent; *CY 1915*) b Feb. 25, 1886, d May 8, 1965

Hardstaff, J. (Notts.) b Nov. 9, 1882, d April 2, 1947

Hardstaff, J. jnr (Notts. and Auckland; *CY 1938*) b July 3, 1911

Harfield, L. (Hants) b Aug. 16, 1905

Harford, N. S. (N. Zealand) b Aug. 30, 1930

Harford, R. I. (N. Zealand) b May 30, 1936

Harisinghani, G. K. (India) (*see* Kishenchand, G.)

Harman, R. (Surrey) b Dec. 28, 1941

Haroon Rashid (Pakistan) b March 25, 1953

Harris, 4th Lord (Oxford U. and Kent; Pres MCC 1895) b Trinidad Feb. 3, 1851, d March 24, 1932

Harris, David (Hants and All-England) b 1755, d May 19, 1803

Harris, C. B. (Notts.) b Dec. 6, 1907, d Aug. 8, 1954

Harris, M. J. (Middx, Notts., E. Province and Wellington) b May 25, 1944

Harris, P. G. Z. (N. Zealand) b July 18, 1927

Harris, R. M. (N. Zealand) b July 27, 1933

Harris, T. A. (S. Africa) b Aug. 27, 1916

Harrison, H. S. (Surrey) b April 12, 1883, d Dec. 10, 1971

Harrison, L. (Hants) b June 8, 1922

Harry, J. (Australia) b Aug. 1, 1857, d Oct. 27, 1919

Hart, G. E. (Middx) b Jan. 13, 1902

Hartigan, G. P. D. (S. Africa) b Dec. 30, 1884, d Jan. 7, 1955

Hartigan, R. J. (Australia) b Dec. 12, 1879, d June 7, 1958

Hartkopf, A. E. V. (Australia) b Dec. 28, 1889, d May 20, 1968

Hartley, A. (Lancs.; *CY 1911*) b April 11, 1879, d Oct. 1918

Hartley, J. C. (Oxford U. and Sussex) b Nov. 15, 1874, d March 8, 1963

Harvey, J. F. (Derby.) b Sept. 27, 1939

Harvey, M. R. (Australia) b April 29, 1918

Harvey, P. F. (Notts.) b Jan. 15, 1923

Harvey, R. L. (S. Africa) b Sept. 14, 1911

Harvey, R. N. (Australia; *CY 1954*) b Oct. 8, 1928

Harvey-Walker, A. J. (Derby.) b July 21, 1944

Haseeb Ahsan (Pakistan) b July 15, 1939

Hassan, B. (Notts.) b March 24, 1944

Hassett, A. L. (Australia; *CY 1949*) b Aug. 28, 1913

Hastings, B. F. (N. Zealand) b March 23, 1940

Hathorn, C. M. H. (S. Africa) b April 7, 1878, d May 17, 1920

Hawke, 7th Lord (Camb. U. and Yorks.; *CY 1909*; Pres. MCC 1914-18) b Aug. 16, 1860, d Oct. 10, 1938

Hawke, N. J. N. (Australia) b Jan. 27, 1939

Hawkins, D. G. (Glos.) b May 18, 1935

Hawtin, A. P. R. (Northants) b Feb. 1, 1883, d Jan. 15, 1975

Hayes, E. G. (Surrey and Leics.; *CY 1907*) b Nov. 6, 1876, d Dec. 2, 1953

Hayes, F. C. (Lancs.) b Dec. 6, 1946

Hayes, J. A. (N. Zealand) b Jan. 11, 1927

Hayes, P. J. (Camb. U.) b May 20, 1954

Haygarth, A. (Sussex; Historian) b Aug. 4, 1825, d May 1, 1903

Haynes, D. L. (W. Indies) b Feb. 15, 1956

Haynes, R. W. (Glos.) b Aug. 27, 1913, d Oct. 16, 1976

Hayward, T. (Cambs. and All-England) b March 21, 1835, d July 21, 1876

Hayward, T. W. (Surrey; *CY 1895*) b March 29, 1871, d July 19, 1939

Haywood, P. R. (Leics.) b March 30, 1947

Hazare, V. S. (India) b March 11, 1915

Hazell, H. L. (Somerset) b Sept. 30, 1909

Hazlerigg, Lord, formerly Hon. A. G. (Camb. U. and Leics.) b Feb. 24, 1910

Hazlitt, G. R. (Australia) b Sept. 4, 1888, d Oct. 30, 1915

Headley, G. A. (W. Indies; *CY 1934*) b Panama May 30, 1909

Headley, R. G. A. (Worcs. and W. Indies) b June 29, 1939

Heal, M. G. (Oxford U.) b Sept. 7, 1948

Hearn, P. (Kent) b Nov. 18, 1925

Hearne, Alec (Kent; *CY 1894*) b July 22, 1863, d May 16, 1952

Hearne, Frank (Kent, England and S. Africa) b Nov. 23, 1858, d July 14, 1949

Hearne, G. A. L. (S. Africa) b March 27, 1888, d Nov. 13, 1978

Hearne, George G. (Kent) b July 7, 1856, d Feb. 13, 1932

Hearne, J. T. (Middx; *CY 1892*) b May 3, 1867, d April 17, 1944

Hearne, J. W. (Middx; *CY 1912*) b Feb. 11, 1891, d Sept. 13, 1965

Hearne, Thos. (Middx) b Sept. 4, 1826, d May 13, 1900

Hearne, Thos. jnr (Lord's Ground Superintendent) b Dec. 29, 1849, d Jan. 29, 1910

Heath, G. E. M. (Hants) b Feb. 20, 1913

Heath, M. (Hants) b March 9, 1934

Hedges, B. (Glam.) b Nov. 10, 1927

Hedges, L. P. (Tonbridge, Oxford U., Kent and Glos.; *CY 1919*) b July 13, 1900, d Jan. 12, 1933

Heine, P. S. (S. Africa) b June 28, 1928

Hemmings, E. E. (Warw. and Notts.) b Feb. 20, 1949

Hemsley, E. J. O. (Worcs.) b Sept. 1, 1943

Henderson, M. (N. Zealand) b Aug. 2, 1895, d June 17, 1970

Henderson, R. (Surrey; *CY 1890*) b March 30, 1865, d Jan. 29, 1931

Hendren, E. H. (Middx; *CY 1920*) b Feb. 5, 1889, d Oct. 4, 1962

Hendrick, M. (Derby.; *CY 1978*) b Oct. 22, 1948

Hendriks, J. L. (W. Indies) b Dec. 21, 1933

Hendry, H. S. T. L. (Australia) b May 24, 1895

Henwood, P. P. (Orange Free State and Natal) b May 22, 1946

Herman, O. W. (Hants) b Sept. 18, 1907

Herman, R. S. (Middx, Border, Griqualand W. and Hants) b Nov. 30, 1946

Heseltine C. (Hants) b Nov. 26, 1869, d June 13, 1944

Hever, N. G. (Middx and Glam.) b Dec. 17 1924

Hewetson, E. P. (Oxford U. and Warw.) b May 27, 1902, d Dec. 26, 1977

Hewett, H. T. (Oxford U. and Somerset; *CY 1893*) b May 25, 1864, d March 4, 1921

Hibbert, P. A. (Australia) b July 23, 1952

Higgins, H. L. (Worcs.) b Feb. 24, 1894, d Sept. 15, 1979

Higgins, J. B. (Worcs.) b Dec. 31, 1885, d Jan. 3, 1970

Higgs, J. D. (Australia) b July 11, 1950

Higgs, K. (Lancs. and Leics.; *CY 1968*) b Jan. 14, 1937

Hignell, A. J. (Camb. U. and Glos.) b Sept. 4, 1955

Hilditch, A. M. J. (Australia) b May 20, 1956

Hill, Alan (Derby. and Orange Free State) b June 29, 1950

Hill, Allen (Yorks.) b Nov. 14, 1845, d Aug. 29, 1910

Hill, A. J. L. (Camb. U. and Hants) b July 26, 1871, d Sept. 6, 1950

Hill, Clement (Australia; *CY 1900*) b March 18, 1877, d Sept. 5, 1945

Hill, E. (Somerset) b July 9, 1923

Hill, G. (Hants) b April 15, 1913

Hill, J. C. (Australia) b June 25, 1923, d Aug. 11, 1974

Hill, L. W. (Glam.) b April 14, 1942

Hill, M. (Notts., Derby. and Somerset) b Sept. 14, 1935

Hill, N. W. (Notts.) b Aug. 22, 1935

Hill, W. A. (Warw.) b April 27, 1910

Hills, R. W. (Kent) b Jan. 8, 1951

Hill-Wood, C. K. B. H. (Oxford U. and Derby.) b June 5, 1907

Hill-Wood, Sir W. W. H. (Camb. U. and Derby.) b Sept. 8, 1901, d Oct. 10, 1980

Hilton, C. (Lancs. and Essex) b Sept. 26, 1937

Hilton, J. (Lancs. and Somerset) b Dec. 29, 1930

Hilton, M. J. (Lancs.; *CY 1957*) b Aug. 2, 1928

Hime, C. F. W. (S. Africa) b Oct. 24, 1869, d Dec. 6, 1940

Hindlekar, D. D. (India) b Jan. 1, 1909, d March 30, 1949

Hirst, G. H. (Yorks.; *CY 1901*) b Sept. 7, 1871, d May 10, 1954

Hitch, J. W. (Surrey; *CY 1914*) b May 7, 1886, d July 7, 1965

Hitchcock, R. E. (Canterbury and Warw.) b Nov. 28, 1929

Hoad, E. L. G. (W. Indies) b Jan. 29, 1896

Hoare, D. E. (Australia) b Oct. 19, 1934

Hobbs, Sir J. B. (Surrey; *CY 1909, special portrait 1926*) b Dec. 16, 1882, d Dec. 21, 1963

Hobbs, R. N. S. (Essex and Glam.) b May 8, 1942

Hobson, D. L. (E. Province and W. Province) b Sept. 3, 1951

Hodges, J. H. (Australia) b July 31, 1856, d Jan. 17, 1933

Hodgkinson, G. F. (Derby.) b Feb. 19, 1914

Hodgson, A. (Northants) b Oct. 27, 1951

Hodson, R. P. (Camb. U.) b April 26, 1951

Hofmeyr, M. B. (Oxford U. and NE Transvaal) b Dec. 9, 1925

Hogg, R. M. (Australia) b March 5, 1951

Hogg, W. (Lancs.) b July 12, 1955

Holder, V. A. (Worcs. and W. Indies) b Oct. 8, 1945

Holding, M. A. (W. Indies; *CY 1977*) b Feb. 16, 1954

Holdsworth, R. L. (Oxford U., Warw. and Sussex) b Feb. 25, 1899, d June 20, 1976

Hole, G. B. (Australia) b Jan. 6, 1931

Holford, D. A. J. (W. Indies) b April 16, 1940

Holliday, D. C. (Camb. U.) b Dec. 20, 1958

Hollies, W. E. (Warw.; *CY 1955*) b June 5, 1912

Hollingdale, R. A. (Sussex) b March 6, 1906

Holmes, E. R. T. (Oxford U. and Surrey; *CY 1936*) b Aug. 21, 1905, d Aug. 16, 1960

Holmes, G. C. (Glam.) b Sept. 16, 1958

Holmes, Percy (Yorks.; *CY 1920*) b Nov. 25, 1886, d Sept. 3, 1971

Holt, A. (Hants) b April 8, 1911

Holt, J. K. jnr (W. Indies) b Aug. 12, 1923

Home of the Hirschel, Lord (Middx; Pres. MCC 1966-67) b July 2, 1903

Hone, Sir B. W. (S. Australia and Oxford U.) b July 1, 1907, d May 28, 1978

Hone, L. (MCC) b Jan. 30, 1853, d Dec. 31, 1896

Hooker, R. W. (Middx) b Feb. 22, 1935

Hookes, D. W. (Australia) b May 3, 1955

Hopkins, A. J. Y. (Australia) b May 4, 1874, d April 25, 1931

Hopkins, H. O. (Oxford U. and Worcs.) b July 6, 1895, d Feb. 23, 1972

Hopkins, J. A. (Glam.) b June 16, 1953

Hopkins, V. (Glos.) b Jan. 21, 1911

Hopwood, J. L. (Lancs.) b Oct. 30, 1903

Horan, T. P. (Australia) b March 8, 1854, d April 16, 1916

Hordern, H. V. (Australia) b Feb. 10, 1884, d June 17, 1938

Hornby, A. N. (Lancs.) b Feb. 10, 1847, d Dec. 17, 1925

Horner, N. F. (Yorks. and Warw.) b May 10, 1926

Hornibrook, P. M. (Australia) b July 27, 1899, d Aug. 25, 1976

Horsfall, R. (Essex and Glam.) b June 26, 1920

Horsley, J. (Notts. and Derby.) b Jan. 4, 1890, d Feb. 13, 1976

Horton, H. (Worcs. and Hants) b April 18, 1923

Horton, J. (Worcs.) b Aug. 12, 1916

Horton, M. J. (Worcs. and N. Districts) b April 21, 1934

Hossell, J. J. (Warw.) b May 25, 1914

Hough, K. W. (N. Zealand) b Oct. 24, 1928

Howard, A. B. (W. Indies) b Aug. 27, 1946

Howard, A. H. (Glam.) b Dec. 11, 1910

Howard, B. J. (Lancs.) b May 21, 1926

Howard, K. (Lancs.) b June 29, 1941

Howard, N. D. (Lancs.) b May 18, 1925, d May 31, 1979

Howard, Major R. (Lancs.; MCC Team Manager) b April 17, 1890, d Sept. 10, 1967

Howarth, G. P. (Surrey and N. Zealand) b March 29, 1951

Howarth, H. J. (N. Zealand) b Dec. 25, 1943

Howat, M. G. (Camb. U.) b March 2, 1958

Howell, H. (Warw.) b Nov. 29, 1890, d July 9, 1932

Howell, M. (Oxford U. and Surrey) b Sept. 9, 1893, d Feb. 23, 1976

Howell, W. P. (Australia) b Dec. 29, 1869, d July 14, 1940

Howland, C. B. (Camb. U., Sussex and Kent) b Feb. 6, 1936

Howorth, R. (Worcs.) b April 26, 1909, d April 2, 1980

Hughes, D. P. (Lancs. and Tasmania) b May 13, 1947

Hughes, K. J. (Australia; *CY 1981*) b Jan. 26, 1954

Huish, F. H. (Kent) b Nov. 15, 1869, d March 16, 1957

Hulme, J. H. A. (Middx) b Aug. 26, 1904

Human, J. H. (Camb. U. and Middx) b Jan. 13, 1912

Humpage, G. W. (Warw.) b April 24, 1954

Humphries, D. J. (Leics. and Worcs.) b Aug. 6, 1953

Humphries, J. (Derby.) b May 17, 1876, d May 8, 1946

Hunt, W. A. (Australia) b Aug. 26, 1908

Hunte, C. C. (W. Indies; *CY 1964*) b May 9, 1932

Hunte, E. A. C. (W. Indies) b Oct. 3, 1905, d Aug. 1967

Hunter, David (Yorks.) b Feb. 23, 1860, d Jan. 11, 1927

Hunter, Joseph (Yorks.) b Aug. 3, 1855, d Jan. 4, 1891

Hurd, A. (Camb. U. and Essex) b Sept. 7, 1937

Hurst, A. G. (Australia) b July 15, 1950

Hurst, R. J. (Middx) b Dec. 29, 1933

Hurwood, A. (Australia) b June 17, 1902

Hussain, M. Dilawar (India) b March 19, 1907, d Aug. 26, 1967

Hutchings, K. L. (Kent; *CY 1907*) b Dec. 7, 1882, d Sept. 3, 1916

Hutchinson, J. M. (Derby.) b Nov. 29, 1896

Hutchinson, P. (S. Africa) b Jan. 26, 1862, d Sept. 30, 1925

Hutton, Sir Leonard (Yorks.; *CY 1938*) b June 23, 1916

Hutton, R. A. (Camb. U., Yorks. and Transvaal) b Sept. 6, 1942

Hylton, L. G. (W. Indies) b March 29, 1905, d May 17, 1955

Ibadulla, K. (Warw., Tasmania, Otago and Pakistan) b Dec. 20, 1935

Ibrahim, K. C. (India) b Jan. 26, 1919

Iddon, J. (Lancs.) b Jan. 8, 1902, d April 17, 1946

Ijaz Butt (Pakistan) b March 10, 1938

Ikin, J. T. (Lancs.) b March 7, 1918

Illingworth, R. (Yorks. and Leics.; *CY 1960*) b June 8, 1932

Imran Khan Niazi (Oxford U., Worcs., Sussex and Pakistan) b Nov. 25, 1952

Imtiaz Ahmed (Pakistan) b Jan. 5, 1928

Imtiaz Ali (W. Indies) b July 28, 1954

Inchmore, J. D. (Worcs. and N. Transvaal) b Feb. 22, 1949

Indrajitsinhji, K. S. (India) b June 15, 1937

Ingle, R. A. (Somerset) b Nov. 5, 1903

Ingleby-Mackenzie, A. C. D. (Hants) b Sept. 15, 1933

Ingram, E. (Middx and Ireland) b Aug. 14, 1910, d March 13, 1973

Inman, C. C. (Ceylon and Leics.) b Jan. 29, 1936

Innes, G. A. S. (W. Province and Transvaal) b Nov. 16, 1931

Inshan Ali (W. Indies) b Sept. 25, 1949

Insole, D. J. (Camb. U. and Essex; *CY 1956*) b April 18, 1926

Intikhab Alam Khan (Surrey and Pakistan) b Dec. 28, 1941

Inverarity, R. J. (Australia) b Jan. 31, 1944

Iqbal Qasim (Pakistan) b Aug. 6, 1953

Irani, J. K. (India) b Aug. 18, 1923

Iredale, F. A. (Australia) b June 19, 1867, d April 15, 1926

Iremonger, J. (Notts.; *CY 1903*) b March 5, 1876, d March 25, 1956

Ironmonger, H. (Australia) b April 7, 1882, d May 31, 1971

Ironside, D. E. J. (S. Africa) b May 2, 1925

Irvine, B. L. (Natal, Essex and Transvaal) b March 9, 1944

Israr Ali (Pakistan) b May 1, 1927

Iverson, J. B. (Australia) b July 27, 1915, d Oct. 24, 1973

Jackman, R. D. (Surrey, W. Province and Rhodesia; *CY 1981*) b Aug. 13, 1945

Jackson, A. (Australia) b Scotland Sept. 5, 1909, d Feb. 16, 1933

Jackson, A. B. (Derby.) b Aug. 21, 1933.

Jackson, Sir A. H. M. (Derby.) b Nov. 9, 1899

Jackson, E. J. W. (Camb. U.) b March 26, 1955

Jackson, Rt Hon. Sir F. S. (Camb. U. and Yorks.; *CY 1894*; Pres. MCC 1921) b Nov. 21, 1870, d March 9, 1947

Jackson, H. L. (Derby.; *CY 1959*) b April 5, 1921

Jackson, John (Notts. and All-England) b May 21, 1833, d Nov. 4, 1901

Jackson, P. F. (Worcs.) b May 11, 1911

Jacques, T. A. (Yorks.) b Feb. 19, 1905

Jahangir Khan, Dr (Camb. U. and India) b Feb. 1, 1910

Jai, L. P. (India) b April 1, 1902, d Jan. 29, 1968

Jaisimha, M. L. (India) b March 3, 1939

Jakeman, F. (Yorks. and Northants) b Jan. 10, 1921

James, A. E. (Sussex) b Aug. 7, 1924

James, K. C. (Northants and N. Zealand) b March 12, 1904, d Aug. 21, 1976

James, R. M. (Camb. U. and Wellington) b Oct. 2, 1934

Jameson, J. A. (Warw.) b June 30, 1941

Jameson, T. E. N. (Camb. U. and Warw.) b July 23, 1946

Jamshedji, R. J. D. (India) b Nov. 18, 1892, d April 5, 1976

Jardine, D. R. (Oxford U. and Surrey; *CY 1928*) b Oct. 23, 1900, d June 18, 1958

Jardine, M. R. (Oxford U. and Middx) b June 8, 1869, d Jan. 16, 1947

Jarman, B. N. (Australia) b Feb. 17, 1936

Jarrett, D. W. (Oxford U. and Cambridge U.) b April 19, 1952

Jarvis, A. H. (Australia) b Oct. 18, 1860, d Nov. 15, 1933

Jarvis, K. B. S. (Kent) b April 23, 1953

Jarvis, T. W. (N. Zealand) b July 29, 1944

Javed Akhtar (Pakistan) b Nov. 21, 1940

Javed Miandad Khan (Sussex, Glam. and Pakistan) b June 12, 1957

Jayantilal, K. (India) b Jan. 13, 1948

Jayasinghe, S. (Ceylon and Leics.) b Jan. 19, 1931

Jefferson, R. I. (Camb. U. and Surrey) b Aug. 15, 1941

Jenkins, R. O. (Worcs.; *CY 1950*) b Nov. 24, 1918

Jenkins, V. G. J. (Oxford U. and Glam.) b Nov. 2, 1911

Jenner, T. J. (Australia) b Sept. 8, 1944

Jennings, D. B. (Australia) b June 5, 1884, d June 20, 1950

Jennings, K. F. (Somerset) b Oct. 5, 1953

Jepson, A. (Notts.) b July 12, 1915

Jessop, G. L. (Camb. U. and Glos.; *CY 1898*) b May 19, 1874, d May 11, 1955

Jesty, T. E. (Hants, Border and Griqualand W.) b June 2, 1948

Jewell, Major M. F. S. (Sussex and Worcs.) b Sept. 15, 1885, d May 28, 1978

Jilani, M. Baga Khan (India) b July 20, 1911, d July 2, 1941

Johns, R. L. (Oxford U. and Northants) b June 30, 1946

Johnson, C. (Yorks.) b Sept. 5, 1947

Johnson, C. L. (S. Africa) b 1871, d May 31, 1908

Johnson, G. W. (Kent) b Nov. 8, 1946

Johnson, H. H. H. (W. Indies) b July 17, 1910

Johnson, H. L. (Derby.) b Nov. 8, 1927

Johnson, I. W. (Australia) b Dec. 8, 1918

Johnson, L. A. (Surrey and Northants) b Aug. 12, 1936

Johnson, L. J. (Australia) b March 18, 1919, d April 20, 1977

Johnson, P. D. (Camb. U. and Notts.) b Nov. 12, 1949

Johnson, T. F. (W. Indies) b Jan. 10, 1917

Johnston, W. A. (Australia; *CY 1949*) b Feb. 26, 1922

Johnstone, C. P. (Camb. U., Kent and Madras) b Aug. 19, 1895, d June 23, 1974

Jones, A. (Glam. W. Australia, N. Transvaal and Natal; *CY 1978*) b Nov. 4, 1938

Jones, A. A. (Sussex, Somerset, Middx, Glam., N. Transvaal and Orange Free State) b Dec. 9, 1947

Jones, A. K. C. (Oxford U. and Warw.) b April 20, 1951

Jones, A. L. (Glam.) b June 1, 1957

Jones, A. O. (Notts. and Camb. U.; *CY 1900*) b Aug. 16, 1872, d Dec. 21, 1914

Jones, B. J. R. (Worcs.) b Nov. 2, 1955

Jones, C. M. (W. Indies) details not known

Jones, Ernest (Australia) b Sept. 30, 1869, d Nov. 23, 1943

Jones, E. C. (Glam.) b Dec. 14, 1912

Jones, E. W. (Glam.) b June 25, 1942

Jones, I. J. (Glam.) b Dec. 10, 1941

Jones, K. V. (Middx) b March 28, 1942

Jones, P. E. (W. Indies) b June 6, 1917

Jones, P. C. H. (Oxford U.) b Aug. 19, 1948

Jones, P. H. (Kent) b June 19, 1935

Jones, S. P. (Australia) b Aug. 1, 1861, d July 14, 1951

Jones, W. E. (Glam.) b Oct. 31, 1916

Jordan, A. B. (C. Districts) b Sept. 5, 1949

Jordan, J. M. (Lancs.) b Feb. 7, 1932

Jorden, A. M. (Camb. U. and Essex) b Jan. 28, 1947

Jordon, R. C. (Victoria) b Feb. 17, 1937

Joshi, P. G. (India) b Oct. 27, 1926

Joshi, U. C. (Gujerat and Sussex) b Dec. 23, 1944

Joslin, L. R. (Australia) b Dec. 13, 1947

Jowett, D. C. P. R. (Oxford U.) b June 24, 1931

Judd, A. K. (Camb. U. and Hants) b Jan. 1, 1904

Judge, P. F. (Middx, Glam. and Bengal) b May 23, 1916

Julian, R. (Leics.) b Aug. 23, 1936

Julien, B. D. (Kent and W. Indies) b March 13, 1950

Jumadeen, R. R. (W. Indies) b April 12, 1948

Jupp, H. (Surrey) b Nov. 19, 1841, d April 8, 1889

Jupp, V. W. C. (Sussex and Northants; *CY 1928*) b March 27, 1891, d July 9, 1960

Kallicharran, A. I. (Warw., Queensland and W. Indies) b March 21, 1949

Kanhai, R. B. (Warw., W. Australia, Tasmania and W. Indies; *CY 1964*) b Dec. 26, 1935

Kanitkar, H. S. (India) b Dec. 8, 1942

Kapil Dev (India) b Jan. 6, 1959

Kaplan, C. J. (Orange Free State) b Jan. 26, 1909

Kardar, A. H. (formerly Abdul Hafeez) (Oxford U., Warw., India and Pakistan) b Jan. 17, 1925

Katz, G. A. (Natal) b Feb. 9, 1947

Kayum, D. A. (Oxford U.) b Oct. 13, 1955

Keeton, W. W. (Notts.; *CY 1940*) b April 30, 1905, d Oct. 9, 1980

Keighley, W. G. (Oxford U. and Yorks.) b Jan. 10, 1925

Keigwin, R. P. (Camb. U., Essex and Glos.) b April 8, 1883, d Nov. 26, 1972

Keith, G. L. (Somerset, W. Province and Hants) b Nov. 19, 1937, d Dec. 26, 1975

Keith, H. J. (S. Africa) b Oct. 25, 1927

Kelleher, H. R. A. (Surrey and Northants) b March 3, 1929

Kelleway, C. (Australia) b April 25, 1889, d Nov. 16, 1944

Kelly, J. (Notts.) b Sept. 15, 1930

Kelly, J. J. (Australia; *CY 1903*) b May 10, 1867, d Aug. 14, 1938

Kelly, J. M. (Lancs. and Derby.) b March 19, 1922, d Nov. 13, 1979

Kelly, T. J. D. (Australia) b Ireland May 3, 1844, d July 20, 1893

Kempis, G. A. (S. Africa) b Aug. 4, 1865, d May 19, 1890

Kendall, M. P. (Camb. U.) b Nov. 10, 1949

Kendall, T. (Australia) b Bedford, England Aug. 24, 1851, d Aug. 17, 1924

Kennedy, A. (Lancs.) b Nov. 4, 1949

Kennedy, A. S. (Hants; *CY 1933*) b Jan. 24, 1891, d Nov. 15, 1959

Kenny, R. B. (India) b Sept. 29, 1930

Kentish, E. S. M. (Oxford U. and W. Indies) b Nov. 21, 1916

Kenyon, D. (Worcs.; *CY 1963*) b May 15, 1924

Kerr, J. (Scotland) b April 8, 1885, d Dec. 27, 1972

Kerr, J. L. (N. Zealand) b Dec. 28, 1910

Kerslake, R. C. (Camb. U. and Somerset) b Dec. 26, 1942

Kettle, M. K. (Northants) b March 18, 1944

Khalid Hassan (Pakistan) b July 14, 1937

Khalid Ibadulla, (*see* Ibadulla, K.)

Khalid Wazir Ali (Pakistan) b April 27, 1936

Khan Mohammad (Somerset and Pakistan) b Jan. 1, 1928

Kidd, E. L. (Camb. U. and Middx) b Oct. 18, 1889

Killick, Rev. E. T. (Camb. U. and Middx) b May 9, 1907, d May 18, 1953

Kilner, Norman (Yorks. and Warw.) b July 21, 1895, d April 28, 1979

Kilner, Roy (Yorks.; *CY 1924*) b Oct. 17, 1890, d April 5, 1928

Kimpton, R. C. M. (Oxford U. and Worcs.) b Sept. 21, 1916

King, B. P. (Worcs. and Lancs.) b April 22, 1915 d March 31, 1970

King, C. L. (Glam. and W. Indies) b June 11, 1951

King, F. McD. (W. Indies) b Dec. 14, 1926

King, I. M. (Warw. and Essex) b Nov. 10, 1931

King, J. B. (Philadelphia) b Oct. 19, 1873, d Oct. 17, 1965

King, J. H. (Leics.) b April 16, 1871, d Nov. 20, 1946

King, L. A. (W. Indies) b Feb. 27, 1939

Kingsley, Sir Patrick (PGT) (Oxford U.) b May 26, 1908

Kinkead-Weekes, R. C. (Oxford U. and Middx) b March 15, 1951

Kinneir, S. (Warw.; *CY 1912*) b May 13, 1871, d Oct. 16, 1928

Kippax, A. F. (Australia) b May 25, 1897, d Sept. 5, 1972

Kirby, D. (Camb. U. and Leics.) b Jan. 18, 1939

Kirmani, S. M. H. (India) b Dec. 29, 1947

Kirsten, P. N. (W. Province, Sussex and Derby.) b May 14, 1955

Kirton, K. N. (Border and E. Province) b Feb. 24, 1928

Kischenchand, G. (India) b April 14, 1925

Kitchen, M. J. (Somerset) b Aug. 1, 1940

Knight, A. E. (Leics.; *CY 1904*) b Oct. 8, 1872, d April 25, 1946

Knight, B. R. (Essex and Leics.) b Feb. 18, 1938

Knight, D. J. (Oxford U. and Surrey; *CY 1915*) b May 12, 1894, d Jan. 5, 1960

Knight, J. M. (Oxford U.) b March 16, 1958

Knight, R. D. V. (Camb. U., Surrey, Glos. and Sussex) b Sept. 6, 1946

Knight, W. H. (Editor of *Wisden* 1870-79) b Nov. 29, 1812, d Aug. 16, 1879

Knott, A. P. E. (Kent and Tasmania; *CY 1970*) b April 9, 1946

Knott, C. H. (Oxford U. and Kent) b March 20, 1901

Knott, C. J. (Hants) b Nov. 26, 1914
Knott, F. H. (Oxford U., Kent and Sussex) b Oct. 30, 1891, d Feb. 10, 1972
Knowles, J. (Notts.) b March 25, 1910
Knox, G. K. (Lancs.) b April 22, 1937
Knox, N. A. (Surrey; *CY 1907*) b Oct. 10, 1884, d March 3, 1935
Kortright, C. J. (Essex) b Jan. 9, 1871, d Dec. 12, 1952
Kotze, J. J. (S. Africa) b Aug. 7, 1879, d July 7, 1931
Kourie, A. J. (Transvaal) b July 30, 1951
Kripal Singh, A. G. (India) b Aug. 6, 1933
Krishnamurthy, P. (India) b July 12, 1947
Kulkarni, U. N. (India) b March 7, 1942
Kumar, V. V. (India) b June 22, 1935
Kunderan, B. K. (India) b Oct. 2, 1939
Kuys, F. (S. Africa) b March 21, 1870, d Sept. 12, 1953

Lacey, Sir F. E. (Camb. U. and Hants; Sec. MCC 1898-1926) b Oct. 19, 1859, d May 26, 1946
Laird, B. M. (Australia) b Nov. 21, 1950
Laker, J. C. (Surrey, Auckland and Essex; *CY 1952*) b Feb. 9, 1922
Lall Singh (India) b Dec. 12, 1909
Lamb, A. J. (W. Province and Northants; *CY 1981*) b June 20, 1954
Lamb, T. M. (Oxford U., Middx and Northants) b March 24, 1953
Lambert, G. E. (Glos. and Somerset) b May 5, 1919
Lambert, R. J. H. (Ireland) b July 14, 1874, d March 24, 1956
Lambert, Wm (Surrey) b 1779, d April 19, 1851
Lampard, A. W. (Victoria and AIF; oldest living Sheffield Shield player) b July 3, 1885
Lance, H. R. (S. Africa) b June 6, 1940
Langdon, W. A. (W. Australia) b 1922
Langdale, G. R. (Derby. and Somerset) b March 11, 1916
Langford, B. A. (Somerset) b Dec. 17, 1935
Langley, G. R. A. (Australia; *CY 1957*) b Sept. 19, 1919
Langridge, James (Sussex; *CY 1932*) b July 10, 1906, d Sept. 10, 1966
Langridge, J. G. (Sussex; *CY 1950*) b Feb. 10, 1910
Langridge, R. J. (Sussex) b April 13, 1939
Langton, A. B. C. (S. Africa) b March 2, 1912, d Nov. 27, 1942
Larkins, W. (Northants) b Nov. 22, 1953
Larter, J. D. F. (Northants) b April 24, 1940
Larwood, H. (Notts.; *CY 1927*) b Nov. 14, 1904
Lashley, P. D. (W. Indies) b Feb. 11, 1937
Latchman, Harichand (Middx and Notts.) b July 26, 1943
Laughlin, T. J. (Australia) b Jan. 30, 1951

Laver, F. (Australia) b Dec. 7, 1869, d Sept. 24, 1919
Lawrence, G. B. (S. Africa) b March 31, 1932
Lawrence, J. (Somerset) b March 29, 1914
Lawry, W. M. (Australia; *CY 1962*) b Feb. 11, 1937
Leadbeater, B. (Yorks.) b Aug. 14, 1943
Leadbeater, E. (Yorks. and Warw.) b Aug. 15, 1927
Leary, S. E. (Kent) b April 30, 1933
Lee, C. (Yorks. and Derby.) b March 17, 1924
Lee, F. S. (Middx and Somerset) b July 24, 1907
Lee, G. M. (Notts. and Derby.) b June 7, 1887, d Feb. 29, 1976
Lee, H. W. (Middlesex) b Oct. 26, 1890
Lee, I. S. (Victoria) b March 24, 1914
Lee, J. W. (Middx and Somerset) b Feb. 1, 1904, d June 20, 1944
Lee, P. G. (Northants and Lancs.; *CY 1976*) b Aug. 27, 1945
Lee, P. K. (Australia) b Sept. 14, 1904, d Aug. 9, 1980
Lee, R. J. (Oxford U.) b March 6, 1950
Lees, W. K. (N. Zealand) b March 19, 1952
Lees, W. S. (Surrey; *CY 1906*) b Dec. 25, 1875, d Sept. 10, 1924
Legall, R. A. (W. Indies) b Dec. 1, 1925
Legard, E. (Warw.) b Aug. 23, 1935
Leggat, I. B. (N. Zealand) b June 7, 1930
Leggat, J. G. (N. Zealand) b May 27, 1926, d March 8, 1973
Lenham, L. J. (Sussex) b May 24, 1936
le Roux, F. L. (S. Africa) b Feb. 5, 1882, d Sept. 22, 1963
le Roux, G. S. (W. Province and Sussex) b Sept. 4, 1955
le Roux, R. A. (Orange Free State) b May 27, 1950
Lester, E. I. (Yorks.) b Feb. 18, 1923
Lester, G. (Leics.) b Dec. 27, 1915
Lester, Dr J. A. (Philadelphia) b Cumberland, England Aug. 1, 1871, d Sept. 3, 1969
L'Estrange, M. G. (Oxford U.) b Oct. 12, 1952
Lever, J. K. (Essex; *CY 1979*) b Feb. 24, 1949
Lever, P. (Lancs. and Tasmania) b Sept. 17, 1940
Leveson Gower, Sir H. D. G. (Oxford U. and Surrey) b May 8, 1873, d Feb. 1, 1954
Levett, W. H. V. (Kent) b Jan. 25, 1908
Lewis, A. R. (Camb. U. and Glam.) b July 6, 1938
Lewis, C. (Kent) b July 27, 1908
Lewis, D. J. (Oxford U. and Rhodesia) b July 27, 1927
Lewis, D. M. (W. Indies) b Feb. 21, 1946
Lewis, E. B. (Warw.) b Jan. 5, 1918

Lewis, E. J. (Glam. and Sussex) b Jan. 31, 1942

Lewis, P. T. (S. Africa) b Oct. 2, 1884, d Jan. 30, 1976

Lewis, R. V. (Hants) b Aug. 6, 1947

Leyland, M. (Yorks.; *CY 1929*) b July 20, 1900, d Jan. 1, 1967

Liaqat Ali Khan (Pakistan) b May 21, 1955

Liddicutt, A. E. (Victoria) b Oct. 17, 1891

Lightfoot, A. (Northants) b Jan. 8, 1936

Lill, J. C. (S. Australia) b Dec. 7, 1933

Lillee, D. K. (Australia; *CY 1973*) b July 18, 1949

Lilley, A. F. A. (Warw.; *CY 1897*) b Nov. 28, 1866, d Nov. 17, 1929

Lilley, B. (Notts.) b Feb. 11, 1895, d Aug. 4, 1950

Lillywhite, Fred (Sussex; Editor of *Lilly-white's Guide to Cricketers*) b July 23, 1829, d Sept. 15, 1866

Lillywhite, F. W. ("William") (Sussex) b June 13, 1792, d Aug. 21 1854

Lillywhite, James, jnr (Sussex) b Feb. 23, 1842, d Oct. 25, 1929

Lindsay, D. T. (S. Africa) b Sept. 4, 1939

Lindsay, J. D. (S. Africa) b Sept. 8, 1909

Lindsay, N. V. (S. Africa) b July 30, 1886, d Feb. 2, 1976

Lindwall, R. R. (Australia; *CY 1949*) b Oct. 3, 1921

Ling, W. V. S. (S. Africa) b Oct. 3, 1891, d Sept. 26, 1960

Lissette, A. F. (N. Zealand) b Nov. 6, 1919, d Jan. 24, 1973

Lister, J. (Yorks. and Worcs.) b May 14, 1930

Lister, W. H. L. (Lancs.) b Oct. 7, 1911

Littlewood, D. J. (Cambridge U.) b Oct. 28, 1955

Livingston, L. (NSW and Northants) b May 3, 1920

Livingstone, D. A. (Hants) b Sept. 21, 1933

Livsey, W. H. (Hants) b Sept. 23, 1893, d Sept. 12, 1978

Llewellyn, C. B. (Hants and S. Africa; *CY 1911*) b Sept. 26, 1876, d June 7, 1964

Llewellyn, M. J. (Glam.) b Nov. 27, 1953

Lloyd, B. J. (Glam.) b Sept. 6, 1953

Lloyd, C. H. (W. Indies and Lancs.; *CY 1971*) b Aug. 31, 1944

Lloyd, D. (Lancs.) b March 18, 1947

Lloyd, M. F. D. (Oxford U.) b June 6, 1954

Lloyd, T. A. (Warw. and Orange Free State) b Nov. 5, 1956

Loader, P. J. (Surrey and W. Australia; *CY 1958*) b Oct. 25, 1929

Lobb, B. (Warw. and Somerset) b Jan. 11, 1931

Lock, G. A. R. (Surrey, Leics. and W. Australia; *CY 1954*) b July 5, 1929

Lock, H. C. (Surrey and Devon) b May 8, 1903, d May 18, 1978

Lockwood, Ephraim (Yorks.) b April 4, 1845, d Dec. 19, 1921

Lockwood, W. H. (Notts. and Surrey; *CY 1899*) b March 25, 1868, d April 26, 1932

Lockyer, T. (Surrey and All-England) b Nov. 1, 1826, d Dec. 22, 1869

Logan, J. D. (S. Africa) b June 24, 1880, d Jan. 3, 1960

Lohmann, G. A. (Surrey, W. Province and Transvaal; *CY 1889*) b June 2, 1865, d Dec. 1, 1901

Lomax, J. G. (Lancs. and Somerset) b May 5, 1925

Long, A. (Surrey and Sussex) b Dec. 18, 1940

Longfield, T. C. (Camb. U. and Kent) b May 12, 1906

Longrigg, E. F. (Camb. U. and Somerset) b April 16, 1906, d July 23, 1974

Lord, Thomas (Middx; founder of Lord's) b Nov. 22, 1757, d Jan. 13, 1832

Louden, G. M. (Essex) b Sept. 6, 1885, d Dec. 28, 1972

Love, H. S. B. (Australia) b Aug. 10, 1895 d July 22, 1969

Love, J. D. (Yorks.) b April 22, 1955

Lowndes, W. G. L. F. (Oxford U. and Hants) b Jan. 24, 1898

Lowry, T. C. (Camb. U., Somerset and N. Zealand) b Feb. 17, 1898, d July 20, 1976

Lowson, F. A. (Yorks.) b July 1, 1925

Loxton, S. J. E. (Australia) b March 29, 1921

Lucas, A. P. (Camb. U., Surrey, Middx and Essex) b Feb. 20, 1857, d Oct. 12, 1923

Luckes, W. T. (Somerset) b Jan. 1, 1901

Luckhurst, B. W. (Kent; *CY 1971*) b Feb. 5, 1939

Lumb, R. G. (Yorks.) b Feb. 27, 1950

Lundie, E. B. (S. Africa) b March 15, 1888, d Sept. 12, 1917

Lyon, B. H. (Oxford U. and Glos.; *CY 1931*) b Jan. 19, 1902, d June 22, 1970

Lyon, J. (Lancs.) b May 17, 1951

Lyon, M. D. (Cambridge U. and Somerset) b April 22, 1898, d Feb. 17, 1964

Lyons, K. J. (Glam.) b Dec. 18, 1946

Lyons, J. J. (Australia) b May 21, 1863, d July 21, 1927

Lyttelton, Rt Hon. Alfred (Camb. U and Middx; Pres. MCC 1898) b Feb. 7, 1857, d July 5, 1913

Lyttelton, Rev. Hon. C. F. (Camb. U. and Worcs.) b Jan. 26, 1887, d Oct. 3, 1931

Lyttelton, Hon. C. J. (*see* 10th Visct Cobham)

Lyttelton, Hon. R. H. (Eton) b Jan. 18, 1854, d Nov. 7, 1939

McAlister, P. A. (Australia) b July 11, 1869, d May 10, 1938

Macartney, C. G. (Australia; *CY 1922*) b June 27, 1886, d Sept. 9, 1958

Macaulay, G. G. (Yorks.; *CY 1924*) b Dec. 7, 1897, d Dec. 14, 1940

Macaulay, M. J. (S. Africa) b April 19, 1939

MacBryan, J. C. W. (Camb. U. and Somerset; *CY 1925*) b July 22, 1892

McCabe, S. J. (Australia; *CY 1935*) b July 16, 1910, d Aug. 25, 1968

McCanlis, M. A. (Oxford U., Surrey and Glos.) b June 17, 1906

McCarthy, C. N. (Camb. U. and S. Africa) b March 24, 1929

McConnon, J. (Glam.) b June 21, 1922

McCool, C. L. (Somerset and Australia) b Dec. 9, 1915

McCorkell, N. T. (Hants) b March 23, 1912

McCormick, E. L. (Australia) b May 16, 1906

McCosker, R. B. (Australia; *CY 1976*) b Dec. 11, 1946

McDonald, C. C. (Australia) b Nov. 17, 1928

McDonald, E. A. (Lancs. and Australia; *CY 1922*) b Jan. 6, 1892, d July 22, 1937

McDonnell, P. S. (Australia) b London Nov. 13, 1860, d Sept. 24, 1896

McEvoy, M. S. A. (Essex) b Jan. 25, 1956

McEwan, K. S. (E. Province, Essex and W. Australia; *CY 1978*) b July 16, 1952

McEwan, P. E. (N. Zealand) b Dec. 19, 1953

McGahey, C. P. (Essex; *CY 1902*) b Feb. 12, 1871, d Jan. 10, 1935

MacGibbon, A. R. (N. Zealand) b Aug. 28, 1924

McGirr, H. M. (N. Zealand) b Nov. 5, 1891, d April 14, 1964

McGlew, D. J. (S. Africa; *CY 1956*) b March 11, 1929

MacGregor, G. (Camb. U. and Middx; *CY 1891*) b Aug. 31, 1869, d Aug. 20, 1919

McGregor, S. N. (N. Zealand) b Dec. 18, 1931

McHugh, F. P. (Yorks. and Glos.) b Nov. 15, 1925

McIlwraith, J. (Australia) b Sept. 7, 1857, d July 5, 1938

Macindoe, D. H. (Oxford U.) b Sept. 1, 1917

McIntyre, A. J. W. (Surrey; *CY 1958*) b May 14, 1918

McIntyre, J. M. (Auckland and Canterbury) b July 4, 1944

MacKay, K. D. (Australia) b Oct. 24, 1925

McKay-Coghill, D. (Transvaal) b Nov. 4, 1941

McKenzie, G. D. (Leics. and Australia; *CY 1965*) b June 24, 1941

McKenzie, K. A. (NE Transvaal and Transvaal) b July 16, 1948

McKibbin, T. R. (Australia) b Dec. 10, 1870, d Dec. 15, 1939

McKinnon, A. H. (S. Africa) b Aug. 20, 1932

McKinnon, F. A. (Camb. U. and Kent) b April 9, 1848, d Feb. 27, 1947

McLachlan, I. M. (Camb. U. and S. Australia) b Oct. 2, 1936

MacLaren, A. C. (Lancs.; *CY 1895*) b Dec. 1, 1871, d Nov. 17, 1944

McLaren, J. W. (Australia) b Dec. 24, 1887, d Nov. 17, 1921

McLaughlin, J. J. (Queensland) b Feb. 18, 1930

Maclean, J. A. (Australia) b April 27, 1946

McLean, R. A. (S. Africa; *CY 1961*) b July 9, 1930

McLeod, C. E. (Australia) b Oct. 24, 1869, d Nov. 26, 1918

McLeod, E. G. (N. Zealand) b Oct. 14, 1900

McLeod, R. W. (Australia) b Jan. 19, 1868, d June 15, 1907

McMahon, J. W. (Surrey and Somerset) b Dec. 28, 1919

McMahon, T. G. (N. Zealand) b Nov. 8, 1929

McMaster, J. E. P. (England) b March 16, 1861, d June 7, 1929

McMillan, Q. (S. Africa) b June 23, 1904, d July 3, 1948

McMorris, E. D. A. (W. Indies) b April 4, 1935

McNally, J. P. (Griqualand W.) b Nov. 27, 1907

McRae, D. A. N. (N. Zealand) b Dec. 25, 1912

McShane, P. G. (Australia) b 1857, d Dec. 11, 1903

McVicker, N. M. (Warw. and Leics.) b Nov. 4, 1940

McWatt, C. A. (W. Indies) b Feb. 1, 1922

Madan Lal, S. (India) b March 20, 1951

Maddocks, L. V. (Australia) b May 24, 1926

Madray, I. S. (W. Indies) b July 2, 1934

Madson, M. B. (Natal) b Sept. 29, 1949

Mahmood Hussain (Pakistan) b April 2, 1932

Mailey, A. A. (Australia) b Jan. 3, 1886, d Dec. 31, 1967

Majid J. Khan (Camb. U., Glam., Queensland and Pakistan; *CY 1970*) b Sept. 28, 1946

Maka, E. S. (India) b March 5, 1922

Makepeace, J. W. H. ("Harry") (Lancs.) b Aug. 22, 1881, d Dec. 19, 1952

Mallett, A. A. (Australia) b July 13, 1945

Mallett, A. W. H. (Oxford U. and Kent) b Aug. 29, 1924

Malone, M. F. (Australia and Lancs.) b Oct. 9, 1950

Manjrekar, V. L. (India) b Sept. 26, 1931

Mankad, A. V. (India) b Oct. 12, 1946

Mankad, M. H. ("Vinoo") (India; *CY 1947*) b April 12, 1917, d Aug. 21, 1978

Mann, A. L. (Australia) b Nov. 8, 1945

Mann, F. G. (Camb. U. and Middx) b Sept. 6, 1917

Mann, F. T. (Camb. U. and Middx) b March 3, 1888, d Oct. 6, 1964

Mann, J. P. (Middx) b June 13, 1919

Mann, N. B. F. (S. Africa) b Dec. 28, 1920, d July 31, 1952

Manning, J. S. (S. Australia and Northants) b June 11, 1924

Manning, T. E. S. (Northants) b Sept. 2, 1884, d Nov. 22, 1975

Mansell, P. N. F. (S. Africa) b Shropshire March 16, 1920

Mantri, M. K. (India) b Sept. 1, 1921

Maqsood Ahmed (Pakistan) b March 26, 1925

Marais, G. G. ("G. Gladstone") (W. Indies) b Jan. 14, 1901, d May 19, 1978

Marie, G. V. (Oxford U.) b Feb. 17, 1945

Markham, L. A. (S. Africa) b Sept. 12, 1924

Marks, V. J. (Oxford U. and Somerset) b June 25, 1955

Marlar, R. G. (Camb. U. and Sussex) b Jan. 2, 1931

Marlow, W. H. (Leics.) b Feb. 13, 1900, d Dec. 16, 1975

Marner, P. T. (Lancs. and Leics.) b March 31, 1936

Marr, A. P. (Australia) b March 28, 1862, d March 15, 1940

Marriott, C. S. (Camb. U., Lancs. and Kent) b Sept. 14, 1895, d Oct. 13, 1966

Marsden, Tom (England) b 1805, d Feb. 27, 1843

Marsh, F. E. (Derby.) b July 7, 1920

Marsh, R. W. (Australia) b Nov. 11, 1947

Marshal, Alan (Queensland and Surrey; *CY 1909*) b June 12, 1883, d July 23, 1915

Marshall, J. M. A. (Warw.) b Oct. 26, 1916

Marshall, M. D. (Hants and W. Indies) b April 18, 1958

Marshall, N. E. (W. Indies) b Feb. 27, 1924

Marshall, R. E. (Hants and W. Indies; *CY 1959*) b April 25, 1930

Martin, E. J. (Notts.) b Aug. 17, 1925

Martin, F. (Kent; *CY 1892*) b Oct. 12, 1861, d Dec. 13, 1921

Martin, F. R. (W. Indies) b Oct. 12, 1893, d Nov. 23, 1967

Martin, J. D. (Oxford U. and Somerset) b Dec. 23, 1941

Martin, J. W. (Australia) b July 28, 1931

Martin, J. W. (Kent) b Feb. 16, 1917

Martin, S. H. (Worcs., Natal and Rhodesia) b Jan. 11, 1909

Martindale, E. A. (W. Indies) b Nov. 25, 1909, d March 17, 1972

Marx, W. F. E. (S. Africa) b July 4, 1895, d June 2, 1974

Mason, J. R. (Kent; *CY 1898*) b March 26, 1874, d Oct. 15, 1958

Massie, H. H. (Australia) b April 11, 1854, d Oct. 12, 1938

Massie, R. A. L. (Australia; *CY 1973*) b April 14, 1947

Matheson, A. M. (N. Zealand) b Feb. 27, 1906

Mathias, Wallis (Pakistan) b Feb. 4, 1935

Matthews, A. D. G. (Northants and Glam.) b May 3, 1905, d July 29, 1977

Matthews, C. S. (Notts.) b Oct. 17, 1929

Matthews, T. J. (Australia) b April 3, 1884, d Oct. 14, 1943

Maudsley, R. H. (Oxford U. and Warw.) b April 8, 1918

May, B. (Oxford U.) b Nov. 1, 1944

May, P. B. H. (Camb. U. and Surrey; *CY 1952*; Pres. MCC 1980-81) b Dec. 31, 1929

Mayer, J. H. (Warw.) b March 2, 1902

Mayes, R. (Kent) b Oct. 7, 1921

Mayne, E. R. (Australia) b July 4, 1884, d Oct. 26, 1961

Mayne, L. C. (Australia) b Jan. 26, 1942

Mead, C. P. (Hants; *CY 1912*) b March 9, 1887, d March 26, 1958

Mead, W. (Essex; *CY 1904*) b March 25, 1869, d March 18, 1954

Meads, E. A. (Notts.) b Aug. 17, 1916

Meale, T. (N. Zealand) b Nov. 11, 1928

Meckiff, I. (Australia) b Jan. 6, 1935

Meherhomji, K. R. (India) b Aug. 9, 1911

Mehra, V. L. (India) b March 12, 1938

Meintjes, D. J. (S. Africa) b June 9, 1890

Melle, M. G. (S. Africa) b June 3, 1930

Melluish, M. E. L. (Camb. U. and Middx) b June 13, 1932

Melville, A. (Oxford U., Sussex and S. Africa; *CY 1948*) b May 19, 1910

Mence, M. D. (Warw. and Glos.) b April 30, 1944

Mendis, G. D. (Sussex) b April 20, 1955

Mendonca, I. L. (W. Indies) b July 13, 1934

Mercer, J. (Sussex, Glam. and Northants; *CY 1927*) b April 22, 1895

Merchant, V. M. (India; *CY 1937*) b Oct. 12, 1911

Merritt, W. E. (Northants and N. Zealand) b Aug. 18, 1908, d June 9, 1977

Merry, C. A. (W. Indies) b Jan. 20, 1911, d April 19, 1964

Meuleman, K. D. (Australia) b Sept. 5, 1923

Meuli, E. M. (N. Zealand) b Feb. 20, 1926

Meyer, B. J. (Glos.) b Aug. 21, 1932

Meyer, R. J. O. (Camb. U., Somerset and W. India) b March 15, 1905

Mian Mohammad Saaed (Pakistan's first captain) b Aug. 31, 1910, d Aug. 23, 1979

Middleton, J. (S. Africa) b Sept. 30, 1865, d Dec. 23, 1913

Midwinter, W. E. (Victoria, Glos., Australia and England) b Forest of Dean, England June 19, 1851, d Dec. 3, 1890

Milburn, B. D. (N. Zealand) b Nov. 24, 1943

Milburn, C. (Northants and W. Australia; *CY 1967*) b Oct. 23, 1941

Milkha Singh, A. G. (India) b Dec. 31, 1941

Miller, A. M. (England) b Oct. 19, 1869, d June 26, 1959

Miller, G. (Derby.) b Sept. 8, 1952

Miller, K. R. (Notts. and Australia; *CY 1954*) b Nov. 28, 1919

Miller, L. S. M. (N. Zealand) b March 31, 1923

Miller, R. (Warw.) b Jan. 6, 1941

Miller, R. C. (W. Indies) b 1911, d 1964. *Dates unconfirmed*

Milligan, F. W. (Yorks.) b March 19, 1870, d March 31, 1900

Millman, G. (Notts.) b Oct. 2, 1934

Mills, C. H. (Surrey and S. Africa) b Nov. 26, 1867, d July 26, 1948

Mills, G. H. (Otago) b Aug. 1, 1916

Mills, J. E. (N. Zealand) b Sept. 3, 1905, d Dec. 11, 1972

Mills, J. P. C. (Camb. U.) b Dec. 6, 1958

Mills, J. M. (Camb. U. and Warw.) b July 27, 1921

Milner, J. (Essex) b Aug. 22, 1937

Milton, C. A. (Glos.; *CY 1959*) b March 10, 1928

Milton, W. H. (S. Africa) b Dec. 3, 1854, d March 6, 1930

Minnett, R. B. (Australia) b June 13, 1888, d Oct. 21, 1955

"Minshull", John (scorer of first recorded century) b *circa* 1741, d Oct. 1793

Miran Bux, M. (Pakistan) b April 20, 1907

Misson, F. M. (Australia) b Nov. 9, 1938

Mitchell, A. (Yorks.) b Sept. 13, 1902, d Dec. 25, 1976

Mitchell, B. (S. Africa; *CY 1936*) b Jan. 8, 1909

Mitchell, C. G. (Somerset) b Jan. 27, 1929

Mitchell, F. (Camb. U., Yorks., England and S. Africa; *CY 1902*) b Aug. 13, 1872, d Oct. 11, 1935

Mitchell, T. B. (Derby.) b Sept. 4, 1902

Mitchell-Innes, N. S. (Oxford U. and Somerset) b Sept. 7, 1914

Mobey, G. S. (Surrey) b March 5, 1904

Modi, R. S. (India) b Nov. 11, 1924

Mohammad Aslam (Pakistan) b Jan. 5, 1920

Mohammad Farooq (Pakistan) b April 8, 1938

Mohammad Ilyas (Pakistan) b March 19, 1946

Mohammad Munaf (Pakistan) b Nov. 2, 1935

Mohammad Nazir (Pakistan) b March 8, 1946

Mohsin Khan (Pakistan) b March 15, 1954

Moir, A. McK. (N. Zealand) b July 17, 1919

Mold, A. W. (Lancs.; *CY 1892*) b May 27, 1863, d April 29, 1921

Moloney, D. A. R. (N. Zealand) b Aug. 11, 1910, d July 15, 1942

Monks, C. I. (Glos.) b March 4, 1912, d Jan. 23, 1974

Moodie, G. H. (W. Indies) b Nov. 25, 1915

Moon, L. J. (Camb. U. and Middx) b Feb. 9, 1878, d Nov. 23, 1916

Mooney, F. L. H. (N. Zealand) b May 26, 1921

Moore, D. N. (Oxford U. and Glos.) b Sept. 26, 1910

Moore, H. I. (Notts.) b Feb. 28, 1941

Moore, R. H. (Hants) b Nov. 14, 1913

Morgan, D. C. (Derby.) b Feb. 26, 1929

Morgan, J. T. (Camb. U. and Glam.) b May 7, 1907, d Dec. 18, 1976

Morgan, M. (Notts.) b May 21, 1936

Morgan, R. W. (N. Zealand) b Feb. 12, 1941

Morkel, D. P. B. (S. Africa) b Jan. 25, 1906, d Oct. 6, 1980

Morley, J. D. (Sussex) b Oct. 20, 1950

Moroney, J. R. (Australia) b Oct. 10, 1919

Morrill, N. D. (Oxford U.) b Dec. 9, 1957

Morris, A. R. (Australia; *CY 1949*) b Jan. 19, 1922

Morris, H. M. (Camb. U. and Essex) b April 16, 1898

Morris, R. E. T. (W. Province) b Jan. 28, 1947

Morris, S. (Australia) b Sept. 15, 1854, d Sept. 20, 1931

Morrisby, R. O. G. (Tasmania) b Jan. 12, 1915

Morrison, B. D. (N. Zealand) b Dec. 17, 1933

Morrison, J. F. M. (N. Zealand) b Aug. 27, 1947

Mortimore, J. B. (Glos.) b May 14, 1933

Mortlock, W. (Surrey and Utd England XI) b July 18, 1832, d Jan. 23, 1884

Moseley, H. R. (Somerset) b May 28, 1948

Moses, G. H. (Camb. U.) b Sept. 24, 1952

Moses, H. (Australia) b Feb. 13, 1858, d Dec. 7, 1938

Moss, A. E. (Middx) b Nov. 14, 1930

Moss, J. K. (Australia) b June 29, 1947

Motz, R. C. (N. Zealand; *CY 1966*) b Jan. 12, 1940

Moulding, R. P. (Oxford U. and Middx) b Jan. 3, 1958

Moule, W. H. (Australia) b Jan. 31, 1858, d Aug. 24, 1939

Moylan, A. C. D. (Camb. U.) b June 26, 1955

Mubarak, A. M. (Camb. U.) b July 4, 1951

Mudassar Nazar (Pakistan) b April 6, 1956

Muddiah, V. M. (India) b June 8, 1929

Mufasir-ul-Haq (Pakistan) b Aug. 16, 1944

Mulholland, Sir Henry (HGH) (Camb. U.) b Dec. 20, 1888, d March 5, 1971

Muncer, B. L. (Middx and Glam.) b Oct. 23, 1913

Munden, V. S. (Leics.) b Jan. 2, 1928

Munir Malik (Pakistan) b July 10, 1934

Murdin, J. V. (Northants) b Aug. 16, 1891, d April 11, 1971

Murdoch, W. L. (Sussex, Australia and England) b Oct. 18, 1854, d Feb. 18, 1911

Murray, A. R. A. (S. Africa) b April 30, 1922

Murray, B. A. G. (N. Zealand) b Sept. 18, 1940

Murray, D. A. (W. Indies) b May 29, 1950

Murray, D. L. (Camb. U., Notts., Warw. and W. Indies) b May 20, 1943

Murray, J. T. (Middx; *CY 1967*) b April 1, 1935

Murray-Willis, P. E. (Worcs. and Northants) b July 14, 1910

Murrell, H. R. (Kent and Middx) b Nov. 19, 1879, d Aug. 15, 1952

Murrills, T. J. (Camb. U.) b Dec. 22, 1953

Musgrove, H. (Australia) b Nov. 27, 1860, d Nov 2, 1931

Mushtaq Ali, S. (India) b Dec. 17, 1914

Mushtaq Mohammad (Northants and Pakistan; *CY 1963*) b Nov. 22, 1943

Muzzell, R. K. (W. Province, Transvaal and E. Province) b Dec. 23, 1945

Mynn, Alfred (Kent and All-England) b Jan. 19, 1807, d Oct. 31, 1861

Nadkarni, R. G. (India) b April 4, 1932

Nagel, L. E. (Australia) b March 6, 1905, d Nov. 23, 1971

Naik, S. S. (India) b Feb. 21, 1945

Naoomal Jaoomal, M. (India) b April 17, 1904, d July 18, 1980

Narasimha Rao, M. V. (India) b Aug. 11, 1954

Nash, J. E. (S. Australia) b April 16, 1950

Nash, L. J. (Australia) b May 2, 1910

Nash, M. A. (Glam.) b May 9, 1945

Nasim-ul-Ghani (Pakistan) b May 14, 1941

Naushad Ali (Pakistan) b Oct. 1, 1943

Navle, J. G. (India) b Dec. 7, 1902

Nayudu, Col. C. K. (India; *CY 1933*) b Oct. 31, 1895, d Nov. 14, 1967

Nayudu, C. S. (India) b April 18, 1914

Nazar Mohammad (Pakistan) b Aug. 5, 1921

Nazir Ali, S. (Sussex and India) b June 8, 1906, d Feb. 18, 1975

Neale, P. A. (Worcs.) b June 5, 1954

Neblett, J. M. (W. Indies) b Nov. 13, 1901, assumed dead

Neilson, D. R. (Transvaal) b Dec. 17, 1948

Nel, J. D. (S. Africa) b July 10, 1928

Nelson, G. W. (Border) b Nov. 14, 1941

Nevell, W. T. (Middx, Surrey and Northants) b Dec. 13, 1916

Newberry, C. (S. Africa) b 1889, d Aug. 1, 1916

Newdick, G. A. (Wellington) b Jan. 11, 1949

Newham, W. (Sussex) b Dec. 12, 1860, d June 26, 1944

Newland, Richard (Sussex) b *circa* 1718, d May 29, 1791

Newman, G. C. (Oxford U. and Middx) b April 26, 1904

Newman, J. (N. Zealand) b July 3, 1902

Newman, J. A. (Hants) b Nov. 12, 1884, d Dec. 21, 1973

Newsom, E. S. (S. Africa) b Dec. 2, 1910

Newstead, J. T. (Yorks; *CY 1909*) b Sept. 8, 1879, d March 25, 1952

Niaz Ahmed (Pakistan) b Nov. 11, 1945

Nicholas, M. C. J. (Hants) b Sept. 29, 1957

Nicholls, D. (Kent) b Dec. 8, 1943

Nicholls, R. B. (Glos.) b Dec. 4, 1933

Nichols, M. S. (Essex; *CY 1934*) b Oct. 6, 1900, d Jan. 26, 1961

Nicholson, A. G. (Yorks.) b June 25, 1938

Nicholson, F. (S. Africa) b Sept. 17, 1909

Nicolson, J. F. W. (S. Africa) b July 19, 1899, d Dec. 13, 1935

Nissar, Mahomed (India) b Aug. 1, 1910, d March 11, 1963

Nitshke, H. C. (Australia) b April 14, 1906

Niven, R. A. (Oxford U.) b April 28, 1948

Noble, M. A. (Australia; *CY 1900*) b Jan. 28, 1873, d June 21, 1940

Noblet, G. (Australia) b Sept. 14, 1916

Noreiga, J. M. (W. Indies) b April 15, 1936

Norman, M. E. J. C. (Northants and Leics.) b Jan. 19, 1933

Norton, N. O. (S. Africa) b May 11, 1881, d June 27, 1968

Nothling, O. E. (Australia) b Aug. 1, 1900, d Sept. 26, 1965

Nourse, A. D. ("Dudley") (S. Africa; *CY 1948*) b Nov. 12, 1910

Nourse, A. W. ("Dave") (S. Africa) b Croydon, Surrey Jan. 26, 1878, d July 8, 1948

Nunes, R. K. (W. Indies) b June 7, 1894, d July 22, 1958

Nupen, E. P. (S. Africa) b Jan. 1, 1902, d Jan. 29, 1977

Nurse, S. M. (W. Indies; *CY 1967*) b Nov. 10, 1933

Nutter, A. E. (Lancs. and Northants) b June 28, 1913

Nyalchand, S. (India) b Sept. 14, 1919

Nye, J. K. (Sussex) b May 23, 1914

Nyren, John (Hants) b Dec. 15, 1764, d June 28, 1837

Nyren, Richard (Hants and Sussex) b 1734, d April 25, 1797

Oakes, C. (Sussex) b Aug. 10, 1912

Oakes, J. (Sussex) b March 3, 1916

Oakman, A. S. M. (Sussex) b April 20, 1930

Oates, T. W. (Notts.) b Aug. 9, 1875, d June 18, 1949

Oates, W. F. (Yorks. and Derby.) b June 11, 1929

O'Brien, F. P. (Canterbury and Northants) b Feb. 11, 1911

O'Brien, L. P. J. (Australia) b July 2, 1907

O'Brien, Sir T. C. (Oxford U. and Middx) b Nov. 5, 1861, d Dec. 9, 1948

Ochse, A. E. (S. Africa) b March 11, 1870, d April 11, 1918

Ochse, A. L. (S. Africa) b Oct. 11, 1899, d May 6, 1949

O'Connor, J. (Essex) b Nov. 6, 1897, d Feb. 22, 1977

O'Connor, J. D. A. (Australia) b Sept. 9, 1875, d Aug. 23, 1941

Odendaal, A. (Camb. U.) b May 4, 1954

Ogilvie, A. D. (Australia) b June 3, 1951

O'Keeffe, K. J. (Somerset and Australia) b Nov. 25, 1949

Old, C. M. (Yorks.; *CY 1979*) b Dec. 22, 1948

Oldfield, N. (Lancs. and Northants) b May 5, 1911

Oldfield, W. A. S. (Australia; *CY 1927*) b Sept. 9, 1894, d Aug. 10, 1976

Oldham, S. (Yorks. and Derby.) b July 26, 1948

Oldroyd, E. (Yorks.) b Oct. 1, 1888, d Dec. 27, 1964

O'Linn, S. (Kent and S. Africa) b May 5, 1927

Oliver, P. R. (Warw.) b May 9, 1956

O'Neill, N. C. (Australia; *CY 1962*) b Feb. 19, 1937

Ontong, R. C. (Border, Transvaal and Glam.) b Sept. 9, 1955

Ord, J. S. (Warw.) b July 12, 1912

Orders, J. O. D. (Oxford U.) b Aug. 12, 1957

O'Reilly, W. J. (Australia; *CY 1935*) b Dec. 20, 1905

Ormrod, J. A. (Worcs.) b Dec. 22, 1942

O'Sullivan, D. R. (Hants and N. Zealand) b Nov. 16, 1944

Outschoorn, L. (Worcs.) b Sept. 26, 1918

Overton, G. W. F. (N. Zealand) b June 8, 1919

Owen-Smith, H. G. O. (Oxford U., Middx and S. Africa; *CY 1930*) b Feb. 18, 1909

Owen-Thomas, D. R. (Camb. U. and Surrey) b Sept. 20, 1948

Oxenham, R. K. (Australia) b July 28, 1891, d Aug. 16, 1939

Packe, M. St J. (Leics.) b Aug. 21, 1916, d Dec. 20, 1978

Padgett, D. E. V. (Yorks.) b July 20, 1934

Padmore, A. L. (W. Indies) b Dec. 17, 1946

Page, J. C. T. (Kent) b May 20, 1930

Page, M. H. (Derby.) b June 17, 1941

Page, M. N. (N. Zealand) b May 8, 1902

Pai, A. M. (India) b April 28, 1945

Paine, G. A. E. (Middx and Warw.; *CY 1935*) b June 11, 1908, d March 30, 1978

Pairaudeau, B. H. (N. Districts NZ and W. Indies) b April 14, 1931

Palairet, L. C. H. (Oxford U. and Somerset; *CY 1893*) b May 27, 1870, d March 27, 1933

Palairet, R. C. N. (Oxford U. and Somerset; Joint-Manager MCC in Australia 1932-33) b June 25, 1871, d Feb. 11, 1955

Palia, P. E. (India) b Sept. 5, 1910

Palm, A. W. (S. Africa) b June 8, 1901, d Aug. 17, 1966

Palmer, C. H. (Worcs. and Leics.; Pres. MCC 1978-79) b May 15, 1919

Palmer, G. E. (Australia) b Feb. 22, 1860, d Aug. 22, 1910

Palmer, K. E. (Somerset) b April 22, 1937

Palmer, R. (Somerset) b July 12, 1942

Pardon, Charles Frederick (Editor of *Wisden* 1887-90) b March 28, 1850, d April 18, 1890

Pardon, Edgar S. (12 years associated with *Wisden*) b Sept. 28, 1859, d July 16, 1898

Pardon, Sydney H. (Editor of *Wisden* 1891-1925) b Sept. 23, 1855, d Nov. 20, 1925

Parfitt, P. H. (Middx; *CY 1963*) b Dec. 8, 1936

Paris, C. G. A. (Hants; Pres. MCC 1975-76) b Aug. 20, 1911

Parish, R. J. (Aust. Administrator) b May 7, 1916

Park, R. L. (Australia) b July 30, 1892, d Jan. 23, 1947

Parkar, R. D. (India) b Oct. 31, 1946

Parker, C. W. L. (Glos.; *CY 1923*) b Oct. 14, 1882, d July 11, 1959

Parker, G. M. (S. Africa) b May 27, 1899, d May 1, 1969

Parker, G. W. (Camb. U. and Glos.) b Feb. 11, 1912

Parker, J. F. (Surrey) b April 23, 1913

Parker, J. M. (Worcs. and N. Zealand) b Feb. 21, 1951

Parker, N. M. (N. Zealand) b Aug. 28, 1948

Parker, P. W. G. (Camb. U. and Sussex) b Jan. 15, 1956

Parkhouse, W. G. A. (Glam.) b Oct. 12, 1925

Parkin, C. H. (Yorks. and Lancs.; *CY 1924*) b Feb. 18, 1886, d June 15, 1943

Parkin, D. C. (S. Africa) b Feb. 18, 1870, d March 20, 1936

Parks, H. W. (Sussex) b July 18, 1906

Parks, J. H. (Sussex and Canterbury; *CY 1938*) b May 12, 1903, d Nov. 21, 1980

Parks, J. M. (Sussex and Somerset; *CY 1968*) b Oct. 21, 1931

Parr, F. D. (Lancs.) b June 1, 1928

Parr, George (Notts. and All-England) b May 22, 1826, d June 23, 1891

Parry, D. R. (W. Indies) b Dec. 22, 1954

Parsana, D. D. (India) b Dec. 2, 1947

Parsons, A. B. D. (Camb. U. and Surrey) b Sept. 20, 1933

Parsons, A. E. W. (Auckland and Sussex) b Glasgow Jan. 9, 1949

Parsons, Canon, J. H. (Warw.) b May 30, 1890

Partridge, J. T. (S. Africa) b Dec. 9, 1932

Partridge, N. E. (Malvern, Camb. U. and Warw.; *CY 1919*) b Aug. 10, 1900

Partridge, R. J. (Northants) b Feb. 11, 1912

Pascoe, L. S. (Australia) b Feb. 13, 1950

Passailaigue, C. C. (W. Indies) b Aug. 1902, d Jan. 7, 1972

Patankar, C. T. (India) b Nov. 24, 1930

Pataudi, Iftikhar Ali, Nawab of (Oxford U., Worcs., England and India; *CY 1932*) b March 16, 1910, d Jan. 5, 1952

Pataudi, Mansur Ali, Nawab of (Oxford U., Sussex and India; *CY 1968*) b Jan. 5, 1941

Patel, B. P. (India) b Nov. 24, 1952

Patel, D. N. (Worcs.) b Oct. 25, 1958

Patel, J. M. (India) b Nov. 26, 1924

Paterson, R. F. T. (Essex) b Sept. 8, 1916, d May 29, 1980

Pathmanathan, G. (Oxford U. and Sri Lanka) b Jan. 23, 1954

Patiala, Yuvraj of (India) b Jan. 17, 1913

Patil, S. R. (India) b Oct. 10, 1933

Paulsen, R. G. (Queensland and W. Australia) b Oct. 18, 1947

Paver, R. G. L. (Oxford U.) b April 4, 1950

Pawson, A. G. (Oxford U. and Worcs.; oldest living Blue) b May 30, 1888

Pawson, H. A. (Oxford U. and Kent) b Aug. 22, 1921

Payn, L. W. (Natal) b May 6, 1915

Paynter, E. (Lancs.; *CY 1938*) b Nov. 5, 1901, d Feb. 5, 1979

Payton, D. H. (C. Districts) b Feb. 19, 1945

Payton, W. R. D. (Notts.) b Feb. 13, 1882, d May 2, 1943

Pearce, G. (Sussex) b Oct. 27, 1908

Pearce, J. P. (Oxford U.) b April 18, 1957

Pearce, T. A. (Kent) b Dec. 18, 1910

Pearce, T. N. (Essex) b Nov. 3, 1905

Pearse, C. O. C. (S. Africa) b Oct. 10, 1884, d May 7, 1953

Pearson, D. B. (Worcs.) b March 29, 1937

Peate, E. (Yorks.) b March 2, 1856, d March 11, 1900

Peck, I. G. (Camb. U. and Northants) b Oct. 18, 1957

Peebles, I. A. R. (Oxford U., Middx and Scotland; *CY 1931*) b Jan. 20, 1908, d Feb. 28, 1980

Peel, R. (Yorks.; *CY 1889*) b Feb. 12, 1857, d Aug. 12, 1941

Pegler, S. J. (S. Africa) b July 28, 1888, d Sept. 10, 1972

Pellew, C. E. (Australia) b Sept. 21, 1893

Penn, F. (Kent) b March 7, 1851, d Dec. 26, 1916

Perkins, C. G. (Northants) b June 4, 1911

Perks, R. T. D. (Worcs.) b Oct. 4, 1911, d Nov. 22, 1977

Perrin, P. A. (Essex; *CY 1905*) b May 26, 1876, d Nov. 20, 1945

Perryman, S. P. (Warw.) b Oct. 22, 1955

Pervez Sajjad (Pakistan) b Aug. 30, 1942

Petherick, P. J. (N. Zealand) b Sept. 25, 1942

Petrie, E. C. (N. Zealand) b May 22, 1927

Pfuhl, G. P. (W. Province) b Aug. 27, 1947

Phadkar, D. G. (India) b Dec. 12, 1925

Phebey, A. H. (Kent) b Oct. 1, 1924

Phelan, P. J. (Essex) b Feb. 9, 1938

Philipson, H. (Oxford U. and Middx) b June 8, 1866, d Dec. 4, 1935

Phillip, N. (Essex and W. Indies) b June 22, 1949

Phillipps, J. H. (N. Zealand Manager 1949, 1958; Manager MCC in N. Zealand 1960-61) b Jan. 1, 1898, d June 8, 1977

Phillipson, C. P. (Sussex) b Feb. 10, 1952

Phillipson, W. E. (Lancs.) b Dec. 3, 1910

Philpott, P. I. (Australia) b Nov. 21, 1934

Piachaud, J. D. (Oxford U., Hants and Ceylon) b March 1, 1937

Pickles, L. (Somerset) b Sept. 17, 1932

Pilch, Fuller (Norfolk and Kent) b March 17, 1804, d May 1, 1870

Pilling, H. (Lancs.) b Feb. 23, 1943

Pilling, R. (Lancs.; *CY 1891*) b July 5, 1855, d March 28, 1891

Pinch, C. L. (NSW and S. Australia) b June 23, 1921

Pithey, A. J. (S. Africa) b July 17, 1933

Pithey, D. B. (Oxford U., Northants and S. Africa) b Oct. 10, 1936

Pitman, R. W. C. (Hants) b Feb. 21, 1933

Place, W. (Lancs.) b Dec. 7, 1914

Platt, R. K. (Yorks. and Northants) b Dec. 21, 1932

Playle, W. R. (W. Australia and N. Zealand) b Dec. 1, 1938

Pleass, J. E. (Glam.) b May 21, 1923

Plimsoll, J. B. (S. Africa) b Oct. 27, 1917

Pocock, N. E. J. (Hants) b Dec. 15, 1951

Pocock, P. I. (Surrey and N. Transvaal) b Sept. 24, 1946

Pollard, R. (Lancs.) b June 19, 1912

Pollard, V. (N. Zealand) b Burnley Sept. 7, 1945

Pollock, P. M. (S. Africa; *CY 1966*) b June 30, 1941

Pollock, R. G. (S. Africa; *CY 1966*) b Feb. 27, 1944

Ponsford, W. H. (Australia; *CY 1935*) b Oct. 19, 1900

Pont, K. R. (Essex) b Jan. 16, 1953

Poole, C. J. (Notts.) b March 13, 1921

Pooley, E. (Surrey and first England tour) b Feb. 13, 1838, d July 18, 1907

Poore, M. B. (N. Zealand) b June 1, 1930

Poore, Brig-Gen. R. M. (Hants and S. Africa; *CY 1900*) b March 20, 1866, d July 14, 1938

Pope, A. V. (Derby.) b Aug. 15, 1909

Pope, G. H. (Derby.) b Jan. 27, 1911

Pope, R. J. (Australia) b Feb. 18, 1864, d July 27, 1952

Popplewell, N. F. M. (Camb. U. and Somerset) b Aug. 8, 1957
Porter, A. (Glam.) b March 25, 1914
Porter, G. D. (W. Australia) b March 18, 1955
Porter, S. R. (Oxford U.) b Aug. 9, 1950
Pothecary, E. A. (Hants) b March 1, 1906
Pothecary, J. E. (S. Africa) b Dec. 6, 1933
Potter, G. (Sussex) b Oct. 26, 1931
Potter, J. (Victoria) b April 13, 1938
Pougher, A. D. (Leics.) b April 19, 1865, d May 20, 1926
Pountain, F. R. (Sussex) b April 23, 1941
Powell, A. G. (Camb. U. and Essex) b Aug. 17, 1912
Powell, A. W. (S. Africa) b July 18, 1873, d Sept. 11, 1948
Prasanna, E. A. S. (India) b May 22, 1940
Pratt, R. C. E. (Surrey) b May 5, 1928, d June 7, 1977
Pratt, R. L. (Leics.) b Nov. 15, 1938
Preece, C. R. (Worcs.) b Dec. 15, 1888, d Feb. 5, 1976
Prentice, F. T. (Leics.) b April 22, 1912, d July 10, 1978
Pressdee, J. S. (Glam. and N. E. Transvaal) b June 19, 1933
Preston, Hubert (Editor of *Wisden* 1944-51) b Dec. 16, 1868, d Aug. 6, 1960
Preston, K. C. (Essex) b Aug. 22, 1925
Preston, Norman, (Editor of *Wisden* 1951-80) b March 18, 1903, d March 6, 1980
Pretlove, J. F. (Camb. U. and Kent) b Nov. 23, 1932
Price, E. J. (Lancs. and Essex) b Oct. 27, 1918
Price, J. S. E. (Middx) b July 22, 1937
Price, V. R. (Oxford U. and Surrey) b May 22, 1895, d May 29, 1973
Price, W. F. F. (Middx) b April 25, 1902, d Jan. 12, 1969
Prideaux, R. M. (Camb. U., Kent, Northants, Sussex and Orange Free State) b July 31, 1939
Pridgeon, A. P. (Worcs.) b Feb. 22, 1954
Prince, C. F. H. (S. Africa) b Sept. 11, 1874, d March 5, 1948
Pringle, D. R. (Camb. U. and Essex) b Sept. 18, 1958
Pritchard, T. L. (Wellington, Warw. and Kent) b March 10, 1917
Procter, M. J. (Glos. and S. Africa; *CY 1970*) b Sept. 15, 1946
Prodger, J. M. (Kent) b Sept. 1, 1935
Promnitz, H. L. E. (S. Africa) b Feb. 23, 1904
Prouton, R. O. (Hants) b March 1, 1926
Puckett, C. W. (W. Australia) b Feb. 21, 1911
Pugh, C. T. M. (Glos.) b March 13, 1937
Pullan, D. A. (Notts.) b May 1, 1944
Pullar, G. (Lancs. and Glos.; *CY 1960*) b Aug. 1, 1935

Pullinger, G. R. (Essex) b March 14, 1920
Puna, N. (N. Zealand) b Oct. 28, 1929
Punjabi, P. H. (India) b Sept. 20, 1921

Quaife, B. W. (Warw. and Worcs.) b Nov. 24, 1899
Quaife, William ("W. G.") (Warw. and Griqualand W.; *CY 1902*) b March 17, 1872, d Oct. 13, 1951
Quick, I. W. (Victoria) b Nov. 5, 1933
Quinn, N. A. (S. Africa) b Feb. 21, 1908, d Aug. 5, 1934

Rabone, G. O. (N. Zealand) b Nov. 6, 1921
Radley, C. T. (Middx; *CY 1979*) b May 13, 1944
Rae, A. F. (W. Indies) b Sept. 30, 1922
Rai Singh, K. (India) b Feb. 24, 1922
Rait Kerr, Col. R. S. (Sec. MCC 1936-52) b April 13, 1891, d April 2, 1961
Rajindernath, V. (India) b Jan. 7, 1928
Rajinder Pal (India) b Nov. 18, 1937
Ralph, L. H. R. (Essex) b May 22, 1920
Ramadhin, S. (Lancs. and W. Indies; *CY 1951*) b May 1, 1930
Ramaswami, C. (India) b June 18, 1896
Ramchand, G. S. (India) b July 26, 1927
Ramji, L. (India) b 1900, d Dec. 20, 1948
Ramsamooj, D. (Trinidad and Northants) b July 5, 1932
Randall, D. W. (Notts.; *CY 1980*) b Feb. 24, 1951
Rangachari, C. R. (India) b April 14, 1916
Rangnekar, K. M. (India) b June 27, 1917
Ranjane, V. B. (India) b July 22, 1937
Ranjitsinhji, Kumar Shri, afterwards H. H. the Jam Saheb of Nawanagar (Camb. U. and Sussex; *CY 1897*) b Sept. 10, 1872, d April 2, 1933
Ransford, V. S. (Australia; *CY 1910*) b March 20, 1885, d March 19, 1958
Ransom, V. J. (Hants and Surrey) b March 17, 1918
Ratcliffe, R. M. (Lancs.) b Nov. 29, 1951
Rayment, A. W. H. (Hants) b May 29, 1928
Raymer, V. N. (Queensland) b May 4, 1918
Read, H. D. (Surrey and Essex) b Jan. 28, 1910
Read, J. M. (Surrey; *CY 1890*) b Feb. 9, 1859, d Feb. 17, 1929
Read, W. W. (Surrey; *CY 1893*) b Nov. 23, 1855, d Jan. 6, 1907
Reddick, T. B. (Middx, Notts. and W. Province) b Feb. 17, 1912
Reddy, B. (India) b Nov. 12, 1954
Redman, J. (Somerset) b March 1, 1926
Redmond, R. E. (N. Zealand) b Dec. 29, 1944
Redpath, I. R. (Australia) b May 11, 1941
Reed, B. L. (Hants) b Sept. 9, 1937
Reedman, J. C. (Australia) b Oct. 9, 1865, d March 25, 1924

Rees, A. (Glam.) b Feb. 17, 1938
Rege, M. R. (India) b March 18, 1924
Rehman, S. F. (Pakistan) b June 11, 1935
Reid, J. F. (N. Zealand) b March 3, 1956
Reid, J. R. (N. Zealand; *CY 1959*) b June 3, 1928
Reid, K. P. (E. Province and Northants) b July 24, 1951
Reid, N. (S. Africa) b Dec. 26, 1890, d June 10, 1947
Reidy, B. W. (Lancs.) b Sept 18, 1953
Relf, A. E. (Sussex and Auckland; *CY 1914*) b June 26, 1874, d March 26, 1937
Renneburg, D. A. (Australia) b Sept. 23, 1942
Revill, A. C. (Derby. and Leics.) b March 27, 1923
Reynolds, B. L. (Northants) b June 10, 1932
Reynolds, G. R. (Queensland) b Aug. 24, 1936
Rhodes, A. E. G. (Derby.) b Oct. 10, 1916
Rhodes, H. J. (Derby.) b July 22, 1936
Rhodes, Wilfred (Yorks.; *CY 1899*) b Oct. 29, 1877, d July 8, 1973
Rice, C. E. B. (Transvaal and Notts.; *CY 1981*) b July 23, 1949
Rice, J. M. (Hants) b Oct. 23, 1949
Richards, A. R. (S. Africa) b 1868, d Jan. 9, 1904
Richards, B. A. (Glos., Hants, S. Australia and S. Africa; *CY 1969*) b July 21, 1945
Richards, C. J. (Surrey) b Aug. 10, 1958
Richards, G. (Glam.) b Nov. 29, 1951
Richards, I. V. A. (Somerset, Queensland and W. Indies; *CY 1977*) b March 7, 1952
Richards, W. H. M. (S. Africa) b August 1862, d Jan. 4, 1903
Richardson, A. J. (Australia) b July 24, 1888, d Dec. 23, 1973
Richardson, A. W. (Derby.) b March 4, 1907
Richardson, D. W. (Worcs.) b Nov. 3, 1934
Richardson, G. W. (Derby.) b April 26, 1938
Richardson, P. E. (Worcs. and Kent; *CY 1957*) b July 4, 1931
Richardson, T. (Surrey and Somerset; *CY 1897*) b Aug. 11, 1870, d July 2, 1912
Richardson, V. Y. (Australia) b Sept. 7, 1894, d Oct. 29, 1969
Riches, N. V. H. (Glam.) b June 9, 1883, d Nov. 6, 1975
Richmond, T. L. (Notts.) b June 23, 1890, d Dec. 29, 1957
Rickards, K. R. (Essex and W. Indies) b Aug. 23, 1923
Riddington, A. (Leics.) b Dec. 22, 1911
Ridgway, F. (Kent) b Aug. 10, 1923
Ridings, P. L. (S. Australia) b Oct. 2, 1917
Rigg, K. E. (Australia) b May 21, 1906
Ridley, G. N. S. (Oxford U. and Kent) b Nov. 27, 1944
Riley, H. (Leics.) b Oct. 3, 1902
Ring, D. T. (Australia) b Oct. 14, 1918

Rist, F. H. (Essex) b March 30, 1914
Ritchie, G. G. (Transvaal) b Sept. 16, 1933
Rixon, S. J. (Australia) b Feb. 25, 1954
Roach, C. A. (W. Indies) b March 13, 1904
Roberts, A. D. G. (N. Zealand) b May 6, 1947
Roberts, A. M. E. (Hants, NSW and W. Indies; *CY 1975*) b Jan. 29, 1951
Roberts, A. T. (W. Indies) b Sept. 18, 1937
Roberts, A. W. (N. Zealand) b Aug. 20, 1909, d May 13, 1978
Roberts, Pascal (Trinidad) b Dec. 15, 1937
Robertson, J. B. (S. Africa) b June 5, 1906
Robertson, J. D. B. (Middx; *CY 1948*) b Feb. 22, 1917
Robertson, S. D. (Rhodesia) b May 1, 1947
Robertson, W. R. (Australia) b Oct. 6, 1861, d June 24, 1938
Robertson-Glasgow, R. C. (Oxford U. and Somerset) b July 15, 1901, d March 4, 1965
Robins, R. V. C. (Middx) b March 13, 1935
Robins, R. W. V. (Camb. U. and Middx; *CY 1930*) b June 3, 1906, d Dec. 12, 1968
Robinson, A. L. (Yorks.) b Aug. 17, 1946
Robinson, Emmott (Yorks.) b Nov. 16, 1883, d Nov. 17, 1969
Robinson, Ellis P. (Yorks. and Somerset) b Aug. 10, 1911
Robinson, G. W. (Oxford U.) b Nov. 3, 1949
Robinson, H. B. O. (Oxford U. and Canada) b March 3, 1919
Robinson, M. (Glam. and Warw.) b July 16, 1921
Robinson, P. J. (Worcs. and Somerset) b Feb. 9, 1943
Robinson, Ray (Writer) b July 8, 1908
Robinson, R. D. (Australia) b June 8, 1946
Robinson, R. H. (Australia) b March 26, 1914, d Aug. 10, 1965
Robson, E. (Somerset) b May 1, 1870, d May 23, 1924
Rochford, P. (Glos.) b Aug. 27, 1928
Rodriguez, W. V. (W. Indies) b June 25, 1934
Roe, B. (Somerset) b Jan. 27, 1939
Roebuck, P. M. (Camb. U. and Somerset) b March 6, 1956
Rogers, J. J. (Oxford U.) b Aug. 20, 1958
Rogers, R. E. (Queensland) b Aug. 24, 1916
Rogers, N. H. (Hants) b March 9, 1918
Roope, G. R. J. (Surrey and Griqualand W.) b July 12, 1946
Root, C. F. (Derby. and Worcs.) b April 16, 1890, d Jan. 20, 1954
Rorke, G. F. (Australia) b June 27, 1938
Rose, B. C. (Somerset; *CY 1980*) b June 4, 1950
Rosebery, 6th Earl of (*See* Dalmeny, Lord)
Rose-Innes, A. (S. Africa) b Feb. 16, 1868, d Nov. 22, 1946
Rosendorff, N. (Orange Free State) b Jan. 22, 1945

Ross, C. J. (Wellington and Oxford U.) b June 24, 1954

Rotherham, G. A. (Rugby, Camb. U., Warw. and Wellington; *CY 1918*) b May 28, 1899

Roundell, J. (Camb. U.) b Oct. 23, 1951

Rouse, S. J. (Warw.) b Jan. 20, 1949

Routledge, R. (Middx) b July 7, 1920

Routledge, T. W. (S. Africa) b April 18, 1867, d May 9, 1927

Rowan, A. M. B. (S. Africa) b Feb. 7, 1921

Rowan, E. A. B. (S. Africa; *CY 1952*) b July 20, 1909

Rowe, C. G. (N. Zealand) b June 30, 1915

Rowe, C. J. C. (Kent) b May 5, 1953

Rowe, E. J. (Notts.) b July 21, 1920

Rowe, G. A. (S. Africa) b June 15, 1874, d Jan. 8, 1950

Rowe, L. G. (Derby. and W. Indies) b Jan. 8, 1949

Roy, A. (India) b June 5, 1945

Roy, P. (India) b May 31, 1928

Royle, Rev. V. P. F. A. (Oxford U. and Lancs.) b Jan. 29, 1854, d May 20, 1929

Rumsey, F. E. (Worcs., Somerset and Derby.) b Dec. 4, 1935

Russell, C. A. G. ("A. C.") (Essex; *CY 1923*) b Oct. 7, 1887, d March 23, 1961

Russell, D. P. (Camb. U.) b June 4, 1951

Russell, P. E. (Derby.) b May 9, 1944

Russell, S. E. J. (Middx and Glos.) b Oct. 4, 1937

Russell, S. G. (Camb. U. and Surrey) b March 11, 1945

Russell, W. E. (Middx) b July 3, 1936

Russom, N. (Camb. U. and Somerset) b Dec. 3, 1958

Rutherford, I. A. (Worcs. and Otago) b June 30, 1957

Rutherford, J. W. (Australia) b Sept. 25, 1929

Ryan, M. (Yorks.) b June 23, 1933

Ryan, M. L. (Canterbury) b June 7, 1943

Ryder, J. (Australia) b Aug. 8, 1889, d April 3, 1977

Sadiq Mohammad (Tasmania, Glos., Essex and Pakistan) b May 3, 1945

Sadler, W. C. H. (Surrey) b Sept. 24, 1896

Saeed Ahmed (Pakistan) b Oct. 1, 1937

Saggers, R. A. (Australia) b May 15, 1917

Sainsbury, P. J. (Hants; *CY 1974*) b June 13, 1934

St Hill, E. L. (W. Indies) b March 9, 1904, d May 21, 1957

St Hill, W. H. (W. Indies) b July 6, 1893, d 1957

Salah-ud-Din (Pakistan) b Feb. 14, 1937

Sale, R. (Oxford U. and Derby.) b June 21, 1889, d Sept. 7, 1970

Sale, R. jnr (Oxford U., Warw. and Derby.) b Oct. 4, 1919

Saleem Altaf (Pakistan) b March 23, 1944

Salter, M. G. (Oxford U. and Glos.) b May 10, 1887, d June 15, 1973

Sampson, H. (Yorkshire and All-England) b March 13, 1813, d March 29, 1885

Samuelson, S. V. (S. Africa) b Nov. 21, 1883, d Nov. 18, 1958

Sanderson, J. F. W. (Oxford U.) b Sept. 10, 1954

Sandham, A. (Surrey; *CY 1923*) b July 6, 1890

Sandman, D. McK. (Canterbury) b Nov. 3, 1889, d Jan. 29, 1973

Sardesai, D. N. (India) b Aug. 8, 1940

Sarfraz Nawaz (Northants and Pakistan) b Dec. 1, 1948

Sarwate, C. T. (India) b June 22, 1920

Saunders, J. V. (Australia) b Feb. 3, 1876, d Dec. 21, 1927

Savage, J. S. (Leics. and Lancs.) b March 3, 1929

Savage, R. Le Q. (Oxford U. and Warw.) b Dec. 10, 1955

Savill, L. A. (Essex) b June 30, 1935

Saville, G. J. (Essex) b Feb. 5, 1944

Saxena, R. C. (India) b Sept. 20, 1944

Sayer, D. M. (Oxford U. and Kent) b Sept. 19, 1936

Scarlett, R. O. (W. Indies) b Aug. 15, 1934

Schofield, R. M. (C. Districts) b Nov. 6, 1939

Schonegevel, D. J. (Orange Free State and Griqualand W.) b Oct. 9, 1934

Schultz, S. S. (Camb. U. and Lancs.) b Aug. 29, 1857, d Dec. 17, 1937

Schwarz, R. O. (Middx and S. Africa; *CY 1908*) b Lee, Kent May 4, 1875, d Nov. 18, 1918

Scott, A. P. H. (W. Indies) b July 29, 1934

Scott, Christopher J. (Lancs.) b Sept. 16, 1959

Scott, Colin J. (Glos.) b May 1, 1919

Scott, H. J. H. (Australia) b Dec. 26, 1858, d Sept. 23, 1910

Scott, M. E. (Northants) b May 8, 1936

Scott, O. C. (W. Indies) b Aug. 25, 1893, d June 16, 1961

Scott, R. H. (N. Zealand) b March 6, 1917

Scott, S. W. (Middx; *CY 1893*) b March 24, 1854, d Dec. 8, 1933

Scott, V. J. (N. Zealand) b July 31, 1916, d Aug. 2, 1980

Scotton, W. H. (Notts.) b Jan. 15, 1856, d July 9, 1893

Seabrook, F. J. (Camb. U. and Glos.) b Jan. 9, 1899, d Aug. 7, 1979

Seager, C. P. (Camb. U.) b April 5, 1951

Sealey, B. J. (W. Indies) b Aug. 12, 1899, d Sept. 12, 1963

Sealy, J. E. D. (W. Indies) b Sept. 11, 1912

Seamer, J. W. (Somerset and Oxford U.) b June 23, 1913

Sebastian, L. C. (Windwards) b Oct. 31, 1955

Seccull, A. W. (S. Africa) b Sept. 14, 1868, d July 20, 1945

Selby, J. (Notts.) b July 1, 1849, d March 11, 1894

Sellers, A. B. (Yorks.; *CY 1940*) b March 5, 1907

Sellers, R. H. D. (Australia) b Aug. 20, 1940

Selvey, M. W. W. (Camb. U., Surrey, Middx and Orange Free State) b April 25, 1948

Sen, P. (India) b May 31, 1926, d Jan. 27, 1970

Sen Gupta, A. K. (India) b Aug. 3, 1939

Serjeant, C. S. (Australia) b Nov. 1, 1951

Seymour, James (Kent) b Oct. 25, 1879, d Sept. 30, 1930

Seymour, M. A. (S. Africa) b June 5, 1936

Shackleton, D. (Hants; *CY 1959*) b Aug. 12, 1924

Shafiq Ahmed (Pakistan) b March 28, 1949

Shafqat Rana (Pakistan) b Aug. 10, 1943

Shahid Israr (Pakistan) b March 1, 1950

Shahid Mahmoud (Pakistan) b March 13, 1939

Shalders, W. A. (S. Africa) b Feb. 12, 1880, d March 18, 1917

Sharma, M. L. (India) (*see* Madan Lal, S.)

Sharma, P. (India) b Jan. 5, 1948

Sharp, A. T. (Leics.) b March 23, 1889, d Feb. 15, 1973

Sharp, G. (Northants) b March 12, 1950

Sharp, H. P. H. (Middx) b Oct. 6, 1917

Sharp, J. (Lancs.) b Feb. 15, 1878, d Jan. 27, 1938

Sharp, K. (Yorks.) b April 6, 1959

Sharpe, D. (Pakistan) b Aug. 3, 1937

Sharpe, J. W. (Surrey and Notts.; *CY 1892*) b Dec. 9, 1866, d June 19, 1936

Sharpe, P. J. (Yorks. and Derby.; *CY 1963*) b Dec. 27, 1936

Shaw, Alfred (Notts. and Sussex) b Aug. 29, 1842, d Jan. 16, 1907

Shaw, J. H. (Victoria) b Oct. 18, 1932

Sheahan, A. P. (Australia) b Sept. 30, 1946

Sheffield, J. R. (Essex) b Nov. 19, 1906

Shepherd, B. K. (Australia) b April 23, 1938

Shepherd, D. J. (Glam.; *CY 1970*) b Aug. 12, 1927

Shepherd, D. R. (Glos.) b Dec. 27, 1940

Shepherd, J. N. (Kent, Rhodesia and W. Indies; *CY 1979*) b Nov. 9, 1943

Shepherd, T. F. (Surrey) b Dec. 5, 1889, d Feb. 13, 1957

Sheppard, Rt Rev. D. S. (Bishop of Liverpool) (Camb. U. and Sussex; *CY 1953*) b March 6, 1929

Shepstone, G. H. (S. Africa) b April 8, 1876, d July 3, 1940

Sherwell, P. W. (S. Africa) b Aug. 17, 1880, d April 17, 1948

Sherwin, M. (Notts.; *CY 1891*) b Feb. 26, 1851, d July 1910

Shillingford, G. C. (W. Indies) b Sept. 25, 1944

Shillingford, I. T. (W. Indies) b April 18, 1944

Shinde, S. G. (India) b Aug. 18, 1923, d June 22, 1955

Shipman, A. W. (Leics.) b March 7, 1901, d Dec. 12, 1979

Shirreff, A. C. (Camb. U., Hants, Kent and Somerset) b Feb. 12, 1919

Shivlal Yadav, N. (India) (*see* Yadav, N. S.)

Shivnarine, S. (W. Indies) b May 13, 1952

Shodhan, R. H. (India) b Oct. 18, 1928

Short, A. M. (Natal) b Sept. 27, 1947

Shortland, N. A. (Warw.) b July 6, 1916, d March 14, 1973

Shrewsbury, Arthur (Notts.; *CY 1890*) b April 11, 1856, d May 19, 1903

Shrimpton, M. J. F. (N. Zealand) b June 23, 1940

Shuja-ud-Din, Col. (Pakistan) b April 10, 1930

Shuter, J. (Kent and Surrey) b Feb. 9, 1855, d July 5, 1920

Shuttleworth, K. (Lancs. and Leics.) b Nov. 13, 1944

Sibbles, F. M. (Lancs.) b March 15, 1904, b July 20, 1973

Sidebottom, A. (Yorks.) b April 1, 1954

Siedle, I. J. (S. Africa) b Jan. 11, 1903

Sievers, M. W. (Australia) b April 13, 1912, d May 10, 1968

Sikander Bakht (Pakistan) b Aug. 25, 1957

Silk, D. R. W. (Camb. U. and Somerset) b Oct. 8, 1931

Sime, W. A. (Notts.) b Feb. 8, 1909

Simmons, J. (Lancs. and Tasmania) b March 28, 1941

Simpson, R. B. (Australia; *CY 1965*) b Feb. 3, 1936

Simpson, R. T. (Notts. and Sind; *CY 1950*) b Feb. 27, 1920

Simpson-Hayward, G. H. T. (Worcs.) b June 7, 1875, d Oct. 2, 1936

Sims, Sir Arthur (Canterbury) b July 22, 1877, d April 27, 1969

Sims, J. M. (Middx) b May 13, 1903, d April 27, 1973

Sinclair, B. W. (N. Zealand) b Oct. 23, 1936

Sinclair, I. McK. (N. Zealand) b June 1, 1933

Sinclair, J. H. (S. Africa) b Oct. 16, 1876, d Feb. 23, 1913

Sincock, D. J. (Australia) b Feb. 1, 1942

Sinfield, R. A. (Glos.) b Dec. 24, 1900

Singh, Charan, K. (West Indies) b 1938

Singh, Swaranjit (Camb. U., Warw., E. Punjab and Bengal) b July 18, 1931

Singleton, A. P. (Oxford U., Worcs. and Rhodesia) b Aug. 5, 1914

Sipahahimalani, R. G. (*see* Ramchand, G. S.)

Siviter, K. (Oxford U.) b Dec. 10, 1953

Skeet, C. H. L. (Oxford U. and Middx) b Aug. 17, 1895, d April 20, 1978

Skelding, Alec (Leics.) b Sept. 5, 1886, d April 17, 1960

Skinner, A. F. (Derby. and Northants) b April 22, 1913

Skinner, D. A. (Derby.) b March 22, 1920

Skinner, L. E. (Surrey and Guyana) b Sept. 7, 1950

Slade, D. N. F. (Worcs.) b Aug. 24, 1940

Slade, W. D. (Glam.) b Sept. 27, 1941

Slater, K. N. (Australia) b March 12, 1935

Sleep, P. R. (Australia) b May 4, 1957

Slight, J. (Australia) b Oct. 20, 1855, d Dec. 9, 1930

Slocombe, P. A. (Somerset) b Sept. 6, 1954

Smailes, T. F. (Yorks.) b March 27, 1910, d Dec. 1, 1970

Smales, K. (Yorks. and Notts.) b Sept. 15, 1927

Small, G. C. (Warw.) b Oct. 18, 1961

Small, John snr (Hants. and All-England) b April 19, 1737, d Dec. 31, 1826

Small, J. A. (W. Indies) b Nov. 3, 1892, d April 26, 1958

Smart, C. C. (Warw. and Glam.) b July 23, 1898, d May 21, 1975

Smart, J. A. (Warw.) b April 12, 1891, d Oct. 3, 1979

Smedley, M. J. (Notts.) b Oct. 28, 1941

Smith, A. C. (Oxford U. and Warw.) b Oct. 25, 1936

Smith, A. J. S. (Natal) b Feb. 8, 1951

Smith, Sir C. Aubrey (Camb. U., Sussex and Transvaal) b July 21, 1863, d Dec. 20, 1948

Smith, C. I. J. ("Jim") (Middx; *CY 1935*) b Aug. 25, 1906, d Feb. 8, 1979

Smith, C. J. E. (S. Africa) b Dec. 25, 1872, d March 27, 1947

Smith, C. L. (Natal, Glam. and Hants) b Oct. 15, 1958

Smith, C. S. (Camb. U. and Lancs.) b Oct. 1, 1932

Smith, C. W. (W. Indies) b July 29, 1933

Smith, Denis (Derby.; *CY 1936*) b Jan. 24, 1907, d Sept. 12, 1979

Smith, D. B. M. (Australia) b Sept. 14, 1884, d July 29, 1974

Smith, D. H. K. (Derby. and Orange Free State) b June 29, 1940

Smith, D. M. (Surrey) b Jan. 9, 1956

Smith, D. R. (Glos.) b Oct. 5, 1934

Smith, D. V. (Sussex) b June 14, 1923

Smith, Edwin (Derby.) b Jan. 2, 1934

Smith, E. J. (Warw.) b Feb. 6, 1886, d Aug. 31, 1979

Smith, F. B. (N. Zealand) b March 13, 1922

Smith, F. W. (S. Africa) No details of birth or death known

Smith, G. (Kent) b Nov. 30, 1925

Smith, G. J. (Essex) b April 2, 1935

Smith, Harry (Glos.) b May 21, 1890, d Nov. 12, 1937

Smith, H. D. (N. Zealand) b Jan. 8, 1913

Smith, K. D. (Warw.) b July 9, 1956

Smith, L. D. (Otago) b Dec. 23, 1914

Smith, M. J. (Middx) b Jan. 4, 1942

Smith, M. J. K. (Oxford U., Leics. and Warw.; *CY 1960*) b June 30, 1933

Smith, N. (Yorks. and Essex) b April 1, 1949

Smith, O. G. (W. Indies; *CY 1958*) b May 5, 1933, d Sept. 9, 1959

Smith, Ray (Essex) b Aug. 10, 1914

Smith, Roy (Somerset) b April 14, 1930

Smith, R. C. (Leics.) b Aug. 3, 1935

Smith, Sydney (Manager Australians in England 1921 and 1926) b March 1, 1880, d April 11, 1972

Smith, S. G. (Trinidad, Northants and Auckland; *CY 1915*) b Jan. 15, 1881, d Oct. 25, 1963

Smith, T. P. B. (Essex; *CY 1947*) b Oct. 30, 1908, d Aug. 4, 1967

Smith, V. I. (S. Africa) b Feb. 23, 1925

Smith, W. A. (Surrey) b Sept. 15, 1937

Smith, W. C. (Surrey; *CY 1911*) b Oct. 4, 1877, d July 16, 1946

Smithson, G. A. (Yorks. and Leics.) b Nov. 1, 1926, d Sept. 6, 1970

Smythe, R. I. (Camb. U.) b Nov. 19, 1951

Snedden, C. A. (N. Zealand) b Jan. 7, 1918

Snellgrove, K. L. (Lancs.) b Nov. 12, 1941

Snooke, S. D. (S. Africa) b Nov. 11, 1878, d April 4, 1959

Snooke, S. J. (S. Africa) b Feb. 1, 1881, d Aug. 14, 1966

Snow, J. A. (Sussex; *CY 1973*) b Oct. 13, 1941

Snowden, A. W. (Northants) b Aug. 15, 1913

Snowden, W. (Camb. U.) b Sept. 27, 1952

Sobers, Sir G. St A. (Notts., S. Australia and W. Indies; *CY 1964*) b July 18, 1936

Sohoni, S. W. (India) b March 5, 1918

Solanky, J. W. (E. Africa and Glam.) b June 30, 1942

Solkar, E. D. (Sussex and India) b March 18, 1948

Solomon, J. S. (W. Indies) b Aug. 26, 1930

Solomon, W. R. T. (S. Africa) b April 23, 1872, d July 12, 1964

Sood, M. M. (India) b July 6, 1939

Southern, J. W. (Hants) b Sept. 2, 1952

Southerton, James (Surrey, Hants and Sussex) b Nov. 16, 1827, d June 16, 1880

Southerton, S. J. (Editor of *Wisden* 1934-35) b July 7, 1874, d March 12, 1935

Sparling, J. T. (N. Zealand) b July 24, 1938

Spencer, C. T. (Leics.) b Aug. 18, 1931

Spencer, J. (Camb. U. and Sussex) b Oct. 6, 1949

Spencer, T. W. (Kent) b March 22, 1914

Sperry, J. (Leics.) b March 19, 1910

Spofforth, F. R. (Australia) b Sept. 9, 1853, d June 4, 1926

Spooner, R. H. (Lancs.; *CY 1905*) b Oct. 21, 1880, d Oct. 2, 1961

Spooner, R. T. (Warw.) b Dec. 30, 1919

Springall, J. D. (Notts.) b Sept. 19, 1932

Squires, H. S. (Surrey) b Feb. 22, 1909, d Jan. 24, 1950

Stackpole, K. R. (Australia; *CY 1973*) b July 10, 1940

Stallibrass, M. J. D. (Oxford U.) b June 28, 1951

Standen, J. A. (Worcs.) b May 30, 1935

Stannard, G. (Sussex) b July 9, 1894, d June 25, 1971

Stanyforth, Lt-Col. R. T. (Yorks.) b May 30, 1892, d Feb. 20, 1964

Staples, S. J. (Notts.; *CY 1929*) b Sept. 18, 1892, d June 4, 1950

Starkie, S. (Northants) b April 4, 1926

Statham, J. B. (Lancs.; *CY 1955*) b June 16, 1930

Stayers, S. C. (W. Indies) b June 9, 1937

Stead, B. (Yorks., Essex, Notts. and N. Transvaal) b June 21, 1939, d April 15, 1980

Steel, A. G. (Camb. U. and Lancs.; Pres. MCC 1902) b Sept. 24, 1858, d June 15, 1914

Steele, D. S. (Northants and Derby.; *CY 1976*) b Sept. 29, 1941

Steele, H. K. C. (Auckland and Camb. U.) b April 6, 1951

Steele, J. F. (Leics. and Natal) b July 23, 1946

Stephens, E. J. (Glos.) b March 23, 1910

Stephens, F. G. (Warw.) b April 26, 1889, d Aug. 9, 1970

Stephenson, G. R. (Derby. and Hants) b Nov. 19, 1942

Stephenson, H. H. (Surrey and All-England) b May 3, 1832, d Dec. 17, 1896

Stephenson, H. W. (Somerset) b July 18, 1920

Stephenson, Lt-Col. J. W. A. (Essex and Worcs.) b Aug. 1, 1907

Stevens, Edward ("Lumpy") (Hants) b *circa* 1735, d Sept. 7, 1819

Stevens, G. B. (Australia) b Feb. 29, 1932

Stevens, G. T. S. (UCS, Oxford U. and Middx; *CY 1918*) b Jan. 7, 1901, d Sept. 19, 1970

Stevenson, G. B. (Yorks.) b Dec. 16, 1955

Stevenson, K. (Derby. and Hants) b Oct. 6, 1950

Stevenson, M. H. (Camb. U. and Derby.) b June 13, 1927

Stewart, M. J. (Surrey; *CY 1958*) b Sept. 16, 1932

Stewart, R. B. (S. Africa) b Sept. 3, 1856, d Sept. 12, 1913

Stewart, R. W. (Glos. and Middx) b Feb. 28, 1945

Stewart, W. J. (Warw. and Northants) b Aug. 31, 1934

Stirling, W. S. (S. Australia and AIF) b March 20, 1891, d July 18, 1971

Stocks, F. W. (Notts.) b Nov. 6, 1917

Stoddart, A. E. (Middx; *CY 1893*) b March 11, 1863, d April 3, 1915

Stollmeyer, J. B. (W. Indies) b April 11, 1921

Stollmeyer, V. H. (W. Indies) b Jan. 24, 1916

Storer, W. (Derby.; *CY 1899*) b Jan. 25, 1867, d March 5, 1912

Storey, S. J. (Surrey and Sussex) b Jan. 6, 1941

Stott, W. B. (Yorks.) b July 18, 1934

Stovold, A. W. (Glos. and Orange Free State) b March 19, 1953

Street, G. B. (Sussex) b Dec. 6, 1889, d April 24, 1924

Stricker, L. A. (S. Africa) b May 26, 1884, d Feb. 5, 1960

Stringer, P. M. (Yorks. and Leics.) b Feb. 23, 1943

Strudwick, H. (Surrey; *CY 1912*) b Jan. 28, 1880, d Feb. 13, 1970

Strydom, W. T. (Orange Free State) b March 21, 1942

Studd, C. T. (Camb. U. and Middx) b Dec. 2, 1860, d July 16, 1931

Studd, G. B. (Camb. U. and Middx) b Oct. 20, 1859, d Feb. 13, 1945

Studd, Sir Peter M. (Camb. U.) b Sept. 15, 1916

Sturt, M. O. C. (Middx) b Sept 12, 1940

Subba Row, R. (Camb. U., Surrey and Northants; *CY 1961*) b Jan. 29, 1932

Subramanya, V. (India) b July 16, 1936

Sueter, T. (Hants and Surrey) b *circa* 1749, d Feb. 17, 1827

Sugg, F. H. (Yorks., Derby. and Lancs.; *CY 1890*) b Jan. 11, 1862, d May 29, 1933

Sullivan, J. (Lancs.) b Feb. 5, 1945

Sully, H. (Somerset and Northants) b Nov. 1, 1939

Sunderram, G. R. (India) b March 29, 1930

Sunnucks, P. R. (Kent) b June 22, 1916

Surendranath, R. (India) b Jan. 4, 1937

Surridge, D. (Camb. U. and Glos.) b Jan. 6, 1956

Surridge, W. S. (Surrey; *CY 1953*) b Sept. 3, 1917

Surti, R. F. (Queensland and India) b May 25, 1936

Susskind, M. J. (Middx and S. Africa) b June 8, 1891, d July 9, 1957

Sutcliffe, B. (N. Zealand; *CY 1950*) b Nov. 17, 1923

Sutcliffe, H. (Yorks.; *CY 1920*) b Nov. 24, 1894, d Jan. 22, 1978

Sutcliffe, S. P. (Oxford U.) b May 22, 1960

Sutcliffe, W. H. H. (Yorks.) b Oct. 10, 1926

Suttle, K. G. (Sussex) b Aug. 25, 1928

Sutton, R. E. (Auckland) b May 30, 1940

Swamy, V. N. (India) b May 23, 1924

Swanton, E. W. (Middx; Writer) b Feb. 11, 1907

Swarbrook, F. W. (Derby., Griqualand W. and Orange Free State) b Dec. 17, 1950

Swart, P. D. (Rhodesia, W. Province and Glam.) b April 27, 1946

Swetman, R. (Surrey, Notts. and Glos.) b Oct. 25, 1933

Sydenham, D. A. D. (Surrey) b April 6, 1934

Symington, S. J. (Leics.) b Sept. 16, 1926

Taber, H. B. (Australia) b April 29, 1940

Taberer, H. M. (S. Africa) b Oct. 7, 1870, d June 5, 1932

Tait, A. (Northants and Glos.) b Dec. 27, 1953

Talat Ali (Pakistan) b May 29, 1950

Talbot, R. O. (Canterbury and Otago) b Nov. 26, 1903

Tallon, D. (Australia; *CY 1949*) b Feb. 17, 1916

Tamhane, N. S. (India) b Aug. 4, 1931

Tancred, A. B. (S. Africa) b Aug. 20, 1865, d Nov. 23, 1911

Tancred, L. J. (S. Africa) b Oct. 7, 1876, d July 28, 1934

Tancred, V. M. (S. Africa) b 1875, d June 3, 1904

Tapscott, G. L. (S. Africa) b Nov. 7, 1889, d Dec. 13, 1940

Tapscott, L. E. (S. Africa) b March 18, 1894, d July 7, 1934

Tarapore, K. K. (India) b Dec. 17, 1910

Tarbox, C. V. (Worcs.) b July 2, 1891, d June 15, 1978

Tarrant, F. A. (Victoria and Middx; *CY 1908*) b Dec. 11, 1880, d Jan. 29, 1951

Tarrant, George (Cambs. and All-England) b Dec. 7, 1838, d July 2, 1870

Taslim Arif (Pakistan) b May 1, 1954

Tate, F. W. (Sussex) b July 24, 1867, d Feb. 24, 1943

Tate, M. W. (Sussex; *CY 1924*) b May 30, 1895, d May 18, 1956

Tattersall, R. (Lancs.) b Aug. 17, 1922

Tausif Ahmed (Pakistan) b May 10, 1960

Tavaré, C. J. (Oxford U. and Kent) b Oct. 27, 1954

Tayfield, A. (Natal, Transvaal and NE Transvaal) b June 21, 1931

Tayfield, H. J. (S. Africa; *CY 1956*) b Jan. 30, 1929

Taylor, A. I. (S. Africa) b July 25, 1925

Taylor, B. (Essex; *CY 1972*) b June 19, 1932

Taylor, B. R. (N. Zealand) b July 12, 1943

Taylor, C. R. V. (Camb. U. and Warw.) b Oct. 3, 1951

Taylor, Daniel (S. Africa) b Jan. 9, 1887, d Jan. 24, 1957

Taylor, D. D. (Warw. and N. Zealand) b March 2, 1923, d Dec. 5, 1980

Taylor, D. J. S. (Surrey, Somerset and Griqualand W.) b Nov. 12, 1942

Taylor, G. R. (Hants) b Nov. 25, 1909

Taylor, H. W. (S. Africa; *CY 1925*) b May 5, 1889, d Feb. 8, 1973

Taylor, J. M. (Australia) b Oct. 10, 1895, d May 12, 1971

Taylor, J. O. (W. Indies) b Jan. 3, 1932

Taylor, K. (Yorks. and Auckland) b Aug. 21, 1935

Taylor, K. A. (Warw.) b Sept. 29, 1916

Taylor, L. B. (Leics.) b Oct. 25, 1953

Taylor, M. L. (Lancs.) b July 16, 1904, d March 14, 1978

Taylor, M. N. S. (Notts. and Hants) b Nov. 12, 1942

Taylor, R. M. (Essex) b Nov. 30, 1909

Taylor, R. W. (Derby.; *CY 1977*) b July 17, 1941

Taylor, T. L. (Camb. U. and Yorks.; *CY 1901*) b May 25, 1878, d March 16, 1960

Taylor, W. (Notts.) b Jan. 24, 1947

Tennekoon, A. P. B. (Sri Lanka) b Oct. 29, 1946

Tennyson, 3rd Lord (Hon. L. H.) (Hants; *CY 1914*) b Nov. 7, 1889, d June 6, 1951

Thackaray, P. R. (Oxford U.) b Sept. 26, 1950

Theunissen, N. H. (S. Africa) b May 4, 1867, d Nov. 9, 1929

Thomas, G. (Australia) b March 21, 1938

Thompson, A. W. (Middx) b April 17, 1916

Thompson, G. J. (Northants; *CY 1906*) b Oct. 27, 1877, d March 3, 1943

Thompson, J. R. (Camb. U. and Warw.) b May 10, 1918

Thompson, Nathaniel (Australia) b Birmingham, England April 21, 1838, d Sept. 2, 1896

Thompson, R. G. (Warw.) b Sept. 26, 1932

Thoms, G. R. (Australia) b March 22, 1927

Thomson, A. L. (Australia) b Dec. 2, 1945

Thomson, J. R. (Australia) b Aug. 16, 1950

Thomson, K. (N. Zealand) b Feb. 26, 1941

Thomson, N. I. (Sussex) b Jan. 23, 1929

Thornton, C. I. (Camb. U., Kent and Middx) b March 20, 1850, d Dec. 10, 1929

Thornton, P. G. (Yorks., Middx and S. Africa) b Dec. 24, 1867, d Jan. 31, 1939

Thurlow, H. M. (Australia) b Jan. 10, 1902, d Dec. 3, 1975

Tilly, H. W. (Middx) b May 25, 1932

Timms, B. S. V. (Hants. and Warw.) b Dec. 17, 1940

Timms, J. E. (Northants) b Nov. 3, 1906, d May 18, 1980

Timms, W. W. (Northants) b Sept. 28, 1902

Tindall, M. (Camb. U. and Middx) b March 31, 1914

Tindall, R. A. E. (Surrey) b Sept. 23, 1935

Tindill, E. W. T. (N. Zealand) b Dec. 18, 1910

Titmus, F. J. (Middx, Surrey and Orange Free State; *CY 1963*) b Nov. 24, 1932

Todd, L. J. (Kent) b June 19, 1907, d Aug. 20, 1967

Todd, P. A. (Notts.) b March 12, 1953

Tolchard, J. G. (Leics.) b March 17, 1944

Tolchard, R. W. (Leics.) b June 15, 1946

Tomlinson, D. S. (S. Africa) b Sept. 4, 1910

Tompkin, M. (Leics.) b Feb. 17, 1919, d Sept. 27, 1956

Toohey, P. M. (Australia) b April 20, 1954

Topham, R. D. N. (Oxford U.) b July 17, 1952

Tordoff, G. G. (Camb. U. and Somerset) b Dec. 6, 1929

Toshack, E. R. H. (Australia) b Dec. 15, 1917

Towell, E. F. (Northants) b July 5, 1901, d June 2, 1972

Townsend, A. (Warw.) b Aug. 26, 1921

Townsend, A. F. (Derby.) b March 29, 1912

Townsend, C. L. (Glos.; *CY 1899*) b Nov. 7, 1876, d Oct. 17, 1958

Townsend, D. C. H. (Oxford U.) b April 20, 1912

Townsend, L. F. (Derby.; *CY 1934*) b June 8, 1903

Traicos, A. J. (S. Africa) b May 17, 1947

Trapnell, B. M. W. (Camb. U. and Middx) b May 18, 1924

Travers, J. P. F. (Australia) b Jan. 10, 1871, d Sept. 15, 1942

Tremlett, M. F. (Somerset and C. Districts) b July 5, 1923

Tremlett, T. M. (Hants) b July 26, 1956

Tribe, G. E. (Northants and Australia; *CY 1955*) b Oct. 4, 1920

Trim, J. (W. Indies) b Jan. 24, 1915, d Nov. 12, 1960

Trimble, S. C. (Queensland) b Aug. 16, 1934

Trimborn, P. H. J. (S. Africa) b May 18, 1940

Trott, A. E. (Middx, Australia and England; *CY 1899*) b Feb. 6, 1873, d July 30, 1914

Trott, G. H. S. (Australia; *CY 1894*) b Aug. 5, 1866, d Nov. 10, 1917

Troup, G. B. (N. Zealand) b Oct. 3, 1952

Trueman, F. S. (Yorks.; *CY 1953*) b Feb. 6, 1931

Trumble, H. (Australia; *CY 1897*) b May 12, 1867, d Aug. 14, 1938

Trumble, J. W. (Australia) b Sept. 16, 1863, d Aug. 17, 1944

Trumper, V. T. (Australia; *CY 1903*) b Nov. 2, 1877, d June 28, 1915

Truscott, P. B. (N. Zealand) b Aug. 14, 1941

Tuckett, L. (S. Africa) b Feb. 6, 1919

Tuckett, L. R. (S. Africa) b April 19, 1885, d April 8, 1963

Tufnell, N. C. (Camb. U. and Surrey) b June 13, 1887, d Aug. 3, 1951

Tunnicliffe, C. J. (Derby.) b Aug. 11, 1951

Tunnicliffe, H. T. (Notts.) b March 4, 1950

Tunnicliffe, J. (Yorks.; *CY 1901*) b Aug. 26, 1866, d July 11, 1948

Turnbull, M. J. L. (Camb. U. and Glam.; *CY 1931*) b March 16, 1906, d Aug. 5, 1944

Turner, A. (Australia) b July 23, 1950

Turner, C. T. B. (Australia; *CY 1889*) b Nov. 16, 1862, d Jan. 1, 1944

Turner, D. R. (Hants and W. Province) b Feb. 5, 1949

Turner, F. M. (Leics.) b Aug. 8, 1934

Turner, G. M. (Worcs. and N. Zealand; *CY 1971*) b May 26, 1947

Turner, S. (Essex and Natal) b July 18, 1943

Twentyman-Jones, P. S. (S. Africa) b Sept. 13, 1876, d March 8, 1954

Twining, R. H. (Oxford U. and Middx; Pres. MCC 1964-65) b Nov. 3, 1889, d Jan. 3, 1979

Tyldesley, G. Ernest (Lancs.; *CY 1920*) b Feb. 5, 1889, d May 5, 1962

Tyldesley, J. T. (Lancs.; *CY 1902*) b Nov. 22, 1873, d Nov. 27, 1930

Tyldesley, R. K. (Lancs.; *CY 1925*) b March 11, 1897, d Sept. 17, 1943

Tylecote, E. F. S. (Oxford U. and Kent) b June 23, 1849, d March 15, 1938

Tyler, E. J. (Somerset) b Oct. 13, 1864, d Jan. 21, 1917

Tyson, F. H. (Northants; *CY 1956*) b June 6, 1930

Ufton, D. G. (Kent) b May 31, 1928

Ulyett, G. (Yorks.) b Oct. 21, 1851, d June 18, 1898

Umrigar, P. R. (India) b March 28, 1926

Underwood, D. L. (Kent; *CY 1969*) b June 8, 1945

Unwin, F. St G. (Essex) b April 23, 1911

Valentine, A. L. (W. Indies; *CY 1951*) b April 29, 1930

Valentine, B. H. (Camb. U. and Kent) b Jan. 17, 1908

Valentine, V. A. (W. Indies) b April 4, 1908, believed dead

van der Bijl, P. G. V. (S. Africa) b Oct. 21, 1907, d Feb. 16, 1973

van der Bijl, V. A. P. (Natal and Middx; *CY 1981*) b March 19, 1948

Van der Gucht, P. I. (Glos.) b Nov. 2, 1911

Van der Merwe, E. A. (S. Africa) b Nov. 9, 1904, d Feb. 28, 1971

Van der Merwe, P. L. (S. Africa) b March 14, 1937

van Geloven, J. (Yorks. and Leics.) b Jan 4, 1934

Van Ryneveld, C. B. (Oxford U. and S. Africa) b March 19, 1928

Varnals, G. D. (S. Africa) b July 24, 1935

Vaulkhard, P. (Notts. and Derby.) b Sept. 15, 1911

Vengsarkar, D. B. (India) b April 6, 1956

Veivers, T. R. (Australia) b April 6, 1937

Venkataraghavan, S. (Derby. and India) b April 21, 1946

Verity, Capt. H. (Yorks.; *CY 1932*) b May 18, 1905, d July 31, 1943

Vernon, G. F. (Middx) b June 20, 1856, d Aug. 10, 1902

Vernon, M. T. (W. Australia) b Feb. 9, 1937

Vials, G. A. T. (Northants) b March 18, 1887, d April 26, 1974

Vigar, F. H. (Essex) b July 7, 1917

Viljoen, K. G. (S. Africa) b May 14, 1910, d Jan. 21, 1974

Vincent, C. L. (S. Africa) b Feb. 16, 1902, d Aug. 24, 1968

Vine, J. (Sussex; *CY 1906*) b May 15, 1875, d April 25, 1946

Vintcent, C. H. (S. Africa) b Sept. 2, 1866, d Sept. 28, 1943

Virgin, R. T. (Somerset and Northants; *CY 1971*) b Aug. 26, 1939

Viswanath, G. R. (India) b Feb. 12, 1949

Vivian, G. E. (N. Zealand) b Feb. 28, 1946

Vivian, H. G. (N. Zealand) b Nov. 4, 1912

Voce, W. (Notts.; *CY 1933*) b Aug. 8, 1909

Vogler, A. E. E. (Middx and S. Africa; *CY 1908*) b Nov. 28, 1876, d Aug. 9, 1946

Vizianagram, Maharaj Sir Vijaya of (India) b Dec. 28, 1905, d Dec. 2, 1965

Waddington, A. (Yorks.) b Feb. 4, 1893, d Oct. 27, 1959

Waddington, J. E. (Griqualand W.) b Dec. 30, 1918

Wade, H. F. (S. Africa) b Sept. 14, 1905, d Nov. 22, 1980

Wade, T. H. (Essex) b Nov. 24, 1910

Wade, W. W. (S. Africa) b June 18, 1914

Wadekar, A. L. (India) b April 1, 1941

Wadsworth, K. J. (N. Zealand) b Nov. 30, 1946, d Aug. 19, 1976

Wagstaffe, M. G. (Oxford U.) b Sept. 26, 1945

Wainwright, E. (Yorks.; *CY 1894*) b April 8, 1865, d Oct. 26, 1919

Waite, J. H. B. (S. Africa) b Jan. 19, 1930

Waite, M. G. (Australia) b Jan. 7, 1911

Walcott, C. L. (W. Indies; *CY 1958*) b Jan. 17, 1926

Walcott, L. A. (W. Indies) b Jan. 18, 1894

Walford, M. M. (Oxford U. and Somerset) b Nov. 27, 1915

Walker, A. K. (NSW and Notts.) b Oct. 4, 1925

Walker, C. (Yorks. and Hants) b June 27, 1920

Walker, I. D. (Middx) b Jan. 8, 1844, d July 6, 1898

Walker, M. H. N. (Australia) b Sept. 12, 1948

Walker, P. M. (Glam., Transvaal and W. Province) b Feb. 17, 1936

Walker, W. (Notts.) b Nov. 24, 1894

Wall, T. W. (Australia) b May 13, 1904

Wallace, W. M. (N. Zealand) b Dec. 19, 1916

Waller, C. E. (Surrey and Sussex) b Oct. 3, 1948

Waller, G. de W. (Oxford U.) b Feb. 10, 1950

Walsh, J. E. (NSW and Leics.) b Dec. 4, 1912, d May 20, 1980

Walter, K. A. (S. Africa) b Nov. 5, 1939

Walters, C. F. (Glam. and Worcs.; *CY 1934*) b Aug. 28, 1905

Walters, F. H. (Australia) b Feb. 9, 1860, d June 1922

Walters, J. (Derby.) b Aug. 7, 1949

Walters, K. D. (Australia) b Dec. 21, 1945

Walton, A. C. (Oxford U. and Middx) b Sept. 26, 1933

Waqar Hassan (Pakistan) b Sept. 12, 1932

Ward, Alan (Derby., Leics. and Border) b Aug. 10, 1947

Ward, Albert (Yorks. and Lancs.; *CY 1890*) b Nov. 21, 1865, d Jan. 6, 1939

Ward, B. (Essex) b Feb. 28, 1944

Ward, D. (Glam.) b Aug. 30, 1934

Ward, F. A. (Australia) b Feb. 23, 1909, d March 25, 1974

Ward, J. M. (Oxford U. and Derby.) b Sept. 14, 1948

Ward, J. T. (N. Zealand) b March 11, 1937

Ward, T. A. (S. Africa) b Aug. 2, 1887, d Feb. 16, 1936

Ward, William (MCC and Hants) b July 24, 1787, d June 30, 1849

Wardle, J. H. (Yorks.; *CY 1954*) b Jan. 8, 1923

Warne, F. B. (Worcs., Victoria and Transvaal) b Oct. 3, 1906

Warner, Sir Pelham (Oxford U. and Middx; *CY 1904, special portrait 1921*) b Oct. 2, 1873, d Jan. 30, 1963

Warr, J. J. (Camb. U. and Middx) b July 16, 1927

Warren, A. (Derby.) b April 2, 1875, d Sept. 3, 1951

Washbrook, C. (Lancs.; *CY 1947*) b Dec. 6, 1914

Wasim Bari (Pakistan) b March 23, 1948

Wasim Raja (Pakistan) b July 3, 1952

Wass, T. G. (Notts.; *CY 1908*) b Dec. 26, 1873, d Oct. 27, 1953

Wassell, A. (Hants) b April 15, 1940

Watkins, A. J. (Glam.) b April 21, 1922

Watkins, J. C. (S. Africa) b April 10, 1923

Watkins, J. R. (Australia) b April 16, 1943

Watson, C. (W. Indies) b July 1, 1938

Watson, F. B. (Lancs.) b Sept. 17, 1898, d Feb. 1, 1976

Watson, G. D. (Australia) b March 8, 1945

Watson, G. G. (NSW and Worcs.) b Jan. 29, 1955

Watson, G. S. (Kent and Leics.) b April 10, 1907, d April 1, 1974

Watson, W. (Yorks. and Leics.; *CY 1954*) b March 7, 1920

Watson, W. (Australia) b Jan. 31, 1931

Watson, W. K. (Border, N. Transvaal, E. Province and Notts.) b May 21, 1955

Watt, A. E. (Kent) b June 19, 1907, d Feb. 3, 1974

Watt, L. (N. Zealand) b Sept. 17, 1924

Watts, E. A. (Surrey) b Aug. 1, 1911

Watts, H. E. (Camb. U. and Somerset) b March 4, 1922

Watts, P. D. (Northants and Notts.) b March 31, 1938

Watts, P. J. (Northants) b June 16, 1940

Wazir Ali, S. (India) b Sept. 15, 1903, d June 17, 1950

Wazir Mohammad (Pakistan) b Dec. 22, 1929

Webb. M. G. (N. Zealand) b June 22, 1947

Webb, P. N. (N. Zealand) b July 14, 1957

Webb, R. T. (Sussex) b July 11, 1922

Webb, S. G. (Manager Australians in England 1961) b Jan. 31, 1900, d Aug. 5, 1976

Webbe, A. J. (Oxford U. and Middx) b Jan. 16, 1855, d Feb. 19, 1941

Webster, J. (Camb. U. and Northants) b Oct. 28, 1917

Webster, Dr R. V. (Warw. and Otago) b June 10, 1939

Webster, W. H. (Camb. U. and Middx; Pres. MCC 1976-77) b Feb. 22, 1910

Weekes, E. D. (W. Indies; *CY 1951*) b Feb. 26, 1925

Weekes, K. H. (W. Indies) b Jan. 24, 1912

Weeks, R. T. (Warw.) b April 30, 1930

Weir, G. L. (N. Zealand) b June 2, 1908

Wellard, A. W. (Somerset; *CY 1936*) b April 8, 1902, d Dec. 31, 1980

Wellings, E. M. (Oxford U. and Surrey) b April 6, 1909

Wells, B. D. (Glos. and Notts.) b July 27, 1930

Wells, C. M. (Sussex) b March 3, 1960

Wenman, E. G. (Kent and England) b Aug. 18, 1803, d Dec. 31, 1879

Wensley, A. F. (Sussex) b May 23, 1898, d June 17, 1970

Wesley, C. (S. Africa) b Sept. 5, 1937

Wessels, K. C. (Orange Free State, W. Province, N. Transvaal, Sussex and Queensland) b Sept. 14, 1957

West, G. H. (Editor of *Wisden* 1880-86) b 1851, d Oct. 6, 1896

Westcott, R. J. (S. Africa) b Sept. 19, 1927

Wharton, A. (Lancs. and Leics.) b April 30, 1923

Whatmore, D. F. (Australia) b March 16, 1954

Wheat, A. B. (Notts.) b May 13, 1898, d May 20, 1973

Wheatley, K. J. (Hants) b Jan. 20, 1946

Wheatley, O. S. (Camb. U., Warw. and Glam.; *CY 1969*) b May 28, 1935

Whitaker, Haddon (Editor of *Wisden* 1940-43) b Aug. 30, 1908

Whitcombe, P. A. (Oxford U. and Middx) b April 23, 1923

White, A. F. T. (Camb. U., Warw. and Worcs.) b Sept. 5, 1915

White, D. W. (Hants. and Glam.) b Dec. 14, 1935

White, E. C. S. (NSW) b July 14, 1913

White, G. C. (S. Africa) b Feb. 5, 1882, d Oct. 17, 1918

White, J. C. (Somerset; *CY 1929*) b Feb. 19, 1891, d May 2, 1961

White, R. A. (Middx and Notts.) b Oct. 6, 1936

White, R. C. (Camb. U., Glos. and Transvaal) b Jan. 29, 1941

White, W. A. (W. Indies) b Nov. 20, 1938

Whitehead, J. P. (Yorks. and Worcs.) b Sept. 3, 1925

Whitehouse, J. (Warw.) b April 8, 1949

Whitelaw, P. E. (N. Zealand) b Feb. 10, 1910

Whitfield, E. W. (Surrey and Northants) b May 31. 1911

Whiting, N. H. (Worcs.) b Oct. 2, 1920

Whittaker, G. J. (Surrey) b May 29, 1916

Whittingham, N. B. (Notts.) b Oct. 22, 1940

Whitty, W. J. (Australia) b Aug. 15, 1886, d Jan. 30, 1974

Whysall, W. W. (Notts.; *CY 1925*) b Oct. 31, 1887, d Nov. 11, 1930

Wiener, J. M. (Australia) b May 1, 1955

Wight, C. V. (W. Indies) b July 28, 1902, assumed dead

Wight, G. L. (W. Indies) b May 28, 1929

Wight, P. B. (B. Guiana, Somerset and Canterbury) b June 25, 1930

Wiles, C. A. (W. Indies) b Aug. 11, 1892

Wilkins, A. H. (Glam. and Glos.) b Aug. 22, 1953

Wilkins, C. P. (Derby. and E. Province) b July 31, 1944

Wilkinson, C. T. A. (Surrey) b Oct. 4, 1884, d Dec. 16, 1970

Wilkinson, L. L. (Lancs.) b Nov. 5, 1916

Wilkinson, P. A. (Notts.) b Aug. 23, 1951

Wilkinson, Col. W. A. C. (Oxford U.) b Dec. 6, 1892

Willatt, G. L. (Camb. U., Notts. and Derby.) b May 7, 1918

Willett, E. T. (W. Indies) b May 1, 1953

Willett, M. D. (Surrey) b April 21, 1933

Willey, P. (Northants) b Dec. 6, 1949

Williams, A. B. (W. Indies) b Nov. 21, 1949

Williams, C. B. (Barbados) b March 8, 1926

Williams, C. C. P. (Oxford U. and Essex) b Feb. 9, 1933

Williams, D. L. (Glam.) b Nov. 20, 1946

Williams, E. A. V. (W. Indies) b April 10, 1914

Williams, R. G. (Northants) b Aug. 10, 1957

Williams, R. J. (S. Africa) b April 12, 1912

Williamson, J. G. (Northants) b April 4, 1936

Willis, R. G. D. (Surrey, Warw. and N. Transvaal; *CY 1978*) b May 30, 1949

Willoughby, J. T. (S. Africa) b Nov. 7, 1874, d *circa* 1955

Willsher, E. (Kent and All-England) b Nov. 22, 1828, d Oct. 7, 1885

Wilmot, A. L. (E. Province) b June 1, 1943

Wilmot, K. (Warw.) b April 3, 1911

Wilson, A. (Lancs.) b April 24, 1921

Wilson, A. E. (Middx and Glos.) b May 5, 1912

Wilson, Rev. C. E. M. (Camb. U. and Yorks.) b May 15, 1875, d Feb. 8, 1944

Wilson, D. (Yorks. and MCC) b Aug. 7, 1937

Wilson, E. F. (Surrey) b June 24, 1907

Wilson, E. R. (Camb. U. and Yorks.) b March 25, 1879, d July 21, 1957

Wilson, J. V. (Yorks.; *CY 1961*) b Jan. 17, 1921

Wilson, J. W. (Australia) b Aug. 20, 1922

Wilson, R. C. (Kent) b Feb. 18, 1928

Wimble, C. S. (S. Africa) b Jan. 9, 1864, d Jan. 28, 1930

Windows, A. R. (Glos. and Camb. U.) b Sept. 25, 1942

Winfield, H. M. (Notts.) b June 13, 1933

Wingfield Digby, A. R. (Oxford U.) b July 25, 1950

Winlaw, Sqd. Ldr R. de W. K. (Camb. U. and Surrey) b March 28, 1912, d Oct. 31, 1942

Winn, C. E. (Oxford U. and Sussex) b Nov. 13, 1926

Winrow, H. F. (Notts.) b Jan. 17, 1916, d Aug. 19, 1973

Winslow, P. L. (Sussex and S. Africa) b May 21, 1929

Wisden John (Sussex; founder John Wisden and Co. and *Wisden's Cricketers' Almanack*) b Sept. 5, 1826, d April 5, 1884

Wishart, K. L. (W. Indies) b Nov. 28, 1908, d Oct. 18, 1972

Wolton, A. V. G. (Warw.) b June 12, 1919

Wood, A. (Yorks.; *CY 1939*) b Aug. 25, 1898, d April 1, 1973

Wood, B. (Yorks., Lancs., Derby. and E. Province) d Dec. 26, 1942

Wood, C. J. B. (Leics.) b Nov. 21, 1875, d June 5, 1960

Wood, D. J. (Sussex) b May 19, 1914

Wood, G. E. C. (Camb. U. and Kent) b Aug. 22, 1893, d March 18, 1971

Wood, G. M. (Australia) b Nov. 6, 1956

Wood, H. (Kent and Surrey; *CY 1891*) b Dec. 14, 1854, d April 30, 1919

Wood, R. (Lancs. and Victoria) b March 7, 1860, d Jan. 6, 1915

Woodcock, A. J. (Australia) b Feb. 27, 1948

Woodfull, W. M. (Australia; *CY 1927*) b Aug. 22, 1897, d Aug. 11, 1965

Woodhead, F. G. (Notts.) b Oct. 30, 1912

Woodhouse, G. E. S. (Somerset) b Feb. 15, 1924

Woods, S. M. J. (Camb. U., Somerset, Australia and England; *CY 1889*) b April 14, 1867, d April 30, 1931

Wookey, S. M. (Camb. U. and Oxford U.) b Sept. 2, 1954

Wooler, C. R. D. (Leics. and Rhodesia) b June 30, 1930

Wooller, W. (Camb. U. and Glam.) b Nov. 20, 1912

Woolley, C. N. (Glos. and Northants) b May 5, 1886, d Nov. 3, 1962

Woolley, F. E. (Kent; *CY 1911*) b May 27, 1887, d Oct. 18, 1978

Woolmer, R. A. (Kent and Natal; *CY 1976*) b May 14, 1948

Worrall, J. (Australia) b May 12, 1863, d Nov. 17, 1937

Worrell, Sir F. M. M. (W. Indies; *CY 1951*) b Aug. 1, 1924, d March 13, 1967

Worsley, D. R. (Oxford U. and Lancs.) b July 18, 1941

Worsley, Sir W. A. 4th Bart. (Yorks.; Pres. MCC 1961-62) b April 5, 1890, d Dec. 4, 1973

Worthington, T. S. (Derby.; *CY 1937*) b Aug. 21, 1905, d Aug. 31, 1973

Wright, A. (Warw.) b Aug. 25, 1941

Wright, C. W. (Camb. U. and Notts.) b May 27, 1863, d Jan. 10, 1936

Wright, D. V. P. (Kent; *CY 1940*) b Aug. 21, 1914

Wright, J. G. (Derby. and N. Zealand) b July 5, 1954

Wright, K. J. (Australia) b Dec. 27, 1953

Wright, L. G. (Derby.; *CY 1906*) b June 15, 1862, d Jun. 11, 1953

Wright, S. (Camb. U.) b Feb. 4, 1952

Wyatt, R. E. S. (Warw. and Worcs.; *CY 1930*) b May 2, 1901

Wynne, O. E. (S. Africa) b June 1, 1919, d July 13, 1975

Wynyard, E. G. (Hants) b April 1, 1861, d Oct. 30, 1936

Yadav, N. Shivlal (India) b Jan. 26, 1957

Yajurvindra Singh, (India) b Aug. 1, 1952

Yallop, G. N. (Australia) b Oct. 7, 1952

Yardley, B. (Australia) b Sept. 7, 1947

Yardley, N. W. D. (Camb. U. and Yorks.; *CY 1948*) b March 19, 1915

Yardley, T. J. (Worcs. and Northants) b Oct. 27, 1946

Yarnold, H. (Worcs.) b July 6, 1917, d Aug. 13, 1974

Yashpal Sharma (India) b Aug. 11, 1954

Yawar Saeed (Somerset and Punjab) b Jan. 22, 1935

Young, D. M. (Worcs. and Glos.) b April 15, 1924

Young, H. I. (Essex) b Feb. 5, 1876, d Dec. 12, 1964

Young, J. A. (Middx) b Oct. 14, 1912

Young, R. A. (Camb. U. and Sussex) b Sept. 16, 1885, d July 1, 1968

Younis Ahmed, M. (Surrey, Worcs. and Pakistan) b Oct. 21, 1947

Yuile, B. W. (N. Zealand) b Oct. 29, 1941

Zaheer Abbas (Glos. and Pakistan; *CY 1972*) b July 24, 1947

Zulch, J. W. (S. Africa) b Jan. 2, 1886, d May 19, 1924

Zulfiqar Ahmed (Pakistan) b Nov. 22, 1926

ENGLAND YOUNG CRICKETERS IN WEST INDIES

A team of fifteen players, sponsored by Agatha Christie Ltd and under the captaincy of Tim Boon and the managership of C. S. Elliott, toured the West Indies for six weeks in January and February 1980. The party consisted of T. J. Boon (Yorkshire) captain, I. P. Butcher (Leicestershire), R. A. Cobb (Leicestershire), N. A. Foster (Essex), C. Gladwin (Essex), G. Hall (Somerset), K. James (Middlesex), J. B. R. Jones (Shropshire), R. Leiper (Essex), G. J. Lord (Warwickshire), N. A. Mallender (Yorkshire), R. Maru (Middlesex), S. J. O'Shaughnessy (Lancashire), G. Tedstone (Warwickshire) and D. Wild (Northamptonshire).

Three Under-19 "Tests" were played; West Indies won the series 2-0, defeating the tourists by 148 runs in the first match and by seven wickets in the third. The second match was drawn. The England Young Cricketers played five other matches, all of which were drawn. Although the results were disappointing, the young team gained much useful experience, playing under totally foreign conditions and against opponents who were more mature and experienced than they were.

The England batting began shakily but, towards the end of the tour, members of the team found their form and batted with confidence, especially Steven O'Shaughnessy who brought respectability to the England innings in both the second and third Tests with 130, 81 and 93. He was well supported by Bob Leiper, who scored an unbeaten century against Barbados Youth. However, Tim Boon's conscientious approach to the responsibilities of captaincy influenced his own batting form. Rajesh Maru was the most effective spinner, with Neil Foster and Neil Mallender also improving towards the end of the tour. Both Kevan James and Bryan Jones suffered minor fractures and were not available for the third Test.

At Chedwin Park, Jamaica, January 3, 4, 5. Drawn. England Young Cricketers 173 (R. Leiper 67; M. Tucker four for 45) and 78 for three; Jamaica Youth 226 (M. Tucker 88; N.A. Mallender four for 54) and 170 for eight dec. (M. Tucker 72, F. Cunningham 40).

At Recreation Ground, St John's, Antigua, January 9, 10, 11. Drawn. England Young Cricketers 150 (I. Liburd four for 33, P. Richards four for 33); Leeward Islands 153 for nine.

At Bourda, Georgetown, January 15, 16, 17. Drawn. Guyana Youth 392 for six dec. (Seeram 186, Jackman 65, Harper 59 not out) and 152 for five; England Young Cricketers 346 (I. P. Butcher 131, T. J. Boon 57, R. A. Cobb 49; R. A. Harper five for 100).

At Queen's Park Oval, Port-of-Spain, January 19, 20, 21. Drawn. England Young Cricketers 121 (S. Pragg four for 35) and 221 for six dec. (T. J. Boon 62, R. A. Cobb 60, R. Leiper 49 not out); Trinidad Youth 170 (A. Logie 61) and 31 for four.

First Test: at Queen's Park Oval, Port-of-Spain, January 24, 25, 26, 27. West Indies U. 19 won by 148 runs. West Indies U. 19 180 (G. Reifer 76) and 225; England U. 19 143 (M. Tucker four for 26) and 114 (R. Joseph four for 45).

Second Test: at Mindoo Phillip Park, St Lucia, January 30, 31, February 1, 2. Drawn. England U. 19 418 (S. J. O'Shaughnessy 130, N. A. Foster 49, G. J. Lord 49, I. P. Butcher 40; R. Harper five for 103) and 120 for four; West Indies U. 19 425 (A. Logie 163, G. Reifer 139; G. Hall four for 115).

At Kensington Oval, Bridgetown, February 4, 5, 6. Drawn. England Young Cricketers 264 for four dec. (R. Leiper 124 not out, R. A. Cobb 43) and 62 for no wicket; Barbados Youth 384 for nine dec. (G. Reifer 98, C. St Hill 81, J. Kirton 68, S. Greaves 49).

Third Test: at Kensington Oval, Bridgetown, February 8, 9, 10, 11. West Indies U. 19 won by seven wickets. England U. 19 192 (S. J. O'Shaughnessy 81; L. Forde four for 47) and 241 (S. J. O'Shaughnessy 93); West Indies U. 19 291 (M. Neita 86, A. Logie 41; N. A. Foster four for 56) and 143 for three (M. Neita 68).

OBITUARIES

ANDERSON, WILLIAM McDOUGAL, who died at Christchurch, New Zealand, on December 21, 1979, played for Canterbury from 1938 to 1949, scoring 1,728 runs with an average of 36.80. An attacking left-hander, in his one Test match, New Zealand's first after the War – against Australia in 1946 – he opened the batting. He was perhaps unlucky not to be picked for the 1949 tour of England. Later he was for a time a New Zealand selector. His son, Robert, has played for New Zealand in recent years.

BANERJEE, SHUTE NATH, who died in Calcutta on October 14, 1980, aged 67, became the first Bengali to play Test cricket when he won his only cap against West Indies in Bombay in 1948. A right-arm fast-medium bowler, he took one for 73 in West Indies' first innings and four for 54 in their second. He is perhaps best remembered for having, in 1946, on the second of his two tours to England, helped C. T. Sarwate add 249 in three hours ten minutes for the Indians' last wicket against Surrey at The Oval. This is still an Indian record and the second-highest last-wicket partnership ever made. Batting at number eleven, he joined Sarwate at 205 for nine and hit 121. Sarwate finished with 124 not out. Surrey's attack included the Bedser twins, Gover, Watts, Squires, Gregory and Parker. Banerjee's best analysis in first-class cricket was his eight for 25 for Nawanagar against Maharashtra in 1941-42, his highest first-class score 135 for Bihar against Bengal in 1952-53 at Calcutta in the Ranji Trophy. He captained Bihar from 1942 until 1958.

BARBER, RAY, who died in the Royal Adelaide Hospital on September 15, 1980, at the age of 64, was cricket correspondent of *The News*, Adelaide's evening paper, for twenty years. In this time he toured England, West Indies and New Zealand and reported regularly on MCC tours to Australia. England teams were assured of a friendly welcome from him.

BARLOW, EDWIN ALAN, died at Gretton, Gloucestershire, on June 27, 1980, aged 68. Captain of Shrewsbury in 1931, he got his Blue at Oxford in the next summer, taking three for 50 and six for 44 against Yorkshire in his first match and playing a valuable innings of 43 not out in the University match, which saved his side from having to follow on. A slow-medium off-spinner who could also swing the ball away, he was an extremely steady bowler and that year and the next was the mainstay of the Oxford attack. In 1934, when he had Schools and was unable to play regularly, he was less successful. He had a trial for Lancashire in 1932.

BOOTH, FRANK STANLEY, died at Shoreham-by-Sea on January 21, 1980, aged 72. First playing for Lancashire in 1927, he had a number of trials in the next few years, but failing to get a regular place went into League cricket. Returning to the county in 1932, he took, in 1933, 89 wickets at 27.43. In 1934, when his bowling had much to do with Lancashire winning the Championship, his figures were 101 at 23.46 and, in 1935, 89 at 19.20. After that, largely owing to injuries, he played less and his connection with the county ceased at the end of 1937. Tall and strong, he bowled fast-medium and came quickly off the pitch; he was an indefatigable trier, who revelled in long spells, and, as the quickest bowler Lancashire had at the time, he was given plenty of them. This, coupled with a long run and a slightly lumbering action, may have shortened his career.

BRIDGEMAN, THE HON. SIR MAURICE, KBE, who died on June 18, 1980, aged 76, was in the Eton XI from 1921 to 1923 and captain in his last year. His father, the first Viscount Bridgeman, was in the Cambridge XI in 1887.

BRINTON, RONALD LEWIS, died at Malvern on April 19, 1980, aged 77. A useful bat and medium-pace swinger, he was in the Shrewsbury XI from 1919 to 1921 and in 1924 made a couple of appearances for Worcestershire.

BURLTON, LT.-COL. ARTHUR TEMPLE, died at Ballochneck, Thornhill, Stirling, on February 10, 1980, aged 79. He was not in the XI at Repton, but in 1922 played five matches for Worcestershire, and against Glamorgan at Cardiff scored 32 and 35 not out, in the first innings saving the side by helping H. L. Higgins to put on 91 for the fifth wicket. He also appeared for Devon. He was author of *Cricketing Courtesy* (1955), a book on cricket manners and etiquette.

BURTON, REGINALD HENRY MARKHAM, who died on October 19, 1980, aged 80, played for Warwickshire v Worcestershire at Edgbaston in 1919, a match not recorded in *Wisden*. Although he made 47 and helped H. Venn to put on over 100 for the third wicket, he never represented the county again.

BUULTJENS, EDWARD W., died in May, 1980. In 1936 he played as a bowler for Ceylon against G. O. Allen's MCC side to Australia and caught and bowled Walter Hammond, his only wicket.

CALDERA, WING COMMANDER KEERTHI, died in England in 1980 at the age of 42, while on a course with the RAF. He played cricket for Ceylon, both at home and abroad, touring India in 1958. He was a left-handed batsman, who could also keep wicket and bowl off-breaks.

CALVERT, EDWARD BUCHANAN, who died on February 24, 1980, aged 65, showed considerable promise for Buckinghamshire as an opening batsman in 1934 and 1935, but played no more county cricket. At St Lawrence, Ramsgate, where he was captain in 1934, he headed the averages for three years. Later he became a master at Cheltenham College, where he worked for many years.

CHEETHAM, JOHN (JACK) ERSKINE, who died in hospital in Johannesburg on August 21, 1980, aged 60, served South African cricket with great distinction, both as player and administrator. In fifteen of his 24 Test matches he captained them with a firm yet understanding touch, and after his retirement he was, from 1969 to 1972, an outstanding President of the South African Cricket Association. He was an Honorary Life President of the Transvaal Cricket Union.

Cheetham was 28 when he first played for South Africa, against F. G. Mann's side in the last Test match of the 1948-49 MCC tour, and 32 when he first led them on the 1952-53 tour of Australia. It was in Australia that he made his reputation as a captain. South Africa were given no chance of holding an Australian side which was led by Hassett and included Harvey, Lindwall, Morris, Miller and Johnston. In the event the Test series was drawn, at two matches all, South Africa winning the final Test at Melbourne after Australia had scored 520 in their first innings. Much of the credit for a notable South African achievement on this tour belonged to Cheetham, not because of the runs he made (he was a batsman pure and simple) but because of the way, with the help of the manager, Ken Viljoen, himself a former Test cricketer, he welded the players into a team. There were those at the time who thought the Cheetham-Viljoen regime too authoritarian; in fact, though, it was a sign of things to come. In his attention to the fitness and fielding of his players Cheetham was the forerunner of the modern captain.

Having led South Africa to victory over New Zealand in South Africa in 1953-54, he brought them to England in 1955 for what was one of the best and most closely fought series since the war. Ironically, in the third and fourth Test matches, which South Africa won, Cheetham was prevented by injury from playing, McGlew leading the side. With the series standing at two-all Cheetham returned for the final Test at The Oval, where England clinched the series thanks to the bowling of Laker and Lock on a wearing pitch and the batting of May, who, early in his innings, survived a memorably close call for leg before wicket against Tayfield.

Cheetham was a dour batsman but a decidedly better one than a top score of 89 from 43 Test innings would suggest. He had the respect of his players and also of the opposition, knowing what he wanted and quietly setting about obtaining it. His 271 not out against Orange Free State at Bloemfontein in 1950-51 remains the highest score ever made for Western Province in the Currie Cup. In his first-class career, which lasted from 1939 to 1955, he scored 5,697 runs at an average of 42.50. In retirement Cheetham continued to give much of his time to cricket, working hard in the interests of non-white cricketers and feeling South Africa's exclusion from the Test scene as acutely as anyone. He was a devout churchman, a determined yet patient administrator, a dutiful host and a conscientious senior executive in a firm of construction engineers. Two of his sons, John and Robert, have both played first-class cricket.

CHILDS-CLARKE, ARTHUR WILLIAM, died suddenly at his home at Mevagissey on February 19, 1980, aged 74. He was a well-known London club cricketer, who played a number of times for Middlesex between 1923 and 1934, his highest score being 58 not out v Glamorgan at Swansea in 1931; he also captained the Middlesex Second XI. In 1947 and

1948 he played for Northamptonshire, captaining the side in both seasons, playing a number of useful innings in the lower order and occasionally picking up a wicket. His highest score for Northamptonshire was 68 v Leicestershire at Leicester in 1947, but more remarkable was his 32 not out against the South Africans in 1947, when he and L. A. Smith added 76 for the last wicket. He was in the Christ's Hospital XI in 1921 and 1922.

COCKELL, W. H., who died in hospital on December 1, 1979, was the regular Cambridgeshire wicket-keeper from 1926 to 1936 and returned in an emergency to help them out as late as 1946. More recently he was the county's scorer.

CRAWFORD, THOMAS ALAN, who died suddenly on December 5, 1979, aged 69, rendered notable service to Kent cricket. A member of the Tonbridge XI for four years and captain in 1929, he made twelve appearances for the county between 1930 and 1951 without particular success. But he scored many runs for Kent's Second XI, including an innings of 175 against Wiltshire in 1931, and captained them from 1950 to 1955, a task for which he was well suited. He had a good knowledge of the game; moreover, at a time when the over-rate was already becoming a problem, he insisted on twenty overs an hour from his bowlers. He was primarily an attacking batsman and a good driver; he also picked up occasional wickets with slow spin. For many years Crawford served on the Kent committee, being President of the club in 1968. He was later appointed Chairman of the Committee, but had to resign almost immediately for reasons of health.

CREEK, FREDERICK NORMAN SMITH, MBE, MC, who died at Folkestone on July 26, 1980, aged 82, was a good bat and a useful change bowler. When available, he played for Wiltshire for some years between the wars, his highest score being 124 not out against Dorset in 1930. He was better known as a footballer: he won a Blue at Cambridge in 1919 and 1921, played constantly for the Corinthians in the FA Cup and gained five amateur international caps and one full one – against France in 1923. Later, besides doing much valuable work as a coach, he became well known as a broadcaster on football as well as a regular correspondent for *The Daily Telegraph*.

DEED, JOHN ARTHUR, who died on October 19, 1980, aged 79, did useful work for Kent as a batsman from 1924 to 1930. A made rather than a natural player, he had been for two years a wholly undistinguished member of the Malvern XI, but had proved a solid and reliable second string to a brilliant stroke-player in a winning rackets pair at Queen's. Much the same qualities appeared in his cricket. He was never in the running for a Blue at Cambridge, and owed his trial for Kent to an innings of 252 for the Second XI at The Oval in May, 1924. In those days the county had no shortage of attacking bats, but, especially in the early part of the season when most of the amateurs were not available, there was a lack of solidity and Deed's steadiness was often valuable. In all he scored 1,996 runs at an average of 23.76, with two centuries, both against Warwickshire at Birmingham, 103 in 1928 and 133 in 1930. He retained to the end his interest in Kent cricket and was President in 1965.

DELANY, VERNON BRIDGE, who died on March 17, 1979, at the age of 86, captained Lancashire Second XI in a number of their matches in 1924.

DENTON, WILLIAM HERBERT, the last survivor of three brothers who played together for Northamptonshire, died on April 23, 1979, aged 88. He and his identical twin, J. S., who between them caused endless confusion to spectators and scorers, first appeared in 1909. By 1912, when the county, calling upon only twelve players in the Championship, came second, they had become essential members of the side. In 1913 both exceeded 1,000 runs and, from August that year until cricket was stopped by the War, they formed the regular opening pair. Both were taken prisoner in the closing months of the War and J. S. played little county cricket afterwards but W. H., after a few appearances between 1919 and 1923, resumed a regular place for the season of 1924. Unfortunately his spell as a prisoner had taken its toll of his health and, though he did much useful work, he was not the player he had been. He did not play for the county again. A small man, he had a sound defence and his footwork was neat: a large proportion of his runs were scored behind the wicket. His highest score was 230 not out, at that time a record for the county, against Essex at Leyton in 1913. Going in first he carried his bat through an innings of five hours forty minutes and was on the field throughout the match. Apart from his batting he was a fine mid-off. When Northamptonshire played Somerset in 1914, the Denton twins opened for Northamptonshire and the Rippon twins, A. D. E. and A. E. S., for Somerset – an occurrence unique in first-class cricket.

DE SILVA, DEVA LOKESH STANLEY, died in a motor cycle accident on April 12, 1980, aged 22. A regular opening bowler on Sri Lanka's tour of England and Ireland in 1979, he was not related to the other two, more successful, de Silvas in the team: all three were Sinhalese. No batsman, he was a medium-fast right-arm swing bowler of real promise. His part in Sri Lanka's impressive win over India in the Prudential Cup match at Old Trafford in 1979 was the capture of the valuable wickets of Gaekwad and Kapil Dev for 36 runs. He came from Mahinda College, Galle, and was an official of the Ceylon Tobacco Company. His early death is a heavy loss to Sri Lanka with their aspirations to be granted full Test status.

DOBSON, FRED, died at his home in Hampshire on October 15, 1980, aged 82. He was an amateur who played three matches for Warwickshire as a slow left-arm bowler in 1928 and, taking seven wickets for 138 runs, came out top of their averages. However, he decided that he preferred club cricket.

DOOLAND, BRUCE, who died in Adelaide, his birthplace, on September 8, 1980, aged 56, was one of the last great leg-spinners in first-class cricket. As early as 1940-41, when only seventeen, he had been asked to play for South Australia, but his employers refused leave. War service with the Australian commandos had intervened before he made his first appearance for them in 1945-46 and, against Victoria, performed the first hat-trick in post-war Australian cricket. In 1946 he was a member of W. A. Brown's team to New Zealand and in 1946-47 was picked for the third Test against England at Melbourne. Taking four for 89 and one for 84 and helping McCool to put on 83 useful runs for the ninth wicket, he did not do badly, especially as his victims were Washbrook (twice), Hammond and Ikin; he was retained for the fourth Test, in which he took three for 133 (Washbrook, Edrich and Ikin) and made 29. For the last Test he was replaced by Tribe. His only other Test was against India at Melbourne in 1948. For the 1948 tour of England, McCool and Ring were preferred to him: his later records suggest that in time he became a better bowler than either, but leg-spinners tend to mature slowly learning from experience, and both were considerably older. The immediate consequence was that he came to England to play in the Lancashire League. In 1950-51 he went with the Commonwealth side to India and made two hundreds in the unofficial Tests. In 1953 he was registered to play for Nottinghamshire. He continued to play for them for five seasons during which he scored 4,782 runs with an average of 24.52 and took 770 wickets at 18.86. Twice he did the double and once he missed it by only 30 runs. He played twice for the Players at Lord's. His batting figures show remarkable consistency as they include only one hundred – 115 not out v Sussex at Worthing in 1957 – a match in which he also took ten for 102. Perhaps his most remarkable bowling performance statistically was sixteen for 83 v Essex at Trent Bridge in 1954. Against Somerset in 1953 he took ten for 49 in the match at Weston-super-Mare and later in the month ten for 48 in the return at Trent Bridge. Standing over six feet he was taller than most leg-spinners and had a long strong arm which had helped him to become one of the best baseball pitchers in his state. Delivering the ball usually with his front foot behind the bowling crease, he was a trifle quicker than many of his predecessors, but like them relied mainly on the leg-break and the top-spinner, keeping the googly in reserve. Probably the chief difference between his bowling in 1948 and in 1953 was that he had become more skilled at varying his pace and his flight. As a batsman, he could cut and drive well and he was also a good fieldsman near the wicket. After 1957 he returned to Australia, as he wished his son to be brought up as an Australian.

DUMINY, DR JOHANNES PETRUS, who played in three Tests for South Africa against England between 1927 and 1929, died in hospital in Cape Town on January 31, 1980, aged 82. "J.P.", as he was known, went as a Rhodes Scholar to Oxford in 1921, where he won a Harlequin as a left-handed batsman and a slow right-arm bowler. Scoring 95 not out, 55 and 74 not out for Transvaal against the 1927-28 MCC team, he was chosen for two of the five Test matches of that series, though without success. Having missed selection for the South African tour to England in 1929, he was holidaying in Switzerland when he was sent for to join a team beset with injuries. He played in the third Test at Headingley, scoring 2 and 12. A distinguished academic, and a man with many friends, he became Vice-Chancellor of the University of Cape Town in 1959. Duminy worked as devotedly as anyone towards the establishment of multi-racial cricket in South Africa.

EBELING, HANS IRVING, MBE, who died on January 12, 1980, aged 75, was a member of the 1934 Australian side in England and was later prominent in administration. It was he who conceived the idea of the 1977 Centenary Test and who, by his persistence, got it carried out. Though he had a long career for Victoria and captained them when they won the Sheffield

Shield twice in four years, he lost four seasons to the claims of work in his early days: otherwise he might have gone further than he did. No less a judge than Jack Hobbs thought highly of his bowling and was surprised that he was ever omitted from a representative side. A tall man, he bowled medium-pace with a sharp in-swing, but he could also make the ball run away. Moreover, he was a useful attacking bat and a particularly good driver and hooker. He owed his selection in 1934 largely to a good performance against Jardine's side in 1933, when his three wickets, which included those of Sutcliffe and Wyatt, combined with an innings of 68 not out, had much to do with Victoria tying the match. In England he was a distinct success: in a side which relied heavily on spin he took 62 wickets with an average of 20.80, and in the final Test at The Oval, the sole Test appearance of his career, took three wickets, including Hammond, and in an admirable second innings of 41 put on 56 in forty minutes with O'Reilly for the last wicket. At the time of his death he was President of the Melbourne Cricket Club.

EDRICH, WILLIAM, who died at his home in Stalham, Norfolk, on November 16, 1979, at the age of 89, was the father of Bill (Middlesex and England), Geoffrey (Lancashire), Eric (Lancashire) and Brian (Kent). John Edrich (Surrey and England) is the son of William's brother, Fred. William himself was a keen Norfolk club cricketer, who kept wicket and scored his first hundred when he was 40.

ELLIOTT, JACK, who had been elected President of the Nottinghamshire County Cricket Club two months earlier, died suddenly on March 8, 1980, aged 69. He did splendid work over many years for cricket in the county.

GANNON, BRIG. JACK ROSE COMPTON, CBE, MVO, who died at Midhurst on April 25, 1980, aged 97, was one of the oldest of first-class cricketers. Elected a member of MCC in 1908, he kept wicket a number of times for the club in that and the two following seasons in first-class matches. Later he was better known in the polo world.

FARRIMOND, WILLIAM, who died at home at Westhoughton, near Bolton, on November 14, 1979, aged 76, had the rare experience of being an England wicket-keeper who had been playing for fourteen years for his county before getting a regular place in the side. This was the more exasperating as for 35 years Lancashire had hardly had a reliable professional 'keeper, merely a succession of men who had to give way when a competent amateur was available. In 1923 they found that great 'keeper, Duckworth, and in 1924 Farrimond appeared. It was only Duckworth's premature retirement at the end of 1937 that gave him an assured place, and after two seasons his career was ended by the war. It speaks volumes for Farrimond's loyalty that during this long period he never accepted any of the offers he received to qualify for another county.

Meanwhile he had kept four times for England, twice in South Africa in 1931, when Duckworth fell ill, once in the West Indies in 1935 and again later that year v South Africa at Lord's. On the last two occasions Ames was playing as a batsman and fielder. In technique Duckworth and Farrimond were poles apart. Duckworth was flamboyant, spectacular and a shrill and tireless appealer. Farrimond was quiet and unobtrusive, but immensely sound and particularly good on the leg. Against Kent at Old Trafford in 1930 he equalled what was then the world's record by claiming seven victims in an innings. He was a considerably better batsman than Duckworth. He scored heavily for the Second XI, and though he never made a century for the county, in 1934 he hit 174 for the Minor Counties against Oxford University. On his tour to South Africa he averaged 30.70. His long and useful service was recognised by a benefit in 1939.

FLEMING, ARTHUR LESLIE, who died on November 7, 1980, aged 88, was a good all-rounder in the Winchester XI for three years and captain in 1910. His younger brother, I. D. K. Fleming, played for Kent.

FOSTER, MAJOR DEREK GEORGE, died at Chipping Camden on October 13, 1980, aged 73. He played for Warwickshire from 1928 to 1934, but only in 1929 and 1931, when he opened the bowling for the Gentlemen at Lord's, was he able to appear at all frequently. A fast-medium bowler with a good action in which he made full use of his height, he could, on a pitch that gave him any help, make the ball lift unpleasantly. His career figures of 150 wickets at 27.47 are not impressive and give an idea of how dangerous he could be is given by some of his analyses – six for 11 v Glamorgan at Cardiff and five for 39 v Kent at Tunbridge Wells in 1929, seven for 42 v Surrey at The Oval in 1930 and seven for 68 v Kent at Folkestone in 1931. Not highly regarded as a batsman, he occasionally hit well and in 1931 made 70 v

Somerset at Taunton in under an hour, including five 6s. He had been in the Shrewsbury XI in 1924.

GRIFFITH, HERMAN C., died at Bridgetown, Barbados, on March 18, 1980, aged 86. He was late in coming to the front, being 35 when he appeared in England in 1928 with the first West Indian team to be granted Test status, but he had played for Barbados as early as 1921, and in 1926 had taken nine for 96 for them against the Hon. F. S. G. Calthorpe's MCC side. In 1928 his final record was not impressive, his 76 wickets costing 27.89 runs each, but there were those who reckoned him the best bowler on the side. Not as fast as Constantine, indeed really fast-medium, he was more of a stock bowler and was an indefatigable trier, a quality less common then in West Indian sides than it has since become. Getting plenty of pace off the pitch and swinging away sharply, he relied greatly on catches in the slips. His best performances were in the final Test at The Oval where, in an innings of 438, he took six for 103 (with a spell of five for 21) and eleven for 118 against Kent at Canterbury, where he was largely responsible for the innings defeat of a strong batting side. In 1930 he took eight wickets against an unrepresentative England side at Port-of-Spain and in the fifth Test at Sydney in 1931 he played an important part in the first West Indian victory over Australia by bowling Bradman for a duck with a slower ball, which he tried to turn to leg and made into a yorker. His second visit to England at the age of 40 in 1933 was perhaps a mistake: he was naturally not the bowler he had been, his 44 wickets costing him over 37 runs each, and he played in only two of the Tests. He continued, however, to play in first-class cricket at home until 1941. Apart from his bowling he had a safe pair of hands in the field.

HATFIELD, LT.-COL. EDWARD JOHN, who died on March 18, 1980, aged 77, made a number of appearances for Devon over a long period. He was a useful batsman.

HOLMES, JOHN RODNEY REAY, was killed in an avalanche in Italy on February 3, 1980, aged 55. A son of the old Sussex captain, Group-Captain A. J. Holmes, he was captain of the Repton XI in 1941 and 1942 and kept wicket for Sussex v Oxford University in 1950 and 1951.

HILL-WOOD, SIR WILFRED WILLIAM HILL, KCVO, died in London on October 10, 1980, aged 79. He was one of the many amateurs who were compelled to give up serious cricket before they had had a chance to fulfil their promise. When his county career for practical purposes ended at 22, some good judges already reckoned him a possible future candidate for England. In technique he was the antithesis of the traditional amateur. With a crouching stance, which he had adopted early in life to counteract a tendency to move away, he was unattractive to watch though he had a good range of strokes: his strength lay in his defence. At Eton, where he was in the XI for three years and captain in 1921, he was an all-rounder and at Lord's in 1919 his leg-breaks, which later in first-class cricket often broke an awkward partnership, brought him four for 40 and seven for 29. Though he played for Derbyshire as early as 1919, he did not get his Blue at Cambridge until his second summer, 1922, and then only secured the last place. He fully justified his selection, going in first on a sodden wicket and batting four and threequarter hours for 81. When the total at lunch was 60 for no wicket after two hours' play, he and his partner, C. A. Fiddian-Green, came in for some criticism: in the end, however, they could justifiably feel that they had made a substantial contribution to an innings victory. That winter Hill-Wood was a member of A. C. MacLaren's MCC side to Australia and New Zealand and accomplished the feat for which he is best remembered. In the return against Victoria at Melbourne, the touring side had been out for 71 and Victoria had declared at 617 for six. Defeat seemed certain, but Hill-Wood and Geoffrey Wilson, later captain of Yorkshire, batted out the rest of the match and after four and threequarter hours were undefeated with 122 and 142 respectively. In 1923 he played throughout the season for Derbyshire, heading their averages with 961 runs at 34.32 and making 107 v Somerset at Bath. He played a few matches in the next two or three seasons and indeed made one appearance as late as 1936, but his serious career was over. Later he served for many years on the MCC Committee. He was one of four brothers who played for Derbyshire, three of them also being awarded Blues. Their father had captained the county at the turn of the century.

HOWORTH, RICHARD, died in hospital on April 2, 1980, aged 70. A slow left-arm bowler, who kept an immaculate length and could spin and flight the ball, an attacking left-handed batsman, who usually appeared in the middle of the order but was prepared to open if wanted, and a good field close to the wicket, he did great service for Worcestershire from 1933 to 1951, scoring for them 10,538 runs at an average of 20.20, taking 1,274 wickets at 21.36 and holding 188 catches. Three times, in 1939, 1946 and 1947 he achieved the double in all matches, and he played five times for England. Born at Bacup, he appeared for Worcestershire in 1933 against the West Indians while qualifying and in the first innings was top scorer with 68. Qualified in 1934, he was disappointing, but in 1935 he jumped right to the front, heading the bowling averages with 121 wickets at 18.94, and from that time he never looked back. In 1936 he played an important part in Worcestershire's sensational victory over Yorkshire, their first since 1909: in the second innings he took five for 21. Later that summer he made the first and highest of his three centuries in county cricket – 114 in two hours and ten minutes v Kent at Dover, scored out of 180 for the first wicket – and followed it by taking, in the two innings, eight for 91. Before the War, with Verity available, there was little chance in the England side for any other slow left-armer, but in 1947 Howorth was picked for the final Test v South Africa at The Oval and proved a great success. He took six wickets in the match, including one with his first ball, and was described in *Wisden* as "far the best England bowler"; he also scored 23 and 45 not out and made two fine catches in the gully. That winter he went with MCC to West Indies under G. O. Allen and played in all four Tests: so important was his steadiness to a weak attack that he was not left out of a single match. But the West Indies is not the ideal place for left-arm spin and his wickets were costly.

In his early days Howorth owed much to his captain, the Hon. C. J. Lyttelton, later Lord Cobham, who, whenever he showed signs of shortening his length and bowling too fast, insisted that he should pitch the ball up and flight it more. When in 1951, at the age of 42, he announced his retirement after a season in which he had headed the Worcestershire bowling averages with 118 wickets at 17.97 and appeared to be bowling as well as ever, Lord Cobham, upon asking him why he was retiring, received the reply, "Because it's not as much fun as it was". Howorth played later for Stourbridge in the Birmingham League, served for many years on the Worcestershire Committee and ran a newsagent's shop across the river from the Worcester ground. He was much liked and respected, though the partial disenchantment which prompted his retirement from the first-class game was never quite thrown off.

JOHNS, DAVID FRANK VICTOR, who died suddenly on November 20, 1979, at High Wycombe, aged 58, was a valuable member of the Buckinghamshire side from 1950 to 1965, captaining it from 1956 to 1958. In 1952, when they won the Minor Counties Championship, he scored three centuries – one of them, 191 against Bedfordshire, the highest score ever made for the county – and also took 39 wickets. He was a slow left-arm bowler. In 1952 and 1953 he played for the representative Minor Counties team.

KEETON, WILLIAM WALLACE, who died on October 9, 1980, aged 75, was a great servant of Nottinghamshire and one of the many candidates for a place in the England side as an opening bat in the years immediately before the Second World War. In fact he played in only two Tests, v Australia at Leeds in 1934 and v West Indies at The Oval in 1939. Probably most people would reckon that the selectors were right, that he was a good county player but not quite Test class. He had a sound defence, was a fine cutter and also had a good cover drive, but what spectators will chiefly remember was his leg-side play and in particular his mastery of that difficult and neglected stroke, the on-drive. Moreover he was, as befitted a first-class soccer forward, a fine outfield. He first played for his county in 1926, but the Nottinghamshire batsmen of that era retained their skill almost undiminished to a patriarchal age and it was not until 1931 that the premature death of Whysall secured him a serious trial. He made the most of his opportunity, scoring his thousand runs with an average of 30 and making two centuries. For most of the season he had the valuable experience of opening with George Gunn. From then for twenty years his career was interrupted only by illness or injuries, of which he had more than his share; in January 1935 he was knocked down by a lorry and was lucky to be able to resume his place in the side late in June. But despite all this and the loss of six seasons in the War he reached his thousand runs on twelve occasions and made 54 hundreds. His highest score, 312 not out in seven and threequarter hours v Middlesex at The Oval (Eton were playing Harrow at Lord's) in 1939, remains the only innings of 300 ever played for Nottinghamshire, and he is also one of the few batsmen to have scored a century against every county. From 1932 to 1948 his regular partner was that eccentric player, Charlie Harris, and a notable pair they were. On 45 occasions they put up three figures, fourteen times they exceeded 150 and five times 200. Twice they put up 100 in each innings. Their highest stand was 277 v Middlesex at Trent Bridge in 1933. Keeton was still as good as ever after the War, but Hutton and Washbrook had now established themselves as England's opening pair. As late as 1949 he scored 2,049 runs with an average of 55.37. In 1951, at 46, he lost his regular place in the side, but against Kent at Trent Bridge helped Simpson to put on 269 for the first wicket. A single match in 1952 concluded his career. In all he had scored 24,276 runs with an average of just under 40. After retiring he had a sports shop for a time and later worked for the National Coal Board.

KOTELAWALA, COLONEL RT. HON. SIR JOHN LIONEL, CH, PC, KBE, who died in 1980 at the age of 82, was Prime Minister of Ceylon from 1953 to 1956. A good schoolboy cricketer, he played for Royal College, Colombo, in 1914 and 1915, and for the Indian Gymkhana while at Cambridge. For many years he was President of the Sinhalese Sports Club, for whom he had also played.

LEE, PHILIP KEITH, who died in Adelaide on August 9, 1980, at the age of 75, played twice for Australia – against South Africa in 1931-32 and against England at Sydney in the body-line series of 1932-33. His four for 111 in England's first innings of 454 included the wickets of Hammond for 101, Paynter for 9 and Allen for 48, in spite of ill-luck with catches. In Australia's first innings, batting at number eight, Lee scored 42. For South Australia in 1930-31, his first innings of 106 (his only first-class century) and five for 57 in the West Indians' second innings had much to do with South Australia gaining an exciting victory. Bowling off-breaks at a slow-medium pace, he had good control of length and his flight could be deceptive. With Wall and Grimmett, he formed the nucleus of a useful South Australian attack. Like Victor Richardson, the great South Australian sportsman, Lee was also a talented footballer and baseball player. In 1933-34 he played in both Test trials, held as a guide to the selection of the Australian side to England in 1934, but although he scored a fifty in the second of them he was never chosen to tour. His 152 first-class wickets cost him 30.16 apiece and he scored 1,669 first-class runs at an average of 18.54.

LE GROS, LT.-COL. PHILIP WALTER, died at the Star and Garter Home, Richmond, on February 27, 1980, aged 87. A good all-rounder, he was in the Rugby XI of 1910, being at that time a dangerous fast bowler who, in the second innings against Marlborough, took nine for 49. From 1911 to 1930 he played for Buckinghamshire and, though he bowled little after the war, was one of their leading batsmen when they won the Minor Counties Championship in 1922, 1923 and 1925. Despite a distinct stoop at the wicket, he was a stylish batsman and a strong hitter. For many years there hung in the High Wycombe pavilion a photograph of a row of cars standing by the pavilion, their windscreens smashed by Le Gros's hits. He was also a first-class squash player.

LEWIS, ARTHUR HAMILTON, who died on August 23, 1978, played one match for Hampshire in 1929 and later, for several seasons, did useful work for Berkshire. A cross-bat hitter with a wonderful eye and a magnificent cover-point, he was credited with some remarkable scoring feats in club cricket.

LEWIS, SIR EDWARD (TED) ROBERTS, KBE, who died on January 29, 1980, was one of that great company whose lifelong devotion to cricket does not stem from personal triumphs on the field. Only a modest player himself at Rugby School and Trinity College, Cambridge, he delighted then, as later he was to do in wider fields, in the skills of others and the traditions of the game and its atmosphere. After the Second World War, when he was well on the way to making Decca a leader in the fields of radio, records and electronics, he was able to give more of his attention to his favourite pastime, becoming in due course a member of the MCC Committee and a Vice-President of Surrey. He was the wisest of counsellors and a most generous benefactor – to more than one generation of county cricketers as well as county clubs and their administrative staffs.

LEWIS, VICTOR, who died in Malta in 1980, at the age of 75, covered the MCC Australian tour of 1946-47 for the *Daily Sketch* and the *Sunday Graphic*. He was at one time editor-in-chief of *The Times* of Ceylon.

LILLEY, AUBREY ROY, who died in an air crash near Johannesburg on August 10, 1979, at the age of 28, was a left-arm seam bowler who took 132 first-class wickets for Natal and Transvaal, four times taking five in an innings. Born at Grahamstown, he was educated at Maritzburg College and played for both the Natal and South African Schools in 1969. He toured England with the Kingsmead Mynahs in 1976. It was after he had had one season for Transvaal that he was killed. When Natal were bowled out for 71 by Transvaal in the Currie Cup of 1978-79, Lilley took four for 9.

MOHANTY, BHAIRAB CHANDRA, who died in 1980 while visiting Moscow with an Indian Parliamentary Delegation to the Olympic Games, was to have succeeded M. Chinnaswamy as President of the Indian Cricket Board in September 1980. He was treasurer of the Indian team to England in 1974.

MOORE, JACK, who died in June, 1980, at the age of 89, was tried for Hampshire as a batsman between 1910 and 1913; but in fifteen matches his highest score was 30 and he never got a regular place in the side.

MORGAN, GEORGE, the Irish scrum-half, who died in Dublin in April, 1979, aged 67, appeared at cricket for his country against MCC at Sion Mills in 1934. Though selected as a batsman he failed to score. For the Clontarf Club, whom he captained for three seasons, he scored 2,360 runs in competitive cricket, including two centuries.

MORKEL, DENYS PAUL BECK, died suddenly in hospital at Nottingham on October 6, 1980, aged 74. He first appeared for South Africa against Capt. R. T. Stanyforth's MCC side in 1927-28, when he played in all five Tests, but, though he made some useful scores, he met with no particular success and his bowling was hardly used. It was on the tour of England in 1929 that he showed his real possibilities. In first-class matches he scored 1,443 runs with an average of 34.35 and took 69 wickets at 26.01. In the Tests he came second both in batting and bowling: at Lord's he made 88 and 17 not out and took seven wickets, at Old Trafford he scored 63 out of a total of 130 and at The Oval 81. Tall and well built, he bowled fast-medium away-swingers with an easy action and plenty of pace off the pitch, and was probably the best bowler in the team. A fine driver on both sides of the wicket, he was inclined to be impetuous but had, as he showed at Lord's, a solid defence when required. He was also a good slip. A great future seemed in store for him and that winter he helped S. S. L. Steyn to put on 222 for the eighth wicket for Western Province v Border, still a South African record. But he had already decided to settle in England and so was not available to play against the MCC side in 1930-31. However he was a member in 1931-32 of the South African team to Australia, where he was a sad disappointment. As a batsman he could never get going in the Tests and his bowling was a complete failure. Only in the last match against Western Australia, not then the power they have since become, did he show his best form, scoring 150 not out and taking eight for 13 in the second innings. In extenuation it must be said that he was in poor health at the beginning of the tour and that he also had trouble with his bowling action. This was the end of his Test career. In 1932 Sir Julien Cahn helped him to establish a business in the motor trade in Nottingham, which became a flourishing concern. For Sir Julien between 1932 and 1939 he made nearly 10,000 runs and took over 400 wickets. During the War he served in the Army. His brother, Ray, also played for Western Province and at one time showed promise of being the better bowler of the two.

MOXLEY, JOHN, who died on April 11, 1980, aged 40, was a well-known figure in Midland sporting circles, running the Birmingham-based sports reporting agency which his father had started and writing about cricket from Edgbaston for many papers, including *The Daily Telegraph*. He contributed the article on Warwickshire to the 1980 *Wisden*.

NAOOMAL JEOOMAL, who died in Bombay on July 18, 1980, aged 76, served the game of cricket for many years, first in India and, after partition, in Pakistan. As a member of the Indian side to England in 1932 he opened their innings at Lord's in their first-ever Test match, scoring 33 and 25, and played twice more against England, in India in 1933-34. His highest score in England was 164 not out against Middlesex in 1932 and in India 203 not out against Nawanagar in 1938. In the 1950s he became Pakistan's national coach. He lived to enjoy the Jubilee Test Match between India and England in Bombay in February 1980.

PACKHAM, HENRY ALFRED, died on November 8, 1980, aged 78. Captain of Rossall in 1920, he later did useful service for some seasons as a batsman for Surrey Second XI.

PARKS, JAMES HORACE, who died on November 21, 1980, aged 77, will be remembered for his feat of scoring 3,003 runs and taking 101 wickets in 1937, a record which, unless the whole pattern of county cricket is radically changed, cannot possibly be equalled. First appearing for Sussex in 1924, he created a sensation by taking seven for 17 in his third match, in the second innings against Leicestershire at Horsham. Naturally, great things were hoped of him, but he was slow to develop and it was not until 1927, when he made 1,036 runs with an average of 23.54 and took 44 wickets at 26.93, that he began to justify the confidence which the county had placed in him. From then until the Second World War he was an indispensable member of the side. In 1928 he made the first of his 41 hundreds and in 1929 helped Bowley to put up 368 in three hours, at that time a Sussex record, for the first wicket against Gloucestershire; his share was 110. In 1935 he did the double and appeared for the Players at Lord's; that winter he was a member of E. R. T. Holmes's MCC side to Australia and New Zealand, which did not play official Tests. His one Test appearance was against New Zealand at Lord's in 1937, when he opened the batting with Hutton, also making his Test début, but, though he scored 22 in the first innings and bowled well, he can never have been a strong candidate for a place against Australia. His first-class career ended in 1939. After the War he went to the Lancashire League and later, for a time in the 1960s, was the county coach at Hove. He was essentially a county player, immensely dependable, but lacking the touch of genius which marks the top class. Indeed, after forty years it is difficult to have any vivid picture of his cricket, except perhaps of his brilliant close fielding. As a batsman he was sound and a particularly good cutter, not very attractive to watch, but capable of scoring fast if wanted. Stockily built, he was for years a formidable opening partner for John Langridge, and had the considerable merit that no fast bowler was likely to intimidate him. He bowled slow-medium in-swingers, which, if there was any bite in the wicket, often moved away after pitching; but again he was normally reliable rather than deadly. He was first of a distinguished cricket family. His younger brother was for years one of the mainstays of the Sussex batting; his son, at one time captain of Sussex, played many times for England both as a batsman and as a wicket-keeper, and his grandson has recently been playing for Hampshire.

PATERSON, ROBERT FRASER TROUTBECK, died in Edinburgh on May 29, 1980, aged 63, after a long illness. He headed the Brighton College averages in 1933 and 1934, when he played for the Public Schools at Lord's, and, making his first appearance for Essex in 1946, was for that season a regular and valuable member of the side. He played many useful innings – the highest of them 80 against Yorkshire, the champion county, at Harrogate – occasionally picked up a wicket as a medium-paced change bowler and in one match at least kept wicket creditably in the absence of T. H. Wade. Apart from one appearance in 1948, this ended his first-class career, though from 1947 to 1950 he was the county's Secretary. He then moved to Scotland where he continued to make many runs and also did notable work as a coach. He was a particularly good off-driver.

PEARE, WILLIAM GEORGE, who died at St Luke's, Cork, on November 16, 1979, aged 74, was a fast-medium bowler and useful batsman who played seven matches for Warwickshire in 1926, but, meeting with little success, abandoned professional cricket and took a job with Dunlop. It was while working for them that he played as an amateur for MCC v Gentlemen of Ireland in 1936.

PEEBLES, IAN ALEXANDER ROSS, who died on February 28, 1980, aged 72, was for a short time one of the most formidable bowlers in the world and one of the few who could make Bradman look fallible. A tall man with a beautifully easy run-up and a high action, which gave him a particularly awkward flight, he bowled leg-breaks and googlies, and in an age of fine leg-spinners he was, for a while, the equal of any.

The start of his career was unusual. Coming south from Scotland in the hope of getting a chance in the cricket world, he was engaged as Secretary at the Aubrey Faulkner School of Cricket and so impressed Faulkner himself (to whose coaching he always acknowledged a great debt) and also Sir Pelham Warner that, when difficulty was found in raising a good enough Gentlemen's side against the Players at The Oval in 1927, he was given a place. On this occasion he bowled Sandham, but that was his only wicket; nor was he more successful later in the season at the Folkestone and Scarborough Festivals. However that winter he was sent with the MCC side to South Africa: ostensibly he went as secretary to the captain, but he bowled well enough to secure a place in the first four Tests and, without doing anything spectacular, made it clear that his possibilities had not been overestimated. In 1928 he played a few matches for Middlesex, but it was in 1929 that he really came to the fore, taking 120 wickets at just under 20 runs each and being one of three amateurs to take 100 wickets for the county that season – a unique performance. In 1930 he was at Oxford, for whom he took 70 wickets, thirteen of them against Cambridge; then, after taking six wickets (including Hobbs, Sutcliffe and Leyland) for 105 for the Gentlemen v the Players, he was picked for the fourth Test at Old Trafford. Here, as soon as Peebles came on, Woodfull, who was well set, became acutely uncomfortable, on one occasion leaving a ball which just went over his middle stump; Bradman, coming in, was all but bowled first ball by Peebles, who then had him dropped in the slips and finally caught at slip for 14. The first three balls Kippax received from

Peebles produced three confident but unsuccessful appeals for lbw. For such bowling three for 150 was a wholly inadequate reward. In the final Test at The Oval six for 204 may not look much, but in an Australian total of 695 it was better than anyone else. That winter Peebles went again with MCC to South Africa and both there and against New Zealand in the following summer he was one of the most effective bowlers. Already, though, the amount of bowling he had had to do in matches, followed by countless hours in the nets in winter, was affecting him: his leg-break was losing its venom, he was becoming increasingly dependent upon his googly, and his great days were passing, though he was picked for the last Test in 1934, an invitation which he had to refuse owing to injury. When, after several seasons of intermittent appearances, he returned to regular county cricket in 1939 to captain Middlesex, Peebles was really no more than a change bowler, and though he played occasionally until 1948, the loss of an eye in a war-time air-raid had, to all intents and purposes, ended his serious cricket career.

After his playing days were over he entered the wine trade and also became a notable cricket writer and journalist. When writing of players he had played with or seen, he was in the top class; to a deep knowledge of the game he added rare charm and humour. For any student of cricket history over the last 60 years, his many books are compulsory and delightful reading.

PEACH, CHARLES WILLIAM, died at Coxheath, near Maidstone, on February 27, 1977, aged 77. After being for many years one of the mainstays of the bowling of the Mote, Maidstone, he was tried for Kent against Yorkshire at Headingley in 1930 and caused some stir by taking six for 93 in the two innings, his victims including Sutcliffe and Leyland twice each. He did some useful work in the later matches and finished the season with 29 wickets at 25.86. However, his action was regarded with suspicion and, although he was never no balled, two matches in 1931 concluded his first-class career. He bowled right-arm, on the quick side of medium, and could produce a sharp off-break.

PEARSON, COLIN HARGREAVES, PC, CBE, a Lord of Appeal in Ordinary, who died on January 31, 1980, aged 80, had been a good cricketer. He was in the St Paul's XI in 1916 and 1917, heading the batting averages in the second year, and later became a member of the Oxford Authentics.

PIGOT, JAMES POOLE MAUNSELL, who died in Dublin on July 20, 1980, aged 79, was a member of a well-known Dublin cricket family. He played as a forcing right-handed batsman and leg-break bowler in two matches for Dublin University against Northamptonshire in 1924 and 1925, scoring 50 on the latter occasion. He also played three times for the Europeans in the Madras Presidency Match between 1926 and 1930. In 1923 he scored 194 for Phoenix CC in a Senior League match in Dublin, still a club record in that competition. His brother, D. R. Pigot, represented Ireland between the wars, as did his nephew, also D. R., more recently.

PILCH, GEORGE EVERETT, a member of the famous Norfolk cricketing family, died at Cringleford on September 12, 1979, aged 67. Between 1935 and 1946 he did useful work for the county as a bowler and was later a great help to it on the administrative side.

POOLE, ARTHUR BERTRAM, who died on November 22, 1979, aged 72, was one of the mainstays of the Bedfordshire batting from 1925 to 1951, and their captain from 1946 to 1951. At the time of his death he was President of Bedfordshire and had previously been Chairman. He was a quick-footed batsman, who played for the Minor Counties, and his 234 v Oxfordshire at Banbury in 1936, made in under three and a half hours, is still a Bedfordshire record.

POULTON, RONALD M., died on October 11, 1979. From 1946 to 1949 he was Assistant Secretary of Nottinghamshire and from 1949 to 1971 Secretary. He had then served the county in one capacity or another for 46 years, including playing frequently for the Second XI and the Club and Ground. He continued to help in various ways until his death.

ROSS, THOMAS DOUGLAS, who died on October 30, 1980, was a useful all-rounder who played for Lincolnshire from 1926 to 1936 and was later President of the Lincolnshire County Cricket Club.

RUTHERFORD, ARNOLD PAGE, who died on July 23, 1980, aged 87, was three years in the Repton XI as a batsman and captain in 1911, and in 1912 played in one match for Hampshire.

SCOTT, VERDUN JOHN, who died suddenly at Devonport, New Zealand, on August 2, 1980, played in ten Tests for New Zealand between 1946 and 1952, and was a member of the side which toured England in 1949. Though overshadowed by Sutcliffe and Donnelly, he was one of their most dependable batsmen, scoring 1,572 runs with an average of 40.30 and making four hundreds. A big man, he had hardly any backlift and was no stylist, but he was very strong in the arms and his strokes travelled deceptively fast. He was an ideal foil to Sutcliffe as an opening partner and their value can be gauged from the fact that in the Tests of 1949 they took part in partnerships of 122 at Leeds, 89 at Lord's and 121 at The Oval. His highest Test score was against West Indies in 1952 when he saved the side with an innings of 84 in rather over four hours. For Auckland in the Plunket Shield he was a heavy scorer.

SEYMOUR, EDWARD NOEL, died in Dublin on February 12, 1980, aged 74. He appeared three times for Ireland in 1927 and 1928. His best work, however, was done for the Clontarf Club. In 1930 he won the Marchant Cup, awarded annually to the batsman who heads the averages in Dublin club cricket.

SHOWERING, RALPH VIVIAN, President of Somerset from 1971 to 1975, died at Beckington, near Bath, on September 20, 1980, aged 70.

SHIPMAN, ALAN WILFRED, who died, aged 79, on December 12, 1979, after years of ill-health, rendered valuable service to Leicestershire from 1920 to 1936, scoring 13,605 runs with an average of 23.26, including fifteen centuries, and taking 597 wickets at 25.37. At first he was regarded almost entirely as a bowler, but by 1925, when he scored his first century, his powers of defence had created such an impression that he had been promoted to go in first, a position he retained until back trouble caused his premature retirement eleven years later. Like many others so promoted, Shipman remained solid and unexciting, scoring chiefly to leg, but he was reliable and there could be no question of his value. His highest score, 226 v Kent at Tonbridge in 1928, took seven hours, but it turned an apparently certain defeat into an honourable draw and almost into a glorious victory. As a brisk medium-pace bowler, he had neither the physique nor the action to achieve greatness, but, for a Leicestershire side which was generally strong enough to save him from being over-bowled, he did much good work. His most notable all-round performance was against Worcestershire at Kidderminster in 1929, when he followed five for 30 by making 183, all on the first day of the match. After his retirement he kept a pub at Ratby, his native place, emerging for one season in 1947 to coach at Tonbridge.

SILLITOE, LT.-COL. WARREN HERBERT, OBE, who was killed in a road accident in Yorkshire on November 1, 1980, at the age of 51, was Secretary of Surrey from 1974 to 1977. Before that he had served as a regular soldier with the Royal Regiment of Fusiliers. He and his wife, Beryl, who was killed with him, made a diligent and attentive partnership at The Oval, though it was Sillitoe's frustration at not being given wider control of affairs there that caused him to leave. When he died he was Public Relations Officer to the North-Eastern Gas Board.

SINGH, LT.-COL. KANWAR SHUMSHERE, died in New Delhi on May 12, 1975, aged 95. A member of the Rugby XI in 1896, he had a trial for Cambridge in 1901 and played three matches for Kent that year and one the next, showing much promise. A batsman with a strong defence and a fine field, he made top score, 45, in the first innings against Worcestershire and against Surrey at The Oval he helped Murrell to add 115 in fifty-five minutes for the seventh wicket. He entered the Indian Medical Service, and at the time of his death was the oldest surviving Kent cricketer.

SNOW, of Leicester, LORD (CHARLES PERCY SNOW), who died on July 1, 1980, was captain of Newton's Grammar School, Leicester, and Leicester University College. He played for Leicester Town and, as a Fellow, for Christ's College, Cambridge, at the time when they were captained by his undergraduate brother, Philip. He eschewed in batting everything but the cut and leg glance and was a useful top-spin bowler. In 1964 C. P. Snow was appointed the House of Lord's ministerial spokesman for Technology. Internationally celebrated as scientist and author, some of his fifty books and innumerable essays include brief cricket scenes and fictitious characters with cricketers' names. His study of G. H. Hardy in *The Saturday Book* (1948) is a classic cricket vignette. As XX he contributed Cambridge notes to *The Cricketer* in the 1930s.

STEAD, BARRY, died on April 7, 1980, aged 40. Born at Leeds, he was a fast-medium left-arm bowler who made a sensational first-class début, taking seven for 76 for Yorkshire v the Indians in 1959. However, so strong at the time was the Yorkshire bowling that he only appeared once more for them before moving to Nottinghamshire for whom he played from 1962 to 1976. He got his cap in 1969 when he took 83 wickets at an average of 23.83. His best season was 1972 when his 98 wickets cost 20.38 each. He had a benefit in 1976. In all for Nottinghamshire he took 604 wickets at 28.04. A left-handed batsman who delighted in hitting 6s, his highest score was 58 for Nottinghamshire v Gloucestershire in 1972. He also played for Northern Transvaal. He died after a long illness and is much missed by his fellow players with whom he was extremely popular.

TARRANT, W. GUY, who died on August 4, 1979, aged 74, scored over 40,000 runs for Spencer, including 86 centuries. An old boy of Emanuel School, he became one of the great figures of the London club scene, playing for Spencer from 1925 until 1960 and being their chairman from 1955 until 1970. A useful wicket-keeper, as well as a successful batsman, he turned down the chance of joining the playing staff at The Oval in order to further his career as a quantity surveyor.

TAYLOR, GORDON MACLAREN, who died on February 9, 1980, at the age of 75, was connected with the Lancashire County Cricket Club for over 50 years. He was still with them when he died, a gentle, well-loved figure known to the highest and the lowest, and to everyone in between, as 'Mac'. There were few off-the-field jobs to which he had not turned his hand at Old Trafford, and from 1946 he had been scorer and baggage master to the First XI.

TIMMS, JOHN EDWARD, who died at his home in Buckingham on May 18, 1980, aged 73, rendered splendid service to Northamptonshire from 1925 to 1949. When he retired he had scored more runs for the county than any other batsman, though he never quite took the place in the cricket world that many had expected. He lacked consistency, and apart from one appearance in a Test trial, in 1932, he remained purely a county player. A member of the Wellingborough XI in 1924, he played originally as an amateur but turned professional in 1927. Short and slightly built, he was a natural cricketer, quick on his feet and severe on the short ball. At the start of his career he was apt to be lackadaisical in the field, but spurred on by his captains he developed into a fine cover point, a not unworthy successor to the great Fanny Walden. At slow-medium, Timms was a rather expensive change bowler, who had no great belief in his own ability, so that when, in 1938, he took six for 18 v Worcestershire and nearly brought about his county's first win in the Championship since 1935, it caused some surprise. In all he scored 20,384 runs for Northamptonshire with an average of 25.07, his highest innings being 213 v Worcestershire at Stourbridge in 1934. His 149 wickets cost 44.42 each. Later he combined a post as professional and green-keeper at the Buckingham Golf Club with coaching cricket at Bloxham School.

TREGLOWN, LT.-COL. CLAUDE JESSE HELBY, MC, died at Worthing on May 7, 1980, aged 87. He played fairly frequently for Essex from 1922 to 1928, sometimes opening the innings. His highest Championship score was 72 not out v Kent at Tunbridge Wells in 1923. He also appeared for Norfolk and Sussex Second XI.

WALSH, JOHN (JACK) EDWARD, who died at Newcastle, New South Wales, on May 20, 1980, aged 67, was for some years one of the most dangerous, if not the most consistent, bowlers in the world, though as an Australian resident in England he never played in a Test. Born in Sydney, he had in 1937 acquired a sufficient reputation in his native state to be invited over to play for Sir Julien Cahn and to qualify for Leicestershire. In three seasons for Sir Julien's XI he took nearly 600 wickets, meanwhile playing occasionally as an amateur for Leicestershire, and in 1938, when he headed their bowling averages, taking seven for 46 against Northamptonshire. In 1946 he joined the Leicestershire staff and for the next ten years was one of the mainstays of the side. A left-arm bowler with tremendous powers of spin, he was of the Fleetwood-Smith type – chinamen and googlies. In fact he had two googlies; one, which could be easily detected, to lull the batsman into a sense of security, when he would unleash the other, which was calculated to deceive even the greatest batsmen. In all for Leicestershire he took 1,127 wickets at an average of 24.25, his best season being 1948 when he took 174 at 19.56. Apart from his bowling he was a good slip and a left-hand batsman of great power with a full range of strokes, who would have scored many more runs had he restrained his passion for straight drives into the pavilion. When he played his highest innings – 106 in 95 minutes against Essex at Loughborough in 1948 – 82 of his runs came in boundaries; seven 6s and ten 4s. In 1952 he performed the double of 1,000 runs and 100 wickets. Outside county cricket he represented the Players at Lord's in 1947. Retiring from first-class cricket at the end of 1956, he captained Leicestershire Second XI in 1957 and was for a time the county's assistant coach. Later he coached both in Tasmania and Scotland.

WILSON, GROUP-CAPTAIN ROBERT G., Secretary of the Nottinghamshire County Cricket Club from 1972 to 1977, died on March 7, 1980, aged 57.

WOLFSON, ANDREW CECIL, who died on July 26, 1978, aged 88, was in the Marlborough XI in 1908 as a medium-paced away-swing bowler, taking nine for 68 in the second innings against Rugby at Lord's. Living mostly abroad, he played little cricket after leaving, but in 1920 appeared for H. D. G. Leveson Gower's XI against both Universities.

YEOMANS, C. RONALD, who died on January 16, 1980, aged 71, had been on the committee of the Yorkshire County Cricket Club for over twenty years, but was perhaps better known as founder in 1948 of the Northern Cricket Society and a contributor on cricket to the columns of *The Daily Telegraph*. He was a useful club cricketer and had been in the XI at St Peter's York.

THE LAWS OF CRICKET

(1980 CODE)

World copyright of MCC and reprinted by permission of MCC. Copies of the "Laws of Cricket" may be obtained from Lord's Cricket Ground.

INDEX TO THE LAWS

LAW 1.   THE PLAYERS

1. Number of Players and Captain

A match is played between two sides each of eleven players, one of whom shall be captain. In the event of the captain not being available at any time, a deputy shall act for him.

2. Nomination of Players

Before the toss for innings, the captain shall nominate his players, who may not thereafter be changed without the consent of the opposing captain.

Note

(a) **More or Less Than Eleven Players a Side**
A match may be played by agreement between sides of more or less than eleven players, but not more than eleven players may field.

LAW 2.   SUBSTITUTES AND RUNNERS: BATSMAN OR FIELDSMAN LEAVING THE FIELD: BATSMAN RETIRING: BATSMAN COMMENCING INNINGS

1. Substitutes

Substitutes shall be allowed by right to field for any player who, during the match, is incapacitated by illness or injury. The consent of the opposing captain must be obtained for the use of a substitute if any player is prevented from fielding for any other reason.

2. Objection to Substitutes

The opposing captain shall have no right of objection to any player acting as substitute in the field, nor as to where he shall field, although he may object to the substitute acting as wicket-keeper.

3. Substitute not to Bat or Bowl

A substitute shall not be allowed to bat or bowl.

4. A Player for whom a Substitute has Acted

A player may bat, bowl or field even though a substitute has acted for him.

5. Runner

A runner shall be allowed for a batsman who, during the match, is incapacitated by illness or injury. The person acting as runner shall be a member of the batting side and shall, if possible, have already batted in that innings.

6. Runner's Equipment

The person acting as runner for an injured batsman shall wear batting gloves and pads if the injured batsman is so equipped.

7. Transgression of the Laws by an Injured Batsman or Runner

An injured batsman may be out should his runner break any one of Laws 33 (Handled the Ball), 37 (Obstructing the Field) or 38 (Run Out). As striker he remains himself subject to the Laws. Furthermore, should he be out of his ground for any purpose and the wicket at the wicket-keeper's end be put down he shall be out under Law 38 (Run Out) or Law 39 (Stumped), irrespective of the position of the other batsman or the runner, and no runs shall be scored.

When not the striker, the injured batsman is out of the game and shall stand where he does not interfere with the play. Should he bring himself into the game in any way, then he shall suffer the penalties that any transgression of the Laws demands.

8. Fieldsman Leaving the Field

No fieldsman shall leave the field or return during a session of play without the consent of the umpire at the bowler's end. The umpire's consent is also necessary if a substitute is required for a fieldsman, when his side returns to the field after an interval. If a member of the fielding side leaves the field or fails to return after an interval and is absent from the field for longer than fifteen minutes, he shall not be permitted to bowl after his return until he has been on the field for at least that length of playing time for which he was absent. This restriction shall not apply at the start of a new day's play.

9. Batsman Leaving the Field or Retiring

A batsman may leave the field or retire at any time owing to illness, injury or other unavoidable cause, having previously notified the umpire at the bowler's end. He may resume his innings at the fall of a wicket, which for the purposes of this Law shall include the retirement of another batsman.

If he leaves the field or retires for any other reason he may resume his innings only with the consent of the opposing captain.

When a batsman has left the field or retired and is unable to return owing to illness, injury or other unavoidable cause, his innings is to be recorded as "retired, not out". Otherwise it is to be recorded as "retired, out".

10. Commencement of a Batsman's Innings

A batsman shall be considered to have commenced his innings once he has stepped on to the field of play.

Note

(a) Substitutes and Runners
For the purpose of these Laws, allowable illnesses or injuries are those which occur at any time after the nomination by the captains of their teams.

LAW 3.   THE UMPIRES

1. Appointment

Before the toss for innings, two umpires shall be appointed, one for each end, to control the game with absolute impartiality as required by the Laws.

2. Change of Umpires

No umpire shall be changed during a match without the consent of both captains.

3. Special Conditions

Before the toss for innings, the umpires shall agree with both captains on any special conditions affecting the conduct of the match.

4. The Wickets

The umpires shall satisfy themselves before the start of the match that the wickets are properly pitched.

5. Clock or Watch

The umpires shall agree between themselves and inform both captains before the start of the match on the watch or clock to be followed during the match.

6. Conduct and Implements

Before and during a match the umpires shall ensure that the conduct of the game and the implements used are strictly in accordance with the Laws.

7. Fair and Unfair Play

The umpires shall be the sole judges of fair and unfair play.

8. Fitness of Ground, Weather and Light

(a) The umpires shall be the sole judges of the fitness of the ground, weather and light for play.

(i) However, before deciding to suspend play, or not to start play, or not to resume play after an interval or stoppage, the umpires shall establish whether both captains (the batsmen at the wicket may deputise for their captain) wish to commence or to continue in the prevailing conditions; if so, their wishes shall be met.

(ii) In addition, if during play the umpires decide that the light is unfit, only the batting side shall have the option of continuing play. After agreeing to continue to play in unfit light conditions, the captain of the batting side (or a batsman at the wicket) may appeal against the light to the umpires, who shall uphold the appeal only if, in their opinion, the light has deteriorated since the agreement to continue was made.

(b) After any suspension of play, the umpires, unaccompanied by any of the players or officials, shall, on their own initiative, carry out an inspection immediately the conditions improve and shall continue to inspect at intervals. Immediately the umpires decide that play is possible they shall call upon the players to resume the game.

9. Exceptional Circumstances

In exceptional circumstances, other than those of weather, ground or light, the umpires may decide to suspend or abandon play. Before making such a decision the umpires shall establish, if the circumstances allow, whether both captains (the batsmen at the wicket may deputise for their captain) wish to continue in the prevailing conditions; if so their wishes shall be met.

10. Position of Umpires

The umpires shall stand where they can best see any act upon which their decision may be required.

Subject to this over-riding consideration, the umpire at the bowler's end shall stand where he does not interfere with either the bowler's run up or the striker's view.

The umpire at the striker's end may elect to stand on the off instead of the leg side of the pitch, provided he informs the captain of the fielding side and the striker of his intention to do so.

11. Umpires Changing Ends

The umpires shall change ends after each side has had one innings.

12. Disputes

All disputes shall be determined by the umpires, and if they disagree the actual state of things shall continue.

13. Signals

The following code of signals shall be used by umpires who will wait until a signal has been answered by a scorer before allowing the game to proceed.

Boundary	– by waving the arm from side to side.
Boundary 6	– by raising both arms above the head.
Bye	– by raising an open hand above the head.
Dead Ball	– by crossing and re-crossing the wrists below the waist.
Leg Bye	– by touching a raised knee with the hand.
No Ball	– by extending one arm horizontally.
Out	– by raising the index finger above the head. If not out, the umpire shall call "not out".
Short run	– by bending the arm upwards and by touching the nearer shoulder with the tips of the fingers.
Wide	– by extending both arms horizontally.

14. Correctness of Scores

The umpires shall be responsible for satisfying themselves on the correctness of the scores throughout and at the conclusion of the match. See Law 21.6 (Correctness of Result).

Notes

(a) Attendance of Umpires
The umpires should be present on the ground and report to the ground executive or the equivalent at least thirty minutes before the start of a day's play.

(b) Consultation between Umpires and Scorers
Consultation between umpires and scorers over doubtful points is essential.

(c) Fitness of Ground
The umpires shall consider the ground as unfit for play when it is so wet or slippery as to deprive the bowlers of a reasonable foothold, the fieldsmen, other than the deep-fielders, of the power of free movement, or the batsmen of the ability to play their strokes or to run between the wickets. Play should not be suspended merely because the grass and the ball are wet and slippery.

(d) Fitness of Weather and Light
The umpires should suspend play only when they consider that the conditions are so bad that it is unreasonable or dangerous to continue.

LAW 4.   THE SCORERS

1. Recording Runs

All runs scored shall be recorded by scorers appointed for the purpose. Where there are two scorers they shall frequently check to ensure that the score sheets agree.

2. Acknowledging Signals

The scorers shall accept and immediately acknowledge all instructions and signals given to them by the umpires.

LAW 5. THE BALL

1. Weight and Size

The ball, when new, shall weigh not less than $5\frac{1}{2}$ ounces/155.9g, nor more than $5\frac{3}{4}$ ounces/163g; and shall measure not less than $8\frac{13}{16}$ inches/22.4cm, nor more than 9 inches/22.9cm in circumference.

2. Approval of Balls

All balls used in matches shall be approved by the umpires and captains before the start of the match.

3. New Ball

Subject to agreement to the contrary, having been made before the toss, either captain may demand a new ball at the start of each innings.

4. New Ball in Match of Three of More Days Duration

In a match of three or more days duration, the captain of the fielding side may demand a new ball after the prescribed number of overs has been bowled with the old one. The Governing Body for cricket in the country concerned shall decide the number of overs applicable in that country, which shall be not less than 75 six-ball overs (55 eight-ball overs).

5. Ball Lost or Becoming Unfit for Play

In the event of a ball during play being lost or, in the opinion of the umpires, becoming unfit for play, the umpires shall allow it to be replaced by one that in their opinion has had a similar amount of wear. If a ball is to be replaced, the umpires shall inform the batsman.

Note

    (a) Specifications

    The specifications, as described in 1 above, shall apply to top-grade balls only. The following degrees of tolerance will be acceptable for other grades of ball.

        (i) *Men's Grades 2–4*
        Weight: $5\frac{5}{16}$ ounces/150g to $5\frac{13}{16}$ ounces/165g.
        Size: $8\frac{11}{16}$ inches/22.0cm to $9\frac{1}{16}$ inches/23.0cm.

        (ii) *Women's*
        Weight: $4\frac{15}{16}$ ounces/140g to $5\frac{5}{16}$ ounces/150g.
        Size: $8\frac{1}{4}$ inches/21.0 cm to $8\frac{7}{8}$ inches/22.5cm.

        (iii) *Junior*
        Weight: $4\frac{5}{16}$ ounces/133g to $5\frac{1}{16}$ ounces/143g.
        Size: $8\frac{1}{16}$ inches/20.5cm to $8\frac{11}{16}$ inches/22.0cm.

LAW 6. THE BAT

1. Width and Length

The bat overall shall not be more than 38 inches/96.5cm in length; the blade of the bat shall be made of wood and shall not exceed $4\frac{1}{4}$ inches/10.8cm at the widest part.

Note

    (a) The blade of the bat may be covered with material for protection, strengthening or repair. Such material shall not exceed $\frac{1}{16}$ inch/1.56mm in thickness.

LAW 7.   THE PITCH

1. Area of Pitch

The pitch is the area between the bowling creases – see Law 9 (The Bowling and Popping Creases). It shall measure 5ft/1.52m in width on either side of a line joining the centre of the middle stumps of the wickets – see Law 8 (The Wickets).

2. Selection and Preparation

Before the toss for innings, the executive of the ground shall be responsible for the selection and preparation of the pitch; thereafter the umpires shall control its use and maintenance.

3. Changing Pitch

The pitch shall not be changed during a match unless it becomes unfit for play, and then only with the consent of both captains.

4. Non-Turf Pitches

In the event of a non-turf pitch being used, the following shall apply:

> (a) Length: That of the playing surface to a minimum of 58ft/17.68m.
>
> (b) Width: That of the playing surface to a minimum of 6ft/1.83m.

See Law 10 (Rolling, Sweeping, Mowing, Watering the Pitch and Re-marking of Creases) Note (a).

LAW 8.   THE WICKETS

1. Width and Pitching

Two sets of wickets, each 9 inches/22.86cm wide, and consisting of three wooden stumps with two wooden bails upon the top, shall be pitched opposite and parallel to each other at a distance of 22 yards/20.12m between the centres of the two middle stumps.

2. Size of Stumps

The stumps shall be of equal and sufficient size to prevent the ball from passing between them. Their tops shall be 28 inches/71.1cm above the ground, and shall be dome-shaped except for the bail grooves.

3. Size of Bails

The bails shall be each 4⅜ inches/11.1cm in length and when in position on the top of the stumps shall not project more than ½ inch/1.3cm above them.

Notes

> **(a) Dispensing with Bails**
> In a high wind the umpires may decide to dispense with the use of bails.
>
> **(b) Junior Cricket**
> For junior cricket, as defined by the local Governing Body, the following measurements for the wickets shall apply:
>
> > Width   – 8 inches/20.32cm.
> > Pitched – 21 yards/19.20m.
> > Height – 27 inches/68.58cm.
> > Bails   – each 3⅞ inches/9.84cm in length and should not project more than ½ inch/1.3cm above the wickets.

LAW 9.   THE BOWLING, POPPING AND RETURN CREASES

1. The Bowling Crease

The bowling crease shall be marked in line with the stumps at each end and shall be 8 feet 8 inches/2.64m in length, with the stumps in the centre.

2. The Popping Crease

The popping crease, which is the back edge of the crease marking, shall be in front of and parallel with the bowling crease. It shall have the back edge of the crease marking 4 feet/1.22m from the centre of the stumps and shall extend to a minimum of 6 feet/1.83m on either side of the line of the wicket.

The popping crease shall be considered to be unlimited in length.

3. The Return Crease

The return crease marking, of which the inside edge is the crease, shall be at each end of the bowling crease and at right angles to it. The return crease shall be marked to a minimum of 4 feet/1.22m behind the wicket and shall be considered to be unlimited in length. A forward extension shall be marked to the popping crease.

LAW 10.   ROLLING, SWEEPING, MOWING, WATERING THE PITCH AND RE-MARKING OF CREASES

1. Rolling

During the match the pitch may be rolled at the request of the captain of the batting side, for a period of not more than seven minutes before the start of each innings, other than the first innings of the match, and before the start of each day's play. In addition, if, after the toss and before the first innings of the match, the start is delayed, the captain of the batting side shall have the right to have the pitch rolled for not more than seven minutes.

The pitch shall not otherwise be rolled during the match.

The seven minutes rolling permitted before the start of a day's play shall take place not earlier than half an hour before the start of play and the captain of the batting side may delay such rolling until ten minutes before the start of play should he so desire.

If a captain declares an innings closed less than fifteen minutes before the resumption of play, and the other captain is thereby prevented from exercising his option of seven minutes rolling or if he is so prevented for any other reason, the time for rolling shall be taken out of the normal playing time.

2. Sweeping

Such sweeping of the pitch as is necessary during the match shall be done so that the seven minutes allowed for rolling the pitch, provided for in 1 above, is not affected.

3. Mowing

(a) Responsibilities of Ground Authority and of Umpires
All mowings which are carried out before the toss for innings shall be the responsibility of the ground authority; thereafter they shall be carried out under the supervision of the umpires. See Law 7.2 (Selection and Preparation).

(b) Initial Mowing
The pitch shall be mown before play begins on the day the match is scheduled to start, or in the case of a delayed start on the day the match is expected to start. See 3(a) above (Responsibilities of Ground Authority and of Umpires).

(c) Subsequent Mowings in a Match of Two or More Days' Duration
In a match of two or more days' duration, the pitch shall be mown daily before play begins. Should this mowing not take place because of weather conditions, rest days or other reasons, the pitch shall be mown on the first day on which the match is resumed.

(d) Mowing of the Outfield in a Match of Two or More Days' Duration
In order to ensure that conditions are as similar as possible for both sides, the outfield shall normally be mown before the commencement of play on each day of the match, if ground and weather conditions allow. See Note (b) to this Law.

4. Watering

The pitch shall not be watered during a match.

5. Re-Marking Creases

Whenever possible the creases shall be re-marked.

6. Maintenance of Foot-Holes

In wet weather, the umpires shall ensure that the holes made by the bowlers and batsmen are cleaned out and dried whenever necessary to facilitate play. In matches of two or more days' duration, the umpires shall allow, if necessary, the re-turfing of foot-holes made by the bowler in his delivery stride, or the use of quick-setting fillings for the same purpose, before the start of each day's play.

7. Securing of Footholds and Maintenance of Pitch

During play, the umpires shall allow either batsman to beat the pitch with his bat and players to secure their footholds by the use of sawdust, provided that no damage to the pitch is so caused, and Law 42 (Unfair Play) is not contravened.

Notes

(a) Non-Turf Pitches
The above Law 10 applies to turf pitches.
  The game is played on non-turf pitches in many countries at various levels. Whilst the conduct of the game on these surfaces should always be in accordance with the Laws of Cricket, it is recognised that it may sometimes be necessary for Governing Bodies to lay down special playing conditions to suit the type of non-turf pitch used in their country.
  In matches played against touring teams, any special playing conditions should be agreed in advance by both parties.

(b) Mowing of the Outfield in a Match of Two or More Days' Duration
If, for reasons other than ground and weather conditions, daily and complete mowing is not possible, the ground authority shall notify the captains and umpires, before the toss for innings, of the procedure to be adopted for such mowing during the match.

(c) Choice of Roller
If there is more than one roller available, the captain of the batting side shall have a choice.

LAW 11.   COVERING THE PITCH

1. Before the Start of a Match

Before the start of a match, complete covering of the pitch shall be allowed.

2. During a Match

The pitch shall not be completely covered during a match unless prior arrangement or regulations so provide.

3. Covering Bowlers' Run-up

Whenever possible, the bowlers' run-up shall be covered, but the covers so used shall not extend further than 4 feet/1.22m in front of the popping crease.

Note

(a) **Removal of Covers**
The covers should be removed as promptly as possible whenever the weather permits.

LAW 12.   INNINGS

1. Number of Innings

A match shall be of one or two innings of each side according to agreement reached before the start of play.

2. Alternate Innings

In a two innings match each side shall take their innings alternately except in the case provided for in Law 13 (The Follow-On).

3. The Toss

The captains shall toss for the choice of innings on the field of play not later than fifteen minutes before the time scheduled for the match to start, or before the time agreed upon for play to start.

4. Choice of Innings

The winner of the toss shall notify his decision to bat or to field to the opposing captain not later than ten minutes before the time scheduled for the match to start, or before the time agreed upon for play to start. The decision shall not thereafter be altered.

5. Continuation after One Innings of Each Side

Despite the terms of 1 above, in a one-innings match, when a result has been reached on the first innings, the captains may agree to the continuation of play if, in their opinion, there is a prospect of carrying the game to a further issue in the time left. See Law 21 (Result).

Notes

(a) **Limited Innings – One-Innings Match**
In a one-innings match, each innings may, by agreement, be limited by a number of overs or by a period of time.

(b) **Limited Innings – Two-Innings Match**
In a two-innings match, the first innings of each side may, by agreement, be limited to a number of overs or by a period of time.

LAW 13.   THE FOLLOW-ON

1. Lead on First Innings

In a two-innings match the side which bats first and leads by 200 runs in a match of five days or more, by 150 runs in a three-day or four-day match, by 100 runs in a two-day match, or by 75 runs in a one-day match, shall have the option of requiring the other side to follow their innings.

2. Day's Play Lost

If no play takes place on the first day of a match of two or more days' duration, 1 above shall apply in accordance with the number of days' play remaining from the actual start of the match.

LAW 14.   DECLARATIONS

1. Time of Declaration

The captain of the batting side may declare an innings closed at any time during a match, irrespective of its duration.

2. Forfeiture of Second Innings

A captain may forfeit his second innings, provided his decision to do so is notified to the opposing captain and umpires in sufficient time to allow seven minutes rolling of the pitch. See Law 10 (Rolling, Sweeping, Mowing, Watering the Pitch and Re-Marking of Creases). The normal ten minute interval between innings shall be applied.

LAW 15.   START OF PLAY

1. Call of Play

At the start of each innings and of each day's play, and on the resumption of play after any interval or interruption, the umpire at the bowler's end shall call "play".

2. Practice on the Field

At no time on any day of the match shall there be any bowling or batting practice on the pitch.
 No practice may take place on the field if, in the opinion of the umpires, it could result in a waste of time.

3. Trial Run-Up

No bowler shall have a trial run-up after "play" has been called in any session of play, except at the fall of a wicket when an umpire may allow such a trial run-up if he is satisfied that it will not cause any waste of time.

LAW 16.   INTERVALS

1. Length

The umpire shall allow such intervals as have been agreed upon for meals, and ten minutes between each innings.

2. Luncheon Interval – Innings Ending or Stoppage within Ten Minutes of Interval

If an innings ends or there is a stoppage caused by weather or bad light within ten minutes of the agreed time for the luncheon interval, the interval shall be taken immediately.
 The time remaining in the session of play shall be added to the agreed length of the interval but no extra allowance shall be made for the ten minute interval between innings.

3. Tea Interval – Innings Ending or Stoppage within Thirty Minutes of Interval

If an innings ends or there is a stoppage caused by weather or bad light within thirty minutes of the agreed time for the tea interval, the interval shall be taken immediately.
 The interval shall be of the agreed length and, if applicable, shall include the ten-minute interval between innings.

4. Tea Interval – Continuation of Play

If, at the agreed time for the tea interval, nine wickets are down, play shall continue for a period not exceeding thirty minutes or until the innings is concluded.

5. Tea Interval – Agreement to Forego

At any time during the match, the captains may agree to forego a tea interval.

6. Intervals for Drinks

If both captains agree before the start of a match that intervals for drinks may be taken, the option to take such intervals shall be available to either side. These intervals shall be restricted to one per session, shall be kept as short as possible, shall not be taken in the last hour of the match, and in any case shall not exceed five minutes.

The agreed times for these intervals shall be strictly adhered to, except that if a wicket falls within five minutes of the agreed time then drinks shall be taken out immediately.

If an innings ends or there is a stoppage caused by weather or bad light within thirty minutes of the agreed time for a drinks interval, there will be no interval for drinks in that session.

At any time during the match the captains may agree to forego any such drinks interval.

Notes

(a) Tea Interval – One-Day Match
In a one-day match, a specific time for the tea interval need not necessarily be arranged, and it may be agreed to take this interval between the innings of a one-innings match.

(b) Changing the Agreed Time of Intervals
In the event of the ground, weather or light conditions causing a suspension of play, the umpires, after consultation with the captains, may decide in the interests of time-saving to bring forward the time of the luncheon or tea interval.

LAW 17.   CESSATION OF PLAY

1. Call of Time

The umpire at the bowler's end shall call "time" on the cessation of play before any interval or interruption of play, at the end of each day's play, and at the conclusion of the match. See Law 27 (Appeals).

2. Removal of Bails

After the call of "time", the umpires shall remove the bails from both wickets.

3. Starting a Last Over

The last over before an interval or the close of play shall be started provided the umpire, after walking at his normal pace, has arrived at his position behind the stumps at the bowler's end before time has been reached.

4. Completion of the Last Over of a Session

The last over before an interval or the close of play shall be completed unless a batsman is out or retires during that over within two minutes of the interval or the close of play or unless the players have occasion to leave the field.

5. Completion of the Last Over of a Match

An over in progress at the close of play on the final day of a match shall be completed at the request of either captain, even if a wicket fall after time has been reached.

If, during the last over, the players have occasion to leave the field, the umpires shall call "time" and there shall be no resumption of play and the match shall be at an end.

6. Last Hour of Match – Number of Overs

The umpires shall indicate when one hour of playing time of the match remains according to the agreed hours of play. The next over after that moment shall be the first of a minimum of 20 six-ball overs (15 eight-ball overs), provided a result is not reached earlier or there is no interval or interruption of play.

7. Last Hour of Match – Intervals between Innings and Interruptions of Play

If, at the commencement of the last hour of the match, an interval or interruption of play is in progress or if, during the last hour, there is an interval between innings or an interruption of play, the minimum number of overs to be bowled on the resumption of play shall be reduced in proportion to the duration, within the last hour of the match, of any such interval or interruption.

The minimum number of overs to be bowled after the resumption of play shall be calculated as follows:

(a) In the case of an interval or interruption of play being in progress at the commencement of the last hour of the match, or in the case of a first interval or interruption, a deduction shall be made from the minimum of 20 six-ball overs (or 15 eight-ball overs).

(b) If there is a later interval or interruption, a further deduction shall be made from the minimum number of overs which should have been bowled following the last resumption of play.

(c) These deductions shall be based on the following factors:

(i) The number of overs already bowled in the last hour of the match or, in the case of a later interval or interruption, in the last session of play.

(ii) The number of overs lost as a result of the interval or interruption allowing one six-ball over for every full three minutes (or one eight-ball over for every full four minutes) of interval or interruption.

(iii) Any over left uncompleted at the end of an innings to be excluded from these calculations.

(iv) Any over left uncompleted at the start of an interruption of play to be completed when play is resumed and to count as one over bowled.

(v) An interval to start with the end of an innings and to end ten minutes later; an interruption to start on the call of "time" and to end on the call of "play".

(d) In the event of an innings being completed and a new innings commencing during the last hour of the match, the number of overs to be bowled in the new innings shall be calculated on the basis of one six-ball over for every three minutes or part thereof remaining for play (or one eight-ball over for every four minutes or part thereof remaining for play); or alternatively on the basis that sufficient overs are bowled to enable the full minimum quota of overs to be completed under circumstances governed by (a), (b) and (c) above. In all such cases the alternative which allows the greater number of overs shall be employed.

8. Bowler Unable to Complete an Over during Last Hour of the Match

If, for any reason, a bowler is unable to complete an over during the period of play referred to in 6 above, Law 22.7 (Bowler Incapacitated or Suspended during an Over) shall apply.

LAW 18.   SCORING

1. A Run

The score shall be reckoned by runs. A run is scored:

(a) So often as the batsmen, after a hit or at any time while the ball is in play, shall have crossed and made good their ground from end to end.

(b) When a boundary is scored. See Law 19 (Boundaries).

(c) When penalty runs are awarded. See 6 below.

2. Short Runs

(a) If either batsman runs a short run, the umpire shall call and signal "one short" as soon as the ball becomes dead and that run shall not be scored. A run is short if a batsman fails to make good his ground on turning for a further run.

(b) Although a short run shortens the succeeding one, the latter, if completed shall count.

(c) If either or both batsmen deliberately run short the umpire shall, as soon as he sees that the fielding side have no chance of dismissing either batsman, call and signal "dead ball" and disallow any runs attempted or previously scored. The batsmen shall return to their original ends.

(d) If both batsmen run short in one and the same run, only one run shall be deducted.

(e) Only if 3 or more runs are attempted can more than one be short and then, subject to (c) and (d) above, all runs so called shall be disallowed. If there has been more than one short run the umpires shall instruct the scorers as to the number of runs disallowed.

3. Striker Caught

If the striker is caught, no run shall be scored.

4. Batsman Run Out

If a batsman is run out, only that run which was being attempted shall not be scored. If, however, an injured striker himself is run out, no runs shall be scored. See Law 2.7 (Transgression of the Laws by an Injured Batsman or Runner).

5. Batsman Obstructing the Field

If a batsman is out Obstructing the Field, any runs completed before the obstruction occurs shall be scored unless such obstruction prevents a catch being made, in which case no runs shall be scored.

6. Runs Scored for Penalties

Runs shall be scored for penalties under Laws 20 (Lost Ball), 24 (No Ball), 25 (Wide Ball), 41.1 (Fielding the Ball) and for boundary allowances under Law 19 (Boundaries).

7. Batsman Returning to Wicket he has Left

If, while the ball is in play, the batsmen have crossed in running, neither shall return to the wicket he has left, even though a short run has been called or no run has been scored as in the case of a catch. Batsmen, however, shall return to the wickets they originally left, in the cases of a boundary and of any disallowance of runs and of an injured batsman being, himself, run out. See Law 2.7 (Transgression by an Injured Batsman or Runner).

Note

(a) Short Run

A striker taking stance in front of his popping crease may run from that point without penalty.

LAW 19.   BOUNDARIES

1. The Boundary of the Playing Area

Before the toss for innings, the umpires shall agree with both captains on the boundary of the playing area. The boundary shall, if possible, be marked by a white line, a rope laid on the ground, or a fence. If flags or posts only are used to mark a boundary, the imaginary line joining such points shall be regarded as the boundary. An obstacle, or person, within the playing area shall not be regarded as a boundary unless so decided by the umpires before the toss for innings. Sight-screens within, or partially within, the playing area shall be regarded as the boundary and when the ball strikes or passes within or under or directly over any part of the screen, a boundary shall be scored.

2. Runs Scored for Boundaries

Before the toss for innings, the umpires shall agree with both captains the runs to be allowed for boundaries, and in deciding the allowance for them, the umpires and captains shall be guided by the prevailing custom of the ground. The allowance for a boundary shall normally be 4 runs, and 6 runs for all hits pitching over and clear of the boundary line or fence, even though the ball has been previously touched by a fieldsman. 6 runs shall also be scored if a fieldsman, after catching a ball, carries it over the boundary. See Law 32 (Caught) Note (a). 6 runs shall not be scored when a ball struck by the striker hits a sight-screen full pitch if the screen is within, or partially within, the playing area, but if the ball is struck directly over a sight-screen so situated, 6 runs shall be scored.

3. A Boundary

A boundary shall be scored and signalled by the umpire at the bowler's end whenever, in his opinion:

    (a) A ball in play touches or crosses the boundary, however marked.

    (b) A fieldsman with ball in hand touches or grounds any part of his person on or over a boundary line.

    (c) A fieldsman with ball in hand grounds any part of his person over a boundary fence or board. This allows the fieldsman to touch or lean on or over a boundary fence or board in preventing a boundary.

4. Runs Exceeding Boundary Allowance

The runs completed at the instant the ball reaches the boundary shall count if they exceed the boundary allowance.

5. Overthrows or Wilful Act of a Fieldsman

If the boundary results from an overthrow or from the wilful act of a fieldsman, any runs already completed and the allowance shall be added to the score. The run in progress shall count provided that the batsmen have crossed at the instant of the throw or act.

Note

    (a) Position of Sight-Screens
    Sight-screens should, if possible, be positioned wholly outside the playing area, as near as possible to the boundary line.

LAW 20.   LOST BALL

1. Runs Scored

If a ball in play cannot be found or recovered, any fieldsman may call "lost ball" when 6 runs shall be added to the score; but if more than 6 have been run before "lost ball" is called, as many runs as have been completed shall be scored. The run in progress shall count provided that the batsmen have crossed at the instant of the call of "lost ball".

2. How Scored

The runs shall be added to the score of the striker if the ball has been struck, but otherwise to the score of byes, leg-byes, no balls or wides as the case may be.

LAW 21.   THE RESULT

1. A Win – Two-Innings Matches

The side which has scored a total of runs in excess of that scored by the opposing side in its two completed innings shall be the winners.

2. A Win – One-Innings Matches

(a) One-innings matches, unless played out as in 1 above, shall be decided on the first innings, but see Law 12.5 (Continuation after One Innings of Each Side).

(b) If the captains agree to continue play after the completion of one innings of each side in accordance with Law 12.5 (Continuation after One Innings of Each Side) and a result is not achieved on the second innings, the first innings result shall stand.

3. Umpires Awarding a Match

(a) A match shall be lost by a side which, during the match, (i) refuses to play, or (ii) concedes defeat, and the umpires shall award the match to the other side.

(b) Should both batsmen at the wickets or the fielding side leave the field at any time without the agreement of the umpires, this shall constitute a refusal to play and, on appeal, the umpires shall award the match to the other side in accordance with (a) above.

4. A Tie

The result of a match shall be a tie when the scores are equal at the conclusion of play, but only if the side batting last has completed its innings.

   If the scores of the completed first innings of a one-day match are equal, it shall be a tie but only if the match has not been played out to a further conclusion.

5. A Draw

A match not determined in any of the ways as in 1, 2, 3 and 4 above shall count as a draw.

6. Correctness of Result

Any decision as to the correctness of the scores shall be the responsibility of the umpires. See Law 3.14 (Correctness of Scores).

   If, after the umpires and players have left the field in the belief that the match has been concluded, the umpires decide that a mistake in scoring has occurred, which affects the result, and provided time has not been reached, they shall order play to resume and to continue until the agreed finishing time unless a result is reached earlier.

   If the umpires decide that a mistake has occurred and time has been reached, the umpires shall immediately inform both captains of the necessary corrections to the scores and, if applicable, to the result.

7. Acceptance of Result

In accepting the scores as notified by the scorers and agreed by the umpires, the captains of both sides thereby accept the result.

Notes

(a) **Statement of Results**
   The result of a finished match is stated as a win by runs, except in the case of a win by the side batting last when it is by the number of wickets still then to fall.

(b) Winning Hit or Extras

As soon as the side has won, see 1 and 2 above, the umpire shall call "time", the match is finished, and nothing that happens thereafter other than as a result of a mistake in scoring (see 6 above) shall be regarded as part of the match.

However, if a boundary constitutes the winning hit – or extras – and the boundary allowance exceeds the number of runs required to win the match, such runs scored shall be credited to the side's total and, in the case of a hit, to the striker's score.

LAW 22.   THE OVER

1. Number of Balls

The ball shall be bowled from each wicket alternately in overs of either six or eight balls according to agreement before the match.

2. Call of "Over"

When the agreed number of balls has been bowled, and as the ball becomes dead or when it becomes clear to the umpire at the bowler's end that both the fielding side and the batsmen at the wicket have ceased to regard the ball as in play, the umpire shall call "over" before leaving the wicket.

3. No Ball or Wide Ball

Neither a no ball nor a wide ball shall be reckoned as one of the over.

4. Umpire Miscounting

If an umpire miscounts the number of balls, the over as counted by the umpire shall stand.

5. Bowler Changing Ends

A bowler shall be allowed to change ends as often as desired, provided only that he does not bowl two overs consecutively in an innings.

6. The Bowler Finishing an Over

A bowler shall finish an over in progress unless he be incapacitated or be suspended under Law 42.8 (The Bowling of Fast Short-Pitched Balls), 9 (The Bowling of Fast High Full Pitches), 10 (Time Wasting) and 11 (Players Damaging the Pitch). If an over is left incomplete for any reason at the start of an interval or interruption of play, it shall be finished on the resumption of play.

7. Bowler Incapacitated or Suspended during an Over

If, for any reason, a bowler is incapacitated while running up to bowl the first ball of an over, or is incapacitated or suspended during an over, the umpire shall call and signal "dead ball" and another bowler shall be allowed to bowl or complete the over from the same end, provided only that he shall not bowl two overs, or part thereof, consecutively in one innings.

8. Position of Non-Striker

The batsman at the bowler's end shall normally stand on the opposite side of the wicket to that from which the ball is being delivered, unless a request to do otherwise is granted by the umpire.

LAW 23.   DEAD BALL

1. The Ball Becomes Dead

When:

(a) It is finally settled in the hands of the wicket-keeper or the bowler.

(b) It reaches or pitches over the boundary.

(c) A batsman is out.

(d) Whether played or not, it lodges in the clothing or equipment of a batsman or the clothing of an umpire.

(e) A ball lodges in a protective helmet worn by a member of the fielding side.

(f) A penalty is awarded under Law 20 (Lost Ball) or Law 41.1 (Fielding the Ball).

(g) The umpire calls "over" or "time".

2. Either Umpire Shall Call and Signal "Dead Ball"

When:

(a) He intervenes in a case of unfair play.

(b) A serious injury to a player or umpire occurs.

(c) He is satisfied that, for an adequate reason, the striker is not ready to receive the ball and makes no attempt to play it.

(d) The bowler drops the ball accidentally before delivery, or the ball does not leave his hand for any reason.

(e) One or both bails fall from the striker's wicket before he receives delivery.

(f) He leaves his normal position for consultation.

(g) He is required to do so under Law 26.3 (Disallowance of Leg Byes).

3. The Ball Ceases to be Dead

When:

(a) The bowler starts his run-up or bowling action.

4. The Ball is Not Dead

When:

(a) It strikes an umpire (unless it lodges in his dress).

(b) The wicket is broken or struck down (unless a batsman is out thereby).

(c) An unsuccessful appeal is made.

(d) The wicket is broken accidentally either by the bowler during his delivery or by a batsman in running.

(e) The umpire has called "no ball" or "wide".

Notes

(a) Ball Finally Settled
Whether the ball is finally settled or not – see 1(a) above – must be a question for the umpires alone to decide.

(b) Action on Call of "Dead Ball"
(i) If "dead ball" is called prior to the striker receiving a delivery, the bowler shall be allowed an additional ball.

(ii) If "dead ball" is called after the striker receives a delivery, the bowler shall not be allowed an additional ball, unless a "no ball" or "wide" has been called.

LAW 24.   NO BALL

1. Mode of Delivery

The umpire shall indicate to the striker whether the bowler intends to bowl over or round the wicket, overarm or underarm, right or left-handed. Failure on the part of the bowler to indicate in advance a change in his mode of delivery is unfair and the umpire shall call and signal "no ball".

2. Fair Delivery – The Arm

For a delivery to be fair the ball must be bowled, not thrown – see Note (a) below. If either umpire is not entirely satisfied with the absolute fairness of a delivery in this respect he shall call and signal "no ball" instantly upon delivery.

3. Fair Delivery – The Feet

The umpire at the bowler's wicket shall call and signal "no ball" if he is not satisfied that in the delivery stride:

(a) The bowler's back foot has landed within and not touching the return crease or its forward extension; or

(b) Some part of the front foot whether grounded or raised was behind the popping crease.

4. Bowler Throwing at Striker's Wicket before Delivery

If the bowler, before delivering the ball, throws it at the striker's wicket in an attempt to run him out, the umpire shall call and signal "no ball". See Law 42.12 (Batsman Unfairly Stealing a Run) and Law 38 (Run Out).

5. Bowler Attempting to Run Out Non-Striker before Delivery

If the bowler, before delivering the ball, attempts to run out the non-striker, any runs which result shall be allowed and shall be scored as no balls. Such an attempt shall not count as a ball in the over. The umpire shall not call "no ball". See Law 42.12 (Batsman Unfairly Stealing a Run).

6. Infringement of Laws by a Wicket-Keeper or a Fieldsman

The umpire shall call and signal "no ball" in the event of the wicket-keeper infringing Law 40.1 (Position of Wicket-Keeper) or a fieldsman infringing Law 41.2 (Limitation of On-side Fieldsmen) or Law 41.3 (Position of Fieldsmen).

7. Revoking a Call

An umpire shall revoke the call "no ball" if the ball does not leave the bowler's hand for any reason. See Law 23.2 (Either Umpire Shall Call and Signal "Dead Ball").

8. Penalty

A penalty of 1 run for a no ball shall be scored if no runs are made otherwise.

9. Runs from a No Ball

The striker may hit a no ball and whatever runs result shall be added to his score. Runs made otherwise from a no ball shall be scored no balls.

10. Out from a No Ball

The striker shall be out from a no ball if he breaks Law 34 (Hit the Ball Twice) and either batsman may be run out or shall be given out if either breaks Law 33 (Handled the Ball) or Law 37 (Obstructing the Field).

11. Batsman Given Out off a No Ball

Should a batsman be given out off a no ball the penalty for bowling it shall stand unless runs are otherwise scored.

Notes

(a) Definition of a Throw

A ball shall be deemed to have been thrown if, in the opinion of either umpire, the process of straightening the bowling arm, whether it be partial or complete, takes place during that part of the delivery swing which directly precedes the ball leaving the hand. This definition shall not debar a bowler from the use of the wrist in the delivery swing.

(b) No Ball Not Counting in Over

A no ball shall not be reckoned as one of the over. See Law 22.3 (No Ball or Wide Ball).

LAW 25.   WIDE BALL

1. Judging a Wide

If the bowler bowls the ball so high over or so wide of the wicket that, in the opinion of the umpire, it passes out of the reach of the striker, standing in a normal guard position, the umpire shall call and signal "wide ball" as soon as it has passed the line of the striker's wicket.

The umpire shall not adjudge a ball as being a wide if:

(a) The striker, by moving from his guard position, causes the ball to pass out of his reach.

(b) The striker moves and thus brings the ball within his reach.

2. Penalty

A penalty of 1 run for a wide shall be scored if no runs are made otherwise.

3. Ball Coming to Rest in Front of the Striker

If a ball which the umpire considers to have been delivered comes to rest in front of the line of the striker's wicket, "wide" shall not be called. The striker has a right, without interference from the fielding side, to make one attempt to hit the ball. If the fielding side interfere, the umpire shall replace the ball where it came to rest and shall order the fieldsmen to resume the places they occupied in the field before the ball was delivered.

The umpire shall call and signal "dead ball" as soon as it is clear that the striker does not intend to hit the ball, or after the striker has made an unsuccessful attempt to hit the ball.

4. Revoking a Call

The umpire shall revoke the call if the striker hits a ball which has been called "wide".

5. Ball Not Dead

The ball does not become dead on the call of "wide ball" – see Law 23.4 (The Ball is Not Dead).

6. Runs Resulting from a Wide

All runs which are run or result from a wide ball which is not a no ball shall be scored wide balls, or if no runs are made 1 shall be scored.

7. Out from a Wide

The striker shall be out from a wide ball if he breaks Law 35 (Hit Wicket), or Law 39 (Stumped). Either batsman may be run out and shall be out if he breaks Law 33 (Handled the Ball), or Law 37 (Obstructing the Field). .

8. Batsman Given Out off a Wide

Should a batsman be given out off a wide, the penalty for bowling it shall stand unless runs are otherwise made.

Note

(a) **Wide Ball Not Counting in Over**
A wide ball shall not be reckoned as one of the over – see Law 22.3 (No Ball or Wide Ball).

LAW 26.   BYE AND LEG-BYE

1. Byes

If the ball, not having been called "wide" or "no ball", passes the striker without touching his bat or person, and any runs are obtained, the umpire shall signal "bye" and the run or runs shall be credited as such to the batting side.

2. Leg-Byes

If the ball, not having been called "wide" or "no ball", is unintentionally deflected by the striker's dress or person, except a hand holding the bat, and any runs are obtained the umpire shall signal "leg-bye" and the run or runs so scored shall be credited as such to the batting side.
  Such leg-byes shall be scored only if, in the opinion of the umpire, the striker has:

(a) Attempted to play the ball with his bat; or

(b) Tried to avoid being hit by the ball.

3. Disallowance of Leg-Byes

In the case of a deflection by the striker's person, other than in 2(a) and (b) above, the umpire shall call and signal "dead ball" as soon as one run has been completed or when it is clear that a run is not being attempted, or the ball has reached the boundary.
  On the call and signal of "dead ball" the batsmen shall return to their original ends and no runs shall be allowed.

LAW 27.   APPEALS

1. Time of Appeals

The umpires shall not give a batsman out unless appealed to by the other side which shall be done prior to the bowler beginning his run-up or bowling action to deliver the next ball. Under Law 23.1 (f) (The Ball Becomes Dead), the ball is dead on "over" being called; this does not, however, invalidate an appeal made prior to the first ball of the following over provided "time" has not been called – see Law 17.1 (Call of Time).

2. An Appeal "How's That?"

An appeal "How's That?" shall cover all ways of being out.

3. Answering Appeals

The umpire at the bowler's wicket shall answer appeals before the other umpire in all cases except those arising out of Law 35 (Hit Wicket) or Law 39 (Stumped) or Law 38 (Run Out) when this occurs at the striker's wicket.

When either umpire has given a batsman not out, the other umpire shall, within his jurisdiction, answer the appeal on a further appeal, provided it is made in time in accordance with 1 above (Time of Appeals).

4. Consultation by Umpires

An umpire may consult with the other umpire on a point of fact which the latter may have been in a better position to see and shall then give his decision. If, after consultation, there is still doubt remaining the decision shall be in favour of the batsman.

5. Batsman Leaving his Wicket under a Misapprehension

The umpires shall intervene if satisfied that a batsman, not having been given out, has left his wicket under a misapprehension that he has been dismissed.

6. Umpire's Decision

The umpire's decision is final. He may alter his decision, provided that such alteration is made promptly.

7. Withdrawal of an Appeal

In exceptional circumstances the captain of the fielding side may seek permission of the umpire to withdraw an appeal provided the outgoing batsman has not left the playing area. If this is allowed, the umpire shall cancel his decision.

LAW 28.   THE WICKET IS DOWN

1. Wicket Down

The wicket is down if:

(a) Either the ball or the striker's bat or person completely removes either bail from the top of the stumps. A disturbance of a bail, whether temporary or not, shall not constitute a complete removal, but the wicket is down if a bail in falling lodges between two of the stumps.

(b) Any player completely removes with his hand or arm a bail from the top of the stumps, provided that the ball is held in that hand or in the hand of the arm so used.

(c) When both bails are off, a stump is struck out of the ground by the ball, or a player strikes or pulls a stump out of the ground, provided that the ball is held in the hand(s) or in the hand of the arm so used.

2. One Bail Off

If one bail is off, it shall be sufficient for the purpose of putting the wicket down to remove the remaining bail, or to strike or pull any of the three stumps out of the ground in any of the ways stated in 1 above.

3. All the Stumps Out of the Ground

If all the stumps are out of the ground, the fielding side shall be allowed to put back one or more stumps in order to have an opportunity of putting the wicket down.

4. Dispensing with Bails

If owing to the strength of the wind, it has been agreed to dispense with the bails in accordance with Law 8, Note (a) (Dispensing with Bails), the decision as to when the wicket is down is one for the umpires to decide on the facts before them. In such circumstances and if the umpires so decide, the wicket shall be held to be down even though a stump has not been struck out of the ground.

Note

(a) Remaking the Wicket

If the wicket is broken while the ball is in play, it is not the umpire's duty to remake the wicket until the ball has become dead – see Law 23 (Dead Ball). A member of the fielding side, however, may remake the wicket in such circumstances.

LAW 29.   BATSMAN OUT OF HIS GROUND

1. When out of his Ground

A batsman shall be considered to be out of his ground unless some part of his bat in his hand or of his person is grounded behind the line of the popping crease.

LAW 30.   BOWLED

1. Out Bowled

The striker shall be out *Bowled* if:

> (a) His wicket is bowled down, even if the ball first touches his bat or person.

> (b) He breaks his wicket by hitting or kicking the ball on to it before the completion of a stroke, or as a result of attempting to guard his wicket. See Law 34.1 (Out Hit the Ball Twice).

Note

(a) Out Bowled – Not LBW

The striker is out bowled if the ball is deflected on to his wicket even though a decision against him would be justified under Law 36 (LBW).

LAW 31.   TIMED OUT

1. Out Timed Out

An incoming batsman shall be out *Timed-Out* if he wilfully takes more than two minutes to come in – the two minutes being timed from the moment a wicket falls until the new batsman steps on to the field of play.

If this is not complied with and if the umpire is satisfied that the delay was wilful and if an appeal is made, the new batsman shall be given out by the umpire at the bowler's end.

2. Time to be Added

The time taken by the umpires to investigate the cause of the delay shall be added at the normal close of play.

Notes

(a) Entry in Score-book

The correct entry in the score-book when a batsman is given out under this Law is "timed out", and the bowler does not get credit for the wicket.

(b) Batsmen Crossing on the Field of Play

It is an essential duty of the captains to ensure that the in-going batsman passes the out-going one before the latter leaves the field of play.

LAW 32. CAUGHT

1. Out Caught

The striker shall be out *Caught* if the ball touches his bat or if it touches below the wrist his hand or glove, holding the bat, and is subsequently held by a fieldsman before it touches the ground.

2. A Fair Catch

A catch shall be considered to have been fairly made if:

    (a) The fieldsman is within the field of play throughout the act of making the catch.

        (i) The act of making the catch shall start from the time when the fieldsman first handles the ball and shall end when he both retains complete control over the further disposal of the ball and remains within the field of play.

        (ii) In order to be within the field of play, the fieldsman may not touch or ground any part of his person on or over a boundary line. When the boundary is marked by a fence or board the fieldsman may not ground any part of his person over the boundary fence or board, but may touch or lean over the boundary fence or board in completing the catch.

    (b) The ball is hugged to the body of the catcher or accidentally lodges in his dress or, in the case of the wicket-keeper, in his pads. However, a striker may not be caught if a ball lodges in a protective helmet worn by a fieldsman, in which case the umpire shall call and signal "dead ball". See Law 23 (Dead Ball).

    (c) The ball does not touch the ground even though a hand holding it does so in effecting the catch.

    (d) A fieldsman catches the ball, after it has been lawfully played a second time by the striker, but only if the ball has not touched the ground since being first struck.

    (e) A fieldsman catches the ball after it has touched an umpire, another fieldsman or the other batsman. However, a striker may not be caught if a ball has touched a protective helmet worn by a fieldsman.

    (f) The ball is caught off an obstruction within the boundary provided it has not previously been agreed to regard the obstruction as a boundary.

3. Scoring of Runs

If a striker is caught, no run shall be scored.

Notes

    (a) Scoring from an Attempted Catch
    When a fieldsman carrying the ball touches or grounds any part of his person on or over a boundary marked by a line, 6 runs shall be scored.

    (b) Ball Still in Play
    If a fieldsman releases the ball before he crosses the boundary, the ball will be considered to be still in play and it may be caught by another fieldsman. However, if the original fieldsman returns to the field of play and handles the ball, a catch may not be made.

LAW 33. HANDLED THE BALL

1. Out Handled the Ball

Either batsman on appeal shall be out *Handled the Ball* if he wilfully touches the ball while in play with the hand not holding the bat unless he does so with the consent of the opposite side.

Note

    (a) Entry in Score-book
    The correct entry in the score-book when a batsman is given out under this Law is "handled the ball", and the bowler does not get credit for the wicket.

LAW 34.   HIT THE BALL TWICE

1. Out Hit the Ball Twice

The striker, on appeal, shall be out *Hit the Ball Twice* if, after the ball is struck or is stopped by any part of his person, he wilfully strikes it again with his bat or person except for the sole purpose of guarding his wicket: this he may do with his bat or any part of his person other than his hands, but see Law 37.2 (Obstructing a Ball From Being Caught).

For the purpose of this Law, a hand holding the bat shall be regarded as part of the bat.

2. Returning the Ball to a Fieldsman

The striker, on appeal, shall be out under this Law if, without the consent of the opposite side, he uses his bat or person to return the ball to any of the fielding side.

3. Runs from Ball Lawfully Struck Twice

No runs except those which result from an overthrow or penalty – see Law 41 (The Fieldsman) – shall be scored from a ball lawfully struck twice.

Notes

(a) Entry in Score-book
The correct entry in the score-book when the striker is given out under this Law is "hit the ball twice", and the bowler does not get credit for the wicket.

(b) Runs Credited to the Batsman
Any runs awarded under 3 above as a result of an overthrow or penalty shall be credited to the striker, provided the ball in the first instance has touched the bat, or, if otherwise, as extras.

LAW 35.   HIT WICKET

1. Out Hit Wicket

The striker shall be out *Hit Wicket* if, while the ball is in play:

(a) His wicket is broken with any part of his person, dress, or equipment as a result of any action taken by him in preparing to receive or in receiving a delivery, or in setting off for his first run, immediately after playing, or playing at, the ball.

(b) He hits down his wicket whilst lawfully making a second stroke for the purpose of guarding his wicket within the provisions of Law 34.1 (Out Hit the Ball Twice).

Notes

(a) Not Out Hit Wicket
A batsman is not out under this Law should his wicket be broken in any of the ways referred to in 1(a) above if:

(i) It occurs while he is in the act of running, other than in setting off for his first run immediately after playing at the ball, or while he is avoiding being run out or stumped.

(ii) The bowler after starting his run-up or bowling action does not deliver the ball; in which case the umpire shall immediately call and signal "dead ball".

(iii) It occurs whilst he is avoiding a throw-in at any time.

LAW 36.   LEG BEFORE WICKET

1. Out LBW

The striker shall be out *LBW* in the circumstances set out below:

(a) Striker Attempting to Play the Ball

The striker shall be out LBW if he first intercepts with any part of his person, dress or equipment a fair ball which would have hit the wicket and which has not previously touched his bat or a hand holding the bat, provided that:

   (i) The ball pitched, in a straight line between wicket and wicket or on the off side of the striker's wicket, or in the case of a ball intercepted full pitch would have pitched in a straight line between wicket and wicket; and

   (ii) The point of impact is in a straight line between wicket and wicket, even if above the level of the bails.

(b) Striker Making No Attempt to Play the Ball

The striker shall be out LBW even if the ball is intercepted outside the line of the off stump if, in the opinion of the umpire, he has made no genuine attempt to play the ball with his bat, but has intercepted the ball with some part of his person and if the circumstances set out in (a) above apply.

LAW 37.   OBSTRUCTING THE FIELD

1. Wilful Obstruction

Either batsman, on appeal, shall be out *Obstructing the Field* if he wilfully obstructs the opposite side by word or action.

2. Obstructing a Ball From Being Caught

The striker, on appeal, shall be out should wilful obstruction by either batsman prevent a catch being made.

   This shall apply even though the striker causes the obstruction in lawfully guarding his wicket under the provisions of Law 34. See Law 34.1 (Out Hit the Ball Twice).

Notes

(a) Accidental Obstruction

The umpires must decide whether the obstruction was wilful or not. The accidental interception of a throw-in by a batsman while running does not break this Law.

(b) Entry in Score-book

The correct entry in the score-book when a batsman is given out under this Law is "obstructing the field", and the bowler does not get credit for the wicket.

LAW 38.   RUN OUT

1. Out Run Out

Either batsman shall be out *Run Out* if in running or at any time while the ball is in play – except in the circumstances described in Law 39 (Stumped) – he is out of his ground and his wicket is put down by the opposite side. If, however, a batsman in running makes good his ground he shall not be out run out if he subsequently leaves his ground, in order to avoid injury, and the wicket is put down.

2. "No Ball" Called

If a no ball has been called, the striker shall not be given run out unless he attempts to run.

3. Which Batsman Is Out

If the batsmen have crossed in running, he who runs for the wicket which is put down shall be out; if they have not crossed, he who has left the wicket which is put down shall be out. If a batsman remains in his ground or returns to his ground and the other batsman joins him there, the latter shall be out if his wicket is put down.

4. Scoring of Runs

If a batsman is run out, only that run which is being attempted shall not be scored. If, however, an injured striker himself is run out, no runs shall be scored. See Law 2.7 (Transgression of the Laws by an Injured Batsman or Runner).

Notes

(a) Ball Played on to Opposite Wicket
If the ball is played on to the opposite wicket, neither batsman is liable to be run out unless the ball has been touched by a fieldsman before the wicket is broken.

(b) Entry in Score-book
The correct entry in the score-book when a batsman is given out under this Law is "run out", and the bowler does not get credit for the wicket.

LAW 39.   STUMPED

1. Out Stumped

The striker shall be out *Stumped* if, in receiving the ball, not being a no ball, he is out of his ground otherwise than in attempting a run and the wicket is put down by the wicket-keeper without the intervention of another fieldsman.

2. Action by the Wicket-Keeper

The wicket-keeper may take the ball in front of the wicket in an attempt to stump the striker only if the ball has touched the bat or person of the striker.

Note

(a) Ball Rebounding from Wicket-Keeper's Person
The striker may be out stumped if, in the circumstances stated in 1 above, the wicket is broken by a ball rebounding from the wicket-keeper's person or equipment or is kicked or thrown by the wicket-keeper on to the wicket.

LAW 40.   THE WICKET-KEEPER

1. Position of Wicket-Keeper

The wicket-keeper shall remain wholly behind the wicket until a ball delivered by the bowler touches the bat or person of the striker, or passes the wicket, or until the striker attempts a run.

In the event of the wicket-keeper contravening this Law, the umpire at the striker's end shall call and signal "no ball" at the instant of delivery or as soon as possible thereafter.

2. Restriction on Actions of the Wicket-Keeper

If the wicket-keeper interferes with the striker's right to play the ball and to guard his wicket, the striker shall not be out except under Laws 33 (Handled the Ball), 34 (Hit the Ball Twice), 37 (Obstructing the Field), 38 (Run Out).

3. Interference with the Wicket-Keeper by the Striker

If in the legitimate defence of his wicket, the striker interferes with the wicket-keeper, he shall not be out, except as provided for in Law 37.2 (Obstructing a Ball From Being Caught).

LAW 41. THE FIELDSMAN

1. Fielding the Ball

The fieldsman may stop the ball with any part of his person, but if he wilfully stops it otherwise, 5 runs shall be added to the run or runs already scored; if no run has been scored 5 penalty runs shall be awarded. The run in progress shall count provided that the batsmen have crossed at the instant of the act. If the ball has been struck, the penalty shall be added to the score of the striker, but otherwise to the scores of byes, leg-byes, no balls or wides as the case may be.

2. Limitation of On-Side Fieldsmen

The number of on-side fieldsmen behind the popping crease at the instant of the bowler's delivery shall not exceed two. In the event of infringement by the fielding side the umpire at the striker's end shall call and signal "no ball" at the instant of delivery or as soon as possible thereafter.

3. Position of Fieldsmen

Whilst the ball is in play and until the ball has made contact with the bat or the striker's person or has passed his bat, no fieldsman, other than the bowler, may stand on or have any part of his person extended over the pitch (measuring 22 yards/20.12m × 10 feet/3.05m). In the event of a fieldsman contravening this Law, the umpire at the bowler's end shall call and signal "no ball" at the instant of delivery or as soon as possible thereafter. See Law 40.1 (Position of Wicket-Keeper).

Note

> **(a) Batsmen Changing Ends**
> The 5 runs referred to in 1 above are a penalty and the batsmen do not change ends solely by reason of this penalty.

LAW 42. UNFAIR PLAY

1. Responsibility of Captains

The captains are responsible at all times for ensuring that play is conducted within the spirit of the game as well as within the Laws.

2. Responsibility of Umpires

The umpires are the sole judges of fair and unfair play.

3. Intervention by the Umpire

The umpires shall intervene without appeal by calling and signalling "dead ball" in the case of unfair play, but should not otherwise interfere with the progress of the game except as required to do so by the Laws.

4. Lifting the Seam

A player shall not lift the seam of the ball for any reason. Should this be done, the umpires shall change the ball for one of similar condition to that in use prior to the contravention. See Note (a).

5. Changing the Condition of the Ball

Any member of the fielding side may polish the ball provided that such polishing wastes no time and that no artificial substance is used. No-one shall rub the ball on the ground or use any artificial substance or take any other action to alter the condition of the ball.

In the event of a contravention of this Law, the umpires, after consultation, shall change the ball for one of similar condition to that in use prior to the contravention.

This Law does not prevent a member of the fielding side from drying a wet ball, or removing mud from the ball. See Note (b).

6. Incommoding the Striker

An umpire is justified in intervening under this Law and shall call and signal "dead ball" if, in his opinion, any player of the fielding side incommodes the striker by any noise or action while he is receiving the ball.

7. Obstruction of a Batsman in Running

It shall be considered unfair if any fieldsman wilfully obstructs a batsman in running. In these circumstances the umpire shall call and signal "dead ball" and allow any completed runs and the run in progress, or alternatively any boundary scored.

8. The Bowling of Fast Short-Pitched Balls

The bowling of fast short-pitched balls is unfair if, in the opinion of the umpire at the bowler's end, it constitutes an attempt to intimidate the striker. See Note (d).

Umpires shall consider intimidation to be the deliberate bowling of fast short-pitched balls which by their length, height and direction are intended or likely to inflict physical injury on the striker. The relative skill of the striker shall also be taken into consideration.

In the event of such unfair bowling, the umpire at the bowler's end shall adopt the following procedure:

(a) In the first instance the umpire shall call and signal "no ball", caution the bowler and inform the other umpire, the captain of the fielding side and the batsmen of what has occurred.

(b) If this caution is ineffective, he shall repeat the above procedure and indicate to the bowler that this is a final warning.

(c) Both the above caution and final warning shall continue to apply even though the bowler may later change ends.

(d) Should the above warnings prove ineffective the umpire at the bowler's end shall:

(i) At the first repetition call and signal "no ball" and when the ball is dead direct the captain to take the bowler off forthwith and to complete the over with another bowler, provided that the bowler does not bowl two overs or part thereof consecutively. See Law 22.7 (Bowler Incapacitated or Suspended during an Over).

(ii) Not allow the bowler, thus taken off, to bowl again in the same innings.

(iii) Report the occurrence to the captain of the batting side as soon as the players leave the field for an interval.

(iv) Report the occurrence to the executive of the fielding side and to any governing body responsible for the match, who shall take any further action which is considered to be appropriate against the bowler concerned.

9. The Bowling of Fast High Full Pitches

The bowling of fast high full pitches is unfair. See Note (e).

In the event of such unfair bowling the umpire at the bowler's end shall adopt the procedures of caution, final warnings, action against the bowler and reporting as set out in 8 above.

10. Time Wasting

Any form of time wasting is unfair.

(a) In the event of the captain of the fielding side wasting time or allowing any member of his side to waste time, the umpire at the bowler's end shall adopt the following procedure:

    (i) In the first instance he shall caution the captain of the fielding side and inform the other umpire of what has occurred.

    (ii) If this caution is ineffective he shall repeat the above procedure and indicate to the captain that this is a final warning.

    (iii) The umpire shall report the occurrence to the captain of the batting side as soon as the players leave the field for an interval.

    (iv) Should the above procedure prove ineffective the umpire shall report the occurrence to the executive of the fielding side and to any governing body responsible for that match, who shall take appropriate action against the captain and the players concerned.

(b) In the event of a bowler taking unnecessarily long to bowl an over the umpire at the bowler's end shall adopt the procedures, other than the calling of "no ball", of caution, final warning, action against the bowler and reporting.

(c) In the event of a batsman wasting time (See Note (f)) other than in the manner described in Law 31 (Timed Out), the umpire at the bowler's end shall adopt the following procedure:

    (i) In the first instance he shall caution the batsman and inform the other umpire at once, and the captain of the batting side, as soon as the players leave the field for an interval, of what has occurred.

    (ii) If this proves ineffective, he shall repeat the caution, indicate to the batsman that this is a final warning and inform the other umpire.

    (iii) The umpire shall report the occurrence to both captains as soon as the players leave the field for an interval.

    (iv) Should the above procedure prove ineffective, the umpire shall report the occurrence to the executive of the batting side and to any governing body responsible for that match, who shall take appropriate action against the player concerned.

11. Players Damaging the Pitch

The umpires shall intervene and prevent players from causing damage to the pitch which may assist the bowlers of either side. See Note (c).

(a) In the event of any member of the fielding side damaging the pitch, the umpire shall follow the procedure of caution, final warning, and reporting as set out in 10(a) above.

(b) In the event of a bowler contravening this Law by running down the pitch after delivering the ball, the umpire at the bowler's end shall first caution the bowler. If this caution is ineffective the umpire shall adopt the procedures, other than the calling of "no ball", of final warning, action against the bowler and reporting.

(c) In the event of a batsman damaging the pitch the umpire at the bowler's end shall follow the procedures of caution, final warning and reporting as set out in 10(c) above.

12. Batsman Unfairly Stealing a Run

Any attempt by the batsman to steal a run during the bowler's run-up is unfair. Unless the bowler attempts to run out either batsman – see Law 24.4 (Bowler Throwing at Striker's Wicket before Delivery) and Law 24.5 (Bowler Attempting to Run Out Non-Striker before Delivery) – the umpire shall call and signal "dead ball" as soon as the batsmen cross in any such attempt to run. The batsmen shall then return to their original wickets.

13. Player's Conduct

In the event of a player failing to comply with the instructions of an umpire, criticising his decisions by word or action, or showing dissent, or generally behaving in a manner which might bring the game into disrepute, the umpire concerned shall, in the first place, report the matter to the other umpire and to the player's captain requesting the latter to take action. If this proves ineffective, the umpire shall report the incident as soon as possible to the executive of the player's team and to any governing body responsible for the match, who shall take any further action which is considered appropriate against the player or players concerned.

Notes

(a) **The Condition of the Ball**
Umpires shall make frequent and irregular inspections of the condition of the ball.

(b) **Drying of a Wet Ball**
A wet ball may be dried on a towel or with sawdust.

(c) **Danger Area**
The danger area on the pitch, which must be protected from damage by a bowler, shall be regarded by the umpires as the area contained by an imaginary line 4 feet/1.22m from the popping crease, and parallel to it, and within two imaginary and parallel lines drawn down the pitch from points on that line 1 foot/30.48cm on either side of the middle stump.

(d) **Fast Short-Pitched Balls**
As a guide, a fast short-pitched ball is one which pitches short and passes, or would have passed, above the shoulder height of the striker standing in a normal batting stance at the crease.

(e) **The Bowling of Fast Full Pitches**
The bowling of one fast, high full pitch shall be considered to be unfair if, in the opinion of the umpire, it is deliberate, bowled at the striker, and if it passes or would have passed above the shoulder height of the striker when standing in a normal batting stance at the crease.

(f) **Time Wasting by Batsmen**
Other than in exceptional circumstances, the batsman should always be ready to take strike when the bowler is ready to start his run-up.

INTERNATIONAL CRICKET CONFERENCE

On June 15, 1909, representatives of cricket in England, Australia and South Africa met at Lord's and founded the Imperial Cricket Conference. Membership was confined to the governing bodies of cricket in countries within the British Commonwealth where Test cricket was played. India, New Zealand and West Indies were elected as members on May 31, 1926, and Pakistan was elected on July 21, 1953. South Africa ceased to be a member of the ICC on leaving the British Commonwealth in 1953.

On July 15, 1965, the Conference was renamed the International Cricket Conference and new rules were adopted to permit the election of countries from outside the British Commonwealth.

CONSTITUTION

Chairman: The President of MCC for the time being or his nominee.
Secretary: The Secretary of MCC.
Foundation members: United Kingdom and Australia.
Full members: India, New Zealand, West Indies and Pakistan.
Associate members*: Argentina (1974), Bangladesh (1977), Bermuda (1966), Canada (1968), Denmark (1966), East Africa (1966), Fiji (1965), Gibraltar (1969), Hong Kong (1969), Israel (1974), Malaysia (1967), Netherlands (1966), Papua New Guinea (1973), Singapore (1974), Sri Lanka (1965), USA (1965) and West Africa (1976).

* *Year of election shown in parentheses.*

MEMBERSHIP

The following governing bodies for cricket shall be eligible for election.

Foundation Members: The governing bodies for cricket in the United Kingdom and Australia are known as Foundation Members, and while being Full Members of the Conference such governing bodies have certain additional rights as set out in the rules of the Conference.

Full Members: The governing body for cricket recognised by the Conference of a country, or countries associated for cricket purposes, of which the representative teams are accepted as qualified to play official Test matches.

Associate Members: The governing body for cricket recognised by the Conference of a country, or countries associated for cricket purposes, not qualifying as Full Members but where cricket is firmly established and organised.

TEST MATCHES

1. Duration of Test Matches

Within a maximum of thirty hours' playing time, the duration of Test matches shall be a matter for negotiation and agreement between the two countries in any particular series of Test matches.

When agreeing the Playing Conditions prior to the commencement of a Test series, the participating countries may:

(a) Extend the playing hours of the last Test beyond the limit of 30 hours, in a series in which, at the conclusion of the penultimate match, one side does not hold a lead of more than one match.

(b) Allow an extension of play by one hour on any of the first four days of a Test match, in the event of play being suspended for one hour or more on that day, owing to weather interference.

(c) Play on the rest day, conditions and circumstances permitting, should a full day's play be lost on either the second or third scheduled days of play.

(d) Make up time lost in excess of five minutes in each day's play owing to circumstances outside the game, other than acts of God.

Note. The umpires shall determine when such time shall be made up. This could, if conditions and circumstances permit, include the following day.

2. Qualification Rules

A cricketer is qualified to play in a Test match either by birth or residence.

(a) Qualification by birth. A cricketer, unless debarred by the Conference, is always eligible to play for the country of his birth.

(b) Qualification by residence. A cricketer, unless debarred by the Conference, shall be eligible to play for any country in which he is residing and has been residing during the four immediately preceding years, provided that he has not played for the country of his birth during that period.

Note. Notwithstanding anything hereinbefore contained, any player who has once played in a Test match for any country shall not afterwards be eligible to play in a Test match against that country, without the consent of its governing body.

FIRST-CLASS MATCHES

1. Definitions

(a) A match of three or more days' duration between two sides of eleven players officially adjudged first-class shall be regarded as a first-class fixture.

(b) In the following Rules the term "governing body" is restricted to Foundation Members, Full Members and Associate Members of the Conference.

2. Rules

(a) Foundation and Full Members of the ICC shall decide the status of matches of three or more days' duration played in their countries.

(b) In matches of three or more days' duration played in countries which are not Foundation or Full Members of the ICC:

  (i) If the visiting team comes from a country which is a Foundation or Full Member of the ICC, that country shall decide the status of matches.

  (ii) If the visiting team does not come from a country which is a Foundation or Full Member of the ICC, or is a Commonwealth team composed of players from different countries, the ICC shall decide the status of matches.

Notes

(a) Governing bodies agree that the interest of first-class cricket will be served by ensuring that first-class status is *not* accorded to any match in which one or other of the teams taking part cannot on a strict interpretation of the definition be adjudged first-class.

(b) In case of any disputes arising from these Rules, the Secretary of the ICC shall refer the matter for decision to the Conference, failing unanimous agreement by postal communication being reached.

3. First-Class Status

The following matches shall be regarded as first-class, subject to the provisions of Definitions (a) being completely complied with:

  (a) In the British Isles and Eire

The following matches of three or more days' duration shall automatically be considered first-class:

  (i) County Championship matches.

  (ii) Official representative tourist matches from Full Member countries unless specifically excluded.

  (iii) MCC v any first-class county.

  (iv) Oxford v Cambridge and either University against first-class counties.

  (v) Scotland v Ireland.

  (b) In Australia

  (i) Sheffield Shield matches.

  (ii) Matches played by teams representing states of the Commonwealth of Australia between each other or against opponents adjudged first-class.

  (c) In India

  (i) Ranji Trophy matches.

  (ii) Duleep Trophy matches.

  (iii) Irani Trophy matches.

    (iv) Matches played by teams representing state or regional associations affiliated to the Board of Control between each other or against opponents adjudged first-class.

    (v) All three-day matches played against representative visiting sides.

(d) In New Zealand

    (i) Shell Trophy matches.

    (ii) Matches played by teams representing provinces or the North or South Islands between each other or against opponents adjudged first-class.

(e) In West Indies

    (i) Texaco Trophy matches.

    (ii) Matches played by teams representing Barbados, Guyana, Jamaica, Trinidad, Windward or Leeward Islands between each other or against opponents adjudged first-class.

    (iii) Inter-county matches in Guyana, between Berbice and Demerara.

(f) In Pakistan

    (i) Matches played by teams representing divisional associations affiliated to the Board of Control, between each other or against teams adjudged first-class.

    (ii) Matches between the divisional associations and the Universities past and present XI.

    (iii) Quaid-e-Azam Trophy matches.

    (iv) Ayub Zonal Cricket Tournament matches.

    (v) BCCP Trophy Tournament matches.

    (vi) Patron's Trophy matches.

    (vii) Pentangular Trophy Tournament matches.

(g) In all Foundation and Full Member Countries represented on the Conference

    (i) Test matches and matches against teams adjudged first-class played by official touring teams.

    (ii) Official Test trial matches.

    (iii) Special matches between teams adjudged first-class by the governing body or bodies concerned.

ADDRESSES OF REPRESENTATIVE BODIES

INTERNATIONAL CRICKET CONFERENCE: J. A. Bailey, Lord's Ground, London, NW8 8QN.

ENGLAND: Test and County Cricket Board, D. B. Carr, Lord's Ground, London, NW8 8QN.

AUSTRALIA: Australian Cricket Board of Control, Alan Barnes, Cricket House, 245 George Street, Sydney, NSW.

SOUTH AFRICA: Cricket Union, Charles Fortune, PO Box 55009. Northlands 2116, Transvaal.

WEST INDIES: West Indies Board of Control, H. Burnett, 9 Appleblossom Avenue, Petit Valley, Diego Martin, Trinidad.

INDIA: Board of Control for Cricket in India, A. W. Kanmadikar, E-4 Radio Colony, Indore (MP).

NEW ZEALAND: New Zealand Cricket Council, R. G. Knowles, PO Box 958, Christchurch.

PAKISTAN: Board of Control for Cricket in Pakistan, A. A. K. Abbasi, Gaddafi Stadium, Lahore.

ARGENTINA: Argentine Cricket Association, I. S. Macgowan, UR1 BUR 405, Adrauge.

BANGLADESH: Bangladesh Cricket Control Board, Raisuddin Ahmed, The Stadium, Dacca.

BERMUDA: Bermuda Cricket Board of Control, Wilton L. Smith, PO Box 992, Hamilton.

CANADA: Canadian Cricket Association, G. Nugent, 574 Alpine Court, North Vancouver, British Columbia.

DENMARK: Danish Cricket Association, Peter S. Hargreaves, Lykkesborg Alle 7, 2860 Soborg.

EAST AFRICA: East African Cricket Conference, A. L. Leigh, PO Box 41968, Nairobi, Kenya.

FIJI: Fiji Cricket Association, P. I. Knight, PO Box 300, Suva.

GIBRALTAR: Gibraltar Cricket Association, T. W. J. Wright, 32/4 Parliament Lane.

HONG KONG: Hong Kong Cricket Association, S. K. Sipahimalani, Centre for Media Research, University of Hong Kong, Knowles Bldg, Pokfulam Road.

ISRAEL: Israel Cricket Association, D. Golding, PO Box 4936, Tel Aviv.

KENYA: Kenya Cricket Association, Jasmer Singh, PO Box 46480, Nairobi.

MALAYSIA: Malaysian Cricket Association, Daljit-Singh Gill, C/o Sessions Court, Jalan Duta, Kuala Lumpur.

NETHERLANDS: Royal Netherlands Cricket Association, P. J. Trijzelaar, Willem de Zwijgerlaan 96A, The Hague.

PAPUA NEW GUINEA: Papua New Guinea Cricket Board of Control, N. R. Agonia, PO Box 2351, Koredobu.

SINGAPORE: Singapore Cricket Association, J. C. Cooke, 147A Block E, Townhouse Apartments, Cavenagh Road, Singapore 0922.

SRI LANKA: Board of Control for Cricket in Sri Lanka, B. S. de Silva, 44 Gregory's Road, Colombo 7.

USA: United States Cricket Association, James J. Reid, 1906 Karen Street, Burbank, California 91504.

WEST AFRICA: West African Cricket Conference, Namseh Eno, C/o Cricket Secretariat, National Sports Commission, PO Box 145, Lagos, Nigeria.

BRITISH UNIVERSITIES SPORTS FEDERATION: 28 Woburn Square, London WC1.

CLUB CRICKET CONFERENCE: 353 West Barnes Lane, New Malden, Surrey, KT3 6JF.

ENGLAND SCHOOLS' CRICKET ASSOCIATION: C. J. Cooper, 68 Hatherley Road, Winchester, Hampshire.

IRISH CRICKET UNION: D. Scott, 45 Foxrock Park, Foxrock, Co. Dublin.

MINOR COUNTIES CRICKET ASSOCIATION: Laurance Hancock, 4 Kingsland Avenue, Oakhill, Stoke-on-Trent, ST4 5LA.

NATIONAL CRICKET ASSOCIATION: B. J. Aspital, Lord's Ground, London, NW8 8QN.

SCARBOROUGH FESTIVAL: Secretary, North Marine Road, Scarborough, Yorkshire.

SCOTTISH CRICKET UNION: R. W. Barclay, Admin. Office, 8 Frederick Street, Edinburgh, EH2 2HB.

THE SPORTS COUNCIL: Emlyn B. Jones, 70 Brompton Road, London, SW3 1EX.

THE SPORTS TURF RESEARCH INSTITUTE: J. R. Escritt, Bingley, Yorkshire, BD16 1AU.

UMPIRES: ASSOCIATION OF CRICKET UMPIRES: L. J. Cheeseman, 16 Ruden Way, Epsom Downs, Surrey, KT17 3LN.

WOMEN'S CRICKET ASSOCIATION: 70 Brompton Road, London, SW3 1HA.

The addresses of MCC, the First-Class Counties, Universities and Minor Counties are given at the head of each separate section.

MEETINGS IN 1980

TCCB SPRING MEETING

CHAMPIONSHIP CHANGES REJECTED

The Test and County Cricket Board rejected a package of changes for the Schweppes County Championship at its Spring Meeting. The Board's cricket sub-committee, containing a wealth of experience under the chairmanship of P. B. H. May, had suggested: the abolition of the 100 overs first innings limitation, total covering of pitches and an increase in win points from twelve to sixteen. The sub-committee believed that such changes in the playing conditions would give encouragement to young batsmen and bring about more positive strategies by captains. The proposals stood or fell as an entity and were narrowly turned down.

FREEDOM OF MOVEMENT

The Board also rejected a move to rescind the previous year's decision that in 1982 each county would be restricted to just one player ineligible to play for England. There was, though, agreement that English players not required by their county could move to another with greater ease.

SESSIONS OF PLAY

Intervals in first-class games were to be altered to ensure that, as far as possible, sessions of play were of similar length.

OVER-RATES

Having noted that the over-rates of England bowlers in Tests had improved since the introduction of fines two years before, the Board intended suggesting to the International Cricket Conference a universal system of penalties, amounting to £50 per player, should a side fail to reach 16.25 overs an hour in Tests. Before the ICC meeting, West Indies were to be asked to agree to such a scheme in the 1980 series, though the Board was not hopeful of its acceptance.

TCCB REGISTRATIONS COMMITTEE

WOOD'S CONTROVERSIAL MOVE

Barry Wood moved from Lancashire to Derbyshire after a prolonged early-season controversy. Wood left Lancashire within 48 hours of banking a benefit cheque of £62,429, but on April 10 the Registrations Committee of the TCCB banned his proposed move to Derbyshire as "not in the best interests of cricket". The Committee added: "In making its decision, the Committee reiterated that it is anxious not to encourage the development of a transfer system."

The Committee told Derbyshire that a further application would not necessarily be refused. But before the county re-applied, Wood took his case to the Appeals Committee of the Cricket Council on April 30. This Committee gave him a date for the resumption of his career – July 30, a lengthy ban by recent precedent. However, within a fortnight the TCCB, faced with the threat of legal action, reduced the ban by two months and allowed Wood's registration on June 4.

ELIGIBLE FOR ENGLAND

In September the Registrations Committee considered the qualifications of four overseas-born players with regard to their eligibility to play for England. It accepted the claims of M. J. Procter (Gloucestershire), B. F. Davison (Leicestershire) and C. L. Smith (Hampshire), but deferred for further examination the case of A. J. Lamb (Northamptonshire). It was not assumed that Procter or Davison would, in fact, be considered for England. Their change of status meant that their counties could have another overseas player when, in 1982, the restriction of one per county came into force. Neither has had a chance of playing Test cricket in the last decade and Davison's birthplace, now Zimbabwe, was no longer part of South Africa for future Test purposes.

Lamb, like Smith, has English parents and needed only to establish a four-year residential qualification. As Lamb has a real chance of playing Test cricket for England, the Committee was concerned with the genuineness of his residence in England.

TCCB DISCIPLINARY COMMITTEE

INCIDENT AT LORD'S

The Disciplinary Committee took the opportunity to remind counties of their duty to ensure high standards of behaviour from their players following an incident between Imran Khan and J. M. Brearley in the Middlesex v Sussex Benson and Hedges Cup quarter-final in June. The Board asked both clubs to hold inquiries into the incident and when these were completed the Board stated:

"The Disciplinary Committee of the TCCB will not be meeting officially to discuss the incident. Both counties have taken action over the matter and fully accept the necessity to maintain the best standards of behaviour on the field of play. The incident occurred during a tense part of the game when Imran questioned the umpire on the amount of short-pitched bowling being delivered. On hearing this, Brearley made a remark to Imran which could be considered provocative and Imran reacted heatedly. Sussex have reprimanded Imran for his part and warned him as to his future conduct. It is accepted that Brearley used no bad language, but both he and Middlesex have expressed regrets that he became involved and thus contributed to an incident which otherwise would not have taken place. Both clubs have stated unequivocally that they fully support the stand taken by the Board on the question of behaviour. At all times it is the object of the Disciplinary Committee to encourage clubs to keep their own house in order in the best interests of the game. In this instance both clubs have acted responsibly and the chairman of the Disciplinary Committee is confident that the point has been made sufficiently clearly to each club."

INTERNATIONAL CRICKET CONFERENCE

SOUTH AFRICA'S ACCEPTABILITY

The re-entry of South Africa and the entry of Sri Lanka into full membership of the Conference became foreseeable possibilities at the ICC meeting held at Lord's on August 14 and 15, 1980. The delegates took the unusual step of engaging in discussions outside the meeting with representatives of the South African Cricket Union, who were asked to make written submissions in support of their re-admission. South Africa's thoughts on the issue – which, it was assumed, would stress the development of multi-racial cricket in their country – would be distributed to all members, whose reactions would be considered in 1981.

South Africa automatically left the old Imperial Cricket Conference when the country became a republic in 1961. Though the Conference's title was altered to its present name in 1965 to allow countries from outside the British Commonwealth to have access, South Africa has remained without a voice in the game's government for two decades. The difficulties that stand in South Africa's way inevitably became clear when the meeting could not agree that there would be no recriminations against any country that resumed cricketing relations with South Africa.

SRI LANKA'S STATUS

The regular review of Sri Lanka's status concluded that the question should be shelved for a further year. But cricket administrators in the island were encouraged when Australia guaranteed that they would send a strong side on their next tour there; and they knew that when the 1981 Conference considered their application their cricketers would be in the middle of a tour of England.

LBW CHANGE PROPOSED

The revolutionary suggestion from J. B. Stollmeyer regarding a change in the lbw law was received favourably and southern hemisphere countries agreed to experiment with the proposal immediately. It was that a batsman should be out lbw to a ball pitching outside the leg stump – provided all normal conditions have been met – if the ball were delivered from the off side; i.e. a left-arm round-the-wicket or right-arm over-the-wicket bowler operating to a right-hander.

NEUTRAL OBSERVERS

New Zealand's radical proposal that a player guilty of wilful assault on an umpire should be banned from the rest of the match was rejected, though great concern was expressed about players' behaviour, especially systematic "pressuring" of umpires. The mood of the meeting took tangible form when Pakistan's resolution that neutral observers should be present at Tests to scrutinise players' conduct and report to ICC was accepted.

TCCB WINTER MEETING

CHANGES IN CHAMPIONSHIP RULES

Significant changes in the playing conditions for the Schweppes County Championship, having been proposed by the TCCB Cricket Committee, were accepted by the full committee at its meeting on Thursday, December 11. These involved full covering of pitches in all Championship matches, the abolition of the 100 overs first innings limitation, an increase from twelve points to sixteen in the value of an outright victory, and a new ball to be available after 85 overs. To compensate spin bowlers for being deprived of drying pitches, groundsmen on all first-class grounds were to be asked to prepare dry pitches, more readily responsive to spin bowling. Bonus points would continue to be available for the first 100 overs of each side's first innings. All decisions were carried by a substantial majority.

NEW BASIC REQUIREMENTS FOR COVERING

On Test grounds and grounds where Prudential Cup and Trophy matches are played, a new set of basic requirements is to be specified. These include the covering of the whole square, as well as twenty yards for the run-ups (with a width of ten yards), and all other compacted and worn areas of the ground. These instructions followed the controversy surrounding the covering arrangements made for the Centenary Test at Lord's in 1980. Warwickshire were reported to be making a "feasibility study" of an automatic cover.

FIELDING CIRCLES

It was agreed to introduce, in the Benson and Hedges Cup limited-overs competition in 1981, an area inside which, at the moment of delivery and throughout a match, four fielders as well as the wicket-keeper and bowler must be. This was a move against the purely defensive field-placing common in one-day cricket. The area is one "boarded by two half-circles centred on each middle stump, each within a radius of 30 yards and joined by a parallel line on each side of the pitch".

TEST MATCH OVER-RATES

A strong recommendation was to be made to the Australian Cricket Board that a system of fines be introduced in the England v Australia series of 1981, in order to maintain a reasonable over-rate. A minimum of 16.25 overs per hour was to be the proposition.

TEST PLAY ON SUNDAYS

Subject to the approval of the Australian Cricket Board it was agreed to make arrangements for Sunday play in three of the six Test matches between England and Australia in 1981 – the first, fourth and fifth – the hours of play to be from twelve until seven. In these three matches there would be no rest day, play starting on Thursdays and ending on Mondays.

LIMITATION OF RUN-UPS

In response to a request from the International Cricket Conference, made at its 1980 annual meeting, for suggestions for improving over-rates worldwide, the TCCB agreed to propose, through the Cricket Council, that bowlers' run-ups should be limited to 25 yards.

FITNESS FOR PLAY

The Board was "very conscious" of the need to get play started whenever reasonably possible. After consultation with captains, umpires and administrators, clearly defined guidelines will be laid down for the 1981 season regarding the fitness of ground, weather and light for play.

FLOODLIT CRICKET

The Board agreed in principle to approve a floodlit competition to be staged after the end of the first-class season.

FEES FOR TEST MATCHES

Players' and umpires' fees would remain unchanged for Test matches in 1981 – at £1,400 and £1,050 respectively.

BOARD'S SURPLUS

The Board declared that in 1979 a surplus of £1,438,539 had been distributed among the first-class and minor counties, MCC, the Irish and Scottish Cricket Unions and the Combined Services.

APPOINTMENTS

M. G. Crawford and A. C. Smith were appointed to the Board's executive committee, where they joined the Chairman of the Board, F. G. Mann, and the chairmen of the four sub-committees, D. J. Insole (cricket), B. Coleman (Marketing), A. G. Waterman (Finance and General Purposes) and O. S. Wheatley (Discipline), plus F. M. Turner.

ERRATA IN WISDEN, 1980

Page 294 There were 229 three-figure innings in 1979, not 228. The list omits 146* by J. S. Johnson for Minor Counties v Indians at Wellington.

Page 508 G. Cook (Northamptonshire) scored 130, not 150, v Warwickshire.

Page 513 P. J. Watts (Northamptonshire) scored 2, not 22, in the first innings v Lancashire.

Page 732 H. P. Cooper (Yorkshire) scored 5, not 15, v Essex.

Page 769 K. Higgs (Leicestershire) scored 3, not 6, v Essex.

Page 948 G. N. Yallop was not the first Australian to hit a century in his maiden Test as captain. G. S. Chappell achieved this feat in 1975-76 when, v West Indies at Brisbane, he became the only player to score a hundred in each innings of his first Test as captain.

Page 965 Javed Miandad's Test batting average should read 5 innings, 3 not outs, average 178.50.

CRICKET BOOKS, 1980

By JOHN ARLOTT

The level of cricket book publications in 1980 was high. Of the 80 books submitted for review, at least eight are valuable additions to the records of the game; and another half-dozen should be in any basically representative collection. It should be noted that several books actually published in 1980 were noticed, under "Cricket Books, 1979", in *Wisden* 1980.

Barclays World of Cricket (Collins; £18) edited by E. W. Swanton, with John Woodcock as associate, is the second, and revised, edition of Messrs Swanton and Melford's *The World of Cricket* of 1966. The pressure of events in modern cricket is such, and its history over the past fifteen years has been so revolutionary, as to demand considerable rewriting to reflect changed historic shape, social and economic balances as distinct from the progress of playing results.

The editors have taken this opportunity of a fresh start to change the general order of the book. Previously it was basically alphabetical; now it has been divided into eleven subject-sections – history, overseas, biographies, international, counties, limited-overs, and so on. That makes for coherent, straight reading on a single theme; meanwhile instant reference, to a more detailed degree than in the earlier edition, is afforded by an index expertly compiled by J. D. Coldham. The best of the previous material has been retained or brought up to date; and, although there are no colour plates, the content is an advance on the first version. The assistant editors are George Plumptre and A. S. R. Winlaw; the statistician, Geoffrey Copinger. There is a long list of distinguished contributors; and Barclays Bank International have rendered the game a considerable service by sponsoring, as the sub-title claims, "The Game from A to Z". It towers above all other works of cricket reference.

Cricket (Hamlyn; £1.75), a "Hamlet Sports Special", is a history, with contributions from Benny Green, Jim Laker, Alan Lee, Maurice Golesworthy, and Martin Tyler. It is most reasonably priced, attractively produced, and generously illustrated.

First-Class Cricket Matches 1864-1876 (The Association of Cricket Statisticians, 127 Davenport Drive, Cleethorpes, S. Humberside; £20) comprises the first five volumes (1864-1866, 1867-1869, 1870-1872, 1873-1874, 1875-1876) of an ambitious and extremely valuable project by the Association. Recognising the difficulties of researchers and statisticians in gaining access to authoritative scores of matches – especially pre-1900 – not included in *Wisden*, they decided to gather, check and reprint them from all available sources. Thus they have gone, not only to *Haygarth's Scores and Biographies*, but to British and overseas annuals and newspapers; while wherever possible, they have checked published versions by comparison with official score-books. As a result they have often corrected even *S & B*. This is a most important and authoritative contribution to the chronicles of cricket. A further five volumes will be published in 1981.

No more serious publication in the sporting field has appeared for many years than *Sport in South Africa; Report of the Sports Council's Fact-Finding Delegation* (Sports Council, 70 Brompton Road, London, SW3 1EX; £3.00). A 184-page quarto, it lays out the evidence submitted to the five-strong British delegation sent to South Africa to study "progress made, at all levels, with multi-racial integration in sport" there. The group made clear some legitimate assumptions, notably the different attitudes of the two sides of the debate ("all are in the fray"). One argues that "each small advance made towards multi-racial sport is a step in the right direction": the other that there can be "no normal sport in an abnormal society". The delegation offered no positive judgement on the issue of apartheid in its relationship to sport in South Africa. That was specifically excluded from their brief. They have, however, collected from the Government, opposition, and the official sports authorities, a wealth of well-arranged and illuminating facts. It is unfortunate that, at a crucial press conference when the party returned to England, Basil D'Oliveira should have been, as he protested, crucially misquoted. Everyone who feels any political or social responsibility for the people of South Africa, and the effect sporting relations with that country may have on them, should study this report.

The Complete Who's Who of Test Cricketers (Orbis Publishing; £10) by Christopher Martin-Jenkins, the result of a simple but good idea, does, in truth, justify use of the old cliché that "it fills a long-felt want". This was one of the few basic books of cricket reference that had been lacking. It consists of a biographical note and statistical record of every cricketer of all the Test-playing countries. It cannot have been easy to compile. Although the essential facts about modern cricketers are easily accessible, there was, for instance, one "England" player (J. E. P. McMaster) whose Test appearance against South Africa in 1888-89 was his only first-class match; while yet another Irishman, Leland Hone, won a cap against Australia but never played county cricket. There has been much patient research, for which J. D. Coldham is credited, and it is most pleasingly presented. The searcher for information is apt to find it compelling reading. There are some 250 illustrations.

The Century Makers (Sidgwick & Jackson; £8.95) by Frank Tyson is sub-titled "The Men Behind The Ashes 1877-1977". It is a substantial and well-produced account of Anglo-Australian Tests, with particular attention to outstanding performers. Mr Tyson is modest, objective but revealing in his reference to his part in the Australian defeat of 1954-55.

Clayton Goodwin, an experienced English member of the West Indian press, is the author of *Caribbean Cricketers From the Pioneers to Packer* (Harrap; £8.50). It is a survey of West Indian cricket from the Barbados-Guyana match of 1865, through the uncertain years, into the great successes, and on to the "Packer and Prudential Age", with a look to the future. A useful statistical appendix includes potted scores of every Test played by West Indies.

Classic Cigarette Cards (Constable; £2) is a reproduction, in full colour and with back-text, of 154 cards of famous cricketers. They range from 1896 to 1938, include virtually all the great players of that period, and are admirably reproduced.

Queensland Cricketers 1892-1979 (Association of Cricket Statisticians, 127 Davenport Drive, Cleethorpes, S. Humberside; £2; gratis to members) is in the Association's established format. It lists every player to appear for the state, giving, wherever possible, full names; birthplace, date of birth and (where applicable) death; present address; playing span, with relevant details, as type of bowler and/or batsman. The register now grows steadily.

One of the early important records of the game, *The English Cricketers' Trip to Canada and the United States in 1859* (World's Work; £4.95) by Fred Lillywhite has been reprinted with an introduction by Robin Marlar. For many years a rarity, this edition now makes generally available a readable, informative, period piece of the game.

Sport in the Market? (Institute of Economic Affairs; £1.50) by Peter J. Sloane, Hobart Paper No. 85, is concerned with "the economic causes and consequences of the 'Packer Revolution'". Professor Sloane had also, perforce, to examine the social significance of cricket, and team spectator sports in general and their relationship with the media and the public. Its objectivity makes it valuable reading, especially for those cricket followers who were not able to stand back and observe the situation vis-à-vis Packer coolly.

Worcestershire County Cricket Club; A Pictorial History (Severn House; £6.95) by M. D. Vockins, secretary of Worcestershire, complements the two-volume history of the club by the Rev. W. R. Chignell. It contains an admirably concise chronology and some neat biographical notes but, as its title suggests, it is primarily – and most successfully – a pictorial record, especially of the outstanding players of the county's first-class history, 1899-1979.

Summer of Success; The Triumph of Essex County Cricket Club in 1979 (Pelham Books; £5.95) by David Lemmon celebrates the great season when, after 103 years without winning a major trophy, Essex won the Championship and the Benson and Hedges Cup. Mr Lemmon, editor of *Pelham Cricket Year*, a lifelong cricket enthusiast and collector, is a schoolteacher in Essex. He begins with a sound and nostalgic historical background, then traces that season through to the ultimate triumph and Keith Fletcher's – "And the great thing was, we all felt part of it".

The Re-opening of the Basin Reserve, 29th November 1980 (Wellington Cricket Association, PO Box 578, Wellington, New Zealand; no price given) is an attractively produced booklet issued to mark the re-shaping of this famous Test ground. The well-chosen illustrations provide a photographic record of social as well as architectural and constructional changes from the latter part of the last century until this re-opening.

An unexpected title, *Demon Bowler* (Nag's Head Press, 385 Memorial

Avenue, Christchurch 5, New Zealand; $NZ8.55) is a small, pleasingly hand-set, limited edition of 225 copies. It reprints, and sympathetically augments, a contemporary newspaper report of the match between Australia and Fifteen of Canterbury played at Hagley Park, Christchurch, in January 1878 which, to the amazement of many people, the fifteen won by six wickets. The title is justified by the fact that Fred Spofforth – "The Demon" – took nine for 77 and four for 29. Absorbing reading – one could do with more – this is likely to become a collectors' item.

Even more unlikely is *Three Ducks on the Trot* (from the author, D. M. Woodhead, 4 Muskoka Avenue, Sheffield, S11 7RL; £1.50). This is an intensely personal, chatty, often funny, adequately statistically appendicized, and in some ways quite idiosyncratic account, of the birth and early childhood of a "A New League Cricket Team".

Poloc Cricket Club Centenary 1878-1978 (The Secretary, Poloc Cricket Club, 2060 Pollokshaws Road, Glasgow G43 1AT; no price given) is the hundred-year story of the club that plays in the pleasant setting of Shawholm, screened by its trees from the skyscrapers of Pollokshaws. There are sidenotes on its lawn tennis, table tennis and golfing sections. Among the club's professionals have been L. N. Devereux (Worcestershire), Gerry Dawson (Hampshire), Gordon Brice (Northamptonshire), Sadiq Mohammad, Hanif Mohammad and Mohammad Ilyas.

In her study, *Playing on Their Nerves* (Stanley Paul; £7.95), Angela Patmore examines the psychological pressure of top-level sport and the way in which it is manipulated, applied and exploited. Cricket – labelled "The Brain Game" – is the first sport dealt with; the argument is, of course, necessarily continued into other fields. Miss Patmore is an experienced journalist; she has mustered her facts, and especially the quotations, well. There is, in the result, much to ponder; but the arguments are not completely convincing because they seem to lack an understanding of the people – professional sportsmen – involved.

Gowerton Cricket Club 1880-1980 (Gowerton Cricket Club, 31 Glanmor Park Road, Sketty, Swansea; no price given) by J. Hywel Rees is a substantial, hard-covered, 148-page quarto history of the club which reached the final of the Haig Village Trophy in 1973, won it in 1975 and reached its centenary in 1980. It is a thorough, parochial, proud, nostalgic, triumphant story, well illustrated.

The centenary of matches between Prince Alfred College and The Collegiate School of St Peter – in Adelaide – is marked by *1878-1978, 100 Years of Intercollegiate Cricket* (Lutheran Publishing House, 205 Halifax Street, Adelaide, SA 5000; no price given). Six authors – and, apparently, two typists – are credited for an obvious labour of love, a record which will be cherished by the surviving generations of this "blood" match.

A Friend of the Family (from the author, The Coach House, Ponsonby, Seascale, Cumbria, CA20 1BX; £5.25) is the sixteenth effusion of the irrepressible Nico Craven, an expatriate Gloucestershireman who hastens back every summer to follow his county and record as many of their doings as he can contrive to watch. He has now been joined as illustrator by Frank

Fisher, another West Country exile to the north-west – this time from Somerset; thus are old rivalries softened by alien parts. The original stream thus diluted, Worcestershire and club cricket creep in; but the main loyalty does not flag.

Cricket is dominant among several sporting themes in *Bowled Over; A Year of Sport with Frank Keating* (André Deutsch; £6.50). It is an account of the impressions, excitements, musings and nostalgias of the annual round of the compulsive writer who has lately won awards both as the sports writer and the columnist of the year. A *Guardian* writer almost by instinct, Mr Keating is deeply but harmlessly biased in favour of Gloucestershire. His book is lively, nostalgic, sentimental, humorous, understanding, enthusiastic; and always, at the core, sharply observed and meaningfully reported. It will sound echoes in the mind of the deep cricket enthusiast.

Wisden Anthology 1900-1940 (Queen Anne Press; £20) is the second of Benny Green's monumental selections and collections from the game's prime source book. Once again he has come up from his enthusiastic delvings with rich material from, as he emphasises, "The Golden Age of Cricket". Mr Green must be set down as a master anthologist. Not only is he a diligent searcher with the gifts of divination and appreciation, but his arrangement is masterly. Thus for the first half of this gathering, he divides his era into two periods, 1900-1914 and 1919-1940; in the second, he lets time have its flow. Walter Robins, who used *Wisden* as a bedside book, claimed, well before his death, to be on his second lap. Few of us have the stamina or – in many cases – the time in hand for such a circuit. For us Mr Green has now compiled the two quite outstanding cricket anthologies, and we await the third.

From Australia comes the sixth edition of *Six and Out* (Jack Pollard Publishing Ltd, 26 Ridge Street, North Sydney, NSW 2060; no price given) edited by Jack Pollard; the classic anthology of Australian cricket. Very widely extended, the 1980 version, at 512 pages, is not far short of twice the length of the first, of 1964. It remains the best of its kind; compulsive reading, well arranged and divertingly illustrated, especially by the caricaturists.

It is a relatively recent development – or, perhaps more accurately, re-development – for active players to weigh in with accounts, or their views, of recent Test series in which they have been involved. In *Put to the Test; England in Australia 1978-79* (Arthur Barker; £4.95) Geoffrey Boycott acknowledges the assistance of as capable a journalist as Terry Brindle. The overall effect is of close observation and first-hand opinion. Perhaps Geoffrey Boycott is introspective; certainly few cricketers have brought their readers quite so close to their playing experience as he – with expert assistance – has done here. The result is absorbing reading.

Bill Frindall's method is more strictly objective. *Frindall's Score Book, Australia v West Indies and England 1979-80* (Queen Anne Press; £15) is based, like the other volumes in his series, on reproduction of his highly informative score sheets, augmented, though, by some workmanlike comments and photographic illustrations. It is worth learning to "read" these scores in order to be able to reconstruct a specific phase of a match.

Cricket Contest 1979-80: The Post-Packer Tests (Queen Anne Press; £6.50) by Christopher Martin-Jenkins is a crowded and busy account. It reports the one-day competitions and the Australia-England and Australia-West Indies Tests which, under the aegis of the Australian Board and Kerry Packer, packed the Australian season and one television channel through the winter of 1979-80, and continues to the England-India match which marked India's Jubilee Test. Mr Martin-Jenkins has presented a commendably balanced and coherent account of a mixed and potentially baffling pattern of cricket. The statistics are workmanlike and the illustrations effective.

Deadly Down Under (Arthur Barker; £5.50) by Derek Underwood is, as collectors of cricketing nicknames will have divined, Derek Underwood's personal account of England in Australia in 1979-80. He is informative about the cricket; revealing about his reasons for joining the Packer operation.

The section of biographies and autobiographies is full of impressive names from recent – and some older – cricket history. In *Compton on Cricketers Past and Present* (Cassell; £6.95) Denis Compton evaluates 25 world-class players of modern times. Most of them were his colleagues or opponents at Test level; he has watched the others in his subsequent career as commentator and reporter. His opinions are his own and he makes no concessions; sometimes he is controversial, always he is readable; and often revealing.

A similar, but localised, survey is David Foot's *From Grace to Botham* (The Redcliffe Press, Bristol; £4.50) which is subtitled "Profiles of 100 West Country Cricketers". Mr Foot is an experienced journalist, working in the West of England, where he has watched Somerset and Gloucestershire cricket for some 30 years. His studies go back much further than that but, whether they are researched and reconstructed, or written from first-hand knowledge, they are perceptive and eminently readable. Indeed, no more felicitously evocative writing is to be found in the year's output. It deserves to be known and enjoyed far beyond its subject boundaries.

Ian Botham, The Great All-Rounder (Cassell; £6.95) by Dudley Doust does credit to both author and subject. Mr Doust came relatively late to cricket writing; but he brought to it a genuine literary ability and an approach completely free from the hackneyed phrases and attitudes of the regular cricket press. He undoubtedly learnt much from writing two Test series accounts with Mike Brearley, and he has put that knowledge to good use here. When Mr Doust wrote, Ian Botham, returning from his phenomenal performance in the Jubilee Test in Bombay, was at the high peak of his career. That was the moment for this book; and, if some discount it because of Botham's lack of success in England in 1980, they do his epic phase – and Mr Doust's account of it – less than justice.

Opening Up (Arthur Barker; £5.95) by Geoffrey Boycott is another book written with Terry Brindle. Semi-autobiographical, it consists mainly of Boycott's opinions on cricket and cricketers. As such it is as penetrating as one would expect from a man who takes much – some would say too much – thought about the game. It is compelling and readable.

Basil D'Oliveira marked his retirement from active play to coach for Worcestershire with *Time to Declare* (Dent; £5.95), a considered autobiography which has been most sympathetically set in order by Patrick Murphy. This is more than a story of a good cricketer playing successful cricket. It is the life of a man who, by rising from a second-class citizen in South Africa to become a British subject who played cricket for England, held out fresh hope for all those of his kind who are oppressed in any country. Importantly, too, it uses the opportunity to correct misquotation of his views on sport in South Africa in relation to apartheid.

Some may think that in publishing *With Time to Spare* (Ward Lock; no price given) the young David Gower was somewhat premature. The argument has two sides. This book (written with Alan Lee) records the entry to the international cricketing scene of a youthful left-handed batsman who excited players and spectators of more than one country. He was to suffer a setback; and at the moment of writing has not yet re-established himself. If he never does so – or if he does – it is worthwhile to record the stimulating effect on him, and on English cricket, of the handsome batting which won him acclaim and an unquestioned Test place. In fact, too, though in a different sense, he has time to spare.

W. G. (The Hambledon Press; £7.50) by W. G. Grace is described in a sub-title typical of its period as "Cricketing Reminiscences and Personal Recollections". As E. W. Swanton points out in his introduction to this reprint (the original edition appeared in 1899) the very existence of the book must be credited to the journalist, Arthur Porritt, who not only wrote it, but wormed the material out of "The Old Man" in the first place. W. G. was not a literary man. He was wont, if he found one of his young players reading, to admonish him for impairing the eyesight he ought to protect for his cricket. At best, he was not forthcoming; but this is probably the best view, largely autobiographical – as distinct from biographical – that we have of the great man. Of biography there is, fortunately, work by Bernard Darwin, Clifford Bax, Methven Brownlee, the various contributors to the *Memorial Biography* and passages of Cardus to compensate for the fact that the eminent Victorian of cricket thought so much more of playing the game than talking about it.

Jack Grant's Story (Lutterworth Press; £5.95) is the autobiography of G. C. (Jackie) Grant. Born in Trinidad, Grant won cricket and soccer Blues at Cambridge and captained West Indies in their first Test series (1930-31) in Australia, where they surprised most people by winning the last Test; and again when they took the series off R. E. S. Wyatt's side in the West Indies in 1934-35. He retired early from cricket – at 27 – became a missionary and, with his wife, as secretaries of the All-Africa Conference of Churches, took the post of principal of Adams College which provided non-state education for Africans in South Africa. When the Government closed the college he stood up to the Special Branch men without fear and went off to run a school for natives in Rhodesia, and to help detainees and their families. He finished this autobiography not long before he died in 1978; and it has been faithfully edited. Alan Paton in his Foreword observes "His sacrifice of cricket career and possessions strengthened his faith" and he ends it with "It is quite a book".

The Man in the Middle (David & Charles; £6.50) is the autobiography of Gordon Greenidge, opening batsman for Hampshire and West Indies, written with Patrick Syme. He is revealing on the subject of going in first with Barry Richards – in, surely, the most exciting opening partnership of modern times. Of its early days he writes: "You may be able to understand my feelings of inadequacy when I say it was not uncommon for me to be still in single figures when the applause was ringing round the ground for his 50." Gordon Greenidge's progress in cricket was by no means easy (it is often forgotten that he was not an imported "star"; that, although born in Barbados, he was brought up in England). He met his challenges, though, characteristically, not by defending but by building his strength – through intensive training, weight-lifting and running – and attacking the bowling. He maintained that aggressive bent through his bad days to success.

My Story (Stanley Paul; £6.95) by Tony Greig (with Alan Lee) will inevitably arouse strong emotions. In text reproduced from tape-recordings, he discusses frankly his epilepsy; his early cricket; his captaincy of England; his decision to join the Packer organisation; and his subsequent aims and ambitions. Although the main text is written in the first person, each chapter has an opening written by Alan Lee which tends to apologia, or even glorification. Nevertheless it should be read by anyone prepared to make an objective judgement of Greig's actions.

Yorkshire and Back (Queen Anne Press; £5.95), the autobiography of Ray Illingworth (written in association with Don Mosey), is as straightforwardly and independently thoughtful as one would expect from the man. It is the story of, virtually, three – or two and a half – cricketing careers. They were, of course, as player with Yorkshire; as captain of Leicestershire and England; and now in its formative stages, that of the manager of Yorkshire. The prophet has returned in honour to his own country.

Clive Lloyd's autobiography (written with Tony Cozier), *Living for Cricket* (Hutchinson; £4.95), is a shrewd story, reflecting the sixteen-year process of the emancipation of the West Indian professional cricketer from relative poverty to his present position of power and some profit. It is succinctly written and most effectively illustrated.

Keith Miller; a Cricketing Biography (Allen & Unwin; £5.50) by Mihir Bose is, quite surprisingly, the first study of one of the most striking characters and brilliant performers in the history of cricket. Mr Bose has considerable experience of journalism in both India and England and although – born in 1947 – he cannot have watched Miller play through a critical eye, he has reconstructed his subject skilfully. If he does not capture the particular charisma of the man, who can say that one who knew him well would be able to do so? In any event this is a welcome publication; well written, thought-provoking and divertingly anecdotal.

Cricketer Militant; The Life of Jack Parsons (North Moreton Press; £5.00) by Gerald Howat is an engaging study of a full man. Canon J. H. Parsons, in his time both professional and amateur cricketer for

Warwickshire, was a refreshingly uninhibited clean and powerful striker of the ball, a clear thinker who drove through to essentials, and a clergyman of high principles and good heart. When he celebrated his 80th birthday on May 30, 1980 he was the last survivor of Warwickshire's Championship-winning side of 1911 – and Warwickshire, most appropriately, even if they were not to stay there long, stood at the top of the County Championship table.

Runs and Catches (Faber; £5.95) by Tony Pawson is the autobiography of a cricketer, soccer player, fly fisherman, sports reporter, industrial relations consultant and immensely zestful man. It is full of life, anecdote and event, all warmly but modestly relished and felicitously recounted.

Scraps from a Cricketer's Memory (Derbyshire County Cricket Supporters' Club; £2.00) consists of the personal reminiscences of L. G. Wright, who played for Derbyshire from 1883 to 1909, written out by hand some 60-odd years ago, with notes and statistics by F. G. Peach. Both a period piece and a human document, which survived by happy accident, it is published as an act of county loyalty. It contains some diverting anecdotes and sidelights on players of the "Golden Age".

Prudential Cup Review (Prudential Assurance Company; 75p) by Ralph Dellor is the official record of that competition – inevitably known as the World Cup – in England in 1979. There is a sound account of every match; competition and national records; and generous illustration.

Pakistan in India 1979-80 (C. K. Haridass & Sons, 57 Kilpauk Gardens, Madras 600 010; Rs. 15) is the 23rd publication in 31 years by C. K. Haridass. A 134-page small quarto, it carries biographical notes and portraits of the players on both sides and an interesting collection of feature articles, caricatures and photographs.

Willow Wood (Eyre Methuen; £6.50) by Mollie Hardwick is a very romantic novel indeed. It tells of the beautiful, invalid, aristocratic heiress who falls in love with the cricketing under-gardener on her uncle's estate, only to fall "deeper and deeper into the trap of Bevis's lethal glamour".

In *Cricket Umpiring and Scoring* (Dent; £5.95), Tom E. Smith, former general-secretary of the Association of Cricket Umpires – and a member of the MCC Laws Committee – has re-written the original (1946) version of Col. R. S. Rait Kerr to include the new, 1980, Laws, with interpretations for umpires, players and scorers.

The Laws of Cricket (EP Publishing; no price given) in the "Know the Game" series, gives the 1980 code and is produced for MCC.

Cricket; The Techniques of the Game (EP Publishing; £4.95) is a National Cricket Association publication written by three of its coaches – Keith Andrew, Bob Carter and Les Lenham. The text is as sound and considered as the names of its authors guarantee, and the photographs and diagrams have been shrewdly chosen. This is a most valuable manual for those concerned with coaching the young.

In the formulation of *Ian Botham on Cricket* (Cassell; £4.95) Ian Botham has the specialist assistance of his Somerset team-mates Vic Marks, Peter Roebuck, Brian Rose and Derek Taylor and the writing of

Ralph Ellis. There is much wisdom, many examples from experience of the famous, and illustrating illustrations.

In *Cricket From Father to Son* (Kaye & Ward; £1.95) T. C. (Dickie) Dodds, the former Essex batsman, sets out to help fathers to teach their sons cricket. He does so intelligently, diligently and purposefully. The diagrams are extremely apposite.

Batting (Pelham Books; £5.50), by Graham Gooch in collaboration with Patrick Murphy, is another in this specialist instructional cricket series. There is much sound first-hand experience and helpful photographic illustrations.

Alf Gover's Cricket Manual (Lutterworth Press; £4.95) is the major instructional study by the man who has made an outstanding reputation as cricket coach and consultant. It is sage and sound; above all, where Mr Gover cannot be at hand to show the young player what to do, he ensures that there is ample illustration to do so.

Captaincy (Pelham Books; £5.50) by Ray Illingworth is also in the specialist instructional series. It is a book characteristic of its author, as profound a tactical thinker as the game has known; and here he gives chapter and verse of his deep experience.

In *Games for Cricket Training* (Pelham; £5.50) by A. S. M. (Alan) Oakman, the former Sussex and England player and present chief coach of Warwickshire is concerned to improve specific skills through group play. Primarily a handbook for coaches, it lays out a sectionalised guide to games intended to build speed, stamina and skills. For most of the games, a scoring system is provided to maintain the keenness of competitive play.

Playfair Cricket Annual 1980 (Queen Anne Press; 90p), edited by Gordon Ross, continues in its now established format as useful pocket-sized reference. The county notes, records and biographies, and the sections of first-class and Test career records are particularly useful.

World of Cricket 1980 (Queen Anne Press; £4.95), edited by Trevor Bailey and compiled by Bill Frindall, and illustrated by Patrick Eagar, again affords a sound balance between news, views, pictures and statistics. The diary of the season, county reviews and register of players are all valuable.

Pelham Cricket Year (Pelham Books; £6.95), edited by David Lemmon, in its second edition again appeared in all its bulk (some 750 pages) hard on the heels of the players walking off the field of the 1980 English season. It covers the world cricket scene from October 1979 and is obviously made up sectionally, the last pages being slotted in hot from someone's typewriter. It is the most topical coverage of cricket in modern times; with authoritative national reviews, scores and statistics in shrewd proportion, it is a considerable editorial and technical achievement.

The Official England Cricket Team Annual (Grandreams, 205/211 Kentish Town Road, London, NW5; £1.95), edited by John Barraclough and Alan Lee, and written by the indefatigable Alan Lee, emanates – "approved by the TCCB" – from the England dressing-room. Part of the communal projection plans inaugurated by Mike Brearley when he captained the Test team, it is a large quarto with features on most of the

England players who toured Australia in 1979-80; lively – even vivid – illustrations and layout.

World Cricket Annual 1979-80 (available in the UK from E. K. Brown, Bevois Mount, Church Street, Liskeard, Cornwall; £2.35 including postage), edited by A. Aziz Rehmatullah, is a Pakistani publication aiming at world coverage. In addition to feature articles – not always up to date – on, and by, players of many countries, it gives, usefully, full scores of the numerous Test series of 1978-79.

Cricket Year (Peter Isaacson Publications, 46 Porter Street, Prahran, 3181, Victoria, Australia; $A5.50) edited by Ken Piesse, is the only Australian annual to appear for the 1980-81 season there. Reviewing the 1979-80 season and looking forward to 1980-81, it is particularly valuable – both domestically and overseas – as affording the only available full coverage of state and grade cricket in Australia. It includes also a complete register of all Australian Test cricketers from 1877, with dates, period and vital – cricketing – statistics.

West Indies Cricket Annual 1980 (Goodyear Gibbs, Caribbean; no price given) edited by Tony Cozier, reaches its eleventh edition. It affords the only complete record of the main – and some of the lesser – domestic competitions of the Caribbean and, for that fact alone, becomes one of the essential archives of the game. There are, too, adequate match reports of all West Indies representative matches in 1979 and 1980. The layout is pleasing, varied, and pictorially enhanced by capable use of colour.

The 1979 Shell Cricket Almanack of New Zealand (available in the UK from E. K. Brown, Bevois Mount, Church Street, Liskeard, Cornwall; £3.50) edited by Arthur H. Carman, is the 32nd issue. Shell's subsidy is helpful in sustaining this annual. Arthur Carman, as ever, discharges his duty conscientiously in providing for the archives a full and sound record of the domestic game in New Zealand. There are biographical notes on the Shell competition players. The choice of batsman of the year falls on Bruce Edgar, and of bowler on Richard Hadlee.

The county and association handbooks and yearbooks which follow may be assumed to be octavo in size, paper-backed and, in the case of counties, to include scores of Championship, Gillette Cup, Benson and Hedges Cup and John Player League matches of 1979; averages for that season, captain's and/or committee's report; and relevant photographs. Only exceptions to this pattern are noted.

Essex County Cricket Club 1980 Handbook (Essex CCC, County Ground, New Whittle Street, Chelmsford, Essex, CM2 0PG; £1) celebrates their dual success of 1979. Every score-detail of those triumphs is included; and there are, too, feature articles. One, by David Acfield, goes to the heart of the matter. "The bare facts, however, do little to convey the sense of relief experienced by the players; that, at last, after several years of threatening to win a major title, we had succeeded." Other pieces are contributed by Peter Baxter, Henry Blofeld, Doug Insole, Ralph Dellor, Keith Fletcher, Tony Lewis, Don Oslear, Bernard Webber and William Franklyn. This issue will make a fine keepsake of a splendid success.

Hampshire Handbook 1980 (Hampshire CCC, The County Ground, Northlands Road, Southampton, SO9 2TY; £1) is edited by Peter Marshall, who has worked with an enthusiasm reminiscent of his predecessor, Desmond Eagar. He was obviously delighted to print a chapter of Desmond Eagar's reminiscences. Other features are by Mike Taylor, Imogen Ginsberg, David Kenny, Mike Neasom, Vic Isaacs and Tony Mitchener. Valuably for distant followers of the county, too, Peter Sainsbury, the club coach, contributed a review of the Second Eleven and Arthur Holt of the Colts.

Surrey County Cricket Club Yearbook 1980 (Surrey CCC, The Oval, Kennington, London, SE11 5SS; £1) has feature articles by John Edrich – on Graham Roope, the beneficiary – Alex Bannister, Alf Gover, and on the long sequence of Surrey's matches against the Australians.

Cricket in Kent Year Book (Association of Kent Cricket Clubs, Coombe Firs, Powdermill Lane, Leigh, Nr Tonbridge, TN11 8PY; 25p) is a working handbook for secretaries and match secretaries of clubs in the county, enthusiastically introduced by the president and chairman.

Midland Club Cricket Conference Year Book 1980 (from Brian F. Jones, "Bleak House", 150 Lordswood Road, Birmingham, B17 9BT; £1) edited by J. W. Jones and Miss M. Wheeldon is the 33rd edition since the late Leslie W. Jones founded it. Primarily a working document for club secretaries, it carries features by Mike Jackson, Alf Tolley, Peter Stevens, Jack Threlfall and Brian F. Jones.

Irish Cricket Union Yearbook 1980 (from Derek Scott, 45 Foxrock Park, Foxrock, Dublin 18; 80p), includes a "Secretary's" (sic; Gaelic?) Report, a salute to their West Indian visitors; a feature on Ossie Colhoun by Sean Pender; and sundry features by Alan Gibson and observers in the various regions of the Union.

New Forest Club Cricket Association Handbook 1980 (NFCCA, "Subtle", Hazel Grove, Ashurst, Hampshire; no price given) contains six remarkable photographs by Roger Loveless of New Forest club cricket pavilions, under the title "Cricket Architecture, Nova Foresta, 1980"; a piece of verse by L. Warren and an essay "New Forest Cricket One Hundred Years Ago" by A. C. Norris.

The Cricketer International (The Cricketer, Beech Hanger, Ashurst, Tunbridge Wells, Kent, TN3 9ST; £9.25 for ten monthly issues plus Spring and Winter annuals) edited by R. J. Hayter, reached its 61st volume in 1980. Traditional, durable, familiar, it has substantial contributions from Alan Gibson (Journal of the Season), Alex Bannister, John Woodcock, H. F. Ellis, Tony Lewis, E. W. Swanton, Mike Brearley, Gordon Ross, Alan Lee, Alf Gover, and Bill Frindall.

Wisden Cricket Monthly (Wisden Cricket Magazines, 313 Kilburn Lane, London, W9 3EQ; twelve monthly issues, 60p per issue; or £9 per year) edited by David Frith, is now two years old. Its contributors include Ted Dexter, Jim Laker, David Gower, Bob Willis, Keith Andrew (coaching), Michael Carey and the editor. Patrick Eagar is the picture editor.

The Cricketer International Quarterly (The Cricketer, Beech Hanger,

Ashurst, Tunbridge Wells, Kent, TN3 9ST; 75p per issue) edited by Gordon Ross, is essentially the statistical supplement to The Cricketer International. Unfortunately, confusedly and stubbornly, it continues to appear dated for instance 'Winter 1980' with no indication as to whether it means winter 1979-80 or 1980-81; when it would be so simple to make it clear. In fact that dating – in complete conflict with the method long employed by Wisden in its list of Test appearances – meant 1979-80. The Quarterly's value lies in its full Test scores; such lists as "Meet the Newcomers", and career records. Statistics were by Michael Fordham, Bill Frindall, Barry McCaully and the late A. H. Wagg; Bill Smith provided the cover-photographs.

The issues of *Nottinghamshire Scorebook* (Nottinghamshire County Cricket Club, Trent Bridge, Nottingham; 35p per copy) compiled by Peter Wynne-Thomas, were dated June, July, August and September 1980. Between them they contain full scores of every match involving a team raised by Nottinghamshire CCC in 1980; plus averages, monthly reviews and the first four parts of a bibliography of books about Nottinghamshire cricket.

Cricketer (Newspress Pty Ltd, 603-611 Little Lonsdale Street, Melbourne 3000, Australia; $A1.20) edited by Ken Piesse, continues monthly through the Australian summer. Regular contributors are Phil Wilkins, Ray Robinson, Frank Tyson, Greg McKie and the editor; Patrick Eagar is the special photographer.

The Cricket Player (PO Box 28-280, Remuera, Auckland, NZ; monthly 85cNZ or $NZ8.75 annual subscription) edited by Don Cameron, continues healthily and positively as a mirror of the game in that country. Main contributors are Dick Brittenden, Martin Horton, Bob Monteith, and Ern Cosgrove.

FIXTURES FOR 1981

Indicates Sunday play; † *Not first-class*

Wednesday, April 22

Cambridge	Univ. v Essex

Saturday, April 25

Cambridge*	Univ. v Hants
Oxford	Univ. v Glam.

Wednesday, April 29

Lord's	MCC v Middx
Cambridge	Univ. v Northants
Oxford	Univ. v Somerset

Saturday, May 2

Cambridge	Univ. v Lancs.
Oxford	Univ. v Yorks.

Wednesday, May 6

Cardiff	Glam. v Glos.
Southampton	Hants v Somerset
Canterbury	Kent v Notts.
Leicester	Leics. v Derby.
Lord's	Middx v Essex
Northampton	Northants v Lancs.
Birmingham	Warw. v Yorks.
Worcester	Worcs. v Sussex
Cambridge	Univ. v Surrey

Saturday, May 9

Benson and Hedges Cup (1 day)

Derby	Derby. v Yorks.
Swansea	Glam. v Essex
Manchester	Lancs. v Warw.
Leicester	Leics. v Glos.
Lord's	Middx v Hants
Northampton	Northants v Notts.

Monday, May 11

Benson and Hedges Cup (1 day)

Canterbury	Kent v Oxford and Cam. U.
Hove	Sussex v Surrey

Wednesday, May 13

Manchester	Lancs. v Somerset
Nottingham	Notts. v Leics.
The Oval	Surrey v Derby.
Hove	Sussex v Glam.
Nuneaton (Griff and Coton)	Warw. v Kent
Leeds	Yorks. v Middx
Cambridge	Univ. v Worcs.
Oxford	Univ. v Glos.

Benson and Hedges Cup (1 day)

Southampton	Hants v Minor C.

Saturday, May 16

Arundel	Lavinia, Duchess of Norfolk's XI v Australians (1 day)

Benson and Hedges Cup (1 day)

Chelmsford	Essex v Somerset
Bristol	Glos. v Northants
Bournemouth	Hants v Surrey
Slough	Minor C. v Middx
Nottingham	Notts. v Worcs.
Oxford	Oxford and Cam. U. v Glam.
Glasgow (Titwood)	Scotland v Lancs.
Birmingham	Warw. v Derby.

Tuesday, May 19

Benson and Hedges Cup (1 day)

Derby	Derby. v Scotland
Cardiff	Glam. v Kent
Lord's	Middx v Sussex
Northampton	Northants v Leics.
Cambridge	Oxford and Cam. U. v Somerset
Birmingham	Warw. v Yorks.
Worcester	Worcs. v Glos.

Wednesday, May 20

Southampton	Hants v Australians

Thursday, May 21

Benson and Hedges Cup (1 day)

Chelmsford	Essex v Oxford and Cam. U.
Bristol	Glos. v Notts.
Manchester	Lancs. v Derby.
Leicester	Leics. v Worcs.
Slough	Minor C. v Sussex
Taunton	Somerset v Kent
The Oval	Surrey v Middx
Bradford	Yorks. v Scotland

Saturday, May 23

Taunton*	Somerset v Australians
Derby	Derby. v Notts.
Chelmsford	Essex v Glos.
Cardiff	Glam. v Kent
Manchester	Lancs. v Yorks.

Lord's	Middx v Sussex
Northampton	Northants v Leics.
The Oval	Surrey v Hants
Birmingham	Warw. v Worcs.
Oxford†	Univ. v Free Foresters

Wednesday, May 27

Swansea	Glam. v Australians
Chelmsford	Essex v Surrey
Bristol	Glos. v Sussex
Dartford	Kent v Yorks.
Leicester	Leics. v Hants
Uxbridge	Middx v Notts.
Northampton	Northants v Derby.
Worcester	Worcs. v Lancs.
Oxford	Univ. v Warw.

Saturday, May 30

Bristol*	Glos. v Australians

Benson and Hedges Cup (1 day)

Dartford	Kent v Essex
Nottingham	Notts. v Leics.
Glasgow (Titwood)	Scotland v Warw.
Taunton	Somerset v Glam.
The Oval	Surrey v Minor C.
Hove	Sussex v Hants
Worcester	Worcs. v Northants
Leeds	Yorks. v Lancs.

Wednesday, June 3

Basingstoke	Hants v Middx
Manchester	Lancs. v Surrey
Nottingham	Notts. v Glos.
Hove	Sussex v Somerset
Birmingham	Warw. v Northants
Hereford	Worcs. v Glam.
Leeds	Yorks. v Essex
Oxford	Univ. v Leics.

Thursday, June 4

Lord's	ENGLAND v AUSTRALIA (1st 1-Day Prudential Trophy)

Saturday, June 6

Birmingham	ENGLAND v AUSTRALIA (2nd 1-Day Prudential Trophy)
Derby	Derby. v Warw.
Swansea	Glam. v Surrey
Bristol	Glos. v Yorks.
Lord's	Middx v Somerset
Northampton	Northants v Kent
Hove	Sussex v Lancs.
Worcester	Worcs. v Essex
Cambridge	Univ. v Notts.
Oxford†	Univ. v MCC

Monday, June 8

Leeds	ENGLAND v AUSTRALIA (3rd 1-Day Prudential Trophy)

Wednesday, June 10

Derby	Derby. v Australians
Bristol	Glos. v Northants
Bournemouth	Hants v Glam.
Tunbridge Wells	Kent v Leics.
Manchester	Lancs. v Warw.
The Oval	Surrey v Worcs.
Cambridge	Univ. v Sussex
Oxford	Univ. v Middx

Saturday, June 13

Lord's*	Middx v Australians
Oxford	Oxford and Cam. U. v Sri Lankans
Derby	Derby. v Essex
Tunbridge Wells	Kent v Sussex
Leicester	Leics. v Glam.
Bath	Somerset v Glos.
Stourport-on-Severn	Worcs. v Hants
Bradford	Yorks. v Notts.

Wednesday, June 17

Bristol	Glos. v Sri Lankans
Ilford	Essex v Middx
Cardiff	Glam. v Warw.
Northampton	Northants v Sussex
Bath	Somerset v Notts.
The Oval	Surrey v Lancs.
Sheffield	Yorks. v Derby.
Leicester	Leics. v Cambridge U.
Oxford	Univ. v Kent

Thursday, June 18

Nottingham*	ENGLAND v AUSTRALIA (1st Cornhill Test, 5 days)

Saturday, June 20

Birmingham	Warw. v Sri Lankans
Derby	Derby. v Northants
Ilford	Essex v Sussex
Southampton	Hants v Glos.
Liverpool	Lancs. v Notts.
Worcester	Worcs. v Somerset
Lord's	Oxford v Cambridge

Wednesday, June 24

Sri Lankans v County not in B & H Cup quarter-final

Benson and Hedges Cup – Quarter-Finals (1 day)

Thursday, June 25

	Australians v County not in B & H Cup quarter-final (1 day)

Saturday, June 27

Canterbury*	Kent v Australians
Hastings	Sussex v Sri Lankans
Swansea	Glam. v Somerset
Gloucester	Glos. v Warw.
Manchester	Lancs. v Hants
Leicester	Leics. v Essex
Nottingham	Notts. v Middx
The Oval	Surrey v Northants
Worcester	Worcs. v Yorks.

Wednesday, July 1

Worcester	Worcs. v Sri Lankans
Derby	Derby. v Lancs.
Chelmsford	Essex v Notts.
Swansea	Glam. v Hants
Maidstone	Kent v Middx
Northampton	Northants v Glos.
Taunton	Somerset v Surrey
Bradford	Yorks. v Leics.

Thursday, July 2

Lord's	ENGLAND v AUSTRALIA (2nd Cornhill Test, 5 days)

Saturday, July 4

Derby	Derby. v Worcs.
Bournemouth	Hants v Notts.
Maidstone	Kent v Lancs.
Leicester	Leics. v Somerset
Northampton	Northants v Glam.
Hove	Sussex v Glos.
Birmingham	Warw. v Essex
Harrogate	Yorks. v Surrey

Wednesday, July 8
Benson and Hedges Cup – Semi-Finals
(1 day)

Nottingham (or Derby)	A Representative XI v Sri Lankans
Harrogate	Tilcon Trophy (Three 1-day matches)

Thursday, July 9

	Australians v County not in B & H Cup semi-final (1 day)

Saturday, July 11

Nottingham	Notts. v Worcs.
Taunton	Somerset v Sussex
The Oval	Surrey v Warw.

NatWest Bank Trophy – First Round
(1 day)

Southampton	Hants v Ches.
Hitchin	Herts. v Essex
Dublin (Clontarf)	Ireland v Glos.
Canterbury	Kent v Yorks.
Manchester	Lancs. v Durham
Oxford (Christ Church)	Oxfords. v Glam.
Bury St Edmunds	Suffolk v Derby.

Saturday, July 11

Northampton*	Northants v Australians
Leicester*	Leics. v Sri Lankans

Wednesday, July 15

Manchester	Lancs. v Sri Lankans
Southend	Essex v Northants
Cardiff	Glam. v Yorks.
Bristol	Glos. v Worcs.
Portsmouth	Hants v Derby.
Lord's	Middx v Kent
Hove	Sussex v Surrey
Coventry (Courtaulds)	Warw. v Leics.

Thursday, July 16

Leeds	ENGLAND v AUSTRALIA (3rd Cornhill Test, 5 days)

Saturday, July 18

Northampton*	Northants v Sri Lankans
Southend	Essex v Lancs.
Bristol	Glos. v Worcs.
Portsmouth	Hants v Surrey
Leicester	Leics. v Kent
Lord's	Middx v Worcs.
Worksop	Notts. v Yorks.
Taunton	Somerset v Derby.
Hove	Sussex v Warw.

Wednesday, July 22

Canterbury (or Sheffield)	Kent v Sri Lankans (or Yorks. v Sri Lankans if Kent in NWB Trophy second round) (2 days if either in B & H Cup final)

NatWest Bank Trophy – Second Round
(1 day)

Chester-le-Street or Manchester	Durham or Lancs. v Middx
Cardiff or Oxford (Christ Church)	Glam. or Oxfords. v Ches. or Hants

Bristol or Belfast (Ormeau)	Glos. or Ireland v Essex or Herts.
Canterbury or Leeds	Kent or Yorks. v Notts.
Northampton	Northants v Somerset
The Oval	Surrey v Leics.
Birmingham	Warw. v Sussex
Worcester	Worcs. v Derby. or Suffolk

Thursday, July 23

Glasgow (Titwood)	Scotland v Australians (1 day)

Saturday, July 25

Lord's	BENSON AND HEDGES CUP FINAL (1 day)
Worcester*	Worcs. v Australians (if Worcs. not in B & H Cup final)
The Oval (or Taunton)	Surrey v Sri Lankans (or Somerset v Sri Lankans if Surrey in B & H Cup final)
Derby	Derby. v Kent (or September 9 if either in B & H Cup final)
Nottingham	Notts. v Lancs. (or August 12 if either in B & H Cup final)
Dublin (Clontarf)*	Ireland v Scotland

Wednesday, July 29

Bournemouth	Hants v Sri Lankans
Derby	Derby. v Glos.
Canterbury	Kent v Essex
Southport	Lancs. v Middx
Leicester	Leics. v Notts.
Taunton	Somerset v Glam.
Guildford	Surrey v Sussex
Stourbridge	Worcs. v Northants
Scarborough	Yorks. v Warw.

Thursday, July 30

Birmingham*	ENGLAND v AUSTRALIA (4th Cornhill Test, 5 days)

Saturday, August 1

Cardiff*	Glam. v Sri Lankans
Chelmsford	Essex v Derby.
Canterbury	Kent v Hants
Manchester	Lancs. v Worcs.
Leicester	Leics. v Sussex
Lord's	Middx v Glos.
Northampton	Northants v Warw.
Nottingham	Notts. v Surrey
Sheffield	Yorks. v Somerset

Tuesday, August 4

Reading	Minor C. v Sri Lankans

Wednesday, August 5

NatWest Bank Trophy – Quarter-Finals (1 day)

(Venue to be decided)†	Scotland v MCC

Thursday, August 6

	Australians v County not in NWB Trophy quarter-finals (1 day)

Saturday, August 8

Chelmsford*	Essex v Australians
Derby	Derby. v Leics.
Cardiff	Glam. v Lancs.
Cheltenham	Glos. v Surrey
Lord's	Middx v Warw.
Weston-super-Mare	Somerset v Northants
Eastbourne	Sussex v Kent
Worcester	Worcs. v Notts.
Middlesbrough	Yorks. v Hants

Wednesday, August 12

Chelmsford	Essex v Kent
Cheltenham	Glos. v Hants
Northampton	Northants v Middx
Nottingham	Notts. v Lancs. (if not played on July 25)
Weston-super-Mare	Somerset v Worcs.
The Oval	Surrey v Leics.
Eastbourne	Sussex v Derby.
Birmingham	Warw. v Glam.

Thursday, August 13

Manchester*	ENGLAND v AUSTRALIA (5th Cornhill Test, 5 days)

Saturday, August 15

Swansea	Glam. v Derby.
Cheltenham	Glos. v Kent
Southampton	Hants v Essex
Leicester	Leics. v Worcs.
Wellingborough	Northants v Yorks.
Nottingham	Notts. v Sussex
The Oval	Surrey v Middx
Birmingham	Warw. v Lancs.

Sunday, August 16

(Venue to be decided)†	Wales v Ireland
	Warwickshire Under-25 Competition Semi-Finals (1 day) (or Sunday, August 23)

Wednesday, August 19

NatWest Bank Trophy – Semi-Finals (1 day)

Thursday, August 20

	Australians v County not in NWB Trophy semi-finals (1 day)

Saturday, August 22

Hove*	Sussex v Australians
Derby	Derby. v Yorks.
Folkestone	Kent v Surrey
Manchester	Lancs. v Leics.
Lord's	Middx v Glam.
Northampton	Northants v Essex
Taunton	Somerset v Hants
Birmingham	Warw. v Notts.
Worcester	Worcs. v Glos.

Sunday, August 23 (if not played on August 16)

	Warwickshire Under-25 Competition Semi-Finals

Wednesday, August 26

Colchester	Essex v Leics.
Swansea	Glam. v Worcs.
Bournemouth	Hants v Sussex
Folkestone	Kent v Somerset
Blackpool	Lancs. v Derby.
Lord's	Middx v Yorks.
Cleethorpes	Notts. v Northants

Thursday, August 27

The Oval	ENGLAND v AUSTRALIA (6th Cornhill Test, 5 days)

Saturday, August 29

Colchester	Essex v Glam.
Bristol	Glos. v Somerset
Bournemouth	Hants v Kent

Leicester	Leics. v Northants
Nottingham	Notts. v Derby.
Hove	Sussex v Middx
Worcester	Worcs. v Warw.
Leeds	Yorks. v Lancs.

Sunday, August 30

Birmingham	Warwickshire Under-25 Competition Final (1 day)

Wednesday, September 2

Leicester	Leics. v Middx
The Oval	Surrey v Kent
Hove	Sussex v Hants
Birmingham	Warw. v Somerset
Scarborough	Fenner Trophy (Three 1-day matches)

Saturday, September 5

Lord's	NATWEST BANK TROPHY FINAL (1 day)

Wednesday, September 9

Derby	Derby. v Kent (if not played on July 25)
Cardiff	Glam. v Leics.
Manchester	Lancs. v Glos.
Lord's or Uxbridge	Middx v Surrey
Taunton	Somerset v Essex
Birmingham	Warw. v Hants
Scarborough	Yorks. v Northants

Saturday, September 12

Derby	Derby. v Middx
Bristol	Glos. v Leics.
Southampton	Hants v Northants
Canterbury	Kent v Worcs.
Nottingham	Notts. v Glam.
Taunton	Somerset v Warw.
The Oval	Surrey v Essex
Hove	Sussex v Yorks.

AUSTRALIAN TOUR, 1981

* Indicates Sunday play.

MAY

16	Arundel	v Lavinia, Duchess of Norfolk's XI (1 day)
20	Southampton	v Hants
23	Taunton*	v Somerset
27	Swansea	v Glam.
30	Bristol*	v Glos.

JUNE

4	Lord's	v ENGLAND (1-day Prudential Trophy)
6	Birmingham	v ENGLAND (1-day Prudential Trophy)
8	Leeds	v ENGLAND (1-day Prudential Trophy)

10	Derby	v Derby.
13	Lord's*	v Middx
18	Nottingham*	v ENGLAND (1st Cornhill Test, 5 days)
25		v County not in B & H Cup quarter-final (1 day)
27	Canterbury*	v Kent

JULY

2	Lord's	v ENGLAND (2nd Cornhill Test, 5 days)
9		v County not in B & H Cup semi-final (1 day)
11	Northampton*	v Northants
16	Leeds	v ENGLAND (3rd Cornhill Test, 5 days)
23	Glasgow (Titwood)	v Scotland (1 day)

| 25 | Worcester* | v Worcs. (if Worcs. not in B & H Cup final) |
| 30 | Birmingham* | v ENGLAND (4th Cornhill Test, 5 days) |

AUGUST

6		v County not in NWB Trophy quarter-finals (1 day)
8	Chelmsford*	v Essex
13	Manchester*	v ENGLAND (5th Cornhill Test, 5 days)
20		v County not in NWB Trophy semi-finals (1 day)
22	Hove*	v Sussex
27	The Oval	v ENGLAND (6th Cornhill Test, 5 days)

SRI LANKAN TOUR, 1981

* Indicates Sunday play.

JUNE

13	Oxford	v Oxford and Cam. U.
17	Bristol	v Glos.
20	Birmingham	v Warw.
24		v County not in B & H Cup quarter-final
27	Hastings	v Sussex

JULY

1	Worcester	v Worcs.
8	Nottingham (or Derby)	v a Representative XI
11	Leicester*	v Leics.
15	Manchester	v Lancs.

18	Northampton*	v Northants
22	Canterbury (or Sheffield)	v Kent (or Yorks. if Kent in NWB Trophy second round) (2 days if either in B & H Cup final)
25	The Oval (or Taunton)	v Surrey (or Somerset if Surrey in B & H Cup final)
29	Bournemouth	v Hants

AUGUST

| 1 | Cardiff* | v Glam. |
| 4 | Reading | v Minor C. |

JOHN PLAYER SUNDAY LEAGUE, 1981

MAY

10 – Glam. v Worcs. (Abergavenny); Glos. v Leics. (Moreton-in-Marsh); Lancs. v Derby. (Manchester); Middx v Hants (Lord's); Northants v Notts. (Northampton); Somerset v Essex (Taunton); Sussex v Surrey (Hove); Warw. v Yorks. (Birmingham).

17 – Hants v Glam. (Bournemouth); Northants v Glos. (Milton Keynes); Notts. v Somerset (Nottingham); Surrey v Middx (The Oval); Worcs. v Sussex (Worcester); Yorks. v Kent (Huddersfield).

24 – Derby. v Notts. (Derby); Essex v Glos. (Chelmsford); Glam. v Kent (Cardiff); Lancs. v Northants (Manchester); Middx v Sussex (Lord's); Warw. v Worcs. (Birmingham); Yorks. v Leics. (Leeds).

31 – Essex v Kent (Chelmsford); Hants v Sussex (Basingstoke); Lancs. v Somerset (Manchester); Northants v Leics. (Northampton); Surrey v Derby. (The Oval); Yorks. v Middx (Bradford).

JUNE

7 – Glam. v Surrey (Swansea); Glos. v Yorks. (Bristol); Kent v Northants (Maidstone); Middx v Somerset (Lord's); Notts. v Essex (Nottingham); Sussex v Lancs. (Hove); Warw. v Leics. (Birmingham).

14 – Derby. v Hants (Derby); Leics. v Glam. (Leicester); Somerset v Glos. (Bath); Surrey v Northants (The Oval); Worcs. v Essex (Worcester).

21 – Essex v Sussex (Ilford); Hants v Glos. (Portsmouth); Lancs. v Notts. (Manchester); Middx v Leics. (Lord's); Somerset v Kent (Bath); Warw. v Derby. (Birmingham); Worcs. v Northants (Worcester); Yorks. v Glam. (Hull).

28 – Glam. v Warw. (Swansea); Glos. v Derby. (Gloucester); Lancs. v Hants (Manchester); Leics. v Essex (Leicester); Notts. v Middx (Nottingham); Sussex v Northants (Hastings); Worcs. v Yorks. (Worcester).

JULY

5 – Derby. v Worcs. (Derby); Hants v Notts. (Portsmouth); Kent v Lancs. (Maidstone); Leics. v Somerset (Leicester); Northants v Glam. (Luton); Sussex v Glos. (Hove); Warw. v Essex (Birmingham); Yorks. v Surrey (Scarborough).

12 – Kent v Notts. (Canterbury); Lancs. v Middx (Manchester); Somerset v Sussex (Taunton); Surrey v Warw. (The Oval); Worcs. v Hants (Worcester).

19 – Essex v Lancs. (Southend); Glos. v Glam. (Bristol); Hants v Surrey (Southampton); Leics. v Kent (Leicester); Middx v Worcs. (Lord's); Notts. v Yorks. (Nottingham); Somerset v Derby. (Taunton); Sussex v Warw. (Horsham).

26 – Derby. v Kent (Derby); Essex v Yorks. (Chelmsford); Glam. v Sussex (Ebbw Vale); Leics. v Notts. (Leicester); Northants v Middx (Tring); Surrey v Lancs. (The Oval); Warw. v Hants (Birmingham).

AUGUST

2 – Essex v Derby. (Chelmsford); Kent v Hants (Canterbury); Lancs. v Worcs. (Manchester); Leics. v Sussex (Leicester); Middx v Glos. (Lord's); Northants v Warw. (Northampton); Notts. v Surrey (Nottingham); Yorks. v Somerset (Scarborough).

9 – Derby. v Leics. (Derby); Glam. v Lancs. (Cardiff); Glos. v Surrey (Cheltenham); Middx v Warw. (Lord's); Somerset v Northants (Weston-super-Mare); Sussex v Kent (Eastbourne); Worcs. v Notts. (Worcester); Yorks. v Hants (Middlesbrough).

16 – Glam. v Derby. (Swansea); Glos. v Kent (Cheltenham); Hants v Essex (Southampton); Leics. v Worcs. (Leicester); Northants v Yorks. (Wellingborough); Notts. v Sussex (Nottingham); Surrey v Somerset (The Oval); Warw. v Lancs. (Birmingham).

23 – Derby. v Yorks. (Derby); Kent v Surrey (Folkestone); Lancs. v Leics. (Manchester); Middx v Glam. (Lord's); Northants v Essex (Northampton); Somerset v Hants (Taunton); Warw. v Notts. (Birmingham); Worcs. v Glos. (Worcester).

30 – Derby. v Northants (Derby); Essex v Glam. (Colchester); Glos. v Warw. (Bristol); Kent v Middx (Canterbury); Leics. v Surrey (Leicester); Worcs. v Somerset (Worcester); Yorks. v Lancs. (Leeds).

SEPTEMBER

6 – Essex v Middx (Chelmsford); Glam. v Somerset (Cardiff); Hants v Leics. (Bournemouth); Kent v Warw. (Canterbury); Notts. v Glos. (Nottingham); Surrey v Worcs. (The Oval); Sussex v Derby. (Hove).

13 – Derby. v Middx (Derby); Glos. v Lancs. (Bristol); Hants v Northants (Southampton); Kent v Worcs. (Canterbury); Notts. v Glam. (Nottingham); Somerset v Warw. (Taunton); Surrey v Essex (The Oval); Sussex v Yorks. (Hove).

MINOR COUNTIES FIXTURES, 1981

MAY

24 – Lincs. v Cambs. (Sleaford).

27 – Ches. v Durham (Alderley Edge).

31 – Northumb. v Lincs. (Jesmond).

JUNE

3 – Staffs. v Shrops. (Bass, Burton upon Trent).

8 – Lancs. II v Ches. (Heywood).

9 – Herts. v Norfolk (Watford).

14 – Ches. v Staffs. (Nantwich); Cumb. v Lincs. (Carlisle); A Minor Counties XI v Lavinia, Duchess of Norfolk's XI (Arundel) (1 day).

15 – Lancs. II v Northumb. (Lytham); Durham v Shrops. (Sunderland).

17 – Camb. v Norfolk (Wisbech).

21 – Cumb. v Northumb. (Netherfield); Lincs. v Staffs. (Cleethorpes).

24 – Herts. v Cambs. (Hitchin).

27 – Oxfords. v Bucks. (Christ Church, Oxford).

28 – Lincs. v Norfolk (Ross, Grimsby); Shrops. v Ches. (St Georges, Telford); Cumb. v Durham (Penrith).

30 – Staffs. v Durham (Longton).

JULY

4 – Herts. v Beds. (Clarence Park, St Albans).

5 – Durham v Northumb. (Durham City); Staffs. v Ches. (Stone); Bucks. v Berks. (Slough); Corn. v Somerset II (Falmouth).

8 – Cambs. v Lincs. (Papworth).

12 – Lincs. v Northumb. (Burghley Park, Stamford); Berks. v Bucks. (to be decided); Corn. v Devon (Truro).

13 – Shrops. v Staffs. (Wellington).

18 – Beds. v Bucks. (Bedford School).

19 – Northumb. v Cumb. (Jesmond); Corn. v Berks. (Penzance).

20 – Wilts. v Oxfords. (Devizes); Cambs. v Suffolk (Fenners).

21 – Devon v Berks. (Sidmouth).

22 – Wilts. v Somerset II (Trowbridge).

24 – Oxfords. v Berks. (Provisional venue; Morris Motors).

25 – Beds. v Cambs. (Goldington Bury, Bedford)

26 – Corn. v Dorset (Camborne); Herts. v Bucks. (Balls Park, Hertford); Ches. v Shrops. (Wallasey).

27 – Staffs. v Northumb. (Brewood); Berks. v Wilts. (Ibis CC, Reading); Lancs. II v Cumb. (Lancaster); Norfolk v Cambs. (Lakenham).

28 – Devon v Dorset (Exmouth).

29 – Ches. v Northumb. (Bowdon); Berks. v Oxfords. (Courage CC, Reading); Norfolk v Lincs. (Lakenham); Somerset II v Wilts. (Keynsham).

AUGUST

1 – Oxfords. v Dorset (St Edward's, Oxford); Suffolk v Bucks. (GRE, Ipswich).

2 – Northumb. v Durham (Jesmond); Berks. v Corn. (Hungerford); Shrops. v Beds. (London Road, Shrewsbury); Cumb. v Lancs. II (Millom).

3 – Dorset v Somerset II (Weymouth); Norfolk v Bucks. (Lakenham); Suffolk v Herts. (Ransomes, Ipswich).

4 – MINOR COUNTIES v SRI LANKANS (Reading) (3 days); Wilts. v Corn. (Salisbury).

5 – Staffs. v Lincs. (Walsall); Devon v Somerset II (Torquay); Norfolk v Herts. (Lakenham).

6 – Dorset v Corn. (Weymouth); Wilts. v Berks. (Swindon).

7 – Bucks. v Oxfords. (Marlow); Beds. v Herts. (Henlow); Norfolk v Suffolk (Lakenham).

9 – Northumb. v Ches. (Jesmond); Bucks. v Suffolk (Chesham).

10 – Wilts. v Dorset (Chippenham); Shrops. v Lancs. II (Bridgnorth); Oxfords. v Devon (Abingdon School).

11 – Beds. v Suffolk (Dunstable); Durham v Ches. (Chester-le-Street).

12 – Berks. v Devon (Reading).

13 – Cambs. v Beds. (March).

14 – Dorset v Devon (Bournemouth); Oxfords. v Wilts. (Shipton under Wychwood).

15 – Bucks. v Beds. (Stowe School, Buckingham); Herts. v Suffolk (Bishop's Stortford).

16 – Lincs. v Cumb. (Lincoln).

17 – Durham v Staffs. (Hartlepool); Somerset II v Corn. (Taunton School).

18 – Dorset v Wilts. (Blandford); Beds. v Shrops. (Wardown Park, Luton); Suffolk v Norfolk (Mildenhall).

19 – Northumb. v Staffs. (Jesmond); Ches. v Lancs. II (Neston); Devon v Corn. (Exeter).

20 – Somerset II v Dorset (Westlands, Weston-super-Mare); Suffolk v Cambs. (Bury St Edmunds).

23 – Bucks. v Norfolk (High Wycombe); Durham v Cumb. (Stockton-on-Tees); Corn. v Wilts. (Wadebridge).

24 – Northumb. v Lancs. II (Jesmond); Devon v Oxfords. (Bovey Tracey).

26 – Dorset v Oxfords. (Poole Park); Shrops. v Durham (Newport).

27 – Cambs. v Herts. (Fenner's); Somerset II v Devon (Taunton).

30 – Bucks. v Herts. (Amersham); Suffolk v Beds. (Ransomes, Ipswich).

31 – Lancs. II v Shrops. (Manchester).

SECOND ELEVEN CHAMPIONSHIP, 1981

All matches are of three days' duration.

APRIL

27 – Lancs. v Notts. (Manchester).

MAY

6 – Glos. v Kent (Bristol), Leics. v Lancs. (Hinckley), Notts. v Surrey (Nottingham), Yorks. v Warw. (Leeds).

13 – Derby. v Warw. (Derby), Kent v Sussex (Maidstone), Leics. v Notts. (Leicester), Middx v Essex (Eton Manor, Leyton), Surrey v Yorks. (Bank of England, Roehampton).

18 – Glos. v Worcs. (Bristol), Leics. v Northants (Leicester), Yorks. v Lancs. (Harrogate).

20 – Kent v Glam. (Folkestone), Notts. v Warw. (Nottingham), Sussex v Middx (Hove).

27 – Derby. v Leics. (Bass, Burton upon Trent), Lancs. v Worcs. (East Lancs, Blackburn), Somerset v Glam. (Taunton), Surrey v Kent (Nat West, Norbury), Warw. v Middx (Griff & Coton, Nuneaton), Yorks. v Notts. (Bradford).

JUNE

3 – Essex v Kent (Chelmsford), Glam. v Yorks. (Llandarcy), Hants v Sussex (Bournemouth), Middx v Surrey (Edmonton), Northants v Derby. (Redwell, Wellingborough), Somerset v Notts. (Taunton), Warw. v Worcs. (Moseley).

10 – Essex v Surrey (Chelmsford), Glam. v Glos. (Cardiff), Northants v Notts. (Finedon), Somerset v Hants (Taunton), Warw. v Lancs. (Birmingham), Yorks. v Derby. (Marske-by-Sea).

17 – Derby. v Notts. (Darley Dale), Lancs. v Northants (Manchester), Middx v Yorks. (Uxbridge), Somerset v Glos. (Taunton), Sussex v Surrey (Hove), Warw. v Glam. (Knowle & Dorridge).

22 – Middx v Kent (Southgate).

24 – Glam. v Worcs. (Abergavenny), Leics. v Derby. (Loughborough), Somerset v Warw. (Victoria, Street), Sussex v Hants (Horsham).

JULY

1 – Glam. v Somerset (Ebbw Vale), Hants v Glos. (Southampton), Kent v Yorks. (Canterbury), Lancs. v Derby. (Fleetwood), Leics. v Warw. (Hinckley), Notts. v Northants (Nottingham), Surrey v Middx (The Oval), Sussex v Essex (Eastbourne).

8 – Glos. v Somerset (Bristol; or at Imperial ground or Keynsham if Glos. at home in B & H Cup), Lancs. v Kent (Manchester), Middx v Hants (Harrow), Notts. v Leics. (Kelham Road, Newark), Surrey v Sussex (Nat West, Norbury), Worcs. v Warw. (Worcester), Yorks. v Glam. (Elland).

15 – Kent v Hants (Canterbury), Middx v Glam. (Harefield), Northants v Leics. (Milton Keynes), Notts. v Lancs. (Steetly, Shireoaks), Surrey v Essex (The Oval), Warw. v Somerset (Studley), Worcs. v Yorks. (Worcester).

22 – Glam. v Hants (Swansea), Kent v Essex (Dartford), Lancs. v Yorks. (Liverpool), Middx v Sussex (Enfield), Warw. v Glos. (Moseley), Worcs. v Notts. (Dudley).

29 – Essex v Sussex (Chelmsford), Middx v Warw. (Hornsey), Northants v Lancs. (Northampton), Notts. v Derby. (Central Ave., Worksop), Worcs. v Glam. (Worcester), Yorks. v Surrey (Bradford).

AUGUST

5 – Hants v Surrey (Bournemouth), Lancs. v Warw. (Southport), Northants v Middx (Northampton), Notts. v Yorks. (Valley Road, Nottingham), Sussex v Kent (Hastings), Worcs. v Leics. (venue to be arranged).

12 – Derby. v Yorks. (Derby), Glam. v Warw. (Pontardulais), Kent v Surrey (Orpington), Leics. v Middx (Leicester), Worcs. v Glos. (Worcester).

19 – Derby. v Northants (Heanor), Glos. v Hants (Bristol), Kent v Middx (Bowaters, Sittingbourne), Sussex v Notts. (Patcham), Warw. v Leics. (Courtaulds, Coventry), Yorks. v Worcs. (Leeds).

24 – Leics. v Worcs. (venue to be arranged), Middx v Northants (Bank of England, Roehampton).

26 – Derby. v Lancs. (Derby), Glam. v Surrey (Cardiff), Hants v Kent (Southampton), Notts. v Sussex (Steetly, Shireoaks), Warw. v Yorks. (Birmingham).

SEPTEMBER

2 – Essex v Middx (Eton Manor, Leyton), Glos. v Glam. (Bristol), Hants v Somerset (Southampton), Lancs. v Leics. (Preston), Warw. v Notts. (Blossomfield), Worcs. v Derby. (Worcester).

9 – Glos. v Warw. (Bristol), Lancs. v Surrey (venue to be arranged), Notts. v Worcs. (Collingham).

WARWICK UNDER 25 COMPETITION

All matches of one day's duration.
* Will be played on Monday if no result achieved on the Sunday.

MAY

11 – Worcs. v Warw. (Worcester).

12 – Warw. v Worcs. (Knowle & Dorridge).

22 – Worcs. v Glos. (Worcester).

26 – Leics. v Middx. (Leicester).

JUNE

1 – Hants v Kent (Southampton), Leics. v Northants (Leicester).

15 – Essex v Leics. (Chigwell), Kent v Hants (Tonbridge School), Northants v Middx (Northampton), Warw. v Glos. (Birmingham).

16 – Glos. v Warw. (Bristol).

22 – Glam. v Glos. (Pontardulais), Lancs. v Derby. (Manchester), Yorks. v Notts. (Doncaster).

23 – Lancs. v Notts. (Manchester), Yorks. v Derby. (York).

26 – Middx v Northants (South Hempstead).

29 – Essex v Middx (Chelmsford), Northants v Leics. (Northampton), Notts. v Lancs. (Worksop College), Surrey v Kent (Barclays Bank, Norbury).

30 – Derby. v Notts. (Derby), Surrey v Hants (Barclays Bank, Norbury), Yorks. v Lancs. (Hull).

10 – Northants v Essex (Horton).

13 – Glos. v Glam. (Bristol), Kent v Surrey (Cornhill, Beckenham), Middx v Essex (Town Ground, Watford), Sussex v Hants (Arundel).

14 – Derby. v Yorks. (Derby), Essex v Northants (Harlow), Glos. v Worcs. (Bristol).

20 – Middx v Leics. (St Albans), Surrey v Sussex (The Oval).

21 – Glam. v Worcs. (Cardiff).

27 – Glam. v Warw. (Barry Island), Hants v Sussex (Southampton).

28 – Kent v Sussex (Midland Bank, Beckenham), Warw. v Glam. (Studley).

JULY

6 – Derby. v Lancs. (Darley Dale), Leics. v Essex (Leicester), Notts. v Yorks. (Colston Bassett), Sussex v Surrey (Horsham).

7 – Lancs. v Yorks. (Manchester), Notts. v Derby. (Caythorpe), Sussex v Kent (Hastings).

AUGUST

2 – Worcs. v Glam. (Worcester).

4 – Hants v Surrey (Southampton).

16* – Semi-finals (to be played on 23rd* i not played on to 16th).

30* – FINAL (Birmingham).

© QUEEN ANNE PRESS

Limp edition ISBN 0362 02032 9   *Cased edition* ISBN 0362 02031 0

Printed in Great Britain by Spottiswoode Ballantyne Ltd.
Colchester and London

CRICKET
CRICKET
GRAY-NICOLLS
Quality within your reach
CRICKET
CRICKET

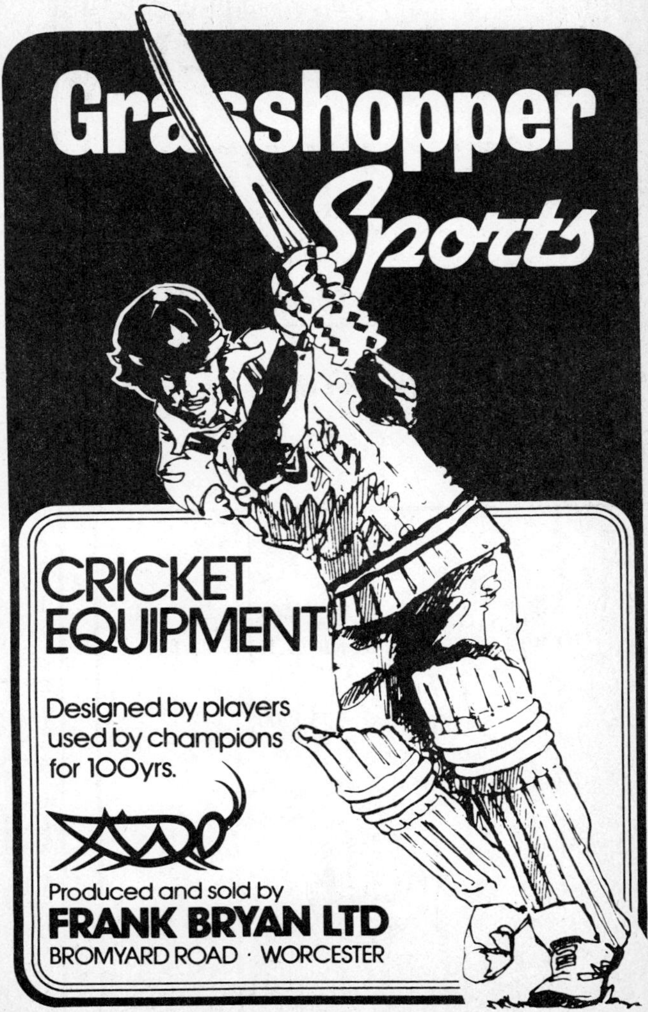
Grasshopper
Sports
CRICKET
EQUIPMENT
Designed by players
used by champions
for 100yrs.
Produced and sold by
FRANK BRYAN LTD
BROMYARD ROAD · WORCESTER

The Prudential Assurance Company Ltd. 142, Holborn Bars, London, EC1N 2NH.